Precalculus

[THIRD EDITION]

Cynthia Y. Young

PROFESSOR OF MATHEMATICS

University of Central Florida

WILEY

VICE PRESIDENT & DIRECTOR Laurie Rosatone
ACQUISITIONS EDITOR Joanna Dingle
DEVELOPMENT EDITOR Ryann Dannelly
EDITORIAL ASSISTANT Giana Milazzo
MARKETING MANAGER John LaVacca III
SENIOR PRODUCT DESIGNER David Dietz
PRODUCT DESIGN MANAGER Thomas Kulesa
PRODUCTION SERVICES Cenveo® Publisher Services
SENIOR CONTENT MANAGER Valerie Zaborski
SENIOR PRODUCTION EDITOR Ken Santor
SENIOR DESIGNER Maureen Eide
SENIOR PHOTO EDITOR Billy Ray
COVER PHOTO Jupiter Images/Getty Images

This book was set in 10/12 Times by Cenveo® Publisher Services, and printed and bound by Quad Graphics/Versailles. The cover was printed by Quad Graphics/Versailles.

This book is printed on acid free paper. ∞

Founded in 1807, John Wiley & Sons, Inc. has been a valued source of knowledge and understanding for more than 200 years, helping people around the world meet their needs and fulfill their aspirations. Our company is built on a foundation of principles that include responsibility to the communities we serve and where we live and work. In 2008, we launched a Corporate Citizenship Initiative, a global effort to address the environmental, social, economic, and ethical challenges we face in our business. Among the issues we are addressing are carbon impact, paper specifications and procurement, ethical conduct within our business and among our vendors, and community and charitable support. For more information, please visit our website: www.wiley.com/go/citizenship.

ISBN: 978-1-119-33951-9 (Enhanced ePUB)

Printed in the United States of America

SKY10029228_081921

FOR

Christopher and Caroline

About the Author

University of Central Florida

University of Central Florida

Cynthia Y. Young is the Pegasus Professor of Mathematics and the Vice Provost for Faculty Excellence and UCF Global at the University of Central Florida (UCF) and the author of *College Algebra, Trigonometry, Algebra and Trigonometry,* and *Precalculus*. She holds a BA in Secondary Mathematics Education from the University of North Carolina (Chapel Hill), an MS in Mathematical Sciences from UCF, and both an MS in Electrical Engineering and a PhD in Applied Mathematics from the University of Washington. She has taught high school in North Carolina and Florida, developmental mathematics at Shoreline Community College in Washington, and undergraduate and graduate students at UCF.

Dr. Young joined the faculty at UCF in 1997 as an assistant professor of mathematics, and her primary research area was the mathematical modeling of the atmospheric effects on propagating laser beams. Her atmospheric propagation research was recognized by the Office of Naval Research Young Investigator Award, and in 2007 she was selected as a fellow of the International Society for Optical Engineering. Her secondary area of research centers on improvement of student learning in mathematics. She has authored or co-authored over 60 books and articles and has served as the principal investigator or co-principal investigator on projects with more than \$2.5 million in federal funding. Dr. Young was on the team at UCF that developed the UCF EXCEL program, which was originally funded by the National Science Foundation to support the increase in the number of students graduating with a degree in science, technology, engineering, and mathematics (STEM). The EXCEL learning community approach centered around core mathematics courses has resulted in a significant increase in STEM graduation rates and has been institutionalized at UCF.

Dr. Young has been the recipient of many of UCF's awards (Excellence in Undergraduate Teaching, Excellence in Research, Teaching Incentive Program, Research Incentive Program, Scholarship of Teaching and Learning award, and UCF's highest honor, UCF Pegasus Professor). She has shared her techniques and experiences with colleagues around the country through talks at colleges, universities, and conferences.

Preface

As a mathematics professor I often heard my students say, "I understand you in class, but when I get home I am lost." When I would probe further, students would continue with "I can't read the book." As a mathematician I always found mathematics textbooks quite easy to read—and then it dawned on me: Don't look at this book through a mathematician's eyes; look at it through the eyes of students who might not view mathematics the same way that I do. What I found was that the books were not at all like my class. Students understood me in class, but when they got home they couldn't understand the book. It was then that the folks at Wiley lured me into writing. My goal was to write a book that is seamless with how we teach and is an ally (not an adversary) to student learning. I wanted to give students a book they could read without sacrificing the rigor needed for conceptual understanding. The following quotation comes from a reviewer who was asked about the rigor of the book:

> *I would say that this text comes across as a little less rigorous than other texts, but I think that stems from how easy it is to read and how clear the author is. When one actually looks closely at the material, the level of rigor is high.*

DISTINGUISHING FEATURES

Four key features distinguish this book from others, and they came directly from my classroom.

PARALLEL WORDS AND MATH

Have you ever looked at your students' notes? I found that my students were only scribbling down the mathematics that I would write—never the words that I would say in class. I started passing out handouts that had two columns: one column for math and one column for words. Each example would have one or the other; either the words were there and students had to fill in the math, or the math was there and students had to fill in the words. If you look at the examples in this book, you will see that the words (your voice) are on the left and the mathematics is on the right. In most math books, when the author illustrates an example, the mathematics is usually down the center of the page, and if the students don't know what mathematical operation was performed, they will look to the right for some brief statement of help. That's not how we teach; we don't write out an example on the board and then say, "Class, guess what I just did!" Instead we lead our students, telling them what step is coming and then performing that mathematical step *together*—and reading naturally from left to right. Student reviewers have said that the examples in this book are easy to read; that's because *your* voice is right there with them, working through problems *together*.

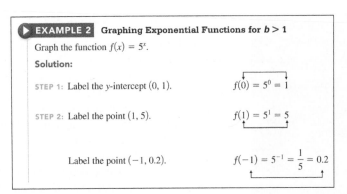

EXAMPLE 2 **Graphing Exponential Functions for $b > 1$**

Graph the function $f(x) = 5^x$.

Solution:

STEP 1: Label the y-intercept $(0, 1)$.	$f(0) = 5^0 = 1$
STEP 2: Label the point $(1, 5)$.	$f(1) = 5^1 = 5$
Label the point $(-1, 0.2)$.	$f(-1) = 5^{-1} = \frac{1}{5} = 0.2$

SKILLS AND CONCEPTS (LEARNING OBJECTIVES AND EXERCISES)

In my experience as a mathematics teacher/instructor/professor, I find skills to be on the micro level and concepts on the macro level of understanding mathematics. I believe that too often skills are emphasized at the expense of conceptual understanding. I have purposely separated *learning objectives* at the beginning of every section into two categories: *skills objectives*—what students should be able to do—and *conceptual objectives*—what students should understand. At the beginning of every class I discuss the learning objectives for the day—both skills and concepts. These are reinforced with both skills exercises and conceptual exercises. Each subsection has a corresponding skill objective and conceptual objective.

3.1 EXPONENTIAL FUNCTIONS AND THEIR GRAPHS

SKILLS OBJECTIVES	CONCEPTUAL OBJECTIVES
▪ Evaluate exponential functions. ▪ Graph exponential functions. ▪ Evaluate exponential functions of base *e*. ▪ Apply exponential functions to economics and the natural sciences.	▪ Understand that irrational exponents lead to approximations. ▪ Understand characteristics of exponential functions (implying domain, range, asymptotes, intercepts, etc.). ▪ Understand that *e* is irrational and why it is the "natural" base. ▪ Understand why compounding continuously results in higher interest than compounding daily.

CATCH THE MISTAKE

Have you ever made a mistake (or had a student bring you his or her homework with a mistake) and you've gone over it and over it and couldn't find the mistake? It's often easier to simply take out a new sheet of paper and solve the problem from scratch than it is to actually find the mistake. Finding the mistake demonstrates a higher level of understanding. I include a few *Catch the Mistake* exercises in each section that demonstrate a common mistake. Using these in class (with individuals or groups) leads to student discussion and offers an opportunity for formative assessment in real time.

• CATCH THE MISTAKE

In Exercises 65 and 66, explain the mistake that is made.

65. Evaluate the function for the given x: $f(x) = 4^x$ for $x = \frac{3}{2}$.

Solution:

$$f\left(\frac{3}{2}\right) = 4^{3/2}$$

$$= \frac{4^3}{4^2} = \frac{64}{16} = 4$$

The correct value is 8. What mistake was made?

66. If \$5000 is invested in a savings account that earns 3% interest compounded continuously, how much will be in the account in 6 months?

Solution:

Write the compound continuous interest formula.	$A = Pe^{rt}$
Substitute $P = 5000$, $r = 0.03$, and $t = 6$.	$A = 5000e^{(0.03)(6)}$
Simplify.	$A = 5986.09$

This is incorrect. What mistake was made?

LECTURE VIDEOS BY THE AUTHOR

I authored the videos to ensure consistency in the students' learning experience. Throughout the book, wherever a student sees the video icon, that indicates a video. These videos provide mini lectures. The chapter openers and chapter summaries act as class discussions. The "Your Turn" problems throughout the book challenge the students to attempt a problem similar to a nearby example. The "worked-out example" videos are intended to come to the rescue for students if they get lost as they read the text and work problems outside the classroom.

NEW TO THE THIRD EDITION

In the third edition, the main upgrades are updated applications throughout the text; new Skills Objectives and Conceptual Objectives mapped to each subsection; new Concept Check questions in each subsection; and the substantially improved version of *WileyPLUS*, including ORION adaptive practice and interactive animations.

LEARNING OBJECTIVES

LEARNING OBJECTIVES

- Graph exponential functions.
- Graph logarithmic functions.
- Apply properties of logarithms.
- Solve exponential and logarithmic equations.
- Use exponential and logarithmic models to represent a variety of real-world phenomena.

APPLICATIONS TO BUSINESS, ECONOMICS, HEALTH SCIENCES, AND MEDICINE

• APPLICATIONS

73. **Health.** After strenuous exercise, Sandy's heart rate R (beats per minute) can be modeled by

$$R(t) = 151e^{-0.055t},\ 0 \le t \le 15$$

where t is the number of minutes that have elapsed after she stops exercising.

a. Find Sandy's heart rate at the end of exercising (when she stops at time $t = 0$).

b. Determine how many minutes it takes after Sandy stops exercising for her heart rate to drop to 100 beats per minute. Round to the nearest minute.

c. Find Sandy's heart rate 15 minutes after she had stopped exercising.

74. **Business.** A local business purchased a new company van for \$45,000. After 2 years the book value of the van is \$30,000.

a. Find an exponential model for the value of the van using $V(t) = V_0e^{kt}$, where V is the value of the van in dollars and t is time in years.

b. Approximately how many years will it take for the book value of the van to drop to \$20,000?

75. **Money.** If money is invested in a savings account earning 3.5% interest compounded yearly, how many years will pass until the money triples?

76. **Money.** If money is invested in a savings account earning 3.5% interest compounded monthly, how many years will pass until the money triples?

77. **Money.** If \$7500 is invested in a savings account earning 5% interest compounded quarterly, how many years will pass until there is \$20,000?

78. **Money.** If \$9000 is invested in a savings account earning 6% interest compounded continuously, how many years will pass until there is \$15,000?

For Exercises 79 and 80, refer to the following:

$$\textbf{Richter scale: } M = \frac{2}{3}\log\left(\frac{E}{E_0}\right) \qquad E_0 = 10^{4.4}\ \textbf{joules}$$

79. **Earthquakes.** On September 25, 2003, an earthquake that measured 7.4 on the Richter scale shook Hokkaido, Japan. How much energy (joules) did the earthquake emit?

80. **Earthquakes.** Again, on that same day (September 25, 2003), a second earthquake that measured 8.3 on the Richter scale shook Hokkaido, Japan. How much energy (joules) did the earthquake emit?

For Exercises 95–96, refer to the following:

An epidemiological study of the spread of malaria in a rural area finds that the total number P of people who contracted malaria t days into an outbreak is modeled by the function

$$P(t) = -\frac{1}{4}t^2 + 7t + 180 \qquad 1 \le t \le 14$$

95. **Medicine/Health.** How many people have contracted malaria 14 days into the outbreak?

96. **Medicine/Health.** How many people have contracted malaria 6 days into the outbreak?

For Exercises 97 and 98, use the following figure:

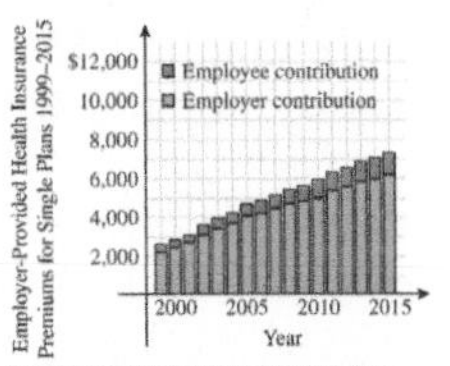

Source: Kaiser Family Foundation Health Research and Education Trust.

97. **Health-Care Costs:** Fill in the following table. Round dollars to the nearest \$1000.

YEAR	TOTAL HEALTH-CARE COST FOR FAMILY PLANS
1999	
2003	
2007	
2011	
2015	

Write the five ordered pairs resulting from the table.

98. **Health-Care Costs.** Using the table found in Exercise 97, let the years correspond to the domain and the total costs correspond to the range. Is this relation a function? Explain.

FEATURE	BENEFIT TO STUDENT
Chapter-Opening Vignette	Piques the student's interest with a real-world application of material presented in the chapter. Later in the chapter, the same concept from the vignette is reinforced.
Chapter Overview, Flow Chart, and Learning Objectives	Students see the big picture of how topics are related, and overarching learning objectives are presented.
Skills and Conceptual Objectives	Skills objectives represent what students should be able to do. Conceptual objectives emphasize a higher-level global perspective on concepts.
Clear, Concise, and Inviting Writing Style, Tone, and Layout	Students are able to *read* this book, which reduces math anxiety and promotes student success.
Parallel Words and Math	Increases students' ability to read and understand examples with a seamless representation of their instructor's class (the instructor's voice and what she or he wrote on the board).
Common Mistakes	Addresses a different learning style: teaching by counterexample. Demonstrates common mistakes so that students understand why a step is incorrect, and reinforces the correct mathematics.
Color for Pedagogical Reasons	Particularly helpful for visual learners when they see a function written in red and then its corresponding graph in red, or a function written in blue and then its corresponding graph in blue.
Study Tips	Reinforces specific notes that you would want to emphasize in class.
Author Videos	Gives students a mini class of several examples worked by the author.
Your Turn	Engages students during class, builds student confidence, and assists instructor in real-time assessment.
Concept Checks	Just as the Your Turn features reinforce the "skills" learning objectives, the Concept Checks reinforce the "conceptual" learning objectives.
Catch the Mistake Exercises	Encourages students to assume the role of teacher—demonstrating a higher mastery level.
Conceptual Exercises	Teaches students to think more globally about a topic.
Inquiry-Based Learning Project (online only)	Lets students *discover* a mathematical identify, formula, or precept that is derived in the book.
Modeling Our World (online only)	Engages students in a modeling project on a timely subject: global climate change.
Chapter Review	Key ideas and formulas are presented section by section in a chart. Improves study skills.
Chapter Review Exercises	Improves study skills.
Chapter Practice Test	Offers self-assessment and improves study skills.
Cumulative Test	Improves retention.

SUPPLEMENTS

INSTRUCTOR SUPPLEMENTS

INSTRUCTOR'S SOLUTIONS MANUAL (Vol. 1: 9781119458098; Vol. 2: 9781119458982)

- Contains worked-out solutions to all exercises in the text.

INSTRUCTOR'S MANUAL

Authored by Cynthia Young, the manual provides practical advice on teaching with the text, including

- sample lesson plans and homework assignments
- suggestions for the effective utilization of additional resources and supplements
- sample syllabi
- Cynthia Young's Top 10 Teaching Tips & Tricks
- online component featuring the author presenting these Tips & Tricks

ANNOTATED INSTRUCTOR'S EDITION (ISBN: 9781119370543)

- Displays, in the back of the book, answers to nearly all the exercises in the text.
- Provides additional classroom examples within the standard difficulty range of the in-text exercises, as well as challenge problems to assess your students' mastery of the material.

POWERPOINT SLIDES

- For each section of the book, corresponding lecture notes and worked-out examples are presented as PowerPoint slides, available on the Book Companion Site (www.wiley.com/college/young) and in *WileyPLUS*.

TEST BANK

- Contains approximately 900 questions and answers from every section of the text.

COMPUTERIZED TEST BANK

Electronically enhanced version of the Test Bank that

- contains approximately 900 algorithmically generated questions.
- enables instructors to freely edit, randomize, and create questions.
- enables instructors to create and print different versions of a quiz or exam.
- recognizes symbolic notation.
- allows for partial credit if used within *WileyPLUS*.

BOOK COMPANION WEBSITE (WWW.WILEY.COM/COLLEGE/YOUNG)

- Contains all instructor supplements listed plus a selection of personal response system questions.

STUDENT SUPPLEMENTS

STUDENT SOLUTIONS MANUAL (ISBN: 9781119458081)

- Includes worked-out solutions for all odd-numbered problems in the text.

BOOK COMPANION WEBSITE (WWW.WILEY.COM/COLLEGE/YOUNG)

- Provides additional resources for students, including Web quizzes, video clips, and audio clips.

WHAT DO STUDENTS RECEIVE WITH *WILEYPLUS*?

WILEYPLUS

- *WileyPLUS* online homework features a full-service, digital learning environment, including additional resources for students, such as lecture videos by the author, self-practice exercises, tutorials, integrated links between the online text and supplements, and new interactive animations and ORION adaptive practice.
- *WileyPLUS* has been substantially revised and improved since the second edition of *Precalculus*. It now includes ORION, an adaptive practice engine built directly into *WileyPLUS* that can connect directly into the *WileyPLUS* gradebook, or into your campus Learning Management System gradebook if you select that option. Wiley has been incorporating ORION into *WileyPLUS* courses for over five years, including the second edition of this program. ORION brings the power of adaptive learning, which will continue to help students and instructors "bridge the gap."

Other new *WileyPLUS* features include:

- Maple TA Math palette and question evaluator (compatible with tablets and Java-free)
- HTML 5 graphing questions
- Interactive animations
- Concept Check questions
- Secure testing enhancements, including IP restriction
- HTML 5 Show Work whiteboard

ACKNOWLEDGMENTS

I want to express my sincerest gratitude to the entire Wiley team. I've said this before, and I will say it again: Wiley is the right partner for me. There is a reason that my dog is named Wiley—she's smart, competitive, a team player, and most of all, a joy to be around. There are several people within Wiley to whom I feel the need to express my appreciation: first and foremost to Laurie Rosatone who convinced Wiley Higher Ed to invest in a young assistant professor's vision for a series and who has been unwavering in her commitment to student learning. To my editor Joanna Dingle whose judgment I trust in both editorial and preschool decisions; thank you for surpassing my greatest expectations for an editor. Special thanks to Mary Sanger who kept me on track throughout the production of this book. To the rest of the math editorial team (Ryann Dannelly, Giana Milazzo, and Kim Eskin), you are all first class! This revision was planned and executed exceptionally well thanks to you. To the math marketing manager, John LaVacca, thank you for helping reps tell my story. To Ken Santor and Laura Abrams, thank you for your attention to detail. To product designer David Dietz, many thanks for your role in developing the online course. Maureen Eide, thank you for the new design! And finally, I'd like to thank all of the Wiley reps: thank you for your commitment to my series and your tremendous efforts to get professors to adopt this book for their students.

I would also like to thank all of the contributors who helped us make this *an even better book*. I'd first like to thank Mark McKibben. He is known as the author of the solutions manuals that accompany this series, but he is much more than that. Mark, thank you for making this series a priority, for being so responsive, and most of all for being my "go-to" person to think through ideas. I'd also like to thank Jodi B.A. McKibben who is a statistician and teamed with Mark to develop the regression material. I'd like to thank Steve Davis who was the inspiration for the Inquiry-Based Learning Projects and a huge thanks to Lyn Riverstone who developed all of the IBLPs. Special thanks to Laura Watkins for finding applications that are real and timely. I'd also like to thank Becky Schantz for her environmental problems (I now use AusPens because of Becky). Many thanks to Jen Blue, Dave Bregenzer, and Kristi Reutzel for accuracy checking the exercises and solutions.

I'd also like to thank the following reviewers whose input helped make this book even better.

Text Reviewers

Piotr Runge, Utah State University
Amy Kong, Helena College University of Montana
Jim Brown, Texas Tech University
Dave Bregenzer, Utah State University
Katherine Cliff, University of Colorado
Elaine Terry, Saint Joseph's University
Richard Andrews, Florida A&M University
Jason Geary, William Rainey Harper College
Brian Loving, New Hope-Solebury High
Sam Needham, Diablo Valley College
Hossein Rostami, Philadelphia University
Jacqueline Lovett, Belmont High School
Victor Padron, Normandale Community College
Stan Stascinsky, Tarrant County College
Jeffrey Brignac, Tarrant County College
John Czaplewski, Western Governors University
Gurcharan Brar, Deleware County Community
Ben Hill, Lane Community College

Animations Reviewers

Monika H. Champion, Ivy Tech Community College
Kim Christensen, Metropolitan Community College
Marissa Ford, Ivy Tech Community College
Yamir DeJesus-Decena, Dutchess Community College
Barbara Hess, California University of Pennsylvania
Christina K. Houston, Community College of Allegheny County
Phyllis Lefton, Manhattanville College
Carrie McCammon, Ivy Tech Community College
Holly J. Middleton, University of North Florida
Becky Moening, Ivy Tech Community College
Denise Race, Eastfield College
Edward Schwartz, Manhattanville College
Mike Shirazi, Germanna Community College
Misty Vorder Bruegge, Hillsborough Community College

Contents

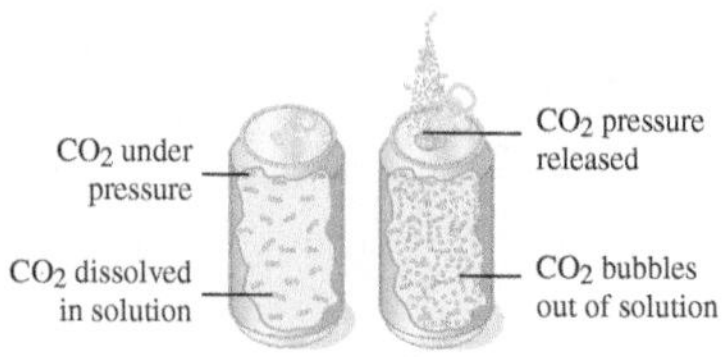

© Catherine Lane

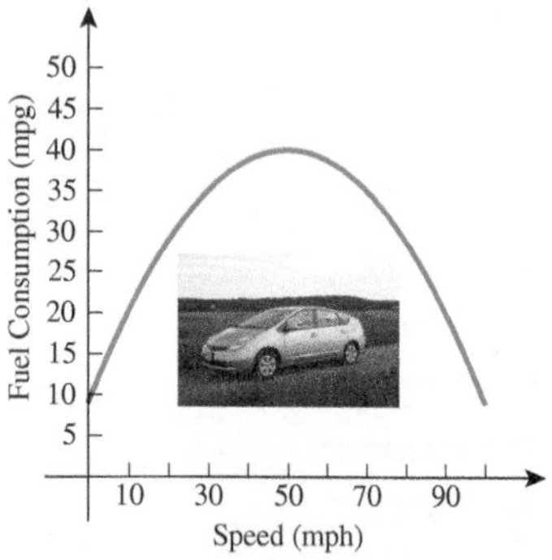

Encore/Alamy

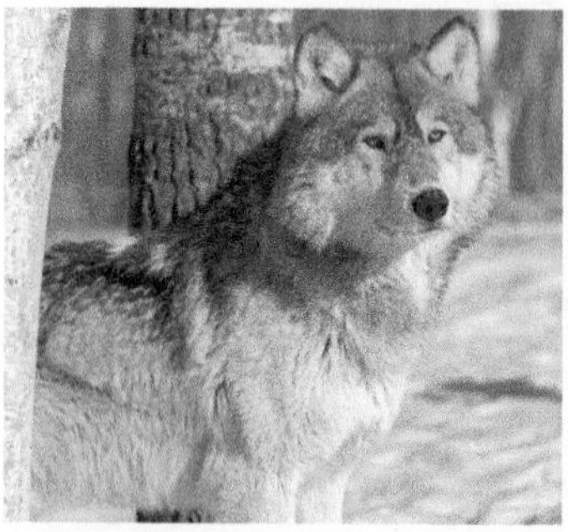
John Pitcher/iStockphoto

[4] Trigonometric Functions of Angles 344

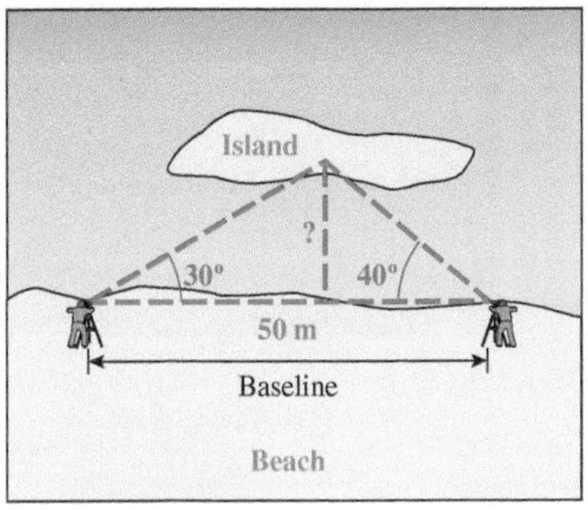

[5] Trigonometric Functions of Real Numbers 432

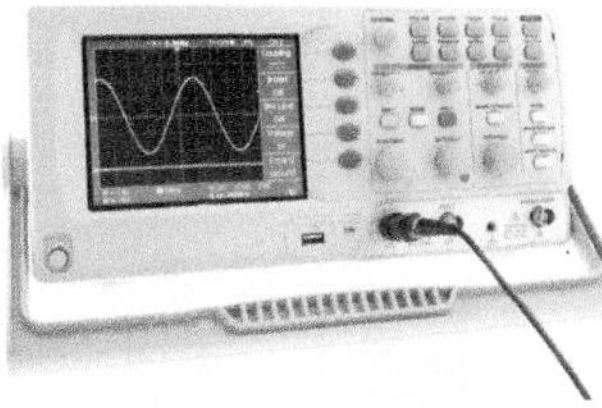

Alexey Filatov/Alamy Stock Photo

[6] Analytic Trigonometry 498

hanibaram

[7] Vectors, the Complex Plane, and Polar Coordinates 594

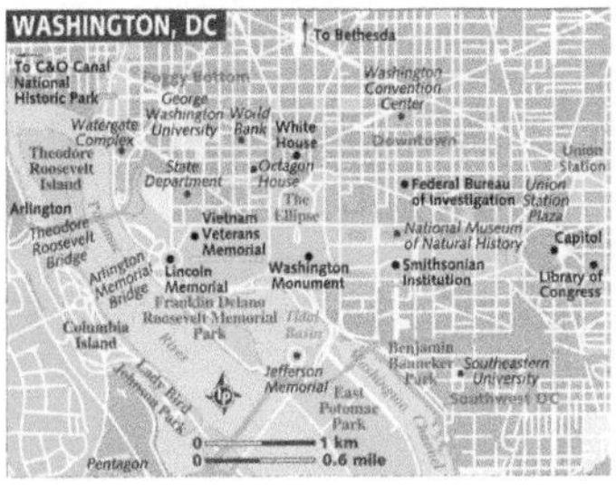

Lonely Planet/Getty Images

[8] Systems of Linear Equations and Inequalities 660

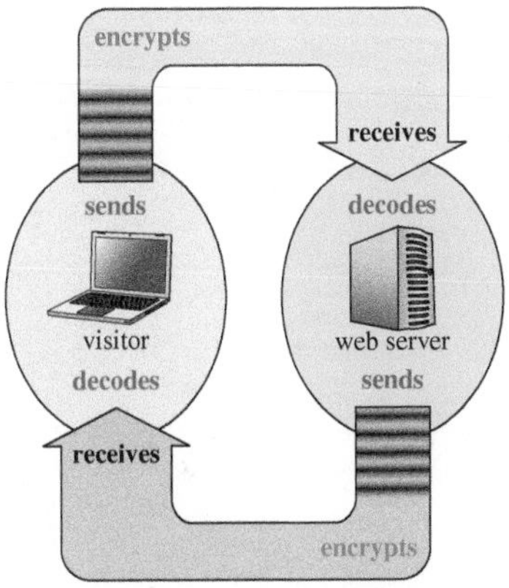

© Photodisc/Age Fotostock America, Inc.

[9] Conics, Systems of Nonlinear Equations and Inequalities, and Parametric Equations 790

Answers to Odd-Numbered Exercises 893

Applications Index 945

Subject Index 948

Gaillardia Flower (55), Kenneth M. Highfil/Photo Researchers, Inc.; Michaelmas Daisy (89), Maxine Adcock/Photo Researchers, Inc.; Yellow Iris (3), Edward Kinsman/Photo Researchers, Inc.; Blue Columbine (5), Jeffrey Lepore/Photo Researchers, Inc.; Gerbera Daisy (34), Bonnie Sue Rauch/Photo Researchers, Inc.; Erect Dayflower (2), Michael Lustbader/Photo Researchers, Inc.; Calla Lilies (1), Adam Jones/Photo Researchers, Inc.; Cosmos Flower (8), Maria Mosolova/Photo Researchers, Inc.; Lemon Symphony (21), Bonnie Sue Rauch/Photo Researchers, Inc.; Black-Eyed Susan (13), Rod Planck/Photo Researchers, Inc.

[10] Sequences and Series (online only)

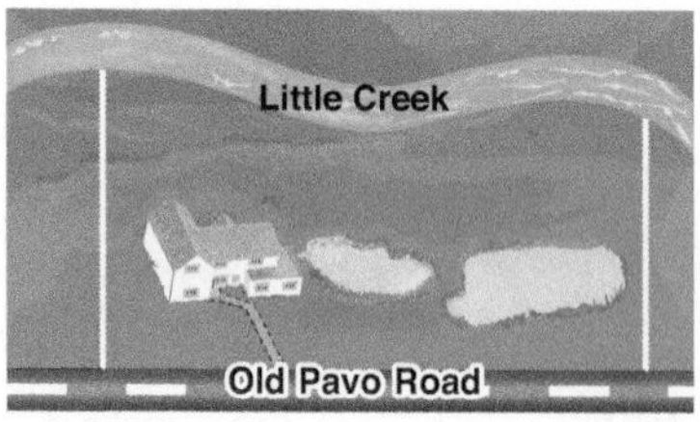

[11] Limits: A Preview to Calculus (online only)

Appendix Prerequisites and Review (online only)

For print options including section 0.8, chapters 10 and 11, and the Appendix, please contact your local Wiley representative.

A Note from the Author

TO THE STUDENT

I wrote this text with careful attention to ways in which to make your learning experience more successful. If you take full advantage of the unique features and elements of this textbook, I believe your experience will be fulfilling and enjoyable. Let's walk through some of the special features that will help you in your study of algebra and trigonometry.

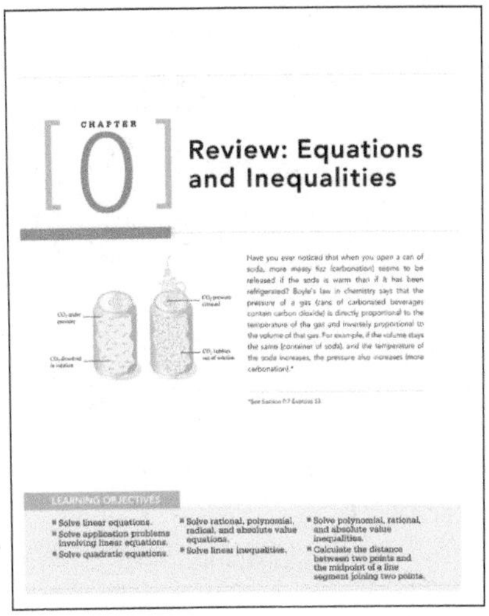

Prerequisites and Review (Chapter 0)

A comprehensive review of prerequisite knowledge (intermediate algebra topics) in Chapter 0 provides a brush-up on knowledge and skills necessary for success in the course.

Clear, Concise, and Inviting Writing

Special efforts have been made to present an engaging, clear, precise narrative in a layout that is easy to use and designed to reduce any math anxiety you may have.

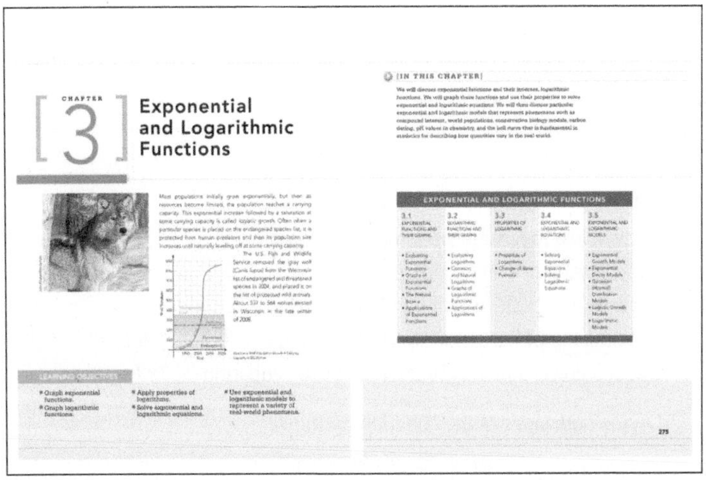

Chapter Introduction, Flow Chart, Section Headings, and Objectives

An opening vignette, flow chart, list of chapter sections, and chapter learning objectives give you an overview of the chapter.

3.1 EXPONENTIAL FUNCTIONS AND THEIR GRAPHS

SKILLS OBJECTIVES	CONCEPTUAL OBJECTIVES
■ Evaluate exponential functions. ■ Graph exponential functions. ■ Evaluate exponential functions of base *e*. ■ Apply exponential functions to economics and the natural sciences.	■ Understand that irrational exponents lead to approximations. ■ Understand characteristics of exponential functions (implying domain, range, asymptotes, intercepts, etc.). ■ Understand that *e* is irrational and why it is the "natural" base. ■ Understand why compounding continuously results in higher interest than compounding daily.

Skills and Conceptual Objectives

For every section, objectives are further subdivided into skills *and* concepts to reflect the difference between solving problems and truly understanding concepts.

EXAMPLE 10 Calculating the Magnitude of an Earthquake

On October 17, 1989, just moments before game 3 of the World Series between the Oakland A's and the San Francisco Giants was about to start—with 60,000 fans in Candlestick Park—a devastating earthquake erupted. Parts of interstates and bridges collapsed, and President George H. W. Bush declared the area a disaster zone. The earthquake released approximately 1.12×10^{15} joules of energy. Calculate the magnitude of the earthquake using the Richter scale.

Solution:

Write the Richter scale formula. $M = \frac{2}{3}\log\left(\frac{E}{E_0}\right)$

Substitute $E = 1.12 \times 10^{15}$ and $E_0 = 10^{4.4}$. $M = \frac{2}{3}\log\left(\frac{1.12 \times 10^{15}}{10^{4.4}}\right)$

Simplify. $M = \frac{2}{3}\log(1.12 \times 10^{10.6})$

Approximate the logarithm using a calculator. $M \approx \frac{2}{3}(10.65) \approx 7.1$

The 1989 earthquake in California measured $\boxed{7.1}$ on the Richter scale.

YOUR TURN On May 3, 1996, Seattle experienced a moderate earthquake. The energy that the earthquake released was approximately 1.12×10^{12} joules. Calculate the magnitude of the 1996 Seattle earthquake using the Richter scale.

ANSWER
5.1

Examples

Examples pose a specific problem using concepts already presented and then work through the solution. These serve to enhance your understanding of the subject matter.

Your Turn

Immediately following many examples, you are given a similar problem to reinforce and check your understanding. This helps build confidence as you progress in the chapter. These are ideal for in-class activity or for preparing for homework later. Answers are provided in the margin for a quick check of your work.

Common Mistake/Correct vs. Incorrect

In addition to standard examples, some problems are worked out both correctly and incorrectly to highlight common errors. Analyzing such counterexamples is often an effective learning approach.

common mistake

A common mistake is to write the sum of the logs as a log of the sum.

$$\log_b M + \log_b N \neq \log_b(M + N)$$

✓CORRECT

Use the power property (7).

$2\log_b 3 + 4\log_b u = \log_b 3^2 + \log_b u^4$

Simplify.

$\log_b 9 + \log_b u^4$

Use the product property (5).

$\boxed{= \log_b(9u^4)}$

✖INCORRECT

$\neq \log_b(9 + u^4)$ **ERROR**

Parallel Words and Math

This text reverses the common textbook presentation of examples by placing the explanation in words *on the left* and the mathematics in parallel *on the right*. This makes it easier for students to read through examples because the material flows more naturally from left to right and as commonly presented in class.

Proof of Change-of-Base Formula

WORDS	MATH
Let y be the logarithm we want to evaluate.	$y = \log_b M$
Write $y = \log_b M$ in exponential form.	$b^y = M$
Let a be any positive real number (where $a \neq 1$).	
Take the log of base a of both sides of the equation.	$\log_a b^y = \log_a M$
Use the power rule on the left side of the equation.	$y \log_a b = \log_a M$
Divide both sides of the equation by $\log_a b$.	$y = \dfrac{\log_a M}{\log_a b}$

Study Tips and Caution Notes

These marginal reminders call out important hints or warnings to be aware of related to the topic or problem.

STUDY TIP

If the number of times per year interest is compounded increases, then the total interest earned that year also increases.

CAUTION

$$\log_b M - \log_b N = \log_b\left(\frac{M}{N}\right)$$

$$\log_b M - \log_b N \neq \frac{\log_b M}{\log_b N}$$

[IN THIS CHAPTER]

We will discuss exponential functions and their inverses, logarithmic functions. We will graph these functions and use their properties to solve exponential and logarithmic equations. We will then discuss particular exponential and logarithmic models that represent phenomena such as

[SECTION 3.1] SUMMARY

In this section, we discussed exponential functions (constant base, variable exponent).

General Exponential Functions: $f(x) = b^x, b \neq 1$, and $b > 0$

1. Evaluating exponential functions
   - Exact (by inspection): $f(x) = 2^x \quad f(3) = 2^3 = 8$.
   - Approximate (with the aid of a calculator): $f(x) = 2^x$ $f(\sqrt{3}) = 2^{\sqrt{3}} \approx 3.322$
2. Graphs of expon

Procedure for Graphing: $f(x) = b^x$

Step 1: Label the point (0, 1) corresponding to the y-intercept $f(0)$.

Step 2: Find and label two additional points corresponding to $f(-1)$ and $f(1)$.

Step 3: Connect the three points with a smooth curve with the x-axis as the horizontal asymptote.

The Natural Exponential Function: $f(x) = e^x$

EXAMPLE 2 Graphing Exponential Functions for $b > 1$

Graph the function $f(x) = 5^x$.

Solution:

$) = 5^0 = 1$

[CHAPTER 3 REVIEW]

SECTION	CONCEPT	KEY IDEAS/FORMULAS
3.1	**Exponential functions and their graphs**	
	Evaluating exponential function	$f(x) = b^x \quad b > 0, b \neq 1$
	Graphs of exponential functions	y-intercept (0, 1) Horizontal asymptote: $y = 0$; the points $(1, b)$ and $(-1, 1/b)$
	The natural base e	$f(x) = e^x$
	Applications of exponential functions	Doubling time: $P = P_0 2^{t/d}$
		Compound interest: $A = P\left(1 + \frac{r}{n}\right)^{nt}$
		Compounded continuously: $A = Pe^{rt}$
3.2	**Logarithmic functions and their graphs**	$y = \log_b x \quad x > 0$ $b > 0, b \neq 1$
	Evaluating logarithms	$y = \log_b x$ and $x = b^y$
	Common and natural logarithms	$y = \log x$ Common (base 10)

CHAPTER 3

[SECTION 3.3] EXERCISES

• **SKILLS**

In Exercises 1–20, apply the properties of logarithms to simplify each expression. Do not use a calculator.

1. $\log_9 1$ 2. $\log_{69} 1$ 3. $\log_{1/2}(\frac{1}{2})$ 4. $\log_{3.3} 3.3$ 5. $\log_{10} 10^8$

• **APPLICATIONS**

59. **Sound.** Sitting in the front row of a rock concert exposes us to a sound pressure (or sound level) of 1×10^{-1} W/m² (or 110 decibels), and a normal conversation is typically around 1×10^{-6} W/m² (or 60 decibels). How many decibels are you exposed to if a friend is talking in your ear at a rock concert? *Note:* 160 decibels causes perforation of the eardrums. *Hint:* Add the sound pressures and convert to decibels.

63. **Photography.** In photographic quality assurance, logarithms are used to determine, for instance, the density. Density is the common logarithm of the opacity, which is the quotient of the amount of incident light and the amount of transmitted light. What is the density of a photographic material that transmits only 90% of the incident light?

64. **pH Scale.** The pH scale measures how acidic or basic a …garithm of the …n, a_H. Thus, if …ine the pH of a

• **CATCH THE MISTAKE**

In Exercises 67–70, simplify if possible and explain the mistake that is made.

67. $3 \log 5 - \log 25$

Solution:

Apply the quotient property (6). $\dfrac{3 \log 5}{\log 25}$

Write $25 = 5^2$. $\dfrac{3 \log 5}{\ldots}$

69. $\log_2 x + \log_3 y - \log_4 z$

Solution:

Apply the product property (5). $\log_6 xy - \log_4 z$

Apply the quotient property (6). $\log_{24} xyz$

This is incorrect. What mistake was made?

• **CONCEPTUAL**

In Exercises 71–76, determine whether each statement is true or false.

71. $\log e = \dfrac{1}{\ln 10}$ 72. $\ln e = \dfrac{1}{\log 10}$ 73. $\ln (xy)^3 = (\ln x + \ln y)^3$

• **CHALLENGE**

77. Prove the quotient rule: $\log_b\left(\frac{M}{N}\right) = \log_b M - \log_b N$.

Hint: Let $u = \log_b M$ and $v = \log_b N$. Write both in exponential form and find the quotient $\log_b\left(\frac{M}{N}\right)$.

78. Prove the power rule: $\log_b M^p = p \log_b M$.

80. Show that $\log_b\left(\frac{1}{x}\right) = -\log_b x$.

81. Show that $\log_b\left(\frac{a^2}{b^3}\right)^{-3} = 9 - \dfrac{6}{\log_a b}$.

82. Given that $\log_b 2 = 0.4307$ and $\log_b 3 = 0.6826$, find $\log_b \sqrt{48}$. Do not use a calculator.

• **PREVIEW TO CALCULUS**

In calculus we prove that the derivative of $f + g$ is $f' + g'$ and that the derivative of $f - g$ is $f' - g'$. It is also shown in calculus that if $f(x) = \ln x$, then $f'(x) = \frac{1}{x}$.

83. Use these properties to find the derivative of $f(x) = \ln x^2$.

84. Find the derivative of $f(x) = \ln \frac{1}{x^2}$.

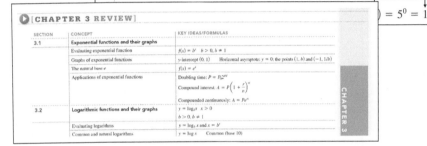

Video Icons

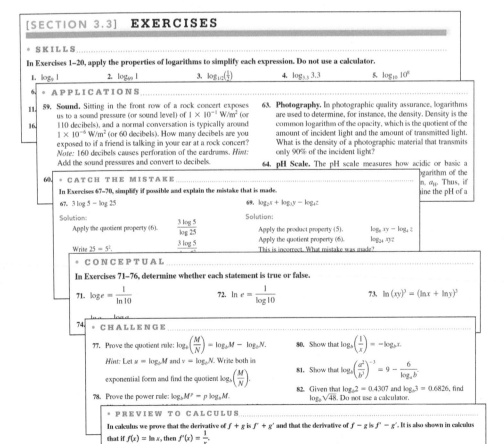

Video icons appear on all chapter introductions, as well as on selected examples throughout the chapter, to indicate that the author has created a video segment for that element. These video clips help you work through the selected examples with the author as your "private tutor."

Six Types of Exercises

Every text section ends with **Skills, Applications, Catch the Mistake, Conceptual, Challenge, and Preview to Calculus** exercises. The exercises gradually increase in difficulty and vary in skill and conceptual emphasis. Catch the Mistake exercises increase your depth of understanding and reinforce what you have learned. Conceptual and Challenge exercises specifically focus on assessing conceptual understanding.

Concept Checks

Just as the Your Turn features reinforce the "skills" learning objectives, the Concept Checks reinforce the "conceptual" learning objectives.

[CONCEPT CHECK]

TRUE OR FALSE In Solution (a) in Example 2 we could have used the log of any base (not just the natural log as shown).

ANSWER True

[CONCEPT CHECK]

TRUE OR FALSE Investments that compound continuously are examples of exponential growth.

ANSWER True

[CONCEPT CHECK]

What threshold score would one have to be at approximately the 98th percentile in IQ?

ANSWER 130

Chapter Review, Review Exercises, Practice Test, and Cumulative Test

At the end of every chapter, a summary review chart organizes the key learning concepts in a one- or two-page layout that's easy to use. This feature includes key ideas and formulas, as well as indicating relevant pages and review exercises so that you can quickly summarize a chapter and "study smarter." Review Exercises, arranged by section heading, are provided for extra study and practice. A Practice Test, without section headings, offers even more self-practice before you move on. A new Cumulative Test feature offers study questions based on all previous chapters' content, thus helping you build on concepts that you learned before.

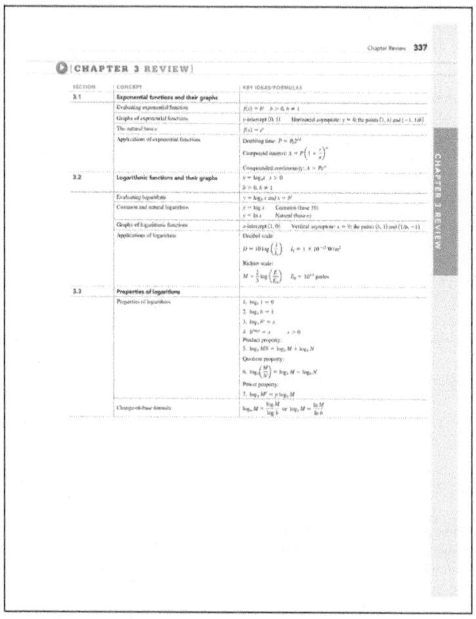

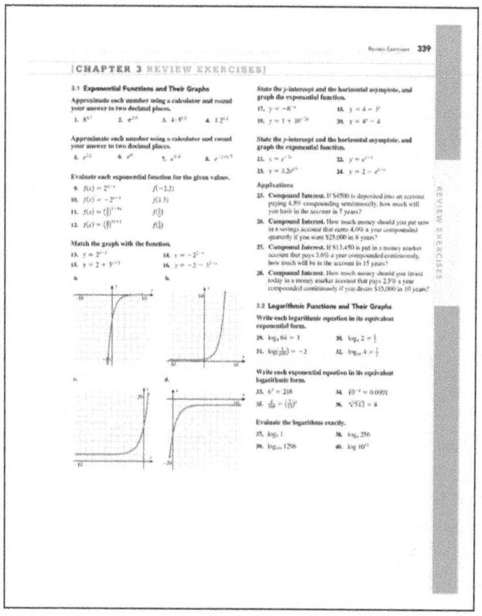

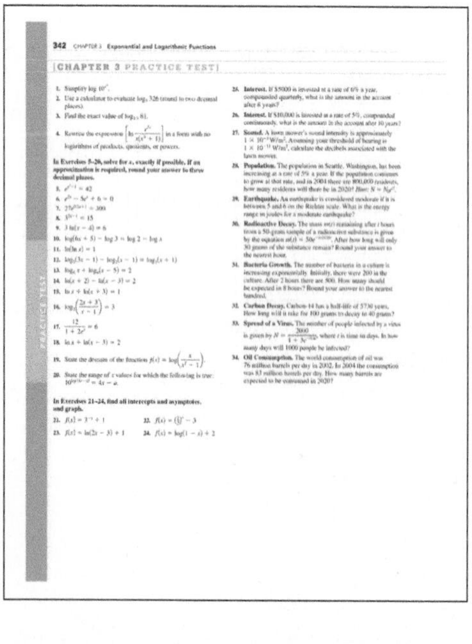

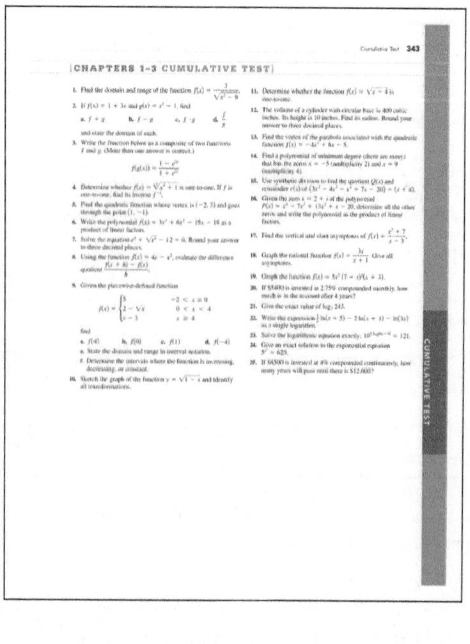

Precalculus

CHAPTER 0

Review: Equations and Inequalities

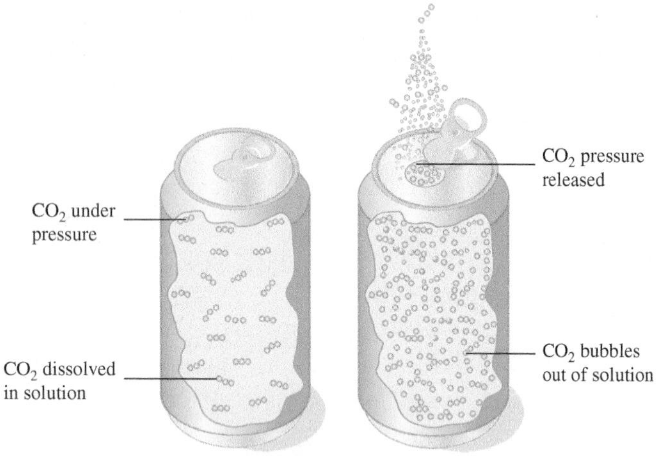

Have you ever noticed that when you open a can of soda, more messy fizz (carbonation) seems to be released if the soda is warm than if it has been refrigerated? Boyle's law in chemistry says that the pressure of a gas (cans of carbonated beverages contain carbon dioxide) is directly proportional to the temperature of the gas and inversely proportional to the volume of that gas. For example, if the volume stays the same (container of soda), and the temperature of the soda increases, the pressure also increases (more carbonation).*

*See Section 0.7 Exercise 53.

LEARNING OBJECTIVES

- Solve linear equations.
- Solve application problems involving linear equations.
- Solve quadratic equations.
- Solve rational, polynomial, radical, and absolute value equations.
- Solve linear inequalities.
- Solve polynomial, rational, and absolute value inequalities.
- Calculate the distance between two points and the midpoint of a line segment joining two points.

[IN THIS CHAPTER]

We will review solving equations in one variable. We will start with linear and quadratic equations and then move on to other types of equations. We will review solving linear, polynomial, rational, and absolute value inequalities in one variable. We will discuss how to graph equations in two variables in the Cartesian plane and specifically discuss circles. Lastly, we will use equations to model variation.

REVIEW: EQUATIONS AND INEQUALITIES

0.1 LINEAR EQUATIONS	0.2 QUADRATIC EQUATIONS	0.3 OTHER TYPES OF EQUATIONS	0.4 INEQUALITIES	0.5 GRAPHING EQUATIONS	0.6 LINES	0.7 MODELING VARIATION
• Solving Linear Equations in One Variable • Applications Involving Linear Equations	• Factoring • Square Root Method • Completing the Square • The Quadratic Formula • Applications Involving Quadratic Equations	• Rational Equations • Radical Equations • Equations Quadratic in Form: *u*-Substitution • Factorable Equations • Absolute Value Equations	• Graphing Inequalities and Interval Notation • Linear Inequalities • Polynomial Inequalities • Rational Inequalities • Absolute Value Inequalities	• Cartesian Plane • The Distance and Midpoint Formulas • Point-Plotting • Using Intercepts as Graphing Aids • Using Symmetry as a Graphing Aid • Circles	• General Form of a Line and Slope • Equations of Lines • Parallel and Perpendicular Lines	• Direct Variation • Inverse Variation • Joint Variation and Combined Variation

- Sketch the graph of an equation using intercepts and symmetry as graphing aids.
- Graph circles.
- Find the equation of a line.
- Model applications with functions using variation.
- Find the line of best fit for a given set of data.

0.1 LINEAR EQUATIONS

SKILLS OBJECTIVES

- Solve linear equations in one variable.
- Solve application problems involving common formulas.
- Solve simple interest problems.
- Solve mixture problems.
- Solve distance–rate–time problems.

CONCEPTUAL OBJECTIVES

- Understand the definition of a linear equation in one variable.
- Understand the mathematical modeling process.
- Use intuition to confirm answers in multiple investment problems.
- Use intuition to confirm answers to mixture problems.
- Estimate distance–rate–time problem solutions prior to solving, and then confirm with a check.

0.1.1 Solving Linear Equations in One Variable

0.1.1 SKILL

Solve linear equations in one variable.

0.1.1 CONCEPTUAL

Understand the definition of a linear equation in one variable.

An **algebraic expression** (see Appendix) consists of one or more terms that are combined through basic operations such as addition, subtraction, multiplication, or division; for example,

$$3x + 2 \qquad 5 - 2y \qquad x + y$$

An **equation** is a statement that says two expressions are equal. For example, the following are all equations in one variable, x:

$$x + 7 = 11 \qquad x^2 = 9 \qquad 7 - 3x = 2 - 3x \qquad 4x + 7 = x + 2 + 3x + 5$$

To **solve** an equation in one variable means to find all the values of that variable that make the equation true. These values are called **solutions**, or **roots**, of the equation. The first of these statements shown above, $x + 7 = 11$, is true when $x = 4$ and false for any other values of x. We say that $x = 4$ is the solution to the equation. Sometimes an equation can have more than one solution, as in $x^2 = 9$. In this case, there are actually two values of x that make this equation true, $x = -3$ and $x = 3$. We say the **solution set** of this equation is $\{-3, 3\}$. In the third equation, $7 - 3x = 2 - 3x$, no values of x make the statement true. Therefore, we say this equation has **no solution**. And the fourth equation, $4x + 7 = x + 2 + 3x + 5$, is true for any values of x. An equation that is true for any value of the variable x is called an **identity**. In this case, we say the solution set is the **set of all real numbers**.

Two equations that have the same solution set are called **equivalent equations**. For example,

$$3x + 7 = 13 \qquad 3x = 6 \qquad x = 2$$

are all equivalent equations because each of them has the solution set $\{2\}$. Note that $x^2 = 4$ is not equivalent to these three equations because it has the solution set $\{-2, 2\}$.

When solving equations, it helps to find a simpler equivalent equation in which the variable is isolated (alone). The following table summarizes the procedures for generating equivalent equations.

Generating Equivalent Equations

ORIGINAL EQUATION	DESCRIPTION	EQUIVALENT EQUATION
$3(x - 6) = 6x - x$	■ Eliminate the parentheses. ■ Combine like terms on one or both sides of the equation.	$3x - 18 = 5x$
$7x + 8 = 29$	Add (or subtract) the same quantity to (from) *both* sides of the equation. $7x + 8 - \mathbf{8} = 29 - \mathbf{8}$	$7x = 21$
$5x = 15$	Multiply (or divide) both sides of the equation by the same nonzero quantity: $\frac{5x}{5} = \frac{15}{5}$.	$x = 3$
$-7 = x$	Interchange the two sides of the equation.	$x = -7$

You probably already know how to solve simple linear equations. Solving a linear equation in one variable is done by finding an equivalent equation. In generating an equivalent equation, remember that whatever operation is performed on one side of an equation must also be performed on the other side of the equation.

EXAMPLE 1 **Solving a Linear Equation**

Solve the equation $3x + 4 = 16$.

Solution:

Subtract 4 from both sides of the equation.

$$\begin{aligned} 3x + 4 &= 16 \\ -4 \quad & -4 \\ \hline 3x \quad &= 12 \end{aligned}$$

Divide both sides by 3.

$$\frac{3x}{3} = \frac{12}{3}$$

The solution is $x = 4$.

$$\boxed{x = 4}$$

The solution set is $\{4\}$.

YOUR TURN Solve the equation $2x + 3 = 9$.

ANSWER
The solution is $x = 3$.
The solution set is $\{3\}$.

Example 1 illustrates solving linear equations in one variable. What is a linear equation in one variable?

DEFINITION **Linear Equation**

A **linear equation in one variable**, x, can be written in the form

$$ax + b = 0$$

where a and b are real numbers and $a \neq 0$.

What makes this equation linear is that x is raised to the first power. We can also classify a linear equation as a **first-degree** equation.

EQUATION	DEGREE	GENERAL NAME
$x - 7 = 0$	First	Linear
$x^2 - 6x - 9 = 0$	Second	Quadratic
$x^3 + 3x^2 - 8 = 0$	Third	Cubic

EXAMPLE 2 **Solving a Linear Equation**

Solve the equation $5x - (7x - 4) - 2 = 5 - (3x + 2)$.

Solution:

Eliminate the parentheses. $5x - (7x - 4) - 2 = 5 - (3x + 2)$

Don't forget to distribute the negative sign through *both* terms inside the parentheses. $5x - 7x + 4 - 2 = 5 - 3x - 2$

Combine like terms on each side. $-2x + 2 = 3 - 3x$

Add $3x$ to both sides. $+3x \quad\quad + 3x$

$x + 2 = 3$

Subtract 2 from both sides. $-2 \quad -2$

$x = 1$

Check to verify that $x = 1$ is a solution to the original equation.

$$5 \cdot 1 - (7 \cdot 1 - 4) - 2 = 5 - (3 \cdot 1 + 2)$$
$$5 - (7 - 4) - 2 = 5 - (3 + 2)$$
$$5 - (3) - 2 = 5 - (5)$$
$$0 = 0$$

Since the solution $x = 1$ makes the equation true, the solution set is $\{1\}$.

YOUR TURN Solve the equation $4(x - 1) - 2 = x - 3(x - 2)$.

ANSWER
The solution is $x = 2$.
The solution set is $\{2\}$.

STUDY TIP
Prime Factors
$2 = 2$
$6 = 2 \cdot 3$
$5 = \quad\quad \cdot 5$
LCD $= 2 \cdot 3 \cdot 5 = 30$

To solve a linear equation involving fractions, find the least common denominator (LCD) of all terms and multiply both sides of the equation by the LCD. We will first review how to find the LCD.

To add the fractions $\frac{1}{2} + \frac{1}{6} + \frac{2}{5}$, we must first find a common denominator. Some people are taught to find the lowest number that 2, 6, and 5 all divide evenly into. Others prefer a more systematic approach in terms of prime factors.

EXAMPLE 3 **Solving a Linear Equation Involving Fractions**

Solve the equation $\frac{1}{2}p - 5 = \frac{3}{4}p$.

Solution:

Write the equation. $\frac{1}{2}p - 5 = \frac{3}{4}p$

Multiply each term in the equation by the LCD, 4. $(4)\frac{1}{2}p - (4)5 = (4)\frac{3}{4}p$

The result is a linear equation with no fractions. $2p - 20 = 3p$

Subtract $2p$ from both sides. $-2p \quad\quad -2p$

$-20 = p$

$\boxed{p = -20}$

Since $p = -20$ satisfies the original equation, the solution set is $\{-20\}$.

YOUR TURN Solve the equation $\frac{1}{4}m = \frac{1}{12}m - 3$.

ANSWER
The solution is $m = -18$.
The solution set is $\{-18\}$.

Solving a Linear Equation in One Variable

STEP	DESCRIPTION	EXAMPLE
1	Simplify the algebraic expressions on both sides of the equation.	$-3(x-2)+5=7(x-4)-1$ $-3x+6+5=7x-28-1$ $-3x+11=7x-29$
2	Gather all variable terms on one side of the equation and all constant terms on the other side.	$-3x+11=7x-29$ $+3x \qquad +3x$ $11=10x-29$ $+29 \qquad +29$ $40=10x$
3	Isolate the variable.	$10x=40$ $\boxed{x=4}$

[CONCEPT CHECK]

Which one of these is a linear equation in one variable?
(A) $3x + 2 = 11$
(B) $x^2 = 9$
(C) $y = x + 1$

ANSWER (A). Option (B) is nonlinear in one variable, and option (C) is linear in two variables.

0.1.2 Applications Involving Linear Equations

0.1.2 SKILL

Solve application problems involving common formulas.

0.1.2 CONCEPTUAL

Understand the mathematical modeling process.

We now use linear equations to solve problems that occur in our day-to-day lives. You typically will read the problem in words, develop a mathematical model (equation) for the problem, solve the equation, and write the answer in words.

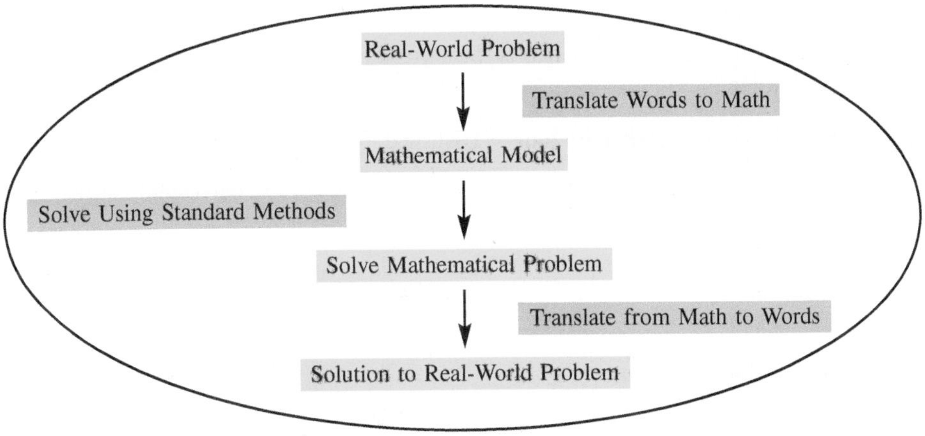

You will have to come up with a unique formula to solve each kind of word problem, but there is a universal *procedure* for approaching all word problems.

PROCEDURE FOR SOLVING WORD PROBLEMS

Step 1: Identify the question. Read the problem *one* time and note what you are asked to find.
Step 2: Make notes. Read until you can note something (an amount, a picture, anything). Continue reading and making notes until you have read the problem a second* time.
Step 3: Assign a variable to whatever is being asked for. If there are two choices, then let it be the smaller of the two.
Step 4: Set up an equation. Assign a variable to represent what you are asked to find.
Step 5: Solve the equation.
Step 6: Check the solution. Substitute the solution for the variable in the equation, and also run the solution past the "common sense department" using estimation.

*Step 2 often requires multiple readings of the problem.

EXAMPLE 4 **How Long Was the Trip?**

During a camping trip in North Bay, Ontario, a couple went one-third of the way by boat, 10 miles by foot, and one-sixth of the way by horse. How long was the trip?

Solution:

STEP 1 **Identify the question.**

How many miles was the trip?

STEP 2 **Make notes.**

Read	Write
... one-third of the way by boat	BOAT: $\frac{1}{3}$ of the trip
... 10 miles by foot	FOOT: 10 miles
... one-sixth of the way by horse	HORSE: $\frac{1}{6}$ of the trip

STEP 3 **Assign a variable.**

Distance of total trip in miles $= x$

STEP 4 **Set up an equation.**

The total distance of the trip is the sum of all the distances by boat, foot, and horse.

Distance by boat + Distance by foot + Distance by horse = Total distance of trip

Distance by boat $= \frac{1}{3}x$

Distance by foot $=$ 10 miles

Distance by horse $= \frac{1}{6}x$

$$\underbrace{\frac{1}{3}x}_{\text{boat}} + \underbrace{10}_{\text{foot}} + \underbrace{\frac{1}{6}x}_{\text{horse}} = \underbrace{x}_{\text{total}}$$

STEP 5 **Solve the equation.**

$$\frac{1}{3}x + 10 + \frac{1}{6}x = x$$

Multiply by the LCD, 6. $\quad 2x + 60 + x = 6x$

Collect x terms on the right. $\quad 60 = 3x$

Divide by 3. $\quad 20 = x$

$x = 20$

The trip was 20 miles.

STEP 6 **Check the solution.**

Estimate: The boating distance, $\frac{1}{3}$ of 20 miles, is approximately 7 miles; the riding distance on horse, $\frac{1}{6}$ of 20 miles, is approximately 3 miles. Adding these two distances to the 10 miles by foot gives a trip distance of 20 miles.

YOUR TURN A family arrives at the Walt Disney World parking lot. To get from their car in the parking lot to the gate at the Magic Kingdom, they walk $\frac{1}{4}$ mile, take a tram for $\frac{1}{3}$ of their total distance, and take a monorail for $\frac{1}{2}$ of their total distance. How far is it from their car to the gate of the Magic Kingdom?

[CONCEPT CHECK]

TRUE OR FALSE In Example 4 we could have stopped at $x = 20$

ANSWER False. A problem that is asked in words "How long was the trip?" needs an answer in words such as "The trip was 20 miles."

ANSWER

The distance from their car to the gate is 1.5 miles.

Geometry Problems

Some problems require geometric formulas in order to be solved.

EXAMPLE 5 Geometry

A rectangle 24 meters long has the same area as a square with 12-meter sides. What are the dimensions of the rectangle?

Solution:

STEP 1 **Identify the question.**

What are the dimensions (length and width) of the rectangle?

STEP 2 **Make notes.**

Read	Write/Draw
A rectangle 24 meters long	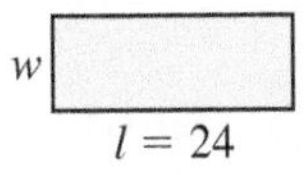
	area of rectangle $= l \cdot w = 24w$
A square with 12-meter sides	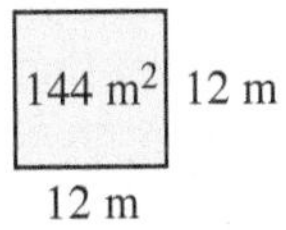
	area of square $= 12 \cdot 12 = 144$

STEP 3 **Assign a variable.** Let w = width of the rectangle.

STEP 4 **Set up an equation.**

The area of the rectangle is equal to the area of the square. rectangle area = square area

Substitute in known quantities. $24w = 144$

STEP 5 **Solve the equation.**

Divide by 24. $w = \frac{144}{24} = 6$

The rectangle is 24 meters long and 6 meters wide.

STEP 6 **Check the solution.**

A 24 meter by 6 meter rectangle has an area of 144 square meters.

YOUR TURN A rectangle 3 inches wide has the same area as a square with 9-inch sides. What are the dimensions of the rectangle?

[CONCEPT CHECK]

If we were to guess an answer to Example 5 what would be our guess?

(A) 24 m by 5 m

(B) 24 m by 20 m

(C) 24 m by 1 m

ANSWER (A). Option (B) cannot be correct because that rectangle would have area much larger than a 12-m square, and (C) cannot be correct because that rectangle would have area much smaller than a 12-m square.

ANSWER

The rectangle is 27 in. long and 3 in. wide.

0.1.3 Interest Problems

In our personal or business financial planning, a particular concern we have is interest. **Interest** is money paid for the use of money; it is the cost of borrowing money. The total amount borrowed is called the **principal**. The principal can be the price of our new car; we pay the bank interest for lending us money to buy the car. The principal can also be the amount we keep in a CD or money market account; the bank uses this money and pays us interest. Typically, interest rate, expressed

0.1.3 SKILL

Solve simple interest problems.

0.1.3 CONCEPTUAL

Use intuition to confirm answers in multiple investment problems.

as a percentage, is the amount charged for the use of the principal for a given time, usually in years.

Simple interest is interest that is paid only on the principal during a period of time. Later we will discuss *compound interest*, which is interest paid on both the principal and the interest accrued over a period of time.

DEFINITION **Simple Interest**

If a principal of P dollars is borrowed for a period of t years at an annual interest rate r (expressed in decimal form), the interest I charged is

$$I = Prt$$

This is the formula for **simple interest**.

EXAMPLE 6 Multiple Investments

Teresa earns a full athletic scholarship for college. Her parents give her the \$20,000 they had saved to pay for her college tuition. She decides to invest that money with an overall goal of earning 11% interest. She wants to put some of the money in a low-risk investment that has been earning 8% a year and the rest of the money in a medium-risk investment that typically earns 12% a year. How much money should she put in each investment to reach her goal?

Solution:

STEP 1 **Identify the question.**
How much money is invested in each (the 8% and the 12%) account?

STEP 2 **Make notes.**

Read

Teresa has \$20,000 to invest.

If part is invested at 8% and the rest at 12%, how much should be invested at each rate to yield 11% on the total amount invested?

Write/Draw

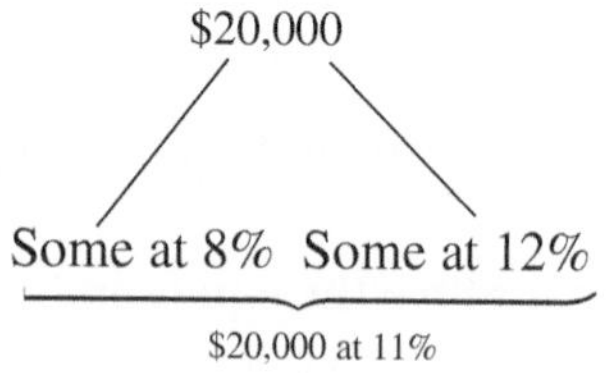

[CONCEPT CHECK]

If Teresa is going to invest in two accounts, one at 8% and one at 12% with a result of an average of 11% earnings, does your intuition tell you she should have (A) more at 8% than at 12% or (B) more at 12% than at 8%?

ANSWER (B) because 11% is closer to 12% than to 8%

STEP 3 **Assign a variable.**
If we let x represent the amount Teresa puts into the 8% investment, how much of the \$20,000 is left for her to put in the 12% investment?

Amount in the 8% investment: x

Amount in the 12% investment: $20{,}000 - x$

STEP 4 **Set up an equation.**

Simple interest formula: $I = Prt$

INVESTMENT	PRINCIPAL	RATE	TIME (YR)	INTEREST
8% Account	x	0.08	1	$0.08x$
12% Account	$20{,}000 - x$	0.12	1	$0.12(20{,}000 - x)$
Total	20,000	0.11	1	$0.11(20{,}000)$

Adding the interest earned in the 8% investment to the interest earned in the 12% investment reveals that she should earn an average of 11% on the total investment.

$$0.08x + 0.12(20{,}000 - x) = 0.11(20{,}000)$$

STEP 5 **Solve the equation.**

Eliminate the parentheses. $0.08x + 2400 - 0.12x = 2200$

Collect x terms on the left, constants on the right. $-0.04x = -200$

Divide by -0.04. $x = \boxed{5000}$

Calculate the amount at 12%. $20{,}000 - 5000 = \boxed{15{,}000}$

Teresa should invest \$5000 at 8% and \$15,000 at 12% to reach her goal.

STEP 6 **Check the solution.**

If money is invested at 8% and 12% with a goal of averaging 11%, our intuition tells us that more should be invested at 12% than 8%, which is what we found. The exact check is as follows:

$$0.08(5000) + 0.12(15{,}000) = 0.11(20{,}000)$$
$$400 + 1800 = 2200$$
$$2200 = 2200$$

YOUR TURN You win \$24,000 and you decide to invest the money in two different investments: one paying 18% and the other paying 12%. A year later you have \$27,480 total. How much did you originally invest in each account?

ANSWER

\$10,000 is invested at 18% and \$14,000 is invested at 12%.

0.1.4 Mixture Problems

0.1.4 SKILL

Solve mixture problems.

0.1.4 CONCEPTUAL

Use intuition to confirm answers to mixture problems.

Mixtures are something we come across every day. Different candies that sell for different prices may make up a movie snack. New blends of coffees are developed by coffee connoisseurs. Chemists mix different concentrations of acids in their labs. Whenever two or more distinct ingredients are combined, the result is a **mixture**.

Our choice at a gas station is typically 87, 89, and 93 octane. The octane number is the number that represents the percentage of iso-octane in fuel. 89 octane is significantly overpriced. Therefore, if your car requires 89 octane, it would be more cost-effective to mix 87 and 93 octane.

EXAMPLE 7 **Mixture Problem**

The manual for your new car suggests using gasoline that is 89 octane. In order to save money, you decide to use some 87 octane and some 93 octane in combination with the 89 octane currently in your tank in order to have an approximate 89 octane mixture. Assuming you have 1 gallon of 89 octane remaining in your tank (your tank capacity is 16 gallons), how many gallons of 87 and how many gallons of 93 octane should be used to fill up your tank to achieve a mixture of 89 octane?

Solution:

STEP 1 **Identify the question.**

How many gallons of 87 octane and how many gallons of 93 octane should be used?

STEP 2 **Make notes.**

Read	Write/Draw
Assuming you have 1 gallon of 89 octane remaining in your tank (your tank capacity is 16 gallons), how many gallons of 87 and of 93 octane should you add?	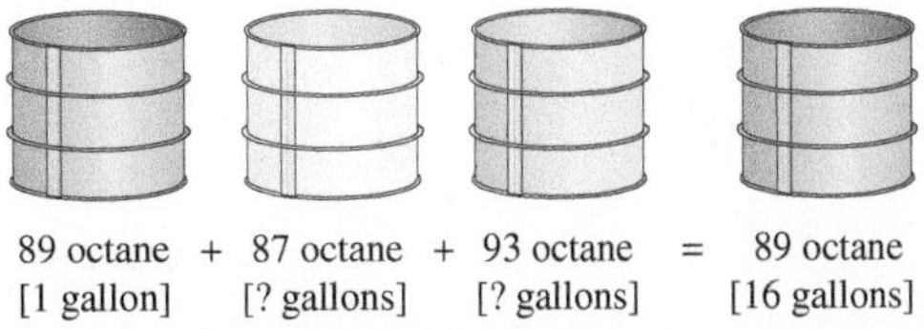

[CONCEPT CHECK]

If a chemistry student has HCl concentrations of 5% and 15% and the desired solution is 11% HCl, which of the following do we expect?

(A) more 15% than 5%

(B) more 5% than 15%

ANSWER (A) because 11% is closer to 15% than to 5%.

STEP 3 **Assign variables.**

$$x = \text{gallons of 87 octane gasoline added at the pump}$$
$$15 - x = \text{gallons of 93 octane gasoline added at the pump}$$
$$1 = \text{gallons of 89 octane gasoline already in the tank}$$

STEP 4 **Set up an equation.**

$$0.89(1) + 0.87x + 0.93(15 - x) = 0.89(16)$$

STEP 5 **Solve the equation.** $0.89(1) + 0.87x + 0.93(15 - x) = 0.89(16)$

Eliminate the parentheses. $0.89 + 0.87x + 13.95 - 0.93x = 14.24$

Collect x terms on the left side. $-0.06x + 14.84 = 14.24$

Subtract 14.84 from both sides of the equation. $-0.06x = -0.6$

Divide both sides by -0.06. $x = 10$

Calculate the amount of 93 octane. $15 - 10 = 5$

Add 10 gallons of 87 octane and 5 gallons of 93 octane.

STEP 6 **Check the solution.**

Estimate: Our intuition tells us that if the desired mixture is 89 octane, then we should add approximately 1 part 93 octane and 2 parts 87 octane. The solution we found, 10 gallons of 87 octane and 5 gallons of 93 octane, agrees with this.

YOUR TURN For a certain experiment, a student requires 100 ml of a solution that is 11% HCl (hydrochloric acid). The storeroom has only solutions that are 5% HCl and 15% HCl. How many milliliters of each available solution should be mixed to get 100 ml of 11% HCl?

ANSWER
40 ml of 5% HCl and
60 ml of 15% HCl

0.1.5 Distance–Rate–Time Problems

0.1.5 SKILL

Solve distance–rate–time problems.

0.1.5 CONCEPTUAL

Estimate distance–rate–time problem solutions prior to solving, and then confirm with a check.

The next example deals with distance, rate, and time. On a road trip, you see a sign that says your destination is 90 miles away, and your speedometer reads 60 miles per hour. Dividing 90 miles by 60 miles per hour tells you that if you continue at this speed, your arrival will be in 1.5 hours. Here is how you know.

If the rate, or speed, is assumed to be constant, then the equation that relates distance (d), rate (r), and time (t) is $d = r \cdot t$. In the above driving example,

$$d = 90 \text{ miles} \qquad r = 60\,\frac{\text{miles}}{\text{hour}}$$

Substituting these into $d = r \cdot t$, we arrive at

$$90 \text{ miles} = \left[60\,\frac{\text{miles}}{\text{hour}}\right] \cdot t$$

Solving for t, we get

$$t = \frac{90 \text{ miles}}{60\,\frac{\text{miles}}{\text{hour}}} = 1.5 \text{ hours}$$

EXAMPLE 8 Distance–Rate–Time

It takes 8 hours to fly from Orlando to London and 9.5 hours to return. If an airplane averages 550 miles per hour (mph) in still air, what is the average rate of the wind blowing in the direction from Orlando to London? Assume the wind speed is constant for both legs of the trip. Round your answer to the nearest mph.

Solution:

STEP 1 **Identify the question.**

At what rate in miles per hour is the wind blowing?

STEP 2 **Make notes.**

Read

It takes 8 hours to fly from Orlando to London and 9.5 hours to return.

If the airplane averages 550 mph in still air ...

Write/Draw

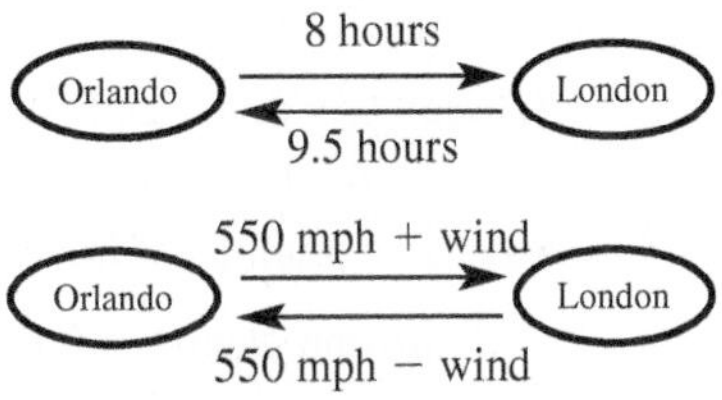

STEP 3 **Assign a variable.** w = wind speed

STEP 4 **Set up an equation.**

The formula relating distance, rate, and time is $d = r \cdot t$. The distance d of each flight is the same. On the Orlando to London flight, the time is 8 hours due to an increased speed from a tailwind. On the London to Orlando flight, the time is 9.5 hours and the speed is decreased due to the headwind.

Orlando to London: $d = (550 + w)8$

London to Orlando: $d = (550 - w)9.5$

These distances are the same, so set them equal to each other:

$$(550 + w)8 = (550 - w)9.5$$

STEP 5 **Solve the equation.**

Eliminate the parentheses. $4400 + 8w = 5225 - 9.5w$

Collect w terms on the left, constants on the right. $17.5w = 825$

Divide by 17.5. $w = 47.1429 \approx 47$

The wind is blowing approximately $\boxed{\text{47 mph}}$ in the direction from Orlando to London.

STEP 6 **Check the solution.**

Estimate: Going from Orlando to London, the tailwind is approximately 50 mph, which when added to the plane's 550 mph speed yields a ground speed of 600 mph. The Orlando to London route took 8 hours. The distance of that flight is (600 mph) (8 hr), which is 4800 miles. The return trip experienced a headwind of approximately 50 mph, so subtracting the 50 from 550 gives an average speed of 500 mph. That route took 9.5 hours, so the distance of the London to Orlando flight was (500 mph)(9.5 hr), which is 4750 miles. Note that the estimates of 4800 and 4750 miles are close together.

YOUR TURN A Cessna 150 averages 150 mph in still air. With a tailwind it is able to make a trip in $2\frac{1}{3}$ hours. Because of the headwind, it is only able to make the return trip in $3\frac{1}{2}$ hours. What is the average wind speed?

ANSWER

The wind is blowing 30 mph.

EXAMPLE 9 Work

Connie can clean her house in 2 hours. If Alvaro helps her, together they can clean the house in 1 hour and 15 minutes. How long would it take Alvaro to clean the house by himself?

Solution:

STEP 1 **Identify the question.**

How long does it take Alvaro to clean the house?

STEP 2 **Make notes.**

- Connie can clean her house in 2 hours, so Connie can clean $\frac{1}{2}$ of the house per hour.
- Together Connie and Alvaro can clean the house in 1 hour and 15 minutes, or $\frac{5}{4}$ of an hour. Therefore together, they can clean $\frac{1}{5/4} = \frac{4}{5}$ of the house per hour.
- Let x = number of hours it takes Alvaro to clean the house by himself. So Alvaro can clean $\frac{1}{x}$ of the house per hour.

	AMOUNT OF TIME TO DO ONE JOB	AMOUNT OF JOB DONE PER UNIT OF TIME
Connie	2	$\frac{1}{2}$
Alvaro	x	$\frac{1}{x}$
Together	$\frac{5}{4}$	$\frac{4}{5}$

STEP 3 **Set up an equation.**

$$\underbrace{\frac{1}{2}}_{\text{Amount of house Connie can clean per hour}} + \underbrace{\frac{1}{x}}_{\text{Amount of house Alvaro can clean per hour}} = \underbrace{\frac{4}{5}}_{\text{Amount of house they can clean per hour if they work together}}$$

STEP 4 **Solve the equation.**

Multiply by the LCD, $10x$. $\quad 5x + 10 = 8x$

Solve for x. $\quad x = \frac{10}{3} = 3\frac{1}{3}$

It takes Alvaro $\boxed{\text{3 hours and 20 minutes}}$ to clean the house by himself.

STEP 5 **Check the solution.**

Estimate: Since Connie can clean the house in 2 hours, and together with Alvaro it takes 1.25 hours, we know it takes Alvaro longer than 2 hours to clean the house himself.

[CONCEPT CHECK]

If Connie cleans her house alone it takes 2 hours, and if Alvaro helps her it takes 1 hour and 15 minutes. Which of the following is true?
(A) Alvaro cleans faster than Connie.
(B) Alvaro and Connie clean at the same rate.
(C) Alvaro cleans slower than Connie.

ANSWER (C). (B) cannot be true or it would take them exactly one hour if they were working together. (A) cannot be true or the combined time would be less than one hour.

[SECTION 0.1] SUMMARY

To solve a linear equation:

1. Simplify the algebraic expressions on both sides of the equation.
2. Gather all variable terms on one side of the equation and all constant terms on the other side.
3. Isolate the variable.

In the real world, many kinds of application problems can be solved through modeling with linear equations. Some problems require the development of a mathematical model, while others rely on common formulas. The following procedure will guide you:

1. Identify the question.
2. Make notes.
3. Assign a variable.
4. Set up an equation.
5. Solve the equation.
6. Check the solution against your intuition.

[SECTION 0.1] EXERCISES

• SKILLS

In Exercises 1–26, solve for the indicated variable.

1. $9m - 7 = 11$
2. $2x + 4 = 5$
3. $5t + 11 = 18$
4. $7x + 4 = 21 + 24x$
5. $3x - 5 = 25 + 6x$
6. $5x + 10 = 25 + 2x$
7. $20n - 30 = 20 - 5n$
8. $14c + 15 = 43 + 7c$
9. $4(x - 3) = 2(x + 6)$
10. $5(2y - 1) = 2(4y - 3)$
11. $-3(4t - 5) = 5(6 - 2t)$
12. $2(3n + 4) = -(n + 2)$
13. $2(x - 1) + 3 = x - 3(x + 1)$
14. $4(y + 6) - 8 = 2y - 4(y + 2)$
15. $5p + 6(p + 7) = 3(p + 2)$
16. $3(z + 5) - 5 = 4z + 7(z - 2)$
17. $7x - (2x + 3) = x - 2$
18. $3x - (4x + 2) = x - 5$
19. $2 - (4x + 1) = 3 - (2x - 1)$
20. $5 - (2x - 3) = 7 - (3x + 5)$
21. $2a - 9(a + 6) = 6(a + 3) - 4a$
22. $25 - [2 + 5y - 3(y + 2)] = -3(2y - 5) - [5(y - 1) - 3y + 3]$
23. $32 - [4 + 6x - 5(x + 4)] = 4(3x + 4) - [6(3x - 4) + 7 - 4x]$
24. $12 - [3 + 4m - 6(3m - 2)] = -7(2m - 8) - 3[(m - 2) + 3m - 5]$
25. $20 - 4[c - 3 - 6(2c + 3)] = 5(3c - 2) - [2(7c - 8) - 4c + 7]$
26. $46 - [7 - 8y + 9(6y - 2)] = -7(4y - 7) - 2[6(2y - 3) - 4 + 6y]$

Exercises 27–38 involve fractions. Clear the fractions by first multiplying by the least common denominator, and then solve the resulting linear equation.

27. $\frac{1}{5}m = \frac{1}{60}m + 1$
28. $\frac{1}{12}z = \frac{1}{24}z + 3$
29. $\frac{x}{7} = \frac{2x}{63} + 4$
30. $\frac{a}{11} = \frac{a}{22} + 9$
31. $\frac{1}{3}p = 3 - \frac{1}{24}p$
32. $\frac{3x}{5} - x = \frac{x}{10} - \frac{5}{2}$
33. $\frac{5y}{3} - 2y = \frac{2y}{84} + \frac{5}{7}$
34. $2m - \frac{5m}{8} = \frac{3m}{72} + \frac{4}{3}$
35. $p + \frac{p}{4} = \frac{5}{2}$
36. $\frac{c}{4} - 2c = \frac{5}{4} - \frac{c}{2}$
37. $\frac{x - 3}{3} - \frac{x - 4}{2} = 1 - \frac{x - 6}{6}$
38. $1 - \frac{x - 5}{3} = \frac{x + 2}{5} - \frac{6x - 1}{15}$

• APPLICATIONS

39. **Puzzle.** Angela is on her way from home in Jersey City to New York City for dinner. She walks 1 mile to the train station, takes the train $\frac{3}{4}$ of the way, and takes a taxi $\frac{1}{6}$ of the way to the restaurant. How far does Angela live from the restaurant?

40. **Puzzle.** An employee at Kennedy Space Center (KSC) lives in Daytona Beach and works in the vehicle assembly building (VAB). She carpools to work with a colleague. On the days that her colleague drives the car pool, she drives 7 miles to the park-and-ride, continues with her colleague to the KSC headquarters building, and then takes the KSC shuttle from the headquarters building to the VAB. The drive from the park-and-ride to the headquarters building is $\frac{5}{6}$ of her total trip and the shuttle ride is $\frac{1}{20}$ of her total trip. How many miles does she travel from her house to the VAB on days when her colleague drives?

41. **Budget.** A company has a total of \$20,000 allocated for monthly costs. Fixed costs are \$15,000 per month and variable costs are \$18.50 per unit. How many units can be manufactured in a month?

42. **Budget.** A woman decides to start a small business making monogrammed cocktail napkins. She can set aside \$1870 for monthly costs. Fixed costs are \$1329.50 per month and variable costs are \$3.70 per set of napkins. How many sets of napkins can she afford to make per month?

43. **Geometry.** Consider two circles, a smaller one and a larger one. If the larger one has a radius that is 3 feet larger than that of the smaller circle and the ratio of the circumferences is 2:1, what are the radii of the two circles?

44. **Geometry.** The length of a rectangle is 2 more than 3 times the width, and the perimeter is 28 inches. What are the dimensions of the rectangle?

45. **Biology: Alligators.** It is common to see alligators in ponds, lakes, and rivers in Florida. The ratio of head size (back of the head to the end of the snout) to the full body length of an alligator is typically constant. If a $3\frac{1}{2}$-foot alligator has a head length of 6 inches, how long would you expect an alligator to be whose head length is 9 inches?

46. **Biology: Snakes.** In the African rainforest there is a snake called a Gaboon viper. The fang size of this snake is proportional to the length of the snake. A 3-foot snake typically has 2-inch fangs. If a herpetologist finds Gaboon viper fangs that are 2.6 inches long, what was the length of the snake they came from?

47. **Investing.** Ashley has \$120,000 to invest and decides to put some in a CD that earns 4% interest per year and the rest in a low-risk stock that earns 7%. How much did she invest in each to earn \$7800 interest in the first year?

48. **Investing.** You inherit \$13,000 and you decide to invest the money in two different investments: one paying 10% and the other paying 14%. A year later your investments are worth \$14,580. How much did you originally invest in each account?

49. **Investing.** Wendy was awarded a volleyball scholarship to the University of Michigan, so on graduation her parents gave her the \$14,000 they had saved for her college tuition. She opted to invest some money in a privately held company that pays 10% per year and to evenly split the remaining money between a money market account yielding 2% and a high-risk stock that yielded 40%. At the end of the first year she had \$16,610 total. How much did she invest in each of the three?

50. **Interest.** A high school student was able to save \$5000 by working a part-time job every summer. He invested half the money in a money market account and half the money in a stock that paid three times as much interest as the money market account. After a year he earned \$150 in interest. What were the interest rates of the money market account and the stock?

51. **Chemistry.** For a certain experiment, a student requires 100 ml of a solution that is 8% HCl (hydrochloric acid). The storeroom has only solutions that are 5% HCl and 15% HCl. How many milliliters of each available solution should be mixed to get 100 ml of 8% HCl?

52. **Chemistry.** How many gallons of pure alcohol must be mixed with 5 gallons of a solution that is 20% alcohol to make a solution that is 50% alcohol?

53. **Communications.** The speed of light is approximately 3.0×10^8 meters per second (670,616,629 miles per hour). The distance from Earth to Mars varies because their orbits around the Sun are independent. On average, Mars is 100 million miles from Earth. If we use laser communication systems, what will be the delay between Houston and NASA astronauts on Mars?

54. **Speed of Sound.** The speed of sound is approximately 760 miles per hour in air. If a gun is fired $\frac{1}{2}$ mile away, how long will it take the sound to reach you?

55. **Medicine.** A patient requires an IV of 0.9% saline solution, also known as normal saline solution. How much distilled water, to the nearest milliliter, must be added to 100 milliliters of a 3% saline solution to produce normal saline?

56. **Medicine.** A patient requires an IV of D5W, a 5% solution of dextrose (sugar) in water. To the nearest milliliter, how much D20W, a 20% solution of dextrose in water, must be added to 100 milliliters of distilled water to produce a D5W solution?

57. **Boating.** A motorboat can maintain a constant speed of 16 miles per hour relative to the water. The boat makes a trip upstream to a marina in 20 minutes. The return trip takes 15 minutes. What is the speed of the current?

58. **Aviation.** A Cessna 175 can average 130 miles per hour. If a trip takes 2 hours one way and the return takes 1 hour and 15 minutes, find the wind speed, assuming it is constant.

59. **Distance–Rate–Time.** A jogger and a walker cover the same distance. The jogger finishes in 40 minutes. The walker takes an hour. How fast is each exerciser moving if the jogger moves 2 miles per hour faster than the walker?

60. **Distance–Rate–Time.** A high school student in Seattle, Washington, attended the University of Central Florida. On the way to UCF he took a southern route. After graduation he returned to Seattle via a northern trip. On both trips he had the same average speed. If the southern trek took 45 hours and the northern trek took 50 hours, and the northern trek was 300 miles longer, how long was each trip?

61. **Distance–Rate–Time.** College roommates leave for their first class in the same building. One walks at 2 miles per hour and the other rides his bike at a slow 6 miles per hour pace. How long will it take each to get to class if the walker takes 12 minutes longer to get to class and they travel on the same path?

62. **Distance–Rate–Time.** A long-distance delivery service sends out a truck with a package at 7 A.M. At 7:30 the manager realizes there was another package going to the same location. He sends out a car to catch the truck. If the truck travels at an average speed of 50 miles per hour and the car travels at 70 miles per hour, how long will it take the car to catch the truck?

63. **Work.** Christopher can paint the interior of his house in 15 hours. If he hires Cynthia to help him, together they can do the same job in 9 hours. If he lets Cynthia work alone, how long will it take her to paint the interior of his house?

64. **Work.** Jay and Morgan work in the summer for a landscaper. It takes Jay 3 hours to complete the company's largest yard alone. If Morgan helps him, it takes only 1 hour. How much time would it take Morgan alone?

65. **Work.** Tracey and Robin deliver soft drinks to local convenience stores. Tracey can complete the deliveries in 4 hours alone. Robin can do it in 6 hours alone. If they decide to work together on a Saturday, how long will it take?

66. **Work.** Joshua can deliver his newspapers in 30 minutes. It takes Amber 20 minutes to do the same route. How long would it take them to deliver the newspapers if they worked together?

67. **Sports.** In Super Bowl XXXVII, the Tampa Bay Buccaneers scored a total of 48 points. All of their points came from field goals and touchdowns. Field goals are worth 3 points and each touchdown was worth 7 points (Martin Gramatica was successful in every extra-point attempt). They scored a total of 8 times. How many field goals and touchdowns were scored?

68. **Sports.** A tight end can run the 100-yard dash in 12 seconds. A defensive back can do it in 10 seconds. The tight end catches a pass at his own 20 yard line with the defensive back at the 15 yard line. If no other players are nearby, at what yard line will the defensive back catch up to the tight end?

69. **Recreation.** How do two children of different weights balance on a seesaw? The heavier child sits closer to the center and the lighter child sits farther away. When the products of the weight of the child and the distance from the center are the same on both sides, the seesaw should be horizontal to the ground. Suppose Max weighs 42 pounds and Maria weighs 60 pounds. If Max sits 5 feet from the center, how far should Maria sit from the center in order to balance the seesaw horizontal to the ground?

70. **Recreation.** Refer to Exercise 69. Suppose Martin, who weighs 33 pounds, sits on the side of the seesaw with Max. If their average distance to the center is 4 feet, how far should Maria sit from the center in order to balance the seesaw horizontal to the ground?

• CATCH THE MISTAKE

In Exercises 71 and 72, explain the mistake that is made.

71. Solve the equation $4x + 3 = 6x - 7$.

Solution:

Subtract $4x$ and add 7 to the equation. $\quad 3 = 6x$

Divide by 3. $\quad x = 2$

This is incorrect. What mistake was made?

72. Solve the equation $3(x + 1) + 2 = x - 3(x - 1)$.

Solution:

$$3x + 3 + 2 = x - 3x - 3$$
$$3x + 5 = -2x - 3$$
$$5x = -8$$
$$x = -\frac{8}{5}$$

This is incorrect. What mistake was made?

• CONCEPTUAL

73. Solve for x, given that a, b, and c are real numbers and $a \neq 0$:

$$ax + b = c$$

74. Find the number a for which $y = 2$ is a solution of the equation $y - a = y + 5 - 3ay$.

In Exercises 75–82, solve each formula for the specified variable.

75. $P = 2l + 2w$ for w

76. $P = 2l + 2w$ for l

77. $A = \frac{1}{2}bh$ for h

78. $C = 2\pi r$ for r

79. $A = lw$ for w

80. $d = rt$ for t

81. $V = lwh$ for h

82. $V = \pi r^2 h$ for h

• CHALLENGE

83. Tricia and Janine are roommates and leave Houston on Interstate 10 at the same time to visit their families for a long weekend. Tricia travels west and Janine travels east. If Tricia's average speed is 12 miles per hour faster than Janine's, find the speed of each if they are 320 miles apart in 2 hours and 30 minutes.

84. Rick and Mike are roommates and leave Gainesville on Interstate 75 at the same time to visit their girlfriends for a long weekend. Rick travels north and Mike travels south. If Mike's average speed is 8 miles per hour faster than Rick's, find the speed of each if they are 210 miles apart in 1 hour and 30 minutes.

0.2 QUADRATIC EQUATIONS

SKILLS OBJECTIVES

- Solve quadratic equations by factoring.
- Use the square root method to solve quadratic equations.
- Solve quadratic equations by completing the square.
- Use the quadratic formula to solve quadratic equations.
- Solve application problems using quadratic equations.

CONCEPTUAL OBJECTIVES

- Understand the zero product property in factoring.
- Understand that the square root method can be used only when there is no linear term in the quadratic equation.
- Understand that completing the square transforms a standard quadratic equation into a perfect square.
- Derive the quadratic formula.
- Understand why it is necessary to eliminate nonphysical answers.

0.2.1 Factoring

0.2.1 SKILL

Solve quadratic equations by factoring.

0.2.1 CONCEPTUAL

Understand the zero product property in factoring.

STUDY TIP

In a quadratic equation the variable is raised to the power of 2, which is the highest power present in the equation.

In a linear equation, the variable is raised only to the first power in any term where it occurs. In a *quadratic equation*, the variable is raised to the second power in at least one term. Examples of *quadratic equations*, also called second-degree equations, are

$$x^2 + 3 = 7 \qquad 5x^2 + 4x - 7 = 0 \qquad x^2 - 3 = 0$$

DEFINITION Quadratic Equation

A **quadratic equation** in x is an equation that can be written in the **standard form**

$$ax^2 + bx + c = 0$$

where a, b, and c are real numbers and $a \neq 0$.

There are several methods for solving quadratic equations: *factoring*, the *square root method*, *completing the square*, and the *quadratic formula*.

FACTORING METHOD

The **factoring method** applies the **zero product property**:

WORDS	MATH
If a product is zero, then at least one of its factors has to be zero.	If $B \cdot C = 0$, then $B = 0$ or $C = 0$ or both.

Consider $(x - 3)(x + 2) = 0$. The zero product property says that $x - 3 = 0$ or $x + 2 = 0$, which leads to $x = -2$ or $x = 3$. The solution set is $\{-2, 3\}$.

When a quadratic equation is written in the standard form $ax^2 + bx + c = 0$, it may be possible to factor the left side of the equation as a product of two first-degree polynomials. We use the zero product property and set each linear factor equal to zero. We solve the resulting two linear equations to obtain the solutions of the quadratic equation.

EXAMPLE 1 Solving a Quadratic Equation by Factoring

Solve the equation $x^2 - 6x - 16 = 0$.

Solution:

The quadratic equation is already in standard form. $x^2 - 6x - 16 = 0$

Factor the left side into a product of two linear factors. $(x - 8)(x + 2) = 0$

If a product equals zero, one of its factors has to be equal to zero. $x - 8 = 0$ or $x + 2 = 0$

Solve both linear equations. $\boxed{x = 8 \text{ or } x = -2}$

The solution set is $\boxed{\{-2, 8\}}$.

YOUR TURN Solve the quadratic equation $x^2 + x - 20 = 0$ by factoring.

ANSWER

The solution is $x = -5, 4$.
The solution set is $\{-5, 4\}$.

EXAMPLE 2 Solving a Quadratic Equation by Factoring

Solve the equation $2x^2 = 3x$.

common mistake

The common mistake here is dividing both sides by x, which is not allowed because x might be 0.

✓CORRECT

Write the equation in standard form by subtracting $3x$.

$$2x^2 - 3x = 0$$

Factor the left side.

$$x(2x - 3) = 0$$

Use the zero product property and set each factor equal to zero.

$$x = 0 \text{ or } 2x - 3 = 0$$

Solve each linear equation.

$$\boxed{x = 0 \text{ or } x = \frac{3}{2}}$$

The solution set is $\boxed{\left\{0, \frac{3}{2}\right\}}$.

✗INCORRECT

Write the original equation.

$$2x^2 = 3x$$

The **error** occurs here when both sides are divided by x.

$$2x = 3$$

CAUTION

Do not divide by a variable (because the value of that variable may be zero). Bring all terms to one side first and then factor.

[CONCEPT CHECK]

If something times something is equal to zero, then ______ must be zero.
(A) one of those somethings
(B) both of those somethings

ANSWER (A) one of those somethings

In Example 2, the root $x = 0$ is lost when the original quadratic equation is divided by x. Remember to put the equation in standard form first and then factor.

0.2.2 Square Root Method

0.2.2 SKILL

Use the square root method to solve quadratic equations.

0.2.2 CONCEPTUAL

Understand that the square root method can be used only when there is no linear term in the quadratic equation.

The square root of 16, $\sqrt{16}$, is 4, *not* ± 4. In the Appendix, the **principal square root** is discussed. The solutions to $x^2 = 16$, however, are $x = -4$ and $x = 4$. Let us now investigate quadratic equations that do not have a first-degree term. They have the form

$$ax^2 + c = 0 \quad a \neq 0$$

The method we use to solve such equations employs the square root property.

SQUARE ROOT PROPERTY

WORDS	MATH
If an expression squared is equal to a constant, then that expression is equal to the positive or negative square root of the constant.	If $x^2 = P$, then $x = \pm\sqrt{P}$.

Note: The variable squared must be isolated first (coefficient equal to 1).

EXAMPLE 3 Using the Square Root Property

Solve the equation $3x^2 - 27 = 0$.

Solution:

Add 27 to both sides. $3x^2 = 27$

Divide both sides by 3. $x^2 = 9$

Apply the square root property. $x = \pm\sqrt{9} = \pm 3$

The solution set is $\boxed{\{-3, 3\}}$.

[CONCEPT CHECK]

Which of the following can be solved using the square root method?
(A) $x^2 = x$
(B) $x^2 = 9$

ANSWER (B). $x^2 = 9$ can be solved by the square root method because it is in the form of $x^2 =$ constant. (A) cannot be solved using the square root method.

If we alter Example 3 by changing subtraction to addition, we see in Example 4 that we get imaginary roots, as opposed to real roots; which is reviewed in the Appendix.

EXAMPLE 4 Using the Square Root Property

Solve the equation $3x^2 + 27 = 0$.

Solution:

Subtract 27 from both sides. $3x^2 = -27$

Divide by 3. $x^2 = -9$

Apply the square root property. $x = \pm\sqrt{-9}$

Simplify. $x = \pm i\sqrt{9} = \pm 3i$

The solution set is $\boxed{\{-3i, 3i\}}$.

YOUR TURN Solve the equations:

a. $y^2 - 147 = 0$ **b.** $v^2 + 64 = 0$

ANSWER

a. The solution is $y = \pm 7\sqrt{3}$. The solution set is $\{-7\sqrt{3}, 7\sqrt{3}\}$.

b. The solution is $v = \pm 8i$. The solution set is $\{-8i, 8i\}$.

EXAMPLE 5 **Using the Square Root Property**

Solve the equation $(x - 2)^2 = 16$.

Solution:

Approach 1: If an expression squared is 16, then the expression equals $\pm\sqrt{16}$. $\quad (x - 2) = \pm\sqrt{16}$

Separate into two equations. $\quad x - 2 = \sqrt{16}$ or $x - 2 = -\sqrt{16}$

$x - 2 = 4 \qquad x - 2 = -4$

$x = 6 \qquad x = -2$

The solution set is $\boxed{\{-2, 6\}}$.

Approach 2: It is acceptable notation to keep the equations together.

$$(x - 2) = \pm\sqrt{16}$$
$$x - 2 = \pm 4$$
$$x = 2 \pm 4$$
$$\boxed{x = -2, 6}$$

0.2.3 Completing the Square

Factoring and the square root method are two efficient, quick procedures for solving many quadratic equations. However, some equations, such as $x^2 - 10x - 3 = 0$, cannot be solved directly by these methods. A more general procedure to solve this kind of equation is called **completing the square**. The idea behind completing the square is to transform any standard quadratic equation $ax^2 + bx + c = 0$ into the form $(x + A)^2 = B$, where A and B are constants, and the left side, $(x + A)^2$, has the form of a **perfect square**. This last equation can then be solved by the square root method. How do we transform the first equation into the second equation?

Note that the above-mentioned example, $x^2 - 10x - 3 = 0$, cannot be factored into expressions in which all numbers are integers (or even rational numbers). We can, however, transform this quadratic equation into a form that contains a perfect square.

0.2.3 SKILL

Solve quadratic equations by completing the square.

0.2.3 CONCEPTUAL

Understand that completing the square transforms a standard quadratic equation into a perfect square.

WORDS	MATH
Write the original equation.	$x^2 - 10x - 3 = 0$
Add 3 to both sides.	$x^2 - 10x = 3$
Add 25 to both sides.*	$x^2 - 10x + 25 = 3 + 25$
The left side can be written as a perfect square.	$(x - 5)^2 = 28$
Apply the square root method.	$x - 5 = \pm\sqrt{28}$
Add 5 to both sides.	$x = 5 \pm 2\sqrt{7}$

*Why did we add 25 to both sides? Recall that $(x - c)^2 = x^2 - 2xc + c^2$. In this case $c = 5$ in order for $-2xc = -10x$. Therefore, the desired perfect square $(x - 5)^2$ results in $x^2 - 10x + 25$. Applying this product, we see that $+25$ is needed.

[CONCEPT CHECK]

The quadratic equation $x^2 - 4x + 3 = 0$ can be transformed into which perfect square?

(A) $(x + 2)^2 = 1$

(B) $(x - 2)^2 = 1$

ANSWER (B). (A), when expanded, is $x^2 + 4x + 3 = 0$.

If the coefficient of x^2 is 1, a systematic approach is to take the coefficient of the first-degree term of $x^2 - 10x - 3 = 0$, which is -10. Divide -10 by 2 to get -5; then square -5 to get 25.

SOLVING A QUADRATIC EQUATION BY COMPLETING THE SQUARE

WORDS	MATH
Express the quadratic equation in the following form.	$x^2 + bx = c$
Divide b by 2 and square the result, then add the square to both sides.	$x^2 + bx + \left(\frac{b}{2}\right)^2 = c + \left(\frac{b}{2}\right)^2$
Write the left side of the equation as a perfect square.	$\left(x + \frac{b}{2}\right)^2 = c + \left(\frac{b}{2}\right)^2$
Solve using the square root method.	

EXAMPLE 6 Completing the Square

Solve the quadratic equation $x^2 + 8x - 3 = 0$ by completing the square.

Solution:

Add 3 to both sides.	$x^2 + 8x = 3$
Add $\left(\frac{1}{2}\cdot 8\right)^2 = 4^2$ to both sides.	$x^2 + 8x + 4^2 = 3 + 4^2$
Write the left side as a perfect square and simplify the right side.	$(x + 4)^2 = 19$
Apply the square root method to solve.	$x + 4 = \pm\sqrt{19}$
Subtract 4 from both sides.	$\boxed{x = -4 \pm \sqrt{19}}$

The solution set is $\boxed{\{-4 - \sqrt{19}, -4 + \sqrt{19}\}}$.

STUDY TIP

When the leading coefficient is not 1, start by first dividing the equation by that leading coefficient.

In Example 6, the leading coefficient (the coefficient of the x^2 term) is 1. When the leading coefficient is not 1, start by first dividing the equation by that leading coefficient.

EXAMPLE 7 Completing the Square When the Leading Coefficient Is Not Equal to 1

Solve the equation $3x^2 - 12x + 13 = 0$ by completing the square.

Solution:

Divide by the leading coefficient, 3. $x^2 - 4x + \frac{13}{3} = 0$

Collect the variables on one side of the equation and constants on the other side. $x^2 - 4x = -\frac{13}{3}$

Add $\left(-\frac{4}{2}\right)^2 = 4$ to both sides. $x^2 - 4x + 4 = -\frac{13}{3} + 4$

Write the left side of the equation as a perfect square and simplify the right side. $(x - 2)^2 = -\frac{1}{3}$

Solve using the square root method. $x - 2 = \pm\sqrt{-\frac{1}{3}}$

Simplify. $x = 2 \pm i\sqrt{\frac{1}{3}}$

Rationalize the denominator (Appendix). $x = 2 \pm \frac{i}{\sqrt{3}} \cdot \frac{\sqrt{3}}{\sqrt{3}}$

Simplify. $x = 2 \pm \frac{i\sqrt{3}}{3}$

$$\boxed{x = 2 - \frac{i\sqrt{3}}{3},\ x = 2 + \frac{i\sqrt{3}}{3}}$$

The solution set is $\boxed{\left\{2 - \frac{i\sqrt{3}}{3}, 2 + \frac{i\sqrt{3}}{3}\right\}}$.

YOUR TURN Solve the equation $2x^2 - 4x + 3 = 0$ by completing the square.

ANSWER

The solution is $x = 1 \pm \frac{i\sqrt{2}}{2}$.

The solution set is

$\left\{1 - \frac{i\sqrt{2}}{2}, 1 + \frac{i\sqrt{2}}{2}\right\}$.

0.2.4 The Quadratic Formula

0.2.4 SKILL

Use the quadratic formula to solve quadratic equations.

0.2.4 CONCEPTUAL

Derive the quadratic formula.

Let us now consider the most general quadratic equation:

$$ax^2 + bx + c = 0 \qquad a \neq 0$$

We can solve this equation by completing the square.

WORDS	MATH
Divide the equation by the leading coefficient a.	$x^2 + \frac{b}{a}x + \frac{c}{a} = 0$
Subtract $\frac{c}{a}$ from both sides.	$x^2 + \frac{b}{a}x = -\frac{c}{a}$
Square half of $\frac{b}{a}$ and add the result $\left(\frac{b}{2a}\right)^2$ to both sides.	$x^2 + \frac{b}{a}x + \left(\frac{b}{2a}\right)^2 = \left(\frac{b}{2a}\right)^2 - \frac{c}{a}$
Write the left side of the equation as a perfect square and the right side as a single fraction.	$\left(x + \frac{b}{2a}\right)^2 = \frac{b^2 - 4ac}{4a^2}$
Solve using the square root method.	$x + \frac{b}{2a} = \pm\sqrt{\frac{b^2 - 4ac}{4a^2}}$
Subtract $\frac{b}{2a}$ from both sides and simplify the radical.	$x = -\frac{b}{2a} \pm \frac{\sqrt{b^2 - 4ac}}{2a}$
Write as a single fraction.	$x = \frac{-b \pm \sqrt{b^2 - 4ac}}{2a}$

We have derived the **quadratic formula**.

[CONCEPT CHECK]

TRUE OR FALSE Completing the square is still necessary in certain cases when the quadratic formula cannot be used to solve a particular quadratic equation.

ANSWER False. The quadratic formula was derived by solving the general quadratic equation by completing the square.

STUDY TIP

$$x = \frac{-b \pm \sqrt{b^2 - 4ac}}{2a}$$

Read as "negative b plus or minus the square root of the quantity b squared minus $4ac$ all over $2a$."

THE QUADRATIC FORMULA

If $ax^2 + bx + c = 0$, $a \neq 0$, then the solution is

$$x = \frac{-b \pm \sqrt{b^2 - 4ac}}{2a}$$

Note: The quadratic equation must be in standard form $(ax^2 + bx + c = 0)$ in order to identify the parameters:

a: coefficient of x^2 $\quad b$: coefficient of x $\quad c$: constant

STUDY TIP

The quadratic formula works for *any* quadratic equation.

We read this formula as *negative b plus or minus the square root of the quantity b squared minus 4ac all over 2a.* It is important to note that negative b can be positive (if b is negative). For this reason, an alternative form is "opposite b. . . ." The quadratic formula should be memorized and used when simpler methods (factoring and the square root method) cannot be used. The quadratic formula works for *any* quadratic equation.

EXAMPLE 8 **Using the Quadratic Formula and Finding Two Distinct Real Roots**

Use the quadratic formula to solve the quadratic equation $x^2 - 4x - 1 = 0$.

Solution:

For this problem, $a = 1$, $b = -4$, and $c = -1$.

Write the quadratic formula. $$x = \frac{-b \pm \sqrt{b^2 - 4ac}}{2a}$$

Use parentheses to avoid losing a minus sign. $$x = \frac{-(\square) \pm \sqrt{(\square)^2 - 4(\square)(\square)}}{2(\square)}$$

Substitute values for a, b, and c into the parentheses. $$x = \frac{-(-4) \pm \sqrt{(-4)^2 - 4(1)(-1)}}{2(1)}$$

Simplify. $$x = \frac{4 \pm \sqrt{16 + 4}}{2} = \frac{4 \pm \sqrt{20}}{2} = \frac{4 \pm 2\sqrt{5}}{2} = \frac{4}{2} \pm \frac{2\sqrt{5}}{2} = \boxed{2 \pm \sqrt{5}}$$

The solution set $\boxed{\{2 - \sqrt{5}, 2 + \sqrt{5}\}}$ contains two distinct real numbers.

YOUR TURN Use the quadratic formula to solve the quadratic equation $x^2 + 6x - 2 = 0$.

STUDY TIP

Using parentheses as placeholders helps avoid $\pm$ errors.

$$x = \frac{-b \pm \sqrt{b^2 - 4ac}}{2a}$$

$$x = \frac{-(\square) \pm \sqrt{(\square)^2 - 4(\square)(\square)}}{2(\square)}$$

ANSWER

The solution is $x = -3 \pm \sqrt{11}$. The solution set is $\{-3 - \sqrt{11}, -3 + \sqrt{11}\}$.

EXAMPLE 9 **Using the Quadratic Formula and Finding Two Complex Roots**

Use the quadratic formula to solve the quadratic equation $x^2 + 8 = 4x$.

Solution:

Write this equation in standard form $x^2 - 4x + 8 = 0$ in order to identify $a = 1$, $b = -4$, and $c = 8$.

Write the quadratic formula. $$x = \frac{-b \pm \sqrt{b^2 - 4ac}}{2a}$$

Use parentheses to avoid overlooking a minus sign. $$x = \frac{-(\square) \pm \sqrt{(\square)^2 - 4(\square)(\square)}}{2(\square)}$$

Substitute the values for a, b, and c into the parentheses. $$x = \frac{-(-4) \pm \sqrt{(-4)^2 - 4(1)(8)}}{2(1)}$$

Simplify. $$x = \frac{4 \pm \sqrt{16 - 32}}{2} = \frac{4 \pm \sqrt{-16}}{2} = \frac{4 \pm 4i}{2} = \frac{4}{2} \pm \frac{4i}{2} = \boxed{2 \pm 2i}$$

The solution set $\boxed{\{2 - 2i, 2 + 2i\}}$ contains two complex numbers. Note that they are complex conjugates of each other.

YOUR TURN Use the quadratic formula to solve the quadratic equation $x^2 + 2 = 2x$.

ANSWER

The solution set is $\{1 - i, 1 + i\}$.

EXAMPLE 10 **Using the Quadratic Formula and Finding One Repeated Real Root**

Use the quadratic formula to solve the quadratic equation $4x^2 - 4x + 1 = 0$.

Solution:

Identify a, b, and c. $a = 4, b = -4, c = 1$

Write the quadratic formula. $x = \dfrac{-b \pm \sqrt{b^2 - 4ac}}{2a}$

Use parentheses to avoid losing a minus sign. $x = \dfrac{-(\square) \pm \sqrt{(\square)^2 - 4(\square)(\square)}}{2(\square)}$

Substitute values $a = 4$, $b = -4$, $c = 1$. $x = \dfrac{-(-4) \pm \sqrt{(-4)^2 - 4(4)(1)}}{2(4)}$

Simplify. $x = \dfrac{4 \pm \sqrt{16 - 16}}{8} = \dfrac{4 \pm 0}{8} = \dfrac{1}{2}$

The solution set is a repeated real root $\boxed{\left\{\dfrac{1}{2}\right\}}$.

Note: This quadratic also could have been solved by factoring: $(2x - 1)^2 = 0$.

YOUR TURN Use the quadratic formula to solve the quadratic equation $9x^2 - 6x + 1 = 0$.

ANSWER
$\{\frac{1}{3}\}$

TYPES OF SOLUTIONS

The expression inside the radical, $b^2 - 4ac$, is called the **discriminant**. The discriminant gives important information about the corresponding solutions or roots of $ax^2 + bx + c = 0$, where a, b, and c are real numbers.

$b^2 - 4ac$	SOLUTIONS (ROOTS)
Positive	Two distinct real roots
0	One real root (a double or repeated root)
Negative	Two complex roots (complex conjugates)

In Example 8, the discriminant is positive and the solution has two distinct real roots. In Example 9, the discriminant is negative and the solution has two complex (conjugate) roots. In Example 10, the discriminant is zero and the solution has one repeated real root.

0.2.5 SKILL

Solve application problems using quadratic equations.

0.2.5 CONCEPTUAL

Understand why it is necessary to eliminate nonphysical answers.

0.2.5 Applications Involving Quadratic Equations

In Section 0.1, we developed a procedure for solving word problems involving linear equations. The procedure is the same for applications involving quadratic equations. The only difference is that the mathematical equations will be quadratic, as opposed to linear.

EXAMPLE 11 **Stock Value**

From March 1 to May 1 the price of Abercrombie & Fitch's (ANF) Stock was approximately given by $P = -3t^2 + 6t + 20$, where P is the price of stock in dollars, t is in months, and $t = 0$ corresponds to March 1. When was the value of the stock worth \$22?

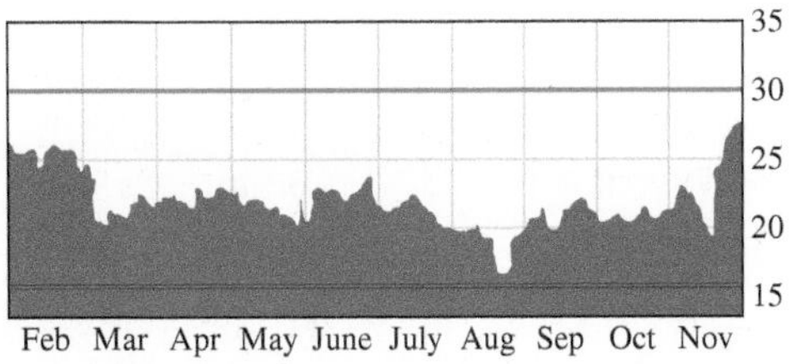

Solution:

STEP 1 **Identify the question.**

When is the price of the stock equal to \$22?

STEP 2 **Make notes.**

Stock price: $P = -3t^2 + 6t + 20$

$P = 22$

STEP 3 **Set up an equation.** $-3t^2 + 6t + 20 = 22$

STEP 4 **Solve the equation.**

Subtract 22 from both sides. $-3t^2 + 6t - 2 = 0$

Solve for t using the quadratic formula.

$$t = \frac{-(6) \pm \sqrt{6^2 - 4(-3)(-2)}}{2(-3)}$$

Simplify.

$$t = \frac{-6 \pm \sqrt{6^2 - 4(-3)(-2)}}{2(-3)} = \frac{-6 \pm \sqrt{12}}{-6} \approx 1.6, 0.4$$

Since $t = 0$ corresponds to March 1, the value of $t = 0.4$ corresponds to March 12, and the value $t = 1.6$ corresponds to April 18.

STEP 5 **Check the solution.**

Look at the figure. The horizontal axis represents the month, and the vertical axis represents the stock price. Estimating when the stock price is approximately \$22, we find March 15 and April 15.

STUDY TIP

Dimensions such as length and width are distances, which are defined as positive quantities. Although the mathematics may yield both positive and negative values, the negative values are excluded.

YOUR TURN When was the stock price \$21?

ANSWER

Approximately March 5 and April 24.

[SECTION 0.2] SUMMARY

The four methods for solving quadratic equations,

$$ax^2 + bx + c = 0 \qquad a \neq 0$$

are *factoring*, the *square root method*, *completing the square*, and the *quadratic formula*. Factoring and the square root method are the quickest and easiest but cannot always be used. The quadratic formula and completing the square work for all quadratic equations.

Quadratic Formula: $x = \dfrac{-b \pm \sqrt{b^2 - 4ac}}{2a}$

A quadratic equation can have three types of solutions: two distinct real roots, one real root (repeated), or two complex roots (conjugates of each other).

[SECTION 0.2] EXERCISES

• SKILLS

In Exercises 1–22, solve by factoring.

1. $x^2 - 5x + 6 = 0$
2. $v^2 + 7v + 6 = 0$
3. $p^2 - 8p + 15 = 0$
4. $u^2 - 2u - 24 = 0$
5. $x^2 = 12 - x$
6. $11x = 2x^2 + 12$
7. $16x^2 + 8x = -1$
8. $3x^2 + 10x - 8 = 0$
9. $9y^2 + 1 = 6y$
10. $4x = 4x^2 + 1$
11. $8y^2 = 16y$
12. $3A^2 = -12A$
13. $9p^2 = 12p - 4$
14. $4u^2 = 20u - 25$
15. $x^2 - 9 = 0$
16. $16v^2 - 25 = 0$
17. $x(x + 4) = 12$
18. $3t^2 - 48 = 0$
19. $2p^2 - 50 = 0$
20. $5y^2 - 45 = 0$
21. $3x^2 = 12$
22. $7v^2 = 28$

In Exercises 23–34, solve using the square root method.

23. $p^2 - 8 = 0$
24. $y^2 - 72 = 0$
25. $x^2 + 9 = 0$
26. $v^2 + 16 = 0$
27. $(x - 3)^2 = 36$
28. $(x - 1)^2 = 25$
29. $(2x + 3)^2 = -4$
30. $(4x - 1)^2 = -16$
31. $(5x - 2)^2 = 27$
32. $(3x + 8)^2 = 12$
33. $(1 - x)^2 = 9$
34. $(1 - x)^2 = -9$

In Exercises 35–46, solve by completing the square.

35. $x^2 + 2x = 3$
36. $y^2 + 8y - 2 = 0$
37. $t^2 - 6t = -5$
38. $x^2 + 10x = -21$
39. $y^2 - 4y + 3 = 0$
40. $x^2 - 7x + 12 = 0$
41. $2p^2 + 8p = -3$
42. $2x^2 - 4x + 3 = 0$
43. $2x^2 - 7x + 3 = 0$
44. $3x^2 - 5x - 10 = 0$
45. $\frac{x^2}{2} - 2x = \frac{1}{4}$
46. $\frac{t^2}{3} + \frac{2t}{3} + \frac{5}{6} = 0$

In Exercises 47–58, solve using the quadratic formula.

47. $t^2 + 3t - 1 = 0$
48. $t^2 + 2t = 1$
49. $s^2 + s + 1 = 0$
50. $2s^2 + 5s = -2$
51. $3x^2 - 3x - 4 = 0$
52. $4x^2 - 2x = 7$
53. $x^2 - 2x + 17 = 0$
54. $4m^2 + 7m + 8 = 0$
55. $5x^2 + 7x = 3$
56. $3x^2 + 5x = -11$
57. $\frac{1}{4}x^2 + \frac{2}{3}x - \frac{1}{2} = 0$
58. $\frac{1}{4}x^2 - \frac{2}{3}x - \frac{1}{3} = 0$

In Exercises 59–74, solve using any method.

59. $v^2 - 8v = 20$
60. $v^2 - 8v = -20$
61. $t^2 + 5t - 6 = 0$
62. $t^2 + 5t + 6 = 0$
63. $(x + 3)^2 = 16$
64. $(x + 3)^2 = -16$
65. $(p - 2)^2 = 4p$
66. $(u + 5)^2 = 16u$
67. $8w^2 + 2w + 21 = 0$
68. $8w^2 + 2w - 21 = 0$
69. $3p^2 - 9p + 1 = 0$
70. $3p^2 - 9p - 1 = 0$
71. $\frac{2}{3}t^2 - \frac{4}{3}t = \frac{1}{5}$
72. $\frac{1}{2}x^2 + \frac{2}{3}x = \frac{2}{5}$
73. $x^2 - 0.1x = 0.12$
74. $y^2 - 0.5y = -0.06$

• APPLICATIONS

75. Stock Value. From June 2003 until April 2004 JetBlue airlines stock (JBLU) was approximately worth $P = -4t^2 + 80t - 360$, where P denotes the price of the stock in dollars and t corresponds to months, with $t = 1$ corresponding to January 2003. During what months was the stock equal to $24?

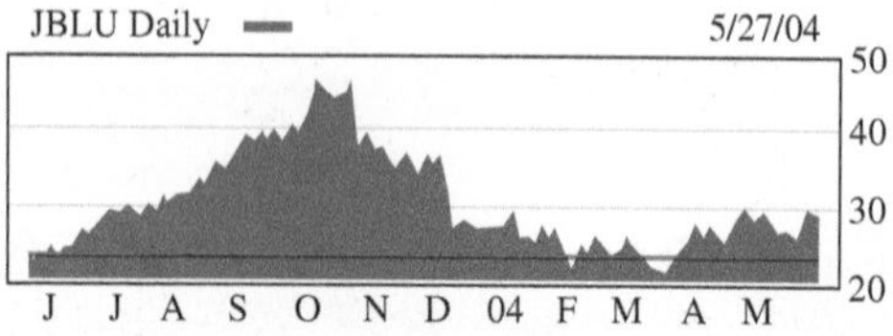

76. **Stock Value.** From November 2014 to November 2015, Apple stock was worth approximately $P = -0.39t^2 + 4.29t + 120.1$, where P is the price of the stock in dollars, t is months, and $t = 0$ corresponds to November 2014. During what months was the stock equal to \$124?

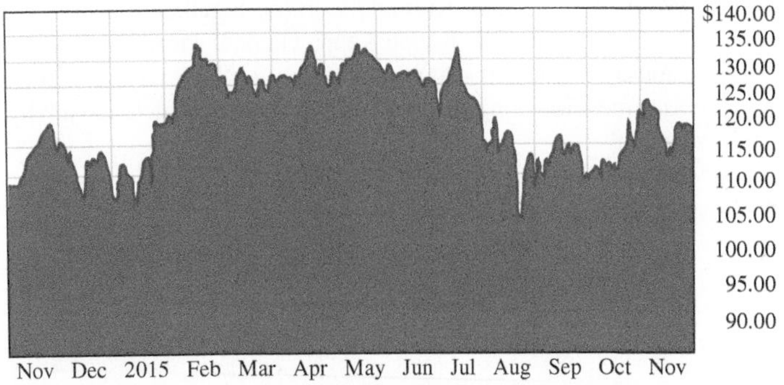

Source: www.nasdaq.com/symbol/aapl/stock-chart

In Exercises 77 and 78 refer to the following:

Research indicates that monthly profit for Widgets R Us is modeled by the function

$$P = -100 + (0.2q - 3)q$$

where P is profit measured in millions of dollars and q is the quantity of widgets produced, measured in thousands.

77. **Business.** Find the break-even point for a month to the nearest unit.

78. **Business.** Find the production level that produces a monthly profit of \$40 million.

In Exercises 79 and 80 refer to the following:

In response to economic conditions, a local business explores the effect of a price increase on weekly profit. The function

$$P = -5(x + 3)(x - 24)$$

models the effect that a price increase of x dollars on a bottle of wine will have on the profit P measured in dollars.

79. **Business/Economics.** What is the smallest price increase that will produce a weekly profit of \$460?

80. **Business/Economics.** What is the smallest price increase that will produce a weekly profit of \$630?

In Exercises 81 and 82 refer to the following:

An epidemiological study of the spread of the flu in a small city finds that the total number P of people who contracted the flu t days into an outbreak is modeled by the function

$$P = -t^2 + 13t + 130 \qquad 1 \le t \le 6$$

81. **Health/Medicine.** After approximately how many days will 160 people have contracted the flu?

82. **Health/Medicine.** After approximately how many days will 172 people have contracted the flu?

83. **Environment: Reduce Your Margins, Save a Tree.** Let's define the *usable area* of an 8.5-inch by 11-inch piece of paper as the rectangular space between the margins of that piece of paper. Assume the default margins in a word processor in a college's computer lab are set up to be 1.25 inches wide (top and bottom) and 1 inch wide (left and right). Answer the following questions using this information.
    a. Determine the amount of usable space, in square inches, on one side of an 8.5-inch by 11-inch piece of paper with the default margins of 1.25 inch and 1 inch.
    b. The Green Falcons, a campus environmental club, has convinced their college's computer lab to reduce the default margins in their word-processing software by x inches. Create and simplify the quadratic expression that represents the new usable area, in square inches, of one side of an 8.5-inch by 11-inch piece of paper if the default margins at the computer lab are each reduced by x inches.
    c. Subtract the usable space in part (a) from the expression in part (b). Explain what this difference represents.
    d. If 10 pages are printed using the new margins and as a result the computer lab saved one whole sheet of paper, then by how much did the computer lab reduce the margins? Round to the nearest tenth of an inch.

84. **Environment: Reduce Your Margins, Save a Tree.** Repeat Exercise 83 assuming the computer lab's default margins are 1 inch all the way around (left, right, top, and bottom). If 15 pages are printed using the new margins and as a result the computer lab saved one whole sheet of paper, then by how much did the computer lab reduce the margins? Round to the nearest tenth of an inch.

85. **Numbers.** Find two consecutive numbers such that their product is 306.

86. **Numbers.** Find two consecutive odd integers such that their product is 143.

87. **Geometry.** The area of a rectangle is 135 square feet. The width is 6 feet less than the length. Find the dimensions of the rectangle.

88. **Geometry.** A rectangle has an area of 31.5 square meters. If the length is 2 meters more than twice the width, find the dimensions of the rectangle.

89. **Geometry.** A triangle has a height that is 2 more than 3 times the base and an area of 60 square units. Find the base and height.

90. **Geometry.** A square's side is increased by 3 yards, which corresponds to an increase in the area by 69 square yards. How many yards is the side of the initial square?

91. **Falling Objects.** If a person drops a water balloon off the rooftop of a 100-foot building, the height of the water balloon is given by the equation $h = -16t^2 + 100$, where t is in seconds. When will the water balloon hit the ground?

92. Falling Objects. If the person in Exercise 85 throws the water balloon downward with a speed of 5 feet per second, the height of the water balloon is given by the equation $h = -16t^2 - 5t + 100$, where t is in seconds. When will the water balloon hit the ground?

93. Gardening. A square garden has an area of 900 square feet. If a sprinkler (with a circular pattern) is placed in the center of the garden, what is the minimum radius of spray the sprinkler would need in order to water all of the garden?

94. Sports. A baseball diamond is a square. The distance from base to base is 90 feet. What is the distance from home plate to second base?

95. Volume. A flat square piece of cardboard is used to construct an open box. Cutting a 1 foot by 1 foot square off of each corner and folding up the edges will yield an open box (assuming these edges are taped together). If the desired volume of the box is 9 cubic feet, what are the dimensions of the original square piece of cardboard?

96. Volume. A rectangular piece of cardboard whose length is twice its width is used to construct an open box. Cutting a 1 foot by 1 foot square off of each corner and folding up the edges will yield an open box. If the desired volume is 12 cubic feet, what are the dimensions of the original rectangular piece of cardboard?

97. Work. Lindsay and Kimmie, working together, can balance the financials for the Kappa Kappa Gamma sorority in 6 days. Lindsay by herself can complete the job in 5 days less than Kimmie. How long will it take Lindsay to complete the job by herself?

98. Work. When Jack cleans the house, it takes him 4 hours. When Ryan cleans the house, it takes him 6 hours. How long would it take both of them if they worked together?

• CATCH THE MISTAKE

In Exercises 99 and 100, explain the mistake that is made.

99.
$$t^2 - 5t - 6 = 0$$
$$(t - 3)(t - 2) = 0$$
$$t = 2, 3$$

100.
$$(2y - 3)^2 = 25$$
$$2y - 3 = 5$$
$$2y = 8$$
$$y = 4$$

• CONCEPTUAL

In Exercises 101–104, determine whether the following statements are true or false.

101. The equation $(3x + 1)^2 = 16$ has the same solution set as the equation $3x + 1 = 4$.

102. The quadratic equation $ax^2 + bx + c = 0$ can be solved by the square root method only if $b = 0$.

103. All quadratic equations can be solved exactly.

104. The quadratic formula can be used to solve any quadratic equation.

105. Write a quadratic equation in standard form that has $x = a$ as a repeated real root. Alternate solutions are possible.

106. Write a quadratic equation in standard form that has $x = bi$ as a root. Alternate solutions are possible.

In Exercises 107–110, solve for the indicated variable in terms of other variables.

107. Solve $s = \frac{1}{2}gt^2$ for t.

108. Solve $A = P(1 + r)^2$ for r.

109. Solve $a^2 + b^2 = c^2$ for c.

110. Solve $P = EI - RI^2$ for I.

• CHALLENGE

111. Show that the sum of the roots of a quadratic equation is equal to $-\frac{b}{a}$.

112. Show that the product of the roots of a quadratic equation is equal to $\frac{c}{a}$.

113. Write a quadratic equation in standard form whose solution set is $\{3 - \sqrt{5}, 3 + \sqrt{5}\}$. Alternative solutions are possible.

114. Write a quadratic equation in standard form whose solution set is $\{2 - i, 2 + i\}$. Alternative solutions are possible.

115. Aviation. An airplane takes 1 hour longer to go a distance of 600 miles flying against a headwind than on the return trip with a tailwind. If the speed of the wind is a constant 50 miles per hour for both legs of the trip, find the speed of the plane in still air.

116. Boating. A speedboat takes 1 hour longer to go 24 miles up a river than to return. If the boat cruises at 10 miles per hour in still water, what is the rate of the current?

117. Find a quadratic equation whose two distinct real roots are the negatives of the two distinct real roots of the equation $ax^2 + bx + c = 0$.

118. Find a quadratic equation whose two distinct real roots are the reciprocals of the two distinct real roots of the equation $ax^2 + bx + c = 0$.

119. A small jet and a 757 leave Atlanta at 1 P.M. The small jet is traveling due west. The 757 is traveling due south. The speed of the 757 is 100 miles per hour faster than that of the small jet. At 3 P.M. the planes are 1000 miles apart. Find the average speed of each plane. (Assume there is no wind.)

120. Two boats leave Key West at noon. The smaller boat is traveling due west. The larger boat is traveling due south. The speed of the larger boat is 10 miles per hour faster than that of the smaller boat. At 3 P.M. the boats are 150 miles apart. Find the average speed of each boat. (Assume there is no current.)

0.3 OTHER TYPES OF EQUATIONS

SKILLS OBJECTIVES

- Solve rational equations.
- Solve radical equations.
- Solve equations that are quadratic in form using u-substitutions.
- Solve equations that are factorable.
- Solve absolute value equations.

CONCEPTUAL OBJECTIVES

- Transform a difficult equation into a simpler linear or quadratic equation.
- Check for extraneous solutions.
- Recognize the u-substitution required to transform the equation into a simpler quadratic equation.
- Recognize when a polynomial equation or an equation with rational exponents can be factored either by grouping or by first factoring out a greatest common factor.
- Understand absolute value in terms of distance on the number line.

0.3.1 Rational Equations

A **rational equation** is an equation that contains one or more rational expressions (Appendix). Some rational equations can be transformed into linear or quadratic equations that you can then solve, but as you will see momentarily, you must be certain that the solution to the resulting linear or quadratic equation also satisfies the original rational equation.

0.3.1 SKILL

Solve rational equations.

0.3.1 CONCEPTUAL

Transform a difficult equation into a simpler linear or quadratic equation.

EXAMPLE 1 **Solving a Rational Equation That Can Be Reduced to a Linear Equation**

Solve the equation $\frac{2}{3x} + \frac{1}{2} = \frac{4}{x} + \frac{4}{3}$.

Solution:

State the excluded values (those that make any denominator equal 0). $\quad \frac{2}{3x} + \frac{1}{2} = \frac{4}{x} + \frac{4}{3} \qquad x \neq 0$

Multiply *each term* by the LCD, $6x$. $\quad 6x\left(\frac{2}{3x}\right) + 6x\left(\frac{1}{2}\right) = 6x\left(\frac{4}{x}\right) + 6x\left(\frac{4}{3}\right)$

Simplify both sides. $\quad 4 + 3x = 24 + 8x$

Subtract 4. $\quad -4 \qquad -4$

$3x = 20 + 8x$

Subtract $8x$. $\quad -8x \qquad -8x$

$-5x = 20$

Divide by -5. $\quad \boxed{x = -4}$

Since $x = -4$ satisfies the original equation, the solution set is $\{-4\}$.

STUDY TIP

Since dividing by 0 is not defined, we exclude values of the variable that correspond to a denominator equaling 0.

YOUR TURN Solve the equation $\frac{3}{y} + 2 = \frac{7}{2y}$.

ANSWER

The solution is $y = \frac{1}{4}$.

The solution set is $\{\frac{1}{4}\}$.

EXAMPLE 2 **Solving Rational Equations: Eliminating Extraneous Solutions**

Solve the equation $\frac{3x}{x-1} + 2 = \frac{3}{x-1}$.

Solution:

State the excluded values (those that make any denominator equal 0).
$$\frac{3x}{x-1} + 2 = \frac{3}{x-1} \qquad x \neq 1$$

Eliminate the fractions by multiplying each term by the LCD, $x - 1$.
$$\frac{3x}{x-1}\cdot(x-1) + 2\cdot(x-1) = \frac{3}{x-1}\cdot(x-1)$$

Simplify.
$$\frac{3x}{\cancel{x-1}}\cdot\cancel{(x-1)} + 2\cdot(x-1) = \frac{3}{\cancel{x-1}}\cdot\cancel{(x-1)}$$

$$3x + 2(x-1) = 3$$

Distribute the 2. $3x + 2x - 2 = 3$

Combine x terms on the left. $5x - 2 = 3$

Add 2 to both sides. $5x = 5$

Divide both sides by 5. $x = 1$

It may seem that $x = 1$ is the solution. However, the original equation had the restriction $x \neq 1$. Therefore, $x = 1$ is an extraneous solution and must be eliminated as a possible solution.

Thus, the equation $\frac{3x}{x-1} + 2 = \frac{3}{x-1}$ has $\boxed{\text{no solution}}$.

YOUR TURN Solve the equation $\frac{2x}{x-2} - 3 = \frac{4}{x-2}$.

ANSWER

no solution

STUDY TIP

When a variable is in the denominator of a fraction, the LCD will contain the variable. This sometimes results in an extraneous solution.

In order to find a *least* common denominator of more complicated expressions, it is useful to first factor the denominators to identify common multiples.

Rational equation: $\frac{1}{3x-3} + \frac{1}{2x-2} = \frac{1}{x^2-x}$

Factor the denominators: $\frac{1}{3(x-1)} + \frac{1}{2(x-1)} = \frac{1}{x(x-1)}$

LCD: $6x(x-1)$

EXAMPLE 3 Solving Rational Equations

Solve the equation $\frac{1}{3x + 18} - \frac{1}{2x + 12} = \frac{1}{x^2 + 6x}$.

Solution:

Factor the denominators. $\frac{1}{3(x + 6)} - \frac{1}{2(x + 6)} = \frac{1}{x(x + 6)}$

State the excluded values. $x \neq 0, -6$

Multiply the equation by the LCD, $6x(x + 6)$.

$$6x(x + 6) \cdot \frac{1}{3(x + 6)} - 6x(x + 6) \cdot \frac{1}{2(x + 6)} = 6x(x + 6) \cdot \frac{1}{x(x + 6)}$$

Divide out the common factors.

$$6x\cancel{(x + 6)} \cdot \frac{1}{3\cancel{(x + 6)}} - 6x\cancel{(x + 6)} \cdot \frac{1}{2\cancel{(x + 6)}} = 6\cancel{x(x + 6)} \cdot \frac{1}{\cancel{x(x + 6)}}$$

Simplify. $2x - 3x = 6$

Solve the linear equation. $x = -6$

Since one of the excluded values is $x \neq -6$, we say that $x = -6$ is an extraneous solution. Therefore, this rational equation has $\boxed{\text{no solution}}$.

YOUR TURN Solve the equation $\frac{2}{x} + \frac{1}{x + 1} = -\frac{1}{x(x + 1)}$.

ANSWER

no solution

EXAMPLE 4 Solving a Rational Equation That Can Be Reduced to a Quadratic Equation

Solve the equation $1 + \frac{3}{x^2 - 2x} = \frac{2}{x - 2}$.

Solution:

Factor the denominators. $1 + \frac{3}{x(x - 2)} = \frac{2}{x - 2}$

State the excluded values (those that make any denominator equal to 0). $x \neq 0, 2$

Multiply each term by the LCD, $x(x - 2)$. $1 \cdot x(x - 2) + \frac{3}{x(x - 2)} \cdot x(x - 2) = \frac{2}{(x - 2)} \cdot x(x - 2)$

Divide out the common factors. $x(x - 2) + \frac{3}{\cancel{x(x - 2)}}\cancel{x(x - 2)} = \frac{2}{\cancel{(x - 2)}}x\cancel{(x - 2)}$

Simplify. $x(x - 2) + 3 = 2x$

Eliminate the parentheses. $x^2 - 2x + 3 = 2x$

Write the quadratic equation in standard form. $x^2 - 4x + 3 = 0$

Factor. $(x - 3)(x - 1) = 0$

Apply the zero product property. $\boxed{x = 3 \quad \text{or} \quad x = 1}$

Since $x = 3$ or $x = 1$ both satisfy the original equation, the solution set is $\{1, 3\}$.

0.3.2 Radical Equations

0.3.2 SKILL

Solve radical equations.

0.3.2 CONCEPTUAL

Check for extraneous solutions.

Radical equations are equations in which the variable is inside a radical (that is, under a square root, cube root, or higher root). Examples of radical equations follow:

$$\sqrt{x-3}=2 \qquad \sqrt{2x+3}=x \qquad \sqrt{x+2}+\sqrt{7x+2}=6$$

Often you can transform a radical equation into a simple linear or quadratic equation. Sometimes the transformation process yields **extraneous solutions**, or apparent solutions that may solve the transformed problem but are not solutions of the original radical equation. Therefore, it is very important to check your answers in the original equation.

EXAMPLE 5 **Solving an Equation Involving a Radical**

Solve the equation $\sqrt{x-3}=2$.

Solution:

Square both sides of the equation. $(\sqrt{x-3})^2 = 2^2$

Simplify. $x - 3 = 4$

Solve the resulting linear equation. $\boxed{x = 7}$

The solution set is $\{7\}$.

Check: $\sqrt{7-3}=\sqrt{4}=2$

STUDY TIP

Extraneous solutions are common when we deal with radical equations, so remember to check your answers.

YOUR TURN Solve the equation $\sqrt{3p+4}=5$.

ANSWER

$p = 7$ or $\{7\}$

EXAMPLE 6 **Solving an Equation Involving a Radical**

Solve the equation $\sqrt{2x+3}=x$.

Solution:

Square both sides of the equation. $(\sqrt{2x+3})^2 = x^2$

Simplify. $2x + 3 = x^2$

Write the quadratic equation in standard form. $x^2 - 2x - 3 = 0$

Factor. $(x-3)(x+1) = 0$

Use the zero product property. $x = 3 \quad \text{or} \quad x = -1$

Check these values to see whether they *both* make the original equation statement true.

$x = 3$: $\sqrt{2(3)+3} = 3 \Rightarrow \sqrt{6+3} = 3 \Rightarrow \sqrt{9} = 3 \Rightarrow 3 = 3$ ✓

$x = -1$: $\sqrt{2(-1)+3} = -1 \Rightarrow \sqrt{-2+3} = -1 \Rightarrow \sqrt{1} = -1 \Rightarrow 1 \neq -1$ ✗

The solution is $\boxed{x = 3}$. The solution set is $\{3\}$.

[CONCEPT CHECK]

Check the extraneous solution in Example 6, $x = -1$, and explain why it does not satisfy the original equation.

ANSWER $\sqrt{2(-1)+3} \stackrel{?}{=} -1$ The square root can never be equal to a negative number.

YOUR TURN Solve the equation $\sqrt{12+t}=t$.

ANSWER

$t = 4$ or $\{4\}$

YOUR TURN Solve the equation $\sqrt{2x+6}=x+3$.

ANSWER

$x = -1$ and $x = -3$ or $\{-3, -1\}$

Examples 5 and 6 contained only one radical each. We transformed the radical equation into a linear (Example 5) or quadratic (Example 6) equation with one step. The next example contains two radicals. Our technique will be to isolate one radical on one side of the equation with the other radical on the other side of the equation.

✓CORRECT	✗INCORRECT
Square the expression. $(3+\sqrt{x+2})^2$	Square the expression. $(3+\sqrt{x+2})^2$
Write the square as a product of two factors. $(3+\sqrt{x+2})(3+\sqrt{x+2})$	The **error** occurs here when only individual terms are squared. $\neq 9+(x+2)$
Use the FOIL method. $9+6\sqrt{x+2}+(x+2)$	

EXAMPLE 7 Solving an Equation with More Than One Radical

Solve the equation $\sqrt{x+2}+\sqrt{7x+2}=6$.

Solution:

Subtract $\sqrt{x+2}$ from both sides. $\sqrt{7x+2}=6-\sqrt{x+2}$

Square both sides. $(\sqrt{7x+2})^2=(6-\sqrt{x+2})^2$

Simplify. $7x+2=(6-\sqrt{x+2})(6-\sqrt{x+2})$

Multiply the expressions on the right side of the equation. $7x+2=36-12\sqrt{x+2}+(x+2)$

Isolate the term with the radical on the left side. $12\sqrt{x+2}=36+x+2-7x-2$

Combine like terms on the right side. $12\sqrt{x+2}=36-6x$

Divide by 6. $2\sqrt{x+2}=6-x$

Square both sides. $4(x+2)=(6-x)^2$

Simplify. $4x+8=36-12x+x^2$

Rewrite the quadratic equation in standard form. $x^2-16x+28=0$

Factor. $(x-14)(x-2)=0$

Solve. $x=14$ and $x=2$

The apparent solutions are 2 and 14. Note that $x = 14$ does not satisfy the original equation; therefore, it is extraneous. The solution is $\boxed{x=2}$. The solution set is $\{2\}$.

YOUR TURN Solve the equation $\sqrt{x-4}=5-\sqrt{x+1}$.

ANSWER

$x=8$ or $\{8\}$

PROCEDURE FOR SOLVING RADICAL EQUATIONS

Step 1: Isolate the term with a radical on one side.
Step 2: Raise both (*entire*) sides of the equation to the power that will eliminate this radical, and simplify the equation.
Step 3: If a radical remains, repeat Steps 1 and 2.
Step 4: Solve the resulting linear or quadratic equation.
Step 5: Check the solutions and eliminate any extraneous solutions.

Note: If there is more than one radical in the equation, it does not matter which radical is isolated first.

0.3.3 Equations Quadratic in Form: *u*-Substitution

0.3.3 SKILL

Solve equations that are quadratic in form using u-substitutions.

0.3.3 CONCEPTUAL

Recognize the u-substitution required to transform the equation into a simpler quadratic equation.

Equations that are higher order or that have fractional powers often can be transformed into a quadratic equation by introducing a u-substitution. When this is the case, we say such equations are **quadratic in form**. In the table below, the two original equations are quadratic in form because they can be transformed into a quadratic equation given the correct substitution.

ORIGINAL EQUATION	SUBSTITUTION	NEW EQUATION
$x^4 - 3x^2 - 4 = 0$	$u = x^2$	$u^2 - 3u - 4 = 0$
$t^{2/3} + 2t^{1/3} + 1 = 0$	$u = t^{1/3}$	$u^2 + 2u + 1 = 0$
$\frac{2}{y} - \frac{1}{\sqrt{y}} + 1 = 0$	$u = y^{-1/2}$	$2u^2 - u + 1 = 0$

For example, the equation $x^4 - 3x^2 - 4 = 0$ is a fourth-degree equation in x. How did we know that $u = x^2$ would transform the original equation into a quadratic equation? If we rewrite the original equation as $(x^2)^2 - 3(x^2) - 4 = 0$, the expression in parentheses is the u-substitution.

Let us introduce the substitution $u = x^2$. Note that squaring both sides implies $u^2 = x^4$. We then replace x^2 in the original equation with u, and x^4 in the original equation with u^2, which leads to a quadratic equation in u: $u^2 - 3u - 4 = 0$.

WORDS	MATH
Solve for x.	$x^4 - 3x^2 - 4 = 0$
Introduce u-substitution.	$u = x^2$ (Note that $u^2 = x^4$.)
Write the quadratic equation in u.	$u^2 - 3u - 4 = 0$
Factor.	$(u - 4)(u + 1) = 0$
Solve for u.	$u = 4$ or $u = -1$
Transform back to x, $u = x^2$.	$x^2 = 4$ or $x^2 = -1$
Solve for x.	$\boxed{x = \pm 2 \text{ or } x = \pm i}$

The solution set is $\{\pm 2, \pm i\}$.

It is important to correctly determine the appropriate substitution in order to arrive at an equation quadratic in form. For example, $t^{2/3} + 2t^{1/3} + 1 = 0$ is an original equation given in the above table. If we rewrite this equation as $(t^{1/3})^2 + 2(t^{1/3}) + 1 = 0$, then it becomes apparent that the correct substitution is $u = t^{1/3}$, which transforms the equation in t into a quadratic equation in u: $u^2 + 2u + 1 = 0$.

PROCEDURE FOR SOLVING EQUATIONS QUADRATIC IN FORM

Step 1: Identify the substitution.
Step 2: Transform the equation into a quadratic equation.
Step 3: Solve the quadratic equation.
Step 4: Apply the substitution to rewrite the solution in terms of the original variable.
Step 5: Solve the resulting equation.
Step 6: Check the solutions in the original equation.

EXAMPLE 8 Solving an Equation Quadratic in Form with Negative Exponents

Find the solutions to the equation $x^{-2} - x^{-1} - 12 = 0$.

Solution:

Rewrite the original equation. $(x^{-1})^2 - (x^{-1}) - 12 = 0$

Determine the u-substitution. $u = x^{-1}$ (Note that $u^2 = x^{-2}$.)

The original equation in x corresponds to a quadratic equation in u. $u^2 - u - 12 = 0$

Factor. $(u - 4)(u + 3) = 0$

Solve for u. $u = 4$ or $u = -3$

The most common mistake is forgetting to transform back to x.

Transform back to x. Let $u = x^{-1}$. $x^{-1} = 4$ or $x^{-1} = -3$

Write x^{-1} as $\frac{1}{x}$. $\frac{1}{x} = 4$ or $\frac{1}{x} = -3$

Solve for x. $\boxed{x = \frac{1}{4}}$ or $\boxed{x = -\frac{1}{3}}$

The solution set is $\left\{-\frac{1}{3}, \frac{1}{4}\right\}$.

STUDY TIP

Remember to transform back to the original variable.

YOUR TURN Find the solutions to the equation $x^{-2} - x^{-1} - 6 = 0$.

ANSWER

The solution is $x = -\frac{1}{2}$ or $x = \frac{1}{3}$.

The solution set is $\left\{-\frac{1}{2}, \frac{1}{3}\right\}$.

EXAMPLE 9 Solving an Equation Quadratic in Form with Fractional Exponents

Find the solutions to the equation $x^{2/3} - 3x^{1/3} - 10 = 0$.

Solution:

Rewrite the original equation. $(x^{1/3})^2 - 3x^{1/3} - 10 = 0$

Identify the substitution as $u = x^{1/3}$. $u^2 - 3u - 10 = 0$

Factor. $(u - 5)(u + 2) = 0$

Solve for u. $u = 5$ or $u = -2$

Let $u = x^{1/3}$ again. $x^{1/3} = 5$ $x^{1/3} = -2$

Cube both sides of the equations. $(x^{1/3})^3 = (5)^3$ $(x^{1/3})^3 = (-2)^3$

Simplify. $\boxed{x = 125}$ $\boxed{x = -8}$

The solution set is $\boxed{\{-8, 125\}}$, which a check will confirm.

[CONCEPT CHECK]

In the Your Turn what do we let u be equal to in order to transform this equation into a quadratic equation?

ANSWER $u = t^{1/2}$

YOUR TURN Find the solutions to the equation $2t - 5t^{1/2} - 3 = 0$.

ANSWER
$t = 9$ or $\{9\}$

0.3.4 Factorable Equations

0.3.4 SKILL

Solve equations that are factorable.

0.3.4 CONCEPTUAL

Recognize when a polynomial equation or an equation with rational exponents can be factored either by grouping or by first factoring out a greatest common factor.

Some equations (both polynomial and with rational exponents) that are factorable can be solved using the zero product property.

EXAMPLE 10 Solving an Equation with Rational Exponents by Factoring

Solve the equation $x^{7/3} - 3x^{4/3} - 4x^{1/3} = 0$.

Solution:

Factor the left side of the equation. $x^{1/3}(x^2 - 3x - 4) = 0$

Factor the quadratic expression. $x^{1/3}(x - 4)(x + 1) = 0$

Apply the zero product property. $x^{1/3} = 0$ or $x - 4 = 0$ or $x + 1 = 0$

Solve for x. $\boxed{x = 0}$ or $\boxed{x = 4}$ or $\boxed{x = -1}$

The solution set is $\{-1, 0, 4\}$.

EXAMPLE 11 **Solving a Polynomial Equation Using Factoring by Grouping**

Solve the equation $x^3 + 2x^2 - x - 2 = 0$.

Solution:

Factor by grouping (Appendix). $(x^3 - x) + (2x^2 - 2) = 0$

Identify the common factors. $x(x^2 - 1) + 2(x^2 - 1) = 0$

Factor. $(x + 2)(x^2 - 1) = 0$

Factor the quadratic expression. $(x + 2)(x - 1)(x + 1) = 0$

Apply the zero product property. $x + 2 = 0$ or $x - 1 = 0$ or $x + 1 = 0$

Solve for x. $\boxed{x = -2}$ or $\boxed{x = 1}$ or $\boxed{x = -1}$

The solution set is $\{-2, -1, 1\}$.

YOUR TURN Solve the equation $x^3 + x^2 - 4x - 4 = 0$.

[CONCEPT CHECK]

For the Your Turn how do we initially group the cubic equation?

ANSWER $(x^3 - 4x) + (x^2 - 4) = 0$

ANSWER

$x = -1$ or $x = \pm 2$ or $\{-2, -1, 2\}$

0.3.5 Absolute Value Equations

The **absolute value** of a real number can be interpreted algebraically and graphically.

0.3.5 SKILL

Solve absolute value equations.

0.3.5 CONCEPTUAL

Understand absolute value in terms of distance on the number line.

DEFINITION **Absolute Value**

The **absolute value** of a real number a, denoted by the symbol $|a|$, is defined by

$$|a| = \begin{cases} a, & \text{if } a \geq 0 \\ -a, & \text{if } a < 0 \end{cases}$$

When absolute value is involved in algebraic equations, we interpret the definition of absolute value as follows.

DEFINITION **Absolute Value Equation**

If $|x| = a$, then $x = -a$ or $x = a$, where $a \geq 0$.

STUDY TIP

Algebraically: $|x| = 5$ implies $x = -5$ or $x = 5$.

Graphically: -5 and 5 are five units from 0.

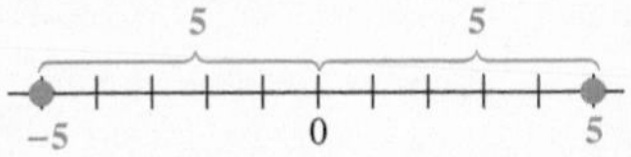

In words, "If the absolute value of a number is a, then that number equals $-a$ or a." For example, the equation $|x| = 7$ is true if $x = -7$ or $x = 7$. We say the equation $|x| = 7$ has the solution set $\{-7, 7\}$. *Note:* $|x| = -3$ does not have a solution because there is no value of x such that its absolute value is -3.

EXAMPLE 12 **Solving an Absolute Value Equation**

Solve the equation $|x - 3| = 8$ algebraically and graphically.

Solution:

Using the definition of an absolute value equation, we see that if the absolute value of an expression is 8, then that expression is either -8 or 8. Rewrite as two equations:

$$x - 3 = -8 \quad \text{or} \quad x - 3 = 8$$

$$x = -5 \qquad\qquad x = 11$$

The solution set is $\boxed{\{-5, 11\}}$.

Graph: The absolute value equation $|x - 3| = 8$ is interpreted as "What numbers are eight units away from 3 on the number line?" We find that eight units to the right of 3 is 11 and eight units to the left of 3 is -5.

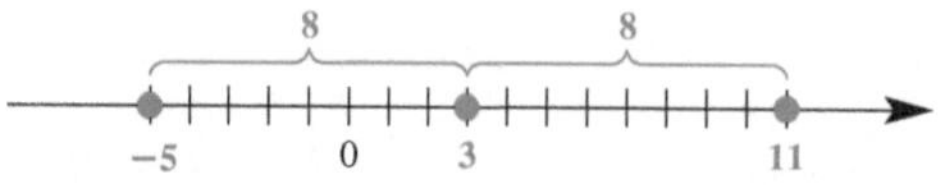

YOUR TURN Solve the equation $|x + 5| = 7$.

ANSWER

$x = 2$ or $x = -12$. The solution set is $\{-12, 2\}$.

EXAMPLE 13 **Solving an Absolute Value Equation**

Solve the equation $2 - 3|x - 1| = -4|x - 1| + 7$.

Solution:

Isolate the absolute value expressions on one side.

Add $4|x - 1|$ to both sides. $\quad 2 + |x - 1| = 7$

Subtract 2 from both sides. $\quad |x - 1| = 5$

If the absolute value of an expression is equal to 5, then the expression is equal to either -5 or 5. $\quad x - 1 = -5$ or $x - 1 = 5$; $x = -4$ $\quad x = 6$

The solution set is $\boxed{\{-4, 6\}}$.

YOUR TURN Solve the equation $3 - 2|x - 4| = -3|x - 4| + 11$.

ANSWER

$x = -4$ or $x = 12$. The solution set is $\{-4, 12\}$.

EXAMPLE 14 **Solving a Quadratic Absolute Value Equation**

Solve the equation $|5 - x^2| = 1$.

Solution:

If the absolute value of an expression is 1, that expression is either -1 or 1, which leads to two equations.

$$5 - x^2 = -1 \quad \text{or} \quad 5 - x^2 = 1$$
$$-x^2 = -6 \qquad -x^2 = -4$$
$$x^2 = 6 \qquad x^2 = 4$$
$$x = \pm\sqrt{6} \qquad x = \pm\sqrt{4} = \pm 2$$

The solution set is $\boxed{\{\pm 2, \pm\sqrt{6}\}}$.

YOUR TURN Solve the equation $|7 - x^2| = 2$.

[CONCEPT CHECK]

$|x - a| = b$ is interpreted on the number line as

(A) b units from a

(B) a units from b

ANSWER (A)

ANSWER

$x = \pm\sqrt{5}$ or $x = \pm 3$. The solution set is $\{\pm\sqrt{5}, \pm 3\}$.

[SECTION 0.3] SUMMARY

Rational equations, radical equations, equations quadratic in form, factorable equations, and absolute value equations can often be solved by transforming them into simpler linear or quadratic equations.

- **Rational Equations:** Multiply the entire equation by the LCD. Solve the resulting equation (if it is linear or quadratic). Check for extraneous solutions.
- **Radical Equations:** Isolate the term containing a radical and raise it to the appropriate power that will eliminate the radical. If there is more than one radical, it does not matter which radical is isolated first. Raising radical equations to powers may cause extraneous solutions, so check each solution.
- **Equations Quadratic in Form:** Identify the u-substitution that transforms the equation into a quadratic equation. Solve the quadratic equation and then remember to transform back to the original variable.
- **Factorable Equations:** Look for a factor common to all terms or factor by grouping.
- **Absolute Value Equations:** Transform the absolute value equation into two equations that do not involve absolute value.

[SECTION 0.3] EXERCISES

• SKILLS

In Exercises 1–20, specify any values that must be excluded from the solution set and then solve the rational equation.

1. $\dfrac{x}{x-2} + 5 = \dfrac{2}{x-2}$
2. $\dfrac{n}{n-5} + 2 = \dfrac{n}{n-5}$
3. $\dfrac{2p}{p-1} = 3 + \dfrac{2}{p-1}$
4. $\dfrac{4t}{t+2} = 3 - \dfrac{8}{t+2}$
5. $\dfrac{3x}{x+2} - 4 = \dfrac{2}{x+2}$
6. $\dfrac{5y}{2y-1} - 3 = \dfrac{12}{2y-1}$
7. $\dfrac{1}{n} + \dfrac{1}{n+1} = \dfrac{-1}{n(n+1)}$
8. $\dfrac{1}{x} + \dfrac{1}{x-1} = \dfrac{1}{x(x-1)}$
9. $\dfrac{3}{a} - \dfrac{2}{a+3} = \dfrac{9}{a(a+3)}$
10. $\dfrac{1}{c-2} + \dfrac{1}{c} = \dfrac{2}{c(c-2)}$
11. $\dfrac{n-5}{6n-6} = \dfrac{1}{9} - \dfrac{n-3}{4n-4}$
12. $\dfrac{5}{m} + \dfrac{3}{m-2} = \dfrac{6}{m(m-2)}$

13. $\frac{2}{5x+1} = \frac{1}{2x-1}$

14. $\frac{3}{4n-1} = \frac{2}{2n-5}$

15. $\frac{t-1}{1-t} = \frac{3}{2}$

16. $\frac{2-x}{x-2} = \frac{3}{4}$

17. $x + \frac{12}{x} = 7$

18. $x - \frac{10}{x} = -3$

19. $\frac{4(x-2)}{x-3} + \frac{3}{x} = \frac{-3}{x(x-3)}$

20. $\frac{5}{y+4} = 4 + \frac{3}{y-2}$

In Exercises 21–60, solve the radical equation for the given variable.

21. $\sqrt{u+1} = -4$

22. $-\sqrt{3-2u} = 9$

23. $\sqrt[3]{5x+2} = 3$

24. $\sqrt[3]{1-x} = -2$

25. $(4y+1)^{1/3} = -1$

26. $(5x-1)^{1/3} = 4$

27. $(x+3)^{5/3} = 32$

28. $(x+2)^{4/3} = 16$

29. $(x+1)^{2/3} = 4$

30. $(x-7)^{4/3} = 81$

31. $\sqrt{12+x} = x$

32. $x = \sqrt{56-x}$

33. $y = 5\sqrt{y}$

34. $\sqrt{y} = \frac{y}{4}$

35. $s = 3\sqrt{s-2}$

36. $-2s = \sqrt{3-s}$

37. $\sqrt{2x+6} = x+3$

38. $\sqrt{8-2x} = 2x-2$

39. $\sqrt{1-3x} = x+1$

40. $\sqrt{2-x} = x-2$

41. $3x - 6\sqrt{x-1} = 3$

42. $5x - 10\sqrt{x+2} = -10$

43. $3x - 6\sqrt{x+2} = 3$

44. $2x - 4\sqrt{x+1} = 4$

45. $3\sqrt{x+4} - 2x = 9$

46. $2\sqrt{x+1} - 3x = -5$

47. $\sqrt{x^2-4} = x-1$

48. $\sqrt{25-x^2} = x+1$

49. $\sqrt{x^2-2x-5} = x+1$

50. $\sqrt{2x^2-8x+1} = x-3$

51. $\sqrt{3x+1} - \sqrt{6x-5} = 1$

52. $\sqrt{2-x} + \sqrt{6-5x} = 6$

53. $\sqrt{x+12} + \sqrt{8-x} = 6$

54. $\sqrt{5-x} + \sqrt{3x+1} = 4$

55. $\sqrt{2x-1} - \sqrt{x-1} = 1$

56. $\sqrt{8-x} = 2 + \sqrt{2x+3}$

57. $\sqrt{3x-5} = 7 - \sqrt{x+2}$

58. $\sqrt{x+5} = 1 + \sqrt{x-2}$

59. $\sqrt{2+\sqrt{x}} = \sqrt{x}$

60. $\sqrt{2-\sqrt{x}} = \sqrt{x}$

In Exercises 61–80, solve the equations by introducing a substitution that transforms these equations to quadratic form.

61. $x^{2/3} + 2x^{1/3} = 0$

62. $x^{1/2} - 2x^{1/4} = 0$

63. $x^4 - 3x^2 + 2 = 0$

64. $x^4 - 8x^2 + 16 = 0$

65. $2x^4 + 7x^2 + 6 = 0$

66. $x^8 - 17x^4 + 16 = 0$

67. $4(t-1)^2 - 9(t-1) = -2$

68. $2(1-y)^2 + 5(1-y) - 12 = 0$

69. $x^{-8} - 17x^{-4} + 16 = 0$

70. $2u^{-2} + 5u^{-1} - 12 = 0$

71. $3y^{-2} + y^{-1} - 4 = 0$

72. $5a^{-2} + 11a^{-1} + 2 = 0$

73. $z^{2/5} - 2z^{1/5} + 1 = 0$

74. $2x^{1/2} + x^{1/4} - 1 = 0$

75. $6t^{-2/3} - t^{-1/3} - 1 = 0$

76. $t^{-2/3} - t^{-1/3} - 6 = 0$

77. $3 = \frac{1}{(x+1)^2} + \frac{2}{(x+1)}$

78. $\frac{1}{(x+1)^2} + \frac{4}{(x+1)} + 4 = 0$

79. $u^{4/3} - 5u^{2/3} = -4$

80. $u^{4/3} + 5u^{2/3} = -4$

In Exercises 81–96, solve by factoring.

81. $x^3 - x^2 - 12x = 0$

82. $2y^3 - 11y^2 + 12y = 0$

83. $4p^3 - 9p = 0$

84. $25x^3 = 4x$

85. $u^5 - 16u = 0$

86. $t^5 - 81t = 0$

87. $x^3 - 5x^2 - 9x + 45 = 0$

88. $2p^3 - 3p^2 - 8p + 12 = 0$

89. $y(y-5)^3 - 14(y-5)^2 = 0$

90. $v(v+3)^3 - 40(v+3)^2 = 0$

91. $x^{9/4} - 2x^{5/4} - 3x^{1/4} = 0$

92. $u^{7/3} + u^{4/3} - 20u^{1/3} = 0$

93. $t^{5/3} - 25t^{-1/3} = 0$

94. $4x^{9/5} - 9x^{-1/5} = 0$

95. $y^{3/2} - 5y^{1/2} + 6y^{-1/2} = 0$

96. $4p^{5/3} - 5p^{2/3} - 6p^{-1/3} = 0$

In Exercises 97–118, solve the absolute value equation.

97. $|p - 7| = 3$

98. $|p + 7| = 3$

99. $|4 - y| = 1$

100. $|2 - y| = 11$

101. $|3t - 9| = 3$

102. $|4t + 2| = 2$

103. $|7 - 2x| = 9$

104. $|6 - 3y| = 12$

105. $|1 - 3y| = 1$

106. $|5 - x| = 2$

107. $\left|\frac{2}{3}x - \frac{4}{7}\right| = \frac{5}{3}$

108. $\left|\frac{1}{2}x + \frac{3}{4}\right| = \frac{1}{16}$

109. $|x - 5| + 4 = 12$

110. $|x + 3| - 9 = 2$

111. $2|p + 3| - 15 = 5$

112. $8 - 3|p - 4| = 2$

113. $5|y - 2| - 10 = 4|y - 2| - 3$

114. $3 - |y + 9| = 11 - 3|y + 9|$

115. $|4 - x^2| = 1$

116. $|7 - x^2| = 3$

117. $|x^2 + 1| = 5$

118. $|x^2 - 1| = 5$

• APPLICATIONS

In Exercises 119 and 120 refer to the following:

An analysis of sales indicates that demand for a product during a calendar year is modeled by

$$d = 3\sqrt{t + 1} - 0.75t$$

where d is demand in millions of units and t is the month of the year where $t = 0$ represents January.

119. Economics. During which month(s) is demand 3 million units?

120. Economics. During which month(s) is demand 4 million units?

In Exercises 121 and 122 refer to the following:

Body Surface Area (BSA) is used in physiology and medicine for many clinical purposes. BSA can be modeled by the function

$$BSA = \sqrt{\frac{wh}{3600}}$$

where w is weight in kilograms and h is height in centimeters.

121. Health. The BSA of a 72-kilogram female is 1.8. Find the height of the female to the nearest centimeter.

122. Health. The BSA of a 177-centimeter tall-male is 2.1. Find the weight of the male to the nearest kilogram.

For Exercises 123–126, refer to this lens law.

The position of the image is found using the thin lens equation

$$\frac{1}{f} = \frac{1}{d_o} + \frac{1}{d_i}$$

where d_o is the distance from the object to the lens, d_i is the distance from the lens to the image, and f is the focal length of the lens.

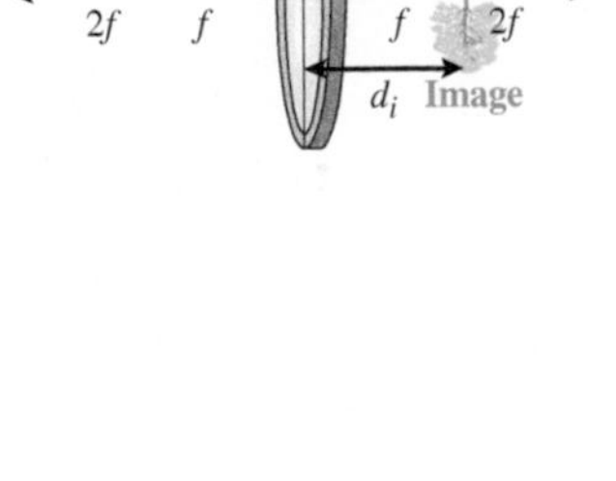

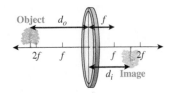

123. Optics. If the focal length of a lens is 3 centimeters and the image distance is 5 centimeters from the lens, what is the distance from the object to the lens?

124. Optics. If the focal length of the lens is 8 centimeters and the image distance is 2 centimeters from the lens, what is the distance from the object to the lens? *Note:* A negative d_i implies that the image is behind the lens.

125. Optics. The focal length of a lens is 2 centimeters. If the image distance from the lens is half the distance from the object to the lens, find the object distance.

126. Optics. The focal length of a lens is 8 centimeters. If the image distance from the lens is half the distance from the object to the lens, find the object distance.

127. Physics: Pendulum. The period (T) of a pendulum is related to the length (L) of the pendulum and acceleration due to gravity (g) by the formula $T = 2\pi\sqrt{\frac{L}{g}}$. If gravity is 9.8 m/s^2 and the period is 1 second, find the approximate length of the pendulum. Round to the nearest centimeter. *Note:* 100 cm = 1 m.

128. Physics: Pendulum. The period (T) of a pendulum is related to the length (L) of the pendulum and acceleration due to gravity (g) by the formula $T = 2\pi\sqrt{\frac{L}{g}}$. If gravity is 32 ft/s^2 and the period is 1 second, find the approximate length of the pendulum. Round to the nearest inch. *Note:* 12 in. = 1 ft.

• CATCH THE MISTAKE

In Exercises 129–132, explain the mistake that is made.

129. Solve the equation $\sqrt{3t+1} = -4$.

Solution:

$$3t + 1 = 16$$
$$3t = 15$$
$$t = 5$$

This is incorrect. What mistake was made?

130. Solve the equation $x = \sqrt{x+2}$.

Solution:

$$x^2 = x + 2$$
$$x^2 - x - 2 = 0$$
$$(x-2)(x+1) = 0$$
$$x = -1, x = 2$$

This is incorrect. What mistake was made?

131. Solve the equation $\frac{4}{p} - 3 = \frac{2}{5p}$.

Solution:

$$(p-3)2 = 4(5p)$$

Cross multiply. $\quad 2p - 6 = 20p$

$$-6 = 18p$$
$$p = -\frac{6}{18}$$
$$p = -\frac{1}{3}$$

This is incorrect. What mistake was made?

132. Solve the equation $\frac{1}{x} + \frac{1}{x-1} = \frac{1}{x(x-1)}$.

Solution:

Multiply by the LCD, $x(x-1)$. $\quad \frac{x(x-1)}{x} + \frac{x(x-1)}{x-1} = \frac{x(x-1)}{x(x-1)}$

Simplify. $\quad (x-1) + x = 1$

$$x - 1 + x = 1$$
$$2x = 2$$
$$x = 1$$

This is incorrect. What mistake was made?

• CONCEPTUAL

In Exercises 133–134, determine whether each statement is true or false.

133. The solution to the equation $x = \frac{1}{1/x}$ is the set of all real numbers.

134. The solution to the equation $\frac{1}{(x-1)(x+2)} = \frac{1}{x^2+x-2}$ is the set of all real numbers.

135. Solve for x, given that a, b, and c are real numbers and $c \neq 0$.

$$\frac{a}{x} - \frac{b}{x} = c$$

136. Solve the equation for y: $\frac{1}{y-a} + \frac{1}{y+a} = \frac{2}{y-1}$. Does y have any restrictions?

• CHALLENGE

137. Solve the equation $\sqrt{x+6} + \sqrt{11+x} = 5\sqrt{3+x}$.

138. Solve the equation $3x^{7/12} - x^{5/6} - 2x^{1/3} = 0$.

139. Solve the equation for x in terms of y: $y = \dfrac{a}{1 + \frac{b}{x} + c}$.

140. Solve for t: $\dfrac{t + \frac{1}{t}}{\frac{1}{t} - 1} = 1$.

0.4 INEQUALITIES

SKILLS OBJECTIVES

- Use interval notation.
- Solve linear inequalities in one variable.
- Solve polynomial inequalities.
- Solve rational inequalities.
- Solve absolute value inequalities.

CONCEPTUAL OBJECTIVES

- Apply intersection and union concepts.
- Understand that a linear inequality in one variable has an interval solution.
- Understand zeros and test intervals.
- Realize that a rational inequality has an implied domain restriction on the variable.
- Apply intersection and union concepts to solutions of linear inequalities in one variable.

0.4.1 Graphing Inequalities and Interval Notation

0.4.1 SKILL

Use interval notation.

0.4.1 CONCEPTUAL

Apply intersection and union concepts.

We will express solutions to inequalities four ways: an inequality, a solution set, an interval, and a graph. The following are ways of expressing all real numbers greater than or equal to a and less than b:

Inequality Notation	Solution Set	Interval Notation	Graph/Number Line
$a \le x < b$	$\{x \mid a \le x < b\}$	$[a, b)$	 or 

In this example, a is referred to as the **left endpoint** and b is referred to as the **right endpoint**. If an inequality is a strict inequality ($<$ or $>$), then the graph and interval notation use *parentheses*. If it includes an endpoint ($\ge$ or $\le$), then the graph and interval notation use *brackets*. Number lines are drawn with either closed/open circles or brackets/parentheses. In this text the brackets/parentheses notation will be used. Intervals are classified as follows:

Open (,) Closed [,] Half open (,] or [,)

LET X BE A REAL NUMBER. X IS...	INEQUALITY	SET NOTATION	INTERVAL	GRAPH
greater than a and less than b	$a < x < b$	$\{x \mid a < x < b\}$	(a, b)	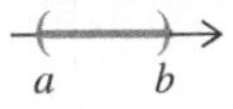
greater than or equal to a and less than b	$a \le x < b$	$\{x \mid a \le x < b\}$	$[a, b)$	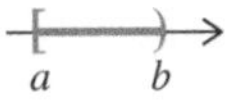
greater than a and less than or equal to b	$a < x \le b$	$\{x \mid a < x \le b\}$	$(a, b]$	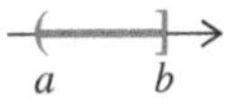
greater than or equal to a and less than or equal to b	$a \le x \le b$	$\{x \mid a \le x \le b\}$	$[a, b]$	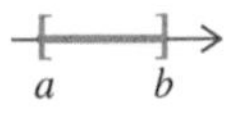
less than a	$x < a$	$\{x \mid x < a\}$	$(-\infty, a)$	
less than or equal to a	$x \le a$	$\{x \mid x \le a\}$	$(-\infty, a]$	
greater than b	$x > b$	$\{x \mid x > b\}$	(b, ∞)	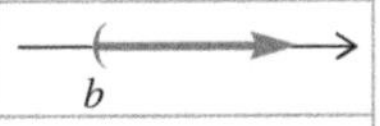
greater than or equal to b	$x \ge b$	$\{x \mid x \ge b\}$	$[b, \infty)$	
all real numbers	$\mathbb{R}$	$\mathbb{R}$	$(-\infty, \infty)$	

1. *Infinity* (∞) is not a number. It is a symbol that means continuing indefinitely to the right on the number line. Similarly, *negative infinity* ($-\infty$) means continuing indefinitely to the left on the number line. Since both are unbounded, we use a parenthesis, never a bracket, to represent them.
2. In interval notation, the lower number is always written to the left. Write the inequality in interval notation: $-1 \leq x < 3$.

✓CORRECT $[-1, 3)$ ✗INCORRECT $(3, -1]$

EXAMPLE 1 Expressing Inequalities Using Interval Notation and a Graph

Express the following as an inequality, an interval, and a graph:

a. x is greater than -3.

b. x is less than or equal to 5.

c. x is greater than or equal to -1 and less than 4.

d. x is greater than or equal to 0 and less than or equal to 4.

Solution:

Inequality	[Interval	Graph
a. $x > -3$	$(-3, \infty)$	
b. $x \leq 5$	$(-\infty, 5]$	
c. $-1 \leq x < 4$	$[-1, 4)$	
d. $0 \leq x \leq 4$	$[0, 4]$	

Since the solutions to inequalities are sets of real numbers, it is useful to discuss two operations on sets called **intersection** and **union**.

[CONCEPT CHECK]

If A is the set of all the students who are enrolled in a math class and B is the set of all students who are enrolled in a history class, then which set is larger?
(A) the intersection of A and B
(B) the union of A and B?
Assume that the two classes are not made up of exactly the same students.

ANSWER (B), the set of students who are enrolled in either a math class or a history class. Option (A) is the smaller set because it consists of the students who are enrolled in both math and history.

DEFINITION Union and Intersection

The **union** of sets A and B, denoted $A \cup B$, is the set formed by combining all the elements in A with all the elements in B.

$$A \cup B = \{x \mid x \text{ is in } A \textbf{ or } B \textbf{ or } \text{both}\}$$

The **intersection** of sets A and B, denoted $A \cap B$, is the set formed by the elements that are in both A and B.

$$A \cap B = \{x \mid x \text{ is in } A \textbf{ and } B\}$$

The notation "$x \mid x$ is in" is read "all x such that x is in." The vertical line represents "such that."

EXAMPLE 2 **Determining Unions and Intersections: Intervals and Graphs**

If $A = [-3, 2]$ and $B = (1, 7)$, determine $A \cup B$ and $A \cap B$. Write these sets in interval notation, and graph them.

Solution:

Set	Interval notation	Graph
A	$[-3, 2]$	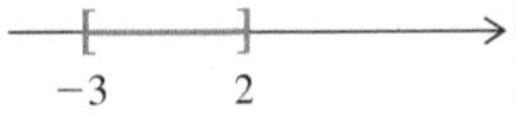
B	$(1, 7)$	
$A \cup B$	$[-3, 7)$	
$A \cap B$	$(1, 2]$	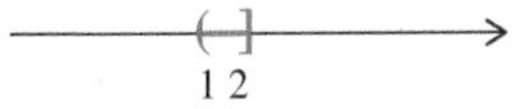

YOUR TURN If $C = [-3, 3)$ and $D = (0, 5]$, find $C \cup D$ and $C \cap D$. Express the intersection and union in interval notation, and graph them.

ANSWER

$C \cup D = [-3, 5]$

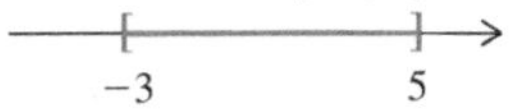

$C \cap D = (0, 3)$

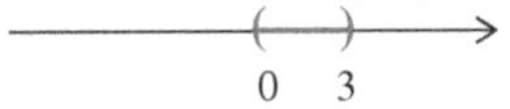

0.4.2 Linear Inequalities

0.4.2 SKILL

Solve linear inequalities in one variable.

0.4.2 CONCEPTUAL

Understand that a linear inequality in one variable has an interval solution.

If we were to solve the linear equation $3x - 2 = 7$, we would add 2 to both sides, divide by 3, and find that $x = 3$ is the solution, the *only* value that makes the equation true. If we were to solve the *linear inequality* $3x - 2 \leq 7$, we would follow the same procedure: Add 2 to both sides, divide by 3, and find that $x \leq 3$, which is an *interval* or *range* of numbers that make the inequality true.

In solving linear inequalities, we follow the same procedures that we used in solving linear equations with one general exception: *If you multiply or divide an inequality by a negative number, then you must change the direction of the inequality sign.*

INEQUALITY PROPERTIES

Procedures That Do Not Change the Inequality Sign

1. Simplifying by eliminating parentheses and collecting like terms.	$3(x - 6) < 6x - x$ $3x - 18 < 5x$
2. Adding or subtracting the same quantity on both sides.	$7x + 8 \geq 29$ $7x \geq 21$
3. Multiplying or dividing by the same *positive* real number.	$5x \leq 15$ $x \leq 3$

Procedures That Change (Reverse) the Inequality Sign

1. Interchanging the two sides of the inequality.	$x \leq 4$ is equivalent to $4 \geq x$
2. Multiplying or dividing by the same *negative* real number.	$-5x \leq 15$ is equivalent to $x \geq -3$

STUDY TIP

If you multiply or divide an inequality by a negative number, remember to change the direction of the inequality sign.

EXAMPLE 3 **Solving a Linear Inequality**

Solve and graph the inequality $5 - 3x < 23$.

Solution:

Write the original inequality.	$5 - 3x < 23$
Subtract 5 from both sides.	$-3x < 18$
Divide both sides by -3 and reverse the inequality sign.	$\frac{-3x}{-3} > \frac{18}{-3}$
Simplify.	$x > -6$

Solution set: $\{x \mid x > -6\}$ Interval notation: $(-6, \infty)$ Graph:

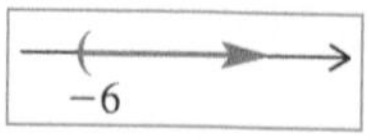

YOUR TURN Solve the inequality $5 \leq 3 - 2x$. Express the solution in set and interval notation, and graph it.

ANSWER

Solution set: $\{x \mid x \leq -1\}$

Interval notation: $(-\infty, -1]$

Graph:

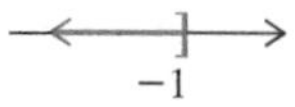

EXAMPLE 4 **Solving a Double Linear Inequality**

Solve the inequality $-2 < 3x + 4 \leq 16$.

Solution:

This double inequality can be written as two inequalities.	$-2 < 3x + 4 \leq 16$
Both inequalities must be satisfied.	$-2 < 3x + 4$ and $3x + 4 \leq 16$
Subtract 4 from both sides of each inequality.	$-6 < 3x$ and $3x \leq 12$
Divide each inequality by 3.	$-2 < x$ and $x \leq 4$

Combining these two inequalities gives us $-2 < x \leq 4$ in inequality notation; in interval notation we have $(-2, \infty) \cap (-\infty, 4)$ or $(-2, 4]$.

Notice that the steps we took in solving these inequalities individually were identical. This leads us to a **shortcut method** in which we solve them together:

Write the combined inequality.	$-2 < 3x + 4 \leq 16$
Subtract 4 from each part.	$-6 < 3x \leq 12$
Divide each part by 3.	$-2 < x \leq 4$

Interval notation: $(-2, 4]$

EXAMPLE 5 **Comparative Shopping**

Two car rental companies have advertised weekly specials on full-size cars. Hertz is advertising an \$80 rental fee plus an additional \$0.10 per mile. Thrifty is advertising \$60 and \$0.20 per mile. How many miles must you drive for the rental car from Hertz to be the better deal?

Solution:

Let x = number of miles driven during the week.

Write the cost for the Hertz rental.	$80 + 0.1x$
Write the cost for the Thrifty rental.	$60 + 0.2x$
Write the inequality if Hertz is less than Thrifty.	$80 + 0.1x < 60 + 0.2x$
Subtract $0.1x$ from both sides.	$80 < 60 + 0.1x$
Subtract 60 from both sides.	$20 < 0.1x$
Divide both sides by 0.1.	$200 < x$

You must drive more than 200 miles for Hertz to be the better deal.

[CONCEPT CHECK]

TRUE OR FALSE When the solution to a linear equation or a linear inequality in one variable is expressed on a number line, a linear equation in one variable has a solution that is a single point, whereas a linear inequality in one variable has a solution that corresponds to a range or interval.

ANSWER True

0.4.3 Polynomial Inequalities

0.4.3 SKILL

Solve polynomial inequalities.

0.4.3 CONCEPTUAL

Understand zeros and test intervals.

A polynomial must pass through zero before its value changes from positive to negative or from negative to positive. **Zeros** of a polynomial are the values of x that make the polynomial equal to zero. These zeros divide the real number line into **test intervals** where the value of the polynomial is either positive or negative. For $x^2 + x - 2 < 0$, if we set the polynomial equal to zero and solve:

$$x^2 + x - 2 = 0$$
$$(x + 2)(x - 1) = 0$$
$$x = -2 \quad \text{or} \quad x = 1$$

we find that $x = -2$ and $x = 1$ are the zeros. These zeros divide the real number line into three test intervals: $(-\infty, -2)$, $(-2, 1)$, and $(1, \infty)$.

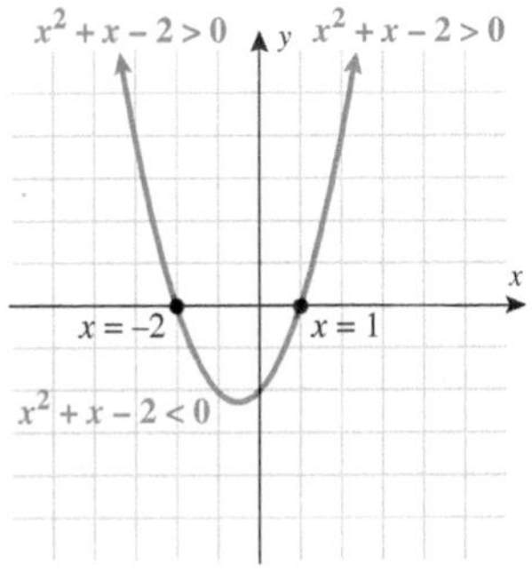

Since the polynomial is equal to zero at $x = -2$ and $x = 1$, we select one real number that lies in each of the three intervals and test to see whether the value of the polynomial at each point is either positive or negative. In this example, we select the real numbers $x = -3$, $x = 0$, and $x = 2$. At this point, there are two ways we can determine whether the value of the polynomial is positive or negative on the interval. One approach is to substitute each of the test points into the polynomial $x^2 + x - 2$.

$x = -3$:	$(-3)^2 + (-3) - 2 = 9 - 3 - 2 = 4$	Positive
$x = 0$:	$(0)^2 + (0) - 2 = 0 - 0 - 2 = -2$	Negative
$x = 2$:	$(2)^2 + (2) - 2 = 4 + 2 - 2 = 4$	Positive

The second approach is to simply determine the sign of the result as opposed to actually calculating the exact number. This alternative approach is often used when the expressions or test points get more complicated to evaluate. The polynomial is written as the product $(x + 2)(x - 1)$; therefore, we simply look for the sign in each set of parentheses.

$$(x + 2)(x - 1)$$

$x = -3$: $\quad (-3 + 2)(-3 - 1) = (-1)(-4) \to (-)(-) = (+)$

$x = 0$: $\quad (0 + 2)(0 - 1) = (2)(-1) \to (+)(-) = (-)$

$x = 2$: $\quad (2 + 2)(2 - 1) = (4)(1) \to (+)(+) = (+)$

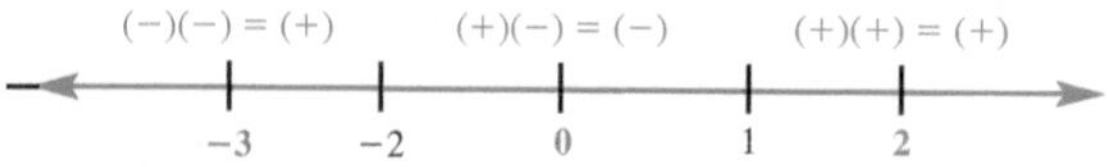

In this second approach we find the same result: $(-\infty, -2)$ and $(1, \infty)$ correspond to a positive value of the polynomial, and $(-2, 1)$ corresponds to a negative value of the polynomial.

In this example, the statement $x^2 + x - 2 < 0$ is true when the value of the polynomial (in factored form), $(x + 2)(x - 1)$, is negative. In the interval $(-2, 1)$, the value of the polynomial is negative. Thus, the solution to the inequality $x^2 + x - 2 < 0$ is $(-2, 1)$. To check the solution, select any number in the interval and substitute it into the original inequality to make sure it makes the statement true. The value $x = -1$ lies in the interval $(-2, 1)$. Upon substituting into the original inequality, we find that $x = -1$ satisfies the inequality $(-1)^2 + (-1) - 2 = -2 < 0$.

STUDY TIP

If the original polynomial is <0, then the interval(s) that yield(s) *negative* products should be selected. If the original polynomial is >0, then the interval(s) that yield(s) *positive* products should be selected.

PROCEDURE FOR SOLVING POLYNOMIAL INEQUALITIES

Step 1: Write the inequality in *standard form.*
Step 2: Identify zeros of the polynomial.
Step 3: Draw the number line with zeros labeled.
Step 4: Determine the sign of the polynomial in each interval.
Step 5: Identify which interval(s) make(s) the inequality true.
Step 6: Write the solution in interval notation.

Note: Be careful in Step 5. If the original polynomial is <0, then the interval(s) that correspond(s) to the value of the polynomial being negative should be selected. If the original polynomial is >0, then the interval(s) that correspond(s) to the value of the polynomial being positive should be selected.

EXAMPLE 6 **Solving a Quadratic Inequality**

Solve the inequality $x^2 - x > 12$.

Solution:

STEP 1: Write the inequality in standard form. $\quad x^2 - x - 12 > 0$

Factor the left side. $\quad (x + 3)(x - 4) > 0$

STEP 2: Identify the zeros. $\quad (x + 3)(x - 4) = 0$

$x = -3 \quad \text{or} \quad x = 4$

STEP 3: Draw the number line with the zeros labeled.

STEP 4: Determine the sign of $(x + 3)(x - 4)$ in each interval.

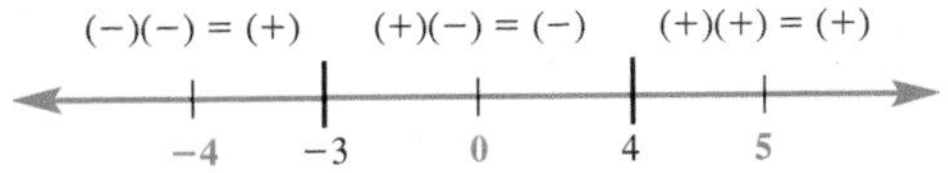

STEP 5: Intervals in which the value of the polynomial is *positive* make this inequality true. $(-\infty, -3)$ or $(4, \infty)$

STEP 6: Write the solution in interval notation. $\boxed{(-\infty, -3) \cup (4, \infty)}$

YOUR TURN Solve the inequality $x^2 - 5x \leq 6$ and express the solution in interval notation.

ANSWER

$[-1, 6]$

The inequality in Example 6, $x^2 - x > 12$, is a strict inequality, so we use parentheses when we express the solution in interval notation $(-\infty, -3) \cup (4, \infty)$. It is important to note that if we change the inequality sign from $>$ to $\geq$, then the zeros $x = -3$ and $x = 4$ also make the inequality true. Therefore, the solution to $x^2 - x \geq 12$ is $(-\infty, -3] \cup [4, \infty)$.

EXAMPLE 7 Solving a Quadratic Inequality

Solve the inequality $x^2 > -5x$.

common mistake

A common mistake is to divide by x. Never divide by a variable, because the value of the variable might be zero. Always start by writing the inequality in standard form and then factor to determine the zeros.

CAUTION

Do not divide inequalities by a variable.

✓CORRECT

STEP 1: Write the inequality in standard form.

$$x^2 + 5x > 0$$

Factor.

$$x(x + 5) > 0$$

STEP 2: Identify the zeros.

$$x = 0, x = -5$$

STEP 3: Draw the number line with the zeros labeled.

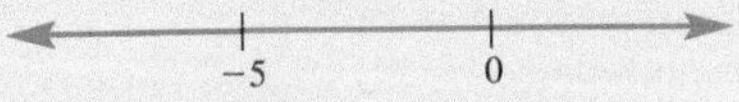

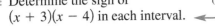

STEP 4: Determine the sign of $x(x + 5)$ in each interval.

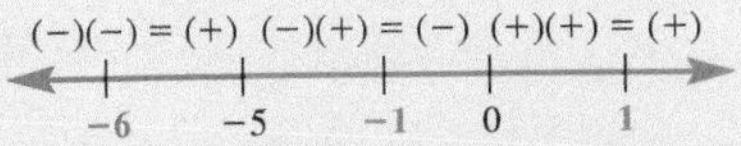

STEP 5: Intervals in which the value of the polynomial is *positive* satisfy the inequality.

$(-\infty, -5)$ and $(0, \infty)$

STEP 6: Express the solution in interval notation.

$\boxed{(-\infty, -5) \cup (0, \infty)}$

✗INCORRECT

Write the original inequality.

$$x^2 > -5x$$

ERROR:

Divide both sides by x.

$$x > -5$$

Dividing by x is the mistake. If x is negative, the inequality sign must be reversed. What if x is zero?

EXAMPLE 8 **Solving a Quadratic Inequality**

Solve the inequality $x^2 + 2x < 1$.

Solution:

Write the inequality in standard form. $x^2 + 2x - 1 < 0$

Identify the zeros. $x^2 + 2x - 1 = 0$

Apply the quadratic formula. $x = \dfrac{-2 \pm \sqrt{2^2 - 4(1)(-1)}}{2(1)}$

Simplify. $x = \dfrac{-2 \pm \sqrt{8}}{2} = \dfrac{-2 \pm 2\sqrt{2}}{2} = -1 \pm \sqrt{2}$

Draw the number line with the intervals labeled.

Note: $-1 - \sqrt{2} \approx -2.41$
$-1 + \sqrt{2} \approx 0.41$

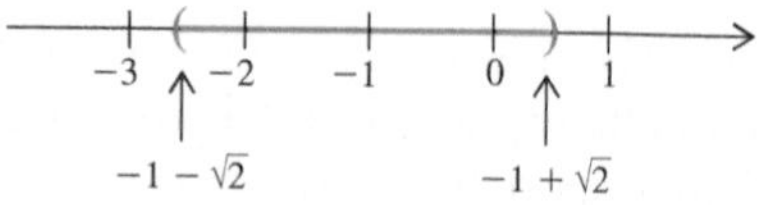

Test each interval.

$(-\infty, -1 - \sqrt{2})$ $x = -3$: $(-3)^2 + 2(-3) - 1 = 2 > 0$

$(-1 - \sqrt{2}, -1 + \sqrt{2})$ $x = 0$: $(0)^2 + 2(0) - 1 = -1 < 0$

$(-1 + \sqrt{2}, \infty)$ $x = 1$: $(1)^2 + 2(1) - 1 = 2 > 0$

Intervals in which the value of the polynomial is *negative* make this inequality true. $\boxed{(-1 - \sqrt{2}, -1 + \sqrt{2})}$

YOUR TURN Solve the inequality $x^2 - 2x \geq 1$.

ANSWER
$(-\infty, 1 - \sqrt{2}] \cup [1 + \sqrt{2}, \infty)$

EXAMPLE 9 **Solving a Polynomial Inequality**

Solve the inequality $x^3 - 3x^2 \geq 10x$.

Solution:

Write the inequality in standard form. $x^3 - 3x^2 - 10x \geq 0$

Factor. $x(x - 5)(x + 2) \geq 0$

Identify the zeros. $x = 0, x = 5, x = -2$

Draw the number line with the zeros (intervals) labeled.

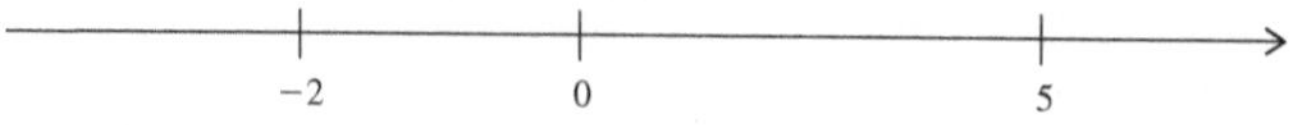

Test each interval.

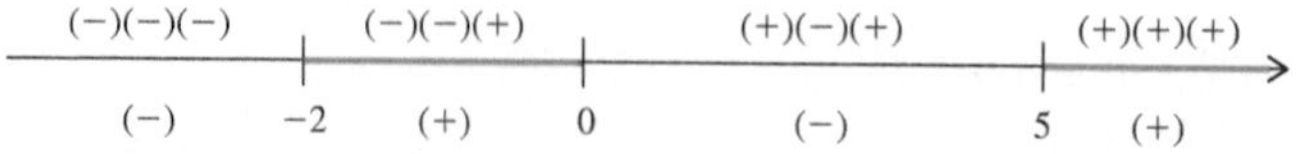

Intervals in which the value of the polynomial is *positive* make this inequality true. $\boxed{[-2, 0] \cup [5, \infty)}$

[CONCEPT CHECK]

Solve: $(x - a)(x + b) < 0$, where $a > 0$ and $b > 0$.

ANSWER $(-b, a)$

YOUR TURN Solve the inequality $x^3 - x^2 - 6x < 0$.

ANSWER
$(-\infty, -2) \cup (0, 3)$

0.4.4 Rational Inequalities

A rational expression can change signs if either the numerator or denominator changes sign. In order to go from positive to negative or vice versa, you must pass through zero. To *solve* rational inequalities such as $\frac{x-3}{x^2-4} \geq 0$, we use a procedure similar to the one used for solving polynomial inequalities, with one exception. You must eliminate from the solution set values for x that make the denominator equal to zero. In this example, we must eliminate $x = -2$ and $x = 2$ because these values make the denominator equal to zero. Rational inequalities have implied domains. In this example, $x \neq \pm 2$ is a domain restriction and these values ($x = -2$ and $x = 2$) must be eliminated from a possible solution.

We will proceed with a similar procedure involving zeros and test intervals that was outlined for polynomial inequalities. However, in rational inequalities, once expressions are combined into a single fraction, any values that make *either* the numerator *or* the denominator equal to zero divide the number line into intervals.

0.4.4 SKILL

Solve rational inequalities.

0.4.4 CONCEPTUAL

Realize that a rational inequality has an implied domain restriction on the variable.

STUDY TIP

Values that make the denominator equal to zero are always excluded.

EXAMPLE 10 **Solving a Rational Inequality**

Solve the inequality $\frac{x-3}{x^2-4} \geq 0$.

Solution:

Factor the denominator. $\frac{(x-3)}{(x-2)(x+2)} \geq 0$

State the domain restrictions on the variable. $x \neq 2, x \neq -2$

Identify the zeros of numerator and denominator. $x = -2, x = 2, x = 3$

Draw the number line and divide into intervals.

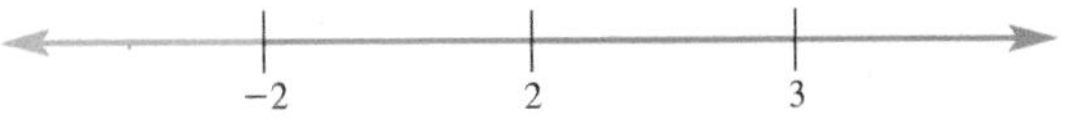

Test the intervals.

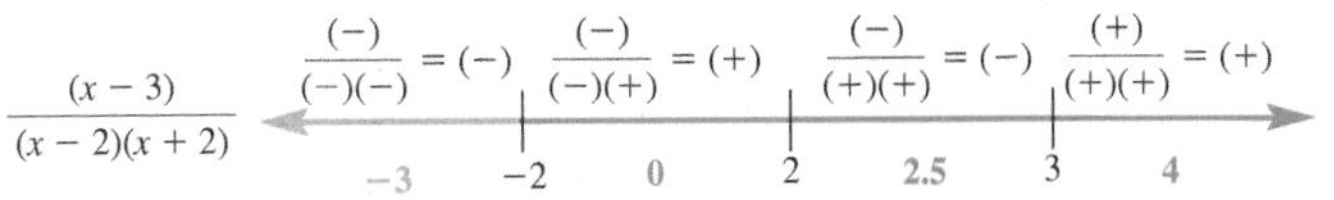

Intervals in which the value of the rational expression is *positive* satisfy this inequality. $(-2, 2)$ and $(3, \infty)$

Since this inequality is greater than or equal to, we include $x = 3$ in our solution because it satisfies the inequality. However, $x = -2$ and $x = 2$ are not included in the solution because they make the denominator equal to zero.

The solution is $\boxed{(-2, 2) \cup [3, \infty)}$.

YOUR TURN Solve the inequality $\frac{x+2}{x-1} \leq 0$.

ANSWER

$[-2, 1)$

EXAMPLE 11 Solving a Rational Inequality

Solve the inequality $\dfrac{x}{x+2} \leq 3$.

CAUTION

Rational inequalities should not be solved using cross multiplication.

common mistake

Do not cross multiply. The LCD or expression by which you are multiplying might be negative for some values of x, and that would require the direction of the inequality sign to be reversed.

✓CORRECT

Subtract 3 from both sides.

$$\frac{x}{x+2} - 3 \leq 0$$

Write as a single rational expression.

$$\frac{x - 3(x+2)}{x+2} \leq 0$$

Eliminate the parentheses.

$$\frac{x - 3x - 6}{x+2} \leq 0$$

Simplify the numerator.

$$\frac{-2x - 6}{x+2} \leq 0$$

Factor the numerator.

$$\frac{-2(x+3)}{x+2} \leq 0$$

Identify the zeros of the numerator and the denominator.

$$x = -3 \text{ and } x = -2$$

Draw the number line and test the intervals.

$$\frac{-2(x+3)}{x+2} \leq 0$$

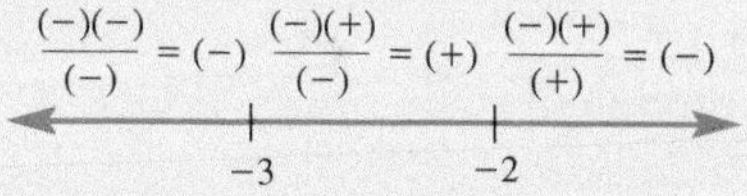

Intervals in which the value of the rational expression is *negative* satisfy the inequality. $(-\infty, -3]$ and $(-2, \infty)$. Note that $x = -2$ is not included in the solution because it makes the denominator zero, and $x = -3$ is included because it satisfies the inequality.

The solution is

$$\boxed{(-\infty, -3] \cup (-2, \infty)}$$

✗INCORRECT

ERROR:

Do not cross multiply.

$$x \leq 3(x+2)$$

0.4.5 Absolute Value Inequalities

To solve the inequality $|x| < 3$, look for all real numbers that make this statement true. If we interpret this inequality as distance, we ask *what numbers are less than three units from the origin?* We can represent the solution in the following ways:

Inequality notation: $-3 < x < 3$

Interval notation: $(-3, 3)$

Graph: 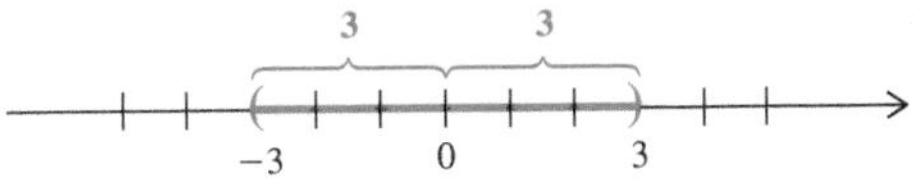

Similarly, to solve the inequality $|x| \geq 3$, look for all real numbers that make the statement true. If we interpret this inequality as a distance, we ask *what numbers are at least three units from the origin?* We can represent the solution in the following ways:

Inequality notation: $x \leq -3$ or $x \geq 3$

Interval notation: $(-\infty, -3] \cup [3, \infty)$

Graph: 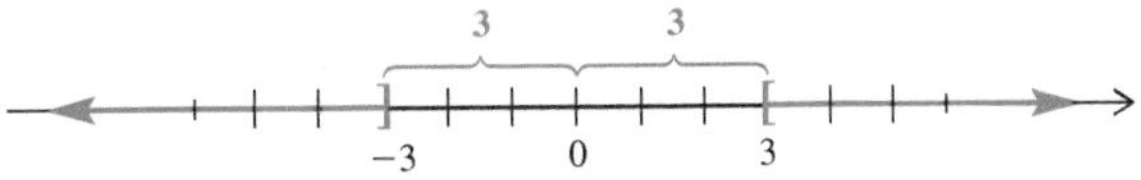

This discussion leads us to the following equivalence relations.

0.4.5 SKILL

Solve absolute value inequalities.

0.4.5 CONCEPTUAL

Apply intersection and union concepts to solutions of linear inequalities in one variable.

PROPERTIES OF ABSOLUTE VALUE INEQUALITIES

1. $|x| < a$ is equivalent to $-a < x < a$ 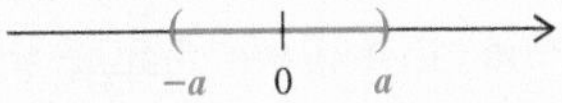

2. $|x| \leq a$ is equivalent to $-a \leq x \leq a$ 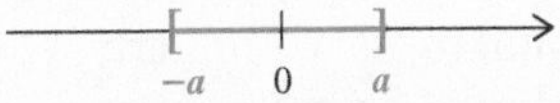

3. $|x| > a$ is equivalent to $x < -a$ or $x > a$ 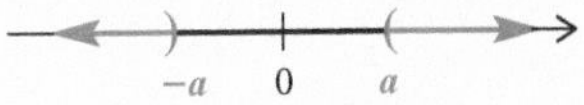

4. $|x| \geq a$ is equivalent to $x \leq -a$ or $x \geq a$ 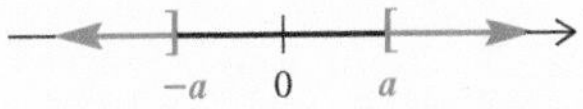

It is important to realize that in the above four properties, the variable x can be any algebraic expression.

EXAMPLE 12 **Solving an Inequality Involving an Absolute Value**

Solve the inequality $|3x - 2| \leq 7$.

Solution:

We apply property (2) and squeeze the absolute value expression between -7 and 7. $\quad -7 \leq 3x - 2 \leq 7$

Add 2 to all three parts. $\quad -5 \leq 3x \leq 9$

Divide all three parts by 3. $\quad -\dfrac{5}{3} \leq x \leq 3$

The solution in interval notation is $\boxed{\left[-\tfrac{5}{3}, 3\right]}$.

Graph: 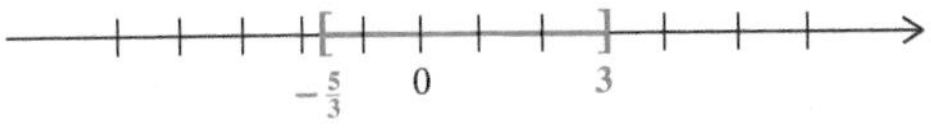

YOUR TURN Solve the inequality $|2x + 1| < 11$.

ANSWER

Inequality notation: $-6 < x < 5$

Interval notation: $(-6, 5)$

STUDY TIP

Less than inequalities can be written as a single statement.

Greater than inequalities must be written as two statements.

It is often helpful to note that for absolute value inequalities,

- *less than* inequalities can be written as a single statement (see Example 12).
- *greater than* inequalities must be written as two statements (see Example 13).

EXAMPLE 13 Solving an Inequality Involving an Absolute Value

Solve the inequality $|1 - 2x| > 5$.

Solution:

Apply property (3).	$1 - 2x < -5$ or $1 - 2x > 5$
Subtract 1 from all expressions.	$-2x < -6$ $\quad$ $-2x > 4$
Divide by -2 and reverse the inequality sign.	$x > 3$ $\quad$ $x < -2$
Express the solution in interval notation.	$\boxed{(-\infty, -2) \cup (3, \infty)}$

Graph:

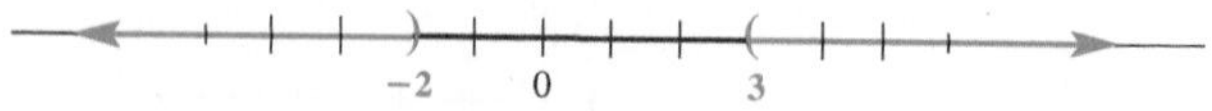

YOUR TURN Solve the inequality $|5 - 2x| \geq 1$.

ANSWER

Inequality notation: $x \leq 2$ or $x \geq 3$
Interval notation: $(-\infty, 2] \cup [3, \infty)$

Notice that if we change the problem in Example 13 to $|1 - 2x| > -5$, the answer is all real numbers because **the absolute value of any expression is greater than or equal to zero.** Similarly, $|1 - 2x| < -5$ would have no solution because **the absolute value of an expression can never be negative.**

EXAMPLE 14 Solving an Inequality Involving an Absolute Value

Solve the inequality $2 - |3x| < 1$.

Solution:

Subtract 2 from both sides.	$-\|3x\| < -1$
Multiply by (-1) and reverse the inequality sign.	$\|3x\| > 1$
Apply property (3).	$3x < -1$ or $3x > 1$
Divide both inequalities by 3.	$x < -\frac{1}{3}$ or $x > \frac{1}{3}$
Express in interval notation.	$\boxed{\left(-\infty, -\frac{1}{3}\right) \cup \left(\frac{1}{3}, \infty\right)}$
Graph.	

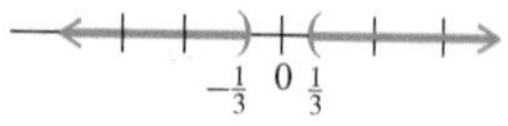

[CONCEPT CHECK]

If the solution to a linear inequality in one variable is all the values less than *a* OR greater than *b* (where *a* and *b* are both positive), then the appropriate notation is
(A) intersection
(B) union.

ANSWER (B) union $(-\infty, a) \cup (b, \infty)$

[SECTION 0.4] SUMMARY

In this section, we used interval notation to represent the solution to inequalities.

- **Linear Inequalities:** Solve linear inequalities similarly to how we solve linear equations with one exception—when you multiply or divide by a negative number, you must reverse the inequality sign.
- **Polynomial Inequalities:** First write the inequality in standard form (zero on one side). Determine the zeros, draw the number line, test the intervals, select the intervals according to the sign of the inequality, and write the solution in interval notation.
- **Rational Inequalities:** Write as a single fraction and then proceed with an approach similar to that used in polynomial inequalities—only the test intervals are determined by finding the zeros of either the numerator or the denominator. Exclude from the solution any values that result in the denominator being equal to zero.
- **Absolute Value Inequalities:** Write an absolute value inequality in terms of two inequalities that do not involve absolute value:
  - $|x| < A$ is equivalent to $-A < x < A$.
  - $|x| > A$ is equivalent to $x < -A$ or $x > A$.

[SECTION 0.4] EXERCISES

• SKILLS

In Exercises 1–10, rewrite in interval notation and graph.

1. $-2 \le x < 3$
2. $-4 \le x \le -1$
3. $-3 < x \le 5$
4. $0 < x < 6$
5. $x \le 6$ and $x \ge 4$
6. $x > -3$ and $x \le 2$
7. $x \le -6$ and $x \ge -8$
8. $x < 8$ and $x < 2$
9. $x > 4$ and $x \le -2$
10. $x \ge -5$ and $x < -6$

In Exercises 11–20, graph the indicated set and write as a single interval, if possible.

11. $(-\infty, 4) \cap [1, \infty)$
12. $(-3, \infty) \cap [-5, \infty)$
13. $[-5, 2) \cap [-1, 3]$
14. $[-4, 5) \cap [-2, 7)$
15. $(-\infty, 4) \cup (4, \infty)$
16. $(-\infty, -3] \cup [-3, \infty)$
17. $(-\infty, -3] \cup [3, \infty)$
18. $(-2, 2) \cap [-3, 1]$
19. $(-\infty, \infty) \cap (-3, 2]$
20. $(-\infty, \infty) \cup (-4, 7)$

In Exercises 21–32, solve each linear inequality and express the solution set in interval notation.

21. $3(t + 1) > 2t$
22. $2(y + 5) \le 3(y - 4)$
23. $7 - 2(1 - x) > 5 + 3(x - 2)$
24. $4 - 3(2 + x) < 5$
25. $\frac{2}{3}y - \frac{1}{2}(5 - y) < \frac{5y}{3} - (2 + y)$
26. $\frac{s}{2} - \frac{(s - 3)}{3} > \frac{s}{4} - \frac{1}{12}$
27. $-3 < 1 - x \le 9$
28. $3 \le -2 - 5x \le 13$
29. $0 < 2 - \frac{1}{3}y < 4$
30. $3 < \frac{1}{2}A - 3 < 7$
31. $\frac{1}{2} \le \frac{1 + y}{3} \le \frac{3}{4}$
32. $-1 < \frac{2 - z}{4} \le \frac{1}{5}$

In Exercises 33–50, solve each polynomial inequality and express the solution set in interval notation.

33. $2t^2 - 3 \le t$
34. $3t^2 \ge -5t + 2$
35. $5v - 1 > 6v^2$
36. $12t^2 < 37t + 10$
37. $2s^2 - 5s \ge 3$
38. $8s + 12 \le -s^2$
39. $y^2 + 2y \ge 4$
40. $y^2 + 3y \le 1$
41. $x^2 - 4x < 6$
42. $x^2 - 2x > 5$
43. $u^2 \ge 3u$
44. $u^2 \le -4u$
45. $x^2 > 9$
46. $t^2 \le 49$
47. $x^3 + x^2 - 2x \le 0$
48. $x^3 + 2x^2 - 3x > 0$
49. $x^3 + x > 2x^2$
50. $x^3 + 4x \le 4x^2$

In Exercises 51–66, solve each rational inequality and express the solution set in interval notation.

51. $\frac{s+1}{4-s^2} \geq 0$ **52.** $\frac{s+5}{4-s^2} \leq 0$ **53.** $\frac{3t^2}{t+2} \geq 5t$ **54.** $\frac{-2t-t^2}{4-t} \geq t$

55. $\frac{3p-2p^2}{4-p^2} < \frac{3+p}{2-p}$ **56.** $-\frac{7p}{p^2-100} \leq \frac{p+2}{p+10}$ **57.** $\frac{x^2+10}{x^2+16} > 0$ **58.** $-\frac{x^2+2}{x^2+4} < 0$

59. $\frac{v^2-9}{v-3} \geq 0$ **60.** $\frac{v^2-1}{v+1} \leq 0$ **61.** $\frac{2}{t-3} + \frac{1}{t+3} \geq 0$ **62.** $\frac{1}{t-2} + \frac{1}{t+2} \leq 0$

63. $\frac{3}{x+4} - \frac{1}{x-2} \leq 0$ **64.** $\frac{2}{x-5} - \frac{1}{x-1} \geq 0$ **65.** $\frac{1}{p-2} - \frac{1}{p+2} \geq \frac{3}{p^2-4}$ **66.** $\frac{2}{2p-3} - \frac{1}{p+1} \leq \frac{1}{2p^2-p-3}$

In Exercises 67–82, solve the absolute value inequality and express the solution set in interval notation.

67. $|x-4| > 2$ **68.** $|x-1| < 3$ **69.** $|4-x| \leq 1$ **70.** $|1-y| < 3$

71. $|2x| > -3$ **72.** $|2x| < -3$ **73.** $|7-2y| \geq 3$ **74.** $|6-5y| \leq 1$

75. $|4-3x| \geq 0$ **76.** $|4-3x| \geq 1$ **77.** $2|4x| - 9 \geq 3$ **78.** $5|x-1| + 2 \leq 7$

79. $9 - |2x| < 3$ **80.** $4 - |x+1| > 1$ **81.** $|x^2 - 1| \leq 8$ **82.** $|x^2 + 4| \geq 29$

• APPLICATIONS

The following table is the 2015 Federal Tax Rate Schedule for people filing as single:

TAX BRACKET #	IF TAXABLE INCOME IS	THE TAX IS
I	\$0 to \$9,225	10% of the amount over \$0
II	\$9,226 to \$37,450	\$922.50 plus 15% of the amount over \$9,225
III	\$37,451 to \$90,750	\$5,156.25 plus 25% of the amount over \$37,450
IV	\$90,751 to \$189,300	\$18,481.25 plus 28% of the amount over \$90,750
V	\$189,301 to \$411,500	\$46,075.25 plus 33% of the amount over \$189,300
VI	\$411,501 to \$413,200	\$119, 401.25 plus 35% of the amount over \$411,500
VII	\$413,201 or more	\$119,996.25 plus 39.6% of the amount over \$413,200

83. Federal Income Tax. What was the range of federal income taxes a person in tax bracket III would pay the IRS?

84. Federal Income Tax. What was the range of federal income taxes a person in tax bracket IV would pay the IRS?

In Exercises 85 and 86 refer to the following:

The annual revenue for a small company is modeled by

$$R = 5000 + 1.75x$$

where x is hundreds of units sold and R is revenue in thousands of dollars.

85. Business. Find the number of units (to the nearest 100) that must be sold to generate at least \$10 million in revenue.

86. Business. Find the number of units (to the nearest 100) that must be sold to generate at least \$7.5 million in revenue.

In Exercises 87 and 88 refer to the following:

The target or training heart rate (THR) is a range of heart rate (measured in beats per minute) that enables a person's heart and lungs to benefit the most from an aerobic workout. THR can be modeled by the formula

$$THR = (HR_{max} - HR_{rest}) \times I + HR_{rest}$$

where HR_{max} is the maximum heart rate that is deemed safe for the individual, HR_{rest} is the resting heart rate, and I is the intensity of the workout that is reported as a percentage.

87. Health. A female with a resting heart rate of 65 beats per minute has a maximum safe heart rate of 170 beats per minute. If her target heart rate is between 100 and 140 beats per minute, what percent intensities of workout can she consider?

88. Health. A male with a resting heart rate of 75 beats per minute has a maximum safe heart rate of 175 beats per minute. If his target heart rate is between 110 and 150 beats per minute, what percent intensities of workout can he consider?

89. Profit. A Web-based embroidery company makes monogrammed napkins. The profit associated with producing x orders of napkins is governed by the equation

$$P(x) = -x^2 + 130x - 3000$$

Determine the range of orders the company should accept in order to make a profit.

90. Profit. Repeat Exercise 89 using $P(x) = x^2 - 130x + 3600$.

91. Car Value. Being "upside down" on car payments means owing more than a car is worth. Assume you buy a new car and finance 100% over 5 years. The difference between the value of the car and what is owed on the car is governed by the expression $\frac{t}{t-3}$, where t is age (in years) of the car. Determine the time period when the car is worth more than you owe $\left(\frac{t}{t-3} > 0\right)$. When do you owe more than it's worth $\left(\frac{t}{t-3} < 0\right)$?

92. **Car Value.** Repeat Exercise 91 using the expression $-\frac{2-t}{4-t}$.

93. **Bullet Speed.** A .22 caliber gun fires a bullet at a speed of 1200 feet per second. If a .22 caliber gun is fired straight upward into the sky, the height of the bullet in feet is given by the equation $h = -16t^2 + 1200t$, where t is the time in seconds with $t = 0$ corresponding to the instant the gun is fired. How long is the bullet in the air?

94. **Bullet Speed.** A .38 caliber gun fires a bullet at a speed of 600 feet per second. If a .38 caliber gun is fired straight upward into the sky, the height of the bullet in feet is given by the equation $h = -16t^2 + 600t$. How many seconds is the bullet in the air?

In Exercises 95 and 96 refer to the following:

A company is reviewing revenue for the prior sales year. The model for projected revenue and the model for actual revenue are

$$R_{\text{projected}} = 200 + 5x$$
$$R_{\text{actual}} = 210 + 4.8x$$

where x represents the number of units sold and R represents the revenue in thousands of dollars. Since the two revenue models are not identical, an error in projected revenue occurred. This error is represented by

$$E = |R_{\text{projected}} - R_{\text{actual}}|$$

95. **Business.** For what number of units sold was the error in projected revenue less than \$5000?

96. **Business.** For what number of units sold was the error in projected revenue less than \$3000?

• CATCH THE MISTAKE

In Exercises 97–100, explain the mistake that is made.

97. Solve the inequality $2 - 3p \le -4$ and express the solution in interval notation.

Solution:

$$2 - 3p \le -4$$
$$-3p \le -6$$
$$p \le 2$$
$$(-\infty, 2]$$

This is incorrect. What mistake was made?

98. Solve the inequality $u^2 < 25$.

Solution:

Take the square root of both sides. $u < -5$

Write the solution in interval notation. $(-\infty, -5)$

This is incorrect. What mistake was made?

99. Solve the inequality $3x < x^2$.

Solution:

Divide by x. $3 < x$

Write the solution in interval notation. $(3, \infty)$

This is incorrect. What mistake was made?

100. Solve the inequality $\frac{x+4}{x} < -\frac{1}{3}$.

Solution:

Cross multiply. $3(x + 4) < -1(x)$

Eliminate the parentheses. $3x + 12 < -x$

Combine like terms. $4x < -12$

Divide both sides by 4. $x < -3$

This is incorrect. What mistake was made?

• CONCEPTUAL

In Exercises 101–104, determine whether each statement is true or false. Assume that *a* is a positive real number.

101. If $x < a$, then $a > x$.

102. If $-x \ge a$, then $x \ge -a$.

103. If $x < a^2$, then the solution is $(-\infty, a)$.

104. If $x \ge a^2$, then the solution is $[a, \infty)$.

• CHALLENGE

In Exercises 105 and 106, solve for *x*, given that *a* and *b* are both positive real numbers.

105. $\frac{x^2 + a^2}{x^2 + b^2} \ge 0$

106. $\frac{x^2 - b^2}{x + b} < 0$

107. For what values of x does the absolute value equation $|x + 1| = 4 + |x - 2|$ hold?

108. Solve the inequality $|3x^2 - 7x + 2| > 8$.

0.5 GRAPHING EQUATIONS

SKILLS OBJECTIVES

- Plot points on the Cartesian plane.
- Calculate the distance between two points in the Cartesian plane, and find the midpoint of a line segment joining two points in the Cartesian plane.
- Sketch graphs of equations by plotting points.
- Find intercepts for graphs of equations.
- Determine whether the graph of an equation is symmetric about the x-axis, y-axis, or origin.
- Graph a circle.

CONCEPTUAL OBJECTIVES

- Expand the concept of a one-dimensional number line to a two-dimensional plane.
- Derive the distance formula using the Pythagorean theorem, and conceptualize the midpoint as the average of the x- and y-coordinates.
- Understand that if a point (a, b) satisfies the equation, then that point lies on its graph.
- Understand that intercepts are points that lie on the graph and either the x-axis or the y-axis.
- Understand how the algebraic definitions of symmetry can be visualized graphically.
- Understand algebraic and graphical representations of circles.

0.5.1 SKILL

Plot points on the Cartesian plane.

0.5.1 CONCEPTUAL

Expand the concept of a one-dimensional number line to a two-dimensional plane.

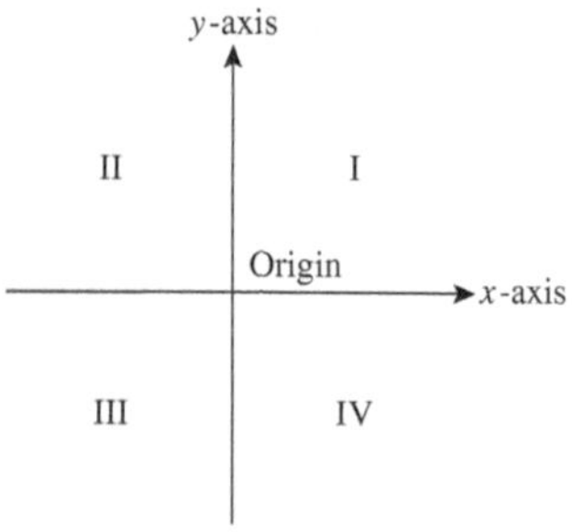

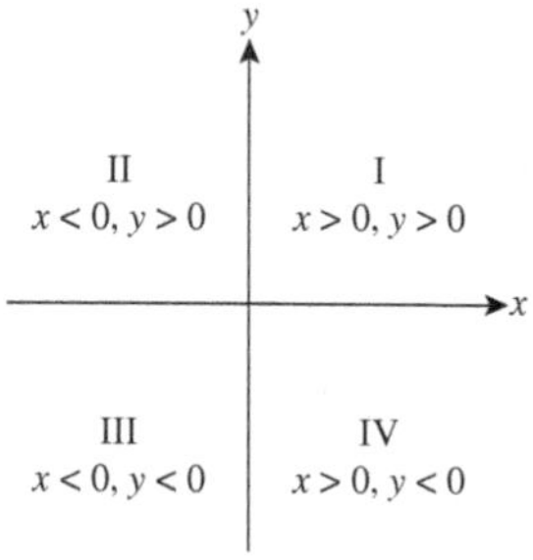

0.5.1 Cartesian Plane

HIV infection rates, stock prices, and temperature conversions are all examples of relationships between two quantities that can be expressed in a two-dimensional graph. Because it is two-dimensional, such a graph lies in a **plane**.

Two perpendicular real number lines, known as the **axes** in the plane, intersect at a point we call the **origin**. Typically, the horizontal axis is called the ***x*-axis** and the vertical axis is known as the ***y*-axis**. The axes divide the plane into four **quadrants**, which are numbered by Roman numerals and ordered counterclockwise.

Points in the plane are represented by **ordered pairs**, denoted (x, y). The first number of the ordered pair indicates the position in the horizontal direction and is often called the **x-coordinate** or **abscissa**. The second number indicates the position in the vertical direction and is often called the **y-coordinate** or **ordinate**. The **origin** is denoted **(0, 0)**.

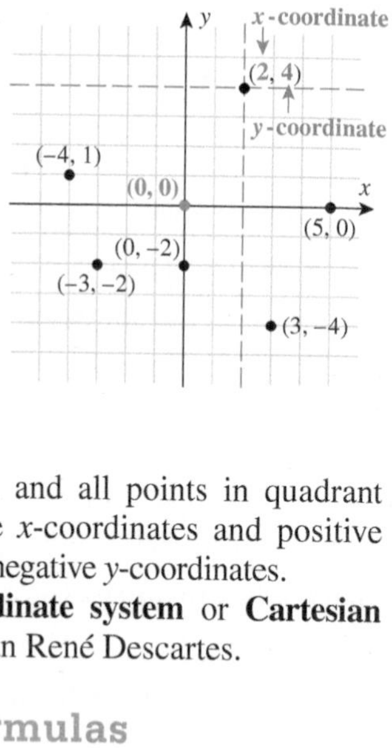

Examples of other coordinates are given on the graph to the left.

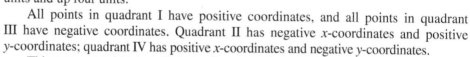

The point (2, 4) lies in quadrant I. To **plot** this point, start at the origin (0, 0) and move to the right two units and up four units.

All points in quadrant I have positive coordinates, and all points in quadrant III have negative coordinates. Quadrant II has negative x-coordinates and positive y-coordinates; quadrant IV has positive x-coordinates and negative y-coordinates.

This representation is called the **rectangular coordinate system** or **Cartesian coordinate system**, named after the French mathematician René Descartes.

0.5.2 SKILL

Calculate the distance between two points in the Cartesian plane, and find the midpoint of a line segment joining two points in the Cartesian plane.

0.5.2 CONCEPTUAL

Derive the distance formula using the Pythagorean theorem, and conceptualize the midpoint as the average of the x- and y-coordinates.

0.5.2 The Distance and Midpoint Formulas

DEFINITION Distance Formula

The **distance *d*** between two points $P_1 = (x_1, y_1)$ and $P_2 = (x_2, y_2)$ is given by

$$d = \sqrt{(x_2 - x_1)^2 + (y_2 - y_1)^2}$$

The distance between two points is the square root of the sum of the square of the difference between the x-coordinates and the square of the difference between the y-coordinates.

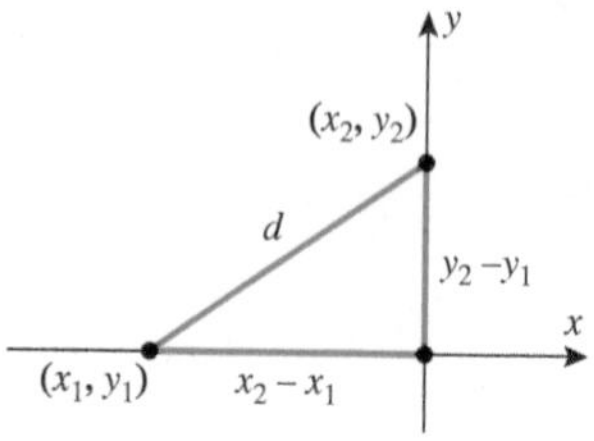

EXAMPLE 1 Using the Distance Formula to Find the Distance Between Two Points

Find the distance between $(-3, 7)$ and $(5, -2)$.

Solution:

Write the distance formula. $d = \sqrt{[x_2 - x_1]^2 + [y_2 - y_1]^2}$

Substitute $(x_1, y_1) = (-3, 7)$ and $(x_2, y_2) = (5, -2)$. $d = \sqrt{[5 - (-3)]^2 + [-2 - 7]^2}$

Simplify. $d = \sqrt{[5 + 3]^2 + [-2 - 7]^2}$

$d = \sqrt{8^2 + (-9)^2} = \sqrt{64 + 81} = \sqrt{145}$

Solve for d. $\boxed{d = \sqrt{145}}$

STUDY TIP

It does not matter which point is taken to be the first point and which to be the second point.

YOUR TURN Find the distance between $(4, -5)$ and $(-3, -2)$.

ANSWER

$d = \sqrt{58}$

DEFINITION Midpoint Formula

The **midpoint**, (x_m, y_m), of the line segment with endpoints (x_1, y_1) and (x_2, y_2) is given by

$$(x_m, y_m) = \left(\frac{x_1 + x_2}{2}, \frac{y_1 + y_2}{2}\right)$$

The midpoint can be found by averaging the x-coordinates and averaging the y-coordinates.

[CONCEPT CHECK]

Which point is P_1 and which point is P_2?

ANSWER It does not matter which point is labeled P_1 and which point is labeled P_2.

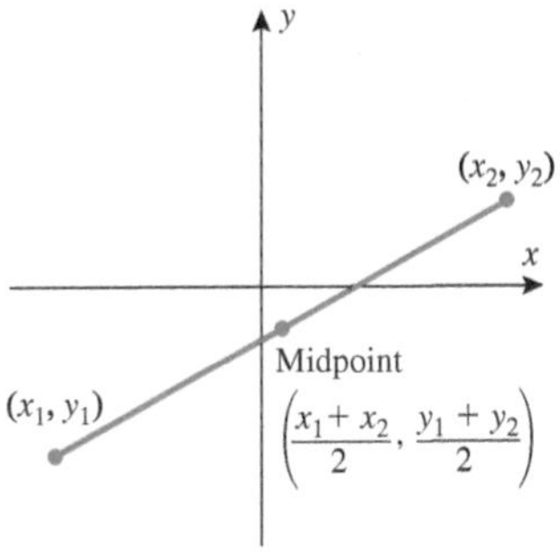

EXAMPLE 2 Finding the Midpoint of a Line Segment

Find the midpoint of the line segment joining the points $(2, 6)$ and $(-4, -2)$.

Solution:

Write the midpoint formula. $(x_m, y_m) = \left(\frac{x_1 + x_2}{2}, \frac{y_1 + y_2}{2}\right)$

Substitute $(x_1, y_1) = (2, 6)$ and $(x_2, y_2) = (-4, -2)$. $(x_m, y_m) = \left(\frac{2 + (-4)}{2}, \frac{6 + (-2)}{2}\right)$

Simplify. $\boxed{(x_m, y_m) = (-1, 2)}$

One way to verify your answer is to plot the given points and the midpoint to make sure your answer looks reasonable.

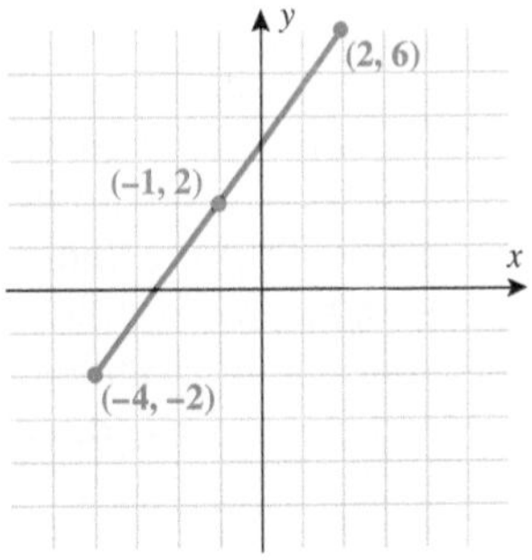

[CONCEPT CHECK]

Find the midpoint of the line segment joining the two points $(-2, -1)$ and $(-4, 1)$.

ANSWER $(-3, 0)$.

YOUR TURN Find the midpoint of the line segment joining the points $(3, -4)$ and $(5, 8)$.

ANSWER

midpoint $= (4, 2)$

0.5.3 Point-Plotting

0.5.3 SKILL

Sketch graphs of equations by plotting points.

0.5.3 CONCEPTUAL

Understand that if a point (a, b) satisfies the equation, then that point lies on its graph.

The **graph of an equation** in two variables, x and y, consists of all the points in the xy-plane whose coordinates (x, y) satisfy the equation. A procedure for plotting the graphs of equations is outlined below and is illustrated with the example $y = x^2$.

WORDS | **MATH**

Step 1: In a table, list several pairs of coordinates for which the equation is true.

x	$y = x^2$	(x, y)
0	0	(0, 0)
−1	1	(−1, 1)
1	1	(1, 1)
−2	4	(−2, 4)
2	4	(2, 4)

Step 2: Plot these points on a graph and connect the points with a smooth curve. Use arrows to indicate that the graph continues.

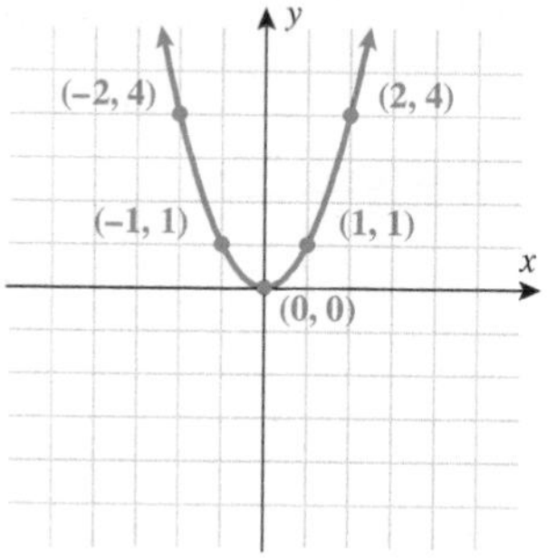

In graphing an equation, first select arbitrary values for x and then use the equation to find the corresponding value of y, or vice versa.

EXAMPLE 3 **Graphing an Equation by Plotting Points**

Graph the equation $y = x^3$.

Solution:

STEP 1 In a table, list several pairs of coordinates that satisfy the equation.

x	$y = x^3$	(x, y)
0	0	(0, 0)
−1	−1	(−1, −1)
1	1	(1, 1)
−2	−8	(−2, −8)
2	8	(2, 8)

STEP 2 Plot these points on a graph and connect the points with a smooth curve, indicating with arrows that the curve continues in both the positive and the negative direction.

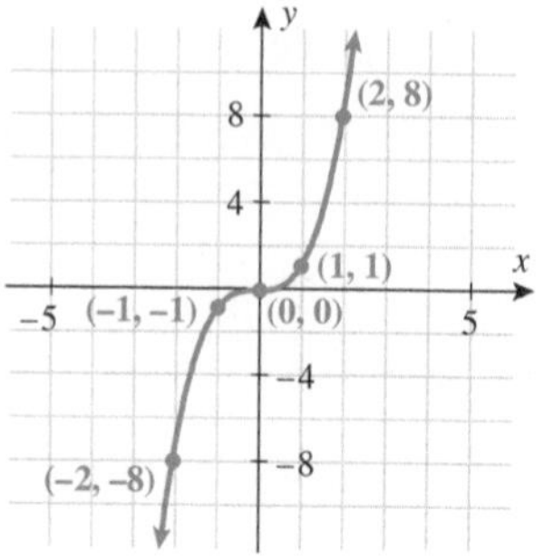

[CONCEPT CHECK]

Show that the points (1, 0) and (2, 3) satisfy the equation $y = x^2 - 1$.

ANSWER (1, 0): $0 = 1 - 1$ and (2, 3): $3 = 2^2 - 1$

0.5.4 Using Intercepts as Graphing Aids

When point-plotting graphs of equations, which points should be selected? Points where a graph crosses (or touches) either the x-axis or y-axis are called **intercepts**, and identifying these points helps define the graph unmistakably.

An ***x*-intercept** of a graph is a point where the graph intersects the x-axis. Specifically, an x-intercept is the x-coordinate of such a point. For example, if a graph intersects the x-axis at the point $(3, 0)$, then we say that 3 is the x-intercept. Since the value for y along the x-axis is zero, all points corresponding to x-intercepts have the form $(a, 0)$.

A ***y*-intercept** of a graph is a point where the graph intersects the y-axis. Specifically, a y-intercept is the y-coordinate of such a point. For example, if a graph intersects the y-axis at the point $(0, 2)$, then we say that 2 is the y-intercept. Since the value for x along the y-axis is zero, all points corresponding to y-intercepts have the form $(0, b)$.

It is important to note that graphs of equations do not have to have intercepts, and if they do have intercepts, they can have one or more of each type.

0.5.4 SKILL

Find intercepts for graphs of equations.

0.5.4 CONCEPTUAL

Understand that intercepts are points that lie on the graph and either the x-axis or the y-axis.

STUDY TIP

Identifying the intercepts helps define the graph unmistakably.

STUDY TIP

- Either the x-coordinate, say a, or the point $(a, 0)$ can be used to denote an x-intercept.
- Either the y-coordinate, say b, or the point $(0, b)$ can be used to denote a y-intercept.

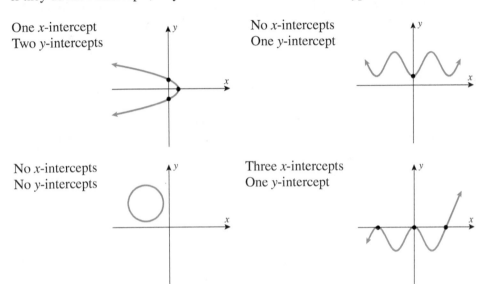

One x-intercept
Two y-intercepts

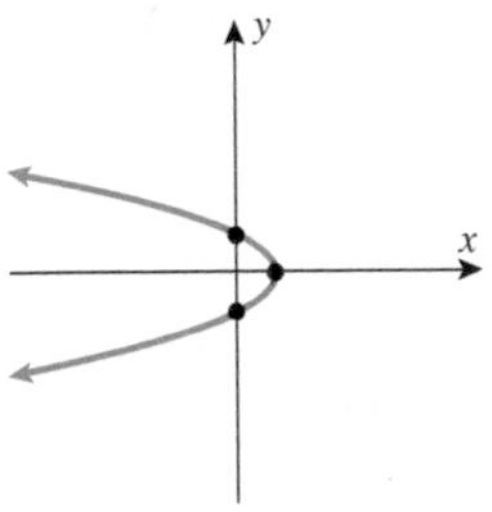

No x-intercepts
One y-intercept

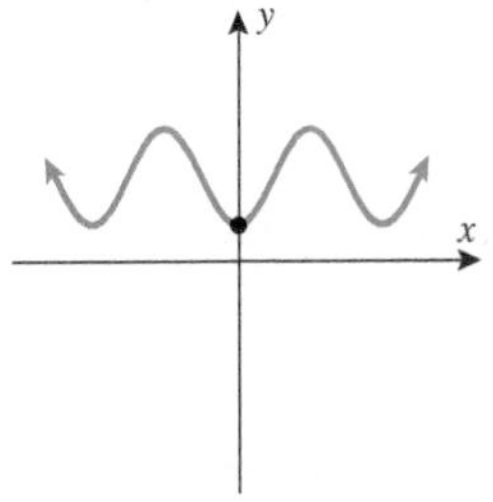

No x-intercepts
No y-intercepts

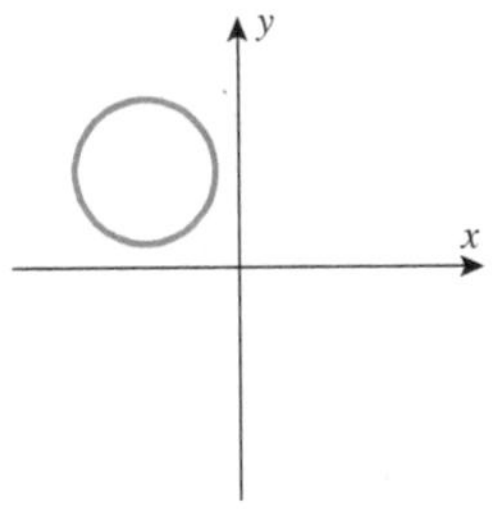

Three x-intercepts
One y-intercept

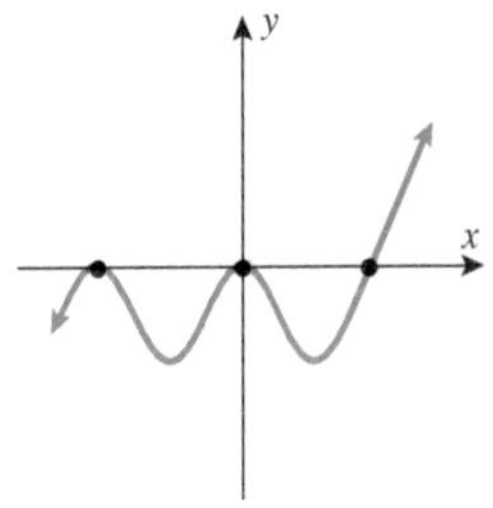

Note: The origin $(0, 0)$ corresponds to both an x-intercept and a y-intercept.

EXAMPLE 4 Finding Intercepts from an Equation

Given the equation $y = x^2 + 1$, find the indicated intercepts of its graph, if any.

a. x-intercept(s) **b.** y-intercept(s)

Solution (a):

Let $y = 0$. $\quad 0 = x^2 + 1$

Solve for x. $\quad x^2 = -1$ no real solution

There are no x-intercepts.

Solution (b):

Let $x = 0$. $\quad y = 0^2 + 1$

Solve for y. $\quad y = 1$

The y-intercept is located at the point $(0, 1)$.

CONCEPT CHECK

If the graph passes through the origin, then the point $(0, 0)$ is
(A) an x-intercept
(B) a y-intercept
or (C) both an x-intercept and a y-intercept

ANSWER (C)

YOUR TURN For the equation $y = x^2 - 4$

a. find the x-intercept(s), if any. **b.** find the y-intercept(s), if any.

ANSWER

a. x-intercepts: -2 and 2
b. y-intercept: -4

0.5.5 Using Symmetry as a Graphing Aid

0.5.5 SKILL

Determine whether the graph of an equation is symmetric about the x-axis, y-axis, or origin.

0.5.5 CONCEPTUAL

Understand how the algebraic definitions of symmetry can be visualized graphically.

STUDY TIP

Symmetry gives us information about the graph "for free."

The word **symmetry** conveys balance. Suppose you have three pictures to hang on a wall. If you space them equal distances apart, then you prefer a symmetric décor. This is an example of symmetry about a line. The word (water) written in the margin is identical if you rotate the word 180 degrees (or turn the page upside down). This is an example of symmetry about a point. Symmetric graphs have the characteristic that their mirror image can be obtained about a reference, typically a line or a point.

Symmetry aids in graphing by giving information "for free." For example, if a graph is symmetric about the y-axis, then once the graph to the right of the y-axis is found, the left side of the graph is the mirror image of that. If a graph is symmetric about the origin, then once the graph is known in quadrant I, the graph in quadrant III is found by rotating the known graph 180 degrees.

It would be beneficial to know whether a graph of an equation is symmetric about a line or point before the graph of the equation is sketched. Although a graph can be symmetric about any line or point, we will discuss only symmetry about the x-axis, y-axis, and origin. These types of symmetry and the algebraic procedures for testing for symmetry are outlined below.

Types and Tests for Symmetry

TYPE OF SYMMETRY	GRAPH	IF THE POINT (a, b) IS ON THE GRAPH, THEN THE POINT . . .	ALGEBRAIC TEST FOR SYMMETRY
Symmetric with respect to the x-axis	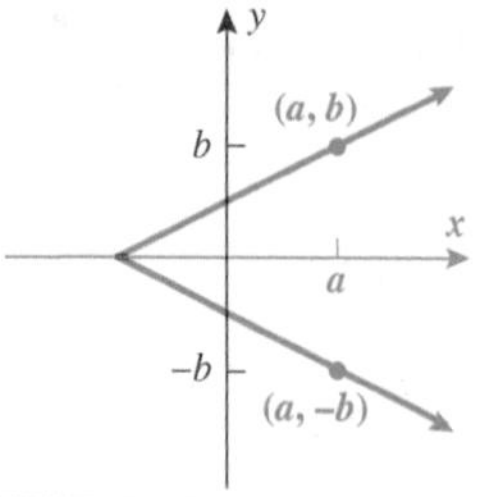	$(a, -b)$ is on the graph.	Replacing y with $-y$ leaves the equation unchanged.
Symmetric with respect to the y-axis	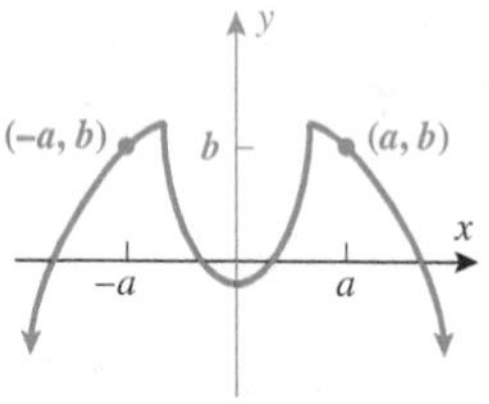	$(-a, b)$ is on the graph.	Replacing x with $-x$ leaves the equation unchanged.
Symmetric with respect to the origin	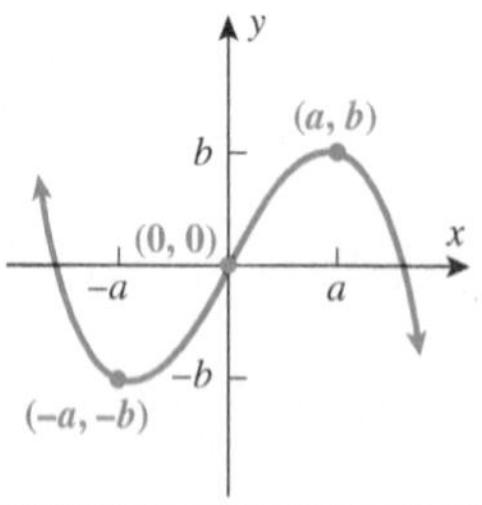	$(-a, -b)$ is on the graph.	Replacing x with $-x$ and y with $-y$ leaves the equation unchanged.

EXAMPLE 5 **Testing for Symmetry**

Determine what type of symmetry (if any) the graphs of the equations exhibit.

a. $y = x^2 + 1$ **b.** $y = x^3 + 1$

Solution (a):

Replace x with $-x$. $y = (-x)^2 + 1$

Simplify. $y = x^2 + 1$

The resulting equation is equivalent to the original equation, so the graph of the equation $y = x^2 + 1$ is **symmetric with respect to the y-axis.**

Replace y with $-y$. $(-y) = x^2 + 1$

Simplify. $y = -x^2 - 1$

The resulting equation $y = -x^2 - 1$ is not equivalent to the original equation $y = x^2 + 1$, so the graph of the equation $y = x^2 + 1$ is **not symmetric with respect to the x-axis.**

Replace x with $-x$ and y with $-y$. $(-y) = (-x)^2 + 1$

Simplify.

$$-y = x^2 + 1$$
$$y = -x^2 - 1$$

The resulting equation $y = -x^2 - 1$ is not equivalent to the original equation $y = x^2 + 1$, so the graph of the equation $y = x^2 + 1$ is **not symmetric with respect to the origin.**

The graph of the equation $y = x^2 + 1$ is **symmetric with respect to the y-axis.**

Solution (b):

Replace x with $-x$. $y = (-x)^3 + 1$

Simplify. $y = -x^3 + 1$

The resulting equation $y = -x^3 + 1$ is not equivalent to the original equation $y = x^3 + 1$. Therefore, the graph of the equation $y = x^3 + 1$ is **not symmetric with respect to the y-axis.**

Replace y with $-y$. $(-y) = x^3 + 1$

Simplify. $y = -x^3 - 1$

The resulting equation $y = -x^3 - 1$ is not equivalent to the original equation $y = x^3 + 1$. Therefore, the graph of the equation $y = x^3 + 1$ is **not symmetric with respect to the x-axis.**

Replace x with $-x$ and y with $-y$. $(-y) = (-x)^3 + 1$

Simplify.

$$-y = -x^3 + 1$$
$$y = x^3 - 1$$

The resulting equation $y = x^3 - 1$ is not equivalent to the original equation $y = x^3 + 1$. Therefore, the graph of the equation $y = x^3 + 1$ is **not symmetric with respect to the origin.**

The graph of the equation $y = x^3 + 1$ exhibits **no symmetry**.

YOUR TURN Determine what type of symmetry (if any) the graph of the equation $x = y^2 - 1$ exhibits.

ANSWER

The graph of the equation is symmetric with respect to the x-axis.

STUDY TIP

When testing for symmetry about the x-axis, y-axis, and origin, there are *five* possibilities:

- No symmetry.
- Symmetry with respect to the x-axis
- Symmetry with respect to the y-axis
- Symmetry with respect to the origin
- Symmetry with respect to the x-axis, y-axis, and origin

CONCEPT CHECK

If both the point (a, b) and the point $(a, -b)$ are on the graph, then the graph is symmetric about

(A) the y-axis

(B) the x-axis

(C) the origin.

ANSWER (B)

EXAMPLE 6 **Using Intercepts and Symmetry as Graphing Aids**

For the equation $x^2 + y^2 = 25$, use intercepts and symmetry to help you graph the equation using the point-plotting technique.

Solution:

STEP 1 **Find the intercepts.**

For the x-intercepts, let $y = 0$. $x^2 + 0^2 = 25$

Solve for x. $x = \pm 5$

The two x-intercepts correspond to the points $(-5, 0)$ and $(5, 0)$.

For the y-intercepts, let $x = 0$. $0^2 + y^2 = 25$

Solve for y. $y = \pm 5$

The two y-intercepts correspond to the points $(0, -5)$ and $(0, 5)$.

STEP 2 **Identify the points on the graph corresponding to the intercepts.**

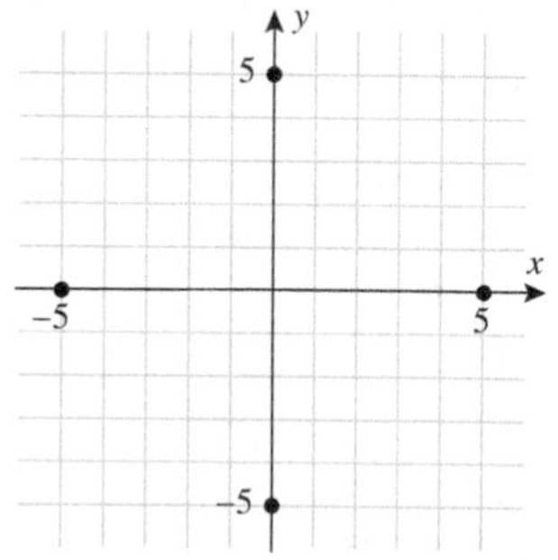

STEP 3 **Test for symmetry with respect to the y-axis, x-axis, and origin.**

Test for symmetry with respect to the y-axis.

Replace x with $-x$. $(-x)^2 + y^2 = 25$

Simplify. $x^2 + y^2 = 25$

The resulting equation is equivalent to the original, so the graph of $x^2 + y^2 = 25$ is **symmetric with respect to the y-axis.**

Test for symmetry with respect to the x-axis.

Replace y with $-y$. $x^2 + (-y)^2 = 25$

Simplify. $x^2 + y^2 = 25$

The resulting equation is equivalent to the original, so the graph of $x^2 + y^2 = 25$ is **symmetric with respect to the x-axis.**

Test for symmetry with respect to the origin.

Replace x with $-x$ and replace y with $-y$. $(-x)^2 + (-y)^2 = 25$

Simplify. $x^2 + y^2 = 25$

The resulting equation is equivalent to the original, so the graph of $x^2 + y^2 = 25$ is **symmetric with respect to the origin.**

We need to determine solutions to the equation on only the positive x- and y-axes and in quadrant I because of the following symmetries:

- **Symmetry with respect to the y-axis gives the solutions in quadrant II.**
- **Symmetry with respect to the origin gives the solutions in quadrant III.**
- **Symmetry with respect to the x-axis gives the solutions in quadrant IV.**

Solutions to $x^2 + y^2 = 25$.

Quadrant I: (3, 4), (4, 3)

Additional points due to symmetry:

Quadrant II: (−3, 4), (−4, 3)

Quadrant III: (−3, −4), (−4, −3)

Quadrant IV: (3, −4), (4, −3)

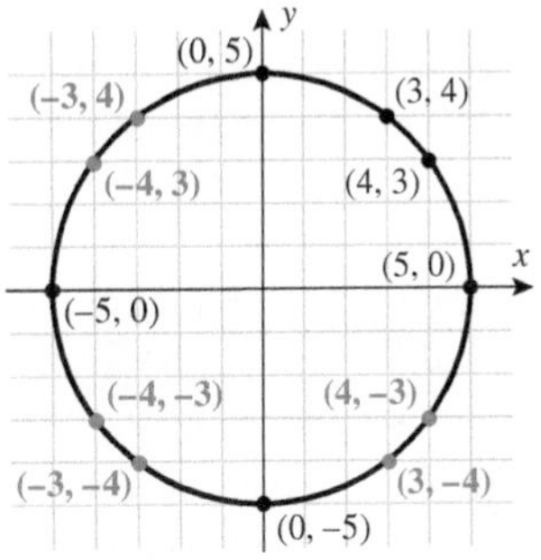

[CONCEPT CHECK]

If the graph is symmetric about the x-axis, the y-axis, and the origin, then once you find a point (a, b) in quadrant I that lies on the graph then what points do you get for free from the symmetry?

(A) (−a, b)
(B) (a, −b)
(C) (−a, −b)
(D) all of these

ANSWER (D)

0.5.6 Circles

0.5.6 SKILL

Graph a circle.

0.5.6 CONCEPTUAL

Understand algebraic and graphical representations of circles.

DEFINITION Circle

A **circle** is the set of all points in a plane that are a fixed distance from a point, the **center**. The center, C, is typically denoted by (h, k), and the fixed distance, or **radius**, is denoted by r.

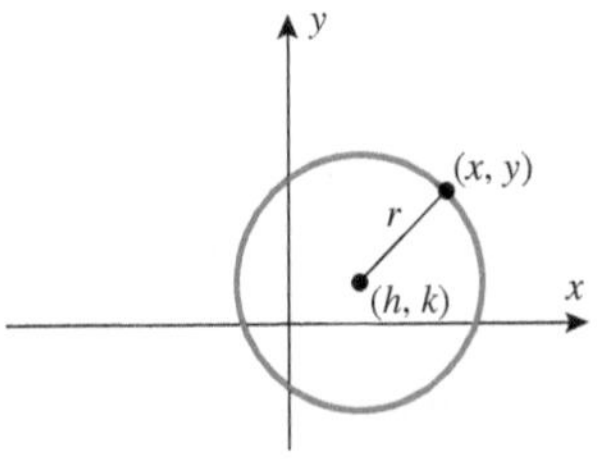

EQUATION OF A CIRCLE

The standard form of the equation of a **circle** with **radius** r and **center** (h, k) is

$$(x - h)^2 + (y - k)^2 = r^2$$

For the special case of a circle with center at the origin (0, 0), the equation simplifies to $x^2 + y^2 = r^2$.

UNIT CIRCLE

A circle with radius 1 and center (0, 0) is called the **unit circle**:

$$x^2 + y^2 = 1$$

The unit circle plays an important role in the study of trigonometry. Note that if $x^2 + y^2 = 0$, the radius is 0, so the "circle" is just a point.

EXAMPLE 7 Finding the Center and Radius of a Circle

Identify the center and radius of the given circle, and graph it.

$$(x - 2)^2 + (y + 1)^2 = 4$$

Solution:

Rewrite this equation in standard form. $[x - 2]^2 + [y - (-1)]^2 = 2^2$

Identify h, k, and r by comparing this equation with the standard form of a circle: $(x - h)^2 + (y - k)^2 = r^2$. $h = 2, k = -1$, and $r = 2$

Center $(2, -1)$ and $r = 2$

To draw the circle, label the center $(2, -1)$. Label four additional points 2 units (the radius) away from the center: $(4, -1)$, $(0, -1)$, $(2, 1)$, and $(2, -3)$.

Note that the easiest four points to get are those obtained by going out from the center both horizontally and vertically. Connect those four points with a smooth curve.

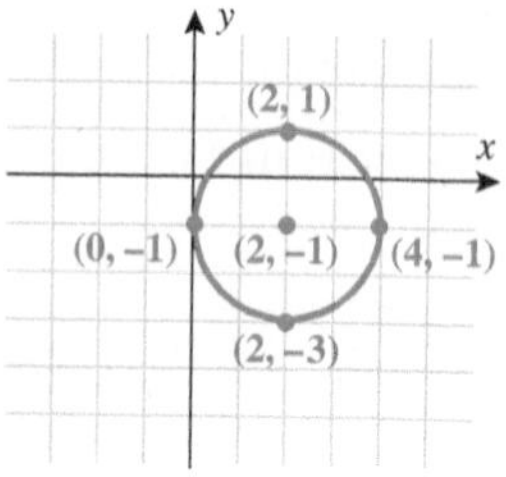

[CONCEPT CHECK]

A circle described algebraically by $(x - h)^2 + (y - k)^2 = r^2$ can be graphed by going first to the center (h, k) and then to the points:

(A) $(-h \pm r, -k \pm r)$

(B) $(h \pm r, k \pm r)$

ANSWER (B)

YOUR TURN Identify the center and radius of the given circle, and graph it.

$$(x + 1)^2 + (y + 2)^2 = 9$$

ANSWER

Center: $(-1, -2)$

Radius: 3

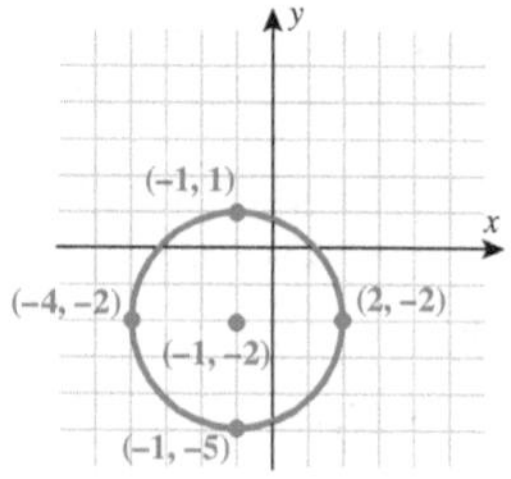

Let's change the look of the equation given in Example 7.

In Example 7, the equation of the circle was given as $(x - 2)^2 + (y + 1)^2 = 4$

Eliminate the parentheses. $x^2 - 4x + 4 + y^2 + 2y + 1 = 4$

Group like terms and subtract 4 from both sides. $x^2 + y^2 - 4x + 2y + 1 = 0$

We have written the *general form* of the equation of the circle in Example 7.

> The **general form** of the **equation of a circle** is
>
> $$x^2 + y^2 + ax + by + c = 0$$

Suppose you are given a point that lies on a circle and the center of the circle. Can you find the equation of the circle?

EXAMPLE 8 Finding the Equation of a Circle Given Its Center and One Point

The point $(10, -4)$ lies on a circle centered at $(7, -8)$. Find the equation of the circle in general form.

Solution:

This circle is centered at $(7, -8)$, so its standard equation is $(x - 7)^2 + (y + 8)^2 = r^2$.

Since the point $(10, -4)$ lies on the circle, it must satisfy the equation of the circle.

Substitute $(x, y) = (10, -4)$. $(10 - 7)^2 + (-4 + 8)^2 = r^2$

Simplify. $3^2 + 4^2 = r^2$

The distance from $(10, -4)$ to $(7, -8)$ is 5 units. $r = 5$

Substitute $r = 5$ into the standard equation. $(x - 7)^2 + (y + 8)^2 = 5^2$

Eliminate the parentheses and simplify. $x^2 - 14x + 49 + y^2 + 16y + 64 = 25$

Write in **general form**. $x^2 + y^2 - 14x + 16y + 88 = 0$

YOUR TURN The point $(1, 11)$ lies on a circle centered at $(-5, 3)$. Find the equation of the circle in general form.

ANSWER

$x^2 + y^2 + 10x - 6y - 66 = 0$

If the equation of a circle is given in general form, it must be rewritten in standard form in order to identify its center and radius. To transform equations of circles from general to standard form, complete the square on both the x- and y-variables.

EXAMPLE 9 Finding the Center and Radius of a Circle by Completing the Square

Find the center and radius of the circle with the equation

$$x^2 - 8x + y^2 + 20y + 107 = 0$$

Solution:

Our goal is to transform this equation into standard form. $\quad (x - h)^2 + (y - k)^2 = r^2$

Group x and y terms, respectively, on the left side of the equation; move constants to the right side. $\quad (x^2 - 8x) + (y^2 + 20y) = -107$

Complete the square on both the x and y expressions. $\quad (x^2 - 8x + \square) + (y^2 + 20y + \square) = -107$

Add $\left(-\frac{8}{2}\right)^2 = 16$ and $\left(\frac{20}{2}\right)^2 = 100$ to both sides.

$$(x^2 - 8x + 16) + (y^2 + 20y + 100) = -107 + 16 + 100$$

Factor the perfect squares on the left side and simplify the right side. $\quad (x - 4)^2 + (y + 10)^2 = 9$

Write in standard form. $\quad (x - 4)^2 + [y - (-10)]^2 = 3^2$

The center is $(4, -10)$ and the radius is 3.

YOUR TURN Find the center and radius of the circle with the equation

$$x^2 + y^2 + 4x - 6y - 12 = 0$$

ANSWER

Center: $(-2, 3)$ Radius: 5

[CONCEPT CHECK]

Show that $(x + 8)^2 + (y + 4)^2 = 6^2$ is equal to $x^2 + y^2 + 16x + 8y + 44 = 0$.

ANSWER $(x + 8)^2 + (y + 4)^2 = 6^2$
$x^2 + 16x + 64 + y^2 + 8y + 16 = 36$
$x^2 + y^2 + 16x + 8y + 80 = 36$
$x^2 + y^2 + 16x + 8y + 44 = 0$

[SECTION 0.5] SUMMARY

Distance between two points

$$d = \sqrt{(x_2 - x_1)^2 + (y_2 - y_1)^2}$$

Midpoint of segment joining two points

$$(x_m, y_m) = \left(\frac{x_1 + x_2}{2}, \frac{y_1 + y_2}{2}\right)$$

Intercepts

- x-intercept: Let $y = 0$ and solve for x.
- y-intercept: Let $x = 0$ and solve for y.

Symmetry

- About the x-axis: Replace y with $-y$, and the resulting equation is the same.
- About the y-axis: Replace x with $-x$, and the resulting equation is the same.
- About the origin: Replace x with $-x$ and y with $-y$, and the resulting equation is the same.

Circles

$(x - h)^2 + (y - k)^2 = r^2 \quad$ center (h, k) and radius r

[SECTION 0.5] EXERCISES

• SKILLS

In Exercises 1–12, calculate the distance between the given points, and find the midpoint of the segment joining them.

1. $(1, 3)$ and $(5, 3)$
2. $(-2, 4)$ and $(-2, -4)$
3. $(-1, 4)$ and $(3, 0)$
4. $(-3, -1)$ and $(1, 3)$
5. $(-10, 8)$ and $(-7, -1)$
6. $(-2, 12)$ and $(7, 15)$
7. $(-3, -1)$ and $(-7, 2)$
8. $(-4, 5)$ and $(-9, -7)$
9. $(-6, -4)$ and $(-2, -8)$
10. $(0, -7)$ and $(-4, -5)$
11. $\left(-\frac{1}{2}, \frac{1}{3}\right)$ and $\left(\frac{7}{2}, \frac{10}{3}\right)$
12. $\left(\frac{1}{5}, \frac{7}{3}\right)$ and $\left(\frac{9}{5}, -\frac{2}{3}\right)$

In Exercises 13–18, graph the equation by plotting points.

13. $y = -3x + 2$
14. $y = 4 - x$
15. $y = x^2 - x - 2$
16. $y = x^2 - 2x + 1$
17. $x = y^2 - 1$
18. $x = |y + 1| + 2$

In Exercises 19–24, find the x-intercept(s) and y-intercepts(s) (if any) of the graphs of the given equations.

19. $2x - y = 6$
20. $y = 4x^2 - 1$
21. $y = \sqrt{x - 4}$
22. $y = \dfrac{x^2 - x - 12}{x}$
23. $4x^2 + y^2 = 16$
24. $x^2 - y^2 = 9$

In Exercises 25–30, test algebraically to determine whether the equation's graph is symmetric with respect to the x-axis, y-axis, or origin.

25. $x = y^2 + 4$
26. $y = x^5 + 1$
27. $x = |y|$
28. $x^2 + 2y^2 = 30$
29. $y = x^{2/3}$
30. $xy = 1$

In Exercises 31–36, plot the graph of the given equation.

31. $y = x^2 - 1$
32. $x = y^2 + 1$
33. $y = \dfrac{1}{x}$
34. $|x| = |y|$
35. $x^2 - y^2 = 16$
36. $\dfrac{x^2}{4} + \dfrac{y^2}{9} = 1$

In Exercises 37–44, write the equation of the circle in standard form.

37. Center $(5, 7)$, $r = 9$
38. Center $(2, 8)$, $r = 6$
39. Center $(-11, 12)$, $r = 13$
40. Center $(6, -7)$, $r = 8$
41. Center $(5, -3)$, $r = 2\sqrt{3}$
42. Center $(-4, -1)$, $r = 3\sqrt{5}$
43. Center $\left(\frac{2}{3}, -\frac{3}{5}\right)$, $r = \frac{1}{4}$
44. Center $\left(-\frac{1}{3}, -\frac{2}{7}\right)$, $r = \frac{2}{5}$

In Exercises 45–50, state the center and radius of the circle with the given equations.

45. $(x - 2)^2 + (y + 5)^2 = 49$
46. $(x + 3)^2 + (y - 7)^2 = 81$
47. $(x - 4)^2 - (y - 9)^2 = 20$
48. $(x + 1)^2 + (y + 2)^2 = 8$
49. $\left(x - \frac{2}{5}\right)^2 + \left(y - \frac{1}{7}\right)^2 = \frac{4}{9}$
50. $\left(x - \frac{1}{2}\right)^2 + \left(y - \frac{1}{3}\right)^2 = \frac{9}{25}$

In Exercises 51–60, find the center and radius of each circle.

51. $x^2 + y^2 - 10x - 14y - 7 = 0$
52. $x^2 + y^2 - 4x - 16y + 32 = 0$
53. $x^2 + y^2 - 2x - 6y + 1 = 0$
54. $x^2 + y^2 - 8x - 6y + 21 = 0$
55. $x^2 + y^2 - 10x + 6y + 22 = 0$
56. $x^2 + y^2 + 8x + 2y - 28 = 0$
57. $x^2 + y^2 - 6x - 4y + 1 = 0$
58. $x^2 + y^2 - 2x - 10y + 2 = 0$
59. $x^2 + y^2 - x + y + \dfrac{1}{4} = 0$
60. $x^2 + y^2 - \dfrac{x}{2} - \dfrac{3y}{2} + \dfrac{3}{8} = 0$

• APPLICATIONS

In Exercises 61 and 62, refer to the following:

It is often useful to display data in visual form by plotting the data as a set of points. This provides a graphical display of the relationship between the two variables. The following table contains data on the average monthly price of gasoline.

U.S. All Grades Conventional Retail Gasoline Prices, 2000–2015 (dollars per gallon)

YEAR	JAN	FEB	MAR	APR	MAY	JUN	JUL	AUG	SEP	OCT	NOV	DEC
2000	1.319	1.409	1.538	1.476	1.496	1.645	1.568	1.480	1.562	1.546	1.533	1.458
2001	1.467	1.471	1.423	1.557	1.689	1.586	1.381	1.422	1.539	1.312	1.177	1.111
2002	1.134	1.129	1.259	1.402	1.394	1.380	1.402	1.398	1.403	1.466	1.424	1.389
2003	1.464	1.622	1.675	1.557	1.477	1.489	1.519	1.625	1.654	1.551	1.512	1.488
2004	1.595	1.654	1.728	1.794	1.981	1.950	1.902	1.880	1.880	1.993	1.973	1.843
2005	1.852	1.927	2.102	2.251	2.155	2.162	2.287	2.489	2.907	2.736	2.265	2.216
2006	2.343	2.293	2.454	2.762	2.873	2.849	2.964	2.952	2.548	2.258	2.254	2.328
2007	2.237	2.276	2.546	2.831	3.157	3.067	2.989	2.821	2.858	2.838	3.110	3.032
2008	3.068	3.064	3.263	3.468	3.783	4.038	4.051	3.789	3.760	3.065	2.153	1.721
2009	1.821	1.942	1.987	2.071	2.289	2.645	2.530	2.613	2.530	2.549	2.665	2.620
2010	2.730	2.657	2.793	2.867	2.847	2.733	2.728	2.733	2.727	2.816	2.866	3.004
2011	3.109	3.219	3.561	3.796	3.900	3.678	3.665	3.664	3.624	3.454	3.385	3.277
2012	3.388	3.576	3.827	3.893	3.698	3.515	3.433	3.724	3.859	3.714	3.444	3.322
2013	3.324	3.668	3.713	3.566	3.621	3.634	3.582	3.583	3.542	3.358	3.263	3.288
2014	3.331	3.382	3.546	3.665	3.678	3.699	3.615	3.501	3.431	3.202	2.957	2.575
2015	2.136	2.235	2.433	2.454	2.661	2.783	2.750	2.608	2.369	2.325	2.188	2.052

Source: U.S. Energy Information Administration (February 2016).

The following graph displays the data for the year 2000.

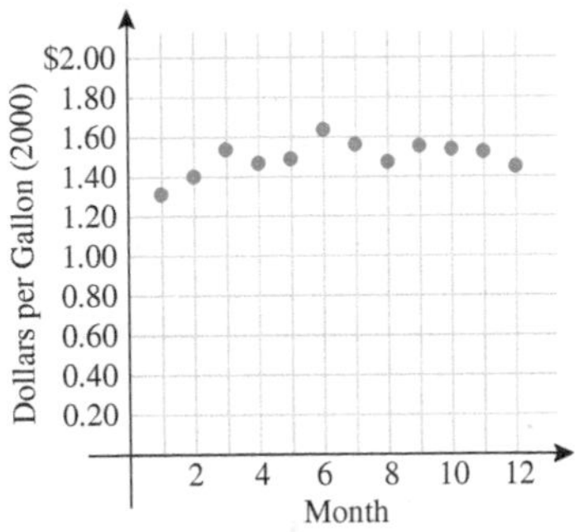

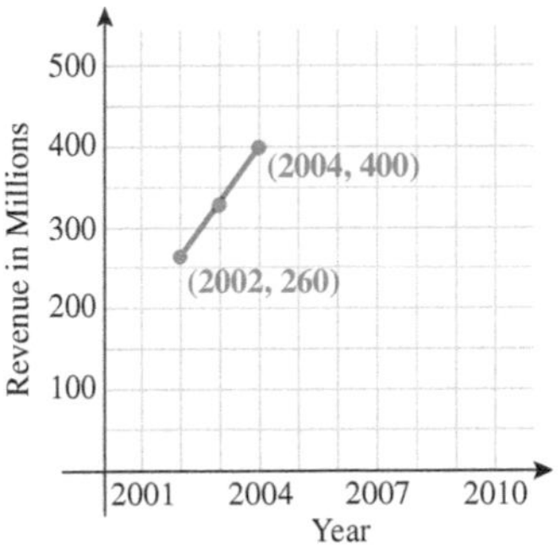

61. Economics. Create a graph displaying the price of gasoline for the year 2012.

62. Economics. Create a graph displaying the price of gasoline for the year 2014.

63. NASCAR Revenue. Action Performance, Inc., the leading seller of NASCAR merchandise, recorded $260 million in revenue in 2002 and $400 million in revenue in 2004. Calculate the midpoint to estimate the revenue Action Performance, Inc. recorded in 2003. Assume the horizontal axis represents the year and the vertical axis represents the revenue in millions.

64. Ticket Price. In 1993 the average Miami Dolphins ticket price was $28 and in 2001 the average price was $56. Find the midpoint of the segment joining these two points to estimate the ticket price in 1997.

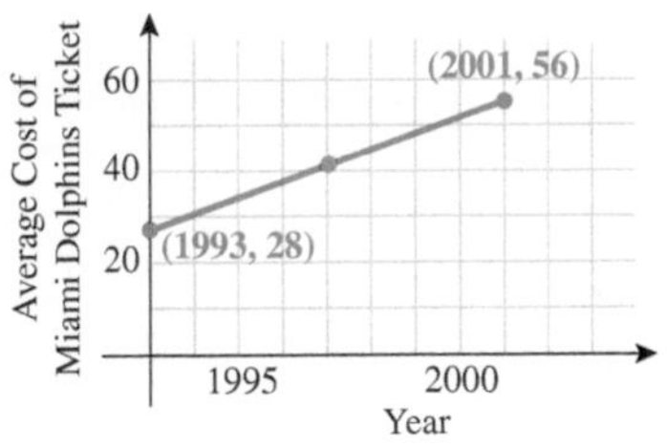

65. Design. A university designs its campus with a master plan of two concentric circles. All of the academic buildings are within the inner circle (so that students can get between classes in less than 10 minutes), and the outer circle contains all the dormitories, the Greek park, cafeterias, the gymnasium, and intramural fields. Assuming the center of campus is the origin, write an equation for the inner circle if the diameter is 3000 feet.

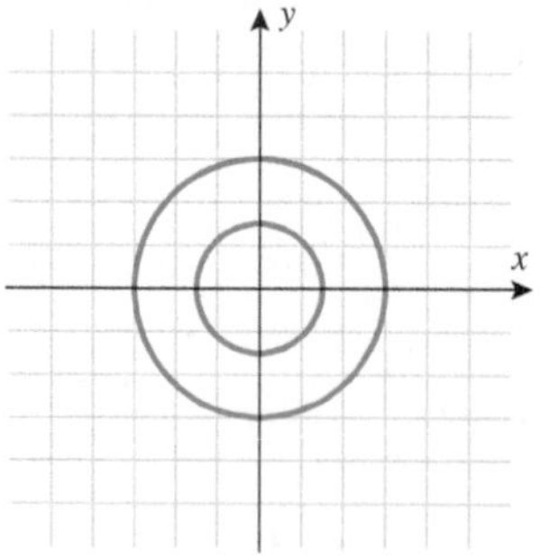

66. Design. Repeat Exercise 65 for the outer circle with a diameter of 6000 feet.

67. Cell Phones. A cellular phone tower has a reception radius of 200 miles. Assuming the tower is located at the origin, write the equation of the circle that represents the reception area.

68. Environment. In a state park, a fire has spread in the form of a circle. If the radius is 2 miles, write an equation for the circle.

• CATCH THE MISTAKE

In Exercises 69–72, explain the mistake that is made.

69. Graph the equation $y = x^2 + 1$.

Solution:

x	$y = x^2 + 1$	(x, y)
0	1	(0, 1)
1	2	(1, 2)

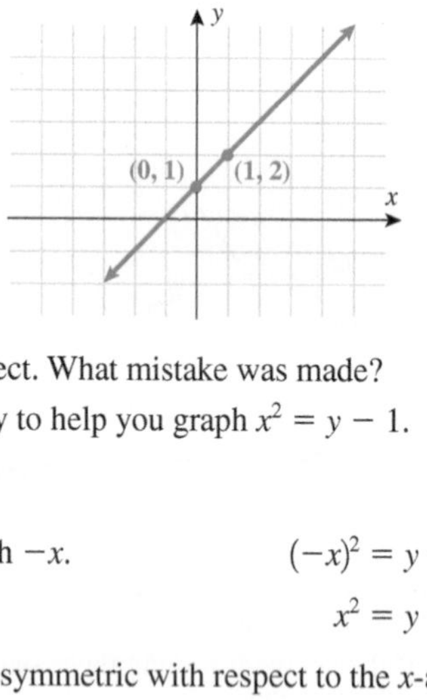

This is incorrect. What mistake was made?

70. Use symmetry to help you graph $x^2 = y - 1$.

Solution:

Replace x with $-x$. $\quad (-x)^2 = y - 1$

Simplify. $\quad x^2 = y - 1$

$x^2 = y - 1$ is symmetric with respect to the x-axis.

Determine points that lie on the graph in quadrant I.

y	$x^2 = y - 1$	(x, y)
1	0	(0, 1)
2	1	(1, 2)
5	2	(2, 5)

Symmetry with respect to the x-axis implies that $(0, -1)$, $(1, -2)$, and $(2, -5)$ are also points that lie on the graph.

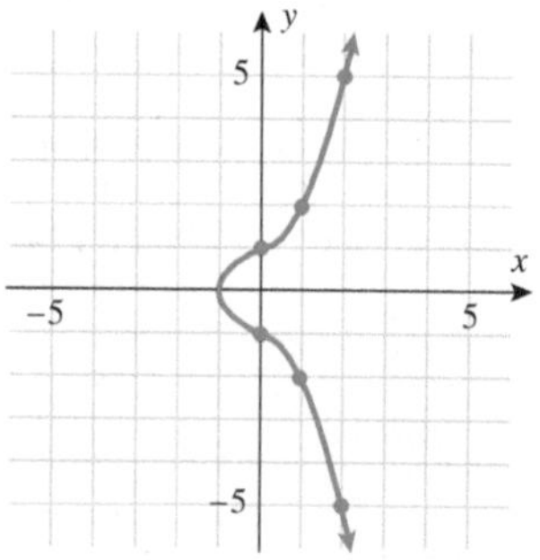

This is incorrect. What mistake was made?

71. Identify the center and radius of the circle with equation $(x - 4)^2 + (y + 3)^2 = 25$.

Solution:

The center is (4, 3) and the radius is 5.

This is incorrect. What mistake was made?

72. Identify the center and radius of the circle with equation $(x - 2)^2 + (y + 3)^2 = 2$.

Solution:

The center is $(2, -3)$ and the radius is 2.

This is incorrect. What mistake was made?

• CONCEPTUAL

In Exercises 73–76, determine whether each statement is true or false.

73. If the point (a, b) lies on a graph that is symmetric about the x-axis, then the point $(-a, b)$ also must lie on the graph.

74. If the point (a, b) lies on a graph that is symmetric about the y-axis, then the point $(-a, b)$ also must lie on the graph.

75. If the point $(a, -b)$ lies on a graph that is symmetric about the x-axis, y-axis, and origin, then the points (a, b), $(-a, -b)$, and $(-a, b)$ must also lie on the graph.

76. Two points are all that is needed to plot the graph of an equation.

77. Describe the graph (if it exists) of

$$x^2 + y^2 + 10x - 6y + 34 = 0$$

78. Describe the graph (if it exists) of

$$x^2 + y^2 - 4x + 6y + 49 = 0$$

• CHALLENGE

79. Determine whether the graph of $y = \dfrac{ax^2 + b}{cx^3}$ has any symmetry, where a, b, and c are real numbers.

80. Find the intercepts of $y = (x - a)^2 - b^2$, where a and b are real numbers.

81. Find the equation of a circle that has a diameter with endpoints $(5, 2)$ and $(1, -6)$.

82. Find the equation of a circle that has a diameter with endpoints $(3, 0)$ and $(-1, -4)$.

83. For the equation $x^2 + y^2 + ax + by + c = 0$, specify conditions on a, b, and c so that the graph is a single point.

84. For the equation $x^2 + y^2 + ax + by + c = 0$, specify conditions on a, b, and c so that there is no corresponding graph.

0.6 LINES

SKILLS OBJECTIVES

- Calculate the slope of a line; graph a line; classify a line as rising, falling, vertical, or horizontal.
- Find the equation of a line, given either slope and a point that lies on the line or two points that lie on the line.
- Find the equation of a line that is parallel or perpendicular to a given line.

CONCEPTUAL OBJECTIVES

- Understand slope as rate of change.
- Understand that the equation of a line given by $y = mx + b$ corresponds to a line with slope m and y-intercept $(0, b)$.
- Understand that parallel lines have the same slope, whereas perpendicular lines have slopes that are negative reciprocals of one another.

0.6.1 General Form of a Line and Slope

First-degree equations such as

$$y = -2x + 4 \qquad 3x + y = 6 \qquad y = 2 \qquad x = -3$$

have graphs that are straight lines. The first two equations given represent inclined or "slant" lines, whereas $y = 2$ represents a horizontal line and $x = -3$ represents a vertical line. One way of writing an equation of a straight line is called *general form.*

0.6.1 SKILL

Calculate the slope of a line; graph a line; classify a line as rising, falling, vertical, or horizontal.

0.6.1 CONCEPTUAL

Understand slope as rate of change.

EQUATION OF A STRAIGHT LINE: GENERAL* FORM

If A, B, and C are constants and x and y are variables, then the equation

$$Ax + By = C$$

is in **general form** and its graph is a straight line.

Note: A or B (but not both) can be zero.

*Some books refer to this as standard form.

The equation $2x - y = -2$ is a first-degree equation, so its graph is a straight line. To graph this line, find the two intercepts, plot those points, and use a straight edge to draw the **line**.

$2x - y = -2$

INTERCEPT	x	y	(x, y)
x-intercept	−1	0	(−1, 0)
y-intercept	0	2	(0, 2)

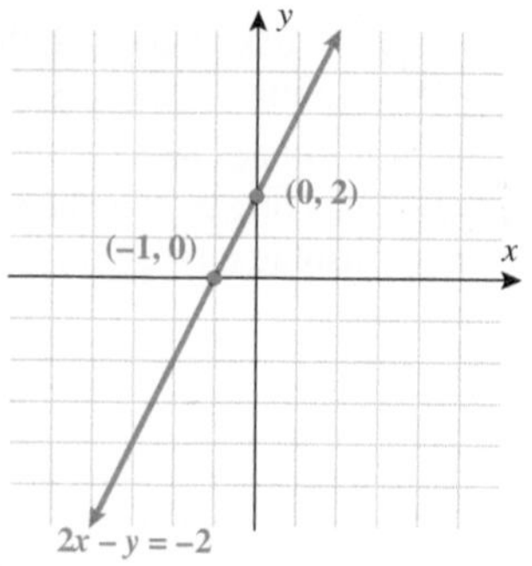

If the graph of $2x - y = -2$ represented an incline that you were about to walk on, would you classify that incline as steep? In the language of mathematics, we use the word **slope** as a measure of steepness. Slope is the ratio of the change in y to the change in x. An easy way to remember this is *rise over run.*

STUDY TIP

To get the correct sign (±) for the slope, remember to start with the same point for both x and y.

SLOPE OF A LINE

A nonvertical line passing through two points (x_1, y_1) and (x_2, y_2) has slope m given by the formula

$$m = \frac{y_2 - y_1}{x_2 - x_1}, \text{ where } x_1 \neq x_2, \text{ or}$$

$$m = \frac{\text{rise}}{\text{run}} = \frac{\text{vertical change}}{\text{horizontal change}}$$

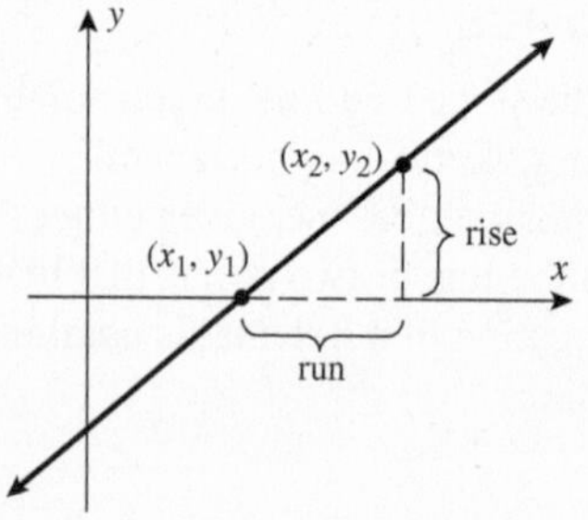

Note: Always start with the same point for both the x-coordinates and the y-coordinates.

Let's find the slope of our graph $2x - y = -2$. Two points that lie on the graph of $2x - y = -2$ are $(x_1, y_1) = (-2, -2)$ and $(x_2, y_2) = (1, 4)$. Substituting these two points into the slope formula yields:

$$m = \frac{y_2 - y_1}{x_2 - x_1} = \frac{[4 - (-2)]}{[1 - (-2)]} = \frac{6}{3} = 2$$

Notice that if we had chosen the two intercepts $(x_1, y_1) = (0, 2)$ and $(x_2, y_2) = (-1, 0)$ instead, we still would have found the slope to be $m = 2$.

common mistake

The most common mistake in calculating slope is writing the coordinates in the wrong order, which results in the slope being opposite in sign.

Find the slope of the line containing the two points (1, 2) and (3, 4).

✓CORRECT

Label the points.

$$(x_1, y_1) = (1, 2)$$
$$(x_2, y_2) = (3, 4)$$

Write the slope formula.

$$m = \frac{y_2 - y_1}{x_2 - x_1}$$

Substitute the coordinates.

$$m = \frac{4 - 2}{3 - 1}$$

Simplify. $m = \frac{2}{2} = \boxed{1}$

✗INCORRECT

The **ERROR** is interchanging the coordinates of the first and second points.

$$m = \frac{4 - 2}{1 - 3}$$

The calculated slope is **INCORRECT** by a negative sign.

$$m = \frac{2}{-2} = -1$$

CAUTION

Interchanging the coordinates will result in a sign error in a nonzero slope.

When interpreting slope, always read the graph from *left to right.* Since we have determined the slope to be 2, or $\frac{2}{1}$, we can interpret this as rising two units and running (to the right) one unit. If we start at the point **(−2, −2)** and move two units up and one unit to the right, we end up at the x-intercept, **(−1, 0)**. Again, moving two units up and one unit to the right puts us at the y-intercept, **(0, 2)**. Another rise of 2 and run of 1 take us to the point **(1, 4)**. See the figure on the left.

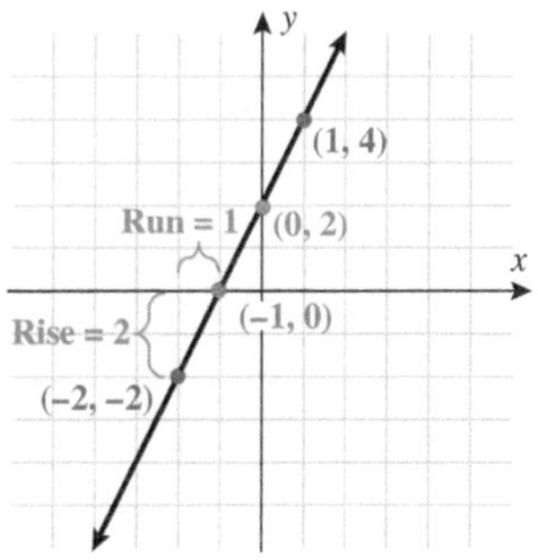

Lines fall into one of four categories: increasing, decreasing, horizontal, or vertical.

Line	Slope
Increasing	Positive ($m > 0$)
Decreasing	Negative ($m < 0$)
Horizontal	Zero ($m = 0$), hence $y = b$
Vertical	Undefined, hence $x = a$

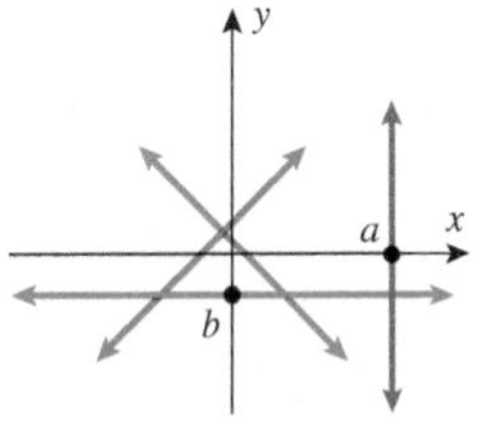

The slope of a horizontal line is 0 because the y-coordinates of any two points on the line are the same. The change in y in the slope formula's numerator is 0, hence $m = 0$. The slope of a vertical line is undefined because the x-coordinates of any two points on the line are the same. The change in x in the slope formula's denominator is zero; hence m is undefined.

EXAMPLE 1 Graph, Classify the Line, and Determine the Slope

Sketch a line through each pair of points, classify the line as increasing, decreasing, vertical, or horizontal, and determine its slope.

a. $(-1, -3)$ and $(1, 1)$ **b.** $(-3, 3)$ and $(3, 1)$

c. $(-1, -2)$ and $(3, -2)$ **d.** $(1, -4)$ and $(1, 3)$

Solution (a): $(-1, -3)$ and $(1, 1)$

This line is **increasing**, so its slope is positive.

$$m = \frac{1 - (-3)}{1 - (-1)} = \frac{4}{2} = \frac{2}{1} = 2.$$

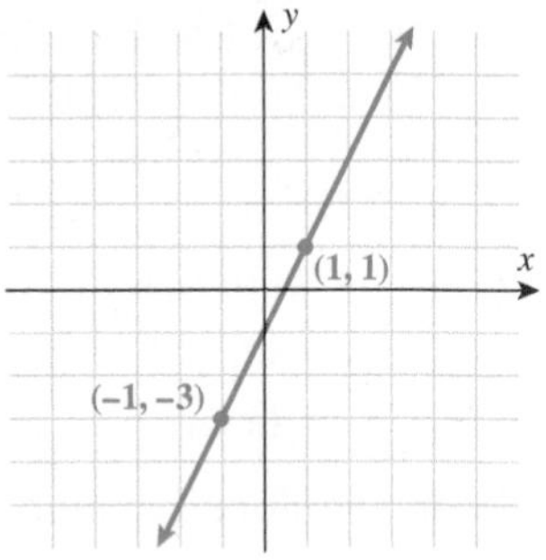

Solution (b): $(-3, 3)$ and $(3, 1)$

This line is **decreasing**, so its slope is negative.

$$m = \frac{3 - 1}{-3 - 3} = -\frac{2}{6} = -\frac{1}{3}.$$

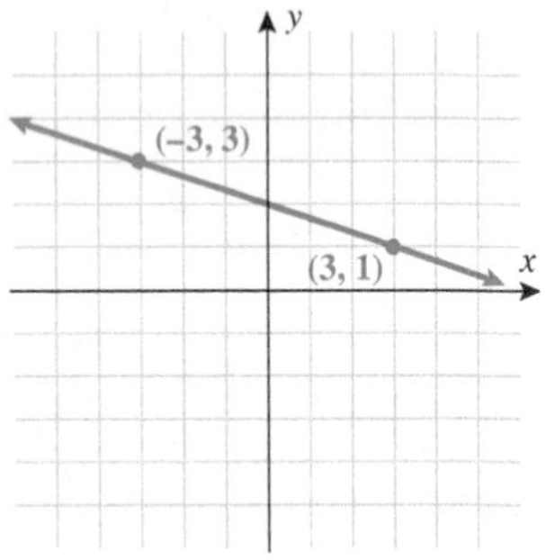

[CONCEPT CHECK]

If two lines are rising from left to right, then the larger slope corresponds to the
(A) steeper incline
(B) less steep incline.

ANSWER (A)

Solution (c): $(-1, -2)$ and $(3, -2)$

This is a **horizontal** line, so its slope is zero.

$$m = \frac{-2 - (-2)}{3 - (-1)} = \frac{0}{4} = 0.$$

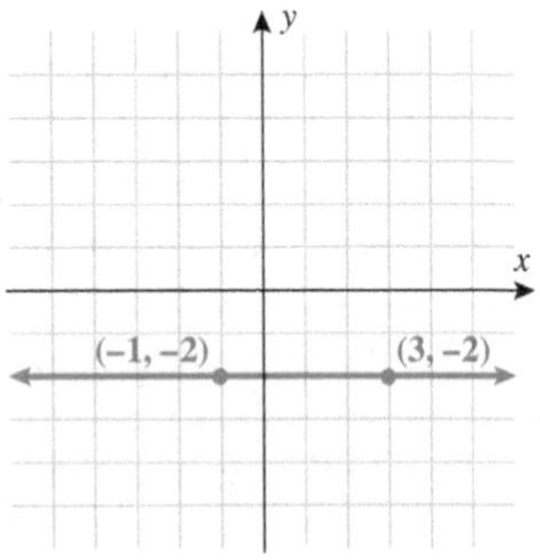

Solution (d): $(1, -4)$ and $(1, 3)$

This is a **vertical** line, so its slope is undefined.

$$m = \frac{3 - (-4)}{1 - 1} = \frac{7}{0}, \text{ which is undefined.}$$

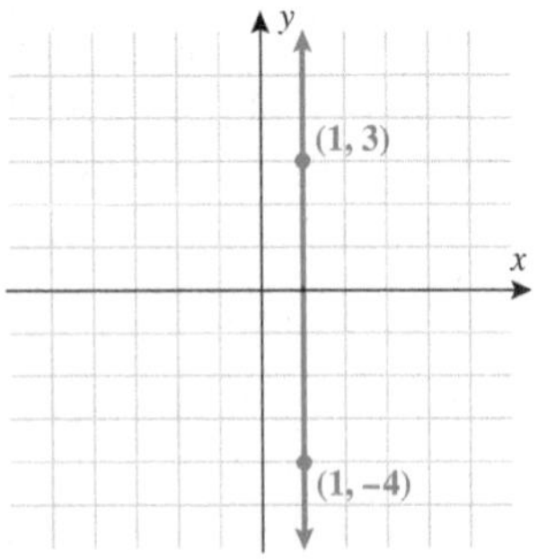

YOUR TURN For each pair of points, classify the line that passes through them as increasing, decreasing, vertical, or horizontal, and determine its slope. Do not graph.

a. $(2, 0)$ and $(1, 5)$ **b.** $(-2, -3)$ and $(2, 5)$

c. $(-3, -1)$ and $(-3, 4)$ **d.** $(-1, 2)$ and $(3, 2)$

ANSWER

a. $m = -5$; decreasing
b. $m = 2$; increasing
c. slope is undefined, vertical
d. $m = 0$, horizontal

0.6.2 Equations of Lines

Slope–Intercept Form

As mentioned earlier, the general form for an equation of a line is $Ax + By = C$. A more standard way to write an equation of a line is in slope–intercept form, because it identifies the slope and the y-intercept.

0.6.2 SKILL

Find the equation of a line, given either slope and a point that lies on the line or two points that lie on the line.

0.6.2 CONCEPTUAL

Understand that the equation of a line given by $y = mx + b$ corresponds to a line with slope m and y-intercept $(0, b)$.

EQUATION OF A STRAIGHT LINE: SLOPE–INTERCEPT FORM

The **slope–intercept form** for the equation of a nonvertical line is

$$y = mx + b$$

Its graph has slope m and y-intercept b.

For example, $2x - y = -3$ is in general form. To write this equation in **slope–intercept form**, we isolate the y variable:

$$y = 2x + 3$$

The slope of this line is 2 and the y-intercept is 3.

EXAMPLE 2 Using Slope–Intercept Form to Graph an Equation of a Line

Write $2x - 3y = 15$ in slope–intercept form and graph it.

Solution:

STEP 1 *Write in slope–intercept form.*

Subtract $2x$ from both sides. $-3y = -2x + 15$

Divide both sides by -3. $\boxed{y = \frac{2}{3}x - 5}$

STEP 2 *Graph.*

Identify the slope and y-intercept. Slope: $m = \frac{2}{3}$ y-intercept: $b = -5$

Plot the point corresponding to the y-intercept $(0, -5)$.

From the point $(0, -5)$, rise two units and run (to the right) three units, which corresponds to the point $(3, -3)$.

Draw the line passing through the two points.

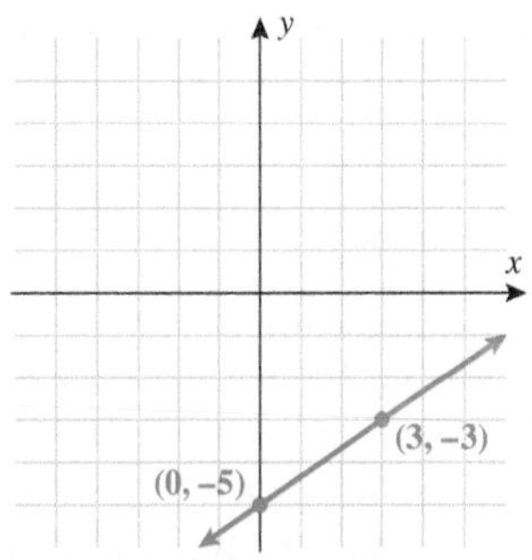

YOUR TURN Write $3x - 2y = 12$ in slope–intercept form and graph it.

ANSWER

$y = \frac{3}{2}x - 6$

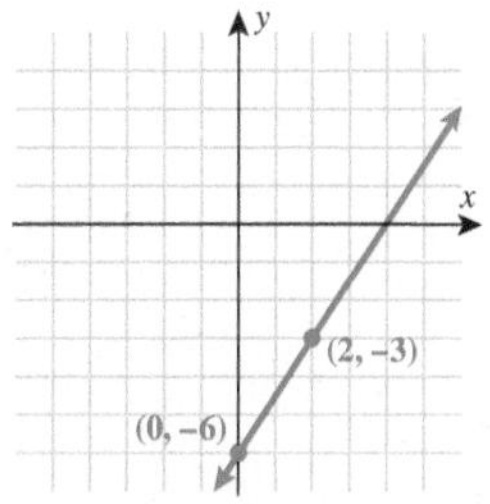

Instead of starting with equations of lines and characterizing them, let us now start with particular features of a line and derive its governing equation. Suppose that you are given the y-intercept and the slope of a line. Using the slope–intercept form of an equation of a line, $y = mx + b$, you could find its equation.

EXAMPLE 3 Using Slope–Intercept Form to Find the Equation of a Line

Find the equation of a line that has slope $\frac{2}{3}$ and y-intercept (0, 1).

Solution:

Write the slope–intercept form of an equation of a line. $y = mx + b$

Label the slope. $m = \dfrac{2}{3}$

Label the y-intercept. $b = 1$

The equation of the line in slope–intercept form is $\boxed{y = \frac{2}{3}x + 1}$.

YOUR TURN Find the equation of the line that has slope $-\frac{3}{2}$ and y-intercept (0, 2).

ANSWER

$y = -\frac{3}{2}x + 2$

Point–Slope Form

Now, suppose that the two pieces of information you are given about an equation are its slope and one point that lies on its graph. You still have enough information to write an equation of the line. Recall the formula for slope:

$$m = \frac{y_2 - y_1}{x_2 - x_1}, \quad \text{where } x_2 \neq x_1$$

We are given the slope m, and we know a particular point that lies on the line (x_1, y_1). We refer to all other points that lie on the line as (x, y). Substituting these values into the slope formula gives us

$$m = \frac{y - y_1}{x - x_1}$$

Cross multiplying yields

$$y - y_1 = m(x - x_1)$$

This is called the *point–slope form* of an equation of a line.

EQUATION OF A STRAIGHT LINE: POINT–SLOPE FORM

The **point–slope form** for the equation of a line is

$$y - y_1 = m(x - x_1)$$

Its graph passes through the point (x_1, y_1), and its slope is m.

Note: This formula does not hold for vertical lines since their slope is undefined.

EXAMPLE 4 Using Point–Slope Form to Find the Equation of a Line

Find the equation of the line that has slope $-\frac{1}{2}$ and passes through the point $(-1, 2)$.

Solution:

Write the point–slope form of an equation of a line. $y - y_1 = m(x - x_1)$

Substitute the values $m = -\frac{1}{2}$ and $(x_1, y_1) = (-1, 2)$. $y - 2 = -\frac{1}{2}[x - (-1)]$

Distribute. $y - 2 = -\frac{1}{2}x - \frac{1}{2}$

Isolate y. $y = -\frac{1}{2}x + \frac{3}{2}$

We can also express the equation in general form $\boxed{x + 2y = 3}$.

YOUR TURN Find the equation of the line that has slope $\frac{1}{4}$ and passes through the point $\left(1, -\frac{1}{2}\right)$.

ANSWER

$y = \frac{1}{4}x - \frac{3}{4}$ or $-x + 4y = -3$

Finding the Equation of a Line Given Two Points

Suppose the slope of a line is not given at all. Instead, two points that lie on the line are given. If we know two points that lie on the line, then we can calculate the slope. Then, using the slope and *either* of the two points, we can derive the equation of the line.

EXAMPLE 5 Finding the Equation of a Line Given Two Points

Find the equation of the line that passes through the points $(-2, -1)$ and $(3, 2)$.

Solution:

Write the equation of a line. $y = mx + b$

Calculate the slope. $m = \dfrac{y_2 - y_1}{x_2 - x_1}$

Substitute $(x_1, y_1) = (-2, -1)$ and $(x_2, y_2) = (3, 2)$. $m = \dfrac{2 - (-1)}{3 - (-2)} = \dfrac{3}{5}$

Proceed using either *slope–intercept* or *point–slope* form (see Study Tip).

Substitute $\frac{3}{5}$ for the slope. $y = \frac{3}{5}x + b$

Let $(x, y) = (3, 2)$. (Either point satisfies the equation.) $2 = \frac{3}{5}(3) + b$

Solve for b. $b = \frac{1}{5}$

Write the equation in slope–intercept form. $y = \frac{3}{5}x + \frac{1}{5}$

Write the equation in general form. $\boxed{-3x + 5y = 1}$

STUDY TIP

When two points that lie on a line are given, first calculate the slope of the line, then use either point and the slope–intercept form (shown in Example 5) or the point–slope form:

$m = \frac{3}{5}, (3, 2)$

$y - y_1 = m(x - x_1)$

$y - 2 = \frac{3}{5}(x - 3)$

$5y - 10 = 3(x - 3)$

$5y - 10 = 3x - 9$

$\boxed{-3x + 5y = 1}$

YOUR TURN Find the equation of the line that passes through the points $(-1, 3)$ and $(2, -4)$.

ANSWER

$y = -\frac{7}{3}x + \frac{2}{3}$ or $7x + 3y = 2$

0.6.3 SKILL

Find the equation of a line that is parallel or perpendicular to a given line.

0.6.3 CONCEPTUAL

Understand that parallel lines have the same slope, whereas perpendicular lines have slopes that are negative reciprocals of one another.

[CONCEPT CHECK]

What order are the slope and *y*-intercept found?
(A) the *y*-intercept and then the slope
(B) the slope and then the *y*-intercept?

ANSWER (B)

0.6.3 Parallel and Perpendicular Lines

Two distinct nonintersecting lines in a plane are *parallel*. How can we tell whether the two lines in the graph on the left are parallel? Parallel lines must have the same steepness. In other words, parallel lines must have the same slope. The two lines shown on the right are parallel because they have the same slope, 2.

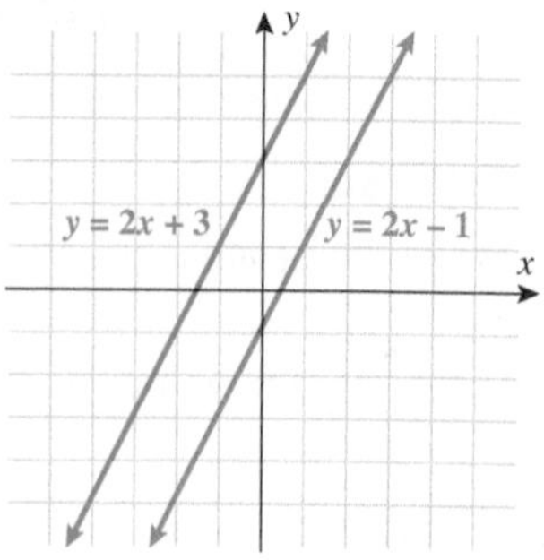

DEFINITION Parallel Lines

Two distinct lines in a plane are **parallel** if and only if their slopes are equal.

In other words, if two lines in a plane are parallel, then their slopes are equal, and if the slopes of two lines in a plane are equal, then the lines are parallel.

WORDS	MATH
Lines L_1 and L_2 are parallel.	$L_1 \| L_2$
Two parallel lines have the same slope.	$m_1 = m_2$

EXAMPLE 6 Finding an Equation of a Parallel Line

Find the equation of the line that passes through the point $(1, 1)$ and is parallel to the line $y = 3x + 1$.

Solution:

Write the slope–intercept equation of a line.	$y = mx + b$
Parallel lines have equal slope.	$m = 3$
Substitute the slope into the equation of the line.	$y = 3x + b$
Since the line passes through (1, 1), this point must satisfy the equation.	$1 = 3(1) + b$
Solve for *b*.	$b = -2$

The equation of the line is $\boxed{y = 3x - 2}$.

YOUR TURN Find the equation of the line parallel to $y = 2x - 1$ that passes through the point $(-1, 3)$.

ANSWER

$y = 2x + 5$

Two *perpendicular* lines form a right angle at their point of intersection. Notice the slopes of the two perpendicular lines in the figure to the left. They are $-\frac{1}{2}$ and 2, negative reciprocals of each other. It turns out that almost all perpendicular lines share this property. Horizontal ($m = 0$) and vertical (m undefined) lines do not share this property.

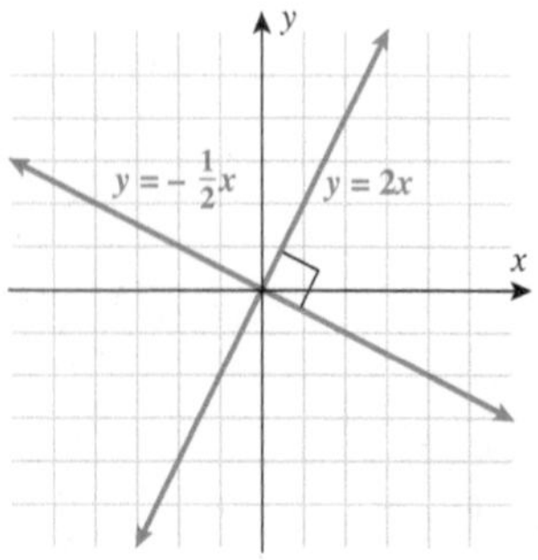

DEFINITION Perpendicular Lines

Except for the special cases of a vertical and a horizontal line, two lines in a plane are **perpendicular** if and only if their slopes are negative reciprocals of each other.

In other words, if two lines in a plane are perpendicular, their slopes are negative reciprocals, provided their slopes are defined. Similarly, if the slopes of two lines in a plane are negative reciprocals, then the lines are perpendicular.

WORDS	MATH
Lines L_1 and L_2 are perpendicular.	$L_1 \perp L_2$
Two perpendicular lines have negative reciprocal slopes.	$m_1 = -\dfrac{1}{m_2} \quad m_1 \neq 0, m_2 \neq 0$

STUDY TIP

If a line has slope equal to 3, then a line perpendicular to it has slope $-\frac{1}{3}$.

EXAMPLE 7 Finding an Equation of a Line That Is Perpendicular to Another Line

Find the equation of the line that passes through the point (3, 0) and is perpendicular to the line $y = 3x + 1$.

Solution:

Identify the slope of the given line $y = 3x + 1$. $\quad m_1 = 3$

The slope of a line perpendicular to the given line is the negative reciprocal of the slope of the given line. $\quad m_2 = -\dfrac{1}{m_1} = -\dfrac{1}{3}$

Write the equation of the line we are looking for in slope–intercept form. $\quad y = m_2x + b$

Substitute $m_2 = -\frac{1}{3}$ into $y = m_2x + b$. $\quad y = -\dfrac{1}{3}x + b$

Since the desired line passes through (3, 0), this point must satisfy the equation. $\quad 0 = -\dfrac{1}{3}(3) + b$

$0 = -1 + b$

Solve for b. $\quad b = 1$

The equation of the line is $\boxed{y = -\frac{1}{3}x + 1}$.

YOUR TURN Find the equation of the line that passes through the point $(1, -5)$ and is perpendicular to the line $y = -\frac{1}{2}x + 4$.

ANSWER

$y = 2x - 7$

[SECTION 0.6] SUMMARY

Lines are often expressed in two forms:

- General Form: $Ax + By = C$
- Slope–Intercept Form: $y = mx + b$

All lines (except horizontal and vertical lines) have exactly one x-intercept and exactly one y-intercept. The slope of a line is a measure of steepness.

- Slope of a line passing through (x_1, y_1) and (x_2, y_2):

$$m = \frac{y_2 - y_1}{x_2 - x_1} = \frac{\text{rise}}{\text{run}} \quad x_1 \neq x_2$$

- Horizontal lines: $m = 0$
- Vertical lines: m is undefined

An equation of a line can be found if either two points or the slope and a point are given. The point–slope form $y - y_1 = m(x - x_1)$ is useful when the slope and a point are given. Parallel lines have the same slope. Perpendicular lines have negative reciprocal (opposite) slopes, provided their slopes are defined.

[SECTION 0.6] EXERCISES

• SKILLS

In Exercises 1–10, find the slope of the line that passes through the given points.

1. $(1, 3)$ and $(2, 6)$
2. $(2, 1)$ and $(4, 9)$
3. $(-2, 5)$ and $(2, -3)$
4. $(-1, -4)$ and $(4, 6)$
5. $(-7, 9)$ and $(3, -10)$
6. $(11, -3)$ and $(-2, 6)$
7. $(0.2, -1.7)$ and $(3.1, 5.2)$
8. $(-2.4, 1.7)$ and $(-5.6, -2.3)$
9. $\left(\frac{2}{3}, -\frac{1}{4}\right)$ and $\left(\frac{5}{6}, -\frac{3}{4}\right)$
10. $\left(\frac{1}{2}, \frac{3}{5}\right)$ and $\left(-\frac{3}{4}, \frac{7}{5}\right)$

For each graph in Exercises 11–16, identify (by inspection) the x- and y-intercepts and slope if they exist, and classify the line as increasing, decreasing, horizontal, or vertical.

11.

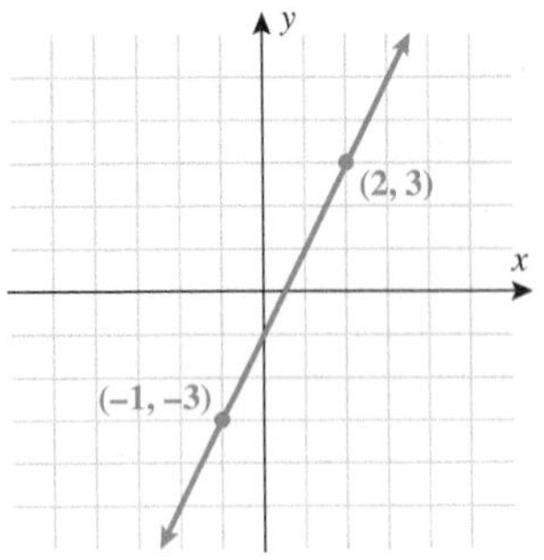

12.

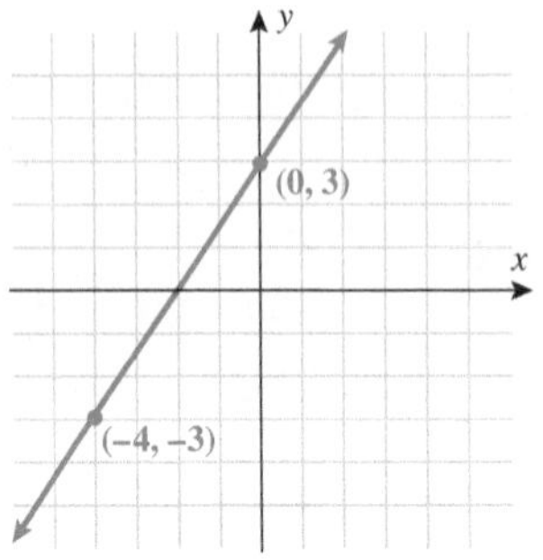

13.

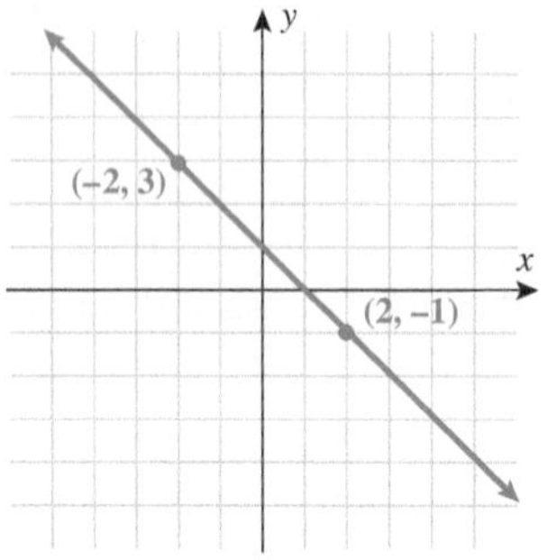

14.

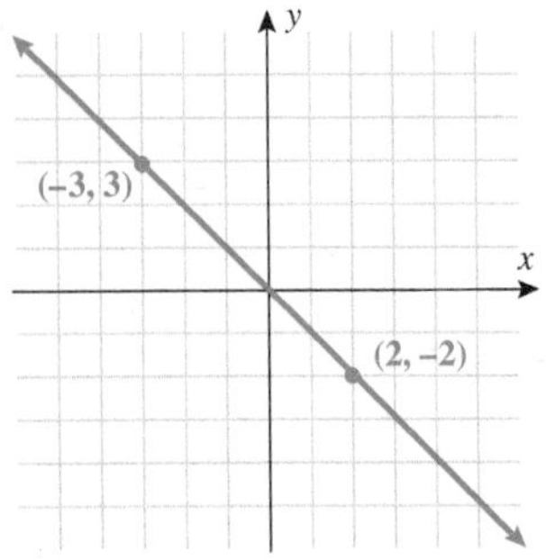

15.

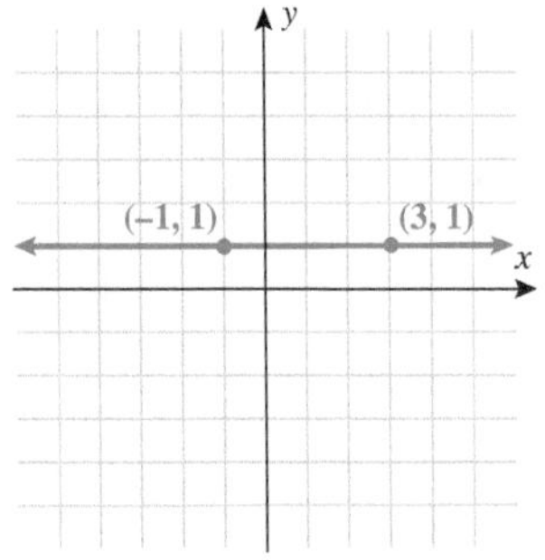

16.

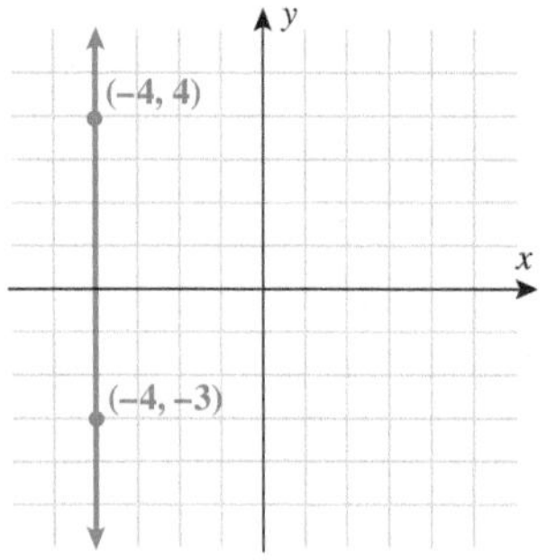

In Exercises 17–30, find the x- and y-intercepts if they exist, and graph the corresponding line.

17. $y = 2x - 3$
18. $y = -3x + 2$
19. $y = -\frac{1}{2}x + 2$
20. $y = \frac{1}{3}x - 1$
21. $2x - 3y = 4$
22. $-x + y = -1$
23. $\frac{1}{2}x + \frac{1}{2}y = -1$
24. $\frac{1}{3}x - \frac{1}{4}y = \frac{1}{12}$
25. $x = -1$
26. $y = -3$
27. $y = 1.5$
28. $x = -7.5$
29. $x = -\frac{7}{2}$
30. $y = \frac{5}{3}$

In Exercises 31–42, write the equation in slope–intercept form. Identify the slope and the y-intercept.

31. $2x - 5y = 10$
32. $3x - 4y = 12$
33. $x + 3y = 6$
34. $x + 2y = 8$
35. $4x - y = 3$
36. $x - y = 5$
37. $12 = 6x + 3y$
38. $4 = 2x - 8y$
39. $0.2x - 0.3y = 0.6$
40. $0.4x + 0.1y = 0.3$
41. $\frac{1}{2}x + \frac{2}{3}y = 4$
42. $\frac{1}{4}x + \frac{2}{5}y = 2$

In Exercises 43–50, write the equation of the line, given the slope and intercept.

43. Slope: $m = 2$
    y-intercept: $(0, 3)$
44. Slope: $m = -2$
    y-intercept: $(0, 1)$
45. Slope: $m = -\frac{1}{3}$
    y-intercept: $(0, 0)$
46. Slope: $m = \frac{1}{2}$
    y-intercept: $(0, -3)$
47. Slope: $m = 0$
    y-intercept: $(0, 2)$
48. Slope: $m = 0$
    y-intercept: $(0, -1.5)$
49. Slope: undefined
    x-intercept: $\left(\frac{3}{2}, 0\right)$
50. Slope: undefined
    x-intercept: $(-3.5, 0)$

In Exercises 51–60, write an equation of the line in slope–intercept form, if possible, given the slope and a point that lies on the line.

51. Slope: $m = 5$ $(-1, -3)$

52. Slope: $m = 2$ $(1, -1)$

53. Slope: $m = -3$ $(-2, 2)$

54. Slope: $m = -1$ $(3, -4)$

55. Slope: $m = \frac{3}{4}$ $(1, -1)$

56. Slope: $m = -\frac{1}{7}$ $(-5, 3)$

57. Slope: $m = 0$ $(-2, 4)$

58. Slope: $m = 0$ $(3, -3)$

59. Slope: undefined $(-1, 4)$

60. Slope: undefined $(4, -1)$

In Exercises 61–80, write the equation of the line that passes through the given points. Express the equation in slope–intercept form or in the form $x = a$ or $y = b$.

61. $(-2, -1)$ and $(3, 2)$

62. $(-4, -3)$ and $(5, 1)$

63. $(-3, -1)$ and $(-2, -6)$

64. $(-5, -8)$ and $(7, -2)$

65. $(20, -37)$ and $(-10, -42)$

66. $(-8, 12)$ and $(-20, -12)$

67. $(-1, 4)$ and $(2, -5)$

68. $(-2, 3)$ and $(2, -3)$

69. $\left(\frac{1}{2}, \frac{3}{4}\right)$ and $\left(\frac{3}{2}, \frac{9}{4}\right)$

70. $\left(-\frac{2}{3}, -\frac{1}{2}\right)$ and $\left(\frac{7}{3}, \frac{1}{2}\right)$

71. $(3, 5)$ and $(3, -7)$

72. $(-5, -2)$ and $(-5, 4)$

73. $(3, 7)$ and $(9, 7)$

74. $(-2, -1)$ and $(3, -1)$

75. $(0, 6)$ and $(-5, 0)$

76. $(0, -3)$ and $(0, 2)$

77. $(-6, 8)$ and $(-6, -2)$

78. $(-9, 0)$ and $(-9, 2)$

79. $\left(\frac{2}{5}, -\frac{3}{4}\right)$ and $\left(\frac{2}{5}, \frac{1}{2}\right)$

80. $\left(\frac{1}{3}, \frac{2}{5}\right)$ and $\left(\frac{1}{3}, \frac{1}{2}\right)$

In Exercises 81–86, write the equation corresponding to each line. Express the equation in slope–intercept form.

81.

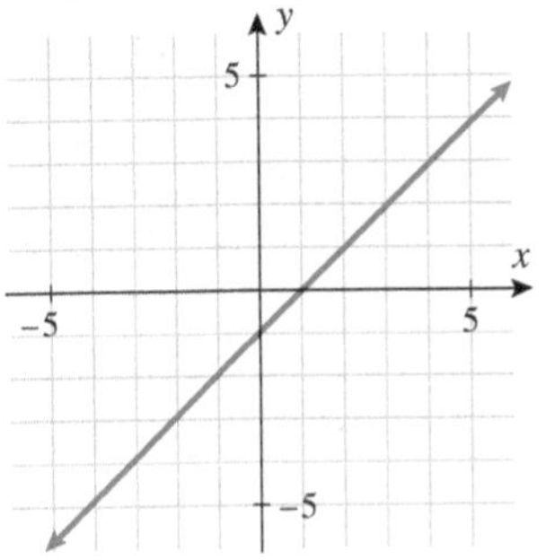

82.

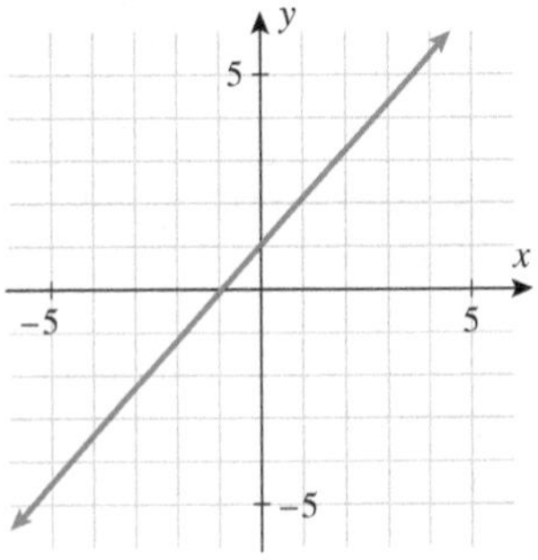

83.

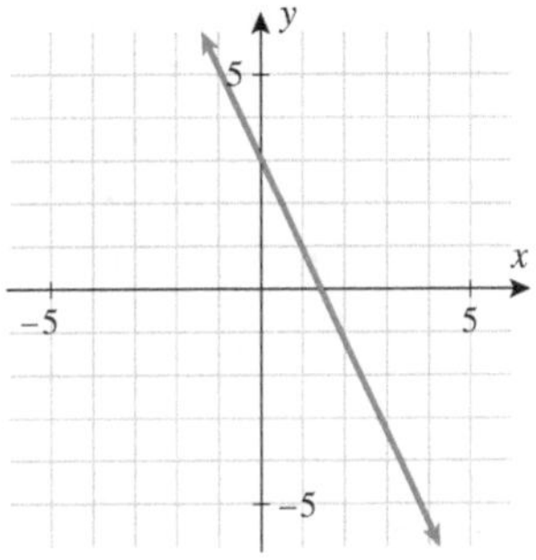

84.

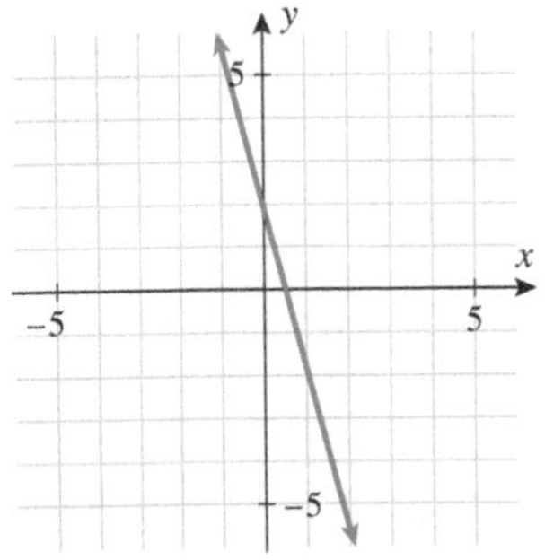

85.

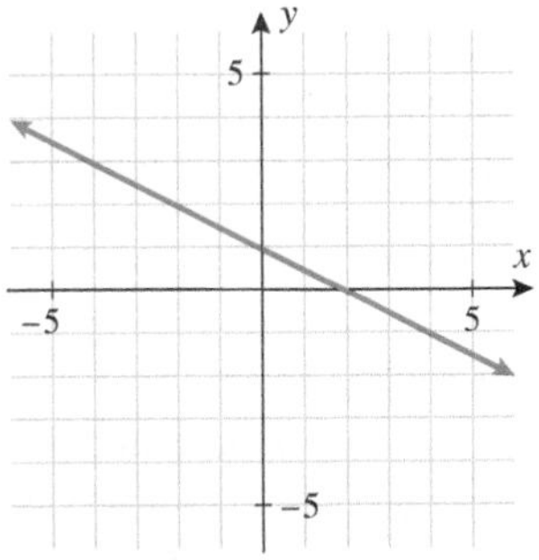

86.

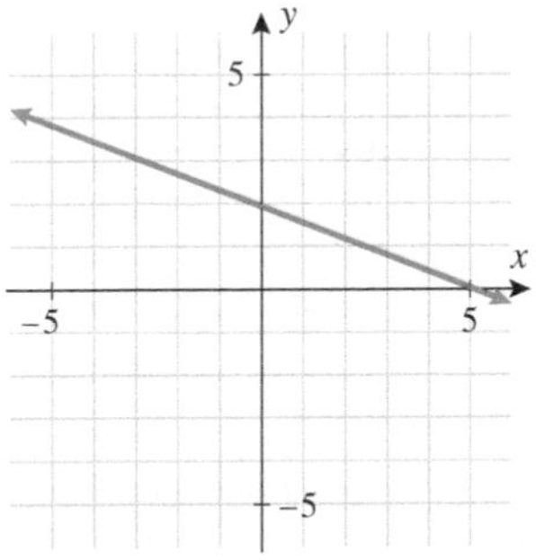

In Exercises 87–100, find the equation of the line that passes through the given point and also satisfies the additional piece of information. Express your answer in slope–intercept form, if possible.

87. $(-3, 1)$; parallel to the line $y = 2x - 1$

88. $(1, 3)$; parallel to the line $y = -x + 2$

89. $(0, 0)$; perpendicular to the line $2x + 3y = 12$

90. $(0, 6)$; perpendicular to the line $x - y = 7$

91. $(3, 5)$; parallel to the x-axis

92. $(3, 5)$; parallel to the y-axis

93. $(-1, 2)$; perpendicular to the y-axis

94. $(-1, 2)$; perpendicular to the x-axis

95. $(-2, -7)$; parallel to the line $\frac{1}{2}x - \frac{1}{3}y = 5$

96. $(1, 4)$; perpendicular to the line $-\frac{2}{3}x + \frac{3}{2}y = -2$

97. $\left(-\frac{2}{3}, \frac{2}{3}\right)$; perpendicular to the line $8x + 10y = -45$

98. $\left(\frac{6}{5}, 3\right)$; perpendicular to the line $6x + 14y = 7$

99. $\left(\frac{7}{2}, 4\right)$; parallel to the line $-15x + 35y = 7$

100. $\left(-\frac{1}{4}, -\frac{13}{9}\right)$; parallel to the line $10x + 45y = -9$

• APPLICATIONS

101. Budget: Home Improvement. The cost of having your bathroom remodeled is the combination of material costs and labor costs. The materials (tile, grout, toilet, fixtures, etc.) cost is \$1200 and the labor cost is \$25 per hour. Write an equation that models the total cost C of having your bathroom remodeled as a function of hours h. How much will the job cost if the worker estimates 32 hours?

102. Budget: Rental Car. The cost of a one-day car rental is the sum of the rental fee, \$50, plus \$0.39 per mile. Write an equation that models the total cost associated with the car rental.

103. Budget: Monthly Driving Costs. The monthly costs associated with driving a new Honda Accord are the monthly loan payment plus \$25 every time you fill up with gasoline. If you fill up 5 times in a month, your total monthly cost is \$500. How much is your loan payment?

104. Budget: Monthly Driving Costs. The monthly costs associated with driving a Ford Explorer are the monthly loan payment plus the cost of filling up your tank with gasoline. If you fill up 3 times in a month, your total monthly cost is \$520. If you fill up 5 times in a month, your total monthly cost is \$600. How much is your monthly loan, and how much does it cost every time you fill up with gasoline?

105. Business. The operating costs for a local business are a fixed amount of \$1300 plus \$3.50 per unit sold, and revenue is \$7.25 per unit sold. How many units does the business have to sell in order to break even?

106. Business. The operating costs for a local business are a fixed amount of \$12,000 plus \$13.50 per unit sold, and revenue is \$27.25 per unit sold. How many units does the business have to sell in order to break even?

107. Weather: Temperature. The National Oceanic and Atmospheric Administration (NOAA) has an online conversion chart that relates degrees Fahrenheit, °F, to degrees Celsius, °C. 77°F is equivalent to 25°C, and 68°F is equivalent to 20°C. Assuming the relationship is linear, write the equation relating degrees Celsius to degrees Fahrenheit. What temperature is the same in both degrees Celsius and degrees Fahrenheit?

108. Weather: Temperature. According to NOAA, a "standard day" is 15°C at sea level, and every 500-feet elevation above sea level corresponds to a 1°C temperature drop. Assuming the relationship between temperature and elevation is linear, write an equation that models this relationship. What is the expected temperature at 2500 feet on a "standard day"?

109. Life Sciences: Height. The average height of a man has increased over the last century. What is the rate of change in inches per year of the average height of men?

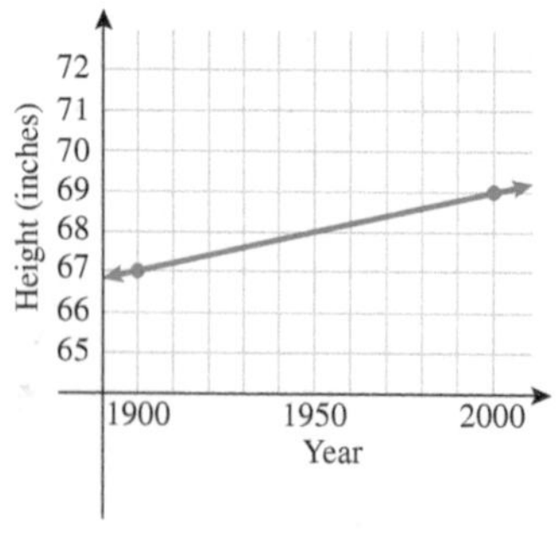

110. Life Sciences: Height. The average height of a woman has increased over the last century. What is the rate of change in inches per year of the average height of women?

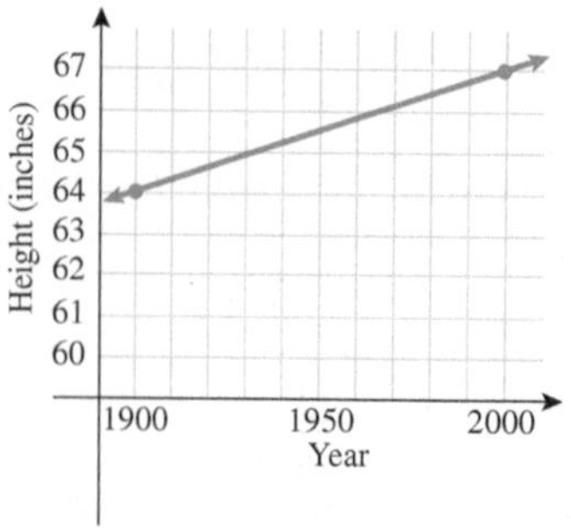

111. Life Sciences: Weight. The average weight of a baby born in 1900 was 6 pounds 4 ounces. In 2000 the average weight of a newborn was 6 pounds 10 ounces. What is the rate of change of birth weight in ounces per year? What do we expect babies will weigh at birth in 2040?

112. Sports. The fastest a man could run a mile in 1906 was 4 minutes and 30 seconds. In 1957 Don Bowden became the first American to break the 4-minute mile. Calculate the rate of change in mile speed per year.

113. Weather: Rainfall. The average rainfall in Norfolk, Virginia, for July was 5.2 inches in 2003. The average July rainfall for Norfolk was 3.8 inches in 2007. What is the rate of change of rainfall in inches per year? If this trend continues, what is the expected average rainfall in 2010?

114. Weather: Temperature. The average temperature for Boston in January 2005 was 43°F. In 2007 the average January temperature was 44.5°F. What is the rate of change of the temperature per year? If this trend continues, what is the expected average temperature in January 2010?

115. Environment. In 2000 Americans used approximately 380 billion plastic bags. In 2005 approximately 392 billion were used. What is the rate of change of plastic bags used per year? How many plastic bags are expected to be used in 2010?

116. Finance: Debt. According to financial reports, the average household credit card debt in 2010 was \$7768 and in 2012 was \$7117. What was the rate of change of the credit card debt per year? If this trend were to continue, how much would you expect the average household credit card debt to be in 2016?

• CATCH THE MISTAKE

In Exercises 117–120, explain the mistake that is made.

117. Find the x- and y-intercepts of the line with equation $2x - 3y = 6$.

Solution:

x-intercept: set $x = 0$ and solve for y. $\quad -3y = 6$

$y = -2$

The x-intercept is $(0, -2)$.

y-intercept: set $y = 0$ and solve for x. $\quad 2x = 6$

$x = 3$

The y-intercept is $(3, 0)$.

This is incorrect. What mistake was made?

118. Find the slope of the line that passes through the points $(-2, 3)$ and $(4, 1)$.

Solution:

Write the slope formula. $\quad m = \dfrac{y_2 - y_1}{x_2 - x_1}$

Substitute $(-2, 3)$ and $(4, 1)$. $\quad m = \dfrac{1 - 3}{-2 - 4} = \dfrac{-2}{-6} = \dfrac{1}{3}$

This is incorrect. What mistake was made?

119. Find the slope of the line that passes through the points $(-3, 4)$ and $(-3, 7)$.

Solution:

Write the slope formula. $\quad m = \dfrac{y_2 - y_1}{x_2 - x_1}$

Substitute $(-3, 4)$ and $(-3, 7)$. $\quad m = \dfrac{-3 - (-3)}{4 - 7} = 0$

This is incorrect. What mistake was made?

120. Given the slope, classify the line as increasing, decreasing, horizontal, or vertical.

a. $m = 0$ **b.** m undefined

c. $m = 2$ **d.** $m = -1$

Solution:

a. vertical line **b.** horizontal line

c. increasing **d.** decreasing

These are incorrect. What mistakes were made?

• CONCEPTUAL

In Exercises 121–124, determine whether each statement is true or false.

121. A nonhorizontal line can have at most one x-intercept.

122. A line must have at least one y-intercept.

123. If the slopes of two lines are $-\frac{1}{5}$ and 5, then the lines are parallel.

124. If the slopes of two lines are -1 and 1, then the lines are perpendicular.

125. If a line has slope equal to zero, describe a line that is perpendicular to it.

126. If a line has no slope (undefined slope), describe a line that is parallel to it.

• CHALLENGE

127. Find an equation of a line that passes through the point $(-B, A + 1)$ and is parallel to the line $Ax + By = C$. Assume that B is not equal to zero.

128. Find an equation of a line that passes through the point $(B, A - 1)$ and is parallel to the line $Ax + By = C$. Assume that B is not equal to zero.

129. Find an equation of a line that passes through the point $(-A, B - 1)$ and is perpendicular to the line $Ax + By = C$. Assume that A and B are both nonzero.

130. Find an equation of a line that passes through the point $(A, B + 1)$ and is perpendicular to the line $Ax + By = C$.

131. Show that two lines with equal slopes and different y-intercepts have no point in common. *Hint:* Let $y_1 = mx + b_1$ and $y_2 = mx + b_2$ with $b_1 \neq b_2$. What equation must be true for there to be a point of intersection? Show that this leads to a contradiction.

132. Let $y_1 = m_1x + b_1$ and $y_2 = m_2x + b_2$ be two nonparallel lines $(m_1 \neq m_2)$. What is the x-coordinate of the point where they intersect?

0.7 MODELING VARIATION

SKILLS OBJECTIVES

- Develop mathematical models using direct variation.
- Develop mathematical models using inverse variation.
- Develop mathematical models using joint variation and combined variation.

CONCEPTUAL OBJECTIVES

- Understand that direct variation implies two things grow with one another (that is, as one increases, the other increases).
- Understand that inverse variation implies two things grow opposite of one another (that is, as one increases, the other decreases).
- Understand the difference between combined variation and joint variation.

In this section, we discuss mathematical models for different applications. Two quantities in the real world often *vary* with respect to one another. Sometimes, they vary *directly*. For example, the more money we make, the more total dollars of federal income tax we expect to pay. Sometimes, quantities vary *inversely*. For example, when interest rates on mortgages decrease, we expect the number of homes purchased to increase, because a buyer can afford "more house" with the same mortgage payment when rates are lower. In this section, we discuss quantities varying *directly*, *inversely*, or *jointly*.

0.7.1 Direct Variation

0.7.1 SKILL

Develop mathematical models using direct variation.

0.7.1 CONCEPTUAL

Understand that direct variation implies two things grow with one another (that is, as one increases, the other increases).

When one quantity is a constant multiple of another quantity, we say that the quantities are *directly proportional* to one another.

DIRECT VARIATION

Let x and y represent two quantities. The following are equivalent statements:

- $y = kx$, where k is a nonzero constant.
- y **varies directly** with x.
- y is **directly proportional** to x.

The constant k is called the **constant of variation** or the **constant of proportionality**.

In 2015 the national average cost of residential electricity was 13.06 ¢/kWh (cents per kilowatt-hour). For example, if a residence used 3400 kWh, then the bill would be \$444.04 and if a residence used 2500 kWh, then the bill would be \$326.50.

EXAMPLE 1 **Finding the Constant of Variation**

In the United States, the cost of electricity is directly proportional to the number of kilowatt-hours (kWh) used. If a household in Tennessee on average used 3098 kWh per month and had an average monthly electric bill of \$320.02, find a mathematical model that gives the cost of electricity in Tennessee in terms of the number of kilowatt-hours used.

Solution:

Write the direct variation model. $y = kx$

Label the variables and constant.

x = number of kWh
y = cost (dollars)
k = cost per kWh

Substitute the given data $x = 3098$ kWh and $y = \$320.02$ into $y = kx$. $320.02 = 3098k$

Solve for k. $k = \frac{320.02}{3098} \approx 0.1033$

$y = 0.1033x$

In Tennessee the cost of electricity is $\boxed{10.33\ ¢/\text{kWh}}$.

YOUR TURN Find a mathematical model that describes the cost of electricity in California if the cost is directly proportional to the number of kWh used and a residence that consumes 4000 kWh is billed \$735.20.

ANSWER

$y = 18.38x$; the cost of electricity in California is 18.38 ¢/kWh.

Not all variation we see in nature is direct variation. Isometric growth, where the various parts of an organism grow in direct proportion to each other, is rare in living organisms. If organisms grew isometrically, young children would look just like adults, only smaller. In contrast, most organisms grow nonisometrically; the various parts of organisms do not increase in size in a one-to-one ratio. The relative proportions of a human body change dramatically as the human grows. Children have proportionately larger heads and shorter legs than adults. *Allometric growth* is the pattern of growth whereby different parts of the body grow at different rates with respect to each other. Some human body characteristics vary directly, and others can be mathematically modeled by *direct variation with powers*.

DIRECT VARIATION WITH POWERS

Let x and y represent two quantities. The following are equivalent statements:

- $y = kx^n$, where k is a nonzero constant.
- **y varies directly with the nth power** of x.
- **y is directly proportional to the nth power** of x.

One example of direct variation with powers is height and weight of humans. Statistics show that weight (in pounds) is directly proportional to the cube of height (in feet):

$$W = kH^3$$

EXAMPLE 2 Direct Variation with Powers

The following is a personal ad:

Single professional male (6 ft/194 lb) *seeks single professional female for long-term relationship. Must be athletic, smart, like the movies and dogs, and have height and weight similarly proportioned to mine.*

Find a mathematical equation that describes the height and weight of the male who wrote the ad. How much would a 5 feet 6 inches woman weigh who has the same proportionality as the male?

Solution:

Write the direct variation (cube) model for height versus weight. $W = kH^3$

Substitute the given data $W = 194$ and $H = 6$ into $W = kH^3$. $194 = k(6)^3$

Solve for k. $k = \frac{194}{216} = 0.898148 \approx 0.90$

$W = 0.9H^3$

Let $H = 5.5$ ft. $W = 0.9(5.5)^3 \approx 149.73$

A woman 5 feet 6 inches tall with the same height and weight proportionality as the male would weigh approximately $\boxed{150 \text{ pounds}}$.

YOUR TURN A brother and sister both have weight (pounds) that varies as the cube of height (feet) and they share the same proportionality constant. The sister is 6 feet tall and weighs 170 pounds. Her brother is 6 feet 4 inches tall. How much does he weigh?

[CONCEPT CHECK]

Most students' final grade in precalculus is directly proportional to
(A) their financial aid amount
(B) how many hours they spend doing homework and in their instructor's office.

ANSWER (B)

ANSWER

≈ 200 pounds

0.7.2 Inverse Variation

0.7.2 SKILL

Develop mathematical models using inverse variation.

0.7.2 CONCEPTUAL

Understand that inverse variation implies two things grow opposite of one another (that is, as one increases, the other decreases).

Two fundamental topics covered in economics are supply and demand. Supply is the quantity that producers are willing to sell at a given price. For example, an artist may be willing to paint and sell 5 portraits if each sells for \$50, but that same artist may be willing to sell 100 portraits if each sells for \$10,000. Demand is the quantity of a good that consumers not only are willing to purchase, but also have the capacity to buy, at a given price. For example, consumers may purchase 1 billion Big Macs from McDonald's every year, but perhaps only 1 million filets mignons are sold at Outback. There may be 1 billion people who want to buy the filet mignon but don't have the financial means to do so. Economists study the equilibrium between supply and demand.

Demand can be modeled with an *inverse variation* of price: When the price increases, demand decreases, and vice versa.

INVERSE VARIATION

Let x and y represent two quantities. The following are equivalent statements:

- $y = \frac{k}{x}$, where k is a nonzero constant.
- y **varies inversely** with x.
- y is **inversely proportional** to x.

The constant k is called the **constant of variation** or the **constant of proportionality**.

EXAMPLE 3 **Inverse Variation**

The number of potential buyers of a house decreases as the price of the house increases (see graph on the right). If the number of potential buyers of a house in a particular city is inversely proportional to the price of the house, find a mathematical equation that describes the demand for houses as it relates to price. How many potential buyers will there be for a $2 million house?

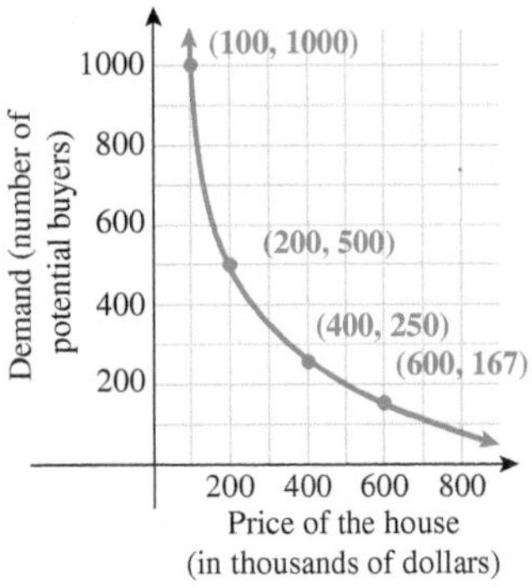

Solution:

Write the inverse variation model. $y = \frac{k}{x}$

Label the variables and constant. x = price of house in thousands of dollars

y = number of buyers

Select *any* point that lies on the curve. (200, 500)

Substitute the given data $x = 200$ and $y = 500$ into $y = \frac{k}{x}$. $500 = \frac{k}{200}$

Solve for k. $k = 200 \cdot 500 = 100{,}000$

$$y = \frac{100{,}000}{x}$$

Let $x = 2000$. $y = \frac{100{,}000}{2000} = 50$

There are only 50 potential buyers for a $2 million house in this city.

YOUR TURN In New York City, the number of potential buyers in the housing market is inversely proportional to the price of a house. If there are 12,500 potential buyers for a $2 million condominium, how many potential buyers are there for a $5 million condominium?

ANSWER 5000

[CONCEPT CHECK]

Given a fixed distance, the time it takes you to drive that distance varies inversely with what?

ANSWER rate (or speed)

Two quantities can vary inversely with the nth power of x.

If x and y are related by the equation $y = \frac{k}{x^n}$, then we say that y varies **inversely with the nth power of x**, or y is **inversely proportional to the nth power of x**.

0.7.3 Joint Variation and Combined Variation

0.7.3 SKILL

Develop mathematical models using joint variation and combined variation.

0.7.3 CONCEPTUAL

Understand the difference between combined variation and joint variation.

We now discuss combinations of variations. When one quantity is directly proportional to the product of two or more other quantities, the variation is called **joint variation**. When direct variation and inverse variation occur at the same time, the variation is called **combined variation**.

An example of a **joint variation** is simple interest (Section 0.1), which is defined as

$$I = Prt$$

where

- I is the interest in dollars.
- P is the principal (initial) in dollars.
- r is the interest rate (expressed in decimal form).
- t is time in years.

The interest earned is directly proportional to the product of three quantities (principal, interest rate, and time). Note that if the interest rate increases, then the interest earned also increases. Similarly, if either the initial investment (principal) or the time the money is invested increases, then the interest earned also increases.

An example of **combined variation** is the combined gas law in chemistry:

$$P = k\frac{T}{V}$$

where

- P is pressure.
- T is temperature (kelvins).
- V is volume.
- k is a gas constant.

This relation states that the pressure of a gas is directly proportional to the temperature and inversely proportional to the volume containing the gas. For example, as the temperature increases, the pressure increases, but when the volume decreases, the pressure increases.

As an example, the gas in the headspace of a soda bottle has a fixed volume. Therefore, as temperature increases, the pressure increases. Compare the different pressures released when you open a twist-off cap on a bottle of soda that is cold versus one that is hot. The hot one feels as though it "releases more pressure."

EXAMPLE 4 Combined Variation

The gas in the headspace of a soda bottle has a volume of 9.0 milliliters, pressure of 2 atm (atmospheres), and a temperature of 298 K (standard room temperature of 77°F). If the soda bottle is stored in a refrigerator, the temperature drops to approximately 279 K (43°F). What is the pressure of the gas in the headspace once the bottle is chilled?

Solution:

Write the combined gas law. $P = k\frac{T}{V}$

Let $P = 2$ atm, $T = 298$ K, and $V = 9.0$ mL. $2 = k\frac{298}{9}$

Solve for k. $k = \frac{18}{298}$

Let $k = \frac{18}{298}$, $T = 279$, and $V = 9.0$ in $P = k\frac{T}{V}$. $P = \frac{18}{298} \cdot \frac{279}{9} \approx 1.87$

Since we used the same physical units for both the chilled and room-temperature soda bottles, the pressure is in atmospheres. $\boxed{P = 1.87 \text{ atm}}$

[CONCEPT CHECK]

The area of a triangle, $A = \frac{1}{2}b \cdot h$ is an example of what type of variation?

(A) combined

(B) joint

ANSWER (B)

[SECTION 0.7] SUMMARY

Direct, inverse, joint, and combined variation can be used to model the relationship between two quantities. For two quantities x and y, we say that

- y is directly proportional to x if $y = kx$.
- y is inversely proportional to x if $y = \frac{k}{x}$.

Joint variation occurs when one quantity is directly proportional to two or more quantities. Combined variation occurs when one quantity is directly proportional to one or more quantities and inversely proportional to one or more other quantities.

[SECTION 0.7] EXERCISES

• SKILLS

In Exercises 1–16, write an equation that describes each variation. Use k as the constant of variation.

1. y varies directly with x.
2. s varies directly with t.
3. V varies directly with x^3.
4. A varies directly with x^2.
5. z varies directly with m.
6. h varies directly with $\sqrt{t}$.
7. f varies inversely with λ.
8. P varies inversely with r^2.
9. F varies directly with w and inversely with L.
10. V varies directly with T and inversely with P.
11. v varies directly with both g and t.
12. S varies directly with both t and d.
13. R varies inversely with both P and T.
14. y varies inversely with both x and z.
15. y is directly proportional to the square root of x.
16. y is inversely proportional to the cube of t.

In Exercises 17–36, write an equation that describes each variation.

17. d is directly proportional to t; $d = r$ when $t = 1$.
18. F is directly proportional to m; $F = a$ when $m = 1$.
19. V is directly proportional to both l and w; $V = 6h$ when $w = 3$ and $l = 2$.
20. A is directly proportional to both b and h; $A = 10$ when $b = 5$ and $h = 4$.
21. A varies directly with the square of r; $A = 9$p when $r = 3$.
22. V varies directly with the cube of r; $V = 36$p when $r = 3$.
23. V varies directly with both h and r^2; $V = 1$ when $r = 2$ and $h = \frac{4}{\pi}$.
24. W is directly proportional to both R and the square of I; $W = 4$ when $R = 100$ and $I = 0.25$.
25. V varies inversely with P; $V = 1000$ when $P = 400$.
26. I varies inversely with the square of d; $I = 42$ when $d = 16$.
27. F varies inversely with both λ and L; $F = 20\pi$ when $\lambda = 1\ \mu$m (micrometers or microns) and $L = 100$ km.
28. y varies inversely with both x and z; $y = 32$ when $x = 4$ and $z = 0.05$.
29. t varies inversely with s; $t = 2.4$ when $s = 8$.
30. W varies inversely with the square of d; $W = 180$ when $d = 0.2$.
31. R varies inversely with the square of I; $R = 0.4$ when $I = 3.5$.
32. y varies inversely with both x and the square root of z; $y = 12$ when $x = 0.2$ and $z = 4$.
33. R varies directly with L and inversely with A; $R = 0.5$ when $L = 20$ and $A = 0.4$.
34. F varies directly with m and inversely with d; $F = 32$ when $m = 20$ and $d = 8$.
35. F varies directly with both m_1 and m_2 and inversely with the square of d; $F = 20$ when $m_1 = 8$, $m_2 = 16$, and $d = 0.4$.
36. w varies directly with the square root of g and inversely with the square of t; $w = 20$ when $g = 16$ and $t = 0.5$.

• APPLICATIONS

37. **Wages.** Jason and Valerie both work at Panera Bread and have the following paycheck information for a certain week. Find an equation that shows their wages W varying directly with the number of hours worked H.

EMPLOYEE	HOURS WORKED	WAGES
Jason	23	\$172.50
Valerie	32	\$240.00

38. **Sales Tax.** The sales taxes in Orange and Seminole Counties in Florida differ by only 0.5%. A new resident knows this but doesn't know which of the counties has the higher tax. The resident lives near the border of the counties and is in the market for a new plasma television and wants to purchase it in the county with the lower tax. If the tax on a pair of \$40 sneakers is \$2.60 in Orange County and the tax on a \$12 T-shirt is \$0.84 in Seminole County, write two equations: one for each county that describes the tax T, which is directly proportional to the purchase price P.

For Exercises 39 and 40, refer to the following:

The ratio of the speed of an object to the speed of sound determines the Mach number. Aircraft traveling at a subsonic speed (less than the speed of sound) have a Mach number less than 1. In other words, the speed of an aircraft is directly proportional to its Mach number. Aircraft traveling at a supersonic speed (greater than the speed of sound) have a Mach number greater than 1. The speed of sound at sea level is approximately 760 miles per hour.

39. **Military.** The U.S. Navy Blue Angels fly F-18 Hornets that are capable of Mach 1.7. How fast can F-18 Hornets fly at sea level?

40. **Military.** The U.S. Air Force's newest fighter aircraft is the F-22A Raptor, which is capable of Mach 1.5. How fast can a F-22A Raptor fly at sea level?

Exercises 41 and 42 are examples of the golden ratio, or phi, a proportionality constant that appears in nature. The numerical approximate value of phi is 1.618 (from www.goldenratio.net).

41. **Human Anatomy.** The length of your forearm F (wrist to elbow) is directly proportional to the length of your hand H (length from wrist to tip of middle finger). Write the equation that describes this relationship if the length of your forearm is 11 inches and the length of your hand is 6.8 inches.

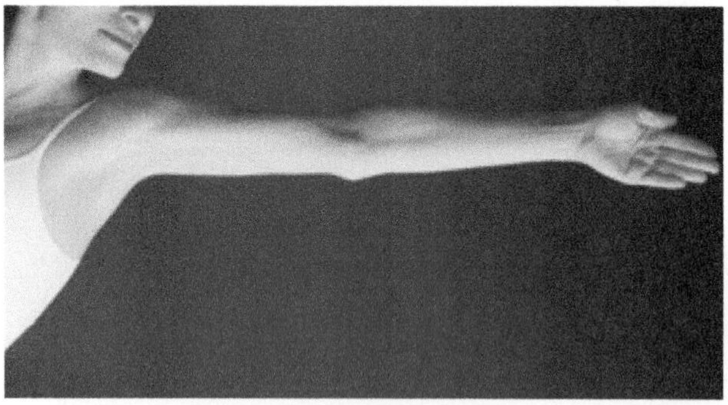

Kim Steele/Getty images, Inc.

42. **Human Anatomy.** Each section of your index finger, from the tip to the base of the wrist, is larger than the preceding one by about the golden (Fibonacci) ratio. Find an equation that represents the ratio of each section of your finger related to the previous one if one section is eight units long and the next section is five units long.

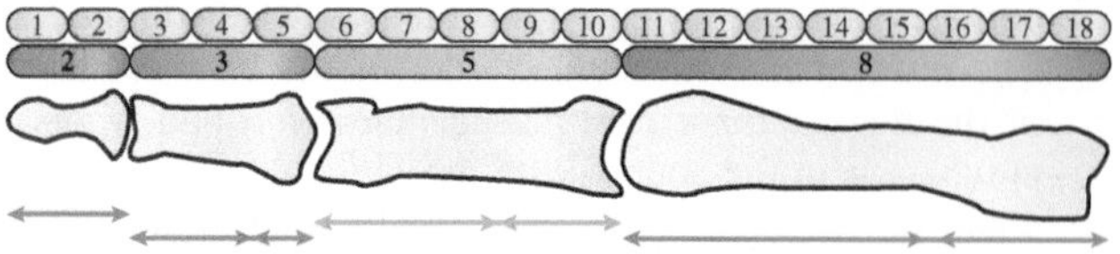

For Exercises 43 and 44, refer to the following:

Hooke's law in physics states that if a spring at rest (equilibrium position) has a weight attached to it, then the distance the spring stretches is directly proportional to the force (weight), according to the formula

$$F = kx$$

where F is the force in Newtons (N), x is the distance stretched in meters (m), and k is the spring constant (N/m).

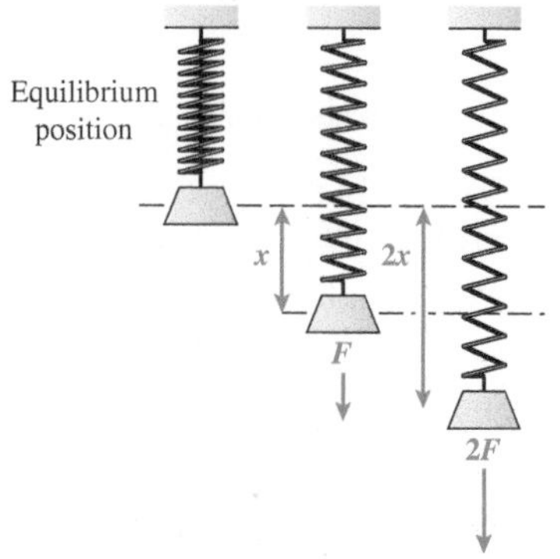

43. **Physics.** A force of 30 N will stretch the spring 10 centimeters. How far will a force of 72 N stretch the spring?

44. **Physics.** A force of 30 N will stretch the spring 10 centimeters. How much force is required to stretch the spring 18 centimeters?

45. **Business.** A cell phone company develops a pay-as-you-go cell phone plan in which the monthly cost varies directly as the number of minutes used. If the company charges $17.70 in a month when 236 minutes are used, what should the company charge for a month in which 500 minutes are used?

46. **Economics.** Demand for a product varies inversely with the price per unit of the product. Demand for the product is 10,000 units when the price is $5.75 per unit. Find the demand for the product (to the nearest hundred units) when the price is $6.50.

47. **Sales.** Levi's makes jeans in a variety of price ranges for juniors. The Flare 519 jeans sell for about $20, whereas the 646 Vintage Flare jeans sell for $300. The demand for Levi's jeans is inversely proportional to the price. If 300,000 pairs of the 519 jeans were bought, approximately how many of the Vintage Flare jeans were bought?

48. **Sales.** Levi's makes jeans in a variety of price ranges for men. The Silver Tab Baggy jeans sell for about $30, whereas the Offender jeans sell for about $160. The demand for Levi's jeans is inversely proportional to the price. If 400,000 pairs of the Silver Tab Baggy jeans were bought, approximately how many of the Offender jeans were bought?

For Exercises 49 and 50, refer to the following:

In physics, the inverse square law states that any physical force or energy flow is inversely proportional to the square of the distance from the source of that physical quantity. In particular, the intensity of light radiating from a point source is inversely proportional to the square of the distance from the source. Below is a table of average distances from the Sun:

PLANET	DISTANCE TO THE SUN
Mercury	58,000 km
Earth	150,000 km
Mars	228,000 km

49. **Solar Radiation.** The solar radiation on Earth is approximately 1400 watts per square meter (W/m^2). How much solar radiation is there on Mars? Round to the nearest hundred watts per square meter.

50. **Solar Radiation.** The solar radiation on Earth is approximately 1400 watts per square meter. How much solar radiation is there on Mercury? Round to the nearest hundred watts per square meter.

51. **Investments.** Marilyn receives a \$25,000 bonus from her company and decides to put the money toward a new car that she will need in 2 years. Simple interest is directly proportional to the principal and the time invested. She compares two different banks' rates on money market accounts. If she goes with Bank of America, she will earn \$750 in interest, but if she goes with the Navy Federal Credit Union, she will earn \$1500. What is the interest rate on money market accounts at each of these banks?

52. **Investments.** Connie and Alvaro sell their house and buy a fixer-upper house. They made \$130,000 on the sale of their previous home. They know it will take 6 months before the general contractor can start their renovation, and they want to take advantage of a 6-month CD that pays simple interest. What is the rate of the 6-month CD if they will make \$3250 in interest?

53. **Chemistry.** A gas contained in a 4-milliliter container at a temperature of 300 K has a pressure of 1 atm. If the temperature decreases to 275 K, what is the resulting pressure?

54. **Chemistry.** A gas contained in a 4-milliliter container at a temperature of 300 K has a pressure of 1 atm. If the container changes to a volume of 3 milliliters, what is the resulting pressure?

• CATCH THE MISTAKE

In Exercises 55 and 56, explain the mistake that is made.

55. y varies directly with t and inversely with x. When $x = 4$ and $t = 2$, then $y = 1$. Find an equation that describes this variation.

Solution:

Write the variation equation. $y = ktx$

Let $x = 4$, $t = 2$, and $y = 1$. $1 = k(2)(4)$

Solve for k. $k = \frac{1}{8}$

Substitute $k = \frac{1}{8}$ into $y = ktx$. $y = \frac{1}{8}x$

This is incorrect. What mistake was made?

56. y varies directly with t and the square of x. When $x = 4$ and $t = 1$, then $y = 8$. Find an equation that describes this variation.

Solution:

Write the variation equation. $y = kt\sqrt{x}$

Let $x = 4$, $t = 1$, and $y = 8$. $8 = k(1)\sqrt{4}$

Solve for k. $k = 4$

Substitute $k = 4$ into $y = kt\sqrt{x}$. $y = 4t\sqrt{x}$

This is incorrect. What mistake was made?

• CONCEPTUAL

In Exercises 57 and 58, determine whether each statement is true or false.

57. The area of a triangle is directly proportional to both the base and the height of the triangle (joint variation).

58. Average speed is directly proportional to both distance and time (joint variation).

In Exercises 59 and 60, match the variation with the graph.

59. Inverse variation

60. Direct variation

a.

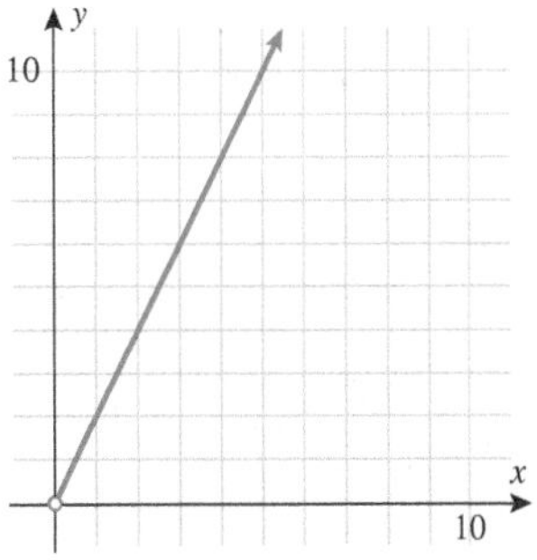

b.

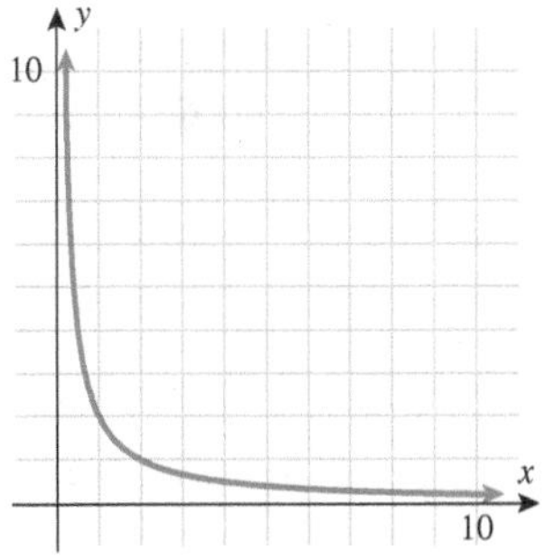

• CHALLENGE

Exercises 61 and 62 involve the theory governing laser propagation through Earth's atmosphere.

The three parameters that help classify the strength of optical turbulence are the following:

- C_n^2, index of refraction structure parameter
- k, wave number of the laser, which is inversely proportional to the wavelength λ of the laser:

$$k = \frac{2\pi}{\lambda}$$

- L, propagation distance

The variance of the irradiance of a laser, σ^2, is directly proportional to C_n^2, $k^{7/6}$, and $L^{11/16}$.

61. When $C_n^2 = 1.0 \times 10^{-13}\,\text{m}^{-2/3}$, $L = 2$ km, and $\lambda = 1.55\ \mu\text{m}$, the variance of irradiance for a plane wave σ_{pl}^2 is 7.1. Find the equation that describes this variation.

62. When $C_n^2 = 1.0 \times 10^{-13}\,\text{m}^{-2/3}$, $L = 2$ km, and $\lambda = 1.55\ \mu\text{m}$, the variance of irradiance for a spherical wave σ_{sp}^2 is 2.3. Find the equation that describes this variation.

CHAPTER 0 REVIEW

SECTION	CONCEPT	KEY IDEAS/FORMULAS
0.1	**Linear equations**	$ax + b = 0$
	Solving linear equations in one variable	Isolate variable on one side and constants on the other side.
	Applications involving linear equations	Six-step procedure: Step 1: Identify the question. Step 2: Make notes. Step 3: Assign a variable. Step 4: Set up an equation. Step 5: Solve the equation. Step 6: Check the solution. **Geometry problems:** Formulas for rectangles, triangles, and circles **Interest problems:** Simple interest: $I = Prt$ **Mixture problems:** Whenever two *distinct* quantities are mixed, the result is a mixture. **Distance–rate–time problems:** $d = r \cdot t$
0.2	**Quadratic equations**	$ax^2 + bx + c = 0$
	Factoring	If $(x - h)(x - k) = 0$, then $x = h$ or $x = k$.
	Square root method	If $x^2 = P$, then $x = \pm\sqrt{P}$.
	Completing the square	Find half of b; square that quantity; add the result to both sides.
	The quadratic formula	$x = \dfrac{-b \pm \sqrt{b^2 - 4ac}}{2a}$
	Applications involving quadratic equations	**Stock value** **Geometry—area and volume of rectangles** **Falling objects** **Work**
0.3	**Other types of equations**	
	Rational equations	Eliminate any values that make the denominator equal to 0.
	Radical equations	Check solutions to avoid extraneous solutions.
	Equations quadratic in form: u-substitution	Use a u-substitution to write the equation in quadratic form.
	Factorable equations	Extract common factor or factor by grouping.
	Absolute value equations	If $\|x\| = a$, then $x = -a$ or $x = a$.
0.4	**Inequalities**	Solutions are a range of real numbers.
	Graphing inequalities and interval notation	■ $a < x < b$ is equivalent to (a, b). ■ $x \leq a$ is equivalent to $(-\infty, a]$. ■ $x > a$ is equivalent to (a, ∞).
	Linear inequalities	If an inequality is multiplied or divided by a *negative* number, the inequality sign must be reversed.
	Polynomial inequalities	Zeros are values that make the polynomial equal to 0.
	Rational inequalities	The number line is divided into intervals. The endpoints of these intervals are values that make either the numerator or denominator equal to 0. Always exclude values that make the denominator equal to 0.
	Absolute value inequalities	■ $\|x\| \leq a$ is equivalent to $-a \leq x \leq a$. ■ $\|x\| > a$ is equivalent to $x < -a$ or $x > a$.

CHAPTER 0 REVIEW

SECTION	CONCEPT	KEY IDEAS/FORMULAS
0.5	**Graphing equations**	
	Cartesian plane	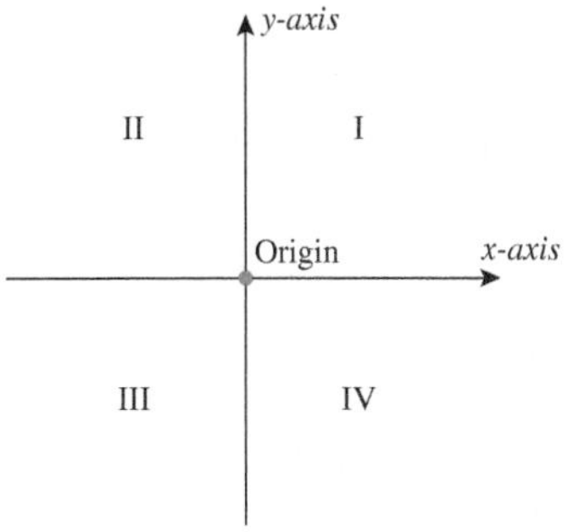
	The distance and midpoint formulas	$d = \sqrt{(x_2 - x_1)^2 + (y_2 - y_1)^2}$ $(x_m, y_m) = \left(\frac{x_1 + x_2}{2}, \frac{y_1 + y_2}{2}\right)$
	Point-plotting	List a table with several coordinates that are solutions to the equation; plot and connect.
	Using intercepts as graphing aids	**Intercepts:** x-intercept: let $y = 0$. y-intercept: let $x = 0$.
	Using symmetry as a graphing aid	If (a, b) is on the graph of the equation, then $(-a, b)$ is on the graph if symmetric about the y-axis, $(a, -b)$ is on the graph if symmetric about the x-axis, and $(-a, -b)$ is on the graph if symmetric about the origin. **Symmetry:** The graph of an equation can be symmetric about the x-axis, y-axis, or origin.
	Circles	Standard equation of a circle with center (h, k) and radius r. $(x - h)^2 + (y - k)^2 = r^2$ General form: $x^2 + y^2 + ax + by + c = 0$ Transform equations of circles into standard form by completing the square
0.6	**Lines**	General form: $Ax + By = C$
	General Form of a Line and Slope	Vertical: $x = a$ Slant: $Ax + By = C$, where $A \neq 0$ and $B \neq 0$ Horizontal: $y = b$ $m = \frac{y_2 - y_1}{x_2 - x_1}$, where $x_1 \neq x_2$ $\frac{\text{"rise"}}{\text{"run"}}$
	Equations of lines	**Slope–intercept form:** $y = mx + b$ m is the slope and b is the y-intercept. **Point–slope form:** $y - y_1 = m(x - x_1)$
	Parallel and perpendicular lines	$L_1 \| L_2$ if and only if $m_1 = m_2$ (slopes are equal). $L_1 \perp L_2$ if and only if $m_1 = -\frac{1}{m_2}$ and $m_1, m_2 \neq 0$ (slopes are negative reciprocals).
0.7	**Modeling variation**	
	Direct variation	$y = kx$
	Inverse variation	$y = \frac{k}{x}$
	Joint variation and combined variation	Joint: One quantity is directly proportional to the product of two or more other quantities. Combined: Direct variation and inverse variation occur at the same time.

[CHAPTER 0 REVIEW EXERCISES]

0.1 Linear Equations

Solve for the variable.

1. $7x - 4 = 12$
2. $13d + 12 = 7d + 6$
3. $20p + 14 = 6 - 5p$
4. $4(x - 7) - 4 = 4$
5. $3(x + 7) - 2 = 4(x - 2)$
6. $7c + 3(c - 5) = 2(c + 3) - 14$
7. $14 - [-3(y - 4) + 9] = [4(2y + 3) - 6] + 4$
8. $[6 - 4x + 2(x - 7)] - 52 = 3(2x - 4) + 6[3(2x - 3) + 6]$
9. $\frac{12}{b} - 3 = \frac{6}{b} + 4$
10. $\frac{g}{3} + g = \frac{7}{9}$
11. $\frac{13x}{7} - x = \frac{x}{4} - \frac{3}{14}$
12. $5b + \frac{b}{6} = \frac{b}{3} - \frac{29}{6}$
13. **Investments.** You win \$25,000 and you decide to invest the money in two different investments: one paying 20% and the other paying 8%. A year later you have \$27,600 total. How much did you originally invest in each account?
14. **Investments.** A college student on summer vacation was able to make \$5000 by working a full-time job every summer. He invested half the money in a mutual fund and half the money in a stock that yielded four times as much interest as the mutual fund. After a year he earned \$250 in interest. What were the interest rates of the mutual fund and the stock?
15. **Chemistry.** For an experiment, a student requires 150 milliliters of a solution that is 8% NaCl (sodium chloride). The storeroom has only solutions that are 10% NaCl and 5% NaCl. How many milliliters of each available solution should be mixed to get 150 milliliters of 8% NaCl?
16. **Chemistry.** A mixture containing 8% salt is to be mixed with 4 ounces of a mixture that is 20% salt, in order to obtain a solution that is 12% salt. How much of the first solution must be used?

0.2 Quadratic Equations

Solve by factoring.

17. $b^2 = 4b + 21$
18. $x(x - 3) = 54$
19. $x^2 = 8x$
20. $6y^2 - 7y - 5 = 0$

Solve by the square root method.

21. $q^2 - 169 = 0$
22. $c^2 + 36 = 0$
23. $(2x - 4)^2 = -64$
24. $(d + 7)^2 - 4 = 0$

Solve by completing the square.

25. $x^2 - 4x - 12 = 0$
26. $2x^2 - 5x - 7 = 0$
27. $\frac{x^2}{2} = 4 + \frac{x}{2}$
28. $8m = m^2 + 15$

Solve by the quadratic formula.

29. $3t^2 - 4t = 7$
30. $4x^2 + 5x + 7 = 0$
31. $8f^2 - \frac{1}{3}f = \frac{7}{6}$
32. $x^2 = -6x + 6$

Solve by any method.

33. $5q^2 - 3q - 3 = 0$
34. $(x - 7)^2 = -12$
35. $2x^2 - 3x - 5 = 0$
36. $(g - 2)(g + 5) = -7$
37. $7x^2 = -19x + 6$
38. $7 = (2b^2 + 1)$
39. **Geometry.** Find the base and height of a triangle with an area of 2 square feet if its base is 3 feet longer than its height.
40. **Falling Objects.** A man is standing on top of a building 500 feet tall. If he drops a penny off the roof, the height of the penny is given by $h = -16t^2 + 500$, where t is in seconds. Determine how many seconds it takes until the penny hits the ground.

0.3 Other Types of Equations

Specify any values that must be excluded from the solution set and then solve the rational equation.

41. $\frac{1}{x} - 4 = 3(x - 7) + 5$
42. $\frac{4}{x + 1} - \frac{8}{x - 1} = 3$
43. $\frac{2}{t + 4} - \frac{7}{t} = \frac{6}{t(t + 4)}$
44. $\frac{3}{2x - 7} = \frac{-2}{3x + 1}$
45. $\frac{3}{2x} - \frac{6}{x} = 9$
46. $\frac{3 - 5/m}{2 + 5/m} = 1$

Solve the radical equation for the given variable.

47. $\sqrt[3]{2x - 4} = 2$
48. $\sqrt{x - 2} = -4$
49. $(2x - 7)^{1/5} = 3$
50. $x = \sqrt{7x - 10}$
51. $x - 4 = \sqrt{x^2 + 5x + 6}$
52. $\sqrt{2x - 7} = \sqrt{x + 3}$
53. $\sqrt{x + 3} = 2 - \sqrt{3x + 2}$
54. $4 + \sqrt{x - 3} = \sqrt{x - 5}$

Solve the equation by introducing a substitution that transforms the equation to quadratic form.

55. $y^{-2} - 5y^{-1} + 4 = 0$
56. $p^{-2} + 4p^{-1} = 12$
57. $3x^{1/3} + 2x^{2/3} = 5$
58. $2x^{2/3} - 3x^{1/3} - 5 = 0$
59. $x^{-2/3} + 3x^{-1/3} + 2 = 0$
60. $y^{-1/2} - 2y^{-1/4} + 1 = 0$
61. $x^4 + 5x^2 = 36$
62. $3 - 4x^{-1/2} + x^{-1} = 0$

Solve the equation by factoring.

63. $x^3 + 4x^2 - 32x = 0$
64. $9t^3 - 25t = 0$
65. $p^3 - 3p^2 - 4p + 12 = 0$
66. $4x^3 - 9x^2 + 4x - 9 = 0$
67. $p(2p - 5)^2 - 3(2p - 5) = 0$
68. $2(t^2 - 9)^3 - 20(t^2 - 9)^2 = 0$
69. $y - 81y^{-1} = 0$
70. $9x^{3/2} - 37x^{1/2} + 4x^{-1/2} = 0$

Solve the absolute value equation.

71. $|x - 3| = -4$
72. $|2 + x| = 5$
73. $|3x - 4| = 1.1$
74. $|x^2 - 6| = 3$

0.4 Inequalities

Graph the indicated set and write as a single interval, if possible.

75. $(4, 6] \cup [5, \infty)$
76. $(-\infty, -3) \cup [-7, 2]$
77. $(3, 12] \cap [8, \infty)$
78. $(-\infty, -2) \cap [-2, 9)$

Solve the linear inequality and express the solution set in interval notation.

79. $2x < 5 - x$
80. $6x + 4 \le 2$
81. $4(x - 1) > 2x - 7$
82. $\frac{x + 3}{3} \ge 6$
83. $6 < 2 + x \le 11$
84. $-6 \le 1 - 4(x + 2) \le 16$
85. $\frac{2}{3} \le \frac{1 + x}{6} \le \frac{3}{4}$
86. $\frac{x}{3} + \frac{x + 4}{9} > \frac{x}{6} - \frac{1}{3}$

Solve the polynomial inequality and express the solution set using interval notation.

87. $x^2 \le 36$
88. $6x^2 - 7x < 20$
89. $4x \le x^2$
90. $-x^2 \ge 9x + 14$
91. $4x^2 - 12 > 13x$
92. $3x \le x^2 + 2$

Solve the rational inequality and express the solution set using interval notation.

93. $\frac{x}{x - 3} < 0$
94. $\frac{x - 1}{x - 4} > 0$
95. $\frac{x^2 - 3x}{3} \ge 18$
96. $\frac{x^2 - 49}{x - 7} \ge 0$
97. $\frac{3}{x - 2} - \frac{1}{x - 4} \le 0$
98. $\frac{4}{x - 1} \le \frac{2}{x + 3}$

Solve the absolute value inequality and express the solution set using interval notation.

99. $|x + 4| > 7$
100. $|-7 + y| \le 4$
101. $|2x| > 6$
102. $\left|\frac{4 + 2x}{3}\right| \ge \frac{1}{7}$
103. $|2 + 5x| \ge 0$
104. $|1 - 2x| \le 4$

0.5 Graphing Equations

Calculate the distance between the two points.

105. $(-2, 0)$ and $(4, 3)$
106. $(1, 4)$ and $(4, 4)$
107. $(-4, -6)$ and $(2, 7)$
108. $\left(\frac{1}{4}, \frac{1}{12}\right)$ and $\left(\frac{1}{3}, -\frac{7}{3}\right)$

Calculate the midpoint of the segment joining the two points.

109. $(2, 4)$ and $(3, 8)$
110. $(-2, 6)$ and $(5, 7)$
111. $(2.3, 3.4)$ and $(5.4, 7.2)$
112. $(-a, 2)$ and $(a, 4)$

Find the *x*-intercept(s) and *y*-intercept(s), if any.

113. $x^2 + 4y^2 = 4$
114. $y = x^2 - x + 2$
115. $y = \sqrt{x^2 - 9}$
116. $y = \frac{x^2 - x - 12}{x - 12}$

Use algebraic tests to determine symmetry with respect to the *x*-axis, *y*-axis, or origin.

117. $x^2 + y^3 = 4$
118. $y = x^2 - 2$
119. $xy = 4$
120. $y^2 = 5 + x$

Use symmetry as a graphing aid and point-plot the given equations.

121. $y = x^2 - 3$
122. $y = |x| - 4$
123. $y = \sqrt[3]{x}$
124. $x = y^2 - 2$
125. $y = x\sqrt{9 - x^2}$
126. $x^2 + y^2 = 36$

Find the center and the radius of the circle given by the equation.

127. $(x + 2)^2 + (y + 3)^2 = 81$
128. $(x - 4)^2 + (y + 2)^2 = 32$
129. $x^2 + y^2 + 2y - 4x + 11 = 0$
130. $3x^2 + 3y^2 - 6x - 7 = 0$

0.6 Lines

Write an equation of the line, given the slope and a point that lies on the line.

131. $m = -2$ $(-3, 4)$
132. $m = \frac{3}{4}$ $(2, 16)$
133. $m = 0$ $(-4, 6)$
134. m is undefined $(2, -5)$

Write the equation of the line that passes through the given points. Express the equation in slope–intercept form or in the form of $x = a$ or $y = b$.

135. $(-4, -2)$ and $(2, 3)$

136. $(-1, 4)$ and $(-2, 5)$

137. $\left(-\frac{3}{4}, \frac{1}{2}\right)$ and $\left(-\frac{7}{4}, \frac{5}{2}\right)$

138. $(3, -2)$ and $(-9, 2)$

Find the equation of the line that passes through the given point and also satisfies the additional piece of information.

139. $(-2, -1)$ parallel to the line $2x - 3y = 6$

140. $(5, 6)$ perpendicular to the line $5x - 3y = 0$

0.7 Modeling Variation

Write an equation that describes each variation.

141. C is directly proportional to r; $C = 2\pi$ when $r = 1$.

142. V is directly proportional to both l and w; $V = 12h$ when $w = 6$ and $l = 2$.

143. A varies directly with the square of r; $A = 25\pi$ when $r = 5$.

144. F varies inversely with both λ and L; $F = 20\pi$ when $\lambda = 10\ \mu\text{m}$ and $L = 10$ km.

[CHAPTER 0 PRACTICE TEST]

Solve the equation.

1. $4p - 7 = 6p - 1$
2. $-2(z - 1) + 3 = -3z + 3(z - 1)$
3. $3t = t^2 - 28$
4. $8x^2 - 13x = 6$
5. $6x^2 - 13x = 8$
6. $\dfrac{3}{x - 1} = \dfrac{5}{x + 2}$
7. $\dfrac{5}{y - 3} + 1 = \dfrac{30}{y^2 - 9}$
8. $x^4 - 5x^2 - 36 = 0$
9. $\sqrt{2x + 1} + x = 7$
10. $2x^{2/3} + 3x^{1/3} - 2 = 0$
11. $\sqrt{3y - 2} = 3 - \sqrt{3y + 1}$
12. $x(3x - 5)^3 - 2(3x - 5)^2 = 0$
13. $x^{7/3} - 8x^{4/3} + 12x^{1/3} = 0$
14. Solve for x: $\left|\frac{1}{5}x + \frac{2}{3}\right| = \frac{7}{15}$.

Solve the inequality and express the solution in interval notation.

15. $3x + 19 \geq 5(x - 3)$
16. $-1 \leq 3x + 5 < 26$
17. $\dfrac{2}{5} < \dfrac{x + 8}{4} \leq \dfrac{1}{2}$
18. $3x \geq 2x^2$
19. $3p^2 \geq p + 4$
20. $|5 - 2x| > 1$
21. $\dfrac{x - 3}{2x + 1} \leq 0$
22. $\dfrac{x + 4}{x^2 - 9} \geq 0$
23. Find the distance between the points $(-7, -3)$ and $(2, -2)$.
24. Find the midpoint between $(-3, 5)$ and $(5, -1)$.

In Exercises 25 and 26, graph the equations.

25. $2x^2 + y^2 = 8$
26. $y = \dfrac{4}{x^2 + 1}$
27. Find the x-intercept and the y-intercept of the line $x - 3y = 6$.
28. Find the x-intercept(s) and the y-intercept(s), if any: $4x^2 - 9y^2 = 36$.
29. Express the line in slope–intercept form: $\frac{2}{3}x - \frac{1}{4}y = 2$.
30. Express the line in slope–intercept form: $4x - 6y = 12$.

In Exercises 31–33, find the equation of the line that is characterized by the given information. Graph the line.

31. Passes through the points $(-3, 2)$ and $(4, 9)$
32. Parallel to the line $y = 4x + 3$ and passes through the point $(1, 7)$
33. Perpendicular to the line $2x - 4y = 5$ and passes through the point $(1, 1)$
34. Determine the center and radius of the circle $x^2 + y^2 - 10x + 6y + 22 = 0$.

In Exercises 35 and 36, use variation to find a model for the given problem.

35. F varies directly with m and inversely with p; $F = 20$ when $m = 2$ and $p = 3$.
36. y varies directly with the square of x; $y = 8$ when $x = 5$.

CHAPTER 1

Functions and Their Graphs

© Catherine Lane

You are buying a pair of running shoes. Their original price was \$100, but they have been discounted 30% as part of a weekend sale. Because you arrived early, you can take advantage of door-buster savings: an additional 20% off the sale price. Naïve shoppers might be lured into thinking these shoes will cost \$50 because they add the 20% and 30% to get 50% off, but they will end up paying more than that. Experienced shoppers know that the store will first take 30% off of \$100, which results in a price of \$70, and then it will take an additional 20% off of the sale price, \$70, which results in a final discounted price of \$56. Experienced shoppers already understand the concept of a function—taking an input (original price) and mapping it to an output (sale price).

A composition of functions can be thought of as a function of a function. One function takes an input (original price, \$100) and maps it to an output (sale price, \$70), and then another function takes that output as its input (sale price, \$70) and maps it to an output (checkout price, \$56).

LEARNING OBJECTIVES

- Find the domain and range of a function.
- Sketch the graphs of common functions.
- Sketch graphs of general functions employing translations of common functions.
- Perform composition of functions.
- Find the inverse of a function.

[IN THIS CHAPTER]

We will establish what a relation is, and then we will determine whether a relation is a function. We will discuss common functions, the domain and range of functions, and graphs of functions. We will determine whether a function is increasing, decreasing, or constant on an interval and calculate the average rate of change of a function. We will perform operations on functions and the composition of functions. Finally, we will discuss one-to-one functions and inverse functions.

FUNCTIONS AND THEIR GRAPHS				
1.1 FUNCTIONS	**1.2** GRAPHS OF FUNCTIONS	**1.3** GRAPHING TECHNIQUES: TRANSFORMATIONS	**1.4** COMBINING FUNCTIONS	**1.5** ONE-TO-ONE FUNCTIONS AND INVERSE FUNCTIONS
• Definition of a Function • Functions Defined by Equations • Function Notation • Domain of a Function	• Recognizing and Classifying Functions • Increasing and Decreasing Functions • Average Rate of Change • Piecewise-Defined Functions	• Horizontal and Vertical Shifts • Reflection about the Axes • Stretching and Compressing	• Adding, Subtracting, Multiplying, and Dividing Functions • Composition of Functions	• One-to-One Functions • Inverse Functions • Graphical Interpretation of Inverse Functions • Finding the Inverse Function

1.1 FUNCTIONS

SKILLS OBJECTIVES

- Determine whether a relation is a function.
- Determine whether an equation represents a function.
- Use function notation to evaluate functions for particular arguments.
- Determine the domain and range of a function.

CONCEPTUAL OBJECTIVES

- Understand that all functions are relations, but not all relations are functions.
- Understand why the vertical line test determines whether a relation is a function.
- Think of function notation as a placeholder or mapping.
- Understand the difference between implicit domain and explicit domain.

1.1.1 Definition of a Function

1.1.1 SKILL

Determine whether a relation is a function.

1.1.1 CONCEPTUAL

Understand that all functions are relations, but not all relations are functions.

What do the following pairs have in common?

- Every person has a blood type.
- Temperature is some typical value at a particular time of day.
- Every working household phone in the United States has a 10-digit phone number.
- First-class postage rates correspond to the weight of a letter.
- Certain times of the day are start times for sporting events at a university.

They all describe a particular correspondence between two groups. A **relation** is a correspondence between two sets. The first set is called the **domain** and the corresponding second set is called the **range**. Members of these sets are called **elements**.

DEFINITION Relation

A **relation** is a correspondence between two sets where each element in the first set, called the **domain**, corresponds to *at least* one element in the second set, called the **range**.

A relation is a set of ordered pairs. The domain is the set of all the first components of the ordered pairs, and the range is the set of all the second components of the ordered pairs.

PERSON	BLOOD TYPE	ORDERED PAIR
Michael	A	(Michael, A)
Tania	A	(Tania, A)
Dylan	AB	(Dylan, AB)
Trevor	O	(Trevor, O)
Megan	O	(Megan, O)

WORDS	MATH
The domain is the set of all the first components.	{Michael, Tania, Dylan, Trevor, Megan}
The range is the set of all the second components.	{A, AB, O}

A relation in which each element in the domain corresponds to exactly one element in the range is a **function**.

DEFINITION **Function**

A **function** is a correspondence between two sets where each element in the first set, called the **domain**, corresponds to *exactly* one element in the second set, called the **range**.

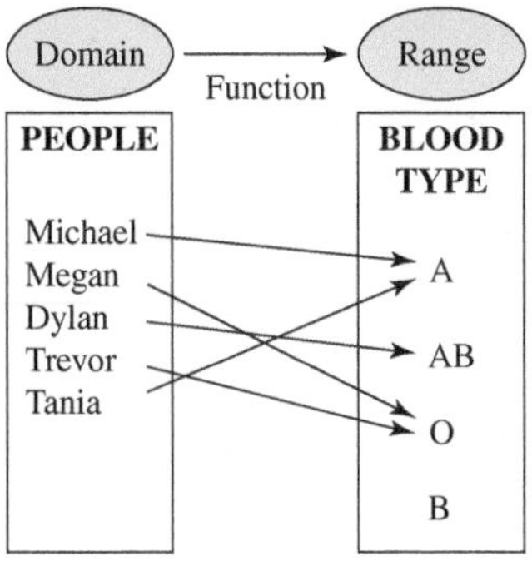

Note that the definition of a function is more restrictive than the definition of a relation. For a relation, each input corresponds to *at least* one output, whereas, for a function, each input corresponds to *exactly* one output. The blood-type example given is both a relation and a function.

Also note that the range (set of values to which the elements of the domain correspond) is a subset of the set of all blood types. Although all functions are relations, not all relations are functions.

For example, at a university, four primary sports typically overlap in the late fall: football, volleyball, soccer, and basketball. On a given Saturday, the table to the right indicates the start times for the competitions.

TIME OF DAY	COMPETITION
1:00 P.M.	Football
2:00 P.M.	Volleyball
7:00 P.M.	Soccer
7:00 P.M.	Basketball

WORDS	MATH
The 1:00 start time corresponds to exactly one event, Football.	(1:00 P.M., Football)
The 2:00 start time corresponds to exactly one event, Volleyball.	(2:00 P.M., Volleyball)
The 7:00 start time corresponds to two events, Soccer and Basketball.	(7:00 P.M., Soccer) (7:00 P.M., Basketball)

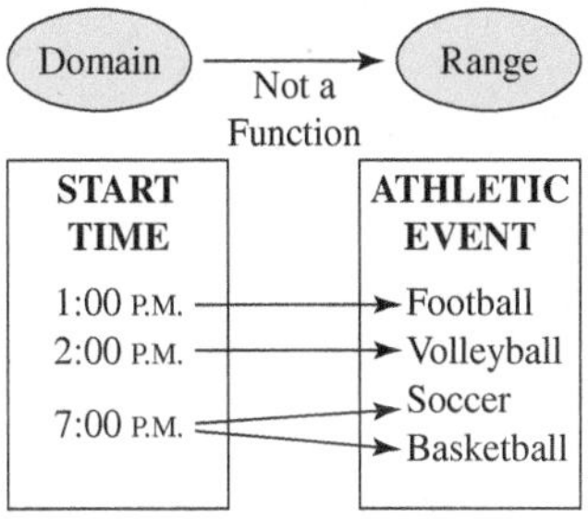

Because an element in the domain, 7:00 P.M., corresponds to more than one element in the range, Soccer and Basketball, this is not a function. It is, however, a relation.

STUDY TIP

All functions are relations but not all relations are functions.

EXAMPLE 1 **Determining Whether a Relation Is a Function**

Determine whether the following relations are functions:

a. $\{(-3, 4), (2, 4), (3, 5), (6, 4)\}$

b. $\{(-3, 4), (2, 4), (3, 5), (2, 2)\}$

c. Domain = Set of all items for sale in a grocery store; Range = Price

Solution:

a. No x-value is repeated. Therefore, each x-value corresponds to exactly one y-value.

This relation is a function.

b. The value $x = 2$ corresponds to *both* $y = 2$ and $y = 4$.

This relation is not a function.

c. Each item in the grocery store corresponds to exactly one price.

This relation is a function.

CONCEPT CHECK

If the domain consists of all physical (home) addresses in a particular county, and the range is the persons living in that county, does this describe a relation? And if so, is that relation a function?

ANSWER This is a relation but not a function.

YOUR TURN Determine whether the following relations are functions:

a. $\{(1, 2), (3, 2), (5, 6), (7, 8)\}$

b. $\{(1, 2), (1, 3), (5, 6), (7, 8)\}$

c. {(11:00 A.M., 83°F), (2:00 P.M., 89°F), (6:00 P.M., 85°F)}

ANSWER

a. function

b. not a function

c. function

All of the examples we have discussed thus far are **discrete** sets in that they represent a countable set of distinct pairs of (x, y). A function can also be defined algebraically by an equation.

1.1.2 Functions Defined by Equations

1.1.2 SKILL

Determine whether an equation represents a function.

1.1.2 CONCEPTUAL

Understand why the vertical line test determines whether a relation is a function.

Let's start with the equation $y = x^2 - 3x$, where x can be any real number. This equation assigns to each x-value exactly one corresponding y-value. For example,

x	$y = x^2 - 3x$	y
1	$y = (1)^2 - 3(1)$	-2
5	$y = (5)^2 - 3(5)$	10
$-\frac{2}{3}$	$y = \left(-\frac{2}{3}\right)^2 - 3\left(-\frac{2}{3}\right)$	$\frac{22}{9}$
1.2	$y = (1.2)^2 - 3(1.2)$	-2.16

Since the variable y *depends* on what value of x is selected, we denote y as the **dependent variable**. The variable x can be any number in the domain; therefore, we denote x as the **independent variable**.

Although functions are defined by equations, it is important to recognize that *not all equations define functions.* The requirement for an equation to define a function is that each element in the domain corresponds to exactly one element in the range. Throughout the ensuing discussion, we assume x to be the independent variable and y to be the dependent variable.

CAUTION

Not all equations are functions.

Equations that represent functions of x: $y = x^2$ $y = |x|$ $y = x^3$

Equations that do not represent functions of x: $x = y^2$ $x^2 + y^2 = 1$ $x = |y|$

In the "equations that represent functions of x," every x-value corresponds to exactly one y-value. Some ordered pairs that correspond to these functions are

STUDY TIP

We say that $x = y^2$ is not a function of x. However, if we reverse the independent and dependent variables, then $x = y^2$ is a function of y.

$y = x^2$: $(-1, 1)\ (0, 0)\ (1, 1)$

$y = |x|$: $(-1, 1)\ (0, 0)\ (1, 1)$

$y = x^3$: $(-1, -1)\ (0, 0)\ (1, 1)$

The fact that $x = -1$ and $x = 1$ both correspond to $y = 1$ in the first two examples does not violate the definition of a function.

In the "equations that do not represent functions of x," some x-values correspond to *more than one* y-value. Some ordered pairs that correspond to these equations are given in the two right-hand columns of the table below.

RELATION	SOLVE RELATION FOR y	POINTS THAT LIE ON GRAPH	
$x = y^2$	$y = \pm\sqrt{x}$	$(1, -1)\ (0, 0)\ (1, 1)$	$x = 1$ maps to **both** $y = -1$ and $y = 1$
$x^2 + y^2 = 1$	$y = \pm\sqrt{1 - x^2}$	$(0, -1)\ (0, 1)\ (-1, 0)\ (1, 0)$	$x = 0$ maps to **both** $y = -1$ and $y = 1$
$x = \|y\|$	$y = \pm x$	$(1, -1)\ (0, 0)\ (1, 1)$	$x = 1$ maps to **both** $y = -1$ and $y = 1$

Let's look at the graphs of the three **functions of x:**

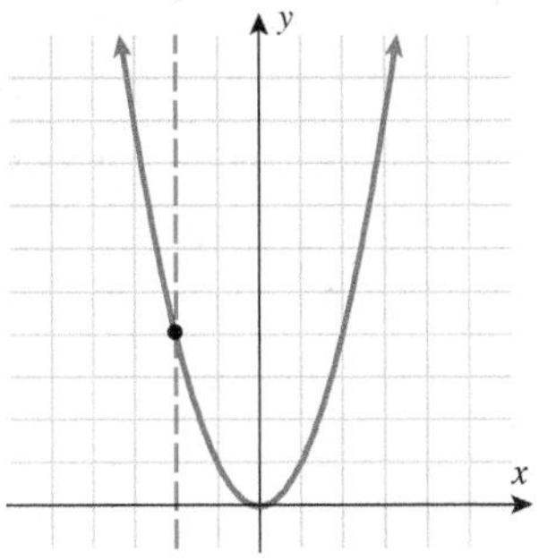

$y = x^2$

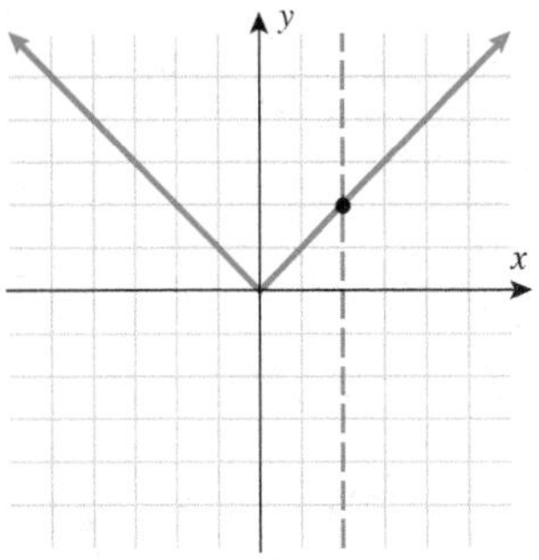

$y = |x|$

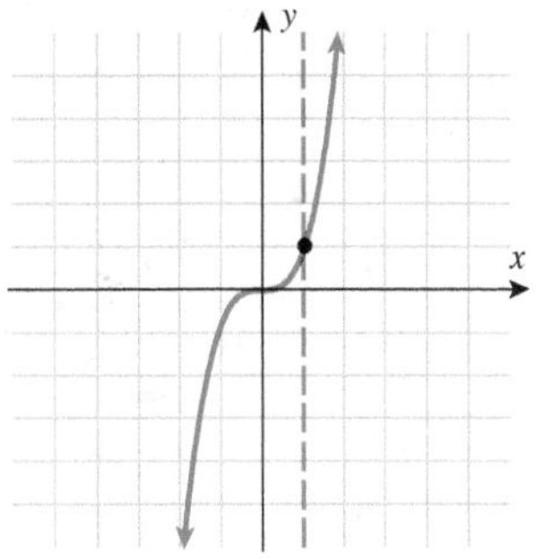

$y = x^3$

Let's take any value for x, say, $x = a$. The graph of $x = a$ corresponds to a vertical line. A function of x maps each x-value to exactly one y-value; therefore, there should be at most one point of intersection with any vertical line. We see in the three graphs of the functions above that if a vertical line is drawn at any value of x on any of the three graphs, the vertical line intersects the graph in only one place. Look at the graphs of the three equations that do **not** represent **functions of x**.

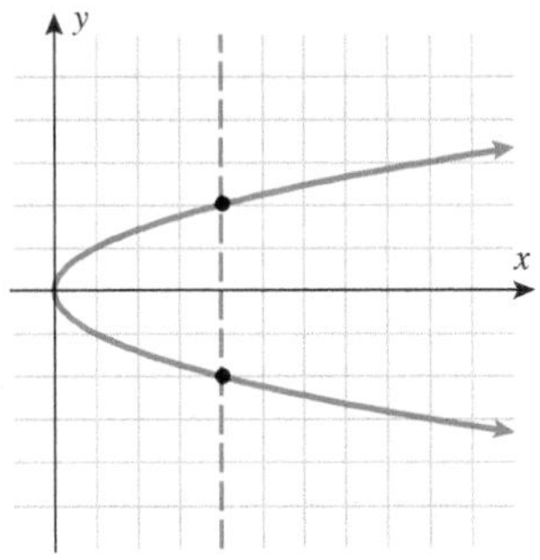

$x = y^2$

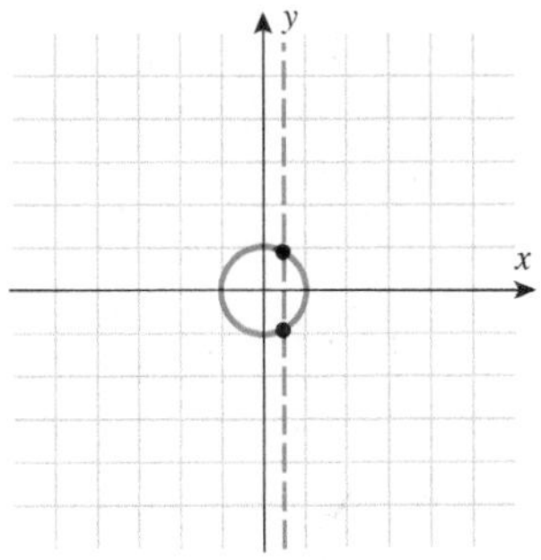

$x^2 + y^2 = 1$

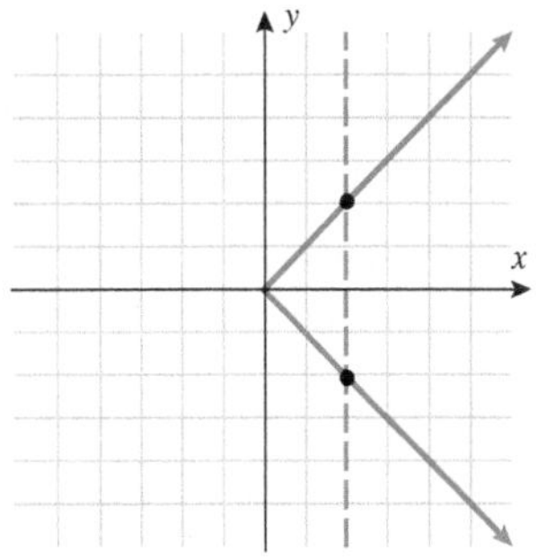

$x = |y|$

[CONCEPT CHECK]

Draw two vertical lines ($x = 0$ and $x = 1$) on the graph of $x = y^2$. At what three points do these lines intersect on the graph of the equation? Explain why the equation $x = y^2$ cannot be a function.

ANSWER (0, 0) (1, −1) and (1, 1): the vertical line $x = 1$ intersects the graph at two places (fails the vertical line test).

A vertical line can be drawn on any of the three graphs such that the vertical line will intersect each of these graphs at two points. Thus, there is more than one y-value that corresponds to some x-value in the domain, which is why these equations do not define y as functions of x.

DEFINITION **Vertical Line Test**

Given the graph of an equation, if any vertical line that can be drawn intersects the graph at no more than one point, the equation defines y as a function of x. This test is called the **vertical line test**.

[STUDY TIP]

If any x-value corresponds to more than one y-value, then y is not a function of x.

EXAMPLE 2 Using the Vertical Line Test

Use the vertical line test to determine whether the graphs of equations define functions of x.

a.

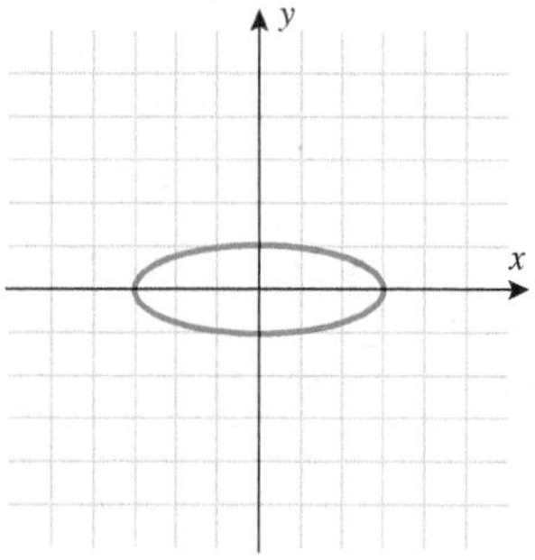

b.

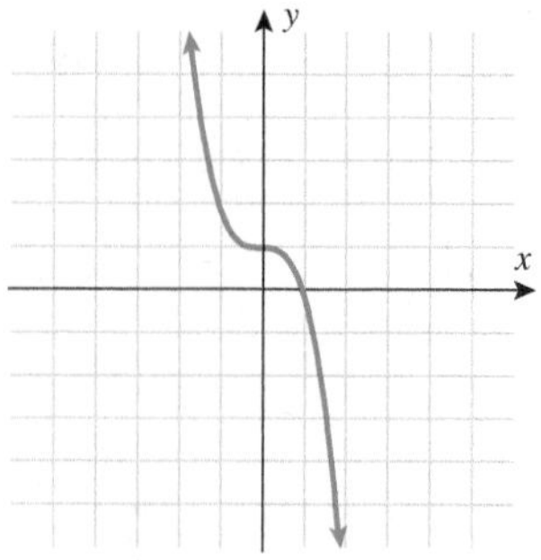

Solution:

Apply the vertical line test.

a.

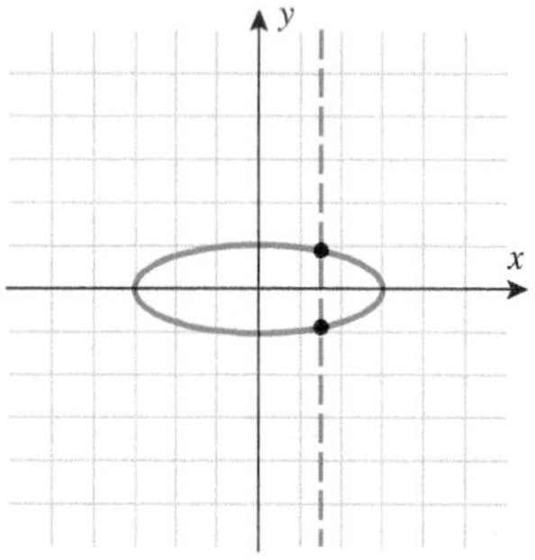

b.

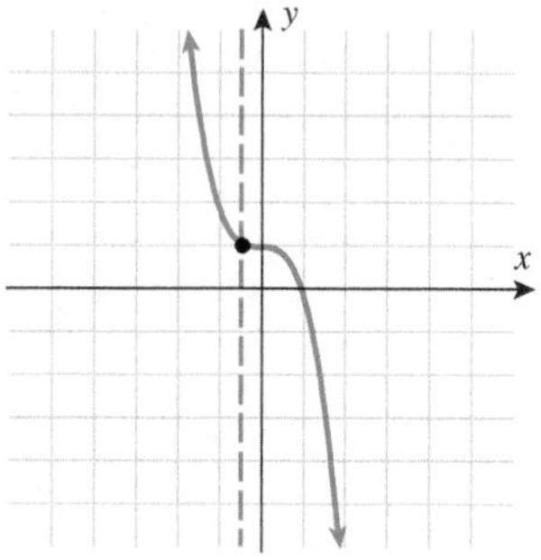

a. Because the vertical line intersects the graph of the equation at two points, this equation does not represent a function.

b. Because any vertical line will intersect the graph of this equation at no more than one point, this equation represents a function.

YOUR TURN Determine whether the equation $(x - 3)^2 + (y + 2)^2 = 16$ defines a function of x.

ANSWER

The graph of the equation is a circle, which does not pass the vertical line test. Therefore, the equation does not define a function.

To recap, a function can be expressed one of four ways: verbally, numerically, algebraically, and graphically. This is sometimes called the Rule of 4.

Expressing a Function

VERBALLY	NUMERICALLY	ALGEBRAICALLY	GRAPHICALLY
Every real number has a corresponding absolute value.	$\{(-3, 3), (-1, 1), (0, 0), (1, 1), (5, 5)\}$	$y = \lvert x \rvert$	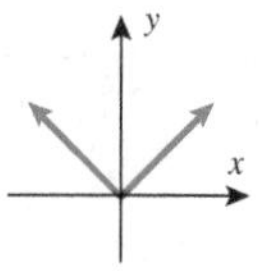

1.1.3 Function Notation

We know that the equation $y = 2x + 5$ defines y as a function of x because its graph is a nonvertical line and thus passes the vertical line test. We can select x-values (input) and determine unique corresponding y-values (output). The output is found by taking 2 times the input and then adding 5. If we give the function a name, say, "f", then we can use **function notation**:

$$f(x) = 2x + 5$$

1.1.3 SKILL

Use function notation to evaluate functions for particular arguments.

1.1.3 CONCEPTUAL

Think of function notation as a placeholder or mapping.

DEFINITION Function Notation

The symbol $f(x)$ is read "f evaluated at x" or "f of x" and represents the y-value that corresponds to a particular x-value. In other words, $y = f(x)$.

INPUT	FUNCTION	OUTPUT	EQUATION
x	f	$f(x)$	$f(x) = 2x + 5$
Independent variable	Mapping	Dependent variable	Mathematical rule

It is important to note that f is the function name, whereas $f(x)$ is the value of the function. In other words, the function f maps some value x in the domain to some value $f(x)$ in the range.

x	$f(x) = 2x + 5$	$f(x)$
0	$f(0) = 2(0) + 5$	$f(0) = 5$
1	$f(1) = 2(1) + 5$	$f(1) = 7$
2	$f(2) = 2(2) + 5$	$f(2) = 9$

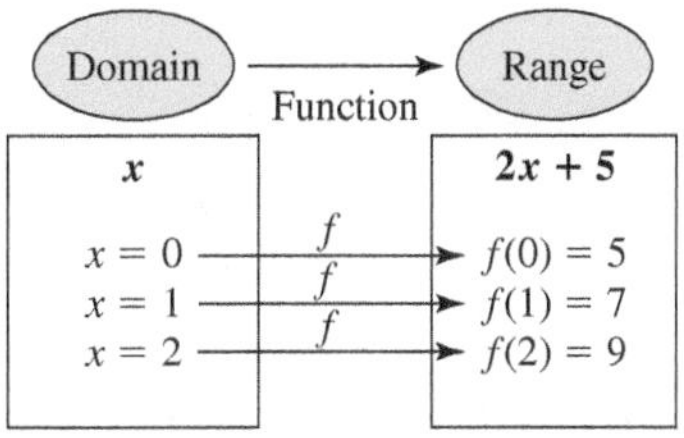

The independent variable is also referred to as the **argument** of a function. To evaluate functions, it is often useful to think of the independent variable or argument as a placeholder. For example, $f(x) = x^2 - 3x$ can be thought of as

$$f(\square) = (\square)^2 - 3(\square)$$

In other words, "f of the argument is equal to the argument squared minus 3 times the argument." Any expression can be substituted for the argument:

$$f(1) = (1)^2 - 3(1)$$
$$f(x + 1) = (x + 1)^2 - 3(x + 1)$$
$$f(-x) = (-x)^2 - 3(-x)$$

It is important to note:

- $f(x)$ does *not* mean f times x.
- The most common function names are f and F since the word function begins with an "f". Other common function names are g and G, but any letter can be used.
- The letter most commonly used for the independent variable is x. The letter t is also common because in real-world applications it represents time, but any letter can be used.
- Although we can think of y and $f(x)$ as interchangeable, the function notation is useful when we want to consider two or more functions of the same independent variable or when we want to evaluate a function at more than one argument.

STUDY TIP

It is important to note that $f(x)$ does not mean f times x.

EXAMPLE 3 Evaluating Functions by Substitution

Given the function $f(x) = 2x^3 - 3x^2 + 6$, find $f(-1)$.

Solution:

Consider the independent variable x to be a placeholder. $\quad f(\square) = 2(\square)^3 - 3(\square)^2 + 6$

To find $f(-1)$, substitute $x = -1$ into the function. $\quad f(-1) = 2(-1)^3 - 3(-1)^2 + 6$

Evaluate the right side. $\quad f(-1) = -2 - 3 + 6$

Simplify. $\quad \boxed{f(-1) = 1}$

[CONCEPT CHECK]

Using the function in Example 3, find f(☺).

ANSWER f(☺) = 2☺^{3} − 3☺^{2} + 6

EXAMPLE 4 Finding Function Values from the Graph of a Function

The graph of f is given on the right.

a. Find $f(0)$.
b. Find $f(1)$.
c. Find $f(2)$.
d. Find $4f(3)$.
e. Find x such that $f(x) = 10$.
f. Find x such that $f(x) = 2$.

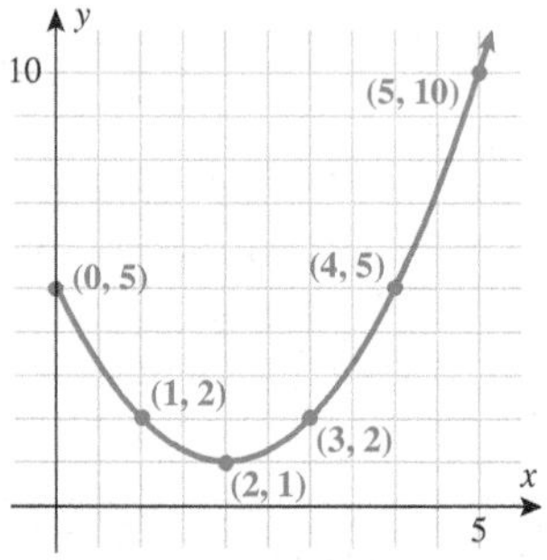

Solution (a): The value $x = 0$ corresponds to the value $y = 5$. $\boxed{f(0) = 5}$

Solution (b): The value $x = 1$ corresponds to the value $y = 2$. $\boxed{f(1) = 2}$

Solution (c): The value $x = 2$ corresponds to the value $y = 1$. $\boxed{f(2) = 1}$

Solution (d): The value $x = 3$ corresponds to the value $y = 2$. $4f(3) = 4 \cdot 2 = \boxed{8}$

Solution (e): The value $y = 10$ corresponds to the value $\boxed{x = 5}$.

Solution (f): The value $y = 2$ corresponds to the values $\boxed{x = 1}$ and $\boxed{x = 3}$.

YOUR TURN For the following graph of a function, find

a. $f(-1)$ **b.** $f(0)$ **c.** $3f(2)$
d. the value of x that corresponds to $f(x) = 0$

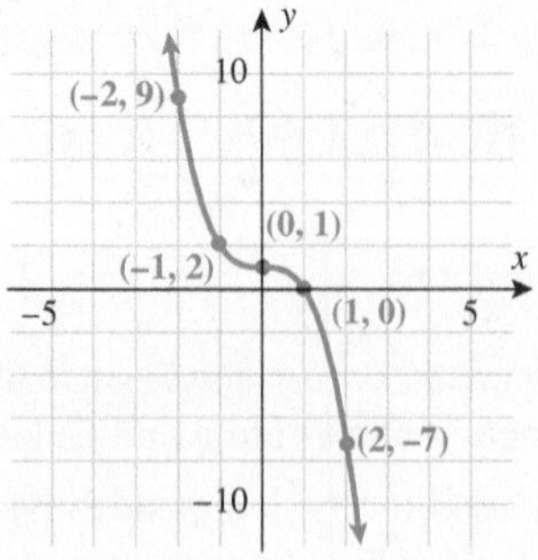

ANSWER

a. $f(-1) = 2$
b. $f(0) = 1$
c. $3f(2) = -21$
d. $x = 1$

EXAMPLE 5 Evaluating Functions with Variable Arguments (Inputs)

For the given function $f(x) = x^2 - 3x$, evaluate $f(x + 1)$ and simplify if possible.

common mistake

A common misunderstanding is to interpret the notation $f(x + 1)$ as a sum: $f(x + 1) \neq f(x) + f(1)$.

✓CORRECT

Write the original function.

$$f(x) = x^2 - 3x$$

Replace the argument x with a placeholder.

$$f(\square) = (\square)^2 - 3(\square)$$

Substitute $x + 1$ for the argument.

$$f(x + 1) = (x + 1)^2 - 3(x + 1)$$

Eliminate the parentheses.

$$f(x + 1) = x^2 + 2x + 1 - 3x - 3$$

Combine like terms.

$$\boxed{f(x + 1) = x^2 - x - 2}$$

✗INCORRECT

The **ERROR** is in interpreting the notation as a sum.

$$f(x + 1) \neq f(x) + f(1)$$

$$f(x + 1) \neq x^2 - 3x - 2$$

CAUTION

$f(x + 1) \neq f(x) + f(1)$

YOUR TURN For the given function $g(x) = x^2 - 2x + 3$, evaluate $g(x - 1)$.

ANSWER

$g(x - 1) = x^2 - 4x + 6$

EXAMPLE 6 Evaluating Functions: Sums

For the given function $H(x) = x^2 + 2x$, evaluate

a. $H(x + 1)$ **b.** $H(x) + H(1)$

Solution (a):

Write the function H in placeholder notation.	$H(\square) = (\square)^2 + 2(\square)$
Substitute $x + 1$ for the argument of H.	$H(x + 1) = (x + 1)^2 + 2(x + 1)$
Eliminate the parentheses on the right side.	$H(x + 1) = x^2 + 2x + 1 + 2x + 2$
Combine like terms on the right side.	$\boxed{H(x + 1) = x^2 + 4x + 3}$

Solution (b):

Write $H(x)$.	$H(x) = x^2 + 2x$
Evaluate H at $x = 1$.	$H(1) = (1)^2 + 2(1) = 3$
Evaluate the sum $H(x) + H(1)$.	$H(x) + H(1) = x^2 + 2x + 3$
	$\boxed{H(x) + H(1) = x^2 + 2x + 3}$

Note: Comparing the results of part (a) and part (b), we see that

$$H(x + 1) \neq H(x) + H(1).$$

EXAMPLE 7 **Evaluating Functions: Negatives**

For the given function $G(t) = t^2 - t$, evaluate

a. $G(-t)$ **b.** $-G(t)$

Solution (a):

Write the function G in placeholder notation. $G(\square) = (\square)^2 - (\square)$

Substitute $-t$ for the argument of G. $G(-t) = (-t)^2 - (-t)$

Eliminate the parentheses on the right side. $\boxed{G(-t) = t^2 + t}$

Solution (b):

Write $G(t)$. $G(t) = t^2 - t$

Multiply by -1. $-G(t) = -(t^2 - t)$

Eliminate the parentheses on the right side. $\boxed{-G(t) = -t^2 + t}$

Note: Comparing the results of part (a) and part (b), we see that $G(-t) \neq -G(t)$. If $G(t)$ were an odd function, then $G(-t) = -G(t)$, but in general this is not true.

EXAMPLE 8 **Evaluating Functions: Quotients**

For the given function $F(x) = 3x + 5$, evaluate

a. $F\left(\frac{1}{2}\right)$ **b.** $\frac{F(1)}{F(2)}$

Solution (a):

Write F in placeholder notation. $F(\square) = 3(\square) + 5$

Replace the argument with $\frac{1}{2}$. $F\left(\frac{1}{2}\right) = 3\left(\frac{1}{2}\right) + 5$

Simplify the right side. $\boxed{F\left(\frac{1}{2}\right) = \frac{13}{2}}$

Solution (b):

Evaluate $F(1)$. $F(1) = 3(1) + 5 = 8$

Evaluate $F(2)$. $F(2) = 3(2) + 5 = 11$

Divide $F(1)$ by $F(2)$. $\boxed{\frac{F(1)}{F(2)} = \frac{8}{11}}$

Note: Comparing the results of part (a) and part (b), we see that $F\left(\frac{1}{2}\right) \neq \frac{F(1)}{F(2)}$.

CAUTION

$f\left(\frac{a}{b}\right) \neq \frac{f(a)}{f(b)}$

YOUR TURN Given the function $G(t) = 3t - 4$, evaluate

a. $G(t - 2)$ **b.** $G(t) - G(2)$ **c.** $\frac{G(1)}{G(3)}$ **d.** $G\left(\frac{1}{3}\right)$

ANSWER

a. $G(t - 2) = 3t - 10$

b. $G(t) - G(2) = 3t - 6$

c. $\frac{G(1)}{G(3)} = -\frac{1}{5}$

d. $G\left(\frac{1}{3}\right) = -3$

Examples 6–8 illustrate the following in general:

$$f(a + b) \neq f(a) + f(b) \qquad f(-t) \neq -f(t) \qquad f\left(\frac{a}{b}\right) \neq \frac{f(a)}{f(b)}$$

1.1.4 Domain of a Function

1.1.4 SKILL

Determine the domain and range of a function.

1.1.4 CONCEPTUAL

Understand the difference between implicit domain and explicit domain.

Sometimes the domain of a function is stated *explicitly*. For example,

$$f(x) = |x| \qquad \underbrace{x < 0}_{\text{domain}}$$

Here, the **explicit domain** is the set of all negative real numbers, $(-\infty, 0)$. Every negative real number in the domain is mapped to a positive real number in the range through the absolute value function.

If the expression that defines the function is given but the domain is not stated explicitly, then the domain is implied. The **implicit domain** is the largest set of real numbers for which the function is defined, and the output value $f(x)$ is a real number. For example,

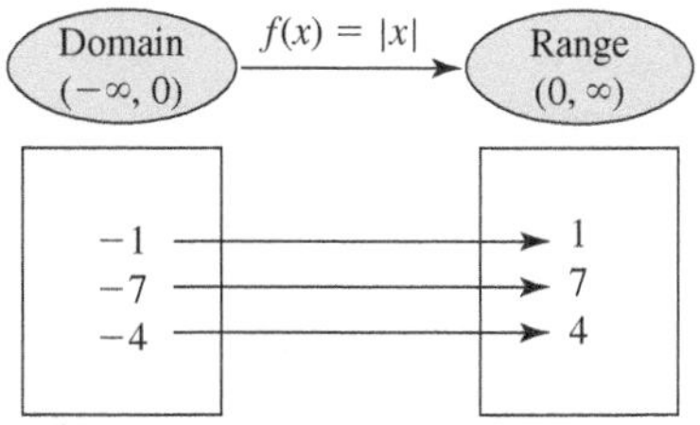

$$f(x) = \sqrt{x}$$

does not have the domain explicitly stated. There is, however, an implicit domain. Note that if the argument is negative, that is, if $x < 0$, then the result is an imaginary number. In order for the output of the function, $f(x)$, to be a real number, we must restrict the domain to nonnegative numbers—that is, $x \geq 0$.

FUNCTION	IMPLICIT DOMAIN
$f(x) = \sqrt{x}$	$[0, \infty)$

In general, we ask the question, "What can x be?" The implicit domain of a function excludes values that cause a function to be undefined or to have outputs that are not real numbers.

EXPRESSION THAT DEFINES THE FUNCTION	EXCLUDED x-VALUES	EXAMPLE	IMPLICIT DOMAIN
Polynomial	None	$f(x) = x^3 - 4x^2$	All real numbers
Rational	x-values that make the denominator equal to 0	$g(x) = \dfrac{2}{x^2 - 9}$	$x \neq \pm 3$ or $(-\infty, -3) \cup (-3, 3) \cup (3, \infty)$
Radical	x-values that result in a square (even) root of a negative number	$h(x) = \sqrt{x - 5}$	$x \geq 5$ or $[5, \infty)$

[CONCEPT CHECK]

Find the implicit domain for $f(x) = \dfrac{1}{\sqrt{x - a}}$.

ANSWER (a, ∞)

EXAMPLE 9 Determining the Domain of a Function

State the domain of the given functions.

a. $F(x) = \dfrac{3}{x^2 - 25}$ **b.** $H(x) = \sqrt[4]{9 - 2x}$ **c.** $G(x) = \sqrt[3]{x - 1}$

Solution (a):

Write the original equation. $F(x) = \dfrac{3}{x^2 - 25}$

Determine any restrictions on the value of x. $x^2 - 25 \neq 0$

Solve the restriction equation. $x^2 \neq 25$ or $x \neq \pm\sqrt{25} = \pm 5$

State the domain restrictions. $x \neq \pm 5$

Write the domain in interval notation. $\boxed{(-\infty, -5) \cup (-5, 5) \cup (5, \infty)}$

Solution (b):

Write the original equation. $H(x) = \sqrt[4]{9 - 2x}$

Determine any restrictions on the value of x. $9 - 2x \geq 0$

Solve the restriction equation. $9 \geq 2x$

State the domain restrictions. $x \leq \dfrac{9}{2}$

Write the domain in interval notation. $\boxed{\left(-\infty, \dfrac{9}{2}\right]}$

Solution (c):

Write the original equation. $G(x) = \sqrt[3]{x - 1}$

Determine any restrictions on the value of x. no restrictions

State the domain. $\mathbb{R}$

Write the domain in interval notation. $\boxed{(-\infty, \infty)}$

YOUR TURN State the domain of the given functions.

a. $f(x) = \sqrt{x - 3}$ **b.** $g(x) = \dfrac{1}{x^2 - 4}$

ANSWER

a. $x \geq 3$ or $[3, \infty)$

b. $x \neq \pm 2$ or $(-\infty, -2) \cup (-2, 2) \cup (2, \infty)$

Applications

Functions that are used in applications often have restrictions on the domains due to physical constraints. For example, the volume of a cube is given by the function $V(x) = x^3$, where x is the length of a side. The function $f(x) = x^3$ has no restrictions on x, and therefore, the domain is the set of all real numbers. However, the volume of any cube has the restriction that the length of a side can never be negative or zero.

EXAMPLE 10 **The Dimensions of a Pool**

Express the volume of a 30 foot by 10 foot rectangular swimming pool as a function of its depth.

Solution:

The volume of any rectangular box is $V = lwh$, where V is the volume, l is the length, w is the width, and h is the height. In this example, the length is 30 feet, the width is 10 feet, and the height represents the depth d of the pool.

Write the volume as a function of depth d. $V(d) = (30)(10)d$

Simplify. $\boxed{V(d) = 300d}$

Determine any restrictions on the domain. $d > 0$

[SECTION 1.1] SUMMARY

Relations and Functions (Let *x* represent the independent variable and *y* the dependent variable.)

TYPE	MAPPING/CORRESPONDENCE	EQUATION	GRAPH
Relation	Every x-value in the domain maps to **at least one** y-value in the range.	$x = y^2$	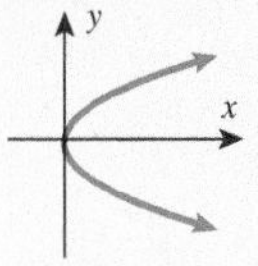
Function	Every x-value in the domain maps to **exactly one** y-value in the range.	$y = x^2$	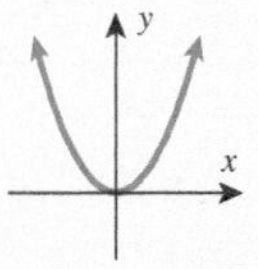 Passes vertical line test

All functions are relations, but not all relations are functions. Functions can be represented by equations. In the following table, each column illustrates an alternative notation.

INPUT	CORRESPONDENCE	OUTPUT	EQUATION
x	Function	y	$y = 2x + 5$
Independent Variable	Mapping	Dependent Variable	Mathematical Rule
Argument	f	$f(x)$	$f(x) = 2x + 5$

The **domain** is the set of all inputs (x-values) and the **range** is the set of all corresponding outputs (y-values). Placeholder notation is useful when evaluating functions.

$$f(x) = 3x^2 + 2x$$

$$f(\square) = 3(\square)^2 + 2(\square)$$

An explicit domain is stated, whereas an **implicit domain** is found by *excluding* ***x*-values that**

- make the function undefined (denominator = 0).
- result in a nonreal output (even roots of negative real numbers).

[SECTION 1.1] EXERCISES

• SKILLS

In Exercises 1–18, determine whether each relation is a function. Assume that the coordinate pair (x, y) represents the independent variable x and the dependent variable y.

1. $\{(0, -3), (0, 3), (-3, 0), (3, 0)\}$
2. $\{(2, -2), (2, 2), (5, -5), (5, 5)\}$
3. $\{(0, 0), (9, -3), (4, -2), (4, 2), (9, 3)\}$
4. $\{(0, 0), (-1, -1), (-2, -8), (1, 1), (2, 8)\}$
5. $\{(0, 1), (1, 0), (2, 1), (-2, 1), (5, 4), (-3, 4)\}$
6. $\{(0, 1), (1, 1), (2, 1), (3, 1)\}$
7. $x^2 + y^2 = 9$
8. $x = |y|$
9. $x = y^2$
10. $y = x^3$
11. $y = |x - 1|$
12. $y = 3$

13.
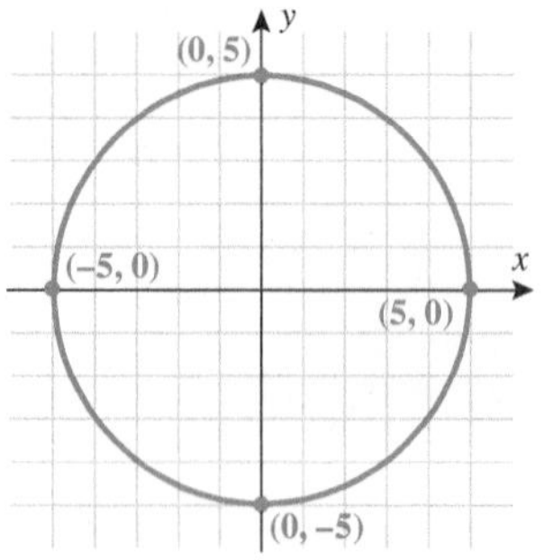

14.
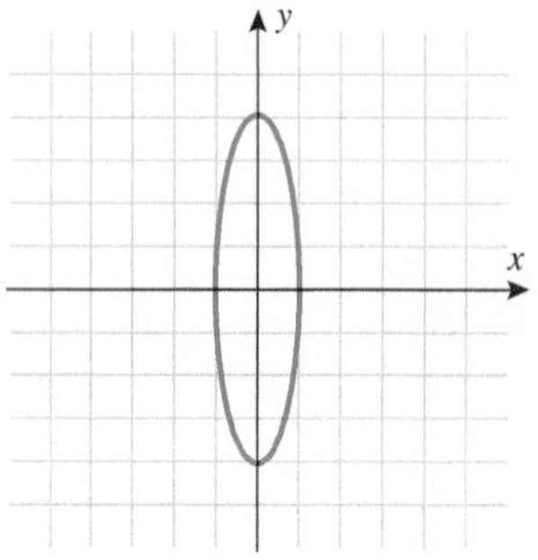

15.
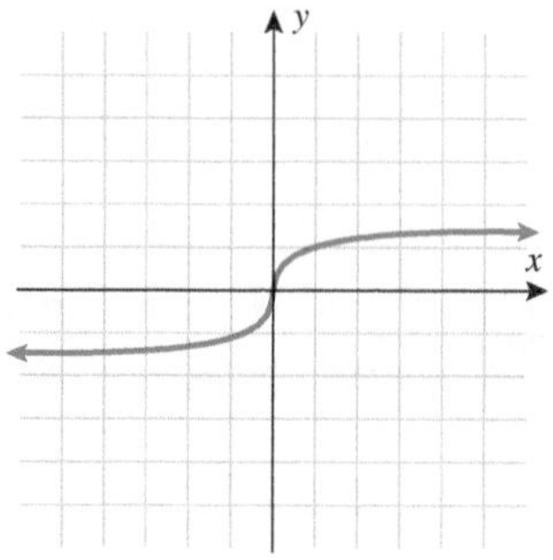

16.
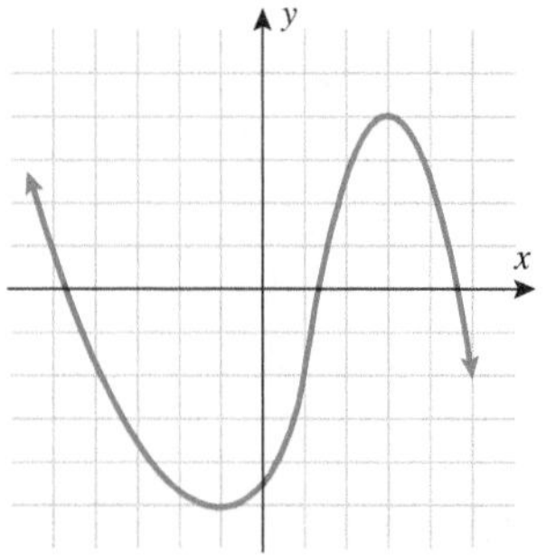

17.
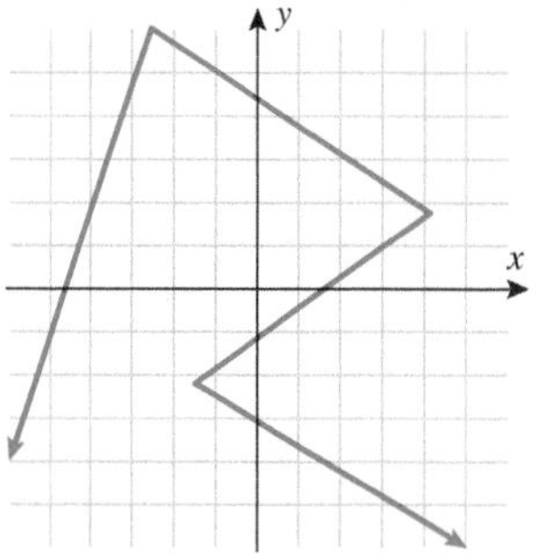

18.
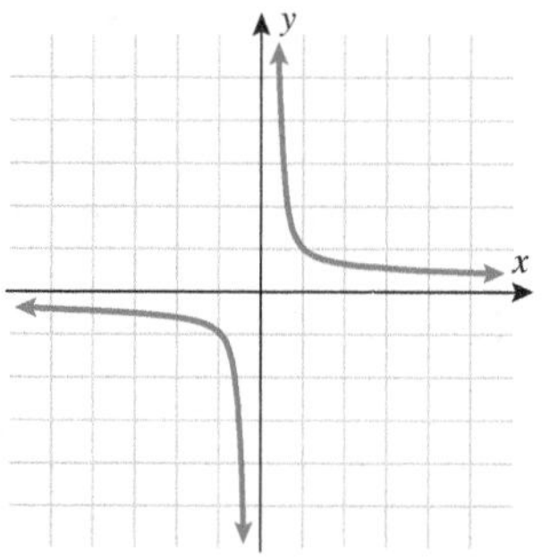

In Exercises 19–26, use each given graph to evaluate the functions listed below it.

19. $y = f(x)$
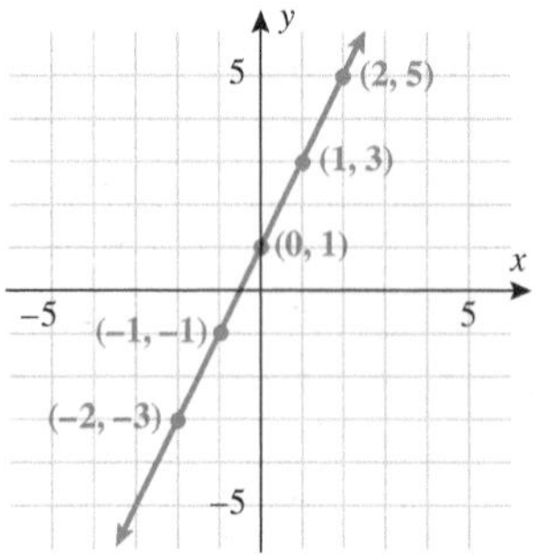

a. $f(2)$ b. $f(0)$ c. $f(-2)$

20. $y = g(x)$
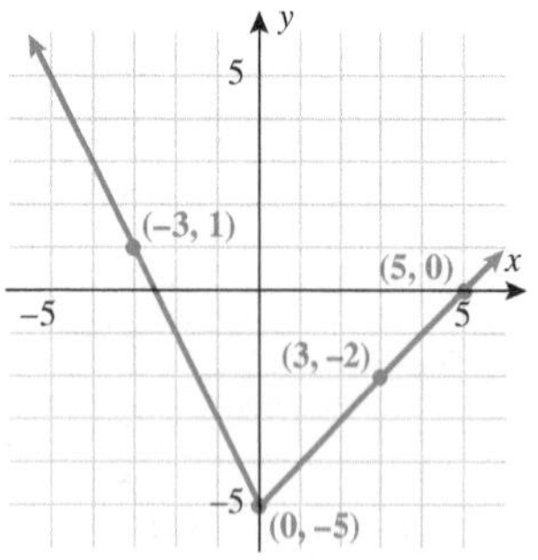

a. $g(-3)$ b. $g(0)$ c. $g(5)$

21. $y = p(x)$
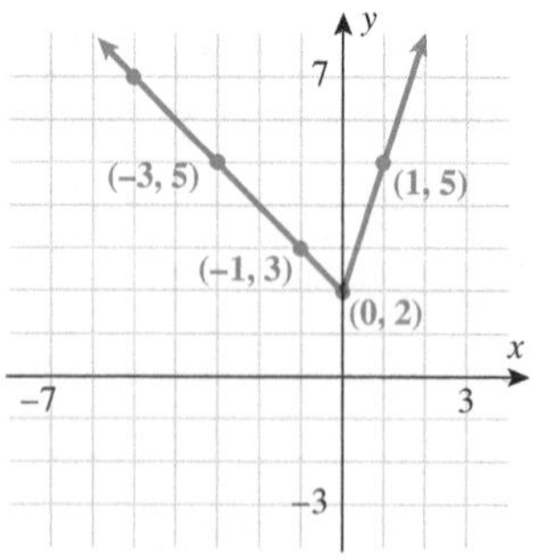

a. $p(-1)$ b. $p(0)$ c. $p(1)$

22. $y = r(x)$
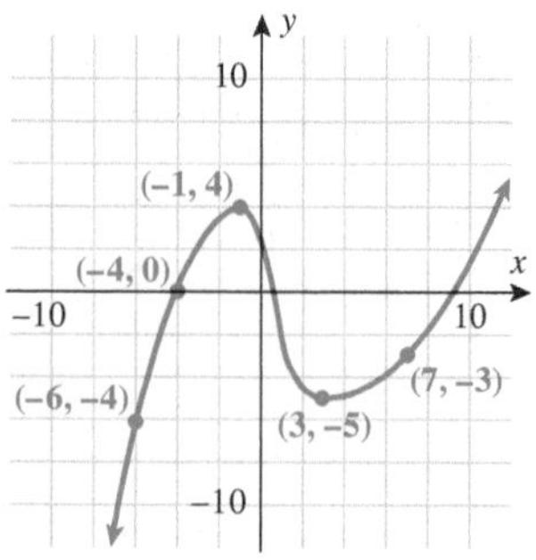

a. $r(-4)$ b. $r(-1)$ c. $r(3)$

23. $y = C(x)$

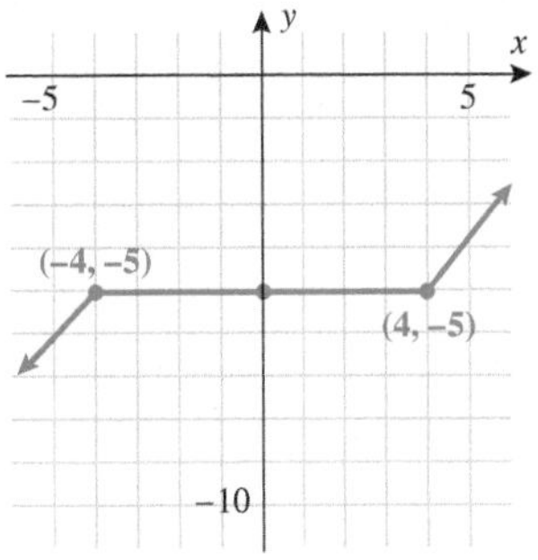

24. $y = q(x)$

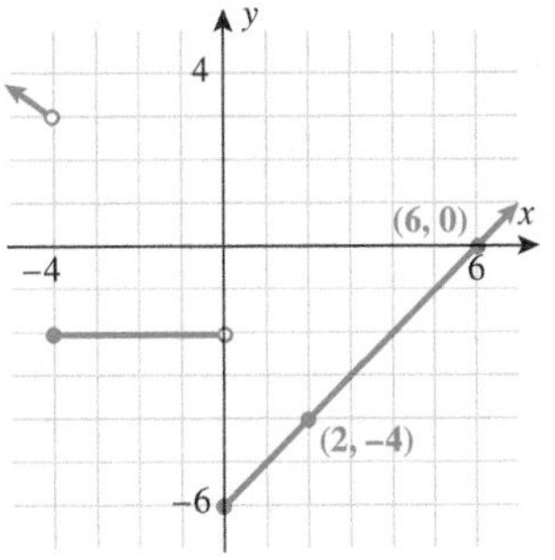

25. $y = S(x)$

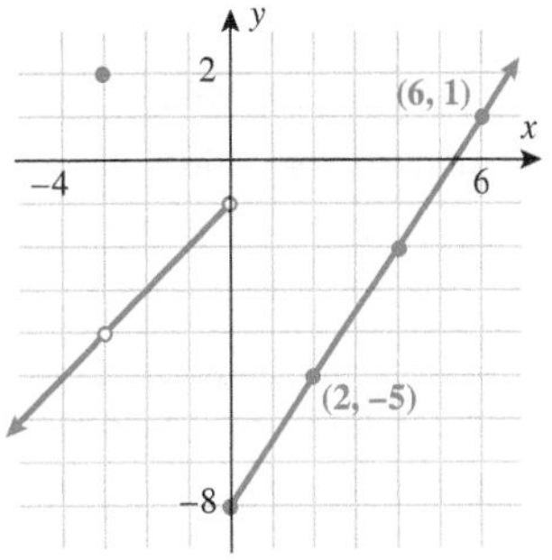

26. $y = T(x)$

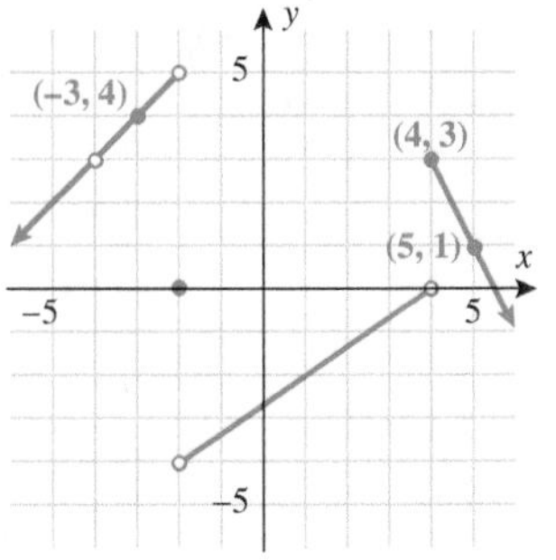

a. $C(2)$ **b.** $C(0)$ **c.** $C(-2)$

a. $q(-4)$ **b.** $q(0)$ **c.** $q(2)$

a. $S(-3)$ **b.** $S(0)$ **c.** $S(2)$

a. $T(-5)$ **b.** $T(-2)$ **c.** $T(4)$

27. Find x if $f(x) = 3$ in Exercise 19.

28. Find x if $g(x) = -2$ in Exercise 20.

29. Find x if $p(x) = 5$ in Exercise 21.

30. Find x if $C(x) = -7$ in Exercise 22.

31. Find x if $C(x) = -5$ in Exercise 23.

32. Find x if $q(x) = -2$ in Exercise 24.

33. Find x if $S(x) = 1$ in Exercise 25.

34. Find x if $T(x) = 4$ in Exercise 26.

In Exercises 35–50, evaluate the given quantity applying the following four functions:

$f(x) = 2x - 3 \qquad F(t) = 4 - t^2 \qquad g(t) = 5 + t \qquad G(x) = x^2 + 2x - 7$

35. $f(-2)$

36. $G(-3)$

37. $g(1)$

38. $F(-1)$

39. $f(-2) + g(1)$

40. $G(-3) - F(-1)$

41. $3f(-2) - 2g(1)$

42. $2F(-1) - 2G(-3)$

43. $\dfrac{f(-2)}{g(1)}$

44. $\dfrac{G(-3)}{F(-1)}$

45. $\dfrac{f(0) - f(-2)}{g(1)}$

46. $\dfrac{G(0) - G(-3)}{F(-1)}$

47. $f(x + 1) - f(x - 1)$

48. $F(t + 1) - F(t - 1)$

49. $g(x + a) - f(x + a)$

50. $G(x + b) + F(b)$

In Exercises 51–82, find the domain of the given function. Express the domain in interval notation.

51. $f(x) = 2x - 5$

52. $f(x) = -2x - 5$

53. $g(t) = t^2 + 3t$

54. $h(x) = 3x^4 - 1$

55. $P(x) = \dfrac{x + 5}{x - 5}$

56. $Q(t) = \dfrac{2 - t^2}{t + 3}$

57. $T(x) = \dfrac{2}{x^2 - 4}$

58. $R(x) = \dfrac{1}{x^2 - 1}$

59. $F(x) = \dfrac{1}{x^2 + 1}$

60. $G(t) = \dfrac{2}{t^2 + 4}$

61. $q(x) = \sqrt{7 - x}$

62. $k(t) = \sqrt{t - 7}$

63. $f(x) = \sqrt{2x + 5}$

64. $g(x) = \sqrt{5 - 2x}$

65. $G(t) = \sqrt{t^2 - 4}$

66. $F(x) = \sqrt{x^2 - 25}$

67. $F(x) = \dfrac{1}{\sqrt{x - 3}}$

68. $G(x) = \dfrac{2}{\sqrt{5 - x}}$

69. $f(x) = \sqrt[3]{1 - 2x}$

70. $g(x) = \sqrt[5]{7 - 5x}$

71. $P(x) = \dfrac{1}{\sqrt[5]{x + 4}}$

72. $Q(x) = \dfrac{x}{\sqrt[3]{x^2 - 9}}$

73. $R(x) = \dfrac{x + 1}{\sqrt[4]{3 - 2x}}$

74. $p(x) = \dfrac{x^2}{\sqrt{25 - x^2}}$

75. $H(t) = \dfrac{t}{\sqrt{t^2 - t - 6}}$

76. $f(t) = \dfrac{t - 3}{\sqrt[4]{t^2 + 9}}$

77. $f(x) = (x^2 - 16)^{1/2}$

78. $g(x) = (2x - 5)^{1/3}$

79. $r(x) = x^2(3 - 2x)^{-1/2}$

80. $p(x) = (x - 1)^2(x^2 - 9)^{-3/5}$

81. $f(x) = \frac{2}{5}x - \frac{2}{4}$

82. $g(x) = \frac{2}{3}x^2 - \frac{1}{6}x - \frac{3}{4}$

83. Let $g(x) = x^2 - 2x - 5$ and find the values of x that correspond to $g(x) = 3$.

84. Let $g(x) = \frac{5}{6}x - \frac{3}{4}$ and find the value of x that corresponds to $g(x) = \frac{2}{3}$.

85. Let $f(x) = 2x(x - 5)^3 - 12(x - 5)^2$ and find the values of x that correspond to $f(x) = 0$.

86. Let $f(x) = 3x(x + 3)^2 - 6(x + 3)^3$ and find the values of x that correspond to $f(x) = 0$.

• APPLICATIONS

87. Temperature. The average temperature in Tampa, Florida in the springtime is given by the function $T(x) = -0.7x^2 + 16.8x - 10.8$, where T is the temperature in degrees Fahrenheit and x is the time of day in military time and is restricted to $6 \le x \le 18$ (sunrise to sunset). What is the temperature at 6 A.M.? What is the temperature at noon?

88. Temperature. The average temperature in Orlando, Florida in the summertime is given by the function $T(x) = -0.5x^2 + 14.2x - 2.8$, where T is the temperature in degrees Fahrenheit and x is the time of the day in military time and is restricted to $7 \le x \le 20$ (sunrise to sunset). What is the temperature at 9 A.M.? What is the temperature at 3 P.M.?

89. Falling Objects: Baseballs. A baseball is hit and its height is a function of time, $h(t) = -16t^2 + 45t + 1$, where h is the height in feet and t is the time in seconds, with $t = 0$ corresponding to the instant the ball is hit. What is the height after 2 seconds? What is the domain of this function?

90. Falling Objects: Firecrackers. A firecracker is launched straight up, and its height is a function of time, $h(t) = -16t^2 + 128t$, where h is the height in feet and t is the time in seconds, with $t = 0$ corresponding to the instant it launches. What is the height 4 seconds after launch? What is the domain of this function?

91. Volume. An open box is constructed from a square 10-inch piece of cardboard by cutting squares of length x inches out of each corner and folding the sides up. Express the volume of the box as a function of x, and state the domain.

92. Volume. A cylindrical water basin will be built to harvest rainwater. The basin is limited in that the largest radius it can have is 10 feet. Write a function representing the volume of water V as a function of height h. How many additional gallons of water will be collected if you increase the height by 2 feet? *Hint:* 1 cu ft = 7.48 gal.

For Exercises 93–94, refer to the following:

The weekly exchange rate of the U.S. dollar to the Japanese yen is shown in the graph as varying over an 8-week period. Assume the exchange rate $E(t)$ is a function of time (week); let $E(1)$ be the exchange rate during Week 1.

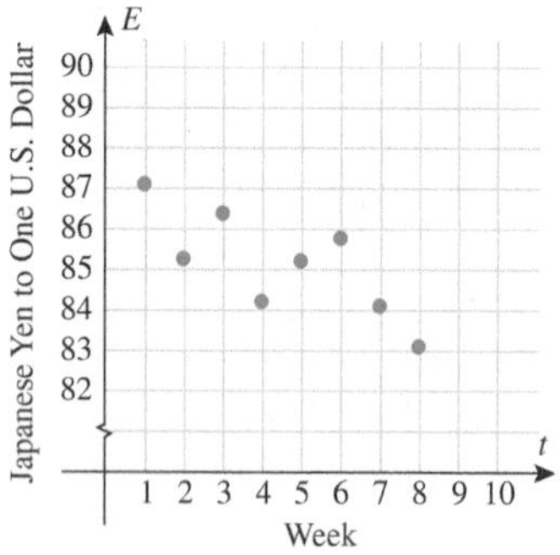

93. Economics. Approximate the exchange rates of the U.S. dollar to the nearest yen during Weeks 4, 7, and 8.

94. Economics. Find the increase or decrease in the number of Japanese yen to the U.S. dollar exchange rate, to the nearest yen, from (a) Week 2 to Week 3 and (b) Week 6 to Week 7.

For Exercises 95–96, refer to the following:

An epidemiological study of the spread of malaria in a rural area finds that the total number P of people who contracted malaria t days into an outbreak is modeled by the function

$$P(t) = -\frac{1}{4}t^2 + 7t + 180 \quad 1 \le t \le 14$$

95. Medicine/Health. How many people have contracted malaria 14 days into the outbreak?

96. Medicine/Health. How many people have contracted malaria 6 days into the outbreak?

For Exercises 97 and 98, use the following figure:

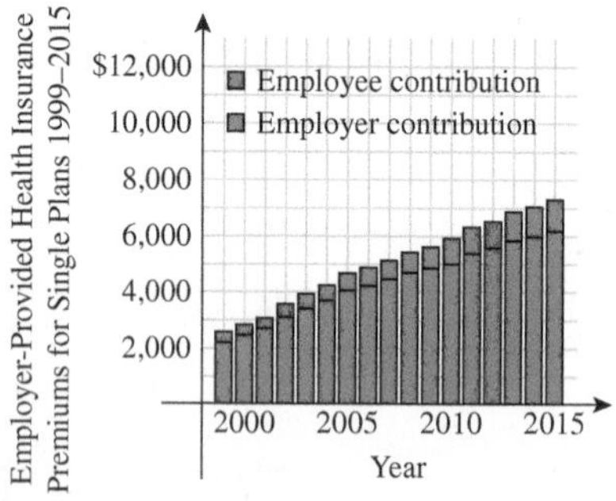

Source: Kaiser Family Foundation Health Research and Education Trust.

97. Health-Care Costs: Fill in the following table. Round dollars to the nearest $1000.

YEAR	TOTAL HEALTH-CARE COST FOR FAMILY PLANS
1999	
2003	
2007	
2011	
2015	

Write the five ordered pairs resulting from the table.

98. Health-Care Costs. Using the table found in Exercise 97, let the years correspond to the domain and the total costs correspond to the range. Is this relation a function? Explain.

For Exercises 99 and 100, use the following information:

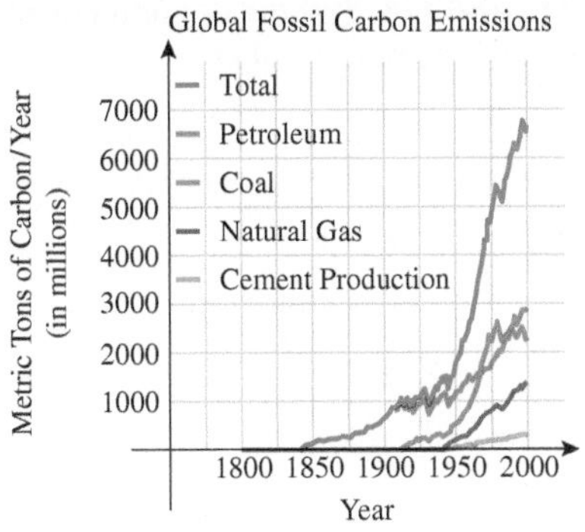

Source: http:/www.nafte.wvu.edu

Let the functions f, F, g, G, and H represent the number of tons of carbon emitted per year as a function of year corresponding to cement production, natural gas, coal, petroleum, and the total amount, respectively. Let t represent the year, with $t = 0$ corresponding to 1900.

99. Environment: Global Climate Change. Estimate (to the nearest thousand) the value of

a. $F(50)$ **b.** $g(50)$ **c.** $H(50)$

100. Environment: Global Climate Change. Explain what the sum $F(100) + g(100) + G(100)$ represents.

• CATCH THE MISTAKE

In Exercises 101–104, explain the mistake that is made.

101. Determine whether the relationship is a function.

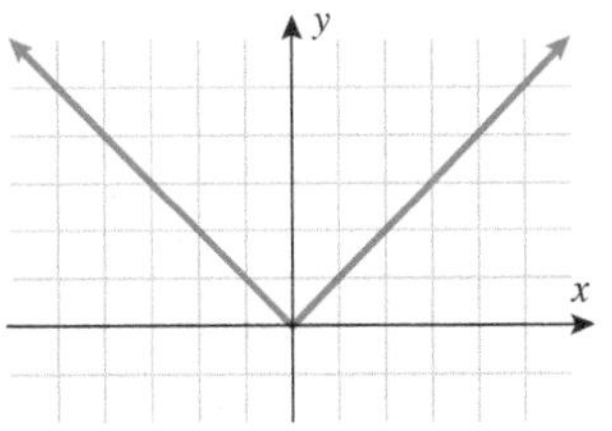

Solution:

Apply the horizontal line test.

Because the horizontal line intersects the graph in two places, this is not a function.

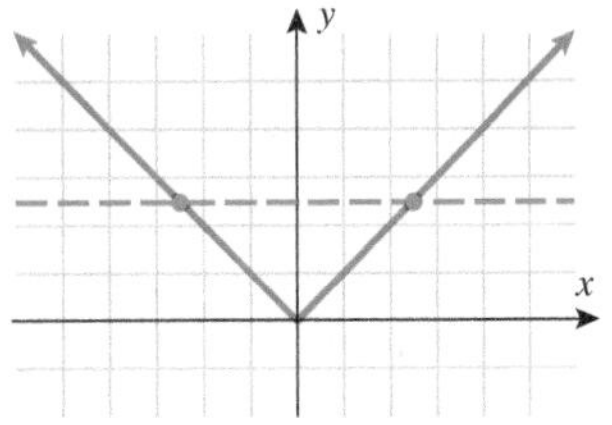

This is incorrect. What mistake was made?

102. Given the function $H(x) = 3x - 2$, evaluate the quantity $H(3) - H(-1)$.

Solution: $H(3) - H(-1) = H(3) + H(1) = 7 + 1 = 8$

This is incorrect. What mistake was made?

103. Given the function $f(x) = x^2 - x$, evaluate the quantity $f(x + 1)$.

Solution: $f(x + 1) = f(x) + f(1) = x^2 - x + 0$

$f(x + 1) = x^2 - x$

This is incorrect. What mistake was made?

104. Determine the domain of the function $g(t) = \sqrt{3 - t}$ and express it in interval notation.

Solution:

What can t be? Any nonnegative real number.

$3 - t > 0$

$3 > t$ or $t < 3$

Domain: $(-\infty, 3)$

This is incorrect. What mistake was made?

• CONCEPTUAL

In Exercises 105–108, determine whether each statement is true or false.

105. If a vertical line does not intersect the graph of an equation, then that equation does not represent a function.

106. If a horizontal line intersects a graph of an equation more than once, the equation does not represent a function.

107. For $x = y^2$, x is a function of y.

108. For $y = x^2$, y is a function of x.

109. If $f(x) = Ax^2 - 3x$ and $f(1) = -1$, find A.

110. If $g(x) = \dfrac{1}{b - x}$ and $g(3)$ is undefined, find b.

• CHALLENGE

111. If $F(x) = \dfrac{C - x}{D - x}$, $F(-2)$ is undefined, and $F(-1) = 4$, find C and D.

112. Construct a function that is undefined at $x = 5$ and whose graph passes through the point $(1, -1)$.

In Exercises 113 and 114, find the domain of each function, where a is any positive real number.

113. $f(x) = \dfrac{-100}{x^2 - a^2}$

114. $f(x) = -5\sqrt{x^2 - a^2}$

• PREVIEW TO CALCULUS

For Exercises 115–118, refer to the following:

In calculus, the difference quotient $\dfrac{f(x+h) - f(x)}{h}$ of a function f is used to find a new function f', called the *derivative of f*. To find f', we let h approach 0, $h \to 0$, in the difference quotient.

For example, if $f(x) = x^2$, $\dfrac{f(x+h) - f(x)}{h} = 2x + h$, and allowing $h = 0$, we have $f'(x) = 2x$.

115. Given $f(x) = x^3 + x$, find $f'(x)$.

116. Given $f(x) = 6x + \sqrt{x}$, find $f'(x)$.

117. Given $f(x) = \dfrac{x - 5}{x + 3}$, find $f'(x)$.

118. Given $f(x) = \sqrt{\dfrac{x + 7}{5 - x}}$, find $f'(x)$.

1.2 GRAPHS OF FUNCTIONS

SKILLS OBJECTIVES

- Classify functions as even, odd, or neither.
- Determine whether functions are increasing, decreasing, or constant.
- Calculate the average rate of change of a function.
- Graph piecewise-defined functions.

CONCEPTUAL OBJECTIVES

- Identify common functions, and understand that even functions have graphs that are symmetric about the y-axis, and odd functions have graphs that are symmetric about the origin.
- Understand that, when applied to functions, the designations increasing, decreasing, and constant refer to the values of the x-coordinates.
- Understand that the difference quotient is just another form of the average rate of change.
- Understand points of discontinuity and domain and range of piecewise-defined functions.

1.2.1 SKILL

Classify functions as even, odd, or neither.

1.2.1 CONCEPTUAL

Identify common functions, and understand that even functions have graphs that are symmetric about the y-axis, and odd functions have graphs that are symmetric about the origin.

1.2.1 Recognizing and Classifying Functions

Common Functions

The nine main functions you will read about in this section will constitute a "library" of functions that you should commit to memory. We will draw on this library of functions in the next section when graphing transformations are discussed.

In Section 0.6, we discussed equations and graphs of lines. All lines (with the exception of vertical lines) pass the vertical line test, and hence are classified as functions. Instead of the traditional notation of a line, $y = mx + b$, we use function notation and classify a function whose graph is a *line* as a *linear* function.

LINEAR FUNCTION

$f(x) = mx + b$ $\quad$ m and b are real numbers.

The domain of a linear function $f(x) = mx + b$ is the set of all real numbers $\mathbb{R}$. The graph of this function has slope m and y-intercept b.

Linear Function
Domain: $(-\infty, \infty)$

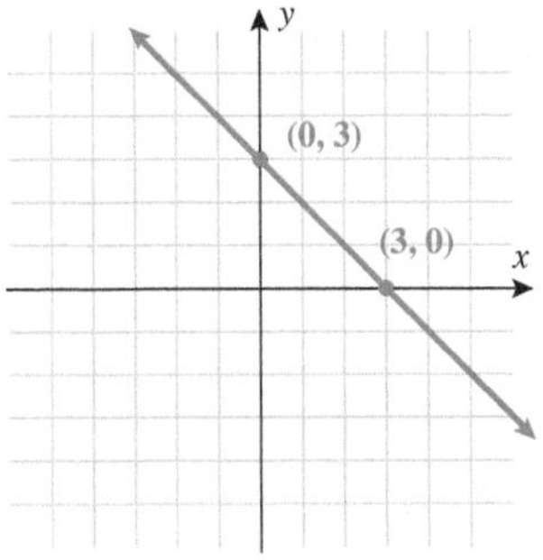

LINEAR FUNCTION: $f(x) = mx + b$	SLOPE: m	y-INTERCEPT: b
$f(x) = 2x - 7$	$m = 2$	$b = -7$
$f(x) = -x + 3$	$m = -1$	$b = 3$
$f(x) = x$	$m = 1$	$b = 0$
$f(x) = 5$	$m = 0$	$b = 5$

One special case of the linear function is the *constant function* $(m = 0)$.

CONSTANT FUNCTION

$f(x) = b$ $\quad$ b is any real number.

The graph of a constant function $f(x) = b$ is a horizontal line. The y-intercept corresponds to the point $(0, b)$. The domain of a constant function is the set of all real numbers $\mathbb{R}$. The range, however, is a single value b. In other words, all x-values correspond to a single y-value.

Points that lie on the graph of a constant function $f(x) = b$ are

$(-5, b)$
$(-1, b)$
$(0, b)$
$(2, b)$
$(4, b)$
...
(x, b)

Domain: $(-\infty, \infty)$ Range: $[b, b]$ or $\{b\}$

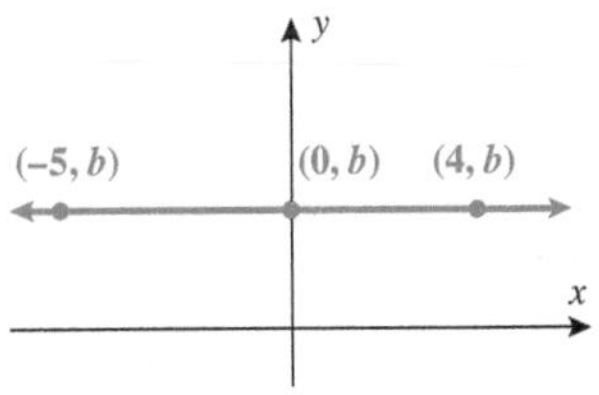

Another specific example of a linear function is the function having a slope of one $(m = 1)$ and a y-intercept of zero $(b = 0)$. This special case is called the *identity function.*

Identity Function
Domain: $(-\infty, \infty)$ Range: $(-\infty, \infty)$

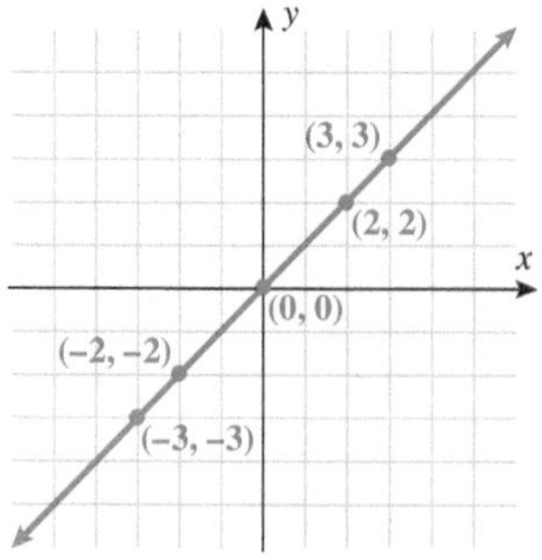

IDENTITY FUNCTION

$$f(x) = x$$

The graph of the identity function has the following properties: It passes through the origin, and every point that lies on the line has equal x- and y-coordinates. Both the domain and the range of the identity function are the set of all real numbers $\mathbb{R}$.

A function that squares the input is called the *square function.*

Square Function
Domain: $(-\infty, \infty)$ Range: $[0, \infty)$

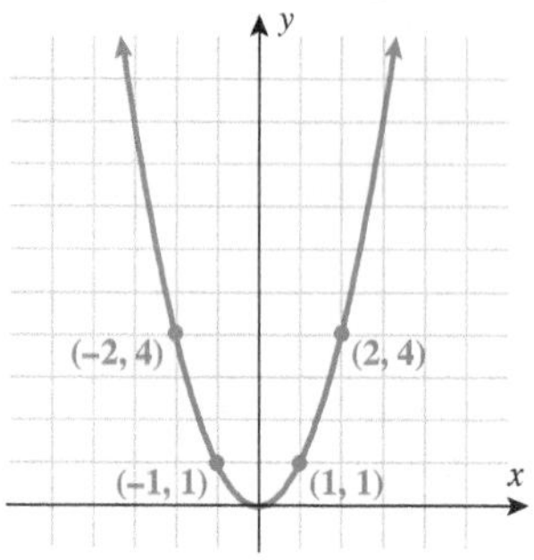

SQUARE FUNCTION

$$f(x) = x^2$$

The graph of the square function is called a parabola and will be discussed in further detail in Chapter 9. The domain of the square function is the set of all real numbers $\mathbb{R}$. Because squaring a real number always yields a positive number or zero, the range of the square function is the set of all nonnegative numbers. Note that the only intercept is the origin and the square function is symmetric about the y-axis. This graph is contained in quadrants I and II.

A function that cubes the input is called the *cube function.*

Cube Function
Domain: $(-\infty, \infty)$ Range: $(-\infty, \infty)$

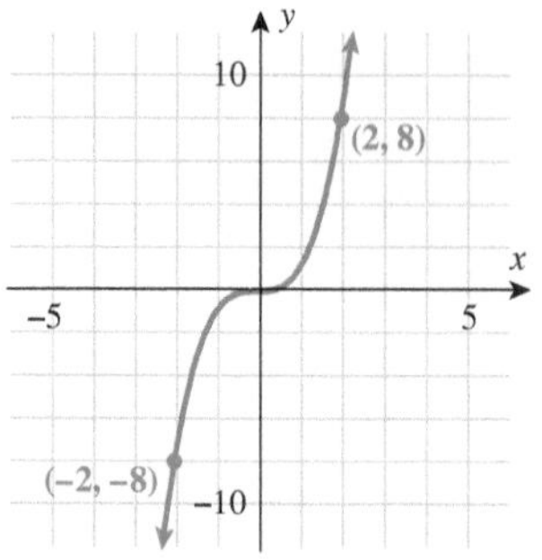

CUBE FUNCTION

$$f(x) = x^3$$

The domain of the cube function is the set of all real numbers $\mathbb{R}$. Because cubing a negative number yields a negative number, cubing a positive number yields a positive number, and cubing 0 yields 0, the range of the cube function is also the set of all real numbers $\mathbb{R}$. Note that the only intercept is the origin and the cube function is symmetric about the origin. This graph extends only into quadrants I and III.

The next two functions are counterparts of the previous two functions: square root and cube root. When a function takes the square root of the input or the cube root of the input, the function is called the *square root function* or the *cube root function*, respectively.

Square Root Function
Domain: $[0, \infty)$ Range: $[0, \infty)$

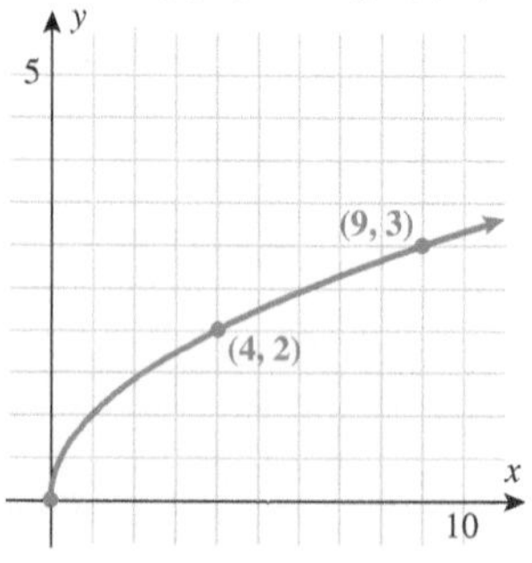

SQUARE ROOT FUNCTION

$$f(x) = \sqrt{x} \quad \text{or} \quad f(x) = x^{1/2}$$

In Section 1.1, we found the domain to be $[0, \infty)$. The output of the function will be all real numbers greater than or equal to zero. Therefore, the range of the square root function is $[0, \infty)$. The graph of this function will be contained in quadrant I.

CUBE ROOT FUNCTION

$$f(x) = \sqrt[3]{x} \quad \text{or} \quad f(x) = x^{1/3}$$

Cube Root Function
Domain: $(-\infty, \infty)$ Range: $(-\infty, \infty)$

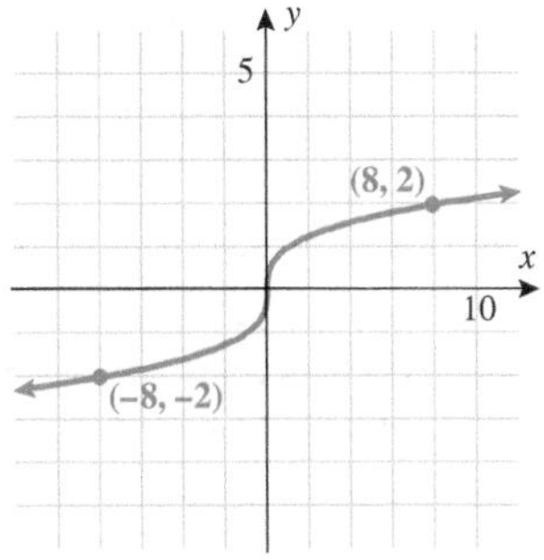

In Section 1.1, we stated the domain of the cube root function to be $(-\infty, \infty)$. We see by the graph that the range is also $(-\infty, \infty)$. This graph is contained in quadrants I and III and passes through the origin. This function is symmetric about the origin.

In Sections 0.3 and 0.4, absolute value equations and inequalities were reviewed. Now we shift our focus to the graph of the *absolute value function.*

ABSOLUTE VALUE FUNCTION

$$f(x) = |x|$$

Absolute Value Function
Domain: $(-\infty, \infty)$ Range: $[0, \infty)$

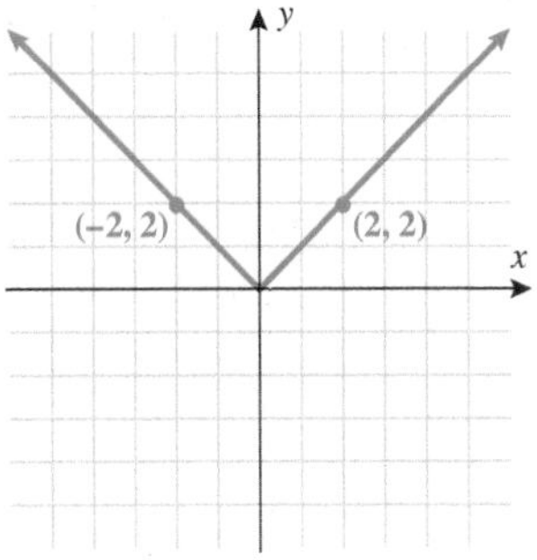

Some points that are on the graph of the absolute value function are $(-1, 1)$, $(0, 0)$, and $(1, 1)$. The domain of the absolute value function is the set of all real numbers $\mathbb{R}$, yet the range is the set of nonnegative real numbers. The graph of this function is symmetric with respect to the y-axis and is contained in quadrants I and II.

A function whose output is the reciprocal of its input is called the *reciprocal function.*

RECIPROCAL FUNCTION

$$f(x) = \frac{1}{x} \qquad x \neq 0$$

Reciprocal Function
Domain: $(-\infty, 0) \cup (0, \infty)$
Range: $(-\infty, 0) \cup (0, \infty)$

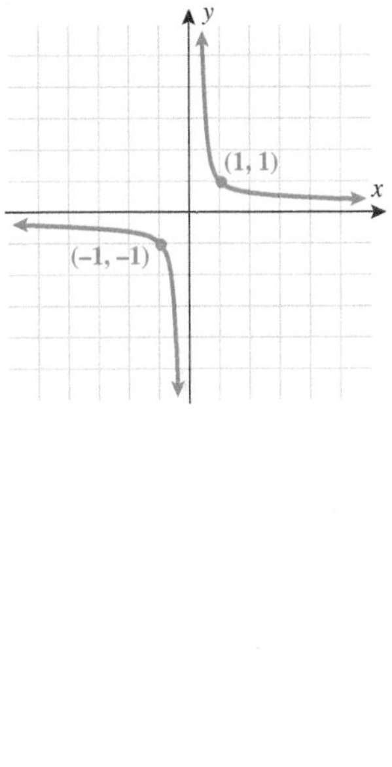

The only restriction on the domain of the reciprocal function is that $x \neq 0$. Therefore, we say the domain is the set of all real numbers excluding zero. The graph of the reciprocal function illustrates that its range is also the set of all real numbers except zero. Note that the reciprocal function is symmetric with respect to the origin and is contained in quadrants I and III.

Even and Odd Functions

Of the nine functions discussed above, several have similar properties of symmetry. The constant function, square function, and absolute value function are all symmetric with respect to the y-axis. The identity function, cube function, cube root function, and reciprocal function are all symmetric with respect to the origin. The term **even** is used to describe functions that are symmetric with respect to the y-axis, or vertical axis, and the term **odd** is used to describe functions that are symmetric with respect to the origin. Recall from Section 0.5 that symmetry can be determined both graphically and algebraically. The box below summarizes the graphical and algebraic characteristics of even and odd functions.

EVEN AND ODD FUNCTIONS

Function	Symmetric with Respect to	On Replacing x with $-x$
Even	y-axis, or vertical axis	$f(-x) = f(x)$
Odd	origin	$f(-x) = -f(x)$

[CONCEPT CHECK]

Classify the functions $f(x) = x^{2n}$ and $g(x) = x^{2n+1}$, where n is a positive integer (1, 2, 3, ...), as even, odd, or neither.

ANSWER $f(x)$ is even; $g(x)$ is odd

The algebraic method for determining symmetry with respect to the y-axis, or vertical axis, is to substitute in $-x$ for x. If the result is an equivalent equation, the function is symmetric with respect to the y-axis. Some examples of even functions are $f(x) = b$, $f(x) = x^2$, $f(x) = x^4$, and $f(x) = |x|$. In any of these equations, if $-x$ is substituted for x, the result is the same, that is, $f(-x) = f(x)$. Also note that, with the exception of the absolute value function, these examples are all even-degree polynomial equations. All constant functions are degree zero and are even functions.

The algebraic method for determining symmetry with respect to the origin is to substitute $-x$ for x. If the result is the negative of the original function, that is, if $f(-x) = -f(x)$, then the function is symmetric with respect to the origin and, hence, classified as an odd function. Examples of odd functions are $f(x) = x$, $f(x) = x^3$, $f(x) = x^5$, and $f(x) = x^{1/3}$. In any of these functions, if $-x$ is substituted for x, the result is the negative of the original function. Note that, with the exception of the cube root function, these equations are odd-degree polynomials.

Be careful, though, because functions that are combinations of even- and odd-degree polynomials can turn out to be neither even nor odd, as we will see in Example 1.

EXAMPLE 1 Determining Whether a Function Is Even, Odd, or Neither

Determine whether the functions are even, odd, or neither.

a. $f(x) = x^2 - 3$ **b.** $g(x) = x^5 + x^3$ **c.** $h(x) = x^2 - x$

Solution (a):

Original function. $f(x) = x^2 - 3$

Replace x with $-x$. $f(-x) = (-x)^2 - 3$

Simplify. $f(-x) = x^2 - 3 = f(x)$

Because $f(-x) = f(x)$, we say that $f(x)$ is an *even* function.

Solution (b):

Original function. $g(x) = x^5 + x^3$

Replace x with $-x$. $g(-x) = (-x)^5 + (-x)^3$

Simplify. $g(-x) = -x^5 - x^3 = -(x^5 + x^3) = -g(x)$

Because $g(-x) = -g(x)$, we say that $g(x)$ is an *odd* function.

Solution (c):

Original function. $h(x) = x^2 - x$

Replace x with $-x$. $h(-x) = (-x)^2 - (-x)$

Simplify. $h(-x) = x^2 + x$

$h(-x)$ is neither $-h(x)$ nor $h(x)$; therefore the function $h(x)$ is neither even nor odd.

In parts (a), (b), and (c), we classified these functions as either even, odd, or neither, using the algebraic test. Look back at them now and reflect on whether these classifications agree with your intuition. In part (a), we combined two functions: the square function and the constant function. Both of these functions are even, and adding even functions yields another even function. In part (b), we combined two odd functions: the fifth-power function and the cube function. Both of these functions are odd, and adding two odd functions yields another odd function. In part (c), we combined two functions: the square function and the identity function. The square function is even, and the identity function is odd. In this part, combining an even function with an odd function yields a function that is neither even nor odd and, hence, has no symmetry with respect to the vertical axis or the origin.

YOUR TURN Classify the functions as even, odd, or neither.

a. $f(x) = |x| + 4$ **b.** $f(x) = x^3 - 1$

ANSWER

a. even b. neither

1.2.2 Increasing and Decreasing Functions

1.2.2 SKILL

Determine whether functions are increasing, decreasing, or constant.

1.2.2 CONCEPTUAL

Understand that, when applied to functions, the designations increasing, decreasing, and constant refer to the values of the x-coordinates.

Look at the figure in the margin. Graphs are read from *left to right*. If we start at the left side of the graph and trace the red curve, we see that the function values (values in the vertical direction) are decreasing until arriving at the point $(-2, -2)$. Then, the function values increase until arriving at the point $(-1, 1)$. The values then remain constant $(y = 1)$ between the points $(-1, 1)$ and $(0, 1)$. Proceeding beyond the point $(0, 1)$, the function values decrease again until the point $(2, -2)$. Beyond the point $(2, -2)$, the function values increase again until the point $(6, 4)$. Finally, the function values decrease and continue to do so.

When specifying a function as increasing, decreasing, or constant, the *intervals are classified according to the x-coordinate*. For instance, in this graph, we say the function is increasing when x is between $x = -2$ and $x = -1$ and again when x is between $x = 2$ and $x = 6$. The graph is classified as decreasing when x is less than -2 and again when x is between 0 and 2 and again when x is greater than 6. The graph is classified as constant when x is between -1 and 0. In interval notation, this is summarized as

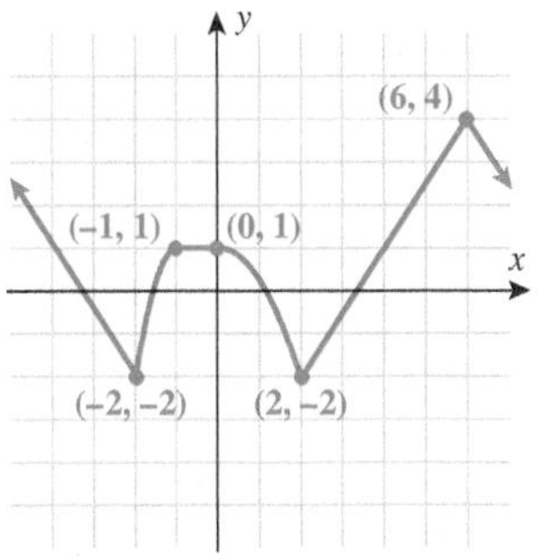

Decreasing	Increasing	Constant
$(-\infty, -2) \cup (0, 2) \cup (6, \infty)$	$(-2, -1) \cup (2, 6)$	$(-1, 0)$

An algebraic test for determining whether a function is increasing, decreasing, or constant is to compare the values $f(x)$ of the function for particular points in the intervals.

INCREASING, DECREASING, AND CONSTANT FUNCTIONS

1. A function f is **increasing** on an open interval I if for any x_1 and x_2 in I, where $x_1 < x_2$, then $f(x_1) < f(x_2)$.
2. A function f is **decreasing** on an open interval I if for any x_1 and x_2 in I, where $x_1 < x_2$, then $f(x_1) > f(x_2)$.
3. A function f is **constant** on an open interval I if for any x_1 and x_2 in I, then $f(x_1) = f(x_2)$.

STUDY TIP

- Graphs are read from left to right.
- Intervals correspond to the x-coordinates.

In addition to classifying a function as increasing, decreasing, or constant, we can also determine the domain and range of a function by inspecting its graph from left to right:

- The domain is the set of all x-values where the function is defined.
- The range is the set of all y-values that the graph of the function corresponds to.
- A solid dot on the left or right end of a graph indicates that the graph terminates there and the point is included in the graph.
- An open dot indicates that the graph terminates there and the point is not included in the graph.
- Unless a dot is present, it is assumed that a graph continues indefinitely in the same direction. (An arrow is used in some books to indicate direction.)

STUDY TIP

Increasing: Graph of function rises from left to right.
Decreasing: Graph of function falls from left to right.
Constant: Graph of function does not change height from left to right.

EXAMPLE 2 Finding Intervals When a Function Is Increasing or Decreasing

Given the graph of a function:

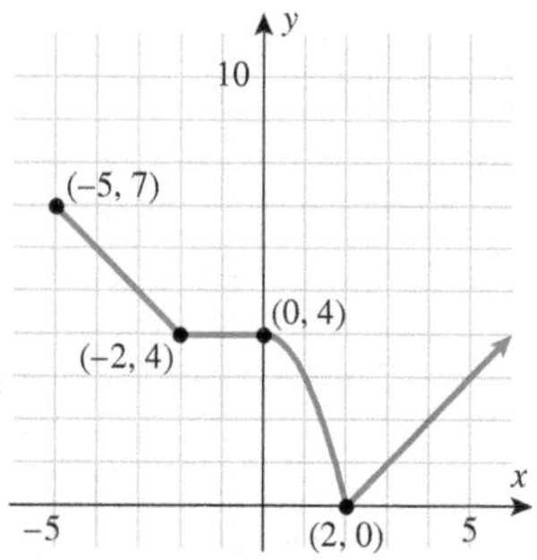

a. State the domain and range of the function.

b. Find the intervals when the function is increasing, decreasing, or constant.

Solution:

Domain: $[-5, \infty)$

Range: $[0, \infty)$

Reading the graph from **left to right**, we see that the graph

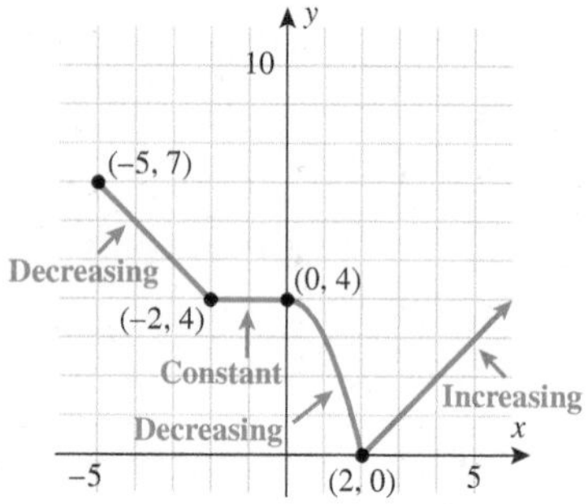

- decreases from the point $(-5, 7)$ to the point $(-2, 4)$.
- is constant from the point $(-2, 4)$ to the point $(0, 4)$.
- decreases from the point $(0, 4)$ to the point $(2, 0)$.
- increases from the point $(2, 0)$ on.

The intervals of increasing and decreasing correspond to the ***x*-coordinates.**

We say that this function is

- increasing on the interval $(2, \infty)$.
- decreasing on the interval $(-5, -2) \cup (0, 2)$.
- constant on the interval $(-2, 0)$.

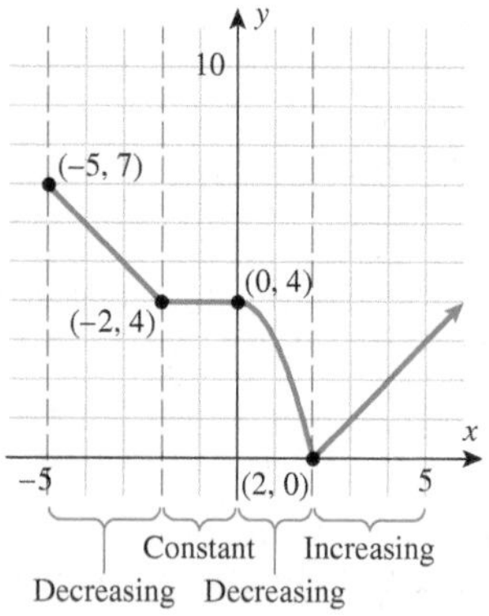

Note: The intervals of increasing or decreasing are defined on *open* intervals. This should not be confused with the domain. For example, the point $x = -5$ is included in the domain of the function but not in the interval where the function is classified as decreasing.

[CONCEPT CHECK]

TRUE OR FALSE An even function has both increasing and decreasing intervals, but an odd function has only one or the other.

ANSWER True

1.2.3 Average Rate of Change

1.2.3 SKILL

Calculate the average rate of change of a function.

1.2.3 CONCEPTUAL

Understand that the difference quotient is just another form of the average rate of change.

How do we know *how much* a function is increasing or decreasing? For example, is the price of a stock slightly increasing or is it doubling every week? One way we determine how much a function is increasing or decreasing is by calculating its *average rate of change.*

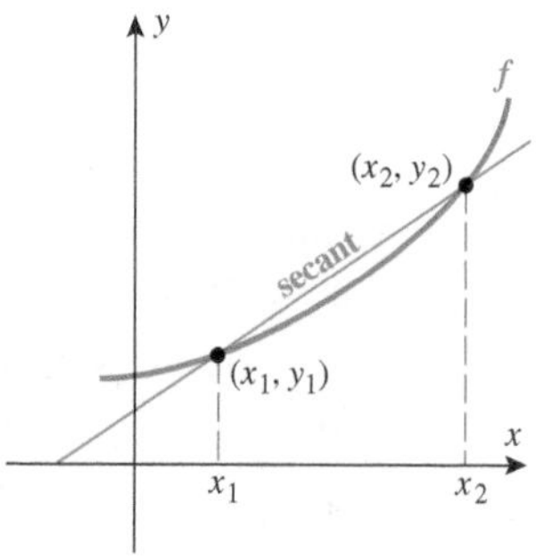

Let (x_1, y_1) and (x_2, y_2) be two points that lie on the graph of a function f. Draw the line that passes through these two points (x_1, y_1) and (x_2, y_2). This line is called a **secant line.**

Note that the slope of the secant line is given by $m = \frac{y_2 - y_1}{x_2 - x_1}$, and recall that the slope of a line is the rate of change of that line. The **slope of the secant line** is used to represent the *average rate of change* of the function.

AVERAGE RATE OF CHANGE

Let $(x_1, f(x_1))$ and $(x_2, f(x_2))$ be two distinct points, $(x_1 \neq x_2)$, on the graph of the function f. The **average rate of change** of f between x_1 and x_2 is given by

$$\textbf{Average rate of change} = \frac{f(x_2) - f(x_1)}{x_2 - x_1}$$

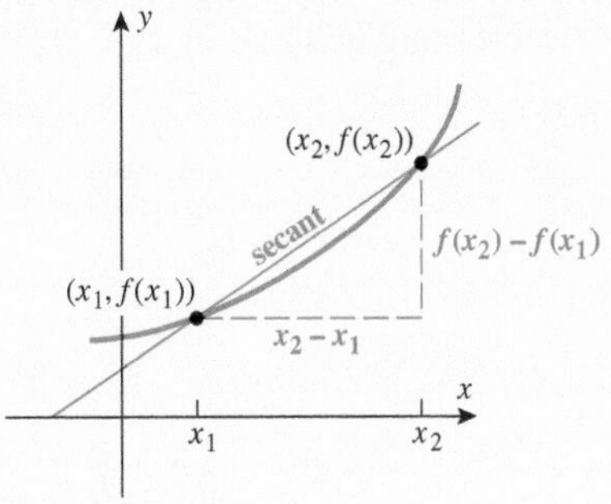

EXAMPLE 3 Average Rate of Change

Find the average rate of change of $f(x) = x^4$ from

a. $x = -1$ to $x = 0$ **b.** $x = 0$ to $x = 1$ **c.** $x = 1$ to $x = 2$

Solution (a):

Write the average rate of change formula. $\dfrac{f(x_2) - f(x_1)}{x_2 - x_1}$

Let $x_1 = -1$ and $x_2 = 0$. $= \dfrac{f(0) - f(-1)}{0 - (-1)}$

Substitute $f(-1) = (-1)^4 = 1$ and $f(0) = 0^4 = 0$. $= \dfrac{0 - 1}{0 - (-1)}$

Simplify. $= \boxed{-1}$

Solution (b):

Write the average rate of change formula. $\dfrac{f(x_2) - f(x_1)}{x_2 - x_1}$

Let $x_1 = 0$ and $x_2 = 1$. $= \dfrac{f(1) - f(0)}{1 - 0}$

Substitute $f(0) = 0^4 = 0$ and $f(1) = (1)^4 = 1$. $= \dfrac{1 - 0}{1 - 0}$

Simplify. $= \boxed{1}$

Solution (c):

Write the average rate of change formula. $\dfrac{f(x_2) - f(x_1)}{x_2 - x_1}$

Let $x_1 = 1$ and $x_2 = 2$. $= \dfrac{f(2) - f(1)}{2 - 1}$

Substitute $f(1) = 1^4 = 1$ and $f(2) = (2)^4 = 16$. $= \dfrac{16 - 1}{2 - 1}$

Simplify. $= \boxed{15}$

Graphical Interpretation: Slope of the Secant Line

a. Between $(-1, 1)$ and $(0, 0)$, this function is decreasing at a rate of 1.

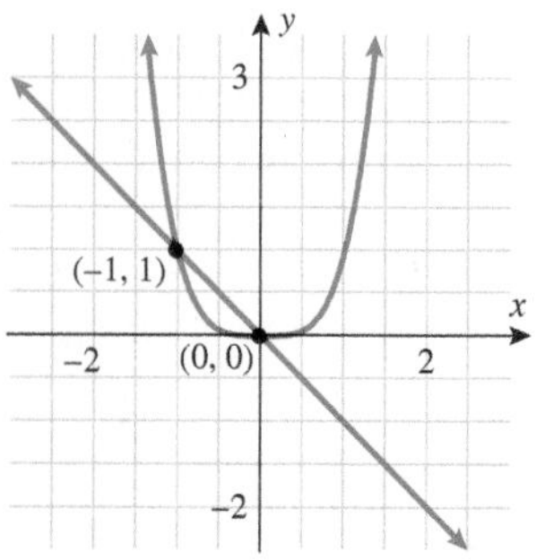

b. Between $(0, 0)$ and $(1, 1)$, this function is increasing at a rate of 1.

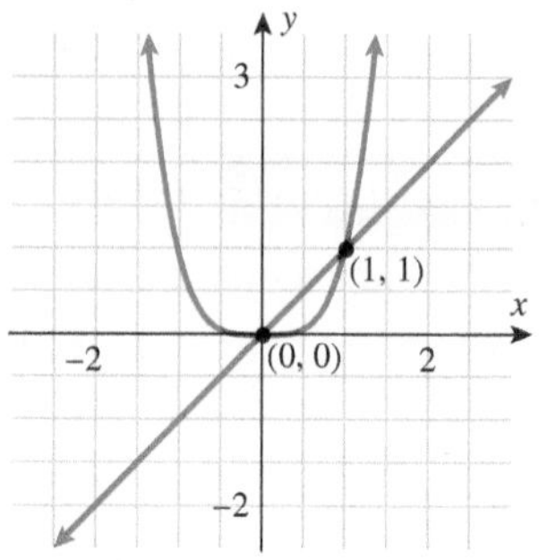

c. Between $(1, 1)$ and $(2, 16)$, this function is increasing at a rate of 15.

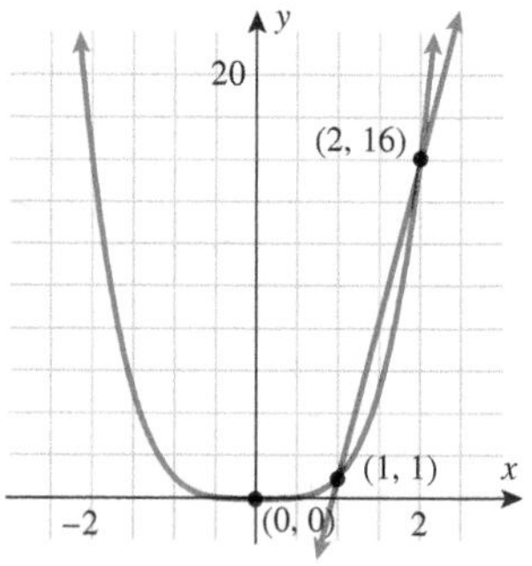

YOUR TURN Find the average rate of change of $f(x) = x^2$ from

a. $x = -2$ to $x = 0$ **b.** $x = 0$ to $x = 2$

ANSWER

a. -2 b. 2

The average rate of change can also be written in terms of the *difference quotient*.

WORDS	**MATH**
Let the distance between x_1 and x_2 be h.	$x_2 - x_1 = h$
Solve for x_2.	$x_2 = x_1 + h$
Substitute $x_2 - x_1 = h$ into the denominator and $x_2 = x_1 + h$ into the numerator of the average rate of change.	Average rate of change $= \dfrac{f(x_2) - f(x_1)}{x_2 - x_1}$ $= \dfrac{f(x_1 + h) - f(x_1)}{h}$
Let $x_1 = x$.	$\boxed{= \dfrac{f(x + h) - f(x)}{h}}$

When written in this form, the average rate of change is called the **difference quotient**.

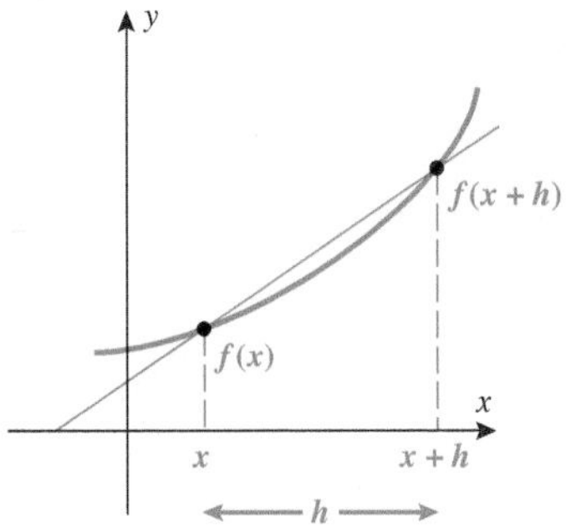

DEFINITION Difference Quotient

The expression $\frac{f(x+h)-f(x)}{h}$, where $h \neq 0$, is called the **difference quotient**.

The difference quotient is more meaningful when h is small. In calculus the difference quotient is used to define a *derivative*.

EXAMPLE 4 **Calculating the Difference Quotient**

Calculate the difference quotient for the function $f(x) = 2x^2 + 1$.

Solution:

Find $f(x+h)$.

$$f(x+h) = 2(x+h)^2 + 1$$
$$= 2(x^2 + 2xh + h^2) + 1$$
$$= 2x^2 + 4xh + 2h^2 + 1$$

Find the difference quotient.

$$\frac{f(x+h)-f(x)}{h} = \frac{\overbrace{2x^2 + 4xh + 2h^2 + 1}^{f(x+h)} - \overbrace{(2x^2+1)}^{f(x)}}{h}$$

Simplify.

$$= \frac{2x^2 + 4xh + 2h^2 + 1 - 2x^2 - 1}{h}$$

$$= \frac{4xh + 2h^2}{h}$$

Factor the numerator.

$$= \frac{h(4x+2h)}{h}$$

Cancel (divide out) the common h.

$$= \boxed{4x + 2h} \qquad h \neq 0$$

YOUR TURN Calculate the difference quotient for the function $f(x) = -x^2 + 2$.

ANSWER
$$\frac{f(x+h)-f(x)}{h} = -2x - h$$

STUDY TIP

Use brackets or parentheses around $f(x)$ to avoid forgetting to distribute the negative sign:

$$\frac{f(x+h) - [f(x)]}{h}$$

CONCEPT CHECK

Find the difference quotient for the line $f(x) = mx + b$.

ANSWER m

EXAMPLE 5 Evaluating the Difference Quotient

For the function $f(x) = x^2 - x$, find $\dfrac{f(x+h) - f(x)}{h}$.

Solution:

Use placeholder notation for the function $f(x) = x^2 - x$. $\quad f(\square) = (\square)^2 - (\square)$

Calculate $f(x+h)$. $\quad f(x+h) = (x+h)^2 - (x+h)$

Write the difference quotient. $\quad \dfrac{f(x+h) - f(x)}{h}$

Let $f(x+h) = (x+h)^2 - (x+h)$ and $f(x) = x^2 - x$.

$$\frac{f(x+h) - f(x)}{h} = \frac{\overbrace{\left[(x+h)^2 - (x+h)\right]}^{f(x+h)} - \overbrace{\left[x^2 - x\right]}^{f(x)}}{h} \qquad h \neq 0$$

Eliminate the parentheses inside the first set of brackets. $\quad = \dfrac{\left[x^2 + 2xh + h^2 - x - h\right] - \left[x^2 - x\right]}{h}$

Eliminate the brackets in the numerator. $\quad = \dfrac{x^2 + 2xh + h^2 - x - h - x^2 + x}{h}$

Combine like terms. $\quad = \dfrac{2xh + h^2 - h}{h}$

Factor the numerator. $\quad = \dfrac{h(2x + h - 1)}{h}$

Divide out the common factor, h. $\quad = \boxed{2x + h - 1} \quad h \neq 0$

YOUR TURN Evaluate the difference quotient for $f(x) = x^2 - 1$.

ANSWER

$2x + h$

1.2.4 SKILL

Graph piecewise-defined functions.

1.2.4 CONCEPTUAL

Understand points of discontinuity and domain and range of piecewise-defined functions.

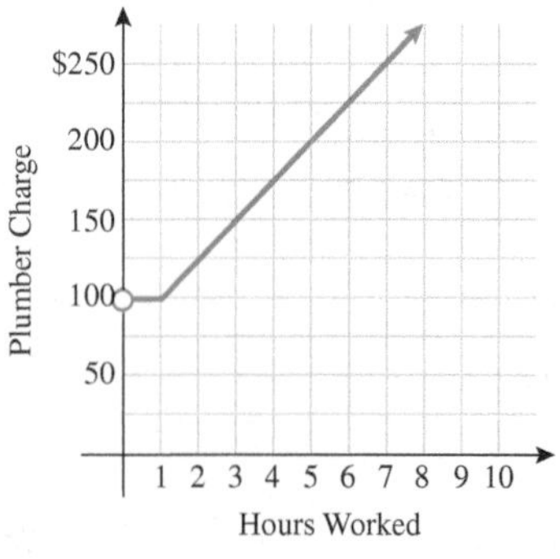

1.2.4 Piecewise-Defined Functions

Most of the functions that we have seen in this text are functions defined by polynomials. Sometimes the need arises to define functions in terms of *pieces*. For example, most plumbers charge a flat fee for a house call and then an additional hourly rate for the job. For instance, if a particular plumber charges \$100 to drive out to your house and work for 1 hour, and then \$25 an hour for every additional hour he or she works on your job, we would define this function in pieces. If we let h be the number of hours worked, then the charge is defined as

$$\text{Plumbing charge} = \begin{cases} 100 & 0 < h \leq 1 \\ 100 + 25(h - 1) & h > 1 \end{cases}$$

We can see in the graph of this function that there is 1 hour that is constant and after that the function continually increases.

The next example is a piecewise-defined function given in terms of pieces of functions from our "library of functions." Because the function is defined in terms of pieces of other functions, we draw the graph of each individual function and, then, for each function darken the piece corresponding to its part of the domain.

EXAMPLE 6 Graphing Piecewise-Defined Functions

Graph the piecewise-defined function, and state the domain, range, and intervals when the function is increasing, decreasing, or constant.

$$G(x) = \begin{cases} x^2 & x < -1 \\ 1 & -1 \le x \le 1 \\ x & x > 1 \end{cases}$$

Solution:

Graph each of the functions on the same plane.

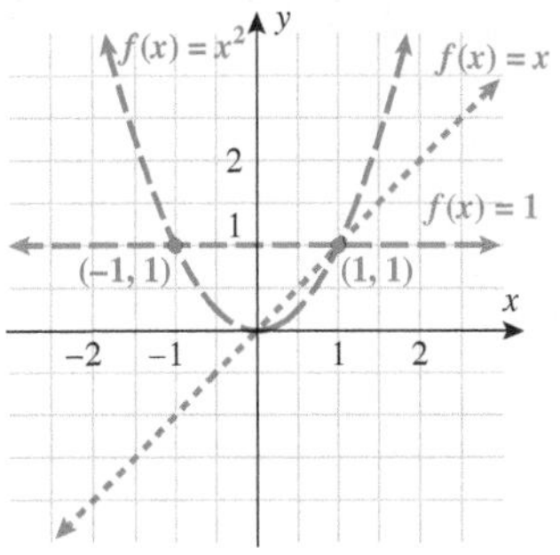

Square function:
$f(x) = x^2$

Constant function:
$f(x) = 1$

Identity function:
$f(x) = x$

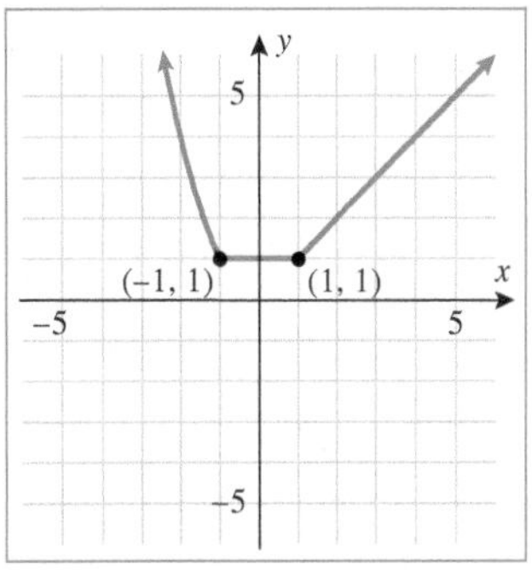

The points to focus on in particular are the x-values where the pieces change over—that is, $x = -1$ and $x = 1$.

Let's now investigate each piece. When $x < -1$, this function is defined by the square function, $f(x) = x^2$, so darken that particular function to the left of $x = -1$. When $-1 \le x \le 1$, the function is defined by the constant function, $f(x) = 1$, so darken that particular function between the x-values of -1 and 1. When $x > 1$, the function is defined by the identity function, $f(x) = x$, so darken that function to the right of $x = 1$. Erase everything that is not darkened, and the resulting graph of the piecewise-defined function is given on the right.

This function is defined for all real values of x, so the domain of this function is the set of all real numbers. The values that this function yields in the vertical direction are all real numbers greater than or equal to 1. Hence, the range of this function is $[1, \infty)$. The intervals of increasing, decreasing, and constant are as follows:

Decreasing: $(-\infty, -1)$

Constant: $(-1, 1)$

Increasing: $(1, \infty)$

The term **continuous** implies that there are no holes or jumps and that the graph can be drawn without picking up your pencil. A function that does have holes or jumps and cannot be drawn in one motion without picking up your pencil is classified as **discontinuous**, and the points where the holes or jumps occur are called *points of discontinuity*.

The previous example illustrates a *continuous* piecewise-defined function. At the $x = -1$ junction, the square function and constant function both pass through the point $(-1, 1)$. At the $x = 1$ junction, the constant function and the identity function both pass through the point $(1, 1)$. Since the graph of this piecewise-defined function has no holes or jumps, we classify it as a continuous function.

The next example illustrates a *discontinuous* piecewise-defined function.

EXAMPLE 7 Graphing a Discontinuous Piecewise-Defined Function

Graph the piecewise-defined function, and state the intervals where the function is increasing, decreasing, or constant, along with the domain and range.

$$f(x) = \begin{cases} 1 - x & x < 0 \\ x & 0 \leq x < 2 \\ -1 & x > 2 \end{cases}$$

Solution:

Graph these functions on the same plane.

Linear function:
$f(x) = 1 - x$

Identity function:
$f(x) = x$

Constant function:
$f(x) = -1$

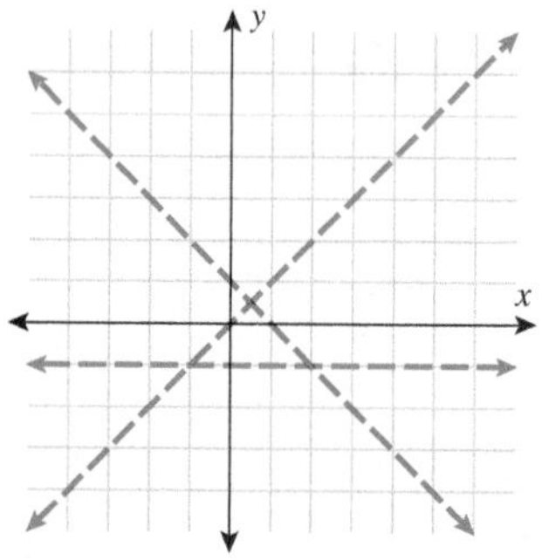

Darken the piecewise-defined function on the graph. For all values less than zero $(x < 0)$, the function is defined by the **linear function**. Note the use of an open circle, indicating up to but not including $x = 0$. For values $0 \leq x < 2$, the function is defined by the **identity function**. The circle is filled in at the left endpoint, $x = 0$. An open circle is used at $x = 2$. For all values greater than 2, $x > 2$, the function is defined by the **constant function**. Because this interval does not include the point $x = 2$, an open circle is used.

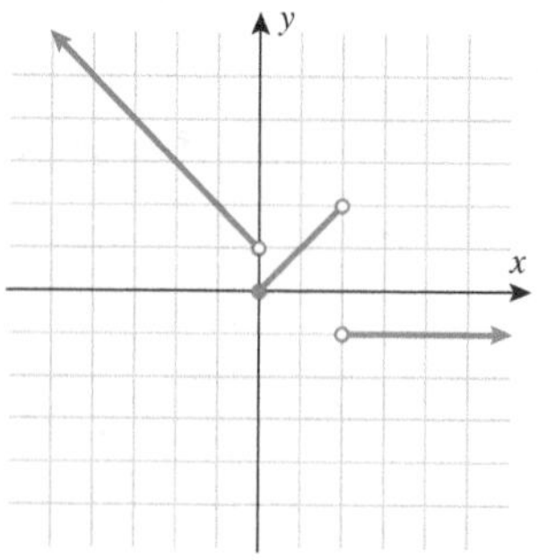

At what intervals is the function increasing, decreasing, or constant? Remember that the intervals correspond to the x-values.

Decreasing: $(-\infty, 0)$ Increasing: $(0, 2)$ Constant: $(2, \infty)$

The function is defined for all values of x except $x = 2$.

$$\text{Domain:} \quad (-\infty, 2) \cup (2, \infty)$$

The output of this function (vertical direction) takes on the y-values $y \geq 0$ and the additional single value $y = -1$.

$$\text{Range:} \quad [-1, -1] \cup [0, \infty) \quad \text{or} \quad \{-1\} \cup [0, \infty)$$

We mentioned earlier that a discontinuous function has a graph that exhibits holes or jumps. In Example 7, the point $x = 0$ corresponds to a jump, because you would have to pick up your pencil to continue drawing the graph. The point $x = 2$ corresponds to both a hole and a jump. The hole indicates that the function is not defined at that point, and there is still a jump because the identity function and the constant function do not meet at the same y-value at $x = 2$.

YOUR TURN Graph the piecewise-defined function, and state the intervals where the function is increasing, decreasing, or constant, along with the domain and range.

$$f(x) = \begin{cases} -x & x \leq -1 \\ 2 & -1 < x < 1 \\ x & x > 1 \end{cases}$$

ANSWER

Increasing: $(1, \infty)$

Decreasing: $(-\infty, -1)$

Constant: $(-1, 1)$

Domain:

$(-\infty, 1) \cup (1, \infty)$

Range: $[1, \infty)$

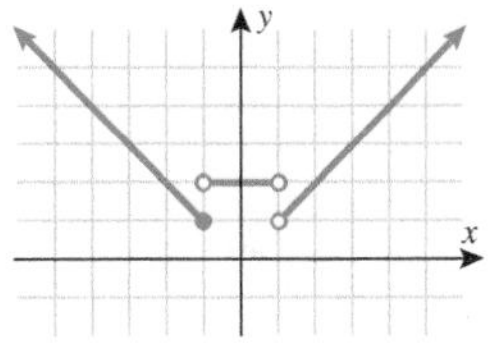

Piecewise-defined functions whose "pieces" are constants are called **step functions**. The reason for this name is that the graph of a step function looks like steps of a staircase. A common step function used in engineering is the **Heaviside step function** (also called the **unit step function**):

$$H(t) = \begin{cases} 0 & t < 0 \\ 1 & t \geq 0 \end{cases}$$

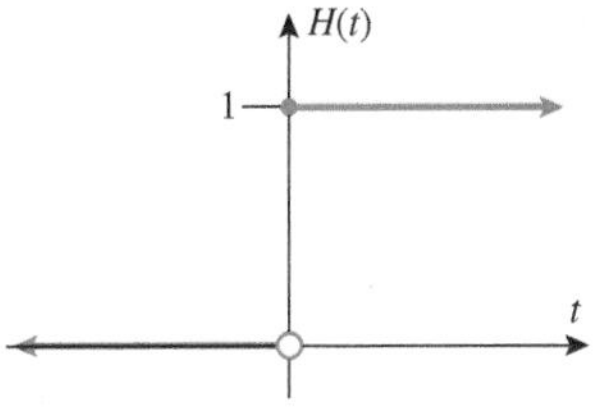

This function is used in signal processing to represent a signal that turns on at some time and stays on indefinitely.

A common step function used in business applications is the *greatest integer function.*

GREATEST INTEGER FUNCTION

$$f(x) = [[x]] = \text{greatest integer less than or equal to } x$$

x	1.0	1.3	1.5	1.7	1.9	2.0
$f(x) = [[x]]$	1	1	1	1	1	2

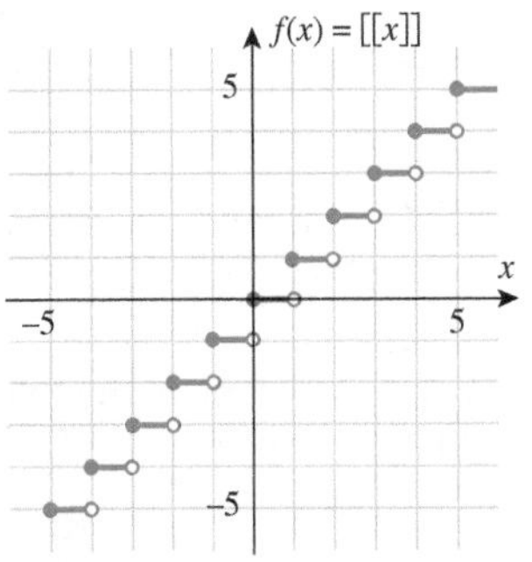

[CONCEPT CHECK]

State the domain, range, and any points of discontinuity for the Heaviside function.

ANSWER Domain: $(-\infty, \infty)$ Range: $[0] \cup [1]$ Point of Discontinuity: $x = 0$.

[SECTION 1.2] SUMMARY

NAME	FUNCTION	DOMAIN	RANGE	GRAPH	EVEN/ODD
Linear	$f(x) = mx + b, m \neq 0$	$(-\infty, \infty)$	$(-\infty, \infty)$	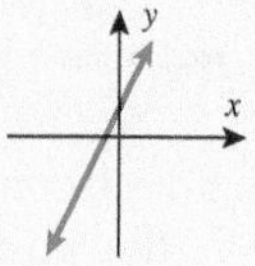	Neither (unless $y = x$)
Constant	$f(x) = c$	$(-\infty, \infty)$	$[c, c]$ or $\{c\}$	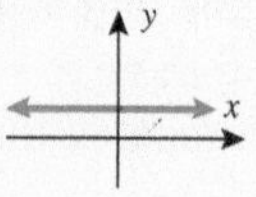	Even
Identity	$f(x) = x$	$(-\infty, \infty)$	$(-\infty, \infty)$	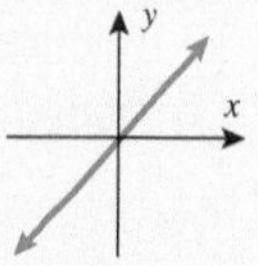	Odd
Square	$f(x) = x^2$	$(-\infty, \infty)$	$[0, \infty)$	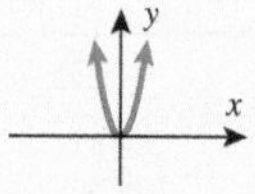	Even
Cube	$f(x) = x^3$	$(-\infty, \infty)$	$(-\infty, \infty)$	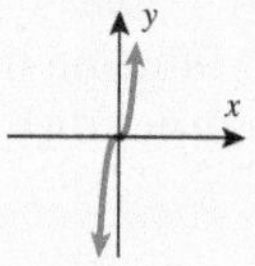	Odd
Square Root	$f(x) = \sqrt{x}$	$[0, \infty)$	$[0, \infty)$	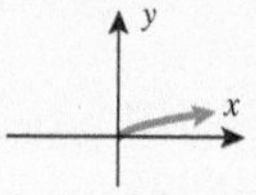	Neither
Cube Root	$f(x) = \sqrt[3]{x}$	$(-\infty, \infty)$	$(-\infty, \infty)$	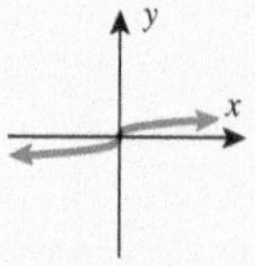	Odd
Absolute Value	$f(x) = \lvert x \rvert$	$(-\infty, \infty)$	$[0, \infty)$	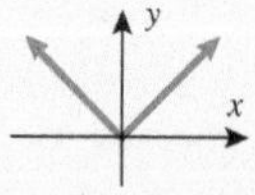	Even
Reciprocal	$f(x) = \dfrac{1}{x}$	$(-\infty, 0) \cup (0, \infty)$	$(-\infty, 0) \cup (0, \infty)$	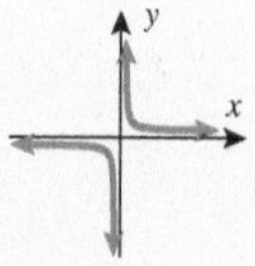	Odd

Domain and Range of a Function

- **Implied Domain:** Exclude any values that lead to the function being undefined (dividing by zero) or to imaginary outputs (even root of a negative real number).
- Inspect the graph to determine the set of all inputs (domain) and the set of all outputs (range).

Finding Intervals Where a Function Is Increasing, Decreasing, or Constant

- **Increasing:** Graph of function rises from left to right.
- **Decreasing:** Graph of function falls from left to right.
- **Constant:** Graph of function does not change height from left to right.

Average Rate of Change $\dfrac{f(x_2) - f(x_1)}{x_2 - x_1}$ $\quad x_1 \neq x_2$

Difference Quotient $\dfrac{f(x + h) - f(x)}{h}$ $\quad h \neq 0$

Piecewise-Defined Functions

- **Continuous:** You can draw the graph of a function without picking up the pencil.
- **Discontinuous:** Graph has holes and/or jumps.

[SECTION 1.2] EXERCISES

• SKILLS

In Exercises 1–16, determine whether the function is even, odd, or neither.

1. $h(x) = x^2 + 2x$
2. $G(x) = 2x^4 + 3x^3$
3. $h(x) = x^{1/3} - x$
4. $g(x) = x^{-1} + x$
5. $f(x) = |x| + 5$
6. $f(x) = |x| + x^2$
7. $f(x) = |x|$
8. $f(x) = |x^3|$
9. $G(t) = |t - 3|$
10. $g(t) = |t + 2|$
11. $G(t) = \sqrt{t - 3}$
12. $f(x) = \sqrt{2 - x}$
13. $g(x) = \sqrt{x^2 + x}$
14. $f(x) = \sqrt{x^2 + 2}$
15. $h(x) = \dfrac{1}{x} + 3$
16. $h(x) = \dfrac{1}{x} - 2x$

In Exercises 17–28, state the (a) domain, (b) range, and (c) x-interval(s) where the function is increasing, decreasing, or constant. Find the values of (d) $f(0)$, (e) $f(-2)$, and (f) $f(2)$.

17.

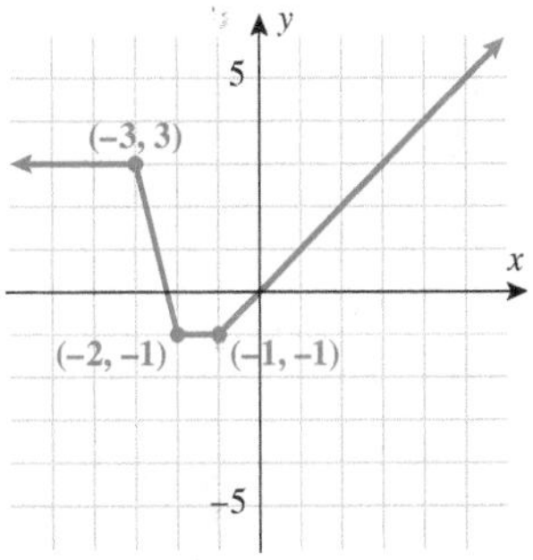

18.

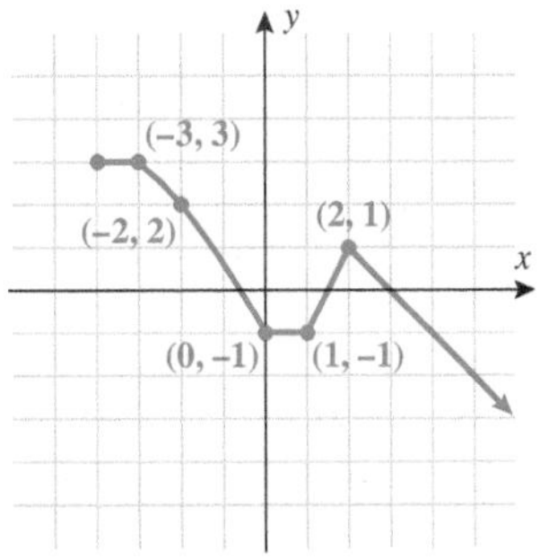

19.

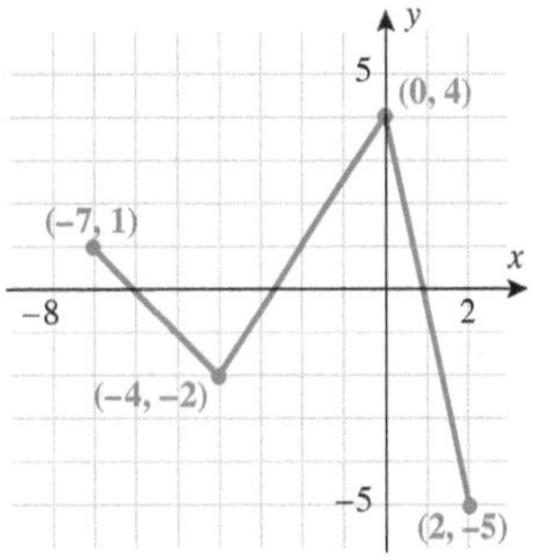

20.

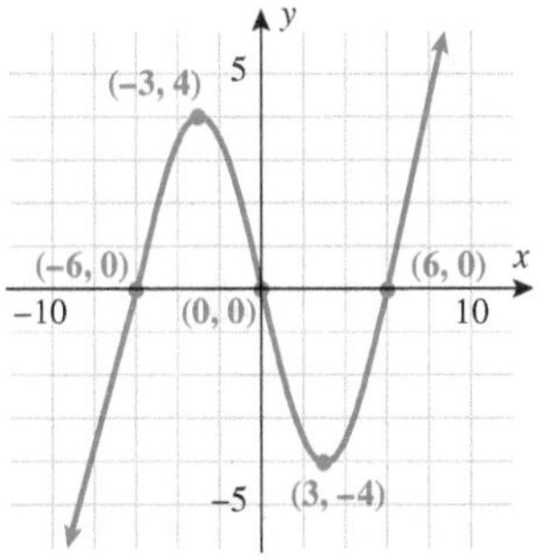

21.

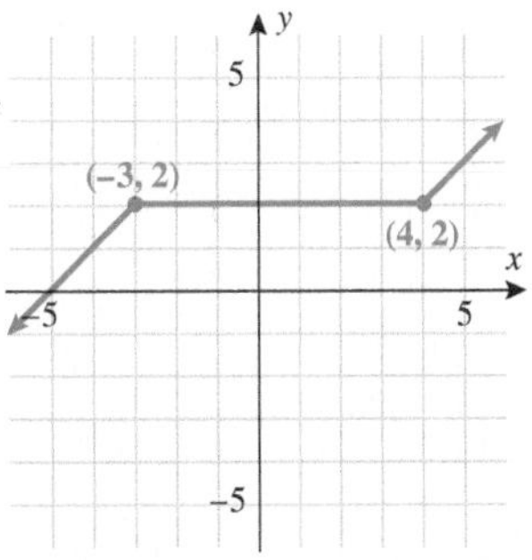

22.

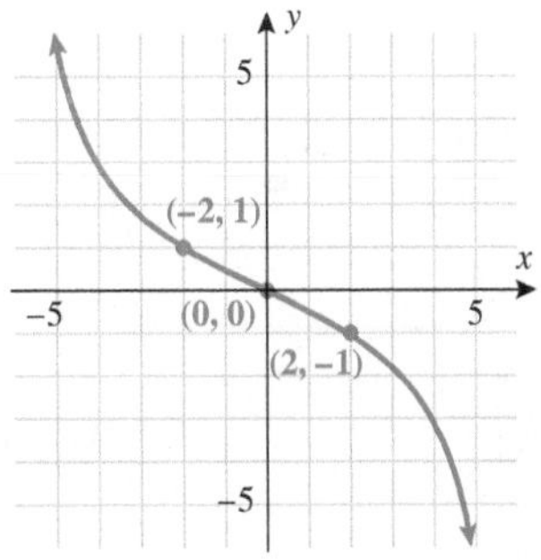

23.

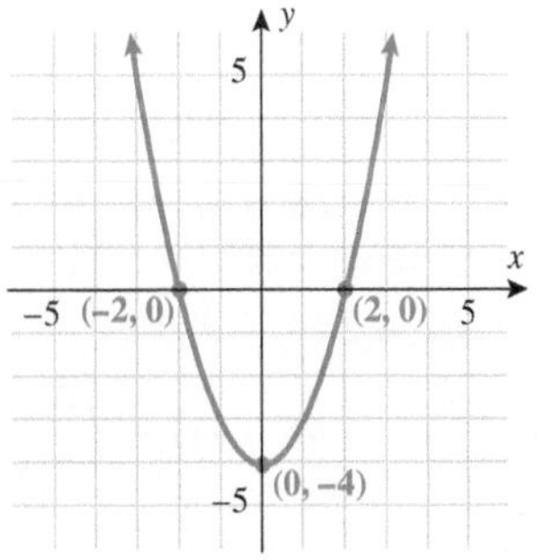

24.

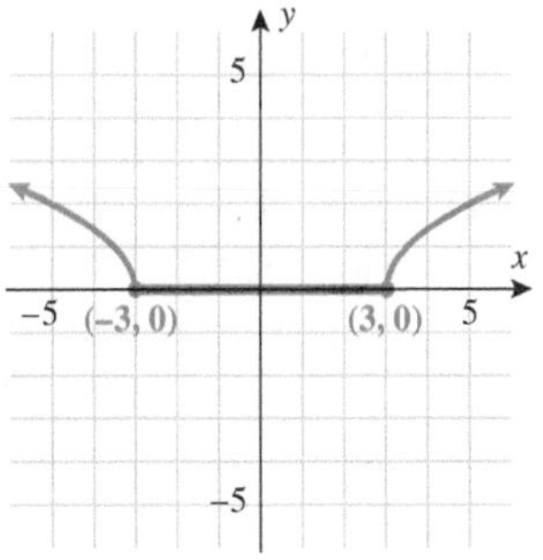

25.

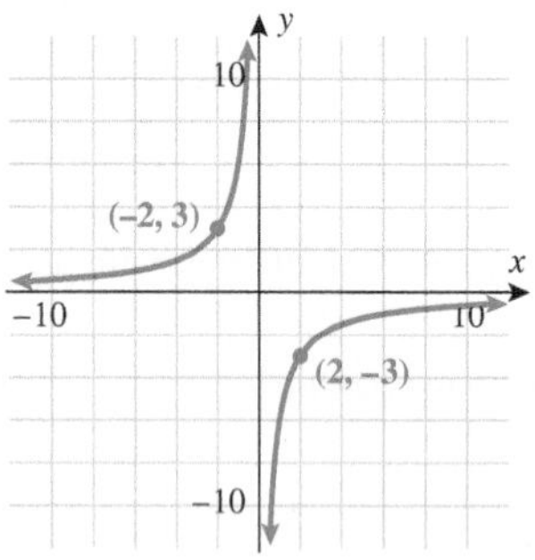

26.

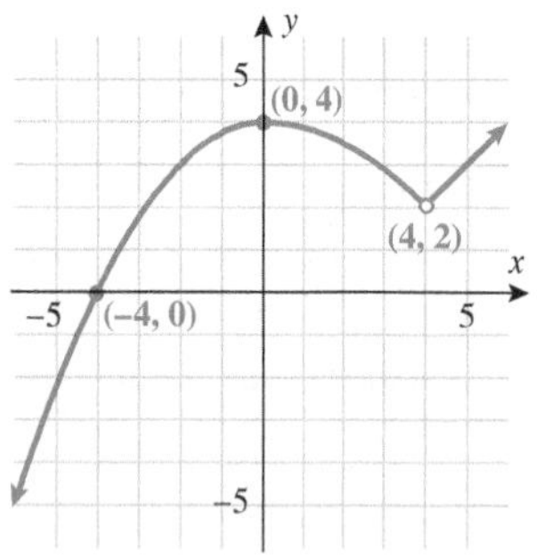

27.

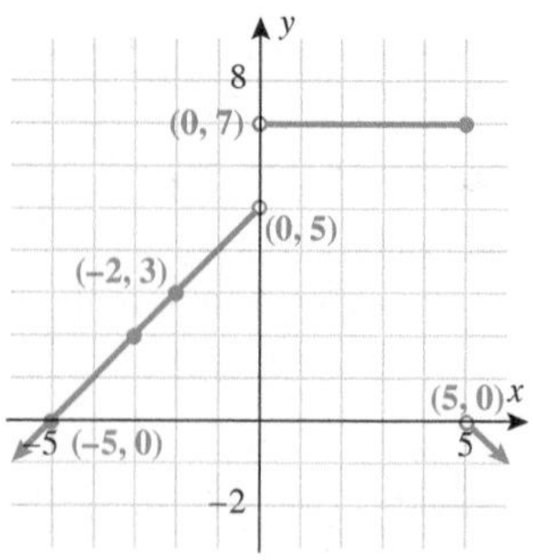

28.

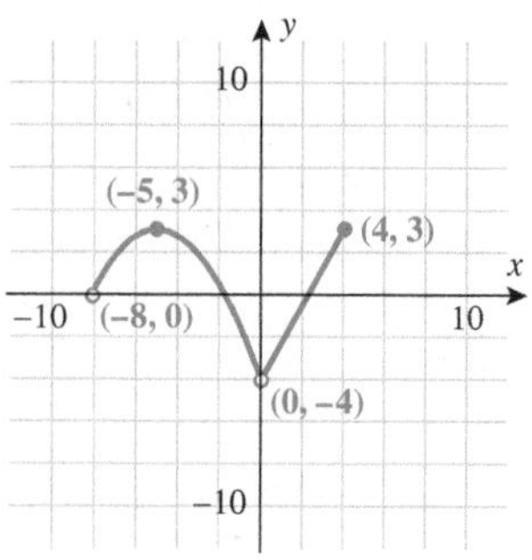

In Exercises 29–44, find the difference quotient $\dfrac{f(x+h)-f(x)}{h}$ for each function.

29. $f(x) = x^2 - x$

30. $f(x) = x^2 + 2x$

31. $f(x) = 3x + x^2$

32. $f(x) = 5x - x^2$

33. $f(x) = x^2 - 3x + 2$

34. $f(x) = x^2 - 2x + 5$

35. $f(x) = -3x^2 + 5x - 4$

36. $f(x) = -4x^2 + 2x - 3$

37. $f(x) = x^3 + x^2$

38. $f(x) = (x - 1)^4$

39. $f(x) = \dfrac{2}{x - 2}$

40. $f(x) = \dfrac{x + 5}{x - 7}$

41. $f(x) = \sqrt{1 - 2x}$

42. $f(x) = \sqrt{x^2 + x + 1}$

43. $f(x) = \dfrac{4}{\sqrt{x}}$

44. $f(x) = \sqrt{\dfrac{x}{x + 1}}$

In Exercises 45–52, find the average rate of change of the function from $x = 1$ to $x = 3$.

45. $f(x) = x^3$

46. $f(x) = \dfrac{1}{x}$

47. $f(x) = |x|$

48. $f(x) = 2x$

49. $f(x) = 1 - 2x$

50. $f(x) = 9 - x^2$

51. $f(x) = |5 - 2x|$

52. $f(x) = \sqrt[3]{x^2 - 1}$

In Exercises 53–78, graph the piecewise-defined functions. State the domain and range in interval notation. Determine the intervals where the function is increasing, decreasing, or constant.

53. $f(x) = \begin{cases} x & x < 2 \\ 2 & x \geq 2 \end{cases}$

54. $f(x) = \begin{cases} -x & x < -1 \\ -1 & x \geq -1 \end{cases}$

55. $f(x) = \begin{cases} 1 & x < -1 \\ x^2 & x \geq -1 \end{cases}$

56. $f(x) = \begin{cases} x^2 & x < 2 \\ 4 & x \geq 2 \end{cases}$

57. $f(x) = \begin{cases} x & x < 0 \\ x^2 & x \geq 0 \end{cases}$

58. $f(x) = \begin{cases} -x & x \leq 0 \\ x^2 & x > 0 \end{cases}$

59. $f(x) = \begin{cases} -x + 2 & x < 1 \\ x^2 & x \geq 1 \end{cases}$

60. $f(x) = \begin{cases} 2 + x & x \leq -1 \\ x^2 & x > -1 \end{cases}$

61. $f(x) = \begin{cases} 5 - 2x & x < 2 \\ 3x - 2 & x > 2 \end{cases}$

62. $f(x) = \begin{cases} 3 - \frac{1}{2}x & x < -2 \\ 4 + \frac{3}{2}x & x > -2 \end{cases}$

63. $G(x) = \begin{cases} -1 & x < -1 \\ x & -1 \leq x \leq 3 \\ 3 & x > 3 \end{cases}$

64. $G(x) = \begin{cases} -1 & x < -1 \\ x & -1 < x < 3 \\ 3 & x > 3 \end{cases}$

65. $G(t) = \begin{cases} 1 & t < 1 \\ t^2 & 1 \leq t \leq 2 \\ 4 & t > 2 \end{cases}$

66. $G(t) = \begin{cases} 1 & t < 1 \\ t^2 & 1 < t < 2 \\ 4 & t > 2 \end{cases}$

67. $f(x) = \begin{cases} -x - 1 & x < -2 \\ x + 1 & -2 < x < 1 \\ -x + 1 & x \geq 1 \end{cases}$

68. $f(x) = \begin{cases} -x - 1 & x \leq -2 \\ x + 1 & -2 < x < 1 \\ -x + 1 & x > 1 \end{cases}$

69. $G(x) = \begin{cases} 0 & x < 0 \\ \sqrt{x} & x \geq 0 \end{cases}$

70. $G(x) = \begin{cases} 1 & x < 1 \\ \sqrt[3]{x} & x > 1 \end{cases}$

71. $G(x) = \begin{cases} 0 & x = 0 \\ \frac{1}{x} & x \neq 0 \end{cases}$

72. $G(x) = \begin{cases} 0 & x = 0 \\ -\frac{1}{x} & x \neq 0 \end{cases}$

73. $G(x) = \begin{cases} -\sqrt[3]{x} & x \leq -1 \\ x & -1 < x < 1 \\ -\sqrt{x} & x > 1 \end{cases}$

74. $G(x) = \begin{cases} -\sqrt[3]{x} & x < -1 \\ x & -1 \leq x < 1 \\ \sqrt{x} & x > 1 \end{cases}$

75. $f(x) = \begin{cases} x + 3 & x \leq -2 \\ |x| & -2 < x < 2 \\ x^2 & x \geq 2 \end{cases}$

76. $f(x) = \begin{cases} |x| & x < -1 \\ 1 & -1 < x < 1 \\ |x| & x > 1 \end{cases}$

77. $f(x) = \begin{cases} x & x \leq -1 \\ x^3 & -1 < x < 1 \\ x^2 & x > 1 \end{cases}$

78. $f(x) = \begin{cases} x^2 & x \leq -1 \\ x^3 & -1 < x < 1 \\ x & x \geq 1 \end{cases}$

• APPLICATIONS

For Exercises 79 and 80, refer to the following:

A manufacturer determines that his *profit* and *cost* functions over one year are represented by the following graphs.

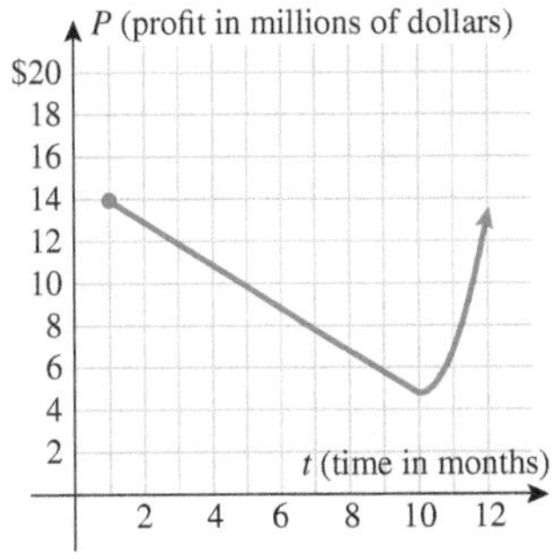

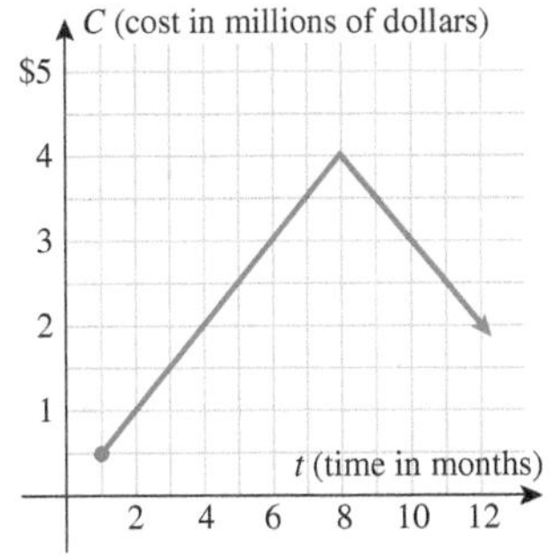

79. **Business.** Find the intervals on which profit is increasing, decreasing, and constant.

80. **Business.** Find the intervals on which cost is increasing, decreasing, and constant.

81. **Budget: Costs.** The Kappa Kappa Gamma sorority decides to order custom-made T-shirts for its *Kappa Krush* mixer with the Sigma Alpha Epsilon fraternity. If the sorority orders 50 or fewer T-shirts, the cost is \$10 per shirt. If it orders more than 50 but fewer than 100, the cost is \$9 per shirt. If it orders 100 or more, the cost is \$8 per shirt. Find the cost function $C(x)$ as a function of the number of T-shirts x ordered.

82. **Budget: Costs.** The marching band at a university is ordering some additional uniforms to replace existing uniforms that are worn out. If the band orders 50 or fewer, the cost is \$176.12 per uniform. If it orders more than 50 but fewer than 100, the cost is \$159.73 per uniform. Find the cost function $C(x)$ as a function of the number of new uniforms x ordered.

83. **Budget: Costs.** The Richmond rowing club is planning to enter the *Head of the Charles* race in Boston and is trying to figure out how much money to raise. The entry fee is \$250 per boat for the first 10 boats and \$175 for each additional boat. Find the cost function $C(x)$ as a function of the number of boats x the club enters.

84. **Phone Cost: Long-Distance Calling.** A phone company charges \$0.39 per minute for the first 10 minutes of an international long-distance phone call and \$0.12 per minute every minute after that. Find the cost function $C(x)$ as a function of the length of the phone call x in minutes.

85. **Sales.** A famous author negotiates with her publisher the monies she will receive for her next suspense novel. She will receive \$50,000 up front and a 15% royalty rate on the first 100,000 books sold, and 20% on any books sold beyond that. If the book sells for \$20 and royalties are based on the selling price, write a royalties function $R(x)$ as a function of total number x of books sold.

86. **Sales.** Rework Exercise 85 if the author receives \$35,000 up front, 15% for the first 100,000 books sold, and 25% on any books sold beyond that.

87. **Postage Rates.** The following table corresponds to first-class postage rates for the U.S. Postal Service. Write a piecewise-defined function in terms of the greatest integer function that models this cost of mailing flat envelopes first class.

WEIGHT LESS THAN (OUNCES)	FIRST-CLASS RATE (FLAT ENVELOPES)
1	\$0.98
2	1.20
3	1.42
4	1.64
5	1.86
6	2.08
7	2.30
8	2.52
9	2.74
10	2.96
11	3.18
12	3.40
13	3.62

88. Postage Rates. The following table corresponds to first-class postage rates for the U.S. Postal Service. Write a piecewise-defined function in terms of the greatest integer function that models this cost of mailing parcels first class.

WEIGHT LESS THAN (OUNCES)	PARCELS
1	\$2.14
2	2.34
3	2.54
4	2.74
5	2.94
6	3.14
7	3.34
8	3.54
9	3.74
10	3.94
11	4.14
12	4.34
13	4.54

For Exercises 89 and 90, refer to the following:

A square wave is a waveform used in electronic circuit testing and signal processing. A square wave alternates regularly and instantaneously between two levels.

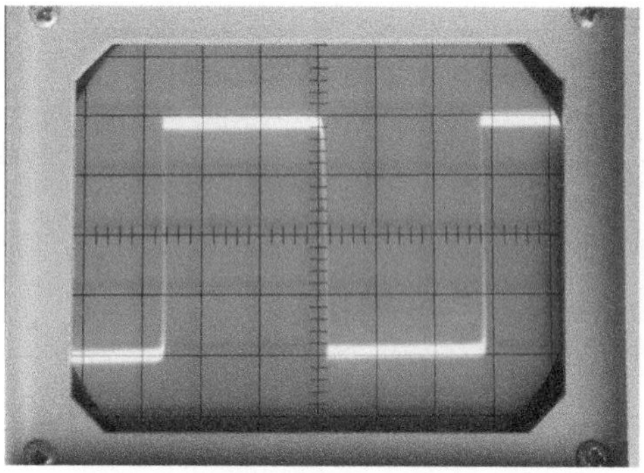

sciencephotos/ Alamy

89. Electronics: Signals. Write a step function $f(t)$ that represents the following square wave:

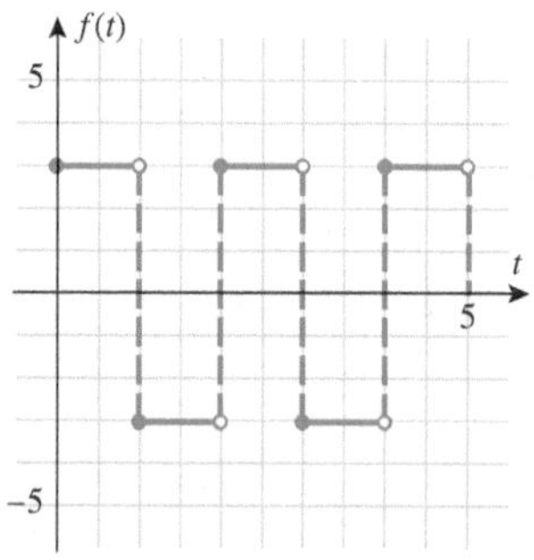

90. Electronics: Signals. Write a step function $f(x)$ that represents the following square wave, where x represents frequency in Hz:

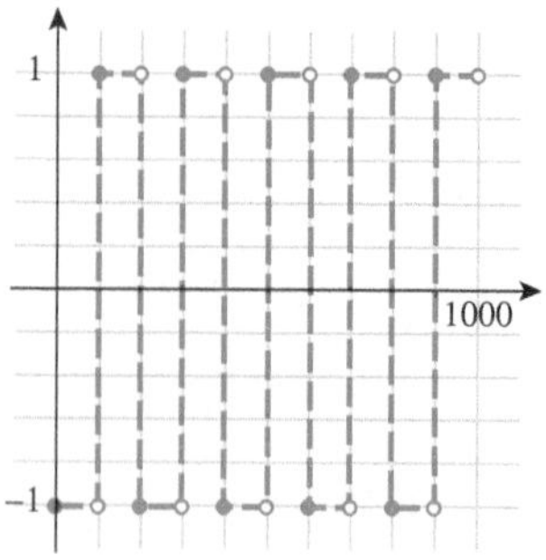

For Exercises 91 and 92, refer to the following table:

Global Carbon Emissions from Fossil Fuel Burning

YEAR	MILLIONS OF TONS OF CARBON
1900	500
1925	1000
1950	1500
1975	5000
2000	7000

91. Climate Change: Global Warming. What is the average rate of change in global carbon emissions from fossil fuel burning from

a. 1900 to 1950? **b.** 1950 to 2000?

92. Climate Change: Global Warming. What is the average rate of change in global carbon emissions from fossil fuel burning from

a. 1950 to 1975? **b.** 1975 to 2000?

For Exercises 93 and 94, use the following information:

The height (in feet) of a falling object with an initial velocity of 48 feet per second launched straight upward from the ground is given by $h(t) = -16t^2 + 48t$, where t is time (in seconds).

93. Falling Objects. What is the average rate of change of the height as a function of time from $t = 1$ to $t = 2$?

94. Falling Objects. What is the average rate of change of the height as a function of time from $t = 1$ to $t = 3$?

For Exercises 95 and 96, refer to the following:

An analysis of sales indicates that demand for a product during a calendar year (no leap year) is modeled by

$$d(t) = 3\sqrt{t^2 + 1} - 2.75t$$

where d is demand in thousands of units and t is the day of the year and $t = 1$ represents January 1.

95. Economics. Find the average rate of change of the demand for of the product over the first quarter.

96. Economics. Find the average rate of change of the demand for of the product over the fourth quarter.

• CATCH THE MISTAKE

In Exercises 97 and 98, explain the mistake that is made.

97. The cost of airport Internet access is \$15 for the first 30 minutes and \$1 per minute for each additional minute. Write a function describing the cost of the service as a function of minutes used online.

Solution: $C(x) = \begin{cases} 15 & x \le 30 \\ 15 + x & x > 30 \end{cases}$

This is incorrect. What mistake was made?

98. Most money market accounts pay a higher interest with a higher principal. If the credit union is offering 2% on accounts with less than or equal to \$10,000 and 4% on the additional money over \$10,000, write the interest function $I(x)$ that represents the interest earned on an account as a function of dollars in the account.

Solution: $I(x) = \begin{cases} 0.02x & x \le 10{,}000 \\ 0.02(10{,}000) + 0.04x & x > 10{,}000 \end{cases}$

This is incorrect. What mistake was made?

• CONCEPTUAL

In Exercises 99 and 100, determine whether each statement is true or false.

99. If an odd function has an interval where the function is increasing, then it also has to have an interval where the function is decreasing.

100. If an even function has an interval where the function is increasing, then it also has to have an interval where the function is decreasing.

In Exercises 101 and 102, for *a* and *b* real numbers, can the function given ever be a continuous function? If so, specify the value for *a* and *b* that would make it so.

101. $f(x) = \begin{cases} ax & x \le 2 \\ bx^2 & x > 2 \end{cases}$

102. $f(x) = \begin{cases} -\dfrac{1}{x} & x < a \\ \dfrac{1}{x} & x \ge a \end{cases}$

• CHALLENGE

In Exercises 103 and 104, find the values of *a* and *b* that make *f* continuous.

103. $f(x) = \begin{cases} -x^2 - 10x - 13 & x \le -2 \\ ax + b & -2 < x < 1 \\ \sqrt{x - 1} - 9 & x \ge 1 \end{cases}$

104. $f(x) = \begin{cases} -2x - a + 2b & x \le -2 \\ \sqrt{x + a} & -2 < x \le 2 \\ x^2 - 4x + a + 4 & x > 2 \end{cases}$

• PREVIEW TO CALCULUS

For Exercises 105–108, refer to the following:

In calculus, the difference quotient $\dfrac{f(x+h) - f(x)}{h}$ of a function f is used to find the derivative f' of f, by allowing h to approach zero, $h \to 0$. Find the derivative of the following functions.

105. $f(x) = k$, where k is a constant

106. $f(x) = mx + b$, where m and b are constants, $m \ne 0$

107. $f(x) = ax^2 + bx + c$, where a, b, and c are constants, $a \ne 0$

108. $f(x) = \begin{cases} 7 & x < 0 \\ 2 - 3x & 0 < x < 4 \\ x^2 + 4x - 6 & x > 4 \end{cases}$

1.3 GRAPHING TECHNIQUES: TRANSFORMATIONS

SKILLS OBJECTIVES

- Sketch the graph of a function using horizontal or vertical shifting of common functions.
- Sketch the graph of a function by reflecting a common function about the x-axis or the y-axis.
- Sketch the graph of a function by stretching or compressing a common function.

CONCEPTUAL OBJECTIVES

- Understand why a shift in the argument inside the function corresponds to a horizontal shift, and a shift outside the function corresponds to a vertical shift.
- Understand why a "negative" argument inside the function corresponds to a reflection about the y-axis, and a negative argument outside the function corresponds to a reflection about the x-axis.
- Understand the difference between rigid and nonrigid transformations.

1.3.1 Horizontal and Vertical Shifts

1.3.1 SKILL

Sketch the graph of a function using horizontal or vertical shifting of common functions.

1.3.1 CONCEPTUAL

Understand why a shift in the argument inside the function corresponds to a horizontal shift, and a shift outside the function corresponds to a vertical shift.

The focus of the previous section was to learn the graphs that correspond to particular functions such as identity, square, cube, square root, cube root, absolute value, and reciprocal. Therefore, at this point, you should be able to recognize and generate the graphs of $y = x$, $y = x^2$, $y = x^3$, $y = \sqrt{x}$, $y = \sqrt[3]{x}$, $y = |x|$, and $y = \frac{1}{x}$. In this section, we will discuss how to sketch the graphs of functions that are very simple modifications of these functions. For instance, a common function may be shifted (horizontally or vertically), reflected, or stretched (or compressed). Collectively, these techniques are called **transformations**.

Let's take the absolute value function as an example. The graphs of $f(x) = |x|$, $g(x) = |x| + 2$, and $h(x) = |x - 1|$ are shown below.

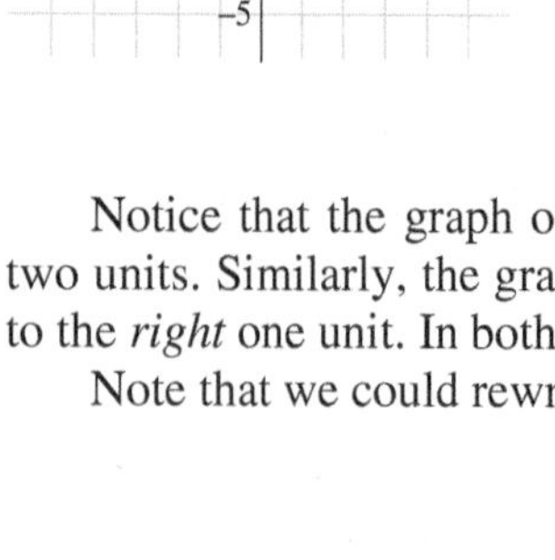

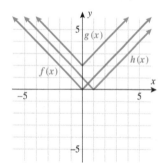

x	$f(x)$
−2	2
−1	1
0	0
1	1
2	2

x	$g(x)$
−2	4
−1	3
0	2
1	3
2	4

x	$h(x)$
−2	3
−1	2
0	1
1	0
2	1

Notice that the graph of $g(x) = |x| + 2$ is the graph of $f(x) = |x|$ shifted *up* two units. Similarly, the graph of $h(x) = |x - 1|$ is the graph of $f(x) = |x|$ shifted to the *right* one unit. In both cases, the base or starting function is $f(x) = |x|$.

Note that we could rewrite the functions $g(x)$ and $h(x)$ in terms of $f(x)$:

$$g(x) = |x| + 2 = f(x) + 2$$

$$h(x) = |x - 1| = f(x - 1)$$

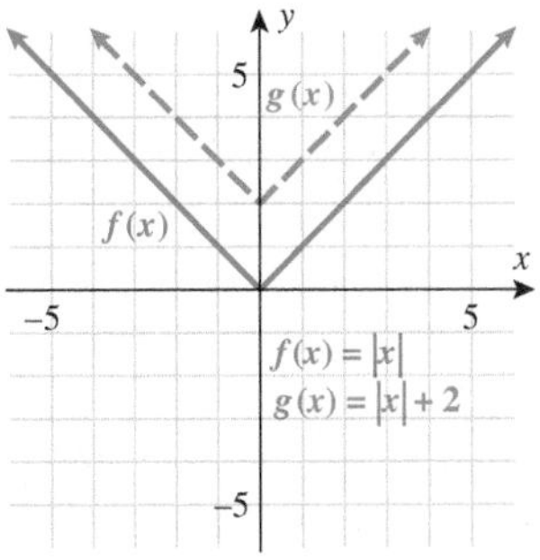

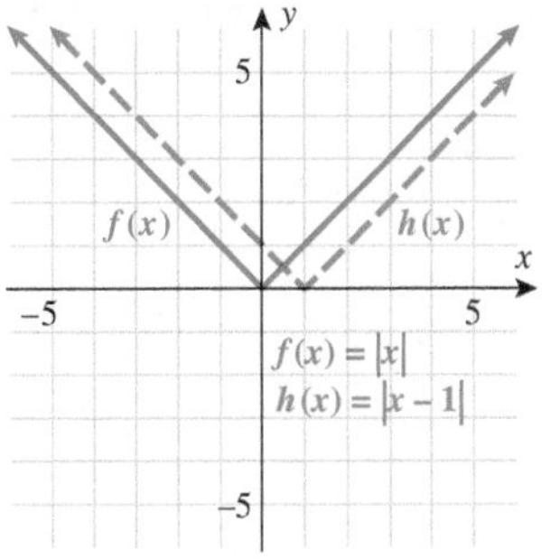

In the case of $g(x)$, the shift $(+2)$ occurs "outside" the function—that is, outside the parentheses showing the argument. Therefore, the output for $g(x)$ is 2 more than the typical output for $f(x)$. Because the output corresponds to the vertical axis, this results in a shift *upward* of two units. In general, shifts that occur *outside* the function correspond to a *vertical* shift corresponding to the sign of the shift. For instance, had the function been $G(x) = |x| - 2$, this graph would have started with the graph of the function $f(x)$ and shifted down two units.

In the case of $h(x)$, the shift occurs "inside" the function—that is, inside the parentheses showing the argument. Note that the point $(0, 0)$ that lies on the graph of $f(x)$ was shifted to the point $(1, 0)$ on the graph of the function $h(x)$. The y-value remained the same, but the x-value shifted to the right one unit. Similarly, the points $(-1, 1)$ and $(1, 1)$ were shifted to the points $(0, 1)$ and $(2, 1)$, respectively. In general, shifts that occur *inside* the function correspond to a *horizontal* shift opposite the sign. In this case, the graph of the function $h(x) = |x - 1|$ shifted the graph of the function $f(x)$ to the right one unit. If, instead, we had the function $H(x) = |x + 1|$, this graph would have started with the graph of the function $f(x)$ and shifted to the left one unit.

VERTICAL SHIFTS

Assuming that c is a positive constant,

To Graph	Shift the Graph of $f(x)$
$f(x) + c$	c units upward
$f(x) - c$	c units downward

Adding or subtracting a constant **outside** the function corresponds to a **vertical** shift that goes **with the sign.**

STUDY TIP

- Shifts *outside* the function are *vertical* shifts with the sign.
- Shifts *inside* the function are *horizontal* shifts opposite the sign.

HORIZONTAL SHIFTS

Assuming that c is a positive constant,

To Graph	Shift the Graph of $f(x)$
$f(x + c)$	c units to the left
$f(x - c)$	c units to the right

Adding or subtracting a constant **inside** the function corresponds to a **horizontal** shift that goes **opposite the sign.**

EXAMPLE 1 Horizontal and Vertical Shifts

Sketch the graphs of the given functions using horizontal and vertical shifts.

a. $g(x) = x^2 - 1$

b. $H(x) = (x + 1)^2$

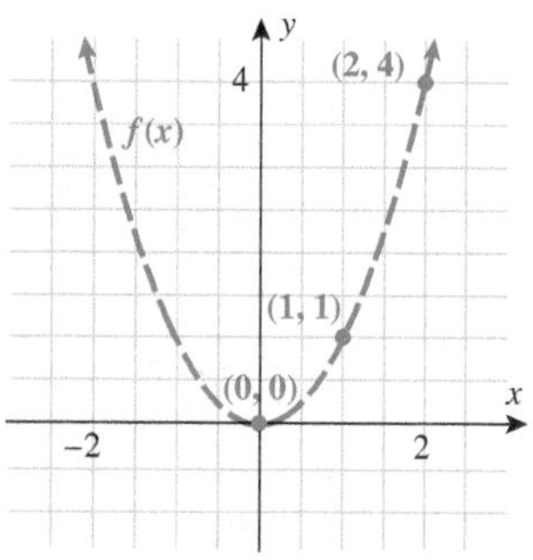

Solution:

In both cases, the function to start with is $f(x) = x^2$.

a. $g(x) = x^2 - 1$ can be rewritten as $g(x) = f(x) - 1$.

1. The shift (one unit) occurs *outside* the function. Therefore, we expect a vertical shift that goes with the sign.
2. Since the sign is *negative*, this corresponds to a *downward* shift.
3. Shifting the graph of the function $f(x) = x^2$ down one unit yields the graph of $g(x) = x^2 - 1$.

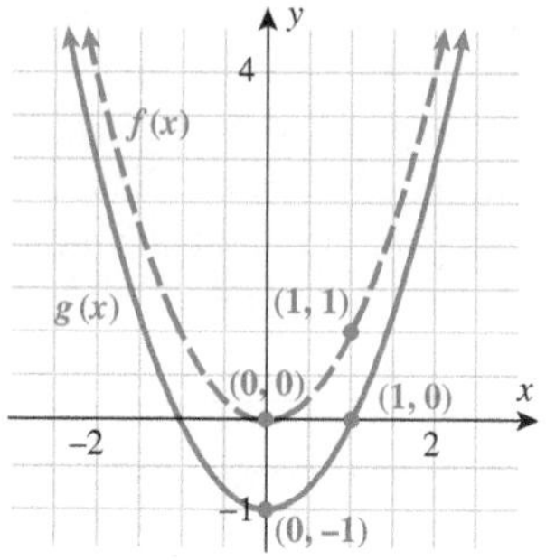

b. $H(x) = (x + 1)^2$ can be rewritten as $H(x) = f(x + 1)$.

1. The shift (one unit) occurs *inside* the function. Therefore, we expect a horizontal shift that goes *opposite* the sign.
2. Since the sign is *positive*, this corresponds to a shift to the *left*.
3. Shifting the graph of the function $f(x) = x^2$ to the left one unit yields the graph of $H(x) = (x + 1)^2$.

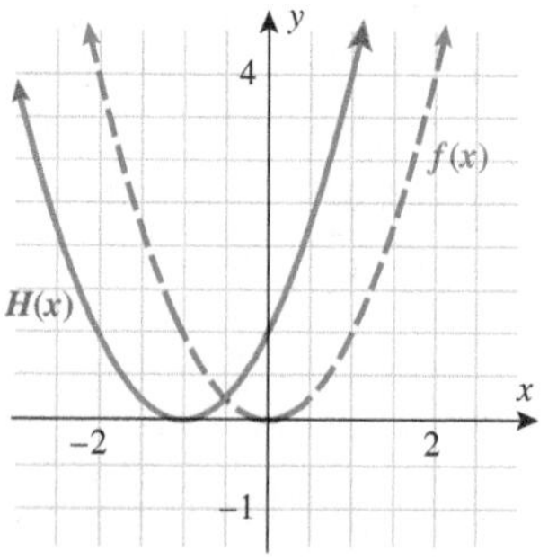

YOUR TURN Sketch the graphs of the given functions using horizontal and vertical shifts.

a. $g(x) = x^2 + 1$ **b.** $H(x) = (x - 1)^2$

ANSWER

a.

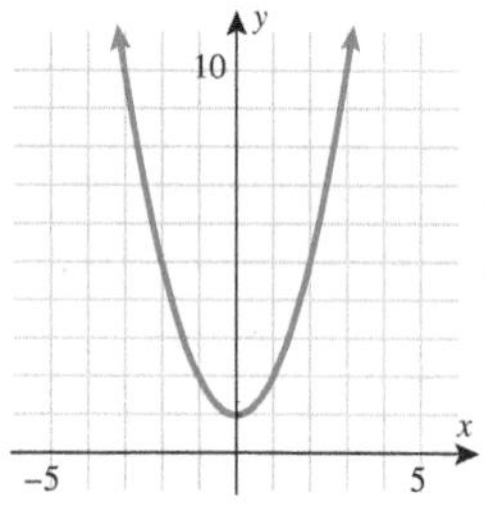

b.

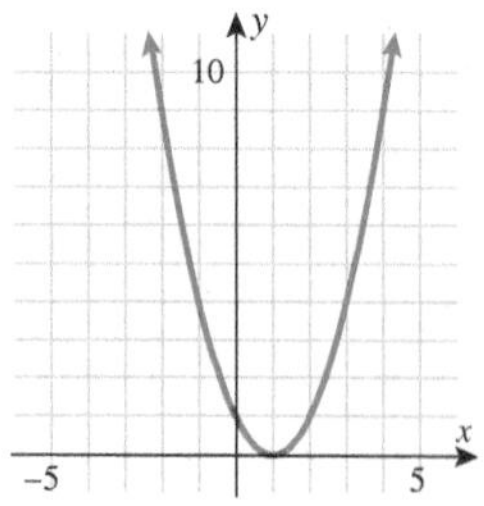

It is important to note that the domain and range of the resulting function can be thought of as also being shifted. Shifts in the domain correspond to horizontal shifts, and shifts in the range correspond to vertical shifts.

EXAMPLE 2 Horizontal and Vertical Shifts and Changes in the Domain and Range

Graph the functions using translations, and state the domain and range of each function.

a. $g(x) = \sqrt{x+1}$

b. $G(x) = \sqrt{x} - 2$

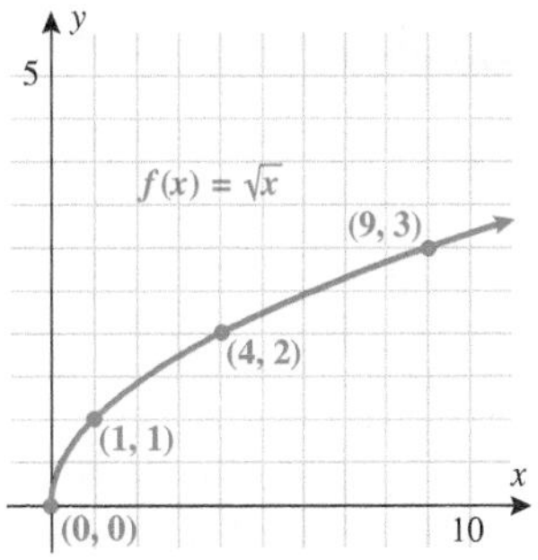

Solution:

In both cases the function to start with is $f(x) = \sqrt{x}$.

Domain: $[0, \infty)$

Range: $[0, \infty)$

a. $g(x) = \sqrt{x+1}$ can be rewritten as $g(x) = f(x+1)$.

1. The shift (one unit) is *inside* the function, which corresponds to a *horizontal* shift *opposite the sign.*
2. Shifting the graph of $f(x) = \sqrt{x}$ to the *left* one unit yields the graph of $g(x) = \sqrt{x+1}$. Notice that the point $(0, 0)$, which lies on the graph of $f(x)$, gets shifted to the point $(-1, 0)$ on the graph of $g(x)$.

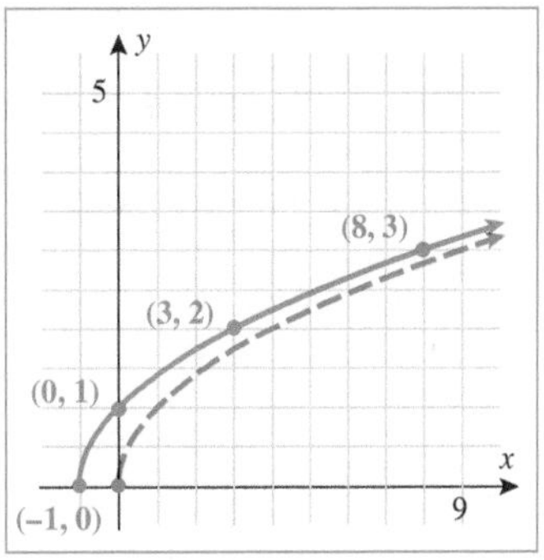

Although the original function $f(x) = \sqrt{x}$ had an implicit restriction on the domain $[0, \infty)$, the function $g(x) = \sqrt{x+1}$ has the implicit restriction that $x \geq -1$. We see that the output or range of $g(x)$ is the same as the output of the original function $f(x)$.

Domain: $[-1, \infty)$ **Range:** $[0, \infty)$

b. $G(x) = \sqrt{x} - 2$ can be rewritten as $G(x) = f(x) - 2$.

1. The shift (two units) is *outside* the function, which corresponds to a *vertical* shift *with the sign.*
2. The graph of $G(x) = \sqrt{x} - 2$ is found by shifting $f(x) = \sqrt{x}$ down two units. Note that the point $(0, 0)$, which lies on the graph of $f(x)$, gets shifted to the point $(0, -2)$ on the graph of $G(x)$.

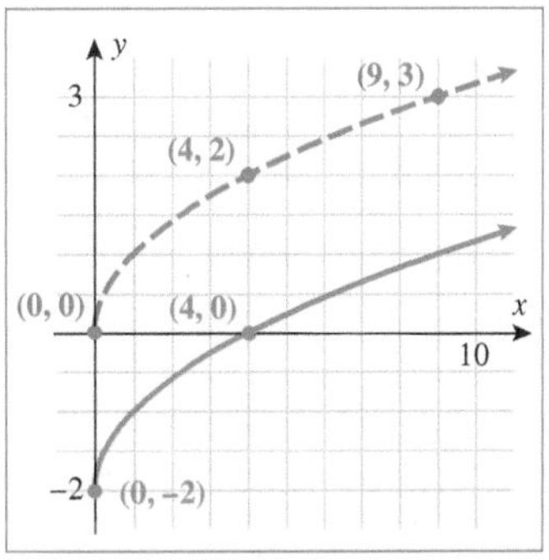

The original function $f(x) = \sqrt{x}$ has an implicit restriction on the domain: $[0, \infty)$. The function $G(x) = \sqrt{x} - 2$ also has the implicit restriction that $x \geq 0$. The output or range of $G(x)$ is always two units less than the output of the original function $f(x)$.

Domain: $[0, \infty)$ **Range:** $[-2, \infty)$

YOUR TURN Sketch the graph of the functions using shifts, and state the domain and range.

a. $G(x) = \sqrt{x-2}$ **b.** $h(x) = |x| + 1$

[CONCEPT CHECK]

For the functions $F(x) = \sqrt{x-a}$ and $G(x) = \sqrt{x} - a$, where $a > 0$ explain the shifts on $y = \sqrt{x}$.

ANSWER $F(x)$ is shifted a units to the right. $G(x)$ is shifted a units down.

ANSWER

a. $G(x) = \sqrt{x-2}$

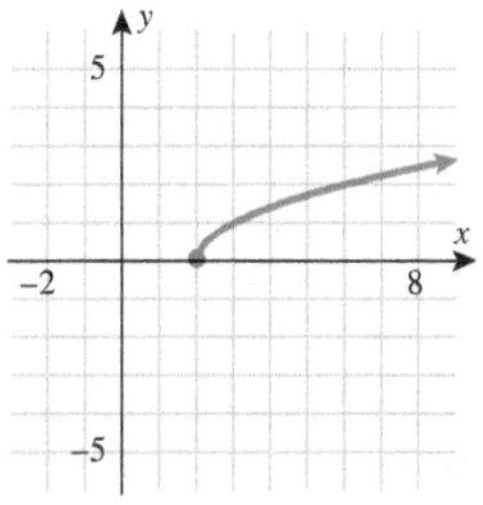

Domain: $[2, \infty)$ Range: $[0, \infty)$

b. $h(x) = |x| + 1$

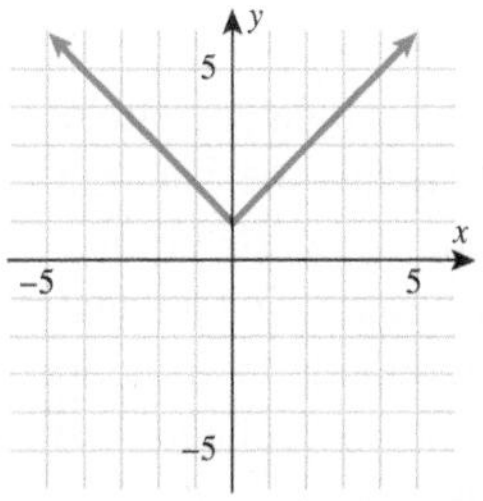

Domain: $(-\infty, \infty)$ Range: $[1, \infty)$

The previous examples have involved graphing functions by shifting a known function either in the horizontal or vertical direction. Let us now look at combinations of horizontal and vertical shifts.

EXAMPLE 3 Combining Horizontal and Vertical Shifts

Sketch the graph of the function $F(x) = (x + 1)^2 - 2$. State the domain and range of F.

Solution:

The base function is $y = x^2$.

1. The shift (one unit) is *inside* the function, so it represents a *horizontal* shift *opposite the sign.*
2. The -2 shift is *outside* the function, which represents a *vertical* shift *with the sign.*
3. Therefore, we shift the graph of $y = x^2$ to the left one unit and down two units. For instance, the point $(0, 0)$ on the graph of $y = x^2$ shifts to the point $(-1, -2)$ on the graph of $F(x) = (x + 1)^2 - 2$.

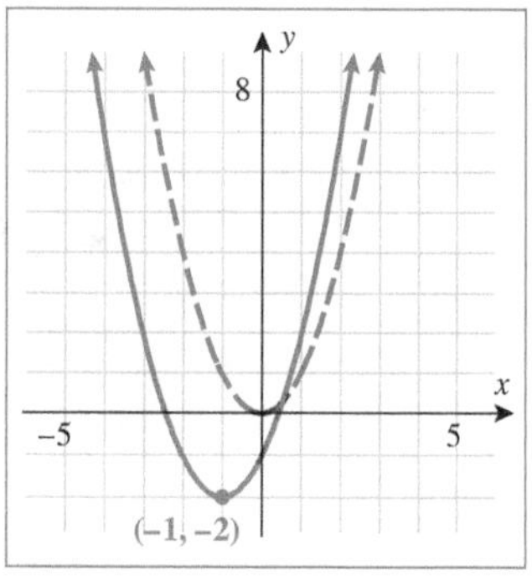

Domain: $(-\infty, \infty)$	Range: $[-2, \infty)$

YOUR TURN Sketch the graph of the function $f(x) = |x - 2| + 1$. State the domain and range of f.

ANSWER

$f(x) = |x - 2| + 1$

$f(x) = |x|$

Domain: $(-\infty, \infty)$

Range: $[1, \infty)$

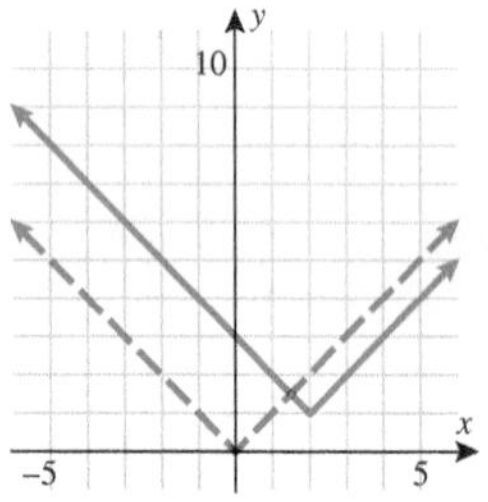

All of the previous transformation examples involve starting with a common function and shifting the function in either the horizontal or the vertical direction (or a combination of both). Now, let's investigate *reflections* of functions about the x-axis or y-axis.

1.3.2 Reflection about the Axes

1.3.2 SKILL

Sketch the graph of a function by reflecting a common function about the x-axis or the y-axis.

1.3.2 CONCEPTUAL

Understand why a "negative" argument inside the function corresponds to a reflection about the y-axis, and a negative argument outside the function corresponds to a reflection about the x-axis.

To sketch the graphs of $f(x) = x^2$ and $g(x) = -x^2$, start by first listing points that are on each of the graphs and then connecting the points with smooth curves.

x	$f(x)$
-2	4
-1	1
0	0
1	1
2	4

x	$g(x)$
-2	-4
-1	-1
0	0
1	-1
2	-4

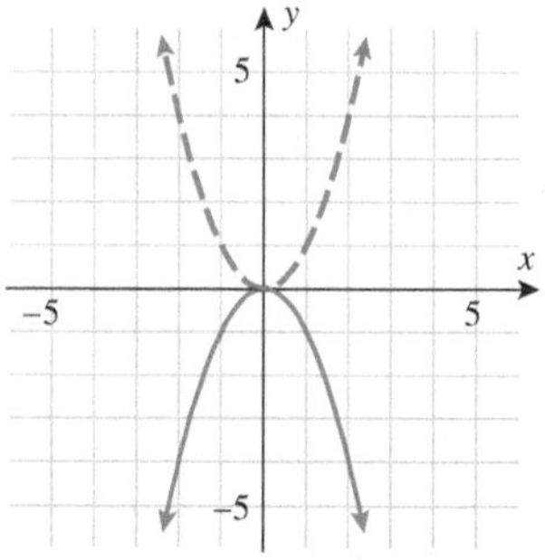

Note that if the graph of $f(x) = x^2$ is reflected about the x-axis, the result is the graph of $g(x) = -x^2$. Also note that the function $g(x)$ can be written as the negative of the function $f(x)$; that is $g(x) = -f(x)$. In general, **reflection about the x-axis** is produced by multiplying a function by -1.

Let's now investigate reflection about the y-axis. To sketch the graphs of $f(x) = \sqrt{x}$ and $g(x) = \sqrt{-x}$, start by listing points that are on each of the graphs and then connecting the points with smooth curves.

x	$f(x)$
0	0
1	1
4	2
9	3

x	$g(x)$
−9	3
−4	2
−1	1
0	0

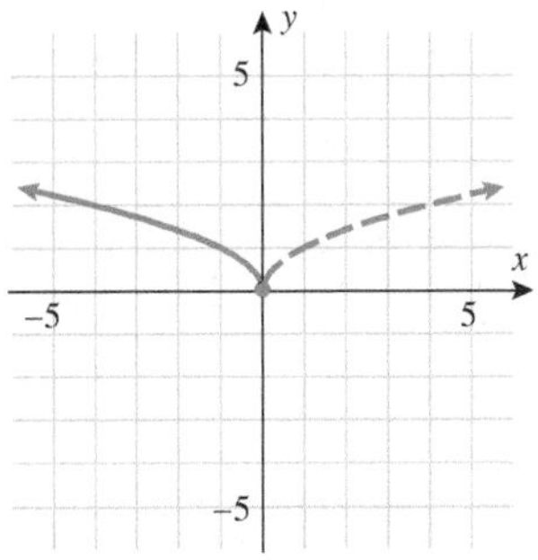

Note that if the graph of $f(x) = \sqrt{x}$ is reflected about the y-axis, the result is the graph of $g(x) = \sqrt{-x}$. Also note that the function $g(x)$ can be written as $g(x) = f(-x)$. In general, **reflection about the *y*-axis** is produced by replacing x with $-x$ in the function. Notice that the domain of f is $[0, \infty)$, whereas the domain of g is $(-\infty, 0]$.

REFLECTION ABOUT THE AXES

The graph of $-f(x)$ is obtained by reflecting the graph of $f(x)$ about the **x-axis**.
The graph of $f(-x)$ is obtained by reflecting the graph of $f(x)$ about the **y-axis**.

EXAMPLE 4 Sketching the Graph of a Function Using Both Shifts and Reflections

Sketch the graph of the function $G(x) = -\sqrt{x+1}$.

Solution:

Start with the square root function. $f(x) = \sqrt{x}$

Shift the graph of $f(x)$ to the left one unit to arrive at the graph of $f(x+1)$. $f(x+1) = \sqrt{x+1}$

Reflect the graph of $f(x+1)$ about the x-axis to arrive at the graph of $-f(x+1)$. $-f(x+1) = -\sqrt{x+1}$

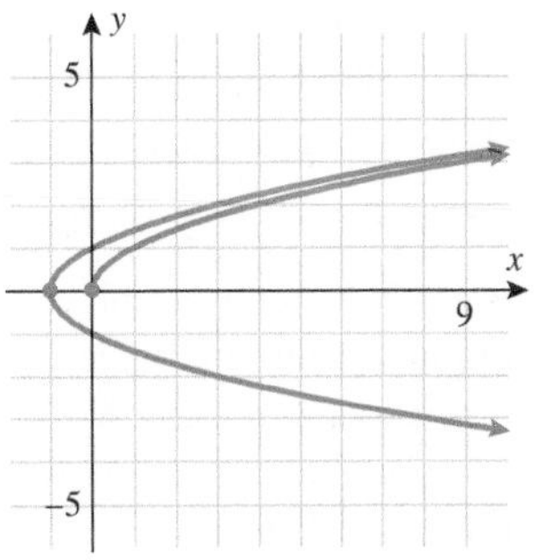

[CONCEPT CHECK]

For any even function $f(x)$, describe the graph of $f(-x)$

ANSWER The graph of $f(-x)$ is the same as the graph of $f(x)$ because for even functions, $f(-x) = f(x)$.

EXAMPLE 5 Sketching the Graph of a Function Using Both Shifts and Reflections

Sketch the graph of the function $f(x) = \sqrt{2 - x} + 1$.

Solution:

Start with the square root function.	$g(x) = \sqrt{x}$
Shift the graph of $g(x)$ to the left two units to arrive at the graph of $g(x + 2)$.	$g(x + 2) = \sqrt{x + 2}$
Reflect the graph of $g(x + 2)$ about the y-axis to arrive at the graph of $g(-x + 2)$.	$g(-x + 2) = \sqrt{-x + 2}$
Shift the graph $g(-x + 2)$ up one unit to arrive at the graph of $g(-x + 2) + 1$.	$g(-x + 2) + 1 = \sqrt{2 - x} + 1$

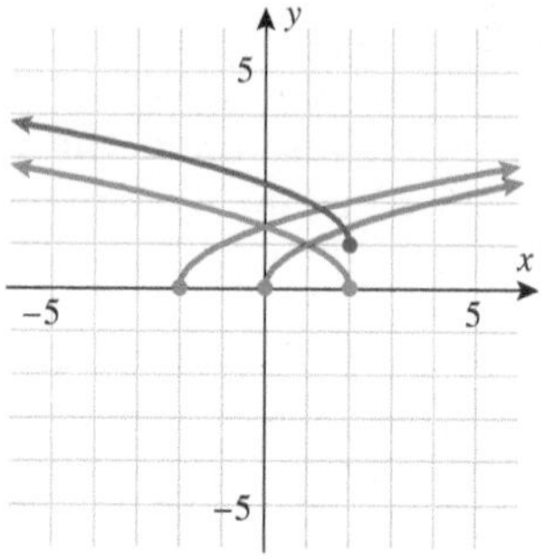

YOUR TURN Use shifts and reflections to sketch the graph of the function $f(x) = -\sqrt{x - 1} + 2$. State the domain and range of $f(x)$.

ANSWER

Domain: $[1, \infty)$

Range: $(-\infty, 2]$

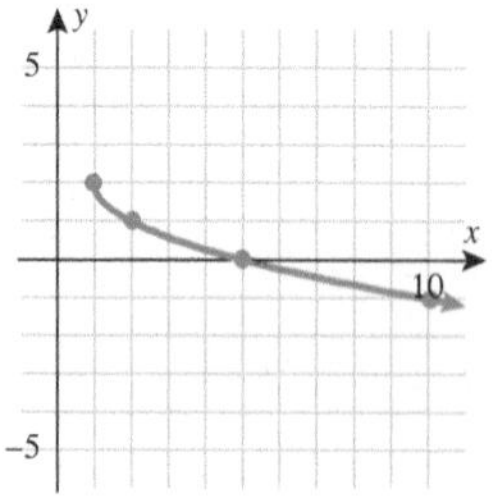

Look back at the order in which transformations were performed in Example 5: horizontal shift, reflection, and then vertical shift. Let's consider an alternative order of transformations.

WORDS	MATH
Start with the square root function.	$g(x) = \sqrt{x}$
Shift the graph of $g(x)$ up one unit to arrive at the graph of $g(x) + 1$.	$g(x) + 1 = \sqrt{x} + 1$
Reflect the graph of $g(x) + 1$ about the y-axis to arrive at the graph of $g(-x) + 1$.	$g(-x) + 1 = \sqrt{-x} + 1$
Replace x with $x - 2$, which corresponds to a shift of the graph of $g(-x) + 1$ to the right two units to arrive at the graph of $g[-(x - 2)] + 1$.	$g(-x + 2) + 1 = \sqrt{2 - x} + 1$

In the last step we replaced x with $x - 2$, which required us to think ahead, knowing the desired result was $2 - x$ inside the radical. To avoid any possible confusion, follow this order of transformations:

1. Horizontal shifts: $f(x \pm c)$
2. Reflection: $f(-x)$ and/or $-f(x)$
3. Vertical shifts: $f(x) \pm c$

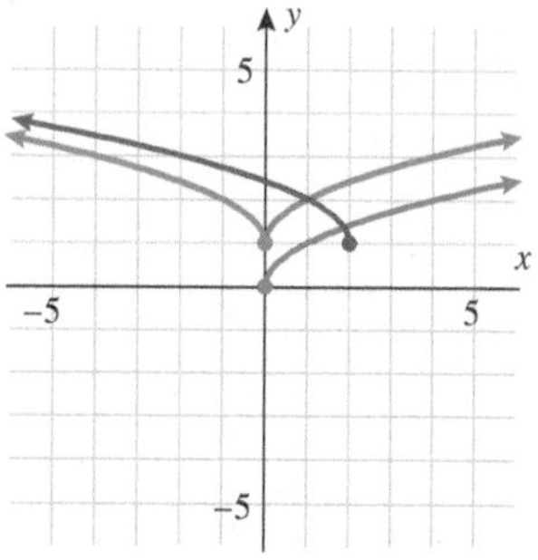

1.3.3 Stretching and Compressing

1.3.3 SKILL

Sketch the graph of a function by stretching or compressing a common function.

1.3.3 CONCEPTUAL

Understand the difference between rigid and nonrigid transformations.

Horizontal shifts, vertical shifts, and reflections change only the position of the graph in the Cartesian plane, leaving the basic shape of the graph unchanged. These transformations (shifts and reflections) are called **rigid transformations** because they alter only the *position*. **Nonrigid transformations**, on the other hand, distort the *shape* of the original graph. We now consider *stretching* and *compressing* of graphs in both the vertical and the horizontal direction.

A vertical stretch or compression of a graph occurs when the function is multiplied by a positive constant. For example, the graphs of the functions $f(x) = x^2$, $g(x) = 2f(x) = 2x^2$, and $h(x) = \frac{1}{2}f(x) = \frac{1}{2}x^2$ are illustrated below. Whether the constant is larger than 1 or smaller than 1 will determine whether it corresponds to a stretch (expansion) or a compression (contraction) in the vertical direction.

x	$f(x)$
-2	4
-1	1
0	0
1	1
2	4

x	$g(x)$
-2	8
-1	2
0	0
1	2
2	8

x	$h(x)$
-2	2
-1	$\frac{1}{2}$
0	0
1	$\frac{1}{2}$
2	2

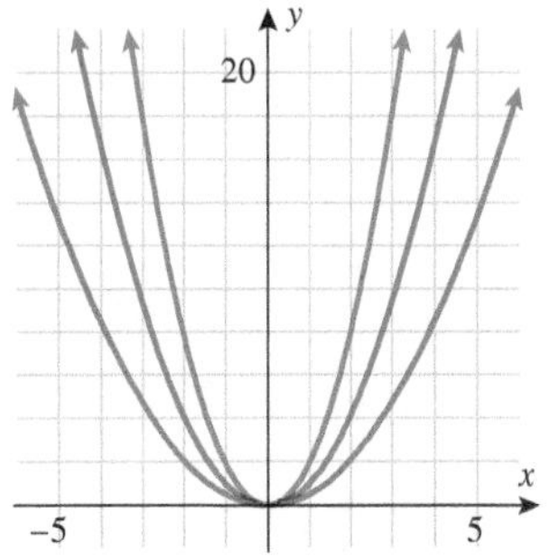

Note that when the function $f(x) = x^2$ is multiplied by 2, so that $g(x) = 2f(x) = 2x^2$, the result is a graph stretched in the vertical direction. When the function $f(x) = x^2$ is multiplied by $\frac{1}{2}$, so that $h(x) = \frac{1}{2}f(x) = \frac{1}{2}x^2$, the result is a graph that is compressed in the vertical direction.

VERTICAL STRETCHING AND VERTICAL COMPRESSING OF GRAPHS

The graph of $cf(x)$ is found by:

- **Vertically stretching** the graph of $f(x)$ if $c > 1$
- **Vertically compressing** the graph of $f(x)$ if $0 < c < 1$

Note: c is any positive real number.

EXAMPLE 6 **Vertically Stretching and Compressing Graphs**

Graph the function $h(x) = \frac{1}{4}x^3$.

Solution:

1. Start with the cube function. $f(x) = x^3$

2. Vertical compression is expected because $\frac{1}{4}$ is less than 1. $h(x) = \frac{1}{4}x^3$

3. Determine a few points that lie on the graph of h.

(0, 0) (2, 2) (−2, −2)

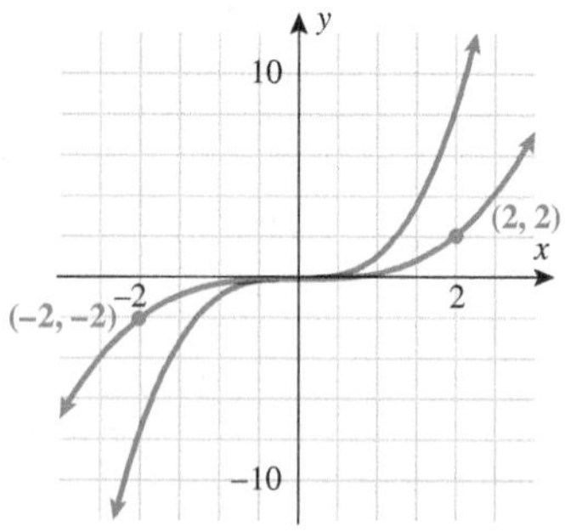

Conversely, if the argument x of a function f is multiplied by a positive real number c, then the result is a *horizontal* stretch of the graph of f if $0 < c < 1$. If $c > 1$, then the result is a *horizontal* compression of the graph of f.

[CONCEPT CHECK]

Describe where the graphs of $f(x)$ and $a \cdot f(x)$ intersect.

ANSWER Only at the points when $f(x) = 0$ (x-intercepts)

HORIZONTAL STRETCHING AND HORIZONTAL COMPRESSING OF GRAPHS

The graph of $f(cx)$ is found by:

- **Horizontally stretching** the graph of $f(x)$ if $0 < c < 1$
- **Horizontally compressing** the graph of $f(x)$ if $c > 1$

Note: c is any positive real number.

EXAMPLE 7 **Vertically Stretching and Horizontally Compressing Graphs**

Given the graph of $f(x)$, graph

a. $2f(x)$ **b.** $f(2x)$

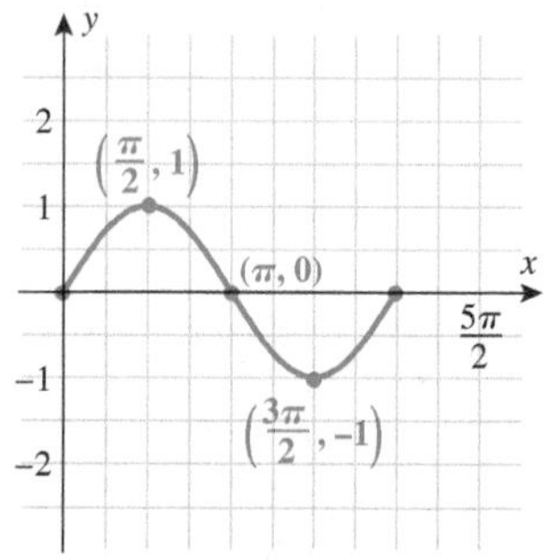

Solution (a):

Since the function is multiplied (on the outside) by 2, the result is that each **y-value** of $f(x)$ is ***multiplied* by 2**, which corresponds to vertical stretching.

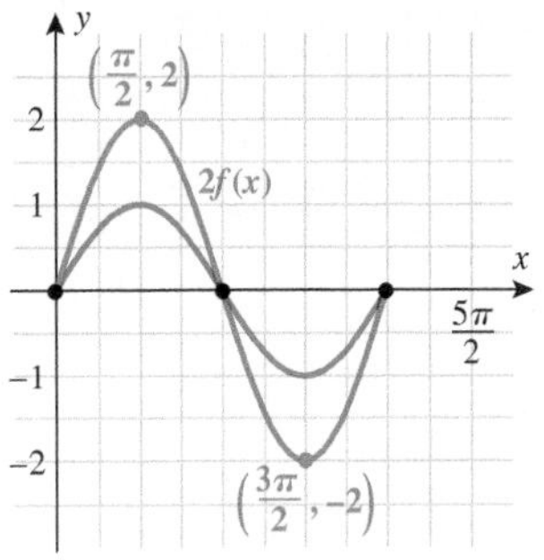

Solution (b):

Since the argument of the function is multiplied (on the inside) by 2, the result is that each **x-value** of $f(x)$ is **divided by 2**, which corresponds to horizontal compression.

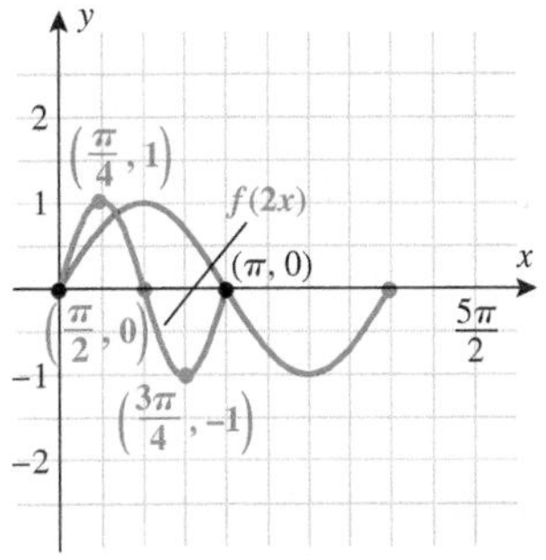

YOUR TURN Graph the function $g(x) = 4x^3$.

ANSWER

Vertical stretch of the graph $f(x) = x^3$.

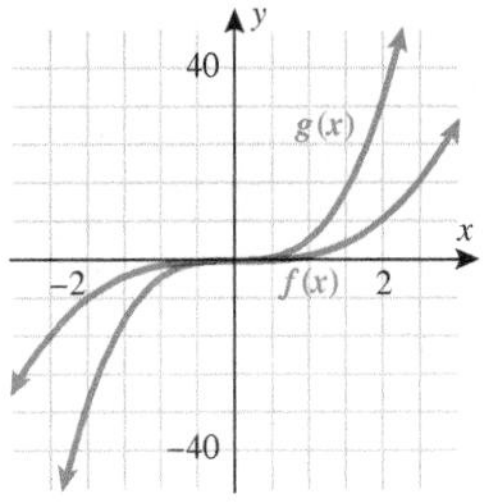

▶ EXAMPLE 8 Sketching the Graph of a Function Using Multiple Transformations

Sketch the graph of the function $H(x) = -2(x - 3)^2$.

Solution:

Start with the square function.	$f(x) = x^2$
Shift the graph of $f(x)$ to the right three units to arrive at the graph of $f(x - 3)$.	$f(x - 3) = (x - 3)^2$
Vertically stretch the graph of $f(x - 3)$ by a factor of 2 to arrive at the graph of $2f(x - 3)$.	$2f(x - 3) = 2(x - 3)^2$
Reflect the graph $2f(x - 3)$ about the x-axis to arrive at the graph of $-2f(x - 3)$.	$-2f(x - 3) = -2(x - 3)^2$

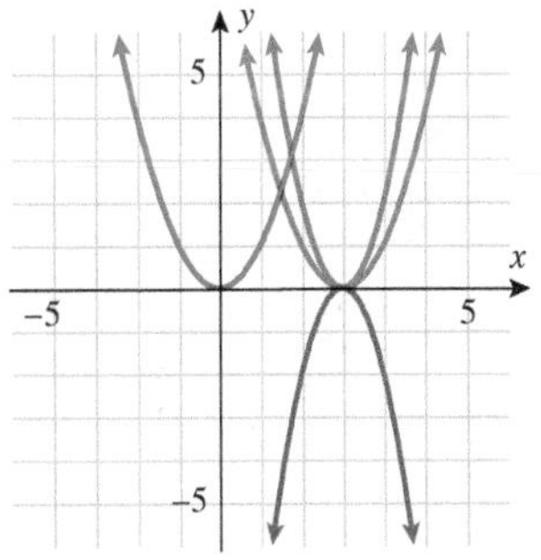

In Example 8 we followed the same "inside out" approach with the functions to determine the order for the transformations: horizontal shift, vertical stretch, and reflection.

[SECTION 1.3] SUMMARY

TRANSFORMATION	TO GRAPH THE FUNCTION...	DRAW THE GRAPH OF *f* AND THEN...	DESCRIPTION
Horizontal shift ($c > 0$)	$f(x + c)$ $f(x - c)$	Shift the graph of f to the left c units. Shift the graph of f to the right c units.	Replace x by $x + c$. Replace x by $x - c$.
Vertical shift ($c > 0$)	$f(x) + c$ $f(x) - c$	Shift the graph of f up c units. Shift the graph of f down c units.	Add c to $f(x)$. Subtract c from $f(x)$.
Reflection about the x-axis	$-f(x)$	Reflect the graph of f about the x-axis.	Multiply $f(x)$ by -1.
Reflection about the y-axis	$f(-x)$	Reflect the graph of f about the y-axis.	Replace x by $-x$.
Vertical stretch	$cf(x)$, where $c > 1$	Vertically stretch the graph of f.	Multiply $f(x)$ by c.
Vertical compression	$cf(x)$, where $0 < c < 1$	Vertically compress the graph of f.	Multiply $f(x)$ by c.
Horizontal stretch	$f(cx)$, where $0 < c < 1$	Horizontally stretch the graph of f.	Replace x by cx.
Horizontal compression	$f(cx)$, where $c > 1$	Horizontally compress the graph of f.	Replace x by cx.

[SECTION 1.3] EXERCISES

• SKILLS

In Exercises 1–6, write the function whose graph is the graph of $y = |x|$, but is transformed accordingly.

1. Shifted up three units
2. Shifted to the left four units
3. Reflected about the y-axis
4. Reflected about the x-axis
5. Vertically stretched by a factor of 3
6. Vertically compressed by a factor of 3

In Exercises 7–12, write the function whose graph is the graph of $y = x^3$, but is transformed accordingly.

7. Shifted down four units
8. Shifted to the right three units
9. Shifted up three units and to the left one unit
10. Reflected about the x-axis
11. Reflected about the y-axis
12. Reflected about both the x-axis and the y-axis

In Exercises 13–28, use the given graph to sketch the graph of the indicated functions.

13.

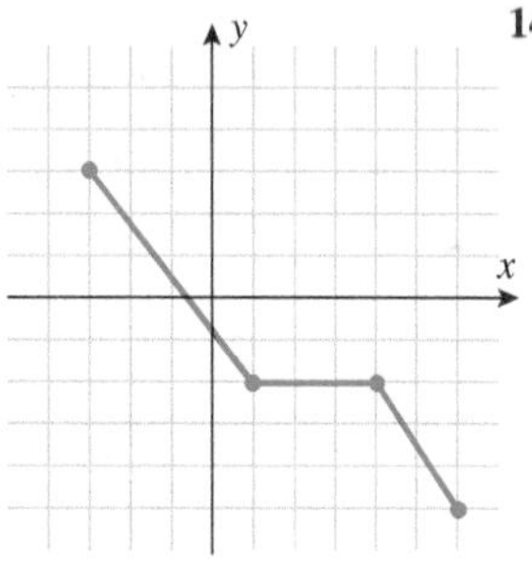

a. $y = f(x - 2)$
b. $y = f(x) - 2$

14.

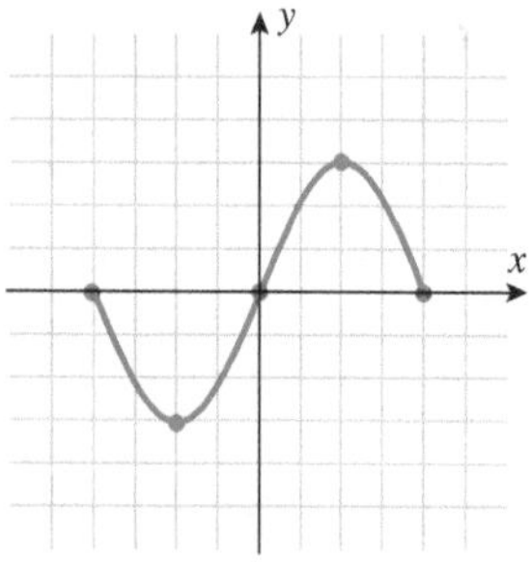

a. $y = f(x + 2)$
b. $y = f(x) + 2$

15.

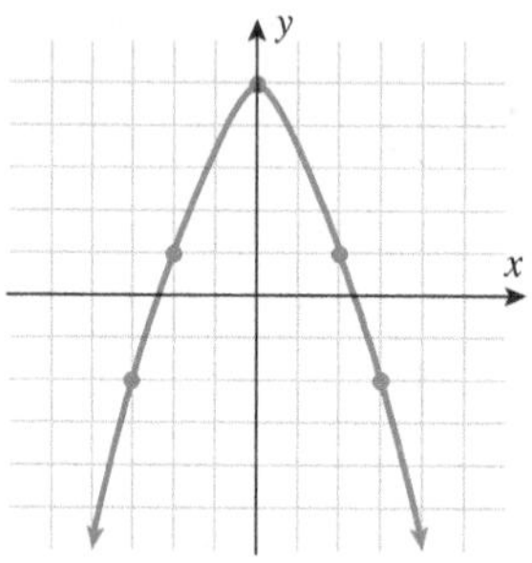

a. $y = f(x) - 3$
b. $y = f(x - 3)$

16.

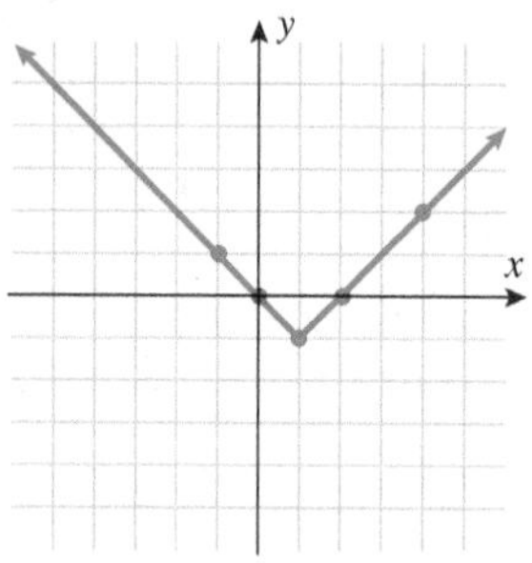

a. $y = f(x) + 3$
b. $y = f(x + 3)$

17.

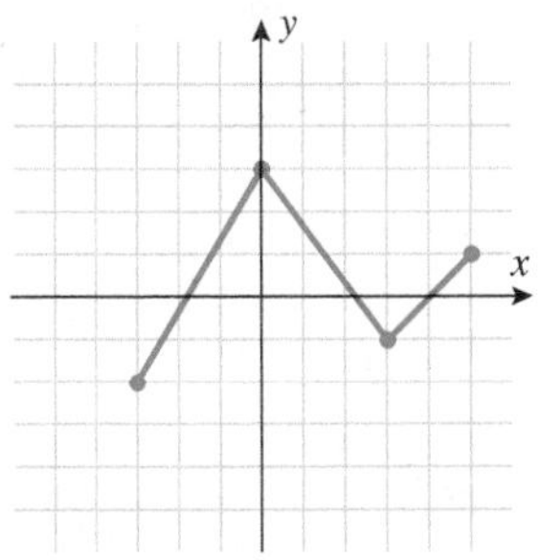

a. $y = -f(x)$
b. $y = f(-x)$

18.

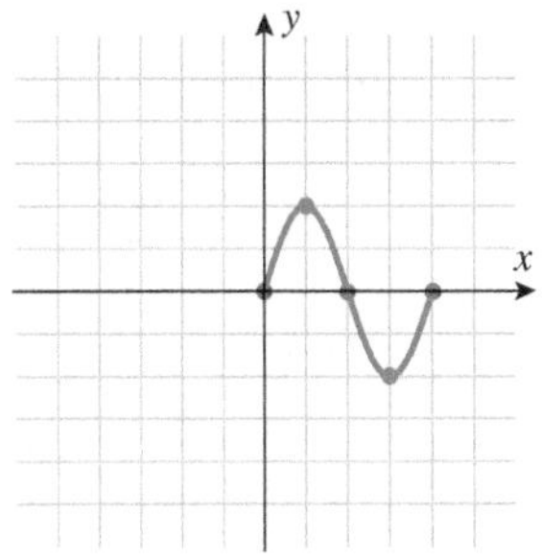

a. $y = -f(x)$
b. $y = f(-x)$

19.

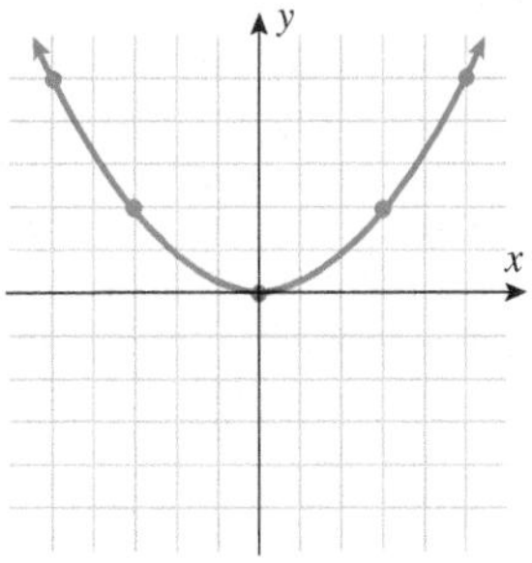

a. $y = 2f(x)$
b. $y = f(2x)$

20.

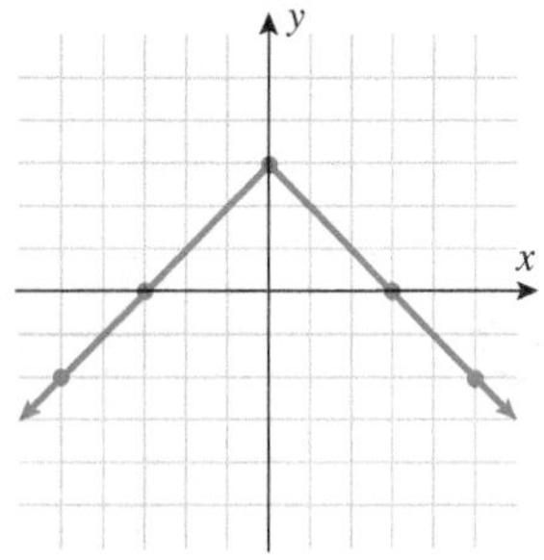

a. $y = 2f(x)$
b. $y = f(2x)$

21. $y = f(x - 2) - 3$

22. $y = f(x + 1) - 2$

23. $y = -f(x - 1) + 2$

24. $y = -2f(x) + 1$

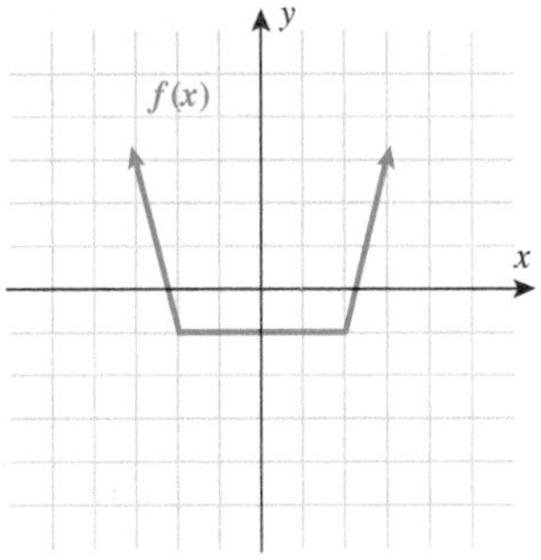

25. $y = -\frac{1}{2}g(x)$

26. $y = \frac{1}{4}g(-x)$

27. $y = -g(2x)$

28. $y = g(\frac{1}{2}x)$

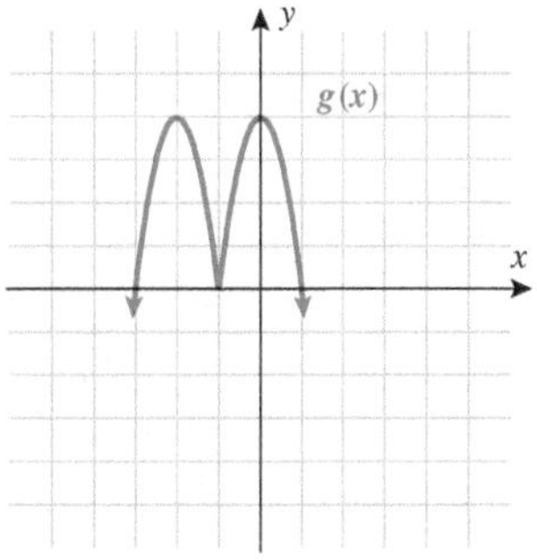

In Exercises 29–52, graph the function using transformations.

29. $y = x^2 - 2$
30. $y = x^2 + 3$
31. $y = (x + 1)^2$
32. $y = (x - 2)^2$
33. $y = (x - 3)^2 + 2$
34. $y = (x + 2)^2 + 1$
35. $y = -(1 - x)^2$
36. $y = -(x + 2)^2$
37. $y = |-x|$
38. $y = -|x|$
39. $y = -|x + 2| - 1$
40. $y = |1 - x| + 2$
41. $y = 2x^2 + 1$
42. $y = 2|x| + 1$
43. $y = -\sqrt{x - 2}$
44. $y = \sqrt{2 - x}$
45. $y = -\sqrt{2 + x} - 1$
46. $y = \sqrt{2 - x} + 3$
47. $y = \sqrt[3]{x - 1} + 2$
48. $y = \sqrt[3]{x + 2} - 1$
49. $y = \dfrac{1}{x + 3} + 2$
50. $y = \dfrac{1}{3 - x}$
51. $y = 2 - \dfrac{1}{x + 2}$
52. $y = 2 - \dfrac{1}{1 - x}$

In Exercises 53–58, transform the function into the form $f(x) = c(x - h)^2 + k$, where c, k, and h are constants, by completing the square. Use graph-shifting techniques to graph the function.

53. $y = x^2 - 6x + 11$
54. $f(x) = x^2 + 2x - 2$
55. $f(x) = -x^2 - 2x$
56. $f(x) = -x^2 + 6x - 7$
57. $f(x) = 2x^2 - 8x + 3$
58. $f(x) = 3x^2 - 6x + 5$

• APPLICATIONS

59. Salary. A manager hires an employee at a rate of \$10 per hour. Write the function that describes the current salary of the employee as a function of the number of hours worked per week, x. After a year, the manager decides to award the employee a raise equivalent to paying him for an additional 5 hours per week. Write a function that describes the salary of the employee after the raise.

60. Profit. The profit associated with St. Augustine sod in Florida is typically $P(x) = -x^2 + 14{,}000x - 48{,}700{,}000$, where x is the number of pallets sold per year in a normal year. In rainy years Sod King gives away 10 free pallets per year. Write the function that describes the profit of x pallets of sod in rainy years.

61. Taxes. Every year in the United States each working American typically pays in taxes a percentage of his or her earnings (minus the standard deduction). Karen's 2005 taxes were calculated based on the formula $T(x) = 0.22(x - 6500)$. That year the standard deduction was \$6500 and her tax bracket paid 22% in taxes. Write the function that will determine her 2006 taxes, assuming she receives a raise that places her in the 33% bracket.

62. **Medication.** The amount of medication that an infant requires is typically a function of the baby's weight. The number of milliliters of an antiseizure medication A is given by $A(x) = \sqrt{x} + 2$, where x is the weight of the infant in ounces. In emergencies there is often not enough time to weigh the infant, so nurses have to estimate the baby's weight. What is the function that represents the actual amount of medication the infant is given if his weight is overestimated by 3 ounces?

63. **Profit.** A company that started in 1900 has made a profit corresponding to $P(t) = t^3 - t^2 + t - 1$, where P is the profit in dollars and t is the year (with $t = 0$ corresponding to 1950). Write the profit function with $t = 0$ corresponding to the year 2000.

64. **Profit.** For the company in Exercise 63, write the profit function with $t = 0$ corresponding to the year 2010.

For Exercises 65 and 66, refer to the following:

Body surface area (BSA) is used in physiology and medicine for many clinical purposes. BSA can be modeled by the function

$$BSA = \sqrt{\frac{wh}{3600}}$$

where w is weight in kilograms and h is height in centimeters. Since BSA depends on weight and height, it is often thought of as a function of both weight and height. However, for an individual adult height is generally considered constant; thus BSA can be thought of as a function of weight alone.

65. **Health/Medicine.** (a) If an adult female is 162 centimeters tall, find her BSA as a function of weight. (b) If she loses 3 kilograms, find a function that represents her new BSA.

66. **Health/Medicine.** (a) If an adult male is 180 centimeters tall, find his BSA as a function of weight. (b) If he gains 5 kilograms, find a function that represents his new BSA.

• CATCH THE MISTAKE

In Exercises 67 and 68, explain the mistake that is made.

67. Describe a procedure for graphing the function $f(x) = \sqrt{x - 3} + 2$.

Solution:

a. Start with the function $f(x) = \sqrt{x}$.

b. Shift the function to the left three units.

c. Shift the function up two units.

This is incorrect. What mistake was made?

68. Describe a procedure for graphing the function $f(x) = -2x^2 + 1$.

Solution:

a. Start with the function $f(x) = x^2$.

b. Reflect the function about the y-axis.

c. Shift the function up one unit.

d. Expand in the vertical direction by a factor of 2.

This is incorrect. What mistake was made?

• CONCEPTUAL

In Exercises 69–74, determine whether each statement is true or false.

69. The graph of $y = |-x|$ is the same as the graph of $y = |x|$.

70. The graph of $y = \sqrt{-x}$ is the same as the graph of $y = \sqrt{x}$.

71. If the graph of an odd function is reflected around the x-axis and then the y-axis, the result is the graph of the original odd function.

72. If the graph of $y = \frac{1}{x}$ is reflected around the x-axis, it produces the same graph as if it had been reflected about the y-axis.

73. If f is a function and $c > 1$ is a constant, then the graph of $-cf$ is a reflection about the x-axis of a vertical stretch of the graph of f.

74. If a and b are positive constants and f is a function, then the graph of $f(x + a) + b$ is obtained by shifting the graph of f to the right a units and then shifting this graph up b units.

• CHALLENGE

75. The point (a, b) lies on the graph of the function $y = f(x)$. What point is guaranteed to lie on the graph of $f(x - 3) + 2$?

76. The point (a, b) lies on the graph of the function $y = f(x)$. What point is guaranteed to lie on the graph of $-f(-x) + 1$?

77. The point (a, b) lies on the graph of the function $y = f(x)$. What point is guaranteed to lie on the graph of $2f(x + 1) - 1$?

78. The point (a, b) lies on the graph of the function $y = f(x)$. What point is guaranteed to lie on the graph of $-2f(x - 3) + 4$?

• **PREVIEW TO CALCULUS**

For Exercises 79–82, refer to the following:

In calculus, the difference quotient $\frac{f(x+h)-f(x)}{h}$ of a function f is used to find the derivative f' of f, by letting h approach 0, $h \to 0$. Find the derivatives of f and g.

79. **Horizontal Shift.** $f(x) = x^2$, $g(x) = (x-1)^2$. How are the graphs of g' and f' related?

80. **Horizontal Shift.** $f(x) = \sqrt{x}$, $g(x) = \sqrt{x+5}$. How are the graphs of g' and f' related?

81. **Vertical Shift.** $f(x) = 2x$, $g(x) = 2x + 7$. How are the graphs of g' and f' related?

82. **Vertical Shift.** $f(x) = x^3$, $g(x) = x^3 - 4$. How are the graphs of g' and f' related?

1.4 COMBINING FUNCTIONS

SKILLS OBJECTIVES

- Add, subtract, multiply, and divide functions.
- Evaluate composite functions and determine the corresponding domains.

CONCEPTUAL OBJECTIVES

- Understand domain restrictions when dividing functions.
- Realize that the domain of a composition of functions excludes the values that are not in the domain of the inside function.

1.4.1 Adding, Subtracting, Multiplying, and Dividing Functions

1.4.1 SKILL

Add, subtract, multiply, and divide functions.

1.4.1 CONCEPTUAL

Understand domain restrictions when dividing functions.

Two functions can be added, subtracted, and multiplied. The domain of the resulting function is the intersection of the domains of the two functions. However, for division, any value of x (input) that makes the denominator equal to zero must be eliminated from the domain.

FUNCTION	NOTATION	DOMAIN
Sum	$(f+g)(x) = f(x) + g(x)$	$\{\text{domain of } f\} \cap \{\text{domain of } g\}$
Difference	$(f-g)(x) = f(x) - g(x)$	$\{\text{domain of } f\} \cap \{\text{domain of } g\}$
Product	$(f \cdot g)(x) = f(x) \cdot g(x)$	$\{\text{domain of } f\} \cap \{\text{domain of } g\}$
Quotient	$\left(\frac{f}{g}\right)(x) = \frac{f(x)}{g(x)}$	$\{\text{domain of } f\} \cap \{\text{domain of } g\} \cap \{g(x) \neq 0\}$

We can think of this in the following way: Any number that is in the domain of *both* the functions is in the domain of the combined function. The exception to this is the quotient function, which also eliminates values that make the denominator equal to zero.

EXAMPLE 1 **Operations on Functions: Determining Domains of New Functions**

For the functions $f(x) = \sqrt{x-1}$ and $g(x) = \sqrt{4-x}$, determine the sum function, difference function, product function, and quotient function. State the domain of these four new functions.

Solution:

Sum function: $f(x) + g(x) = \sqrt{x-1} + \sqrt{4-x}$

Difference function: $f(x) - g(x) = \sqrt{x-1} - \sqrt{4-x}$

Product function: $f(x) \cdot g(x) = \sqrt{x-1} \cdot \sqrt{4-x}$

$$= \sqrt{(x-1)(4-x)} = \sqrt{-x^2 + 5x - 4}$$

Quotient function: $\dfrac{f(x)}{g(x)} = \dfrac{\sqrt{x-1}}{\sqrt{4-x}} = \sqrt{\dfrac{x-1}{4-x}}$

The domain of the square root function is determined by setting the argument under the radical greater than or equal to zero.

Domain of $f(x)$: $[1, \infty)$

Domain of $g(x)$: $(-\infty, 4]$

The domain of the sum, difference, and product functions is

$$[1, \infty) \cap (-\infty, 4] = [1, 4]$$

The quotient function has the additional constraint that the denominator cannot be zero. This implies that $x \neq 4$, so the domain of the quotient function is $[1, 4)$.

[CONCEPT CHECK]

Let $f(x) = \sqrt{x+1}$ and $g(x) = \frac{1}{x}$, and find the domain of $\frac{g(x)}{f(x)}$.

ANSWER $(-1, 0) \cup (0, \infty)$

YOUR TURN Given the functions $f(x) = \sqrt{x+3}$ and $g(x) = \sqrt{1-x}$, find $(f+g)(x)$ and state its domain.

ANSWER

$(f+g)(x) = \sqrt{x+3} + \sqrt{1-x}$

Domain: $[-3, 1]$

EXAMPLE 2 **Quotient Function and Domain Restrictions**

Given the functions $F(x) = \sqrt{x}$ and $G(x) = |x-3|$, find the quotient function $\left(\frac{F}{G}\right)(x)$, and state its domain.

Solution:

The quotient function is written as

$$\left(\frac{F}{G}\right)(x) = \frac{F(x)}{G(x)} = \frac{\sqrt{x}}{|x-3|}$$

Domain of $F(x)$: $[0, \infty)$ Domain of $G(x)$: $(-\infty, \infty)$

The real numbers that are in both the domain for $F(x)$ and the domain for $G(x)$ are represented by the intersection $[0, \infty) \cap (-\infty, \infty) = [0, \infty)$. Also, the denominator of the quotient function is equal to zero when $x = 3$, so we must eliminate this value from the domain.

$$\text{Domain of } \left(\frac{F}{G}\right)(x)\text{: } [0, 3) \cup (3, \infty)$$

YOUR TURN For the functions given in Example 2, determine the quotient function $\left(\frac{G}{F}\right)(x)$, and state its domain.

ANSWER

$\left(\frac{G}{F}\right)(x) = \frac{G(x)}{F(x)} = \frac{|x-3|}{\sqrt{x}}$

Domain: $(0, \infty)$

1.4.2 Composition of Functions

1.4.2 SKILL

Evaluate composite functions and determine the corresponding domains.

1.4.2 CONCEPTUAL

Realize that the domain of a composition of functions excludes the values that are not in the domain of the inside function.

Recall that a function maps every element in the domain to exactly one corresponding element in the range as shown in the figure below.

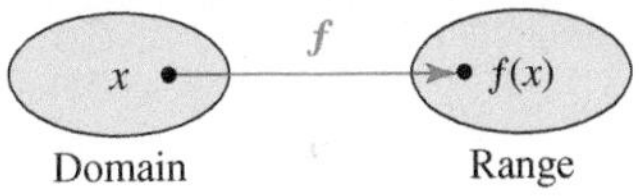

Suppose there is a sales rack of clothes in a department store. Let x correspond to the original price of each item on the rack. These clothes have recently been marked down 20%. Therefore, the function $g(x) = 0.80x$ represents the current sale price of each item. You have been invited to a special sale that lets you take 10% off the current sale price and an additional \$5 off every item at checkout. The function $f(g(x)) = 0.90g(x) - 5$ determines the checkout price. Note that the output of the function g is the input of the function f as shown in the figure below.

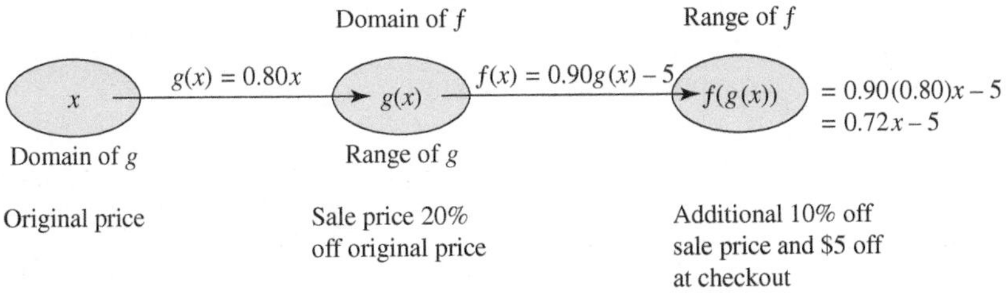

The "checkout" price is found by taking 28% off the original price and subtracting an additional \$5.

This is an example of a **composition of functions**, when the output of one function is the input of another function. It is commonly referred to as a function of a function.

An algebraic example of this is the function $y = \sqrt{x^2 - 2}$. Suppose we let $g(x) = x^2 - 2$ and $f(x) = \sqrt{x}$. Recall that the independent variable in function notation is a placeholder. Since $f(\square) = \sqrt{(\square)}$, then $f(g(x)) = \sqrt{(g(x))}$. Substituting the expression for $g(x)$, we find $f(g(x)) = \sqrt{x^2 - 2}$. The function $y = \sqrt{x^2 - 2}$ is said to be a composite function, $y = f(g(x))$.

Note that the domain of $g(x)$ is the set of all real numbers, and the domain of $f(x)$ is the set of all nonnegative numbers. The domain of a composite function is the set of all x such that $g(x)$ is in the domain of f. For instance, in the composite function $y = f(g(x))$, we know that the allowable inputs into f are all numbers greater than or equal to zero. Therefore, we restrict the outputs of $g(x) \geq 0$ and find the corresponding x-values. Those x-values are the only allowable inputs and constitute the domain of the composite function $y = f(g(x))$.

The symbol that represents composition of functions is a small open circle; thus $(f \circ g)(x) = f(g(x))$ and is read aloud as "f of g." It is important not to confuse this with the multiplication sign: $(f \cdot g)(x) = f(x)g(x)$.

CAUTION

$f \circ g \neq f \cdot g$

COMPOSITION OF FUNCTIONS

Given two functions f and g, there are two **composite functions** that can be formed.

NOTATION	WORDS	DEFINITION	DOMAIN
$f \circ g$	f composed with g	$f(g(x))$	The set of all real numbers x in the domain of g such that $g(x)$ is also in the domain of f
$g \circ f$	g composed with f	$g(f(x))$	The set of all real numbers x in the domain of f such that $f(x)$ is also in the domain of g

STUDY TIP

Order is important:

$(f \circ g)(x) = f(g(x))$
$(g \circ f)(x) = g(f(x))$

STUDY TIP

The domain of $f \circ g$ is always a subset of the domain of g, and the range of $f \circ g$ is always a subset of the range of f.

It is important to realize that there are two "filters" that allow certain values of x into the domain. The first filter is $g(x)$. If x is not in the domain of $g(x)$, it cannot be in the domain of $(f \circ g)(x) = f(g(x))$. Of those values for x that are in the domain of $g(x)$, only some pass through, because we restrict the output of $g(x)$ to values that are allowable as input into f. This adds an additional filter.

The domain of $f \circ g$ is always a subset of the domain of g, and the range of $f \circ g$ is always a subset of the range of f.

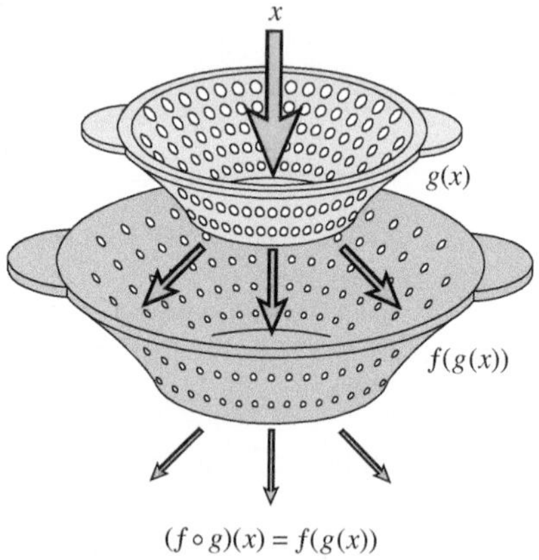

EXAMPLE 3 Finding a Composite Function

Given the functions $f(x) = x^2 + 1$ and $g(x) = x - 3$, find $(f \circ g)(x)$.

Solution:

Write $f(x)$ using placeholder notation. $\quad f(\square) = (\square)^2 + 1$

Express the composite function $f \circ g$. $\quad f(g(x)) = (g(x))^2 + 1$

Substitute $g(x) = x - 3$ into f. $\quad f(g(x)) = (x - 3)^2 + 1$

Eliminate the parentheses on the right side. $\quad f(g(x)) = x^2 - 6x + 10$

$$\boxed{(f \circ g)(x) = f(g(x)) = x^2 - 6x + 10}$$

YOUR TURN Given the functions in Example 3, find $(g \circ f)(x)$.

ANSWER

$g \circ f = g(f(x)) = x^2 - 2$

EXAMPLE 4 Determining the Domain of a Composite Function

Given the functions $f(x) = \dfrac{1}{x-1}$ and $g(x) = \dfrac{1}{x}$, determine $f \circ g$, and state its domain.

Solution:

Write $f(x)$ using placeholder notation. $\quad f(\square) = \dfrac{1}{(\square) - 1}$

Express the composite function $f \circ g$. $\quad f(g(x)) = \dfrac{1}{g(x) - 1}$

Substitute $g(x) = \dfrac{1}{x}$ into f. $\quad f(g(x)) = \dfrac{1}{\frac{1}{x} - 1}$

Multiply the right side by $\dfrac{x}{x}$. $\quad f(g(x)) = \dfrac{1}{\frac{1}{x} - 1} \cdot \dfrac{x}{x} = \dfrac{x}{1-x}$

$$\boxed{(f \circ g) = f(g(x)) = \frac{x}{1-x}}$$

What is the domain of $(f \circ g)(x) = f(g(x))$? By inspecting the final result of $f(g(x))$, we see that the denominator is zero when $x = 1$. Therefore, $x \neq 1$. Are there any other values for x that are not allowed? The function $g(x)$ has the domain $x \neq 0$; therefore, we must also exclude zero.

The domain of $(f \circ g)(x) = f(g(x))$ excludes $x = 0$ and $x = 1$ or, in interval notation,

$$\boxed{(-\infty, 0) \cup (0, 1) \cup (1, \infty)}$$

YOUR TURN For the functions f and g given in Example 4, determine the composite function $g \circ f$, and state its domain.

ANSWER
$g(f(x)) = x - 1$. Domain of $g \circ f$ is $x \neq 1$ or, in interval notation, $(-\infty, 1) \cup (1, \infty)$.

The domain of the composite function cannot always be determined by examining the final form of $f \circ g$, as illustrated in Example 4.

EXAMPLE 5 Determining the Domain of a Composite Function (Without Finding the Composite Function)

Let $f(x) = \dfrac{1}{x-2}$ and $g(x) = \sqrt{x+3}$. Find the domain of $f(g(x))$. Do not find the composite function.

Solution:

Find the domain of g. $\quad [-3, \infty)$

Find the range of g. $\quad [0, \infty)$

In $f(g(x))$, the output of g becomes the input for f. Since the domain of f is the set of all real numbers except 2, we eliminate any values of x in the domain of g that correspond to $g(x) = 2$.

Let $g(x) = 2$. $\quad \sqrt{x+3} = 2$

Square both sides. $\quad x + 3 = 4$

Solve for x. $\quad x = 1$

Eliminate $x = 1$ from the domain of g, $[-3, \infty)$.

State the domain of $f(g(x))$. $\quad \boxed{[-3, 1) \cup (1, \infty)}$

CAUTION
The domain of the composite function cannot always be determined by examining the final form of $f \circ g$.

[CONCEPT CHECK]
For the functions $f(x) = x - a$ and $g(x) = \dfrac{1}{(x+a)}$, find $g(f(x))$ and state its domain.

ANSWER $g(f(x)) = \frac{1}{x}$; domain is all real numbers except $x = 0$.

EXAMPLE 6 **Evaluating a Composite Function**

Given the functions $f(x) = x^2 - 7$ and $g(x) = 5 - x^2$, evaluate

a. $f(g(1))$ **b.** $f(g(-2))$ **c.** $g(f(3))$ **d.** $g(f(-4))$

Solution:

One way of evaluating these composite functions is to calculate the two individual composites in terms of x: $f(g(x))$ and $g(f(x))$. Once those functions are known, the values can be substituted for x and evaluated.

Another way of proceeding is as follows:

a. Write the desired quantity. $f(g(1))$

Find the value of the inner function g. $g(1) = 5 - 1^2 = 4$

Substitute $g(1) = 4$ into f. $f(g(1)) = f(4)$

Evaluate $f(4)$. $f(4) = 4^2 - 7 = 9$

$$\boxed{f(g(1)) = 9}$$

b. Write the desired quantity. $f(g(-2))$

Find the value of the inner function g. $g(-2) = 5 - (-2)^2 = 1$

Substitute $g(-2) = 1$ into f. $f(g(-2)) = f(1)$

Evaluate $f(1)$. $f(1) = 1^2 - 7 = -6$

$$\boxed{f(g(-2)) = -6}$$

c. Write the desired quantity. $g(f(3))$

Find the value of the inner function f. $f(3) = 3^2 - 7 = 2$

Substitute $f(3) = 2$ into g. $g(f(3)) = g(2)$

Evaluate $g(2)$. $g(2) = 5 - 2^2 = 1$

$$\boxed{g(f(3)) = 1}$$

d. Write the desired quantity. $g(f(-4))$

Find the value of the inner function f. $f(-4) = (-4)^2 - 7 = 9$

Substitute $f(-4) = 9$ into g. $g(f(-4)) = g(9)$

Evaluate $g(9)$. $g(9) = 5 - 9^2 = -76$

$$\boxed{g(f(-4)) = -76}$$

YOUR TURN Given the functions $f(x) = x^3 - 3$ and $g(x) = 1 + x^3$, evaluate $f(g(1))$ and $g(f(1))$.

ANSWER
$f(g(1)) = 5$
$g(f(1)) = -7$

Application Problems

Recall the example at the beginning of this section involving the clothes that are on sale. Often, real-world applications are modeled with composite functions. In the clothes example, x is the original price of each item. The first function maps its input (original price) to an output (sale price). The second function maps its input (sale price) to an output (checkout price). Example 7 is another real-world application of composite functions.

Three temperature scales are commonly used:

- The Celsius (°C) scale
  - This scale was devised by dividing the range between the freezing (0°C) and boiling (100°C) points of pure water at sea level into 100 equal parts. This scale is used in science and is one of the standards of the "metric" (SI) system of measurements.

- The Kelvin (K) temperature scale
  - This scale shifts the Celsius scale down so that the zero point is equal to absolute zero (about −273.15°C), a hypothetical temperature at which there is a complete absence of heat energy.
  - Units of temperature on the Kelvin scale are called **kelvins**, *not* degrees Kelvin, and the word *kelvin* is not capitalized when it refers to the unit. The symbol for the kelvin is K.
- The Fahrenheit (°F) scale
  - This scale evolved over time and is still widely used mainly in the United States, although Celsius is the preferred "metric" scale.
  - With respect to pure water at sea level, the **degrees Fahrenheit** are gauged by the spread from 32°F (freezing) to 212°F (boiling).

The equations that relate these temperature scales are

$$F = \frac{9}{5}C + 32 \qquad C = K - 273.15$$

EXAMPLE 7 **Applications Involving Composite Functions**

Determine degrees Fahrenheit as a function of kelvins.

Solution:

Degrees Fahrenheit is a function of degrees Celsius. $F = \frac{9}{5}C + 32$

Now substitute $C = K - 273.15$ into the equation for F. $F = \frac{9}{5}(K - 273.15) + 32$

Simplify. $F = \frac{9}{5}K - 491.67 + 32$

$$\boxed{F = \frac{9}{5}K - 459.67}$$

[SECTION 1.4] SUMMARY

Operations on Functions

Function	Notation	
Sum	$(f + g)(x) = f(x) + g(x)$	
Difference	$(f - g)(x) = f(x) - g(x)$	
Product	$(f \cdot g)(x) = f(x) \cdot g(x)$	
Quotient	$\left(\frac{f}{g}\right)(x) = \frac{f(x)}{g(x)}$	$g(x) \neq 0$

The domain of the sum, difference, and product functions is the intersection of the domains, or common domain shared by both f and g. The domain of the quotient function is also the intersection of the domain shared by both f and g with an additional restriction that $g(x) \neq 0$.

Composition of Functions

$$(f \circ g)(x) = f(g(x))$$

The domain restrictions cannot always be determined simply by inspecting the final form of $f(g(x))$. Rather, the domain of the composite function is a subset of the domain of $g(x)$. Values of x must be eliminated if their corresponding values of $g(x)$ are not in the domain of f.

[SECTION 1.4] EXERCISES

• SKILLS

In Exercises 1–10, given the functions f and g, find $f+g$, $f-g$, $f\cdot g$, and $\frac{f}{g}$, and state the domain of each.

1. $f(x)=2x+1$, $g(x)=1-x$
2. $f(x)=3x+2$, $g(x)=2x-4$
3. $f(x)=2x^2-x$, $g(x)=x^2-4$
4. $f(x)=3x+2$, $g(x)=x^2-25$
5. $f(x)=\frac{1}{x}$, $g(x)=x$
6. $f(x)=\frac{2x+3}{x-4}$, $g(x)=\frac{x-4}{3x+2}$
7. $f(x)=\sqrt{x}$, $g(x)=2\sqrt{x}$
8. $f(x)=\sqrt{x-1}$, $g(x)=2x^2$
9. $f(x)=\sqrt{4-x}$, $g(x)=\sqrt{x+3}$
10. $f(x)=\sqrt{1-2x}$, $g(x)=\frac{1}{x}$

In Exercises 11–20, for the given functions f and g, find the composite functions $f\circ g$ and $g\circ f$, and state their domains.

11. $f(x)=2x+1$, $g(x)=x^2-3$
12. $f(x)=x^2-1$, $g(x)=2-x$
13. $f(x)=\frac{1}{x-1}$, $g(x)=x+2$
14. $f(x)=\frac{2}{x-3}$, $g(x)=2+x$
15. $f(x)=|x|$, $g(x)=\frac{1}{x-1}$
16. $f(x)=|x-1|$, $g(x)=\frac{1}{x}$
17. $f(x)=\sqrt{x-1}$, $g(x)=x+5$
18. $f(x)=\sqrt{2-x}$, $g(x)=x^2+2$
19. $f(x)=x^3+4$, $g(x)=(x-4)^{1/3}$
20. $f(x)=\sqrt[3]{x^2-1}$, $g(x)=x^{2/3}+1$

In Exercises 21–38, evaluate the functions for the specified values, if possible.

$$f(x)=x^2+10 \qquad g(x)=\sqrt{x-1}$$

21. $(f+g)(2)$
22. $(f+g)(10)$
23. $(f-g)(2)$
24. $(f-g)(5)$
25. $(f\cdot g)(4)$
26. $(f\cdot g)(5)$
27. $\left(\frac{f}{g}\right)(10)$
28. $\left(\frac{f}{g}\right)(2)$
29. $f(g(2))$
30. $f(g(1))$
31. $g(f(-3))$
32. $g(f(4))$
33. $f(g(0))$
34. $g(f(0))$
35. $f(g(-3))$
36. $g(f(\sqrt{7}))$
37. $(f\circ g)(4)$
38. $(g\circ f)(-3)$

In Exercises 39–50, evaluate $f(g(1))$ and $g(f(2))$, if possible.

39. $f(x)=\frac{1}{x}$, $g(x)=2x+1$
40. $f(x)=x^2+1$, $g(x)=\frac{1}{2-x}$
41. $f(x)=\sqrt{1-x}$, $g(x)=x^2+2$
42. $f(x)=\sqrt{3-x}$, $g(x)=x^2+1$
43. $f(x)=\frac{1}{|x-1|}$, $g(x)=x+3$
44. $f(x)=\frac{1}{x}$, $g(x)=|2x-3|$
45. $f(x)=\sqrt{x-1}$, $g(x)=x^2+5$
46. $f(x)=\sqrt[3]{x-3}$, $g(x)=\frac{1}{x-3}$
47. $f(x)=\frac{1}{x^2-3}$, $g(x)=\sqrt{x-3}$
48. $f(x)=\frac{x}{2-x}$, $g(x)=4-x^2$
49. $f(x)=(x-1)^{1/3}$, $g(x)=x^2+2x+1$
50. $f(x)=(1-x^2)^{1/2}$, $g(x)=(x-3)^{1/3}$

In Exercises 51–60, show that $f(g(x))=x$ and $g(f(x))=x$.

51. $f(x)=2x+1$, $g(x)=\frac{x-1}{2}$
52. $f(x)=\frac{x-2}{3}$, $g(x)=3x+2$
53. $f(x)=\sqrt{x-1}$, $g(x)=x^2+1$ for $x\geq 1$
54. $f(x)=2-x^2$, $g(x)=\sqrt{2-x}$ for $x\leq 2$
55. $f(x)=\frac{1}{x}$, $g(x)=\frac{1}{x}$ for $x\neq 0$
56. $f(x)=(5-x)^{1/3}$, $g(x)=5-x^3$
57. $f(x)=4x^2-9$, $g(x)=\frac{\sqrt{x+9}}{2}$ for $x\geq 0$
58. $f(x)=\sqrt[3]{8x-1}$, $g(x)=\frac{x^3+1}{8}$
59. $f(x)=\frac{1}{x-1}$, $g(x)=\frac{x+1}{x}$ for $x\neq 0$, $x\neq 1$
60. $f(x)=\sqrt{25-x^2}$, $g(x)=\sqrt{25-x^2}$ for $0\leq x\leq 5$

In Exercises 61–66, write the function as a composite of two functions f and g. (More than one answer is correct.)

61. $f(g(x)) = 2(3x - 1)^2 + 5(3x - 1)$

62. $f(g(x)) = \dfrac{1}{1 + x^2}$

63. $f(g(x)) = \dfrac{2}{|x - 3|}$

64. $f(g(x)) = \sqrt{1 - x^2}$

65. $f(g(x)) = \dfrac{3}{\sqrt{x + 1} - 2}$

66. $f(g(x)) = \dfrac{\sqrt{x}}{3\sqrt{x} + 2}$

• APPLICATIONS

Exercises 67 and 68 depend on the relationship between degrees Fahrenheit, degrees Celsius, and kelvins:

$$F = \frac{9}{5}C + 32 \qquad C = K - 273.15$$

67. Temperature. Write a composite function that converts kelvins into degrees Fahrenheit.

68. Temperature. Convert the following degrees Fahrenheit to kelvins: 32°F and 212°F.

69. Market Price. Typical supply and demand relationships state that as the number of units for sale increases, the market price decreases. Assume that the market price p and the number of units for sale x are related by the demand equation:

$$p = 3000 - \frac{1}{2}x$$

Assume that the cost $C(x)$ of producing x items is governed by the equation

$$C(x) = 2000 + 10x$$

and the revenue $R(x)$ generated by selling x units is governed by

$$R(x) = 100x$$

a. Write the cost as a function of price p.
b. Write the revenue as a function of price p.
c. Write the profit as a function of price p.

70. Market Price. Typical supply and demand relationships state that as the number of units for sale increases, the market price decreases. Assume that the market price p and the number of units for sale x are related by the demand equation:

$$p = 10{,}000 - \frac{1}{4}x$$

Assume that the cost $C(x)$ of producing x items is governed by the equation

$$C(x) = 30{,}000 + 5x$$

and the revenue $R(x)$ generated by selling x units is governed by

$$R(x) = 1000x$$

a. Write the cost as a function of price p.
b. Write the revenue as a function of price p.
c. Write the profit as a function of price p.

In Exercises 71 and 72, refer to the following:

The cost of manufacturing a product is a function of the number of hours t the assembly line is running per day. The number of products manufactured n is a function of the number of hours t the assembly line is operating and is given by the function $n(t)$. The cost of manufacturing the product C measured in thousands of dollars is a function of the quantity manufactured, that is, the function $C(n)$.

71. Business. If the quantity of a product manufactured during a day is given by

$$n(t) = 50t - t^2$$

and the cost of manufacturing the product is given by

$$C(n) = 10n + 1375$$

a. Find a function that gives the cost of manufacturing the product in terms of the number of hours t the assembly line was functioning, $C(n(t))$.
b. Find the cost of production on a day when the assembly line was running for 16 hours. Interpret your answer.

72. Business. If the quantity of a product manufactured during a day is given by

$$n(t) = 100t - 4t^2$$

and the cost of manufacturing the product is given by

$$C(n) = 8n + 2375$$

a. Find a function that gives the cost of manufacturing the product in terms of the number of hours t the assembly line was functioning, $C(n(t))$.
b. Find the cost of production on a day when the assembly line was running for 24 hours. Interpret your answer.

In Exercises 73 and 74, refer to the following:

Surveys performed immediately following an accidental oil spill at sea indicate the oil moved outward from the source of the spill in a nearly circular pattern. The radius of the oil spill r measured in miles is a function of time t measured in days from the start of the spill, while the area of the oil spill is a function of radius, that is, the function $A(r)$.

73. Environment: Oil Spill. If the radius of the oil spill is given by

$$r(t) = 10t - 0.2t^2$$

and the area of the oil spill is given by

$$A(r) = \pi r^2$$

a. Find a function that gives the area of the oil spill in terms of the number of days since the start of the spill, $A(r(t))$.
b. Find the area of the oil spill to the nearest square mile 7 days after the start of the spill.

74. Environment: Oil Spill. If the radius of the oil spill is given by

$$r(t) = 8t - 0.1t^2$$

and the area of the oil spill is given by

$$A(r) = \pi r^2$$

a. Find a function that gives the area of the oil spill in terms of the number of days since the start of the spill, $A(r(t))$.
b. Find the area of the oil spill to the nearest square mile 5 days after the start of the spill.

• CATCH THE MISTAKE

In Exercises 75–79, for the functions $f(x) = x + 2$ and $g(x) = x^2 - 4$, find the indicated function and state its domain. Explain the mistake that is made in each problem.

75. $\dfrac{g}{f}$

Solution: $$\frac{g(x)}{f(x)} = \frac{x^2 - 4}{x + 2} = \frac{(x-2)(x+2)}{x+2} = x - 2$$

Domain: $(-\infty, \infty)$

This is incorrect. What mistake was made?

76. $\dfrac{f}{g}$

Solution: $$\frac{f(x)}{g(x)} = \frac{x+2}{x^2-4} = \frac{x+2}{(x-2)(x+2)} = \frac{1}{x-2} = \frac{1}{x-2}$$

Domain: $(-\infty, 2) \cup (2, \infty)$

This is incorrect. What mistake was made?

77. $f \circ g$

Solution: $$f \circ g = f(x)g(x)$$
$$= (x + 2)(x^2 - 4)$$
$$= x^3 + 2x^2 - 4x - 8$$

Domain: $(-\infty, \infty)$

This is incorrect. What mistake was made?

78. $f(x) - g(x)$

Solution: $$f(x) - g(x) = x + 2 - x^2 - 4$$
$$= -x^2 + x - 2$$

Domain: $(-\infty, \infty)$

This is incorrect. What mistake was made?

79. $(f + g)(2)$

Solution: $$(f + g)(2) = (x + 2 + x^2 - 4)(2)$$
$$= (x^2 + x - 2)(2)$$
$$= 2x^2 + 2x - 4$$

Domain: $(-\infty, \infty)$

This is incorrect. What mistake was made?

80. Given the function $f(x) = x^2 + 7$ and $g(x) = \sqrt{x - 3}$, find $f \circ g$, and state the domain.

Solution: $$f \circ g = f(g(x)) = (\sqrt{x-3})^2 + 7$$
$$= f(g(x)) = x - 3 + 7$$
$$= x - 4$$

Domain: $(-\infty, \infty)$

This is incorrect. What mistake was made?

• CONCEPTUAL

In Exercises 81–84, determine whether each statement is true or false.

81. When adding, subtracting, multiplying, or dividing two functions, the domain of the resulting function is the union of the domains of the individual functions.

82. For any functions f and g, $f(g(x)) = g(f(x))$ for all values of x that are in the domain of both f and g.

83. For any functions f and g, $(f \circ g)(x)$ exists for all values of x that are in the domain of $g(x)$, provided the range of g is a subset of the domain of f.

84. The domain of a composite function can be found by inspection, without knowledge of the domain of the individual functions.

• CHALLENGE

85. For the functions $f(x) = x + a$ and $g(x) = \frac{1}{x - a}$, find $g \circ f$ and state its domain.

86. For the functions $f(x) = ax^2 + bx + c$ and $g(x) = \frac{1}{x - c}$, find $g \circ f$ and state its domain.

87. For the functions $f(x) = \sqrt{x + a}$ and $g(x) = x^2 - a$ find $g \circ f$ and state its domain.

88. For the functions $f(x) = \frac{1}{x^a}$ and $g(x) = \frac{1}{x^b}$, find $g \circ f$ and state its domain. Assume $a > 1$ and $b > 1$.

• PREVIEW TO CALCULUS

For Exercises 89–92, refer to the following:

In calculus, the difference quotient $\frac{f(x + h) - f(x)}{h}$ of a function f is used to find the derivative f' of f by letting h approach 0, $h \to 0$.

89. **Addition.** Find the derivatives of $F(x) = x$, $G(x) = x^2$, and $H(x) = (F + G)(x) = x + x^2$. What do you observe?

90. **Subtraction.** Find the derivatives of $F(x) = \sqrt{x}$, $G(x) = x^3 + 1$, and $H(x) = (F - G)(x) = \sqrt{x} - x^3 - 1$. What do you observe?

91. **Multiplication.** Find the derivatives of $F(x) = 5$, $G(x) = \sqrt{x - 1}$, and $H(x) = (FG)(x) = 5\sqrt{x - 1}$. What do you observe?

92. **Division.** Find the derivatives of $F(x) = x$, $G(x) = \sqrt{x + 1}$, and $H(x) = \left(\frac{F}{G}\right)(x) = \frac{x}{\sqrt{x + 1}}$. What do you observe?

1.5 ONE-TO-ONE FUNCTIONS AND INVERSE FUNCTIONS

SKILLS OBJECTIVES

- Determine whether a function is a one-to-one function.
- Verify that two functions are inverses of one another.
- Graph the inverse function given the graph of the function.
- Find the inverse of a function.

CONCEPTUAL OBJECTIVES

- Understand why a function that passes the horizontal line test is one-to-one.
- Visualize the relationships between the domain and range of a function and the domain and range of its inverse.
- Understand why functions and their inverses are symmetric about the line $y = x$.
- Understand why a function must be one-to-one in order for its inverse to exist.

1.5.1 One-to-One Functions

Every human being has a blood type, and every human being has a DNA sequence. These are examples of functions, where a person is the input and the output is blood type or DNA sequence. These relationships are classified as functions because each person can have one and only one blood type or DNA strand. The difference between these functions is that many people have the same blood type, but DNA is unique to each individual. Can we map backwards? For instance, if you know the blood type, do you know specifically which person it came from? No, but if you know the DNA sequence, you know that the sequence belongs to only one person. When a function has a one-to-one correspondence, like the DNA example, then mapping backwards is possible. The map back is called the *inverse function.*

In Section 1.1, we defined a function as a relationship that maps an input (contained in the domain) to exactly one output (found in the range). Algebraically, each value for x can correspond to only a single value for y. Recall the square, identity, absolute value, and reciprocal functions from our library of functions in Section 1.3.

1.5.1 SKILL

Determine whether a function is a one-to-one function.

1.5.1 CONCEPTUAL

Understand why a function that passes the horizontal line test is one-to-one.

All of the graphs of these functions satisfy the vertical line test. Although the square function and the absolute value function map each value of x to exactly one value for y, these two functions map two values of x to the same value for y. For example, $(-1, 1)$ and $(1, 1)$ lie on both graphs. The identity and reciprocal functions, on the other hand, map each x to a single value for y, and no two x-values map to the same y-value. These two functions are examples of *one-to-one functions.*

DEFINITION One-to-One Function

A function $f(x)$ is **one-to-one** if no two elements in the domain correspond to the same element in the range; that is,

$$\text{if } x_1 \neq x_2, \text{then } f(x_1) \neq f(x_2).$$

In other words, it is one-to-one if no two inputs map to the same output.

EXAMPLE 1 **Determining Whether a Function Defined as a Set of Points Is a One-to-One Function**

For each of the three relations, determine whether the relation is a function. If it is a function, determine whether it is a one-to-one function.

$$f = \{(0, 0), (1, 2), (1, 3)\}$$
$$g = \{(2, 1), (0, 0), (3, 1)\}$$
$$h = \{(-1, -1), (0, 0), (1, 1)\}$$

Solution:

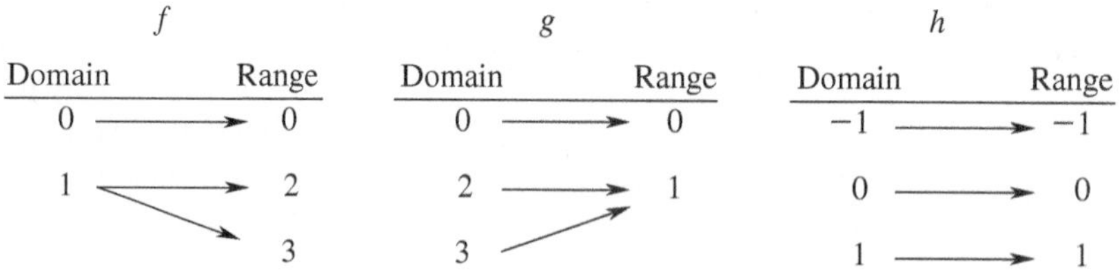

f is not a function.

g is a function, but not one-to-one.

h is a one-to-one function.

Just as there is a graphical test for functions, the vertical line test, there is a graphical test for one-to-one functions, the *horizontal line test.* Note that a horizontal line can be drawn on the square and absolute value functions so that it intersects the graph of each function at two points. The identity and reciprocal functions, however, will intersect a horizontal line at only one point. This leads us to the horizontal line test for one-to-one functions.

DEFINITION **Horizontal Line Test**

If every horizontal line intersects the graph of a function at only one point, then the function is classified as a one-to-one function.

EXAMPLE 2 Using the Horizontal Line Test to Determine Whether a Function Is One-to-One

For each of the three relations, determine whether the relation is a function. If it is a function, determine whether it is a one-to-one function. Assume that x is the independent variable and y is the dependent variable.

$$x = y^2 \qquad y = x^2 \qquad y = x^3$$

Solution:

$x = y^2$ | $y = x^2$ | $y = x^3$

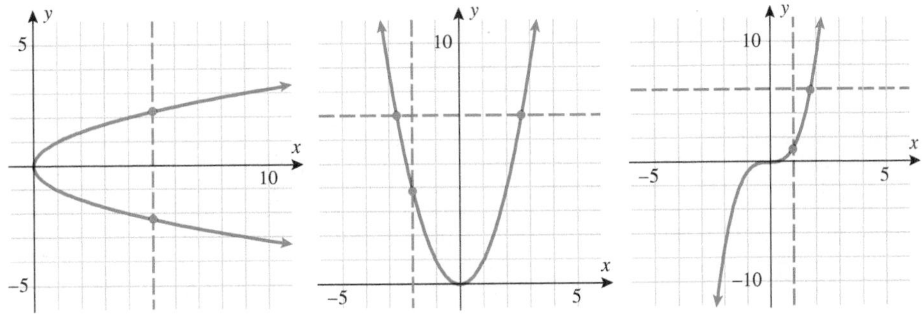

Not a function (fails vertical line test)

Function, but not one-to-one (passes vertical line test, but fails horizontal line test)

One-to-one function (passes both vertical and horizontal line tests)

[CONCEPT CHECK]

Draw a horizontal line at $y = 4$ on the graph of $y = x^2$. What are the two points of intersection? Explain why the equation $y = x^2$ cannot be a one-to-one function.

ANSWER $(-2, 4)$ and $(2, 4)$: Two different x-values map to the same y-value so this graph fails the horizontal line test.

YOUR TURN Determine whether each of the functions is a one-to-one function.

a. $f(x) = x + 2$ **b.** $f(x) = x^2 + 1$

ANSWER

a. yes

b. no

Another way of writing the definition of a one-to-one function is

$$\text{If } f(x_1) = f(x_2), \text{ then } x_1 = x_2.$$

In the Your Turn following Example 2, we found (using the horizontal line test) that $f(x) = x + 2$ is a one-to-one function, but that $f(x) = x^2 + 1$ is not a one-to-one function. We can also use this alternative definition to determine algebraically whether a function is one-to-one.

WORDS	MATH
State the function.	$f(x) = x + 2$
Let there be two real numbers, x_1 and x_2, such that $f(x_1) = f(x_2)$.	$x_1 + 2 = x_2 + 2$
Subtract 2 from both sides of the equation.	$x_1 = x_2$

$f(x) = x + 2$ is a one-to-one function.

WORDS	MATH
State the function.	$f(x) = x^2 + 1$
Let there be two real numbers, x_1 and x_2, such that $f(x_1) = f(x_2)$.	$x_1^2 + 1 = x_2^2 + 1$
Subtract 1 from both sides of the equation.	$x_1^2 = x_2^2$
Solve for x_1.	$x_1 = \pm x_2$

$f(x) = x^2 + 2$ is *not* a one-to-one function.

EXAMPLE 3 Determining Algebraically Whether a Function Is One-to-One

Determine algebraically whether the functions are one-to-one.

a. $f(x) = 5x^3 - 2$ **b.** $f(x) = |x + 1|$

Solution (a):

Find $f(x_1)$ and $f(x_2)$.	$f(x_1) = 5x_1^3 - 2$ and $f(x_2) = 5x_2^3 - 2$
Let $f(x_1) = f(x_2)$.	$5x_1^3 - 2 = 5x_2^3 - 2$
Add 2 to both sides of the equation.	$5x_1^3 = 5x_2^3$
Divide both sides of the equation by 5.	$x_1^3 = x_2^3$
Take the cube root of both sides of the equation.	$(x_1^3)^{1/3} = (x_2^3)^{1/3}$
Simplify.	$x_1 = x_2$

$f(x) = 5x^3 - 2$ is a one-to-one function.

Solution (b):

Find $f(x_1)$ and $f(x_2)$.	$f(x_1) = |x_1 + 1|$ and $f(x_2) = |x_2 + 1|$
Let $f(x_1) = f(x_2)$.	$|x_1 + 1| = |x_2 + 1|$
Solve the absolute value equation.	$(x_1 + 1) = (x_2 + 1)$ or $(x_1 + 1) = -(x_2 + 1)$
	$x_1 = x_2$ or $x_1 = -x_2 - 2$

$f(x) = |x + 1|$ is **not** a one-to-one function.

1.5.2 Inverse Functions

1.5.2 SKILL

Verify that two functions are inverses of one another.

1.5.2 CONCEPTUAL

Visualize the relationships between the domain and range of a function and the domain and range of its inverse.

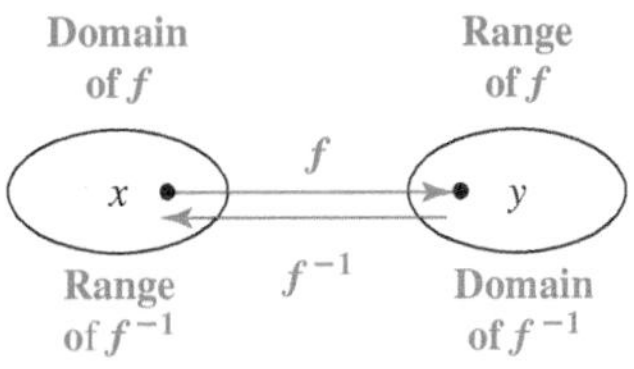

If a function is one-to-one, then the function maps each x to exactly one y, and no two x-values map to the same y-value. This implies that there is a one-to-one correspondence between the inputs (domain) and outputs (range) of a one-to-one function $f(x)$. In the special case of a one-to-one function, it would be possible to map from the output (range of f) back to the input (domain of f), and this mapping would also be a function. The function that maps the output back to the input of a function f is called the **inverse function** and is denoted $f^{-1}(x)$.

A one-to-one function f maps every x in the domain to a unique and distinct corresponding y in the range. Therefore, the inverse function f^{-1} maps every y back to a unique and distinct x.

The function notations $f(x) = y$ and $f^{-1}(y) = x$ indicate that if the point (x, y) satisfies the function, then the point (y, x) satisfies the inverse function.

For example, let the function $h(x) = \{(-1, 0), (1, 2), (3, 4)\}$.

$$h = \{(-1, 0), (1, 2), (3, 4)\}$$

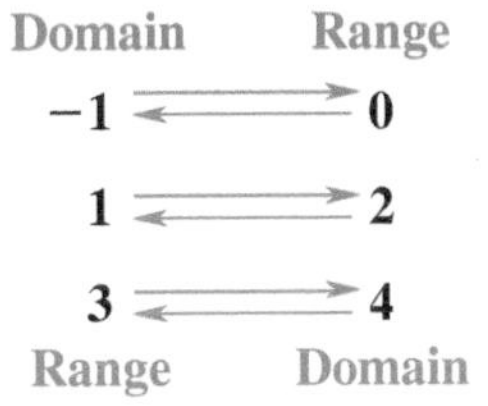

h is a one-to-one function

$$h^{-1} = \{(0, -1), (2, 1), (4, 3)\}$$

The inverse function undoes whatever the function does. For example, if $f(x) = 5x$, then the function f maps any value x in the domain to a value $5x$ in the range. If we want to map backwards, or undo the $5x$, we develop a function called the inverse function that takes $5x$ as input and maps back to x as output. The inverse function is $f^{-1}(x) = \frac{1}{5}x$. Note that if we input $5x$ into the inverse function, the output is x: $f^{-1}(5x) = \frac{1}{5}(5x) = x$.

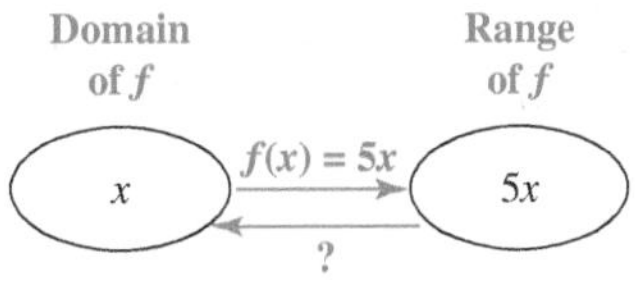

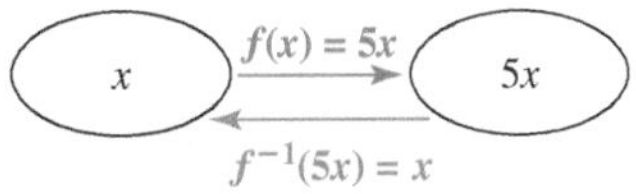

DEFINITION Inverse Function

If f and g denote two one-to-one functions such that

$$f(g(x)) = x \text{ for every } x \text{ in the domain of } g$$

and

$$g(f(x)) = x \text{ for every } x \text{ in the domain of } f,$$

then g is the **inverse** of the function f. The function g is denoted by f^{-1} (read "f-inverse").

CAUTION

$$f^{-1} \neq \frac{1}{f}$$

Note: f^{-1} is used to denote the inverse of f. The superscript -1 is not used as an exponent and, therefore, does not represent the reciprocal of f: $\frac{1}{f}$.

Two properties hold true in the relationships between one-to-one functions and their inverses: (1) The range of the function is the domain of the inverse, and the range of the inverse is the domain of the function, and (2) the composite function that results with a function and its inverse (and vice versa) is the identity function x.

$$\text{Domain of } f = \text{range of } f^{-1} \text{ and range of } f = \text{domain of } f^{-1}$$

$$f^{-1}(f(x)) = x \quad \text{and} \quad f(f^{-1}(x)) = x$$

EXAMPLE 4 **Verifying Inverse Functions**

Verify that $f^{-1}(x) = \frac{1}{2}x - 2$ is the inverse of $f(x) = 2x + 4$.

Solution:

Show that $f^{-1}(f(x)) = x$ and $f(f^{-1}(x)) = x$.

Write f^{-1} using placeholder notation. $\quad f^{-1}(\square) = \frac{1}{2}(\square) - 2$

Substitute $f(x) = 2x + 4$ into f^{-1}. $\quad f^{-1}(f(x)) = \frac{1}{2}(2x + 4) - 2$

Simplify. $\quad f^{-1}(f(x)) = x + 2 - 2 = x$

$f^{-1}(f(x)) = x$

Write f using placeholder notation. $\quad f(\square) = 2(\square) + 4$

Substitute $f^{-1}(x) = \frac{1}{2}x - 2$ into f. $\quad f(f^{-1}(x)) = 2\left(\frac{1}{2}x - 2\right) + 4$

Simplify. $\quad f(f^{-1}(x)) = x - 4 + 4 = x$

$f(f^{-1}(x)) = x$

Note the relationship between the domain and range of f and f^{-1}.

	DOMAIN	RANGE
$f(x) = 2x + 4$	$(-\infty, \infty)$	$(-\infty, \infty)$
$f^{-1}(x) = \frac{1}{2}x - 2$	$(-\infty, \infty)$	$(-\infty, \infty)$

EXAMPLE 5 **Verifying Inverse Functions with Domain Restrictions**

Verify that $f^{-1}(x) = x^2$, for $x \geq 0$, is the inverse of $f(x) = \sqrt{x}$.

Solution:

Show that $f^{-1}(f(x)) = x$ and $f(f^{-1}(x)) = x$.

Write f^{-1} using placeholder notation. $\quad f^{-1}(\square) = (\square)^2$

Substitute $f(x) = \sqrt{x}$ into f^{-1}. $\quad f^{-1}(f(x)) = (\sqrt{x})^2 = x$

$f^{-1}(f(x)) = x$ for $x \geq 0$

Write f using placeholder notation. $\quad f(\square) = \sqrt{(\square)}$

Substitute $f^{-1}(x) = x^2, x \geq 0$ into f. $\quad f(f^{-1}(x)) = \sqrt{x^2} = x, x \geq 0$

$f(f^{-1}(x)) = x$ for $x \geq 0$

	DOMAIN	RANGE
$f(x) = \sqrt{x}$	$[0, \infty)$	$[0, \infty)$
$f^{-1}(x) = x^2, x \geq 0$	$[0, \infty)$	$[0, \infty)$

[CONCEPT CHECK]

If a one-to-one function f has domain $[a, \infty)$ and range $[b, \infty)$, then what are the domain and range of its inverse, $f^{-1}(-1)$?

ANSWER The inverse function, f^{-1}, has domain $[b, \infty)$ and range $[a, \infty)$

1.5.3 Graphical Interpretation of Inverse Functions

In Example 4, we showed that $f^{-1}(x) = \frac{1}{2}x - 2$ is the inverse of $f(x) = 2x + 4$. Let's now investigate the graphs that correspond to the function f and its inverse f^{-1}.

$f(x)$	
x	y
−3	−2
−2	0
−1	2
0	4

$f^{-1}(x)$	
x	y
−2	−3
0	−2
2	−1
4	0

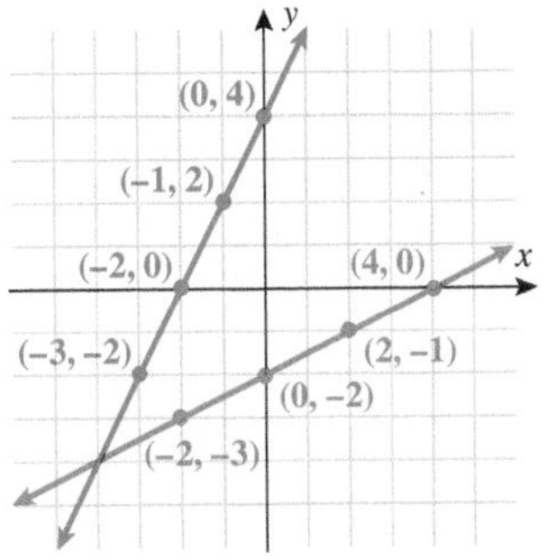

Note that the point $(-3, -2)$ lies on the function and the point $(-2, -3)$ lies on the inverse. In fact, every point (a, b) that lies on the function corresponds to a point (b, a) that lies on the inverse.

Draw the line $y = x$ on the graph. In general, the point (b, a) on the inverse $f^{-1}(x)$ is the reflection (about $y = x$) of the point (a, b) on the function $f(x)$.

In general, if the point (a, b) is on the graph of a function, then the point (b, a) is on the graph of its inverse.

1.5.3 SKILL

Graph the inverse function given the graph of the function.

1.5.3 CONCEPTUAL

Understand why functions and their inverses are symmetric about the line $y = x$.

STUDY TIP

If the point (a, b) is on the function, then the point (b, a) is on the inverse. Notice the interchanging of the x- and y-coordinates.

[CONCEPT CHECK]

If the point (A, B) lies on the graph of a one-to-one function f, what point must lie on the graph of its inverse, f^{-1}?

ANSWER (B, A)

EXAMPLE 6 Graphing the Inverse Function

Given the graph of the function $f(x)$, plot the graph of its inverse, $f^{-1}(x)$.

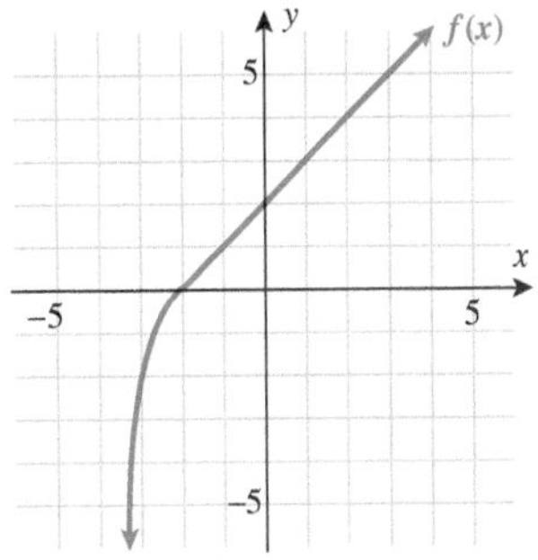

Solution:

Because the points $(-3, -2)$, $(-2, 0)$, $(0, 2)$, and $(2, 4)$ lie on the graph of f, the points $(-2, -3)$, $(0, -2)$, $(2, 0)$, and $(4, 2)$ lie on the graph of f^{-1}.

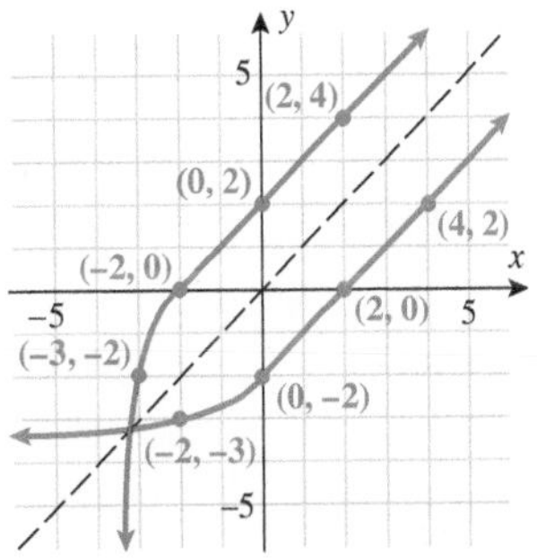

YOUR TURN Given the graph of a function f, plot the inverse function.

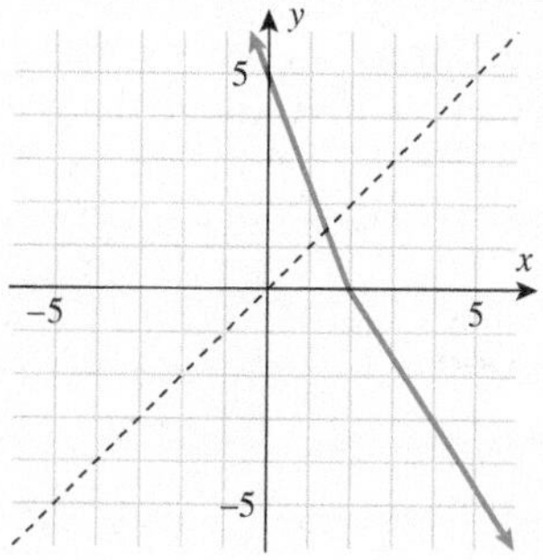

ANSWER

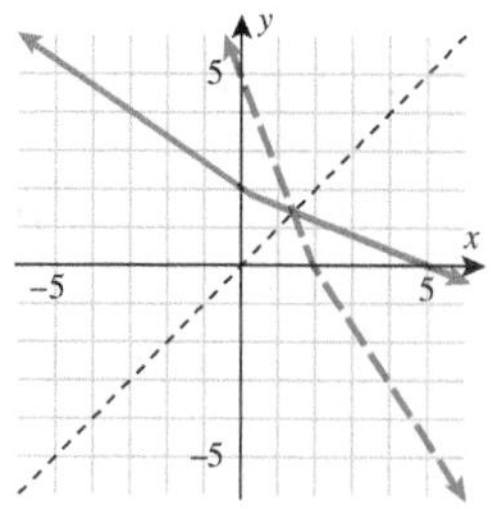

We have developed the definition of an inverse function, and properties of inverses. At this point, you should be able to determine whether two functions are inverses of one another. Let's turn our attention to another problem: How do you find the inverse of a function?

1.5.4 Finding the Inverse Function

1.5.4 SKILL

Find the inverse of a function.

1.5.4 CONCEPTUAL

Understand why a function must be one-to-one in order for its inverse to exist.

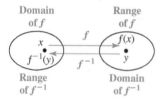

If the point (a, b) lies on the graph of a function, then the point (b, a) lies on the graph of the inverse function. The symmetry about the line $y = x$ tells us that the roles of x and y interchange. Therefore, if we start with every point (x, y) that lies on the graph of a function, then every point (y, x) lies on the graph of its inverse. Algebraically, this corresponds to interchanging x and y. Finding the inverse of a finite set of ordered pairs is easy: Simply interchange the x- and y-coordinates. Earlier, we found that if $h(x) = \{(-1, 0), (1, 2), (3, 4)\}$, then $h^{-1}(x) = \{(0, -1), (2, 1), (4, 3)\}$. But how do we find the inverse of a function defined by an equation?

Recall the mapping relationship if f is a one-to-one function. This relationship implies that $f(x) = y$ and $f^{-1}(y) = x$. Let's use these two identities to find the inverse. Now consider the function defined by $f(x) = 3x - 1$. To find f^{-1}, we let $f(x) = y$, which yields $y = 3x - 1$. Solve for the variable x: $x = \frac{1}{3}y + \frac{1}{3}$.

Recall that $f^{-1}(y) = x$, so we have found the inverse to be $f^{-1}(y) = \frac{1}{3}y + \frac{1}{3}$. It is customary to write the independent variable as x, so we write the inverse as $f^{-1}(x) = \frac{1}{3}x + \frac{1}{3}$. Now that we have found the inverse, let's confirm that the properties $f^{-1}(f(x)) = x$ and $f(f^{-1}(x)) = x$ hold.

$$f(f^{-1}(x)) = 3\left(\frac{1}{3}x + \frac{1}{3}\right) - 1 = x + 1 - 1 = x$$

$$f^{-1}(f(x)) = \frac{1}{3}(3x - 1) + \frac{1}{3} = x - \frac{1}{3} + \frac{1}{3} = x$$

FINDING THE INVERSE OF A FUNCTION

Let f be a one-to-one function. Then the following procedure can be used to find the inverse function f^{-1} if the inverse exists.

STEP	PROCEDURE	EXAMPLE
1	Let $y = f(x)$.	$f(x) = -3x + 5$ $y = -3x + 5$
2	Solve the resulting equation for x in terms of y (if possible).	$3x = -y + 5$ $x = -\frac{1}{3}y + \frac{5}{3}$
3	Let $x = f^{-1}(y)$.	$f^{-1}(y) = -\frac{1}{3}y + \frac{5}{3}$
4	Let $y = x$ (interchange x and y).	$f^{-1}(x) = -\frac{1}{3}x + \frac{5}{3}$

The same result is found if we first interchange x and y and then solve for y in terms of x.

STEP	PROCEDURE	EXAMPLE
1	Let $y = f(x)$.	$f(x) = -3x + 5$ $y = -3x + 5$
2	Interchange x and y.	$x = -3y + 5$
3	Solve for y in terms of x.	$3y = -x + 5$ $y = -\frac{1}{3}x + \frac{5}{3}$
4	Let $y = f^{-1}(x)$.	$f^{-1}(x) = -\frac{1}{3}x + \frac{5}{3}$

Note the following:

- Verify that a function is one-to-one before finding an inverse (if it is not one-to-one, then the inverse does not exist).
- State the domain restrictions on the inverse function. The domain of f is the range of f^{-1}, and vice versa.
- To verify that you have found the inverse, show that $f(f^{-1}(x)) = x$ for all x in the domain of f^{-1} and that $f^{-1}(f(x)) = x$ for all x in the domain of f.

EXAMPLE 7 The Inverse of a Square Root Function

Find the inverse of the function $f(x) = \sqrt{x + 2}$, and state the domain and range of both f and f^{-1}.

Solution:

$f(x)$ is a one-to-one function because it passes the horizontal line test.

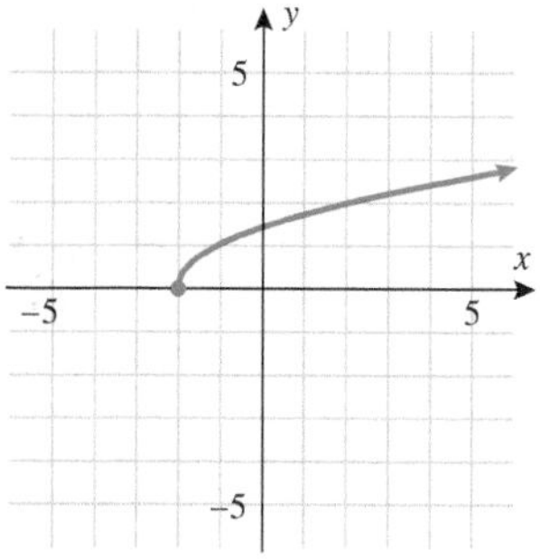

STEP 1 Let $y = f(x)$. $\quad y = \sqrt{x + 2}$

STEP 2 Interchange x and y. $\quad x = \sqrt{y + 2}$

STEP 3 Solve for y.

Square both sides of the equation. $\quad x^2 = y + 2$

Subtract 2 from both sides. $\quad x^2 - 2 = y$ or $y = x^2 - 2$

STEP 4 Let $y = f^{-1}(x)$. $\quad f^{-1}(x) = x^2 - 2$

Note any domain restrictions. (State the domain and range of both f and f^{-1}.)

f:	Domain: $[-2, \infty)$	Range: $[0, \infty)$
f^{-1}:	Domain: $[0, \infty)$	Range: $[-2, \infty)$

The inverse of $f(x) = \sqrt{x + 2}$ is $\boxed{f^{-1}(x) = x^2 - 2 \text{ for } x \geq 0}$.

Check.

$f^{-1}(f(x)) = x$ for all x in the domain of f.

$$f^{-1}(f(x)) = \left(\sqrt{x + 2}\right)^2 - 2$$
$$= x + 2 - 2 \text{ for } x \geq -2$$
$$= x$$

$f(f^{-1}(x)) = x$ for all x in the domain of f^{-1}.

$$f(f^{-1}(x)) = \sqrt{(x^2 - 2) + 2}$$
$$= \sqrt{x^2} \text{ for } x \geq 0$$
$$= x$$

Note that the function $f(x) = \sqrt{x + 2}$ and its inverse $f^{-1}(x) = x^2 - 2$ for $x \geq 0$ are symmetric about the line $y = x$.

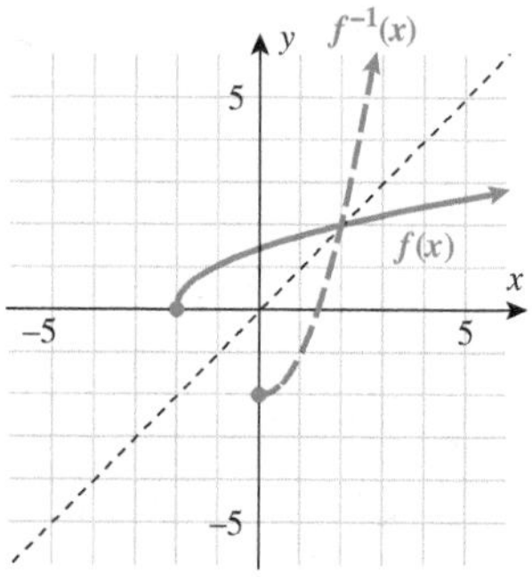

YOUR TURN Find the inverse of the given function, and state the domain and range of the inverse function.

a. $f(x) = 7x - 3$ **b.** $g(x) = \sqrt{x - 1}$

STUDY TIP

Had we ignored the domain and range in Example 7, we would have found the inverse function to be the square function $f(x) = x^2 - 2$, which is not a one-to-one function. It is only when we restrict the domain of the square function that we get a one-to-one function.

ANSWER

a. $f^{-1}(x) = \dfrac{x + 3}{7}$, Domain: $(-\infty, \infty)$, Range: $(-\infty, \infty)$

b. $g^{-1}(x) = x^2 + 1$, Domain: $[0, \infty)$, Range: $[1, \infty)$

EXAMPLE 8 **A Function That Does Not Have an Inverse Function**

Find the inverse of the function $f(x) = |x|$ if it exists.

Solution:

The function $f(x) = |x|$ fails the horizontal line test and therefore is not a one-to-one function. Because f is not a one-to-one function, its inverse function does not exist.

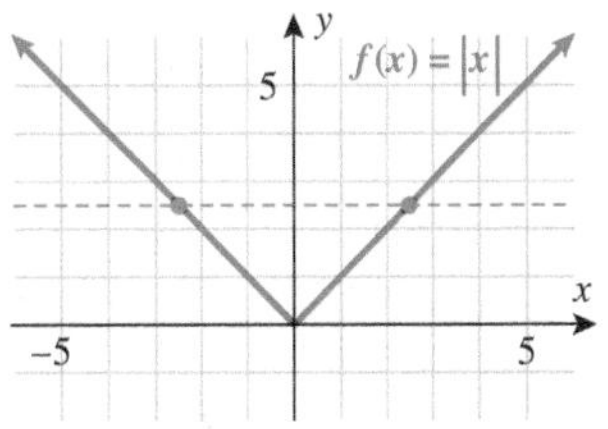

EXAMPLE 9 **Finding the Inverse Function**

The function $f(x) = \dfrac{2}{x+3}$, $x \neq -3$, is a one-to-one function. Find its inverse.

Solution:

STEP 1 Let $y = f(x)$. $\qquad y = \dfrac{2}{x+3}$

STEP 2 Interchange x and y. $\qquad x = \dfrac{2}{y+3}$

STEP 3 Solve for y.

Multiply the equation by $(y + 3)$. $\qquad x(y+3) = 2$

Eliminate the parentheses. $\qquad xy + 3x = 2$

Subtract $3x$ from both sides. $\qquad xy = -3x + 2$

Divide the equation by x. $\qquad y = \dfrac{-3x+2}{x} = -3 + \dfrac{2}{x}$

STEP 4 Let $y = f^{-1}(x)$. $\qquad f^{-1}(x) = -3 + \dfrac{2}{x}$

Note any domain restrictions on $f^{-1}(x)$. $\qquad x \neq 0$

The inverse of the function $f(x) = \dfrac{2}{x+3}$, $x \neq -3$, is $\boxed{f^{-1}(x) = -3 + \dfrac{2}{x}, x \neq 0}$.

Check.

$$f^{-1}(f(x)) = -3 + \frac{2}{\left(\dfrac{2}{x+3}\right)} = -3 + (x+3) = x, x \neq -3$$

$$f(f^{-1}(x)) = \frac{2}{\left(-3 + \dfrac{2}{x}\right) + 3} = \frac{2}{\left(\dfrac{2}{x}\right)} = x, x \neq 0$$

YOUR TURN The function $f(x) = \dfrac{4}{x-1}$, $x \neq 1$, is a one-to-one function. Find its inverse.

STUDY TIP

The range of a function is equal to the domain of its inverse function.

CONCEPT CHECK

Explain why you cannot find the inverse of $f(x) = x^2$ without restricting the domain?

ANSWER $f(x) = x^2$ is not a one-to-one function.

ANSWER

$f^{-1}(x) = 1 + \dfrac{4}{x}, x \neq 0$

Note in Example 9 that the domain of f is $(-\infty, -3)\cup(-3, \infty)$ and the domain of f^{-1} is $(-\infty, 0)\cup(0, \infty)$. Therefore, we know that the range of f is $(-\infty, 0)\cup(0, \infty)$ and the range of f^{-1} is $(-\infty, -3)\cup(-3, \infty)$.

EXAMPLE 10 **Finding the Inverse of a Piecewise-Defined Function**

Determine whether the function $f(x) = \begin{cases} x^2 & x < 0 \\ -x & x \geq 0 \end{cases}$ is a one-to-one function. If it is a one-to-one function, find its inverse.

Solution:

The graph of the function f passes the horizontal line test, so f is a one-to-one function.

STEP 1 Let $y = f(x)$.

Let $y_1 = x_1^2$ for $x_1 < 0$ and $y_2 = -x_2$ for $x_2 \geq 0$ represent the two pieces of f. Note the domain and range for each piece.

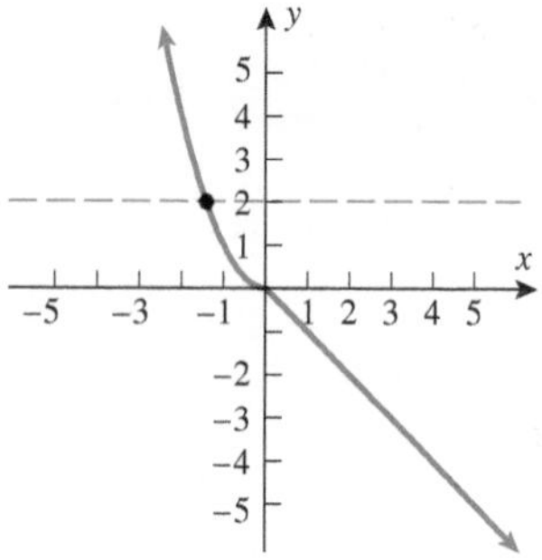

EQUATION	DOMAIN	RANGE
$y_1 = x_1^2$	$x_1 < 0$	$y_1 > 0$
$y_2 = -x_2$	$x_2 \geq 0$	$y_2 \leq 0$

STEP 2 Solve for x in terms of y.

Solve for x_1. $x_1 = \pm\sqrt{y_1}$

Select the negative root since $x_1 < 0$. $x_1 = -\sqrt{y_1}$

Solve for x_2. $x_2 = -y_2$

STEP 3 Let $x = f^{-1}(y)$.

$x_1 = f^{-1}(y_1) = -\sqrt{y_1}$	$x_1 < 0$	$y_1 > 0$
$x_2 = f^{-1}(y_2) = -y_2$	$x_2 \geq 0$	$y_2 \leq 0$

Express the two "pieces" in terms of a piecewise-defined function.

$$f^{-1}(y) = \begin{cases} -\sqrt{y} & y > 0 \\ -y & y \leq 0 \end{cases}$$

STEP 4 Let $y = x$ (interchange x and y).

$$f^{-1}(x) = \begin{cases} -\sqrt{x} & x > 0 \\ -x & x \leq 0 \end{cases}$$

[SECTION 1.5] SUMMARY

One-to-One Functions

Each input in the domain corresponds to exactly one output in the range, and no two inputs map to the same output. There are three ways to test a function to determine whether it is a one-to-one function.

1. **Discrete points:** For the set of all points (a, b), verify that no y-values are repeated.
2. **Algebraic equations:** Let $f(x_1) = f(x_2)$; if it can be shown that $x_1 = x_2$, then the function is one-to-one.
3. **Graphs:** Use the horizontal line test; if any horizontal line intersects the graph of the function in more than one point, then the function is not one-to-one.

Properties of Inverse Functions

1. If f is a one-to-one function, then f^{-1} exists.
2. Domain and range
   - Domain of f = range of f^{-1}
   - Domain of f^{-1} = range of f
3. Composition of inverse functions
   - $f^{-1}(f(x)) = x$ for all x in the domain of f
   - $f(f^{-1}(x)) = x$ for all x in the domain of f^{-1}
4. The graphs of f and f^{-1} are symmetric with respect to the line $y = x$.

Procedure for Finding the Inverse of a Function

1. Let $y = f(x)$.
2. Interchange x and y.
3. Solve for y.
4. Let $y = f^{-1}(x)$.

[SECTION 1.5] EXERCISES

• SKILLS

In Exercises 1–10, determine whether the given relation is a function. If it is a function, determine whether it is a one-to-one function.

1. $\{(0, 0), (9, -3), (4, -2), (4, 2), (9, 3)\}$
2. $\{(0, 1), (1, 1), (2, 1), (3, 1)\}$
3. $\{(0, 1), (1, 0), (2, 1), (-2, 1), (5, 4), (-3, 4)\}$
4. $\{(0, 0), (-1, -1), (-2, -8), (1, 1), (2, 8)\}$

5.
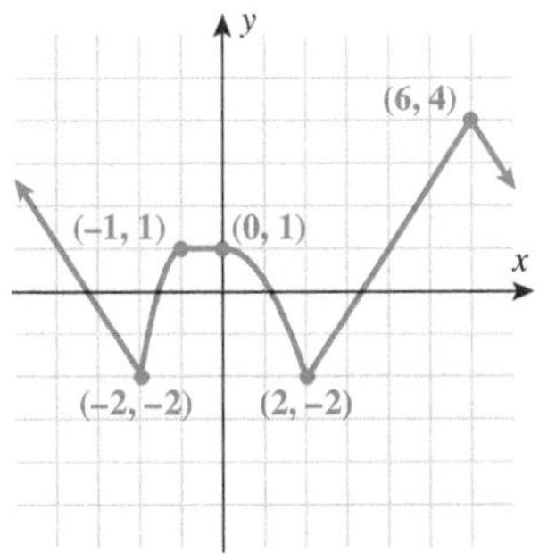

6.
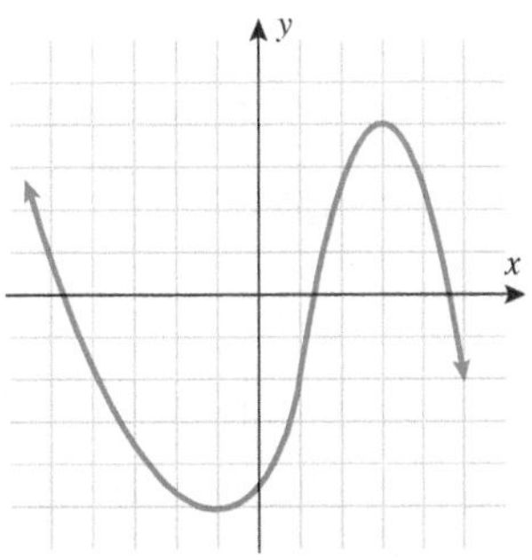

7.
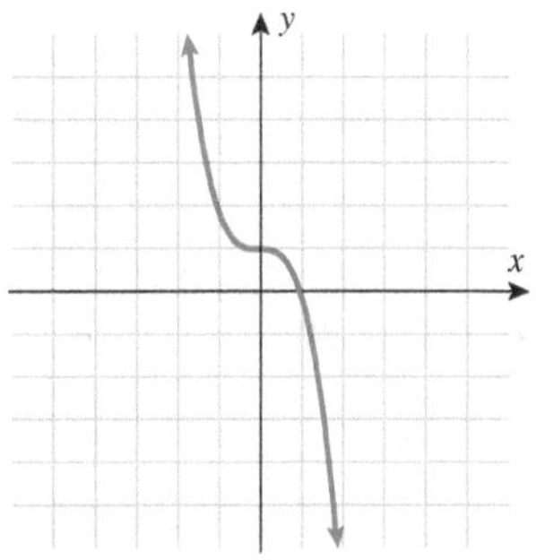

8.
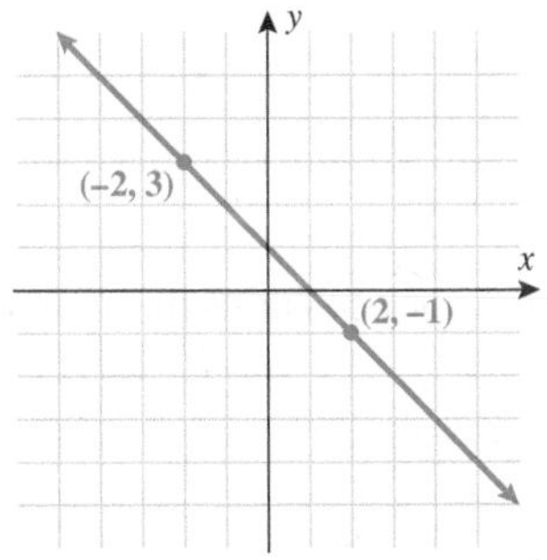

9.
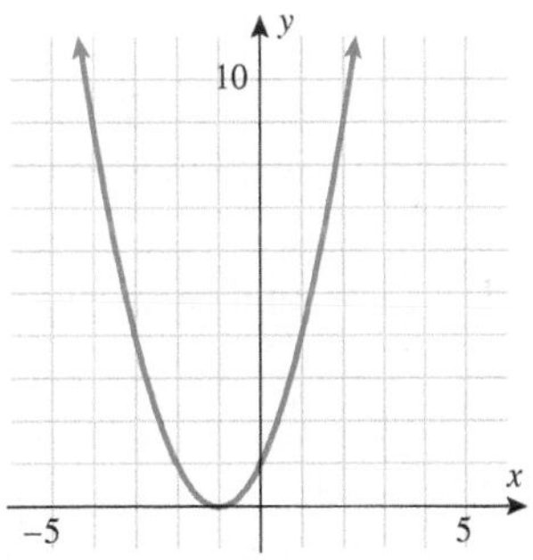

10.
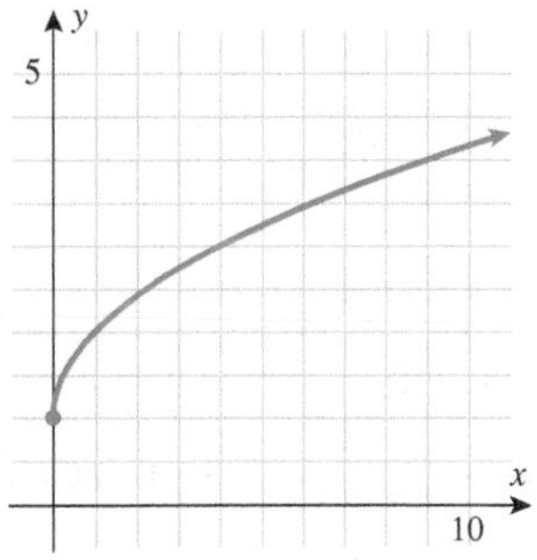

In Exercises 11–18, determine algebraically and graphically whether the function is one-to-one.

11. $f(x) = |x - 3|$

12. $f(x) = (x - 2)^2 + 1$

13. $f(x) = \dfrac{1}{x - 1}$

14. $f(x) = \sqrt[3]{x}$

15. $f(x) = x^2 - 4$

16. $f(x) = \sqrt{x + 1}$

17. $f(x) = x^3 - 1$

18. $f(x) = \dfrac{1}{x + 2}$

In Exercises 19–28, verify that the function $f^{-1}(x)$ is the inverse of $f(x)$ by showing that $f(f^{-1}(x)) = x$ and $f^{-1}(f(x)) = x$. Graph $f(x)$ and $f^{-1}(x)$ on the same axes to show the symmetry about the line $y = x$.

19. $f(x) = 2x + 1;\ f^{-1}(x) = \dfrac{x - 1}{2}$

20. $f(x) = \dfrac{x - 2}{3};\ f^{-1}(x) = 3x + 2$

21. $f(x) = \sqrt{x - 1},\ x \geq 1;\ f^{-1}(x) = x^2 + 1,\ x \geq 0$

22. $f(x) = 2 - x^2,\ x \geq 0;\ f^{-1}(x) = \sqrt{2 - x},\ x \leq 2$

23. $f(x) = \dfrac{1}{x};\ f^{-1}(x) = \dfrac{1}{x},\ x \neq 0$

24. $f(x) = (5 - x)^{1/3};\ f^{-1}(x) = 5 - x^3$

25. $f(x) = \dfrac{1}{2x + 6},\ x \neq -3;\ f^{-1}(x) = \dfrac{1}{2x} - 3,\ x \neq 0$

26. $f(x) = \dfrac{3}{4 - x},\ x \neq 4;\ f^{-1}(x) = 4 - \dfrac{3}{x},\ x \neq 0$

27. $f(x) = \dfrac{x + 3}{x + 4},\ x \neq -4;\ f^{-1}(x) = \dfrac{3 - 4x}{x - 1},\ x \neq 1$

28. $f(x) = \dfrac{x - 5}{3 - x},\ x \neq 3;\ f^{-1}(x) = \dfrac{3x + 5}{x + 1},\ x \neq -1$

In Exercises 29–36, graph the inverse of the one-to-one function that is given.

29.

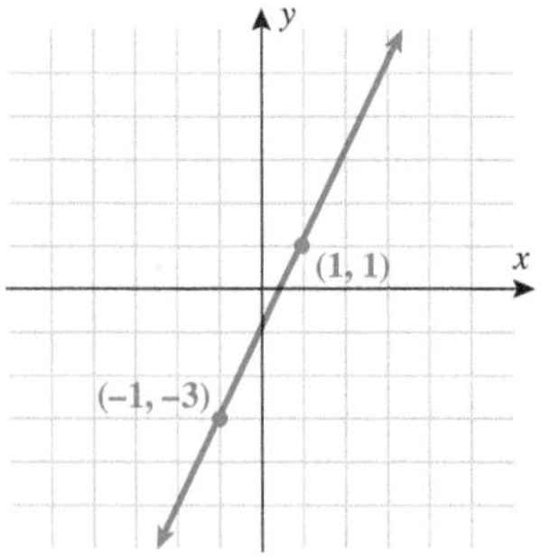

30.

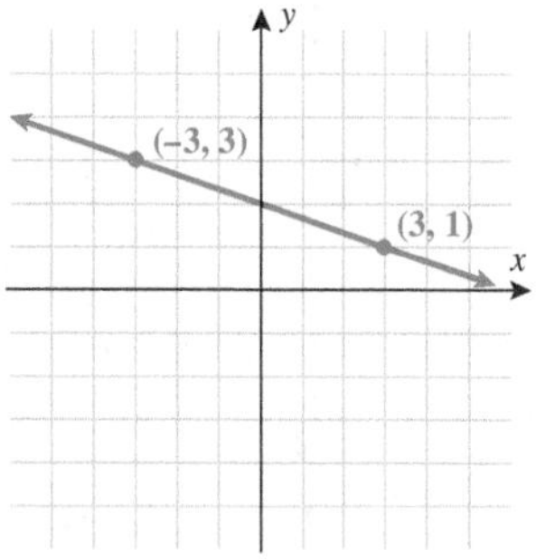

31.

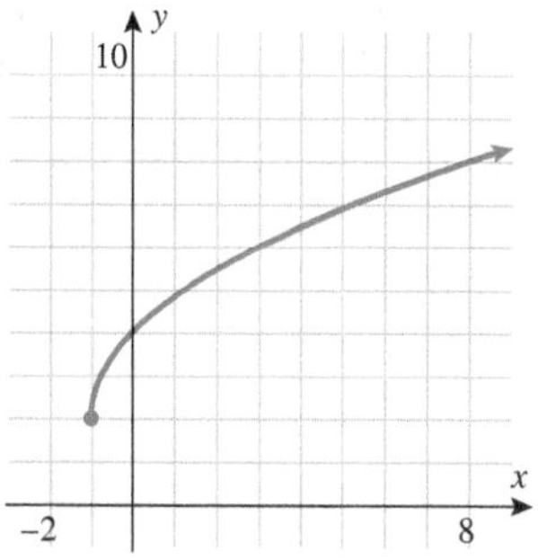

32.

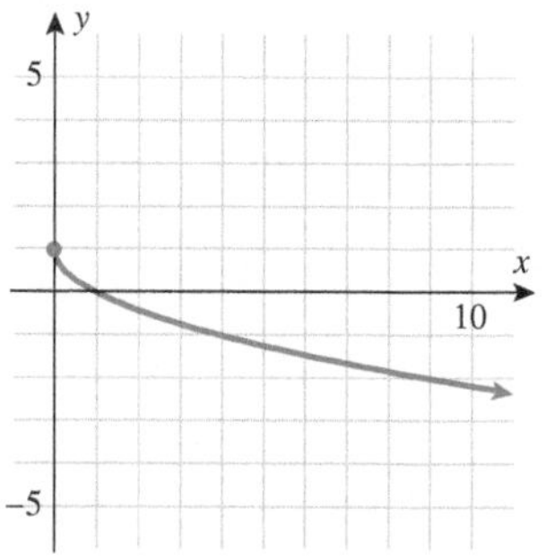

33.

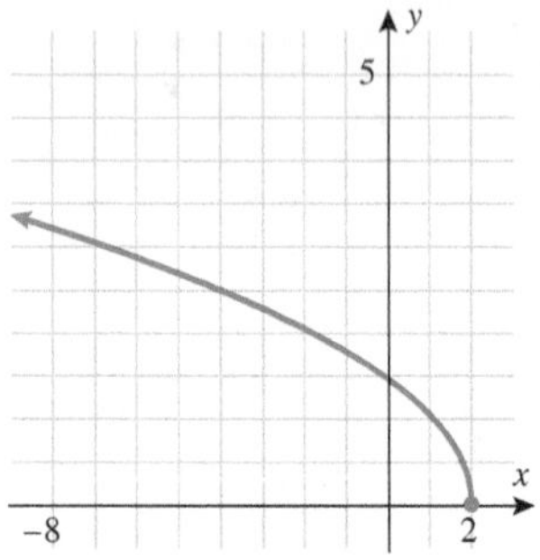

34.

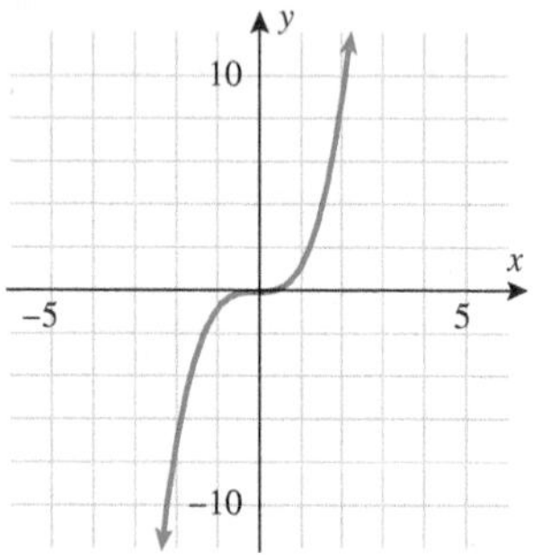

35.

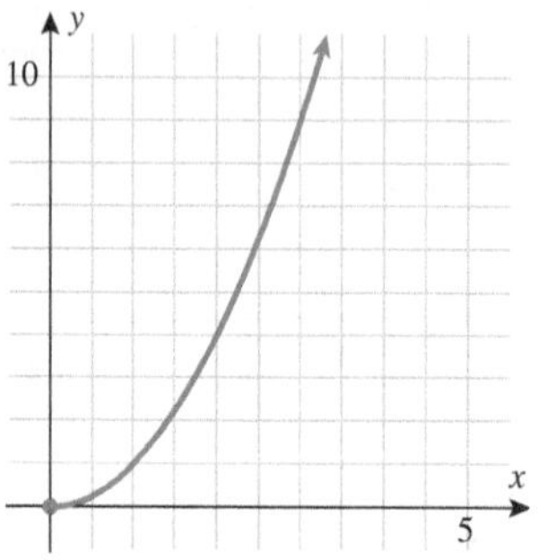

36.

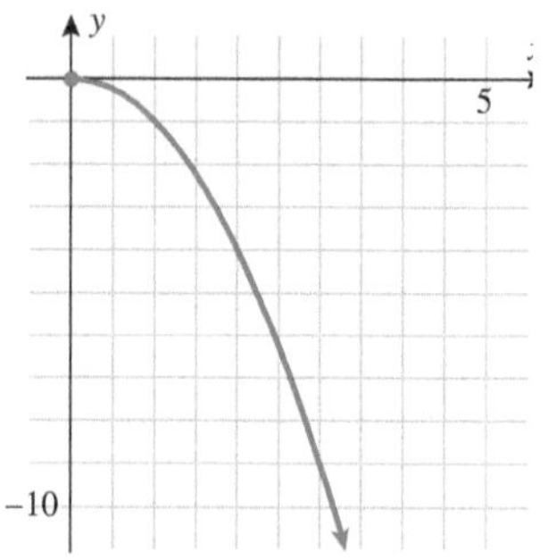

In Exercises 37–56, the function f is one-to-one. Find its inverse, and check your answer. State the domain and range of both f and f^{-1}.

37. $f(x) = -3x + 2$

38. $f(x) = 2x + 3$

39. $f(x) = x^3 + 1$

40. $f(x) = x^3 - 1$

41. $f(x) = \sqrt{x - 3}$

42. $f(x) = \sqrt{3 - x}$

43. $f(x) = x^2 - 1,\ x \geq 0$

44. $f(x) = 2x^2 + 1,\ x \geq 0$

45. $f(x) = (x + 2)^2 - 3,\ x \geq -2$

46. $f(x) = (x - 3)^2 - 2,\ x \geq 3$

47. $f(x) = \dfrac{2}{x}$

48. $f(x) = -\dfrac{3}{x}$

49. $f(x) = \dfrac{2}{3 - x}$

50. $f(x) = \dfrac{7}{x + 2}$

51. $f(x) = \dfrac{7x + 1}{5 - x}$

52. $f(x) = \dfrac{2x + 5}{7 + x}$

53. $f(x) = \dfrac{1}{\sqrt{x}}$

54. $f(x) = \dfrac{x}{\sqrt{x + 1}}$

55. $f(x) = \sqrt{\dfrac{x + 1}{x - 2}}$

56. $f(x) = \sqrt{x^2 - 1}, x \geq 1$

In Exercises 57–62, graph the piecewise-defined function to determine whether it is a one-to-one function. If it is a one-to-one function, find its inverse.

57. $G(x) = \begin{cases} 0 & x < 0 \\ \sqrt{x} & x \geq 0 \end{cases}$

58. $G(x) = \begin{cases} \dfrac{1}{x} & x < 0 \\ \sqrt{x} & x \geq 0 \end{cases}$

59. $f(x) = \begin{cases} \sqrt[3]{x} & x \leq -1 \\ x^2 + 2x & -1 < x \leq 1 \\ \sqrt{x} + 2 & x > 1 \end{cases}$

60. $f(x) = \begin{cases} -x & x < -2 \\ \sqrt{4 - x^2} & -2 \leq x \leq 0 \\ -\dfrac{1}{x} & x > 0 \end{cases}$

61. $f(x) = \begin{cases} x & x \leq -1 \\ x^3 & -1 < x < 1 \\ x & x \geq 1 \end{cases}$

62. $f(x) = \begin{cases} x + 3 & x \leq -2 \\ |x| & -2 < x < 2 \\ x^2 & x \geq 2 \end{cases}$

• APPLICATIONS

63. **Temperature.** The equation used to convert from degrees Celsius to degrees Fahrenheit is $f(x) = \frac{9}{5}x + 32$. Determine the inverse function $f^{-1}(x)$. What does the inverse function represent?

64. **Temperature.** The equation used to convert from degrees Fahrenheit to degrees Celsius is $C(x) = \frac{5}{9}(x - 32)$. Determine the inverse function $C^{-1}(x)$. What does the inverse function represent?

65. **Budget.** The Richmond rowing club is planning to enter the *Head of the Charles* race in Boston and is trying to figure out how much money to raise. The entry fee is \$250 per boat for the first 10 boats and \$175 for each additional boat. Find the cost function $C(x)$ as a function of the number of boats x the club enters. Find the inverse function that will yield how many boats the club can enter as a function of how much money it will raise.

66. **Long-Distance Calling Plans.** A phone company charges \$0.39 per minute for the first 10 minutes of a long-distance phone call and \$0.12 per minute every minute after that. Find the cost function $C(x)$ as a function of length x of the phone call in minutes. Suppose you buy a "prepaid" phone card that is planned for a single call. Find the inverse function that determines how many minutes you can talk as a function of how much you prepaid.

67. **Salary.** A student works at Target making \$7 per hour and the weekly number of hours worked per week x varies. If Target withholds 25% of his earnings for taxes and Social Security, write a function $E(x)$ that expresses the student's take-home pay each week. Find the inverse function $E^{-1}(x)$. What does the inverse function tell you?

68. **Salary.** A grocery store pays you \$8 per hour for the first 40 hours per week and time and a half for overtime. Write a piecewise-defined function that represents your weekly earnings $E(x)$ as a function of the number of hours worked x. Find the inverse function $E^{-1}(x)$. What does the inverse function tell you?

In Exercises 69–72, refer to the following:

By analyzing available empirical data it was determined that during an illness, a patient's body temperature fluctuated over one 24-hour period according to the function

$$T(t) = 0.0003(t - 24)^3 + 101.70$$

where T represents that patient's temperature in degrees Fahrenheit and t represents the time of day in hours measured from 12:00 A.M. (midnight).

69. **Health/Medicine.** Find the domain and range of the function $T(t)$.

70. **Health/Medicine.** Find time as a function of temperature, that is, the inverse function $t(T)$.

71. **Health/Medicine.** Find the domain and range of the function $t(T)$ found in Exercise 70.

72. **Health/Medicine.** At what time, to the nearest hour, was the patient's temperature 99.5°F?

• CATCH THE MISTAKE

In Exercises 73 and 74, explain the mistake that is made.

73. Is $x = y^2$ a one-to-one function?

Solution:

Yes, this graph represents a one-to-one function because it passes the horizontal line test.

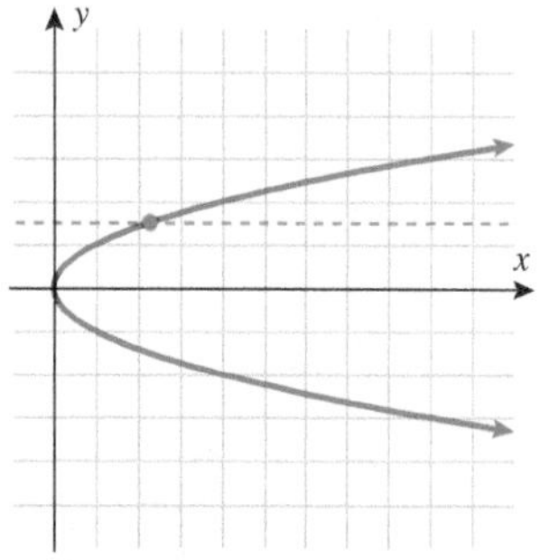

This is incorrect. What mistake was made?

74. Given the function $f(x) = \sqrt{x - 2}$, find the inverse function $f^{-1}(x)$, and state the domain restrictions on $f^{-1}(x)$.

Solution:

Step 1: Let $y = f(x)$. $y = \sqrt{x - 2}$

Step 2: Interchange x and y. $x = \sqrt{y - 2}$

Step 3: Solve for y. $y = x^2 + 2$

Step 4: Let $f^{-1}(x) = y$. $f^{-1}(x) = x^2 + 2$

Step 5: Domain restrictions $f(x) = \sqrt{x - 2}$ has the domain restriction that $x \geq 2$.

The inverse of $f(x) = \sqrt{x - 2}$ is $f^{-1}(x) = x^2 + 2$.

The domain of $f^{-1}(x)$ is $x \geq 2$.

This is incorrect. What mistake was made?

• CONCEPTUAL

In Exercises 75–78, determine whether each statement is true or false.

75. Every even function is a one-to-one function.

76. Every odd function is a one-to-one function.

77. It is not possible that $f = f^{-1}$.

78. A function f has an inverse. If the function lies in quadrant II, then its inverse lies in quadrant IV.

79. If $(0, b)$ is the y-intercept of a one-to-one function f, what is the x-intercept of the inverse f^{-1}?

80. If $(a, 0)$ is the x-intercept of a one-to-one function f, what is the y-intercept of the inverse f^{-1}?

• CHALLENGE

81. The unit circle is not a function. If we restrict ourselves to the semicircle that lies in quadrants I and II, the graph represents a function, but it is not a one-to-one function. If we further restrict ourselves to the quarter circle lying in quadrant I, the graph does represent a one-to-one function. Determine the equations of both the one-to-one function and its inverse. State the domain and range of both.

82. Find the inverse of $f(x) = \frac{c}{x}$, $c \neq 0$.

83. Under what conditions is the linear function $f(x) = mx + b$ a one-to-one function?

84. Assuming that the conditions found in Exercise 83 are met, determine the inverse of the linear function.

85. Determine the value of a that makes $f(x) = \frac{x - 2}{x^2 - a}$ a one-to-one function. Determine $f^{-1}(x)$ and its domain.

86. The point (a, b) lies on the graph of the one-to-one function $y = f(x)$. What other points are guaranteed to lie on the graph of $y = f^{-1}(x)$?

• PREVIEW TO CALCULUS

For Exercises 87–90, refer to the following:

In calculus, the difference quotient $\frac{f(x + h) - f(x)}{h}$ of a function f is used to find the derivative f' of f, by allowing h to approach zero, $h \to 0$. The derivative of the inverse function $(f^{-1})'$ can be found using the formula

$$(f^{-1})'(x) = \frac{1}{f'(f^{-1}(x))}$$

provided that the denominator is not 0 and both f and f^{-1} are differentiable. For the following one-to-one function, find (a) f^{-1}, (b) f', (c) $(f^{-1})'$, and (d) verify the formula above. For (b) and (c), use the difference quotient.

87. $f(x) = 2x + 1$

88. $f(x) = x^2, x > 0$

89. $f(x) = \sqrt{x + 2}, x > -2$

90. $f(x) = \frac{1}{x + 1}, x > -1$

[CHAPTER 1 REVIEW]

SECTION	CONCEPT	KEY IDEAS/FORMULAS
1.1	**Functions**	
	Definition of a function	All functions are relations, but not all relations are functions.
	Functions defined by equations	A vertical line can intersect a function in at most one point.
	Function notation	Placeholder notation Difference quotient: $\frac{f(x+h)-f(x)}{h}$, $h \neq 0$
	Domain of a function	Are there any restrictions on x?
1.2	**Graphs of functions**	
	Recognizing and classifying functions	**Common functions** $f(x) = mx + b$, $f(x) = x$, $f(x) = x^2$, $f(x) = x^3$, $f(x) = \sqrt{x}$, $f(x) = \sqrt[3]{x}$, $f(x) = \|x\|$, $f(x) = \frac{1}{x}$ **Even and odd functions:** *Even:* $f(-x) = f(x)$ Symmetry about y-axis *Odd:* $f(-x) = -f(x)$ Symmetry about origin
	Increasing and decreasing functions	■ Increasing: rises (left to right) ■ Decreasing: falls (left to right)
	Average rate of change	$\frac{f(x_2)-f(x_1)}{x_2-x_1}$ $x_1 \neq x_2$
	Piecewise-defined functions	Points of discontinuity
1.3	**Graphing techniques: Transformations**	Shift the graph of $f(x)$.
	Horizontal and vertical shifts	$f(x+c)$ c units to the left where $c > 0$ $f(x-c)$ c units to the right where $c > 0$ $f(x)+c$ c units upward where $c > 0$ $f(x)-c$ c units downward where $c > 0$
	Reflection about the axes	$-f(x)$ Reflection about the x-axis $f(-x)$ Reflection about the y-axis
	Stretching and compressing	$cf(x)$ if $c > 1$ stretch vertically $cf(x)$ if $0 < c < 1$ compress vertically $f(cx)$ if $c > 1$ compress horizontally $f(cx)$ if $0 < c < 1$ stretch horizontally

SECTION	CONCEPT	KEY IDEAS/FORMULAS
1.4	**Combining functions**	
	Adding, subtracting, multiplying, and dividing functions	$(f+g)(x) = f(x) + g(x)$ $(f-g)(x) = f(x) - g(x)$ $(f \cdot g)(x) = f(x) \cdot g(x)$ Domain of the resulting function is the intersection of the individual domains. $\left(\frac{f}{g}\right)(x) = \frac{f(x)}{g(x)}, \quad g(x) \neq 0$ Domain of the quotient is the intersection of the domains of f and g, and any points where $g(x) = 0$ must be eliminated.
	Composition of functions	$(f \circ g)(x) = f(g(x))$ The domain of the composite function is a subset of the domain of $g(x)$. Values for x must be eliminated if their corresponding values $g(x)$ are not in the domain of f. 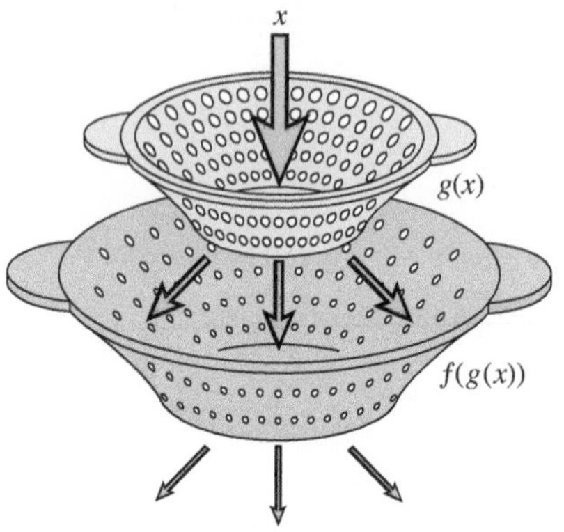 $(f \circ g)(x) = f(g(x))$
1.5	**One-to-one functions and inverse functions**	
	One-to-one functions	■ No two x-values map to the same y-value. If $f(x_1) = f(x_2)$, then $x_1 = x_2$. ■ A horizontal line may intersect a one-to-one function in at most one point.
	Inverse functions	■ Only one-to-one functions have inverses. ■ $f^{-1}(f(x)) = x$ for all x in the domain of f. ■ $f(f^{-1}(x)) = x$ for all x in the domain of f^{-1}. ■ Domain of f = range of f^{-1}. Range of f = domain of f^{-1}.
	Graphical interpretation of inverse functions	■ The graph of a function and its inverse are symmetric about the line $y = x$. ■ If the point (a, b) lies on the graph of a function, then the point (b, a) lies on the graph of its inverse.
	Finding the inverse function	1. Let $y = f(x)$. 2. Interchange x and y. 3. Solve for y. 4. Let $y = f^{-1}(x)$.

[CHAPTER 1 REVIEW EXERCISES]

1.1 Functions

Determine whether each relation is a function. Assume that the coordinate pair (x, y) represents independent variable x and dependent variable y.

1. $\{(-2, 3), (1, -3), (0, 4), (2, 6)\}$
2. $\{(4, 7), (2, 6), (3, 8), (1, 7)\}$
3. $x^2 + y^2 = 36$
4. $x = 4$
5. $y = |x + 2|$
6. $y = \sqrt{x}$
7.

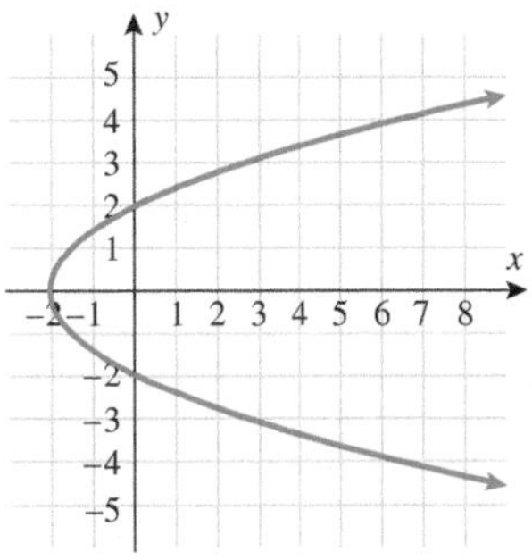

8.

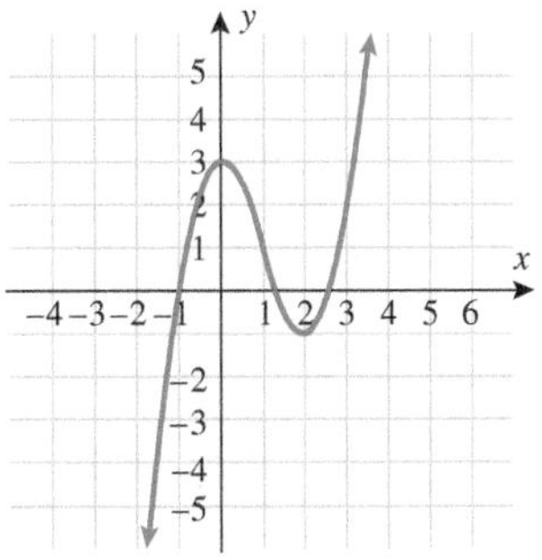

Use the graphs of the functions to find:

9.

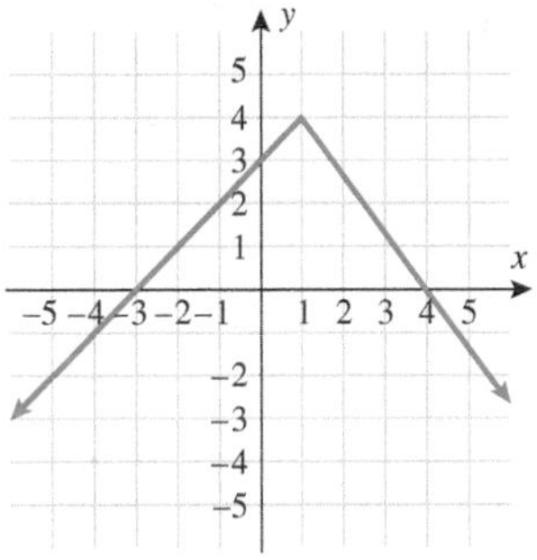

a. $f(-1)$ b. $f(1)$
c. x, where $f(x) = 0$

10.

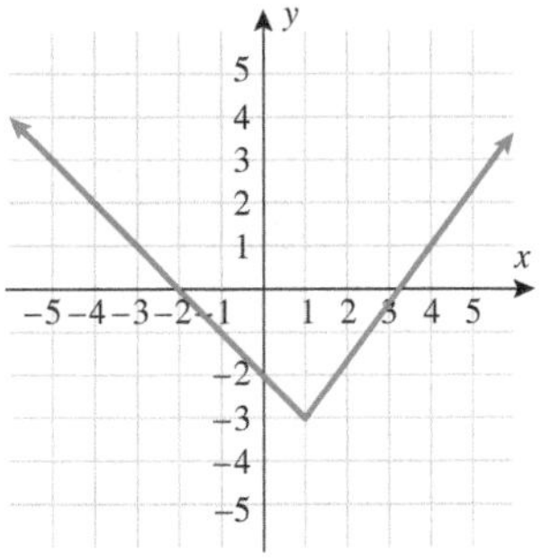

a. $f(-4)$ b. $f(0)$
c. x, where $f(x) = 0$

11.

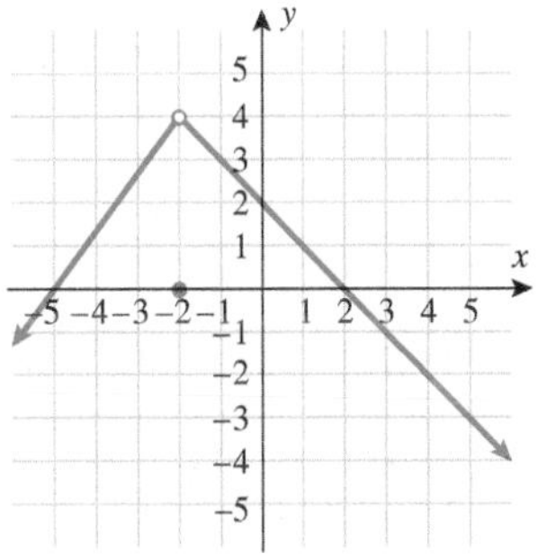

a. $f(-2)$ b. $f(4)$
c. x, where $f(x) = 0$

12.

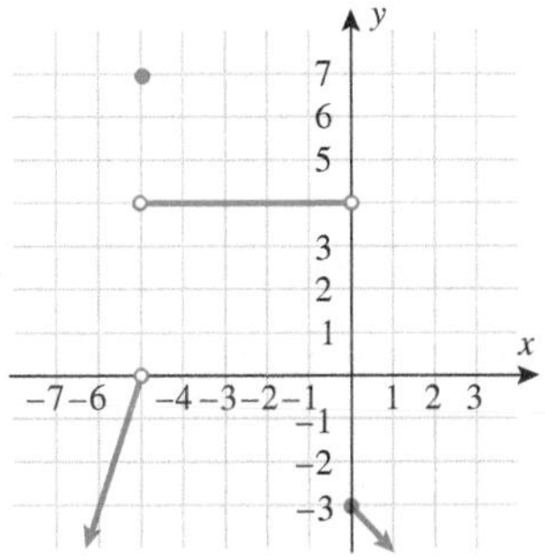

a. $f(-5)$ b. $f(0)$
c. x, where $f(x) = 0$

Evaluate the given quantities using the following three functions:

$f(x) = 4x - 7 \qquad F(t) = t^2 + 4t - 3 \qquad g(x) = |x^2 + 2x + 4|$

13. $f(3)$
14. $F(4)$
15. $f(-7) \cdot g(3)$
16. $\dfrac{F(0)}{g(0)}$
17. $\dfrac{f(2) - F(2)}{g(0)}$
18. $f(3 + h)$
19. $\dfrac{f(3 + h) - f(3)}{h}$
20. $\dfrac{F(t + h) - F(t)}{h}$

Find the domain of the given function. Express the domain in interval notation.

21. $f(x) = -3x - 4$
22. $g(x) = x^2 - 2x + 6$
23. $h(x) = \dfrac{1}{x + 4}$
24. $F(x) = \dfrac{7}{x^2 + 3}$
25. $G(x) = \sqrt{x - 4}$
26. $H(x) = \dfrac{1}{\sqrt{2x - 6}}$

Challenge

27. If $f(x) = \dfrac{D}{x^2 - 16}$, $f(4)$ and $f(-4)$ are undefined, and $f(5) = 2$, find D.

38. Construct a function that is undefined at $x = -3$ and $x = 2$ such that the point $(0, -4)$ lies on the graph of the function.

1.2 Graphs of Functions

Determine whether the function is even, odd, or neither.

29. $h(x) = x^3 - 7x$
30. $f(x) = x^4 + 3x^2$
31. $f(x) = \dfrac{1}{x^3} + 3x$
32. $f(x) = \dfrac{1}{x^2} + 3x^4 + |x|$

In Exercises 33–36, state the (a) domain, (b) range, and (c) x-interval(s) where the function is increasing, decreasing, or constant. Find the values of (d) $f(0)$, (e) $f(-3)$, and (f) $f(3)$.

33.

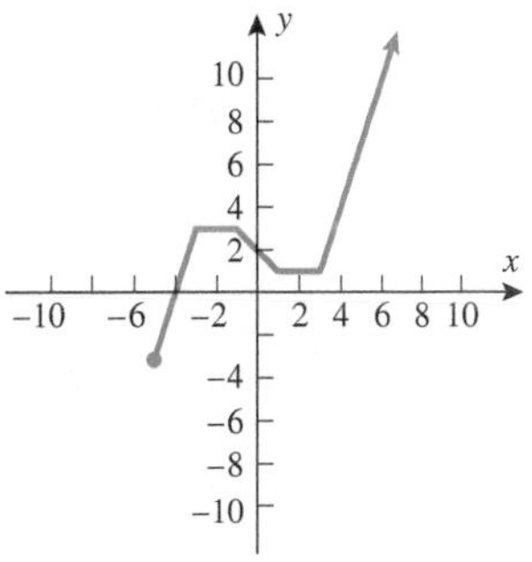

34.

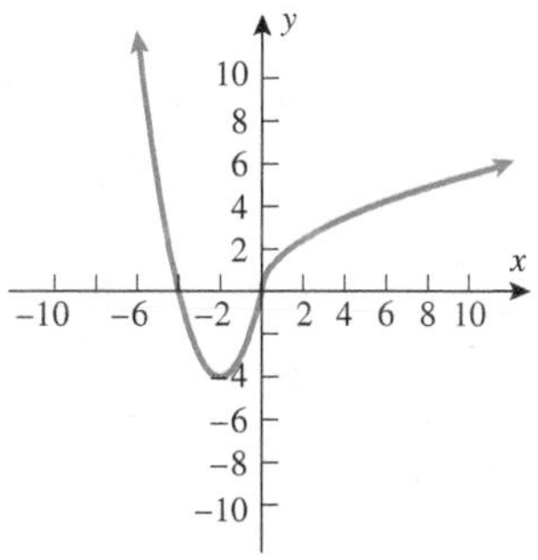

35.

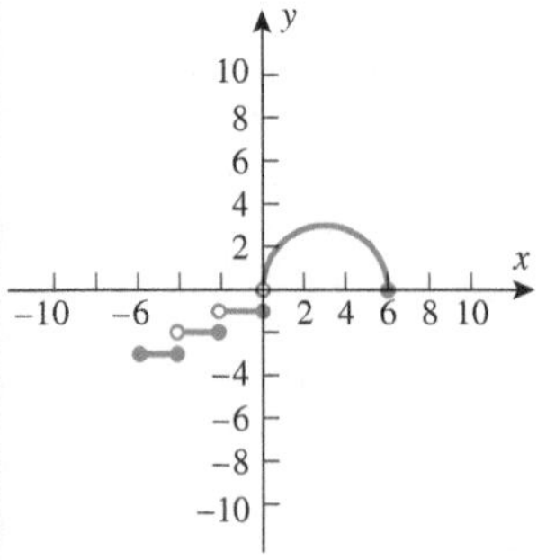

36.

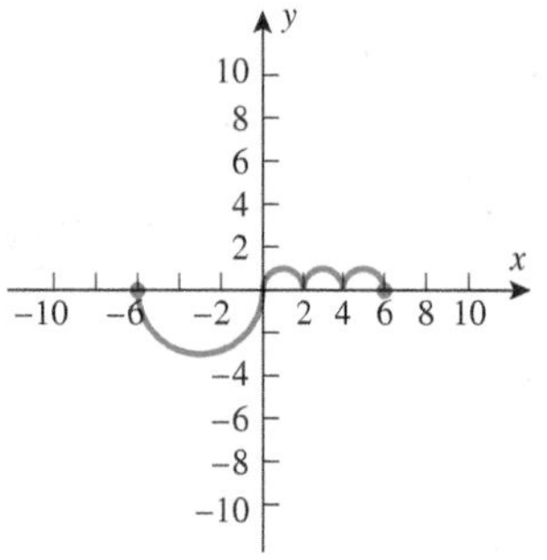

In Exercises 37–40, find the difference quotient $\dfrac{f(x+h)-f(x)}{h}$ for each function.

37. $f(x) = x^3 - 1$

38. $f(x) = \dfrac{x-1}{x+2}$

39. $f(x) = x + \dfrac{1}{x}$

40. $f(x) = \sqrt{\dfrac{x}{x+1}}$

41. Find the average rate of change of $f(x) = 4 - x^2$ from $x = 0$ to $x = 2$.

42. Find the average rate of change of $f(x) = |2x - 1|$ from $x = 1$ to $x = 5$.

Graph the piecewise-defined function. State the domain and range in interval notation.

43. $F(x) = \begin{cases} x^2 & x < 0 \\ 2 & x \geq 0 \end{cases}$

44. $f(x) = \begin{cases} -2x - 3 & x \leq 0 \\ 4 & 0 < x \leq 1 \\ x^2 + 4 & x > 1 \end{cases}$

45. $f(x) = \begin{cases} x^2 & x \leq 0 \\ -\sqrt{x} & 0 < x \leq 1 \\ |x + 2| & x > 1 \end{cases}$

46. $F(x) = \begin{cases} x^2 & x < 0 \\ x^3 & 0 < x < 1 \\ -|x| - 1 & x \geq 1 \end{cases}$

Applications

47. Housing Cost. In 2001 the market value of a house was \$135,000; in 2006 the market price of the same house was \$280,000. What is the average rate of change of the market price as a function of the time (in years), where $t = 0$ corresponds to 2001.

48. Digital TV Conversion. A newspaper reported that by February 2009, only 38% of the urban population was ready for the conversion to digital TV. Ten weeks later, the newspaper reported that 64% of the population was prepared for the broadcasting change. Find the average rate of change of the population percent as a function of the time (in weeks).

1.3 Graphing Techniques: Transformations

Graph the following functions using graphing aids:

49. $y = -(x - 2)^2 + 4$

50. $y = |-x + 5| - 7$

51. $y = \sqrt[3]{x - 3} + 2$

52. $y = \dfrac{1}{x - 2} - 4$

53. $y = -\frac{1}{2}x^3$

54. $y = 2x^2 + 3$

Use the given graph to graph the following:

55.

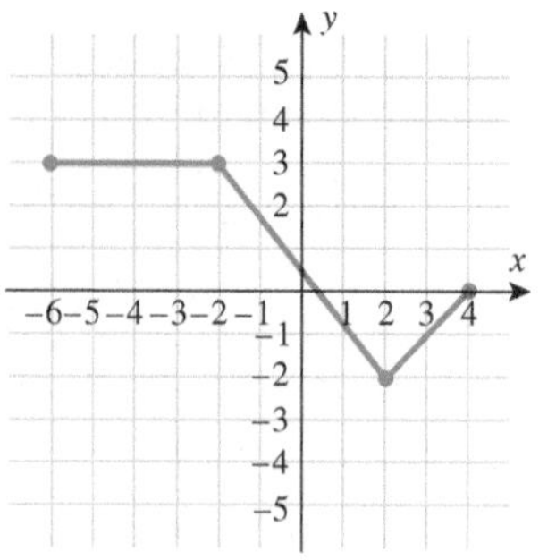

$y = f(x - 2)$

56.

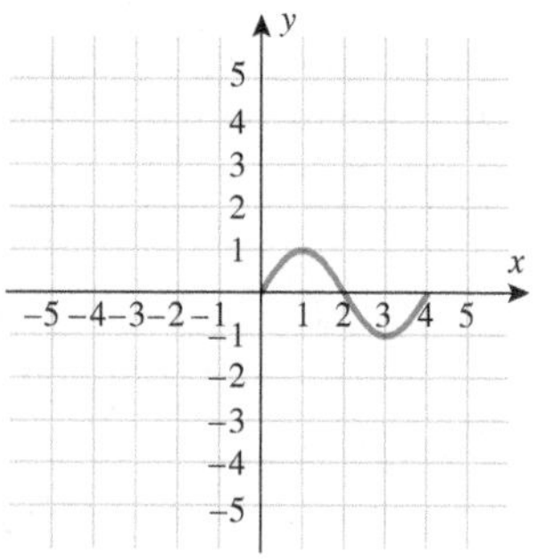

$y = 3f(x)$

57.

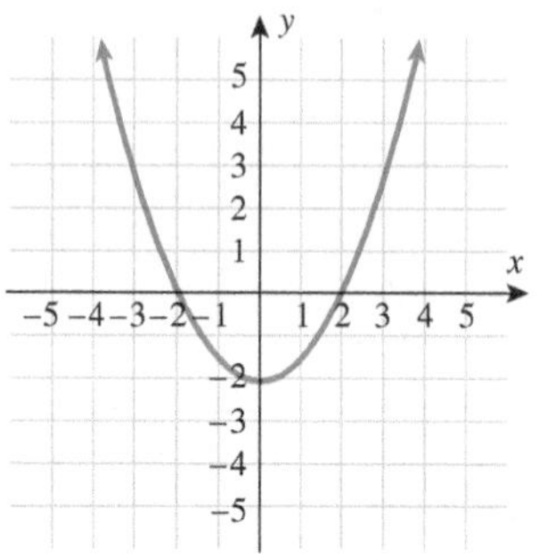

$y = -2f(x)$

58.

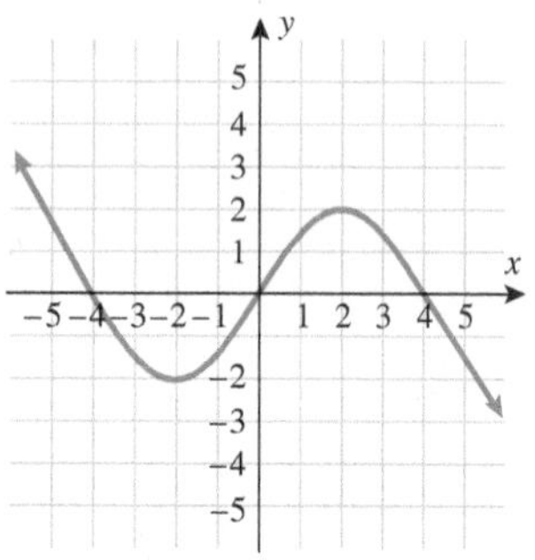

$y = f(x) + 3$

Write the function whose graph is the graph of $y = \sqrt{x}$, but is transformed as indicated, and state the domain of the resulting function.

59. Shifted to the left three units

60. Shifted down four units

61. Shifted to the right two units and up three units

62. Reflected about the y-axis

63. Stretched by a factor of 5 and shifted vertically down six units

64. Compressed by a factor of 2 and shifted vertically up three units

Transform the function into the form $f(x) = c(x - h)^2 + k$ by completing the square, and graph the resulting function using transformations.

65. $y = x^2 + 4x - 8$

66. $y = 2x^2 + 6x - 5$

1.4 Combining Functions

Given the functions g and h, find $g + h$, $g - h$, $g \cdot h$, and $\dfrac{g}{h}$, and state the domain.

67. $g(x) = -3x - 4$
$h(x) = x - 3$

68. $g(x) = 2x + 3$
$h(x) = x^2 + 6$

69. $g(x) = \dfrac{1}{x^2}$
$h(x) = \sqrt{x}$

70. $g(x) = \dfrac{x + 3}{2x - 4}$
$h(x) = \dfrac{3x - 1}{x - 2}$

71. $g(x) = \sqrt{x - 4}$
$h(x) = \sqrt{2x + 1}$

72. $g(x) = x^2 - 4$
$h(x) = x + 2$

For the given functions f and g, find the composite functions $f \circ g$ and $g \circ f$, and state the domains.

73. $f(x) = 3x - 4$, $g(x) = 2x + 1$

74. $f(x) = x^3 + 2x - 1$, $g(x) = x + 3$

75. $f(x) = \dfrac{2}{x+3}$, $g(x) = \dfrac{1}{4-x}$

76. $f(x) = \sqrt{2x^2 - 5}$, $g(x) = \sqrt{x+6}$

77. $f(x) = \sqrt{x-5}$, $g(x) = x^2 - 4$

78. $f(x) = \dfrac{1}{\sqrt{x}}$, $g(x) = \dfrac{1}{x^2 - 4}$

Evaluate $f(g(3))$ and $g(f(-1))$, if possible.

79. $f(x) = 4x^2 - 3x + 2$, $g(x) = 6x - 3$

80. $f(x) = \sqrt{4 - x}$, $g(x) = x^2 + 5$

81. $f(x) = \dfrac{x}{|2x - 3|}$, $g(x) = |5x + 2|$

82. $f(x) = \dfrac{1}{x - 1}$, $g(x) = x^2 - 1$

83. $f(x) = x^2 - x + 10$, $g(x) = \sqrt[3]{x - 4}$

84. $f(x) = \dfrac{4}{x^2 - 2}$, $g(x) = \dfrac{1}{x^2 - 9}$

Write the function as a composite $f(g(x))$ of two functions f and g.

85. $h(x) = 3(x-2)^2 + 4(x-2) + 7$

86. $h(x) = \dfrac{\sqrt[3]{x}}{1 - \sqrt[3]{x}}$

87. $h(x) = \dfrac{1}{\sqrt{x^2 + 7}}$

88. $h(x) = \sqrt{|3x + 4|}$

Applications

89. **Rain.** A rain drop hitting a lake makes a circular ripple. If the radius, in inches, grows as a function of time, in minutes, $r(t) = 25\sqrt{t+2}$, find the area of the ripple as a function of time.

90. **Geometry.** Let the area of a rectangle be given by $42 = l \cdot w$, and let the perimeter be $36 = 2 \cdot l + 2 \cdot w$. Express the perimeter in terms of w.

1.5 One-to-One Functions and Inverse Functions

Determine whether the given function is a one-to-one function.

91. $\{(-2, 0), (4, 5), (3, 7)\}$

92. $\{(-8, -6), (-4, 2), (0, 3), (2, -8), (7, 4)\}$

93. $y = \sqrt{x}$

94. $y = x^2$

95. $f(x) = x^3$

96. $f(x) = \dfrac{1}{x^2}$

In Exercises 97–100, determine whether the function is one-to-one.

97.

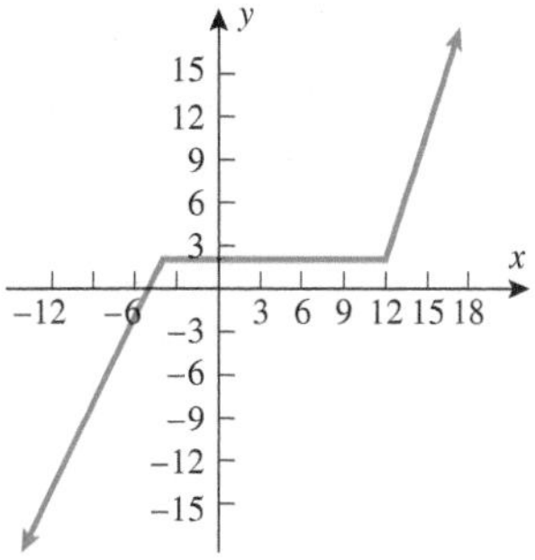

98.

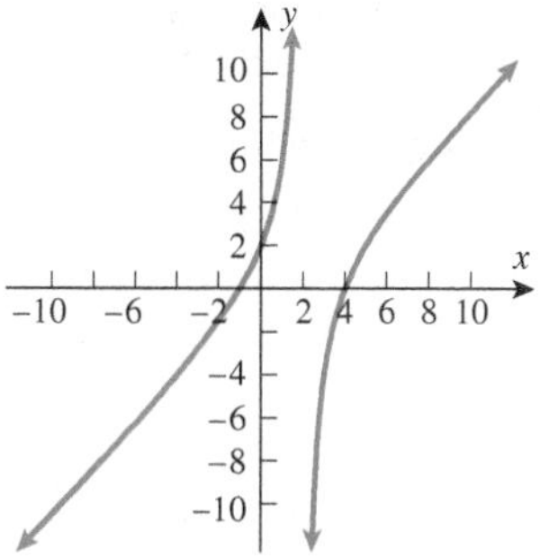

99.

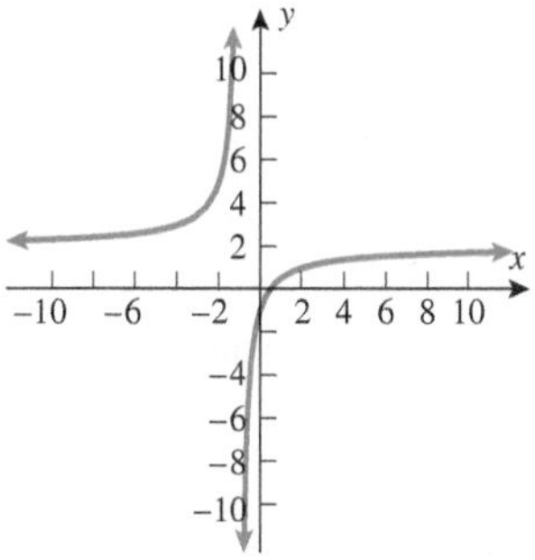

100.

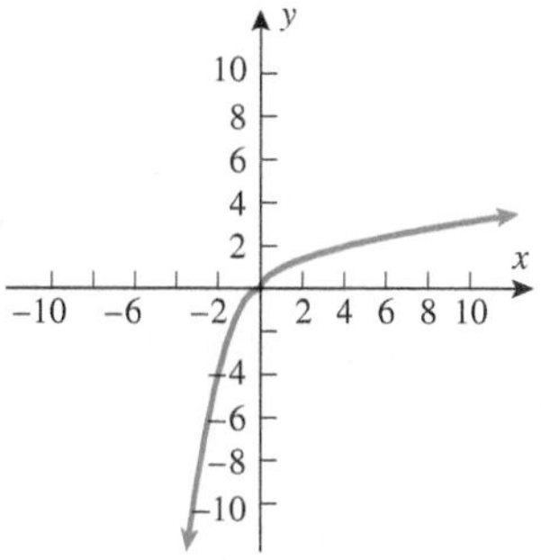

Verify that the function $f^{-1}(x)$ is the inverse of $f(x)$ by showing that $f(f^{-1}(x)) = x$. Graph $f(x)$ and $f^{-1}(x)$ on the same graph, and show the symmetry about the line $y = x$.

101. $f(x) = 3x + 4$; $f^{-1}(x) = \dfrac{x-4}{3}$

102. $f(x) = \dfrac{1}{4x - 7}$; $f^{-1}(x) = \dfrac{1 + 7x}{4x}$

103. $f(x) = \sqrt{x + 4}$; $f^{-1}(x) = x^2 - 4 \quad x \geq 0$

104. $f(x) = \dfrac{x+2}{x-7}$; $f^{-1}(x) = \dfrac{7x + 2}{x - 1}$

The function f is one-to-one. Find its inverse and check your answer. State the domain and range of both f and f^{-1}.

105. $f(x) = 2x + 1$

106. $f(x) = x^5 + 2$

107. $f(x) = \sqrt{x + 4}$

108. $f(x) = (x+4)^2 + 3 \quad x \geq -4$

109. $f(x) = \dfrac{x+6}{x+3}$

110. $f(x) = 2\sqrt[3]{x - 5} - 8$

Applications

111. **Salary.** A pharmaceutical salesperson makes $22,000 base salary a year plus 8% of the total dollars worth of products sold. Write a function $S(x)$ that represents her yearly salary as a function of the total dollars x worth of products sold. Find $S^{-1}(x)$. What does this inverse function tell you?

112. **Volume.** Express the volume V of a rectangular box that has a square base of length s and is 3 feet high as a function of the square length. Find V^{-1}. If a certain volume is desired, what does the inverse tell you?

[CHAPTER 1 PRACTICE TEST]

Assuming that x represents the independent variable and y represents the dependent variable, classify the relationships as:

a. not a function

b. a function, but not one-to-one

c. a one-to-one function

1. $f(x) = |2x + 3|$ 2. $x = y^2 + 2$ 3. $y = \sqrt[3]{x + 1}$

Use $f(x) = \sqrt{x - 2}$ and $g(x) = x^2 + 11$, and determine the desired quantity or expression. In the case of an expression, state the domain.

4. $f(11) - 2g(-1)$
5. $\left(\frac{f}{g}\right)(x)$
6. $\left(\frac{g}{f}\right)(x)$
7. $g(f(x))$
8. $(f + g)(6)$
9. $f(g(\sqrt{7}))$

Determine whether the function is odd, even, or neither.

10. $f(x) = |x| - x^2$
11. $f(x) = 9x^3 + 5x - 3$
12. $f(x) = \frac{2}{x}$

Graph the functions. State the domain and range of each function.

13. $f(x) = -\sqrt{x - 3} + 2$
14. $f(x) = -2(x - 1)^2$
15. $f(x) = \begin{cases} -x & x < -1 \\ 1 & -1 < x < 2 \\ x^2 & x \geq 2 \end{cases}$

Use the graph of each function to find the values listed below it.

16. $y = f(x)$

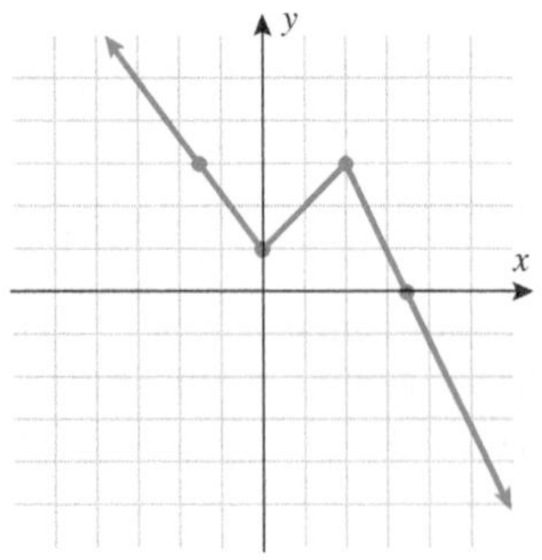

a. $f(3)$ b. $f(0)$ c. $f(-4)$

d. x, where $f(x) = 3$ e. x, where $f(x) = 0$

17. $y = g(x)$

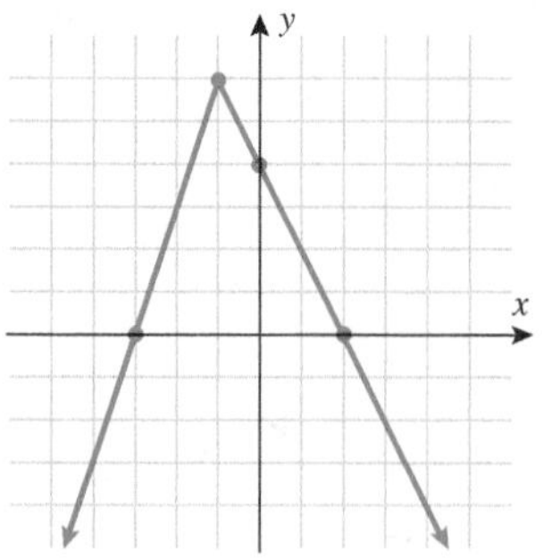

a. $g(3)$ b. $g(0)$ c. $g(-4)$

d. x, where $g(x) = 0$

18. $y = f(x)$

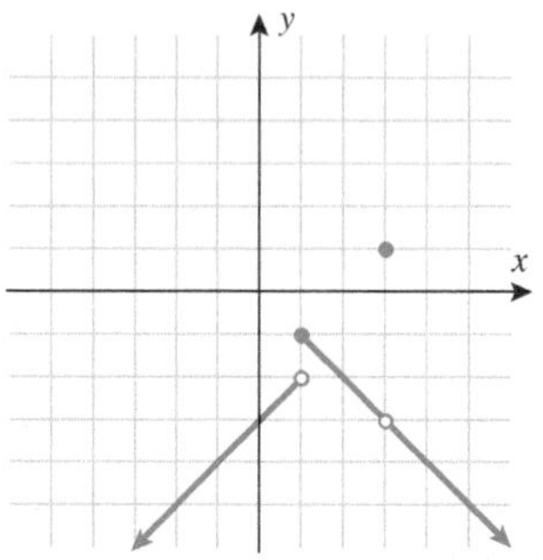

a. $p(0)$ b. x, where $p(x) = 0$

c. $p(1)$ d. $p(3)$

Find the difference equation, $\frac{f(x + h) - f(x)}{h}$, for:

19. $f(x) = 3x^2 - 4x + 1$ 20. $f(x) = x^3 - \frac{1}{\sqrt{x}}$

Find the average rate of change of the given functions.

21. $f(x) = 64 - 16x^2$ for $x = 0$ to $x = 2$
22. $f(x) = \sqrt{x - 1}$ for $x = 2$ to $x = 10$

In Exercises 23–26, given the function f, find the inverse if it exists. State the domain and range of both f and f^{-1}.

23. $f(x) = \sqrt{x - 5}$
24. $f(x) = x^2 + 5$
25. $f(x) = \frac{2x + 1}{5 - x}$
26. $f(x) = \begin{cases} -x & x \leq 0 \\ -x^2 & x > 0 \end{cases}$

27. What domain restriction can be made so that $f(x) = x^2$ has an inverse?

28. If the point $(-2, 5)$ lies on the graph of a function, what point lies on the graph of its inverse function?

29. **Pressure.** A mini-submarine descends at a rate of 5 feet per second. The pressure on the submarine structure is a linear function of the depth. When the submarine is on the surface, the pressure is 10 pounds per square inch, and when it is 100 feet under water, the pressure is 28 pounds per square inch. Write a function that describes the pressure P as a function of the time t in seconds.

30. **Geometry.** Both the volume V and the surface area S of a sphere are functions of the radius R. Write the volume as a function of the surface area.

31. **Circles.** If a quarter circle is drawn by tracing the unit circle in quadrant III, what does the inverse of that function look like? Where is it located?

32. **Sprinkler.** A sprinkler head malfunctions at midfield in an NFL football field. The puddle of water forms a circular pattern around the sprinkler head with a radius, in yards, that grows as a function of time, in hours: $r(t) = 10\sqrt{t}$. When will the puddle reach the sidelines? (A football field is 30 yards from sideline to sideline.)

33. **Internet.** The cost of airport Internet access is \$15 for the first 30 minutes and \$1 per minute for each minute after that. Write a function describing the cost of the service as a function of minutes used.

34. **Temperature and CO_2 Emissions.** The following table shows average yearly temperature in degrees Fahrenheit (°F) and carbon dioxide emissions in parts per million (ppm) for Mauna Loa, Hawaii. Scientists discovered that both temperature and CO_2 emissions are linear functions of the time in years since 2000. Write a function that describes the temperature T as a function of the CO_2 emissions x. Use this function to determine the temperature when CO_2 emissions reach the level of 375 ppm.

Year	2000	2005
Temperature (°F)	45.86	46.23
CO_2 emissions (ppm)	369.4	379.7

CHAPTER 2

Polynomial and Rational Functions

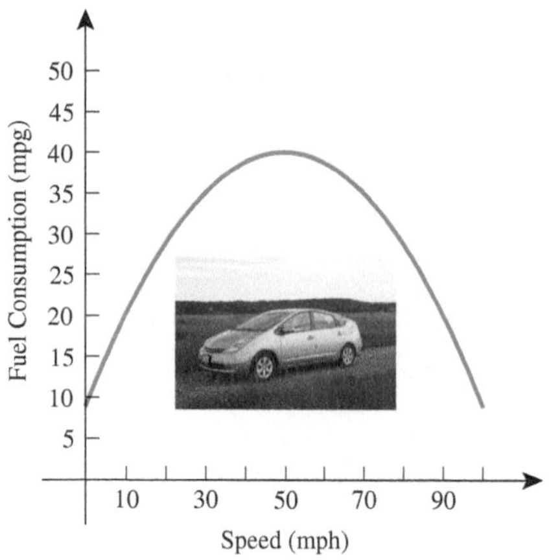

Encore/Alamy

The gas mileage you achieve (in whatever vehicle you drive) is a function of speed, which can be modeled by a *polynomial function*. The number of turning points in the graph of a polynomial function is related to the degree of that polynomial.

We can approximate gas mileage as a function of speed with a simple second-degree polynomial function, called a *quadratic function*, the graph of which is a parabola. We see from the graph why hypermilers do not drive above posted speed limits (and often drive below them).

LEARNING OBJECTIVES

- Find the vertex (maximum or minimum) of the graph of a quadratic function.
- Graph polynomial functions.
- Divide polynomials using long division and synthetic division.
- Develop strategies for searching for zeros of a polynomial function.
- Understand that complex zeros come in conjugate pairs.
- Graph rational functions.

[IN THIS CHAPTER]

We will start by discussing quadratic functions (polynomial functions of degree 2), whose graphs are parabolas. We will find the vertex, which is the maximum or minimum point on the graph. Then we will expand our discussion to higher degree polynomial functions. We will discuss techniques to find zeros of polynomial functions and strategies for graphing polynomial functions. Finally, we will discuss rational functions, which are ratios of polynomial functions.

POLYNOMIAL AND RATIONAL FUNCTIONS

2.1 QUADRATIC FUNCTIONS	2.2 POLYNOMIAL FUNCTIONS OF HIGHER DEGREE	2.3 DIVIDING POLYNOMIALS	2.4 THE REAL ZEROS OF A POLYNOMIAL FUNCTION	2.5 COMPLEX ZEROS: THE FUNDAMENTAL THEOREM OF ALGEBRA	2.6 RATIONAL FUNCTIONS
• Graphs of Quadratic Functions: Parabolas • Finding the Equation of a Parabola	• Identifying Polynomial Functions • Graphing Polynomial Functions Using Transformations of Power Functions • Real Zeros of a Polynomial Function • Graphing General Polynomial Functions	• Long Division of Polynomials • Synthetic Division of Polynomials	• The Remainder Theorem and the Factor Theorem • The Rational Zero Theorem and Descartes' Rule of Signs • Factoring Polynomials • The Intermediate Value Theorem • Graphing Polynomial Functions	• Complex Zeros • Factoring Polynomials	• Domain of Rational Functions • Vertical, Horizontal, and Slant Asymptotes • Graphing Rational Functions

2.1 QUADRATIC FUNCTIONS

SKILLS OBJECTIVES

- Graph a quadratic function given in either standard or general form.
- Find the equation of a parabola.

CONCEPTUAL OBJECTIVES

- Recognize characteristics of graphs of quadratic functions (parabolas): whether the parabola opens up or down; whether the vertex is a maximum or a minimum; the axis of symmetry.
- Understand that as long as you know the vertex and a point that lies on the graph of a parabola, you can determine the equation of the parabola.

2.1.1 Graphs of Quadratic Functions: Parabolas

2.1.1 SKILL

Graph a quadratic function given in either standard or general form.

2.1.1 CONCEPTUAL

Recognize characteristics of graphs of quadratic functions (parabolas): whether the parabola opens up or down; whether the vertex is a maximum or a minimum; the axis of symmetry.

In Chapter 1, we studied functions in general. In this chapter, we will learn about a special group of functions called *polynomial functions*. Polynomial functions are simple functions; often, more complicated functions are approximated by polynomial functions. Polynomial functions model many real-world applications, such as the stock market, football punts, business costs, revenues and profits, and the flight path of NASA's "vomit comet." Let's start by defining a polynomial function.

DEFINITION Polynomial Function

Let n be a nonnegative integer, and let $a_n, a_{n-1}, \ldots, a_2, a_1, a_0$ be real numbers with $a_n \neq 0$. The function

$$f(x) = a_n x^n + a_{n-1}x^{n-1} + \cdots + a_2x^2 + a_1x + a_0$$

is called a **polynomial function of x with degree n**. The coefficient a_n is called the **leading coefficient**, and a_0 is the constant.

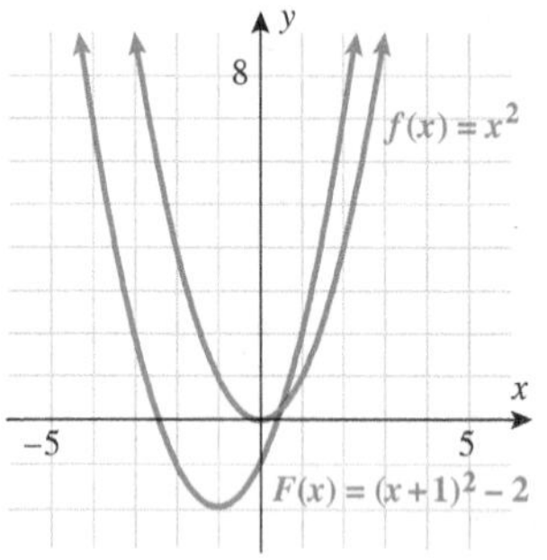

Polynomials of particular degrees have special names. In Chapter 1, the library of functions included the constant function $f(x) = b$, which is a horizontal line; the linear function $f(x) = mx + b$, which is a line with slope m and y-intercept $(0, b)$; the square function $f(x) = x^2$; and the cube function $f(x) = x^3$. These are all special cases of a polynomial function.

In Section 1.3, using transformation techniques, we graphed functions such as $F(x) = (x + 1)^2 - 2$, which can be graphed by starting with the square function $y = x^2$ and shifting one unit to the left and down two units. See the graph on the left.

Note that if we eliminate the parentheses in $F(x) = (x + 1)^2 - 2$ to get

$$F(x) = x^2 + 2x + 1 - 2$$
$$= x^2 + 2x - 1$$

the result is a function defined by a second-degree polynomial (a polynomial with x^2 as the highest degree term), which is also called a *quadratic function*.

DEFINITION Quadratic Function

Let a, b, and c be real numbers with $a \neq 0$. The function

$$f(x) = ax^2 + bx + c$$

is called a **quadratic function**.

The graph of any quadratic function is a **parabola**. If the leading coefficient a is *positive*, then the parabola opens *upward.* If the leading coefficient a is *negative*, then the parabola opens *downward.* The **vertex** (or turning point) is the *minimum* point, or low point, on the graph if the parabola opens upward, whereas it is the *maximum* point, or high point, on the graph if the parabola opens downward. The vertical line that intersects the parabola at the vertex is called the **axis of symmetry**.

The axis of symmetry is the line $x = h$, and the vertex is located at the point (h, k), as shown in the following two figures:

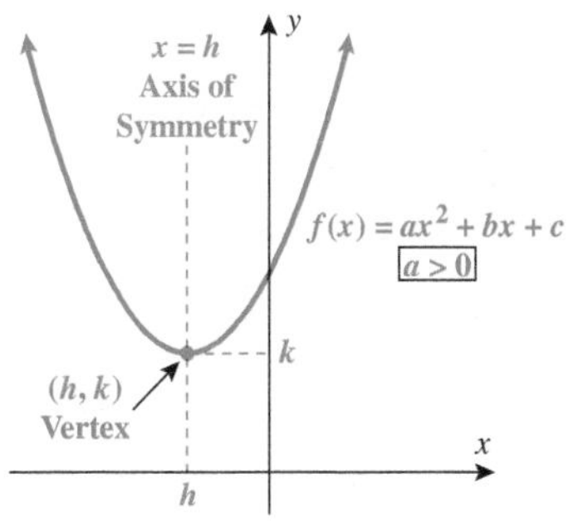

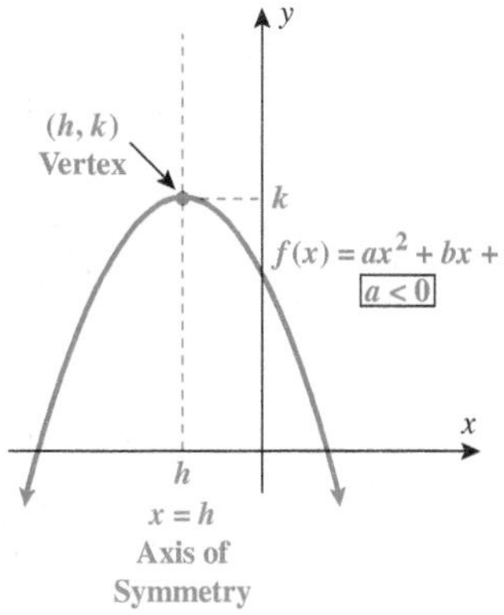

Graphing Quadratic Functions in Standard Form

In general, writing a quadratic function in the form

$$f(x) = a(x - h)^2 + k$$

allows the vertex (h, k) and the axis of symmetry $x = h$ to be determined by inspection. This form is a convenient way to express a quadratic function in order to quickly determine its corresponding graph. Hence, this form is called *standard form.*

QUADRATIC FUNCTION: STANDARD FORM

The quadratic function

$$f(x) = a(x - h)^2 + k$$

is in **standard form**. The graph of f is a parabola whose vertex is the point (h, k). The parabola is symmetric with respect to the line $x = h$. If $a > 0$, the parabola opens up. If $a < 0$, the parabola opens down.

Recall that graphing linear functions requires finding two points on the line, or a point and the slope of the line. However, for a quadratic function, simply knowing two points that lie on its graph is no longer sufficient. Below is a general step-by-step procedure for graphing quadratic functions given in standard form.

GRAPHING QUADRATIC FUNCTIONS

To graph $f(x) = a(x - h)^2 + k$

Step 1: Determine whether the parabola opens up or down.

$$a > 0 \quad \text{up}$$
$$a < 0 \quad \text{down}$$

Step 2: Determine the vertex (h, k).

Step 3: Find the y-intercept (by setting $x = 0$).

Step 4: Find any x-intercepts [by setting $f(x) = 0$ and solving for x].

Step 5: Plot the vertex and intercepts and connect them with a smooth curve.

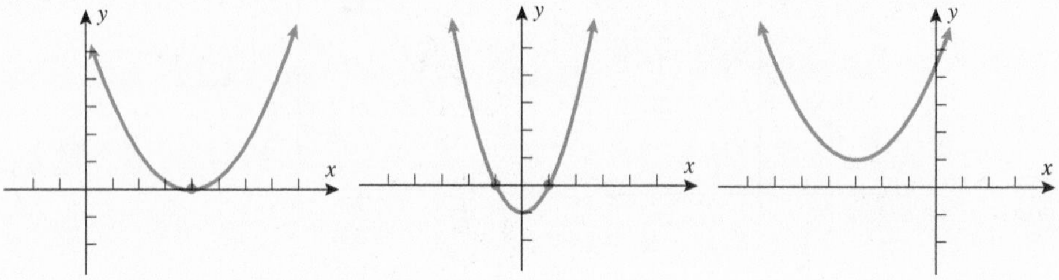

Note that Step 4 says to "find any x-intercepts." Parabolas opening up or down will always have a y-intercept. However, they can have **one**, **two**, or **no** x-intercepts. The figures above illustrate this for parabolas opening up, and the same can be said about parabolas opening down.

EXAMPLE 1 **Graphing a Quadratic Function Given in Standard Form**

Graph the quadratic function $f(x) = (x - 3)^2 - 1$.

Solution:

STEP 1 The parabola opens up. $a = 1$, so $a > 0$

STEP 2 Determine the vertex. $(h, k) = (3, -1)$

STEP 3 Find the y-intercept. $f(0) = (-3)^2 - 1 = 8$

(0, 8) corresponds to the y-intercept

STEP 4 Find any x-intercepts. $f(x) = (x - 3)^2 - 1 = 0$

$(x - 3)^2 = 1$

Use the square root method. $x - 3 = \pm 1$

Solve. $x = 2$ or $x = 4$

(2, 0) and (4, 0) correspond to the x-intercepts

STEP 5 Plot the vertex and intercepts (3, −1), (0, 8), (2, 0), (4, 0).

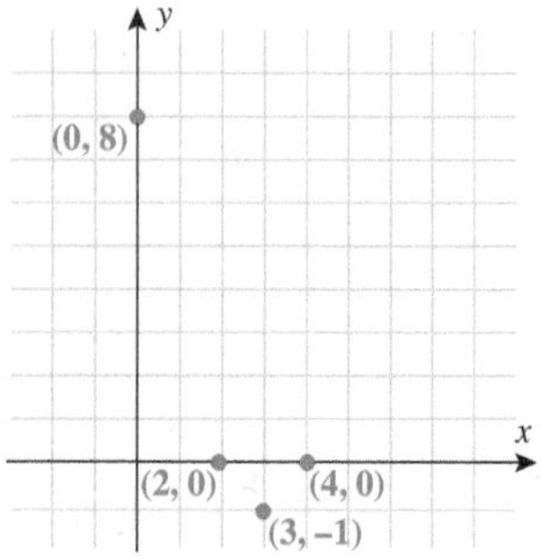

[CONCEPT CHECK]

Will the parabola $y = -(x - 2)^2 + 1$ open up or down? Will it have x-intercepts?

ANSWER down; yes

Connect the points with a smooth curve opening up.

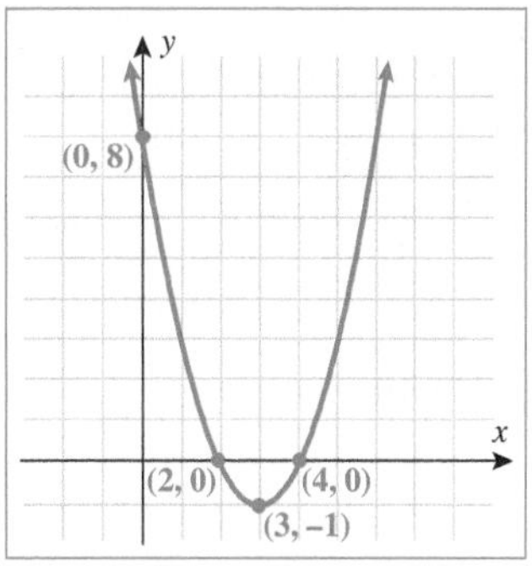

The graph in Example 1 could also have been found by shifting the square function to the right three units and down one unit.

STUDY TIP

A quadratic function given in standard form can be graphed using the transformation techniques shown in Section 1.3 for the square function.

YOUR TURN Graph the quadratic function $f(x) = (x - 1)^2 - 4$.

ANSWER

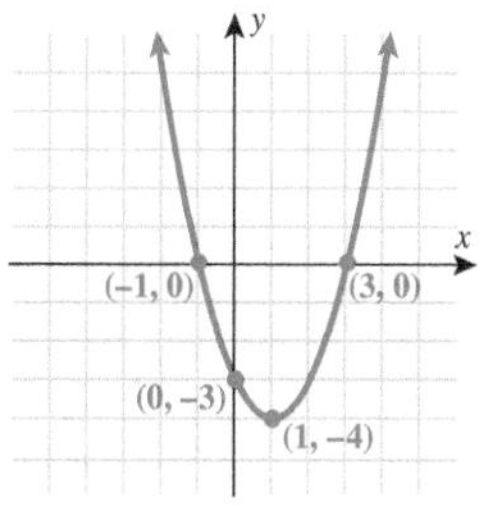

EXAMPLE 2 Graphing a Quadratic Function Given in Standard Form with a Negative Leading Coefficient

Graph the quadratic function $f(x) = -2(x - 1)^2 - 3$.

Solution:

STEP 1 The parabola opens down. $a = -2$, so $a < 0$

STEP 2 Determine the vertex. $(h, k) = (1, -3)$

STEP 3 Find the y-intercept. $f(0) = -2(-1)^2 - 3 = -2 - 3 = -5$

$(0, -5)$ corresponds to the y-intercept

STEP 4 Find any x-intercepts.

$$f(x) = -2(x - 1)^2 - 3 = 0$$
$$-2(x - 1)^2 = 3$$
$$(x - 1)^2 = -\frac{3}{2}$$

A real quantity squared cannot be negative, so there are no real solutions. There are no x-intercepts.

STEP 5 Plot the vertex $(1, -3)$ and y-intercept $(0, -5)$. Connect the points with a smooth curve.

Note that the axis of symmetry is $x = 1$. Because the point $(0, -5)$ lies on the parabola, we know that, by symmetry with respect to $x = 1$, the point $(2, -5)$ also lies on the graph.

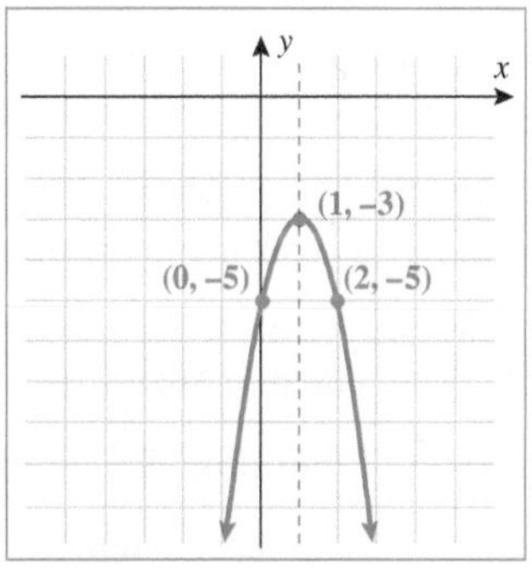

YOUR TURN Graph the quadratic function $f(x) = -3(x + 1)^2 - 2$.

ANSWER

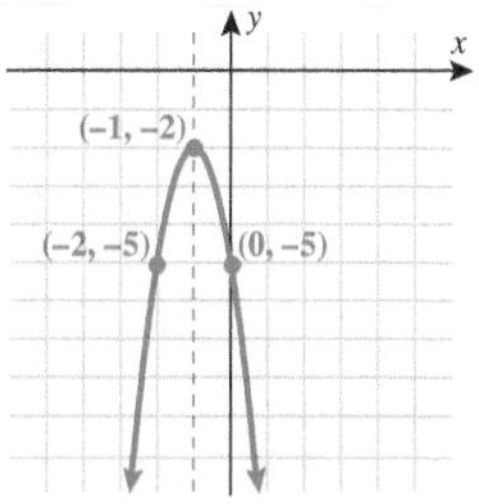

When graphing quadratic functions (parabolas), have *at least three points* labeled on the graph.

- When there are x-intercepts (Example 1), label the vertex, y-intercept, and x-intercepts.
- When there are no x-intercepts (Example 2), label the vertex, y-intercept, and another point.

Graphing Quadratic Functions in General Form

A quadratic function is often written in one of two forms:

$$\text{Standard form: } f(x) = a(x - h)^2 + k$$

$$\text{General form: } f(x) = ax^2 + bx + c$$

When the quadratic function is expressed in standard form, the graph is easily obtained by identifying the vertex (h, k) and the intercepts and drawing a smooth curve that opens either up or down, depending on the sign of a.

Typically, quadratic functions are expressed in general form and a graph is the ultimate goal, so we must first express the quadratic function in standard form. One technique for transforming a quadratic function from general form to standard form was reviewed in Section 0.2 and is called *completing the square.*

EXAMPLE 3 Graphing a Quadratic Function Given in General Form

Write the quadratic function $f(x) = x^2 - 6x + 4$ in standard form and graph f.

Solution:

Express the quadratic function in standard form by completing the square.

Write the original function. $f(x) = x^2 - 6x + 4$

Group the variable terms together. $= (x^2 - 6x) + 4$

Complete the square.

Half of -6 is -3; -3 squared is 9.

Add and subtract 9 within the parentheses. $= (x^2 - 6x + 9 - 9) + 4$

Write the -9 outside the parentheses. $= (x^2 - 6x + 9) - 9 + 4$

Write the expression inside the parentheses as a perfect square and simplify. $= (x - 3)^2 - 5$

Now that the quadratic function is written in standard form, $f(x) = (x - 3)^2 - 5$, follow the step-by-step procedure for graphing a quadratic function in standard form.

STEP 1 The parabola opens up. $a = 1$, so $a > 0$

STEP 2 Determine the vertex. $(h, k) = (3, -5)$

STEP 3 Find the y-intercept. $f(x) = x^2 - 6x + 4$

$f(0) = (0)^2 - 6(0) + 4 = 4$

$(0, 4)$ corresponds to the y-intercept

STEP 4 Find any x-intercepts. $f(x) = 0$

Using the standard form:

$$f(x) = (x - 3)^2 - 5 = 0$$
$$(x - 3)^2 = 5$$
$$x - 3 = \pm\sqrt{5}$$
$$x = 3 \pm \sqrt{5}$$

Using the general form:

$$f(x) = x - 6x + 4 = 0$$
$$x = \frac{-(-6) \pm \sqrt{(-6)^2 - 4(1)(4)}}{2(1)}$$
$$x = 3 \pm \sqrt{5}$$

$(3 + \sqrt{5}, 0)$ and $(3 - \sqrt{5}, 0)$ correspond to the x-intercepts.

STEP 5 Plot the vertex and intercepts $(3, -5)$, $(0, 4)$, $(3 + \sqrt{5}, 0)$, and $(3 - \sqrt{5}, 0)$.

Connect the points with a smooth parabolic curve.

Note: $3 + \sqrt{5} \approx 5.24$ and $3 - \sqrt{5} \approx 0.76$.

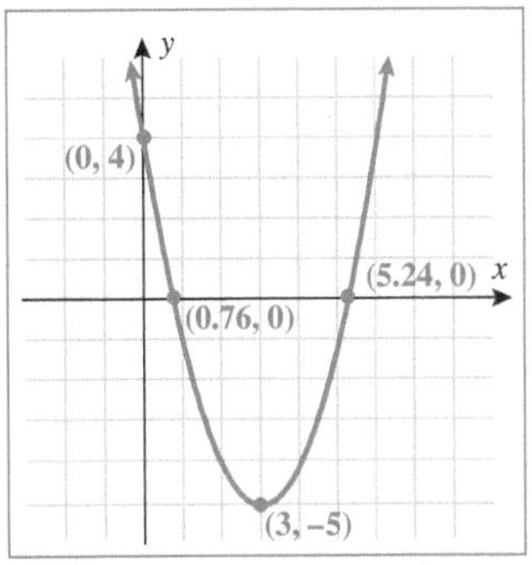

> **STUDY TIP**
> Although either form (standard or general) can be used to find the intercepts, it is often more convenient to use the general form when finding the y-intercept and the standard form when finding the x-intercept.

YOUR TURN Write the quadratic function $f(x) = x^2 - 8x + 14$ in standard form and graph f.

ANSWER

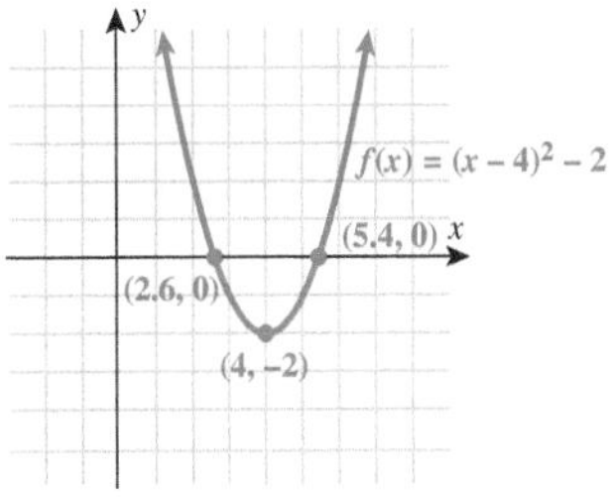

When the leading coefficient of a quadratic function is not equal to 1, the leading coefficient must be factored out before completing the square.

EXAMPLE 4 Graphing a Quadratic Function Given in General Form with a Negative Leading Coefficient

Graph the quadratic function $f(x) = -3x^2 + 6x + 2$.

Solution:

Express the function in standard form by completing the square.

Write the original function.	$f(x) = -3x^2 + 6x + 2$
Group the variable terms together.	$= (-3x^2 + 6x) + 2$
Factor out -3 in order to make the coefficient of x^2 equal to 1 inside the parentheses.	$= -3(x^2 - 2x) + 2$
Add and subtract 1 inside the parentheses to create a perfect square.	$= -3(x^2 - 2x + 1 - 1) + 2$
Regroup the terms.	$= -3(x^2 - 2x + 1) - 3(-1) + 2$
Write the expression inside the parentheses as a perfect square and simplify.	$= -3(x - 1)^2 + 5$

Now that the quadratic function is written in standard form, $f(x) = -3(x - 1)^2 + 5$, *follow the step-by-step procedure for graphing a quadratic function in standard form.*

STEP 1 The parabola opens down. $a = -3$; therefore, $a < 0$

STEP 2 Determine the vertex. $(h, k) = (1, 5)$

STEP 3 Find the y-intercept using the general form. $f(0) = -3(0)^2 + 6(0) + 2 = 2$

(0, 2) corresponds to the y-intercept

STEP 4 Find any x-intercepts using the standard form.

$$f(x) = -3(x-1)^2 + 5 = 0$$
$$-3(x-1)^2 = -5$$
$$(x-1)^2 = \frac{5}{3}$$
$$x - 1 = \pm\sqrt{\frac{5}{3}}$$
$$x = 1 \pm \sqrt{\frac{5}{3}}$$
$$= 1 \pm \frac{\sqrt{15}}{3}$$

The x-intercepts are $\left(1 + \frac{\sqrt{15}}{3}, 0\right)$ and $\left(1 - \frac{\sqrt{15}}{3}, 0\right)$.

STEP 5 Plot the vertex and intercepts

$(1, 5)$, $(0, 2)$, $\left(1 + \frac{\sqrt{15}}{3}, 0\right)$, and $\left(1 - \frac{\sqrt{15}}{3}, 0\right)$.

Connect the points with a smooth curve.

Note: $1 + \frac{\sqrt{15}}{3} \approx 2.3$ and

$1 - \frac{\sqrt{15}}{3} \approx -0.3$.

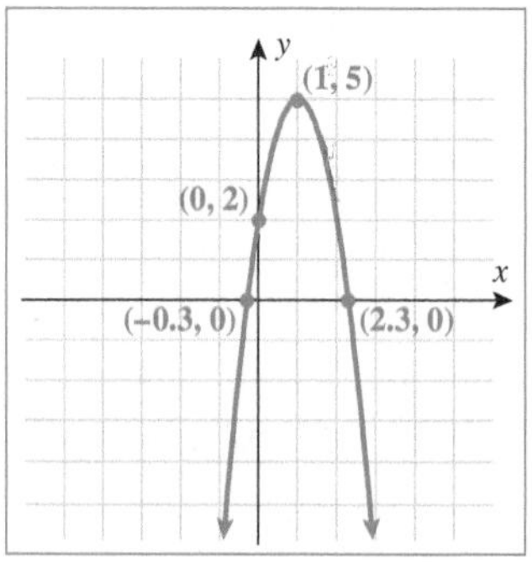

YOUR TURN Graph the quadratic function $f(x) = -2x^2 - 4x + 1$.

ANSWER

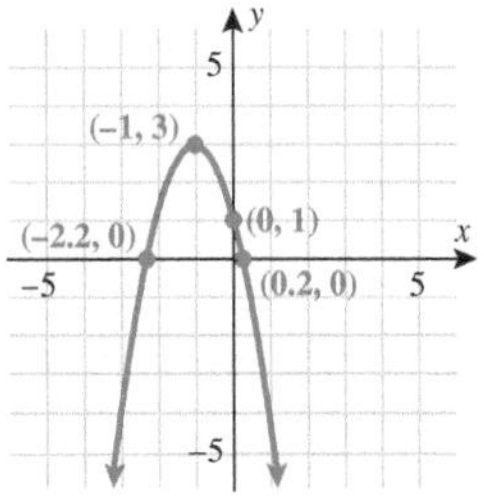

In Examples 3 and 4, the quadratic functions were given in general form and they were transformed into standard form by completing the square. It can be shown (by completing the square) that the vertex of a quadratic function in general form, $f(x) = ax^2 + bx + c$, is located at $x = -\frac{b}{2a}$.

Another approach to sketching the graphs of quadratic functions is to first find the vertex and then find additional points through point-plotting.

VERTEX OF A PARABOLA

The graph of a quadratic function $f(x) = ax^2 + bx + c$ is a parabola with the **vertex** located at the point

$$\left(-\frac{b}{2a}, f\left(-\frac{b}{2a}\right)\right)$$

GRAPHING A QUADRATIC FUNCTION IN GENERAL FORM

Step 1: Find the vertex.

Step 2: Determine whether the parabola opens up or down.

- If $a > 0$, the parabola opens up.
- If $a < 0$, the parabola opens down.

Step 3: Find additional points near the vertex.

Step 4: Sketch the graph with a parabolic curve.

[CONCEPT CHECK]

TRUE OR FALSE If you know the vertex and a point (other than the vertex) that lies on the graph you can determine the *y*-intercept.

ANSWER True

EXAMPLE 5 Graphing a Quadratic Function Given in General Form

Sketch the graph of $f(x) = -2x^2 + 4x + 5$.

Solution: Let $a = -2$, $b = 4$, and $c = 5$.

STEP 1 Find the vertex.

$$x = -\frac{b}{2a} = -\frac{4}{2(-2)} = 1$$

$$f(1) = -2(1)^2 + 4(1) + 5 = 7$$

Vertex: $(1, 7)$

STEP 2 The parabola opens down. $a = -2$

STEP 3 Find additional points near the vertex.

x	-1	0	1	2	3
$f(x)$	$f(-1) = -1$	$f(0) = 5$	$f(1) = 7$	$f(2) = 5$	$f(3) = -1$

STEP 4 Label the vertex and additional points then sketch the graph.

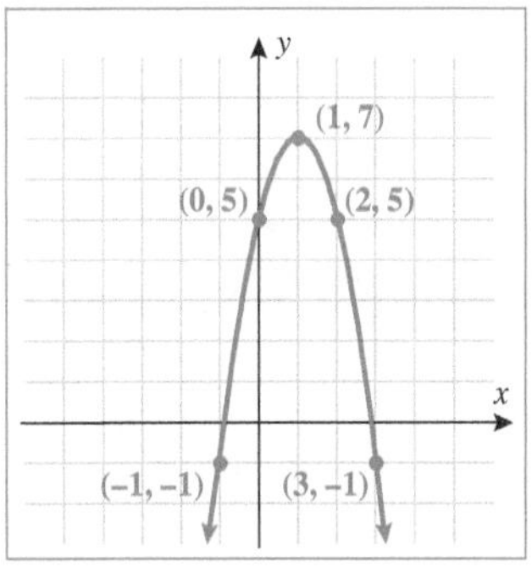

YOUR TURN Sketch the graph of $f(x) = 3x^2 - 6x + 4$.

ANSWER

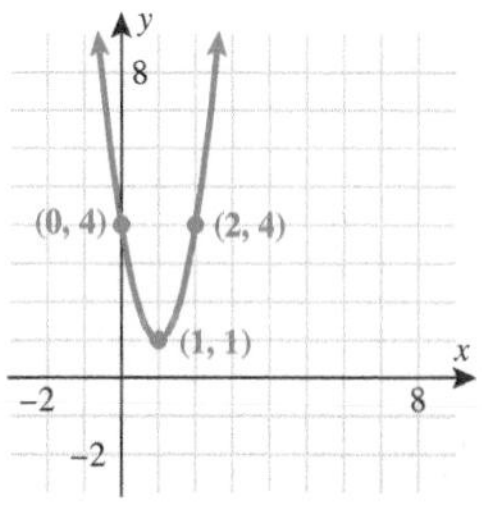

2.1.2 Finding the Equation of a Parabola

It is important to understand that the equation $y = x^2$ is equivalent to the quadratic function $f(x) = x^2$. Both have the same parabolic graph. Thus far, we have been given the function and then asked to find characteristics (vertex and intercepts) in order to graph. We now turn our attention to the problem of determining the function, given certain characteristics.

2.1.2 SKILL

Find the equation of a parabola.

2.1.2 CONCEPTUAL

Understand that as long as you know the vertex and a point that lies on the graph of a parabola, you can determine the equation of the parabola.

EXAMPLE 6 **Finding the Quadratic Function Given the Vertex and a Point That Lies on Its Graph**

Find the quadratic function whose graph has a vertex at (3, 4) and which passes through the point (2, 3). Express the quadratic function in both standard and general forms.

Solution:

Write the standard form of a quadratic function. $f(x) = a(x - h)^2 + k$

Substitute the coordinates of the vertex $(h, k) = (3, 4)$. $f(x) = a(x - 3)^2 + 4$

Use the point (2, 3) to find a.

The point (2, 3) implies $f(2) = 3$. $f(2) = a(2 - 3)^2 + 4 = 3$

Solve for a.

$$a(2 - 3)^2 + 4 = 3$$
$$a(-1)^2 + 4 = 3$$
$$a + 4 = 3$$
$$a = -1$$

Write both forms of the quadratic function.

Standard form: $\boxed{f(x) = -(x - 3)^2 + 4}$ General form: $\boxed{f(x) = -x^2 + 6x - 5}$

YOUR TURN Find the standard form of the equation of a parabola whose graph has a vertex at $(-3, -5)$ and which passes through the point $(-2, -4)$.

ANSWER

Standard form:

$f(x) = (x + 3)^2 - 5$

As we have seen in Example 6, once the vertex is known, the leading coefficient a can be found from any point that lies on the parabola.

Application Problems That Involve Quadratic Functions

Because the vertex of a parabola represents either the minimum or the maximum value of the quadratic function, in application problems it often suffices simply to find the vertex.

EXAMPLE 7 **Finding the Minimum Cost of Manufacturing a Motorcycle**

A company that produces motorcycles has a per-unit production cost of

$$C(x) = 2000 - 15x + 0.05x^2$$

where C is the cost in dollars to manufacture a motorcycle and x is the number of motorcycles produced. How many motorcycles should be produced in order to minimize the cost of each motorcycle? What is the corresponding minimum cost?

Solution:

The graph of the quadratic function is a parabola.

Rewrite the quadratic function in general form. $C(x) = 0.05x^2 - 15x + 2000$

The parabola opens up, because a is positive. $a = 0.05 > 0$

Because the parabola opens up, the vertex of the parabola is a *minimum*.

Find the x-coordinate of the vertex. $x = -\dfrac{b}{2a} = -\dfrac{(-15)}{2(0.05)} = 150$

The company keeps per-unit cost to a minimum when 150 motorcycles are produced.

The minimum cost is \$875 per motorcycle. $C(150) = 875$

YOUR TURN The revenue associated with selling vitamins is

$$R(x) = 500x - 0.001x^2$$

where R is the revenue in dollars and x is the number of bottles of vitamins sold. Determine how many bottles of vitamins should be sold to maximize the revenue.

ANSWER
250,000 bottles

EXAMPLE 8 Finding the Dimensions That Yield a Maximum Area

You have just bought a puppy and want to fence in an area in the backyard for her. You buy 100 linear feet of fence from Home Depot and have decided to make a rectangular fenced-in area using the back of your house as one side. Determine the dimensions of the rectangular pen that will maximize the area in which your puppy may roam. What is the maximum area of the rectangular pen?

Solution:

STEP 1 **Identify the question.**
Find the dimensions of the rectangular pen.

STEP 2 **Draw a picture.**

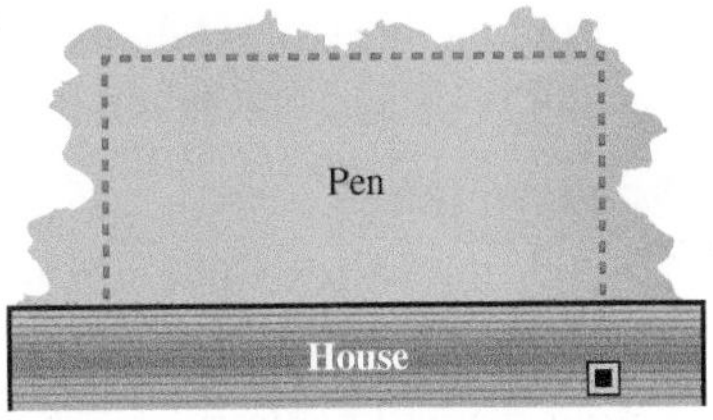

STEP 3 **Set up a function.**
If we let x represent the length of one side of the rectangle, then the opposite side is also of length x. Because there are 100 feet of fence, the remaining fence left for the side opposite the house is $100 - 2x$.

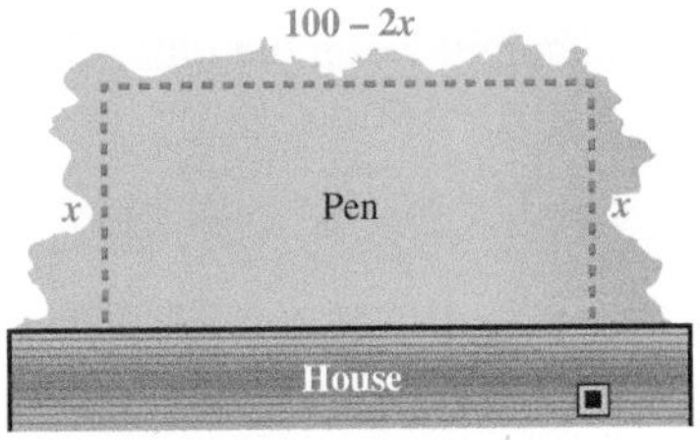

The area of a rectangle is equal to length times width:

$$A(x) = x(100 - 2x)$$

STEP 4 **Find the maximum value of the function.**

$$A(x) = x(100 - 2x) = -2x^2 + 100x$$

Find the maximum of the parabola that corresponds to the quadratic function for area $A(x) = -2x^2 + 100x$.
$a = -2$ and $b = 100$; therefore, the maximum occurs when

$$x = -\frac{b}{2a} = -\frac{100}{2(-2)} = 25$$

Replacing x with 25 in our original diagram:

The dimensions of the rectangle are 25 feet by 50 feet.

The maximum area $A(25) = 1250$ is 1250 square feet.

STEP 5 **Check the solution.**
Two sides are 25 feet and one side is 50 feet, and together they account for all 100 feet of fence.

YOUR TURN Suppose you have 200 linear feet of fence to enclose a rectangular garden. Determine the dimensions of the rectangle that will yield the greatest area.

ANSWER
50 ft by 50 ft

EXAMPLE 9 Path of a Punted Football

The path of a particular punt follows the quadratic function $h(x) = -\frac{1}{8}(x - 5)^2 + 50$, where $h(x)$ is the height of the ball in yards and x corresponds to the horizontal distance in yards. Assume $x = 0$ corresponds to midfield (the 50 yard line). For example, $x = -20$ corresponds to the punter's own 30 yard line, whereas $x = 20$ corresponds to the other team's 30 yard line.

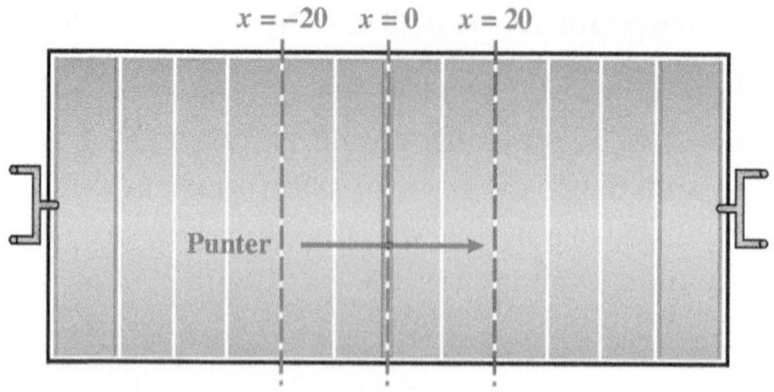

a. Find the maximum height the ball achieves.

b. Find the horizontal distance the ball covers. Assume the height is zero when the ball is kicked and when the ball is caught.

Solution (a):

Identify the vertex since it is given in standard form. $(h, k) = (5, 50)$

The maximum height of the punt occurs at the other team's 45 yard line, and the height the ball achieves is $\boxed{50 \text{ yards } (150 \text{ feet})}$.

Solution (b):

The height when the ball is kicked or caught is zero.

$$h(x) = -\frac{1}{8}(x - 5)^2 + 50 = 0$$

Solve for x.

$$\frac{1}{8}(x - 5)^2 = 50$$

$$(x - 5)^2 = 400$$

$$(x - 5) = \pm\sqrt{400}$$

$$x = 5 \pm 20$$

$$x = -15 \text{ and } x = 25$$

The horizontal distance is the distance between these two points:

$|25 - (-15)| = \boxed{40 \text{ yd}}$.

[SECTION 2.1] SUMMARY

All quadratic functions $f(x) = ax^2 + bx + c$ or $f(x) = a(x - h)^2 + k$ have graphs that are parabolas:

- If $a > 0$, the parabola opens up.
- If $a < 0$, the parabola opens down.
- The vertex is at the point

$$(h, k) = \left(-\frac{b}{2a}, f\left(-\frac{b}{2a}\right)\right) = \left(-\frac{b}{2a}, \frac{4ac - b^2}{4a}\right)$$

- When the quadratic function is given in general form, completing the square can be used to rewrite the function in standard form.
- At least three points are needed to graph a quadratic function:
  - vertex
  - y-intercept
  - x-intercept(s) or other point(s)

[SECTION 2.1] EXERCISES

• SKILLS

In Exercises 1–4, match the quadratic function with its graph.

1. $f(x) = 3(x + 2)^2 - 5$
2. $f(x) = 2(x - 1)^2 + 3$
3. $f(x) = -\frac{1}{2}(x + 3)^2 + 2$
4. $f(x) = -\frac{1}{3}(x - 2)^2 + 3$

a.

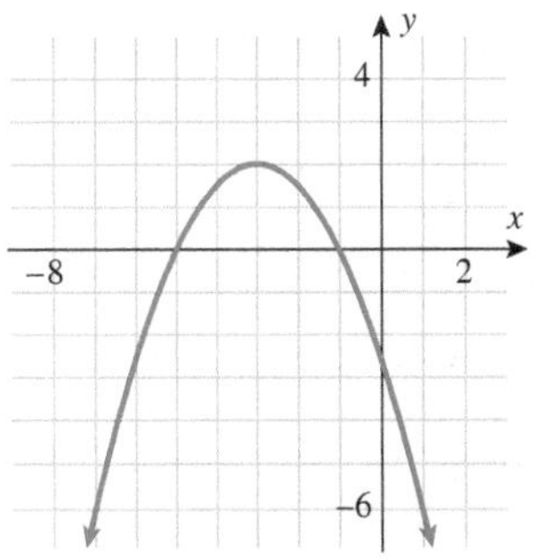

b.

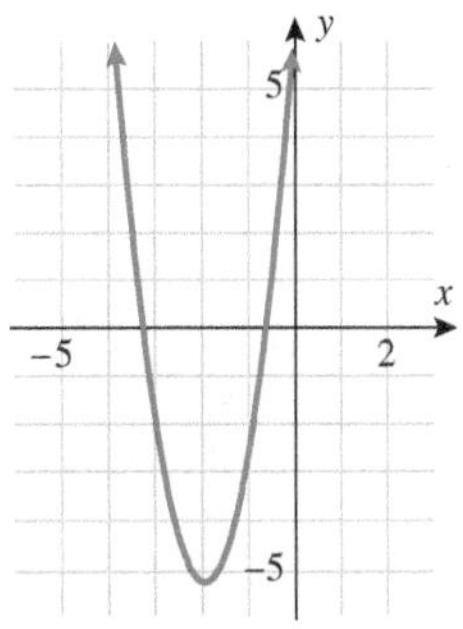

c.

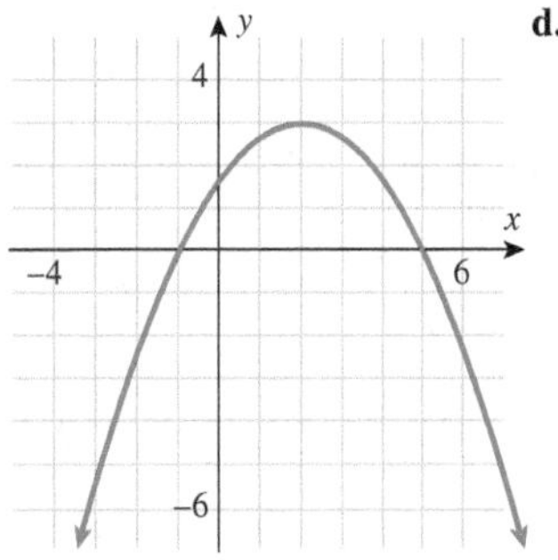

d.

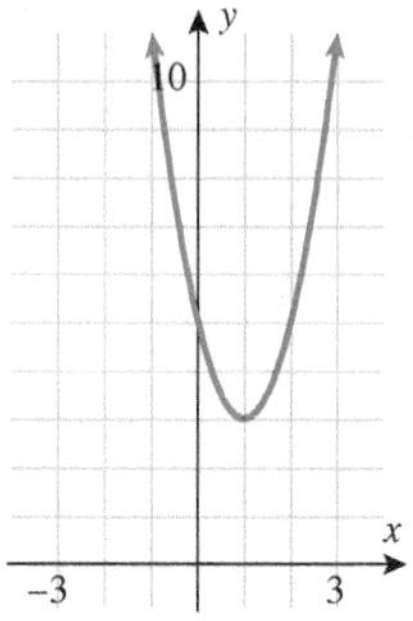

In Exercises 5–8, match the quadratic function with its graph.

5. $f(x) = 3x^2 + 5x - 2$
6. $f(x) = 3x^2 - x - 2$
7. $f(x) = -x^2 + 2x - 1$
8. $f(x) = -2x^2 - x + 3$

a.

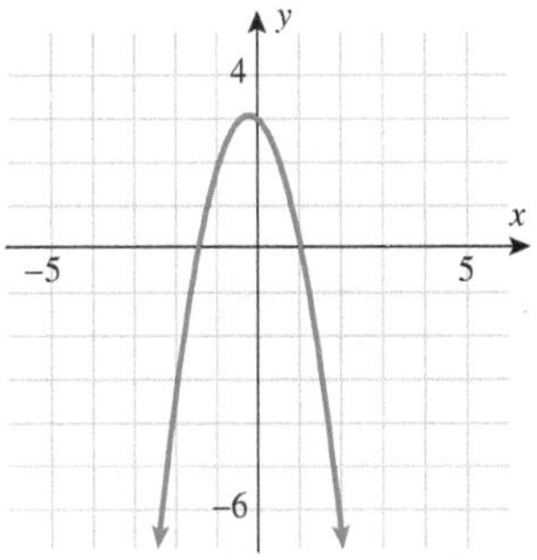

b.

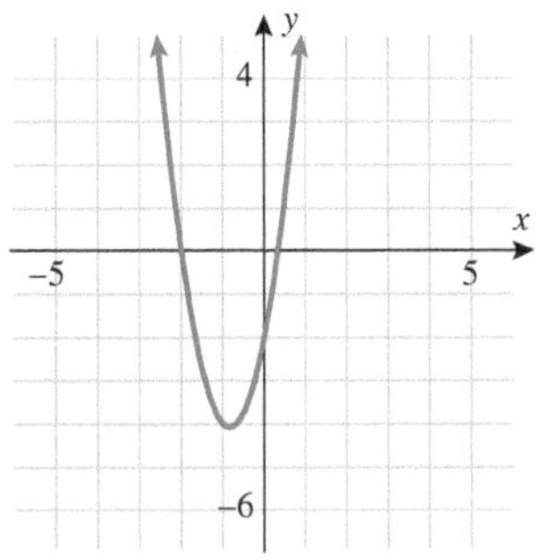

c.

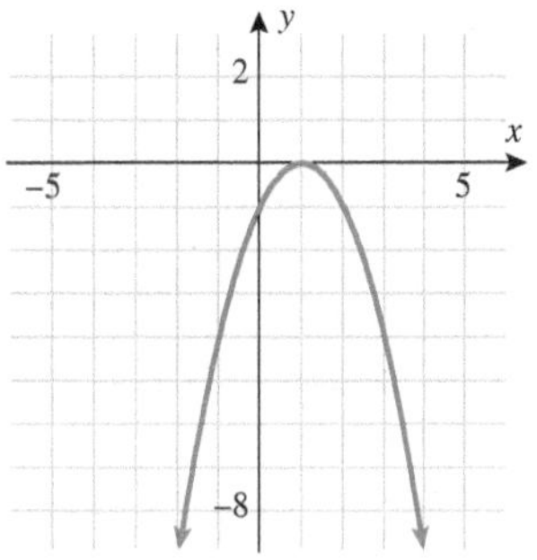

d.

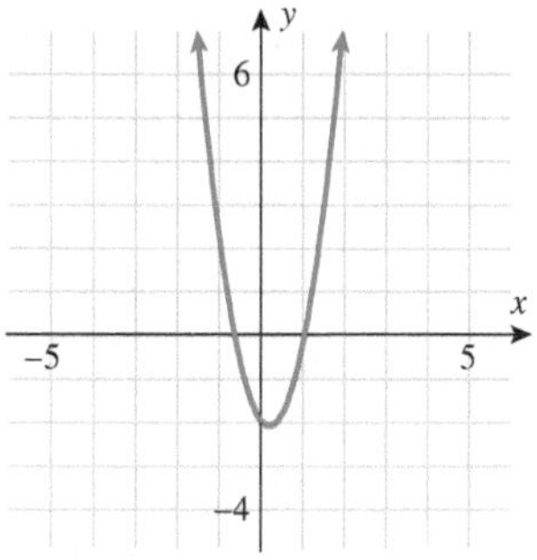

In Exercises 9–20, graph the quadratic function, which is given in standard form.

9. $f(x) = (x + 1)^2 - 2$
10. $f(x) = (x + 2)^2 - 1$
11. $f(x) = (x - 2)^2 - 3$
12. $f(x) = (x - 4)^2 + 2$
13. $f(x) = -(x - 3)^2 + 9$
14. $f(x) = -(x - 5)^2 - 4$
15. $f(x) = -(x + 1)^2 - 3$
16. $f(x) = -(x - 2)^2 + 6$
17. $f(x) = 2(x - 2)^2 + 2$
18. $f(x) = -3(x + 2)^2 - 15$
19. $f(x) = (x - \frac{1}{3})^2 + \frac{1}{9}$
20. $f(x) = (x + \frac{1}{4})^2 - \frac{1}{2}$

In Exercises 21–32, rewrite the quadratic function in standard form by completing the square.

21. $f(x) = x^2 + 6x - 3$
22. $f(x) = x^2 + 8x + 2$
23. $f(x) = -x^2 - 10x + 3$
24. $f(x) = -x^2 - 12x + 6$
25. $f(x) = 2x^2 + 8x - 2$
26. $f(x) = 3x^2 - 9x + 11$
27. $f(x) = -4x^2 + 16x - 7$
28. $f(x) = -5x^2 + 100x - 36$
29. $f(x) = x^2 + 10x$
30. $f(x) = -4x^2 + 12x - 2$
31. $f(x) = \frac{1}{2}x^2 - 4x + 3$
32. $f(x) = -\frac{1}{3}x^2 + 6x + 4$

In Exercises 33–40, graph the quadratic function.

33. $f(x) = x^2 + 6x - 7$
34. $f(x) = x^2 - 3x + 10$
35. $f(x) = -x^2 - 5x + 6$
36. $f(x) = -x^2 + 3x + 4$
37. $f(x) = 4x^2 - 5x + 10$
38. $f(x) = 3x^2 + 9x - 1$
39. $f(x) = -2x^2 - 12x - 16$
40. $f(x) = -3x^2 + 12x - 12$

In Exercises 41–46, find the vertex of the parabola associated with each quadratic function.

41. $f(x) = 33x^2 - 2x + 15$
42. $f(x) = 17x^2 + 4x - 3$
43. $f(x) = \frac{1}{2}x^2 - 7x + 5$
44. $f(x) = -\frac{1}{3}x^2 + \frac{2}{5}x + 4$
45. $f(x) = 0.06x^2 - 2.6x + 3.52$
46. $f(x) = -3.2x^2 + 0.8x - 0.14$

In Exercises 47–56, find the quadratic function that has the given vertex and goes through the given point.

47. vertex: $(-1, 4)$ point: $(0, 2)$
48. vertex: $(2, -3)$ point: $(0, 1)$
49. vertex: $(2, 5)$ point: $(3, 0)$
50. vertex: $(1, 3)$ point: $(-2, 0)$
51. vertex: $(-1, -3)$ point: $(-4, 2)$
52. vertex: $(0, -2)$ point: $(3, 10)$
53. vertex: $(-2, -4)$ point: $(-1, 6)$
54. vertex: $(5, 4)$ point: $(2, -5)$
55. vertex: $(\frac{1}{2}, -\frac{3}{4})$ point: $(\frac{3}{4}, 0)$
56. vertex: $(-\frac{5}{6}, \frac{2}{3})$ point: $(0, 0)$

• APPLICATIONS

57. **Business.** The annual profit for a company that manufactures cell phone accessories can be modeled by the function

$$P(x) = -0.0001x^2 + 70x + 12{,}500$$

where x is the number of units sold and P is the total profit in dollars.

a. What sales level maximizes the company's annual profit?
b. Find the maximum annual profit for the company.

58. **Business.** A manufacturer of office supplies has daily production costs of

$$C(x) = 0.5x^2 - 20x + 1600$$

where x is the number of units produced, measured in thousands, and C is cost in hundreds of dollars.

a. What production level will minimize the manufacturer's daily production costs?
b. Find the minimum daily production costs for the manufacturer.

For Exercises 59 and 60, refer to the following:

An adult male's weight, in kilograms, can be modeled by the function

$$W(t) = -\frac{2}{3}t^2 + \frac{13}{5}t + \frac{433}{5}; \quad 1 \le t \le 18$$

where t measures months ($t = 1$ is January 2010, $t = 2$ is February 2010, etc.) and W is the male's weight.

59. **Health/Medicine.** During which months was the male losing weight and during which gaining weight?

60. **Health/Medicine.** Find the maximum weight to the nearest kilogram of the adult male during the 18 months.

Exercises 61 and 62 concern the path of a punted football. Refer to the diagram in Example 9.

61. **Sports.** The path of a particular punt follows the quadratic function

$$h(x) = -\frac{8}{125}(x + 5)^2 + 40$$

where $h(x)$ is the height of the ball in yards and x corresponds to the horizontal distance in yards. Assume $x = 0$ corresponds to midfield (the 50 yard line). For example, $x = -20$ corresponds to the punter's own 30 yard line, whereas $x = 20$ corresponds to the other team's 30 yard line.

a. Find the maximum height the ball achieves.
b. Find the horizontal distance the ball covers. Assume the height is zero when the ball is kicked and when the ball is caught.

62. **Sports.** The path of a particular punt follows the quadratic function

$$h(x) = -\frac{5}{40}(x - 30)^2 + 50$$

where $h(x)$ is the height of the ball in yards and x corresponds to the horizontal distance in yards. Assume $x = 0$ corresponds to midfield (the 50 yard line). For example, $x = -20$ corresponds to the punter's own 30 yard line, whereas $x = 20$ corresponds to the other team's 30 yard line.

a. Find the maximum height the ball achieves.
b. Find the horizontal distance the ball covers. Assume the height is zero when the ball is kicked and when the ball is caught.

63. **Ranching.** A rancher has 10,000 linear feet of fencing and wants to enclose a rectangular field and then divide it into two equal pastures with an internal fence parallel to the shorter sides of the rectangle. What is the maximum area of each pasture? Round to the nearest square foot.

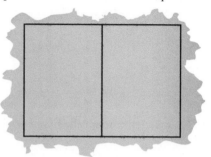

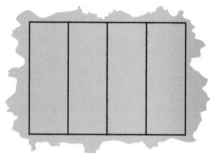

64. **Ranching.** A rancher has 30,000 linear feet of fencing and wants to enclose a rectangular field and then divide it into four equal pastures with three internal fences parallel to the shorter sides of the rectangle. What is the maximum area of each pasture?

65. **Gravity.** A person standing near the edge of a cliff 100 feet above a lake throws a rock upward with an initial speed of 32 feet per second. The height of the rock above the lake at the bottom of the cliff is a function of time and is described by

$$h(t) = -16t^2 + 32t + 100$$

a. How many seconds will it take until the rock reaches its maximum height? What is that height?
b. At what time will the rock hit the water?
c. Over what time interval is the rock higher than the cliff?

66. **Gravity.** A person holds a pistol straight upward and fires. The initial velocity of most bullets is around 1200 feet per second. The height of the bullet is a function of time and is described by

$$h(t) = -16t^2 + 1200t$$

How long, after the gun is fired, does the person have to get out of the way of the bullet falling from the sky?

67. **Zero Gravity.** As part of their training, astronauts rode the "vomit comet," NASA's reduced-gravity KC 135A aircraft that performed parabolic flights to simulate weightlessness. The plane started at an altitude of 20,000 feet and made a steep climb at 528 with the horizon for 20–25 seconds and then dove at that same angle back down, repeatedly. The equation governing the altitude of the flight is

$$A(x) = -0.0003x^2 + 9.3x - 46{,}075$$

where $A(x)$ is altitude and x is horizontal distance in feet.

a. What is the maximum altitude the plane attains?
b. Over what horizontal distance is the entire maneuver performed? (Assume the starting and ending altitude is 20,000 feet.)

Courtesy NASA

68. **Environment: Fuel Economy.** Gas mileage (miles per gallon, mpg) can be approximated by a quadratic function of speed. For a particular automobile, assume the vertex occurs when the speed is 50 miles per hour (the mpg will be 30).

a. Write a quadratic function that models this relationship, assuming 70 miles per hour corresponds to 25 mpg.
b. What gas mileage would you expect for this car driving 90 miles per hour?

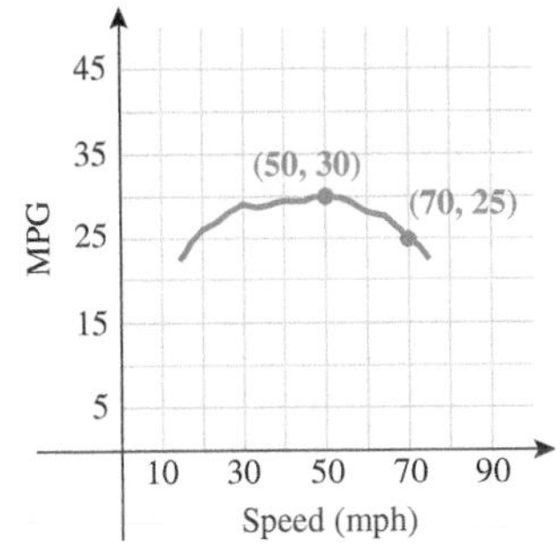

For Exercises 69 and 70, use the following information:

One function of particular interest in economics is the **profit function**. We denote this function by $P(x)$. It is defined to be the difference between revenue $R(x)$ and cost $C(x)$ so that

$$P(x) = R(x) - C(x)$$

The total revenue received from the sale of x goods at price p is given by

$$R(x) = px$$

The total cost function relates the cost of production to the level of output x. This includes both fixed costs C_f and variable costs C_v (costs per unit produced). The total cost in producing x goods is given by

$$C(x) = C_f + C_v x$$

Thus, the profit function is

$$P(x) = px - C_f - C_v x$$

Assume fixed costs are \$1000, variable costs per unit are \$20, and the demand function is

$$p = 100 - x$$

69. **Profit.** How many units should the company produce to break even?

70. **Profit.** What is the maximum profit?

71. **Drug Concentration.** The concentration of a drug in the bloodstream, measured in parts per million, can be modeled with a quadratic function. In 50 minutes the concentration is 93.75 parts per million. The maximum concentration of the drug in the bloodstream occurs in 225 minutes and is 400 parts per million.

a. Find a quadratic function that models the concentration of the drug as a function of time in minutes.
b. After the concentration peaks, eventually the drug will be eliminated from the body. How many minutes will it take until the concentration finally reaches 0?

72. **Revenue.** Jeff operates a mobile car-washing business. When he charged \$20 a car, he washed 70 cars a month. He raised the price to \$25 a car and his business dropped to 50 cars a month.

a. Find a linear function that represents the demand equation (the price per car as a function of the number of cars washed).
b. Find the revenue function $R(x) = xp$.
c. How many cars should he wash to maximize the revenue?
d. What price should he charge to maximize revenue?

• CATCH THE MISTAKE

In Exercises 73 and 74, explain the mistake that is made. There may be a single mistake or more than one mistake.

73. Plot the quadratic function $f(x) = (x + 3)^2 - 1$.

Solution:

STEP 1: The parabola opens up because $a = 1 > 0$.

STEP 2: The vertex is $(3, -1)$.

STEP 3: The y-intercept is $(0, 8)$.

STEP 4: The x-intercepts are $(2, 0)$ and $(4, 0)$.

STEP 5: Plot the vertex and intercepts, and connect the points with a smooth curve.

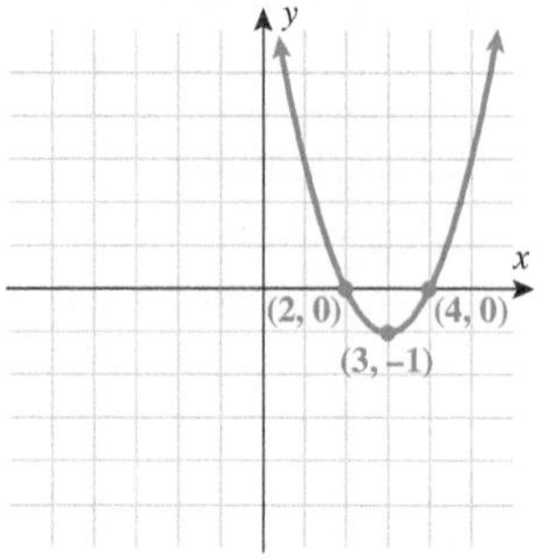

This is incorrect. What mistake(s) were made?

74. Find the quadratic function whose vertex is $(2, -3)$ and whose graph passes through the point $(9, 0)$.

Solution:

STEP 1: Write the quadratic function in standard form. $f(x) = a(x - h)^2 + k$

STEP 2: Substitute $(h, k) = (2, -3)$. $f(x) = a(x - 2)^2 - 3$

STEP 3: Substitute the point $(9, 0)$ and solve for a.

$$f(0) = a(0 - 2)^2 - 3 = 9$$
$$4a - 3 = 9$$
$$4a = 12$$
$$a = 3$$

The quadratic function sought is $f(x) = 3(x - 2)^2 - 3$.

This is incorrect. What mistake(s) was(were) made?

• CONCEPTUAL

In Exercises 75–78, determine whether each statement is true or false.

75. A quadratic function must have a y-intercept.
76. A quadratic function must have an x-intercept.
77. A quadratic function may have more than one y-intercept.
78. A quadratic function may have more than one x-intercept.
79. For the general quadratic equation, $f(x) = ax^2 + bx + c$, show that the vertex is $(h, k) = \left(-\frac{b}{2a}, f\left(-\frac{b}{2a}\right)\right)$.
80. Given the quadratic function $f(x) = a(x - h)^2 + k$, determine the x- and y-intercepts in terms of a, h, and k.

• CHALLENGE

81. A rancher has 1000 feet of fence to enclose a pasture.
    a. Determine the maximum area if a rectangular fence is used.
    b. Determine the maximum area if a circular fence is used.
82. A 600-room hotel in Orlando is filled to capacity every night when the rate is \$90 per night. For every \$5 increase in the rate, 10 fewer rooms are filled. How much should the hotel charge to produce the maximum income? What is its maximum income?
83. The speed of the river current is $\frac{1}{x + 4}$ mph. In quiet waters, the speed of a swimmer is $\frac{1}{x + 11}$ mph. When the swimmer swims down the river, her speed is $\frac{25}{144}$ mph. What is the value of x?
84. When a rectangle is reduced 25% (length and width each reduced by 25%), the new length equals the original width. Find the dimensions of the original rectangle given that the area of the reduced rectangle is 36 sq ft.

• PREVIEW TO CALCULUS

Parabolas, ellipses, and hyperbolas form a family of curves called conic sections. These curves are studied later in Chapter 9 and in calculus. The general equation of each curve is given below.

Parabola: $(x - h)^2 = 4p(y - k)$

Ellipse: $\dfrac{(x - h)^2}{a^2} + \dfrac{(y - k)^2}{b^2} = 1$

Hyperbola: $\dfrac{(x - h)^2}{a^2} - \dfrac{(y - k)^2}{b^2} = 1$

In Exercises 85–88, write the general equation of each conic section and identify the curve.

85. $4x^2 + 9y^2 = 36y$
86. $x^2 + 16y = 4y^2 + 2x + 19$
87. $x^2 + 6x - 20y + 5 = 0$
88. $x^2 + 105 = 6x - 40y + 4y^2$

2.2 POLYNOMIAL FUNCTIONS OF HIGHER DEGREE

SKILLS OBJECTIVES

- Identify a polynomial function and determine its degree.
- Graph polynomial functions using transformations.
- Identify real zeros of a polynomial function and their multiplicities.
- Graph polynomial functions using x-intercepts, multiplicity of each zero, and end behavior.

CONCEPTUAL OBJECTIVES

- Understand that polynomial functions are both continuous and smooth.
- Understand that power functions of even power have similar shapes, and power functions of odd power have similar shapes.
- Understand that the real zeros of a polynomial function correspond to x-intercepts on its graph.
- Understand that odd multiplicity of a zero corresponds to the graph crossing the x-axis; that even multiplicity of a zero corresponds to the graph touching the x-axis; and that end behavior is a result of the leading term dominating.

2.2.1 Identifying Polynomial Functions

2.2.1 SKILL

Identify a polynomial function and determine its degree.

2.2.1 CONCEPTUAL

Understand that polynomial functions are both continuous and smooth.

DEFINITION Polynomial Function

Let n be a nonnegative integer and let $a_n, a_{n-1}, \ldots, a_2, a_1, a_0$ be real numbers with $a_n \neq 0$. The function

$$f(x) = a_n x^n + a_{n-1}x^{n-1} + \cdots + a_2x^2 + a_1x + a_0$$

is called a **polynomial function of x with degree n**. The coefficient a_n is called the leading coefficient.

EXAMPLE 1 Identifying Polynomials and Their Degree

For each of the functions given, determine whether the function is a polynomial function. If it is a polynomial function, then state the degree of the polynomial. If it is not a polynomial function, justify your answer.

a. $f(x) = 3 - 2x^5$ **b.** $F(x) = \sqrt{x} + 1$

c. $g(x) = 2$ **d.** $h(x) = 3x^2 - 2x + 5$

e. $H(x) = 4x^5(2x - 3)^2$ **f.** $G(x) = 2x^4 - 5x^3 - 4x^{-2}$

Solution:

a. $f(x)$ is a polynomial function of degree 5.

b. $F(x)$ is not a polynomial function. The variable x is raised to the power of $\frac{1}{2}$, which is not an integer.

c. $g(x)$ is a polynomial function of degree zero, also known as a constant function. Note that $g(x) = 2$ can also be written as $g(x) = 2x^0$ (assuming $x \neq 0$).

d. $h(x)$ is a polynomial function of degree 2. A polynomial function of degree 2 is called a quadratic function.

e. $H(x)$ is a polynomial function of degree 7.
Note: $4x^5(4x^2 - 12x + 9) = 16x^7 - 48x^6 + 36x^5$.

f. $G(x)$ is not a polynomial function. $-4x^{-2}$ has an exponent that is negative.

YOUR TURN For each of the functions given, determine whether the function is a polynomial function. If it is a polynomial function, then state the degree of the polynomial. If it is not a polynomial function, justify your answer.

a. $f(x) = \dfrac{1}{x} + 2$ **b.** $g(x) = 3x^8(x - 2)^2(x + 1)^3$

ANSWER

a. $f(x)$ is not a polynomial function because x is raised to the power of -1, which is a negative integer.

b. $g(x)$ is a polynomial function of degree 13.

Whenever we have discussed a particular polynomial function of degree 0, 1, or 2, we have graphed it too. These functions are summarized in the table below.

POLYNOMIAL	DEGREE	SPECIAL NAME	GRAPH
$f(x) = c$	0	Constant function	Horizontal line
$f(x) = mx + b$	1	Linear function	Line • Slope $= m$ • y-intercept: $(0, b)$
$f(x) = ax^2 + bx + c$	2	Quadratic function	Parabola • Opens up if $a > 0$. • Opens down if $a < 0$.

How do we graph polynomial functions that are of degree 3 or higher, and why do we care? Polynomial functions model real-world applications. One example is the percentage of fat in our bodies as we age. We can model the weight of a baby after it comes home from the hospital as a function of time. When a baby comes home from the hospital, it usually experiences weight loss. Then typically there is an increase in the percent of body fat when the baby is nursing. When infants start to walk, the increase in exercise is associated with a drop in the percentage of fat. Growth spurts in children are examples of the percent of body fat increasing and decreasing. Later in life, our metabolism slows down, and typically, the percent of body fat increases. We will model this with a polynomial function. Other examples are stock prices, the federal funds rate, and yo-yo dieting as functions of time.

Graphs of all polynomial functions are both *continuous* and *smooth.* A **continuous** graph is one you can draw completely without picking up your pencil (the graph has no jumps or holes). A **smooth** graph has no sharp corners. The following graphs illustrate what it means to be smooth (no sharp corners or cusps) and continuous (no holes or jumps).

STUDY TIP

All polynomial functions have graphs that are both continuous and smooth.

The graph is *not continuous.*

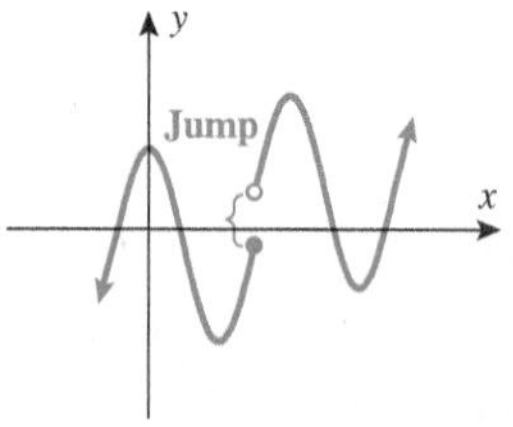

The graph is *not continuous.*

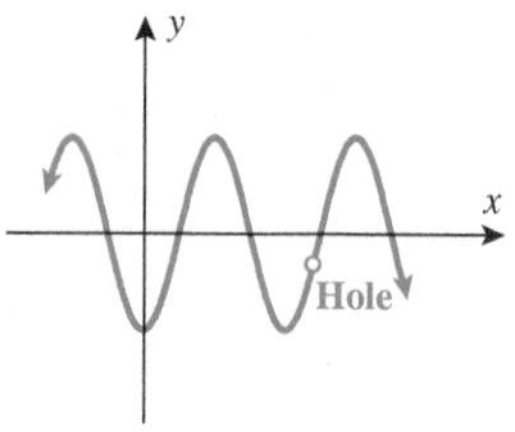

CONCEPT CHECK

TRUE OR FALSE It is possible for the graph of a polynomial function to have a hole.

ANSWER False

The graph is *continuous* but *not smooth.*

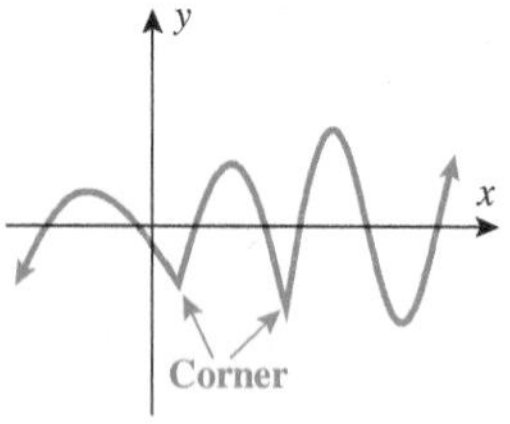

The graph is *continuous* and *smooth.*

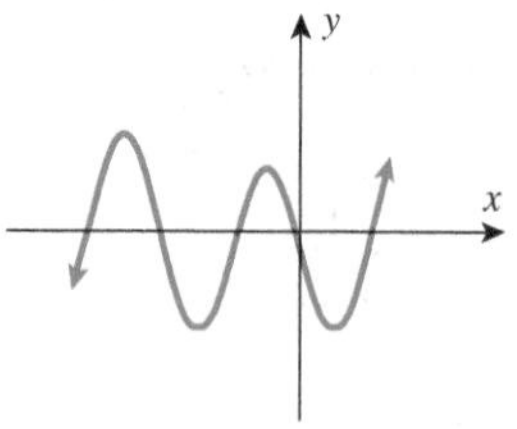

2.2.2 SKILL

Graph polynomial functions using transformations.

2.2.2 CONCEPTUAL

Understand that power functions of even power have similar shapes, and power functions of odd power have similar shapes.

2.2.2 Graphing Polynomial Functions Using Transformations of Power Functions

Recall from Chapter 1 that graphs of functions can be drawn by hand using graphing aids such as intercepts and symmetry. The graphs of polynomial functions can be graphed using these same aids. Let's start with the simplest types of polynomial functions, called

power functions. Power functions are monomial functions (Appendix) of the form $f(x) = x^n$, where n is a positive integer.

DEFINITION **Power Function**

Let n be a positive integer and let the coefficient $a \neq 0$ be a real number. The function

$$f(x) = ax^n$$

is called a **power function of degree n**.

Power functions with *even* powers look similar to the square function.

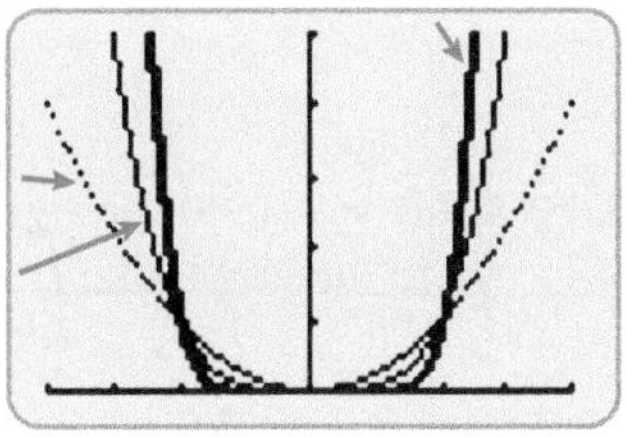

Power functions with *odd* powers (other than $n = 1$) look similar to the cube function.

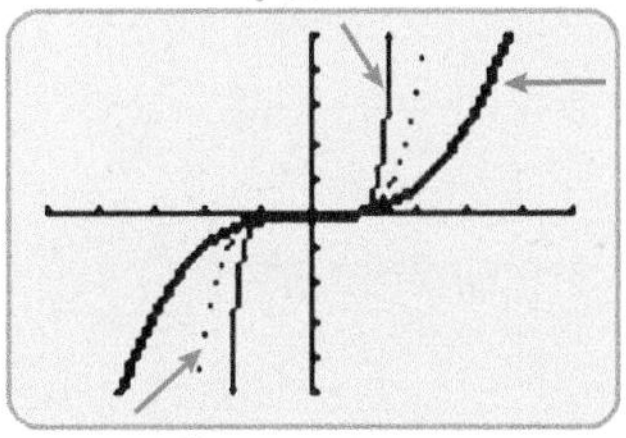

[CONCEPT CHECK]

An even power function has a domain and range that are both the set of all real numbers.

ANSWER False

All even power functions have similar characteristics to a quadratic function (parabola), and all odd $(n > 1)$ power functions have similar characteristics to a cubic function. For example, all even functions are symmetric with respect to the y-axis, whereas all odd functions are symmetric with respect to the origin. This table summarizes their characteristics.

CHARACTERISTICS OF POWER FUNCTIONS: $f(x) = x^n$

	n EVEN	n ODD
Symmetry	y-axis	Origin
Domain	$(-\infty, \infty)$	$(-\infty, \infty)$
Range	$[0, \infty)$	$(-\infty, \infty)$
Some key points that lie on the graph	$(-1, 1)$, $(0, 0)$, and $(1, 1)$	$(-1, -1)$, $(0, 0)$, and $(1, 1)$
Increasing	$(0, \infty)$	$(-\infty, \infty)$
Decreasing	$(-\infty, 0)$	Nowhere

We now have the tools to graph polynomial functions that are transformations of power functions. We will use the power functions combined with graphing techniques such as horizontal and vertical shifting and reflection (Section 1.3).

EXAMPLE 2 **Graphing Transformations of Power Functions**

Graph the function $f(x) = (x - 1)^3$.

Solution:

STEP 1 Start with the graph of $y = x^3$.

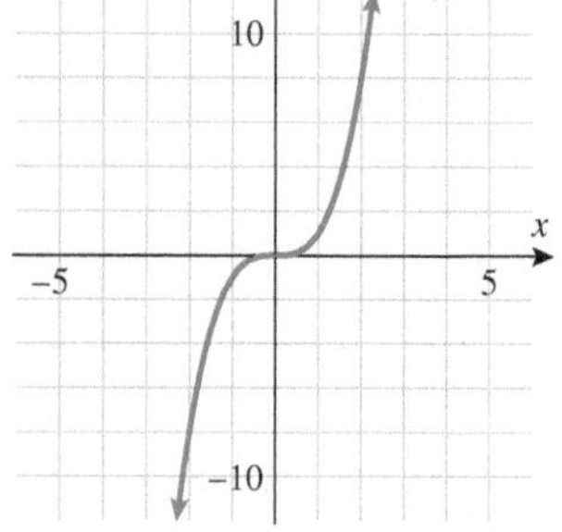

STEP 2 Shift $y = x^3$ to the right one unit to yield the graph of $f(x) = (x - 1)^3$.

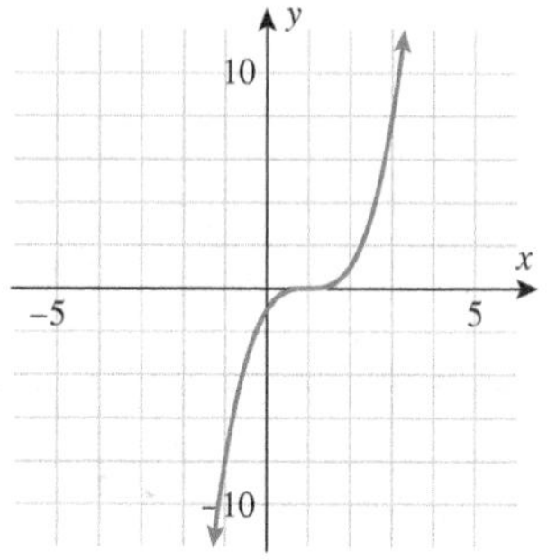

YOUR TURN Graph the function $f(x) = 1 - x^4$.

ANSWER

$f(x) = 1 - x^4$

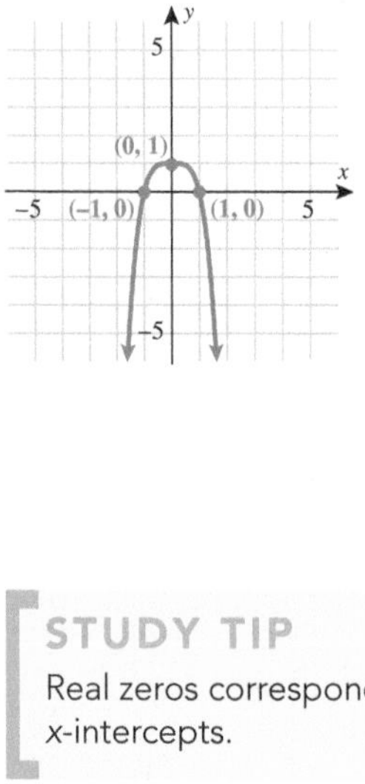

2.2.3 Real Zeros of a Polynomial Function

How do we graph general polynomial functions of degree greater than or equal to 3 if they cannot be written as transformations of power functions? We start by identifying the x-intercepts of the polynomial function. Recall that we determine the x-intercepts by setting the function equal to *zero* and solving for x. Therefore, an alternative name for an x-intercept of a function is a *zero* of the function. In our experience, to set a quadratic function equal to zero, the first step is to factor the quadratic expression into linear factors and then set each factor equal to zero. Therefore, there are four equivalent relationships that are summarized in the following box.

STUDY TIP

Real zeros correspond to x-intercepts.

REAL ZEROS OF POLYNOMIAL FUNCTIONS

If $f(x)$ is a polynomial function and a is a *real* number, then the following statements are equivalent.

- $x = a$ is a **solution,** or **root,** of the equation $f(x) = 0$.
- $(a, 0)$ is an **x-intercept** of the graph of $f(x)$.
- $x = a$ is a **zero** of the function $f(x)$.
- $(x - a)$ is a **factor** of $f(x)$.

2.2.3 SKILL

Identify real zeros of a polynomial function and their multiplicities.

2.2.3 CONCEPTUAL

Understand that the real zeros of a polynomial function correspond to x-intercepts on its graph.

Let's use a simple polynomial function to illustrate these four relationships. We'll focus on the quadratic function $f(x) = x^2 - 1$. The graph of this function is a parabola that opens up and has as its vertex the point $(0, -1)$.

<table>
<tr><th>SOLUTION</th><th colspan="2">X-INTERCEPT</th><th>ZERO</th><th>FACTOR</th></tr>
<tr><td>$x = -1$ and $x = 1$ are solutions, or roots, of the equation $x^2 - 1 = 0$.</td><td>The x-intercepts correspond to the points $(-1, 0)$ and $(1, 0)$.</td><td>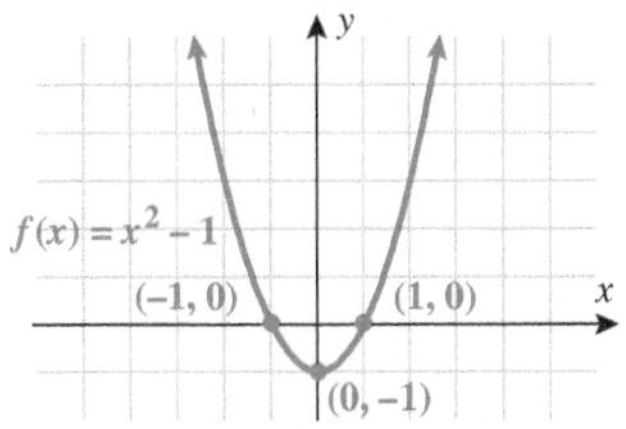
</td><td>$f(-1) = 0$
$f(1) = 0$</td><td>$f(x) = (x - 1)(x + 1)$</td></tr>
</table>

We have a good reason for wanting to know the x-intercepts, or zeros. When the value of a continuous function transitions from negative to positive, and vice versa, it must pass through zero.

DEFINITION Intermediate Value Theorem

Let a and b be real numbers such that $a < b$ and let f be a polynomial function. If $f(a)$ and $f(b)$ have opposite signs, then there is at least one zero between a and b.

[CONCEPT CHECK]

For the graph of a polynomial function $f(x) = (x - a)(x - b)$, what do a and b correspond to?.

ANSWER x-intercepts

The **intermediate value theorem** will be used later in this chapter to assist us in finding the real zeros of a polynomial function. For now, it tells us that in order to change signs, the graph of a polynomial function must pass through the x-axis. In other words, once we know the zeros, then we know that between two consecutive zeros the graph of a polynomial function is either entirely above the x-axis or entirely below the x-axis. This enables us to break down the x-axis into intervals that we can test, which will assist us in graphing polynomial functions. Keep in mind, though, that the existence of a zero does not imply that the function will change signs—as you will see in the subsection on graphing general polynomial functions.

EXAMPLE 3 Identifying the Real Zeros of a Polynomial Function

Find the zeros of the polynomial function $f(x) = x^3 + x^2 - 2x$.

Solution:

Set the function equal to zero. $\quad x^3 + x^2 - 2x = 0$

Factor out an x common to all three terms. $\quad x(x^2 + x - 2) = 0$

Factor the quadratic expression inside the parentheses. $\quad x(x + 2)(x - 1) = 0$

Apply the zero product property. $\quad x = 0$ or $(x + 2) = 0$ or $(x - 1) = 0$

Solve. $\quad x = -2, x = 0$, and $x = 1$

The zeros are $\boxed{-2, 0, \text{and } 1}$.

YOUR TURN Find the zeros of the polynomial function $f(x) = x^3 - 7x^2 + 12x$.

ANSWER

The zeros are 0, 3, and 4.

When a quadratic equation is factored, if the factor is raised to a power greater than 1, the corresponding root, or zero, is repeated. For example, the quadratic equation $x^2 - 2x + 1 = 0$ when factored is written as $(x - 1)^2 = 0$. The solution, or root, in this case is $x = 1$, and we say that it is a **repeated** root. Similarly, when determining zeros of higher order polynomial functions, if a factor is repeated, we say that the zero is a repeated, or **multiple**, zero of the function. The number of times that a zero repeats is called its *multiplicity*.

DEFINITION **Multiplicity of a Zero**

If $(x - a)^n$ is a factor of a polynomial f, then a is called a **zero of multiplicity n** of f.

EXAMPLE 4 **Finding the Multiplicities of Zeros of a Polynomial Function**

Find the zeros, and state their multiplicities, of the polynomial function $g(x) = (x - 1)^2(x + \frac{3}{5})^7(x + 5)$.

Solution:

1 is a zero of multiplicity 2.

$-\frac{3}{5}$ is a zero of multiplicity 7.

-5 is a zero of multiplicity 1.

Note: Adding the multiplicities yields the degree of the polynomial. The polynomial $g(x)$ is of degree 10, since $2 + 7 + 1 = 10$.

YOUR TURN For the polynomial $h(x)$, determine the zeros and state their multiplicities.

$$h(x) = x^2(x - 2)^3\left(x + \frac{1}{2}\right)^5$$

ANSWER

0 is a zero of multiplicity 2.
2 is a zero of multiplicity 3.
$-\frac{1}{2}$ is a zero of multiplicity 5.

EXAMPLE 5 **Finding a Polynomial from Its Zeros**

Find a polynomial of degree 7 whose zeros are

$$-2 \text{ (multiplicity 2)} \quad 0 \text{ (multiplicity 4)} \quad 1 \text{ (multiplicity 1)}$$

STUDY TIP

It is not always possible to find x-intercepts. Sometimes there are no x-intercepts (for some even-degree polynomial functions).

Solution:

If $x = a$ is a zero, then $(x - a)$ is a factor.	$f(x) = (x + 2)^2(x - 0)^4(x - 1)^1$
Simplify.	$= x^4(x + 2)^2(x - 1)$
Square the binomial.	$= x^4(x^2 + 4x + 4)(x - 1)$
Multiply the two polynomials.	$= x^4(x^3 + 3x^2 - 4)$
Distribute x^4.	$= \boxed{x^7 + 3x^6 - 4x^4}$

2.2.4 SKILL

Graph polynomial functions using x-intercepts, multiplicity of each zero, and end behavior.

2.2.4 CONCEPTUAL

Understand that odd multiplicity of a zero corresponds to the graph crossing the x-axis; that even multiplicity of a zero corresponds to the graph touching the x-axis; and that end behavior is a result of the leading term dominating.

2.2.4 Graphing General Polynomial Functions

Let's develop a strategy for sketching an approximate graph of any polynomial function. First, we determine the x- and y-intercepts. Then we use the x-intercepts, or zeros, to divide the domain into intervals where the value of the polynomial is positive or negative so that we can find points in those intervals to assist in sketching a smooth and continuous graph. *Note:* It is not always possible to find x-intercepts. Some even-degree polynomial functions have no x-intercepts on their graph.

EXAMPLE 6 Using a Strategy for Sketching the Graph of a Polynomial Function

Sketch the graph of $f(x) = (x + 2)(x - 1)^2$.

Solution:

STEP 1 Find the y-intercept. (Let $x = 0$.)

$f(0) = (2)(-1)^2 = 2$

$(0, 2)$ is the y-intercept

STEP 2 Find any x-intercepts. (Set $f(x) = 0$.)

$f(x) = (x + 2)(x - 1)^2 = 0$

$x = -2$ or $x = 1$

$(-2, 0)$ and $(1, 0)$ are the x-intercepts

STEP 3 Plot the intercepts.

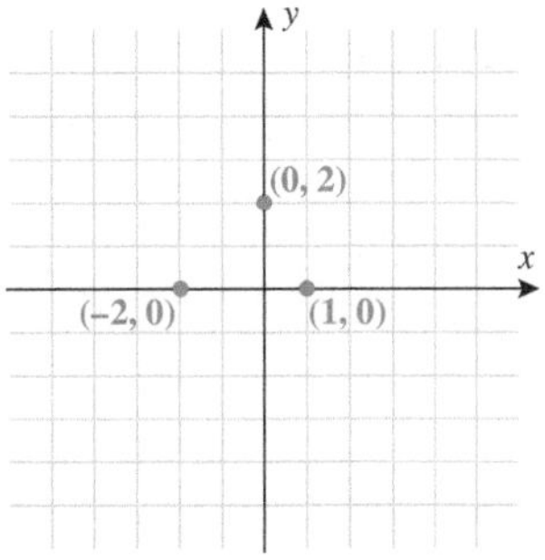

STEP 4 Divide the x-axis into intervals: $(-\infty, -2)$, $(-2, 1)$, and $(1, \infty)$

STEP 5 Select a number in each interval and test each interval. The function $f(x)$ either *crosses* the x-axis at an x-intercept or *touches* the x-axis at an x-intercept. Therefore, we need to check each of these intervals to determine whether the function is positive (above the x-axis) or negative (below the x-axis). We do so by selecting numbers in the intervals and determining the value of the function at the corresponding points.

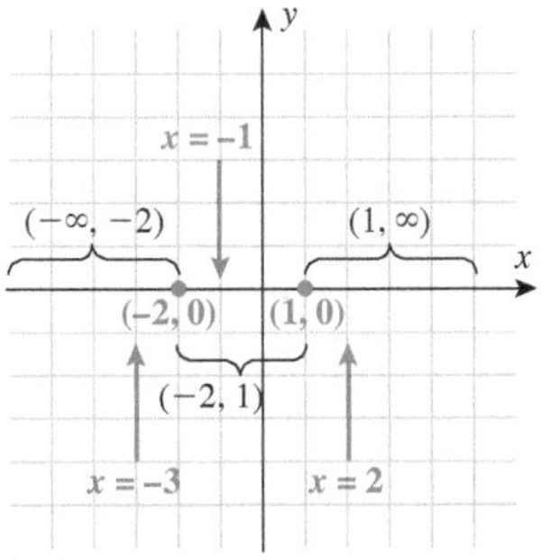

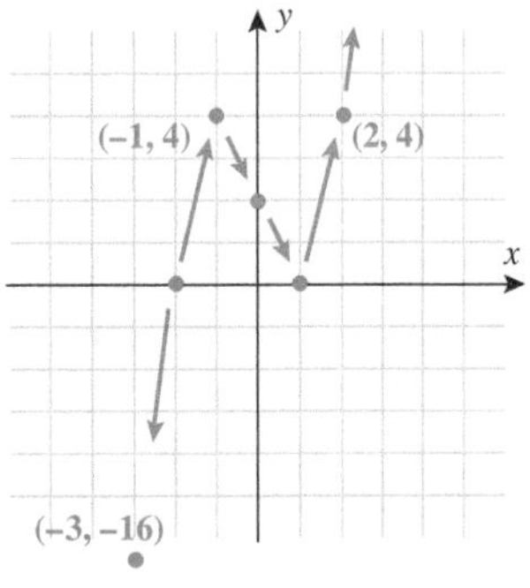

INTERVAL	$(-\infty, -2)$	$(-2, 1)$	$(1, \infty)$
NUMBER SELECTED IN INTERVAL	-3	-1	2
VALUE OF FUNCTION	$f(-3) = -16$	$f(-1) = 4$	$f(2) = 4$
POINT ON GRAPH	$(-3, -16)$	$(-1, 4)$	$(2, 4)$
INTERVAL RELATION TO x-AXIS	Below x-axis	Above x-axis	Above x-axis

From the table, we find three additional points on the graph: $(-3, -16)$, $(-1, 4)$, and $(2, 4)$. The point $(-2, 0)$ is an intercept where the function *crosses* the x-axis, because the graph is below the x-axis to the left of -2 and above the x-axis to the right of -2. The point $(1, 0)$ is an intercept where the function *touches* the x-axis, because the graph is above the x-axis on both sides of $x = 1$. Connecting these points with a smooth curve yields the graph.

STUDY TIP

Although there may be up to n x-intercepts for the graph of a polynomial function of degree n, there will always be exactly one y-intercept.

STUDY TIP

We do not know for sure that the points $(-1, 4)$ and $(1, 0)$ are turning points. We will see later that $(1, 0)$ is a turning point because the graph touches the x-axis at $(1, 0)$, but a graphing utility suggests that $(-1, 4)$ is a turning point, and later in calculus you will learn how to find relative maximum points and relative minimum points.

STEP 6 Sketch a plot of the function.

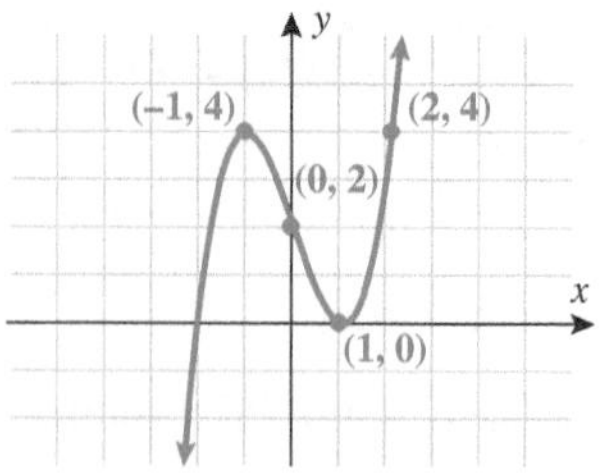

YOUR TURN Sketch the graph of $f(x) = x^2(x + 3)^2$.

ANSWER

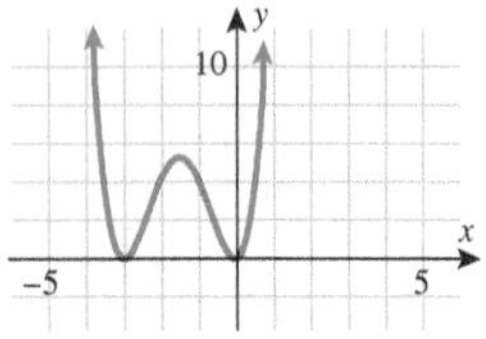

In Example 6, we found that the function crosses the x-axis at the point $(-2, 0)$. Note that -2 is a zero of multiplicity 1. We also found that the function touches the x-axis at the point $(1, 0)$. Note that 1 is a zero of multiplicity 2. In general, zeros with even multiplicity correspond to intercepts where the function touches the x-axis, and zeros with odd multiplicity correspond to intercepts where the function crosses the x-axis.

STUDY TIP

In general, zeros with *even* multiplicity correspond to intercepts where the function *touches* the x-axis, and zeros with *odd* multiplicity correspond to intercepts where the function *crosses* the x-axis.

MULTIPLICITY OF A ZERO AND RELATION TO THE GRAPH OF A POLYNOMIAL FUNCTION

If a is a zero of $f(x)$, then

MULTIPLICITY OF a	$f(x)$ ON EITHER SIDE OF $x = a$	GRAPH OF FUNCTION AT THE INTERCEPT
Even	Does not change sign	Touches the x-axis (turns around) at point $(a, 0)$
Odd	Changes sign	Crosses the x-axis at point $(a, 0)$

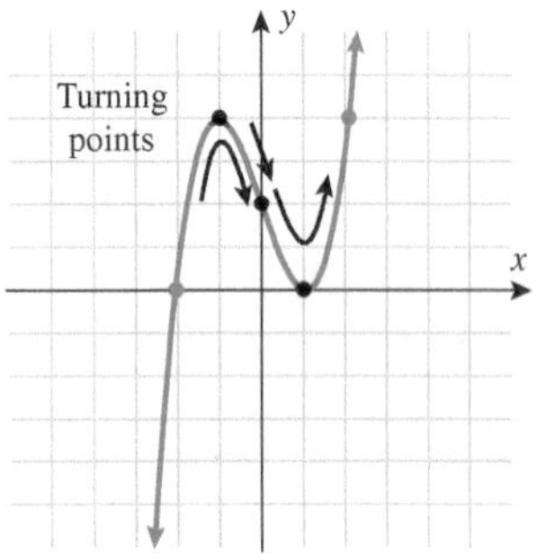

Also in Example 6, we know that somewhere in the interval $(-2, 1)$ the function must reach a relative or local maximum and then turn back toward the x-axis, because both points $(-2, 0)$ and $(1, 0)$ correspond to x-intercepts. When we sketch the graph, it "appears" that the point $(-1, 4)$ is a *turning point*. The point $(1, 0)$ also corresponds to a turning point. In general, if f is a polynomial of degree n, then the graph of f has at most $n - 1$ turning points.

The point $(-1, 4)$, which we call a turning point, is also a relative or local "high point" on the graph in the vicinity of the point $(-1, 4)$. Also note that the point $(1, 0)$, which we call a turning point, is a relative or local "low point" on the graph in the vicinity of the point $(1, 0)$. We call a "high point" on a graph a **local (relative) maximum** and a "low point" on a graph a **local (relative) minimum**. For quadratic functions we can find the maximum or minimum point by finding the vertex. However, for higher degree polynomial functions, we rely on graphing utilities to assist us in locating such points. Later in calculus, techniques will be developed for finding such points exactly. For now, we use the [zoom] and [trace] features to locate such points on a graph, and we can use the [table] feature of a graphing utility to approximate relative minima or maxima.

STUDY TIP

If f is a polynomial of degree n, then the graph of f has at most $n - 1$ turning points.

Let us take the polynomial $f(x) = x^3 - 2x^2 - 5x + 6$. Using methods discussed thus far, we can find that the x-intercepts of its graph are $(-2, 0)$, $(1, 0)$, and $(3, 0)$ and the y-intercept is the point $(0, 6)$. We can also find additional points that lie on the graph, such as $(-1, 8)$ and $(2, -4)$. Plotting these points, we might "think" that the points $(-1, 8)$ and $(2, -4)$ might be turning points, but a graphing utility reveals an approximate relative maximum at the point $(-0.7863, 8.2088207)$ and an approximate relative minimum at the point $(2.1196331, -4.060673)$.

Intercepts and turning points assist us in sketching graphs of polynomial functions. Another piece of information that will assist us in graphing polynomial functions is knowledge of the *end behavior.* All polynomials eventually rise or fall without bound as x gets large in both the positive $(x \to \infty)$ and negative $(x \to -\infty)$ directions. The highest degree monomial within the polynomial dominates the *end behavior.* In other words, the highest power term is eventually going to overwhelm the other terms as x grows without bound.

END BEHAVIOR

As x gets large in the positive ($x \to \infty$) and negative ($x \to -\infty$) directions, the graph of the polynomial

$$f(x) = a_n x^n + a_{n-1} x^{n-1} + \cdots + a_2 x^2 + a_1 x + a_0$$

has the same behavior as the power function

$$y = a_n x^n$$

Power functions behave much like a quadratic function (parabola) for even-degree polynomial functions and much like a cubic function for odd-degree polynomial functions. There are four possibilities because the leading coefficient can be positive or negative with either an odd or an even power.

Let $y = a_n x^n$ then

n	Even	Even	Odd	Odd
a_n	Positive	Negative	Negative	Positive
$x \to -\infty$ (LEFT)	The graph of the function *rises.*	The graph of the function *falls.*	The graph of the function *rises.*	The graph of the function *falls.*
$x \to \infty$ (RIGHT)	The graph of the function *rises.*	The graph of the function *falls.*	The graph of the function *falls.*	The graph of the function *rises.*
GRAPH	$a_n > 0$ 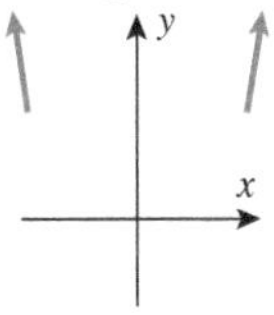	$a_n < 0$ 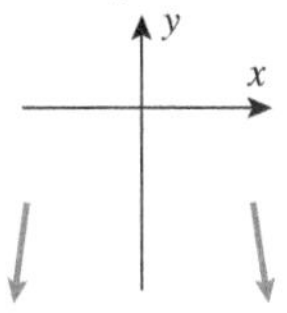	$a_n < 0$ 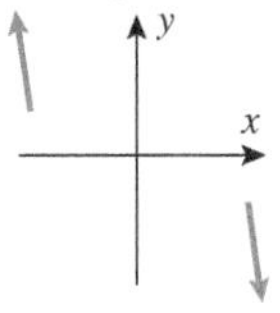	$a_n > 0$ 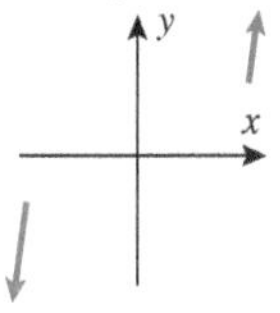

EXAMPLE 7 **Graphing a Polynomial Function**

Sketch a graph of the polynomial function $f(x) = 2x^4 - 8x^2$.

Solution:

STEP 1 Determine the y-intercept: ($x = 0$). $f(0) = 0$

The y-intercept corresponds to the point $(0, 0)$.

STEP 2 Find the zeros of the polynomial. $f(x) = 2x^4 - 8x^2$

Factor out the common $2x^2$. $= 2x^2(x^2 - 4)$

Factor the quadratic binomial. $= 2x^2(x - 2)(x + 2)$

Set $f(x) = 0$. $= 2x^2(x - 2)(x + 2) = 0$

0 is a zero of multiplicity 2. The graph will *touch* the x-axis.

2 is a zero of multiplicity 1. The graph will *cross* the x-axis.

−2 is a zero of multiplicity 1. The graph will *cross* the x-axis.

STEP 3 Determine the end behavior. $f(x) = 2x^4 - 8x^2$ behaves like $y = 2x^4$.

$y = 2x^4$ is of even degree, and the leading coefficient is positive, so the graph rises without bound as x gets large in both the positive and negative directions.

STEP 4 Sketch the intercepts and end behavior.

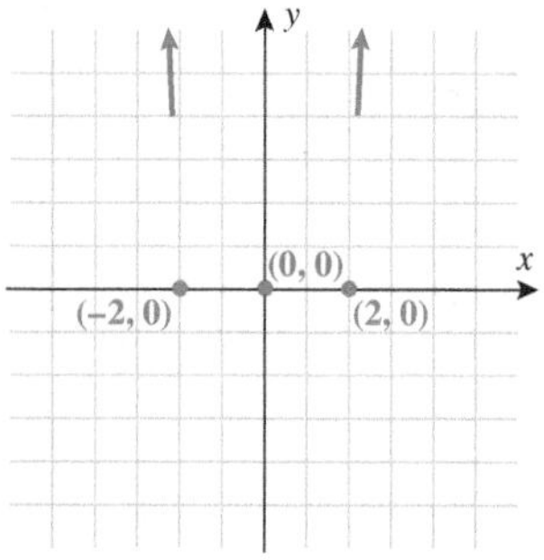

[CONCEPT CHECK]

Does the graph of the function $f(x) = (x - a)^3(x - b)^2$ cross or touch the x-axis at $(a, 0)$? at $(b, 0)$?

ANSWER crosses at $(a, 0)$ and touches at $(b, 0)$.

STEP 5 Find additional points.

x	-1	$-\frac{1}{2}$	$\frac{1}{2}$	1
$f(x)$	-6	$-\frac{15}{8}$	$-\frac{15}{8}$	-6

STEP 6 Sketch the graph.

- estimate additional points
- connect with a smooth curve

Note the symmetry about the y-axis. This function is an even function: $f(-x) = f(x)$.

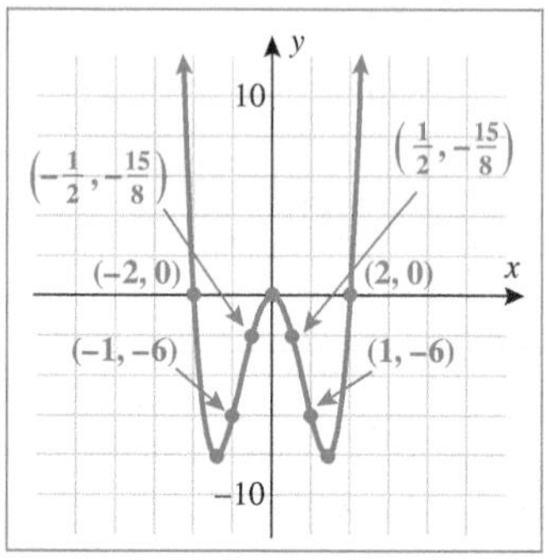

It is important to note that the absolute minimum occurs when $x = \pm\sqrt{2} \approx \pm 1.14$ but, at this time, can be illustrated only using a graphing utility.

YOUR TURN Sketch a graph of the polynomial function $f(x) = x^5 - 4x^3$.

ANSWER

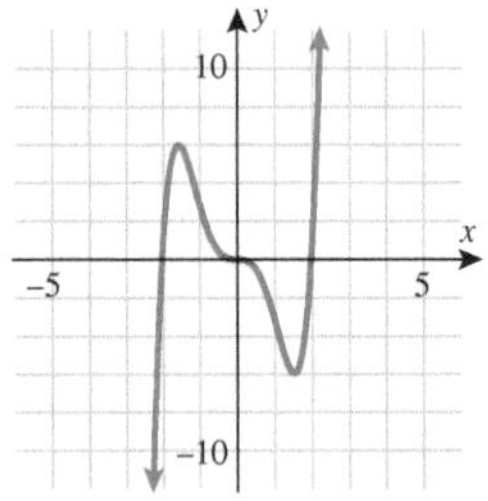

[SECTION 2.2] SUMMARY

Polynomials can sometimes by graphed using graph-shifting techniques with power functions. For more general polynomials, use the following steps:

1. Identify intercepts.
2. Determine each real zero and its multiplicity, and ascertain whether the graph crosses or touches the x-axis there.
3. x-intercepts (real zeros) divide the x-axis into intervals. Test points in the intervals to determine whether the graph is above or below the x-axis.
4. Determine the end behavior by investigating the end behavior of the highest degree monomial.
5. Sketch the graph with a smooth curve.

[SECTION 2.2] EXERCISES

• SKILLS

In Exercises 1–10, determine which functions are polynomials, and for those that are, state their degree.

1. $g(x) = (x + 2)^3(x - \frac{3}{5})^2$ **2.** $g(x) = (x - \frac{1}{4})^4(x + \sqrt{7})^2$ **3.** $g(x) = x^5(x + 2)(x - 6.4)$ **4.** $g(x) = x^4(x - 1)^2(x + 2.5)^3$

5. $h(x) = \sqrt{x} + 1$ **6.** $h(x) = (x - 1)^{1/2} + 5x$ **7.** $F(x) = x^{1/3} + 7x^2 - 2$ **8.** $F(x) = 3x^2 + 7x - \dfrac{2}{3x}$

9. $G(x) = \dfrac{x + 1}{x^2}$ **10.** $H(x) = \dfrac{x^2 + 1}{2}$

In Exercises 11–18, match the polynomial function with its graph.

11. $f(x) = -3x + 1$ **12.** $f(x) = -3x^2 - x$ **13.** $f(x) = x^2 + x$ **14.** $f(x) = -2x^3 + 4x^2 - 6x$

15. $f(x) = x^3 - x^2$ **16.** $f(x) = 2x^4 - 18x^2$ **17.** $f(x) = -x^4 + 5x^3$ **18.** $f(x) = x^5 - 5x^3 + 4x$

a.

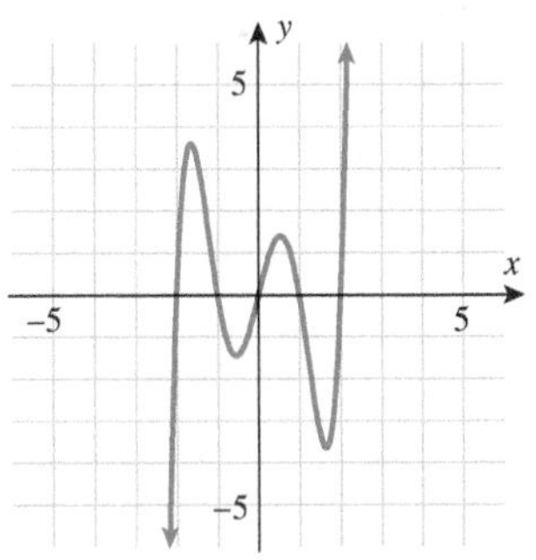

b.

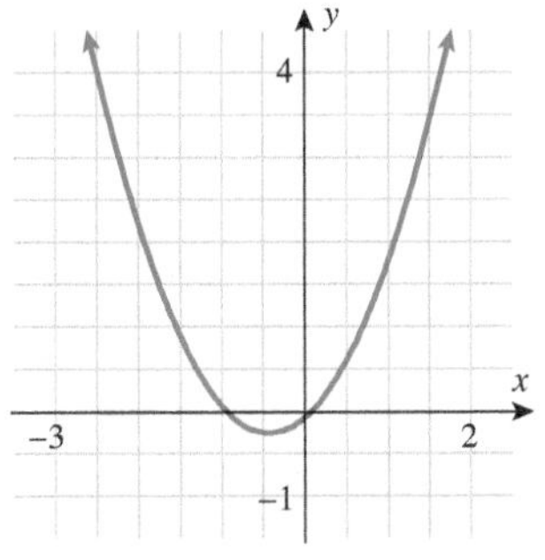

c.

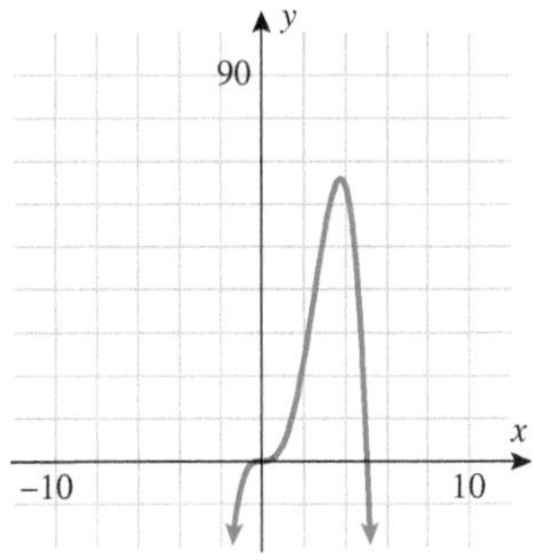

d.

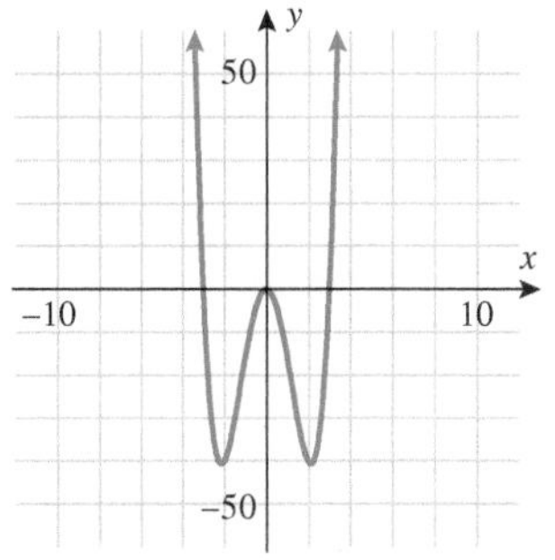

e.

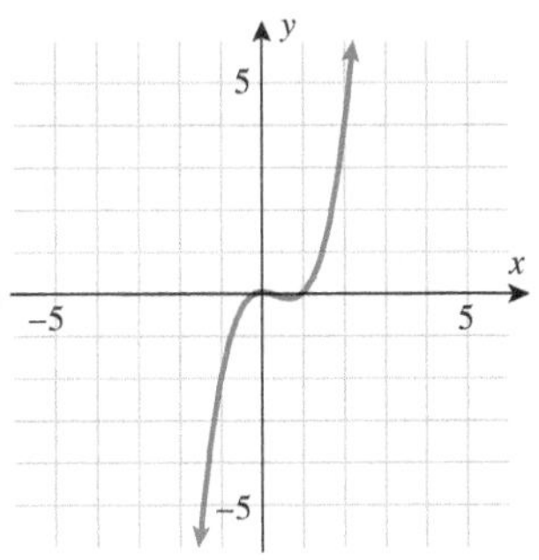

f.

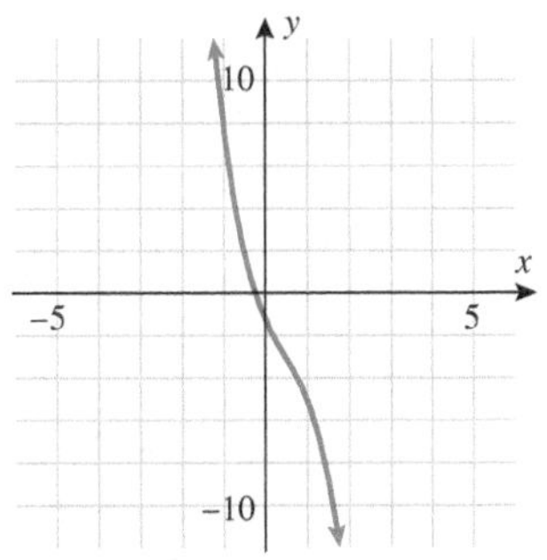

g.

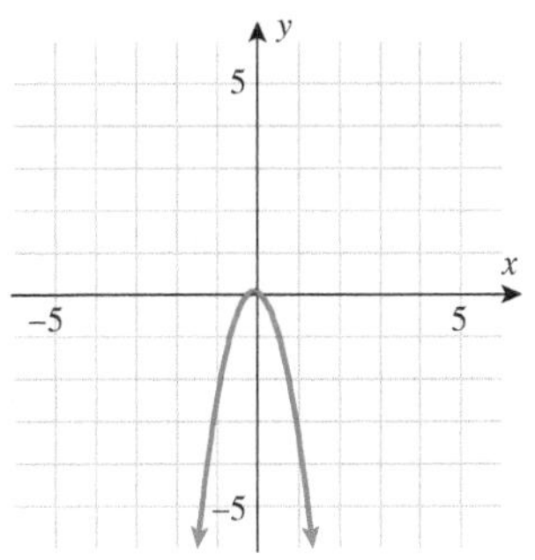

h.

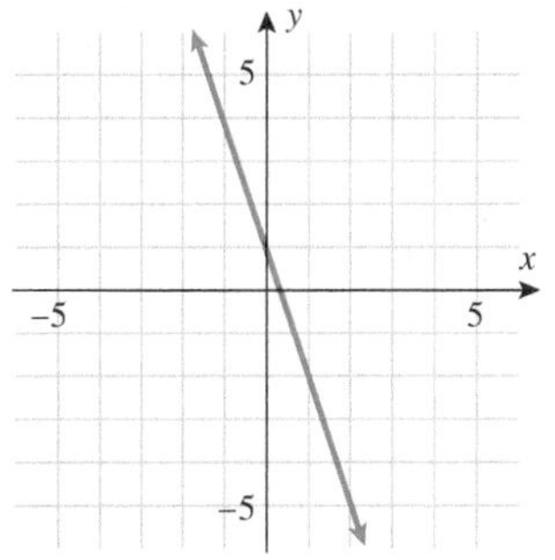

In Exercises 19–24, graph each function by transforming a power function $y = x^n$.

19. $f(x) = (x - 2)^4$ **20.** $f(x) = (x + 2)^5$ **21.** $f(x) = x^5 + 3$

22. $f(x) = -x^4 - 3$ **23.** $f(x) = 3 - (x + 1)^4$ **24.** $f(x) = (x - 3)^5 - 2$

In Exercises 25–32, find all the real zeros of each polynomial function (and state their multiplicities).

25. $f(x) = 2(x - 3)(x + 4)^3$ **26.** $f(x) = -3(x + 2)^3(x - 1)^2$ **27.** $f(x) = 4x^2(x - 7)^2(x + 4)$

28. $f(x) = 5x^3(x + 1)^4(x - 6)$ **29.** $f(x) = 4x^2(x - 1)^2(x^2 + 4)$ **30.** $f(x) = 4x^2(x^2 - 1)(x^2 + 9)$

31. $f(x) = 8x^3 + 6x^2 - 27x$ **32.** $f(x) = 2x^4 + 5x^3 - 3x^2$

In Exercises 33–46, find a polynomial (there are many) of minimum degree that has the given zeros.

33. $-3, 0, 1, 2$ **34.** $-2, 0, 2$ **35.** $-5, -3, 0, 2, 6$

36. $0, 1, 3, 5, 10$ **37.** $-\frac{1}{2}, \frac{2}{3}, \frac{3}{4}$ **38.** $-\frac{3}{4}, -\frac{1}{3}, 0, \frac{1}{2}$

39. $1 - \sqrt{2}, 1 + \sqrt{2}$ **40.** $1 - \sqrt{3}, 1 + \sqrt{3}$

41. -2 (multiplicity 3), 0 (multiplicity 2) **42.** -4 (multiplicity 2), 5 (multiplicity 3)

43. -3 (multiplicity 2), 7 (multiplicity 5) **44.** 0 (multiplicity 1), 10 (multiplicity 3)

45. $-\sqrt{3}$ (multiplicity 2), -1 (multiplicity 1), 0 (multiplicity 2), $\sqrt{3}$ (multiplicity 2)

46. $-\sqrt{5}$ (multiplicity 2), 0 (multiplicity 1), 1 (multiplicity 2), $\sqrt{5}$ (multiplicity 2)

In Exercises 47–64, for each polynomial function given: (a) list each real zero and its multiplicity; (b) determine whether the graph touches or crosses at each x-intercept; (c) find the y-intercept and a few points on the graph; (d) determine the end behavior; and (e) sketch the graph.

47. $f(x) = (x - 2)^3$

48. $f(x) = -(x + 3)^3$

49. $f(x) = x^3 - 9x$

50. $f(x) = -x^3 + 4x^2$

51. $f(x) = -x^3 + x^2 + 2x$

52. $f(x) = x^3 - 6x^2 + 9x$

53. $f(x) = -x^4 - 3x^3$

54. $f(x) = x^5 - x^3$

55. $f(x) = 12x^6 - 36x^5 - 48x^4$

56. $f(x) = 7x^5 - 14x^4 - 21x^3$

57. $f(x) = 2x^5 - 6x^4 - 8x^3$

58. $f(x) = -5x^4 + 10x^3 - 5x^2$

59. $f(x) = x^3 - x^2 - 4x + 4$

60. $f(x) = x^3 - x^2 - x + 1$

61. $f(x) = -(x + 2)^2(x - 1)^2$

62. $f(x) = (x - 2)^3(x + 1)^3$

63. $f(x) = x^2(x - 2)^3(x + 3)^2$

64. $f(x) = -x^3(x - 4)^2(x + 2)^2$

In Exercises 65–68, for each graph given: (a) list each real zero and its smallest possible multiplicity; (b) determine whether the degree of the polynomial is even or odd; (c) determine whether the leading coefficient of the polynomial is positive or negative; (d) find the y-intercept; and (e) write an equation for the polynomial function (assume the least degree possible).

65.

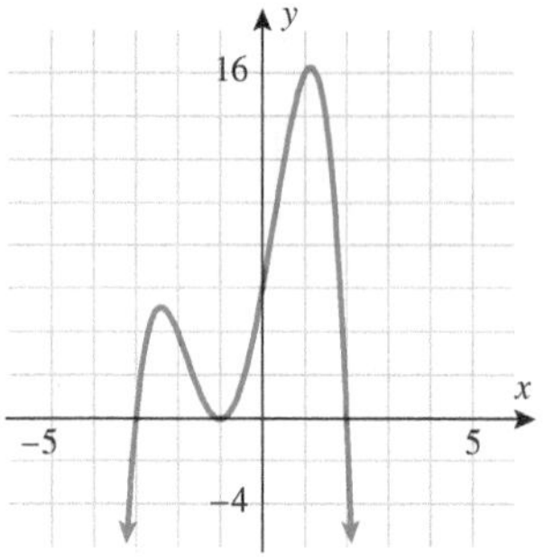

66.

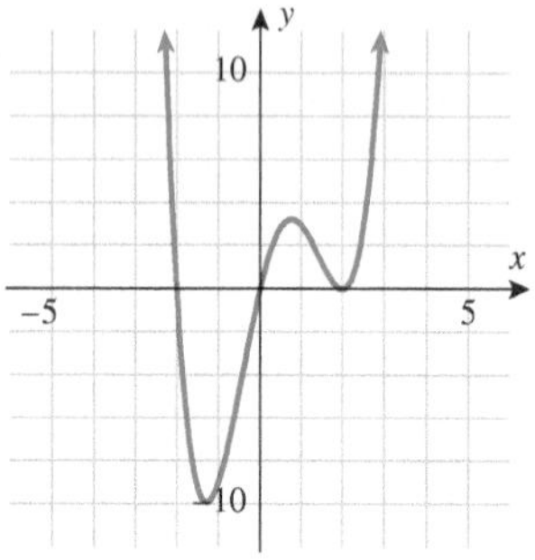

67.

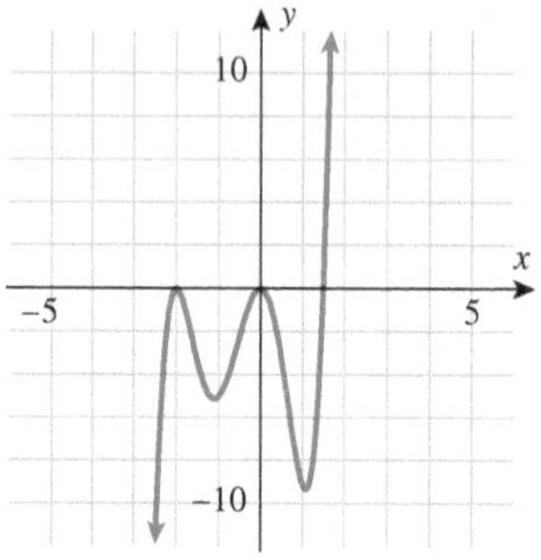

68.

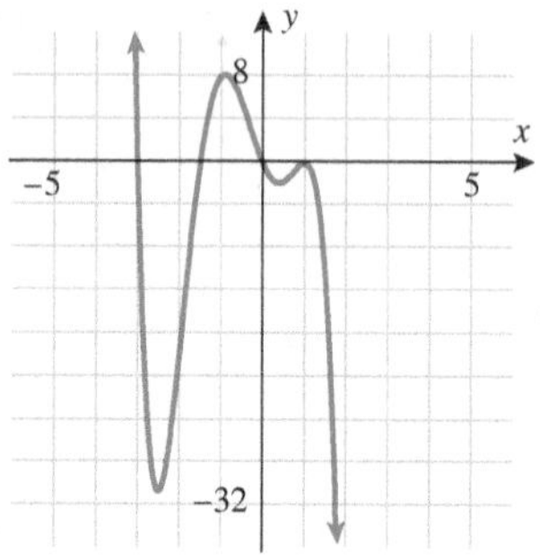

• APPLICATIONS

For Exercises 69 and 70, refer to the following:

A company's total revenue R (in millions of dollars) is related to its advertising costs x (in thousands of dollars). The relationship between revenue R and advertising costs x is illustrated in the graph.

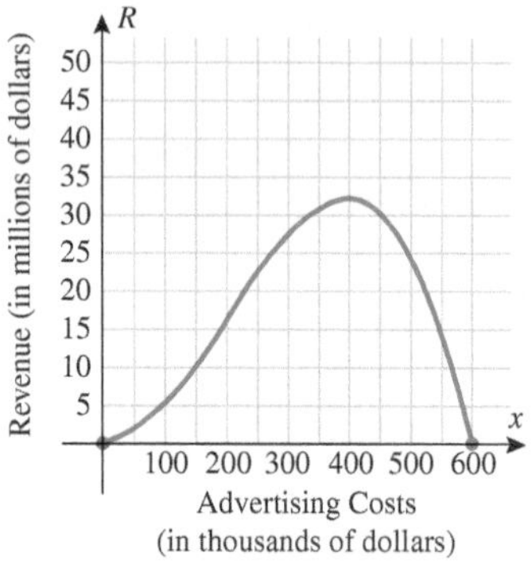

69. Business. Analyze the graph of the revenue function.

a. Determine the intervals on which revenue is increasing and those on which it is decreasing.

b. Identify the zeros of the function. Interpret the meaning of zeros for this function.

70. Business. Use the graph to identify the maximum revenue for the company and the corresponding advertising costs that produce maximum revenue.

For Exercises 71 and 72, refer to the following:

During a cough, the velocity v (in meters per second) of air in the trachea may be modeled by the function

$$v(r) = -120r^3 + 80r^2$$

where r is the radius of the trachea (in centimeters) during the cough.

71. Health/Medicine. Graph the velocity function and estimate the intervals on which the velocity of air in the trachea is increasing and those on which it is decreasing.

72. Health/Medicine. Estimate the radius of the trachea that produces the maximum velocity of air in the trachea. Use this radius to estimate the maximum velocity of air in the trachea.

73. Stock Value. The price of Tommy Hilfiger stock during a 4-hour period is given below. If a third-degree polynomial models this stock, do you expect the stock to go up or down in the fifth period?

PERIOD WATCHING STOCK MARKET	PRICE
1	\$15.10
2	\$14.76
3	\$15.50
4	\$14.85

74. Stock Value. The stock prices for Coca-Cola during a 4-hour period on another day yield the following results. If a third-degree polynomial models this stock, do you expect the stock to go up or down in the fifth period?

PERIOD WATCHING STOCK MARKET	PRICE
1	\$52.80
2	\$53.00
3	\$56.00
4	\$52.70

For Exercises 75 and 76, the following graph illustrates the average federal funds rate in the month of January (2006 to 2014):

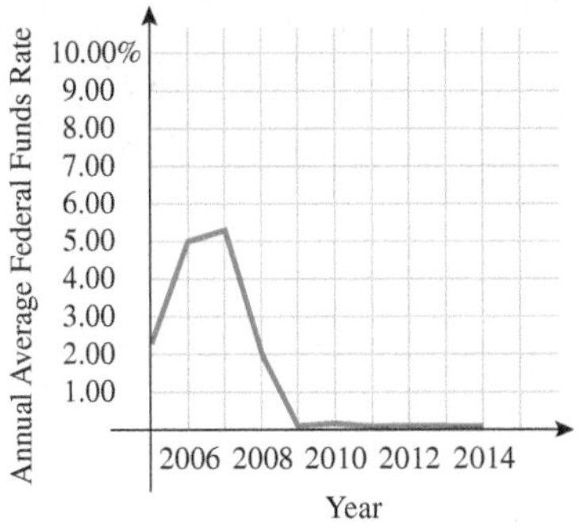

75. Finance. If a polynomial function is used to model the federal funds rate data shown in the graph, determine the degree of the lowest degree polynomial that can be used to model those data.

76. Finance. Should the leading coefficient in the polynomial found in Exercise 75 be positive or negative? Explain.

77. Air Travel. An airline has a daily flight Chicago–Miami. The number of passengers per flight is given in the table below. Which would be the minimum degree of a polynomial that models the number of passengers on the airline?

DAY	PASSENGERS
Monday	180
Tuesday	150
Wednesday	175
Thursday	160
Friday	100
Saturday	98
Sunday	120

78. Air Travel. The airline in Exercise 77 discovered that the information about the number of passengers corresponding to Monday and Sunday was mixed. On Sunday, they have 180 passengers, while on Monday, they have 120 passengers. Determine the degree of the lowest degree polynomial that can be used to model those data.

• CATCH THE MISTAKE

In Exercises 79 and 80, explain the mistake that is made.

79. Find a fourth-degree polynomial function with zeros -2, $-1, 3, 4$.

Solution:

$f(x) = (x - 2)(x - 1)(x + 3)(x + 4)$

This is incorrect. What mistake was made?

80. Determine the end behavior of the polynomial function $f(x) = x(x - 2)^3$.

Solution:

This polynomial has similar end behavior to the graph of $y = x^3$.

End behavior falls to the left and rises to the right.

This is incorrect. What mistake was made?

• CONCEPTUAL

In Exercises 81–84, determine whether each statement is true or false.

81. The graph of a polynomial function might not have any y-intercepts.

82. The graph of a polynomial function might not have any x-intercepts.

83. The domain of all polynomial functions is $(-\infty, \infty)$.

84. The range of all polynomial functions is $(-\infty, \infty)$.

85. What is the maximum number of zeros that a polynomial of degree n can have?

86. What is the maximum number of turning points a graph of an nth-degree polynomial can have?

• CHALLENGE

87. Find a seventh-degree polynomial that has the following graph characteristics: The graph touches the x-axis at $x = -1$, and the graph crosses the x-axis at $x = 3$. Plot this polynomial function.

88. Find a fifth-degree polynomial that has the following graph characteristics: The graph touches the x-axis at $x = 0$ and crosses the x-axis at $x = 4$. Plot the polynomial function.

89. Determine the zeros of the polynomial $f(x) = x^3 + (b - a)x^2 - abx$ for the positive real numbers a and b.

90. Graph the function $f(x) = x^2(x - a)^2(x - b)^2$ for the positive real numbers a, b, where $b > a$.

• PREVIEW TO CALCULUS

In calculus we study the extreme values of functions; in order to find these values we need to solve different types of equations.

In Exercises 91–94, use the Intermediate Value Theorem to find all the zeros of the polynomial functions in the given interval. Round all your answers to three decimal places.

91. $x^3 + 3x - 5 = 0, [0, 2]$

92. $x^5 - x + 0.5 = 0, [0, 1]$

93. $x^4 - 3x^3 + 6x^2 - 7 = 0, [-2, 2]$

94. $x^3 + x^2 - 2x - 2 = 0, [1, 2]$

2.3 DIVIDING POLYNOMIALS

SKILLS OBJECTIVES

- Divide polynomials with long division.
- Divide polynomials with synthetic division.

CONCEPTUAL OBJECTIVES

- Extend long division of real numbers to polynomials.
- Understand that synthetic division can only be used when dividing a polynomial by a linear factor.

2.3.1 Long Division of Polynomials

2.3.1 SKILL

Divide polynomials with long division.

2.3.1 CONCEPTUAL

Extend long division of real numbers to polynomials.

Let's start with an example whose answer we already know. We know that a quadratic expression can be factored into the product of two linear factors: $x^2 + 4x - 5 = (x + 5)(x - 1)$. Therefore, if we divide both sides of the equation by $(x - 1)$, we get

$$\frac{x^2 + 4x - 5}{x - 1} = x + 5$$

We can state this by saying $x^2 + 4x - 5$ divided by $x - 1$ is equal to $x + 5$. Confirm this statement by long division:

$$x - 1\overline{)x^2 + 4x - 5}$$

Note that although this is standard division notation, the **dividend**, $x^2 + 4x - 5$, and the **divisor**, $x - 1$, are both polynomials that consist of multiple terms. The *leading* terms of each algebraic expression will guide us.

WORDS	MATH
Q: x times what quantity gives x^2? A: x	$\begin{array}{r} \boxed{x} \\ \boxed{x} - 1\overline{)\boxed{x^2} + 4x - 5} \end{array}$ $\begin{array}{r} x \\ x - 1\overline{)x^2 + 4x - 5} \end{array}$
Multiply $x(x - 1) = x^2 - x$.	$x^2 - \quad x$
Subtract $(x^2 - x)$ from $x^2 + 4x - 5$. *Note:* $-(x^2 - x) = -x^2 + x$. Bring down the -5.	$\begin{array}{r} x \\ x - 1\overline{)x^2 + 4x - 5} \\ \underline{-x^2 + \quad x} \\ 5x - 5 \end{array}$
Q: x times what quantity is $5x$? A: 5 Multiply $5(x - 1) = 5x - 5$.	$\begin{array}{r} x + \boxed{5} \\ \boxed{x} - 1\overline{)x^2 + 4x - 5} \\ \underline{-x^2 + \quad x} \\ \boxed{5x} - 5 \end{array}$
Subtract $(5x - 5)$. *Note:* $-(5x - 5) = -5x + 5$.	$\begin{array}{r} x + 5 \\ x - 1\overline{)x^2 + 4x - 5} \\ \underline{-x^2 + \quad x} \\ 5x - 5 \\ \underline{-5x + 5} \\ 0 \end{array}$

The **quotient** is $x + 5$, and, as expected, the **remainder** is 0. By long division we have shown that

$$\boxed{\frac{x^2 + 4x - 5}{x - 1} = x + 5}$$

Check: Multiplying the equation by $x - 1$ yields $x^2 + 4x - 5 = (x + 5)(x - 1)$, which we knew to be true.

EXAMPLE 1 Dividing Polynomials Using Long Division; Zero Remainder

Divide $2x^3 - 9x^2 + 7x + 6$ by $2x + 1$.

Solution:

$$\begin{array}{r} x^2 - 5x + 6 \\ 2x + 1 \overline{)2x^3 - 9x^2 + 7x + 6} \end{array}$$

Multiply: $x^2(2x + 1)$.	$-(2x^3 + x^2)$
Subtract: Bring down the $7x$.	$-10x^2 + 7x$
Multiply: $-5x(2x + 1)$.	$-(-10x^2 - 5x)$
Subtract: Bring down the 6.	$12x + 6$
Multiply: $6(2x + 1)$.	$-(12x + 6)$
Subtract.	0
Quotient:	$\boxed{x^2 - 5x + 6}$

Check: $(2x + 1)(x^2 - 5x + 6) = 2x^3 - 9x^2 + 7x + 6$.

Note: The divisor cannot be equal to zero, $2x + 1 \neq 0$, so we say $x \neq -\frac{1}{2}$.

YOUR TURN Divide $4x^3 + 13x^2 - 2x - 15$ by $4x + 5$.

ANSWER

$x^2 + 2x - 3$, remainder 0.

Why are we interested in dividing polynomials? Because it helps us find zeros of polynomials. In Example 1, using long division, we found that

$$2x^3 - 9x^2 + 7x + 6 = (2x + 1)(x^2 - 5x + 6)$$

Factoring the quadratic expression enables us to write the cubic polynomial as a product of three linear factors:

$$2x^3 - 9x^2 + 7x + 6 = (2x + 1)(x^2 - 5x + 6) = (2x + 1)(x - 3)(x - 2)$$

Set the value of the polynomial equal to zero, $(2x + 1)(x - 3)(x - 2) = 0$, and solve for x. The zeros of the polynomial are $-\frac{1}{2}$, 2, and 3. In Example 1 and in the Your Turn, the remainder was 0. Sometimes there is a nonzero remainder (Example 2).

EXAMPLE 2 **Dividing Polynomials Using Long Division; Nonzero Remainder**

Divide $6x^2 - x - 2$ by $x + 1$.

Solution:

	$6x - 7$
Multiply $6x(x + 1)$.	$x + 1\overline{)6x^2 - x - 2}$
	$-(6x^2 + 6x)$
Subtract and bring down -2.	$-7x - 2$
Multiply $-7(x + 1)$.	$-(-7x - 7)$
Subtract and identify the remainder.	$+5$

Dividend Quotient Remainder

$$\frac{6x^2 - x - 2}{x + 1} = 6x - 7 + \frac{5}{x + 1} \qquad \boxed{x \neq -1}$$

Divisor Divisor

Check: Multiply equation by $x + 1$.

$$6x^2 - x - 2 = (6x - 7)(x + 1) + \frac{5}{(x + 1)} \cdot (x + 1)$$
$$= 6x^2 - x - 7 + 5$$
$$= 6x^2 - x - 2 \checkmark$$

YOUR TURN Divide $2x^3 + x^2 - 4x - 3$ by $x - 1$.

ANSWER

$2x^2 + 3x - 1$ R:-4 or

$2x^2 + 3x - 1 - \frac{4}{x - 1}$

In general, when a polynomial is divided by another polynomial, we express the result in the following form:

$$\frac{P(x)}{d(x)} = Q(x) + \frac{r(x)}{d(x)}$$

where $P(x)$ is the **dividend**, $d(x) \neq 0$ is the **divisor**, $Q(x)$ is the **quotient**, and $r(x)$ is the **remainder**. Multiplying this equation by the divisor $d(x)$ leads us to the division algorithm.

[CONCEPT CHECK]

For long division to be used to divide two polynomials, the degree of the numerator must be (greater/less) than or equal to the degree of the denominator.

ANSWER greater

THE DIVISION ALGORITHM

If $P(x)$ and $d(x)$ are polynomials with $d(x) \neq 0$, and if the degree of $P(x)$ is greater than or equal to the degree of $d(x)$, then unique polynomials $Q(x)$ and $r(x)$ exist such that

$$P(x) = d(x) \cdot Q(x) + r(x)$$

If the remainder $r(x) = 0$, then we say that $d(x)$ divides $P(x)$ and that $d(x)$ and $Q(x)$ are factors of $P(x)$.

EXAMPLE 3 Long Division of Polynomials with "Missing" Terms

Divide $3x^4 + 2x^3 + x^2 + 4$ by $x^2 + 1$.

Solution:

$$\begin{array}{r}
3x^2 + 2x \quad - 2 \\
x^2 + 0x + 1 \overline{)3x^4 + 2x^3 + x^2 + 0x + 4} \\
\underline{-(3x^4 + 0x^3 + 3x^2)} \\
2x^3 - 2x^2 + 0x \\
\underline{-(2x^3 + 0x^2 + 2x)} \\
-2x^2 - 2x + 4 \\
\underline{-(-2x^2 + 0x - 2)} \\
-2x + 6
\end{array}$$

Insert $0x$ as a placeholder in both the divisor and the dividend.

Multiply $3x^2(x^2 + 0x + 1)$.

Subtract and bring down $0x$.

Multiply $2x(x^2 + 0x + 1)$.

Subtract and bring down 4.

Multiply $-2(x^2 - 2x + 1)$.

Subtract and get remainder $-2x + 6$.

$$\boxed{\frac{3x^4 + 2x^3 + x^2 + 4}{x^2 + 1} = 3x^2 + 2x - 2 + \frac{-2x + 6}{x^2 + 1}}$$

YOUR TURN Divide $2x^5 + 3x^2 + 12$ by $x^3 - 3x - 4$.

ANSWER

$2x^2 + 6 + \dfrac{11x^2 + 18x + 36}{x^3 - 3x - 4}$

EXAMPLE 4 Long Division of Polynomials Resulting in Quotients with Rational Coefficients

Divide $8x^4 - 5x^3 + 7x - 2$ by $2x^2 + 1$.

Solution:

$$\begin{array}{r}
4x^2 - \frac{5}{2}x - 2 \\
2x^2 + 0x + 1 \overline{)8x^4 - 5x^3 + 0x^2 + 7x - 2} \\
\underline{-(8x^4 + 0x^3 + 4x^2)} \\
-5x^3 - 4x^2 + 7x \\
\underline{-(-5x^3 + 0x^2 - \frac{5}{2}x)} \\
-4x^2 + \frac{19}{2}x - 2 \\
\underline{-(-4x^2 + 0x - 2)} \\
\frac{19}{2}x
\end{array}$$

Insert $0x^2$ as a placeholder in the dividend and $0x$ as a placeholder in the divisor.

Multiply $4x^2(2x^2 + 0x + 1)$.

Subtract and bring down $7x$.

Multiply $-\frac{5}{2}x(2x^2 + 0x + 1)$.

Subtract and bring down -2.

Multiply $-2(2x^2 + 0x + 1)$.

Subtract and bring down the remainder $\frac{19}{2}x$.

$$\frac{8x^4 - 5x^3 + 7x - 2}{2x^2 + 1} = 4x^2 - \frac{5}{2}x - 2 + \frac{\frac{19}{2}x}{2x^2 + 1}$$

YOUR TURN Divide $10x^4 - 3x^3 + 5x - 4$ by $2x^2 - 1$.

ANSWER

$5x^2 - \frac{3}{2}x + \frac{5}{2} + \dfrac{\frac{7}{2}x - \frac{3}{2}}{2x^2 - 1}$

2.3.2 Synthetic Division of Polynomials

2.3.2 SKILL

Divide polynomials with synthetic division.

2.3.2 CONCEPTUAL

Understand that synthetic division can only be used when dividing a polynomial by a linear factor.

In the special case when the *divisor is a linear factor* of the form $x - a$ or $x + a$, there is another, more efficient way to divide polynomials. This method is called **synthetic division**. It is called synthetic because it is a contrived shorthand way of dividing a polynomial by a linear factor. A detailed step-by-step procedure is given below for synthetic division. Let's divide $x^4 - x^3 - 2x + 2$ by $x + 1$ using synthetic division.

STUDY TIP

If $(x - a)$ is a divisor, then a is the number used in synthetic division.

Step 1: Write the division in synthetic form.

- List the coefficients of the dividend. **Remember to use 0 for a placeholder.**
- The divisor is $x + 1$, so $x = -1$ is used.

Coefficients of Dividend

$$\begin{array}{r|rrrrr} -1 & 1 & -1 & 0 & -2 & 2 \\ & & & & & \\ \hline \end{array}$$

Step 2: *Bring down* the first term (1) in the dividend.

$$\begin{array}{r|rrrrr} -1 & 1 & -1 & 0 & -2 & 2 \\ & \downarrow & \multicolumn{4}{l}{\text{Bring down the 1}} \\ \hline & 1 & & & & \end{array}$$

Step 3: *Multiply* the -1 by this leading coefficient (1), and place the product up and to the right in the second column.

$$\begin{array}{r|rrrrr} -1 & 1 & -1 & 0 & -2 & 2 \\ & & -1 & & & \\ \hline & 1 & & & & \end{array}$$

Step 4: *Add* the values in the second column.

$$\begin{array}{r|rrrrr} -1 & 1 & -1 & 0 & -2 & 2 \\ & & \downarrow -1 & \text{ADD} & & \\ \hline & 1 & -2 & & & \end{array}$$

Step 5: Repeat Steps 3 and 4 until all columns are filled.

$$\begin{array}{r|rrrrr} -1 & 1 & -1 & 0 & -2 & 2 \\ & & -1 & 2\downarrow & -2\downarrow & 4\downarrow \\ \hline & 1 & -2 & 2 & -4 & 6 \end{array}$$

STUDY TIP

Synthetic division can be used only when the divisor is of the form $x - a$. Realize that a may be negative, as in the divisor $x + 2$.

Step 6: Identify the **quotient** by assigning powers of x in descending order, beginning with $x^{n-1} = x^{4-1} = x^3$. The last term is the **remainder**.

$$\begin{array}{r|rrrrr} -1 & 1 & -1 & 0 & -2 & 2 \\ & & -1 & 2 & -2 & 4 \\ \hline & 1 & -2 & 2 & -4 & 6 \end{array}$$

Quotient Coefficients: $x^3 - 2x^2 + 2x - 4$ Remainder: 6

We know that the degree of the first term of the quotient is 3, because a fourth-degree polynomial was divided by a first-degree polynomial. Let's compare dividing $x^4 - x^3 - 2x + 2$ by $x + 1$ using both long division and synthetic division.

Long Division

$$\begin{array}{r} x^3 - 2x^2 + 2x - 4 \\ x + 1\overline{)x^4 - x^3 + 0x^2 - 2x + 2} \\ \underline{x^4 + x^3} \qquad\qquad\qquad \\ -2x^3 + 0x^2 \qquad\quad \\ \underline{-(-2x^3 - 2x^2)} \qquad\quad \\ 2x^2 - 2x \quad \\ \underline{-(2x^2 + 2x)} \quad \\ -4x + 2 \\ \underline{-(-4x - 4)} \\ +6 \end{array}$$

Synthetic Division

$$\begin{array}{r|rrrrr} -1 & 1 & -1 & 0 & -2 & 2 \\ & & -1 & 2 & -2 & 4 \\ \hline & 1 & -2 & 2 & -4 & 6 \end{array}$$

$x^3 - 2x^2 + 2x - 4$

Both long division and synthetic division yield the same answer.

$$\frac{x^4 - x^3 - 2x + 2}{x + 1} = x^3 - 2x^2 + 2x - 4 + \frac{6}{x + 1}$$

EXAMPLE 5 Synthetic Division

Use synthetic division to divide $3x^5 - 2x^3 + x^2 - 7$ by $x + 2$.

Solution:

STEP 1 Write the division in synthetic form.

- List the coefficients of the dividend. Remember to use 0 for a placeholder.
- The divisor of the original problem is $x + 2$. If we set $x + 2 = 0$, we find that $x = -2$, so -2 is the divisor for synthetic division.

$$\begin{array}{r|rrrrrr} -2 & 3 & 0 & -2 & 1 & 0 & -7 \\ \hline \end{array}$$

STEP 2 Perform the synthetic division steps.

$$\begin{array}{r|rrrrrr} -2 & 3 & 0 & -2 & 1 & 0 & -7 \\ & & -6 & 12 & -20 & 38 & -76 \\ \hline & 3 & -6 & 10 & -19 & 38 & -83 \end{array}$$

STEP 3 Identify the quotient and remainder.

$$\begin{array}{r|rrrrrr} -2 & 3 & 0 & -2 & 1 & 0 & -7 \\ & & -6 & 12 & -20 & 38 & -76 \\ \hline & 3 & -6 & 10 & -19 & 38 & \boxed{-83} \end{array}$$

$$3x^4 - 6x^3 + 10x^2 - 19x + 38$$

$$\frac{3x^5 - 2x^3 + x^2 - 7}{x + 2} = 3x^4 - 6x^3 + 10x^2 - 19x + 38 - \frac{83}{x + 2}$$

YOUR TURN Use synthetic division to divide $2x^3 - x + 3$ by $x - 1$.

ANSWER $2x^2 + 2x + 1 + \frac{4}{x - 1}$

[CONCEPT CHECK]

Can synthetic division be used to divide $f(x) = x^4 - 1$ by $g(x) = x^3 + 1$?

ANSWER No; the degree of the divisor has to be 1.

[SECTION 2.3] SUMMARY

Division of Polynomials

- Long division can always be used.
- Synthetic division can be used only when the divisor is of the form $x - a$ or $x + a$.

Expressing Results

- $\frac{\text{Dividend}}{\text{Divisor}} = \text{quotient} + \frac{\text{remainder}}{\text{divisor}}$
- Dividend = (quotient)(divisor) + remainder

When Remainder Is Zero

- Dividend = (quotient)(divisor)
- Quotient and divisor are factors of the dividend.

[SECTION 2.3] EXERCISES

• SKILLS

In Exercises 1–22, divide the polynomials using long division. Use exact values and express the answer in the form $Q(x) = ?, r(x) = ?$.

1. $(3x^2 - 9x - 5) \div (x - 2)$
2. $(x^2 + 4x - 3) \div (x - 1)$
3. $(3x^2 - 13x - 10) \div (x + 5)$
4. $(3x^2 - 13x - 10) \div (x - 5)$
5. $(x^2 - 4) \div (x + 4)$
6. $(x^2 - 9) \div (x - 2)$
7. $(9x^2 - 25) \div (3x - 5)$
8. $(5x^2 - 3) \div (x + 1)$
9. $(4x^2 - 9) \div (2x + 3)$
10. $(8x^3 + 27) \div (2x + 3)$
11. $(11x + 20x^2 + 12x^3 + 2) \div (3x + 2)$
12. $(12x^3 + 2 + 11x + 20x^2) \div (2x + 1)$
13. $(4x^3 - 2x + 7) \div (2x + 1)$
14. $(6x^4 - 2x^2 + 5) \div (-3x + 2)$
15. $(4x^3 - 12x^2 - x + 3) \div (x - \frac{1}{2})$
16. $(12x^3 + 1 + 7x + 16x^2) \div (x + \frac{1}{3})$
17. $(-2x^5 + 3x^4 - 2x^2) \div (x^3 - 3x^2 + 1)$
18. $(-9x^6 + 7x^4 - 2x^3 + 5) \div (3x^4 - 2x + 1)$
19. $\dfrac{x^4 - 1}{x^2 - 1}$
20. $\dfrac{x^4 - 9}{x^2 + 3}$
21. $\dfrac{40 - 22x + 7x^3 + 6x^4}{6x^2 + x - 2}$
22. $\dfrac{-13x^2 + 4x^4 + 9}{4x^2 - 9}$

In Exercises 23–42, divide the polynomial by the linear factor with synthetic division. Indicate the quotient $Q(x)$ and the remainder $r(x)$.

23. $(3x^2 + 7x + 2) \div (x + 2)$
24. $(2x^2 + 7x - 15) \div (x + 5)$
25. $(7x^2 - 3x + 5) \div (x + 1)$
26. $(4x^2 + x + 1) \div (x - 2)$
27. $(3x^2 + 4x - x^4 - 2x^3 - 4) \div (x + 2)$
28. $(3x^2 - 4 + x^3) \div (x - 1)$
29. $(x^4 + 1) \div (x + 1)$
30. $(x^4 + 9) \div (x + 3)$
31. $(x^4 - 16) \div (x + 2)$
32. $(x^4 - 81) \div (x - 3)$
33. $(2x^3 - 5x^2 - x + 1) \div (x + \frac{1}{2})$
34. $(3x^3 - 8x^2 + 1) \div (x + \frac{1}{3})$
35. $(2x^4 - 3x^3 + 7x^2 - 4) \div (x - \frac{2}{3})$
36. $(3x^4 + x^3 + 2x - 3) \div (x - \frac{3}{4})$
37. $(2x^4 + 9x^3 - 9x^2 - 81x - 81) \div (x + 1.5)$
38. $(5x^3 - x^2 + 6x + 8) \div (x + 0.8)$
39. $\dfrac{x^7 - 8x^4 + 3x^2 + 1}{x - 1}$
40. $\dfrac{x^6 + 4x^5 - 2x^3 + 7}{x + 1}$
41. $(x^6 - 49x^4 - 25x^2 + 1225) \div (x - \sqrt{5})$
42. $(x^6 - 4x^4 - 9x^2 + 36) \div (x - \sqrt{3})$

In Exercises 43–56, divide the polynomials by either long division or synthetic division.

43. $(6x^2 - 23x + 7) \div (3x - 1)$
44. $(6x^2 + x - 2) \div (2x - 1)$
45. $(x^3 - x^2 - 9x + 9) \div (x - 1)$
46. $(x^3 + 2x^2 - 6x - 12) \div (x + 2)$
47. $(x^3 + 6x^2 - 2x - 5) \div (x^2 - 1)$
48. $(3x^5 - x^3 + 2x^2 - 1) \div (x^3 + x^2 - x + 1)$
49. $(x^6 - 2x^5 + x^4 - 6x^3 + 7x^2 - 4x + 7) \div (x^2 + 1)$
50. $(x^6 - 1) \div (x^2 + x + 1)$
51. $(x^5 + 4x^3 + 2x^2 - 1) \div (x - 2)$
52. $(x^4 - x^2 + 3x - 10) \div (x + 5)$
53. $(x^4 - 25) \div (x^2 - 1)$
54. $(x^3 - 8) \div (x^2 - 2)$
55. $(x^7 - 1) \div (x - 1)$
56. $(x^6 - 27) \div (x - 3)$

• APPLICATIONS

57. **Geometry.** The area of a rectangle is $6x^4 + 4x^3 - x^2 - 2x - 1$ square feet. If the length of the rectangle is $2x^2 - 1$ feet, what is the width of the rectangle?

58. **Geometry.** If the rectangle in Exercise 61 is the base of a rectangular box with volume $18x^5 + 18x^4 + x^3 - 7x^2 - 5x - 1$ cubic feet, what is the height of the box?

59. **Travel.** If a car travels a distance of $x^3 + 60x^2 + x + 60$ miles at an average speed of $x + 60$ miles per hour, how long does the trip take?

60. **Sports.** If a quarterback throws a ball $-x^2 - 5x + 50$ yards in $5 - x$ seconds, how fast is the football traveling?

• CATCH THE MISTAKE

In Exercises 61–64, explain the mistake that is made.

61. Divide $x^3 - 4x^2 + x + 6$ by $x^2 + x + 1$.

Solution:

$$\begin{array}{r} x - 3 \\ x^2 + x + 1 \overline{) x^3 - 4x^2 + x + 6} \\ \underline{x^3 + x^2 + x} \\ -3x^2 + 2x + 6 \\ \underline{-3x^2 - 3x - 3} \\ -x + 3 \end{array}$$

This is incorrect. What mistake was made?

62. Divide $x^4 - 3x^2 + 5x + 2$ by $x - 2$.

Solution:

$$\begin{array}{r|rrrr} -2 & 1 & -3 & 5 & 2 \\ & & -2 & 10 & -30 \\ \hline & 1 & -5 & 15 & \boxed{-28} \end{array}$$

$$x^2 - 5x + 15$$

This is incorrect. What mistake was made?

63. Divide $x^3 + 4x - 12$ by $x - 3$.

Solution:

$$\begin{array}{r|rrr} 3 & 1 & 4 & -12 \\ & & 3 & 21 \\ \hline & 1 & 7 & \boxed{9} \end{array}$$

$$x + 7$$

This is incorrect. What mistake was made?

64. Divide $x^3 + 3x^2 - 2x + 1$ by $x^2 + 1$.

Solution:

$$\begin{array}{r|rrrr} -1 & 1 & 3 & -2 & 1 \\ & & -1 & -2 & 4 \\ \hline & 1 & 2 & -4 & \boxed{5} \end{array}$$

$$x^2 - 2x - 4$$

This is incorrect. What mistake was made?

• CONCEPTUAL

In Exercises 65–70, determine whether each statement is true or false.

65. A fifth-degree polynomial divided by a third-degree polynomial will yield a quadratic quotient.

66. A third-degree polynomial divided by a linear polynomial will yield a linear quotient.

67. Synthetic division can be used whenever the degree of the dividend is exactly one more than the degree of the divisor.

68. When the remainder is zero, the divisor is a factor of the dividend.

69. When both the dividend and the divisor have the same degree, the quotient equals one.

70. Long division must be used whenever the degree of the divisor is greater than one.

• CHALLENGE

71. Is $x + b$ a factor of $x^3 + (2b - a)x^2 + (b^2 - 2ab)x - ab^2$?

72. Is $x + b$ a factor of $x^4 + (b^2 - a^2)x^2 - a^2b^2$?

73. Divide $x^{3n} + x^{2n} - x^n - 1$ by $x^n - 1$.

74. Divide $x^{3n} + 5x^{2n} + 8x^n + 4$ by $x^n + 1$.

• PREVIEW TO CALCULUS

For some of the operations in calculus it is convenient to write rational fractions $\frac{P(x)}{d(x)}$ in the form $Q(x) + \frac{r(x)}{d(x)}$, where

$$\frac{P(x)}{d(x)} = Q(x) + \frac{r(x)}{d(x)}.$$

In Exercises 75–78, write each rational function $\frac{P(x)}{d(x)}$ in the form $Q(x) + \frac{r(x)}{d(x)}$.

75. $\dfrac{2x^2 - x}{x + 2}$

76. $\dfrac{5x^3 + 2x^2 - 3x}{x - 3}$

77. $\dfrac{2x^4 + 3x^2 + 6}{x^2 + x + 1}$

78. $\dfrac{3x^5 - 2x^3 + x^2 + x - 6}{x^2 + x + 5}$

2.4 THE REAL ZEROS OF A POLYNOMIAL FUNCTION

SKILLS OBJECTIVES

- Apply the remainder theorem to evaluate a polynomial function, and use the factor theorem to factor polynomials.
- Use the rational zero (root) theorem to list possible rational zeros, and use Descartes' rule of signs to determine the possible combination of positive and negative real zeros.
- Express polynomials as a product of linear or irreducible quadratic factors.
- Employ the intermediate value theorem to approximate an irrational zero.
- Graph any polynomial function.

CONCEPTUAL OBJECTIVES

- Understand that a polynomial of degree n has at most n real zeros.
- Understand that a real zero can be either rational or irrational and that irrational zeros will not be listed as possible zeros through the rational zero test.
- Recognize that irreducible factors are quadratic expressions that are not factorable over the real numbers.
- Realize that rational zeros can be found exactly, whereas irrational zeros must be approximated.
- Understand that the rational root test and the intermediate value theorem make it possible for us to graph any polynomial function and that Descartes' rule of signs and upper and lower bound rules help us determine the graphs more efficiently.

2.4.1 The Remainder Theorem and the Factor Theorem

2.4.1 SKILL

Apply the remainder theorem to evaluate a polynomial function, and use the factor theorem to factor polynomials.

2.4.1 CONCEPTUAL

Understand that a polynomial of degree n has at most n real zeros.

The zeros of a polynomial function assist us in finding the x-intercepts of the graph of a polynomial function. How do we find the zeros of a polynomial function if we cannot factor them easily? For polynomial functions of degree 2, we have the quadratic formula, which allows us to find the two zeros. For polynomial functions whose degree is greater than 2, much more work is required.* In this section, we focus our attention on finding the *real* zeros of a polynomial function. Later, in Section 2.5, we expand our discussion to *complex* zeros of polynomial functions.

In this section, we start by listing possible rational zeros. As you will see, there are sometimes many possibilities. We can then narrow the search using Descartes' rule of signs, which tells us possible combinations of positive and negative real zeros. We can narrow the search even further with the upper and lower bound rules. Once we have tested possible values and determined a zero, we will employ synthetic division to divide the polynomial by the linear factor associated with the zero. We will continue the process until we have factored the polynomial function into a product of either linear factors or irreducible quadratic factors. Last, we will discuss how to find irrational real zeros using the intermediate value theorem.

If we divide the polynomial function $f(x) = x^3 - 2x^2 + x - 3$ by $x - 2$ using synthetic division, we find the remainder is -1.

$$\begin{array}{r|rrrr} 2 & 1 & -2 & 1 & -3 \\ & & 2 & 0 & 2 \\ \hline & 1 & 0 & 1 & -1 \end{array}$$

Notice that if we evaluate the function at $x = 2$, the result is -1. $\quad f(2) = -1$

*There are complicated formulas for finding the zeros of polynomial functions of degree 3 and 4, but there are no such formulas for polynomial functions of degree 5 and higher (according to the Abel–Ruffini theorem).

WORDS	MATH
Recall the Division Algorithm.	$P(x) = d(x) \cdot Q(x) + r(x)$
Let $d(x) = x - a$ for any real number a.	$P(x) = (x - a) \cdot Q(x) + r(x)$
The degree of the remainder is always less than the degree of the divisor, so the remainder must be a constant (call it r, $r(x) = r$).	$P(x) = (x - a) \cdot Q(x) + r$
Let $x = a$.	$P(a) = \underbrace{(a - a)}_{0} \cdot Q(x) + r$
Simplify.	$\boxed{P(a) = r}$

This leads us to the *remainder theorem.*

REMAINDER THEOREM

If a polynomial $P(x)$ is divided by $x - a$, then the remainder is $r = P(a)$.

The remainder theorem tells you that polynomial division can be used to evaluate a polynomial function at a particular point.

EXAMPLE 1 **Two Methods for Evaluating Polynomials**

Let $P(x) = 4x^5 - 3x^4 + 2x^3 - 7x^2 + 9x - 5$ and evaluate $P(2)$ by

a. evaluating $P(2)$ directly.

b. the remainder theorem and synthetic division.

Solution:

a.
$$\begin{aligned} P(2) &= 4(2)^5 - 3(2)^4 + 2(2)^3 - 7(2)^2 + 9(2) - 5 \\ &= 4(32) - 3(16) + 2(8) - 7(4) + 9(2) - 5 \\ &= 128 - 48 + 16 - 28 + 18 - 5 \\ &= \boxed{81} \end{aligned}$$

b.
$$\begin{array}{r|rrrrrr} 2 & 4 & -3 & 2 & -7 & 9 & -5 \\ & & 8 & 10 & 24 & 34 & 86 \\ \hline & 4 & 5 & 12 & 17 & 43 & \boxed{81} \end{array}$$

YOUR TURN Let $P(x) = -x^3 + 2x^2 - 5x + 2$ and evaluate $P(-2)$ using the remainder theorem and synthetic division.

ANSWER

$P(-2) = 28$

Recall that when a polynomial is divided by $x - a$, if the remainder is zero, we say that $x - a$ is a factor of the polynomial. Through the remainder theorem, we now know that the remainder is related to evaluation of the polynomial at the point $x = a$. We are then led to the *factor theorem.*

FACTOR THEOREM

If $P(a) = 0$, then $x - a$ is a factor of $P(x)$. Conversely, if $x - a$ is a factor of $P(x)$, then $P(a) = 0$.

EXAMPLE 2 Using the Factor Theorem to Factor a Polynomial

Determine whether $x + 2$ is a factor of $P(x) = x^3 - 2x^2 - 5x + 6$. If so, factor $P(x)$ completely.

Solution:

STEP 1 Divide $P(x) = x^3 - 2x^2 - 5x + 6$ by $x + 2$ using synthetic division.

$$\begin{array}{r|rrrr} -2 & 1 & -2 & -5 & 6 \\ & & -2 & 8 & -6 \\ \hline & 1 & -4 & 3 & \boxed{0} \end{array}$$

$x^2 - 4x + 3$

Since the remainder is zero, $P(-2) = 0$, $\boxed{x + 2 \text{ is a factor}}$ of $P(x) = x^3 - 2x^2 - 5x + 6$.

STEP 2 Write $P(x)$ as a product. $P(x) = (x + 2)(x^2 - 4x + 3)$

STEP 3 Factor the quadratic polynomial. $\boxed{P(x) = (x + 2)(x - 3)(x - 1)}$

YOUR TURN Determine whether $x - 1$ is a factor of $P(x) = x^3 - 4x^2 - 7x + 10$. If so, factor $P(x)$ completely.

ANSWER

$(x - 1)$ is a factor; $P(x) = (x - 5)(x - 1)(x + 2)$

EXAMPLE 3 Using the Factor Theorem to Factor a Polynomial

Determine whether $x - 3$ and $x + 2$ are factors of $P(x) = x^4 - 13x^2 + 36$. If so, factor $P(x)$ completely.

Solution:

STEP 1 With synthetic division, divide $P(x) = x^4 - 13x^2 + 36$ by $x - 3$.

$$\begin{array}{r|rrrrr} 3 & 1 & 0 & -13 & 0 & 36 \\ & & 3 & 9 & -12 & -36 \\ \hline & 1 & 3 & -4 & -12 & \boxed{0} \end{array}$$

$x^3 + 3x^2 - 4x - 12$

Because the remainder is 0, $\boxed{x - 3 \text{ is a factor}}$, and we can write the polynomial as

$$P(x) = (x - 3)(x^3 + 3x^2 - 4x - 12)$$

STEP 2 With synthetic division, divide the remaining cubic polynomial $(x^3 + 3x^2 - 4x - 12)$ by $x + 2$.

$$\begin{array}{r|rrrr} -2 & 1 & 3 & -4 & -12 \\ & & -2 & -2 & 12 \\ \hline & 1 & 1 & -6 & \boxed{0} \end{array}$$

$x^2 + x - 6$

Because the remainder is 0, $\boxed{x + 2 \text{ is a factor}}$, and we can now write the polynomial as

$$P(x) = (x - 3)(x + 2)(x^2 + x - 6)$$

STEP 3 Factor the quadratic polynomial: $x^2 + x - 6 = (x + 3)(x - 2)$.

STEP 4 Write $P(x)$ as a product of linear factors:

$$\boxed{P(x) = (x - 3)(x - 2)(x + 2)(x + 3)}$$

[CONCEPT CHECK]

If a fourth-degree polynomial can be factored into four distinct linear factors $P(x) = (x - a)(x - b)(x - c)(x - d)$, what are the x-intercepts of the graph of this polynomial?

ANSWER $(a, 0)$, $(b, 0)$, $(c, 0)$, $(d, 0)$

YOUR TURN Determine whether $x - 3$ and $x + 2$ are factors of $P(x) = x^4 - x^3 - 7x^2 + x + 6$. If so, factor $P(x)$ completely.

ANSWER

$(x - 3)$ and $(x + 2)$ are factors; $P(x) = (x - 3)(x + 2)(x - 1)(x + 1)$

The Search for Real Zeros

In all of the examples thus far, the polynomial function and one or more real zeros (or linear factors) were given. Now, we will not be given any real zeros to start with. Instead, we will develop methods to search for them.

Each real zero corresponds to a linear factor, and each linear factor is of degree 1. Therefore, the largest number of real zeros that a polynomial function can have is equal to the degree of the polynomial.

THE NUMBER OF REAL ZEROS

A polynomial function cannot have more real zeros than its degree.

STUDY TIP

The largest number of zeros a polynomial can have is equal to the degree of the polynomial.

The following functions illustrate that a polynomial function of degree n can have at most n real zeros:

POLYNOMIAL FUNCTION	DEGREE	REAL ZEROS	COMMENTS
$f(x) = x^2 - 9$	2	$x = \pm 3$	**Two** real zeros
$f(x) = x^2 + 4$	2	None	**No** real zeros
$f(x) = x^3 - 1$	3	$x = 1$	**One** real zero
$f(x) = x^3 - x^2 - 6x$	3	$x = -2, 0, 3$	**Three** real zeros

Now that we know the *maximum* number of real zeros a polynomial function can have, let us discuss how to find these zeros.

2.4.2 The Rational Zero Theorem and Descartes' Rule of Signs

When the coefficients of a polynomial are integers, the *rational zero theorem* (*rational root test*) gives us a list of possible rational zeros. We can then test these possible values to determine whether they really do correspond to actual zeros. *Descartes' rule of signs* tells us the possible combinations of *positive* real zeros and *negative* real zeros. Using Descartes' rule of signs will help us narrow down the large list of possible zeros generated through the rational zero theorem to a shorter list of possible zeros. First, let's look at the rational zero theorem; then we'll turn to Descartes' rule of signs.

2.4.2 SKILL

Use the rational zero (root) theorem to list possible rational zeros, and use Descartes' rule of signs to determine the possible combination of positive and negative real zeros.

2.4.2 CONCEPTUAL

Understand that a real zero can be either rational or irrational and that irrational zeros will not be listed as possible zeros through the rational zero test.

THE RATIONAL ZERO THEOREM (RATIONAL ROOT TEST)

If the polynomial function $P(x) = a_n x^n + a_{n-1}x^{n-1} + \cdots + a_2 x^2 + a_1 x + a_0$ has *integer* coefficients, then every rational zero of $P(x)$ has the form

$$\text{Rational zero} = \frac{\text{integer factors of } a_0}{\text{integer factors of } a_n} = \frac{\text{integer factors of constant term}}{\text{integer factors of leading coefficient}}$$

$$= \pm\frac{\text{positive integer factors of constant term}}{\text{positive integer factors of leading coefficient}}$$

To use this theorem, simply list all combinations of integer factors of both the constant term a_0 and the leading coefficient term a_n and take all appropriate combinations of ratios. This procedure is illustrated in Example 4. Notice that when the leading coefficient is 1, the possible rational zeros will simply be the possible integer factors of the constant term.

EXAMPLE 4 Using the Rational Zero Theorem

Determine possible rational zeros for the polynomial $P(x) = x^4 - x^3 - 5x^2 - x - 6$ by the rational zero theorem. Test each one to find all rational zeros.

Solution:

STEP 1 List factors of the constant and leading coefficient terms.

$a_0 = -6$ $\quad \pm 1, \pm 2, \pm 3, \pm 6$

$a_n = 1$ $\quad \pm 1$

STEP 2 List possible rational zeros $\frac{a_0}{a_n}$.

$$\frac{\pm 1}{\pm 1}, \frac{\pm 2}{\pm 1}, \frac{\pm 3}{\pm 1}, \frac{\pm 6}{\pm 1} = \pm 1, \pm 2, \pm 3, \pm 6$$

There are three ways to test whether any of these are zeros: Substitute these values into the polynomial to see which ones yield zero, or use either polynomial division or synthetic division to divide the polynomial by these possible zeros, and look for a zero remainder.

STEP 3 Test possible zeros by looking for zero remainders.

1 is not a zero: $P(1) = (1)^4 - (1)^3 - 5(1)^2 - (1) - 6 = -12$

-1 is not a zero: $P(-1) = (-1)^4 - (-1)^3 - 5(-1)^2 - (-1) - 6 = -8$

We could continue testing with direct substitution, but let us now use synthetic division as an alternative.

2 is not a zero:

2	1	−1	−5	−1	−6
		2	2	−6	−14
	1	1	−3	−7	[−20]

-2 is a zero:

−2	1	−1	−5	−1	−6
		−2	6	−2	−6
	1	−3	1	−3	[0]

Since -2 is a zero, then $x + 2$ is a factor of $P(x)$, and the remaining quotient is $x^3 - 3x^2 + x - 3$. Therefore, if there are any other real roots remaining, we can now use the simpler $x^3 - 3x^2 + x - 3$ for the dividend. Also note that the rational zero theorem can be applied to the new dividend, and doing so may shorten the list of possible rational zeros. In this case, the possible rational zeros of $F(x) = x^3 - 3x^2 + x - 3$ are ± 1 and ± 3.

3 is a zero:

3	1	−3	1	−3
		3	0	3
	1	0	1	[0]

We now know that [−2] and [3] are confirmed zeros. If we continue testing, we will find that the other possible zeros fail. This is a fourth-degree polynomial, and we have found two rational real zeros. We see in the graph on the right that these two real zeros correspond to the x-intercepts.

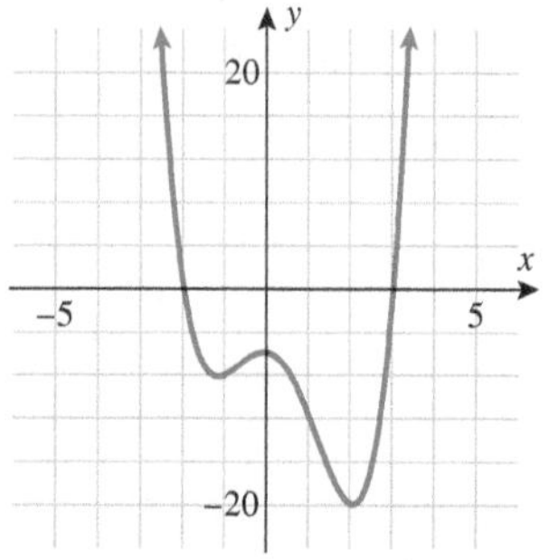

STUDY TIP

The remainder can be found by evaluating the function or synthetic division. For simple values like $x = \pm 1$, it is easier to evaluate the polynomial function. For other values, it is often easier to use synthetic division.

STUDY TIP

Notice in Step 3 that the polynomial $F(x) = x^3 - 3x^2 + x - 3$ can be factored by grouping: $F(x) = (x - 3)(x^2 + 1)$.

YOUR TURN List the possible rational zeros of the polynomial $P(x) = x^4 + 2x^3 - 2x^2 + 2x - 3$, and determine rational real zeros.

ANSWER

Possible rational zeros: ± 1 and ± 3.

Rational real zeros: 1 and -3.

Notice in Example 4 that the polynomial function $P(x) = x^4 - x^3 - 5x^2 - x - 6$ had two rational real zeros, -2 and 3. This implies that $x + 2$ and $x - 3$ are factors of $P(x)$. Also note that in the last step, when we divided by the zero 3, the quotient was $x^2 + 1$. Thus, we can write the polynomial in factored form as

$$P(x) = \underbrace{(x+2)}_{\substack{\text{linear}\\\text{factor}}}\underbrace{(x-3)}_{\substack{\text{linear}\\\text{factor}}}\underbrace{(x^2+1)}_{\substack{\text{irreducible}\\\text{quadratic}\\\text{factor}}}$$

Notice that the first two factors are of degree 1, so we call them **linear factors**. The third expression, $x^2 + 1$, is of degree 2 and cannot be factored in terms of real numbers. We will discuss complex zeros in the next section. For now, we say that a quadratic expression, $ax^2 + bx + c$, is called **irreducible** if it cannot be factored over the real numbers.

EXAMPLE 5 Factoring a Polynomial Function

Write the following polynomial function as a product of linear and/or irreducible quadratic factors:

$$P(x) = x^4 - 4x^3 + 4x^2 - 36x - 45$$

Solution:

Use the rational zero theorem to list possible rational roots. $x = \pm 1, \pm 3, \pm 5, \pm 9, \pm 15, \pm 45$

Test possible zeros by evaluating the function or by utilizing synthetic division.

$x = 1$ is not a zero. $P(1) = -80$

$x = -1$ is a zero. $P(-1) = 0$

Divide $P(x)$ by $x + 1$.

$$\begin{array}{r|rrrrr} -1 & 1 & -4 & 4 & -36 & -45 \\ & & -1 & 5 & -9 & 45 \\ \hline & 1 & -5 & 9 & -45 & \boxed{0} \end{array}$$

$x = 5$ is a zero.

$$\begin{array}{r|rrrr} 5 & 1 & -5 & 9 & -45 \\ & & 5 & 0 & 45 \\ \hline & \underbrace{1 \quad 0 \quad 9}_{x^2+9} & & & \boxed{0} \end{array}$$

The factor $x^2 + 9$ is irreducible.

Write the polynomial as a product of linear and/or irreducible quadratic factors. $\boxed{P(x) = (x - 5)(x + 1)(x^2 + 9)}$

The graph of this polynomial function will have x-intercepts at $x = -1$ and $x = 5$.

YOUR TURN Write the following polynomial function as a product of linear and/or irreducible quadratic factors:

$$P(x) = x^4 - 2x^3 - x^2 - 4x - 6$$

ANSWER

$P(x) = (x + 1)(x - 3)(x^2 + 2)$

The rational zero theorem lists possible zeros. It would be helpful if we could narrow that list. Descartes' rule of signs determines the possible combinations of positive real zeros and negative real zeros through variations of sign. A *variation in sign* is a sign difference seen between consecutive coefficients.

Sign Change − to +

$$P(x) = 2x^6 - 5x^5 - 3x^4 + 2x^3 - x^2 - x - 1$$

Sign Change + to − Sign Change + to −

This polynomial exhibits three sign changes, or variations in sign.

DESCARTES' RULE OF SIGNS

If the polynomial function $P(x) = a_n x^n + a_{n-1}x^{n-1} + \cdots + a_2x^2 + a_1x + a_0$ has real coefficients and $a_0 \neq 0$, then:

- The number of **positive** real zeros of the polynomial is either equal to the number of variations in sign in $P(x)$ or less than that number by an even integer.
- The number of **negative** real zeros of the polynomial is either equal to the number of variations in sign of $P(-x)$ or less than that number by an even integer.

Descartes' rule of signs narrows our search for real zeros, because we don't have to test all of the possible rational zeros. For example, if we know there is one positive real zero, then if we find a positive rational zero, we no longer need to continue to test possible positive zeros.

EXAMPLE 6 Using Descartes' Rule of Signs to Find Possible Combinations of Real Zeros

Determine the possible combinations of real zeros for

$$P(x) = x^4 - 2x^3 + x^2 + 2x - 2$$

Solution:

$P(x)$ has three variations in sign.

Sign Change

$$P(x) = x^4 - 2x^3 + x^2 + 2x - 2$$

Sign Change Sign Change

Apply Descartes' rule of signs. $P(x)$ has *either* three or one **positive** real zero.

Find $P(-x)$. $P(-x) = (-x)^4 - 2(-x)^3 + (-x)^2 + 2(-x) - 2$

$= x^4 + 2x^3 + x^2 - 2x - 2$

$P(-x)$ has one variation in sign. $P(-x) = x^4 + 2x^3 + x^2 - 2x - 2$

Sign Change

Apply Descartes' rule of signs. $P(x)$ has one **negative** real zero.

Since $P(x) = x^4 - 2x^3 + x^2 + 2x - 2$ is a *fourth*-degree polynomial, there are at most four real zeros. One zero is a negative real number.

> $P(x)$ has one negative real zero and could have three positive real zeros or one positive real zero.

YOUR TURN Determine the possible combinations of zeros for

$$P(x) = x^4 + 2x^3 + x^2 + 8x - 12$$

[CONCEPT CHECK]

TRUE OR FALSE The rational zeros are a subset of the real zeros.

ANSWER True

ANSWER

Positive real zeros: 1

Negative real zeros: 3 or 1

2.4.3 Factoring Polynomials

Now let's draw on the tests discussed in this section thus far to help us in finding all real zeros of a polynomial function. Doing so will enable us to factor polynomials.

2.4.3 SKILL

Express polynomials as a product of linear or irreducible quadratic factors.

2.4.3 CONCEPTUAL

Recognize that irreducible factors are quadratic expressions that are not factorable over the real numbers.

EXAMPLE 7 Factoring a Polynomial

Write the polynomial $P(x) = x^5 + 2x^4 - x - 2$ as a product of linear and/or irreducible quadratic factors.

Solution:

STEP 1 Determine variations in sign.

$P(x)$ has one sign change. $P(x) = x^5 + 2x^4 - x - 2$

$P(-x)$ has two sign changes. $P(-x) = -x^5 + 2x^4 + x - 2$

STEP 2 Apply Descartes' rule of signs.

Positive Real Zeros: 1

Negative Real Zeros: 2 or 0

STEP 3 Use the rational zero theorem to determine the possible rational zeros. $\pm 1, \pm 2$

We know (Step 2) that there is one positive real zero, so test the possible positive rational zeros first.

STEP 4 Test possible rational zeros.

$$\begin{array}{r|rrrrrr} 1 & 1 & 2 & 0 & 0 & -1 & -2 \\ & & 1 & 3 & 3 & 3 & 2 \\ \hline & 1 & 3 & 3 & 3 & 2 & \boxed{0} \end{array}$$

1 is a zero:

Now that we have found *the* positive zero, we can test the other two possible negative zeros—because either they both are zeros or neither is a zero (or one is a double root).

$$\begin{array}{r|rrrrr} -1 & 1 & 3 & 3 & 3 & 2 \\ & & -1 & -2 & -1 & -2 \\ \hline & 1 & 2 & 1 & 2 & \boxed{0} \end{array}$$

-1 is a zero:

Let's now try the other possible negative zero, -2.

-2 is a zero:

$$\begin{array}{r|rrrr} -2 & 1 & 2 & 1 & 2 \\ & & -2 & 0 & -2 \\ \hline & 1 & 0 & 1 & \boxed{0} \end{array}$$

$$\underbrace{1 \quad 0 \quad 1}_{x^2 + 1}$$

STEP 5 Three zeros are: -1, -2, and 1.

STEP 6 Write the fifth-degree polynomial as a product of three linear factors and an irreducible quadratic factor.

$$\boxed{P(x) = (x - 1)(x + 1)(x + 2)(x^2 + 1)}$$

[CONCEPT CHECK]

TRUE OR FALSE An irreducible quadratic factor corresponds to two additional x-intercepts.

ANSWER False

YOUR TURN Write the polynomial $P(x) = x^5 - 2x^4 + x^3 - 2x^2 - 2x + 4$ as a product of linear and/or irreducible quadratic factors.

ANSWER

$(x - 2)(x + 1)(x - 1)(x^2 + 2)$

EXAMPLE 8 Factoring a Polynomial

Write the polynomial $P(x) = 2x^4 + 3x^3 - 12x^2 - 7x + 6$ as a product of linear and/or irreducible quadratic factors.

Solution:

STEP 1 Determine variations in sign.

$P(x)$ has two sign changes. $\quad P(x) = 2x^4 + 3x^3 - 12x^2 - 7x + 6$

$P(-x)$ has two sign changes. $\quad P(-x) = 2x^4 - 3x^3 - 12x^2 + 7x + 6$

STEP 2 Apply Descartes' rule of signs. Positive Real Zeros: 2 or 0

Negative Real Zeros: 2 or 0

STEP 3 Use the rational zero theorem to determine the possible rational zeros. $\pm 1, \pm 2, \pm 3, \pm 6, \pm\frac{1}{2}, \pm\frac{3}{2}$

STEP 4 Test possible rational zeros.

$$\begin{array}{r|rrrrr} -1 & 2 & 3 & -12 & -7 & 6 \\ & & -2 & -1 & 13 & -6 \\ \hline & 2 & 1 & -13 & 6 & \boxed{0} \end{array}$$

-1 is a zero:

Since there are either two or no negative real zeros and we have found one of the negative zeros, try the other negative real zeros.

$$\begin{array}{r|rrrr} -3 & 2 & 1 & -13 & 6 \\ & & -6 & 15 & -6 \\ \hline & 2 & -5 & +2 & \boxed{0} \end{array}$$

$\underbrace{2 \quad -5 \quad +2}_{2x^2 - 5x + 2}$

-3 is a zero:

Factor $2x^2 - 5x + 2$ to find the remaining two zeros. $\quad (2x - 1)(x - 2)$

STEP 5 Write the fourth-degree polynomial as a product of four linear factors.

$$\boxed{P(x) = (2x - 1)(x - 2)(x + 3)(x + 1)}$$

YOUR TURN Write the polynomial $P(x) = 3x^4 - 5x^3 - 17x^2 + 13x + 6$ as a product of linear and/or irreducible quadratic factors.

ANSWER

$(3x + 1)(x - 1)(x + 2)(x - 3)$

STUDY TIP

If f(x) has a common monomial factor, cancel it before applying the bound rules.

The rational zero theorem gives us possible rational zeros of a polynomial, and Descartes' rule of signs gives us possible combinations of positive and negative real zeros. Additional aids that help eliminate possible zeros are the *upper* and *lower bound rules.* These rules can give you an upper and a lower bound on the real zeros of a polynomial function. If $f(x)$ has a common monomial factor, you should factor it out first, and then follow the upper and lower bound rules.

UPPER AND LOWER BOUND RULES

Let $f(x)$ be a polynomial with real coefficients and a positive leading coefficient. Suppose $f(x)$ is divided by $x - c$ using synthetic division.

1. If $c > 0$ and each number in the bottom row is either positive or zero, then c is an **upper bound** for the real zeros of f.
2. If $c < 0$ and the numbers in the bottom row are alternately positive and negative (zero entries count as either positive or negative), then c is a **lower bound** for the real zeros of f.

EXAMPLE 9 **Using Upper and Lower Bounds to Eliminate Possible Zeros**

Find the real zeros of $f(x) = 4x^3 - x^2 + 36x - 9$.

Solution:

STEP 1 The rational zero theorem gives possible rational zeros.

$$\frac{\text{Factors of 9}}{\text{Factors of 4}} = \frac{\pm 1, \pm 3, \pm 9}{\pm 1, \pm 2, \pm 4}$$

$$= \pm 1, \pm\frac{1}{2}, \pm\frac{1}{4}, \pm\frac{3}{4}, \pm\frac{3}{2}, \pm\frac{9}{4}, \pm 3, \pm\frac{9}{2}, \pm 9$$

STEP 2 Apply Descartes' rule of signs:

$f(x)$ has three sign variations. three or one positive real zeros

$f(-x)$ has no sign variations. no negative real zeros

STEP 3 Try $x = 1$.

$$\begin{array}{r|rrrr} 1 & 4 & -1 & 36 & -9 \\ & & 4 & 3 & 39 \\ \hline & 4 & 3 & 39 & 30 \end{array}$$

$x = 1$ is not a zero, but because the last row contains all positive entries, $x = 1$ is an *upper* bound. Since we know there are no negative real zeros, we restrict our search to between 0 and 1.

STEP 4 Try $x = \frac{1}{4}$.

$$\begin{array}{r|rrrr} \frac{1}{4} & 4 & -1 & 36 & -9 \\ & & 1 & 0 & 9 \\ \hline & 4 & 0 & 36 & 0 \end{array}$$

$\frac{1}{4}$ is a zero and the quotient $4x^2 + 36$ has all positive coefficients; therefore, $\frac{1}{4}$ is an upper bound, so $\boxed{\frac{1}{4} \text{ is the only real zero}}$.

Note: If $f(x)$ has a common monomial factor, you should factor it out before applying the bound rules.

STUDY TIP

In Example 9, Steps 3 and 4, long division can be used as well as evaluating the function at $x = 1$ and $x = \frac{1}{4}$ to determine whether these are zeros.

2.4.4 The Intermediate Value Theorem

2.4.4 SKILL

Employ the intermediate value theorem to approximate an irrational zero.

2.4.4 CONCEPTUAL

Realize that rational zeros can be found exactly, whereas irrational zeros must be approximated.

In our search for zeros, we sometimes encounter irrational zeros, as in, for example, the polynomial

$$f(x) = x^5 - x^4 - 1$$

Descartes' rule of signs tells us there is exactly one real positive zero. However, the rational zero test yields only $x = \pm 1$, neither of which is a zero. So if we know there is a real positive zero and we know it's not rational, it must be irrational. Notice that $f(1) = -1$ and $f(2) = 15$. Since polynomial functions are continuous and the function goes from negative to positive between $x = 1$ and $x = 2$, we expect a zero somewhere in that interval. Generating a graph with a graphing utility, we find that there is a zero around $x = 1.3$.

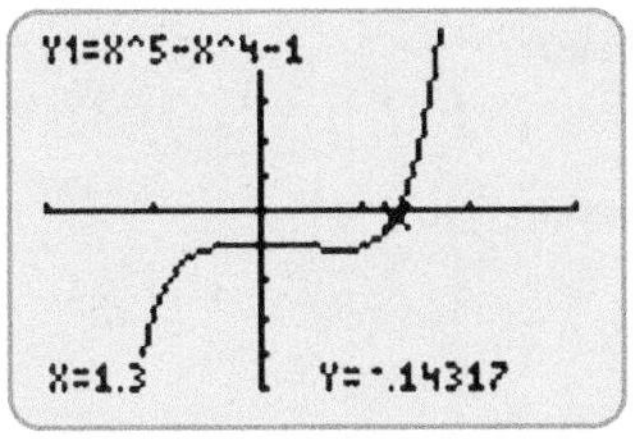

The *intermediate value theorem* is based on the fact that polynomial functions are continuous.

INTERMEDIATE VALUE THEOREM

Let a and b be real numbers such that $a < b$ and $f(x)$ is a polynomial function. If $f(a)$ and $f(b)$ have opposite signs, then there is at least one real zero between a and b.

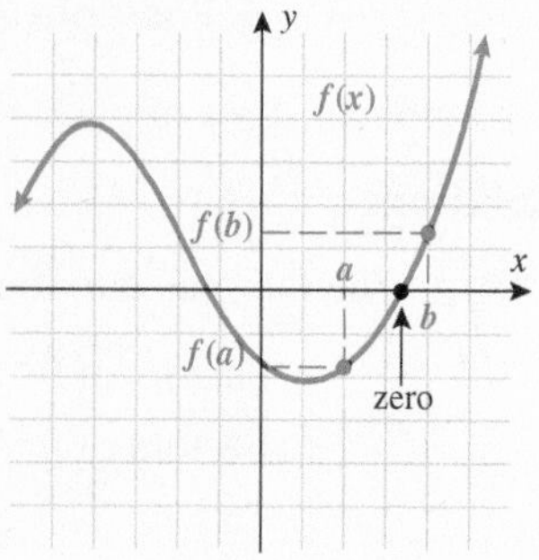

If the intermediate value theorem tells us that there is a real zero in the interval (a, b), how do we approximate that zero? The **bisection method*** is a root-finding algorithm that approximates the solution to the equation $f(x) = 0$. In the bisection method the interval is divided in half, and then the subinterval that contains the zero is selected. This is repeated until the bisection method converges to an approximate root of f.

EXAMPLE 10 **Approximating Real Zeros of a Polynomial Function**

Approximate the real zero of $f(x) = x^5 - x^4 - 1$.

Note: Descartes' rule of signs tells us that there are no real negative zeros and that there is exactly one real positive zero.

Solution:

Find two consecutive integer values for x that have corresponding function values opposite in sign.

x	$f(x)$
1	−1
2	15

Note that a graphing utility would have shown an x-intercept between $x = 1$ and $x = 2$.

Apply the bisection method, with $a = 1$ and $b = 2$. $\quad c = \dfrac{a+b}{2} = \dfrac{1+2}{2} = \dfrac{3}{2}$

Evaluate the function at $x = c$. $\quad f(1.5) \approx 1.53$

Compare the values of f at the endpoints and midpoint. $\quad f(1) = -1, f(1.5) \approx 1.53, f(2) = 15$

Select the subinterval corresponding to the *opposite* signs of f. $\quad (1, 1.5)$

Apply the bisection method again (repeat the algorithm). $\quad \dfrac{1+1.5}{2} = 1.25$

Evaluate the function at $x = 1.25$. $\quad f(1.25) \approx -0.38965$

Compare the values of f at the endpoints and midpoint. $\quad f(1) = -1, f(1.25) \approx -0.38965, f(1.5) \approx 1.53$

Select the subinterval corresponding to the *opposite* signs of f. $\quad (1.25, 1.5)$

[CONCEPT CHECK]

TRUE OR FALSE If we know there is one positive zero, and all of the potential rational roots have been found not to be zeros, then the real zero must be irrational.

ANSWER: True

*In calculus you will learn Newton's method, which is a more efficient approximation technique for finding zeros.

Apply the bisection method again (repeat the algorithm). $\dfrac{1.25 + 1.5}{2} = 1.375$

Evaluate the function at $x = 1.375$. $f(1.375) \approx 0.3404$

Compare the values of f at the endpoints and midpoint. $f(1.25) \approx -0.38965,\ f(1.375) \approx 0.3404,\ f(1.5) \approx 1.53$

Select the subinterval corresponding to the *opposite* signs of f. $(1.25, 1.375)$

We can continue this procedure (*applying the bisection method*) to find that the zero is somewhere between $x = 1.32$ and $x = 1.33$, since $f(1.32) \approx -0.285$ and $f(1.33) \approx 0.0326$.

We find that, to three significant digits, $\boxed{1.32}$ is an approximation to the real zero.

2.4.5 Graphing Polynomial Functions

In Section 2.2, we graphed simple polynomial functions that were easily factored. Now that we have procedures for finding real zeros of polynomial functions (rational zero theorem, Descartes' rule of signs, the upper and lower bound rules for rational zeros, and the intermediate value theorem and the bisection method for irrational zeros), let us return to the topic of graphing polynomial functions. Since a real zero of a polynomial function corresponds to an x-intercept of its graph, we now have methods for finding (or estimating) any x-intercepts of the graph of any polynomial function.

2.4.5 SKILL

Graph any polynomial function.

2.4.5 CONCEPTUAL

Understand that the rational root test and the intermediate value theorem make it possible for us to graph any polynomial function and that Descartes' rule of signs and the upper and lower bound rules help us determine the graphs more efficiently.

EXAMPLE 11 **Graphing a Polynomial Function**

Graph the function $f(x) = 2x^4 - 2x^3 + 5x^2 + 17x - 22$.

Solution:

STEP 1 **Find the y-intercept.** $f(0) = -22$

STEP 2 **Find any x-intercepts (real zeros).**

Apply Descartes' rule of signs.

Three sign changes correspond to three or one positive real zeros. $f(x) = 2x^4 - 2x^3 + 5x^2 + 17x - 22$

One sign change corresponds to one negative real zero. $f(-x) = 2x^4 + 2x^3 + 5x^2 - 17x - 22$

Apply the rational zero theorem.

Let $a_0 = -22$ and $a_n = 2$. $\dfrac{\text{Factors of } a_0}{\text{Factors of } a_n} = \pm\dfrac{1}{2}, \pm 1, \pm 2, \pm\dfrac{11}{2}, \pm 11, \pm 22$

Test the possible zeros.

$x = 1$ is a zero. $f(1) = 0$

There are no other rational zeros.

Apply the upper bound rule.

$$\begin{array}{r|rrrrr} 1 & 2 & -2 & 5 & 17 & -22 \\ & & 2 & 0 & 5 & 22 \\ \hline & 2 & 0 & 5 & 22 & \boxed{0} \end{array}$$

[CONCEPT CHECK]

TRUE OR FALSE We now have the tools to find all x-intercepts (exactly or approximated)

ANSWER: True

Since $x = 1$ is positive and all of the numbers in the bottom row are positive (or zero), $x = 1$ is an upper bound for the real zeros. We know there is exactly one negative real zero, but none of the possible zeros from the rational zero theorem is a zero. Therefore, the negative real zero is irrational.

Apply the intermediate value theorem and the bisection method.

f is positive at $x = -2$. $\quad f(-2) = 12$

f is negative at $x = -1$. $\quad f(-1) = -30$

Use the bisection method to find the negative real zero between -2 and -1. $\quad x \approx -1.85$

STEP 3 **Determine the end behavior.** $\quad y = 2x^4$

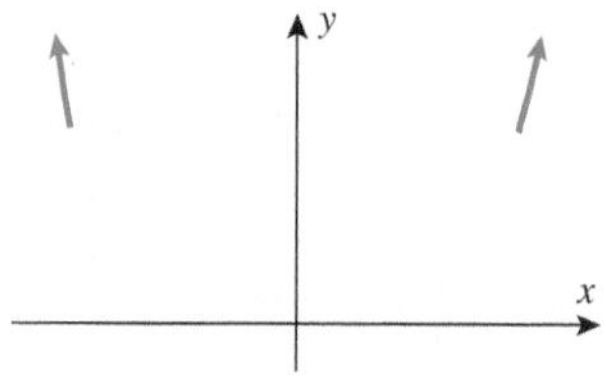

STEP 4 **Find additional points.**

x	−2	−1.85	−1	0	1	2
f(x)	12	0	−30	−22	0	48
Point	(−2, 12)	(−1.85, 0)	(−1, −30)	(0, −22)	(1, 0)	(2, 48)

STEP 5 **Sketch the graph.**

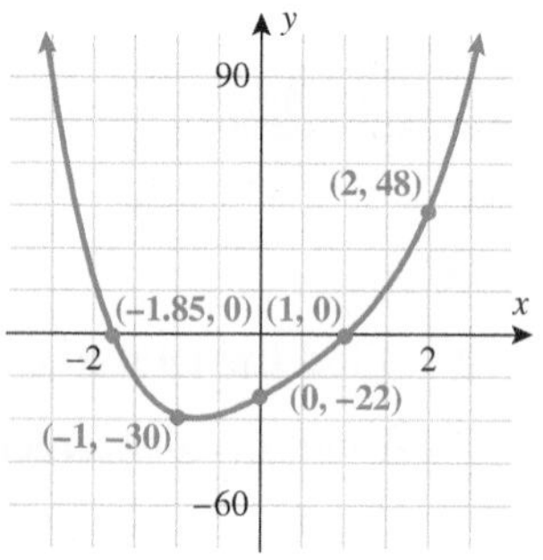

[SECTION 2.4] SUMMARY

In this section, we discussed how to find the real zeros of a polynomial function. Once real zeros are known, it is possible to write the polynomial function as a product of linear and/or irreducible quadratic factors.

The Number of Zeros

- A polynomial of degree n has *at most* n real zeros.
- *Descartes' rule of signs* determines the possible combinations of positive and negative real zeros.
- *Upper and lower bounds* help narrow the search for zeros.

How to Find Zeros

- *Rational zero theorem:* List possible rational zeros:

$$\frac{\text{Factors of constant, } a_0}{\text{Factors of leading coefficient, } a_n}$$

- *Irrational zeros:* Approximate zeros by determining when the polynomial function changes sign (intermediate value theorem).

Procedure for Factoring a Polynomial Function

- List possible rational zeros (rational zero theorem).
- List possible combinations of positive and negative real zeros (Descartes' rule of signs).
- Test possible values until a zero is found.*
- Once a real zero is found, repeat testing on the quotient until linear and/or irreducible quadratic factors remain.
- If there is a real zero but all possible rational roots have failed, then approximate the zero using the *intermediate value theorem* and the *bisection method.*

*Depending on the form of the quotient, upper and lower bounds may eliminate possible zeros.

[SECTION 2.4] EXERCISES

• SKILLS

In Exercises 1–10, given a real zero of the polynomial, determine all other real zeros, and write the polynomial in terms of a product of linear and/or irreducible quadratic factors.

	Polynomial	Zero		Polynomial	Zero
1.	$P(x) = x^3 - 13x + 12$	1	**2.**	$P(x) = x^3 + 3x^2 - 10x - 24$	3
3.	$P(x) = 2x^3 + x^2 - 13x + 6$	$\frac{1}{2}$	**4.**	$P(x) = 3x^3 - 14x^2 + 7x + 4$	$-\frac{1}{3}$

	Polynomial	Zero		Polynomial	Zero
5.	$P(x) = x^4 - 2x^3 - 11x^2 - 8x - 60$	$-3, 5$	**6.**	$P(x) = x^4 - x^3 + 7x^2 - 9x - 18$	$-1, 2$
7.	$P(x) = x^4 - 5x^2 + 10x - 6$	$1, -3$	**8.**	$P(x) = x^4 - 4x^3 + x^2 + 6x - 40$	$4, -2$
9.	$P(x) = x^4 + 6x^3 + 13x^2 + 12x + 4$	-2 (multiplicity 2)	**10.**	$P(x) = x^4 + 4x^3 - 2x^2 - 12x + 9$	1 (multiplicity 2)

In Exercises 11–18, use the rational zero theorem to list the *possible* rational zeros.

11. $P(x) = x^4 + 3x^2 - 8x + 4$

12. $P(x) = -x^4 + 2x^3 - 5x + 4$

13. $P(x) = x^5 - 14x^3 + x^2 - 15x + 12$

14. $P(x) = x^5 - x^3 - x^2 + 4x + 9$

15. $P(x) = 2x^6 - 7x^4 + x^3 - 2x + 8$

16. $P(x) = 3x^5 + 2x^4 - 5x^3 + x - 10$

17. $P(x) = 5x^5 + 3x^4 + x^3 - x - 20$

18. $P(x) = 4x^6 - 7x^4 + 4x^3 + x - 21$

In Exercises 19–22, list the possible rational zeros, and test to determine all rational zeros.

19. $P(x) = x^4 + 2x^3 - 9x^2 - 2x + 8$

20. $P(x) = x^4 + 2x^3 - 4x^2 - 2x + 3$

21. $P(x) = 2x^3 - 9x^2 + 10x - 3$

22. $P(x) = 3x^3 - 5x^2 - 26x - 8$

In Exercises 23–34, use Descartes' rule of signs to determine the possible number of positive real zeros and negative real zeros.

23. $P(x) = x^4 - 32$

24. $P(x) = x^4 + 32$

25. $P(x) = x^5 - 1$

26. $P(x) = x^5 + 1$

27. $P(x) = x^5 - 3x^3 - x + 2$

28. $P(x) = x^4 + 2x^2 - 9$

29. $P(x) = 9x^7 + 2x^5 - x^3 - x$

30. $P(x) = 16x^7 - 3x^4 + 2x - 1$

31. $P(x) = x^6 - 16x^4 + 2x^2 + 7$

32. $P(x) = -7x^6 - 5x^4 - x^2 + 2x + 1$

33. $P(x) = -3x^4 + 2x^3 - 4x^2 + x - 11$

34. $P(x) = 2x^4 - 3x^3 + 7x^2 + 3x + 2$

For each polynomial in Exercises 35–52: (a) use Descartes' rule of signs to determine the possible combinations of positive real zeros and negative real zeros; (b) use the rational zero test to determine possible rational zeros; (c) test for rational zeros; and (d) factor as a product of linear and/or irreducible quadratic factors.

35. $P(x) = x^3 + 6x^2 + 11x + 6$

36. $P(x) = x^3 - 6x^2 + 11x - 6$

37. $P(x) = x^3 - 7x^2 - x + 7$

38. $P(x) = x^3 - 5x^2 - 4x + 20$

39. $P(x) = x^4 + 6x^3 + 3x^2 - 10x$

40. $P(x) = x^4 - x^3 - 14x^2 + 24x$

41. $P(x) = x^4 - 7x^3 + 27x^2 - 47x + 26$

42. $P(x) = x^4 - 5x^3 + 5x^2 + 25x - 26$

43. $P(x) = 10x^3 - 7x^2 - 4x + 1$

44. $P(x) = 12x^3 - 13x^2 + 2x - 1$

45. $P(x) = 6x^3 + 17x^2 + x - 10$

46. $P(x) = 6x^3 + x^2 - 5x - 2$

47. $P(x) = x^4 - 2x^3 + 5x^2 - 8x + 4$

48. $P(x) = x^4 + 2x^3 + 10x^2 + 18x + 9$

49. $P(x) = x^6 + 12x^4 + 23x^2 - 36$

50. $P(x) = x^4 - x^2 - 16x^2 + 16$

51. $P(x) = 4x^4 - 20x^3 + 37x^2 - 24x + 5$

52. $P(x) = 4x^4 - 8x^3 + 7x^2 + 30x + 50$

In Exercises 53–56, use the information found in Exercises 37, 41, 45, and 51 to assist in sketching a graph of each polynomial function.

53. Exercise 37

54. Exercise 41

55. Exercise 45

56. Exercise 51

In Exercises 57–62, use the intermediate value theorem and the bisection method to approximate the real zero in the indicated interval. Approximate to two decimal places.

57. $f(x) = x^4 - 3x^3 + 4 \quad [1, 2]$

58. $f(x) = x^5 - 3x^3 + 1 \quad [0, 1]$

59. $f(x) = 7x^5 - 2x^2 + 5x - 1 \quad [0, 1]$

60. $f(x) = -2x^3 + 3x^2 + 6x - 7 \quad [-2, -1]$

61. $f(x) = x^3 - 2x^2 - 8x - 3 \quad [-1, 0]$

62. $f(x) = x^4 + 4x^2 - 7x - 13 \quad [-2, -1]$

• APPLICATIONS

63. **Geometry.** The distances (in inches) from one vertex of a rectangle to the other three vertices are x, $x + 2$, and $x + 4$. Find the dimensions of the rectangle.

64. **Geometry.** A box is constructed to contain a volume of 97.5 cubic inches. The length of the base is 3.5 inches larger than the width, and the height is 0.5 inch larger than the length. Find the dimensions of the box.

65. **Agriculture.** The weekly volume (in liters) of milk produced in a farm is given by $v(x) = x^3 + 21x^2 - 1480x$, where x is the number of cows. Find the number of cows that corresponds to a total production of 1500 liters of milk in a week.

66. **Profit.** A bakery uses the formula $f(x) = 2x^4 - 7x^3 + 3x^2 + 8x$ to determine the profit of selling x loaves of bread. How many loaves of bread must be sold to have a profit of \$4? Assume $x \geq 1$.

For Exercises 67 and 68, refer to the following:

The demand function for a product is

$$p(x) = 28 - 0.0002x$$

where p is the unit price (in dollars) of the product and x is the number of units produced and sold. The cost function for the product is

$$C(x) = 20x + 1500$$

where C is the total cost (in dollars) and x is the number of units produced. The total profit obtained by producing and selling x units is

$$P(x) = xp(x) - C(x)$$

67. **Business.** Find the total profit function when x units are produced and sold. Use Descartes' rule of signs to determine possible combinations of positive zeros for the profit function.

68. **Business.** Find the break-even point(s) for the product to the nearest unit. Discuss the significance of the break-even point(s) for the product.

69. **Health/Medicine.** During the course of treatment of an illness the concentration of a dose of a drug (in mcg/mL) in the bloodstream fluctuates according to the model

$$C(t) = 15.4 - 0.05t^2$$

where $t = 0$ is when the drug was administered. Assuming a single dose of the drug is administered, in how many hours (to the nearest hour) after being administered will the drug be eliminated from the bloodstream?

70. **Health/Medicine.** During the course of treatment of an illness, the concentration of a dose of a drug (in mcg/mL) in the bloodstream fluctuates according to the model

$$C(t) = 60 - 0.75t^2$$

where $t = 0$ is when the drug was administered. Assuming a single dose of the drug is administered, in how many hours (to the nearest hour) after being administered will the drug be eliminated from the bloodstream?

• CATCH THE MISTAKE

In Exercises 71 and 72, explain the mistake that is made.

71. Use Descartes' rule of signs to determine the possible combinations of zeros of

$$P(x) = 2x^5 + 7x^4 + 9x^3 + 9x^2 + 7x + 2$$

Solution:

No sign changes, so no positive real zeros.

$$P(x) = 2x^5 + 7x^4 + 9x^3 + 9x^2 + 7x + 2$$

Five sign changes, so five negative real zeros.

$$P(-x) = -2x^5 + 7x^4 - 9x^3 + 9x^2 - 7x + 2$$

This is incorrect. What mistake was made?

72. Determine whether $x - 2$ is a factor of

$$P(x) = x^3 - 2x^2 - 5x + 6$$

Solution:

$$\begin{array}{r|rrrr} -2 & 1 & -2 & -5 & 6 \\ & & -2 & 8 & -6 \\ \hline & 1 & -4 & 3 & \boxed{0} \end{array}$$

Yes, $x - 2$ is a factor of $P(x)$.

This is incorrect. What mistake was made?

• CONCEPTUAL

In Exercises 73–78, determine whether each statement is true or false.

73. All real zeros of a polynomial correspond to x-intercepts.

74. A polynomial of degree n, $n > 0$, must have at least one zero.

75. A polynomial of degree n, $n > 0$, can be written as a product of n linear factors over real numbers.

76. The number of sign changes in a polynomial is equal to the number of positive real zeros of that polynomial.

77. A polynomial of degree n, $n > 0$, must have exactly n x-intercepts.

78. A polynomial with an odd number of zeros must have odd degree.

• CHALLENGE

79. Given that $x = a$ is a zero of $P(x) = x^3 - (a + b + c)x^2 + (ab + ac + bc)x - abc$, find the other two zeros, given that a, b, and c are real numbers and $a > b > c$.

80. Given that $x = a$ is a zero of $p(x) = x^3 + (-a + b - c)x^2 - (ab + bc - ac)x + abc$, find the other two real zeros, given that a, b, and c are real positive numbers.

81. Given that b is a zero of

$$P(x) = x^4 - (a + b)x^3 + (ab - c^2)x^2 + (a + b)c^2x - abc^2,$$

find the other three real zeros, given that a, b, and c are real positive numbers.

82. Given that a is a zero of $P(x) =$

$$x^4 + 2(b - a)x^3 + (a^2 - 4ab + b^2)x^2 + 2ab(a - b)x + a^2b^2,$$

find the other three real zeros, given that a and b are real positive numbers.

• PREVIEW TO CALCULUS

In calculus we use the zeros of the derivative f' of a function f to determine whether the function f is increasing or decreasing around the zeros.

In Exercises 83–86, find the zeros of each polynomial function and determine the intervals over which $f(x) > 0$.

83. $f(x) = x^3 - 4x^2 - 7x + 10$

84. $f(x) = 6x^3 - 13x^2 - 11x + 8$

85. $f(x) = -2x^4 + 5x^3 + 7x^2 - 10x - 6$

86. $f(x) = -3x^4 + 14x^3 - 11x^2 + 14x - 8$

2.5 COMPLEX ZEROS: THE FUNDAMENTAL THEOREM OF ALGEBRA

SKILLS OBJECTIVES

- Factor a polynomial function given certain zeros.
- Factor a polynomial function of degree n into n linear factors.

CONCEPTUAL OBJECTIVES

- Understand why complex zeros occur in conjugate pairs.
- Understand why an odd-degree polynomial must have at least one real zero.

2.5.1 Complex Zeros

2.5.1 SKILL

Factor a polynomial function given certain zeros.

2.5.1 CONCEPTUAL

Understand why complex zeros occur in conjugate pairs.

In Section 2.4, we found the *real* zeros of a polynomial function. In this section, we find the *complex* zeros of a polynomial function. The domain of polynomial functions has thus far been the set of all real numbers. Now, we consider a more general case, where the domain of a polynomial function is the set of *complex numbers*. Note that the set of real numbers is a subset of the complex numbers. (Choose the imaginary part to be zero.)

It is important to note, however, that when we are discussing *graphs* of polynomial functions, we restrict the domain to the set of real numbers.

A *zero* of a polynomial $P(x)$ is the *solution* or *root* of the equation $P(x) = 0$. The *zeros of a polynomial can be complex numbers.* However, since the axes of the xy-plane represent real numbers, we interpret zeros as x-intercepts only when the zeros are real numbers.

STUDY TIP

The zeros of a polynomial can be complex numbers. Only when the zeros are real numbers do we interpret zeros as x-intercepts.

We can illustrate the relationship between real and complex zeros of polynomial functions and their graphs with two similar examples. Let's take the two quadratic functions $f(x) = x^2 - 4$ and $g(x) = x^2 + 4$. The graphs of these two functions are parabolas that open upward with $f(x)$ shifted down four units and $g(x)$ shifted up four units as shown on the left. Setting each function equal to zero and solving for x, we find that the zeros for $f(x)$ are -2 and 2 and the zeros for $g(x)$ are $-2i$ and $2i$. Notice that the x-intercepts for $f(x)$ are $(-2, 0)$ and $(2, 0)$ and that $g(x)$ has **no x-intercepts.**

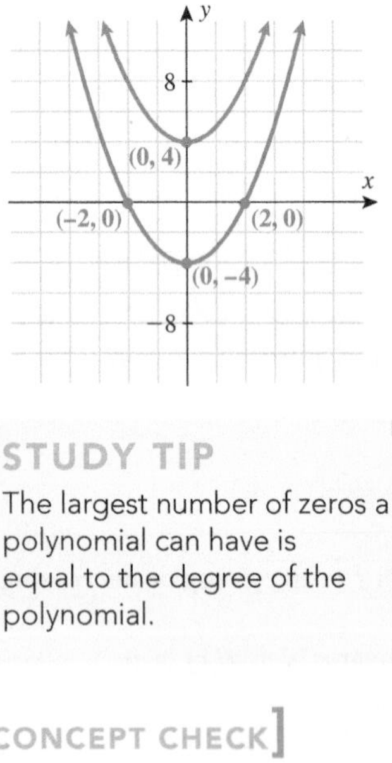

The Fundamental Theorem of Algebra

In Section 2.4, we were able to write a polynomial function as a product of linear and/or irreducible quadratic factors. Now, we consider factors over complex numbers. Therefore, what were irreducible quadratic factors over real numbers will now be a product of two linear factors over the complex numbers.

What are the minimum and maximum number of zeros a polynomial can have? Every polynomial has *at least one zero* (provided the degree is greater than zero). The largest number of zeros a polynomial can have is equal to the degree of the polynomial.

STUDY TIP

The largest number of zeros a polynomial can have is equal to the degree of the polynomial.

THE FUNDAMENTAL THEOREM OF ALGEBRA

Every polynomial $P(x)$ of degree $n > 0$ has *at least one zero* in the complex number system.

[CONCEPT CHECK]

TRUE OR FALSE Complex zeros correspond to x-intercepts.

ANSWER: False

The fundamental theorem of algebra and the factor theorem are used to prove the following n zeros theorem.

n ZEROS THEOREM

Every polynomial $P(x)$ of degree $n > 0$ can be expressed as the product of n linear factors in the complex number system. Hence, $P(x)$ has exactly n zeros, not necessarily distinct.

STUDY TIP

A polynomial of degree n has exactly n zeros (provided we count multiplicities).

These two theorems are illustrated with five polynomials below:

a. The **first**-degree polynomial $f(x) = x + 3$ has exactly **one** zero: $x = -3$.

b. The **second**-degree polynomial $f(x) = x^2 + 10x + 25 = (x + 5)(x + 5)$ has exactly **two** zeros: $x = -5$ and $x = -5$. It is customary to write this as a single zero of multiplicity 2 or refer to it as a repeated root.

c. The **third**-degree polynomial $f(x) = x^3 + 16x = x(x^2 + 16) = x(x + 4i)(x - 4i)$ has exactly **three** zeros: $x = 0$, $x = -4i$, and $x = 4i$.

d. The **fourth**-degree polynomial $f(x) = x^4 - 1 = (x^2 - 1)(x^2 + 1)$ $= (x - 1)(x + 1)(x - i)(x + i)$ has exactly **four** zeros: $x = 1$, $x = -1$, $x = i$, and $x = -i$.

e. The **fifth**-degree polynomial $f(x) = x^5 = x \cdot x \cdot x \cdot x \cdot x$ has exactly **five** zeros: $x = 0$, which has multiplicity 5.

The fundamental theorem of algebra and the n zeros theorem tell you only that the zeros *exist*—not how to find them. We must rely on the techniques discussed in Section 2.4 and the additional strategies discussed in this section to determine the zeros.

Complex Conjugate Pairs

Often, at a grocery store or a drugstore, we see signs for special offers—"buy one, get one free." A similar phenomenon occurs for complex zeros of a polynomial function with real coefficients! If we restrict the coefficients of a polynomial to real numbers, complex zeros always come in conjugate pairs. In other words, if a zero of a polynomial function is a complex number, then another zero will always be its complex conjugate. Look at the third-degree polynomial in the above illustration, part (c), where two of the zeros were $-4i$ and $4i$, and in part (d), where two of the zeros were i and $-i$. In general, if we restrict the coefficients of a polynomial to real numbers, complex zeros always come in conjugate pairs.

STUDY TIP

If we restrict the coefficients of a polynomial to real numbers, complex zeros always come in conjugate pairs.

COMPLEX CONJUGATE ZEROS THEOREM

If a polynomial $P(x)$ has real coefficients, and if $a + bi$ is a zero of $P(x)$, then its complex conjugate $a - bi$ is also a zero of $P(x)$.

We use the complex zeros theorem to assist us in factoring a higher degree polynomial.

EXAMPLE 1 **Factoring a Polynomial with Complex Zeros**

Factor the polynomial $P(x) = x^4 - x^3 - 5x^2 - x - 6$ given that i is a zero of $P(x)$.

Since $P(x)$ is a *fourth*-degree polynomial, we expect *four* zeros. The goal in this problem is to write $P(x)$ as a product of four linear factors: $P(x) = (x - a)(x - b)(x - c)(x - d)$, where a, b, c, and d are complex numbers and represent the zeros of the polynomial.

Solution:

Write known zeros and linear factors.

Since i is a zero, we know that $-i$ is a zero. $\quad x = i$ and $x = -i$

We now know two linear factors of $P(x)$. $\quad (x - i)$ and $(x + i)$

Write $P(x)$ as a product of four factors. $\quad P(x) = (x - i)(x + i)(x - c)(x - d)$

Multiply the two known factors.

$$\begin{aligned}(x + i)(x - i) &= x^2 - i^2 \\ &= x^2 - (-1) \\ &= x^2 + 1\end{aligned}$$

Rewrite the polynomial. $\quad P(x) = (x^2 + 1)(x - c)(x - d)$

Divide both sides of the equation by $x^2 + 1$. $\quad \dfrac{P(x)}{x^2 + 1} = (x - c)(x - d)$

Divide $P(x)$ by $x^2 + 1$ using long division.

$$\begin{array}{r} x^2 - x - 6 \\ x^2 + 0x + 1 \overline{\smash{)}\, x^4 - x^3 - 5x^2 - x - 6} \\ \underline{-(x^4 + 0x^3 + x^2)} \\ -x^3 - 6x^2 - x \\ \underline{-(-x^3 + 0x^2 + x)} \\ -6x^2 + 0x - 6 \\ \underline{-(-6x^2 + 0x - 6)} \\ 0 \end{array}$$

Since the remainder is 0, $x^2 - x - 6$ is a factor. $\quad P(x) = (x^2 + 1)(x^2 - x - 6)$

Factor the quotient $x^2 - x - 6$. $\quad x^2 - x - 6 = (x - 3)(x + 2)$

Write $P(x)$ as a product of four linear factors. $\quad \boxed{P(x) = (x - i)(x + i)(x - 3)(x + 2)}$

Check: $P(x)$ is a *fourth*-degree polynomial and we found *four* zeros, two of which are complex conjugates.

YOUR TURN Factor the polynomial $P(x) = x^4 - 3x^3 + 6x^2 - 12x + 8$ given that $x - 2i$ is a factor.

ANSWER

$P(x) = (x - 2i)(x + 2i)(x - 1)(x - 2)$

Note: The zeros of $P(x)$ are 1, 2, $2i$, and $-2i$.

EXAMPLE 2 Factoring a Polynomial with Complex Zeros

Factor the polynomial $P(x) = x^4 - 2x^3 + x^2 + 2x - 2$ given that $1 + i$ is a zero of $P(x)$.

Since $P(x)$ is a *fourth*-degree polynomial, we expect *four* zeros. The goal in this problem is to write $P(x)$ as a product of four linear factors: $P(x) = (x - a)(x - b)(x - c)(x - d)$, where a, b, c, and d are complex numbers and represent the zeros of the polynomial.

Solution:

STEP 1 Write known zeros and linear factors.

Since $1 + i$ is a zero, we know that $1 - i$ is a zero. $\quad x = 1 + i$ and $x = 1 - i$

We now know two linear factors of $P(x)$. $\quad [x - (1 + i)]$ and $[x - (1 - i)]$

STEP 2 Write $P(x)$ as a product of four factors. $\quad P(x) = [x - (1 + i)][x - (1 - i)](x - c)(x - d)$

STEP 3 Multiply the first two terms. $\quad [x - (1 + i)][x - (1 - i)]$

First regroup the expressions in each bracket. $\quad [(x - 1) - i][(x - 1) + i]$

Use the special product $(a - b)(a + b) = a^2 - b^2$, where a is $(x - 1)$ and b is i.

$$(x - 1)^2 - i^2$$
$$(x^2 - 2x + 1) - (-1)$$
$$x^2 - 2x + 2$$

STEP 4 Rewrite the polynomial. $\quad P(x) = (x^2 - 2x + 2)(x - c)(x - d)$

STEP 5 Divide both sides of the equation by $x^2 - 2x + 2$, and substitute in the original polynomial $P(x) = x^4 - 2x^3 + x^2 + 2x - 2$.

$$\frac{x^4 - 2x^3 + x^2 + 2x - 2}{x^2 - 2x + 2} = (x - c)(x - d)$$

STEP 6 Divide the left side of the equation using long division.

$$\frac{x^4 - 2x^3 + x^2 + 2x - 2}{x^2 - 2x + 2} = x^2 - 1$$

STEP 7 Factor $x^2 - 1$. $\quad (x - 1)(x + 1)$

STEP 8 Write $P(x)$ as a product of four linear factors.

$$\boxed{P(x) = [x - (1 + i)][x - (1 - i)][x - 1][x + 1]}$$

or

$$\boxed{P(x) = (x - 1 - i)(x - 1 + i)(x - 1)(x + 1)}$$

YOUR TURN Factor the polynomial $P(x) = x^4 - 2x^2 + 16x - 15$ given that $1 + 2i$ is a zero.

ANSWER

$P(x) = [x - (1 + 2i)] \cdot [x - (1 - 2i)](x - 1)(x + 3)$

Note: The zeros of $P(x)$ are $1, -3, 1 + 2i$, and $1 - 2i$.

Because an n-degree polynomial function has exactly n zeros and since complex zeros always come in conjugate pairs, if the degree of the polynomial is **odd**, there is guaranteed to be **at least one zero that is a real number**. If the degree of the polynomial is even, there is no guarantee that a zero will be real—all the zeros could be complex.

STUDY TIP

Odd-degree polynomials have at least one real zero.

EXAMPLE 3 Finding Possible Combinations of Real and Complex Zeros

List the possible combinations of real and complex zeros for the given polynomials.

a. $17x^5 + 2x^4 - 3x^3 + x^2 - 5$ **b.** $5x^4 + 2x^3 - x + 2$

Solution:

a. Since this is a *fifth*-degree polynomial, there are *five* zeros. Because complex zeros come in conjugate pairs, the table describes the possible five zeros.

REAL ZEROS	COMPLEX ZEROS
1	4
3	2
5	0

Applying Descartes' rule of signs, we find that there are three or one positive real zeros and two or no negative real zeros.

POSITIVE REAL ZEROS	NEGATIVE REAL ZEROS	COMPLEX ZEROS
1	0	4
3	0	2
1	2	2
3	2	0

b. Because this is a *fourth*-degree polynomial, there are *four* zeros. Since complex zeros come in conjugate pairs, the table describes the possible four zeros.

REAL ZEROS	COMPLEX ZEROS
0	4
2	2
4	0

Applying Descartes' rule of signs, we find that there are two or no positive real zeros and two or no negative real zeros.

POSITIVE REAL ZEROS	NEGATIVE REAL ZEROS	COMPLEX ZEROS
0	0	4
2	0	2
0	2	2
2	2	0

YOUR TURN List the possible combinations of real and complex zeros for

$$P(x) = x^6 - 7x^5 + 8x^3 - 2x + 1$$

ANSWER

REAL ZEROS	COMPLEX ZEROS
0	6
2	4
4	2
6	0

2.5.2 Factoring Polynomials

2.5.2 SKILL

Factor a polynomial function of degree n into n linear factors.

2.5.2 CONCEPTUAL

Understand why an odd-degree polynomial must have at least one real zero.

Now let's draw on the tests discussed in this chapter to help us find all the zeros of a polynomial. Doing so will enable us to write polynomials as a product of linear factors. Before reading Example 4, reread Section 2.4, Example 7.

EXAMPLE 4 Factoring a Polynomial

Factor the polynomial $P(x) = x^5 + 2x^4 - x - 2$.

Solution:

STEP 1 Determine variations in sign.

$P(x)$ has one sign change. $P(x) = x^5 + 2x^4 - x - 2$

$P(-x)$ has two sign changes. $P(-x) = -x^5 + 2x^4 + x - 2$

STEP 2 Apply Descartes' rule of signs and summarize the results in a table.

POSITIVE REAL ZEROS	NEGATIVE REAL ZEROS	COMPLEX ZEROS
1	2	2
1	0	4

STUDY TIP

From Step 2 we know there is one positive real zero, so test the positive possible rational zeros first in Step 4.

STEP 3 Utilize the rational zero theorem to determine the possible rational zeros. $\pm1, \pm2$

[CONCEPT CHECK]

A polynomial of the form $P(x) = (x^2 + a^2)(x^2 - b^2)$, where a and b are real numbers, has how many real and how many imaginary zeros?

ANSWER two real ($\pm b$) and two imaginary ($\pm ai$)

STEP 4 Test possible rational zeros.

1 is a zero:

$$\begin{array}{r|rrrrrr} 1 & 1 & 2 & 0 & 0 & -1 & -2 \\ & & 1 & 3 & 3 & 3 & 2 \\ \hline & 1 & 3 & 3 & 3 & 2 & \boxed{0} \end{array}$$

-1 is a zero:

$$\begin{array}{r|rrrrr} -1 & 1 & 3 & 3 & 3 & 2 \\ & & -1 & -2 & -1 & -2 \\ \hline & 1 & 2 & 1 & 2 & \boxed{0} \end{array}$$

-2 is a zero:

$$\begin{array}{r|rrrr} -2 & 1 & 2 & 1 & 2 \\ & & -2 & 0 & -2 \\ \hline & 1 & 0 & 1 & \boxed{0} \end{array}$$

$$\underbrace{1 \quad 0 \quad 1}_{x^2+1} = (x - i)(x + i)$$

STUDY TIP

In Step 4 we could have evaluated the function to show that 1, -1, and -2 are all zeros of $P(x)$.

STEP 5 Write $P(x)$ as a product of linear factors.

$$\boxed{P(x) = (x - 1)(x + 1)(x + 2)(x - i)(x + i)}$$

[SECTION 2.5] SUMMARY

In this section, we discussed **complex zeros** of polynomial functions. A polynomial function $P(x)$ of degree n with real coefficients has the following properties:

- $P(x)$ has at least one zero (if $n > 0$) and no more than n zeros.
- If $a + bi$ is a zero, then $a - bi$ is also a zero.
- The polynomial can be written as a product of linear factors, not necessarily distinct.

[SECTION 2.5] EXERCISES

• SKILLS

In Exercises 1–8, find all zeros (real and complex). Factor the polynomial as a product of linear factors.

1. $P(x) = x^2 + 4$
2. $P(x) = x^2 + 9$
3. $P(x) = x^2 - 2x + 2$
4. $P(x) = x^2 - 4x + 5$
5. $P(x) = x^4 - 16$
6. $P(x) = x^4 - 81$
7. $P(x) = x^4 - 25$
8. $P(x) = x^4 - 9$

In Exercises 9–16, a polynomial function is described. Find all remaining zeros.

9. Degree: 3 Zeros: $-1, i$
10. Degree: 3 Zeros: $1, -i$
11. Degree: 4 Zeros: $2i, 3 - i$
12. Degree: 4 Zeros: $3i, 2 + i$
13. Degree: 6 Zeros: 2 (multiplicity 2), $1 - 3i, 2 + 5i$
14. Degree: 6 Zeros: -2 (multiplicity 2), $1 - 5i, 2 + 3i$
15. Degree: 6 Zeros: $-i, 1 - i$ (multiplicity 2)
16. Degree: 6 Zeros: $2i, 1 + i$ (multiplicity 2)

In Exercises 17–22, find a polynomial of minimum degree that has the given zeros.

17. $0, 1 - 2i, 1 + 2i$
18. $0, 2 - i, 2 + i$
19. $1, 1 - 5i, 1 + 5i$
20. $2, 4 - i, 4 + i$
21. $1 - i, 1 + i, -3i, 3i$
22. $-i, i, 1 - 2i, 1 + 2i$

In Exercises 23–34, given a zero of the polynomial, determine all other zeros (real and complex) and write the polynomial in terms of a product of linear factors.

Polynomial	Zero	Polynomial	Zero
23. $P(x) = x^4 - 2x^3 - 11x^2 - 8x - 60$	$-2i$	24. $P(x) = x^4 - x^3 + 7x^2 - 9x - 18$	$3i$
25. $P(x) = x^4 - 4x^3 + 4x^2 - 4x + 3$	i	26. $P(x) = x^4 - x^3 + 2x^2 - 4x - 8$	$-2i$
27. $P(x) = x^4 - 2x^3 + 10x^2 - 18x + 9$	$-3i$	28. $P(x) = x^4 - 3x^3 + 21x^2 - 75x - 100$	$5i$
29. $P(x) = x^4 - 9x^2 + 18x - 14$	$1 + i$	30. $P(x) = x^4 - 4x^3 + x^2 + 6x - 40$	$1 - 2i$
31. $P(x) = x^4 - 6x^3 + 6x^2 + 24x - 40$	$3 - i$	32. $P(x) = x^4 - 4x^3 + 4x^2 + 4x - 5$	$2 + i$
33. $P(x) = x^4 - 9x^3 + 29x^2 - 41x + 20$	$2 - i$	34. $P(x) = x^4 - 7x^3 + 14x^2 + 2x - 20$	$3 + i$

In Exercises 35–58, factor each polynomial as a product of linear factors.

35. $P(x) = x^3 - x^2 + 9x - 9$
36. $P(x) = x^3 - 2x^2 + 4x - 8$
37. $P(x) = x^3 - 5x^2 + x - 5$
38. $P(x) = x^3 - 7x^2 + x - 7$
39. $P(x) = x^3 + x^2 + 4x + 4$
40. $P(x) = x^3 + x^2 - 2$
41. $P(x) = x^3 - x^2 - 18$
42. $P(x) = x^4 - 2x^3 - 2x^2 - 2x - 3$
43. $P(x) = x^4 - 2x^3 - 11x^2 - 8x - 60$
44. $P(x) = x^4 - x^3 + 7x^2 - 9x - 18$
45. $P(x) = x^4 - 4x^3 - x^2 - 16x - 20$
46. $P(x) = x^4 - 3x^3 + 11x^2 - 27x + 18$
47. $P(x) = x^4 - 7x^3 + 27x^2 - 47x + 26$
48. $P(x) = x^4 - 5x^3 + 5x^2 + 25x - 26$
49. $P(x) = -x^4 - 3x^3 + x^2 + 13x + 10$
50. $P(x) = -x^4 - x^3 + 12x^2 + 26x + 24$
51. $P(x) = x^4 - 2x^3 + 5x^2 - 8x + 4$
52. $P(x) = x^4 + 2x^3 + 10x^2 + 18x + 9$
53. $P(x) = x^6 + 12x^4 + 23x^2 - 36$
54. $P(x) = x^6 - 2x^5 + 9x^4 - 16x^3 + 24x^2 - 32x + 16$
55. $P(x) = 4x^4 - 20x^3 + 37x^2 - 24x + 5$
56. $P(x) = 4x^4 - 44x^3 + 145x^2 - 114x + 26$
57. $P(x) = 3x^5 - 2x^4 + 9x^3 - 6x^2 - 12x + 8$
58. $P(x) = 2x^5 - 5x^4 + 4x^3 - 26x^2 + 50x - 25$

• APPLICATIONS

In Exercises 59–62, assume the profit model is given by a polynomial function $P(x)$, where x is the number of units sold by the company per year.

59. Profit. If the profit function of a given company has all imaginary zeros and the leading coefficient is positive, would you invest in this company? Explain.

60. Profit. If the profit function of a given company has all imaginary zeros and the leading coefficient is negative, would you invest in this company? Explain.

61. Profit. If the profit function of a company is modeled by a third-degree polynomial with a negative leading coefficient and this polynomial has two complex conjugates as zeros and one positive real zero, would you invest in this company? Explain.

62. Profit. If the profit function of a company is modeled by a third-degree polynomial with a positive leading coefficient and this polynomial has two complex conjugates as zeros and one positive real zero, would you invest in this company? Explain.

For Exercises 63 and 64, refer to the following:

The following graph models the profit P of a company, where t is months and $t \geq 0$.

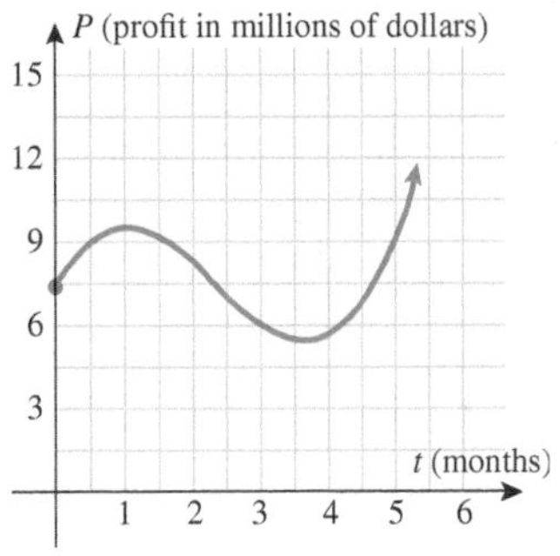

63. Business. If the profit function pictured is a third-degree polynomial, how many real and how many complex zeros does the function have? Discuss the implications of these zeros.

64. Business. If the profit function pictured is a fourth-degree polynomial with a negative leading coefficient, how many real and how many complex zeros does the function have? Discuss the implications of these zeros.

For Exercises 65 and 66, refer to the following:

The following graph models the concentration, C (in μg/mL), of a drug in the bloodstream; and t is time in hours after the drug is administered, where $t \geq 0$.

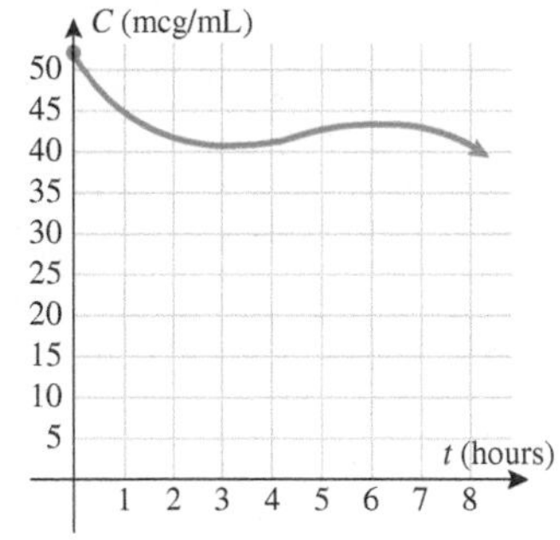

65. Health/Medicine. If the concentration function pictured is a third-degree polynomial, how many real and how many complex zeros does the function have? Discuss the implications of these zeros.

66. Health/Medicine. If the concentration function pictured is a fourth-degree polynomial with a negative leading coefficient, how many real and how many complex zeros does the function have? Discuss the implications of these zeros.

• CATCH THE MISTAKE

In Exercises 67 and 68, explain the mistake that is made.

67. Given that 1 is a zero of $P(x) = x^3 - 2x^2 + 7x - 6$, find all other zeros.

Solution:

STEP 1: $P(x)$ is a third-degree polynomial, so we expect three zeros.

STEP 2: Because 1 is a zero, -1 is a zero, so two linear factors are $(x - 1)$ and $(x + 1)$.

STEP 3: Write the polynomial as a product of three linear factors.

$$P(x) = (x - 1)(x + 1)(x - c)$$
$$P(x) = (x^2 - 1)(x - c)$$

STEP 4: To find the remaining linear factor, we divide $P(x)$ by $x^2 - 1$.

$$\frac{x^3 - 2x^2 + 7x - 6}{x^2 - 1} = x - 2 + \frac{6x - 8}{x^2 - 1}$$

Which has a nonzero remainder? What went wrong?

68. Factor the polynomial $P(x) = 2x^3 + x^2 + 2x + 1$.

Solution:

STEP 1: Since $P(x)$ is an odd-degree polynomial, we are guaranteed one real zero (since complex zeros come in conjugate pairs).

STEP 2: Apply the rational zero test to develop a list of potential rational zeros.

Possible zeros: ± 1

STEP 3: Test possible zeros.

1 is not a zero: $P(x) = 2(1)^3 + (1)^2 + 2(1) + 1$
$= 6$

-1 is not a zero: $P(x) = 2(-1)^3 + (-1)^2 + 2(-1) + 1$
$= -2$

Note: $-\frac{1}{2}$ is the real zero. Why did we not find it?

• CONCEPTUAL

In Exercises 69–72, determine whether each statement is true or false.

69. If $x = 1$ is a zero of a polynomial function, then $x = -1$ is also a zero of the polynomial function.

70. All zeros of a polynomial function correspond to x-intercepts.

71. A polynomial function of degree n, $n > 0$ must have at least one zero.

72. A polynomial function of degree n, $n > 0$, can be written as a product of n linear factors.

73. Is it possible for an odd-degree polynomial to have all imaginary complex zeros? Explain.

74. Is it possible for an even-degree polynomial to have all imaginary zeros? Explain.

• CHALLENGE

In Exercises 75–78, assume *a* and *b* are nonzero real numbers.

75. Find a polynomial function that has degree 6 and for which bi is a zero of multiplicity 3.

76. Find a polynomial function that has degree 4 and for which $a + bi$ is a zero of multiplicity 2.

77. Find a polynomial function that has degree 6 and for which ai and bi are zeros, where ai has multiplicity 2. Assume $|a| \neq |b|$.

78. Assuming $|a| \neq |b|$, find a polynomial function of lowest degree for which ai and bi are zeros of equal multiplicity.

• PREVIEW TO CALCULUS

In Exercises 79–82, refer to the following:

In calculus we study the integration of rational functions by partial fractions.

a. Factor each polynomial into linear factors. Use complex numbers when necessary.

b. Factor each polynomial using only real numbers.

79. $f(x) = x^3 + x^2 + x + 1$

80. $f(x) = x^3 - 6x^2 + 21x - 26$

81. $f(x) = x^4 + 5x^2 + 4$

82. $f(x) = x^4 - 2x^3 - 7x^2 + 18x - 18$

2.6 RATIONAL FUNCTIONS

SKILLS OBJECTIVES

- Find the domain of a rational function.
- Determine vertical, horizontal, and slant asymptotes of rational functions.
- Graph rational functions.

CONCEPTUAL OBJECTIVES

- Understand that the domain of a rational function is the set of all real numbers except those that correspond to the denominator being equal to zero.
- Understand that the graph of a rational function can have either a horizontal asymptote or a slant asymptote, but not both.
- Recognize that any real number excluded from the domain of a rational function corresponds either to a vertical asymptote or to a hole on the graph.

2.6.1 Domain of Rational Functions

So far in this chapter, we have discussed polynomial functions. We now turn our attention to *rational functions*, which are *ratios* of polynomial functions. Ratios of integers are called *rational numbers*. Similarly, ratios of polynomial functions are called *rational functions*.

2.6.1 SKILL

Find the domain of a rational function.

2.6.1 CONCEPTUAL

Understand that the domain of a rational function is the set of all real numbers except those that correspond to the denominator being equal to zero.

DEFINITION Rational Function

A function $f(x)$ is a **rational function** if

$$f(x) = \frac{n(x)}{d(x)} \qquad d(x) \neq 0$$

where the numerator $n(x)$ and the denominator $d(x)$ are polynomial functions. The domain of $f(x)$ is the set of all real numbers x such that $d(x) \neq 0$.

Note: If $d(x)$ is a constant, then $f(x)$ is a polynomial function.

The domain of any polynomial function is the set of all real numbers. When we divide two polynomial functions, the result is a *rational function*, and we must exclude any values of x that make the denominator equal to zero.

EXAMPLE 1 Finding the Domain of a Rational Function

Find the domain of the rational function $f(x) = \dfrac{x+1}{x^2 - x - 6}$. Express the domain in interval notation.

Solution:

Set the denominator equal to zero.	$x^2 - x - 6 = 0$
Factor.	$(x + 2)(x - 3) = 0$
Solve for x.	$x = -2$ or $x = 3$
Eliminate these values from the domain.	$x \neq -2$ or $x \neq 3$
State the domain in interval notation.	$\boxed{(-\infty, -2)\cup(-2, 3)\cup(3, \infty)}$

YOUR TURN Find the domain of the rational function $f(x) = \dfrac{x-2}{x^2 - 3x - 4}$. Express the domain in interval notation.

ANSWER

The domain is the set of all real numbers such that $x \neq -1$ or $x \neq 4$.

Interval notation: $(-\infty, -1)\cup(-1, 4)\cup(4, \infty)$

It is important to note that there are not always restrictions on the domain. For example, if the denominator is never equal to zero, the domain is the set of all real numbers.

EXAMPLE 2 **When the Domain of a Rational Function Is the Set of All Real Numbers**

Find the domain of the rational function $g(x) = \frac{3x}{x^2 + 9}$. Express the domain in interval notation.

Solution:

Set the denominator equal to zero. $x^2 + 9 = 0$

Subtract 9 from both sides. $x^2 = -9$

Solve for x. $x = -3i$ or $x = 3i$

There are no *real* solutions; therefore, the domain has no restrictions. $\mathbb{R}$, the set of all real numbers

State the domain in interval notation. $\boxed{(-\infty, \infty)}$

YOUR TURN Find the domain of the rational function $g(x) = \frac{5x}{x^2 + 4}$. Express the domain in interval notation.

ANSWER
The domain is the set of all real numbers. Interval notation: $(-\infty, \infty)$

[CONCEPT CHECK]

TRUE OR FALSE The domain of $f(x) = \frac{1}{x^2 + a^2}$ and the domain of $g(x) = \frac{1}{x^2 + b^2}$ are equal.

ANSWER True

It is important to note that $f(x) = \frac{x^2 - 4}{x + 2}$, where $x \neq -2$, and $g(x) = x - 2$ are *not* the same function. Even though $f(x)$ can be written in the factored form $f(x) = \frac{(x - 2)(x + 2)}{x + 2} = x - 2$, its domain is different. The domain of $g(x)$ is the set of all real numbers, whereas the domain of $f(x)$ is the set of all real numbers such that $x \neq -2$. If we were to plot $f(x)$ and $g(x)$, they would both look like the line $y = x - 2$. However, $f(x)$ would have a hole, or discontinuity, at the point $x = -2$.

2.6.2 Vertical, Horizontal, and Slant Asymptotes

2.6.2 SKILL

Determine vertical, horizontal, and slant asymptotes of rational functions.

2.6.2 CONCEPTUAL

Understand that the graph of a rational function can have either a horizontal asymptote or a slant asymptote, but not both.

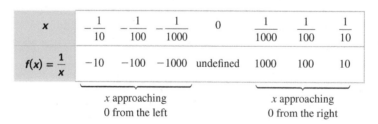

If a function is not defined at a point, then it is still useful to know how the function behaves near that point. Let's start with a simple rational function, the reciprocal function $f(x) = \frac{1}{x}$. This function is defined everywhere except at $x = 0$.

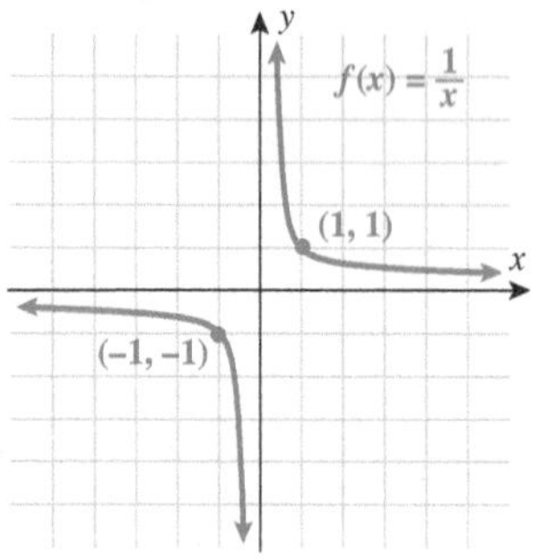

x	$-\frac{1}{10}$	$-\frac{1}{100}$	$-\frac{1}{1000}$	0	$\frac{1}{1000}$	$\frac{1}{100}$	$\frac{1}{10}$
$f(x) = \frac{1}{x}$	-10	-100	-1000	undefined	1000	100	10
	x approaching 0 from the left				*x* approaching 0 from the right		

x	$f(x) = \frac{1}{x}$
-10	$-\frac{1}{10}$
-1	-1
1	1
10	$\frac{1}{10}$

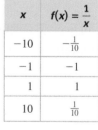

We cannot let $x = 0$, because that point is not in the domain of the function. We should, however, ask the question, "How does $f(x)$ behave as *x approaches* zero?" Let us take values that get closer and closer to $x = 0$, such as $\frac{1}{10}, \frac{1}{100}, \frac{1}{1000}, \ldots$ (See the table above.) We use an *arrow* to represent the word *approach*, a *positive* superscript to represent from the *right*, and a *negative* superscript to represent from the *left*. A plot of this function can be generated using point-plotting techniques. The following are observations of the graph for $f(x) = \frac{1}{x}$.

WORDS	MATH
As x approaches zero from the *right*, the function $f(x)$ increases without bound.	$x \to 0^+$ $\frac{1}{x} \to \infty$
As x approaches zero from the *left*, the function $f(x)$ decreases without bound.	$x \to 0^-$ $\frac{1}{x} \to -\infty$
As x approaches infinity (increases without bound), the function $f(x)$ approaches zero from *above*.	$x \to \infty$ $\frac{1}{x} \to 0^+$
As x approaches negative infinity (decreases without bound), the function $f(x)$ approaches zero from *below*.	$x \to -\infty$ $\frac{1}{x} \to 0^-$

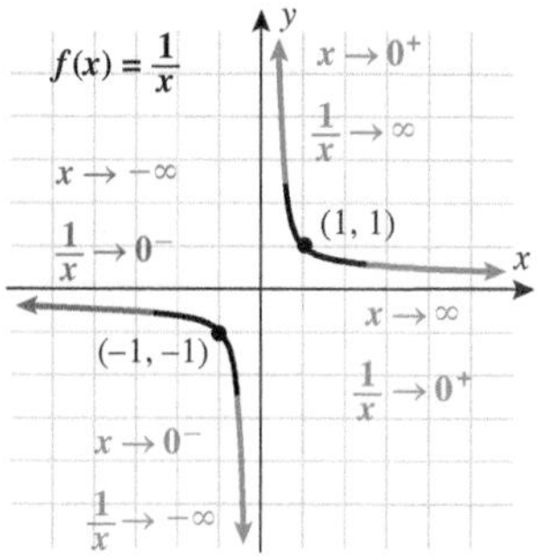

The symbol ∞ does not represent an actual real number. This symbol represents growing without bound.

1. Notice that the function is not defined at $x = 0$. The y-axis, or the vertical line $x = 0$, represents the *vertical asymptote.*
2. Notice that the value of the function is never equal to zero. The x-axis is approached but not actually reached by the function. The x-axis, or $y = 0$, is a *horizontal asymptote.*

Asymptotes are lines that the graph of a function approaches. Suppose a football team's defense is on its own 8 yard line and the team gets an "offsides" penalty that results in loss of "half the distance to the goal." Then the offense would get the ball on the 4 yard line. Suppose the defense gets another penalty on the next play that results in "half the distance to the goal." The offense would then get the ball on the 2 yard line. If the defense received 10 more penalties all resulting in "half the distance to the goal," would the referees *give* the offense a touchdown? No, because although the offense may appear to be snapping the ball from the goal line, technically it has not actually reached the goal line. Asymptotes utilize the same concept.

We will start with *vertical asymptotes.* Although the function $f(x) = \frac{1}{x}$ had one vertical asymptote, in general, rational functions can have *none, one,* or *several* vertical asymptotes. We will first formally define what a vertical asymptote is and then discuss how to find it.

DEFINITION **Vertical Asymptotes**

The line $x = a$ is a **vertical asymptote** for the graph of a function if $f(x)$ either increases or decreases without bound as x approaches a from either the left or the right.

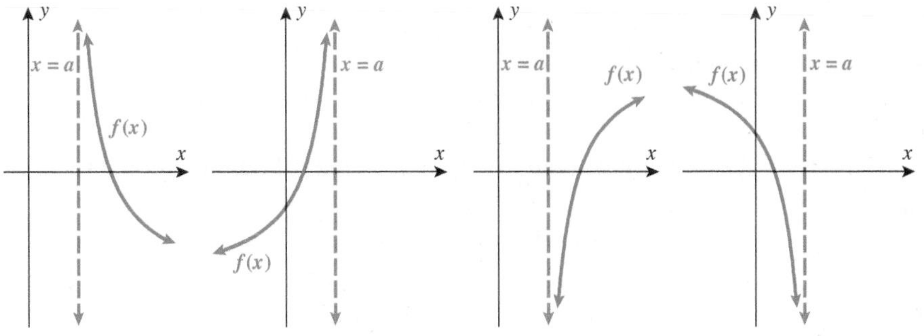

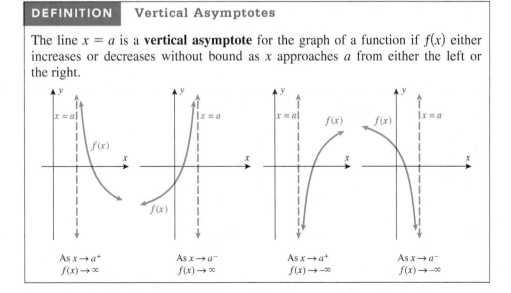

As $x \to a^+$, $f(x) \to \infty$ | As $x \to a^-$, $f(x) \to \infty$ | As $x \to a^+$, $f(x) \to -\infty$ | As $x \to a^-$, $f(x) \to -\infty$

Vertical asymptotes assist us in graphing rational functions because they essentially "steer" the function in the vertical direction. How do we locate the vertical asymptotes of a rational function? Set the denominator equal to zero. If the numerator and denominator have no common factors, then any numbers that are excluded from the domain of a rational function locate vertical asymptotes.

A rational function $f(x) = \frac{n(x)}{d(x)}$ is said to be in **lowest terms** if the numerator $n(x)$ and denominator $d(x)$ have no common factors. Let $f(x) = \frac{n(x)}{d(x)}$ be a rational function in lowest terms; then any zeros of the numerator $n(x)$ correspond to x-intercepts of the graph of f, and any zeros of the denominator $d(x)$ correspond to vertical asymptotes of the graph of f. If a rational function does have a common factor (is not in lowest terms), then the common factor(s) should be canceled, resulting in an equivalent rational function $R(x)$ in lowest terms. If $(x - a)^p$ is a factor of the numerator and $(x - a)^q$ is a factor of the denominator, then there is a *hole* in the graph at $x = a$, provided $p \geq q$ and $x = a$ is a vertical asymptote if $p < q$.

STUDY TIP

The vertical asymptotes of a rational function in *lowest terms* occur at x-values that make the denominator equal to zero.

LOCATING VERTICAL ASYMPTOTES

Let $f(x) = \frac{n(x)}{d(x)}$ be a rational function in lowest terms (that is, assume $n(x)$ and $d(x)$ are polynomials with no common factors); then the graph of f has a vertical asymptote at any real zero of the denominator $d(x)$. That is, if $d(a) = 0$, then $x = a$ corresponds to a vertical asymptote on the graph of f.

Note: If f is a rational function that is not in lowest terms, then divide out the common factors, resulting in a rational function R that is in lowest terms. Any common factor $x - a$ of the function f corresponds to a hole in the graph of f at $x = a$, provided that the multiplicity of a in the numerator is greater than or equal to the multiplicity of a in the denominator.

EXAMPLE 3 Determining Vertical Asymptotes

Locate any vertical asymptotes of the rational function $f(x) = \frac{5x + 2}{6x^2 - x - 2}$.

Solution:

Factor the denominator. $f(x) = \frac{5x + 2}{(2x + 1)(3x - 2)}$

The numerator and denominator have no common factors, which means that all zeros of the denominator correspond to vertical asymptotes.

Set the denominator equal to zero. $2x + 1 = 0$ and $3x - 2 = 0$

Solve for x. $x = -\frac{1}{2}$ and $x = \frac{2}{3}$

The vertical asymptotes are $\boxed{x = -\frac{1}{2}}$ and $\boxed{x = \frac{2}{3}}$.

YOUR TURN Locate any vertical asymptotes of the following rational function:

$$f(x) = \frac{3x - 1}{2x^2 - x - 15}$$

ANSWER

$x = -\frac{5}{2}$ and $x = 3$

EXAMPLE 4 **Determining Vertical Asymptotes When the Rational Function Is Not in Lowest Terms**

Locate any vertical asymptotes of the rational function $f(x) = \dfrac{x+2}{x^3 - 3x^2 - 10x}$.

Solution:

Factor the denominator. $x^3 - 3x^2 - 10x = x(x^2 - 3x - 10)$
$= x(x-5)(x+2)$

Write the rational function in factored form. $f(x) = \dfrac{(x+2)}{x(x-5)(x+2)}$

Cancel (divide out) the common factor $(x + 2)$. $R(x) = \dfrac{1}{x(x-5)} \quad x \neq -2$

Find the values when the denominator of R is equal to zero. $x = 0$ and $x = 5$

The vertical asymptotes are $\boxed{x = 0}$ and $\boxed{x = 5}$.

Note: $x = -2$ is not in the domain of $f(x)$, even though there is no vertical asymptote there. There is a "hole" in the graph at $x = -2$. Graphing calculators do not always show such "holes."

YOUR TURN Locate any vertical asymptotes of the following rational function:

$$f(x) = \frac{x^2 - 4x}{x^2 - 7x + 12}$$

ANSWER
$x = 3$

We now turn our attention to *horizontal asymptotes.* As we have seen, rational functions can have several vertical asymptotes. However, rational functions can have *at most* one horizontal asymptote. Horizontal asymptotes imply that a function approaches a constant value as x becomes large in the positive or negative direction. Another difference between vertical and horizontal asymptotes is that the graph of a function never touches a vertical asymptote but, as you will see in the next box, the graph of a function may cross a horizontal asymptote, just not at the "ends" $(x \to \pm\infty)$.

DEFINITION **Horizontal Asymptote**

The line $y = b$ is a **horizontal asymptote** of the graph of a function if $f(x)$ approaches b as x increases or decreases without bound. The following are three examples:

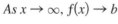

As $x \to \infty$, $f(x) \to b$

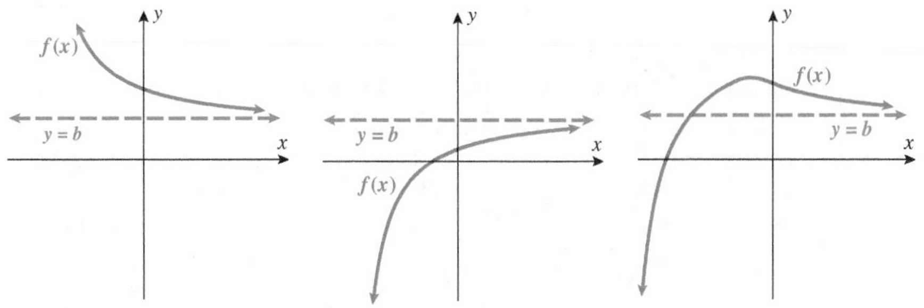

Note: A horizontal asymptote steers a function as x gets large. Therefore, when x is not large, the function may cross the asymptote.

How do we determine whether a horizontal asymptote exists? And if it does, how do we locate it? We investigate the value of the rational function as $x \to \infty$ or as $x \to -\infty$.One of two things will happen: Either the rational function will increase or decrease without bound or the rational function will approach a constant value.

We say that a rational function is **proper** if the degree of the numerator is less than the degree of the denominator. Proper rational functions, like $f(x) = \frac{1}{x}$, approach zero as x gets large. Therefore, all proper rational functions have the specific horizontal asymptote $y = 0$ (see Example 5a).

We say that a rational function is **improper** if the degree of the numerator is greater than or equal to the degree of the denominator. In this case, we can divide the numerator by the denominator and determine how the quotient behaves as x increases without bound.

- If the quotient is a constant (resulting when the degrees of the numerator and denominator are equal), then as $x \to \infty$ or as $x \to -\infty$, the rational function approaches the constant quotient (see Example 5b).
- If the quotient is a polynomial function of degree 1 or higher, then the quotient depends on x and does not approach a constant value as x increases (see Example 5c). In this case, we say that there is no horizontal asymptote.

We find horizontal asymptotes by comparing the degree of the numerator and the degree of the denominator. There are three cases to consider:

1. The degree of the numerator is less than the degree of the denominator.
2. The degree of the numerator is equal to the degree of the denominator.
3. The degree of the numerator is greater than the degree of the denominator.

LOCATING HORIZONTAL ASYMPTOTES

Let f be a rational function given by

$$f(x) = \frac{n(x)}{d(x)} = \frac{a_n x^n + a_{n-1}x^{n-1} + \cdots + a_1 x + a_0}{b_m x^m + b_{m-1}x^{m-1} + \cdots + b_1 x + b_0}$$

where $n(x)$ and $d(x)$ are polynomials.

1. When $n < m$, the x-axis ($y = 0$) is the horizontal asymptote.
2. When $n = m$, the line $y = \frac{a_n}{b_m}$ (ratio of leading coefficients) is the horizontal asymptote.
3. When $n > m$, there is no horizontal asymptote.

In other words:

1. When the degree of the numerator is less than the degree of the denominator, $y = 0$ is the horizontal asymptote.
2. When the degree of the numerator is the same as the degree of the denominator, the horizontal asymptote is the ratio of the leading coefficients.
3. When the degree of the numerator is greater than the degree of the denominator, there is no horizontal asymptote.

EXAMPLE 5 Finding Horizontal Asymptotes

Determine whether a horizontal asymptote exists for the graph of each of the given rational functions. If it does, locate the horizontal asymptote.

a. $f(x) = \dfrac{8x + 3}{4x^2 + 1}$ **b.** $g(x) = \dfrac{8x^2 + 3}{4x^2 + 1}$ **c.** $h(x) = \dfrac{8x^3 + 3}{4x^2 + 1}$

Solution (a):

The degree of the numerator $8x + 3$ is 1. $n = 1$

The degree of the denominator $4x^2 + 1$ is 2. $m = 2$

The degree of the numerator is less than the degree of the denominator. $n < m$

The x-axis is the horizontal asymptote for the graph of $f(x)$. $y = 0$

The line $\boxed{y = 0}$ is the horizontal asymptote for the graph of $f(x)$.

Solution (b):

The degree of the numerator $8x^2 + 3$ is 2. $n = 2$

The degree of the denominator $4x^2 + 1$ is 2. $m = 2$

The degree of the numerator is equal to the degree of the denominator. $n = m$

The ratio of the leading coefficients is the horizontal asymptote for the graph of $g(x)$. $y = \dfrac{8}{4} = 2$

The line $\boxed{y = 2}$ is the horizontal asymptote for the graph of $g(x)$.

If we divide the numerator by the denominator, the resulting quotient is the constant 2. $g(x) = \dfrac{8x^2 + 3}{4x^2 + 1} = 2 + \dfrac{1}{4x^2 + 1}$

Solution (c):

The degree of the numerator $8x^3 + 3$ is 3. $n = 3$

The degree of the denominator $4x^2 + 1$ is 2. $m = 2$

The degree of the numerator is greater than the degree of the denominator. $n > m$

The graph of the rational function $h(x)$ has $\boxed{\text{no horizontal asymptote}}$.

If we divide the numerator by the denominator, the resulting quotient is a linear function and corresponds to the slant asymptote $y = 2x$. $h(x) = \dfrac{8x^3 + 3}{4x^2 + 1} = 2x + \dfrac{-2x + 3}{4x^2 + 1}$

YOUR TURN Find the horizontal asymptote (if one exists) for the graph of the rational function $f(x) = \dfrac{7x^3 + x - 2}{-4x^3 + 1}$.

ANSWER

$y = -\frac{7}{4}$ is the horizontal asymptote.

STUDY TIP

There are three types of linear asymptotes: horizontal, vertical, and *slant*.

There are three types of lines: horizontal (slope is zero), vertical (slope is undefined), and slant (nonzero slope). Similarly, there are three types of linear asymptotes: horizontal, vertical, and *slant*.

Recall that in dividing polynomials, the degree of the quotient is always the difference between the degree of the numerator and the degree of the denominator. For example, a cubic (third-degree) polynomial divided by a quadratic (second-degree) polynomial results in a linear (first-degree) polynomial. A fifth-degree polynomial divided by a fourth-degree polynomial results in a first-degree (linear) polynomial. When the degree of the numerator is exactly one more than the degree of the denominator, the quotient is linear and represents a *slant asymptote.*

[CONCEPT CHECK]

TRUE OR FALSE A rational function can have both a horizontal and a slant asymptote.

ANSWER False

SLANT ASYMPTOTES

Let f be a rational function given by $f(x) = \frac{n(x)}{d(x)}$, where $n(x)$ and $d(x)$ are polynomials and the degree of $n(x)$ is *one more than* the degree of $d(x)$. When dividing $n(x)$ by $d(x)$, the rational function can be expressed as

$$f(x) = mx + b + \frac{r(x)}{d(x)}$$

where the degree of the remainder $r(x)$ is less than the degree of $d(x)$ and the line $y = mx + b$ is a **slant asymptote** for the graph of f.

Note that as $x \to -\infty$ or $x \to \infty$, $f(x) \to mx + b$.

EXAMPLE 6 Finding Slant Asymptotes

Determine the slant asymptote of the rational function $f(x) = \frac{4x^3 + x^2 + 3}{x^2 - x + 1}$.

Solution:

Divide the numerator by the denominator with long division.

$$\begin{array}{r} 4x + 5 \\ x^2 - x + 1 \overline{)\,4x^3 + x^2 + 0x + 3} \\ -(4x^3 - 4x^2 + 4x) \\ \hline 5x^2 - 4x + 3 \\ -(5x^2 - 5x + 5) \\ \hline x - 2 \end{array}$$

$$f(x) = 4x + 5 + \frac{x - 2}{x^2 - x + 1}$$

Note that as $x \to \pm\infty$, the rational expression approaches 0.

$$\frac{x - 2}{x^2 - x + 1} \to 0 \text{ as } x \to \pm\infty$$

The quotient is the slant asymptote.

$$\boxed{y = 4x + 5}$$

YOUR TURN Find the slant asymptote of the rational function $f(x) = \frac{x^2 + 3x + 2}{x - 2}$.

ANSWER

$y = x + 5$

2.6.3 Graphing Rational Functions

We can now graph rational functions using asymptotes as graphing aids. The following box summarizes the six-step procedure for graphing rational functions.

2.6.3 SKILL

Graph rational functions.

2.6.3 CONCEPTUAL

Any real number excluded from the domain of a rational function corresponds either to a vertical asymptote or to a hole on the graph.

STUDY TIP

Common factors need to be divided out first; then the remaining x-values corresponding to a denominator value of 0 are vertical asymptotes.

GRAPHING RATIONAL FUNCTIONS

Let f be a rational function given by $f(x) = \frac{n(x)}{d(x)}$.

Step 1: Find the domain of the rational function f.

Step 2: Find the **intercept(s)**.
- y-intercept: evaluate $f(0)$.
- x-intercept: solve the equation $n(x) = 0$ for x in the domain of f.

Step 3: Find any **holes**.
- Factor the numerator and denominator.
- Divide out common factors.
- A common factor $x - a$ corresponds to a hole on the graph of f at $x = a$ if the multiplicity of a in the numerator is greater than or equal to the multiplicity of a in the denominator.
- The result is an equivalent rational function $R(x) = \frac{p(x)}{q(x)}$ in lowest terms.

Step 4: Find any **asymptotes**.
- Vertical asymptotes: solve $q(x) = 0$.
- Compare the degree of the numerator and the degree of the denominator to determine whether either a horizontal or a slant asymptote exists. If one exists, find it.

Step 5: Find **additional points** on the graph of f—particularly near asymptotes.

Step 6: **Sketch** the graph; draw the asymptotes, label the intercept(s) and additional points, and complete the graph with a smooth curve between and beyond the vertical asymptotes.

STUDY TIP

Any real number excluded from the domain of a rational function corresponds to either a vertical asymptote or a hole on its graph.

It is important to note that any real number eliminated from the domain of a rational function corresponds to either a vertical asymptote or a hole on its graph.

EXAMPLE 7 Graphing a Rational Function

Graph the rational function $f(x) = \dfrac{x}{x^2 - 4}$.

Solution:

STEP 1 Find the **domain**.

Set the denominator equal to zero.	$x^2 - 4 = 0$
Solve for x.	$x = \pm 2$
State the domain.	$(-\infty, -2) \cup (-2, 2) \cup (2, \infty)$

STEP 2 Find the **intercepts**.

y-intercept: $f(0) = \dfrac{0}{-4} = 0 \quad y = 0$

x-intercepts: $f(x) = \dfrac{x}{x^2 - 4} = 0 \quad x = 0$

The only intercept is at the point $\boxed{(0, 0)}$.

STEP 3 Find any holes. $f(x) = \dfrac{x}{(x + 2)(x - 2)}$

There are no common factors, so f is in lowest terms.

Since there are no common factors, there are no holes on the graph of f.

STEP 4 Find any **asymptotes**.

Vertical asymptotes: $d(x) = (x + 2)(x - 2) = 0$

$\boxed{x = -2}$ and $\boxed{x = 2}$

Horizontal asymptote: $\dfrac{\text{Degree of numerator}}{\text{Degree of denominator}} = \dfrac{1}{2}$

Degree of numerator < Degree of denominator $\boxed{y = 0}$

STEP 5 Find **additional points** on the graph.

x	-3	-1	1	3
$f(x)$	$-\frac{3}{5}$	$\frac{1}{3}$	$-\frac{1}{3}$	$\frac{3}{5}$

STEP 6 **Sketch** the graph; label the intercepts, asymptotes, and additional points; and complete with a smooth curve approaching the asymptotes.

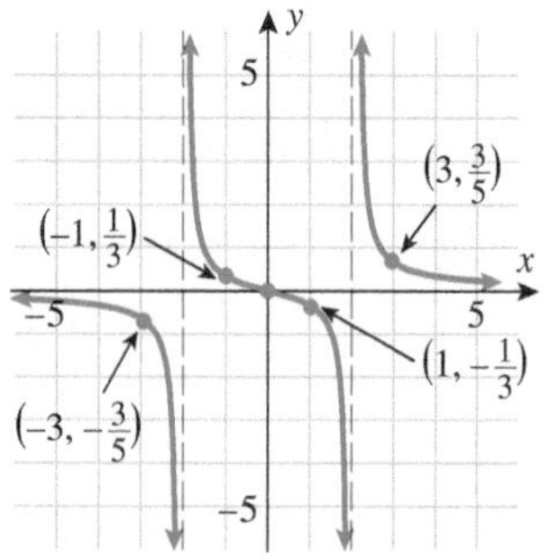

YOUR TURN Graph the rational function $f(x) = \dfrac{x}{x^2 - 1}$.

ANSWER

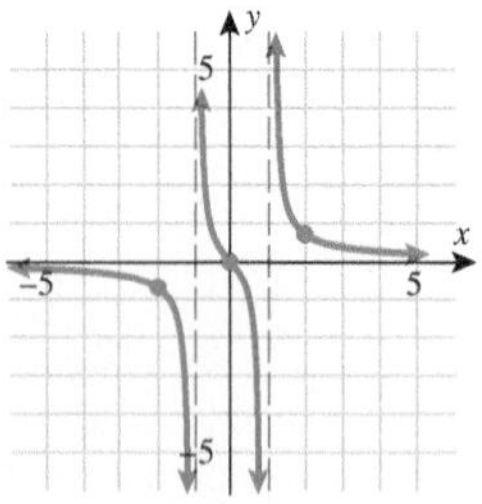

EXAMPLE 8 Graphing a Rational Function with No Horizontal or Slant Asymptotes

State the asymptotes (if there are any) and graph the rational function $f(x) = \dfrac{x^4 - x^3 - 6x^2}{x^2 - 1}$.

Solution:

STEP 1 Find the domain.

Set the denominator equal to zero. $x^2 - 1 = 0$

Solve for x. $x = \pm 1$

State the domain. $(-\infty, -1)\cup(-1, 1)\cup(1, \infty)$

STEP 2 Find the **intercepts**.

y-intercept: $f(0) = \dfrac{0}{-1} = 0$

x-intercepts: $n(x) = x^4 - x^3 - 6x^2 = 0$

Factor. $x^2(x - 3)(x + 2) = 0$

Solve. $x = 0$, $x = 3$, and $x = -2$

The intercepts are the points $(0, 0)$, $(3, 0)$, and $(-2, 0)$.

STEP 3 Find any **holes**. $f(x) = \dfrac{x^2(x - 3)(x + 2)}{(x - 1)(x + 1)}$

There are no common factors, so f is in lowest terms.

Since there are no common factors, there are no holes on the graph of f.

STEP 4 Find the **asymptotes**.

Vertical asymptote: $d(x) = x^2 - 1 = 0$

Factor. $(x + 1)(x - 1) = 0$

Solve. $x = -1$ and $x = 1$

No horizontal asymptote: degree of $n(x)$ > degree of $d(x)$ $[4 > 2]$

No slant asymptote: degree of $n(x)$ − degree of $d(x) > 1$ $[4 - 2 = 2 > 1]$

The asymptotes are $x = -1$ and $x = 1$.

STEP 5 Find **additional points** on the graph.

x	−3	−0.5	0.5	2	4
f(x)	6.75	1.75	2.08	−5.33	6.4

STEP 6 **Sketch** the graph; label the intercepts and asymptotes, and complete with a smooth curve between and beyond the vertical asymptote.

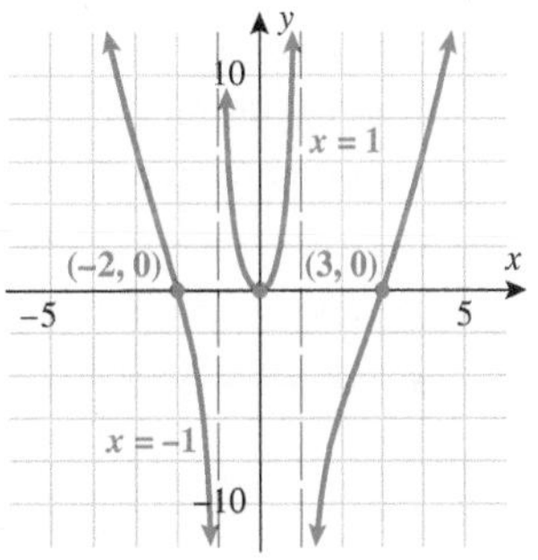

YOUR TURN State the asymptotes (if there are any) and graph the rational function:

$$f(x) = \frac{x^3 - 2x^2 - 3x}{x + 2}$$

ANSWER

Vertical asymptote: $x = -2$. No horizontal or slant asymptotes.

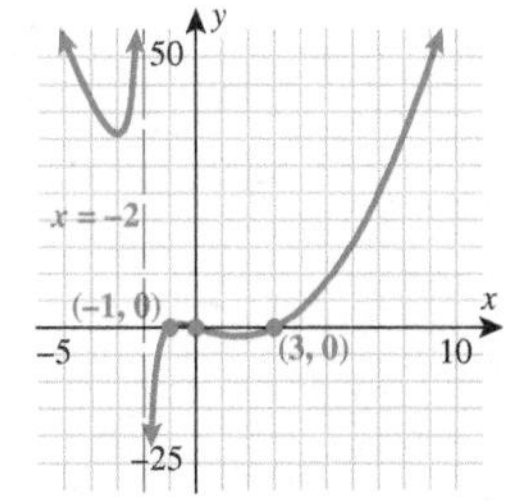

EXAMPLE 9 Graphing a Rational Function with a Horizontal Asymptote

State the asymptotes (if there are any) and graph the rational function

$$f(x) = \frac{4x^3 + 10x^2 - 6x}{8 - x^3}$$

Solution:

STEP 1 Find the **domain**.

Set the denominator equal to zero. $8 - x^3 = 0$

Solve for x. $x = 2$

State the domain. $(-\infty, 2)\cup(2, \infty)$

STEP 2 Find the **intercepts**.

y-intercept: $f(0) = \frac{0}{8} = 0$

x-intercepts: $n(x) = 4x^3 + 10x^2 - 6x = 0$

Factor. $2x(2x - 1)(x + 3) = 0$

Solve. $x = 0, x = \frac{1}{2}$, and $x = -3$

The intercepts are the points $(0, 0)$, $(\frac{1}{2}, 0)$, and $(-3, 0)$.

STEP 3 Find the **holes**. $f(x) = \dfrac{2x(2x - 1)(x + 3)}{(2 - x)(x^2 + 2x + 4)}$

There are no common factors, so f is in lowest terms (no holes).

STEP 4 Find the **asymptotes**.

Vertical asymptote: $d(x) = 8 - x^3 = 0$

Solve. $x = 2$

Horizontal asymptote: degree of $n(x)$ = degree of $d(x)$

Use leading coefficients. $y = \frac{4}{-1} = -4$

The asymptotes are $x = 2$ and $y = -4$.

STEP 5 Find **additional points** on the graph.

x	-4	-1	$\frac{1}{4}$	1	3
$f(x)$	-1	1.33	-0.10	1.14	-9.47

STEP 6 **Sketch** the graph; label the intercepts and asymptotes, and complete with a smooth curve.

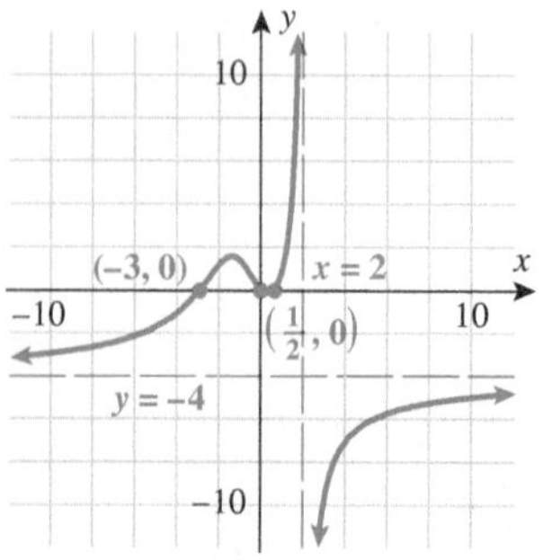

ANSWER

Vertical asymptotes: $x = 4, x = -1$
Horizontal asymptote: $y = 2$
Intercepts: $(0, -\frac{3}{2})$, $(\frac{3}{2}, 0)$, $(2, 0)$

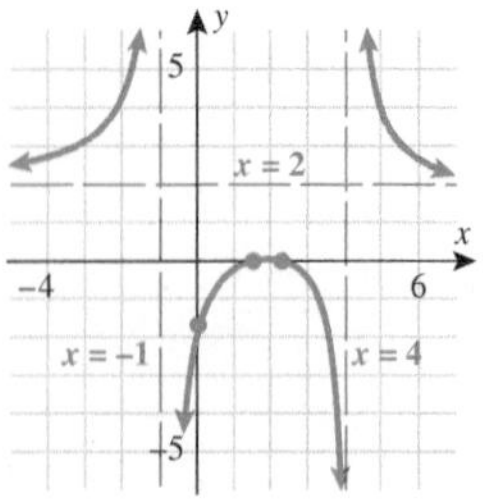

YOUR TURN Graph the rational function $f(x) = \dfrac{2x^2 - 7x + 6}{x^2 - 3x - 4}$. Give equations of the vertical and horizontal asymptotes, and state the intercepts.

EXAMPLE 10 Graphing a Rational Function with a Slant Asymptote

Graph the rational function $f(x) = \dfrac{x^2 - 3x - 4}{x + 2}$.

Solution:

STEP 1 Find the **domain**.

Set the denominator equal to zero. $x + 2 = 0$

Solve for x. $x = -2$

State the domain. $(-\infty, -2)\cup(-2, \infty)$

STEP 2 Find the **intercepts**.

y-intercept: $f(0) = -\dfrac{4}{2} = -2$

x-intercepts: $n(x) = x^2 - 3x - 4 = 0$

Factor. $(x + 1)(x - 4) = 0$

Solve. $x = -1$ and $x = 4$

The intercepts are the points $(0, -2)$, $(-1, 0)$, and $(4, 0)$.

STEP 3 Find any **holes**. $f(x) = \dfrac{(x - 4)(x + 1)}{(x + 2)}$

There are no common factors, so f is in lowest terms.

Since there are no common factors, there are no holes on the graph of f.

STEP 4 Find the **asymptotes**.

Vertical asymptote: $d(x) = x + 2 = 0$

Solve. $x = -2$

Slant asymptote: degree of $n(x)$ − degree of $d(x) = 1$

Divide $n(x)$ by $d(x)$. $f(x) = \dfrac{x^2 - 3x - 4}{x + 2} = x - 5 + \dfrac{6}{x + 2}$

Write the equation of the asymptote. $y = x - 5$

The asymptotes are $x = -2$ and $y = x - 5$.

STEP 5 Find **additional points** on the graph.

x	−6	−5	−3	5	6
f(x)	−12.5	−12	−14	0.86	1.75

STEP 6 **Sketch** the graph; label the intercepts and asymptotes, and complete with a smooth curve between and beyond the vertical asymptote.

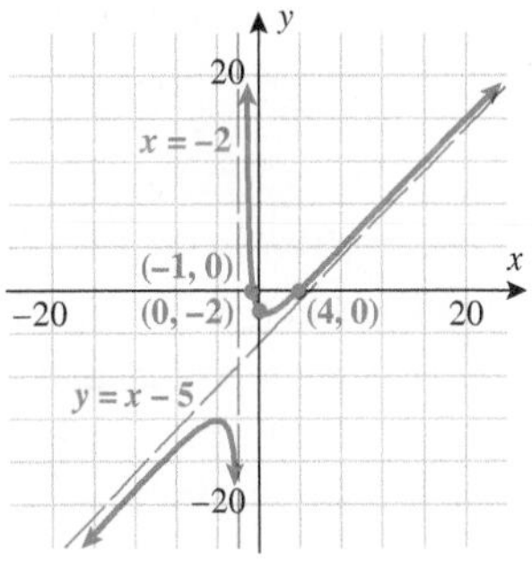

YOUR TURN For the function $f(x) = \dfrac{x^2 + x - 2}{x - 3}$, state the asymptotes (if any exist) and graph the function.

ANSWER

Vertical asymptote: $x = 3$

Slant asymptote: $y = x + 4$

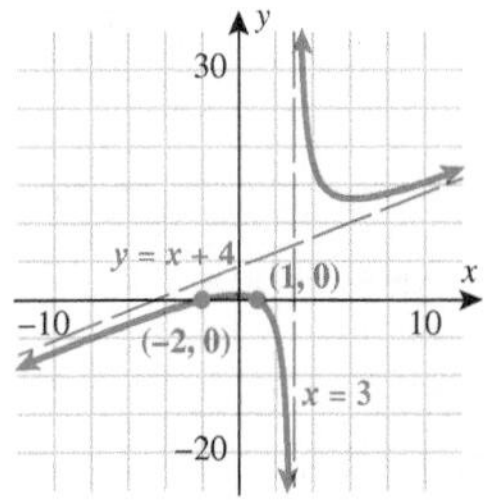

EXAMPLE 11 Graphing a Rational Function with a Hole on the Graph

Graph the rational function $f(x) = \dfrac{x^2 + x - 6}{x^2 - x - 2}$.

Solution:

STEP 1 Find the **domain**.

Set the denominator equal to zero. $x^2 - x - 2 = 0$

Solve for x. $(x - 2)(x + 1) = 0$

$x = -1$ or $x = 2$

State the domain. $(-\infty, -1)\cup(-1, 2)\cup(2, \infty)$

STEP 2 Find the **intercepts**.

y-intercept: $f(0) = \dfrac{-6}{-2} = 3 \quad y = 3$

x-intercepts: $n(x) = x^2 + x - 6 = 0$

$(x + 3)(x - 2) = 0$

$x = -3$ or $x = 2$

The intercepts correspond to the points $\boxed{(0, 3)}$ and $\boxed{(-3, 0)}$. The point $(2, 0)$ appears to be an x-intercept; however, $x = 2$ is not in the domain of the function.

STEP 3 Find any **holes**. $f(x) = \dfrac{(x - 2)(x + 3)}{(x - 2)(x + 1)}$

Since $x - 2$ is a common factor, there is a *hole* on the graph of f at $x = 2$.

Dividing out the common factor generates an equivalent rational function in lowest terms. $R(x) = \dfrac{(x + 3)}{(x + 1)}$

STEP 4 Find the **asymptotes**.

Vertical asymptotes: $x + 1 = 0$

$\boxed{x = -1}$

Horizontal asymptote: $\dfrac{\text{Degree of numerator}}{\text{Degree of denominator}} = \overbrace{\dfrac{2}{2}}^{f} = \overbrace{\dfrac{1}{1}}^{R}$

Since the degree of the numerator equals the degree of the denominator, use the leading coefficients. $\boxed{y = \dfrac{1}{1} = 1}$

STEP 5 Find **additional points** on the graph.

x	-4	-2	$-\frac{1}{2}$	1	3
$f(x)$ or $R(x)$	$\frac{1}{3}$	-1	5	2	$\frac{3}{2}$

STEP 6 **Sketch** the graph; label the intercepts, asymptotes, and additional points; and complete with a smooth curve approaching asymptotes.

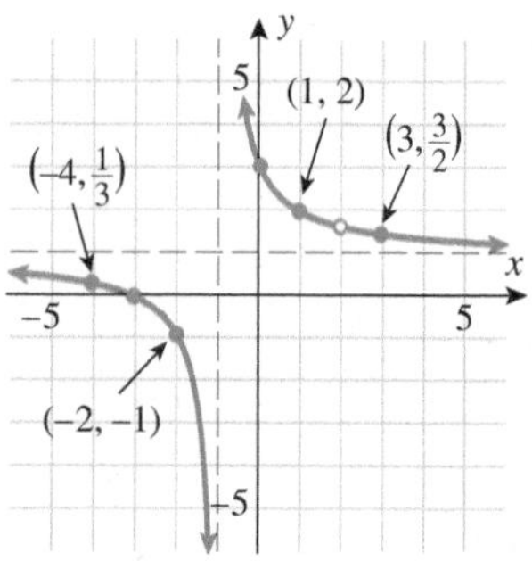

YOUR TURN Graph the rational function $f(x) = \dfrac{x^2 - x - 2}{x^2 + x - 6}$.

[CONCEPT CHECK]

TRUE OR FALSE The only time a hole will exist on the graph of a rational function is when the numerator and the denominator have a common factor.

ANSWER True

ANSWER

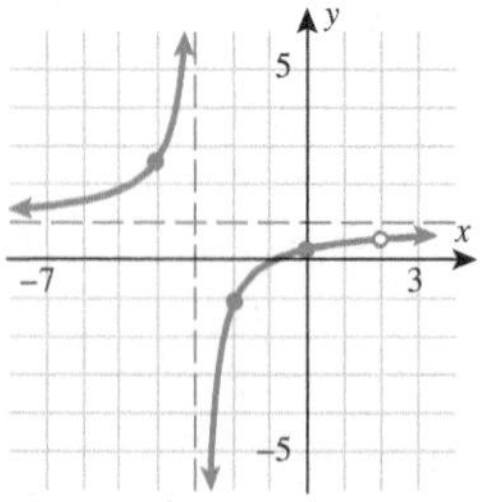

[SECTION 2.6] SUMMARY

In this section, rational functions were discussed.

$$f(x) = \frac{n(x)}{d(x)}$$

- **Domain:** All real numbers except the x-values that make the denominator equal to zero, $d(x) = 0$.
- **Vertical Asymptotes:** Vertical lines, $x = a$, where $d(a) = 0$, after all common factors have been divided out. Vertical asymptotes steer the graph and are never touched.
- **Horizontal Asymptote:** Horizontal line, $y = b$, that steers the graph as $x \to \pm\infty$.
  1. If degree of the numerator < degree of the denominator, then $y = 0$ is a horizontal asymptote.
  2. If degree of the numerator = degree of the denominator, then $y = c$ is a horizontal asymptote, where c is the ratio of the leading coefficients of the numerator and denominator, respectively.
  3. If degree of the numerator > degree of the denominator, then there is no horizontal asymptote.
- **Slant Asymptote:** Slant line, $y = mx + b$, that steers the graph as $x \to \pm\infty$.
  1. If degree of the numerator − degree of the denominator = 1, then there is a slant asymptote.
  2. Divide the numerator by the denominator. The quotient corresponds to the equation of the line (slant asymptote).

Procedure for Graphing Rational Functions

1. Find the domain of the function.
2. Find the intercept(s).
   - y-intercept (does not exist if $x = 0$ is a vertical asymptote)
   - x-intercepts (if any)
3. Find any holes.
   - If $x - a$ is a common factor of the numerator and denominator, then $x = a$ corresponds to a hole on the graph of the rational function if the multiplicity of a in the numerator is greater than or equal to the multiplicity of a in the denominator. The result after the common factor is canceled is an equivalent rational function in lowest terms (no common factor).
4. Find any asymptotes.
   - Vertical asymptotes
   - Horizontal/slant asymptotes
5. Find additional points on the graph.
6. Sketch the graph: Draw the asymptotes, label the intercepts and points, and connect with a smooth curve.

[SECTION 2.6] EXERCISES

• SKILLS

In Exercises 1–8, find the domain of each rational function.

1. $f(x) = \dfrac{x+4}{x^2 + x - 12}$
2. $f(x) = \dfrac{x-1}{x^2 + 2x - 3}$
3. $f(x) = \dfrac{x-2}{x^2 - 4}$
4. $f(x) = \dfrac{x+7}{2(x^2 - 49)}$
5. $f(x) = \dfrac{7x}{x^2 + 16}$
6. $f(x) = -\dfrac{2x}{x^2 + 9}$
7. $f(x) = -\dfrac{3(x^2 + x - 2)}{2(x^2 - x - 6)}$
8. $f(x) = \dfrac{5(x^2 - 2x - 3)}{(x^2 - x - 6)}$

In Exercises 9–16, find all vertical asymptotes and horizontal asymptotes (if there are any).

9. $f(x) = \dfrac{1}{x+2}$
10. $f(x) = \dfrac{1}{5-x}$
11. $f(x) = \dfrac{7x^3 + 1}{x + 5}$
12. $f(x) = \dfrac{2 - x^3}{2x - 7}$
13. $f(x) = \dfrac{6x^5 - 4x^2 + 5}{6x^2 + 5x - 4}$
14. $f(x) = \dfrac{6x^2 + 3x + 1}{3x^2 - 5x - 2}$
15. $f(x) = \dfrac{\frac{1}{3}x^2 + \frac{1}{3}x - \frac{1}{4}}{x^2 + \frac{1}{9}}$
16. $f(x) = \dfrac{\frac{1}{10}\left(x^2 - 2x + \frac{3}{10}\right)}{2x - 1}$

In Exercises 17–22, find the slant asymptote corresponding to the graph of each rational function.

17. $f(x) = \dfrac{x^2 + 10x + 25}{x + 4}$

18. $f(x) = \dfrac{x^2 + 9x + 20}{x - 3}$

19. $f(x) = \dfrac{2x^2 + 14x + 7}{x - 5}$

20. $f(x) = \dfrac{3x^3 + 4x^2 - 6x + 1}{x^2 - x - 30}$

21. $f(x) = \dfrac{8x^4 + 7x^3 + 2x - 5}{2x^3 - x^2 + 3x - 1}$

22. $f(x) = \dfrac{2x^6 + 1}{x^5 - 1}$

In Exercises 23–28, match the function to the graph.

23. $f(x) = \dfrac{3}{x - 4}$

24. $f(x) = \dfrac{3x}{x - 4}$

25. $f(x) = \dfrac{3x^2}{x^2 - 4}$

26. $f(x) = -\dfrac{3x^2}{x^2 + 4}$

27. $f(x) = \dfrac{3x^2}{4 - x^2}$

28. $f(x) = \dfrac{3x^2}{x + 4}$

a.

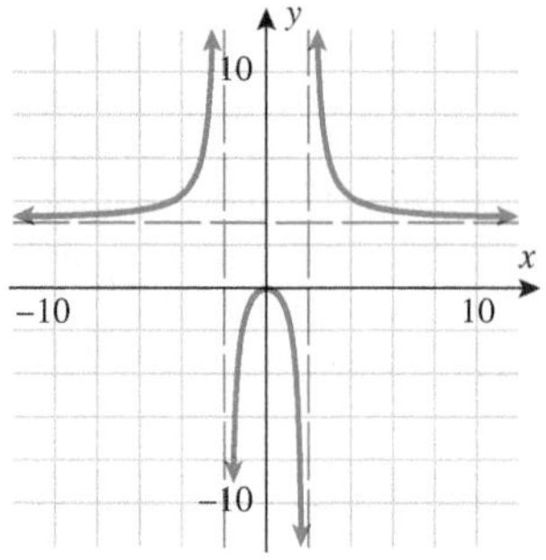

b.

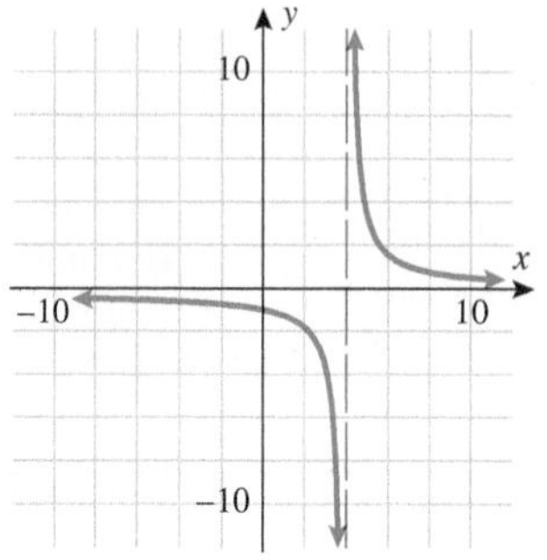

c.

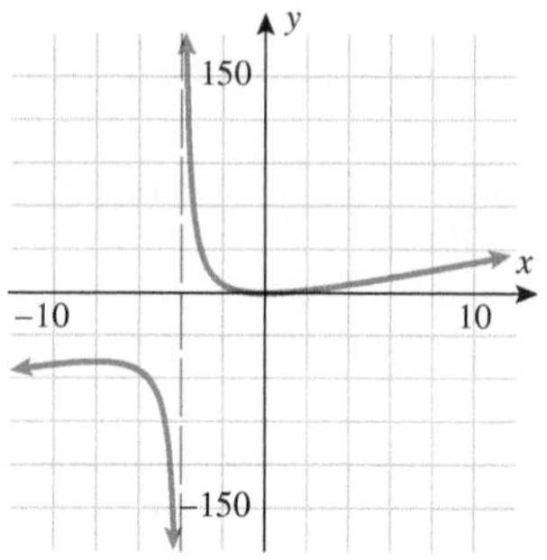

d.

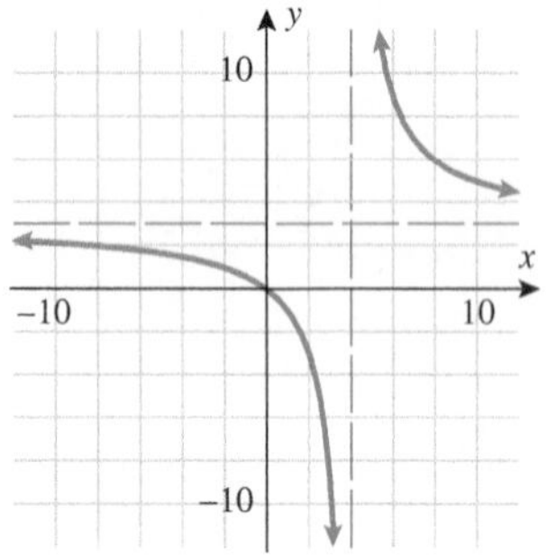

e.

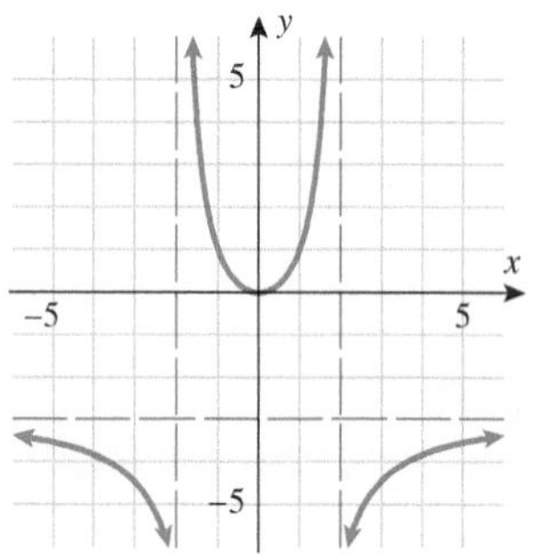

f.

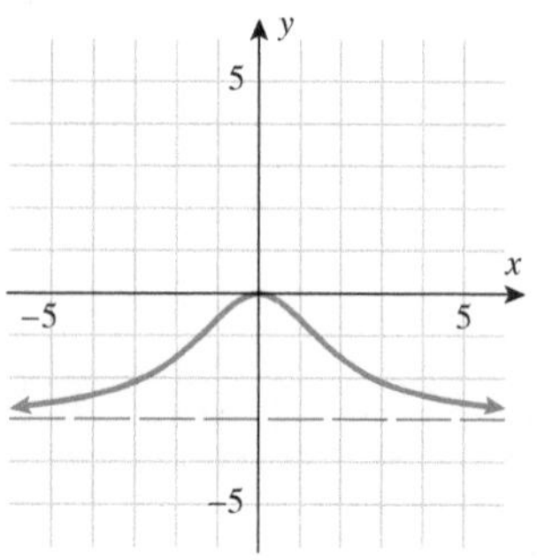

In Exercises 29–56, graph the rational functions. Locate any asymptotes on the graph.

29. $f(x) = \dfrac{2}{x + 1}$

30. $f(x) = \dfrac{4}{x - 2}$

31. $f(x) = \dfrac{2x}{x - 1}$

32. $f(x) = \dfrac{4x}{x + 2}$

33. $f(x) = \dfrac{x - 1}{x}$

34. $f(x) = \dfrac{2 + x}{x - 1}$

35. $f(x) = \dfrac{2(x^2 - 2x - 3)}{x^2 + 2x}$

36. $f(x) = \dfrac{3(x^2 - 1)}{x^2 - 3x}$

37. $f(x) = \dfrac{x^2}{x + 1}$

38. $f(x) = \dfrac{x^2 - 9}{x + 2}$

39. $f(x) = \dfrac{2x^3 - x^2 - x}{x^2 - 4}$

40. $f(x) = \dfrac{3x^3 + 5x^2 - 2x}{x^2 + 4}$

41. $f(x) = \dfrac{x^2 + 1}{x^2 - 1}$

42. $f(x) = \dfrac{1 - x^2}{x^2 + 1}$

43. $f(x) = \dfrac{7x^2}{(2x + 1)^2}$

44. $f(x) = \dfrac{12x^4}{(3x + 1)^4}$

45. $f(x) = \dfrac{1 - 9x^2}{(1 - 4x^2)^3}$

46. $f(x) = \dfrac{25x^2 - 1}{(16x^2 - 1)^2}$

47. $f(x) = 3x + \dfrac{4}{x}$

48. $f(x) = x - \dfrac{4}{x}$

49. $f(x) = \dfrac{(x - 1)^2}{(x^2 - 1)}$

50. $f(x) = \dfrac{(x + 1)^2}{(x^2 - 1)}$

51. $f(x) = \dfrac{(x - 1)(x^2 - 4)}{(x - 2)(x^2 + 1)}$

52. $f(x) = \dfrac{(x - 1)(x^2 - 9)}{(x - 3)(x^2 + 1)}$

53. $f(x) = \dfrac{3x(x - 1)}{x(x^2 - 4)}$

54. $f(x) = \dfrac{-2x(x - 3)}{x(x^2 + 1)}$

55. $f(x) = \dfrac{x^2(x + 5)}{2x(x^2 + 3)}$

56. $f(x) = \dfrac{4x(x - 1)(x + 2)}{x^2(x^2 - 4)}$

In Exercises 57–60, for each graph of the rational function given, determine: (a) all intercepts, (b) all asymptotes, and (c) an equation of the rational function.

57.

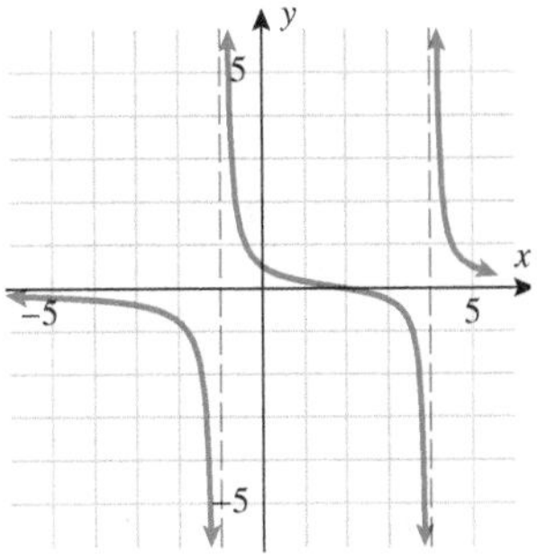

58.

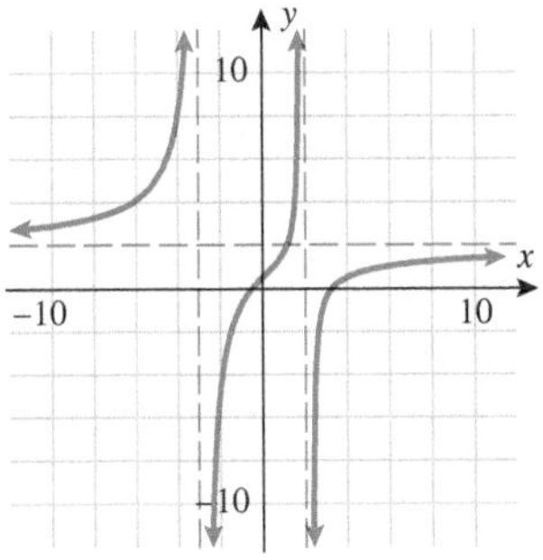

59.

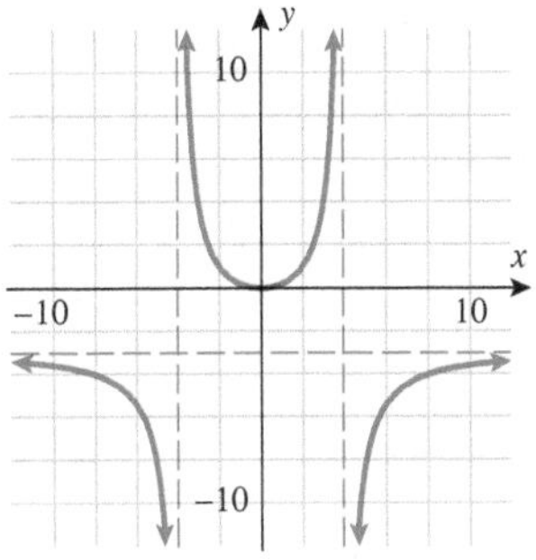

60.

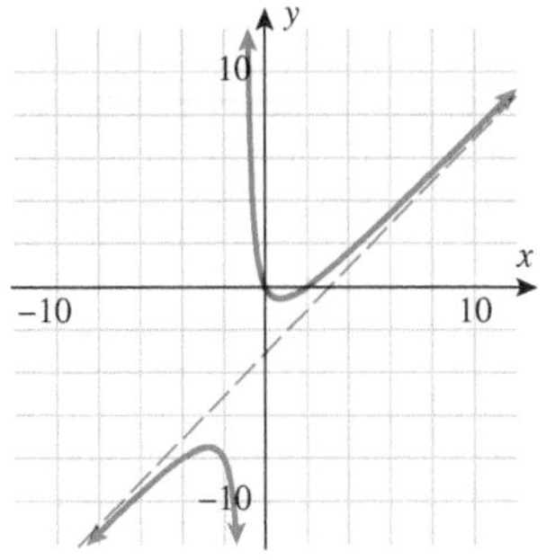

• APPLICATIONS

61. Epidemiology. Suppose the number of individuals infected by a virus can be determined by the formula

$$n(t) = \frac{9500t - 2000}{4 + t}$$

where $t > 0$ is the time in months.

a. Find the number of infected people by the end of the fourth month.
b. After how many months are there 5500 infected people?
c. What happens with the number of infected people if the trend continues?

62. Investment. A financial institution offers to its investors a variable annual interest rate using the formula

$$r(x) = \frac{4x^2}{x^2 + 2x + 5}$$

where x is the amount invested, in thousands of dollars.

a. What is the annual interest rate for an investment of \$8000?
b. What is the annual interest rate for an investment of \$20,000?
c. What is the maximum annual interest rate offered here?

63. Medicine. The concentration C of a particular drug in a person's bloodstream t minutes after injection is given by

$$C(t) = \frac{2t}{t^2 + 100}$$

a. What is the concentration in the bloodstream after 1 minute?
b. What is the concentration in the bloodstream after 1 hour?
c. What is the concentration in the bloodstream after 5 hours?
d. Find the horizontal asymptote of $C(t)$. What do you expect the concentration to be after several days?

64. Medicine. The concentration C of aspirin in the bloodstream t hours after consumption is given by $C(t) = \frac{t}{t^2 + 40}$.

a. What is the concentration in the bloodstream after $\frac{1}{2}$ hour?
b. What is the concentration in the bloodstream after 1 hour?
c. What is the concentration in the bloodstream after 4 hours?
d. Find the horizontal asymptote for $C(t)$. What do you expect the concentration to be after several days?

65. Typing. An administrative assistant is hired after graduating from high school and learns to type on the job. The number of words he can type per minute is given by

$$N(t) = \frac{130t + 260}{t + 5} \qquad t \geq 0$$

where t is the number of months he has been on the job.

a. How many words per minute can he type the day he starts?
b. How many words per minute can he type after 12 months?
c. How many words per minute can he type after 3 years?
d. How many words per minute would you expect him to type if he worked there until he retired?

66. Memorization. A professor teaching a large lecture course tries to learn students' names. The number of names she can remember $N(t)$ increases with each week in the semester t and is given by the rational function

$$N(t) = \frac{600t}{t + 20}$$

How many students' names does she know by the third week in the semester? How many students' names should she know by the end of the semester (16 weeks)? According to this function, what are the most names she can remember?

For Exercises 67 and 68, refer to the following:

The monthly profit function for a product is given by

$$P(x) = -x^3 + 10x^2$$

where x is the number of units sold measured in thousands and P is profit measured in thousands of dollars. The average profit, which represents the profit per thousand units sold, for this product is given by

$$\overline{P}(x) = \frac{-x^3 + 10x^2}{x}$$

where x is units sold measured in thousands and $\overline{P}$ is profit measured in thousands of dollars.

67. **Business.** Find the number of units that must be sold to produce an average profit of \$16,000 per thousand units. Then find the average profit (in dollars per unit) for the number sold.

68. **Business.** Find the number of units that must be sold to produce an average profit of \$25,000 per thousand units. Then find the average profit (in dollars per unit) for the number sold.

For Exercises 69 and 70, refer to the following:

Some medications, such as Synthroid, are prescribed as a maintenance drug because they are taken regularly for an ongoing condition, such as hypothyroidism. Maintenance drugs function by maintaining a therapeutic drug level in the bloodstream over time. The concentration of a maintenance drug over a 24-hour period is modeled by the function

$$C(t) = \frac{22(t-1)}{t^2+1} + 24$$

where t is time in hours after the dose was administered and C is the concentration of the drug in the bloodstream measured in μg/mL. This medication is designed to maintain a consistent concentration in the bloodstream of approximately 25 μg/mL. *Note:* This drug will become inert; that is, the concentration will drop to 0 μg/mL, during the 25th hour after taking the medication.

69. **Health/Medicine.** Find the concentration of the drug, to the nearest tenth of μg/mL, in the bloodstream 15 hours after the dose is administered. Is this the only time this concentration of the drug is found in the bloodstream? At what other times is this concentration reached? Round to the nearest hour. Discuss the significance of this answer.

70. **Health/Medicine.** Find the time, after the first hour and a half, at which the concentration of the drug in the bloodstream has dropped to 25 μg/mL. Find the concentration of the drug 24 hours after taking a dose to the nearest tenth of a μg/mL. Discuss the importance of taking the medication every 24 hours rather than every day.

• CATCH THE MISTAKE

In Exercises 71 and 72, explain the mistake that is made.

71. Determine the vertical asymptotes of the function $f(x) = \dfrac{x-1}{x^2-1}$.

Solution:

Set the denominator equal to zero. $x^2 - 1 = 0$

Solve for x. $x = \pm 1$

The vertical asymptotes are $x = -1$ and $x = 1$.

The following is a correct graph of the function:

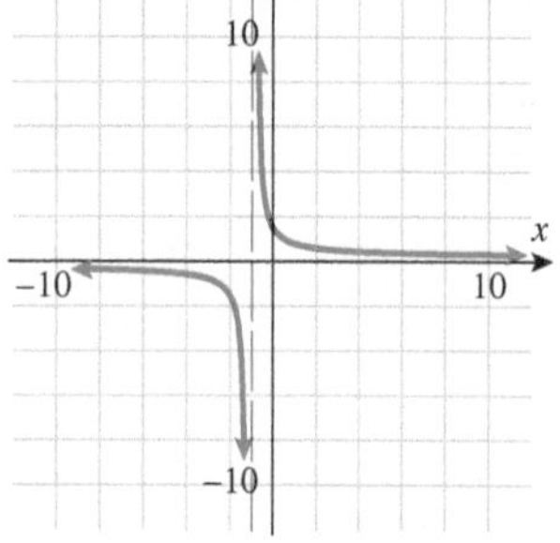

Note that only $x = -1$ is an asymptote. What went wrong?

72. Determine whether a horizontal or a slant asymptote exists for the function $f(x) = \dfrac{x^2 + 2x - 1}{3x^3 - 2x^2 - 1}$. If one does, find it.

Solution:

STEP 1: The degree of the denominator is exactly one more than the degree of the numerator, so there is a slant asymptote.

STEP 2: Divide.

$$\begin{array}{r} 3x - 8 \\ x^2+2x-1\,\overline{)\,3x^3 - 2x^2 + 0x - 1} \\ 3x^3 + 6x^2 - 3x \\ \hline -8x^2 + 3x - 1 \\ 8x^2 - 16x + 8 \\ \hline 19x - 9 \end{array}$$

The slant asymptote is $y = 3x - 8$.

The following is the correct graph of the function.

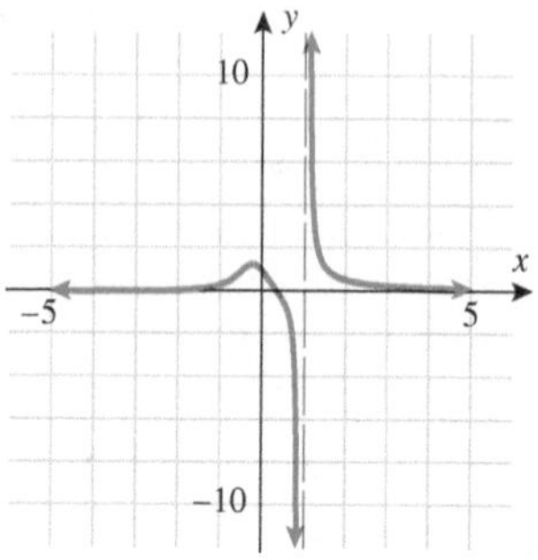

Note that $y = 3x - 8$ is not an asymptote. What went wrong?

• CONCEPTUAL

For Exercises 73–76, determine whether each statement is true or false.

73. A rational function can have either a horizontal asymptote or an oblique asymptote, but not both.

74. A rational function can have at most one vertical asymptote.

75. A rational function can cross a vertical asymptote.

76. A rational function can cross a horizontal or an oblique asymptote.

77. Determine the asymptotes of the rational function

$$f(x) = \frac{(x-a)(x+b)}{(x-c)(x+d)}.$$

78. Determine the asymptotes of the rational function

$$f(x) = \frac{3x^2+b^2}{x^2+a^2}.$$

• CHALLENGE

79. Write a rational function that has vertical asymptotes at $x = -3$ and $x = 1$ and a horizontal asymptote at $y = 4$.

80. Write a rational function that has no vertical asymptotes, approaches the x-axis as a horizontal asymptote, and has an x-intercept of $(3, 0)$.

81. Write a rational function that has no vertical asymptotes and oblique asymptote $y = x$, y-intercept $(0, 1)$, and x-intercept $(-1, 0)$. Round your answers to two decimal places.

82. Write a rational function that has vertical asymptotes at $x = -3$ and $x = 1$ and oblique asymptote $y = 3x$, y-intercept $(0, 2)$, and x-intercept $(2, 0)$. Round your answers to two decimal places.

• PREVIEW TO CALCULUS

In calculus the integral of a rational function f on an interval $[a, b]$ might not exist if f has a vertical asymptote in $[a, b]$.

In Exercises 83–86, find the vertical asymptotes of each rational function.

83. $f(x) = \dfrac{x-1}{x^3-2x^2-13x-10}$ $[0, 3]$

84. $f(x) = \dfrac{x^2+x+2}{x^3+2x^2-25x-50}$ $[-3, 2]$

85. $f(x) = \dfrac{5x+2}{6x^2-x-2}$ $[-2, 0]$

86. $f(x) = \dfrac{6x-2x^2}{x^3+x}$ $[-1, 1]$

[CHAPTER 2 REVIEW]

SECTION	CONCEPT	KEY IDEAS/FORMULAS
2.1	**Quadratic functions**	
	Graphs of quadratic functions: parabolas	**Graphing quadratic functions in standard form** $f(x) = a(x - h)^2 + k$ ■ Vertex: (h, k) ■ Opens up: $a > 0$ ■ Opens down: $a < 0$ **Graphing quadratic functions in general form** $f(x) = ax^2 + bx + c$, vertex is $(h, k) = \left(-\frac{b}{2a}, f\left(-\frac{b}{2a}\right)\right)$
	Finding the equation of a parabola	Applications
2.2	**Polynomial functions of higher degree**	
	Identifying polynomial functions	$P(x) = a_n x^n + a_{n-1}x^{n-1} + \cdots + a_2x^2 + a_1x + a_0$ is a polynomial of degree n.
	Graphing polynomial functions using transformations of power functions	$y = x^n$ behave similar to ■ $y = x^2$, when n is even. ■ $y = x^3$, when n is odd.
	Real zeros of a polynomial function	$P(x) = (x - a)(x - b)^n = 0$ ■ a is a zero of multiplicity 1. ■ b is a zero of multiplicity n.
	Graphing general polynomial functions	Intercepts; zeros and multiplicities; end behavior
2.3	**Dividing polynomials**	Use zero placeholders for missing terms.
	Long division of polynomials	Can be used for all polynomial division.
	Synthetic division of polynomials	Can be used only when dividing by $(x \pm a)$.
2.4	**The real zeros of a polynomial function**	$P(x) = a_n x^n + a_{n-1}x^{n-1} + \cdots + a_2x^2 + a_1x + a_0$ If $P(c) = 0$, then c is a zero of $P(x)$.
	The remainder theorem and the factor theorem	If $P(x)$ is divided by $x - a$, then the remainder r is $r = P(a)$.
	The rational zero theorem and Descartes' rule of signs	Possible zeros $= \pm\frac{\text{Factors of } a_0}{\text{Factors of } a_n}$ Number of positive or negative real zeros is related to the number of sign variations in $P(x)$ or $P(-x)$.

SECTION	CONCEPT	KEY IDEAS/FORMULAS
	Factoring polynomials	1. List possible rational zeros (rational zero theorem). 2. List possible combinations of positive and negative real zeros (Descartes' rule of signs). 3. Test possible values until a zero is found. 4. Once a real zero is found, use synthetic division. Then repeat testing on the quotient until linear and/or irreducible quadratic factors are reached. 5. If there is a real zero but all possible rational roots have failed, then approximate the real zero using the intermediate value theorem/bisection method.
	The intermediate value theorem	The intermediate value theorem and the bisection method are used to approximate irrational zeros.
	Graphing polynomial functions	1. Find the intercepts. 2. Determine end behavior. 3. Find additional points. 4. Sketch a smooth curve.
2.5	**Complex zeros: The fundamental theorem of algebra**	$P(x) = a_n x^n + a_{n-1}x^{n-1} + \cdots + a_2 x^2 + a_1 x + a_0$ $P(x) = \underbrace{(x - c_1)(x - c_2)\cdots(x - c_n)}_{n \text{ factors}}$ where the c's represent complex (not necessarily distinct) zeros.
	Complex zeros	**The fundamental theorem of algebra** $P(x)$ of degree n has at least one zero and at most n zeros. $(n > 0)$
	Factoring polynomials	If $a + bi$ is a zero of $P(x)$, then $a - bi$ is also a zero. The polynomial can be written as a product of linear factors, not necessarily distinct.
2.6	**Rational functions**	$f(x) = \dfrac{n(x)}{d(x)} \qquad d(x) \neq 0$
	Domain of rational functions	**Domain:** All real numbers except x-values that make the denominator equal to zero; that is, $d(x) = 0$. A rational function $f(x) = \dfrac{n(x)}{d(x)}$ is said to be in *lowest terms* if $n(x)$ and $d(x)$ have no common factors.
	Vertical, horizontal, and slant asymptotes	A rational function that has a common factor $x - a$ in both the numerator and the denominator has a hole at $x = a$ on its graph if the multiplicity of a in the numerator is greater than or equal to the multiplicity of a in the denominator. *Vertical Asymptotes* A rational function in lowest terms has a vertical asymptote corresponding to any x-values that make the denominator equal to zero.

CHAPTER 2 REVIEW

SECTION	CONCEPT	KEY IDEAS/FORMULAS
		Horizontal Asymptote ■ $y = 0$ if degree of $n(x) <$ degree of $d(x)$. ■ No horizontal asymptote if degree of $n(x) >$ degree of $d(x)$. ■ $y = \dfrac{\text{Leading coefficient of } n(x)}{\text{Leading coefficient of } d(x)}$ if degree of $n(x) =$ degree of $d(x)$. *Slant Asymptote* If degree of $n(x) -$ degree of $d(x) = 1$. Divide $n(x)$ by $d(x)$ and the quotient determines the slant asymptote; that is, $y =$ quotient.
	Graphing rational functions	1. Find the domain of the function. 2. Find the intercept(s). 3. Find any holes. 4. Find any asymptotes. 5. Find additional points on the graph. 6. *Sketch the graph:* Draw the asymptotes, label the intercepts and points, and connect with a smooth curve.

[CHAPTER 2 REVIEW EXERCISES]

2.1 Quadratic Functions

Match the quadratic function with its graph.

1. $f(x) = -2(x + 6)^2 + 3$
2. $f(x) = \frac{1}{4}(x - 4)^2 + 2$
3. $f(x) = x^2 + x - 6$
4. $f(x) = -3x^2 - 10x + 8$

a.

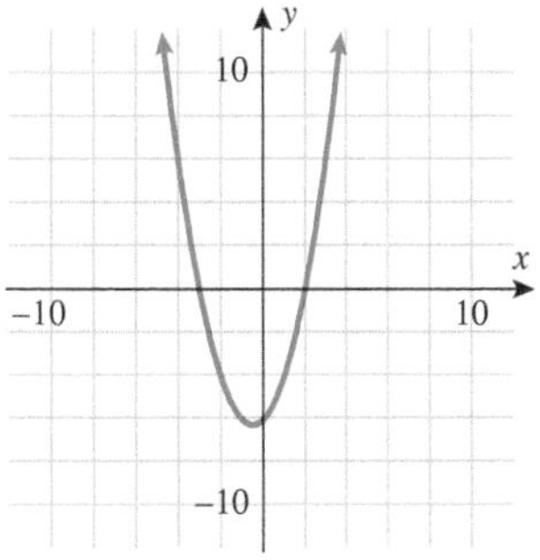

b.

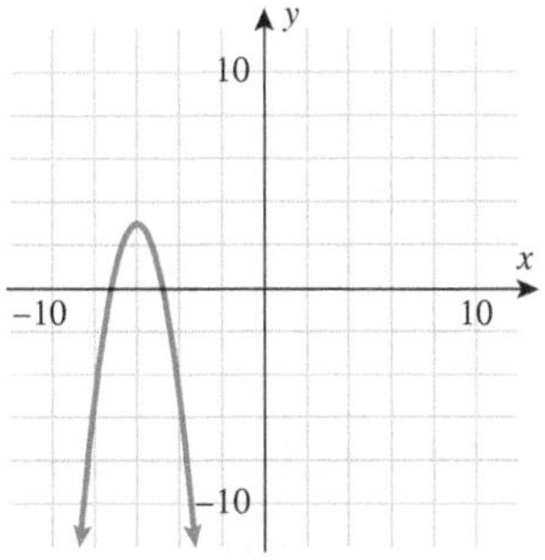

c.

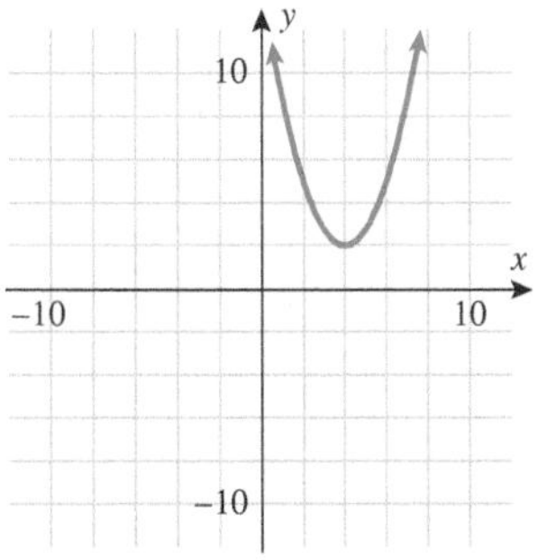

d.

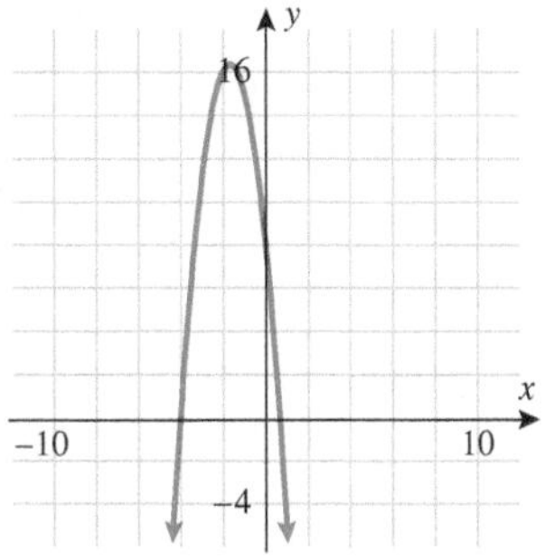

Graph the quadratic function given in standard form.

5. $f(x) = -(x - 7)^2 + 4$
6. $f(x) = (x + 3)^2 - 5$
7. $f(x) = -\frac{1}{2}(x - \frac{1}{3})^2 + \frac{2}{5}$
8. $f(x) = 0.6(x - 0.75)^2 + 0.5$

Rewrite the quadratic function in standard form by completing the square.

9. $f(x) = x^2 - 3x - 10$
10. $f(x) = x^2 - 2x - 24$
11. $f(x) = 4x^2 + 8x - 7$
12. $f(x) = -\frac{1}{4}x^2 + 2x - 4$

Graph the quadratic function given in general form.

13. $f(x) = x^2 - 3x + 5$
14. $f(x) = -x^2 + 4x + 2$
15. $f(x) = -4x^2 + 2x + 3$
16. $f(x) = -0.75x^2 + 2.5$

Find the vertex of the parabola associated with each quadratic function.

17. $f(x) = 13x^2 - 5x + 12$
18. $f(x) = \frac{2}{5}x^2 - 4x + 3$
19. $f(x) = -0.45x^2 - 0.12x + 3.6$
20. $f(x) = -\frac{3}{4}x^2 + \frac{2}{5}x + 4$

Find the quadratic function that has the given vertex and goes through the given point.

21. vertex: $(-2, 3)$ point: $(1, 4)$
22. vertex: $(4, 7)$ point: $(-3, 1)$
23. vertex: $(2.7, 3.4)$ point: $(3.2, 4.8)$
24. vertex: $\left(-\frac{5}{2}, \frac{7}{4}\right)$ point: $\left(\frac{1}{2}, \frac{3}{5}\right)$

Applications

25. **Profit.** The revenue and the cost of a local business are given below as functions of the number of units x in thousands produced and sold. Use the cost and the revenue to answer the questions that follow.

$$C(x) = \frac{1}{3}x + 2 \quad \text{and} \quad R(x) = -2x^2 + 12x - 12$$

   a. Determine the profit function.
   b. State the break-even points.
   c. Graph the profit function.
   d. What is the range of units to make and sell that will correspond to a profit?

26. **Geometry.** Given that the length of a rectangle is $2x - 4$ and the width is $x + 7$, find the area of the rectangle. What dimensions correspond to the largest area?

27. **Geometry.** A triangle has a base of $x + 2$ units and a height of $4 - x$ units. Determine the area of the triangle. What dimensions correspond to the largest area?

28. **Geometry.** A person standing at a ridge in the Grand Canyon throws a penny upward and toward the pit of the canyon. The height of the penny is given by the function

$$h(t) = -12t^2 + 80t$$

   a. What is the maximum height that the penny will reach?
   b. How many seconds will it take the penny to hit the ground below?

2.2 Polynomial Functions of Higher Degree

Determine which functions are polynomials, and for those, state their degree.

29. $f(x) = x^6 - 2x^5 + 3x^2 + 9x - 42$
30. $f(x) = (3x - 4)^3(x + 6)^2$
31. $f(x) = 3x^4 - x^3 + x^2 + \sqrt[4]{x} + 5$
32. $f(x) = 5x^3 - 2x^2 + \frac{4x}{7} - 3$

Match the polynomial function with its graph.

33. $f(x) = 2x - 5$
34. $f(x) = -3x^2 + x - 4$
35. $f(x) = x^4 - 2x^3 + x^2 - 6$
36. $f(x) = x^7 - x^5 + 3x^4 + 3x + 7$

a.

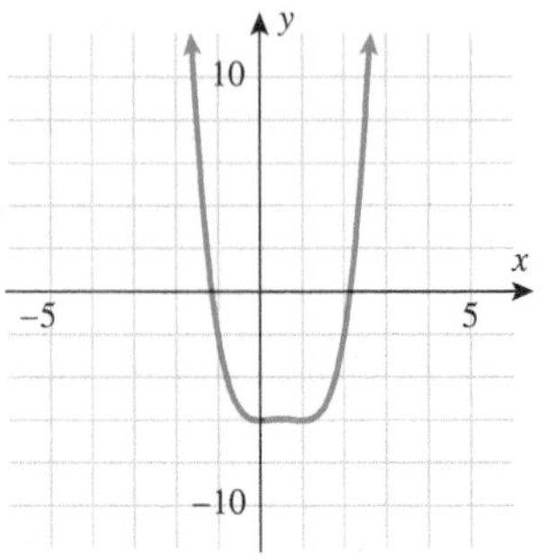

b.

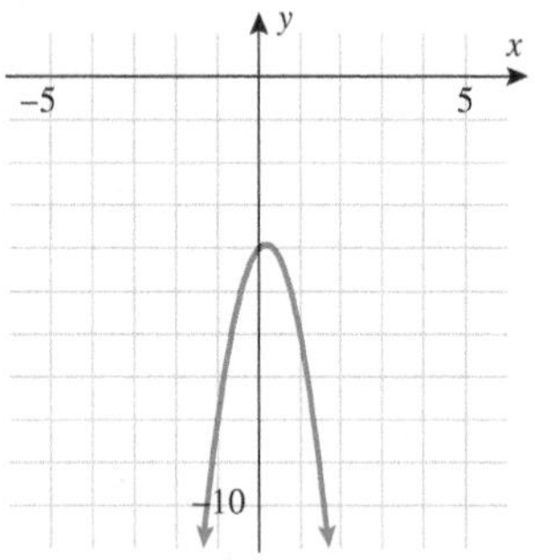

c.

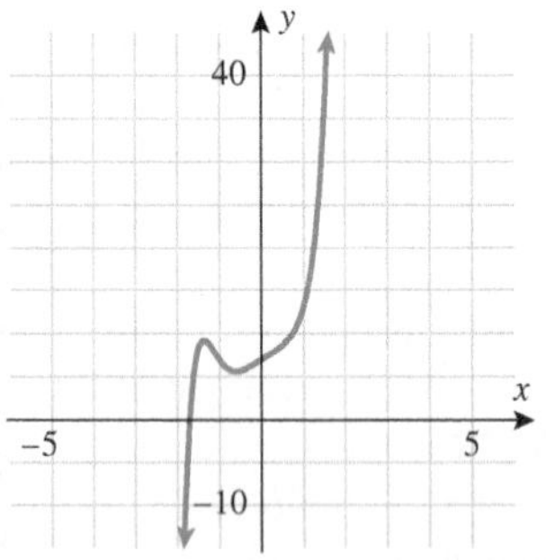

d.

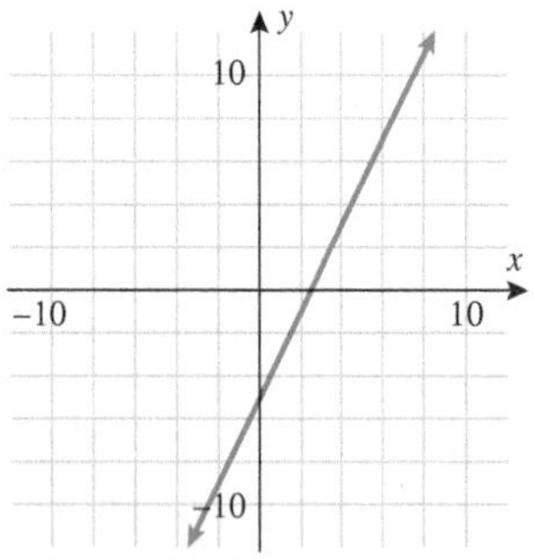

Graph each function by transforming a power function $y = x^n$.

37. $f(x) = -x^7$
38. $f(x) = (x - 3)^3$
39. $f(x) = x^4 - 2$
40. $f(x) = -6 - (x + 7)^5$

Find all the real zeros of each polynomial function, and state their multiplicities.

41. $f(x) = 3(x + 4)^2(x - 6)^5$
42. $f(x) = 7x(2x - 4)^3(x + 5)$
43. $f(x) = x^5 - 13x^3 + 36x$
44. $f(x) = 4.2x^4 - 2.6x^2$

Find a polynomial of minimum degree that has the given zeros.

45. $-3, 0, 4$
46. $2, 4, 6, -8$
47. $-\frac{2}{5}, \frac{3}{4}, 0$
48. $2 - \sqrt{5}, 2 + \sqrt{5}$
49. -2 (multiplicity of 2), 3 (multiplicity of 2)
50. 3 (multiplicity of 2), -1 (multiplicity of 2), 0 (multiplicity of 3)

For each polynomial function given: (a) list each real zero and its multiplicity; (b) determine whether the graph touches or crosses at each x-intercept; (c) find the y-intercept and a few points on the graph; (d) determine the end behavior; and (e) sketch the graph.

51. $f(x) = x^2 - 5x - 14$
52. $f(x) = -(x - 5)^5$
53. $f(x) = 6x^7 + 3x^5 - x^2 + x - 4$
54. $f(x) = -x^4(3x + 6)^3(x - 7)^3$

Applications

55. **Salary.** Tiffany has started tutoring students x hours per week. The tutoring job corresponds to the following additional income:

$$f(x) = (x - 1)(x - 3)(x - 7)$$

   a. Graph the polynomial function.
   b. Give any real zeros that occur.
   c. How many hours of tutoring are financially beneficial to Tiffany?

56. **Profit.** The following function is the profit for Walt Disney World, where $P(x)$ represents profit in millions of dollars and x represents the month ($x = 1$ corresponds to January):

$$P(x) = 3(x - 2)^2(x - 5)^2(x - 10)^2 \quad 1 \leq x \leq 12$$

Graph the polynomial. When are the peak seasons?

2.3 Dividing Polynomials

Divide the polynomials with long division. If you choose to use a calculator, do not round off. Keep the exact values instead. Express the answer in the form $Q(x) = ?,\ r(x) = ?$.

57. $(x^2 + 2x - 6) \div (x - 2)$
58. $(2x^2 - 5x - 1) \div (2x - 3)$
59. $(4x^4 - 16x^3 + x - 9 + 12x^2) \div (2x - 4)$
60. $(6x^2 + 2x^3 - 4x^4 + 2 - x) \div (2x^2 + x - 4)$

Use synthetic division to divide the polynomial by the linear factor. Indicate the quotient $Q(x)$ and the remainder $r(x)$.

61. $(x^4 + 4x^3 + 5x^2 - 2x - 8) \div (x + 2)$
62. $(x^3 - 10x + 3) \div (2 + x)$
63. $(x^6 - 64) \div (x + 8)$
64. $(2x^5 + 4x^4 - 2x^3 + 7x + 5) \div (x - \frac{3}{4})$

Divide the polynomials with either long division or synthetic division.

65. $(5x^3 + 8x^2 - 22x + 1) \div (5x^2 - 7x - 3)$
66. $(x^4 + 2x^3 - 5x^2 + 4x + 2) \div (x - 3)$
67. $(x^3 - 4x^2 + 2x - 8) \div (x + 1)$
68. $(x^3 - 5x^2 + 4x - 20) \div (x^2 + 4)$

Applications

69. **Geometry.** The area of a rectangle is given by the polynomial $6x^4 - 8x^3 - 10x^2 + 12x - 16$. If the width is $2x - 4$, what is the length of the rectangle?

70. **Volume.** A 10 inch by 15 inch rectangular piece of cardboard is used to make a box. Square pieces x inches on a side are cut out from the corners of the cardboard, and then the sides are folded up. Find the volume of the box.

2.4 The Real Zeros of a Polynomial Function

Find the following values by applying synthetic division. Check by substituting the value into the function.

$$f(x) = 6x^5 + x^4 - 7x^2 + x - 1 \qquad g(x) = x^3 + 2x^2 - 3$$

71. $f(-2)$
72. $f(1)$
73. $g(1)$
74. $g(-1)$

Determine whether the number given is a zero of the polynomial.

75. -3, $P(x) = x^3 - 5x^2 + 4x + 2$
76. 2 and -2, $P(x) = x^4 - 16$
77. 1, $P(x) = 2x^4 - 2x$
78. 4, $P(x) = x^4 - 2x^3 - 8x$

Given a zero of the polynomial, determine all other real zeros, and write the polynomial in terms of a product of linear and/or irreducible factors.

Polynomial	Zero
79. $P(x) = x^4 - 6x^3 + 32x$	-2
80. $P(x) = x^3 - 7x^2 + 36$	3
81. $P(x) = x^5 - x^4 - 8x^3 + 12x^2$	0
82. $P(x) = x^4 - 32x^2 - 144$	6

Use Descartes' rule of signs to determine the possible number of positive real zeros and negative real zeros.

83. $P(x) = x^4 + 3x^3 - 16$
84. $P(x) = x^5 + 6x^3 - 4x - 2$
85. $P(x) = x^9 - 2x^7 + x^4 - 3x^3 + 2x - 1$
86. $P(x) = 2x^5 - 4x^3 + 2x^2 - 7$

Use the rational zero theorem to list the possible rational zeros.

87. $P(x) = x^3 - 2x^2 + 4x + 6$
88. $P(x) = x^5 - 4x^3 + 2x^2 - 4x - 8$
89. $P(x) = 2x^4 + 2x^3 - 36x^2 - 32x + 64$
90. $P(x) = -4x^5 - 5x^3 + 4x + 2$

List the possible rational zeros, and test to determine all rational zeros.

91. $P(x) = 2x^3 - 5x^2 + 1$
92. $P(x) = 12x^3 + 8x^2 - 13x + 3$
93. $P(x) = x^4 - 5x^3 + 20x - 16$
94. $P(x) = 24x^4 - 4x^3 - 10x^2 + 3x - 2$

For each polynomial: (a) use Descartes' rule of signs to determine the possible combinations of positive real zeros and negative real zeros; (b) use the rational zero test to determine possible rational zeros; (c) determine, if possible, the smallest value in the list of possible rational zeros for $P(x)$ that serves as a lower bound for all real zeros; (d) test for rational zeros; (e) factor as a product of linear and/or irreducible quadratic factors; and (f) graph the polynomial function.

95. $P(x) = x^3 + 3x - 5$
96. $P(x) = x^3 + 3x^2 - 6x - 8$
97. $P(x) = x^3 - 9x^2 + 20x - 12$
98. $P(x) = x^4 - x^3 - 7x^2 + x + 6$
99. $P(x) = x^4 - 5x^3 - 10x^2 + 20x + 24$
100. $P(x) = x^5 - 3x^3 - 6x^2 + 8x$

2.5 Complex Zeros: The Fundamental Theorem of Algebra

Find all zeros. Factor the polynomial as a product of linear factors.

101. $P(x) = x^2 + 25$
102. $P(x) = x^2 + 16$
103. $P(x) = x^2 - 2x + 5$
104. $P(x) = x^2 + 4x + 5$

A polynomial function is described. Find all remaining zeros.

105. Degree: 4 Zeros: $-2i$, $3 + i$
106. Degree: 4 Zeros: $3i$, $2 - i$
107. Degree: 6 Zeros: i, $2 - i$ (multiplicity 2)
108. Degree: 6 Zeros: $2i$, $1 - i$ (multiplicity 2)

Given a zero of the polynomial, determine all other zeros (real and complex) and write the polynomial in terms of a product of linear factors.

Polynomial	Zero
109. $P(x) = x^4 - 3x^3 - 3x^2 - 3x - 4$	i
110. $P(x) = x^4 - 4x^3 + x^2 + 16x - 20$	$2 - i$
111. $P(x) = x^4 - 2x^3 + 11x^2 - 18x + 18$	$-3i$
112. $P(x) = x^4 - 5x^2 + 10x - 6$	$1 + i$

Factor each polynomial as a product of linear factors.

113. $P(x) = x^4 - 81$
114. $P(x) = x^3 - 6x^2 + 12x$
115. $P(x) = x^3 - x^2 + 4x - 4$
116. $P(x) = x^4 - 5x^3 + 12x^2 - 2x - 20$

2.6 Rational Functions

Determine the vertical, horizontal, or slant asymptotes (if they exist) for the following rational functions.

117. $f(x) = \dfrac{7 - x}{x + 2}$
118. $f(x) = \dfrac{2 - x^2}{(x - 1)^3}$
119. $f(x) = \dfrac{4x^2}{x + 1}$
120. $f(x) = \dfrac{3x^2}{x^2 + 9}$
121. $f(x) = \dfrac{2x^2 - 3x + 1}{x^2 + 4}$
122. $f(x) = \dfrac{-2x^2 + 3x + 5}{x + 5}$

Graph the rational functions.

123. $f(x) = -\dfrac{2}{x - 3}$
124. $f(x) = \dfrac{5}{x + 1}$
125. $f(x) = \dfrac{x^2}{x^2 + 4}$
126. $f(x) = \dfrac{x^2 - 36}{x^2 + 25}$
127. $f(x) = \dfrac{x^2 - 49}{x + 7}$
128. $f(x) = \dfrac{2x^2 - 3x - 2}{2x^2 - 5x - 3}$

[CHAPTER 2 PRACTICE TEST]

1. Graph the quadratic function $f(x) = -(x - 4)^2 + 1$.
2. Write the quadratic function in standard form $f(x) = -x^2 + 4x - 1$.
3. Find the vertex of the parabola $f(x) = -\frac{1}{2}x^2 + 3x - 4$.
4. Find a quadratic function whose graph has a vertex at $(-3, -1)$ and whose graph passes through the point $(-4, 1)$.
5. Find a sixth-degree polynomial function with the given zeros: 2 of multiplicity 3; 1 of multiplicity 2; 0 of multiplicity 1
6. For the polynomial function $f(x) = x^4 + 6x^3 - 7x$:
   a. List each real zero and its multiplicity.
   b. Determine whether the graph touches or crosses at each x-intercept.
   c. Find the y-intercept and a few points on the graph.
   d. Determine the end behavior.
   e. Sketch the graph.
7. Divide $-4x^4 + 2x^3 - 7x^2 + 5x - 2$ by $2x^2 - 3x + 1$.
8. Divide $17x^5 - 4x^3 + 2x - 10$ by $x + 2$.
9. Is $x - 3$ a factor of $x^4 + x^3 - 13x^2 - x + 12$?
10. Determine whether -1 is a zero of $P(x) = x^{21} - 2x^{18} + 5x^{12} + 7x^3 + 3x^2 + 2$.
11. Given that $x - 7$ is a factor of $P(x) = x^3 - 6x^2 - 9x + 14$, factor the polynomial in terms of linear factors.
12. Given that $3i$ is a zero of $P(x) = x^4 - 3x^3 + 19x^2 - 27x + 90$, find all other zeros.
13. Can a polynomial have zeros that are not x-intercepts? Explain.
14. Apply Descartes' rule of signs to determine the possible combinations of positive real zeros, negative real zeros, and complex zeros of $P(x) = 3x^5 + 2x^4 - 3x^3 + 2x^2 - x + 1$.
15. From the rational zero test, list all possible rational zeros of $P(x) = 3x^4 - 7x^2 + 3x + 12$.

In Exercises 16–18, determine all zeros of the polynomial function, and graph it.

16. $P(x) = -x^3 + 4x$
17. $P(x) = 2x^3 - 3x^2 + 8x - 12$
18. $P(x) = x^4 - 6x^3 + 10x^2 - 6x + 9$
19. **Sports.** A football player shows up in August at 300 pounds. After 2 weeks of practice in the hot sun, he is down to 285 pounds. Ten weeks into the season he is up to 315 pounds because of weight training. In the spring he does not work out, and he is back to 300 pounds by the next August. Plot these points on a graph. What degree polynomial could this be?
20. **Profit.** The profit of a company is governed by the polynomial $P(x) = x^3 - 13x^2 + 47x - 35$, where x is the number of units sold in thousands. How many units does the company have to sell to break even?
21. **Interest Rate.** The interest rate for a 30-year fixed mortgage fluctuates with the economy. In 1970 the mortgage interest rate was 8%, and in 1988 it peaked at 13%. In 2002 it dipped down to 4%, and in 2005 it was up to 6%. What is the lowest degree polynomial that can represent this function?

In Exercises 22–25, determine (if any) the:

a. x- and y-intercepts
b. vertical asymptotes
c. horizontal asymptotes
d. slant asymptotes
e. graph

22. $f(x) = \dfrac{2x - 9}{x + 3}$
23. $g(x) = \dfrac{x}{x^2 - 4}$
24. $h(x) = \dfrac{3x^3 - 3}{x^2 - 4}$
25. $F(x) = \dfrac{x - 3}{x^2 - 2x - 8}$
26. **Food.** After a sugary snack, the glucose level of the average body almost doubles. The percentage increase in glucose level y can be approximated by the rational function $y = \dfrac{25x}{x^2 + 50}$, where x represents the number of minutes after eating the snack. Graph the function.

PRACTICE TEST

[CHAPTERS 1–2 CUMULATIVE TEST]

1. If $f(x) = 4x - \dfrac{1}{\sqrt{x+2}}$, find $f(2)$, $f(-1)$, $f(1+h)$, and $f(-x)$.
2. If $f(x) = (x-1)^4 - \sqrt{2x+3}$, find $f(1)$, $f(3)$, and $f(x+h)$.
3. If $f(x) = \dfrac{3x-5}{2-x-x^2}$, find $f(-3)$, $f(0)$, $f(1)$, and $f(4)$.
4. If $f(x) = 4x^3 - 3x^2 + 5$, evaluate the difference quotient $\dfrac{f(x+h)-f(x)}{h}$.
5. If $f(x) = \sqrt{x} - \dfrac{1}{x^2}$, evaluate the difference quotient $\dfrac{f(x+h)-f(x)}{h}$.
6. If $f(x) = \begin{cases} 0 & x < 0 \\ 3x + x^2 & 0 \le x \le 4 \\ |2x - x^3| & x > 4 \end{cases}$

   find $f(-5)$, $f(0)$, $f(3)$, $f(4)$, and $f(5)$.

In Exercises 7 and 8: (a) Graph the piecewise-defined functions. (b) State the domain and range in interval notation. (c) Determine the intervals where the function is increasing, decreasing, or constant.

7. $f(x) = \begin{cases} |6 - 2x| & x \le 8 \\ 10 & 8 < x < 10 \\ \dfrac{1}{x-10} & x > 10 \end{cases}$
8. $f(x) = \begin{cases} (x+5)^2 - 6 & x < -2 \\ \sqrt{x-1} + 3 & -2 \le x < 10 \\ 26 - 2x & 10 \le x \le 14 \end{cases}$
9. The position of a particle is described by the curve $y = \dfrac{2t}{t^2+3}$, where t is time (in seconds). What is the average rate of change of the position as a function of time from $t = 5$ to $t = 9$?
10. Express the domain of the function $f(x) = \sqrt{6x-7}$ with interval notation.
11. Determine whether the function $g(x) = \sqrt{x+10}$ is even, odd, or neither.
12. For the function $y = -(x+1)^2 + 2$, identify all of the transformations of $y = x^2$.
13. Sketch the graph of $y = \sqrt{x-1} + 3$ and identify all transformations.
14. Find the composite function $f \circ g$ and state the domain for $f(x) = x^2 - 3$ and $g(x) = \sqrt{x+2}$.
15. Evaluate $g(f(-1))$ for $f(x) = 7 - 2x^2$ and $g(x) = 2x - 10$.
16. Find the inverse of the function $f(x) = (x-4)^2 + 2$, where $x \ge 4$.
17. Find a quadratic function whose graph has a vertex at $(-2, 3)$ and passes through the point $(-1, 4)$.
18. Find all of the real zeros (and state their multiplicity) of the function $f(x) = -3.7x^4 - 14.8x^3$.
19. Use long division to find the quotient $Q(x)$ and the remainder $r(x)$ of $(-20x^3 - 8x^2 + 7x - 5) \div (-5x + 3)$.
20. Use synthetic division to find the quotient $Q(x)$ and the remainder $r(x)$ of $(2x^3 + 3x^2 - 11x + 6) \div (x - 3)$.
21. List the possible rational zeros, and test to determine all rational zeros, for $P(x) = 12x^3 + 29x^2 + 7x - 6$.
22. Given the real zero $x = 5$ of the polynomial $P(x) = 2x^3 - 3x^2 - 32x - 15$, determine all the other zeros, and write the polynomial in terms of a product of linear factors.
23. Factor the polynomial $P(x) = x^3 - 5x^2 + 2x + 8$ completely.
24. Factor the polynomial $P(x) = x^5 + 7x^4 + 15x^3 + 5x^2 - 16x - 12$ completely.
25. Find all vertical and horizontal asymptotes of $f(x) = \dfrac{3x-5}{x^2-4}$.
26. Graph the function $f(x) = \dfrac{2x^3 - x^2 - x}{x^2 - 1}$.

CHAPTER 3

Exponential and Logarithmic Functions

John Pitcher/iStockphoto

Most populations initially grow *exponentially*, but then as resources become limited, the population reaches a *carrying capacity*. This exponential increase followed by a saturation at some carrying capacity is called *logistic growth*. Often when a particular species is placed on the endangered species list, it is protected from human predators and then its population size increases until naturally leveling off at some carrying capacity.

The U.S. Fish and Wildlife Service removed the gray wolf (*Canis lupus*) from the Wisconsin list of endangered and threatened species in 2004, and placed it on the list of protected wild animals. About 537 to 564 wolves existed in Wisconsin in the late winter of 2008.

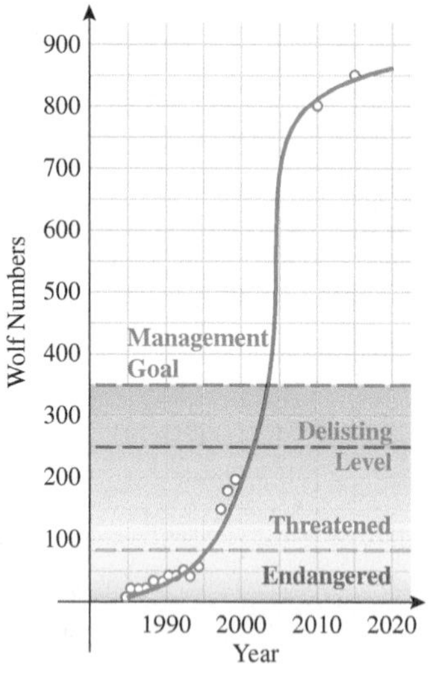

Wisconsin Wolf Population Growth if Carrying Capacity is 500 Wolves

LEARNING OBJECTIVES

- Graph exponential functions.
- Graph logarithmic functions.
- Apply properties of logarithms.
- Solve exponential and logarithmic equations.
- Use exponential and logarithmic models to represent a variety of real-world phenomena.

[IN THIS CHAPTER]

We will discuss exponential functions and their inverses, logarithmic functions. We will graph these functions and use their properties to solve exponential and logarithmic equations. We will then discuss particular exponential and logarithmic models that represent phenomena such as compound interest, world populations, conservation biology models, carbon dating, pH values in chemistry, and the bell curve that is fundamental in statistics for describing how quantities vary in the real world.

EXPONENTIAL AND LOGARITHMIC FUNCTIONS				
3.1 EXPONENTIAL FUNCTIONS AND THEIR GRAPHS	3.2 LOGARITHMIC FUNCTIONS AND THEIR GRAPHS	3.3 PROPERTIES OF LOGARITHMS	3.4 EXPONENTIAL AND LOGARITHMIC EQUATIONS	3.5 EXPONENTIAL AND LOGARITHMIC MODELS
• Evaluating Exponential Functions • Graphs of Exponential Functions • The Natural Base *e* • Applications of Exponential Functions	• Evaluating Logarithms • Common and Natural Logarithms • Graphs of Logarithmic Functions • Applications of Logarithms	• Properties of Logarithms • Change-of-Base Formula	• Solving Exponential Equations • Solving Logarithmic Equations	• Exponential Growth Models • Exponential Decay Models • Gaussian (Normal) Distribution Models • Logistic Growth Models • Logarithmic Models

3.1 EXPONENTIAL FUNCTIONS AND THEIR GRAPHS

SKILLS OBJECTIVES

- Evaluate exponential functions.
- Graph exponential functions.
- Evaluate exponential functions of base *e*.
- Apply exponential functions to economics and the natural sciences.

CONCEPTUAL OBJECTIVES

- Understand that irrational exponents lead to approximations.
- Understand characteristics of exponential functions (implying domain, range, asymptotes, intercepts, etc.).
- Understand that *e* is irrational and why it is the "natural" base.
- Understand why compounding continuously results in higher interest than compounding daily.

3.1.1 Evaluating Exponential Functions

3.1.1 SKILL

Evaluate exponential functions.

3.1.1 CONCEPTUAL

Understand that irrational exponents lead to approximations.

Most of the functions (polynomial, rational, radical, etc.) we have studied thus far have been **algebraic functions**. Algebraic functions involve basic operations, powers, and roots. In this chapter, we discuss *exponential functions* and *logarithmic functions*. The following table illustrates the difference between algebraic functions and *exponential functions*:

FUNCTION	VARIABLE IS IN THE	CONSTANT IS IN THE	EXAMPLE	EXAMPLE
Algebraic	Base	Exponent	$f(x) = x^2$	$g(x) = x^{1/3}$
Exponential	Exponent	Base	$F(x) = 2^x$	$G(x) = \left(\frac{1}{3}\right)^x$

DEFINITION Exponential Function

An **exponential function** with **base *b*** is denoted by

$$f(x) = b^x$$

where b and x are any real numbers such that $b > 0$ and $b \neq 1$.

Note:

- We eliminate $b = 1$ as a value for the base because it merely yields the constant function $f(x) = 1^x = 1$.
- We eliminate negative values for b because they would give non–real-number values such as $(-9)^{1/2} = \sqrt{-9} = 3i$.
- We eliminate $b = 0$ because 0^x corresponds to an undefined value when x is negative.

Our experience with integer exponents has implied a constant multiplication:

$$2^5 = 2 \cdot 2 \cdot 2 \cdot 2 \cdot 2 = 32$$

We can now think of $f(x) = 2^x$ as a continuous function that for positive integers will result in a constant multiplication.

Sometimes the value of an exponential function for a specific argument can be found by inspection as an *exact* number.

x	-3	-1	0	1	3
$F(x) = 2^x$	$2^{-3} = \frac{1}{2^3} = \frac{1}{8}$	$2^{-1} = \frac{1}{2^1} = \frac{1}{2}$	$2^0 = 1$	$2^1 = 2$	$2^3 = 8$

If an exponential function cannot be evaluated exactly, then we find the decimal *approximation* using a calculator.

x	-2.7	$-\frac{4}{5}$	$\frac{5}{7}$	2.7
$F(x) = 2^x$	$2^{-2.7} \approx 0.154$	$2^{-4/5} \approx 0.574$	$2^{5/7} \approx 1.641$	$2^{2.7} \approx 6.498$

The domain of exponential functions, $f(x) = b^x$, is the set of all real numbers. All of the arguments discussed in the first two tables have been rational numbers. What happens if x is irrational? We can approximate the irrational number with a decimal approximation such as $b^\pi \approx b^{3.14}$ or $b^{\sqrt{2}} \approx b^{1.41}$.

Consider $7^{\sqrt{3}}$, and realize that the irrational number $\sqrt{3}$ is a decimal that never terminates or repeats: $\sqrt{3} \approx 1.7320508$. We can show in advanced mathematics that there is a number $7^{\sqrt{3}}$, and although we cannot write it exactly, we can approximate the number. In fact, the closer the exponent is to $\sqrt{3}$, the closer the approximation is to $7^{\sqrt{3}}$.

$$7^{1.7} \approx 27.3317$$
$$7^{1.73} \approx 28.9747$$
$$7^{1.732} \approx 29.0877$$
$$\ldots$$
$$7^{\sqrt{3}} \approx 29.0906$$

It is important to note that the properties of exponents (Appendix) hold when the exponent is any real number (rational or irrational).

EXAMPLE 1 Evaluating Exponential Functions

Let $f(x) = 3^x$, $g(x) = \left(\frac{1}{4}\right)^x$, and $h(x) = 10^{x-2}$. Find the following values:

a. $f(2)$ **b.** $f(\pi)$ **c.** $g\left(-\frac{3}{2}\right)$ **d.** $h(2.3)$ **e.** $f(0)$ **f.** $g(0)$

If an approximation is required, approximate to four decimal places.

Solution:

a. $f(2) = 3^2 = \boxed{9}$

b. $f(\pi) = 3^\pi \approx \boxed{31.5443}^*$

c. $g\left(-\frac{3}{2}\right) = \left(\frac{1}{4}\right)^{-3/2} = 4^{3/2} = \left(\sqrt{4}\right)^3 = 2^3 = \boxed{8}$

d. $h(2.3) = 10^{2.3-2} = 10^{0.3} \approx \boxed{1.9953}$

e. $f(0) = 3^0 = \boxed{1}$

f. $g(0) = \left(\frac{1}{4}\right)^0 = \boxed{1}$

Notice that parts (a) and (c) were evaluated exactly, whereas parts (b) and (d) required approximation using a calculator.

YOUR TURN Let $f(x) = 2^x$ and $g(x) = \left(\frac{1}{9}\right)^x$ and $h(x) = 5^{x-2}$. Find the following values:

a. $f(4)$ **b.** $f(\pi)$ **c.** $g\left(-\frac{3}{2}\right)$ **d.** $h(2.9)$

Evaluate exactly when possible, and round to four decimal places when a calculator is needed.

ANSWER
a. 16 **b.** 8.8250
c. 27 **d.** 4.2567

[CONCEPT CHECK]

Find the approximation to $f(x) = \pi^x$ for $f(-2.3)$; round to four decimal places.

ANSWER 0.0719

*In part (b) of the Your Turn, the π button on the calculator is selected. If we instead approximate π by 3.14, we get a slightly different approximation for the function value:

$$f(\pi) = 3^\pi \approx 3^{3.14} \approx 31.4891$$

3.1.2 Graphs of Exponential Functions

3.1.2 SKILL

Graph exponential functions.

3.1.2 CONCEPTUAL

Understand characteristics of exponential functions (implying domain, range, asymptotes, intercepts, etc.).

Let's graph two exponential functions, $y = 2^x$ and $y = 2^{-x} = \left(\frac{1}{2}\right)^x$, by plotting points.

x	$y = 2^x$	(x, y)
-2	$2^{-2} = \frac{1}{2^2} = \frac{1}{4}$	$\left(-2, \frac{1}{4}\right)$
-1	$2^{-1} = \frac{1}{2^1} = \frac{1}{2}$	$\left(-1, \frac{1}{2}\right)$
0	$2^0 = 1$	$(0, 1)$
1	$2^1 = 2$	$(1, 2)$
2	$2^2 = 4$	$(2, 4)$
3	$2^3 = 8$	$(3, 8)$

x	$y = 2^{-x}$	(x, y)
-3	$2^{-(-3)} = 2^3 = 8$	$(-3, 8)$
-2	$2^{-(-2)} = 2^2 = 4$	$(-2, 4)$
-1	$2^{-(-1)} = 2^1 = 2$	$(-1, 2)$
0	$2^0 = 1$	$(0, 1)$
1	$2^{-1} = \frac{1}{2^1} = \frac{1}{2}$	$\left(1, \frac{1}{2}\right)$
2	$2^{-2} = \frac{1}{2^2} = \frac{1}{4}$	$\left(2, \frac{1}{4}\right)$

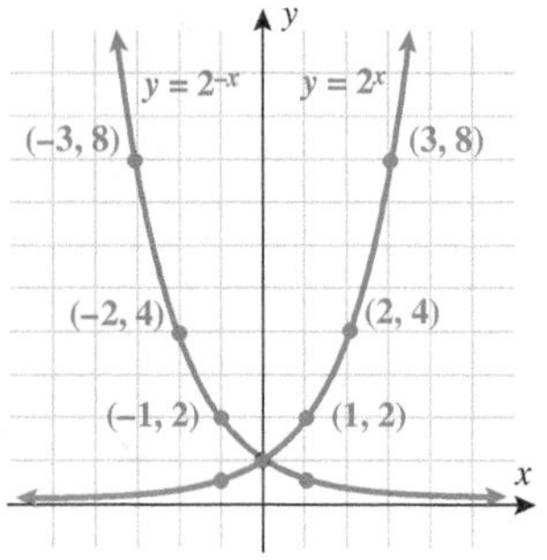

Notice that both graphs' y-intercept is $(0, 1)$ (as shown to the left) and neither graph has an x-intercept. The x-axis is a horizontal asymptote for both graphs. The following box summarizes general characteristics of the graphs of exponential functions.

CHARACTERISTICS OF GRAPHS OF EXPONENTIAL FUNCTIONS

$$f(x) = b^x, \qquad b > 0, \qquad b \neq 1$$

- Domain: $(-\infty, \infty)$
- Range: $(0, \infty)$
- x-intercepts: none
- y-intercept: $(0, 1)$
- Horizontal asymptote: x-axis
- The graph passes through $(1, b)$ and $\left(-1, \frac{1}{b}\right)$.
- As x increases, $f(x)$ increases if $b > 1$ and decreases if $0 < b < 1$.
- The function f is one-to-one.

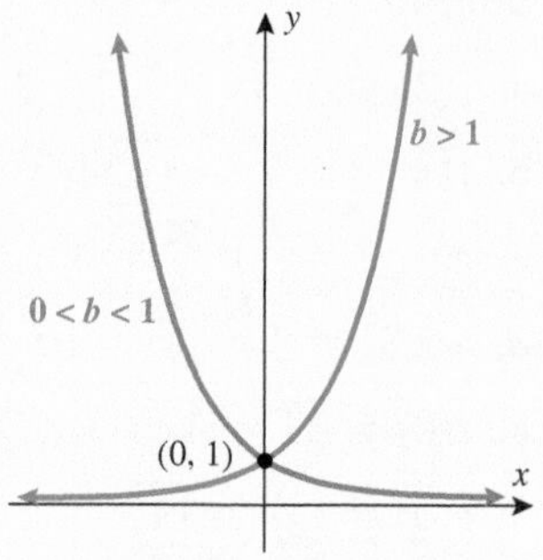

Since exponential functions, $f(x) = b^x$, all go through the point $(0, 1)$ and have the x-axis as a horizontal asymptote, we can find the graph by finding two additional points as outlined in the following procedure.

PROCEDURE FOR GRAPHING $f(x) = b^x$

Step 1: Label the point $(0, 1)$ corresponding to the y-intercept $f(0)$.

Step 2: Find and label two additional points corresponding to $f(-1)$ and $f(1)$.

Step 3: Connect the three points with a *smooth* curve with the x-axis as the horizontal asymptote.

EXAMPLE 2 **Graphing Exponential Functions for $b > 1$**

Graph the function $f(x) = 5^x$.

Solution:

STEP 1: Label the y-intercept $(0, 1)$. $\quad f(0) = 5^0 = 1$

STEP 2: Label the point $(1, 5)$. $\quad f(1) = 5^1 = 5$

Label the point $(-1, 0.2)$. $\quad f(-1) = 5^{-1} = \frac{1}{5} = 0.2$

STEP 3: Sketch a smooth curve through the three points with the x-axis as a horizontal asymptote.

Domain: $(-\infty, \infty)$

Range: $(0, \infty)$

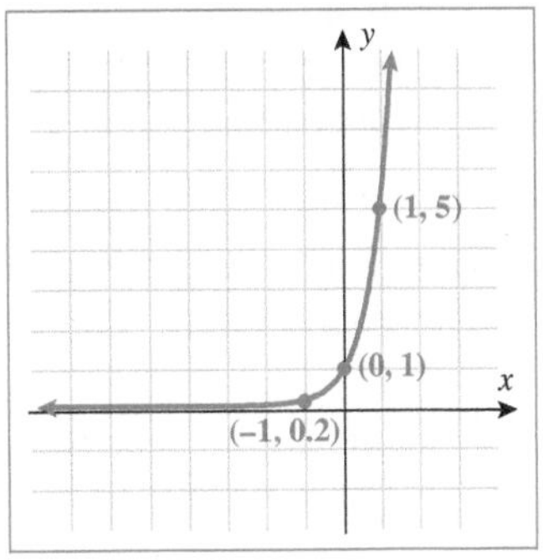

YOUR TURN Graph the function $f(x) = 5^{-x}$.

ANSWER

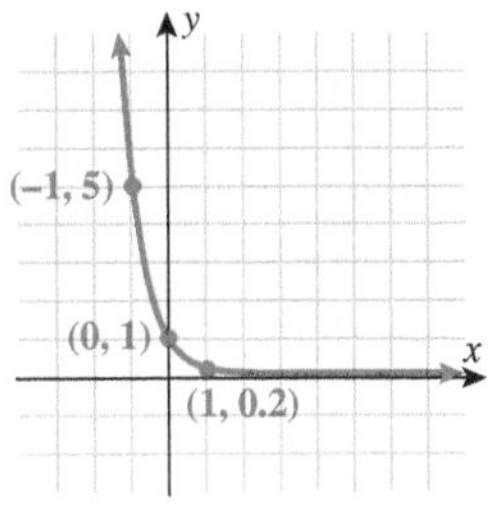

EXAMPLE 3 **Graphing Exponential Functions for $b < 1$**

Graph the function $f(x) = \left(\frac{2}{5}\right)^x$.

Solution:

STEP 1: Label the y-intercept $(0, 1)$. $\quad f(0) = \left(\frac{2}{5}\right)^0 = 1$

STEP 2: Label the point $(-1, 2.5)$. $\quad f(-1) = \left(\frac{2}{5}\right)^{-1} = \frac{5}{2} = 2.5$

Label the point $(1, 0.4)$. $\quad f(1) = \left(\frac{2}{5}\right)^1 = \frac{2}{5} = 0.4$

STEP 3: Sketch a smooth curve through the three points with the x-axis as a horizontal asymptote.

Domain: $(-\infty, \infty)$

Range: $(0, \infty)$

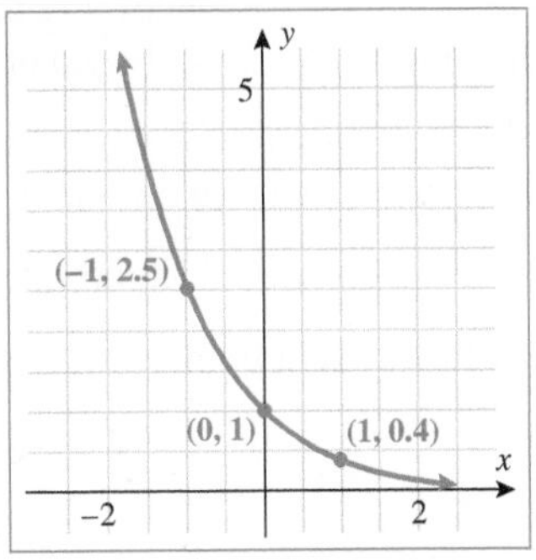

Exponential functions, like all functions, can be graphed by point-plotting. We can also use transformations (horizontal and vertical shifting and reflection; Section 1.3) to graph exponential functions.

EXAMPLE 4 Graphing Exponential Functions Using a Horizontal or Vertical Shift

a. Graph the function $F(x) = 2^{x-1}$. State the domain and range of F.

b. Graph the function $G(x) = 2^x + 1$. State the domain and range of G.

Solution (a):

Identify the base function. $\quad f(x) = 2^x$

Identify the base function y-intercept and horizontal asymptote. $\quad (0, 1)$ and $y = 0$

The graph of the function F is found by shifting the graph of the function f to the right one unit. $\quad F(x) = f(x - 1)$

Shift the y-intercept to the right one unit. $\quad (0, 1)$ shifts to $(1, 1)$

The horizontal asymptote is not altered by a horizontal shift. $\quad y = 0$

Find additional points on the graph. $\quad F(0) = 2^{0-1} = 2^{-1} = \frac{1}{2}$

y-intercept: $\left(0, \frac{1}{2}\right)$

$F(2) = 2^{2-1} = 2^1 = 2$

[CONCEPT CHECK]

State the y-intercept, domain, and range of $F(x) = b^x + 2$, where $b > 0$.

ANSWER y-intercept: $(0, 3)$; Domain: $(-\infty, \infty)$; Range: $(2, \infty)$

Sketch the graph of $F(x) = 2^{x-1}$ with a *smooth* curve.

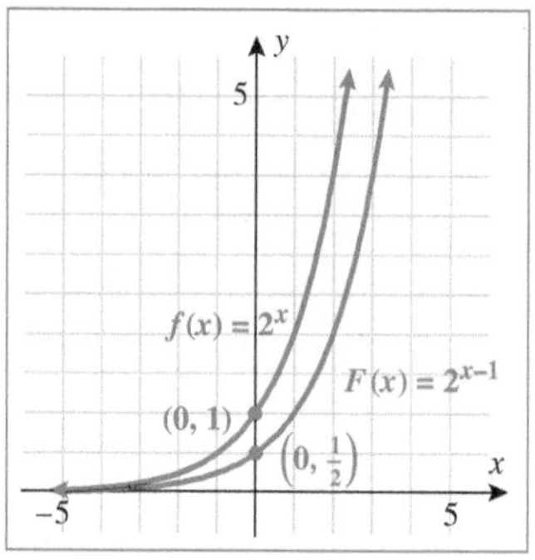

Domain: $(-\infty, \infty)$
Range: $(0, \infty)$

Solution (b):

Identify the base function. $\quad f(x) = 2^x$

Identify the base function y-intercept and horizontal asymptote. $\quad (0, 1)$ and $y = 0$

The graph of the function G is found by shifting the graph of the function f up one unit. $\quad G(x) = f(x) + 1$

Shift the y-intercept up one unit. $\quad (0, 1)$ shifts to $(0, 2)$

Shift the horizontal asymptote up one unit. $\quad y = 0$ shifts to $y = 1$

Find additional points on the graph. $\quad G(1) = 2^1 + 1 = 2 + 1 = 3$

$G(-1) = 2^{-1} + 1 = \frac{1}{2} + 1 = \frac{3}{2}$

Sketch the graph of $G(x) = 2^x + 1$ with a *smooth* curve.

Domain: $(-\infty, \infty)$
Range: $(1, \infty)$

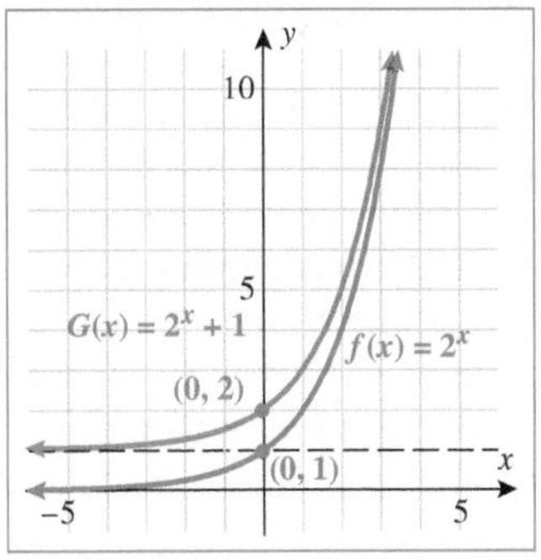

EXAMPLE 5 Graphing Exponential Functions Using Both Horizontal and Vertical Shifts

Graph the function $F(x) = 3^{x+1} - 2$. State the domain and range of F.

Solution:

Identify the base function. $f(x) = 3^x$

Identify the base function y-intercept and horizontal asymptote. $(0, 1)$ and $y = 0$

The graph of the function F is found by shifting the graph of the function f to the left one unit and down two units. $F(x) = f(x + 1) - 2$

Shift the y-intercept to the left one unit and down two units. $(0, 1)$ shifts to $(-1, -1)$

Shift the horizontal asymptote down two units. $y = 0$ shifts to $y = -2$

Find additional points on the graph.

$F(0) = 3^{0+1} - 2 = 3 - 2 = 1$

$F(1) = 3^{1+1} - 2 = 9 - 2 = 7$

Sketch the graph of $F(x) = 3^{x+1} - 2$ with a *smooth* curve.

Domain: $(-\infty, \infty)$
Range: $(-2, \infty)$

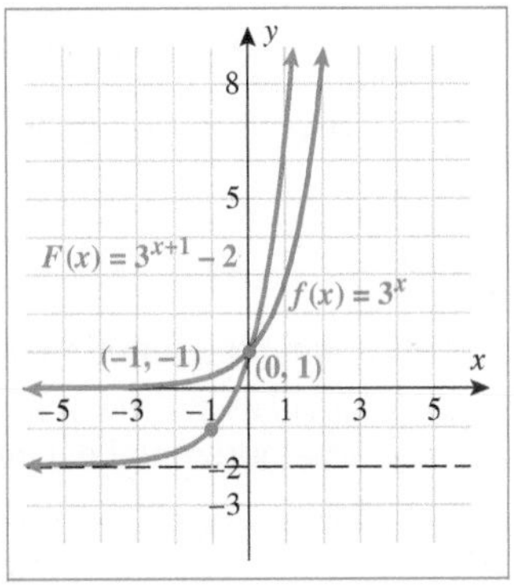

YOUR TURN Graph $f(x) = 2^{x+3} - 1$. State the domain and range of f.

ANSWER

Domain: $(-\infty, \infty)$
Range: $(-1, \infty)$

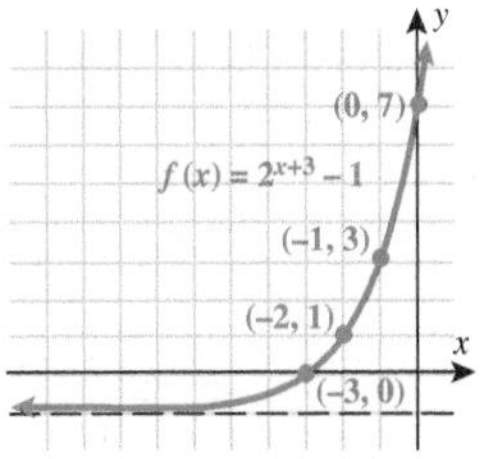

3.1.3 The Natural Base *e*

3.1.3 SKILL

Evaluate exponential functions of base *e*.

3.1.3 CONCEPTUAL

Understand that *e* is irrational and why it is the "natural" base.

Any positive real number can serve as the base for an exponential function. A particular irrational number, denoted by the letter *e*, appears as the base in many applications, as you will soon see when we discuss continuous compounded interest. Although you will see 2 and 10 as common bases, the base that appears most often is *e*, because ***e***, as you will come to see in your further studies of mathematics, is the **natural base.** The exponential function with base *e*, $f(x) = e^x$, is called the **exponential function** or the **natural exponential function.** Mathematicians did not pull this irrational number out of a hat. The number *e* has many remarkable properties, but most simply, it comes from evaluating the expression $\left(1 + \frac{1}{m}\right)^m$ as *m* gets large (increases without bound).

$e \approx 2.71828$

m	$\left(1 + \frac{1}{m}\right)^m$
1	2
10	2.59374
100	2.70481
1000	2.71692
10,000	2.71815
100,000	2.71827
1,000,000	**2.71828**

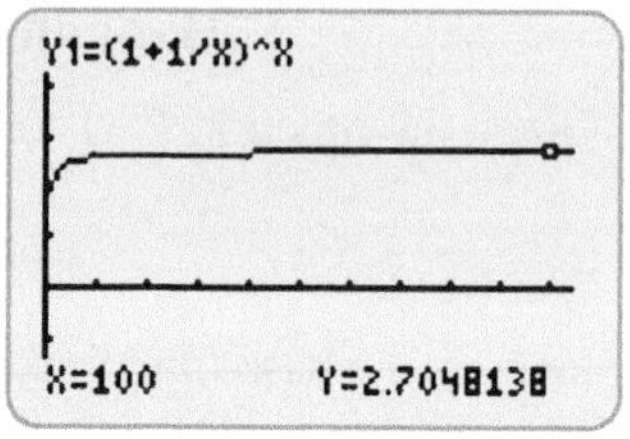

Calculators have an e^x button for approximating the natural exponential function.

EXAMPLE 6 **Evaluating the Natural Exponential Function**

Evaluate $f(x) = e^x$ for the given *x*-values. Round your answers to four decimal places.

a. $x = 1$ **b.** $x = -1$ **c.** $x = 1.2$ **d.** $x = -0.47$

Solution:

a. $f(1) = e^1 \approx 2.718281828 \approx \boxed{2.7183}$

b. $f(-1) = e^{-1} \approx 0.367879441 \approx \boxed{0.3679}$

c. $f(1.2) = e^{1.2} \approx 3.320116923 \approx \boxed{3.3201}$

d. $f(-0.47) = e^{-0.47} \approx 0.625002268 \approx \boxed{0.6250}$

STUDY TIP

A common base is 10, that is, $f(x) = 10^x$. The *natural base* is e, that is, $f(x) = e^x$.

Like all exponential functions of the form $f(x) = b^x$, $f(x) = e^x$ and $f(x) = e^{-x}$ have (0, 1) as their *y*-intercept and the *x*-axis as a horizontal asymptote as shown in the figure on the right.

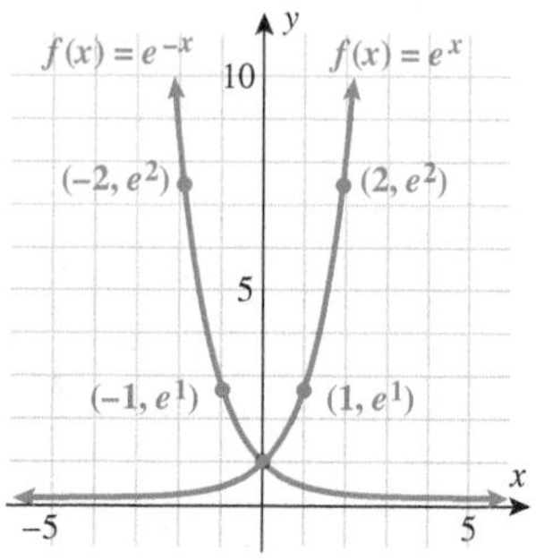

EXAMPLE 7 **Graphing Exponential Functions with Base *e***

Graph the function $f(x) = 3 + e^{2x}$.

Solution:

x	$f(x) = 3 + e^{2x}$	(x, y)
−2	3.02	(−2, 3.02)
−1	3.14	(1, 3.14)
0	4	(0, 4)
1	10.39	(1, 10.39)
2	57.60	(2, 57.60)

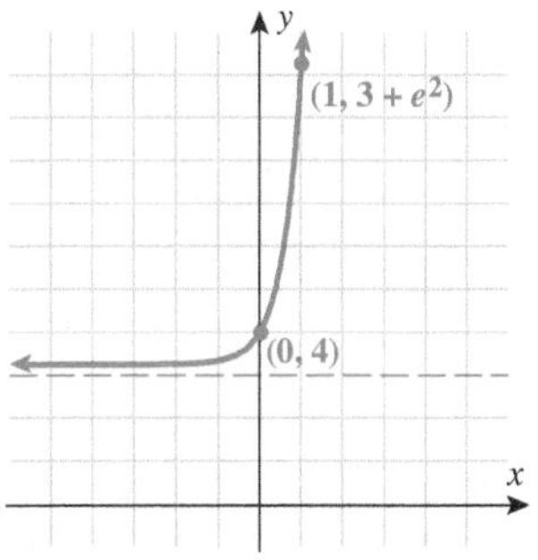

Note: The y-intercept is (0, 4), and the line $y = 3$ is the horizontal asymptote.

YOUR TURN Graph the function $f(x) = e^{x+1} - 2$.

[CONCEPT CHECK]

Since $2 < e < 3$ what would $\frac{1}{e}$ lie between?

ANSWER $\frac{1}{3}$ and $\frac{1}{2}$

ANSWER

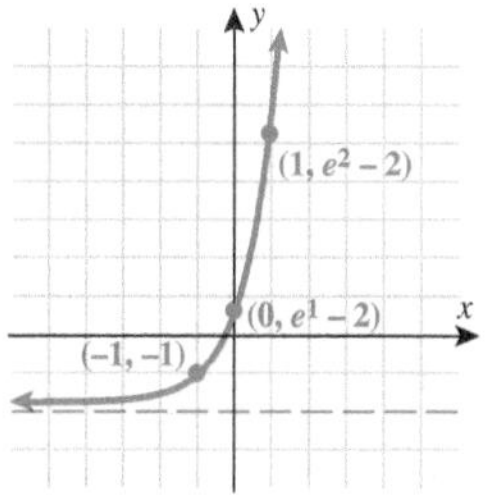

3.1.4 Applications of Exponential Functions

3.1.4 SKILL

Apply exponential functions to economics and the natural sciences.

3.1.4 CONCEPTUAL

Understand why compounding continuously results in higher interest than compounding daily.

Exponential functions describe either *growth* or *decay.* Populations and investments are often modeled with exponential growth functions, while the declining value of a used car and the radioactive decay of isotopes are often modeled with exponential decay functions. In Section 3.5, various exponential models will be discussed. In this section, we discuss doubling time, half-life, and compound interest.

A successful investment program, growing at about 7.2% per year, will double in size every 10 years. Let's assume that you will retire at the age of 65. There is a saying: *It's not the first time your money doubles, it's the last time that makes such a difference.* As you may already know or as you will soon find, it is important to start investing early.

Suppose Maria invests \$5000 at age 25 and David invests \$5000 at age 35. Let's calculate how much will accrue from the initial \$5000 investment by the time they each retire, assuming that their money doubles every 10 years and that they both retire at age 65.

AGE	MARIA	DAVID
25	\$5,000	
35	\$10,000	\$5,000
45	\$20,000	\$10,000
55	\$40,000	\$20,000
65	**\$80,000**	**\$40,000**

They each made a one-time investment of \$5000. By investing 10 years sooner, Maria made twice what David made.

A measure of growth rate is the *doubling time*, the time it takes for something to double. Often doubling time is used to describe populations.

DOUBLING TIME GROWTH MODEL

The doubling time growth model is given by

$$P = P_0 2^{t/d}$$

where P = Population at time t
P_0 = Population at time $t = 0$
d = Doubling time

Note that when $t = d$, $P = 2P_0$ (population is equal to twice the original).

The units for P and P_0 are the same and can be any quantity (people, dollars, etc.). The units for t and d must be the same (years, weeks, days, hours, seconds, etc.).

In the investment scenario with Maria and David, P_0 = \$5000 and d = 10 years, so the model used to predict how much money the original \$5000 investment yielded is $P = 5000(2)^{t/10}$. Maria retired 40 years after the original investment, $t = 40$, and David retired 30 years after the original investment, $t = 30$.

$$\text{Maria: } P = 5000(2)^{40/10} = 5000(2)^4 = 5000(16) = 80{,}000$$
$$\text{David: } P = 5000(2)^{30/10} = 5000(2)^3 = 5000(8) = 40{,}000$$

EXAMPLE 8 Doubling Time of Populations

In 2004 the population in Kazakhstan, a country in Asia, reached 15 million. It is estimated that the population doubles in 30 years. If the population continues to grow at the same rate, what will the population be in 2024? Round to the nearest million.

Solution:

Write the doubling model. $P = P_0 2^{t/d}$

Substitute P_0 = 15 million, d = 30 years, and t = 20 years. $P = 15(2)^{20/30}$

Simplify. $P = 15(2)^{2/3} \approx 23.8110$

In 2024, there will be approximately **24 million people** in Kazakhstan.

YOUR TURN What will the approximate population in Kazakhstan be in 2044? Round to the nearest million.

ANSWER
38 million

We now turn our attention from exponential growth to exponential decay, or negative growth. Suppose you buy a brand-new car from a dealership for \$24,000. The value of a car decreases over time according to an exponential decay function. The **half-life** of this particular car, or the time it takes for the car to depreciate 50%, is approximately 3 years. The exponential decay is described by

$$A = A_0\left(\frac{1}{2}\right)^{t/h}$$

where A_0 is the amount the car is worth (in dollars) when new (that is, when $t = 0$), A is the amount the car is worth (in dollars) after t years, and h is the half-life in years. In our car scenario, $A_0 = 24{,}000$ and $h = 3$:

$$A = 24{,}000\left(\frac{1}{2}\right)^{t/3}$$

How much is the car worth after three years? Six years? Nine years? Twenty-four years?

$$t = 3: \quad A = 24{,}000\left(\frac{1}{2}\right)^{3/3} = 24{,}000\left(\frac{1}{2}\right) = 12{,}000$$

$$t = 6: \quad A = 24{,}000\left(\frac{1}{2}\right)^{6/3} = 24{,}000\left(\frac{1}{2}\right)^{2} = 6000$$

$$t = 9: \quad A = 24{,}000\left(\frac{1}{2}\right)^{9/3} = 24{,}000\left(\frac{1}{2}\right)^{3} = 3000$$

$$t = 24: \quad A = 24{,}000\left(\frac{1}{2}\right)^{24/3} = 24{,}000\left(\frac{1}{2}\right)^{8} = 93.75 \approx 100$$

The car that was worth \$24,000 new is worth \$12,000 in 3 years, \$6000 in 6 years, \$3000 in 9 years, and about \$100 in the junkyard in 24 years.

EXAMPLE 9 Radioactive Decay

The radioactive isotope of potassium ^{42}K, which is used in the diagnosis of brain tumors, has a half-life of 12.36 hours. If 500 milligrams of potassium-42 are taken, how many milligrams will remain after 24 hours? Round to the nearest milligram.

Solution:

Write the half-life formula. $\quad A = A_0\left(\frac{1}{2}\right)^{t/h}$

Substitute $A_0 = 500$ mg, $h = 12.36$ hours, and $t = 24$ hours. $\quad A = 500\left(\frac{1}{2}\right)^{24/12.36}$

Simplify. $\quad A \approx 500(0.2603) \approx 130.15$

After 24 hours, there are approximately **130 milligrams** of potassium-42 left.

YOUR TURN How many milligrams of potassium-42 are expected to be left in the body after 1 week?

ANSWER

0.04 mg (less than 1 mg)

In Section 0.1, *simple interest* was defined where the interest I is calculated based on the principal P, the annual interest rate r, and the time t in years, using the formula $I = Prt$.

If the interest earned in a period is then reinvested at the same rate, future interest is earned on both the principal and the reinvested interest during the next period. Interest paid on both the principal and interest is called *compound interest.*

COMPOUND INTEREST

If a **principal** P is invested at an annual **rate** r **compounded** n times a year, then the **amount** A in the account at the end of t years is given by

$$A = P\left(1 + \frac{r}{n}\right)^{nt}$$

The annual interest rate r is expressed as a decimal.

The following list shows the typical number of times interest is compounded:

Annually	$n = 1$	Monthly	$n = 12$
Semiannually	$n = 2$	Weekly	$n = 52$
Quarterly	$n = 4$	Daily	$n = 365$

EXAMPLE 10 Compound Interest

If \$3000 is deposited in an account paying 3% compounded quarterly, how much will you have in the account in 7 years?

Solution:

Write the compound interest formula. $A = P\left(1 + \frac{r}{n}\right)^{nt}$

Substitute $P = 3000$, $r = 0.03$, $n = 4$, and $t = 7$. $A = 3000\left(1 + \frac{0.03}{4}\right)^{(4)(7)}$

Simplify. $A = 3000(1.0075)^{28} \approx 3698.14$

You will have \$3698.14 in the account.

YOUR TURN If \$5000 is deposited in an account paying 6% compounded annually, how much will you have in the account in 4 years?

ANSWER

\$6312.38

[CONCEPT CHECK]

If we were to repeat Example 10 using interest compounded continuously, would you expect more or less money than if it were compounded quarterly?

ANSWER More. See Example 11.

Notice in the compound interest formula that as n increases the amount A also increases. In other words, the more times the interest is compounded per year, the more money you make. Ideally, your bank will compound your interest infinitely many times. This is called *compounding continuously.* We will now show the development of the continuous compounding formula, $A = Pe^{rt}$.

WORDS	MATH
Write the compound interest formula.	$A = P\left(1 + \frac{r}{n}\right)^{nt}$
Note that $\frac{r}{n} = \frac{1}{n/r}$ and $nt = \left(\frac{n}{r}\right)rt$.	$A = P\left(1 + \frac{1}{n/r}\right)^{(n/r)rt}$
Let $m = \frac{n}{r}$.	$A = P\left(1 + \frac{1}{m}\right)^{mrt}$
Use the exponential property: $x^{mrt} = (x^m)^{rt}$.	$A = P\left[\left(1 + \frac{1}{m}\right)^{m}\right]^{rt}$

Recall that as m increases, $\left(1 + \frac{1}{m}\right)^{m}$ approaches e. Therefore, as the number of times the interest is compounded approaches infinity, or as $n \to \infty$, the amount in an account $A = P\left(1 + \frac{r}{n}\right)^{nt}$ approaches $A = Pe^{rt}$.

CONTINUOUS COMPOUND INTEREST

If a **principal** P is invested at an annual **rate** r **compounded continuously**, then the **amount** A in the account at the end of t years is given by

$$A = Pe^{rt}$$

The annual interest rate r is expressed as a decimal.

It is important to note that for a given interest rate, the highest return you can earn is by compounding continuously.

EXAMPLE 11 **Continuously Compounded Interest**

If \$3000 is deposited in a savings account paying 3% a year compounded continuously, how much will you have in the account in 7 years?

Solution:

Write the continuous compound interest formula. $A = Pe^{rt}$

Substitute $P = 3000$, $r = 0.03$, and $t = 7$. $A = 3000e^{(0.03)(7)}$

Simplify. $A \approx 3701.034$

There will be \$3701.03 in the account in 7 years.

Note: In Example 10, we worked this same problem compounding *quarterly*, and the result was \$3698.14.

If the number of times per year interest is compounded increases, then the total interest earned that year also increases.

STUDY TIP

If the number of times per year interest is compounded increases, then the total interest earned that year also increases.

YOUR TURN If \$5000 is deposited in an account paying 6% compounded continuously, how much will be in the account in 4 years?

ANSWER

\$6356.25

[SECTION 3.1] SUMMARY

In this section, we discussed exponential functions (constant base, variable exponent).

General Exponential Functions: $f(x) = b^x, b \neq 1$, and $b > 0$

1. Evaluating exponential functions
   - Exact (by inspection): $f(x) = 2^x$ $f(3) = 2^3 = 8$.
   - Approximate (with the aid of a calculator): $f(x) = 2^x$ $f(\sqrt{3}) = 2^{\sqrt{3}} \approx 3.322$
2. Graphs of exponential functions
   - Domain: $(-\infty, \infty)$ and range: $(0, \infty)$.
   - The point $(0, 1)$ corresponds to the y-intercept.
   - The graph passes through the points $(1, b)$ and $\left(-1, \frac{1}{b}\right)$.
   - The x-axis is a horizontal asymptote.
   - The function f is one-to-one.

$f(x) = b^x, \quad b > 0, \quad b \neq 1$

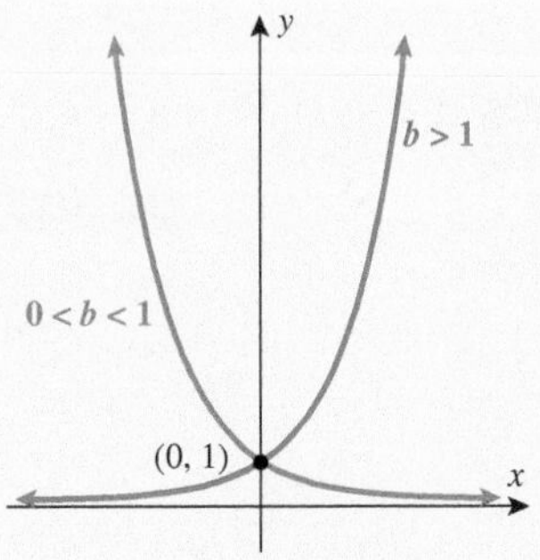

Procedure for Graphing: $f(x) = b^x$

Step 1: Label the point $(0, 1)$ corresponding to the y-intercept $f(0)$.

Step 2: Find and label two additional points corresponding to $f(-1)$ and $f(1)$.

Step 3: Connect the three points with a smooth curve with the x-axis as the horizontal asymptote.

The Natural Exponential Function: $f(x) = e^x$

- The irrational number e is called the natural base.
- $e = \left(1 + \frac{1}{m}\right)^m$ as $m \to \infty$
- $e \approx 2.71828$

Applications of Exponential Functions (all variables expressed in consistent units)

1. Doubling time: $P = P_0 2^{t/d}$
   - d is doubling time.
   - P is population at time t.
   - P_0 is population at time $t = 0$.
2. Half-life: $A = A_0\left(\frac{1}{2}\right)^{t/h}$
   - h is the half-life.
   - A is amount at time t.
   - A_0 is amount at time $t = 0$.
3. Compound interest (P = principal, A = amount after t years, r = interest rate)
   - Compounded n times a year: $A = P\left(1 + \frac{r}{n}\right)^{nt}$
   - Compounded continuously: $A = Pe^{rt}$

[SECTION 3.1] EXERCISES

• SKILLS

In Exercises 1–6, evaluate *exactly* (without using a calculator). For rational exponents, consider converting to radical form first.

1. 5^{-2}
2. 4^{-3}
3. $8^{2/3}$
4. $27^{2/3}$
5. $\left(\frac{1}{9}\right)^{-3/2}$
6. $\left(\frac{1}{16}\right)^{-3/2}$

In Exercises 7–12, approximate with a calculator. Round your answer to four decimal places.

7. $5^{\sqrt{2}}$
8. $6^{\sqrt{3}}$
9. e^2
10. $e^{1/2}$
11. $e^{-\pi}$
12. $e^{-\sqrt{2}}$

In Exercises 13–20, for the functions $f(x) = 3^x$, $g(x) = \left(\frac{1}{16}\right)^x$, and $h(x) = 10^{x+1}$, find the function value at the indicated points.

13. $f(3)$
14. $h(1)$
15. $g(-1)$
16. $f(-2)$
17. $g\left(-\frac{1}{2}\right)$
18. $g\left(-\frac{3}{2}\right)$
19. $f(e)$
20. $g(\pi)$

In Exercises 21–26, match each function with the correct graph.

21. $y = 5^{x-1}$
22. $y = 5^{1-x}$
23. $y = -5^x$
24. $y = -5^{-x}$
25. $y = 1 - 5^{-x}$
26. $y = 5^x - 1$

a.

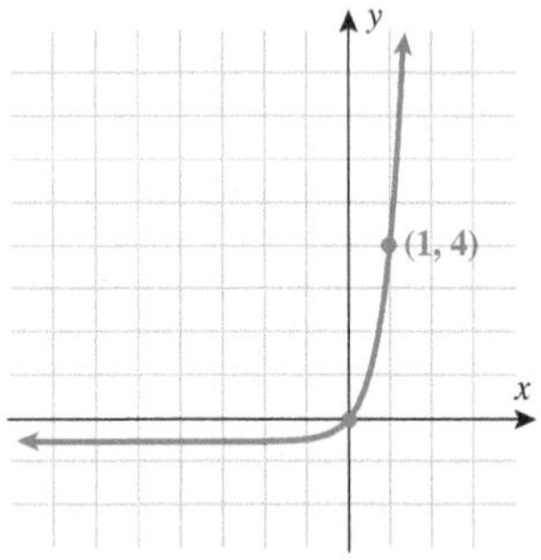

b.

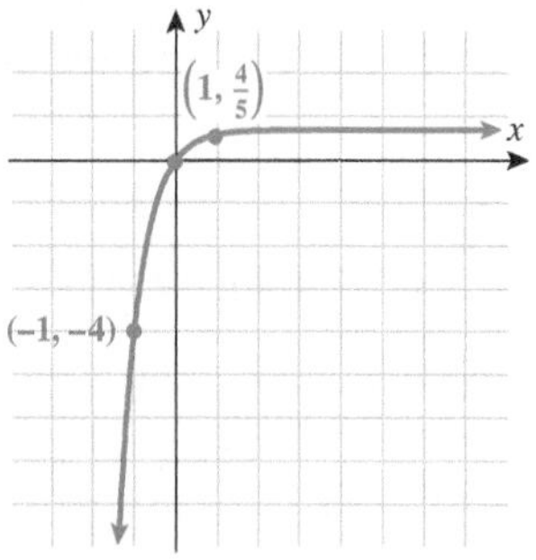

c.

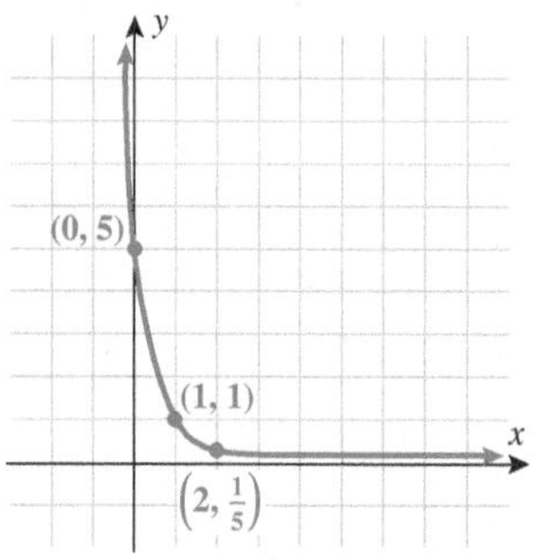

d.

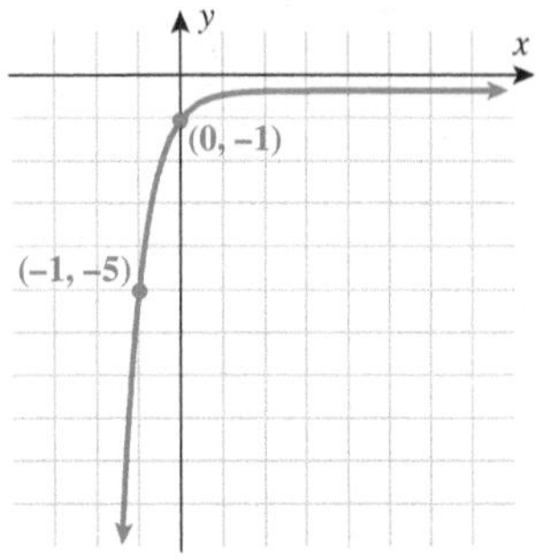

e.

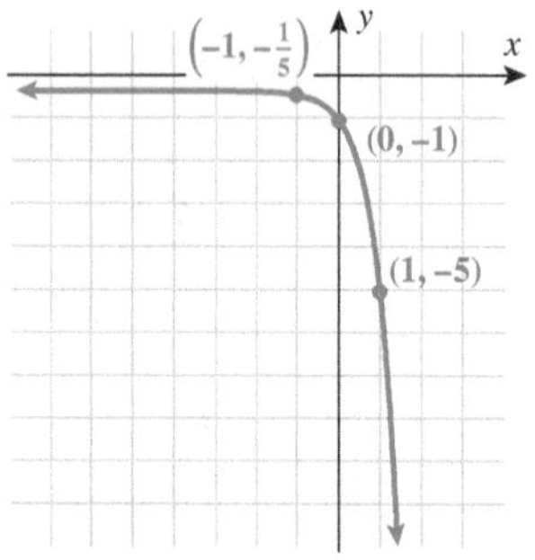

f.

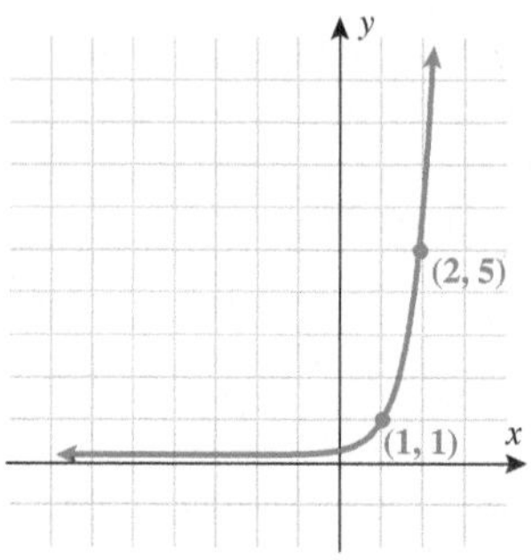

In Exercises 27–46, graph the exponential function using transformations. State the *y*-intercept, two additional points, the domain, the range, and the horizontal asymptote.

27. $f(x) = 6^x$
28. $f(x) = 7^x$
29. $f(x) = 10^{-x}$
30. $f(x) = 4^{-x}$
31. $f(x) = e^x$
32. $f(x) = -e^{-x}$
33. $f(x) = e^{-x}$
34. $f(x) = -e^x$
35. $f(x) = 2^x - 1$
36. $f(x) = 3^x - 1$
37. $f(x) = 2 - e^x$
38. $f(x) = 1 + e^{-x}$
39. $f(x) = 5 + 4^{-x}$
40. $f(x) = 5^x - 2$
41. $f(x) = e^{x+1} - 4$
42. $f(x) = e^{x-1} + 2$
43. $f(x) = 3e^{x/2}$
44. $f(x) = 2e^{-x}$
45. $f(x) = 1 + \left(\frac{1}{2}\right)^{x-2}$
46. $f(x) = 2 - \left(\frac{1}{3}\right)^{x+1}$

• APPLICATIONS

47. **Population Doubling Time.** In 2002 there were 7.1 million people living in London, England. If the population is expected to double by 2090, what is the expected population in London in 2050?

48. **Population Doubling Time.** In 2004 the population in Morganton, Georgia, was 43,000. The population in Morganton doubled by 2010. If the growth rate remains the same, what is the expected population in Morganton in 2020?

49. **Investments.** Suppose an investor buys land in a rural area for \$1500 an acre and sells some of it 5 years later at \$3000 an acre and the rest of it 10 years later at \$6000. Write a function that models the value of land in that area, assuming the growth rate stays the same. What would the expected cost per acre be 30 years after the initial investment of \$1500?

50. **Salaries.** Twin brothers, Collin and Cameron, get jobs immediately after graduating from college at the age of 22. Collin opts for the higher starting salary, \$55,000, and stays with the same company until he retires at 65. His salary doubles every 15 years. Cameron opts for a lower starting salary, \$35,000, but moves to a new job every 5 years; he doubles his salary every 10 years until he retires at 65. What is the annual salary of each brother upon retirement?

51. **Radioactive Decay.** A radioactive isotope of selenium, ^{75}Se, which is used in medical imaging of the pancreas, has a half-life of 119.77 days. If 200 milligrams are given to a patient, how many milligrams are left after 30 days?

52. **Radioactive Decay.** The radioactive isotope indium-111 (^{111}In), used as a diagnostic tool for locating tumors associated with prostate cancer, has a half-life of 2.807 days. If 300 milligrams are given to a patient, how many milligrams will be left after a week?

53. **Radioactive Decay.** A radioactive isotope of beryllium-11 decays to boron-11 with a half-life of 13.81 seconds. Beryllium is given to patients who have chronic beryllium disease (CBD). If 800 milligrams are given to a CBD patient, how much beryllium is present after 2 minutes? Round your answer to the nearest milligram.

54. **Radioactive Decay.** If the CBD patient in Exercise 53 is given 1000 milligrams, how much beryllium is present after 1 minute? Round your answer to the nearest milligram.

55. **Compound Interest.** If you put \$3200 in a savings account that earns 2.5% interest per year compounded quarterly, how much would you expect to have in that account in 3 years?

56. **Compound Interest.** If you put \$10,000 in a savings account that earns 3.5% interest per year compounded annually, how much would you expect to have in that account in 5 years?

57. **Compound Interest.** How much money should you put in a savings account now that earns 5% a year compounded daily if you want to have \$32,000 in 18 years?

58. **Compound Interest.** How much money should you put in a savings account now that earns 3.0% a year compounded weekly if you want to have \$80,000 in 15 years?

59. **Compound Interest.** If you put \$3200 in a savings account that pays 2% a year compounded continuously, how much will you have in the account in 15 years?

60. **Compound Interest.** If you put \$7000 in a money market account that pays 4.3% a year compounded continuously, how much will you have in the account in 10 years?

61. **Compound Interest.** How much money should you deposit into a money market account that pays 5% a year compounded continuously to have \$38,000 in the account in 20 years?

62. **Compound Interest.** How much money should you deposit into a certificate of deposit that pays 6% a year compounded continuously to have \$80,000 in the account in 18 years?

For Exercises 63 and 64, refer to the following:

Exponential functions can be used to model the concentration of a drug in a patient's body. Suppose the concentration of Drug X in a patient's bloodstream is modeled by

$$C(t) = C_0 e^{-rt}$$

where $C(t)$ represents the concentration at time t (in hours), C_0 is the concentration of the drug in the blood immediately after injection, and $r > 0$ is a constant indicating the removal of the drug by the body through metabolism and/or excretion. The rate constant r has units of 1/time (1/hr). It is important to note that this model assumes that the blood concentration of the drug C_0 peaks immediately when the drug is injected.

63. **Health/Medicine.** After an injection of Drug Y, the concentration of the drug in the bloodstream drops at the rate of 0.020 1/hr. Find the concentration, to the nearest tenth, of the drug 20 hours after receiving an injection with initial concentration of 5.0 mg/L.

64. **Health/Medicine.** After an injection of Drug Y, the concentration of the drug in the bloodstream drops at the rate of 0.009 1/hr. Find the concentration, to the nearest tenth, of the drug 4 hours after receiving an injection with initial concentration of 4.0 mg/L.

• CATCH THE MISTAKE

In Exercises 65 and 66, explain the mistake that is made.

65. Evaluate the function for the given x: $f(x) = 4^x$ for $x = \frac{3}{2}$.

Solution: $f\left(\frac{3}{2}\right) = 4^{3/2}$

$= \frac{4^3}{4^2} = \frac{64}{16} = 4$

The correct value is 8. What mistake was made?

66. If \$5000 is invested in a savings account that earns 3% interest compounded continuously, how much will be in the account in 6 months?

Solution:

Write the compound continuous interest formula. $A = Pe^{rt}$

Substitute $P = 5000$, $r = 0.03$, and $t = 6$. $A = 5000e^{(0.03)(6)}$

Simplify. $A = 5986.09$

This is incorrect. What mistake was made?

• CONCEPTUAL

In Exercises 67–70, determine whether each statement is true or false.

67. The function $f(x) = -e^{-x}$ has the y-intercept $(0, 1)$.

68. The function $f(x) = -e^{-x}$ has a horizontal asymptote along the x-axis.

69. The functions $y = 3^{-x}$ and $y = \left(\frac{1}{3}\right)^x$ have the same graphs.

70. $e = 2.718$.

71. Plot $f(x) = 3^x$ and its inverse on the same graph.

72. Plot $f(x) = e^x$ and its inverse on the same graph.

73. Graph $f(x) = e^{|x|}$.

74. Graph $f(x) = e^{-|x|}$.

• CHALLENGE

75. Find the y-intercept and horizontal asymptote of $f(x) = be^{-x+1} - a$.

76. Find the y-intercept and horizontal asymptote of $f(x) = a + be^{x+1}$.

77. Graph $f(x) = b^{|x|}$, $b > 1$, and state the domain.

78. Graph the function $f(x) = \begin{cases} a^x & x < 0 \\ a^{-x} & x \geq 0 \end{cases}$ where $a > 1$.

79. Graph the function

$$f(x) = \begin{cases} -a^x & x < 0 \\ -a^{-x} & x \geq 0 \end{cases} \quad \text{where } 0 < a < 1.$$

80. Find the y-intercept and horizontal asymptote(s) of $f(x) = 2^x + 3^x$.

• PREVIEW TO CALCULUS

In calculus the following two functions are studied:

$$\sinh x = \frac{e^x - e^{-x}}{2} \quad \text{and} \quad \cosh x = \frac{e^x + e^{-x}}{2}$$

81. Determine whether $f(x) = \sinh x$ is an even function or an odd function.

82. Determine whether $f(x) = \cosh x$ is an even function or an odd function.

83. Show that $\cosh^2 x - \sinh^2 x = 1$.

84. Show that $\cosh x - \sinh x = e^x$.

3.2 LOGARITHMIC FUNCTIONS AND THEIR GRAPHS

SKILLS OBJECTIVES

- Evaluate logarithmic expressions.
- Approximate common and natural logarithms using a calculator.
- Graph logarithmic functions.
- Apply logarithmic functions to problems in the natural sciences and engineering.

CONCEPTUAL OBJECTIVES

- Interpret logarithmic functions as inverses of exponential functions.
- Recognize when a logarithm or the value of a logarithmic function can be evaluated exactly and when it must be approximated.
- Understand the inverse relationship between the characteristics of logarithmic functions and exponential functions.
- Understand that logarithmic functions allow very large ranges of numbers in science and engineering applications to be represented on a smaller scale.

3.2.1 Evaluating Logarithms

In Section 3.1, we found that the graph of an exponential function, $f(x) = b^x$, passes through the point (0, 1), with the x-axis as a horizontal asymptote. The graph passes both the vertical line test (for a function) and the horizontal line test (for a one-to-one function), and therefore an inverse exists. We will now apply the technique outlined in Section 1.5 to find the inverse of $f(x) = b^x$:

WORDS	MATH
Let $y = f(x)$.	$y = b^x$
Interchange x and y.	$x = b^y$
Solve for y.	$y = ?$

3.2.1 SKILL

Evaluate logarithmic expressions.

3.2.1 CONCEPTUAL

Interpret logarithmic functions as inverses of exponential functions.

DEFINITION Logarithmic Function

For $x > 0$, $b > 0$, and $b \neq 1$, the **logarithmic function with base b** is denoted $f(x) = \log_b x$, where

$$y = \log_b x \qquad \text{if and only if} \qquad x = b^y$$

We read $\log_b x$ as "log base b of x."

STUDY TIP

- $\log_b x = y$ is equivalent to $b^y = x$.
- The exponent y is called a logarithm (or "log" for short).

This definition says that $x = b^y$ (**exponential form**) and $y = \log_b x$ (**logarithmic form**) are equivalent. One way to remember this relationship is by adding arrows to the logarithmic form:

$$\log_b x = y \Leftrightarrow b^y = x$$

EXAMPLE 1 **Changing from Logarithmic Form to Exponential Form**

Express each equation in its equivalent exponential form.

a. $\log_2 8 = 3$ **b.** $\log_9 3 = \frac{1}{2}$ **c.** $\log_5\left(\frac{1}{25}\right) = -2$

Solution:

a. $\log_2 8 = 3$ is equivalent to $\boxed{2^3 = 8}$

b. $\log_9 3 = \frac{1}{2}$ is equivalent to $\boxed{9^{1/2} = 3}$

c. $\log_5\left(\frac{1}{25}\right) = -2$ is equivalent to $\boxed{5^{-2} = \frac{1}{25}}$

YOUR TURN Write each equation in its equivalent exponential form.

a. $\log_3 9 = 2$ **b.** $\log_{16} 4 = \frac{1}{2}$ **c.** $\log_2\left(\frac{1}{8}\right) = -3$

ANSWER

a. $9 = 3^2$

b. $4 = 16^{1/2}$

c. $\frac{1}{8} = 2^{-3}$

EXAMPLE 2 **Changing from Exponential Form to Logarithmic Form**

Write each equation in its equivalent logarithmic form.

a. $16 = 2^4$ **b.** $9 = \sqrt{81}$ **c.** $\frac{1}{9} = 3^{-2}$ **d.** $x^a = z$

Solution:

a. $16 = 2^4$ is equivalent to $\boxed{\log_2 16 = 4}$

b. $9 = \sqrt{81} = 81^{1/2}$ is equivalent to $\boxed{\log_{81} 9 = \frac{1}{2}}$

c. $\frac{1}{9} = 3^{-2}$ is equivalent to $\boxed{\log_3\left(\frac{1}{9}\right) = -2}$

d. $x^a = z$ is equivalent to $\boxed{\log_x z = a \quad \text{for } x > 0}$

YOUR TURN Write each equation in its equivalent logarithmic form.

a. $81 = 9^2$ **b.** $12 = \sqrt{144}$ **c.** $\frac{1}{49} = 7^{-2}$ **d.** $y^b = w$

ANSWER

a. $\log_9 81 = 2$

b. $\log_{144} 12 = \frac{1}{2}$

c. $\log_7\left(\frac{1}{49}\right) = -2$

d. $\log_y w = b$ for $y > 0$

Some logarithms can be found exactly, while others must be approximated. Example 3 illustrates how to find the exact value of a logarithm. Example 4 illustrates approximating values of logarithms with a calculator.

EXAMPLE 3 **Finding the Exact Value of a Logarithm**

Find the exact value of

a. $\log_3 81$ **b.** $\log_{169} 13$ **c.** $\log_5\left(\frac{1}{5}\right)$

Solution (a):

The logarithm has some value. Let's call it x. $\log_3 81 = x$

Change from logarithmic to exponential form. $3^x = 81$

3 raised to what power is 81? $3^4 = 81 \quad x = 4$

Change from exponential to logarithmic form. $\boxed{\log_3 81 = 4}$

Solution (b):

The logarithm has some value. Let's call it x. $\log_{169} 13 = x$

Change from logarithmic to exponential form. $169^x = 13$

169 raised to what power is 13? $169^{1/2} = \sqrt{169} = 13 \quad x = \frac{1}{2}$

Change from exponential to logarithmic form. $\boxed{\log_{169} 13 = \frac{1}{2}}$

[CONCEPT CHECK]

Write $\log_a x = 5$ in exponential form.

ANSWER $a^5 = x$

Solution (c):

The logarithm has some value. Let's call it x. $\log_5\left(\frac{1}{5}\right) = x$

Change from logarithmic to exponential form. $5^x = \frac{1}{5}$

5 raised to what power is $\frac{1}{5}$? $5^{-1} = \frac{1}{5}$ $x = -1$

Change from exponential to logarithmic form. $\boxed{\log_5\left(\frac{1}{5}\right) = -1}$

YOUR TURN Evaluate the given logarithms exactly.

a. $\log_2 \frac{1}{2}$ **b.** $\log_{100} 10$ **c.** $\log_{10} 1000$

ANSWER

a. $\log_2 \frac{1}{2} = -1$

b. $\log_{100} 10 = \frac{1}{2}$

c. $\log_{10} 1000 = 3$

3.2.2 Common and Natural Logarithms

Two logarithmic bases that arise frequently are base 10 and base e. The logarithmic function of base 10 is called the **common logarithmic function**. Since it is common, $f(x) = \log_{10}x$ is often expressed as $f(x) = \log x$. Thus, if no explicit base is indicated, base 10 is implied. The logarithmic function of base e is called the **natural logarithmic function**. The natural logarithmic function $f(x) = \log_e x$ is often expressed as $f(x) = \ln x$. Both the LOG and LN buttons appear on scientific and graphing calculators. For the ***logarithms*** (not the functions), we say "the log" (for base 10) and "the natural log" (for base e).

Earlier in this section, we evaluated logarithms exactly by converting to exponential form and identifying the exponent. For example, to evaluate $\log_{10} 100$, we ask the question, 10 raised to what power is 100? The answer is 2.

Calculators enable us to approximate logarithms. For example, evaluate $\log_{10} 233$. We are unable to evaluate this exactly by asking the question, 10 raised to what power is 233? Since $10^2 < 10^x < 10^3$, we know the answer x must lie between 2 and 3. Instead, we use a calculator to find an approximate value, 2.367.

3.2.2 SKILL

Approximate common and natural logarithms using a calculator.

3.2.2 CONCEPTUAL

Recognize when a logarithm or the value of a logarithmic function can be evaluated exactly and when it must be approximated.

STUDY TIP

- $\log_{10} x = \log x$. No explicit base implies base 10.
- $\log_e x = \ln x$

EXAMPLE 4 Using a Calculator to Evaluate Common and Natural Logarithms

Use a calculator to evaluate the common and natural logarithms. Round your answers to four decimal places.

a. $\log 415$ **b.** $\ln 415$ **c.** $\log 1$ **d.** $\ln 1$ **e.** $\log(-2)$ **f.** $\ln(-2)$

Solution:

a. $\log(415) \approx 2.618048097 \approx \boxed{2.6180}$ **b.** $\ln(415) \approx 6.02827852 \approx \boxed{6.0283}$

c. $\log(1) = \boxed{0}$ **d.** $\ln(1) = \boxed{0}$

e. $\log(-2)$ $\boxed{\text{undefined}}$ **f.** $\ln(-2)$ $\boxed{\text{undefined}}$

CONCEPT CHECK

Find log(10), log(50), and log(100).

ANSWER 1; 1.699; 2

Parts (c) and (d) in Example 4 illustrate that all logarithmic functions pass through the point (1, 0). Parts (e) and (f) in Example 4 illustrate that the domains of logarithmic functions are positive real numbers.

STUDY TIP

Logarithms can be evaluated only for positive arguments.

3.2.3 Graphs of Logarithmic Functions

3.2.3 SKILL

Graph logarithmic functions.

3.2.3 CONCEPTUAL

Understand the inverse relationship between the characteristics of logarithmic functions and exponential functions.

The general logarithmic function $y = \log_b x$ is defined as the inverse of the exponential function $y = b^x$. Therefore, when these two functions are plotted on the same graph, they are symmetric about the line $y = x$. Notice the symmetry about the line $y = x$ when $y = b^x$ and $y = \log_b x$ are plotted on the same graph.

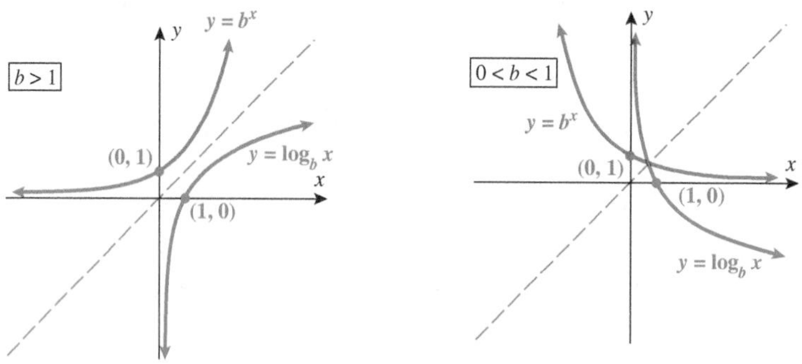

Comparison of Inverse Functions: $f(x) = \log_b x$ and $f^{-1}(x) = b^x$

EXPONENTIAL FUNCTION	LOGARITHMIC FUNCTION
$y = b^x$	$y = \log_b x$
y-intercept: (0, 1)	x-intercept: (1, 0)
Domain: $(-\infty, \infty)$	Domain: $(0, \infty)$
Range: $(0, \infty)$	Range: $(-\infty, \infty)$
Horizontal asymptote: x-axis	Vertical asymptote: y-axis
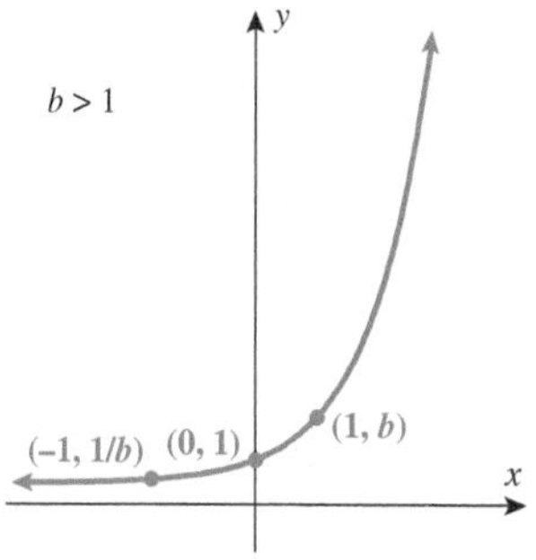	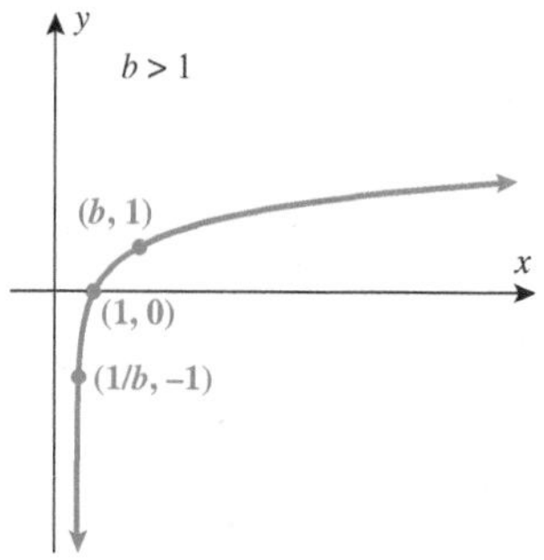

Additionally, the domain of one function is the range of the other, and vice versa. When dealing with logarithmic functions, special attention must be paid to the domain of the function. The domain of $y = \log_b x$ is $(0, \infty)$. In other words, you can only take the log of a positive real number, $x > 0$.

EXAMPLE 5 **Finding the Domain of a Shifted Logarithmic Function**

Find the domain of each of the given logarithmic functions.

a. $f(x) = \log_b(x - 4)$ **b.** $g(x) = \log_b(5 - 2x)$

Solution (a):

Set the argument greater than zero. $x - 4 > 0$

Solve the inequality. $x > 4$

Write the domain in interval notation. $\boxed{(4, \infty)}$

Solution (b):

Set the argument greater than zero. $5 - 2x > 0$

Solve the inequality. $-2x > -5$

$2x < 5$

$x < \frac{5}{2}$

Write the domain in interval notation. $\boxed{\left(-\infty, \frac{5}{2}\right)}$

YOUR TURN Find the domain of the given logarithmic functions.

a. $f(x) = \log_b(x + 2)$ **b.** $g(x) = \log_b(3 - 5x)$

ANSWER

a. $(-2, \infty)$

b. $\left(-\infty, \frac{3}{5}\right)$

It is important to note that when finding the domain of a logarithmic function, we set the argument strictly greater than zero and solve.

STUDY TIP

Review solving inequalities in Section 0.4.

EXAMPLE 6 Finding the Domain of a Logarithmic Function with a Complicated Argument

Find the domain of each of the given logarithmic functions.

a. $\ln(x^2 - 9)$ **b.** $\log(|x + 1|)$

Solution (a):

Set the argument greater than zero. $x^2 - 9 > 0$

Solve the inequality. $\boxed{(-\infty, -3) \cup (3, \infty)}$

Solution (b):

Set the argument greater than zero. $|x + 1| > 0$

Solve the inequality. $x \neq -1$

Write the domain in interval notation. $\boxed{(-\infty, -1) \cup (-1, \infty)}$

YOUR TURN Find the domain of each of the given logarithmic functions.

a. $\ln(x^2 - 4)$ **b.** $\log(|x - 3|)$

ANSWER

a. $(-\infty, -2) \cup (2, \infty)$

b. $(-\infty, 3) \cup (3, \infty)$

Recall from Section 1.3 that a technique for graphing general functions is transformations of known functions. For example, to graph $f(x) = (x - 3)^2 + 1$, we start with the known parabola $y = x^2$, whose vertex is at $(0, 0)$, and we shift that graph to the right three units and up one unit. We use the same techniques for graphing logarithmic functions. To graph $y = \log_b(x + 2) - 1$, we start with the graph of $y = \log_b(x)$ and shift the graph to the left two units and down one unit.

EXAMPLE 7 **Graphing Logarithmic Functions Using Horizontal and Vertical Shifts**

Graph the functions, and state the domain and range of each.

a. $y = \log_2(x - 3)$ **b.** $\log_2 x - 3$

Solution:

Identify the base function. $y = \log_2 x$

Label key features of $y = \log_2 x$.

x-intercept: $(1, 0)$

Vertical asymptote: $x = 0$

Additional points: $(2, 1), (4, 2)$

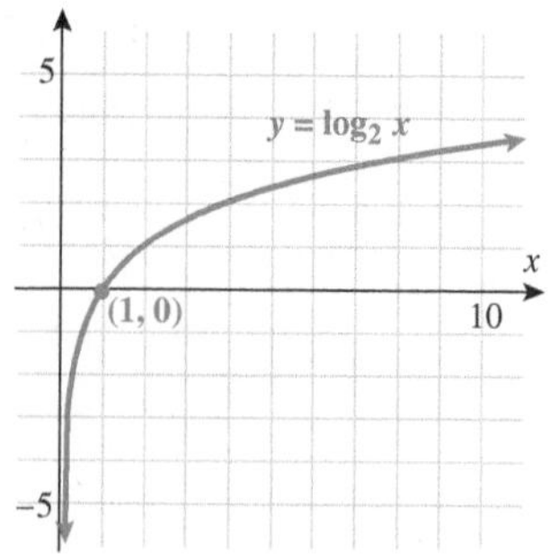

a. Shift base function to the *right* three units.
x-intercept: $(4, 0)$

Vertical asymptote: $x = 3$

Additional points: $(5, 1), (7, 2)$

Domain: $(3, \infty)$ Range: $(-\infty, \infty)$

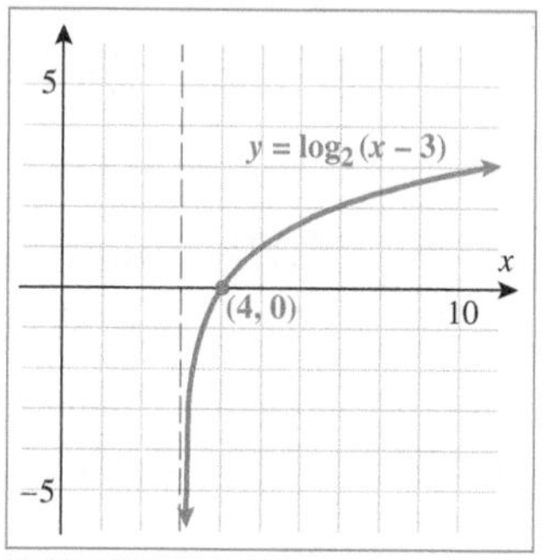

b. Shift base function *down* three units.

x-intercept: $(1, -3)$

Vertical asymptote: $x = 0$

Additional points: $(2, -2), (4, -1)$

Domain: $(0, \infty)$ Range: $(-\infty, \infty)$

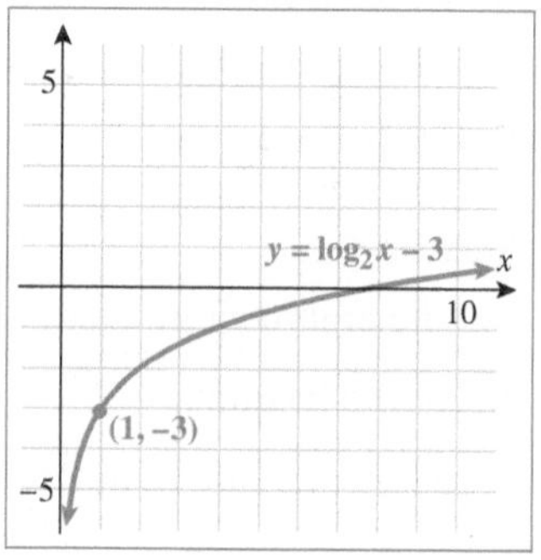

YOUR TURN Graph the functions and state the domain and range of each.

a. $y = \log_3 x$ **b.** $y = \log_3(x + 3)$ **c.** $\log_3 x + 1$

ANSWER

a. Domain: $(0, \infty)$ Range: $(-\infty, \infty)$

b. Domain: $(-3, \infty)$ Range: $(-\infty, \infty)$

c. Domain: $(0, \infty)$ Range: $(-\infty, \infty)$

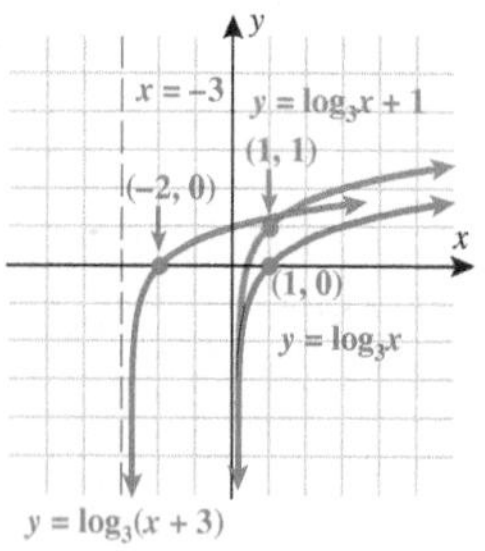

All of the transformation techniques (shifting, reflection, and compression) discussed in Chapter 1 also apply to logarithmic functions. For example, the graphs of $-\log_2 x$ and $\log_2(-x)$ are found by reflecting the graph of $y = \log_2 x$ about the x-axis and y-axis, respectively.

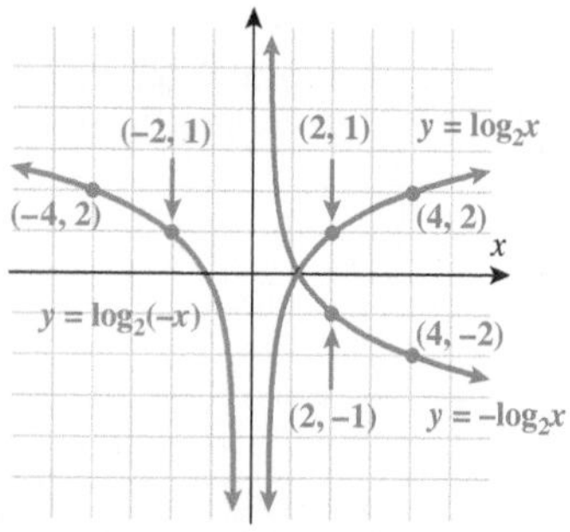

EXAMPLE 8 **Graphing Logarithmic Functions Using Transformations**

Graph the function $f(x) = -\log_2(x - 3)$ and state its domain and range.

Solution:

Graph $y = \log_2 x$.

x-intercept: $(1, 0)$

Vertical asymptote: $x = 0$

Additional points: $(2, 1)$, $(4, 2)$

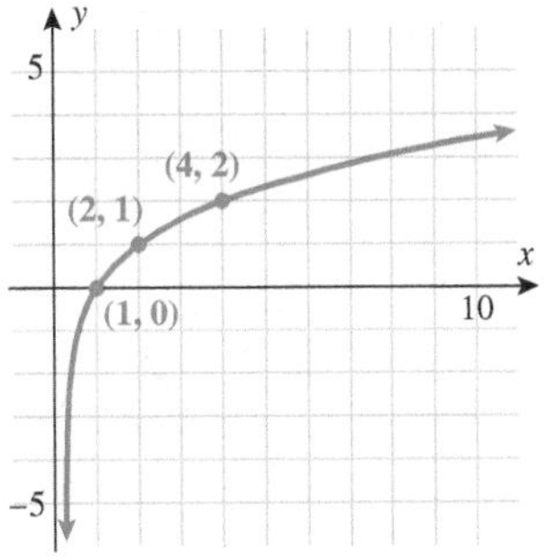

Graph $y = \log_2(x - 3)$ by shifting $y = \log_2 x$ to the *right* three units.

x-intercept: $(4, 0)$

Vertical asymptote: $x = 3$

Additional points: $(5, 1)$, $(7, 2)$

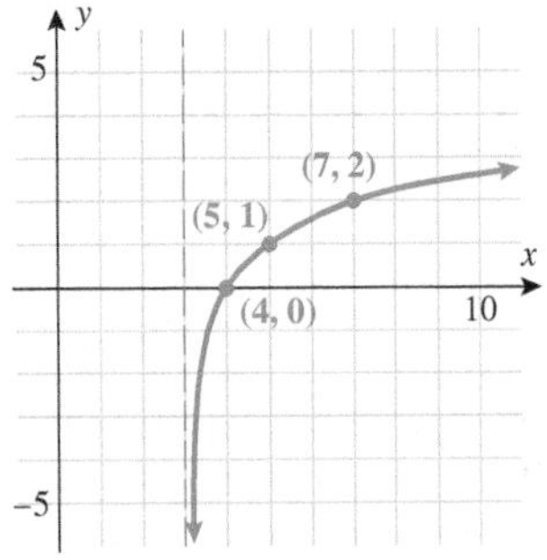

Graph $y = -\log_2(x - 3)$ by reflecting $y = \log_2(x - 3)$ about the x-axis.

x-intercept: $(4, 0)$

Vertical asymptote: $x = 3$

Additional points: $(5, -1)$, $(7, -2)$

Domain: $(3, \infty)$	Range: $(-\infty, \infty)$

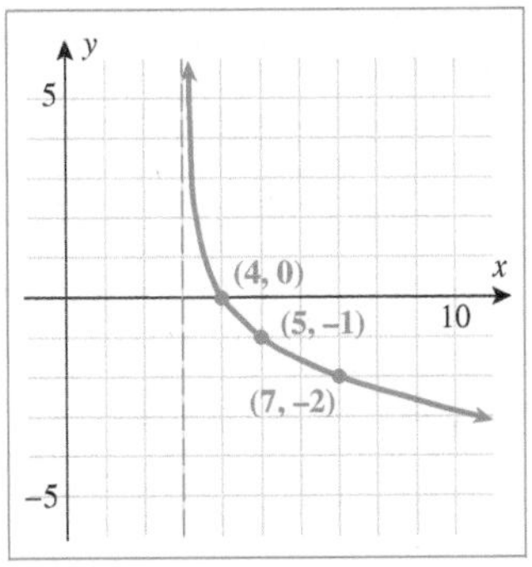

[CONCEPT CHECK]

Find the x-intercept, domain, and range of $\log_b(x - 1)$.

ANSWER x-intercept: $(2, 0)$; Domain: $(1, \infty)$; Range: $(-\infty, \infty)$

3.2.4 Applications of Logarithms

Logarithms are used to make a large range of numbers manageable. For example, to create a scale to measure a human's ability to hear, we must have a way to measure the sound intensity of an explosion, even though that intensity can be more than a trillion (10^{12}) times greater than that of a soft whisper. Decibels in engineering and physics, pH in chemistry, and the Richter scale for earthquakes are all applications of logarithmic functions.

The **decibel** is a logarithmic unit used to measure the magnitude of a physical quantity relative to a specified reference level. The *decibel* (dB) is employed in many engineering and science applications. The most common application is the intensity of sound.

3.2.4 SKILL

Apply logarithmic functions to problems in the natural sciences and engineering.

3.2.4 CONCEPTUAL

Understand that logarithmic functions allow very large ranges of numbers in science and engineering applications to be represented on a smaller scale.

DEFINITION Decibel (Sound)

The **decibel** is defined as $D = 10 \log\left(\frac{I}{I_T}\right)$

where D is the decibel level (dB), I is the intensity of the sound measured in watts per square meter, and I_T is the intensity threshold of the least audible sound a human can hear.

The human average threshold is $I_T = 1 \times 10^{-12}$ W/m^2.

Notice that when $I = I_T$, then $D = 10 \overbrace{\log 1}^{0} = 0$ dB. People who work professionally with sound, such as acoustics engineers and medical hearing specialists, refer to this threshold level I_T as "0 dB." The following table illustrates typical sounds we hear and their corresponding decibel levels.

[CONCEPT CHECK]

The sound intensity of a jet engine is ________ times the sound intensity of an iPod, but it's only ________ more decibels.

ANSWER 100,000; 50

SOUND SOURCE	SOUND INTENSITY (W/m^2)	DECIBELS (dB)
Threshold of hearing	1.0×10^{-12}	0
Vacuum cleaner	1.0×10^{-4}	80
iPod	1.0×10^{-2}	100
Jet engine	1.0×10^{3}	150

For example, a whisper (approximately 0 dB) from someone standing next to a jet engine (150 dB) might go unheard because when these are added, we get approximately 150 dB (the jet engine).

EXAMPLE 9 Calculating Decibels of Sounds

Suppose you have seats to a concert given by your favorite musical artist. Calculate the approximate decibel level associated with the typical sound intensity, given $I = 1 \times 10^{-2}$ W/m^2.

Solution:

Write the decibel-scale formula. $D = 10 \log\left(\frac{I}{I_T}\right)$

Substitute $I = 1 \times 10^{-2}$ W/m^2 and $I_T = 1 \times 10^{-12}$ W/m^2. $D = 10 \log\left(\frac{1 \times 10^{-2}}{1 \times 10^{-12}}\right)$

Simplify. $D = 10 \log(10^{10})$

Recall that the implied base for log is 10. $D = 10 \log_{10}(10^{10})$

Evaluate the right side. $[\log_{10}(10^{10}) = 10]$ $D = 10 \cdot 10$

$D = 100$

The typical sound level on the front row of a rock concert is 100 dB.

YOUR TURN Calculate the approximate decibels associated with a sound so loud it will cause instant perforation of the eardrums, $I = 1 \times 10^4$ W/m^2.

ANSWER

160 dB

The Richter scale (earthquakes) is another application of logarithms.

DEFINITION **Richter Scale**

The magnitude M of an earthquake is measured using the **Richter scale**

$$M = \frac{2}{3}\log\left(\frac{E}{E_0}\right)$$

where

M is the magnitude
E is the seismic energy released by the earthquake (in joules)
E_0 is the energy released by a reference earthquake $E_0 = 10^{4.4}$ joules

EXAMPLE 10 **Calculating the Magnitude of an Earthquake**

On October 17, 1989, just moments before game 3 of the World Series between the Oakland A's and the San Francisco Giants was about to start—with 60,000 fans in Candlestick Park—a devastating earthquake erupted. Parts of interstates and bridges collapsed, and President George H. W. Bush declared the area a disaster zone. The earthquake released approximately 1.12×10^{15} joules of energy. Calculate the magnitude of the earthquake using the Richter scale.

Solution:

Write the Richter scale formula. $M = \frac{2}{3}\log\left(\frac{E}{E_0}\right)$

Substitute $E = 1.12 \times 10^{15}$ and $E_0 = 10^{4.4}$. $M = \frac{2}{3}\log\left(\frac{1.12 \times 10^{15}}{10^{4.4}}\right)$

Simplify. $M = \frac{2}{3}\log\left(1.12 \times 10^{10.6}\right)$

Approximate the logarithm using a calculator. $M \approx \frac{2}{3}(10.65) \approx 7.1$

The 1989 earthquake in California measured $\boxed{7.1}$ on the Richter scale.

YOUR TURN On May 3, 1996, Seattle experienced a moderate earthquake. The energy that the earthquake released was approximately 1.12×10^{12} joules. Calculate the magnitude of the 1996 Seattle earthquake using the Richter scale.

ANSWER

5.1

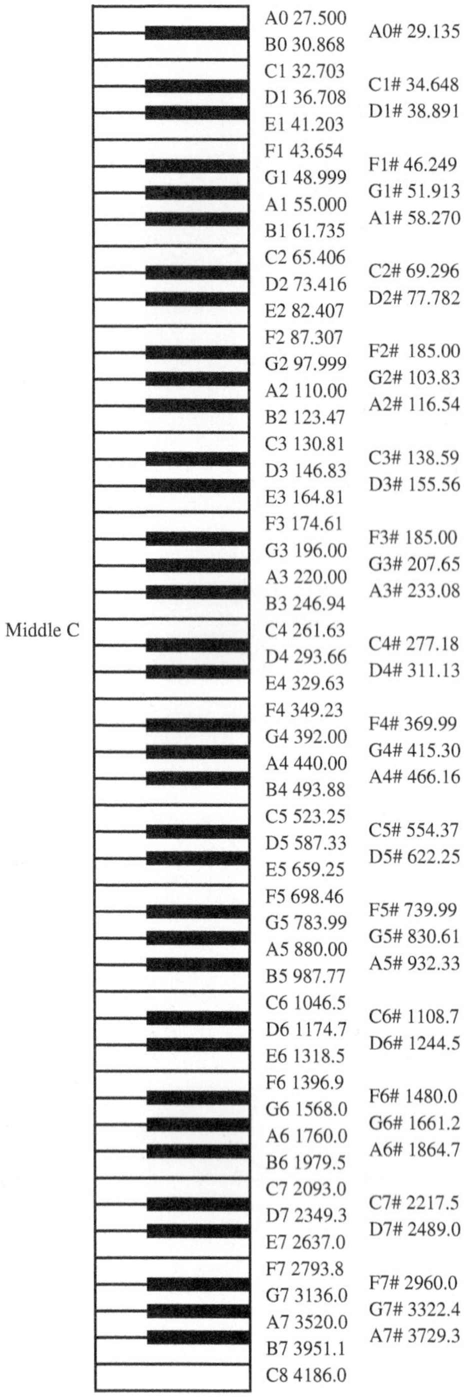

A **logarithmic scale** expresses the logarithm of a physical quantity instead of the quantity itself. In music, the pitch is the perceived fundamental frequency of sound. The note A above middle C on a piano has the pitch associated with a pure tone of 440 hertz. An octave is the interval between one musical pitch and another with either double or half its frequency. For example, if a note has a frequency of 440 hertz, then the note an octave above it has a frequency of 880 hertz, and the note an octave below it has a frequency of 220 hertz. Therefore, the ratio of two notes an octave apart is 2:1.

The following table lists the frequencies associated with A notes.

NOTE	A_1	A_2	A_3	A_4	A_5	A_6	A_7
Frequency (Hz)	55	110	220	440	880	1760	3520
Octave with respect to A_4	-3	-2	-1	0	$+1$	$+2$	$+3$

We can graph $\dfrac{\text{Frequency of note}}{440\text{ Hz}}$ on the horizontal axis and the octave (with respect to A_4) on the vertical axis.

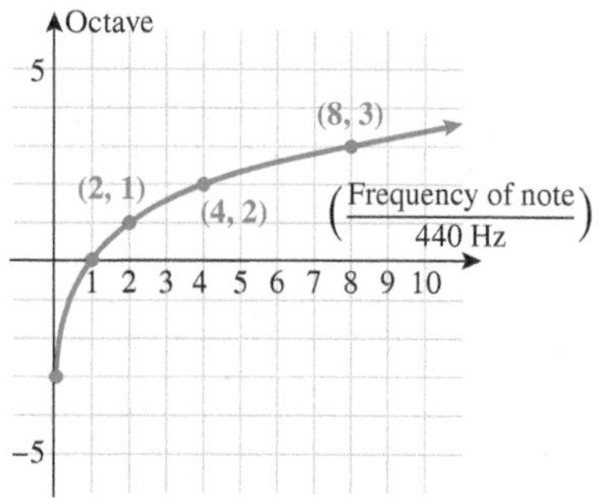

If we instead graph the logarithm of this quantity, $\log\left[\dfrac{\text{Frequency of note}}{440\text{ Hz}}\right]$, we see that using a logarithmic scale expresses octaves linearly (up or down an octave). In other words, an "octave" is a purely logarithmic concept.

When a logarithmic scale is used we typically classify a graph one of two ways:

- Log-log plot (both the horizontal and vertical axes use logarithmic scales)
- Semilog plot (one of the axes uses a logarithmic scale)

The second graph, with octaves on the vertical axis and the log of the ratio of frequencies on the horizontal axis, is called a semilog plot.

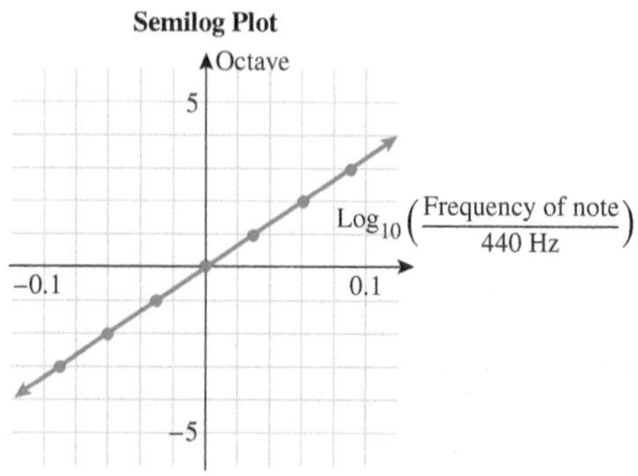

EXAMPLE 11 Graphing Using a Logarithmic Scale

Frequency is inversely proportional to the wavelength: In a vacuum, $f = \frac{c}{\lambda}$, where f is the frequency (in hertz), $c = 3.0 \times 10^8$ m/s is the speed of light in a vacuum, and λ is the wavelength in meters. Graph frequency versus wavelength using a log-log plot.

Solution:

Let wavelength range from microns (10^{-6}) to hundreds of meters (10^2) by powers of 10 along the horizontal axis.

λ	$f = \frac{3.0 \times 10^8}{\lambda}$	
10^{-6}	3.0×10^{14}	
10^{-5}	3.0×10^{13}	
10^{-4}	3.0×10^{12}	(Terahertz: THz)
10^{-3}	3.0×10^{11}	
10^{-2}	3.0×10^{10}	
10^{-1}	3.0×10^{9}	(Gigahertz: GHz)
10^{0}	3.0×10^{8}	
10^{1}	3.0×10^{7}	
10^{2}	3.0×10^{6}	(Megahertz: MHz)

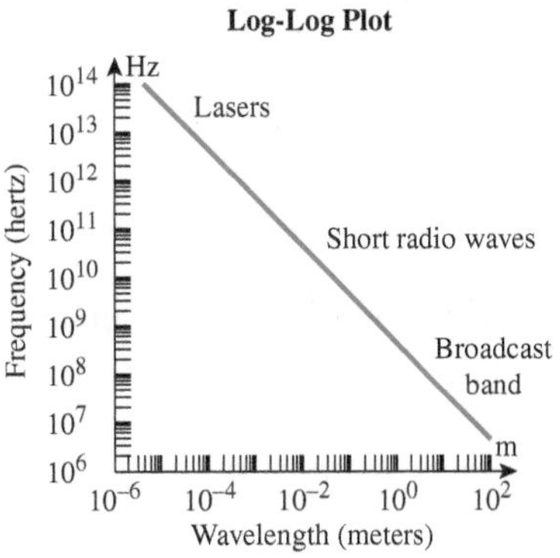

The logarithmic scales allow us to represent a large range of numbers. In this graph, the x-axis ranges from microns, 10^{-6} meters, to hundreds of meters, and the y-axis ranges from megahertz (MHz), 10^6 hertz, to hundreds of terahertz (THz), 10^{12} hertz.

[SECTION 3.2] SUMMARY

In this section, logarithmic functions were defined as inverses of exponential functions.

$$y = \log_b x \text{ is equivalent to } x = b^y$$

NAME	EXPLICIT BASE	IMPLICIT BASE
Common logarithm	$f(x) = \log_{10} x$	$f(x) = \log x$
Natural logarithm	$f(x) = \log_e x$	$f(x) = \ln x$

Evaluating Logarithms

- *Exact:* Convert to exponential form first, then evaluate.
- *Approximate:* Find the natural and common logarithms with calculators.

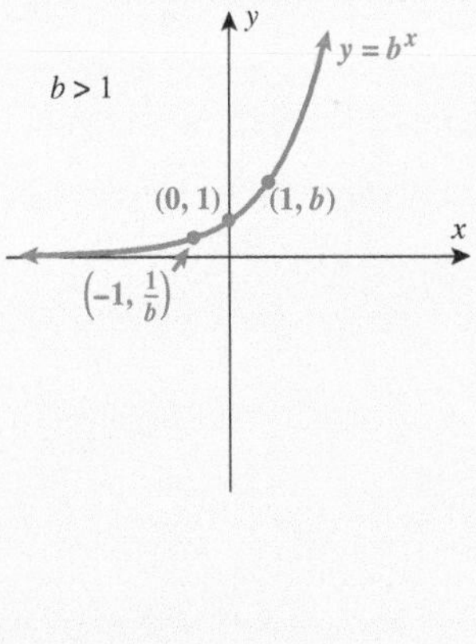

Graphs of Logarithmic Functions

EXPONENTIAL FUNCTION	LOGARITHMIC FUNCTION
$y = b^x$	$y = \log_b x$
y-intercept: (0, 1)	x-intercept: (1, 0)
Domain: $(-\infty, \infty)$	Domain: $(0, \infty)$
Range: $(0, \infty)$	Range: $(-\infty, \infty)$
Horizontal asymptote: x-axis	Vertical asymptote: y-axis

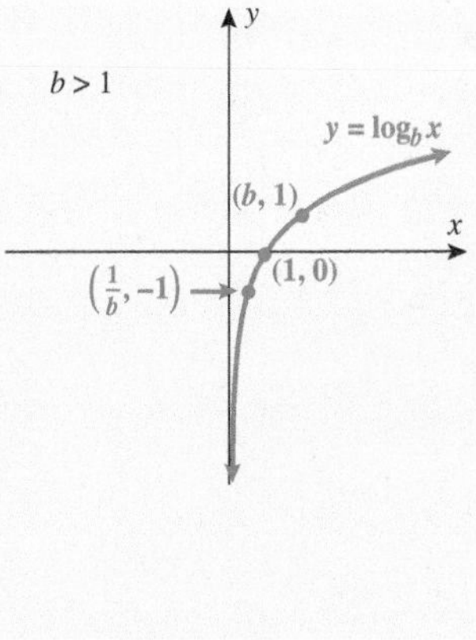

[SECTION 3.2] EXERCISES

• SKILLS

In Exercises 1–20, write each logarithmic equation in its equivalent exponential form.

1. $\log_{81} 3 = \frac{1}{4}$
2. $\log_{121} 11 = \frac{1}{2}$
3. $\log_2\left(\frac{1}{32}\right) = -5$
4. $\log_3\left(\frac{1}{81}\right) = -4$
5. $\log 0.01 = -2$
6. $\log 0.0001 = -4$
7. $\log 10{,}000 = 4$
8. $\log 1000 = 3$
9. $\log_{1/4}(64) = -3$
10. $\log_{1/6}(36) = -2$
11. $-1 = \ln\left(\frac{1}{e}\right)$
12. $1 = \ln e$
13. $\ln 1 = 0$
14. $\log 1 = 0$
15. $\ln 5 = x$
16. $\ln 4 = y$
17. $z = \log_x y$
18. $y = \log_x z$
19. $x = \log_y(x + y)$
20. $z = \ln x^y$

In Exercises 21–34, write each exponential equation in its equivalent logarithmic form.

21. $0.00001 = 10^{-5}$
22. $3^6 = 729$
23. $78{,}125 = 5^7$
24. $100{,}000 = 10^5$
25. $15 = \sqrt{225}$
26. $7 = \sqrt[3]{343}$
27. $\frac{8}{125} = \left(\frac{2}{5}\right)^3$
28. $\frac{8}{27} = \left(\frac{2}{3}\right)^3$
29. $3 = \left(\frac{1}{27}\right)^{-1/3}$
30. $4 = \left(\frac{1}{1024}\right)^{-1/5}$
31. $e^x = 6$
32. $e^{-x} = 4$
33. $x = y^z$
34. $z = y^x$

In Exercises 35–46, evaluate the logarithms exactly (if possible).

35. $\log_2 1$
36. $\log_5 1$
37. $\log_5 3125$
38. $\log_3 729$
39. $\log 10^7$
40. $\log 10^{-2}$
41. $\log_{1/4} 4096$
42. $\log_{1/7} 2401$
43. $\log 0$
44. $\ln 0$
45. $\log(-100)$
46. $\ln(-1)$

In Exercises 47–54, approximate (if possible) the common and natural logarithms using a calculator. Round to two decimal places.

47. $\log 29$
48. $\ln 29$
49. $\ln 380$
50. $\log 380$
51. $\log 0$
52. $\ln 0$
53. $\ln 0.0003$
54. $\log 0.0003$

In Exercises 55–66, state the domain of the logarithmic function in interval notation.

55. $f(x) = \log_2(x + 5)$
56. $f(x) = \log_2(4x - 1)$
57. $f(x) = \log_3(5 - 2x)$
58. $f(x) = \log_3(5 - x)$
59. $f(x) = \ln(7 - 2x)$
60. $f(x) = \ln(3 - x)$
61. $f(x) = \log|x|$
62. $f(x) = \log|x + 1|$
63. $f(x) = \log(x^2 + 1)$
64. $f(x) = \log(1 - x^2)$
65. $f(x) = \log(10 + 3x - x^2)$
66. $f(x) = \log_3(x^3 - 3x^2 + 3x - 1)$

In Exercises 67–72, match the graph with the function.

67. $y = \log_5 x$
68. $y = \log_5(-x)$
69. $y = -\log_5(-x)$
70. $y = \log_5(x + 3) - 1$
71. $y = \log_5(1 - x) - 2$
72. $y = -\log_5(3 - x) + 2$

a.

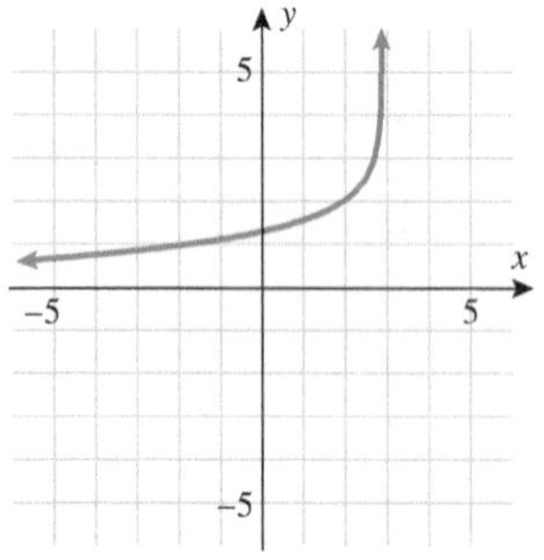

b.

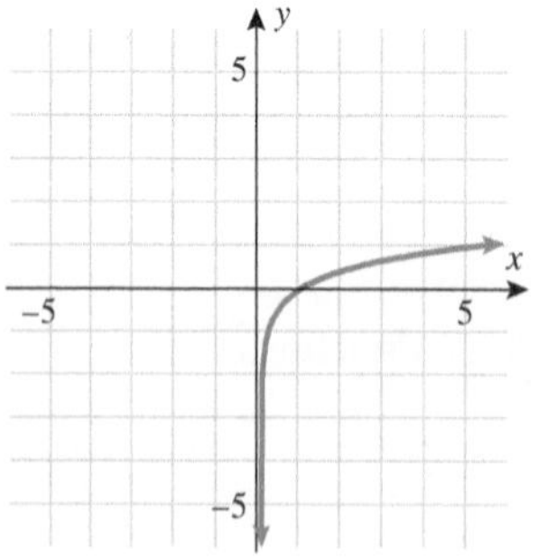

c.

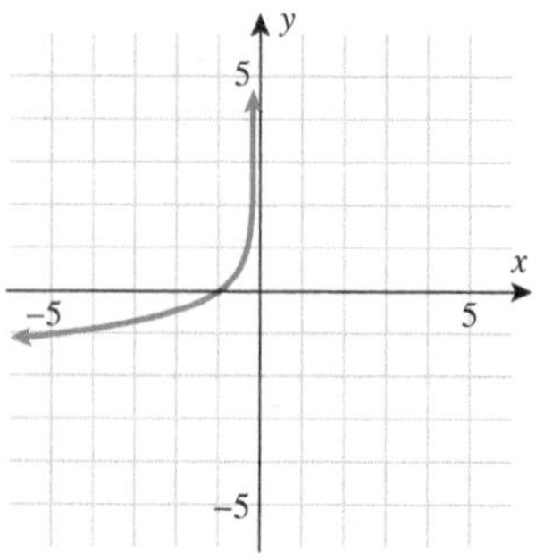

d.

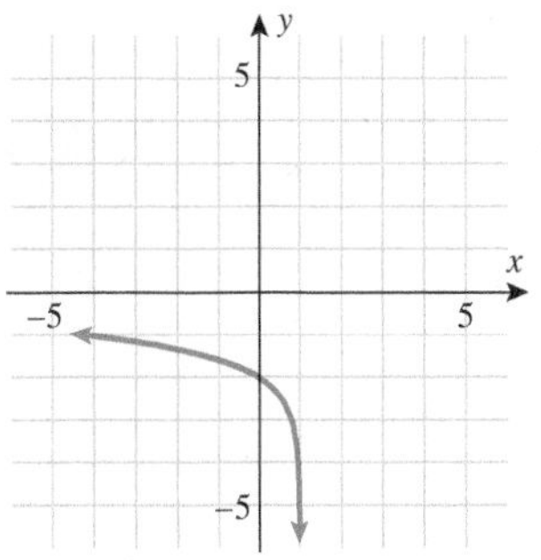

e.

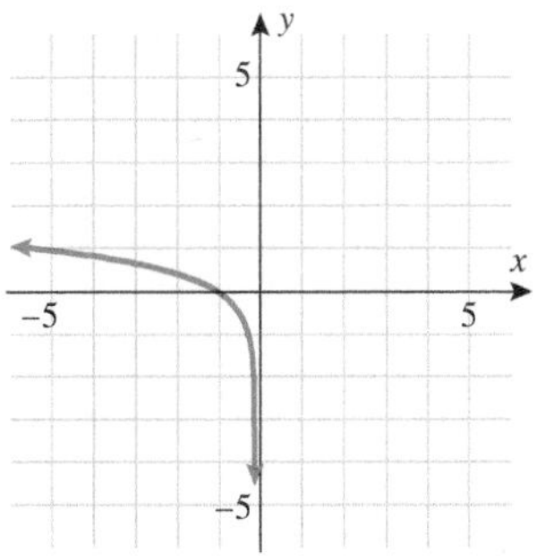

f.

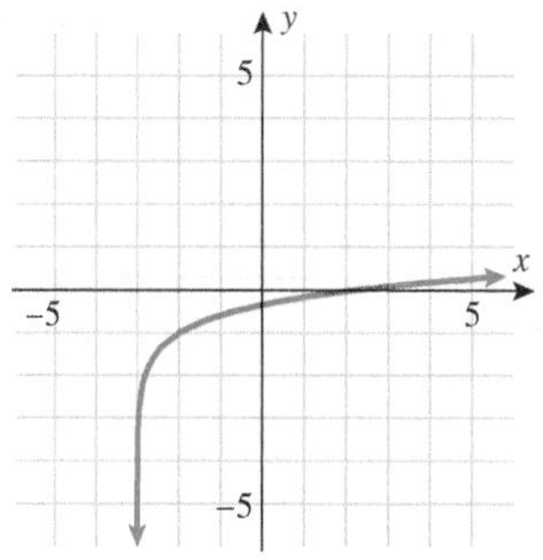

In Exercises 73–84, graph the logarithmic function using transformation techniques. State the domain and range of *f*.

73. $f(x) = \log(x - 1)$ **74.** $f(x) = \log(x + 2)$ **75.** $\ln(x + 2)$ **76.** $\ln(x - 1)$

77. $f(x) = \log_3(x + 2) - 1$ **78.** $f(x) = \log_3(x + 1) - 2$ **79.** $f(x) = -\log(x) + 1$ **80.** $f(x) = \log(-x) + 2$

81. $f(x) = \ln(x + 4)$ **82.** $f(x) = \ln(4 - x)$ **83.** $f(x) = \log(2x)$ **84.** $f(x) = 2\ln(-x)$

• APPLICATIONS

For Exercises 85–88, refer to the following:

Decibel: $D = 10\log\left(\frac{I}{I_T}\right) \qquad I_T = 1 \times 10^{-12}\ \text{W/m}^2$

85. Sound. Calculate the decibels associated with *normal conversation* if the intensity is $I = 1 \times 10^{-6}$ W/m^2.

86. Sound. Calculate the decibels associated with the *onset of pain* if the intensity is $I = 1 \times 10^1$ W/m^2.

87. Sound. Calculate the decibels associated with attending *a football game in a loud college stadium* if the intensity is $I = 1 \times 10^{-0.3}$ W/m^2.

88. Sound. Calculate the decibels associated with a *doorbell* if the intensity is $I = 1 \times 10^{-4.5}$ W/m^2.

For Exercises 89–92, refer to the following:

Richter Scale: $M = \frac{2}{3}\log\left(\frac{E}{E_0}\right) \qquad E_0 = 10^{4.4}$ **joules**

89. Earthquakes. On Good Friday 1964, one of the most severe North American earthquakes ever recorded struck Alaska. The energy released measured 1.41×10^{17} joules. Calculate the magnitude of the 1964 Alaska earthquake using the Richter scale.

90. Earthquakes. On January 22, 2003, Colima, Mexico, experienced a major earthquake. The energy released measured 6.31×10^{15} joules. Calculate the magnitude of the 2003 Mexican earthquake using the Richter scale.

91. Earthquakes. On December 26, 2003, a major earthquake rocked southeastern Iran. In Bam, 30,000 people were killed, and 85% of buildings were damaged or destroyed. The energy released measured 2×10^{14} joules. Calculate the magnitude of the 2003 Iran earthquake with the Richter scale.

92. Earthquakes. On November 1, 1755, Lisbon was destroyed by an earthquake, which killed 90,000 people and destroyed 85% of the city. It was one of the most destructive earthquakes in history. The energy released measured 8×10^{17} joules. Calculate the magnitude of the 1755 Lisbon earthquake with the Richter scale.

For Exercises 93–98, refer to the following:

The pH of a solution is a measure of the molar concentration of hydrogen ions, H^+, in moles per liter, in the solution, which means that it is a measure of the acidity or basicity of the solution. The letters pH stand for "power of hydrogen," and the numerical value is defined as

$$\text{pH} = -\log_{10}[H^+]$$

Very acidic corresponds to pH values near 1, neutral corresponds to a pH near 7 (pure water), and very basic corresponds to values near 14. In the next six exercises you will be asked to calculate the pH value of wine, Pepto-Bismol, normal rainwater, bleach, and fruit. List these six liquids and use your intuition to classify them as neutral, acidic, very acidic, basic, or very basic before you calculate their actual pH values.

93. Chemistry. If wine has an approximate hydrogen ion concentration of 5.01×10^{-4}, calculate its pH value.

94. Chemistry. Pepto-Bismol has a hydrogen ion concentration of about 5.01×10^{-11}. Calculate its pH value.

95. Chemistry. Normal rainwater is slightly acidic and has an approximate hydrogen ion concentration of $10^{-5.6}$. Calculate its pH value. Acid rain and tomato juice have similar approximate hydrogen ion concentrations of 10^{-4}. Calculate the pH value of acid rain and tomato juice.

96. **Chemistry.** Bleach has an approximate hydrogen ion concentration of 5.0×10^{-13}. Calculate its pH value.

97. **Chemistry.** An apple has an approximate hydrogen ion concentration of $10^{-3.6}$. Calculate its pH value.

98. **Chemistry.** An orange has an approximate hydrogen ion concentration of $10^{-4.2}$. Calculate its pH value.

99. **Archaeology.** Carbon dating is a method used to determine the age of a fossil or other organic remains. The age t in years is related to the mass C (in milligrams) of carbon-14 through a logarithmic equation:

$$t = -\frac{\ln\left(\frac{C}{500}\right)}{0.0001216}$$

How old is a fossil that contains 100 milligrams of carbon-14?

100. **Archaeology.** Repeat Exercise 99, only now the fossil contains 40 milligrams of carbon-14.

101. **Broadcasting.** Decibels are used to quantify losses associated with atmospheric interference in a communication system. The ratio of the power (watts) received to the power transmitted (watts) is often compared. Often, *watts* are transmitted, but losses due to the atmosphere typically correspond to *milliwatts* being received:

$$\text{dB} = 10 \log\left(\frac{\text{Power received}}{\text{Power transmitted}}\right)$$

If 1 watt of power is transmitted and 3 megawatts is received, calculate the power loss in decibels.

102. **Broadcasting.** Repeat Exercise 101, assuming 3 watts of power is transmitted and 0.2 megawatt is received.

For Exercises 103 and 104, refer to the following:

The range of all possible frequencies of electromagnetic radiation is called the electromagnetic spectrum. In a vacuum the frequency of electromagnetic radiation is modeled by

$$f = \frac{c}{\lambda}$$

where c is 3.0×10^8 m/s and λ is wavelength in meters.

103. **Physics/Electromagnetic Spectrum.** The *radio spectrum* is the portion of the electromagnetic spectrum that corresponds to radio frequencies. The radio spectrum is used for various transmission technologies and is government regulated. Ranges of the radio spectrum are often allocated based on usage; for example, AM radio, cell phones, and television. (Source: http://en.wikipedia.org/wiki/Radio_spectrum)

a. Complete the following table for the various usages of the radio spectrum.

USAGE	WAVELENGTH	FREQUENCY
Super Low Frequency—Communication with Submarines	10,000,000 m	30 Hz
Ultra Low Frequency—Communication within Mines	1,000,000 m	
Very Low Frequency—Avalanche Beacons	100,000 m	
Low Frequency—Navigation, AM Longwave Broadcasting	10,000 m	
Medium Frequency—AM Broadcasts, Amateur Radio	1000 m	
High Frequency—Shortwave broadcasts, Citizens Band Radio	100 m	
Very High Frequency—FM Radio, Television	10 m	
Ultra High Frequency—Television, Mobile Phones	0.050 m	

b. Graph the frequency within the radio spectrum (in hertz) as a function of wavelength (in meters).

104. **Physics/Electromagnetic Spectrum.** The *visible spectrum* is the portion of the electromagnetic spectrum that is visible to the human eye. Typically, the human eye can see wavelengths between 390 and 750 nm (nanometers, or 10^{-9} m).

a. Complete the following table for the following colors of the visible spectrum.

COLOR	WAVELENGTH	FREQUENCY
Violet	400 nm	750×10^{12} Hz
Cyan	470 nm	
Green	480 nm	
Yellow	580 nm	
Orange	610 nm	
Red	630 nm	

b. Graph the frequency (in hertz) of the colors as a function of wavelength (in meters) on a log-log plot.

• CATCH THE MISTAKE

In Exercises 105–108, explain the mistake that is made.

105. Evaluate the logarithm $\log_2 4$.

Solution:

Set the logarithm equal to x.	$\log_2 4 = x$
Write the logarithm in exponential form.	$x = 2^4$
Simplify.	$x = 16$
Answer:	$\log_2 4 = 16$

This is incorrect. The correct answer is $\log_2 4 = 2$. What went wrong?

106. Evaluate the logarithm $\log_{100} 10$.

Solution:

Set the logarithm equal to x.	$\log_{100} 10 = x$
Express the equation in exponential form.	$10^x = 100$
Solve for x.	$x = 2$
Answer:	$\log_{100} 10 = 2$

This is incorrect. The correct answer is $\log_{100} 10 = \frac{1}{2}$. What went wrong?

107. State the domain of the logarithmic function $f(x) = \log_2(x + 5)$ in interval notation.

Solution:

The domain of all logarithmic functions is $x > 0$.

Interval notation: $(0, \infty)$

This is incorrect. What went wrong?

108. State the domain of the logarithmic function $f(x) = \ln|x|$ in interval notation.

Solution:

Since the absolute value eliminates all negative numbers, the domain is the set of all real numbers.

Interval notation: $(-\infty, \infty)$

This is incorrect. What went wrong?

• CONCEPTUAL

In Exercises 109–112, determine whether each statement is true or false.

109. The domain of the standard logarithmic function, $y = \ln x$, is the set of nonnegative real numbers.

110. The horizontal axis is the horizontal asymptote of the graph of $y = \ln x$.

111. The graphs of $y = \log x$ and $y = \ln x$ have the same x-intercept $(1, 0)$.

112. The graphs of $y = \log x$ and $y = \ln x$ have the same vertical asymptote, $x = 0$.

• CHALLENGE

113. State the domain, range, and x-intercept of the function $f(x) = -\ln(x - a) + b$ for a and b real positive numbers.

114. State the domain, range, and x-intercept of the function $f(x) = \log(a - x) - b$ for a and b real positive numbers.

115. Graph the function $f(x) = \begin{cases} \ln(-x) & x < 0 \\ \ln(x) & x > 0 \end{cases}$.

116. Graph the function $f(x) = \begin{cases} -\ln(-x) & x < 0 \\ -\ln(x) & x > 0 \end{cases}$.

• PREVIEW TO CALCULUS

In Exercises 117–118, refer to the following:

Recall that the derivative of f can be found by letting $h \to 0$ in the difference quotient $\frac{f(x + h) - f(x)}{h}$. In calculus we prove that $\frac{e^h - 1}{h} = 1$ when h approaches 0; that is, for really small values of h, $\frac{e^h - 1}{h}$ gets very close to 1.

117. Use this information to find the derivative of $f(x) = e^x$.

118. Use this information to find the derivative of $f(x) = e^{2x}$. *Hint:* $e^{2h} - 1 = (e^h - 1)(e^h + 1)$

We also prove in calculus that the derivative of the inverse function f^{-1} is given by $(f^{-1})'(x) = \frac{1}{f'(f^{-1}(x))}$.

119. Given $f(x) = e^x$, find

a. $f^{-1}(x)$ **b.** $(f^{-1})'(x)$

120. Given $f(x) = e^{2x}$, find

a. $f^{-1}(x)$ **b.** $(f^{-1})'(x)$

3.3 PROPERTIES OF LOGARITHMS

SKILLS OBJECTIVES

- Use properties of logarithms to simplify logarithmic expressions.
- Use the change-of-base formula to evaluate a logarithm of a general base (other than base 10 or e).

CONCEPTUAL OBJECTIVES

- Understand that the properties of logarithms are derived from the properties of exponents and the properties of inverse functions.
- Understand that it does not matter which logarithm (natural or common) is used in the change-of-base formula.

3.3.1 Properties of Logarithms

3.3.1 SKILL

Use properties of logarithms to simplify logarithmic expressions.

3.3.1 CONCEPTUAL

Understand that the properties of logarithms are derived from the properties of exponents and the properties of inverse functions.

Since exponential functions and logarithmic functions are inverses of one another, properties of exponents are related to properties of logarithms. We will start by reviewing properties of exponents (Appendix), and then proceed to properties of logarithms.

PROPERTIES OF EXPONENTS

Let a, b, m, and n be any real numbers and $m > 0$, $n > 0$, and $b \neq 0$; then the following are true:

1. $b^m \cdot b^n = b^{m+n}$
2. $b^{-m} = \dfrac{1}{b^m} = \left(\dfrac{1}{b}\right)^m$
3. $\dfrac{b^m}{b^n} = b^{m-n}$
4. $(b^m)^n = b^{mn}$
5. $(ab)^m = a^m \cdot b^m$
6. $b^0 = 1$
7. $b^1 = b$

From these properties of exponents, we can develop similar properties for logarithms. We list seven basic properties.

PROPERTIES OF LOGARITHMS

If b, M, and N are positive real numbers, where $b \neq 1$, and p and x are real numbers, then the following are true:

1. $\log_b 1 = 0$
2. $\log_b b = 1$
3. $\log_b b^x = x$
4. $b^{\log_b x} = x \qquad x > 0$
5. $\log_b MN = \log_b M + \log_b N$ — *Product rule:* Log of a product is the sum of the logs.
6. $\log_b \left(\dfrac{M}{N}\right) = \log_b M - \log_b N$ — *Quotient rule:* Log of a quotient is the difference of the logs.
7. $\log_b M^p = p \log_b M$ — *Power rule:* Log of a number raised to an exponent is the exponent times the log of the number.

We will devote this section to proving and illustrating these seven properties.

The first two properties follow directly from the definition of a logarithmic function and properties of exponentials.

Property (1): $\log_b 1 = 0$ since $b^0 = 1$

Property (2): $\log_b b = 1$ since $b^1 = b$

The third and fourth properties follow from the fact that exponential functions and logarithmic functions are inverses of one another. Recall that inverse functions satisfy the relationship that $f^{-1}(f(x)) = x$ for all x in the domain of $f(x)$, and $f(f^{-1}(x)) = x$ for all x in the domain of f^{-1}. Let $f(x) = b^x$ and $f^{-1}(x) = \log_b x$.

Property (3):

Write the inverse identity.	$f^{-1}(f(x)) = x$
Substitute $f^{-1}(x) = \log_b x$.	$\log_b(f(x)) = x$
Substitute $f(x) = b^x$.	$\log_b b^x = x$

Property (4):

Write the inverse identity.	$f(f^{-1}(x)) = x$
Substitute $f(x) = b^x$.	$b^{f^{-1}(x)} = x$
Substitute $f^{-1}(x) = \log_b x$ $\quad x > 0$.	$b^{\log_b x} = x$

The first four properties are summarized below for common and natural logarithms:

COMMON AND NATURAL LOGARITHM PROPERTIES

Common Logarithm (base 10)	Natural Logarithm (base e)
1. $\log 1 = 0$	**1.** $\ln 1 = 0$
2. $\log 10 = 1$	**2.** $\ln e = 1$
3. $\log 10^x = x$	**3.** $\ln e^x = x$
4. $10^{\log x} = x \quad x > 0$	**4.** $e^{\ln x} = x \quad x > 0$

EXAMPLE 1 Using Logarithmic Properties

Use properties (1)–(4) to simplify the expressions.

a. $\log_{10} 10$ **b.** $\ln 1$ **c.** $10^{\log(x+8)}$

d. $e^{\ln(2x+5)}$ **e.** $\log 10^{x^2}$ **f.** $\ln e^{x+3}$

Solution:

a. Use property (2).	$\log_{10} 10 = \boxed{1}$	
b. Use property (1).	$\ln 1 = \boxed{0}$	
c. Use property (4).	$10^{\log(x+8)} = \boxed{x + 8}$	$x > -8$
d. Use property (4).	$e^{\ln(2x+5)} = \boxed{2x + 5}$	$x > -\frac{5}{2}$
e. Use property (3).	$\log 10^{x^2} = \boxed{x^2}$	
f. Use property (3).	$\ln e^{x+3} = \boxed{x + 3}$	

The fifth through seventh properties follow from the properties of exponents and the definition of logarithms. We will prove the product rule and leave the proofs of the quotient and power rules for the exercises.

$$\text{Property (5): } \log_b MN = \log_b M + \log_b N$$

WORDS	MATH
Assume two logs that have the same base.	Let $u = \log_b M$ and $v = \log_b N$. $M > 0, N > 0$
Change to equivalent exponential forms.	$b^u = M$ and $b^v = N$
Write the log of a product.	$\log_b MN$
Substitute $M = b^u$ and $N = b^v$.	$= \log_b(b^u b^v)$
Use properties of exponents.	$= \log_b(b^{u+v})$
Apply property 3.	$= u + v$
Substitute $u = \log_b M$, $v = \log_b N$.	$= \log_b M + \log_b N$

$$\boxed{\log_b MN = \log_b M + \log_b N}$$

[CONCEPT CHECK]

When we multiply exponential functions with the same base we add their arguments (exponents), but when we add two logarithms with the same bases we _______ their arguments.

ANSWER multiply

In other words, the log of a product is the sum of the logs. Let us illustrate this property with a simple example.

$$\underbrace{\log_2 8}_{3} + \underbrace{\log_2 4}_{2} = \underbrace{\log_2 32}_{5}$$

Notice that $\log_2 8 + \log_2 4 \neq \log_2 12$.

EXAMPLE 2 Writing a Logarithmic Expression as a Sum of Logarithms

Use the logarithmic properties to write the expression $\log_b(u^2\sqrt{v})$ as a sum of simpler logarithms.

Solution:

Convert the radical to exponential form. $\log_b(u^2\sqrt{v}) = \log_b(u^2v^{1/2})$

Use the product property (5). $= \log_b u^2 + \log_b v^{1/2}$

Use the power property (7). $= \boxed{2\log_b u + \frac{1}{2}\log_b v}$

YOUR TURN Use the logarithmic properties to write the expression $\log_b(x^4\sqrt[3]{y})$ as a sum of simpler logarithms.

ANSWER

$\log_b(x^4\sqrt[3]{y}) = 4\log_b x + \frac{1}{3}\log_b y$

EXAMPLE 3 Writing a Sum of Logarithms as a Single Logarithmic Expression: The Right Way and the Wrong Way

Use properties of logarithms to write the expression $2\log_b 3 + 4\log_b u$ as a single logarithmic expression.

common mistake

A common mistake is to write the sum of the logs as a log of the sum.

$$\log_b M + \log_b N \neq \log_b(M + N)$$

✓CORRECT

Use the power property (7).

$2\log_b 3 + 4\log_b u = \log_b 3^2 + \log_b u^4$

Simplify.

$\log_b 9 + \log_b u^4$

Use the product property (5).

$\boxed{= \log_b(9u^4)}$

✗INCORRECT

$\neq \log_b(9 + u^4)$ **ERROR**

CAUTION

$\log_b M + \log_b N = \log_b(MN)$

$\log_b M + \log_b N \neq \log_b(M + N)$

YOUR TURN Express $2\ln x + 3\ln y$ as a single logarithm.

ANSWER

$\ln(x^2y^3)$

EXAMPLE 4 Writing a Logarithmic Expression as a Difference of Logarithms

Write the expression $\ln\left(\frac{x^3}{y^2}\right)$ as a difference of logarithms.

Solution:

Apply the quotient property (6). $\ln\left(\frac{x^3}{y^2}\right) = \ln(x^3) - \ln(y^2)$

Apply the power property (7). $= \boxed{3\ln x - 2\ln y}$

YOUR TURN Write the expression $\log\left(\frac{a^4}{b^5}\right)$ as a difference of logarithms.

ANSWER

$4\log a - 5\log b$

Another common mistake is misinterpreting the quotient rule.

EXAMPLE 5 Writing the Difference of Logarithms as a Logarithm of a Quotient

Write the expression $\frac{2}{3}\ln x - \frac{1}{2}\ln y$ as a logarithm of a quotient.

common mistake

$$\log_b M - \log_b N \neq \frac{\log_b M}{\log_b N}$$

✓CORRECT	✗INCORRECT
Use the power property (7).	
$\frac{2}{3}\ln x - \frac{1}{2}\ln y = \ln x^{2/3} - \ln y^{1/2}$	
Use the quotient property (6).	
$\boxed{\ln\left(\frac{x^{2/3}}{y^{1/2}}\right)}$	$\frac{\ln x^{2/3}}{\ln y^{1/2}}$ **ERROR**

CAUTION

$\log_b M - \log_b N = \log_b\left(\frac{M}{N}\right)$

$\log_b M - \log_b N \neq \frac{\log_b M}{\log_b N}$

YOUR TURN Write the expression $\frac{1}{2}\log a - 3\log b$ as a single logarithm.

ANSWER

$\log\left(\frac{a^{1/2}}{b^3}\right)$

EXAMPLE 6 Combining Logarithmic Expressions into a Single Logarithm

Write the expression $3\log_b x + \log_b(2x+1) - 2\log_b 4$ as a single logarithm.

Solution:

Use the power property (7) on the first and third terms. $= \log_b x^3 + \log_b(2x+1) - \log_b 4^2$

Use the product property (5) on the first two terms. $= \log_b[x^3(2x+1)] - \log_b 16$

Use the quotient property (6). $= \boxed{\log_b\left[\frac{x^3(2x+1)}{16}\right]}$

YOUR TURN Write the expression $2\ln x - \ln(3y) + 3\ln z$ as a single logarithm.

ANSWER

$\ln\left(\frac{x^2z^3}{3y}\right)$

EXAMPLE 7 Expanding a Logarithmic Expression into a Sum or Difference of Logarithms

Write $\ln\left(\frac{x^2 - x - 6}{x^2 + 7x + 6}\right)$ as a sum or difference of logarithms.

Solution:

Factor the numerator and denominator. $= \ln\left[\frac{(x-3)(x+2)}{(x+6)(x+1)}\right]$

Use the quotient property (6). $= \ln[(x-3)(x+2)] - \ln[(x+6)(x+1)]$

Use the product property (5). $= \ln(x-3) + \ln(x+2) - [\ln(x+6) + \ln(x+1)]$

Eliminate brackets. $= \boxed{\ln(x-3) + \ln(x+2) - \ln(x+6) - \ln(x+1)}$

3.3.2 Change-of-Base Formula

3.3.2 SKILL

Use the change-of-base formula to evaluate a logarithm of a general base (other than base 10 or *e*).

3.3.2 CONCEPTUAL

Understand that it does not matter which logarithm (natural or common) is used in the change-of-base formula.

Recall that in the last section, we were able to evaluate logarithms two ways: (1) exactly by writing the logarithm in exponential form and identifying the exponent and (2) using a calculator if the logarithms were base 10 or *e*. How do we evaluate a logarithm of general base if we cannot identify the exponent? We use the *change-of-base formula.*

EXAMPLE 8 Using Properties of Logarithms to Change the Base to Evaluate a General Logarithm

Evaluate $\log_3 8$. Round the answer to four decimal places.

Solution:

Let $y = \log_3 8$. $y = \log_3 8$

Write the logarithm in exponential form. $3^y = 8$

Take the log of both sides. $\log 3^y = \log 8$

Use the power property (7). $y \log 3 = \log 8$

Divide both sides by log 3. $y = \frac{\log 8}{\log 3}$

Let $y = \log_3 8$. $\boxed{\log_3 8 = \frac{\log 8}{\log 3}}$

Example 8 illustrated our ability to use properties of logarithms to change from base 3 to base 10, which our calculators can handle. This leads to the general change-of-base formula.

CHANGE-OF-BASE FORMULA

For any logarithmic bases a and b and any positive number M, the change-of-base formula says that

$$\log_b M = \frac{\log_a M}{\log_a b}$$

In the special case when a is either 10 or e, this relationship becomes

Common Logarithms		Natural Logarithms
$\log_b M = \dfrac{\log M}{\log b}$	or	$\log_b M = \dfrac{\ln M}{\ln b}$

It does not matter what base we select (10, e, or any other base); the ratio will be the same.

Proof of Change-of-Base Formula

WORDS	MATH
Let y be the logarithm we want to evaluate.	$y = \log_b M$
Write $y = \log_b M$ in exponential form.	$b^y = M$
Let a be any positive real number (where $a \neq 1$).	
Take the log of base a of both sides of the equation.	$\log_a b^y = \log_a M$
Use the power rule on the left side of the equation.	$y \log_a b = \log_a M$
Divide both sides of the equation by $\log_a b$.	$y = \dfrac{\log_a M}{\log_a b}$

EXAMPLE 9 **Using the Change-of-Base Formula**

Use the change-of-base formula to evaluate $\log_4 17$. Round to four decimal places.

Solution:

We will illustrate this in two ways (choosing common and natural logarithms) using a scientific calculator.

Common Logarithms

Use the change-of-base formula with base 10. $\log_4 17 = \dfrac{\log 17}{\log 4}$

Approximate with a calculator. ≈ 2.043731421

$\approx \boxed{2.0437}$

Natural Logarithms

Use the change-of-base formula with base e. $\log_4 17 = \dfrac{\ln 17}{\ln 4}$

Approximate with a calculator. ≈ 2.043731421

$\approx \boxed{2.0437}$

YOUR TURN Use the change-of-base formula to approximate $\log_7 34$. Round to four decimal places.

ANSWER

$\log_7 34 \approx 1.8122$

[CONCEPT CHECK]

TRUE OR FALSE if $\frac{\ln(a)}{\ln(b)} = \frac{\log(a)}{\log(b)}$, then $\ln(a) = \log(a)$ and $\ln(b) = \log(b)$.

ANSWER False

[SECTION 3.3] SUMMARY

Properties of Logarithms

If b, M, and N are positive real numbers, where $b \neq 1$, and p and x are real numbers, then the following are true:

- Product Property: $\log_b MN = \log_b M + \log_b N$
- Quotient Property: $\log_b\left(\frac{M}{N}\right) = \log_b M - \log_b N$
- Power Property: $\log_b M^p = p \log_b M$

GENERAL LOGARITHM	COMMON LOGARITHM	NATURAL LOGARITHM
$\log_b 1 = 0$	$\log 1 = 0$	$\ln 1 = 0$
$\log_b b = 1$	$\log 10 = 1$	$\ln e = 1$
$\log_b b^x = x$	$\log 10^x = x$	$\ln e^x = x$
$b^{\log_b x} = x \quad x > 0$	$10^{\log x} = x \quad x > 0$	$e^{\ln x} = x \quad x > 0$
$\log_b M = \dfrac{\log_a M}{\log_a b}$	$\log_b M = \dfrac{\log M}{\log b}$	$\log_b M = \dfrac{\ln M}{\ln b}$

[SECTION 3.3] EXERCISES

• SKILLS

In Exercises 1–20, apply the properties of logarithms to simplify each expression. Do not use a calculator.

1. $\log_9 1$
2. $\log_{69} 1$
3. $\log_{1/2}\left(\frac{1}{2}\right)$
4. $\log_{3.3} 3.3$
5. $\log_{10} 10^8$
6. $\ln e^3$
7. $\log_{10} 0.001$
8. $\log_3 3^7$
9. $\log_2 \sqrt{8}$
10. $\log_5 \sqrt[3]{5}$
11. $8^{\log_8 5}$
12. $2^{\log_2 5}$
13. $e^{\ln(x+5)}$
14. $10^{\log(3x^2+2x+1)}$
15. $5^{3\log_5 2}$
16. $7^{2\log_7 5}$
17. $7^{-2\log_7 3}$
18. $e^{-2\ln 10}$
19. $7e^{-3\ln x}$
20. $-19e^{-2\ln x^2}$

In Exercises 21–36, write each expression as a sum or difference of logarithms.

Example: $\log(m^2n^5) = 2\log m + 5\log n$

21. $\log_b(x^3y^5)$
22. $\log_b(x^{-3}y^{-5})$
23. $\log_b(x^{1/2}y^{1/3})$
24. $\log_b(\sqrt{r}\,\sqrt[3]{t})$
25. $\log_b\left(\frac{r^{1/3}}{s^{1/2}}\right)$
26. $\log_b\left(\frac{r^4}{s^2}\right)$
27. $\log_b\left(\frac{x}{yz}\right)$
28. $\log_b\left(\frac{xy}{z}\right)$
29. $\log(x^2\sqrt{x+5})$
30. $\log[(x-3)(x+2)]$
31. $\ln\left[\frac{x^3(x-2)^2}{\sqrt{x^2+5}}\right]$
32. $\ln\left[\frac{\sqrt{x+3}\,\sqrt[3]{x-4}}{(x+1)^4}\right]$
33. $\log\left(\frac{x^2-2x+1}{x^2-9}\right)$
34. $\log\left(\frac{x^2-x-2}{x^2+3x-4}\right)$
35. $\ln\sqrt{\frac{x^2+3x-10}{x^2-3x+2}}$
36. $\ln\left[\frac{\sqrt[3]{x-1}(3x-2)^4}{(x+1)\sqrt{x-1}}\right]^2$

In Exercises 37–48, write each expression as a single logarithm.

Example: $2\log m + 5\log n = \log(m^2n^5)$

37. $3\log_b x + 5\log_b y$
38. $2\log_b u + 3\log_b v$
39. $5\log_b u - 2\log_b v$
40. $3\log_b x - \log_b y$
41. $\frac{1}{2}\log_b x + \frac{2}{3}\log_b y$
42. $\frac{1}{2}\log_b x - \frac{2}{3}\log_b y$
43. $2\log u - 3\log v - 2\log z$
44. $3\log u - \log 2v - \log z$
45. $\ln(x+1) + \ln(x-1) - 2\ln(x^2+3)$
46. $\ln\sqrt{x-1} + \ln\sqrt{x+1} - 2\ln(x^2-1)$
47. $\frac{1}{2}\ln(x+3) - \frac{1}{3}\ln(x+2) - \ln(x)$
48. $\frac{1}{3}\ln(x^2+4) - \frac{1}{2}\ln(x^2-3) - \ln(x-1)$

In Exercises 49–58, evaluate the logarithms using the change-of-base formula. Round to four decimal places.

49. $\log_5 7$
50. $\log_4 19$
51. $\log_{1/2} 5$
52. $\log_5 \frac{1}{2}$
53. $\log_{2.7} 5.2$
54. $\log_{7.2} 2.5$
55. $\log_\pi 10$
56. $\log_\pi 2.7$
57. $\log_{\sqrt{3}} 8$
58. $\log_{\sqrt{2}} 9$

• APPLICATIONS

59. **Sound.** Sitting in the front row of a rock concert exposes us to a sound pressure (or sound level) of 1×10^{-1} W/m^2 (or 110 decibels), and a normal conversation is typically around 1×10^{-6} W/m^2 (or 60 decibels). How many decibels are you exposed to if a friend is talking in your ear at a rock concert? *Note:* 160 decibels causes perforation of the eardrums. *Hint:* Add the sound pressures and convert to decibels.

60. **Sound.** A whisper corresponds to 1×10^{-10} W/m^2 (or 20 decibels) and a normal conversation is typically around 1×10^{-6} W/m^2 (or 60 decibels). How many decibels are you exposed to if one friend is whispering in your ear, while the other one is talking at a normal level? *Hint:* Add the sound pressures and convert to decibels.

For Exercises 61 and 62, refer to the following:

There are two types of waves associated with an earthquake: *compression* and *shear.* The compression, or longitudinal, waves displace material behind the earthquake's path. Longitudinal waves travel at great speeds and are often called "primary waves" or simply "P" waves. Shear, or transverse, waves displace material at right angles to the earthquake's path. Transverse waves do not travel as rapidly through the Earth's crust and mantle as do longitudinal waves, and they are called "secondary" or "S" waves.

61. **Earthquakes.** If a seismologist records the energy of P waves as 4.5×10^{12} joules and the energy of S waves as 7.8×10^{8} joules, what is the total energy (sum the two energies)? What would the combined effect be on the Richter scale?

62. **Earthquakes.** Repeat Exercise 61, assuming the energy associated with the P waves is 5.2×10^{11} joules and the energy associated with the S waves is 4.1×10^{9} joules.

63. **Photography.** In photographic quality assurance, logarithms are used to determine, for instance, the density. Density is the common logarithm of the opacity, which is the quotient of the amount of incident light and the amount of transmitted light. What is the density of a photographic material that transmits only 90% of the incident light?

64. **pH Scale.** The pH scale measures how acidic or basic a substance is. pH is defined as the negative logarithm of the hydrogen ion activity in an aqueous solution, a_H. Thus, if $a_H = 0.01$, then pH $= -\log 0.01 = 2$. Determine the pH of a liquid with $a_H = 0.00407$. Round your answer to the nearest hundredth.

65. **pH Scale.** How many times more acidic is a substance with pH $= 3.2$ than a substance with pH $= 4.4$? Round your answer to the nearest integer.

66. **Information Theory.** In information theory, logarithms in base 2 are often used. The capacity C of a noisy channel with bandwidth W and signal and noise powers S and N is $C = W\log_2\left(1 + \frac{S}{N}\right)$. The signal noise ratio R is given by $R = 10\log\left(\frac{S}{N}\right)$. Assuming a channel with a bandwidth of 3 megahertz and a signal noise ratio $R = 2$ dB, calculate the channel capacity.

• CATCH THE MISTAKE

In Exercises 67–70, simplify if possible and explain the mistake that is made.

67. $3\log 5 - \log 25$

Solution:

Apply the quotient property (6).	$\frac{3\log 5}{\log 25}$
Write $25 = 5^2$.	$\frac{3\log 5}{\log 5^2}$
Apply the power property (7).	$\frac{3\log 5}{2\log 5}$
Simplify.	$\frac{3}{2}$

This is incorrect. The correct answer is log 5. What mistake was made?

68. $\ln 3 + 2\ln 4 - 3\ln 2$

Solution:

Apply the power property (7).	$\ln 3 + \ln 4^2 - \ln 2^3$
Simplify.	$\ln 3 + \ln 16 - \ln 8$
Apply property (5).	$\ln(3 + 16 - 8)$
Simplify.	$\ln 11$

This is incorrect. The correct answer is ln 6. What mistake was made?

69. $\log_2 x + \log_3 y - \log_4 z$

Solution:

Apply the product property (5).	$\log_6 xy - \log_4 z$
Apply the quotient property (6).	$\log_{24} xyz$

This is incorrect. What mistake was made?

70. $2(\log 3 - \log 5)$

Solution:

Apply the quotient property (6).	$2\left(\log\frac{3}{5}\right)$
Apply the power property (7).	$\left(\log\frac{3}{5}\right)^2$
Apply a calculator to approximate.	≈ 0.0492

This is incorrect. What mistake was made?

• CONCEPTUAL

In Exercises 71–76, determine whether each statement is true or false.

71. $\log e = \dfrac{1}{\ln 10}$

72. $\ln e = \dfrac{1}{\log 10}$

73. $\ln (xy)^3 = (\ln x + \ln y)^3$

74. $\dfrac{\ln a}{\ln b} = \dfrac{\log a}{\log b}$

75. $\log 12x^3 = 36 \log x$

76. $e^{\ln x^2} = x^2$

• CHALLENGE

77. Prove the quotient rule: $\log_b\left(\dfrac{M}{N}\right) = \log_b M - \log_b N$.

Hint: Let $u = \log_b M$ and $v = \log_b N$. Write both in exponential form and find the quotient $\log_b\left(\dfrac{M}{N}\right)$.

78. Prove the power rule: $\log_b M^p = p \log_b M$.

Hint: Let $u = \log_b M$. Write this log in exponential form, and find $\log_b M^p$.

79. Write in terms of simpler logarithmic forms.

$$\log_b\left(\sqrt{\frac{x^2}{y^3 z^{-5}}}\right)^6$$

80. Show that $\log_b\left(\dfrac{1}{x}\right) = -\log_b x$.

81. Show that $\log_b\left(\dfrac{a^2}{b^3}\right)^{-3} = 9 - \dfrac{6}{\log_a b}$.

82. Given that $\log_b 2 = 0.4307$ and $\log_b 3 = 0.6826$, find $\log_b \sqrt{48}$. Do not use a calculator.

• PREVIEW TO CALCULUS

In calculus we prove that the derivative of $f + g$ is $f' + g'$ and that the derivative of $f - g$ is $f' - g'$. It is also shown in calculus that if $f(x) = \ln x$, then $f'(x) = \dfrac{1}{x}$.

83. Use these properties to find the derivative of $f(x) = \ln x^2$.

84. Find the derivative of $f(x) = \ln \dfrac{1}{x^2}$.

85. Use these properties to find the derivative of $f(x) = \ln \dfrac{1}{x}$.

86. Find the derivative of $f(x) = \ln x^2 + \ln x^3$.

3.4 EXPONENTIAL AND LOGARITHMIC EQUATIONS

SKILLS OBJECTIVES

- Use properties of one-to-one functions and properties of inverses to solve exponential equations.
- Use properties of one-to-one functions and properties of inverses to solve logarithmic equations.
- Solve application problems that involve exponential and logarithmic equations.

CONCEPTUAL OBJECTIVES

- Understand that properties of one-to-one functions enable us to solve some simple exponential equations, and for other exponential equations the properties of inverses must be used.
- Understand why extraneous solutions can arise in logarithmic equations and how to eliminate extraneous solutions.
- Use the rule of 70 to guide intuition on investment questions.

3.4.1 Solving Exponential Equations

To solve algebraic equations such as $x^2 - 9 = 0$, the goal is to solve for the variable, x, by finding the values of x that make the statement true. Exponential and logarithmic equations have the variable (x) buried within an exponent or a logarithm, but the goal is the same. Find the value(s) of x that make(s) the statement true.

Exponential equation: $e^{2x+1} = 5$

Logarithmic equation: $\log(3x - 1) = 7$

There are two methods for solving exponential and logarithmic equations that are based on the properties of one-to-one functions and inverses. To solve simple exponential and logarithmic equations, we will use one-to-one properties. To solve more complicated exponential and logarithmic equations, we will use properties of inverses. The following box summarizes the one-to-one and inverse properties that hold true when $b > 0$ and $b \neq 1$.

3.4.1 SKILL

Use properties of one-to-one functions and properties of inverses to solve exponential equations.

3.4.1 CONCEPTUAL

Understand that properties of one-to-one functions enable us to solve some simple exponential equations, and for other exponential equations the properties of inverses must be used.

ONE-TO-ONE PROPERTIES

$b^x = b^y$ if and only if $x = y$

$\log_b x = \log_b y$ if and only if $x = y$

INVERSE PROPERTIES

$b^{\log_b x} = x$ $\quad x > 0$

$\log_b b^x = x$

The following strategies are outlined for solving simple and complicated exponential equations using the one-to-one and inverse properties.

STRATEGIES FOR SOLVING EXPONENTIAL EQUATIONS

TYPE OF EQUATION	STRATEGY	EXAMPLE
Simple	1. Rewrite both sides of the equation in terms of the same base.	$2^{x-3} = 32$ $2^{x-3} = 2^5$
	2. Use the one-to-one property to equate the exponents.	$x - 3 = 5$
	3. Solve for the variable.	$\boxed{x = 8}$
Complicated	1. Isolate the exponential expression.	$3e^{2x} - 2 = 7$ $3e^{2x} = 9$ $e^{2x} = 3$
	2. Take the same logarithm* of both sides.	$\ln e^{2x} = \ln 3$
	3. Simplify using the inverse properties.	$2x = \ln 3$
	4. Solve for the variable.	$\boxed{x = \frac{1}{2}\ln 3}$

*Take the logarithm with base that is equal to the base of the exponent and use the property $\log_b b^x = x$, or take the natural logarithm and use the property $\ln M^p = p \ln M$.

EXAMPLE 1 Solving a Simple Exponential Equation

Solve the exponential equations using the one-to-one property.

a. $3^x = 81$ **b.** $5^{7-x} = 125$ **c.** $\left(\frac{1}{2}\right)^{4y} = 16$

Solution (a):

Substitute $81 = 3^4$. $3^x = 3^4$

Use the one-to-one property to identify x. $\boxed{x = 4}$

Solution (b):

Substitute $125 = 5^3$. $5^{7-x} = 5^3$

Use the one-to-one property. $7 - x = 3$

Solve for x. $\boxed{x = 4}$

Solution (c):

Substitute $\left(\frac{1}{2}\right)^{4y} = \left(\frac{1}{2^{4y}}\right) = 2^{-4y}$. $2^{-4y} = 16$

Substitute $16 = 2^4$. $2^{-4y} = 2^4$

Use the one-to-one property to identify y. $\boxed{y = -1}$

YOUR TURN Solve the following equations:

a. $2^{x-1} = 8$ **b.** $\left(\frac{1}{3}\right)^y = 27$

ANSWER

a. $x = 4$ b. $y = -3$

In Example 1, we were able to rewrite the equation in a form with the same bases so that we could use the one-to-one property. In Example 2, we will not be able to write both sides in a form with the same bases. Instead, we will use properties of inverses.

EXAMPLE 2 **Solving a More Complicated Exponential Equation with a Base Other Than 10 or *e***

Solve the exponential equations exactly and then approximate the answers to four decimal places.

a. $5^{3x} = 16$ **b.** $4^{3x+2} = 71$

Solution (a):

Take the natural logarithm of both sides of the equation. $\ln 5^{3x} = \ln 16$

Use the power property on the left side of the equation. $3x \ln 5 = \ln 16$

Divide both sides of the equation by 3 ln 5. $\boxed{x = \dfrac{\ln 16}{3 \ln 5}}$

Use a calculator to approximate x to four decimal places. $\boxed{x \approx 0.5742}$

Solution (b):

Rewrite in logarithmic form. $3x + 2 = \log_4 71$

Subtract 2 from both sides. $3x = \log_4 71 - 2$

Divide both sides by 3. $x = \dfrac{\log_4 71 - 2}{3}$

Use the change-of-base formula, $\log_4 71 = \dfrac{\ln 71}{\ln 4}$. $\boxed{x = \dfrac{\frac{\ln 71}{\ln 4} - 2}{3}}$

Use a calculator to approximate x to four decimal places. $x \approx \dfrac{3.07487356 - 2}{3} \approx \boxed{0.3583}$

We could have proceeded in an alternative way by taking either the natural log or the common log of both sides and using the power property (instead of using the change-of-base formula) to evaluate the logarithm with base 4.

Take the natural logarithm of both sides. $\ln(4^{3x+2}) = \ln 71$

Use the power property (7). $(3x + 2)\ln 4 = \ln 71$

Divide by ln 4. $3x + 2 = \dfrac{\ln 71}{\ln 4}$

Subtract 2 and divide by 3. $\boxed{x = \dfrac{\frac{\ln 71}{\ln 4} - 2}{3}}$

Use a calculator to approximate x. $x \approx \dfrac{3.07487356 - 2}{3} \approx \boxed{0.3583}$

YOUR TURN Solve the equation $5^{y^2} = 27$ exactly and then approximate the answer to four decimal places.

ANSWER $y = \pm\sqrt{\log_5 27} \approx \pm 1.4310$

[CONCEPT CHECK]

TRUE OR FALSE In Solution (a) in Example 2 we could have used the log of any base (not just the natural log as shown).

ANSWER True

EXAMPLE 3 **Solving a More Complicated Exponential Equation with Base 10 or *e***

Solve the exponential equation $4e^{x^2} = 64$ exactly and then approximate the answer to four decimal places.

Solution:

Divide both sides by 4. $e^{x^2} = 16$

Take the natural logarithm (ln) of both sides. $\ln\left(e^{x^2}\right) = \ln 16$

Simplify the left side with the property of inverses. $x^2 = \ln 16$

Solve for x using the square-root method. $\boxed{x = \pm\sqrt{\ln 16}}$

Use a calculator to approximate x to four decimal places. $\boxed{x \approx \pm 1.6651}$

YOUR TURN Solve the equation $10^{2x-3} = 7$ exactly and then approximate the answer to four decimal places.

ANSWER

$x = \dfrac{\log_{10} 7 + 3}{2} \approx 1.9225$

EXAMPLE 4 **Solving an Exponential Equation Quadratic in Form**

Solve the equation $e^{2x} - 4e^x + 3 = 0$ exactly and then approximate the answer to four decimal places.

Solution:

Let $u = e^x$. $\left(\textit{Note: } u^2 = e^x \cdot e^x = e^{2x}.\right)$ $u^2 - 4u + 3 = 0$

Factor. $(u - 3)(u - 1) = 0$

Solve for u. $u = 3$ or $u = 1$

Substitute $u = e^x$. $e^x = 3$ or $e^x = 1$

Take the natural logarithm (ln) of both sides. $\ln(e^x) = \ln 3$ or $\ln(e^x) = \ln 1$

Simplify with the properties of logarithms. $\boxed{x = \ln 3 \quad \text{or} \quad x = \ln 1}$

Approximate or evaluate exactly the right sides. $\boxed{x \approx 1.0986}$ or $\boxed{x = 0}$

YOUR TURN Solve the equation $100^x - 10^x - 2 = 0$ exactly and then approximate the answer to four decimal places.

ANSWER

$x = \log 2 \approx 0.3010$

3.4.2 SKILL

Use properties of one-to-one functions and properties of inverses to solve logarithmic equations.

3.4.2 CONCEPTUAL

Understand why extraneous solutions can arise in logarithmic equations and how to eliminate extraneous solutions.

3.4.2 Solving Logarithmic Equations

We can solve simple logarithmic equations using the property of one-to-one functions. For more complicated logarithmic equations, we can employ properties of logarithms and properties of inverses. **Solutions must be checked to eliminate extraneous solutions.**

STRATEGIES FOR SOLVING LOGARITHMIC EQUATIONS

TYPE OF EQUATION	STRATEGY	EXAMPLE
Simple	1. Combine logarithms on each side of the equation using properties.	$\log(x-3)+\log x=\log 4$ $\log x(x-3)=\log 4$
	2. Use the one-to-one property to equate the arguments.	$x(x-3)=4$
	3. Solve for the variable.	$x^2-3x-4=0$ $(x-4)(x+1)=0$ $x=-1, 4$
	4. Check the results and eliminate any extraneous solutions.	Eliminate $x=-1$ because $\log(-1)$ is undefined. $\boxed{x=4}$
Complicated	1. Combine and isolate the logarithmic expressions.	$\log_5(x+2)-\log_5 x=2$ $\log_5\left(\frac{x+2}{x}\right)=2$
	2. Rewrite the equation in exponential form.	$\frac{x+2}{x}=5^2$
	3. Solve for the variable.	$x+2=25x$ $24x=2$ $\boxed{x=\frac{1}{12}}$
	4. Check the results and eliminate any extraneous solutions.	$\log_5\left(\frac{1}{12}+2\right)-\log_5\left(\frac{1}{12}\right)$ $=\log_5\left(\frac{25}{12}\right)-\log_5\left(\frac{1}{12}\right)$ $=\log_5\left[\frac{25/12}{1/12}\right]=\log_5[25]=2$ ✓

[CONCEPT CHECK]

TRUE OR FALSE ALL of the logarithms must be undefined for a particular value in order for that value to be eliminated from the domain of the solution.

ANSWER False

EXAMPLE 5 Solving a Simple Logarithmic Equation

Solve the equation $\log_4(2x-3)=\log_4(x)+\log_4(x-2)$.

Solution:

Apply the product property (5) on the right side. $\log_4(2x-3)=\log_4[x(x-2)]$

Apply the property of one-to-one functions. $2x-3=x(x-2)$

Distribute and simplify. $x^2-4x+3=0$

Factor. $(x-3)(x-1)=0$

Solve for x. $x=3$ or $x=1$

The possible solution $x=1$ must be eliminated because it is not in the domain of two of the logarithmic functions.

$$x=1:\ \underbrace{\log_4(-1)}_{\text{undefined}}\stackrel{?}{=}\log_4(1)+\underbrace{\log_4(-1)}_{\text{undefined}}$$

$\boxed{x=3}$

[STUDY TIP]

Solutions should be checked in the original equation to eliminate extraneous solutions.

YOUR TURN Solve the equation $\ln(x+8)=\ln(x)+\ln(x+3)$.

ANSWER
$x=2$

EXAMPLE 6 Solving a More Complicated Logarithmic Equation

Solve the equation $\log_3(9x) - \log_3(x - 8) = 4$.

Solution:

Employ the quotient property (6) on the left side. $\log_3\left(\frac{9x}{x-8}\right) = 4$

Write in exponential form. $\log_b x = y \Rightarrow x = b^y$ $\frac{9x}{x-8} = 3^4$

Simplify the right side. $\frac{9x}{x-8} = 81$

Multiply the equation by the LCD, $x - 8$. $9x = 81(x - 8)$

Eliminate parentheses. $9x = 81x - 648$

Solve for x. $-72x = -648$

$\boxed{x = 9}$

Check: $\log_3[9 \cdot 9] - \log_3[9 - 8] = \log_3[81] - \log_3 1 = 4 - 0 = 4$

YOUR TURN Solve the equation $\log_2(4x) - \log_2(2) = 2$.

ANSWER
$x = 2$

EXAMPLE 7 Solving a Logarithmic Equation with No Solution

Solve the equation $\ln(3 - x^2) = 7$.

Solution:

Write in exponential form. $3 - x^2 = e^7$

Simplify. $x^2 = 3 - e^7$

$3 - e^7$ is negative. $x^2 =$ negative real number

There are no real numbers that when squared yield a negative real number. Therefore, there is $\boxed{\text{no real solution}}$.

3.4.3 Applications

3.4.3 SKILL

Solve application problems that involve exponential and logarithmic equations.

3.4.3 CONCEPTUAL

Use the rule of 70 to guide intuition on investment questions.

Archaeologists determine the age of a fossil by how much carbon-14 is present at the time of discovery. The number of grams of carbon-14 based on the radioactive decay of the isotope is given by

$$A = A_0 e^{-0.000124t}$$

where A is the number of grams of carbon-14 at the present time, A_0 is the number of grams of carbon-14 while alive, and t is the number of years since death. Using the inverse properties, we can isolate t.

WORDS	MATH
Divide by A_0.	$\frac{A}{A_0} = e^{-0.000124t}$
Take the natural logarithm of both sides.	$\ln\left(\frac{A}{A_0}\right) = \ln\left(e^{-0.000124t}\right)$
Simplify the right side utilizing properties of inverses.	$\ln\left(\frac{A}{A_0}\right) = -0.000124t$
Solve for t.	$t = -\frac{1}{0.000124}\ln\left(\frac{A}{A_0}\right)$

Let's assume that animals have approximately 1000 mg of carbon-14 in their bodies when they are alive. If a fossil has 200 mg of carbon-14, approximately how old is the fossil? Substituting $A = 200$ and $A_0 = 1000$ into our equation for t, we find

$$t = -\frac{1}{0.000124}\ln\left(\frac{1}{5}\right) \approx 12{,}979.338$$

The fossil is approximately 13,000 years old.

EXAMPLE 8 **Calculating How Many Years It Will Take for Money to Double**

You save \$1000 from a summer job and put it in a CD earning 5% compounding continuously. How many years will it take for your money to double? Round to the nearest year.

Solution:

Recall the compound continuous interest formula. $A = Pe^{rt}$

Substitute $P = 1000$, $A = 2000$, and $r = 0.05$. $2000 = 1000e^{0.05t}$

Divide by 1000. $2 = e^{0.05t}$

Take the natural logarithm of both sides. $\ln 2 = \ln\left(e^{0.05t}\right)$

Simplify with the property $\ln e^x = x$. $\ln 2 = 0.05t$

Solve for t. $t = \dfrac{\ln 2}{0.05} \approx 13.8629$

It will take almost $\boxed{14 \text{ years}}$ for your money to double.

YOUR TURN How long will it take \$1000 to triple (become \$3000) in a savings account earning 10% a year compounding continuously? Round your answer to the nearest year.

ANSWER approximately 11 years

When an investment is compounded continuously, how long will it take for that investment to double?

WORDS	MATH
Write the interest formula for compounding continuously.	$A = Pe^{rt}$
Let $A = 2P$ (investment doubles).	$2P = Pe^{rt}$
Divide both sides of the equation by P.	$2 = e^{rt}$
Take the natural log of both sides of the equation.	$\ln 2 = \ln e^{rt}$
Simplify the right side by applying the property $\ln e^x = x$.	$\ln 2 = rt$
Divide both sides by r to get the exact value for t.	$t = \dfrac{\ln 2}{r}$
Now, approximate $\ln 2 \approx 0.7$.	$t \approx \dfrac{0.7}{r}$
Multiply the numerator and denominator by 100.	$t \approx \dfrac{70}{100r}$
This is the "rule of 70."	

[CONCEPT CHECK]

TRUE OR FALSE If we know the interest rate and how interest is compounded, we do not need to know the principal in order to determine how long until an investment doubles.

ANSWER True

If we divide 70 by the interest rate (compounding continuously), we get the approximate time for an investment to double. In Example 8, the interest rate (compounding continuously) is 5%. Dividing 70 by 5 yields 14 years.

[SECTION 3.4] SUMMARY

Strategy for Solving Exponential Equations

TYPE OF EQUATION	STRATEGY
Simple	1. Rewrite both sides of the equation in terms of the same base. 2. Use the one-to-one property to equate the exponents. 3. Solve for the variable.
Complicated	1. Isolate the exponential expression. 2. Take the same logarithm* of both sides. 3. Simplify using the inverse properties. 4. Solve for the variable.

*Take the logarithm with the base that is equal to the base of the exponent and use the property $\log_b b^x = x$, or take the natural logarithm and use the property $\ln M^p = p \ln M$.

Strategy for Solving Logarithmic Equations

TYPE OF EQUATION	STRATEGY
Simple	1. Combine logarithms on each side of the equation using properties. 2. Use the one-to-one property to equate the arguments. 3. Solve for the variable. 4. Check the results and eliminate any extraneous solutions.
Complicated	1. Combine and isolate the logarithmic expressions. 2. Rewrite the equation in exponential form. 3. Solve for the variable. 4. Check the results and eliminate any extraneous solutions.

[SECTION 3.4] EXERCISES

• SKILLS

In Exercises 1–14, solve the exponential equations exactly for x.

1. $2^{x^2} = 16$
2. $169^x = 13$
3. $\left(\frac{2}{3}\right)^{x+1} = \frac{27}{8}$
4. $\left(\frac{3}{5}\right)^{x+1} = \frac{25}{9}$
5. $e^{2x+3} = 1$
6. $10^{x^2-1} = 1$
7. $7^{2x-5} = 7^{3x-4}$
8. $125^x = 5^{2x-3}$
9. $2^{x^2+12} = 2^{7x}$
10. $5^{x^2-3} = 5^{2x}$
11. $9^x = 3^{x^2-4x}$
12. $16^{x-1} = 2^{x^2}$
13. $e^{5x-1} = e^{x^2+3}$
14. $10^{x^2-8} = 100^x$

In Exercises 15–40, solve the exponential equations exactly and then approximate your answers to three decimal places.

15. $27 = 2^{3x-1}$
16. $15 = 7^{3-2x}$
17. $3e^x - 8 = 7$
18. $5e^x + 12 = 27$
19. $9 - 2e^{0.1x} = 1$
20. $21 - 4e^{0.1x} = 5$
21. $2(3^x) - 11 = 9$
22. $3(2^x) + 8 = 35$
23. $e^{3x+4} = 22$
24. $e^{x^2} = 73$
25. $3e^{2x} = 18$
26. $4(10^{3x}) = 20$
27. $4e^{2x+1} = 17$
28. $5\left(10^{x^2+2x+1}\right) = 13$
29. $3\left(4^{x^2-4}\right) = 16$
30. $7 \cdot \left(\frac{1}{4}\right)^{6-5x} = 3$
31. $e^{2x} + 7e^x - 3 = 0$
32. $e^{2x} - 4e^x - 5 = 0$
33. $(3^x - 3^{-x})^2 = 0$
34. $(3^x - 3^{-x})(3^x + 3^{-x}) = 0$
35. $\frac{2}{e^x - 5} = 1$
36. $\frac{17}{e^x + 4} = 2$
37. $\frac{20}{6 - e^{2x}} = 4$
38. $\frac{4}{3 - e^{3x}} = 8$
39. $\frac{4}{10^{2x} - 7} = 2$
40. $\frac{28}{10^x + 3} = 4$

In Exercises 41–58, solve the logarithmic equations exactly.

41. $\log_3(2x+1) = 4$
42. $\log_2(3x-1) = 3$
43. $\log_2(4x-1) = -3$
44. $\log_4(5-2x) = -2$
45. $\ln x^2 - \ln 9 = 0$
46. $\log x^2 + \log x = 3$
47. $\log_5(x-4) + \log_5 x = 1$
48. $\log_2(x-1) + \log_2(x-3) = 3$
49. $\log(x-3) + \log(x+2) = \log(4x)$
50. $\log_2(x+1) + \log_2(4-x) = \log_2(6x)$
51. $\log(4-x) + \log(x+2) = \log(3-2x)$
52. $\log(3-x) + \log(x+3) = \log(1-2x)$
53. $\log_4(4x) - \log_4\left(\frac{x}{4}\right) = 3$
54. $\log_3(7-2x) - \log_3(x+2) = 2$
55. $\log(2x-5) - \log(x-3) = 1$
56. $\log_3(10-x) - \log_3(x+2) = 1$
57. $\log_4(x^2+5x+4) - 2\log_4(x+1) = 2$
58. $\log_2(x+1) + \log_2(x+5) - \log_2(2x+5) = 2$

In Exercises 59–72, solve the logarithmic equations exactly and then approximate your answers, if possible, to three decimal places.

59. $\log(2x+5) = 2$
60. $\ln(4x-7) = 3$
61. $\ln(x^2+1) = 4$
62. $\log(x^2+4) = 2$
63. $\ln(2x+3) = -2$
64. $\log(3x-5) = -1$
65. $\log(2-3x) + \log(3-2x) = 1.5$
66. $\log_2(3-x) + \log_2(1-2x) = 5$
67. $\ln(x) + \ln(x-2) = 4$
68. $\ln(4x) + \ln(2+x) = 2$
69. $\log_7(1-x) - \log_7(x+2) = \log_7 x$
70. $\log_5(x+1) - \log_5(x-1) = \log_5 x$
71. $\ln\sqrt{x+4} - \ln\sqrt{x-2} = \ln\sqrt{x+1}$
72. $\log(\sqrt{1-x}) - \log(\sqrt{x+2}) = \log x$

• APPLICATIONS

73. **Health.** After strenuous exercise, Sandy's heart rate R (beats per minute) can be modeled by

$$R(t) = 151e^{-0.055t},\ 0 \leq t \leq 15$$

where t is the number of minutes that have elapsed after she stops exercising.

a. Find Sandy's heart rate at the end of exercising (when she stops at time $t = 0$).
b. Determine how many minutes it takes after Sandy stops exercising for her heart rate to drop to 100 beats per minute. Round to the nearest minute.
c. Find Sandy's heart rate 15 minutes after she had stopped exercising.

74. **Business.** A local business purchased a new company van for \$45,000. After 2 years the book value of the van is \$30,000.

a. Find an exponential model for the value of the van using $V(t) = V_0e^{kt}$, where V is the value of the van in dollars and t is time in years.
b. Approximately how many years will it take for the book value of the van to drop to \$20,000?

75. **Money.** If money is invested in a savings account earning 3.5% interest compounded yearly, how many years will pass until the money triples?

76. **Money.** If money is invested in a savings account earning 3.5% interest compounded monthly, how many years will pass until the money triples?

77. **Money.** If \$7500 is invested in a savings account earning 5% interest compounded quarterly, how many years will pass until there is \$20,000?

78. **Money.** If \$9000 is invested in a savings account earning 6% interest compounded continuously, how many years will pass until there is \$15,000?

For Exercises 79 and 80, refer to the following:

Richter scale: $M = \frac{2}{3}\log\left(\frac{E}{E_0}\right) \qquad E_0 = 10^{4.4}$ **joules**

79. **Earthquakes.** On September 25, 2003, an earthquake that measured 7.4 on the Richter scale shook Hokkaido, Japan. How much energy (joules) did the earthquake emit?

80. **Earthquakes.** Again, on that same day (September 25, 2003), a second earthquake that measured 8.3 on the Richter scale shook Hokkaido, Japan. How much energy (joules) did the earthquake emit?

For Exercises 81 and 82, refer to the following:

$$\textbf{Decibel: } D = 10\log\left(\frac{I}{I_T}\right) \qquad I_T = 1 \times 10^{-12}\ \text{W/m}^2$$

81. **Sound.** Matt likes to drive around campus in his classic Mustang with the stereo blaring. If his boom stereo has a sound intensity of 120 decibels, how many watts per square meter does the stereo emit?

82. **Sound.** The New York Philharmonic has a sound intensity of 100 decibels. How many watts per square meter does the orchestra emit?

83. **Anesthesia.** When a person has a cavity filled, the dentist typically administers a local anesthetic. After one leaves the dentist's office, one's mouth may remain numb for several more hours. If a shot of anesthesia is injected into the bloodstream at the time of the procedure ($t = 0$), and the amount of anesthesia still in the bloodstream t hours after the initial injection is given by $A = A_0 e^{-0.5t}$, in how many hours will only 10% of the original anesthetic still be in the bloodstream?

84. **Investments.** Money invested in an account that compounds interest continuously at a rate of 3% a year is modeled by $A = A_0 e^{0.03t}$, where A is the amount in the investment after t years and A_0 is the initial investment. How long will it take the initial investment to double?

85. **Biology.** The U.S. Fish and Wildlife Service is releasing a population of the endangered Mexican gray wolf in a protected area along the New Mexico and Arizona border. They estimate the population of the Mexican gray wolf to be approximated by

$$P(t) = \frac{200}{1 + 24e^{-0.2t}}$$

How many years will it take for the population to reach 100 wolves?

86. **Introducing a New Car Model.** If the number of new model Honda Accord hybrids purchased in North America is given by $N = \dfrac{100{,}000}{1 + 10e^{-2t}}$, where t is the number of weeks after Honda releases the new model, how many weeks will it take after the release until there are 50,000 Honda hybrids from that batch on the road?

• CATCH THE MISTAKE

In Exercises 87 and 88, explain the mistake that is made.

87. Solve the equation: $4e^x = 9$.

Solution:

Take the natural log of both sides.	$\ln(4e^x) = \ln 9$
Apply the property of inverses.	$4x = \ln 9$
Solve for x.	$x = \dfrac{\ln 9}{4} \approx 0.55$

This is incorrect. What mistake was made?

88. Solve the equation: $\log(x) + \log(3) = 1$.

Solution:

Apply the product property (5).	$\log(3x) = 1$
Exponentiate (base 10).	$10^{\log(3x)} = 1$
Apply the properties of inverses.	$3x = 1$
Solve for x.	$x = \dfrac{1}{3}$

This is incorrect. What mistake was made?

• CONCEPTUAL

In Exercises 89–94, determine whether each statement is true or false.

89. The sum of logarithms with the same base is equal to the logarithm of the product.

90. A logarithm squared is equal to two times the logarithm.

91. $e^{\log x} = x$

92. $e^x = -2$ has no solution.

93. $\log_3(x^2 + x - 6) = 1$ has two solutions.

94. The division of two logarithms with the same base is equal to the logarithm of the subtraction.

• CHALLENGE

95. Solve for x in terms of b:

$$\frac{1}{3}\log_b(x^3) + \frac{1}{2}\log_b(x^2 - 2x + 1) = 2$$

96. Solve exactly:

$$2\log_b(x) + 2\log_b(1 - x) = 4$$

97. Solve $y = \dfrac{3000}{1 + 2e^{-0.2t}}$ for t in terms of y.

98. State the range of values of x that the following identity holds: $e^{\ln(x^2 - a)} = x^2 - a$.

99. A function called the hyperbolic cosine is defined as the average of exponential growth and exponential decay by $f(x) = \dfrac{e^x + e^{-x}}{2}$. If we restrict the domain of f to $[0, \infty)$, find its inverse.

100. A function called the hyperbolic sine is defined by $f(x) = \dfrac{e^x - e^{-x}}{2}$. Find its inverse.

• PREVIEW TO CALCULUS

101. The hyperbolic sine function is defined by $\sinh x = \dfrac{e^x - e^{-x}}{2}$. Find its inverse function $\sinh^{-1} x$.

102. The hyperbolic tangent is defined by $\tanh x = \dfrac{e^x - e^{-x}}{e^x + e^{-x}}$. Find its inverse function $\tanh^{-1} x$.

In Exercises 103 and 104, refer to the following:

In calculus, to find the derivative of a function of the form $y = k^x$, where k is a constant, we apply logarithmic differentiation. The first step in this process consists of writing $y = k^x$ in an equivalent form using the natural logarithm. Use the properties of this section to write an equivalent form of the following implicitly defined functions.

103. $y = 2^x$

104. $y = 4^x \cdot 3^{x+1}$

3.5 EXPONENTIAL AND LOGARITHMIC MODELS

SKILLS OBJECTIVES

- Use exponential growth functions to model populations, economic applications of assets, and initial spreading of diseases.
- Use exponential decay functions to model scenarios in medicine, economic depreciation of assets, archaeology, and forensic science.
- Represent distributions using a Gaussian (normal) model.
- Represent restricted growth with logistic models.
- Use logistic growth models to determine time to pay off debt.

CONCEPTUAL OBJECTIVES

- Understand that exponential growth models assume "uninhibited" growth.
- Understand that the horizontal asymptote corresponds to a limiting value, often zero.
- Understand that the bell curve is used to represent standardized tests (IQ/SAT), as well as height/weight charts.
- Understand that the asymptote of a logistic model corresponds to the carrying capacity of the system.
- Understand why doubling your monthly payment will reduce the life of the loan by more than half.

The following table summarizes the five primary models that involve exponential and logarithmic functions:

NAME	MODEL	GRAPH	APPLICATIONS
Exponential growth	$f(t) = ce^{kt} \quad k > 0$	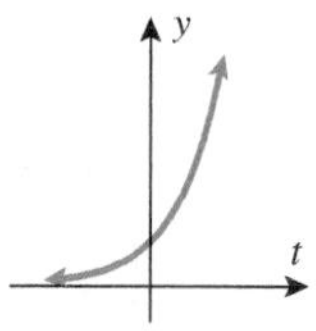	World populations, bacteria growth, appreciation, global spread of the HIV virus
Exponential decay	$f(t) = ce^{-kt} \quad k > 0$	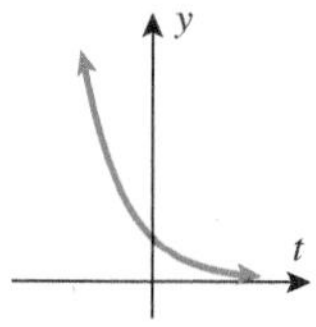	Radioactive decay, carbon dating, depreciation
Gaussian (normal) distribution	$f(x) = ce^{-(x-a)^2/k}$	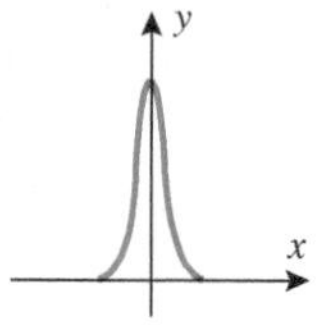	Bell curve (grade distribution), life expectancy, height/weight charts, intensity of a laser beam, IQ tests
Logistic growth	$f(t) = \dfrac{a}{1 + ce^{-kt}}$	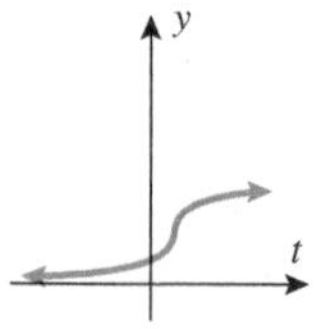	Conservation biology, learning curve, spread of virus on an island, carrying capacity
Logarithmic	$f(t) = a + c \log t$ $f(t) = a + c \ln t$	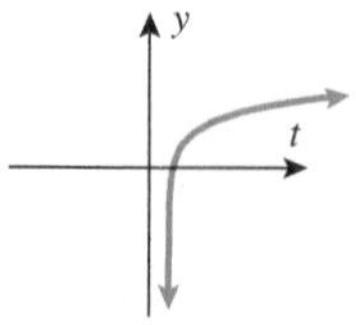	Population of species, anesthesia wearing off, time to pay off credit cards

3.5.1 Exponential Growth Models

Quite often one will hear that something "grows exponentially," meaning that it grows very fast and at increasing speed. In mathematics, the precise meaning of **exponential growth** is a *growth rate of a function that is proportional to its current size*. Let's assume you get a 5% raise every year in a government job. If your annual starting salary out of college is \$40,000, then your first raise will be \$2000. Fifteen years later your annual salary will be approximately \$83,000 and your next 5% raise will be around \$4150. The raise is always 5% of the current salary, so the larger the current salary, the larger the raise.

In Section 3.1, we saw that interest that is compounded continuously is modeled by $A = Pe^{rt}$. Here A stands for amount and P stands for principal. There are similar models for populations; these take the form $N(t) = N_0e^{rt}$, where N_0 represents the number of people at time $t = 0$, r is the annual growth rate, t is time in years, and N represents the number of people at time t. In general, any model of the form $f(x) = ce^{kx}$, $k > 0$, models exponential growth.

3.5.1 SKILL

Use exponential growth functions to model populations, economic applications of assets, and initial spreading of diseases.

3.5.1 CONCEPTUAL

Understand that exponential growth models assume "uninhibited" growth.

EXAMPLE 1 **World Population Projections**

The world population is the total number of humans on Earth at a given time. In 2000 the world population was 6.1 billion and in 2005 the world population was 6.5 billion. Find the annual growth rate and determine in what year the population will reach 9 billion.

Solution:

Assume an exponential growth model. $N(t) = N_0e^{rt}$

Let $t = 0$ correspond to 2000. $N(0) = N_0 = 6.1$

In 2005, $t = 5$, the population was 6.5 billion. $6.5 = 6.1e^{5r}$

Solve for r.

$$\frac{6.5}{6.1} = e^{5r}$$

$$\ln\left(\frac{6.5}{6.1}\right) = \ln\left(e^{5r}\right)$$

$$\ln\left(\frac{6.5}{6.1}\right) = 5r$$

$$r \approx 0.012702681$$

The annual growth rate is approximately $\boxed{1.3\%}$ per year.

Assuming the growth rate stays the same, write a population model. $N(t) = 6.1e^{0.013t}$

Let $N(t) = 9$. $9 = 6.1e^{0.013t}$

Solve for t.

$$e^{0.013t} = \frac{9}{6.1}$$

$$\ln\left(e^{0.013t}\right) = \ln\left(\frac{9}{6.1}\right)$$

$$0.013t = \ln\left(\frac{9}{6.1}\right)$$

$$t \approx 29.91813894$$

The world population will reach 9 billion in $\boxed{2030}$ if the same growth rate is maintained.

[CONCEPT CHECK]

TRUE OR FALSE Investments that compound continuously are examples of exponential growth.

ANSWER True

YOUR TURN The population of North America (United States and Canada) was 300 million in 1995, and in 2005 the North American population was 332 million. Find the annual growth rate (round to the nearest percent) and use that rounded growth rate to determine what year the population will reach 1 billion.

ANSWER

1% per year; 2115

3.5.2 Exponential Decay Models

3.5.2 SKILL

Use exponential decay functions to model scenarios in medicine, economic depreciation of assets, archaeology, and forensic science.

3.5.2 CONCEPTUAL

Understand that the horizontal asymptote corresponds to a limiting value, often zero.

We mentioned radioactive decay briefly in Section 3.1. Radioactive decay is the process in which a radioactive isotope of an element (atoms) loses energy by emitting radiation in the form of particles. This results in loss of mass of the isotope, which we measure as a reduction in the rate of radioactive emission. This process is random, but given a large number of atoms, the decay rate is directly proportional to the mass of the radioactive substance. Since the mass is decreasing, we say this represents *exponential decay*, $m = m_0 e^{-rt}$, where m_0 represents the initial mass at time $t = 0$, r is the decay rate, t is time, and m represents the mass at time t. In general, any model of the form $f(x) = ce^{-kx}$, $k > 0$, models **exponential decay**.

Typically, the decay rate r is expressed in terms of the half-life h. Recall (Section 3.1) that half-life is the time it takes for a quantity to decrease by half.

WORDS	MATH
Write the radioactive decay model.	$m = m_0 e^{-rt}$
Divide both sides by m_0.	$\dfrac{m}{m_0} = e^{-rt}$
The remaining mass of the radioactive isotope is half of the initial mass when $t = h$.	$\dfrac{1}{2} = e^{-rh}$
Solve for r.	
Take the natural logarithm of both sides.	$\ln\left(\dfrac{1}{2}\right) = \ln(e^{-rh})$
Simplify.	$\underbrace{\ln 1}_{0} - \ln 2 = -rh$
	$rh = \ln 2$
	$\boxed{r = \dfrac{\ln 2}{h}}$

[CONCEPT CHECK]

TRUE OR FALSE The value of a car in age (how old the car is) is an example of exponential decay.

ANSWER True

EXAMPLE 2 **Radioactive Decay**

The radioactive isotope of potassium ^{42}K, which is vital in the diagnosis of brain tumors, has a half-life of 12.36 hours.

a. Determine the exponential decay model that represents the mass of ^{42}K.

b. If 500 milligrams of potassium-42 are taken, how many milligrams of this isotope will remain after 48 hours?

c. How long will it take for the original 500-milligram sample to decay to a mass of 5 milligrams?

Solution (a):

Write the relationship between rate of decay and half-life. $r = \dfrac{\ln 2}{h}$

Let $h = 12.36$. $r \approx 0.056$

Write the exponential decay model for the mass of ^{42}K. $\boxed{m = m_0 e^{-0.056t}}$

Solution (b):

Let $m_0 = 500$ and $t = 48$. $\quad m = 500e^{-(0.056)(48)} \approx 34.00841855$

There are approximately $\boxed{\text{34 milligrams}}$ of ^{42}K still in the body after 48 hours.

Note: Had we used the full value of $r = 0.056079868$, the resulting mass would have been $m = 33.8782897$, which is approximately 34 milligrams.

Solution (c):

Write the exponential decay model for the mass of ^{42}K. $\quad m = m_0e^{-0.056t}$

Let $m = 5$ and $m_0 = 500$. $\quad 5 = 500e^{-0.056t}$

Solve for t.

Divide by 500. $\quad e^{-0.056t} = \frac{5}{500} = \frac{1}{100}$

Take the natural logarithm of both sides. $\quad \ln\left(e^{-0.056t}\right) = \ln\left(\frac{1}{100}\right)$

Simplify. $\quad -0.056t = \ln\left(\frac{1}{100}\right)$

Divide by -0.056 and approximate with a calculator. $\quad t \approx 82.2352$

It will take approximately $\boxed{\text{82 hours}}$ for the original 500-milligram substance to decay to a mass of 5 milligrams.

YOUR TURN The radioactive element radon-222 has a half-life of 3.8 days.

a. Determine the exponential decay model that represents the mass of radon-222.

b. How much of a 64-gram sample of radon-222 will remain after 7 days? Round to the nearest gram.

c. How long will it take for the original 64-gram sample to decay to a mass of 4 grams? Round to the nearest day.

ANSWER

a. $m = m_0e^{-0.1824t}$

b. 18 g

c. 15 days

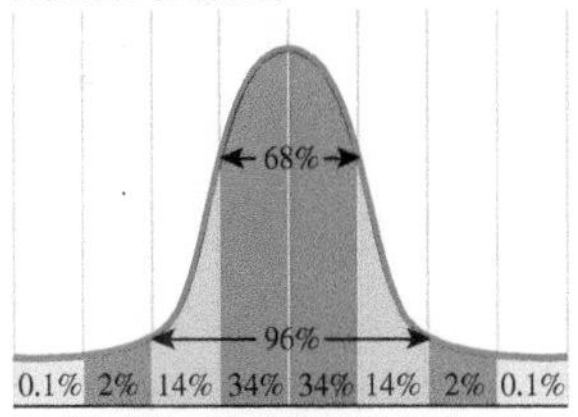

3.5.3 Gaussian (Normal) Distribution Models

If your instructor plots the grades from the last test, typically you will see a **Gaussian (normal) distribution** of scores, otherwise known as the *bell-shaped curve*. Other examples of phenomena that tend to follow a Gaussian distribution are SAT scores, height distributions of adults, and standardized tests like IQ assessments.

The graph to the right represents a Gaussian distribution of IQ scores. The average score, which for IQ is 100, is the x-value at which the maximum occurs. The typical probability distribution is

$$F(x) = \frac{1}{\sigma\sqrt{2\pi}}e^{-(x-\mu)^2/2\sigma^2}$$

where μ is the average or mean value and the variance is σ^2.

Any model of the form $f(x) = ce^{-(x-a)^2/k}$ is classified as a **Gaussian model**.

3.5.3 SKILL

Represent distributions using a Gaussian (normal) model.

3.5.3 CONCEPTUAL

Understand that the bell curve is used to represent standardized tests (IQ/SAT), as well as height/weight charts.

[CONCEPT CHECK]

What threshold score would one have to be at approximately the 98th percentile in IQ?

ANSWER 130

EXAMPLE 3 Weight Distributions

Suppose each member of a Little League football team is weighed and the weight distribution follows the Gaussian model $f(x) = 10e^{-(x-100)^2/25}$.

a. Graph the weight distribution.

b. What is the average weight of a member of this team?

c. Approximately how many boys weigh 95 pounds?

Solution:

a.

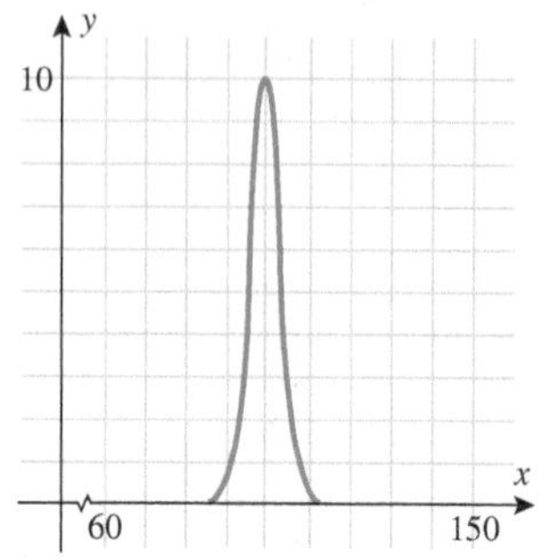

b. 100 pounds

c. $f(95) = 10e^{-(95-100)^2/25}$

$= 10^{-25/25}$

$= 10e^{-1}$

≈ 3.6788

Approximately 4 boys weigh 95 pounds.

3.5.4 SKILL

Represent restricted growth with logistic models.

3.5.4 CONCEPTUAL

Understand that the asymptote of a logistic model corresponds to the carrying capacity of the system.

3.5.4 Logistic Growth Models

Earlier in this section, we discussed exponential growth models for populations that experience uninhibited growth. Now we will turn our attention to *logistic growth*, which models population growth when there are factors that impact the ability to grow, such as food and space. For example, if 10 rabbits are dropped off on an uninhabited island, they will reproduce and the population of rabbits on that island will experience rapid growth. The population will continue to increase rapidly until the rabbits start running out of space or food on the island. In other words, under favorable conditions the growth is not restricted, while under less favorable conditions the growth becomes restricted. This type of growth is represented by **logistic growth models**, $f(x) = \dfrac{a}{1 + ce^{-kx}}$. Ultimately, the population of rabbits reaches the island's *carrying capacity, a*.

EXAMPLE 4 Number of Students on a College Campus

In 2008 the University of Central Florida was the sixth largest university in the country. The number of undergraduate students can be modeled by the function $f(t) = \dfrac{50{,}000}{1 + 5e^{-0.12t}}$, where t is time in years and $t = 0$ corresponds to 1970.

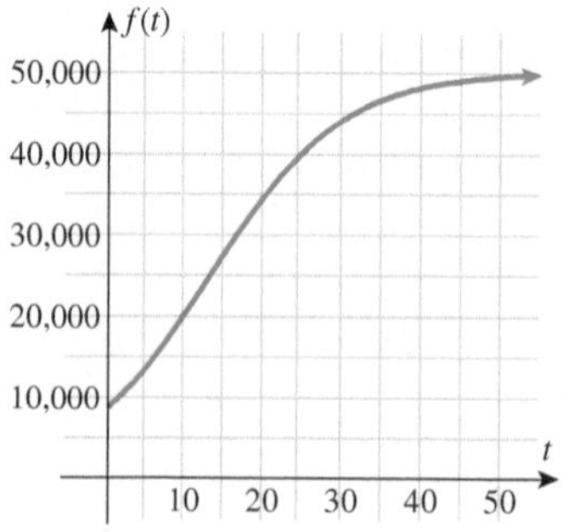

a. How many students attended UCF in 1990? Round to the nearest thousand.

b. How many students attended UCF in 2000?

c. What is the carrying capacity of the UCF main campus?

Round all answers to the nearest thousand.

Solution (a): Let $t = 20$. $f(20) = \dfrac{50{,}000}{1 + 5e^{-0.12(20)}} \approx \boxed{34{,}000}$

Solution (b): Let $t = 30$. $f(30) = \dfrac{50{,}000}{1 + 5e^{-0.12(30)}} \approx \boxed{44{,}000}$

Solution (c): As t increases, the UCF student population approaches $\boxed{50{,}000}$.

[CONCEPT CHECK]

Why would the spread of a disease on an island be modeled with a logistic growth model, rather than an exponential growth model?

ANSWER Once everyone on the island is infected, there are no more people to infect.

3.5.5 Logarithmic Models

3.5.5 SKILL

Use logistic growth models to determine time to pay off debt.

3.5.5 CONCEPTUAL

Understand why doubling your monthly payment will reduce the life of the loan by more than half.

Homeowners typically ask the question, "If I increase my payment, how long will it take to pay off my current mortgage?" In general, a loan over t years with an annual interest rate r with n periods per year corresponds to an interest rate per period of $i = \frac{r}{n}$. Typically, loans are paid in equal payments consisting of the principal P plus total interest divided by the total number of periods over the life of the loan nt. The periodic payment R is given by

$$R = P\frac{i}{1 - (1 + i)^{-nt}}$$

We can find the time (in years) it will take to pay off the loan as a function of periodic payment by solving for t.

WORDS	MATH
Multiply both sides by $1 - (1 + i)^{-nt}$.	$R[1 - (1 + i)^{-nt}] = Pi$
Eliminate the brackets.	$R - R(1 + i)^{-nt} = Pi$
Subtract R.	$-R(1 + i)^{-nt} = Pi - R$
Divide by $-R$.	$(1 + i)^{-nt} = 1 - \dfrac{Pi}{R}$
Take the natural log of both sides.	$\ln(1 + i)^{-nt} = \ln\left(1 - \dfrac{Pi}{R}\right)$
Use the power property for logarithms.	$-nt\ln(1 + i) = \ln\left(1 - \dfrac{Pi}{R}\right)$
Isolate t.	$t = -\dfrac{\ln\left(1 - \dfrac{Pi}{R}\right)}{n\ln(1 + i)}$
Let $i = \dfrac{r}{n}$.	$\boxed{t = -\dfrac{\ln\left(1 - \dfrac{Pr}{nR}\right)}{n\ln\left(1 + \dfrac{r}{n}\right)}}$

EXAMPLE 5 Paying Off Credit Cards

James owes \$15,000 on his credit card. The annual interest rate is 13% compounded monthly.

a. Find the time it will take to pay off his credit card if he makes payments of \$200 per month.

b. Find the time it will take to pay off his credit card if he makes payments of \$400 per month.

Let $P = 15{,}000$, $r = 0.13$, and $n = 12$.

$$t = -\frac{\ln\left(1 - \frac{15{,}000(0.13)}{12R}\right)}{12\ln\left(1 + \frac{0.13}{12}\right)}$$

Solution (a): Let $R = 200$.

$$t = -\frac{\ln\left(1 - \frac{15{,}000(0.13)}{12(200)}\right)}{12\ln\left(1 + \frac{0.13}{12}\right)} \approx 13$$

\$200 monthly payments will allow James to pay off his credit card in about $\boxed{\text{13 years}}$.

Solution (b): Let $R = 400$.

$$t = -\frac{\ln\left(1 - \frac{15{,}000(0.13)}{12(400)}\right)}{12\ln\left(1 + \frac{0.13}{12}\right)} \approx 4$$

\$400 monthly payments will allow James to pay off the balance in approximately $\boxed{\text{4 years}}$. It is important to note that doubling the payment reduced the time to pay off the balance by two-thirds.

[CONCEPT CHECK]

TRUE OR FALSE If you double your payments on a loan, you will pay off the loan in half the time.

ANSWER False

[SECTION 3.5] SUMMARY

In this section, we discussed five main types of models that involve exponential and logarithmic functions.

NAME	MODEL	APPLICATIONS
Exponential growth	$f(t) = ce^{kt}, k > 0$	Uninhibited growth (populations/inflation)
Exponential decay	$f(t) = ce^{-kt}, k > 0$	Carbon dating, depreciation
Gaussian (normal) distributions	$f(x) = ce^{-(x-a)^2/k}$	Bell curves (standardized tests, height/weight charts, distribution of power flux of laser beams)
Logistic growth	$f(t) = \dfrac{a}{1 + ce^{-kt}}$	Conservation biology (growth limited by factors like food and space), learning curve
Logarithmic	$f(t) = a + c\log t$ $f(t) = a + c\ln t$ or quotients of logarithmic functions	Time to pay off credit cards, annuity planning

[SECTION 3.5] EXERCISES

• SKILLS

In Exercises 1–6, match each function with the correct graph (a to f) and model name (i to v).

1. $f(t) = 5e^{2t}$
2. $N(t) = 28e^{-t/2}$
3. $T(x) = 4e^{-(x-80)^2/10}$
4. $P(t) = \dfrac{200}{1 + 5e^{-0.4t}}$
5. $D(x) = 4 + \log(x - 1)$
6. $h(t) = 2 + \ln(t + 3)$

Model Names

i. Logarithmic **ii.** Logistic **iii.** Gaussian **iv.** Exponential growth **v.** Exponential decay

Graphs

a.

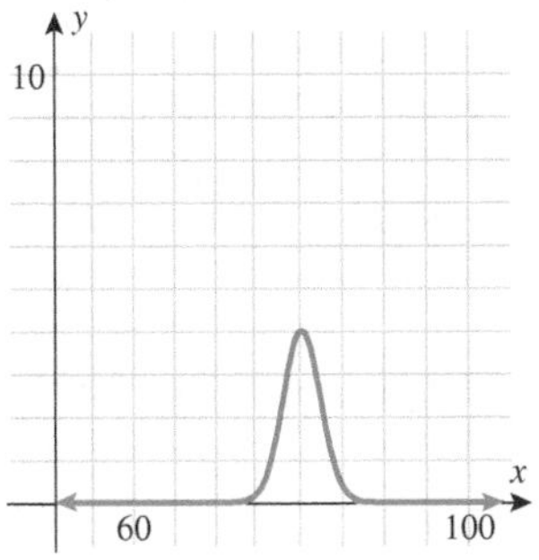

b.

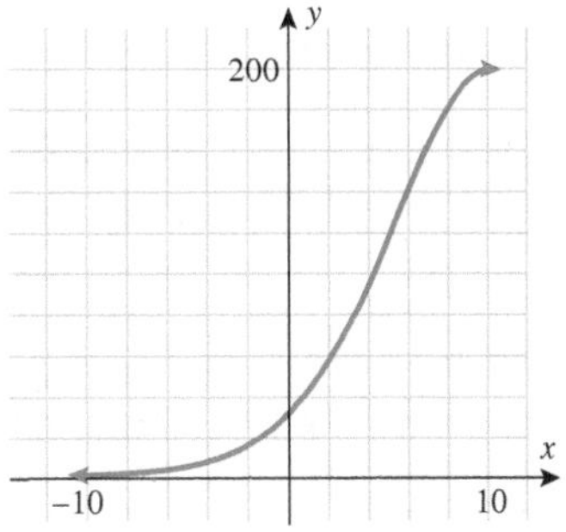

c.

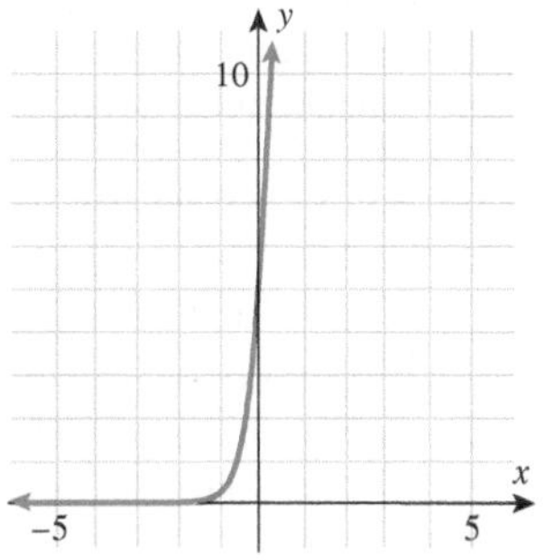

d.

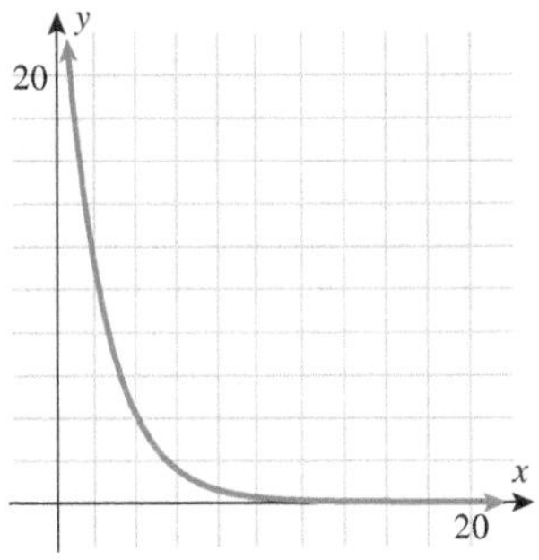

e.

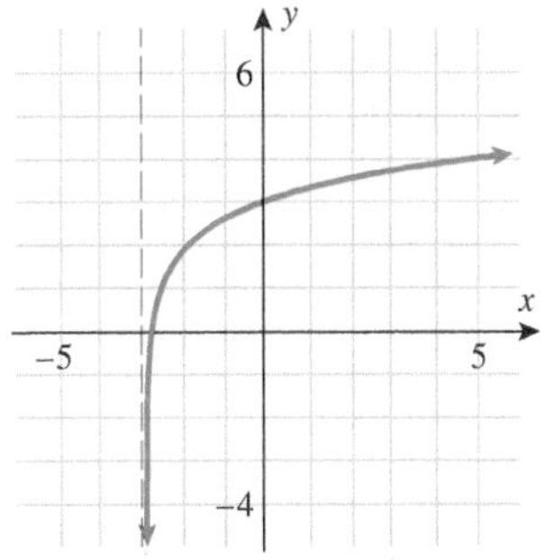

f.

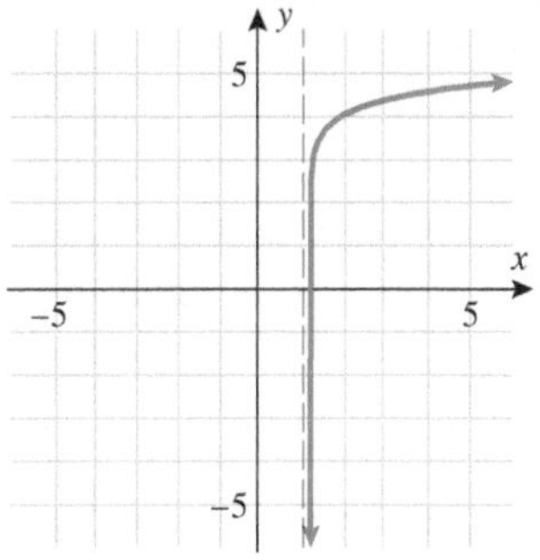

• APPLICATIONS

7. **Population Growth.** The population of the Philippines in 2003 was 80 million. It increases 2.36% per year. What was the expected population of the Philippines in 2020? Apply the formula $N = N_0e^{rt}$, where N represents the number of people.

8. **Population Growth.** China's urban population is growing at 2.5% a year, compounding continuously. If there were 13.7 million people in Shanghai in 1996, approximately how many people will there be in 2020? Apply the formula $N = N_0e^{rt}$, where N represents the number of people.

9. **Population Growth.** Port St. Lucie, Florida, had the United States' fastest growth rate among cities with a population of 100,000 or more between 2003 and 2004. In 2003 the population was 103,800 and increasing at a rate of 12% per year. In what year should the population reach 260,000? (Let $t = 0$ correspond to 2003.) Apply the formula $N = N_0e^{rt}$, where N represents the number of people.

10. **Population Growth.** San Francisco's population has been declining since the "dot com" bubble burst. In 2002 the population was 776,000. If the population is declining at a rate of 1.5% per year, in what year will the population be 600,000? (Let $t = 0$ correspond to 2002.) Apply the formula $N = N_0e^{-rt}$, where N represents the number of people.

11. **Cellular Phone Plans.** The number of cell phones in China is exploding. In 2007 there were 487.4 million cell phone subscribers, and the number is increasing at a rate of 16.5% per year. How many cell phone subscribers were there in 2016 according to this model? Use the formula $N = N_0e^{rt}$, where N represents the number of cell phone subscribers. Let $t = 0$ correspond to 2007.

12. **Bacteria Growth.** A colony of bacteria is growing exponentially. Initially, 500 bacteria were in the colony. The growth rate is 20% per hour. (a) How many bacteria should be in the colony in 12 hours? (b) How many in 1 day? Use the formula $N = N_0e^{rt}$, where N represents the number of bacteria.

13. **Real Estate Appreciation.** In 2004 the average house in Birmingham, AL cost \$185,000, and real estate prices were increasing at an amazing rate of 30% per year. What was the expected cost of an average house in Birmingham in 2016? Use the formula $N = N_0e^{rt}$, where N represents the average cost of a home. Round to the nearest thousand.

14. **Real Estate Appreciation.** The average cost of a single family home in Seattle, WA in 2004 was \$230,000. In 2005 the average cost was \$252,000. If this trend continued, what was the expected cost in 2016? Use the formula $N = N_0e^{rt}$, where N represents the average cost of a home. Round to the nearest thousand.

15. **Oceanography (Growth of Phytoplankton).** Phytoplankton are microscopic plants that live in the ocean. Phytoplankton grow abundantly in oceans around the world and are the foundation of the marine food chain. One variety of phytoplankton growing in tropical waters is increasing at a rate of 20% per month. If it is estimated that there are 100 million in the water, how many will there be in 6 months? Utilize formula $N = N_0e^{rt}$, where N represents the population of phytoplankton.

16. **Oceanography (Growth of Phytoplankton).** In Arctic waters there are an estimated 50,000,000 phytoplankton. The growth rate is 12% per month. How many phytoplankton will there be in 3 months? Utilize formula $N = N_0e^{rt}$, where N represents the population of phytoplankton.

17. **HIV/AIDS.** In 2003 an estimated 1 million people had been infected with HIV in the United States. If the infection rate increases at an annual rate of 2.5% a year compounding continuously, how many Americans will be infected with the HIV virus by 2020?

18. **HIV/AIDS.** In 2003 there were an estimated 25 million people who have been infected with HIV in sub-Saharan Africa. If the infection rate increases at an annual rate of 9% a year compounding continuously, how many Africans will be infected with the HIV virus by 2020?

19. **Anesthesia.** When a person has a cavity filled, the dentist typically gives a local anesthetic. After leaving the dentist's office, one's mouth often is numb for several more hours. If 100 milliliters of anesthesia is injected into the local tissue at the time of the procedure ($t = 0$), and the amount of anesthesia still in the local tissue t hours after the initial injection is given by $A = 100e^{-0.5t}$, how much remains in the local tissue 4 hours later?

20. **Anesthesia.** When a person has a cavity filled, the dentist typically gives a local anesthetic. After leaving the dentist's office, one's mouth often is numb for several more hours. If 100 milliliters of anesthesia is injected into the local tissue at the time of the procedure ($t = 0$), and the amount of anesthesia still in the local tissue t hours after the initial injection is given by $A = 100e^{-0.5t}$, how much remains in the local tissue 12 hours later?

21. **Business.** The sales S (in thousands of units) of a new mp3 player after it has been on the market for t years can be modeled by

$$S(t) = 750\left(1 - e^{-kt}\right)$$

   a. If 350,000 units of the mp3 player were sold in the first year, find k to four decimal places.
   b. Use the model found in part (a) to estimate the sales of the mp3 player after it has been on the market for 3 years.

22. **Business.** During an economic downturn the annual profits of a company dropped from \$850,000 in 2013 to \$525,000 in 2015. Assume the exponential model $P(t) = P_0e^{kt}$ for the annual profit where P is profit in thousands of dollars, and t is time in years.
   a. Find the exponential model for the annual profit.
   b. Assuming the exponential model was applicable in the year 2018, estimate the profit (to the nearest thousand dollars) for the year 2018.

23. **Radioactive Decay.** Carbon-14 has a half-life of 5730 years. How long will it take 5 grams of carbon-14 to be reduced to 2 grams?

24. **Radioactive Decay.** Radium-226 has a half-life of 1600 years. How long will it take 5 grams of radium-226 to be reduced to 2 grams?

25. **Radioactive Decay.** The half-life of uranium-238 is 4.5 billion years. If 98% of uranium-238 remains in a fossil, how old is the fossil?

26. **Decay Levels in the Body.** A drug has a half-life of 12 hours. If the initial dosage is 5 milligrams, how many milligrams will be in the patient's body in 16 hours?

In Exercises 27–30, use the following formula for Newton's Law of Cooling:

If you take a hot dinner out of the oven and place it on the kitchen countertop, the dinner cools until it reaches the temperature of the kitchen. Likewise, a glass of ice set on a table in a room eventually melts into a glass of water at that room temperature. The rate at which the hot dinner cools or the ice in the glass melts at any given time is proportional to the difference between its temperature and the temperature of its surroundings (in this case, the room). This is called **Newton's law of cooling** (or warming) and is modeled by

$$T = T_S + (T_0 - T_S)e^{-kt}$$

where T is the temperature of an object at time t, T_s is the temperature of the surrounding medium, T_0 is the temperature of the object at time $t = 0$, t is the time, and k is a constant.

27. **Newton's Law of Cooling.** An apple pie is taken out of the oven with an internal temperature of 325°F. It is placed on a rack in a room with a temperature of 72°F. After 10 minutes, the temperature of the pie is 200°F. What will the temperature of the pie be 30 minutes after coming out of the oven?

28. **Newton's Law of Cooling.** A cold drink is taken out of an ice chest with a temperature of 38°F and placed on a picnic table with a surrounding temperature of 75°F. After 5 minutes, the temperature of the drink is 45°F. What will the temperature of the drink be 20 minutes after it is taken out of the chest?

29. **Forensic Science (Time of Death).** A body is discovered in a hotel room. At 7:00 A.M. a police detective found the body's temperature to be 85°F. At 8:30 A.M. a medical examiner measures the body's temperature to be 82°F. Assuming the room in which the body was found had a constant temperature of 74°F, how long has the victim been dead? (Normal body temperature is 98.6°F.)

30. **Forensic Science (Time of Death).** At 4 A.M. a body is found in a park. The police measure the body's temperature to be 90°F. At 5 A.M. the medical examiner arrives and determines the temperature to be 86°F. Assuming the temperature of the park was constant at 60°F, how long has the victim been dead?

31. **Depreciation of Automobile.** A new Lexus IS250 has a book value of \$38,000, and after 1 year has a book value of \$32,000. What is the car's value in 4 years? Apply the formula $N = N_0e^{-rt}$, where N represents the value of the car. Round to the nearest hundred.

32. **Depreciation of Automobile.** A new Hyundai Triburon has a book value of \$22,000, and after 2 years a book value of \$14,000. What is the car's value in 4 years? Apply the formula $N = N_0e^{-rt}$, where N represents the value of the car. Round to the nearest hundred.

33. **Automotive.** A new model BMW convertible coupe is designed and produced in time to appear in North America in the fall. BMW Corporation has a limited number of new models available. The number of new model BMW convertible coupes purchased in North America is given by $N = \dfrac{100{,}000}{1 + 10e^{-2t}}$, where t is the number of weeks after the BMW is released.
   a. How many new model BMW convertible coupes will have been purchased 2 weeks after the new model becomes available?
   b. How many after 30 weeks?
   c. What is the maximum number of new model BMW convertible coupes that will be sold in North America?

34. **iPhone.** The number of iPhones purchased is given by $N = \dfrac{2{,}000{,}000}{1 + 2e^{-4t}}$, where t is the time in weeks after they are made available for purchase.
   a. How many iPhones are purchased within the first 2 weeks?
   b. How many iPhones are purchased within the first month?

35. **Spread of a Disease.** The number of MRSA (methicillin-resistant *Staphylococcus aureus*) cases has been rising sharply in England and Wales since 1997. In 1997, 2422 cases were reported. The number of cases reported in 2003 was 7684. How many cases might be expected in 2020? (Let $t = 0$ correspond to 1997.) Use the formula $N = N_0e^{-rt}$, where N represents the number of cases reported.

36. **Spread of a Virus.** Dengue fever, an illness carried by mosquitoes, is occurring in one of the worst outbreaks in decades across Latin America and the Caribbean. In 2004, 300,000 cases were reported, and 630,000 cases in 2007. How many cases in 2020? (Let $t = 0$ be 2004.) Use the formula $N = N_0e^{-rt}$, where N represents the number of cases.

37. **Carrying Capacity.** The Virginia Department of Fish and Game stock a mountain lake with 500 trout. Officials believe the lake can support no more than 10,000 trout. The number of trout is given by $N = \dfrac{10{,}000}{1 + 19e^{-1.56t}}$, where t is time in years. How many years will it take for the trout population to reach 5000?

38. **Carrying Capacity.** The World Wildlife Fund has placed 1000 rare pygmy elephants in a conservation area in Borneo. They believe 1600 pygmy elephants can be supported in this environment. The number of elephants is given by $N = \dfrac{1600}{1 + 0.6e^{-0.14t}}$, where t is time in years. How many years will it take the herd to reach 1200 elephants?

39. **Time to Pay Off Debt.** Diana just graduated from medical school owing \$80,000 in student loans. The annual interest rate is 9%.
   a. Approximately how many years will it take to pay off her student loan if she makes a monthly payment of \$750?
   b. Approximately how many years will it take to pay off her loan if she makes a monthly payment of \$1000?

40. **Time to Pay Off Debt.** Victor owes \$20,000 on his credit card. The annual interest rate is 17%.
   a. Approximately how many years will it take him to pay off this credit card if he makes a monthly payment of \$300?
   b. Approximately how many years will it take him to pay off this credit card if he makes a monthly payment of \$400?

For Exercises 41 and 42, refer to the following:

A local business borrows \$200,000 to purchase property. The loan has an annual interest rate of 8% compounded monthly and a minimum monthly payment of \$1467.

41. **Time to Pay Off Debt/Business.**
   a. Approximately how many years will it take the business to pay off the loans if only the minimum payment is made?
   b. How much interest will the business pay over the life of the loan if only the minimum payment is made?

42. **Time to Pay Off Debt/Business.**
   a. Approximately how many years will it take the business to pay off the loan if the minimum payment is doubled?
   b. How much interest will the business pay over the life of the loan if the minimum payment is doubled?
   c. How much in interest will the business save by doubling the minimum payment (see Exercise 41, part b)?

• CATCH THE MISTAKE

In Exercises 43 and 44, explain the mistake that is made.

43. The city of Orlando, Florida, has a population that is growing at 7% a year, compounding continuously. If there were 1.1 million people in greater Orlando in 2006, approximately how many people will there be in 2018? Apply the formula $N = N_0e^{rt}$, where N represents the number of people.

Solution:

Use the population growth model.	$N = N_0e^{rt}$
Let $N_0 = 1.1$, $r = 7$, and $t = 12$.	$N = 1.1e^{(7)(12)}$
Approximate with a calculator.	2.8×10^{30}

This is incorrect. What mistake was made?

44. The city of San Antonio, Texas, has a population that is growing at 5% a year, compounding continuously. If there were 1.3 million people in the greater San Antonio area in 2006, approximately how many people will there be in 2018? Apply the formula $N = N_0e^{rt}$, where N represents the number of people.

Solution:

Use the population growth model.	$N = N_0e^{rt}$
Let $N_0 = 1.3$, $r = 5$, and $t = 12$.	$N = 1.3e^{(5)(12)}$
Approximate with a calculator.	6.7×10^{21}

This is incorrect. What mistake was made?

• CONCEPTUAL

In Exercises 45–48, determine whether each statement is true or false.

45. When a species gets placed on an endangered species list, the species begins to grow rapidly, and then reaches a carrying capacity. This can be modeled by logistic growth.

46. A professor has 400 students one semester. The number of names (of her students) she is able to memorize can be modeled by a logarithmic function.

47. The spread of lice at an elementary school can be modeled by exponential growth.

48. If you purchase a laptop computer this year ($t = 0$), then the value of the computer can be modeled with exponential decay.

• CHALLENGE

In Exercises 49 and 50, refer to the logistic model $f(t) = \dfrac{a}{1 + ce^{-kt}}$, where a is the carrying capacity.

49. As c increases, does the model reach the carrying capacity in less time or more time?

50. As k increases, does the model reach the carrying capacity in less time or more time?

51. A culture of 100 bacteria grows at a rate of 20% every day. Two days later, 60 of the same type of bacteria are placed in a culture that allows a 30% daily growth rate. After how many days do both cultures have the same population?

52. Consider the quotient $Q = \dfrac{P_1e^{r_1t}}{P_2e^{r_2t}}$ of two models of exponential growth.

a. If $r_1 > r_2$, what can you say about Q?

b. If $r_1 < r_2$, what can you say about Q?

53. Consider the models of exponential decay $f(t) = (2 + c)e^{-k_1t}$ and $g(t) = ce^{-k_2t}$. Suppose that $f(1) = g(1)$, what is the relationship between k_1 and k_2?

54. Suppose that both logistic growth models $f(t) = \dfrac{a_1}{1 + c_1e^{-k_1t}}$ and $g(t) = \dfrac{a_2}{1 + c_2e^{-k_2t}}$ have horizontal asymptote $y = 100$. What can you say about the corresponding carrying capacities?

• PREVIEW TO CALCULUS

In Exercises 55–58, refer to the following:

In calculus, we find the derivative, $f'(x)$, of a function $f(x)$ by allowing h to approach 0 in the difference quotient $\dfrac{f(x + h) - f(x)}{h}$ of functions involving exponential functions.

55. Find the difference quotient of the exponential growth model $f(x) = Pe^{kx}$, where P and k are positive constants.

56. Find the difference quotient of the exponential decay model $f(x) = Pe^{-kx}$, where P and k are positive constants.

57. Use the fact that $\dfrac{e^h - 1}{h} = 1$ when h is close to zero to find the derivative of $f(x) = e^x + x$.

58. Find the difference quotient of $f(x) = \cosh x$ and use it to prove that $(\cosh x)' = \sinh x$.

[CHAPTER 3 REVIEW]

SECTION	CONCEPT	KEY IDEAS/FORMULAS
3.1	**Exponential functions and their graphs**	
	Evaluating exponential function	$f(x) = b^x \quad b > 0, b \neq 1$
	Graphs of exponential functions	y-intercept $(0, 1)$ Horizontal asymptote: $y = 0$; the points $(1, b)$ and $(-1, 1/b)$
	The natural base e	$f(x) = e^x$
	Applications of exponential functions	Doubling time: $P = P_0 2^{t/d}$ Compound interest: $A = P\left(1 + \frac{r}{n}\right)^{nt}$ Compounded continuously: $A = Pe^{rt}$
3.2	**Logarithmic functions and their graphs**	$y = \log_b x \quad x > 0$ $b > 0, b \neq 1$
	Evaluating logarithms	$y = \log_b x$ and $x = b^y$
	Common and natural logarithms	$y = \log x$ Common (base 10) $y = \ln x$ Natural (base e)
	Graphs of logarithmic functions	x-intercept $(1, 0)$ Vertical asymptote: $x = 0$; the points $(b, 1)$ and $(1/b, -1)$
	Applications of logarithms	Decibel scale: $D = 10 \log\left(\frac{I}{I_T}\right) \quad I_T = 1 \times 10^{-12}$ W/m^2 Richter scale: $M = \frac{2}{3}\log\left(\frac{E}{E_0}\right) \quad E_0 = 10^{4.4}$ joules
3.3	**Properties of logarithms**	
	Properties of logarithms	1. $\log_b 1 = 0$ 2. $\log_b b = 1$ 3. $\log_b b^x = x$ 4. $b^{\log_b x} = x \quad x > 0$ Product property: 5. $\log_b MN = \log_b M + \log_b N$ Quotient property: 6. $\log_b\left(\frac{M}{N}\right) = \log_b M - \log_b N$ Power property: 7. $\log_b M^p = p \log_b M$
	Change-of-base formula	$\log_b M = \frac{\log M}{\log b}$ or $\log_b M = \frac{\ln M}{\ln b}$

CHAPTER 3 REVIEW

SECTION	CONCEPT	KEY IDEAS/FORMULAS
3.4	**Exponential and logarithmic equations**	
	Solving exponential equations	*Simple exponential equations* 1. Rewrite both sides of the equation in terms of the same base. 2. Use the one-to-one property to equate the exponents. 3. Solve for the variable. *Complicated exponential equations* 1. Isolate the exponential expression. 2. Take the same logarithm of both sides. 3. Simplify using the inverse properties. 4. Solve for the variable.
	Solving logarithmic equations	*Simple logarithmic equations* 1. Combine logarithms on each side of the equation using properties. 2. Use the one-to-one property to equate the exponents. 3. Solve for the variable. 4. Check the results and eliminate any extraneous solutions. *Complicated logarithmic equations* 1. Combine and isolate the logarithmic expressions. 2. Rewrite the equation in exponential form. 3. Solve for the variable. 4. Check the results and eliminate any extraneous solutions.
3.5	**Exponential and logarithmic models**	
	Exponential growth models	$f(x) = ce^{kx} \quad k > 0$
	Exponential decay models	$f(x) = ce^{-kx} \quad k > 0$
	Gaussian (normal) distribution models	$f(x) = ce^{-(x-a)^2/k}$
	Logistic growth models	$f(x) = \dfrac{a}{1 + ce^{-kx}}$
	Logarithmic models	$f(x) = a + c \log x$ $f(x) = a + c \ln x$

[CHAPTER 3 REVIEW EXERCISES]

3.1 Exponential Functions and Their Graphs

Approximate each number using a calculator and round your answer to two decimal places.

1. $8^{4.7}$
2. $\pi^{2/5}$
3. $4 \cdot 5^{0.2}$
4. $1.2^{1.2}$

Approximate each number using a calculator and round your answer to two decimal places.

5. $e^{3.2}$
6. e^{π}
7. $e^{\sqrt{\pi}}$
8. $e^{-2.5\sqrt{3}}$

Evaluate each exponential function for the given values.

9. $f(x) = 2^{4-x}$ $\quad f(-2.2)$
10. $f(x) = -2^{x+4}$ $\quad f(1.3)$
11. $f(x) = \left(\frac{2}{5}\right)^{1-6x}$ $\quad f\left(\frac{1}{2}\right)$
12. $f(x) = \left(\frac{4}{7}\right)^{5x+1}$ $\quad f\left(\frac{1}{5}\right)$

Match the graph with the function.

13. $y = 2^{x-2}$
14. $y = -2^{2-x}$
15. $y = 2 + 3^{x+2}$
16. $y = -2 - 3^{2-x}$

a.

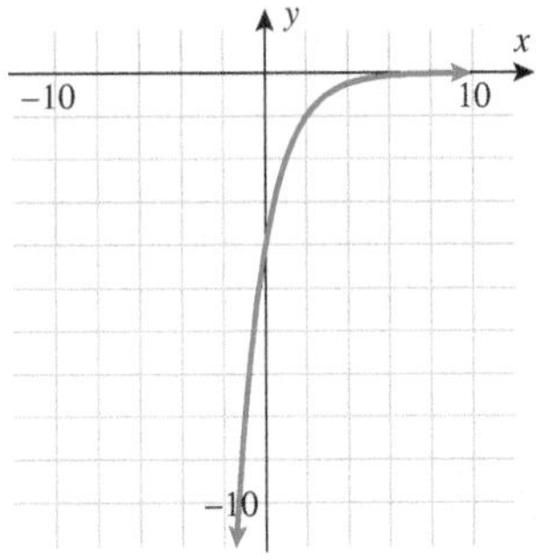

b.

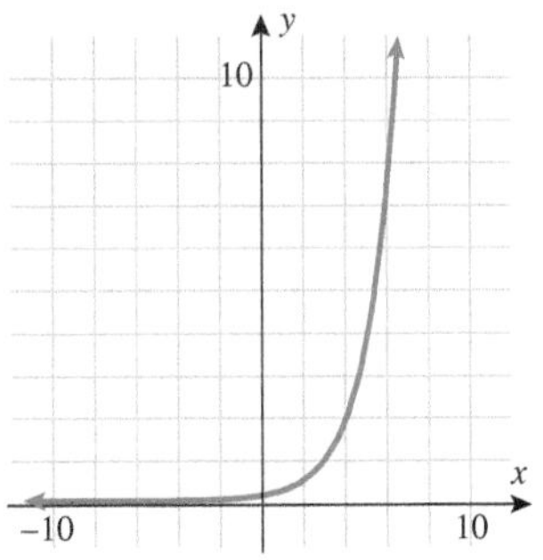

c.

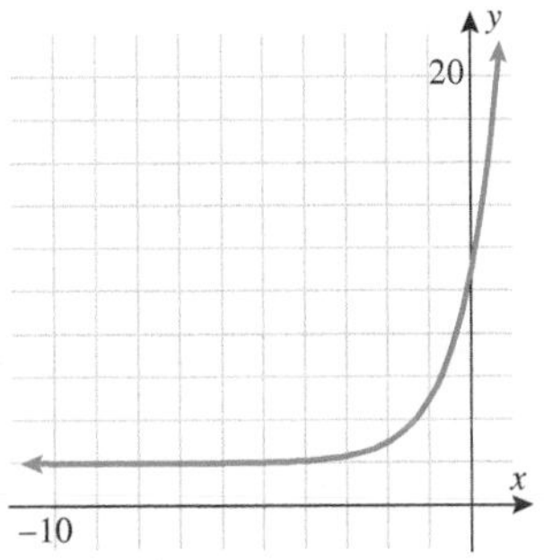

d.

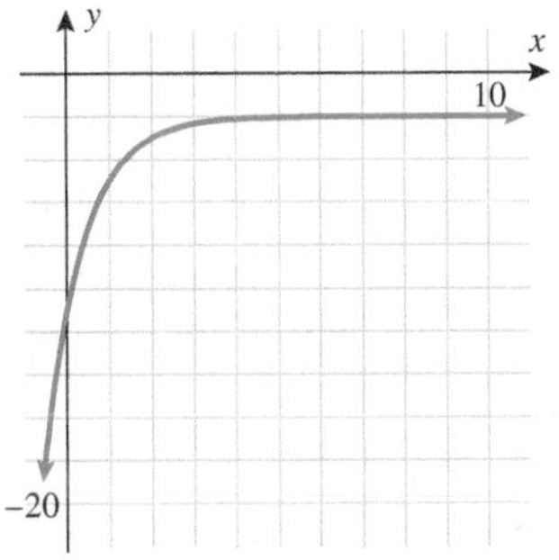

State the *y*-intercept and the horizontal asymptote, and graph the exponential function.

17. $y = -6^{-x}$
18. $y = 4 - 3^x$
19. $y = 1 + 10^{-2x}$
20. $y = 4^x - 4$

State the *y*-intercept and the horizontal asymptote, and graph the exponential function.

21. $y = e^{-2x}$
22. $y = e^{x-1}$
23. $y = 3.2e^{x/3}$
24. $y = 2 - e^{1-x}$

Applications

25. **Compound Interest.** If \$4500 is deposited into an account paying 4.5% compounding semiannually, how much will you have in the account in 7 years?
26. **Compound Interest.** How much money should you put now in a savings account that earns 4.0% a year compounded quarterly if you want \$25,000 in 8 years?
27. **Compound Interest.** If \$13,450 is put in a money market account that pays 3.6% a year compounded continuously, how much will be in the account in 15 years?
28. **Compound Interest.** How much money should you invest today in a money market account that pays 2.5% a year compounded continuously if you desire \$15,000 in 10 years?

3.2 Logarithmic Functions and Their Graphs

Write each logarithmic equation in its equivalent exponential form.

29. $\log_4 64 = 3$
30. $\log_4 2 = \frac{1}{2}$
31. $\log\left(\frac{1}{100}\right) = -2$
32. $\log_{16} 4 = \frac{1}{2}$

Write each exponential equation in its equivalent logarithmic form.

33. $6^3 = 216$
34. $10^{-4} = 0.0001$
35. $\frac{4}{169} = \left(\frac{2}{13}\right)^2$
36. $\sqrt[3]{512} = 8$

Evaluate the logarithms exactly.

37. $\log_7 1$
38. $\log_4 256$
39. $\log_{1/6} 1296$
40. $\log 10^{12}$

Approximate the common and natural logarithms utilizing a calculator. Round to two decimal places.

41. $\log 32$
42. $\ln 32$
43. $\ln 0.125$
44. $\log 0.125$

State the domain of the logarithmic function in interval notation.

45. $f(x) = \log_3(x + 2)$
46. $f(x) = \log_2(2 - x)$
47. $f(x) = \log(x^2 + 3)$
48. $f(x) = \log(3 - x^2)$

Match the graph with the function.

49. $y = \log_7 x$
50. $y = -\log_7(-x)$
51. $y = \log_7(x + 1) - 3$
52. $y = -\log_7(1 - x) + 3$

a.

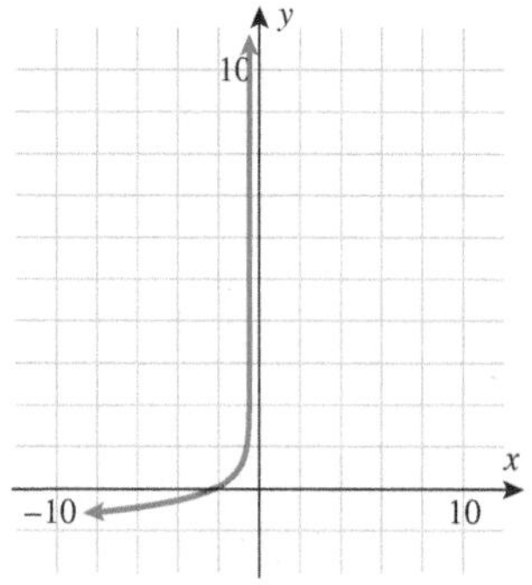

b.

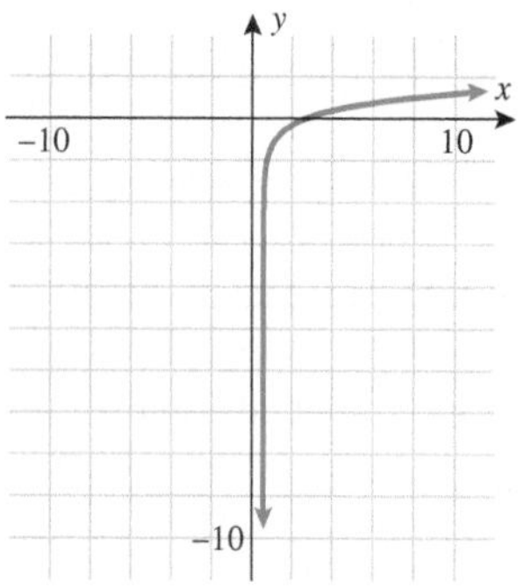

c.

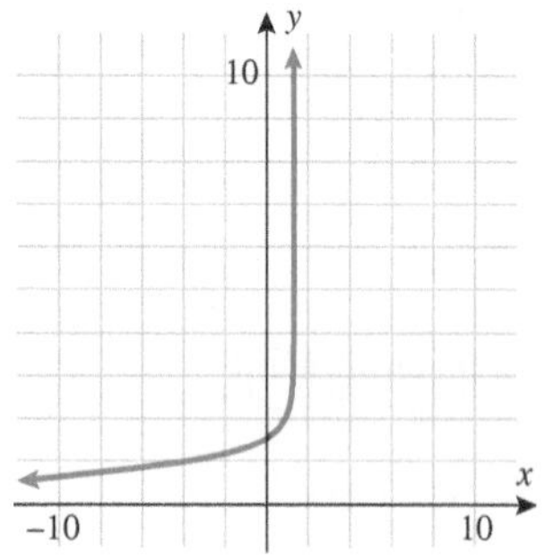

d.

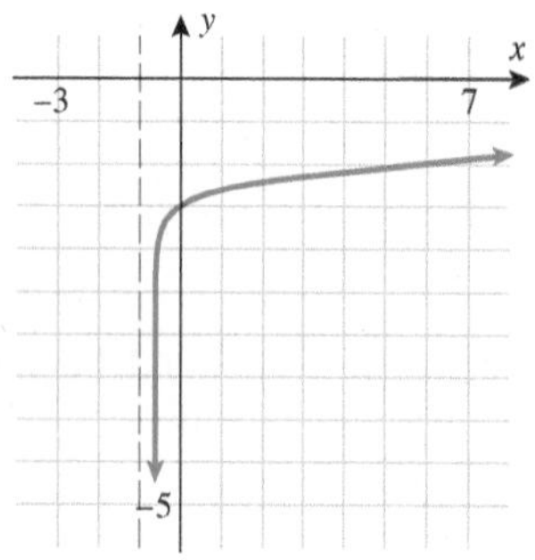

Graph the logarithmic function with transformation techniques.

53. $f(x) = \log_4(x - 4) + 2$
54. $f(x) = \log_4(x + 4) - 3$
55. $f(x) = -\log_4(x) - 6$
56. $f(x) = -2\log_4(-x) + 4$

Applications

57. **Chemistry.** Calculate the pH value of milk, assuming it has a concentration of hydrogen ions given by $H^+ = 3.16 \times 10^{-7}$.

58. **Chemistry.** Calculate the pH value of Coca-Cola, assuming it has a concentration of hydrogen ions given by $H^+ = 2.0 \times 10^{-3}$.

59. **Sound.** Calculate the decibels associated with a teacher speaking to a medium-sized class if the sound intensity is 1×10^{-7} W/m^2.

60. **Sound.** Calculate the decibels associated with an alarm clock if the sound intensity is 1×10^{-4} W/m^2.

3.3 Properties of Logarithms

Use the properties of logarithms to simplify each expression.

61. $\log_{2.5} 2.5$
62. $\log_2\sqrt{16}$
63. $2.5^{\log_{2.5} 6}$
64. $e^{-3\ln 6}$

Write each expression as a sum or difference of logarithms.

65. $\log_c x^a y^b$
66. $\log_3 x^2 y^{-3}$
67. $\log_j\left(\frac{rs}{t^3}\right)$
68. $\log x^c\sqrt{x + 5}$
69. $\log\left[\frac{a^{1/2}}{b^{3/2}c^{2/5}}\right]$
70. $\log_7\left[\frac{c^3 d^{1/3}}{e^6}\right]^{1/3}$

Evaluate the logarithms using the change-of-base formula.

71. $\log_8 3$
72. $\log_5 \frac{1}{2}$
73. $\log_\pi 1.4$
74. $\log_{\sqrt{3}} 2.5$

3.4 Exponential and Logarithmic Equations

Solve the exponential equations exactly for *x*.

75. $4^x = \frac{1}{256}$
76. $3^{x^2} = 81$
77. $e^{3x-4} = 1$
78. $e^{\sqrt{x}} = e^{4.8}$
79. $\left(\frac{1}{3}\right)^{x+2} = 81$
80. $100^{x^2-3} = 10$

Solve the exponential equation. Round your answer to three decimal places.

81. $e^{2x+3} - 3 = 10$
82. $2^{2x-1} + 3 = 17$
83. $e^{2x} + 6e^x + 5 = 0$
84. $4e^{0.1x} = 64$
85. $(2^x - 2^{-x})(2^x + 2^{-x}) = 0$
86. $5(2^x) = 25$

Solve the logarithmic equations exactly.

87. $\log(3x) = 2$
88. $\log_3(x + 2) = 4$
89. $\log_4 x + \log_4 2x = 8$
90. $\log_6 x + \log_6(2x - 1) = \log_6 3$

Solve the logarithmic equations. Round your answers to three decimal places.

91. $\ln x^2 = 2.2$
92. $\ln(3x - 4) = 7$
93. $\log_3(2 - x) - \log_3(x + 3) = \log_3 x$
94. $4\log(x + 1) - 2\log(x + 1) = 1$

3.5 Exponential and Logarithmic Models

95. Compound Interest. If Tania needs \$30,000 a year from now for a down payment on a new house, how much should she put in a 1-year CD earning 5% a year compounding continuously so that she will have exactly \$30,000 a year from now?

96. Stock Prices. Jeremy is tracking the stock value of Best Buy (BBY on the NYSE). In 2003 he purchased 100 shares at \$28 a share. The stock did not pay dividends because the company reinvested all earnings. In 2005 Jeremy cashed out and sold the stock for \$4000. What was the annual rate of return on BBY?

97. Compound Interest. Money is invested in a savings account earning 4.2% interest compounded quarterly. How many years will pass until the money doubles?

98. Compound Interest. If \$9000 is invested in an investment earning 8% interest compounded continuously, how many years will pass until there is \$22,500?

99. Population. Nevada has the fastest-growing population according to the U.S. Census Bureau. In 2004 the population of Nevada was 2.62 million and was increasing at an annual rate of 3.5%. What is the expected population in 2020? (Let $t = 0$ be 2004.) Apply the formula $N = N_0e^{rt}$, where N is the population.

100. Population. The Hispanic population in the United States is the fastest growing of any ethnic group. In 1996 there were an estimated 28.3 million Hispanics in the United States, and in 2000 there were an estimated 32.5 million. What is the expected population of Hispanics in the United States in 2020? (Let $t = 0$ be 1996.) Apply the formula $N = N_0e^{rt}$, where N is the population.

101. Bacteria Growth. Bacteria are growing exponentially. Initially, there were 1000 bacteria; after 3 hours there were 2500. How many bacteria should be expected in 6 hours? Apply the formula $N = N_0e^{rt}$, where N is the number of bacteria.

102. Population. In 2003 the population of Phoenix, Arizona, was 1,388,215. In 2004 the population was 1,418,041. What is the expected population in 2020? (Let $t = 0$ be 2003.) Apply the formula $N = N_0e^{rt}$, where N is the population.

103. Radioactive Decay. Strontium-90 has a half-life of 28 years. How long will it take for 20 grams of this to decay to 5 grams? Apply the formula $N = N_0e^{-rt}$, where N is the number of grams.

104. Radioactive Decay. Plutonium-239 has a half-life of 25,000 years. How long will it take for 100 grams to decay to 20 grams? Apply the formula $N = N_0e^{-rt}$, where N is the number of grams.

105. Wild Life Population. The *Boston Globe* reports that the fish population of the Essex River in Massachusetts is declining. In 2003 it was estimated there were 5600 fish in the river, and in 2004 there were only 2420 fish. How many fish should there have been in 2010 if this trend continued? Apply the formula $N = N_0e^{-rt}$, where N is the number of fish.

106. Car Depreciation. A new Acura TSX costs \$28,200. In 2 years the value will be \$24,500. What is the expected value in 6 years? Apply the formula $N = N_0e^{-rt}$, where N is the value of the car.

107. Carrying Capacity. The carrying capacity of a species of beach mice in St. Croix is given by $M = 1000(1 - e^{-0.035t})$, where M is the number of mice and t is time in years ($t = 0$ corresponds to 1998). How many mice should there have been in 2010?

108. Population. The city of Brandon, Florida, had 50,000 residents in 1970, and since the crosstown expressway was built, its population has increased 2.3% per year. If the growth continues at the same rate, how many residents will Brandon have in 2030?

[CHAPTER 3 PRACTICE TEST]

1. Simplify $\log 10^{x^3}$.
2. Use a calculator to evaluate $\log_5 326$ (round to two decimal places).
3. Find the exact value of $\log_{1/3} 81$.
4. Rewrite the expression $\left[\ln \frac{e^{5x}}{x(x^4+1)}\right]$ in a form with no logarithms of products, quotients, or powers.

In Exercises 5–20, solve for *x*, exactly if possible. If an approximation is required, round your answer to three decimal places.

5. $e^{x^2-1} = 42$
6. $e^{2x} - 5e^x + 6 = 0$
7. $27e^{0.2x+1} = 300$
8. $3^{2x-1} = 15$
9. $3\ln(x-4) = 6$
10. $\log(6x+5) - \log 3 = \log 2 - \log x$
11. $\ln(\ln x) = 1$
12. $\log_2(3x-1) - \log_2(x-1) = \log_2(x+1)$
13. $\log_6 x + \log_6(x-5) = 2$
14. $\ln(x+2) - \ln(x-3) = 2$
15. $\ln x + \ln(x+3) = 1$
16. $\log_2\left(\frac{2x+3}{x-1}\right) = 3$
17. $\frac{12}{1+2e^x} = 6$
18. $\ln x + \ln(x-3) = 2$
19. State the domain of the function $f(x) = \log\left(\frac{x}{x^2-1}\right)$.
20. State the range of x values for which the following is true: $10^{\log(4x-a)} = 4x - a$.

In Exercises 21–24, find all intercepts and asymptotes, and graph.

21. $f(x) = 3^{-x} + 1$
22. $f(x) = \left(\frac{1}{2}\right)^x - 3$
23. $f(x) = \ln(2x-3) + 1$
24. $f(x) = \log(1-x) + 2$
25. **Interest.** If \$5000 is invested at a rate of 6% a year, compounded quarterly, what is the amount in the account after 8 years?
26. **Interest.** If \$10,000 is invested at a rate of 5%, compounded continuously, what is the amount in the account after 10 years?
27. **Sound.** A lawn mower's sound intensity is approximately 1×10^{-3} W/m^2. Assuming your threshold of hearing is 1×10^{-12} W/m^2, calculate the decibels associated with the lawn mower.
28. **Population.** The population in Seattle, Washington, has been increasing at a rate of 5% a year. If the population continues to grow at that rate, and in 2004 there are 800,000 residents, how many residents will there be in 2020? *Hint:* $N = N_0e^{rt}$.
29. **Earthquake.** An earthquake is considered moderate if it is between 5 and 6 on the Richter scale. What is the energy range in joules for a moderate earthquake?
30. **Radioactive Decay.** The mass $m(t)$ remaining after t hours from a 50-gram sample of a radioactive substance is given by the equation $m(t) = 50e^{-0.0578t}$. After how long will only 30 grams of the substance remain? Round your answer to the nearest hour.
31. **Bacteria Growth.** The number of bacteria in a culture is increasing exponentially. Initially, there were 200 in the culture. After 2 hours there are 500. How many should be expected in 8 hours? Round your answer to the nearest hundred.
32. **Carbon Decay.** Carbon-14 has a half-life of 5730 years. How long will it take for 100 grams to decay to 40 grams?
33. **Spread of a Virus.** The number of people infected by a virus is given by $N = \frac{2000}{1+3e^{-0.4t}}$, where t is time in days. In how many days will 1000 people be infected?
34. **Oil Consumption.** The world consumption of oil was 76 million barrels per day in 2002. In 2004 the consumption was 83 million barrels per day. How many barrels are expected to be consumed in 2020?

[CHAPTERS 1–3 CUMULATIVE TEST]

1. Find the domain and range of the function $f(x) = \dfrac{3}{\sqrt{x^2 - 9}}$.

2. If $f(x) = 1 + 3x$ and $g(x) = x^2 - 1$, find

   a. $f + g$ b. $f - g$ c. $f \cdot g$ d. $\dfrac{f}{g}$

   and state the domain of each.

3. Write the function below as a composite of two functions f and g. (More than one answer is correct.)

$$f(g(x)) = \frac{1 - e^{2x}}{1 + e^{2x}}$$

4. Determine whether $f(x) = \sqrt[5]{x^3 + 1}$ is one-to-one. If f is one-to-one, find its inverse f^{-1}.

5. Find the quadratic function whose vertex is $(-2, 3)$ and goes through the point $(1, -1)$.

6. Write the polynomial $f(x) = 3x^3 + 6x^2 - 15x - 18$ as a product of linear factors.

7. Solve the equation $e^x + \sqrt{e^x} - 12 = 0$. Round your answer to three decimal places.

8. Using the function $f(x) = 4x - x^2$, evaluate the difference quotient $\dfrac{f(x + h) - f(x)}{h}$.

9. Given the piecewise-defined function

$$f(x) = \begin{cases} 5 & -2 < x \le 0 \\ 2 - \sqrt{x} & 0 < x < 4 \\ x - 3 & x \ge 4 \end{cases}$$

   find

   a. $f(4)$ b. $f(0)$ c. $f(1)$ d. $f(-4)$

   e. State the domain and range in interval notation.

   f. Determine the intervals where the function is increasing, decreasing, or constant.

10. Sketch the graph of the function $y = \sqrt{1 - x}$ and identify all transformations.

11. Determine whether the function $f(x) = \sqrt{x - 4}$ is one-to-one.

12. The volume of a cylinder with circular base is 400 cubic inches. Its height is 10 inches. Find its radius. Round your answer to three decimal places.

13. Find the vertex of the parabola associated with the quadratic function $f(x) = -4x^2 + 8x - 5$.

14. Find a polynomial of minimum degree (there are many) that has the zeros $x = -5$ (multiplicity 2) and $x = 9$ (multiplicity 4).

15. Use synthetic division to find the quotient $Q(x)$ and remainder $r(x)$ of $(3x^2 - 4x^3 - x^4 + 7x - 20) \div (x + 4)$.

16. Given the zero $x = 2 + i$ of the polynomial $P(x) = x^4 - 7x^3 + 13x^2 + x - 20$, determine all the other zeros and write the polynomial as the product of linear factors.

17. Find the vertical and slant asymptotes of $f(x) = \dfrac{x^2 + 7}{x - 3}$.

18. Graph the rational function $f(x) = \dfrac{3x}{x + 1}$. Give all asymptotes.

19. Graph the function $f(x) = 5x^2(7 - x)^2(x + 3)$.

20. If \$5400 is invested at 2.75% compounded monthly, how much is in the account after 4 years?

21. Give the exact value of $\log_3 243$.

22. Write the expression $\frac{1}{2}\ln(x + 5) - 2\ln(x + 1) - \ln(3x)$ as a single logarithm.

23. Solve the logarithmic equation exactly: $10^{2\log(4x+9)} = 121$.

24. Give an exact solution to the exponential equation $5^{x^2} = 625$.

25. If \$8500 is invested at 4% compounded continuously, how many years will pass until there is \$12,000?

CHAPTER 4

Trigonometric Functions of Angles

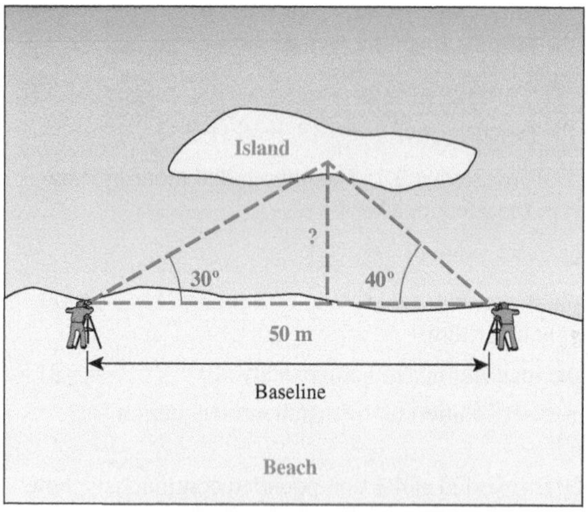

Surveyors use trigonometry to indirectly measure distances. Since angles are easier to measure than distances, surveyors set up a baseline between two stations and measure the distance between the two stations and the angles made by the baseline and some third station.

Here there are two stations along the shoreline, the distance along the beach between the two stations is 50 meters, and the angles between the baseline (beach) and the line of sight to the island are 30° and 40°. Then the Law of Sines can be used to find the shortest distance from the beach to the island.*

*See Section 4.4, Exercises 43 and 44.

LEARNING OBJECTIVES

- Understand degree measure.
- Define the six trigonometric functions as ratios of lengths of the sides of right triangles.
- Solve right triangles.
- Define the six trigonometric functions as ratios of x- and y-coordinates and distances in the Cartesian plane.
- Evaluate trigonometric functions for nonacute angles.
- Relate degree and radian measure.

[IN THIS CHAPTER]

Angle measure will be defined in terms of both degrees and radians. Then the six trigonometric functions will be defined for acute angles in terms of right triangle ratios. Next the trigonometric functions will be defined for nonacute angles. Last, the Law of Sines and the Law of Cosines will be used to solve oblique triangles.

TRIGONOMETRIC FUNCTIONS OF ANGLES

4.1 ANGLE MEASURE	4.2 RIGHT TRIANGLE TRIGONOMETRY	4.3 TRIGONOMETRIC FUNCTIONS OF ANGLES	4.4 THE LAW OF SINES	4.5 THE LAW OF COSINES
• Angles and Their Measure • Radian Measure • Angles in Standard Position • Coterminal Angles • Arc Length • Area of a Circular Sector • Linear and Angular Speeds • Relationship between Linear and Angular Speeds	• Right Triangle Ratios • Trigonometric Ratios of General Acute Angles • Reciprocal Identities • Evaluating Trigonometric Functions Exactly for Special Angle Measures • Using Calculators to Evaluate (Approximate) Trigonometric Functions • Solving Right Triangles	• Trigonometric Functions: The Cartesian Plane • Algebraic Signs of Trigonometric Functions • Ranges of the Trigonometric Functions • Reference Angles and Reference Right Triangles • Evaluating Trigonometric Functions for Nonacute Angles	• Solving Oblique Triangles	• Solving Oblique Triangles Using the Law of Cosines • The Area of a Triangle

- Solve oblique triangles using the Law of Sines.
- Solve oblique triangles using the Law of Cosines.

4.1 ANGLE MEASURE

SKILLS OBJECTIVES

- Find the complement and supplement of an angle.
- Calculate the radian measure of an angle.
- Sketch angles in standard position.
- Identify coterminal angles.
- Calculate the length of an arc along a circle.
- Calculate the area of a circular sector.
- Calculate linear speed and angular speed.
- Solve application problems involving both angular and linear speeds.

CONCEPTUAL OBJECTIVES

- Understand that degrees are a measure of an angle.
- Understand that degrees and radians are both units for measuring angles.
- Understand that rotation in the counterclockwise direction corresponds to a positive angle measure, whereas rotation in the clockwise direction corresponds to a negative angle measure.
- Understand that the measures of coterminal angles must differ by an integer multiple of 360 degrees.
- Understand why the angle in the arc length formula must be in radian measure.
- Understand that the central angle must be given in radians in order for the formula for the area of a circular sector to be used.
- Understand that linear speed has units of length/time and that angular speed has units of radians/time.
- Understand that angular speed and linear speed are related through the radius.

4.1.1 Angles and Their Measure

4.1.1 SKILL

Find the complement and supplement of an angle.

4.1.1 CONCEPTUAL

Understand that degrees are a measure of an angle.

An **angle** is formed when a ray is rotated around its endpoint. The common endpoint is called the **vertex**.

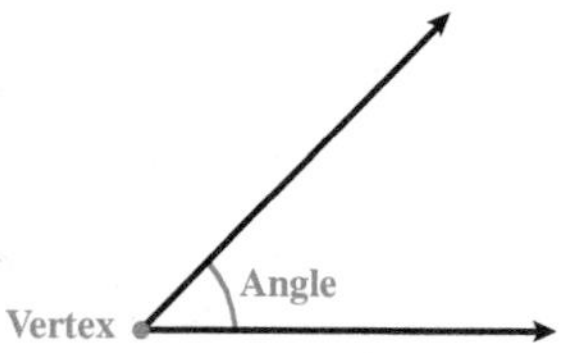

The ray in its original position is called the **initial ray** or the **initial side** of an angle. In the Cartesian plane, we assume the initial side of an angle is the positive x-axis. The ray after it is rotated is called the **terminal ray** or the **terminal side** of an angle. Rotation in a counterclockwise direction corresponds to a **positive angle**, whereas rotation in a clockwise direction corresponds to a **negative angle**.

STUDY TIP

Positive angle: counterclockwise
Negative angle: clockwise

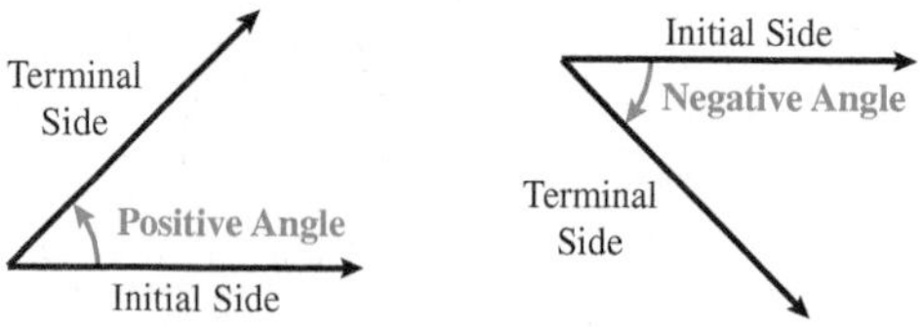

Lengths, or distances, can be measured in different units: feet, miles, and meters are three common units. In order to compare angles of different sizes, we need a standard unit of measure. One way to measure the size of an angle is with **degree measure**.

CONCEPT CHECK

TRUE OR FALSE The measure of an acute angle is greater than the measure of an obtuse angle.

ANSWER False

DEFINITION **Degree Measure of Angles**

An angle formed by one complete counterclockwise rotation has **measure 360 degrees,** denoted 360°.

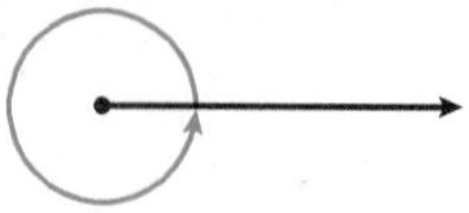

One complete counterclockwise revolution = 360°

WORDS	MATH
360° represents 1 complete counterclockwise rotation.	$\frac{360°}{360°} = 1$
180° represents a $\frac{1}{2}$ counterclockwise rotation.	$\frac{180°}{360°} = \frac{1}{2}$
90° represents a $\frac{1}{4}$ counterclockwise rotation.	$\frac{90°}{360°} = \frac{1}{4}$
1° represents a $\frac{1}{360}$ counterclockwise rotation.	$\frac{1°}{360°} = \frac{1}{360}$

The Greek letter θ (theta) is the most common name for an angle in mathematics. Other common names of angles are α (alpha), β (beta), and γ (gamma).

STUDY TIP

Greek letters are often used to denote angles in trigonometry.

WORDS	MATH
An angle measuring exactly 90° is called a **right angle**. A right angle is often represented by the adjacent sides of a rectangle, indicating that the two rays are ***perpendicular***.	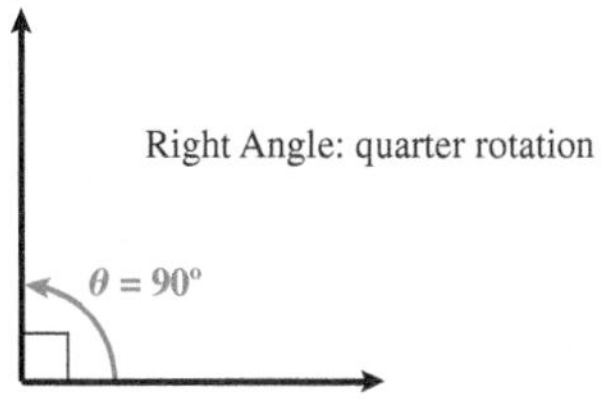
An angle measuring exactly 180° is called a **straight angle**.	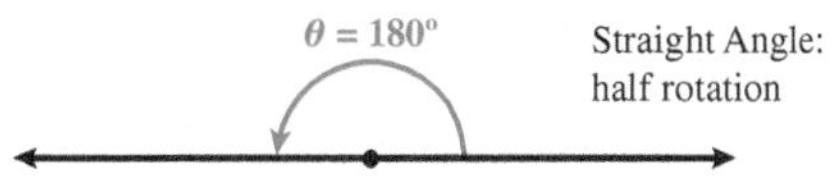
An angle measuring greater than 0°, but less than 90°, is called an **acute angle**.	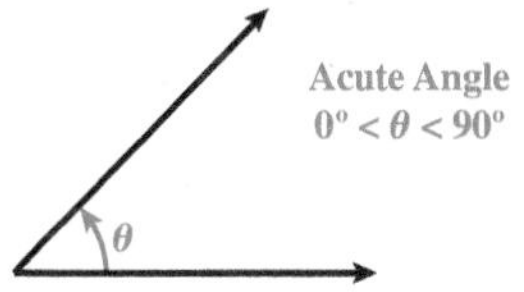
An angle measuring greater than 90°, but less than 180°, is called an **obtuse angle**.	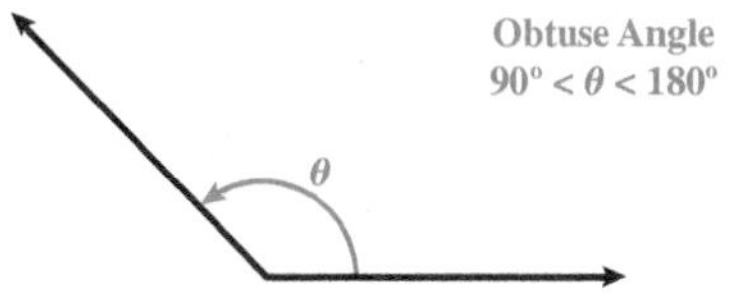
If the sum of the measures of two positive angles is 90°, the angles are called **complementary**. We say that α is the **complement** of β (and vice versa).	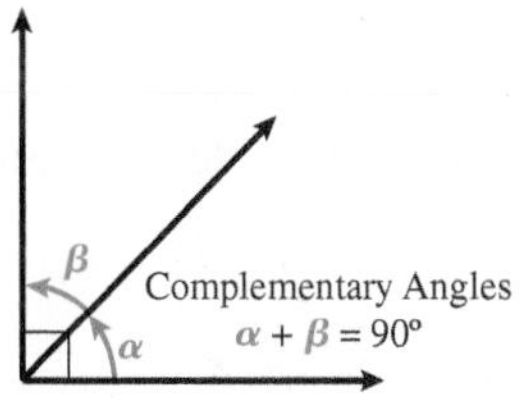
If the sum of the measures of two positive angles is 180°, the angles are called **supplementary**. We say that α is the **supplement** of β (and vice versa).	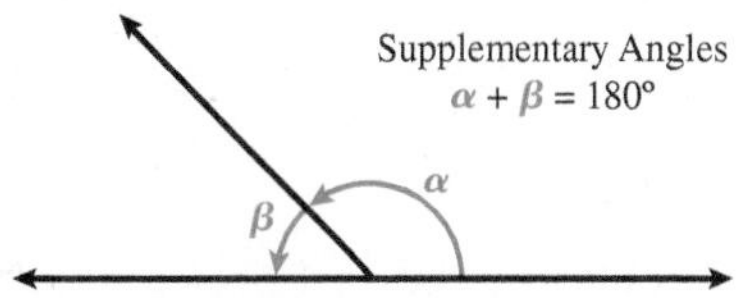

EXAMPLE 1 Finding Measures of Complementary and Supplementary Angles

Find the measure of each angle.

a. Find the complement of 50°.

b. Find the supplement of 110°.

c. Represent the complement of α in terms of α.

d. Find two supplementary angles such that the first angle is twice as large as the second angle.

Solution:

a. The sum of complementary angles is 90°. $\theta + 50° = 90°$

Solve for θ. $\theta = \boxed{40°}$

b. The sum of supplementary angles is 180°. $\theta + 110° = 180°$

Solve for θ. $\theta = \boxed{70°}$

c. Let β be the complement of α.

The sum of complementary angles is 90°. $\alpha + \beta = 90°$

Solve for β. $\beta = \boxed{90° - \alpha}$

d. The sum of supplementary angles is 180°. $\alpha + \beta = 180°$

Let $\beta = 2\alpha$. $\alpha + 2\alpha = 180°$

Solve for α. $3\alpha = 180°$

$\alpha = 60°$

Substitute $\alpha = 60°$ into $\beta = 2\alpha$. $\beta = 120°$

The angles have measures $\boxed{60°}$ and $\boxed{120°}$.

YOUR TURN Find two supplementary angles such that the first angle is 3 times as large as the second angle.

ANSWER

The angles have measures 45° and 135°.

It is important not to confuse an angle with its measure. In Example 1(d), angle α is a rotation and the measure of that rotation is 60°.

4.1.2 Radian Measure

4.1.2 SKILL

Calculate the radian measure of an angle.

4.1.2 CONCEPTUAL

Understand that degrees and radians are both units for measuring angles.

In geometry and most everyday applications, angles are measured in degrees. However, in calculus a more natural angle measure is *radian measure*. Using radian measure allows us to write trigonometric functions as functions not only of angles but also of real numbers in general.

Now we think of the angle in the context of a circle. A **central angle** is an angle that has its vertex at the center of a circle. When the intercepted arc's length is equal to the radius, the measure of the central angle is 1 **radian**.

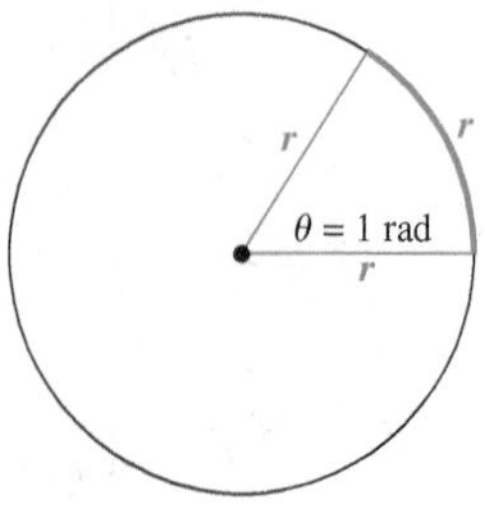

DEFINITION Radian Measure

If a central angle θ in a circle with radius r intercepts an arc on the circle of length s (**arc length**), then the measure of θ, in **radians**, is given by

$$\theta\ (\text{in radians}) = \frac{s}{r}$$

Note: The formula is valid only if s (arc length) and r (radius) are expressed in the same units.

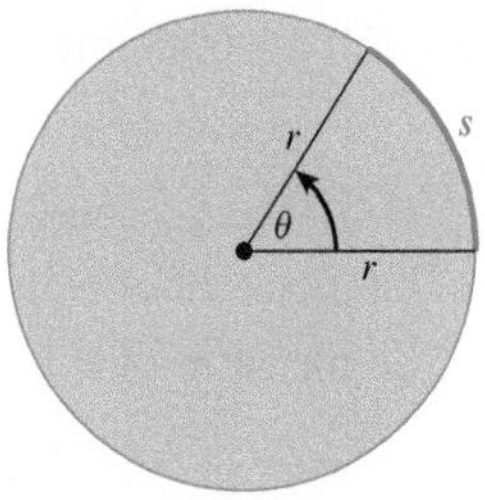

CAUTION

To correctly calculate radians from the formula $\theta = \frac{s}{r}$, the radius and arc length must be expressed in the same units.

Note that both s and r are measured in units of length. When both are given in the same units, the units cancel, giving the number of radians as a *dimensionless* (unitless) real number. One full rotation corresponds to an arc length equal to the circumference $2\pi r$ of the circle with radius r. We see then that one full rotation is equal to 2π radians.

$$\theta_{\text{full rotation}} = \frac{2\pi r}{r} = 2\pi$$

[CONCEPT CHECK]

What is the measure (in radians) of a central angle θ that intercepts an arc of length A cm on a circle with radius A mm?

ANSWER 10 radians, or 10 rad

EXAMPLE 2 Finding the Radian Measure of an Angle

What is the measure (in radians) of a central angle θ that intercepts an arc of length 6 centimeters on a circle with radius 2 meters?

common mistake

A common mistake is to forget to first put the radius and arc length in the same units.

✓CORRECT	✗INCORRECT
Write the formula relating radian measure to arc length and radius. $\theta\ (\text{in radians}) = \frac{s}{r}$	
Substitute $s = 6$ cm and $r = 2$ m into the radian expression. $\theta = \frac{6\text{ cm}}{2\text{ m}}$	Substitute $s = 6$ cm and $r = 2$ m into the radian expression. $\theta = \frac{6\text{ cm}}{2\text{ m}}$
Convert the radius (2) meters to centimeters: 2 m = 200 cm. $\theta = \frac{6\text{ cm}}{200\text{ cm}}$	Simplify. $\theta = 3$ rad **ERROR**
The units, cm, cancel and the result is a unitless real number. $\theta = 0.03$ rad	

CAUTION

Units for arc length and radius must be the same to use $\theta = \frac{s}{r}$.

YOUR TURN What is the measure (in radians) of a central angle θ that intercepts an arc of length 12 millimeters on a circle with radius 4 centimeters?

ANSWER

0.3 rad

STUDY TIP

If an angle measure is given as a real number, then radians are implied.

STUDY TIP

If we let

- θ_d = angle measure in degrees
- θ_R = angle measure in radians

then

- $\theta_R = \theta_d \cdot \frac{\pi}{180°}$
- $\theta_d = \theta_R \cdot \frac{180°}{\pi}$

In the previous example, the units, cm, canceled, therefore correctly giving *radians* as a unitless real number. Because radians are unitless, the word radians (or rad) is often omitted. If an angle measure is given simply as a real number, then radians are implied.

WORDS	MATH
The measure of θ is 4 degrees.	$\theta = 4°$
The measure of θ is 4 radians.	$\theta = 4$

Converting between Degrees and Radians

An angle corresponding to one full rotation is said to have measure 360° or 2π radians. Therefore, $180° = \pi$ rad.

- To convert degrees to radians, multiply the degree measure by $\frac{\pi}{180°}$.
- To convert radians to degrees, multiply the radian measure by $\frac{180°}{\pi}$.

EXAMPLE 3 **Converting between Degrees and Radians**

Convert:

a. 45° to radians **b.** 472° to radians **c.** $\frac{2\pi}{3}$ to degrees

Solution (a):

Multiply 45° by $\frac{\pi}{180°}$. $\quad (45°)\left(\frac{\pi}{180°}\right) = \frac{45°\pi}{180°}$

Simplify. $\quad = \frac{\pi}{4}$ radians

Note: $\frac{\pi}{4}$ is the exact value. A calculator can be used to approximate this expression. Scientific and graphing calculators have a π button (on most scientific calculators, it requires using a shift or second command). The decimal approximation rounded to three decimal places is 0.785.

Exact value: $\boxed{\frac{\pi}{4}}$

Approximate value: $\boxed{0.785}$

Solution (b):

Multiply 472° by $\frac{\pi}{180°}$. $\quad 472°\left(\frac{\pi}{180°}\right)$

Simplify (factor out the common 4). $\quad = \boxed{\frac{118}{45}\pi}$

Approximate with a calculator. $\quad \boxed{\approx 8.238}$

Solution (c):

Multiply $\frac{2\pi}{3}$ by $\frac{180°}{\pi}$. $\quad \frac{2\pi}{3} \cdot \frac{180°}{\pi}$

Simplify. $\quad = \boxed{120°}$

YOUR TURN Convert:

a. 60° to radians **b.** 460° to radians **c.** $\frac{3\pi}{2}$ to degrees

ANSWER

a. $\frac{\pi}{3}$ or approximately 1.047

b. $\frac{23}{9}\pi$ or approximately 8.029

c. 270°

4.1.3 Angles in Standard Position

If the *initial side* of an angle is aligned along the *positive x-axis* and the *vertex* of the angle is positioned at the *origin*, then the angle is said to be in *standard position.*

4.1.3 SKILL

Sketch angles in standard position.

DEFINITION **Standard Position**

An angle is said to be in **standard position** if its initial side is along the positive x-axis and its vertex is at the origin.

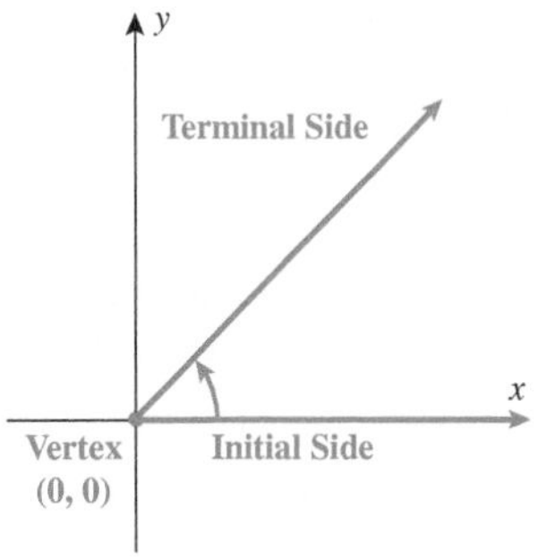

4.1.3 CONCEPTUAL

Understand that rotation in the counterclockwise direction corresponds to a positive angle measure, whereas rotation in the clockwise direction corresponds to a negative angle measure.

STUDY TIP

Both the initial side (initial ray) and the terminal side (terminal ray) of an angle are rays.

We say that an angle lies in the quadrant in which its terminal side lies. Angles in standard position with terminal sides along the x-axis or y-axis (90°, 180°, 270°, 360°, etc.) are called **quadrantal angles**.

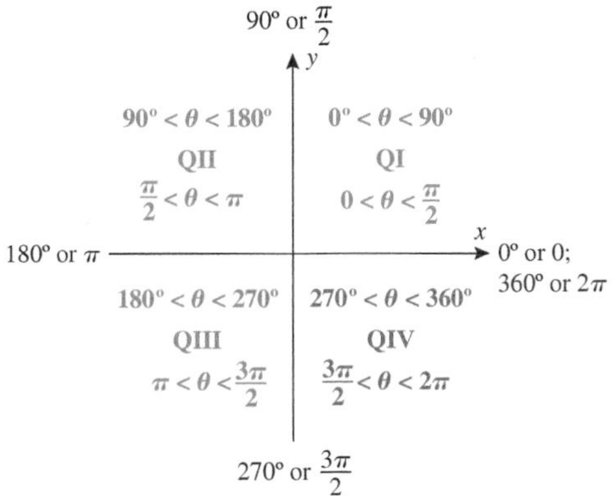

[CONCEPT CHECK]

Match the following: When the angle is formed using a clockwise/counterclockwise rotation, that corresponds to an angle with positive/negative measure.

ANSWER Clockwise—Negative
Counterclockwise—Positive

4.1.4 Coterminal Angles

4.1.4 SKILL

Identify coterminal angles.

DEFINITION **Coterminal Angles**

Two angles in standard position with the same terminal side are called **coterminal angles**.

4.1.4 CONCEPTUAL

Understand that the measures of coterminal angles must differ by an integer multiple of 360 degrees.

For example, −40° and 320° are measures of coterminal angles; their terminal rays are identical even though they are formed by rotations in opposite directions. The angles 60° and 420° are also coterminal; angles larger than 360° or less than −360° are generated by continuing the rotation beyond one full circle. Thus, all coterminal angles have the same initial side (positive x-axis) and the same terminal side, just different amounts and/or direction of rotation.

[CONCEPT CHECK]

TRUE OR FALSE If an angle α has measure 50°, then the angle β that has measure 410° is coterminal with angle α.

ANSWER True

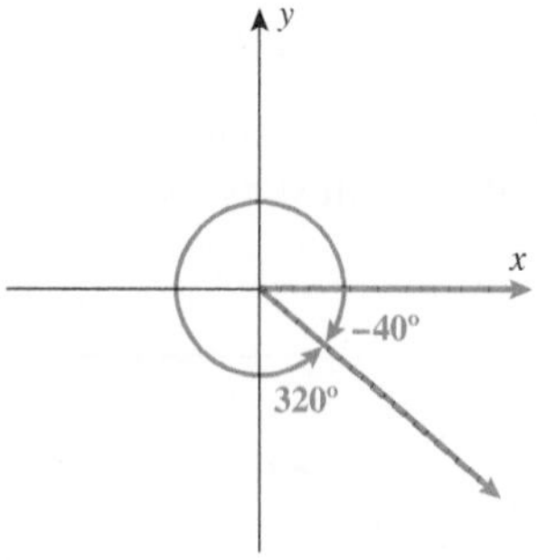

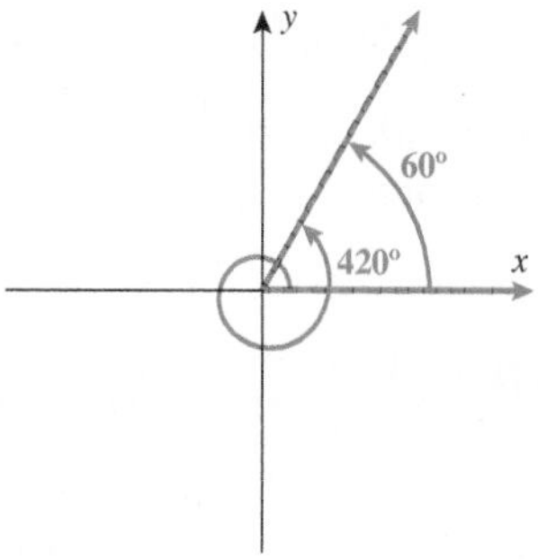

To find the measure of the smallest nonnegative coterminal angle of a given angle measured in degrees, follow this procedure:

- If the given angle is positive, subtract 360° (repeatedly until the result is a positive angle less than or equal to 360°).
- If the given angle is negative, add 360° (repeatedly until the result is a positive angle less than or equal to 360°).

Similarly, if the angle is measured in radians, subtract or add equivalently 2π until your result is a positive angle less than or equal to 2π.

EXAMPLE 4 Finding Measures of Coterminal Angles

Determine the angle with the smallest possible positive measure that is coterminal with each of the following angles:

a. 830° **b.** −520° **c.** $\frac{11\pi}{3}$

Solution (a):

Since 830° is positive, subtract 360°. $830° - 360° = 470°$

Subtract 360° again. $470° - 360° = \boxed{110°}$

Solution (b):

Since −520° is negative, add 360°. $-520° + 360° = -160°$

Add 360° again. $-160° + 360° = \boxed{200°}$

Solution (c):

Since $\frac{11\pi}{3}$ is positive, subtract 2π. $\frac{11\pi}{3} - 2\pi = \boxed{\frac{5\pi}{3}}$

YOUR TURN Determine the angle with the smallest possible positive measure that is coterminal with each of the following angles:

a. 900° **b.** −430° **c.** $-\frac{13\pi}{6}$

ANSWER

a. 180°

b. 290°

c. $\frac{11\pi}{6}$

STUDY TIP

To use the relationship

$s = r\theta$

the angle θ must be in radians.

Applications of Radian Measure

We now look at applications of radian measure that involve calculating *arc lengths*, *areas of circular sectors*, and *angular and linear speeds*. All of these applications are related to the definition of radian measure.

4.1.5 Arc Length

DEFINITION Arc Length

If a central angle θ in a circle with radius r intercepts an arc on the circle of length s, then the **arc length** s is given by

$$s = r\theta \qquad \theta \text{ is given in radians}$$

EXAMPLE 5 **Finding Arc Length When the Angle Has Degree Measure**

The International Space Station (ISS) is in an approximately circular orbit 400 kilometers above the surface of the Earth. If the ground station tracks the space station when it is within a 45° central angle of this circular orbit above the tracking antenna, how many kilometers does the ISS cover while it is being tracked by the ground station? Assume that the radius of the Earth is 6400 kilometers. Round to the nearest kilometer.

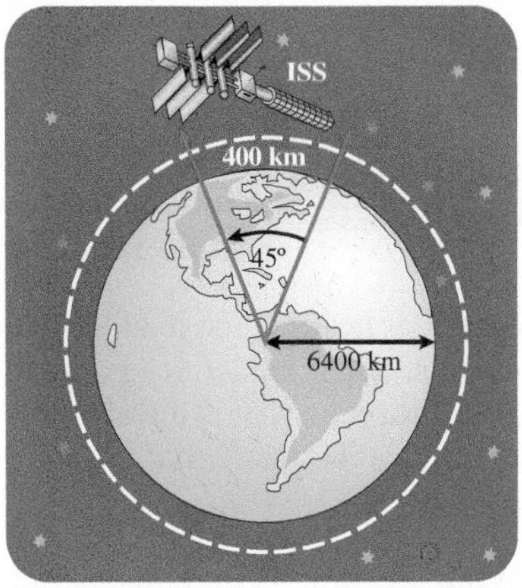

Solution:

Write the formula for arc length when the angle has degree measure. $s = r\theta_d\left(\frac{\pi}{180°}\right)$

Substitute $r = 6400 + 400 = 6800$ km and $\theta_d = 45°$. $s = (6800\text{ km})(45°)\left(\frac{\pi}{180°}\right)$

Evaluate with a calculator. $s \approx 5340.708$ km

Round to the nearest kilometer. $s \approx \boxed{5341\text{ km}}$

The ISS travels approximately 5341 kilometers during the ground station tracking.

YOUR TURN If the ground station in Example 5 could track the ISS within a 60° central angle, how far would the ISS travel during the tracking?

4.1.6 Area of a Circular Sector

DEFINITION Area of a Circular Sector

The **area of a sector of a circle** with radius r and central angle θ is given by

$$A = \frac{1}{2}r^2\theta \qquad \theta \text{ is given in radians}$$

4.1.5 SKILL

Calculate the length of an arc along a circle.

4.1.5 CONCEPTUAL

Understand why the angle in the arc length formula must be in radian measure.

STUDY TIP

When the angle is given in degrees, the arc length formula becomes

$$s = r \cdot \theta_d\left(\frac{\pi}{180°}\right)$$

CONCEPT CHECK

What are the units of arc length s if $s = r\theta_d\frac{\pi}{180°}$ where r is given in feet and θ_d is given in degrees?

ANSWER feet

STUDY TIP

To use the relationship

$$A = \frac{1}{2}r^2\theta$$

the angle θ must be in radians.

CONCEPT CHECK

If the area of a circular sector A is given by $A = \frac{1}{2}r^2\theta_r$ and r is given in feet, then what are the units of A?

ANSWER square feet

ANSWER

7121 km

4.1.6 SKILL

Calculate the area of a circular sector.

4.1.6 CONCEPTUAL

Understand that the central angle must be given in radians in order for the formula for the area of a circular sector to be used.

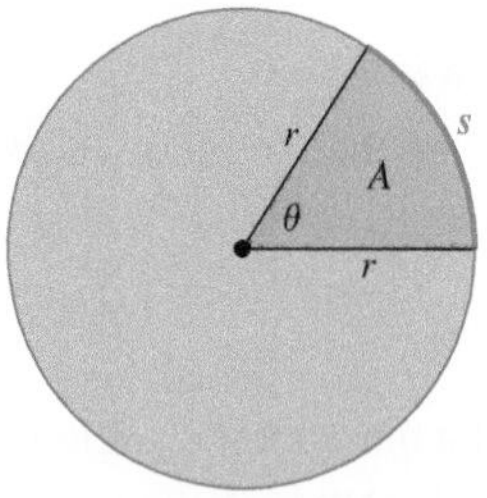

WORDS	MATH
Write the ratio of the area of the sector to the area of the entire circle.	$\frac{A}{\pi r^2}$
Write the ratio of the central angle θ to the measure of one full rotation.	$\frac{\theta}{2\pi}$
The ratios must be equal (proportionality of sector to circle).	$\frac{A}{\pi r^2} = \frac{\theta}{2\pi}$
Multiply both sides of the equation by πr^2.	$\pi r^2 \cdot \frac{A}{\pi r^2} = \frac{\theta}{2\pi} \cdot \pi r^2$
Simplify.	$A = \frac{1}{2} r^2 \theta$

EXAMPLE 6 Finding the Area of a Sector When the Angle Has Degree Measure

Sprinkler heads come in all different sizes depending on the angle of rotation desired. If a sprinkler head rotates 90° and has enough pressure to keep a constant 25-foot spray, what is the area of the sector of the lawn that gets watered? Round to the nearest square foot.

Solution:

Write the formula for circular sector area in degrees. $A = \frac{1}{2} r^2 \theta_d \left(\frac{\pi}{180°}\right)$

Substitute $r = 25$ ft and $\theta_d = 90°$ into the area equation. $A = \frac{1}{2}(25 \text{ ft})^2(90°)\left(\frac{\pi}{180°}\right)$

Simplify. $A = \left(\frac{625\pi}{4}\right) \text{ft}^2 \approx 490.87 \text{ ft}^2$

Round to the nearest square foot. $A \approx \boxed{491 \text{ ft}^2}$

STUDY TIP

When the angle is given in degrees, the area of a circular sector becomes

$$A = \frac{1}{2} r^2 \theta_d \left(\frac{\pi}{180°}\right)$$

YOUR TURN If a sprinkler head rotates 180° and has enough pressure to keep a constant 30-foot spray, what is the area of the sector of the lawn it can water? Round to the nearest square foot.

ANSWER

$450\pi \text{ ft}^2 \approx 1414 \text{ ft}^2$

4.1.7 Linear and Angular Speeds

4.1.7 SKILL

Calculate linear speed and angular speed.

4.1.7 CONCEPTUAL

Understand that linear speed has units of length/time and that angular speed has units of radians/time.

Recall the relationship between distance, rate (assumed to be constant), and time: $d = rt$. Rate is speed, and in words this formula can be rewritten as

$$\text{distance} = \text{speed} \cdot \text{time} \quad \text{or} \quad \text{speed} = \frac{\text{distance}}{\text{time}}$$

It is important to note that we assume speed is constant. If we think of a car driving around a circular track, the distance it travels is the arc length s; and if we let v represent speed and t represent time, we have the formula for speed along a circular path (*linear speed*):

$$v = \frac{s}{t}$$

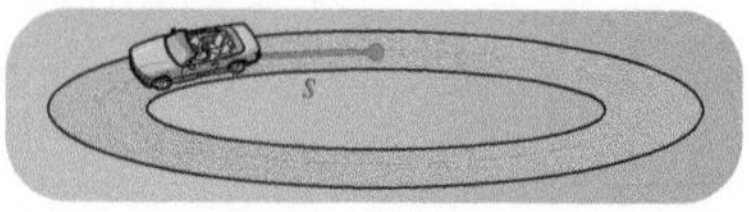

DEFINITION **Linear Speed**

If a point P moves along the circumference of a circle at a constant speed, then the **linear speed** v is given by

$$v = \frac{s}{t}$$

where s is the arc length and t is the time.

EXAMPLE 7 **Linear Speed**

A car travels at a constant speed around a circular track with circumference equal to 2 miles. If the car records a time of 15 minutes for 9 laps, what is the linear speed of the car in miles per hour?

Solution:

Calculate the distance traveled around the circular track.

$$s = (9 \text{ laps})\left(\frac{2 \text{ mi}}{\text{lap}}\right) = 18 \text{ mi}$$

Substitute $t = 15$ min and $s = 18$ mi into $v = \frac{s}{t}$.

$$v = \frac{18 \text{ mi}}{15 \text{ min}}$$

Convert the linear speed from miles per minute to miles per hour.

$$v = \left(\frac{18 \text{ mi}}{15 \text{ min}}\right)\left(\frac{60 \text{ min}}{1 \text{ hr}}\right)$$

Simplify.

$$v = \boxed{72 \text{ mph}}$$

YOUR TURN A car travels at a constant speed around a circular track with circumference equal to 3 miles. If the car records a time of 12 minutes for 7 laps, what is the linear speed of the car in miles per hour?

ANSWER
105 mph

To calculate linear speed, we find how fast a position along the circumference of a circle is changing. To calculate *angular speed*, we find how fast the central angle is changing.

[CONCEPT CHECK]

Which of the following is not a measure of linear speed?

(A) miles per hour

(B) feet per second

(C) degrees per second

(D) meters per minute

ANSWER (C)

DEFINITION **Angular Speed**

If a point P moves along the circumference of a circle at a constant speed, then the central angle θ that is formed with the terminal side passing through point P also changes over some time t at a constant speed. The **angular speed** ω (omega) is given by

$$\omega = \frac{\theta}{t} \quad \text{where } \theta \text{ is given in radians}$$

EXAMPLE 8 Angular Speed

A lighthouse in the middle of a channel rotates its light in a circular motion with constant speed. If the beacon of light completes 1 rotation every 10 seconds, what is the angular speed of the beacon in radians per minute?

Solution:

Calculate the angle measure in radians associated with 1 rotation. $\theta = 2\pi$

Substitute $\theta = 2\pi$ and $t = 10$ sec into $\omega = \frac{\theta}{t}$. $\omega = \frac{2\pi \text{ (rad)}}{10 \text{ sec}}$

Convert the angular speed from radians per second to radians per minute. $\omega = \frac{2\pi \text{ (rad)}}{10 \text{ sec}} \cdot \frac{60 \text{ sec}}{1 \text{ min}}$

Simplify. $\boxed{\omega = 12\pi \text{ rad/min}}$

[CONCEPT CHECK]

If we know that it takes a beacon A minutes to complete one full rotation, then what is its angular speed?

ANSWER $\frac{2\pi}{A}$ rad/min

YOUR TURN If the lighthouse in Example 8 is adjusted so that the beacon rotates 1 time every 40 seconds, what is the angular speed of the beacon in radians per minute?

ANSWER $\omega = 3\pi$ rad/min

4.1.8 Relationship between Linear and Angular Speeds

4.1.8 SKILL

Solve application problems involving both angular and linear speeds.

4.1.8 CONCEPTUAL

Understand that angular speed and linear speed are related through the radius.

Angular speed and *linear speed* are related through the *radius*.

WORDS	MATH
Write the definition of radian measure.	$\theta = \frac{s}{r}$
Write the definition of arc length (θ in radians).	$s = r\theta$
Divide both sides by t.	$\frac{s}{t} = \frac{r\theta}{t}$
Rewrite the right side of the equation.	$\frac{s}{t} = r\frac{\theta}{t}$
Recall the definitions of **linear** and **angular** speeds.	$v = \frac{s}{t}$ and $\omega = \frac{\theta}{t}$
Substitute $v = \frac{s}{t}$ and $\omega = \frac{\theta}{t}$ into $\frac{s}{t} = r\frac{\theta}{t}$.	$v = r\omega$

STUDY TIP

This relationship between linear and angular speed assumes the angle is given in radians.

[CONCEPT CHECK]

For a fixed angular speed, if the radius is increased, then the linear speed (increases/decreases)?

ANSWER increases

RELATING LINEAR AND ANGULAR SPEEDS

If a point P moves at a constant speed along the circumference of a circle with radius r, then the **linear speed** v and the **angular speed** ω are related by

$$v = r\omega \quad \text{or} \quad \omega = \frac{v}{r}$$

Note: This relationship is true only when θ is given in radians.

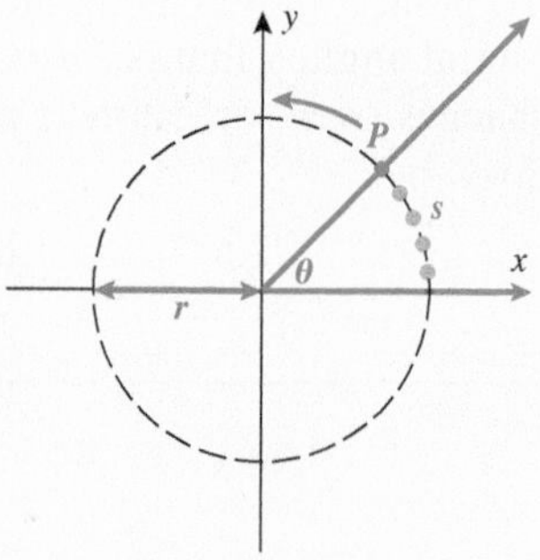

Notice that tires of two different radii with the same angular speed have different linear speeds. The larger tire has the faster linear speed.

EXAMPLE 9 Relating Linear and Angular Speeds

A 2016 Lexus RX 450 h comes standard with wheels that have a rim diameter of 18 inches and tire diameter of 28 inches. If the owner upgrades the wheels with a rim diameter of 20 inches (tire diameter of 30 inches) without having the onboard computer updated, how fast will the car *actually* be traveling when the speedometer reads 75 miles per hour?

Solution:

The computer in the 2016 Lexus RX "thinks" the tires are 28 inches in diameter and knows the angular speed. Use the programmed tire diameter and speedometer reading to calculate the angular speed. Then use that angular speed and the upgraded tire diameter to get the actual speed (linear speed).

STEP 1 Calculate the angular speed of the tires.

Write the formula for the angular speed. $\omega = \frac{v}{r}$

Substitute $v = 75$ miles per hour and $r = \frac{28}{2} = 14$ inches into the formula. $\omega = \frac{75 \text{ mi/hr}}{14 \text{ in.}}$

1 mile = 5280 feet = 63,360 inches. $\omega = \frac{75(63{,}360) \text{ in./hr}}{14 \text{ in.}}$

Simplify. $\omega \approx 339{,}429 \frac{\text{rad}}{\text{hr}}$

STEP 2 Calculate the actual linear speed of the car.

Write the linear speed formula. $v = r\omega$

Substitute $r = \frac{30}{2} = 15$ inches and $\omega \approx 339{,}429$ radians per hour. $v = (15 \text{ in.})\left(339{,}429 \frac{\text{rad}}{\text{hr}}\right)$

Simplify. $v \approx 5{,}091{,}435 \frac{\text{in.}}{\text{hr}}$

1 mile = 5280 feet = 63,360 inches. $v \approx 5{,}091{,}435 \frac{\cancel{\text{in.}}}{\text{hr}} \cdot \frac{1 \text{ mi}}{63{,}360 \cancel{\text{in.}}}$

$\boxed{v \approx 80 \text{ mph}}$

Although the speedometer indicates a speed of 75 miles per hour, the actual speed is approximately 80 miles per hour.

STUDY TIP

We could have solved Example 9 the following way:

$$\frac{75 \text{ mph}}{14 \text{ in.}} = \frac{x}{15 \text{ in.}}$$

$$x = \frac{15 \text{ in.}}{14 \text{ in.}} \times 75 \text{ mph}$$

$$\approx 80 \text{ mph}$$

YOUR TURN Suppose the owner of the 2016 Lexus RX in Example 9 decides to downsize the tires from their original 18-inch rims (28-inch tires) to a wheel with 17-inch rims (27-inch tires). If the speedometer indicates a speed of 65 miles per hour, what is the actual speed of the car?

ANSWER

Approximately 63 mph

[SECTION 4.1] SUMMARY

Angle measures can be converted between degrees and radians in the following way:

- To convert degrees to radians, multiply the degree measure by $\frac{\pi}{180°}$.
- To convert radians to degrees, multiply the radian measure by $\frac{180°}{\pi}$.

(Remember that $\pi = 180°$.)

Coterminal angles in standard position have terminal sides that coincide.

The length of a circular arc is given by $s = r\theta$, where θ is the central angle given in radians and r is the radius of the circle.

The area of a circular sector is given by $A = \frac{1}{2}r^2\theta$, where θ is the central angle given in radians and r is the radius of the circle.

Linear speed, $v = \frac{s}{t}$, and angular speed, $\omega = \frac{\theta}{t}$, are related through the radius: $v = r\omega$.

[SECTION 4.1] EXERCISES

• SKILLS

In Exercises 1–6, find (*a*) the complement and (*b*) the supplement of the given angles.

1. 18° **2.** 39° **3.** 42° **4.** 57° **5.** 89° **6.** 75°

In Exercises 7–12, find the measure (in radians) of a central angle θ that intercepts an arc of length s on a circle with radius r.

7. $r = 22$ in., $s = 4$ in. **8.** $r = 6$ in., $s = 1$ in. **9.** $r = 100$ cm, $s = 20$ mm

10. $r = 1$ m, $s = 2$ cm **11.** $r = \frac{1}{4}$ in., $s = \frac{1}{32}$ in. **12.** $r = \frac{3}{4}$ cm, $s = \frac{3}{14}$ cm

In Exercises 13–28, convert from degrees to radians. Leave the answers in terms of π.

13. 30° **14.** 60° **15.** 45° **16.** 90° **17.** 315° **18.** 270°

19. 75° **20.** 100° **21.** 170° **22.** 340° **23.** 780° **24.** 540°

25. −210° **26.** −320° **27.** −3600° **28.** 1800°

In Exercises 29–42, convert from radians to degrees.

29. $\frac{\pi}{6}$ **30.** $\frac{\pi}{4}$ **31.** $\frac{3\pi}{4}$ **32.** $\frac{7\pi}{6}$ **33.** $\frac{3\pi}{8}$ **34.** $\frac{11\pi}{9}$ **35.** $\frac{5\pi}{12}$

36. $\frac{7\pi}{3}$ **37.** 9π **38.** -6π **39.** $\frac{19\pi}{20}$ **40.** $\frac{13\pi}{36}$ **41.** $-\frac{7\pi}{15}$ **42.** $-\frac{8\pi}{9}$

In Exercises 43–50, convert from radians to degrees. Round your answers to the nearest hundredth of a degree.

43. 4 **44.** 3 **45.** 0.85 **46.** 3.27

47. −2.7989 **48.** −5.9841 **49.** $2\sqrt{3}$ **50.** $5\sqrt{7}$

In Exercises 51–56, convert from degrees to radians. Round your answers to three significant digits.

51. 47° **52.** 65° **53.** 112° **54.** 172° **55.** 56.5° **56.** 298.7°

In Exercises 57–68, state in which quadrant or on which axis each angle with the given measure in standard position would lie.

57. 145° **58.** 175° **59.** 270° **60.** 180° **61.** −540° **62.** −450°

63. $\frac{2\pi}{5}$ **64.** $\frac{4\pi}{7}$ **65.** $\frac{13\pi}{4}$ **66.** $\frac{18\pi}{11}$ **67.** 2.5 **68.** 11.4

In Exercises 69–80, determine the angle of the smallest possible positive measure that is coterminal with each of the angles whose measure is given. Use degree or radian measure accordingly.

69. $412°$ **70.** $379°$ **71.** $-92°$ **72.** $-187°$ **73.** $-390°$ **74.** $945°$

75. $\frac{29\pi}{3}$ **76.** $\frac{47\pi}{7}$ **77.** $-\frac{313\pi}{9}$ **78.** $-\frac{217\pi}{4}$ **79.** -30 **80.** 42

In Exercises 81–88, find the exact length of the arc made by the indicated central angle and radius of each circle.

81. $\theta = \frac{\pi}{12}, r = 8 \text{ ft}$ **82.** $\theta = \frac{\pi}{8}, r = 6 \text{ yd}$ **83.** $\theta = \frac{1}{2}, r = 5 \text{ in.}$ **84.** $\theta = \frac{3}{4}, r = 20 \text{ m}$

85. $\theta = 22°, r = 18 \,\mu\text{m}$ **86.** $\theta = 14°, r = 15 \,\mu\text{m}$ **87.** $\theta = 8°, r = 1500 \text{ km}$ **88.** $\theta = 3°, r = 1800 \text{ km}$

In Exercises 89–94, find the area of the circular sector given the indicated radius and central angle. Round your answers to three significant digits.

89. $\theta = \frac{3\pi}{8}, r = 2.2 \text{ km}$ **90.** $\theta = \frac{5\pi}{6}, r = 13 \text{ mi}$ **91.** $\theta = 56°, r = 4.2 \text{ cm}$

92. $\theta = 27°, r = 2.5 \text{ mm}$ **93.** $\theta = 1.2°, r = 1.5 \text{ ft}$ **94.** $\theta = 14°, r = 3.0 \text{ ft}$

In Exercises 95–98, find the linear speed of a point that moves with constant speed in a circular motion if the point travels along the circle of arc length *s* in time *t*.

95. $s = 2 \text{ m}, t = 5 \text{ sec}$ **96.** $s = 12 \text{ ft}, t = 3 \text{ min}$ **97.** $s = 68{,}000 \text{ km}, t = 250 \text{ hr}$ **98.** $s = 7524 \text{ mi}, t = 12 \text{ days}$

In Exercises 99–102, find the distance traveled (arc length) of a point that moves with constant speed *v* along a circle in time *t*.

99. $v = 2.8 \text{ m/sec}, t = 3.5 \text{ sec}$ **100.** $v = 6.2 \text{ km/hr}, t = 4.5 \text{ hr}$

101. $v = 4.5 \text{ mi/hr}, t = 20 \text{ min}$ **102.** $v = 5.6 \text{ ft/sec}, t = 2 \text{ min}$

In Exercises 103–106, find the angular speed (radians/second) associated with rotating a central angle θ in time *t*.

103. $\theta = 25\pi, t = 10 \text{ sec}$ **104.** $\theta = \frac{3\pi}{4}, t = \frac{1}{6} \text{ sec}$ **105.** $\theta = 200°, t = 5 \text{ sec}$ **106.** $\theta = 60°, t = 0.2 \text{ sec}$

In Exercises 107–110, find the linear speed of a point traveling at a constant speed along the circumference of a circle with radius *r* and angular speed ω.

107. $\omega = \frac{2\pi \text{ rad}}{3 \text{ sec}}, r = 9 \text{ in.}$ **108.** $\omega = \frac{3\pi \text{ rad}}{4 \text{ sec}}, r = 8 \text{ cm}$ **109.** $\omega = \frac{\pi \text{ rad}}{20 \text{ sec}}, r = 5 \text{ mm}$ **110.** $\omega = \frac{5\pi \text{ rad}}{16 \text{ sec}}, r = 24 \text{ ft}$

In Exercises 111–114, find the distance a point travels along a circle over a time *t*, given the angular speed ω and radius *r* of the circle. Round your answers to three significant digits.

111. $r = 5 \text{ cm}, \omega = \frac{\pi \text{ rad}}{6 \text{ sec}}, t = 10 \text{ sec}$ **112.** $r = 2 \text{ mm}, \omega = 6\pi \frac{\text{rad}}{\text{sec}}, t = 11 \text{ sec}$

113. $r = 5.2 \text{ in.}, \omega = \frac{\pi \text{ rad}}{15 \text{ sec}}, t = 10 \text{ min}$ **114.** $r = 3.2 \text{ ft}, \omega = \frac{\pi \text{ rad}}{4 \text{ sec}}, t = 3 \text{ min}$

• APPLICATIONS

For Exercises 115 and 116, refer to the following:

A common school locker combination lock is shown. The lock has a dial with 40 calibration marks numbered 0 to 39. A combination consists of three of these numbers (e.g., 5-35-20). To open the lock, the steps below are taken:

Tacojim/iStockphoto

- Turn the dial clockwise two full turns.
- Continue turning clockwise until the first number of the combination.
- Turn the dial counterclockwise one full turn.
- Continue turning counterclockwise until the second number is reached.
- Turn the dial clockwise again until the third number is reached.
- Pull the shank and the lock will open.

115. Combination Lock. Given that the initial position of the dial is at zero (shown in the illustration), how many degrees is the dial rotated in total (sum of clockwise and counterclockwise rotations) in opening the lock if the combination is 35-5-20?

116. Combination Lock. Given that the initial position of the dial is at zero (shown in the illustration), how many degrees is the dial rotated in total (sum of clockwise and counterclockwise rotations) in opening the lock if the combination is 20-15-5?

117. Tires. A car owner decides to upgrade from tires with a diameter of 24.3 inches to tires with a diameter of 26.1 inches. If she doesn't update the onboard computer, how fast will she actually be traveling when the speedometer reads 65 miles per hour? Round to the nearest mile per hour.

118. Tires. A car owner decides to upgrade from tires with a diameter of 24.8 inches to tires with a diameter of 27.0 inches. If she doesn't update the onboard computer, how fast will she actually be traveling when the speedometer reads 70 miles per hour? Round to the nearest miles per hour.

For Exercises 119 and 120, refer to the following:

NASA explores artificial gravity as a way to counter the physiologic effects of extended weightlessness for future space exploration. NASA's centrifuge has a 58-foot-diameter arm.

Courtesy NASA

119. NASA. If two humans are on opposite (red and blue) ends of the centrifuge and their linear speed is 200 miles per hour, how fast is the arm rotating? Express the answer in radians per second to two significant digits.

120. NASA. If two humans are on opposite (red and blue) ends of the centrifuge and they rotate one full rotation every second, what is their linear speed in feet per second?

For Exercises 121–124, refer to the following:

A collimator is a device used in radiation treatment that narrows beams or waves, causing the waves to be more aligned in a specific direction. The use of a collimator facilitates the focusing of radiation to treat an affected region of tissue beneath the skin. In the figure, d_s is the distance from the radiation source to the skin, and d_t is the distance from the outer layer of skin to the targeted tissue. The field size on the skin (diameter of the circular treated skin) is $2f_s$, and $2f_d$ is the targeted field size at depth d_t (the diameter of the targeted tissue at the specified depth beneath the skin surface).

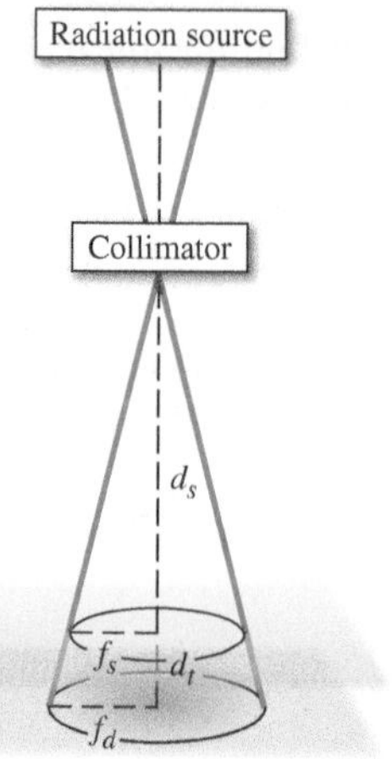

121. Health/Medicine. Radiation treatment is applied to a field size of 8 centimeters at a depth 2.5 centimeters below the skin surface. If the treatment head is positioned 80 centimeters from the skin, find the targeted field size to the nearest millimeter.

122. Health/Medicine. Radiation treatment is applied to a field size of 4 centimeters lying at a depth of 3.5 centimeters below the skin surface. If the field size on the skin is required to be 3.8 centimeters, find the distance from the skin that the radiation source must be located to the nearest millimeter.

123. Health/Medicine. Radiation treatment is applied to a field size on the skin of 3.75 centimeters to reach an affected region of tissue with field size of 4 centimeters at some depth below the skin. If the treatment head is positioned 60 centimeters from the skin surface, find the desired depth below the skin to the target area to the nearest millimeter.

124. Health/Medicine. Radiation treatment is applied to a field size on the skin of 4.15 centimeters to reach an affected area lying 4.5 centimeters below the skin surface. If the treatment head is positioned 60 centimeters from the skin surface, find the field size of the targeted area to the nearest millimeter.

• CATCH THE MISTAKE

In Exercises 125 and 126, explain the mistake that is made.

125. If the radius of a set of tires on a car is 15 inches and the tires rotate 180° per second, how fast is the car traveling (linear speed) in miles per hour?

Solution:

Write the formula for linear speed. $v = r\omega$

Let $r = 15$ in. and $\omega = 180°$ per sec. $v = (15\text{ in.})\left(\dfrac{180°}{\text{sec}}\right)$

Simplify. $v = 2700\,\dfrac{\text{in.}}{\text{sec}}$

Let 1 mi = 5280 ft = 63,360 in. and 1 hr = 3600 sec. $v = \left(\dfrac{2700 \cdot 3600}{63{,}360}\right)\text{mph}$

Simplify. $v \approx 153.4$ mph

This is incorrect. The correct answer is approximately 2.7 miles per hour. What mistake was made?

126. If a bicycle has tires with radius 10 inches and the tires rotate 90° per $\frac{1}{2}$ second, how fast is the bicycle traveling (linear speed) in miles per hour?

Solution:

Write the formula for linear speed. $v = r\omega$

Let $r = 10$ in. and $\omega = 180°$ per sec. $v = (10\text{ in.})\left(\dfrac{180°}{\text{sec}}\right)$

Simplify. $v = \dfrac{1800\text{ in.}}{\text{sec}}$

Let 1 mi = 5280 ft = 63,360 in. and 1 hr = 3600 sec. $v = \left(\dfrac{1800 \cdot 3600}{63{,}360}\right)\text{mph}$

Simplify. $v \approx 102.3$ mph

This is incorrect. The correct answer is approximately 1.8 miles per hour. What mistake was made?

• CONCEPTUAL

In Exercises 127–130, determine whether each statement is true or false.

127. If the radius of a circle doubles, then the arc length (associated with a fixed central angle) doubles.

128. If the radius of a circle doubles, then the area of the sector (associated with a fixed central angle) doubles.

129. If the angular speed doubles, then the number of revolutions doubles.

130. If the central angle of a sector doubles, then the area corresponding to the sector is double the area of the original sector.

• CHALLENGE

131. What is the measure (in degrees) of the smaller angle the hour and minute hands make when the time is 12:20?

132. What is the measure (in degrees) of the smaller angle the hour and minute hands make when the time is 9:10?

133. Find the area of the shaded region below:

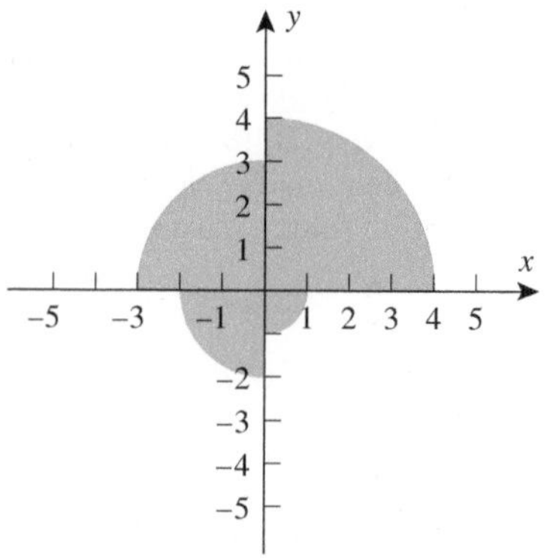

134. Find the perimeter of the shaded region in Exercise 133.

• PREVIEW TO CALCULUS

In calculus we work with real numbers; thus, the measure of an angle must be in radians.

135. What is the measure (in radians) of a central angle θ that intercepts an arc of length 2π centimeters on a circle of radius 10 centimeters?

136. Determine the angle of the smallest possible positive measure (in radians) that is coterminal with the angle 750°.

137. The area of a sector of a circle with radius 3 inches and central angle θ is $\frac{3\pi}{2}$ in.^{2}. What is the radian measure of θ?

138. An object is rotating at 600° per second, find the central angle θ, in radians, when $t = 3$ sec.

4.2 RIGHT TRIANGLE TRIGONOMETRY

SKILLS OBJECTIVES

- Use the Pythagorean theorem to solve a right triangle.
- Calculate trigonometric ratios of general acute angles.
- Calculate cosecant, secant, and cotangent functions as reciprocals of sine, cosine, and tangent functions, respectively.
- Evaluate trigonometric functions exactly for special angles.
- Evaluate (approximate) trigonometric functions using a calculator.
- Solve right triangles given the measure of an acute angle and the length of a side, or two side lengths.

CONCEPTUAL OBJECTIVES

- Understand that the Pythagorean theorem applies only to right triangles.
- Understand that right triangle ratios are based on the properties of similar triangles.
- Understand that if you learn the three main trigonometric functions (sine, cosine, and tangent), the other three trigonometric functions can always be calculated as reciprocals of these main three for any acute angle.
- Learn the trigonometric functions as ratios of sides of a right triangle.
- Understand the difference between evaluating trigonometric functions exactly and using a calculator.
- Understand that when an acute angle is given, the third angle can be found exactly. The remaining unknown side lengths can be found using right triangle trigonometry and the Pythagorean theorem.

The word **trigonometry** stems from the Greek words *trigonon*, which means "triangle," and *metrein*, which means "to measure." Trigonometry began as a branch of geometry and was utilized extensively by early Greek mathematicians to determine unknown distances. The major *trigonometric functions*, including *sine*, *cosine*, and *tangent*, were first defined as ratios of sides in a right triangle. This is the way we will define them in this section. Since the two angles, besides the right angle, in a right triangle have to be acute, a second kind of definition was needed to extend the domain of trigonometric functions to nonacute angles in the Cartesian plane (Section 4.3). Starting in the eighteenth century, broader definitions of the trigonometric functions came into use, under which the functions are associated with points along the unit circle (Section 5.1).

4.2.1 Right Triangle Ratios

Similar Triangles

The word *similar* in mathematics means identical in shape, although not necessarily the same size. It is important to note that two triangles can have the exact same shape (same angles) but differ in size.

4.2.1 SKILL

Use the Pythagorean theorem to solve a right triangle.

4.2.1 CONCEPTUAL

Understand that the Pythagorean theorem applies only to right triangles.

DEFINITION Similar Triangles

Similar triangles are triangles with equal corresponding angle measures (equal angles).

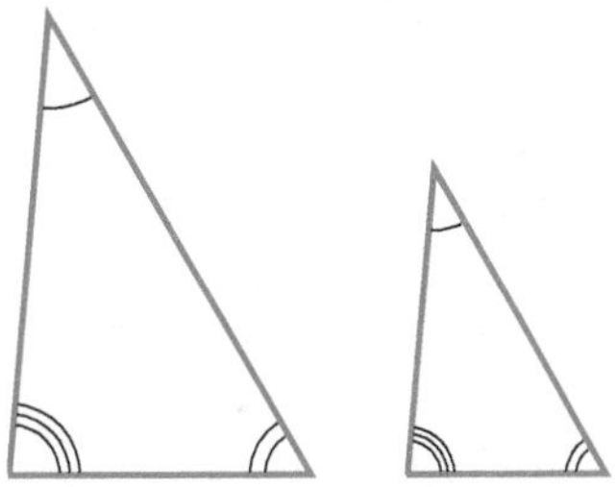

STUDY TIP

Although an angle and its measure are fundamentally different, out of convenience, the phrase "equal angles" implies "equal angle measures."

Right Triangles

A **right triangle** is a triangle in which one of the angles is a 90° right angle. Since one angle is 90°, the other two angles must be complementary (sum to 90°), so that the sum of all three angles is 180°. The longest side of a right triangle, called the **hypotenuse**, is opposite the right angle. The other two sides are called the **legs** of the right triangle.

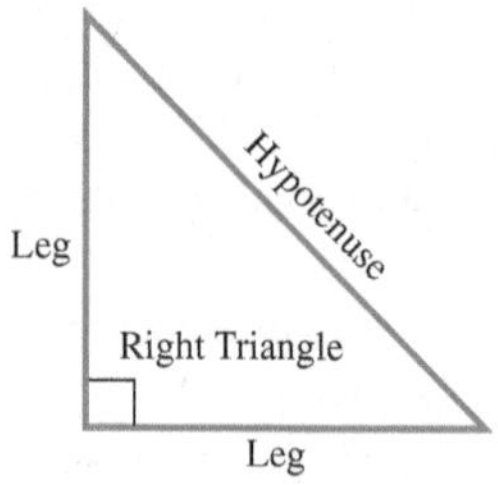

The *Pythagorean theorem* relates the sides of a right triangle. It says that the sum of the squares of the lengths of the two legs is equal to the square of the length of the hypotenuse. It is important to note that length (a synonym of distance) is always positive.

PYTHAGOREAN THEOREM

In any right triangle, the square of the length of the longest side (hypotenuse) is equal to the sum of the squares of the lengths of the other two sides (legs).

$$a^2 + b^2 = c^2$$

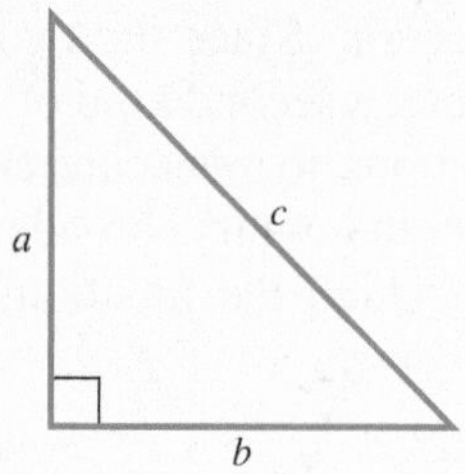

STUDY TIP

The Pythagorean theorem applies only to *right* triangles.

It is important to note that the Pythagorean theorem applies *only* to right triangles. It is also important to note that it does not matter which side is called a or b, as long as the square of the longest side is equal to the sum of the squares of the shorter sides.

Right triangle trigonometry relies on the properties of similar triangles. Since similar triangles have the same shape (equal corresponding angles), the sides opposite the corresponding angles must be proportional.

4.2.2 Trigonometric Ratios of General Acute Angles

4.2.2 SKILL

Calculate trigonometric ratios of general acute angles.

4.2.2 CONCEPTUAL

Understand that right triangle ratios are based on the properties of similar triangles.

The concept of similar triangles, one of the basic insights in trigonometry, allows us to determine the length of a side of one triangle if we know the length of certain sides of a similar triangle. Consider the following similar triangles:

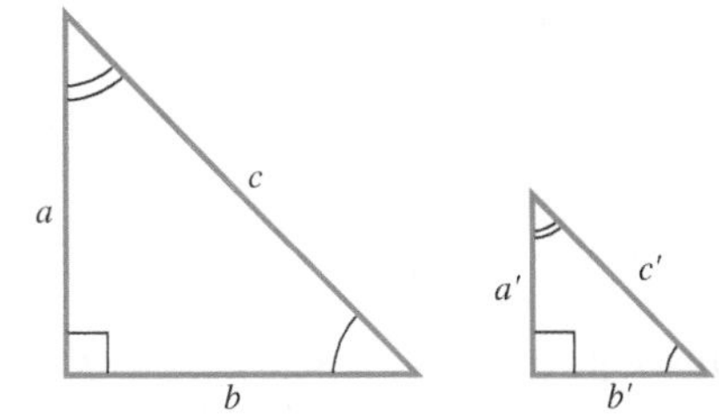

In similar triangles, the sides opposite corresponding angles must be proportional, so the following ratios hold true:

$$\frac{a}{a'} = \frac{b}{b'} = \frac{c}{c'}$$

Separate the common ratios into three equations:

$$\frac{a}{a'} = \frac{b}{b'} \qquad \frac{b}{b'} = \frac{c}{c'} \qquad \frac{a}{a'} = \frac{c}{c'}$$

For any right triangle, there are six possible ratios of sides that can be calculated for each acute angle θ:

$$\frac{b}{c} \quad \frac{a}{c} \quad \frac{b}{a} \quad \frac{c}{b} \quad \frac{c}{a} \quad \frac{a}{b}$$

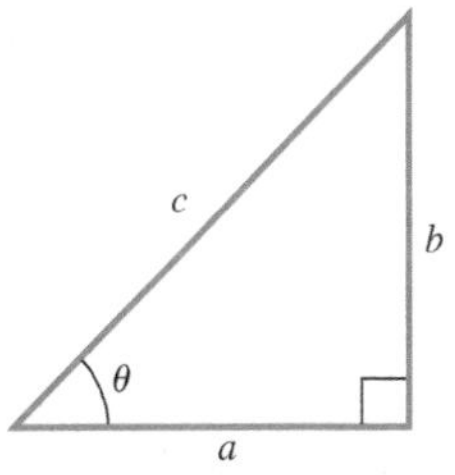

[CONCEPT CHECK]

How many possible ratios of the lengths of the sides of a right triangle are there for an acute angle in a right triangle?

ANSWER six

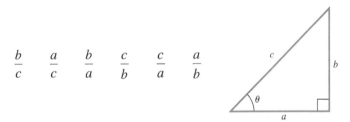

These ratios are referred to as **trigonometric ratios** or **trigonometric functions**, since they depend on the angle θ, and each is given a name:

FUNCTION NAME	ABBREVIATION
Sine	sin
Cosine	cos
Tangent	tan
Cosecant	csc
Secant	sec
Cotangent	cot

WORDS	MATH
The sine of θ	$\sin\theta$
The cosine of θ	$\cos\theta$
The tangent of θ	$\tan\theta$
The cosecant of θ	$\csc\theta$
The secant of θ	$\sec\theta$
The cotangent of θ	$\cot\theta$

Sine, cosine, tangent, cotangent, secant, and cosecant are names given to specific ratios of the lengths of sides of right triangles.

STUDY TIP

Notice that

$\csc\theta = \dfrac{1}{\sin\theta}$

$\sec\theta = \dfrac{1}{\cos\theta}$

$\cot\theta = \dfrac{1}{\tan\theta}$

DEFINITION Trigonometric Functions

Let θ be an acute angle in a right triangle, then

$$\sin\theta = \frac{b}{c} \quad \cos\theta = \frac{a}{c} \quad \tan\theta = \frac{b}{a}$$

$$\csc\theta = \frac{c}{b} \quad \sec\theta = \frac{c}{a} \quad \cot\theta = \frac{a}{b}$$

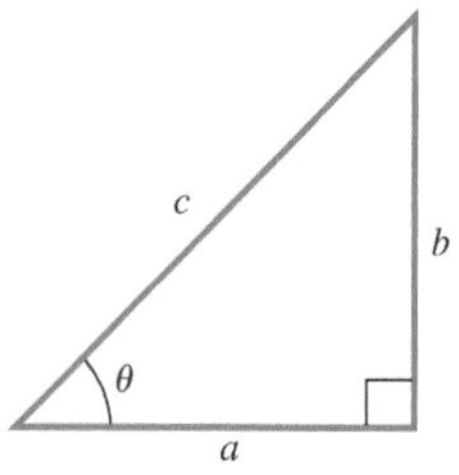

STUDY TIP

Trigonometric functions are functions of a specified angle. Always specify the angle. "sin" alone means nothing. $\sin\theta$ specifies the angle dependency. The same is true for the other five trigonometric functions.

The following terminology will be used throughout this text (refer to the right triangle above):

- The **hypotenuse** is always opposite the right angle.
- One leg (b) is **opposite** the angle θ.
- One leg (a) is **adjacent** to the angle θ.

Also notice that since $\sin\theta = \frac{b}{c}$ and $\cos\theta = \frac{a}{c}$, then $\tan\theta = \dfrac{\sin\theta}{\cos\theta} = \dfrac{\frac{b}{c}}{\frac{a}{c}} = \dfrac{b}{a}$.

STUDY TIP

SOHCAHTOA

SOH: $\sin\theta = \dfrac{\text{Opposite}}{\text{Hypotenuse}}$

CAH: $\cos\theta = \dfrac{\text{Adjacent}}{\text{Hypotenuse}}$

TOA: $\tan\theta = \dfrac{\text{Opposite}}{\text{Adjacent}}$

Using this terminology, we arrive at an alternative definition that is easier to remember.

DEFINITION Trigonometric Functions (Alternative Form)

For an acute angle θ in a right triangle:

$$\sin\theta = \frac{\text{opposite}}{\text{hypotenuse}} \quad \cos\theta = \frac{\text{adjacent}}{\text{hypotenuse}} \quad \tan\theta = \frac{\text{opposite}}{\text{adjacent}}$$

and their reciprocals:

$$\csc\theta = \frac{1}{\sin\theta} = \frac{\text{hypotenuse}}{\text{opposite}}$$

$$\sec\theta = \frac{1}{\cos\theta} = \frac{\text{hypotenuse}}{\text{adjacent}}$$

$$\cot\theta = \frac{1}{\tan\theta} = \frac{\text{adjacent}}{\text{opposite}}$$

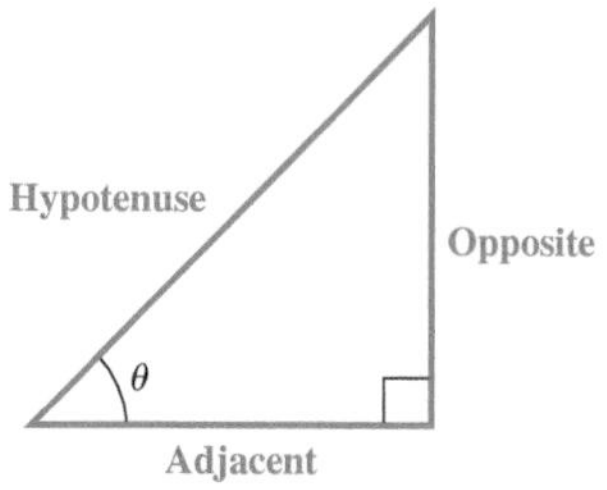

STUDY TIP

You need to learn only the three main trigonometric ratios: $\sin\theta$, $\cos\theta$, and $\tan\theta$. The other three can always be calculated as reciprocals of these main three for an acute angle θ.

4.2.3 SKILL

Calculate cosecant, secant, and cotangent functions as reciprocals of sine, cosine, and tangent functions, respectively.

4.2.3 CONCEPTUAL

Understand that if you learn the three main trigonometric functions (sine, cosine, and tangent), the other three trigonometric functions can always be calculated as reciprocals of these main three for any acute angle.

4.2.3 Reciprocal Identities

The three main trigonometric functions should be learned in terms of the following ratios:

$$\sin\theta = \frac{\textbf{opposite}}{\textbf{hypotenuse}} \quad \cos\theta = \frac{\textbf{adjacent}}{\textbf{hypotenuse}} \quad \tan\theta = \frac{\textbf{opposite}}{\textbf{adjacent}}$$

The remaining three trigonometric functions can be derived from $\sin\theta$, $\cos\theta$, and $\tan\theta$ using the *reciprocal identities*. Recall that the **reciprocal** of x is $\frac{1}{x}$ for $x \neq 0$.

RECIPROCAL IDENTITIES

$$\csc\theta = \frac{1}{\sin\theta} \qquad \sec\theta = \frac{1}{\cos\theta} \qquad \cot\theta = \frac{1}{\tan\theta}$$

4.2.4 Evaluating Trigonometric Functions Exactly for Special Angle Measures

4.2.4 SKILL

Evaluate trigonometric functions exactly for special angles.

4.2.4 CONCEPTUAL

Learn the trigonometric functions as ratios of sides of a right triangle.

There are three special acute angles that are very important in trigonometry: 30°, 45°, and 60°. We can combine the relationships governing their side lengths

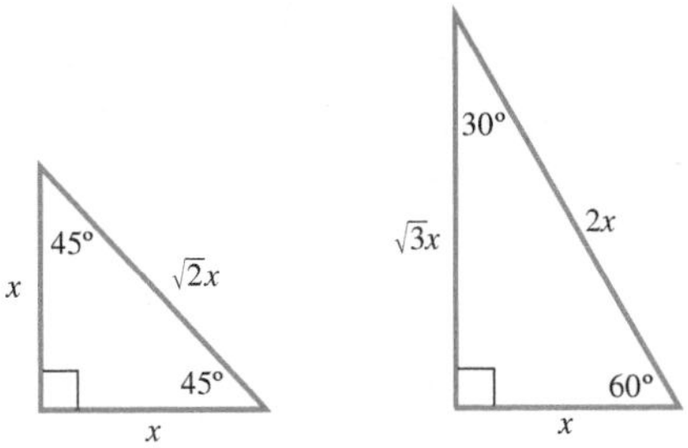

with the trigonometric ratios developed in this section to evaluate the trigonometric functions for the special angle measures of 30°, 45°, and 60°.

Consider a 45°-45°-90° triangle.

WORDS / **MATH**

A 45°-45°-90° triangle is an isosceles (two legs are equal) right triangle.

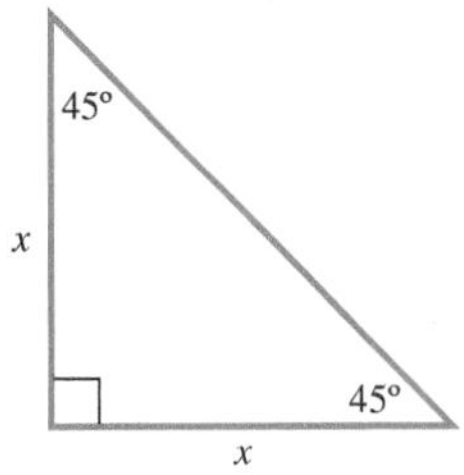

Apply the Pythagorean theorem. $\quad x^2 + x^2 = (\text{hypotenuse})^2$

Simplify the left side of the equation. $\quad 2x^2 = (\text{hypotenuse})^2$

Solve for the hypotenuse. $\quad \text{hypotenuse} = \pm\sqrt{2x^2} = \pm\sqrt{2}\,|x|$

x and the hypotenuse are lengths and must be positive. $\quad \text{hypotenuse} = \sqrt{2}\,x$

The hypotenuse of a 45°-45°-90 triangle is $\sqrt{2}$ times the length of either leg.

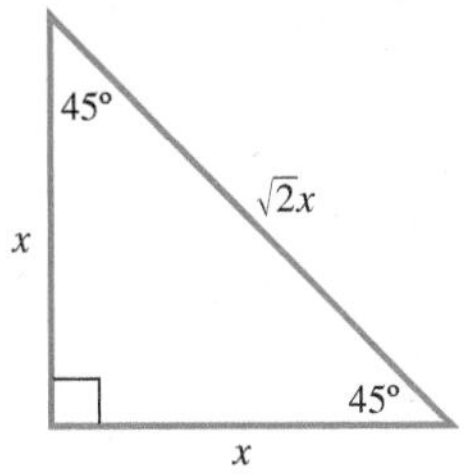

[CONCEPT CHECK]

TRUE OR FALSE If you learn the values of sine and cosine for the special angles 30°, 45°, and 60°, then you can calculate the other values (secant, cosecant, tangent, and cotangent) using the reciprocal and quotient identities.

ANSWER True

Let us now determine the relationship of the sides of a 30°-60°-90° triangle. We start with an equilateral triangle (equal sides and equal angles of measure 60°).

WORDS | **MATH**

Draw an equilateral triangle with sides $2x$.

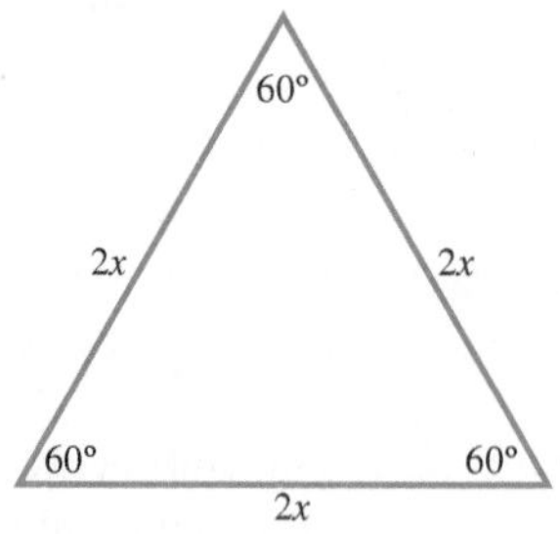

Draw a line segment from one vertex that is perpendicular to the opposite side; this line segment represents the height of the triangle, h, and bisects the base. There are now two identical 30°-60°-90° triangles.

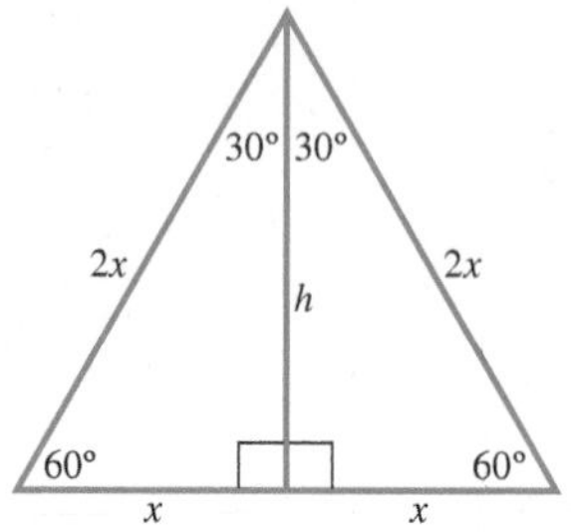

Notice that in each triangle the hypotenuse is twice the shortest leg, which is opposite the 30° angle.

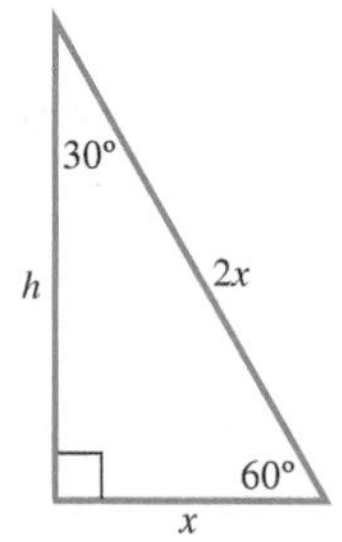

To find the length h, use the Pythagorean theorem. $h^2 + x^2 = (2x)^2$

$$h^2 + x^2 = 4x^2$$

Solve for h. $h^2 = 3x^2$

$$h = \pm\sqrt{3x^2} = \pm\sqrt{3}|x|$$

h and x are lengths and must be positive. $h = \sqrt{3}x$

The hypotenuse of a 30°-60°-90° is twice the length of the leg opposite the 30° angle, the shortest leg.

The leg opposite the 60° angle is $\sqrt{3}$ times the length of the leg opposite the 30° angle, the shortest leg.

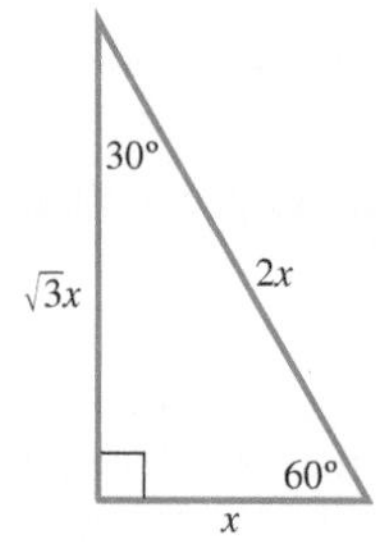

EXAMPLE 1 Evaluating the Trigonometric Functions Exactly for 30°

Evaluate the six trigonometric functions for an angle that measures 30°.

Solution:

Label the sides (opposite, adjacent, and hypotenuse) of the 30°-60°-90° triangle with respect to the 30° angle.

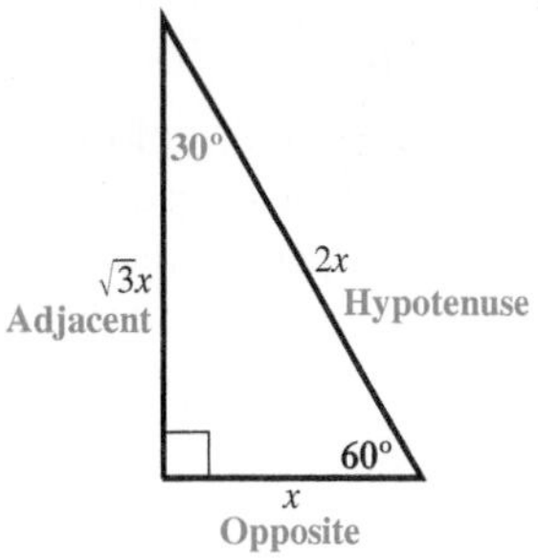

Use the right triangle ratio definitions of sine, cosine, and tangent.

$$\sin 30° = \frac{\text{opposite}}{\text{hypotenuse}} = \frac{x}{2x} = \frac{1}{2}$$

$$\cos 30° = \frac{\text{adjacent}}{\text{hypotenuse}} = \frac{\sqrt{3}x}{2x} = \frac{\sqrt{3}}{2}$$

$$\tan 30° = \frac{\text{opposite}}{\text{adjacent}} = \frac{x}{\sqrt{3}x} = \frac{1}{\sqrt{3}} = \frac{1}{\sqrt{3}} \cdot \frac{\sqrt{3}}{\sqrt{3}} = \frac{\sqrt{3}}{3}$$

Use the reciprocal identities to obtain the value of the cosecant, secant, and cotangent functions.

$$\csc 30° = \frac{1}{\sin 30°} = \frac{1}{\frac{1}{2}} = 2$$

$$\sec 30° = \frac{1}{\cos 30°} = \frac{1}{\frac{\sqrt{3}}{2}} = \frac{2}{\sqrt{3}} = \frac{2}{\sqrt{3}} \cdot \frac{\sqrt{3}}{\sqrt{3}} = \frac{2\sqrt{3}}{3}$$

$$\cot 30° = \frac{1}{\tan 30°} = \frac{1}{\frac{\sqrt{3}}{3}} = \frac{3}{\sqrt{3}} = \frac{3}{\sqrt{3}} \cdot \frac{\sqrt{3}}{\sqrt{3}} = \sqrt{3}$$

The six trigonometric functions evaluated for an angle measuring 30° are

$\boxed{\sin 30° = \frac{1}{2}}$ $\boxed{\cos 30° = \frac{\sqrt{3}}{2}}$ $\boxed{\tan 30° = \frac{\sqrt{3}}{3}}$

$\boxed{\csc 30° = 2}$ $\boxed{\sec 30° = \frac{2\sqrt{3}}{3}}$ $\boxed{\cot 30° = \sqrt{3}}$

YOUR TURN Evaluate the six trigonometric functions for an angle that measures 60°.

ANSWER

$\sin 60° = \frac{\sqrt{3}}{2}$ $\cos 60° = \frac{1}{2}$

$\tan 60° = \sqrt{3}$ $\csc 60° = \frac{2\sqrt{3}}{3}$

$\sec 60° = 2$ $\cot 60° = \frac{\sqrt{3}}{3}$

In comparing our answers in Example 1 and Your Turn, we see that the following cofunction relationships are true. We call these *cofunction* relationships.

$$\sin 30° = \cos 60° \quad \sec 30° = \csc 60° \quad \tan 30° = \cot 60°$$

$$\sin 60° = \cos 30° \quad \sec 60° = \csc 30° \quad \tan 60° = \cot 30°$$

Notice that 30° and 60° are complementary angles.

EXAMPLE 2 Evaluating the Trigonometric Functions Exactly for 45°

Evaluate the six trigonometric functions for an angle that measures 45°.

Solution:

Label the sides of the 45°-45°-90° triangle as opposite, adjacent, or hypotenuse with respect to one of the 45° angles.

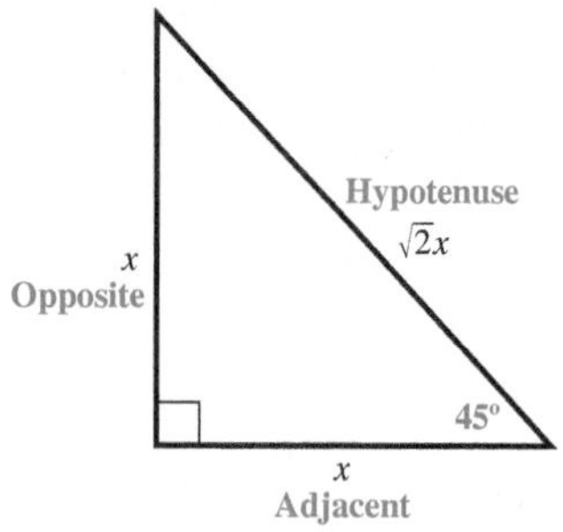

Use the right triangle ratio definitions of sine, cosine, and tangent.

$$\sin 45° = \frac{\text{opposite}}{\text{hypotenuse}} = \frac{x}{\sqrt{2}x} = \frac{1}{\sqrt{2}} = \frac{1}{\sqrt{2}} \cdot \frac{\sqrt{2}}{\sqrt{2}} = \frac{\sqrt{2}}{2}$$

$$\cos 45° = \frac{\text{adjacent}}{\text{hypotenuse}} = \frac{x}{\sqrt{2}x} = \frac{1}{\sqrt{2}} = \frac{1}{\sqrt{2}} \cdot \frac{\sqrt{2}}{\sqrt{2}} = \frac{\sqrt{2}}{2}$$

$$\tan 45° = \frac{\text{opposite}}{\text{adjacent}} = \frac{x}{x} = 1$$

Use the reciprocal identities to obtain the values of the cosecant, secant, and cotangent functions.

$$\csc 45° = \frac{1}{\sin 45°} = \frac{1}{\frac{\sqrt{2}}{2}} = \frac{2}{\sqrt{2}} = \frac{2}{\sqrt{2}} \cdot \frac{\sqrt{2}}{\sqrt{2}} = \sqrt{2}$$

$$\sec 45° = \frac{1}{\cos 45°} = \frac{1}{\frac{\sqrt{2}}{2}} = \frac{2}{\sqrt{2}} = \frac{2}{\sqrt{2}} \cdot \frac{\sqrt{2}}{\sqrt{2}} = \sqrt{2}$$

$$\cot 45° = \frac{1}{\tan 45°} = \frac{1}{1} = 1$$

The six trigonometric functions evaluated for an angle measuring 45° are

$$\boxed{\sin 45° = \frac{\sqrt{2}}{2}} \quad \boxed{\cos 45° = \frac{\sqrt{2}}{2}} \quad \boxed{\tan 45° = 1}$$

$$\boxed{\csc 45° = \sqrt{2}} \quad \boxed{\sec 45° = \sqrt{2}} \quad \boxed{\cot 45° = 1}$$

We see that the following *cofunction* relationships are true

$$\sin 45° = \cos 45° \quad \sec 45° = \csc 45° \quad \tan 45° = \cot 45°$$

since 45° and 45° are complementary angles.

STUDY TIP

$\sin 45° = \frac{\sqrt{2}}{2}$ is exact, whereas if we evaluate with a calculator, we get an approximation:

$\sin 45° \approx 0.7071$

The trigonometric function values for the three special angle measures, 30°, 45°, and 60°, are summarized in the following table.

Trigonometric Function Values for Special Angles

θ							
DEGREES	RADIANS	$\sin\theta$	$\cos\theta$	$\tan\theta$	$\cot\theta$	$\sec\theta$	$\csc\theta$
30°	$\frac{\pi}{6}$	$\frac{1}{2}$	$\frac{\sqrt{3}}{2}$	$\frac{\sqrt{3}}{3}$	$\sqrt{3}$	$\frac{2\sqrt{3}}{3}$	2
45°	$\frac{\pi}{4}$	$\frac{\sqrt{2}}{2}$	$\frac{\sqrt{2}}{2}$	1	1	$\sqrt{2}$	$\sqrt{2}$
60°	$\frac{\pi}{3}$	$\frac{\sqrt{3}}{2}$	$\frac{1}{2}$	$\sqrt{3}$	$\frac{\sqrt{3}}{3}$	2	$\frac{2\sqrt{3}}{3}$

It is important to **learn** the special values in **red** for sine and cosine. All other values in the table can be found through reciprocals or quotients of these two functions. Remember that the tangent function is the ratio of the sine to cosine functions.

$$\sin\theta = \frac{\text{opposite}}{\text{hypotenuse}} \quad \cos\theta = \frac{\text{adjacent}}{\text{hypotenuse}} \quad \tan\theta = \frac{\sin\theta}{\cos\theta} = \frac{\frac{\text{opposite}}{\text{hypotenuse}}}{\frac{\text{adjacent}}{\text{hypotenuse}}} = \frac{\text{opposite}}{\text{adjacent}}$$

STUDY TIP

If you memorize the values for sine and cosine for the angles given in the table, then the other trigonometric function values in the table can be found using the quotient and reciprocal identities.

4.2.5 Using Calculators to Evaluate (Approximate) Trigonometric Functions

4.2.5 SKILL

Evaluate (approximate) trigonometric functions using a calculator.

4.2.5 CONCEPTUAL

Understand the difference between evaluating trigonometric functions exactly and using a calculator.

We now turn our attention to using calculators to evaluate trigonometric functions, which often results in an approximation. Scientific and graphing calculators have buttons for sine (sin), cosine (cos), and tangent (tan) functions.

EXAMPLE 3 Evaluating Trigonometric Functions with a Calculator

Use a calculator to find the values of

a. $\sin 75°$ **b.** $\tan 67°$ **c.** $\sec 52°$ **d.** $\cos\left(\frac{\pi}{6}\right)$ **e.** $\tan\left(\frac{\pi}{8}\right)$

Round your answers to four decimal places.

Solution:

a. 0.965925826 $\boxed{\approx 0.9659}$

b. 2.355852366 $\boxed{\approx 2.3559}$

c. $\cos 52° \approx 0.615661475$ $1/x$ (or x^{-1}) 1.624269245 $\boxed{\approx 1.6243}$

d. 0.866025404 $\boxed{\approx 0.8660}$

e. 0.414213562 $\boxed{\approx 0.4142}$

Note: We know $\cos\left(\frac{\pi}{6}\right) = \frac{\sqrt{3}}{2} \approx 0.8660$.

STUDY TIP

In calculating secant, cosecant, and cotangent function values with a calculator, it is important not to round the number until after using the reciprocal function key 1/x.

YOUR TURN Use a calculator to find the values of

a. $\cos 22°$ **b.** $\tan 81°$ **c.** $\csc 37°$ **d.** $\sin\left(\frac{\pi}{4}\right)$ **e.** $\cot\left(\frac{\pi}{12}\right)$

Round your answers to four decimal places.

ANSWER

a. 0.9272 **b.** 6.3138
c. 1.6616 **d.** 0.7071
e. 3.7321

[CONCEPT CHECK]

TRUE OR FALSE
sin(45°) = 0.07071

ANSWER False

STUDY TIP

To solve a right triangle means to find the lengths of the sides and the angle measures.

4.2.6 SKILL

Solve right triangles given the measure of an acute angle and the length of a side, or two side lengths.

4.2.6 CONCEPTUAL

Understand that when an acute angle is given, the third angle can be found exactly. The remaining unknown side lengths can be found using right triangle trigonometry and the Pythagorean theorem.

When calculating secant, cosecant, and cotangent function values with a calculator, it is important not to round the number until after using the reciprocal function key $1/x$ or x^{-1} in order to be as accurate as possible.

4.2.6 Solving Right Triangles

A triangle has three angles and three sides. To *solve a triangle* means to find the length of all three sides and the measures of all three angles.

EXAMPLE 4 Solving a Right Triangle Given an Angle and a Side

Solve the right triangle—find a, b, and α.

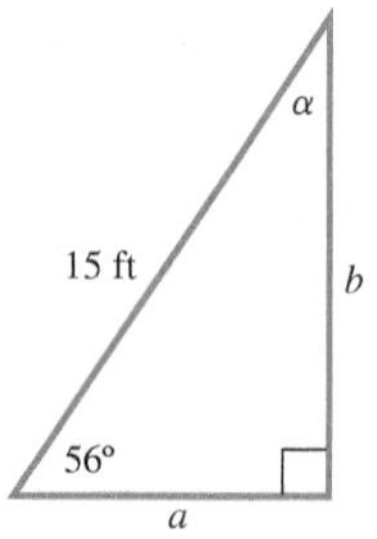

Solution:

STEP 1 Solve for α.

The two acute angles in a right triangle are complementary. $\alpha + 56° = 90°$

Solve for α. $\boxed{\alpha = 34°}$

STEP 2 Solve for a.

Cosine of an angle is equal to the adjacent side over the hypotenuse. $\cos 56° = \dfrac{a}{15}$

Solve for a. $a = 15\cos 56°$

Evaluate the right side of the expression using a calculator. $a \approx 8.38789$

Round a to two significant digits. $\boxed{a \approx 8.4 \text{ ft}}$

STEP 3 Solve for b.

Notice that there are two ways to solve for b: trigonometric functions or the Pythagorean theorem. Although it is tempting to use the Pythagorean theorem, it is better to use the given information with trigonometric functions than to use a value that has already been rounded, which could make results less accurate.

Sine of an angle is equal to the opposite side over the hypotenuse. $\sin 56° = \dfrac{b}{15}$

Solve for b. $b = 15\sin 56°$

Evaluate the right side of the expression using a calculator. $b \approx 12.43556$

Round b to two significant digits. $\boxed{b \approx 12 \text{ ft}}$

STEP 4 **Check.**

Check the trigonometric values of the specific angles by calculating the trigonometric ratios.

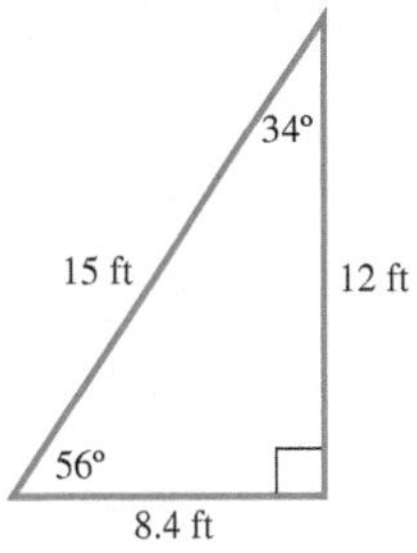

$$\sin 34° \stackrel{?}{=} \frac{8.4}{15} \qquad \cos 34° \stackrel{?}{=} \frac{12}{15} \qquad \tan 34° \stackrel{?}{=} \frac{8.4}{12}$$

$$0.5592 \approx 0.56 \qquad 0.8290 \approx 0.80 \qquad 0.6745 \approx 0.70$$

[CONCEPT CHECK]

In the Your Turn, θ can be calculated exactly. Can the side lengths be calculated exactly?

ANSWER No, they must be approximated.

YOUR TURN Solve the right triangle—find a, b, and θ.

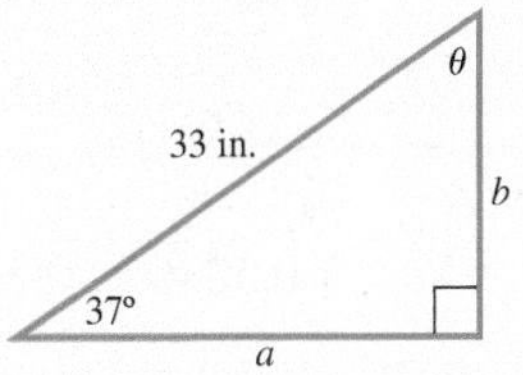

ANSWER
$\theta = 53°$, $a \approx 26$ in., $b \approx 20$ in.

Sometimes in solving a right triangle, the side lengths are given and we need to find the angles. To do this, we can work backwards from the table of known values. For example, if $\cos\theta = \frac{1}{2}$, what is θ? We see from the table of exact values that $\theta = 60°$ or $\frac{\pi}{3}$. To find an angle that is not listed in the table, we use the inverse cosine function, $\cos^{-1}$, key on a calculator. In a later section, we will discuss inverse trigonometric functions, but for now we will simply use the inverse trigonometric function keys on a calculator to determine the unknown angle.

EXAMPLE 5 **Solving a Right Triangle Given Two Sides**

Solve the right triangle—find a, α, and β.

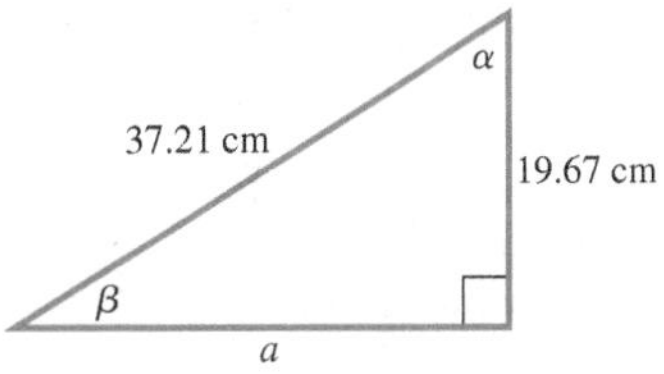

Solution:

STEP 1 **Solve for α.**

Cosine of an angle is equal to the adjacent side over the hypotenuse. $\cos\alpha = \dfrac{19.67 \text{ cm}}{37.21 \text{ cm}}$

Evaluate the right side using a calculator. $\cos\alpha \approx 0.528621338$

Write the angle α in terms of the inverse cosine function. $\alpha \approx \cos^{-1} 0.528621338$

Use a calculator to evaluate the inverse cosine function. $\alpha \approx 58.08764854°$

Round α to the nearest hundredth of a degree. $\boxed{\alpha \approx 58.09°}$

STEP 2 **Solve for β.**

The two acute angles in a right triangle are complementary. $\alpha + \beta = 90°$

Substitute $\alpha \approx 58.09°$. $58.09 + \beta \approx 90°$

Solve for β. $\boxed{\beta \approx 31.91°}$

The answer is already rounded to the nearest hundredth of a degree.

STEP 3 Solve for *a*.

Use the Pythagorean theorem. $a^2 + b^2 = c^2$

Substitute the given values for b and c. $a^2 + 19.67^2 = 37.21^2$

Solve for a. $a \approx 31.5859969$

Round a to four significant digits. $\boxed{a \approx 31.59 \text{ cm}}$

STEP 4 Check.

Check the trigonometric values of the specific angles by calculating the trigonometric ratio.

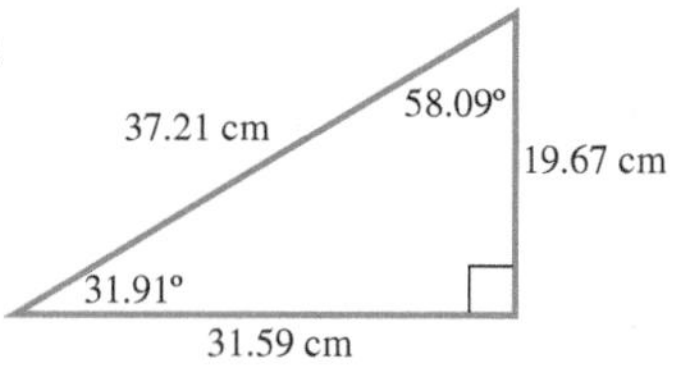

$$\sin 31.91° \stackrel{?}{=} \frac{19.67}{37.21} \qquad \sin 58.09° \stackrel{?}{=} \frac{31.59}{37.21}$$

$$0.5286 \approx 0.5286 \qquad 0.8489 \approx 0.8490$$

YOUR TURN Solve the right triangle—find a, α, and β.

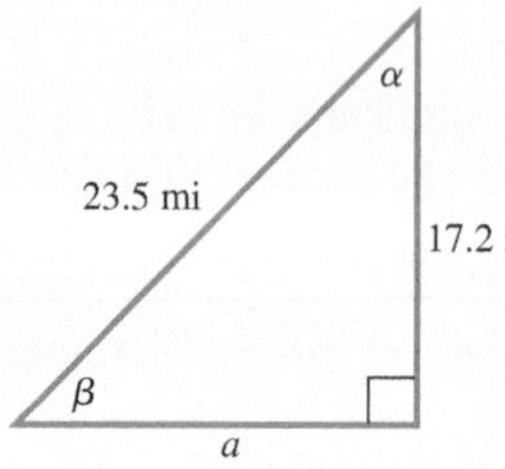

ANSWER

$a \approx 16.0$ mi, $\alpha \approx 43.0°$, $\beta \approx 47.0°$

STUDY TIP

To find a length in a right triangle, use the sine, cosine, or tangent function. To find an angle measure in a right triangle, given the proper ratio of side lengths, use the inverse sine, inverse cosine, or inverse tangent function.

Applications

Suppose NASA wants to talk with the International Space Station (ISS), which is traveling at a speed of 17,700 miles per hour (7900 meters per second), 400 kilometers (250 miles) above the surface of Earth. If the antennas at the ground station in Houston have a pointing error of even 1/100 of a degree, that is, 0.01°, the ground station will miss the chance to talk with the astronauts.

EXAMPLE 6 Pointing Error

Assume that the ISS (which is 108 meters long and 73 meters wide) is in a 400-kilometer low Earth orbit. If the communications antennas have a 0.01° pointing error, how many meters off will the communications link be?

Solution:

Draw a right triangle that depicts this scenario.

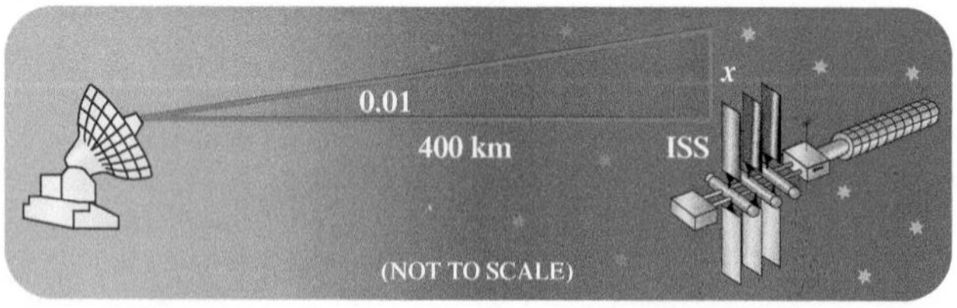

Identify the tangent ratio. $\tan 0.01° = \dfrac{x}{400}$

Solve for x. $x = (400 \text{ km}) \tan 0.01°$

Evaluate the expression on the right. $x \approx 0.06981317$ km

400 kilometers is accurate to three significant digits, so we express the answer to three significant digits.

The pointing error causes the signal to be off by $\boxed{69.8 \text{ meters}}$. Since the ISS is only 108 meters long, it is possible that the signal will be missed by the astronaut crew.

In navigation, the word **bearing** means the direction in which a vessel is pointed. **Heading** is the direction in which the vessel is actually traveling. Heading and bearing are synonyms only when there is no wind. Direction is often given as a bearing, which is the measure of an acute angle with respect to the north–south vertical line. "The plane has a bearing of N 20° E" means that the plane is pointed 20° to the east of due north.

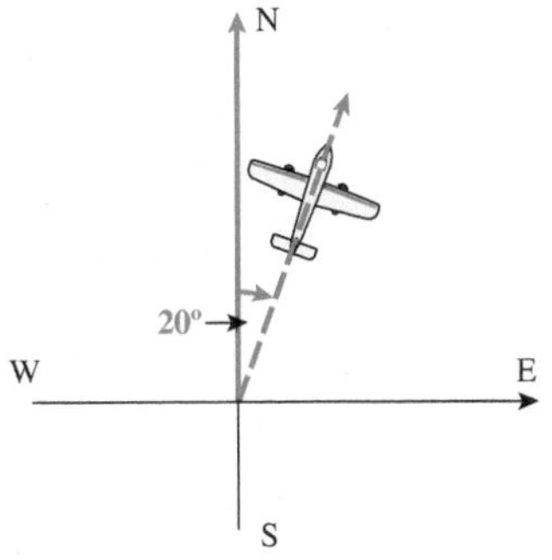

EXAMPLE 7 **Bearing (Navigation)**

A jet takes off bearing N 28° E and flies 5 miles, and then makes a left (90°) turn and flies 12 miles farther. If the control tower operator wants to locate the plane, what bearing should she use?

Solution:

Draw a picture that represents this scenario.

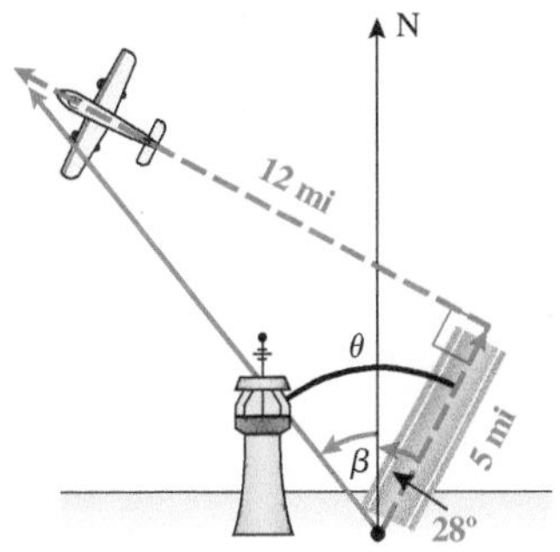

Identify the tangent ratio. $\tan\theta = \dfrac{12}{5}$

Use the inverse tangent function to solve for θ. $\theta = \tan^{-1}\left(\dfrac{12}{5}\right) \approx 67.4°$

Subtract 28° from θ to find the bearing, β. $\beta \approx 67.4° - 28° \approx 39.4°$

Round to the nearest degree. $\boxed{\beta \approx \text{N } 39° \text{ W}}$

[SECTION 4.2] SUMMARY

The trigonometric functions defined in terms of ratios of side lengths of right triangles are given by

$$\sin\theta = \frac{\text{opposite}}{\text{hypotenuse}}$$

$$\cos\theta = \frac{\text{adjacent}}{\text{hypotenuse}}$$

$$\tan\theta = \frac{\text{opposite}}{\text{adjacent}}$$

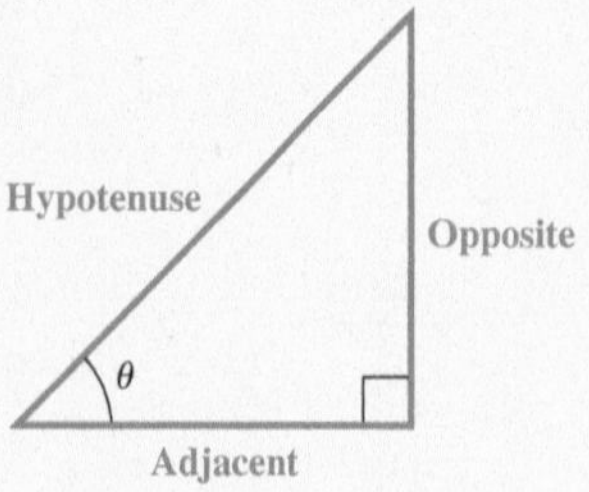

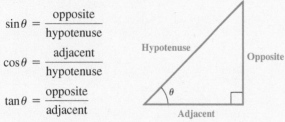

And the remaining three trigonometric functions can be found using the reciprocal identities:

$$\csc\theta = \frac{1}{\sin\theta} \qquad \sin\theta \neq 0$$

$$\sec\theta = \frac{1}{\cos\theta} \qquad \cos\theta \neq 0$$

$$\cot\theta = \frac{1}{\tan\theta} \qquad \tan\theta \neq 0$$

The following table lists the values of the sine and cosine functions for special acute angles:

θ (DEGREES)	**θ (RADIANS)**	**$\sin\theta$**	**$\cos\theta$**	**$\tan\theta$**
30°	$\frac{\pi}{6}$	$\frac{1}{2}$	$\frac{\sqrt{3}}{2}$	$\frac{\sqrt{3}}{3}$
45°	$\frac{\pi}{4}$	$\frac{\sqrt{2}}{2}$	$\frac{\sqrt{2}}{2}$	1
60°	$\frac{\pi}{3}$	$\frac{\sqrt{3}}{2}$	$\frac{1}{2}$	$\sqrt{3}$

[SECTION 4.2] EXERCISES

• SKILLS

In Exercises 1–6, refer to the triangle in the drawing to find the indicated trigonometric function values. Rationalize any denominators containing radicals that you encounter in the answers.

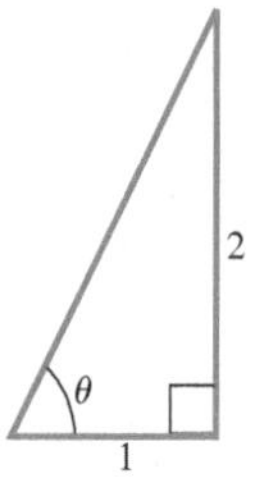

1. $\cos\theta$ **2.** $\sin\theta$ **3.** $\sec\theta$

4. $\csc\theta$ **5.** $\tan\theta$ **6.** $\cot\theta$

For Exercises 7–12, refer to the triangle in the drawing to find the indicated trigonometric function values. Rationalize any denominators containing radicals that you encounter in the answers.

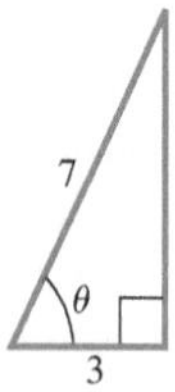

7. $\sin\theta$ **8.** $\cos\theta$ **9.** $\sec\theta$

10. $\csc\theta$ **11.** $\cot\theta$ **12.** $\tan\theta$

In Exercises 13–18, match the trigonometric function values.

a. $\frac{1}{2}$ **b.** $\frac{\sqrt{3}}{2}$ **c.** $\frac{\sqrt{2}}{2}$

13. $\sin 30°$ **14.** $\sin 60°$ **15.** $\cos\left(\frac{\pi}{6}\right)$ **16.** $\cos\left(\frac{\pi}{3}\right)$ **17.** $\sin 45°$ **18.** $\cos\left(\frac{\pi}{4}\right)$

In Exercises 19–21, use the results in Exercises 13–18 and the trigonometric quotient identity $\tan\theta = \dfrac{\sin\theta}{\cos\theta}$ to calculate the following values:

19. $\tan 30°$ **20.** $\tan\left(\frac{\pi}{4}\right)$ **21.** $\tan 60°$

In Exercises 22–30, use the results in Exercises 13–21 and the reciprocal identities $\csc\theta = \dfrac{1}{\sin\theta}$, $\sec\theta = \dfrac{1}{\cos\theta}$, and $\cot\theta = \dfrac{1}{\tan\theta}$ to calculate the following values:

22. $\csc 30°$ **23.** $\sec 30°$ **24.** $\cot\left(\frac{\pi}{6}\right)$ **25.** $\csc\left(\frac{\pi}{3}\right)$ **26.** $\sec 60°$ **27.** $\cot 60°$

28. $\csc 45°$ **29.** $\sec\left(\frac{\pi}{4}\right)$ **30.** $\cot\left(\frac{\pi}{4}\right)$

In Exercises 31–46, use a calculator to evaluate the trigonometric functions for the indicated angle values. Round your answers to four decimal places.

31. $\sin 37°$ **32.** $\sin 17.8°$ **33.** $\cos 82°$ **34.** $\cos 21.9°$ **35.** $\sin\left(\frac{\pi}{12}\right)$ **36.** $\sin\left(\frac{5\pi}{9}\right)$

37. $\cos\left(\frac{6\pi}{5}\right)$ **38.** $\cos\left(\frac{13\pi}{7}\right)$ **39.** $\tan 54°$ **40.** $\tan 43.2°$ **41.** $\tan\left(\frac{\pi}{8}\right)$ **42.** $\cot\left(\frac{3\pi}{5}\right)$

43. $\csc\left(\frac{10\pi}{19}\right)$ **44.** $\sec\left(\frac{4\pi}{9}\right)$ **45.** $\cot 55°$ **46.** $\cot 29°$

In Exercises 47–54, refer to the right triangle diagram and the given information to find the indicated measure. Write your answers for angle measures in decimal degrees.

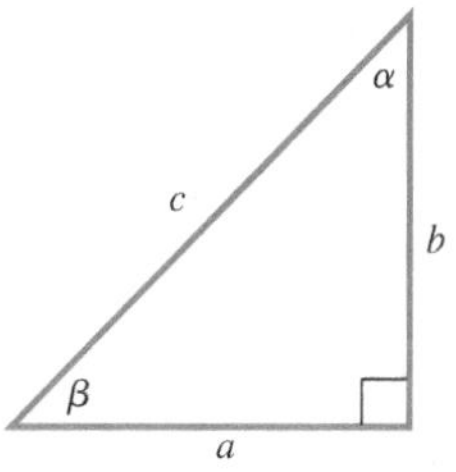

47. $\alpha = 55°$, $c = 22$ ft; find a. **48.** $\alpha = 55°$, $c = 22$ ft; find b.

49. $\alpha = 20.5°$, $b = 14.7$ mi; find a. **50.** $\beta = 69.3°$, $a = 0.752$ mi; find b.

51. $\beta = 25°$, $a = 11$ km; find c. **52.** $\beta = 75°$, $b = 26$ km; find c.

53. $b = 2.3$ m, $c = 4.9$ m; find α. **54.** $b = 7.8$ m, $c = 13$ m; find β.

In Exercises 55–66, refer to the right triangle diagram and the given information to solve the right triangle. Write your answers for angle measures in decimal degrees.

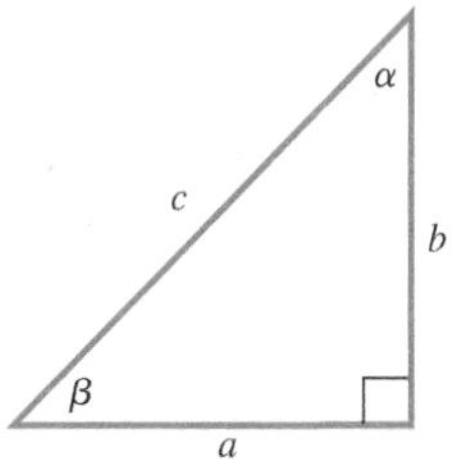

55. $\alpha = 32°$ and $c = 12$ ft **56.** $\alpha = 65°$ and $c = 37$ ft

57. $\beta = 72°$ and $c = 9.7$ mm **58.** $\beta = 45°$ and $c = 7.8$ mm

59. $\alpha = 54.2°$ and $a = 111$ mi **60.** $\beta = 47.2°$ and $a = 9.75$ mi

61. $a = 42.5$ ft and $b = 28.7$ ft **62.** $a = 19.8$ ft and $c = 48.7$ ft

63. $a = 35{,}236$ km and $c = 42{,}766$ km **64.** $b = 0.1245$ mm and $c = 0.8763$ mm

65. $\beta = 25.4°$ and $b = 11.6$ in. **66.** $\beta = 39.21°$ and $b = 6.3$ m

• APPLICATIONS

Exercises 67 and 68 illustrate a mid-air refueling scenario that military aircraft often enact. Assume the elevation angle that the hose makes with the plane being fueled is $\theta = 30°$.

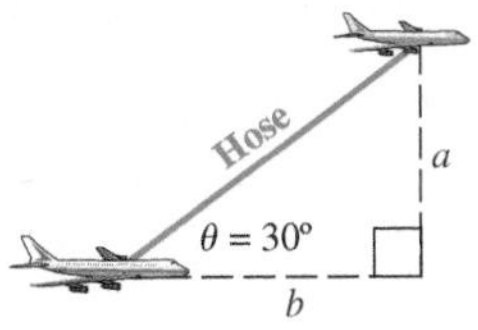

67. Mid-Air Refueling. If the hose is 150 feet long, what should be the altitude difference a between the two planes? Round to the nearest foot.

68. Mid-Air Refueling. If the smallest acceptable altitude difference a between the two planes is 100 feet, how long should the hose be? Round to the nearest foot.

Exercises 69 and 70 are based on the idea of a glide slope (the angle the flight path makes with the ground).

Precision Approach Path Indicator (PAPI) lights are used as a visual approach slope aid for pilots landing aircraft. A typical glide path for commercial jet airliners is 3°. The space shuttle has an outer glide approach of 18°–20°. PAPI lights are typically configured as a row of four lights. All four lights are on, but in different combinations of red and/or white. If all four lights are white, then the angle of descent is too high; if all four lights are red, then the angle of descent is too low; if there are two white and two red, then the approach is perfect.

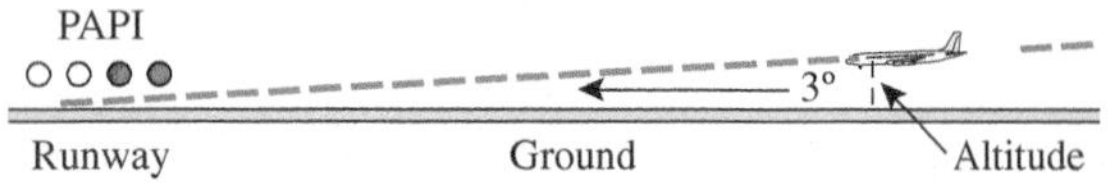

69. **Glide Path of a Commercial Jet Airliner.** If a commercial jetliner is 5000 feet (about 1 mile) ground distance from the runway, what should the altitude of the plane be to achieve two red and two white PAPI lights? (Assume this corresponds to a 3° glide path.)

70. **Glide Path of a Commercial Jet Airliner.** If a commercial jetliner is at an altitude of 450 feet when it is 5200 feet from the runway (approximately 1 mile ground distance), what is the glide slope angle? Will the pilot see white lights, red lights, or both?

In Exercises 71 and 72, refer to the illustration below, which shows a search and rescue helicopter with a 30° field of view with a searchlight.

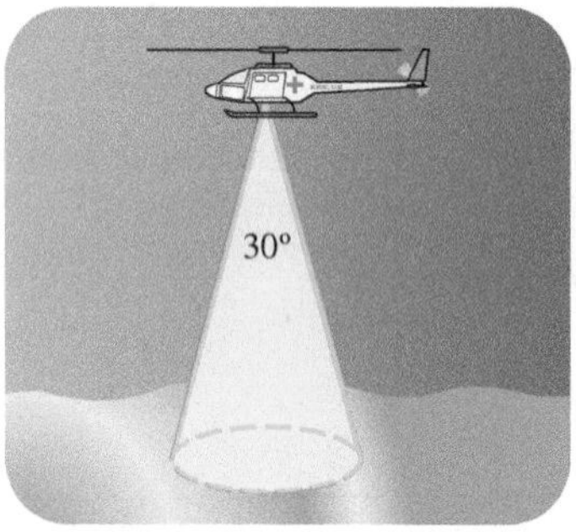

71. **Search and Rescue.** If the search and rescue helicopter is flying at an altitude of 150 feet above sea level, what is the diameter of the circle illuminated on the surface of the water?

72. **Search and Rescue.** If the search and rescue helicopter is flying at an altitude of 500 feet above sea level, what is the diameter of the circle illuminated on the surface of the water?

For Exercises 73–76, refer to the following:

Geostationary orbits are useful because they cause a satellite to appear stationary with respect to a fixed point on the rotating Earth. As a result, an antenna (dish TV) can point in a fixed direction and maintain a link with the satellite. The satellite orbits in the direction of Earth's rotation at an altitude of approximately 35,000 kilometers.

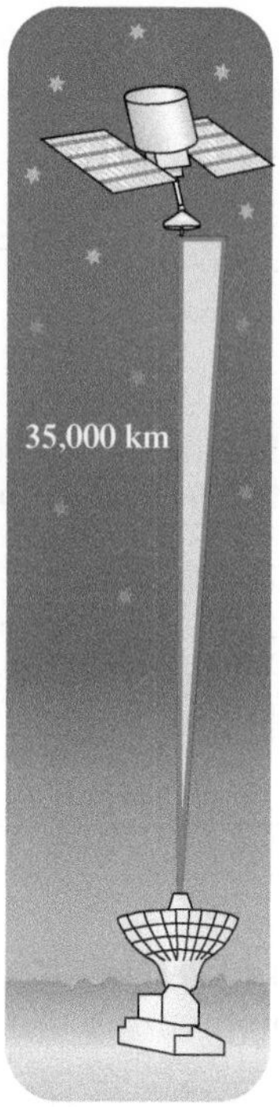

73. **Dish TV.** If your dish TV antenna has a pointing error of 0.000278°, how long would the satellite have to be in order to maintain a link? Round your answer to the nearest meter.

74. **Dish TV.** If your dish TV antenna has a pointing error of 0.000139°, how long would the satellite have to be in order to maintain a link? Round your answer to the nearest meter.

75. **Dish TV.** If the satellite in a geostationary orbit (at 35,000 kilometers) was only 10 meters long, about how accurate would the pointing of the dish have to be? Give the answer in degrees to two significant digits.

76. **Dish TV.** If the satellite in a geostationary orbit (at 35,000 kilometers) was only 30 meters long, about how accurate would the pointing of the dish have to be? Give the answer in degrees to two significant digits.

77. **Angle of Inclination (Skiing).** The angle of inclination of a mountain with triple black diamond ski trails is 65°. If a skier at the top of the mountain is at an elevation of 4000 feet, how long is the ski run from the top to the base of the mountain? Round to the nearest foot.

78. **Bearing (Navigation).** If a plane takes off bearing N 33° W and flies 6 miles and then makes a right (90°) turn and flies 10 miles further, what bearing will the traffic controller use to locate the plane?

For Exercises 79 and 80, refer to the following:

The structure of molecules is critical to the study of materials science and organic chemistry, and has countless applications to a variety of interesting phenomena. Trigonometry plays a critical role in determining the bonding angles of molecules. For instance, the structure of the $(FeCl_4Br_2)^{-3}$ ion (dibromatetetrachlorideferrate III) is shown in the figure below.

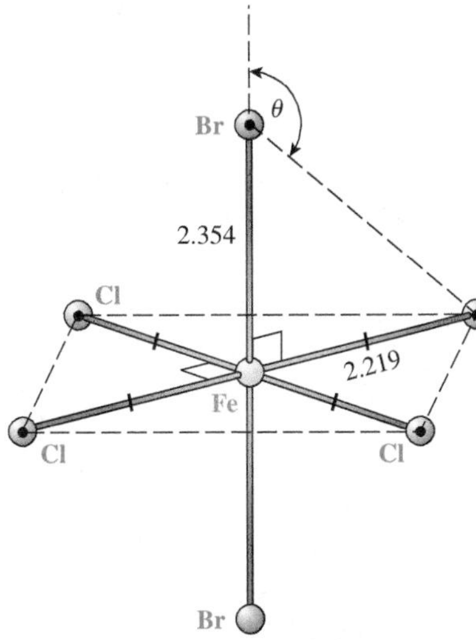

79. Chemistry. Determine the angle θ [i.e., the angle between the axis containing the apical bromide atom (Br) and the segment connecting Br to Cl].

80. Chemistry. Now, suppose one of the chlorides (Cl) is removed. The resulting structure is triagonal in nature, resulting in the following structure. Does the angle θ change? If so, what is its new value?

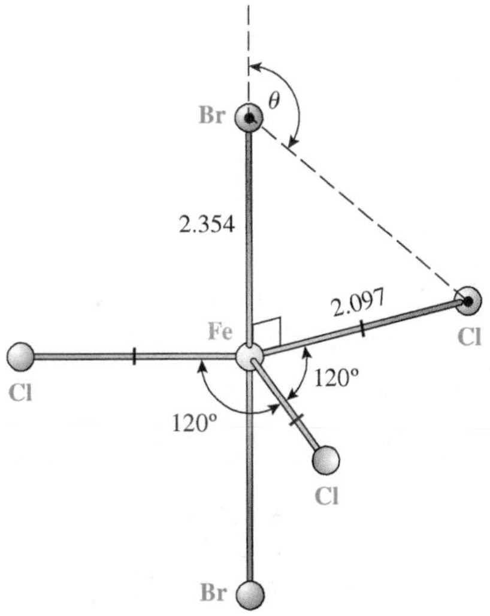

For Exercises 81 and 82, refer to the following:

A canal constructed by a water-users association can be approximated by an isosceles triangle (see the figure below). When the canal was originally constructed, the depth of the canal was 5.0 feet and the angle defining the shape of the canal was 60°.

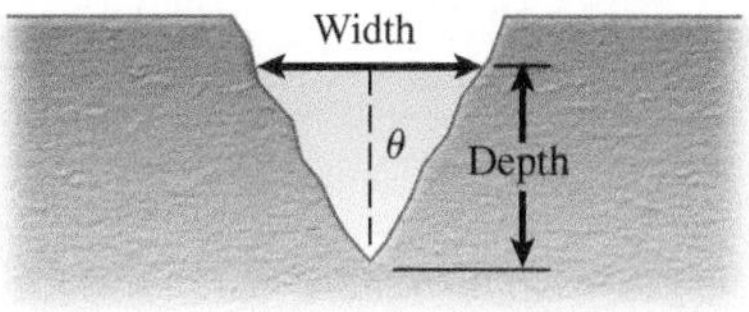

81. Environmental Science. If the width of the water surface today is 4.0 feet, find the depth of the water running through the canal.

82. Environmental Science. One year later a survey is performed to measure the effects of erosion on the canal. It is determined that when the water depth is 4.0 feet, the width of the water surface is 5.0 feet. Find the angle θ defining the shape of the canal to the nearest degree. Has erosion affected the shape of the canal? Explain.

For Exercises 83 and 84, refer to the following:

After breaking a femur, a patient is placed in traction. The end of a femur of length l is lifted to an elevation forming an angle θ with the horizontal (angle of elevation).

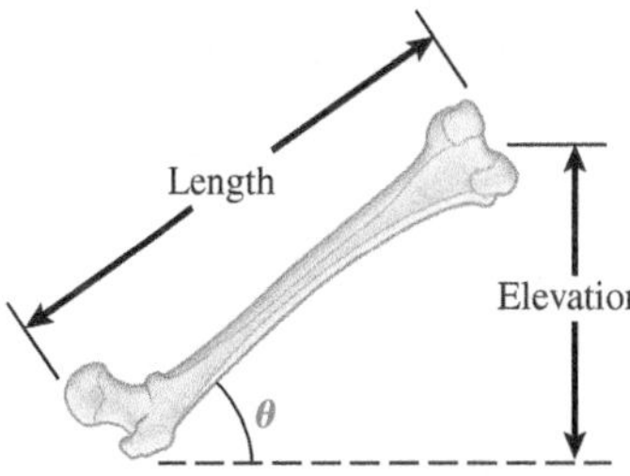

83. Health/Medicine. A femur 18 inches long is placed into traction, forming an angle of 15° with the horizontal. Find the height of elevation at the end of the femur.

84. Health/Medicine. A femur 18 inches long is placed in traction with an elevation of 6.2 inches. What is the angle of elevation of the femur?

• CATCH THE MISTAKE

For Exercises 85 and 86, explain the mistake that is made.

For the triangle in the drawing, calculate the indicated trigonometric function values.

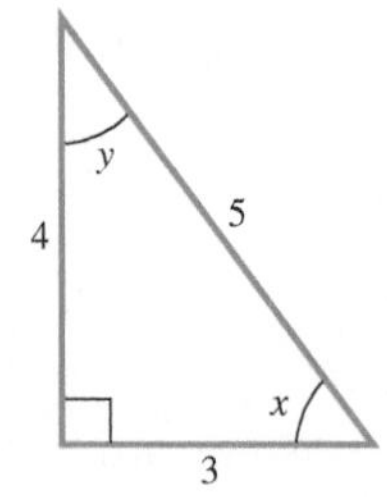

85. Calculate $\sin y$.

Solution:

Formulate sine in terms of trigonometric ratios. $\sin y = \dfrac{\text{opposite}}{\text{hypotenuse}}$

The opposite side is 4, and the hypotenuse is 5. $\sin y = \dfrac{4}{5}$

This is incorrect. What mistake was made?

86. Calculate $\tan x$.

Solution:

Formulate tangent in terms of trigonometric ratios. $\tan x = \dfrac{\text{adjacent}}{\text{opposite}}$

The adjacent side is 3, and the opposite side is 4. $\tan x = \dfrac{3}{4}$

This is incorrect. What mistake was made?

• CONCEPTUAL

In Exercises 87–90, determine whether each statement is true or false.

87. If you are given the measures of two sides of a right triangle, you can solve the right triangle.

88. If you are given the measures of one side and one acute angle of a right triangle, you can solve the right triangle.

89. If you are given the two acute angles of a right triangle, you can solve the right triangle.

90. If you are given the hypotenuse of a right triangle and the angle opposite the hypotenuse, you can solve the right triangle.

In Exercises 91–94, use trignometric ratios and the assumption that *a* is much larger than *b*.

Thus far in this text, we have discussed trigonometric values only for acute angles, or for $0° < \theta < 90°$. How do we determine these values when θ is approximately 0° or 90°? We will formally consider these cases in the next section, but for now, draw and label a right triangle that has one angle very close to 0°, so that the opposite side is very small compared to the adjacent side. Then the hypotenuse and the adjacent side will be very close to the same length.

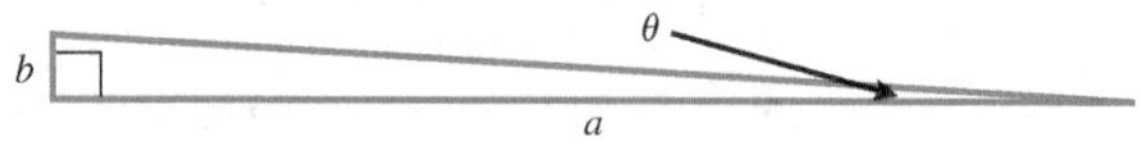

91. Approximate $\sin 0°$ without using a calculator.

92. Approximate $\cos 0°$ without using a calculator.

93. Approximate $\cos 90°$ without using a calculator.

94. Approximate $\sin 90°$ without using a calculator.

• CHALLENGE

For Exercises 95 and 96, consider the following diagram:

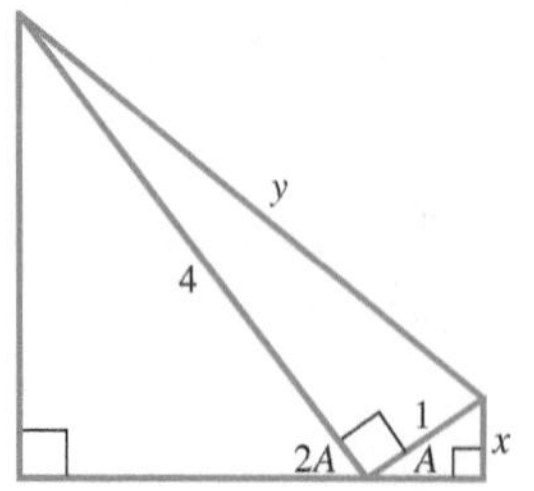

95. Determine x.

96. Determine y.

• PREVIEW TO CALCULUS

In calculus, the value of $F(b) - F(a)$ of a function $F(x)$ at $x = a$ and $x = b$ plays an important role in the calculation of definite integrals. In Exercises 97–100, find the exact value of $F(b) - F(a)$.

97. $F(x) = \sec x, a = \frac{\pi}{6}, b = \frac{\pi}{3}$

98. $F(x) = \sin^3 x, a = 0, b = \frac{\pi}{4}$

99. $F(x) = \tan x + 2\cos x, a = 0, b = \frac{\pi}{3}$

100. $F(x) = \dfrac{\cot x - 4\sin x}{\cos x}, a = \frac{\pi}{4}, b = \frac{\pi}{3}$

4.3 TRIGONOMETRIC FUNCTIONS OF ANGLES

SKILLS OBJECTIVES

- Calculate the trigonometric function values for nonacute and quadrantal angles.
- Determine the reference angle of a nonacute angle.
- Determine the ranges of the six trigonometric functions.
- Determine the reference angle for any angle whose terminal side lies in one of the four quadrants.
- Evaluate trigonometric functions for nonacute and quadrantal angles.

CONCEPTUAL OBJECTIVES

- Recognize that right triangle definitions of trigonometric functions for acute angles are consistent with definitions of trigonometric functions for all angles in the Cartesian plane.
- Understand which trigonometric functions are positive or negative in each of the four quadrants.
- Understand why sine and cosine range between -1 and 1.
- Recognize that reference angles are acute and have positive measure.
- Understand that the value of a trigonometric function at an angle is the same as the trigonometric value of its reference angle, except that there may be a difference in its algebraic sign $(+/-)$.

In Section 4.2, we defined trigonometric functions as ratios of side lengths of right triangles. This definition holds only for acute $(0° < \theta < 90°)$ angles, since the two angles in a right triangle other than the right angle must be acute. We now define trigonometric functions as ratios of x- and y-coordinates and distances in the Cartesian plane, which for acute angles is consistent with right triangle trigonometry. However, this second approach also enables us to formulate trigonometric functions for quadrantal angles (whose terminal side lies along an axis) and nonacute angles.

4.3.1 Trigonometric Functions: The Cartesian Plane

4.3.1 SKILL

Calculate the trigonometric function values for nonacute and quadrantal angles.

4.3.1 CONCEPTUAL

Recognize that right triangle definitions of trigonometric functions for acute angles are consistent with definitions of trigonometric functions for all angles in the Cartesian plane.

To define the trigonometric functions in the Cartesian plane, let us start with an acute angle θ in standard position. Choose any point (x, y) on the terminal side of the angle as long as it is not the vertex (the origin).

A right triangle can be drawn so that the right angle is made when a perpendicular segment connects the point (x, y) to the x-axis. Notice that the side opposite θ has length y and the other leg of the right triangle has length x.

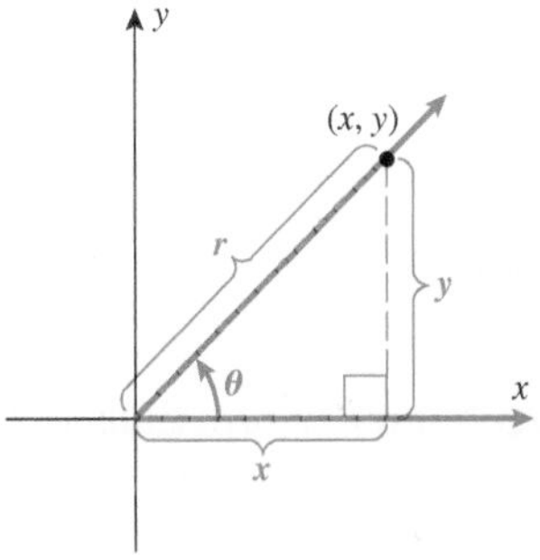

The distance r from the origin $(0, 0)$ to the point (x, y) can be found using the distance formula.

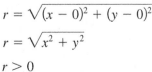

$$r = \sqrt{(x - 0)^2 + (y - 0)^2}$$

$$r = \sqrt{x^2 + y^2}$$

Since r is a distance and x and y are not both zero, r is always positive. $\quad r > 0$

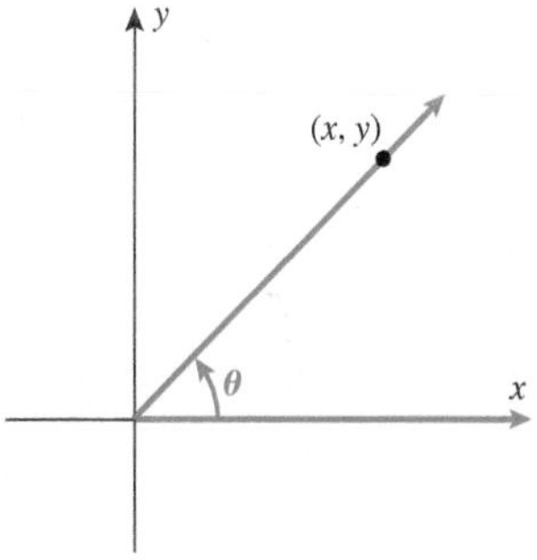

Using our first definition of trigonometric functions in terms of right triangle ratios (Section 4.2), we know that $\sin\theta = \frac{\text{opposite}}{\text{hypotenuse}}$. From this picture, we see that sine can also be defined by the relation $\sin\theta = \frac{y}{r}$. Similar reasoning holds for all six trigonometric functions and leads us to the second definition of the trigonometric functions, in terms of ratios of coordinates of a point and distances in the Cartesian plane.

[CONCEPT CHECK]

TRUE OR FALSE The trigonometric function values for nonacute angles can be found using right triangle trigonometry for acute angles and then changing the algebraic sign (+/−) depending on the quadrant in which the terminal side lies.

ANSWER True

DEFINITION Trigonometric Functions

Let (x, y) be a point, other than the origin, on the terminal side of an angle θ in standard position. Let r be the distance from the point (x, y) to the origin. Then the six trigonometric functions are defined as

$$\sin\theta = \frac{y}{r} \qquad \cos\theta = \frac{x}{r} \qquad \tan\theta = \frac{y}{x}\ (x \neq 0)$$

$$\csc\theta = \frac{r}{y}\ (y \neq 0) \qquad \sec\theta = \frac{r}{x}\ (x \neq 0) \qquad \cot\theta = \frac{x}{y}\ (y \neq 0)$$

where $r = \sqrt{x^2 + y^2}$, or $x^2 + y^2 = r^2$. The distance r is positive: $r > 0$.

EXAMPLE 1 Calculating Trigonometric Function Values for Acute Angles

The terminal side of an angle θ in standard position passes through the point $(2, 5)$. Calculate the values of the six trigonometric functions for angle θ.

Solution:

STEP 1 **Draw the angle and label the point (2, 5).**

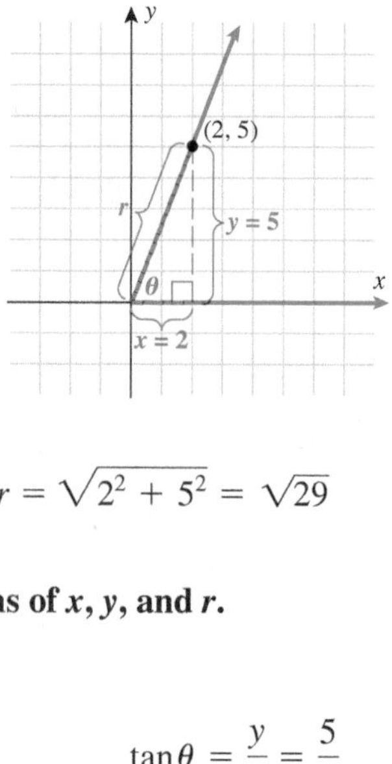

STEP 2 **Calculate the distance r.** $r = \sqrt{2^2 + 5^2} = \sqrt{29}$

STEP 3 **Formulate the trigonometric functions in terms of x, y, and r.**

Let $x = 2, y = 5, r = \sqrt{29}$.

$$\sin\theta = \frac{y}{r} = \frac{5}{\sqrt{29}} \qquad \cos\theta = \frac{x}{r} = \frac{2}{\sqrt{29}} \qquad \tan\theta = \frac{y}{x} = \frac{5}{2}$$

$$\csc\theta = \frac{r}{y} = \frac{\sqrt{29}}{5} \qquad \sec\theta = \frac{r}{x} = \frac{\sqrt{29}}{2} \qquad \cot\theta = \frac{x}{y} = \frac{2}{5}$$

STEP 4 **Rationalize any denominators containing a radical.**

$$\sin\theta = \frac{5}{\sqrt{29}} \cdot \frac{\sqrt{29}}{\sqrt{29}} = \frac{5\sqrt{29}}{29} \qquad \cos\theta = \frac{2}{\sqrt{29}} \cdot \frac{\sqrt{29}}{\sqrt{29}} = \frac{2\sqrt{29}}{29}$$

STEP 5 **Write the values of the six trigonometric functions for θ.**

$$\sin\theta = \frac{5\sqrt{29}}{29} \qquad \cos\theta = \frac{2\sqrt{29}}{29} \qquad \tan\theta = \frac{5}{2}$$

$$\csc\theta = \frac{\sqrt{29}}{5} \qquad \sec\theta = \frac{\sqrt{29}}{2} \qquad \cot\theta = \frac{2}{5}$$

Note: In Example 1, we could have used the values of the sine, cosine, and tangent functions along with the reciprocal identities to calculate the cosecant, secant, and cotangent function values.

STUDY TIP

There is no need to memorize definitions for secant, cosecant, and cotangent functions, because their values can be derived from the reciprocals of the sine, cosine, and tangent function values.

YOUR TURN The terminal side of an angle θ in standard position passes through the point $(3, 7)$. Calculate the values of the six trigonometric functions for angle θ.

ANSWER

$$\sin\theta = \frac{7\sqrt{58}}{58} \qquad \cos\theta = \frac{3\sqrt{58}}{58}$$

$$\tan\theta = \frac{7}{3} \qquad \csc\theta = \frac{\sqrt{58}}{7}$$

$$\sec\theta = \frac{\sqrt{58}}{3} \qquad \cot\theta = \frac{3}{7}$$

We can now find values for nonacute angles (angles with measure greater than or equal to 90°) as well as negative angles.

EXAMPLE 2 Calculating Trigonometric Function Values for Nonacute Angles

The terminal side of an angle θ in standard position passes through the point $(-4, -7)$. Calculate the values of the six trigonometric functions for angle θ.

Solution:

STEP 1 **Draw the angle and label the point $(-4, -7)$.**

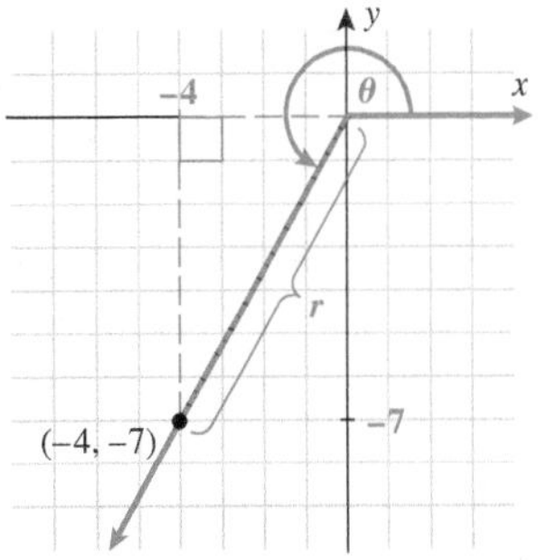

STEP 2 **Calculate the distance r.** $$r = \sqrt{(-4)^2 + (-7)^2} = \sqrt{65}$$

STEP 3 **Formulate the trigonometric functions in terms of x, y, and r.**

Let $x = -4$, $y = -7$, and $r = \sqrt{65}$.

$$\sin\theta = \frac{y}{r} = \frac{-7}{\sqrt{65}} \qquad \cos\theta = \frac{x}{r} = \frac{-4}{\sqrt{65}} \qquad \tan\theta = \frac{y}{x} = \frac{-7}{-4} = \frac{7}{4}$$

$$\csc\theta = \frac{r}{y} = \frac{\sqrt{65}}{-7} \qquad \sec\theta = \frac{r}{x} = \frac{\sqrt{65}}{-4} \qquad \cot\theta = \frac{x}{y} = \frac{-4}{-7} = \frac{4}{7}$$

STEP 4 **Rationalize the radical denominators in the sine and cosine functions.**

$$\sin\theta = \frac{y}{r} = \frac{-7}{\sqrt{65}} \cdot \frac{\sqrt{65}}{\sqrt{65}} = -\frac{7\sqrt{65}}{65}$$

$$\cos\theta = \frac{x}{r} = \frac{-4}{\sqrt{65}} \cdot \frac{\sqrt{65}}{\sqrt{65}} = -\frac{4\sqrt{65}}{65}$$

STEP 5 **Write the values of the six trigonometric functions for θ.**

$$\sin\theta = -\frac{7\sqrt{65}}{65} \qquad \cos\theta = -\frac{4\sqrt{65}}{65} \qquad \tan\theta = \frac{7}{4}$$

$$\csc\theta = -\frac{\sqrt{65}}{7} \qquad \sec\theta = -\frac{\sqrt{65}}{4} \qquad \cot\theta = \frac{4}{7}$$

YOUR TURN The terminal side of an angle θ in standard position passes through the point $(-3, -5)$. Calculate the values of the six trigonometric functions for angle θ.

ANSWER

$$\sin\theta = -\frac{5\sqrt{34}}{34} \qquad \cos\theta = -\frac{3\sqrt{34}}{34}$$

$$\tan\theta = \frac{5}{3} \qquad \csc\theta = -\frac{\sqrt{34}}{5}$$

$$\sec\theta = -\frac{\sqrt{34}}{3} \qquad \cot\theta = \frac{3}{5}$$

4.3.2 Algebraic Signs of Trigonometric Functions

4.3.2 SKILL

Determine the reference angle of a nonacute angle.

4.3.2 CONCEPTUAL

Understand which trigonometric functions are positive or negative in each of the four quadrants.

We have defined trigonometric functions as ratios of x, y, and r. Since r is the distance from the origin to the point (x, y) and distance is never negative, r is always taken as the positive solution to $r^2 = x^2 + y^2$, so $r = \sqrt{x^2 + y^2}$.

The x-coordinate is positive in quadrants **I** and **IV** and negative in quadrants **II** and **III**.

The y-coordinate is positive in quadrants **I** and **II** and negative in quadrants **III** and **IV**.

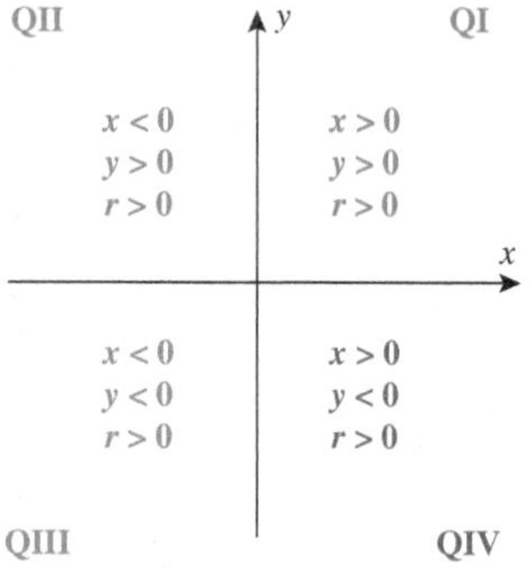

[CONCEPT CHECK]

In what quadrant are the sine and cosine functions both negative?

ANSWER quadrant III

Recall the definition of the six trigonometric functions in the Cartesian plane:

$$\sin\theta = \frac{y}{r} \qquad \cos\theta = \frac{x}{r} \qquad \tan\theta = \frac{y}{x}\ (x \neq 0)$$

$$\csc\theta = \frac{r}{y}\ (y \neq 0) \qquad \sec\theta = \frac{r}{x}\ (x \neq 0) \qquad \cot\theta = \frac{x}{y}\ (y \neq 0)$$

Therefore, the algebraic sign, + or −, of each trigonometric function will depend on which quadrant contains the terminal side of angle θ. Let us look at the three main trigonometric functions: sine, cosine, and tangent. In quadrant I, all three functions are positive since x, y, and r are all positive. However, in quadrant II, only sine is positive since y and r are both positive. In quadrant III, only tangent is positive, and in quadrant IV, only cosine is positive. The expression "**A**ll **S**tudents **T**ake **C**alculus" helps us remember which of the three main trigonometric functions are positive in each quadrant.

STUDY TIP

All Students Take Calculus is an expression that helps us remember which of the three (sine, cosine, tangent) functions are positive in quadrants I, II, III, and IV.

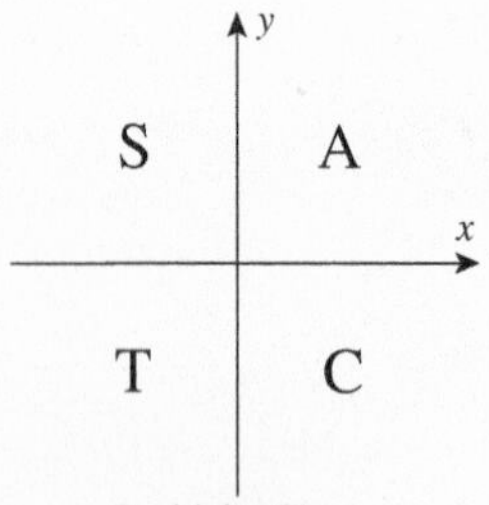

Positivity Chart

PHRASE	QUADRANT	POSITIVE TRIGONOMETRIC FUNCTION
All	I	**A**ll three: sine, cosine, and tangent
Students	II	**S**ine
Take	III	**T**angent
Calculus	IV	**C**osine

The following table indicates the algebraic sign of all six trigonometric functions according to the quadrant in which the terminal side of an angle θ lies. Notice that the reciprocal functions have the same sign.

TERMINAL SIDE OF θ IS IN QUADRANT	$\sin\theta$	$\cos\theta$	$\tan\theta$	$\cot\theta$	$\sec\theta$	$\csc\theta$
I	+	+	+	+	+	+
II	+	−	−	−	−	+
III	−	−	+	+	−	−
IV	−	+	−	−	+	−

EXAMPLE 3 **Evaluating a Trigonometric Function When One Trigonometric Function Value and the Quadrant of the Terminal Side Is Known**

If $\cos\theta = -\frac{3}{5}$ and the terminal side of angle θ lies in quadrant III, find $\sin\theta$.

Solution:

STEP 1 **Draw some angle θ in quadrant III.**

STEP 2 **Identify known quantities from the information given.**

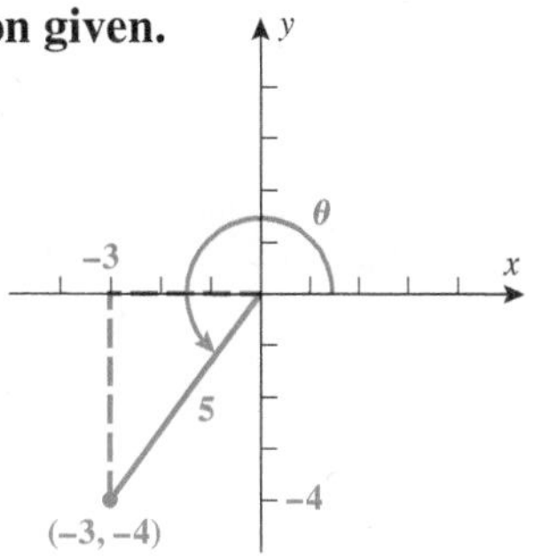

Recall that $\cos\theta = \frac{x}{r}$ and $r > 0$. $\quad \cos\theta = -\frac{3}{5} = \frac{-3}{5} = \frac{x}{r}$

Identify x and r. $\quad x = -3$ and $r = 5$

STEP 3 **Since x and r are known, find y.**

Substitute $x = -3$ and $r = 5$ into $x^2 + y^2 = r^2$. $\quad (-3)^2 + y^2 = 5^2$

Solve for y.

$$9 + y^2 = 25$$
$$y^2 = 16$$
$$y = \pm 4$$

STEP 4 **Select the sign of y based on quadrant information.**

Since the terminal side of angle θ lies in quadrant III, $y < 0$. $\quad y = -4$

STEP 5 **Find $\sin\theta$.** $\quad \sin\theta = \frac{y}{r} = \frac{-4}{5}$

$$\boxed{\sin\theta = -\frac{4}{5}}$$

YOUR TURN If $\sin\theta = -\frac{3}{4}$ and the terminal side of angle θ lies in quadrant III, find $\cos\theta$.

ANSWER

$\cos\theta = -\frac{\sqrt{7}}{4}$

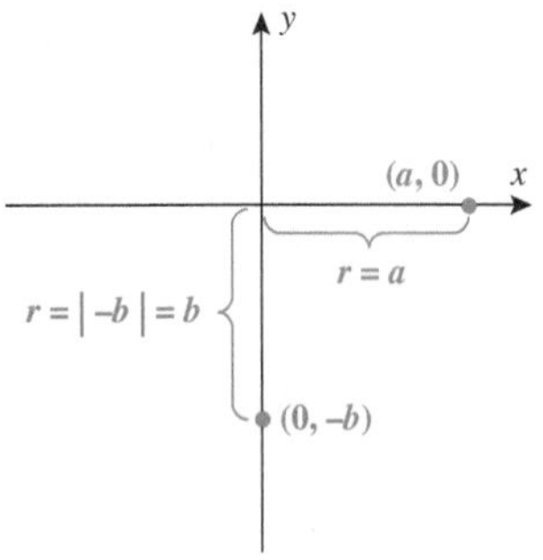

We can also make a table showing the values of the trigonometric functions when the terminal side of angle θ lies along each axis (i.e., when θ is any of the quadrantal angles).

When the terminal side lies along the x-axis, then $y = 0$. When $y = 0$, notice that $r = \sqrt{x^2 + y^2} = \sqrt{x^2} = |x|$. When the terminal side lies along the positive x-axis, $x > 0$; and when the terminal side lies along the negative x-axis, $x < 0$. Therefore, when the terminal side of the angle lies on the positive x-axis, then $y = 0$, $x > 0$, and $r = x$; and when the terminal side lies along the negative x-axis, then $y = 0$, $x < 0$, and $r = |x|$. A similar argument can be made when the terminal side lies along the y-axis, which results in $r = |y|$.

TERMINAL SIDE OF θ LIES ALONG THE	$\sin\theta$	$\cos\theta$	$\tan\theta$	$\cot\theta$	$\sec\theta$	$\csc\theta$
Positive x-axis (e.g., 0° or 360° or 0 or 2π)	0	1	0	undefined	1	undefined
Positive y-axis $\left(\text{e.g., } 90° \text{ or } \frac{\pi}{2}\right)$	1	0	undefined	0	undefined	1
Negative x-axis (e.g., 180° or π)	0	−1	0	undefined	−1	undefined
Negative y-axis $\left(\text{e.g., } 270° \text{ or } \frac{3\pi}{2}\right)$	−1	0	undefined	0	undefined	−1

EXAMPLE 4 **Working with Values of the Trigonometric Functions for Quadrantal Angles**

Evaluate each of the following expressions, if possible:

a. $\cos 540° + \sin 270°$ **b.** $\cot\left(\frac{\pi}{2}\right) + \tan\left(-\frac{\pi}{2}\right)$

Solution (a):

The terminal side of an angle with measure 540° lies along the negative x-axis. $540° - 360° = 180°$

Evaluate cosine of an angle whose terminal side lies along the negative x-axis. $\cos 540° = -1$

Evaluate sine of an angle whose terminal side lies along the negative y-axis. $\sin 270° = -1$

Sum the sine and cosine values. $\cos 540° + \sin 270° = -1 + (-1)$

$$\cos 540° + \sin 270° = \boxed{-2}$$

Check: Evaluate this expression with a calculator.

Solution (b):

Evaluate cotangent of an angle whose terminal side lies along the positive y-axis. $\cot\left(\frac{\pi}{2}\right) = 0$

The terminal side of an angle with measure $-\frac{\pi}{2}$ lies along the negative y-axis. $\tan\left(-\frac{\pi}{2}\right) = \tan\left(\frac{3\pi}{2}\right)$

The tangent function is undefined for an angle whose terminal side lies along the negative y-axis. $\tan\left(-\frac{\pi}{2}\right)$ is $\boxed{\text{undefined}}$

Even though $\cot\left(\frac{\pi}{2}\right)$ is defined, since $\tan\left(-\frac{\pi}{2}\right)$ is undefined, the sum of the two expressions is also undefined.

YOUR TURN Evaluate each of the following expressions, if possible:

a. $\csc\left(\frac{\pi}{2}\right) + \sec\pi$ **b.** $\csc(-630°) + \sec(-630°)$

ANSWER

a. 0 **b.** undefined

4.3.3 Ranges of the Trigonometric Functions

4.3.3 SKILL

Determine the ranges of the six trigonometric functions.

4.3.3 CONCEPTUAL

Understand why sine and cosine range between -1 and 1.

Thus far, we have discussed the algebraic sign of a trigonometric function value for an angle in a particular quadrant, but we haven't discussed how to find actual values of the trigonometric functions for nonacute angles. We will need to define *reference angles* and reference right triangles. However, before we proceed, let's get a feel for the ranges (set of values of the functions) we will expect.

Let us start with an angle θ in quadrant I and the sine function defined as the ratio $\sin\theta = \frac{y}{r}$.

$$\sin\theta = \frac{y}{r}$$

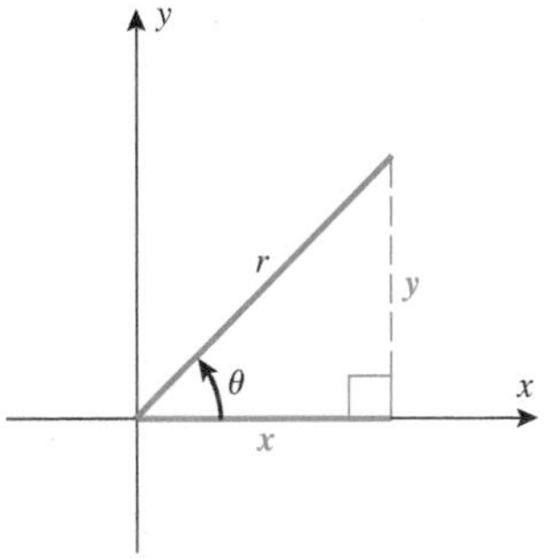

If we keep the value of r constant, then as the measure of θ increases toward 90° or $\frac{\pi}{2}$, y increases. Notice that the value of y approaches the value of r until they are equal when $\theta = 90°\left(\text{or } \frac{\pi}{2}\right)$, and y can never be larger than r.

[CONCEPT CHECK]

The value of r is always (greater than/less than) the values of both x and y.

ANSWER greater than

$$y \leq r$$

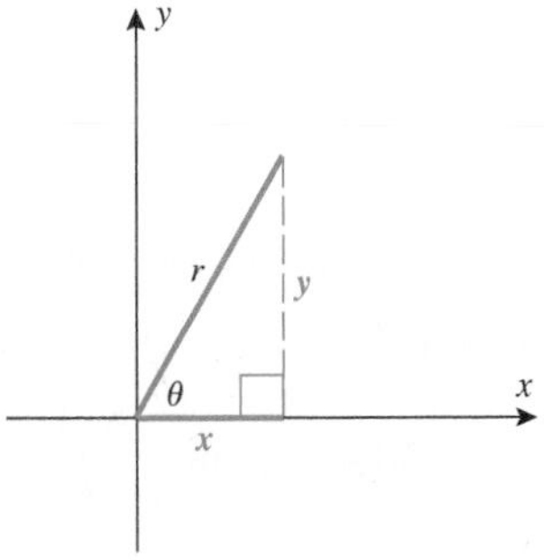

A similar analysis can be conducted in quadrant IV as θ approaches $-90°$ from $0°$ (note that y is negative in quadrant IV). A result that is valid in all four quadrants is $|y| \le r$.

WORDS	MATH
Write the absolute value inequality as a double inequality.	$-r \le y \le r$
Divide both sides by r.	$-1 \le \frac{y}{r} \le 1$
Let $\sin\theta = \frac{y}{r}$.	$-1 \le \sin\theta \le 1$

Similarly, by allowing θ to approach $0°$ and $180°$, we can show that $|x| \le r$, which leads to the range of the cosine function: $-1 \le \cos\theta \le 1$. Sine and cosine values range between -1 and 1, and since secant and cosecant are reciprocals of the cosine and sine functions, respectively, their ranges are stated as

$$\sec\theta \le -1 \text{ or } \sec\theta \ge 1 \qquad \csc\theta \le -1 \text{ or } \csc\theta \ge 1$$

Since $\tan\theta = \frac{y}{x}$ and $\cot\theta = \frac{x}{y}$ and since $x < y, x = y$, and $x > y$ are all possible, the values of the tangent and cotangent functions can be any real numbers (positive, negative, or zero). The following box summarizes the ranges of the trigonometric functions.

RANGES OF THE TRIGONOMETRIC FUNCTIONS

For any angle θ for which the trigonometric functions are defined, the six trigonometric functions have the following ranges:

- $-1 \le \sin\theta \le 1$
- $-1 \le \cos\theta \le 1$
- $\tan\theta$ and $\cot\theta$ can equal any real number.
- $\sec\theta \le -1$ or $\sec\theta \ge 1$
- $\csc\theta \le -1$ or $\csc\theta \ge 1$

EXAMPLE 5 Determining Whether a Value Is within the Range of a Trigonometric Function

Determine whether each statement is possible or not.

a. $\cos\theta = 1.001$

b. $\cot\theta = 0$

c. $\sec\theta = \frac{\sqrt{3}}{2}$

Solution (a): Not possible, because $1.001 > 1$.

Solution (b): Possible, because $\cot 90° = 0$.

Solution (c): Not possible, because $\frac{\sqrt{3}}{2} \approx 0.866 < 1$.

YOUR TURN Determine whether each statement is possible or not.

a. $\sin\theta = -1.1$ **b.** $\tan\theta = 2$ **c.** $\csc\theta = \sqrt{3}$

ANSWER

a. not possible
b. possible
c. possible

4.3.4 Reference Angles and Reference Right Triangles

Now that we know the trigonometric function ranges and their algebraic signs in each of the four quadrants, we can evaluate the trigonometric functions of nonacute angles. Before we do that, however, we first must discuss *reference angles* and *reference right triangles*.

Every nonquadrantal angle in standard position has a corresponding *reference angle* and *reference right triangle*. We have already calculated the trigonometric function values for quadrantal angles.

4.3.4 SKILL

Determine the reference angle for any angle whose terminal side lies in one of the four quadrants.

4.3.4 CONCEPTUAL

Recognize that reference angles are acute and have positive measure.

DEFINITION Reference Angle

For angle θ, $0° < \theta < 360°$ or $0 < \theta < 2\pi$, in standard position, whose terminal side lies in one of the four quadrants, there exists a **reference angle** α, which is the acute angle formed by the terminal side of angle θ and the x-axis.

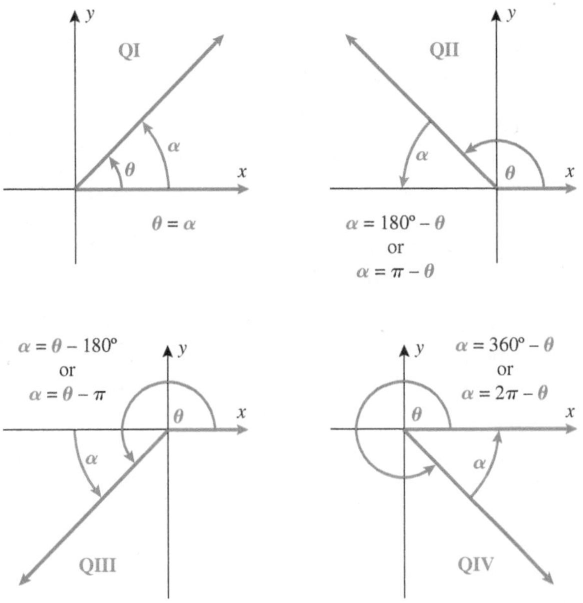

STUDY TIP

The reference angle is the acute angle that the terminal side makes with the x-axis, not the y-axis.

CONCEPT CHECK

Which of the following statements is(are) true of the reference angle?

(A) It is the angle made by the terminal side and the x-axis.
(B) It is positive.
(C) It is an acute angle.
(D) all of these

ANSWER (D)

The reference angle is the positive, acute angle that the terminal side makes with the x-axis.

EXAMPLE 6 Finding Reference Angles

Find the reference angle for each angle given.

a. 210° **b.** $\dfrac{3\pi}{4}$ **c.** 422°

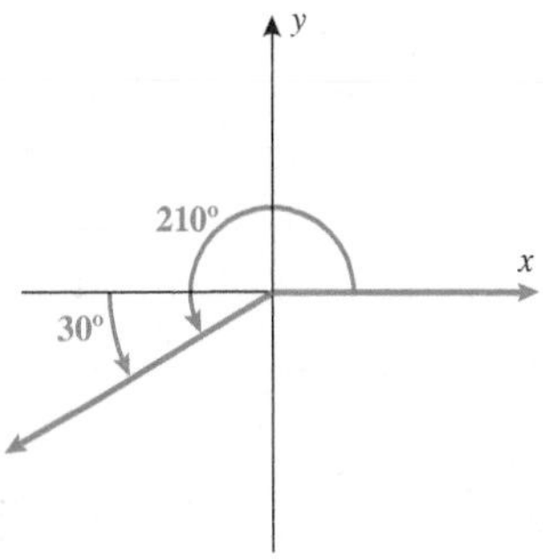

Solution (a):

The terminal side of angle θ lies in quadrant III.

The reference angle is formed by the terminal side and the negative x-axis.

$210° - 180° = \boxed{30°}$

Solution (b):

The terminal side of angle θ lies in quadrant II.

The reference angle is formed by the terminal side and the negative x-axis.

$$\pi - \frac{3\pi}{4} = \boxed{\frac{\pi}{4}}$$

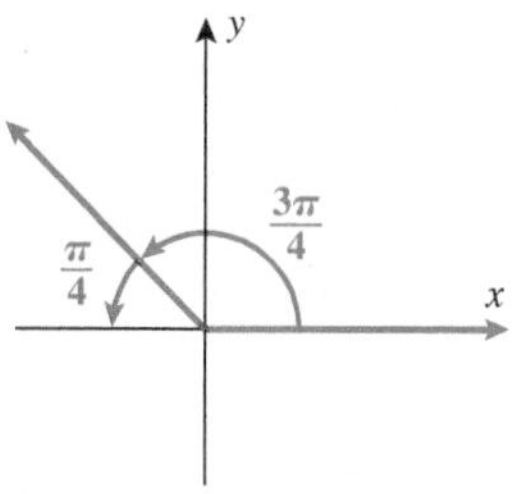

Solution (c):

The terminal side of angle θ lies in quadrant I.

The reference angle is formed by the terminal side and the positive x-axis.

$$422° - 360° = \boxed{62°}$$

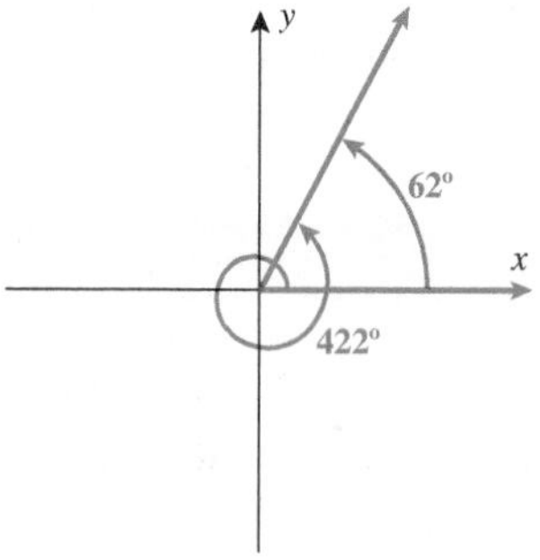

ANSWER

a. 20° b. $\frac{\pi}{4}$ c. 60°

YOUR TURN Find the reference angle for each angle given.

a. 160° **b.** $\frac{7\pi}{4}$ **c.** 600°

DEFINITION Reference Right Triangle

To form a **reference right** triangle for angle θ, where $0° < \theta < 360°$ or $0 < \theta < 2\pi$, drop a perpendicular line from the terminal side of the angle to the x-axis. The right triangle now has reference angle α as one of its acute angles.

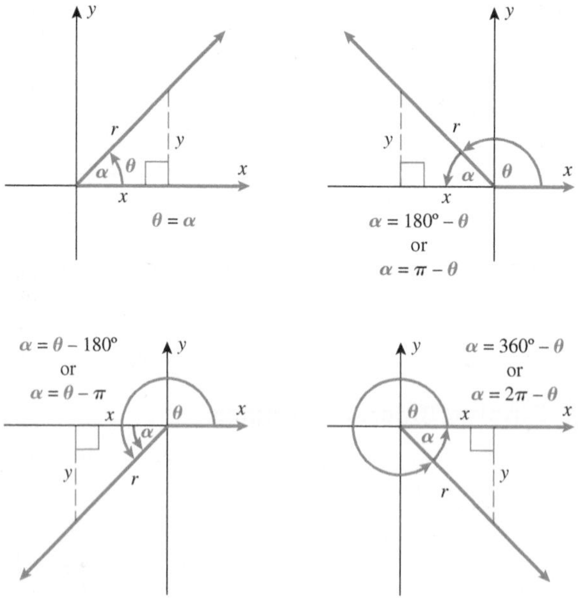

In Section 4.2, we first defined the trigonometric functions of an acute angle as ratios of lengths of sides of a right triangle. For example, $\sin\theta = \dfrac{\text{opposite}}{\text{hypotenuse}}$. The lengths of the sides of triangles are always positive.

In this section, we defined the sine function of any angle as $\sin\theta = \dfrac{y}{r}$. Notice in the previous definition box that for a nonacute angle θ, $\sin\theta = \dfrac{y}{r}$; and for the acute reference angle α, $\sin\alpha = \dfrac{|y|}{r}$. The only difference between these two expressions is the algebraic sign, since r is always positive and y is positive or negative depending on the quadrant.

Therefore, to calculate the trigonometric function values for a nonacute angle, simply find the trigonometric values for the reference angle and determine the correct algebraic sign according to the quadrant in which the terminal side lies.

STUDY TIP

To find the trigonometric function values of nonacute angles, first find the trigonometric values of the reference angle and then use the quadrant information to determine the algebraic sign.

4.3.5 Evaluating Trigonometric Functions for Nonacute Angles

4.3.5 SKILL

Evaluate trigonometric functions for nonacute and quadrantal angles.

4.3.5 CONCEPTUAL

Understand that the value of a trigonometric function at an angle is the same as the trigonometric value of its reference angle, except that there may be a difference in its algebraic sign (+/−).

Let's look at a specific example before we generalize a procedure for evaluating trigonometric function values for nonacute angles.

Suppose we have the angles in standard position with measures 60°, 120°, 240°, and 300° or $\frac{\pi}{3}, \frac{2\pi}{3}, \frac{4\pi}{3}$, and $\frac{5\pi}{3}$, respectively. Notice that the reference angle for all of these angles is 60° or $\frac{\pi}{3}$.

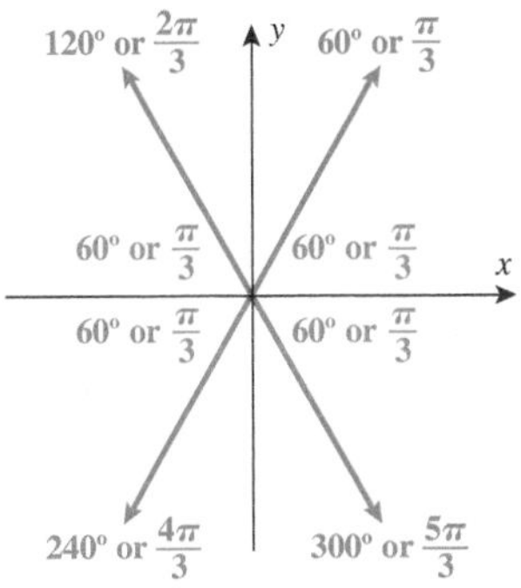

If we draw reference triangles and let the shortest leg have length 1, we find that the other leg has length $\sqrt{3}$ and the hypotenuse has length 2. (Recall the relationships for side lengths of a 30°–60°–90° triangle.)

Notice that the legs of the triangles have lengths (always positive) 1 and $\sqrt{3}$; however, the coordinates are $(\pm 1, \pm\sqrt{3})$. Therefore, when we calculate the trigonometric functions for any of the angles, $60°\left(\frac{\pi}{3}\right), 120°\left(\frac{2\pi}{3}\right), 240°\left(\frac{4\pi}{3}\right)$, and $300°\left(\frac{5\pi}{3}\right)$, we can simply calculate the trigonometric functions for the reference angle, $60°\left(\frac{\pi}{3}\right)$, and determine the algebraic sign (+ or −) for the particular trigonometric function and quadrant.

[CONCEPT CHECK]

If the terminal side lies in a quadrant other than I, the cosine is positive, and the sine is the negative of the reference angle, then the terminal side lies in which quadrant?

ANSWER quadrant IV

STUDY TIP

The value of a trigonometric function of an angle is the same as the trigonometric value of its reference angle, except there may be an algebraic sign (+ or −) difference between the two values.

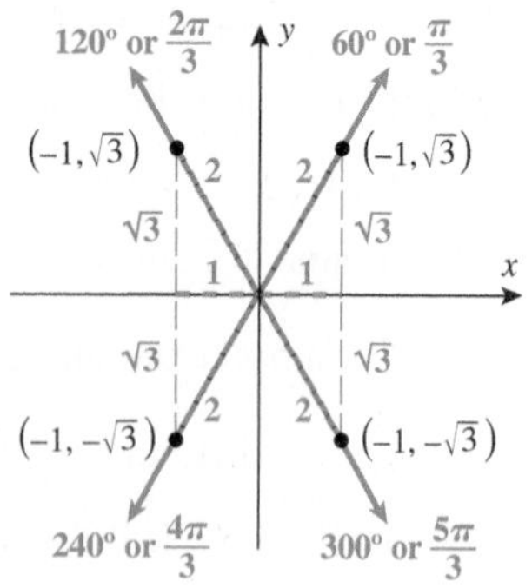

To find the value of $\cos 120°$, we first recognize that the terminal side of an angle with 120° measure lies in quadrant II. We also know that cosine is negative in quadrant II. We then calculate the cosine of the reference angle, 60°.

$$\cos 60° = \frac{\text{adjacent}}{\text{hypotenuse}} = \frac{1}{2}$$

Since we know $\cos 120°$ is negative because it lies in quadrant II, we know that

$$\cos 120° = -\frac{1}{2}$$

Similarly, we know that $\cos 240° = -\frac{1}{2}$ and $\cos 300° = \frac{1}{2}$.

For any angle whose terminal side lies along one of the axes, we consult the table in this section for the values of the trigonometric functions for quadrantal angles. If the terminal side lies in one of the four quadrants, then the angle is said to be nonquadrantal and the following procedure can be used.

PROCEDURE FOR EVALUATING FUNCTION VALUES FOR ANY NONQUADRANTAL ANGLE θ

Step 1:
- If $0° < \theta < 360°$ or $0 < \theta < 2\pi$, proceed to Step 2.
- If $\theta < 0°$, add 360° as many times as needed to get a coterminal angle with measure between 0° and 360°. Similarly, if $\theta < 0$, add 2π as many times as needed to get a coterminal angle with measure between 0 and 2π.
- If $\theta > 360°$, subtract 360° as many times as needed to get a coterminal angle with measure between 0° and 360°. Similarly, if $\theta > 2\pi$, subtract 2π as many times as needed to get a coterminal angle with measure between 0 and 2π.

Step 2: Find the quadrant in which the terminal side of the angle in Step 1 lies.
Step 3: Find the reference angle α of the angle found in Step 1.
Step 4: Find the trigonometric function values for the reference angle α.
Step 5: Determine the correct algebraic signs (+ or −) for the trigonometric function values based on the quadrant identified in Step 2.
Step 6: Combine the trigonometric values found in Step 4 with the algebraic signs in Step 5 to get the trigonometric function values of θ.

We follow the above procedure for all angles except when we get to Step 4. In Step 4, we evaluate exactly, if possible, the special angles $\left(30°, 45°, 60° \text{ or } \frac{\pi}{6}, \frac{\pi}{4}, \frac{\pi}{3}\right)$; otherwise, we use a calculator to approximate.

EXAMPLE 7 Evaluating the Cosine Function of a Special Angle Exactly

Find the exact value of $\cos 210°$.

Solution:

The terminal side of $\theta = 210°$ lies in quadrant III.

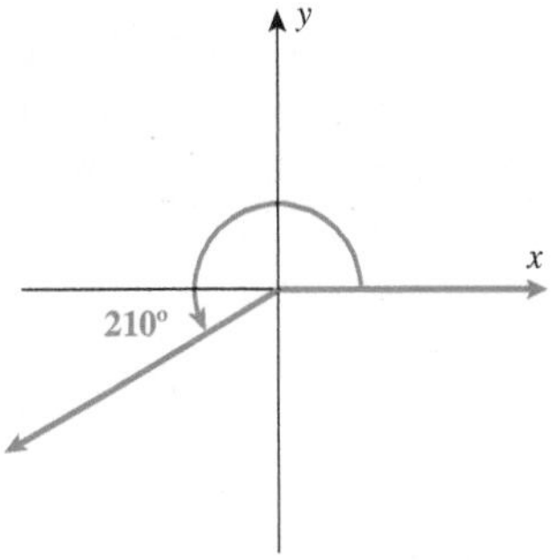

Find the reference angle for $\theta = 210°$. $\quad 210° - 180° = 30°$

Find the value of the cosine of the reference angle. $\quad \cos 30° = \dfrac{\sqrt{3}}{2}$

Determine the algebraic sign for the cosine in quadrant III. $\quad$ Negative $(-)$

Combine the algebraic sign of the cosine in quadrant III with the value of the cosine of the reference angle. $\quad \cos 210° = -\dfrac{\sqrt{3}}{2}$

YOUR TURN Find the exact value of $\sin 330°$.

ANSWER
$-\frac{1}{2}$

EXAMPLE 8 Evaluating the Cosecant Function of a Special Angle Exactly

Find the exact value of $\csc\left(-\dfrac{7\pi}{6}\right)$.

Solution:

Add 2π to get a coterminal angle between 0 and 2π. $\quad -\dfrac{7\pi}{6} + 2\pi = \dfrac{5\pi}{6}$

The terminal side of the angle lies in quadrant II.

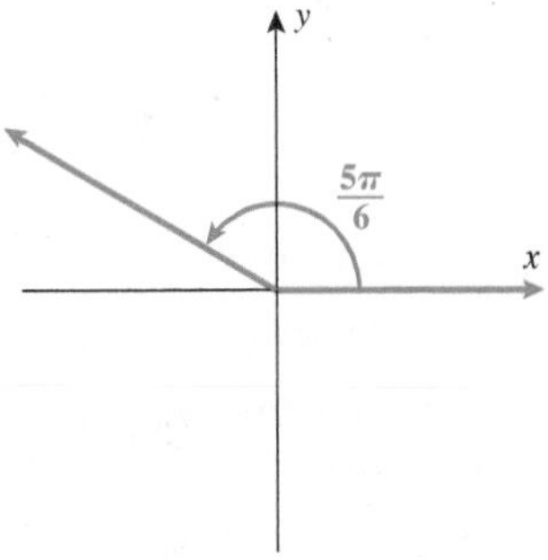

Find the reference angle for the angle with measure $\dfrac{5\pi}{6}$. $\quad \pi - \dfrac{5\pi}{6} = \dfrac{\pi}{6}$

Find the value of the cosecant of the reference angle. $\quad \csc\left(\dfrac{\pi}{6}\right) = \dfrac{1}{\sin\left(\dfrac{\pi}{6}\right)} = \dfrac{1}{\frac{1}{2}} = 2$

Determine the algebraic sign for the cosecant in quadrant II. — Positive (+)

Combine the algebraic sign of the cosecant in quadrant II with the value of the cosecant of the reference angle. — $\csc\left(-\frac{7\pi}{6}\right) = \boxed{2}$

YOUR TURN Find the exact value of $\sec\left(-\frac{11\pi}{6}\right)$.

ANSWER
$\frac{2\sqrt{3}}{3}$

EXAMPLE 9 Finding Exact Angle Measures Given Trigonometric Function Values

Find all values of θ, where $0° \leq \theta \leq 360°$, when $\sin\theta = -\frac{\sqrt{3}}{2}$.

Solution:

Determine in which quadrants sine is negative. — QIII and QIV

Since the absolute value of $\sin\theta$ is $\frac{\sqrt{3}}{2}$, the reference angle has measure 60°. — $\sin 60° = \frac{\sqrt{3}}{2}$

Determine the angles between 180° and 360° in quadrants III and IV with reference angle 60°.

Quadrant III: — $180° + 60° = 240°$

Quadrant IV: — $360° - 60° = 300°$

The two angles are $\boxed{240°}$ and $\boxed{300°}$.

YOUR TURN Find all values of θ, where $0° \leq \theta \leq 360°$, when $\cos\theta = -\frac{\sqrt{3}}{2}$.

ANSWER
150° and 210°

EXAMPLE 10 Finding Approximate Angle Measures Given Trigonometric Function Values

Find the measure of an angle θ (rounded to the nearest degree) if $\sin\theta = -0.6293$ and the terminal side of θ (in standard position) lies in quadrant III, where $0° \leq \theta \leq 360°$.

Solution:

The sine of the reference angle is 0.6293. — $\sin\alpha = 0.6293$

Find the reference angle. — $\alpha = \sin^{-1}(0.6293) \approx 38.998°$

Round the reference angle to the nearest degree. — $\alpha \approx 39°$

Find θ, which lies in quadrant III. — $\theta \approx 180° + 39° \approx 219°$

$\boxed{\theta \approx 219°}$

Check with a calculator. — $\sin 219° \approx -0.6293$

YOUR TURN Find the measure of θ, the smallest positive angle (rounded to the nearest degree), if $\cos\theta = -0.5299$ and the terminal side of θ (in standard position) lies in quadrant II.

ANSWER
122°

[SECTION 4.3] SUMMARY

The trigonometric functions are defined in the Cartesian plane for any angle as follows:

Let (x, y) be a point, other than the origin, on the terminal side of an angle θ in standard position. Let r be the distance from the point (x, y) to the origin. Then the sine, cosine, and tangent functions are defined as

$$\sin\theta = \frac{y}{r} \qquad \cos\theta = \frac{x}{r} \qquad \tan\theta = \frac{y}{x} \quad (x \neq 0)$$

The range of the sine and cosine functions is $[-1, 1]$, whereas the range of the secant and cosecant functions is $(-\infty, -1] \cup [1, \infty)$.

Reference angles and reference right triangles can be used to evaluate trigonometric functions for nonacute angles.

[SECTION 4.3] EXERCISES

• SKILLS

In Exercises 1–14, the terminal side of an angle θ in standard position passes through the indicated point. Calculate the values of the six trigonometric functions for angle θ.

1. $(3, 6)$
2. $(8, 4)$
3. $\left(\frac{1}{2}, \frac{2}{5}\right)$
4. $\left(\frac{4}{7}, \frac{2}{3}\right)$
5. $(-2, 4)$
6. $(-1, 3)$
7. $(-4, -7)$
8. $(-9, -5)$
9. $(-\sqrt{2}, \sqrt{3})$
10. $(-\sqrt{3}, \sqrt{2})$
11. $(-\sqrt{5}, -\sqrt{3})$
12. $(-\sqrt{6}, -\sqrt{5})$
13. $\left(-\frac{10}{3}, -\frac{4}{3}\right)$
14. $\left(-\frac{2}{9}, -\frac{1}{3}\right)$

In Exercises 15–24, indicate the quadrant in which the terminal side of θ must lie in order for the information to be true.

15. $\cos\theta$ is positive and $\sin\theta$ is negative.
16. $\cos\theta$ is negative and $\sin\theta$ is positive.
17. $\tan\theta$ is negative and $\sin\theta$ is positive.
18. $\tan\theta$ is positive and $\cos\theta$ is negative.
19. $\sec\theta$ and $\csc\theta$ are both positive.
20. $\sec\theta$ and $\csc\theta$ are both negative.
21. $\cot\theta$ and $\cos\theta$ are both positive.
22. $\cot\theta$ and $\sin\theta$ are both negative.
23. $\tan\theta$ is positive and $\sec\theta$ is negative.
24. $\cot\theta$ is negative and $\csc\theta$ is positive.

In Exercises 25–36, find the indicated trigonometric function values.

25. If $\cos\theta = -\frac{3}{5}$, and the terminal side of θ lies in quadrant III, find $\sin\theta$.

26. If $\tan\theta = -\frac{5}{12}$, and the terminal side of θ lies in quadrant II, find $\cos\theta$.

27. If $\sin\theta = \frac{60}{61}$, and the terminal side of θ lies in quadrant II, find $\tan\theta$.

28. If $\cos\theta = \frac{40}{41}$, and the terminal side of θ lies in quadrant IV, find $\tan\theta$.

29. If $\tan\theta = \frac{84}{13}$, and the terminal side of θ lies in quadrant III, find $\sin\theta$.

30. If $\sin\theta = -\frac{7}{25}$, and the terminal side of θ lies in quadrant IV, find $\cos\theta$.

31. If $\sec\theta = -2$, and the terminal side of θ lies in quadrant III, find $\tan\theta$.

32. If $\cot\theta = 1$, and the terminal side of θ lies in quadrant I, find $\sin\theta$.

33. If $\csc\theta = \frac{2}{\sqrt{3}}$, and the terminal side of θ lies in quadrant II, find $\cot\theta$.

34. If $\sec\theta = -\frac{13}{5}$, and the terminal side of θ lies in quadrant II, find $\csc\theta$.

35. If $\cot\theta = -\sqrt{3}$, and the terminal side of θ lies in quadrant IV, find $\sec\theta$.

36. If $\cot\theta = -\frac{13}{84}$, and the terminal side of θ lies in quadrant II, find $\csc\theta$.

In Exercises 37–46, evaluate each expression, if possible.

37. $\cos(-270°) + \sin 450°$ **38.** $\sin(-270°) + \cos 450°$ **39.** $\sin 630° + \tan(-540°)$ **40.** $\cos(-720°) + \tan 720°$

41. $\cos(3\pi) - \sec(-3\pi)$ **42.** $\sin\left(-\frac{5\pi}{2}\right) + \csc\left(\frac{3\pi}{2}\right)$ **43.** $\csc\left(-\frac{7\pi}{2}\right) - \cot\left(\frac{7\pi}{2}\right)$ **44.** $\sec(-3\pi) + \tan(3\pi)$

45. $\tan 720° + \sec 720°$ **46.** $\cot 450° - \cos(-450°)$

In Exercises 47–56, determine whether each statement is possible or not.

47. $\sin\theta = -0.999$ **48.** $\cos\theta = 1.0001$ **49.** $\cos\theta = \frac{2\sqrt{6}}{3}$ **50.** $\sin\theta = \frac{\sqrt{2}}{10}$ **51.** $\tan\theta = 4\sqrt{5}$

52. $\cot\theta = -\frac{\sqrt{6}}{7}$ **53.** $\sec\theta = -\frac{4}{\sqrt{7}}$ **54.** $\csc\theta = \frac{\pi}{2}$ **55.** $\cot\theta = 500$ **56.** $\sec\theta = 0.9996$

In Exercises 57–68, evaluate the following expressions *exactly*:

57. $\cos 240°$ **58.** $\cos 120°$ **59.** $\sin\left(\frac{5\pi}{3}\right)$ **60.** $\sin\left(\frac{7\pi}{4}\right)$

61. $\tan 210°$ **62.** $\sec 135°$ **63.** $\tan(-315°)$ **64.** $\sec(-330°)$

65. $\csc\left(\frac{11\pi}{6}\right)$ **66.** $\csc\left(-\frac{4\pi}{3}\right)$ **67.** $\cot(-315°)$ **68.** $\cot 150°$

In Exercises 69–76, find all possible values of θ, where $0° \leq \theta \leq 360°$.

69. $\cos\theta = \frac{\sqrt{3}}{2}$ **70.** $\sin\theta = \frac{\sqrt{3}}{2}$ **71.** $\sin\theta = -\frac{1}{2}$ **72.** $\cos\theta = -\frac{1}{2}$

73. $\cos\theta = 0$ **74.** $\sin\theta = 0$ **75.** $\sin\theta = -1$ **76.** $\cos\theta = -1$

In Exercises 77–90, find the smallest positive measure of θ (rounded to the nearest degree) if the indicated information is true.

77. $\sin\theta = 0.9397$ and the terminal side of θ lies in quadrant II.

78. $\cos\theta = 0.7071$ and the terminal side of θ lies in quadrant IV.

79. $\cos\theta = -0.7986$ and the terminal side of θ lies in quadrant II.

80. $\sin\theta = -0.1746$ and the terminal side of θ lies in quadrant III.

81. $\tan\theta = -0.7813$ and the terminal side of θ lies in quadrant IV.

82. $\cos\theta = -0.3420$ and the terminal side of θ lies in quadrant III.

83. $\tan\theta = -0.8391$ and the terminal side of θ lies in quadrant II.

84. $\tan\theta = 11.4301$ and the terminal side of θ lies in quadrant III.

85. $\sin\theta = -0.3420$ and the terminal side of θ lies in quadrant IV.

86. $\sin\theta = -0.4226$ and the terminal side of θ lies in quadrant III.

87. $\sec\theta = 1.0001$ and the terminal side of θ lies in quadrant I.

88. $\sec\theta = -3.1421$ and the terminal side of θ lies in quadrant II.

89. $\csc\theta = -2.3604$ and the terminal side of θ lies in quadrant IV.

90. $\csc\theta = -1.0001$ and the terminal side of θ lies in quadrant III.

• APPLICATIONS

In Exercises 91–94, refer to the following:

When light passes from one substance to another, such as from air to water, its path bends. This is called refraction and is what is seen in eyeglass lenses, camera lenses, and gems. The rule governing the change in the path is called *Snell's law*, named after a Dutch astronomer: $n_1 \sin\theta_1 = n_2 \sin\theta_2$, where n_1 and n_2 are the indices of refraction of the different substances, and θ_1 and θ_2 are the respective angles that light makes with a line perpendicular to the surface at the boundary between substances. The figure shows the path of light rays going from air to water. Assume that the index of refraction in air is 1.

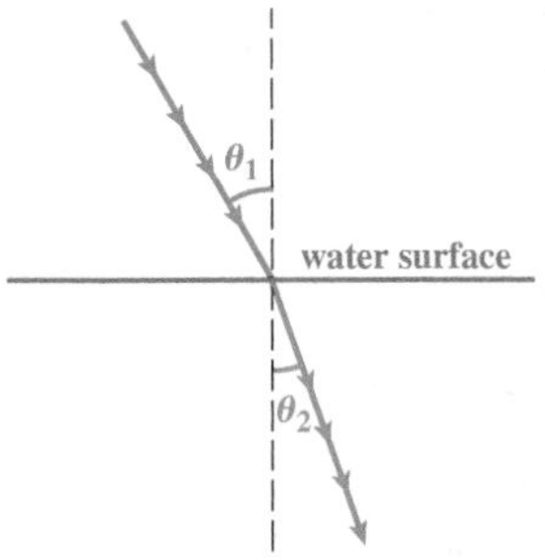

91. If light rays hit the water's surface at an angle of 30° from the perpendicular and are refracted to an angle of 22° from the perpendicular, then what is the refraction index for water? Round the answer to two significant digits.

92. If light rays hit a glass surface at an angle of 30° from the perpendicular and are refracted to an angle of 18° from the perpendicular, then what is the refraction index for that glass? Round the answer to two significant digits.

93. If the refraction index for a diamond is 2.4, then to what angle is light refracted if it enters the diamond at an angle of 30°? Round the answer to two significant digits.

94. If the refraction index for a rhinestone is 1.9, then to what angle is light refracted if it enters the rhinestone at an angle of 30°? Round the answer to two significant digits.

For Exercises 95 and 96, refer to the following:

An orthotic knee brace can be used to treat knee injuries by locking the knee at an angle θ chosen to facilitate healing. The angle θ is measured from the metal bar on the side of the brace on the thigh to the metal bar on the side of the brace on the calf (see the figure on the left above). To make working with the brace more convenient, rotate the image such that the thigh aligns with the positive x-axis (see the figure on the right below).

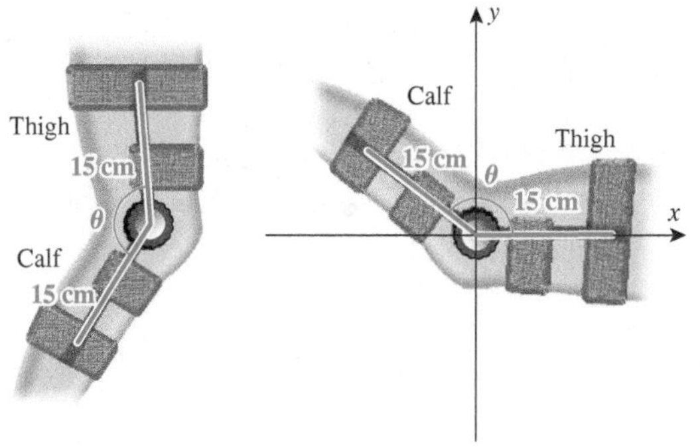

95. Health/Medicine. If $\theta = 165°$, find the measure of the reference angle. What is the physical meaning of the reference angle?

96. Health/Medicine. If $\theta = 160°$, find the measure of the reference angle. What would an angle greater than 180° represent?

For Exercises 97 and 98, refer to the following:

Water covers two-thirds of the Earth's surface, and every living thing is dependent on it. For example, the human body is over 70% water. The water molecule is composed of one oxygen atom and two hydrogen atoms and exhibits a bent shape with the oxygen molecule at the center. The angle θ between the O-H bonds is 104.5°.

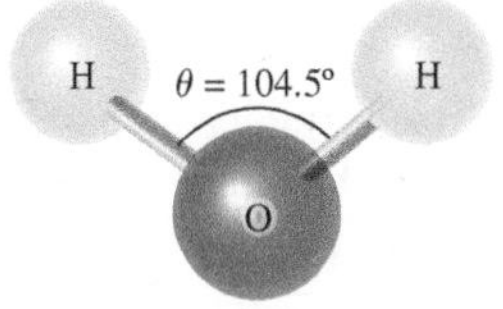

(*Source:* http://www.wiley.com/college/boyer/0470003790/reviews/pH/ph_water.htm.)

97. Chemistry. Sketch the water molecule in the xy-coordinate system in a convenient manner for illustrating angles. Find the reference angle. Illustrate both the angle θ and the reference angle on the sketch.

98. Chemistry. Find $\cos(104.5°)$ using the reference angle found in Exercise 97.

• CATCH THE MISTAKE

In Exercises 99 and 100, explain the mistake that is made.

99. Evaluate the expression $\sec 120°$ exactly.

Solution:

120° lies in quadrant II.
The reference angle is 30°.

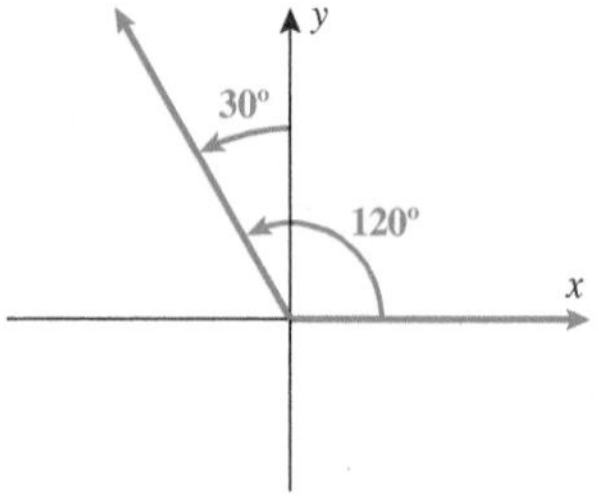

Find the cosine of the reference angle. $\cos 30° = \frac{\sqrt{3}}{2}$

Cosine is negative in quadrant II. $\cos 120° = -\frac{\sqrt{3}}{2}$

Secant is the reciprocal of cosine. $\sec 120° = -\frac{2}{\sqrt{3}} = -\frac{2\sqrt{3}}{3}$

This is incorrect. What mistake was made?

100. Find the measure of the smallest positive angle θ (rounded to the nearest degree) if $\cos\theta = -0.2388$ and the terminal side of θ (in standard position) lies in quadrant III.

Solution:

Evaluate with a calculator. $\theta = \cos^{-1}(-0.2388) = 103.8157°$

Approximate to the nearest degree. $\theta \approx 104°$

This is incorrect. What mistake was made?

• CONCEPTUAL

In Exercises 101–108, determine whether each statement is true or false.

101. It is possible for all six trigonometric functions of the same angle to have positive values.

102. It is possible for all six trigonometric functions of the same angle to have negative values.

103. The trigonometric function value for any angle with negative measure must be negative.

104. The trigonometric function value for any angle with positive measure must be positive.

105. $\sec^2\theta - 1$ can be negative for some value of θ.

106. $(\sec\theta)(\csc\theta)$ is negative only when the terminal side of θ lies in quadrant II or IV.

107. $\cos\theta = \cos(\theta + 360°n)$, where n is an integer.

108. $\sin\theta = \sin(\theta + 2\pi n)$, where n is an integer.

• CHALLENGE

109. If the terminal side of angle θ passes through the point $(-3a, 4a)$, find $\cos\theta$. Assume $a > 0$.

110. If the terminal side of angle θ passes through the point $(-3a, 4a)$, find $\sin\theta$. Assume $a > 0$.

111. Find the equation of the line with negative slope that passes through the point $(a, 0)$ and makes an acute angle θ with the x-axis. The equation of the line will be in terms of x, a, and a trigonometric function of θ. Assume $a > 0$.

112. Find the equation of the line with positive slope that passes through the point $(a, 0)$ and makes an acute angle θ with the x-axis. The equation of the line will be in terms of x, a, and a trigonometric function of θ. Assume $a > 0$.

113. If $\tan\theta = \frac{a}{b}$, where a and b are positive, and if θ lies in quadrant III, find $\sin\theta$.

114. If $\tan\theta = -\frac{a}{b}$, where a and b are positive, and if θ lies in quadrant II, find $\cos\theta$.

115. If $\csc\theta = -\frac{a}{b}$, where a and b are positive, and if θ lies in quadrant IV, find $\cot\theta$.

116. If $\sec\theta = -\frac{a}{b}$, where a and b are positive, and if θ lies in quadrant III, find $\tan\theta$.

• **PREVIEW TO CALCULUS**

In calculus, the value $F(b) - F(a)$ of a function $F(x)$ at $x = a$ and $x = b$ plays an important role in the calculation of definite integrals.

In Exercises 117–120, find the exact value of $F(b) - F(a)$.

117. $F(x) = 2\tan x + \cos x, a = -\frac{\pi}{6}, b = \frac{\pi}{4}$

118. $F(x) = \sin^2 x + \cos^2 x, a = \frac{3\pi}{4}, b = \frac{7\pi}{6}$

119. $F(x) = \sec^2 x + 1, a = \frac{5\pi}{6}, b = \frac{4\pi}{3}$

120. $F(x) = \cot x - \csc^2 x, a = \frac{7\pi}{6}, b = \frac{7\pi}{4}$

4.4 THE LAW OF SINES

SKILLS OBJECTIVE

- Solve the AAS, ASA, and SSA right triangles using the Law of Sines.

CONCEPTUAL OBJECTIVE

- Understand why an AAA case cannot be solved.

4.4.1 Solving Oblique Triangles

Thus far we have discussed only *right* triangles. There are, however, two types of triangles, right and *oblique*. An **oblique triangle** is any triangle that does not have a right angle. An oblique triangle is either an **acute triangle**, having three acute angles, or an **obtuse triangle**, having one obtuse (between 90° and 180°) angle.

4.4.1 SKILL

Solve the AAS, ASA, and SSA right triangles using the Law of Sines.

4.4.1 CONCEPTUAL

Understand why an AAA case cannot be solved.

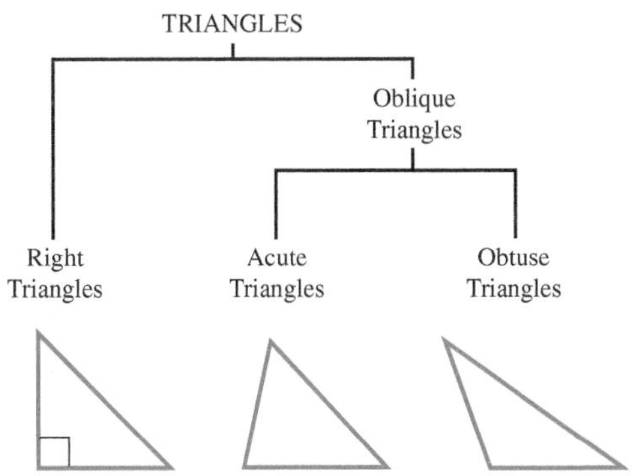

It is customary to label oblique triangles in the following way:

- angle α (alpha) opposite side a
- angle β (beta) opposite side b
- angle γ (gamma) opposite side c

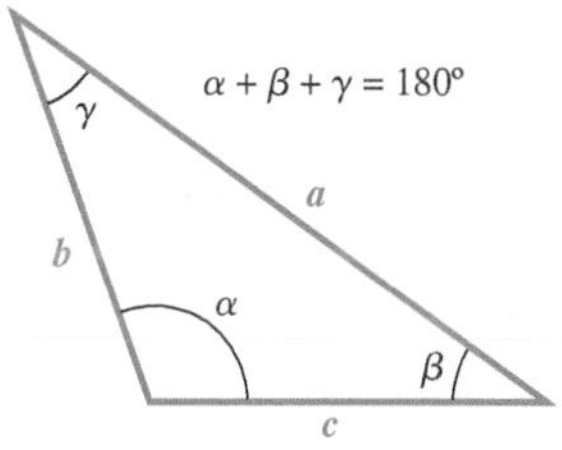

Remember that the sum of the three angles of any triangle must equal 180°. In Section 4.3, we solved right triangles. In this section, we solve oblique triangles, which means we find the lengths of all three sides and the measures of all three angles.

Four Cases

To solve an oblique triangle, *we need to know the length of one side* and one of the following three:

- two angles
- one angle and another side
- the other two sides

This requirement leads to the following four possible cases to consider:

INFORMATION REQUIRED TO SOLVE OBLIQUE TRIANGLES

CASE	WHAT'S GIVEN	EXAMPLES/NAMES	
Case 1	Measures of one side and two angles	**AAS: Angle-Angle-Side** 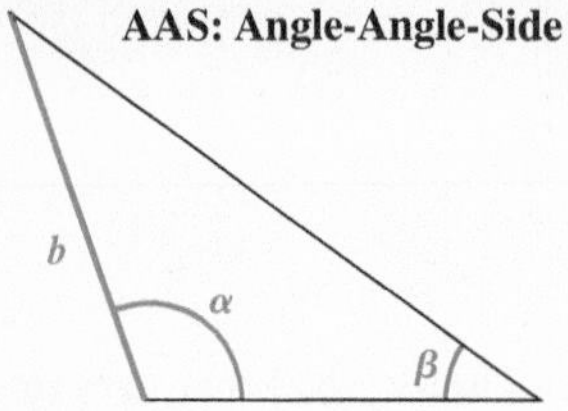	**ASA: Angle-Side-Angle** 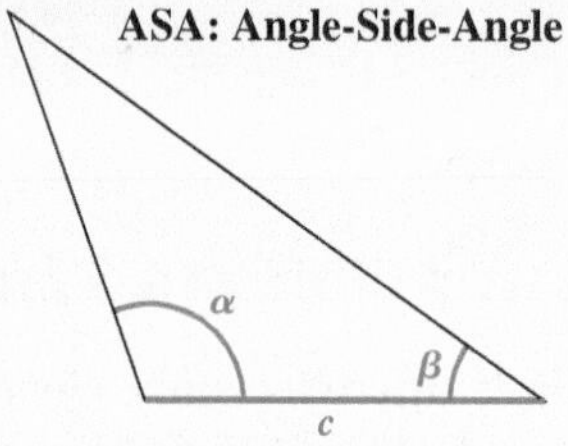
Case 2	Measures of two sides and the angle opposite one of them	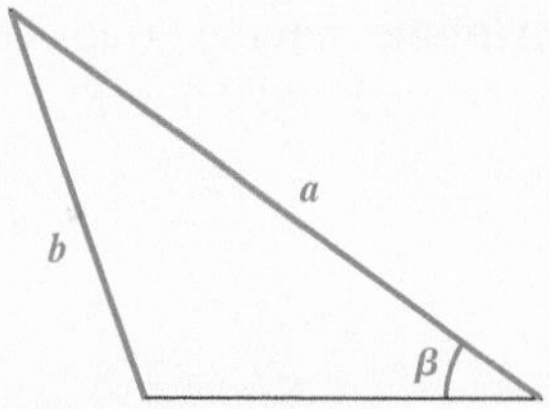	**SSA: Side-Side-Angle**
Case 3	Measures of two sides and the angle between them	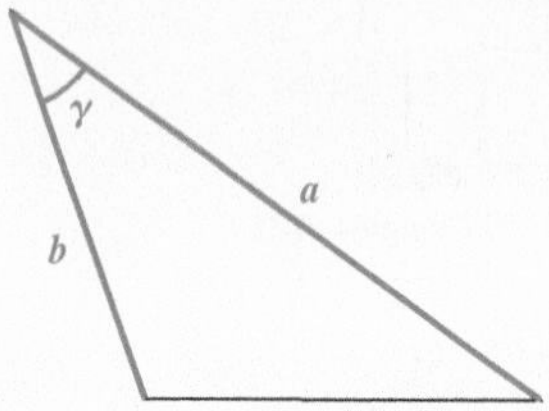	**SAS: Side-Angle-Side**
Case 4	Measures of three sides	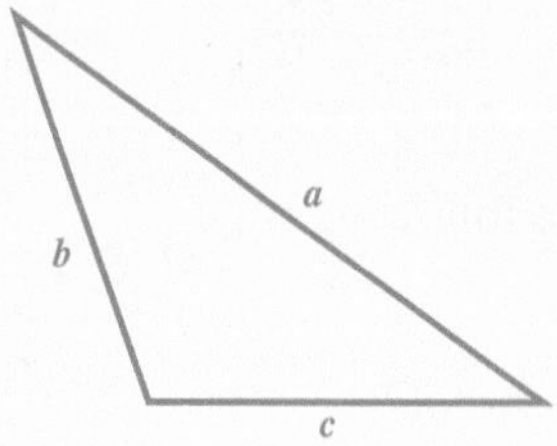	**SSS: Side-Side-Side**

Notice that there is **no AAA case**, because two similar triangles can have the same angle measures but different side lengths.

STUDY TIP

To solve triangles, at least one side must be known.

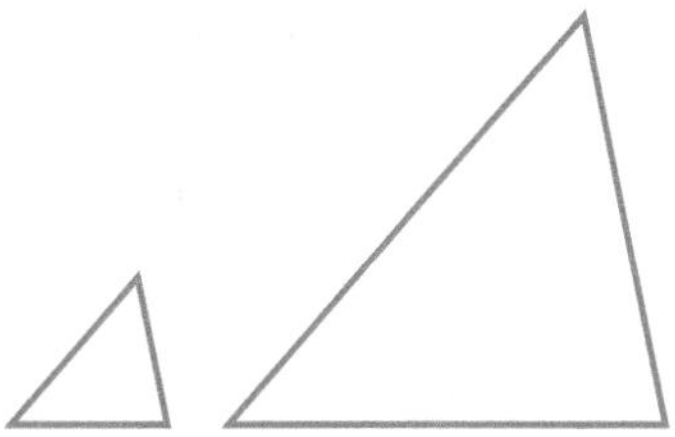

That is why at least the length of one side must be known.

In this section, we will derive the Law of Sines, which will enable us to solve Case 1 and Case 2 problems. In the next section, we will derive the Law of Cosines, which will enable us to solve Case 3 and Case 4 problems.

The Law of Sines

Let us start with two oblique triangles: an acute triangle and an obtuse triangle.

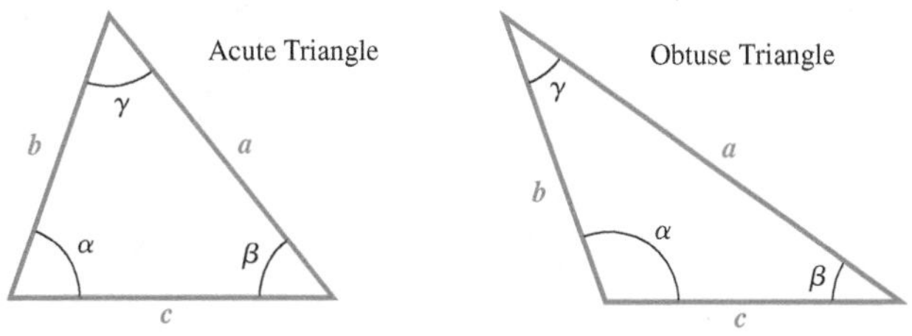

The following discussion applies to both triangles. First, construct an altitude (perpendicular) h from the vertex at angle γ to the side (or its extension) opposite γ.

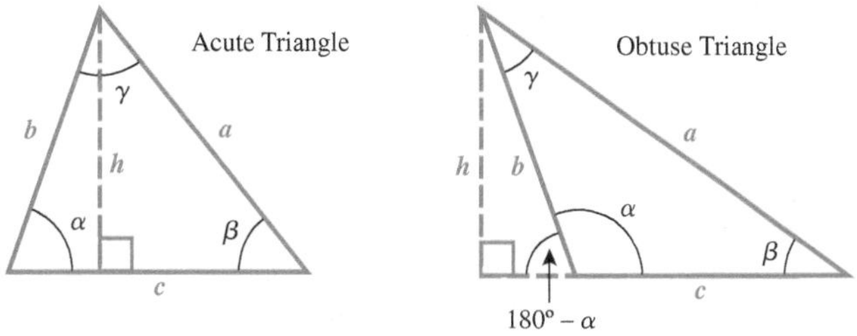

WORDS	MATH
Formulate sine ratios for the acute triangle.	$\sin\alpha = \frac{h}{b}$ and $\sin\beta = \frac{h}{a}$
Formulate sine ratios for the obtuse triangle.	$\sin(180° - \alpha) = \frac{h}{b}$ and $\sin\beta = \frac{h}{a}$
For the obtuse triangle, apply the sine difference identity.*	$\sin(180° - \alpha) = \sin 180° \cos\alpha - \cos 180° \sin\alpha$ $= 0 \cdot \cos\alpha - (-1)\sin\alpha$ $= \sin\alpha$
Therefore, in either triangle we find the same equation.	$\sin\alpha = \frac{h}{b}$ and $\sin\beta = \frac{h}{a}$
Solve for h in both equations.	$h = b\sin\alpha$ and $h = a\sin\beta$
Since h is equal to itself, equate the expressions for h.	$b\sin\alpha = a\sin\beta$

*The sine difference identity, $\sin(x - y) = \sin x \cdot \cos y - \cos x \cdot \sin y$, is derived in Section 6.2.

Divide both sides by *ab*. $\frac{b\sin\alpha}{ab} = \frac{a\sin\beta}{ab}$

Divide out common factors. $\boxed{\frac{\sin\alpha}{a} = \frac{\sin\beta}{b}}$

In a similar manner, we can extend an altitude (perpendicular) from angle α, and we will find that $\boxed{\frac{\sin\gamma}{c} = \frac{\sin\beta}{b}}$. Equating these two expressions leads us to the third ratio of the *Law of Sines*: $\boxed{\frac{\sin\alpha}{a} = \frac{\sin\gamma}{c}}$.

STUDY TIP

When an angle and the side opposite that angle are known, the Law of Sines can be used, provided one other piece of information (side length/angle measure) is known.

THE LAW OF SINES

For a triangle with sides of lengths *a*, *b*, and *c*, and opposite angles of measures α, β, and γ, the following is true:

$$\frac{\sin\alpha}{a} = \frac{\sin\beta}{b} = \frac{\sin\gamma}{c}$$

In other words, the ratio of the sine of an angle in a triangle to its opposite side is equal to the ratios of the sines of the other two angles to their opposite sides.

STUDY TIP

Remember that the longest side is opposite the largest angle; the shortest side is opposite the smallest angle.

Notice that in both Cases 1 and 2, where an angle and the side opposite that angle are known, the Law of Sines can be used as long as one other piece of information is known (i.e., side length or angle measure).

Some things to note before we begin solving oblique triangles:

- The angles and sides share the same progression of magnitude:
  - The longest side of a triangle is opposite the largest angle.
  - The shortest side of a triangle is opposite the smallest angle.
- Draw the triangle and label the angles and sides.
- If two angle measures are known, start by determining the third angle.
- Whenever possible, in successive steps always return to given values rather than referring to calculated (approximate) values.

STUDY TIP

Always use given values rather than calculated (approximated) values for better accuracy.

Keeping these pointers in mind will help you determine whether your answers are reasonable.

Case 1: Two Angles and One Side (AAS or ASA)

EXAMPLE 1 **Using the Law of Sines to Solve a Triangle (AAS)**

Solve the triangle.

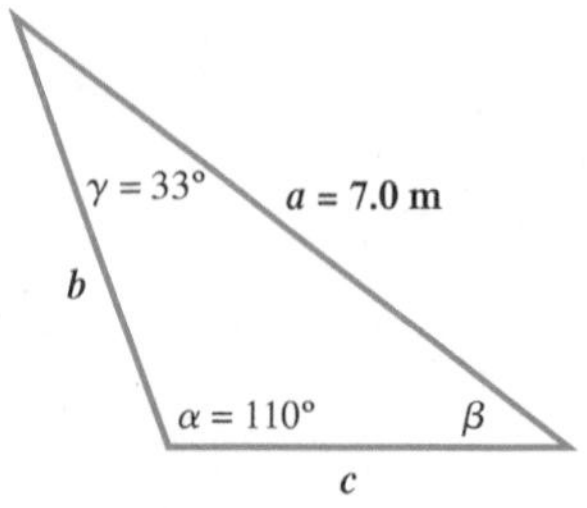

Solution:

This is an AAS (angle-angle-side) case because two angles and a side are given, and the side is opposite one of the angles.

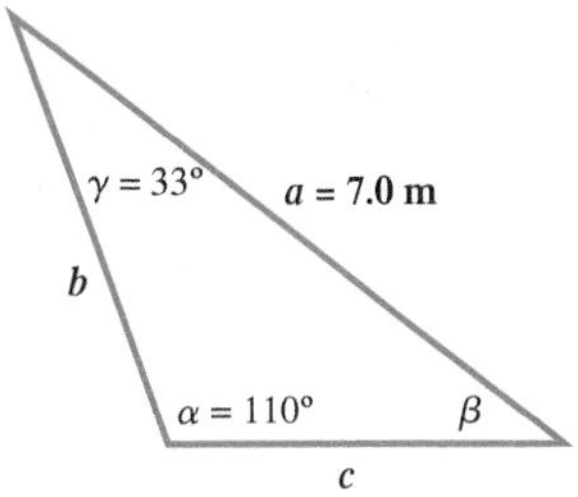

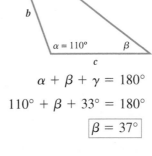

STEP 1 Find β.

The sum of the measures of the angles in a triangle is 180°. $\alpha + \beta + \gamma = 180°$

Let $\alpha = 110°$ and $\gamma = 33°$. $110° + \beta + 33° = 180°$

Solve for β. $\boxed{\beta = 37°}$

STEP 2 Find b.

Use the Law of Sines with the known side a. $\dfrac{\sin\alpha}{a} = \dfrac{\sin\beta}{b}$

Isolate b. $b = \dfrac{a\sin\beta}{\sin\alpha}$

Let $\alpha = 110°$, $\beta = 37°$, and $a = 7$ m. $b = \dfrac{(7\text{ m})\sin 37°}{\sin 110°}$

Use a calculator to approximate b. $b \approx 4.483067$ m

Round b to two significant digits. $\boxed{b \approx 4.5\text{ m}}$

STEP 3 Find c.

Use the Law of Sines with the known side a. $\dfrac{\sin\alpha}{a} = \dfrac{\sin\gamma}{c}$

Isolate c. $c = \dfrac{a\sin\gamma}{\sin\alpha}$

Let $\alpha = 110°$, $\gamma = 33°$, and $a = 7$ m. $c = \dfrac{(7\text{ m})\sin 33°}{\sin 110°}$

Use a calculator to approximate c. $c \approx 4.057149$ m

Round c to two significant digits. $\boxed{c \approx 4.1\text{ m}}$

STUDY TIP

Notice in Step 3 that we used *a* that is given, as opposed to *b* that has been calculated (approximated).

STEP 4 Draw and label the triangle.

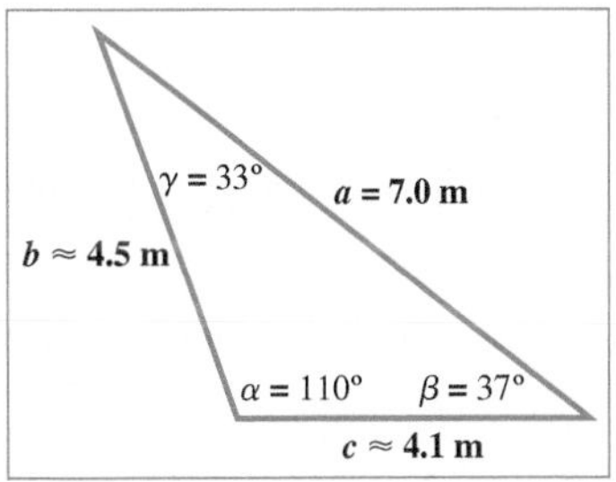

YOUR TURN Solve the triangle.

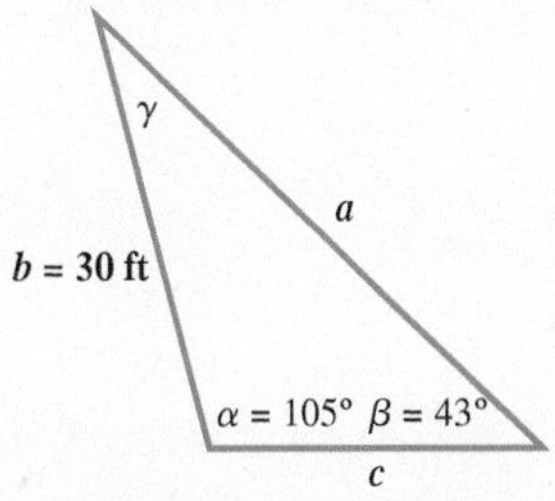

ANSWER

$\gamma = 32°$, $a \approx 42$ ft, $c \approx 23$ ft

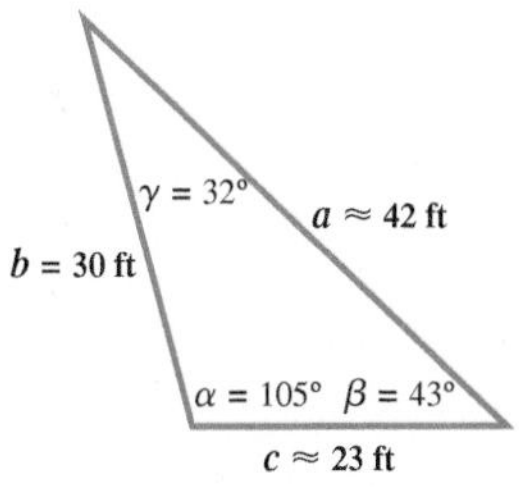

EXAMPLE 2 Using the Law of Sines to Solve a Triangle (ASA)

Solve the triangle.

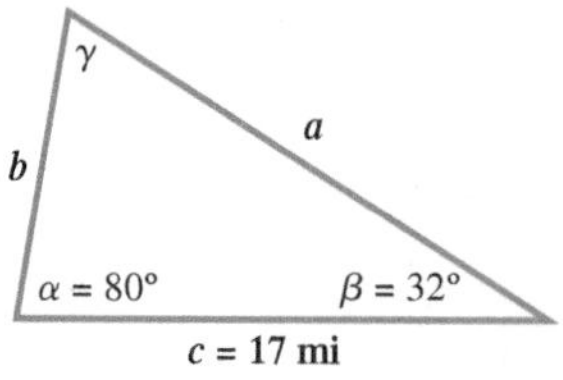

Solution:

This is an ASA (angle-side-angle) case because two angles and a side are given, and the side is not opposite one of the angles.

STEP 1 Find γ.

The sum of the measures of the angles in a triangle is 180°. $\quad \alpha + \beta + \gamma = 180°$

Let $\alpha = 80°$ and $\beta = 32°$. $\quad 80° + 32° + \gamma = 180°$

Solve for γ. $\quad \boxed{\gamma = 68°}$

STEP 2 Find b.

Write the Law of Sines to include the known side c. $\quad \dfrac{\sin\beta}{b} = \dfrac{\sin\gamma}{c}$

Isolate b. $\quad b = \dfrac{c\sin\beta}{\sin\gamma}$

Let $\beta = 32°$, $\gamma = 68°$, and $c = 17$ mi. $\quad b = \dfrac{(17 \text{ mi})\sin 32°}{\sin 68°}$

Use a calculator to approximate b. $\quad b \approx 9.7161177$ mi

Round b to two significant digits. $\quad \boxed{b \approx 9.7 \text{ mi}}$

STEP 3 Find a.

Write the Law of Sines again, incorporating the known side c. $\quad \dfrac{\sin\alpha}{a} = \dfrac{\sin\gamma}{c}$

Isolate a. $\quad a = \dfrac{c\sin\alpha}{\sin\gamma}$

Let $\alpha = 80°$, $\gamma = 68°$, and $c = 17$ mi. $\quad a = \dfrac{(17 \text{ mi})\sin 80°}{\sin 68°}$

Use a calculator to approximate a. $\quad a \approx 18.056539$ mi

Round a to two significant digits. $\quad \boxed{a \approx 18 \text{ mi}}$

STEP 4 Draw and label the triangle.

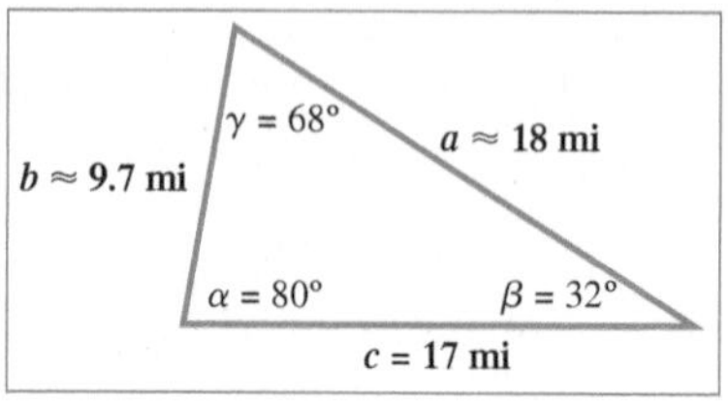

[CONCEPT CHECK]

TRUE OR FALSE If you know all three angles (AAA), then you can solve the triangle using the Law of Sines.

ANSWER False

YOUR TURN Solve the triangle.

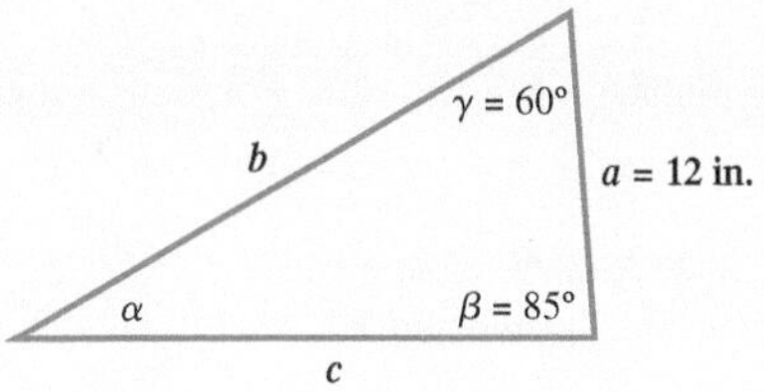

ANSWER
$\alpha = 35°, b \approx 21$ in.,
$c \approx 18$ in.

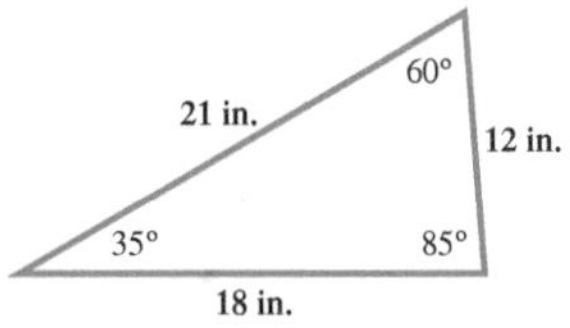

Case 2 (Ambiguous Case): Two Sides and One Angle (SSA)

If we are given the measures of two sides and an angle opposite one of the sides, then we call that Case 2, SSA (side-side-angle). This case is called the ambiguous case, because the given information by itself can represent one triangle, two triangles, or no triangle at all. If the angle given is acute, then the possibilities are zero, one, or two triangles. If the angle given is obtuse, then the possibilities are zero or one triangle. The possibilities come from the fact that $\sin\alpha = k$, where $0 < k < 1$, has two solutions for α: one in quadrant I (acute angle) and one in quadrant II (obtuse angle).

In the figure on the left, note that

- $h = b\sin\alpha$ by the definition of the sine ratio, and
- a may turn out to be smaller than, equal to, or larger than h.

Since $0 < \sin\alpha < 1$, then $h < b$.

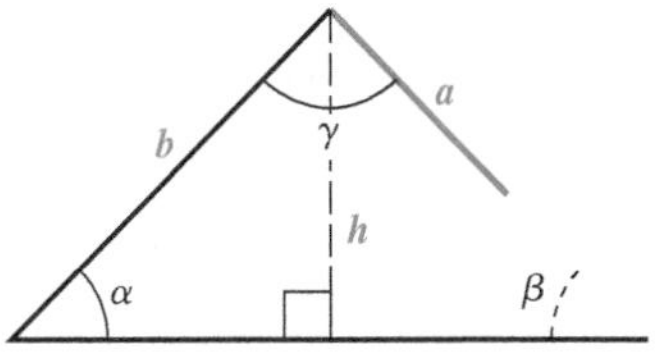

Given Angle (α) Is Acute

CONDITION	PICTURE	NUMBER OF TRIANGLES
$0 < a < h$, in this case, $\sin\beta > 1$ (impossible)	No Triangle 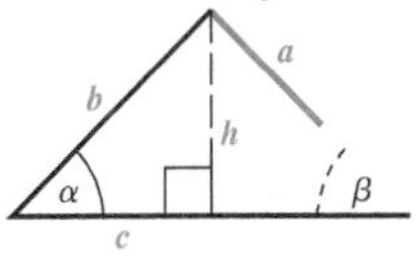	0
$a = h$, in this case, $\sin\beta = 1$	Right Triangle 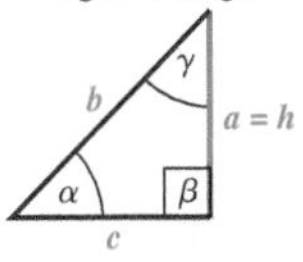	1
$h < a < b$, in this case, $0 < \sin\beta < 1$	Acute Triangle 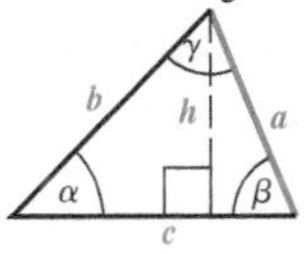 Obtuse Triangle 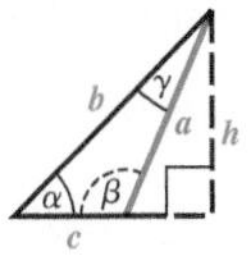	2
$a \geq b$, in this case, $0 < \sin\beta < 1$	Acute Triangle 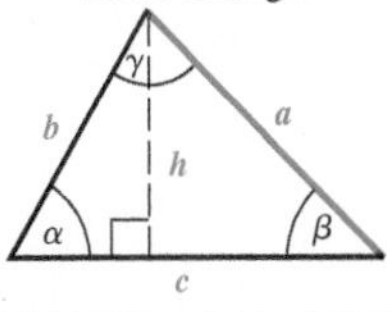	1

> **STUDY TIP**
> If an angle given is obtuse, then the side opposite that angle must be longer than the other sides (longest side opposite largest angle).

Given Angle (α) Is Obtuse

CONDITION	PICTURE	NUMBER OF TRIANGLES
$a \leq b$, in this case, $\sin\beta \geq 1$ (impossible)	No Triangle 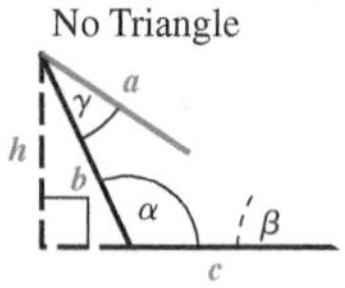	0
$a > b$, in this case, $0 < \sin\beta < 1$	One Triangle 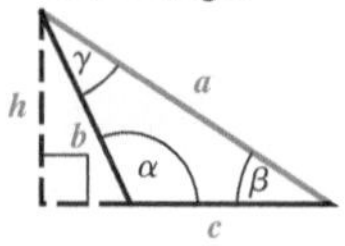	1

EXAMPLE 3 **Solving the Ambiguous Case (SSA)—One Triangle**

Solve the triangle $a = 23$ ft, $b = 11$ ft, and $\alpha = 122°$.

Solution:

This is the ambiguous case because the measures of two sides and an angle opposite one of those sides are given. Since the given angle α is obtuse and $a > b$, we expect one triangle.

STEP 1 Find β.

Use the Law of Sines. $$\frac{\sin\alpha}{a} = \frac{\sin\beta}{b}$$

Isolate $\sin\beta$. $$\sin\beta = \frac{b\sin\alpha}{a}$$

Let $a = 23$ ft, $b = 11$ ft, and $\alpha = 122°$. $$\sin\beta = \frac{(11 \text{ ft})\sin 122°}{23 \text{ ft}}$$

Use a calculator to evaluate the right side. $$\sin\beta \approx 0.40558822$$

Use a calculator to approximate β. $$\beta \approx \sin^{-1}(0.40558822) \approx \boxed{24°}$$

STEP 2 Find γ.

The measures of angles in a triangle sum to 180°. $$\alpha + \beta + \gamma = 180°$$

Substitute $\alpha = 122°$ and $\beta \approx 24°$. $$122° + 24° + \gamma \approx 180°$$

Solve for γ. $$\boxed{\gamma \approx 34°}$$

STEP 3 Find c.

Use the Law of Sines. $$\frac{\sin\alpha}{a} = \frac{\sin\gamma}{c}$$

Isolate c. $$c = \frac{a\sin\gamma}{\sin\alpha}$$

Substitute $a = 23$ ft, $\alpha = 122°$, and $\gamma \approx 34°$. $$c \approx \frac{(23 \text{ ft})\sin 34°}{\sin 122°}$$

Use a calculator to evaluate c. $$\boxed{c \approx 15 \text{ ft}}$$

STEP 4 Draw and label the triangle.

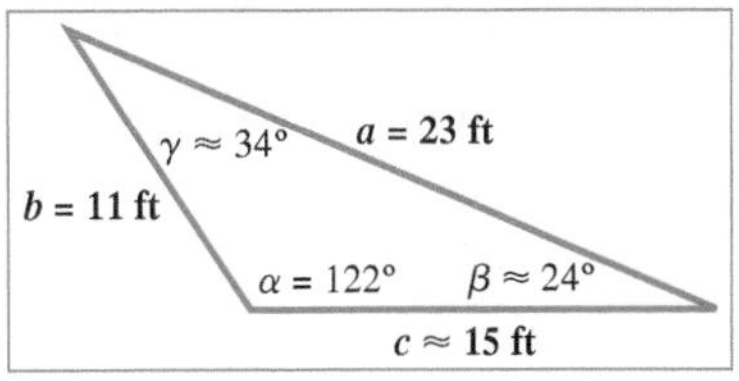

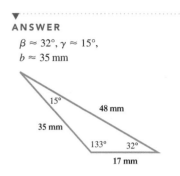

YOUR TURN Solve the triangle $\alpha = 133°$, $a = 48$ mm, and $c = 17$ mm.

ANSWER

$\beta \approx 32°$, $\gamma \approx 15°$, $b \approx 35$ mm

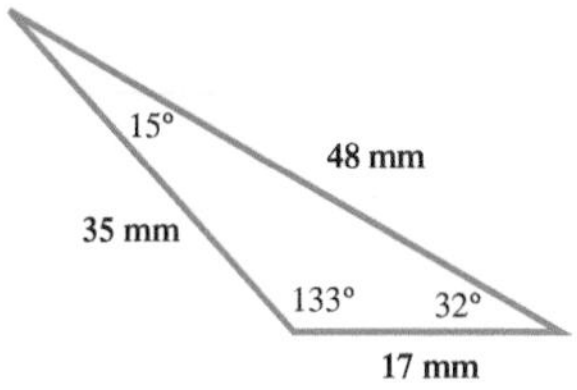

EXAMPLE 4 Solving the Ambiguous Case (SSA)—Two Triangles

Solve the triangle $a = 8.1$ m, $b = 8.3$ m, and $\alpha = 72°$.

Solution:

This is the ambiguous case because the measures of two sides and an angle opposite one of those sides are given. Since the given angle α is acute and $a < b$, we expect two triangles.

STEP 1 Find β.

Write the Law of Sines for the given information. $\quad \dfrac{\sin\alpha}{a} = \dfrac{\sin\beta}{b}$

Isolate $\sin\beta$. $\quad \sin\beta = \dfrac{b\sin\alpha}{a}$

Let $a = 8.1$ m, $b = 8.3$ m, and $\alpha = 72°$. $\quad \sin\beta = \dfrac{(8.3\text{ m})\sin 72°}{8.1\text{ m}}$

Use a calculator to evaluate the right side. $\quad \sin\beta \approx 0.974539393$

Use a calculator to approximate β. Note that β can be acute or obtuse. $\quad \beta \approx \sin^{-1}(0.974539393) \approx 77°$

This is the quadrant I solution (β is acute). $\quad \boxed{\beta_1 \approx 77°}$

The quadrant II solution (β is obtuse) is $\beta_2 = 180 - \beta_1$. $\quad \boxed{\beta_2 \approx 103°}$

STEP 2 Find γ.

The measures of the angles in a triangle sum to 180°. $\quad \alpha + \beta + \gamma = 180°$

Substitute $\alpha = 72°$ and $\beta_1 \approx 77°$. $\quad 72° + 77° + \gamma_1 \approx 180°$

Solve for γ_1. $\quad \boxed{\gamma_1 \approx 31°}$

Substitute $\alpha = 72°$ and $\beta_2 \approx 103°$. $\quad 72° + 103° + \gamma_2 \approx 180°$

Solve for γ_2. $\quad \boxed{\gamma_2 \approx 5°}$

STEP 3 Find c.

Use the Law of Sines. $\quad \dfrac{\sin\alpha}{a} = \dfrac{\sin\gamma}{c}$

Isolate c. $\quad c = \dfrac{a\sin\gamma}{\sin\alpha}$

Substitute $a = 8.1$ m, $\alpha = 72°$, and $\gamma_1 \approx 31°$. $\quad c_1 \approx \dfrac{(8.1\text{ m})\sin 31°}{\sin 72°}$

Use a calculator to evaluate c_1. $\quad \boxed{c_1 \approx 4.4\text{ m}}$

Substitute $a = 8.1$ m, $\alpha = 72°$, and $\gamma_2 \approx 5°$. $\quad c_2 \approx \dfrac{(8.1\text{ m})\sin 5°}{\sin 72°}$

Use a calculator to evaluate c_2. $\quad \boxed{c_2 \approx 0.74\text{ m}}$

STUDY TIP

Notice that when there are two solutions in the SSA case, one triangle will be obtuse.

STEP 4 Draw and label the two triangles.

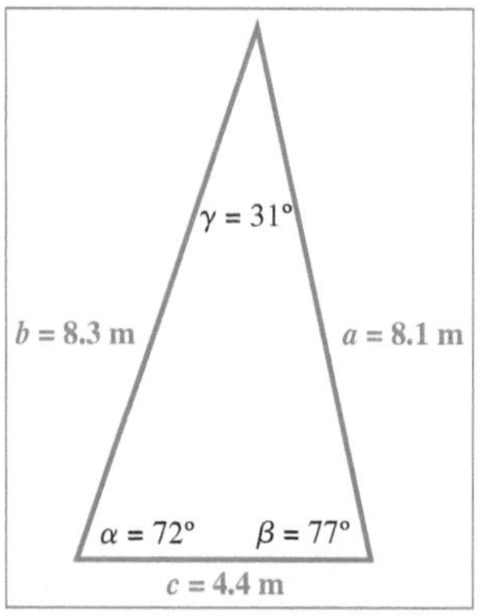

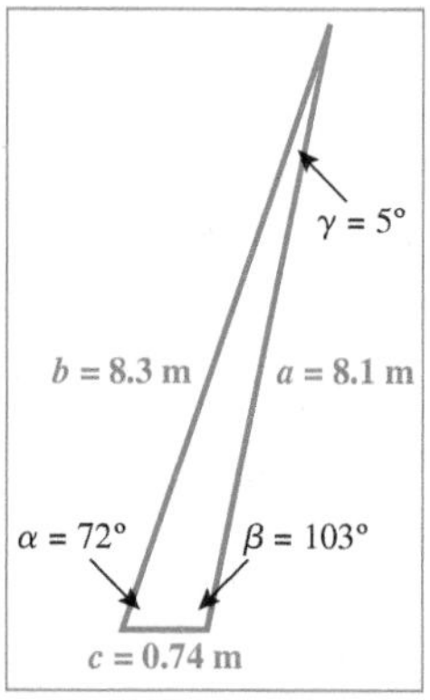

EXAMPLE 5 Solving the Ambiguous Case (SSA)—No Triangle

Solve the triangle $\alpha = 107°$, $a = 6$, and $b = 8$.

Solution:

This is the ambiguous case because the measures of two sides and an angle opposite one of those sides are given. Since the given angle α is obtuse and $a < b$, we expect no triangle since the longer side is not opposite the largest angle.

Write the Law of Sines. $\quad \dfrac{\sin\alpha}{a} = \dfrac{\sin\beta}{b}$

Isolate $\sin\beta$. $\quad \sin\beta = \dfrac{b\sin\alpha}{a}$

Let $\alpha = 107°$, $a = 6$, and $b = 8$. $\quad \sin\beta = \dfrac{8\sin 107°}{6}$

Use a calculator to evaluate the right side. $\quad \sin\beta \approx 1.28 > 1$

Since the range of the sine function is $[-1,1]$, there is no angle β such that $\sin\beta \approx 1.28$. Therefore, there is $\boxed{\text{no triangle}}$ with the given measurements.

Note: Had the geometric contradiction not been noticed, your work analytically will show a contradiction of $\sin\beta > 1$.

[SECTION 4.4] SUMMARY

In this section, we solved oblique triangles. When given the measures of three parts of a triangle, we classify the triangle according to the given data (sides and angles). Four cases arise:

- one side and two angles (AAS or ASA)
- two sides and the angle opposite one of the sides (SSA)
- two sides and the angle between sides (SAS)
- three sides (SSS)

The Law of Sines

$$\frac{\sin\alpha}{a} = \frac{\sin\beta}{b} = \frac{\sin\gamma}{c}$$

can be used to solve the first two cases (AAS or ASA, and SSA). It is important to note that the SSA case is called the ambiguous case because any one of three results is possible: no triangle, one triangle, or two triangles.

[SECTION 4.4] EXERCISES

• SKILLS

In Exercises 1–6, classify each triangle problem as case AAS, ASA, SAS, SSA, or SSS on the basis of the given information.

1. c, a, and α
2. c, a, and γ
3. a, b, and c
4. a, b, and γ
5. α, β, and c
6. β, γ, and a

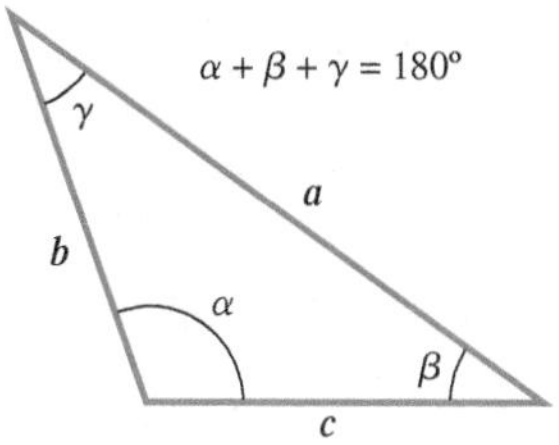

In Exercises 7–16, solve each of the following triangles with the given measures.

7. $\alpha = 45°, \beta = 60°, a = 10$ m
8. $\beta = 75°, \gamma = 60°, b = 25$ in.
9. $\alpha = 46°, \gamma = 72°, b = 200$ cm
10. $\gamma = 100°, \beta = 40°, a = 16$ ft
11. $\alpha = 16.3°, \gamma = 47.6°, c = 211$ yd
12. $\beta = 104.2°, \gamma = 33.6°, a = 26$ in.
13. $\alpha = 30°, \beta = 30°, c = 12$ m
14. $\alpha = 45°, \gamma = 75°, c = 9$ in.
15. $\beta = 26°, \gamma = 57°, c = 100$ yd
16. $\alpha = 80°, \gamma = 30°, b = 3$ ft

In Exercises 17–34, the measures of two sides and an angle are given. Determine whether a triangle (or two) exist, and if so, solve the triangle(s).

17. $a = 4, b = 5, \alpha = 16°$
18. $b = 30, c = 20, \beta = 70°$
19. $a = 12, c = 12, \gamma = 40°$
20. $b = 111, a = 80, \alpha = 25°$
21. $a = 21, b = 14, \beta = 100°$
22. $a = 13, b = 26, \alpha = 120°$
23. $\alpha = 30°, b = 18, a = 9$
24. $\alpha = 45°, b = \sqrt{2}, a = 1$
25. $\alpha = 34°, b = 7, a = 10$
26. $\alpha = 71°, b = 5.2, a = 5.2$
27. $\alpha = 21.3°, b = 6.18, a = 6.03$
28. $\alpha = 47.3°, b = 7.3, a = 5.32$
29. $\alpha = 116°, b = 4\sqrt{3}, a = 5\sqrt{2}$
30. $\alpha = 51°, b = 4\sqrt{3}, a = 4\sqrt{5}$
31. $b = 500, c = 330, \gamma = 40°$
32. $b = 16, a = 9, \beta = 137°$
33. $a = \sqrt{2}, b = \sqrt{7}, \beta = 106°$
34. $b = 15.3, c = 27.2, \gamma = 11.6°$

• APPLICATIONS

35. **Hot-Air Balloon.** A hot-air balloon is sighted at the same time by two friends who are 1.0 mile apart on the same side of the balloon. The angles of elevation from the two friends are 20.5° and 25.5°. How high is the balloon?

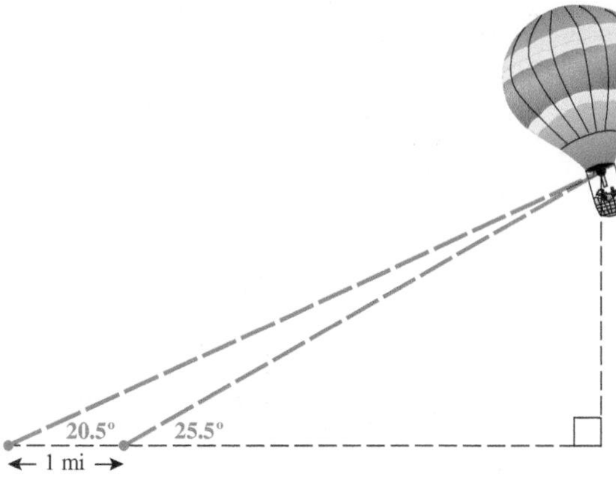

36. **Hot-Air Balloon.** A hot-air balloon is sighted at the same time by two friends who are 2 miles apart on the same side of the balloon. The angles of elevation from the two friends are 10° and 15°. How high is the balloon?

37. **Rocket Tracking.** A tracking station has two telescopes that are 1.0 mile apart. The telescopes can lock onto a rocket after it is launched and record the angles of elevation to the rocket. If the angles of elevation from telescopes A and B are 30° and 80°, respectively, then how far is the rocket from telescope A?

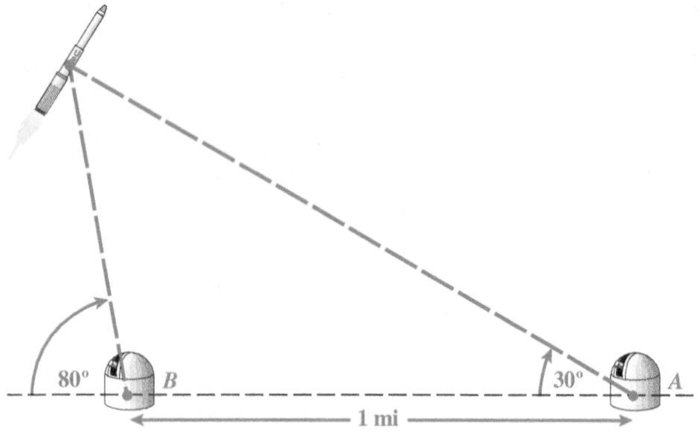

38. **Rocket Tracking.** Given the data in Exercise 37, how far is the rocket from telescope B?

39. **Distance across River.** An engineer wants to construct a bridge across a fast-moving river. Using a straight-line segment between two points that are 100 feet apart along his side of the river, she measures the angles formed when sighting the point on the other side where she wants to have the bridge end. If the angles formed at points A and B are 65° and 15°, respectively, how far is it from point A to the point on the other side of the river? Round to the nearest foot.

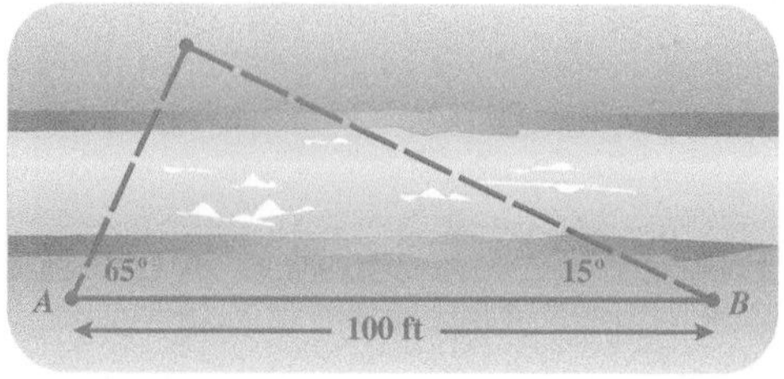

40. **Distance across River.** Given the data in Exercise 39, how far is it from point B to the point on the other side of the river? Round to the nearest foot.

41. **Lifeguard Posts.** Two lifeguard chairs, labeled P and Q, are located 400 feet apart. A troubled swimmer is spotted by both lifeguards. If the lifeguard at P reports the swimmer at angle 35° (with respect to the line segment connecting P and Q) and the lifeguard at Q reports the swimmer at angle 41°, how far is the swimmer from P?

42. **Rock Climbing.** A rock climbing enthusiast is creating a climbing route rated as 5.8 level (i.e., medium difficulty) on the wall at the local rock gym. Given the difficulty of the route, he wants to avoid placing any two holds on the same vertical or horizontal line on the wall. If he places holds at P, Q, and R such that $\angle QPR = 40°$, $QR = 6$ feet, and $QP = 4.5$ feet, how far is the hold at P from the hold at R?

43. **Surveying.** There are two stations along the shoreline, and the distance along the beach between the two stations is 50 meters. The angles between the baseline (beach) and the line of sight to the island are 30° and 40°. Find the shortest distance from the beach to the island. Round to the nearest meter.

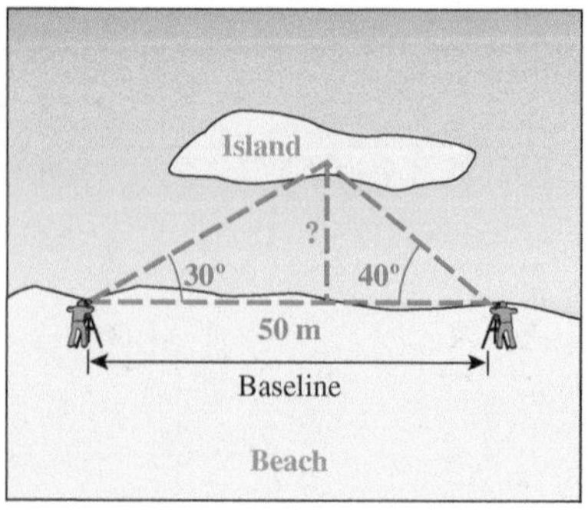

44. **Surveying.** There are two stations along a shoreline, and the distance along the beach between the two stations is 200 feet. The angles between the baseline (beach) and the line of sight to the island are 30° and 50°. Find the shortest distance from the beach to the island. Round to the nearest foot.

45. **Bowling.** The 6-8 split is common in bowling. To make this split, a bowler stands dead center and throws the ball hard and straight directly toward the right of the 6 pin. The distance from the ball at the point of release to the 8 pin is 63.2 feet. See the diagram. How far does the ball travel from the bowler to the 6 pin?

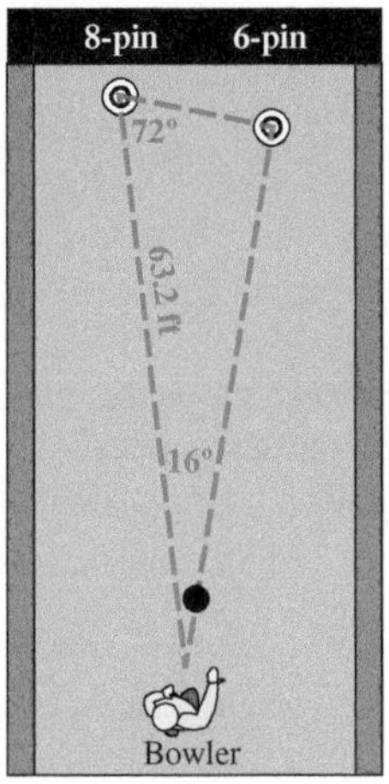

46. **Bowling.** A bowler is said to get a strike on the "Brooklyn side" of the head pin if he hits the head pin on the side opposite the pocket. (For a right-handed bowler, the pocket is to the right of the head pin.) There is a small range for the angle at which the ball must contact the head pin in order to convert all of the pins. If the measurements are as shown, how far does the ball travel (assuming it is thrown straight with no hook) before it contacts the head pin?

For Exercises 47 and 48, refer to the following:

To quantify the torque (rotational force) of the elbow joint of a human arm (see the figure to the right), it is necessary to identify angles A, B, and C as well as lengths a, b, and c. Measurements performed on an arm determine that the measure of angle C is 95°, the measure of angle A is 82°, and the length of the muscle a is 23 centimeters.

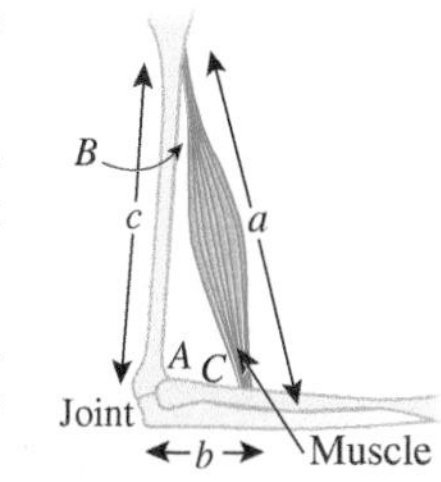

47. **Health/Medicine.** Find the length of the forearm from the elbow joint to the muscle attachment b.

48. **Health/Medicine.** Find the length of the upper arm from the muscle attachment to the elbow joint c.

• CATCH THE MISTAKE

In Exercises 49 and 50, explain the mistake that is made.

49. Solve the triangle $\alpha = 120°, a = 7$, and $b = 9$.

Solution:

Use the Law of Sines to find β. $\quad \dfrac{\sin\alpha}{a} = \dfrac{\sin\beta}{b}$

Let $\alpha = 120°, a = 7$, and $b = 9$. $\quad \dfrac{\sin 120°}{7} = \dfrac{\sin\beta}{9}$

Solve for $\sin\beta$. $\quad \sin\beta = 1.113$

Solve for β. $\quad \beta = 42°$

Sum the angle measures to 180°. $\quad 120° + 42° + \gamma = 180°$

Solve for γ. $\quad \gamma = 18°$

Use the Law of Sines to find c. $\quad \dfrac{\sin\alpha}{a} = \dfrac{\sin\gamma}{c}$

Let $\alpha = 120°, a = 7$, and $\gamma = 18°$. $\quad \dfrac{\sin 120°}{7} = \dfrac{\sin 18°}{c}$

Solve for c. $\quad c = 2.5$

$\alpha = 120°, \beta = 42°, \gamma = 18°, a = 7, b = 9$, and $c = 2.5$.

This is incorrect. The longest side is not opposite the longest angle. There is no triangle that makes the original measurements work. What mistake was made?

50. Solve the triangle $\alpha = 40°, a = 7$, and $b = 9$.

Solution:

Use the Law of Sines to find β. $\quad \dfrac{\sin\alpha}{a} = \dfrac{\sin\beta}{b}$

Let $\alpha = 40°, a = 7$, and $b = 9$. $\quad \dfrac{\sin 40°}{7} = \dfrac{\sin\beta}{9}$

Solve for $\sin\beta$. $\quad \sin\beta = 0.826441212$

Solve for β. $\quad \beta = 56°$

Find γ. $\quad 40° + 56° + \gamma = 180°$

$\gamma = 84°$

Use the Law of Sines to find c. $\quad \dfrac{\sin\alpha}{a} = \dfrac{\sin\gamma}{c}$

Let $\alpha = 40°, a = 7$, and $\gamma = 84°$. $\quad \dfrac{\sin 40°}{7} = \dfrac{\sin 84°}{c}$

Solve for c. $\quad c = 11$

$\alpha = 40°, \beta = 56°, \gamma = 84°, a = 7, b = 9$ and $c = 11$.

This is incorrect. What mistake was made?

• CONCEPTUAL

In Exercises 51–56, determine whether each statement is true or false.

51. The Law of Sines applies only to right triangles.

52. If you are given the measures of two sides and any angle, there is a unique solution for the triangle.

53. An acute triangle is an oblique triangle.

54. An obtuse triangle is an oblique triangle.

55. If you are given two sides that have the same length in a triangle, then there can be at most one triangle.

56. If α is obtuse and $\beta = \frac{\alpha}{2}$, then the situation is unambiguous.

• CHALLENGE

The following identities are useful in Exercises 57–60, and will be derived in Chapter 6.

$$\sin x + \sin y = 2\sin\left(\frac{x+y}{2}\right)\cos\left(\frac{x-y}{2}\right)$$

$$\sin(2x) = 2\sin x\cos x$$

$$\sin(x \pm y) = \sin x\cos y \pm \cos x\sin y$$

$$\cos(x \pm y) = \cos x\cos y \mp \sin x\sin y$$

57. Mollweide's Identity. For any triangle, the following identity is true. It is often used to check the solution of a triangle since all six pieces of information (three sides and three angles) are involved. Derive the identity using the Law of Sines.

$$(a+b)\sin\left(\tfrac{1}{2}\gamma\right) = c\cos\left[\tfrac{1}{2}(\alpha-\beta)\right]$$

58. The Law of Tangents. Use the Law of Sines and trigonometric identities to show that for any triangle, the following is true:

$$\frac{a-b}{a+b} = \frac{\tan\left[\frac{1}{2}(\alpha-\beta)\right]}{\tan\left[\frac{1}{2}(\alpha+\beta)\right]}$$

59. Use the Law of Sines to prove that all angles in an equilateral triangle must have the same measure.

60. Suppose that you have a triangle with side lengths a, b, and c, and angles α, β, and γ, respectively, directly across from them. If it is known that $a = \frac{1}{\sqrt{2}}b$, $c = 2$, α is an acute angle, and $\beta = 2\alpha$, solve the triangle.

• PREVIEW TO CALCULUS

In calculus, some applications of the derivative require the solution of triangles. In Exercises 61–64, solve each triangle using the Law of Sines.

61. In an oblique triangle ABC, $\beta = 45°$, $\gamma = 60°$, and $b = 20$ in. Find the length of a. Round your answer to the nearest unit.

62. In an oblique triangle ABC, $\beta = \frac{2\pi}{9}$, $\gamma = \frac{5\pi}{9}$, and $a = 200$ ft. Find the length of c. Round your answer to the nearest unit.

63. In an oblique triangle ABC, $b = 14$ m, $c = 14$ m, and $\alpha = \frac{4\pi}{7}$. Find the length of a. Round your answer to the nearest unit.

64. In an oblique triangle ABC, $b = 30$ cm, $c = 45$ cm, and $\gamma = 35°$. Find the length of a. Round your answer to the nearest unit.

4.5 THE LAW OF COSINES

SKILLS OBJECTIVES

- Solve SAS and SSS triangles using the Law of Cosines.
- Find the area of a non-right triangle.

CONCEPTUAL OBJECTIVES

- Understand that the Pythagorean theorem is a special case of the Law of Cosines.
- Develop a formula for finding the area of a non-right triangle.

4.5.1 Solving Oblique Triangles Using the Law of Cosines

4.5.1 SKILL

Solve SAS and SSS triangles using the Law of Cosines.

4.5.1 CONCEPTUAL

Understand that the Pythagorean theorem is a special case of the Law of Cosines.

In Section 4.4, we learned that to solve oblique triangles means to find all three side lengths and angle measures, and that at least one side length must be known. We need two additional pieces of information to solve an oblique triangle (combinations of side lengths and/or angles). We found that there are four cases:

- Case 1: AAS or ASA (measures of two angles and a side are given)
- Case 2: SSA (measures of two sides and an angle opposite one of the sides are given)
- Case 3: SAS (measures of two sides and the angle between them are given)
- Case 4: SSS (measures of three sides are given)

We used the Law of Sines to solve Case 1 and Case 2 triangles. Now we need the *Law of Cosines* to solve Case 3 and Case 4 triangles.

WORDS	MATH
Start with an oblique (acute) triangle.	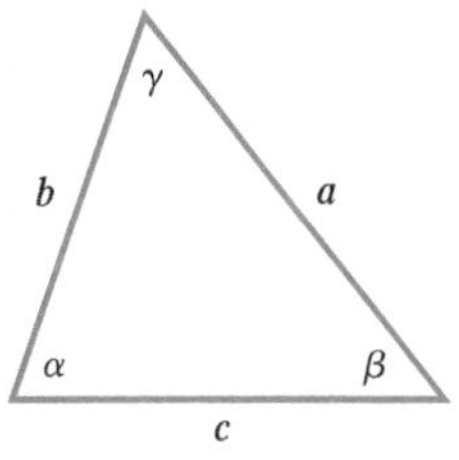
Drop a perpendicular line segment from γ to side c with height h. The result is two right triangles within the larger triangle.	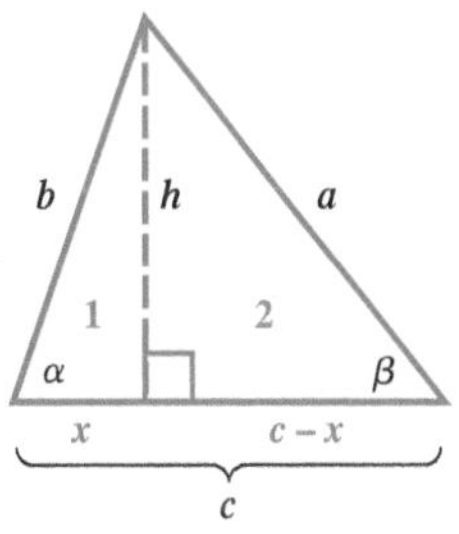
Use the Pythagorean theorem to write the relationship between the side lengths in both right triangles.	
Triangle 1:	$x^2 + h^2 = b^2$
Triangle 2:	$(c - x)^2 + h^2 = a^2$

[CONCEPT CHECK]

TRUE OR FALSE The Pythagorean theorem applies only to right triangles, whereas the Law of Sines and the Law of Cosines can be applied to acute and obtuse triangles.

ANSWER True

Solve for h^2 in both equations.	
Triangle 1:	$h^2 = b^2 - x^2$
Triangle 2:	$h^2 = a^2 - (c - x)^2$
Since the segment of length h is shared, set $h^2 = h^2$, for the two triangles.	$b^2 - x^2 = a^2 - (c - x)^2$
Multiply out the squared binomial on the right.	$b^2 - x^2 = a^2 - (c^2 - 2cx + x^2)$
Eliminate the parentheses.	$b^2 - x^2 = a^2 - c^2 + 2cx - x^2$
Add x^2 to both sides.	$b^2 = a^2 - c^2 + 2cx$
Isolate a^2.	$a^2 = b^2 + c^2 - 2cx$
Notice that $\cos\alpha = \frac{x}{b}$. Let $x = b\cos\alpha$.	$\boxed{a^2 = b^2 + c^2 - 2bc\cos\alpha}$

Note: If we instead drop the perpendicular line segment with length h from the angle α or the angle β, we can derive the other two parts of the Law of Cosines:

$$\boxed{b^2 = a^2 + c^2 - 2ac\cos\beta} \quad \text{and} \quad \boxed{c^2 = a^2 + b^2 - 2ab\cos\gamma}$$

THE LAW OF COSINES

For a triangle with sides of length a, b, and c, and opposite angle measures α, β, and γ, the following equations are true:

$$a^2 = b^2 + c^2 - 2bc\cos\alpha$$
$$b^2 = a^2 + c^2 - 2ac\cos\beta$$
$$c^2 = a^2 + b^2 - 2ab\cos\gamma$$

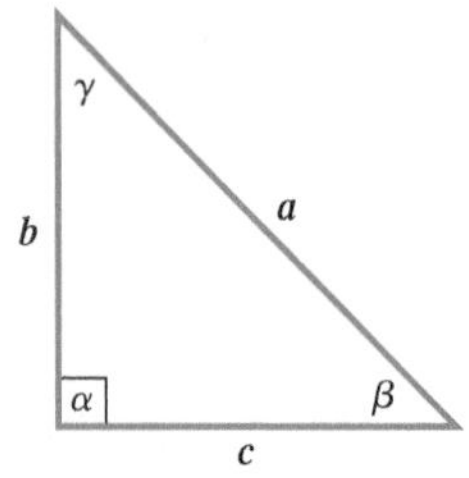

It is important to note that the Law of Cosines can be used to find side lengths or angles in any triangle in cases SAS and SSS; as long as three of the four variables in any of the equations are known, the fourth can be calculated.

Notice that in the special case of a right triangle (say, $\alpha = 90°$),

$$a^2 = b^2 + c^2 - 2bc\underbrace{\cos 90°}_{0}$$

one of the equations of the Law of Cosines reduces to the Pythagorean theorem:

$$\underbrace{a^2}_{\text{hyp}} = \underbrace{b^2}_{\text{leg}} + \underbrace{c^2}_{\text{leg}}$$

The Pythagorean theorem can thus be regarded as a special case of the Law of Cosines.

STUDY TIP

The Pythagorean theorem is a special case of the Law of Cosines.

Case 3: Solving Oblique Triangles (SAS)

We now solve SAS triangle problems where the measures of two sides and the angle between them are given. We start by using the Law of Cosines to solve for the length of the side opposite the given angle. We then can apply either the Law of Sines or the Law of Cosines to find the second angle measure.

EXAMPLE 1 **Using the Law of Cosines to Solve a Triangle (SAS)**

Solve the triangle $a = 13$, $c = 6.0$, and $\beta = 20°$.

Solution:

The measures of two sides and the angle between them are given (SAS).

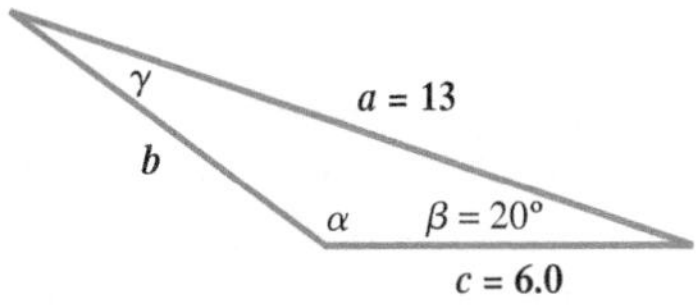

Notice that the Law of Sines can't be used, because it requires the measures of at least one angle and the side opposite that angle.

STEP 1 Find b.

Apply the Law of Cosines that involves β. $b^2 = a^2 + c^2 - 2ac\cos\beta$

Let $a = 13$, $c = 6.0$, and $\beta = 20°$. $b^2 = 13^2 + 6^2 - 2(13)(6)\cos 20°$

Evaluate the right side with a calculator. $b^2 \approx 58.40795$

Solve for b. $b \approx \pm 7.6425$

Round to two significant digits; b can only be positive. $\boxed{b \approx 7.6}$

STEP 2 Find γ.

Use the Law of Sines to find the smaller angle γ. $\dfrac{\sin\gamma}{c} = \dfrac{\sin\beta}{b}$

Isolate $\sin\gamma$. $\sin\gamma = \dfrac{c\sin\beta}{b}$

Let $b \approx 7.6$, $c = 6.0$, and $\beta = 20°$. $\sin\gamma \approx \dfrac{6\sin 20°}{7.6}$

Apply the inverse sine function. $\gamma \approx \sin^{-1}\left(\dfrac{6\sin 20°}{7.6}\right)$

Evaluate the right side with a calculator. $\gamma \approx 15.66521°$

Round to the nearest degree. $\boxed{\gamma \approx 16°}$

STEP 3 Find α.

The angle measures must sum to 180°. $\alpha + 20° + 16° \approx 180°$

Solve for α. $\boxed{\alpha \approx 144°}$

YOUR TURN Solve the triangle $b = 4.2$, $c = 1.8$, and $\alpha = 35°$.

ANSWER

$a \approx 2.9$, $\gamma \approx 21°$, $\beta \approx 124°$

Notice the steps we took in solving a SAS triangle:

1. Find the length of the side opposite the given angle using the Law of Cosines.
2. Solve for the smaller angle using the Law of Sines.
3. Solve for the larger angle using the fact that angles of a triangle sum to 180°.

You may be thinking, "Would it matter if we had solved for α before solving for γ?" Yes, it does matter—in this problem you cannot solve for α by the Law of Sines

STUDY TIP

Although the Law of Sines is sometimes ambiguous, the Law of Cosines is never ambiguous.

before finding γ. The Law of Sines can be used only on the smaller angle (opposite the shortest side). If we had tried to use the Law of Sines with the obtuse angle α, the inverse sine would have resulted in $\alpha = 36°$. Since the sine function is positive in QI and QII, we would not know whether that angle was $\alpha = 36°$ or its supplementary angle $\alpha = 144°$. Notice that $c < a$; therefore, the angles opposite those sides must have the same relationship, $\gamma < \alpha$. We choose the smaller angle first. Alternatively, if we want to solve for the obtuse angle first, we can use the Law of Cosines to solve for α. If you use the Law of Cosines to find the second angle, you can choose either angle. The Law of Cosines can be used to find the measure of either acute or obtuse angles.

Case 4: Solving Oblique Triangles (SSS)

We now solve oblique triangles when all three side lengths are given (the SSS case). In this case, start by finding the largest angle (opposite the largest side) using the Law of Cosines. Then apply the Law of Sines to find either of the remaining two angles. Last, find the third angle with the triangle angle sum identity.

EXAMPLE 2 Using the Law of Cosines to Solve a Triangle (SSS)

Solve the triangle $a = 8, b = 6$, and $c = 7$.

Solution:

STEP 1 Identify the largest angle, which is α.

Write the equation of the Law of Cosines that involves α.
$$a^2 = b^2 + c^2 - 2bc\cos\alpha$$

Let $a = 8, b = 6$, and $c = 7$.
$$8^2 = 6^2 + 7^2 - 2(6)(7)\cos\alpha$$

Simplify and isolate $\cos\alpha$.
$$\cos\alpha = \frac{6^2 + 7^2 - 8^2}{2(6)(7)} = 0.25$$

Approximate with a calculator.
$$\alpha = \cos^{-1}(0.25) \approx \boxed{75.5°}$$

STEP 2 Find either of the remaining angles. We will solve for β.

Write the Law of Sines.
$$\frac{\sin\alpha}{a} = \frac{\sin\beta}{b}$$

Isolate $\sin\beta$.
$$\sin\beta = \frac{b\sin\alpha}{a}$$

Let $a = 8, b = 6$, and $\alpha = 75.5°$.
$$\sin\beta \approx \frac{6\sin 75.5°}{8}$$

Approximate with a calculator.
$$\beta \approx \sin^{-1}\left(\frac{6\sin 75.5°}{8}\right) \approx \boxed{46.6°}$$

STEP 3 Find the third angle, γ.

The sum of the angle measures is 180°.
$$75.5° + 46.6° + \gamma \approx 180°$$

Solve for γ.
$$\boxed{\gamma \approx 57.9°}$$

YOUR TURN Solve the triangle $a = 5, b = 7$, and $c = 8$.

ANSWER
$\alpha \approx 38.2°, \beta \approx 60.0°,$
$\gamma \approx 81.8°$

4.5.2 The Area of a Triangle

The general formula for the area of a triangle and the sine function together can be used to develop a formula for the area of a triangle when the measures of two sides and the angle between them are given.

4.5.2 SKILL

Find the area of a non-right triangle.

4.5.2 CONCEPTUAL

Develop a formula for finding the area of a non-right triangle.

WORDS	MATH
Start with an acute triangle, given b, c, and α.	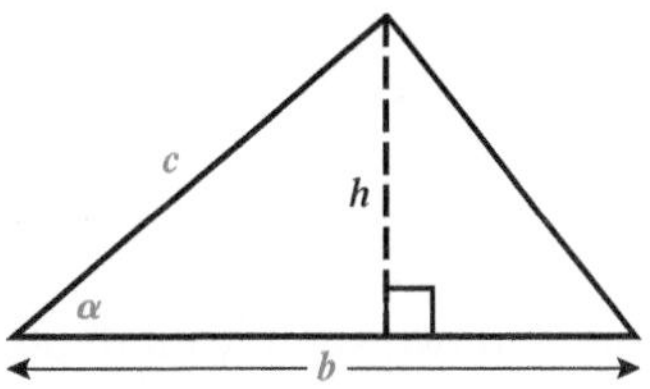
Write the sine ratio in the right triangle for the acute angle α.	$\sin\alpha = \frac{h}{c}$
Solve for h.	$h = c\sin\alpha$
Write the formula for area of a triangle.	$A_{\text{triangle}} = \frac{1}{2}bh$
Substitute $h = c\sin\alpha$.	$\boxed{A_{\text{SAS}} = \frac{1}{2}bc\sin\alpha}$

Now we can calculate the area of this triangle with the given information (the measures of two sides and the angle between them: b, c, and α). Similarly, it can be shown that the other formulas for SAS triangles are

$$\boxed{A_{\text{SAS}} = \frac{1}{2}ab\sin\gamma} \quad \text{and} \quad \boxed{A_{\text{SAS}} = \frac{1}{2}ac\sin\beta}$$

AREA OF A TRIANGLE (SAS)

For any triangle where the measures of two sides and the angle between them are known, the area for that triangle is given by one of the following formulas (depending on which angle and sides measures are given):

$A_{\text{SAS}} = \frac{1}{2}bc\sin\alpha$ when b, c, and α are known

$A_{\text{SAS}} = \frac{1}{2}ab\sin\gamma$ when a, b, and γ are known

$A_{\text{SAS}} = \frac{1}{2}ac\sin\beta$ when a, c, and β are known

In other words, the area of a triangle equals one-half the product of two of its sides and the sine of the angle between them.

EXAMPLE 3 Finding the Area of a Triangle (SAS Case)

Find the area of the triangle $a = 7.0$ ft, $b = 9.3$ ft, and $\gamma = 86°$.

Solution:

Use the area formula where a, b, and γ are given. $A = \frac{1}{2}ab\sin\gamma$

Substitute $a = 7.0$ ft, $b = 9.3$ ft, and $\gamma = 86°$. $A = \frac{1}{2}(7.0 \text{ ft})(9.3 \text{ ft})\sin 86°$

Approximate with a calculator. $A \approx 32.47071 \text{ ft}^2$

Round to two significant digits. $\boxed{A \approx 32 \text{ ft}^2}$

YOUR TURN Find the area of the triangle $a = 3.2$ m, $c = 5.1$ m, and $\beta = 49°$.

ANSWER
6.2 m^2

The Law of Cosines can be used to develop a formula for the area of an SSS triangle, called **Heron's formula**.

WORDS	MATH
Start with any of the formulas for SAS triangles.	$A = \frac{1}{2}ab\sin\gamma$
Square both sides.	$A^2 = \frac{1}{4}a^2b^2\sin^2\gamma$
Isolate $\sin^2\gamma$.	$\frac{4A^2}{a^2b^2} = \sin^2\gamma$
Apply the Pythagorean identity.	$\frac{4A^2}{a^2b^2} = 1 - \cos^2\gamma$
Factor the difference of the two squares on the right.	$\frac{4A^2}{a^2b^2} = (1 - \cos\gamma)(1 + \cos\gamma)$
Solve the Law of Cosines, $c^2 = a^2 + b^2 - 2ab\cos\gamma$, for $\cos\gamma$.	$\cos\gamma = \frac{a^2 + b^2 - c^2}{2ab}$
Substitute $\cos\gamma = \frac{a^2 + b^2 - c^2}{2ab}$ into $\frac{4A^2}{a^2b^2} = (1 - \cos\gamma)(1 + \cos\gamma)$.	$\frac{4A^2}{a^2b^2} = \left[1 - \frac{a^2 + b^2 - c^2}{2ab}\right]\left[1 + \frac{a^2 + b^2 - c^2}{2ab}\right]$
Combine the expressions in brackets.	$\frac{4A^2}{a^2b^2} = \left[\frac{2ab - a^2 - b^2 + c^2}{2ab}\right]\left[\frac{2ab + a^2 + b^2 - c^2}{2ab}\right]$
Group the terms in the numerators on the right.	$\frac{4A^2}{a^2b^2} = \left[\frac{-(a^2 - 2ab + b^2) + c^2}{2ab}\right]\left[\frac{(a^2 + 2ab + b^2) - c^2}{2ab}\right]$

Write the numerators on the right as the difference of two squares.

$$\frac{4A^2}{a^2b^2} = \left[\frac{c^2 - (a - b)^2}{2ab}\right]\left[\frac{(a + b)^2 - c^2}{2ab}\right]$$

Factor the numerators on the right. Recall: $x^2 - y^2 = (x - y)(x + y)$.

$$\frac{4A^2}{a^2b^2} = \left[\frac{(c - [a - b])(c + [a - b])}{2ab}\right]\left[\frac{([a + b] - c)([a + b] + c)}{2ab}\right]$$

Simplify.

$$\frac{4A^2}{a^2b^2} = \left[\frac{(c - a + b)(c + a - b)}{2ab}\right]\left[\frac{(a + b - c)(a + b + c)}{2ab}\right]$$

$$\frac{4A^2}{a^2b^2} = \frac{(c - a + b)(c + a - b)(a + b - c)(a + b + c)}{4a^2b^2}$$

Solve for A^2 by multiplying both sides by $\frac{a^2b^2}{4}$.

$$A^2 = \frac{1}{16}(c - a + b)(c + a - b)(a + b - c)(a + b + c)$$

The semiperimeter s is half the perimeter of the triangle.

$$s = \frac{a + b + c}{2}$$

Manipulate each of the four factors:

$$c - a + b = a + b + c - 2a = 2s - 2a = 2(s - a)$$

$$c + a - b = a + b + c - 2b = 2s - 2b = 2(s - b)$$

$$a + b - c = a + b + c - 2c = 2s - 2c = 2(s - c)$$

$$a + b + c = 2s$$

Substitute these values for the four factors.

$$A^2 = \frac{1}{16} \cdot 2(s - a) \cdot 2(s - b) \cdot 2(s - c) \cdot 2s$$

Simplify.

$$A^2 = s(s - a)(s - b)(s - c)$$

Solve for A (area is always positive).

$$A = \boxed{\sqrt{s(s - a)(s - b)(s - c)}}$$

AREA OF A TRIANGLE (SSS CASE—HERON'S FORMULA)

For any triangle where the lengths of the three sides are known, the area for that triangle is given by the following formula:

$$A_{SSS} = \sqrt{s(s - a)(s - b)(s - c)}$$

where a, b, and c are the lengths of the sides of the triangle, and s is half the perimeter of the triangle, called the semiperimeter.

$$s = \frac{a + b + c}{2}$$

EXAMPLE 4 Finding the Area of a Triangle (SSS Case)

Find the area of the triangle $a = 5$, $b = 6$, and $c = 9$.

Solution:

Find the semiperimeter s. $s = \dfrac{a + b + c}{2}$

Substitute $a = 5$, $b = 6$, and $c = 9$. $s = \dfrac{5 + 6 + 9}{2}$

Simplify. $s = 10$

Write the formula for the area of a triangle in the SSS case (Heron's formula). $A = \sqrt{s(s - a)(s - b)(s - c)}$

Substitute $a = 5$, $b = 6$, $c = 9$, and $s = 10$. $A = \sqrt{10(10 - 5)(10 - 6)(10 - 9)}$

Simplify the radicand. $A = \sqrt{10 \cdot 5 \cdot 4 \cdot 1}$

Evaluate the radical. $\boxed{A = 10\sqrt{2} \approx 14 \text{ sq units}}$

YOUR TURN Find the area of the triangle $a = 3$, $b = 5$, and $c = 6$.

ANSWER
$2\sqrt{14} \approx 7.5$ sq units

[SECTION 4.5] SUMMARY

We can solve any triangle given three measures, as long as one of the measures is a side length. Depending on the information given, either we apply the **Law of Sines**

$$\frac{\sin\alpha}{a} = \frac{\sin\beta}{b} = \frac{\sin\gamma}{c}$$

and the angle sum identity, or we apply a combination of the **Law of Cosines**,

$$a^2 = b^2 + c^2 - 2bc\cos\alpha \qquad b^2 = a^2 + c^2 - 2ac\cos\beta \qquad c^2 = a^2 + b^2 - 2ab\cos\gamma$$

the Law of Sines, and the angle sum identity. The table below summarizes the strategies for solving oblique triangles covered in Sections 4.4 and 4.5.

OBLIQUE TRIANGLE	WHAT'S KNOWN	PROCEDURE FOR SOLVING
AAS or ASA	Two angles and a side	Step 1: Find the remaining angle with $\alpha + \beta + \gamma = 180°$. Step 2: Find the remaining sides with the Law of Sines.
SSA	Two sides and an angle opposite one of the sides	This is the ambiguous case, so there is either no triangle, one triangle, or two triangles. If the given angle is obtuse, then there is either one or no triangles. If the given angle is acute, then there is no triangle, one triangle, or two triangles. Step 1: Apply the Law of Sines to find one of the angles. Step 2: Find the remaining angle with $\alpha + \beta + \gamma = 180°$. Step 3: Find the remaining side with the Law of Sines. If two triangles exist, then the angle found in Step 1 can be either acute or obtuse, and Steps 2 and 3 must be performed for each triangle.
SAS	Two sides and an angle between the sides	Step 1: Find the third side with the Law of Cosines. Step 2: Find the smaller angle with the Law of Sines. Step 3: Find the remaining angle with $\alpha + \beta + \gamma = 180°$.
SSS	Three sides	Step 1: Find the largest angle with the Law of Cosines. Step 2: Find either remaining angle with the Law of Sines. Step 3: Find the last remaining angle with $\alpha + \beta + \gamma = 180°$.

Formulas for calculating the areas of triangles (SAS and SSS cases) were derived. The three area formulas for the SAS case depend on which angles and sides are given.

$$A_{SAS} = \frac{1}{2}bc\sin\alpha \qquad A_{SAS} = \frac{1}{2}ab\sin\gamma \qquad A_{SAS} = \frac{1}{2}ac\sin\beta$$

The Law of Cosines was instrumental in developing a formula for the area of a triangle (SSS case) when all three sides are given.

$$(\textit{Heron's formula}) \quad A_{SSS} = \sqrt{s(s-a)(s-b)(s-c)} \quad \text{where} \quad s = \frac{a+b+c}{2}$$

[SECTION 4.5] EXERCISES

• SKILLS

In Exercises 1–28, solve each triangle.

1. $a = 4, c = 3, \beta = 100°$
2. $a = 6, b = 10, \gamma = 80°$
3. $b = 7, c = 2, \alpha = 16°$
4. $b = 5, a = 6, \gamma = 170°$
5. $b = 5, c = 5, \alpha = 20°$
6. $a = 4.2, b = 7.3, \gamma = 25°$
7. $a = 9, c = 12, \beta = 23°$
8. $b = 6, c = 13, \alpha = 16°$
9. $a = 4, c = 8, \beta = 60°$
10. $b = 3, c = \sqrt{18}, \alpha = 45°$
11. $a = 8, b = 5, c = 6$
12. $a = 6, b = 9, c = 12$
13. $a = 4, b = 4, c = 5$
14. $a = 17, b = 20, c = 33$
15. $a = 8.2, b = 7.1, c = 6.3$
16. $a = 1492, b = 2001, c = 1776$
17. $a = 4, b = 5, c = 10$
18. $a = 1.3, b = 2.7, c = 4.2$
19. $a = 12, b = 5, c = 13$
20. $a = 4, b = 5, c = \sqrt{41}$
21. $\alpha = 40°, \beta = 35°, a = 6$
22. $b = 11.2, a = 19.0, \gamma = 13.3°$
23. $\alpha = 31°, b = 5, a = 12$
24. $a = 11, c = 12, \gamma = 60°$
25. $a = \sqrt{7}, b = \sqrt{8}, c = \sqrt{3}$
26. $\beta = 106°, \gamma = 43°, a = 1$
27. $b = 11, c = 2, \beta = 10°$
28. $\alpha = 25°, a = 6, c = 9$

In Exercises 29–50, find the area of each triangle with measures given.

29. $a = 8, c = 16, \beta = 60°$
30. $b = 6, c = 4\sqrt{3}, \alpha = 30°$
31. $a = 1, b = \sqrt{2}, \alpha = 45°$
32. $b = 2\sqrt{2}, c = 4, \beta = 45°$
33. $a = 6, b = 8, \gamma = 80°$
34. $b = 9, c = 10, \alpha = 100°$
35. $a = 4, c = 7, \beta = 27°$
36. $a = 6.3, b = 4.8, \gamma = 17°$
37. $b = 100, c = 150, \alpha = 36°$
38. $c = 0.3, a = 0.7, \beta = 145°$
39. $a = 15, b = 15, c = 15$
40. $a = 1, b = 1, c = 1$
41. $a = 7, b = \sqrt{51}, c = 10$
42. $a = 9, b = 40, c = 41$
43. $a = 6, b = 10, c = 9$
44. $a = 40, b = 50, c = 60$
45. $a = 14.3, b = 15.7, c = 20.1$
46. $a = 146.5, b = 146.5, c = 100$
47. $a = 14{,}000, b = 16{,}500, c = 18{,}700$
48. $a = \sqrt{2}, b = \sqrt{3}, c = \sqrt{5}$
49. $a = 80, b = 75, c = 160$
50. $a = 19, b = 23, c = 3$

• APPLICATIONS

51. **Aviation.** A plane flew due north at 500 miles per hour for 3 hours. A second plane, starting at the same point and at the same time, flew southeast at an angle 150° clockwise from due north at 435 miles per hour for 3 hours. At the end of the 3 hours, how far apart were the two planes? Round to the nearest mile.

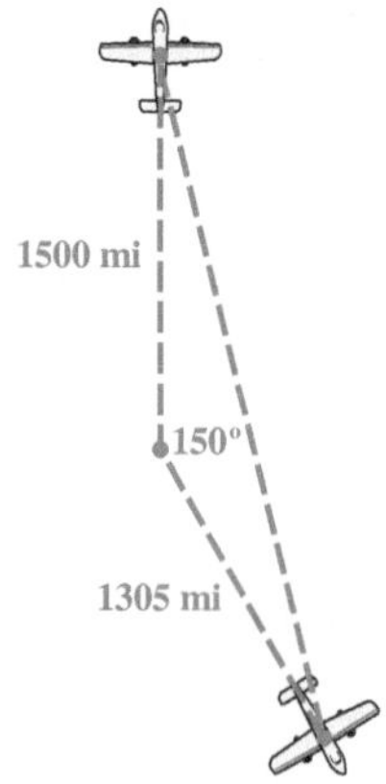

52. **Aviation.** A plane flew due north at 400 miles per hour for 4 hours. A second plane, starting at the same point and at the same time, flew southeast at an angle 120° clockwise from due north at 300 miles per hour for 4 hours. At the end of the 4 hours, how far apart were the two planes? Round to the nearest mile.

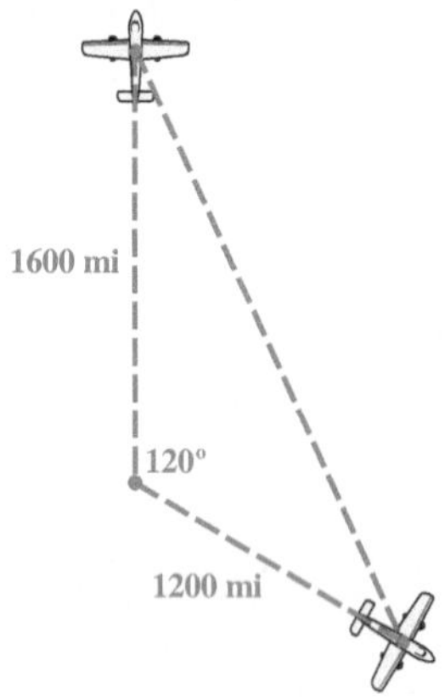

53. **Aviation.** A plane flew N30°W at 350 miles per hour for 2.5 hours. A second plane, starting at the same point and at the same time, flew 35° at an angle clockwise from due north at 550 miles per hour for 2.5 hours. At the end of 2.5 hours, how far apart were the two planes? Round to the nearest mile.

54. **Aviation.** A plane flew N30°W at 350 miles per hour for 3 hours. A second plane starts at the same point and takes off at the same time. It is known that after 3 hours, the two planes are 2100 miles apart. Find the original bearing of the second plane, to the nearest hundredth of a degree.

55. **Sliding Board.** A 40-foot slide leaning against the bottom of a building's window makes a 55° angle with the building. The angle formed with the building by the line of sight from the top of the window to the point on the ground where the slide ends is 40°. How tall is the window?

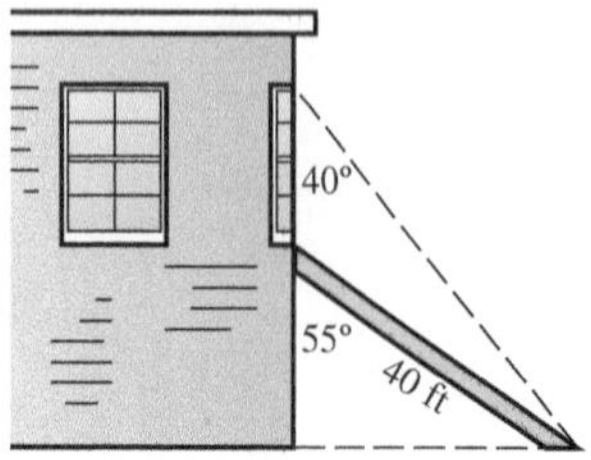

56. **Airplane Slide.** An airplane door is 6 feet high. If a slide attached to the bottom of the open door is at an angle of 40° with the ground, and the angle formed by the line of sight from where the slide touches the ground to the top of the door is 45°, how long is the slide?

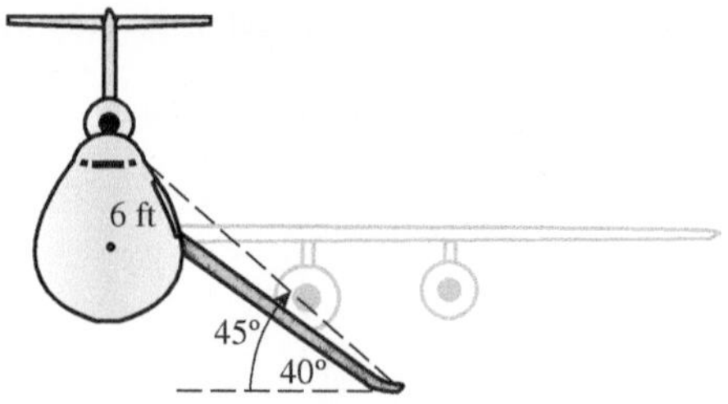

For Exercises 57 and 58, refer to the following:

To quantify the torque (rotational force) of the elbow joint of a human arm (see the figure to the right), it is necessary to identify angles A, B, and C as well as lengths a, b, and c. Measurements performed on an arm determine that the measure of angle C is 105°, the length of the muscle a is 25.5 centimeters, and the length of the forearm from the elbow joint to the muscle attachment b is 1.76 centimeters.

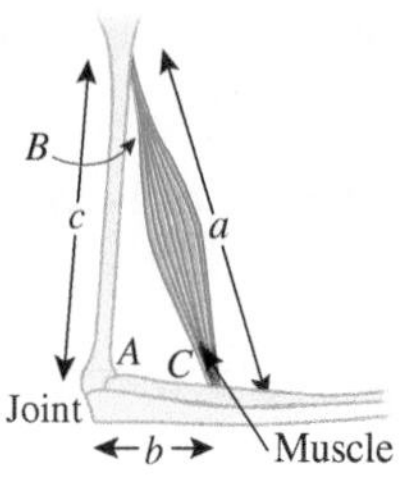

57. **Health/Medicine.** Find the length of the upper arm from the muscle attachment to the elbow joint c.

58. **Health/Medicine.** Find the measure of angle B.

59. **Surveying.** A glaciologist needs to determine the length across a certain crevice on Mendenhall glacier in order to circumvent it with his team. He has the following measurements:

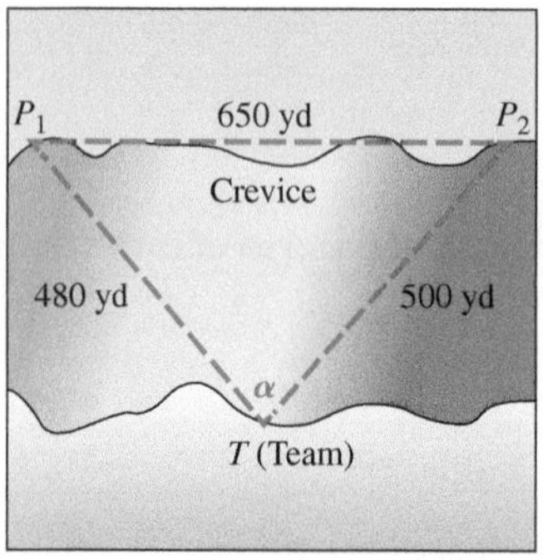

Find α.

60. **Surveying.** A glaciologist needs to determine the length across a certain crevice on Mendenhall glacier in order to circumvent it with her team. She has the following measurements:

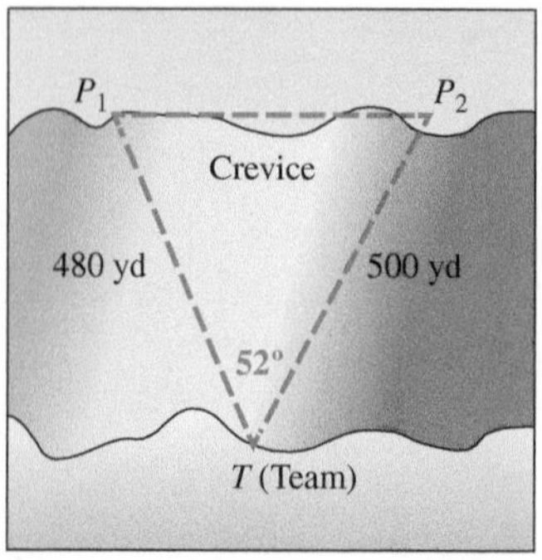

Find the approximate length across the crevice.

61. Parking Lot. A parking lot is to have the shape of a parallelogram that has adjacent sides measuring 200 feet and 260 feet. The acute angle between two adjacent sides is 65°. What is the area of the parking lot?

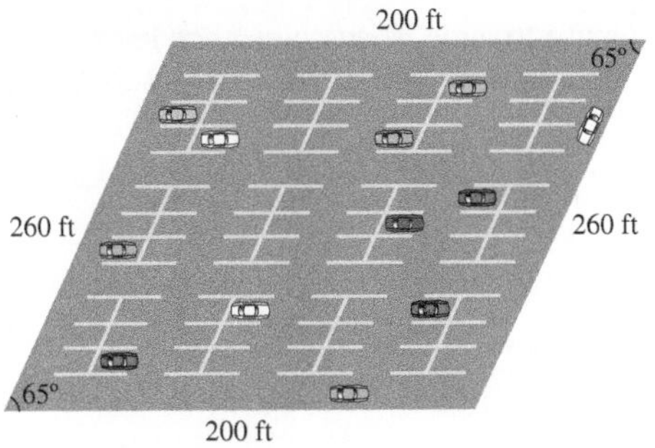

62. Parking Lot. A parking lot is to have the shape of a parallelogram that has adjacent sides measuring 250 feet and 300 feet. The acute angle between two adjacent sides is 55°. What is the area of the parking lot?

63. Regular Hexagon. A regular hexagon has sides measuring 3 feet. What is its area? Recall that the measure of an angle of a regular n-gon is given by the formula angle $= \dfrac{180°(n-2)}{n}$.

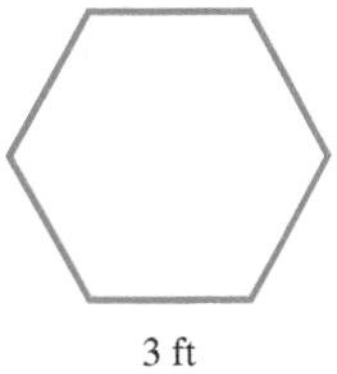

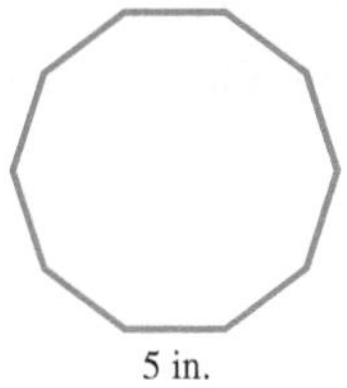

64. Regular Decagon. A regular decagon has sides measuring 5 inches. What is its area?

65. Geometry. A quadrilateral $ABCD$ has sides of lengths $AB = 2$, $BC = 3$, $CD = 4$, and $DA = 5$. The angle between AB and BC is 135°. Find the area of $ABCD$.

66. Geometry. A quadrilateral $ABCD$ has sides of lengths $AB = 5$, $BC = 6$, $CD = 7$, and $DA = 8$. The angle between AB and BC is 135°. Find the area of $ABCD$.

• CATCH THE MISTAKE

In Exercises 67 and 68, explain the mistake that is made.

67. Solve the triangle $b = 3$, $c = 4$, and $\alpha = 30°$.

Solution:

STEP 1: Find a.

Apply the Law of Cosines. $\quad a^2 = b^2 + c^2 - 2bc\cos\alpha$

Let $b = 3$, $c = 4$, and $\alpha = 30°$. $\quad a^2 = 3^2 + 4^2 - 2(3)(4)\cos 30°$

Solve for a. $\quad a \approx 2.1$

STEP 2: Find γ.

Apply the Law of Sines. $\quad \dfrac{\sin\alpha}{a} = \dfrac{\sin\gamma}{c}$

Solve for $\sin\gamma$. $\quad \sin\gamma = \dfrac{c\sin\alpha}{a}$

Solve for γ. $\quad \gamma = \sin^{-1}\left(\dfrac{c\sin\alpha}{a}\right)$

Let $a = 2.1$, $c = 4$, and $\alpha = 30°$. $\quad \gamma \approx 72°$

STEP 3: Find β.

$\alpha + \beta + \gamma = 180° \quad 30° + \beta + 72° = 180°$

Solve for β. $\quad \beta \approx 78°$

$a \approx 2.1$, $b = 3$, $c = 4$, $\alpha = 30°$, $\beta \approx 78°$, and $\gamma \approx 72°$.

This is incorrect. The longest side is not opposite the largest angle. What mistake was made?

68. Solve the triangle $a = 6$, $b = 2$, and $c = 5$.

Solution:

STEP 1: Find β.

Apply the Law of Cosines. $\quad b^2 = a^2 + c^2 - 2ac\cos\beta$

Solve for β. $\quad \beta = \cos^{-1}\left(\dfrac{a^2 + c^2 - b^2}{2ac}\right)$

Let $a = 6$, $b = 2$, and $c = 5$. $\quad \beta \approx 18°$

STEP 2: Find α.

Apply the Law of Sines. $\quad \dfrac{\sin\alpha}{a} = \dfrac{\sin\beta}{b}$

Solve for α. $\quad \alpha = \sin^{-1}\left(\dfrac{a\sin\beta}{b}\right)$

Let $a = 6$, $b = 2$, and $\beta = 18°$. $\quad \alpha \approx 68°$

STEP 3: Find γ. $\quad \alpha + \beta + \gamma = 180°$

$68° + 18° + \gamma = 180°$

$\gamma \approx 94°$

$a = 6$, $b = 2$, $c = 5$, $\alpha \approx 68°$, $\beta \approx 18°$, and $\gamma \approx 94°$.

This is incorrect. The longest side is not opposite the largest angle. What mistake was made?

• CONCEPTUAL

In Exercises 69–74, determine whether each statement is true or false.

69. Given the lengths of all three sides of a triangle, there is insufficient information to solve the triangle.

70. Given three angles of a triangle, there is insufficient information to solve the triangle.

71. The Pythagorean theorem is a special case of the Law of Cosines.

72. The Law of Cosines is a special case of the Pythagorean theorem.

73. If an obtuse triangle is isosceles, then knowing the measure of the obtuse angle and a side adjacent to it is sufficient to solve the triangle.

74. All acute triangles can be solved using the Law of Cosines.

• CHALLENGE

75. Show that $\dfrac{\cos\alpha}{a} + \dfrac{\cos\beta}{b} + \dfrac{\cos\gamma}{c} = \dfrac{a^2 + b^2 + c^2}{2abc}$.
Hint: Use the Law of Cosines.

76. Show that $a = c\cos\beta + b\cos\gamma$. *Hint:* Use the Law of Cosines.

The following half-angle identities are useful in Exercises 77 and 78 and will be derived in Chapter 6.

$$\cos\left(\frac{x}{2}\right) = \sqrt{\frac{1 + \cos x}{2}} \qquad \tan\left(\frac{x}{2}\right) = \sqrt{\frac{1 - \cos x}{1 + \cos x}}$$

77. Consider the following diagram and express $\cos\left(\dfrac{X}{2}\right)$ in terms of a.

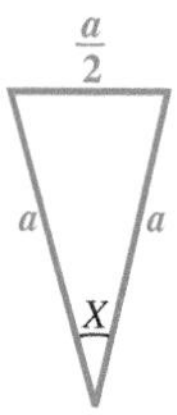

78. Using the diagram in Exercise 77, express $\tan\left(\dfrac{X}{2}\right)$ in terms of a.

79. Show that the area for an SAA triangle is given by

$$A = \frac{a^2 \sin\beta \sin\gamma}{2\sin\alpha}$$

Assume that α, β, and a are given.

80. Show that the area of an isosceles triangle with equal sides of length s is given by

$$A_{\text{isosceles}} = \frac{1}{2}s^2 \sin\theta$$

where θ is the angle between the two equal sides.

81. Find the area of the shaded region.

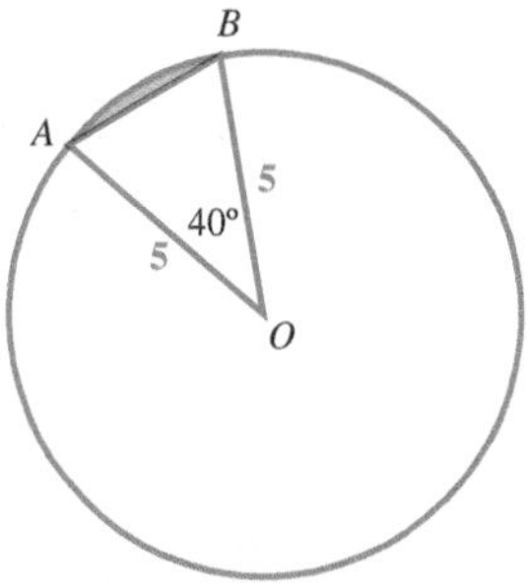

82. Find the area of the shaded region.

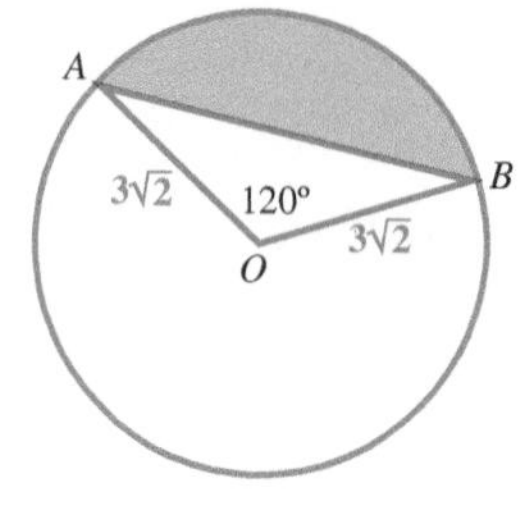

• PREVIEW TO CALCULUS

In calculus, some applications of the derivative require the solution of triangles. In Exercises 83–86, solve each triangle using the Law of Cosines.

83. Two ships start moving from the same port at the same time. One moves north at 40 miles per hour, while the other moves southeast at 50 miles per hour. Find the distance between the ships 4 hours later. Round your answer to the nearest mile.

84. An airport radar detects two planes approaching. The distance between the planes is 80 miles; the closest plane is 60 miles from the airport and the other plane is 70 miles from the airport. What is the angle (in degrees) formed by the planes and the airport?

85. An athlete runs along a circular track, of radius 100 meters, runs from A to B and then decides to take a shortcut to go to C. If the measure of angle BAC is $\dfrac{2\pi}{9}$, find the distance covered by the athlete if the distance from A to B is 153 meters. Round your answer to the nearest integer.

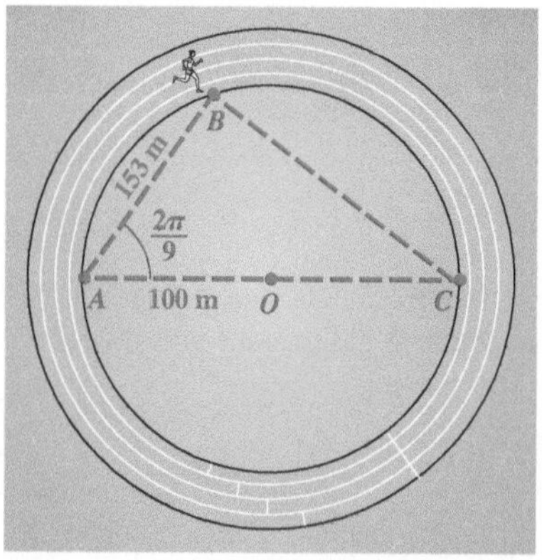

86. A regular pentagon is inscribed in a circle of radius 10 feet. Find its perimeter. Round your answer to the nearest tenth.

[CHAPTER 4 REVIEW]

SECTION	CONCEPT	KEY IDEAS/FORMULAS
4.1	**Angle measure**	
	Angles and their measure	*Degrees and Radians* 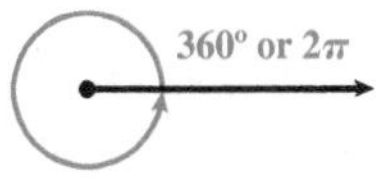 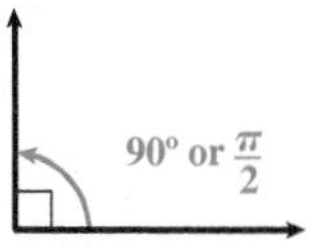 Converting between degrees and radians (Remember that $\pi = 180°$.)
	Radian measure	■ Degrees to radians: Multiply by $\frac{\pi}{180°}$ ■ Radians to degrees: Multiply by $\frac{180°}{\pi}$
	Angles in standard position	An angle is said to be in **standard position** if its initial side is along the positive x-axis and its vertex is at the origin. 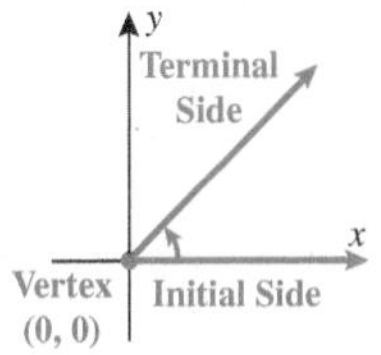
	Coterminal angles	Two angles in standard position with the same terminal side
	Arc length	$s = r\theta$ θ is in radians.
	Area of a circular sector	$A = \frac{1}{2}r^2\theta$ θ is in radians.
	Linear and angular speeds	**Linear speed** v is given by $$v = \frac{s}{t}$$ where s is the arc length (or distance along the arc) and t is time. **Angular speed** ω is given by $$\omega = \frac{\theta}{t}$$ where θ is given in radians.
	Relationship between linear and angular speeds	Linear and angular speeds are related through the radius of the circle: $$v = r\omega \quad \text{or} \quad \omega = \frac{v}{r}$$
4.2	**Right triangle trigonometry**	
	Right triangle ratios	**Pythagorean Theorem** 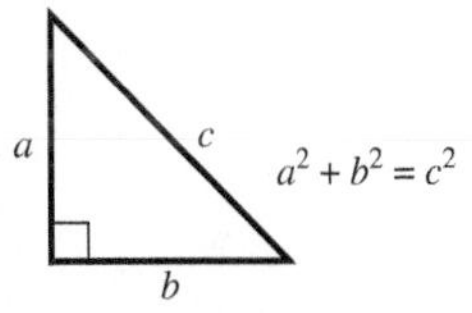
	Trigonometric ratios of general acute angles	$\sin\theta = \frac{\text{opposite}}{\text{hypotenuse}}$ (SOH) $\cos\theta = \frac{\text{adjacent}}{\text{hypotenuse}}$ (CAH) $\tan\theta = \frac{\text{opposite}}{\text{adjacent}}$ (TOA) 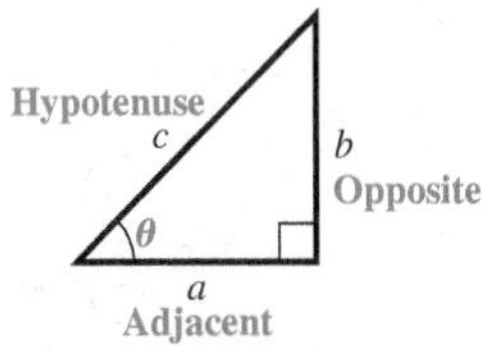

SECTION	CONCEPT	KEY IDEAS/FORMULAS
	Reciprocal identities	$\cot\theta = \frac{1}{\tan\theta}$ $\csc\theta = \frac{1}{\sin\theta}$ $\sec\theta = \frac{1}{\cos\theta}$
	Evaluating trigonometric functions exactly for special angle measures	See table below. The other trigonometric functions can be found for these values using $\tan\theta = \frac{\sin\theta}{\cos\theta}$ and the reciprocal identities.
	Using calculators to evaluate (approximate) trigonometric functions	Scientific and graphing calculators have buttons for sine, cosine, and tangent functions. When calculating the cotangent, secant, and cosecant functions of an angle, use the reciprocal button.
	Solving right triangles	
4.3	**Trigonometric functions of angles**	
	Trigonometric functions: The Cartesian plane	See below.
	Ranges of the trigonometric functions	$\sin\theta$ and $\cos\theta$: $[-1, 1]$ $\tan\theta$ and $\cot\theta$: $(-\infty, \infty)$ $\sec\theta$ and $\csc\theta$: $(-\infty, -1] \cup [1, \infty)$

Special angle measures:

θ	$\sin\theta$	$\cos\theta$
30°	$\frac{1}{2}$	$\frac{\sqrt{3}}{2}$
45°	$\frac{\sqrt{2}}{2}$	$\frac{\sqrt{2}}{2}$
60°	$\frac{\sqrt{3}}{2}$	$\frac{1}{2}$

Trigonometric functions: The Cartesian plane

$\sin\theta = \frac{y}{r}$ $\cos\theta = \frac{x}{r}$ $\tan\theta = \frac{y}{x}, x \neq 0$

$\csc\theta = \frac{r}{y}$ $\sec\theta = \frac{r}{x}$ $\cot\theta = \frac{x}{y}, y \neq 0$

where $x^2 + y^2 = r^2 \Rightarrow r = \sqrt{x^2 + y^2}$

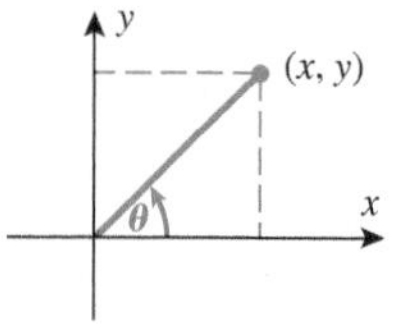

The distance r is positive: $r > 0$.

Algebraic signs of trigonometric functions

θ	QI	QII	QIII	QIV
$\sin\theta$	+	+	−	−
$\cos\theta$	+	−	−	+
$\tan\theta$	+	−	+	−

Trigonometric function values for quadrantal angles.

θ	0°	90°	180°	270°
$\sin\theta$	0	1	0	−1
$\cos\theta$	1	0	−1	0
$\tan\theta$	0	undefined	0	undefined
$\cot\theta$	undefined	0	undefined	0
$\sec\theta$	1	undefined	−1	undefined
$\csc\theta$	undefined	1	undefined	−1

SECTION	CONCEPT	KEY IDEAS/FORMULAS

Algebraic signs of trigonometric functions

TERMINAL SIDE OF θ IS IN QUADRANT	$\sin\theta$	$\cos\theta$	$\tan\theta$	$\cot\theta$	$\sec\theta$	$\csc\theta$
I	+	+	+	+	+	+
II	+	−	−	−	−	+
III	−	−	+	+	−	−
IV	−	+	−	−	+	−

Reference angles and reference right triangles

The reference angle α for angle θ (between 0° and 360°) is given by

- QI: $\alpha = \theta$
- QII: $\alpha = 180° - \theta$ or $\pi - \theta$
- QIII: $\alpha = \theta - 180°$ or $\theta - \pi$
- QIV: $\alpha = 360° - \theta$ or $2\pi - \theta$

Evaluating trigonometric functions for nonacute angles

4.4 The Law of Sines

Solving oblique triangles

Oblique (Nonright) Triangles

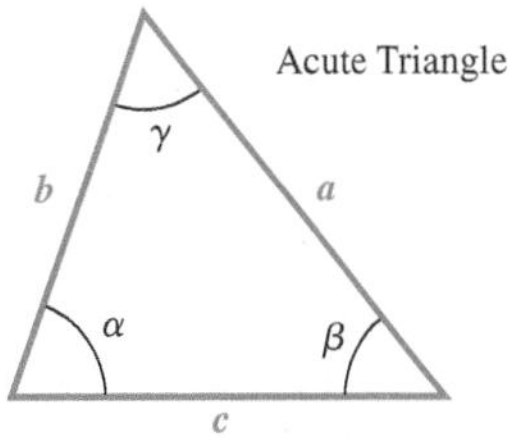

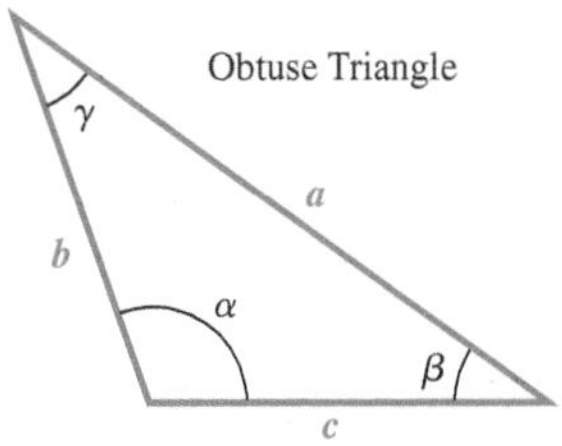

The Law of Sines

$$\frac{\sin\alpha}{a} = \frac{\sin\beta}{b} = \frac{\sin\gamma}{c}$$

Use for:

- AAS (or ASA) triangles
- SSA triangles (ambiguous case)

4.5 The Law of Cosines

Solving oblique triangles using the Law of Cosines

$$a^2 = b^2 + c^2 - 2bc\cos\alpha$$
$$b^2 = a^2 + c^2 - 2ac\cos\beta$$
$$c^2 = a^2 + b^2 - 2ab\cos\gamma$$

Use for:

- SAS triangles
- SSS triangles

The area of a triangle

The area of a triangle (SAS case)

$A_{SAS} = \frac{1}{2}bc\sin\alpha$ when b, c, and α are known.

$A_{SAS} = \frac{1}{2}ab\sin\gamma$ when a, b, and γ are known.

$A_{SAS} = \frac{1}{2}ac\sin\beta$ when a, c, and β are known.

The area of a triangle (SSS case)

Use Heron's formula for the SSS case:

$$A_{SSS} = \sqrt{s(s-a)(s-b)(s-c)}$$

where a, b, and c are the lengths of the sides of the triangle, and s is half the perimeter of the triangle, called the semiperimeter.

$$s = \frac{a+b+c}{2}$$

[CHAPTER 4 REVIEW EXERCISES]

4.1 Angle Measure

Find (a) the complement and (b) the supplement of the given angles.

1. $28°$
2. $17°$
3. $35°$
4. $78°$
5. $89.01°$
6. $0.013°$

Convert from degrees to radians. Leave your answers in terms of π.

7. $135°$
8. $240°$
9. $330°$
10. $180°$
11. $216°$
12. $108°$
13. $1620°$
14. $900°$

Convert from radians to degrees.

15. $\frac{\pi}{3}$
16. $\frac{11\pi}{6}$
17. $\frac{5\pi}{4}$
18. $\frac{2\pi}{3}$
19. $\frac{5\pi}{9}$
20. $\frac{17\pi}{10}$
21. 10π
22. $\frac{31\pi}{2}$

Applications

23. **Clock.** What is the measure (in degrees) of the angle that the minute hand sweeps in exactly 25 minutes?
24. **Clock.** What is the measure (in degrees) of the angle that the second hand sweeps in exactly 15 seconds?
25. A ladybug is clinging to the outer edge of a child's spinning disk. The disk is 4 inches in diameter and is spinning at 60 revolutions per minute. How fast is the ladybug traveling in inches/minute?
26. How fast is a motorcyclist traveling in miles per hour if his tires are 30 inches in diameter and the angular speed of the tire is 10π radians per second?

4.2 Right Triangle Trigonometry

Use the following triangle to find the indicated trigonometric functions. Rationalize any denominators that you encounter in the answers.

27. $\cos\theta$
28. $\sin\theta$
29. $\sec\theta$
30. $\csc\theta$
31. $\tan\theta$
32. $\cot\theta$

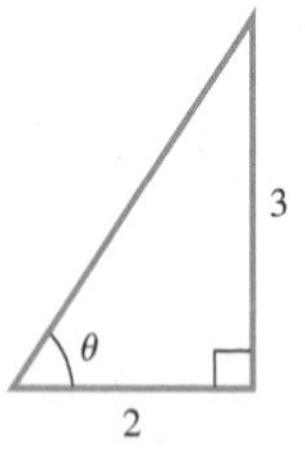

Label each trigonometric function value with the corresponding value (a, b, or c).

a. $\frac{\sqrt{3}}{2}$ **b.** $\frac{1}{2}$ **c.** $\frac{\sqrt{2}}{2}$

33. $\sin 30°$
34. $\cos 30°$
35. $\cos 60°$
36. $\sin 60°$
37. $\sin 45°$
38. $\cos 45°$

Use a calculator to approximate the following trigonometric function values. Round the answers to four decimal places.

39. $\sin 42°$
40. $\cos 57°$
41. $\cos 17.3°$
42. $\tan 25.2°$
43. $\cot 33°$
44. $\sec 16.8°$
45. $\csc 40.25°$
46. $\cot 19.76°$

The following exercises illustrate a mid-air refueling scenario that U.S. military aircraft often use. Assume the elevation angle that the hose makes with the plane being fueled is $\theta = 30°$.

47. **Mid-Air Refueling.** If the hose is 150 feet long, what should the altitude difference a be between the two planes?

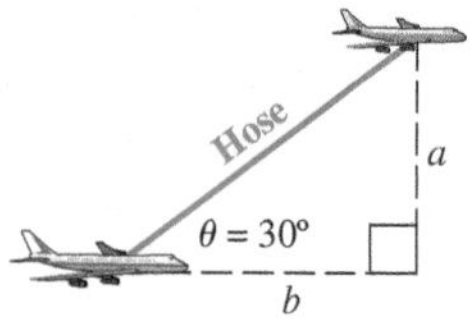

48. **Mid-Air Refueling.** If the smallest acceptable altitude difference, a, between the two planes is 100 feet, how long should the hose be?

4.3 Trigonometric Functions of Angles

In the following exercises, the terminal side of an angle θ in standard position passes through the indicated point. Calculate the values of the six trigonometric functions for angle θ.

49. $(6, -8)$
50. $(-24, -7)$
51. $(-6, 2)$
52. $(-40, 9)$
53. $(\sqrt{3}, 1)$
54. $(-9, -9)$
55. $(\frac{1}{2}, -\frac{1}{4})$
56. $(-\frac{3}{4}, \frac{5}{6})$
57. $(-1.2, -2.4)$
58. $(0.8, -2.4)$

Evaluate the following expressions exactly:

59. $\sin 330°$
60. $\cos(-300°)$
61. $\tan 150°$
62. $\cot 315°$
63. $\sec(-150°)$
64. $\csc 210°$
65. $\sin\left(\frac{7\pi}{4}\right)$
66. $\cos\left(\frac{7\pi}{6}\right)$
67. $\tan\left(-\frac{2\pi}{3}\right)$
68. $\cot\left(\frac{4\pi}{3}\right)$
69. $\sec\left(\frac{5\pi}{4}\right)$
70. $\csc\left(-\frac{8\pi}{3}\right)$
71. $\sec\left(\frac{5\pi}{6}\right)$
72. $\cos\left(-\frac{11\pi}{6}\right)$

4.4 The Law of Sines

Solve the given triangles.

73. $\alpha = 10°, \beta = 20°, a = 4$

74. $\beta = 40°, \gamma = 60°, b = 10$

75. $\alpha = 5°, \beta = 45°, c = 10$

76. $\beta = 60°, \gamma = 70°, a = 20$

77. $\gamma = 11°, \alpha = 11°, c = 11$

78. $\beta = 20°, \gamma = 50°, b = 8$

79. $\alpha = 45°, \gamma = 45°, b = 2$

80. $\alpha = 60°, \beta = 20°, c = 17$

81. $\alpha = 12°, \gamma = 22°, a = 99$

82. $\beta = 102°, \gamma = 27°, a = 24$

Two sides and an angle are given. Determine whether a triangle (or two) exist(s), and if so, solve the triangle.

83. $a = 7, b = 9, \alpha = 20°$

84. $b = 24, c = 30, \beta = 16°$

85. $a = 10, c = 12, \alpha = 24°$

86. $b = 100, c = 116, \beta = 12°$

87. $a = 40, b = 30, \beta = 150°$

88. $b = 2, c = 3, \gamma = 165°$

89. $a = 4, b = 6, \alpha = 10°$

90. $c = 25, a = 37, \gamma = 4°$

4.5 The Law of Cosines

Solve each triangle.

91. $a = 40, b = 60, \gamma = 50°$

92. $b = 15, c = 12, \alpha = 140°$

93. $a = 24, b = 25, c = 30$

94. $a = 6, b = 6, c = 8$

95. $a = \sqrt{11}, b = \sqrt{14}, c = 5$

96. $a = 22, b = 120, c = 122$

97. $b = 7, c = 10, \alpha = 14°$

98. $a = 6, b = 12, \gamma = 80°$

99. $b = 10, c = 4, \alpha = 90°$

100. $a = 4, b = 5, \gamma = 75°$

101. $a = 10, b = 11, c = 12$

102. $a = 22, b = 24, c = 25$

103. $b = 16, c = 18, \alpha = 100°$

104. $a = 25, c = 25, \beta = 9°$

105. $b = 12, c = 40, \alpha = 10°$

106. $a = 26, b = 20, c = 10$

107. $a = 26, b = 40, c = 13$

108. $a = 1, b = 2, c = 3$

109. $a = 6.3, b = 4.2, \alpha = 15°$

110. $b = 5, c = 6, \beta = 35°$

Find the area of each triangle described.

111. $b = 16, c = 18, \alpha = 100°$

112. $a = 25, c = 25, \beta = 9°$

113. $a = 10, b = 11, c = 12$

114. $a = 22, b = 24, c = 25$

115. $a = 26, b = 20, c = 10$

116. $a = 24, b = 32, c = 40$

117. $b = 12, c = 40, \alpha = 10°$

118. $a = 21, c = 75, \beta = 60°$

Applications

119. Area of Inscribed Triangle. The area of a triangle inscribed in a circle can be found if you know the lengths of the sides of the triangle and the radius of the circle: $A = \frac{abc}{4r}$. Find the radius of the circle that circumscribes the triangle if all the sides of the triangle measure 9.0 inches and the area of the triangle is 35 square inches.

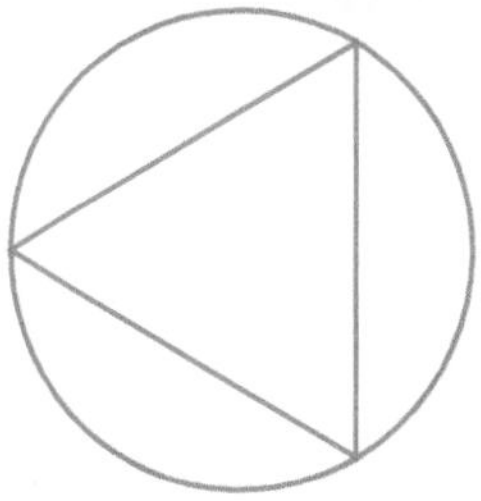

120. Area of Inscribed Triangle. The area of a triangle inscribed in a circle can be found if you know the lengths of the sides of the triangle and the radius of the circle: $A = \frac{abc}{4r}$. Find the radius of the circle that circumscribes the triangle if the sides of the triangle measure 9, 12, and 15 inches and the area of the triangle is 54 square inches.

[CHAPTER 4 PRACTICE TEST]

1. A 5-foot girl is standing *in* the Grand Canyon, and she wants to estimate the depth of the canyon. The sun casts her shadow 6 inches along the ground. To measure the shadow cast by the top of the canyon, she walks the length of the shadow. She takes 200 steps and estimates that each step is roughly 3 feet. Approximately how tall is the Grand Canyon?
2. Fill in the values in the table.

θ	$\sin\theta$	$\cos\theta$	$\tan\theta$	$\cot\theta$	$\sec\theta$	$\csc\theta$
30°						
45°						
60°						

3. What is the difference between $\cos\theta = \frac{2}{3}$ and $\cos\theta \approx 0.6\overline{6}$?
4. Fill in the table with exact values for the quadrantal angles and the algebraic signs for the quadrants.

	0°	QI	90°	QII	180°	QIII	270°	QIV	360°
$\sin\theta$									
$\cos\theta$									

5. If $\cot\theta < 0$ and $\sec\theta > 0$, in which quadrant does the terminal side of θ lie?
6. Evaluate $\sin 210°$ exactly.
7. Convert $\frac{13\pi}{4}$ to degree measure.
8. Convert 260° to radian measure. Leave the answer in terms of π.
9. What is the area of the sector swept by the second hand of a clock in 25 seconds? Assume the radius of the sector is 3 inches.
10. What is the measure in radians of the smaller angle between the hour and minute hands at 10:10?

Solve the triangles if possible.

11. $\alpha = 30°, \beta = 40°, b = 10$
12. $\alpha = 47°, \beta = 98°, \gamma = 35°$
13. $a = 7, b = 9, c = 12$
14. $\alpha = 45°, a = 8, b = 10$
15. $a = 1, b = 1, c = 2$
16. $a = \frac{23}{7}, c = \frac{5}{7}, \beta = 61.2°$
17. $\alpha = 110°, \beta = 20°, a = 5$
18. $b = \frac{\sqrt{5}}{2}, c = 3\sqrt{5}, \alpha = 45°$

In Exercises 19 and 20, find the areas of the given triangles.

19. $\gamma = 72°, a = 10, b = 12$
20. $a = 7, b = 10, c = 13$

[CHAPTERS 1–4 CUMULATIVE TEST]

1. Find the average rate of change for $f(x) = \frac{5}{x}$ from $x = 2$ to $x = 4$.
2. Use interval notation to express the domain of the function $f(x) = \sqrt{x^2 - 25}$.
3. Using the function $f(x) = 5 - x^2$, evaluate the difference quotient $\frac{f(x+h) - f(x)}{h}$.
4. Given the piecewise-defined function
$$f(x) = \begin{cases} x^2 & x < 0 \\ 2x - 1 & 0 \le x < 5 \\ 5 - x & x \ge 5 \end{cases}$$
find:
   a. $f(0)$ **b.** $f(4)$ **c.** $f(5)$ **d.** $f(-4)$
   e. State the domain and range in interval notation.
   f. Determine the intervals where the function is increasing, decreasing, or constant.
5. Evaluate $g(f(-1))$ for $f(x) = \sqrt[3]{x - 7}$ and $g(x) = \frac{5}{3 - x}$.
6. Find the inverse of the function $f(x) = \frac{5x + 2}{x - 3}$.
7. Find the quadratic function that has the vertex $(0, 7)$ and goes through the point $(2, -1)$.
8. Find all of the real zeros, and state the multiplicity of each, for the function $f(x) = \frac{1}{7}x^5 + \frac{2}{9}x^3$.
9. Graph the rational function $f(x) = \frac{x^2 + 3}{x - 2}$. Give all asymptotes.
10. Factor the polynomial $P(x) = 4x^4 - 4x^3 + 13x^2 + 18x + 5$ as a product of linear factors.
11. How much money should you put now in a savings account that earns 5.5% a year compounded continuously, if you want to have $85,000 in 15 years?
12. Evaluate $\log_{4.7} 8.9$ using the change-of-base formula. Round the answer to three decimal places.
13. Solve the equation $5(10^{2x}) = 37$ for x. Round the answer to three decimal places.
14. Solve for x: $\ln\sqrt{6 - 3x} - \frac{1}{2}\ln(x + 2) = \ln(x)$.
15. In a 45°-45°-90° triangle, if the two legs have a length of 15 feet, how long is the hypotenuse?
16. **Height of a Tree.** The shadow of a tree measures $15\frac{1}{3}$ feet. At the same time of day, the shadow of a 6-foot pole measures 2.3 feet. How tall is the tree?
17. Convert 432° to radians.
18. Convert $\frac{5\pi}{9}$ to degrees.
19. Find the exact value of $\tan\left(\frac{4\pi}{3}\right)$.
20. Find the exact value of $\sec\left(-\frac{7\pi}{6}\right)$.
21. Use a calculator to find the value of $\csc 37°$. Round your answer to four decimal places.
22. In the right triangle below, find a, b, and θ. Round each to the nearest tenth.

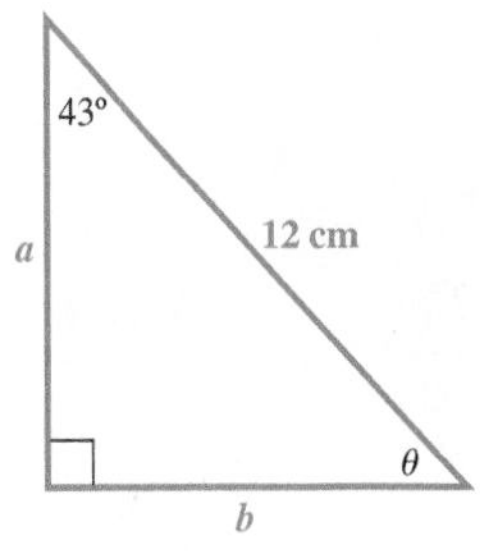

23. Solve the triangle below. Round the side lengths to the nearest centimeter.

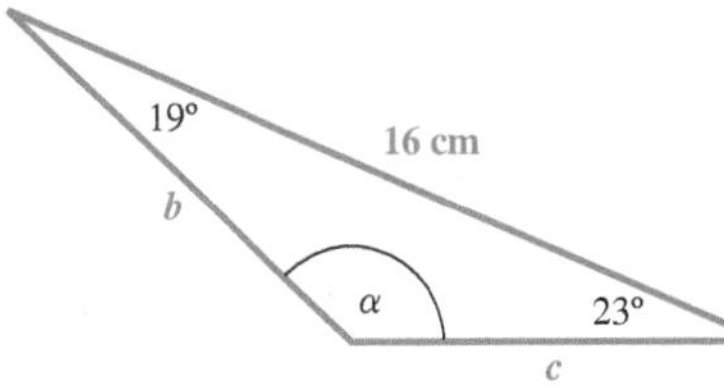

24. Solve the triangle $a = 2$, $b = 4$, and $c = 5$. Round your answer to the nearest degree.

CHAPTER 5

Trigonometric Functions of Real Numbers

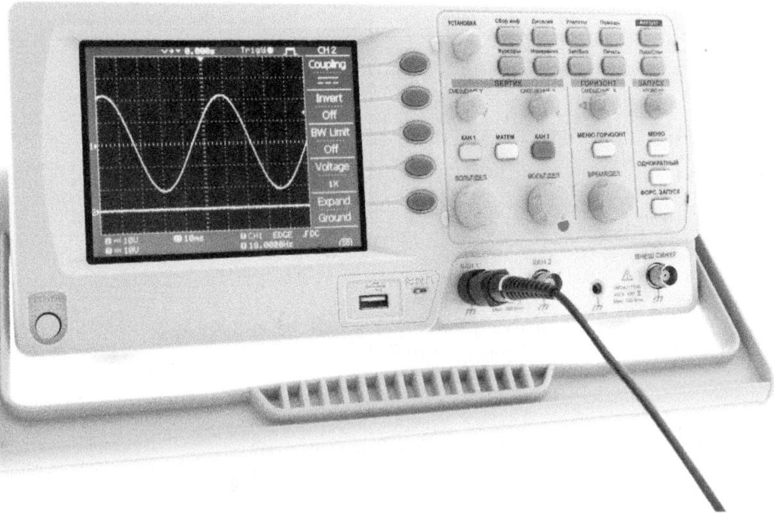

Alexey Filatov/Alamy Stock Photo

An oscilloscope displays voltage (vertical axis) as a function of time (horizontal axis) of an electronic signal. The electronic signal is an electric representation of some periodic process that occurs in the real world, such as a human pulse or a sound wave. Oscilloscopes are used in medicine, the sciences, and engineering. They allow the shape of a signal to be displayed, which allows the amplitude and frequency of the repetitive signal to then be determined. The oscilloscope above displays a *sine* wave.

LEARNING OBJECTIVES

- Draw the unit circle, and label the sine and cosine values for special angles (in both degrees and radians).
- Graph sine and cosine functions (amplitude, period, and translations).
- Graph tangent, cotangent, secant, and cosecant functions.

[IN THIS CHAPTER]

We will use the unit circle approach to define trigonometric functions. We will graph the sine and cosine functions and find periods, amplitudes, and phase shifts. Applications such as harmonic motion will be discussed. Combinations of sinusoidal functions will be discussed through a technique called the addition of ordinates. Last, we will discuss the graphs of the other trigonometric functions (tangent, cotangent, secant, and cosecant).

TRIGONOMETRIC FUNCTIONS OF REAL NUMBERS

5.1 TRIGONOMETRIC FUNCTIONS: THE UNIT CIRCLE APPROACH	5.2 GRAPHS OF SINE AND COSINE FUNCTIONS	5.3 GRAPHS OF OTHER TRIGONOMETRIC FUNCTIONS
• Trigonometric Functions and the Unit Circle • Properties of Trigonometric (Circular) Functions	• The Graphs of Sinusoidal Functions • Graphing a Shifted Sinusoidal Function: $y = A\sin(Bx + C) + D$ and $y = A\cos(Bx + C) + D$ • Harmonic Motion • Graphing Sums of Functions: Addition of Ordinates	• Graphing the Tangent, Cotangent, Secant, and Cosecant Functions • Translations of Trigonometric Functions

5.1 TRIGONOMETRIC FUNCTIONS: THE UNIT CIRCLE APPROACH

SKILLS OBJECTIVES

- Draw the unit circle illustrating the special angles, and label cosine and sine values.
- Classify circular functions as even or odd.

CONCEPTUAL OBJECTIVES

- Relate x-coordinates and y-coordinates of points on the unit circle to the values of cosine and sine functions.
- Visualize the periodic properties of circular functions.

5.1.1 SKILL

Draw the unit circle illustrating the special angles, and label cosine and sine values.

5.1.1 CONCEPTUAL

Relate x-coordinates and y-coordinates of points on the unit circle to the values of cosine and sine functions.

The first definition of trigonometric functions we developed was in terms of ratios of sides of right triangles (Section 4.2). Then in Section 4.3 we superimposed right triangles on the Cartesian plane, which led to a second definition of trigonometric functions (for any angle) in terms of ratios of x- and y-coordinates of a point and the distance from the origin to that point. In this section, we inscribe the right triangles into the unit circle in the Cartesian plane, which will yield a third definition of trigonometric functions. It is important to note that all three definitions are consistent with one another.

5.1.1 Trigonometric Functions and the Unit Circle

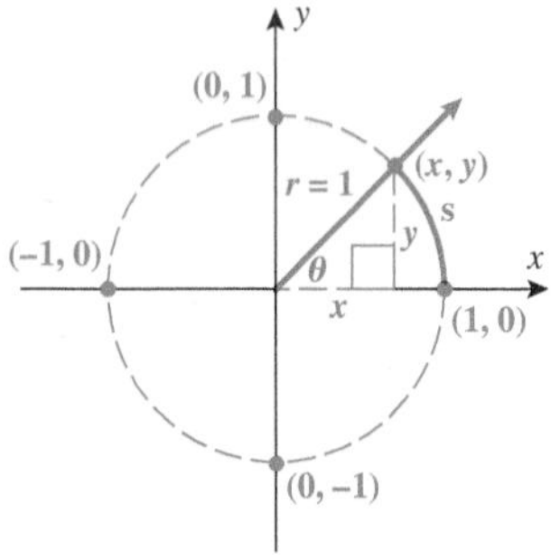

Note: In radians, $\theta = \frac{s}{r}$, and since $r = 1$, we know that $\theta = s$.

The equation for the **unit circle** centered at the origin is given by $x^2 + y^2 = 1$. The term *circular function* is often used as a synonym for *trigonometric function*, but it is important to note that a circle is not a function (it does not pass the vertical line test).

If we form a central angle θ in the unit circle such that the terminal side lies in quadrant I, we can use the previous two definitions of the sine and cosine functions when $r = 1$ (i.e., in the unit circle).

TRIGONOMETRIC FUNCTION	RIGHT TRIANGLE TRIGONOMETRY	CARTESIAN PLANE
$\sin\theta$	$\frac{\text{opposite}}{\text{hypotenuse}} = \frac{y}{1} = y$	$\frac{y}{r} = \frac{y}{1} = y$
$\cos\theta$	$\frac{\text{adjacent}}{\text{hypotenuse}} = \frac{x}{1} = x$	$\frac{x}{r} = \frac{x}{1} = x$

STUDY TIP

$(\cos\theta, \sin\theta)$ represents a unique point (x, y) on the unit circle.

Notice that the point (x, y) on the unit circle can be written as $(\cos\theta, \sin\theta)$. We can now summarize the exact values for **sine** and **cosine** in the illustration that follows.

The following observations are consistent with properties of trigonometric functions we've studied already:

- $\sin\theta > 0$ in QI and QII.
- $\cos\theta > 0$ in QI and QIV.
- The unit circle equation $x^2 + y^2 = 1$ leads to the Pythagorean identity $\cos^2\theta + \sin^2\theta = 1$.

CONCEPT CHECK

If the point $(-A, -B)$ lies in quadrant III, then what must be true so that $\cos\theta = -A$ and $\sin\theta = -B$?

ANSWER $A^2 + B^2 = 1$

$(x, y) = (\cos\theta, \sin\theta)$, where θ is the central angle whose terminal side intersects the unit circle at (x, y).

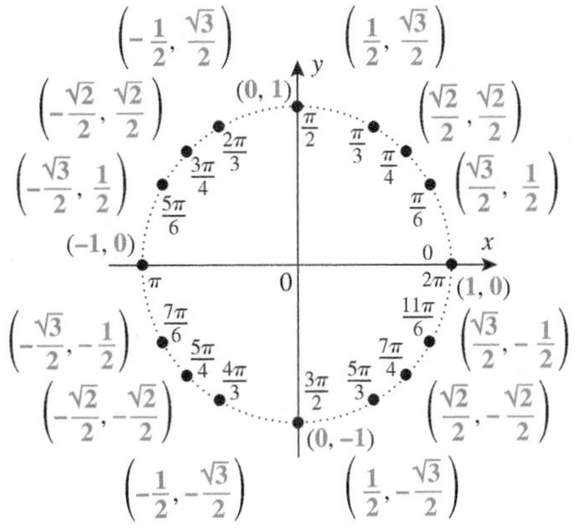

Trigonometric (Circular) Functions

Using the unit circle relationship, $(x, y) = (\cos\theta, \sin\theta)$, where θ is the central angle whose terminal side intersects the unit circle at the point (x, y), we can now define the remaining trigonometric functions using this unit circle approach and the quotient and reciprocal identities. Because the trigonometric functions are defined in terms of the unit *circle*, the trigonometric functions are often called **circular functions.**

DEFINITION Trigonometric Functions

Unit Circle Approach

Let (x, y) be any point on the unit circle. If θ is a real number that represents the distance from the point $(1, 0)$ along the circumference to the point (x, y), then

$$\sin\theta = y \qquad \cos\theta = x \qquad \tan\theta = \frac{y}{x} \quad x \neq 0$$

$$\csc\theta = \frac{1}{y} \quad y \neq 0 \qquad \sec\theta = \frac{1}{x} \quad x \neq 0 \qquad \cot\theta = \frac{x}{y} \quad y \neq 0$$

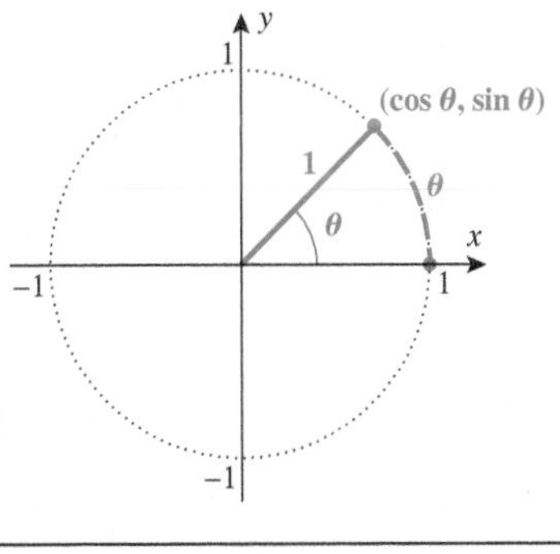

EXAMPLE 1 Finding Exact Trigonometric (Circular) Function Values

Find the exact values for

a. $\sin\left(\frac{7\pi}{4}\right)$ **b.** $\cos\left(\frac{5\pi}{6}\right)$ **c.** $\tan\left(\frac{3\pi}{2}\right)$

Solution (a):

The angle $\frac{7\pi}{4}$ corresponds to the coordinates $\left(\frac{\sqrt{2}}{2}, -\frac{\sqrt{2}}{2}\right)$ on the unit circle.

The value of the sine function is the y-coordinate. $\boxed{\sin\left(\frac{7\pi}{4}\right) = -\frac{\sqrt{2}}{2}}$

Solution (b):

The angle $\frac{5\pi}{6}$ corresponds to the coordinate $\left(-\frac{\sqrt{3}}{2}, \frac{1}{2}\right)$ on the unit circle.

The value of the cosine function is the x-coordinate. $\boxed{\cos\left(\frac{5\pi}{6}\right) = -\frac{\sqrt{3}}{2}}$

Solution (c):

The angle $\frac{3\pi}{2}$ corresponds to the coordinate $(0, -1)$ on the unit circle.

The value of the cosine function is the x-coordinate. $\cos\left(\frac{3\pi}{2}\right) = 0$

The value of the sine function is the y-coordinate. $\sin\left(\frac{3\pi}{2}\right) = -1$

Tangent is the ratio of sine to cosine. $\tan\left(\frac{3\pi}{2}\right) = \frac{\sin\left(\frac{3\pi}{2}\right)}{\cos\left(\frac{3\pi}{2}\right)}$

Let $\cos\left(\frac{3\pi}{2}\right) = 0$ and $\sin\left(\frac{3\pi}{2}\right) = -1$. $\tan\left(\frac{3\pi}{2}\right) = \frac{-1}{0}$

$\boxed{\tan\left(\frac{3\pi}{2}\right) \text{ is undefined.}}$

YOUR TURN Find the exact values for

a. $\sin\left(\frac{5\pi}{6}\right)$ **b.** $\cos\left(\frac{7\pi}{4}\right)$ **c.** $\tan\left(\frac{2\pi}{3}\right)$

ANSWER

a. $\frac{1}{2}$ b. $\frac{\sqrt{2}}{2}$ c. $-\sqrt{3}$

EXAMPLE 2 **Solving Equations That Involve Trigonometric (Circular) Functions**

Use the unit circle to find all values of θ, $0 \le \theta \le 2\pi$, for which $\sin\theta = -\frac{1}{2}$.

Solution:

The value of sine is the y-coordinate.

Since the value of sine is negative, θ must lie in quadrant III or quadrant IV.

There are two values for θ that are greater than or equal to zero and less than or equal to 2π that correspond to $\sin\theta = -\frac{1}{2}$.

$$\theta = \frac{7\pi}{6}, \frac{11\pi}{6}$$

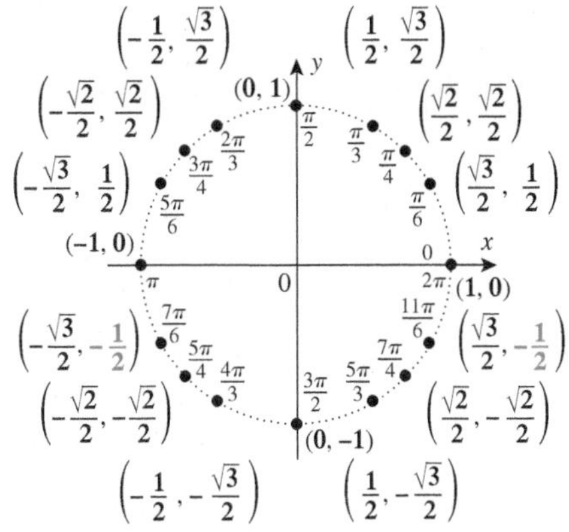

YOUR TURN Find all values of θ, $0 \le \theta \le 2\pi$, for which $\cos\theta = -\frac{1}{2}$.

ANSWER

$\theta = \frac{2\pi}{3}, \frac{4\pi}{3}$

5.1.2 Properties of Trigonometric (Circular) Functions

5.1.2 SKILL

Classify circular functions as even or odd.

5.1.2 CONCEPTUAL

Visualize the periodic properties of circular functions.

WORDS	MATH
For a point (x, y) that lies on the unit circle, $x^2 + y^2 = 1$.	$-1 \le x \le 1$ and $-1 \le y \le 1$
Since $(x, y) = (\cos\theta, \sin\theta)$, the following holds.	$-1 \le \cos\theta \le 1$ and $-1 \le \sin\theta \le 1$
State the **domain and range of the cosine and sine functions**.	Domain: $(-\infty, \infty)$ Range: $[-1, 1]$
Since $\cot\theta = \frac{\cos\theta}{\sin\theta}$ and $\csc\theta = \frac{1}{\sin\theta}$, the values for θ that make $\sin\theta = 0$ must be eliminated from the **domain of the cotangent and cosecant functions**. (The integer multiples of π (i.e., $\pm\pi, \pm 2\pi, \pm 3\pi, \ldots$) can be written as $n\pi$.)	Domain: $\theta \ne n\pi$, n an integer
Since $\tan\theta = \frac{\sin\theta}{\cos\theta}$ and $\sec\theta = \frac{1}{\cos\theta}$, the values for θ that make $\cos\theta = 0$ must be eliminated from the **domain of the tangent and secant functions**.	Domain: $\theta \ne \frac{(2n+1)\pi}{2}$, n an integer

[CONCEPT CHECK]

Which of the following is NOT equivalent to the others for all values of angle A?

(A) $\sin(2\pi + A)$
(B) $\sin(A - 2\pi)$
(C) $\sin(\pi + A)$
(D) $\sin(A + 8\pi)$

ANSWER (C)

The following box summarizes the domains and ranges of the trigonometric functions.

DOMAINS AND RANGES OF THE TRIGONOMETRIC (CIRCULAR) FUNCTIONS

For any real number θ and integer n:

FUNCTION	DOMAIN	RANGE
$\sin\theta$	$(-\infty, \infty)$	$[-1, 1]$
$\cos\theta$	$(-\infty, \infty)$	$[-1, 1]$
$\tan\theta$	all real numbers such that $\theta \neq \frac{(2n+1)\pi}{2}$	$(-\infty, \infty)$
$\cot\theta$	all real numbers such that $\theta \neq n\pi$	$(-\infty, \infty)$
$\sec\theta$	all real numbers such that $\theta \neq \frac{(2n+1)\pi}{2}$	$(-\infty, -1] \cup [1, \infty)$
$\csc\theta$	all real numbers such that $\theta \neq n\pi$	$(-\infty, -1] \cup [1, \infty)$

STUDY TIP

- The sine function is an odd function.
- The cosine function is an even function.

Recall from algebra that **even functions** are functions for which $f(-x) = f(x)$, and **odd functions** are functions for which $f(-x) = -f(x)$.

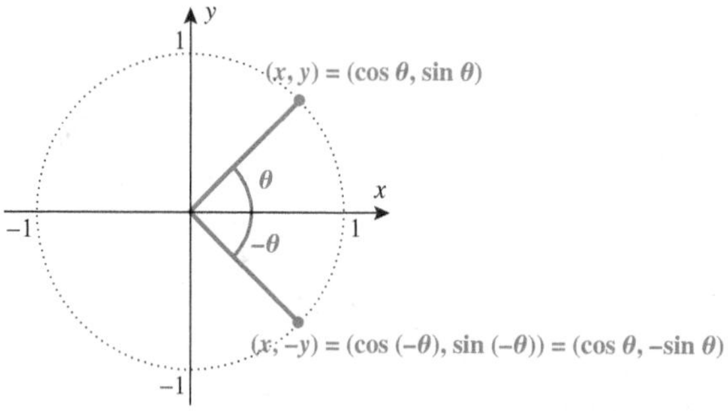

The **cosine function is an even function.** $\boxed{\cos\theta = \cos(-\theta)}$

The **sine function is an odd function.** $\boxed{\sin(-\theta) = -\sin\theta}$

EXAMPLE 3 Using Properties of Trigonometric (Circular) Functions

Evaluate $\cos\left(-\frac{5\pi}{6}\right)$.

Solution:

The cosine function is an even function. $\cos\left(-\frac{5\pi}{6}\right) = \cos\left(\frac{5\pi}{6}\right)$

Use the unit circle to evaluate cosine. $\cos\left(\frac{5\pi}{6}\right) = -\frac{\sqrt{3}}{2}$

$$\cos\left(-\frac{5\pi}{6}\right) = \boxed{-\frac{\sqrt{3}}{2}}$$

YOUR TURN Evaluate $\sin\left(-\frac{5\pi}{6}\right)$.

ANSWER

$-\frac{1}{2}$

It is important to note that although trigonometric functions can be evaluated exactly for some special angles, a calculator can be used to approximate trigonometric functions for any angle. When approximating trigonometric function values, set the calculator to radian mode first, since θ is a real number.

STUDY TIP

Set the calculator in radian mode before evaluating trigonometric functions in radians. Alternatively, convert the radian measure to degrees before evaluating the trigonometric function.

EXAMPLE 4 Evaluating Trigonometric (Circular) Functions with a Calculator

Use a calculator to evaluate $\sin\left(\frac{7\pi}{12}\right)$. Round the answer to four decimal places.

✓CORRECT

Evaluate with a calculator.

0.965925826

Round to four decimal places.

$\sin\left(\frac{7\pi}{12}\right) \approx \boxed{0.9659}$

✗INCORRECT

Evaluate with a calculator.

0.031979376 **ERROR**

(Calculator in degree mode)

Many calculators automatically reset to degree mode after every calculation, so make sure to always check what mode the calculator indicates.

YOUR TURN Use a calculator to evaluate $\tan\left(\frac{9\pi}{5}\right)$. Round the answer to four decimal places.

ANSWER

-0.7265

EXAMPLE 5 Even and Odd Trigonometric (Circular) Functions

Show that the secant function is an even function.

Solution:

Show that $\sec(-\theta) = \sec\theta$.

Secant is the reciprocal of cosine. $\quad \sec(-\theta) = \dfrac{1}{\cos(-\theta)}$

Cosine is an even function, $\cos(-\theta) = \cos\theta$. $\quad \sec(-\theta) = \dfrac{1}{\cos\theta}$

Secant is the reciprocal of cosine, $\sec\theta = \dfrac{1}{\cos\theta}$. $\quad \sec(-\theta) = \dfrac{1}{\cos\theta} = \sec\theta$

Since $\sec(-\theta) = \sec\theta$, $\boxed{\text{the secant function is an even function}}$.

[SECTION 5.1] SUMMARY

In this section, we have defined trigonometric functions as circular functions. Any point (x, y) that lies on the unit circle satisfies the equation $x^2 + y^2 = 1$. The Pythagorean identity $\cos^2\theta + \sin^2\theta = 1$ can also be represented on the unit circle, where $(x, y) = (\cos\theta, \sin\theta)$, and where θ is the central angle whose terminal side intersects the unit circle at the point (x, y). The cosine function is an even function, $\cos(-\theta) = \cos\theta$; the sine function is an odd function, $\sin(-\theta) = -\sin\theta$.

[SECTION 5.1] EXERCISES

• SKILLS

In Exercises 1–14, find the *exact* values of the indicated trigonometric functions using the unit circle.

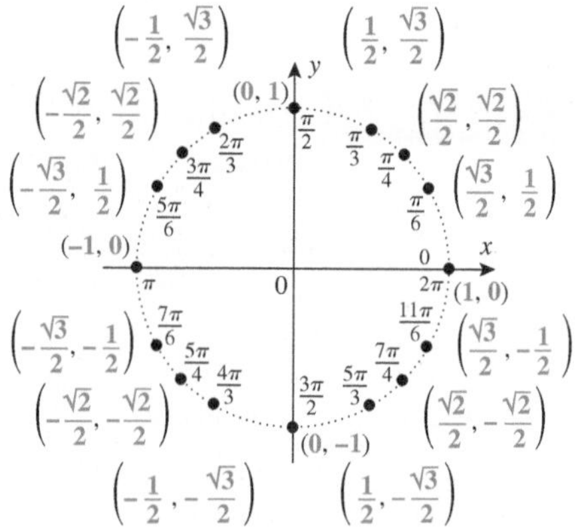

1. $\sin\left(\frac{5\pi}{3}\right)$ 2. $\cos\left(\frac{5\pi}{3}\right)$ 3. $\cos\left(\frac{7\pi}{6}\right)$ 4. $\sin\left(\frac{7\pi}{6}\right)$

5. $\sin\left(\frac{3\pi}{4}\right)$ 6. $\cos\left(\frac{3\pi}{4}\right)$ 7. $\tan\left(\frac{7\pi}{4}\right)$ 8. $\cot\left(\frac{7\pi}{4}\right)$

9. $\sec\left(\frac{5\pi}{4}\right)$ 10. $\csc\left(\frac{5\pi}{3}\right)$ 11. $\tan\left(\frac{4\pi}{3}\right)$ 12. $\cot\left(\frac{11\pi}{6}\right)$

13. $\csc\left(\frac{5\pi}{6}\right)$ 14. $\cot\left(\frac{2\pi}{3}\right)$

In Exercises 15–34, use the unit circle and the facts that sine is an odd function and cosine is an even function to find the *exact* values of the indicated functions.

15. $\sin\left(-\frac{2\pi}{3}\right)$ 16. $\sin\left(-\frac{5\pi}{4}\right)$ 17. $\sin\left(-\frac{\pi}{3}\right)$ 18. $\sin\left(-\frac{7\pi}{6}\right)$ 19. $\cos\left(-\frac{3\pi}{4}\right)$

20. $\cos\left(-\frac{5\pi}{3}\right)$ 21. $\cos\left(-\frac{5\pi}{6}\right)$ 22. $\cos\left(-\frac{7\pi}{4}\right)$ 23. $\sin\left(-\frac{5\pi}{4}\right)$ 24. $\sin(-\pi)$

25. $\sin\left(-\frac{3\pi}{2}\right)$ 26. $\sin\left(-\frac{\pi}{3}\right)$ 27. $\cos\left(-\frac{\pi}{4}\right)$ 28. $\cos\left(-\frac{3\pi}{4}\right)$ 29. $\cos\left(-\frac{\pi}{2}\right)$

30. $\cos\left(-\frac{7\pi}{6}\right)$ 31. $\csc\left(-\frac{5\pi}{6}\right)$ 32. $\sec\left(-\frac{7\pi}{4}\right)$ 33. $\tan\left(-\frac{11\pi}{6}\right)$ 34. $\cot\left(-\frac{11\pi}{6}\right)$

In Exercises 35–54, use the unit circle to find all of the exact values of θ that make the equation true in the indicated interval.

35. $\cos\theta = \frac{\sqrt{3}}{2}, 0 \le \theta \le 2\pi$ 36. $\cos\theta = -\frac{\sqrt{3}}{2}, 0 \le \theta \le 2\pi$ 37. $\sin\theta = -\frac{\sqrt{3}}{2}, 0 \le \theta \le 2\pi$

38. $\sin\theta = \frac{\sqrt{3}}{2}, 0 \le \theta \le 2\pi$ 39. $\sin\theta = 0, 0 \le \theta \le 4\pi$ 40. $\sin\theta = -1, 0 \le \theta \le 4\pi$

41. $\cos\theta = -1, 0 \le \theta \le 4\pi$ 42. $\cos\theta = 0, 0 \le \theta \le 4\pi$ 43. $\tan\theta = -1, 0 \le \theta \le 2\pi$

44. $\cot\theta = 1, 0 \le \theta \le 2\pi$ 45. $\sec\theta = -\sqrt{2}, 0 \le \theta \le 2\pi$ 46. $\csc\theta = \sqrt{2}, 0 \le \theta \le 2\pi$

47. $\csc\theta$ is undefined, $0 \le \theta \le 2\pi$ 48. $\sec\theta$ is undefined, $0 \le \theta \le 2\pi$ 49. $\tan\theta$ is undefined, $0 \le \theta \le 2\pi$

50. $\cot\theta$ is undefined, $0 \le \theta \le 2\pi$ 51. $\csc\theta = -2, 0 \le \theta \le 2\pi$ 52. $\cot\theta = -\sqrt{3}, 0 \le \theta \le 2\pi$

53. $\sec\theta = \frac{2\sqrt{3}}{3}, 0 \le \theta \le 2\pi$ 54. $\tan\theta = \frac{\sqrt{3}}{3}, 0 \le \theta \le 2\pi$

• APPLICATIONS

For Exercises 55 and 56, refer to the following:

The average daily temperature in Peoria, Illinois, can be predicted by the formula $T = 50 - 28\cos\left[\frac{2\pi(x-31)}{365}\right]$, where x is the number of the day in the year (January 1 = 1, February 1 = 32, etc.) and T is in degrees Fahrenheit.

55. **Atmospheric Temperature.** What is the expected temperature on February 15?

56. **Atmospheric Temperature.** What is the expected temperature on August 15? (Assume it is not a leap year.)

For Exercises 57 and 58, refer to the following:

The human body temperature normally fluctuates during the day. A person's body temperature can be predicted by the formula $T = 99.1 - 0.5\sin\left(x + \frac{\pi}{12}\right)$, where x is the number of hours since midnight and T is in degrees Fahrenheit.

57. **Body Temperature.** According to this model, what is a person's temperature at 6:00 A.M.?

58. **Body Temperature.** According to this model, what is a person's temperature at 9:00 P.M.?

For Exercises 59 and 60, refer to the following:

The height of the water in a harbor changes with the tides. The height of the water at a particular hour during the day can be determined by the formula $h(x) = 5 + 4.8\sin\left[\frac{\pi}{6}(x + 4)\right]$, where x is the number of hours since midnight and h is the height of the tide in feet.

Bill Brooks/Alamy

Bill Brooks/Alamy

59. **Tides.** What is the height of the tide at 3:00 P.M.?

60. **Tides.** What is the height of the tide at 5:00 A.M.?

61. **Yo-Yo Dieting.** A woman has been yo-yo dieting for years. Her weight changes throughout the year as she gains and loses weight. Her weight in a particular month can be determined by the formula $w(x) = 145 + 10\cos\left(\frac{\pi}{6}x\right)$, where x is the month and w is in pounds. If $x = 1$ corresponds to January, how much does she weigh in June?

62. **Yo-Yo Dieting.** How much does the woman in Exercise 61 weigh in December?

63. **Seasonal Sales.** The average number of guests visiting the Magic Kingdom at Walt Disney World per day is given by $n(x) = 30{,}000 + 20{,}000\sin\left[\frac{\pi}{2}(x + 1)\right]$, where n is the number of guests and x is the month. If January corresponds to $x = 1$, how many people on average are visiting the Magic Kingdom per day in February?

64. **Seasonal Sales.** How many guests are visiting the Magic Kingdom in Exercise 63 in December?

For Exercises 65 and 66, refer to the following:

During the course of treatment of an illness, the concentration of a drug in the bloodstream in micrograms per microliter fluctuates during the dosing period of 8 hours according to the model

$$C(t) = 15.4 - 4.7\sin\left(\frac{\pi}{4}t + \frac{\pi}{2}\right), \quad 0 \le t \le 8$$

Note: This model does not apply to the first dose of the medication.

65. **Health/Medicine.** Find the concentration of the drug in the bloodstream at the beginning of a dosing period.

66. **Health/Medicine.** Find the concentration of the drug in the bloodstream 6 hours after taking a dose of the drug.

In Exercises 67 and 68, refer to the following:

By analyzing available empirical data, it has been determined that the body temperature of a particular species fluctuates during a 24-hour day according to the model

$$T(t) = 36.3 - 1.4\cos\left[\frac{\pi}{12}(t - 2)\right], \quad 0 \le t \le 24$$

where T represents temperature in degrees Celsius and t represents time in hours measured from 12:00 A.M. (midnight).

67. **Biology.** Find the approximate body temperature at midnight. Round your answer to the nearest degree.

68. **Biology.** Find the approximate body temperature at 2:45 P.M. Round your answer to the nearest degree.

• CATCH THE MISTAKE

In Exercises 69 and 70, explain the mistake that is made.

69. Use the unit circle to evaluate $\tan\left(\frac{5\pi}{6}\right)$ exactly.

Solution:

Tangent is the ratio of sine to cosine. $\tan\left(\frac{5\pi}{6}\right) = \dfrac{\sin\left(\frac{5\pi}{6}\right)}{\cos\left(\frac{5\pi}{6}\right)}$

Use the unit circle to identify sine and cosine. $\sin\left(\frac{5\pi}{6}\right) = -\frac{\sqrt{3}}{2}$ and $\cos\left(\frac{5\pi}{6}\right) = \frac{1}{2}$

Substitute values for sine and cosine. $\tan\left(\frac{5\pi}{6}\right) = \dfrac{-(\sqrt{3}/2)}{1/2}$

Simplify. $\tan\left(\frac{5\pi}{6}\right) = -\sqrt{3}$

This is incorrect. What mistake was made?

70. Use the unit circle to evaluate $\sec\left(\frac{11\pi}{6}\right)$ exactly.

Solution:

Secant is the reciprocal of cosine. $\sec\left(\frac{11\pi}{6}\right) = \dfrac{1}{\cos\left(\frac{11\pi}{6}\right)}$

Use the unit circle to evaluate cosine. $\cos\left(\frac{11\pi}{6}\right) = -\frac{1}{2}$

Substitute the value for cosine. $\sec\left(\frac{11\pi}{6}\right) = \dfrac{1}{-\frac{1}{2}}$

Simplify. $\sec\left(\frac{11\pi}{6}\right) = -2$

This is incorrect. What mistake was made?

• CONCEPTUAL

In Exercises 71–76, determine whether each statement is true or false.

71. $\sin(2n\pi + \theta) = \sin\theta$, n an integer.

72. $\cos(2n\pi + \theta) = \cos\theta$, n an integer.

73. $\sin\theta = 1$ when $\theta = \frac{(2n+1)\pi}{2}$, n an integer.

74. $\cos\theta = 1$ when $\theta = n\pi$, n an integer.

75. $\tan(\theta + 2n\pi) = \tan\theta$, n an integer.

76. $\tan\theta = 0$ if and only if $\theta = \frac{(2n+1)\pi}{2}$, n an integer.

77. Is cosecant an even or an odd function? Justify your answer.

78. Is tangent an even or an odd function? Justify your answer.

• CHALLENGE

79. Find all the values of θ, $0 \le \theta \le 2\pi$, for which the equation $\sin\theta = \cos\theta$ is true.

80. Find all the values of θ (θ is any real number) for which the equation $\sin\theta = \cos\theta$ is true.

81. Find all the values of θ, $0 \le \theta \le 2\pi$, for which the equation $2\sin\theta = \csc\theta$ is true.

82. Find all the values of θ, $0 \le \theta \le 2\pi$, for which the equation $\cos\theta = \frac{1}{4}\sec\theta$ is true.

83. Find all the values of θ (θ is any real number) for which the equation $3\csc\theta = 4\sin\theta$ is true.

84. Find all the values of θ (θ is any real number) for which the equation $4\cos\theta = 3\sec\theta$ is true.

85. Does there exist an angle $0 \le \theta < 2\pi$ such that $\tan\theta = \cot\theta$?

86. Does there exist an angle $0 \le \theta < 2\pi$ such that $\sec\theta = \csc(-\theta)$?

• PREVIEW TO CALCULUS

The Fundamental Theorem of Calculus establishes that the definite integral $\int_a^b f(x)dx$ equals $F(b) - F(a)$, where F is any antiderivative of a continuous function f.

In Exercises 87–90, use the information below to find the exact value of each definite integral.

FUNCTION	$\sin x$	$\cos x$	$\sec^2 x$	$\csc x \cot x$
ANTIDERIVATIVE	$-\cos x$	$\sin x$	$\tan x$	$-\csc x$

87. $\displaystyle\int_0^{\pi} \sin x\,dx$

88. $\displaystyle\int_{\pi/4}^{5\pi/6} \cos x\,dx$

89. $\displaystyle\int_{7\pi/6}^{5\pi/4} \sec^2 x\,dx$

90. $\displaystyle\int_{5\pi/3}^{11\pi/6} \csc x \cot x\,dx$

5.2 GRAPHS OF SINE AND COSINE FUNCTIONS

SKILLS OBJECTIVES

- Determine the amplitude and period of sinusoidal functions.
- Determine the phase shift of a sinusoidal function.
- Solve harmonic motion problems.
- Graph sums of trigonometric and other algebraic functions.

CONCEPTUAL OBJECTIVES

- Understand why the graphs of the sine and cosine functions are called sinusoidal graphs.
- Recognize that rewriting the sinusoidal function in standard form makes identifying the phase shift easier.
- Visualize harmonic motion as a sinusoidal function.
- Understand that the y-coordinates of the combined function are found by adding the y-coordinates of the individual functions.

5.2.1 The Graphs of Sinusoidal Functions

5.2.1 SKILL

Determine the amplitude and period of sinusoidal functions.

5.2.1 CONCEPTUAL

Understand why the graphs of the sine and cosine functions are called sinusoidal graphs.

The following are examples of things that repeat in a predictable way (are roughly periodic):

- heartbeat
- tide levels
- time of sunrise
- average outdoor temperature for the time of year

The trigonometric functions are *strictly* periodic. In the unit circle, the value of any of the trigonometric functions is the same for any coterminal angle (same initial and terminal sides no matter how many full rotations the angle makes). For example, if we add (or subtract) multiples of 2π to (from) the angle θ, the values for sine and cosine are unchanged.

$$\sin(\theta + 2n\pi) = \sin\theta \qquad \text{and} \qquad \cos(\theta + 2n\pi) = \cos\theta \quad (n \text{ is any integer})$$

DEFINITION **Periodic Function**

A function f is called a **periodic function** if there is a positive number p such that

$$f(x + p) = f(x) \qquad \text{for all } x \text{ in the domain of } f$$

If p is the smallest such number for which this equation holds, then p is called the **fundamental period**.

You will see in this chapter that sine, cosine, secant, and cosecant have fundamental period 2π, but tangent and cotangent have fundamental period π.

The Graph of $f(x) = \sin x$

Let us start by point-plotting the sine function. We select special values for the sine function that we already know.

STUDY TIP

Note that either notation, $y = \sin x$ or $f(x) = \sin x$, can be used.

x	$f(x) = \sin x$	(x, y)
0	$\sin 0 = 0$	$(0, 0)$
$\frac{\pi}{4}$	$\sin\left(\frac{\pi}{4}\right) = \frac{\sqrt{2}}{2}$	$\left(\frac{\pi}{4}, \frac{\sqrt{2}}{2}\right)$
$\frac{\pi}{2}$	$\sin\left(\frac{\pi}{2}\right) = 1$	$\left(\frac{\pi}{2}, 1\right)$
$\frac{3\pi}{4}$	$\sin\left(\frac{3\pi}{4}\right) = \frac{\sqrt{2}}{2}$	$\left(\frac{3\pi}{4}, \frac{\sqrt{2}}{2}\right)$
π	$\sin \pi = 0$	$(\pi, 0)$
$\frac{5\pi}{4}$	$\sin\left(\frac{5\pi}{4}\right) = -\frac{\sqrt{2}}{2}$	$\left(\frac{5\pi}{4}, -\frac{\sqrt{2}}{2}\right)$
$\frac{3\pi}{2}$	$\sin\left(\frac{3\pi}{2}\right) = -1$	$\left(\frac{3\pi}{2}, -1\right)$
$\frac{7\pi}{4}$	$\sin\left(\frac{7\pi}{4}\right) = -\frac{\sqrt{2}}{2}$	$\left(\frac{7\pi}{4}, -\frac{\sqrt{2}}{2}\right)$
2π	$\sin 2\pi = 0$	$(2\pi, 0)$

[CONCEPT CHECK]

Which of the following is NOT a sinusoidal function?

(A) $f(x) = \tan(x)$
(B) $g(x) = \sin(x)$
(C) $h(x) = \cos(x)$

ANSWER (A)

STUDY TIP

Looking at the graph of $f(x) = \sin x$, we are reminded that $\sin x > 0$ when $0 < x < \pi$, and $\sin x < 0$ when $\pi < x < 2\pi$. We also see that when $x = \frac{3\pi}{4}, \frac{5\pi}{4}$, or $\frac{7\pi}{4}$, the reference angle is $\frac{\pi}{4}$.

By plotting the above coordinates (x, y), we can obtain the graph of one **period**, or **cycle**, of the graph of $y = \sin x$. Note that $\frac{\sqrt{2}}{2} \approx 0.7$.

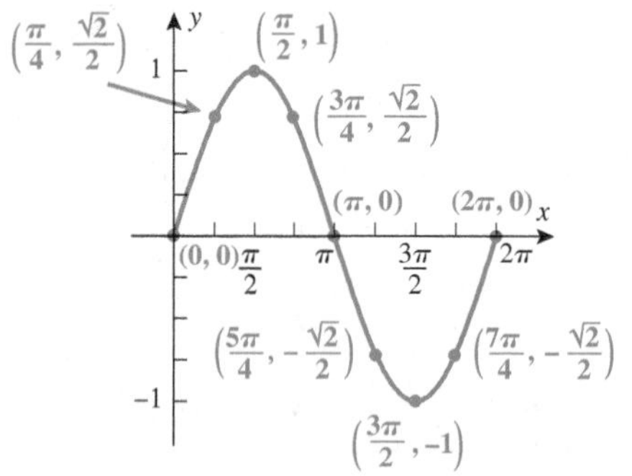

We can extend the graph horizontally in both directions (left and right) since the domain of the sine function is the set of all real numbers.

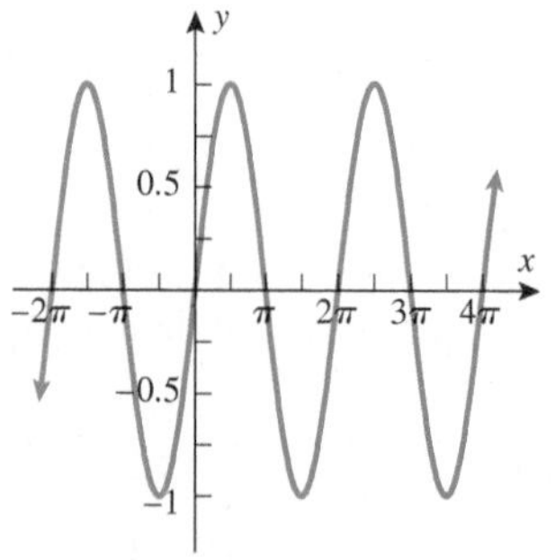

From here on, we are no longer showing angles on the unit circle but are now showing angles as *real numbers* in radians on the x-axis of the *Cartesian* graph. Therefore, we no longer illustrate a "terminal side" to an angle—the physical arcs and angles no longer exist. Only their measures exist, as values of the x-coordinate.

If we graph the function $f(x) = \sin x$, the x-intercepts correspond to values of x at which the sine function is equal to zero.

x	f(x) = sin x	(x, y)
0	$\sin 0 = 0$	$(0, 0)$
π	$\sin \pi = 0$	$(\pi, 0)$
2π	$\sin(2\pi) = 0$	$(2\pi, 0)$
3π	$\sin(3\pi) = 0$	$(3\pi, 0)$
4π	$\sin(4\pi) = 0$	$(4\pi, 0)$
...		
$n\pi$	$\sin(n\pi) = 0$	$(n\pi, 0)$, n is an integer.

Notice that the point $(0, 0)$ is both a y-intercept and an x-intercept, but all x-intercepts have the form $(n\pi, 0)$. The maximum value of the sine function is 1, and the minimum value of the sine function is -1, which occurs at odd multiples of $\frac{\pi}{2}$.

x	f(x) = sin x	(x, y)
$\frac{\pi}{2}$	$\sin\left(\frac{\pi}{2}\right) = 1$	$\left(\frac{\pi}{2}, 1\right)$
$\frac{3\pi}{2}$	$\sin\left(\frac{3\pi}{2}\right) = -1$	$\left(\frac{3\pi}{2}, -1\right)$
$\frac{5\pi}{2}$	$\sin\left(\frac{5\pi}{2}\right) = 1$	$\left(\frac{5\pi}{2}, 1\right)$
$\frac{7\pi}{2}$	$\sin\left(\frac{7\pi}{2}\right) = -1$	$\left(\frac{7\pi}{2}, -1\right)$
...	...	...
$\frac{(2n+1)\pi}{2}$	$\sin\left(\frac{(2n+1)\pi}{2}\right) = \pm 1$	$\left(\frac{(2n+1)\pi}{2}, \pm 1\right)$, n is an integer.

The following box summarizes the sine function.

SINE FUNCTION $f(x) = \sin x$

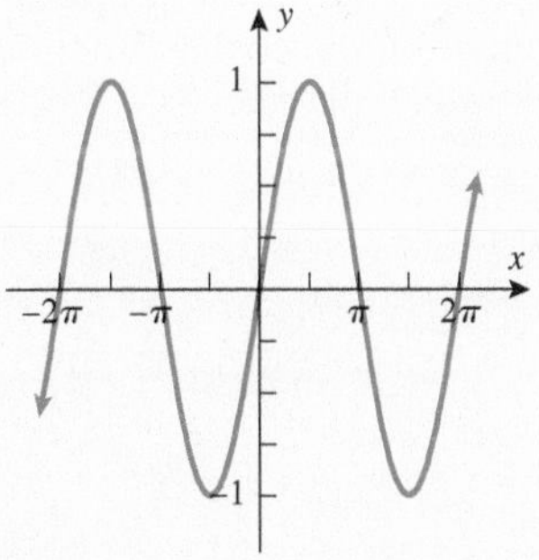

- Domain: $(-\infty, \infty)$ or $-\infty < x < \infty$
- Range: $[-1, 1]$ or $-1 \le y \le 1$
- The sine function is an odd function:
  - symmetric about the origin
  - $\sin(-x) = -\sin x$
- The sine function is a periodic function with fundamental period 2π.
- The x-intercepts, $0, \pm\pi, \pm 2\pi, \ldots$, are of the form $n\pi$, where n is an integer.
- The maximum (1) and minimum (-1) values of the sine function correspond to x-values of the form $\frac{(2n+1)\pi}{2}$, such as $\pm\frac{\pi}{2}, \pm\frac{3\pi}{2}, \pm\frac{5\pi}{2}, \ldots$.

STUDY TIP

Note that either notation, $y = \cos x$ or $f(x) = \cos x$, can be used.

The Graph of $f(x) = \cos x$

Let us start by point-plotting the cosine function.

x	$f(x) = \cos x$	(x, y)
0	$\cos 0 = 1$	$(0, 1)$
$\frac{\pi}{4}$	$\cos\left(\frac{\pi}{4}\right) = \frac{\sqrt{2}}{2}$	$\left(\frac{\pi}{4}, \frac{\sqrt{2}}{2}\right)$
$\frac{\pi}{2}$	$\cos\left(\frac{\pi}{2}\right) = 0$	$\left(\frac{\pi}{2}, 0\right)$
$\frac{3\pi}{4}$	$\cos\left(\frac{3\pi}{4}\right) = -\frac{\sqrt{2}}{2}$	$\left(\frac{3\pi}{4}, -\frac{\sqrt{2}}{2}\right)$
π	$\cos \pi = -1$	$(\pi, -1)$
$\frac{5\pi}{4}$	$\cos\left(\frac{5\pi}{4}\right) = -\frac{\sqrt{2}}{2}$	$\left(\frac{5\pi}{4}, -\frac{\sqrt{2}}{2}\right)$
$\frac{3\pi}{2}$	$\cos\left(\frac{3\pi}{2}\right) = 0$	$\left(\frac{3\pi}{2}, 0\right)$
$\frac{7\pi}{4}$	$\cos\left(\frac{7\pi}{4}\right) = \frac{\sqrt{2}}{2}$	$\left(\frac{7\pi}{4}, \frac{\sqrt{2}}{2}\right)$
2π	$\cos(2\pi) = 1$	$(2\pi, 1)$

STUDY TIP

Looking at the graph of $f(x) = \cos x$, we are reminded that $\cos x > 0$ when $0 < \pi < \frac{\pi}{2}$ and $\frac{3\pi}{2} < x < 2\pi$, and $\cos x < 0$ when $\frac{\pi}{2} < x < \frac{3\pi}{2}$.

By plotting the above coordinates (x, y), we can obtain the graph of one period, or cycle, of the graph of $y = \cos x$. Note that $\frac{\sqrt{2}}{2} \approx 0.7$.

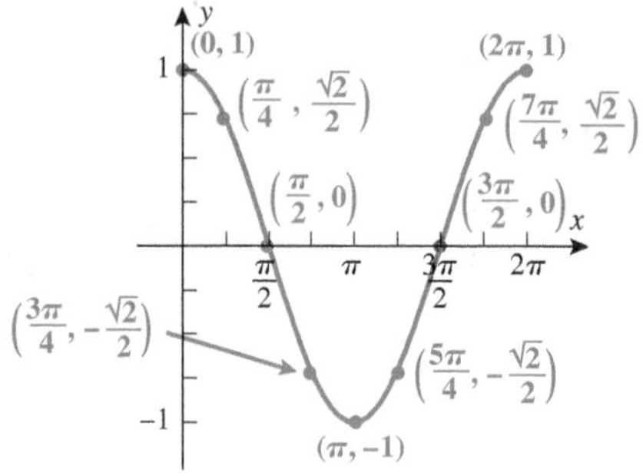

We can extend the graph horizontally in both directions (left and right) since the domain of the cosine function is all real numbers.

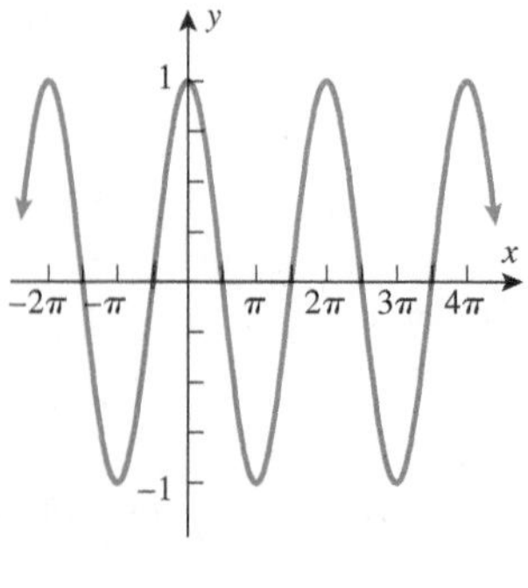

If we graph the function $f(x) = \cos x$, the x-intercepts correspond to values of x at which the cosine function is equal to zero.

x	$f(x) = \cos x$	(x, y)
$\frac{\pi}{2}$	$\cos\left(\frac{\pi}{2}\right) = 0$	$\left(\frac{\pi}{2}, 0\right)$
$\frac{3\pi}{2}$	$\cos\left(\frac{3\pi}{2}\right) = 0$	$\left(\frac{3\pi}{2}, 0\right)$
$\frac{5\pi}{2}$	$\cos\left(\frac{5\pi}{2}\right) = 0$	$\left(\frac{5\pi}{2}, 0\right)$
$\frac{7\pi}{2}$	$\cos\left(\frac{7\pi}{2}\right) = 0$	$\left(\frac{7\pi}{2}, 0\right)$
...	...	...
$\frac{(2n+1)\pi}{2}$	$\cos\left(\frac{(2n+1)\pi}{2}\right) = 0$	$\left(\frac{(2n+1)\pi}{2}, 0\right)$, n is an integer.

The point $(0, 1)$ is the y-intercept, and all x-intercepts have the form $\left(\frac{(2n+1)\pi}{2}, 0\right)$. The maximum value of the cosine function is 1, and the minimum value of the cosine function is -1; these values occur at integer multiples of π, i.e., $n\pi$.

x	$f(x) = \cos x$	(x, y)
0	$\cos 0 = 1$	$(0, 1)$
π	$\cos \pi = -1$	$(\pi, -1)$
2π	$\cos(2\pi) = 1$	$(2\pi, 1)$
3π	$\cos(3\pi) = -1$	$(3\pi, -1)$
4π	$\cos(4\pi) = 1$	$(4\pi, 1)$
...	...	...
$n\pi$	$\cos(n\pi) = \pm 1$	$(n\pi, \pm 1)$, n is an integer.

The following box summarizes the cosine function.

COSINE FUNCTION $f(x) = \cos x$

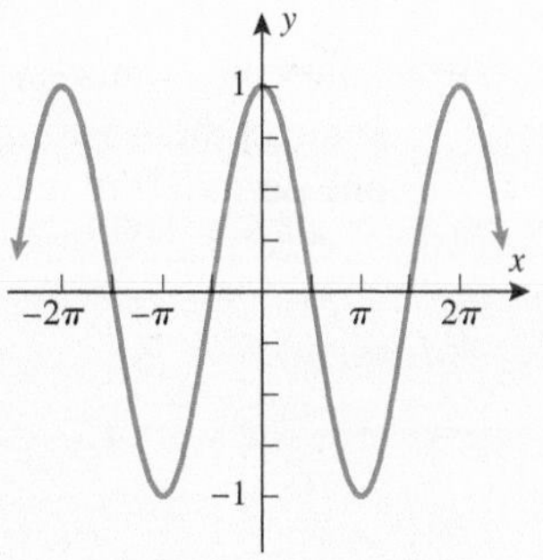

- Domain: $(-\infty, \infty)$ or $-\infty < x < \infty$
- Range: $[-1, 1]$ or $-1 \le y \le 1$
- The cosine function is an even function:
  - symmetric about the y-axis
  - $\cos(-x) = \cos x$
- The cosine function is a periodic function with fundamental period 2π.
- The x-intercepts, $\pm\frac{\pi}{2}, \pm\frac{3\pi}{2}, \pm\frac{5\pi}{2}, \ldots$, are odd integer multiples of $\frac{\pi}{2}$ that have the form $\frac{(2n+1)\pi}{2}$, where n is an integer.
- The maximum (1) and minimum (-1) values of the cosine function correspond to x-values of the form $n\pi$, such as $0, \pm\pi, \pm 2\pi, \ldots$.

The Amplitude and Period of Sinusoidal Graphs

In mathematics, the word **sinusoidal** means "resembling the sine function." Let us start by graphing $f(x) = \sin x$ and $f(x) = \cos x$ on the same graph. Notice that they have similar characteristics (domain, range, period, and shape).

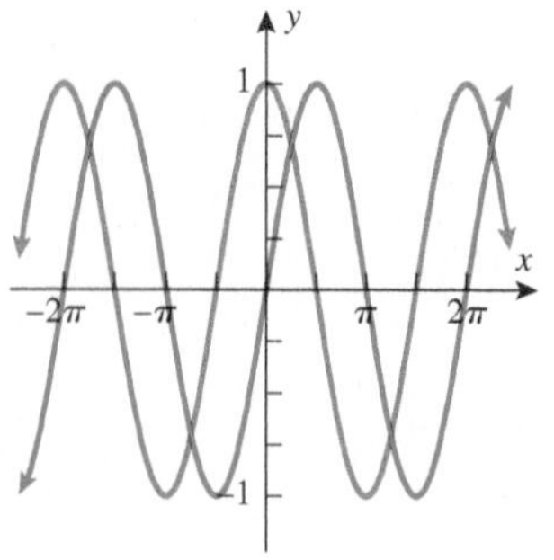

In fact, if we were to shift the cosine graph to the right $\frac{\pi}{2}$ units, the two graphs would be identical. For that reason we refer to any graphs of the form $y = \cos x$ or $y = \sin x$ as **sinusoidal functions**.

We now turn our attention to graphs of the form $y = A\sin(Bx)$ and $y = A\cos(Bx)$, which are graphs like $y = \sin x$ and $y = \cos x$ that have been stretched or compressed vertically and horizontally.

EXAMPLE 1 Vertical Stretching and Compressing

Plot the functions $y = 2\sin x$ and $y = \frac{1}{2}\sin x$ on the same graph with $y = \sin x$ on the interval $-4\pi \leq x \leq 4\pi$.

Solution:

STEP 1 Make a table with the coordinate values of the graphs.

x	0	$\frac{\pi}{2}$	π	$\frac{3\pi}{2}$	2π
$\sin x$	0	1	0	-1	0
$2\sin x$	0	2	0	-2	0
$\frac{1}{2}\sin x$	0	$\frac{1}{2}$	0	$-\frac{1}{2}$	0

STEP 2 Label the points on the graph, and connect them with a smooth curve over one period, $0 \leq x \leq 2\pi$.

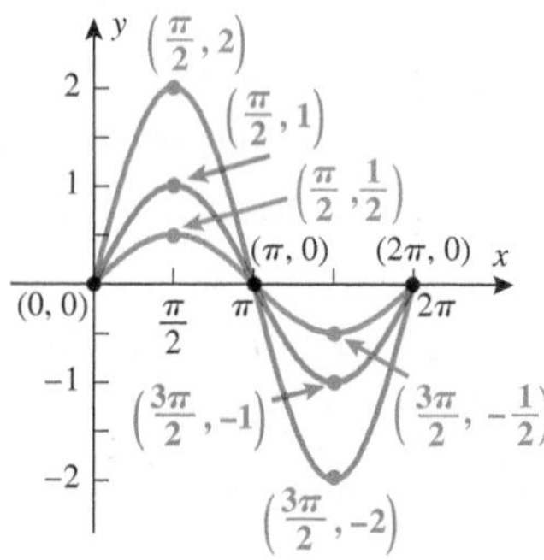

STEP 3 Extend the graph in both directions (repeat every 2π).

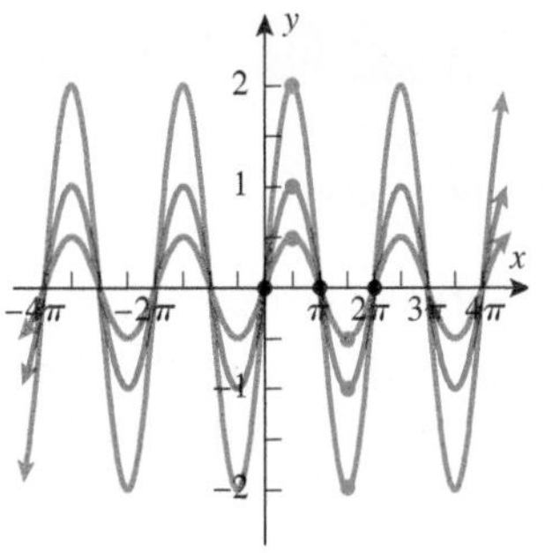

YOUR TURN Plot the functions $y = 3\cos x$ and $y = \frac{1}{3}\cos x$ on the same graph with $y = \cos x$ on the interval $-2\pi \le x \le 2\pi$.

ANSWER

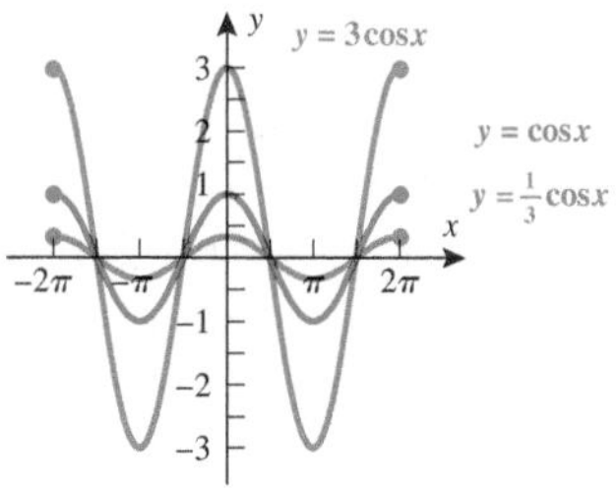

Notice in Example 1 and the corresponding Your Turn that:

- $y = 2\sin x$ has the shape and period of $y = \sin x$ but is stretched vertically.
- $y = \frac{1}{2}\sin x$ has the shape and period of $y = \sin x$ but is compressed vertically.
- $y = 3\cos x$ has the shape and period of $y = \cos x$ but is stretched vertically.
- $y = \frac{1}{3}\cos x$ has the shape and period of $y = \cos x$ but is compressed vertically.

In general, functions of the form $y = A\sin x$ and $y = A\cos x$ are stretched vertically when $|A| > 1$ and compressed vertically when $|A| < 1$.

The **amplitude** of a periodic function is half the difference between the maximum value of the function and the minimum value of the function. For the functions $y = \sin x$ and $y = \cos x$, the maximum value is 1 and the minimum value is -1. Therefore, the amplitude of each of these two functions is $|A| = \frac{1}{2}|1 - (-1)| = 1$.

AMPLITUDE OF SINUSOIDAL FUNCTIONS

For sinusoidal functions of the form $y = A\sin(Bx)$ and $y = A\cos(Bx)$, the **amplitude** is $|A|$. When $|A| < 1$, the graph is compressed vertically, and when $|A| > 1$, the graph is stretched vertically.

EXAMPLE 2 Finding the Amplitude of Sinusoidal Functions

State the amplitude of

a. $f(x) = -4\cos x$

b. $g(x) = \frac{1}{5}\sin x$

Solution (a): The amplitude is the magnitude of -4. $A = |-4| = \boxed{4}$

Solution (b): The amplitude is the magnitude of $\frac{1}{5}$. $A = \left|\frac{1}{5}\right| = \boxed{\frac{1}{5}}$

EXAMPLE 3 Horizontal Stretching and Compressing

Plot the functions $y = \cos(2x)$ and $y = \cos(\frac{1}{2}x)$ on the same graph with $y = \cos x$ on the interval $-2\pi \le x \le 2\pi$.

Solution:

STEP 1 Make a table with the coordinate values of the graphs. It is necessary only to select the points that correspond to x-intercepts, ($y = 0$), and maximum and minimum points, ($y = \pm 1$). Usually, the period is divided into four subintervals (which you will see in Examples 5 to 7).

x	0	$\frac{\pi}{4}$	$\frac{\pi}{2}$	$\frac{3\pi}{4}$	π	$\frac{5\pi}{4}$	$\frac{3\pi}{2}$	$\frac{7\pi}{4}$	2π
$\cos x$	1		0		−1		0		1
$\cos(2x)$	1	0	−1	0	1	0	−1	0	1
$\cos(\frac{1}{2}x)$	1				0				−1

STEP 2 Label the points on the graph, and connect them with a smooth curve.

$y = \cos x$

$y = \cos(2x)$

$y = \cos\left(\frac{1}{2}x\right)$

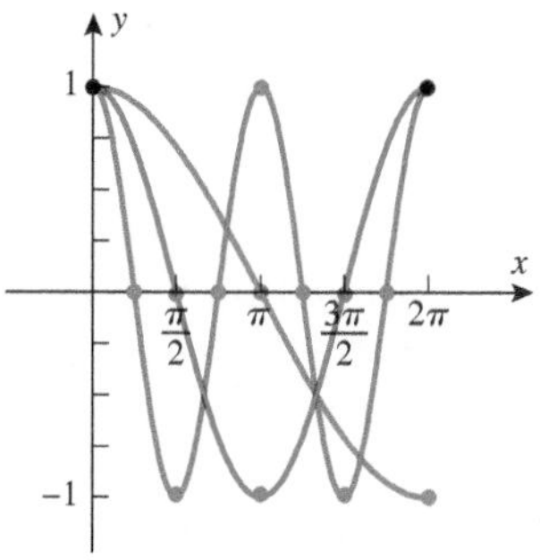

STEP 3 Extend the graph to cover the entire interval: $-2\pi \le x \le 2\pi$.

$y = \cos x$

$y = \cos(2x)$

$y = \cos\left(\frac{1}{2}x\right)$

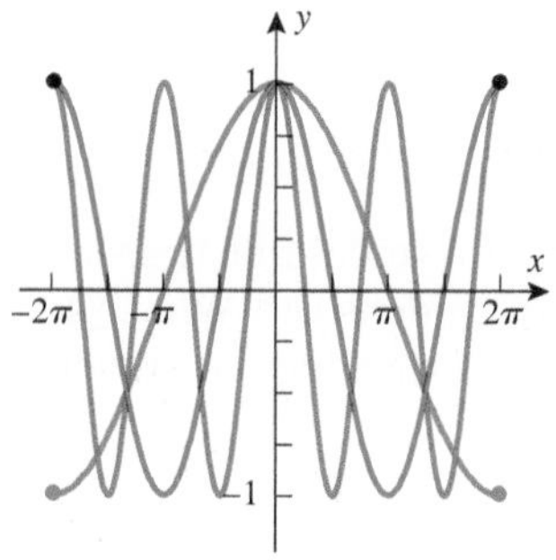

YOUR TURN Plot the functions $y = \sin(2x)$ and $y = \sin(\frac{1}{2}x)$ on the same graph with $y = \sin x$ on the interval $-2\pi \le x \le 2\pi$.

ANSWER

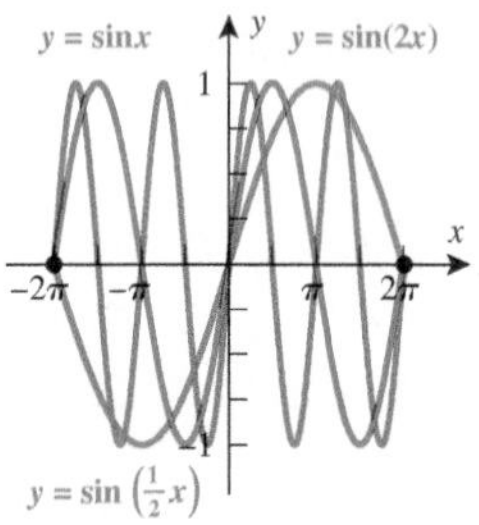

Notice in Example 3 and the corresponding Your Turn that:

- $y = \cos(2x)$ has the shape and amplitude of $y = \cos x$ but is compressed horizontally.
- $y = \cos(\frac{1}{2}x)$ has the shape and amplitude of $y = \cos x$ but is stretched horizontally.
- $y = \sin(2x)$ has the shape and amplitude of $y = \sin x$ but is compressed horizontally.
- $y = \sin(\frac{1}{2}x)$ has the shape and amplitude of $y = \sin x$ but is stretched horizontally.

In general, functions of the form $y = \sin(Bx)$ and $y = \cos(Bx)$, with $B > 0$, are compressed horizontally when $B > 1$ and stretched horizontally when $0 < B < 1$. Negative arguments ($B < 0$) are included in the context of *reflections*.

The period of the functions $y = \sin x$ and $y = \cos x$ is 2π. To find the period of a function of the form $y = A\sin(Bx)$ or $y = A\cos(Bx)$, set Bx equal to 2π and solve for x.

$$Bx = 2\pi$$

$$x = \frac{2\pi}{B}$$

PERIOD OF SINUSOIDAL FUNCTIONS

For sinusoidal functions of the form $y = A\sin(Bx)$ and $y = A\cos(Bx)$, with $B > 0$, the **period** is $\frac{2\pi}{B}$. When $0 < B < 1$, the graph is stretched horizontally, and when $B > 1$, the graph is compressed horizontally since the period is smaller than 2π.

STUDY TIP

When B is negative, the period is $\frac{2\pi}{|B|}$.

EXAMPLE 4 Finding the Period of a Sinusoidal Function

State the period of

a. $y = \cos(4x)$

b. $y = \sin(\frac{1}{3}x)$

Solution (a):

Compare $\cos(4x)$ with $\cos(Bx)$ to identify B. $\quad B = 4$

Calculate the period of $\cos(4x)$, using $p = \frac{2\pi}{B}$. $\quad p = \frac{2\pi}{4} = \frac{\pi}{2}$

The period of $\cos(4x)$ is $\boxed{p = \frac{\pi}{2}}$.

Solution (b):

Compare $\sin(\frac{1}{3}x)$ with $\sin(Bx)$ to identify B. $\quad B = \frac{1}{3}$

Calculate the period of $\sin(\frac{1}{3}x)$, using $p = \frac{2\pi}{B}$. $\quad p = \frac{2\pi}{\frac{1}{3}} = 6\pi$

The period of $\sin(\frac{1}{3}x)$ is $\boxed{p = 6\pi}$.

YOUR TURN State the period of

a. $y = \sin(3x)$ **b.** $y = \cos(\frac{1}{2}x)$

ANSWER

a. $p = \frac{2\pi}{3}$ **b.** $p = 4\pi$

STUDY TIP

Divide the period by 4 to get the key values along the x-axis for graphing.

Now that you know the basic graphs of $y = \sin x$ and $y = \cos x$, you can sketch one cycle (period) of these graphs with the following x-values: $0, \frac{\pi}{2}, \pi, \frac{3\pi}{2}, 2\pi$. For a period of 2π, we used steps of $\frac{\pi}{2}$. Therefore, for functions of the form $y = A\sin(Bx)$ or $y = A\cos(Bx)$, when we start at the origin and as long as we include these four basic values during one period, we are able to sketch the graphs.

STRATEGY FOR SKETCHING GRAPHS OF SINUSOIDAL FUNCTIONS

To graph $y = A\sin(Bx)$ or $y = A\cos(Bx)$ with $B > 0$:

Step 1: Find the amplitude $|A|$ and period $\frac{2\pi}{B}$.

Step 2: Divide the period into four subintervals of equal lengths.

Step 3: Make a table and evaluate the function for x-values from Step 2 starting at $x = 0$.

Step 4: Draw the xy-plane (label the y-axis from $-|A|$ to $|A|$) and plot the points found in Step 3.

Step 5: Connect the points with a sinusoidal curve (with amplitude $|A|$).

Step 6: Extend the graph over one or two additional periods in both directions (left and right).

EXAMPLE 5 **Graphing Sinusoidal Functions of the Form $y = A\sin(Bx)$**

Use the strategy for graphing a sinusoidal function to graph $y = 3\sin(2x)$.

Solution:

STEP 1 Find the amplitude and period for $A = 3$ and $B = 2$. $\quad |A| = |3| = 3$ and $p = \frac{2\pi}{B} = \frac{2\pi}{2} = \pi$

STEP 2 Divide the period π into four equal steps. $\quad \frac{\pi}{4}$

STEP 3 Make a table from $x = 0$ to the period $x = \pi$ in steps of $\frac{\pi}{4}$.

x	$y = 3\sin(2x)$	(x, y)
0	$3[\sin 0] = 3[0] = 0$	$(0, 0)$
$\frac{\pi}{4}$	$3\left[\sin\left(\frac{\pi}{2}\right)\right] = 3[1] = 3$	$\left(\frac{\pi}{4}, 3\right)$
$\frac{\pi}{2}$	$3[\sin \pi] = 3[0] = 0$	$\left(\frac{\pi}{2}, 0\right)$
$\frac{3\pi}{4}$	$3\left[\sin\left(\frac{3\pi}{2}\right)\right] = 3[-1] = -3$	$\left(\frac{3\pi}{4}, -3\right)$
π	$3[\sin(2\pi)] = 3[0] = 0$	$(\pi, 0)$

STEP 4 Draw the *xy*-plane and label the points in the table.

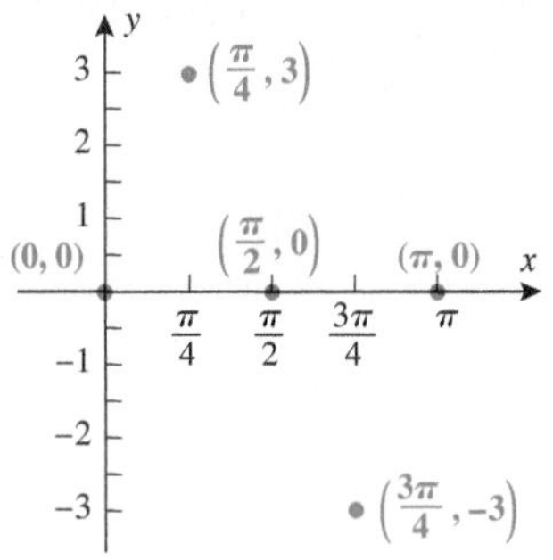

STEP 5 Connect the points with a sinusoidal curve.

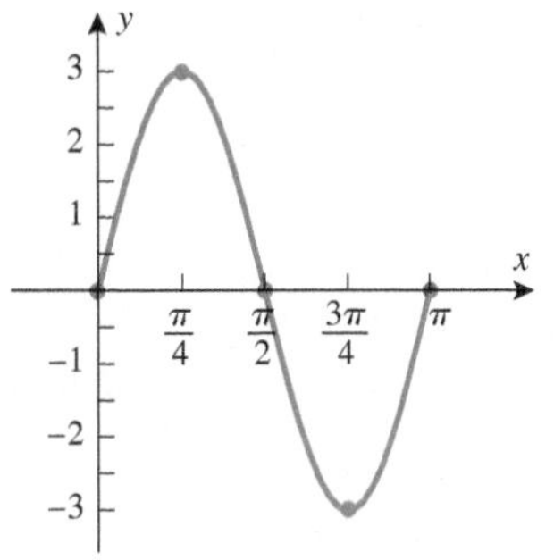

STEP 6 Repeat over several periods (to the left and right).

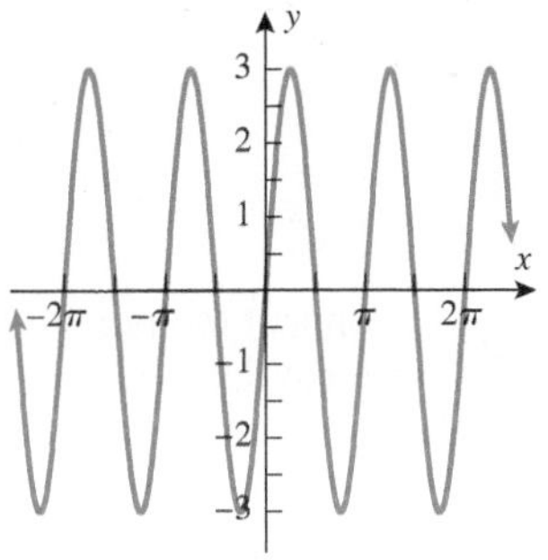

YOUR TURN Use the strategy for graphing sinusoidal functions to graph $y = 2\sin(3x)$.

ANSWER

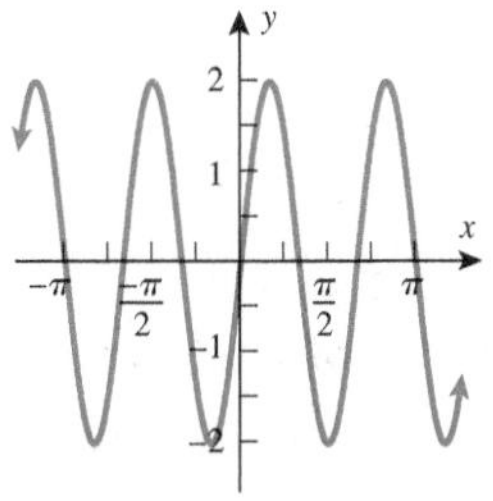

EXAMPLE 6 Graphing Sinusoidal Functions of the Form $y = A\cos(Bx)$

Use the strategy for graphing a sinusoidal function to graph $y = -2\cos\left(\frac{1}{3}x\right)$.

Solution:

STEP 1 Find the amplitude for $A = -2$. $\quad |A| = |-2| = 2$

Find the period for $B = \frac{1}{3}$. $\quad p = \dfrac{2\pi}{B} = \dfrac{2\pi}{\frac{1}{3}} = 6\pi$

STEP 2 Divide the period 6π into four equal steps. $\quad \dfrac{6\pi}{4} = \dfrac{3\pi}{2}$

STEP 3 Make a table starting at $x = 0$ and completing one period of 6π in steps of $\dfrac{3\pi}{2}$.

x	$y = -2\cos\left(\dfrac{1}{3}x\right)$	(x, y)
0	$-2[\cos 0] = -2[1] = -2$	$(0, -2)$
$\dfrac{3\pi}{2}$	$-2\left[\cos\left(\dfrac{\pi}{2}\right)\right] = -2[0] = 0$	$\left(\dfrac{3\pi}{2}, 0\right)$
3π	$-2[\cos\pi] = -2[-1] = 2$	$(3\pi, 2)$
$\dfrac{9\pi}{2}$	$-2\left[\cos\left(\dfrac{3\pi}{2}\right)\right] = -2[0] = 0$	$\left(\dfrac{9\pi}{2}, 0\right)$
6π	$-2[\cos(2\pi)] = -2[1] = -2$	$(6\pi, -2)$

STEP 4 Draw the xy-plane and label the points in the table.

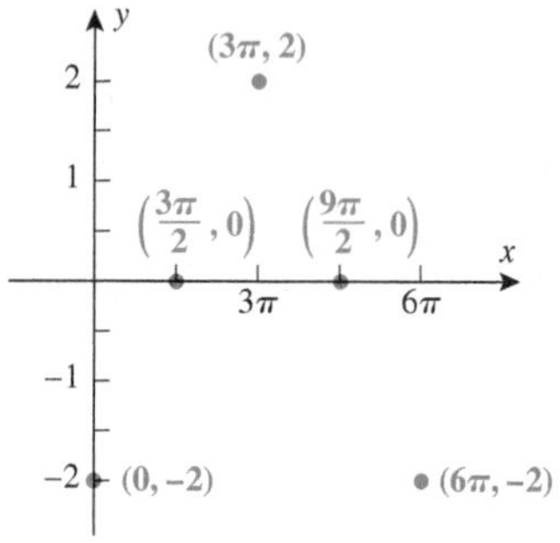

STEP 5 Connect the points with a sinusoidal curve.

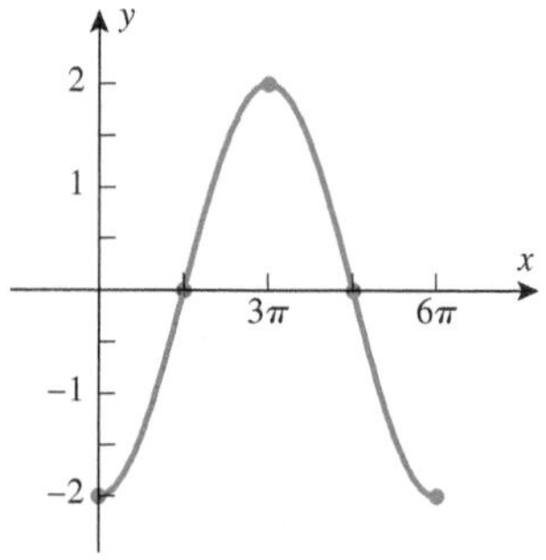

STEP 6 Repeat over several periods (to the left and right).

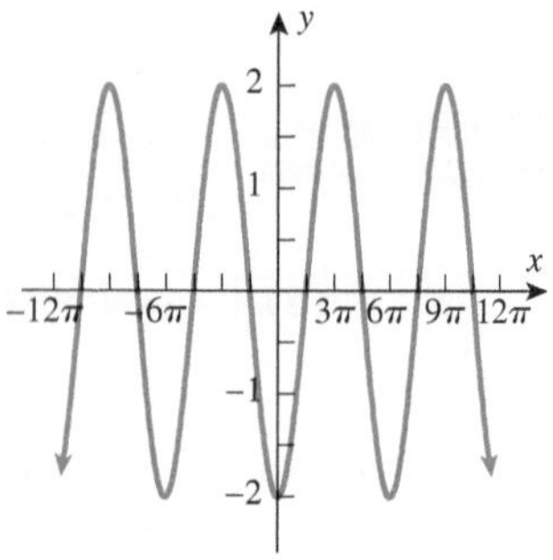

ANSWER

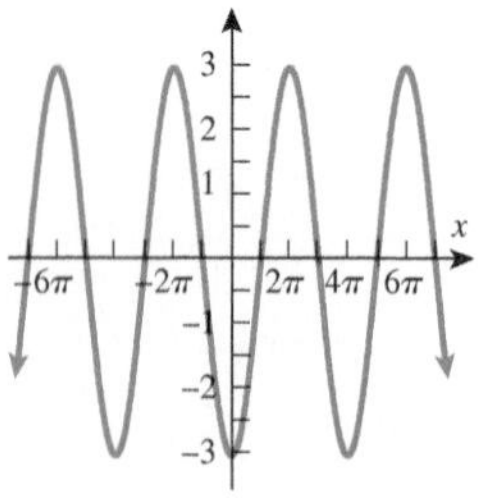

YOUR TURN Use the strategy for graphing a sinusoidal function to graph $y = -3\cos\left(\frac{1}{2}x\right)$.

Notice in Example 6 and the corresponding Your Turn that when A is negative, the result is a reflection of the original function (sine or cosine) about the x-axis.

EXAMPLE 7 **Finding an Equation for a Sinusoidal Graph**

Find an equation for the graph.

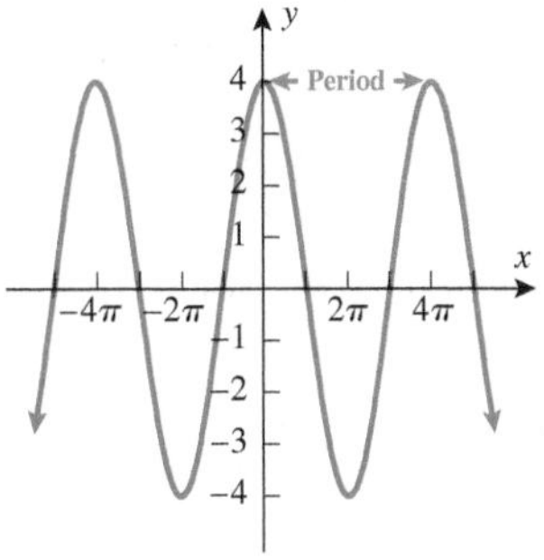

Solution:

This graph represents a cosine function. $y = A\cos(Bx)$

The amplitude is 4 (half the maximum spread). $|A| = 4$

The period $\frac{2\pi}{B}$ is equal to 4π. $\frac{2\pi}{B} = 4\pi$

Solve for B. $B = \frac{1}{2}$

Substitute $A = 4$ and $B = \frac{1}{2}$ into $y = A\cos(Bx)$. $\boxed{y = 4\cos\left(\frac{1}{2}x\right)}$

YOUR TURN Find an equation for the graph.

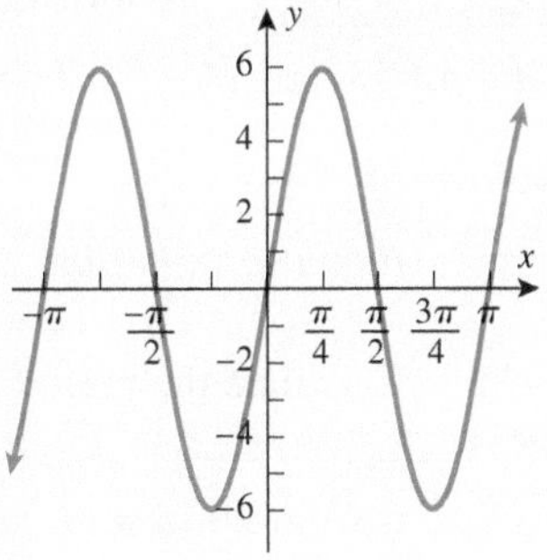

ANSWER

$y = 6\sin(2x)$

5.2.2 Graphing a Shifted Sinusoidal Function: $y = A\sin(Bx + C) + D$ and $y = A\cos(Bx + C) + D$

5.2.2 SKILL

Determine the phase shift of a sinusoidal function.

5.2.2 CONCEPTUAL

Recognize that rewriting the sinusoidal function in standard form makes identifying the phase shift easier.

Recall from Section 1.3 that we graph functions using horizontal and vertical translations (shifts) in the following way ($c > 0$):

- To graph $f(x + c)$, shift $f(x)$ to the **left** c units.
- To graph $f(x - c)$, shift $f(x)$ to the **right** c units.
- To graph $f(x) + c$, shift $f(x)$ **up** c units.
- To graph $f(x) - c$, shift $f(x)$ **down** c units.

To graph functions of the form $y = A\sin(Bx + C) + D$ and $y = A\cos(Bx + C) + D$, utilize the strategy below.

STRATEGY FOR GRAPHING $y = A\sin(Bx + C) + D$ AND $y = A\cos(Bx + C) + D$

A strategy for graphing $y = A\sin(Bx + C) + D$ is outlined below. The same strategy can be used to graph $y = A\cos(Bx + C) + D$.

Step 1: Find the amplitude $|A|$.

Step 2: Find the period $\frac{2\pi}{B}$ and the **phase shift** $-\frac{C}{B}$.

Step 3: Graph $y = A\sin(Bx + C)$ over one period $\left(\text{from } -\frac{C}{B} \text{ to } -\frac{C}{B} + \frac{2\pi}{B}\right)$.

Step 4: Extend the graph over several periods.

Step 5: Shift the graph of $y = A\sin(Bx + C)$ vertically D units.

Note: If we rewrite the function in **standard form**, we get

$$y = A\sin\left[B\left(x + \frac{C}{B}\right)\right] + D$$

which makes it easier to identify the **phase shift**.

If $B < 0$, we can use properties of even and odd functions

$$\sin(-x) = -\sin x \qquad \cos(-x) = -\cos x$$

to rewrite the function with $B > 0$.

STUDY TIP

Rewriting in standard form

$$y = A\sin\left[B\left(x + \frac{C}{B}\right)\right]$$

makes identifying the phase shift easier.

STUDY TIP

An alternative method for finding the period and phase shift is first to write the function in standard form.

$$y = 5\cos\left[4\left(x + \frac{\pi}{4}\right)\right]$$

$B = 4$

Period $= \frac{2\pi}{B} = \frac{2\pi}{4} = \frac{\pi}{2}$.

Phase shift $= \frac{\pi}{4}$ units to the left.

EXAMPLE 8 Graphing Functions of the Form $y = A\cos(Bx \pm C)$

Graph $y = 5\cos(4x + \pi)$ over one period.

Solution:

STEP 1 Find the amplitude. $\quad |A| = |5| = 5$

STEP 2 Calculate the period and phase shift.

The interval for one period is from 0 to 2π. $\quad 4x + \pi = 0$ to $4x + \pi = 2\pi$

Solve for x. $\quad x = -\frac{\pi}{4}$ to $x = -\frac{\pi}{4} + \frac{\pi}{2}$

Identify the phase shift. $\quad -\frac{C}{B} = -\frac{\pi}{4}$

Identify the period $\frac{2\pi}{B}$. $\quad \frac{2\pi}{B} = \frac{2\pi}{4} = \frac{\pi}{2}$

STEP 3 Graph.

Draw a cosine function starting at $x = -\frac{\pi}{4}$ with period $\frac{\pi}{2}$ and amplitude 5.

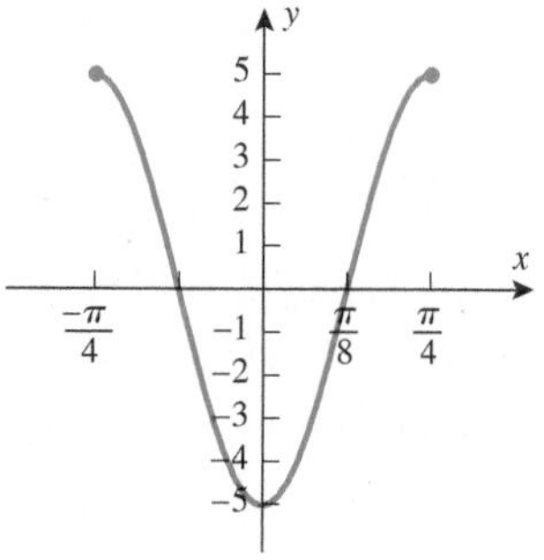

YOUR TURN Graph $y = 3\cos(2x - \pi)$ over one period.

[CONCEPT CHECK]

Rewrite $y = A\sin(Bx \pm C)$ in standard form.

ANSWER $y = A\sin\left[B\left(x \pm \frac{C}{B}\right)\right]$

ANSWER

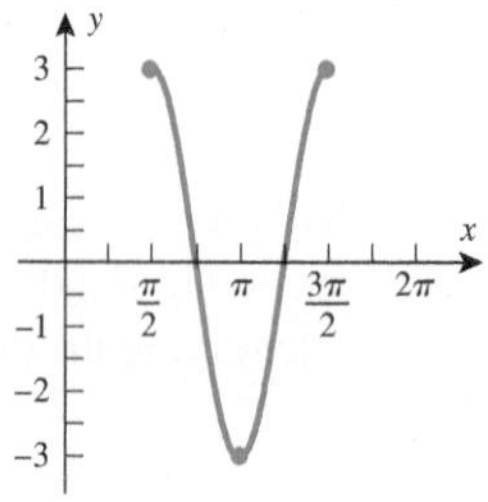

EXAMPLE 9 Graphing Sinusoidal Functions

Graph $y = -3 + 2\cos(2x - \pi)$.

Solution:

STEP 1 Find the amplitude. $|A| = |2| = 2$

STEP 2 Find the phase shift and period.

Set $2x - \pi$ equal to 0 and 2π. $2x - \pi = 0$ to $2x - \pi = 2\pi$

Solve for x. $x = \frac{\pi}{2}$ to $x = \frac{\pi}{2} + \pi$

Identify phase shift and period. $-\frac{C}{B} = \frac{\pi}{2}$

$\frac{2\pi}{B} = \pi$

STEP 3 Graph $y = 2\cos(2x - \pi)$ starting at $x = \frac{\pi}{2}$ over one period, π.

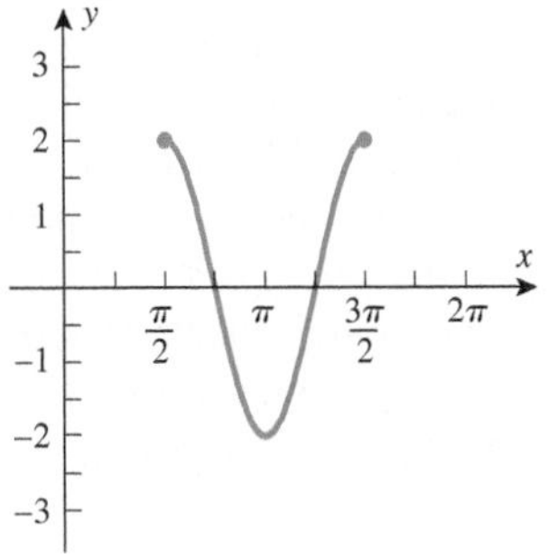

STEP 4 Extend the graph of $y = 2\cos(2x - \pi)$ over several periods.

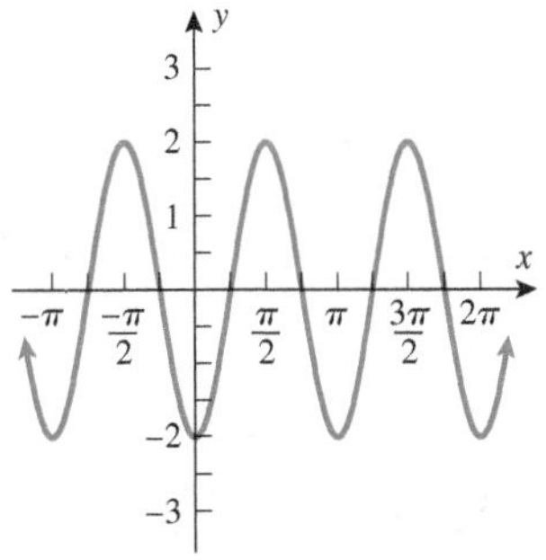

STEP 5 Shift the graph of $y = 2\cos(2x - \pi)$ down three units to arrive at the graph of $y = -3 + 2\cos(2x - \pi)$.

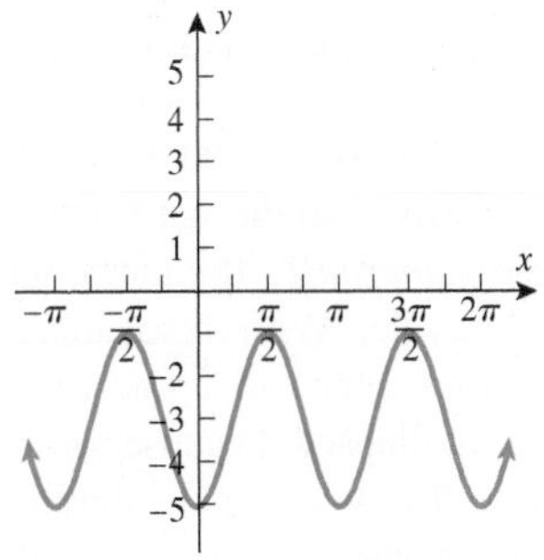

YOUR TURN Graph $y = -2 + 3\sin(2x + \pi)$.

ANSWER

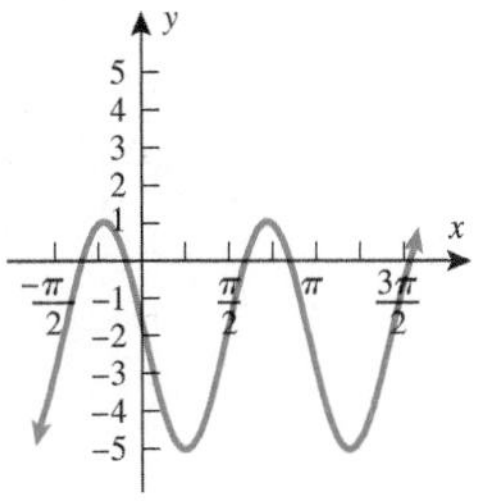

5.2.3 Harmonic Motion

5.2.3 SKILL

Solve harmonic motion problems.

5.2.3 CONCEPTUAL

Visualize harmonic motion as a sinusoidal function.

One of the most important applications of sinusoidal functions is in describing *harmonic motion*, which we define as the symmetric periodic movement of an object or quantity about a center (equilibrium) position or value. The oscillation of a pendulum is a form of harmonic motion. Other examples are the recoil of a spring balance scale when a weight is placed on the tray and the variation of current or voltage within an AC circuit.

There are three types of harmonic motion: **simple harmonic motion**, **damped harmonic motion**, and **resonance**.

Simple Harmonic Motion

Simple harmonic motion is the kind of *unvarying* periodic motion that would occur in an ideal situation in which no resistive forces, such as friction, cause the amplitude of oscillation to decrease over time: The amplitude stays in exactly the same range in each period as time—the variable on the horizontal axis—increases. It will also occur if energy is being supplied at the correct rate to overcome resistive forces. Simple harmonic motion occurs, for example, in an AC electric circuit when a power source is consistently supplying energy. When you are swinging on a swing and "pumping" energy into the swing to keep it in motion at a constant period and amplitude, you are sustaining simple harmonic motion.

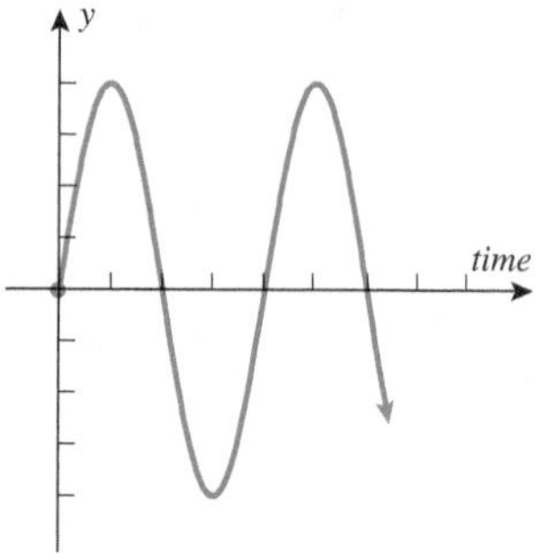

Damped Harmonic Motion

In damped harmonic motion, the amplitude of the periodic motion decreases as time increases. If you are on a moving swing and stop "pumping" new energy into the swing, the swing will continue moving with a constant period, but the amplitude—the height to which the swing will rise—will diminish with each cycle as the swing is slowed down by friction with the air or between its own moving parts.

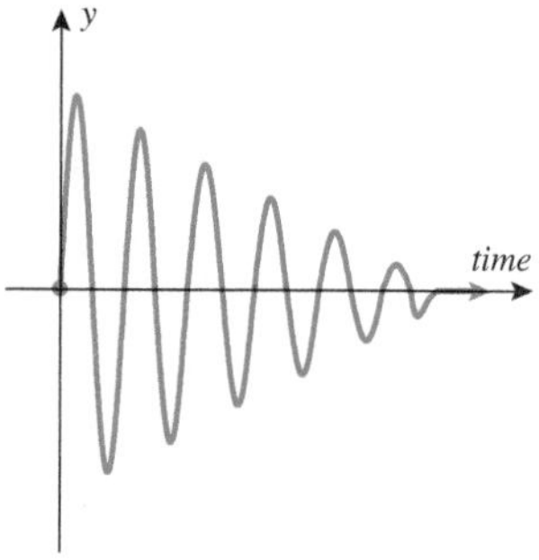

Resonance

Resonance is what occurs when the amplitude of periodic motion increases as time increases. It is caused when the energy applied to an oscillating object or system is more than what is needed to oppose friction or other forces and sustain simple harmonic motion; instead, the applied energy *increases* the amplitude of harmonic motion with each cycle. With resonance, eventually, the amplitude becomes unbounded and the result is disastrous. Bridges have collapsed because of resonance. Military soldiers know that when they march across a bridge, they must break cadence to prevent resonance. Below are two pictures of the Tacoma Narrows Bridge (near Seattle, Washington) that opened to traffic on July 1, 1940, and collapsed into Puget Sound on November 7, 1940. The collapsing of the Tacoma Narrows Bridge is often presented as an example of resonance (the wind providing an external periodic frequency that coincided with the bridge's natural frequency), but many believe the actual angle of failure was torsional motion that twisted cubes.

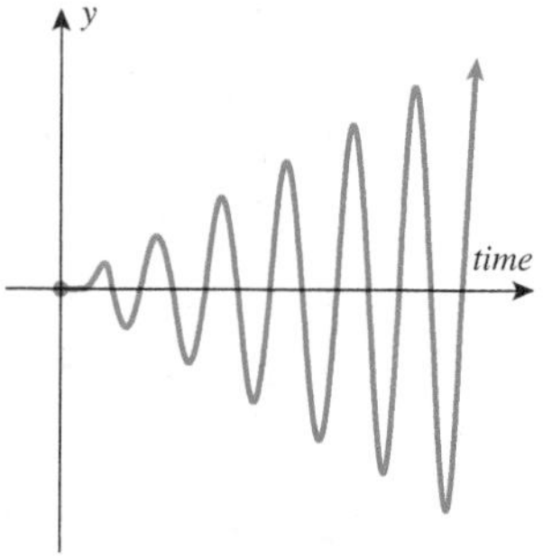

Keystone/Stringer/Getty Images

Topham/The Image Works

Examples of Harmonic Motion

If we hang a weight from a spring, then while the resulting "system" is at rest, we say it is in the equilibrium position.

If we then pull down on the weight and release it, the elasticity in the spring pulls the weight up and causes it to start oscillating up and down.

If we neglect friction and air resistance, we can imagine that the combination of the weight and the spring will oscillate indefinitely; the height of the weight with respect to the equilibrium position can be modeled by a simple sinusoidal function. This is an example of **simple harmonic motion**.

SIMPLE HARMONIC MOTION

The position of a point oscillating around an equilibrium position at time t is modeled by the sinusoidal function

$$y = A\sin(\omega t) \qquad \text{or} \qquad y = A\cos(\omega t)$$

Here $|A|$ is the amplitude and the period is $\frac{2\pi}{\omega}$, where $\omega > 0$.

Note: The symbol ω (Greek lowercase omega) represents the angular frequency.

[CONCEPT CHECK]

The scenario of a tennis ball being dropped vertically onto the ground, and continuing to bounce a few times before eventually coming to rest, is an example of:

(A) simple harmonic motion

(B) damped harmonic motion

(C) resonance

ANSWER (B)

EXAMPLE 10 Simple Harmonic Motion

Let the height of the seat of a swing be equal to zero when the swing is at rest. Assume that a child starts swinging until she reaches the highest she can swing and keeps her effort constant. Suppose the height $h(t)$ of the seat can be given by

$$h(t) = 8\sin\left(\frac{\pi}{2}t\right)$$

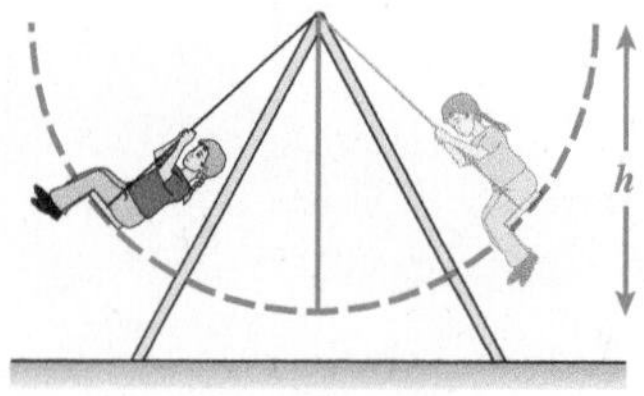

where t is time in seconds and h is the height in feet. Note that positive h indicates height reached swinging forward, and negative h indicates height reached swinging backward. Assume that $t = 0$ when the child passes through the equilibrium position swinging forward.

a. Graph the height function $h(t)$ for $0 \leq t \leq 4$.

b. What is the maximum height above the resting level reached by the seat of the swing?

c. What is the period of the swinging child?

Solution (a):

Make a table with integer values of t. $\quad 0 \leq t \leq 4$

t (SECONDS)	$y = h(t) = 8\sin\left(\frac{\pi}{2}t\right)$ (FEET)	(t, y)
0	$8\sin 0 = 0$	$(0, 0)$
1	$8\sin\left(\frac{\pi}{2}\right) = 8$	$(1, 8)$
2	$8\sin\pi = 0$	$(2, 0)$
3	$8\sin\left(\frac{3\pi}{2}\right) = -8$	$(3, -8)$
4	$8\sin(2\pi) = 0$	$(4, 0)$

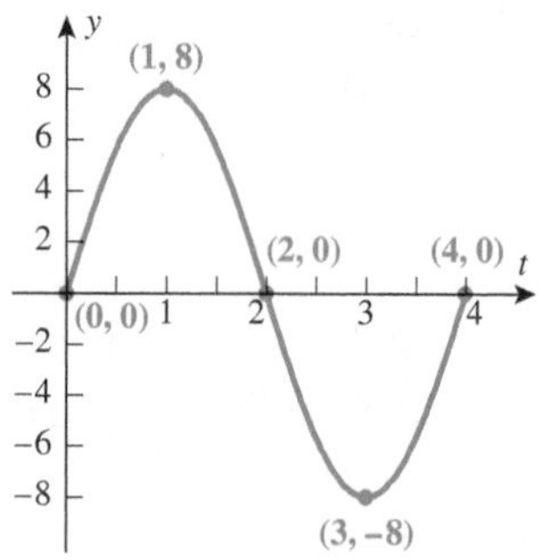

Labeling the time and height on the original diagram, we see that the maximum height is 8 feet and the period is 4 seconds.

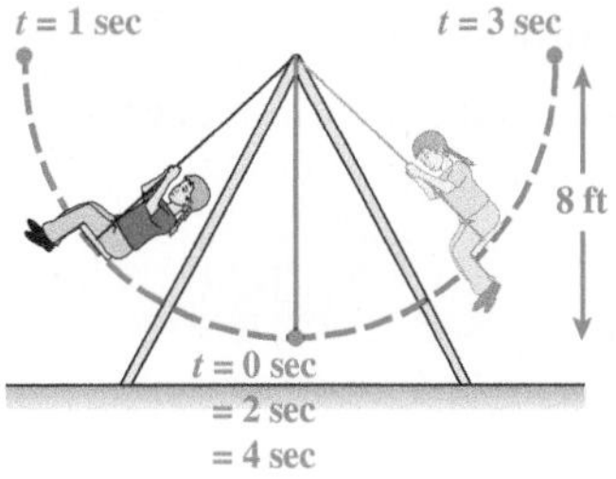

Solutions (b) and (c):

$$h(t) = 8\sin\left(\frac{\pi}{2}t\right)$$

The maximum height above the equilibrium is the amplitude.

$$\boxed{A = 8 \text{ ft}}$$

The period is $\frac{2\pi}{\omega}$.

$$\boxed{p = \frac{2\pi}{\frac{\pi}{2}} = 4 \text{ sec}}$$

Damped harmonic motion can be modeled by a sinusoidal function whose amplitude decreases as time increases. If we again hang a weight from a spring so that it is suspended at rest, and then pull down on the weight and release, the weight will oscillate about the equilibrium point. This time we will not neglect friction and air resistance: The weight will oscillate closer and closer to the equilibrium point over time until the weight eventually comes to rest at the equilibrium point. This is an example of damped harmonic motion.

The product of any decreasing function and the original periodic function will describe damped oscillatory motion. Here are two examples of functions that describe damped harmonic motion:

$$y = \frac{1}{t}\sin(\omega t) \qquad y = e^{-t}\cos(\omega t)$$

where e^{-t} is a decreasing exponential function (exponential decay).

EXAMPLE 11 **Damped Harmonic Motion**

If the child in Example 10 decides to stop pumping and allows the swing to continue until she eventually comes to rest. Assume the height function is given by

$$h(t) = \frac{8}{t}\cos\left(\frac{\pi}{2}t\right)$$

where t is time in seconds and h is the height in feet above the resting position. Note that positive h indicates height reached swinging forward and that negative h indicates height reached swinging backward, assuming that $t = 1$ when the child passes through the equilibrium position swinging backward and stops "pumping."

a. Graph the height function $h(t)$ for $1 \leq t \leq 8$.

b. What is the height above the resting level at 4 seconds? At 8 seconds? After 1 minute?

Solution (a):

Make a table with integer values of t. $1 \le t \le 8$

t (SECONDS)	$y = h(t) = \frac{8}{t}\cos\left(\frac{\pi}{2}t\right)$ (FEET)	(t, y)
1	$\frac{8}{1}\cos\left(\frac{\pi}{2}\right) = 0$	$(1, 0)$
2	$\frac{8}{2}\cos\pi = -4$	$(2, -4)$
3	$\frac{8}{3}\cos\left(\frac{3\pi}{2}\right) = 0$	$(3, 0)$
4	$\frac{8}{4}\cos(2\pi) = 2$	$(4, 2)$
5	$\frac{8}{5}\cos\left(\frac{5\pi}{2}\right) = 0$	$(5, 0)$
6	$\frac{8}{6}\cos(3\pi) = -\frac{4}{3}$	$\left(6, -\frac{4}{3}\right)$
7	$\frac{8}{7}\cos\left(\frac{7\pi}{2}\right) = 0$	$(7, 0)$
8	$\frac{8}{8}\cos(4\pi) = 1$	$(8, 1)$

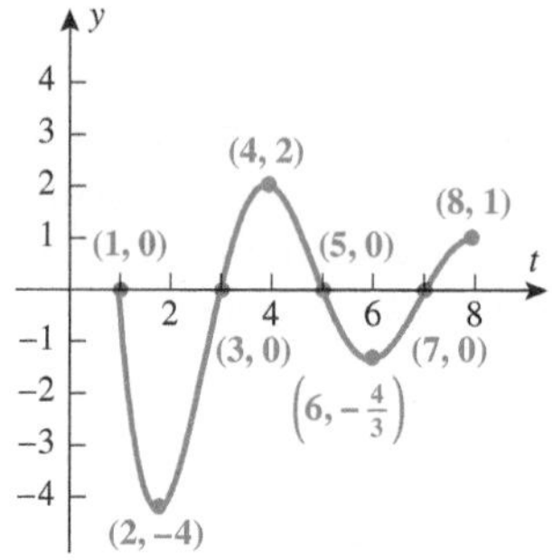

Solution (b):

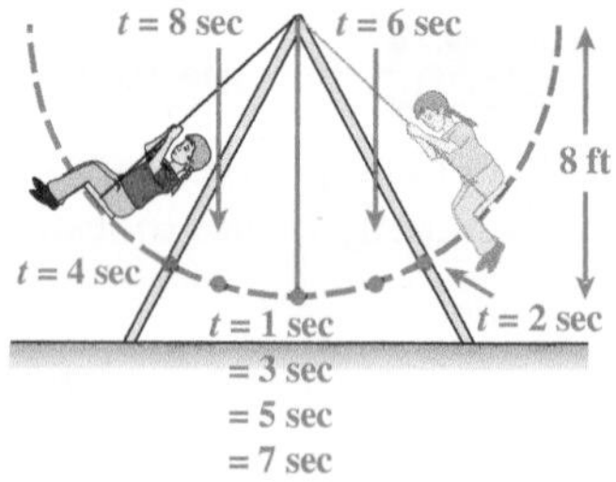

The height is 2 feet when t is 4 seconds. $\frac{8}{4}\cos(2\pi) = 2$

The height is 1 foot when t is 8 seconds. $\frac{8}{8}\cos(4\pi) = 1$

The height is 0.13 foot when t is 1 minute (60 seconds). $\frac{8}{60}\cos(30\pi) = 0.1333$

Resonance can be represented by the product of any increasing function and the original sinusoidal function. Here are two examples of functions that result in resonance as time increases:

$$y = t\cos(\omega t) \qquad y = e^t\sin(\omega t)$$

5.2.4 Graphing Sums of Functions: Addition of Ordinates

5.2.4 SKILL

Graph sums of trigonometric and other algebraic functions.

5.2.4 CONCEPTUAL

Understand that the y-coordinates of the combined function are found by adding the y-coordinates of the individual functions.

Now that you have the ability to graph sinusoidal functions, let us consider graphing sums of functions such as

$$y = x - \sin\left(\frac{\pi x}{2}\right) \qquad y = \sin x + \cos x \qquad y = 3\sin x + \cos(2x)$$

The method for graphing these sums is called the **addition of ordinates**, because we add the corresponding y-values (ordinates). The following table illustrates the ordinates (y-values) of the two sinusoidal functions $\sin x$ and $\cos x$; adding the corresponding ordinates leads to the y-values of $y = \sin x + \cos x$.

x	$\sin x$	$\cos x$	$y = \sin x + \cos x$
0	0	1	1
$\frac{\pi}{4}$	$\frac{\sqrt{2}}{2}$	$\frac{\sqrt{2}}{2}$	$\sqrt{2}$
$\frac{\pi}{2}$	1	0	1
$\frac{3\pi}{4}$	$\frac{\sqrt{2}}{2}$	$-\frac{\sqrt{2}}{2}$	0
π	0	-1	-1
$\frac{5\pi}{4}$	$-\frac{\sqrt{2}}{2}$	$-\frac{\sqrt{2}}{2}$	$-\sqrt{2}$
$\frac{3\pi}{2}$	-1	0	-1
$\frac{7\pi}{4}$	$-\frac{\sqrt{2}}{2}$	$\frac{\sqrt{2}}{2}$	0
2π	0	1	1

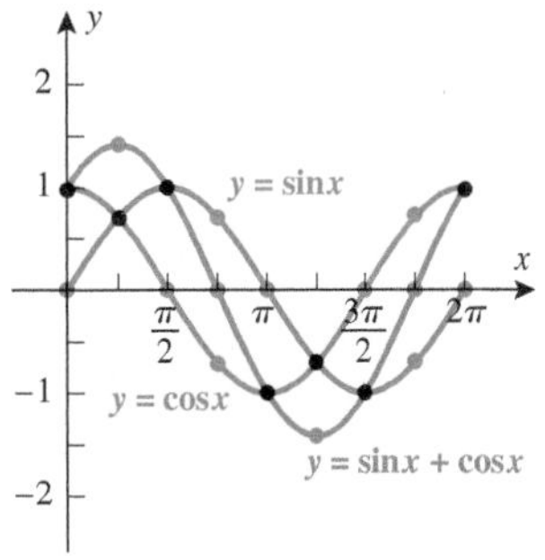

Using a graphing utility, we can graph $Y_1 = \sin X$, $Y_2 = \cos X$, and $Y_3 = Y_1 + Y_2$.

EXAMPLE 12 **Graphing Sums of Functions**

Graph $y = x - \sin\left(\frac{\pi x}{2}\right)$ on the interval $0 \leq x \leq 4$.

Solution:

Let $y_1 = x$ and $y_2 = -\sin\left(\frac{\pi x}{2}\right)$.

State the amplitude and period of the graph of y_2. $|A| = |-1| = 1, p = 4$

Make a table of x-values and y-values of y_1, y_2, and $y = y_1 + y_2$.

x	$y_1 = x$	$y_2 = -\sin\left(\frac{\pi x}{2}\right)$	$y = x + \left[-\sin\left(\frac{\pi x}{2}\right)\right]$
0	0	0	0
1	1	−1	0
2	2	0	2
3	3	1	4
4	4	0	4

Graph $y_1 = x$, $y_2 = -\sin\left(\frac{\pi x}{2}\right)$, and $y = x - \sin\left(\frac{\pi x}{2}\right)$.

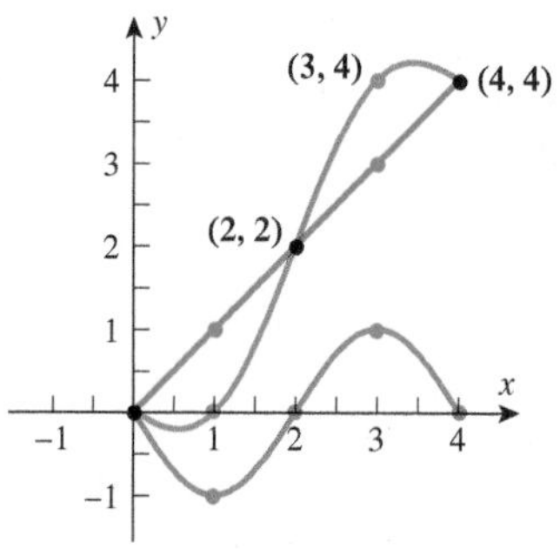

EXAMPLE 13 Graphing Sums of Sine and Cosine Functions

Graph $y = 3\sin x + \cos(2x)$ on the interval $0 \le x \le 2\pi$.

Solution:

Let $y_1 = 3\sin x$, and state the amplitude and period of its graph.

$|A| = 3, p = 2\pi$

Let $y_2 = \cos(2x)$, and state the amplitude and period of its graph.

$|A| = 1, p = \pi$

Make a table of x-values and y-values of y_1, y_2, and $y = y_1 + y_2$.

x	$y_1 = 3\sin x$	$y_2 = \cos(2x)$	$y = 3\sin x + \cos(2x)$
0	0	1	1
$\frac{\pi}{4}$	$\frac{3\sqrt{2}}{2}$	0	$\frac{3\sqrt{2}}{2}$
$\frac{\pi}{2}$	3	-1	2
$\frac{3\pi}{4}$	$\frac{3\sqrt{2}}{2}$	0	$\frac{3\sqrt{2}}{2}$
π	0	1	1
$\frac{5\pi}{4}$	$-\frac{3\sqrt{2}}{2}$	0	$-\frac{3\sqrt{2}}{2}$
$\frac{3\pi}{2}$	-3	-1	-4
$\frac{7\pi}{4}$	$-\frac{3\sqrt{2}}{2}$	0	$-\frac{3\sqrt{2}}{2}$
2π	0	1	1

Graph $y_1 = 3\sin x$, $y_2 = \cos(2x)$, and $y = 3\sin x + \cos(2x)$.

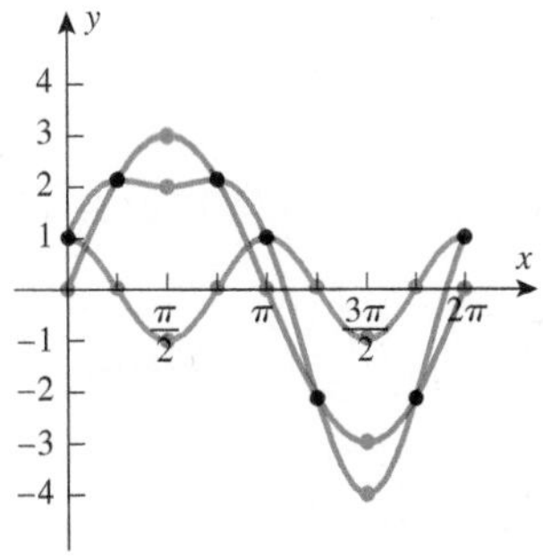

[CONCEPT CHECK]

For addition of ordinates, divide the smallest period of the periodic functions by ______ in order to get the corresponding ordinates to add.

ANSWER 4

EXAMPLE 14 Graphing Sums of Cosine Functions

Graph $y = \cos\left(\frac{x}{2}\right) - \cos x$ on the interval $0 \le x \le 4\pi$.

Solution:

Let $y_1 = \cos\left(\frac{x}{2}\right)$ and state the amplitude and period of its graph. $|A| = 1, p = 4\pi$

Let $y_2 = -\cos x$ and state the amplitude and period of its graph. $|A| = |-1| = 1, p = 2\pi$

Make a table of x-values and y-values of y_1, y_2, and $y = y_1 + y_2$.

x	$y_1 = \cos\left(\frac{x}{2}\right)$	$y_2 = -\cos x$	$y = \cos\left(\frac{x}{2}\right) + (-\cos x)$
0	1	−1	0
$\frac{\pi}{2}$	$\frac{\sqrt{2}}{2}$	0	$\frac{\sqrt{2}}{2}$
π	0	1	1
$\frac{3\pi}{2}$	$-\frac{\sqrt{2}}{2}$	0	$-\frac{\sqrt{2}}{2}$
2π	−1	−1	−2
$\frac{5\pi}{2}$	$-\frac{\sqrt{2}}{2}$	0	$-\frac{\sqrt{2}}{2}$
3π	0	1	1
$\frac{7\pi}{2}$	$\frac{\sqrt{2}}{2}$	0	$\frac{\sqrt{2}}{2}$
4π	1	−1	0

Graph $y_1 = \cos\left(\frac{x}{2}\right)$, $y_2 = -\cos x$, and $y = \cos\left(\frac{x}{2}\right) - \cos x$.

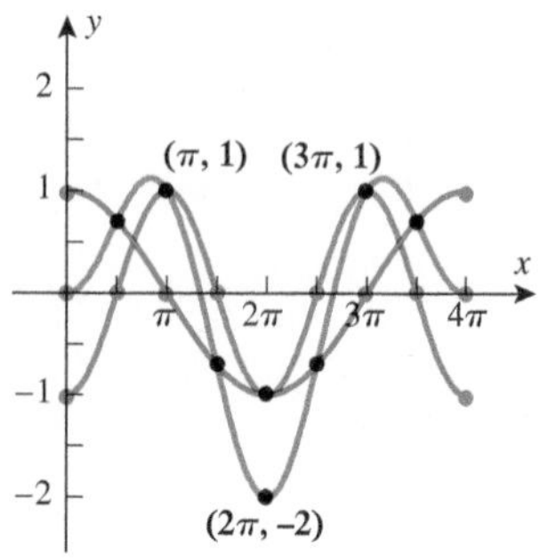

[SECTION 5.2] SUMMARY

The sine function is an odd function, and its graph is symmetric about the origin. The cosine function is an even function, and its graph is symmetric about the y-axis. Graphs of the form $y = A\sin(Bx)$ and $y = A\cos(Bx)$ have amplitude $|A|$ and period $\frac{2\pi}{B}$.

To graph sinusoidal functions, point-plotting can be used. A more efficient way is first to determine the amplitude and period. Divide the period into four equal parts and choose the values of the division points starting at 0 for x. Make a table of those four points and graph them (this is the graph of one period) by labeling the four coordinates and drawing a smooth sinusoidal curve. Extend the graph to the left and right.

To find an equation of a sinusoidal function given its graph, start by finding the amplitude (half the distance between the maximum and minimum values) so you can find A. Then determine the period so you can find B. Graphs of the form $y = A\sin(Bx + C) + D$ and $y = A\cos(Bx + C) + D$ can be graphed using graph-shifting techniques.

Harmonic motion is one of the primary applications of sinusoidal functions. To graph combinations of trigonometric functions, add the corresponding y-values of the individual functions.

[SECTION 5.2] EXERCISES

• SKILLS

In Exercises 1–10, match the function with its graph (a–j).

1. $y = -\sin x$
2. $y = \sin x$
3. $y = \cos x$
4. $y = -\cos x$
5. $y = 2\sin x$
6. $y = 2\cos x$
7. $y = \sin\left(\frac{1}{2}x\right)$
8. $y = \cos\left(\frac{1}{2}x\right)$
9. $y = -2\cos\left(\frac{1}{2}x\right)$
10. $y = -2\sin\left(\frac{1}{2}x\right)$

a.

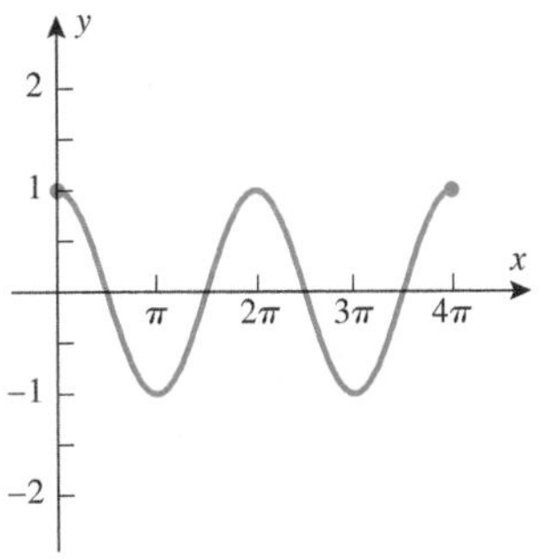

b.

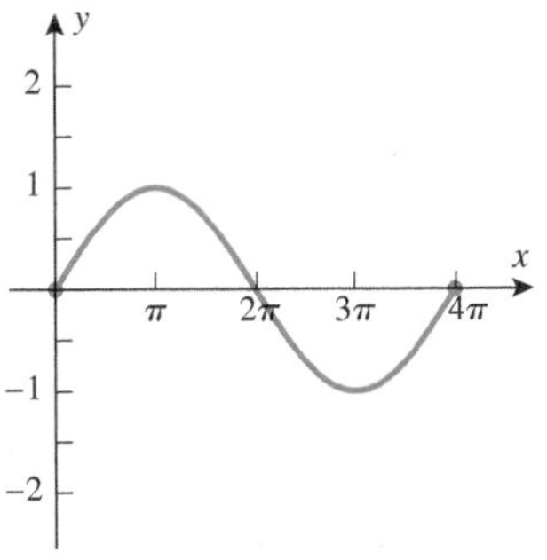

c.

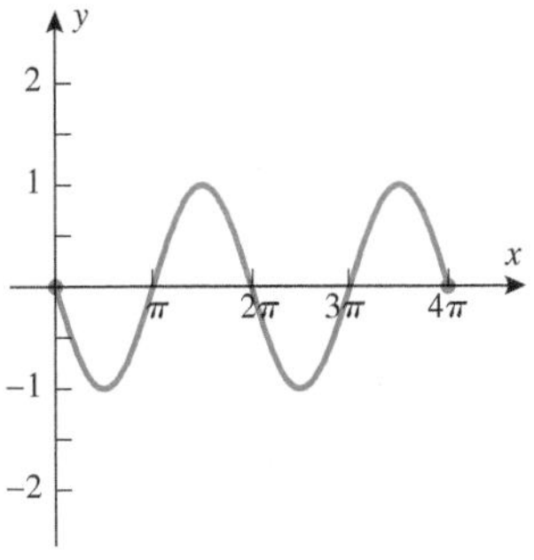

d.

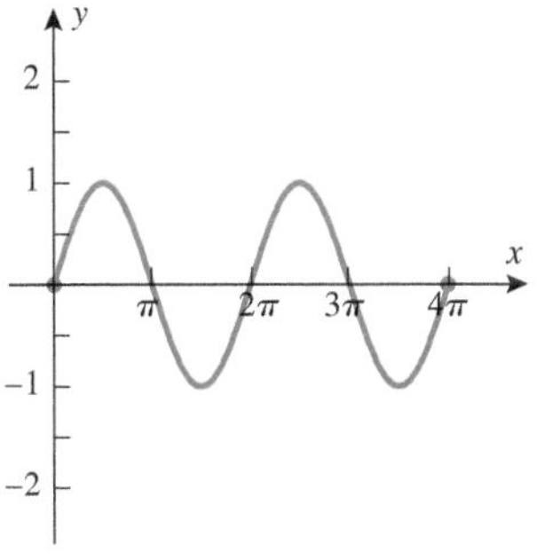

e.

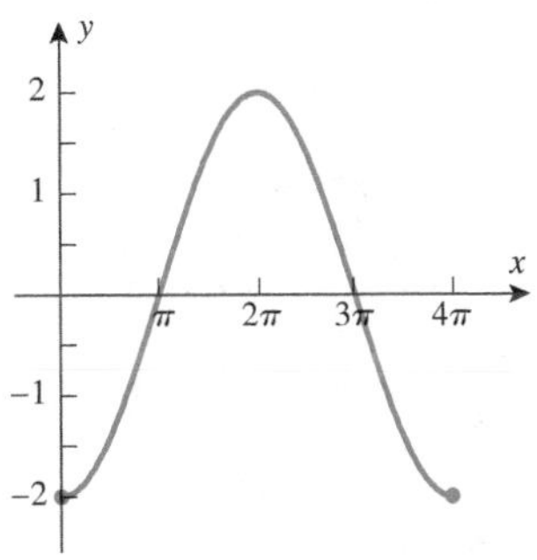

f.

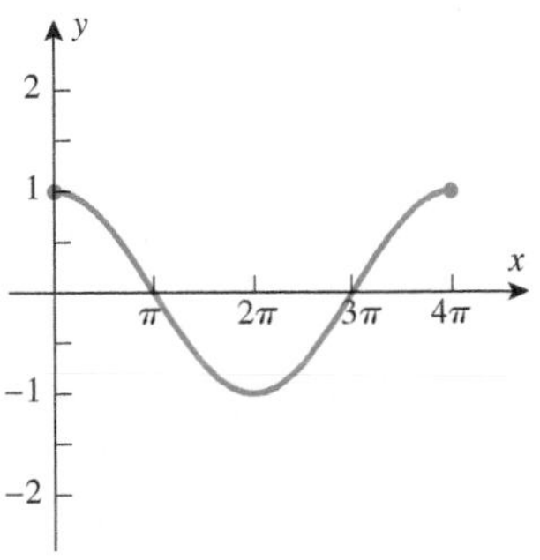

g.

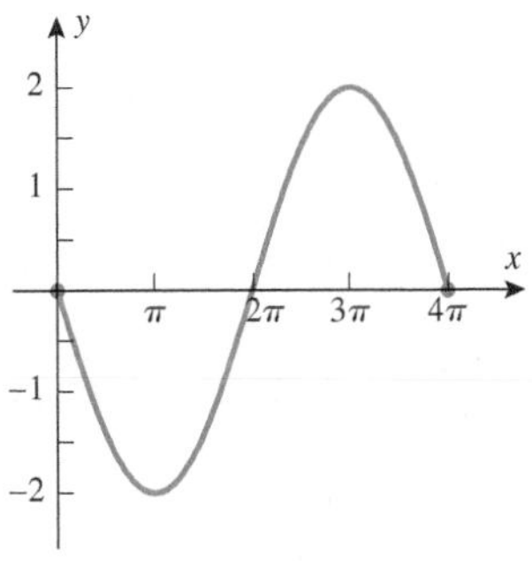

h.

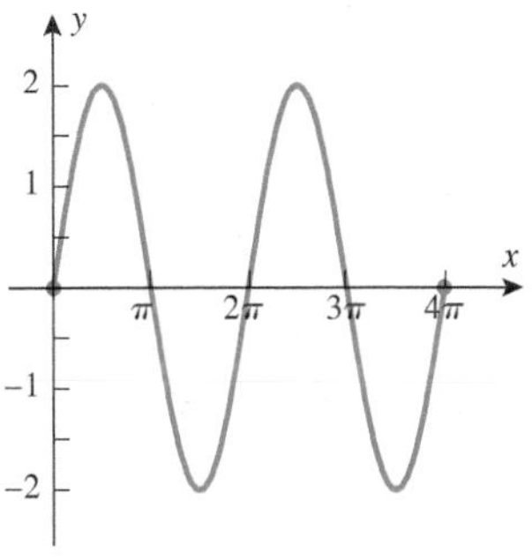

i.

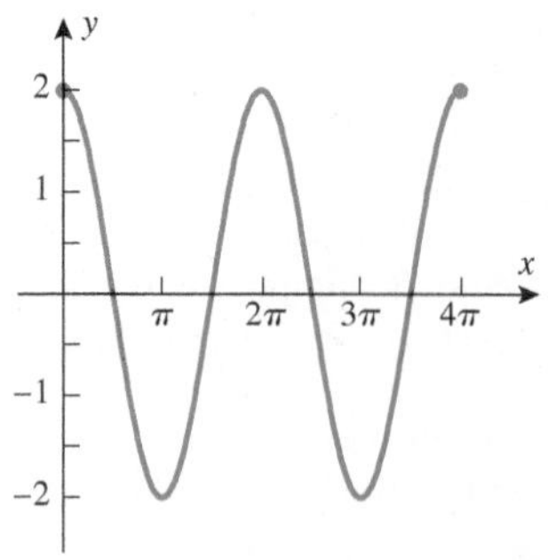

j.

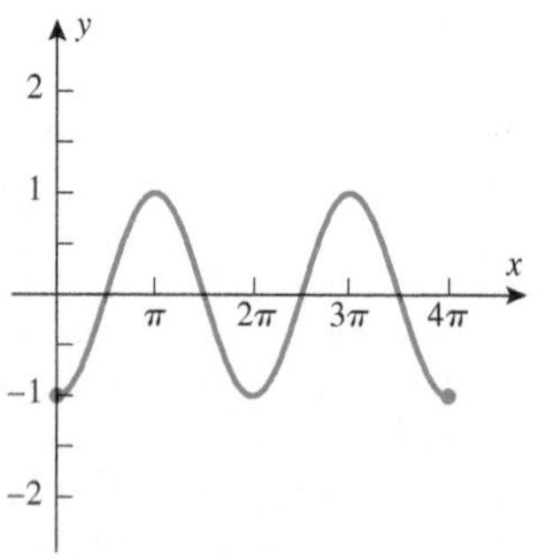

In Exercises 11–20, state the amplitude and period of each function.

11. $y = \frac{3}{2}\cos(3x)$ **12.** $y = \frac{2}{3}\sin(4x)$ **13.** $y = -\sin(5x)$ **14.** $y = -\cos(7x)$ **15.** $y = \frac{2}{3}\cos\left(\frac{3}{2}x\right)$

16. $y = \frac{3}{2}\sin\left(\frac{2}{3}x\right)$ **17.** $y = -3\cos(\pi x)$ **18.** $y = -2\sin(\pi x)$ **19.** $y = 5\sin\left(\frac{\pi}{3}x\right)$ **20.** $y = 4\cos\left(\frac{\pi}{4}x\right)$

In Exercises 21–32, graph the given function over one period.

21. $y = 8\cos x$ **22.** $y = 7\sin x$ **23.** $y = \sin(4x)$ **24.** $y = \cos(3x)$

25. $y = -3\cos\left(\frac{1}{2}x\right)$ **26.** $y = -2\sin\left(\frac{1}{4}x\right)$ **27.** $y = -3\sin(\pi x)$ **28.** $y = -2\cos(\pi x)$

29. $y = 5\cos(2\pi x)$ **30.** $y = 4\sin(2\pi x)$ **31.** $y = -3\sin\left(\frac{\pi}{4}x\right)$ **32.** $y = -4\sin\left(\frac{\pi}{2}x\right)$

In Exercises 33–40, graph the given function over the interval $[-2p, 2p]$, where p is the period of the function.

33. $y = -4\cos\left(\frac{1}{2}x\right)$ **34.** $y = -5\sin\left(\frac{1}{2}x\right)$ **35.** $y = -\sin(6x)$ **36.** $y = -\cos(4x)$

37. $y = 3\cos\left(\frac{\pi}{4}x\right)$ **38.** $y = 4\sin\left(\frac{\pi}{4}x\right)$ **39.** $y = \sin(4\pi x)$ **40.** $y = \cos(6\pi x)$

In Exercises 41–48, find the equation for each graph.

41.

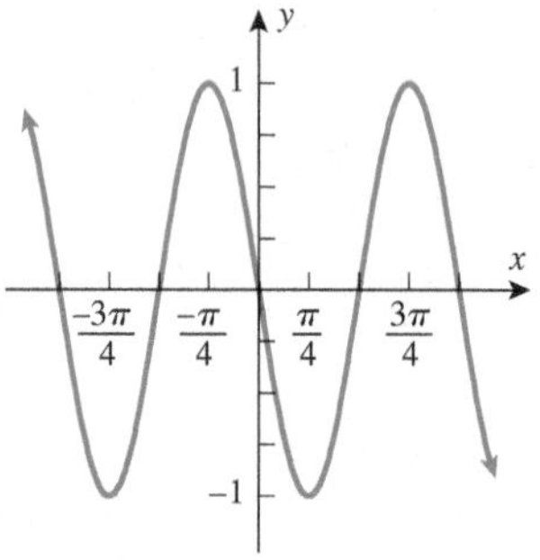

42.

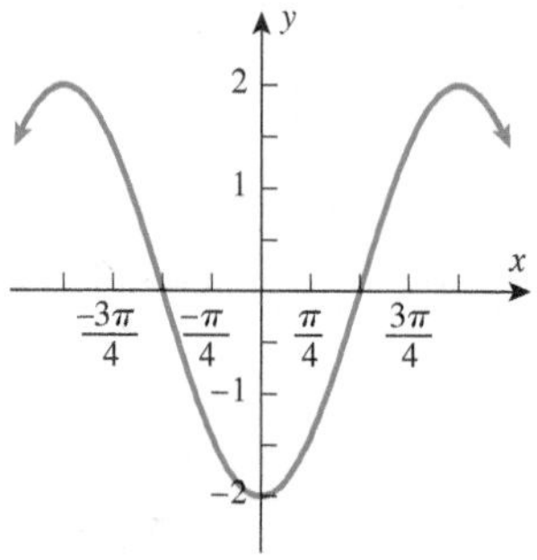

43.

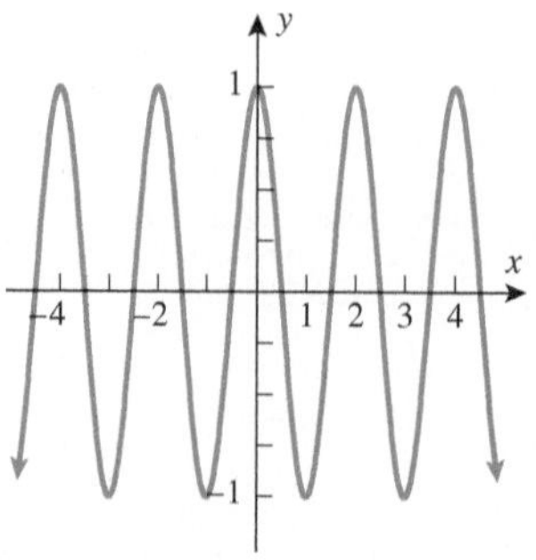

44.

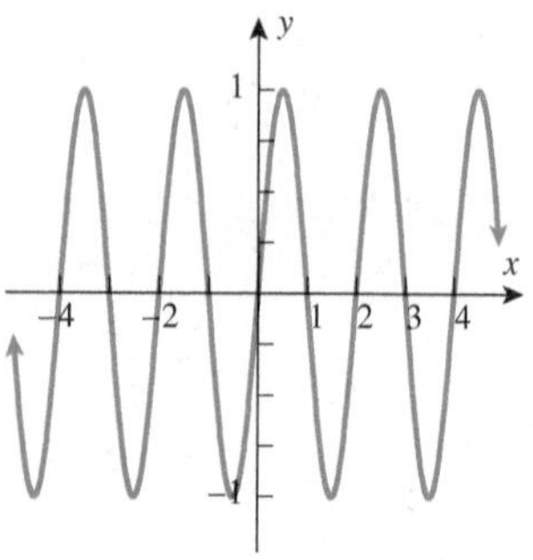

45.

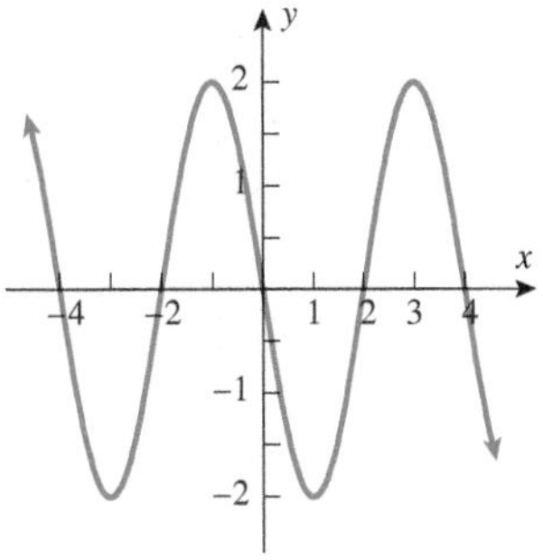

46.

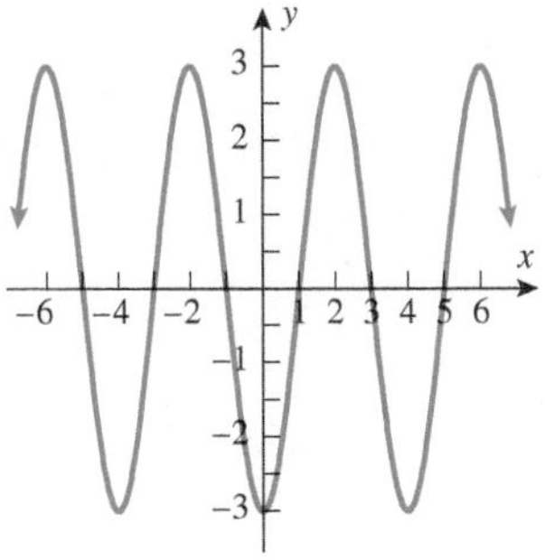

47.

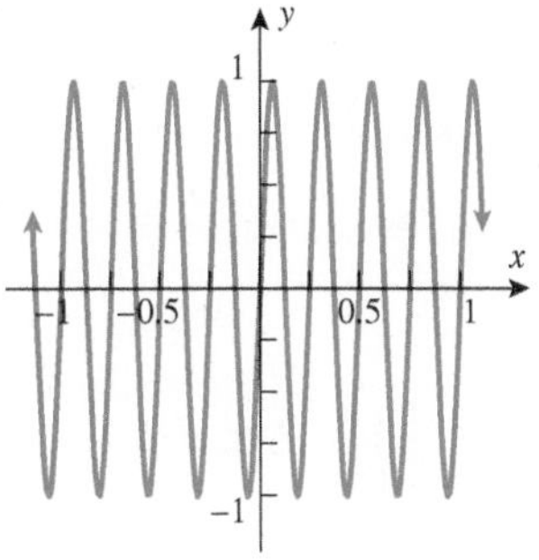

48.

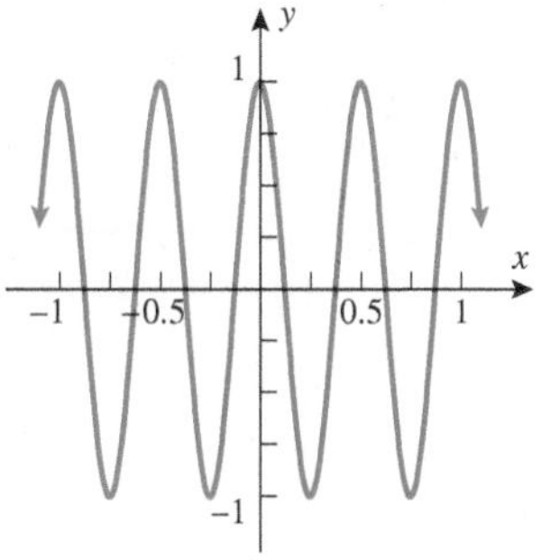

In Exercises 49–60, state the amplitude, period, and phase shift (including direction) of the given function and graph.

49. $y = 2\sin(\pi x - 1)$

50. $y = 4\cos(x + \pi)$

51. $y = -5\cos(3x + 2)$

52. $y = -7\sin(4x - 3)$

53. $y = 6\sin[-\pi(x + 2)]$

54. $y = 3\sin\left[-\frac{\pi}{2}(x - 1)\right]$

55. $y = 3\sin(2x + \pi)$

56. $y = -4\cos(2x - \pi)$

57. $y = -\frac{1}{4}\cos\left(\frac{1}{4}x - \frac{\pi}{2}\right)$

58. $y = \frac{1}{2}\sin\left(\frac{1}{3}x + \pi\right)$

59. $y = 2\cos\left[\frac{\pi}{2}(x - 4)\right]$

60. $y = -5\sin[-\pi(x + 1)]$

In Exercises 61–66, sketch the graph of the function over the indicated interval.

61. $y = \frac{1}{2} + \frac{3}{2}\cos(2x + \pi), \left[-\frac{3\pi}{2}, \frac{3\pi}{2}\right]$

62. $y = \frac{1}{3} + \frac{2}{3}\sin(2x - \pi), \left[-\frac{3\pi}{2}, \frac{3\pi}{2}\right]$

63. $y = \frac{1}{2} - \frac{1}{2}\sin\left(\frac{1}{2}x - \frac{\pi}{4}\right), \left[-\frac{7\pi}{2}, \frac{9\pi}{2}\right]$

64. $y = -\frac{1}{2} + \frac{1}{2}\cos\left(\frac{1}{2}x + \frac{\pi}{4}\right), \left[-\frac{9\pi}{2}, \frac{7\pi}{2}\right]$

65. $y = -3 + 4\sin[\pi(x - 2)], [0, 4]$

66. $y = 4 - 3\cos[\pi(x + 1)], [-1, 3]$

In Exercises 67–94, add the ordinates of the individual functions to graph each summed function on the indicated interval.

67. $y = 2x - \cos(\pi x), 0 \le x \le 4$

68. $y = 3x - 2\cos(\pi x), 0 \le x \le 4$

69. $y = \frac{1}{3}x + 2\cos(2x), 0 \le x \le 2\pi$

70. $y = \frac{1}{4}x + 3\cos\left(\frac{x}{2}\right), 0 \le x \le 4\pi$

71. $y = x - \cos\left(\frac{3\pi}{2}x\right), 0 \le x \le 6$

72. $y = -2x + 2\sin\left(\frac{\pi}{2}x\right), -2 \le x \le 2$

73. $y = \frac{1}{4}x - \frac{1}{2}\cos[\pi(x - 1)], 2 \le x \le 6$

74. $y = -\frac{1}{3}x + \frac{1}{3}\sin\left[\frac{\pi}{6}(x + 2)\right], -2 \le x \le 10$

75. $y = \sin x - \cos x, 0 \le x \le 2\pi$

76. $y = \cos x - \sin x, 0 \le x \le 2\pi$

77. $y = 3\cos x + \sin x, 0 \le x \le 2\pi$

78. $y = 3\sin x - \cos x, 0 \le x \le 2\pi$

79. $y = 4\cos x - \sin(2x), 0 \le x \le 2\pi$

80. $y = \frac{1}{2}\sin x + 2\cos(4x), -\pi \le x \le \pi$

81. $y = 2\sin[\pi(x - 1)] - 2\cos[\pi(x + 1)], -1 \le x \le 2$

82. $y = \sin\left[\frac{\pi}{4}(x + 2)\right] + 3\cos\left[\frac{3\pi}{3}(x - 1)\right], 1 \le x \le 5$

83. $y = \cos\left(\frac{x}{2}\right) + \cos(2x), 0 \le x \le 4\pi$

84. $y = \sin(2x) + \sin(3x), -\pi \le x \le \pi$

85. $y = \sin\left(\frac{x}{2}\right) + \sin(2x), 0 \le x \le 4\pi$

86. $y = -\sin\left(\frac{\pi}{4}x\right) - 3\sin\left(\frac{5\pi}{4}x\right), 0 \le x \le 4$

87. $y = -\frac{1}{3}\sin\left(\frac{\pi}{6}x\right) + \frac{2}{3}\sin\left(\frac{5\pi}{6}x\right),\ 0 \le x \le 3$

88. $y = 8\cos x - 6\cos\left(\frac{1}{2}x\right),\ -2\pi \le x \le 2\pi$

89. $y = -\frac{1}{4}\cos\left(\frac{\pi}{6}x\right) - \frac{1}{2}\cos\left(\frac{\pi}{3}x\right),\ 0 \le x \le 12$

90. $y = 2\cos\left(\frac{3}{2}x\right) - \cos\left(\frac{1}{2}x\right),\ -2\pi \le x \le 2\pi$

91. $y = 2\sin\left(\frac{x}{2}\right) - \cos(2x),\ 0 \le x \le 4\pi$

92. $y = 2\cos\left(\frac{x}{2}\right) + \sin(2x),\ 0 \le x \le 4\pi$

93. $y = 2\sin[\pi(x-1)] + 3\sin\left[2\pi\left(x + \frac{1}{2}\right)\right],\ -2 \le x \le 2$

94. $y = -\frac{1}{2}\cos\left(x + \frac{\pi}{3}\right) - 2\cos\left(x - \frac{\pi}{6}\right),\ -\pi \le x \le \pi$

• APPLICATIONS

For Exercises 95 and 96, refer to the following:

An analysis of demand d for widgets manufactured by WidgetsRUs (measured in thousands of units per week) indicates that demand can be modeled by the graph below, where t is time in months since January 2010 (note that $t = 0$ corresponds to January 2010).

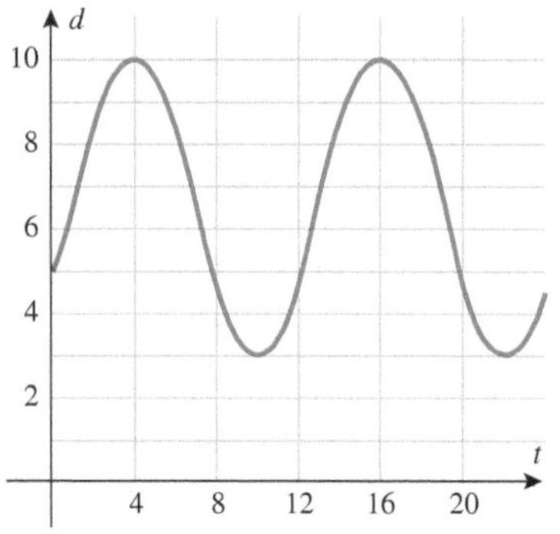

95. Business. Find the amplitude of the graph.

96. Business. Find the period of the graph.

For Exercises 97 and 98, refer to the following:

Researchers have been monitoring oxygen levels (milligrams per liter) in the water of a lake and have found that the oxygen levels fluctuate with an eight-week period. The following tables illustrate data from eight weeks.

97. Environment. Find the amplitude of the oxygen level fluctuations.

WEEK: t	0 (initial measurement)	1	2	3	4	5	6	7	8
OXYGEN LEVEL: mg/L	7	7.7	8	7.7	7	6.3	6	6.3	7

98. Environment. Find the amplitude of the oxygen level fluctuations.

WEEK: t	0 (initial measurement)	1	2	3	4	5	6	7	8
OXYGEN LEVEL: mg/L	7	8.4	9	8.4	7	5.6	5	5.6	7

For Exercises 99–102, refer to the following:

A weight hanging on a spring will oscillate up and down about its equilibrium position after it is pulled down and released.

This is an example of simple harmonic motion. This motion would continue forever if there were not any friction or air resistance. Simple harmonic motion can be described with the function $y = A\cos\left(t\sqrt{\frac{k}{m}}\right)$, where $|A|$ is the amplitude, t is the time in seconds, m is the mass of the weight, and k is a constant particular to the spring.

99. Simple Harmonic Motion. If the height of the spring is measured in centimeters and the mass in grams, then what are the amplitude and mass if $y = 4\cos\left(\frac{t\sqrt{k}}{2}\right)$?

100. Simple Harmonic Motion. If a spring is measured in centimeters and the mass in grams, then what are the amplitude and mass if $y = 3\cos(3t\sqrt{k})$?

101. Frequency of Oscillations. The frequency of the oscillations in cycles per second is determined by $f = \frac{1}{p}$, where p is the period. What is the frequency for the oscillation modeled by $y = 3\cos\left(\frac{t}{2}\right)$?

102. Frequency of Oscillations. The frequency of the oscillations f is given by $f = \frac{1}{p}$, where p is the period. What is the frequency of oscillation modeled by $y = 3.5\cos(3t)$?

103. Sound Waves. A pure tone created by a vibrating tuning fork shows up as a sine wave on an oscilloscope's screen. A tuning fork vibrating at 256 hertz(Hz) gives the tone middle C and can have the equation $y = 0.005\sin[(2\pi)(256t)]$, where the amplitude is in centimeters (cm) and the time t in seconds. What are the amplitude and frequency of the wave where the frequency is $\frac{1}{p}$ in cycles per second?

Note: 1 hertz = 1 cycle per second.

104. Sound Waves. A pure tone created by a vibrating tuning fork shows up as a sine wave on an oscilloscope's screen. A tuning fork vibrating at 288 hertz gives the tone D and can have the equation $y = 0.005\sin[(2\pi)(288t)]$, where the amplitude is in centimeters (cm) and the time t in seconds. What are the amplitude and frequency of the wave where the frequency is $\frac{1}{p}$ in cycles per second?

105. Sound Waves. If a sound wave is represented by $y = 0.008\sin(750\,\pi t)$ cm, what are its amplitude and frequency? See Exercise 103.

106. Sound Waves. If a sound wave is represented by $y = 0.006\,\cos(1000\pi t)$ cm, what are its amplitude and frequency? See Exercise 103.

For Exercises 107–110, refer to the following:

When an airplane flies faster than the speed of sound, the sound waves that are formed take on a cone shape, and where the cone hits the ground, a sonic boom is heard. If θ is the angle of the vertex of the cone, then $\sin\left(\frac{\theta}{2}\right) = \frac{330\text{ m/sec}}{V} = \frac{1}{M}$, where V is the speed of the plane and M is the Mach number.

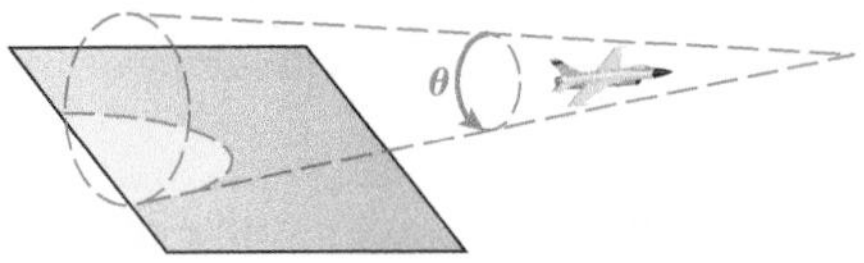

107. Sonic Booms. What is the speed of the plane if the plane is flying at Mach 2?

108. Sonic Booms. What is the Mach number if the plane is flying at 990 meters per second?

109. Sonic Booms. What is the speed of the plane if the cone angle is 60°?

110. Sonic Booms. What is the speed of the plane if the cone angle is 30°?

• CATCH THE MISTAKE

In Exercises 111 and 112, explain the mistake that is made.

111. Graph the function $y = -2\cos x$.

Solution:

Find the amplitude. $|A| = |-2| = 2$

The graph of $y = -2\cos x$ is similar to the graph of $y = \cos x$ with amplitude 2.

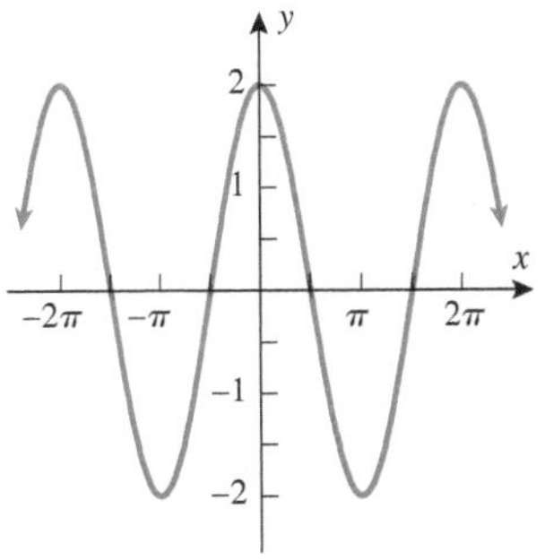

This is incorrect. What mistake was made?

112. Graph the function $y = -\sin(2x)$.

Solution:

Make a table with values.

x	$y = -\sin(2x)$	(x, y)
0	$y = -\sin 0 = 0$	$(0, 0)$
$\frac{\pi}{2}$	$y = -\sin \pi = 0$	$(0, 0)$
π	$y = -\sin(2\pi) = 0$	$(0, 0)$
$\frac{3\pi}{2}$	$y = -\sin(3\pi) = 0$	$(0, 0)$
2π	$y = -\sin(4\pi) = 0$	$(0, 0)$

Graph the function by plotting these points and connecting them with a sinusoidal curve.

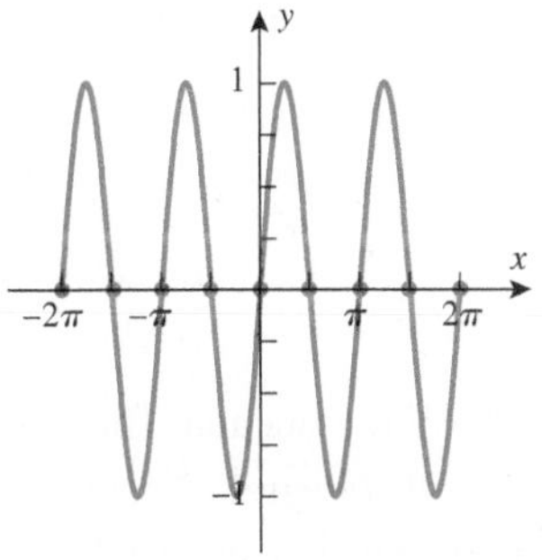

This is incorrect. What mistake was made?

• CONCEPTUAL

In Exercises 113–116, determine whether each statement is true or false. (A and B are positive real numbers.)

113. The graph of $y = -A\cos(Bx)$ is the graph of $y = A\cos(Bx)$ reflected about the x-axis.

114. The graph of $y = A\sin(-Bx)$ is the graph of $y = A\sin(Bx)$ reflected about the x-axis.

115. The graph of $y = -A\cos(-Bx)$ is the graph of $y = A\cos(Bx)$.

116. The graph of $y = -A\sin(-Bx)$ is the graph of $y = A\sin(Bx)$.

In Exercises 117–120, A and B are positive real numbers.

117. Find the y-intercept of the function $y = A\cos(Bx)$.

118. Find the y-intercept of the function $y = A\sin(Bx)$.

119. Find the x-intercepts of the function $y = A\sin(Bx)$.

120. Find the x-intercepts of the function $y = A\cos(Bx)$.

• CHALLENGE

121. Find the y-intercept of $y = -A\sin\left(Bx + \frac{\pi}{6}\right)$.

122. Find the y-intercept of $y = A\cos(Bx - \pi) + C$.

123. Find the x-intercept(s) of $y = A\sin(Bx) + A$.

124. Find an expression involving C and A that describes the values of C for which the graph of $y = A\cos(Bx) + C$ does not cross the x-axis. (Assume that $A > 0$.)

125. What is the range of $y = 2A\sin(Bx + C) - \frac{A}{2}$?

126. Can the y-coordinate of a point on the graph of $y = A\sin(Bx) + 3A\cos\left(\frac{B}{2}x\right)$ exceed $4A$? Explain. (Assume that $A > 0$.)

• PREVIEW TO CALCULUS

In calculus, the definite integral $\int_a^b f(x)dx$ is used to find the area below the graph of f, above the x-axis, between $x = a$ and $x = b$. For example, $\int_0^2 x\,dx = 2$, as you can see in the following figure:

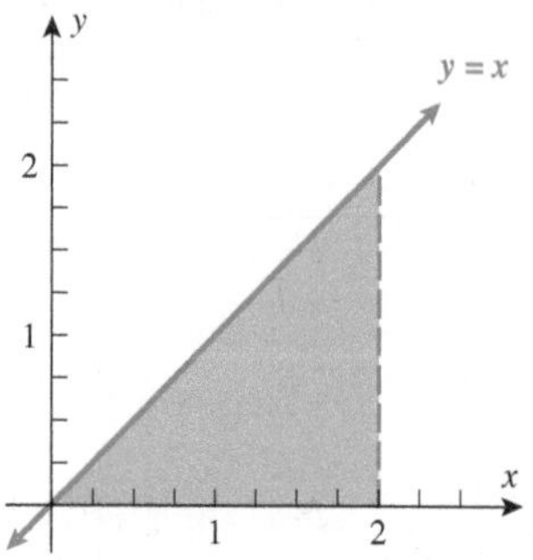

The Fundamental Theorem of Calculus establishes that the definite integral $\int_a^b f(x)dx$ equals $F(b) - F(a)$, where F is any antiderivative of a continuous function f.

In Exercises 127–130, first shade the area corresponding to the definite integral, and then use the information below to find the exact value of the area.

FUNCTION	$\sin x$	$\cos x$
ANTIDERIVATIVE	$-\cos x$	$\sin x$

127. $\int_0^{\pi} \sin x\,dx$

128. $\int_{-\pi/2}^{\pi/2} \cos x\,dx$

129. $\int_0^{\pi/2} \cos x\,dx$

130. $\int_0^{\pi/2} \sin x\,dx$

5.3 GRAPHS OF OTHER TRIGONOMETRIC FUNCTIONS

SKILLS OBJECTIVES

- Graph basic tangent, cotangent, secant, and cosecant functions.
- Graph translated tangent, cotangent, secant, and cosecant functions.

CONCEPTUAL OBJECTIVES

- Understand the relationships between the graphs of the cosine and secant functions, and those of the sine and cosecant functions.
- Understand that graph-shifting techniques for tangent and cotangent are consistent with translations used for sinusoidal functions, but that for secant and cosecant functions, we first graph the horizontally translated sinusoidal functions and then shift up or down, depending on the vertical translations.

5.3.1 Graphing the Tangent, Cotangent, Secant, and Cosecant Functions

5.3.1 SKILL

Graph basic tangent, cotangent, secant, and cosecant functions.

5.3.1 CONCEPTUAL

Understand the relationships between the graphs of the cosine and secant functions, and those of the sine and cosecant functions.

Section 5.2 focused on graphing sinusoidal functions (sine and cosine). We now turn our attention to graphing the other trigonometric functions: tangent, cotangent, secant, and cosecant. We know the graphs of the sine and cosine functions, and we can get the graphs of the other trigonometric functions from the sinusoidal functions. Recall the reciprocal and quotient identities:

$$\tan x = \frac{\sin x}{\cos x} \qquad \cot x = \frac{\cos x}{\sin x} \qquad \sec x = \frac{1}{\cos x} \qquad \csc x = \frac{1}{\sin x}$$

Recall that in graphing rational functions, a *vertical asymptote* is found by setting the denominator of the rational function equal to zero (as long as the numerator and denominator have no common factors). As you will see in this section, tangent and secant functions have graphs with vertical asymptotes at the x-values where cosine is equal to zero, and cotangent and cosecant functions have graphs with vertical asymptotes at the x-values where sine is equal to zero.

One important difference between the sinusoidal functions, $y = \sin x$ and $y = \cos x$, and the other four trigonometric functions ($y = \tan x$, $y = \sec x$, $y = \csc x$, and $y = \cot x$) is that the sinusoidal functions have defined amplitudes, whereas the other four trigonometric functions do not (since they are unbounded vertically).

[CONCEPT CHECK]

If the range of the graph of a sinusoidal function is $[-A, A]$, what is the range of the corresponding secant or cosecant functions?

ANSWER $(-\infty, -A] \cup [A, \infty)$

The Tangent Function

Since the tangent function is a quotient that relies on the sine and cosine functions, let us start with a table of values for the quadrantal angles.

x	$\sin x$	$\cos x$	$\tan x = \frac{\sin x}{\cos x}$	(x, y) OR ASYMPTOTE
0	0	1	0	$(0, 0)$
$\frac{\pi}{2}$	1	0	undefined	vertical asymptote: $x = \frac{\pi}{2}$
π	0	-1	0	$(\pi, 0)$
$\frac{3\pi}{2}$	-1	0	undefined	vertical asymptote: $x = \frac{3\pi}{2}$
2π	0	1	0	$(2\pi, 0)$

Notice that the x-intercepts correspond to integer multiples of π and the vertical asymptotes correspond to odd integer multiples of $\frac{\pi}{2}$.

We know that the graph of the tangent function is undefined at the odd integer multiples of $\frac{\pi}{2}$, so its graph cannot cross the vertical asymptotes. The question is, what happens between the asymptotes? We know the x-intercepts, so let us now make a table for special values of x.

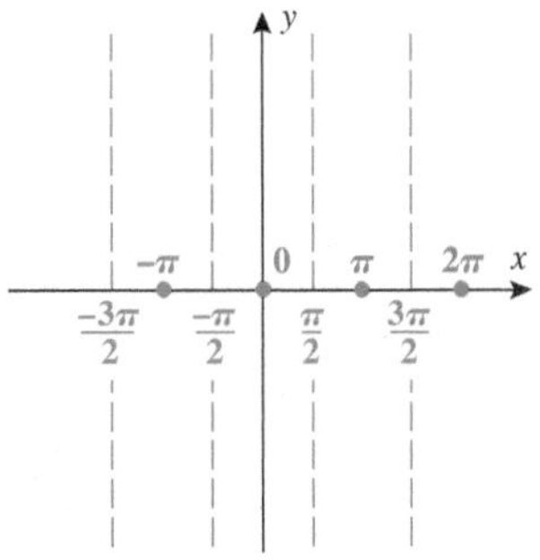

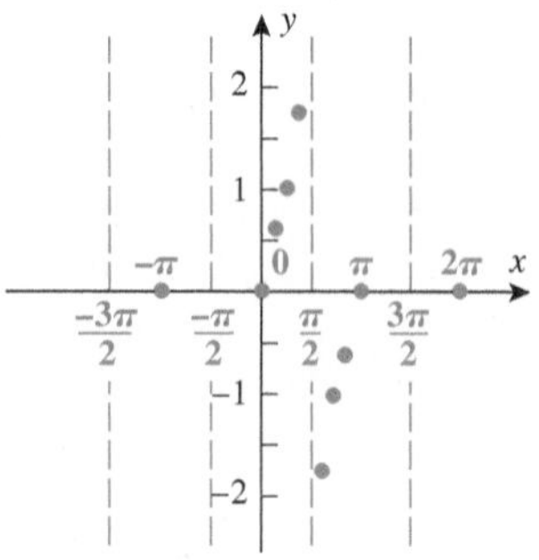

x	$\sin x$	$\cos x$	$\tan x = \dfrac{\sin x}{\cos x}$	(x, y)
$\frac{\pi}{6}$	$\frac{1}{2}$	$\frac{\sqrt{3}}{2}$	$\frac{1}{\sqrt{3}} = \frac{\sqrt{3}}{3} \approx 0.577$	$\left(\frac{\pi}{6}, 0.577\right)$
$\frac{\pi}{4}$	$\frac{\sqrt{2}}{2}$	$\frac{\sqrt{2}}{2}$	1	$\left(\frac{\pi}{4}, 1\right)$
$\frac{\pi}{3}$	$\frac{\sqrt{3}}{2}$	$\frac{1}{2}$	$\sqrt{3} \approx 1.732$	$\left(\frac{\pi}{3}, 1.732\right)$
$\frac{2\pi}{3}$	$\frac{\sqrt{3}}{2}$	$-\frac{1}{2}$	$-\sqrt{3} \approx -1.732$	$\left(\frac{2\pi}{3}, -1.732\right)$
$\frac{3\pi}{4}$	$\frac{\sqrt{2}}{2}$	$-\frac{\sqrt{2}}{2}$	-1	$\left(\frac{3\pi}{4}, -1\right)$
$\frac{5\pi}{6}$	$\frac{1}{2}$	$-\frac{\sqrt{3}}{2}$	$\frac{1}{-\sqrt{3}} = -\frac{\sqrt{3}}{3} \approx -0.577$	$\left(\frac{5\pi}{6}, -0.577\right)$

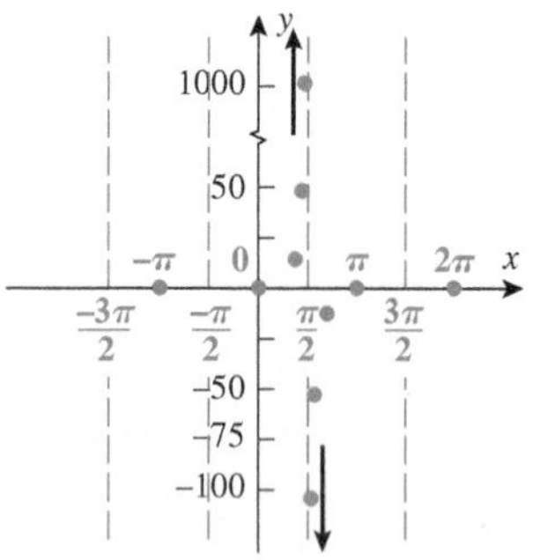

What happens to $\tan x$ as x approaches $\frac{\pi}{2}$? We know $\tan x$ is undefined at $x = \frac{\pi}{2}$ but we must consider x-values both larger and smaller than $\frac{\pi}{2} \approx 1.571$.

approaching from the left → $\frac{\pi}{2}$ ← approaching from the right

x	1.5	1.55	1.57	1.571	1.58	1.59	1.65
$\tan x$	14.1	48.1	1255.8	undefined	−108.6	−52.1	−12.6

$\tan x$ gets larger (for 1.5, 1.55, 1.57); $\tan x$ gets more negative (for 1.58, 1.59, 1.65)

The arrows on the graph in the margin indicate increasing without bound (in the positive and negative directions).

GRAPH OF $y = \tan x$

1. The x-intercepts occur at integer multiples of π. $(n\pi, 0)$
2. Vertical asymptotes occur at odd integer multiples of $\frac{\pi}{2}$. $x = \dfrac{(2n+1)\pi}{2}$
3. The domain is the set of all real numbers except odd integer multiples of $\frac{\pi}{2}$. $x \neq \dfrac{(2n+1)\pi}{2}$
4. The range is the set of all real numbers. $(-\infty, \infty)$
5. $y = \tan x$ has period π.
6. $y = \tan x$ is an odd function (symmetric about the origin). $\tan(-x) = -\tan x$
7. The graph has no defined amplitude, since the function is unbounded.

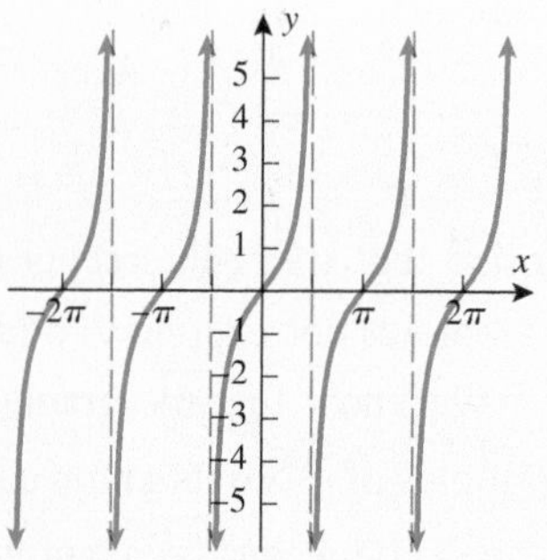

Note: n is an integer.

The Cotangent Function

The cotangent function is similar to the tangent function in that it is a quotient involving the sine and cosine functions. The difference is that cotangent has cosine in the numerator and sine in the denominator: $\cot x = \dfrac{\cos x}{\sin x}$. The graph of $y = \tan x$ has x-intercepts corresponding to integer multiples of π and vertical asymptotes corresponding to odd integer multiples of $\dfrac{\pi}{2}$. The graph of the cotangent function is the reverse in that it has x-intercepts corresponding to odd integer multiples of $\dfrac{\pi}{2}$ and vertical asymptotes corresponding to integer multiples of π. This is because the x-intercepts occur when the numerator, $\cos x$, is equal to 0, and the vertical asymptotes occur when the denominator, $\sin x$, is equal to 0.

STUDY TIP

The graphs of $y = \tan x$ and $y = \cot x$ both have period π, and neither of them has defined amplitude.

GRAPH OF $y = \cot x$

1. The x-intercepts occur at odd integer multiples of $\dfrac{\pi}{2}$. $\left(\dfrac{(2n+1)\pi}{2}, 0\right)$
2. Vertical asymptotes occur at integer multiples of π. $x = n\pi$
3. The domain is the set of all real numbers except integer multiples of π. $x \neq n\pi$
4. The range is the set of all real numbers. $(-\infty, \infty)$
5. $y = \cot x$ has period π.
6. $y = \cot x$ is an odd function (symmetric about the origin). $\cot(-x) = -\cot x$
7. The graph has no defined amplitude, since the function is unbounded.

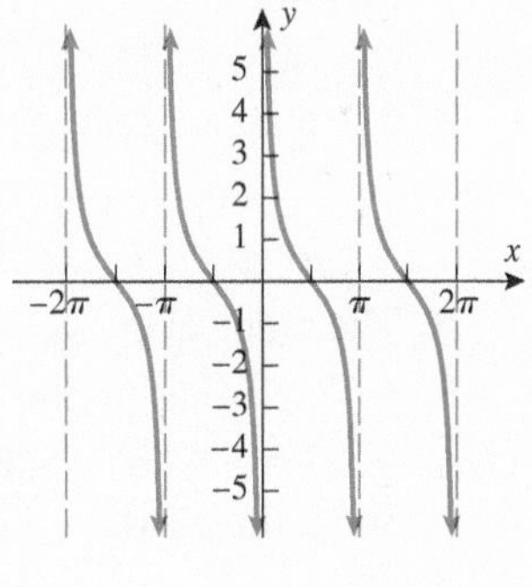

Note: n is an integer.

The Secant Function

Since $y = \cos x$ has period 2π, the secant function, which is the reciprocal of the cosine function, $\sec x = \dfrac{1}{\cos x}$, also has period 2π. We now illustrate values of the secant function with a table.

x	$\cos x$	$\sec x = \dfrac{1}{\cos x}$	(x, y) OR ASYMPTOTE
0	1	1	$(0, 1)$
$\dfrac{\pi}{2}$	0	undefined	vertical asymptote: $x = \dfrac{\pi}{2}$
π	-1	-1	$(\pi, -1)$
$\dfrac{3\pi}{2}$	0	undefined	vertical asymptote: $x = \dfrac{3\pi}{2}$
2π	1	1	$(2\pi, 1)$

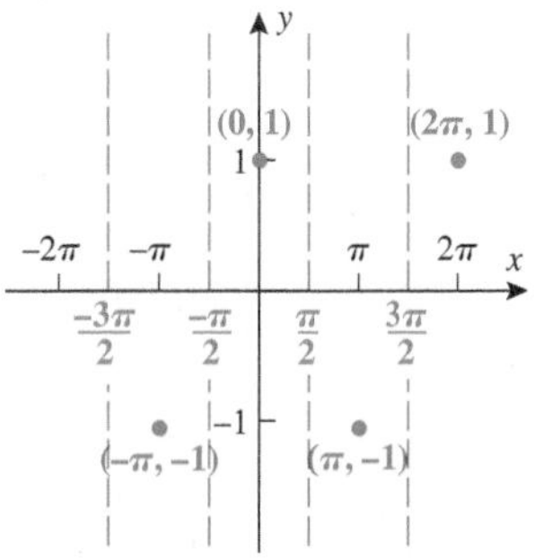

Again, we ask the same question: What happens as x approaches the vertical asymptotes? The secant function grows without bound in either the positive or the negative direction.

If we graph $y = \cos x$ (the "guide" function) and $y = \sec x$ on the same graph, we notice the following:

- The x-intercepts of $y = \cos x$ correspond to the vertical asymptotes of $y = \sec x$.
- The range of cosine is $[-1, 1]$ and the range of secant is $(-\infty, -1] \cup [1, \infty)$.
- When cosine is positive, secant is positive, and when cosine is negative, secant is negative.

The cosine function is used as the guide function to graph the secant function.

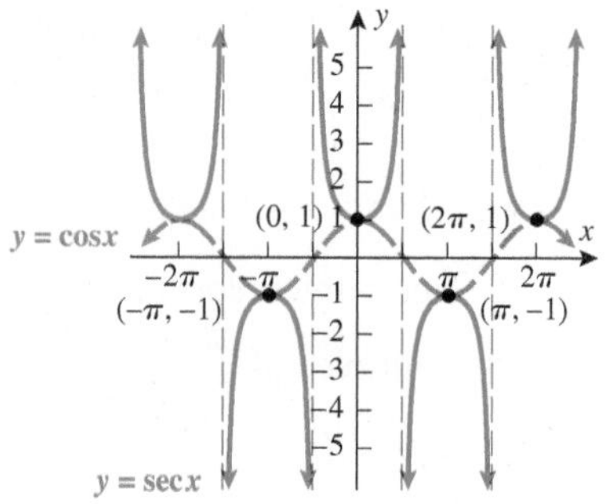

GRAPH OF $y = \sec x$

1. There are no x-intercepts. $\quad \dfrac{1}{\cos x} \neq 0$
2. Vertical asymptotes occur at odd integer multiples of $\dfrac{\pi}{2}$. $\quad x = \dfrac{(2n + 1)\pi}{2}$
3. The domain is the set of all real numbers except odd integer multiples of $\dfrac{\pi}{2}$. $\quad x \neq \dfrac{(2n + 1)\pi}{2}$
4. The range is $(-\infty, -1] \cup [1, \infty)$.
5. $y = \sec x$ has period 2π.
6. $y = \sec x$ is an even function (symmetric about the y-axis). $\quad \sec(-x) = \sec x$
7. The graph has no defined amplitude, since the function is unbounded.

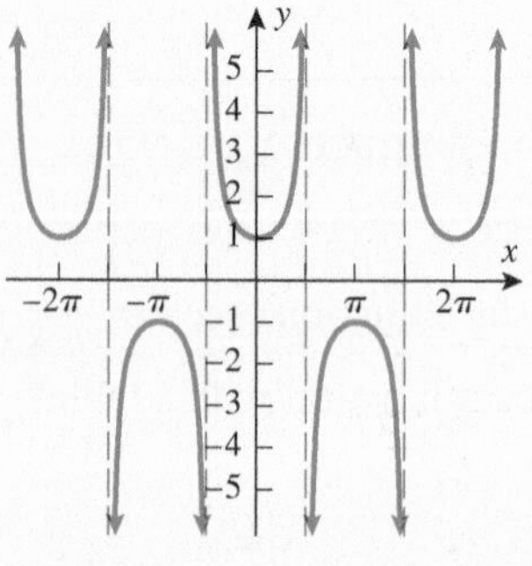

Note: n is an integer.

The Cosecant Function

Since $y = \sin x$ has period 2π, the cosecant function, which is the reciprocal of the sine function, $\csc x = \dfrac{1}{\sin x}$, also has period 2π. We now illustrate values of cosecant with a table.

x	$\sin x$	$\csc x = \frac{1}{\sin x}$	(x, y) OR ASYMPTOTE
0	0	undefined	vertical asymptote: $x = 0$
$\frac{\pi}{2}$	1	1	$\left(\frac{\pi}{2}, 1\right)$
π	0	undefined	vertical asymptote: $x = \pi$
$\frac{3\pi}{2}$	-1	-1	$\left(\frac{3\pi}{2}, -1\right)$
2π	0	undefined	vertical asymptote: $x = 2\pi$

Again, we ask the same question: What happens as x approaches the vertical asymptotes? The cosecant function grows without bound in either the positive or the negative direction.

If we graph $y = \sin x$ (the "guide" function) and $y = \csc x$ on the same graph, we notice the following:

- The x-intercepts of $y = \sin x$ correspond to the vertical asymptotes of $y = \csc x$.
- The range of sine is $[-1, 1]$ and the range of cosecant is $(-\infty, -1] \cup [1, \infty)$.
- When sine is positive, cosecant is positive, and when sine is negative, cosecant is negative.

The sine function is used as the guide function to graph the cosecant function.

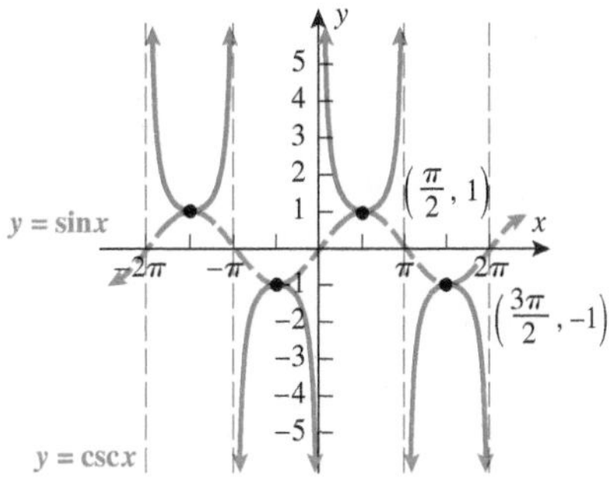

GRAPH OF $y = \csc x$

1. There are no x-intercepts. $\frac{1}{\sin x} \neq 0$
2. Vertical asymptotes occur at integer multiples of π. $x = n\pi$
3. The domain is the set of all real numbers except integer multiples of π. $x \neq n\pi$
4. The range is $(-\infty, -1] \cup [1, \infty)$.
5. $y = \csc x$ has period 2π.
6. $y = \csc x$ is an odd function (symmetric about the origin). $\csc(-x) = -\csc x$
7. The graph has no defined amplitude, since the function is unbounded.

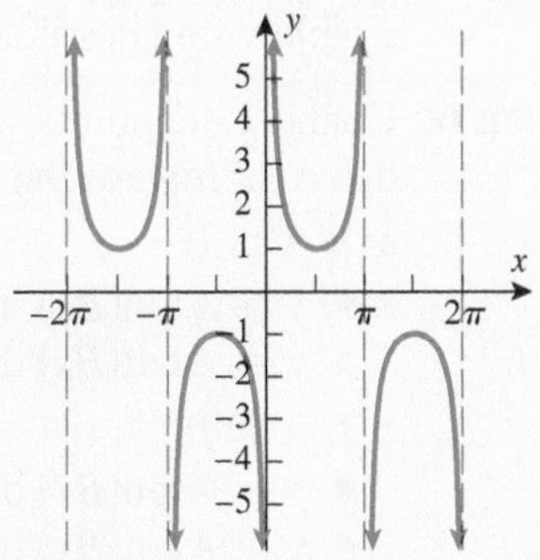

Note: n is an integer.

Graphing More General Tangent, Cotangent, Secant, and Cosecant Functions

FUNCTION	$y = \sin x$	$y = \cos x$	$y = \tan x$	$y = \cot x$	$y = \sec x$	$y = \csc x$
Graph of One Period	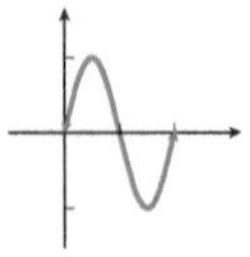	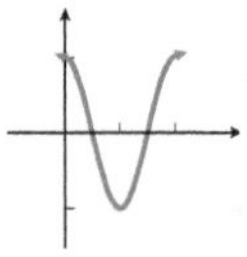	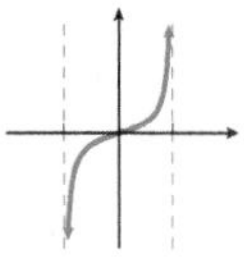	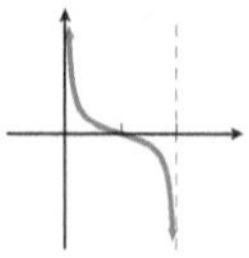	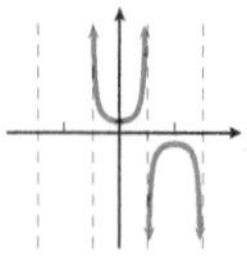	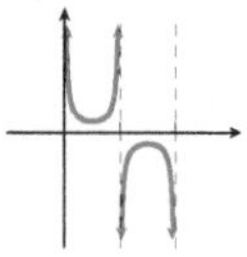
Domain	$(-\infty, \infty)$	$(-\infty, \infty)$	$x \neq \frac{(2n+1)\pi}{2}$	$x \neq n\pi$	$x \neq \frac{(2n+1)\pi}{2}$	$x \neq n\pi$
Range	$[-1, 1]$	$[-1, 1]$	$(-\infty, \infty)$	$(-\infty, \infty)$	$(-\infty, -1] \cup [1, \infty)$	$(-\infty, -1] \cup [1, \infty)$
Amplitude	1	1	none	none	none	none
Period	2π	2π	π	π	2π	2π
x-intercepts	$(n\pi, 0)$	$\left(\frac{(2n+1)\pi}{2}, 0\right)$	$(n\pi, 0)$	$\left(\frac{(2n+1)\pi}{2}, 0\right)$	none	none
Vertical Asymptotes	none	none	$x = \frac{(2n+1)\pi}{2}$	$x = n\pi$	$x = \frac{(2n+1)\pi}{2}$	$x = n\pi$

Note: n is an integer.

We use these basic functions as the starting point for graphing general tangent, cotangent, secant, and cosecant functions.

GRAPHING TANGENT AND COTANGENT FUNCTIONS

Graphs of $y = A\tan(Bx)$ and $y = A\cot(Bx)$ can be obtained using the following steps (assume $B > 0$).

Step 1: Calculate the period: $\frac{\pi}{B}$.

Step 2: Find two neighboring vertical asymptotes.

For $y = A\tan(Bx)$: $\quad Bx = -\frac{\pi}{2}$ and $Bx = \frac{\pi}{2}$

For $y = A\cot(Bx)$: $\quad Bx = 0$ and $Bx = \pi$

Step 3: Find the x-intercept between the two asymptotes.

For $y = A\tan(Bx)$: $\quad$ Solve for x: $Bx = 0 \Rightarrow x = 0$

For $y = A\cot(Bx)$: $\quad$ Solve for x: $Bx = \frac{\pi}{2} \Rightarrow x = \frac{\pi}{2B}$

Step 4: Draw the vertical asymptotes and label the x-intercept.

Step 5: Divide the interval between the asymptotes into four equal parts. Set up a table with coordinates corresponding to the points in the interval.

Step 6: Connect the points with a smooth curve. Use arrows to indicate the behavior toward the asymptotes.

- If $A > 0$
  - $y = A\tan(Bx)$ increases from left to right.
  - $y = A\cot(Bx)$ decreases from left to right.
- If $A < 0$
  - $y = A\tan(Bx)$ decreases from left to right.
  - $y = A\cot(Bx)$ increases from left to right.

EXAMPLE 1 Graphing $y = A\tan(Bx)$

Graph $y = -3\tan(2x)$ on the interval $-\frac{\pi}{2} \le x \le \frac{\pi}{2}$.

Solution: $A = -3, B = 2$

STEP 1 Calculate the period. $\frac{\pi}{B} = \frac{\pi}{2}$

STEP 2 Find two vertical asymptotes. $Bx = -\frac{\pi}{2}$ and $Bx = \frac{\pi}{2}$

Substitute $B = 2$ and solve for x. $x = -\frac{\pi}{4}$ and $x = \frac{\pi}{4}$

STEP 3 Find the x-intercept between the asymptotes. $Bx = 0$
$x = 0$

STEP 4 Draw the vertical asymptotes $x = -\frac{\pi}{4}$ and $x = \frac{\pi}{4}$ and label the x-intercept $(0, 0)$.

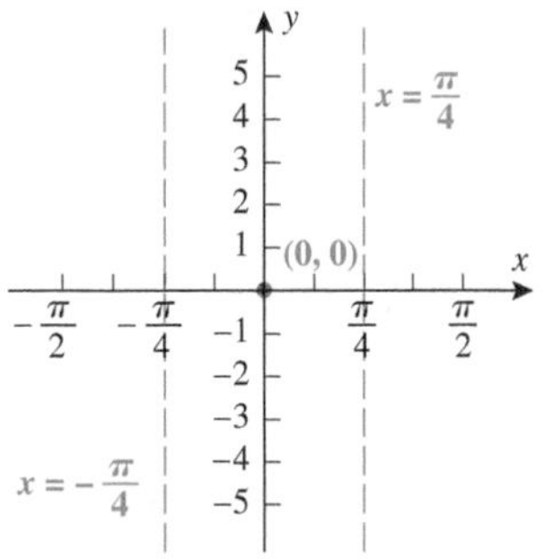

STEP 5 Divide the period $\frac{\pi}{2}$ into four equal parts, in steps of $\frac{\pi}{8}$. Set up a table with coordinates corresponding to values of $y = -3\tan(2x)$.

x	$y = -3\tan(2x)$	(x, y)
$-\frac{\pi}{4}$	undefined	vertical asymptote, $x = -\frac{\pi}{4}$
$-\frac{\pi}{8}$	3	$\left(-\frac{\pi}{8}, 3\right)$
0	0	$(0, 0)$
$\frac{\pi}{8}$	-3	$\left(\frac{\pi}{8}, -3\right)$
$\frac{\pi}{4}$	undefined	vertical asymptote, $x = \frac{\pi}{4}$

STEP 6 Graph the points from the table and connect with a smooth curve. Repeat to the right and left until you reach the interval endpoints. Note that the distance between the vertical asymptotes is the period length $\frac{\pi}{2}$.

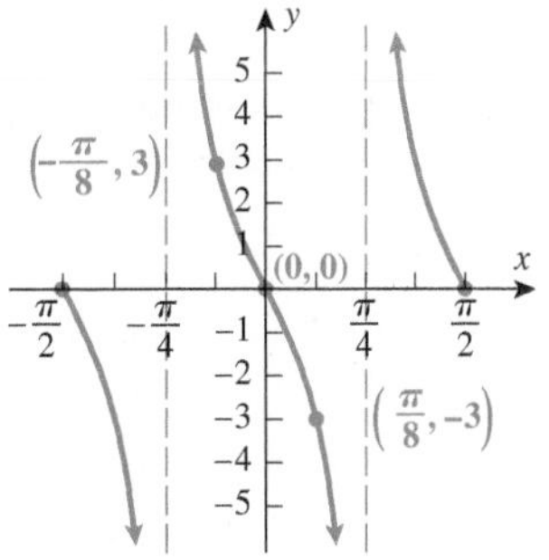

YOUR TURN Graph $y = \frac{1}{3}\tan\left(\frac{1}{2}x\right)$ on the interval $-\pi \le x \le \pi$.

ANSWER

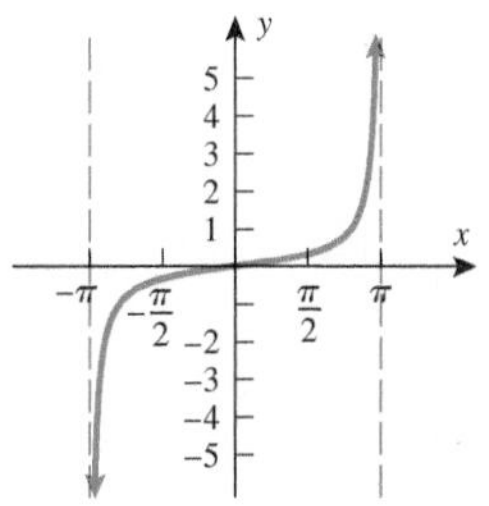

EXAMPLE 2 Graphing $y = A\cot(Bx)$

Graph $y = 4\cot\left(\frac{1}{2}x\right)$ on the interval $-2\pi \leq x \leq 2\pi$.

Solution: $A = 4$, $B = \frac{1}{2}$

STEP 1 Calculate the period. $\frac{\pi}{B} = 2\pi$

STEP 2 Find two vertical asymptotes. $Bx = 0$ and $Bx = \pi$

Substitute $B = \frac{1}{2}$ and solve for x. $x = 0$ and $x = 2\pi$

STEP 3 Find the x-intercept between the asymptotes. $Bx = \frac{\pi}{2}$

$x = \pi$

STEP 4 Draw the vertical asymptotes $x = 0$ and $x = 2\pi$ and label the x-intercept $(\pi, 0)$.

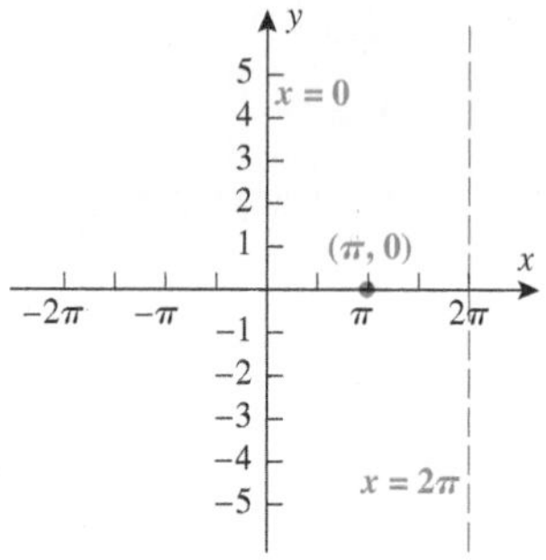

STEP 5 Divide the period 2π into four equal parts, in steps of $\frac{\pi}{2}$. Set up a table with coordinates corresponding to values of $y = 4\cot\left(\frac{1}{2}x\right)$.

x	$y = 4\cot\left(\frac{1}{2}x\right)$	(x, y)
0	undefined	vertical asymptote, $x = 0$
$\frac{\pi}{2}$	4	$\left(\frac{\pi}{2}, 4\right)$
π	0	$(\pi, 0)$
$\frac{3\pi}{2}$	-4	$\left(\frac{3\pi}{2}, -4\right)$
2π	undefined	vertical asymptote, $x = 2\pi$

STEP 6 Graph the points from the table and connect them with a smooth curve. Repeat to the right and left until you reach the interval endpoints.

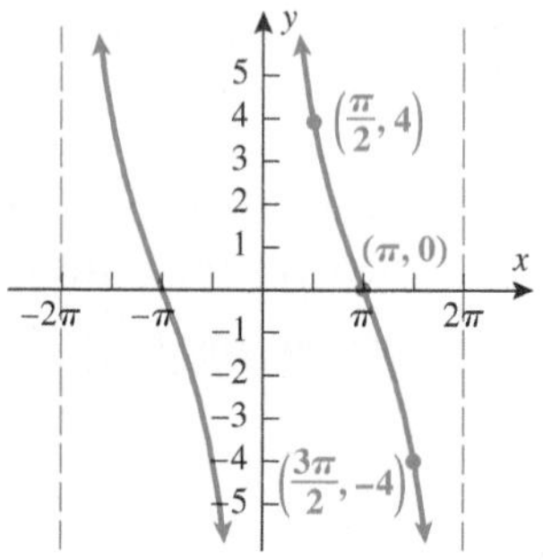

ANSWER

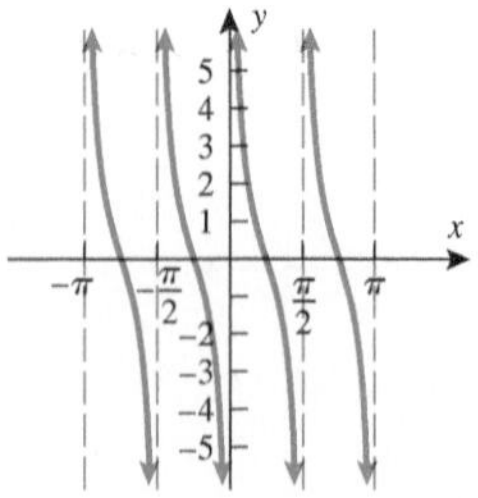

YOUR TURN Graph $y = 2\cot(2x)$ on the interval $-\pi \leq x \leq \pi$.

GRAPHING SECANT AND COSECANT FUNCTIONS

Graphs of $y = A\sec(Bx)$ and $y = A\csc(Bx)$ can be obtained using the following steps.

Step 1: Graph the corresponding guide function with a dashed curve.

For $y = A\sec(Bx)$, use $y = A\cos(Bx)$ as a guide.
For $y = A\csc(Bx)$, use $y = A\sin(Bx)$ as a guide.

Step 2: Draw the vertical asymptotes which correspond to the x-intercepts of the guide function.

Step 3: Draw the U shapes between the asymptotes. If the guide function has a positive value between the asymptotes, the U opens upward; and if the guide function has a negative value, the U opens downward.

EXAMPLE 3 Graphing $y = A\sec(Bx)$

Graph $y = 2\sec(\pi x)$ on the interval $-2 \le x \le 2$.

Solution:

STEP 1 Graph the corresponding guide function with a dashed curve.

For $y = 2\sec(\pi x)$, use $y = 2\cos(\pi x)$ as a guide.

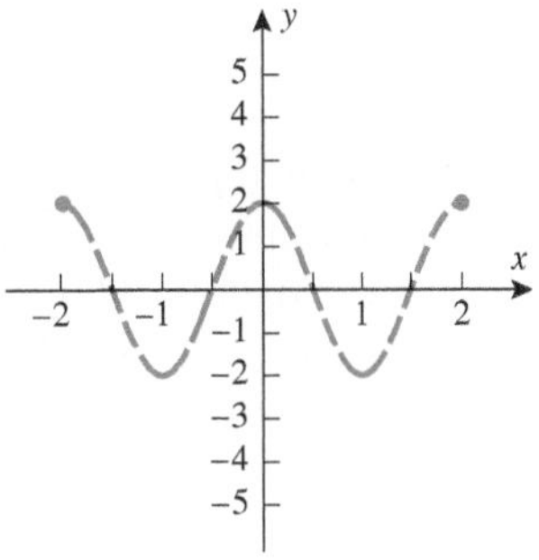

STEP 2 Draw the **asymptotes**, which correspond to the x-intercepts of the guide function.

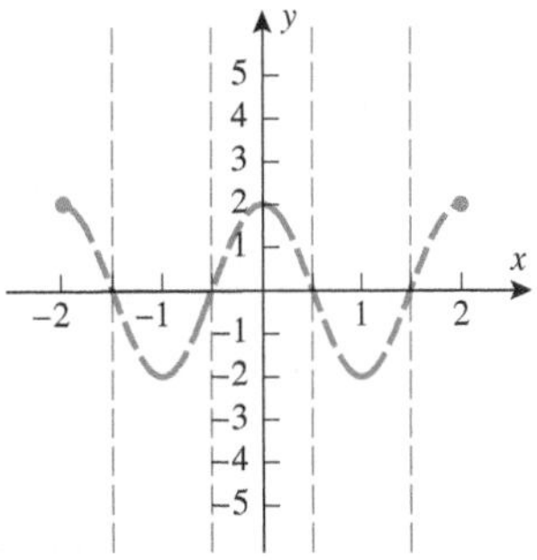

STEP 3 Draw the U shape between the asymptotes. If the guide function is positive, the U opens upward, and if the guide function is negative, the U opens downward.

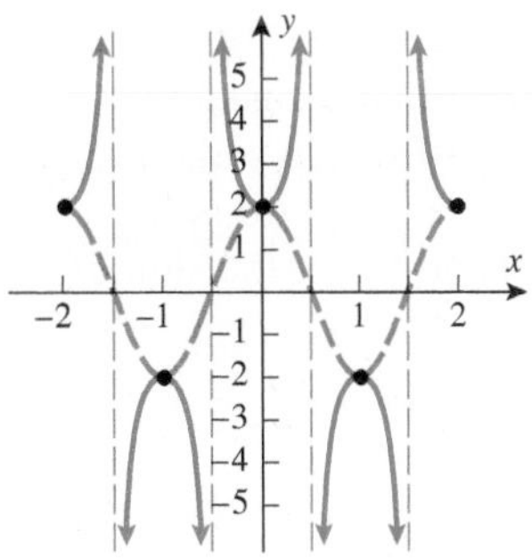

YOUR TURN Graph $y = -\sec(2\pi x)$ on the interval $-1 \le x \le 1$.

ANSWER

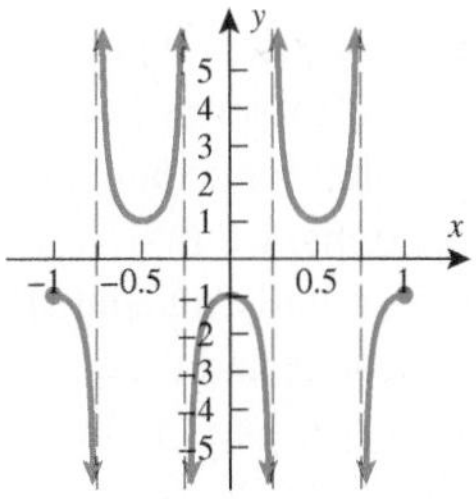

EXAMPLE 4 **Graphing $y = A\csc(Bx)$**

Graph $y = -3\csc(2\pi x)$ on the interval $-1 \le x \le 1$.

Solution:

STEP 1 Graph the corresponding guide function with a dashed curve.

For $y = -3\csc(2\pi x)$, use $y = -3\sin(2\pi x)$ as a guide.

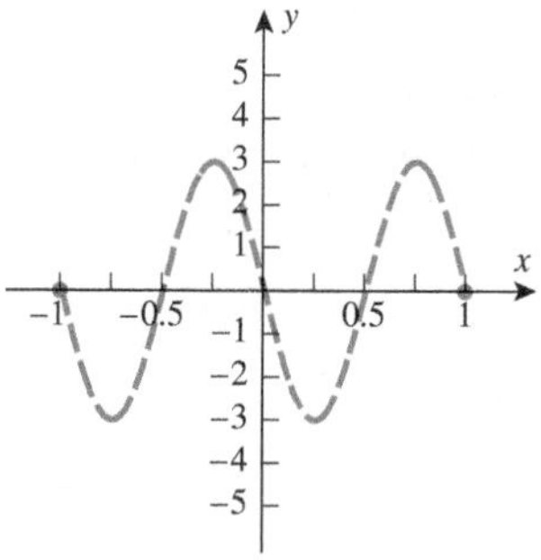

STEP 2 Draw the asymptotes, which correspond to the x-intercepts of the guide function.

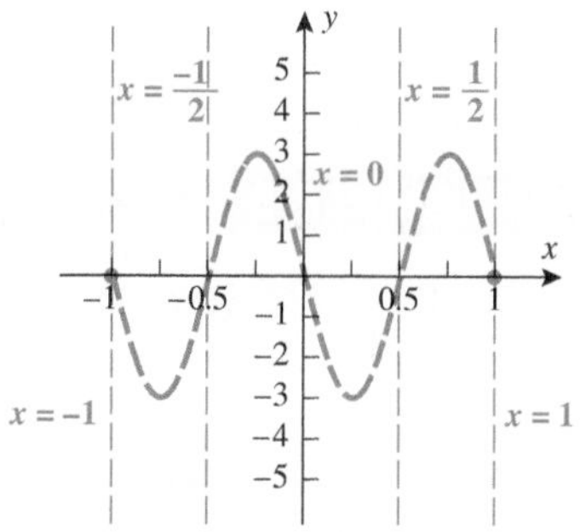

STEP 3 Draw the U shape between the asymptotes. If the guide function is positive, the U opens upward, and if the guide function is negative, the U opens downward.

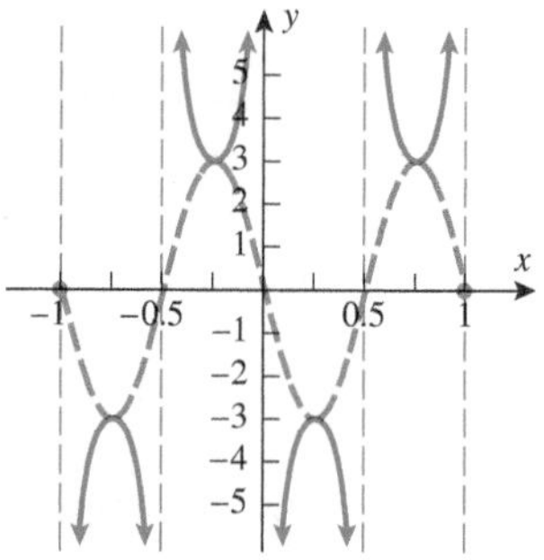

ANSWER

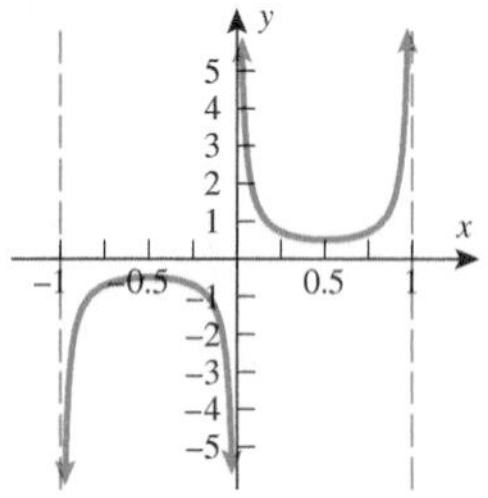

YOUR TURN Graph $y = \frac{1}{2}\csc(\pi x)$ on the interval $-1 \le x \le 1$.

5.3.2 SKILL

Graph translated tangent, cotangent, secant, and cosecant functions.

5.3.2 CONCEPTUAL

Understand that graph-shifting techniques for tangent and cotangent are consistent with translations used for sinusoidal functions, but that for secant and cosecant functions, we first graph the horizontally translated sinusoidal functions and then shift up or down, depending on the vertical translations.

5.3.2 Translations of Trigonometric Functions

Vertical translations and horizontal translations (phase shifts) of the tangent, cotangent, secant, and cosecant functions are graphed the same way as vertical and horizontal translations of sinusoidal graphs. For tangent and cotangent functions, we follow the same procedure as we did with sinusoidal functions. For secant and cosecant functions, we graph the guide function first and then translate up or down, depending on the sign of the vertical shift.

EXAMPLE 5 Graphing $y = A\tan(Bx + C) + D$

Graph $y = 1 - \tan\left(x - \frac{\pi}{2}\right)$ on $-\pi \le x \le \pi$. State the domain and range on the interval. There are two ways to approach graphing this function. Both will be illustrated.

Solution (1):

Plot $y = \tan x$, and then do the following:

- Shift the curve to the right $\frac{\pi}{2}$ units. $\quad y = \tan\left(x - \frac{\pi}{2}\right)$
- Reflect the curve about the x-axis (because of the negative sign). $\quad y = -\tan\left(x - \frac{\pi}{2}\right)$
- Shift the entire graph up one unit. $\quad y = 1 - \tan\left(x - \frac{\pi}{2}\right)$

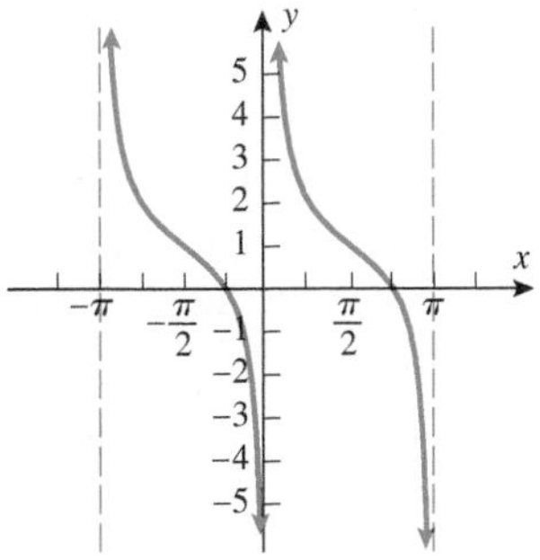

Solution (2): Graph $y = -\tan\left(x - \frac{\pi}{2}\right)$, and then shift the entire graph up one unit, because $D = 1$.

STEP 1 Calculate the period. $\quad \frac{\pi}{B} = \pi$

STEP 2 Find two vertical asymptotes. $\quad x - \frac{\pi}{2} = -\frac{\pi}{2}$ and $x - \frac{\pi}{2} = \frac{\pi}{2}$

Solve for x. $\quad x = 0$ and $x = \pi$

STEP 3 Find the x-intercept between the asymptotes. $\quad x - \frac{\pi}{2} = 0$

$$x = \frac{\pi}{2}$$

STEP 4 Draw the vertical asymptotes $x = 0$ and $x = \pi$ and label the x-intercept $\left(\frac{\pi}{2}, 0\right)$.

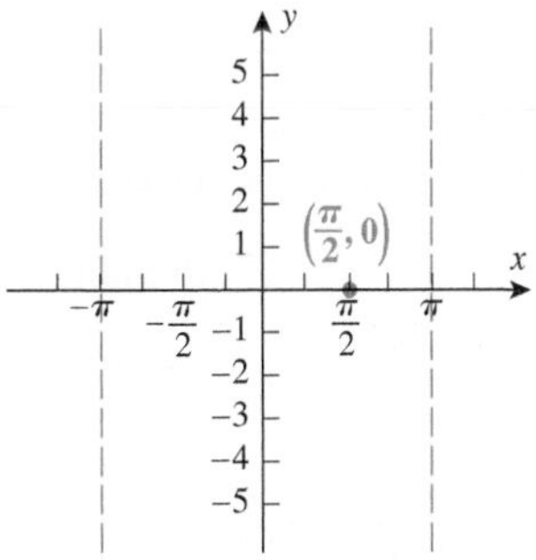

STEP 5 Divide the period π into four equal parts, in steps of $\frac{\pi}{4}$. Set up a table with coordinates corresponding to values of $y = -\tan\left(x - \frac{\pi}{2}\right)$ between the two asymptotes.

x	$y = -\tan\left(x - \frac{\pi}{2}\right)$	(x, y)
$x = 0$	undefined	vertical asymptote, $x = 0$
$\frac{\pi}{4}$	1	$\left(\frac{\pi}{4}, 1\right)$
$\frac{\pi}{2}$	0	$\left(\frac{\pi}{2}, 0\right)$ (x-intercept)
$\frac{3\pi}{4}$	-1	$\left(\frac{3\pi}{4}, -1\right)$
$x = \pi$	undefined	vertical asymptote, $x = \pi$

STEP 6 Graph the points from the table and connect them with a smooth curve. Repeat to the right and left until you reach the interval endpoints.

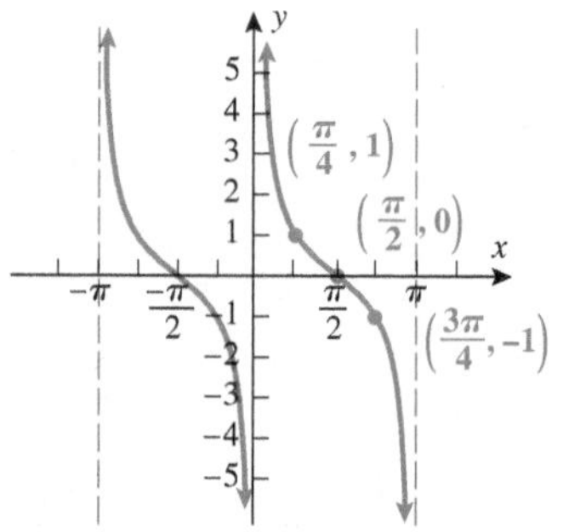

STEP 7 Shift the entire graph up one unit to arrive at the graph of

$$y = 1 - \tan\left(x - \frac{\pi}{2}\right).$$

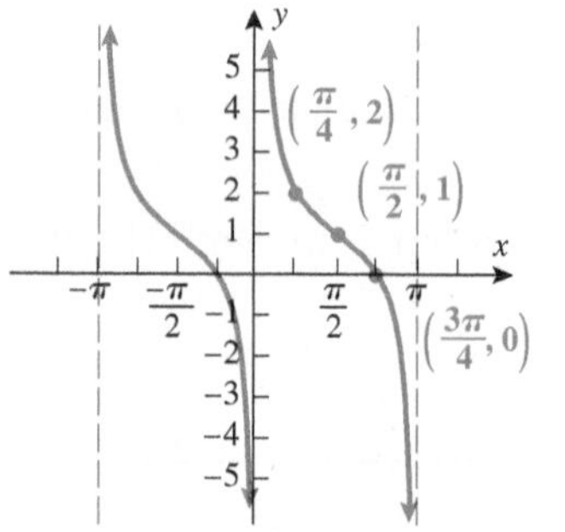

STEP 8 State the domain and range on the interval. Domain: $(-\pi, 0) \cup (0, \pi)$
Range: $(-\infty, \infty)$

YOUR TURN Graph $y = -1 + \cot\left(x + \frac{\pi}{2}\right)$ on $-\pi \le x \le \pi$. State the domain and range on the interval.

ANSWER

Domain:
$\left[-\pi, -\frac{\pi}{2}\right) \cup \left(-\frac{\pi}{2}, \frac{\pi}{2}\right) \cup \left(\frac{\pi}{2}, \pi\right]$

Range: $(-\infty, \infty)$

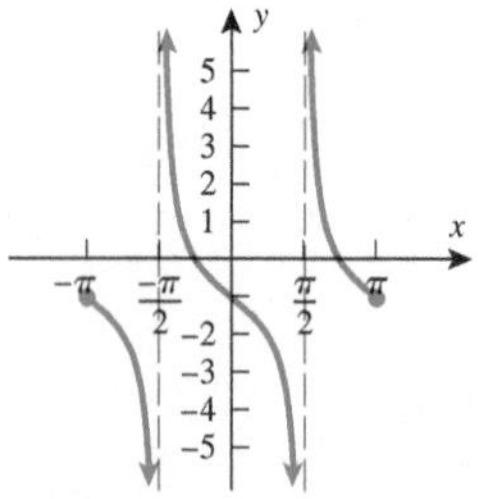

EXAMPLE 6 Graphing $y = A\csc(Bx + C) + D$

Graph $y = 1 - \csc(2x - \pi)$ on $-\pi \le x \le \pi$. State the domain and range on the interval.

Solution:

Graph $y = -\csc(2x - \pi)$, and shift the entire graph up one unit to arrive at the graph of $y = 1 - \csc(2x - \pi)$.

STEP 1 Draw the guide function, $y = -\sin(2x - \pi)$.

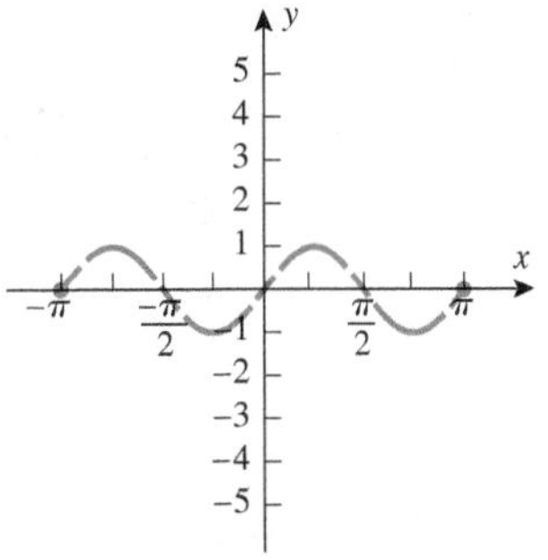

STEP 2 Draw the vertical asymptotes of $y = -\csc(2x - \pi)$ that correspond to the x-intercepts of $y = -\sin(2x - \pi)$.

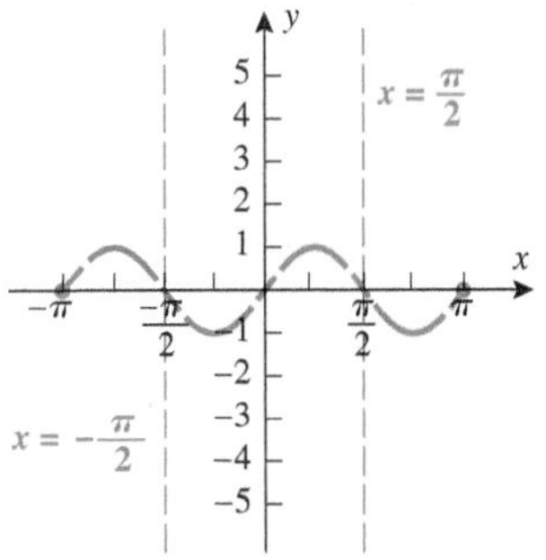

STEP 3 Draw the U shape between the asymptotes. If the guide function is positive, the U opens upward, and if the guide function is negative, the U opens downward.

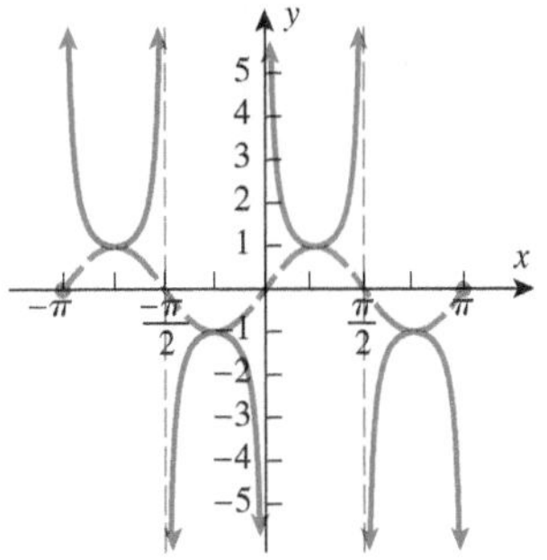

STEP 4 Shift the entire graph up one unit to arrive at the graph of $y = 1 - \csc(2x - \pi)$.

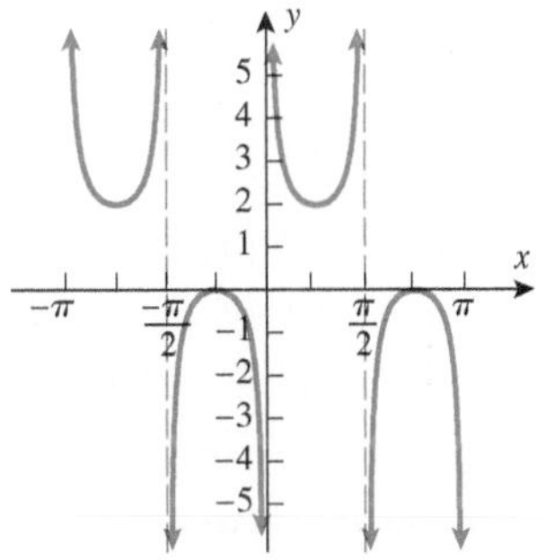

STEP 5 State the domain and range on the interval.

$$\text{Domain: } \left(-\pi, -\frac{\pi}{2}\right) \cup \left(-\frac{\pi}{2}, 0\right) \cup \left(0, \frac{\pi}{2}\right) \cup \left(\frac{\pi}{2}, \pi\right)$$

$$\text{Range: } (-\infty, 0] \cup [2, \infty)$$

YOUR TURN Graph $y = -2 + \sec(\pi x - \pi)$ on $-1 \le x \le 1$. State the domain and range on the interval.

[CONCEPT CHECK]

If $k > 0$, what is the last step in graphing the function $y = -k + \sec(\pi x)$?

ANSWER Shift the graph of $\sec(\pi x)$ down k units.

ANSWER

Domain: $\left[-1, -\frac{1}{2}\right) \cup \left(-\frac{1}{2}, \frac{1}{2}\right) \cup \left(\frac{1}{2}, 1\right]$

Range: $(-\infty, -3] \cup [-1, \infty)$

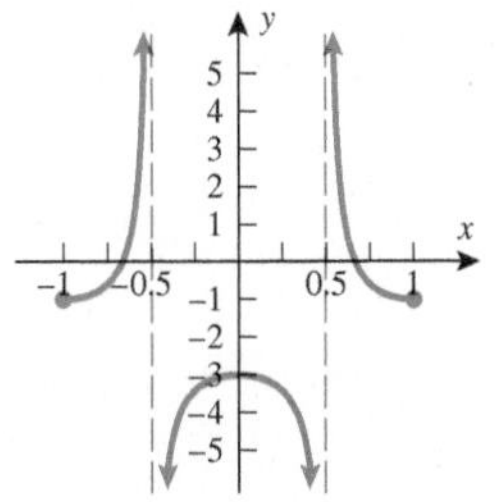

[SECTION 5.3] SUMMARY

The tangent and cotangent functions have period π, whereas the secant and cosecant functions have period 2π. To graph the tangent and cotangent functions, first identify the vertical asymptotes and x-intercepts, and then find values of the function within a period (i.e., between the asymptotes). To find graphs of secant and cosecant functions, first graph their guide functions (cosine and sine, respectively), and then label vertical asymptotes that correspond to x-intercepts of the guide function. The graphs of the secant and cosecant functions resemble the letter U opening up or down. The secant and cosecant functions are positive when their guide function is positive and negative when their guide function is negative.

[SECTION 5.3] EXERCISES

• SKILLS

In Exercises 1–8, match the graphs to the functions (a–h).

1. $y = -\tan x$

2. $y = -\csc x$

3. $y = \sec(2x)$

4. $y = \csc(2x)$

5. $y = \cot(\pi x)$

6. $y = -\cot(\pi x)$

7. $y = 3\sec x$

8. $y = 3\csc x$

a.

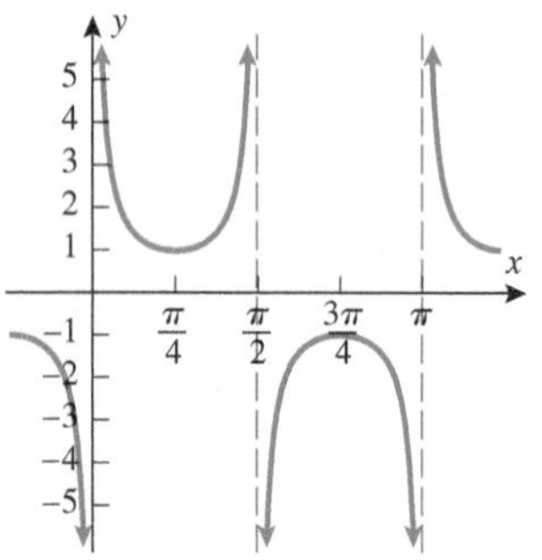

b.

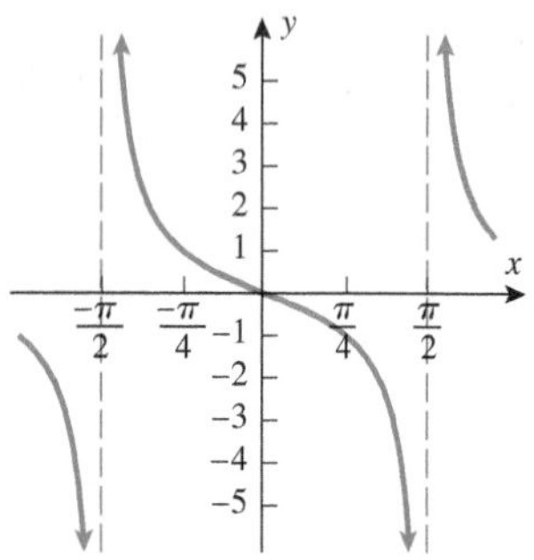

c.

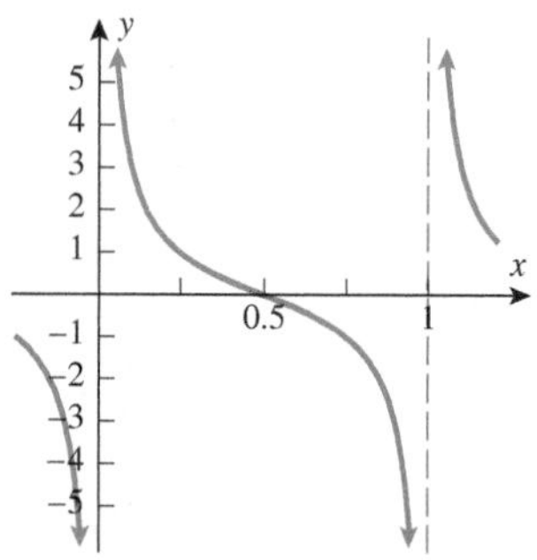

d.

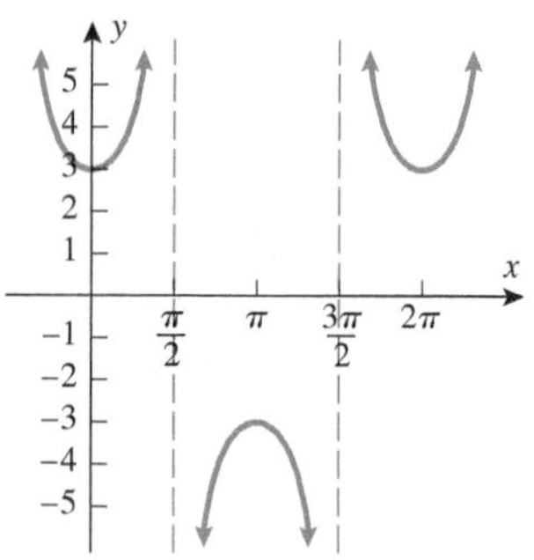

e.

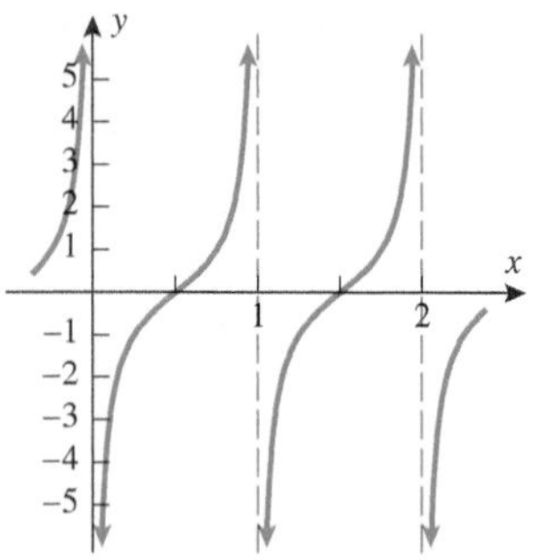

f.

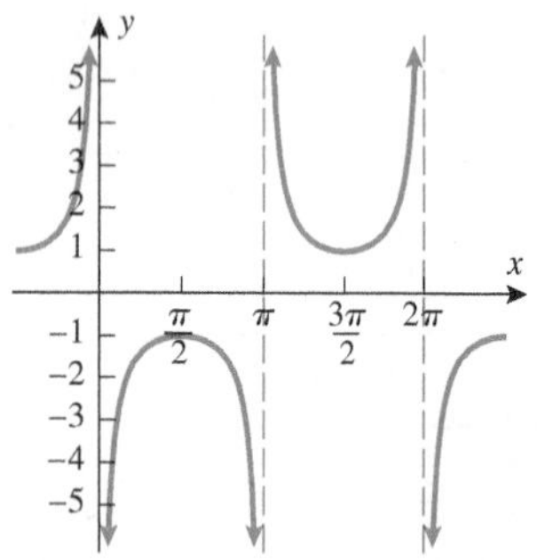

g.

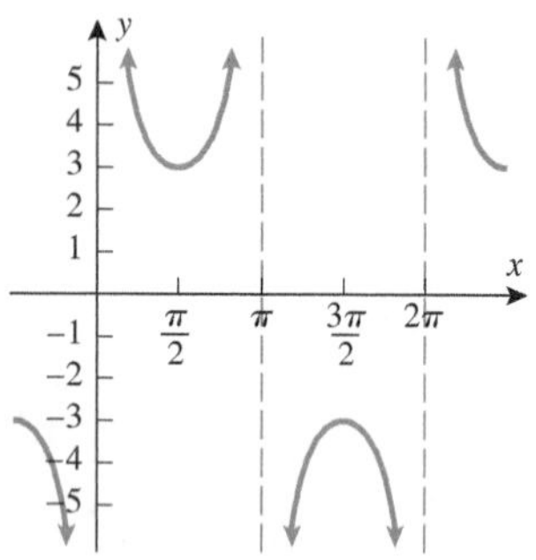

h.

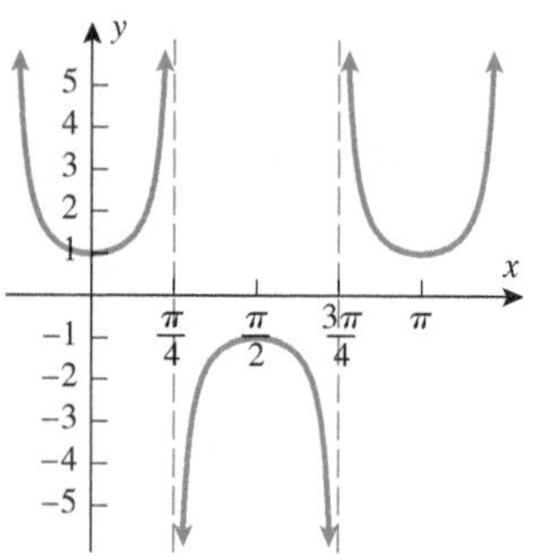

In Exercises 9–28, graph the functions over the indicated intervals.

9. $y = \tan\left(\frac{1}{2}x\right),\ -2\pi \le x \le 2\pi$

10. $y = \cot\left(\frac{1}{2}x\right),\ -2\pi \le x \le 2\pi$

11. $y = -\cot(2\pi x),\ -1 \le x \le 1$

12. $y = -\tan(2\pi x),\ -1 \le x \le 1$

13. $y = 2\tan(3x),\ -\pi \le x \le \pi$

14. $y = 2\tan\left(\frac{1}{3}x\right),\ -3\pi \le x \le 3\pi$

15. $y = -\frac{1}{4}\cot\left(\frac{x}{2}\right), -2\pi \le x \le 2\pi$

16. $y = -\frac{1}{2}\tan\left(\frac{x}{4}\right), -4\pi \le x \le 4\pi$

17. $y = -\tan\left(x - \frac{\pi}{2}\right), -\pi \le x \le \pi$

18. $y = \tan\left(x + \frac{\pi}{4}\right), -\pi \le x \le \pi$

19. $y = 2\tan\left(x + \frac{\pi}{6}\right), -\pi \le x \le \pi$

20. $y = -\frac{1}{2}\tan(x + \pi), -\pi \le x \le \pi$

21. $y = \cot\left(x - \frac{\pi}{4}\right), -\pi \le x \le \pi$

22. $y = -\cot\left(x + \frac{\pi}{2}\right), -\pi \le x \le \pi$

23. $y = -\frac{1}{2}\cot\left(x + \frac{\pi}{3}\right), -\pi \le x \le \pi$

24. $y = 3\cot\left(x - \frac{\pi}{6}\right), -\pi \le x \le \pi$

25. $y = \tan(2x - \pi), -2\pi \le x \le 2\pi$

26. $y = \cot(2x - \pi), -2\pi \le x \le 2\pi$

27. $y = \cot\left(\frac{x}{2} + \frac{\pi}{4}\right), -\pi \le x \le \pi$

28. $y = \tan\left(\frac{x}{3} - \frac{\pi}{3}\right), -\pi \le x \le \pi$

In Exercises 29–46, graph the functions over the indicated intervals.

29. $y = \sec(\frac{1}{2}x), -2\pi \le x \le 2\pi$

30. $y = \csc(\frac{1}{2}x), -2\pi \le x \le 2\pi$

31. $y = -\csc(2\pi x), -1 \le x \le 1$

32. $y = -\sec(2\pi x), -1 \le x \le 1$

33. $y = \frac{1}{3}\sec\left(\frac{\pi}{2}x\right), -4 \le x \le 4$

34. $y = \frac{1}{2}\csc\left(\frac{\pi}{3}x\right), -6 \le x \le 6$

35. $y = -3\csc\left(\frac{x}{3}\right), -6\pi \le x \le 0$

36. $y = -4\sec\left(\frac{x}{2}\right), -4\pi \le x \le 4\pi$

37. $y = 2\sec(3x), 0 \le x \le 2\pi$

38. $y = 2\csc\left(\frac{1}{3}x\right), -3\pi \le x \le 3\pi$

39. $y = -3\csc\left(x - \frac{\pi}{2}\right)$, over at least one period

40. $y = 5\sec\left(x + \frac{\pi}{4}\right)$, over at least one period

41. $y = \frac{1}{2}\sec(x - \pi)$, over at least one period

42. $y = -4\csc(x + \pi)$, over at least one period

43. $y = 2\sec(2x - \pi), -2\pi \le x \le 2\pi$

44. $y = 2\csc(2x + \pi), -2\pi \le x \le 2\pi$

45. $y = -\frac{1}{4}\sec(3x + \pi)$

46. $y = -\frac{2}{3}\csc\left(4x - \frac{\pi}{2}\right), -\pi \le x \le \pi$

In Exercises 47–56, graph the functions over at least one period.

47. $y = 3 - 2\sec\left(x - \frac{\pi}{2}\right)$

48. $y = -3 + 2\csc\left(x + \frac{\pi}{2}\right)$

49. $y = \frac{1}{2} + \frac{1}{2}\tan\left(x - \frac{\pi}{2}\right)$

50. $y = \frac{3}{4} - \frac{1}{4}\cot\left(x + \frac{\pi}{2}\right)$

51. $y = -2 + 3\csc(2x - \pi)$

52. $y = -1 + 4\sec(2x + \pi)$

53. $y = -1 - \sec\left(\frac{1}{2}x - \frac{\pi}{4}\right)$

54. $y = -2 + \csc\left(\frac{1}{2}x + \frac{\pi}{4}\right)$

55. $y = -2 - 3\cot\left(2x - \frac{\pi}{4}\right), -\pi \le x \le \pi$

56. $y = -\frac{1}{4} + \frac{1}{2}\sec\left(\pi x + \frac{\pi}{4}\right), -2 \le x \le 2$

In Exercises 57–66, state the domain and range of the functions.

57. $y = \tan\left(\pi x - \frac{\pi}{2}\right)$

58. $y = \cot\left(x - \frac{\pi}{2}\right)$

59. $y = 2\sec(5x)$

60. $y = -4\sec(3x)$

61. $y = 2 - \csc(\frac{1}{2}x - \pi)$

62. $y = 1 - 2\sec(\frac{1}{2}x + \pi)$

63. $y = -3\tan\left(\frac{\pi}{4}x - \pi\right) + 1$

64. $y = \frac{1}{4}\cot\left(2\pi x + \frac{\pi}{3}\right) - 3$

65. $y = -2 + \frac{1}{2}\sec\left(\pi x + \frac{\pi}{2}\right)$

66. $y = \frac{1}{2} - \frac{1}{3}\csc\left(3x - \frac{\pi}{2}\right)$

• APPLICATIONS

67. Tower of Pisa. The angle between the ground and the Tower of Pisa is about 85°. Its inclination measured at the base is 4.2 meters. What is the vertical distance from the top of the tower to the ground?

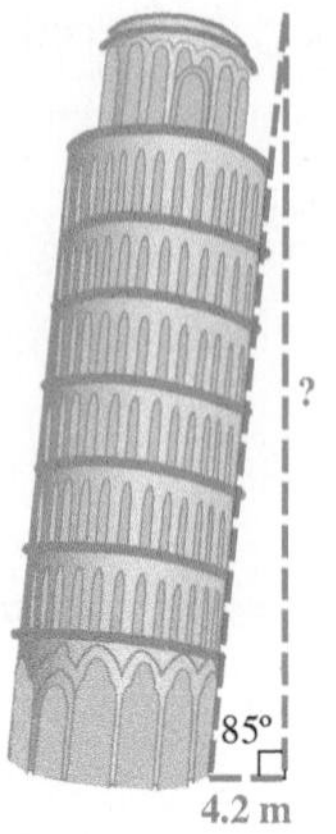

68. Architecture. The angle of elevation from the top of a building 40 feet tall to the top of another building 75 feet tall is $\frac{\pi}{6}$. What is the distance between the buildings?

69. Lighthouse. A lighthouse is located on a small island 3 miles offshore. The distance x is given by $x = 3\tan(\pi t)$, where t is the time measured in seconds. Suppose that at midnight the light beam forms a straight angle with the shoreline. Find x at

a. $t = \frac{2}{3}$ s **b.** $t = \frac{3}{4}$ s **c.** 1 s

d. $t = \frac{5}{4}$ s **e.** $t = \frac{4}{3}$ s

Round to the nearest mile.

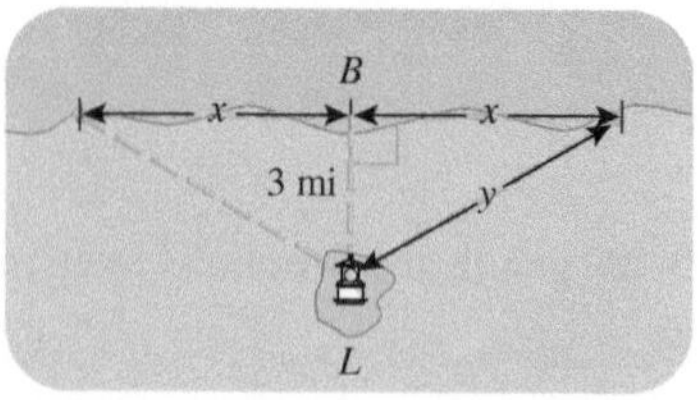

70. Lighthouse. If the length of the light beam is determined by $y = 3|\sec(\pi t)|$, find y at

a. $t = \frac{2}{3}$ s **b.** $t = \frac{3}{4}$ s **c.** 1 s

d. $t = \frac{5}{4}$ s **e.** $t = \frac{4}{3}$ s

Round to the nearest mile.

• CATCH THE MISTAKE

In Exercises 71 and 72, explain the mistake that is made.

71. Graph $y = 3\csc(2x)$.

Solution:

Graph the guide function, $y = \sin(2x)$.

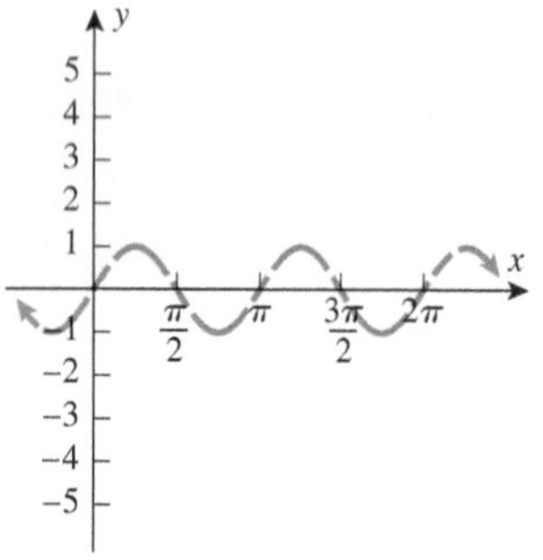

Draw vertical asymptotes at x-values that correspond to x-intercepts of the guide function.

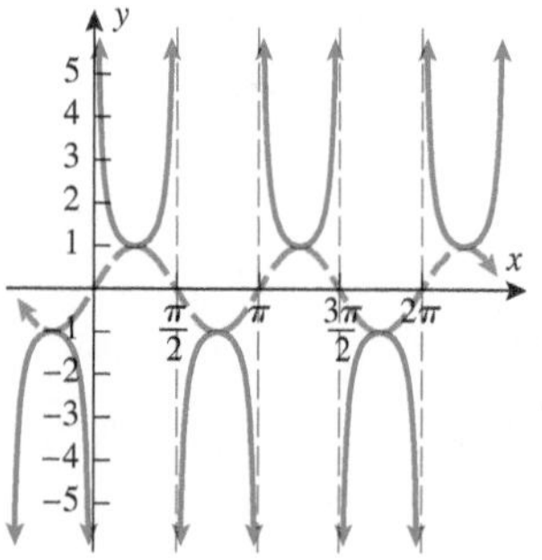

Draw the cosecant function.

This is incorrect. What mistake was made?

72. Graph $y = \tan(4x)$.

Solution:

STEP 1: Calculate the period. $\frac{\pi}{B} = \frac{\pi}{4}$

STEP 2: Find two vertical asymptotes. $4x = 0$ and $4x = \pi$

Solve for x. $x = 0$ and $x = \frac{\pi}{4}$

STEP 3: Find the x-intercept between the asymptotes. $4x = \frac{\pi}{2}$

$x = \frac{\pi}{8}$

STEP 4: Draw the vertical asymptotes, $x = 0$ and $x = \frac{\pi}{4}$ and label the x-intercept $\left(\frac{\pi}{8}, 0\right)$.

STEP 5: Graph.

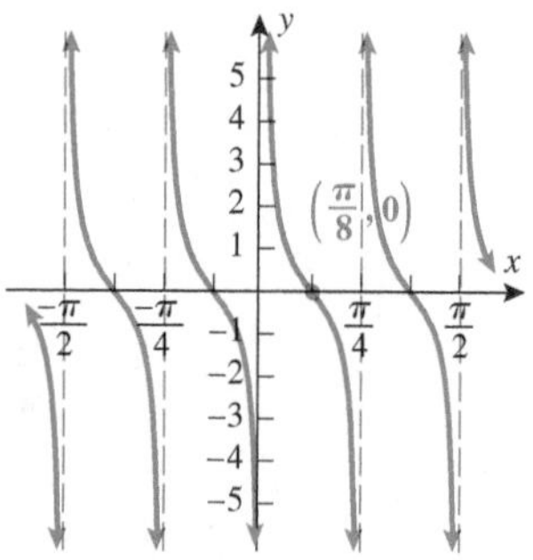

This is incorrect. What mistake was made?

• CONCEPTUAL

In Exercises 73 and 74, determine whether each statement is true or false.

73. $\sec\left(x - \frac{\pi}{2}\right) = \csc x$

74. $\csc\left(x - \frac{\pi}{2}\right) = \sec x$

75. For what values of n do $y = \tan x$ and $y = \tan(x - n\pi)$ have the same graph?

76. For what values of n do $y = \csc x$ and $y = \csc(x - n\pi)$ have the same graph?

77. Solve the equation $\tan(2x - \pi) = 0$ for x in the interval $[-\pi, \pi]$ by graphing.

78. Solve the equation $\csc(2x + \pi) = 0$ for x in the interval $[-\pi, \pi]$ by graphing.

79. Find the x-intercepts of $y = A\tan(Bx + C)$.

80. For what x-values does the graph of $y = -A\sec\left(\frac{\pi}{2}x\right)$ lie above the x-axis? (Assume $A > 0$.)

81. How many solutions are there to the equation $\tan x = x$? Explain.

82. For what values of A do the graphs of $y = A\sin(Bx + C)$ and $y = -2\csc\left(\frac{\pi}{6}x - \pi\right)$ never intersect?

• PREVIEW TO CALCULUS

In calculus, the definite integral $\int_a^b f(x)\,dx$ is used to find the area below the graph of a continuous function f, above the x-axis, and between $x = a$ and $x = b$. The Fundamental Theorem of Calculus establishes that the definite integral $\int_a^b f(x)\,dx$ equals $F(b) - F(a)$, where F is any antiderivative of a continuous function f.

In Exercises 83–86, first shade the area corresponding to the definite integral and then use the information below to find the exact value of the area.

FUNCTION	$\tan x$	$\cot x$	$\sec x$	$\csc x$
ANTIDERIVATIVE	$-\ln\lvert\cos x\rvert$	$\ln\lvert\sin x\rvert$	$\ln\lvert\sec x + \tan x\rvert$	$-\ln\lvert\csc x + \cot x\rvert$

83. $\int_0^{\pi/4} \tan x\,dx$

84. $\int_{\pi/4}^{\pi/2} \cot x\,dx$

85. $\int_0^{\pi/4} \sec x\,dx$

86. $\int_{\pi/4}^{\pi/2} \csc x\,dx$

CHAPTER 5 REVIEW

SECTION	CONCEPT	KEY IDEAS/FORMULAS
5.1	**Trigonometric functions: The unit circle approach**	
	Trigonometric functions and the unit circle	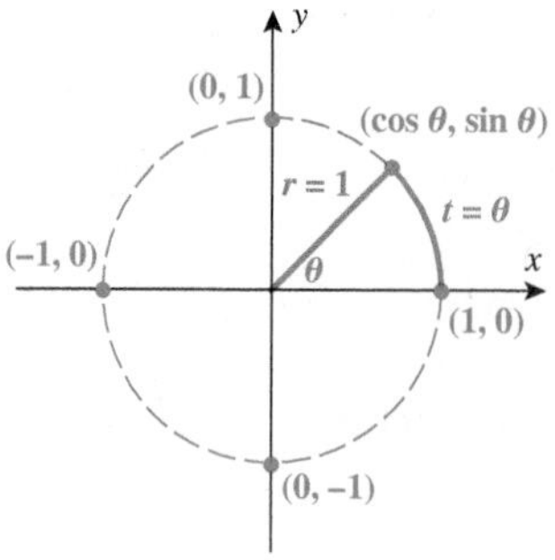 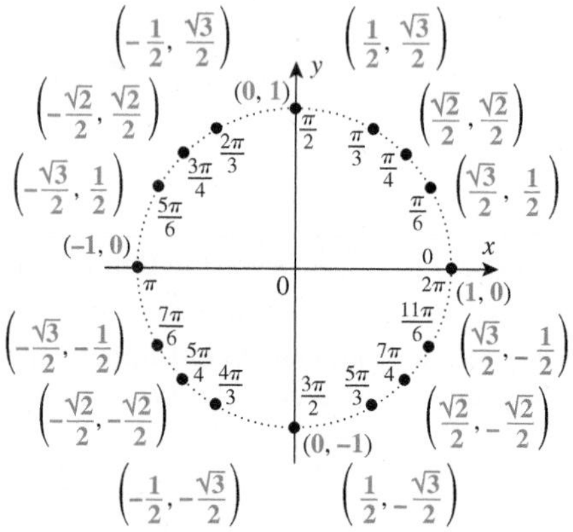
	Properties of trigonometric (circular) functions	Cosine is an even function. $\cos(-\theta) = \cos\theta$ Sine is an odd function. $\sin(-\theta) = -\sin\theta$

SECTION	CONCEPT	KEY IDEAS/FORMULAS
5.2	**Graphs of sine and cosine functions**	

The graphs of sinusoidal functions

$f(x) = \sin x$

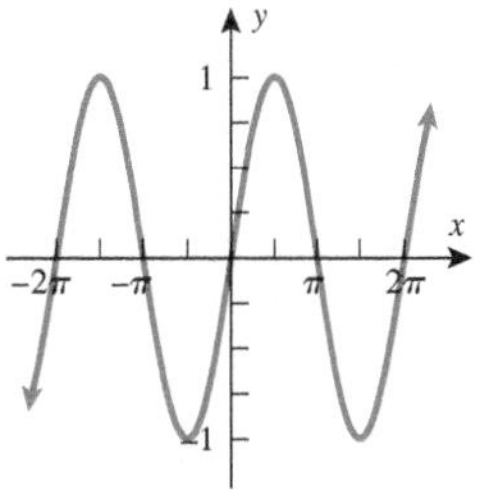

Odd Function

$\sin(-x) = -\sin x$

$f(x) = \cos x$

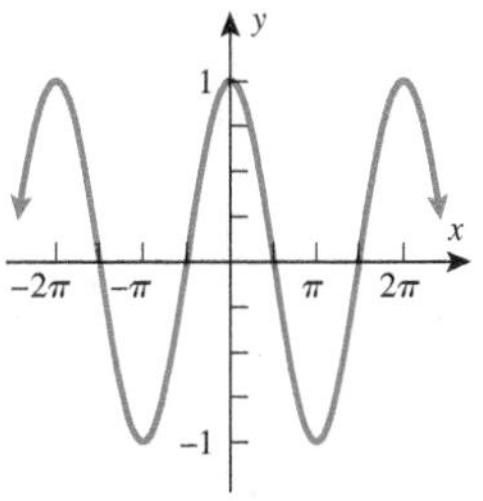

Even Function

$\cos(-x) = \cos(x)$

The amplitude and period of sinusoidal graphs

$y = A\sin(Bx)$ or $y = A\cos(Bx)$, $B > 0$

Amplitude $= |A|$

- $|A| > 1$ stretch vertically.
- $|A| < 1$ compress vertically.

Period $= \dfrac{2\pi}{B}$

- $B > 1$ compress horizontally.
- $B < 1$ stretch horizontally.

Graphing a shifted sinusoidal function:

$y = A\sin(Bx + C) + D$

and

$y = A\cos(Bx + C) + D$

- $y = A\sin(Bx \pm C) = A\sin\left[B\left(x \pm \dfrac{C}{B}\right)\right]$ has period $\dfrac{2\pi}{B}$ and a phase shift of $\dfrac{C}{B}$ units to the left (+) or the right (−).
- $y = A\cos(Bx \pm C) = A\cos\left[B\left(x \pm \dfrac{C}{B}\right)\right]$ has period $\dfrac{2\pi}{B}$ and a phase shift of $\dfrac{C}{B}$ units to the left (+) or the right (−).
- To graph $y = A\sin(Bx + C) + D$ or $y = A\cos(Bx + C) + D$, start with the graph of $y = A\sin(Bx + C)$ or $y = A\cos(Bx + C)$ and shift up or down D units.

SECTION	CONCEPT	KEY IDEAS/FORMULAS
	Harmonic motion	■ Simple ■ Damped ■ Resonance
	Graphing sums of functions: Addition of ordinates	
5.3	**Graphs of other trigonometric functions**	
	Graphing the tangent, cotangent, secant, and cosecant functions	**The tangent function** 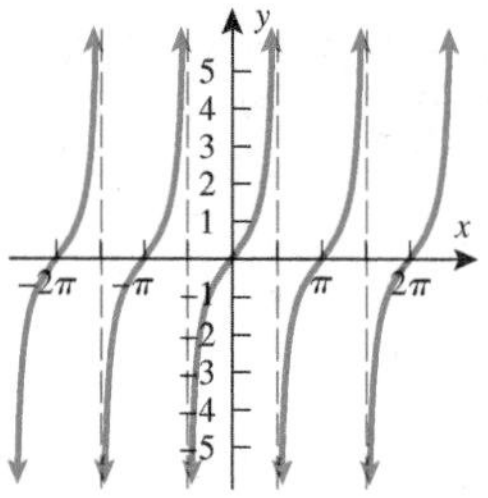 x-intercepts: $(n\pi, 0)$, n = integer Asymptotes: $x = \frac{(2n+1)\pi}{2}$ Period: π Amplitude: none **The cotangent function** 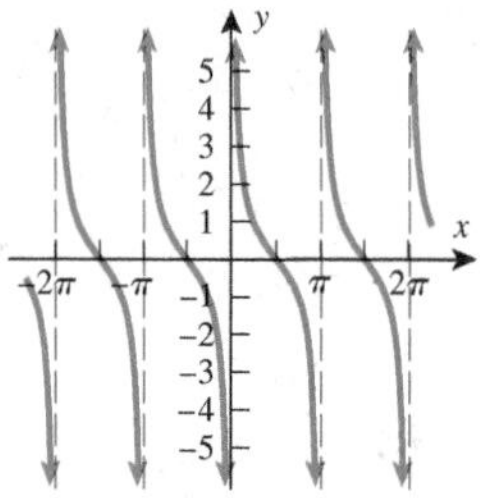 Asymptotes: $x = n\pi$, n = integer x-intercepts: $\left(\frac{(2n+1)\pi}{2}, 0\right)$ Period: π Amplitude: none

SECTION	CONCEPT	KEY IDEAS/FORMULAS
		The secant function 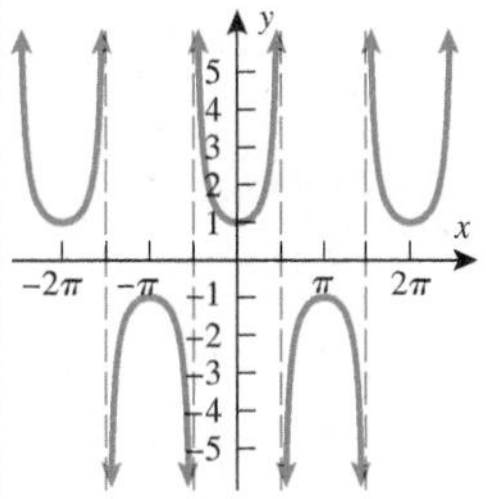 Asymptotes: $x = \frac{(2n + 1)\pi}{2}$, n = integer Period: 2π Amplitude: none x-intercepts: none **The cosecant function** 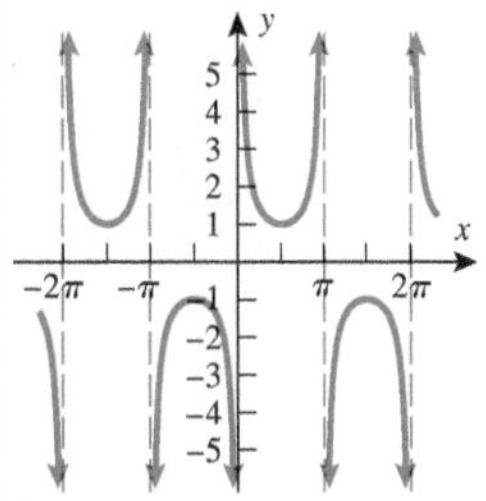 Asymptotes: $x = n\pi$, n = integer Period: 2π Amplitude: none x-intercepts: none **Graphing more general tangent, cotangent, secant, and cosecant functions** $y = A\tan(Bx)$, $y = A\cot(Bx)$, $y = A\sec(Bx)$, $y = A\csc(Bx)$
	Translations of trigonometric functions	$y = A\tan(Bx + C)$ or $y = A\cot(Bx + C)$ To find asymptotes, set $Bx + C$ equal to ■ $-\frac{\pi}{2}$ and $\frac{\pi}{2}$ for tangent. ■ 0 and π for cotangent. To find x-intercepts, set $Bx + C$ equal to ■ 0 for tangent. ■ $\frac{\pi}{2}$ for cotangent. $y = A\sec(Bx + C)$ or $y = A\csc(Bx + C)$ To graph $y = A\sec(Bx + C)$, use $y = A\cos(Bx + C)$ as the guide. To graph $y = A\csc(Bx + C)$, use $y = A\sin(Bx + C)$ as the guide. Intercepts on the guide function correspond to vertical asymptotes of secant or cosecant functions.

[CHAPTER 5 REVIEW EXERCISES]

5.1 Trigonometric Functions: The Unit Circle Approach

Find each trigonometric function value in *exact* form.

1. $\tan\left(\frac{5\pi}{6}\right)$
2. $\cos\left(\frac{5\pi}{6}\right)$
3. $\sin\left(\frac{11\pi}{6}\right)$
4. $\sec\left(\frac{11\pi}{6}\right)$
5. $\cot\left(\frac{5\pi}{4}\right)$
6. $\csc\left(\frac{5\pi}{4}\right)$
7. $\sin\left(\frac{3\pi}{2}\right)$
8. $\cos\left(\frac{3\pi}{2}\right)$
9. $\cos\pi$
10. $\tan\left(\frac{7\pi}{4}\right)$
11. $\cos\left(\frac{\pi}{3}\right)$
12. $\sin\left(\frac{11\pi}{6}\right)$
13. $\sin\left(-\frac{7\pi}{4}\right)$
14. $\tan\left(-\frac{2\pi}{3}\right)$
15. $\csc\left(-\frac{3\pi}{2}\right)$
16. $\cot\left(-\frac{5\pi}{6}\right)$
17. $\cos\left(-\frac{7\pi}{6}\right)$
18. $\sec\left(-\frac{3\pi}{4}\right)$
19. $\tan\left(-\frac{13\pi}{6}\right)$
20. $\cos\left(-\frac{14\pi}{3}\right)$

5.2 Graphs of Sine and Cosine Functions

Refer to the graph of the sinusoidal function to answer the questions.

21. Determine the period of the function.
22. Determine the amplitude of the function.
23. Write an equation for the sinusoidal function.

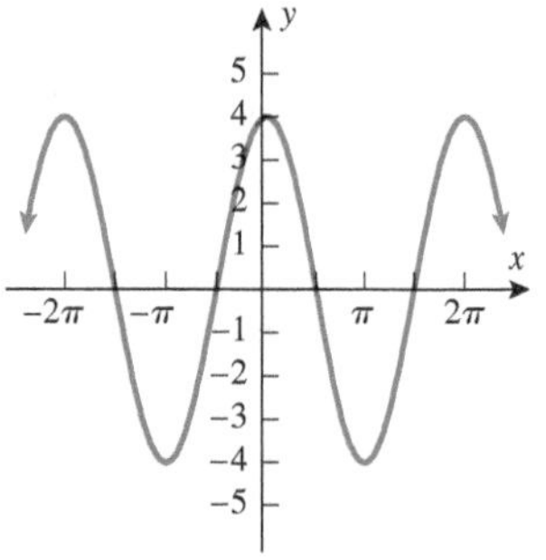

Refer to the graph of the sinusoidal function to answer the questions.

24. Determine the period of the function.
25. Determine the amplitude of the function.
26. Write an equation for the sinusoidal function.

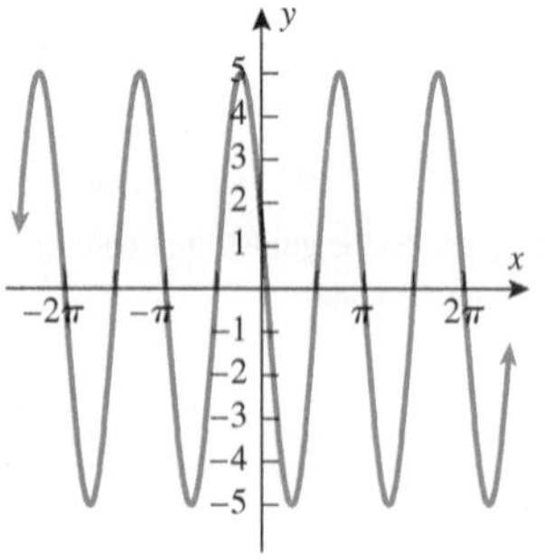

Determine the amplitude and period of each function.

27. $y = -2\cos(2\pi x)$
28. $y = \frac{1}{3}\sin\left(\frac{\pi}{2}x\right)$
29. $y = \frac{1}{5}\sin(3x)$
30. $y = -\frac{7}{6}\cos(6x)$

Graph each function from -2π to 2π.

31. $y = -2\sin\left(\frac{x}{2}\right)$
32. $y = 3\sin(3x)$
33. $y = \frac{1}{2}\cos(2x)$
34. $y = -\frac{1}{4}\cos\left(\frac{x}{2}\right)$

State the amplitude, period, phase shift, and vertical shift of each function.

35. $y = 2 + 3\sin\left(x - \frac{\pi}{2}\right)$
36. $y = 3 - \frac{1}{2}\sin\left(x + \frac{\pi}{4}\right)$
37. $y = -2 - 4\cos\left[3\left(x + \frac{\pi}{4}\right)\right]$
38. $y = -1 + 2\cos\left[2\left(x - \frac{\pi}{3}\right)\right]$
39. $y = -\frac{1}{2} + \frac{1}{3}\cos\left(\pi x - \frac{1}{2}\right)$
40. $y = \frac{3}{4} - \frac{1}{6}\sin\left(\frac{\pi}{6}x + \frac{\pi}{3}\right)$

Graph each function from $-\pi$ to π.

41. $y = 3x - \cos(2x)$
42. $y = -\frac{1}{2}\cos(4x) + \frac{1}{2}\cos(2x)$
43. $y = 2\sin\left(\frac{1}{3}x\right) - 3\sin(3x)$
44. $y = 5\cos x + 3\sin\left(\frac{x}{2}\right)$

5.3 Graphs of Other Trigonometric Functions

State the domain and range of each function.

45. $y = 4\tan\left(x + \frac{\pi}{2}\right)$

46. $y = \cot 2\left(x - \frac{\pi}{2}\right)$

47. $y = 3\sec(2x)$

48. $y = 1 + 2\csc x$

49. $y = -\frac{1}{2} + \frac{1}{4}\sec\left(\pi x - \frac{2\pi}{3}\right)$

50. $y = 3 - \frac{1}{2}\csc(2x - \pi)$

Graph each function on the interval $[-2\pi, 2\pi]$.

51. $y = -\tan\left(x - \frac{\pi}{4}\right)$

52. $y = 1 + \cot(2x)$

53. $y = 2 + \sec(x - \pi)$

54. $y = -\csc\left(x + \frac{\pi}{4}\right)$

55. $y = \frac{1}{2} + 2\csc\left(2x - \frac{\pi}{2}\right)$

56. $y = -1 - \frac{1}{2}\sec\left(\pi x - \frac{3\pi}{4}\right)$

[CHAPTER 5 PRACTICE TEST]

1. State the amplitude and period of $y = -5\sin(3x)$.
2. Graph $y = -2\cos(\frac{1}{2}x)$ on the interval $-4\pi \leq x \leq 4\pi$.
3. Graph $y = 1 + 3\sin(x + \pi)$ on the interval $-3\pi \leq x \leq 3\pi$.
4. Graph $y = 4 - \sin\left(x - \frac{\pi}{2}\right)$ on the interval $-6\pi \leq x \leq 6\pi$.
5. Graph $y = -2 - \cos\left(x + \frac{\pi}{2}\right)$ on the interval $-4\pi \leq x \leq 4\pi$.
6. Graph $y = 3 + 2\cos\left(x + \frac{3\pi}{2}\right)$ on the interval $-5\pi \leq x \leq 5\pi$.
7. Graph $y = \tan\left(\pi x - \frac{\pi}{2}\right)$ over two periods.
8. The vertical asymptotes of $y = 2\csc(3x - \pi)$ correspond to the ________ of $y = 2\sin(3x - \pi)$.
9. State the x-intercepts of $y = \tan(2x)$ for all x.
10. State the phase shift and vertical shift for $y = -\cot\left(\frac{\pi}{3}x - \pi\right)$.
11. State the range of $y = -3\sec\left(2x + \frac{\pi}{3}\right) - 1$.
12. State the domain of $y = \tan\left(2x - \frac{\pi}{6}\right) + 3$.
13. Graph $y = -2\csc\left(x + \frac{\pi}{2}\right)$ over two periods.
14. Find the x-intercept(s) of $y = \frac{6}{\sqrt{3}} - 3\sec\left(6x - \frac{5\pi}{6}\right)$.
15. True or false: The equation $2\sin\theta = 2.0001$ has no solution.
16. On what x-intervals does the graph of $y = \cos(2x)$ lie below the x-axis?
17. Write the equation of a sine function that has amplitude 4, vertical shift $\frac{1}{2}$ down, phase shift $\frac{3}{2}$ to the left, and period π.
18. Write the equation of a cotangent function that has period π, vertical shift 0.01 up, and no phase shift.
19. Graph $y = \cos(3x) - \frac{1}{2}\sin(3x)$ for $0 \leq x \leq \pi$.
20. $y = -\frac{1}{5}\cos\left(\frac{x}{3}\right)$
    a. Graph the function over one period.
    b. Determine the amplitude, period, and phase shift.
21. $y = 4\sin(2\pi x)$
    a. Graph the function over one period.
    b. Determine the amplitude, period, and phase shift.
22. $y = -2\sin(3x + 4\pi) + 1$
    a. Write the sinusoidal function in standard form.
    b. Determine its amplitude, period, and phase shift.
    c. Graph the function over one period.
23. $y = 6 + 5\cos(2x - \pi)$
    a. Write the sinusoidal function in standard form.
    b. Determine its amplitude, period, and phase shift.
    c. Graph the function over one period.
24. Graph the function $y = 2\cos x - \sin x$ on the interval $[-\pi, \pi]$ by adding the ordinates of each individual function.

[CHAPTERS 1–5 CUMULATIVE TEST]

1. Find the domain of $f(x) = \dfrac{4}{\sqrt{15 + 3x}}$. Express the domain in interval notation.
2. On February 24, the gasoline price (per gallon) was \$1.94; on May 24, its price per gallon was \$2.39. Find the average rate of change per month in the gasoline price from February 24 to May 24.
3. Write the function whose graph is the graph of $y = |x|$, but stretched by a factor of 2, shifted up four units, and shifted to the left six units. Graph the function on the interval $[-10, 10]$.
4. Given $f(x) = 2x - 5$ and $g(x) = x^2 + 7$, find
   a. $f + g$
   b. $f - g$
   c. $f \cdot g$
   d. f/g
   e. $f \circ g$
5. Find the inverse function of the one-to-one function $f(x) = \dfrac{x - 2}{3x + 5}$. Find the domain and range of both f and f^{-1}.
6. $f(x) = -x^2(2x - 6)^3(x + 5)^4$
   a. List each zero and its multiplicity.
   b. Sketch the graph.
7. Divide $(6x^4 - 5x^3 + 6x^2 + 7x - 4)$ by $(2x^2 - 1)$ using long division. Express the answer in the form $Q(x) = ?$ and $r(x) = ?$.
8. $f(x) = x^4 + x^3 - 7x^2 - x + 6$
   a. Factor the polynomial function as a product of linear and/or irreducible quadratic factors.
   b. Graph the function.
9. Factor the polynomial $P(x) = x^4 - 4x^2 - 5$ as a product of linear factors.
10. $f(x) = \dfrac{x^2 - 5x - 14}{2x^2 + 14x + 20}$,
    a. Determine the vertical, horizontal, or slant asymptotes (if they exist).
    b. Graph the function.
11. If you deposit \$3000 into an account paying 1.2% compounded quarterly, how much will you have in the account in 10 years?
12. Approximate $\log_2 19$ utilizing a calculator. Round to two decimal places.
13. Write $\ln\left(\dfrac{a^3}{b^2c^5}\right)$ as a sum or difference of constant multiples of logarithms.
14. Solve the exponential equation $4^{3x-2} + 5 = 23$. Round your answer to three decimal places.
15. Solve the exponential equation $\log(x + 2) + \log(x + 3) = \log(2x + 10)$. Round your answer to three decimal places.
16. Find the area of a circular sector with radius $r = 6.5$ cm and central angle $\theta = \dfrac{4\pi}{5}$. Round your answer to the nearest integer.
17. Solve the right triangle $\beta = 27°$, $c = 14$ in. Round your answer to the nearest hundredth.
18. The terminal side of an angle θ in standard position passes through the point $(3, -2)$. Calculate the exact value of the six trigonometric functions for angle θ.
19. Solve the triangle $\alpha = 68°$, $a = 24$ m, and $b = 24.5$ m.
20. Solve the triangle $a = 5$, $b = 6$, and $c = 7$.
21. Given that $\sin\theta = \dfrac{1}{2}$ and $\dfrac{\pi}{2} < \theta < \pi$, find the exact value of all the other trigonometric functions.
22. Graph the function $y = 4\cos(2x + \pi)$ over one period.
23. The frequency of the oscillations f is given by $f = \dfrac{1}{p}$, where p is the period. What is the frequency of the oscillations modeled by $y = 1.14\sin(4t)$?
24. Graph the function $y = -2 + 5\csc\left(4x - \dfrac{\pi}{2}\right)$ over two periods. State the range of the function.

CHAPTER 6

Analytic Trigonometry

hanibaram

When you press a touch-tone button to dial a phone number, how does the phone system know which key you have pressed? Dual Tone Multi-Frequency (DTMF), also known as Touch-Tone dialing, was developed by Bell Labs in the 1960s. The Touch-Tone system also introduced a standardized *keypad* layout.

The keypad is laid out in a 4×3 matrix, with each row representing a low frequency and each column representing a high frequency.

FREQUENCY	1209 Hz	1336 Hz	1477 Hz
697 Hz	1	2	3
770 Hz	4	5	6
852 Hz	7	8	9
941 Hz	*	0	#

When you press the number 8, the phone sends a sinusoidal tone that combines a low-frequency tone of 852 hertz and a high-frequency tone of 1336 hertz. The result can be found using sum-to-product *trigonometric identities.*

LEARNING OBJECTIVES

- Review basic identities.
- Verify a trigonometric identity.
- Apply the sum and difference identities.
- Apply the double-angle identities.
- Apply the half-angle identities.
- Apply the product-to-sum and sum-to-product identities.
- Graph inverse trigonometric functions.
- Solve trigonometric identities.

[IN THIS CHAPTER]

We will verify trigonometric identities. Specific identities that we will discuss are sum and difference, double-angle and half-angle, and product-to-sum and sum-to-product. Inverse trigonometric functions will be defined. Trigonometric identities and inverse trigonometric functions will be used to solve trigonometric equations.

ANALYTIC TRIGONOMETRY					
6.1 VERIFYING TRIGONOMETRIC IDENTITIES	**6.2** SUM AND DIFFERENCE IDENTITIES	**6.3** DOUBLE-ANGLE AND HALF-ANGLE IDENTITIES	**6.4** PRODUCT-TO-SUM AND SUM-TO-PRODUCT IDENTITIES	**6.5** INVERSE TRIGONOMETRIC FUNCTIONS	**6.6** TRIGONOMETRIC EQUATIONS
• Fundamental Identities • Simplifying Trigonometric Expressions Using Identities • Verifying Identities	• Sum and Difference Identities for the Cosine Function • Sum and Difference Identities for the Sine Function • Sum and Difference Identities for the Tangent Function	• Double-Angle Identities • Half-Angle Identities	• Product-to-Sum Identities • Sum-to-Product Identities	• Inverse Sine Function • Inverse Cosine Function • Inverse Tangent Function • Remaining Inverse Trigonometric Functions • Finding Exact Values for Expressions Involving Inverse Trigonometric Functions	• Solving Trigonometric Equations by Inspection • Solving Trigonometric Equations Using Algebraic Techniques • Solving Trigonometric Equations That Require the Use of Inverse Functions • Using Trigonometric Identities to Solve Trigonometric Equations

6.1 VERIFYING TRIGONOMETRIC IDENTITIES

SKILLS OBJECTIVES

- Apply the reciprocal, quotient, and Pythagorean identities.
- Simplify trigonometric expressions using identities.
- Verify trigonometric expressions using identities.

CONCEPTUAL OBJECTIVES

- Understand that trigonometric reciprocal and quotient identities are not always defined.
- Understand that there is more than one way to simplify trigonometric expressions.
- Understand that there is more than one way to verify an identity.

6.1.1 Fundamental Identities

6.1.1 SKILL

Apply the reciprocal, quotient, and Pythagorean identities.

6.1.1 CONCEPTUAL

Understand that trigonometric reciprocal and quotient identities are not always defined.

In mathematics, an **identity** is an equation that is true for *all* values of the variable for which the expressions in the equation are defined. If an equation is true for only *some* values of the variable, it is a **conditional equation.**

The following boxes summarize trigonometric identities that have been discussed in Chapters 4 and 5.

STUDY TIP

Just because an equation is true for *some* values of x does not mean it is an identity. An equation has to be true for **all** values of the variable for it to be an **identity**.

RECIPROCAL IDENTITIES

RECIPROCAL IDENTITIES	EQUIVALENT FORMS	DOMAIN RESTRICTIONS
$\csc x = \dfrac{1}{\sin x}$	$\sin x = \dfrac{1}{\csc x}$	$x \neq n\pi \quad n = \text{integer}$
$\sec x = \dfrac{1}{\cos x}$	$\cos x = \dfrac{1}{\sec x}$	$x \neq \dfrac{n\pi}{2} \quad n = \text{odd integer}$
$\cot x = \dfrac{1}{\tan x}$	$\tan x = \dfrac{1}{\cot x}$	$x \neq \dfrac{n\pi}{2} \quad n = \text{integer}$

QUOTIENT IDENTITIES

QUOTIENT IDENTITIES	DOMAIN RESTRICTIONS
$\tan x = \dfrac{\sin x}{\cos x}$	$\cos x \neq 0 \quad x \neq \dfrac{n\pi}{2} \quad n = \text{odd integer}$
$\cot x = \dfrac{\cos x}{\sin x}$	$\sin x \neq 0 \quad x \neq n\pi \quad n = \text{integer}$

CONCEPT CHECK

(A) For what values of θ is $\csc\theta$ not defined?

(B) For what values of θ is $\tan\theta$ not defined?

(C) True or False: $\sin^2 x + \cos^2 y = 1$, for all values of x and y.

ANSWER (A) $\theta = \pm n\pi, n = 0, 1, 2, \ldots$

(B) $\theta = \pm\dfrac{(2n+1)\pi}{2}, n = 0, 1, 2, \ldots$

(C) False

PYTHAGOREAN IDENTITIES

$$\sin^2 x + \cos^2 x = 1 \qquad \tan^2 x + 1 = \sec^2 x \qquad 1 + \cot^2 x = \csc^2 x$$

In Chapter 5, we discussed even and odd trigonometric functions, which, like even and odd functions in general, have these respective properties:

TYPE OF FUNCTION	ALGEBRAIC IDENTITY	GRAPH
Even	$f(-x) = f(x)$	Symmetry about the y-axis
Odd	$f(-x) = -f(x)$	Symmetry about the origin

We learned in Chapter 5 that the sine function is an odd function and the cosine function is an even function. Combining this knowledge with the reciprocal and quotient identities, we arrive at the *even-odd identities*, which we can add to our list of basic identities.

EVEN–ODD IDENTITIES

$$\text{Odd}\begin{cases}\sin(-x) = -\sin x\\ \csc(-x) = -\csc x\\ \tan(-x) = -\tan x\\ \cot(-x) = -\cot x\end{cases} \qquad \text{Even}\begin{cases}\cos(-x) = \cos x\\ \sec(-x) = \sec x\end{cases}$$

Cofunctions

Recall complementary angles (Section 4.1). Notice the *co* in *co*sine, *co*secant, and *co*tangent functions. These *cofunctions* are based on the relationship of *co*mplementary angles. Let us look at a right triangle with labeled sides and angles.

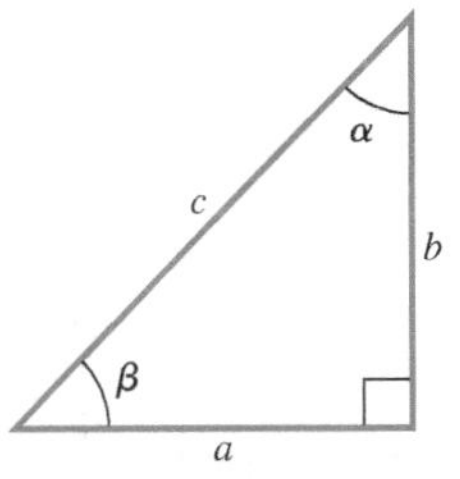

$$\left.\begin{aligned}\sin\beta &= \frac{\text{opposite of } \beta}{\text{hypotenuse}} = \frac{b}{c}\\ \cos\alpha &= \frac{\text{adjacent to } \alpha}{\text{hypotenuse}} = \frac{b}{c}\end{aligned}\right\}\ \sin\beta = \cos\alpha$$

Recall that the sum of the measures of the three angles in a triangle is 180°. In a right triangle, one angle is 90°; therefore, the two acute angles are complementary angles (the measures sum to 90°). You can see in the triangle above that β and α are complementary angles. In other words, the sine of an angle is the same as the *co*sine of the *co*mplement of that angle. This is true for all *trigonometric cofunction* pairs.

COFUNCTION THEOREM

A trigonometric function of an angle is always equal to the cofunction of the complement of the angle. If $\alpha + \beta = 90°\left(\text{or } \alpha + \beta = \frac{\pi}{2}\right)$, then

$$\sin\beta = \cos\alpha$$
$$\sec\beta = \csc\alpha$$
$$\tan\beta = \cot\alpha$$

STUDY TIP

Alternate form of cofunction identities:

$\sin\theta = \cos\left(\frac{\pi}{2} - \theta\right)$

$\cos\theta = \sin\left(\frac{\pi}{2} - \theta\right)$

$\tan\theta = \cot\left(\frac{\pi}{2} - \theta\right)$

$\cot\theta = \tan\left(\frac{\pi}{2} - \theta\right)$

$\sec\theta = \csc\left(\frac{\pi}{2} - \theta\right)$

$\csc\theta = \sec\left(\frac{\pi}{2} - \theta\right)$

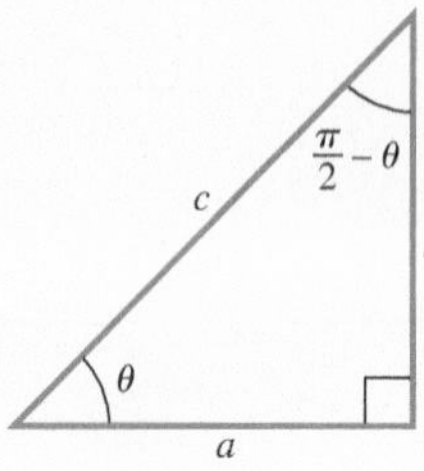

COFUNCTION IDENTITIES

$$\sin\theta = \cos(90° - \theta) \qquad \cos\theta = \sin(90° - \theta)$$
$$\tan\theta = \cot(90° - \theta) \qquad \cot\theta = \tan(90° - \theta)$$
$$\sec\theta = \csc(90° - \theta) \qquad \csc\theta = \sec(90° - \theta)$$

EXAMPLE 1 Writing Trigonometric Function Values in Terms of Their Cofunctions

Write each function or function value in terms of its cofunction.

a. $\sin 30°$ **b.** $\tan x$ **c.** $\csc 40°$

Solution (a):

Cosine is the cofunction of sine. $\sin\theta = \cos(90° - \theta)$

Substitute $\theta = 30°$. $\sin 30° = \cos(90° - 30°)$

Simplify. $\boxed{\sin 30° = \cos 60°}$

Solution (b):

Cotangent is the cofunction of tangent. $\tan\theta = \cot(90° - \theta)$

Substitute $\theta = x$. $\boxed{\tan x = \cot(90° - x)}$

Solution (c):

Cosecant is the cofunction of secant. $\csc\theta = \sec(90° - \theta)$

Substitute $\theta = 40°$. $\csc 40° = \sec(90° - 40°)$

Simplify. $\boxed{\csc 40° = \sec 50°}$

YOUR TURN Write each function or function value in terms of its cofunction.

a. $\cos 45°$ **b.** $\csc y$

ANSWER

a. $\sin 45°$

b. $\sec(90° - y)$

6.1.2 Simplifying Trigonometric Expressions Using Identities

6.1.2 SKILL

Simplify trigonometric expressions using identities.

6.1.2 CONCEPTUAL

Understand that there is more than one way to simplify trigonometric expressions.

We can use the fundamental identities and algebraic manipulation to simplify more complicated trigonometric expressions. In simplifying trigonometric expressions, one approach is first to convert all expressions into sines and cosines and then to simplify.

EXAMPLE 2 Simplifying Trigonometric Expressions

Simplify $\tan x \sin x + \cos x$.

Solution:

Write the tangent function in terms of the sine and cosine functions: $\tan x = \dfrac{\sin x}{\cos x}$.

$$\tan x \cdot \sin x + \cos x$$
$$= \frac{\sin x}{\cos x}\sin x + \cos x$$

Simplify.

$$= \frac{\sin^2 x}{\cos x} + \cos x$$

Write as a fraction with a single quotient by finding a common denominator, $\cos x$. $\quad = \dfrac{\sin^2 x + \cos^2 x}{\cos x}$

Use the Pythagorean identity: $\sin^2 x + \cos^2 x = 1$. $\quad = \dfrac{1}{\cos x}$

Use the reciprocal identity $\sec x = \dfrac{1}{\cos x}$. $\quad = \boxed{\sec x}$

YOUR TURN Simplify $\cot x \cos x + \sin x$.

ANSWER

$\csc x$

In Example 2, $\tan x$ and $\sec x$ are not defined for odd integer multiples of $\frac{\pi}{2}$. In the Your Turn, $\cot x$ and $\csc x$ are not defined for integer multiples of π. Both the original expression and the simplified form are governed by the same restrictions. There are times when the original expression is subject to more domain restrictions than the simplified form, and thus special attention must be given to domain restrictions.

For example, the algebraic expression $\dfrac{x^2 - 1}{x + 1}$ is under the domain restriction $x \neq -1$ because that value for x makes the value of the denominator equal to zero. If we forget to state the domain restrictions, we might simplify the algebraic expression as $\dfrac{x^2 - 1}{x + 1} = \dfrac{(x - 1)(x + 1)}{(x + 1)} = x - 1$ and assume that this is true for all values of x. The correct simplification is $\dfrac{x^2 - 1}{x + 1} = x - 1$ for $x \neq -1$. In fact, if we were to graph both the original expression $y = \dfrac{x^2 - 1}{x + 1}$ and the line $y = x - 1$, they would coincide, except that the graph of the original expression would have a "hole" or discontinuity at $x = -1$. In this chapter, it is assumed that the domain of the simplified expression is the same as the domain of the original expression.

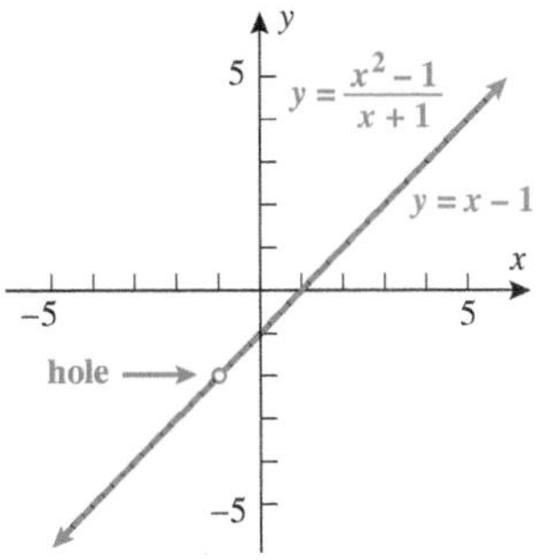

EXAMPLE 3 Simplifying Trigonometric Expressions

Simplify $\dfrac{1}{\csc^2 x} + \dfrac{1}{\sec^2 x}$.

Solution:

Rewrite the expression in terms of quotients squared. $\quad \dfrac{1}{\csc^2 x} + \dfrac{1}{\sec^2 x} = \left(\dfrac{1}{\csc x}\right)^2 + \left(\dfrac{1}{\sec x}\right)^2$

Use the reciprocal identities to write the cosecant and secant functions in terms of sines and cosines: $\sin x = \dfrac{1}{\csc x}$ and $\cos x = \dfrac{1}{\sec x}$. $\quad = \sin^2 x + \cos^2 x$

Use the Pythagorean identity: $\sin^2 x + \cos^2 x = 1$. $\quad = \boxed{1}$

YOUR TURN Simplify $\dfrac{1}{\cos^2 x} - 1$.

ANSWER

$\tan^2 x$

[CONCEPT CHECK]

TRUE OR FALSE In the Your Turn following Example 3, you can first combine into a single fraction and then use the first Pythagorean theorem, or you can first use the reciprocal identity and then use the second Pythagorean identity.

ANSWER True

6.1.3 Verifying Identities

6.1.3 SKILL

Verify trigonometric expressions using identities.

6.1.3 CONCEPTUAL

Understand that there is more than one way to verify an identity.

We will now use the trigonometric identities to verify, or establish, other trigonometric identities. For example, verify that

$$(\sin x - \cos x)^2 - 1 = -2\sin x \cos x$$

The good news is that we will know we are done when we get there, since we know the desired identity. But how do we get there? How do we verify that the identity is true? Remember that it must be true for *all* x, not just some x. Therefore, it is not enough to simply select values for x and show that the identity is true for those specific values.

WORDS	MATH
Start with one side of the equation (the more complicated side).	$(\sin x - \cos x)^2 - 1$
Remember that $(a - b)^2 = a^2 - 2ab + b^2$ and expand $(\sin x - \cos x)^2$.	$= \sin^2 x - 2\sin x \cos x + \cos^2 x - 1$
Group the $\sin^2 x$ and $\cos^2 x$ terms and use the Pythagorean identity.	$= -2\sin x \cos x + \underbrace{(\sin^2 x + \cos^2 x)}_{1} - 1$
Simplify.	$= -2\sin x \cos x$

When we arrive at the right side of the equation, we will have succeeded in verifying the identity. In verifying trigonometric identities, there is no one procedure that works for all identities. You must manipulate one side of the equation until it looks like the other side.

The following suggestions help guide the way in verifying trigonometric identities.

GUIDELINES FOR VERIFYING TRIGONOMETRIC IDENTITIES

- Start with the more complicated side of the equation.
- Combine all sums and differences of fractions (quotients) into a single fraction (quotient).
- Use fundamental trigonometric identities.
- Use algebraic techniques to manipulate one side of the equation until the other side of the equation is achieved.
- Sometimes it is helpful to convert all trigonometric functions into sines and cosines.

It is important to note that trigonometric identities must be valid for all values of the independent variable (usually, x or θ) for which the expressions in the equation are defined (domain of the equation).

EXAMPLE 4 Verifying Trigonometric Identities

Verify the identity $\dfrac{\tan x - \cot x}{\tan x + \cot x} = \sin^2 x - \cos^2 x$.

Solution:

Start with the more complicated side of the equation.

$$\frac{\tan x - \cot x}{\tan x + \cot x}$$

Use the quotient identity to write the tangent and cotangent functions in terms of the sine and cosine functions.

$$= \frac{\dfrac{\sin x}{\cos x} - \dfrac{\cos x}{\sin x}}{\dfrac{\sin x}{\cos x} + \dfrac{\cos x}{\sin x}}$$

Multiply by $\dfrac{\sin x \cos x}{\sin x \cos x}$.

$$= \left(\frac{\dfrac{\sin x}{\cos x} - \dfrac{\cos x}{\sin x}}{\dfrac{\sin x}{\cos x} + \dfrac{\cos x}{\sin x}}\right)\left(\frac{\sin x \cos x}{\sin x \cos x}\right)$$

Simplify.

$$= \frac{\sin^2 x - \cos^2 x}{\sin^2 x + \cos^2 x}$$

Use the Pythagorean identity: $\sin^2 x + \cos^2 x = 1$.

$$= \boxed{\sin^2 x - \cos^2 x}$$

EXAMPLE 5 Determining Whether a Trigonometric Equation Is an Identity

Determine whether $(1 - \cos^2 x)(1 + \cot^2 x) = 0$ is an identity, a conditional equation, or a contradiction.

Solution:

Use the quotient identity to write the cotangent function in terms of the sine and cosine functions.

$$(1 - \cos^2 x)(1 + \cot^2 x)$$

$$= (1 - \cos^2 x)\left(1 + \frac{\cos^2 x}{\sin^2 x}\right)$$

Combine the expression in the second parentheses so that it is a single quotient.

$$= (1 - \cos^2 x)\left(\frac{\sin^2 x + \cos^2 x}{\sin^2 x}\right)$$

Use the Pythagorean identity.

$$= \underbrace{(1 - \cos^2 x)}_{\sin^2 x}\left(\frac{\overbrace{\sin^2 x + \cos^2 x}^{1}}{\sin^2 x}\right)$$

Eliminate the parentheses.

$$= \frac{\sin^2 x}{\sin^2 x}$$

Simplify.

$$= 1$$

Since $1 \neq 0$, this is not an identity, but rather a $\boxed{\text{contradiction}}$.

[CONCEPT CHECK]

TRUE OR FALSE There is only one approach that can be used to verify an identity.

ANSWER False

EXAMPLE 6 Determine Whether a Trigonometric Equation Is an Identity

Determine whether $\sin^4 x - \cos^4 x = 0$ is an identity, a conditional equation, or a contradiction.

Solution:

Factor the left side of the equation.

$$\sin^4 x - \cos^4 x$$
$$= (\sin^2 x + \cos^2 x)(\sin^2 x - \cos^2 x) = 0$$

Apply the Pythagorean identity: $\sin^2 x + \cos^2 x = 1$.

$$= (\sin^2 x - \cos^2 x) = 0$$

Factor the left side of the equation again.

$$= (\sin x - \cos x)(\sin x + \cos x) = 0$$

Solve.

$$\sin x = \cos x \quad \text{or} \quad \sin x = -\cos x$$

Notice that when $x = \frac{\pi}{4}$ and $x = \frac{5\pi}{4}$ the equation is satisfied, but for $x = \frac{3\pi}{4}$ and $x = \frac{7\pi}{4}$ the equation is not satisfied. Since this equation is true for some (but not all values) of x, it is a **conditional equation**.

EXAMPLE 7 Verifying Trigonometric Identities

Verify that $\dfrac{\sin(-x)}{\cos(-x)\tan(-x)} = 1$.

Solution:

Start with the left side of the equation.

$$\frac{\sin(-x)}{\cos(-x)\tan(-x)}$$

Use the even-odd identities.

$$= \frac{-\sin x}{-\cos x \tan x}$$

Simplify.

$$= \frac{\sin x}{\cos x \tan x}$$

Use the quotient identity to write the tangent function in terms of the sine and cosine functions.

$$= \frac{\sin x}{\cos x\left(\frac{\sin x}{\cos x}\right)}$$

Divide out the cosine term in the denominator.

$$= \frac{\sin x}{\sin x}$$

Simplify.

$$= 1$$

We have verified that $\dfrac{\sin(-x)}{\cos(-x)\tan(-x)} = 1$.

STUDY TIP

Start with the more complicated expression (side) and manipulate until you arrive at the simpler expression (on the other side).

So far we have discussed working with only one side of the identity until we arrive at the other side. Another method for verifying identities is to work with (simplify) each side separately and use identities and algebraic techniques to arrive at the same result on both sides.

EXAMPLE 8 **Verifying an Identity by Simplifying Both Sides Separately**

Verify that $\dfrac{\sin x + 1}{\sin x} = -\dfrac{\cot^2 x}{1 - \csc x}$.

Solution:

Left-hand side: $\dfrac{\sin x + 1}{\sin x} = \dfrac{\sin x}{\sin x} + \dfrac{1}{\sin x} = 1 + \csc x$

Right-hand side: $\dfrac{-\cot^2 x}{1 - \csc x} = \dfrac{1 - \csc^2 x}{1 - \csc x} = \dfrac{(1 - \csc x)(1 + \csc x)}{(1 - \csc x)} = 1 + \csc x$

Since the left-hand side equals the right-hand side, the equation is an identity.

[SECTION 6.1] SUMMARY

We combined the fundamental trigonometric identities—reciprocal, quotient, Pythagorean, even-odd, and cofunction—with algebraic techniques to simplify trigonometric expressions and to verify more complex trigonometric identities. Two steps that we often use both in simplifying trigonometric expressions and in verifying trigonometric identities are (1) writing all trigonometric functions in terms of the sine and cosine functions, and (2) combining sums or differences of quotients into a single quotient.

When verifying trigonometric identities, we typically work with the more complicated side (keeping the other side in mind as our goal). Another approach to verifying trigonometric identities is to work on each side separately and arrive at the same result.

[SECTION 6.1] EXERCISES

• SKILLS

In Exercises 1–6, use the cofunction identities to fill in the blanks.

1. $\sin 60° = \cos$ ______
2. $\sin 45° = \cos$ ______
3. $\cos x = \sin$ ______
4. $\cot A = \tan$ ______
5. $\csc 30° = \sec$ ______
6. $\sec B = \csc$ ______

In Exercises 7–14, write each trigonometric function value in terms of its cofunction.

7. $\sin(x + y)$
8. $\sin(60° - x)$
9. $\cos(20° + A)$
10. $\cos(A + B)$
11. $\cot(45° - x)$
12. $\sec(30° - \theta)$
13. $\csc(60° - \theta)$
14. $\tan(40° + \theta)$

In Exercises 15–38, simplify each of the trigonometric expressions.

15. $\sin x \csc x$
16. $\tan x \cot x$
17. $\sec(-x)\cot x$
18. $\tan(-x)\cos(-x)$
19. $\csc(-x)\sin x$
20. $\cot(-x)\tan x$
21. $\sec x \cos(-x) + \tan^2 x$
22. $\sec(-x)\tan(-x)\cos(-x)$
23. $(\sin^2 x)(\cot^2 x + 1)$
24. $(\cos^2 x)(\tan^2 x + 1)$
25. $(\sin x - \cos x)(\sin x + \cos x)$
26. $(\sin x + \cos x)^2$
27. $\dfrac{\csc x}{\cot x}$
28. $\dfrac{\sec x}{\tan x}$
29. $\dfrac{1 - \cot(-x)}{1 + \cot x}$
30. $\sec^2 x - \tan^2(-x)$
31. $\dfrac{1 - \cos^4 x}{1 + \cos^2 x}$
32. $\dfrac{1 - \sin^4 x}{1 + \sin^2 x}$
33. $\dfrac{1 - \cot^4 x}{1 - \cot^2 x}$
34. $\dfrac{1 - \tan^4(-x)}{1 - \tan^2 x}$
35. $1 - \dfrac{\sin^2 x}{1 - \cos x}$
36. $1 - \dfrac{\cos^2 x}{1 + \sin x}$
37. $\dfrac{\tan x - \cot x}{\tan x + \cot x} + 2\cos^2 x$
38. $\dfrac{\tan x - \cot x}{\tan x + \cot x} + \cos^2 x$

In Exercises 39–64, verify each of the trigonometric identities.

39. $(\sin x + \cos x)^2 + (\sin x - \cos x)^2 = 2$

40. $(1 - \sin x)(1 + \sin x) = \cos^2 x$

41. $(\csc x + 1)(\csc x - 1) = \cot^2 x$

42. $(\sec x + 1)(\sec x - 1) = \tan^2 x$

43. $\tan x + \cot x = \csc x \sec x$

44. $\csc x - \sin x = \cot x \cos x$

45. $\dfrac{2 - \sin^2 x}{\cos x} = \sec x + \cos x$

46. $\dfrac{2 - \cos^2 x}{\sin x} = \csc x + \sin x$

47. $[\cos(-x) - 1][1 + \cos x] = -\sin^2 x$

48. $\tan(-x)\cot x = -1$

49. $\dfrac{\sec(-x)\cot x}{\csc(-x)} = -1$

50. $\csc(-x) - 1 = \dfrac{\cot^2 x}{\csc(-x) + 1}$

51. $\dfrac{1}{\csc^2 x} + \dfrac{1}{\sec^2 x} = 1$

52. $\dfrac{1}{\cot^2 x} - \dfrac{1}{\tan^2 x} = \sec^2 x - \csc^2 x$

53. $\dfrac{1}{1 - \sin x} + \dfrac{1}{1 + \sin x} = 2\sec^2 x$

54. $\dfrac{1}{1 - \cos x} + \dfrac{1}{1 + \cos x} = 2\csc^2 x$

55. $\dfrac{\sin^2 x}{1 - \cos x} = 1 + \cos x$

56. $\dfrac{\cos^2 x}{1 - \sin x} = 1 + \sin x$

57. $\sec x + \tan x = \dfrac{1}{\sec x - \tan x}$

58. $\csc x + \cot x = \dfrac{1}{\csc x - \cot x}$

59. $\dfrac{\csc x - \tan x}{\sec x + \cot x} = \dfrac{\cos x - \sin^2 x}{\sin x + \cos^2 x}$

60. $\dfrac{\sec x + \tan x}{\csc x + 1} = \tan x$

61. $\dfrac{\cos^2 x + 1 + \sin x}{\cos^2 x + 3} = \dfrac{1 + \sin x}{2 + \sin x}$

62. $\dfrac{\sin x + 1 - \cos^2 x}{\cos^2 x} = \dfrac{\sin x}{1 - \sin x}$

63. $\sec x(\tan x + \cot x) = \dfrac{\csc x}{\cos^2 x}$

64. $\tan x(\csc x - \sin x) = \cos x$

In Exercises 65–78, determine whether each equation is a conditional equation or an identity.

65. $\cos^2 x(\tan x - \sec x)(\tan x + \sec x) = 1$

66. $\cos^2 x(\tan x - \sec x)(\tan x + \sec x) = \sin^2 x - 1$

67. $\dfrac{\csc x \cot x}{\sec x \tan x} = \cot^3 x$

68. $\sin x \cos x = 0$

69. $\sin x + \cos x = \sqrt{2}$

70. $\sin^2 x + \cos^2 x = 1$

71. $\tan^2 x - \sec^2 x = 1$

72. $\sec^2 x - \tan^2 x = 1$

73. $\sin x = \sqrt{1 - \cos^2 x}$

74. $\csc x = \sqrt{1 + \cot^2 x}$

75. $\sqrt{\sin^2 x + \cos^2 x} = 1$

76. $\sqrt{\sin^2 x + \cos^2 x} = \sin x + \cos x$

77. $(\sin x - \cos x)^2 = \sin^2 x - \cos^2 x$

78. $[\sin(-x) - 1][\sin(-x) + 1] = \cos^2 x$

• APPLICATIONS

79. Area of a Circle. Show that the area of a circle with radius $r = \sec x$ is equal to $\pi + \pi(\tan x)^2$.

80. Area of a Triangle. Show that the area of a triangle with base $b = \cos x$ and height $h = \sec x$ is equal to $\frac{1}{2}$.

81. Pythagorean Theorem. Find the length of the hypotenuse of a right triangle whose legs have lengths 1 and $\tan\theta$.

82. Pythagorean Theorem. Find the length of the hypotenuse of a right triangle whose legs have lengths 1 and $\cot\theta$.

• CATCH THE MISTAKE

In Exercises 83 and 84, explain the mistake that is made.

83. Verify the identity $\dfrac{\cos x}{1 - \tan x} + \dfrac{\sin x}{1 - \cot x} = \sin x + \cos x$.

Solution:

Start with the left side of the equation. $\qquad \dfrac{\cos x}{1 - \tan x} + \dfrac{\sin x}{1 - \cot x}$

Write the tangent and cotangent functions in terms of sines and cosines. $\qquad = \dfrac{\cos x}{1 - \dfrac{\sin x}{\cos x}} + \dfrac{\sin x}{1 - \dfrac{\cos x}{\sin x}}$

Cancel the common cosine in the first term and sine in the second term. $\qquad = \dfrac{1}{1 - \sin x} + \dfrac{1}{1 - \cos x}$

This is incorrect. What mistake was made?

84. Determine whether the equation is a conditional equation or an identity: $|\sin x| - \cos x = 1$.

Solution:

Start with the left side of the equation. $\qquad |\sin x| - \cos x$

Let $x = \dfrac{n\pi}{2}$, where n is an odd integer. $\qquad \left|\sin\left(\dfrac{n\pi}{2}\right)\right| - \cos\left(\dfrac{n\pi}{2}\right)$

Simplify. $\qquad |\pm 1| - 0 = 1$

Since $|\sin x| - \cos x = 1$, this is an identity.

This is incorrect. What mistake was made?

• CONCEPTUAL

In Exercises 85 and 86, determine whether each statement is true or false.

85. If an equation is true for some values (but not all values), then it is still an identity.

86. If an equation has an infinite number of solutions, then it is an identity.

87. In which quadrants is the equation $\cos\theta = \sqrt{1 - \sin^2\theta}$ true?

88. In which quadrants is the equation $-\cos\theta = \sqrt{1 - \sin^2\theta}$ true?

89. In which quadrants is the equation $\csc\theta = -\sqrt{1 + \cot^2\theta}$ true?

90. In which quadrants is the equation $\sec\theta = \sqrt{1 + \tan^2\theta}$ true?

91. Do you think that $\sin(A + B) = \sin A + \sin B$? Why?

92. Do you think that $\cos(\frac{1}{2}A) = \frac{1}{2}\cos A$? Why?

93. Do you think $\tan(2A) = 2\tan A$? Why?

94. Do you think that $\cot(A^2) = (\cot A)^2$? Why?

• CHALLENGE

95. Simplify $(a\sin x + b\cos x)^2 + (b\sin x - a\cos x)^2$.

96. Simplify $\dfrac{1 + \cot^3 x}{1 + \cot x} + \cot x$.

97. Show that $\csc\left(\dfrac{\pi}{2} + \theta + 2n\pi\right) = \sec\theta$, n an integer.

98. Show that $\sec\left(\dfrac{\pi}{2} - \theta - 2n\pi\right) = \csc\theta$, n an integer.

99. Simplify $\csc\left(2\pi - \dfrac{\pi}{2} - \theta\right) \cdot \sec\left(\theta - \dfrac{\pi}{2}\right) \cdot \sin(-\theta)$.

100. Simplify $\tan\theta \cdot \cot(2\pi - \theta)$.

• PREVIEW TO CALCULUS

For Exercises 101–104, refer to the following:

In calculus, when integrating expressions such as $\sqrt{a^2 - x^2}$, $\sqrt{a^2 + x^2}$, and $\sqrt{x^2 - a^2}$, we use trigonometric functions as "dummy" functions to eliminate the radical. Once the integration is performed, the trigonometric function is "unsubstituted." Such trigonometric substitutions (and corresponding trigonometric identities) are used to simplify these types of expressions.

When simplifying, it is important to remember that

$$|x| = \begin{cases} x & \text{if } x \geq 0 \\ -x & \text{if } x < 0 \end{cases}$$

EXPRESSIONS	SUBSTITUTION		TRIGONOMETRIC IDENTITY
$\sqrt{a^2 - x^2}$	$x = a\sin\theta$	$-\frac{\pi}{2} \leq \theta \leq \frac{\pi}{2}$	$1 - \sin^2\theta = \cos^2\theta$
$\sqrt{a^2 + x^2}$	$x = a\tan\theta$	$-\frac{\pi}{2} \leq \theta \leq \frac{\pi}{2}$	$1 + \tan^2\theta = \sec^2\theta$
$\sqrt{x^2 - a^2}$	$x = a\sec\theta$	$0 \leq \theta < \frac{\pi}{2}$ or $\pi \leq \theta < \frac{3\pi}{2}$	$\sec^2\theta - 1 = \tan^2\theta$

101. Start with the expression $\sqrt{a^2 - x^2}$ and let $x = a\sin\theta$, assuming $-\frac{\pi}{2} \leq \theta \leq \frac{\pi}{2}$. Simplify the original expression so that it contains no radicals.

102. Start with the expression $\sqrt{a^2 + x^2}$ and let $x = a\tan\theta$, assuming $-\frac{\pi}{2} < \theta < \frac{\pi}{2}$. Simplify the original expression so that it contains no radicals.

103. Start with the expression $\sqrt{x^2 - a^2}$ and let $x = a\sec\theta$, assuming $0 \leq \theta < \frac{\pi}{2}$. Simplify the original expression so that it contains no radicals.

104. Use a trigonometric substitution to simplify the expression $\sqrt{9 - x^2}$ so that it contains no radicals.

6.2 SUM AND DIFFERENCE IDENTITIES

SKILLS OBJECTIVES

- Find exact values for the cosine function using sum and difference identities.
- Find exact values for the sine function using sum and difference identities.
- Find exact values for the tangent function using the sum and difference identities for the tangent function.

CONCEPTUAL OBJECTIVES

- Understand that some sums or differences of trigonometric functions can be written as a single cosine expression.
- Understand that some sums or differences of trigonometric functions can be written as a single sine expression.
- Understand that the sum and difference identities for sine and cosine functions are used to derive the sum and difference identities for the tangent function.

In this section, we will consider trigonometric functions with arguments that are sums and differences. In general, $f(A + B) \neq f(A) + f(B)$. First, it is important to note that function notation is not distributive:

$$\cos(A + B) \neq \cos A + \cos B$$

This principle is easy to prove. Let $A = \pi$ and $B = 0$; then

$$\cos(A + B) = \cos(\pi + 0) = \cos(\pi) = -1$$

$$\cos A + \cos B = \cos\pi + \cos 0 = -1 + 1 = 0$$

In this section, we will derive some new and important identities.

- Sum and difference identities for the cosine, sine, and tangent functions
- Cofunction identities

We begin with the familiar distance formula, from which we can derive the sum and difference identities for the cosine function. From there we can derive the sum and difference formulas for the sine and tangent functions.

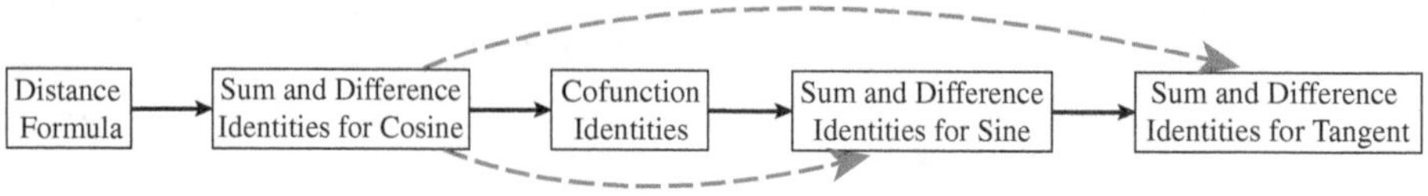

Before we start deriving and working with trigonometric sum and difference identities, let us first discuss why these are important. Sum and difference (and later product-to-sum and sum-to-product) identities are important because they allow calculation in functional (analytic) form and often lead to evaluating expressions *exactly* (as opposed to approximating them with calculators). The identities developed in this chapter are useful in such applications as musical sound, where they make it possible to determine the "beat" frequency. In calculus, these identities simplify the integration and differentiation processes.

6.2.1 SKILL

Find exact values for the cosine function using sum and difference identities.

6.2.1 CONCEPTUAL

Understand that some sums or differences of trigonometric functions can be written as a single cosine expression.

6.2.1 Sum and Difference Identities for the Cosine Function

Recall from Section 5.1 that the unit circle approach gave the relationship between the coordinates along the unit circle and the sine and cosine functions. Specifically, the x-coordinate corresponds to the value of the cosine function, and the y-coordinate corresponds to the value of the sine function.

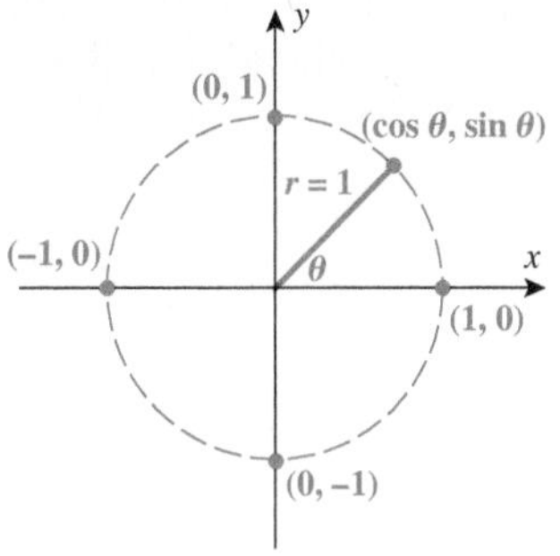

Let us now draw the unit circle with two angles α and β, realizing that the two terminal sides of these angles form a third angle, $\alpha - \beta$.

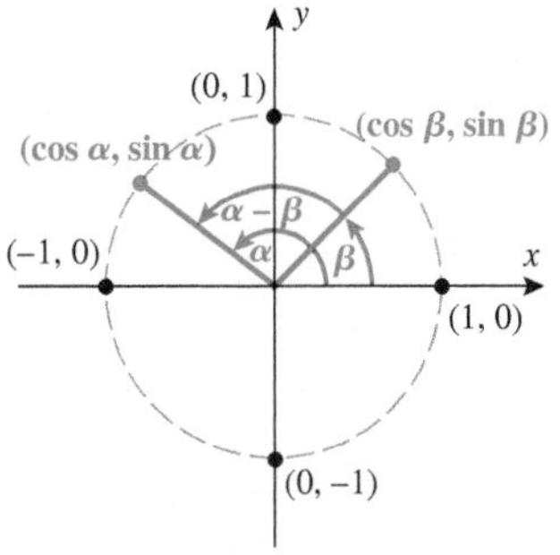

If we label the points $P_1 = (\cos\alpha, \sin\alpha)$ and $P_2 = (\cos\beta, \sin\beta)$, we can then draw a **segment** connecting points P_1 and P_2.

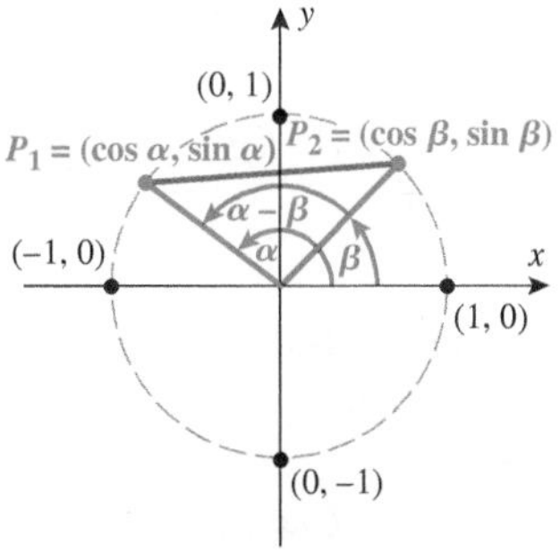

If we rotate the angle clockwise so the central angle $\alpha - \beta$ is in standard position, then the two points where the initial and terminal sides intersect the unit circle are $P_4 = (1, 0)$ and $P_3 = (\cos(\alpha - \beta), \sin(\alpha - \beta))$, respectively.

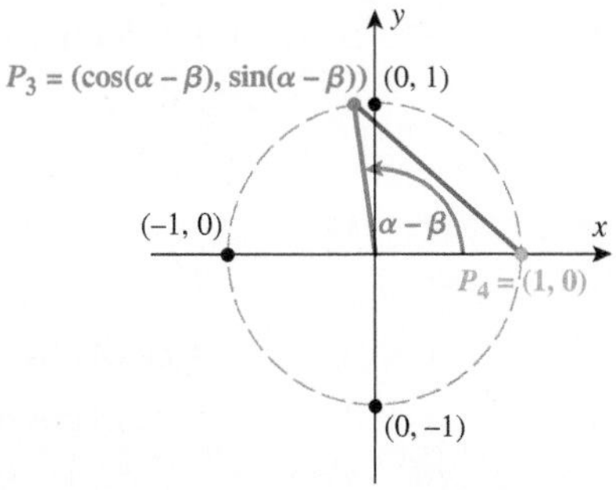

STUDY TIP

The distance from point $P_1 = (x_1, y_1)$ to point $P_2 = (x_2, y_2)$ is given by the distance formula $d(P_1, P_2) = \sqrt{(x_2 - x_1)^2 + (y_2 - y_1)^2}$.

The distance from P_1 to P_2 is equal to the length of the **segment** joining the points. Similarly, the distance from P_3 to P_4 is equal to the length of the **segment** joining the points. Since the lengths of the **segments** are equal, we say that the distances are equal: $d(P_1, P_2) = d(P_3, P_4)$.

WORDS	MATH
Set the distances (segment lengths) equal.	$d(P_1, P_2) = d(P_3, P_4)$
Apply the distance formula.	$\sqrt{(x_2 - x_1)^2 + (y_2 - y_1)^2} = \sqrt{(x_4 - x_3)^2 + (y_4 - y_3)^2}$

Substitute $P_1 = (x_1, y_1) = (\cos\alpha, \sin\alpha)$ and $P_2 = (x_2, y_2) = (\cos\beta, \sin\beta)$ into the left side of the equation and $P_3 = (x_3, y_3) = (\cos(\alpha - \beta), \sin(\alpha - \beta))$ and $P_4 = (x_4, y_4) = (1, 0)$ into the right side of the equation.

$$\sqrt{[\cos\beta - \cos\alpha]^2 + [\sin\beta - \sin\alpha]^2} = \sqrt{[1 - \cos(\alpha - \beta)]^2 + [0 - \sin(\alpha - \beta)]^2}$$

WORDS	MATH
Square both sides of the equation.	$[\cos\beta - \cos\alpha]^2 + [\sin\beta - \sin\alpha]^2 = [1 - \cos(\alpha - \beta)]^2 + [0 - \sin(\alpha - \beta)]^2$
Eliminate the brackets.	$\cos^2\beta - 2\cos\beta\cos\alpha + \cos^2\alpha + \sin^2\beta - 2\sin\beta\sin\alpha + \sin^2\alpha = 1 - 2\cos(\alpha - \beta) + \cos^2(\alpha - \beta) + \sin^2(\alpha - \beta)$
Regroup terms on each side and use the Pythagorean identity.	$\underbrace{\cos^2\alpha + \sin^2\alpha}_{1} - 2\cos\alpha\cos\beta - 2\sin\alpha\sin\beta + \underbrace{\cos^2\beta + \sin^2\beta}_{1} = 1 - 2\cos(\alpha - \beta) + \underbrace{\cos^2(\alpha - \beta) + \sin^2(\alpha - \beta)}_{1}$
Simplify.	$2 - 2\cos\alpha\cos\beta - 2\sin\alpha\sin\beta = 2 - 2\cos(\alpha - \beta)$
Subtract 2 from both sides.	$-2\cos\alpha\cos\beta - 2\sin\alpha\sin\beta = -2\cos(\alpha - \beta)$
Divide by -2.	$\cos\alpha\cos\beta + \sin\alpha\sin\beta = \cos(\alpha - \beta)$
Write the **difference identity for the cosine function**.	$\boxed{\cos(\alpha - \beta) = \cos\alpha\cos\beta + \sin\alpha\sin\beta}$

We can now derive the sum identity for the cosine function from the difference identity for the cosine function and the properties of even and odd functions.

WORDS	MATH
Apply the difference identity.	$\cos(\alpha + \beta) = \cos[\alpha - (-\beta)]$ $\cos(\alpha + \beta) = \cos\alpha\cos(-\beta) + \sin\alpha\sin(-\beta)$
Simplify the left side and use properties of even and odd functions on the right side.	$\cos(\alpha + \beta) = \cos\alpha(\cos\beta) + \sin\alpha(-\sin\beta)$
Write the **sum identity for the cosine function.**	$\boxed{\cos(\alpha + \beta) = \cos\alpha\cos\beta - \sin\alpha\sin\beta}$

SUM AND DIFFERENCE IDENTITIES FOR THE COSINE FUNCTION

Sum	$\cos(A + B) = \cos A\cos B - \sin A\sin B$
Difference	$\cos(A - B) = \cos A\cos B + \sin A\sin B$

EXAMPLE 1 Finding Exact Values for the Cosine Function

Evaluate each of the following cosine expressions exactly:

a. $\cos\left(\frac{7\pi}{12}\right)$

b. $\cos 15°$

Solution (a):

Write $\frac{7\pi}{12}$ as a sum of known "special" angles. $\cos\left(\frac{7\pi}{12}\right) = \cos\left(\frac{4\pi}{12} + \frac{3\pi}{12}\right)$

Simplify. $\cos\left(\frac{7\pi}{12}\right) = \cos\left(\frac{\pi}{3} + \frac{\pi}{4}\right)$

Write the sum identity for the cosine function. $\cos(A + B) = \cos A \cos B - \sin A \sin B$

Substitute $A = \frac{\pi}{3}$ and $B = \frac{\pi}{4}$. $\cos\left(\frac{7\pi}{12}\right) = \cos\left(\frac{\pi}{3}\right)\cos\left(\frac{\pi}{4}\right) - \sin\left(\frac{\pi}{3}\right)\sin\left(\frac{\pi}{4}\right)$

Evaluate the expressions on the right exactly. $\cos\left(\frac{7\pi}{12}\right) = \frac{1}{2}\frac{\sqrt{2}}{2} - \frac{\sqrt{3}}{2}\frac{\sqrt{2}}{2}$

Simplify. $\boxed{\cos\left(\frac{7\pi}{12}\right) = \frac{\sqrt{2} - \sqrt{6}}{4}}$

Solution (b):

Write 15° as a difference of known "special" angles. $\cos 15° = \cos(45° - 30°)$

Write the difference identity for the cosine function. $\cos(A - B) = \cos A \cos B + \sin A \sin B$

Substitute $A = 45°$ and $B = 30°$. $\cos 15° = \cos 45° \cos 30° + \sin 45° \sin 30°$

Evaluate the expressions on the right exactly. $\cos 15° = \frac{\sqrt{2}}{2}\frac{\sqrt{3}}{2} + \frac{\sqrt{2}}{2}\frac{1}{2}$

Simplify. $\boxed{\cos 15° = \frac{\sqrt{6} + \sqrt{2}}{4}}$

YOUR TURN Use the sum or difference identities for the cosine function to evaluate each cosine expression exactly.

a. $\cos\left(\frac{5\pi}{12}\right)$ **b.** $\cos 75°$

ANSWER

a. $\frac{\sqrt{6} - \sqrt{2}}{4}$

b. $\frac{\sqrt{6} - \sqrt{2}}{4}$

[CONCEPT CHECK]

TRUE OR FALSE

$\sin A \sin B - \cos A \cos B = -\cos(A + B)$

ANSWER True

Example 1 illustrates an important characteristic of the sum and difference identities: We can now find the exact trigonometric function value of angles that are multiples of $15°\left(\text{or, equivalently, } \frac{\pi}{12}\right)$, since each of these can be written as a sum or difference of angles for which we know the trigonometric function values exactly.

EXAMPLE 2 **Writing a Sum or Difference as a Single Cosine Expression**

Use the sum or the difference identity for the cosine function to write each of the following expressions as a single cosine expression:

a. $\sin(5x)\sin(2x) + \cos(5x)\cos(2x)$

b. $\cos x\cos(3x) - \sin x\sin(3x)$

Solution (a):

Because of the positive sign, this will be a cosine of a difference.

Reverse the expression and write the formula. $\cos A\cos B + \sin A\sin B = \cos(A - B)$

Identify A and B. $A = 5x$ and $B = 2x$

Substitute $A = 5x$ and $B = 2x$ into the difference identity. $\cos(5x)\cos(2x) + \sin(5x)\sin(2x) = \cos(5x - 2x)$

Simplify. $\cos(5x)\cos(2x) + \sin(5x)\sin(2x) = \boxed{\cos(3x)}$

Notice that if we had selected $A = 2x$ and $B = 5x$ instead, the result would have been $\cos(-3x)$, but since the cosine function is an even function, this would have simplified to $\cos(3x)$.

Solution (b):

Because of the negative sign, this will be a cosine of a sum.

Reverse the expression and write the formula. $\cos A\cos B - \sin A\sin B = \cos(A + B)$

Identify A and B. $A = x$ and $B = 3x$

Substitute $A = x$ and $B = 3x$ into the sum identity. $\cos x\cos(3x) - \sin x\sin(3x) = \cos(x + 3x)$

Simplify. $\cos x\cos(3x) - \sin x\sin(3x) = \boxed{\cos(4x)}$

ANSWER
$\cos(3x)$

YOUR TURN Write as a single cosine expression.

$$\cos(4x)\cos(7x) + \sin(4x)\sin(7x)$$

6.2.2 Sum and Difference Identities for the Sine Function

6.2.2 SKILL

Find exact values for the sine function using sum and difference identities.

6.2.2 CONCEPTUAL

Understand that some sums or differences of trigonometric functions can be written as a single sine expression.

We can now use the cofunction identities (Section 6.1) together with the sum and difference identities for the cosine function to develop the sum and difference identities for the sine function.

WORDS	MATH
Start with the cofunction identity.	$\sin\theta = \cos\left(\frac{\pi}{2} - \theta\right)$
Let $\theta = A + B$.	$\sin(A + B) = \cos\left[\frac{\pi}{2} - (A + B)\right]$
Regroup the terms in the cosine expression.	$\sin(A + B) = \cos\left[\left(\frac{\pi}{2} - A\right) - B\right]$
Use the difference identity for the cosine function.	$\sin(A + B) = \cos\left(\frac{\pi}{2} - A\right)\cos B + \sin\left(\frac{\pi}{2} - A\right)\sin B$
Use the cofunction identities.	$\sin(A + B) = \underbrace{\cos\left(\frac{\pi}{2} - A\right)}_{\sin A}\cos B + \underbrace{\sin\left(\frac{\pi}{2} - A\right)}_{\cos A}\sin B$
Simplify.	$\boxed{\sin(A + B) = \sin A\cos B + \cos A\sin B}$

Now we can derive the difference identity for the sine function using the sum identity for the sine function and the properties of even and odd functions.

WORDS	MATH
Replace B with $-B$ in the sum identity.	$\sin(A + (-B)) = \sin A\cos(-B) + \cos A\sin(-B)$
Simplify using even and odd identities.	$\boxed{\sin(A - B) = \sin A\cos B - \cos A\sin B}$

SUM AND DIFFERENCE IDENTITIES FOR THE SINE FUNCTION

Sum	$\sin(A + B) = \sin A\cos B + \cos A\sin B$
Difference	$\sin(A - B) = \sin A\cos B - \cos A\sin B$

EXAMPLE 3 Finding Exact Values for the Sine Function

Use the sum or the difference identity for the sine function to evaluate each sine expression exactly.

a. $\sin\left(\frac{5\pi}{12}\right)$ **b.** $\sin 75°$

Solution (a):

Write $\frac{5\pi}{12}$ as a sum of known "special" angles. $\sin\left(\frac{5\pi}{12}\right) = \sin\left(\frac{2\pi}{12} + \frac{3\pi}{12}\right)$

Simplify. $\sin\left(\frac{5\pi}{12}\right) = \sin\left(\frac{\pi}{6} + \frac{\pi}{4}\right)$

Write the sum identity for the sine function. $\sin(A + B) = \sin A\cos B + \cos A\sin B$

Substitute $A = \frac{\pi}{6}$ and $B = \frac{\pi}{4}$. $\sin\left(\frac{5\pi}{12}\right) = \sin\left(\frac{\pi}{6}\right)\cos\left(\frac{\pi}{4}\right) + \cos\left(\frac{\pi}{6}\right)\sin\left(\frac{\pi}{4}\right)$

[CONCEPT CHECK]

TRUE OR FALSE
$\sin(A - B) = \sin(B - A)$

ANSWER False

Evaluate the expressions on the right exactly.	$\sin\left(\frac{5\pi}{12}\right) = \left(\frac{1}{2}\right)\left(\frac{\sqrt{2}}{2}\right) + \left(\frac{\sqrt{3}}{2}\right)\left(\frac{\sqrt{2}}{2}\right)$
Simplify.	$\boxed{\sin\left(\frac{5\pi}{12}\right) = \frac{\sqrt{2}+\sqrt{6}}{4}}$

Solution (b):

Write 75° as a sum of known "special" angles.	$\sin 75° = \sin(45° + 30°)$
Write the sum identity for the sine function.	$\sin(A + B) = \sin A \cos B + \cos A \sin B$
Substitute $A = 45°$ and $B = 30°$.	$\sin 75° = \sin 45° \cos 30° + \cos 45° \sin 30°$
Evaluate the expressions on the right exactly.	$\sin 75° = \left(\frac{\sqrt{2}}{2}\right)\left(\frac{\sqrt{3}}{2}\right) + \left(\frac{\sqrt{2}}{2}\right)\left(\frac{1}{2}\right)$
Simplify.	$\boxed{\sin 75° = \frac{\sqrt{6}+\sqrt{2}}{4}}$

YOUR TURN Use the sum or the difference identity for the sine function to evaluate the sine expressions exactly.

a. $\sin\left(\frac{7\pi}{12}\right)$ **b.** $\sin 15°$

ANSWER

a. $\frac{\sqrt{6}+\sqrt{2}}{4}$

b. $\frac{\sqrt{6}-\sqrt{2}}{4}$

We see in Example 3 that the sum and difference identities allow us to calculate exact values for trigonometric functions of angles that are multiples of $15°\left(\text{or, equivalently, } \frac{\pi}{12}\right)$, as we saw with the cosine function.

EXAMPLE 4 **Writing a Sum or Difference as a Single Sine Expression**

Graph $y = 3\sin x \cos(3x) + 3\cos x \sin(3x)$.

Solution:

Use the sum identity for the sine function to write the expression as a single sine expression.

Factor out the common 3.	$y = 3[\sin x \cos(3x) + \cos x \sin(3x)]$
Write the sum identity for the sine function.	$\sin A \cos B + \cos A \sin B = \sin(A + B)$
Identify A and B.	$A = x \quad \text{and} \quad B = 3x$
Substitute $A = x$ and $B = 3x$ into the sum identity.	$\sin x \cos(3x) + \cos x \sin(3x) = \sin(x + 3x) = \sin(4x)$
Simplify.	$y = 3[\underbrace{\sin x \cos(3x) + \cos x \sin(3x)}_{\sin(4x)}]$

Graph $y = 3\sin(4x)$.

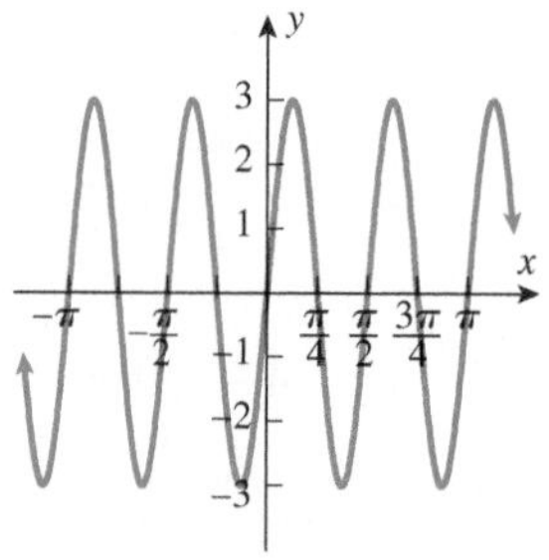

6.2.3 Sum and Difference Identities for the Tangent Function

We now develop the sum and difference identities for the tangent function.

WORDS	MATH
Start with the quotient identity.	$\tan x = \dfrac{\sin x}{\cos x}$
Let $x = A + B$.	$\tan(A + B) = \dfrac{\sin(A + B)}{\cos(A + B)}$
Use the sum identities for the sine and cosine functions.	$\tan(A + B) = \dfrac{\sin A \cos B + \cos A \sin B}{\cos A \cos B - \sin A \sin B}$
Multiply the numerator and denominator by $\dfrac{1}{\cos A \cos B}$.	$\tan(A + B) = \dfrac{\dfrac{\sin A \cos B + \cos A \sin B}{\cos A \cos B}}{\dfrac{\cos A \cos B - \sin A \sin B}{\cos A \cos B}} = \dfrac{\dfrac{\sin A \cancel{\cos B}}{\cos A \cancel{\cos B}} + \dfrac{\cancel{\cos A} \sin B}{\cancel{\cos A} \cos B}}{\dfrac{\cancel{\cos A \cos B}}{\cancel{\cos A \cos B}} - \dfrac{\sin A \sin B}{\cos A \cos B}}$
Simplify.	$\tan(A + B) = \dfrac{\left(\dfrac{\sin A}{\cos A}\right) + \left(\dfrac{\sin B}{\cos B}\right)}{1 - \left(\dfrac{\sin A}{\cos A}\right)\left(\dfrac{\sin B}{\cos B}\right)}$
Write the expressions inside the parentheses in terms of the tangent function.	$\boxed{\tan(A + B) = \dfrac{\tan A + \tan B}{1 - \tan A \tan B}}$
Replace B with $-B$.	$\tan(A - B) = \dfrac{\tan A + \tan(-B)}{1 - \tan A \tan(-B)}$
Since the tangent function is an odd function, $\tan(-B) = -\tan B$.	$\boxed{\tan(A - B) = \dfrac{\tan A - \tan B}{1 + \tan A \tan B}}$

SUM AND DIFFERENCE IDENTITIES FOR THE TANGENT FUNCTION

Sum	$\tan(A + B) = \dfrac{\tan A + \tan B}{1 - \tan A \tan B}$
Difference	$\tan(A - B) = \dfrac{\tan A - \tan B}{1 + \tan A \tan B}$

6.2.3 SKILL

Find exact values for the tangent function using the sum and difference identities for the tangent function.

6.2.3 CONCEPTUAL

Understand that the sum and difference identities for sine and cosine functions are used to derive the sum and difference identities for the tangent function.

EXAMPLE 5 Finding Exact Values for the Tangent Function

Find the exact value of $\tan(\alpha + \beta)$ if $\sin\alpha = -\frac{1}{3}$ and $\cos\beta = -\frac{1}{4}$, and the terminal side of α lies in quadrant III and the terminal side of β lies in quadrant II.

Solution:

STEP 1 Write the sum identity for the tangent function.

$$\tan(\alpha + \beta) = \frac{\tan\alpha + \tan\beta}{1 - \tan\alpha\tan\beta}$$

STEP 2 Find $\tan\alpha$.

The terminal side of α lies in quadrant III.

$$\sin\alpha = \frac{y}{r} = -\frac{1}{3}.$$

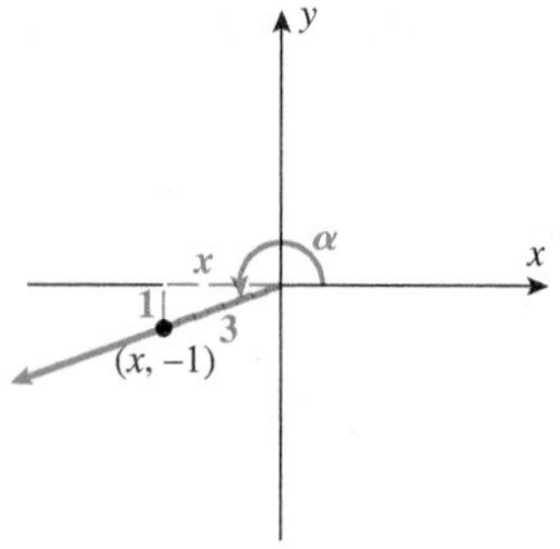

Solve for x. (Recall $x^2 + y^2 = r^2$.)

$$x^2 + (-1)^2 = 3^2$$
$$x = \pm\sqrt{8}$$

Take the negative sign since x is negative in quadrant III.

$$x = -2\sqrt{2}$$

Find $\tan\alpha$.

$$\tan\alpha = \frac{y}{x} = \frac{-1}{-2\sqrt{2}} = \frac{1}{2\sqrt{2}}\cdot\frac{\sqrt{2}}{\sqrt{2}} = \frac{\sqrt{2}}{4}$$

[CONCEPT CHECK]

TRUE OR FALSE

$\tan(A - B) = -\tan(B - A)$

ANSWER True

STEP 3 Find $\tan\beta$.

The terminal side of β lies in quadrant II.

$$\cos\beta = -\frac{1}{4} = \frac{x}{r}.$$

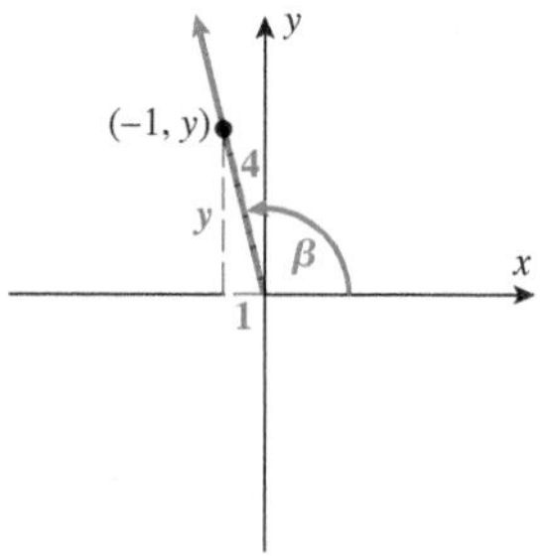

Solve for y. (Recall $x^2 + y^2 = r^2$.)

$$(-1)^2 + y^2 = 4^2$$
$$y = \pm\sqrt{15}$$

Take the positive sign since y is positive in quadrant II.

$$y = \sqrt{15}$$

Find $\tan\beta$.

$$\tan\beta = \frac{y}{x} = \frac{\sqrt{15}}{-1} = -\sqrt{15}$$

STEP 4 Substitute $\tan\alpha = \frac{\sqrt{2}}{4}$ and $\tan\beta = -\sqrt{15}$ into the sum identity for the tangent function.

$$\tan(\alpha + \beta) = \frac{\frac{\sqrt{2}}{4} - \sqrt{15}}{1 - \left(\frac{\sqrt{2}}{4}\right)(-\sqrt{15})}$$

Multiply the numerator and the denominator by 4.

$$\tan(\alpha + \beta) = \frac{4}{4}\frac{\left(\frac{\sqrt{2}}{4} - \sqrt{15}\right)}{\left(1 + \frac{\sqrt{30}}{4}\right)}$$

$$= \frac{\sqrt{2} - 4\sqrt{15}}{4 + \sqrt{30}}$$

The expression $\boxed{\tan(\alpha + \beta) = \frac{\sqrt{2} - 4\sqrt{15}}{4 + \sqrt{30}}}$ can be simplified further if we rationalize the denominator.

It is important to note in Example 5 that right triangles have been superimposed in the Cartesian plane. The coordinate pair (x, y) can have positive or negative values, but the radius r is always positive. When right triangles are superimposed, with one vertex at the point (x, y) and another vertex at the origin, it is important to understand that triangles have positive side lengths.

[SECTION 6.2] SUMMARY

In this section, we derived the sum and difference identities for the cosine function using the distance formula. The cofunction identities and sum and difference identities for the cosine function were used to derive the sum and difference identities for the sine function. We combined the sine and cosine sum and difference identities to determine the tangent sum and difference identities. The sum and difference identities enabled us to evaluate a trigonometric expression exactly for any multiple of $15°\left(\text{i.e.}, \frac{\pi}{12}\right)$.

$$\cos(A + B) = \cos A \cos B - \sin A \sin B$$
$$\cos(A - B) = \cos A \cos B + \sin A \sin B$$
$$\sin(A + B) = \sin A \cos B + \cos A \sin B$$
$$\sin(A - B) = \sin A \cos B - \cos A \sin B$$
$$\tan(A + B) = \frac{\tan A + \tan B}{1 - \tan A \tan B}$$
$$\tan(A - B) = \frac{\tan A - \tan B}{1 + \tan A \tan B}$$

[SECTION 6.2] EXERCISES

• SKILLS

In Exercises 1–16, find the exact value for each trigonometric expression.

1. $\sin\left(\frac{\pi}{12}\right)$
2. $\cos\left(\frac{\pi}{12}\right)$
3. $\cos\left(-\frac{5\pi}{12}\right)$
4. $\sin\left(-\frac{5\pi}{12}\right)$
5. $\tan\left(-\frac{\pi}{12}\right)$
6. $\tan\left(\frac{13\pi}{12}\right)$
7. $\sin 105°$
8. $\cos 195°$
9. $\tan(-105°)$
10. $\tan 165°$
11. $\cot\left(\frac{\pi}{12}\right)$
12. $\cot\left(-\frac{5\pi}{12}\right)$
13. $\sec\left(-\frac{11\pi}{12}\right)$
14. $\sec\left(-\frac{13\pi}{12}\right)$
15. $\csc(-255°)$
16. $\csc(-15°)$

In Exercises 17–28, write each expression as a single trigonometric function.

17. $\sin(2x)\sin(3x) + \cos(2x)\cos(3x)$
18. $\sin x\sin(2x) - \cos x\cos(2x)$
19. $\sin x\cos(2x) - \cos x\sin(2x)$
20. $\sin(2x)\cos(3x) + \cos(2x)\sin(3x)$
21. $\cos(\pi - x)\sin x + \sin(\pi - x)\cos x$
22. $\sin\left(\frac{\pi}{3}x\right)\cos\left(-\frac{\pi}{2}x\right) - \cos\left(\frac{\pi}{3}x\right)\sin\left(-\frac{\pi}{2}x\right)$
23. $(\sin A - \sin B)^2 + (\cos A - \cos B)^2 - 2$
24. $(\sin A + \sin B)^2 + (\cos A + \cos B)^2 - 2$
25. $2 - (\sin A + \cos B)^2 - (\cos A + \sin B)^2$
26. $2 - (\sin A - \cos B)^2 - (\cos A + \sin B)^2$
27. $\frac{\tan 49° - \tan 23°}{1 + \tan 49° \tan 23°}$
28. $\frac{\tan 49° + \tan 23°}{1 - \tan 49° \tan 23°}$

In Exercises 29–34, find the exact value of the indicated expression using the given information and identities.

29. Find the exact value of $\cos(\alpha + \beta)$ if $\cos\alpha = -\frac{1}{3}$ and $\cos\beta = -\frac{1}{4}$, and the terminal side of α lies in quadrant III and the terminal side of β lies in quadrant II.

30. Find the exact value of $\cos(\alpha - \beta)$ if $\cos\alpha = \frac{1}{3}$ and $\cos\beta = -\frac{1}{4}$, and the terminal side of α lies in quadrant IV and the terminal side of β lies in quadrant II.

31. Find the exact value of $\sin(\alpha - \beta)$ if $\sin\alpha = -\frac{3}{5}$ and $\sin\beta = \frac{1}{5}$, and the terminal side of α lies in quadrant III and the terminal side of β lies in quadrant I.

32. Find the exact value of $\sin(\alpha + \beta)$ if $\sin\alpha = -\frac{3}{5}$ and $\sin\beta = \frac{1}{5}$, and the terminal side of α lies in quadrant III and the terminal side of β lies in quadrant II.

33. Find the exact value of $\tan(\alpha + \beta)$ if $\sin\alpha = -\frac{3}{5}$ and $\cos\beta = -\frac{1}{4}$, and the terminal side of α lies in quadrant III and the terminal side of β lies in quadrant II.

34. Find the exact value of $\tan(\alpha - \beta)$ if $\sin\alpha = -\frac{3}{5}$ and $\cos\beta = -\frac{1}{4}$, and the terminal side of α lies in quadrant III and the terminal side of β lies in quadrant II.

In Exercises 35–52, determine whether each equation is a conditional equation or an identity.

35. $\sin(A + B) + \sin(A - B) = 2\sin A\cos B$

36. $\cos(A + B) + \cos(A - B) = 2\cos A\cos B$

37. $\sin\left(x - \frac{\pi}{2}\right) = \cos\left(x + \frac{\pi}{2}\right)$

38. $\sin\left(x + \frac{\pi}{2}\right) = \cos\left(x + \frac{\pi}{2}\right)$

39. $\frac{\sqrt{2}}{2}(\sin x + \cos x) = \sin\left(x + \frac{\pi}{4}\right)$

40. $\sqrt{3}\cos x + \sin x = 2\cos\left(x + \frac{\pi}{3}\right)$

41. $\sin^2 x = \frac{1 - \cos(2x)}{2}$

42. $\cos^2 x = \frac{1 + \cos(2x)}{2}$

43. $\sin(2x) = 2\sin x\cos x$

44. $\cos(2x) = \cos^2 x - \sin^2 x$

45. $\sin(A + B) = \sin A + \sin B$

46. $\cos(A + B) = \cos A + \cos B$

47. $\tan(\pi + B) = \tan B$

48. $\tan(A - \pi) = \tan A$

49. $\cot(3\pi + x) = \frac{1}{\tan x}$

50. $\csc(2x) = 2\sec x\csc x$

51. $\frac{1 + \tan x}{1 - \tan x} = \tan\left(x - \frac{\pi}{4}\right)$

52. $\cot\left(x + \frac{\pi}{4}\right) = \frac{1 - \tan x}{1 + \tan x}$

In Exercises 53–62, graph each of the functions by first rewriting it as a sine, cosine, or tangent of a difference or sum.

53. $y = \cos\left(\frac{\pi}{3}\right)\sin x + \cos x\sin\left(\frac{\pi}{3}\right)$

54. $y = \cos\left(\frac{\pi}{3}\right)\sin x - \cos x\sin\left(\frac{\pi}{3}\right)$

55. $y = \sin x\sin\left(\frac{\pi}{4}\right) + \cos x\cos\left(\frac{\pi}{4}\right)$

56. $y = \sin x\sin\left(\frac{\pi}{4}\right) - \cos x\cos\left(\frac{\pi}{4}\right)$

57. $y = -\sin x\cos(3x) - \cos x\sin(3x)$

58. $y = \sin x\sin(3x) + \cos x\cos(3x)$

59. $y = \frac{1 + \tan x}{1 - \tan x}$

60. $y = \frac{\sqrt{3} - \tan x}{1 + \sqrt{3}\tan x}$

61. $y = \frac{1 + \sqrt{3}\tan x}{\sqrt{3} - \tan x}$

62. $y = \frac{1 - \tan x}{1 + \tan x}$

• APPLICATIONS

In Exercises 63 and 64, refer to the following:

Sum and difference identities can be used to simplify more complicated expressions. For instance, the sine and cosine function can be represented by infinite polynomials called power series.

$$\cos x = 1 - \frac{x^2}{2!} + \frac{x^4}{4!} - \frac{x^6}{6!} + \frac{x^8}{8!} - \cdots$$

$$\sin x = x - \frac{x^3}{3!} + \frac{x^5}{5!} - \frac{x^7}{7!} + \frac{x^9}{9!} - \cdots$$

63. Power Series. Find the power series that represents $\cos\left(x - \frac{\pi}{4}\right)$.

64. Power Series. Find the power series that represents $\sin\left(x + \frac{3\pi}{2}\right)$.

For Exercises 65 and 66, use the following:

A nonvertical line makes an angle with the x-axis. In the figure, we see that the line L_1 makes an acute angle θ_1 with the x-axis. Similarly, the line L_2 makes an acute angle θ_2 with the x-axis.

$\tan\theta_1 = \text{slope of } L_1 = m_1$

$\tan\theta_2 = \text{slope of } L_2 = m_2$

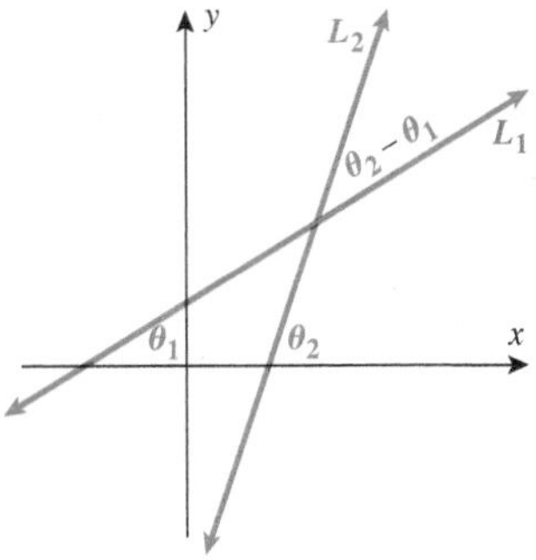

65. Angle between Two Lines. Show that

$$\tan(\theta_2 - \theta_1) = \frac{m_2 - m_1}{1 + m_1 m_2}$$

66. Relating Tangent and Slope. Show that

$$\tan(\theta_1 - \theta_2) = \frac{m_1 - m_2}{1 + m_1 m_2}$$

For Exercises 67 and 68, refer to the following:

An electric field E of a wave with constant amplitude A, propagating a distance z, is given by

$$E = A\cos(kz - ct)$$

where k is the propagation wave number, which is related to the wavelength λ by $k = \frac{2\pi}{\lambda}$, and where $c = 3.0 \times 10^8$ m/s is the speed of light in a vacuum, and t is time in seconds.

67. Electromagnetic Wave Propagation. Use the cosine difference identity to express the electric field in terms of both sine and cosine functions. When the quotients of the propagation distance z and the wavelength λ are equal to an integer, what do you notice?

68. Electromagnetic Wave Propagation. Use the cosine difference identity to express the electric field in terms of both sine and cosine functions. When $t = 0$, what do you notice?

69. Biology. By analyzing available empirical data, it has been determined that the body temperature of a species fluctuates according to the model

$$T(t) = 38 - 2.5\cos\left[\frac{\pi}{6}(t - 3)\right], \quad 0 \le t \le 24$$

where T represents temperature in degrees Celsius and t represents time (in hours) measured from 12:00 P.M. (noon). Use an identity to express $T(t)$ in terms of the sine function.

70. Health/Medicine. During the course of treatment of an illness, the concentration of a drug (in micrograms per milliliter) in the bloodstream fluctuates during the dosing period of 8 hours according to the model

$$C(t) = 15.4 - 4.7\sin\left(\frac{\pi}{4}t + \frac{\pi}{2}\right), \quad 0 \le t \le 8$$

Use an identity to express the concentration $C(t)$ in terms of the cosine function.

Note: This model does not apply to the first dose of the medication, because there will be no medication in the bloodstream.

• CATCH THE MISTAKE

In Exercises 71 and 72, explain the mistake that is made.

71. Find the exact value of $\tan\left(\frac{5\pi}{12}\right)$.

Solution:

Write $\frac{5\pi}{12}$ as a sum. $\quad \tan\left(\frac{\pi}{4}+\frac{\pi}{6}\right)$

Distribute. $\quad \tan\left(\frac{\pi}{4}\right)+\tan\left(\frac{\pi}{6}\right)$

Evaluate the tangent function for $\frac{\pi}{4}$ and $\frac{\pi}{6}$. $\quad 1+\frac{\sqrt{3}}{3}$

This is incorrect. What mistake was made?

72. Find the exact value of $\tan\left(-\frac{7\pi}{6}\right)$.

Solution:

The tangent function is an even function. $\quad \tan\left(\frac{7\pi}{6}\right)$

Write $\frac{7\pi}{6}$ as a sum. $\quad \tan\left(\pi+\frac{\pi}{6}\right)$

Use the tangent sum identity: $\tan(A+B)=\frac{\tan A+\tan B}{1-\tan A\tan B}$. $\quad \frac{\tan\pi+\tan\left(\frac{\pi}{6}\right)}{1-\tan\pi\tan\left(\frac{\pi}{6}\right)}$

Evaluate the tangent functions on the right. $\quad \frac{0+\frac{1}{\sqrt{3}}}{1-0}$

Simplify. $\quad \frac{\sqrt{3}}{3}$

This is incorrect. What mistake was made?

• CONCEPTUAL

In Exercises 73–76, determine whether each statement is true or false.

73. $\cos 15° = \cos 45° - \cos 30°$

74. $\sin\left(\frac{\pi}{2}\right) = \sin\left(\frac{\pi}{3}\right)+\sin\left(\frac{\pi}{6}\right)$

75. $\tan\left(x+\frac{\pi}{4}\right) = 1+\tan x$

76. $\cot\left(\frac{\pi}{4}-x\right) = \frac{1+\tan x}{1-\tan x}$

• CHALLENGE

77. Verify that $\sin(A+B+C) = \sin A\cos B\cos C + \cos A\sin B\cos C + \cos A\cos B\sin C - \sin A\sin B\sin C$.

78. Verify that $\cos(A+B+C) = \cos A\cos B\cos C - \sin A\sin B\cos C - \sin A\cos B\sin C - \cos A\sin B\sin C$.

79. Although in general the statement $\sin(A-B) = \sin A - \sin B$ is not true, it is true for some values. Determine some values of A and B that make this statement true.

80. Although in general the statement $\sin(A+B) = \sin A + \sin B$ is not true, it is true for some values. Determine some values of A and B that make this statement true.

• PREVIEW TO CALCULUS

In calculus, one technique used to solve differential equations consists of the separation of variables. For example, consider the equation $x^2 + 3y\frac{f(y)}{g(x)} = 0$, which is equivalent to $3yf(y) = -x^2g(x)$. Here each side of the equation contains only one type of variable, either x or y.

In Exercises 81–84, use the sum and difference identities to separate the variables in each equation.

81. $\sin(x+y) = 0$

82. $\cos(x-y) = 0$

83. $\tan(x+y) = 2$

84. $\cos(x+y) = \sin y$

6.3 DOUBLE-ANGLE AND HALF-ANGLE IDENTITIES

SKILLS OBJECTIVES

- Use double-angle identities in simplifying some trigonometric expressions.
- Use half-angle identities in simplifying some trigonometric expressions.

CONCEPTUAL OBJECTIVES

- Understand that the double-angle identities are derived from the sum identities.
- Understand that the half-angle identities are derived from the double-angle identities.

6.3.1 Double-Angle Identities

Previously, we could only evaluate trigonometric functions exactly for reference angles of 30°, 45°, and 60° or $\frac{\pi}{6}, \frac{\pi}{4}$, and $\frac{\pi}{3}$. We now can include multiples of $\frac{\pi}{12}$ among these "special" angles. We can use *double-angle identities* to also evaluate the trigonometric function values for other angles that are even integer multiples of the special angles or to verify other trigonometric identities. One important distinction now is that we will be able to find exact values of many functions using the double-angle identities without needing to know the value of the angle.

6.3.1 SKILL

Use double-angle identities in simplifying some trigonometric expressions.

6.3.1 CONCEPTUAL

Understand that the double-angle identities are derived from the sum identities.

Derivation of Double-Angle Identities

To derive the double-angle identities, we let $A = B$ in the sum identities.

WORDS	MATH
Write the identity for the sine of a sum.	$\sin(A + B) = \sin A \cos B + \cos A \sin B$
Let $B = A$.	$\sin(A + A) = \sin A \cos A + \cos A \sin A$
Simplify.	$\boxed{\sin(2A) = 2\sin A \cos A}$
Write the identity for the cosine of a sum.	$\cos(A + B) = \cos A \cos B - \sin A \sin B$
Let $B = A$.	$\cos(A + A) = \cos A \cos A - \sin A \sin A$
Simplify.	$\boxed{\cos(2A) = \cos^2 A - \sin^2 A}$

We can write the double-angle identity for the cosine function two other ways if we use the Pythagorean identity:

1. Write the identity for the cosine function of a double angle. $\quad \cos(2A) = \cos^2 A - \sin^2 A$

   Use the Pythagorean identity for the cosine function. $\quad \cos(2A) = \underbrace{\cos^2 A}_{1 - \sin^2 A} - \sin^2 A$

   Simplify. $\quad \boxed{\cos(2A) = 1 - 2\sin^2 A}$

2. Write the identity for the cosine function of a double angle. $\cos(2A) = \cos^2 A - \sin^2 A$

   Use the Pythagorean identity for the sine function. $\cos(2A) = \cos^2 A - \underbrace{\sin^2 A}_{1-\cos^2 A}$

   Simplify. $\boxed{\cos(2A) = 2\cos^2 A - 1}$

The tangent function can always be written as a quotient, $\tan(2A) = \dfrac{\sin(2A)}{\cos(2A)}$, if $\sin(2A)$ and $\cos(2A)$ are known. Here we write the double-angle identity for the tangent function in terms of only the tangent function.

[CONCEPT CHECK]

TRUE OR FALSE The double-angle identities are derived by using the sum identities with $B = A$.

ANSWER True

Write the tangent of a sum identity. $\tan(A + B) = \dfrac{\tan A + \tan B}{1 - \tan A \tan B}$

Let $B = A$. $\tan(A + A) = \dfrac{\tan A + \tan A}{1 - \tan A \tan A}$

Simplify. $\boxed{\tan(2A) = \dfrac{2\tan A}{1 - \tan^2 A}}$

DOUBLE-ANGLE IDENTITIES

SINE	COSINE	TANGENT
$\sin(2A) = 2\sin A\cos A$	$\cos(2A) = \cos^2 A - \sin^2 A$	$\tan(2A) = \dfrac{2\tan A}{1 - \tan^2 A}$
	$\cos(2A) = 1 - 2\sin^2 A$	
	$\cos(2A) = 2\cos^2 A - 1$	

Applying Double-Angle Identities

EXAMPLE 1 **Finding Exact Values Using Double-Angle Identities**

If $\cos x = \frac{2}{3}$, find $\sin(2x)$ given $\sin x < 0$.

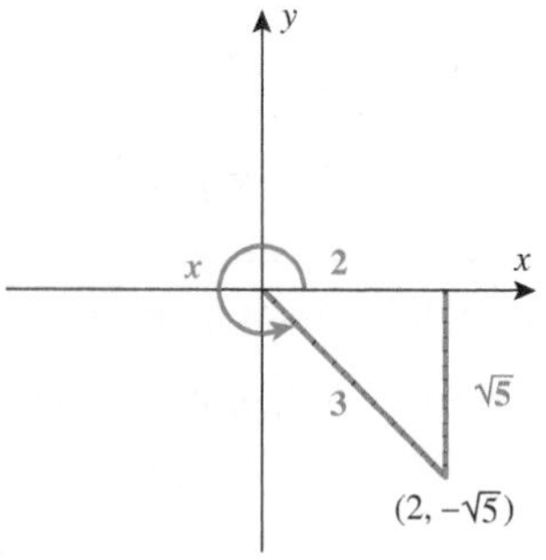

Solution:

Find $\sin x$.

Use the Pythagorean identity. $\sin^2 x + \cos^2 x = 1$

Substitute $\cos x = \frac{2}{3}$. $\sin^2 x + \left(\dfrac{2}{3}\right)^2 = 1$

Solve for $\sin x$, which is negative. $\sin x = -\sqrt{1 - \dfrac{4}{9}}$

Simplify. $\sin x = -\dfrac{\sqrt{5}}{3}$

Find $\sin(2x)$.

Use the double-angle formula for the sine function. $\sin(2x) = 2\sin x \cos x$

Substitute $\sin x = -\frac{\sqrt{5}}{3}$ and $\cos x = \frac{2}{3}$. $\sin(2x) = 2\left(-\frac{\sqrt{5}}{3}\right)\left(\frac{2}{3}\right)$

Simplify. $\boxed{\sin(2x) = -\frac{4\sqrt{5}}{9}}$

YOUR TURN If $\cos x = -\frac{1}{3}$, find $\sin(2x)$ given $\sin x < 0$.

ANSWER

$\sin(2x) = \frac{4\sqrt{2}}{9}$

EXAMPLE 2 Finding Exact Values Using Double-Angle Identities

If $\sin x = -\frac{4}{5}$ and $\cos x < 0$, find $\sin(2x)$, $\cos(2x)$, and $\tan(2x)$.

Solution:

Solve for $\cos x$.

Use the Pythagorean identity. $\sin^2 x + \cos^2 x = 1$

Substitute $\sin x = -\frac{4}{5}$. $\left(-\frac{4}{5}\right)^2 + \cos^2 x = 1$

Simplify. $\cos^2 x = \frac{9}{25}$

Solve for $\cos x$, which is negative. $\cos x = -\sqrt{\frac{9}{25}} = -\frac{3}{5}$

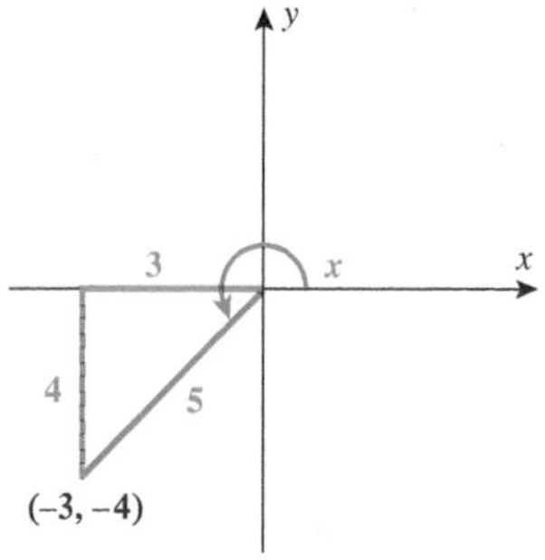

Find $\sin(2x)$.

Use the double-angle identity for the sine function. $\sin(2x) = 2\sin x \cos x$

Substitute $\sin x = -\frac{4}{5}$ and $\cos x = -\frac{3}{5}$. $\sin(2x) = 2\left(-\frac{4}{5}\right)\left(-\frac{3}{5}\right)$

Simplify. $\boxed{\sin(2x) = \frac{24}{25}}$

Find $\cos(2x)$.

Use the double-angle identity for the cosine function. $\cos(2x) = \cos^2 x - \sin^2 x$

Substitute $\sin x = -\frac{4}{5}$ and $\cos x = -\frac{3}{5}$. $\cos(2x) = \left(-\frac{3}{5}\right)^2 - \left(-\frac{4}{5}\right)^2$

Simplify. $\boxed{\cos(2x) = -\frac{7}{25}}$

Find $\tan(2x)$.

Use the quotient identity.	$\tan\theta = \dfrac{\sin\theta}{\cos\theta}$
Let $\theta = 2x$.	$\tan(2x) = \dfrac{\sin(2x)}{\cos(2x)}$
Substitute $\sin(2x) = \frac{24}{25}$ and $\cos(2x) = -\frac{7}{25}$.	$\tan(2x) = \dfrac{\frac{24}{25}}{-\frac{7}{25}}$
Simplify.	$\boxed{\tan(2x) = -\dfrac{24}{7}}$

Note: We could also have found $\tan(2x)$ first by finding $\tan x = \dfrac{\sin x}{\cos x}$ and then using the value for $\tan x$ in the double-angle identity, $\tan(2A) = \dfrac{2\tan A}{1 - \tan^2 A}$.

YOUR TURN If $\cos x = \frac{3}{5}$ and $\sin x < 0$, find $\sin(2x)$, $\cos(2x)$, and $\tan(2x)$.

ANSWER
$\sin(2x) = -\frac{24}{25}$,
$\cos(2x) = -\frac{7}{25}$, $\tan(2x) = \frac{24}{7}$

EXAMPLE 3 Verifying Trigonometric Identities Using Double-Angle Identities

Verify the identity $(\sin x - \cos x)^2 = 1 - \sin(2x)$.

Solution:

Start with the left side of the equation.	$\boxed{(\sin x - \cos x)^2}$
Expand by squaring.	$= \sin^2 x - 2\sin x\cos x + \cos^2 x$
Group the $\sin^2 x$ and $\cos^2 x$ terms.	$= \sin^2 x + \cos^2 x - 2\sin x\cos x$
Apply the Pythagorean identity.	$= \underbrace{\sin^2 x + \cos^2 x}_{1} - 2\sin x\cos x$
Apply the sine double-angle identity.	$= 1 - \underbrace{2\sin x\cos x}_{\sin(2x)}$
Simplify.	$= \boxed{1 - \sin(2x)}$

EXAMPLE 4 Verifying Multiple-Angle Identities

Verify the identity $\cos(3x) = (1 - 4\sin^2 x)\cos x$.

Solution:

Write the cosine of a sum identity.	$\cos(A + B) = \cos A\cos B - \sin A\sin B$
Let $A = 2x$ and $B = x$.	$\cos(2x + x) = \cos(2x)\cos x - \sin(2x)\sin x$
Apply the double-angle identities.	$\cos(3x) = \underbrace{\cos(2x)}_{1-2\sin^2 x}\cos x - \underbrace{\sin(2x)}_{2\sin x\cos x}\sin x$
Simplify.	$\cos(3x) = \cos x - 2\sin^2 x\cos x - 2\sin^2 x\cos x$
	$\cos(3x) = \cos x - 4\sin^2 x\cos x$
Factor out the common cosine term.	$\boxed{\cos(3x) = (1 - 4\sin^2 x)\cos x}$

EXAMPLE 5 Simplifying Trigonometric Expressions Using Double-Angle Identities

Graph $y = \dfrac{\cot x - \tan x}{\cot x + \tan x}$.

Solution:

Simplify $y = \dfrac{\cot x - \tan x}{\cot x + \tan x}$ first.

Write the cotangent and tangent functions in terms of the sine and cosine functions.

$$y = \frac{\dfrac{\cos x}{\sin x} - \dfrac{\sin x}{\cos x}}{\dfrac{\cos x}{\sin x} + \dfrac{\sin x}{\cos x}}$$

Multiply the numerator and the denominator by $\sin x \cos x$.

$$y = \left(\frac{\dfrac{\cos x}{\sin x} - \dfrac{\sin x}{\cos x}}{\dfrac{\cos x}{\sin x} + \dfrac{\sin x}{\cos x}}\right)\left(\frac{\sin x \cos x}{\sin x \cos x}\right)$$

Simplify.

$$y = \frac{\cos^2 x - \sin^2 x}{\cos^2 x + \sin^2 x}$$

Use the double-angle and Pythagorean identities.

$$y = \frac{\overbrace{\cos^2 x - \sin^2 x}^{\cos(2x)}}{\underbrace{\cos^2 x + \sin^2 x}_{1}}$$

$$\boxed{y = \cos(2x)}$$

Graph $y = \cos(2x)$.

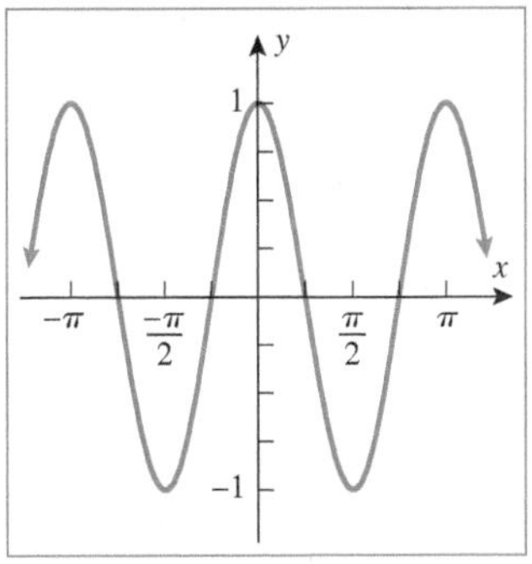

6.3.2 Half-Angle Identities

We now use the *double-angle identities* to develop the *half-angle identities*. Like the double-angle identities, the half-angle identities will enable us to find certain exact values of trigonometric functions and to verify other trigonometric identities. The *half-angle identities* come directly from the double-angle identities. We start by rewriting the second and third forms of the cosine double-angle identity to obtain identities for the square of the sine and cosine functions, $\sin^2$ and $\cos^2$.

6.3.2 SKILL

Use half-angle identities in simplifying some trigonometric expressions.

6.3.2 CONCEPTUAL

Understand that the half-angle identities are derived from the double-angle identities.

WORDS	MATH
Write the second form of the cosine double-angle identity.	$\cos(2A) = 1 - 2\sin^2 A$
Find $\sin^2 A$.	
Isolate the $2\sin^2 A$ term on one side of the equation.	$2\sin^2 A = 1 - \cos(2A)$
Divide both sides by 2.	$\boxed{\sin^2 A = \dfrac{1 - \cos(2A)}{2}}$

Find $\cos^2 A$.

Write the third form of the cosine double-angle identity.

$$\cos(2A) = 2\cos^2 A - 1$$

Isolate the $2\cos^2 A$ term on one side of the equation.

$$2\cos^2 A = 1 + \cos^2 A$$

Divide both sides by 2.

$$\boxed{\cos^2 A = \frac{1 + \cos(2A)}{2}}$$

Find $\tan^2 A$.

Taking the quotient of these leads us to another identity.

$$\tan^2 A = \frac{\sin^2 A}{\cos^2 A} = \frac{\frac{1 - \cos(2A)}{2}}{\frac{1 + \cos(2A)}{2}}$$

Simplify.

$$\boxed{\tan^2 A = \frac{1 - \cos(2A)}{1 + \cos(2A)}}$$

These three identities for the squared functions—really, alternative forms of the double-angle identities—are used in calculus as power reduction formulas (identities that allow us to reduce the power of the trigonometric function from 2 to 1):

$$\boxed{\sin^2 A = \frac{1 - \cos(2A)}{2}} \qquad \boxed{\cos^2 A = \frac{1 + \cos(2A)}{2}} \qquad \boxed{\tan^2 A = \frac{1 - \cos(2A)}{1 + \cos(2A)}}$$

We can now use these forms of the double-angle identities to derive the *half-angle identities*.

WORDS	MATH
For the *sine half-angle identity*, start with the double-angle formula involving both the sine and cosine functions, $\cos(2x) = 1 - 2\sin^2 x$, and solve for $\sin^2 x$.	$\sin^2 x = \frac{1 - \cos(2x)}{2}$
Solve for $\sin x$.	$\sin x = \pm\sqrt{\frac{1 - \cos(2x)}{2}}$
Let $x = \frac{A}{2}$.	$\sin\left(\frac{A}{2}\right) = \pm\sqrt{\frac{1 - \cos\left(2 \cdot \frac{A}{2}\right)}{2}}$
Simplify.	$\boxed{\sin\left(\frac{A}{2}\right) = \pm\sqrt{\frac{1 - \cos A}{2}}}$

For the *cosine half-angle identity*, start with the double-angle formula involving only the cosine function, $\cos(2x) = 2\cos^2 x - 1$, and solve for $\cos^2 x$.

$$\cos^2 x = \frac{1 + \cos(2x)}{2}$$

Solve for $\cos x$.

$$\cos x = \pm\sqrt{\frac{1 + \cos(2x)}{2}}$$

Let $x = \frac{A}{2}$.

$$\cos\left(\frac{A}{2}\right) = \pm\sqrt{\frac{1 + \cos\left(2 \cdot \frac{A}{2}\right)}{2}}$$

Simplify.

$$\boxed{\cos\left(\frac{A}{2}\right) = \pm\sqrt{\frac{1 + \cos A}{2}}}$$

For the *tangent half-angle identity*, start with the quotient identity.

$$\tan\left(\frac{A}{2}\right) = \frac{\sin\left(\frac{A}{2}\right)}{\cos\left(\frac{A}{2}\right)}$$

Substitute half-angle identities for the sine and cosine functions.

$$\tan\left(\frac{A}{2}\right) = \frac{\pm\sqrt{\frac{1 - \cos A}{2}}}{\pm\sqrt{\frac{1 + \cos A}{2}}}$$

Simplify.

$$\boxed{\tan\left(\frac{A}{2}\right) = \pm\sqrt{\frac{1 - \cos A}{1 + \cos A}}}$$

Note: We can also find $\tan\left(\frac{A}{2}\right)$ by starting with the identity $\tan^2 x = \frac{1 - \cos(2x)}{1 + \cos(2x)}$, solving for $\tan x$, and letting $x = \frac{A}{2}$. The tangent function also has two other, similar forms for $\tan\left(\frac{A}{2}\right)$ (see Exercises 129 and 130).

HALF-ANGLE IDENTITIES

SINE	COSINE	TANGENT
$\sin\left(\frac{A}{2}\right) = \pm\sqrt{\frac{1 - \cos A}{2}}$	$\cos\left(\frac{A}{2}\right) = \pm\sqrt{\frac{1 + \cos A}{2}}$	$\tan\left(\frac{A}{2}\right) = \pm\sqrt{\frac{1 - \cos A}{1 + \cos A}}$
		$\tan\left(\frac{A}{2}\right) = \frac{\sin A}{1 + \cos A}$
		$\tan\left(\frac{A}{2}\right) = \frac{1 - \cos A}{\sin A}$

STUDY TIP

The sign + or − is determined by what quadrant contains $\frac{A}{2}$ and what the sign of the particular trigonometric function is in that quadrant.

It is important to note that these identities hold for any real number A or any angle with either degree measure or radian measure A as long as both sides of the equation are defined. The sign (+ or −) is determined by the sign of the trigonometric function in the quadrant that contains $\frac{A}{2}$.

EXAMPLE 6 Finding Exact Values Using Half-Angle Identities

Use a half-angle identity to find $\cos 15°$.

Solution:

Write $\cos 15°$ in terms of a half-angle. $\cos 15° = \cos\left(\frac{30°}{2}\right)$

Write the half-angle identity for the cosine function. $\cos\left(\frac{A}{2}\right) = \pm\sqrt{\frac{1+\cos A}{2}}$

Substitute $A = 30°$. $\cos\left(\frac{30°}{2}\right) = \pm\sqrt{\frac{1+\cos 30°}{2}}$

Simplify. $\cos 15° = \pm\sqrt{\frac{1+\frac{\sqrt{3}}{2}}{2}}$

$15°$ is in quadrant I, where the cosine function is positive. $\cos 15° = \sqrt{\frac{2+\sqrt{3}}{4}} = \boxed{\frac{\sqrt{2+\sqrt{3}}}{2}}$

ANSWER

$\sin 22.5° = \frac{\sqrt{2-\sqrt{2}}}{2}$

YOUR TURN Use a half-angle identity to find $\sin 22.5°$.

EXAMPLE 7 Finding Exact Values Using Half-Angle Identities

Use a half-angle identity to find $\tan\left(\frac{11\pi}{12}\right)$.

Solution:

Write $\tan\left(\frac{11\pi}{12}\right)$ in terms of a half-angle. $\tan\left(\frac{11\pi}{12}\right) = \tan\left(\frac{\frac{11\pi}{6}}{2}\right)$

Write the half-angle identity for the tangent function.* $\tan\left(\frac{A}{2}\right) = \frac{1-\cos A}{\sin A}$

Substitute $A = \frac{11\pi}{6}$. $\tan\left(\frac{\frac{11\pi}{6}}{2}\right) = \frac{1-\cos\left(\frac{11\pi}{6}\right)}{\sin\left(\frac{11\pi}{6}\right)}$

Simplify. $\tan\left(\frac{11\pi}{12}\right) = \frac{1-\frac{\sqrt{3}}{2}}{-\frac{1}{2}}$

$\tan\left(\frac{11\pi}{12}\right) = \boxed{\sqrt{3}-2}$

$\frac{11\pi}{12}$ is in quadrant II, where tangent is negative. Notice that if we approximate $\tan\left(\frac{11\pi}{12}\right)$ with a calculator, we find that $\tan\left(\frac{11\pi}{12}\right) \approx -0.2679$ and $\sqrt{3}-2 \approx -0.2679$.

*This form of the tangent half-angle identity was selected because of mathematical simplicity. If we had selected either of the other forms, we would have obtained an expression that had a square root within a square root or a radical in the denominator (requiring rationalization).

[CONCEPT CHECK]

If angle A corresponds to a terminal side that lies in quadrant III, then $\sin\frac{A}{2}$ is positive.

ANSWER True

ANSWER

$\frac{\sqrt{2}}{2+\sqrt{2}}$ or $\sqrt{2}-1$

YOUR TURN Use a half-angle identity to find $\tan\left(\frac{\pi}{8}\right)$.

EXAMPLE 8 Finding Exact Values Using Half-Angle Identities

If $\cos x = \frac{3}{5}$ and $\frac{3\pi}{2} < x < 2\pi$, find $\sin\left(\frac{x}{2}\right)$, $\cos\left(\frac{x}{2}\right)$, and $\tan\left(\frac{x}{2}\right)$.

Solution:

Determine in which quadrant $\frac{x}{2}$ lies.

Since $\frac{3\pi}{2} < x < 2\pi$, we divide by 2. $\frac{3\pi}{4} < \frac{x}{2} < \pi$

$\frac{x}{2}$ lies in quadrant II; therefore, the sine function is positive and both the cosine and tangent functions are negative.

Write the half-angle identity for the sine function. $\sin\left(\frac{x}{2}\right) = \pm\sqrt{\frac{1 - \cos x}{2}}$

Substitute $\cos x = \frac{3}{5}$. $\sin\left(\frac{x}{2}\right) = \pm\sqrt{\frac{1 - \frac{3}{5}}{2}}$

Simplify. $\sin\left(\frac{x}{2}\right) = \pm\sqrt{\frac{1}{5}} = \pm\frac{\sqrt{5}}{5}$

Since $\frac{x}{2}$ lies in quadrant II, choose the positive value for the sine function. $\boxed{\sin\left(\frac{x}{2}\right) = \frac{\sqrt{5}}{5}}$

Write the half-angle identity for the cosine function. $\cos\left(\frac{x}{2}\right) = \pm\sqrt{\frac{1 + \cos x}{2}}$

Substitute $\cos x = \frac{3}{5}$. $\cos\left(\frac{x}{2}\right) = \pm\sqrt{\frac{1 + \frac{3}{5}}{2}}$

Simplify. $\cos\left(\frac{x}{2}\right) = \pm\sqrt{\frac{4}{5}} = \pm\frac{2\sqrt{5}}{5}$

Since $\frac{x}{2}$ lies in quadrant II, choose the negative value for the cosine function. $\boxed{\cos\left(\frac{x}{2}\right) = -\frac{2\sqrt{5}}{5}}$

Use the quotient identity for tangent. $\tan\left(\frac{x}{2}\right) = \frac{\sin\left(\frac{x}{2}\right)}{\cos\left(\frac{x}{2}\right)}$

Substitute $\sin\left(\frac{x}{2}\right) = \frac{\sqrt{5}}{5}$ and $\cos\left(\frac{x}{2}\right) = -\frac{2\sqrt{5}}{5}$. $\tan\left(\frac{x}{2}\right) = \frac{\frac{\sqrt{5}}{5}}{-\frac{2\sqrt{5}}{5}}$

Simplify. $\boxed{\tan\left(\frac{x}{2}\right) = -\frac{1}{2}}$

YOUR TURN If $\cos x = -\frac{3}{5}$ and $\pi < x < \frac{3\pi}{2}$, find $\sin\left(\frac{x}{2}\right)$, $\cos\left(\frac{x}{2}\right)$, and $\tan\left(\frac{x}{2}\right)$.

ANSWER

$\sin\left(\frac{x}{2}\right) = \frac{2\sqrt{5}}{5}$, $\cos\left(\frac{x}{2}\right) = -\frac{\sqrt{5}}{5}$, $\tan\left(\frac{x}{2}\right) = -2$

EXAMPLE 9 **Using Half-Angle Identities to Verify Other Identities**

Verify the identity $\cos^2\left(\frac{x}{2}\right) = \frac{\tan x + \sin x}{2\tan x}$.

Solution:

Write the cosine half-angle identity. $\cos\left(\frac{x}{2}\right) = \pm\sqrt{\frac{1 + \cos x}{2}}$

Square both sides of the equation. $\cos^2\left(\frac{x}{2}\right) = \frac{1 + \cos x}{2}$

Multiply the numerator and denominator on the right side by $\tan x$. $\cos^2\left(\frac{x}{2}\right) = \left(\frac{1 + \cos x}{2}\right)\left(\frac{\tan x}{\tan x}\right)$

Simplify. $\cos^2\left(\frac{x}{2}\right) = \frac{\tan x + \cos x \tan x}{2\tan x}$

Note that $\cos x \tan x = \sin x$. $\boxed{\cos^2\left(\frac{x}{2}\right) = \frac{\tan x + \sin x}{2\tan x}}$

An alternative solution is to start with the right-hand side.

Solution (alternative):

Start with the right-hand side. $\frac{\tan x + \sin x}{2\tan x}$

Write this expression as the sum of two expressions. $= \frac{\tan x}{2\tan x} + \frac{\sin x}{2\tan x}$

Simplify. $= \frac{1}{2} + \frac{1}{2}\frac{\sin x}{\tan x}$

Write $\tan x = \frac{\sin x}{\cos x}$. $= \frac{1}{2} + \frac{1}{2}\frac{\sin x}{\left(\frac{\sin x}{\cos x}\right)}$

$= \frac{1}{2}(1 + \cos x)$

$= \cos^2\left(\frac{x}{2}\right)$

EXAMPLE 10 **Using Half-Angle Identities to Verify Other Trigonometric Identities**

Verify the identity $\tan x = \csc(2x) - \cot(2x)$.

Solution:

Write the third half-angle formula for the tangent function. $\tan\left(\frac{A}{2}\right) = \frac{1 - \cos A}{\sin A}$

Write the right side as a difference of two expressions having the same denominator. $\tan\left(\frac{A}{2}\right) = \frac{1}{\sin A} - \frac{\cos A}{\sin A}$

Substitute the reciprocal and quotient identities, respectively, on the right. $\tan\left(\frac{A}{2}\right) = \csc A - \cot A$

Let $A = 2x$. $\boxed{\tan x = \csc(2x) - \cot(2x)}$

Notice that in Example 10 we started with the third half-angle identity for the tangent function. In Example 11 we will start with the second half-angle identity for the tangent function. In general, you select the form that appears to lead to the desired expression.

EXAMPLE 11 **Using Half-Angle Identities to Simplify Trigonometric Expressions**

Graph $y = \dfrac{\sin(2\pi x)}{1 + \cos(2\pi x)}$.

Solution:

Simplify the trigonometric expression using a half-angle identity for the tangent function.

Write the second half-angle identity for the tangent function. $\tan\left(\dfrac{A}{2}\right) = \dfrac{\sin A}{1 + \cos A}$

Let $A = 2\pi x$. $\tan(\pi x) = \dfrac{\sin(2\pi x)}{1 + \cos(2\pi x)}$

Graph $y = \tan(\pi x)$.

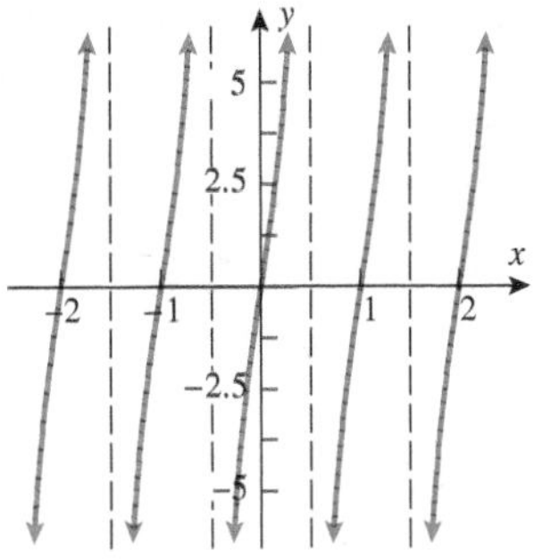

$y = \tan(\pi x)$ $y = \dfrac{\sin(2\pi x)}{1 + \cos(2\pi x)}$

YOUR TURN Graph $y = \dfrac{1 - \cos(\pi x)}{\sin(\pi x)}$.

ANSWER

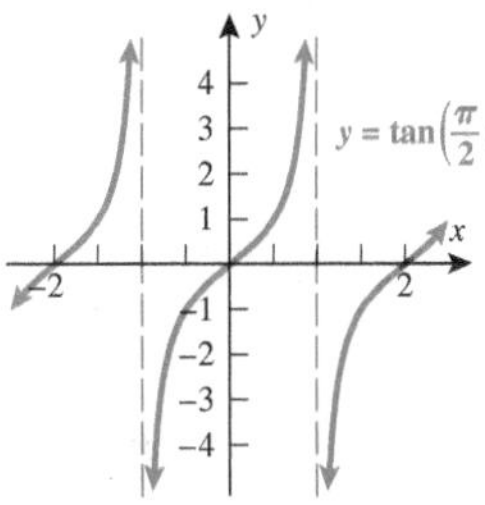

$y = \tan\left(\dfrac{\pi}{2}x\right)$

[SECTION 6.3] SUMMARY

In this section, we derived the double-angle identities from the sum identities. We then used the double-angle identities to find exact values of trigonometric functions, to verify other trigonometric identities, and to simplify trigonometric expressions.

$$\sin(2A) = 2\sin A\cos A$$
$$\cos(2A) = \cos^2 A - \sin^2 A$$
$$= 1 - 2\sin^2 A$$
$$= 2\cos^2 A - 1$$
$$\tan(2A) = \frac{2\tan A}{1 - \tan^2 A}$$

The double-angle identities were used to derive the half-angle identities. We then used the half-angle identities to find certain exact values of trigonometric functions, verify other trigonometric identities, and simplify trigonometric expressions.

$$\sin\left(\frac{A}{2}\right) = \pm\sqrt{\frac{1 - \cos A}{2}} \qquad \cos\left(\frac{A}{2}\right) = \pm\sqrt{\frac{1 + \cos A}{2}}$$

$$\tan\left(\frac{A}{2}\right) = \pm\sqrt{\frac{1 - \cos A}{1 + \cos A}}$$

We determine the sign, + or −, by first deciding which quadrant contains $\frac{A}{2}$ and then finding the sign of the indicated trigonometric function in that quadrant.

Recall that there are three forms of the tangent half-angle identity. There is no need to memorize the other forms of the tangent half-angle identity, because they can be derived by first using the Pythagorean identity and algebraic manipulation.

[SECTION 6.3] EXERCISES

• SKILLS

In Exercises 1–12, use the double-angle identities to answer the following questions:

1. If $\sin x = \frac{1}{\sqrt{5}}$ and $\cos x < 0$, find $\sin(2x)$.
2. If $\sin x = \frac{1}{\sqrt{5}}$ and $\cos x < 0$, find $\cos(2x)$.
3. If $\cos x = \frac{5}{13}$ and $\sin x < 0$, find $\tan(2x)$.
4. If $\cos x = -\frac{5}{13}$ and $\sin x < 0$, find $\tan(2x)$.
5. If $\tan x = \frac{12}{5}$ and $\pi < x < \frac{3\pi}{2}$, find $\sin(2x)$.
6. If $\tan x = \frac{12}{5}$ and $\pi < x < \frac{3\pi}{2}$, find $\cos(2x)$.
7. If $\sec x = \sqrt{5}$ and $\sin x > 0$, find $\tan(2x)$.
8. If $\sec x = \sqrt{3}$ and $\sin x < 0$, find $\tan(2x)$.
9. If $\csc x = -2\sqrt{5}$ and $\cos x < 0$, find $\sin(2x)$.
10. If $\csc x = -\sqrt{13}$ and $\cos x > 0$, find $\sin(2x)$.
11. If $\cos x = -\frac{12}{13}$ and $\csc x < 0$, find $\cot(2x)$.
12. If $\sin x = \frac{12}{13}$ and $\cot x < 0$, find $\csc(2x)$.

In Exercises 13–24, simplify each expression. Evaluate the resulting expression exactly, if possible.

13. $\dfrac{2\tan 15°}{1 - \tan^2 15°}$
14. $\dfrac{2\tan\left(\frac{\pi}{8}\right)}{1 - \tan^2\left(\frac{\pi}{8}\right)}$
15. $\sin\left(\frac{\pi}{8}\right)\cos\left(\frac{\pi}{8}\right)$
16. $\sin 15° \cos 15°$
17. $\cos^2(2x) - \sin^2(2x)$
18. $\cos^2(x + 2) - \sin^2(x + 2)$
19. $\dfrac{2\tan\left(\frac{5\pi}{12}\right)}{1 - \tan^2\left(\frac{5\pi}{12}\right)}$
20. $\dfrac{2\tan\left(\frac{x}{2}\right)}{1 - \tan^2\left(\frac{x}{2}\right)}$
21. $1 - 2\sin^2\left(\frac{7\pi}{12}\right)$
22. $2\sin^2\left(-\frac{5\pi}{8}\right) - 1$
23. $2\cos^2\left(-\frac{7\pi}{12}\right) - 1$
24. $1 - 2\cos^2\left(-\frac{\pi}{8}\right)$

In Exercises 25–40, use the double-angle identities to verify each identity.

25. $\csc(2A) = \frac{1}{2}\csc A \sec A$
26. $\cot(2A) = \frac{1}{2}(\cot A - \tan A)$
27. $(\sin x - \cos x)(\cos x + \sin x) = -\cos(2x)$
28. $(\sin x + \cos x)^2 = 1 + \sin(2x)$
29. $\cos^2 x = \dfrac{1 + \cos(2x)}{2}$
30. $\sin^2 x = \dfrac{1 - \cos(2x)}{2}$
31. $\cos^4 x - \sin^4 x = \cos(2x)$
32. $\cos^4 x + \sin^4 x = 1 - \frac{1}{2}\sin^2(2x)$
33. $8\sin^2 x \cos^2 x = 1 - \cos(4x)$
34. $[\cos(2x) - \sin(2x)][\sin(2x) + \cos(2x)] = \cos(4x)$
35. $-\frac{1}{2}\sec^2 x = -2\sin^2 x \csc^2(2x)$
36. $4\csc(4x) = \dfrac{\sec x \csc x}{\cos(2x)}$
37. $\sin(3x) = \sin x(4\cos^2 x - 1)$
38. $\tan(3x) = \dfrac{\tan x(3 - \tan^2 x)}{(1 - 3\tan^2 x)}$
39. $\frac{1}{2}\sin(4x) = 2\sin x \cos x - 4\sin^3 x \cos x$
40. $\cos(4x) = [\cos(2x) - \sin(2x)][(\cos(2x) + \sin(2x)]$

In Exercises 41–50, graph the functions.

41. $y = \dfrac{\sin(2x)}{1 - \cos(2x)}$

42. $y = \dfrac{2\tan x}{2 - \sec^2 x}$

43. $y = \dfrac{\cot x + \tan x}{\cot x - \tan x}$

44. $y = \frac{1}{2}\tan x \cot x \sec x \csc x$

45. $y = \sin(2x)\cos(2x)$

46. $y = 3\sin(3x)\cos(-3x)$

47. $y = 1 - \dfrac{\tan x \cot x}{\sec x \csc x}$

48. $y = 3 - 2\dfrac{\sec(2x)}{\csc(2x)}$

49. $y = \dfrac{\sin(2x)}{\cos x} - 3\cos(2x)$

50. $y = 2 + \dfrac{\sin(2x)}{\cos x} - 3\cos(2x)$

In Exercises 51–66, use the half-angle identities to find the exact values of the trigonometric expressions.

51. $\sin 15°$

52. $\cos 22.5°$

53. $\cos\left(\dfrac{11\pi}{12}\right)$

54. $\sin\left(\dfrac{\pi}{8}\right)$

55. $\cos 75°$

56. $\sin 75°$

57. $\tan 67.5°$

58. $\tan 202.5°$

59. $\sec\left(-\dfrac{9\pi}{8}\right)$

60. $\csc\left(\dfrac{9\pi}{8}\right)$

61. $\cot\left(\dfrac{13\pi}{8}\right)$

62. $\cot\left(\dfrac{7\pi}{8}\right)$

63. $\sec\left(\dfrac{5\pi}{8}\right)$

64. $\csc\left(-\dfrac{5\pi}{8}\right)$

65. $\cot(-135°)$

66. $\cot 105°$

In Exercises 67–82, use the half-angle identities to find the desired function values.

67. If $\cos x = \dfrac{5}{13}$ and $\sin x < 0$, find $\sin\left(\dfrac{x}{2}\right)$.

68. If $\cos x = -\dfrac{5}{13}$ and $\sin x < 0$, find $\cos\left(\dfrac{x}{2}\right)$.

69. If $\tan x = \dfrac{12}{5}$ and $\pi < x < \dfrac{3\pi}{2}$, find $\sin\left(\dfrac{x}{2}\right)$.

70. If $\tan x = \dfrac{12}{5}$ and $\pi < x < \dfrac{3\pi}{2}$, find $\cos\left(\dfrac{x}{2}\right)$.

71. If $\sec x = \sqrt{5}$ and $\sin x > 0$, find $\tan\left(\dfrac{x}{2}\right)$.

72. If $\sec x = \sqrt{3}$ and $\sin x < 0$, find $\tan\left(\dfrac{x}{2}\right)$.

73. If $\csc x = 3$ and $\cos x < 0$, find $\sin\left(\dfrac{x}{2}\right)$.

74. If $\csc x = -3$ and $\cos x > 0$, find $\cos\left(\dfrac{x}{2}\right)$.

75. If $\cos x = -\dfrac{1}{4}$ and $\csc x < 0$, find $\cot\left(\dfrac{x}{2}\right)$.

76. If $\cos x = \dfrac{1}{4}$ and $\cot x < 0$, find $\csc\left(\dfrac{x}{2}\right)$.

77. If $\cot x = -\dfrac{24}{5}$ and $\dfrac{\pi}{2} < x < \pi$, find $\cos\left(\dfrac{x}{2}\right)$.

78. If $\cot x = -\dfrac{24}{5}$ and $\dfrac{\pi}{2} < x < \pi$, find $\sin\left(\dfrac{x}{2}\right)$.

79. If $\sin x = -0.3$ and $\sec x > 0$, find $\tan\left(\dfrac{x}{2}\right)$.

80. If $\sin x = -0.3$ and $\sec x < 0$, find $\cot\left(\dfrac{x}{2}\right)$.

81. If $\sec x = 2.5$ and $\tan x > 0$, find $\cot\left(\dfrac{x}{2}\right)$.

82. If $\sec x = -3$ and $\cot x < 0$, find $\tan\left(\dfrac{x}{2}\right)$.

In Exercises 83–88, simplify each expression using half-angle identities. Do not evaluate.

83. $\sqrt{\dfrac{1 + \cos\left(\dfrac{5\pi}{6}\right)}{2}}$

84. $\sqrt{\dfrac{1 - \cos\left(\dfrac{\pi}{4}\right)}{2}}$

85. $\dfrac{\sin 150°}{1 + \cos 150°}$

86. $\dfrac{1 - \cos 150°}{\sin 150°}$

87. $\sqrt{\dfrac{1 - \cos\left(\dfrac{5\pi}{4}\right)}{1 + \cos\left(\dfrac{5\pi}{4}\right)}}$

88. $\sqrt{\dfrac{1 - \cos 15°}{1 + \cos 15°}}$

In Exercises 89–100, use the half-angle identities to verify the identities.

89. $\sin^2\left(\frac{x}{2}\right) + \cos^2\left(\frac{x}{2}\right) = 1$

90. $\cos^2\left(\frac{x}{2}\right) - \sin^2\left(\frac{x}{2}\right) = \cos x$

91. $\sin(-x) = -2\sin\left(\frac{x}{2}\right)\cos\left(\frac{x}{2}\right)$

92. $2\cos^2\left(\frac{x}{4}\right) = 1 + \cos\left(\frac{x}{2}\right)$

93. $\tan^2\left(\frac{x}{2}\right) = \frac{1 - \cos x}{1 + \cos x}$

94. $\tan^2\left(\frac{x}{2}\right) = (\csc x - \cot x)^2$

95. $\tan\left(\frac{A}{2}\right) + \cot\left(\frac{A}{2}\right) = 2\csc A$

96. $\cot\left(\frac{A}{2}\right) - \tan\left(\frac{A}{2}\right) = 2\cot A$

97. $\csc^2\left(\frac{A}{2}\right) = \frac{2(1 + \cos A)}{\sin^2 A}$

98. $\sec^2\left(\frac{A}{2}\right) = \frac{2(1 - \cos A)}{\sin^2 A}$

99. $\csc\left(\frac{A}{2}\right) = \pm|\csc A|\sqrt{2 + 2\cos A}$

100. $\sec\left(\frac{A}{2}\right) = \pm|\csc A|\sqrt{2 - 2\cos A}$

In Exercises 101–108, graph the functions.

101. $y = 4\cos^2\left(\frac{x}{2}\right)$

102. $y = -6\sin^2\left(\frac{x}{2}\right)$

103. $y = \dfrac{1 - \tan^2\left(\frac{x}{2}\right)}{1 + \tan^2\left(\frac{x}{2}\right)}$

104. $y = 1 - \left[\sin\left(\frac{x}{2}\right) + \cos\left(\frac{x}{2}\right)\right]^2$

105. $y = 4\sin^2\left(\frac{x}{2}\right) - 1$

106. $y = -\frac{1}{6}\cos^2\left(\frac{x}{2}\right) + 2$

107. $y = \sqrt{\dfrac{1 - \cos(2x)}{1 + \cos(2x)}} \quad 0 \le x < \pi$

108. $y = \sqrt{\dfrac{1 + \cos(3x)}{2}} + 3 \quad 0 \le x \le \frac{\pi}{3}$

• APPLICATIONS

109. Business/Economics. Annual cash flow of a stock fund (measured as a percentage of total assets) has fluctuated in cycles. The highs were roughly $+12\%$ of total assets and the lows were roughly -8% of total assets. This cash flow can be modeled by the function

$$C(t) = 12 - 20\sin^2 t$$

Use a double-angle identity to express $C(t)$ in terms of the cosine function.

110. Business. Computer sales are generally subject to seasonal fluctuations. An analysis by a computer manufacturer has determined that during 2008–2010, its sales were approximated by the function

$$s(t) = 0.098\cos^2 t + 0.387 \qquad 1 \le t \le 12$$

where t represents time in quarters ($t = 1$ represents the end of the first quarter of 2008), and $s(t)$ represents computer sales (quarterly revenue) in millions of dollars. Use a double-angle identity to express $s(t)$ in terms of the cosine function.

For Exercises 111 and 112, refer to the following:

An ore-crusher wheel consists of a heavy disk spinning on its axle. The normal (crushing) force F, in pounds, between the wheel and the inclined track is determined by

$$F = W\sin\theta + \frac{1}{2}\psi^2\left[\frac{C}{R}(1 - \cos 2\theta) + \frac{A}{l}\sin 2\theta\right]$$

where W is the weight of the wheel in pounds, θ is the angle of the axis, C and A are moments of inertia, R is the radius of the wheel, l is the distance from the wheel to the pin where the axle is attached, and ψ is the speed in rpm at which the wheel is spinning. The optimum crushing force occurs when the angle θ is between 45° and 90°.

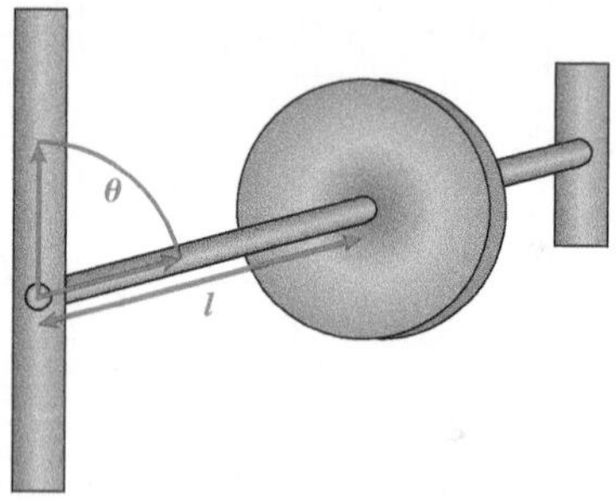

111. Ore-Crusher Wheel. Find F if the angle is 60°, W is 500 lb, ψ is 200 rpm, $\frac{C}{R} = 750$, and $\frac{A}{l} = 3.75$.

112. Ore-Crusher Wheel. Find F if the angle is 75°, W is 500 lb, ψ is 200 rpm, $\frac{C}{R} = 750$, and $\frac{A}{l} = 3.75$.

113. **Area of an Isosceles Triangle.** Consider the triangle below, where the vertex angle measures θ, the equal sides measure a, the height is h, and half the base is b. (In an isosceles triangle, the perpendicular dropped from the vertex angle divides the triangle into two congruent triangles.) The two triangles formed are right triangles.

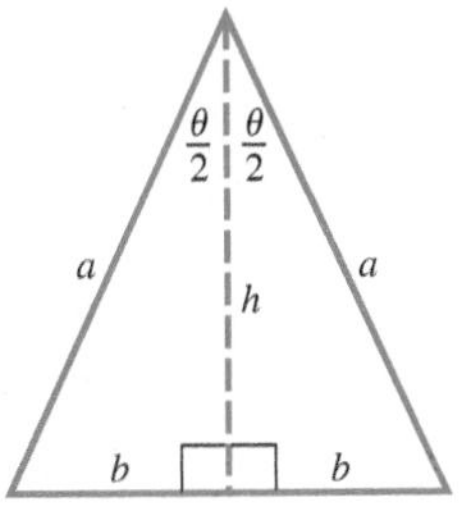

In the right triangles, $\sin\left(\frac{\theta}{2}\right) = \frac{b}{a}$ and $\cos\left(\frac{\theta}{2}\right) = \frac{h}{a}$. Multiply each side of each equation by a to get $b = a\sin\left(\frac{\theta}{2}\right)$, $h = a\cos\left(\frac{\theta}{2}\right)$.

The area of the entire isosceles triangle is $A = \frac{1}{2}(2b)h = bh$. Substitute the values for b and h into the area formula. Show that the area is equivalent to $\left(\frac{a^2}{2}\right)\sin\theta$.

114. **Area of an Isosceles Triangle.** Use the results from Exercise 113 to find the area of an isosceles triangle whose equal sides measure 7 inches and whose base angles each measure 75°.

115. With the information given in the diagram below, compute y.

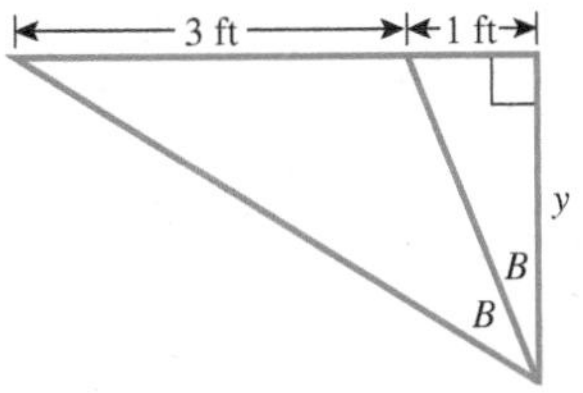

116. With the information given in the diagram below, compute x.

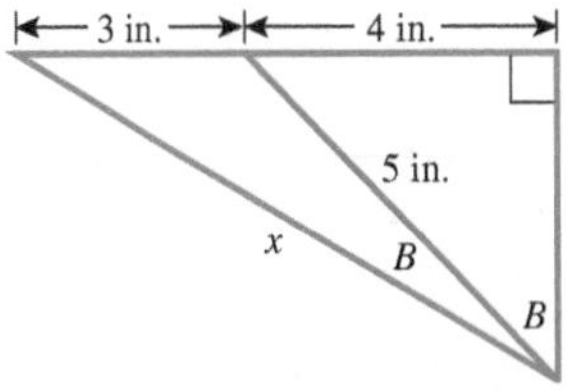

For Exercises 117 and 118, refer to the following:

Monthly profits can be expressed as a function of sales, that is, $p(s)$. A financial analysis of a company has determined that the sales s in thousands of dollars are also related to monthly profits p in thousands of dollars by the relationship:

$$\tan\theta = \frac{p}{s} \quad \text{for } 0 \le s \le 50,\ 0 \le p < 40$$

Based on sales and profits, it can be determined that the domain for angle θ is $0 \le \theta \le 38°$.

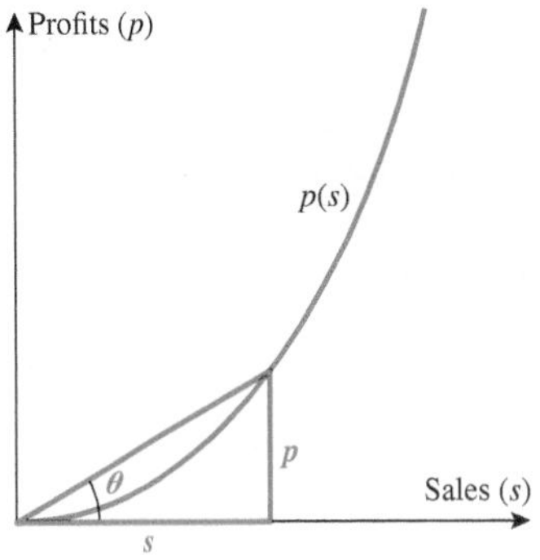

117. **Business.** If monthly profits are \$3000 and monthly sales are \$4000, find $\tan\left(\frac{\theta}{2}\right)$.

118. **Business.** If monthly profits are p and monthly sales are s (where $p < s$), find $\tan\left(\frac{\theta}{2}\right)$.

• CATCH THE MISTAKE

In Exercises 119 and 120, explain the mistake that is made.

119. If $\cos x = \frac{1}{3}$, find $\sin(2x)$ given $\sin x < 0$.

Solution:

Write the double-angle identity for the sine function. $\sin(2x) = 2\sin x\cos x$

Solve for $\sin x$ using the Pythagorean identity. $\sin^2 x + \left(\frac{1}{3}\right)^2 = 1$

$\sin x = \frac{2\sqrt{2}}{3}$

Substitute $\cos x = \frac{1}{3}$ and $\sin x = \frac{2\sqrt{2}}{3}$. $\sin(2x) = 2\left(\frac{2\sqrt{2}}{3}\right)\left(\frac{1}{3}\right)$

Simplify. $\sin(2x) = \frac{4\sqrt{2}}{9}$

This is incorrect. What mistake was made?

120. If $\sin x = \frac{1}{3}$, find $\tan(2x)$ given $\cos x < 0$.

Solution:

Use the quotient identity. $\tan(2x) = \frac{\sin(2x)}{\cos x}$

Use the double-angle formula for the sine function. $\tan(2x) = \frac{2\sin x\cos x}{\cos x}$

Cancel the common cosine factors. $\tan(2x) = 2\sin x$

Substitute $\sin x = \frac{1}{3}$. $\tan(2x) = \frac{2}{3}$

This is incorrect. What mistake was made?

• CONCEPTUAL

For Exercises 121–128, determine whether each statement is true or false.

121. $\sin(2A) + \sin(2A) = \sin(4A)$

122. $\cos(4A) - \cos(2A) = \cos(2A)$

123. If $\tan x > 0$, then $\tan(2x) > 0$.

124. If $\sin x > 0$, then $\sin(2x) > 0$.

125. $\sin\left(\frac{A}{2}\right) + \sin\left(\frac{A}{2}\right) = \sin A$

126. $\cos\left(\frac{A}{2}\right) + \cos\left(\frac{A}{2}\right) = \cos A$

127. If $\tan x > 0$, then $\tan\left(\frac{x}{2}\right) > 0$.

128. If $\sin x > 0$, then $\sin\left(\frac{x}{2}\right) > 0$.

129. Given $\tan\left(\frac{A}{2}\right) = \pm\sqrt{\frac{1-\cos A}{1+\cos A}}$, verify $\tan\left(\frac{A}{2}\right) = \frac{\sin A}{1+\cos A}$. Substitute $A = \pi$ into the identity and explain your results.

130. Given $\tan\left(\frac{A}{2}\right) = \pm\sqrt{\frac{1-\cos A}{1+\cos A}}$, verify $\tan\left(\frac{A}{2}\right) = \frac{1-\cos A}{\sin A}$. Substitute $A = \pi$ into the identity and explain your results.

• CHALLENGE

131. Is the identity $\tan(2x) = \frac{2\tan x}{1-\tan^2 x}$ true for $x = \frac{\pi}{4}$? Explain.

132. Is the identity $2\csc(2x) = \frac{1+\tan^2 x}{\tan x}$ true for $x = \frac{\pi}{2}$? Explain.

133. Prove that $\cot\left(\frac{A}{4}\right) = \pm\sqrt{\frac{1+\cos\left(\frac{A}{2}\right)}{1-\cos\left(\frac{A}{2}\right)}}$.

134. Prove that $\cot\left(-\frac{A}{2}\right)\sec\left(\frac{A}{2}\right)\csc\left(-\frac{A}{2}\right)\tan\left(\frac{A}{2}\right) = 2\csc A$.

135. Find the values of x in the interval $[0, 2\pi]$ for which $\tan\left(\frac{x}{2}\right) > 0$.

136. Find the values of x in the interval $[0, 2\pi]$ for which $\cot\left(\frac{x}{2}\right) \leq 0$.

• PREVIEW TO CALCULUS

In calculus, we work with the derivative of expressions containing trigonometric functions. Usually, it is better to work with a simplified version of these expressions.

In Exercises 137–140, simplify each expression using the double-angle and half-angle identities.

137. $\dfrac{\frac{2\sin x}{\cos x}}{\frac{\cos^2 x - \sin^2 x}{\cos^2 x}}$

138. $\cos^4 x - 6\sin^2 x\cos^2 x + \sin^4 x$

139. $3\sin x\cos^2 x - \sin^3 x$

140. $\sqrt{\dfrac{1-\sqrt{\frac{1+\cos x}{2}}}{1+\sqrt{\frac{1+\cos x}{2}}}}$

6.4 PRODUCT-TO-SUM AND SUM-TO-PRODUCT IDENTITIES

SKILLS OBJECTIVES

- Express products of trigonometric functions as sums of trigonometric functions.
- Express sums of trigonometric functions as products of trigonometric functions.

CONCEPTUAL OBJECTIVES

- Understand that the sum and difference identities are used to derive product-to-sum identities.
- Understand that the product-to-sum identities are used to derive the sum-to-product identities.

In calculus, often it is helpful to write products of trigonometric functions as sums of other trigonometric functions, and vice versa. In this section, we discuss the *product-to-sum identities*, which convert products to sums, and the *sum-to-product identities*, which convert sums to products.

6.4.1 SKILL

Express products of trigonometric functions as sums of trigonometric functions.

6.4.1 Product-to-Sum Identities

6.4.1 CONCEPTUAL

Understand that the sum and difference identities are used to derive product-to-sum identities.

The *product-to-sum identities* are derived from the sum and difference identities.

WORDS	MATH
Write the identity for the cosine of a sum.	$\cos A \cos B - \sin A \sin B = \cos(A + B)$
Write the identity for the cosine of a difference.	$\cos A \cos B + \sin A \sin B = \cos(A - B)$
Add the two identities.	$2\cos A \cos B = \cos(A + B) + \cos(A - B)$
Divide both sides by 2.	$\boxed{\cos A \cos B = \frac{1}{2}[\cos(A + B) + \cos(A - B)]}$
Write the identity for the cosine of a difference.	$\cos A \cos B + \sin A \sin B = \cos(A - B)$
Subtract the sum identity from the difference identity.	$-\cos A \cos B + \sin A \sin B = -\cos(A + B)$
	$2\sin A \sin B = \cos(A - B) - \cos(A + B)$
Divide both sides by 2.	$\boxed{\sin A \sin B = \frac{1}{2}[\cos(A - B) - \cos(A + B)]}$
Write the identity for the sine of a sum.	$\sin A \cos B + \cos A \sin B = \sin(A + B)$
Write the identity for the sine of a difference.	$\sin A \cos B - \cos A \sin B = \sin(A - B)$
Add the two identities.	$2\sin A \cos B = \sin(A + B) + \sin(A - B)$
Divide both sides by 2.	$\boxed{\sin A \cos B = \frac{1}{2}[\sin(A + B) + \sin(A - B)]}$

PRODUCT-TO-SUM IDENTITIES

1. $\cos A \cos B = \frac{1}{2}[\cos(A + B) + \cos(A - B)]$
2. $\sin A \sin B = \frac{1}{2}[\cos(A - B) - \cos(A + B)]$
3. $\sin A \cos B = \frac{1}{2}[\sin(A + B) + \sin(A - B)]$

[CONCEPT CHECK]

TRUE OR FALSE
$\sin(A)\cos(B) = \cos(A)\sin(B)$, for angles A and B.

ANSWER False

EXAMPLE 1 **Illustrating a Product-to-Sum Identity for Specific Values**

Show that product-to-sum identity (3) is true when $A = 30°$ and $B = 90°$.

Solution:

Write product-to-sum identity (3). $\sin A \cos B = \frac{1}{2}[\sin(A + B) + \sin(A - B)]$

Let $A = 30°$ and $B = 90°$. $\sin 30° \cos 90° = \frac{1}{2}[\sin(30° + 90°) + \sin(30° - 90°)]$

Simplify. $\sin 30° \cos 90° = \frac{1}{2}[\sin 120° + \sin(-60°)]$

Evaluate the trigonometric functions. $\frac{1}{2} \cdot 0 = \frac{1}{2}\left[\frac{\sqrt{3}}{2} - \frac{\sqrt{3}}{2}\right]$

Simplify. $0 = 0$

EXAMPLE 2 **Convert a Product to a Sum**

Convert the product $\cos(4x)\cos(3x)$ to a sum.

Solution:

Write product-to-sum identity (1). $\cos A \cos B = \frac{1}{2}[\cos(A + B) + \cos(A - B)]$

Let $A = 4x$ and $B = 3x$. $\cos(4x)\cos(3x) = \frac{1}{2}[\cos(4x + 3x) + \cos(4x - 3x)]$

Simplify. $\boxed{\cos(4x)\cos(3x) = \frac{1}{2}[\cos(7x) + \cos x]}$

YOUR TURN Convert the product $\cos(2x)\cos(5x)$ to a sum.

ANSWER
$\frac{1}{2}[\cos(7x) + \cos(3x)]$

EXAMPLE 3 Converting Products to Sums

Express $\sin(2x)\sin(3x)$ in terms of cosines.

common mistake

A common mistake that is often made is calling the product of two sines the square of a sine.

✓CORRECT

Write product-to-sum identity (2).

$\sin A \sin B$

$= \frac{1}{2}[\cos(A - B) - \cos(A + B)]$

Let $A = 2x$ and $B = 3x$.

$\sin(2x)\sin(3x)$

$= \frac{1}{2}[\cos(2x - 3x) - \cos(2x + 3x)]$

Simplify.

$\sin(2x)\sin(3x)$

$= \frac{1}{2}[\cos(-x) - \cos(5x)]$

The cosine function is an even function; thus,

$\sin(2x)\sin(3x) = \frac{1}{2}[\cos x - \cos(5x)]$.

✗INCORRECT

Multiply the two sine functions.

$\sin(2x)\sin(3x) = \sin^2(6x^2)$ **ERROR**

CAUTION

1. $\sin A \sin B \neq \sin^2(AB)$.
2. The argument must be the same in order to use the identity: $\sin A \sin A = (\sin A)^2 = \sin^2 A$.

YOUR TURN Express $\sin x \sin(2x)$ in terms of cosines.

ANSWER

$\frac{1}{2}[\cos x - \cos(3x)]$

6.4.2 Sum-to-Product Identities

The *sum-to-product identities* can be obtained from the product-to-sum identities.

6.4.2 SKILL

Express sums of trigonometric functions as products of trigonometric functions.

6.4.2 CONCEPTUAL

Understand that the product-to-sum identities are used to derive the sum-to-product identities.

WORDS	MATH
Write the identity for the product of the sine and cosine functions.	$\frac{1}{2}[\sin(x + y) + \sin(x - y)] = \sin x \cos y$
Let $x + y = A$ and $x - y = B$; then $x = \frac{A + B}{2}$ and $y = \frac{A - B}{2}$.	
Substitute these values into the identity.	$\frac{1}{2}[\sin A + \sin B] = \sin\left(\frac{A + B}{2}\right)\cos\left(\frac{A - B}{2}\right)$
Multiply by 2.	$\sin A + \sin B = 2\sin\left(\frac{A + B}{2}\right)\cos\left(\frac{A - B}{2}\right)$

The other three *sum-to-product* identities can be found similarly. All are summarized in the box below.

[CONCEPT CHECK]

TRUE OR FALSE
If $B = -A$, then $\cos(A) - \cos(B) = 0$ and $\sin(A) - \sin(B) = 2\sin(A)$.

ANSWER True

SUM-TO-PRODUCT IDENTITIES

4. $\sin A + \sin B = 2\sin\left(\frac{A+B}{2}\right)\cos\left(\frac{A-B}{2}\right)$

5. $\sin A - \sin B = 2\sin\left(\frac{A-B}{2}\right)\cos\left(\frac{A+B}{2}\right)$

6. $\cos A + \cos B = 2\cos\left(\frac{A+B}{2}\right)\cos\left(\frac{A-B}{2}\right)$

7. $\cos A - \cos B = -2\sin\left(\frac{A+B}{2}\right)\sin\left(\frac{A-B}{2}\right)$

EXAMPLE 4 Illustrating a Sum-to-Product Identity for Specific Values

Show that sum-to-product identity (7) is true when $A = 30°$ and $B = 90°$.

Solution:

Write the sum-to-product identity (7). $\cos A - \cos B = -2\sin\left(\frac{A+B}{2}\right)\sin\left(\frac{A-B}{2}\right)$

Let $A = 30°$ and $B = 90°$. $\cos 30° - \cos 90° = -2\sin\left(\frac{30° + 90°}{2}\right)\sin\left(\frac{30° - 90°}{2}\right)$

Simplify. $\cos 30° - \cos 90° = -2\sin 60° \sin(-30°)$

The sine function is an odd function. $\cos 30° - \cos 90° = 2\sin 60° \sin 30°$

Evaluate the trigonometric functions. $\frac{\sqrt{3}}{2} - 0 = 2\left(\frac{\sqrt{3}}{2}\right)\left(\frac{1}{2}\right)$

Simplify. $\frac{\sqrt{3}}{2} = \frac{\sqrt{3}}{2}$

EXAMPLE 5 Convert a Sum to a Product

Convert $-9[\sin(2x) - \sin(10x)]$, a trigonometric expression containing a sum, to a product.

Solution:

The expression inside the brackets is in the form of identity (5). $\sin A - \sin B = 2\sin\left(\frac{A-B}{2}\right)\cos\left(\frac{A+B}{2}\right)$

Let $A = 2x$ and $B = 10x$. $\sin(2x) - \sin(10x) = 2\sin\left(\frac{2x - 10x}{2}\right)\cos\left(\frac{2x + 10x}{2}\right)$

Simplify. $\sin(2x) - \sin(10x) = 2\sin(-4x)\cos(6x)$

The sine function is an odd function. $\sin(2x) - \sin(10x) = -2\sin(4x)\cos(6x)$

Multiply both sides by -9. $\boxed{-9[\sin(2x) - \sin(10x)] = 18\sin(4x)\cos(6x)}$

EXAMPLE 6 Simplifying a Trigonometric Expression

Simplify the expression $\sin\left(\frac{x+y}{2}\right)\cos\left(\frac{x-y}{2}\right) + \sin\left(\frac{x-y}{2}\right)\cos\left(\frac{x+y}{2}\right)$.

Solution:

Use identities (4) and (5).

$$\underbrace{\sin\left(\frac{x+y}{2}\right)\cos\left(\frac{x-y}{2}\right)}_{\frac{1}{2}[\sin x + \sin y]} + \underbrace{\sin\left(\frac{x-y}{2}\right)\cos\left(\frac{x+y}{2}\right)}_{\frac{1}{2}[\sin x - \sin y]}$$

$$= \frac{1}{2}\sin x + \frac{1}{2}\sin y + \frac{1}{2}\sin x - \frac{1}{2}\sin y$$

Simplify. $= \boxed{\sin x}$

Applications

In music, a note is a fixed pitch (frequency) that is given a name. If two notes are sounded simultaneously, then they combine to produce another note often called a "beat." The beat frequency is the difference of the two frequencies. The more rapid the beat, the further apart the two frequencies of the notes are. When musicians "tune" their instruments, they use a tuning fork to sound a note and then tune the instrument until the beat is eliminated; hence, the fork and instrument are in tune with each other. Mathematically, a note or tone is represented as $A\cos(2\pi ft)$, where A is the amplitude (loudness), f is the frequency in hertz, and t is time in seconds. The following figure summarizes common notes and frequencies:

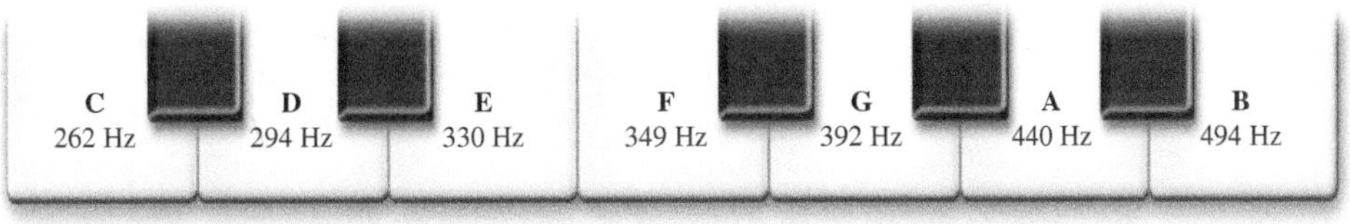

EXAMPLE 7 Music

Express the musical tone when a C and a G are simultaneously struck (assume with the same loudness).

Find the beat frequency $f_2 - f_1$. Assume uniform loudness, $A = 1$.

Solution:

Write the mathematical description of a C note. $\cos(2\pi f_1 t),\ f_1 = 262\,\text{Hz}$

Write the mathematical description of a G note. $\cos(2\pi f_2 t),\ f_2 = 392\,\text{Hz}$

Add the two notes. $\cos(524\pi t) + \cos(784\pi t)$

Use a sum-to-product identity: $\cos(524\pi t) + \cos(784\pi t)$.

$$= 2\cos\left(\frac{524\pi t + 784\pi t}{2}\right)\cos\left(\frac{524\pi t - 784\pi t}{2}\right)$$

Simplify. $= 2\cos(654\pi t)\cos(-130\pi t)$

Cosine is an even function: $\cos(-x) = \cos x$. $= 2\cos(654\pi t)\cos(130\pi t)$

Identify the average frequency and beat of the tone.

$$= 2\cos(\underbrace{327\pi t}_{\text{average frequency}})\cos(\underbrace{130\pi t}_{\text{beats per second}})$$

The beat frequency can also be found by subtracting f_1 from f_2.

$$f_2 - f_1 = 392 - 262 = 130 \text{ Hz}$$

Therefore, the tone of average frequency, 327 hertz, has a beat of 130 hertz (beats/per second).

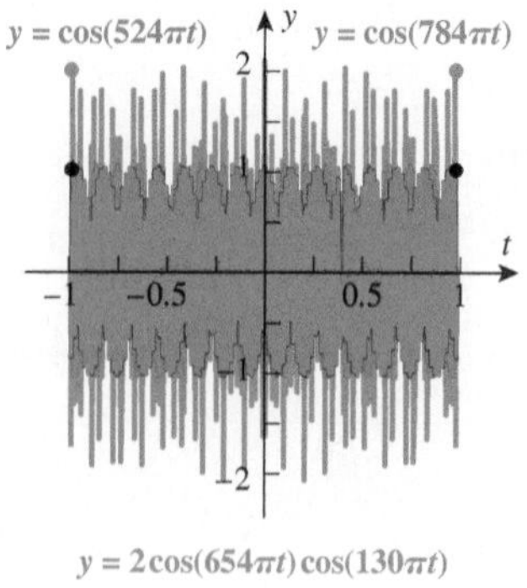

[SECTION 6.4] SUMMARY

In this section, we used the sum and difference identities to derive the product-to-sum identities. The product-to-sum identities allowed us to express products as sums.

$$\cos A \cos B = \frac{1}{2}[\cos(A + B) + \cos(A - B)]$$

$$\sin A \sin B = \frac{1}{2}[\cos(A - B) - \cos(A + B)]$$

$$\sin A \cos B = \frac{1}{2}[\sin(A + B) + \sin(A - B)]$$

We then used the product-to-sum identities to derive the sum-to-product identities. The sum-to-product identities allow us to express sums as products.

$$\sin A + \sin B = 2\sin\left(\frac{A + B}{2}\right)\cos\left(\frac{A - B}{2}\right)$$

$$\sin A - \sin B = 2\sin\left(\frac{A - B}{2}\right)\cos\left(\frac{A + B}{2}\right)$$

$$\cos A + \cos B = 2\cos\left(\frac{A + B}{2}\right)\cos\left(\frac{A - B}{2}\right)$$

$$\cos A - \cos B = -2\sin\left(\frac{A + B}{2}\right)\sin\left(\frac{A - B}{2}\right)$$

[SECTION 6.4] EXERCISES

• SKILLS

In Exercises 1–14, write each product as a sum or difference of sines and/or cosines.

1. $\sin(2x)\cos x$
2. $\cos(10x)\sin(5x)$
3. $5\sin(4x)\sin(6x)$
4. $-3\sin(2x)\sin(4x)$
5. $4\cos(-x)\cos(2x)$
6. $-8\cos(3x)\cos(5x)$
7. $\sin\left(\frac{3x}{2}\right)\sin\left(\frac{5x}{2}\right)$
8. $\sin\left(\frac{\pi x}{2}\right)\sin\left(\frac{5\pi x}{2}\right)$
9. $\cos\left(\frac{2x}{3}\right)\cos\left(\frac{4x}{3}\right)$
10. $\sin\left(-\frac{\pi}{4}x\right)\cos\left(-\frac{\pi}{2}x\right)$
11. $-3\cos(0.4x)\cos(1.5x)$
12. $2\sin(2.1x)\sin(3.4x)$
13. $4\sin(-\sqrt{3}x)\cos(3\sqrt{3}x)$
14. $-5\cos\left(-\frac{\sqrt{2}}{3}x\right)\sin\left(\frac{5\sqrt{2}}{3}x\right)$

In Exercises 15–28, write each expression as a product of sines and/or cosines.

15. $\cos(5x) + \cos(3x)$
16. $\cos(2x) - \cos(4x)$
17. $\sin(3x) - \sin x$
18. $\sin(10x) + \sin(5x)$
19. $\sin\left(\frac{x}{2}\right) - \sin\left(\frac{5x}{2}\right)$
20. $\cos\left(\frac{x}{2}\right) - \cos\left(\frac{5x}{2}\right)$
21. $\cos\left(\frac{2}{3}x\right) + \cos\left(\frac{7}{3}x\right)$
22. $\sin\left(\frac{2}{3}x\right) + \sin\left(\frac{7}{3}x\right)$
23. $\sin(0.4x) + \sin(0.6x)$

24. $\cos(0.3x) - \cos(0.5x)$

25. $\sin(\sqrt{5}x) - \sin(3\sqrt{5}x)$

26. $\cos(-3\sqrt{7}x) - \cos(2\sqrt{7}x)$

27. $\cos\left(-\frac{\pi}{4}x\right) + \cos\left(\frac{\pi}{6}x\right)$

28. $\sin\left(\frac{3\pi}{4}x\right) + \sin\left(\frac{5\pi}{4}x\right)$

In Exercises 29–34, simplify the trigonometric expressions.

29. $\dfrac{\cos(3x) - \cos x}{\sin(3x) + \sin x}$

30. $\dfrac{\sin(4x) + \sin(2x)}{\cos(4x) - \cos(2x)}$

31. $\dfrac{\cos x - \cos(3x)}{\sin(3x) - \sin x}$

32. $\dfrac{\sin(4x) + \sin(2x)}{\cos(4x) + \cos(2x)}$

33. $\dfrac{\cos(5x) + \cos(2x)}{\sin(5x) - \sin(2x)}$

34. $\dfrac{\sin(7x) - \sin(2x)}{\cos(7x) - \cos(2x)}$

In Exercises 35–42, verify the identities.

35. $\dfrac{\sin A + \sin B}{\cos A + \cos B} = \tan\left(\dfrac{A+B}{2}\right)$

36. $\dfrac{\sin A - \sin B}{\cos A + \cos B} = \tan\left(\dfrac{A-B}{2}\right)$

37. $\dfrac{\cos A - \cos B}{\sin A + \sin B} = -\tan\left(\dfrac{A-B}{2}\right)$

38. $\dfrac{\cos A - \cos B}{\sin A - \sin B} = -\tan\left(\dfrac{A+B}{2}\right)$

39. $\dfrac{\sin A + \sin B}{\sin A - \sin B} = \tan\left(\dfrac{A+B}{2}\right)\cot\left(\dfrac{A-B}{2}\right)$

40. $\dfrac{\cos A - \cos B}{\cos A + \cos B} = -\tan\left(\dfrac{A+B}{2}\right)\tan\left(\dfrac{A-B}{2}\right)$

41. $\dfrac{\cos(A+B) + \cos(A-B)}{\sin(A+B) + \sin(A-B)} = \cot A$

42. $\dfrac{\cos(A-B) - \cos(A+B)}{\sin(A+B) + \sin(A-B)} = \tan B$

• APPLICATIONS

43. **Business.** An analysis of the monthly costs and monthly revenues of a toy store indicates that monthly costs fluctuate (increase and decrease) according to the function

$$C(t) = \sin\left(\frac{\pi}{6}t + \pi\right)$$

and monthly revenues fluctuate (increase and decrease) according to the function

$$R(t) = \sin\left(\frac{\pi}{6}t + \frac{5\pi}{3}\right)$$

Find the function that describes how the monthly profits fluctuate: $P(t) = R(t) - C(t)$. Using identities in this section, express $P(t)$ in terms of a cosine function.

44. **Business.** An analysis of the monthly costs and monthly revenues of an electronics manufacturer indicates that monthly costs fluctuate (increase and decrease) according to the function

$$C(t) = \cos\left(\frac{\pi}{3}t + \frac{\pi}{3}\right)$$

and monthly revenues fluctuate (increase and decrease) according to the function

$$R(t) = \cos\left(\frac{\pi}{3}t\right)$$

Find the function that describes how the monthly profits fluctuate: $P(t) = R(t) - C(t)$. Using identities in this section, express $P(t)$ in terms of a sine function.

45. **Music.** Write a mathematical description of a tone that results from simultaneously playing a G and a B. What is the beat frequency? What is the average frequency?

46. **Music.** Write a mathematical description of a tone that results from simultaneously playing an F and an A. What is the beat frequency? What is the average frequency?

47. **Optics.** Two optical signals with uniform ($A = 1$) intensities and wavelengths of 1.55 μm and 0.63 μm are "beat" together. What is the resulting sum if their individual signals are given by $\sin\left(\dfrac{2\pi tc}{1.55\,\mu\text{m}}\right)$ and $\sin\left(\dfrac{2\pi tc}{0.63\,\mu\text{m}}\right)$, where $c = 3.0 \times 10^8$ m/s?

Note: $1\,\mu\text{m} = 10^{-6}$ m.

48. **Optics.** The two optical signals in Exercise 47 are beat together. What are the average frequency and the beat frequency?

For Exercises 49 and 50, refer to the following:

Touch-tone keypads have the following simultaneous low and high frequencies.

FREQUENCY	1209 Hz	1336 Hz	1477 Hz
697 Hz	1	2	3
770 Hz	4	5	6
852 Hz	7	8	9
941 Hz	*	0	#

The signal given when a key is pressed is $\sin(2\pi f_1 t) + \sin(2\pi f_2 t)$, where f_1 is the low frequency and f_2 is the high frequency.

49. **Touch-Tone Dialing.** What is the mathematical function that models the sound of dialing 4?

50. **Touch-Tone Dialing.** What is the mathematical function that models the sound of dialing 3?

• CATCH THE MISTAKE

In Exercises 51 and 52, explain the mistake that is made.

51. Simplify the expression $(\cos A - \cos B)^2 + (\sin A - \sin B)^2$.

Solution:

Expand by squaring.

$\cos^2 A - 2\cos A\cos B + \cos^2 B + \sin^2 A - 2\sin A\sin B + \sin^2 B$

Group terms.

$\cos^2 A + \sin^2 A - 2\cos A\cos B - 2\sin A\sin B + \cos^2 B + \sin^2 B$

Simplify using the Pythagorean identity.

$\underbrace{\cos^2 A + \sin^2 A}_{1} - 2\cos A\cos B - 2\sin A\sin B + \underbrace{\cos^2 B + \sin^2 B}_{1}$

Factor the common 2. $2(1 - \cos A\cos B - \sin A\sin B)$

Simplify. $2(1 - \cos AB - \sin AB)$

This is incorrect. What mistakes were made?

52. Simplify the expression $(\sin A - \sin B)(\cos A + \cos B)$.

Solution:

Multiply the expressions using the distributive property.

$\sin A\cos A + \sin A\cos B - \sin B\cos A - \sin B\cos B$

Cancel the second and third terms.

$\sin A\cos A - \sin B\cos B$

Use the product-to-sum identity.

$\underbrace{\sin A\cos A}_{\frac{1}{2}[\sin(A+A)+\sin(A-A)]} - \underbrace{\sin B\cos B}_{\frac{1}{2}[\sin(B+B)+\sin(B-B)]}$

Simplify. $= \frac{1}{2}\sin(2A) - \frac{1}{2}\sin(2B)$

This is incorrect. What mistake was made?

• CONCEPTUAL

In Exercises 53–56, determine whether each statement is true or false.

53. $\cos A\cos B = \cos AB$

54. $\sin A\sin B = \sin AB$

55. The product of two cosine functions is a sum of two other cosine functions.

56. The product of two sine functions is a difference of two cosine functions.

57. Write $\sin A\sin B\sin C$ as a sum or difference of sines and cosines.

58. Write $\cos A\cos B\cos C$ as a sum or difference of sines and cosines.

• CHALLENGE

59. Prove the addition formula
$\cos(A + B) = \cos A\cos B - \sin A\sin B$
using the identities of this section.

60. Prove the difference formula
$\sin(A - B) = \sin A\cos B - \sin B\cos A$
using the identities of this section.

61. Graph $y = 1 - 3\sin(\pi x)\sin\left(-\frac{\pi}{6}x\right)$.

62. Graph $y = 4\sin(2x - 1)\cos(2 - x)$.

63. Graph $y = -\cos\left(\frac{2\pi}{3}x\right)\cos\left(\frac{5\pi}{6}x\right)$.

64. Graph $y = x - \cos(2x)\sin(3x)$.

• PREVIEW TO CALCULUS

In calculus, the method of separation of variables is used to solve certain differential equations. Given an equation with two variables, the method consists of writing the equation in such a way that each side of the equation contains only one type of variable.

In Exercises 65–68, use the product-to-sum and sum-to-product identities to separate the variables *x* and *y* in each equation.

65. $\sin\left(\frac{x+y}{2}\right)\sin\left(\frac{x-y}{2}\right) = \frac{1}{5}$

66. $\frac{1}{2} = \sin\left(\frac{x+y}{2}\right)\cos\left(\frac{x-y}{2}\right)$

67. $\sin(x + y) = 1 + \sin(x - y)$

68. $2 + \cos(x + y) = \cos(x - y)$

6.5 INVERSE TRIGONOMETRIC FUNCTIONS

SKILLS OBJECTIVES

- Find exact values of an inverse sine function.
- Find exact values of an inverse cosine function.
- Find exact values of an inverse tangent function.
- Find exact values of the cotangent, cosecant, and secant inverse functions.
- Use identities to find exact values of trigonometric expressions involving inverse trigonometric functions.

CONCEPTUAL OBJECTIVES

- Understand that the domain of the sine function is restricted to $\left[-\frac{\pi}{2}, \frac{\pi}{2}\right]$ in order for the inverse sine function to exist.
- Understand that the domain of the cosine function is restricted to $[0, \pi]$ in order for the inverse cosine function to exist.
- Understand that the domain of the tangent function is restricted to $\left(-\frac{\pi}{2}, \frac{\pi}{2}\right)$ in order for the inverse tangent function to exist.
- Understand that the cotangent, cosecant, and secant inverse functions are not found from the reciprocal of the tangent, sine, and cosine, respectively, but rather from the inverse secant, inverse cosecant, and inverse cotangent identities.
- Visualize the quadrants in order to find exact values of trigonometric expressions involving inverse trigonometric functions.

In Section 1.5, we discussed one-to-one functions and inverse functions. Here we present a summary of that section. A function is one-to-one if it passes the horizontal line test: No two x-values map to the same y-value.

Notice that the sine function does not pass the horizontal line test. However, if we restrict the domain to $-\frac{\pi}{2} \leq x \leq \frac{\pi}{2}$, then the restricted function is one-to-one.

Recall that if $y = f(x)$, then $x = f^{-1}(y)$.

The following are the properties of inverse functions:

1. If f is a one-to-one function, then the inverse function f^{-1} exists.
2. The domain of f^{-1} = the range of f.
   The range of f^{-1} = the domain of f.
3. $f^{-1}(f(x)) = x$ for all x in the domain of f.
   $f(f^{-1}(x)) = x$ for all x in the domain of f^{-1}.
4. The graph of f^{-1} is the reflection of the graph of f about the line $y = x$. If the point (a, b) lies on the graph of a function, then the point (b, a) lies on the graph of its inverse.

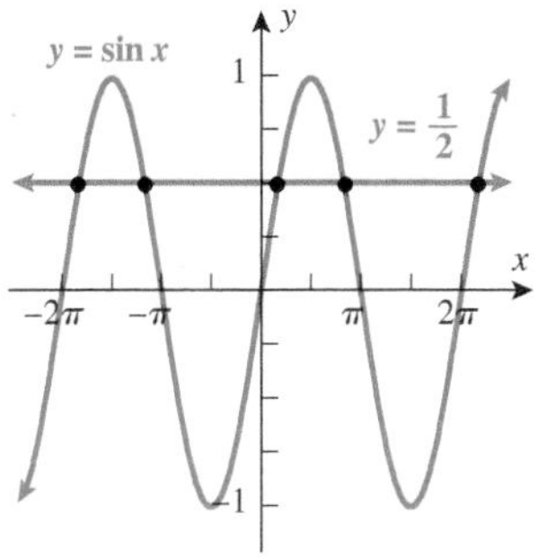

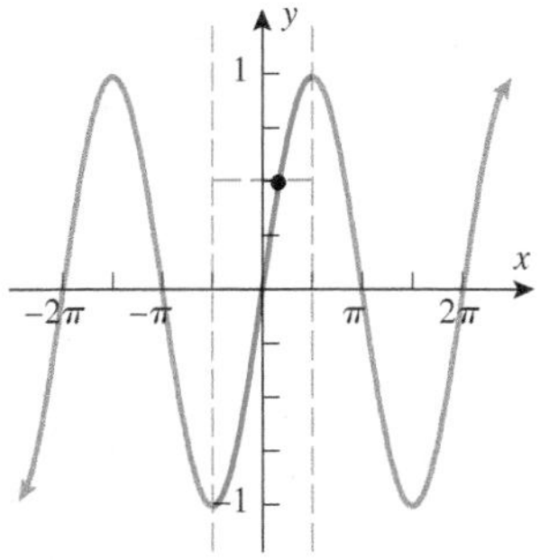

6.5.1 Inverse Sine Function

Let us start with the sine function with the restricted domain $\left[-\frac{\pi}{2}, \frac{\pi}{2}\right]$.

$$y = \sin x \quad \text{Domain: } \left[-\frac{\pi}{2}, \frac{\pi}{2}\right] \quad \text{Range: } [-1, 1]$$

x	y
$-\frac{\pi}{2}$	-1
$-\frac{\pi}{4}$	$-\frac{\sqrt{2}}{2}$
0	0
$\frac{\pi}{4}$	$\frac{\sqrt{2}}{2}$
$\frac{\pi}{2}$	1

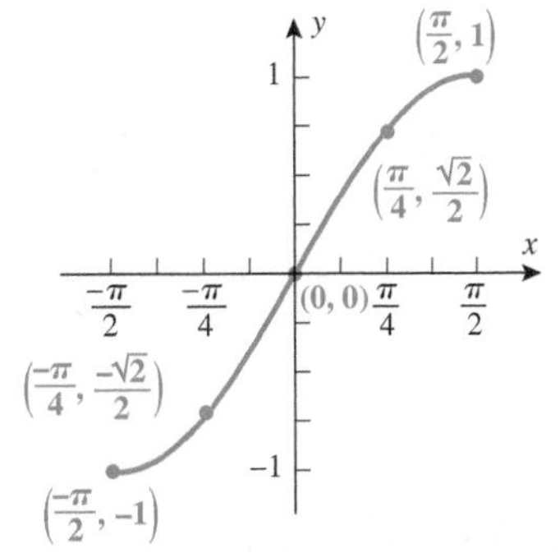

6.5.1 SKILL

Find exact values of an inverse sine function.

6.5.1 CONCEPTUAL

Understand that the domain of the sine function is restricted to $\left[-\frac{\pi}{2}, \frac{\pi}{2}\right]$ in order for the inverse sine function to exist.

STUDY TIP

The inverse sine function gives an angle on the right half of the unit circle (QI and QIV).

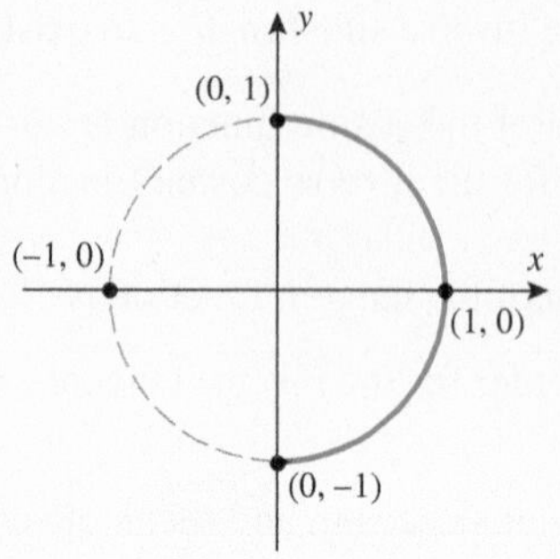

By the properties of inverse functions, the inverse sine function will have a domain of $[-1, 1]$ and a range of $\left[-\frac{\pi}{2}, \frac{\pi}{2}\right]$. To find the inverse sine function, we interchange the x- and y-values of $y = \sin x$.

$$y = \sin^{-1}x \quad \text{Domain: } [-1, 1] \quad \text{Range: } \left[-\frac{\pi}{2}, \frac{\pi}{2}\right]$$

x	y
-1	$-\frac{\pi}{2}$
$-\frac{\sqrt{2}}{2}$	$-\frac{\pi}{4}$
0	0
$\frac{\sqrt{2}}{2}$	$\frac{\pi}{4}$
1	$\frac{\pi}{2}$

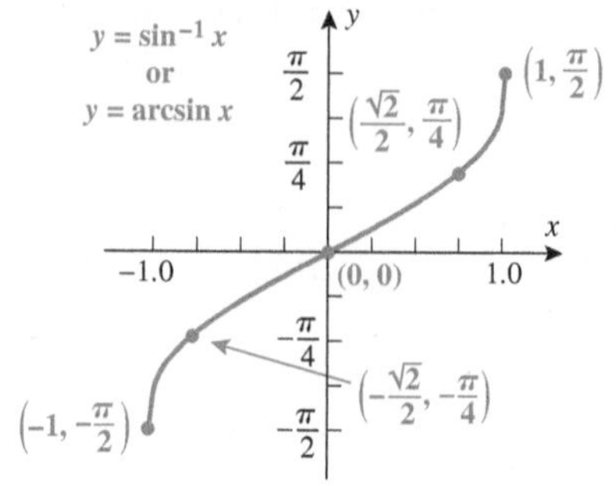

Notice that the inverse sine function, like the sine function, is an odd function (symmetric about the origin).

If the sine of an angle is known, and the angle is between $-\frac{\pi}{2}$ and $\frac{\pi}{2}$, what is the measure of that angle? The inverse sine function determines that angle measure. Another notation for the inverse sine function is $\arcsin x$.

INVERSE SINE FUNCTION

$$\underbrace{y = \sin^{-1}x \quad \text{or} \quad y = \arcsin x}_{\text{"}y\text{ is the inverse sine of }x\text{"}} \qquad \text{means} \qquad \underbrace{x = \sin y}_{\text{"}y\text{ is the angle measure whose sine equals }x\text{"}}$$

$$\text{where} \quad -1 \le x \le 1 \quad \text{and} \quad -\frac{\pi}{2} \le y \le \frac{\pi}{2}$$

STUDY TIP

Trigonometric functions take angle measures and return real numbers. Inverse trigonometric functions take real numbers and return angle measures.

It is important to note that the -1 as the superscript indicates an inverse function. Therefore, the inverse sine function should not be interpreted as a reciprocal:

$$\sin^{-1}x \neq \frac{1}{\sin x}$$

EXAMPLE 1 **Finding Exact Values of an Inverse Sine Function**

Find the exact value of each of the following expressions:

a. $\sin^{-1}\left(\frac{\sqrt{3}}{2}\right)$ **b.** $\arcsin\left(-\frac{1}{2}\right)$

Solution (a):

Let $\theta = \sin^{-1}\left(\frac{\sqrt{3}}{2}\right)$. $\sin\theta = \frac{\sqrt{3}}{2}$ for $-\frac{\pi}{2} \le \theta \le \frac{\pi}{2}$

Which value of θ, in the range $-\frac{\pi}{2} \le \theta \le \frac{\pi}{2}$, corresponds to a sine value of $\frac{\sqrt{3}}{2}$?

- The range $-\frac{\pi}{2} \le \theta \le \frac{\pi}{2}$ corresponds to quadrants I and IV.
- The sine function is positive in quadrant I.
- We look for a value of θ in quadrant I that has a sine value of $\frac{\sqrt{3}}{2}$. $\theta = \frac{\pi}{3}$

$\sin\frac{\pi}{3} = \frac{\sqrt{3}}{2}$ and $\frac{\pi}{3}$ is in the interval $\left[-\frac{\pi}{2}, \frac{\pi}{2}\right]$. $\boxed{\sin^{-1}\left(\frac{\sqrt{3}}{2}\right) = \frac{\pi}{3}}$

Calculator Confirmation: Since $\frac{\pi}{3} = 60°$, if our calculator is set in degree mode, we should find that $\sin^{-1}\left(\frac{\sqrt{3}}{2}\right)$ is equal to $60°$.

Solution (b):

Let $\theta = \arcsin\left(-\frac{1}{2}\right)$. $\sin\theta = -\frac{1}{2}$ for $-\frac{\pi}{2} \le \theta \le \frac{\pi}{2}$

Which value of θ, in the range $-\frac{\pi}{2} \le \theta \le \frac{\pi}{2}$, corresponds to a sine value of $-\frac{1}{2}$?

- The range $-\frac{\pi}{2} \le \theta \le \frac{\pi}{2}$ corresponds to quadrants I and IV.
- The sine function is negative in quadrant IV.
- We look for a value of θ in quadrant IV that has a sine value of $-\frac{1}{2}$. $\theta = -\frac{\pi}{6}$

$\sin\left(-\frac{\pi}{6}\right) = -\frac{1}{2}$ and $-\frac{\pi}{6}$ is in the interval $\left[-\frac{\pi}{2}, \frac{\pi}{2}\right]$. $\boxed{\arcsin\left(-\frac{1}{2}\right) = -\frac{\pi}{6}}$

Calculator Confirmation: Since $-\frac{\pi}{6} = -30°$, if our calculator is set in degree mode, we should find that $\sin^{-1}\left(-\frac{1}{2}\right)$ is equal to $-30°$.

STUDY TIP

In Example 1, note that the graphs help identify the desired angles.

a.

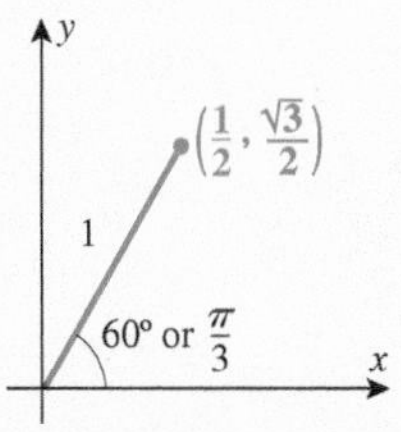

b.

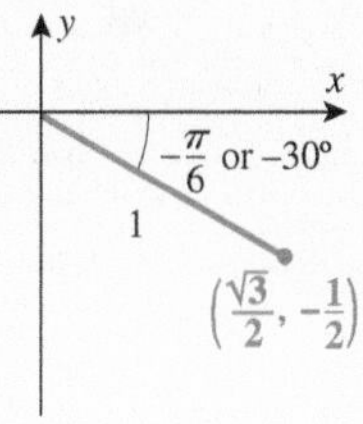

YOUR TURN Find the exact value of each of the following expressions:

a. $\sin^{-1}\left(-\frac{\sqrt{3}}{2}\right)$ **b.** $\arcsin\left(\frac{1}{2}\right)$

ANSWER

a. $-\frac{\pi}{3}$ b. $\frac{\pi}{6}$

In Example 1, we see in part (a), both 60° and 120° correspond to the sine function equal to $\frac{\sqrt{3}}{2}$, and only one of them is valid, which is why the domain restrictions are necessary for inverse functions except for quadrantal angles. There are always two angles (values) from 0 to 360° or 0 to 2π (except that only 90°, or $\frac{\pi}{2}$, and 270°, or $\frac{3\pi}{2}$, correspond to 1 and -1, respectively) that correspond to the sine function equal to a particular value.

It is important to note that the inverse sine function has a domain $[-1, 1]$. For example, $\sin^{-1}3$ does not exist because 3 is not in the domain of the inverse sine function. Notice that calculator evaluation of $\sin^{-1}3$ says *error*. Calculators can be used to evaluate inverse sine functions when an exact evaluation is not feasible, just as they are for the basic trigonometric functions. For example, $\sin^{-1}0.3 \approx 17.46°$, or 0.305 radian.

We now state the properties relating the sine function and the inverse sine function that follow directly from properties of inverse functions.

SINE–INVERSE SINE IDENTITIES

$$\sin^{-1}(\sin x) = x \quad \text{for} \quad -\frac{\pi}{2} \leq x \leq \frac{\pi}{2}$$

$$\sin(\sin^{-1}x) = x \quad \text{for} \quad -1 \leq x \leq 1$$

For example, $\sin^{-1}\left[\sin\left(\frac{\pi}{12}\right)\right] = \frac{\pi}{12}$, since $\frac{\pi}{12}$ is in the interval $\left[-\frac{\pi}{2}, \frac{\pi}{2}\right]$. However, you must be careful not to overlook the domain restriction for which these identities hold, as illustrated in the next example.

[CONCEPT CHECK]

Evaluate (if possible) $\sin(\sin^{-1}(A))$ when (A) $A > 1$, (B) $A = 0$, (C) $A = -1$.

ANSWER (A) DNE (B) 0 (C) -1

EXAMPLE 2 Using Inverse Identities to Evaluate Expressions Involving Inverse Sine Functions

Find the exact value of each of the following trigonometric expressions:

a. $\sin\left[\sin^{-1}\left(\frac{\sqrt{2}}{2}\right)\right]$ **b.** $\sin^{-1}\left[\sin\left(\frac{3\pi}{4}\right)\right]$

Solution (a):

Write the appropriate identity. $\sin(\sin^{-1}x) = x$ for $-1 \leq x \leq 1$

Let $x = \frac{\sqrt{2}}{2}$, which is in the interval $[-1, 1]$.

Since the domain restriction is met, the identity can be used. $\boxed{\sin\left[\sin^{-1}\left(\frac{\sqrt{2}}{2}\right)\right] = \frac{\sqrt{2}}{2}}$

Solution (b):

common mistake

Ignoring the domain restrictions on inverse identities.

✓CORRECT

Write the appropriate identity.

$\sin^{-1}(\sin x) = x$ for $-\frac{\pi}{2} \le x \le \frac{\pi}{2}$

Let $x = \frac{3\pi}{4}$, which is *not* in the interval $\left[-\frac{\pi}{2}, \frac{\pi}{2}\right]$.

Since the domain restriction is not met, the identity cannot be used. Instead, we look for a value in the domain that corresponds to the same value of sine.

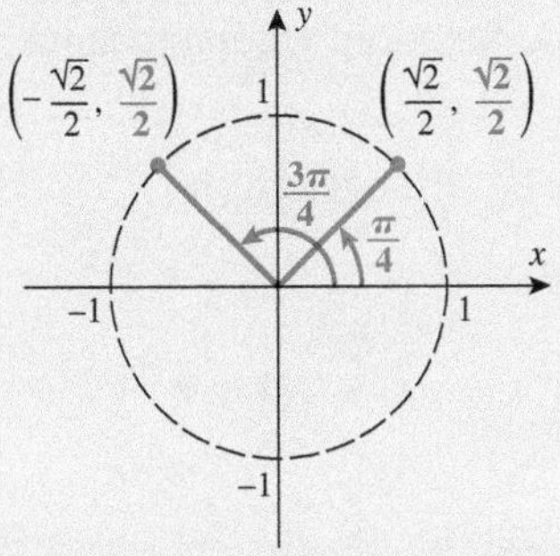

Substitute $\sin\frac{3\pi}{4} = \sin\frac{\pi}{4}$ into the expression.

$$\sin^{-1}\left[\sin\left(\frac{3\pi}{4}\right)\right] = \sin^{-1}\left[\sin\left(\frac{\pi}{4}\right)\right]$$

Since $\frac{\pi}{4}$ is in the interval $\left[-\frac{\pi}{2}, \frac{\pi}{2}\right]$, we can use the identity.

$$\sin^{-1}\left[\sin\left(\frac{3\pi}{4}\right)\right] = \sin^{-1}\left[\sin\left(\frac{\pi}{4}\right)\right] = \boxed{\frac{\pi}{4}}$$

✗INCORRECT

$\sin^{-1}(\sin x) = x$ **ERROR**

Let $x = \frac{3\pi}{4}$.

(Forgot the domain restriction.)

$$\sin^{-1}\left[\sin\left(\frac{3\pi}{4}\right)\right] = \frac{3\pi}{4}$$

INCORRECT

YOUR TURN Find the exact value of each of the following trigonometric expressions:

a. $\sin\left[\sin^{-1}\left(-\frac{1}{2}\right)\right]$ **b.** $\sin^{-1}\left[\sin\left(\frac{5\pi}{6}\right)\right]$

ANSWER

a. $-\frac{1}{2}$ b. $\frac{\pi}{6}$

6.5.2 Inverse Cosine Function

6.5.2 SKILL

Find exact values of an inverse cosine function.

6.5.2 CONCEPTUAL

Understand that the domain of the cosine function is restricted to $[0, \pi]$ in order for the inverse cosine function to exist.

The cosine function is also not a one-to-one function, so we must restrict the domain in order to develop the inverse cosine function.

$$y = \cos x \quad \text{Domain: } [0, \pi] \quad \text{Range: } [-1, 1]$$

x	y
0	1
$\frac{\pi}{4}$	$\frac{\sqrt{2}}{2}$
$\frac{\pi}{2}$	0
$\frac{3\pi}{4}$	$-\frac{\sqrt{2}}{2}$
π	-1

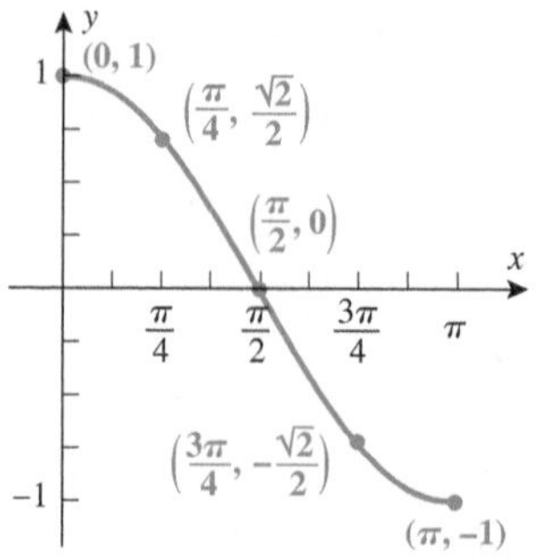

By the properties of inverses, the inverse cosine function will have a domain of $[-1,1]$ and a range of $[0, \pi]$. To find the inverse cosine function, we interchange the x- and y-values of $y = \cos x$.

$$y = \cos^{-1}x \quad \text{Domain: } [-1, 1] \quad \text{Range: } [0, \pi]$$

x	y
-1	π
$-\frac{\sqrt{2}}{2}$	$\frac{3\pi}{4}$
0	$\frac{\pi}{2}$
$\frac{\sqrt{2}}{2}$	$\frac{\pi}{4}$
1	0

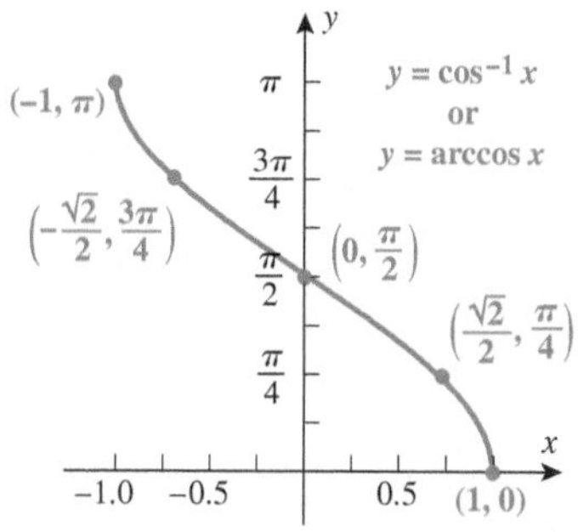

STUDY TIP

The inverse cosine function gives an angle on the top half of the unit circle (QI and QII).

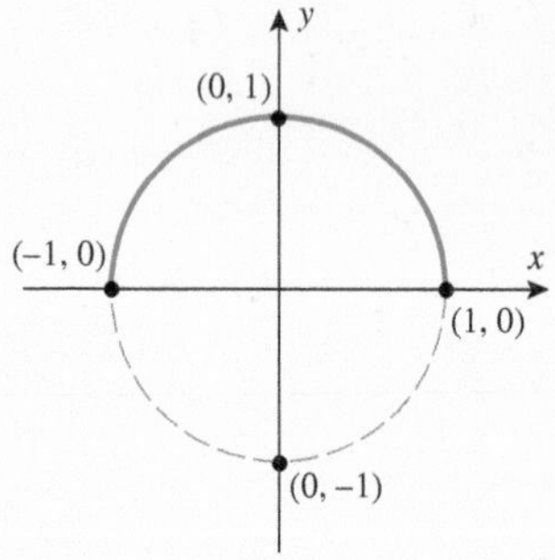

Notice that the inverse cosine function, unlike the cosine function, is not symmetric about the y-axis or the origin. Although the inverse sine and inverse cosine functions have the same domain, they behave differently. The inverse sine function increases on its domain (from left to right), whereas the inverse cosine function decreases on its domain (from left to right).

If the cosine of an angle is known and the angle is between 0 and π, what is the measure of that angle? The inverse cosine function determines that angle measure. Another notation for the inverse cosine function is $\arccos x$.

STUDY TIP

$$\cos^{-1}x \neq \frac{1}{\cos x}$$

INVERSE COSINE FUNCTION

$$\underbrace{y = \cos^{-1}x \quad \text{or} \quad y = \arccos x}_{\text{"}y\text{ is the inverse cosine of }x\text{"}} \qquad \text{means} \qquad \underbrace{x = \cos y}_{\text{"}y\text{ is the angle measure whose cosine equals }x\text{"}}$$

where $-1 \leq x \leq 1$ and $0 \leq y \leq \pi$

EXAMPLE 3 **Finding Exact Values of an Inverse Cosine Function**

Find the exact value of each of the following expressions:

a. $\cos^{-1}\left(-\frac{\sqrt{2}}{2}\right)$ **b.** $\arccos 0$

Solution (a):

Let $\theta = \cos^{-1}\left(-\frac{\sqrt{2}}{2}\right)$. $\cos\theta = -\frac{\sqrt{2}}{2}$ when $0 \le \theta \le \pi$

Which value of θ, in the range $0 \le \theta \le \pi$, corresponds to a cosine value of $-\frac{\sqrt{2}}{2}$?

- The range $0 \le \theta \le \pi$ corresponds to quadrants I and II.
- The cosine function is negative in quadrant II.
- We look for a value of θ in quadrant II that has a cosine value of $-\frac{\sqrt{2}}{2}$. $\theta = \frac{3\pi}{4}$

$\cos\left(\frac{3\pi}{4}\right) = -\frac{\sqrt{2}}{2}$ and $\frac{3\pi}{4}$ is in the interval $[0, \pi]$. $\boxed{\cos^{-1}\left(-\frac{\sqrt{2}}{2}\right) = \frac{3\pi}{4}}$

Calculator Confirmation: Since $\frac{3\pi}{4} = 135°$, if our calculator is set in degree mode, we should find that $\cos^{-1}\left(-\frac{\sqrt{2}}{2}\right)$ is equal to 135°.

Solution (b):

Let $\theta = \arccos 0$. $\cos\theta = 0$ when $0 \le \theta \le \pi$

Which value of θ, in the range $0 \le \theta \le \pi$, corresponds to a cosine value of 0? $\theta = \frac{\pi}{2}$

$\cos\left(\frac{\pi}{2}\right) = 0$ and $\frac{\pi}{2}$ is in the interval $[0, \pi]$. $\boxed{\arccos 0 = \frac{\pi}{2}}$

Calculator Confirmation: Since $\frac{\pi}{2} = 90°$, if our calculator is set in degree mode, we should find that $\cos^{-1} 0$ is equal to 90°.

YOUR TURN Find the exact value of each of the following expressions:

a. $\cos^{-1}\left(\frac{\sqrt{2}}{2}\right)$ **b.** $\arccos 1$

ANSWER

a. $\frac{\pi}{4}$ b. 0

We now state the properties relating the cosine function and the inverse cosine function that follow directly from the properties of inverses.

COSINE–INVERSE COSINE IDENTITIES

$$\cos^{-1}(\cos x) = x \quad \text{for} \quad 0 \le x \le \pi$$

$$\cos(\cos^{-1} x) = x \quad \text{for} \quad -1 \le x \le 1$$

As was the case with inverse identities for the sine function, you must be careful not to overlook the domain restrictions governing when each of these identities holds.

EXAMPLE 4 Using Inverse Identities to Evaluate Expressions Involving Inverse Cosine Functions

Find the exact value of each of the following trigonometric expressions:

a. $\cos\left[\cos^{-1}\left(-\frac{1}{2}\right)\right]$ **b.** $\cos^{-1}\left[\cos\left(\frac{7\pi}{4}\right)\right]$

Solution (a):

Write the appropriate identity. $\cos(\cos^{-1}x) = x$ for $-1 \le x \le 1$

Let $x = -\frac{1}{2}$, which is in the interval $[-1, 1]$.

Since the domain restriction is met, the identity can be used. $\cos\left[\cos^{-1}\left(-\frac{1}{2}\right)\right] = \boxed{-\frac{1}{2}}$

Solution (b):

Write the appropriate identity. $\cos^{-1}(\cos x) = x$ for $0 \le x \le \pi$

Let $x = \frac{7\pi}{4}$, which is *not* in the interval $[0, \pi]$.

Since the domain restriction is not met, the identity cannot be used.

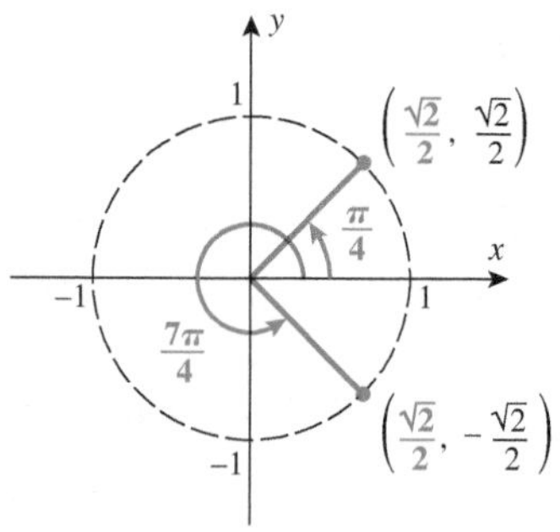

Instead, we find another angle in the interval that has the same cosine value. $\cos\left(\frac{7\pi}{4}\right) = \cos\left(\frac{\pi}{4}\right)$

Substitute $\cos\left(\frac{7\pi}{4}\right) = \cos\left(\frac{\pi}{4}\right)$ into the expression. $\cos^{-1}\left[\cos\left(\frac{7\pi}{4}\right)\right] = \cos^{-1}\left[\cos\left(\frac{\pi}{4}\right)\right]$

Since $\frac{\pi}{4}$ is in the interval $[0, \pi]$, we can use the identity. $= \boxed{\frac{\pi}{4}}$

YOUR TURN Find the exact value of each of the following trigonometric expressions:

a. $\cos\left[\cos^{-1}\left(\frac{1}{2}\right)\right]$ **b.** $\cos^{-1}\left[\cos\left(-\frac{\pi}{6}\right)\right]$

[CONCEPT CHECK]

Evaluate (if possible) $\cos^{-1}(\cos(A))$ when

(A) $A = \frac{\pi}{2}$

(B) $A = 2n\pi - \frac{\pi}{4}$, where n is an integer.

ANSWER (A) $\frac{\pi}{2}$ (B) $\frac{\pi}{4}$

ANSWER

a. $\frac{1}{2}$ b. $\frac{\pi}{6}$

6.5.3 Inverse Tangent Function

6.5.3 SKILL

Find exact values of an inverse tangent function.

6.5.3 CONCEPTUAL

Understand that the domain of the tangent function is restricted to $\left(-\frac{\pi}{2}, \frac{\pi}{2}\right)$ in order for the inverse tangent function to exist.

The tangent function, too, is not a one-to-one function (it fails the horizontal line test). Let us start with the tangent function with a restricted domain:

$$y = \tan x \quad \text{Domain: } \left(-\frac{\pi}{2}, \frac{\pi}{2}\right) \quad \text{Range: } (-\infty, \infty)$$

x	y
$-\frac{\pi}{2}$	$-\infty$
$-\frac{\pi}{4}$	-1
0	0
$\frac{\pi}{4}$	1
$\frac{\pi}{2}$	∞

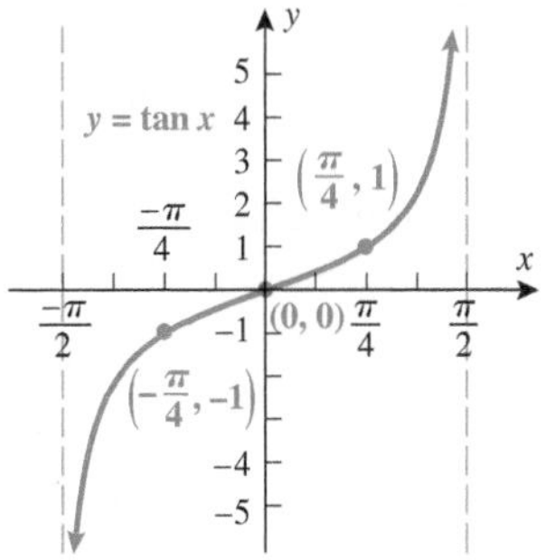

By the properties of inverse functions, the inverse tangent function will have a domain of $(-\infty, \infty)$ and a range of $\left(-\frac{\pi}{2}, \frac{\pi}{2}\right)$. To find the inverse tangent function, interchange x- and y-values.

$$y = \tan^{-1} x \quad \text{Domain: } (-\infty, \infty) \quad \text{Range: } \left(-\frac{\pi}{2}, \frac{\pi}{2}\right)$$

x	y
$-\infty$	$-\frac{\pi}{2}$
-1	$-\frac{\pi}{4}$
0	0
1	$\frac{\pi}{4}$
∞	$\frac{\pi}{2}$

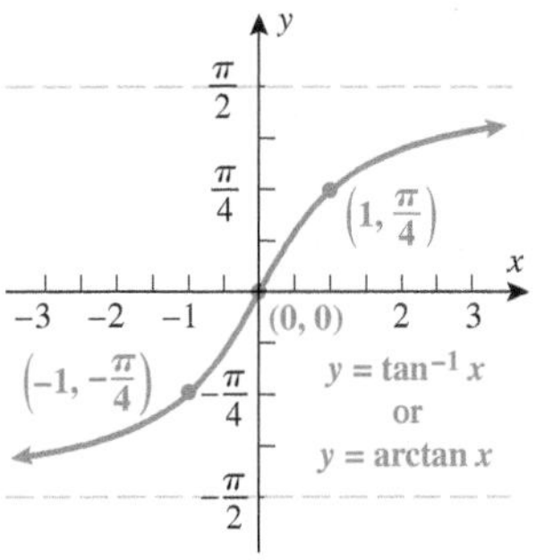

STUDY TIP

The inverse tangent function gives an angle on the right half of the unit circle (QI and QIV).

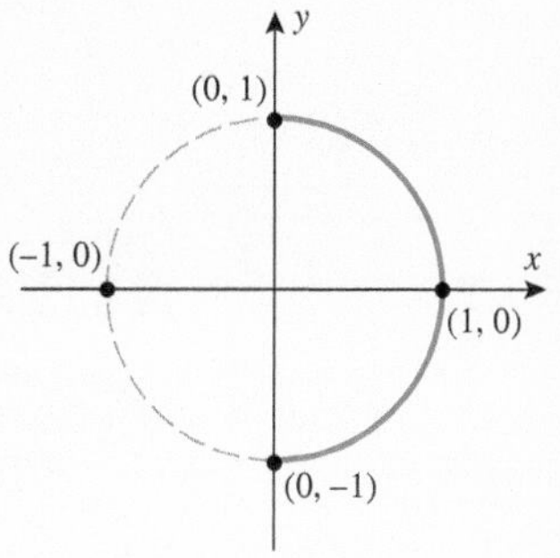

Notice that the inverse tangent function, like the tangent function, is an odd function (it is symmetric about the origin).

The inverse tangent function allows us to answer the question: If the tangent of an angle is known, what is the measure of that angle? Another notation for the inverse tangent function is $\arctan x$.

INVERSE TANGENT FUNCTION

$\underbrace{y = \tan^{-1} x \quad \text{or} \quad y = \arctan x}_{\text{"y is the inverse tangent of x"}}$ means $\underbrace{x = \tan y}_{\text{"y is the angle measure whose tangent equals x"}}$

where $-\frac{\pi}{2} < y < \frac{\pi}{2}$

EXAMPLE 5 Finding Exact Values of an Inverse Tangent Function

Find the exact value of each of the following expressions:

a. $\tan^{-1}(\sqrt{3})$ **b.** $\arctan 0$

Solution (a):

Let $\theta = \tan^{-1}(\sqrt{3})$. $\tan\theta = \sqrt{3}$ when $-\frac{\pi}{2} < \theta < \frac{\pi}{2}$

Which value of θ, in the range $-\frac{\pi}{2} < \theta < \frac{\pi}{2}$, corresponds to a tangent value of $\sqrt{3}$? $\theta = \frac{\pi}{3}$

$\tan\left(\frac{\pi}{3}\right) = \sqrt{3}$ and $\frac{\pi}{3}$ is in the interval $\left(-\frac{\pi}{2}, \frac{\pi}{2}\right)$. $\boxed{\tan^{-1}(\sqrt{3}) = \frac{\pi}{3}}$

Calculator Confirmation: Since $\frac{\pi}{3} = 60°$, if our calculator is set in degree mode, we should find that $\tan^{-1}(\sqrt{3})$ is equal to $60°$.

Solution (b):

Let $\theta = \arctan 0$. $\tan\theta = 0$ when $-\frac{\pi}{2} < \theta < \frac{\pi}{2}$

Which value of θ, in the range $-\frac{\pi}{2} < \theta < \frac{\pi}{2}$, corresponds to a tangent value of 0? $\theta = 0$

$\tan 0 = 0$, and 0 is in the interval $\left(-\frac{\pi}{2}, \frac{\pi}{2}\right)$. $\boxed{\arctan 0 = 0}$

Calculator Confirmation: $\tan^{-1} 0$ is equal to 0.

We now state the properties relating the tangent function and the inverse tangent function that follow directly from the properties of inverses.

TANGENT–INVERSE TANGENT IDENTITIES

$$\tan^{-1}(\tan x) = x \quad \text{for} \quad -\frac{\pi}{2} < x < \frac{\pi}{2}$$

$$\tan(\tan^{-1} x) = x \quad \text{for} \quad -\infty < x < \infty$$

EXAMPLE 6 **Using Inverse Identities to Evaluate Expressions Involving Inverse Tangent Functions**

Find the exact value of each of the following trigonometric expressions:

a. $\tan(\tan^{-1}17)$ **b.** $\tan^{-1}\left[\tan\left(\frac{2\pi}{3}\right)\right]$

Solution (a):

Write the appropriate identity. $\tan(\tan^{-1}x) = x$ for $-\infty < x < \infty$

Let $x = 17$, which is in the interval $(-\infty, \infty)$.

Since the domain restriction is met, the identity can be used. $\boxed{\tan(\tan^{-1}17) = 17}$

Solution (b):

Write the appropriate identity. $\tan^{-1}(\tan x) = x$ for $-\frac{\pi}{2} < x < \frac{\pi}{2}$

Let $x = \frac{2\pi}{3}$, which is *not* in the interval $\left(-\frac{\pi}{2}, \frac{\pi}{2}\right)$.

Since the domain restriction is not met, the identity cannot be used.

Instead, we find another angle in the interval that has the same tangent value. $\tan\left(\frac{2\pi}{3}\right) = \tan\left(-\frac{\pi}{3}\right)$

Substitute $\tan\left(\frac{2\pi}{3}\right) = \tan\left(-\frac{\pi}{3}\right)$ into the expression. $\tan^{-1}\left[\tan\left(\frac{2\pi}{3}\right)\right] = \tan^{-1}\left[\tan\left(-\frac{\pi}{3}\right)\right]$

Since $-\frac{\pi}{3}$ is in the interval $\left(-\frac{\pi}{2}, \frac{\pi}{2}\right)$, we can use the identity. $\tan^{-1}\left[\tan\left(\frac{2\pi}{3}\right)\right] = \boxed{-\frac{\pi}{3}}$

YOUR TURN Find the exact value of $\tan^{-1}\left[\tan\left(\frac{7\pi}{6}\right)\right]$.

ANSWER

$\frac{\pi}{6}$

[CONCEPT CHECK]

Evaluate $\arctan\left(\tan\left(2n\pi + \frac{5\pi}{4}\right)\right)$, where n is an integer.

ANSWER $\frac{\pi}{4}$

6.5.4 Remaining Inverse Trigonometric Functions

6.5.4 SKILL

Find exact values of the cotangent, cosecant, and secant inverse functions.

6.5.4 CONCEPTUAL

Understand that the cotangent, cosecant, and secant inverse functions are not found from the reciprocal of the tangent, sine, and cosine, respectively, but rather from the inverse secant, inverse cosecant, and inverse cotangent identities.

The remaining three inverse trigonometric functions are defined similarly to the previous ones.

- Inverse cotangent function: $\cot^{-1}x$ or $\operatorname{arccot} x$
- Inverse secant function: $\sec^{-1}x$ or $\operatorname{arcsec} x$
- Inverse cosecant function: $\csc^{-1}x$ or $\operatorname{arccsc} x$

A table summarizing all six of the inverse trigonometric functions is given below.

INVERSE FUNCTION	$y = \sin^{-1}x$	$y = \cos^{-1}x$	$y = \tan^{-1}x$	$y = \cot^{-1}x$	$y = \sec^{-1}x$	$y = \csc^{-1}x$
DOMAIN	$[-1, 1]$	$[-1, 1]$	$(-\infty, \infty)$	$(-\infty, \infty)$	$(-\infty, -1] \cup [1, \infty)$	$(-\infty, -1] \cup [1, \infty)$
RANGE	$\left[-\frac{\pi}{2}, \frac{\pi}{2}\right]$	$[0, \pi]$	$\left(-\frac{\pi}{2}, \frac{\pi}{2}\right)$	$(0, \pi)$	$\left[0, \frac{\pi}{2}\right) \cup \left(\frac{\pi}{2}, \pi\right]$	$\left[-\frac{\pi}{2}, 0\right) \cup \left(0, \frac{\pi}{2}\right]$
GRAPH	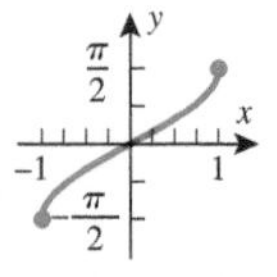	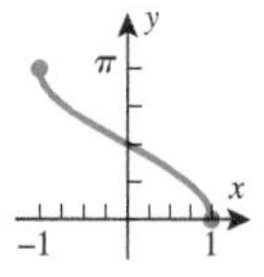	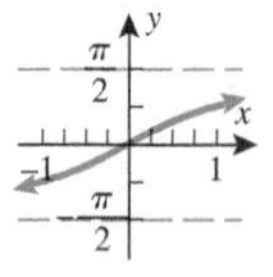	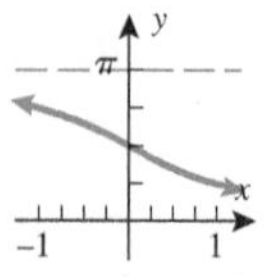	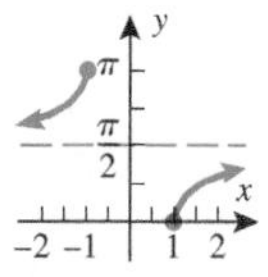	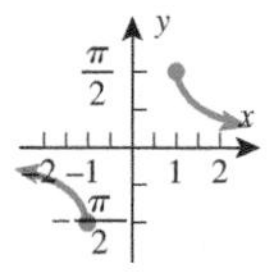

EXAMPLE 7 **Finding the Exact Value of Inverse Trigonometric Functions**

Find the exact value of the following expressions:

a. $\cot^{-1}(\sqrt{3})$ **b.** $\csc^{-1}(\sqrt{2})$ **c.** $\sec^{-1}(-\sqrt{2})$

Solution (a):

Let $\theta = \cot^{-1}(\sqrt{3})$. $\cot\theta = \sqrt{3}$ when $0 < \theta < \pi$

Which value of θ, in the range $0 < \theta < \pi$, corresponds to a cotangent value of $\sqrt{3}$? $\theta = \frac{\pi}{6}$

$\cot\left(\frac{\pi}{6}\right) = \sqrt{3}$ and $\frac{\pi}{6}$ is in the interval $(0, \pi)$. $\boxed{\cot^{-1}(\sqrt{3}) = \frac{\pi}{6}}$

Solution (b):

Let $\theta = \csc^{-1}(\sqrt{2})$. $\csc\theta = \sqrt{2}$

Which value of θ, in the range $\left[-\frac{\pi}{2}, 0\right) \cup \left(0, \frac{\pi}{2}\right]$, corresponds to a cosecant value of $\sqrt{2}$? $\theta = \frac{\pi}{4}$

$\csc\left(\frac{\pi}{4}\right) = \sqrt{2}$ and $\frac{\pi}{4}$ is in the interval $\left[-\frac{\pi}{2}, 0\right) \cup \left(0, \frac{\pi}{2}\right]$. $\boxed{\csc^{-1}(\sqrt{2}) = \frac{\pi}{4}}$

Solution (c):

Let $\theta = \sec^{-1}(-\sqrt{2})$. $\sec\theta = -\sqrt{2}$

Which value of θ, in the range $\left[0, \frac{\pi}{2}\right) \cup \left(\frac{\pi}{2}, \pi\right]$, corresponds to a secant value of $-\sqrt{2}$? $\theta = \frac{3\pi}{4}$

$\sec\left(\frac{3\pi}{4}\right) = -\sqrt{2}$ and $\frac{3\pi}{4}$ is in the interval $\left[0, \frac{\pi}{2}\right) \cup \left(\frac{\pi}{2}, \pi\right]$. $\boxed{\sec^{-1}(-\sqrt{2}) = \frac{3\pi}{4}}$

[CONCEPT CHECK]

Find the exact value (if possible) of $\csc^{-1}(A)$ for (A) $A = 0$ and (B) $A = 2$.

ANSWER (A) DNE (B) $\frac{\pi}{6}$

How do we approximate the inverse secant, inverse cosecant, and inverse cotangent functions with a calculator? Scientific calculators have keys ($\sin^{-1}$, $\cos^{-1}$, and $\tan^{-1}$) for three of the inverse trigonometric functions but not for the other three. Recall that we find the cosecant, secant, and cotangent function values by taking sine, cosine, or tangent, and finding the reciprocal.

$$\csc x = \frac{1}{\sin x} \qquad \sec x = \frac{1}{\cos x} \qquad \cot x = \frac{1}{\tan x}$$

However, *the reciprocal approach cannot be used for inverse functions.* The three inverse trigonometric functions $\csc^{-1}x$, $\sec^{-1}x$, and $\cot^{-1}x$ cannot be found by finding the reciprocal of $\sin^{-1}x$, $\cos^{-1}x$, or $\tan^{-1}x$.

$$\csc^{-1}x \neq \frac{1}{\sin^{-1}x} \qquad \sec^{-1}x \neq \frac{1}{\cos^{-1}x} \qquad \cot^{-1}x \neq \frac{1}{\tan^{-1}x}$$

Instead, we seek the equivalent $\sin^{-1}x$, $\cos^{-1}x$, or $\tan^{-1}x$ values by algebraic means, always remembering to look within the correct domain and range.

STUDY TIP

$$\sec^{-1}x \neq \frac{1}{\cos^{-1}x}$$
$$\csc^{-1}x \neq \frac{1}{\sin^{-1}x}$$
$$\cot^{-1}x \neq \frac{1}{\tan^{-1}x}$$

WORDS	MATH
Start with the inverse secant function.	$y = \sec^{-1}x$ for $x \le -1$ or $x \ge 1$
Write the equivalent secant expression.	$\sec y = x$ for $0 \le y < \frac{\pi}{2}$ or $\frac{\pi}{2} < y \le \pi$
Apply the reciprocal identity.	$\frac{1}{\cos y} = x$
Simplify using algebraic techniques.	$\cos y = \frac{1}{x}$
Write the result in terms of the inverse cosine function.	$y = \cos^{-1}\left(\frac{1}{x}\right)$
Therefore, we have the following relationship:	$\sec^{-1}x = \cos^{-1}\left(\frac{1}{x}\right)$ for $x \le -1$ or $x \ge 1$

The other relationships will be found in the exercises and are summarized below.

INVERSE SECANT, INVERSE COSECANT, AND INVERSE COTANGENT IDENTITIES

$$\sec^{-1}x = \cos^{-1}\left(\frac{1}{x}\right) \quad \text{for} \quad x \le -1 \text{ or } x \ge 1$$

$$\csc^{-1}x = \sin^{-1}\left(\frac{1}{x}\right) \quad \text{for} \quad x \le -1 \text{ or } x \ge 1$$

$$\cot^{-1}x = \begin{cases} \tan^{-1}\left(\frac{1}{x}\right) & \text{for} \quad x > 0 \\ \pi + \tan^{-1}\left(\frac{1}{x}\right) & \text{for} \quad x < 0 \end{cases}$$

EXAMPLE 8 **Using Inverse Identities**

a. Find the exact value of $\sec^{-1}2$.

b. Use a calculator to find the value of $\cot^{-1}7$.

Solution (a):

Let $\theta = \sec^{-1}2$. $\quad \sec\theta = 2$ on $\left[0, \frac{\pi}{2}\right) \cup \left(\frac{\pi}{2}, \pi\right]$

Substitute the reciprocal identity. $\quad \frac{1}{\cos\theta} = 2$

Solve for $\cos\theta$. $\quad \cos\theta = \frac{1}{2}$

The restricted interval $\left[0, \frac{\pi}{2}\right) \cup \left(\frac{\pi}{2}, \pi\right]$ corresponds to quadrants I and II.

The cosine function is positive in quadrant I. $\quad \theta = \frac{\pi}{3}$

$$\boxed{\sec^{-1}2 = \cos^{-1}\left(\frac{1}{2}\right) = \frac{\pi}{3}}$$

Solution (b):

Since we do not know an exact value that would correspond to the cotangent function equal to 7, we proceed using identities and a calculator.

Select the correct identity, given that $x = 7 > 0$. $\quad \cot^{-1}x = \tan^{-1}\left(\frac{1}{x}\right)$

Let $x = 7$. $\quad \cot^{-1}7 = \tan^{-1}\left(\frac{1}{7}\right)$

Evaluate the right side with a calculator. $\quad \boxed{\cot^{-1}7 \approx 8.13°}$

6.5.5 Finding Exact Values for Expressions Involving Inverse Trigonometric Functions

6.5.5 SKILL

Use identities to find exact values of trigonometric expressions involving inverse trigonometric functions.

6.5.5 CONCEPTUAL

Visualize the quadrants in order to find exact values of trigonometric expressions involving inverse trigonometric functions.

We will now find exact values of trigonometric expressions that involve inverse trigonometric functions.

EXAMPLE 9 **Finding Exact Values of Trigonometric Expressions Involving Inverse Trigonometric Functions**

Find the exact value of $\cos\left[\sin^{-1}\left(\frac{2}{3}\right)\right]$.

Solution:

STEP 1 Let $\theta = \sin^{-1}\left(\frac{2}{3}\right)$. $\quad \sin\theta = \frac{2}{3}$ when $-\frac{\pi}{2} \le \theta \le \frac{\pi}{2}$

The range $-\frac{\pi}{2} \le \theta \le \frac{\pi}{2}$ corresponds to quadrants I and IV.

The sine function is positive in quadrant I.

STEP 2 Draw angle θ in quadrant I.

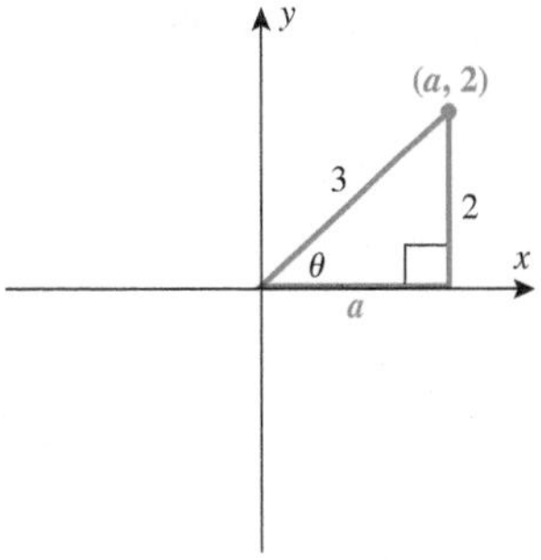

Label the sides known from the sine value. $\quad \sin\theta = \frac{2}{3} = \frac{\text{opposite}}{\text{hypotenuse}}$

STEP 3 Find the unknown side length a. $\quad a^2 + 2^2 = 3^2$

Solve for a. $\quad a = \pm\sqrt{5}$

Since θ is in quadrant I, a is positive. $\quad a = \sqrt{5}$

STEP 4 Find $\cos\left[\sin^{-1}\left(\frac{2}{3}\right)\right]$.

Substitute $\theta = \sin^{-1}\left(\frac{2}{3}\right)$. $\quad \cos\left[\sin^{-1}\left(\frac{2}{3}\right)\right] = \cos\theta$

Find $\cos\theta$.

$$\cos\theta = \frac{\text{adjacent}}{\text{hypotenuse}} = \frac{\sqrt{5}}{3}$$

$$\boxed{\cos\left[\sin^{-1}\left(\frac{2}{3}\right)\right] = \frac{\sqrt{5}}{3}}$$

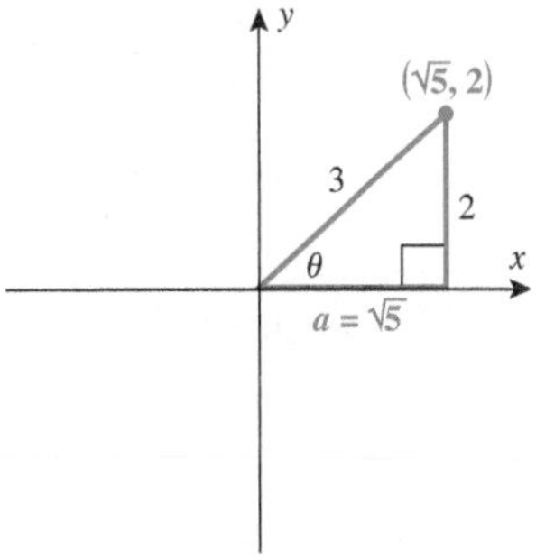

YOUR TURN Find the exact value of $\sin\left[\cos^{-1}\left(\frac{1}{3}\right)\right]$.

ANSWER

$\frac{2\sqrt{2}}{3}$

EXAMPLE 10 Finding Exact Values of Trigonometric Expressions Involving Inverse Trigonometric Functions

Find the exact value of $\tan\left[\cos^{-1}\left(-\frac{7}{12}\right)\right]$.

Solution:

STEP 1 Let $\theta = \cos^{-1}\left(-\frac{7}{12}\right)$. $\quad \cos\theta = -\dfrac{7}{12}$ when $0 \le \theta \le \pi$

The range $0 \le \theta \le \pi$ corresponds to quadrants I and II.

The cosine function is negative in quadrant II.

STEP 2 Draw angle θ in quadrant II.

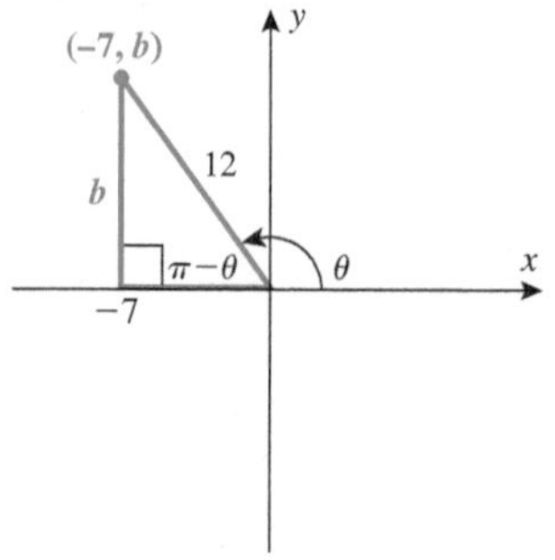

Label the sides known from the cosine value. $\quad \cos\theta = -\dfrac{7}{12} = \dfrac{\text{adjacent}}{\text{hypotenuse}}$

[CONCEPT CHECK]

TRUE OR FALSE
sin(arctan(A)) < 0 if $A < 0$.

ANSWER True

STEP 3 Find the length of the unknown side b. $\quad b^2 + (-7)^2 = 12^2$

Solve for b. $\quad b = \pm\sqrt{95}$

Since θ is in quadrant II, b is positive. $\quad b = \sqrt{95}$

STEP 4 Find $\tan\left[\cos^{-1}\left(-\frac{7}{12}\right)\right]$.

Substitute $\theta = \cos^{-1}\left(-\frac{7}{12}\right)$. $\quad \tan\left[\cos^{-1}\left(-\dfrac{7}{12}\right)\right] = \tan\theta$

Find $\tan\theta$.

$$\tan\theta = \frac{\text{opposite}}{\text{adjacent}} = \frac{\sqrt{95}}{-7}$$

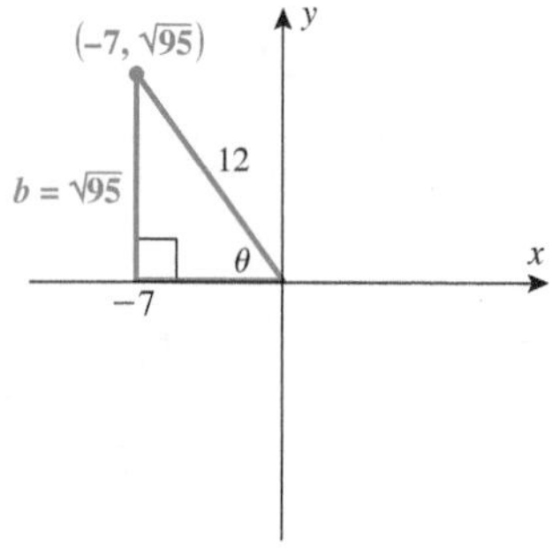

$$\boxed{\tan\left[\cos^{-1}\left(-\frac{7}{12}\right)\right] = -\frac{\sqrt{95}}{7}}$$

YOUR TURN Find the exact value of $\tan\left[\sin^{-1}\left(-\frac{3}{7}\right)\right]$.

ANSWER
$-\dfrac{3\sqrt{10}}{20}$

EXAMPLE 11 **Using Identities to Find Exact Values of Trigonometric Expressions Involving Inverse Trigonometric Functions**

Find the exact value of $\cos\left[\sin^{-1}\left(\frac{3}{5}\right) + \tan^{-1}1\right]$.

Solution:

Recall the cosine sum identity: $\cos(A + B) = \cos A \cos B - \sin A \sin B$

Let $A = \sin^{-1}\left(\frac{3}{5}\right)$ and $B = \tan^{-1}1$.

$$\cos\left[\sin^{-1}\left(\frac{3}{5}\right) + \tan^{-1}1\right] = \cos\left[\sin^{-1}\left(\frac{3}{5}\right)\right]\cos(\tan^{-1}1) - \sin\left[\sin^{-1}\left(\frac{3}{5}\right)\right]\sin(\tan^{-1}1)$$

From the figure,

$$A = \sin^{-1}\left(\tfrac{3}{5}\right) \Rightarrow \sin A = \tfrac{3}{5}$$

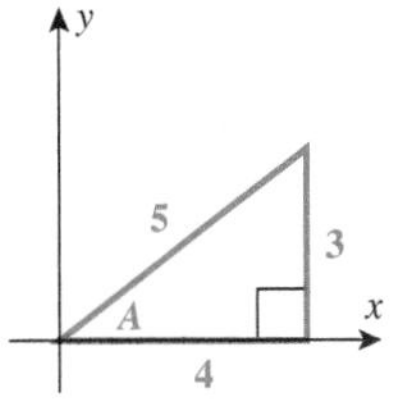

we see that

$$\cos\left[\sin^{-1}\left(\frac{3}{5}\right)\right] = \cos A = \frac{4}{5}$$
$$\sin\left[\sin^{-1}\left(\frac{3}{5}\right)\right] = \sin A = \frac{3}{5}$$

From the figure,

$$B = \tan^{-1}(1) \Rightarrow \tan B = 1$$

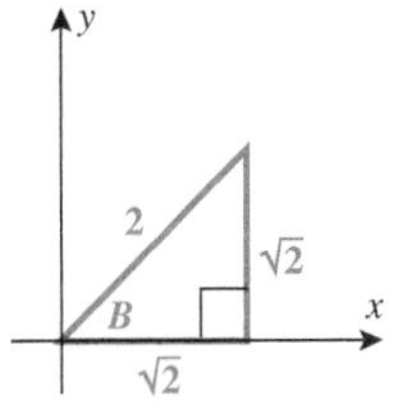

we see that

$$\cos(\tan^{-1}1) = \cos B = \frac{\sqrt{2}}{2}$$
$$\sin(\tan^{-1}1) = \sin B = \frac{\sqrt{2}}{2}$$

Substitute these values into the cosine sum identity.

$$\cos\left[\sin^{-1}\left(\frac{3}{5}\right) + \tan^{-1}1\right] = \left(\frac{4}{5}\right)\left(\frac{\sqrt{2}}{2}\right) - \left(\frac{3}{5}\right)\left(\frac{\sqrt{2}}{2}\right)$$

Simplify.

$$= \boxed{\frac{\sqrt{2}}{10}}$$

YOUR TURN Find the exact value of $\sin\left[\cos^{-1}\left(\frac{3}{5}\right) + \tan^{-1}1\right]$.

ANSWER

$\frac{7\sqrt{2}}{10}$

EXAMPLE 12 **Writing Trigonometric Expressions Involving Inverse Trigonometric Functions in Terms of a Single Variable**

Write the expression $\cos(\tan^{-1}u)$ as an equivalent expression in terms of only the variable u.

Solution: Let $\theta = \tan^{-1}u$; therefore, $\tan\theta = u = \frac{u}{1}$. Realize that u can be positive or negative. Since the range of the inverse tangent function is $\left(-\frac{\pi}{2}, \frac{\pi}{2}\right)$, sketch the angle θ in both quadrants I and IV and draw the corresponding two right triangles. Recalling that the tangent ratio is opposite over adjacent, we label those corresponding sides with u and 1, respectively. Then solving for the hypotenuse using the Pythagorean theorem gives $\sqrt{u^2 + 1}$.

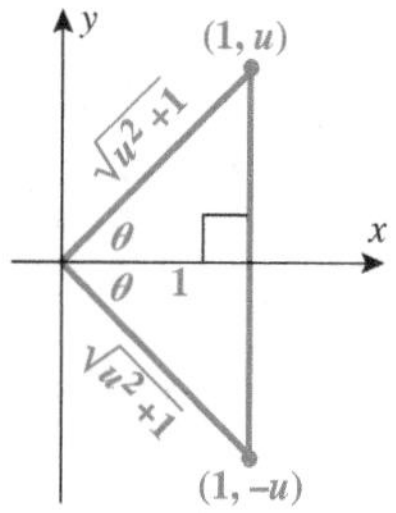

Substitute $\theta = \tan^{-1}u$ into $\cos(\tan^{-1}u)$. $\qquad \cos(\tan^{-1}u) = \cos\theta$

Use the right triangle ratio for cosine: adjacent over hypotenuse. $\qquad = \dfrac{1}{\sqrt{u^2 + 1}}$

Rationalize the denominator. $\qquad \cos(\tan^{-1}u) = \dfrac{1}{\sqrt{u^2 + 1}} \cdot \dfrac{\sqrt{u^2 + 1}}{\sqrt{u^2 + 1}}$

$$= \boxed{\dfrac{\sqrt{u^2 + 1}}{u^2 + 1}}$$

YOUR TURN Write the expression $\sin(\tan^{-1}u)$ as an equivalent expression in terms of only the variable u.

ANSWER

$\dfrac{u\sqrt{u^2 + 1}}{u^2 + 1}$

[SECTION 6.5] SUMMARY

If a trigonometric function value of an angle or of a real number is known, what is that number, as defined by the domain restriction? Inverse trigonometric functions determine the angle measure (or the value of the argument). To define the inverse trigonometric relations as functions, we first restrict the trigonometric functions to domains in which they are one-to-one functions.

Exact values for inverse trigonometric functions can be found when the function values are those of the special angles. Inverse trigonometric functions also provide a means for evaluating one trigonometric function when we are given the value of another. It is important to note that the -1 as a superscript indicates an inverse function, not a reciprocal.

INVERSE FUNCTION	$y = \sin^{-1}x$	$y = \cos^{-1}x$	$y = \tan^{-1}x$	$y = \cot^{-1}x$	$y = \sec^{-1}x$	$y = \csc^{-1}x$
DOMAIN	$[-1, 1]$	$[-1, 1]$	$(-\infty, \infty)$	$(-\infty, \infty)$	$(-\infty, -1] \cup [1, \infty)$	$(-\infty, -1] \cup [1, \infty)$
RANGE	$\left[-\frac{\pi}{2}, \frac{\pi}{2}\right]$	$[0, \pi]$	$\left(-\frac{\pi}{2}, \frac{\pi}{2}\right)$	$(0, \pi)$	$\left[0, \frac{\pi}{2}\right) \cup \left(\frac{\pi}{2}, \pi\right]$	$\left[-\frac{\pi}{2}, 0\right) \cup \left(0, \frac{\pi}{2}\right]$
GRAPH	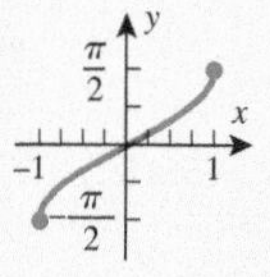	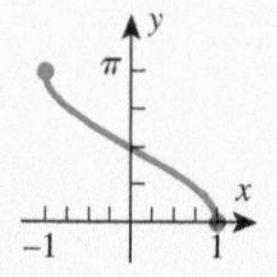	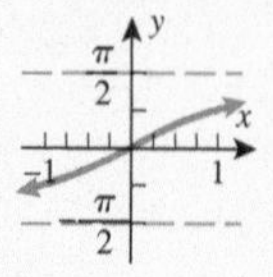	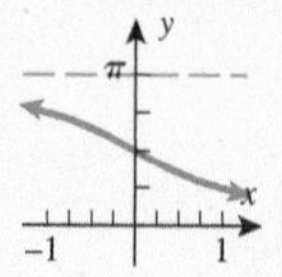	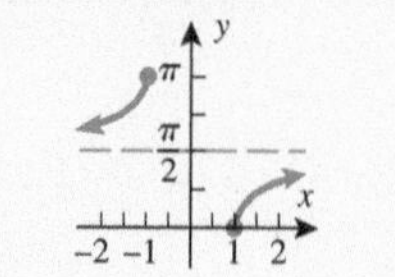	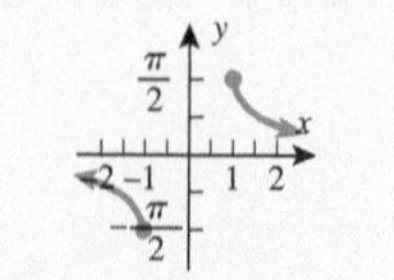

[SECTION 6.5] EXERCISES

• SKILLS

In Exercises 1–16, find the exact value of each expression. Give the answer in radians.

1. $\arccos\left(\frac{\sqrt{2}}{2}\right)$
2. $\arccos\left(-\frac{\sqrt{2}}{2}\right)$
3. $\arcsin\left(-\frac{\sqrt{3}}{2}\right)$
4. $\arcsin\left(\frac{1}{2}\right)$
5. $\cot^{-1}(-1)$
6. $\tan^{-1}\left(\frac{\sqrt{3}}{3}\right)$
7. $\operatorname{arcsec}\left(\frac{2\sqrt{3}}{3}\right)$
8. $\operatorname{arccsc}(-1)$
9. $\csc^{-1}2$
10. $\sec^{-1}(-2)$
11. $\arctan(-\sqrt{3})$
12. $\operatorname{arccot}(\sqrt{3})$
13. $\sin^{-1}0$
14. $\tan^{-1}1$
15. $\sec^{-1}(-1)$
16. $\cot^{-1}0$

In Exercises 17–32, find the exact value of each expression. Give the answer in degrees.

17. $\cos^{-1}\left(\frac{1}{2}\right)$
18. $\cos^{-1}\left(-\frac{\sqrt{3}}{2}\right)$
19. $\sin^{-1}\left(\frac{\sqrt{2}}{2}\right)$
20. $\sin^{-1}0$
21. $\cot^{-1}\left(-\frac{\sqrt{3}}{3}\right)$
22. $\tan^{-1}(-\sqrt{3})$
23. $\arctan\left(\frac{\sqrt{3}}{3}\right)$
24. $\operatorname{arccot}1$
25. $\operatorname{arccsc}(-2)$
26. $\csc^{-1}\left(-\frac{2\sqrt{3}}{3}\right)$
27. $\operatorname{arcsec}(-\sqrt{2})$
28. $\operatorname{arccsc}(-\sqrt{2})$
29. $\sin^{-1}(-1)$
30. $\arctan(-1)$
31. $\operatorname{arccot}0$
32. $\operatorname{arcsec}(-1)$

In Exercises 33–42, use a calculator to evaluate each expression. Give the answer in degrees and round it to two decimal places.

33. $\cos^{-1}(0.5432)$
34. $\sin^{-1}(0.7821)$
35. $\tan^{-1}(1.895)$
36. $\tan^{-1}(3.2678)$
37. $\sec^{-1}(1.4973)$
38. $\sec^{-1}(2.7864)$
39. $\csc^{-1}(-3.7893)$
40. $\csc^{-1}(-6.1324)$
41. $\cot^{-1}(-4.2319)$
42. $\cot^{-1}(-0.8977)$

In Exercises 43–52, use a calculator to evaluate each expression. Give the answer in radians and round it to two decimal places.

43. $\sin^{-1}(-0.5878)$
44. $\sin^{-1}(0.8660)$
45. $\cos^{-1}(0.1423)$
46. $\tan^{-1}(-0.9279)$
47. $\tan^{-1}(1.3242)$
48. $\cot^{-1}(2.4142)$
49. $\cot^{-1}(-0.5774)$
50. $\sec^{-1}(-1.0422)$
51. $\csc^{-1}(3.2361)$
52. $\csc^{-1}(-2.9238)$

In Exercises 53–76, evaluate each expression exactly, if possible. If not possible, state why.

53. $\sin^{-1}\left[\sin\left(\frac{5\pi}{12}\right)\right]$
54. $\sin^{-1}\left[\sin\left(-\frac{5\pi}{12}\right)\right]$
55. $\sin[\sin^{-1}(1.03)]$
56. $\sin[\sin^{-1}(1.1)]$
57. $\sin^{-1}\left[\sin\left(-\frac{7\pi}{6}\right)\right]$
58. $\sin^{-1}\left[\sin\left(\frac{7\pi}{6}\right)\right]$
59. $\cos^{-1}\left[\cos\left(\frac{4\pi}{3}\right)\right]$
60. $\cos^{-1}\left[\cos\left(-\frac{5\pi}{3}\right)\right]$
61. $\cot[\cot^{-1}(\sqrt{3})]$
62. $\cot^{-1}\left[\cot\left(\frac{5\pi}{4}\right)\right]$
63. $\sec^{-1}\left[\sec\left(-\frac{\pi}{3}\right)\right]$
64. $\sec\left[\sec^{-1}\left(\frac{1}{2}\right)\right]$
65. $\csc\left[\csc^{-1}\left(\frac{1}{2}\right)\right]$
66. $\csc^{-1}\left[\csc\left(\frac{7\pi}{6}\right)\right]$
67. $\cot(\cot^{-1}0)$
68. $\cot^{-1}\left[\cot\left(-\frac{\pi}{4}\right)\right]$
69. $\tan^{-1}\left[\tan\left(-\frac{\pi}{4}\right)\right]$
70. $\tan^{-1}\left[\tan\left(\frac{\pi}{4}\right)\right]$
71. $\sec(\sec^{-1}0)$
72. $\csc^{-1}(\csc\pi)$
73. $\cot^{-1}\left[\cot\left(\frac{8\pi}{3}\right)\right]$
74. $\tan^{-1}[\tan(8\pi)]$
75. $\csc^{-1}\left[\csc\left(\frac{15\pi}{4}\right)\right]$
76. $\sec^{-1}\left[\sec\left(\frac{17\pi}{2}\right)\right]$

In Exercises 77–96, evaluate each expression exactly.

77. $\cos\left[\sin^{-1}\left(\frac{3}{4}\right)\right]$

78. $\sin\left[\cos^{-1}\left(\frac{2}{3}\right)\right]$

79. $\sin\left[\tan^{-1}\left(\frac{12}{5}\right)\right]$

80. $\cos\left[\tan^{-1}\left(\frac{7}{24}\right)\right]$

81. $\tan\left[\sin^{-1}\left(\frac{3}{5}\right)\right]$

82. $\tan\left[\cos^{-1}\left(\frac{2}{5}\right)\right]$

83. $\sec\left[\sin^{-1}\left(\frac{\sqrt{2}}{5}\right)\right]$

84. $\sec\left[\cos^{-1}\left(\frac{\sqrt{7}}{4}\right)\right]$

85. $\csc\left[\cos^{-1}\left(\frac{1}{4}\right)\right]$

86. $\csc\left[\sin^{-1}\left(\frac{1}{4}\right)\right]$

87. $\cot\left[\sin^{-1}\left(\frac{60}{61}\right)\right]$

88. $\cot\left[\sec^{-1}\left(\frac{41}{9}\right)\right]$

89. $\cos\left[\tan^{-1}\left(\frac{3}{4}\right) - \sin^{-1}\left(\frac{4}{5}\right)\right]$

90. $\cos\left[\tan^{-1}\left(\frac{12}{5}\right) + \sin^{-1}\left(\frac{3}{5}\right)\right]$

91. $\sin\left[\cos^{-1}\left(\frac{5}{13}\right) + \tan^{-1}\left(\frac{4}{3}\right)\right]$

92. $\sin\left[\cos^{-1}\left(\frac{3}{5}\right) - \tan^{-1}\left(\frac{5}{12}\right)\right]$

93. $\sin\left[2\cos^{-1}\left(\frac{3}{5}\right)\right]$

94. $\cos\left[2\sin^{-1}\left(\frac{3}{5}\right)\right]$

95. $\tan\left[2\sin^{-1}\left(\frac{5}{13}\right)\right]$

96. $\tan\left[2\cos^{-1}\left(\frac{5}{13}\right)\right]$

For each of the following expressions, write an equivalent expression in terms of only the variable *u*.

97. $\cos(\sin^{-1}u)$

98. $\sin(\cos^{-1}u)$

99. $\tan(\cos^{-1}u)$

100. $\tan(\sin^{-1}u)$

• APPLICATIONS

For Exercises 101 and 102, refer to the following:

Annual sales of a product are generally subject to seasonal fluctuations and are approximated by the function

$$s(t) = 4.3\cos\left(\frac{\pi}{6}t\right) + 56.2 \quad 0 \le t \le 11$$

where t represents time in months ($t = 0$ represents January) and $s(t)$ represents monthly sales of the product in thousands of dollars.

101. Business. Find the month(s) in which monthly sales are \$56,200.

102. Business. Find the month(s) in which monthly sales are \$51,900.

For Exercises 103 and 104, refer to the following:

Allergy sufferers' symptoms fluctuate with pollen levels. Pollen levels are often reported to the public on a scale of 0–12, which is meant to reflect the levels of pollen in the air. For example, a pollen level between 4.9 and 7.2 indicates that pollen levels will likely cause symptoms for many individuals allergic to the predominant pollen of the season (*Source*: http://www.pollen.com). The pollen levels at a single location were measured and averaged for each month. Over a period of 6 months, the levels fluctuated according to the model

$$p(t) = 5.5 + 1.5\sin\left(\frac{\pi}{6}t\right) \quad 0 \le t \le 6$$

where t is measured in months and $p(t)$ is the pollen level.

103. Biology/Health. In which month(s) was the monthly average pollen level 7.0?

104. Biology/Health. In which month(s) was the monthly average pollen level 6.25?

105. Alternating Current. Alternating electrical current in amperes (A) is modeled by the equation $i = I\sin(2\pi f t)$, where i is the current, I is the maximum current, t is time in seconds, and f is the frequency in hertz, which is the number of cycles per second. If the frequency is 5 hertz and maximum current is 115 amperes, what time t corresponds to a current of 85 amperes? Find the smallest positive value of t.

106. Alternating Current. If the frequency is 100 hertz and maximum current is 240 amperes, what time t corresponds to a current of 100 amperes? Find the smallest positive value of t.

107. Hours of Daylight. The number of hours of daylight in San Diego, California, can be modeled with $H(t) = 12 + 2.4\sin(0.017t - 1.377)$, where t is the day of the year (January 1, $t = 1$, etc.). For what value of t is the number of hours of daylight equal to 14.4? If May 31 is the 151st day of the year, what month and day correspond to that value of t?

108. Hours of Daylight. Repeat Exercise 107. For what value of t is the number of hours of daylight equal to 9.6? What month and day correspond to the value of t? (You may have to count backwards.)

109. Money. A young couple get married and immediately start saving money. They renovate a house and are left with less and less saved money. They have children after 10 years and are in debt until their children are in college. They then save until retirement. A formula that represents the percentage of their annual income that they either save (positive) or are in debt (negative) is given by $P(t) = 12.5\cos(0.157t) + 2.5$, where $t = 0$ corresponds to the year they were married. How many years into their marriage do they first incur debt?

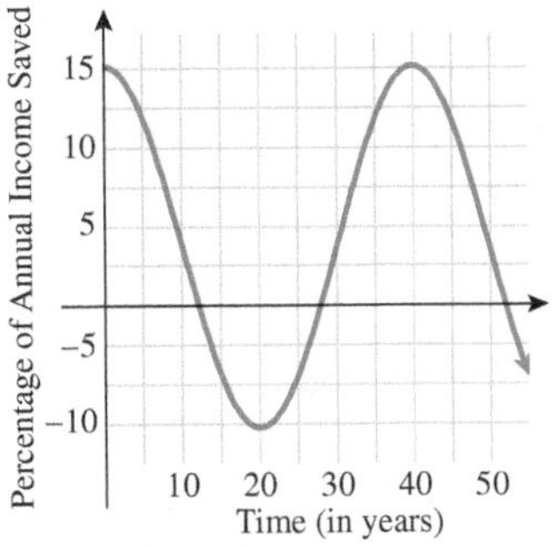

110. **Money.** For the couple in Exercise 109, how many years into their marriage are they back to saving 15% of their annual income?

111. **Earthquake Movement.** The horizontal movement of a point that is k kilometers away from an earthquake's fault line can be estimated with

$$M = \frac{f}{2}\left[1 - \frac{2\tan^{-1}\left(\frac{k}{d}\right)}{\pi}\right]$$

where M is the movement of the point in meters, f is the total horizontal displacement occurring along the fault line, k is the distance of the point from the fault line, and d is the depth in kilometers of the focal point of the earthquake. If an earthquake produces a displacement f of 2 meters and the depth of the focal point is 4 kilometers, what is the movement M of a point that is 2 kilometers from the fault line? of a point 10 kilometers from the fault line?

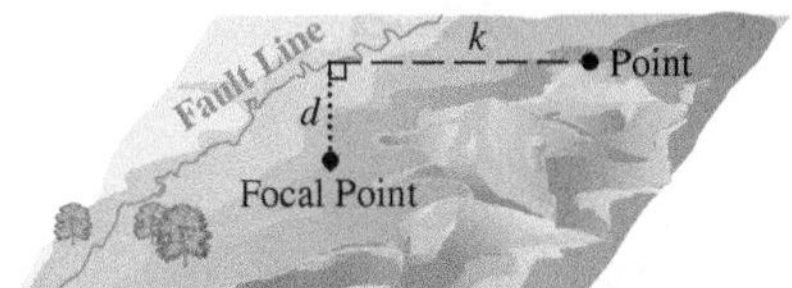

112. **Earthquake Movement.** Repeat Exercise 111. If an earthquake produces a displacement f of 3 meters and the depth of the focal point is 2.5 kilometers, what is the movement M of a point that is 5 kilometers from the fault line? of a point 10 kilometers from the fault line?

• CATCH THE MISTAKE

In Exercises 113–116, explain the mistake that is made.

113. Evaluate the expression exactly: $\sin^{-1}\left[\sin\left(\frac{3\pi}{5}\right)\right]$.

Solution:

Use the identity $\sin^{-1}(\sin x) = x$ on $0 \le x \le \pi$.

Since $\frac{3\pi}{5}$ is in the interval $[0, \pi]$, the identity can be used. $\sin^{-1}\left[\sin\left(\frac{3\pi}{5}\right)\right] = \frac{3\pi}{5}$

This is incorrect. What mistake was made?

114. Evaluate the expression exactly: $\cos^{-1}\left[\cos\left(-\frac{\pi}{5}\right)\right]$.

Solution:

Use the identity $\cos^{-1}(\cos x) = x$ on $-\frac{\pi}{2} \le x \le \frac{\pi}{2}$.

Since $-\frac{\pi}{5}$ is in the interval $\left[-\frac{\pi}{2}, \frac{\pi}{2}\right]$, the identity can be used. $\cos^{-1}\left[\cos\left(-\frac{\pi}{5}\right)\right] = -\frac{\pi}{5}$

This is incorrect. What mistake was made?

115. Evaluate the expression exactly: $\cot^{-1}(2.5)$.

Solution:

Use the reciprocal identity. $\cot^{-1}(2.5) = \frac{1}{\tan^{-1}(2.5)}$

Evaluate $\tan^{-1}(2.5) = 1.19$. $\cot^{-1}(2.5) = \frac{1}{1.19}$

Simplify. $\cot^{-1}(2.5) = 0.8403$

This is incorrect. What mistake was made?

116. Evaluate the expression exactly: $\csc^{-1}\left(\frac{1}{4}\right)$.

Solution:

Use the reciprocal identity. $\csc^{-1}\left(\frac{1}{4}\right) = \frac{1}{\sin^{-1}\left(\frac{1}{4}\right)}$

Evaluate $\sin^{-1}\left(\frac{1}{4}\right) = 14.478$. $\csc^{-1}\left(\frac{1}{4}\right) = \frac{1}{14.478}$

Simplify. $\csc^{-1}\left(\frac{1}{4}\right) = 0.0691$

This is incorrect. What mistake was made?

• CONCEPTUAL

In Exercises 117–120, determine whether each statement is true or false.

117. The inverse secant function is an even function.

118. The inverse cosecant function is an odd function.

119. $\csc^{-1}(\csc\theta) = \theta$, for all θ in the domain of cosecant.

120. $\sin^{-1}(2x)\cdot\csc^{-1}(2x) = 1$, for all x for which both functions are defined.

121. Explain why $\sec^{-1}\left(\frac{1}{2}\right)$ does not exist.

122. Explain why $\csc^{-1}\left(\frac{1}{2}\right)$ does not exist.

• CHALLENGE

123. Evaluate exactly: $\sin\left[\cos^{-1}\left(\frac{\sqrt{2}}{2}\right) + \sin^{-1}\left(-\frac{1}{2}\right)\right]$.

124. Determine the x-values for which

$$\sin^{-1}\left[2\sin\left(\frac{3x}{2}\right)\cos\left(\frac{3x}{2}\right)\right] = 3x$$

125. Evaluate exactly: $\sin(2\sin^{-1}1)$.

126. Let $f(x) = 2 - 4\sin\left(x - \frac{\pi}{2}\right)$.

a. State an accepted domain of $f(x)$ so that $f(x)$ is a one-to-one function.

b. Find $f^{-1}(x)$ and state its domain.

127. Let $f(x) = 3 + \cos\left(x - \frac{\pi}{4}\right)$.

a. State an accepted domain of $f(x)$ so that $f(x)$ is a one-to-one function.

b. Find $f^{-1}(x)$ and state its domain.

128. Let $f(x) = 1 - \tan\left(x + \frac{\pi}{3}\right)$.

a. State an accepted domain of $f(x)$ so that $f(x)$ is a one-to-one function.

b. Find $f^{-1}(x)$ and state its domain.

• PREVIEW TO CALCULUS

In calculus, we study the derivatives of inverse trigonometric functions. In order to obtain these formulas, we use the definitions of the functions and a right triangle. Thus, if $y = \sin^{-1}x$, then $\sin y = x$; the right triangle associated with this equation is given below, where we can see that $\cos y = \sqrt{1 - x^2}$.

In Exercises 129–132, use this idea to find the indicated expression.

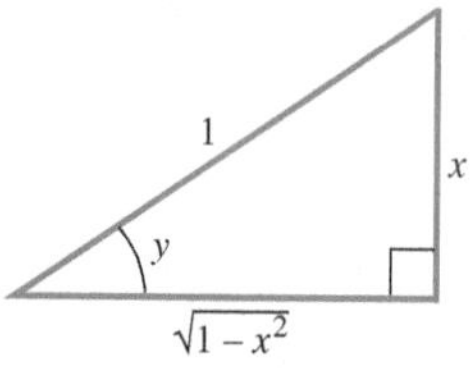

129. If $y = \tan^{-1}x$, find $\sec^2 y$.

130. If $y = \cos^{-1}x$, find $\sin y$.

131. If $y = \sec^{-1}x$, find $\sec y \tan y$.

132. If $y = \cot^{-1}x$, find $\csc^2 y$.

6.6 TRIGONOMETRIC EQUATIONS

SKILLS OBJECTIVES

- Solve trigonometric equations by inspection.
- Solve trigonometric equations by using algebraic techniques.
- Solve trigonometric equations using inverse functions.
- Solve trigonometric equations (involving more than one trigonometric function) using trigonometric identities.

CONCEPTUAL OBJECTIVES

- When solving trigonometric equations by inspection, remember to find all solutions, not just the solutions within a single period.
- Utilize the concept of substitution in solving trigonometric equations when the results are simple linear or quadratic equations.
- Utilize a calculator to approximate solutions when solving trigonometric equations using inverse functions.
- Using trigonometric identities can often help convert a trigonometric equation involving more than one trigonometric function into trigonometric equations involving a single trigonometric function.

6.6.1 SKILL

Solve trigonometric equations by inspection.

6.6.1 CONCEPTUAL

When solving trigonometric equations by inspection, remember to find all solutions, not just the solutions within a single period.

6.6.1 Solving Trigonometric Equations by Inspection

The goal in solving equations in one variable is to find the values for that variable which make the equation true. For example, $9x = 72$ can be solved by inspection by asking the question, "9 times what is 72?" The answer is $x = 8$. We approach simple trigonometric equations the same way we approach algebraic equations: We inspect the equation and determine the solution.

EXAMPLE 1 Solving a Trigonometric Equation by Inspection

Solve each of the following equations on the interval $[0, 2\pi]$:

a. $\sin x = \frac{1}{2}$ **b.** $\cos(2x) = \frac{1}{2}$

Solution (a):

Ask the question, "sine of what angles is $\frac{1}{2}$?"

$$\boxed{x = \frac{\pi}{6} \quad \text{or} \quad x = \frac{5\pi}{6}}$$

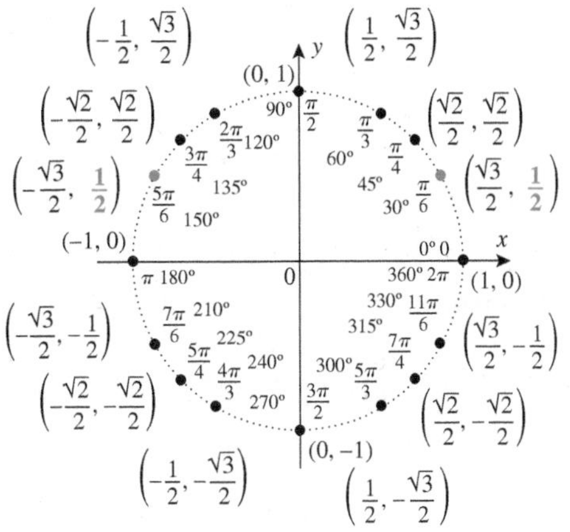

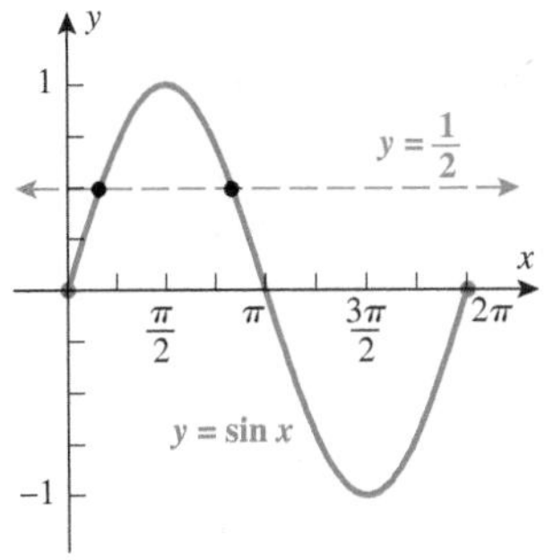

> **STUDY TIP**
>
> Recall the special triangle.
>
> 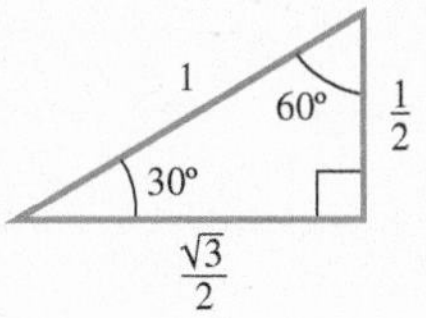
>
>
> $\sin 30° = \frac{1}{2}$

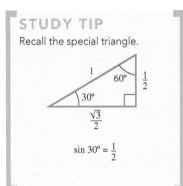

Solution (b):

Ask the question, "cosine of what angles is $\frac{1}{2}$?"

In this case, the angle is equal to $2x$.

$$2x = \frac{\pi}{3} \quad \text{or} \quad 2x = \frac{5\pi}{3}$$

Solve for x: $\boxed{x = \frac{\pi}{6} \quad \text{or} \quad x = \frac{5\pi}{6}}$.

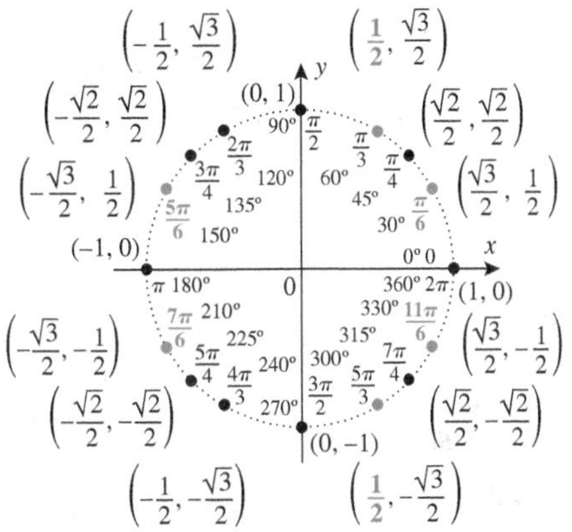

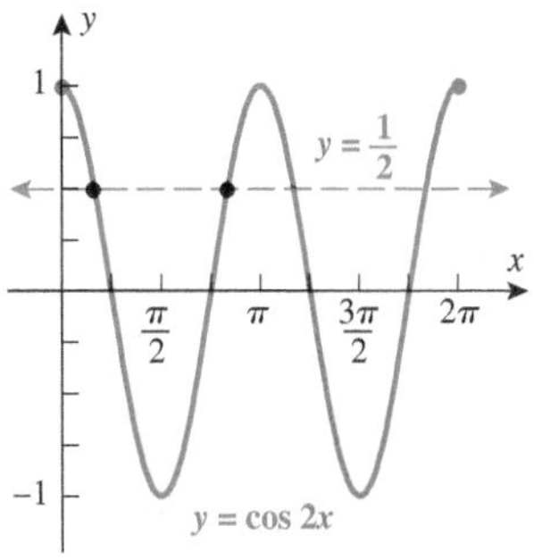

If the solution set for x is over $[0, 2\pi)$, then the solution set for $2x$ is over $[0, 4\pi)$.

Notice that $\boxed{x = \frac{7\pi}{6} \quad \text{or} \quad x = \frac{11\pi}{6}}$ also satisfy the equation $\cos(2x) = \frac{1}{2}$.

YOUR TURN Solve each of the following equations on the interval $[0, 2\pi)$:

a. $\cos x = \frac{1}{2}$ **b.** $\sin(2x) = \frac{1}{2}$

ANSWER

a. $x = \frac{\pi}{3}, \frac{5\pi}{3}$

b. $x = \frac{\pi}{12}, \frac{5\pi}{12}, \frac{13\pi}{12}, \frac{17\pi}{12}$

EXAMPLE 2 Solving a Trigonometric Equation by Inspection

Solve the equation $\sin x = \frac{\sqrt{2}}{2}$.

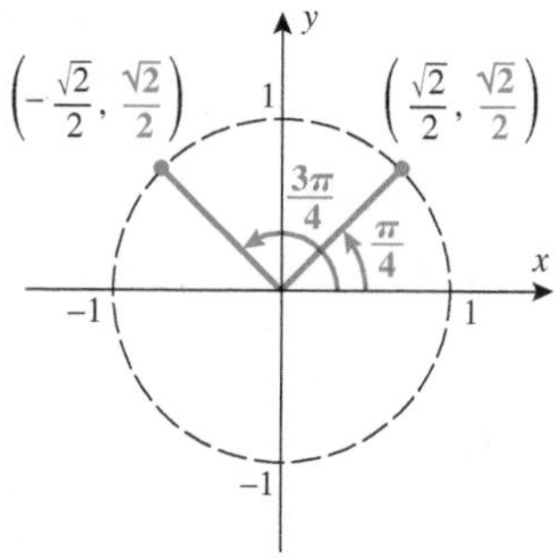

[CONCEPT CHECK]

Solve $\sin(x) = 0$.

ANSWER $x = n\pi$, where n is an integer.

Solution:

STEP 1 Solve over one period, $[0, 2\pi)$.

Ask the question, "sine of what angles is $\frac{\sqrt{2}}{2}$?"

The sine function is positive in quadrants I and II.

DEGREES	$x = 45°$ or $x = 135°$	
RADIANS	$x = \frac{\pi}{4}$ or $x = \frac{3\pi}{4}$	

STUDY TIP

Find *all* solutions unless the domain is restricted.

STEP 2 Solve over all real numbers.

Since the sine function has a period of $360°$ or 2π, adding integer multiples of $360°$ or 2π will give the other (infinitely many) solutions.

DEGREES	$x = 45° + 360°n$ or $x = 135° + 360°n$
RADIANS	$x = \frac{\pi}{4} + 2n\pi$ or $x = \frac{3\pi}{4} + 2n\pi$, where n is any integer

YOUR TURN Solve the equation $\cos x = \frac{1}{2}$.

ANSWER

DEGREES	$x = 60° + 360°n$ or $x = 300° + 360°n$
RADIANS	$x = \frac{\pi}{3} + 2n\pi$ or $x = \frac{5\pi}{3} + 2n\pi$, where n is any integer

Notice that the equations in Example 2 and Your Turn have an infinite number of solutions. Unless the domain is restricted, you must find *all* solutions.

EXAMPLE 3 Solving a Trigonometric Equation by Inspection

Solve the equation $\tan(2x) = -\sqrt{3}$.

Solution:

STEP 1 Solve over one period, $[0, \pi)$.

Ask the question, "tangent of what angles is $-\sqrt{3}$?" Note that the angle in this case is $2x$.

DEGREES	$2x = 120°$
RADIANS	$2x = \frac{2\pi}{3}$

The tangent function is negative in quadrants II and IV. Since $[0, \pi)$ includes quadrants I and II, we find only the angle in quadrant II. (The solution corresponding to quadrant IV will be found when we extend the solution over all real numbers.)

STEP 2 Solve over all x.

Since the tangent function has a period of 180°, or π, adding integer multiples of 180° or π will give all of the other solutions.

DEGREES	$2x = 120° + 180°n$
RADIANS	$2x = \frac{2\pi}{3} + n\pi$, where n is any integer

Solve for x by dividing by 2.

DEGREES	$x = 60° + 90°n$
RADIANS	$x = \frac{\pi}{3} + \frac{n}{2}\pi$, where n is any integer

Note:

- There are infinitely many solutions. If we graph $y = \tan(2x)$ and $y = -\sqrt{3}$, we see that there are infinitely many points of intersection.

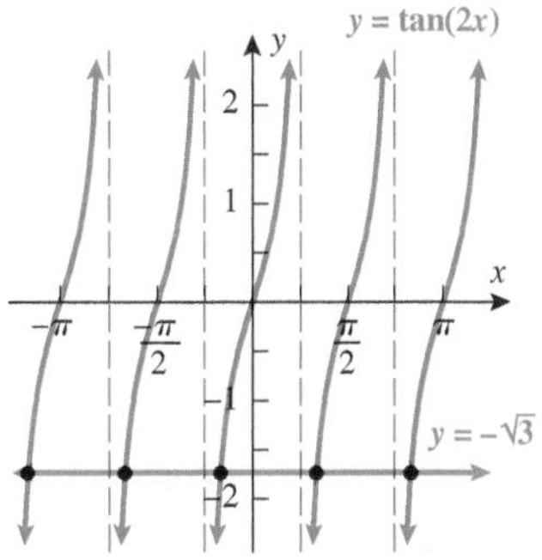

- Had we restricted the domain to $0 \le x < 2\pi$, the solutions (in radians) would have been the values given in the table to the right.

n	$x = \frac{\pi}{3} + \frac{n}{2}\pi$
0	$x = \frac{\pi}{3}$
1	$x = \frac{5\pi}{6}$
2	$x = \frac{4\pi}{3}$
3	$x = \frac{11\pi}{6}$

Notice that only $n = 0, 1, 2, 3$ yield x-values in the domain $0 \le x < 2\pi$.

Notice that in Step 2 of Example 2, $2n\pi$ was added to get all of the solutions, whereas in Step 2 of Example 3, we added $n\pi$ to the argument of the tangent function. The reason why we added $2n\pi$ in Example 2 and $n\pi$ in Example 3 is that the sine function has period 2π, whereas the tangent function has period π.

6.6.2 SKILL

Solve trigonometric equations by using algebraic techniques.

6.6.2 CONCEPTUAL

Utilize the concept of substitution in solving trigonometric equations when the results are simple linear or quadratic equations.

6.6.2 Solving Trigonometric Equations Using Algebraic Techniques

We now will utilize algebraic techniques to solve trigonometric equations. Let us begin with linear and quadratic equations. For linear equations, we solve for the variable by isolating it. For quadratic equations, we often employ factoring or the quadratic formula. If we can let x represent the trigonometric function and the resulting equation is either linear or quadratic, then we use techniques learned in solving algebraic equations.

TYPE	EQUATION	SUBSTITUTION	ALGEBRAIC EQUATION
Linear trigonometric equation	$4\sin\theta - 2 = -4$	$u = \sin\theta$	$4u - 2 = -4$
Quadratic trigonometric equation	$2\cos^2\theta + \cos\theta - 1 = 0$	$u = \cos\theta$	$2u^2 + u - 1 = 0$

It is not necessary to make the substitution, though it is convenient. Frequently, one can see how to factor a quadratic trigonometric equation without first converting it to an algebraic equation. In Example 4, we will not use a substitution. However, in Example 5, we will illustrate the use of a substitution.

EXAMPLE 4 **Solving a Linear Trigonometric Equation**

Solve $4\sin\theta - 2 = -4$ on $0 \le \theta < 2\pi$.

Solution:

STEP 1 Solve for $\sin\theta$. $\quad 4\sin\theta - 2 = -4$

Add 2. $\quad 4\sin\theta = -2$

Divide by 4. $\quad \sin\theta = -\dfrac{1}{2}$

STEP 2 Find the values of θ on $0 \le \theta < 2\pi$ that satisfy the equation $\sin\theta = -\frac{1}{2}$.

The sine function is negative in quadrants III and IV.

$$\sin\left(\frac{7\pi}{6}\right) = -\frac{1}{2} \quad \text{and} \quad \sin\left(\frac{11\pi}{6}\right) = -\frac{1}{2}. \qquad \boxed{\theta = \frac{7\pi}{6}} \text{ or } \boxed{\theta = \frac{11\pi}{6}}$$

YOUR TURN Solve $2\cos\theta + 1 = 2$ on $0 \le \theta < 2\pi$.

ANSWER

$\theta = \dfrac{\pi}{3}$ or $\dfrac{5\pi}{3}$

EXAMPLE 5 Solving a Quadratic Trigonometric Equation

Solve $2\cos^2\theta + \cos\theta - 1 = 0$ on $0 \le \theta < 2\pi$.

Solution:

STEP 1 Solve for $\cos\theta$. $$2\cos^2\theta + \cos\theta - 1 = 0$$

Let $u = \cos\theta$. $$2u^2 + u - 1 = 0$$

Factor the quadratic equation. $$(2u - 1)(u + 1) = 0$$

Set each factor equal to 0. $$2u - 1 = 0 \quad \text{or} \quad u + 1 = 0$$

Solve each for u. $$u = \frac{1}{2} \quad \text{or} \quad u = -1$$

Substitute $u = \cos\theta$. $$\cos\theta = \frac{1}{2} \quad \text{or} \quad \cos\theta = -1$$

STEP 2 Find the values of θ on $0 \le \theta < 2\pi$ that satisfy the equation $\cos\theta = \frac{1}{2}$.

The cosine function is positive in quadrants I and IV.

$$\cos\left(\frac{\pi}{3}\right) = \frac{1}{2} \quad \text{and} \quad \cos\left(\frac{5\pi}{3}\right) = \frac{1}{2}. \qquad \boxed{\theta = \frac{\pi}{3}} \quad \text{or} \quad \boxed{\theta = \frac{5\pi}{3}}$$

STEP 3 Find the values of θ on $0 \le \theta < 2\pi$ that satisfy the equation $\cos\theta = -1$.

$$\cos\pi = -1. \qquad \boxed{\theta = \pi}$$

The solutions to $2\cos^2\theta + \cos\theta - 1 = 0$ on $0 \le \theta < 2\pi$ are $\theta = \frac{\pi}{3}$, $\theta = \frac{5\pi}{3}$, and $\theta = \pi$.

YOUR TURN Solve $2\sin^2\theta - \sin\theta - 1 = 0$ on $0 \le \theta < 2\pi$.

[CONCEPT CHECK]

Solve $\cos^2(x) = 1$.

ANSWER $x = n\pi$, where n is an integer.

STUDY TIP

If Example 5 asked for the solution to the trigonometric equation over all real numbers, then the solutions would be $\theta = \frac{\pi}{3} \pm 2n\pi$, $\frac{5\pi}{3} \pm 2n\pi$, and $\pi \pm 2n\pi$.

ANSWER

$\theta = \frac{\pi}{2}, \frac{7\pi}{6}$, or $\frac{11\pi}{6}$

6.6.3 Solving Trigonometric Equations That Require the Use of Inverse Functions

Thus far, we have been able to solve the trigonometric equations exactly. Now we turn our attention to situations that require using a calculator and inverse functions to approximate a solution to a trigonometric equation.

6.6.3 SKILL

Solve trigonometric equations using inverse functions.

6.6.3 CONCEPTUAL

Utilize a calculator to approximate solutions when solving trigonometric equations using inverse functions.

EXAMPLE 6 **Solving a Trigonometric Equation That Requires the Use of Inverse Functions**

Solve $\tan^2\theta - \tan\theta = 6$ on $0° \le \theta < 180°$.

Solution:

STEP 1 Solve for $\tan\theta$.

Subtract 6. $\tan^2\theta - \tan\theta - 6 = 0$

Factor the quadratic trigonometric expression on the left. $(\tan\theta - 3)(\tan\theta + 2) = 0$

Set the factors equal to 0. $\tan\theta - 3 = 0$ or $\tan\theta + 2 = 0$

Solve for $\tan\theta$. $\tan\theta = 3$ or $\tan\theta = -2$

STEP 2 Solve $\tan\theta = 3$ on $0° \le \theta < 180°$.

The tangent function is positive on $0° \le \theta < 180°$ only in quadrant I.

Write the equivalent inverse notation to $\tan\theta = 3$. $\theta = \tan^{-1}3$

Use a calculator to evaluate (approximate) θ. $\boxed{\theta \approx 71.6°}$

STEP 3 Solve $\tan\theta = -2$ on $0° \le \theta < 180°$.

The tangent function is negative on $0° \le \theta < 180°$ only in quadrant II.

A calculator gives values of the inverse tangent in quadrants I and IV.

We will call the reference angle in quadrant IV "α."

Write the equivalent inverse notation to $\tan\alpha = -2$. $\alpha = \tan^{-1}(-2)$

Use a calculator to evaluate (approximate) α. $\alpha \approx -63.4°$

To find the value of θ in quadrant II, add 180°. $\theta = \alpha + 180°$

$\boxed{\theta \approx 116.6°}$

The solutions to $\tan^2\theta - \tan\theta = 6$ on $0° \le \theta < 180°$ are $\theta \approx 71.6°$ and $\theta \approx 116.6°$.

YOUR TURN Solve $\tan^2\theta + \tan\theta = 6$ on $0° \le \theta < 180°$.

ANSWER

$\theta \approx 63.4°$ or $108.4°$

[CONCEPT CHECK]

Explain why $\cos^2(x) + \cos(x) = 6$ does not have a solution.

ANSWER The range of cosine is $[-1, 1]$. The largest the left side of the equation can be is 2, which does not equal 6.

Recall that in solving algebraic quadratic equations, one method (when factoring is not obvious or possible) is to use the Quadratic Formula.

$$ax^2 + bx + c = 0 \text{ has solutions } x = \frac{-b \pm \sqrt{b^2 - 4ac}}{2a}$$

EXAMPLE 7 Solving a Quadratic Trigonometric Equation That Requires the Use of the Quadratic Formula and Inverse Functions

Solve $2\cos^2\theta + 5\cos\theta - 6 = 0$ on $0° \le \theta < 360°$.

Solution:

STEP 1 Solve for $\cos\theta$. $\quad 2\cos^2\theta + 5\cos\theta - 6 = 0$

Let $u = \cos\theta$. $\quad 2u^2 + 5u - 6 = 0$

Use the Quadratic Formula, $a = 2, b = 5, c = -6$. $\quad u = \dfrac{-5 \pm \sqrt{5^2 - 4(2)(-6)}}{2(2)}$

Simplify. $\quad u = \dfrac{-5 \pm \sqrt{73}}{4}$

Use a calculator to approximate the solution. $\quad u \approx -3.3860 \quad$ or $\quad u \approx 0.8860$

Let $u = \cos\theta$. $\quad \cos\theta \approx -3.3860 \quad$ or $\quad \cos\theta \approx 0.8860$

STEP 2 Solve $\cos\theta = -3.3860$ on $0° \le \theta < 360°$.

Recall that the range of the cosine function is $[-1, 1]$; therefore, the cosine function can never equal a number outside that range.

Since $-3.3860 < -1$, the equation $\cos\theta = -3.3860$ has *no solution.*

STEP 3 Solve $\cos\theta = 0.8860$ on $0° \le \theta < 360°$.

The cosine function is positive in quadrants I and IV. Since a calculator gives inverse cosine values only in quadrants I and II, we will have to use a reference angle to get the quadrant IV solution.

Write the equivalent inverse notation for $\cos\theta = 0.8860$. $\quad \theta = \cos^{-1}(0.8860)$

Use a calculator to evaluate (approximate) the solution. $\quad \boxed{\theta \approx 27.6°}$

To find the second solution (in quadrant IV), subtract the reference angle from 360°. $\quad \theta = 360° - 27.6°$

$\boxed{\theta \approx 332.4°}$

The solutions to $2\cos^2\theta + 5\cos\theta - 6 = 0$ on $0° \le \theta < 360°$ are $\theta \approx 27.6°$ and $\theta \approx 332.4°$.

YOUR TURN Solve $2\sin^2\theta - 5\sin\theta - 6 = 0$ on $0° \le \theta < 360°$.

ANSWER

$\theta \approx 242.4°$ or $297.6°$

6.6.4 Using Trigonometric Identities to Solve Trigonometric Equations

6.6.4 SKILL

Solve trigonometric equations (involving more than one trigonometric function) using trigonometric identities.

6.6.4 CONCEPTUAL

Using trigonometric identities can often help convert a trigonometric equation involving more than one trigonometric function into trigonometric equations involving a single trigonometric function.

We now consider trigonometric equations that involve more than one trigonometric function. Trigonometric identities are an important part of solving these types of equations.

EXAMPLE 8 **Using Trigonometric Identities to Solve Trigonometric Equations**

Solve $\sin x + \cos x = 1$ on $0 \le x < 2\pi$.

Solution:

Square both sides. $\sin^2 x + 2\sin x\cos x + \cos^2 x = 1$

Label the Pythagorean identity. $\underbrace{\sin^2 x + \cos^2 x}_{1} + 2\sin x\cos x = 1$

Subtract 1 from both sides. $2\sin x\cos x = 0$

Use the Zero Product Property. $\sin x = 0 \quad \text{or} \quad \cos x = 0$

Solve for x on $0 \le x < 2\pi$. $x = 0 \quad \text{or} \quad x = \pi \quad \text{or} \quad x = \frac{\pi}{2} \quad \text{or} \quad x = \frac{3\pi}{2}$

Because we squared the equation, we have to check for extraneous solutions.

Check $x = 0$. $\sin 0 + \cos 0 = 0 + 1 = 1$ ✓

Check $x = \pi$. $\sin\pi + \cos\pi = 0 - 1 = -1$ ✗

Check $x = \frac{\pi}{2}$. $\sin\left(\frac{\pi}{2}\right) + \cos\left(\frac{\pi}{2}\right) = 1 + 0 = 1$ ✓

Check $x = \frac{3\pi}{2}$. $\sin\left(\frac{3\pi}{2}\right) + \cos\left(\frac{3\pi}{2}\right) = -1 + 0 = -1$ ✗

The solutions to $\sin x + \cos x = 1$ on $0 \le x < 2\pi$ are $\boxed{x = 0}$ and $\boxed{x = \frac{\pi}{2}}$.

YOUR TURN Solve $\sin x - \cos x = 1$ on $0 \le x < 2\pi$.

ANSWER

$x = \frac{\pi}{2}$ or $x = \pi$

EXAMPLE 9 Using Trigonometric Identities to Solve Trigonometric Equations

Solve $\sin(2x) = \sin x$ on $0 \le x < 2\pi$.

common mistake

Dividing by a trigonometric function (which could be equal to zero).

✓CORRECT	✗INCORRECT
Use the double-angle formula for sine.	
$\underbrace{\sin(2x)}_{2\sin x\cos x} = \sin x$	$2\sin x\cos x = \sin x$
Subtract $\sin x$.	Divide by $\sin x$. **ERROR**
$2\sin x\cos x - \sin x = 0$	$2\cos x = 1$
Factor out the common $\sin x$.	
$(\sin x)(2\cos x - 1) = 0$	
Set each factor equal to 0.	
$\sin x = 0$ or $2\cos x - 1 = 0$	Solve for $\cos x$
$\sin x = 0$ or $\cos x = \frac{1}{2}$	$\cos x = \frac{1}{2}$
Solve $\sin x = 0$ for x on $0 \le x < 2\pi$.	
$\boxed{x = 0}$ or $\boxed{x = \pi}$	Missing solutions from $\sin x = 0$.
Solve $\cos x = \frac{1}{2}$ for x on $0 \le x < 2\pi$.	
$\boxed{x = \frac{\pi}{3}}$ or $\boxed{x = \frac{5\pi}{3}}$	

The solutions to $\sin(2x) = \sin x$ are $x = 0, \frac{\pi}{3}, \pi$, and $\frac{5\pi}{3}$.

YOUR TURN Solve $\sin(2x) = \cos x$ on $0 \le x < 2\pi$.

[CONCEPT CHECK]

TRUE OR FALSE $\sin(2A) = \cos(A)$ has the same solution as $\sin(2A) = \cos(-A)$.

ANSWER True

CAUTION

Do not divide equations by trigonometric functions, because they can sometimes equal zero.

ANSWER

$x = \frac{\pi}{2}, \frac{3\pi}{2}, \frac{\pi}{6}$, or $\frac{5\pi}{6}$

EXAMPLE 10 **Using Trigonometric Identities to Solve Trigonometric Equations**

Solve $\sin x + \csc x = -2$.

Solution:

Use the reciprocal identity. $\sin x + \underbrace{\csc x}_{\frac{1}{\sin x}} = -2$

Add 2. $\sin x + 2 + \dfrac{1}{\sin x} = 0$

Multiply by $\sin x$. *Note*: $\sin x \neq 0$. $\sin^2 x + 2\sin x + 1 = 0$

Factor as a perfect square. $(\sin x + 1)^2 = 0$

Solve for $\sin x$. $\sin x = -1$

Solve for x on one period of the sine function, $[0, 2\pi)$. $x = \dfrac{3\pi}{2}$

Add integer multiples of 2π to obtain all solutions. $\boxed{x = \dfrac{3\pi}{2} + 2n\pi}$

STUDY TIP

In Example 10 the equation $\sin x + \csc x = -2$ has an implied domain restriction of $\sin x \neq 0$.

EXAMPLE 11 **Using Trigonometric Identities and Inverse Functions to Solve Trigonometric Equations**

Solve $3\cos^2\theta + \sin\theta = 3$ on $0° \leq \theta < 360°$.

Solution:

Use the Pythagorean identity. $3\underbrace{\cos^2\theta}_{1-\sin^2\theta} + \sin\theta = 3$

Subtract 3. $3(1 - \sin^2\theta) + \sin\theta - 3 = 0$

Eliminate the parentheses. $3 - 3\sin^2\theta + \sin\theta - 3 = 0$

Simplify. $-3\sin^2\theta + \sin\theta = 0$

Factor the common $\sin\theta$. $\sin\theta(1 - 3\sin\theta) = 0$

Set each factor equal to 0. $\sin\theta = 0$ or $1 - 3\sin\theta = 0$

Solve for $\sin\theta$. $\sin\theta = 0$ or $\sin\theta = \dfrac{1}{3}$

Solve $\sin\theta = 0$ for x on $0° \leq \theta < 360°$. $\boxed{\theta = 0°}$ or $\boxed{\theta = 180°}$

Solve $\sin\theta = \frac{1}{3}$ for x on $0° \leq \theta < 360°$.

The sine function is positive in quadrants I and II.

A calculator gives inverse values only in quadrant I.

Write the equivalent inverse notation for $\sin\theta = \frac{1}{3}$. $\theta = \sin^{-1}\left(\dfrac{1}{3}\right)$

Use a calculator to approximate the quadrant I solution. $\boxed{\theta \approx 19.5°}$

To find the quadrant II solution, subtract the reference angle from 180°. $\theta \approx 180° - 19.5°$

$\boxed{\theta \approx 160.5°}$

Applications

EXAMPLE 12 Applications Involving Trigonometric Equations

Light bends (refracts) according to Snell's law, which states

$$n_i \sin(\theta_i) = n_r \sin(\theta_r)$$

where

- n_i is the refractive index of the medium the light is leaving.
- θ_i is the incident angle between the light ray and the normal (perpendicular) to the interface between mediums.
- n_r is the refractive index of the medium the light is entering.
- θ_r is the refractive angle between the light ray and the normal (perpendicular) to the interface between mediums.

Janis Christie/Getty Images, Inc.

Assume that light is going from air into a diamond. Calculate the refractive angle θ_r if the incidence angle is $\theta_i = 32°$ and the index-of-refraction values for air and diamond are $n_i = 1.00$ and $n_r = 2.417$, respectively.

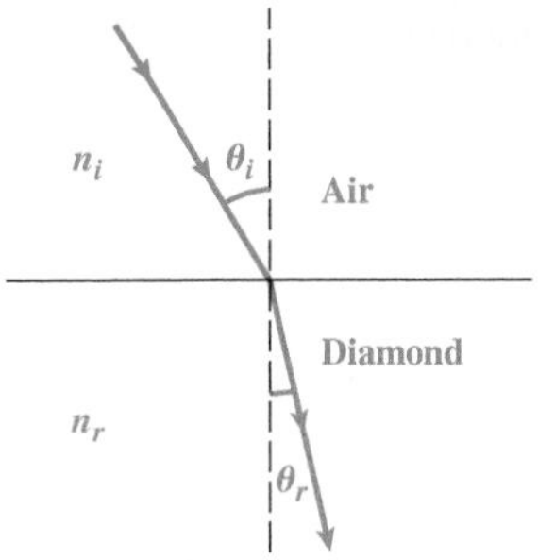

Solution:

Write Snell's law. $\quad n_i \sin(\theta_i) = n_r \sin(\theta_r)$

Substitute $\theta_i = 32°$, $n_i = 1.00$, and $n_r = 2.417$. $\quad \sin 32° = 2.417 \sin\theta_r$

Isolate $\sin\theta_r$ and simplify. $\quad \sin\theta_r = \dfrac{\sin 32°}{2.417} \approx 0.21925$

Solve for θ_r using the inverse sine function. $\quad \theta_r \approx \sin^{-1}(0.21925) \approx 12.665°$

Round to the nearest degree. $\quad \boxed{\theta_r \approx 13°}$

[SECTION 6.6] SUMMARY

In this section, we began by solving basic trigonometric equations that contained only one trigonometric function. Some such equations can be solved exactly by inspection, and others can be solved exactly using algebraic techniques similar to those for linear and quadratic equations. Calculators and inverse functions are needed when exact values are not known. It is important to note that calculators give the inverse function in only one of the two relevant quadrants. The other quadrant solutions must be found using reference angles. Trigonometric identities are useful for solving equations that involve more than one trigonometric function. With trigonometric identities we can transform such equations into equations involving only one trigonometric function, and then we can apply algebraic techniques.

[SECTION 6.6] EXERCISES

• SKILLS

In Exercises 1–20, solve the given trigonometric equation exactly over the indicated interval.

1. $\cos\theta = -\frac{\sqrt{2}}{2}, 0 \le \theta < 2\pi$
2. $\sin\theta = -\frac{\sqrt{2}}{2}, 0 \le \theta < 2\pi$
3. $\csc\theta = -2, 0 \le \theta < 4\pi$
4. $\sec\theta = -2, 0 \le \theta < 4\pi$
5. $\tan\theta = 0$, all real numbers
6. $\cot\theta = 0$, all real numbers
7. $\sin(2\theta) = -\frac{1}{2}, 0 \le \theta < 2\pi$
8. $\cos(2\theta) = \frac{\sqrt{3}}{2}, 0 \le \theta < 2\pi$
9. $\sin\left(\frac{\theta}{2}\right) = -\frac{1}{2}$, all real numbers
10. $\cos\left(\frac{\theta}{2}\right) = -1$, all real numbers
11. $\tan(2\theta) = \sqrt{3}, -2\pi \le \theta < 2\pi$
12. $\tan(2\theta) = -\sqrt{3}$, all real numbers
13. $\sec\theta = -2, -2\pi \le \theta < 0$
14. $\csc\theta = \frac{2\sqrt{3}}{3}, -\pi \le \theta < \pi$
15. $\cot(4\theta) = -\frac{\sqrt{3}}{3}$, all real numbers
16. $\tan(5\theta) = 1$, all real numbers
17. $\sec(3\theta) = -1, -2\pi \le \theta \le 0$
18. $\sec(4\theta) = \sqrt{2}, 0 \le \theta \le \pi$
19. $\csc(3\theta) = 1, -2\pi \le \theta \le 0$
20. $\csc(6\theta) = -\frac{2\sqrt{3}}{3}, 0 \le \theta \le \pi$

In Exercises 21–40, solve the given trigonometric equation exactly on $0 \le \theta < 2\pi$.

21. $2\sin(2\theta) = \sqrt{3}$
22. $2\cos\left(\frac{\theta}{2}\right) = -\sqrt{2}$
23. $3\tan(2\theta) - \sqrt{3} = 0$
24. $4\tan\left(\frac{\theta}{2}\right) - 4 = 0$
25. $2\cos(2\theta) + 1 = 0$
26. $4\csc(2\theta) + 8 = 0$
27. $\sqrt{3}\cot\left(\frac{\theta}{2}\right) - 3 = 0$
28. $\sqrt{3}\sec(2\theta) + 2 = 0$
29. $\tan^2\theta - 1 = 0$
30. $\sin^2\theta + 2\sin\theta + 1 = 0$
31. $2\cos^2\theta - \cos\theta = 0$
32. $\tan^2\theta - \sqrt{3}\tan\theta = 0$
33. $\csc^2\theta + 3\csc\theta + 2 = 0$
34. $\cot^2\theta = 1$
35. $\sin^2\theta + 2\sin\theta - 3 = 0$
36. $2\sec^2\theta + \sec\theta - 1 = 0$
37. $\sec^2\theta - 1 = 0$
38. $\csc^2\theta - 1 = 0$
39. $\sec^2(2\theta) - \frac{4}{3} = 0$
40. $\csc^2(2\theta) - 4 = 0$

In Exercises 41–60, solve the given trigonometric equation on $0° \le \theta < 360°$, and express the answer in degrees rounded to two decimal places.

41. $\sin(2\theta) = -0.7843$
42. $\cos(2\theta) = 0.5136$
43. $\tan\left(\frac{\theta}{2}\right) = -0.2343$
44. $\sec\left(\frac{\theta}{2}\right) = 1.4275$
45. $5\cot\theta - 9 = 0$
46. $5\sec\theta + 6 = 0$
47. $4\sin\theta + \sqrt{2} = 0$
48. $3\cos\theta - \sqrt{5} = 0$
49. $4\cos^2\theta + 5\cos\theta - 6 = 0$
50. $6\sin^2\theta - 13\sin\theta - 5 = 0$
51. $6\tan^2\theta - \tan\theta - 12 = 0$
52. $6\sec^2\theta - 7\sec\theta - 20 = 0$
53. $15\sin^2(2\theta) + \sin(2\theta) - 2 = 0$
54. $12\cos^2\left(\frac{\theta}{2}\right) - 13\cos\left(\frac{\theta}{2}\right) + 3 = 0$
55. $\cos^2\theta - 6\cos\theta + 1 = 0$
56. $\sin^2\theta + 3\sin\theta - 3 = 0$
57. $2\tan^2\theta - \tan\theta - 7 = 0$
58. $3\cot^2\theta + 2\cot\theta - 4 = 0$
59. $\csc^2(3\theta) - 2 = 0$
60. $\sec^2\left(\frac{\theta}{2}\right) - 2 = 0$

In Exercises 61–88, solve the trigonometric equations exactly on the interval $0 \le x < 2\pi$.

61. $\sin x = \cos x$
62. $\sin x = -\cos x$
63. $\sec x + \cos x = -2$
64. $\sin x + \csc x = 2$
65. $\sec x - \tan x = \frac{\sqrt{3}}{3}$
66. $\sec x + \tan x = 1$
67. $\csc x + \cot x = \sqrt{3}$
68. $\csc x - \cot x = \frac{\sqrt{3}}{3}$
69. $2\sin x - \csc x = 0$
70. $2\sin x + \csc x = 3$
71. $\sin(2x) = 4\cos x$
72. $\sin(2x) = \sqrt{3}\sin x$
73. $\sqrt{2}\sin x = \tan x$
74. $\cos(2x) = \sin x$
75. $\tan(2x) = \cot x$
76. $3\cot(2x) = \cot x$

77. $\sqrt{3}\sec x = 4\sin x$

78. $\sqrt{3}\tan x = 2\sin x$

79. $\sin^2 x - \cos(2x) = -\frac{1}{4}$

80. $\sin^2 x - 2\sin x = 0$

81. $\cos^2 x + 2\sin x + 2 = 0$

82. $2\cos^2 x = \sin x + 1$

83. $2\sin^2 x + 3\cos x = 0$

84. $4\cos^2 x - 4\sin x = 5$

85. $\cos(2x) + \cos x = 0$

86. $2\cot x = \csc x$

87. $\frac{1}{4}\sec(2x) = \sin(2x)$

88. $-\frac{1}{4}\csc(\frac{1}{2}x) = \cos(\frac{1}{2}x)$

In Exercises 89–98, solve each trigonometric equation on $0° \leq \theta < 360°$. Express solutions in degrees and round to two decimal places.

89. $\cos(2x) + \frac{1}{2}\sin x = 0$

90. $\sec^2 x = \tan x + 1$

91. $6\cos^2 x + \sin x = 5$

92. $\sec^2 x = 2\tan x + 4$

93. $\cot^2 x - 3\csc x - 3 = 0$

94. $\csc^2 x + \cot x = 7$

95. $2\sin^2 x + 2\cos x - 1 = 0$

96. $\sec^2 x + \tan x - 2 = 0$

97. $\frac{1}{16}\csc^2\left(\frac{x}{4}\right) - \cos^2\left(\frac{x}{4}\right) = 0$

98. $-\frac{1}{4}\sec^2\left(\frac{x}{8}\right) + \sin^2\left(\frac{x}{8}\right) = 0$

• APPLICATIONS

For Exercises 99 and 100, refer to the following:

Computer sales are generally subject to seasonal fluctuations. The sales of QualComp computers during 2008–2010 is approximated by the function

$$s(t) = 0.120\sin(0.790t - 2.380) + 0.387 \quad 1 \leq t \leq 12$$

where t represents time in quarters ($t = 1$ represents the end of the first quarter of 2008), and $s(t)$ represents computer sales (quarterly revenue) in millions of dollars.

99. **Business.** Find the quarter(s) in which the quarterly sales are \$472,000.

100. **Business.** Find the quarter(s) in which the quarterly sales are \$507,000.

For Exercises 101 and 102, refer to the following:

Allergy sufferers' symptoms fluctuate with the concentration of pollen in the air. At one location the pollen concentration, measured in grains per cubic meter, of grasses fluctuates throughout the day according to the function

$$p(t) = 35 - 26\cos\left(\frac{\pi}{12}t - \frac{7\pi}{6}\right), \quad 0 \leq t \leq 24$$

where t is measured in hours and $t = 0$ is 12:00 A.M.

101. **Biology/Health.** Find the time(s) of day when the grass pollen level is 41 grains per cubic meter. Round to the nearest hour.

102. **Biology/Health.** Find the time(s) of day when the grass pollen level is 17 grains per cubic meter. Round to the nearest hour.

103. **Sales.** Monthly sales of soccer balls are approximated by $S = 400\sin\left(\frac{\pi}{6}x\right) + 2000$, where x is the number of the month (January is $x = 1$, etc.). During which month do sales reach 2400?

104. **Sales.** Monthly sales of soccer balls are approximated by $S = 400\sin\left(\frac{\pi}{6}x\right) + 2000$, where x is the number of the month (January is $x = 1$, etc.). During which two months do sales reach 1800?

105. **Deer Population.** The number of deer on an island is given by $D = 200 + 100\sin\left(\frac{\pi}{2}x\right)$, where x is the number of years since 2000. Which is the first year after 2000 that the number of deer reaches 300?

106. **Deer Population.** The number of deer on an island is given by $D = 200 + 100\sin\left(\frac{\pi}{6}x\right)$, where x is the number of years since 2000. Which is the first year after 2000 that the number of deer reaches 150?

107. **Optics.** Assume that light is going from air into a diamond. Calculate the refractive angle θ_r if the incidence angle is $\theta_i = 75°$ and the index-of-refraction values for air and diamond are $n_i = 1.00$ and $n_r = 2.417$, respectively. Round to the nearest degree. (See Example 12 for Snell's law.)

108. **Optics.** Assume that light is going from a diamond into air. Calculate the refractive angle θ_r if the incidence angle is $\theta_i = 15°$ and the index-of-refraction values for diamond and air are $n_i = 2.417$ and $n_r = 1.00$, respectively. Round to the nearest degree. (See Example 12 for Snell's law.)

109. **Air in Lungs.** If a person breathes in and out every 3 seconds, the volume of air in the lungs can be modeled by $A = 2\sin\left(\frac{\pi}{3}x\right)\cos\left(\frac{\pi}{3}x\right) + 3$, where A is in liters of air and x is in seconds. How many seconds into the cycle is the volume of air equal to 4 liters?

110. **Air in Lungs.** For the function given in Exercise 109, how many seconds into the cycle is the volume of air equal to 2 liters?

For Exercises 111 and 112, refer to the following:

The figure below shows the graph of $y = 2\cos x - \cos(2x)$ between -2π and 2π. The maximum and minimum values of the curve occur at the *turning points* and are found in the solutions of the equation $-2\sin x + 2\sin(2x) = 0$.

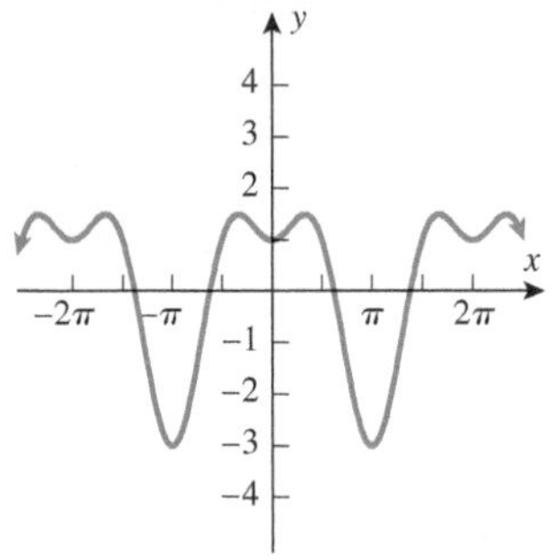

111. **Finding Turning Points.** Solve for the coordinates of the turning points of the curve between 0 and 2π.

112. **Finding Turning Points.** Solve for the coordinates of the turning points of the curve between -2π and 0.

113. **Business.** An analysis of a company's costs and revenue shows that the annual costs of producing its product, and the annual revenues from the sale of that product, are generally subject to seasonal fluctuations and are approximated by the functions

$$C(t) = 2.3 + 0.25\sin\left(\frac{\pi}{6}t\right) \quad 0 \le t \le 11$$

$$R(t) = 2.3 + 0.5\cos\left(\frac{\pi}{6}t\right) \quad 0 \le t \le 11$$

where t represents time in months ($t = 0$ represents January), $C(t)$ represents the monthly costs of producing the product in millions of dollars, and $R(t)$ represents monthly revenue from sales of the product in millions of dollars. Find the month(s) in which the company breaks even. *Hint:* A company breaks even when its profit is zero.

114. **Business.** An analysis of a company's costs and revenues shows that the annual costs of producing its product, and the annual revenues from the sale of that product, are generally subject to seasonal fluctuations and are approximated by the functions

$$C(t) = 25.7 + 0.2\sin\left(\frac{\pi}{6}t\right) \quad 0 \le t \le 11$$

$$R(t) = 25.7 + 9.6\cos\left(\frac{\pi}{6}t\right) \quad 0 \le t \le 11$$

where t represents time in months ($t = 0$ represents January), $C(t)$ represents the monthly costs of producing the product in millions of dollars, and $R(t)$ represents monthly revenue from sales of the product in millions of dollars. Find the month(s) in which the company breaks even. *Hint:* A company breaks even when its profit is zero.

For Exercises 115 and 116, refer to the following:

By analyzing available empirical data, it has been determined that the body temperature of a species fluctuates according to the model

$$T(t) = 37.10 + 1.40\sin\left(\frac{\pi}{24}t\right)\cos\left(\frac{\pi}{24}t\right) \quad 0 \le t \le 24$$

where T represents temperature in degrees Celsius and t represents time (in hours) measured from 12:00 A.M. (midnight).

115. **Biology/Health.** Find the time(s) of day when the body temperature is 37.28°C. Round to the nearest hour.

116. **Biology/Health.** Find the time(s) of day when the body temperature is 36.75°C. Round to the nearest hour.

• CATCH THE MISTAKE

In Exercises 117–120, explain the mistake that is made.

117. Solve $\sqrt{2 + \sin\theta} = \sin\theta$ on $0 \le \theta \le 2\pi$.

Solution:

Square both sides.	$2 + \sin\theta = \sin^2\theta$
Gather all terms to one side.	$\sin^2\theta - \sin\theta - 2 = 0$
Factor.	$(\sin\theta - 2)(\sin\theta + 1) = 0$
Set each factor equal to zero.	$\sin\theta - 2 = 0$ or $\sin\theta + 1 = 0$
Solve for $\sin\theta$.	$\sin\theta = 2$ or $\sin\theta = -1$
Solve $\sin\theta = 2$ for θ.	no solution
Solve $\sin\theta = -1$ for θ.	$\theta = \frac{3\pi}{2}$

This is incorrect. What mistake was made?

118. Solve $\sqrt{3\sin\theta - 2} = -\sin\theta$ on $0 \le \theta \le 2\pi$.

Solution:

Square both sides.	$3\sin\theta - 2 = \sin^2\theta$
Gather all terms to one side.	$\sin^2\theta - 3\sin\theta + 2 = 0$
Factor.	$(\sin\theta - 2)(\sin\theta - 1) = 0$
Set each factor equal to zero.	$\sin\theta - 2 = 0$ or $\sin\theta - 1 = 0$
Solve for $\sin\theta$.	$\sin\theta = 2$ or $\sin\theta = 1$
Solve $\sin\theta = 2$ for θ.	no solution
Solve $\sin\theta = 1$ for θ.	$\theta = \frac{\pi}{2}$

This is incorrect. What mistake was made?

119. Solve $3\sin(2x) = 2\cos x$ on $0° \leq \theta \leq 180°$.

Solution:

Use the double-angle identity for the sine function.	$3\underbrace{\sin(2x)}_{2\sin x\cos x} = 2\cos x$
Simplify.	$6\sin x\cos x = 2\cos x$
Divide by $2\cos x$.	$3\sin x = 1$
Divide by 3.	$\sin x = \frac{1}{3}$
Write the equivalent inverse notation.	$x = \sin^{-1}\left(\frac{1}{3}\right)$
Use a calculator to approximate the solution.	$x \approx 19.47°$, QI solution
The QII solution is:	$x \approx 180° - 19.47° \approx 160.53°$

This is incorrect. What mistake was made?

120. Solve $\sqrt{1 + \sin x} = \cos x$ on $0 \leq x \leq 2\pi$.

Solution:

Square both sides.	$1 + \sin x = \cos^2 x$
Use the Pythagorean identity.	$1 + \sin x = \underbrace{\cos^2 x}_{1-\sin^2 x}$
Simplify.	$\sin^2 x + \sin x = 0$
Factor.	$\sin x(\sin x + 1) = 0$
Set each factor equal to zero.	$\sin x = 0$ or $\sin x + 1 = 0$
Solve for $\sin x$.	$\sin x = 0$ or $\sin x = -1$
Solve for x.	$x = 0, \pi, \frac{3\pi}{2}, 2\pi$

This is incorrect. What mistake was made?

• CONCEPTUAL

In Exercises 121–124, determine whether each statement is true or false.

121. Linear trigonometric equations always have one solution on $[0, 2\pi]$.

122. Quadratic trigonometric equations always have two solutions on $[0, 2\pi]$.

123. If a trigonometric equation has all real numbers as its solution, then it is an identity.

124. If a trigonometric equation has an infinite number of solutions, then it is an identity.

• CHALLENGE

125. Solve $16\sin^4\theta - 8\sin^2\theta = -1$ over $0 \leq \theta \leq 2\pi$.

126. Solve $\left|\cos\left(\theta + \frac{\pi}{4}\right)\right| = \frac{\sqrt{3}}{2}$ over all real numbers.

127. Solve for the smallest positive x that makes this statement true:

$$\sin\left(x + \frac{\pi}{4}\right) + \sin\left(x - \frac{\pi}{4}\right) = \frac{\sqrt{2}}{2}$$

128. Solve for the smallest positive x that makes this statement true:

$$\cos x\cos 15° + \sin x\sin 15° = 0.7$$

129. Find all real numbers x such that $\dfrac{1 - \cos\left(\frac{x}{3}\right)}{1 + \cos\left(\frac{x}{3}\right)} + 1 = 0.$

130. Find all real numbers θ such that $\sec^4\left(\frac{1}{3}\theta\right) - 1 = 0.$

131. Find all real numbers θ such that $\csc^4\left(\frac{\pi}{4}\theta - \pi\right) - 4 = 0.$

132. Find all real numbers x such that $2\tan(3x) = \sqrt{3} - \sqrt{3}\tan^2(3x)$.

• PREVIEW TO CALCULUS

In calculus, the definite integral is used to find the area between two intersecting curves (functions). When the curves correspond to trigonometric functions, we need to solve trigonometric equations.

In Exercises 133–136, solve each trigonometric equation within the indicated interval.

133. $\cos x = 2 - \cos x,\ 0 \leq x \leq 2\pi$

134. $\cos(2x) = \sin x,\ -\frac{\pi}{2} \leq x \leq \frac{\pi}{6}$

135. $2\sin x = \tan x,\ -\frac{\pi}{3} \leq x \leq \frac{\pi}{3}$

136. $\sin(2x) - \cos(2x) = 0,\ 0 < x \leq \pi$

[CHAPTER 6 REVIEW]

SECTION	CONCEPT	KEY IDEAS/FORMULAS
6.1	**Verifying trigonometric identities**	Identities must hold for *all* values of x (not just some values of x) for which both sides of the equation are defined.
	Fundamental identities	*Reciprocal identities* $\csc\theta = \dfrac{1}{\sin\theta}$ $\sec\theta = \dfrac{1}{\cos\theta}$ $\cot\theta = \dfrac{1}{\tan\theta}$ *Quotient identities* $\tan\theta = \dfrac{\sin\theta}{\cos\theta}$ $\cot\theta = \dfrac{\cos\theta}{\sin\theta}$ *Pythagorean identities* $\sin^2\theta + \cos^2\theta = 1$ $\tan^2\theta + 1 = \sec^2\theta$ $1 + \cot^2\theta = \csc^2\theta$ *Cofunction identities* $\sin\theta = \cos\left(\dfrac{\pi}{2} - \theta\right)$ $\csc\theta = \sec\left(\dfrac{\pi}{2} - \theta\right)$ $\cos\theta = \sin\left(\dfrac{\pi}{2} - \theta\right)$ $\sec\theta = \csc\left(\dfrac{\pi}{2} - \theta\right)$ $\tan\theta = \cot\left(\dfrac{\pi}{2} - \theta\right)$ $\cot\theta = \tan\left(\dfrac{\pi}{2} - \theta\right)$
	Simplifying trigonometric expressions using identities	Use the reciprocal, quotient, or Pythagorean identities to simplify trigonometric expressions.
	Verifying identities	■ Convert all trigonometric expressions to sines and cosines. ■ Write all sums or differences of fractions as a single fraction.
6.2	**Sum and difference identities**	$f(A \pm B) \neq f(A) \pm f(B)$ For trigonometric functions, we have the sum and difference identities.
	Sum and difference identities for the cosine function	$\cos(A + B) = \cos A\cos B - \sin A\sin B$ $\cos(A - B) = \cos A\cos B + \sin A\sin B$
	Sum and difference identities for the sine function	$\sin(A + B) = \sin A\cos B + \cos A\sin B$ $\sin(A - B) = \sin A\cos B - \cos A\sin B$
	Sum and difference identities for the tangent function	$\tan(A + B) = \dfrac{\tan A + \tan B}{1 - \tan A\tan B}$ $\tan(A - B) = \dfrac{\tan A - \tan B}{1 + \tan A\tan B}$
6.3	**Double-angle and half-angle identities**	
	Double-angle identities	$\sin(2A) = 2\sin A\cos A$ $\cos(2A) = \cos^2 A - \sin^2 A$ $= 1 - 2\sin^2 A = 2\cos^2 A - 1$ $\tan(2A) = \dfrac{2\tan A}{1 - \tan^2 A}$

SECTION	CONCEPT	KEY IDEAS/FORMULAS
	Half-angle identities	$\sin\left(\frac{A}{2}\right) = \pm\sqrt{\frac{1-\cos A}{2}}$ $\cos\left(\frac{A}{2}\right) = \pm\sqrt{\frac{1+\cos A}{2}}$ $\tan\left(\frac{A}{2}\right) = \pm\sqrt{\frac{1-\cos A}{1+\cos A}} = \frac{\sin A}{1+\cos A} = \frac{1-\cos A}{\sin A}$
6.4	**Product-to-sum and sum-to-product identities**	
	Product-to-sum identities	$\cos A\cos B = \frac{1}{2}[\cos(A+B) + \cos(A-B)]$ $\sin A\sin B = \frac{1}{2}[\cos(A-B) - \cos(A+B)]$ $\sin A\cos B = \frac{1}{2}[\sin(A+B) + \sin(A-B)]$
	Sum-to-product identities	$\sin A + \sin B = 2\sin\left(\frac{A+B}{2}\right)\cos\left(\frac{A-B}{2}\right)$ $\sin A - \sin B = 2\sin\left(\frac{A-B}{2}\right)\cos\left(\frac{A+B}{2}\right)$ $\cos A + \cos B = 2\cos\left(\frac{A+B}{2}\right)\cos\left(\frac{A-B}{2}\right)$ $\cos A - \cos B = -2\sin\left(\frac{A+B}{2}\right)\sin\left(\frac{A-B}{2}\right)$
6.5	**Inverse trigonometric functions**	$\sin^{-1}x$ or $\arcsin x$ $\quad\cos^{-1}x$ or $\arccos x$ $\tan^{-1}x$ or $\arctan x$ $\quad\cot^{-1}x$ or $\operatorname{arccot} x$ $\sec^{-1}x$ or $\operatorname{arcsec} x$ $\quad\csc^{-1}x$ or $\operatorname{arccsc} x$
	Inverse sine function	**Definition** $y = \sin^{-1}x$ means $x = \sin y$ $-1 \le x \le 1$ and $-\frac{\pi}{2} \le y \le \frac{\pi}{2}$ **Identities** $\sin^{-1}(\sin x) = x$ for $-\frac{\pi}{2} \le x \le \frac{\pi}{2}$ $\sin(\sin^{-1}x) = x$ for $-1 \le x \le 1$ 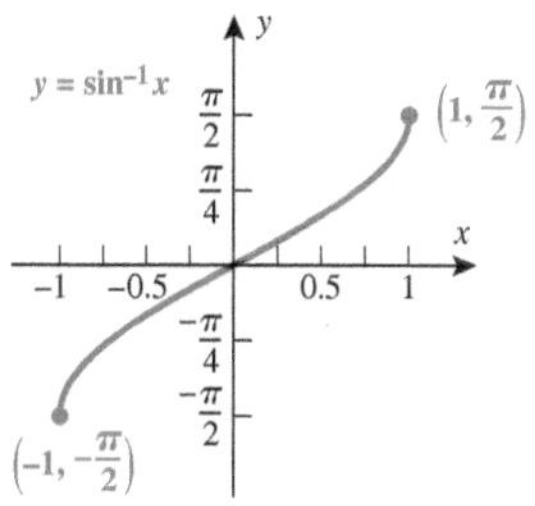
	Inverse cosine function	**Definition** $y = \cos^{-1}x$ means $x = \cos y$ $-1 \le x \le 1$ and $0 \le y \le \pi$ **Identities** $\cos^{-1}(\cos x) = x$ for $0 \le x \le \pi$ $\cos(\cos^{-1}x) = x$ for $-1 \le x \le 1$ 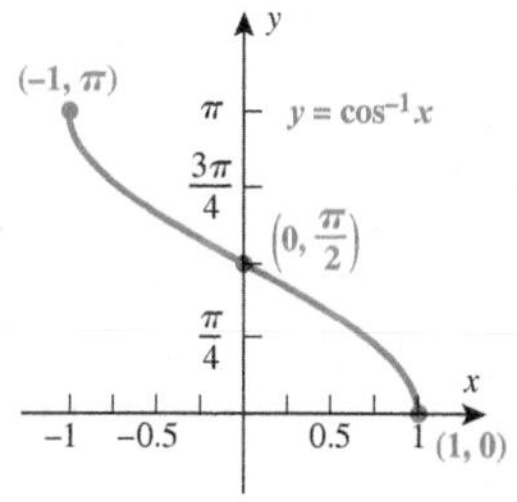

SECTION	CONCEPT	KEY IDEAS/FORMULAS
	Inverse tangent function	**Definition** $y = \tan^{-1}x$ means $x = \tan y$ $-\infty < x < \infty$ and $-\frac{\pi}{2} < y < \frac{\pi}{2}$ **Identities** $\tan^{-1}(\tan x) = x$ for $-\frac{\pi}{2} < x < \frac{\pi}{2}$ $\tan(\tan^{-1}x) = x$ for $-\infty < x < \infty$ 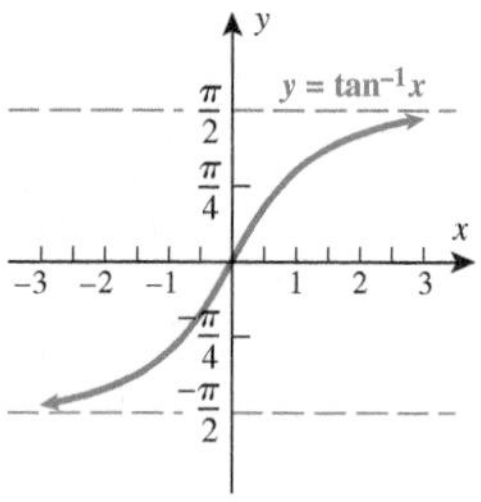
	Remaining inverse trigonometric functions	**Inverse cotangent function** **Definition** $y = \cot^{-1}x$ means $x = \cot y$ $-\infty < x < \infty$ and $0 < y < \pi$ **Identity** $\cot^{-1}x = \begin{cases} \tan^{-1}\left(\frac{1}{x}\right), x > 0 \\ \pi + \tan^{-1}\left(\frac{1}{x}\right), x < 0 \end{cases}$ 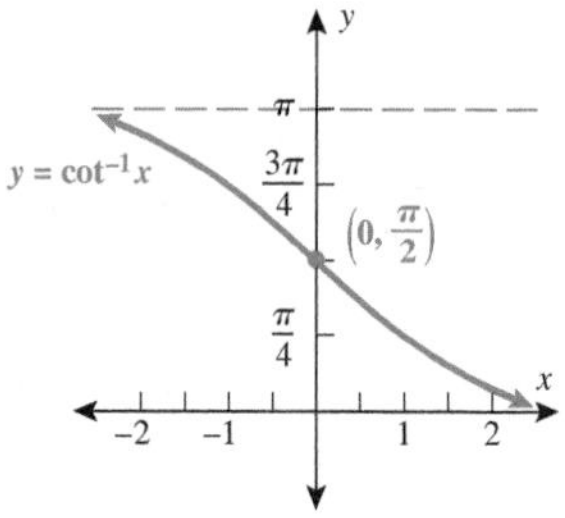 **Inverse secant function** **Definition** $y = \sec^{-1}x$ means $x = \sec y$ $x \le -1$ or $x \ge 1$ and $0 \le y < \frac{\pi}{2}$ or $\frac{\pi}{2} < y \le \pi$ **Identity** $\sec^{-1}x = \cos^{-1}\left(\frac{1}{x}\right)$ for $x \le -1$ or $x \ge 1$ 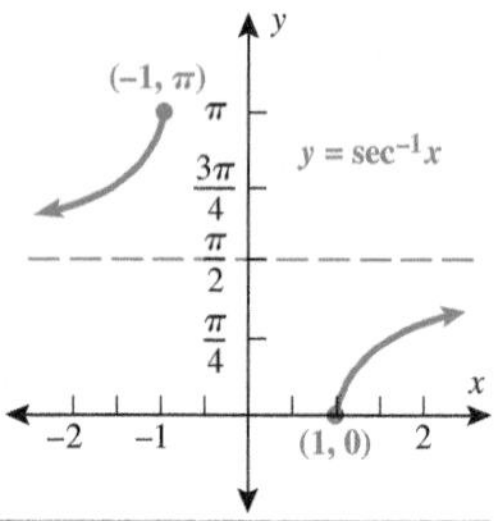

SECTION	CONCEPT	KEY IDEAS/FORMULAS
		Inverse cosecant function **Definition** $y = \csc^{-1}x$ means $x = \csc y$ $x \leq -1$ or $x \geq 1$ and $-\frac{\pi}{2} \leq y < 0$ or $0 < y \leq \frac{\pi}{2}$ **Identity** $\csc^{-1}x = \sin^{-1}\left(\frac{1}{x}\right)$ for $x \leq -1$ or $x \geq 1$ 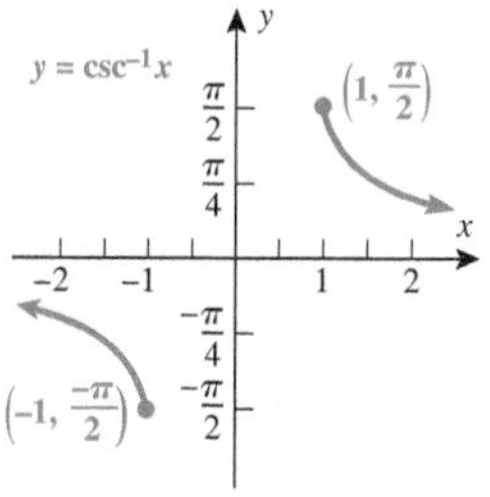
	Finding exact values for expressions involving inverse trigonometric functions	
6.6	**Trigonometric equations**	Goal: Find the values of the variable that make the equation true.
	Solving trigonometric equations by inspection	Solve: $\sin\theta = \frac{\sqrt{2}}{2}$ on $0 \leq \theta \leq 2\pi$. Answer: $\theta = \frac{\pi}{4}$ or $\theta = \frac{3\pi}{4}$. Solve: $\sin\theta = \frac{\sqrt{2}}{2}$ on all real numbers. Answer: $\theta = \begin{cases} \frac{\pi}{4} + 2n\pi \\ \frac{3\pi}{4} + 2n\pi \end{cases}$ where n is an integer.
	Solving trigonometric equations using algebraic techniques	Transform trigonometric equations into linear or quadratic algebraic equations by making a substitution such as $x = \sin\theta$. Then use algebraic methods for solving linear and quadratic equations. If an expression is squared, always check for extraneous solutions.
	Solving trigonometric equations that require the use of inverse functions	Follow the same procedures outlined by inspection or algebraic methods. Finding the solution requires the use of inverse functions and a calculator. Be careful: Calculators give only one solution (the one in the range of the inverse function).
	Using trigonometric identities to solve trigonometric equations	Use trigonometric identities to transform an equation with multiple trigonometric functions into an equation with only one trigonometric function. Then use the methods outlined above.

[CHAPTER 6 REVIEW EXERCISES]

6.1 Verifying Trigonometric Identities

Use the cofunction identities to fill in the blanks.

1. $\sin 30° = \cos$ ______
2. $\cos A = \sin$ ______
3. $\tan 45° = \cot$ ______
4. $\csc 60° = \sec$ ______
5. $\sec 30° = \csc$ ______
6. $\cot 60° = \tan$ ______

Simplify the following trigonometric expressions:

7. $\tan x(\cot x + \tan x)$
8. $(\sec x + 1)(\sec x - 1)$
9. $\dfrac{\tan^4 x - 1}{\tan^2 x - 1}$
10. $\sec^2 x(\cot^2 x - \cos^2 x)$
11. $\cos x[\cos(-x) - \tan(-x)] - \sin x$
12. $\dfrac{\tan^2 x + 1}{2\sec^2 x}$
13. $\dfrac{\csc^3(-x) + 8}{\csc x - 2}$
14. $\dfrac{\csc^2 x - 1}{\cot x}$

Verify the trigonometric identities.

15. $(\tan x + \cot x)^2 - 2 = \tan^2 x + \cot^2 x$
16. $\csc^2 x - \cot^2 x = 1$
17. $\dfrac{1}{\sin^2 x} - \dfrac{1}{\tan^2 x} = 1$
18. $\dfrac{1}{\csc x + 1} + \dfrac{1}{\csc x - 1} = \dfrac{2\tan x}{\cos x}$
19. $\dfrac{\tan^2 x - 1}{\sec^2 x + 3\tan x + 1} = \dfrac{\tan x - 1}{\tan x + 2}$
20. $\cot x(\sec x - \cos x) = \sin x$

Determine whether each of the following equations is a conditional equation or an identity:

21. $2\tan^2 x + 1 = \dfrac{1 + \sin^2 x}{\cos^2 x}$
22. $\sin x - \cos x = 0$
23. $\cot^2 x - 1 = \tan^2 x$
24. $\cos^2 x(1 + \cot^2 x) = \cot^2 x$
25. $\left(\cot x - \dfrac{1}{\tan x}\right)^2 = 0$
26. $\csc x + \sec x = \dfrac{1}{\sin x + \cos x}$

6.2 Sum and Difference Identities

Find the exact value for each trigonometric expression.

27. $\cos\left(\dfrac{7\pi}{12}\right)$
28. $\sin\left(\dfrac{\pi}{12}\right)$
29. $\tan(-15°)$
30. $\cot 105°$

Write each expression as a single trigonometric function.

31. $\sin(4x)\cos(3x) - \cos(4x)\sin(3x)$
32. $\sin(-x)\sin(-2x) + \cos(-x)\cos(-2x)$
33. $\dfrac{\tan(5x) - \tan(4x)}{1 + \tan(5x)\tan(4x)}$
34. $\dfrac{\tan\left(\frac{\pi}{4}\right) + \tan\left(\frac{\pi}{3}\right)}{1 - \tan\left(\frac{\pi}{4}\right)\tan\left(\frac{\pi}{3}\right)}$

Find the exact value of the indicated expression using the given information and identities.

35. Find the exact value of $\tan(\alpha - \beta)$ if $\sin\alpha = -\frac{3}{5}$, $\sin\beta = -\frac{24}{25}$, the terminal side of α lies in quadrant IV, and the terminal side of β lies in quadrant III.
36. Find the exact value of $\cos(\alpha + \beta)$ if $\cos\alpha = -\frac{5}{13}$, $\sin\beta = \frac{7}{25}$, the terminal side of α lies in quadrant II, and the terminal side of β also lies in quadrant II.
37. Find the exact value of $\cos(\alpha - \beta)$ if $\cos\alpha = \frac{9}{41}$, $\cos\beta = \frac{7}{25}$, the terminal side of α lies in quadrant IV, and the terminal side of β lies in quadrant I.
38. Find the exact value of $\sin(\alpha - \beta)$ if $\sin\alpha = -\frac{5}{13}$, $\cos\beta = -\frac{4}{5}$, the terminal side of α lies in quadrant III, and the terminal side of β lies in quadrant II.

Determine whether each of the following equations is a conditional equation or an identity:

39. $2\cos A\cos B = \cos(A + B) + \cos(A - B)$
40. $2\sin A\sin B = \cos(A - B) - \cos(A + B)$

Graph the following functions:

41. $y = \cos\left(\frac{\pi}{2}\right)\cos x - \sin\left(\frac{\pi}{2}\right)\sin x$

42. $y = \sin\left(\frac{2\pi}{3}\right)\cos x + \cos\left(\frac{2\pi}{3}\right)\sin x$

43. $y = \dfrac{2\tan\left(\frac{x}{3}\right)}{1 - \tan^2\left(\frac{x}{3}\right)}$

44. $y = \dfrac{\tan(\pi x) - \tan x}{1 + \tan(\pi x)\tan x}$

6.3 Double-Angle and Half-Angle Identities

Use double-angle identities to answer the following questions:

45. If $\sin x = \frac{3}{5}$ and $\frac{\pi}{2} < x < \pi$, find $\cos(2x)$.

46. If $\cos x = \frac{7}{25}$ and $\frac{3\pi}{2} < x < 2\pi$, find $\sin(2x)$.

47. If $\cot x = -\frac{11}{61}$ and $\frac{3\pi}{2} < x < 2\pi$, find $\tan(2x)$.

48. If $\tan x = -\frac{12}{5}$ and $\frac{\pi}{2} < x < \pi$, find $\cos(2x)$.

49. If $\sec x = \frac{25}{24}$ and $0 < x < \frac{\pi}{2}$, find $\sin(2x)$.

50. If $\csc x = \frac{5}{4}$ and $\frac{\pi}{2} < x < \pi$, find $\tan(2x)$.

Simplify each of the following expressions. Evaluate exactly, if possible.

51. $\cos^2 15° - \sin^2 15°$

52. $\dfrac{2\tan\left(-\frac{\pi}{12}\right)}{1 - \tan^2\left(-\frac{\pi}{12}\right)}$

53. $6\sin\left(\frac{\pi}{12}\right)\cos\left(\frac{\pi}{12}\right)$

54. $1 - 2\sin^2\left(\frac{\pi}{8}\right)$

Verify the following identities:

55. $\sin^3 A - \cos^3 A = (\sin A - \cos A)\left[1 + \frac{1}{2}\sin(2A)\right]$

56. $2\sin A\cos^3 A - 2\sin^3 A\cos A = \cos(2A)\sin(2A)$

57. $\tan A = \dfrac{\sin(2A)}{1 + \cos(2A)}$

58. $\tan A = \dfrac{1 - \cos(2A)}{\sin(2A)}$

59. Launching a Missile. When a missile is launched for a given range, the minimum velocity needed is related to the angle θ of the launch, and the velocity is determined by $V = \dfrac{2\cos(2\theta)}{1 + \cos(2\theta)}$. Show that V is equivalent to $1 - \tan^2\theta$.

60. Launching a Missile. When a missile is launched for a given range, the minimum velocity needed is related to the angle θ of the launch, and the velocity is determined by $V = \dfrac{2\cos(2\theta)}{1 + \cos(2\theta)}$. Find the value of V when $\theta = \frac{\pi}{6}$.

Use half-angle identities to find the exact value of each of the following trigonometric expressions:

61. $\sin(-22.5°)$

62. $\cos 67.5°$

63. $\cot\left(\frac{3\pi}{8}\right)$

64. $\csc\left(-\frac{7\pi}{8}\right)$

65. $\sec(-165°)$

66. $\tan(-75°)$

Use half-angle identities to find each of the following values:

67. If $\sin x = -\frac{7}{25}$ and $\pi < x < \frac{3\pi}{2}$, find $\sin\left(\frac{x}{2}\right)$.

68. If $\cos x = -\frac{4}{5}$ and $\frac{\pi}{2} < x < \pi$, find $\cos\left(\frac{x}{2}\right)$.

69. If $\tan x = \frac{40}{9}$ and $\pi < x < \frac{3\pi}{2}$, find $\tan\left(\frac{x}{2}\right)$.

70. If $\sec x = \frac{17}{15}$ and $\frac{3\pi}{2} < x < 2\pi$, find $\sin\left(\frac{x}{2}\right)$.

Simplify each expression using half-angle identities. Do not evaluate.

71. $\sqrt{\dfrac{1 - \cos\left(\frac{\pi}{6}\right)}{2}}$

72. $\sqrt{\dfrac{1 - \cos\left(\frac{11\pi}{6}\right)}{1 + \cos\left(\frac{11\pi}{6}\right)}}$

Verify each of the following identities:

73. $\left[\sin\left(\frac{A}{2}\right) + \cos\left(\frac{A}{2}\right)\right]^2 = 1 + \sin A$

74. $\sec^2\left(\frac{A}{2}\right) + \tan^2\left(\frac{A}{2}\right) = \dfrac{3 - \cos A}{1 + \cos A}$

75. $\csc^2\left(\frac{A}{2}\right) + \cot^2\left(\frac{A}{2}\right) = \dfrac{3 + \cos A}{1 - \cos A}$

76. $\tan^2\left(\frac{A}{2}\right) + 1 = \sec^2\left(\frac{A}{2}\right)$

Graph each of the following functions.
***Hint:* Use trigonometric identities first.**

77. $y = \sqrt{\dfrac{1 - \cos\left(\frac{\pi}{12}x\right)}{2}}$

78. $y = \cos^2\left(\dfrac{x}{2}\right) - \sin^2\left(\dfrac{x}{2}\right)$

79. $y = -\sqrt{\dfrac{1 - \cos x}{1 + \cos x}}$

80. $y = \sqrt{\dfrac{1 + \cos(3x - 1)}{2}}$

6.4 Product-to-Sum and Sum-to-Product Identities

Write each product as a sum or difference of sines and/or cosines.

81. $6\sin(5x)\cos(2x)$

82. $3\sin(4x)\sin(2x)$

Write each expression as a product of sines and/or cosines.

83. $\cos(5x) - \cos(3x)$

84. $\sin\left(\dfrac{5x}{2}\right) + \sin\left(\dfrac{3x}{2}\right)$

85. $\sin\left(\dfrac{4x}{3}\right) - \sin\left(\dfrac{2x}{3}\right)$

86. $\cos(7x) + \cos x$

Simplify each trigonometric expression.

87. $\dfrac{\cos(8x) + \cos(2x)}{\sin(8x) - \sin(2x)}$

88. $\dfrac{\sin(5x) + \sin(3x)}{\cos(5x) + \cos(3x)}$

Verify the identities.

89. $\dfrac{\sin A + \sin B}{\cos A - \cos B} = -\cot\left(\dfrac{A - B}{2}\right)$

90. $\dfrac{\sin A - \sin B}{\cos A - \cos B} = -\cot\left(\dfrac{A + B}{2}\right)$

91. $\csc\left(\dfrac{A - B}{2}\right) = \dfrac{2\sin\left(\frac{A + B}{2}\right)}{\cos B - \cos A}$

92. $\sec\left(\dfrac{A + B}{2}\right) = \dfrac{2\sin\left(\frac{A - B}{2}\right)}{\sin A - \sin B}$

6.5 Inverse Trigonometric Functions

Find the exact value of each expression. Give the answer in radians.

93. $\arctan 1$

94. $\text{arccsc}(-2)$

95. $\cos^{-1} 0$

96. $\sin^{-1}(-1)$

97. $\sec^{-1}\left(\dfrac{2}{\sqrt{3}}\right)$

98. $\cot^{-1}(-\sqrt{3})$

Find the exact value of each expression. Give the answer in degrees.

99. $\csc^{-1}(-1)$

100. $\arctan(-1)$

101. $\text{arccot}\left(\dfrac{\sqrt{3}}{3}\right)$

102. $\cos^{-1}\left(\dfrac{\sqrt{2}}{2}\right)$

103. $\sin^{-1}\left(-\dfrac{\sqrt{3}}{2}\right)$

104. $\sec^{-1} 1$

Use a calculator to evaluate each expression. Give the answer in degrees and round to two decimal places.

105. $\sin^{-1}(-0.6088)$

106. $\tan^{-1}(1.1918)$

107. $\sec^{-1}(1.0824)$

108. $\cot^{-1}(-3.7321)$

Use a calculator to evaluate each expression. Give the answer in radians and round to two decimal places.

109. $\cos^{-1}(-0.1736)$

110. $\tan^{-1}(0.1584)$

111. $\csc^{-1}(-10.0167)$

112. $\sec^{-1}(-1.1223)$

Evaluate each expression exactly, if possible. If not possible, state why.

113. $\sin^{-1}\left[\sin\left(-\dfrac{\pi}{4}\right)\right]$

114. $\cos\left[\cos^{-1}\left(-\dfrac{\sqrt{2}}{2}\right)\right]$

115. $\tan[\tan^{-1}(-\sqrt{3})]$

116. $\cot^{-1}\left[\cot\left(\dfrac{11\pi}{6}\right)\right]$

117. $\csc^{-1}\left[\csc\left(\dfrac{2\pi}{3}\right)\right]$

118. $\sec\left[\sec^{-1}\left(-\dfrac{2\sqrt{3}}{3}\right)\right]$

Evaluate each expression exactly.

119. $\sin\left[\cos^{-1}\left(\dfrac{11}{61}\right)\right]$

120. $\cos\left[\tan^{-1}\left(\dfrac{40}{9}\right)\right]$

121. $\tan\left[\cot^{-1}\left(\dfrac{6}{7}\right)\right]$

122. $\cot\left[\sec^{-1}\left(\dfrac{25}{7}\right)\right]$

123. $\sec\left[\sin^{-1}\left(\dfrac{1}{6}\right)\right]$

124. $\csc\left[\cot^{-1}\left(\dfrac{5}{12}\right)\right]$

6.6 Trigonometric Equations

Solve the given trigonometric equation on the indicated interval.

125. $\sin(2\theta) = -\frac{\sqrt{3}}{2}, 0 \le \theta \le 2\pi$

126. $\sec\left(\frac{\theta}{2}\right) = 2, -2\pi \le \theta \le 2\pi$

127. $\sin\left(\frac{\theta}{2}\right) = -\frac{\sqrt{2}}{2}, -2\pi \le \theta \le 2\pi$

128. $\csc(2\theta) = 2, 0 \le \theta \le 2\pi$

129. $\tan\left(\frac{1}{3}\theta\right) = -1, 0 \le \theta \le 6\pi$

130. $\cot(4\theta) = -\sqrt{3}, -\pi \le \theta \le \pi$

Solve each trigonometric equation exactly on $0 \le \theta \le 2\pi$.

131. $4\cos(2\theta) + 2 = 0$

132. $\sqrt{3}\tan\left(\frac{\theta}{2}\right) - 1 = 0$

133. $2\tan(2\theta) + 2 = 0$

134. $2\sin^2\theta + \sin\theta - 1 = 0$

135. $\tan^2\theta + \tan\theta = 0$

136. $\sec^2\theta - 3\sec\theta + 2 = 0$

Solve the given trigonometric equations on $0° \le \theta \le 360°$ and express the answer in degrees to two decimal places.

137. $\tan(2\theta) = -0.3459$

138. $6\sin\theta - 5 = 0$

139. $4\cos^2\theta + 3\cos\theta = 0$

140. $12\cos^2\theta - 7\cos\theta + 1 = 0$

141. $\csc^2\theta - 3\csc\theta - 1 = 0$

142. $2\cot^2\theta + 5\cot\theta - 4 = 0$

Solve each trigonometric equation exactly on the interval $0 \le \theta \le 2\pi$.

143. $\sec x = 2\sin x$

144. $3\tan x + \cot x = 2\sqrt{3}$

145. $\sqrt{3}\tan x - \sec x = 1$

146. $2\sin(2x) = \cot x$

147. $\sqrt{3}\tan x = 2\sin x$

148. $2\sin x = 3\cot x$

149. $\cos^2 x + \sin x + 1 = 0$

150. $2\cos^2 x - \sqrt{3}\cos x = 0$

151. $\cos(2x) + 4\cos x + 3 = 0$

152. $\sin(2x) + \sin x = 0$

153. $\tan^2(\frac{1}{2}x) - 1 = 0$

154. $\cot^2(\frac{1}{3}x) - 1 = 0$

Solve each trigonometric equation on $0° \le \theta \le 360°$. Give the answers in degrees and round to two decimal places.

155. $\csc^2 x + \cot x = 1$

156. $8\cos^2 x + 6\sin x = 9$

157. $\sin^2 x + 2 = 2\cos x$

158. $\cos(2x) = 3\sin x - 1$

159. $\cos x - 1 = \cos(2x)$

160. $12\cos^2 x + 4\sin x = 11$

[CHAPTER 6 PRACTICE TEST]

1. For what values of x does the quotient identity $\tan x = \dfrac{\sin x}{\cos x}$ not hold?
2. Is the equation $\sqrt{\sin^2 x + \cos^2 x} = \sin x + \cos x$ a conditional equation or an identity?
3. Evaluate $\sin\left(-\dfrac{\pi}{8}\right)$ exactly.
4. Evaluate $\tan\left(\dfrac{7\pi}{12}\right)$ exactly.
5. If $\cos x = \dfrac{2}{5}$ and $\dfrac{3\pi}{2} < x < 2\pi$, find $\sin\left(\dfrac{x}{2}\right)$.
6. If $\sin x = -\dfrac{1}{5}$ and $\pi < x < \dfrac{3\pi}{2}$, find $\cos(2x)$.
7. Write $\cos(7x)\cos(3x) - \sin(3x)\sin(7x)$ as a cosine or sine of a sum or difference.
8. Write $\dfrac{2\tan x}{1 - \tan^2 x}$ as a single tangent function.
9. Write $\sqrt{\dfrac{1 + \cos(a + b)}{2}}$ as a single cosine function if $a + b$ is an angle in quadrant II. $\left(\text{Assume } \dfrac{\pi}{2} < a + b < \pi.\right)$
10. Write $2\sin\left(\dfrac{x+3}{2}\right)\cos\left(\dfrac{x-3}{2}\right)$ as a sum of two sine functions.
11. Write $10\cos(3 - x) + 10\cos(x + 3)$ as a product of two cosine functions.
12. In the expression $\sqrt{9 - u^2}$, let $u = 3\sin x$. What is the resulting expression?

Solve the trigonometric equations exactly, if possible. Otherwise, use a calculator to approximate solution(s).

13. $2\sin\theta = -\sqrt{3}$ on all real numbers.
14. $2\cos^2\theta + \cos\theta - 1 = 0$ on $0 \le \theta \le 2\pi$
15. $\sin 2\theta = \dfrac{1}{2}\cos\theta$ over $0 \le \theta \le 360°$
16. $\sqrt{\sin x + \cos x} = -1$ over $0 \le \theta \le 2\pi$
17. Determine whether $(1 + \cot x)^2 = \csc^2 x$ is a conditional equation or an identity.
18. Evaluate $\csc\left(-\dfrac{\pi}{12}\right)$ exactly.
19. If $\sin x = -\dfrac{5}{13}$ and $\pi < x < \dfrac{3\pi}{2}$, find $\cos\left(\dfrac{x}{2}\right)$.
20. If $\cos x = -0.26$ and $\dfrac{\pi}{2} < x < \pi$, find $\sin(2x)$.
21. Express $y = \sqrt{\dfrac{1 + \dfrac{\sqrt{2}}{2}\left[\cos\left(\dfrac{\pi}{3}x\right) + \sin\left(\dfrac{\pi}{3}x\right)\right]}{1 - \dfrac{\sqrt{2}}{2}\left[\cos\left(\dfrac{\pi}{3}x\right) + \sin\left(\dfrac{\pi}{3}x\right)\right]}}$ as a cotangent function.
22. Calculate $\csc\left(\csc^{-1}\sqrt{2}\right)$.
23. Determine an interval on which $f(x) = a + b\csc(\pi x + c)$ is one-to-one, and determine the inverse of $f(x)$ on this interval. Assume that a, b, and c are all positive.
24. Find the range of $y = -\dfrac{\pi}{4} + \arctan(2x - 3)$.
25. Solve $\cos\left(\dfrac{\pi}{4}\theta\right) = -\dfrac{1}{2}$, for all real numbers.
26. Solve $\sqrt{\dfrac{1 - \cos(2\pi x)}{1 + \cos(2\pi x)}} = -\dfrac{1}{\sqrt{3}}$, for all real numbers.
27. Solve $\dfrac{\sqrt{3}}{\csc\left(\dfrac{x}{3}\right)} = \cos\left(\dfrac{x}{3}\right)$, for all real numbers.

PRACTICE TEST

[CHAPTERS 1–6 CUMULATIVE TEST]

1. Find the exact value of the following trigonometric functions:
   a. $\sin\left(\frac{7\pi}{3}\right)$
   b. $\tan\left(-\frac{5\pi}{3}\right)$
   c. $\csc\left(\frac{11\pi}{6}\right)$
2. Find the exact value of the following trigonometric functions:
   a. $\sec\left(\frac{5\pi}{6}\right)$
   b. $\cos\left(-\frac{3\pi}{4}\right)$
   c. $\cot\left(\frac{7\pi}{6}\right)$
3. Find the exact value of the following inverse trigonometric functions:
   a. $\cos^{-1}\left(-\frac{1}{2}\right)$
   b. $\csc^{-1}(-2)$
   c. $\cot(-\sqrt{3})$
4. For the relation $x^2 - y^2 = 25$, determine whether y is a function of x.
5. Determine whether the function $g(x) = \sqrt{2 - x^2}$ is odd or even.
6. For the function $y = 5(x - 4)^2$, identify all of the transformations of $y = x^2$.
7. Find the composite function, $f \circ g$, and state the domain for $f(x) = x^3 - 1$ and $g(x) = \frac{1}{x}$.
8. Find the inverse of the function $f(x) = \sqrt[3]{x} - 1$.
9. Find the vertex of the parabola associated with the quadratic function $f(x) = \frac{1}{4}x^2 + \frac{3}{5}x - \frac{6}{25}$.
10. Find a polynomial of minimum degree that has the zeros $x = -\sqrt{7}$ (multiplicity 2), $x = 0$ (multiplicity 3), $x = \sqrt{7}$ (multiplicity 2).
11. Use long division to find the quotient $Q(x)$ and the remainder $r(x)$ of $(5x^3 - 4x^2 + 3) \div (x^2 + 1)$.
12. Given the zero $x = 4i$ of the polynomial $P(x) = x^4 + 2x^3 + x^2 + 32x - 240$, determine all the other zeros and write the polynomial in terms of a product of linear factors.
13. Find the vertical and horizontal asymptotes of the function $$f(x) = \frac{0.7x^2 - 5x + 11}{x^2 - x - 6}.$$
14. If \$5400 is invested at 2.25% compounded continuously, how much is in the account after 4 years?
15. Use interval notation to express the domain of the function $f(x) = \log_4(x + 3)$.
16. Use properties of logarithms to simplify the expression $\log_\pi 1$.
17. Give an exact solution to the logarithmic equation $\log_5(x + 2) + \log_5(6 - x) = \log_5(3x)$.
18. If money is invested in a savings account earning 4% compounded continuously, how many years will it take for the money to triple?
19. Use a calculator to evaluate $\cos 62°$. Round the answer to four decimal places.
20. **Angle of Inclination (Skiing).** The angle of inclination of a mountain with triple black diamond ski trails is 63°. If a skier at the top of the mountain is at an elevation of 4200 feet, how long is the ski run from the top to the base of the mountain?
21. Convert $-105°$ to radians. Leave the answer in terms of π.
22. Find all of the exact values of θ, when $\tan\theta = 1$ and $0 \le \theta \le 2\pi$.
23. Determine whether the equation $\cos^2 x - \sin^2 x = 1$ is a conditional equation or an identity.
24. Simplify $\dfrac{2\tan\left(-\frac{\pi}{8}\right)}{1 - \tan^2\left(-\frac{\pi}{8}\right)}$ and evaluate exactly.
25. Evaluate exactly the expression $\tan\left[\sin^{-1}\left(\frac{5}{13}\right)\right]$.

CHAPTER 7

Vectors, the Complex Plane, and Polar Coordinates

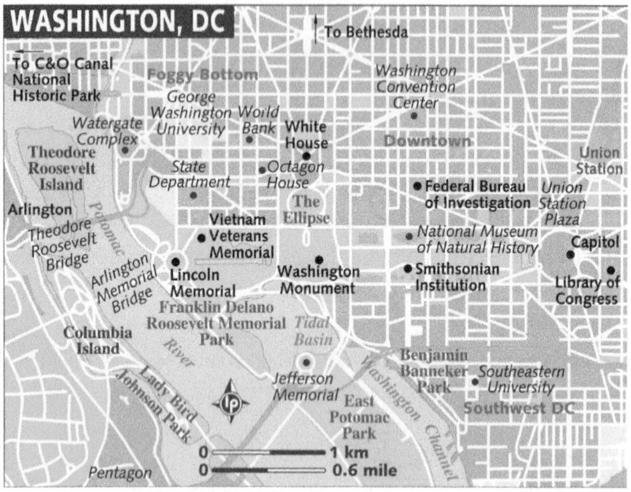

Lonely Planet/Getty Images

A coordinate system is used to locate a point in a plane. In the Cartesian plane, rectangular coordinates (x, y) are used to describe the location of a point. For example, we can say that the Museum of Natural History in Washington, D.C., is at the corner of Constitution Avenue and 12th Street. But we can also describe the location of the Museum of Natural History as being $\frac{1}{4}$ mile east-northeast of the Washington Monument. Instead of using a grid of streets running east-west and north-south, it is sometimes more convenient to give a location with respect to a distance and direction from a fixed point. In the *polar coordinate system*, the location of a point is given in *polar coordinates* as (r, θ), where r is the distance and θ is the direction angle of the point from a fixed reference point (origin).

LEARNING OBJECTIVES

- Find the magnitude and direction of a vector; add and subtract vectors.
- Perform scalar multiplication and dot products.
- Express complex numbers in polar form.
- Use DeMoivre's theorem to find a complex number raised to a power.
- Graph polar equations.

[IN THIS CHAPTER]

Vectors will be defined and combined with the Law of Sines and the Law of Cosines to find resulting velocity and force vectors. The dot product (product of two vectors) is defined and used in physical problems like calculating work. Trigonometric functions are then used to define complex numbers in polar form. Last, we define polar coordinates and examine polar equations and their corresponding graphs.

VECTORS, THE COMPLEX PLANE, AND POLAR COORDINATES

7.1 VECTORS	7.2 THE DOT PRODUCT	7.3 POLAR (TRIGONOMETRIC) FORM OF COMPLEX NUMBERS	7.4 PRODUCTS, QUOTIENTS, POWERS, AND ROOTS OF COMPLEX NUMBERS	7.5 POLAR COORDINATES AND GRAPHS OF POLAR EQUATIONS
• Magnitude and Direction of Vectors • Vector Operations • Horizontal and Vertical Components of a Vector • Unit Vectors • Resultant Vectors	• The Dot Product • Angle between Two Vectors • Work	• Complex Numbers in Rectangular Form • Complex Numbers in Polar Form	• Products of Complex Numbers • Quotients of Complex Numbers • Powers of Complex Numbers • Roots of Complex Numbers	• Polar Coordinates • Converting between Polar and Rectangular Coordinates • Graphs of Polar Equations

7.1 VECTORS

SKILLS OBJECTIVES

- Find the magnitude and direction of a vector.
- Add and subtract vectors, and perform scalar multiplication of a vector.
- Express a vector in terms of its horizontal and vertical components.
- Find unit vectors.
- Find resultant vectors in application problems.

CONCEPTUAL OBJECTIVES

- Understand the differences between scalars and vectors.
- Relate the geometric and algebraic representations of operations on vectors.
- Relate the right triangle trigonometric definitions of sine and cosine to the vertical and horizontal components of a vector.
- Recognize that unit vectors have a magnitude (length) equal to one.
- Understand how resultant vectors are used to find actual velocities or actual forces.

7.1.1 Magnitude and Direction of Vectors

7.1.1 SKILL

Find the magnitude and direction of a vector.

7.1.1 CONCEPTUAL

Understand the differences between scalars and vectors.

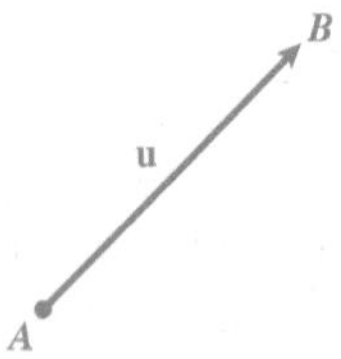

What is the difference between velocity and speed? Speed (55 miles per hour) has only *magnitude*, whereas velocity (55 miles per hour west) has both *magnitude* and *direction*. We use **scalars**, which are real numbers, to denote magnitudes such as speed and mass. We use **vectors**, which have magnitude *and* direction, to denote quantities such as velocity (speed in a certain direction) and force (weight in a certain direction).

A vector quantity is geometrically denoted by a **directed line segment**, which is a line segment with an arrow representing direction. There are many ways to denote a vector. For example, the vector shown in the margin can be denoted as $\mathbf{u}$, $\vec{u}$, or $\overrightarrow{AB}$, where A is the **initial point** and B is the **terminal point**.

It is customary in books to use the bold letter to represent a vector and when handwritten (as in your class notes and homework) to use the arrow on top to denote a vector.

In this section, we will limit our discussion to vectors in a plane (two-dimensional). It is important to note that geometric representation can be extended to three dimensions and algebraic representation can be extended to any higher dimension, as you will see in the exercises.

STUDY TIP

The magnitude of a vector is the distance between the initial and terminal points of the vector.

Geometric Interpretation of Vectors

The *magnitude* of a vector can be denoted one of two ways: $|\mathbf{u}|$ or $\|\mathbf{u}\|$. We will use the former notation.

MAGNITUDE: $|\mathbf{u}|$

The **magnitude** of a vector $\mathbf{u}$, denoted $|\mathbf{u}|$, is the length of the directed line segment—that is, the distance between the initial and terminal points of the vector.

Two vectors have the **same direction** if they are parallel and point in the same direction. Two vectors have **opposite direction** if they are parallel and point in opposite directions.

[CONCEPT CHECK]

Match: (1) speed and (2) velocity to (A) vector or (B) scalar

ANSWER (1) B (2) A

EQUAL VECTORS: $\mathbf{u} = \mathbf{v}$

Two vectors $\mathbf{u}$ and $\mathbf{v}$ are **equal** ($\mathbf{u} = \mathbf{v}$) if and only if they have the same magnitude ($|\mathbf{u}| = |\mathbf{v}|$) and the same direction.

Equal Vectors $\mathbf{u} = \mathbf{v}$	Same Magnitude but Opposite Direction $\mathbf{u} = -\mathbf{v}$	Same Magnitude $\lvert\mathbf{u}\rvert = \lvert\mathbf{v}\rvert$	Different Magnitude	Same Direction but Different Magnitude

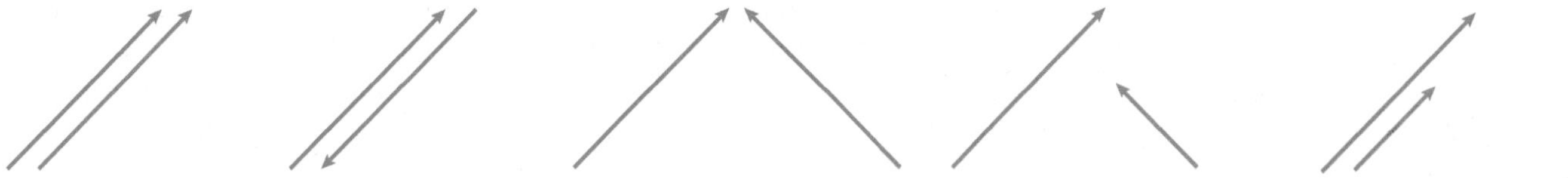

It is important to note that vectors do not have to coincide to be equal.

VECTOR ADDITION: u + v

Two vectors, **u** and **v**, can be added together using either of the following approaches:

- The **tail-to-tip** (or head-to-tail) method: Sketch the initial point of one vector at the terminal point of the other vector. The **sum**, **u** + **v**, is the **resultant** vector from the tail end of **u** to the tip end of **v**.

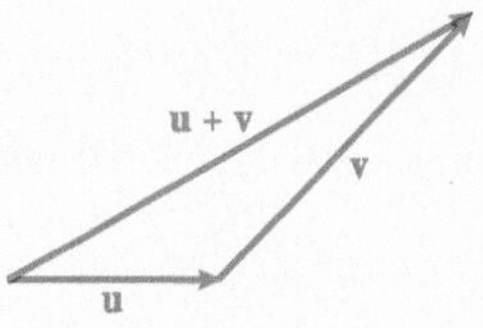

  [or]

- The parallelogram method: Sketch the initial points of the vectors at the same point. The sum **u** + **v** is the diagonal of the parallelogram formed by **u** and **v**.

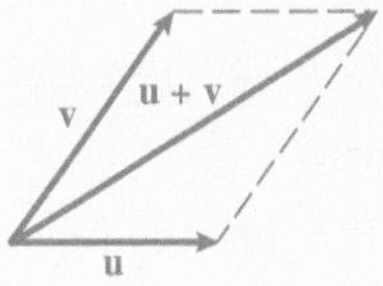

The difference, **u** − **v**, is

- The resultant vector from the tip of **v** to the tip of **u**, when the tails of **v** and **u** coincide.

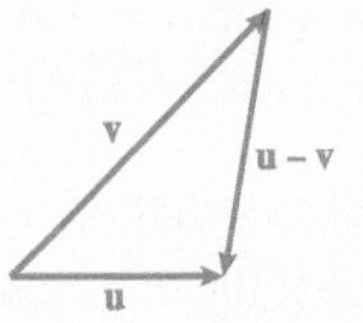

  [or]

- The other diagonal formed by the parallelogram method.

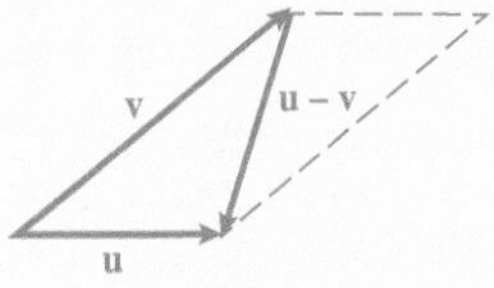

STUDY TIP

Equal vectors can be translated (shifted) so that they coincide.

Algebraic Interpretation of Vectors

Since vectors that have the same direction and magnitude are equal, any vector can be translated to an equal vector with its initial point located at the origin in the Cartesian plane. Therefore, we will now consider vectors in a rectangular coordinate system.

A vector with its initial point at the origin is called a **position vector**, or a vector in **standard position**. A position vector **u** with its terminal point at the point (a, b) is denoted

$$\mathbf{u} = \langle a, b \rangle$$

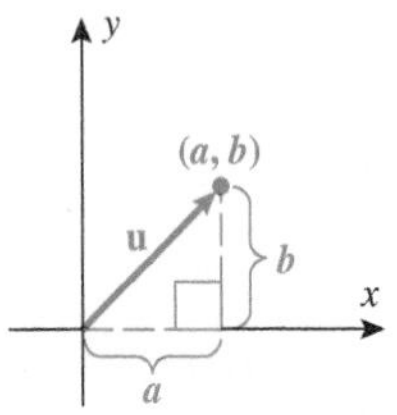

where the real numbers a and b are called the **components** of vector **u**.

STUDY TIP

$\langle a, b \rangle$ denotes a vector.
(a, b) denotes a point.

Notice the subtle difference between coordinate notation and vector notation. The point is denoted with parentheses, (a, b), whereas the vector is denoted with angled brackets, $\langle a, b \rangle$. The notation $\langle a, b \rangle$ denotes a vector whose initial point is $(0, 0)$ and terminal point is (a, b).

The vector with initial point $(3, 4)$ and terminal point $(8, 10)$ is equal to the vector $\langle 5, 6 \rangle$, which has initial point $(0, 0)$ and terminal point $(5, 6)$.

Recall that the geometric definition of the *magnitude* of a vector is the *length* of the vector.

MAGNITUDE: $|\mathbf{u}|$

The **magnitude** (or norm) of a vector, $\mathbf{u} = \langle a, b \rangle$, is

$$|\mathbf{u}| = \sqrt{a^2 + b^2}$$

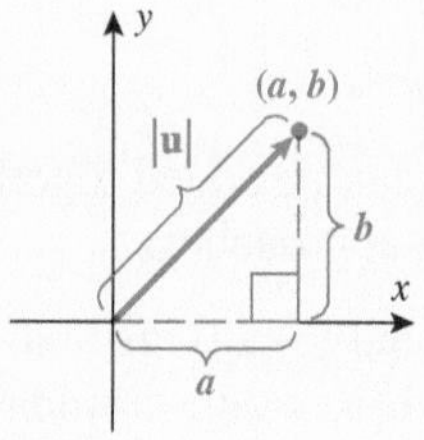

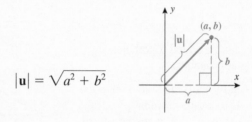

EXAMPLE 1 Finding the Magnitude of a Vector

Find the magnitude of the vector $\mathbf{u} = \langle 3, -4 \rangle$.

Solution:

Write the formula for magnitude of a vector. $|\mathbf{u}| = \sqrt{a^2 + b^2}$

Let $a = 3$ and $b = -4$. $|\mathbf{u}| = \sqrt{3^2 + (-4)^2}$

Simplify. $|\mathbf{u}| = \boxed{\sqrt{25} = 5}$

Note: If we graph the vector $\mathbf{u} = \langle 3, -4 \rangle$, we see that the distance from the origin to the point $(3, -4)$ is five units.

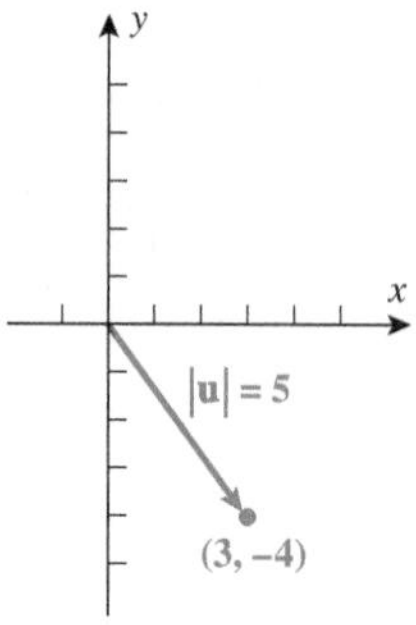

YOUR TURN Find the magnitude of the vector $\mathbf{v} = \langle -1, 5 \rangle$.

ANSWER

$\sqrt{26}$

DIRECTION ANGLE OF A VECTOR

The positive angle between the x-axis and a position vector is called the **direction angle**, denoted θ.

$$\tan\theta = \frac{b}{a}, \text{ where } a \neq 0$$

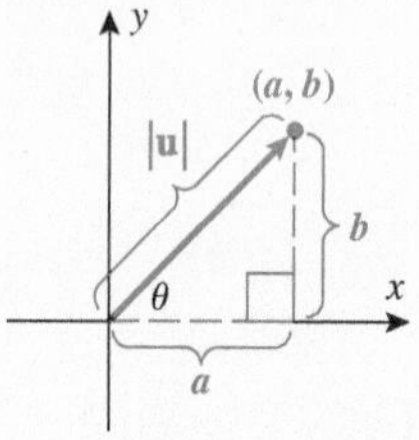

EXAMPLE 2 **Finding the Direction Angle of a Vector**

Find the direction angle of the vector $\mathbf{v} = \langle -1, 5 \rangle$.

Solution:

Start with $\tan\theta = \frac{b}{a}$ and let $a = -1$ and $b = 5$. $\tan\theta = \frac{5}{-1}$

With a calculator, approximate $\tan^{-1}(-5)$. $\tan^{-1}(-5) \approx -78.7°$

The calculator gives a **quadrant IV** angle.

The point $(-1, 5)$ lies in quadrant II.

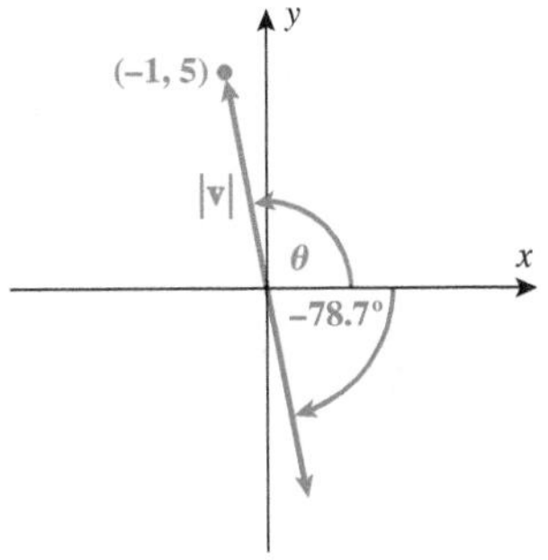

Add 180°. $\theta = -78.7° + 180° = 101.3°$

$\boxed{\theta = 101.3°}$

YOUR TURN Find the direction angle of the vector $\mathbf{u} = \langle 3, -4 \rangle$.

ANSWER

306.9°

Recall that two vectors are equal if they have the same magnitude and direction. Algebraically, this corresponds to their corresponding vector components (a and b) being equal.

EQUAL VECTORS: u = v

The vectors $\mathbf{u} = \langle a, b \rangle$ and $\mathbf{v} = \langle c, d \rangle$ are **equal** (that is, $\mathbf{u} = \mathbf{v}$) if and only if $a = c$ and $b = d$.

7.1.2 Vector Operations

Vector addition is done geometrically with the tail-to-tip rule. Algebraically, vector addition is performed component by component.

7.1.2 SKILL

Add and subtract vectors, and perform scalar multiplication of a vector.

7.1.2 CONCEPTUAL

Relate the geometric and algebraic representations of operations on vectors.

VECTOR ADDITION: u + v

If $\mathbf{u} = \langle a, b \rangle$ and $\mathbf{v} = \langle c, d \rangle$, then $\mathbf{u} + \mathbf{v} = \langle a + c, b + d \rangle$.

EXAMPLE 3 **Adding Vectors**

Let $\mathbf{u} = \langle 2, -7 \rangle$ and $\mathbf{v} = \langle -3, 4 \rangle$. Find $\mathbf{u} + \mathbf{v}$.

Solution:

Let $\mathbf{u} = \langle 2, -7 \rangle$ and $\mathbf{v} = \langle -3, 4 \rangle$ in the addition formula. $\mathbf{u} + \mathbf{v} = \langle 2 + (-3), -7 + 4 \rangle$

Simplify. $\mathbf{u} + \mathbf{v} = \boxed{\langle -1, -3 \rangle}$

YOUR TURN Let $\mathbf{u} = \langle 1, 2 \rangle$ and $\mathbf{v} = \langle -5, -4 \rangle$. Find $\mathbf{u} + \mathbf{v}$.

ANSWER

$\mathbf{u} + \mathbf{v} = \langle -4, -2 \rangle$

We now summarize vector operations. As we have seen, addition and subtraction are performed algebraically component by component. Multiplication, however, is not as straightforward. To perform **scalar multiplication** of a vector (to multiply a vector by a real number), we multiply each component by the scalar. In Section 7.2, we will study a form of multiplication for two vectors that is defined as long as the vectors have the same number of components; it gives a result known as the *dot product* and is useful in solving common problems in physics.

SCALAR MULTIPLICATION: $k\mathbf{u}$

If k is a scalar (real number) and $\mathbf{u} = \langle a, b \rangle$, then

$$k\mathbf{u} = k\langle a, b \rangle = \langle ka, kb \rangle$$

Scalar multiplication corresponds to

- Increasing the length of the vector: $|k| > 1$
- Decreasing the length of the vector: $|k| < 1$
- Changing the direction of the vector: $k < 0$

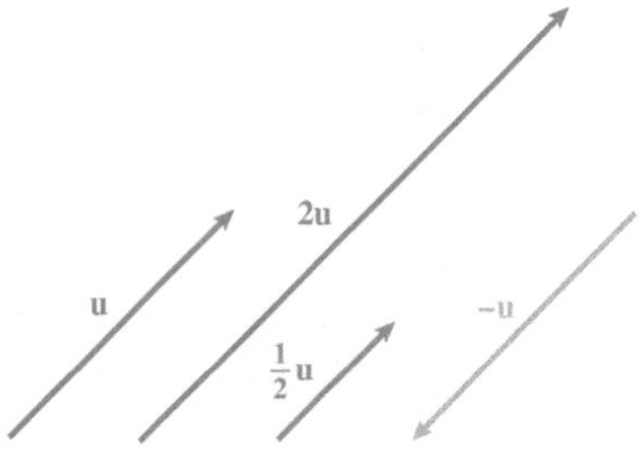

The following box is a summary of vector operations:

[CONCEPT CHECK]

If $a > c$ and $b < d$, then if a, b, c, and d are positive, then $u - v$ is a vector pointing into which quadrant?

ANSWER IV

VECTOR OPERATIONS

If $\mathbf{u} = \langle a, b \rangle$, $\mathbf{v} = \langle c, d \rangle$, and k is a scalar, then

$$\mathbf{u} + \mathbf{v} = \langle a + c, b + d \rangle$$

$$\mathbf{u} - \mathbf{v} = \langle a - c, b - d \rangle$$

$$k\mathbf{u} = k\langle a, b \rangle = \langle ka, kb \rangle$$

The zero vector, $\mathbf{0} = \langle 0, 0 \rangle$, is a vector in any direction with a magnitude equal to zero. We now can state the algebraic properties (associative, commutative, and distributive) of vectors.

ALGEBRAIC PROPERTIES OF VECTORS

$$\mathbf{u} + \mathbf{v} = \mathbf{v} + \mathbf{u}$$

$$(\mathbf{u} + \mathbf{v}) + \mathbf{w} = \mathbf{u} + (\mathbf{v} + \mathbf{w})$$

$$(k_1 k_2)\mathbf{u} = k_1(k_2\mathbf{u})$$

$$k(\mathbf{u} + \mathbf{v}) = k\mathbf{u} + k\mathbf{v}$$

$$(k_1 + k_2)\mathbf{u} = k_1\mathbf{u} + k_2\mathbf{u}$$

$$0\mathbf{u} = \mathbf{0} \qquad 1\mathbf{u} = \mathbf{u} \qquad -1\mathbf{u} = -\mathbf{u}$$

$$\mathbf{u} + (-\mathbf{u}) = \mathbf{0}$$

7.1.3 Horizontal and Vertical Components of a Vector

The **horizontal component** a and **vertical component** b of a vector **u** are related to the magnitude of the vector, $|\mathbf{u}|$, through the sine and cosine of the direction angle.

$$\cos\theta = \frac{a}{|\mathbf{u}|} \qquad \sin\theta = \frac{b}{|\mathbf{u}|}$$

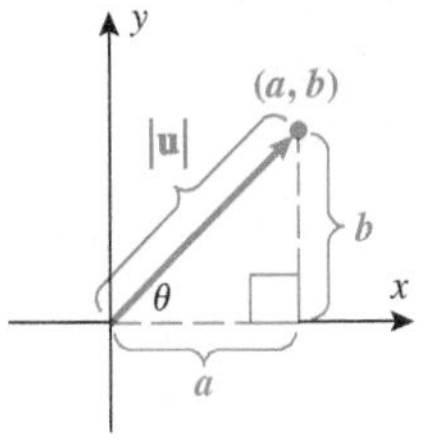

7.1.3 SKILL

Express a vector in terms of its horizontal and vertical components.

7.1.3 CONCEPTUAL

Relate the right triangle trigonometric definitions of sine and cosine to the vertical and horizontal components of a vector.

HORIZONTAL AND VERTICAL COMPONENTS OF A VECTOR

The horizontal and vertical components of vector **u**, with magnitude $|\mathbf{u}|$ and direction angle θ, are given by

$$\text{horizontal component: } a = |\mathbf{u}|\cos\theta$$

$$\text{vertical component: } b = |\mathbf{u}|\sin\theta$$

The vector **u** can then be written as $\mathbf{u} = \langle a, b\rangle = \langle|\mathbf{u}|\cos\theta, |\mathbf{u}|\sin\theta\rangle$.

[CONCEPT CHECK]

Match:

(1) $\theta = n\frac{\pi}{2}$, n even

(2) $\theta = n\pi + \frac{\pi}{2}$ to

(A) vertical vector

(B) horizontal vector

ANSWER (1) B (2) A

EXAMPLE 4 Finding the Horizontal and Vertical Components of a Vector

Find the vector that has a magnitude of 6 and a direction angle of 15°.

Solution:

Write the horizontal and vertical components of a vector **u**. $\quad a = |\mathbf{u}|\cos\theta$ and $b = |\mathbf{u}|\sin\theta$

Let $|\mathbf{u}| = 6$ and $\theta = 15°$. $\quad a = 6\cos 15°$ and $b = 6\sin 15°$

Use a calculator to approximate the sine and cosine functions of 15°. $\quad a \approx 5.8$ and $b \approx 1.6$

Let $\mathbf{u} = \langle a, b\rangle$. $\quad \mathbf{u} = \boxed{\langle 5.8, 1.6\rangle}$

YOUR TURN Find the vector that has a magnitude of 3 and direction angle of 75°.

ANSWER

$\mathbf{u} = \langle 0.78, 2.9\rangle$

7.1.4 Unit Vectors

A **unit vector** is any vector with magnitude equal to 1 or $|\mathbf{u}| = 1$. It is often useful to be able to find a unit vector in the same direction of some vector **v**. A unit vector can be formed from any nonzero vector as follows:

7.1.4 SKILL

Find unit vectors.

7.1.4 CONCEPTUAL

Recognize that unit vectors have a magnitude (length) equal to one.

FINDING A UNIT VECTOR

If **v** is a nonzero vector, then

$$\mathbf{u} = \frac{\mathbf{v}}{|\mathbf{v}|} = \frac{1}{|\mathbf{v}|}\cdot\mathbf{v}$$

is a **unit vector** in the same direction as **v**. In other words, multiplying any nonzero vector by the reciprocal of its magnitude results in a unit vector.

[STUDY TIP]

Multiplying a nonzero vector by the reciprocal of its magnitude results in a unit vector.

[CONCEPT CHECK]

TRUE OR FALSE A unit circle has radius equal to 1, and a unit vector has length equal to 1.

ANSWER True

It is important to notice that because the magnitude is always a scalar, the reciprocal of the magnitude is always a scalar. A scalar times a vector is a vector.

EXAMPLE 5 Finding a Unit Vector

Find a unit vector in the same direction as $\mathbf{v} = \langle -3, -4 \rangle$.

Solution:

Find the magnitude of the vector $\mathbf{v} = \langle -3, -4 \rangle$. $\quad |\mathbf{v}| = \sqrt{(-3)^2 + (-4)^2}$

Simplify. $\quad |\mathbf{v}| = 5$

Multiply $\mathbf{v}$ by the reciprocal of its magnitude. $\quad \dfrac{1}{|\mathbf{v}|} \cdot \mathbf{v}$

Let $|\mathbf{v}| = 5$ and $\mathbf{v} = \langle -3, -4 \rangle$. $\quad \dfrac{1}{5}\langle -3, -4 \rangle$

Simplify. $\quad \boxed{\left\langle -\dfrac{3}{5}, -\dfrac{4}{5} \right\rangle}$

Check: The unit vector, $\left\langle -\frac{3}{5}, -\frac{4}{5} \right\rangle$, should have a magnitude of 1.

$$\sqrt{\left(-\frac{3}{5}\right)^2 + \left(-\frac{4}{5}\right)^2} = \sqrt{\frac{25}{25}} = 1$$

YOUR TURN Find a unit vector in the same direction as $\mathbf{v} = \langle 5, -12 \rangle$.

ANSWER

$\left\langle \dfrac{5}{13}, -\dfrac{12}{13} \right\rangle$

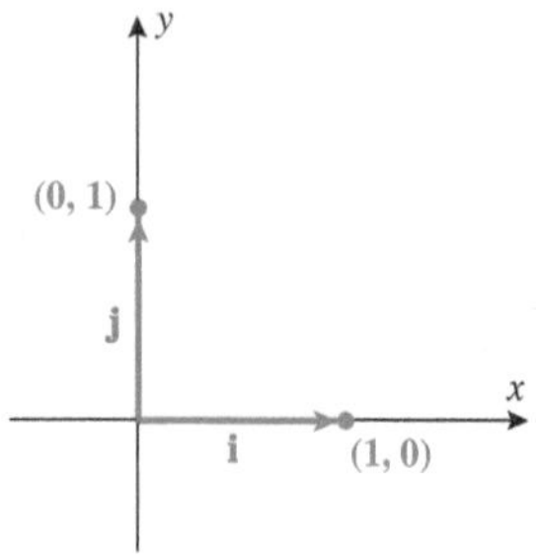

Two important unit vectors are the horizontal and vertical unit vectors **i** and **j**. The unit vector **i** has an initial point at the origin and terminal point at $(1, 0)$. The unit vector **j** has an initial point at the origin and terminal point at $(0, 1)$. We can use these unit vectors to represent vectors algebraically. For example, the vector $\langle 3, -4 \rangle = 3\mathbf{i} - 4\mathbf{j}$.

7.1.5 Resultant Vectors

7.1.5 SKILL

Find resultant vectors in application problems.

7.1.5 CONCEPTUAL

Understand how resultant vectors are used to find actual velocities or actual forces.

Vectors arise in many applications. **Velocity vectors** and **force vectors** are two that we will discuss. For example, suppose that you are at the beach and "think" that you are swimming straight out at a certain speed (magnitude and direction). This is your **apparent velocity** with respect to the water. After a few minutes you turn around to look at the shore, and you are farther out than you thought and appear to have drifted down the beach. This is because of the current of the water. When the **current velocity** and the apparent velocity are added together, the result is the **actual** or **resultant velocity**.

EXAMPLE 6 **Resultant Velocities**

A boat's speedometer reads 25 miles per hour (which is relative to the water) and its course is set due east (90° from due north). If the river is moving 10 miles per hour due north, what is the resultant (actual) velocity of the boat?

Solution:

Draw a picture.

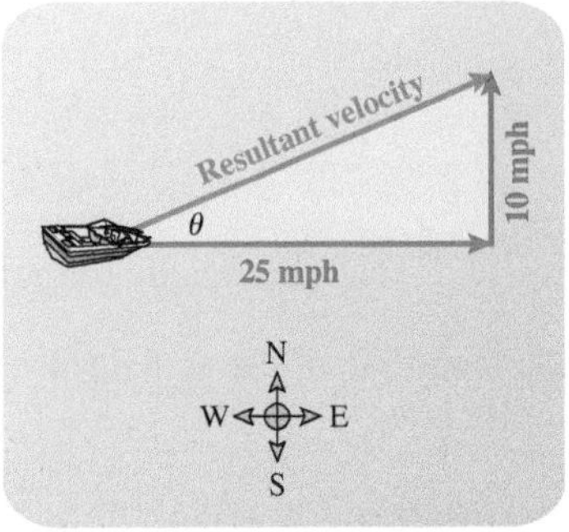

[CONCEPT CHECK]

The speedometer on a boat will correspond to the magnitude of which velocity, apparent or actual?

ANSWER apparent

Label the horizontal and vertical components of the resultant vector. $\langle 25, 10\rangle$

Determine the magnitude of the resultant vector. $\sqrt{25^2 + 10^2} = 5\sqrt{29} \approx 27\text{ mph}$

Determine the direction angle. $\tan\theta = \dfrac{10}{25}$

Solve for θ. $\theta = \tan^{-1}\left(\dfrac{2}{5}\right) \approx 22°$

The actual velocity of the boat has magnitude **27 miles per hour** and the boat is headed **22° north of east or 68° east of north**.

In Example 6, the three vectors formed a right triangle. In Example 7, the three vectors form an oblique triangle.

EXAMPLE 7 **Resultant Velocities**

A speedboat traveling 30 miles per hour has a compass heading of 100° east of north. The current velocity has a magnitude of 15 miles per hour and its heading is 22° east of north. Find the resultant (actual) velocity of the boat.

Solution:

Draw a picture.

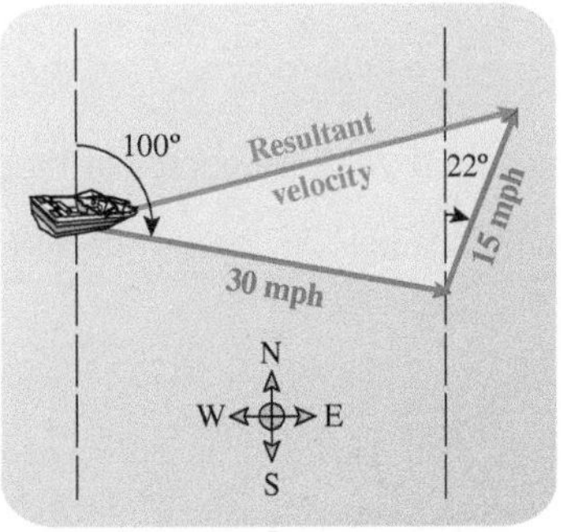

Label the angles supplementary to 100°.

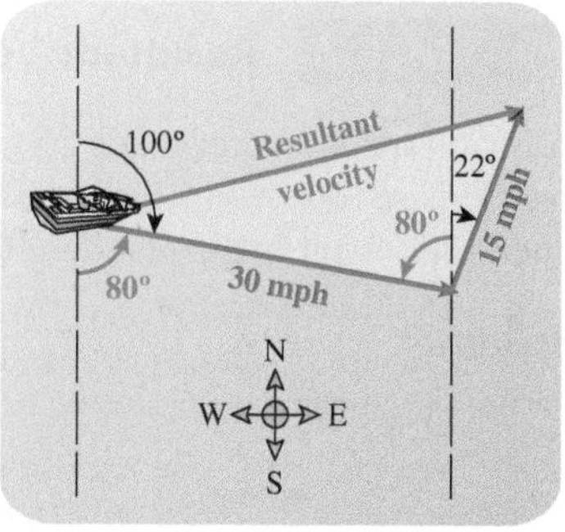

Draw and label the oblique triangle.

The magnitude of the actual (resultant) velocity is b.

The heading of the actual (resultant) velocity is $100° - \alpha$.

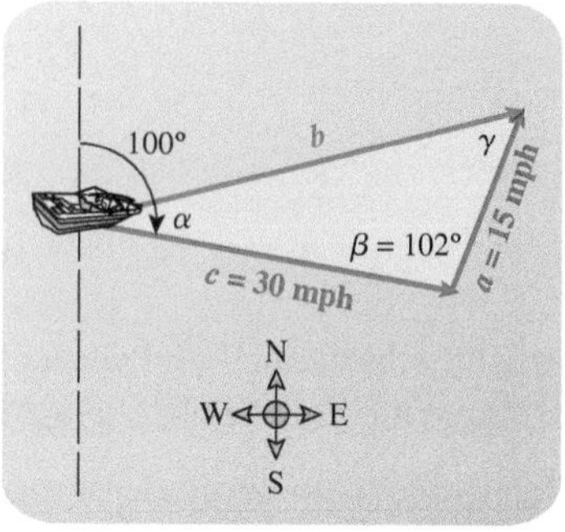

Use the Law of Sines and the Law of Cosines to solve for α and b.

Find b: Apply the Law of Cosines. $b^2 = a^2 + c^2 - 2ac\cos\beta$

Let $a = 15$, $c = 30$, and $\beta = 102°$. $b^2 = 15^2 + 30^2 - 2(15)(30)\cos 102°$

Solve for b. $\boxed{b \approx 36 \text{ mph}}$

Find α: Apply the Law of Sines. $\dfrac{\sin\alpha}{a} = \dfrac{\sin\beta}{b}$

Isolate $\sin\alpha$. $\sin\alpha = \dfrac{a}{b}\sin\beta$

Let $a = 15$, $b = 36$, and $\beta = 102°$. $\sin\alpha = \dfrac{15}{36}\sin 102°$

Apply the inverse sine function to solve for α. $\alpha = \sin^{-1}\left(\dfrac{15}{36}\sin 102°\right)$

Approximate α with a calculator. $\alpha \approx 24°$

Actual heading: $100° - \alpha = 100° - 24° = \boxed{76°}$

The actual velocity vector of the boat has magnitude $\boxed{\text{36 miles per hour}}$ and the boat is headed $\boxed{\text{76° east of north}}$.

Two vectors combine to yield a resultant vector. The opposite vector to the resultant vector is called the **equilibrant**.

EXAMPLE 8 Finding an Equilibrant

A skier is being pulled up a slope by a handle lift. Let $\mathbf{F}_1$ represent the vertical force due to gravity and $\mathbf{F}_2$ represent the force of the skier pushing against the side of the mountain, at an angle of 35° to the horizontal. If the weight of the skier is 145 pounds, that is, $|\mathbf{F}_1| = 145$, find the magnitude of the equilibrant force $\mathbf{F}_3$ required to hold the skier in place (i.e., to keep the skier from sliding down the mountain). Assume that the side of the mountain is a frictionless surface.

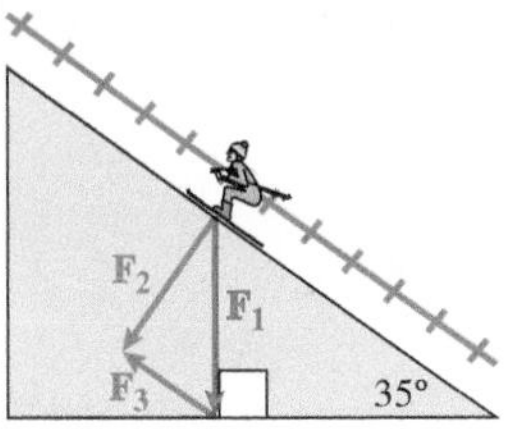

Solution:

The angle between vectors $\mathbf{F}_1$ and $\mathbf{F}_2$ is 35°.

The magnitude of vector $\mathbf{F}_3$ is the force required to hold the skier in place.

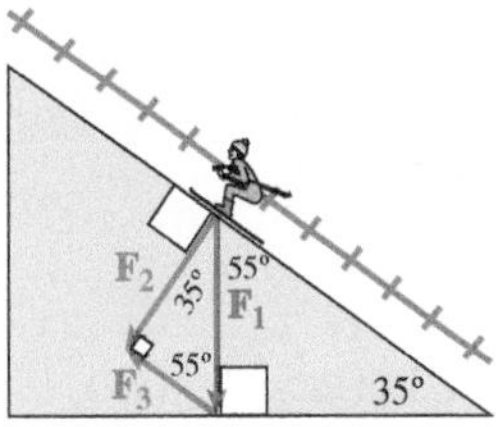

Relate the magnitudes (side lengths) to the given angle using the sine ratio.

$$\sin 35° = \frac{|\mathbf{F}_3|}{|\mathbf{F}_1|}$$

Solve for $|\mathbf{F}_3|$.

$$|\mathbf{F}_3| = |\mathbf{F}_1| \sin 35°$$

Let $|\mathbf{F}_1| = 145$.

$$|\mathbf{F}_3| = 145 \sin 35°$$

$$|\mathbf{F}_3| = 83.16858$$

A force of approximately 83 pounds is required to keep the skier from sliding down the hill.

EXAMPLE 9 Resultant Forces

A barge runs aground outside the channel. A single tugboat cannot generate enough force to pull the barge off the sandbar. A second tugboat comes to assist. The following diagram illustrates the force vectors, $\mathbf{F}_1$ and $\mathbf{F}_2$, from the tugboats. What is the resultant force vector of the two tugboats?

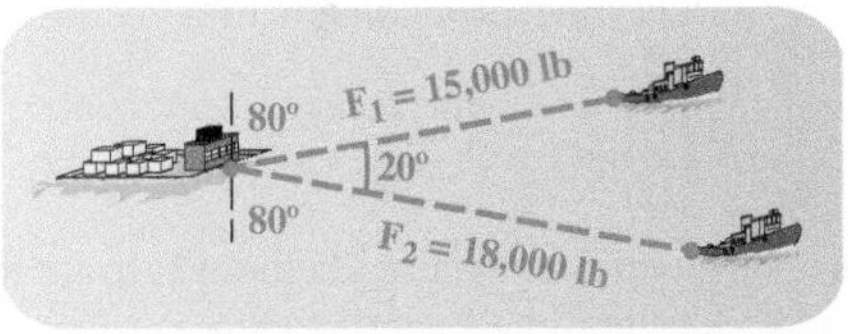

STUDY TIP

In Example 9, $\beta = 160°$ because the angle between the paths of the tugboats is 20°.

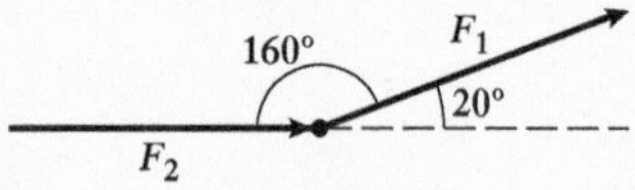

Solution:

Using the tail-to-tip rule, we can add these two vectors and form a triangle:

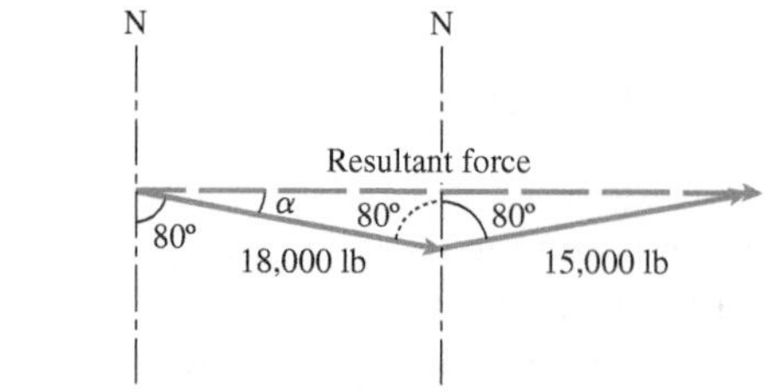

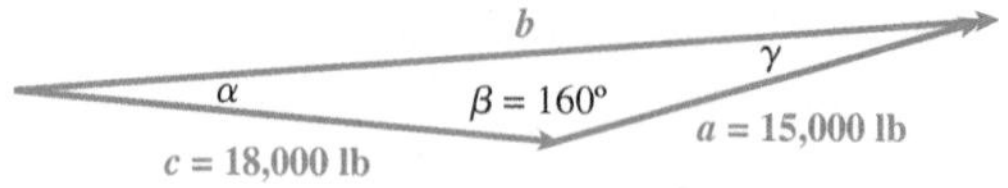

Find b: Apply the Law of Cosines. $\quad b^2 = a^2 + c^2 - 2ac\cos\beta$

Let $a = 15{,}000$, $c = 18{,}000$, and $\beta = 160°$. $\quad b^2 = 15{,}000^2 + 18{,}000^2 - 2(15{,}000)(18{,}000)\cos 160°$

Solve for b. $\quad \boxed{b = 32{,}503 \text{ lb}}$

Find α: Apply the Law of Sines. $\quad \dfrac{\sin\alpha}{a} = \dfrac{\sin\beta}{b}$

Isolate $\sin\alpha$. $\quad \sin\alpha = \dfrac{a}{b}\sin\beta$

Let $a = 15{,}000$, $b = 32{,}503$, and $\beta = 160°$. $\quad \sin\alpha = \dfrac{15{,}000}{32{,}503}\sin 160°$

Apply the inverse sine function to solve for α. $\quad \alpha = \sin^{-1}\left(\dfrac{15{,}000}{32{,}503}\sin 160°\right)$

Approximate α with a calculator. $\quad \boxed{\alpha \approx 9.08°}$

The resulting force is **32,503 pounds** at an angle of **9° from the tug pulling with a force of 18,000 pounds**.

[SECTION 7.1] SUMMARY

In this section, we discussed scalars (real numbers) and vectors. Scalars have only magnitude, whereas vectors have both magnitude and direction.

$$\text{Vector:} \quad \mathbf{u} = \langle a, b\rangle$$

$$\text{Magnitude:} \quad |\mathbf{u}| = \sqrt{a^2 + b^2}$$

$$\text{Direction } (\theta)\text{:} \quad \tan\theta = \frac{b}{a}$$

We defined vectors both algebraically and geometrically and gave interpretations of magnitude and vector addition in both methods.

Vector addition is performed algebraically component by component.

$$\langle a, b\rangle + \langle c, d\rangle = \langle a + c, b + d\rangle.$$

The trigonometric functions are used to express the horizontal and vertical components of a vector.

$$\text{Horizontal component:} \quad a = |\mathbf{u}|\cos\theta$$

$$\text{Vertical component:} \quad b = |\mathbf{u}|\sin\theta$$

Velocity and force vectors illustrate applications of the Law of Sines and the Law of Cosines.

[SECTION 7.1] EXERCISES

• SKILLS

In Exercises 1–6, find the magnitude of the vector $\overrightarrow{AB}$.

1. $A = (2, 7)$ and $B = (5, 9)$
2. $A = (-2, 3)$ and $B = (3, -4)$
3. $A = (4, 1)$ and $B = (-3, 0)$
4. $A = (-1, -1)$ and $B = (2, -5)$
5. $A = (0, 7)$ and $B = (-24, 0)$
6. $A = (-2, 1)$ and $B = (4, 9)$

In Exercises 7–16, find the magnitude and direction angle of the given vector.

7. $\mathbf{u} = \langle 3, 8\rangle$
8. $\mathbf{u} = \langle 4, 7\rangle$
9. $\mathbf{u} = \langle 5, -1\rangle$
10. $\mathbf{u} = \langle -6, -2\rangle$
11. $\mathbf{u} = \langle -4, 1\rangle$
12. $\mathbf{u} = \langle -6, 3\rangle$
13. $\mathbf{u} = \langle -8, 0\rangle$
14. $\mathbf{u} = \langle 0, 7\rangle$
15. $\mathbf{u} = \langle \sqrt{3}, 3\rangle$
16. $\mathbf{u} = \langle -5, -5\rangle$

In Exercises 17–24, perform the indicated vector operation, given $\mathbf{u} = \langle -4, 3\rangle$ and $\mathbf{v} = \langle 2, -5\rangle$.

17. $\mathbf{u} + \mathbf{v}$
18. $\mathbf{u} - \mathbf{v}$
19. $3\mathbf{u}$
20. $-2\mathbf{u}$
21. $2\mathbf{u} + 4\mathbf{v}$
22. $5(\mathbf{u} + \mathbf{v})$
23. $6(\mathbf{u} - \mathbf{v})$
24. $2\mathbf{u} - 3\mathbf{v} + 4\mathbf{u}$

In Exercises 25–34, find the vector, given its magnitude and direction angle.

25. $|\mathbf{u}| = 7, \theta = 25°$
26. $|\mathbf{u}| = 5, \theta = 75°$
27. $|\mathbf{u}| = 16, \theta = 100°$
28. $|\mathbf{u}| = 8, \theta = 200°$
29. $|\mathbf{u}| = 4, \theta = 310°$
30. $|\mathbf{u}| = 8, \theta = 225°$
31. $|\mathbf{u}| = 9, \theta = 335°$
32. $|\mathbf{u}| = 3, \theta = 315°$
33. $|\mathbf{u}| = 2, \theta = 120°$
34. $|\mathbf{u}| = 6, \theta = 330°$

In Exercises 35–44, find a unit vector in the direction of the given vector.

35. $\mathbf{v} = \langle -5, -12\rangle$
36. $\mathbf{v} = \langle 3, 4\rangle$
37. $\mathbf{v} = \langle 60, 11\rangle$
38. $\mathbf{v} = \langle -7, 24\rangle$
39. $\mathbf{v} = \langle 24, -7\rangle$
40. $\mathbf{v} = \langle -10, 24\rangle$
41. $\mathbf{v} = \langle -9, -12\rangle$
42. $\mathbf{v} = \langle 40, -9\rangle$
43. $\mathbf{v} = \langle \sqrt{2}, 3\sqrt{2}\rangle$
44. $\mathbf{v} = \langle -4\sqrt{3}, -2\sqrt{3}\rangle$

In Exercises 45–50, express the vector in terms of unit vectors i and j.

45. $\langle 7, 3\rangle$
46. $\langle -2, 4\rangle$
47. $\langle 5, -3\rangle$
48. $\langle -6, -2\rangle$
49. $\langle -1, 0\rangle$
50. $\langle 0, 2\rangle$

In Exercises 51–56, perform the indicated vector operation.

51. $(5\mathbf{i} - 2\mathbf{j}) + (-3\mathbf{i} + 2\mathbf{j})$
52. $(4\mathbf{i} - 2\mathbf{j}) + (3\mathbf{i} - 5\mathbf{j})$
53. $(-3\mathbf{i} + 3\mathbf{j}) - (2\mathbf{i} - 2\mathbf{j})$
54. $(\mathbf{i} - 3\mathbf{j}) - (-2\mathbf{i} + \mathbf{j})$
55. $(5\mathbf{i} + 3\mathbf{j}) + (2\mathbf{i} - 3\mathbf{j})$
56. $(-2\mathbf{i} + \mathbf{j}) + (2\mathbf{i} - 4\mathbf{j})$

• APPLICATIONS

57. **Bullet Speed.** A bullet is fired from ground level at a speed of 2200 feet per second at an angle of 30° from the horizontal. Find the magnitude of the horizontal and vertical components of the velocity vector.

58. **Weightlifting.** A 50-pound weight lies on an inclined bench that makes an angle of 40° with the horizontal. Find the component of the weight directed perpendicular to the bench and also the component of the weight parallel to the inclined bench.

59. **Weight of a Boat.** A force of 630 pounds is needed to pull a speedboat and its trailer up a ramp that has an incline of 13°. What is the combined weight of the boat and its trailer?

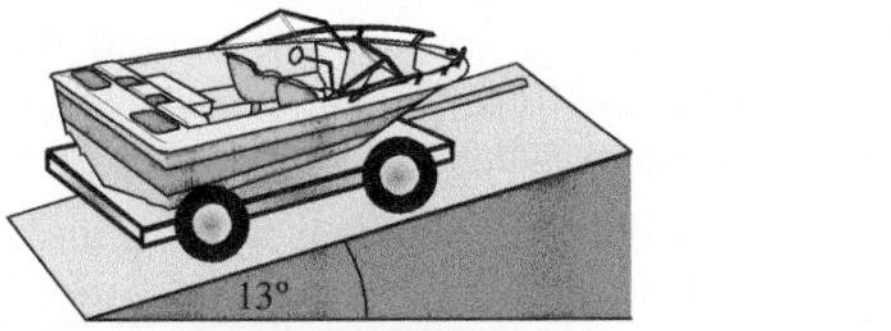

60. **Weight of a Boat.** A force of 500 pounds is needed to pull a speedboat and its trailer up a ramp that has an incline of 16°. What is the weight of the boat and its trailer?

61. **Speed and Direction of a Ship.** A ship's captain sets a course due north at 10 miles per hour. The water is moving at 6 miles per hour due west. What is the actual velocity of the ship, and in what direction is it traveling?

62. **Speed and Direction of a Ship.** A ship's captain sets a course due west at 12 miles per hour. The water is moving at 3 miles per hour due north. What is the actual velocity of the ship, and in what direction is it traveling?

63. **Heading and Airspeed.** A plane has a compass heading of 60° east of due north and an airspeed of 300 miles per hour. The wind is blowing at 40 miles per hour with a heading of 30° west of due north. What are the plane's actual heading and airspeed?

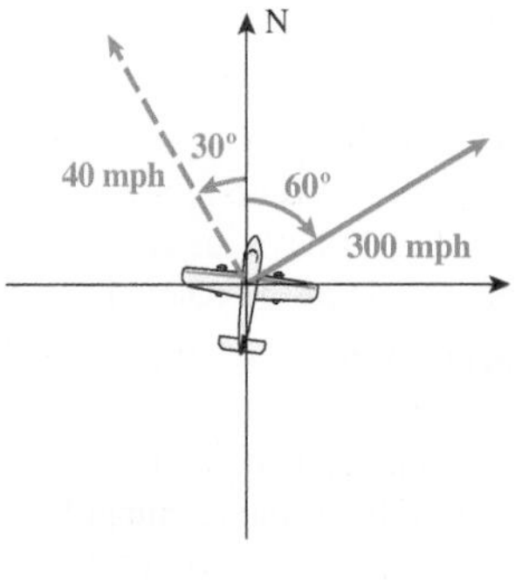

64. **Heading and Airspeed.** A plane has a compass heading of 30° east of due north and an airspeed of 400 miles per hour. The wind is blowing at 30 miles per hour with a heading of 60° west of due north. What are the plane's actual heading and airspeed?

65. **Sliding Box.** A box weighing 500 pounds is held in place on an inclined plane that has an angle of 30°. What force is required to hold it in place?

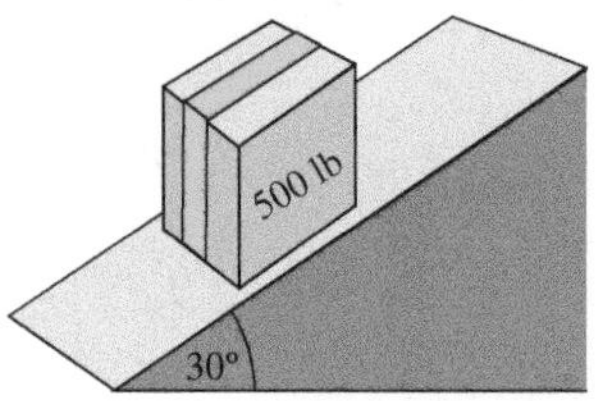

66. **Sliding Box.** A box weighing 500 pounds is held in place on an inclined plane that has an angle of 10°. What force is required to hold it in place?

67. **Baseball.** A baseball player throws a ball with an initial velocity of 80 feet per second at an angle of 40° with the horizontal. What are the vertical and horizontal components of the velocity?

68. **Baseball.** A baseball pitcher throws a ball with an initial velocity of 100 feet per second at an angle of 5° with the horizontal. What are the vertical and horizontal components of the velocity?

For Exercises 69 and 70, refer to the following:

In a post pattern in football, the receiver in motion runs past the quarterback parallel to the line of scrimmage (A), runs perpendicular to the line of scrimmage (B), and then cuts toward the goal post (C).

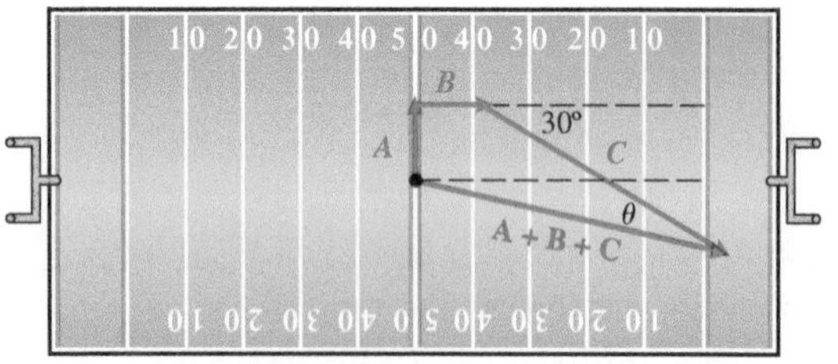

69. **Football.** A receiver runs the post pattern. If the magnitudes of the vectors are $|A| = 4$ yd, $|B| = 12$ yd, and $|C| = 20$ yd, find the magnitude of the resultant vector $\mathbf{A} + \mathbf{B} + \mathbf{C}$.

70. **Football.** A receiver runs the post pattern. If the magnitudes of the vectors are $|A| = 4$ yd, $|B| = 12$ yd, and $|C| = 20$ yd, find the direction angle θ.

71. **Resultant Force.** A force with a magnitude of 100 pounds and another with a magnitude of 400 pounds are acting on an object. The two forces have an angle of 60° between them. What is the direction of the resultant force with respect to the force of 400 pounds?

72. **Resultant Force.** A force with a magnitude of 100 pounds and another with a magnitude of 400 pounds are acting on an object. The two forces have an angle of 60° between them. What is the magnitude of the resultant force?

73. **Resultant Force.** A force of 1000 pounds is acting on an object at an angle of 45° from the horizontal. Another force of 500 pounds is acting at an angle of −40° from the horizontal. What is the magnitude of the resultant force?

74. **Resultant Force.** A force of 1000 pounds is acting on an object at an angle of 45° from the horizontal. Another force of 500 pounds is acting at an angle of −40° from the horizontal. What is the angle of the resultant force?

75. **Resultant Force.** Forces with magnitudes of 200 N and 180 N act on a hook. The angle between these two forces is 45°. Find the direction and magnitude of the resultant of these forces.

76. **Resultant Force.** Forces with magnitudes of 100 N and 50 N act on a hook. The angle between these two forces is 30°. Find the direction and magnitude of the resultant of these forces.

77. **Exercise Equipment.** A tether ball weighing 5 pounds is pulled outward from a pole by a horizontal force **u** until the rope makes a 45° angle with the pole. Determine the resulting tension (in pounds) on the rope and the magnitude of **u**.

78. **Exercise Equipment.** A tether ball weighing 8 pounds is pulled outward from a pole by a horizontal force **u** until the rope makes a 60° angle with the pole. Determine the resulting tension (in pounds) on the rope and the magnitude of **u**.

79. **Torque.** *Torque* is the tendency for an arm to rotate about a pivot point. If a force **F** is applied at an angle θ to turn an arm of length L, as pictured below, then the magnitude of the torque $= L|\mathbf{F}|\sin\theta$.

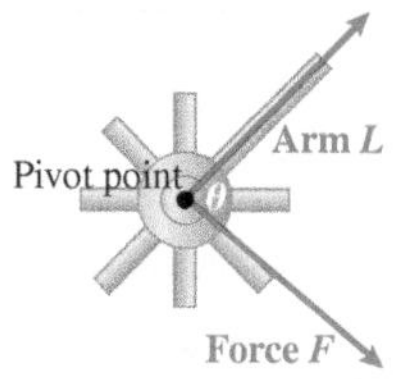

Assume that a force of 45 N is applied to a bar 0.2 meter wide on a sewer shut-off valve at an angle 85°. What is the magnitude of the torque in N-m?

80. **Torque.** You walk through a swinging mall door to enter a department store. You exert a force of 40 N applied perpendicular to the door. The door is 0.85 meter wide. Assuming that you pushed the door at its edge and the hinge is the pivot point, find the magnitude of the torque.

81. **Torque.** You walk through a swinging mall door to enter a department store. You exert a force of 40 N applied at an angle 110° to the door. The door is 0.85 meter wide. Assuming that you pushed the door at its edge and the hinge is the pivot point, find the magnitude of the torque.

82. **Torque.** Suppose that within the context of Exercises 80 and 81, the magnitude of the torque turned out to be 0 N-m. When can this occur?

83. **Resultant Force.** A person is walking two dogs fastened to separate leashes that meet in a connective hub, leading to a single leash that she is holding. Dog 1 applies a force N 60° W with a magnitude of 8, and Dog 2 applies a force N 45° E with a magnitude of 6. Find the magnitude and direction of the force **w** that the walker applies to the leash in order to counterbalance the total force exerted by the dogs.

84. **Resultant Force.** A person is walking three dogs fastened to separate leashes that meet in a connective hub, leading to a single leash that she is holding. Dog 1 applies a force N 60° W with a magnitude of 8, Dog 2 applies a force N 45° E with a magnitude of 6, and Dog 3 moves directly N with a magnitude of 12. Find the magnitude and direction of the force **w** that the walker applies to the leash in order to counterbalance the total force exerted by the dogs.

For Exercises 85 and 86, refer to the following:

Muscle A and muscle B are attached to a bone as indicated in the figure below. Muscle A exerts a force on the bone at angle α, while muscle B exerts a force on the bone at angle β.

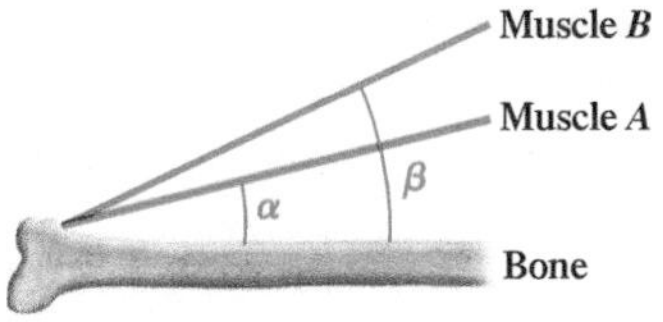

85. Health/Medicine. Assume muscle A exerts a force of 900 N on the bone at angle $\alpha = 8°$, while muscle B exerts a force of 750 N on the bone at angle $\beta = 33°$. Find the resultant force and the angle of the force due to muscle A and muscle B on the bone.

86. Health/Medicine. Assume muscle A exerts a force of 1000 N on the bone at angle $\alpha = 9°$, while muscle B exerts a force of 820 N on the bone at angle $\beta = 38°$. Find the resultant force and the angle of the force due to muscle A and muscle B on the bone.

• CATCH THE MISTAKE

In Exercises 87 and 88, explain the mistake that is made.

87. Find the magnitude of the vector $\langle -2, -8 \rangle$.

Solution:

Factor the -1. $\quad -\langle 2, 8 \rangle$

Find the magnitude of $\langle 2, 8 \rangle$. $\quad |\langle 2, 8 \rangle| = \sqrt{2^2 + 8^2} = \sqrt{68} = 2\sqrt{17}$

Write the magnitude of $\langle -2, -8 \rangle$. $\quad |\langle -2, -8 \rangle| = -2\sqrt{17}$

This is incorrect. What mistake was made?

88. Find the direction angle of the vector $\langle -2, -8 \rangle$.

Solution:

Write the formula for the direction angle of $\langle a, b \rangle$. $\quad \tan\theta = \dfrac{b}{a}$

Let $a = -2$ and $b = -8$. $\quad \tan\theta = \dfrac{-8}{-2}$

Apply the inverse tangent function. $\quad \theta = \tan^{-1}4$

Evaluate with a calculator. $\quad \theta = 76°$

This is incorrect. What mistake was made?

• CONCEPTUAL

In Exercises 89–92, determine whether each statement is true or false.

89. The magnitude of the vector **i** is the imaginary number i.

90. The arrow components of equal vectors must coincide.

91. The magnitude of a vector is always greater than or equal to the magnitude of its horizontal component.

92. The magnitude of a vector is always greater than or equal to the magnitude of its vertical component.

93. Would a scalar or a vector represent the following? *The car is driving 72 miles per hour due east (90° with respect to north).*

94. Would a scalar or vector represent the following? *The granite has a mass of 131 kilograms.*

95. Find the magnitude of the vector $\langle -a, b \rangle$ if $a > 0$ and $b > 0$.

96. Find the direction angle of the vector $\langle -a, b \rangle$ if $a > 0$ and $b > 0$.

• CHALLENGE

97. Show that if $\mathbf{u}$ is a unit vector in the direction of $\mathbf{v}$, then $\mathbf{v} = |\mathbf{u}|\,\mathbf{u}$.

98. Show that if $\mathbf{u} = a\mathbf{i} + b\mathbf{j}$ is a unit vector, then (a, b) lies on the unit circle.

99. A vector $\mathbf{u}$ is a *linear combination* of $\mathbf{p}$ and $\mathbf{q}$ if there exist constants c_1 and c_2 such that $\mathbf{u} = c_1\mathbf{p} + c_2\mathbf{q}$. Show that $\langle -6, 4 \rangle$ is a linear combination of $\langle -8, 4 \rangle$ and $\langle 1, -1 \rangle$.

100. Show that $\langle -\frac{2}{9}a, \frac{8}{9}b \rangle$ is a linear combination of $\langle a, 3b \rangle$ and $\langle -a, -b \rangle$, for any real constants a and b.

101. Prove that $\mathbf{u} + 3(2\mathbf{v} - \mathbf{u}) = 6\mathbf{v} - 2\mathbf{u}$, showing carefully how all relevant properties and definitions enter the proof.

102. Let $\mathbf{u} = \langle 2a, a \rangle$, $\mathbf{v} = \langle -a, -2a \rangle$. Compute $\left|\dfrac{2\mathbf{u}}{|\mathbf{v}|} - \dfrac{3\mathbf{v}}{|\mathbf{u}|}\right|$.

• PREVIEW TO CALCULUS

There is a branch of calculus devoted to the study of vector-valued functions; these are functions that map real numbers onto vectors. For example, $\mathbf{v}(t) = \langle t, 2t \rangle$.

103. Find the magnitude of the vector-valued function $\mathbf{v}(t) = \langle \cos t, \sin t \rangle$.

104. Find the direction of the vector-valued function $\mathbf{v}(t) = \langle -3t, -4t \rangle$.

The difference quotient for the vector-valued function $\mathbf{v}(t)$ is defined as $\dfrac{\mathbf{v}(t+h) - \mathbf{v}(t)}{h}$. In Exercises 105 and 106, find the difference quotient of the vector-valued function.

105. $\mathbf{v}(t) = \langle t, t^2 \rangle$

106. $\mathbf{v}(t) = \langle t^2 + 1, t^3 \rangle$

7.2 THE DOT PRODUCT

SKILLS OBJECTIVES

- Find the dot product of two vectors.
- Use the dot product to find the angle between two vectors.
- Use the dot product to calculate the amount of work associated with a physical problem.

CONCEPTUAL OBJECTIVES

- Understand that the dot product of two vectors is a scalar.
- Understand why the dot product of two orthogonal (perpendicular) vectors is equal to zero.
- Understand that work is done when a force causes an object to move a certain distance.

7.2.1 The Dot Product

7.2.1 SKILL

Find the dot product of two vectors.

7.2.1 CONCEPTUAL

Understand that the dot product of two vectors is a scalar.

With two-dimensional vectors, there are two types of multiplication defined for vectors: scalar multiplication and the dot product. Scalar multiplication (which we already demonstrated in Section 7.1) is multiplication of a vector by a scalar; the result is a vector. Now we discuss the *dot product* of two vectors. In this case, there are two important things to note: (1) The dot product of two vectors is defined only if the vectors have the same number of components and (2) if the dot product does exist, then the result is a scalar.

[CONCEPT CHECK]

TRUE OR FALSE The dot product of two vectors is a scalar, and the product of two scalars is a vector.

ANSWER False

DOT PRODUCT

The **dot product** of two vectors $\mathbf{u} = \langle a, b\rangle$ and $\mathbf{v} = \langle c, d\rangle$ is given by

$$\mathbf{u} \cdot \mathbf{v} = ac + bd$$

$\mathbf{u} \cdot \mathbf{v}$ is pronounced "u dot v."

EXAMPLE 1 Finding the Dot Product of Two Vectors

Find the dot product $\langle -7, 3\rangle \cdot \langle 2, 5\rangle$.

Solution:

Sum the products of the first components and the products of the second components. $\langle -7, 3\rangle \cdot \langle 2, 5\rangle = (-7)(2) + (3)(5)$

Simplify. $= -14 + 15$

$= \boxed{1}$

STUDY TIP

The dot product of two vectors is a scalar.

YOUR TURN Find the dot product $\langle 6, 1\rangle \cdot \langle -2, 3\rangle$.

ANSWER

-9

The following box summarizes the properties of the dot product:

PROPERTIES OF THE DOT PRODUCT

1. $\mathbf{u} \cdot \mathbf{v} = \mathbf{v} \cdot \mathbf{u}$
2. $\mathbf{u} \cdot \mathbf{u} = |\mathbf{u}|^2$
3. $\mathbf{0} \cdot \mathbf{u} = 0$
4. $k(\mathbf{u} \cdot \mathbf{v}) = (k\mathbf{u}) \cdot \mathbf{v} = \mathbf{u} \cdot (k\mathbf{v})$
5. $(\mathbf{u} + \mathbf{v}) \cdot \mathbf{w} = \mathbf{u} \cdot \mathbf{w} + \mathbf{v} \cdot \mathbf{w}$
6. $\mathbf{u} \cdot (\mathbf{v} + \mathbf{w}) = \mathbf{u} \cdot \mathbf{v} + \mathbf{u} \cdot \mathbf{w}$

These properties are verified in the exercises.

7.2.2 Angle between Two Vectors

We can use the properties of the dot product to develop an equation that relates the angle between two vectors and the dot product of the vectors.

7.2.2 SKILL

Use the dot product to find the angle between two vectors.

7.2.2 CONCEPTUAL

Understand why the dot product of two orthogonal (perpendicular) vectors is equal to zero.

WORDS	MATH
Let **u** and **v** be two vectors with the same initial point, and let θ be the angle between them.	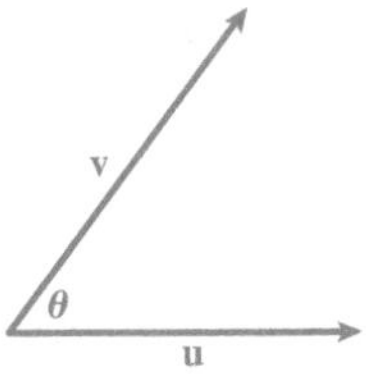
The vector $\mathbf{u} - \mathbf{v}$ is opposite angle θ.	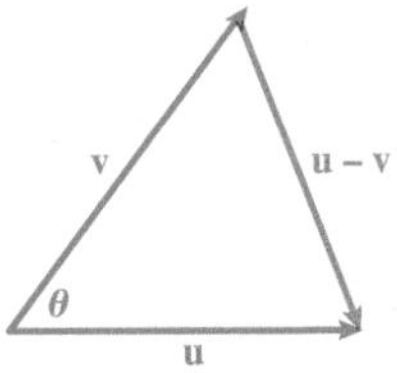
A triangle is formed with side lengths equal to the magnitudes of the three vectors.	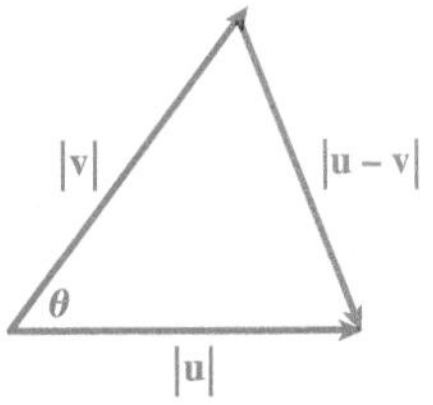
Apply the Law of Cosines.	$\boxed{\lvert\mathbf{u}-\mathbf{v}\rvert^2 = \lvert\mathbf{u}\rvert^2 + \lvert\mathbf{v}\rvert^2 - 2\lvert\mathbf{u}\rvert\lvert\mathbf{v}\rvert\cos\theta}$
Use properties of the dot product to rewrite the left side of the equation.	
Property (2):	$\lvert\mathbf{u}-\mathbf{v}\rvert^2 = (\mathbf{u}-\mathbf{v})\cdot(\mathbf{u}-\mathbf{v})$
Property (6):	$= \mathbf{u}\cdot(\mathbf{u}-\mathbf{v}) - \mathbf{v}\cdot(\mathbf{u}-\mathbf{v})$
Property (6):	$= \mathbf{u}\cdot\mathbf{u} - \mathbf{u}\cdot\mathbf{v} - \mathbf{v}\cdot\mathbf{u} + \mathbf{v}\cdot\mathbf{v}$
Property (2):	$= \lvert\mathbf{u}\rvert^2 - \mathbf{u}\cdot\mathbf{v} - \mathbf{v}\cdot\mathbf{u} + \lvert\mathbf{v}\rvert^2$
Property (1):	$\boxed{= \lvert\mathbf{u}\rvert^2 - 2(\mathbf{u}\cdot\mathbf{v}) + \lvert\mathbf{v}\rvert^2}$
Substitute this last expression for the left side of the original Law of Cosines equation.	$\lvert\mathbf{u}\rvert^2 - 2(\mathbf{u}\cdot\mathbf{v}) + \lvert\mathbf{v}\rvert^2 = \lvert\mathbf{u}\rvert^2 + \lvert\mathbf{v}\rvert^2 - 2\lvert\mathbf{u}\rvert\lvert\mathbf{v}\rvert\cos\theta$
Simplify.	$-2(\mathbf{u}\cdot\mathbf{v}) = -2\lvert\mathbf{u}\rvert\lvert\mathbf{v}\rvert\cos\theta$
Isolate $\cos\theta$.	$\boxed{\cos\theta = \dfrac{\mathbf{u}\cdot\mathbf{v}}{\lvert\mathbf{u}\rvert\lvert\mathbf{v}\rvert}}$

Notice that **u** and **v** have to be nonzero vectors, since we divided by them in the last step.

ANGLE BETWEEN TWO VECTORS

If θ is the angle between two nonzero vectors **u** and **v**, where $0° \leq \theta \leq 180°$, then

$$\cos\theta = \frac{\mathbf{u}\cdot\mathbf{v}}{\lvert\mathbf{u}\rvert\lvert\mathbf{v}\rvert}$$

[CONCEPT CHECK]

Determine the relationship between a and b that guarantees that the vectors $u = <a, b>$ and $v = <a, -b>$ are orthogonal.

ANSWER $a = \pm b$

STUDY TIP

The angle between two vectors $\theta = \cos^{-1}\left(\frac{\mathbf{u}\cdot\mathbf{v}}{\lvert\mathbf{u}\rvert\lvert\mathbf{v}\rvert}\right)$ is an angle between 0° and 180° (the range of the inverse cosine function).

In the Cartesian plane, there are two angles between two vectors, θ and $360° - \theta$. **We assume that θ is the "smaller" angle.**

EXAMPLE 2 Finding the Angle between Two Vectors

Find the angle between $\langle 2, -3 \rangle$ and $\langle -4, 3 \rangle$.

Solution:

Let $\mathbf{u} = \langle 2, -3 \rangle$ and $\mathbf{v} = \langle -4, 3 \rangle$.

STEP 1 Find $\mathbf{u} \cdot \mathbf{v}$.

$$\mathbf{u} \cdot \mathbf{v} = \langle 2, -3 \rangle \cdot \langle -4, 3 \rangle = (2)(-4) + (-3)(3) = -17$$

STEP 2 Find $|\mathbf{u}|$.

$$|\mathbf{u}| = \sqrt{\mathbf{u} \cdot \mathbf{u}} = \sqrt{2^2 + (-3)^2} = \sqrt{13}$$

STEP 3 Find $|\mathbf{v}|$.

$$|\mathbf{v}| = \sqrt{\mathbf{v} \cdot \mathbf{v}} = \sqrt{(-4)^2 + 3^2} = \sqrt{25} = 5$$

STEP 4 Find θ.

$$\cos\theta = \frac{\mathbf{u} \cdot \mathbf{v}}{|\mathbf{u}||\mathbf{v}|} = \frac{-17}{5\sqrt{13}}$$

Approximate θ with a calculator.

$$\theta = \cos^{-1}\left(-\frac{17}{5\sqrt{13}}\right) \approx 160.559965°$$

$$\boxed{\theta \approx 161°}$$

STEP 5 Draw a picture to confirm the answer.

Draw the vectors $\langle 2, -3 \rangle$ and $\langle -4, 3 \rangle$.

161° appears to be correct.

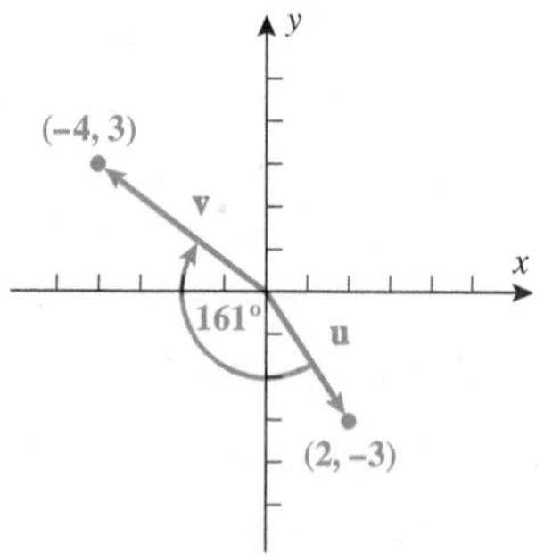

YOUR TURN Find the angle between $\langle 1, 5 \rangle$ and $\langle -2, 4 \rangle$.

ANSWER

38°

When two vectors are **parallel**, the angle between them is 0° or 180°.

When two vectors are **perpendicular (orthogonal)**, the angle between them is 90°.

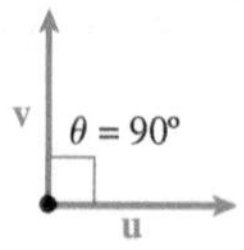

Note: We did not include 270° because the angle $0° \le \theta \le 180°$ between two vectors is taken to be the smaller angle.

WORDS	MATH
When two vectors **u** and **v** are perpendicular, $\theta = 90°$.	$\cos 90° = \dfrac{\mathbf{u} \cdot \mathbf{v}}{\lvert\mathbf{u}\rvert\lvert\mathbf{v}\rvert}$
Substitute $\cos 90° = 0$.	$0 = \dfrac{\mathbf{u} \cdot \mathbf{v}}{\lvert\mathbf{u}\rvert\lvert\mathbf{v}\rvert}$
Therefore, the dot product of **u** and **v** must be zero.	$\mathbf{u} \cdot \mathbf{v} = 0$

ORTHOGONAL VECTORS

Two vectors **u** and **v** are **orthogonal** (perpendicular) if and only if their dot product is zero.

$$\mathbf{u} \cdot \mathbf{v} = 0$$

EXAMPLE 3 Determining Whether Vectors Are Orthogonal

Determine whether each pair of vectors is orthogonal.

a. $\mathbf{u} = \langle 2, -3 \rangle$ and $\mathbf{v} = \langle 3, 2 \rangle$ **b.** $\mathbf{u} = \langle -7, -3 \rangle$ and $\mathbf{v} = \langle 7, 3 \rangle$

Solution (a):

Find the dot product $\mathbf{u} \cdot \mathbf{v}$. $\mathbf{u} \cdot \mathbf{v} = (2)(3) + (-3)(2)$

Simplify. $\mathbf{u} \cdot \mathbf{v} = 0$

Vectors **u** and **v** are orthogonal, since $\mathbf{u} \cdot \mathbf{v} = 0$.

Solution (b):

Find the dot product $\mathbf{u} \cdot \mathbf{v}$. $\mathbf{u} \cdot \mathbf{v} = (-7)(7) + (-3)(3)$

Simplify. $\mathbf{u} \cdot \mathbf{v} = -58$

Vectors **u** and **v** are not orthogonal, since $\mathbf{u} \cdot \mathbf{v} \neq 0$.

7.2.3 Work

If you had to carry barbells with weights or pillows for 1 mile, which would you choose? You would probably pick the pillows over the barbell with weights, because the pillows are lighter. It requires less work to carry the pillows than it does to carry the weights. If asked to carry either of them 1 mile or 10 miles, you would probably pick 1 mile, because it's a shorter distance and requires less work. **Work** is done when a *force causes an object to move a certain distance.*

The simplest case is when the force is in the same direction as the displacement—for example, a stagecoach (the horses pull with a force in the same direction). In this case the work is defined as the magnitude of the force times the magnitude of the displacement, distance *d*.

$$W = \lvert\mathbf{F}\rvert d$$

Notice that the magnitude of the force is a scalar, the distance *d* is a scalar, and hence the product is a scalar.

If the horses pull with a force of 1000 pounds and they move the stagecoach 100 feet, the work done by the force is

$$W = (1000 \text{ lb})(100 \text{ ft}) = 100{,}000 \text{ ft-lb}$$

7.2.3 SKILL

Use the dot product to calculate the amount of work associated with a physical problem.

7.2.3 CONCEPTUAL

Understand that work is done when a force causes an object to move a certain distance.

[CONCEPT CHECK]

TRUE OR FALSE Work increases only if either the magnitude of the force or the distance or both increases.

ANSWER True

In many physical applications, however, the force is not in the same direction as the displacement, and hence vectors (not just their magnitudes) are required.

We often want to know how much of a force is applied in a certain direction. For example, when your car runs out of gasoline and you try to push it, some of the force vector $\mathbf{F}_1$ you generate from pushing translates into the horizontal component $\mathbf{F}_2$; hence, the car moves horizontally.

If we let θ be the angle between the vectors $\mathbf{F}_1$ and $\mathbf{F}_2$, then the horizontal component of $\mathbf{F}_1$ is $\mathbf{F}_2$, where $|F_2| = |F_1|\cos\theta$.

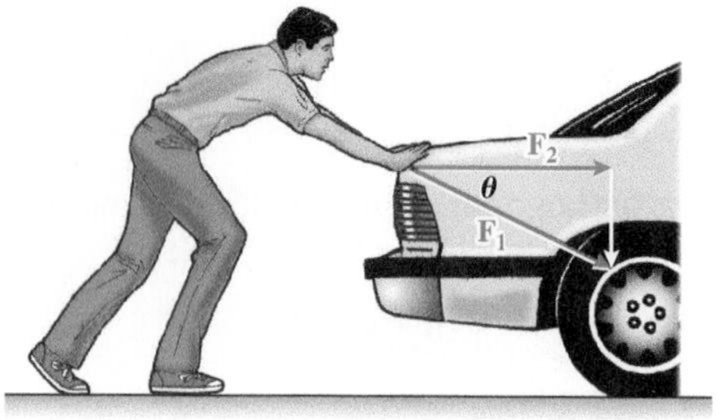

If the man in the picture pushes at an angle of 25° with a force of 150 pounds, then the horizontal component of the force vector $\mathbf{F}_1$ is

$$(150\text{ lb})(\cos 25°) \approx \boxed{136\text{ lb}}$$

WORDS	MATH
To develop a generalized formula when the force exerted and the displacement are not in the same direction, we start with the formula for the angle between two vectors.	$\cos\theta = \dfrac{\mathbf{u}\cdot\mathbf{v}}{\lvert\mathbf{u}\rvert\lvert\mathbf{v}\rvert}$
We then isolate the dot product $\mathbf{u}\cdot\mathbf{v}$.	$\mathbf{u}\cdot\mathbf{v} = \lvert\mathbf{u}\rvert\lvert\mathbf{v}\rvert\cos\theta$
Let $\mathbf{u} = \mathbf{F}$ and $\mathbf{v} = \mathbf{d}$.	$W = \mathbf{F}\cdot\mathbf{d} = \lvert\mathbf{F}\rvert\lvert\mathbf{d}\rvert\cos\theta = \underbrace{\lvert\mathbf{F}\rvert\cos\theta}_{\text{magnitude of force in direction of displacement}} \cdot \underbrace{\lvert\mathbf{d}\rvert}_{\text{distance}}$

WORK

If an object is moved from point A to point B by a constant force, then the work associated with this displacement is

$$W = \mathbf{F}\cdot\mathbf{d}$$

where $\mathbf{d}$ is the displacement vector and $\mathbf{F}$ is the force vector.

Work is typically expressed in one of two units:

SYSTEM	FORCE	DISTANCE	WORK
U.S. customary	pound	foot	ft-lb
SI	newton	meter	N-m

EXAMPLE 4 **Calculating Work**

How much work is done when a force (in pounds) $\mathbf{F} = \langle 2, 4 \rangle$ moves an object from $(0, 0)$ to $(5, 9)$? (The distance is in feet.)

Solution:

Find the displacement vector **d**. $\mathbf{d} = \langle 5, 9 \rangle$

Apply the work formula, $W = \mathbf{F} \cdot \mathbf{d}$. $W = \langle 2, 4 \rangle \cdot \langle 5, 9 \rangle$

Calculate the dot product. $W = (2)(5) + (4)(9)$

Simplify. $\boxed{W = 46 \text{ ft-lb}}$

YOUR TURN How much work is done when a force (in newtons) $\mathbf{F} = \langle 1, 3 \rangle$ moves an object from $(0, 0)$ to $(4, 7)$? (The distance is in meters.)

ANSWER

25 N-m

[SECTION 7.2] SUMMARY

In this section, we defined the dot product as a form of multiplication of two vectors. A scalar times a vector results in a vector, whereas the dot product of two vectors is a scalar.

$$\langle a, b \rangle \cdot \langle c, d \rangle = ac + bd$$

We developed a formula that determines the angle θ between two vectors **u** and **v**.

$$\cos\theta = \frac{\mathbf{u} \cdot \mathbf{v}}{|\mathbf{u}||\mathbf{v}|}$$

Orthogonal (perpendicular) vectors have an angle of 90° between them, and consequently, the dot product of two orthogonal vectors is equal to zero. Work is the result of a force displacing an object. When the force and displacement are in the same direction, the work is equal to the product of the magnitude of the force and the distance (magnitude of the displacement). When the force and displacement are not in the same direction, work is the dot product of the force vector and displacement vector, $\mathbf{W} = \mathbf{F} \cdot \mathbf{d}$.

[SECTION 7.2] EXERCISES

• SKILLS

In Exercises 1–12, find the indicated dot product.

1. $\langle 4, -2 \rangle \cdot \langle 3, 5 \rangle$
2. $\langle 7, 8 \rangle \cdot \langle 2, -1 \rangle$
3. $\langle -5, 6 \rangle \cdot \langle 3, 2 \rangle$
4. $\langle 6, -3 \rangle \cdot \langle 2, 1 \rangle$
5. $\langle -7, -4 \rangle \cdot \langle -2, -7 \rangle$
6. $\langle 5, -2 \rangle \cdot \langle -1, -1 \rangle$
7. $\langle \sqrt{3}, -2 \rangle \cdot \langle 3\sqrt{3}, -1 \rangle$
8. $\langle 4\sqrt{2}, \sqrt{7} \rangle \cdot \langle -\sqrt{2}, -\sqrt{7} \rangle$
9. $\langle 5, a \rangle \cdot \langle -3a, 2 \rangle$
10. $\langle 4x, 3y \rangle \cdot \langle 2y, -5x \rangle$
11. $\langle 0.8, -0.5 \rangle \cdot \langle 2, 6 \rangle$
12. $\langle -18, 3 \rangle \cdot \langle 10, -300 \rangle$

In Exercises 13–24, find the angle (round to the nearest degree) between each pair of vectors.

13. $\langle -4, 3 \rangle$ and $\langle -5, -9 \rangle$
14. $\langle 2, -4 \rangle$ and $\langle 4, -1 \rangle$
15. $\langle -2, -3 \rangle$ and $\langle -3, 4 \rangle$
16. $\langle 6, 5 \rangle$ and $\langle 3, -2 \rangle$
17. $\langle -4, 6 \rangle$ and $\langle -6, 8 \rangle$
18. $\langle 1, 5 \rangle$ and $\langle -3, -2 \rangle$
19. $\langle -2, 2\sqrt{3} \rangle$ and $\langle -\sqrt{3}, 1 \rangle$
20. $\langle -3\sqrt{3}, -3 \rangle$ and $\langle -2\sqrt{3}, 2 \rangle$
21. $\langle -5\sqrt{3}, -5 \rangle$ and $\langle \sqrt{2}, -\sqrt{2} \rangle$
22. $\langle -5, -5\sqrt{3} \rangle$ and $\langle 2, -\sqrt{2} \rangle$
23. $\langle 4, 6 \rangle$ and $\langle -6, -9 \rangle$
24. $\langle 2, 8 \rangle$ and $\langle -12, 3 \rangle$

In Exercises 25–36, determine whether each pair of vectors is orthogonal.

25. $\langle -6, 8 \rangle$ and $\langle -8, 6 \rangle$
26. $\langle 5, -2 \rangle$ and $\langle -5, 2 \rangle$
27. $\langle 6, -4 \rangle$ and $\langle -6, -9 \rangle$
28. $\langle 8, 3 \rangle$ and $\langle -6, 16 \rangle$
29. $\langle 0.8, 4 \rangle$ and $\langle 3, -6 \rangle$
30. $\langle -7, 3 \rangle$ and $\langle \frac{1}{7}, -\frac{1}{3} \rangle$
31. $\langle 5, -0.4 \rangle$ and $\langle 1.6, 20 \rangle$
32. $\langle 12, 9 \rangle$ and $\langle 3, -4 \rangle$
33. $\langle \sqrt{3}, \sqrt{6} \rangle$ and $\langle -\sqrt{2}, 1 \rangle$
34. $\langle \sqrt{7}, -\sqrt{3} \rangle$ and $\langle 3, 7 \rangle$
35. $\langle \frac{4}{3}, \frac{8}{15} \rangle$ and $\langle -\frac{1}{12}, \frac{5}{24} \rangle$
36. $\langle \frac{5}{6}, \frac{6}{7} \rangle$ and $\langle \frac{36}{25}, -\frac{49}{36} \rangle$

• APPLICATIONS

37. **Lifting Weights.** How much work does it take to lift 100 pounds vertically 4 feet?

38. **Lifting Weights.** How much work does it take to lift 150 pounds vertically 3.5 feet?

39. **Raising Wrecks.** How much work is done by a crane to lift a 2-ton car to a level of 20 feet?

40. **Raising Wrecks.** How much work is done by a crane to lift a 2.5-ton car to a level of 25 feet?

41. **Work.** To slide a crate across the floor, a force of 50 pounds at a 30° angle is needed. How much work is done if the crate is dragged 30 feet?

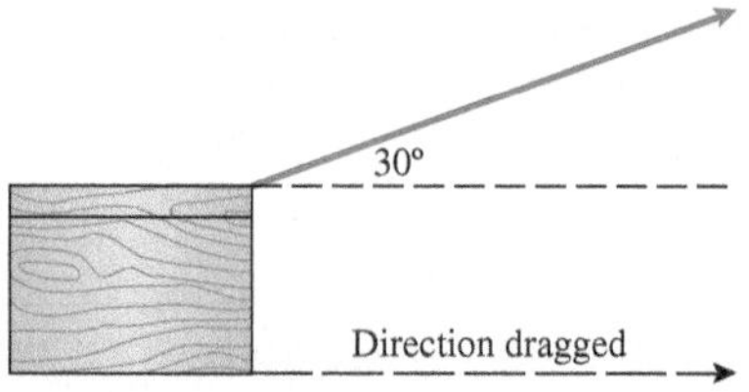

42. **Work.** To slide a crate across the floor, a force of 800 pounds at a 20° angle is needed. How much work is done if the crate is dragged 50 feet?

43. **Close a Door.** A sliding door is closed by pulling a cord with a constant force of 35 pounds at a constant angle of 45°. The door is moved 6 feet to close it. How much work is done?

44. **Close a Door.** A sliding door is closed by pulling a cord with a constant force of 45 pounds at a constant angle of 55°. The door is moved 6 feet to close it. How much work is done?

45. **Braking Power.** A car that weighs 2500 pounds is parked on a hill in San Francisco with a slant of 40° from the horizontal. How much force will keep it from rolling down the hill?

46. **Towing Power.** A car that weighs 2500 pounds is parked on a hill in San Francisco with a slant of 40° from the horizontal. A tow truck has to remove the car from its parking spot and move it 120 feet up the hill. How much work is required?

47. **Towing Power.** A semitrailer truck that weighs 40,000 pounds is parked on a hill in San Francisco with a slant of 10° from the horizontal. A tow truck has to remove the truck from its parking spot and move it 100 feet up the hill. How much work is required?

48. **Braking Power.** A truck that weighs 40,000 pounds is parked on a hill in San Francisco with a slant of 10° from the horizontal. How much force will keep it from rolling down the hill?

49. **Business.** Suppose that $\mathbf{u} = \langle 2000, 5000 \rangle$ represents the number of batteries A and B, respectively, produced by a company, and $\mathbf{v} = \langle 8.40, 6.50 \rangle$ represents the price (in dollars) of a 10-pack of battery A and a 10-pack of B, respectively. Compute and interpret $\mathbf{u} \cdot \mathbf{v}$.

50. **Demographics.** Suppose that $\mathbf{u} = \langle 120, 80 \rangle$ represents the number of males and females in a high school class, and $\mathbf{v} = \langle 7.2, 5.3 \rangle$ represents the average number of minutes it takes a male and a female, respectively, to register. Compute and interpret $\mathbf{u} \cdot \mathbf{v}$.

51. **Geometry.** Use vector methods to show that the diagonals of a rhombus are perpendicular to each other.

52. **Geometry.** Let $\mathbf{u}$ be a unit vector, and consider the following diagram:

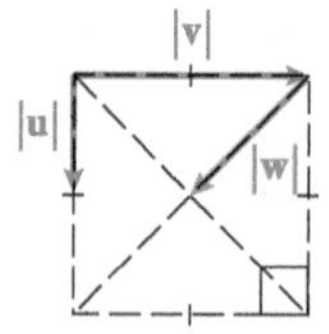

Compute $\mathbf{u} \cdot \mathbf{v}$ and $\mathbf{u} \cdot \mathbf{w}$.

53. **Geometry.** Consider the following diagram:

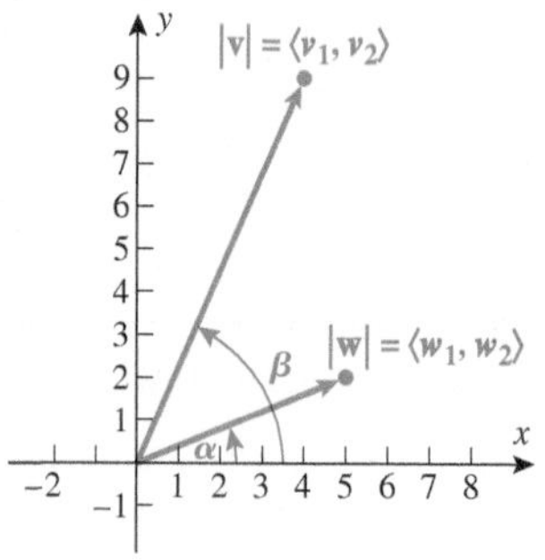

a. Compute $\cos\beta$, $\sin\beta$, $\cos\alpha$, and $\sin\alpha$.

b. Use (a) to show that $\cos(\alpha - \beta) = \dfrac{\mathbf{v} \cdot \mathbf{w}}{\sqrt{\mathbf{v} \cdot \mathbf{v}}\sqrt{\mathbf{w} \cdot \mathbf{w}}}$.

54. **Geometry.** Consider the diagram in Exercise 53.

a. Compute $\cos\beta$, $\sin\beta$, $\cos\alpha$, and $\sin\alpha$.

b. Use (a) to show that $\cos(\alpha + \beta) = \dfrac{\mathbf{v} \cdot \langle w_1, -w_2 \rangle}{\sqrt{\mathbf{v} \cdot \mathbf{v}}\sqrt{\mathbf{w} \cdot \mathbf{w}}}$.

55. **Optimization.** Let $\mathbf{u} = \langle a, b \rangle$ be a given vector, and suppose that the head of $\mathbf{n} = \langle n_1, n_2 \rangle$ lies on the circle $x^2 + y^2 = r^2$. Find the vector $\mathbf{n}$ such that $\mathbf{u} \cdot \mathbf{n}$ is as big as possible. Find the actual value of $\mathbf{u} \cdot \mathbf{n}$ in this case.

56. **Optimization.** Let $\mathbf{u} = \langle a, b \rangle$ be a given vector, and suppose that the head of $\mathbf{n} = \langle n_1, n_2 \rangle$ lies on the circle $x^2 + y^2 = r^2$. Find the vector $\mathbf{n}$ such that $\mathbf{u} \cdot \mathbf{n}$ is as small as possible. Find the actual value of $\mathbf{u} \cdot \mathbf{n}$ in this case.

57. **Pursuit Theory.** Assume that the head of $\mathbf{u}$ is restricted so that its tail is at the origin and its head is on the unit circle in quadrant II or quadrant III. A vector $\mathbf{v}$ has its tail at the origin, and its head must lie on the line $y = 2 - x$ in quadrant I. Find the least value of $\mathbf{u} \cdot \mathbf{v}$.

58. **Pursuit Theory.** Assume that the head of $\mathbf{u}$ is restricted so that its tail is at the origin and its head is on the unit circle in quadrant I or quadrant IV. A vector $\mathbf{v}$ has its tail at the origin, and its head must lie on the line $y = 2 - x$ in quadrant I. Find the largest value of $\mathbf{u} \cdot \mathbf{v}$.

• CATCH THE MISTAKE

In Exercises 59 and 60, explain the mistake that is made.

59. Find the dot product $\langle -3, 2\rangle \cdot \langle 2, 5\rangle$.

Solution:

Multiply component by component. $\langle -3, 2\rangle \cdot \langle 2, 5\rangle = \langle (-3)(2), (2)(5)\rangle$

Simplify. $\langle -3, 2\rangle \cdot \langle 2, 5\rangle = \langle -6, 10\rangle$

This is incorrect. What mistake was made?

60. Find the dot product $\langle 11, 12\rangle \cdot \langle -2, 3\rangle$.

Solution:

Multiply the outer and inner components.

$\langle 11, 12\rangle \cdot \langle -2, 3\rangle = (11)(3) + (12)(-2)$

Simplify. $\langle 11, 12\rangle \cdot \langle -2, 3\rangle = 9$

This is incorrect. What mistake was made?

• CONCEPTUAL

In Exercises 61–64, determine whether each statement is true or false.

61. A dot product of two vectors is a vector.

62. A dot product of two vectors is a scalar.

63. Orthogonal vectors have a dot product equal to zero.

64. If the dot product of two nonzero vectors is equal to zero, then the vectors must be perpendicular.

For Exercises 65 and 66, refer to the following to find the dot product:

The dot product of vectors with n components is

$\langle a_1, a_2, \ldots, a_n\rangle \cdot \langle b_1, b_2, \ldots, b_n\rangle = a_1b_1 + a_2b_2 + \cdots + a_nb_n.$

65. $\langle 3, 7, -5\rangle \cdot \langle -2, 4, 1\rangle$

66. $\langle 1, 0, -2, 3\rangle \cdot \langle 5, 2, 3, 1\rangle$

In Exercises 67–70, given $u = \langle a, b\rangle$ and $v = \langle c, d\rangle$, show that the following properties are true:

67. $\mathbf{u} \cdot \mathbf{v} = \mathbf{v} \cdot \mathbf{u}$

68. $\mathbf{u} \cdot \mathbf{u} = |\mathbf{u}|^2$

69. $\mathbf{0} \cdot \mathbf{u} = 0$

70. $k(\mathbf{u} \cdot \mathbf{v}) = (k\mathbf{u}) \cdot \mathbf{v} = \mathbf{u} \cdot (k\mathbf{v})$, k is a scalar

• CHALLENGE

71. Show that $\mathbf{u} \cdot (\mathbf{v} + \mathbf{w}) = \mathbf{u} \cdot \mathbf{v} + \mathbf{u} \cdot \mathbf{w}$.

72. Show that $|\mathbf{u} - \mathbf{v}|^2 = |\mathbf{u}|^2 + |\mathbf{v}|^2 - 2(\mathbf{u} \cdot \mathbf{v})$.

73. The *projection of* **v** *onto* **u** is defined by $\text{proj}_{\mathbf{u}}\mathbf{v} = \left(\dfrac{\mathbf{u} \cdot \mathbf{v}}{|\mathbf{u}|^2}\right)\mathbf{u}$.

This vector is depicted below. Heuristically, this is the "shadow" of **v** on **u**.

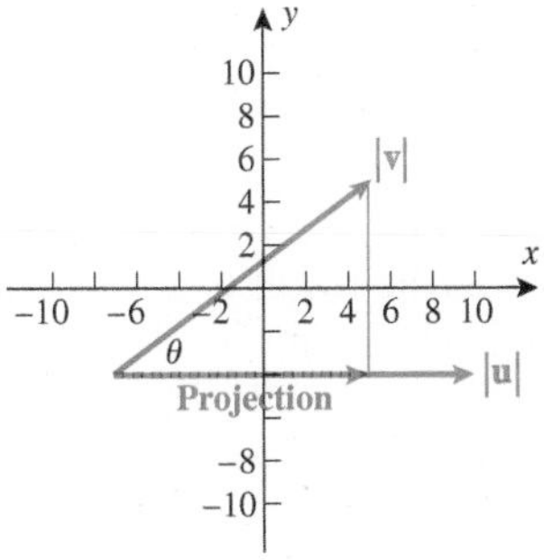

a. Compute $\text{proj}_{\mathbf{u}}2\mathbf{u}$.

b. What is $\text{proj}_{\mathbf{u}}c\mathbf{u}$ for any $c > 0$?

74. a. Compute $\text{proj}_{\mathbf{u}}2\mathbf{u}$.

b. What is $\text{proj}_{\mathbf{u}}c\mathbf{u}$ for any $c > 0$?

75. Suppose that you are given a vector **u**. For what vectors **v** does $\text{proj}_{\mathbf{u}}\mathbf{v} = \mathbf{0}$?

76. True or false: $\text{proj}_{\mathbf{u}}(\mathbf{v} + \mathbf{w}) = \text{proj}_{\mathbf{u}}\mathbf{v} + \text{proj}_{\mathbf{u}}\mathbf{w}$.

77. If **u** and **v** are unit vectors, determine the maximum and minimum value of $(-2\mathbf{u}) \cdot (3\mathbf{v})$.

78. Assume that the angle between **u** and **v** is $\theta = \dfrac{\pi}{3}$. Show that

$$\frac{(\mathbf{u} \cdot \mathbf{v})\mathbf{u}}{|\mathbf{v}|} - \frac{(\mathbf{v} \cdot \mathbf{u})\mathbf{v}}{|\mathbf{u}|} = \frac{|\mathbf{u}|\mathbf{u} - |\mathbf{v}|\mathbf{v}}{2}.$$

• PREVIEW TO CALCULUS

There is a branch of calculus devoted to the study of vector-valued functions; these are functions that map real numbers onto vectors. For example, $\mathbf{v}(t) = \langle t, 2t \rangle$.

79. Calculate the dot product of the vector-valued functions $\mathbf{u}(t) = \langle 2t, t^2 \rangle$ and $\mathbf{v}(t) = \langle t, -3t \rangle$.

80. Calculate the dot product of the vector-valued functions $\mathbf{u}(t) = \langle \cos t, \sin t \rangle$ and $\mathbf{v}(t) = \langle \cos t, -\sin t \rangle$.

81. Find the angle between the vector-valued functions $\mathbf{u}(t) = \langle \sin t, \cos t \rangle$ and $\mathbf{v}(t) = \langle \csc t, -\cos t \rangle$ when $t = \frac{\pi}{6}$.

82. Find the values of t that make the vector-valued functions $\mathbf{u}(t) = \langle \sin t, \sin t \rangle$ and $\mathbf{v}(t) = \langle \cos t, -\sin t \rangle$ orthogonal.

7.3 POLAR (TRIGONOMETRIC) FORM OF COMPLEX NUMBERS

SKILLS OBJECTIVES

- Calculate the modulus of a complex number.
- Convert complex numbers from rectangular form to polar form, and vice versa.

CONCEPTUAL OBJECTIVES

- Understand that the modulus, or magnitude, of a complex number is the distance from the origin to the point in the complex plane.
- Understand that imaginary numbers lie along the vertical axis and real numbers lie along the horizontal axis of the complex plane.

7.3.1 Complex Numbers in Rectangular Form

7.3.1 SKILL

Calculate the modulus of a complex number.

7.3.1 CONCEPTUAL

Understand that the modulus, or magnitude, of a complex number is the distance from the origin to the point in the complex plane.

We are already familiar with the **rectangular coordinate system**, where the horizontal axis is called the x-axis and the vertical axis is called the y-axis. In our study of complex numbers, we refer to the **standard (rectangular) form** as $a + bi$, where a represents the real part and b represents the imaginary part. If we let the horizontal axis be the **real axis** and the vertical axis be the **imaginary axis**, the result is the **complex plane**. The point $a + bi$ is located in the complex plane by finding the coordinates (a, b).

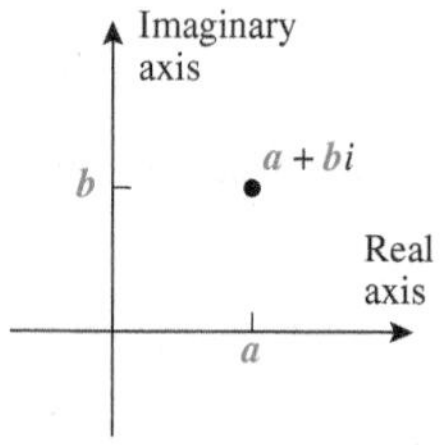

When $b = 0$, the result is a real number, and therefore any numbers along the horizontal axis are real numbers. When $a = 0$, the result is an imaginary number, so any numbers along the vertical axis are imaginary numbers.

The variable z is often used to represent a complex number: $z = x + iy$. Complex numbers are analogous to vectors. Suppose we define a vector $\mathbf{z} = \langle x, y \rangle$, whose initial point is the origin and whose terminal point is (x, y); then the magnitude of that vector is $|\mathbf{z}| = \sqrt{x^2 + y^2}$. Similarly, the magnitude, or *modulus*, of a complex number is defined like the magnitude of a position vector in the xy-plane, as the distance from the origin $(0, 0)$ to the point (x, y) in the complex plane.

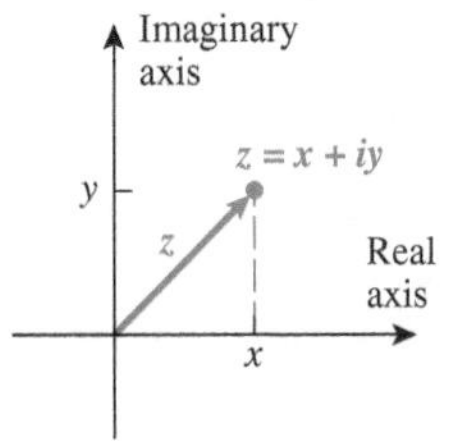

DEFINITION **Modulus of a Complex Number**

The **modulus**, or magnitude, of a complex number $z = x + iy$ is the distance from the origin to the point (x, y) in the complex plane, which is given by

$$|z| = \sqrt{x^2 + y^2}$$

Recall that a complex number $z = x + iy$ has a complex conjugate $\bar{z} = x - iy$. The bar above a complex number denotes its conjugate. Notice that

$$z\bar{z} = (x + iy)(x - iy) = x^2 - i^2y^2 = x^2 + y^2$$

and therefore the modulus can also be written as

$$\boxed{|z| = \sqrt{z\bar{z}}}$$

EXAMPLE 1 **Finding the Modulus of a Complex Number**

Find the modulus of $z = -3 + 2i$.

common mistake

Including the i in the imaginary part.

✓CORRECT

Let $x = -3$ and $y = 2$ in $|z| = \sqrt{x^2 + y^2}$.

$$|-3 + 2i| = \sqrt{(-3)^2 + 2^2}$$

Eliminate the parentheses.

$$|-3 + 2i| = \sqrt{9 + 4}$$

Simplify.

$$\boxed{|z| = |-3 + 2i| = \sqrt{13}}$$

✗INCORRECT

Let $x = -3$ and $y = 2i$ **ERROR**

$$|-3 + 2i| = \sqrt{(-3)^2 + (2i)^2}$$

The i is not included in the formula. Only the imaginary part (the coefficient of i) is used.

YOUR TURN Find the modulus of $z = 2 - 5i$.

[CONCEPT CHECK]

TRUE OR FALSE The modulus of a complex number is greater than or equal to the sum of the real part and the imaginary part of the complex number.

ANSWER False

ANSWER

$|z| = |2 - 5i| = \sqrt{29}$

7.3.2 Complex Numbers in Polar Form

7.3.2 SKILL

Convert complex numbers from rectangular form to polar form, and vice versa.

7.3.2 CONCEPTUAL

Understand that imaginary numbers lie along the vertical axis and real numbers lie along the horizontal axis of the complex plane.

We say that a complex number $z = x + iy$ is in *rectangular* form because it is located at the point (x, y), which is expressed in rectangular coordinates, in the complex plane. Another convenient way of expressing complex numbers is in *polar* form. Recall from our study of vectors (Section 7.1) that vectors have both magnitude and a direction angle. The same is true of numbers in the complex plane. Let r represent the magnitude, or distance from the origin to the point (x, y), and let θ represent the direction angle; then we have the following relationships:

$$r = \sqrt{x^2 + y^2}$$

$$\sin\theta = \frac{y}{r} \qquad \cos\theta = \frac{x}{r} \qquad \text{and} \qquad \tan\theta = \frac{y}{x} \quad (x \neq 0)$$

Isolating x and y in the sinusoidal functions, we find

$$x = r\cos\theta \qquad y = r\sin\theta$$

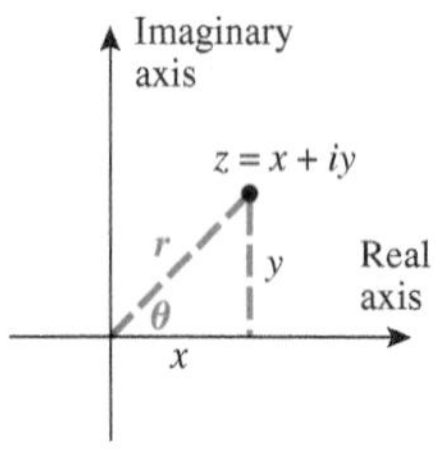

When we use these expressions for x and y, a complex number can be written in *polar* form.

$$z = x + yi = (r\cos\theta) + (r\sin\theta)i = r(\cos\theta + i\sin\theta)$$

POLAR (TRIGONOMETRIC) FORM OF COMPLEX NUMBERS

The following expression is the **polar form** of a complex number:

$$z = r(\cos\theta + i\sin\theta)$$

where r represents the **modulus** (magnitude) of the complex number and θ represents the **argument** of z.

The following is standard notation for modulus and argument:

$$r = \text{mod}\,z = |z| \quad \text{and} \quad \theta = \text{Arg}\,z, \quad 0 \leq \theta < 2\pi \quad \text{or} \quad 0° \leq \theta < 360°$$

[CONCEPT CHECK]

TRUE OR FALSE In the complex plane, a real number or purely imaginary complex number lies along one of the axes, and all other complex numbers lie in one of the four quadrants.

ANSWER True

Converting Complex Numbers between Rectangular and Polar Forms

We can convert back and forth between rectangular and polar (trigonometric) forms of complex numbers using the modulus and trigonometric ratios.

$$r = \sqrt{x^2 + y^2} \qquad \sin\theta = \frac{y}{r} \qquad \cos\theta = \frac{x}{r} \qquad \text{and} \qquad \tan\theta = \frac{y}{x} \quad (x \neq 0)$$

CONVERTING COMPLEX NUMBERS FROM RECTANGULAR FORM TO POLAR FORM

Step 1: Plot the point $z = x + iy$ in the complex plane (note the quadrant).

Step 2: Find r. Use $r = \sqrt{x^2 + y^2}$.

Step 3: Find θ. Apply $\tan\theta = \frac{y}{x}$, $x \neq 0$, where θ is in the quadrant found in Step 1.

Step 4: Write the complex number in polar form: $z = r(\cos\theta + i\sin\theta)$.

Notice that imaginary numbers, $z = bi$, lie on the imaginary axis. Therefore, $\theta = 90°$ if $b > 0$ and $\theta = 270°$ if $b < 0$.

EXAMPLE 2 **Converting from Rectangular to Polar Form**

Express the complex number $z = \sqrt{3} - i$ in polar form.

Solution:

STEP 1 Plot the point.

The point lies in quadrant IV.

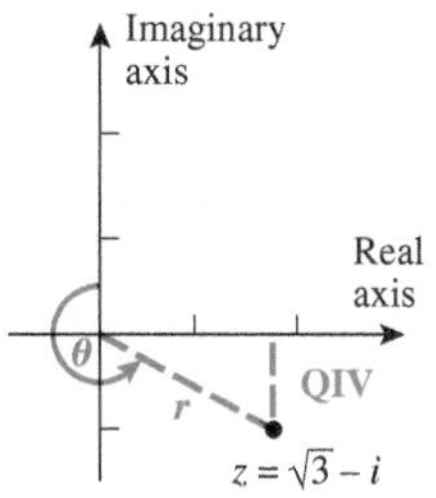

STEP 2 Find r.

Let $x = \sqrt{3}$ and $y = -1$ in $r = \sqrt{x^2 + y^2}$. $\quad r = \sqrt{(\sqrt{3})^2 + (-1)^2}$

Eliminate the parentheses. $\quad r = \sqrt{3 + 1}$

Simplify. $\quad \boxed{r = 2}$

STEP 3 Find θ.

Let $x = \sqrt{3}$ and $y = -1$ in $\tan\theta = \frac{y}{x}$. $\quad \tan\theta = -\frac{1}{\sqrt{3}}$

Solve for θ. $\quad \theta = \tan^{-1}\left(-\frac{1}{\sqrt{3}}\right) = -\frac{\pi}{6}$

Find the reference angle. $\quad \text{reference angle} = \frac{\pi}{6}$

The complex number lies in quadrant IV. $\quad \boxed{\theta = \frac{11\pi}{6}}$

STEP 4 Write the complex number in polar form. $z = r(\cos\theta + i\sin\theta)$ $\quad \boxed{z = 2\left[\cos\left(\frac{11\pi}{6}\right) + i\sin\left(\frac{11\pi}{6}\right)\right]}$

Note: An alternative form is in degrees: $z = 2(\cos 330° + i\sin 330°)$.

YOUR TURN Express the complex number $z = 1 - i\sqrt{3}$ in polar form.

ANSWER

$z = 2\left[\cos\left(\frac{5\pi}{3}\right) + i\sin\left(\frac{5\pi}{3}\right)\right]$ or $2(\cos 300° + i\sin 300°)$

You must be very careful in converting from rectangular to polar form. Remember that the inverse tangent function is a one-to-one function and will yield values in quadrants I and IV. If the point lies in quadrant II or III, add 180° to the angle found through the inverse tangent function.

EXAMPLE 3 Converting from Rectangular to Polar Form

common mistake

Forgetting to confirm the quadrant, which results in using the reference angle instead of the actual angle.

Express the complex number $z = -2 + i$ in polar form.

✓CORRECT

Step 1: Plot the point.

The point lies in **quadrant II**.

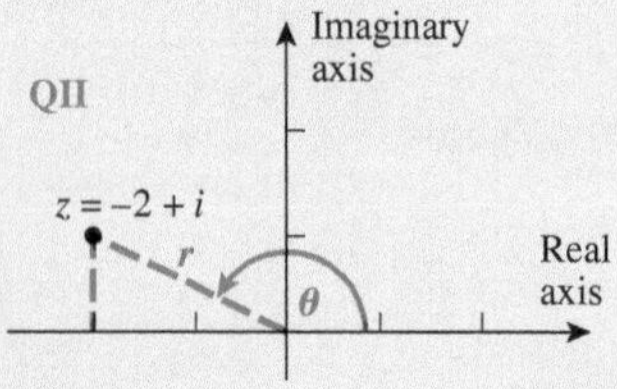

Step 2: Find r.

Let $x = -2$ and $y = 1$ in.

$r = \sqrt{x^2 + y^2}$.

$$r = \sqrt{(-2)^2 + 1^2}$$

Simplify.

$$\boxed{r = \sqrt{5}}$$

Step 3: Find θ.

Let $x = -2$ and $y = 1$ in.

$$\tan\theta = \frac{y}{x}.$$

$$\tan\theta = -\frac{1}{2}$$

$$\theta = \tan^{-1}\left(-\frac{1}{2}\right)$$

$$= -26.565°$$

The complex number lies in quadrant II.

$$\boxed{\theta = -26.6° + 180° = 153.4°}$$

Step 4: Write the complex number in polar form: $z = r(\cos\theta + i\sin\theta)$.

$$\boxed{z = \sqrt{5}(\cos 153.4° + i\sin 153.4°)}$$

✗INCORRECT

Evaluate the inverse function with a calculator.

$$\theta = \tan^{-1}\left(-\frac{1}{2}\right) = -26.565°$$

Write the complex number in polar form.

$z = r(\cos\theta + i\sin\theta)$

$z = \sqrt{5}[\cos(-26.6°) + i\sin(-26.6°)]$

Note: $\theta = -26.565°$ lies in quadrant IV, whereas the original point lies in quadrant II. Therefore, we should have added 180° to θ in order to arrive at a point in quadrant II.

YOUR TURN Express the complex number $z = -1 + 2i$ in polar form.

ANSWER

$z = \sqrt{5}(\cos 116.6° + i\sin 116.6°)$

To convert from polar to rectangular form, simply evaluate the trigonometric functions.

EXAMPLE 4 Converting from Polar to Rectangular Form

Express $z = 4(\cos 120° + i \sin 120°)$ in rectangular form.

Solution:

Evaluate the trigonometric functions exactly. $z = 4\left(\underbrace{\cos 120°}_{-\frac{1}{2}} + i \underbrace{\sin 120°}_{\frac{\sqrt{3}}{2}}\right)$

Distribute the 4. $z = 4\left(-\frac{1}{2}\right) + 4\left(\frac{\sqrt{3}}{2}\right)i$

Simplify. $\boxed{z = -2 + 2\sqrt{3}i}$

YOUR TURN Express $z = 2(\cos 210° + i \sin 210°)$ in rectangular form.

ANSWER

$z = -\sqrt{3} - i$

EXAMPLE 5 Using a Calculator to Convert from Polar to Rectangular Form

Express $z = 3(\cos 109° + i \sin 109°)$ in rectangular form. Round to four decimal places.

Solution:

Use a calculator to evaluate the trigonometric functions. $z = 3\left(\underbrace{\cos 109°}_{-0.325568} + i \underbrace{\sin 109°}_{0.945519}\right)$

Simplify. $\boxed{z = -0.9767 + 2.8366i}$

YOUR TURN Express $z = 7(\cos 217° + i \sin 217°)$ in rectangular form. Round to four decimal places.

ANSWER

$z = -5.5904 - 4.2127i$

[SECTION 7.3] SUMMARY

In the complex plane, the horizontal axis is the real axis and the vertical axis is the imaginary axis. We can express complex numbers in either rectangular or polar form.

rectangular form: $z = x + iy$

or

polar form: $z = r(\cos\theta + i \sin\theta)$

The modulus of a complex number, $z = x + iy$, is given by

$$|z| = \sqrt{x^2 + y^2}$$

To convert from rectangular to polar form, we use the relationships

$$r = \sqrt{x^2 + y^2} \quad \text{and} \quad \tan\theta = \frac{y}{x},\ x \neq 0 \text{ and } 0 \leq \theta < 2\pi$$

It is important to note in which quadrant the point lies. To convert from polar to rectangular form, simply evaluate the trigonometric functions.

$$x = r\cos\theta \quad \text{and} \quad y = r\sin\theta$$

[SECTION 7.3] EXERCISES

• SKILLS

In Exercises 1–8, graph each complex number in the complex plane.

1. $7 + 8i$ **2.** $3 + 5i$ **3.** $-2 - 4i$ **4.** $-3 - 2i$

5. 2 **6.** 7 **7.** $-3i$ **8.** $-5i$

In Exercises 9–24, express each complex number in polar form.

9. $1 - i$ **10.** $2 + 2i$ **11.** $1 + \sqrt{3}i$ **12.** $-3 - \sqrt{3}i$

13. $-4 + 4i$ **14.** $\sqrt{5} - \sqrt{5}i$ **15.** $\sqrt{3} - 3i$ **16.** $-\sqrt{3} + i$

17. $3 + 0i$ **18.** $-2 + 0i$ **19.** $-\frac{1}{2} - \frac{1}{2}i$ **20.** $\frac{1}{6} - \frac{1}{6}i$

21. $-\sqrt{6} - \sqrt{6}i$ **22.** $\frac{1}{3} - \frac{1}{3}i$ **23.** $-5 + 5i$ **24.** $3 + 3i$

In Exercises 25–40, use a calculator to express each complex number in polar form.

25. $3 - 7i$ **26.** $2 + 3i$ **27.** $-6 + 5i$ **28.** $-4 - 3i$

29. $-5 + 12i$ **30.** $24 + 7i$ **31.** $8 - 6i$ **32.** $-3 + 4i$

33. $-\frac{1}{2} + \frac{3}{4}i$ **34.** $-\frac{5}{8} - \frac{11}{4}i$ **35.** $5.1 + 2.3i$ **36.** $1.8 - 0.9i$

37. $-2\sqrt{3} - \sqrt{5}i$ **38.** $-\frac{4\sqrt{5}}{3} + \frac{\sqrt{5}}{2}i$ **39.** $4.02 - 2.11i$ **40.** $1.78 - 0.12i$

In Exercises 41–52, express each complex number in rectangular form.

41. $5(\cos 180° + i\sin 180°)$ **42.** $2(\cos 135° + i\sin 135°)$ **43.** $2(\cos 315° + i\sin 315°)$

44. $3(\cos 270° + i\sin 270°)$ **45.** $-4(\cos 60° + i\sin 60°)$ **46.** $-4(\cos 210° + i\sin 210°)$

47. $\sqrt{3}(\cos 150° + i\sin 150°)$ **48.** $\sqrt{3}(\cos 330° + i\sin 330°)$ **49.** $\sqrt{2}\left[\cos\left(\frac{\pi}{4}\right) + i\sin\left(\frac{\pi}{4}\right)\right]$

50. $2\left[\cos\left(\frac{5\pi}{6}\right) + i\sin\left(\frac{5\pi}{6}\right)\right]$ **51.** $6\left[\cos\left(\frac{3\pi}{4}\right) + i\sin\left(\frac{3\pi}{4}\right)\right]$ **52.** $4\left[\cos\left(\frac{11\pi}{6}\right) + i\sin\left(\frac{11\pi}{6}\right)\right]$

In Exercises 53–64, use a calculator to express each complex number in rectangular form.

53. $5(\cos 295° + i\sin 295°)$ **54.** $4(\cos 35° + i\sin 35°)$ **55.** $3(\cos 100° + i\sin 100°)$

56. $6(\cos 250° + i\sin 250°)$ **57.** $-7(\cos 140° + i\sin 140°)$ **58.** $-5(\cos 320° + i\sin 320°)$

59. $3\left[\cos\left(\frac{11\pi}{12}\right) + i\sin\left(\frac{11\pi}{12}\right)\right]$ **60.** $2\left[\cos\left(\frac{4\pi}{7}\right) + i\sin\left(\frac{4\pi}{7}\right)\right]$ **61.** $-2\left[\cos\left(\frac{3\pi}{5}\right) + i\sin\left(\frac{3\pi}{5}\right)\right]$

62. $-4\left[\cos\left(\frac{15\pi}{11}\right) + i\sin\left(\frac{15\pi}{11}\right)\right]$ **63.** $-5\left[\cos\left(\frac{4\pi}{9}\right) + i\sin\left(\frac{4\pi}{9}\right)\right]$ **64.** $6\left[\cos\left(\frac{13\pi}{8}\right) + i\sin\left(\frac{13\pi}{8}\right)\right]$

• APPLICATIONS

65. Road Construction. Engineers are planning the construction of a bypass in a north–south highway to connect cities *B* and *C*.

a. What is the distance from *A* to *C*?

b. Write the vector *AC* as a complex number in polar form. (Use degrees for the angle.)

c. What is the angle *BAC*?

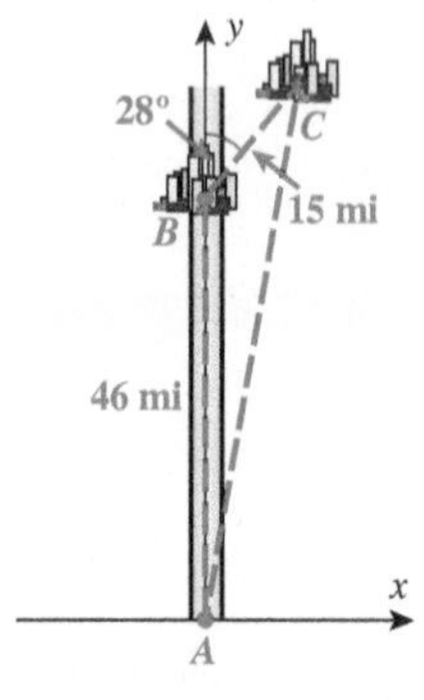

66. Road Construction. Engineers are planning the construction of a bypass in a north–south highway to connect cities *B* and *C*.

a. What is the distance from *A* to *C*?

b. Write the vector *AC* as a complex number in polar form. (Use degrees for the angle.)

c. What is the angle *BAC*?

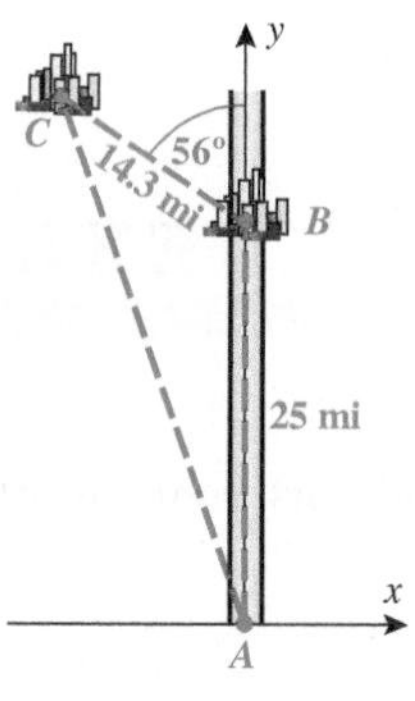

67. City Map Barcelona. The city of Barcelona is crossed by Diagonal Avenue as shown in the map.

a. Which complex numbers, in rectangular form, represent the street segments $\overline{AB}$, $\overline{BC}$, and $\overline{CD}$?

b. Which complex number, in polar form, represents $\overline{AD}$?

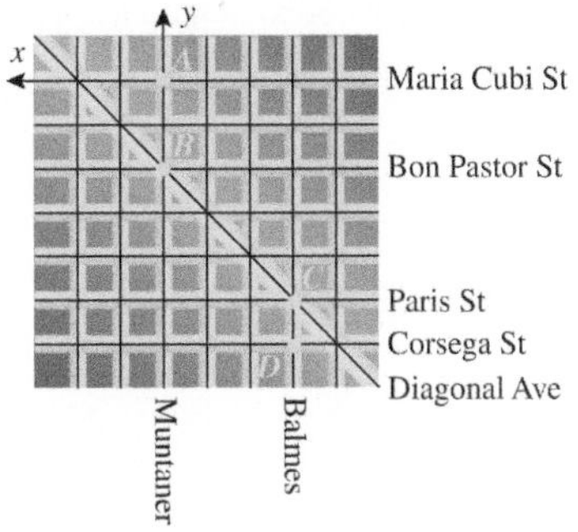

68. City Map Washington, D.C. A simplified map of Washington, D.C., is shown below.

a. Which complex numbers, in rectangular form, represent the street segments $\overline{AB}$, $\overline{BC}$, and $\overline{CD}$?

b. Which complex number, in polar form, represents $\overline{AD}$?

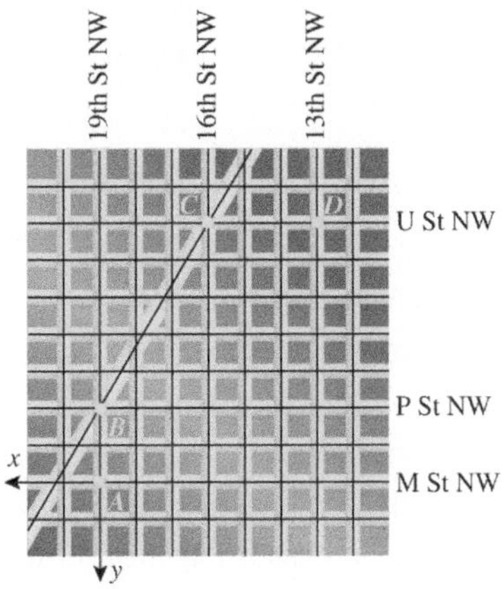

For Exercises 69 and 70, refer to the following:

In the design of AC circuits, the voltage across a resistance is regarded as a real number. When the voltage goes across an inductor or a capacitor, it is considered an imaginary number: positive ($I > 0$) in the inductor case and negative ($I < 0$) in the capacitor case. The impedance results from the combination of the voltages in the circuit and is given by the formula

$$z = |z|(\cos\theta + i\sin\theta), \text{ where } |z| = \sqrt{R^2 + I^2}$$

$$\text{and } \theta = \tan^{-1}\left(\frac{I}{R}\right)$$

where z is impedance, R is resistance, and I is inductance.

69. AC Circuits. Find the impedance of a circuit with resistance 4 ohms and inductor of 6 ohms. Write your answer in polar form.

70. AC Circuits. Find the impedance of a circuit with resistance 7 ohms and capacitor of 5 ohms. Write your answer in polar form.

• CATCH THE MISTAKE

In Exercises 71 and 72, explain the mistake that is made.

71. Express $z = -3 - 8i$ in polar form.

Solution:

Find r. $\quad r = \sqrt{x^2 + y^2} = \sqrt{9 + 64} = \sqrt{73}$

Find θ. $\quad \tan\theta = \frac{8}{3}$

$$\theta = \tan^{-1}\left(\frac{8}{3}\right) = 69.44^\circ$$

Write the complex number in polar form.

$$z = \sqrt{73}(\cos 69.44^\circ + i\sin 69.44^\circ)$$

This is incorrect. What mistake was made?

72. Express $z = -3 + 8i$ in polar form.

Solution:

Find r. $\quad r = \sqrt{x^2 + y^2} = \sqrt{9 + 64} = \sqrt{73}$

Find θ. $\quad \tan\theta = -\frac{8}{3}$

$$\theta = \tan^{-1}\left(-\frac{8}{3}\right) = -69.44^\circ$$

Write the complex number in polar form.

$$z = \sqrt{73}[\cos(-69.44^\circ) + i\sin(-69.44^\circ)]$$

This is incorrect. What mistake was made?

• CONCEPTUAL

In Exercises 73–76, determine whether each statement is true or false.

73. In the complex plane, any point that lies along the horizontal axis is a real number.

74. In the complex plane, any point that lies along the vertical axis is an imaginary number.

75. The modulus of z and the modulus of $\bar{z}$ are equal.

76. The argument of z and the argument of $\bar{z}$ are equal.

77. Find the argument of $z = a$, where a is a positive real number.

78. Find the argument of $z = bi$, where b is a positive real number.

79. Find the modulus of $z = bi$, where b is a negative real number.

80. Find the modulus of $z = a$, where a is a negative real number.

In Exercises 81 and 82, use a calculator to express the complex number in polar form.

81. $a - 2ai$, where $a > 0$

82. $-3a - 4ai$, where $a > 0$

• CHALLENGE

83. Suppose that a complex number z lies on the circle $x^2 + y^2 = \pi^2$. If $\cos\left(\frac{\theta}{2}\right) = \frac{1}{2}$ and $\sin\theta < 0$, find the rectangular form of z.

84. Suppose that a complex number z lies on the circle $x^2 + y^2 = 8$. If $\sin\left(\frac{\theta}{2}\right) = -\frac{\sqrt{3}}{2}$ and $\cos\theta < 0$, find the rectangular form of z.

85. Consider the following diagram:

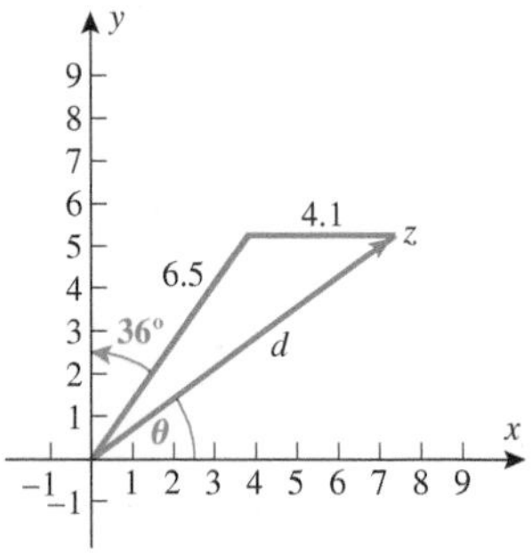

Find z in trigonometric form.

Hint: Use the Law of Cosines.

86. Consider the following diagram:

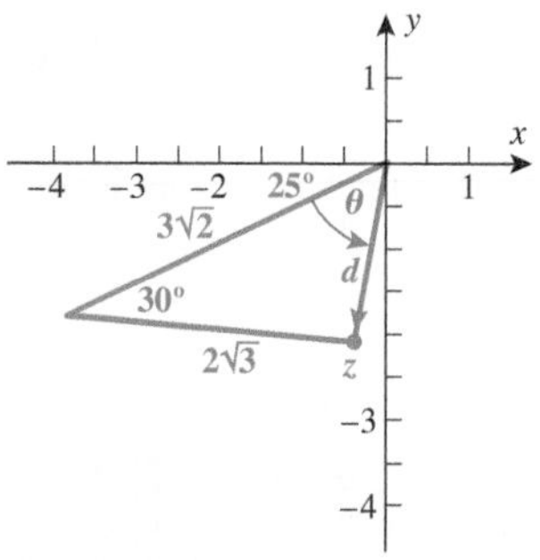

Find z in trigonometric form.

Hint: Use the Law of Cosines.

87. Consider the complex number in polar form $z = r(\cos\theta + i\sin\theta)$. What is the polar form of $-z$?

88. Consider the complex number in polar form $z = r(\cos\theta + i\sin\theta)$. What is the polar form of $\bar{z}$?

• PREVIEW TO CALCULUS

In Exercises 89–92, refer to the following:

The use of a different system of coordinates simplifies many mathematical expressions, and some calculations are performed in an easier way. The rectangular coordinates (x, y) are transformed into polar coordinates by the equations

$$x = r\cos\theta \quad \text{and} \quad y = r\sin\theta$$

where $r = \sqrt{x^2 + y^2}$ $(r \neq 0)$ and $\tan\theta = \frac{y}{x}$ $(x \neq 0)$. In polar coordinates, the equation of the unit circle $x^2 + y^2 = 1$ is just $r = 1$. In calculus, we use polar coordinates extensively. Transform the rectangular equation to polar form.

89. $x^2 + y^2 = 25$

90. $x^2 + y^2 = 4x$

91. $y^2 - 2y = -x^2$

92. $(x^2 + y^2)^2 - 16(x^2 - y^2) = 0$

7.4 PRODUCTS, QUOTIENTS, POWERS, AND ROOTS OF COMPLEX NUMBERS

SKILLS OBJECTIVES

- Find the product of two complex numbers.
- Find the quotient of two complex numbers.
- Raise a complex number to an integer power.
- Find the nth root of a complex number.

CONCEPTUAL OBJECTIVES

- Understand that when two complex numbers are multiplied, the magnitudes are multiplied and the arguments are added.
- Understand that when two complex numbers are divided, the magnitudes are divided and the arguments are subtracted.
- Understand that when a complex number is raised to an integer power n, the magnitude is raised to the power and the argument is multiplied by n.
- Understand that a polynomial equation can often be solved by finding complex roots.

7.4.1 SKILL

Find the product of two complex numbers.

7.4.1 CONCEPTUAL

Understand that when two complex numbers are multiplied, the magnitudes are multiplied and the arguments are added.

In this section, we will multiply complex numbers, divide complex numbers, raise complex numbers to powers, and find roots of complex numbers.

7.4.1 Products of Complex Numbers

First, we will derive a formula for the product of two complex numbers.

WORDS	MATH
Start with two complex numbers z_1 and z_2.	$z_1 = r_1(\cos\theta_1 + i\sin\theta_1)$ and $z_2 = r_2(\cos\theta_2 + i\sin\theta_2)$
Multiply z_1 and z_2.	$z_1z_2 = r_1r_2(\cos\theta_1 + i\sin\theta_1)(\cos\theta_2 + i\sin\theta_2)$
Use the FOIL method to multiply the expressions in parentheses.	$z_1z_2 = r_1r_2(\cos\theta_1\cos\theta_2 + i\cos\theta_1\sin\theta_2 + i\sin\theta_1\cos\theta_2 + \underbrace{i^2}_{-1}\sin\theta_1\sin\theta_2)$
Group the real parts and the imaginary parts.	$z_1z_2 = r_1r_2[(\cos\theta_1\cos\theta_2 - \sin\theta_1\sin\theta_2) + i(\cos\theta_1\sin\theta_2 + \sin\theta_1\cos\theta_2)]$
Apply the cosine and sine sum identities.	$z_1z_2 = r_1r_2\left[\underbrace{(\cos\theta_1\cos\theta_2 - \sin\theta_1\sin\theta_2)}_{\cos(\theta_1+\theta_2)} + i\underbrace{(\cos\theta_1\sin\theta_2 + \sin\theta_1\cos\theta_2)}_{\sin(\theta_1+\theta_2)}\right]$
Simplify.	$z_1z_2 = r_1r_2[\cos(\theta_1 + \theta_2) + i\sin(\theta_1 + \theta_2)]$

PRODUCT OF TWO COMPLEX NUMBERS

Let $z_1 = r_1(\cos\theta_1 + i\sin\theta_1)$ and $z_2 = r_2(\cos\theta_2 + i\sin\theta_2)$ be two complex numbers. The complex product z_1z_2 is given by

$$z_1z_2 = r_1r_2[\cos(\theta_1 + \theta_2) + i\sin(\theta_1 + \theta_2)]$$

In other words, *when multiplying two complex numbers, multiply the magnitudes and add the arguments.*

STUDY TIP

When two complex numbers are multiplied, the magnitudes are multiplied and the arguments are added.

[CONCEPT CHECK]

TRUE OR FALSE When two complex numbers are multiplied, their magnitudes and arguments are multiplied, respectively.

ANSWER False

EXAMPLE 1 Multiplying Complex Numbers

Find the product of $z_1 = 3(\cos 35° + i\sin 35°)$ and $z_2 = 2(\cos 10° + i\sin 10°)$.

Solution:

Set up the product. $z_1z_2 = 3(\cos 35° + i\sin 35°)\cdot 2(\cos 10° + i\sin 10°)$

Multiply the magnitudes and add the arguments. $z_1z_2 = 3\cdot 2[\cos(35° + 10°) + i\sin(35° + 10°)]$

Simplify. $z_1z_2 = 6(\cos 45° + i\sin 45°)$

The product is in polar form. To express the product in rectangular form, evaluate the trigonometric functions. $z_1z_2 = 6\left(\frac{\sqrt{2}}{2} + i\frac{\sqrt{2}}{2}\right) = 3\sqrt{2} + 3i\sqrt{2}$

Product in polar form: $\boxed{z_1z_2 = 6(\cos 45° + i\sin 45°)} = 6\left[\cos\left(\frac{\pi}{4}\right) + i\sin\left(\frac{\pi}{4}\right)\right]$

Product in rectangular form: $\boxed{z_1z_2 = 3\sqrt{2} + 3i\sqrt{2}}$

YOUR TURN Find the product of $z_1 = 2(\cos 55° + i\sin 55°)$ and $z_2 = 5(\cos 65° + i\sin 65°)$. Express the answer in both polar and rectangular form.

ANSWER
$z_1z_2 = 10(\cos 120° + i\sin 120°)$ or
$z_1z_2 = -5 + 5i\sqrt{3}$

7.4.2 SKILL

Find the quotient of two complex numbers.

7.4.2 CONCEPTUAL

Understand that when two complex numbers are divided, the magnitudes are divided and the arguments are subtracted.

7.4.2 Quotients of Complex Numbers

We now derive a formula for the quotient of two complex numbers.

WORDS	MATH
Start with two complex numbers z_1 and z_2.	$z_1 = r_1(\cos\theta_1 + i\sin\theta_1)$ and $z_2 = r_2(\cos\theta_2 + i\sin\theta_2)$
Divide z_1 by z_2.	$\frac{z_1}{z_2} = \frac{r_1(\cos\theta_1 + i\sin\theta_1)}{r_2(\cos\theta_2 + i\sin\theta_2)} = \left(\frac{r_1}{r_2}\right)\left(\frac{\cos\theta_1 + i\sin\theta_1}{\cos\theta_2 + i\sin\theta_2}\right)$
Multiply the numerator and the denominator of the second expression in parentheses by the conjugate of the denominator, $\cos\theta_2 - i\sin\theta_2$.	$\frac{z_1}{z_2} = \left(\frac{r_1}{r_2}\right)\left(\frac{\cos\theta_1 + i\sin\theta_1}{\cos\theta_2 + i\sin\theta_2}\right)\left(\frac{\cos\theta_2 - i\sin\theta_2}{\cos\theta_2 - i\sin\theta_2}\right)$
Use the FOIL method to multiply the expressions in parentheses in the last two expressions.	$\frac{z_1}{z_2} = \left(\frac{r_1}{r_2}\right)\left(\frac{\cos\theta_1\cos\theta_2 - i^2\sin\theta_1\sin\theta_2 + i\sin\theta_1\cos\theta_2 - i\sin\theta_2\cos\theta_1}{\cos^2\theta_2 - i^2\sin^2\theta_2}\right)$
Substitute $i^2 = -1$ and group the real parts and the imaginary parts.	$\frac{z_1}{z_2} = \left(\frac{r_1}{r_2}\right)\left[\frac{(\cos\theta_1\cos\theta_2 + \sin\theta_1\sin\theta_2) + i(\sin\theta_1\cos\theta_2 - \sin\theta_2\cos\theta_1)}{\underbrace{\cos^2\theta_2 + \sin^2\theta_2}_{1}}\right]$
Simplify.	$\frac{z_1}{z_2} = \left(\frac{r_1}{r_2}\right)[(\cos\theta_1\cos\theta_2 + \sin\theta_1\sin\theta_2) + i(\sin\theta_1\cos\theta_2 - \sin\theta_2\cos\theta_1)]$

Use the cosine and sine difference identities.

$$\frac{z_1}{z_2} = \left(\frac{r_1}{r_2}\right)\underbrace{(\cos\theta_1\cos\theta_2 + \sin\theta_1\sin\theta_2)}_{\cos(\theta_1 - \theta_2)} + i\underbrace{(\sin\theta_1\cos\theta_2 - \sin\theta_2\cos\theta_1)}_{\sin(\theta_1 - \theta_2)}$$

Simplify.

$$\frac{z_1}{z_2} = \frac{r_1}{r_2}[\cos(\theta_1 - \theta_2) + i\sin(\theta_1 - \theta_2)]$$

It is important to notice that the argument difference is the argument of the numerator minus the argument of the denominator.

QUOTIENT OF TWO COMPLEX NUMBERS

Let $z_1 = r_1(\cos\theta_1 + i\sin\theta_1)$ and $z_2 = r_2(\cos\theta_2 + i\sin\theta_2)$ be two complex numbers. The complex quotient $\frac{z_1}{z_2}$ is given by

$$\frac{z_1}{z_2} = \frac{r_1}{r_2}[\cos(\theta_1 - \theta_2) + i\sin(\theta_1 - \theta_2)]$$

In other words, *when dividing two complex numbers, divide the magnitudes and subtract the arguments. It is important to note that the argument difference is the argument of the complex number in the numerator minus the argument of the complex number in the denominator.*

EXAMPLE 2 Dividing Complex Numbers

Let $z_1 = 6(\cos 125° + i\sin 125°)$ and $z_2 = 3(\cos 65° + i\sin 65°)$. Find $\frac{z_1}{z_2}$.

Solution:

Set up the quotient.

$$\frac{z_1}{z_2} = \frac{6(\cos 125° + i\sin 125°)}{3(\cos 65° + i\sin 65°)}$$

Divide the magnitudes and subtract the arguments.

$$\frac{z_1}{z_2} = \frac{6}{3}[\cos(125° - 65°) + i\sin(125° - 65°)]$$

Simplify.

$$\frac{z_1}{z_2} = 2(\cos 60° + i\sin 60°)$$

The quotient is in polar form. To express the quotient in rectangular form, evaluate the trigonometric functions.

$$\frac{z_1}{z_2} = 2\left(\frac{1}{2} + i\frac{\sqrt{3}}{2}\right) = 1 + i\sqrt{3}$$

Polar form: $\boxed{\frac{z_1}{z_2} = 2(\cos 60° + i\sin 60°)}$

Rectangular form: $\boxed{\frac{z_1}{z_2} = 1 + i\sqrt{3}}$

YOUR TURN Let $z_1 = 10(\cos 275° + i\sin 275°)$ and $z_2 = 5(\cos 65° + i\sin 65°)$. Find $\frac{z_1}{z_2}$. Express the answers in both polar and rectangular form.

[CONCEPT CHECK]

TRUE OR FALSE When two complex numbers are divided, their magnitudes and arguments are divided, respectively.

ANSWER False

ANSWER

$\frac{z_1}{z_2} = 2(\cos 210° + i\sin 210°)$ or

$\frac{z_1}{z_2} = -\sqrt{3} - i$

When multiplying or dividing complex numbers, we have considered only those values of θ such that $0° \le \theta < 360°$. When the value of θ is negative or greater than or equal to $360°$, find the coterminal angle in the interval $[0°, 360°)$.

7.4.3 Powers of Complex Numbers

7.4.3 SKILL

Raise a complex number to an integer power.

7.4.3 CONCEPTUAL

Understand that when a complex number is raised to an integer power n, the magnitude is raised to the power and the argument is multiplied by n.

Raising a number to a positive integer power is the same as multiplying that number by itself repeated times.

$$x^3 = x \cdot x \cdot x \qquad (a + b)^2 = (a + b)(a + b)$$

Therefore, raising a complex number to a power that is a positive integer is the same as multiplying the complex number by itself multiple times. Let us illustrate this with the complex number $z = r(\cos\theta + i\sin\theta)$, which we will raise to positive integer powers (n).

WORDS	MATH
Take the case $n = 2$.	$z^2 = [r(\cos\theta + i\sin\theta)][r(\cos\theta + i\sin\theta)]$
Apply the product rule (multiply the magnitudes and add the arguments).	$z^2 = r^2[\cos(2\theta) + i\sin(2\theta)]$
Take the case $n = 3$.	$z^3 = z^2 z = \{r^2[\cos(2\theta) + i\sin(2\theta)]\}[r(\cos\theta + i\sin\theta)]$
Apply the product rule (multiply the magnitudes and add the arguments).	$z^3 = r^3[\cos(3\theta) + i\sin(3\theta)]$
Take the case $n = 4$.	$z^4 = z^3 z = \{r^3[\cos(3\theta) + i\sin(3\theta)]\}[r(\cos\theta + i\sin\theta)]$
Apply the product rule (multiply the magnitudes and add the arguments).	$z^4 = r^4[\cos(4\theta) + i\sin(4\theta)]$
The pattern observed for any n is	$z^n = r^n[\cos(n\theta) + i\sin(n\theta)]$

[CONCEPT CHECK]

TRUE OR FALSE When a complex number is raised to a positive integer power n, the magnitude is raised to the nth power and the argument is multiplied by n.

ANSWER True

Although we will not prove this generalized representation of a complex number raised to a power, it was proved by Abraham De Moivre, and hence its name.

DE MOIVRE'S THEOREM

If $z = r(\cos\theta + i\sin\theta)$ is a complex number, then

$$z^n = r^n[\cos(n\theta) + i\sin(n\theta)]$$

when n is a positive integer ($n \ge 1$).

In other words, when raising a complex number to a power n, raise the magnitude to the same power n and multiply the argument by n.

Although De Moivre's theorem was proved for all real numbers n, we will only use it for positive integer values of n and their reciprocals (nth roots). This is a very powerful theorem. For example, if asked to find $(\sqrt{3} + i)^{10}$, you have two choices: (1) Multiply out the expression algebraically, which we will call the long way, or (2) convert to polar coordinates and use De Moivre's theorem, which we will call the short way. We will use De Moivre's theorem.

EXAMPLE 3 Finding a Power of a Complex Number

Find $(\sqrt{3} + i)^{10}$ and express the answer in rectangular form.

Solution:

STEP 1 Convert to polar form. $(\sqrt{3} + i)^{10} = [2(\cos 30^\circ + i\sin 30^\circ)]^{10}$

STEP 2 Apply De Moivre's theorem with $n = 10$.

$$(\sqrt{3} + i)^{10} = [2(\cos 30^\circ + i\sin 30^\circ)]^{10} = 2^{10}[\cos(10\cdot 30^\circ) + i\sin(10\cdot 30^\circ)]$$

STEP 3 Simplify. $(\sqrt{3} + i)^{10} = 2^{10}(\cos 300^\circ + i\sin 300^\circ)$

Evaluate 2^{10} and the sine and cosine functions. $= 1024\left(\frac{1}{2} - i\frac{\sqrt{3}}{2}\right)$

Simplify. $\boxed{= 512 - 512i\sqrt{3}}$

YOUR TURN Find $(1 + i\sqrt{3})^{10}$ and express the answer in rectangular form.

ANSWER

$-512 - 512i\sqrt{3}$

7.4.4 SKILL

Find the *n*th root of a complex number.

7.4.4 CONCEPTUAL

Understand that a polynomial equation can often be solved by finding complex roots.

7.4.4 Roots of Complex Numbers

De Moivre's theorem is the basis for the *nth root theorem*. Before we proceed, let us motivate it with a problem: Solve $x^3 - 1 = 0$. Recall that a polynomial of degree n has n solutions (roots in the complex number system). So the polynomial $P(x) = x^3 - 1$ is of degree 3 and has three solutions (roots). We can solve it algebraically.

WORDS	MATH
List the potential rational roots of the polynomial $P(x) = x^3 - 1$.	$x = \pm 1$
Use synthetic division to test $x = 1$.	$\begin{array}{r\|rrrr} 1 & 1 & 0 & 0 & -1 \\ & & 1 & 1 & 1 \\ \hline & 1 & 1 & 1 & \boxed{0} \end{array}$ $\underbrace{1 \quad 1 \quad 1}_{x^2 + x + 1}$
Since $x = 1$ is a zero, the polynomial can be written as a product of the linear factor $(x - 1)$ and a quadratic factor.	$P(x) = (x - 1)(x^2 + x + 1)$
Use the quadratic formula on $x^2 + x + 1 = 0$ to solve for x.	$x = \frac{-1 \pm \sqrt{1 - 4}}{2} = \frac{-1 \pm \sqrt{-3}}{2} = -\frac{1}{2} \pm \frac{i\sqrt{3}}{2}$

So the three solutions to the equation $x^3 - 1 = 0$ are $\boxed{x = 1, x = -\frac{1}{2} + \frac{i\sqrt{3}}{2}, \text{ and } x = -\frac{1}{2} - \frac{i\sqrt{3}}{2}}$.

An alternative approach to solving $x^3 - 1 = 0$ is to use the *nth root theorem* to find the additional complex cube roots of 1.

Derivation of the *n*th Root Theorem

WORDS	MATH
Let z and w be complex numbers such that w is the nth root of z.	$w = z^{1/n}$ or $w = \sqrt[n]{z}$, where n is a positive integer
Raise both sides of the equation to the nth power.	$w^n = z$
Let $z = r(\cos\theta + i\sin\theta)$ and $w = s(\cos\alpha + i\sin\alpha)$.	$[s(\cos\alpha + i\sin\alpha)]^n = r(\cos\theta + i\sin\theta)$
Apply De Moivre's theorem to the left side of the equation.	$s^n[\cos(n\alpha) + i\sin(n\alpha)] = r(\cos\theta + i\sin\theta)$
For these two expressions to be equal, their magnitudes must be equal and their angles must be coterminal.	$s^n = r$ and $n\alpha = \theta + 2k\pi$, where k is any integer
Solve for s and α.	$s = r^{1/n}$ and $\alpha = \dfrac{\theta + 2k\pi}{n}$
Substitute $s = r^{1/n}$ and $\alpha = \dfrac{\theta + 2k\pi}{n}$ into $w = z^{1/n}$.	$z^{1/n} = r^{1/n}\left[\cos\left(\dfrac{\theta + 2k\pi}{n}\right) + i\sin\left(\dfrac{\theta + 2k\pi}{n}\right)\right]$

Notice that when $k = n$, the arguments $\frac{\theta}{n} + 2\pi$ and $\frac{\theta}{n}$ are coterminal. Therefore, to get distinct roots, let $k = 0, 1, \ldots, n - 1$. If we let z be a given complex number and w be any complex number that satisfies the relationship $z^{1/n} = w$ or $z = w^n$, where $n \geq 2$, then we say that w is a **complex *n*th root** of z.

*n*TH ROOT THEOREM

The ***n*th roots** of the complex number $z = r(\cos\theta + i\sin\theta)$ are given by

$$w_k = r^{1/n}\left[\cos\left(\frac{\theta}{n} + \frac{2k\pi}{n}\right) + i\sin\left(\frac{\theta}{n} + \frac{2k\pi}{n}\right)\right] \qquad \theta \text{ in radians}$$

or

$$w_k = r^{1/n}\left[\cos\left(\frac{\theta}{n} + \frac{k\cdot 360^\circ}{n}\right) + i\sin\left(\frac{\theta}{n} + \frac{k\cdot 360^\circ}{n}\right)\right] \qquad \theta \text{ in degrees}$$

where $k = 0, 1, 2, \ldots, n - 1$ and $n =$ integer.

EXAMPLE 4 Finding Roots of Complex Numbers

Find the three distinct cube roots of $-4 - 4i\sqrt{3}$, and plot the roots in the complex plane.

Solution:

STEP 1 Write $-4 - 4i\sqrt{3}$ in polar form. $\quad 8(\cos 240^\circ + i\sin 240^\circ)$

STEP 2 Find the three cube roots.

$$w_k = r^{1/n}\left[\cos\left(\frac{\theta}{n} + \frac{k\cdot 360^\circ}{n}\right) + i\sin\left(\frac{\theta}{n} + \frac{k\cdot 360^\circ}{n}\right)\right]$$

$$\theta = 240^\circ, r = 8, n = 3, k = 0, 1, 2$$

$k = 0$: $\quad w_0 = 8^{1/3}\left[\cos\left(\dfrac{240^\circ}{3} + \dfrac{0\cdot 360^\circ}{3}\right) + i\sin\left(\dfrac{240^\circ}{3} + \dfrac{0\cdot 360^\circ}{3}\right)\right]$

Simplify. $\quad \boxed{w_0 = 2(\cos 80^\circ + i\sin 80^\circ)}$

$k = 1$: $\quad w_1 = 8^{1/3}\left[\cos\left(\dfrac{240°}{3} + \dfrac{1 \cdot 360°}{3}\right) + i\sin\left(\dfrac{240°}{3} + \dfrac{1 \cdot 360°}{3}\right)\right]$

Simplify. $\quad \boxed{w_1 = 2(\cos 200° + i\sin 200°)}$

$k = 2$: $\quad w_2 = 8^{1/3}\left[\cos\left(\dfrac{240°}{3} + \dfrac{2 \cdot 360°}{3}\right) + i\sin\left(\dfrac{240°}{3} + \dfrac{2 \cdot 360°}{3}\right)\right]$

Simplify. $\quad \boxed{w_2 = 2(\cos 320° + i\sin 320°)}$

STEP 3 Plot the three cube roots in the complex plane.

Notice the following:

- The roots all have a magnitude of 2.
- The roots lie on a circle of radius 2.
- The roots are equally spaced around the circle (120° apart).

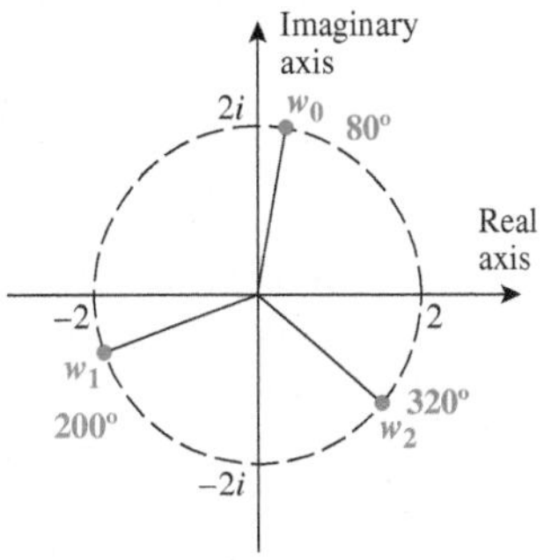

YOUR TURN Find the three distinct cube roots of $4 - 4i\sqrt{3}$, and plot the roots in the complex plane.

ANSWER

$w_0 = 2(\cos 100° + i\sin 100°)$
$w_1 = 2(\cos 220° + i\sin 220°)$
$w_2 = 2(\cos 340° + i\sin 340°)$

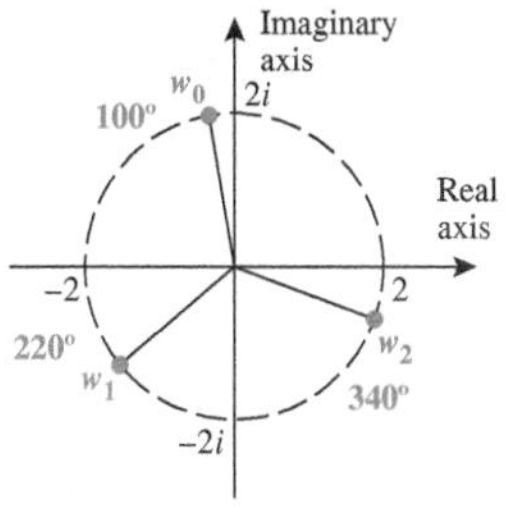

Solving Equations Using Roots of Complex Numbers

Let us return to solving the equation $x^3 - 1 = 0$. As stated, $x = 1$ is the real solution to this cubic equation. However, there are two additional (complex) solutions. Since we are finding the zeros of a third-degree polynomial, we expect three solutions. Furthermore, when complex solutions arise in finding the roots of polynomials with real coefficients, they come in conjugate pairs.

EXAMPLE 5 Solving Equations Using Complex Roots

Find all complex solutions to $x^3 - 1 = 0$.

Solution: $x^3 = 1$

STEP 1 Write 1 in polar form. $\quad 1 = 1 + 0i = \cos 0° + i\sin 0°$

STEP 2 Find the three cube roots of 1.

$$w_k = r^{1/n}\left[\cos\left(\frac{\theta}{n} + \frac{k \cdot 360°}{n}\right) + i\sin\left(\frac{\theta}{n} + \frac{k \cdot 360°}{n}\right)\right]$$

$$r = 1, \theta = 0°, n = 3, k = 0, 1, 2$$

$k = 0$: $\quad w_0 = 1^{1/3}\left[\cos\left(\dfrac{0°}{3} + \dfrac{0 \cdot 360°}{3}\right) + i\sin\left(\dfrac{0°}{3} + \dfrac{0 \cdot 360°}{3}\right)\right]$

Simplify. $\quad w_0 = \cos 0° + i\sin 0°$

$k = 1$: $\quad w_1 = 1^{1/3}\left[\cos\left(\dfrac{0°}{3} + \dfrac{1 \cdot 360°}{3}\right) + i\sin\left(\dfrac{0°}{3} + \dfrac{1 \cdot 360°}{3}\right)\right]$

Simplify. $\quad w_1 = \cos 120° + i\sin 120°$

$k = 2$: $\quad w_2 = 1^{1/3}\left[\cos\left(\dfrac{0°}{3} + \dfrac{2 \cdot 360°}{3}\right) + i\sin\left(\dfrac{0°}{3} + \dfrac{2 \cdot 360°}{3}\right)\right]$

Simplify. $\quad w_2 = \cos 240° + i\sin 240°$

STEP 3 Write the roots in rectangular form.

w_0: $$w_0 = \underbrace{\cos 0°}_{1} + i\underbrace{\sin 0°}_{0} = 1$$

w_1: $$w_1 = \underbrace{\cos 120°}_{-\frac{1}{2}} + i\underbrace{\sin 120°}_{\frac{\sqrt{3}}{2}} = -\frac{1}{2} + i\frac{\sqrt{3}}{2}$$

w_2: $$w_2 = \underbrace{\cos 240°}_{-\frac{1}{2}} + i\underbrace{\sin 240°}_{-\frac{\sqrt{3}}{2}} = -\frac{1}{2} - i\frac{\sqrt{3}}{2}$$

STEP 4 Write the solutions to the equation $x^3 - 1 = 0$.

$$\boxed{x = 1} \quad \boxed{x = -\frac{1}{2} + i\frac{\sqrt{3}}{2}} \quad \boxed{x = -\frac{1}{2} - i\frac{\sqrt{3}}{2}}$$

[CONCEPT CHECK]

TRUE OR FALSE The n distinct roots are equally spread around the circle: The angle between consecutive roots is $\frac{\theta}{n}$.

ANSWER True

Notice that there is one real solution, there are two (nonreal) complex solutions, and the two complex solutions are complex conjugates.

It is always a good idea to check that the solutions indeed satisfy the equation. The equation $x^3 - 1 = 0$ can also be written as $x^3 = 1$, so the check in this case is to cube each of the three solutions and confirm that the result is 1.

$x = 1$: $$1^3 = 1$$

$x = -\frac{1}{2} + \frac{i\sqrt{3}}{2}$:
$$\left(-\frac{1}{2} + i\frac{\sqrt{3}}{2}\right)^3 = \left(-\frac{1}{2} + i\frac{\sqrt{3}}{2}\right)^2\left(-\frac{1}{2} + i\frac{\sqrt{3}}{2}\right)$$
$$= \left(-\frac{1}{2} - i\frac{\sqrt{3}}{2}\right)\left(-\frac{1}{2} + i\frac{\sqrt{3}}{2}\right)$$
$$= \frac{1}{4} + \frac{3}{4}$$
$$= 1$$

$x = -\frac{1}{2} - \frac{i\sqrt{3}}{2}$:
$$\left(-\frac{1}{2} - i\frac{\sqrt{3}}{2}\right)^3 = \left(-\frac{1}{2} - i\frac{\sqrt{3}}{2}\right)^2\left(-\frac{1}{2} - i\frac{\sqrt{3}}{2}\right)$$
$$= \left(-\frac{1}{2} + i\frac{\sqrt{3}}{2}\right)\left(-\frac{1}{2} - i\frac{\sqrt{3}}{2}\right)$$
$$= \frac{1}{4} + \frac{3}{4}$$
$$= 1$$

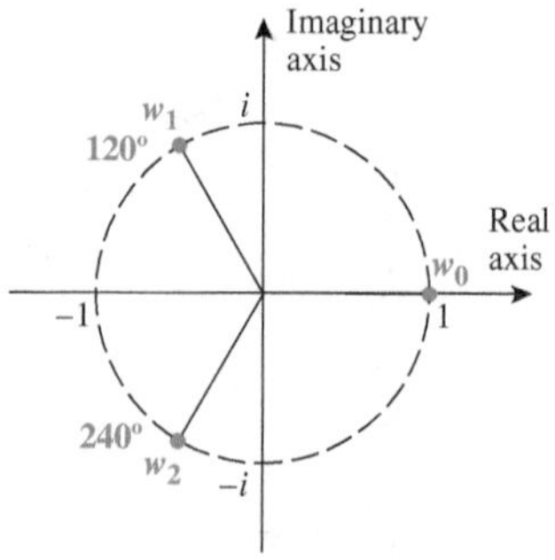

[SECTION 7.4] SUMMARY

In this section, we multiplied and divided complex numbers and, using De Moivre's theorem, raised complex numbers to integer powers and found the nth roots of complex numbers, as follows:

Let $z_1 = r_1(\cos\theta_1 + i\sin\theta_1)$ and
$z_2 = r_2(\cos\theta_2 + i\sin\theta_2)$ be two complex numbers.

The **product** z_1z_2 is given by

$$z_1z_2 = r_1r_2[\cos(\theta_1 + \theta_2) + i\sin(\theta_1 + \theta_2)]$$

The **quotient** $\frac{z_1}{z_2}$ is given by

$$\frac{z_1}{z_2} = \frac{r_1}{r_2}[\cos(\theta_1 - \theta_2) + i\sin(\theta_1 - \theta_2)]$$

Let $z = r(\cos\theta + i\sin\theta)$ be a complex number. Then, for a positive integer n,

z raised to a **power** n is given by

$$z^n = r^n[\cos(n\theta) + i\sin(n\theta)]$$

The ***n*th roots** of z are given by

$$w_k = r^{1/n}\left[\cos\left(\frac{\theta}{n} + \frac{k \cdot 360°}{n}\right) + i\sin\left(\frac{\theta}{n} + \frac{k \cdot 360°}{n}\right)\right]$$

where θ is in degrees and $k = 0, 1, 2, \ldots, n - 1$

or

$$w_k = r^{1/n}\left[\cos\left(\frac{\theta}{n} + \frac{k \cdot 2\pi}{n}\right) + i\sin\left(\frac{\theta}{n} + \frac{k \cdot 2\pi}{n}\right)\right]$$

where θ is in radians and $k = 0, 1, 2, \ldots, n - 1$.

[SECTION 7.4] EXERCISES

• SKILLS

In Exercises 1–10, find the product z_1z_2 and express it in rectangular form.

1. $z_1 = 4(\cos 40° + i\sin 40°)$ and $z_2 = 3(\cos 80° + i\sin 80°)$
2. $z_1 = 2(\cos 100° + i\sin 100°)$ and $z_2 = 5(\cos 50° + i\sin 50°)$
3. $z_1 = 4(\cos 80° + i\sin 80°)$ and $z_2 = 2(\cos 145° + i\sin 145°)$
4. $z_1 = 3(\cos 130° + i\sin 130°)$ and $z_2 = 4(\cos 170° + i\sin 170°)$
5. $z_1 = 2(\cos 10° + i\sin 10°)$ and $z_2 = 4(\cos 80° + i\sin 80°)$
6. $z_1 = 3(\cos 190° + i\sin 190°)$ and $z_2 = 5(\cos 80° + i\sin 80°)$
7. $z_1 = \sqrt{3}\left[\cos\left(\frac{\pi}{12}\right) + i\sin\left(\frac{\pi}{12}\right)\right]$ and $z_2 = \sqrt{27}\left[\cos\left(\frac{\pi}{6}\right) + i\sin\left(\frac{\pi}{6}\right)\right]$
8. $z_1 = \sqrt{5}\left[\cos\left(\frac{\pi}{15}\right) + i\sin\left(\frac{\pi}{15}\right)\right]$ and $z_2 = \sqrt{5}\left[\cos\left(\frac{4\pi}{15}\right) + i\sin\left(\frac{4\pi}{15}\right)\right]$
9. $z_1 = 4\left[\cos\left(\frac{3\pi}{8}\right) + i\sin\left(\frac{3\pi}{8}\right)\right]$ and $z_2 = 3\left[\cos\left(\frac{\pi}{8}\right) + i\sin\left(\frac{\pi}{8}\right)\right]$
10. $z_1 = 6\left[\cos\left(\frac{2\pi}{9}\right) + i\sin\left(\frac{2\pi}{9}\right)\right]$ and $z_2 = 5\left[\cos\left(\frac{\pi}{9}\right) + i\sin\left(\frac{\pi}{9}\right)\right]$

In Exercises 11–20, find the quotient $\frac{z_1}{z_2}$ and express it in rectangular form.

11. $z_1 = 6(\cos 100° + i\sin 100°)$ and $z_2 = 2(\cos 40° + i\sin 40°)$
12. $z_1 = 8(\cos 80° + i\sin 80°)$ and $z_2 = 2(\cos 35° + i\sin 35°)$
13. $z_1 = 10(\cos 200° + i\sin 200°)$ and $z_2 = 5(\cos 65° + i\sin 65°)$
14. $z_1 = 4(\cos 280° + i\sin 280°)$ and $z_2 = 4(\cos 55° + i\sin 55°)$
15. $z_1 = \sqrt{12}(\cos 350° + i\sin 350°)$ and $z_2 = \sqrt{3}(\cos 80° + i\sin 80°)$
16. $z_1 = \sqrt{40}(\cos 110° + i\sin 110°)$ and $z_2 = \sqrt{10}(\cos 20° + i\sin 20°)$
17. $z_1 = 9\left[\cos\left(\frac{5\pi}{12}\right) + i\sin\left(\frac{5\pi}{12}\right)\right]$ and $z_2 = 3\left[\cos\left(\frac{\pi}{12}\right) + i\sin\left(\frac{\pi}{12}\right)\right]$
18. $z_1 = 8\left[\cos\left(\frac{5\pi}{8}\right) + i\sin\left(\frac{5\pi}{8}\right)\right]$ and $z_2 = 4\left[\cos\left(\frac{3\pi}{8}\right) + i\sin\left(\frac{3\pi}{8}\right)\right]$

19. $z_1 = 45\left[\cos\left(\frac{22\pi}{15}\right) + i\sin\left(\frac{22\pi}{15}\right)\right]$ and $z_2 = 9\left[\cos\left(\frac{2\pi}{15}\right) + i\sin\left(\frac{2\pi}{15}\right)\right]$

20. $z_1 = 22\left[\cos\left(\frac{11\pi}{18}\right) + i\sin\left(\frac{11\pi}{18}\right)\right]$ and $z_2 = 11\left[\cos\left(\frac{5\pi}{18}\right) + i\sin\left(\frac{5\pi}{18}\right)\right]$

In Exercises 21–30, find the result of each expression using De Moivre's theorem. Write the answer in rectangular form.

21. $(-1 + i)^5$
22. $(1 - i)^4$
23. $(-\sqrt{3} + i)^6$
24. $(\sqrt{3} - i)^8$
25. $(1 - \sqrt{3}i)^4$
26. $(-1 + \sqrt{3}i)^5$
27. $(4 - 4i)^8$
28. $(-3 + 3i)^{10}$
29. $(4\sqrt{3} + 4i)^7$
30. $(-5 + 5\sqrt{3}i)^7$

In Exercises 31–40, find all *n*th roots of *z*. Write the answers in polar form, and plot the roots in the complex plane.

31. $2 - 2i\sqrt{3}, n = 2$
32. $2 + 2\sqrt{3}i, n = 2$
33. $\sqrt{18} - \sqrt{18}i, n = 2$
34. $-\sqrt{2} + \sqrt{2}i, n = 2$
35. $4 + 4\sqrt{3}i, n = 3$
36. $-\frac{27}{2} + \frac{27\sqrt{3}}{2}i, n = 3$
37. $\sqrt{3} - i, n = 3$
38. $4\sqrt{2} + 4\sqrt{2}i, n = 3$
39. $8\sqrt{2} - 8\sqrt{2}i, n = 4$
40. $-\sqrt{128} + \sqrt{128}i, n = 4$

In Exercises 41–56, find all complex solutions to the given equations.

41. $x^4 - 16 = 0$
42. $x^3 - 8 = 0$
43. $x^3 + 8 = 0$
44. $x^3 + 1 = 0$
45. $x^4 + 16 = 0$
46. $x^6 + 1 = 0$
47. $x^6 - 1 = 0$
48. $4x^2 + 1 = 0$
49. $x^2 + i = 0$
50. $x^2 - i = 0$
51. $x^4 - 2i = 0$
52. $x^4 + 2i = 0$
53. $x^5 + 32 = 0$
54. $x^5 - 32 = 0$
55. $x^7 - \pi^{14}i = 0$
56. $x^7 + \pi^{14} = 0$

• APPLICATIONS

57. Complex Pentagon. When you graph the five fifth roots of $-\frac{\sqrt{2}}{2} - \frac{\sqrt{2}}{2}i$ and connect the points, you form a pentagon. Find the roots and draw the pentagon.

58. Complex Square. When you graph the four fourth roots of $16i$ and connect the points, you form a square. Find the roots and draw the square.

59. Hexagon. Compute the six sixth roots of $\frac{1}{2} - \frac{\sqrt{3}}{2}i$, and form a hexagon by connecting successive roots.

60. Octagon. Compute the eight eighth roots of $2i$, and form an octagon by connecting successive roots.

• CATCH THE MISTAKE

In Exercises 61–64, explain the mistake that is made.

61. Let $z_1 = 6(\cos 65° + i\sin 65°)$ and $z_2 = 3(\cos 125° + i\sin 125°)$. Find $\frac{z_1}{z_2}$.

Solution:

Use the quotient formula.

$$\frac{z_1}{z_2} = \frac{r_1}{r_2}[\cos(\theta_1 - \theta_2) + i\sin(\theta_1 - \theta_2)]$$

Substitute values.

$$\frac{z_1}{z_2} = \frac{6}{3}[\cos(125° - 65°) + i\sin(125° - 65°)]$$

Simplify. $\frac{z_1}{z_2} = 2(\cos 60° + i\sin 60°)$

Evaluate the trigonometric functions.

$$\frac{z_1}{z_2} = 2\left(\frac{1}{2} + i\frac{\sqrt{3}}{2}\right) = 1 + i\sqrt{3}$$

This is incorrect. What mistake was made?

62. Let $z_1 = 6(\cos 65° + i\sin 65°)$ and $z_2 = 3(\cos 125° + i\sin 125°)$. Find z_1z_2.

Solution:

Write the product.

$$z_1z_2 = 6(\cos 65° + i\sin 65°)\cdot 3(\cos 125° + i\sin 125°)$$

Multiply the magnitudes.

$$z_1z_2 = 18(\cos 65° + i\sin 65°)(\cos 125° + i\sin 125°)$$

Multiply the cosine terms and sine terms (add the arguments).

$$z_1z_2 = 18[\cos(65° + 125°) + i^2\sin(65° + 125°)]$$

Simplify ($i^2 = -$).

$$z_1z_2 = 18(\cos 190° - \sin 190°)$$

This is incorrect. What mistake was made?

63. Find $(\sqrt{2} + i\sqrt{2})^6$.

Solution:

Raise each term to the sixth power. $(\sqrt{2})^6 + i^6(\sqrt{2})^6$

Simplify. $8 + 8i^6$

Let $i^6 = i^4 \cdot i^2 = -1$. $8 - 8 = 0$

This is incorrect. What mistake was made?

64. Find all complex solutions to $x^5 - 1 = 0$.

Solution:

Add 1 to both sides. $x^5 = 1$

Raise both sides to the fifth power. $x = 1^{1/5}$

Simplify. $x = 1$

This is incorrect. What mistake was made?

• CONCEPTUAL

In Exercises 65–72, determine whether the statement is true or false.

65. The product of two complex numbers is a complex number.

66. The quotient of two complex numbers is a complex number.

67. There are always n distinct real solutions of the equation $x^n - a = 0$, where a is not zero.

68. There are always n distinct complex solutions of the equation $x^n - a = 0$, where a is not zero.

69. There are n distinct complex zeros of $\dfrac{1}{a + bi}$, where a and b are positive real numbers.

70. There exists a complex number for which there is no complex square root.

71. The distance between any consecutive pair of the n complex roots of a number is a constant.

72. If $2\left[\cos\left(\frac{\pi}{2}\right) + i\sin\left(\frac{\pi}{2}\right)\right]$ is one of the n complex roots of a number, then n is even.

• CHALLENGE

In Exercises 73–76, use the following identity:

In calculus you will see an identity called Euler's formula or identity, $e^{i\theta} = \cos\theta + i\sin\theta$. Notice that when $\theta = \pi$, the identity reduces to $e^{i\pi} + 1 = 0$, which is a beautiful identity in that it relates the five fundamental numbers (e, π, 1, i, and 0) and the fundamental operations (multiplication, addition, exponents, and equality) in mathematics.

73. Let $z_1 = r_1(\cos\theta_1 + i\sin\theta_1) = r_1 e^{i\theta_1}$ and $z_2 = r_2(\cos\theta_2 + i\sin\theta_2) = r_2 e^{i\theta_2}$ be two complex numbers. Use the properties of exponentials to show that $z_1 z_2 = r_1 r_2[\cos(\theta_1 + \theta_2) + i\sin(\theta_1 + \theta_2)]$.

74. Let $z_1 = r_1(\cos\theta_1 + i\sin\theta_1) = r_1 e^{i\theta_1}$ and $z_2 = r_2(\cos\theta_2 + i\sin\theta_2) = r_2 e^{i\theta_2}$ be two complex numbers. Use the properties of exponentials to show that $\dfrac{z_1}{z_2} = \dfrac{r_1}{r_2}[\cos(\theta_1 - \theta_2) + i\sin(\theta_1 - \theta_2)]$.

75. Let $z = r(\cos\theta + i\sin\theta) = re^{i\theta}$. Use the properties of exponents to show that $z^n = r^n[\cos(n\theta) + i\sin(n\theta)]$.

76. Let $z = r(\cos\theta + i\sin\theta) = re^{i\theta}$. Use the properties of exponents to show that

$$w_k = r^{1/n}\left[\cos\left(\frac{\theta}{n} + \frac{2k\pi}{n}\right) + i\sin\left(\frac{\theta}{n} + \frac{2k\pi}{n}\right)\right].$$

77. Use De Moivre's theorem to prove the identity $\cos 2\theta = \cos^2\theta - \sin^2\theta$.

78. Use De Moivre's theorem to derive an expression for $\sin(3\theta)$.

79. Use De Moivre's theorem to derive an expression for $\cos(3\theta)$.

80. Calculate $\dfrac{\left(\frac{1}{2} + \frac{\sqrt{3}}{2}i\right)^{14}}{\left(\frac{1}{2} - \frac{\sqrt{3}}{2}i\right)^{20}}$.

81. Calculate $(1 - i)^n \cdot (1 + i)^m$, where n and m are positive integers.

82. Calculate $\dfrac{(1 + i)^n}{(1 - i)^m}$, where n and m are positive integers.

• PREVIEW TO CALCULUS

In advanced calculus, complex numbers in polar form are used extensively. Use De Moivre's formula to show that

83. $\cos(2\theta) = \cos^2\theta - \sin^2\theta$

84. $\sin(2\theta) = 2\sin\theta\cos\theta$

85. $\cos(3\theta) = 4\cos^3\theta - 3\cos\theta$

86. $\sin(3\theta) = 3\sin\theta - 4\sin^3\theta$

7.5 POLAR COORDINATES AND GRAPHS OF POLAR EQUATIONS

SKILLS OBJECTIVES

- Plot points in the polar coordinate system.
- Convert between rectangular and polar coordinates.
- Graph polar equations.

CONCEPTUAL OBJECTIVES

- Understand that the name of a point (r, θ) in the polar coordinate system is not unique.
- Relate the rectangular coordinate system to the polar coordinate system.
- Classify common shapes that arise from plotting certain types of polar equations.

We have discussed the rectangular and the trigonometric (polar) form of complex numbers in the complex plane. We now turn our attention back to the familiar Cartesian plane, where the horizontal axis represents the x-variable, the vertical axis represents the y-variable, and points in this plane represent pairs of real numbers. It is often convenient to represent real-number plots in the *polar coordinate system* instead.

7.5.1 Polar Coordinates

7.5.1 SKILL

Plot points in the polar coordinate system.

7.5.1 CONCEPTUAL

Understand that the name of a point (r, θ) in the polar coordinate system is not unique.

The **polar coordinate system** is anchored by a point, called the **pole** (taken to be the **origin**), and a ray with a vertex at the pole, called the **polar axis**. The polar axis is normally shown where we expect to find the positive x-axis in Cartesian coordinates.

If you align the pole with the origin on the rectangular graph and the polar axis with the positive x-axis, you can label a point either with rectangular coordinates (x, y) or with an ordered pair (r, θ) in **polar coordinates**.

Typically, polar graph paper is used that gives the angles and radii. The graph below gives the angles in radians (the angles also can be given in degrees) and shows the radii from 0 through 5.

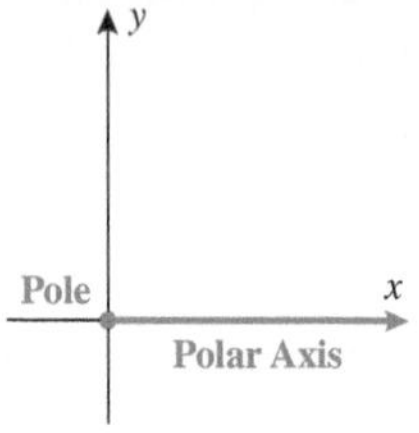

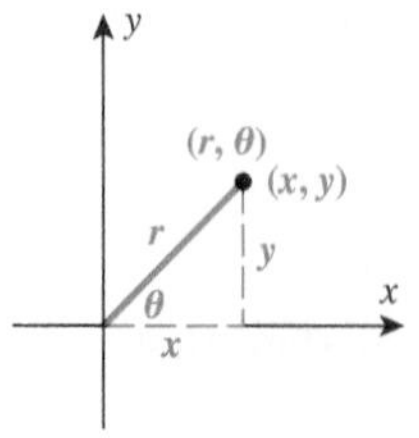

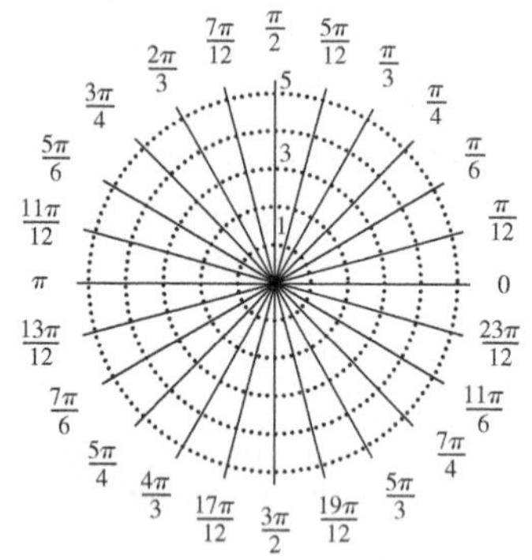

When points are plotted in the polar coordinate system, $|r|$ represents the distance from the origin to the point. The following procedure guides us in plotting points in the polar coordinate system.

POINT-PLOTTING POLAR COORDINATES

To plot a point (r, θ):

1. Start on the polar axis and rotate the terminal side of an angle to the value θ.
2. If $r > 0$, the point is r units from the origin in the *same direction* as the terminal side of θ.
3. If $r < 0$, the point is $|r|$ units from the origin in the *opposite direction* from the terminal side of θ.

EXAMPLE 1 Plotting Points in the Polar Coordinate System

Plot the points in a polar coordinate system.

a. $\left(3, \dfrac{3\pi}{4}\right)$ **b.** $(-2, 60°)$

Solution (a):

Start by placing a pencil along the polar axis.

Rotate the pencil to the angle $\dfrac{3\pi}{4}$.

Go out (in the direction of the pencil) three units.

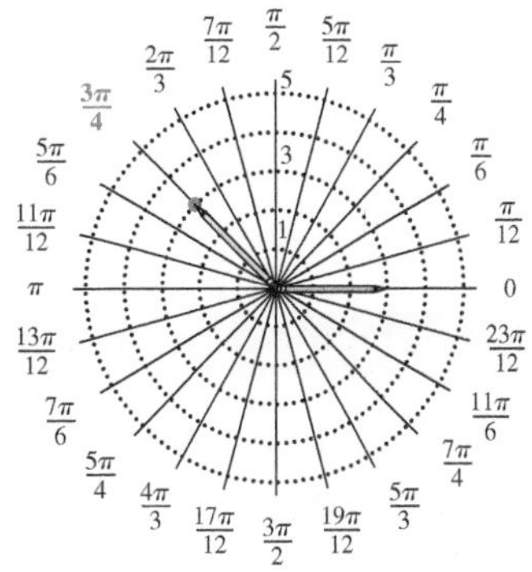

Solution (b):

Start by placing a pencil along the polar axis.

Rotate the pencil to the angle 60°.

Go out (opposite the direction of the pencil) two units.

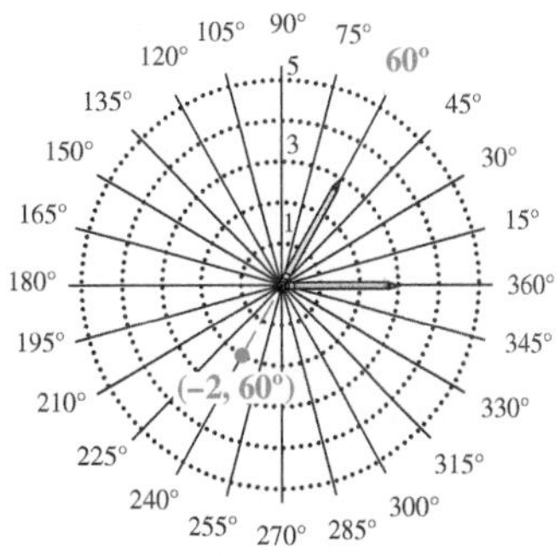

[CONCEPT CHECK]

Match the following:

(1) (x, y)

(2) (r, θ)

(A) not unique

(B) unique

ANSWER (1) B (2) A

YOUR TURN Plot the points in the polar coordinate system.

a. $\left(-4, \dfrac{3\pi}{2}\right)$ **b.** $(3, 330°)$

ANSWER

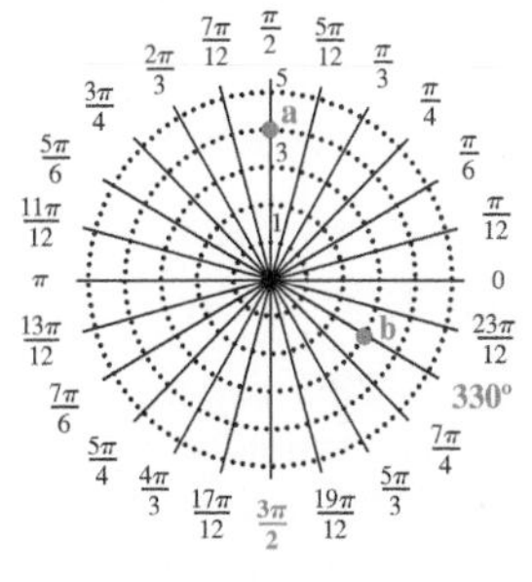

It is important to note that (r, θ), the name of the point, is not unique in polar form, whereas in rectangular form (x, y) it is unique. For example, $(2, 30°) = (-2, 210°)$.

7.5.2 Converting between Polar and Rectangular Coordinates

7.5.2 SKILL

Convert between rectangular and polar coordinates.

7.5.2 CONCEPTUAL

Relate the rectangular coordinate system to the polar coordinate system.

The relationships between polar and rectangular coordinates are the familiar ones:

$$\sin\theta = \frac{y}{r}$$

$$\cos\theta = \frac{x}{r} \qquad r^2 = x^2 + y^2$$

$$\tan\theta = \frac{y}{x} \quad (x \neq 0)$$

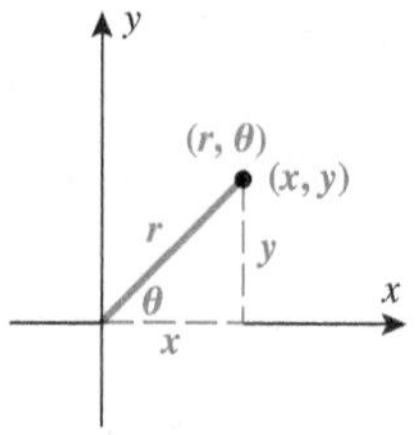

CONVERTING BETWEEN POLAR AND RECTANGULAR COORDINATES

FROM	TO	IDENTITIES
Polar (r, θ)	Rectangular (x, y)	$x = r\cos\theta \qquad y = r\sin\theta$
Rectangular (x, y)	Polar (r, θ)	$r = \sqrt{x^2 + y^2} \qquad \tan\theta = \frac{y}{x} \quad (x \neq 0)$ Make sure that θ is in the correct quadrant.

EXAMPLE 2 **Converting between Polar and Rectangular Coordinates**

a. Convert $\left(-1, \sqrt{3}\right)$ to polar coordinates.

b. Convert $\left(6\sqrt{2}, 135°\right)$ to rectangular coordinates.

Solution (a): $\left(-1, \sqrt{3}\right)$ lies in quadrant II.

Identify x and y. $\qquad x = -1, \quad y = \sqrt{3}$

Find r. $\qquad r = \sqrt{x^2 + y^2} = \sqrt{(-1)^2 + \left(\sqrt{3}\right)^2} = \sqrt{4} = 2$

Find θ. $\qquad \tan\theta = \frac{\sqrt{3}}{-1} \quad (\theta \text{ lies in quadrant II})$

Identify θ from the unit circle. $\qquad \theta = \frac{2\pi}{3}$

Write the point in polar coordinates. $\qquad \boxed{\left(2, \frac{2\pi}{3}\right)}$

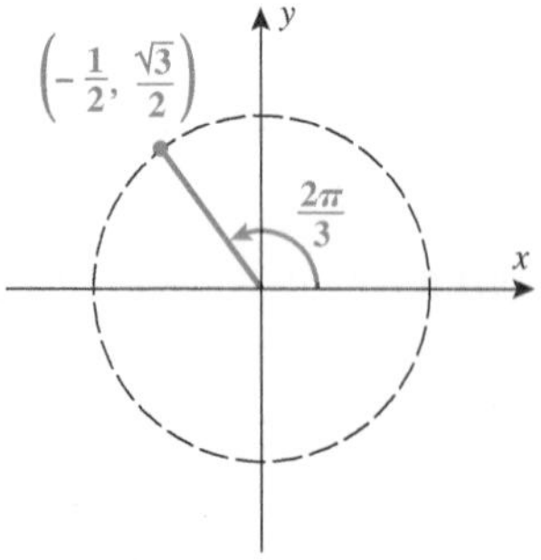

Note: Other polar coordinates, such as $\left(2, -\frac{4\pi}{3}\right)$ and $\left(-2, \frac{5\pi}{3}\right)$, also correspond to the point $\left(-1, \sqrt{3}\right)$.

Solution (b): $\left(6\sqrt{2}, 135°\right)$ lies in quadrant II.

Identify r and θ. $\qquad r = 6\sqrt{2} \quad \theta = 135°$

Find x. $\qquad x = r\cos\theta = 6\sqrt{2}\cos 135° = 6\sqrt{2}\left(-\frac{\sqrt{2}}{2}\right) = -6$

Find y. $\qquad y = r\sin\theta = 6\sqrt{2}\sin 135° = 6\sqrt{2}\left(\frac{\sqrt{2}}{2}\right) = 6$

Write the point in rectangular coordinates. $\qquad \boxed{(-6, 6)}$

[CONCEPT CHECK]

TRUE OR FALSE The point $(-a, -b)$ in rectangular coordinates can correspond to the point (r, θ) when r and θ are both positive.

ANSWER True

7.5.3 Graphs of Polar Equations

7.5.3 SKILL

Graph polar equations.

7.5.3 CONCEPTUAL

Classify common shapes that arise from plotting certain types of polar equations.

We are familiar with equations in rectangular form, such as

$y = 3x + 5$	$y = x^2 + 2$	$x^2 + y^2 = 9$
(line)	(parabola)	(circle)

We now discuss equations in polar form (known as **polar equations**) such as

$$r = 5\theta \qquad r = 2\cos\theta \qquad r = \sin(5\theta)$$

which you will learn to recognize in this section as typical equations whose plots are some general shapes.

Our first example deals with two of the simplest forms of polar equations: when r or θ is constant. The results are a circle centered at the origin and a line that passes through the origin, respectively.

EXAMPLE 3 **Graphing a Polar Equation of the Form r = Constant or θ = Constant**

Graph the polar equations.

a. $r = 3$ **b.** $\theta = \dfrac{\pi}{4}$

Solution (a): Constant value of r

Approach 1 (polar coordinates): $r = 3$ (θ can take on any value),

Plot points for arbitrary θ and $r = 3$.

Connect the points; a circle with radius 3.

Approach 2 (rectangular coordinates): $r = 3$

Square both sides. $r^2 = 9$

Remember that in rectangular coordinates, $r^2 = x^2 + y^2$. $x^2 + y^2 = 3^2$

This is a circle, centered at the origin, with radius 3.

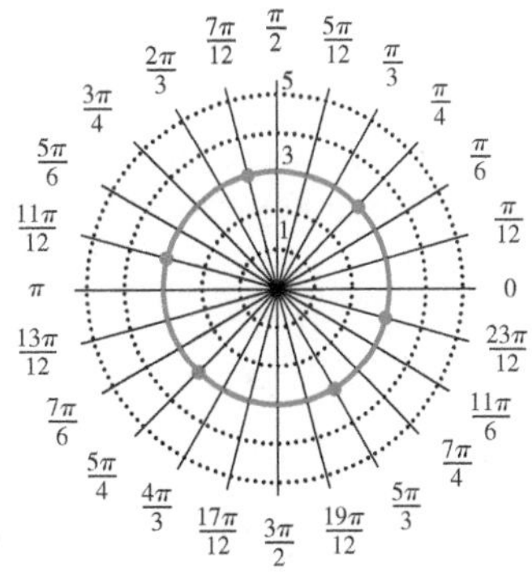

Solution (b): Constant value of θ

Approach 1: $\theta = \dfrac{\pi}{4}$ (r can take on any value, positive or negative.)

Plot points for $\theta = \dfrac{\pi}{4}$ at several arbitrary values of r.

Connect the points. The result is a line passing through the origin with slope $= 1 \left[m = \tan\left(\dfrac{\pi}{4}\right)\right]$.

Approach 2: $\theta = \dfrac{\pi}{4}$

Take the tangent of both sides. $\tan\theta = \underbrace{\tan\left(\dfrac{\pi}{4}\right)}_{1}$

Use the identity $\tan\theta = \dfrac{y}{x}$. $\dfrac{y}{x} = 1$

Multiply by x. $y = x$

The result is a line passing through the origin with slope $= 1$.

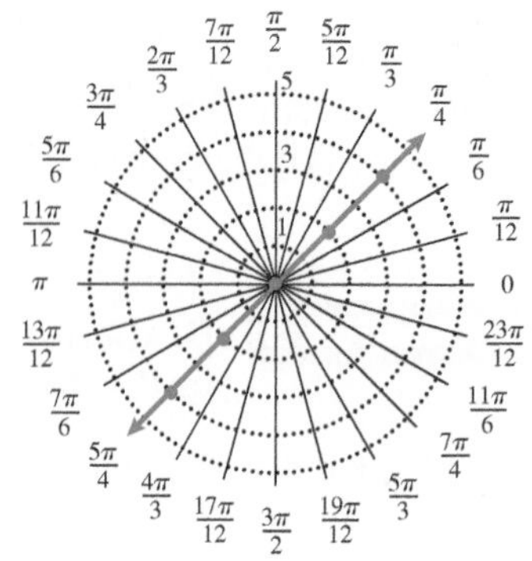

[CONCEPT CHECK]

Match the polar equations with their graphs:

(1) $r =$ constant

(2) $\theta =$ constant

(3) $r =$ constant $\cdot\,\theta$

(A) spiral

(B) circle

(C) line

ANSWER (1) B (2) C (3) A

Rectangular equations that depend on varying (not constant) values of x or y can be graphed by point-plotting (making a table and plotting the points). We will use this same procedure for graphing polar equations that depend on varying (not constant) values of r or θ.

EXAMPLE 4 Graphing a Polar Equation of the Form $r = c \cdot \cos\theta$ or $r = c \cdot \sin\theta$

Graph $r = 4\cos\theta$.

Solution:

STEP 1 Make a table and find several key values.

θ	$r = 4\cos\theta$	(r, θ)
0	$4(1) = 4$	$(4, 0)$
$\frac{\pi}{4}$	$4\left(\frac{\sqrt{2}}{2}\right) \approx 2.8$	$\left(2.8, \frac{\pi}{4}\right)$
$\frac{\pi}{2}$	$4(0) = 0$	$\left(0, \frac{\pi}{2}\right)$
$\frac{3\pi}{4}$	$4\left(-\frac{\sqrt{2}}{2}\right) \approx -2.8$	$\left(-2.8, \frac{3\pi}{4}\right)$
π	$4(-1) = -4$	$(-4, \pi)$
$\frac{5\pi}{4}$	$4\left(-\frac{\sqrt{2}}{2}\right) \approx -2.8$	$\left(-2.8, \frac{5\pi}{4}\right)$
$\frac{3\pi}{2}$	$4(0) = 0$	$\left(0, \frac{3\pi}{2}\right)$
$\frac{7\pi}{4}$	$4\left(\frac{\sqrt{2}}{2}\right) \approx 2.8$	$\left(2.8, \frac{7\pi}{4}\right)$
2π	$4(1) = 4$	$(4, 2\pi)$

STEP 2 Plot the points in polar coordinates.

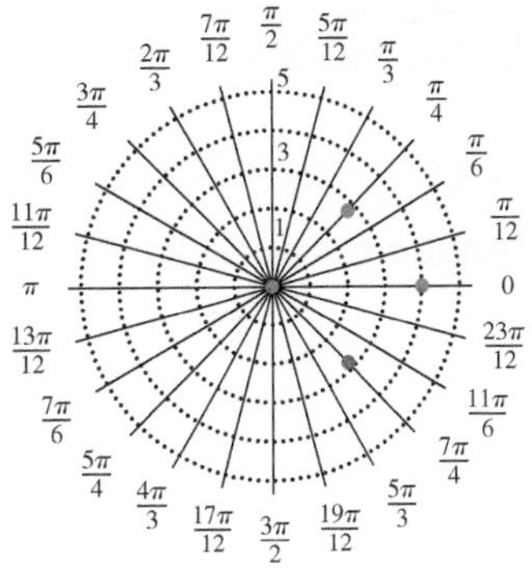

STEP 3 Connect the points with a smooth curve.

Notice that $(4, 0)$ and $(-4, \pi)$ correspond to the same point. There is no need to continue with angles beyond π, because the result would be to go around the same circle again.

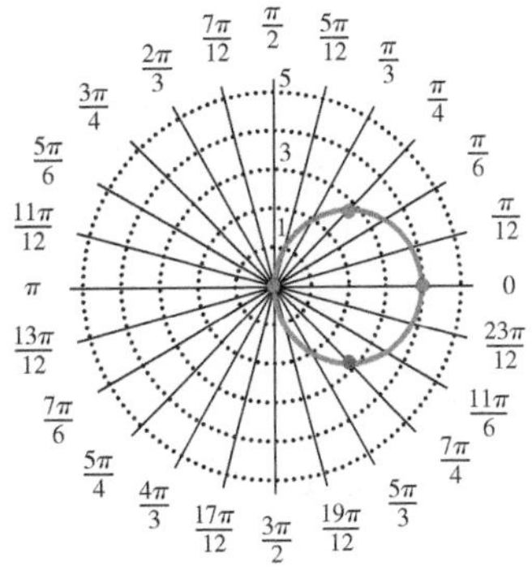

YOUR TURN Graph $r = 4\sin\theta$.

ANSWER

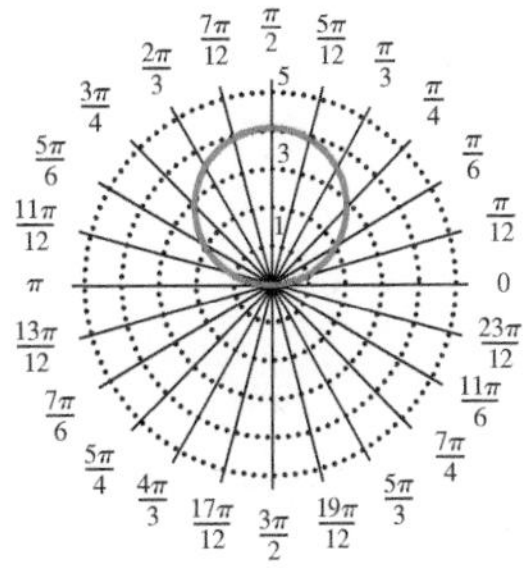

Compare the result of Example 4, the graph of $r = 4\cos\theta$, with the Your Turn result, the graph of $r = 4\sin\theta$. Notice that they are 90° out of phase (we simply rotate one graph 90° about the pole to get the other graph).

In general, graphs of polar equations of the form $r = a\sin\theta$ and $r = a\cos\theta$ are circles.

STUDY TIP

Graphs of $r = a\sin\theta$ and $r = a\cos\theta$ are circles.

WORDS	MATH	
Start with the polar form.	$r = a\sin\theta$	$r = a\cos\theta$
Apply trigonometric ratios: $\sin\theta = \frac{y}{r}$ and $\cos\theta = \frac{x}{r}$.	$r = a\frac{y}{r}$	$r = a\frac{x}{r}$
Multiply the equations by r.	$r^2 = ay$	$r^2 = ax$
Let $r^2 = x^2 + y^2$.	$x^2 + y^2 = ay$	$x^2 + y^2 = ax$
Group x terms together and y terms together.	$x^2 + (y^2 - ay) = 0$	$(x^2 - ax) + y^2 = 0$
Complete the square.	$x^2 + \left[y^2 - ay + \left(\frac{a}{2}\right)^2\right] = \left(\frac{a}{2}\right)^2$	$\left[x^2 - ax + \left(\frac{a}{2}\right)^2\right] + y^2 = \left(\frac{a}{2}\right)^2$
	$x^2 + \left(y - \frac{a}{2}\right)^2 = \left(\frac{a}{2}\right)^2$	$\left(x - \frac{a}{2}\right)^2 + y^2 = \left(\frac{a}{2}\right)^2$
Identify the center and radius.	Center: $\left(0, \frac{a}{2}\right)$ Radius: $\frac{a}{2}$	Center: $\left(\frac{a}{2}, 0\right)$ Radius: $\frac{a}{2}$

EXAMPLE 5 **Graphing a Polar Equation of the Form $r = c \cdot \sin(2\theta)$ or $r = c \cdot \cos(2\theta)$**

Graph $r = 5\sin(2\theta)$.

Solution:

STEP 1 Make a table and find key values. Since the argument of the sine function is doubled, the period is halved. Therefore, instead of steps of $\frac{\pi}{4}$, take steps of $\frac{\pi}{8}$.

θ	$r = 5\sin(2\theta)$	(r, θ)
0	$5(0) = 0$	$(0, 0)$
$\frac{\pi}{8}$	$5\left(\frac{\sqrt{2}}{2}\right) \approx 3.5$	$\left(3.5, \frac{\pi}{8}\right)$
$\frac{\pi}{4}$	$5(1) = 5$	$\left(5, \frac{\pi}{4}\right)$
$\frac{3\pi}{8}$	$5\left(\frac{\sqrt{2}}{2}\right) \approx 3.5$	$\left(3.5, \frac{3\pi}{8}\right)$
$\frac{\pi}{2}$	$5(0) = 0$	$\left(0, \frac{\pi}{2}\right)$

STEP 2 Label the polar coordinates.

The values in the table represent what happens in quadrant I. The same pattern repeats in the other three quadrants. The result is a **four-leaved rose**.

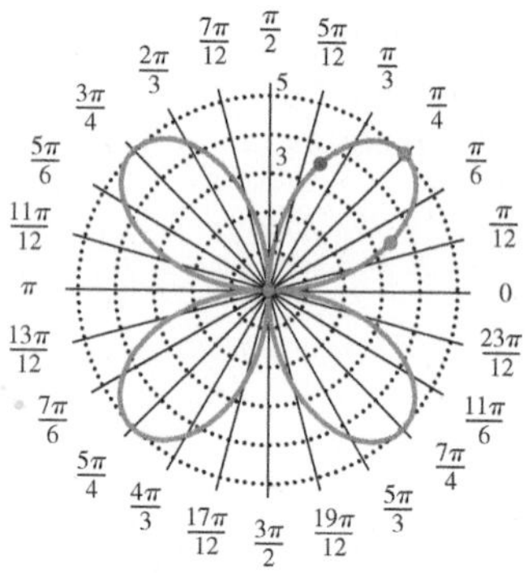

STEP 3 Connect the points with smooth curves.

YOUR TURN Graph $r = 5\cos(2\theta)$.

ANSWER

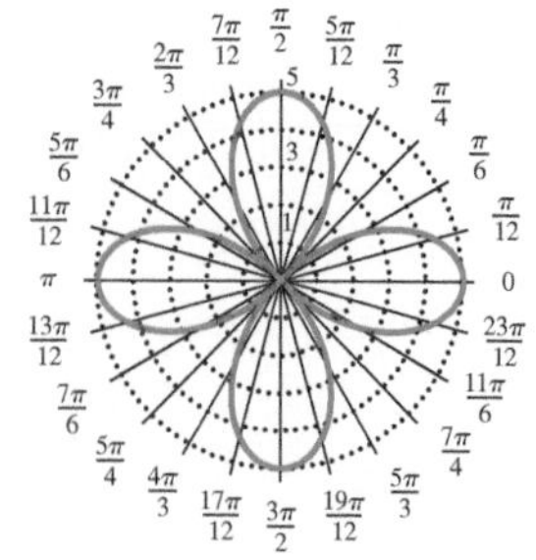

Compare the result of Example 5, the graph of $r = 5\sin(2\theta)$, with the Your Turn result, the graph of $r = 5\cos(2\theta)$. Notice that they are 45° out of phase (we rotate one graph 45° about the pole to get the other graph).

In general, for $r = a\sin(n\theta)$ or $r = a\cos(n\theta)$, the graph has n leaves (petals) if n is odd and $2n$ leaves (petals) if n is even. As a increases, the leaves (petals) get longer.

STUDY TIP

Graphs of $r = a\sin(n\theta)$ and $r = a\cos(n\theta)$ are roses with n leaves if n is odd and $2n$ leaves if n is even.

The next class of graphs are called **limaçons**, which have equations of the form $r = a \pm b\cos\theta$ or $r = a \pm b\sin\theta$. When $a = b$, the result is a **cardioid** (heart shape).

EXAMPLE 6 The Cardioid as a Polar Equation

Graph $r = 2 + 2\cos\theta$.

Solution:

STEP 1 Make a table and find key values.

This behavior repeats in quadrant III and quadrant IV, because the cosine function has corresponding values in quadrant I and quadrant IV and in quadrant II and quadrant III.

θ	$r = 2 + 2\cos\theta$	(r, θ)
0	$2 + 2(1) = 4$	$(4, 0)$
$\frac{\pi}{4}$	$2 + 2\left(\frac{\sqrt{2}}{2}\right) = 3.4$	$\left(3.4, \frac{\pi}{4}\right)$
$\frac{\pi}{2}$	$2 + 2(0) = 2$	$\left(2, \frac{\pi}{2}\right)$
$\frac{3\pi}{4}$	$2 + 2\left(-\frac{\sqrt{2}}{2}\right) \approx 0.6$	$\left(0.6, \frac{3\pi}{4}\right)$
π	$2 + 2(-1) = 0$	$(0, \pi)$

STEP 2 Plot the points in polar coordinates.

STEP 3 Connect the points with a smooth curve. The curve is a *cardioid*, a term formed from Greek roots meaning "heart-shaped."

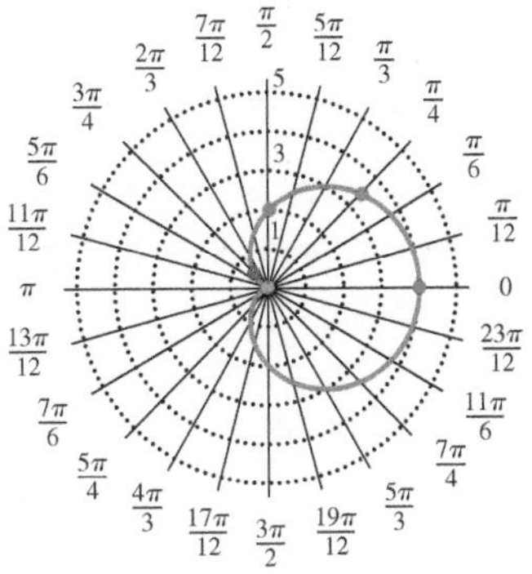

EXAMPLE 7 Graphing a Polar Equation of the Form $r = c \cdot \theta$

Graph $r = 0.5\theta$.

Solution:

STEP 1 Make a table and find key values.

θ	$r = 0.5\theta$	(r, θ)
0	$0.5(0) = 0$	$(0, 0)$
$\frac{\pi}{2}$	$0.5\left(\frac{\pi}{2}\right) = 0.8$	$\left(0.8, \frac{\pi}{2}\right)$
π	$0.5(\pi) = 1.6$	$(1.6, \pi)$
$\frac{3\pi}{2}$	$0.5\left(\frac{3\pi}{2}\right) = 2.4$	$\left(2.4, \frac{3\pi}{2}\right)$
2π	$0.5(2\pi) = 3.1$	$(3.1, 2\pi)$

STEP 2 Plot the points in polar coordinates.

STEP 3 Connect the points with a smooth curve. The curve is a *spiral*.

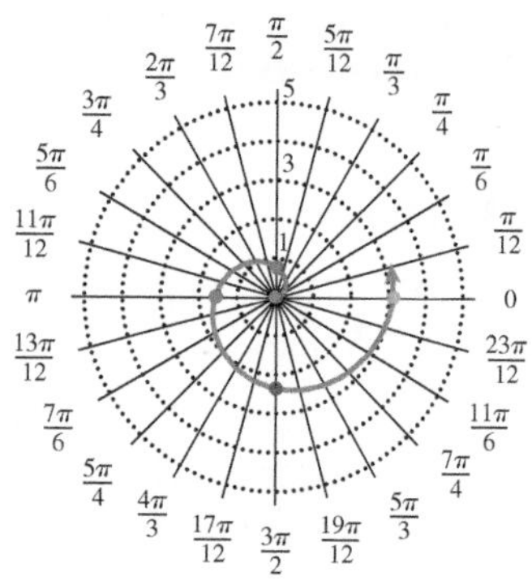

EXAMPLE 8 Graphing a Polar Equation of the Form $r^2 = c \cdot \sin(2\theta)$ or $r^2 = c \cdot \cos(2\theta)$

Graph $r^2 = 4\cos(2\theta)$.

Solution:

STEP 1 Make a table and find key values.

Solving for r yields $r = \pm 2\sqrt{\cos(2\theta)}$. All coordinates $(-r, \theta)$ can be expressed as $(r, \theta + \pi)$. The following table does not have values for $\frac{\pi}{4} < \theta < \frac{3\pi}{4}$, because the corresponding values of $\cos(2\theta)$ are negative and hence r is an imaginary number. The table also does not have values for $\theta > \pi$, because $2\theta > 2\pi$ and the corresponding points are repeated.

θ	$\cos(2\theta)$	$r = \pm 2\sqrt{\cos(2\theta)}$	(r, θ)
0	1	$r = \pm 2$	$(2, 0)$ and $(-2, 0) = (2, \pi)$
$\frac{\pi}{6}$	0.5	$r = \pm 1.4$	$\left(1.4, \frac{\pi}{6}\right)$ and $\left(-1.4, \frac{\pi}{6}\right) = \left(1.4, \frac{7\pi}{6}\right)$
$\frac{\pi}{4}$	0	$r = 0$	$\left(0, \frac{\pi}{4}\right)$
$\frac{3\pi}{4}$	0	$r = 0$	$\left(0, \frac{3\pi}{4}\right)$
$\frac{5\pi}{6}$	0.5	$r = \pm 1.4$	$\left(1.4, \frac{5\pi}{6}\right)$ and $\left(-1.4, \frac{5\pi}{6}\right) = \left(1.4, \frac{11\pi}{6}\right)$
π	1	$r = \pm 2$	$(2, \pi)$ and $(-2, \pi) = (2, 2\pi)$

STEP 2 Plot the points in polar coordinates.

STEP 3 Connect the points with a smooth curve. The resulting curve is known as a *lemniscate*.

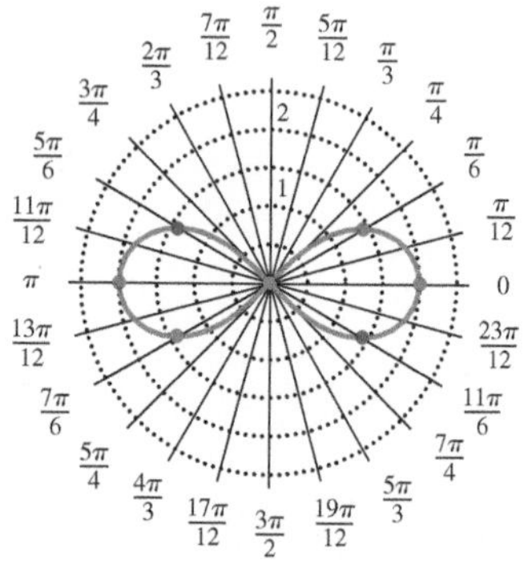

Converting Equations between Polar and Rectangular Forms

It is not always advantageous to plot an equation in the form in which it is given. It is sometimes easier to first convert to rectangular form and then plot. For example, to plot $r = \frac{2}{\cos\theta + \sin\theta}$, we could make a table of values. However, as you will see in Example 9, it is much easier to convert this equation to rectangular coordinates.

EXAMPLE 9 Converting an Equation from Polar Form to Rectangular Form

Graph $r = \frac{2}{\cos\theta + \sin\theta}$.

Solution:

Multiply the equation by $\cos\theta + \sin\theta$. $\quad r(\cos\theta + \sin\theta) = 2$

Eliminate parentheses. $\quad r\cos\theta + r\sin\theta = 2$

Convert the result to rectangular form. $\quad \underbrace{r\cos\theta}_{x} + \underbrace{r\sin\theta}_{y} = 2$

Simplify. The result is a straight line. $\quad \boxed{y = -x + 2}$

Graph the line.

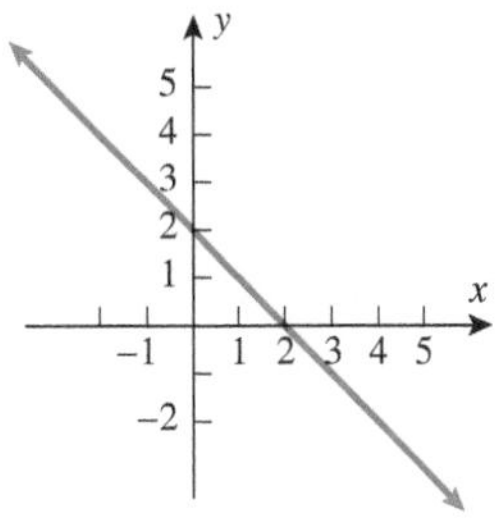

YOUR TURN Graph $r = \frac{2}{\cos\theta - \sin\theta}$.

ANSWER

$y = x - 2$

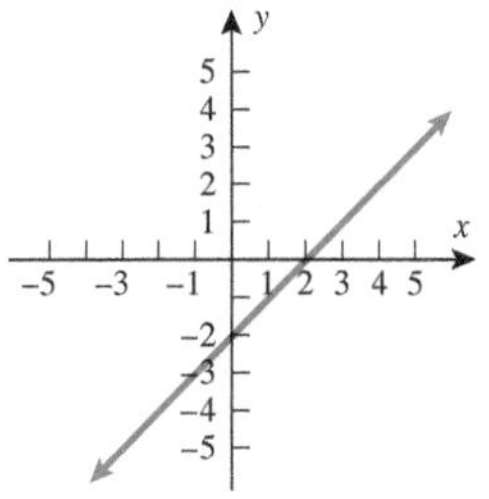

[SECTION 7.5] SUMMARY

Graph polar coordinates (r, θ) in the polar coordinate system first by rotating a ray to get the terminal side of the angle. Then, if r is positive, go out r units from the origin in the direction of the terminal side. If r is negative, go out $|r|$ units in the opposite direction from the terminal side. Conversions between polar and rectangular forms are given below.

FROM	TO	IDENTITIES
Polar (r, θ)	Rectangular (x, y)	$x = r\cos\theta \quad y = r\sin\theta$
Rectangular (x, y)	Polar (r, θ)	$r = \sqrt{x^2 + y^2} \quad \tan\theta = \frac{y}{x}, x \neq 0$ Be careful to note the proper quadrant for θ.

We can graph polar equations by point-plotting. Common shapes that arise are given in the following table. Sine and cosine curves have the same shapes (just rotated). If more than one equation is given, then the top equation corresponds to the actual graph. In this table, a and b are assumed to be positive.

CLASSIFICATION	DESCRIPTION	POLAR EQUATIONS	GRAPH
Line	Radial line	$\theta = a$	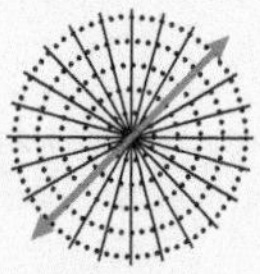
Circle	Circle centered at the origin	$r = a$	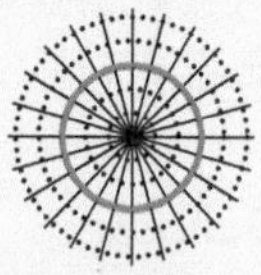
Circle	Circle that touches the pole and whose center is on the polar axis	$r = a\cos\theta$	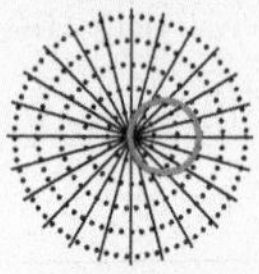
Circle	Circle that touches the pole and whose center is on the line $\theta = \frac{\pi}{2}$	$r = a\sin\theta$	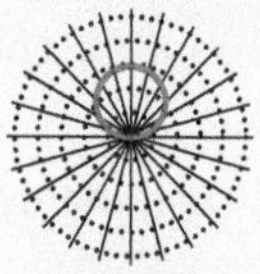
Limaçon	Cardioid $a = b$	$r = a + b\cos\theta$ $r = a + b\sin\theta$	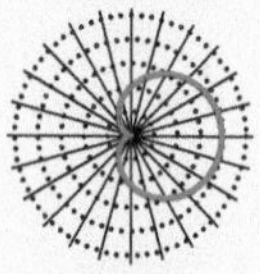
Limaçon	Without inner loop $a > b$	$r = -a - b\cos\theta$ $r = a + b\sin\theta$	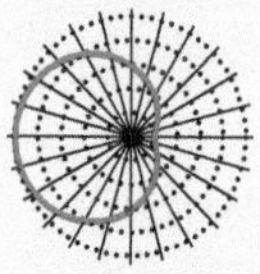
Limaçon	With inner loop $a < b$	$r = a + b\sin\theta$ $r = a + b\cos\theta$	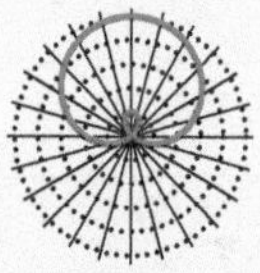
Lemniscate		$r^2 = a^2\cos(2\theta)$ $r^2 = a^2\sin(2\theta)$	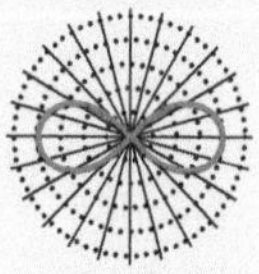
Rose	Three* rose petals	$r = a\sin(3\theta)$ $r = a\cos(3\theta)$	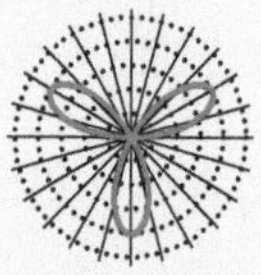

CLASSIFICATION	DESCRIPTION	POLAR EQUATIONS	GRAPH
Rose	Four* rose petals	$r = a\sin(2\theta)$ $r = a\cos(2\theta)$	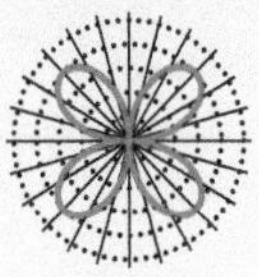
Spiral		$r = a\theta$	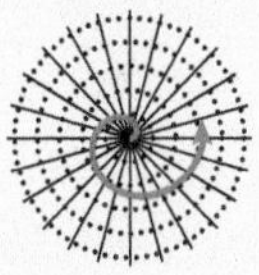

*In the argument $n\theta$, if n is odd, there are n petals (leaves), and if n is even, there are $2n$ petals (leaves).

[SECTION 7.5] EXERCISES

• SKILLS

In Exercises 1–10, plot each indicated point in a polar coordinate system.

1. $\left(3, \frac{5\pi}{6}\right)$ **2.** $\left(2, \frac{5\pi}{4}\right)$ **3.** $\left(4, \frac{11\pi}{6}\right)$ **4.** $\left(1, \frac{2\pi}{3}\right)$ **5.** $\left(-2, \frac{\pi}{6}\right)$

6. $\left(-4, \frac{7\pi}{4}\right)$ **7.** $(-4, 270°)$ **8.** $(3, 135°)$ **9.** $(4, 225°)$ **10.** $(-2, 60°)$

In Exercises 11–20, convert each point to exact polar coordinates. Assume that $0 \le \theta < 2\pi$.

11. $(2, 2\sqrt{3})$ **12.** $(3, -3)$ **13.** $(-1, -\sqrt{3})$ **14.** $(6, 6\sqrt{3})$ **15.** $(-4, 4)$

16. $(0, \sqrt{2})$ **17.** $(3, 0)$ **18.** $(-7, -7)$ **19.** $(-\sqrt{3}, -1)$ **20.** $(2\sqrt{3}, -2)$

In Exercises 21–30, convert each point to exact rectangular coordinates.

21. $\left(4, \frac{5\pi}{3}\right)$ **22.** $\left(2, \frac{3\pi}{4}\right)$ **23.** $\left(-1, \frac{5\pi}{6}\right)$ **24.** $\left(-2, \frac{7\pi}{4}\right)$ **25.** $\left(0, \frac{11\pi}{6}\right)$

26. $(6, 0)$ **27.** $(2, 240°)$ **28.** $(-3, 150°)$ **29.** $(-1, 135°)$ **30.** $(5, 315°)$

In Exercises 31–34, match each polar graph with its corresponding equation.

31. $r = 4\cos\theta$ **32.** $r = 2\theta$ **33.** $r = 3 + 3\sin\theta$ **34.** $r = 3\sin(2\theta)$

a.

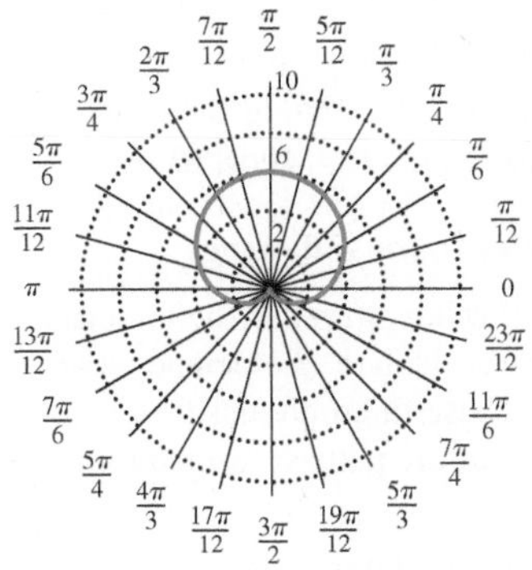

b.

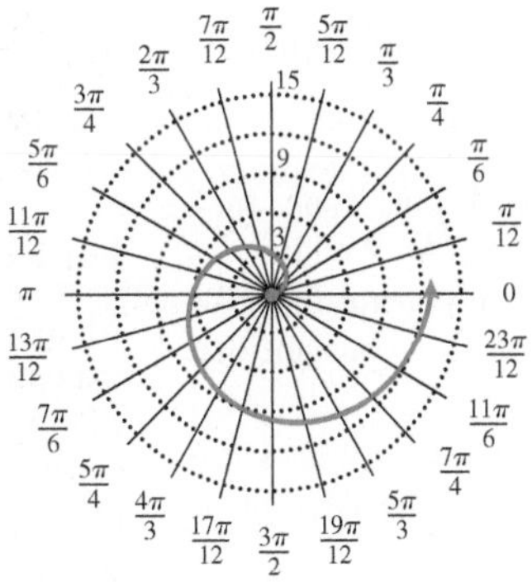

c.

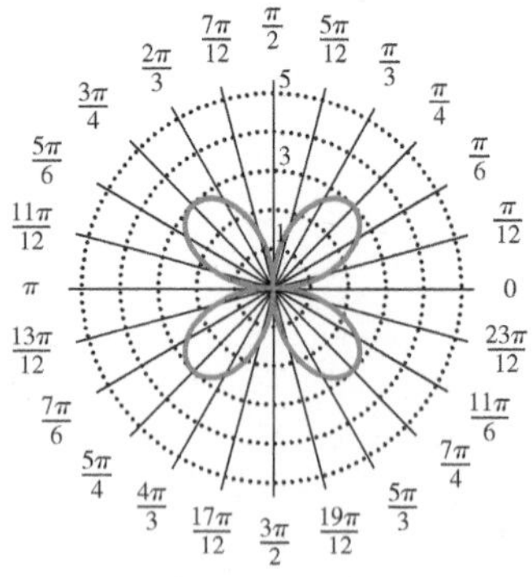

d.

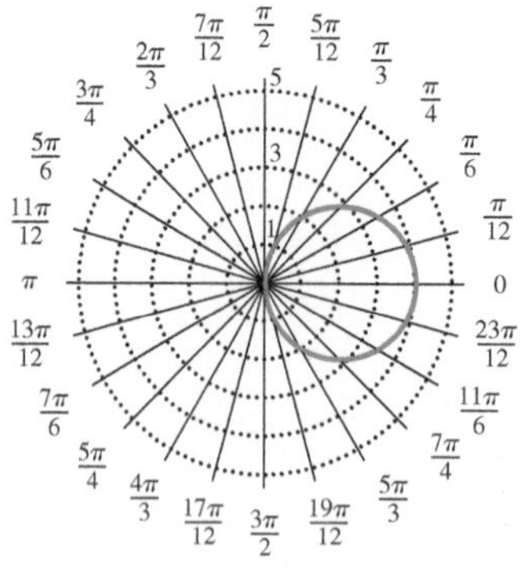

In Exercises 35–50, graph each equation.

35. $r = 5$

36. $\theta = -\frac{\pi}{3}$

37. $r = 2\cos\theta$

38. $r = 3\sin\theta$

39. $r = 4\sin(2\theta)$

40. $r = 5\cos(2\theta)$

41. $r = 3\sin(3\theta)$

42. $r = 4\cos(3\theta)$

43. $r^2 = 9\cos(2\theta)$

44. $r^2 = 16\sin(2\theta)$

45. $r = -2\cos\theta$

46. $r = -3\sin(3\theta)$

47. $r = 4\theta$

48. $r = -2\theta$

49. $r = -3 + 2\cos\theta$

50. $r = 2 + 3\sin\theta$

In Exercises 51–54, convert the equation from polar to rectangular form. Identify the resulting equation as a line, parabola, or circle.

51. $r(\sin\theta + 2\cos\theta) = 1$

52. $r(\sin\theta - 3\cos\theta) = 2$

53. $r^2\cos^2\theta - 2r\cos\theta + r^2\sin^2\theta = 8$

54. $r^2\cos^2\theta - r\sin\theta = -2$

In Exercises 55–60, graph the polar equation.

55. $r = -\frac{1}{3}\theta$

56. $r = \frac{1}{4}\theta$

57. $r = 4\sin(5\theta)$

58. $r = -3\cos(4\theta)$

59. $r = -2 - 3\cos\theta$

60. $r = 4 - 3\sin\theta$

• APPLICATIONS

61. Halley's Comet. Halley's comet travels an elliptical path that can be modeled with the polar equation $r = \frac{0.587(1 + 0.967)}{1 - 0.967\cos\theta}$. Sketch the graph of the path of Halley's comet.

62. Dwarf Planet Pluto. The planet Pluto travels in an elliptical orbit that can be modeled with the polar equation $r = \frac{29.62(1 + 0.249)}{1 - 0.249\cos\theta}$. Sketch the graph of Pluto's orbit.

For Exercises 63 and 64, refer to the following:

Spirals are seen in nature, as in the swirl of a pine cone; they are also used in machinery to convert motions. An Archimedes spiral has the general equation $r = a\theta$. A more general form for the equation of a spiral is $r = a\theta^{1/n}$, where n is a constant that determines how tightly the spiral is wrapped.

63. Archimedes Spiral. Compare the Archimedes spiral $r = \theta$ with the spiral $r = \theta^{1/2}$ by graphing both on the same polar graph.

64. Archimedes Spiral. Compare the Archimedes spiral $r = \theta$ with the spiral $r = \theta^{4/3}$ by graphing both on the same polar graph.

For Exercises 65 and 66, refer to the following:

The *lemniscate motion* occurs naturally in the flapping of birds' wings. The bird's vertical lift and wing sweep create the distinctive figure-eight pattern. The patterns vary with the different wing profiles.

65. Flapping Wings of Birds. Compare the following two possible lemniscate patterns by graphing them on the same polar graph: $r^2 = 4\cos(2\theta)$ and $r^2 = \frac{1}{4}\cos(2\theta)$.

66. Flapping Wings of Birds. Compare the following two possible lemniscate patterns by graphing them on the same polar graph: $r^2 = 4\cos(2\theta)$ and $r^2 = 4\cos(2\theta + 2)$.

For Exercises 67 and 68, refer to the following:

Many microphone manufacturers advertise that their microphones' exceptional pickup capabilities isolate the sound source and minimize background noise. These microphones are described as cardioid microphones because of the pattern formed by the range of the pickup.

67. Cardioid Pickup Pattern. Graph the cardioid curve $r = 2 + 2\sin\theta$ to see what the range looks like.

68. Cardioid Pickup Pattern. Graph the cardioid curve $r = -4 - 4\sin\theta$ to see what the range looks like.

For Exercises 69 and 70, refer to the following:

The sword artistry of the Samurai is legendary in Japanese folklore and myth. The elegance with which a samurai could wield a sword rivals the grace exhibited by modern figure skaters. In more modern times, such legends have been rendered digitally in many different video games (e.g., *Onimusha*). In order to make the characters realistically move across the screen and, in particular, wield various sword motions true to the legends, trigonometric functions are extensively used in constructing the underlying graphics module. One famous movement is a figure eight, swept out with two hands on the sword. The actual path of the tip of the blade as the movement progresses in this figure-eight motion depends essentially on the length L of the sword and the speed with which it is swept out. Such a path is modeled using a polar equation of the form

$$r^2\theta = L\cos(A\theta) \quad \text{or} \quad r^2\theta = L\sin(A\theta),\ \theta_1 \le \theta \le \theta_2$$

whose graphs are called *lemniscates*.

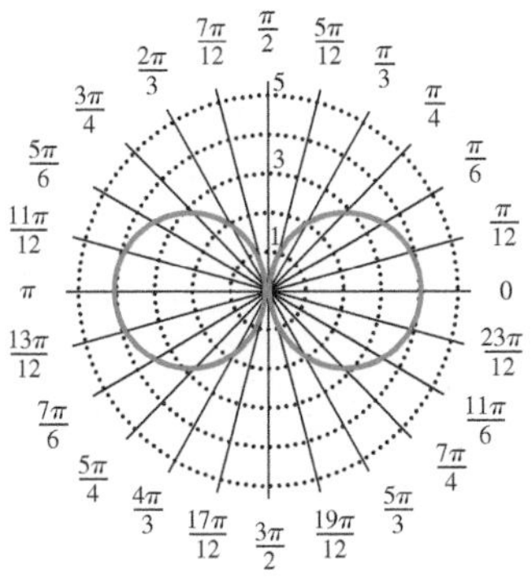

69. Video Games. Graph the following equations:

a. $r^2\theta = 5\cos\theta,\ 0 \le \theta \le 2\pi$

b. $r^2\theta = 5\cos(2\theta),\ 0 \le \theta \le \pi$

c. $r^2\theta = 5\cos(4\theta),\ 0 \le \theta \le \dfrac{\pi}{2}$

What do you notice about all of these graphs? Suppose that the movement of the tip of the sword in a game is governed by these graphs. Describe what happens if you change the domain in (b) and (c) to $0 \le \theta \le 2\pi$.

70. Video Games. Write a polar equation that would describe the motion of a sword 12 units long that makes 8 complete motions in $[0, 2\pi]$.

71. Magnetic Pendulum. A magnetic bob is affixed to an arm of length L, which is fastened to a pivot point. Three magnets of equal strength are positioned on a plane 8 inches from the center; one is placed on the x-axis, one at 120° with respect to the positive x-axis, and the other at 240° with respect to the positive x-axis. The path swept out is a three-petal rose, as shown below:

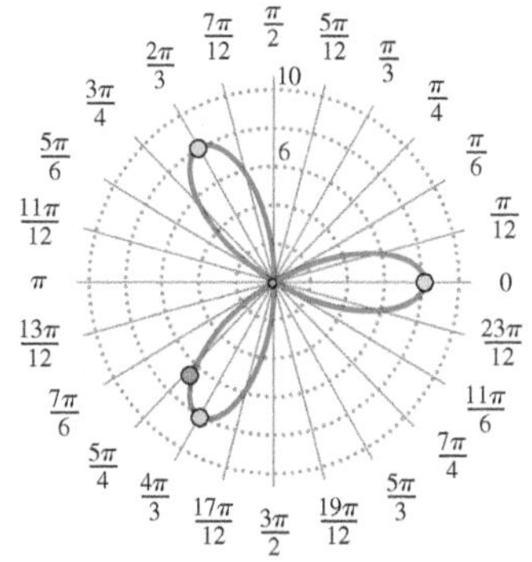

a. Find the equation of this path.

b. How many times does the path retrace itself on the interval $[0, 100\pi]$?

72. Magnetic Pendulum. In reference to the context of Exercise 71, now position 8 magnets, each 8 units from the origin and at the vertices of a regular octagon, one being on the x-axis. Assume that the path of the pendulum is an eight-petal rose.

a. Find the equation of this path.

b. Graph this equation.

• CATCH THE MISTAKE

In Exercises 73 and 74, explain the mistake that is made.

73. Convert $(-2, -2)$ to polar coordinates.

Solution:

Label x and y. $\quad x = -2,\ y = -2$

Find r. $\quad r = \sqrt{x^2 + y^2} = \sqrt{4+4} = \sqrt{8} = 2\sqrt{2}$

Find θ. $\quad \tan\theta = \dfrac{-2}{-2} = 1$

$$\theta = \tan^{-1}(1) = \frac{\pi}{4}$$

Write the point in polar coordinates. $\quad \left(2\sqrt{2}, \dfrac{\pi}{4}\right)$

This is incorrect. What mistake was made?

74. Convert $(-\sqrt{3}, 1)$ to polar coordinates.

Solution:

Label x and y. $\quad x = -\sqrt{3},\ y = 1$

Find r. $\quad r = \sqrt{x^2 + y^2} = \sqrt{3+1} = \sqrt{4} = 2$

Find θ. $\quad \tan\theta = \dfrac{1}{-\sqrt{3}} = -\dfrac{1}{\sqrt{3}}$

$$\theta = \tan^{-1}\left(-\frac{1}{\sqrt{3}}\right) = -\frac{\pi}{4}$$

Write the point in polar coordinates. $\quad \left(2, -\dfrac{\pi}{4}\right)$

This is incorrect. What mistake was made?

• CONCEPTUAL

In Exercises 75 and 76, determine whether each statement is true or false.

75. All cardioids are limaçons, but not all limaçons are cardioids.

76. All limaçons are cardioids, but not all cardioids are limaçons.

77. Find the polar equation that is equivalent to a vertical line, $x = a$.

78. Find the polar equation that is equivalent to a horizontal line, $y = b$.

79. Give another pair of polar coordinates for the point (a, θ).

80. Convert $(-a, b)$ to polar coordinates. Assume that $a > 0, b > 0$.

• CHALLENGE

81. Determine the values of θ at which $r = 4\cos\theta$ and $r\cos\theta = 1$ intersect. Graph both equations.

82. Find the Cartesian equation for $r = a\sin\theta + b\cos\theta$, where a and b are positive. Identify the type of graph.

83. Find the Cartesian equation for $r = \dfrac{a\sin(2\theta)}{\cos^3\theta - \sin^3\theta}$.

84. Identify an equation for the following graph:

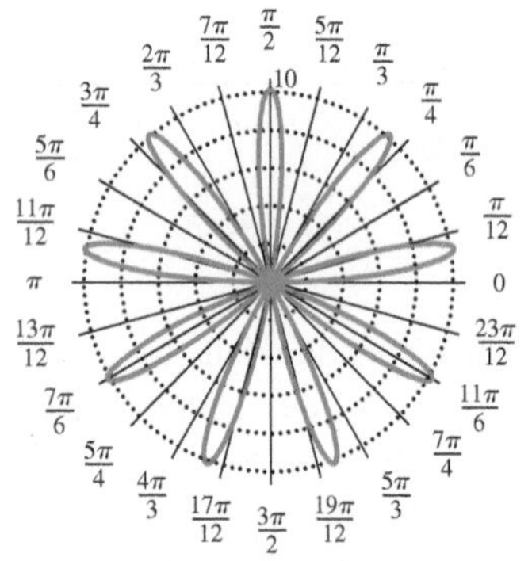

85. Consider the equation $r = 2a\cos(\theta - b)$. Sketch the graph for various values of a and b, and then give a general description of the graph.

86. Consider the equation $r = a\sin(b\theta)$, where $a, b > 0$. Determine the smallest number M for which the graph starts to repeat.

• PREVIEW TO CALCULUS

In calculus, when we need to find the area enclosed by two polar curves, the first step consists of finding the points where the curves coincide.

In Exercises 87–90, find the points of intersection of the given curves.

87. $r = 4\sin\theta$ and $r = 4\cos\theta$

88. $r = \cos\theta$ and $r = 2 + 3\cos\theta$

89. $r = 1 - \sin\theta$ and $r = 1 + \cos\theta$

90. $r = 1 + \sin\theta$ and $r = 1 + \cos\theta$

[CHAPTER 7 REVIEW]

SECTION	CONCEPT	KEY IDEAS/FORMULAS
7.1	**Vectors**	Vector **u** or $\overrightarrow{AB}$ 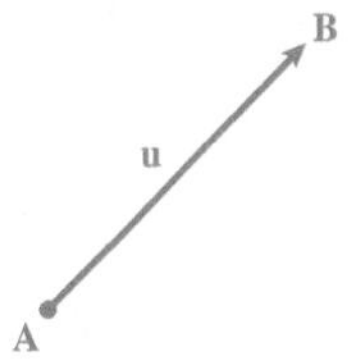
	Magnitude and direction of vectors	$\mathbf{u} = \langle a, b \rangle$ $\tan\theta = \frac{b}{a}$ Magnitude (length of a vector): $\lvert\mathbf{u}\rvert = \sqrt{a^2 + b^2}$ Geometric: tail-to-tip 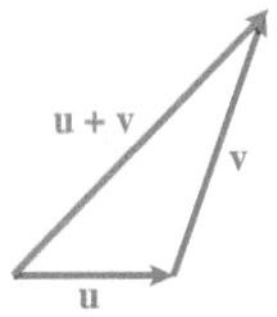 $\mathbf{u} = \langle a, b \rangle$ and $\mathbf{v} = \langle c, d \rangle$ $\mathbf{u} + \mathbf{v} = \langle a + c, b + d \rangle$
	Vector operations	Scalar multiplication: $k\langle a, b \rangle = \langle ka, kb \rangle$
	Horizontal and vertical components of a vector	Horizontal component: $a = \lvert\mathbf{u}\rvert\cos\theta$ Vertical component: $b = \lvert\mathbf{u}\rvert\sin\theta$
	Unit vectors	$\mathbf{u} = \frac{\mathbf{v}}{\lvert\mathbf{v}\rvert}$
	Resultant vectors	■ Resultant velocities ■ Resultant forces
7.2	**The dot product**	■ The product of a scalar and a vector is a vector. ■ The dot product of two vectors is a scalar.
	The dot product	$\mathbf{u} = \langle a, b \rangle$ and $\mathbf{v} = \langle c, d \rangle$ $\mathbf{u} \cdot \mathbf{v} = ac + bd$
	Angle between two vectors	If θ is the angle between two nonzero vectors **u** and **v**, where $0° \leq \theta \leq 180°$, then $\cos\theta = \frac{\mathbf{u} \cdot \mathbf{v}}{\lvert\mathbf{u}\rvert\lvert\mathbf{v}\rvert}$ Orthogonal (perpendicular) vectors: $\mathbf{u} \cdot \mathbf{v} = 0$
	Work	When force and displacement are in the same direction: $W = \lvert\mathbf{F}\rvert\lvert\mathbf{d}\rvert$. When force and displacement are not in the same direction: $W = \mathbf{F} \cdot \mathbf{d}$.

SECTION	CONCEPT	KEY IDEAS/FORMULAS
7.3	**Polar (trigonometric) form of complex numbers**	
	Complex numbers in rectangular form	The **modulus**, or magnitude, of a complex number $z = x + iy$ is the distance from the origin to the point (x, y) in the complex plane given by $$\lvert z \rvert = \sqrt{x^2 + y^2}$$
	Complex numbers in polar form	The **polar form** of a complex number is $$z = r(\cos\theta + i\sin\theta)$$ where r represents the **modulus** (magnitude) of the complex number and θ represents the **argument** of z. **Converting complex numbers between rectangular and polar forms** Step 1: Plot the point $z = x + yi$ in the complex plane (note the quadrant). Step 2: Find r. Use $r = \sqrt{x^2 + y^2}$. Step 3: Find θ. Use $\tan\theta = \frac{y}{x}$, $x \neq 0$, where θ is in the quadrant found in Step 1.
7.4	**Products, quotients, powers, and roots of complex numbers**	
	Products of complex numbers	Let $z_1 = r_1(\cos\theta_1 + i\sin\theta_1)$ and $z_2 = r_2(\cos\theta_2 + i\sin\theta_2)$ be two complex numbers. The product z_1z_2 is given by $$z_1z_2 = r_1r_2[\cos(\theta_1 + \theta_2) + i\sin(\theta_1 + \theta_2)]$$ Multiply the magnitudes and add the arguments.
	Quotients of complex numbers	Let $z_1 = r_1(\cos\theta_1 + i\sin\theta_1)$ and $z_2 = r_2(\cos\theta_2 + i\sin\theta_2)$ be two complex numbers. The quotient $\frac{z_1}{z_2}$ is given by $$\frac{z_1}{z_2} = \frac{r_1}{r_2}[\cos(\theta_1 - \theta_2) + i\sin(\theta_1 - \theta_2)]$$ Divide the magnitudes and subtract the arguments.
	Powers of complex numbers	**De Moivre's theorem** If $z = r(\cos\theta + i\sin\theta)$ is a complex number, then $z^n = r^n[\cos(n\theta) + i\sin(n\theta)]$, $n \geq 1$, where n is an integer.
	Roots of complex numbers	The ***n*th roots** of the complex number $z = r(\cos\theta + i\sin\theta)$ are given by $$w_k = r^{1/n}\left[\cos\left(\frac{\theta}{n} + \frac{k\cdot 360^\circ}{n}\right) + i\sin\left(\frac{\theta}{n} + \frac{k\cdot 360^\circ}{n}\right)\right]$$ θ in degrees, where $k = 0, 1, 2, \ldots, n - 1$; $n =$ integer

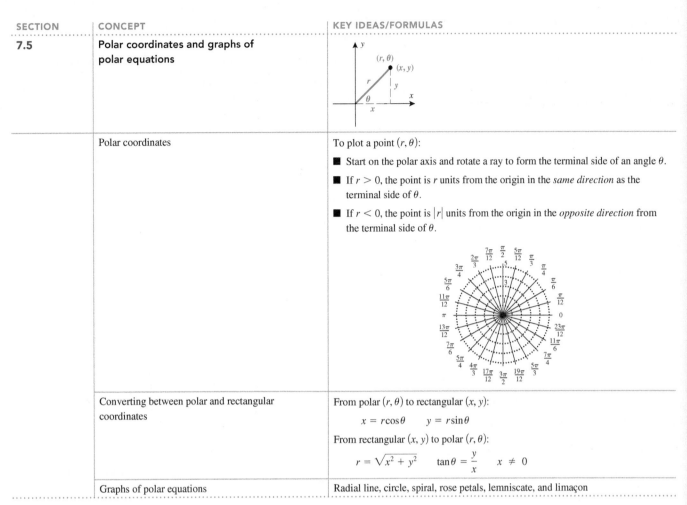

SECTION	CONCEPT	KEY IDEAS/FORMULAS
7.5	**Polar coordinates and graphs of polar equations**	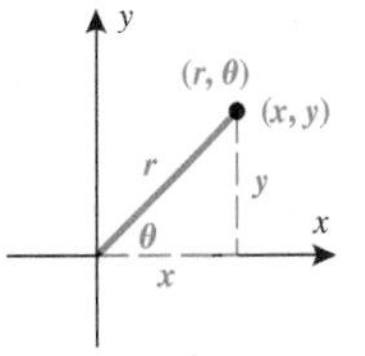
	Polar coordinates	To plot a point (r, θ): ■ Start on the polar axis and rotate a ray to form the terminal side of an angle θ. ■ If $r > 0$, the point is r units from the origin in the *same direction* as the terminal side of θ. ■ If $r < 0$, the point is $\lvert r \rvert$ units from the origin in the *opposite direction* from the terminal side of θ. 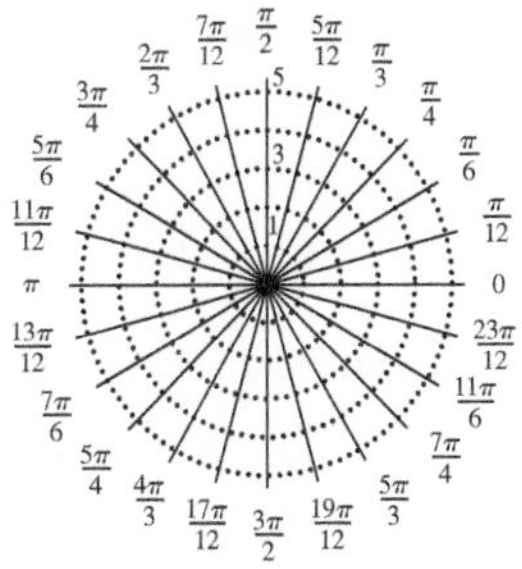
	Converting between polar and rectangular coordinates	From polar (r, θ) to rectangular (x, y): $x = r\cos\theta \qquad y = r\sin\theta$ From rectangular (x, y) to polar (r, θ): $r = \sqrt{x^2 + y^2} \qquad \tan\theta = \frac{y}{x} \qquad x \neq 0$
	Graphs of polar equations	Radial line, circle, spiral, rose petals, lemniscate, and limaçon

[CHAPTER 7 REVIEW EXERCISES]

7.1 Vectors

Find the magnitude of vector $\overrightarrow{AB}$.

1. $A = (4, -3)$ and $B = (-8, 2)$
2. $A = (-2, 11)$ and $B = (2, 8)$
3. $A = (0, -3)$ and $B = (5, 9)$
4. $A = (3, -11)$ and $B = (9, -3)$

Find the magnitude and direction angle of the given vector.

5. $\mathbf{u} = \langle -10, 24 \rangle$
6. $\mathbf{u} = \langle -5, -12 \rangle$
7. $\mathbf{u} = \langle 16, -12 \rangle$
8. $\mathbf{u} = \langle 0, 3 \rangle$

Perform the vector operation, given that $\mathbf{u} = \langle 7, -2 \rangle$ and $\mathbf{v} = \langle -4, 5 \rangle$.

9. $2\mathbf{u} + 3\mathbf{v}$
10. $\mathbf{u} - \mathbf{v}$
11. $6\mathbf{u} + \mathbf{v}$
12. $-3(\mathbf{u} + 2\mathbf{v})$

Find the vector, given its magnitude and direction angle.

13. $|\mathbf{u}| = 10, \theta = 75°$
14. $|\mathbf{u}| = 8, \theta = 225°$
15. $|\mathbf{u}| = 12, \theta = 105°$
16. $|\mathbf{u}| = 20, \theta = 15°$

Find a unit vector in the direction of the given vector.

17. $\mathbf{v} = \langle \sqrt{6}, -\sqrt{6} \rangle$
18. $\mathbf{v} = \langle -11, 60 \rangle$

Perform the indicated vector operation.

19. $(3\mathbf{i} - 4\mathbf{j}) + (2\mathbf{i} + 5\mathbf{j})$
20. $(-6\mathbf{i} + \mathbf{j}) - (9\mathbf{i} - \mathbf{j})$

7.2 The Dot Product

Find the indicated dot product.

21. $\langle 6, -3 \rangle \cdot \langle 1, 4 \rangle$
22. $\langle -6, 5 \rangle \cdot \langle -4, 2 \rangle$
23. $\langle 3, 3 \rangle \cdot \langle 3, -6 \rangle$
24. $\langle -2, -8 \rangle \cdot \langle -1, 1 \rangle$
25. $\langle 0, 8 \rangle \cdot \langle 1, 2 \rangle$
26. $\langle 4, -3 \rangle \cdot \langle -1, 0 \rangle$

Find the angle (round to the nearest degree) between each pair of vectors.

27. $\langle 3, 4 \rangle$ and $\langle -5, 12 \rangle$
28. $\langle -4, 5 \rangle$ and $\langle 5, -4 \rangle$
29. $\langle 1, \sqrt{2} \rangle$ and $\langle -1, 3\sqrt{2} \rangle$
30. $\langle 7, -24 \rangle$ and $\langle -6, 8 \rangle$
31. $\langle 3, 5 \rangle$ and $\langle -4, -4 \rangle$
32. $\langle -1, 6 \rangle$ and $\langle 2, -2 \rangle$

Determine whether each pair of vectors is orthogonal.

33. $\langle 8, 3 \rangle$ and $\langle -3, 12 \rangle$
34. $\langle -6, 2 \rangle$ and $\langle 4, 12 \rangle$
35. $\langle 5, -6 \rangle$ and $\langle -12, -10 \rangle$
36. $\langle 1, 1 \rangle$ and $\langle -4, 4 \rangle$
37. $\langle 0, 4 \rangle$ and $\langle 0, -4 \rangle$
38. $\langle -7, 2 \rangle$ and $\langle \frac{1}{7}, -\frac{1}{2} \rangle$
39. $\langle 6z, a - b \rangle$ and $\langle a + b, -6z \rangle$
40. $\langle a - b, -1 \rangle$ and $\langle a + b, a^2 - b^2 \rangle$

7.3 Polar (Trigonometric) Form of Complex Numbers

Graph each complex number in the complex plane.

41. $-6 + 2i$
42. $5i$

Express each complex number in polar form.

43. $\sqrt{2} - \sqrt{2}i$
44. $\sqrt{3} + i$
45. $-8i$
46. $-8 - 8i$

With a calculator, express each complex number in polar form.

47. $-60 + 11i$
48. $9 - 40i$
49. $15 + 8i$
50. $-10 - 24i$

Express each complex number in rectangular form.

51. $6(\cos 300° + i\sin 300°)$
52. $4(\cos 210° + i\sin 210°)$
53. $\sqrt{2}(\cos 135° + i\sin 135°)$
54. $4(\cos 150° + i\sin 150°)$

With a calculator, express each complex number in rectangular form.

55. $4(\cos 200° + i\sin 200°)$
56. $3(\cos 350° + i\sin 350°)$

7.4 Products, Quotients, Powers, and Roots of Complex Numbers

Find the product z_1z_2.

57. $z_1 = 3(\cos 200° + i\sin 200°)$ and $z_2 = 4(\cos 70° + i\sin 70°)$
58. $z_1 = 3(\cos 20° + i\sin 20°)$ and $z_2 = 4(\cos 220° + i\sin 220°)$
59. $z_1 = 7(\cos 100° + i\sin 100°)$ and $z_2 = 3(\cos 140° + i\sin 140°)$
60. $z_1 = (\cos 290° + i\sin 290°)$ and $z_2 = 4(\cos 40° + i\sin 40°)$

Find the quotient $\dfrac{z_1}{z_2}$.

61. $z_1 = \sqrt{6}(\cos 200° + i\sin 200°)$ and $z_2 = \sqrt{6}(\cos 50° + i\sin 50°)$
62. $z_1 = 18(\cos 190° + i\sin 190°)$ and $z_2 = 2(\cos 100° + i\sin 100°)$
63. $z_1 = 24(\cos 290° + i\sin 290°)$ and $z_2 = 4(\cos 110° + i\sin 110°)$
64. $z_1 = \sqrt{200}(\cos 93° + i\sin 93°)$ and $z_2 = \sqrt{2}(\cos 48° + i\sin 48°)$

Find the result of each expression using De Moivre's theorem. Write the answer in rectangular form.

65. $(3 + 3i)^4$
66. $(3 + \sqrt{3}i)^4$
67. $(1 + \sqrt{3}i)^5$
68. $(-2 - 2i)^7$

REVIEW EXERCISES

Find all nth roots of z. Write the answers in polar form, and plot the roots in the complex plane.

69. $2 + 2\sqrt{3}i,\ n = 2$
70. $-8 + 8\sqrt{3}i,\ n = 4$
71. $-256,\ n = 4$
72. $-18i,\ n = 2$

Find all complex solutions to the given equations.

73. $x^3 + 216 = 0$
74. $x^4 - 1 = 0$
75. $x^4 + 1 = 0$
76. $x^3 - 125 = 0$

7.5 Polar Coordinates and Graphs of Polar Equations

Convert each point to exact polar coordinates (assuming that $0 \leq \theta < 2\pi$), and then graph the point in the polar coordinate system.

77. $(-2, 2)$
78. $(4, -4\sqrt{3})$
79. $(-5\sqrt{3}, -5)$
80. $(\sqrt{3}, \sqrt{3})$
81. $(0, -2)$
82. $(11, 0)$

Convert each polar point to exact rectangular coordinates.

83. $\left(-3, \frac{5\pi}{3}\right)$
84. $\left(4, \frac{5\pi}{4}\right)$
85. $\left(2, \frac{\pi}{3}\right)$
86. $\left(6, \frac{7\pi}{6}\right)$
87. $\left(1, \frac{4\pi}{3}\right)$
88. $\left(-3, \frac{7\pi}{4}\right)$

Graph each equation.

89. $r = 4\cos(2\theta)$
90. $r = \sin(3\theta)$
91. $r = -\theta$
92. $r = 4 - 3\sin\theta$

[CHAPTER 7 PRACTICE TEST]

1. Find the magnitude and direction angle of the vector $\mathbf{u} = \langle -5, 12 \rangle$.

2. Find a unit vector pointing in the same direction as $\mathbf{v} = \langle -3, -4 \rangle$.

3. Perform the indicated operations:

a. $2\langle -1, 4 \rangle - 3\langle 4, 1 \rangle$

b. $\langle -7, -1 \rangle \cdot \langle 2, 2 \rangle$

4. In a post pattern in football, the receiver in motion runs past the quarterback parallel to the line of scrimmage (A), runs 12 yards perpendicular to the line of scrimmage (B), and then cuts toward the goal post (C).

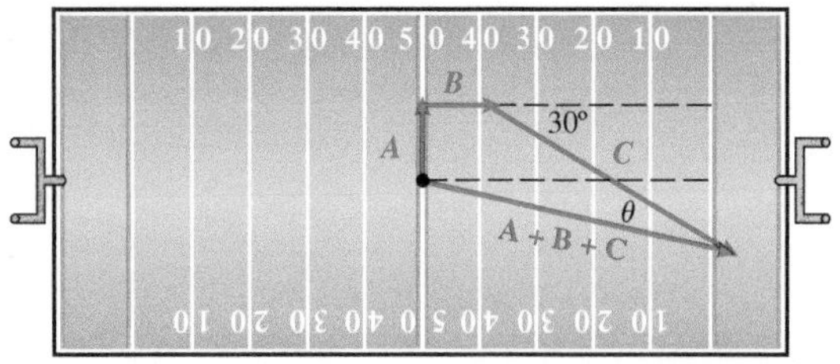

A receiver runs the post pattern. If the magnitudes of the vectors are $|A| = 3$ yd, $|B| = 12$ yd, and $|C| = 18$ yd, find the magnitude of the resultant vector $\mathbf{A} + \mathbf{B} + \mathbf{C}$ and the direction angle θ.

5. Find the dot product $\langle 4, -51 \rangle \cdot \langle -2, -\frac{1}{3} \rangle$.

6. If the dot product $\langle a, -2a \rangle \cdot \langle 4, 5 \rangle = 18$, find the value of a.

For Exercises 7 and 8, use the complex number $z = 16(\cos 120° + i \sin 120°)$.

7. Find z^4.

8. Find the four distinct fourth roots of z.

9. Convert the point $(3, 210°)$ to rectangular coordinates.

10. Convert the polar point $\left(4, \frac{5\pi}{4}\right)$ to rectangular coordinates.

11. Convert the point $(30, -15)$ to polar coordinates.

12. Graph $r = 6\sin(2\theta)$.

13. Graph $r^2 = 9\cos(2\theta)$.

14. Find x such that $\langle x, 1 \rangle$ is perpendicular to $3\mathbf{i} - 4\mathbf{j}$.

15. Prove that $\mathbf{u} \cdot (\mathbf{v} - \mathbf{w}) = \mathbf{u} \cdot \mathbf{v} - \mathbf{u} \cdot \mathbf{w}$.

16. Construct a unit vector in the opposite direction from $\langle 3, 5 \rangle$.

17. Compute $\mathbf{u} \cdot \mathbf{v}$ if $|\mathbf{u}| = 4$, $|\mathbf{v}| = 10$, and $\theta = \frac{2\pi}{3}$.

18. Determine whether $\mathbf{u}$ and $\mathbf{v}$ are parallel, perpendicular, or neither: $\mathbf{u} = \langle \sin\theta, \cos\theta \rangle$, and $\mathbf{v} = \langle -\cos\theta, \sin\theta \rangle$.

19. Find the magnitude of $-\mathbf{i} - \mathbf{j}$.

20. Determine θ, when a streetlight is formed as follows:

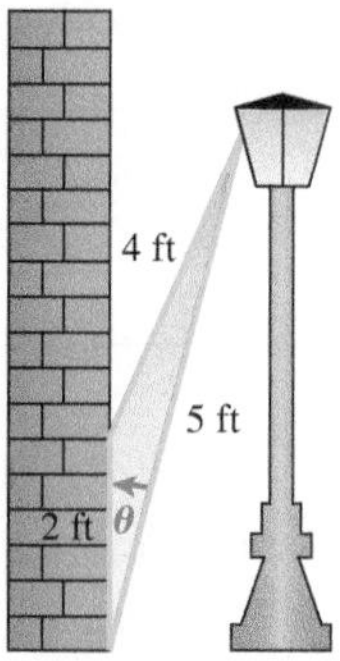

21. Two tugboats pull a cruiser off the port of Miami. The first one pulls with a force of 25,000 pounds and the second one pulls with a force of 27,000 pounds. If the angle between the lines connecting the cruiser with the tugboats is 25°, what is the resultant force vector of the two tugboats?

22. True or false: If $\mathbf{u} + \mathbf{v}$ is perpendicular to $\mathbf{u} - \mathbf{v}$, then $|\mathbf{u}| = |\mathbf{v}|$.

23. Solve $z^4 + 256i = 0$.

24. Convert to a Cartesian equation: $r^2 = \tan\theta$.

[CHAPTERS 1–7 CUMULATIVE TEST]

1. Given $f(x) = x^2 - 4$ and $g(x) = \dfrac{1}{\sqrt{3x+5}}$, find $(f \circ g)(x)$ and the domain of f, g, and $f \circ g$.
2. Determine whether the function $f(x) = |x^3|$ is even, odd, or neither.
3. Find the quadratic function whose graph has a vertex at $(-1, 2)$ and passes through the point $(2, -1)$. Express the quadratic function in both standard and general forms.
4. For the polynomial function $f(x) = x^5 - 4x^4 + x^3 + 10x^2 - 4x - 8$
   a. List each real zero and its multiplicity.
   b. Determine whether the graph touches or crosses at each x-intercept.
5. Find all vertical and horizontal or slant asymptotes (if any) in the following:
$$f(x) = \frac{x^3 - 3x^2 + 2x - 1}{x^2 - 2x + 1}$$
6. How much money should you invest today in a money market account that pays 1.4% a year compounded continuously if you desire \$5000 in 8 years?
7. Write the exponential equation $\sqrt[4]{625} = 5$ in its equivalent logarithmic form.
8. What is the radian measure of an angle of 305°? Express your answer in terms of π.
9. Find all trigonometric functions of the angle θ. Rationalize any denominators containing radicals that you encounter in your answers.

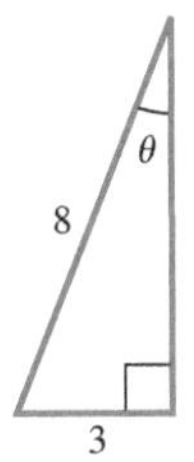

10. Solve the triangle $\alpha = 30°$, $\beta = 30°$, and $c = 4$ in.
11. Solve the triangle $a = 14.2$ m, $b = 16.5$ m, and $\gamma = 50°$.
12. Find the exact value of each trigonometric function:
    a. $\sin\left(\dfrac{3\pi}{2}\right)$
    b. $\cos 0$
    c. $\tan\left(\dfrac{5\pi}{4}\right)$
    d. $\cot\left(\dfrac{11\pi}{6}\right)$
    e. $\sec\left(\dfrac{2\pi}{3}\right)$
    f. $\csc\left(\dfrac{5\pi}{6}\right)$
13. State the amplitude, period, phase shift, and vertical shift of the function $y = 4 - \frac{1}{3}\sin(4x - \pi)$.
14. If $\sin x = \dfrac{1}{\sqrt{3}}$ and $\cos x < 0$, find $\cos(2x)$.
15. Find the exact value of $\tan\left[\cos^{-1}\left(-\frac{3}{5}\right) + \sin^{-1}\left(\frac{1}{2}\right)\right]$.
16. Find $(1 + \sqrt{3}i)^8$. Express the answer in rectangular form.

CUMULATIVE TEST

CHAPTER 8

Systems of Linear Equations and Inequalities

Cryptography is the practice and study of encryption and decryption—encoding data so that it can be decoded only by specific individuals. In other words, it turns a message into gibberish so that only the person who has the deciphering tools can turn that gibberish back into the original message. ATM cards, online shopping sites, and secure military communications all depend on coding and decoding of information. Matrices are used extensively in cryptography. A *matrix* is used as the "key" to encode the data, and then its *inverse matrix* is used as the key to decode the data.*

*Section 8.4, Exercises 87–92.

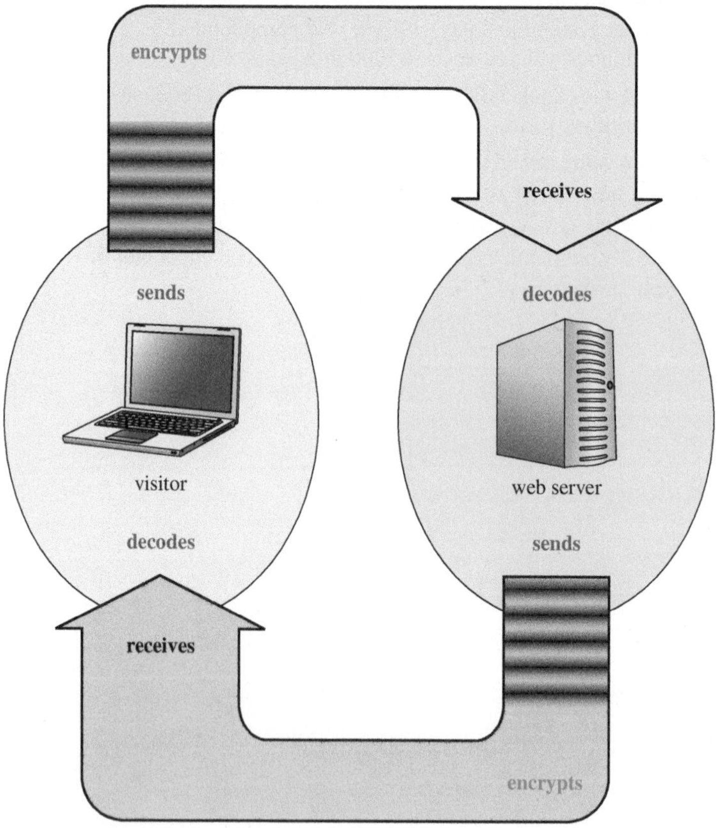

LEARNING OBJECTIVES

- Solve systems of linear equations in two variables with the substitution method and the elimination method.
- Solve systems of linear equations in three variables employing a combination of the elimination and substitution methods.
- Use Gauss–Jordan elimination to solve systems of linear equations.
- Perform matrix operations: addition, subtraction, and multiplication.

[IN THIS CHAPTER]

We will solve systems of linear equations using the elimination and substitution methods. We will then solve systems of linear equations by employing matrices three different ways: using augmented matrices (Gauss–Jordan elimination), matrix algebra (inverse matrices), and determinants (Cramer's rule). We will next discuss an application of systems of linear equations that is useful in calculus called partial-fraction decomposition. Finally, we will solve systems of linear inequalities.

SYSTEMS OF LINEAR EQUATIONS AND INEQUALITIES						
8.1 SYSTEMS OF LINEAR EQUATIONS IN TWO VARIABLES	**8.2** SYSTEMS OF LINEAR EQUATIONS IN THREE VARIABLES	**8.3** SYSTEMS OF LINEAR EQUATIONS AND MATRICES	**8.4** MATRIX ALGEBRA	**8.5** THE DETERMINANT OF A SQUARE MATRIX AND CRAMER'S RULE	**8.6** PARTIAL FRACTIONS	**8.7** SYSTEMS OF LINEAR INEQUALITIES IN TWO VARIABLES
• Solving Systems of Linear Equations in Two Variables • Three Methods and Three Types of Solutions	• Solving Systems of Linear Equations in Three Variables • Types of Solutions	• Matrices • Augmented Matrices • Row Operations on a Matrix • Row–Echelon Form of a Matrix • Gaussian Elimination with Back-Substitution • Gauss–Jordan Elimination • Inconsistent and Dependent Systems	• Equality of Matrices • Matrix Addition and Subtraction • Scalar and Matrix Multiplication • Matrix Equations • Finding the Inverse of a Square Matrix • Solving Systems of Linear Equations Using Matrix Algebra and Inverses of Square Matrices	• Determinant of a 2×2 Matrix • Determinant of an $n \times n$ Matrix • Cramer's Rule: Systems of Linear Equations in Two Variables • Cramer's Rule: Systems of Linear Equations in Three Variables	• Performing Partial-Fraction Decomposition	• Linear Inequalities in Two Variables • Systems of Linear Inequalities in Two Variables • The Linear Programming Model

- Utilize matrix algebra and inverses of matrices to solve systems of linear equations.
- Use Cramer's rule (determinants) to solve systems of linear equations.
- Perform partial-fraction decomposition.
- Solve a system of linear inequalities by finding the overlapping shaded regions.
- Use the linear programming model to solve optimization problems subject to constraints.

8.1 SYSTEMS OF LINEAR EQUATIONS IN TWO VARIABLES

SKILLS OBJECTIVES

- Solve systems of linear equations in two variables.
- Solve applications involving systems of linear equations.

CONCEPTUAL OBJECTIVES

- Understand that a system of linear equations has either one solution (two lines intersecting at a single point), no solution (parallel lines), or infinitely many solutions (same line).
- Understand how to model a real-world problem using systems of linear equations in two variables.

8.1.1 Solving Systems of Linear Equations in Two Variables

8.1.1 SKILL

Solve systems of linear equations in two variables.

8.1.1 CONCEPTUAL

Understand that a system of linear equations has either one solution (two lines intersecting at a single point), no solution (parallel lines), or infinitely many solutions (same line).

Overview

A linear equation in two variables is given in standard form by

$$Ax + By = C$$

and the graph of this linear equation is a line, provided that A and B are not both equal to zero. In this section, we discuss **systems of linear equations**, which can be thought of as simultaneous equations. To **solve** a system of linear equations in two variables means to find the solution that satisfies *both* equations. Suppose we are given the following system of equations:

$$\begin{aligned} x + 2y &= 6 \\ 3x - y &= 11 \end{aligned}$$

We can interpret the solution to this system of equations both algebraically and graphically.

	ALGEBRAIC		GRAPHICAL
Solution	$x = 4$ and $y = 1$		$(4, 1)$
Check	**Equation 1** $x + 2y = 6$ $(4) + 2(1) = 6$ ✓	**Equation 2** $3x - y = 11$ $3(4) - 1 = 11$ ✓	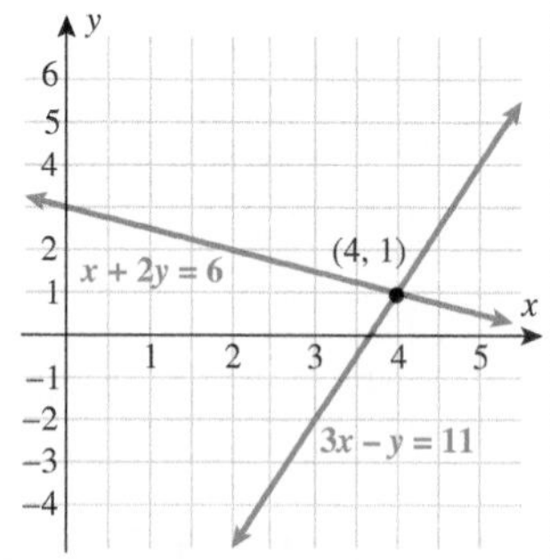
Interpretation	$x = 4$ and $y = 1$ satisfy both equations.		The point $(4, 1)$ lies on both lines.

This particular example had *one solution*. There are systems of equations that have *no solution* or *infinitely many solutions*. We give these systems special names: **independent**, **inconsistent**, and **dependent**, respectively.

INDEPENDENT SYSTEM	INCONSISTENT SYSTEM	DEPENDENT SYSTEM
One solution	No solution	Infinitely many solutions
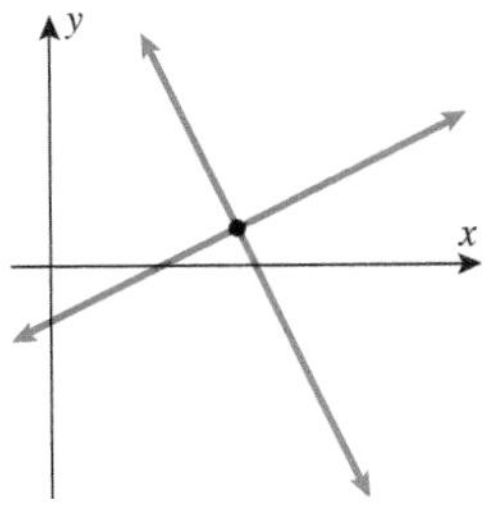	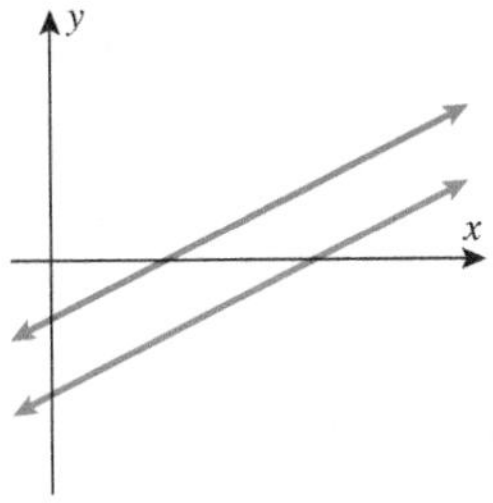	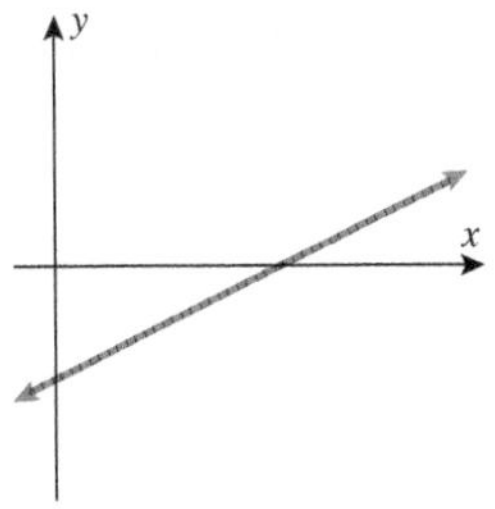
Lines have different slopes.	Lines are parallel (same slope and different y-intercepts).	Lines coincide (same slope and same y-intercept).

In this section, we discuss three methods for solving systems of two linear equations in two variables: *substitution*, *elimination*, and *graphing*. We use the algebraic methods—substitution and elimination—to find solutions exactly; we then look at a graphical interpretation of the solution (two lines that intersect at one point, parallel lines, or coinciding lines).

We will illustrate each method with the same example given earlier:

$$x + 2y = 6 \qquad \text{Equation (1)}$$
$$3x - y = 11 \qquad \text{Equation (2)}$$

Substitution Method

The following box summarizes the substitution method for solving systems of two linear equations in two variables.

SUBSTITUTION METHOD

Step 1: **Solve** one of the equations for one variable in terms of the other variable.	Equation (2): $y = 3x - 11$
Step 2: **Substitute** the expression found in Step 1into the *other* equation. The result is an equation in one variable.	Equation (1): $x + 2(3x - 11) = 6$
Step 3: **Solve** the equation obtained in Step 2.	$x + 6x - 22 = 6$ $7x = 28$ $\boxed{x = 4}$
Step 4: **Back-substitute** the value found in Step 3 into the expression found in Step 1.	$y = 3(4) - 11$ $\boxed{y = 1}$
Step 5: **Check** that the solution satisfies *both* equations. Substitute (4, 1) into both equations.	Equation (1): $x + 2y = 6$ $(4) + 2(1) = 6$ ✓ Equation (2): $3x - y = 11$ $3(4) - 1 = 11$ ✓

EXAMPLE 1 **Determining by Substitution That a System Has One Solution**

Use the substitution method to solve the following system of linear equations:

$$x + y = 8 \quad \text{Equation (1)}$$
$$3x - y = 4 \quad \text{Equation (2)}$$

Solution:

STEP 1 Solve Equation (2) for y in terms of x. $y = 3x - 4$

STEP 2 Substitute $y = 3x - 4$ into Equation (1). $x + (3x - 4) = 8$

STEP 3 Solve for x.

$$x + 3x - 4 = 8$$
$$4x = 12$$
$$\boxed{x = 3}$$

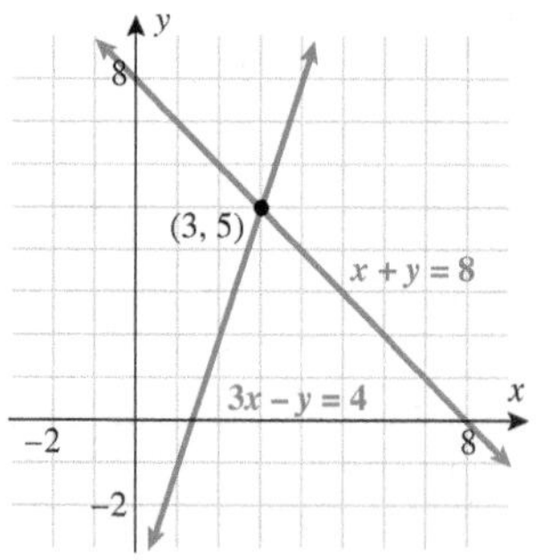

STEP 4 Back-substitute $x = 3$ into Equation (1).

$$3 + y = 8$$
$$\boxed{y = 5}$$

STEP 5 Check that $(3, 5)$ satisfies *both* equations.

Equation (1): $x + y = 8$
$3 + 5 = 8$

Equation (2): $3x - y = 4$
$3(3) - 5 = 4$

Note: The graphs of the two equations are two lines that intersect at the point $(3, 5)$.

EXAMPLE 2 **Determining by Substitution That a System Has No Solution**

Use the substitution method to solve the following system of linear equations:

$$x - y = 2 \quad \text{Equation (1)}$$
$$2x - 2y = 10 \quad \text{Equation (2)}$$

Solution:

STEP 1 Solve Equation (1) for y in terms of x. $y = x - 2$

STEP 2 Substitute $y = x - 2$ into Equation (2). $2x - 2(x - 2) = 10$

STEP 3 Solve for x.

$$2x - 2x + 4 = 10$$
$$4 = 10$$

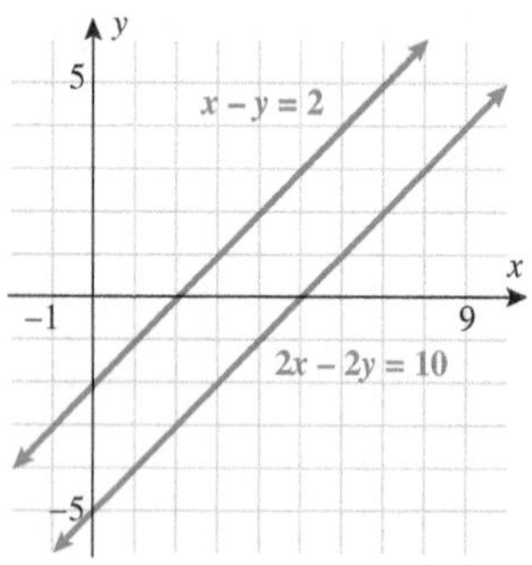

$4 = 10$ is never true, so this is called an inconsistent system. There is $\boxed{\text{no solution}}$ to this system of linear equations.

Note: The graphs of the two equations are parallel lines.

EXAMPLE 3 **Determining by Substitution That a System Has Infinitely Many Solutions**

Use the substitution method to solve the following system of linear equations:

$$x - y = 2 \quad \text{Equation (1)}$$
$$-x + y = -2 \quad \text{Equation (2)}$$

Solution:

STEP 1 Solve Equation (1) for y in terms of x. $\quad y = x - 2$

STEP 2 Substitute $y = x - 2$ into Equation (2). $\quad -x + (x - 2) = -2$

STEP 3 Solve for x. $\quad -x + x - 2 = -2$

$$-2 = -2$$

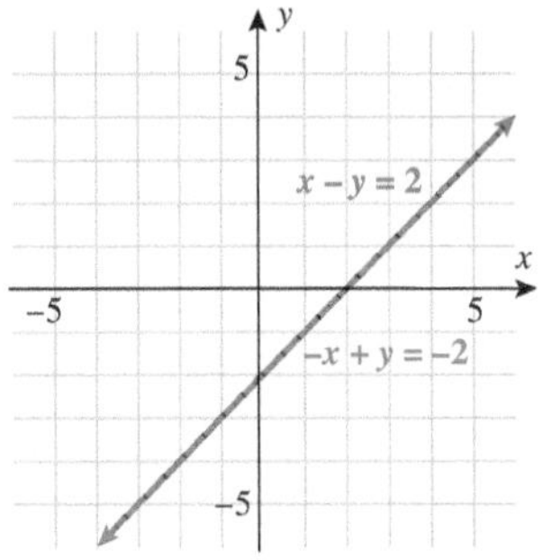

$-2 = -2$ is always true, so this is called a dependent system. Notice, for instance, that the points (2, 0), (4, 2), and (7, 5) all satisfy both equations. In fact, there are infinitely many solutions to this system of linear equations. All solutions are in the form (x, y), where $y = x - 2$. (The graphs of these two equations are the same line.) If we let $x = a$, then $y = a - 2$. In other words, all of the points $(a, a - 2)$, where a is any real number, are solutions to this system of linear equations.

YOUR TURN Use the substitution method to solve each system of linear equations.

a. $2x + y = 3$, $4x + 2y = 4$ **b.** $x - y = 2$, $4x - 3y = 10$ **c.** $x + 2y = 1$, $2x + 4y = 2$

ANSWER

a. no solution
b. (4, 2)
c. infinitely many solutions where $y = -\frac{1}{2}x + \frac{1}{2}$ or $\left(a, \frac{1 - a}{2}\right)$.

Elimination Method

We now turn our attention to another method, *elimination*, which is often preferred over substitution and will later be used in higher order systems. In a system of two linear equations in two variables, the equations can be combined, resulting in a third equation in one variable, thus *eliminating* one of the variables. The following is an example of when elimination would be preferred because the y terms sum to zero when the two equations are added together:

$$\begin{array}{r} 2x - y = 5 \\ -x + y = -2 \\ \hline x \quad = 3 \end{array}$$

When you cannot eliminate a variable simply by *adding* the two equations, multiply one equation by a constant that will cause the coefficients of some variable in the two equations to match and be opposite in sign.

The following box summarizes the *elimination method*, also called the *addition method*, for solving systems of two linear equations in two variables using the same example given earlier:

$$x + 2y = 6 \quad \text{Equation (1)}$$
$$3x - y = 11 \quad \text{Equation (2)}$$

ELIMINATION METHOD

Step 1*:	**Multiply** the coefficients of one (or both) of the equations so that one of the variables will be eliminated when the two equations are added.	Multiply Equation (2) by 2: $6x - 2y = 22$
Step 2:	**Eliminate** one of the variables by adding the equation found in Step 1 to the *other* original equation. The result is an equation in one variable.	$x + 2y = 6$ $6x - 2y = 22$ $7x = 28$
Step 3:	**Solve** the equation obtained in Step 2.	$7x = 28$ $\boxed{x = 4}$
Step 4:	**Back-substitute** the value found in Step 3 into either of the two original equations.	$(4) + 2y = 6$ $2y = 2$ $\boxed{y = 1}$
Step 5:	**Check** that the solution satisfies *both* equations. Substitute $\boxed{(4, 1)}$ into both equations.	Equation (1): $x + 2y = 6$ $(4) + 2(1) = 6$ ✓ Equation (2): $3x - y = 11$ $3(4) - 1 = 11$ ✓

*Step 1 is not necessary in cases where a pair of corresponding terms already sum to zero.

EXAMPLE 4 Applying the Elimination Method When One Variable Is Eliminated by Adding the Two Original Equations

Use the elimination method to solve the following system of linear equations:

$$2x - y = -5 \qquad \text{Equation (1)}$$
$$4x + y = 11 \qquad \text{Equation (2)}$$

Solution:

STEP 1 Not necessary.

STEP 2 Eliminate y by adding Equation (1) to Equation (2).

$$\begin{aligned} 2x - y &= -5 \\ 4x + y &= 11 \\ \hline 6x &= 6 \end{aligned}$$

STEP 3 Solve for x. $\boxed{x = 1}$

STEP 4 Back-substitute $x = 1$ into Equation (2). $4(1) + y = 11$

Solve for y. $\boxed{y = 7}$

STEP 5 Check that $(1, 7)$ satisfies both equations.

Equation (1): $2x - y = -5$
$2(1) - (7) = -5$ ✓

Equation (2): $4x + y = 11$
$4(1) + (7) = 11$ ✓

Note: The graphs of the two given equations correspond to two lines that intersect at the point $(1, 7)$.

STUDY TIP

You can eliminate one variable from the system by addition when (1) the coefficients are equal and (2) the signs are opposite.

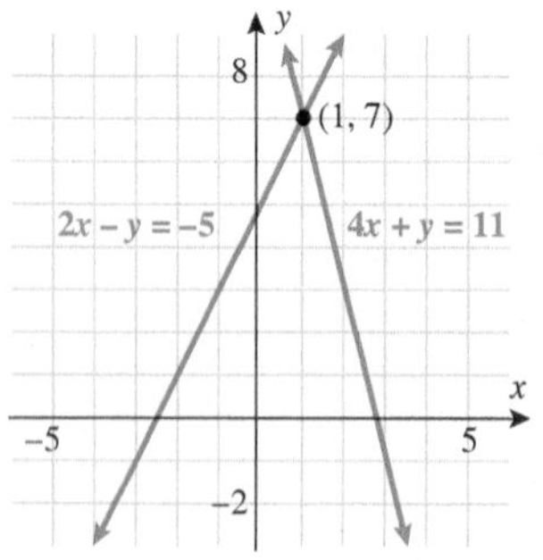

In Example 4, we eliminated the variable y simply by adding the two equations. Sometimes it is necessary to multiply one equation (Example 5) or both equations (Example 6) by constants prior to adding.

EXAMPLE 5 Applying the Elimination Method When Multiplying One Equation by a Constant Is Necessary

Use the elimination method to solve the following system of linear equations:

$$-4x + 3y = 23 \quad \text{Equation (1)}$$
$$12x + 5y = 1 \quad \text{Equation (2)}$$

Solution:

STEP 1 Multiply Equation (1) by 3. $\quad -12x + 9y = 69$

STEP 2 Eliminate x by adding the modified Equation (1) to Equation (2).

$$\begin{aligned} -12x + 9y &= 69 \\ 12x + 5y &= 1 \\ \hline 14y &= 70 \end{aligned}$$

STEP 3 Solve for y. $\quad \boxed{y = 5}$

STEP 4 Back-substitute $y = 5$ into Equation (2).

Solve for x.

$$\begin{aligned} 12x + 5(5) &= 1 \\ 12x + 25 &= 1 \\ 12x &= -24 \\ \boxed{x = -2} \end{aligned}$$

STEP 5 Check that $(-2, 5)$ satisfies both equations.

Equation (1): $-4(-2) + 3(5) = 23$
$8 + 15 = 23$ ✓

Equation (2): $12(-2) + 5(5) = 1$
$-24 + 25 = 1$ ✓

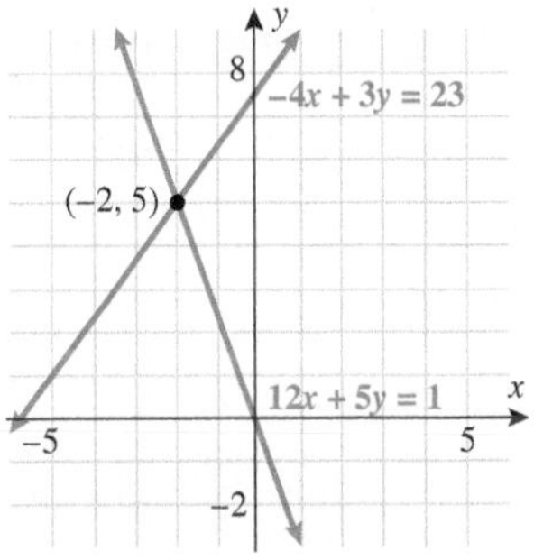

Note: The graphs of the two given equations correspond to two lines that intersect at the point $(-2, 5)$.

STUDY TIP

Be sure to multiply the **entire** equation by the constant.

In Example 5, we eliminated x simply by multiplying the first equation by a constant and adding the result to the second equation. In order to eliminate either of the variables in Example 6, we will have to multiply *both* equations by constants prior to adding.

EXAMPLE 6 **Applying the Elimination Method When Multiplying Both Equations by Constants Is Necessary**

Use the elimination method to solve the following system of linear equations:

$$3x + 2y = 1 \quad \text{Equation (1)}$$
$$5x + 7y = 9 \quad \text{Equation (2)}$$

Solution:

STEP 1 Multiply Equation (1) by 5 and Equation (2) by -3.

$$15x + 10y = 5$$
$$-15x - 21y = -27$$

STEP 2 Eliminate x by adding the modified Equation (1) to the modified Equation (2).

$$15x + 10y = 5$$
$$-15x - 21y = -27$$
$$-11y = -22$$

STEP 3 Solve for y.

$$\boxed{y = 2}$$

STEP 4 Back-substitute $y = 2$ into Equation (1). Solve for x.

$$3x + 2(2) = 1$$
$$3x = -3$$
$$\boxed{x = -1}$$

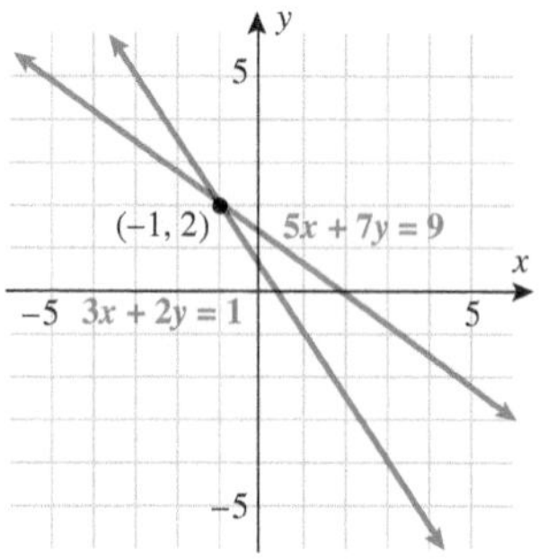

STEP 5 Check that $(-1, 2)$ satisfies both equations.

Equation (1): $3x + 2y = 1$
$3(-1) + 2(2) = 1$ ✓

Equation (2): $5x + 7y = 9$
$5(-1) + 7(2) = 9$ ✓

Note: The graphs of the two given equations correspond to two lines that intersect at the point $(-1, 2)$.

Note that in Example 6 we could have eliminated y instead by multiplying the first equation by 7 and the second equation by -2. Typically, the choice is dictated by which approach will keep the coefficients as simple as possible. In the event that the original coefficients contain fractions or decimals, first rewrite the equations in standard form with integer coefficients and then make the decision.

EXAMPLE 7 **Determining by the Elimination Method That a System Has No Solution**

Use the elimination method to solve the following system of linear equations:

$$-x + y = 7 \quad \text{Equation (1)}$$
$$2x - 2y = 4 \quad \text{Equation (2)}$$

Solution:

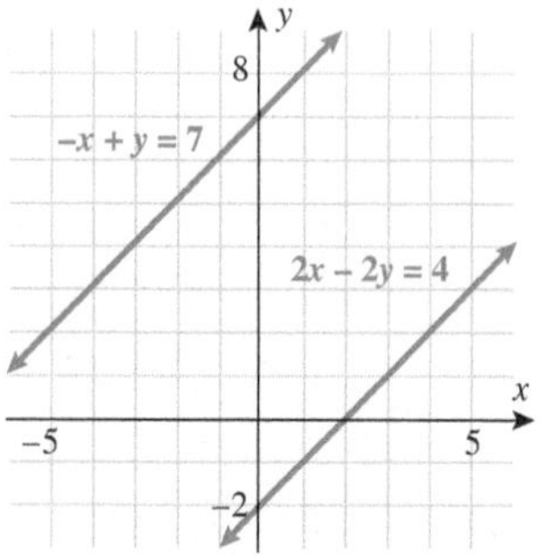

STEP 1 Multiply Equation (1) by 2.

$$-2x + 2y = 14$$

STEP 2 Eliminate y by adding the modified Equation (1) found in Step 1 to Equation (2).

$$-2x + 2y = 14$$
$$2x - 2y = 4$$
$$0 = 18$$

This system is inconsistent since $0 = 18$ is never true. Therefore, there are no values of x and y that satisfy both equations. We say that there is $\boxed{\text{no solution}}$ to this system of linear equations.

Note: The graphs of the two equations are two parallel lines.

EXAMPLE 8 **Determining by the Elimination Method That a System Has Infinitely Many Solutions**

Use the elimination method to solve the following system of linear equations:

$$7x + y = 2 \qquad \text{Equation (1)}$$
$$-14x - 2y = -4 \qquad \text{Equation (2)}$$

Solution:

STEP 1 Multiply Equation (1) by 2. $14x + 2y = 4$

STEP 2 Add the modified Equation (1) found in Step 1 to Equation (2).

$$\begin{array}{r} 14x + 2y = 4 \\ -14x - 2y = -4 \\ \hline 0 = 0 \end{array}$$

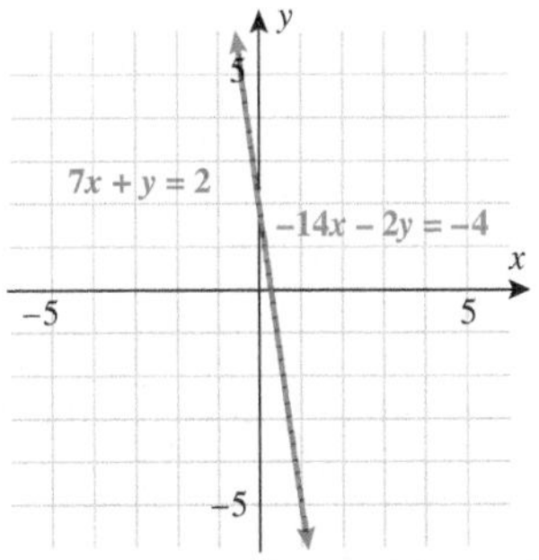

This system is dependent since $0 = 0$ is always true. We say that there are infinitely many solutions to this system of linear equations of the form $y = -7x + 2$ and these can be represented by the points $(a, 2 - 7a)$.

Note: The graphs of the two equations are the same line.

STUDY TIP

Systems of linear equations in two variables have either one solution, no solution, or infinitely many solutions.

YOUR TURN Apply the elimination method to solve each system of linear equations.

a. $2x + 3y = 1$, $4x - 3y = -7$ **b.** $x - 5y = 2$, $-10x + 50y = -20$ **c.** $x - y = 14$, $-x + y = 9$

ANSWER

a. $(-1, 1)$
b. infinitely many solutions of the form $y = \frac{1}{5}x - \frac{2}{5}$ or $\left(a, \frac{a-2}{5}\right)$.
c. no solution

Graphing Method

A third way to solve a system of linear equations in two variables is to graph the two lines. If the two lines intersect, then the point of intersection is the solution. Graphing is the most labor-intensive method for solving systems of linear equations in two variables. The graphing method is typically not used to solve systems of linear equations when an exact solution is desired. Instead, it is used to interpret or confirm the solution(s) found by the other two methods (substitution and elimination). If you are using a graphing calculator, however, you will get as accurate an answer using the graphing method as you will when applying the other methods.

The following box summarizes the graphing method for solving systems of linear equations in two variables using the same example given earlier:

$$x + 2y = 6 \qquad \text{Equation (1)}$$
$$3x - y = 11 \qquad \text{Equation (2)}$$

GRAPHING METHOD

Step 1*: Write the equations in slope–intercept form.

Equation (1): $y = -\frac{1}{2}x + 3$

Equation (2): $y = 3x - 11$

Step 2: Graph the two lines.

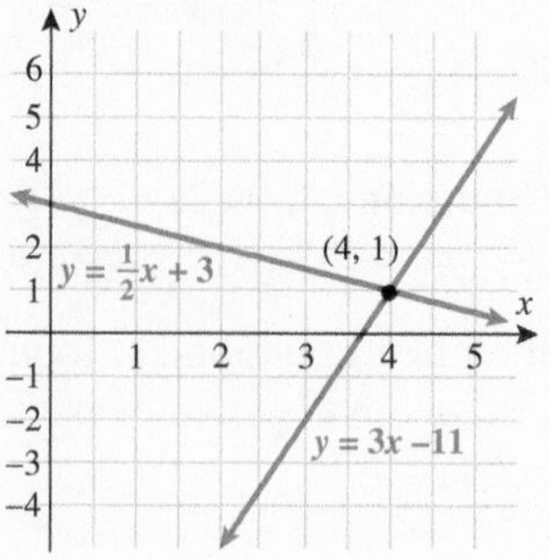

Step 3: Identify the point of intersection.

(4, 1)

Step 4: Check that the solution satisfies *both* equations.

Equation (1):
$x + 2y = 6$
$(4) + 2(1) = 6$ ✓

Equation (2):
$3x - y = 11$
$3(4) - 1 = 11$ ✓

*Step 1 is not necessary when the lines are already in slope–intercept form.

EXAMPLE 9 **Determining by Graphing That a System Has One Solution**

Use graphing to solve the following system of linear equations:

$x + y = 2$ Equation (1)

$3x - y = 2$ Equation (2)

Solution:

STEP 1 Write each equation in slope–intercept form.

$y = -x + 2$ Equation (1)
$y = 3x - 2$ Equation (2)

STEP 2 Plot both lines on the same graph.

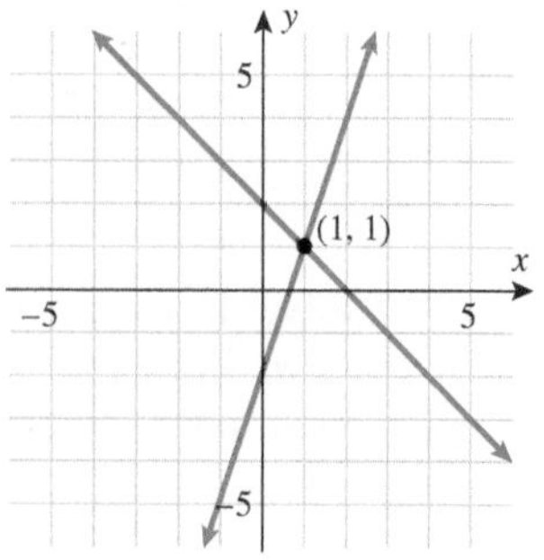

STEP 3 Identify the point of intersection.

(1, 1)

STEP 4 Check that the point (1, 1) satisfies both equations.

$x + y = 2$
$1 + 1 = 2$ ✓ Equation (1)

$3x - y = 2$
$3(1) - (1) = 2$ ✓ Equation (2)

Note: There is one solution, because the two lines intersect at one point.

EXAMPLE 10 **Determining by Graphing That a System Has No Solution**

Use graphing to solve the following system of linear equations:

$$2x - 3y = 9 \qquad \text{Equation (1)}$$
$$-4x + 6y = 12 \qquad \text{Equation (2)}$$

Solution:

STEP 1 Write each equation in slope–intercept form.

$$y = \frac{2}{3}x - 3 \qquad \text{Equation (1)}$$
$$y = \frac{2}{3}x + 2 \qquad \text{Equation (2)}$$

STEP 2 Plot both lines on the same graph.

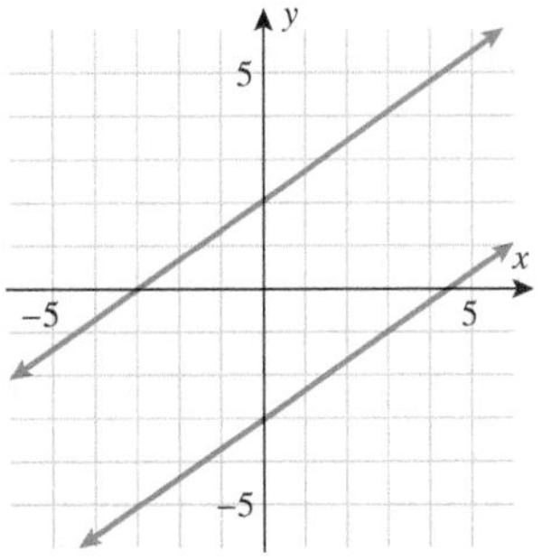

STEP 3 Identify the point of intersection. None

The two lines are parallel because they have the same slope but different y-intercepts. For this reason there is **no solution**—two parallel lines do not intersect.

EXAMPLE 11 **Determining by Graphing That a System Has Infinitely Many Solutions**

Use graphing to solve the following system of linear equations:

$$3x + 4y = 12 \qquad \text{Equation (1)}$$
$$\frac{3}{4}x + y = 3 \qquad \text{Equation (2)}$$

Solution:

STEP 1 Write each equation in slope–intercept form.

$$y = -\frac{3}{4}x + 3 \quad y = -\frac{3}{4}x + 3$$

STEP 2 Plot both lines on the same graph.

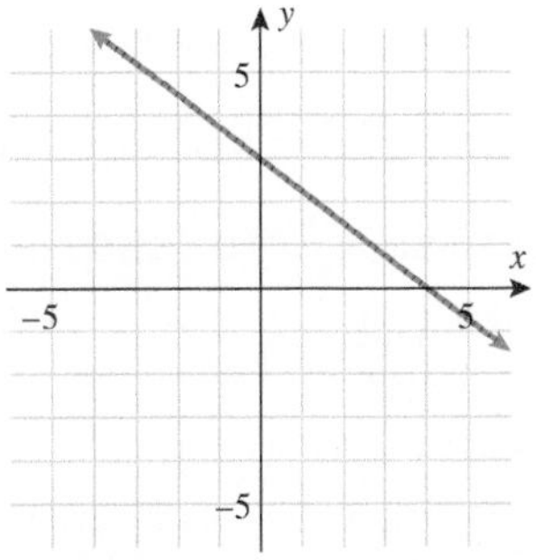

[CONCEPT CHECK]

TRUE OR FALSE If the solution to a system of linear equations in two variables is "infinitely many solutions," then every point in the Cartesian plane is a solution.

ANSWER False

STEP 3 Identify the point of intersection. Infinitely many points

There are infinitely many solutions, $y = -\frac{3}{4}x + 3$, since the two lines are identical and coincide. The points that lie along the line are $\left(a, -\frac{3}{4}a + 3\right)$.

YOUR TURN Utilize graphing to solve each system of linear equations.

a. $x - 2y = 1$
$2x - 4y = 2$

b. $x - 2y = 1$
$2x + y = 7$

c. $2x + y = 3$
$2x + y = 7$

ANSWER

a. infinitely many solutions of the form $y = \frac{1}{2}x - \frac{1}{2}$

b. $(3, 1)$

c. no solution

8.1.2 Three Methods and Three Types of Solutions

8.1.2 SKILL

Solve applications involving systems of linear equations.

8.1.2 CONCEPTUAL

Understand how to model a real-world problem using systems of linear equations in two variables.

Given any system of two linear equations in two variables, any of the three methods (substitution, elimination, or graphing) can be utilized. If you find that it is easy to eliminate a variable by adding multiples of the two equations, then elimination is the preferred choice. If you do not see an obvious elimination, then solve the system by substitution. For exact solutions, choose one of these two algebraic methods. You should typically use graphing to confirm the solution(s) you have found by applying the other two methods or when you are using a graphing utility.

EXAMPLE 12 Identifying Which Method to Use

State which of the two algebraic methods (elimination or substitution) would be the preferred method to solve each system of linear equations.

a. $x - 2y = 1$
$-x + y = 2$

b. $x = 2y - 1$
$2x - y = 4$

c. $7x - 20y = 1$
$5x + 3y = 18$

Solution:

a. Elimination: Because the x variable is eliminated when the two equations are added.

b. Substitution: Because the first equation is easily substituted into the second equation (for x).

c. Either: There is no preferred method, because both elimination and substitution require substantial work.

Regardless of which method is used to solve systems of two linear equations in two variables, in general, we can summarize the three types of solutions both algebraically and graphically.

THREE TYPES OF SOLUTIONS TO SYSTEMS OF LINEAR EQUATIONS

NUMBER OF SOLUTIONS	GRAPHICAL INTERPRETATION
One solution	The two lines intersect at one point.
No solution	The two lines are parallel. (*Same* slope/*different* y-intercepts.)
Infinitely many solutions	The two lines coincide. (*Same* slope/*same* y-intercept.)

Applications

Suppose you have two job offers that require sales. One pays a higher base, and the other pays a higher commission. Which job do you take?

EXAMPLE 13 Deciding Which Job to Take

Suppose that upon graduation you are offered a job selling biomolecular devices to laboratories studying DNA. The Beckman-Coulter Company offers you a job selling its DNA sequencer with an annual base salary of \$20,000 plus 5% commission on total sales. The MJ Research Corporation offers you a job selling its PCR Machine that makes copies of DNA with an annual base salary of \$30,000 plus 3% commission on sales. Determine what the total sales would have to be to make the Beckman-Coulter job the better offer.

Solution:

STEP 1 **Identify the question.**

When would these two jobs offer the same compensation?

STEP 2 **Make notes.**

Beckman-Coulter salary	20,000 + 5% of sales
MJ Research salary	30,000 + 3% of sales

STEP 3 **Set up the equations.**

Let x = total sales and y = compensation.

Equation (1) Beckman-Coulter: $y = 20{,}000 + 0.05x$

Equation (2) MJ Research: $y = 30{,}000 + 0.03x$

STEP 4 **Solve the system of equations.**

*Substitution method**

Substitute Equation (1) into Equation (2). $20{,}000 + 0.05x = 30{,}000 + 0.03x$

Solve for x. $0.02x = 10{,}000$

$x = 500{,}000$

If you make \$500,000 worth of sales per year, the jobs will offer the same compensation. If you make sales worth less than \$500,000, the MJ Research job is the better offer, and if you make sales worth more than \$500,000, the Beckman-Coulter job is the better offer.

*The elimination method could also have been used.

STEP 5 **Check the solution.**

Equation (1) Beckman-Coulter: $y = 20{,}000 + 0.05(500{,}000) = \$45{,}000$

Equation (2) MJ Research: $y = 30{,}000 + 0.03(500{,}000) = \$45{,}000$

[CONCEPT CHECK]

When determining which sales job will result in more money, the higher base/lower commission job is better if sales are low, and the lower base/higher commission job is better if sales are high. The point of intersection of the two linear salary models corresponds to __________.

ANSWER The sales at which both models will yield the same salary

[SECTION 8.1] SUMMARY

In this section, we discussed two algebraic techniques for solving systems of two linear equations in two variables:

- Substitution method
- Elimination method

The algebraic methods are preferred for exact solutions, and the graphing method is typically used to give a visual interpretation and confirmation of the solution. There are three possible outcomes in solving systems of two linear equations in two variables: one solution, no solution, or infinitely many solutions.

INDEPENDENT SYSTEM	INCONSISTENT SYSTEM	DEPENDENT SYSTEM
One solution	No solution	Infinitely many solutions
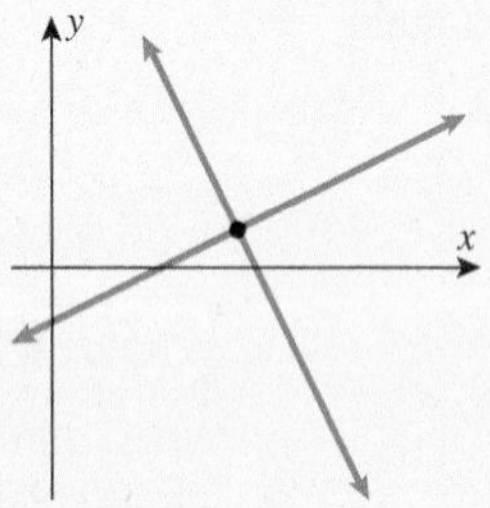	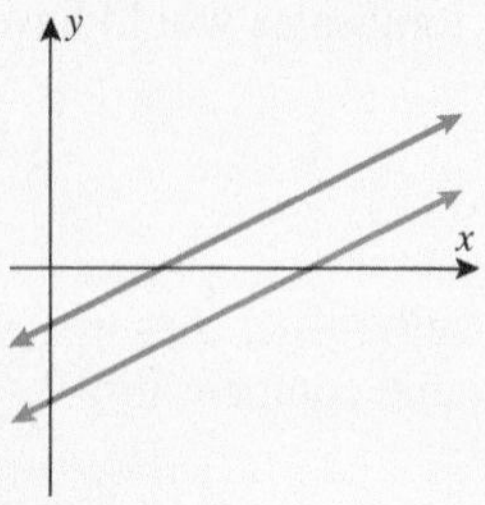	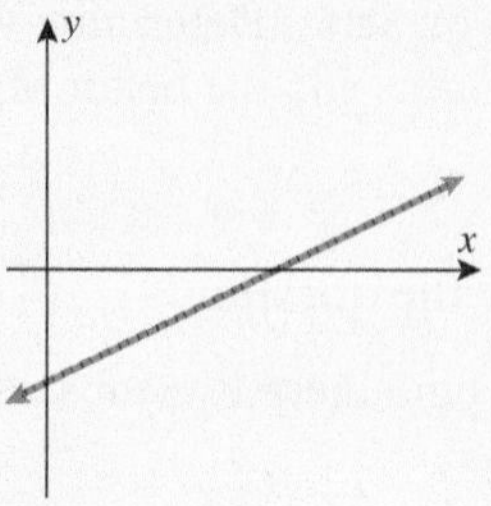
Lines have different slopes.	Lines are parallel (same slope and different y-intercepts).	Lines coincide (same slope and same y-intercept).

[SECTION 8.1] EXERCISES

• SKILLS

In Exercises 1–20, solve each system of linear equations by substitution.

1. $x + y = 7$
$x - y = 9$

2. $x - y = -10$
$x + y = 4$

3. $2x - y = 3$
$x - 3y = 4$

4. $4x + 3y = 3$
$2x + y = 1$

5. $3x + y = 5$
$2x - 5y = -8$

6. $6x - y = -15$
$2x - 4y = -16$

7. $2u + 5v = 7$
$3u - v = 5$

8. $m - 2n = 4$
$3m + 2n = 1$

9. $2x + y = 7$
$-2x - y = 5$

10. $3x - y = 2$
$3x - y = 4$

11. $4r - s = 1$
$8r - 2s = 2$

12. $-3p + q = -4$
$6p - 2q = 8$

13. $5r - 3s = 15$
$-10r + 6s = -30$

14. $-5p - 3q = -1$
$10p + 6q = 2$

15. $2x - 3y = -7$
$3x + 7y = 24$

16. $4x - 5y = -7$
$3x + 8y = 30$

17. $\frac{1}{3}x - \frac{1}{4}y = 0$
$-\frac{2}{3}x + \frac{3}{4}y = 2$

18. $\frac{1}{5}x + \frac{2}{3}y = 10$
$-\frac{1}{2}x - \frac{1}{6}y = -7$

19. $-3.9x + 4.2y = 15.3$
$-5.4x + 7.9y = 16.7$

20. $6.3x - 7.4y = 18.6$
$2.4x + 3.5y = 10.2$

In Exercises 21–40, solve each system of linear equations by elimination.

21. $\begin{aligned} x - y &= -3 \\ x + y &= 7 \end{aligned}$

22. $\begin{aligned} x - y &= -10 \\ x + y &= 8 \end{aligned}$

23. $\begin{aligned} 5x + 3y &= -3 \\ 3x - 3y &= -21 \end{aligned}$

24. $\begin{aligned} -2x + 3y &= 1 \\ 2x - y &= 7 \end{aligned}$

25. $\begin{aligned} 2x - 7y &= 4 \\ 5x + 7y &= 3 \end{aligned}$

26. $\begin{aligned} 3x + 2y &= 6 \\ -3x + 6y &= 18 \end{aligned}$

27. $\begin{aligned} 2x + 5y &= 7 \\ 3x - 10y &= 5 \end{aligned}$

28. $\begin{aligned} 6x - 2y &= 3 \\ -3x + 2y &= -2 \end{aligned}$

29. $\begin{aligned} 2x + 5y &= 5 \\ -4x - 10y &= -10 \end{aligned}$

30. $\begin{aligned} 11x + 3y &= 3 \\ 22x + 6y &= 6 \end{aligned}$

31. $\begin{aligned} 3x - 2y &= 12 \\ 4x + 3y &= 16 \end{aligned}$

32. $\begin{aligned} 5x - 2y &= 7 \\ 3x + 5y &= 29 \end{aligned}$

33. $\begin{aligned} 6x - 3y &= -15 \\ 7x + 2y &= -12 \end{aligned}$

34. $\begin{aligned} 7x - 4y &= -1 \\ 3x - 5y &= 16 \end{aligned}$

35. $\begin{aligned} 4x - 5y &= 22 \\ 3x + 4y &= 1 \end{aligned}$

36. $\begin{aligned} 6x - 5y &= 32 \\ 2x - 6y &= 2 \end{aligned}$

37. $\begin{aligned} \tfrac{1}{3}x + \tfrac{1}{2}y &= 1 \\ \tfrac{1}{5}x + \tfrac{7}{2}y &= 2 \end{aligned}$

38. $\begin{aligned} \tfrac{1}{2}x - \tfrac{1}{3}y &= 0 \\ \tfrac{3}{2}x + \tfrac{1}{2}y &= \tfrac{3}{4} \end{aligned}$

39. $\begin{aligned} 3.4x + 1.7y &= 8.33 \\ -2.7x - 7.8y &= 15.96 \end{aligned}$

40. $\begin{aligned} -0.04x + 1.12y &= 9.815 \\ 2.79x + 1.19y &= -0.165 \end{aligned}$

In Exercises 41–44, match each system of equations with the appropriate graph.

41. $\begin{aligned} 3x - y &= 1 \\ 3x + y &= 5 \end{aligned}$

42. $\begin{aligned} -x + 2y &= -1 \\ 2x + y &= 7 \end{aligned}$

43. $\begin{aligned} 2x + y &= 3 \\ 2x + y &= 7 \end{aligned}$

44. $\begin{aligned} x - 2y &= 1 \\ 2x - 4y &= 2 \end{aligned}$

a.

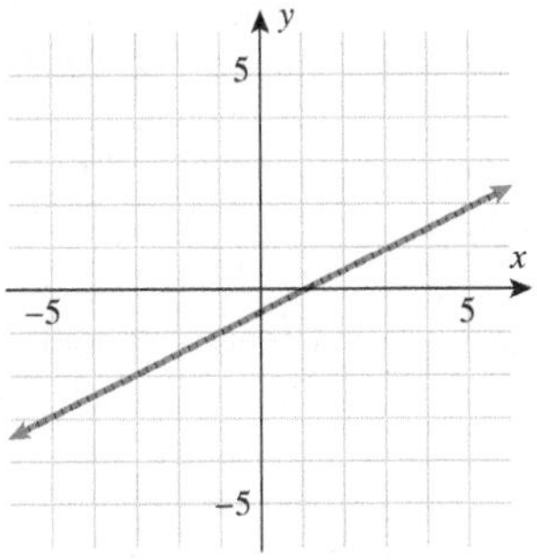

b.

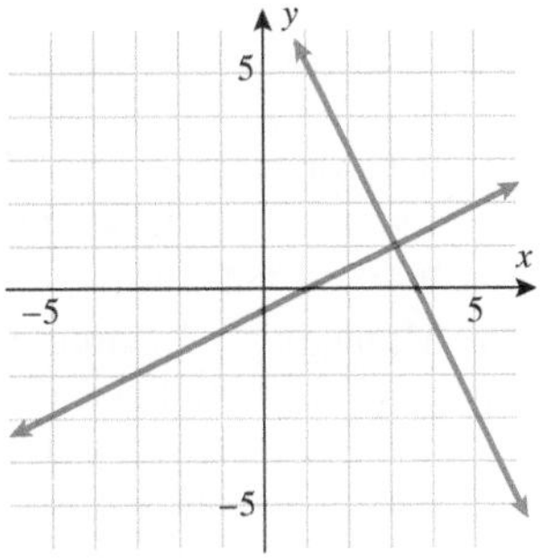

c.

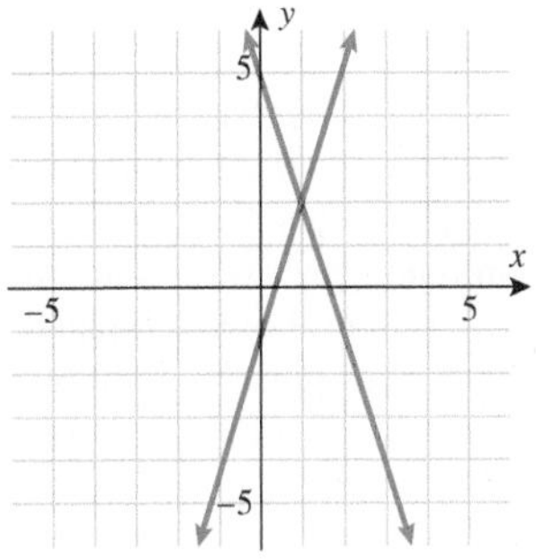

d.

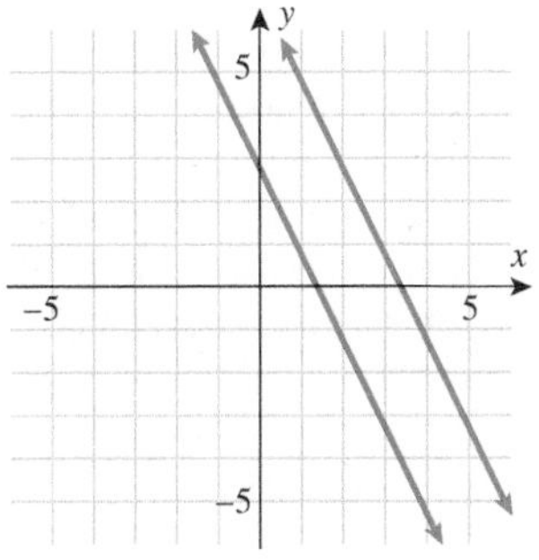

In Exercises 45–52, solve each system of linear equations by graphing.

45. $\begin{aligned} y &= -x \\ y &= x \end{aligned}$

46. $\begin{aligned} x - 3y &= 0 \\ x + 3y &= 0 \end{aligned}$

47. $\begin{aligned} 2x + y &= -3 \\ x + y &= -2 \end{aligned}$

48. $\begin{aligned} x - 2y &= -1 \\ -x - y &= -5 \end{aligned}$

49. $\begin{aligned} \tfrac{1}{2}x - \tfrac{2}{3}y &= 4 \\ \tfrac{1}{4}x - y &= 6 \end{aligned}$

50. $\begin{aligned} \tfrac{1}{5}x - \tfrac{5}{2}y &= 10 \\ \tfrac{1}{15}x - \tfrac{5}{6}y &= \tfrac{10}{3} \end{aligned}$

51. $\begin{aligned} 1.6x - y &= 4.8 \\ -0.8x + 0.5y &= 1.5 \end{aligned}$

52. $\begin{aligned} 1.1x - 2.2y &= 3.3 \\ -3.3x + 6.6y &= -6.6 \end{aligned}$

In Exercises 53–58, use any method to solve each system of linear equations.

53. $\begin{aligned} x - y &= 2 \\ x + y &= 4 \end{aligned}$

54. $\begin{aligned} -0.5x + 0.3y &= 0.8 \\ -1.5x + 0.9y &= 2.4 \end{aligned}$

55. $\begin{aligned} x - y &= 1 \\ x + y &= 1 \end{aligned}$

56. $\begin{aligned} x + y &= 2 \\ x - y &= -2 \end{aligned}$

57. $\begin{aligned} 0.02x + 0.05y &= 1.25 \\ -0.06x - 0.15y &= -3.75 \end{aligned}$

58. $\begin{aligned} x - y &= 2 \\ x + y &= -2 \end{aligned}$

• APPLICATIONS

59. **Mixture.** In chemistry lab, Stephanie has to make a 37-milliliter solution that is 12% HCl. All that is in the lab is 8% and 15% HCl. How many milliliters of each solution should she use to obtain the desired mix?

60. **Mixture.** A mechanic has 340 gallons of gasoline and 10 gallons of oil to make gas/oil mixtures. He wants one mixture to be 4% oil and the other mixture to be 2.5% oil. If he wants to use all of the gas and oil, how many gallons of gas and oil will be in each of the resulting mixtures?

61. **Salary Comparison.** Upon graduation with a degree in management of information systems (MIS), you decide to work for a company that buys data from states' departments of motor vehicles and sells to banks and car dealerships customized reports detailing how many cars at each dealership are financed through particular banks. Autocount Corporation offers you a $15,000 base salary and 10% commission on your total annual sales. Polk Corporation offers you a base salary of $30,000 plus a 5% commission on your total annual sales. How many total sales would you have to make per year to earn more money at Autocount?

62. **Salary Comparison.** Two types of residential real estate agents are those who sell existing houses (resale) and those who sell new homes for developers. Resale of existing homes typically earns 6% commission on every sale, and representing developers in selling new homes typically earns a base salary of $15,000 per year plus an additional 1.5% commission, because agents are required to work 5 days a week on site in a new development. Find the total value (dollars) an agent would have to sell per year to make more money in resale than in new homes?

63. **Gas Mileage.** Your Honda Accord gets approximately 26 mpg on the highway and 19 mpg in the city. You drove 349.5 miles on a full tank (16 gallons) of gasoline. Approximately how many miles did you drive in the city and how many on the highway?

64. **Wireless Plans.** AT&T is offering a 600-minute peak plan with free mobile-to-mobile and weekend minutes at $59 per month plus $0.13 per minute for every minute over 600. The next plan up is the 800-minute plan that costs $79 per month. You think you may go over 600 minutes, but you are not sure you need 800 minutes. How many minutes would you have to talk for the 800-minute plan to be the better deal?

65. **Distance/Rate/Time.** A direct flight on Delta Air Lines from Atlanta to Paris is 4000 miles and takes approximately 8 hours going east (Atlanta to Paris) and 10 hours going west (Paris to Atlanta). Although the plane averages the same airspeed, there is a headwind while traveling west and a tailwind while traveling east, resulting in different air speeds. What is the average air speed of the plane, and what is the average wind speed?

66. **Distance/Rate/Time.** A private pilot flies a Cessna 172 on a trip that is 500 miles each way. It takes her approximately 3 hours to get there and 4 hours to return. What is the approximate average air speed of the Cessna, and what is the approximate wind speed?

67. **Investment Portfolio.** Leticia has been tracking two volatile stocks. Over the last year, stock A has increased 10%, and stock B has increased 14% (using a simple interest model). She has $10,000 to invest and would like to split it between these two stocks. If the stocks continue to perform at the same rate, how much should she invest in each for one year to result in a balance of $11,260?

68. **Investment Portfolio.** Toby split his savings into two different investments, one earning 5% and the other earning 7%. He put twice as much in the investment earning the higher rate. In one year, he earned $665 in interest. How much money did he invest in each account?

69. **Break-Even Analysis.** A company produces CD players for a unit cost of $15 per CD player. The company has fixed costs of $120. If each CD player can be sold for $30, how many CD players must be sold to break even? Determine the cost equation first. Next, determine the revenue equation. Use the two equations you have found to determine the break-even point.

70. **Managing a Lemonade Stand.** An elementary-school-age child wants to have a lemonade stand. She would sell each glass of lemonade for $0.25. She has determined that each glass of lemonade costs about $0.10 to make (for lemons and sugar). It costs her $15.00 for materials to make the lemonade stand. How many glasses of lemonade must she sell to break even?

71. **Population.** The U.S. Census Bureau reports that Florida's population in the year 2008 was 18,328,340 habitants. The number of females exceeded the number of males by 329,910. What was the number of habitants, by gender, in Florida in 2008?

72. **Population.** According to the U.S. Census Bureau, in 2000, the U.S. population was 281,420,906 habitants. Some projections indicate that by 2020 there will be 341,250,007 habitants. The number of senior citizens will increase 30%, while the number of citizens under the age of 65 will increase 20%. Find the number of senior citizens and the number of nonsenior citizens in 2000. Round your answer to the nearest integer.

• CATCH THE MISTAKE

In Exercises 73 and 74, explain the mistake that is made.

73. Solve the system of equations by elimination.

$$\begin{aligned} 2x + y &= -3 \\ 3x + y &= 8 \end{aligned}$$

Solution:

Multiply Equation (1) by -1. $\quad 2x - y = -3$

Add the result to Equation (2). $\quad 3x + y = 8$

$5x = 5$

Solve for x. $\quad x = 1$

Substitute $x = 1$ into Equation (2). $\quad 3(1) + y = 8$

$y = 5$

The answer $(1, 5)$ is incorrect. What mistake was made?

74. Solve the system of equations by elimination.

$$\begin{aligned} 4x - y &= 12 \\ 4x - y &= 24 \end{aligned}$$

Solution:

Multiply Equation (1) by -1. $\quad -4x + y = -12$

Add the result to Equation (2).

$$\begin{aligned} -4x + y &= -12 \\ 4x - y &= 24 \\ \hline 0 &= 12 \end{aligned}$$

Answer: Infinitely many solutions.

This is incorrect. What mistake was made?

• CONCEPTUAL

In Exercises 75–78, determine whether each statement is true or false on the *xy*-plane.

75. A system of equations represented by a graph of two lines with the same slope always has no solution.

76. A system of equations represented by a graph of two lines with slopes that are negative reciprocals always has one solution.

77. If two lines do not have exactly one point of intersection, then they must be parallel.

78. The system of equations $Ax - By = 1$ and $-Ax + By = -1$ has no solution.

79. The point $(2, -3)$ is a solution to the system of equations

$$\begin{aligned} Ax + By &= -29 \\ Ax - By &= 13 \end{aligned}$$

Find A and B.

80. If you graph the lines

$$\begin{aligned} x - 50y &= 100 \\ x - 48y &= -98 \end{aligned}$$

they appear to be parallel lines. However, there is a unique solution. Explain how this might be possible.

• CHALLENGE

81. Energy Drinks. A nutritionist wishes to market a new vitamin-enriched fruit drink and is preparing two versions of it to distribute at a local health club. She has 100 cups of pineapple juice and 4 cups of super vitamin-enriched pomegranate concentrate. One version of the drink is to contain 2% pomegranate and the other version 4% pomegranate. How much of each drink can she create if drinks are 1 cup and she uses all of the ingredients?

82. Easter Eggs. A family is coloring Easter eggs and wants to make 2 shades of purple, "light purple" and "deep purple." They have 30 tablespoons of deep red solution and 2 tablespoons of blue solution. If "light purple" consists of 2% blue solution and "deep purple" consists of 10% blue solution, how much of each version of purple solution can be created?

83. The line $y = mx + b$ connects the points $(-2, 4)$ and $(4, -2)$. Find the values of m and b.

84. Find b and c such that the parabola $y = x^2 + bx + c$ goes through the points $(2, 7)$ and $(-6, 7)$.

85. Find b and c such that the parabola $y = bx^2 + bx + c$ goes through the points $(4, 46)$ and $(-2, 10)$.

86. The system of equations

$$\begin{aligned} x^2 + y^2 &= 4 \\ x^2 - y^2 &= 2 \end{aligned}$$

can be solved by a change of variables. Taking $u = x^2$ and $v = y^2$, we can transform the system into

$$\begin{aligned} u + v &= 4 \\ u - v &= 2 \end{aligned}$$

Find the solutions of the original system.

87. The system of equations

$$\begin{aligned} x^2 + 2y^2 &= 11 \\ 4x^2 + 2y^2 &= 16 \end{aligned}$$

can be solved by a change of variables. Taking $u = x^2$ and $v = y^2$, we can transform the system into

$$\begin{aligned} u + 2v &= 11 \\ 4u + v &= 16 \end{aligned}$$

Find the solutions of the original system.

88. The parabola $y = bx^2 - 2x - a$ goes through the points $(-2, a)$ and $(-1, b - 2)$. Find a and b.

• PREVIEW TO CALCULUS

For Exercises 89–92, refer to the following:

In calculus, when integrating rational functions, we decompose the function into partial fractions. This technique involves the solution of systems of equations. For example, suppose

$$\frac{1}{x^2 + x - 2} = \frac{1}{(x-1)(x+2)} = \frac{A}{x-1} + \frac{B}{x+2} = \frac{A(x+2) + B(x-1)}{(x-1)(x+2)}$$

and we want to find A and B such that $1 = A(x+2) + B(x-1)$, which is equivalent to $1 = (A+B)x + (2A - B)$. From this equation, we obtain the system of equations

$$\begin{aligned} A + B &= 0 \\ 2A - B &= 1 \end{aligned}$$

the solution of which is $\left(\frac{1}{3}, -\frac{1}{3}\right)$.

Find the values of A and B that make each equation true.

89. $x + 5 = A(x+2) + B(x-4)$

90. $6x = A(x+1) + B(x-2)$

91. $x + 1 = A(x+2) + B(x-3)$

92. $5 = A(x-2) + B(2x+1)$

8.2 SYSTEMS OF LINEAR EQUATIONS IN THREE VARIABLES

SKILLS OBJECTIVES

- Solve systems of linear equations in three variables using a combination of the elimination method and the substitution method.
- Identify three types of solutions: one solution (point), no solution, or infinitely many solutions (a single line or a plane in three-dimensional space).

CONCEPTUAL OBJECTIVES

- Understand that a graph of a linear equation in three variables corresponds to a plane.
- Understand the parametric representation of a line in three dimensions.

8.2.1 Solving Systems of Linear Equations in Three Variables

8.2.1 SKILL

Solve systems of linear equations in three variables using a combination of the elimination method and the substitution method.

8.2.1 CONCEPTUAL

Understand that a graph of a linear equation in three variables corresponds to a plane.

In Section 8.1, we solved systems of two linear equations in two variables. Graphs of linear equations in two variables correspond to lines. Now we turn our attention to linear equations in *three* variables. A **linear equation in three variables**, x, y, and z, is given by

$$Ax + By + Cz = D$$

where A, B, C, and D are real numbers that are not all equal to zero. All three variables have degree equal to one, which is why this is called a linear equation in three variables. The graph of any equation in three variables requires a three-dimensional coordinate system.

The x-axis, y-axis, and z-axis are each perpendicular to the other two. For the three-dimensional coordinate system on the right, a point $(x, y, z) = (2, 3, 1)$ is found by starting at the origin, moving two units to the right, three units up, and one unit out toward you.

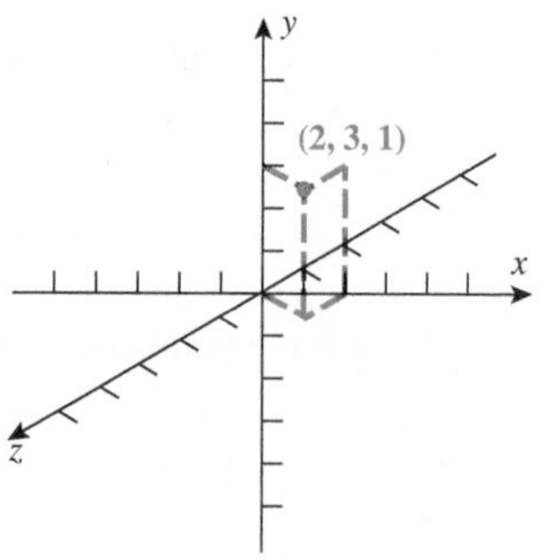

In two variables, the graph of a linear equation is a line. In three variables, however, the graph of a linear equation is a **plane**. A plane can be thought of as an infinite sheet of paper. When solving systems of linear equations in three variables, we find one of three possibilities: one solution, no solution, or infinitely many solutions.

STUDY TIP

If all three planes are coplaner (the same plane), there are infinitely many solutions.

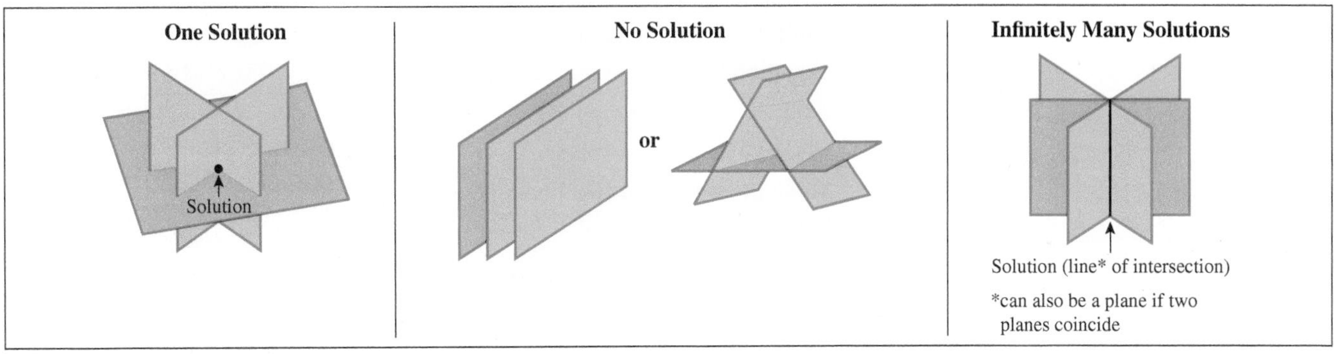

There are many ways to solve systems of linear equations in more than two variables. One method is to combine the elimination and substitution methods, which will be discussed in this section. Other methods involve matrices, which will be discussed in Sections 8.3–8.5. We now outline a procedure for solving systems of linear equations in three variables, which can be extended to solve systems of more than three variables. Solutions are sometimes given as ordered triples of the form (x, y, z).

SOLVING SYSTEMS OF LINEAR EQUATIONS IN THREE VARIABLES USING ELIMINATION AND SUBSTITUTION

Step 1: Reduce the system of three equations in three variables to two equations in two (of the same) variables by applying elimination.

Step 2: Solve the resulting system of two linear equations in two variables by applying elimination or substitution.

Step 3: Substitute the solutions in Step 2 into *any* one of the original equations and solve for the third variable.

Step 4: Check that the solution satisfies *all* three original equations.

EXAMPLE 1 Solving a System of Linear Equations in Three Variables

Solve the system:

$$\begin{aligned} 2x + y + 8z &= -1 \quad &\text{Equation (1)} \\ x - y + z &= -2 \quad &\text{Equation (2)} \\ 3x - 2y - 2z &= 2 \quad &\text{Equation (3)} \end{aligned}$$

Solution:

Inspecting the three equations, we see that y is easily eliminated when Equations (1) and (2) are added, because the coefficients of y, $+1$ and -1, are equal in magnitude and opposite in sign. We can also eliminate y from Equation (3) by adding Equation (3) to *either* 2 times Equation (1) *or* -2 times Equation (2). Therefore, our plan of attack is to eliminate y from the system of equations, so the result will be two equations in two variables x and z.

STUDY TIP

First eliminate the *same* variable from two different pairs of equations.

STEP 1 Eliminate y in Equation (1) and Equation (2).

Equation (1):	$2x + y + 8z = -1$
Equation (2):	$x - y + z = -2$
Add.	$3x + 9z = -3$

Eliminate y in Equation (2) and Equation (3).

Multiply Equation (2) by -2.	$-2x + 2y - 2z = 4$
Equation (3):	$3x - 2y - 2z = 2$
Add.	$x - 4z = 6$

STEP 2 Solve the system of two linear equations in two variables.

$$3x + 9z = -3$$
$$x - 4z = 6$$

Substitution* method: $x = 4z + 6$	$3(4z + 6) + 9z = -3$
Distribute.	$12z + 18 + 9z = -3$
Combine like terms.	$21z = -21$
Solve for z.	$\boxed{z = -1}$
Substitute $z = -1$ into $x = 4z + 6$.	$x = 4(-1) + 6 = 2$

$\boxed{x = 2}$ and $\boxed{z = -1}$ are the solutions to the system of two equations.

STEP 3 Substitute $x = 2$ and $z = -1$ into any one of the three original equations and solve for y.

Substitute $x = 2$ and $z = -1$ into Equation (2).	$2 - y - 1 = -2$
Solve for y.	$\boxed{y = 3}$

STEP 4 Check that $x = 2$, $y = 3$, and $z = -1$ satisfy all three equations.

Equation (1): $2(2) + 3 + 8(-1) = 4 + 3 - 8 = -1$

Equation (2): $2 - 3 - 1 = -2$

Equation (3): $3(2) - 2(3) - 2(-1) = 6 - 6 + 2 = 2$

The solution is $\boxed{x = 2, y = 3, z = -1, \text{ or } (2, 3, -1)}$.

*Elimination method could also be used.

YOUR TURN Solve the system:

$$\begin{aligned} 2x - y + 3z &= -1 \\ x + y - z &= 0 \\ 3x + 3y - 2z &= 1 \end{aligned}$$

ANSWER

$x = -1, y = 2, z = 1$

In Example 1 and the Your Turn, the variable y was eliminated by adding the first and second equations. In practice, any of the three variables can be eliminated, but typically we select the most convenient variable to eliminate. If a variable is missing from one of the equations (has a coefficient of 0), then we eliminate that variable from the other two equations.

EXAMPLE 2 Solving a System of Linear Equations in Three Variables When One Variable Is Missing

Solve the system:

$$\begin{aligned} x \quad\quad + z &= 1 \quad \text{Equation (1)} \\ 2x + y - z &= -3 \quad \text{Equation (2)} \\ x + 2y - z &= -1 \quad \text{Equation (3)} \end{aligned}$$

Solution:

Since y is missing from Equation (1), y is the variable to be eliminated in Equation (2) and Equation (3).

STEP 1 Eliminate y.

Multiply Equation (2) by -2.	$-4x - 2y + 2z = 6$
Equation (3):	$x + 2y - z = -1$
Add.	$-3x + z = 5$

STEP 2 Solve the system of two equations.

Equation (1) and the resulting equation in Step 1.	$x + z = 1$ $-3x + z = 5$
Multiply the second equation by (-1) and add it to the first equation.	$x + z = 1$ $3x - z = -5$ $4x = -4$
Solve for x.	$x = -1$
Substitute $x = -1$ into Equation (1).	$-1 + z = 1$
Solve for z.	$z = 2$

STEP 3 Substitute $x = -1$ and $z = 2$ into one of the original equations [Equation (2) or Equation (3)] and solve for y.

Substitute $x = -1$ and $z = 2$ into $x + 2y - z = -1$.	$(-1) + 2y - 2 = -1$
Gather like terms.	$2y = 2$
Solve for y.	$y = 1$

STEP 4 Check that $x = -1$, $y = 1$, and $z = 2$ satisfy all three equations.

Equation (1): $(-1) + 2 = 1$

Equation (2): $2(-1) + (1) - (2) = -3$

Equation (3): $(-1) + 2(1) - (2) = -1$

The solution is $\boxed{x = -1, y = 1, z = 2}$.

YOUR TURN Solve the system:

$$\begin{aligned} x + y + z &= 0 \\ 2x \quad\quad + z &= -1 \\ x - y - z &= 2 \end{aligned}$$

ANSWER

$x = 1, y = 2, z = -3$

8.2.2 Types of Solutions

8.2.2 SKILL

Identify three types of solutions: one solution (point), no solution, or infinitely many solutions (a single line or a plane in three-dimensional space).

8.2.2 CONCEPTUAL

Understand parametric representation of a line in three dimensions.

Systems of linear equations in three variables have three possible solutions: one solution, infinitely many solutions, or no solution. Examples 1 and 2 each had one solution. Examples 3 and 4 illustrate systems with infinitely many solutions and no solution, respectively.

EXAMPLE 3 A Dependent System of Linear Equations in Three Variables (Infinitely Many Solutions)

Solve the system:

$$2x + y - z = 4 \quad \text{Equation (1)}$$
$$x + y = 2 \quad \text{Equation (2)}$$
$$3x + 2y - z = 6 \quad \text{Equation (3)}$$

Solution:

Since z is missing from Equation (2), z is the variable to be eliminated from Equation (1) and Equation (3).

STEP 1 Eliminate z.

Multiply Equation (1) by (-1). $\quad -2x - y + z = -4$

Equation (3): $\quad 3x + 2y - z = 6$

Add. $\quad x + y = 2$

STEP 2 Solve the system of two equations: Equation (2) and the resulting equation in Step 1.

$$x + y = 2$$
$$x + y = 2$$

Multiply the first equation by (-1) and add it to the second equation.

$$-x - y = -2$$
$$x + y = 2$$
$$0 = 0$$

This statement is always true; therefore, there are infinitely many solutions. The original system has been reduced to a system of two identical linear equations. Therefore, the equations are dependent (share infinitely many solutions). Typically, to define those infinitely many solutions, we let $z = a$, where a stands for any real number, and then find x and y in terms of a. The resulting ordered triple showing the three variables in terms of a is called a **parametric representation** of a line in three dimensions.

STEP 3 Let $z = a$ and find x and y in terms of a.

Solve Equation (2) for y. $\quad y = 2 - x$

Let $y = 2 - x$ and $z = a$ in Equation (1). $\quad 2x + (2 - x) - a = 4$

Solve for x. $\quad 2x + 2 - x - a = 4$

$$x - a = 2$$
$$x = a + 2$$

Let $x = a + 2$ in Equation (2). $\quad (a + 2) + y = 2$

Solve for y. $\quad y = -a$

The infinitely many solutions are written as $(a + 2, -a, a)$.

[CONCEPT CHECK]

For Example 3, the infinitely many points that lie along a line are given by the parametric representation: $(a + 2, -a, a)$. Find four points that lie along the line. (Use $a = 0, 1, 2,$ and 3.)

ANSWER (2, 0, 0), (3, −1, 1), (4, −2, 2), and (5, −3, 3)

STEP 4 Check that $x = a + 2$, $y = -a$, and $z = a$ satisfy all three equations.

Equation (1): $2(a + 2) + (-a) - a = 2a + 4 - a - a = 4$ ✓

Equation (2): $(a + 2) + (-a) = a + 2 - a = 2$ ✓

Equation (3): $3(a + 2) + 2(-a) - a = 3a + 6 - 2a - a = 6$ ✓

YOUR TURN Solve the system:

$$\begin{aligned} x + y - 2z &= 0 \\ x - z &= -1 \\ x - 2y + z &= -3 \end{aligned}$$

ANSWER

$(a - 1, a + 1, a)$

EXAMPLE 4 An Inconsistent System of Linear Equations in Three Variables (No Solution)

Solve the system:

$$\begin{aligned} x + 2y - z &= 3 && \text{Equation (1)} \\ 2x + y + 2z &= -1 && \text{Equation (2)} \\ -2x - 4y + 2z &= 5 && \text{Equation (3)} \end{aligned}$$

Solution:

STEP 1 Eliminate x.

Multiply Equation (1) by -2. $\quad -2x - 4y + 2z = -6$

Equation (2): $\quad 2x + y + 2z = -1$

Add. $\quad -3y + 4z = -7$

Equation (2): $\quad 2x + y + 2z = -1$

Equation (3): $\quad -2x - 4y + 2z = 5$

Add. $\quad -3y + 4z = 4$

STEP 2 Solve the system of two equations:

$$\begin{aligned} -3y + 4z &= -7 \\ -3y + 4z &= 4 \end{aligned}$$

Multiply the top equation by (-1) and add it to the second equation.

$$\begin{aligned} 3y - 4z &= 7 \\ -3y + 4y &= 4 \\ \hline 0 &= 11 \end{aligned}$$

This is a contradiction, or inconsistent statement, so there is **no solution**.

So far in this section, we have discussed only systems of *three* linear equations in *three* variables. What happens if we have a system of *two* linear equations in *three* variables? The two linear equations in three variables will always correspond to two planes in three dimensions. The possibilities are no solution (the two planes are parallel) or infinitely many solutions (the two planes either intersect in a line or are coplanar).

NO SOLUTION

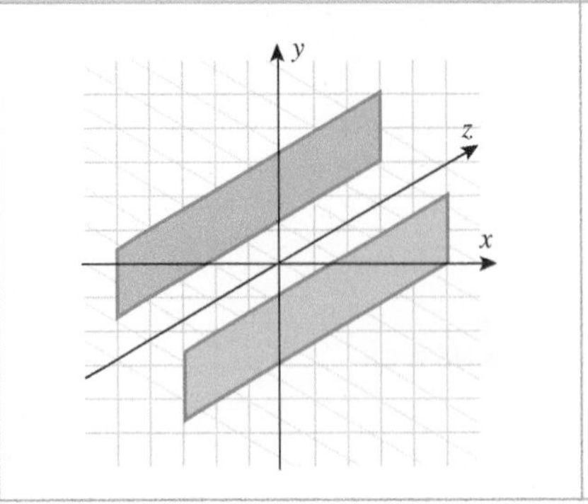

INFINITELY MANY SOLUTIONS (LINE)

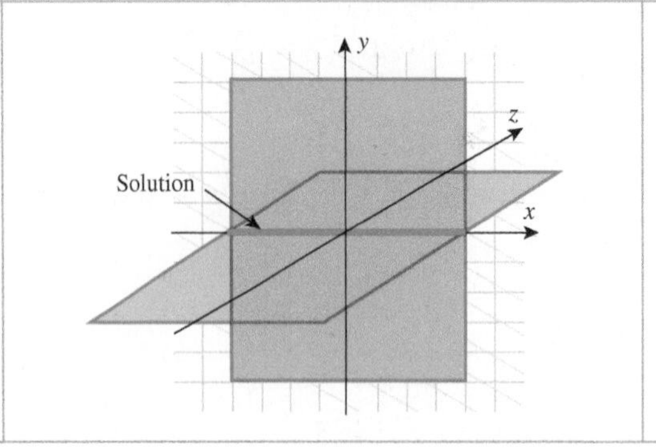

COPLANAR

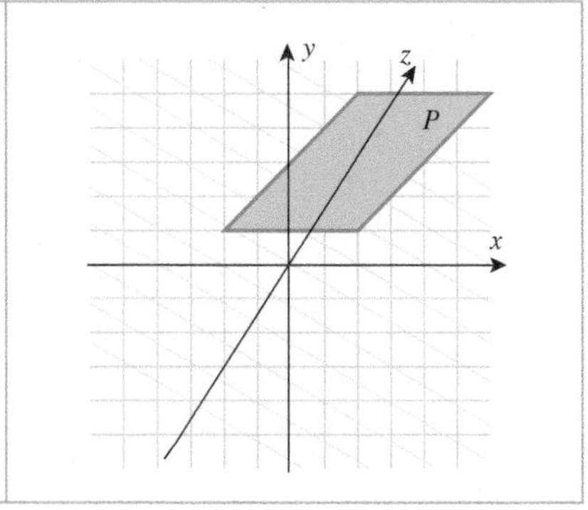

EXAMPLE 5 **Solving a System of Two Linear Equations in Three Variables**

Solve the system of linear equations:

$$x - y + z = 7 \qquad \text{Equation (1)}$$
$$x + y + 2z = 2 \qquad \text{Equation (2)}$$

Solution:

Eliminate y by adding the two equations.

$$\begin{array}{r} x - y + z = 7 \\ x + y + 2z = 2 \\ \hline 2x \quad + 3z = 9 \end{array}$$

Therefore, Equation (1) and Equation (2) are both true if $2x + 3z = 9$. Since we know there is a solution, it must be a line. To define the line of intersection, we again turn to parametric representation.

Let $\boxed{z = a}$, where a is any real number. $2x + 3a = 9$

Solve for x. $\boxed{x = \frac{9}{2} - \frac{3}{2}a}$

Substitute $z = a$ and $x = \frac{9}{2} - \frac{3}{2}a$ into Equation (1). $\left(\frac{9}{2} - \frac{3}{2}a\right) - y + a = 7$

Solve for y. $\boxed{y = -\frac{1}{2}a - \frac{5}{2}}$

The solution is the line in three dimensions given by $\boxed{\left(\frac{9}{2} - \frac{3}{2}a, -\frac{1}{2}a - \frac{5}{2}, a\right)}$, where a is any real number.

Note: Every real number a corresponds to a point on the line of intersection.

a	$\left(\frac{9}{2} - \frac{3}{2}a, -\frac{1}{2}a - \frac{5}{2}, a\right)$
-1	$(6, -2, -1)$
0	$\left(\frac{9}{2}, -\frac{5}{2}, 0\right)$
1	$(3, -3, 1)$

Modeling with a System of Three Linear Equations

Many times in the real world we see a relationship that looks like a particular function such as a quadratic function and we know particular data points, but we do not know the function. We start with the general function, fit the curve to particular data points, and solve a system of linear equations to determine the specific function parameters.

Suppose you want to model a stock price as a function of time, and, judging on the basis of the data, you feel a quadratic model would be the best fit.

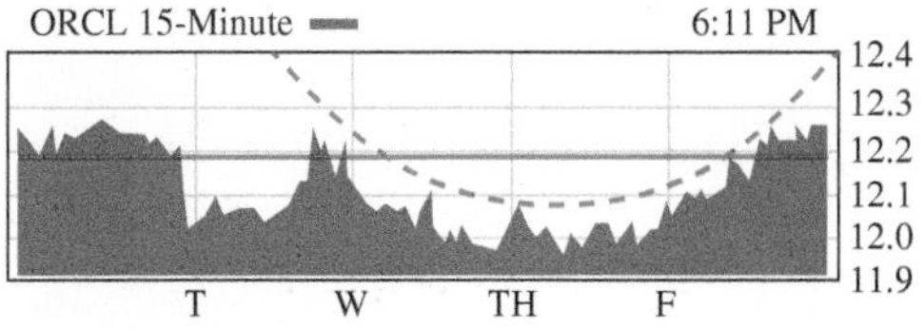

Therefore, the model is given by

$$P(t) = at^2 + bt + c$$

where $P(t)$ is the price of the stock at time t. If we have data corresponding to three distinct points $(t, P(t))$, the result is a system of three linear equations in three variables a, b, and c. We can solve the resulting system of linear equations, which determines the coefficients a, b, and c of the quadratic model for stock price.

EXAMPLE 6 **Stock Value**

The Oracle Corporation's stock (ORCL) over 3 days (Wednesday, October 13, to Friday, October 15, 2004) can be approximately modeled by a quadratic function: $f(t) = at^2 + bt + c$. If Wednesday corresponds to $t = 1$, where t is in days, then the following data points approximately correspond to the stock value:

t	$f(t)$	DAYS
1	\$12.20	Wednesday
2	\$12.00	Thursday
3	\$12.20	Friday

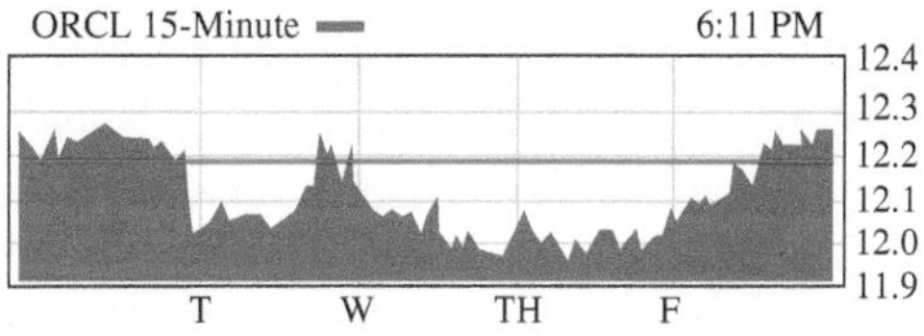

Determine the function that models this behavior.

Solution:

Substitute the points $(1, 12.20)$, $(2, 12.00)$, and $(3, 12.20)$ into $f(t) = at^2 + bt + c$.

$$a(1)^2 + b(1) + c = 12.20$$
$$a(2)^2 + b(2) + c = 12.00$$
$$a(3)^2 + b(3) + c = 12.20$$

Simplify to a system of three equations in three variables $(a, b, \text{and } c)$.

$$a + b + c = 12.20 \quad \text{Equation (1)}$$
$$4a + 2b + c = 12.00 \quad \text{Equation (2)}$$
$$9a + 3b + c = 12.20 \quad \text{Equation (3)}$$

Solve for a, b, and c by applying the technique of this section.

STEP 1 Eliminate c.

Multiply Equation (1) by (-1).	$-a - b - c = -12.20$
Equation (2):	$4a + 2b + c = 12.00$
Add.	$3a + b = -0.20$
Multiply Equation (1) by -1.	$-a - b - c = -12.20$
Equation (3):	$9a + 3b + c = 12.20$
Add.	$8a + 2b = 0$

STEP 2 Solve the system of two equations.

$$3a + b = -0.20$$
$$8a + 2b = 0$$

Multiply the first equation by -2 and add to the second equation.	$-6a - 2b = 0.40$ $8a + 2b = 0$
Add.	$2a = 0.4$
Solve for a.	$a = 0.2$
Substitute $a = 0.2$ into $8a + 2b = 0$.	$8(0.2) + 2b = 0$
Simplify.	$2b = -1.6$
Solve for b.	$b = -0.8$

STEP 3 Substitute $a = 0.2$ and $b = -0.8$ into one of the original three equations.

Substitute $a = 0.2$ and $b = -0.8$ into $a + b + c = 12.20$.	$0.2 - 0.8 + c = 12.20$
Gather like terms.	$-0.6 + c = 12.20$
Solve for c.	$c = 12.80$

STEP 4 Check that $a = 0.2$, $b = -0.8$, and $c = 12.80$ satisfy all three equations.

Equation (1): $a + b + c = 0.2 - 0.8 + 12.8 = 12.20$

Equation (2): $4a + 2b + c = 4(0.2) + 2(-0.8) + 12.80 = 0.8 - 1.6 + 12.8 = 12.00$

Equation (3): $9a + 3b + c = 9(0.2) + 3(-0.8) + 12.80 = 1.8 - 2.4 + 12.8 = 12.20$

The model is given by $\boxed{f(t) = 0.2t^2 - 0.8t + 12.80}$.

[SECTION 8.2] SUMMARY

Graphs of linear equations in *two* variables are *lines*, whereas graphs of linear equations in *three* variables are *planes*. Systems of linear equations in three variables have one of three solutions:

- One solution (the intersection point of the three planes)
- No solution (no intersection of all three planes)
- Infinitely many solutions (planes intersect along a line or a plane)

When the solution to a system of three linear equations is a line in three dimensions, we use parametric representation to express the solution.

[SECTION 8.2] EXERCISES

• SKILLS

In Exercises 1–32, solve each system of linear equations.

1. $x - y + z = 6$, $-x + y + z = 3$, $-x - y - z = 0$

2. $-x - y + z = -1$, $-x + y - z = 3$, $x - y - z = 5$

3. $x + y - z = 2$, $-x - y - z = -3$, $-x + y - z = 6$

4. $x + y + z = -1$, $-x + y - z = 3$, $-x - y + z = 8$

5. $-x + y - z = -1$, $x - y - z = 3$, $x + y - z = 9$

6. $x - y - z = 2$, $-x - y + z = 4$, $-x + y - z = 6$

7. $2x - 3y + 4z = -3$, $-x + y + 2z = 1$, $5x - 2y - 3z = 7$

8. $x - 2y + z = 0$, $-2x + y - z = -5$, $13x + 7y + 5z = 6$

9. $3y - 4x + 5z = 2$, $2x - 3y - 2z = -3$, $3z + 4y - 2x = 1$

10. $2y + z - x = 5$, $2x + 3z - 2y = 0$, $-2z + y - 4x = 3$

11. $x - y + z = -1$, $y - z = -1$, $-x + y + z = 1$

12. $-y + z = 1$, $x - y + z = -1$, $x - y - z = -1$

13. $3x - 2y - 3z = -1$, $x - y + z = -4$, $2x + 3y + 5z = 14$

14. $3x - y + z = 2$, $x - 2y + 3z = 1$, $2x + y - 3z = -1$

15. $-3x - y - z = 2$, $x + 2y - 3z = 4$, $2x - y + 4z = 6$

16. $2x - 3y + z = 1$, $x + 4y - 2z = 2$, $3x - y + 4z = -3$

17. $3x + 2y + z = 4$, $-4x - 3y - z = -15$, $x - 2y + 3z = 12$

18. $3x - y + 4z = 13$, $-4x - 3y - z = -15$, $x - 2y + 3z = 12$

19. $-x + 2y + z = -2$, $3x - 2y + z = 4$, $2x - 4y - 2z = 4$

20. $2x - y = 1$, $-x + z = -2$, $-2x + y = -1$

21. $x - z - y = 10$, $2x - 3y + z = -11$, $y - x + z = -10$

22. $2x + z + y = -3$, $2y - z + x = 0$, $x + y + 2z = 5$

23. $3x_1 + x_2 - x_3 = 1$, $x_1 - x_2 + x_3 = -3$, $2x_1 + x_2 + x_3 = 0$

24. $2x_1 + x_2 + x_3 = -1$, $x_1 + x_2 - x_3 = 5$, $3x_1 - x_2 - x_3 = 1$

25. $2x + 5y = 9$, $x + 2y - z = 3$, $-3x - 4y + 7z = 1$

26. $x - 2y + 3z = 1$, $-2x + 7y - 9z = 4$, $x + z = 9$

27. $2x_1 - x_2 + x_3 = 3$, $x_1 - x_2 + x_3 = 2$, $-2x_1 + 2x_2 - 2x_3 = -4$

28. $x_1 - x_2 - 2x_3 = 0$, $-2x_1 + 5x_2 + 10x_3 = -3$, $3x_1 + x_2 = 0$

29. $2x + y - z = 2$, $x - y - z = 6$

30. $3x + y - z = 0$, $x + y + 7z = 4$

31. $4x + 3y - 3z = 5$, $6x + 2z = 10$

32. $x + 2y + 4z = 12$, $-3x - 4y + 7z = 21$

• APPLICATIONS

33. Business. A small company has an assembly line that produces three types of widgets. The basic widget is sold for \$10 per unit, the midprice widget for \$12 per unit, and the top-of-the-line widget for \$15 per unit. The assembly line has a daily capacity of producing 300 widgets that may be sold for a total of \$3700. Find the quantity of each type of widget produced on a day when the number of basic widgets and the number of top-of-the-line widgets are the same.

34. Business. A small company has an assembly line that produces three types of widgets. The basic widget is sold for \$10 per unit, the midprice widget for \$12 per unit, and the top-of-the-line widget for \$15 per unit. The assembly line has a daily capacity of producing 325 widgets that may be sold for a total of \$3825. Find the quantity of each type of widget produced on a day when twice as many basic widgets as top-of-the-line widgets are produced.

Exercises 35 and 36 rely on a selection of sandwiches whose nutrition information is given in the table.

Suppose you are going to eat only sandwiches for a week (seven days) for lunch and dinner (total of 14 meals).

SANDWICH	CALORIES	FAT (GRAMS)
Chicken	350	18
Tuna	430	19
Roast beef	290	5

35. Diet. Your goal is a total of 4840 calories and 190 grams of fat. How many of each sandwich would you eat that week to obtain this goal?

36. Diet. Your goal is a total of 4380 calories and 123 grams of fat. How many of each sandwich would you eat that week to obtain this goal?

Exercises 37 and 38 involve vertical motion and the effect of gravity on an object.

Because of gravity, an object that is projected upward will eventually reach a maximum height and then fall to the ground. The equation that determines the height h of a projectile t seconds after it is shot upward is given by

$$h = \frac{1}{2}at^2 + v_0t + h_0$$

where a is the acceleration due to gravity, h_0 is the initial height of the object at time $t = 0$, and v_0 is the initial velocity of the object at time $t = 0$. Note that a projectile follows the path of a parabola opening down, so $a < 0$.

37. **Vertical Motion.** An object is thrown upward, and the following table depicts the height of the ball t seconds after the projectile is released. Find the initial height, initial velocity, and acceleration due to gravity.

t SECONDS	HEIGHT (FEET)
1	36
2	40
3	12

38. **Vertical Motion.** An object is thrown upward, and the following table depicts the height of the ball t seconds after the projectile is released. Find the initial height, initial velocity, and acceleration due to gravity.

t SECONDS	HEIGHT (FEET)
1	84
2	136
3	156

39. **Data Curve-Fitting.** The number of minutes that an average person of age x spends driving a car can be modeled by a quadratic function $y = ax^2 + bx + c$, where $a < 0$ and $18 \leq x \leq 65$. The following table gives the average number of minutes per day that a person spends driving a car. Determine the quadratic function that models this quantity.

AGE	AVERAGE DAILY MINUTES DRIVING
20	30
40	60
60	40

40. **Data Curve-Fitting.** The average age when a woman gets married began increasing during the last century. In 1930 the average age was 18.6, in 1950 the average age was 20.2, and in 2002 the average age was 25.3. Find a quadratic function $y = ax^2 + bx + c$, where $a > 0$ and $18 < y < 35$, that models the average age y when a woman gets married as a function of the year $x (x = 0$ corresponds to 1930). What will the average age be in 2010?

41. **Money.** Tara and Lamar decide to place \$20,000 of their savings into investments. They put some in a money market account earning 3% interest, some in a mutual fund that has been averaging 7% a year, and some in a stock that rose 10% last year. If they put \$6000 more in the money market account than in the mutual fund, and the mutual fund and stocks experience the same growth the next year as they did the previous year, they will earn \$1180 in a year. How much money did Tara and Lamar put in each of the three investments?

42. **Money.** Tara talks Lamar into putting less money in the money market account and more money in the stock (see Exercise 41). They place \$20,000 of their savings into investments. They put some in a money market account earning 3% interest, some in a mutual fund that has been averaging 7% a year, and some in a stock that rose 10% last year. If they put \$6000 more in the stock than in the mutual fund, and the mutual fund and stock experience the same growth the next year as they did the previous year, they will earn \$1680 in a year. How much money did Tara and Lamar put in each of the three investments?

43. **Ski Production.** A company produces three types of skis: regular model, trick ski, and slalom ski. They need to fill a customer order of 110 pairs of skis. There are two major production divisions within the company: labor and finishing. Each regular model of skis requires 2 hours of labor and 1 hour of finishing. Each trick ski model requires 3 hours of labor and 2 hours of finishing. Finally, each slalom ski model requires 3 hours of labor and 5 hours of finishing. Suppose the company has only 297 labor hours and 202 finishing hours. How many of each type of ski can be made under these restrictions?

44. **Automobile Production.** An automobile manufacturing company produces three types of automobiles: compact car, intermediate, and luxury model. The company has the capability of producing 500 automobiles. Suppose that each compact-model car requires 200 units of steel and 30 units of rubber, each intermediate model requires 300 units of steel and 20 units of rubber, and each luxury model requires 250 units of steel and 45 units of rubber. The number of units of steel available is 128,750, and the number of units of rubber available is 15,625. How many of each type of automobile can be produced with these restraints?

45. **Computer versus Man.** *The Seattle Times* reported a story on November 18, 2006, about a game of Scrabble played between a human and a computer. The best Scrabble player in the United States was pitted against a computer program designed to play the game. Remarkably, the human beat the computer in the best of two out of three games competition. The total points scored by both computer and man for all three games was 2591. The difference between the first game's total and the second game's total was 62 points. The difference between the first game's total and the third game's total was only 2 points. Determine the total number of points scored by both the computer and the man for each of the three contests.

46. **Brain versus Computer.** Can the human brain perform more calculations per second than a supercomputer? The calculating speed of the three top supercomputers, IBM's Blue Gene/L, IBM's BGW, and IBM's ASC Purple, has been determined. The speed of IBM's Blue Gene/L is 245 teraflops more than that of IBM's BGW. The computing speed of IBM's BGW is 22 teraflops more than that of IBM's ASC Purple. The combined speed of all three top supercomputers is 568 teraflops. Determine the computing speed (in teraflops) of each supercomputer. A **teraflop** is a measure of a computer's speed and can be expressed as 1 trillion floating-point operations per second. By comparison, it is estimated that the human brain can perform 10 quadrillion calculations per second.

• CATCH THE MISTAKE

In Exercises 47 and 48, explain the mistake that is made.

47. Solve the system of equations.

Equation (1):	$2x - y + z = 2$
Equation (2):	$x - y \quad = 1$
Equation (3):	$x \quad + z = 1$

Solution:

Equation (2):	$x - y \quad = 1$
Equation (3):	$x \quad + z = 1$
Add Equation (2) and Equation (3).	$-y + z = 2$
Multiply Equation (1) by (-1).	$-2x + y - z = -2$
Add.	$-2x \quad = 0$
Solve for x.	$x = 0$
Substitute $x = 0$ into Equation (2).	$0 - y = 1$
Solve for y.	$y = -1$
Substitute $x = 0$ into Equation (3).	$0 + z = 1$
Solve for z.	$z = 1$

The answer is $x = 0$, $y = -1$, and $z = 1$.

This is incorrect. Although $x = 0$, $y = -1$, and $z = 1$ does satisfy the three original equations, it is only one of infinitely many solutions. What mistake was made?

48. Solve the system of equations.

Equation (1):	$x + 3y + 2z = 4$
Equation (2):	$3x + 10y + 9z = 17$
Equation (3):	$2x + 7y + 7z = 17$

Solution:

Multiply Equation (1) by -3.	$-3x - 9y - 6z = -12$
Equation (2):	$3x + 10y + 9z = 17$
Add.	$y + 3z = 5$
Multiply Equation (1) by -2.	$-2x - 6y - 4z = -8$
Equation (3):	$2x + 7y + 7z = 17$
Add.	$y + 3z = 9$
Solve the system of two equations.	$y + 3z = 5$
	$y + 3z = 9$

Infinitely many solutions.

Let $z = a$; then $y = 5 - 3a$.

Substitute $z = a$ and $y = 5 - 3a$ into Equation (1).	$x + 3y + 2z = 4$
	$x + 3(5 - 3a) + 2a = 4$
Eliminate parentheses.	$x + 15 - 9a + 2a = 4$
Solve for x.	$x = 7a - 11$

The answer is $x = 7a - 11$, $y = 5 - 3a$, and $z = a$.

This is incorrect. There is no solution. What mistake was made?

• CONCEPTUAL

In Exercises 49–52, determine whether each statement is true or false.

49. A system of linear equations that has more variables than equations cannot have a unique solution.

50. A system of linear equations that has the same number of equations as variables always has a unique solution.

51. The linear equation $Ax + By = C$ always represents a straight line.

52. If the system of linear equations

$$\begin{aligned} x + 2y + 3z &= a \\ 2x + 3y + z &= b \\ 3x + y + 2z &= c \end{aligned}$$

has a unique solution $\left(\frac{1}{6}, \frac{1}{6}, \frac{1}{6}\right)$, then the system of equations

$$\begin{aligned} x + 2y + 3z &= 2a \\ 2x + 3y + z &= 2b \\ 3x + y + 2z &= 2c \end{aligned}$$

has a unique solution $\left(\frac{1}{3}, \frac{1}{3}, \frac{1}{3}\right)$.

53. The circle given by the equation $x^2 + y^2 + ax + by + c = 0$ passes through the points $(-2, 4)$, $(1, 1)$, and $(-2, -2)$. Find a, b, and c.

54. The circle given by the equation $x^2 + y^2 + ax + by + c = 0$ passes through the points $(0, 7)$, $(6, 1)$ and $(5, 4)$. Find a, b, and c.

• CHALLENGE

55. A fourth-degree polynomial, $f(x) = ax^4 + bx^3 + cx^2 + dx + e$, with $a < 0$, can be used to represent the following data on the number of deaths per year due to lightning strikes. Assume that 1999 corresponds to $x = -2$ and 2003 corresponds to $x = 2$. Use the data to determine a, b, c, d, and e.

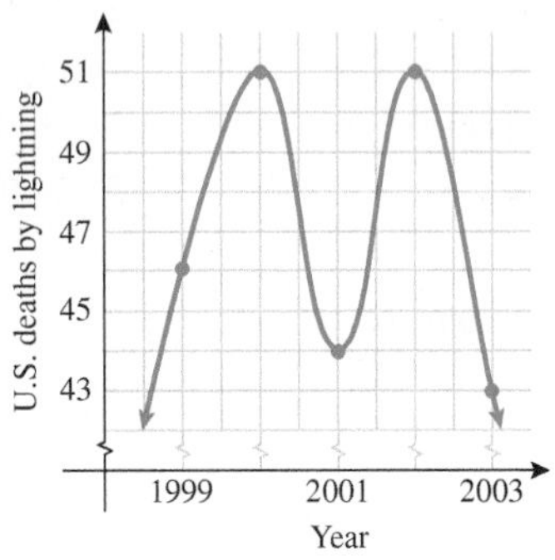

56. A copy machine accepts nickels, dimes, and quarters. After 1 hour, there are 30 coins total and their value is \$4.60. If there are four more quarters than nickels, how many nickels, quarters, and dimes are in the machine?

In Exercises 57–60, solve the system of linear equations.

57.
$$\begin{aligned} 2y + z &= 3 \\ 4x - z &= -3 \\ 7x - 3y - 3z &= 2 \\ x - y - z &= -2 \end{aligned}$$

58.
$$\begin{aligned} -2x - y + 2z &= 3 \\ 3x - 4z &= 2 \\ 2x + y &= -1 \\ -x + y - z &= -8 \end{aligned}$$

59.
$$\begin{aligned} 3x_1 - 2x_2 + x_3 + 2x_4 &= -2 \\ -x_1 + 3x_2 + 4x_3 + 3x_4 &= 4 \\ x_1 + x_2 + x_3 + x_4 &= 0 \\ 5x_1 + 3x_2 + x_3 + 2x_4 &= -1 \end{aligned}$$

60.
$$\begin{aligned} 5x_1 + 3x_2 + 8x_3 + x_4 &= 1 \\ x_1 + 2x_2 + 5x_3 + 2x_4 &= 3 \\ 4x_1 + x_3 - 2x_4 &= -3 \\ x_2 + x_3 + x_4 &= 0 \end{aligned}$$

61. Find the values of A, B, C, and D such that the following equation is true:

$$x^3 + x^2 + 2x + 3 = (Ax + B)(x^2 + 3) + (Cx + D)(x^2 + 2)$$

62. Find the values of A, B, C, D, and E such that the following equation is true:

$$Ax^3(x + 1) + Bx^2(x + 1) + Cx(x + 1) + D(x + 1) + Ex^4 = 4x^4 + x + 1$$

• PREVIEW TO CALCULUS

In calculus, when integrating rational functions, we decompose the function into partial fractions. This technique involves the solution of systems of equations.

In Exercises 63–66, find the values of A, B, and C that make each equation true.

63. $5x^2 + 6x + 2 = A(x^2 + 2x + 5) + (Bx + C)(x + 2)$

64. $2x^2 - 3x + 2 = A(x^2 + 1) + (Bx + C)x$

65. $3x + 8 = A(x^2 + 5x + 6) + B(x^2 + 3x) + C(x^2 + 2x)$

66. $x^2 + x + 1 = A(x^2 + 5x + 6) + B(x^2 + 4x + 3) + C(x^2 + 3x + 2)$

8.3 SYSTEMS OF LINEAR EQUATIONS AND MATRICES

SKILLS OBJECTIVES

- Determine the order of a matrix.
- Write a system of linear equations as an augmented matrix.
- Perform row operations on an augmented matrix.
- Write a matrix in reduced row–echelon form.
- Solve systems of linear equations using Gaussian elimination with back-substitution.
- Solve systems of linear equations using Gauss–Jordan elimination.
- Recognize matrices that correspond to inconsistent and dependent systems.

CONCEPTUAL OBJECTIVES

- Understand that a_{ij} corresponds to the element in row i and column j of matrix A.
- Visualize an augmented matrix as a system of linear equations.
- Understand that row operations correspond to generating equivalent systems of linear equations.
- Understand the difference between row–echelon and reduced row–echelon forms.
- Recognize that solving systems with augmented matrices is equivalent to solving by the method of elimination.
- Understand that when you move down an augmented matrix, you use rows above, and that on the way back up, you use rows below.
- Understand the difference between matrices that correspond to inconsistent systems and those that correspond to dependent systems.

8.3.1 Matrices

Some information is best displayed in a table. For example, the number of calories burned per half hour of exercise depends on the person's weight, as illustrated in the following table. Note that the rows correspond to activities and the columns correspond to weight.

8.3.1 SKILL

Determine the order of a matrix.

8.3.1 CONCEPTUAL

Understand that a_{ij} corresponds to the element in row i and column j of matrix A.

ACTIVITY	127–137 LB	160–170 LB	180–200 LB
Walking/4 mph	156	183	204
Volleyball	267	315	348
Jogging/5 mph	276	345	381

Another example is the driving distance in miles from cities in Arizona (columns) to cities outside the state (rows).

CITY	FLAGSTAFF	PHOENIX	TUCSON	YUMA
Albuquerque, NM	325	465	440	650
Las Vegas, NV	250	300	415	295
Los Angeles, CA	470	375	490	285

[CONCEPT CHECK]

How many calories correspond to the a_{23} element?

ANSWER 348

If we selected only the numbers in each of the preceding tables and placed brackets around them, the result would be a *matrix*.

$$\text{Calories: } \begin{bmatrix} 156 & 183 & 204 \\ 267 & 315 & 348 \\ 276 & 345 & 381 \end{bmatrix} \qquad \text{Miles: } \begin{bmatrix} 325 & 465 & 440 & 650 \\ 250 & 300 & 415 & 295 \\ 470 & 375 & 490 & 285 \end{bmatrix}$$

A ***matrix*** is a rectangular array of numbers written within brackets.

$$\begin{bmatrix} a_{11} & a_{12} & \cdots & a_{1j} & \cdots & a_{1n} \\ a_{21} & a_{22} & \cdots & a_{2j} & \cdots & a_{2n} \\ \vdots & \vdots & \cdots & \vdots & \cdots & \vdots \\ a_{i1} & a_{i2} & \cdots & a_{ij} & \cdots & a_{in} \\ \vdots & \vdots & \cdots & \vdots & \cdots & \vdots \\ a_{m1} & a_{m2} & \cdots & a_{mj} & \cdots & a_{mn} \end{bmatrix}$$

Each number a_{ij} in the matrix is called an **entry** (or **element**) of the matrix. The first subscript i is the **row index**, and the second subscript j is the **column index**. This matrix contains m rows and n columns, so it is said to be of **order** $m \times n$.

STUDY TIP

The order of a matrix is always given as the number of rows by the number of columns.

When the number of rows equals the number of columns (i.e., when $m = n$), the matrix is a **square matrix** of order n. In a square matrix, the entries $a_{11}, a_{22}, a_{33}, \ldots, a_{nn}$ are the **main diagonal** entries.

The matrix

$$A_{4\times 3} = \begin{bmatrix} * & * & * \\ * & * & * \\ * & a_{32} & * \\ * & * & * \end{bmatrix}$$

has order (dimensions) 4×3, since there are four rows and three columns. The entry a_{32} is in the third row and the second column.

EXAMPLE 1 **Finding the Order of a Matrix**

Determine the order of each matrix given.

a. $\begin{bmatrix} 2 & 1 \\ 3 & 0 \end{bmatrix}$ **b.** $\begin{bmatrix} 1 & -2 & 5 \\ -1 & 3 & 4 \end{bmatrix}$ **c.** $\begin{bmatrix} -2 & 5 & 4 \\ 1 & -\frac{1}{3} & 0 \\ 3 & 8 & 1 \end{bmatrix}$

d. $\begin{bmatrix} 4 & 9 & -\frac{1}{2} & 3 \end{bmatrix}$ **e.** $\begin{bmatrix} 3 & -2 \\ 5 & 1 \\ 0 & -\frac{2}{3} \\ 7 & 6 \end{bmatrix}$

Solution:

a. This matrix has **2** rows and **2** columns, so the order of the matrix is $\boxed{2 \times 2}$.

b. This matrix has **2** rows and **3** columns, so the order of the matrix is $\boxed{2 \times 3}$.

c. This matrix has **3** rows and **3** columns, so the order of the matrix is $\boxed{3 \times 3}$ or 3 since it is a square matrix.

d. This matrix has **1** row and **4** columns, so the order of the matrix is $\boxed{1 \times 4}$.

e. This matrix has **4** rows and **2** columns, so the order of the matrix is $\boxed{4 \times 2}$.

A matrix with only one column is called a **column matrix**, and a matrix that has only one row is called a **row matrix**. Notice that in Example 1 the matrices given in parts (a) and (c) are square matrices and the matrix given in part (d) is a row matrix.

You can use matrices as a shorthand way of writing systems of linear equations. There are two ways we can represent systems of linear equations with matrices: as *augmented matrices* or with *matrix equations*. In this section, we will discuss *augmented matrices* and solve systems of linear equations using two methods: *Gaussian elimination with back-substitution* and *Gauss–Jordan elimination*.

8.3.2 Augmented Matrices

A **coefficient matrix** is a matrix whose elements are the coefficients of a system of linear equations. A particular type of matrix that is used in representing a system of linear equations is an **augmented matrix**. It resembles a coefficient matrix with an additional vertical line and column of numbers, hence the name *augmented*. The following table illustrates examples of augmented matrices that represent systems of linear equations.

8.3.2 SKILL

Write a system of linear equations as an augmented matrix.

8.3.2 CONCEPTUAL

Visualize an augmented matrix as a system of linear equations.

SYSTEM OF LINEAR EQUATIONS	AUGMENTED MATRIX
$\begin{aligned} 3x + 4y &= 1 \\ x - 2y &= 7 \end{aligned}$	$\left[\begin{array}{cc\|c} 3 & 4 & 1 \\ 1 & -2 & 7 \end{array}\right]$
$\begin{aligned} x - y + z &= 2 \\ 2x + 2y - 3z &= -3 \\ x + y + z &= 6 \end{aligned}$	$\left[\begin{array}{ccc\|c} 1 & -1 & 1 & 2 \\ 2 & 2 & -3 & -3 \\ 1 & 1 & 1 & 6 \end{array}\right]$
$\begin{aligned} x + y + z &= 0 \\ 3x \quad - z &= 2 \end{aligned}$	$\left[\begin{array}{ccc\|c} 1 & 1 & 1 & 0 \\ 3 & 0 & -1 & 2 \end{array}\right]$

Note the following:

- Each row represents an equation.
- The vertical line represents the equal sign.
- The first column represents the coefficients of the variable x.
- The second column represents the coefficients of the variable y.
- The third column (in the second and third systems) represents the coefficients of the variable z.
- The coefficients of the variables are on the left of the equal sign (vertical line), and the constants are on the right.
- Any variable that does not appear in an equation has an implied coefficient of 0.

[CONCEPT CHECK]

TRUE OR FALSE The entries to the right of the solid vertical line in an augmented matrix correspond to the constants in the system of linear equations.

ANSWER True

EXAMPLE 2 **Writing a System of Linear Equations as an Augmented Matrix**

Write each system of linear equations as an augmented matrix.

a. $\begin{aligned} 2x - y &= 5 \\ -x + 2y &= 3 \end{aligned}$ **b.** $\begin{aligned} 3x - 2y + 4z &= 5 \\ y - 3z &= -2 \\ 7x \quad\quad - z &= 1 \end{aligned}$ **c.** $\begin{aligned} x_1 - x_2 + 2x_3 - 3 &= 0 \\ x_1 + x_2 - 3x_3 + 5 &= 0 \\ x_1 - x_2 + x_3 - 2 &= 0 \end{aligned}$

Solution:

a. $\left[\begin{array}{rr|r} 2 & -1 & 5 \\ -1 & 2 & 3 \end{array}\right]$

b. Note that all missing terms have a 0 coefficient.

$$\begin{aligned} 3x - 2y + 4z &= 5 \\ 0x + y - 3z &= -2 \\ 7x + 0y - z &= 1 \end{aligned}$$

$$\left[\begin{array}{rrr|r} 3 & -2 & 4 & 5 \\ 0 & 1 & -3 & -2 \\ 7 & 0 & -1 & 1 \end{array}\right]$$

c. Write the constants on the right side of the vertical line in the matrix.

$$\begin{aligned} x_1 - x_2 + 2x_3 &= 3 \\ x_1 + x_2 - 3x_3 &= -5 \\ x_1 - x_2 + x_3 &= 2 \end{aligned}$$

$$\left[\begin{array}{rrr|r} 1 & -1 & 2 & 3 \\ 1 & 1 & -3 & -5 \\ 1 & -1 & 1 & 2 \end{array}\right]$$

YOUR TURN Write each system of linear equations as an augmented matrix.

a. $\begin{aligned} 2x + y - 3 &= 0 \\ x - y &= 5 \end{aligned}$ **b.** $\begin{aligned} y - x + z &= 7 \\ x - y - z &= 2 \\ z - y &= -1 \end{aligned}$

ANSWER

a. $\left[\begin{array}{rr|r} 2 & 1 & 3 \\ 1 & -1 & 5 \end{array}\right]$

b. $\left[\begin{array}{rrr|r} -1 & 1 & 1 & 7 \\ 1 & -1 & -1 & 2 \\ 0 & -1 & 1 & -1 \end{array}\right]$

8.3.3 Row Operations on a Matrix

8.3.3 SKILL

Perform row operations on an augmented matrix.

8.3.3 CONCEPTUAL

Understand that row operations correspond to generating equivalent systems of linear equations.

Row operations on a matrix are used to solve a system of linear equations when the system is written as an augmented matrix. Recall from the elimination method in Sections 8.1 and 8.2 that we could interchange equations, multiply an entire equation by a nonzero constant, and add a multiple of one equation to another equation to produce equivalent systems. Because each row in a matrix represents an equation, the operations that produced equivalent systems of equations that were used in the elimination method will also produce equivalent augmented matrices.

ROW OPERATIONS

The following operations on an augmented matrix will yield an equivalent matrix:

1. Interchange any two rows.
2. Multiply a row by a nonzero constant.
3. Add a multiple of one row to another row.

The following symbols describe these row operations:

1. $R_i \leftrightarrow R_j$ Interchange row i with row j.
2. $cR_i \rightarrow R_i$ Multiply row i by the constant c.
3. $cR_i + R_j \rightarrow R_j$ Multiply row i by the constant c and add to row j, writing the results in row j.

STUDY TIP

Each missing term in an equation of the system of linear equations is represented with a zero in the augmented matrix.

EXAMPLE 3 Applying a Row Operation to an Augmented Matrix

For each matrix, perform the given operation.

a. $\left[\begin{array}{cc|c} 2 & -1 & 3 \\ 0 & 2 & 1 \end{array}\right]$ $R_1 \leftrightarrow R_2$

b. $\left[\begin{array}{ccc|c} -1 & 0 & 1 & -2 \\ 3 & -1 & 2 & 3 \\ 0 & 1 & 3 & 1 \end{array}\right]$ $2R_3 \rightarrow R_3$

c. $\left[\begin{array}{cccc|c} 1 & 2 & 0 & 2 & 2 \\ 0 & 1 & 2 & 3 & 5 \end{array}\right]$ $R_1 - 2R_2 \rightarrow R_1$

Solution:

a. Interchange the first row with the second row.

$$\left[\begin{array}{cc|c} 2 & -1 & 3 \\ 0 & 2 & 1 \end{array}\right] \quad R_1 \leftrightarrow R_2 \quad \boxed{\left[\begin{array}{cc|c} 0 & 2 & 1 \\ 2 & -1 & 3 \end{array}\right]}$$

b. Multiply the third row by 2.

$$\left[\begin{array}{ccc|c} -1 & 0 & 1 & -2 \\ 3 & -1 & 2 & 3 \\ 0 & 1 & 3 & 1 \end{array}\right] \quad 2R_3 \rightarrow R_3 \quad \boxed{\left[\begin{array}{ccc|c} -1 & 0 & 1 & -2 \\ 3 & -1 & 2 & 3 \\ 0 & 2 & 6 & 2 \end{array}\right]}$$

c. From row 1 subtract 2 times row 2, and write the answer in row 1. Note that finding row 1 minus 2 times row 2 is the same as adding row 1 to the product of -2 with row 2.

$$R_1 - 2R_2 \rightarrow R_1 \quad \left[\begin{array}{cccc|c} 1-2(0) & 2-2(1) & 0-2(2) & 2-2(3) & 2-2(5) \\ 0 & 1 & 2 & 3 & 5 \end{array}\right]$$

$$\boxed{\left[\begin{array}{cccc|c} 1 & 0 & -4 & -4 & -8 \\ 0 & 1 & 2 & 3 & 5 \end{array}\right]}$$

YOUR TURN Perform the operation $R_1 + 2R_3 \rightarrow R_1$ on the matrix.

$$\left[\begin{array}{ccc|c} 1 & 0 & -2 & -3 \\ 0 & 1 & 2 & 3 \\ 0 & 0 & 1 & 2 \end{array}\right]$$

ANSWER

$$\left[\begin{array}{ccc|c} 1 & 0 & 0 & 1 \\ 0 & 1 & 2 & 3 \\ 0 & 0 & 1 & 2 \end{array}\right]$$

[CONCEPT CHECK]

The notation $R_1 + 2R_3 \rightarrow R_1$ corresponds to what row operations?

ANSWER Add row 1 to 2 times row 3, and put the result in row 1.

8.3.4 Row–Echelon Form of a Matrix

8.3.4 SKILL

Write a matrix in reduced row–echelon form.

8.3.4 CONCEPTUAL

Understand the difference between row–echelon and reduced row–echelon forms.

We can solve systems of linear equations using augmented matrices with two procedures: *Gaussian elimination with back-substitution*, which uses row operations to transform a matrix into *row–echelon form*, and *Gauss–Jordan elimination*, which uses row operations to transform a matrix into *reduced row–echelon form*.

Row–Echelon Form

A matrix is in **row–echelon** form if it has all three of the following properties:

1. Any rows consisting entirely of 0s are at the bottom of the matrix.
2. For each row that does not consist entirely of 0s, the first (leftmost) nonzero entry is 1 (called the leading 1).
3. For two successive nonzero rows, the leading 1 in the higher row is farther to the left than the leading 1 in the lower row.

Reduced Row–Echelon Form

If a matrix in row–echelon form has the following additional property, then the matrix is in **reduced row–echelon form**:

4. Every column containing a leading 1 has zeros in every position above and below the leading 1.

[CONCEPT CHECK]

TRUE OR FALSE A matrix that does not satisfy row–echelon form does not satisfy reduced row–echelon form.

ANSWER True

EXAMPLE 4 **Determining Whether a Matrix Is in Row–Echelon Form**

Determine whether each matrix is in row–echelon form. If it is in row–echelon form, determine whether it is in reduced row–echelon form.

a. $\left[\begin{array}{ccc|c} 1 & 3 & 2 & 3 \\ 0 & 1 & 4 & 2 \\ 0 & 0 & 1 & -1 \end{array}\right]$ **b.** $\left[\begin{array}{ccc|c} 1 & 3 & 2 & 3 \\ 0 & 1 & 1 & 3 \\ 0 & 0 & 0 & 0 \end{array}\right]$ **c.** $\left[\begin{array}{ccc|c} 1 & 0 & 3 & 2 \\ 0 & 1 & -1 & 5 \end{array}\right]$

d. $\left[\begin{array}{cc|c} 1 & 0 & 1 \\ 0 & 3 & 1 \end{array}\right]$ **e.** $\left[\begin{array}{ccc|c} 1 & 0 & 0 & 3 \\ 0 & 1 & 0 & 5 \\ 0 & 0 & 1 & 7 \end{array}\right]$ **f.** $\left[\begin{array}{ccc|c} 1 & 3 & 2 & 3 \\ 0 & 0 & 1 & 2 \\ 0 & 1 & 0 & -3 \end{array}\right]$

Solution:

The matrices in (a), (b), (c), and (e) are in row–echelon form. The matrix in (d) is not in row–echelon form, by condition 2; the leading nonzero entry is not a 1 in each row. If the "3" were a "1," the matrix would be in reduced row–echelon form. The matrix in (f) is not in row–echelon form, because of condition 3; the leading 1 in row 2 is not to the left of the leading 1 in row 3. The matrices in (c) and (e) are in reduced row–echelon form, because in the columns containing the leading 1s there are zeros in every position above and below the leading 1.

8.3.5 Gaussian Elimination with Back-Substitution

8.3.5 SKILL

Solve systems of linear equations using Gaussian elimination with back-substitution.

8.3.5 CONCEPTUAL

Recognize that solving systems with augmented matrices is equivalent to solving by the method of elimination.

STUDY TIP

For row–echelon form, get 1s along the main diagonal and 0s below these 1s.

Gaussian elimination with back-substitution is a method that uses row operations to transform an augmented matrix into row–echelon form and then uses back-substitution to find the solution to the system of linear equations.

GAUSSIAN ELIMINATION WITH BACK-SUBSTITUTION

Step 1: Write the system of linear equations as an augmented matrix.

Step 2: Use row operations to rewrite the augmented matrix in row–echelon form.

Step 3: Write the system of linear equations that corresponds to the matrix in row–echelon form found in Step 2.

Step 4: Use the system of linear equations found in Step 3 together, with back-substitution, to find the solution of the system.

The order in which we perform row operations is important. You should move from left to right. Here is an example of Step 2 in the procedure:

$$\left[\begin{array}{ccc|c} 1 & * & * & * \\ * & * & * & * \\ * & * & * & * \end{array}\right] \rightarrow \left[\begin{array}{ccc|c} 1 & * & * & * \\ 0 & * & * & * \\ 0 & * & * & * \end{array}\right] \rightarrow \left[\begin{array}{ccc|c} 1 & * & * & * \\ 0 & 1 & * & * \\ 0 & * & * & * \end{array}\right] \rightarrow \left[\begin{array}{ccc|c} 1 & * & * & * \\ 0 & 1 & * & * \\ 0 & 0 & * & * \end{array}\right] \rightarrow \left[\begin{array}{ccc|c} 1 & * & * & * \\ 0 & 1 & * & * \\ 0 & 0 & 1 & * \end{array}\right]$$

Matrices are not typically used for systems of linear equations in two variables because the methods from Section 8.1 (substitution and elimination) are more efficient. Example 5 illustrates this procedure with a simple system of linear equations in two variables.

EXAMPLE 5 **Using Gaussian Elimination with Back-Substitution to Solve a System of Two Linear Equations in Two Variables**

Apply Gaussian elimination with back-substitution to solve the system of linear equations.

$$\begin{aligned} 2x + y &= -8 \\ x + 3y &= 6 \end{aligned}$$

Solution:

STEP 1 Write the system of linear equations as an augmented matrix. $\left[\begin{array}{cc|c} 2 & 1 & -8 \\ 1 & 3 & 6 \end{array}\right]$

STEP 2 Use row operations to rewrite the matrix in row–echelon form.

Get a 1 at the top left. Interchange rows 1 and 2.

$$\left[\begin{array}{cc|c} 2 & 1 & -8 \\ 1 & 3 & 6 \end{array}\right] \quad R_1 \leftrightarrow R_2 \quad \left[\begin{array}{cc|c} 1 & 3 & 6 \\ 2 & 1 & -8 \end{array}\right]$$

Get a 0 below the leading 1 in row 1.

$$\left[\begin{array}{cc|c} 1 & 3 & 6 \\ 2 & 1 & -8 \end{array}\right] \quad R_2 - 2R_1 \rightarrow R_2 \quad \left[\begin{array}{cc|c} 1 & 3 & 6 \\ 0 & -5 & -20 \end{array}\right]$$

Get a leading 1 in row 2. Make the "-5" a "1" by dividing by -5. Dividing by -5 is the same as multiplying by its reciprocal $-\frac{1}{5}$.

$$\left[\begin{array}{cc|c} 1 & 3 & 6 \\ 0 & -5 & -20 \end{array}\right] \quad -\tfrac{1}{5}R_2 \rightarrow R_2 \quad \left[\begin{array}{cc|c} 1 & 3 & 6 \\ 0 & 1 & 4 \end{array}\right]$$

The resulting matrix is in row–echelon form.

STEP 3 Write the system of linear equations corresponding to the row–echelon form of the matrix resulting in Step 2.

$$\left[\begin{array}{cc|c} 1 & 3 & 6 \\ 0 & 1 & 4 \end{array}\right] \rightarrow \begin{aligned} x + 3y &= 6 \\ y &= 4 \end{aligned}$$

STEP 4 Use back-substitution to find the solution to the system.

Let $y = 4$ in the first equation $x + 3y = 6$. $\quad x + 3(4) = 6$

Solve for x. $\quad x = -6$

The solution to the system of linear equations is $\boxed{x = -6, y = 4}$.

[CONCEPT CHECK]

Solve the system of linear equations in Example 5 using the elimination method.

ANSWER $x = -6, y = 4$

EXAMPLE 6 **Using Gaussian Elimination with Back-Substitution to Solve a System of Three Linear Equations in Three Variables**

Use Gaussian elimination with back-substitution to solve the system of linear equations.

$$\begin{aligned} 2x + y + 8z &= -1 \\ x - y + z &= -2 \\ 3x - 2y - 2z &= 2 \end{aligned}$$

Solution:

STEP 1 Write the system of linear equations as an augmented matrix.

$$\left[\begin{array}{ccc|c} 2 & 1 & 8 & -1 \\ 1 & -1 & 1 & -2 \\ 3 & -2 & -2 & 2 \end{array}\right]$$

STEP 2 Use row operations to rewrite the matrix in row–echelon form.

Get a 1 at the top left. Interchange rows 1 and 2.

$$R_1 \leftrightarrow R_2 \quad \left[\begin{array}{ccc|c} 1 & -1 & 1 & -2 \\ 2 & 1 & 8 & -1 \\ 3 & -2 & -2 & 2 \end{array}\right]$$

Get 0s below the leading 1 in row 1.

$$R_2 - 2R_1 \rightarrow R_2 \quad \left[\begin{array}{ccc|c} 1 & -1 & 1 & -2 \\ 0 & 3 & 6 & 3 \\ 3 & -2 & -2 & 2 \end{array}\right]$$

$$R_3 - 3R_1 \rightarrow R_3 \quad \left[\begin{array}{ccc|c} 1 & -1 & 1 & -2 \\ 0 & 3 & 6 & 3 \\ 0 & 1 & -5 & 8 \end{array}\right]$$

Get a leading 1 in row 2. Make the "3" a "1" by dividing by 3.

$$\tfrac{1}{3}R_2 \rightarrow R_2 \quad \left[\begin{array}{ccc|c} 1 & -1 & 1 & -2 \\ 0 & 1 & 2 & 1 \\ 0 & 1 & -5 & 8 \end{array}\right]$$

Get a zero below the leading 1 in row 2.

$$R_3 - R_2 \rightarrow R_3 \quad \left[\begin{array}{ccc|c} 1 & -1 & 1 & -2 \\ 0 & 1 & 2 & 1 \\ 0 & 0 & -7 & 7 \end{array}\right]$$

Get a leading 1 in row 3. Make the "−7" a "1" by dividing by −7.

$$-\tfrac{1}{7}R_3 \rightarrow R_3 \quad \left[\begin{array}{ccc|c} 1 & -1 & 1 & -2 \\ 0 & 1 & 2 & 1 \\ 0 & 0 & 1 & -1 \end{array}\right]$$

STEP 3 Write the system of linear equations corresponding to the row–echelon form of the matrix resulting in Step 2.

$$\begin{aligned} x - y + z &= -2 \\ y + 2z &= 1 \\ z &= -1 \end{aligned}$$

STEP 4 Use back-substitution to find the solution to the system.

Let $\boxed{z = -1}$ in the second equation $y + 2z = 1$. $\quad y + 2(-1) = 1$

Solve for y. $\quad \boxed{y = 3}$

Let $y = 3$ and $z = -1$ in the first equation $x - y + z = -2$. $\quad x - (3) + (-1) = -2$

Solve for x. $\quad \boxed{x = 2}$

The solution to the system of linear equations is $\boxed{x = 2, y = 3, \text{ and } z = -1}$.

ANSWER

$x = -1, y = 2, z = 1$

YOUR TURN Use Gaussian elimination with back-substitution to solve the system of linear equations.

$$\begin{aligned} x + y - z &= 0 \\ 2x + y + z &= 1 \\ 2x - y + 3z &= -1 \end{aligned}$$

8.3.6 Gauss–Jordan Elimination

In Gaussian elimination with back-substitution, we used row operations to rewrite the matrix in an equivalent row–echelon form. If we continue using row operations until the matrix is in *reduced* row–echelon form, this eliminates the need for back-substitution, and we call this process *Gauss–Jordan elimination*.

8.3.6 SKILL

Solve systems of linear equations using Gauss–Jordan elimination.

8.3.6 CONCEPTUAL

Understand that when you move down an augmented matrix, you use rows above, and that on the way back up, you use rows below.

GAUSS–JORDAN ELIMINATION

Step 1: Write the system of linear equations as an augmented matrix.

Step 2: Use row operations to rewrite the augmented matrix in *reduced* row–echelon form.

Step 3: Write the system of linear equations that corresponds to the matrix in reduced row–echelon form found in Step 2. The result is the solution to the system.

The order in which we perform row operations is important. You should move from left to right. Think of this process as climbing *down* a set of stairs first and then back up the stairs second. On the way *down* the stairs, always use operations with rows *above* where you currently are, and on the way back *up* the stairs, always use rows *below* where you currently are.

STUDY TIP

For reduced row–echelon form, get 1s along the main diagonal and 0s above and below these 1s.

Down the stairs:

$$\left[\begin{array}{ccc|c} 1 & * & * & * \\ * & * & * & * \\ * & * & * & * \end{array}\right] \rightarrow \left[\begin{array}{ccc|c} 1 & * & * & * \\ 0 & * & * & * \\ 0 & * & * & * \end{array}\right] \rightarrow \left[\begin{array}{ccc|c} 1 & * & * & * \\ 0 & 1 & * & * \\ 0 & * & * & * \end{array}\right] \rightarrow \left[\begin{array}{ccc|c} 1 & * & * & * \\ 0 & 1 & * & * \\ 0 & 0 & * & * \end{array}\right] \rightarrow \left[\begin{array}{ccc|c} 1 & * & * & * \\ 0 & 1 & * & * \\ 0 & 0 & 1 & * \end{array}\right]$$

Up the stairs:

$$\left[\begin{array}{ccc|c} 1 & * & * & * \\ 0 & 1 & * & * \\ 0 & 0 & 1 & * \end{array}\right] \rightarrow \left[\begin{array}{ccc|c} 1 & * & * & * \\ 0 & 1 & 0 & * \\ 0 & 0 & 1 & * \end{array}\right] \rightarrow \left[\begin{array}{ccc|c} 1 & * & 0 & * \\ 0 & 1 & 0 & * \\ 0 & 0 & 1 & * \end{array}\right] \rightarrow \left[\begin{array}{ccc|c} 1 & 0 & 0 & * \\ 0 & 1 & 0 & * \\ 0 & 0 & 1 & * \end{array}\right]$$

[CONCEPT CHECK]

TRUE OR FALSE Going down the stairs corresponds to transforming the augmented matrix to row–echelon form, and going up the stairs corresponds to transforming the augmented matrix to reduced row–echelon form.

ANSWER True

EXAMPLE 7 **Using Gauss–Jordan Elimination to Solve a System of Linear Equations in Three Variables**

Apply Gauss–Jordan elimination to solve the system of linear equations.

$$\begin{aligned} x - y + 2z &= -1 \\ 3x + 2y - 6z &= 1 \\ 2x + 3y + 4z &= 8 \end{aligned}$$

Solution:

STEP 1 Write the system as an augmented matrix.

$$\left[\begin{array}{ccc|c} 1 & -1 & 2 & -1 \\ 3 & 2 & -6 & 1 \\ 2 & 3 & 4 & 8 \end{array}\right]$$

STEP 2 Utilize row operations to rewrite the matrix in reduced row–echelon form.

There is already a 1 in the first row/first column.

Get 0s below the leading 1 in row 1.

$$\begin{array}{l} R_2 - 3R_1 \to R_2 \\ R_3 - 2R_1 \to R_3 \end{array} \quad \left[\begin{array}{ccc|c} 1 & -1 & 2 & -1 \\ 0 & 5 & -12 & 4 \\ 0 & 5 & 0 & 10 \end{array}\right]$$

Get a 1 in row 2/column 2.

$$R_2 \leftrightarrow R_3 \quad \left[\begin{array}{ccc|c} 1 & -1 & 2 & -1 \\ 0 & 5 & 0 & 10 \\ 0 & 5 & -12 & 4 \end{array}\right]$$

$$\tfrac{1}{5}R_2 \to R_2 \quad \left[\begin{array}{ccc|c} 1 & -1 & 2 & -1 \\ 0 & 1 & 0 & 2 \\ 0 & 5 & -12 & 4 \end{array}\right]$$

Get a 0 in row 3/column 2.

$$R_3 - 5R_2 \to R_3 \quad \left[\begin{array}{ccc|c} 1 & -1 & 2 & -1 \\ 0 & 1 & 0 & 2 \\ 0 & 0 & -12 & -6 \end{array}\right]$$

Get a 1 in row 3/column 3.

$$-\tfrac{1}{12}R_3 \to R_3 \quad \left[\begin{array}{ccc|c} 1 & -1 & 2 & -1 \\ 0 & 1 & 0 & 2 \\ 0 & 0 & 1 & \frac{1}{2} \end{array}\right]$$

Now go back up the stairs.

Get 0s above the 1 in row 3/column 3.

$$R_1 - 2R_3 \to R_1 \quad \left[\begin{array}{ccc|c} 1 & -1 & 0 & -2 \\ 0 & 1 & 0 & 2 \\ 0 & 0 & 1 & \frac{1}{2} \end{array}\right]$$

Get a 0 in row 1/column 2.

$$R_1 + R_2 \to R_1 \quad \left[\begin{array}{ccc|c} 1 & 0 & 0 & 0 \\ 0 & 1 & 0 & 2 \\ 0 & 0 & 1 & \frac{1}{2} \end{array}\right]$$

STEP 3 Identify the solution. $\boxed{x = 0, y = 2, z = \frac{1}{2}}$

YOUR TURN Use an augmented matrix and Gauss–Jordan elimination to solve the system of equations.

$$\begin{aligned} x + y - z &= -2 \\ 3x + y - z &= -4 \\ 2x - 2y + 3z &= 3 \end{aligned}$$

ANSWER

$x = -1, y = 2, z = 3$

EXAMPLE 8 Solving a System of Four Linear Equations in Four Variables

Solve the system of equations with Gauss–Jordan elimination.

$$\begin{aligned} x_1 + x_2 - x_3 + 3x_4 &= 3 \\ 3x_2 \qquad - 2x_4 &= 4 \\ 2x_1 \qquad - 3x_3 \qquad &= -1 \\ 2x_1 \qquad\qquad + 4x_4 &= -6 \end{aligned}$$

Solution:

STEP 1 Write the system as an augmented matrix.

$$\left[\begin{array}{cccc|c} 1 & 1 & -1 & 3 & 3 \\ 0 & 3 & 0 & -2 & 4 \\ 2 & 0 & -3 & 0 & -1 \\ 2 & 0 & 0 & 4 & -6 \end{array}\right]$$

> **STUDY TIP**
> Careful attention should be paid to the order of terms, and zeros should be used for missing terms.

STEP 2 Use row operations to rewrite the matrix in reduced row–echelon form.

There is already a 1 in the first row/first column.

Get 0s below the 1 in row 1/column 1.

$$\begin{array}{r} R_3 - 2R_1 \to R_3 \\ R_4 - 2R_1 \to R_4 \end{array} \quad \left[\begin{array}{cccc|c} 1 & 1 & -1 & 3 & 3 \\ 0 & 3 & 0 & -2 & 4 \\ 0 & -2 & -1 & -6 & -7 \\ 0 & -2 & 2 & -2 & -12 \end{array}\right]$$

Get a 1 in row 2/column 2.

$$R_2 \leftrightarrow R_4 \quad \left[\begin{array}{cccc|c} 1 & 1 & -1 & 3 & 3 \\ 0 & -2 & 2 & -2 & -12 \\ 0 & -2 & -1 & -6 & -7 \\ 0 & 3 & 0 & -2 & 4 \end{array}\right]$$

$$-\tfrac{1}{2}R_2 \leftrightarrow R_2 \quad \left[\begin{array}{cccc|c} 1 & 1 & -1 & 3 & 3 \\ 0 & 1 & -1 & 1 & 6 \\ 0 & -2 & -1 & -6 & -7 \\ 0 & 3 & 0 & -2 & 4 \end{array}\right]$$

Get 0s below the 1 in row 2/column 2.

$$\begin{array}{r} R_3 + 2R_2 \to R_3 \\ R_4 - 3R_2 \to R_4 \end{array} \quad \left[\begin{array}{cccc|c} 1 & 1 & -1 & 3 & 3 \\ 0 & 1 & -1 & 1 & 6 \\ 0 & 0 & -3 & -4 & 5 \\ 0 & 0 & 3 & -5 & -14 \end{array}\right]$$

Get a 1 in row 3/column 3.

$$-\tfrac{1}{3}R_3 \to R_3 \quad \left[\begin{array}{cccc|c} 1 & 1 & -1 & 3 & 3 \\ 0 & 1 & -1 & 1 & 6 \\ 0 & 0 & 1 & \frac{4}{3} & -\frac{5}{3} \\ 0 & 0 & 3 & -5 & -14 \end{array}\right]$$

Get a 0 in row 4/column 3.

$$R_4 - 3R_3 \to R_4 \quad \left[\begin{array}{cccc|c} 1 & 1 & -1 & 3 & 3 \\ 0 & 1 & -1 & 1 & 6 \\ 0 & 0 & 1 & \frac{4}{3} & -\frac{5}{3} \\ 0 & 0 & 0 & -9 & -9 \end{array}\right]$$

Get a 1 in row 4/column 4.

$$-\tfrac{1}{9}R_4 \to R_4 \quad \left[\begin{array}{cccc|c} 1 & 1 & -1 & 3 & 3 \\ 0 & 1 & -1 & 1 & 6 \\ 0 & 0 & 1 & \frac{4}{3} & -\frac{5}{3} \\ 0 & 0 & 0 & 1 & 1 \end{array}\right]$$

Now go back up the stairs.

Get 0s above the 1 in row 4/column 4.

$$\begin{array}{l} R_3 - \tfrac{4}{3}R_4 \to R_3 \\ R_2 - R_4 \to R_2 \\ R_1 - 3R_4 \to R_1 \end{array} \quad \left[\begin{array}{cccc|c} 1 & 1 & -1 & 0 & 0 \\ 0 & 1 & -1 & 0 & 5 \\ 0 & 0 & 1 & 0 & -3 \\ 0 & 0 & 0 & 1 & 1 \end{array}\right]$$

Get 0s above the 1 in row 3/column 3.

$$\begin{array}{l} R_2 + R_3 \to R_2 \\ R_1 + R_3 \to R_1 \end{array} \quad \left[\begin{array}{cccc|c} 1 & 1 & 0 & 0 & -3 \\ 0 & 1 & 0 & 0 & 2 \\ 0 & 0 & 1 & 0 & -3 \\ 0 & 0 & 0 & 1 & 1 \end{array}\right]$$

Get a 0 in row 1/column 2.

$$R_1 - R_2 \to R_1 \quad \left[\begin{array}{cccc|c} 1 & 0 & 0 & 0 & -5 \\ 0 & 1 & 0 & 0 & 2 \\ 0 & 0 & 1 & 0 & -3 \\ 0 & 0 & 0 & 1 & 1 \end{array}\right]$$

STEP 3 Identify the solution. $\boxed{x_1 = -5, x_2 = 2, x_3 = -3, x_4 = 1}$

8.3.7 SKILL

Recognize matrices that correspond to inconsistent and dependent systems.

8.3.7 CONCEPTUAL

Understand the difference between matrices that correspond to inconsistent systems and those that correspond to dependent systems.

8.3.7 Inconsistent and Dependent Systems

Recall from Section 8.1 that systems of linear equations can be independent, inconsistent, or dependent systems and can therefore have *one solution*, *no solution*, or *infinitely many solutions*. All of the systems we have solved so far in this section have been independent systems (unique solution). The following table indicates the three possible types of solutions when a system of linear equations is solved using Gaussian elimination or Gauss–Jordan elimination.

SYSTEM	TYPE OF SOLUTION	MATRIX DURING GAUSS–JORDAN ELIMINATION	EXAMPLE
Independent	One (unique) solution	Diagonal entries are all 1s, and the 0s occupy all other coefficient positions.	$\left[\begin{array}{ccc\|c} 1 & 0 & 0 & 1 \\ 0 & 1 & 0 & -3 \\ 0 & 0 & 1 & 2 \end{array}\right]$ or $\begin{array}{l} x = 1 \\ y = -3 \\ z = 2 \end{array}$
Inconsistent	No solution	One row will have only zero entries for coefficients and a nonzero entry for the constant.	$\left[\begin{array}{ccc\|c} 1 & 0 & 0 & 1 \\ 0 & 1 & 0 & -3 \\ 0 & 0 & 0 & 2 \end{array}\right]$ or $\begin{array}{l} x = 1 \\ y = -3 \\ 0 \neq 2 \end{array}$
Dependent	Infinitely many solutions	One row will be entirely 0s when the number of equations is less than the number of variables.	$\left[\begin{array}{ccc\|c} 1 & 0 & -2 & 1 \\ 0 & 1 & 1 & -3 \\ 0 & 0 & 0 & 0 \end{array}\right]$ or $\begin{array}{r} x - 2z = 1 \\ y + z = -3 \\ 0 = 0 \end{array}$

EXAMPLE 9 Determining That a System Is Inconsistent: No Solution

Solve the system of equations.

$$\begin{aligned} x + 2y - z &= 3 \\ 2x + y + 2z &= -1 \\ -2x - 4y + 2z &= 5 \end{aligned}$$

Solution:

STEP 1 Write the system of equations as an augmented matrix.

$$\left[\begin{array}{ccc|c} 1 & 2 & -1 & 3 \\ 2 & 1 & 2 & -1 \\ -2 & -4 & 2 & 5 \end{array}\right]$$

STEP 2 Apply row operations to rewrite the matrix in row–echelon form.

Get 0s below the 1 in column 1.

$$\begin{array}{r} R_2 - 2R_1 \to R_2 \\ R_3 + 2R_1 \to R_3 \end{array} \left[\begin{array}{ccc|c} 1 & 2 & -1 & 3 \\ 0 & -3 & 4 & -7 \\ 0 & 0 & 0 & 11 \end{array}\right]$$

There is no need to continue because row 3 is a contradiction. $0x + 0y + 0z = 11$ or $0 = 11$

Since this is inconsistent, there is *no solution* to this system of equations.

[CONCEPT CHECK]

TRUE OR FALSE An inconsistent system of linear equations in three variables corresponds to three planes that do not have a common point or line of intersection, whereas dependent systems of linear equations in three variables correspond to three planes that intersect along a line or a plane.

ANSWER True

EXAMPLE 10 Determining That a System Is Dependent: Infinitely Many Solutions

Solve the system of equations.

$$\begin{aligned} x + z &= 3 \\ 2x + y + 4z &= 8 \\ 3x + y + 5z &= 11 \end{aligned}$$

Solution:

STEP 1 Write the system of equations as an augmented matrix.

$$\left[\begin{array}{ccc|c} 1 & 0 & 1 & 3 \\ 2 & 1 & 4 & 8 \\ 3 & 1 & 5 & 11 \end{array}\right]$$

STEP 2 Use row operations to rewrite the matrix in reduced row–echelon form.

Get the 0s below the 1 in column 1.

$$\begin{array}{r} R_2 - 2R_1 \to R_2 \\ R_3 - 3R_1 \to R_3 \end{array} \left[\begin{array}{ccc|c} 1 & 0 & 1 & 3 \\ 0 & 1 & 2 & 2 \\ 0 & 1 & 2 & 2 \end{array}\right]$$

Get a 0 in row 3/column 2.

$$R_3 - R_2 \to R_3 \left[\begin{array}{ccc|c} 1 & 0 & 1 & 3 \\ 0 & 1 & 2 & 2 \\ 0 & 0 & 0 & 0 \end{array}\right]$$

This matrix is in reduced row–echelon form. This matrix corresponds to a dependent system of linear equations and has infinitely many solutions.

STEP 3 Write the augmented matrix as a system of linear equations.

$$\begin{aligned} x + z &= 3 \\ y + 2z &= 2 \end{aligned}$$

Let $z = a$, where a is any real number, and substitute this into the two equations.

We find that $x = 3 - a$ and $y = 2 - 2a$. The general solution is $\boxed{x = 3 - a, y = 2 - 2a, z = a}$ for a any real number. Note that $(2, 0, 1)$ and $(3, 2, 0)$ are particular solutions when $a = 1$ and $a = 0$, respectively.

[STUDY TIP]

In a system with three variables, say x, y, and z, we typically let $z = a$ (where a is called a parameter) and then solve for x and y in terms of a.

A common mistake that is made is to identify a unique solution as no solution when one of the variables is equal to zero. For example, what is the difference between the following two matrices?

$$\left[\begin{array}{ccc|c} 1 & 0 & 2 & 1 \\ 0 & 1 & 3 & 2 \\ 0 & 0 & 3 & 0 \end{array}\right] \quad \text{and} \quad \left[\begin{array}{ccc|c} 1 & 0 & 2 & 1 \\ 0 & 1 & 3 & 2 \\ 0 & 0 & 0 & 3 \end{array}\right]$$

The first matrix has a *unique solution*, whereas the second matrix has *no solution*. The third row of the first matrix corresponds to the equation $3z = 0$, which implies that $z = 0$. The third row of the second matrix corresponds to the equation $0x + 0y + 0z = 3$ or $0 = 3$, which is inconsistent, and therefore the system has no solution.

EXAMPLE 11 **Determining That a System Is Dependent: Infinitely Many Solutions**

Solve the system of linear equations.

$$\begin{aligned} 2x + y + z &= 8 \\ x + y - z &= -3 \end{aligned}$$

Solution:

STEP 1 Write the system of equations as an augmented matrix.

$$\left[\begin{array}{ccc|c} 2 & 1 & 1 & 8 \\ 1 & 1 & -1 & -3 \end{array}\right]$$

STEP 2 Use row operations to rewrite the matrix in reduced row–echelon form.

Get a 1 in row 1/column 1.

$$R_1 \leftrightarrow R_2 \quad \left[\begin{array}{ccc|c} 1 & 1 & -1 & -3 \\ 2 & 1 & 1 & 8 \end{array}\right]$$

Get a 0 in row 2/column 1.

$$R_2 - 2R_1 \rightarrow R_2 \quad \left[\begin{array}{ccc|c} 1 & 1 & -1 & -3 \\ 0 & -1 & 3 & 14 \end{array}\right]$$

Get a 1 in row 2/column 2.

$$-R_2 \rightarrow R_2 \quad \left[\begin{array}{ccc|c} 1 & 1 & -1 & -3 \\ 0 & 1 & -3 & -14 \end{array}\right]$$

Get a 0 in row 1/column 2.

$$R_1 - R_2 \rightarrow R_1 \quad \left[\begin{array}{ccc|c} 1 & 0 & 2 & 11 \\ 0 & 1 & -3 & -14 \end{array}\right]$$

This matrix is in reduced row–echelon form.

STEP 3 Identify the solution.

$$\begin{aligned} x + 2z &= 11 \\ y - 3z &= -14 \end{aligned}$$

Let $z = a$, where a is any real number. Substituting $z = a$ into these two equations gives the infinitely many solutions $\boxed{x = 11 - 2a,\ y = 3a - 14,\ z = a}$.

YOUR TURN Solve the system of equations using an augmented matrix.

$$\begin{aligned} x + y + z &= 0 \\ 3x + 2y - z &= 2 \end{aligned}$$

ANSWER

$x = 3a + 2,\ y = -4a - 2,\ z = a$, where a is any real number.

In Example 10 there were three equations and three unknowns (x, y, and z). In Example 11 there were two equations and three unknowns. Whenever there are more unknowns than equations, the system is dependent; that is, it has infinitely many solutions.

Applications

The following table gives nutritional information for sandwiches offered at a local cafe.

SANDWICH	CALORIES	FAT (g)	CARBOHYDRATES (g)	PROTEIN (g)
Vegetable	350	18	17	36
Oven-roasted chicken breast	430	19	46	20
Ham (Black Forest without cheese)	290	5	45	19

EXAMPLE 12 **Sandwich Diet**

Suppose you are going to eat only sandwiches for a week (seven days) for both lunch and dinner (total of 14 meals). If your goal is to eat 388 grams of protein and 4900 calories in those 14 sandwiches, how many of each sandwich should you eat that week?

Solution:

STEP 1 Determine the system of linear equations.

Let three variables represent the number of each type of sandwich you eat in a week.

x = number of vegetable sandwiches

y = number of chicken breast sandwiches

z = number of ham sandwiches

The total number of sandwiches eaten is 14. $x + y + z = 14$

The total number of calories consumed is 4900. $350x + 430y + 290z = 4900$

The total number of grams of protein consumed is 388. $36x + 20y + 19z = 388$

Write an augmented matrix representing this system of linear equations.

$$\left[\begin{array}{ccc|c} 1 & 1 & 1 & 14 \\ 350 & 430 & 290 & 4900 \\ 36 & 20 & 19 & 388 \end{array}\right]$$

STEP 2 Utilize row operations to rewrite the matrix in reduced row–echelon form.

$$\begin{array}{l} R_2 - 350R_1 \to R_2 \\ R_3 - 36R_1 \to R_3 \end{array} \left[\begin{array}{ccc|c} 1 & 1 & 1 & 14 \\ 0 & 80 & -60 & 0 \\ 0 & -16 & -17 & -116 \end{array}\right]$$

$$\tfrac{1}{80}R_2 \to R_2 \left[\begin{array}{ccc|c} 1 & 1 & 1 & 14 \\ 0 & 1 & -\frac{3}{4} & 0 \\ 0 & -16 & -17 & -116 \end{array}\right]$$

$$R_3 + 16R_2 \to R_3 \left[\begin{array}{ccc|c} 1 & 1 & 1 & 14 \\ 0 & 1 & -\frac{3}{4} & 0 \\ 0 & 0 & -29 & -116 \end{array}\right]$$

$$-\tfrac{1}{29}R_3 \to R_3 \quad \left[\begin{array}{ccc|c} 1 & 1 & 1 & 14 \\ 0 & 1 & -\frac{3}{4} & 0 \\ 0 & 0 & 1 & 4 \end{array}\right]$$

$$\begin{array}{l} R_2 + \frac{3}{4}R_3 \to R_2 \\ R_1 - R_3 \to R_1 \end{array} \quad \left[\begin{array}{ccc|c} 1 & 1 & 0 & 10 \\ 0 & 1 & 0 & 3 \\ 0 & 0 & 1 & 4 \end{array}\right]$$

$$R_1 - R_2 \to R_1 \quad \left[\begin{array}{ccc|c} 1 & 0 & 0 & 7 \\ 0 & 1 & 0 & 3 \\ 0 & 0 & 1 & 4 \end{array}\right]$$

STEP 3 Identify the solution. $\boxed{x = 7, y = 3, z = 4}$

You should eat 7 vegetable, 3 oven-roasted chicken breast, and 4 ham sandwiches.

EXAMPLE 13 Fitting a Curve to Data

The amount of money awarded in medical malpractice suits is rising. This can be modeled with a quadratic function $y = at^2 + bt + c$, where $t > 0$ and $a > 0$. Determine a quadratic function that passes through the three points shown on the graph. Based on this trend, how much money will be spent on malpractice in 2011?

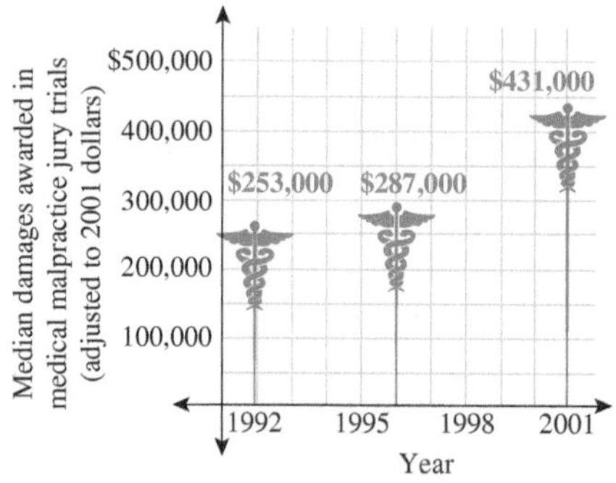

Solution:

Let 1991 correspond to $t = 0$ and y represent the number of dollars awarded for malpractice suits. The following data are reflected in the illustration above:

YEAR	t	y (THOUSANDS OF DOLLARS)	(t, y)
1992	1	253	(1, 253)
1996	5	287	(5, 287)
2001	10	431	(10, 431)

Substitute the three points (1, 253), (5, 287), and (10, 431) into the general quadratic equation: $y = at^2 + bt + c$.

POINT	$y = at^2 + bt + c$	SYSTEM OF EQUATIONS
(1, 253)	$253 = a(1)^2 + b(1) + c$	$a + b + c = 253$
(5, 287)	$287 = a(5)^2 + b(5) + c$	$25a + 5b + c = 287$
(10, 431)	$431 = a(10)^2 + b(10) + c$	$100a + 10b + c = 431$

STEP 1 Write this system of linear equations as an augmented matrix.

$$\left[\begin{array}{ccc|c} 1 & 1 & 1 & 253 \\ 25 & 5 & 1 & 287 \\ 100 & 10 & 1 & 431 \end{array}\right]$$

STEP 2 Apply row operations to rewrite the matrix in reduced row–echelon form.

$$R_2 - 25R_1 \to R_2 \quad \left[\begin{array}{ccc|c} 1 & 1 & 1 & 253 \\ 0 & -20 & -24 & -6038 \\ 100 & 10 & 1 & 431 \end{array}\right]$$

$$R_3 - 100R_1 \to R_3 \quad \left[\begin{array}{ccc|c} 1 & 1 & 1 & 253 \\ 0 & -20 & -24 & -6038 \\ 0 & -90 & -99 & -24{,}869 \end{array}\right]$$

$$-\tfrac{1}{20}R_2 \to R_2 \quad \left[\begin{array}{ccc|c} 1 & 1 & 1 & 253 \\ 0 & 1 & \frac{6}{5} & \frac{3019}{10} \\ 0 & -90 & -99 & -24{,}869 \end{array}\right]$$

$$R_3 + 90R_2 \to R_3 \quad \left[\begin{array}{ccc|c} 1 & 1 & 1 & 253 \\ 0 & 1 & \frac{6}{5} & \frac{3019}{10} \\ 0 & 0 & 9 & 2302 \end{array}\right]$$

$$\tfrac{1}{9}R_3 \to R_3 \quad \left[\begin{array}{ccc|c} 1 & 1 & 1 & 253 \\ 0 & 1 & \frac{6}{5} & \frac{3019}{10} \\ 0 & 0 & 1 & \frac{2302}{9} \end{array}\right]$$

$$R_2 - \tfrac{6}{5}R_3 \to R_2 \quad \left[\begin{array}{ccc|c} 1 & 1 & 1 & 253 \\ 0 & 1 & 0 & -\frac{151}{30} \\ 0 & 0 & 1 & \frac{2302}{9} \end{array}\right]$$

$$R_1 - R_3 \to R_1 \quad \left[\begin{array}{ccc|c} 1 & 1 & 0 & -\frac{25}{9} \\ 0 & 1 & 0 & -\frac{151}{30} \\ 0 & 0 & 1 & \frac{2302}{9} \end{array}\right]$$

$$R_1 - R_2 \to R_1 \quad \left[\begin{array}{ccc|c} 1 & 0 & 0 & \frac{203}{90} \\ 0 & 1 & 0 & -\frac{151}{30} \\ 0 & 0 & 1 & \frac{2302}{9} \end{array}\right]$$

STEP 3 Identify the solution.

$$a = \frac{203}{90}, \quad b = -\frac{151}{30}, \quad c = \frac{2302}{9}$$

Substituting $a = \frac{203}{90}$, $b = -\frac{151}{30}$, $c = \frac{2302}{9}$ into $y = at^2 + bt + c$, we find that the thousands of dollars spent on malpractice suits as a function of year is given by

$$\boxed{y = \frac{203}{90}t^2 - \frac{151}{30}t + \frac{2302}{9}} \qquad 1991 \text{ is } t = 0$$

Notice that all three points lie on this curve.

For 2011, we let $t = 20$, which results in approximately $\boxed{\$1.06\text{ M}}$ in malpractice.

[SECTION 8.3] SUMMARY

In this section, we used augmented matrices to represent a system of linear equations.

$$\begin{array}{l} a_1x + b_1y + c_1z = d_1 \\ a_2x + b_2y + c_2z = d_2 \\ a_3x + b_3y + c_3z = d_3 \end{array} \Leftrightarrow \left[\begin{array}{ccc|c} a_1 & b_1 & c_1 & d_1 \\ a_2 & b_2 & c_2 & d_2 \\ a_3 & b_3 & c_3 & d_3 \end{array}\right]$$

Any missing terms correspond to a 0 in the matrix. A matrix is in **row–echelon** form if it has all three of the following properties:

1. Any rows consisting entirely of 0s are at the bottom of the matrix.
2. For each row that does not consist entirely of 0s, the first (leftmost) nonzero entry is 1 (called the leading 1).
3. For two successive nonzero rows, the leading 1 in the higher row is farther to the left than the leading 1 in the lower row.

If a matrix in row–echelon form has the following additional property, then the matrix is in **reduced row–echelon form:**

4. Every column containing a leading 1 has zeros in every position above and below the leading 1.

The two methods used for solving systems of linear equations represented as augmented matrices are Gaussian elimination with back-substitution and Gauss–Jordan elimination. In both cases, we represent the system of linear equations as an augmented matrix and then use row operations to rewrite in row–echelon form. With Gaussian elimination we then stop and perform back-substitution to solve the system, and with Gauss–Jordan elimination we continue with row operations until the matrix is in reduced row–echelon form and then identify the solution to the system.

[SECTION 8.3] EXERCISES

• SKILLS

In Exercises 1–6, determine the order of each matrix.

1. $\begin{bmatrix} -1 & 3 & 4 \\ 2 & 7 & 9 \end{bmatrix}$

2. $\begin{bmatrix} 0 & 1 \\ 3 & 9 \\ 7 & 8 \end{bmatrix}$

3. $\begin{bmatrix} 1 & 2 & 3 & 4 \end{bmatrix}$

4. $\begin{bmatrix} 3 \\ 7 \\ -1 \\ 10 \end{bmatrix}$

5. $\begin{bmatrix} 0 \end{bmatrix}$

6. $\begin{bmatrix} -1 & 3 & 6 & 8 \\ 2 & 9 & 7 & 3 \\ 5 & 4 & -2 & -10 \\ 6 & 3 & 1 & 5 \end{bmatrix}$

In Exercises 7–14, write the augmented matrix for each system of linear equations.

7. $\begin{aligned} 3x - 2y &= 7 \\ -4x + 6y &= -3 \end{aligned}$

8. $\begin{aligned} -x + y &= 2 \\ x - y &= -4 \end{aligned}$

9. $\begin{aligned} 2x - 3y + 4z &= -3 \\ -x + y + 2z &= 1 \\ 5x - 2y - 3z &= 7 \end{aligned}$

10. $\begin{aligned} x - 2y + z &= 0 \\ -2x + y - z &= -5 \\ 13x + 7y + 5z &= 6 \end{aligned}$

11. $\begin{aligned} x + y &= 3 \\ x - z &= 2 \\ y + z &= 5 \end{aligned}$

12. $\begin{aligned} x - y &= -4 \\ x + z &= 3 \end{aligned}$

13. $\begin{aligned} 3y - 4x + 5z - 2 &= 0 \\ 2x - 3y - 2z &= -3 \\ 3z + 4y - 2x - 1 &= 0 \end{aligned}$

14. $\begin{aligned} 2y + z - x - 3 &= 2 \\ 2x + 3z - 2y &= 0 \\ -2z + y - 4x - 3 &= 0 \end{aligned}$

In Exercises 15–20, write the system of linear equations represented by the augmented matrix. Utilize the variables *x*, *y*, and *z*.

15. $\left[\begin{array}{cc|c} -3 & 7 & 2 \\ 1 & 5 & 8 \end{array}\right]$

16. $\left[\begin{array}{ccc|c} -1 & 2 & 4 & 4 \\ 7 & 9 & 3 & -3 \\ 4 & 6 & -5 & 8 \end{array}\right]$

17. $\left[\begin{array}{ccc|c} -1 & 0 & 0 & 4 \\ 7 & 9 & 3 & -3 \\ 4 & 6 & -5 & 8 \end{array}\right]$

18. $\left[\begin{array}{ccc|c} 2 & 3 & -4 & 6 \\ 7 & -1 & 5 & 9 \end{array}\right]$

19. $\left[\begin{array}{cc|c} 1 & 0 & a \\ 0 & 1 & b \end{array}\right]$

20. $\left[\begin{array}{ccc|c} 3 & 0 & 5 & 1 \\ 0 & -4 & 7 & -3 \\ 2 & -1 & 0 & 8 \end{array}\right]$

In Exercises 21–30, indicate whether each matrix is in row–echelon form. If it is, determine whether it is in reduced row–echelon form.

21. $\left[\begin{array}{cc|c} 1 & 0 & 3 \\ 1 & 1 & 2 \end{array}\right]$

22. $\left[\begin{array}{cc|c} 0 & 1 & 3 \\ 1 & 0 & 2 \end{array}\right]$

23. $\left[\begin{array}{ccc|c} 1 & 0 & -1 & -3 \\ 0 & 1 & 3 & 14 \end{array}\right]$

24. $\left[\begin{array}{ccc|c} 1 & 0 & 0 & -3 \\ 0 & 1 & 3 & 14 \end{array}\right]$

25. $\left[\begin{array}{ccc|c} 1 & 0 & 1 & 3 \\ 0 & 0 & 0 & 0 \\ 0 & 1 & 2 & 2 \end{array}\right]$

26. $\left[\begin{array}{ccc|c} 1 & 0 & 1 & 3 \\ 0 & 1 & 2 & 2 \\ 0 & 0 & 0 & 0 \end{array}\right]$

27. $\left[\begin{array}{ccc|c} 1 & 0 & 0 & 3 \\ 0 & 1 & 0 & 2 \\ 0 & 0 & 1 & 5 \end{array}\right]$

28. $\left[\begin{array}{ccc|c} -1 & 0 & 0 & 3 \\ 0 & -1 & 0 & 2 \\ 0 & 0 & -1 & 5 \end{array}\right]$

29. $\left[\begin{array}{cccc|c} 1 & 0 & 0 & 1 & 3 \\ 0 & 1 & 0 & 3 & 2 \\ 0 & 0 & 1 & 0 & 5 \\ 0 & 0 & 0 & 1 & 0 \end{array}\right]$

30. $\left[\begin{array}{cccc|c} 1 & 0 & 0 & 1 & 3 \\ 0 & 1 & 0 & 3 & 2 \\ 0 & 0 & 1 & 0 & 5 \\ 0 & 0 & 0 & 0 & 0 \end{array}\right]$

In Exercises 31–40, perform the indicated row operations on each augmented matrix.

31. $\left[\begin{array}{cc|c} 1 & -2 & -3 \\ 2 & 3 & -1 \end{array}\right]$ $\quad R_2 - 2R_1 \to R_2$

32. $\left[\begin{array}{cc|c} 2 & -3 & -4 \\ 1 & 2 & 5 \end{array}\right]$ $\quad R_1 \leftrightarrow R_2$

33. $\left[\begin{array}{ccc|c} 1 & -2 & -1 & 3 \\ 2 & 1 & -3 & 6 \\ 3 & -2 & 5 & -8 \end{array}\right]$ $\quad R_2 - 2R_1 \to R_2$

34. $\left[\begin{array}{ccc|c} 1 & -2 & 1 & 3 \\ 0 & 1 & -2 & 6 \\ -3 & 0 & -1 & -5 \end{array}\right]$ $\quad R_3 + 3R_1 \to R_3$

35. $\left[\begin{array}{cccc|c} 1 & -2 & 5 & -1 & 2 \\ 0 & 3 & 0 & -1 & -2 \\ 0 & -2 & 1 & -2 & 5 \\ 0 & 0 & 1 & -1 & -6 \end{array}\right]$ $\quad R_3 + R_2 \to R_2$

36. $\left[\begin{array}{cccc|c} 1 & 0 & 5 & -10 & 15 \\ 0 & 1 & 2 & -3 & 4 \\ 0 & 2 & -3 & 0 & -1 \\ 0 & 0 & 1 & -1 & -3 \end{array}\right]$ $\quad R_2 - \frac{1}{2}R_3 \to R_3$

37. $\left[\begin{array}{cccc|c} 1 & 0 & 5 & -10 & -5 \\ 0 & 1 & 2 & -3 & -2 \\ 0 & 2 & -3 & 0 & -1 \\ 0 & -3 & 2 & -1 & -3 \end{array}\right]$ $\quad \begin{array}{l} R_3 - 2R_2 \to R_3 \\ R_4 + 3R_2 \to R_4 \end{array}$

38. $\left[\begin{array}{cccc|c} 1 & 0 & 4 & 0 & 1 \\ 0 & 1 & 2 & 0 & -2 \\ 0 & 0 & 1 & 0 & 0 \\ 0 & 0 & 0 & 1 & -3 \end{array}\right]$ $\quad \begin{array}{l} R_2 - 2R_3 \to R_2 \\ R_1 - 4R_3 \to R_1 \end{array}$

39. $\left[\begin{array}{cccc|c} 1 & 0 & 4 & 8 & 3 \\ 0 & 1 & 2 & -3 & -2 \\ 0 & 0 & 1 & 6 & 3 \\ 0 & 0 & 0 & 1 & -3 \end{array}\right]$ $\quad \begin{array}{l} R_3 - 6R_4 \to R_3 \\ R_2 + 3R_4 \to R_2 \\ R_1 - 8R_4 \to R_1 \end{array}$

40. $\left[\begin{array}{cccc|c} 1 & 0 & -1 & 5 & 2 \\ 0 & 1 & 2 & 3 & -5 \\ 0 & 0 & 1 & -2 & 2 \\ 0 & 0 & 0 & 1 & 1 \end{array}\right]$ $\quad \begin{array}{l} R_3 + 2R_4 \to R_3 \\ R_2 - 3R_4 \to R_2 \\ R_1 - 5R_4 \to R_1 \end{array}$

In Exercises 41–50, use row operations to transform each matrix to reduced row–echelon form.

41. $\left[\begin{array}{cc|c} 1 & 2 & 4 \\ 2 & 3 & 2 \end{array}\right]$

42. $\left[\begin{array}{cc|c} 1 & -1 & 3 \\ -3 & 2 & 2 \end{array}\right]$

43. $\left[\begin{array}{ccc|c} 1 & -1 & 1 & -1 \\ 0 & 1 & -1 & -1 \\ -1 & 1 & 1 & 1 \end{array}\right]$

44. $\left[\begin{array}{ccc|c} 0 & -1 & 1 & 1 \\ 1 & -1 & 1 & -1 \\ 1 & -1 & -1 & -1 \end{array}\right]$

45. $\left[\begin{array}{ccc|c} 3 & -2 & -3 & -1 \\ 1 & -1 & 1 & -4 \\ 2 & 3 & 5 & 14 \end{array}\right]$

46. $\left[\begin{array}{ccc|c} 3 & -1 & 1 & 2 \\ 1 & -2 & 3 & 1 \\ 2 & 1 & -3 & -1 \end{array}\right]$

47. $\left[\begin{array}{ccc|c} 2 & 1 & -6 & 4 \\ 1 & -2 & 2 & -3 \end{array}\right]$

48. $\left[\begin{array}{ccc|c} -3 & -1 & 2 & -1 \\ -1 & -2 & 1 & -3 \end{array}\right]$

49. $\left[\begin{array}{ccc|c} -1 & 2 & 1 & -2 \\ 3 & -2 & 1 & 4 \\ 2 & -4 & -2 & 4 \end{array}\right]$

50. $\left[\begin{array}{ccc|c} 2 & -1 & 0 & 1 \\ -1 & 0 & 1 & -2 \\ -2 & 1 & 0 & -1 \end{array}\right]$

In Exercises 51–70, solve the system of linear equations using Gaussian elimination with back-substitution.

51. $\begin{aligned} 2x + 3y &= 1 \\ x + y &= -2 \end{aligned}$

52. $\begin{aligned} 3x + 2y &= 11 \\ x - y &= 12 \end{aligned}$

53. $\begin{aligned} -x + 2y &= 3 \\ 2x - 4y &= -6 \end{aligned}$

54. $\begin{aligned} 3x - y &= -1 \\ 2y + 6y &= 2 \end{aligned}$

55. $\begin{aligned} \tfrac{2}{3}x + \tfrac{1}{3}y &= \tfrac{8}{9} \\ \tfrac{1}{2}x + \tfrac{1}{4}y &= \tfrac{3}{4} \end{aligned}$

56. $\begin{aligned} 0.4x - 0.5y &= 2.08 \\ -0.3x + 0.7y &= 1.88 \end{aligned}$

57. $\begin{aligned} x - z - y &= 10 \\ 2x - 3y + z &= -11 \\ y - x + z &= -10 \end{aligned}$

58. $\begin{aligned} 2x + z + y &= -3 \\ 2y - z + x &= 0 \\ x + y + 2z &= 5 \end{aligned}$

59. $\begin{aligned} 3x_1 + x_2 - x_3 &= 1 \\ x_1 - x_2 + x_3 &= -3 \\ 2x_1 + x_2 + x_3 &= 0 \end{aligned}$

60. $\begin{aligned} 2x_1 + x_2 + x_3 &= -1 \\ x_1 + x_2 - x_3 &= 5 \\ 3x_1 - x_2 - x_3 &= 1 \end{aligned}$

61. $\begin{aligned} 2x + 5y &= 9 \\ x + 2y - z &= 3 \\ -3x - 4y + 7z &= 1 \end{aligned}$

62. $\begin{aligned} x - 2y + 3z &= 1 \\ -2x + 7y - 9z &= 4 \\ x + z &= 9 \end{aligned}$

63. $\begin{aligned} 2x_1 - x_2 + x_3 &= 3 \\ x_1 - x_2 + x_3 &= 2 \\ -2x_1 + 2x_2 - 2x_3 &= -4 \end{aligned}$

64. $\begin{aligned} x_1 - x_2 - 2x_3 &= 0 \\ -2x_1 + 5x_2 + 10x_3 &= -3 \\ 3x_1 + x_2 &= 0 \end{aligned}$

65. $\begin{aligned} 2x + y - z &= 2 \\ x - y - z &= 6 \end{aligned}$

66. $\begin{aligned} 3x + y - z &= 0 \\ x + y + 7z &= 4 \end{aligned}$

67. $\begin{aligned} 2y + z &= 3 \\ 4x - z &= -3 \\ 7x - 3y - 3z &= 2 \\ x - y - z &= -2 \end{aligned}$

68. $\begin{aligned} -2x - y + 2z &= 3 \\ 3x - 4z &= 2 \\ 2x + y &= -1 \\ -x + y - z &= -8 \end{aligned}$

69. $\begin{aligned} 3x_1 - 2x_2 + x_3 + 2x_4 &= -2 \\ -x_1 + 3x_2 + 4x_3 + 3x_4 &= 4 \\ x_1 + x_2 + x_3 + x_4 &= 0 \\ 5x_1 + 3x_2 + x_3 + 2x_4 &= -1 \end{aligned}$

70. $\begin{aligned} 5x_1 + 3x_2 + 8x_3 + x_4 &= 1 \\ x_1 + 2x_2 + 5x_3 + 2x_4 &= 3 \\ 4x_1 + x_3 - 2x_4 &= -3 \\ x_2 + x_3 + x_4 &= 0 \end{aligned}$

In Exercises 71–86, solve the system of linear equations using Gauss–Jordan elimination.

71. $\begin{aligned} x + 3y &= -5 \\ -2x - y &= 0 \end{aligned}$

72. $\begin{aligned} 5x - 4y &= 31 \\ 3x + 7y &= -19 \end{aligned}$

73. $\begin{aligned} x + y &= 4 \\ -3x - 3y &= 10 \end{aligned}$

74. $\begin{aligned} 3x - 4y &= 12 \\ -6x + 8y &= -24 \end{aligned}$

75. $\begin{aligned} x - 2y + 3z &= 5 \\ 3x + 6y - 4z &= -12 \\ -x - 4y + 6z &= 16 \end{aligned}$

76. $\begin{aligned} x + 2y - z &= 6 \\ 2x - y + 3z &= -13 \\ 3x - 2y + 3z &= -16 \end{aligned}$

77. $\begin{aligned} x + y + z &= 3 \\ x - z &= 1 \\ y - z &= -4 \end{aligned}$

78. $\begin{aligned} x - 2y + 4z &= 2 \\ 2x - 3y - 2z &= -3 \\ \tfrac{1}{2}x + \tfrac{1}{4}y + z &= -2 \end{aligned}$

79. $\begin{aligned} x + 2y + z &= 3 \\ 2x - y + 3z &= 7 \\ 3x + y + 4z &= 5 \end{aligned}$

80. $\begin{aligned} x + 2y + z &= 3 \\ 2x - y + 3z &= 7 \\ 3x + y + 4z &= 10 \end{aligned}$

81. $\begin{aligned} 3x - y + z &= 8 \\ x + y - 2z &= 4 \end{aligned}$

82. $\begin{aligned} x - 2y + 3z &= 10 \\ -3x + z &= 9 \end{aligned}$

83. $\begin{aligned} 4x - 2y + 5z &= 20 \\ x + 3y - 2z &= 6 \end{aligned}$

84. $\begin{aligned} y + z &= 4 \\ x + y &= 8 \end{aligned}$

85. $\begin{aligned} x - y - z - w &= 1 \\ 2x + y + z + 2w &= 3 \\ x - 2y - 2z - 3w &= 0 \\ 3x - 4y + z + 5w &= -3 \end{aligned}$

86. $\begin{aligned} x - 3y + 3z - 2w &= 4 \\ x + 2y - z &= -3 \\ x + 3z + 2w &= 3 \\ y + z + 5w &= 6 \end{aligned}$

• APPLICATIONS

87. Astronomy. Astronomers have determined the number of stars in a small region of the universe to be 2,880,968 classified as red dwarfs, yellow, and blue stars. For every blue star there are 120 red dwarfs; for every red dwarf there are 3000 yellow stars. Determine the number of stars of each type in that region of the universe.

88. Orange Juice. Orange juice producers use three varieties of oranges: Hamlin, Valencia, and navel. They want to make a juice mixture to sell at $3.00 per gallon. The prices per gallon of these varieties of juice are $2.50, $3.40, and $2.80, respectively. To maintain their quality standards, they use the same amount of Valencia and navel oranges. Determine the quantity of each juice used to produce 1 gallon of mixture.

Suppose you are only going to eat sandwiches from a local cafe for a week (seven days) for lunch and dinner (a total of 14 meals). The nutritional information is given in the table:

SANDWICH	CALORIES	FAT (g)	CARBOHYDRATES (g)	PROTEIN (g)
Chicken	350	18	17	36
Tuna	430	19	46	20
Roast beef	290	5	45	19
Turkey–bacon	430	27	20	34

89. Diet. Your goal is a low-fat diet consisting of 526 grams of carbohydrates, 168 grams of fat, and 332 grams of protein. How many of each sandwich would you eat that week to attain this goal?

90. Diet. Your goal is a low-carb diet consisting of 5180 calories, 335 grams of carbohydrates, and 263 grams of fat. How many of each sandwich would you eat that week to attain this goal?

Exercises 91 and 92 involve vertical motion and the effect of gravity on an object.

Because of gravity, an object that is projected upward will eventually reach a maximum height and then fall to the ground. The equation that relates the height h of a projectile to the number of seconds t after it is projected upward is given by

$$h = \frac{1}{2}at^2 + v_0 t + h_0$$

where a is the acceleration due to gravity, h_0 is the initial height of the object at time $t = 0$, and v_0 is the initial velocity of the object at time $t = 0$. Note that a projectile follows the path of a parabola opening down, so $a < 0$.

91. Vertical Motion. An object is thrown upward, and the table below depicts the height of the ball t seconds after it is released. Find the initial height, initial velocity, and acceleration due to gravity.

t (SECONDS)	HEIGHT (FEET)
1	34
2	36
3	6

92. Vertical Motion. An object is thrown upward, and the table below depicts the height of the ball t seconds after it is released. Find the initial height, initial velocity, and acceleration due to gravity.

t (SECONDS)	HEIGHT (FEET)
1	54
2	66
3	46

93. Data Curve-Fitting. The average number of minutes that a person spends driving a car can be modeled by a quadratic function $y = ax^2 + bx + c$, where $a < 0$ and $15 < x < 65$. The table below gives the average number of minutes a day that a person spends driving a car. Determine a quadratic function that models this quantity.

AGE	AVERAGE DAILY MINUTES DRIVING
16	25
40	64
65	40

94. Data Curve-Fitting. The average age when a woman gets married has been increasing during the last century. In 1920 the average age was 18.4, in 1960 the average age was 20.3, and in 2002 the average age was 25.30. Find a quadratic function $y = ax^2 + bx + c$, where $a > 0$ and $18 < x < 35$, that models the average age y when a woman gets married as a function of the year $x (x = 0$ corresponds to 1920). What will the average age be in 2010?

95. Chemistry/Pharmacy. A pharmacy receives an order for 100 milliliters of 5% hydrogen peroxide solution. The pharmacy has a 1.5% and a 30% solution on hand. A technician will mix the 1.5% and 30% solutions to make the 5% solution. How much of the 1.5% and 30% solutions, respectively, will be needed to fill this order? Round to the nearest milliliter.

96. Chemistry/Pharmacy. A pharmacy receives an order for 60 grams of a 0.7% hydrocortisone cream. The pharmacy has 1% and 0.5% hydrocortisone creams as well as a Eucerin cream for use as a base (0% hydrocortisone). The technician must use twice as much 0.5% hydrocortisone cream as Eucerin base. How much of the 1% and 0.5% hydrocortisone creams and Eucerin cream are needed to fill this order?

97. Money. Gary and Ginger decide to place $10,000 of their savings into investments. They put some in a money market account earning 3% interest, some in a mutual fund that has been averaging 7% a year, and some in a stock that rose 10% last year. If they put $3000 more in the money market account than in the mutual fund, and the mutual fund and stocks have the same growth in the next year as they did in the previous year, they will earn $540 in a year. How much money did they put in each of the three investments?

98. Money. Ginger talks Gary into putting less money in the money market account and more money in the stock (see Exercise 99). They place $10,000 of their savings into investments. They put some in a money market account earning 3% interest, some in a mutual fund that has been averaging 7% a year, and some in a stock that rose 10% last year. If they put $3000 more in the stock than in the mutual fund, and the mutual fund and stock have the same growth in the next year as they did in the previous year, they will earn $840 in a year. How much money did they put in each of the three investments?

99. **Manufacturing.** A company produces three products: x, y, and z. Each item of product x requires 20 units of steel, 2 units of plastic, and 1 unit of glass. Each item of product y requires 25 units of steel, 5 units of plastic, and no units of glass. Each item of product z requires 150 units of steel, 10 units of plastic, and 0.5 units of glass. The available units of steel, plastic, and glass are 2400, 310, and 28, respectively. How many items of each type can the company produce and utilize all the available raw materials?

100. **Geometry.** Find the values of a, b, and c such that the graph of the quadratic function $y = ax^2 + bx + c$ passes through the points $(1, 5)$, $(-2, -10)$, and $(0, 4)$.

101. **Geometry.** The circle given by the equation $x^2 + y^2 + ax + by + c = 0$ passes through the points $(4, 4)$, $(-3, -1)$, and $(1, -3)$. Find a, b, and c.

102. **Geometry.** The circle given by the equation $x^2 + y^2 + ax + by + c = 0$ passes through the points $(0, 7)$, $(6, 1)$, and $(5, 4)$. Find a, b, and c.

• CATCH THE MISTAKE

In Exercises 103–106, explain the mistake that is made.

103. Solve the system of equations using the augmented matrix.

$$\begin{aligned} y - x + z &= 2 \\ x - 2z + y &= -3 \\ x + y + z &= 6 \end{aligned}$$

Solution:

Step 1: Write as an augmented matrix.
$$\left[\begin{array}{ccc|c} 1 & -1 & 1 & 2 \\ 1 & -2 & 1 & -3 \\ 1 & 1 & 1 & 6 \end{array}\right]$$

Step 2: Reduce the matrix using Gaussian elimination.
$$\left[\begin{array}{ccc|c} 1 & -1 & 1 & 2 \\ 0 & 1 & 0 & 5 \\ 0 & 0 & 0 & -6 \end{array}\right]$$

Step 3: Identify the solution. Row 3 is inconsistent, so there is no solution.

This is incorrect. The correct answer is $x = 1$, $y = 2$, $z = 3$. What mistake was made?

104. Perform the indicated row operations on the matrix.

$$\left[\begin{array}{ccc|c} 1 & -1 & 1 & 2 \\ 2 & -3 & 1 & 4 \\ 3 & 1 & 2 & -6 \end{array}\right]$$

a. $R_2 - 2R_1 \rightarrow R_2$
b. $R_3 - 3R_1 \rightarrow R_3$

Solution:

a. $\left[\begin{array}{ccc|c} 1 & -1 & 1 & 2 \\ 0 & -3 & 1 & 4 \\ 3 & 1 & 2 & -6 \end{array}\right]$

b. $\left[\begin{array}{ccc|c} 1 & -1 & 1 & 2 \\ 2 & -3 & 1 & 4 \\ 0 & 1 & 2 & -6 \end{array}\right]$

This is incorrect. What mistake was made?

105. Solve the system of equations using an augmented matrix.

$$\begin{aligned} 3x - 2y + z &= -1 \\ x + y - z &= 3 \\ 2x - y + 3z &= 0 \end{aligned}$$

Solution:

Step 1: Write the system as an augmented matrix.
$$\left[\begin{array}{ccc|c} 3 & -2 & 1 & -1 \\ 1 & 1 & -1 & 3 \\ 2 & -1 & 3 & 0 \end{array}\right]$$

Step 2: Reduce the matrix using Gaussian elimination.
$$\left[\begin{array}{ccc|c} 1 & 0 & 0 & 1 \\ 0 & 1 & 0 & 2 \\ 0 & 0 & 1 & 0 \end{array}\right]$$

Step 3: Identify the answer. Row 3 is inconsistent $1 = 0$, so there is no solution.

This is incorrect. What mistake was made?

106. Solve the system of equations using an augmented matrix.

$$\begin{aligned} x + 3y + 2z &= 4 \\ 3x + 10y + 9z &= 17 \\ 2x + 7y + 7z &= 17 \end{aligned}$$

Solution:

Step 1: Write the system as an augmented matrix.
$$\left[\begin{array}{ccc|c} 1 & 3 & 2 & 4 \\ 3 & 10 & 9 & 17 \\ 2 & 7 & 7 & 17 \end{array}\right]$$

Step 2: Reduce the matrix using Gaussian elimination.
$$\left[\begin{array}{ccc|c} 1 & 0 & -7 & -11 \\ 0 & 1 & 3 & 5 \\ 0 & 0 & 0 & 4 \end{array}\right]$$

Step 3: Identify the answer: Infinitely many solutions.
$$\begin{aligned} x &= 7t - 11 \\ y &= -3t + 5 \\ z &= t \end{aligned}$$

This is incorrect. What mistake was made?

• CONCEPTUAL

In Exercises 107–114, determine whether each of the following statements is true or false:

107. A system of equations represented by a nonsquare coefficient matrix cannot have a unique solution.

108. The procedure for Gaussian elimination can be used only for a system of linear equations represented by a square matrix.

109. A system of linear equations represented by a square coefficient matrix that has a unique solution has a reduced matrix with 1s along the main diagonal and 0s above and below the 1s.

110. A system of linear equations represented by a square coefficient matrix with an all-zero row has infinitely many solutions.

111. When a system of linear equations is represented by a square augmented matrix, the system of equations always has a unique solution.

112. Gauss–Jordan elimination produces a matrix in reduced row–echelon form.

113. An inconsistent system of linear equations has infinitely many solutions.

114. Every system of linear equations with a unique solution is represented by an augmented matrix of order $n \times (n + 1)$. (Assume no two rows are identical.)

• CHALLENGE

115. A fourth-degree polynomial $f(x) = ax^4 + bx^3 + cx^2 + dx + k$, with $a < 0$, can be used to represent the data on the number of deaths per year due to lightning strikes (assume 1999 corresponds to $x = 0$).

Use the data below to determine a, b, c, d, and k.

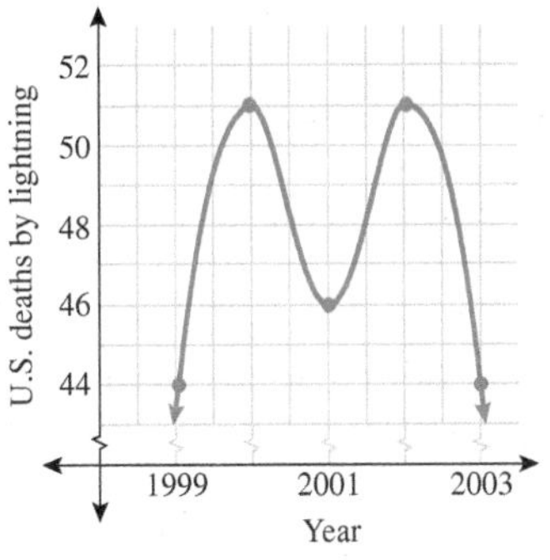

116. A copy machine accepts nickels, dimes, and quarters. After one hour, it holds 30 coins, and their value is \$4.60. How many nickels, quarters, and dimes are in the machine?

117. A ferry goes down a river from city A to city B in 5 hours. The return trip takes 7 hours. How long will a canoe take to make the trip from A to B if it moves at the river speed?

118. Solve the system of equations.

$$\frac{3}{x} - \frac{4}{y} + \frac{6}{z} = 1$$

$$\frac{9}{x} + \frac{8}{y} - \frac{12}{z} = 3$$

$$\frac{9}{x} - \frac{4}{y} + \frac{12}{z} = 4$$

119. The sides of a triangle are formed by the lines $x - y = -3$, $3x + 4y = 5$, and $6x + y = 17$. Find the vertices of the triangle.

120. A winery has three barrels, A, B, and C, containing mixtures of three different wines, w_1, w_2, and w_3. In barrel A, the wines are in the ratio 1:2:3. In barrel B, the wines are in the ratio 3:5:7. In barrel C, the wines are in the ratio 3:7:9. How much wine must be taken from each barrel to get a mixture containing 17 liters of w_1, 35 liters of w_2, and 47 liters of w_3?

• PREVIEW TO CALCULUS

In calculus, when solving systems of linear differential equations with initial conditions, the solution of a system of linear equations is required. In Exercises 121–124, solve each system of equations.

121.
$$\begin{aligned} c_1 + c_2 &= 0 \\ c_1 + 5c_2 &= -3 \end{aligned}$$

122.
$$\begin{aligned} 3c_1 + 3c_2 &= 0 \\ 2c_1 + 3c_2 &= 0 \end{aligned}$$

123.
$$\begin{aligned} 2c_1 + 2c_2 + 2c_3 &= 0 \\ 2c_1 \qquad - 2c_3 &= 2 \\ c_1 - c_2 + c_3 &= 6 \end{aligned}$$

124.
$$\begin{aligned} c_1 + c_4 &= 1 \\ c_3 &= 1 \\ c_2 + 3c_4 &= 1 \\ c_1 - 2c_3 &= 1 \end{aligned}$$

8.4 MATRIX ALGEBRA

SKILLS OBJECTIVES

- Determine if two matrices are equal.
- Add and subtract matrices.
- Perform scalar and matrix multiplication.
- Write a system of linear equations as a matrix equation.
- Find the inverse of a square matrix.
- Solve systems of linear equations using inverse matrices.

CONCEPTUAL OBJECTIVES

- Recognize that only matrices of the same order can be equal.
- Understand that matrices of the same order are added or subtracted element by element.
- Understand why matrix multiplication is not commutative.
- Understand that only a system of linear equations can be represented with a matrix equation.
- Understand that only a square matrix can have an inverse, and that not all square matrices have inverses.
- Matrix algebra can be used to solve only systems of linear equations that have a unique solution.

8.4.1 Equality of Matrices

8.4.1 SKILL

Determine if two matrices are equal.

8.4.1 CONCEPTUAL

Recognize that only matrices of the same order can be equal.

In Section 8.3, we defined a matrix with m rows and n columns to have order $m \times n$.

$$A = \begin{bmatrix} a_{11} & a_{12} & \cdots & a_{1n} \\ a_{21} & a_{22} & \cdots & a_{2n} \\ \vdots & \vdots & \cdots & \vdots \\ a_{m1} & a_{m2} & \cdots & a_{mn} \end{bmatrix}$$

Capital letters are used to represent (or name) a matrix, and lowercase letters are used to represent the entries (elements) of the matrix. The subscripts are used to denote the location (row/column) of each entry. The order of a matrix is often written as a subscript of the matrix name: $A_{m \times n}$. Other words like "size" and "dimension" are used as synonyms of "order." Matrices are a convenient way to represent data.

There is an entire field of study called **matrix algebra** that treats matrices similarly to functions and variables in traditional algebra. This section serves as an introduction to matrix algebra. It is important to pay special attention to the *order* of a matrix, because it determines whether certain operations are defined.

Two matrices are equal if and only if they have the same order, $m \times n$, and all of their corresponding entries are equal.

DEFINITION **Equality of Matrices**

Two matrices, A and B, are **equal**, written as $A = B$, if and only if *both* of the following are true:

- A and B have the same order $m \times n$.
- Every pair of corresponding entries is equal: $a_{ij} = b_{ij}$ for all $i = 1, 2, \ldots, m$ and all $j = 1, 2, \ldots, n$.

[CONCEPT CHECK]

TRUE OR FALSE A matrix with three rows and two columns can be equal to a matrix with two rows and three columns.

ANSWER False

EXAMPLE 1 **Equality of Matrices**

Referring to the definition of equality of matrices, find the indicated entries.

$$\begin{bmatrix} a_{11} & a_{12} & a_{13} \\ a_{21} & a_{22} & a_{23} \\ a_{31} & a_{32} & a_{33} \end{bmatrix} = \begin{bmatrix} 2 & -7 & 1 \\ 0 & 5 & -3 \\ -1 & 8 & 9 \end{bmatrix}$$

Find the main diagonal entries: a_{11}, a_{22}, and a_{33}.

Solution:

Since the matrices are equal, their corresponding entries are equal. $\boxed{a_{11} = 2}$ $\boxed{a_{22} = 5}$ $\boxed{a_{33} = 9}$

8.4.2 Matrix Addition and Subtraction

Two matrices, A and B, can be added or subtracted only if they have the *same order*. Suppose A and B are both of order $m \times n$; then the *sum* $A + B$ is found by adding corresponding entries, or taking $a_{ij} + b_{ij}$. The *difference* $A - B$ is found by subtracting the entries in B from the corresponding entries in A, or finding $a_{ij} - b_{ij}$.

8.4.2 SKILL

Add and subtract matrices.

8.4.2 CONCEPTUAL

Understand that matrices of the same order are added or subtracted element by element.

DEFINITION **Matrix Addition and Matrix Subtraction**

If A is an $m \times n$ matrix and B is an $m \times n$ matrix, then their **sum** $A + B$ is an $m \times n$ matrix whose entries are given by

$$a_{ij} + b_{ij}$$

and their **difference** $A - B$ is an $m \times n$ matrix whose entries are given by

$$a_{ij} - b_{ij}$$

EXAMPLE 2 Adding and Subtracting Matrices

Given that $A = \begin{bmatrix} -1 & 3 & 4 \\ -5 & 2 & 0 \end{bmatrix}$ and $B = \begin{bmatrix} 2 & 1 & -3 \\ 0 & -5 & 4 \end{bmatrix}$, find:

a. $A + B$ **b.** $A - B$

Solution:

Since $A_{2\times 3}$ and $B_{2\times 3}$ have the same order, they can be added or subtracted.

a. Write the sum. $A + B = \begin{bmatrix} -1 & 3 & 4 \\ -5 & 2 & 0 \end{bmatrix} + \begin{bmatrix} 2 & 1 & -3 \\ 0 & -5 & 4 \end{bmatrix}$

Add the corresponding entries. $= \begin{bmatrix} -1+2 & 3+1 & 4+(-3) \\ -5+0 & 2+(-5) & 0+4 \end{bmatrix}$

Simplify. $= \boxed{\begin{bmatrix} 1 & 4 & 1 \\ -5 & -3 & 4 \end{bmatrix}}$

b. Write the difference. $A - B = \begin{bmatrix} -1 & 3 & 4 \\ -5 & 2 & 0 \end{bmatrix} - \begin{bmatrix} 2 & 1 & -3 \\ 0 & -5 & 4 \end{bmatrix}$

Subtract the corresponding entries. $= \begin{bmatrix} -1-2 & 3-1 & 4-(-3) \\ -5-0 & 2-(-5) & 0-4 \end{bmatrix}$

Simplify. $= \boxed{\begin{bmatrix} -3 & 2 & 7 \\ -5 & 7 & -4 \end{bmatrix}}$

CONCEPT CHECK

TRUE OR FALSE When performing matrix subtraction $A - B$, we subtract each element in B, b_{ij}, from each corresponding element in A, a_{ij}.

ANSWER True

YOUR TURN Perform the indicated matrix operations, if possible.

$A = \begin{bmatrix} -4 & 0 \\ 1 & 2 \end{bmatrix}$ $B = \begin{bmatrix} 2 & 3 \\ -4 & 0 \end{bmatrix}$ $C = \begin{bmatrix} 2 & 9 & 5 & -1 \end{bmatrix}$ $D = \begin{bmatrix} 0 \\ -3 \\ 4 \\ 2 \end{bmatrix}$

a. $B - A$ **b.** $C + D$ **c.** $A + B$ **d.** $A + D$

ANSWER

a. $\begin{bmatrix} 6 & 3 \\ -5 & -2 \end{bmatrix}$ **b.** not defined

c. $\begin{bmatrix} -2 & 3 \\ -3 & 2 \end{bmatrix}$ **d.** not defined

STUDY TIP

Only matrices of the same order can be added or subtracted.

It is important to note that only matrices of the same order can be added or subtracted. For example, if $A = \begin{bmatrix} -1 & 3 & 4 \\ -5 & 2 & 0 \end{bmatrix}$ and $B = \begin{bmatrix} 5 & -3 \\ 12 & 1 \end{bmatrix}$, the sum and difference of these matrices are undefined because $A_{2\times 3}$ and $B_{2\times 2}$ do not have the same order.

A matrix whose entries are all equal to 0 is called a **zero matrix**, denoted **0**. The following are examples of zero matrices:

2×2 square zero matrix $\begin{bmatrix} 0 & 0 \\ 0 & 0 \end{bmatrix}$

3×2 zero matrix $\begin{bmatrix} 0 & 0 \\ 0 & 0 \\ 0 & 0 \end{bmatrix}$

1×4 zero matrix $\begin{bmatrix} 0 & 0 & 0 & 0 \end{bmatrix}$

If A, an $m \times n$ matrix, is added to the $m \times n$ zero matrix, the result is A.

$$A + \mathbf{0} = A$$

For example,

$$\begin{bmatrix} 1 & -3 \\ 2 & 5 \end{bmatrix} + \begin{bmatrix} 0 & 0 \\ 0 & 0 \end{bmatrix} = \begin{bmatrix} 1 & -3 \\ 2 & 5 \end{bmatrix}$$

Because of this result, an $m \times n$ zero matrix is called the **additive identity** for $m \times n$ matrices. Similarly, for any matrix A, there exists an **additive inverse**, $-A$, such that each entry of $-A$ is the negative of the corresponding entry of A.

For example, $A = \begin{bmatrix} 1 & -3 \\ 2 & 5 \end{bmatrix}$ and $-A = \begin{bmatrix} -1 & 3 \\ -2 & -5 \end{bmatrix}$, and adding these two matrices results in a zero matrix: $A + (-A) = \mathbf{0}$.

The same properties that hold for adding real numbers also hold for adding matrices, provided that addition of matrices is defined.

PROPERTIES OF MATRIX ADDITION

If A, B, and C are all $m \times n$ matrices and $\mathbf{0}$ is the $m \times n$ zero matrix, then the following are true.

Commutative property:	$A + B = B + A$
Associative property:	$(A + B) + C = A + (B + C)$
Additive identity property:	$A + \mathbf{0} = A$
Additive inverse property:	$A + (-A) = \mathbf{0}$

8.4.3 Scalar and Matrix Multiplication

There are two types of multiplication involving matrices: *scalar multiplication* and *matrix multiplication*. A **scalar** is any real number. *Scalar multiplication* is the multiplication of a matrix by a scalar, or real number, and is defined for all matrices. *Matrix multiplication* is the multiplication of two matrices and is defined only for certain pairs of matrices, depending on the order of each matrix.

8.4.3 SKILL

Perform scalar and matrix multiplication.

8.4.3 CONCEPTUAL

Understand why matrix multiplication is not commutative.

Scalar Multiplication

To multiply a matrix A by a scalar k, multiply every entry in A by k.

$$3\begin{bmatrix} -1 & 0 & 4 \\ 7 & 5 & -2 \end{bmatrix} = \begin{bmatrix} 3(-1) & 3(0) & 3(4) \\ 3(7) & 3(5) & 3(-2) \end{bmatrix} = \begin{bmatrix} -3 & 0 & 12 \\ 21 & 15 & -6 \end{bmatrix}$$

Here, the scalar is $k = 3$.

DEFINITION **Scalar Multiplication**

If A is an $m \times n$ matrix and k is any real number, then their product kA is an $m \times n$ matrix whose entries are given by

$$ka_{ij}$$

In other words, every entry a_{ij} of A is multiplied by k.

In general, uppercase letters are used to denote a matrix, and lowercase letters are used to denote scalars. Note that the elements of each matrix are also represented with lowercase letters, since they are real numbers.

EXAMPLE 3 **Multiplying a Matrix by a Scalar**

Given that $A = \begin{bmatrix} -1 & 2 \\ -3 & 4 \end{bmatrix}$ and $B = \begin{bmatrix} 0 & 1 \\ -2 & 3 \end{bmatrix}$, perform:

a. $2A$ **b.** $-3B$ **c.** $2A - 3B$

Solution (a):

Write the scalar multiplication. $2A = 2\begin{bmatrix} -1 & 2 \\ -3 & 4 \end{bmatrix}$

Multiply all entries of A by 2. $2A = \begin{bmatrix} 2(-1) & 2(2) \\ 2(-3) & 2(4) \end{bmatrix}$

Simplify. $\boxed{2A = \begin{bmatrix} -2 & 4 \\ -6 & 8 \end{bmatrix}}$

Solution (b):

Write the scalar multiplication. $-3B = -3\begin{bmatrix} 0 & 1 \\ -2 & 3 \end{bmatrix}$

Multiply all entries of B by -3. $-3B = \begin{bmatrix} -3(0) & -3(1) \\ -3(-2) & -3(3) \end{bmatrix}$

Simplify. $\boxed{-3B = \begin{bmatrix} 0 & -3 \\ 6 & -9 \end{bmatrix}}$

Solution (c):

Add the results of parts (a) and (b). $2A - 3B = 2A + (-3B)$

$2A - 3B = \begin{bmatrix} -2 & 4 \\ -6 & 8 \end{bmatrix} + \begin{bmatrix} 0 & -3 \\ 6 & -9 \end{bmatrix}$

Add the corresponding entries. $2A - 3B = \begin{bmatrix} -2 + 0 & 4 + (-3) \\ -6 + 6 & 8 + (-9) \end{bmatrix}$

Simplify. $\boxed{2A - 3B = \begin{bmatrix} -2 & 1 \\ 0 & -1 \end{bmatrix}}$

YOUR TURN For the matrices A and B given in Example 3, find $-5A + 2B$.

ANSWER

$-5A + 2B = \begin{bmatrix} 5 & -8 \\ 11 & -14 \end{bmatrix}$

STUDY TIP

When we multiply matrices, we *do not* multiply corresponding entries.

Matrix Multiplication

Scalar multiplication is straightforward in that it is defined for all matrices and is performed by multiplying every entry in the matrix by the scalar. Addition of matrices is also an entry-by-entry operation. *Matrix multiplication*, on the other hand, is not as straightforward in that we *do not multiply the corresponding entries* and it is not defined for all matrices. Matrices are multiplied using a row-by-column method.

Before we even try to find the product AB of two matrices A and B, we first have to determine whether the product is defined. For the product AB to exist, **the number of columns in the first matrix A must equal the number of rows in the second matrix B**. In other words, if the matrix $A_{m\times n}$ has m rows and n columns and the matrix $B_{n\times p}$ has n rows and p columns, then the product $(AB)_{m\times p}$ is defined and has m rows and p columns.

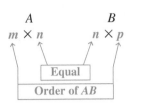

Matrix:	A	B	AB
Order:	$m \times n$	$n \times p$	$m \times p$

Equal

Order of AB

> **STUDY TIP**
> For the product AB of two matrices A and B to be defined, the number of columns in the first matrix must equal the number of rows in the second matrix.

EXAMPLE 4 Determining Whether the Product of Two Matrices Is Defined

Given the matrices

$$A = \begin{bmatrix} 1 & -2 & 0 \\ 5 & -1 & 3 \end{bmatrix} \quad B = \begin{bmatrix} 2 & 3 \\ 0 & 7 \\ 4 & 9 \end{bmatrix} \quad C = \begin{bmatrix} 6 & -1 \\ 5 & 2 \end{bmatrix} \quad D = \begin{bmatrix} -3 & -2 \end{bmatrix}$$

state whether each of the following products exists. If the product exists, state the order of the product matrix.

a. AB **b.** AC **c.** BC **d.** CD **e.** DC

Solution:

Label the order of each matrix: $A_{2\times 3}$, $B_{3\times 2}$, $C_{2\times 2}$, and $D_{1\times 2}$.

a. AB is defined, because A has 3 columns and B has 3 rows. $A_{2\times 3}B_{3\times 2}$

AB is order $\boxed{2 \times 2}$. $(AB)_{2\times 2}$

b. AC is $\boxed{\text{not defined}}$, because A has 3 columns and C has 2 rows.

c. BC is defined, because B has 2 columns and C has 2 rows. $B_{3\times 2}C_{2\times 2}$

BC is order $\boxed{3 \times 2}$. $(BC)_{3\times 2}$

d. CD is $\boxed{\text{not defined}}$, because C has 2 columns and D has 1 row.

e. DC is defined, because D has 2 columns and C has 2 rows. $D_{1\times 2}C_{2\times 2}$

DC is order $\boxed{1 \times 2}$. $(DC)_{1\times 2}$

Notice that in part (d) we found that CD is not defined, but in part (e) we found that DC is defined. **Matrix multiplication is not commutative**. Therefore, the order in which matrices are multiplied is important in determining whether the product is defined or undefined. For the product of two matrices to exist, the number of *columns* in the *first* matrix A must equal the number of *rows* in the *second* matrix B.

YOUR TURN For the matrices given in Example 4, state whether the following products exist. If the product exists, state the order of the product matrix.

a. DA **b.** CB **c.** BA

ANSWER

a. DA exists and is order 1×3.

b. CB does not exist.

c. BA exists and is order 3×3

Now that we can determine whether a product of two matrices is defined and, if so, what the order of the resulting product is, let us turn our attention to how to multiply two matrices.

DEFINITION Matrix Multiplication

If A is an $m \times n$ matrix and B is an $n \times p$ matrix, then their product AB is an $m \times p$ matrix whose entries are given by

$$(ab)_{ij} = a_{i1}b_{1j} + a_{i2}b_{2j} + \cdots + a_{in}b_{nj}$$

In other words, the entry $(ab)_{ij}$, which is in the ith row and the jth column of AB, is the sum of the products of the corresponding entries in the ith row of A and the jth column of B. Multiply *across* the row and *down* the column.

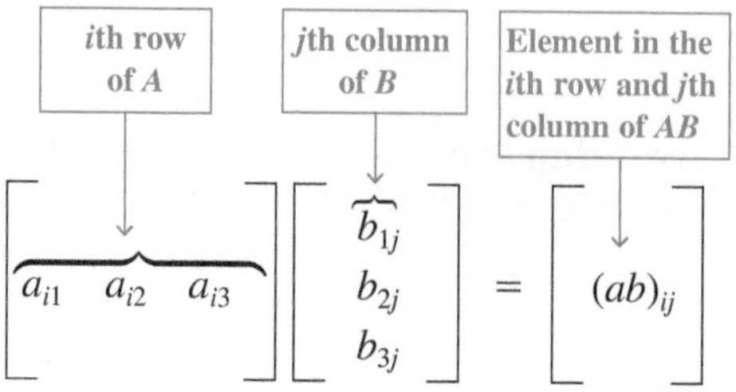

$$(ab)_{ij} = a_{i1}b_{1j} + a_{i2}b_{2j} + a_{i3}b_{3j}$$

EXAMPLE 5 Multiplication of Two 2 × 2 Matrices

Given $A = \begin{bmatrix} 1 & 2 \\ 3 & 4 \end{bmatrix}$ and $B = \begin{bmatrix} 5 & 6 \\ 7 & 8 \end{bmatrix}$, find AB.

common mistake

Do not multiply entry by entry.

✓CORRECT

Write the product of the two matrices A and B.

$$AB = \begin{bmatrix} 1 & 2 \\ 3 & 4 \end{bmatrix}\begin{bmatrix} 5 & 6 \\ 7 & 8 \end{bmatrix}$$

Perform the row-by-column multiplication.

$$AB = \begin{bmatrix} (1)(5) + (2)(7) & (1)(6) + (2)(8) \\ (3)(5) + (4)(7) & (3)(6) + (4)(8) \end{bmatrix}$$

Simplify.

$$\boxed{AB = \begin{bmatrix} 19 & 22 \\ 43 & 50 \end{bmatrix}}$$

✖INCORRECT

Multiply the corresponding entries.

ERROR

$$AB \neq \begin{bmatrix} (1)(5) & (2)(6) \\ (3)(7) & (4)(8) \end{bmatrix}$$

YOUR TURN For matrices A and B given in Example 5, find BA.

ANSWER

$$BA = \begin{bmatrix} 5 & 6 \\ 7 & 8 \end{bmatrix}\begin{bmatrix} 1 & 2 \\ 3 & 4 \end{bmatrix} = \begin{bmatrix} 23 & 34 \\ 31 & 46 \end{bmatrix}$$

Compare the products obtained in Example 5 and the preceding Your Turn. Note that $AB \neq BA$. Therefore, there is **no commutative property for matrix multiplication.**

EXAMPLE 6 Multiplying Matrices

For $A = \begin{bmatrix} -1 & 2 & -3 \\ -2 & 0 & 4 \end{bmatrix}$ and $B = \begin{bmatrix} 2 & 0 \\ 1 & 3 \\ -1 & -2 \end{bmatrix}$, find AB.

Solution:

Since A is order 2×3 and B is order 3×2, the product AB is defined and has order 2×2.

$$A_{2\times 3}B_{3\times 2} = (AB)_{2\times 2}$$

Write the product of the two matrices.

$$AB = \begin{bmatrix} -1 & 2 & -3 \\ -2 & 0 & 4 \end{bmatrix}\begin{bmatrix} 2 & 0 \\ 1 & 3 \\ -1 & -2 \end{bmatrix}$$

Perform the row-by-column multiplication.

$$AB = \begin{bmatrix} (-1)(2) + (2)(1) + (-3)(-1) & (-1)(0) + (2)(3) + (-3)(-2) \\ (-2)(2) + (0)(1) + (4)(-1) & (-2)(0) + (0)(3) + (4)(-2) \end{bmatrix}$$

Simplify.

$$\boxed{AB = \begin{bmatrix} 3 & 12 \\ -8 & -8 \end{bmatrix}}$$

YOUR TURN For $A = \begin{bmatrix} 1 & 0 & 2 \\ -3 & -1 & 4 \end{bmatrix}$ and $B = \begin{bmatrix} 0 & -1 \\ 1 & 2 \\ 0 & -2 \end{bmatrix}$, find AB.

ANSWER

$AB = \begin{bmatrix} 0 & -5 \\ -1 & -7 \end{bmatrix}$

EXAMPLE 7 Multiplying Matrices

For $A = \begin{bmatrix} 1 & 0 & 3 \\ -2 & 5 & -1 \end{bmatrix}$ and $B = \begin{bmatrix} -2 & 0 & 1 \\ -3 & -1 & 4 \\ 0 & 2 & 5 \end{bmatrix}$, find AB.

Solution:

Since A is order 2×3 and B is order 3×3, the product AB is defined and has order 2×3.

$$A_{2\times 3}B_{3\times 3} = (AB)_{2\times 3}$$

Write the product of the two matrices.

$$AB = \begin{bmatrix} 1 & 0 & 3 \\ -2 & 5 & -1 \end{bmatrix}\begin{bmatrix} -2 & 0 & 1 \\ -3 & -1 & 4 \\ 0 & 2 & 5 \end{bmatrix}$$

Perform the row-by-column multiplication.

$$AB = \begin{bmatrix} (1)(-2) + (0)(-3) + (3)(0) & (1)(0) + (0)(-1) + (3)(2) & (1)(1) + (0)(4) + (3)(5) \\ (-2)(-2) + (5)(-3) + (-1)(0) & (-2)(0) + (5)(-1) + (-1)(2) & (-2)(1) + (5)(4) + (-1)(5) \end{bmatrix}$$

Simplify.

$$\boxed{AB = \begin{bmatrix} -2 & 6 & 16 \\ -11 & -7 & 13 \end{bmatrix}}$$

YOUR TURN Given $A = \begin{bmatrix} 1 \\ 2 \\ 3 \end{bmatrix}$ and $B = \begin{bmatrix} 4 & 5 \end{bmatrix}$, find:

a. AB, if it exists **b.** BA, if it exists

ANSWER

a. $AB = \begin{bmatrix} 4 & 5 \\ 8 & 10 \\ 12 & 15 \end{bmatrix}$

b. does not exist

Although we have shown repeatedly that there is no commutative property of multiplication for matrices, matrices do have an associative property of multiplication, as well as a distributive property of multiplication similar to real numbers.

PROPERTIES OF MATRIX MULTIPLICATION

If A, B, and C are all matrices for which AB, AC, BC, $A + B$, and $B + C$ are all defined, then the following properties are true.

Associative property: $A(BC) = (AB)C$

Distributive property: $A(B + C) = AB + AC$ or $(A + B)C = AC + BC$

EXAMPLE 8 Application of Matrix Multiplication

The following table gives fuel and electric requirements per mile associated with gasoline and electric automobiles:

	NUMBER OF GALLONS/MILE	NUMBER OF kW-hr/MILE
Gas car	0.05	0
Hybrid car	0.02	0.1
Electric car	0	0.25

The following table gives an average cost for gasoline and electricity.

Cost per gallon of gasoline	\$3.00
Cost per kW-hr of electricity	\$0.05

a. Let matrix A represent the gasoline and electricity consumption and matrix B represent the costs of gasoline and electricity.

b. Find AB and describe what the entries of the product matrix represent.

c. Assume you drive 12,000 miles per year. What are the yearly costs associated with driving the three types of cars?

Solution (a):

A has order 3×2.

$$A = \begin{bmatrix} 0.05 & 0 \\ 0.02 & 0.1 \\ 0 & 0.25 \end{bmatrix}$$

B has order 2×1.

$$B = \begin{bmatrix} \$3.00 \\ \$0.05 \end{bmatrix}$$

Solution (b):

Find the order of the product matrix AB.

$$A_{3\times2}B_{2\times1} = (AB)_{3\times1}$$

$$AB = \begin{bmatrix} 0.05 & 0 \\ 0.02 & 0.1 \\ 0 & 0.25 \end{bmatrix}\begin{bmatrix} \$3.00 \\ \$0.05 \end{bmatrix}$$

Calculate AB.

$$= \begin{bmatrix} (0.05)(\$3.00) + (0)(\$0.05) \\ (0.02)(\$3.00) + (0.1)(\$0.05) \\ (0)(\$3.00) + (0.25)(\$0.05) \end{bmatrix}$$

$$AB = \begin{bmatrix} \$0.15 \\ \$0.065 \\ \$0.0125 \end{bmatrix}$$

Interpret the product matrix.

$$AB = \begin{bmatrix} \text{Cost per mile to drive the gas car} \\ \text{Cost per mile to drive the hybrid car} \\ \text{Cost per mile to drive the electric car} \end{bmatrix}$$

Solution (c):

Find 12,000AB.

$$12{,}000\begin{bmatrix} \$0.15 \\ \$0.065 \\ \$0.0125 \end{bmatrix} = \begin{bmatrix} \$1800 \\ \$780 \\ \$150 \end{bmatrix}$$

	GAS/ELECTRIC COSTS PER YEAR ($)
Gas car	1800
Hybrid car	780
Electric car	150

8.4.4 Matrix Equations

Matrix equations are another way of writing systems of linear equations.

8.4.4 SKILL

Write a system of linear equations as a matrix equation.

8.4.4 CONCEPTUAL

Understand that only a system of linear equations can be represented with a matrix equation.

WORDS	MATH
Start with a matrix equation.	$\begin{bmatrix} 2 & -3 \\ 1 & 5 \end{bmatrix}\begin{bmatrix} x \\ y \end{bmatrix} = \begin{bmatrix} -7 \\ 9 \end{bmatrix}$
Multiply the two matrices on the left.	$\begin{bmatrix} 2x - 3y \\ x + 5y \end{bmatrix} = \begin{bmatrix} -7 \\ 9 \end{bmatrix}$
Apply equality of two matrices.	$2x - 3y = -7$ $x + 5y = 9$

Let A be a matrix with m rows and n columns, which represents the coefficients in the system. Also, let X be a column matrix of order $n \times 1$ that represents the variables in the system and let B be a column matrix of order $m \times 1$ that represents the constants in the system. Then a system of linear equations can be written as $AX = B$.

SYSTEM OF LINEAR EQUATIONS	*A*	*X*	*B*	MATRIX EQUATION: *AX* = *B*
$3x + 4y = 1$ $x - 2y = 7$	$\begin{bmatrix} 3 & 4 \\ 1 & -2 \end{bmatrix}$	$\begin{bmatrix} x \\ y \end{bmatrix}$	$\begin{bmatrix} 1 \\ 7 \end{bmatrix}$	$\begin{bmatrix} 3 & 4 \\ 1 & -2 \end{bmatrix}\begin{bmatrix} x \\ y \end{bmatrix} = \begin{bmatrix} 1 \\ 7 \end{bmatrix}$
$x - y + z = 2$ $2x + 2y - 3z = -3$ $x + y + z = 6$	$\begin{bmatrix} 1 & -1 & 1 \\ 2 & 2 & -3 \\ 1 & 1 & 1 \end{bmatrix}$	$\begin{bmatrix} x \\ y \\ z \end{bmatrix}$	$\begin{bmatrix} 2 \\ -3 \\ 6 \end{bmatrix}$	$\begin{bmatrix} 1 & -1 & 1 \\ 2 & 2 & -3 \\ 1 & 1 & 1 \end{bmatrix}\begin{bmatrix} x \\ y \\ z \end{bmatrix} = \begin{bmatrix} 2 \\ -3 \\ 6 \end{bmatrix}$
$x + y + z = 0$ $3x + 2y - z = 2$	$\begin{bmatrix} 1 & 1 & 1 \\ 3 & 2 & -1 \end{bmatrix}$	$\begin{bmatrix} x \\ y \\ z \end{bmatrix}$	$\begin{bmatrix} 0 \\ 2 \end{bmatrix}$	$\begin{bmatrix} 1 & 1 & 1 \\ 3 & 2 & -1 \end{bmatrix}\begin{bmatrix} x \\ y \\ z \end{bmatrix} = \begin{bmatrix} 0 \\ 2 \end{bmatrix}$

[CONCEPT CHECK]

TRUE OR FALSE Matrices can be used to solve systems of linear and nonlinear equations.

ANSWER False

EXAMPLE 9 **Writing a System of Linear Equations as a Matrix Equation**

Write each system of linear equations as a matrix equation.

a. $\begin{aligned} 2x - y &= 5 \\ -x + 2y &= 3 \end{aligned}$ **b.** $\begin{aligned} 3x - 2y + 4z &= 5 \\ y - 3z &= -2 \\ 7x \quad - z &= 1 \end{aligned}$ **c.** $\begin{aligned} x_1 - x_2 + 2x_3 - 3 &= 0 \\ x_1 + x_2 - 3x_3 + 5 &= 0 \\ x_1 - x_2 + x_3 - 2 &= 0 \end{aligned}$

Solution:

a. $$\begin{bmatrix} 2 & -1 \\ -1 & 2 \end{bmatrix}\begin{bmatrix} x \\ y \end{bmatrix} = \begin{bmatrix} 5 \\ 3 \end{bmatrix}$$

b. Note that all missing terms have 0 coefficients.

$$\begin{aligned} 3x - 2y + 4z &= 5 \\ 0x + y - 3z &= -2 \\ 7x + 0y - z &= 1 \end{aligned}$$

$$\begin{bmatrix} 3 & -2 & 4 \\ 0 & 1 & -3 \\ 7 & 0 & -1 \end{bmatrix}\begin{bmatrix} x \\ y \\ z \end{bmatrix} = \begin{bmatrix} 5 \\ -2 \\ 1 \end{bmatrix}$$

c. Write the constants on the right side of the equal sign.

$$\begin{aligned} x_1 - x_2 + 2x_3 &= 3 \\ x_1 + x_2 - 3x_3 &= -5 \\ x_1 - x_2 + x_3 &= 2 \end{aligned}$$

$$\begin{bmatrix} 1 & -1 & 2 \\ 1 & 1 & -3 \\ 1 & -1 & 1 \end{bmatrix}\begin{bmatrix} x_1 \\ x_2 \\ x_3 \end{bmatrix} = \begin{bmatrix} 3 \\ -5 \\ 2 \end{bmatrix}$$

YOUR TURN Write each system of linear equations as a matrix equation.

a. $\begin{aligned} 2x + y - 3 &= 0 \\ x - y \quad &= 5 \end{aligned}$ **b.** $\begin{aligned} y - x + z &= 7 \\ x - y - z &= 2 \\ z - y &= -1 \end{aligned}$

ANSWER

a. $\begin{bmatrix} 2 & 1 \\ 1 & -1 \end{bmatrix}\begin{bmatrix} x \\ y \end{bmatrix} = \begin{bmatrix} 3 \\ 5 \end{bmatrix}$

b. $\begin{bmatrix} -1 & 1 & 1 \\ 1 & -1 & -1 \\ 0 & -1 & 1 \end{bmatrix}\begin{bmatrix} x \\ y \\ z \end{bmatrix} = \begin{bmatrix} 7 \\ 2 \\ -1 \end{bmatrix}$

8.4.5 Finding the Inverse of a Square Matrix

8.4.5 SKILL

Find the inverse of a square matrix.

8.4.5 CONCEPTUAL

Understand that only a square matrix can have an inverse, and that not all square matrices have inverses.

Before we discuss solving systems of linear equations in the form $AX = B$, let us first recall how we solve $ax = b$, where a and b are real numbers (not matrices).

WORDS	MATH
Write the linear equation in one variable.	$ax = b$
Multiply both sides by a^{-1} (same as dividing by a), provided $a \neq 0$.	$a^{-1}ax = a^{-1}b$
Simplify.	$\underbrace{a^{-1}a}_{1}x = a^{-1}b$
	$x = a^{-1}b$

Recall that a^{-1}, or $\frac{1}{a}$, is the *multiplicative inverse* of a because $a^{-1}a = 1$. And we call 1 the *multiplicative identity*, because any number multiplied by 1 is itself. Before we solve matrix equations, we need to define the *multiplicative identity matrix* and the *multiplicative inverse matrix*.

A square matrix of order $n \times n$ with 1s along the **main diagonal** (a_{ii}) and 0s for all other elements is called the **multiplicative identity matrix I_n**.

$$I_2 = \begin{bmatrix} 1 & 0 \\ 0 & 1 \end{bmatrix} \quad I_3 = \begin{bmatrix} 1 & 0 & 0 \\ 0 & 1 & 0 \\ 0 & 0 & 1 \end{bmatrix} \quad I_4 = \begin{bmatrix} 1 & 0 & 0 & 0 \\ 0 & 1 & 0 & 0 \\ 0 & 0 & 1 & 0 \\ 0 & 0 & 0 & 1 \end{bmatrix}$$

Since a real number multiplied by 1 is itself $(a \cdot 1 = a)$, we expect that a matrix multiplied by the appropriate identity matrix should result in itself. Remember, the order in which matrices are multiplied makes a difference. Note that the appropriate identity matrix may differ, depending on the order of multiplication, but the identity matrix will always be square.

$$A_{m \times n} I_n = A_{m \times n} \quad \text{and} \quad I_m A_{m \times n} = A_{m \times n}$$

EXAMPLE 10 **Multiplying a Matrix by the Multiplicative Identity Matrix I_n**

For $A = \begin{bmatrix} -2 & 4 & 1 \\ 3 & 7 & -1 \end{bmatrix}$, find I_2A.

Solution:

Write the two matrices. $A = \begin{bmatrix} -2 & 4 & 1 \\ 3 & 7 & -1 \end{bmatrix} \quad I_2 = \begin{bmatrix} 1 & 0 \\ 0 & 1 \end{bmatrix}$

Find the product I_2A. $I_2A = \begin{bmatrix} 1 & 0 \\ 0 & 1 \end{bmatrix}\begin{bmatrix} -2 & 4 & 1 \\ 3 & 7 & -1 \end{bmatrix}$

$$I_2A = \begin{bmatrix} (1)(-2) + (0)(3) & (1)(4) + (0)(7) & (1)(1) + (0)(-1) \\ (0)(-2) + (1)(3) & (0)(4) + (1)(7) & (0)(1) + (1)(-1) \end{bmatrix}$$

$$I_2A = \boxed{\begin{bmatrix} -2 & 4 & 1 \\ 3 & 7 & -1 \end{bmatrix}} = A$$

YOUR TURN For A in Example 10, find AI_3.

ANSWER

$AI_3 = \begin{bmatrix} -2 & 4 & 1 \\ 3 & 7 & -1 \end{bmatrix} = A$

The identity matrix I_n will assist us in developing the concept of an *inverse of a square matrix.*

DEFINITION **Inverse of a Square Matrix**

Let A be a square $n \times n$ matrix. If there exists a square $n \times n$ matrix A^{-1} such that

$$AA^{-1} = I_n \quad \text{and} \quad A^{-1}A = I_n$$

then A^{-1}, stated as "A inverse," is the **inverse** of A.

STUDY TIP

- Only a *square* matrix can have an inverse.
- Not all square matrices have inverses.

It is important to note that only a square matrix can have an inverse. Even then, not all square matrices have inverses.

EXAMPLE 11 Multiplying a Matrix by Its Inverse

Verify that the inverse of $A = \begin{bmatrix} 1 & 3 \\ 2 & 5 \end{bmatrix}$ is $A^{-1} = \begin{bmatrix} -5 & 3 \\ 2 & -1 \end{bmatrix}$.

Solution:

Show that $AA^{-1} = I_2$ and $A^{-1}A = I_2$.

Find the product AA^{-1}.

$$AA^{-1} = \begin{bmatrix} 1 & 3 \\ 2 & 5 \end{bmatrix}\begin{bmatrix} -5 & 3 \\ 2 & -1 \end{bmatrix}$$

$$= \begin{bmatrix} (1)(-5) + (3)(2) & (1)(3) + (3)(-1) \\ (2)(-5) + (5)(2) & (2)(3) + (5)(-1) \end{bmatrix}$$

$$= \begin{bmatrix} 1 & 0 \\ 0 & 1 \end{bmatrix} = I_2$$

Find the product $A^{-1}A$.

$$A^{-1}A = \begin{bmatrix} -5 & 3 \\ 2 & -1 \end{bmatrix}\begin{bmatrix} 1 & 3 \\ 2 & 5 \end{bmatrix}$$

$$= \begin{bmatrix} (-5)(1) + (3)(2) & (-5)(3) + (3)(5) \\ (2)(1) + (-1)(2) & (2)(3) + (-1)(5) \end{bmatrix}$$

$$= \begin{bmatrix} 1 & 0 \\ 0 & 1 \end{bmatrix} = I_2$$

YOUR TURN Verify that the inverse of $A = \begin{bmatrix} 1 & 4 \\ 2 & 9 \end{bmatrix}$ is $A^{-1} = \begin{bmatrix} 9 & -4 \\ -2 & 1 \end{bmatrix}$.

ANSWER

$AA^{-1} = A^{-1}A = I_2$

Now that we can show two matrices are inverses of one another, let us describe the process for finding an inverse, if it exists. If an inverse A^{-1} exists, then the matrix A is said to be **nonsingular**. If the inverse does not exist, then the matrix A is said to be **singular**.

Let $A = \begin{bmatrix} 1 & -1 \\ 2 & -3 \end{bmatrix}$ and the inverse be $A^{-1} = \begin{bmatrix} w & x \\ y & z \end{bmatrix}$, where w, x, y, and z are variables to be determined. A matrix and its inverse must satisfy the identity $AA^{-1} = I_2$.

WORDS	MATH
The product of a matrix and its inverse is the identity matrix.	$\begin{bmatrix} 1 & -1 \\ 2 & -3 \end{bmatrix}\begin{bmatrix} w & x \\ y & z \end{bmatrix} = \begin{bmatrix} 1 & 0 \\ 0 & 1 \end{bmatrix}$
Multiply the two matrices on the left.	$\begin{bmatrix} w - y & x - z \\ 2w - 3y & 2x - 3z \end{bmatrix} = \begin{bmatrix} 1 & 0 \\ 0 & 1 \end{bmatrix}$
Equate corresponding matrix elements.	$\begin{aligned} w - y &= 1 \\ 2w - 3y &= 0 \end{aligned}$ and $\begin{aligned} x - z &= 0 \\ 2x - 3z &= 1 \end{aligned}$

Notice that there are two systems of equations, both of which can be solved by several methods (elimination, substitution, or augmented matrices). We will find that $w = 3, x = -1, y = 2$, and $z = -1$. Therefore, we know the inverse is $A^{-1} = \begin{bmatrix} 3 & -1 \\ 2 & -1 \end{bmatrix}$. But instead, let us use augmented matrices in order to develop the general procedure.

Write the two systems of equations as two augmented matrices:

$$\begin{array}{c} \quad w \quad y \\ \left[\begin{array}{cc|c} 1 & -1 & 1 \\ 2 & -3 & 0 \end{array}\right] \end{array} \qquad \begin{array}{c} \quad x \quad z \\ \left[\begin{array}{cc|c} 1 & -1 & 0 \\ 2 & -3 & 1 \end{array}\right] \end{array}$$

Since the left side is the same for each augmented matrix, we can combine these two matrices into one matrix, thereby simultaneously solving both systems of equations.

$$\left[\begin{array}{cc|cc} 1 & -1 & 1 & 0 \\ 2 & -3 & 0 & 1 \end{array}\right]$$

Notice that the right side of the vertical line is the identity matrix I_2.

Using Gauss–Jordan elimination, transform the matrix on the left to the identity matrix.

$$\left[\begin{array}{cc|cc} 1 & -1 & 1 & 0 \\ 2 & -3 & 0 & 1 \end{array}\right]$$

$$R_2 - 2R_1 \to R_2 \quad \left[\begin{array}{cc|cc} 1 & -1 & 1 & 0 \\ 0 & -1 & -2 & 1 \end{array}\right]$$

$$-R_2 \to R_2 \quad \left[\begin{array}{cc|cc} 1 & -1 & 1 & 0 \\ 0 & 1 & 2 & -1 \end{array}\right]$$

$$R_1 + R_2 \to R_1 \quad \left[\begin{array}{cc|cc} 1 & 0 & 3 & -1 \\ 0 & 1 & 2 & -1 \end{array}\right]$$

The matrix on the right of the vertical line is the inverse $A^{-1} = \begin{bmatrix} 3 & -1 \\ 2 & -1 \end{bmatrix}$.

FINDING THE INVERSE OF A SQUARE MATRIX

To find the inverse of an $n \times n$ matrix A:

Step 1: Form the matrix $[A \mid I_n]$.

Step 2: Use row operations to transform this entire augmented matrix to $[I_n \mid A^{-1}]$. This is done by applying Gauss–Jordan elimination to reduce A to the identity matrix I_n. If this is not possible, then A is a singular matrix and no inverse exists.

Step 3: Verify the result by showing that $AA^{-1} = I_n$ and $A^{-1}A = I_n$.

EXAMPLE 12 Finding the Inverse of a 2 × 2 Matrix

Find the inverse of $A = \begin{bmatrix} 1 & 2 \\ 3 & 5 \end{bmatrix}$.

Solution:

STEP 1 Form the matrix $[A \mid I_2]$. $\left[\begin{array}{cc|cc} 1 & 2 & 1 & 0 \\ 3 & 5 & 0 & 1 \end{array}\right]$

STEP 2 Use row operations to transform A into I_2. $R_2 - 3R_1 \to R_2$ $\left[\begin{array}{cc|cc} 1 & 2 & 1 & 0 \\ 0 & -1 & -3 & 1 \end{array}\right]$

$$-R_2 \to R_2 \quad \left[\begin{array}{cc|cc} 1 & 2 & 1 & 0 \\ 0 & 1 & 3 & -1 \end{array}\right]$$

$$R_1 - 2R_2 \to R_1 \quad \left[\begin{array}{cc|cc} 1 & 0 & -5 & 2 \\ 0 & 1 & 3 & -1 \end{array}\right]$$

Identify the inverse. $A^{-1} = \begin{bmatrix} -5 & 2 \\ 3 & -1 \end{bmatrix}$

STEP 3 Check.

$$AA^{-1} = \begin{bmatrix} 1 & 2 \\ 3 & 5 \end{bmatrix}\begin{bmatrix} -5 & 2 \\ 3 & -1 \end{bmatrix} = \begin{bmatrix} 1 & 0 \\ 0 & 1 \end{bmatrix} = I_2$$

$$A^{-1}A = \begin{bmatrix} -5 & 2 \\ 3 & -1 \end{bmatrix}\begin{bmatrix} 1 & 2 \\ 3 & 5 \end{bmatrix} = \begin{bmatrix} 1 & 0 \\ 0 & 1 \end{bmatrix} = I_2$$

YOUR TURN Find the inverse of $A = \begin{bmatrix} 2 & 3 \\ 5 & 8 \end{bmatrix}$.

ANSWER

$A^{-1} = \begin{bmatrix} 8 & -3 \\ -5 & 2 \end{bmatrix}$

This procedure for finding an inverse of a square matrix is used for all square matrices of order $n \times n$. For the special case of a 2×2 matrix, there is a formula (that will be derived in Exercises 113 and 114) for finding the inverse.

Let $A = \begin{bmatrix} a & b \\ c & d \end{bmatrix}$ represent any 2×2 matrix; then the inverse matrix is given by

$$A^{-1} = \frac{1}{ad - bc}\begin{bmatrix} d & -b \\ -c & a \end{bmatrix} \qquad ad - bc \neq 0$$

The denominator $ad - bc$ is called the *determinant* of the matrix A and will be discussed in Section 8.5.

We found the inverse of $A = \begin{bmatrix} 1 & 2 \\ 3 & 5 \end{bmatrix}$ in Example 12. Let us now find the inverse using this formula.

WORDS	MATH
Write the formula for A^{-1}.	$A^{-1} = \frac{1}{ad - bc}\begin{bmatrix} d & -b \\ -c & a \end{bmatrix}$
Substitute $a = 1, b = 2, c = 3,$ and $d = 5$ into the formula.	$A^{-1} = \frac{1}{(1)(5) - (2)(3)}\begin{bmatrix} 5 & -2 \\ -3 & 1 \end{bmatrix}$
Simplify.	$A^{-1} = (-1)\begin{bmatrix} 5 & -2 \\ -3 & 1 \end{bmatrix}$
	$A^{-1} = \begin{bmatrix} -5 & 2 \\ 3 & -1 \end{bmatrix}$

The result is the same as that we found in Example 12.

STUDY TIP

If the determinant of a 2×2 matrix is equal to 0, then its inverse does not exist.

EXAMPLE 13 Finding That No Inverse Exists: Singular Matrix

Find the inverse of $A = \begin{bmatrix} 1 & -5 \\ -1 & 5 \end{bmatrix}$.

Solution:

STEP 1 Form the matrix $[A \mid I_2]$. $\left[\begin{array}{cc|cc} 1 & -5 & 1 & 0 \\ -1 & 5 & 0 & 1 \end{array}\right]$

STEP 2 Apply row operations to transform A into I_2. $R_2 + R_1 \rightarrow R_2$ $\left[\begin{array}{cc|cc} 1 & -5 & 1 & 0 \\ 0 & 0 & 1 & 1 \end{array}\right]$

We cannot convert the left-hand side of the augmented matrix to I_2 because of the all-zero row on the left-hand side. Therefore, $\boxed{A \text{ is not invertible}}$; that is, A has no inverse, or A^{-1} does not exist. We say that A is **singular**.

[CONCEPT CHECK]

TRUE OR FALSE A matrix must be square in order for its inverse to exist, and some square matrices are singular and do not have an inverse.

ANSWER True

EXAMPLE 14 **Finding the Inverse of a 3 × 3 Matrix**

Find the inverse of $A = \begin{bmatrix} 1 & 2 & -1 \\ 0 & 1 & -1 \\ -1 & 0 & -2 \end{bmatrix}$.

Solution:

STEP 1 Form the matrix $[A \mid I_3]$.

$$\left[\begin{array}{ccc|ccc} 1 & 2 & -1 & 1 & 0 & 0 \\ 0 & 1 & -1 & 0 & 1 & 0 \\ -1 & 0 & -2 & 0 & 0 & 1 \end{array}\right]$$

STEP 2 Apply row operations to transform A into I_3.

$$R_3 + R_1 \to R_3 \quad \left[\begin{array}{ccc|ccc} 1 & 2 & -1 & 1 & 0 & 0 \\ 0 & 1 & -1 & 0 & 1 & 0 \\ 0 & 2 & -3 & 1 & 0 & 1 \end{array}\right]$$

$$R_3 - 2R_2 \to R_3 \quad \left[\begin{array}{ccc|ccc} 1 & 2 & -1 & 1 & 0 & 0 \\ 0 & 1 & -1 & 0 & 1 & 0 \\ 0 & 0 & -1 & 1 & -2 & 1 \end{array}\right]$$

$$-R_3 \to R_3 \quad \left[\begin{array}{ccc|ccc} 1 & 2 & -1 & 1 & 0 & 0 \\ 0 & 1 & -1 & 0 & 1 & 0 \\ 0 & 0 & 1 & -1 & 2 & -1 \end{array}\right]$$

$$\begin{array}{l} R_2 + R_3 \to R_2 \\ R_1 + R_3 \to R_1 \end{array} \quad \left[\begin{array}{ccc|ccc} 1 & 2 & 0 & 0 & 2 & -1 \\ 0 & 1 & 0 & -1 & 3 & -1 \\ 0 & 0 & 1 & -1 & 2 & -1 \end{array}\right]$$

$$R_1 - 2R_2 \to R_1 \quad \left[\begin{array}{ccc|ccc} 1 & 0 & 0 & 2 & -4 & 1 \\ 0 & 1 & 0 & -1 & 3 & -1 \\ 0 & 0 & 1 & -1 & 2 & -1 \end{array}\right]$$

Identify the inverse.

$$A^{-1} = \begin{bmatrix} 2 & -4 & 1 \\ -1 & 3 & -1 \\ -1 & 2 & -1 \end{bmatrix}$$

STEP 3 Check.

$$AA^{-1} = \begin{bmatrix} 1 & 2 & -1 \\ 0 & 1 & -1 \\ -1 & 0 & -2 \end{bmatrix}\begin{bmatrix} 2 & -4 & 1 \\ -1 & 3 & -1 \\ -1 & 2 & -1 \end{bmatrix} = \begin{bmatrix} 1 & 0 & 0 \\ 0 & 1 & 0 \\ 0 & 0 & 1 \end{bmatrix} = I_3$$

$$A^{-1}A = \begin{bmatrix} 2 & -4 & 1 \\ -1 & 3 & -1 \\ -1 & 2 & -1 \end{bmatrix}\begin{bmatrix} 1 & 2 & -1 \\ 0 & 1 & -1 \\ -1 & 0 & -2 \end{bmatrix} = \begin{bmatrix} 1 & 0 & 0 \\ 0 & 1 & 0 \\ 0 & 0 & 1 \end{bmatrix} = I_3$$

YOUR TURN Find the inverse of $A = \begin{bmatrix} 1 & 1 & 0 \\ -1 & 0 & 1 \\ 2 & 0 & -1 \end{bmatrix}$.

ANSWER

$$A^{-1} = \begin{bmatrix} 0 & 1 & 1 \\ 1 & -1 & -1 \\ 0 & 2 & 1 \end{bmatrix}$$

8.4.6 Solving Systems of Linear Equations Using Matrix Algebra and Inverses of Square Matrices

8.4.6 SKILL

Solve systems of linear equations using inverse matrices.

8.4.6 CONCEPTUAL

Matrix algebra can be used to solve only systems of linear equations that have a unique solution.

We can solve systems of linear equations using matrix algebra. We will use a system of three equations and three variables to demonstrate the procedure. However, it can be extended to any square system (n equations and n variables).

Linear System of Equations

$$a_1x + b_1y + c_1z = d_1$$
$$a_2x + b_2y + c_2z = d_2$$
$$a_3x + b_3y + c_3z = d_3$$

Matrix Form of the System

$$\underbrace{\begin{bmatrix} a_1 & b_1 & c_1 \\ a_2 & b_2 & c_2 \\ a_3 & b_3 & c_3 \end{bmatrix}}_{A} \underbrace{\begin{bmatrix} x \\ y \\ z \end{bmatrix}}_{X} = \underbrace{\begin{bmatrix} d_1 \\ d_2 \\ d_3 \end{bmatrix}}_{B}$$

Recall that a system of linear equations has a unique solution, no solution, or infinitely many solutions. If a system of n equations in n variables has a unique solution, it can be found using the following procedure:

WORDS	MATH
Write the system of linear equations as a matrix equation.	$A_{n\times n} X_{n\times 1} = B_{n\times 1}$
Multiply both sides of the equation by A^{-1}.	$A^{-1}AX = A^{-1}B$
A matrix times its inverse is the identity matrix.	$I_n X = A^{-1}B$
A matrix times the identity matrix is equal to itself.	$X = A^{-1}B$

Notice the order in which the right side is multiplied, $X_{n\times 1} = A^{-1}_{n\times n}B_{n\times 1}$, and remember that matrix multiplication is not commutative. Therefore, you multiply both sides of the matrix equation in the same order.

[CONCEPT CHECK]

TRUE OR FALSE Matrix algebra can be used to solve any system of linear equations.

ANSWER False

SOLVING A SYSTEM OF LINEAR EQUATIONS USING MATRIX ALGEBRA: UNIQUE SOLUTION

If a system of linear equations is represented by the matrix equation $AX = B$, where A is a nonsingular square matrix, then the system has a unique solution given by

$$X = A^{-1}B$$

EXAMPLE 15 Solving a System of Linear Equations Using Matrix Algebra

Solve the system of equations using matrix algebra.

$$\begin{aligned} x + y + z &= 2 \\ x \quad\;\; + z &= 1 \\ x - y - z &= -4 \end{aligned}$$

Solution:

Write the system in matrix form.

$$AX = B$$

$$A = \begin{bmatrix} 1 & 1 & 1 \\ 1 & 0 & 1 \\ 1 & -1 & -1 \end{bmatrix} \quad X = \begin{bmatrix} x \\ y \\ z \end{bmatrix} \quad B = \begin{bmatrix} 2 \\ 1 \\ -4 \end{bmatrix}$$

Find the inverse of A.

Form the matrix $[A \mid I_3]$.

$$\left[\begin{array}{ccc|ccc} 1 & 1 & 1 & 1 & 0 & 0 \\ 1 & 0 & 1 & 0 & 1 & 0 \\ 1 & -1 & -1 & 0 & 0 & 1 \end{array}\right]$$

$$\begin{matrix} R_2 - R_1 \to R_2 \\ R_3 - R_1 \to R_3 \end{matrix} \left[\begin{array}{ccc|ccc} 1 & 1 & 1 & 1 & 0 & 0 \\ 0 & -1 & 0 & -1 & 1 & 0 \\ 0 & -2 & -2 & -1 & 0 & 1 \end{array}\right]$$

$$-R_2 \to R_2 \left[\begin{array}{ccc|ccc} 1 & 1 & 1 & 1 & 0 & 0 \\ 0 & 1 & 0 & 1 & -1 & 0 \\ 0 & -2 & -2 & -1 & 0 & 1 \end{array}\right]$$

$$R_3 + 2R_2 \to R_3 \left[\begin{array}{ccc|ccc} 1 & 1 & 1 & 1 & 0 & 0 \\ 0 & 1 & 0 & 1 & -1 & 0 \\ 0 & 0 & -2 & 1 & -2 & 1 \end{array}\right]$$

$$-\tfrac{1}{2}R_3 \to R_3 \left[\begin{array}{ccc|ccc} 1 & 1 & 1 & 1 & 0 & 0 \\ 0 & 1 & 0 & 1 & -1 & 0 \\ 0 & 0 & 1 & -\frac{1}{2} & 1 & -\frac{1}{2} \end{array}\right]$$

$$R_1 - R_3 \to R_1 \left[\begin{array}{ccc|ccc} 1 & 1 & 0 & \frac{3}{2} & -1 & \frac{1}{2} \\ 0 & 1 & 0 & 1 & -1 & 0 \\ 0 & 0 & 1 & -\frac{1}{2} & 1 & -\frac{1}{2} \end{array}\right]$$

$$R_1 - R_2 \to R_1 \left[\begin{array}{ccc|ccc} 1 & 0 & 0 & \frac{1}{2} & 0 & \frac{1}{2} \\ 0 & 1 & 0 & 1 & -1 & 0 \\ 0 & 0 & 0 & -\frac{1}{2} & 1 & -\frac{1}{2} \end{array}\right]$$

Identify the inverse.

$$A^{-1} = \begin{bmatrix} \frac{1}{2} & 0 & \frac{1}{2} \\ 1 & -1 & 0 \\ -\frac{1}{2} & 1 & -\frac{1}{2} \end{bmatrix}$$

The solution to the system is $X = A^{-1}B$.

$$X = A^{-1}B = \begin{bmatrix} \frac{1}{2} & 0 & \frac{1}{2} \\ 1 & -1 & 0 \\ -\frac{1}{2} & 1 & -\frac{1}{2} \end{bmatrix} \begin{bmatrix} 2 \\ 1 \\ -4 \end{bmatrix}$$

Simplify. $X = \begin{bmatrix} x \\ y \\ z \end{bmatrix} = \begin{bmatrix} -1 \\ 1 \\ 2 \end{bmatrix}$

$\boxed{x = -1, y = 1, z = 2}$

ANSWER

$x = 0, y = 2, z = -1$

YOUR TURN Solve the system of equations using matrix algebra.

$$\begin{aligned} x + y - z &= 3 \\ y + z &= 1 \\ 2x + 3y + z &= 5 \end{aligned}$$

Cryptography Applications

Cryptography is the practice of hiding information, or secret communication. Let's assume you want to send your ATM PIN code over the Internet, but you don't want hackers to be able to retrieve it. You can represent the PIN code in a matrix and then multiply that PIN matrix by a "key" matrix so that it is encrypted. If the person you send it to has the "inverse key" matrix, he can multiply the encrypted matrix he receives by the inverse key matrix, and the result will be the original PIN matrix. Although PIN numbers are typically four digits, we will assume two digits to illustrate the process.

STUDY TIP

$K = \begin{bmatrix} 2 & 3 \\ 5 & 8 \end{bmatrix}$

$K^{-1} = \dfrac{1}{(2)(8) - (3)(5)} \begin{bmatrix} 8 & -3 \\ -5 & 2 \end{bmatrix} = \begin{bmatrix} 8 & -3 \\ -5 & 2 \end{bmatrix}$

WORDS	MATH
Suppose the two-digit ATM PIN is 13.	$P = [1 \quad 3]$
Apply any 2×2 nonsingular matrix as the "key" (encryption) matrix.	$K = \begin{bmatrix} 2 & 3 \\ 5 & 8 \end{bmatrix}$
Multiply the PIN and encryption matrices.	$PK = [1 \quad 3]\begin{bmatrix} 2 & 3 \\ 5 & 8 \end{bmatrix}$
	$= [1(2) + 3(5) \quad 1(3) + 3(8)]$
	$= [17 \quad 27]$
The receiver of the encrypted matrix sees only $[17 \quad 27]$.	
The decoding "key" is the inverse matrix K^{-1}.	$K^{-1} = \begin{bmatrix} 8 & -3 \\ -5 & 2 \end{bmatrix}$

Any receiver who has the decoding key can multiply the received encrypted matrix by the decoding "key" matrix. The result is the original transmitted PIN number.

$$[17 \quad 27]\begin{bmatrix} 8 & -3 \\ -5 & 2 \end{bmatrix} = [17(8) + 27(-5) \quad 17(-3) + 27(2)] = [1 \quad 3]$$

[SECTION 8.4] SUMMARY

Matrices can be used to represent data. Operations such as equality, addition, subtraction, and scalar multiplication are performed entry by entry. Two matrices can be added or subtracted only if they have the same order. Matrix multiplication, however, requires that the number of columns in the first matrix be equal to the number of rows in the second matrix; it is performed using a row-by-column procedure.

Matrix Multiplication Is Not Commutative: $AB \neq BA$

OPERATION	ORDER REQUIREMENT
Equality	Same: $A_{m\times n} = B_{m\times n}$
Addition	Same: $A_{m\times n} + B_{m\times n}$
Subtraction	Same: $A_{m\times n} - B_{m\times n}$
Scalar multiplication	None: $kA_{m\times n}$
Matrix multiplication	$A_{m\times n}B_{n\times p} = (AB)_{m\times p}$

Systems of linear equations can be solved using matrix equations.

SYSTEM OF LINEAR EQUATIONS	A	X	B	MATRIX EQUATION: $AX = B$
$x - y + z = 2$ $2x + 2y - 3z = -3$ $x + y + z = 6$	$\begin{bmatrix} 1 & -1 & 1 \\ 2 & 2 & -3 \\ 1 & 1 & 1 \end{bmatrix}$	$\begin{bmatrix} x \\ y \\ z \end{bmatrix}$	$\begin{bmatrix} 2 \\ -3 \\ 6 \end{bmatrix}$	$\begin{bmatrix} 1 & -1 & 1 \\ 2 & 2 & -3 \\ 1 & 1 & 1 \end{bmatrix}\begin{bmatrix} x \\ y \\ z \end{bmatrix} = \begin{bmatrix} 2 \\ -3 \\ 6 \end{bmatrix}$

If this system of linear equations has a unique solution, then the solution is represented by

$$X = A^{-1}B \text{ (where } A \text{ is a square matrix)}$$

A^{-1} is the inverse of A, that is, $AA^{-1} = A^{-1}A = I$, and is found by

$$[A_{n\times n} \mid I_n] \rightarrow [I_n \mid A^{-1}_{n\times n}]$$

[SECTION 8.4] EXERCISES

• SKILLS

In Exercises 1–8, state the order of each matrix.

1. $\begin{bmatrix} -1 & 2 & 4 \\ 7 & -3 & 9 \end{bmatrix}$

2. $\begin{bmatrix} 3 & 5 \\ 2 & 6 \\ -1 & -4 \end{bmatrix}$

3. $\begin{bmatrix} -4 & 5 \\ 0 & 1 \end{bmatrix}$

4. $\begin{bmatrix} -4 & 5 & 3 & 7 \end{bmatrix}$

5. $\begin{bmatrix} -3 & 4 & 1 \\ 10 & 8 & 0 \\ -2 & 5 & 7 \end{bmatrix}$

6. $\begin{bmatrix} 1 \\ 2 \\ 3 \\ 4 \end{bmatrix}$

7. $\begin{bmatrix} -3 & 6 & 0 & 5 \\ 4 & -9 & 2 & 7 \\ 1 & 8 & 3 & 6 \\ 5 & 0 & -4 & 11 \end{bmatrix}$

8. $\begin{bmatrix} -1 & 3 & 6 & 9 \\ 2 & 5 & -7 & 8 \end{bmatrix}$

In Exercises 9–14, solve for the indicated variables.

9. $\begin{bmatrix} 2 & x \\ y & 3 \end{bmatrix} = \begin{bmatrix} 2 & -5 \\ 1 & 3 \end{bmatrix}$

10. $\begin{bmatrix} -3 & 17 \\ x & y \end{bmatrix} = \begin{bmatrix} -3 & 17 \\ 10 & 12 \end{bmatrix}$

11. $\begin{bmatrix} x+y & 3 \\ x-y & 9 \end{bmatrix} = \begin{bmatrix} -5 & z \\ -1 & 9 \end{bmatrix}$

12. $\begin{bmatrix} x & -4 \\ y & 7 \end{bmatrix} = \begin{bmatrix} 2+y & -4 \\ 5 & 7 \end{bmatrix}$

13. $\begin{bmatrix} 3 & 4 \\ 0 & 12 \end{bmatrix} = \begin{bmatrix} x-y & 4 \\ 0 & 2y+x \end{bmatrix}$

14. $\begin{bmatrix} 9 & 2b+1 \\ -5 & 16 \end{bmatrix} = \begin{bmatrix} a^2 & 9 \\ 2a+1 & b^2 \end{bmatrix}$

In Exercises 15–24, perform the indicated operations for each expression, if possible.

$$A = \begin{bmatrix} -1 & 3 & 0 \\ 2 & 4 & 1 \end{bmatrix} \quad B = \begin{bmatrix} 0 & 2 & 1 \\ 3 & -2 & 4 \end{bmatrix} \quad C = \begin{bmatrix} 0 & 1 \\ 2 & -1 \\ 3 & 1 \end{bmatrix} \quad D = \begin{bmatrix} 2 & -3 \\ 0 & 1 \\ 4 & -2 \end{bmatrix}$$

15. $A + B$ **16.** $C + D$ **17.** $C - D$ **18.** $A - B$ **19.** $B + C$

20. $A + D$ **21.** $D - B$ **22.** $C - A$ **23.** $2A + 3B$ **24.** $2B - 3A$

In Exercises 25–44, perform the indicated operations for each expression, if possible.

$$A = \begin{bmatrix} 1 & 2 & -1 \\ 0 & 3 & 1 \\ 5 & 0 & -2 \end{bmatrix} \quad B = \begin{bmatrix} 2 & 0 & -3 \end{bmatrix} \quad C = \begin{bmatrix} -1 & 7 & 2 \\ 3 & 0 & 1 \end{bmatrix} \quad D = \begin{bmatrix} 3 & 0 \\ 1 & -1 \\ 2 & 5 \end{bmatrix}$$

$$E = \begin{bmatrix} -1 & 0 & 1 \\ 2 & 1 & 4 \\ -3 & 1 & 5 \end{bmatrix} \quad F = \begin{bmatrix} 1 \\ 0 \\ -1 \end{bmatrix} \quad G = \begin{bmatrix} 1 & 2 \\ 3 & 4 \end{bmatrix}$$

25. CD **26.** BF **27.** DC **28.** $(A + E)D$

29. DG **30.** $2A + 3E$ **31.** GD **32.** $ED + C$

33. $-4BD$ **34.** $-3ED$ **35.** $B(A + E)$ **36.** $GC + 5C$

37. $FB + 5A$ **38.** A^2 **39.** $G^2 + 5G$ **40.** $C \cdot (2E)$

41. $(2E) \cdot F$ **42.** $CA + 5C$ **43.** DF **44.** AE

In Exercises 45–50, determine whether *B* is the multiplicative inverse of *A* using $AA^{-1} = I$.

45. $A = \begin{bmatrix} 8 & -11 \\ -5 & 7 \end{bmatrix} \quad B = \begin{bmatrix} 7 & 11 \\ 5 & 8 \end{bmatrix}$

46. $A = \begin{bmatrix} 7 & -9 \\ -3 & 4 \end{bmatrix} \quad B = \begin{bmatrix} 4 & 9 \\ 3 & 7 \end{bmatrix}$

47. $A = \begin{bmatrix} 3 & 1 \\ 1 & -2 \end{bmatrix} \quad B = \begin{bmatrix} \frac{2}{7} & \frac{1}{7} \\ \frac{1}{7} & -\frac{3}{7} \end{bmatrix}$

48. $A = \begin{bmatrix} 2 & 3 \\ 1 & -1 \end{bmatrix} \quad B = \begin{bmatrix} \frac{1}{5} & \frac{3}{5} \\ \frac{1}{5} & -\frac{2}{5} \end{bmatrix}$

49. $A = \begin{bmatrix} 1 & -1 & 1 \\ 1 & 0 & -1 \\ 0 & 1 & -1 \end{bmatrix} \quad B = \begin{bmatrix} 1 & 0 & 1 \\ 1 & -1 & 2 \\ 1 & -1 & 1 \end{bmatrix}$

50. $A = \begin{bmatrix} -1 & 0 & -1 \\ -1 & 1 & -2 \\ -1 & 1 & -1 \end{bmatrix} \quad B = \begin{bmatrix} -1 & 1 & -1 \\ -1 & 0 & 1 \\ 0 & -1 & 1 \end{bmatrix}$

In Exercises 51–62, find A^{-1}, if possible.

51. $A = \begin{bmatrix} 2 & 1 \\ -1 & 0 \end{bmatrix}$

52. $A = \begin{bmatrix} 3 & 1 \\ 2 & 1 \end{bmatrix}$

53. $A = \begin{bmatrix} \frac{1}{3} & 2 \\ 5 & \frac{3}{4} \end{bmatrix}$

54. $A = \begin{bmatrix} \frac{1}{4} & 2 \\ \frac{1}{3} & \frac{2}{3} \end{bmatrix}$

55. $A = \begin{bmatrix} 1 & 1 & 1 \\ 1 & -1 & -1 \\ -1 & 1 & -1 \end{bmatrix}$

56. $A = \begin{bmatrix} 1 & -1 & 1 \\ 1 & 1 & 1 \\ -1 & 2 & -3 \end{bmatrix}$

57. $A = \begin{bmatrix} 1 & 0 & 1 \\ 0 & 1 & 1 \\ 1 & -1 & 0 \end{bmatrix}$

58. $A = \begin{bmatrix} 1 & 2 & -3 \\ 1 & -1 & -1 \\ 1 & 0 & -4 \end{bmatrix}$

59. $A = \begin{bmatrix} 2 & 4 & 1 \\ 1 & 1 & -1 \\ 1 & 1 & 0 \end{bmatrix}$

60. $A = \begin{bmatrix} 1 & 0 & 1 \\ 1 & 1 & -1 \\ 2 & 1 & -1 \end{bmatrix}$

61. $A = \begin{bmatrix} 1 & 1 & -1 \\ 1 & -1 & 1 \\ 2 & -1 & -1 \end{bmatrix}$

62. $A = \begin{bmatrix} 1 & -1 & -1 \\ 1 & 1 & -3 \\ 3 & -5 & 1 \end{bmatrix}$

In Exercises 63–74, apply matrix algebra to solve the system of linear equations.

63. $\begin{aligned} 2x - y &= 5 \\ x + y &= 1 \end{aligned}$

64. $\begin{aligned} 2x - 3y &= 12 \\ x + y &= 1 \end{aligned}$

65. $\begin{aligned} 4x - 9y &= -1 \\ 7x - 3y &= \tfrac{5}{2} \end{aligned}$

66. $\begin{aligned} 7x - 3y &= 1 \\ 4x - 5y &= -\tfrac{7}{5} \end{aligned}$

67. $\begin{aligned} x + y + z &= 1 \\ x - y - z &= -1 \\ -x + y - z &= -1 \end{aligned}$

68. $\begin{aligned} x - y + z &= 0 \\ x + y + z &= 2 \\ -x + 2y - 3z &= 1 \end{aligned}$

69. $\begin{aligned} x \quad + z &= 3 \\ y + z &= 1 \\ x - y \quad &= 2 \end{aligned}$

70. $\begin{aligned} x + 2y - 3z &= 1 \\ x - y - z &= 3 \\ x \quad - 4z &= 0 \end{aligned}$

71. $\begin{aligned} 2x + 4y + z &= -5 \\ x + y - z &= 7 \\ x + y \quad &= 0 \end{aligned}$

72. $\begin{aligned} x \quad + z &= 3 \\ x + y - z &= -3 \\ 2x + y - z &= -5 \end{aligned}$

73. $\begin{aligned} x + y - z &= 4 \\ x - y + z &= 2 \\ 2x - y - z &= -3 \end{aligned}$

74. $\begin{aligned} x - y - z &= 0 \\ x + y - 3z &= 2 \\ 3x - 5y + z &= 4 \end{aligned}$

• APPLICATIONS

75. Smoking. On January 6 and 10, 2000, the Harris Poll conducted a survey of adult smokers in the United States. When asked, "Have you ever tried to quit smoking?", 70% said yes and 30% said no. Write a 2×1 matrix—call it A—that represents those smokers. When asked what consequences smoking would have on their lives, 89% believed it would increase their chance of getting lung cancer and 84% believed smoking would shorten their lives. Write a 2×1 matrix—call it B—that represents those smokers. Say there are 46 million adult smokers in the United States.

a. What does $46A$ tell us?

b. What does $46B$ tell us?

76. Women in Science. According to a study of science and engineering indicators by the National Science Foundation (www.nsf.gov), the number of female graduate students in science and engineering disciplines has increased over the last 30 years. In 1981, 24% of mathematics graduate students were female and 23% of graduate students in computer science were female. In 1991, 32% of mathematics graduate students and 21% of computer science graduate students were female. In 2001, 38% of mathematics graduate students and 30% of computer science graduate students were female. Write three 2×1 matrices representing the percentage of female graduate students.

$$A = \begin{bmatrix} \text{\% female–math–1981} \\ \text{\% female–C.S.–1981} \end{bmatrix}$$

$$B = \begin{bmatrix} \text{\% female–math–1991} \\ \text{\% female–C.S.–1991} \end{bmatrix}$$

$$C = \begin{bmatrix} \text{\% female–math–2001} \\ \text{\% female–C.S.–2001} \end{bmatrix}$$

What does $C - B$ tell us? What does $B - A$ tell us? What can you conclude about the number of women pursuing mathematics and computer science graduate degrees?

Note: C.S. = computer science.

77. Registered Voters. According to the U.S. Census Bureau (www.census.gov), in the 2000 national election, 58.9% of men over the age of 18 were registered voters, but only 41.4% voted; and 62.8% of women over 18 were registered voters, but only 43% voted. Write a 2×2 matrix with the following data:

$$A = \begin{bmatrix} \text{Percentage of registered male voters} & \text{Percentage of registered female voters} \\ \text{Percent of males who voted} & \text{Percent of females who voted} \end{bmatrix}$$

If we let B be a 2×1 matrix representing the total population of males and females over the age of 18 in the United States, or $B = \begin{bmatrix} 100 \text{ M} \\ 110 \text{ M} \end{bmatrix}$, what does AB tell us?

78. Job Application. A company has two rubrics for scoring job applicants based on weighting education, experience, and the interview differently.

Matrix A

	Rubric 1	Rubric 2
Education	0.5	0.6
Experience	0.3	0.1
Interview	0.2	0.3

Applicants receive a score from 1 to 10 in each category (education, experience, and interview). Two applicants are shown in matrix B.

Matrix B

	Education	Experience	Interview
Applicant 1	8	7	5
Applicant 2	6	8	8

What is the order of BA? What does each entry in BA tell us?

79. **Taxes.** The IRS allows an individual to deduct business expenses in the following way: \$0.45 per mile driven, 50% of entertainment costs, and 100% of actual expenses. Represent these deductions in the given order as a row matrix A. In 2006, Jamie had the following business expenses: \$2700 entertainment and \$15,200 actual expenses, and he drove 7523 miles. Represent Jamie's expenses in the given order as a column matrix B. Multiply these two matrices to find the total amount of business expenses Jamie can claim on his 2006 federal tax form: AB.

80. **Tips on Service.** Marilyn decides to go to the Safety Harbor Spa for a day of pampering. She is treated to a hot stone massage (\$85), a manicure and pedicure (\$75), and a haircut (\$100). Represent the costs of the individual services as a row matrix A (in the given order). She decides to tip her masseur 25%, her nail tech 20%, and her hair stylist 15%. Represent the tipping percentages as a column matrix B (in the given order). Multiply these matrices to find the total amount in tips AB she needs to add to her final bill.

Use the following tables for Exercises 81 and 82:

The following table gives fuel and electric requirements per mile associated with gasoline and electric automobiles:

	NUMBER OF GALLONS/MILE	NUMBER OF kW-hr/MILE
SUV full size	0.06	0
Hybrid car	0.02	0.1
Electric car	0	0.3

The following table gives an average cost for gasoline and electricity:

Cost per gallon of gasoline	\$3.80
Cost per kW-hr of electricity	\$0.05

81. **Environment.** Let matrix A represent the gasoline and electricity consumption and matrix B represent the costs of gasoline and electricity. Find AB and describe what the elements of the product matrix represent. *Hint:* A has order 3×2 and B has order 2×1.

82. **Environment.** Assume you drive 12,000 miles per year. What are the yearly costs associated with driving the three types of cars in Exercise 81?

For Exercises 83 and 84, refer to the following:

The results of a nutritional analysis of one serving of three foods A, B, and C were

$$\begin{array}{c} \\ X = \end{array} \begin{array}{ccc} \text{Carbohydrates (g)} & \text{Protein (g)} & \text{Fat (g)} \\ \end{array}$$

$$X = \begin{bmatrix} 5 & 0 & 2 \\ 5 & 6 & 5 \\ 8 & 4 & 4 \end{bmatrix} \begin{matrix} \text{A} \\ \text{B} \\ \text{C} \end{matrix}$$

It is possible to find the nutritional content of a meal consisting of a combination of the foods A, B, and C by multiplying the matrix X by a second matrix $N = \begin{bmatrix} r \\ s \\ t \end{bmatrix}$, that is, XN, where r is the number of servings of food A, s is the number of servings of food B, and t is the number of servings of food C.

83. **Health/Nutrition.** Find the matrix N that represents a meal consisting of two servings of food A and one serving of food B. Find the nutritional content of that meal.

84. **Health/Nutrition.** Find the matrix N that represents a meal consisting of one serving of food A and two servings of food C. Find the nutritional content of that meal.

For Exercises 85 and 86, refer to the following:

Cell phone companies charge users based on the number of minutes talked, the number of text messages sent, and the number of megabytes of data used. The costs for three cell phone providers are given in the following table:

	MINUTES	TEXT MESSAGES	MEGABYTES OF DATA
C_1	\$0.04	\$0.05	\$0.15
C_2	\$0.06	\$0.05	\$0.18
C_3	\$0.07	\$0.07	\$0.13

It is possible to find the cost to a cell phone user for each of the three providers by creating a matrix X whose rows are the rows of data in the table and multiplying the matrix X by a second matrix $N = \begin{bmatrix} m \\ t \\ d \end{bmatrix}$, that is, XN, where m is the number of minutes talked, t is the number of text messages sent, and d is the megabytes of data used.

85. **Telecommunications/Business.** A local business is looking at providing an employee a cell phone for business use. Find the matrix N that represents expected normal cell phone usage of 200 minutes, 25 text messages, and no data usage. Find and interpret XN. Which is the best cell phone provider for this employee?

86. **Telecommunications/Business.** A local business is looking at providing an employee a cell phone for business use. Find the matrix N that represents expected normal cell phone usage of 125 minutes, 125 text messages, and 320 megabytes of data usage. Find and interpret XN. Which is the best cell phone provider for this employee?

For Exercises 87–92, apply the following decoding scheme:

1	A	10	J	19	S
2	B	11	K	20	T
3	C	12	L	21	U
4	D	13	M	22	V
5	E	14	N	23	W
6	F	15	O	24	X
7	G	16	P	25	Y
8	H	17	Q	26	Z
9	I	18	R		

The encoding matrix is $\begin{bmatrix} 1 & 1 & 0 \\ -1 & 0 & 1 \\ 2 & 0 & -1 \end{bmatrix}$. The encrypted matrices are given below. For each of the following, determine the 3-letter word that is originally transmitted. *Hint:* All six words are parts of the body.

87. Cryptography. $[55 \quad 10 \quad -22]$

88. Cryptography. $[31 \quad 8 \quad -7]$

89. Cryptography. $[21 \quad 12 \quad -2]$

90. Cryptography. $[9 \quad 1 \quad 5]$

91. Cryptography. $[-10 \quad 5 \quad 20]$

92. Cryptography. $[40 \quad 5 \quad -17]$

For Exercises 93 and 94, refer to the following:

The results of a nutritional analysis of one serving of three foods A, B, and C follow.

$$\begin{array}{cccc} & \text{Carbohydrates (g)} & \text{Protein (g)} & \text{Fat (g)} \\ Y = & \left[\begin{array}{c} 8 \\ 6 \\ 10 \end{array}\right. & \begin{array}{c} 4 \\ 10 \\ 4 \end{array} & \left.\begin{array}{c} 6 \\ 5 \\ 8 \end{array}\right] \begin{array}{c} \text{A} \\ \text{B} \\ \text{C} \end{array} \end{array}$$

The nutritional content of a meal consisting of a combination of the foods A, B, and C is the product of the matrix Y and a second matrix $N = \begin{bmatrix} r \\ s \\ t \end{bmatrix}$, that is, YN, where r is the number of servings of food A, s is the number of servings of food B, and t is the number of servings of food C.

93. Health/Nutrition. Use the inverse matrix technique to find the number of servings of foods A, B, and C necessary to create a meal of 18 grams of carbohydrates, 21 grams of protein, and 22 grams of fat.

94. Health/Nutrition. Use the inverse matrix technique to find the number of servings of foods A, B, and C necessary to create a meal of 14 grams of carbohydrates, 25 grams of protein, and 16 grams of fat.

• CATCH THE MISTAKE

In Exercises 95–98, explain the mistake that is made.

95. Multiply $\begin{bmatrix} 3 & 2 \\ 1 & 4 \end{bmatrix}\begin{bmatrix} -1 & 3 \\ -2 & 5 \end{bmatrix}$.

Solution:

Multiply corresponding elements.

$$\begin{bmatrix} 3 & 2 \\ 1 & 4 \end{bmatrix}\begin{bmatrix} -1 & 3 \\ -2 & 5 \end{bmatrix} = \begin{bmatrix} (3)(-1) & (2)(3) \\ (1)(-2) & (4)(5) \end{bmatrix}$$

Simplify. $\begin{bmatrix} 3 & 2 \\ 1 & 4 \end{bmatrix}\begin{bmatrix} -1 & 3 \\ -2 & 5 \end{bmatrix} = \begin{bmatrix} -3 & 6 \\ -2 & 20 \end{bmatrix}$

This is incorrect. What mistake was made?

96. Multiply $\begin{bmatrix} 3 & 2 \\ 1 & 4 \end{bmatrix}\begin{bmatrix} -1 & 3 \\ -2 & 5 \end{bmatrix}$.

Solution:

Multiply using the column-by-row method.

$$\begin{bmatrix} 3 & 2 \\ 1 & 4 \end{bmatrix}\begin{bmatrix} -1 & 3 \\ -2 & 5 \end{bmatrix} = \begin{bmatrix} (3)(-1) + (1)(3) & (2)(-1) + (4)(3) \\ (3)(-2) + (1)(5) & (2)(-2) + (4)(5) \end{bmatrix}$$

Simplify. $\begin{bmatrix} 3 & 2 \\ 1 & 4 \end{bmatrix}\begin{bmatrix} -1 & 3 \\ -2 & 5 \end{bmatrix} = \begin{bmatrix} 0 & 10 \\ -1 & 16 \end{bmatrix}$

This is incorrect. What mistake was made?

97. Find the inverse of $A = \begin{bmatrix} 1 & 0 & 1 \\ -1 & 0 & -1 \\ 1 & 2 & 0 \end{bmatrix}$.

Solution:

Write the matrix $[A \mid I_3]$. $\left[\begin{array}{ccc|ccc} 1 & 0 & 1 & 1 & 0 & 0 \\ -1 & 0 & -1 & 0 & 1 & 0 \\ 1 & 2 & 0 & 0 & 0 & 1 \end{array}\right]$

Use Gaussian elimination to reduce A.

$\begin{array}{l} R_2 + R_1 \to R_2 \\ R_3 - R_1 \to R_3 \end{array}$ $\left[\begin{array}{ccc|ccc} 1 & 0 & 1 & 1 & 0 & 0 \\ 0 & 0 & 0 & 1 & 1 & 0 \\ 0 & 2 & -1 & -1 & 0 & 1 \end{array}\right]$

$R_2 \leftrightarrow R_3$ $\left[\begin{array}{ccc|ccc} 1 & 0 & 1 & 1 & 0 & 0 \\ 0 & 2 & -1 & -1 & 0 & 1 \\ 0 & 0 & 0 & 1 & 1 & 0 \end{array}\right]$

$\frac{1}{2}R_2 \to R_2$ $\left[\begin{array}{ccc|ccc} 1 & 0 & 1 & 1 & 0 & 0 \\ 0 & 1 & -\frac{1}{2} & -\frac{1}{2} & 0 & \frac{1}{2} \\ 0 & 0 & 0 & 1 & 1 & 0 \end{array}\right]$

$A^{-1} = \begin{bmatrix} 1 & 0 & 0 \\ -\frac{1}{2} & 0 & \frac{1}{2} \\ 1 & 1 & 0 \end{bmatrix}$ is incorrect because $AA^{-1} \neq I_3$.

What mistake was made?

98. Find the inverse of A given that $A = \begin{bmatrix} 2 & 5 \\ 3 & 10 \end{bmatrix}$.

Solution: $A^{-1} = \dfrac{1}{A} \quad A^{-1} = \dfrac{1}{\begin{bmatrix} 2 & 5 \\ 3 & 10 \end{bmatrix}}$

Simplify. $A^{-1} = \begin{bmatrix} \frac{1}{2} & \frac{1}{5} \\ \frac{1}{3} & \frac{1}{10} \end{bmatrix}$

This is incorrect. What mistake was made?

• CONCEPTUAL

In Exercises 99–104, determine whether the statements are true or false.

99. If $A = \begin{bmatrix} a_{11} & a_{12} \\ a_{21} & a_{22} \end{bmatrix}$ and $B = \begin{bmatrix} b_{11} & b_{12} \\ b_{21} & b_{22} \end{bmatrix}$, then $AB = \begin{bmatrix} a_{11}b_{11} & a_{12}b_{12} \\ a_{21}b_{21} & a_{22}b_{22} \end{bmatrix}$.

100. If AB is defined, then $AB = BA$.

101. AB is defined only if the number of columns in A equals the number of rows in B.

102. $A + B$ is defined only if A and B have the same order.

103. If $A = \begin{bmatrix} a_{11} & a_{12} \\ a_{21} & a_{22} \end{bmatrix}$, then $A^{-1} = \begin{bmatrix} \frac{1}{a_{11}} & \frac{1}{a_{12}} \\ \frac{1}{a_{21}} & \frac{1}{a_{22}} \end{bmatrix}$.

104. All square matrices have inverses.

105. For $A = \begin{bmatrix} a_{11} & a_{12} \\ a_{21} & a_{22} \end{bmatrix}$, find A^2.

106. In order for $A^2_{m \times n}$ to be defined, what condition (with respect to m and n) must be met?

107. For what values of x does the inverse of A not exist, given $A = \begin{bmatrix} x & 6 \\ 3 & 2 \end{bmatrix}$?

108. Let $A = \begin{bmatrix} a & 0 & 0 \\ 0 & b & 0 \\ 0 & 0 & c \end{bmatrix}$. Find A^{-1}. Assume $abc \neq 0$.

• CHALLENGE

109. For $A = \begin{bmatrix} 1 & 1 \\ 1 & 1 \end{bmatrix}$ find $A, A^2, A^3, \ldots$. What is A^n?

110. For $A = \begin{bmatrix} 1 & 0 \\ 0 & 1 \end{bmatrix}$ find $A, A^2, A^3, \ldots$. What is A^n?

111. If $A_{m \times n} B_{n \times p}$ is defined, explain why $(A_{m \times n} B_{n \times p})^2$ is not defined for $m \neq p$.

112. Given $C_{n \times m}$ and $A_{m \times n} = B_{m \times n}$, explain why $AC \neq CB$, if $m \neq n$.

113. Verify that $A^{-1} = \frac{1}{ad - bc}\begin{bmatrix} d & -b \\ -c & a \end{bmatrix}$ is the inverse of $A = \begin{bmatrix} a & b \\ c & d \end{bmatrix}$, provided $ad - bc \neq 0$.

114. Let $A = \begin{bmatrix} a & b \\ c & d \end{bmatrix}$ and form the matrix $[A \mid I_2]$. Apply row operations to transform into $[I_2 \mid A^{-1}]$. Show $A^{-1} = \frac{1}{ad - bc}\begin{bmatrix} d & -b \\ -c & a \end{bmatrix}$ such that $ad - bc \neq 0$.

115. Why does the square matrix $A = \begin{bmatrix} 2 & 3 \\ 4 & 6 \end{bmatrix}$ not have an inverse?

116. Why does the square matrix $A = \begin{bmatrix} 1 & 2 & -1 \\ 2 & 4 & -2 \\ 0 & 1 & 3 \end{bmatrix}$ not have an inverse?

• PREVIEW TO CALCULUS

In calculus, when finding the inverse of a vector function, it is fundamental that the matrix of partial derivatives not be singular.

In Exercises 117–120, find the inverse of each matrix.

117. $\begin{bmatrix} 2x & 2y \\ 2x & -2y \end{bmatrix}$

118. $\begin{bmatrix} 1 & 1 \\ uy & ux \end{bmatrix}$

119. $\begin{bmatrix} \cos\theta & \sin\theta \\ -\sin\theta & \cos\theta \end{bmatrix}$

120. $\begin{bmatrix} \cos\theta & -r\sin\theta & 0 \\ \sin\theta & r\cos\theta & 0 \\ 0 & 0 & 1 \end{bmatrix}$

8.5 THE DETERMINANT OF A SQUARE MATRIX AND CRAMER'S RULE

SKILLS OBJECTIVES

- Find the determinant of a 2×2 matrix.
- Find the determinant of an $n \times n$ matrix.
- Use Cramer's rule to solve a square system of linear equations in two variables.
- Use Cramer's rule to solve a square system of linear equations in three variables.

CONCEPTUAL OBJECTIVES

- Understand that only a square matrix has a determinant.
- Understand that it does not matter which row or which column is chosen to expand the determinant.
- Derive Cramer's rule.
- Recognize that if the determinant of the coefficient matrix is equal to zero, then the system has no unique solution.

In Section 8.3, we discussed Gauss–Jordan elimination as a way to solve systems of linear equations using augmented matrices. Then in Section 8.4, we employed matrix algebra and inverses to solve systems of linear equations that are square (same number of equations as variables). In this section, we will describe another method, called Cramer's rule, for solving systems of linear equations. Cramer's rule is applicable only to square systems. *Determinants* of square matrices play a vital role in Cramer's rule and indicate whether a matrix has an inverse.

8.5.1 Determinant of a 2 × 2 Matrix

Every square matrix A has a number associated with it called its *determinant*, which is denoted $\det(A)$ or $|A|$.

8.5.1 SKILL

Find the determinant of a 2×2 matrix.

8.5.1 CONCEPTUAL

Understand that only a square matrix has a determinant.

DEFINITION **Determinant of a 2 × 2 Matrix**

The **determinant** of the 2×2 matrix $A = \begin{bmatrix} a & b \\ c & d \end{bmatrix}$ is given by

$$\det(A) = |A| = \begin{vmatrix} a & b \\ c & d \end{vmatrix} = ad - bc$$

Although the symbol for determinant, $|\,|$, looks like absolute value bars, the determinant can be any real number (positive, negative, or zero). The determinant of a 2×2 matrix is found by finding the product of the main diagonal entries (top left to bottom right) and subtracting the product of the entries along the other diagonal (bottom left to top right).

STUDY TIP

The determinant of a 2×2 matrix is found by finding the product of the main diagonal entries and subtracting the product of the other diagonal entries.

$$\begin{vmatrix} a & b \\ c & d \end{vmatrix} = ad - bc$$

EXAMPLE 1 **Finding the Determinant of a 2 × 2 Matrix**

Find the determinant of each matrix.

a. $\begin{bmatrix} 2 & -5 \\ -1 & 3 \end{bmatrix}$ **b.** $\begin{bmatrix} 0.5 & 0.2 \\ -3 & -4.2 \end{bmatrix}$ **c.** $\begin{bmatrix} \frac{2}{3} & 1 \\ 2 & 3 \end{bmatrix}$

Solution:

a. $\begin{vmatrix} 2 & -5 \\ -1 & 3 \end{vmatrix} = (2)(3) - (-1)(-5) = 6 - 5 = \boxed{1}$

b. $\begin{vmatrix} 0.5 & 0.2 \\ -3 & -4.2 \end{vmatrix} = (0.5)(-4.2) - (-3)(0.2) = -2.1 + 0.6 = \boxed{-1.5}$

c. $\begin{vmatrix} \frac{2}{3} & 1 \\ 2 & 3 \end{vmatrix} = \left(\frac{2}{3}\right)(3) - (2)(1) = 2 - 2 = \boxed{0}$

In Example 1, we see that determinants are real numbers that can be positive, negative, or zero. Although evaluating determinants of 2 × 2 matrices is a simple process, one **common mistake** is reversing the difference: $\begin{vmatrix} a & b \\ c & d \end{vmatrix} \neq bc - ad$.

[CONCEPT CHECK]

A determinant of a 2 × 2 matrix can be positive, negative, or zero.

ANSWER True

YOUR TURN Evaluate the determinant $\begin{vmatrix} -2 & 1 \\ -3 & 2 \end{vmatrix}$.

ANSWER
−1

8.5.2 Determinant of an $n \times n$ Matrix

8.5.2 SKILL

Find the determinant of an $n \times n$ matrix.

8.5.2 CONCEPTUAL

Understand that it does not matter which row or which column is chosen to expand the determinant.

To define the *determinant* of a 3 × 3 or a general $n \times n$ (where $n \geq 3$) matrix, we first define *minors* and *cofactors* of a square matrix.

DEFINITION **Minor and Cofactor**

Let A be a square matrix of order $n \times n$. Then:

- The **minor** M_{ij} of the entry a_{ij} is the determinant of the $(n-1) \times (n-1)$ matrix obtained when the ith row and jth column of A are deleted.
- The **cofactor** C_{ij} of the entry a_{ij} is given by $C_{ij} = (-1)^{i+j} M_{ij}$.

The following table illustrates entries, minors, and cofactors of the matrix

$$A = \begin{bmatrix} 1 & -3 & 2 \\ 4 & -1 & 0 \\ 5 & -2 & 3 \end{bmatrix}$$

ENTRY a_{ij}	MINOR M_{ij}	COFACTOR C_{ij}
$a_{11} = 1$	For M_{11}, delete the first row and first column: $\begin{bmatrix} 1 & -3 & 2 \\ 4 & -1 & 0 \\ 5 & -2 & 3 \end{bmatrix}$ $M_{11} = \begin{vmatrix} -1 & 0 \\ -2 & 3 \end{vmatrix} = -3 - 0 = -3$	$C_{11} = (-1)^{1+1}M_{11}$ $= (1)(-3)$ $= -3$
$a_{32} = -2$	For M_{32}, delete the third row and second column: $\begin{bmatrix} 1 & -3 & 2 \\ 4 & -1 & 0 \\ 5 & -2 & 3 \end{bmatrix}$ $M_{32} = \begin{vmatrix} 1 & 2 \\ 4 & 0 \end{vmatrix} = 0 - 8 = -8$	$C_{32} = (-1)^{3+2}M_{32}$ $= (-1)(-8)$ $= 8$

Notice that the cofactor is simply the minor multiplied by either 1 or -1, depending on whether $i + j$ is even or odd. Therefore, we can make the following sign pattern for 3×3 and 4×4 matrices and obtain the cofactor by multiplying the minor with the appropriate sign ($+1$ or -1):

$$\begin{bmatrix} + & - & + \\ - & + & - \\ + & - & + \end{bmatrix} \qquad \begin{bmatrix} + & - & + & - \\ - & + & - & + \\ + & - & + & - \\ - & + & - & + \end{bmatrix}$$

DEFINITION Determinant of an $n \times n$ Matrix

Let A be an $n \times n$ matrix. Then the **determinant** of A is found by summing the entries in *any* row of A (or column of A) multiplied by each entry's respective cofactor.

If A is a 3×3 matrix, the determinant can be given by

$$\det(A) = a_{11}C_{11} + a_{12}C_{12} + a_{13}C_{13}$$

This is called **expanding the determinant by the first row**. It is important to note that any row or column can be used. Typically, the row or column with the most zeros is selected because it makes the arithmetic simpler.

Combining the definitions of minors, cofactors, and determinants, we now give a general definition for the determinant of a 3×3 matrix.

Row 1 expansion: $\begin{vmatrix} a_1 & b_1 & c_1 \\ a_2 & b_2 & c_2 \\ a_3 & b_3 & c_3 \end{vmatrix} = a_1\begin{vmatrix} b_2 & c_2 \\ b_3 & c_3 \end{vmatrix} - b_1\begin{vmatrix} a_2 & c_2 \\ a_3 & c_3 \end{vmatrix} + c_1\begin{vmatrix} a_2 & b_2 \\ a_3 & b_3 \end{vmatrix}$

Column 1 expansion: $\begin{vmatrix} a_1 & b_1 & c_1 \\ a_2 & b_2 & c_2 \\ a_3 & b_3 & c_3 \end{vmatrix} = a_1\begin{vmatrix} b_2 & c_2 \\ b_3 & c_3 \end{vmatrix} - a_2\begin{vmatrix} b_1 & c_1 \\ b_3 & c_3 \end{vmatrix} + a_3\begin{vmatrix} b_1 & c_1 \\ b_2 & c_2 \end{vmatrix}$

Whichever row or column is expanded, an alternating sign scheme is used (see sign arrays above). Notice that in either of the expansions above, each 2×2 determinant obtained is found by crossing out the row and column containing the entry that is multiplying the determinant.

EXAMPLE 2 Finding the Determinant of a 3 × 3 Matrix

For the given matrix, expand the determinant by the *first row*.

$$\begin{bmatrix} 2 & 1 & 3 \\ -1 & 5 & -2 \\ -3 & 7 & 4 \end{bmatrix}$$

Solution:

Expand the determinant by the **first** row. Remember the alternating **sign**.

$$\begin{vmatrix} 2 & 1 & 3 \\ -1 & 5 & -2 \\ -3 & 7 & 4 \end{vmatrix} = +2\begin{vmatrix} 5 & -2 \\ 7 & 4 \end{vmatrix} - 1\begin{vmatrix} -1 & -2 \\ -3 & 4 \end{vmatrix} + 3\begin{vmatrix} -1 & 5 \\ -3 & 7 \end{vmatrix}$$

Evaluate the resulting 2 × 2 determinants.

$$= 2[(5)(4) - (7)(-2)] - 1[(-1)(4) - (-3)(-2)] + 3[(-1)(7) - (-3)(5)]$$

$$= 2[20 + 14] - [-4 - 6] + 3[-7 + 15]$$

Simplify.

$$= 2(34) - (-10) + 3(8)$$

$$= 68 + 10 + 24$$

$$= \boxed{102}$$

STUDY TIP

The determinant by the third column is also 102. It does not matter on which row or column the expansion occurs.

YOUR TURN For the given matrix, expand the determinant by the first row.

$$\begin{bmatrix} 1 & 3 & -2 \\ 2 & 5 & 4 \\ 7 & -1 & 6 \end{bmatrix}$$

ANSWER

156

Determinants can be expanded by any row *or* column. Typically, the row or column with the most zeros is selected to simplify the arithmetic.

EXAMPLE 3 Finding the Determinant of a 3 × 3 Matrix

Find the determinant of the matrix $\begin{vmatrix} -1 & 2 & 0 \\ 4 & 7 & 1 \\ 5 & 3 & 0 \end{vmatrix}$.

Solution:

Since there are two 0s in the third column, expand the determinant by the third column. Recall the sign array.

$$\begin{bmatrix} + & - & + \\ - & + & - \\ + & - & + \end{bmatrix}$$

$$\begin{vmatrix} -1 & 2 & 0 \\ 4 & 7 & 1 \\ 5 & 3 & 0 \end{vmatrix} = +0\begin{vmatrix} 4 & 7 \\ 5 & 3 \end{vmatrix} - 1\begin{vmatrix} -1 & 2 \\ 5 & 3 \end{vmatrix} + 0\begin{vmatrix} -1 & 2 \\ 4 & 7 \end{vmatrix}$$

There is no need to calculate the two determinants that are multiplied by 0s, since 0 times any real number is zero.

$$\begin{vmatrix} -1 & 2 & 0 \\ 4 & 7 & 1 \\ 5 & 3 & 0 \end{vmatrix} = 0 - 1\underbrace{\begin{vmatrix} -1 & 2 \\ 5 & 3 \end{vmatrix}}_{-3-10} + 0$$

Simplify.

$$= -1(-13) = \boxed{13}$$

YOUR TURN Evaluate the determinant $\begin{vmatrix} 1 & -2 & 1 \\ -1 & 0 & 3 \\ -4 & 0 & 2 \end{vmatrix}$.

ANSWER

20

EXAMPLE 4 Finding the Determinant of a 4 × 4 Matrix

Find the determinant of the matrix $\begin{vmatrix} 1 & -2 & 3 & 4 \\ -4 & 0 & -1 & 0 \\ -3 & 9 & 6 & 5 \\ -5 & 7 & 2 & 1 \end{vmatrix}$.

Solution:

Since there are two 0s in the second row, expand the determinant by the second row. Recall the sign array for a 4 × 4 matrix.

$$\begin{bmatrix} + & - & + & - \\ - & + & - & + \\ + & - & + & - \\ - & + & - & + \end{bmatrix}$$

$$\begin{bmatrix} 1 & -2 & 3 & 4 \\ -4 & 0 & -1 & 0 \\ -3 & 9 & 6 & 5 \\ -5 & 7 & 2 & 1 \end{bmatrix} = -(-4)\begin{vmatrix} -2 & 3 & 4 \\ 9 & 6 & 5 \\ 7 & 2 & 1 \end{vmatrix} + 0 - (-1)\begin{vmatrix} 1 & -2 & 4 \\ -3 & 9 & 5 \\ -5 & 7 & 1 \end{vmatrix} + 0$$

Evaluate the two 3 × 3 determinants.

$$\begin{aligned} \begin{vmatrix} -2 & 3 & 4 \\ 9 & 6 & 5 \\ 7 & 2 & 1 \end{vmatrix} &= -2\begin{vmatrix} 6 & 5 \\ 2 & 1 \end{vmatrix} - 3\begin{vmatrix} 9 & 5 \\ 7 & 1 \end{vmatrix} + 4\begin{vmatrix} 9 & 6 \\ 7 & 2 \end{vmatrix} \\ &= -2(6 - 10) - 3(9 - 35) + 4(18 - 42) \\ &= -2(-4) - 3(-26) + 4(-24) \\ &= 8 + 78 - 96 \\ &= -10 \end{aligned}$$

$$\begin{aligned} \begin{vmatrix} 1 & -2 & 4 \\ -3 & 9 & 5 \\ -5 & 7 & 1 \end{vmatrix} &= 1\begin{vmatrix} 9 & 5 \\ 7 & 1 \end{vmatrix} - (-2)\begin{vmatrix} -3 & 5 \\ -5 & 1 \end{vmatrix} + 4\begin{vmatrix} -3 & 9 \\ -5 & 7 \end{vmatrix} \\ &= 1(9 - 35) + 2(-3 + 25) + 4(-21 + 45) \\ &= -26 + 2(22) + 4(24) \\ &= -26 + 44 + 96 \\ &= 114 \end{aligned}$$

$$\begin{bmatrix} 1 & -2 & 3 & 4 \\ -4 & 0 & -1 & 0 \\ -3 & 9 & 6 & 5 \\ -5 & 7 & 2 & 1 \end{bmatrix} = 4\underbrace{\begin{vmatrix} -2 & 3 & 4 \\ 9 & 6 & 5 \\ 7 & 2 & 1 \end{vmatrix}}_{-10} + \underbrace{\begin{vmatrix} 1 & -2 & 4 \\ -3 & 9 & 5 \\ -5 & 7 & 1 \end{vmatrix}}_{114} = 4(-10) + 114 = \boxed{74}$$

[CONCEPT CHECK]

TRUE OR FALSE When finding the determinant of an $n \times n$ matrix, only the first row or first column can be chosen for expanding.

ANSWER False

8.5.3 Cramer's Rule: Systems of Linear Equations in Two Variables

8.5.3 SKILL

Use Cramer's rule to solve a square system of linear equations in two variables.

8.5.3 CONCEPTUAL

Derive Cramer's rule.

Let's now apply determinants of 2×2 matrices to solve systems of linear equations in two variables. We begin by solving the general system of two linear equations in two variables:

$$(1) \quad a_1x + b_1y = c_1$$

$$(2) \quad a_2x + b_2y = c_2$$

Solve for x using elimination (eliminate y).

Multiply (1) by b_2. $\qquad b_2a_1x + b_2b_1y = b_2c_1$

Multiply (2) by $-b_1$. $\qquad -b_1a_2x - b_1b_2y = -b_1c_2$

Add the two new equations to eliminate y. $\qquad (a_1b_2 - a_2b_1)x = (b_2c_1 - b_1c_2)$

Divide both sides by $(a_1b_2 - a_2b_1)$. $\qquad x = \dfrac{(b_2c_1 - b_1c_2)}{(a_1b_2 - a_2b_1)}$

Write both the numerator and the denominator as determinants.

$$x = \frac{\begin{vmatrix} c_1 & b_1 \\ c_2 & b_2 \end{vmatrix}}{\begin{vmatrix} a_1 & b_1 \\ a_2 & b_2 \end{vmatrix}}$$

Solve for y using elimination (eliminate x).

Multiply (1) by $-a_2$. $\qquad -a_2a_1x - a_2b_1y = -a_2c_1$

Multiply (2) by a_1. $\qquad a_1a_2x + a_1b_2y = a_1c_2$

Add the two new equations to eliminate x. $\qquad (a_1b_2 - a_2b_1)y = (a_1c_2 - a_2c_1)$

Divide both sides by $(a_1b_2 - a_2b_1)$. $\qquad y = \dfrac{(a_1c_2 - a_2c_1)}{(a_1b_2 - a_2b_1)}$

Write both the numerator and the denominator as determinants.

$$y = \frac{\begin{vmatrix} a_1 & c_1 \\ a_2 & c_2 \end{vmatrix}}{\begin{vmatrix} a_1 & b_1 \\ a_2 & b_2 \end{vmatrix}}$$

The solutions for x and y involve three determinants. If we let

$$D = \begin{vmatrix} a_1 & b_1 \\ a_2 & b_2 \end{vmatrix} \quad D_x = \begin{vmatrix} c_1 & b_1 \\ c_2 & b_2 \end{vmatrix} \quad D_y = \begin{vmatrix} a_1 & c_1 \\ a_2 & c_2 \end{vmatrix},$$

$$\text{then} \quad x = \frac{D_x}{D} \quad \text{and} \quad y = \frac{D_y}{D}.$$

Notice that the real number D is the determinant of the coefficient matrix of the system and cannot equal zero ($D \neq 0$) or there will be no unique solution. These formulas for solving a system of two linear equations in two variables are known as *Cramer's rule*.

CRAMER'S RULE FOR SOLVING SYSTEMS OF TWO LINEAR EQUATIONS IN TWO VARIABLES

For the system of linear equations

$$a_1x + b_1y = c_1$$
$$a_2x + b_2y = c_2$$

let

$$D = \begin{vmatrix} a_1 & b_1 \\ a_2 & b_2 \end{vmatrix} \qquad D_x = \begin{vmatrix} c_1 & b_1 \\ c_2 & b_2 \end{vmatrix} \qquad D_y = \begin{vmatrix} a_1 & c_1 \\ a_2 & c_2 \end{vmatrix}$$

If $D \neq 0$, then the solution to the system of linear equations is

$$x = \frac{D_x}{D} \qquad y = \frac{D_y}{D}$$

If $D = 0$, then the system of linear equations has either no solution or infinitely many solutions.

Notice that the determinants D_x and D_y are similar to the determinant D. A three-step procedure is outlined for setting up the three determinants for a system of two linear equations in two variables:

$$a_1x + b_1y = c_1$$
$$a_2x + b_2y = c_2$$

Step 1: Set up D.

Apply the coefficients of x and y.

$$D = \begin{vmatrix} a_1 & b_1 \\ a_2 & b_2 \end{vmatrix}$$

Step 2: Set up D_x.

Start with D and replace the coefficients of x (column 1) with the constants on the right side of the equal sign.

$$D_x = \begin{vmatrix} c_1 & b_1 \\ c_2 & b_2 \end{vmatrix}$$

Step 3: Set up D_y.

Start with D and replace the coefficients of y (column 2) with the constants on the right side of the equal sign.

$$D_y = \begin{vmatrix} a_1 & c_1 \\ a_2 & c_2 \end{vmatrix}$$

STUDY TIP

Cramer's rule is applicable only to square systems of linear equations.

EXAMPLE 5 Using Cramer's Rule to Solve a System of Two Linear Equations

Apply Cramer's rule to solve the system.

$$\begin{aligned} x + 3y &= 1 \\ 2x + y &= -3 \end{aligned}$$

[CONCEPT CHECK]

Cramer's rule for systems of linear equations in two variables is derived by solving a general system of equations in two variables using the elimination method.

ANSWER True

Solution:

Set up the three determinants.

$$D = \begin{vmatrix} 1 & 3 \\ 2 & 1 \end{vmatrix}$$

$$D_x = \begin{vmatrix} 1 & 3 \\ -3 & 1 \end{vmatrix}$$

$$D_y = \begin{vmatrix} 1 & 1 \\ 2 & -3 \end{vmatrix}$$

Evaluate the determinants.

$$D = 1 - 6 = -5$$

$$D_x = 1 - (-9) = 10$$

$$D_y = -3 - 2 = -5$$

Solve for x and y.

$$x = \frac{D_x}{D} = \frac{10}{-5} = -2$$

$$y = \frac{D_y}{D} = \frac{-5}{-5} = 1$$

$$\boxed{x = -2, y = 1}$$

YOUR TURN Apply Cramer's rule to solve the system.

$$\begin{aligned} 5x + 4y &= 1 \\ -3x - 2y &= -3 \end{aligned}$$

ANSWER
$x = 5, y = -6$

Recall from Section 8.1 that systems of two linear equations in two variables led to one of three possible outcomes: a unique solution, no solution, and infinitely many solutions. When $D = 0$, Cramer's rule does not apply and the system is either inconsistent (has no solution) or contains dependent equations (has infinitely many solutions).

8.5.4 Cramer's Rule: Systems of Linear Equations in Three Variables

8.5.4 SKILL

Use Cramer's rule to solve a square system of linear equations in three variables.

8.5.4 CONCEPTUAL

Recognize that if the determinant of the coefficient matrix is equal to zero, then the system has no unique solution.

Cramer's rule can also be used to solve higher order systems of linear equations. The following box summarizes Cramer's rule for solving a system of three equations in three variables.

CRAMER'S RULE: SOLUTION FOR SYSTEMS OF THREE EQUATIONS IN THREE VARIABLES

The system of linear equations

$$\begin{aligned} a_1x + b_1y + c_1z &= d_1 \\ a_2x + b_2y + c_2z &= d_2 \\ a_3x + b_3y + c_3z &= d_3 \end{aligned}$$

has the solution

$$x = \frac{D_x}{D} \qquad y = \frac{D_y}{D} \qquad z = \frac{D_z}{D} \qquad D \neq 0$$

where the determinants are given as follows:

Display the coefficients of x, y, and z.
$$D = \begin{vmatrix} a_1 & b_1 & c_1 \\ a_2 & b_2 & c_2 \\ a_3 & b_3 & c_3 \end{vmatrix}$$

Replace the coefficients of x (column 1) in D with the constants on the right side of the equal sign.
$$D_x = \begin{vmatrix} d_1 & b_1 & c_1 \\ d_2 & b_2 & c_2 \\ d_3 & b_3 & c_3 \end{vmatrix}$$

Replace the coefficients of y (column 2) in D with the constants on the right side of the equal sign.
$$D_y = \begin{vmatrix} a_1 & d_1 & c_1 \\ a_2 & d_2 & c_2 \\ a_3 & d_3 & c_3 \end{vmatrix}$$

Replace the coefficients of z (column 3) in D with the constants on the right side of the equal sign.
$$D_z = \begin{vmatrix} a_1 & b_1 & d_1 \\ a_2 & b_2 & d_2 \\ a_3 & b_3 & d_3 \end{vmatrix}$$

EXAMPLE 6 Using Cramer's Rule to Solve a System of Three Linear Equations

Use Cramer's rule to solve the system.
$$\begin{aligned} 3x - 2y + 3z &= -3 \\ 5x + 3y + 8z &= -2 \\ x + y + 3z &= 1 \end{aligned}$$

Solution:

Set up the four determinants.

D contains the coefficients of x, y, and z.
$$D = \begin{vmatrix} 3 & -2 & 3 \\ 5 & 3 & 8 \\ 1 & 1 & 3 \end{vmatrix}$$

Replace a column with constants on the right side of the equation.
$$D_x = \begin{vmatrix} -3 & -2 & 3 \\ -2 & 3 & 8 \\ 1 & 1 & 3 \end{vmatrix} \qquad D_y = \begin{vmatrix} 3 & -3 & 3 \\ 5 & -2 & 8 \\ 1 & 1 & 3 \end{vmatrix} \qquad D_z = \begin{vmatrix} 3 & -2 & -3 \\ 5 & 3 & -2 \\ 1 & 1 & 1 \end{vmatrix}$$

Evaluate the determinants.
$$\begin{aligned} D &= 3(9-8) - (-2)(15-8) + 3(5-3) = 23 \\ D_x &= -3(9-8) - (-2)(-6-8) + 3(-2-3) = -46 \\ D_y &= 3(-6-8) - (-3)(15-8) + 3(5+2) = 0 \\ D_z &= 3(3+2) - (-2)(5+2) - 3(5-3) = 23 \end{aligned}$$

Solve for x, y, and z.
$$x = \frac{D_x}{D} = \frac{-46}{23} = -2 \qquad y = \frac{D_y}{D} = \frac{0}{23} = 0 \qquad z = \frac{D_z}{D} = \frac{23}{23} = 1$$

$$\boxed{x = -2, y = 0, z = 1}$$

YOUR TURN Use Cramer's rule to solve the system.
$$\begin{aligned} 2x + 3y + z &= -1 \\ x - y - z &= 0 \\ -3x - 2y + 3z &= 10 \end{aligned}$$

[CONCEPT CHECK]

TRUE OR FALSE Cramer's rule can be used to solve a system of linear equations only if there is a unique solution. If $D = 0$, then there is either no solution or infinitely many solutions.

ANSWER True

ANSWER

$x = 1, y = -2, z = 3$

As was the case in two equations, when $D = 0$, Cramer's rule does not apply and the system of three equations either is inconsistent (no solution) or contains dependent equations (infinitely many solutions).

[SECTION 8.5] SUMMARY

In this section, **determinants** were discussed for square matrices.

ORDER	DETERMINANT	ARRAY
2×2	$\det(A) = \lvert A \rvert = \begin{vmatrix} a & b \\ c & d \end{vmatrix} = ad - bc$	
3×3	$\begin{vmatrix} a_1 & b_1 & c_1 \\ a_2 & b_2 & c_2 \\ a_3 & b_3 & c_3 \end{vmatrix} = a_1 \begin{vmatrix} b_2 & c_2 \\ b_3 & c_3 \end{vmatrix} - b_1 \begin{vmatrix} a_2 & c_2 \\ a_3 & c_3 \end{vmatrix} + c_1 \begin{vmatrix} a_2 & b_2 \\ a_3 & b_3 \end{vmatrix}$ Expansion by first row (any row or column can be used)	$\begin{bmatrix} + & - & + \\ - & + & - \\ + & - & + \end{bmatrix}$

Cramer's rule was developed for 2×2 and 3×3 matrices, but it can be extended to general $n \times n$ matrices. When the coefficient determinant is equal to zero ($D = 0$), the system either is inconsistent (and has no solution) or represents dependent equations (and has infinitely many solutions), and Cramer's rule does not apply.

SYSTEM	ORDER	SOLUTION	DETERMINANTS
$a_1x + b_1y = c_1$ $a_2x + b_2y = c_2$	2×2	$x = \dfrac{D_x}{D} \quad y = \dfrac{D_y}{D}$	$D = \begin{vmatrix} a_1 & b_1 \\ a_2 & b_2 \end{vmatrix} \neq 0$ $D_x = \begin{vmatrix} c_1 & b_1 \\ c_2 & b_2 \end{vmatrix}$ $D_y = \begin{vmatrix} a_1 & c_1 \\ a_2 & c_2 \end{vmatrix}$
$a_1x + b_1y + c_1z = d_1$ $a_2x + b_2y + c_2z = d_2$ $a_3x + b_3y + c_3z = d_3$	3×3	$x = \dfrac{D_x}{D} \quad y = \dfrac{D_y}{D} \quad z = \dfrac{D_z}{D}$	$D = \begin{vmatrix} a_1 & b_1 & c_1 \\ a_2 & b_2 & c_2 \\ a_3 & b_3 & c_3 \end{vmatrix} \neq 0$ $D_x = \begin{vmatrix} d_1 & b_1 & c_1 \\ d_2 & b_2 & c_2 \\ d_3 & b_3 & c_3 \end{vmatrix}$ $D_y = \begin{vmatrix} a_1 & d_1 & c_1 \\ a_2 & d_2 & c_2 \\ a_3 & d_3 & c_3 \end{vmatrix}$ $D_z = \begin{vmatrix} a_1 & b_1 & d_1 \\ a_2 & b_2 & d_2 \\ a_3 & b_3 & d_3 \end{vmatrix}$

[SECTION 8.5] EXERCISES

• SKILLS

In Exercises 1–10, evaluate each 2 × 2 determinant.

1. $\begin{vmatrix} 1 & 2 \\ 3 & 4 \end{vmatrix}$

2. $\begin{vmatrix} 1 & -2 \\ -3 & -4 \end{vmatrix}$

3. $\begin{vmatrix} 7 & 9 \\ -5 & -2 \end{vmatrix}$

4. $\begin{vmatrix} -3 & -11 \\ 7 & 15 \end{vmatrix}$

5. $\begin{vmatrix} 0 & 7 \\ 4 & -1 \end{vmatrix}$

6. $\begin{vmatrix} 0 & 0 \\ 1 & 0 \end{vmatrix}$

7. $\begin{vmatrix} -1.2 & 2.4 \\ -0.5 & 1.5 \end{vmatrix}$

8. $\begin{vmatrix} -1.0 & 1.4 \\ 1.5 & -2.8 \end{vmatrix}$

9. $\begin{vmatrix} \frac{3}{4} & \frac{1}{3} \\ 2 & \frac{8}{9} \end{vmatrix}$

10. $\begin{vmatrix} -\frac{1}{2} & \frac{1}{4} \\ \frac{2}{3} & -\frac{8}{9} \end{vmatrix}$

In Exercises 11–30, use Cramer's rule to solve each system of equations, if possible.

11. $\begin{aligned} x + y &= -1 \\ x - y &= 11 \end{aligned}$

12. $\begin{aligned} x + y &= -1 \\ x - y &= -9 \end{aligned}$

13. $\begin{aligned} 3x + 2y &= -4 \\ -2x + y &= 5 \end{aligned}$

14. $\begin{aligned} 5x + 3y &= 1 \\ 4x - 7y &= -18 \end{aligned}$

15. $\begin{aligned} 3x - 2y &= -1 \\ 5x + 4y &= -31 \end{aligned}$

16. $\begin{aligned} x - 4y &= -7 \\ 3x + 8y &= 19 \end{aligned}$

17. $\begin{aligned} 7x - 3y &= -29 \\ 5x + 2y &= 0 \end{aligned}$

18. $\begin{aligned} 6x - 2y &= 24 \\ 4x + 7y &= 41 \end{aligned}$

19. $\begin{aligned} 3x + 5y &= 16 \\ y - x &= 0 \end{aligned}$

20. $\begin{aligned} -2x - 3y &= 15 \\ 7y + 4x &= -33 \end{aligned}$

21. $\begin{aligned} 3x - 5y &= 7 \\ -6x + 10y &= -21 \end{aligned}$

22. $\begin{aligned} 3x - 5y &= 7 \\ 6x - 10y &= 14 \end{aligned}$

23. $\begin{aligned} 2x - 3y &= 4 \\ -10x + 15y &= -20 \end{aligned}$

24. $\begin{aligned} 2x - 3y &= 2 \\ 10x - 15y &= 20 \end{aligned}$

25. $\begin{aligned} 3x + \tfrac{1}{2}y &= 1 \\ 4x + \tfrac{1}{3}y &= \tfrac{5}{3} \end{aligned}$

26. $\begin{aligned} \tfrac{3}{2}x + \tfrac{9}{4}y &= \tfrac{9}{8} \\ \tfrac{1}{3}x + \tfrac{1}{4}y &= \tfrac{1}{12} \end{aligned}$

27. $\begin{aligned} 0.3x - 0.5y &= -0.6 \\ 0.2x + y &= 2.4 \end{aligned}$

28. $\begin{aligned} 0.5x - 0.4y &= -3.6 \\ 10x + 3.6y &= -14 \end{aligned}$

29. $\begin{aligned} y &= 17x + 7 \\ y &= -15x + 7 \end{aligned}$

30. $\begin{aligned} 9x &= -45 - 2y \\ 4x &= -3y - 20 \end{aligned}$

In Exercises 31–42, evaluate each 3 × 3 determinant.

31. $\begin{vmatrix} 3 & 1 & 0 \\ 2 & 0 & -1 \\ -4 & 1 & 0 \end{vmatrix}$

32. $\begin{vmatrix} 1 & 1 & 0 \\ 0 & 2 & -1 \\ 0 & -3 & 5 \end{vmatrix}$

33. $\begin{vmatrix} 2 & 1 & -5 \\ 3 & 0 & -1 \\ 4 & 0 & 7 \end{vmatrix}$

34. $\begin{vmatrix} 2 & 1 & -5 \\ 3 & -7 & 0 \\ 4 & -6 & 0 \end{vmatrix}$

35. $\begin{vmatrix} 1 & 1 & -5 \\ 3 & -7 & -4 \\ 4 & -6 & 9 \end{vmatrix}$

36. $\begin{vmatrix} -3 & 2 & -5 \\ 1 & 8 & 2 \\ 4 & -6 & 9 \end{vmatrix}$

37. $\begin{vmatrix} 1 & 3 & 4 \\ 2 & -1 & 1 \\ 3 & -2 & 1 \end{vmatrix}$

38. $\begin{vmatrix} -7 & 2 & 5 \\ \frac{7}{8} & 3 & 4 \\ -1 & 4 & 6 \end{vmatrix}$

39. $\begin{vmatrix} -3 & 1 & 5 \\ 2 & 0 & 6 \\ 4 & 7 & -9 \end{vmatrix}$

40. $\begin{vmatrix} 1 & -1 & 5 \\ 3 & -3 & 6 \\ 4 & 9 & 0 \end{vmatrix}$

41. $\begin{vmatrix} -2 & 1 & -7 \\ 4 & -2 & 14 \\ 0 & 1 & 8 \end{vmatrix}$

42. $\begin{vmatrix} 5 & -2 & -1 \\ 4 & -9 & -3 \\ 2 & 8 & -6 \end{vmatrix}$

In Exercises 43–58, apply Cramer's rule to solve each system of equations, if possible.

43. $\begin{aligned} x + y - z &= 0 \\ x - y + z &= 4 \\ x + y + z &= 10 \end{aligned}$

44. $\begin{aligned} -x + y + z &= -4 \\ x + y - z &= 0 \\ x + y + z &= 2 \end{aligned}$

45. $\begin{aligned} 3x + 8y + 2z &= 28 \\ -2x + 5y + 3z &= 34 \\ 4x + 9y + 2z &= 29 \end{aligned}$

46. $\begin{aligned} 7x + 2y - z &= -1 \\ 6x + 5y + z &= 16 \\ -5x - 4y + 3z &= -5 \end{aligned}$

47. $\begin{aligned} 3x \phantom{{}-y} + 5z &= 11 \\ 4y + 3z &= -9 \\ 2x - y \phantom{{}+3z} &= 7 \end{aligned}$

48. $\begin{aligned} 3x \phantom{{}-2y} - 2z &= 7 \\ 4x \phantom{{}-2y} + z &= 24 \\ 6x - 2y \phantom{{}+z} &= 10 \end{aligned}$

49. $\begin{aligned} x + y - z &= 5 \\ x - y + z &= -1 \\ -2x - 2y + 2z &= -10 \end{aligned}$

50. $\begin{aligned} x + y - z &= 3 \\ x - y + z &= -2 \\ -2x - 2y + 2z &= -6 \end{aligned}$

51. $\begin{aligned} x + y + z &= 9 \\ x - y + z &= 3 \\ -x + y - z &= 5 \end{aligned}$

52. $\begin{aligned} x + y + z &= 6 \\ x - y - z &= 0 \\ -x + y + z &= 7 \end{aligned}$

53. $\begin{aligned} x + 2y + 3z &= 11 \\ -2x + 3y + 5z &= 29 \\ 4x - y + 8z &= 19 \end{aligned}$

54. $\begin{aligned} 8x - 2y + 5z &= 36 \\ 3x + y - z &= 17 \\ 2x - 6y + 4z &= -2 \end{aligned}$

55. $\begin{aligned} x - 4y + 7z &= 49 \\ -3x + 2y - z &= -17 \\ 5x + 8y - 2z &= -24 \end{aligned}$

56. $\begin{aligned} \tfrac{1}{2}x - 2y + 7z &= 25 \\ x + \tfrac{1}{4}y - 4z &= -2 \\ -4x + 5y &= -56 \end{aligned}$

57. $\begin{aligned} 2x + 7y - 4z &= -5.5 \\ -x - 4y - 5z &= -19 \\ 4x - 2y - 9z &= -38 \end{aligned}$

58. $\begin{aligned} 4x - 2y + z &= -15 \\ 3x + y - 2z &= -20 \\ -6x + y + 5z &= 51 \end{aligned}$

• APPLICATIONS

In Exercises 59 and 60, three points, (x_1, y_1), (x_2, y_2), and (x_3, y_3), are collinear if and only if

$$\begin{vmatrix} x_1 & y_1 & 1 \\ x_2 & y_2 & 1 \\ x_3 & y_3 & 1 \end{vmatrix} = 0$$

59. Geometry. Apply determinants to determine whether the points $(-2, -1)$, $(1, 5)$, and $(3, 9)$, are collinear.

60. Geometry. Apply determinants to determine whether the points $(2, -6)$, $(-7, 30)$, and $(5, -18)$, are collinear.

For Exercises 61–64, the area of a triangle with vertices (x_1, y_1), (x_2, y_2), and (x_3, y_3) is given by

$$\text{Area} = \pm\frac{1}{2}\begin{vmatrix} x_1 & y_1 & 1 \\ x_2 & y_2 & 1 \\ x_3 & y_3 & 1 \end{vmatrix}$$

where the sign is chosen so that the area is positive.

61. Geometry. Apply determinants to find the area of a triangle with vertices $(3, 2)$, $(5, 2)$, and $(3, -4)$. Check your answer by plotting these vertices in a Cartesian plane and using the formula for area of a right triangle.

62. Geometry. Apply determinants to find the area of a triangle with vertices $(2, 3)$, $(7, 3)$, and $(7, 7)$. Check your answer by plotting these vertices in a Cartesian plane and using the formula for area of a right triangle.

63. Geometry. Apply determinants to find the area of a triangle with vertices $(1, 2)$, $(3, 4)$, and $(-2, 5)$.

64. Geometry. Apply determinants to find the area of a triangle with vertices $(-1, -2)$, $(3, 4)$, and $(2, 1)$.

65. Geometry. An equation of a line that passes through two points (x_1, y_1) and (x_2, y_2) can be expressed as a determinant equation as follows:

$$\begin{vmatrix} x & y & 1 \\ x_1 & y_1 & 1 \\ x_2 & y_2 & 1 \end{vmatrix} = 0$$

Apply the determinant to write an equation of the line passing through the points $(1, 2)$ and $(2, 4)$. Expand the determinant and express the equation of the line in slope–intercept form.

66. Geometry. If three points (x_1, y_1), (x_2, y_2), and (x_3, y_3) are collinear (lie on the same line), then the following determinant equation must be satisfied:

$$\begin{vmatrix} x_1 & y_1 & 1 \\ x_2 & y_2 & 1 \\ x_3 & y_3 & 1 \end{vmatrix} = 0$$

Determine whether $(0, 5)$, $(2, 0)$, and $(1, 2)$ are collinear.

67. Electricity: Circuit Theory. The following equations come from circuit theory. Find the currents I_1, I_2, and I_3.

$$\begin{aligned} I_1 &= I_2 + I_3 \\ 16 &= 4I_1 + 2I_3 \\ 24 &= 4I_1 + 4I_2 \end{aligned}$$

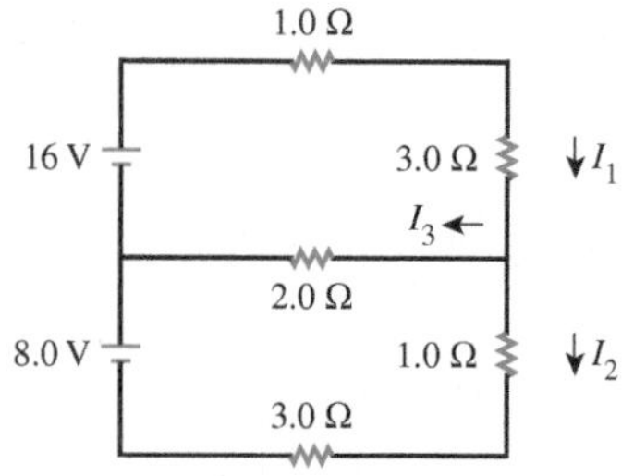

68. Electricity: Circuit Theory. The following equations come from circuit theory. Find the currents I_1, I_2, and I_3.

$$\begin{aligned} I_1 &= I_2 + I_3 \\ 24 &= 6I_1 + 3I_3 \\ 36 &= 6I_1 + 6I_2 \end{aligned}$$

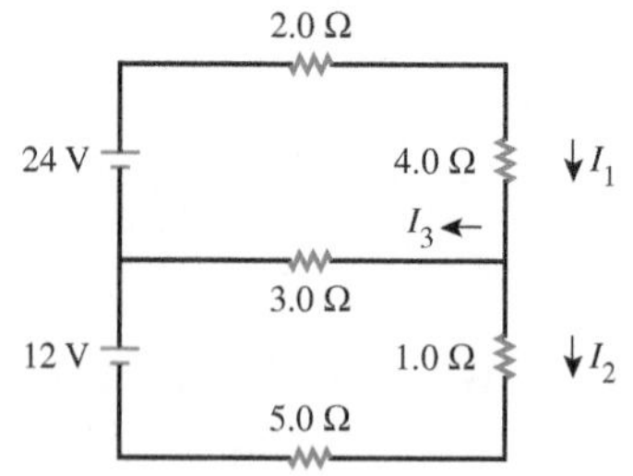

• CATCH THE MISTAKE

In Exercises 69–72, explain the mistake that is made.

69. Evaluate the determinant $\begin{vmatrix} 2 & 1 & 3 \\ -3 & 0 & 2 \\ 1 & 4 & -1 \end{vmatrix}$.

Solution:

Expand the 3×3 determinant in terms of the 2×2 determinants.

$$\begin{vmatrix} 2 & 1 & 3 \\ -3 & 0 & 2 \\ 1 & 4 & -1 \end{vmatrix} = 2\begin{vmatrix} 0 & 2 \\ 4 & -1 \end{vmatrix} + 1\begin{vmatrix} -3 & 2 \\ 1 & -1 \end{vmatrix} + 3\begin{vmatrix} -3 & 0 \\ 1 & 4 \end{vmatrix}$$

Expand the 2×2 determinants. $= 2(0 - 8) + 1(3 - 2) + 3(-12 - 0)$

Simplify. $= -16 + 1 - 36 = -51$

This is incorrect. What mistake was made?

70. Evaluate the determinant $\begin{vmatrix} 2 & 1 & 3 \\ -3 & 0 & 2 \\ 1 & 4 & -1 \end{vmatrix}$.

Solution:

Expand the 3×3 determinant in terms of the 2×2 determinants.

$$\begin{vmatrix} 2 & 1 & 3 \\ -3 & 0 & 2 \\ 1 & 4 & -1 \end{vmatrix} = 2\begin{vmatrix} 0 & 2 \\ 4 & -1 \end{vmatrix} - 1\begin{vmatrix} -3 & 2 \\ 1 & -1 \end{vmatrix} + 3\begin{vmatrix} -3 & 2 \\ 1 & -1 \end{vmatrix}$$

Expand the 2×2 determinants. $= 2(0 - 8) - 1(3 - 2) + 3(3 - 2)$

Simplify. $= -16 - 1 + 3 = -14$

This is incorrect. What mistake was made?

71. Solve the system of linear equations.

$$\begin{aligned} 2x + 3y &= 6 \\ -x - y &= -3 \end{aligned}$$

Solution:

Set up the determinants.

$$D = \begin{vmatrix} 2 & 3 \\ -1 & -1 \end{vmatrix}, D_x = \begin{vmatrix} 2 & 6 \\ -1 & -3 \end{vmatrix}, \text{ and } D_y = \begin{vmatrix} 6 & 3 \\ -3 & -1 \end{vmatrix}$$

Evaluate the determinants. $D = 1, D_x = 0, \text{ and } D_y = 3$

Solve for x and y. $x = \dfrac{D_x}{D} = \dfrac{0}{1} = 0 \text{ and } y = \dfrac{D_y}{D} = \dfrac{3}{1} = 3$

$x = 0, y = 3$ is incorrect. What mistake was made?

72. Solve the system of linear equations.

$$\begin{aligned} 4x - 6y &= 0 \\ 4x + 6y &= 4 \end{aligned}$$

Solution:

Set up the determinants.

$$D = \begin{vmatrix} 4 & -6 \\ 4 & 6 \end{vmatrix}, D_x = \begin{vmatrix} 0 & -6 \\ 4 & 6 \end{vmatrix}, \text{ and } D_y = \begin{vmatrix} 4 & 0 \\ 4 & 4 \end{vmatrix}$$

Evaluate the determinants. $D = 48, D_x = 24, \text{ and } D_y = 16$

Solve for x and y. $x = \dfrac{D}{D_x} = \dfrac{48}{24} = 2 \text{ and } y = \dfrac{D_y}{D} = \dfrac{48}{16} = 3$

$x = 2, y = 3$ is incorrect. What mistake was made?

• CONCEPTUAL

In Exercises 73–76, determine whether each statement is true or false.

73. The value of a determinant changes sign if any two rows are interchanged.

74. If all the entries in any column are equal to zero, the value of the determinant is 0.

75. $\begin{vmatrix} 2 & 6 & 4 \\ 0 & 2 & 8 \\ 4 & 0 & 10 \end{vmatrix} = 2\begin{vmatrix} 1 & 3 & 2 \\ 0 & 1 & 4 \\ 2 & 0 & 5 \end{vmatrix}$

76. $\begin{vmatrix} 3 & 1 & 2 \\ 0 & 2 & 8 \\ 3 & 1 & 2 \end{vmatrix} = 0$

77. Calculate the determinant $\begin{vmatrix} a & 0 & 0 \\ 0 & b & 0 \\ 0 & 0 & c \end{vmatrix}$.

78. Calculate the determinant $\begin{vmatrix} a_1 & b_1 & c_1 \\ 0 & b_2 & c_2 \\ 0 & 0 & c_3 \end{vmatrix}$.

• CHALLENGE

79. Evaluate the determinant:

$$\begin{vmatrix} 1 & -2 & -1 & 3 \\ 4 & 0 & 1 & 2 \\ 0 & 3 & 2 & 4 \\ 1 & -3 & 5 & -4 \end{vmatrix}$$

80. For the system of equations

$$\begin{aligned} 3x + 2y &= 5 \\ ax - 4y &= 1 \end{aligned}$$

find a that guarantees no unique solution.

81. Show that

$$\begin{vmatrix} a_1 & b_1 & c_1 \\ a_2 & b_2 & c_2 \\ a_3 & b_3 & c_3 \end{vmatrix} = \begin{matrix} a_1b_2c_3 + b_1c_2a_3 + c_1a_2b_3 \\ -a_3b_2c_1 - b_3c_2a_1 - b_1a_2c_3 \end{matrix}$$

by expanding down the second column.

82. Show that

$$\begin{vmatrix} a_1 & b_1 & c_1 \\ a_2 & b_2 & c_2 \\ a_3 & b_3 & c_3 \end{vmatrix} = \begin{matrix} a_1b_2c_3 + b_1c_2a_3 + c_1a_2b_3 \\ -a_3b_2c_1 - b_3c_2a_1 - c_3b_1a_2 \end{matrix}$$

by expanding across the third row.

83. Show that

$$\begin{vmatrix} a^2 & a & 1 \\ b^2 & b & 1 \\ c^2 & c & 1 \end{vmatrix} = (a - b)(a - c)(b - c)$$

84. For the system of equations

$$\begin{aligned} x + 3y + 2z &= 0 \\ x + ay + 4z &= 0 \\ 2y + az &= 0 \end{aligned}$$

find the value(s) of a that guarantee(s) no unique solution.

• PREVIEW TO CALCULUS

In calculus, determinants are used when evaluating double and triple integrals through a change of variables. In these cases, the elements of the determinant are functions.

In Exercises 85–88, find each determinant.

85. $\begin{vmatrix} \cos\theta & -r\sin\theta \\ \sin\theta & r\cos\theta \end{vmatrix}$

86. $\begin{vmatrix} 2x & 2y \\ 2x & 2y - 2 \end{vmatrix}$

87. $\begin{vmatrix} \sin\phi\cos\theta & -\rho\sin\phi\sin\theta & \rho\cos\phi\cos\theta \\ \sin\phi\sin\theta & \rho\sin\phi\cos\theta & \rho\cos\phi\sin\theta \\ \cos\phi & 0 & -\rho\sin\phi \end{vmatrix}$

88. $\begin{vmatrix} \cos\theta & -r\sin\theta & 0 \\ \sin\theta & r\cos\theta & 0 \\ 0 & 0 & 1 \end{vmatrix}$

8.6 PARTIAL FRACTIONS

SKILLS OBJECTIVE

- Decompose rational expressions into sums of partial fractions when the denominators contain distinct linear factors, repeated linear factors, distinct irreducible quadratic factors, or repeated irreducible quadratic factors.

CONCEPTUAL OBJECTIVE

- Understand the connection between partial-fraction decomposition and systems of linear equations.

8.6.1 Performing Partial-Fraction Decomposition

8.6.1 SKILL

Decompose rational expressions into sums of partial fractions when the denominators contain distinct linear factors, repeated linear factors, distinct irreducible quadratic factors, or repeated irreducible quadratic factors.

8.6.1 CONCEPTUAL

Understand the connection between partial-fraction decomposition and systems of linear equations.

In Chapter 2, we studied polynomial functions, and in Section 2.6, we discussed ratios of polynomial functions, called rational functions. Rational expressions are of the form

$$\frac{n(x)}{d(x)} \qquad d(x) \neq 0$$

where the numerator $n(x)$ and the denominator $d(x)$ are polynomials. Examples of rational expressions are

$$\frac{4x-1}{2x+3} \qquad \frac{2x+5}{x^2-1} \qquad \frac{3x^4-2x+5}{x^2+2x+4}$$

Suppose we are asked to add two rational expressions: $\frac{2}{x+1} + \frac{5}{x-3}$.

We already possess the skills to accomplish this. We first identify the least common denominator $(x+1)(x-3)$ and combine the fractions into a single expression.

$$\frac{2}{x+1} + \frac{5}{x-3} = \frac{2(x-3)+5(x+1)}{(x+1)(x-3)} = \frac{2x-6+5x+5}{(x+1)(x-3)} = \frac{7x-1}{x^2-2x-3}$$

How do we do this in reverse? For example, how do we start with $\frac{7x-1}{x^2-2x-3}$ and write this expression as a sum of two simpler expressions?

$$\frac{7x-1}{x^2-2x-3} = \overbrace{\underbrace{\frac{2}{x+1}}_{\text{Partial Fraction}} + \underbrace{\frac{5}{x-3}}_{\text{Partial Fraction}}}^{\text{Partial-Fraction Decomposition}}$$

Each of the two expressions on the right is called a **partial fraction**. The sum of these fractions is called the **partial-fraction decomposition** of $\frac{7x-1}{x^2-2x-3}$.

Partial-fraction decomposition is an important tool in calculus. Calculus operations such as differentiation and integration are often made simpler by applying partial fractions. The reason why partial fractions were not discussed until now is that partial-fraction decomposition *requires the ability to solve systems of linear equations*. Since partial-fraction decomposition is made possible by the techniques of solving systems of linear equations, we consider partial fractions an important application of systems of linear equations.

As mentioned earlier, a rational expression is the ratio of two polynomial expressions $n(x)/d(x)$ and we assume that $n(x)$ and $d(x)$ are polynomials with no common factors other than 1. If the degree of $n(x)$ is less than the degree of $d(x)$, then the rational expression $n(x)/d(x)$ is said to be **proper**. If the degree of $n(x)$ is greater than or equal to the degree of $d(x)$, the rational expression is said to be **improper**. If the rational expression is improper, it should first be divided using long division.

$$\frac{n(x)}{d(x)} = Q(x) + \frac{r(x)}{d(x)}$$

The result is the sum of a quotient $Q(x)$ and a rational expression, which is the ratio of the remainder $r(x)$ and the divisor $d(x)$. The rational expression $r(x)/d(x)$ is proper, and the techniques outlined in this section can be applied to its partial-fraction decomposition.

Partial-fraction decomposition of proper rational expressions always begins with factoring the denominator $d(x)$. The goal is to write $d(x)$ as a product of distinct linear factors, but that may not always be possible. Sometimes $d(x)$ can be factored into a product of linear factors, where one or more are repeated. And sometimes the factored form of $d(x)$ contains irreducible quadratic factors, such as $x^2 + 1$. There are times when the irreducible quadratic factors are repeated, such as $(x^2 + 1)^2$. A procedure is now outlined for partial-fraction decomposition.

PARTIAL-FRACTION DECOMPOSITION

To write a rational expression $\frac{n(x)}{d(x)}$ as a sum of partial fractions:

Step 1: Determine whether the rational expression is proper or improper.

- Proper: degree of $n(x) <$ degree of $d(x)$
- Improper: degree of $n(x) \geq$ degree of $d(x)$

Step 2: If proper, proceed to Step 3.

If improper, divide $\frac{n(x)}{d(x)}$ using polynomial (long) division, write the result as $\frac{n(x)}{d(x)} = Q(x) + \frac{r(x)}{d(x)}$, and proceed to Step 3 with $\frac{r(x)}{d(x)}$.

Step 3: Factor $d(x)$. Four possible cases:

Case 1 Distinct (nonrepeated) *linear* factors: $(ax + b)$

Example: $d(x) = (3x - 1)(x + 2)$

Case 2 One or more repeated linear factors: $(ax + b)^m$ $m \geq 2$

Example: $d(x) = (x + 5)^2(x - 3)$

Case 3 One or more distinct irreducible ($ax^2 + bx + c = 0$ has no real roots) quadratic factors: $(ax^2 + bx + c)$

Example: $d(x) = (x^2 + 4)(x + 1)(x - 2)$

Case 4 One or more repeated irreducible quadratic factors: $(ax^2 + bx + c)^m$

Example: $d(x) = (x^2 + x + 1)^2(x + 1)(x - 2)$

Step 4: Decompose the rational expression into a sum of partial fractions according to the procedure outlined in each case in this section.

Step 4 depends on which cases, or types of factors, arise. It is important to note that these four cases are not exclusive and combinations of different types of factors will appear.

Distinct Linear Factors

CASE 1: $d(x)$ HAS ONLY DISTINCT (NONREPEATED) LINEAR FACTORS

If $d(x)$ is a polynomial of degree p, and it can be factored into p linear factors

$$d(x) = \underbrace{(ax + b)(cx + d)\ldots}_{p \text{ linear factors}}$$

where no two factors are the same, then the partial-fraction decomposition of $\frac{n(x)}{d(x)}$ can be written as

$$\frac{n(x)}{d(x)} = \frac{A}{(ax + b)} + \frac{B}{(cx + d)} + \cdots$$

where the numerators A, B, and so on are constants to be determined.

The goal is to write a proper rational expression as the sum of proper rational expressions. Therefore, if the denominator is a linear factor (degree 1), then the numerator is a constant (degree 0).

EXAMPLE 1 Partial-Fraction Decomposition with Distinct Linear Factors

Find the partial-fraction decomposition of $\frac{5x + 13}{x^2 + 4x - 5}$.

Solution:

Factor the denominator. $\frac{5x + 13}{(x - 1)(x + 5)}$

Express as a sum of two partial fractions. $\frac{5x + 13}{(x - 1)(x + 5)} = \frac{A}{(x - 1)} + \frac{B}{(x + 5)}$

Multiply the two sides of the equation by the LCD $(x - 1)(x + 5)$. $5x + 13 = A(x + 5) + B(x - 1)$

Eliminate the parentheses. $5x + 13 = Ax + 5A + Bx - B$

Group the x's and constants on the right. $5x + 13 = (A + B)x + (5A - B)$

Identify like terms. $5x + 13 = (A + B)x + (5A - B)$

Equate the coefficients of x. $5 = A + B$

Equate the constant terms. $13 = 5A - B$

Solve the system of two linear equations using any method to solve for A and B. $A = 3, B = 2$

Substitute $A = 3, B = 2$ into the partial-fraction decomposition. $\boxed{\frac{5x + 13}{(x - 1)(x + 5)} = \frac{3}{(x - 1)} + \frac{2}{(x + 5)}}$

Check by adding the partial fractions.

$$\frac{3}{(x - 1)} + \frac{2}{(x + 5)} = \frac{3(x + 5) + 2(x - 1)}{(x - 1)(x + 5)} = \frac{5x + 13}{x^2 + 4x - 5}$$

YOUR TURN Find the partial-fraction decomposition of $\frac{4x - 13}{x^2 - 3x - 10}$.

ANSWER

$\frac{4x - 13}{x^2 - 3x - 10} = \frac{3}{x + 2} + \frac{1}{x - 5}$

In Example 1, we started with a rational expression that had a numerator of degree 1 and a denominator of degree 2. Partial-fraction decomposition enabled us to write that rational expression as a sum of two rational expressions with degree 0 numerators and degree 1 denominators.

Repeated Linear Factors

CASE 2: $d(x)$ HAS AT LEAST ONE REPEATED LINEAR FACTOR

If $d(x)$ can be factored into a product of linear factors, then the partial-fraction decomposition will proceed as in Case 1, with the exception of a repeated factor $(ax + b)^m$, $m \geq 2$. Any linear factor repeated m times will result in the sum of m partial fractions

$$\frac{A}{(ax+b)} + \frac{B}{(ax+b)^2} + \frac{C}{(ax+b)^3} + \cdots + \frac{M}{(ax+b)^m}$$

where the numerators, $A, B, C, \ldots, M$ are constants to be determined.

Note that if $d(x)$ is of degree p, the general form of the decomposition will have p partial fractions. If some numerator constants turn out to be zero, then the final decomposition may have fewer than p partial fractions.

EXAMPLE 2 Partial-Fraction Decomposition with a Repeated Linear Factor

Find the partial-fraction decomposition of $\dfrac{-3x^2 + 13x - 12}{x^3 - 4x^2 + 4x}$.

Solution:

Factor the denominator.
$$\frac{-3x^2 + 13x - 12}{x(x-2)^2}$$

Express as a sum of three partial fractions.
$$\frac{-3x^2 + 13x - 12}{x(x-2)^2} = \frac{A}{x} + \frac{B}{(x-2)} + \frac{C}{(x-2)^2}$$

Multiply both sides by the LCD $x(x-2)^2$.
$$-3x^2 + 13x - 12 = A(x-2)^2 + Bx(x-2) + Cx$$

Eliminate the parentheses.
$$-3x^2 + 13x - 12 = Ax^2 - 4Ax + 4A + Bx^2 - 2Bx + Cx$$

Group like terms on the right.
$$-3x^2 + 13x - 12 = (A + B)x^2 + (-4A - 2B + C)x + 4A$$

Identify like terms on both sides.
$$\mathbf{-3x^2 + 13x - 12 = (A + B)x^2 + (-4A - 2B + C)x + 4A}$$

Equate the coefficients of x^2. $\quad -3 = A + B \quad$ (1)

Equate the coefficients of x. $\quad 13 = -4A - 2B + C \quad$ (2)

Equate the constant terms. $\quad -12 = 4A \quad$ (3)

Solve the system of three equations for A, B, and C.

Solve Equation (3) for A.	$A = -3$
Substitute $A = -3$ into (1).	$B = 0$
Substitute $A = -3$ and $B = 0$ into (2).	$C = 1$

Substitute $A = -3$, $B = 0$, $C = 1$ into the partial-fraction decomposition.

$$\frac{-3x^2 + 13x - 12}{x(x-2)^2} = \frac{-3}{x} + \frac{0}{(x-2)} + \frac{1}{(x-2)^2}$$

$$\boxed{\frac{-3x^2 + 13x - 12}{x^3 - 4x^2 + 4x} = \frac{-3}{x} + \frac{1}{(x-2)^2}}$$

Check by adding the partial fractions.

$$\frac{-3}{x} + \frac{1}{(x-2)^2} = \frac{-3(x-2)^2 + 1(x)}{x(x-2)^2} = \frac{-3x^2 + 13x - 12}{x^3 - 4x^2 + 4x}$$

YOUR TURN Find the partial-fraction decomposition of $\dfrac{x^2 + 1}{x^3 + 2x^2 + x}$.

ANSWER

$$\frac{x^2 + 1}{x^3 + 2x^2 + x} = \frac{1}{x} - \frac{2}{(x+1)^2}$$

EXAMPLE 3 Partial-Fraction Decomposition with Multiple Repeated Linear Factors

Find the partial-fraction decomposition of $\dfrac{2x^3 + 6x^2 + 6x + 9}{x^4 + 6x^3 + 9x^2}$.

Solution:

Factor the denominator.

$$\frac{2x^3 + 6x^2 + 6x + 9}{x^2(x+3)^2}$$

Express as a sum of four partial fractions.

$$\frac{2x^3 + 6x^2 + 6x + 9}{x^2(x+3)^2} = \frac{A}{x} + \frac{B}{x^2} + \frac{C}{(x+3)} + \frac{D}{(x+3)^2}$$

Multiply both sides by the LCD $x^2(x+3)^2$.

$$2x^3 + 6x^2 + 6x + 9 = Ax(x+3)^2 + B(x+3)^2 + Cx^2(x+3) + Dx^2$$

Eliminate the parentheses.

$$2x^3 + 6x^2 + 6x + 9 = Ax^3 + 6Ax^2 + 9Ax + Bx^2 + 6Bx + 9B + Cx^3 + 3Cx^2 + Dx^2$$

Group like terms on the right.

$$2x^3 + 6x^2 + 6x + 9 = (A + C)x^3 + (6A + B + 3C + D)x^2 + (9A + 6B)x + 9B$$

Identify like terms on both sides.

$$2x^3 + 6x^2 + 6x + 9 = (A + C)x^3 + (6A + B + 3C + D)x^2 + (9A + 6B)x + 9B$$

Equate the coefficients of x^3.	$2 = A + C$	(1)
Equate the coefficients of x^2.	$6 = 6A + B + 3C + D$	(2)
Equate the coefficients of x.	$6 = 9A + 6B$	(3)
Equate the constant terms.	$9 = 9B$	(4)

Solve the system of four equations for A, B, C, and D.

Solve Equation (4) for B.	$B = 1$
Substitute $B = 1$ into Equation (3) and solve for A.	$A = 0$
Substitute $A = 0$ into Equation (1) and solve for C.	$C = 2$
Substitute $A = 0$, $B = 1$, and $C = 2$ into Equation (2) and solve for D.	$D = -1$

Substitute $A = 0, B = 1, C = 2, D = -1$ into the partial-fraction decomposition.

$$\frac{2x^3 + 6x^2 + 6x + 9}{x^2(x+3)^2} = \frac{0}{x} + \frac{1}{x^2} + \frac{2}{(x+3)} + \frac{-1}{(x+3)^2}$$

$$\boxed{\frac{2x^3 + 6x^2 + 6x + 9}{x^2(x+3)^2} = \frac{1}{x^2} + \frac{2}{(x+3)} - \frac{1}{(x+3)^2}}$$

Check by adding the partial fractions.

$$\frac{1}{x^2} + \frac{2}{(x+3)} - \frac{1}{(x+3)^2} = \frac{(x+3)^2 + 2x^2(x+3) - 1(x^2)}{x^2(x+3)^2}$$

$$= \frac{2x^3 + 6x^2 + 6x + 9}{x^4 + 6x^3 + 9x^2}$$

YOUR TURN Find the partial-fraction decomposition of $\frac{2x^3 + 2x + 1}{x^4 + 2x^3 + x^2}$.

ANSWER

$$\frac{2x^3 + 2x + 1}{x^4 + 2x^3 + x^2} = \frac{1}{x^2} + \frac{2}{(x+1)} - \frac{3}{(x+1)^2}$$

Distinct Irreducible Quadratic Factors

There will be times when a polynomial cannot be factored into a product of linear factors with real coefficients. For example, $x^2 + 4$, $x^2 + x + 1$, and $9x^2 + 3x + 2$ are all examples of *irreducible quadratic* expressions. The general form of an **irreducible quadratic factor** is given by

$$ax^2 + bx + c \quad \text{where } ax^2 + bx + c = 0 \text{ has no real roots}$$

CASE 3: $d(x)$ HAS A DISTINCT IRREDUCIBLE QUADRATIC FACTOR

If the factored form of $d(x)$ contains an irreducible quadratic factor $ax^2 + bx + c$, then the partial-fraction decomposition will contain a term of the form

$$\frac{Ax + B}{ax^2 + bx + c}$$

where A and B are constants to be determined.

STUDY TIP

In a partial-fraction decomposition, the degree of the numerator is always 1 less than the degree of the denominator.

Recall that for a proper rational expression, the degree of the numerator is less than the degree of the denominator. For irreducible quadratic (degree 2) denominators, we assume a linear (degree 1) numerator. For example,

$$\frac{7x^2 + 2}{(2x+1)(x^2+1)} = \underbrace{\frac{A}{(2x+1)}}_{} + \underbrace{\frac{Bx + C}{(x^2+1)}}_{}$$

$$\frac{\text{Constant numerator}}{\text{Linear factor}} + \frac{\text{Linear numerator}}{\text{Quadratic factor}}$$

A constant is used in the numerator when the denominator consists of a linear expression, and a linear expression is used in the numerator when the denominator consists of a quadratic expression.

EXAMPLE 4 **Partial-Fraction Decomposition with an Irreducible Quadratic Factor**

Find the partial-fraction decomposition of $\dfrac{7x^2 + 2}{(2x + 1)(x^2 + 1)}$.

Solution:

The denominator is already in factored form. $\dfrac{7x^2 + 2}{(2x + 1)(x^2 + 1)}$

Express as a sum of two partial fractions. $\dfrac{7x^2 + 2}{(2x + 1)(x^2 + 1)} = \dfrac{A}{(2x + 1)} + \dfrac{Bx + C}{(x^2 + 1)}$

Multiply both sides by the LCD $(2x + 1)(x^2 + 1)$. $7x^2 + 2 = A(x^2 + 1) + (Bx + C)(2x + 1)$

Eliminate the parentheses. $7x^2 + 2 = Ax^2 + A + 2Bx^2 + Bx + 2Cx + C$

Group like terms on the right. $7x^2 + 2 = (A + 2B)x^2 + (B + 2C)x + (A + C)$

Identify like terms on both sides. $7x^2 + 0x + 2 = (A + 2B)x^2 + (B + 2C)x + (A + C)$

Equate the coefficients of x^2. $7 = A + 2B$

Equate the coefficients of x. $0 = B + 2C$

Equate the constant terms. $2 = A + C$

Solve the system of three equations for A, B, and C. $A = 3, B = 2, C = -1$

Substitute $A = 3$, $B = 2$, $C = -1$ into the partial-fraction decomposition.

$$\boxed{\frac{7x^2 + 2}{(2x + 1)(x^2 + 1)} = \frac{3}{(2x + 1)} + \frac{2x - 1}{(x^2 + 1)}}$$

Check by adding the partial fractions.

$$\frac{3}{(2x + 1)} + \frac{2x - 1}{(x^2 + 1)} = \frac{3(x^2 + 1) + (2x - 1)(2x + 1)}{(2x + 1)(x^2 + 1)} = \frac{7x^2 + 2}{(2x + 1)(x^2 + 1)}$$

YOUR TURN Find the partial-fraction decomposition of $\dfrac{-2x^2 + x + 6}{(x - 1)(x^2 + 4)}$.

ANSWER

$$\frac{-2x^2 + x + 6}{(x - 1)(x^2 + 4)} = \frac{1}{x - 1} - \frac{3x + 2}{x^2 + 4}$$

Repeated Irreducible Quadratic Factors

CASE 4: $d(x)$ HAS A REPEATED IRREDUCIBLE QUADRATIC FACTOR

If the factored form of $d(x)$ contains an irreducible quadratic factor $(ax^2 + bx + c)^m$, where $b^2 - 4ac < 0$, then the partial-fraction decomposition will contain a series of terms of the form

$$\frac{A_1x + B_1}{ax^2 + bx + c} + \frac{A_2x + B_2}{(ax^2 + bx + c)^2} + \frac{A_3x + B_3}{(ax^2 + bx + c)^3} + \cdots + \frac{A_mx + B_m}{(ax^2 + bx + c)^m}$$

where A_i and B_i with $i = 1, 2, \ldots, m$, are constants to be determined.

EXAMPLE 5 **Partial-Fraction Decomposition with a Repeated Irreducible Quadratic Factor**

Find the partial-fraction decomposition of $\dfrac{x^3 - x^2 + 3x + 2}{(x^2+1)^2}$.

Solution:

The denominator is already in factored form. $\dfrac{x^3 - x^2 + 3x + 2}{(x^2+1)^2}$

Express as a sum of two partial fractions. $\dfrac{x^3 - x^2 + 3x + 2}{(x^2+1)^2} = \dfrac{Ax+B}{x^2+1} + \dfrac{Cx+D}{(x^2+1)^2}$

Multiply both sides by the LCD $(x^2+1)^2$. $x^3 - x^2 + 3x + 2 = (Ax+B)(x^2+1) + Cx + D$

Eliminate the parentheses. $x^3 - x^2 + 3x + 2 = Ax^3 + Bx^2 + Ax + B + Cx + D$

Group like terms on the right. $x^3 - x^2 + 3x + 2 = Ax^3 + Bx^2 + (A+C)x + (B+D)$

Identify like terms on both sides. $x^3 - x^2 + 3x + 2 = Ax^3 + Bx^2 + (A+C)x + (B+D)$

Equate the coefficients of x^3. $1 = A$ (1)

Equate the coefficients of x^2. $-1 = B$ (2)

Equate the coefficients of x. $3 = A + C$ (3)

Equate the constant terms. $2 = B + D$ (4)

Substitute $A = 1$ into Equation (3) and solve for C. $C = 2$

Substitute $B = -1$ into Equation (4) and solve for D. $D = 3$

Substitute $A = 1$, $B = -1$, $C = 2$, $D = 3$ into the partial-fraction decomposition.

$$\boxed{\dfrac{x^3 - x^2 + 3x + 2}{(x^2+1)^2} = \dfrac{x-1}{x^2+1} + \dfrac{2x+3}{(x^2+1)^2}}$$

Check by adding the partial fractions.

$$\dfrac{x-1}{x^2+1} + \dfrac{2x+3}{(x^2+1)^2} = \dfrac{(x-1)(x^2+1) + (2x+3)}{(x^2+1)^2} = \dfrac{x^3 - x^2 + 3x + 2}{(x^2+1)^2}$$

YOUR TURN Find the partial-fraction decomposition of $\dfrac{3x^3 + x^2 + 4x - 1}{(x^2+4)^2}$.

ANSWER

$$\dfrac{3x^3 + x^2 + 4x - 1}{(x^2+4)^2} = \dfrac{3x+1}{x^2+4} - \dfrac{8x+5}{(x^2+4)^2}$$

Combinations of All Four Cases

As you probably can imagine, there are rational expressions that have combinations of all four cases, which can lead to a system of several equations when solving for the unknown constants in the numerators of the partial fractions.

EXAMPLE 6 Partial-Fraction Decomposition

Find the partial-fraction decomposition of $\dfrac{x^5 + x^4 + 4x^3 - 3x^2 + 4x - 8}{x^2(x^2 + 2)^2}$.

Solution:

The denominator is already in factored form.

$$\frac{x^5 + x^4 + 4x^3 - 3x^2 + 4x - 8}{x^2(x^2 + 2)^2}$$

Express as a sum of partial fractions.

There are repeated linear and irreducible quadratic factors.

$$\frac{x^5 + x^4 + 4x^3 - 3x^2 + 4x - 8}{x^2(x^2 + 2)^2} = \frac{A}{x} + \frac{B}{x^2} + \frac{Cx + D}{(x^2 + 2)} + \frac{Ex + F}{(x^2 + 2)^2}$$

Multiply both sides by the LCD $x^2(x^2 + 2)^2$.

$$x^5 + x^4 + 4x^3 - 3x^2 + 4x - 8$$
$$= Ax(x^2 + 2)^2 + B(x^2 + 2)^2 + (Cx + D)x^2(x^2 + 2) + (Ex + F)x^2$$

Eliminate the parentheses.

$$x^5 + x^4 + 4x^3 - 3x^2 + 4x - 8$$
$$= Ax^5 + 4Ax^3 + 4Ax + Bx^4 + 4Bx^2 + 4B + Cx^5 + 2Cx^3$$
$$+ Dx^4 + 2Dx^2 + Ex^3 + Fx^2$$

Group like terms on the right.

$$x^5 + x^4 + 4x^3 - 3x^2 + 4x - 8$$
$$= (A + C)x^5 + (B + D)x^4 + (4A + 2C + E)x^3$$
$$+ (4B + 2D + F)x^2 + 4Ax + 4B$$

Equating the coefficients of like terms leads to six equations.

$$A + C = 1$$
$$B + D = 1$$
$$4A + 2C + E = 4$$
$$4B + 2D + F = -3$$
$$4A = 4$$
$$4B = -8$$

Solve this system of equations.

$$A = 1, \quad B = -2, \quad C = 0, \quad D = 3, \quad E = 0, \quad F = -1$$

Substitute $A = 1, B = -2, C = 0, D = 3, E = 0, F = -1$ into the partial-fraction decomposition.

$$\frac{x^5 + x^4 + 4x^3 - 3x^2 + 4x - 8}{x^2(x^2 + 2)^2} = \frac{1}{x} + \frac{-2}{x^2} + \frac{0x + 3}{(x^2 + 2)} + \frac{0x + -1}{(x^2 + 2)^2}$$

$$\boxed{\frac{x^5 + x^4 + 4x^3 - 3x^2 + 4x - 8}{x^2(x^2 + 2)^2} = \frac{1}{x} - \frac{2}{x^2} + \frac{3}{(x^2 + 2)} - \frac{1}{(x^2 + 2)^2}}$$

Check by adding the partial fractions.

[CONCEPT CHECK]

TRUE OR FALSE Partial-fraction decomposition relies on solving systems of linear equations in order to determine the unknown coefficients.

ANSWER True

[SECTION 8.6] SUMMARY

A rational expression $\frac{n(x)}{d(x)}$ is

- **Proper:** If the degree of the numerator is less than the degree of the denominator.
- **Improper:** If the degree of the numerator is equal to or greater than the degree of the denominator.

Partial-Fraction Decomposition of Proper Rational Expressions

1. Distinct (nonrepeated) linear factors

Example: $\frac{3x-10}{(x-5)(x+4)} = \frac{A}{x-5} + \frac{B}{x+4}$

2. Repeated linear factors

Example: $\frac{2x+5}{(x-3)^2(x+1)} = \frac{A}{x-3} + \frac{B}{(x-3)^2} + \frac{C}{x+1}$

3. Distinct irreducible quadratic factors

Example: $\frac{1-x}{(x^2+1)(x^2+8)} = \frac{Ax+B}{x^2+1} + \frac{Cx+D}{x^2+8}$

4. Repeated irreducible quadratic factors

Example: $\frac{4x^2-3x+2}{(x^2+1)^2} = \frac{Ax+B}{x^2+1} + \frac{Cx+D}{(x^2+1)^2}$

[SECTION 8.6] EXERCISES

• SKILLS

In Exercises 1–6, match each rational expression (1–6) with the appropriate form of the partial-fraction decomposition (a–f).

1. $\frac{3x+2}{x(x^2-25)}$
2. $\frac{3x+2}{x(x^2+25)}$
3. $\frac{3x+2}{x^2(x^2+25)}$
4. $\frac{3x+2}{x^2(x^2-25)}$
5. $\frac{3x+2}{x(x^2+25)^2}$
6. $\frac{3x+2}{x^2(x^2+25)^2}$

a. $\frac{A}{x} + \frac{B}{x^2} + \frac{Cx+D}{x^2+25}$

b. $\frac{A}{x} + \frac{Bx+C}{x^2+25} + \frac{Dx+E}{(x^2+25)^2}$

c. $\frac{A}{x} + \frac{Bx+C}{x^2+25}$

d. $\frac{A}{x} + \frac{B}{x+5} + \frac{C}{x-5}$

e. $\frac{A}{x} + \frac{B}{x^2} + \frac{Cx+D}{x^2+25} + \frac{Ex+F}{(x^2+25)^2}$

f. $\frac{A}{x} + \frac{B}{x^2} + \frac{C}{x+5} + \frac{D}{x-5}$

In Exercises 7–14, write the form of the partial-fraction decomposition. Do not solve for the constants.

7. $\frac{9}{x^2-x-20}$
8. $\frac{8}{x^2-3x-10}$
9. $\frac{2x+5}{x^3-4x^2}$
10. $\frac{x^2+2x-1}{x^4-9x^2}$
11. $\frac{2x^3-4x^2+7x+3}{(x^2+x+5)}$
12. $\frac{2x^3+5x^2+6}{(x^2-3x+7)}$
13. $\frac{3x^3-x+9}{(x^2+10)^2}$
14. $\frac{5x^3+2x^2+4}{(x^2+13)^2}$

In Exercises 15–40, find the partial-fraction decomposition for each rational function.

15. $\frac{1}{x(x+1)}$
16. $\frac{1}{x(x-1)}$
17. $\frac{x}{x(x-1)}$
18. $\frac{x}{x(x+1)}$
19. $\frac{9x-11}{(x-3)(x+5)}$
20. $\frac{8x-13}{(x-2)(x+1)}$
21. $\frac{3x+1}{(x-1)^2}$
22. $\frac{9y-2}{(y-1)^2}$
23. $\frac{4x-3}{x^2+6x+9}$
24. $\frac{3x+1}{x^2+4x+4}$
25. $\frac{4x^2-32x+72}{(x+1)(x-5)^2}$
26. $\frac{4x^2-7x-3}{(x+2)(x-1)^2}$
27. $\frac{5x^2+28x-6}{(x+4)(x^2+3)}$
28. $\frac{x^2+5x+4}{(x-2)(x^2+2)}$
29. $\frac{-2x^2-17x+11}{(x-7)(3x^2-7x+5)}$
30. $\frac{14x^2+8x+40}{(x+5)(2x^2-3x+5)}$

31. $\dfrac{x^3}{(x^2+9)^2}$

32. $\dfrac{x^2}{(x^2+9)^2}$

33. $\dfrac{2x^3-3x^2+7x-2}{(x^2+1)^2}$

34. $\dfrac{-x^3+2x^2-3x+15}{(x^2+8)^2}$

35. $\dfrac{3x+1}{x^4-1}$

36. $\dfrac{2-x}{x^4-81}$

37. $\dfrac{5x^2+9x-8}{(x-1)(x^2+2x-1)}$

38. $\dfrac{10x^2-5x+29}{(x-3)(x^2+4x+5)}$

39. $\dfrac{3x}{x^3-1}$

40. $\dfrac{5x+2}{x^3-8}$

• APPLICATIONS

41. **Optics.** The relationship among the distance of an object to a lens d_o, the distance to the image d_i, and the focal length f of the lens is given by

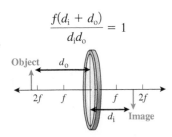

$$\frac{f(d_i+d_o)}{d_i d_o}=1$$

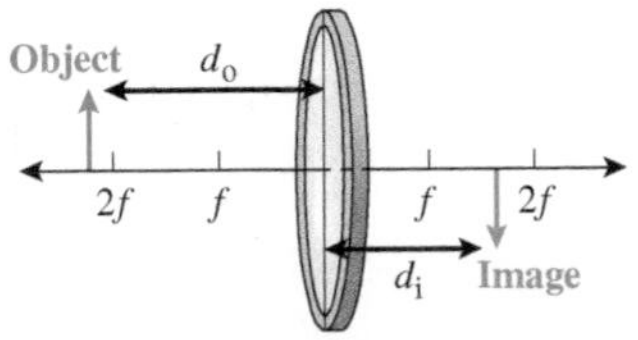

Use partial-fraction decomposition to write the lens law in terms of sums of fractions. What does each term represent?

42. **Sums.** Find the partial-fraction decomposition of $\dfrac{1}{n(n+1)}$, and apply it to find the sum of

$$\frac{1}{1\cdot 2}+\frac{1}{2\cdot 3}+\frac{1}{3\cdot 4}+\cdots+\frac{1}{999\cdot 1000}$$

In Exercises 43 and 44, refer to the following:

Laplace transforms are used to solve differential equations. The Laplace transform of $f(t)$ is denoted by $L\{f(t)\}$; thus, $L\{e^{3t}\}$ is the Laplace transform of $f(t)=e^{3t}$. It is known that $L\{e^{kt}\}=\dfrac{1}{s-k}$ and $L\{e^{-kt}\}=\dfrac{1}{s+k}$. Then the inverse Laplace transform of $g(s)=\dfrac{1}{s-k}$ is $L^{-1}\left\{\dfrac{1}{s-k}\right\}=e^{kt}$. Inverse Laplace transforms are linear:

$$L^{-1}\{f(t)+g(t)\}=L^{-1}\{f(t)\}+L^{-1}\{g(t)\}$$

43. **Laplace Transform.** Use partial fractions to find the inverse Laplace transform of $\dfrac{9+s}{4-s^2}$.

44. **Laplace Transform.** Use partial fractions to find the inverse Laplace transform of $\dfrac{2s^2+3s-2}{s(s+1)(s-2)}$.

• CATCH THE MISTAKE

In Exercises 45 and 46, explain the mistake that is made.

45. Find the partial-fraction decomposition of $\dfrac{3x^2+3x+1}{x(x^2+1)}$.

Solution:

Write the partial-fraction decomposition form.	$\dfrac{3x^2+3x+1}{x(x^2+1)}=\dfrac{A}{x}+\dfrac{B}{x^2+1}$
Multiply both sides by the LCD $x(x^2+1)$.	$3x^2+3x+1=A(x^2+1)+Bx$
Eliminate the parentheses.	$3x^2+3x+1=Ax^2+Bx+A$
Matching like terms leads to three equations.	$A=3$, $B=3$, and $A=1$

This is incorrect. What mistake was made?

46. Find the partial-fraction decomposition of $\dfrac{3x^4-x-1}{x(x-1)}$.

Solution:

Write the partial-fraction decomposition form.	$\dfrac{3x^4-x-1}{x(x-1)}=\dfrac{A}{x}+\dfrac{B}{x-1}$
Multiply both sides by the LCD $x(x-1)$.	$3x^4-x-1=A(x-1)+Bx$
Eliminate the parentheses and group like terms.	$3x^4-x-1=(A+B)x-A$
Compare like coefficients.	$A=1, B=-2$

This is incorrect. What mistake was made?

• CONCEPTUAL

In Exercises 47–52, determine whether each statement is true or false.

47. Partial-fraction decomposition can be employed only when the degree of the numerator is greater than the degree of the denominator.

48. The degree of the denominator of a proper rational expression is equal to the number of partial fractions in its decomposition.

49. Partial-fraction decomposition depends on the factors of the denominator.

50. A rational function can always be decomposed into partial fractions with linear or irreducible quadratic factors in each denominator.

51. The partial-fraction decomposition of a rational function $\dfrac{f(x)}{(x-a)^n}$ has the form $\dfrac{A_1}{(x-a)} + \dfrac{A_2}{(x-a)^2} + \cdots + \dfrac{A_n}{(x-a)^n}$, where all the numbers A_i are nonzero.

52. The rational function $\dfrac{1}{x^3+1}$ cannot be decomposed into partial fractions.

• CHALLENGE

For Exercises 53–58, find the partial-fraction decomposition.

53. $\dfrac{x^2+4x-8}{x^3-x^2-4x+4}$

54. $\dfrac{ax+b}{x^2-c^2}$ a, b, c are real numbers.

55. $\dfrac{2x^3+x^2-x-1}{x^4+x^3}$

56. $\dfrac{-x^3+2x-2}{x^5-x^4}$

57. $\dfrac{x^5+2}{(x^2+1)^3}$

58. $\dfrac{x^2-4}{(x^2+1)^3}$

• PREVIEW TO CALCULUS

In calculus, partial fractions are used to calculate the sums of infinite series. In Exercises 59–62, find the partial-fraction decomposition of the summand.

59. $\displaystyle\sum_{k=1}^{\infty} \frac{9}{k(k+3)}$

60. $\displaystyle\sum_{k=1}^{\infty} \frac{1}{k(k+1)}$

61. $\displaystyle\sum_{k=1}^{\infty} \frac{2k+1}{k^2(k+1)^2}$

62. $\displaystyle\sum_{k=1}^{\infty} \frac{4}{k(k+1)(k+2)}$

8.7 SYSTEMS OF LINEAR INEQUALITIES IN TWO VARIABLES

SKILLS OBJECTIVES

- Graph a linear inequality in two variables.
- Graph a system of linear inequalities in two variables.
- Solve the optimization problem, which combines minimizing or maximizing a function subject to constraints, using linear programming.

CONCEPTUAL OBJECTIVES

- Interpret the difference between solid and dashed lines.
- Interpret an overlapped shaded region as a solution.
- Understand that linear programming is a graphical method for solving optimization problems in which vertices represent maxima or minima.

8.7.1 Linear Inequalities in Two Variables

8.7.1 SKILL

Graph a linear inequality in two variables.

8.7.1 CONCEPTUAL

Interpret the difference between solid and dashed lines.

We saw in Section 0.6 that $y = 2x + 1$ is an *equation in two variables* whose graph is a line in the *xy*-plane. We now turn our attention to **linear inequalities in two variables**. For example, if we change the = in $y = 2x + 1$ to <, we get $y < 2x + 1$. The solution to this inequality in two variables is the set of all points (x, y) that make this inequality true. Some solutions to this inequality are $(-2, -5)$, $(0, 0)$, $(3, 4)$, $(5, -1)$, ...

In fact, the entire region *below* the line $y = 2x + 1$ satisfies the inequality $y < 2x + 1$. If we reverse the sign of the inequality to get $y > 2x + 1$, then the entire region *above* the line $y = 2x + 1$ represents the solution to the inequality.

Any line divides the *xy*-plane into two **half-planes**. For example, the line $y = 2x + 1$ divides the *xy*-plane into two half-planes represented as $y > 2x + 1$ and $y < 2x + 1$. Recall that with inequalities in one variable, we used the notation of parentheses and brackets to denote the type of inequality (strict or nonstrict). We use a similar notation with linear inequalities in two variables. If the inequality is a strict inequality, < or >, then the line is *dashed*, and if the inequality includes the equal sign, ≤ or ≥, then a *solid* line is used. The following box summarizes the procedure for graphing a linear inequality in two variables.

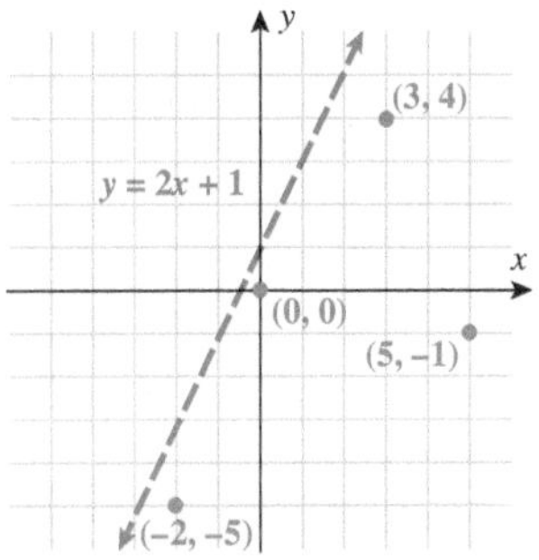

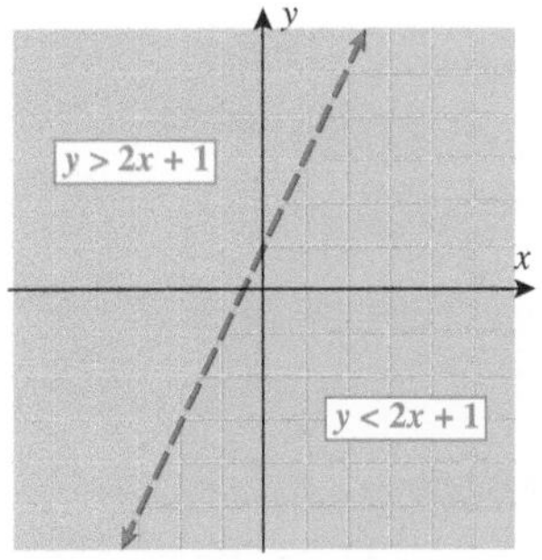

GRAPHING A LINEAR INEQUALITY IN TWO VARIABLES

Step 1: Change the inequality sign, <, ≤, ≥, or >, to an equal sign, =.

Step 2: Draw the line that corresponds to the resulting equation in Step 1.
- If the inequality is strict, < or >, use a **dashed** line.
- If the inequality is not strict, ≤ or ≥, use a **solid** line.

Step 3: Test a point.
- Select a point in one half-plane and test to see whether it satisfies the inequality. If it does, then so do all the points in that region (half-plane). If not, then none of the points in that half-plane satisfy the inequality.
- Repeat this step for the other half-plane.

Step 4: Shade the half-plane that satisfies the inequality.

STUDY TIP

A dashed line means that the points that lie on the line are not included in the solution of the linear inequality.

EXAMPLE 1 **Graphing a Strict Linear Inequality in Two Variables**

Graph the inequality $3x + y < 2$.

Solution:

STEP 1 Change the inequality sign to an equal sign. $3x + y = 2$

STEP 2 Draw the line.

Convert from standard form to slope–intercept form. $y = -3x + 2$

Since the inequality $<$ is a strict inequality, use a **dashed** line.

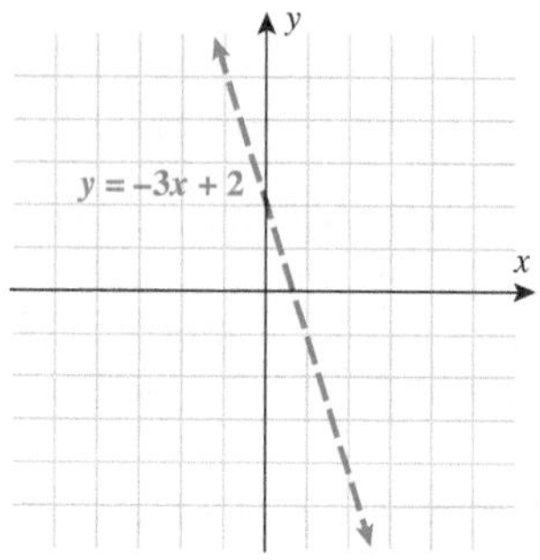

STEP 3 Test points in each half-plane.

Substitute $(3, 0)$ into $3x + y < 2$. $3(3) + 0 < 2$

The point $(3, 0)$ does not satisfy the inequality. $9 < 2$

Substitute $(-2, 0)$ into $3x + y < 2$. $3(-2) + 0 < 2$

The point $(-2, 0)$ does satisfy the inequality. $-6 < 2$

STEP 4 Shade the region containing the point $(-2, 0)$.

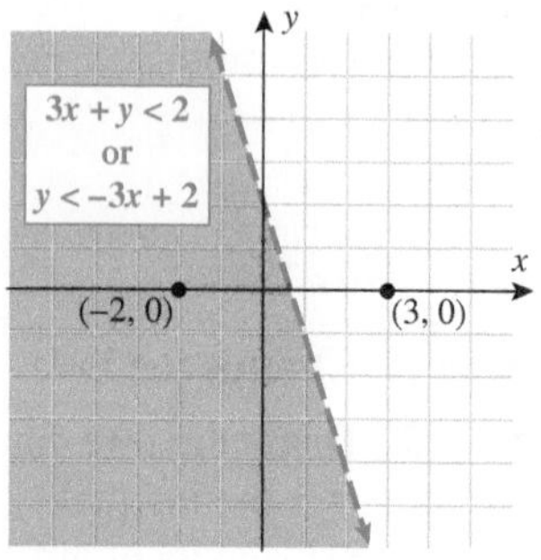

YOUR TURN Graph the inequality $-x + y > -1$.

ANSWER

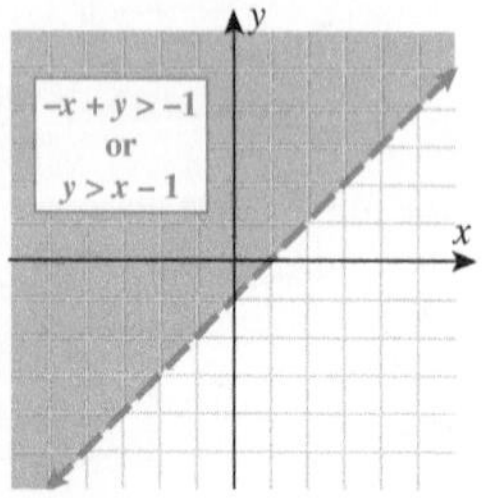

EXAMPLE 2 **Graphing a Nonstrict Linear Inequality in Two Variables**

Graph the inequality $2x - 3y \geq 6$.

Solution:

STEP 1 Change the inequality sign to an equal sign. $2x - 3y = 6$

STEP 2 Draw the line.

Convert from standard form to slope–intercept form. $y = \frac{2}{3}x - 2$

Since the inequality $\geq$ is not a strict inequality, use a **solid** line.

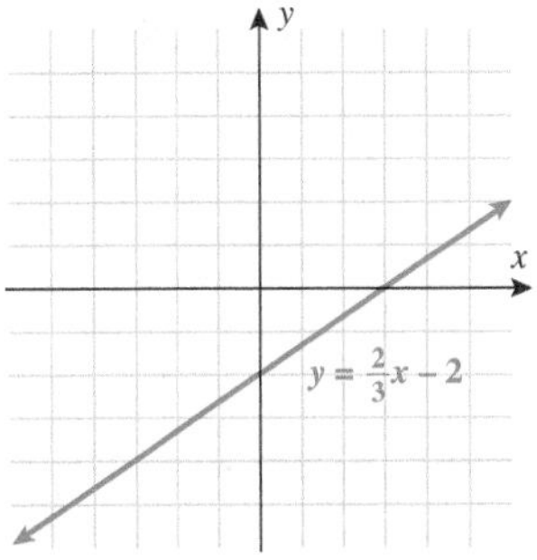

STEP 3 Test points in each half-plane.

Substitute $(5, 0)$ into $2x - 3y \geq 6$. $2(5) - 3(0) \geq 6$

The point $(5, 0)$ satisfies the inequality. $10 \geq 6$

Substitute $(0, 0)$ into $2x - 3y \geq 6$. $2(0) - 3(0) \geq 6$

$0 \geq 6$

The point $(0, 0)$ does not satisfy the inequality.

STEP 4 Shade the region containing the point $(5, 0)$.

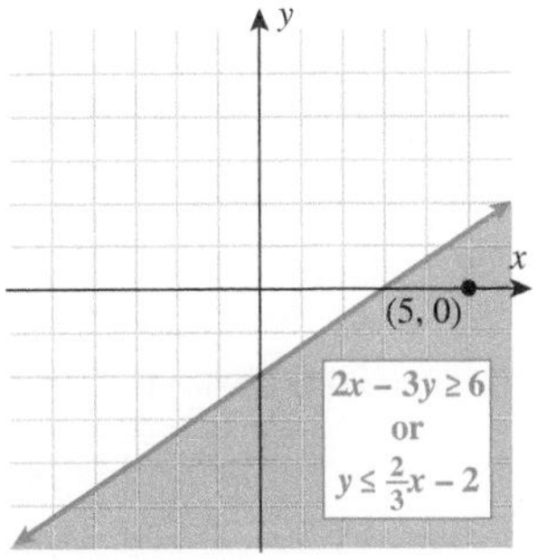

YOUR TURN Graph the inequality $x - 2y \leq 6$.

ANSWER

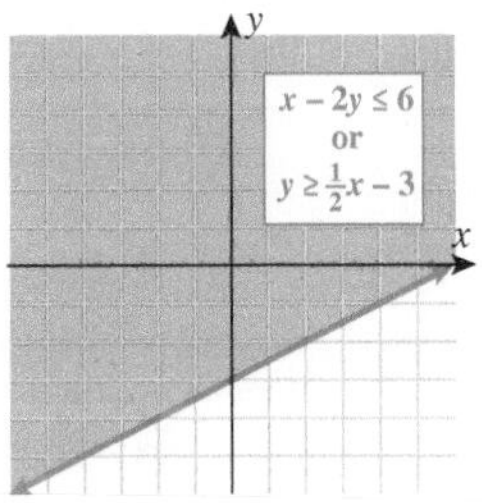

8.7.2 Systems of Linear Inequalities in Two Variables

8.7.2 SKILL

Graph a system of linear inequalities in two variables.

8.7.2 CONCEPTUAL

Interpret an overlapped shaded region as a solution.

Systems of linear inequalities are similar to *systems of linear equations.* In systems of linear equations we sought the points that satisfied *all* of the equations. The **solution set of a system of inequalities** contains the points that satisfy *all* of the inequalities. The graph of a system of inequalities can be obtained by simultaneously graphing each individual inequality and finding where the shaded regions intersect (or overlap), if at all.

EXAMPLE 3 Solving a System of Two Linear Inequalities

Graph the system of inequalities: $x + y \geq -2$
$x + y \leq 2$

Solution:

STEP 1 Change the inequality signs to equal signs. $x + y = -2$
$x + y = 2$

STEP 2 Draw the two lines.

Because the inequality signs are not strict, use solid lines.

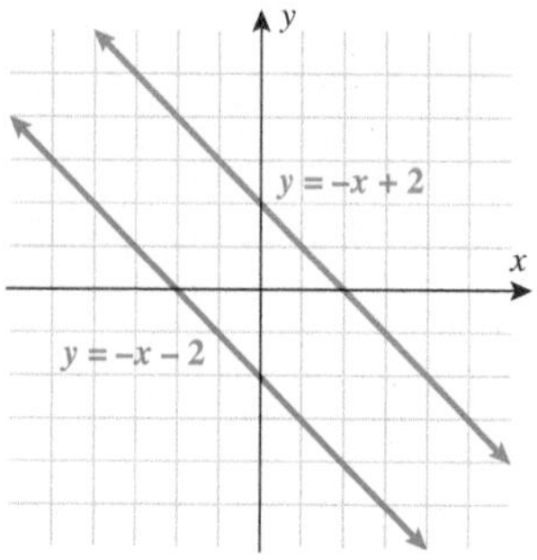

STEP 3 Test points for each inequality.

$x + y \geq -2$

Substitute $(-4, 0)$ into $x + y \geq -2$. $-4 \geq -2$
The point $(-4, 0)$ does not satisfy the inequality.
Substitute $(0, 0)$ into $x + y \geq -2$. $0 \geq -2$
The point $(0, 0)$ does satisfy the inequality.

$x + y \leq 2$

Substitute $(0, 0)$ into $x + y \leq 2$. $0 \leq 2$
The point $(0, 0)$ does satisfy the inequality.
Substitute $(4, 0)$ into $x + y \leq 2$. $4 \leq 2$
The point $(4, 0)$ does not satisfy the inequality.

STEP 4 For $x + y \geq -2$, shade the region *above* that includes $(0, 0)$.

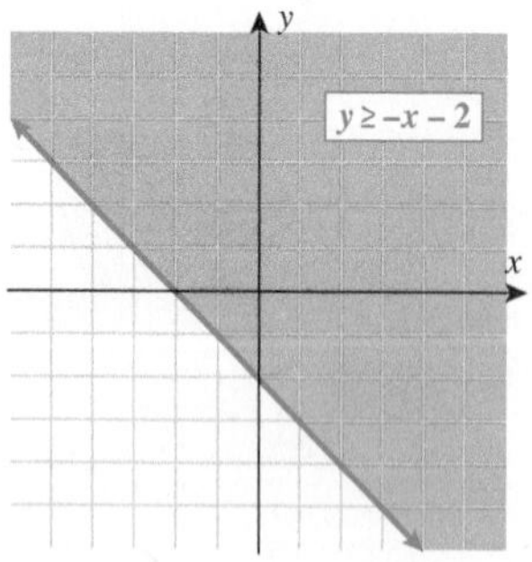

For $x + y \leq 2$, shade the region *below* that includes $(0, 0)$.

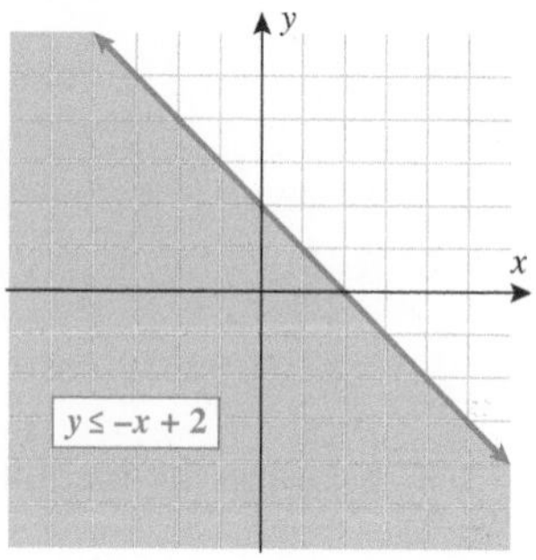

STEP 5 All of the points in the overlapping region and on the lines constitute the solution.

Notice that the points $(0, 0)$, $(-1, 1)$, and $(1, -1)$ all lie in the shaded region and all three satisfy both inequalities.

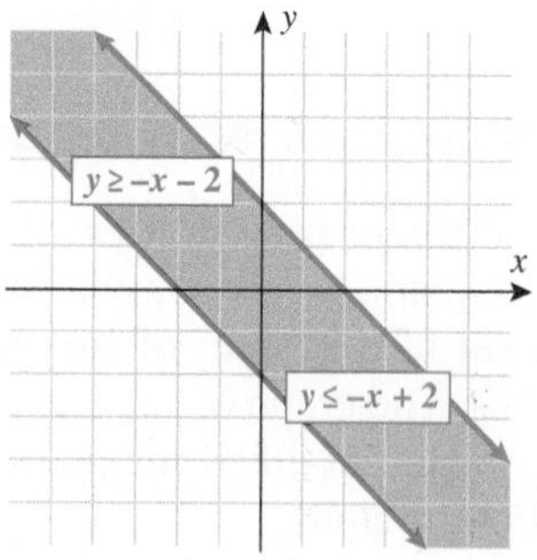

EXAMPLE 4 Solving a System of Two Linear Inequalities with No Solution

Graph the system of inequalities: $x + y \leq -2$
$x + y \geq 2$

Solution:

STEP 1 Change the inequality signs to equal signs. $x + y = -2$
$x + y = 2$

STEP 2 Draw the two lines.

Because the inequality signs are not strict, use solid lines.

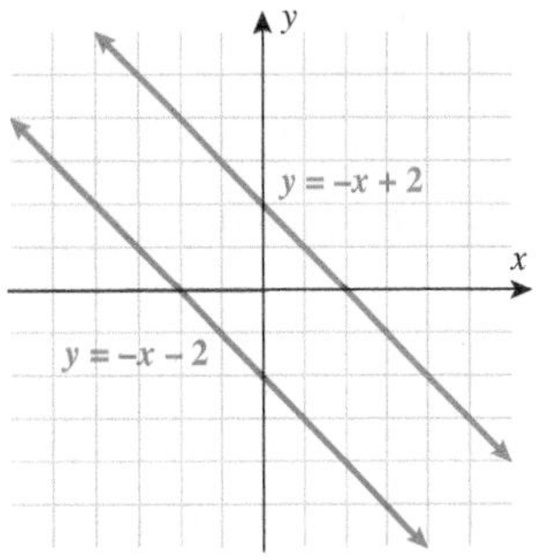

[CONCEPT CHECK]

TRUE OR FALSE Only the points that lie in the shaded region satisfy both linear inequalities.

ANSWER True

STEP 3 Test points for each inequality.

$x + y \leq -2$

Substitute $(-4, 0)$ into $x + y \leq -2$. $-4 \leq -2$

The point $(-4, 0)$ does satisfy the inequality.

Substitute $(0, 0)$ into $x + y \leq -2$. $0 \leq -2$

The point $(0, 0)$ does not satisfy the inequality.

$x + y \geq 2$

Substitute $(0, 0)$ into $x + y \geq 2$. $0 \geq 2$

The point $(0, 0)$ does not satisfy the inequality.

Substitute $(4, 0)$ into $x + y \geq 2$. $4 \geq 2$

The point $(4, 0)$ does satisfy the inequality.

STEP 4 For $x + y \leq -2$, shade the region *below* that includes $(-4, 0)$.

For $x + y \geq 2$, shade the region *above* that includes $(4, 0)$.

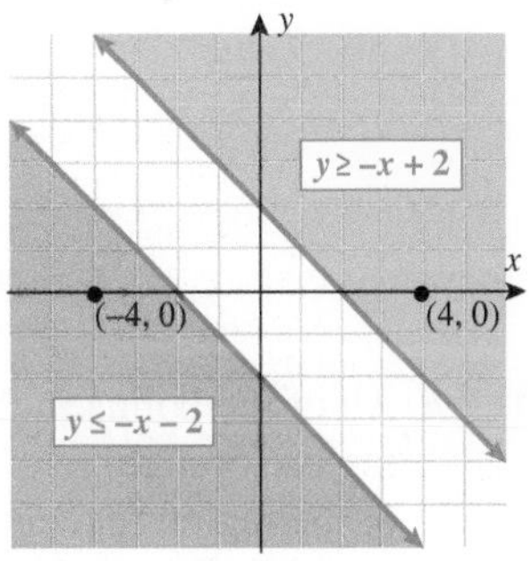

STEP 5 There is no overlapping region. Therefore, no points satisfy both inequalities. We say there is **no solution**.

YOUR TURN Graph the solution to the system of inequalities.

a. $y > x + 1$
$y < x - 1$

b. $y < x + 1$
$y > x - 1$

ANSWER

a. no solution

b.

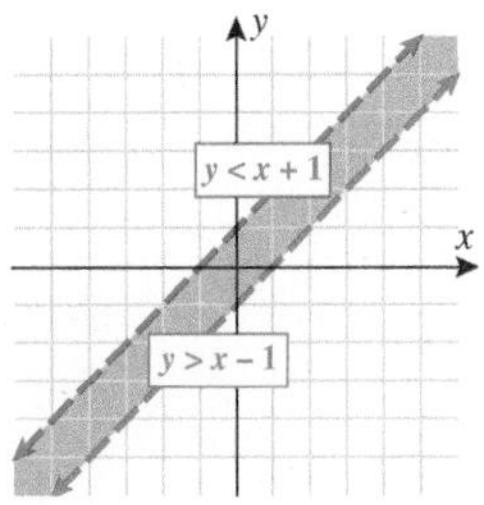

Thus far we have addressed only systems of two linear inequalities. Systems with more than two inequalities are treated in a similar manner. The solution is the set of all points that satisfy *all* of the inequalities. When there are more than two linear inequalities, the solution may be a **bounded** region. We can algebraically determine where the lines intersect by setting the y-values equal to each other.

EXAMPLE 5 Solving a System of Multiple Linear Inequalities

Solve the system of inequalities:

$$\begin{aligned} y &\le x \\ y &\ge -x \\ y &< 3 \end{aligned}$$

Solution:

STEP 1 Change the inequalities to equal signs.

$$\begin{aligned} y &= x \\ y &= -x \\ y &= 3 \end{aligned}$$

STEP 2 Draw the three lines.

To determine the points of intersection, set the y-values equal.

Point where $y = x$ and $y = -x$ intersect: $x = -x$

$x = 0$

Substitute $x = 0$ into $y = x$. $(0, 0)$

Point where $y = -x$ and $y = 3$ intersect: $-x = 3$

$x = -3$

$(-3, 3)$

Point where $y = 3$ and $y = x$ intersect: $x = 3$

$(3, 3)$

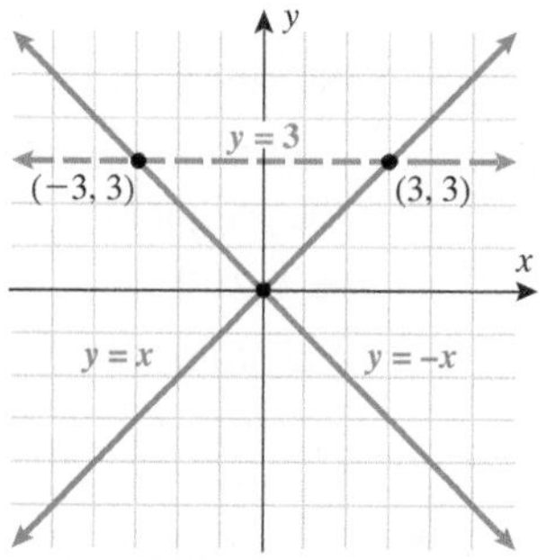

STEP 3 Test points to determine the shaded half-planes corresponding to $y \le x$, $y \ge -x$, and $y < 3$.

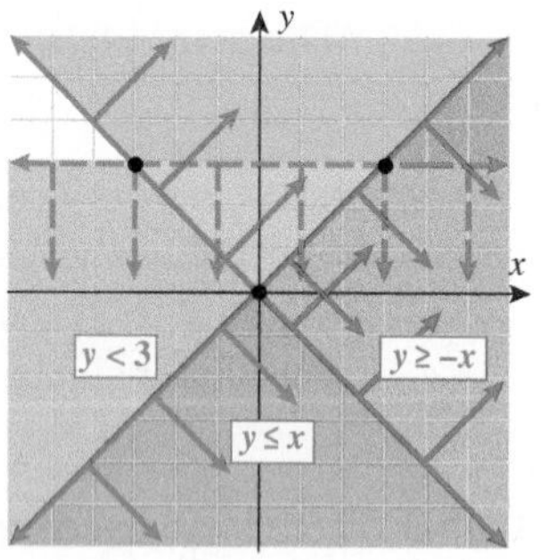

STEP 4 All of the points in the overlapping region (orange) and along the boundaries of the region (except (3, 3) because of strict inequality) corresponding to the lines $y = -x$ and $y = x$ constitute the solution.

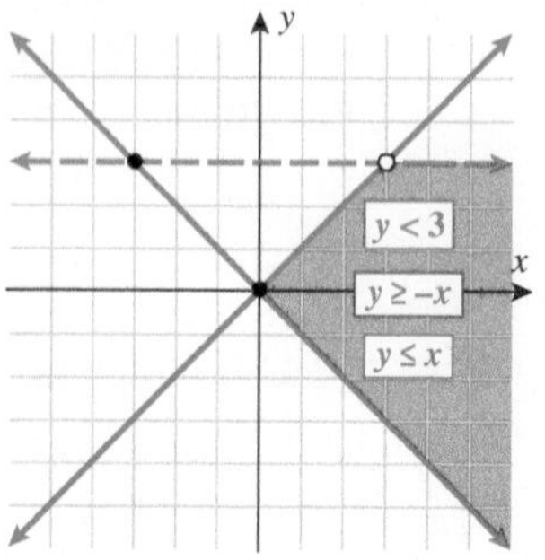

Applications

In economics, the point where the supply and demand curves intersect is called the **equilibrium point**. **Consumer surplus** is a measure of the amount that consumers benefit by being able to purchase a product for a price less than the maximum they would be willing to pay. **Producer surplus** is a measure of the amount that producers benefit by selling at a market price that is higher than the least they would be willing to sell for.

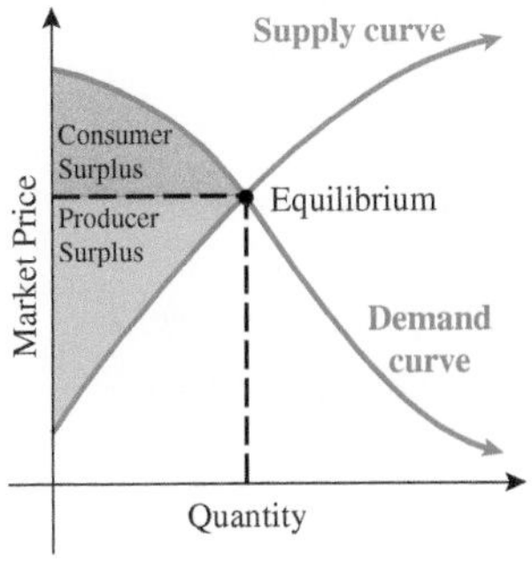

EXAMPLE 6 Consumer Surplus and Producer Surplus

The Tesla Motors Roadster is the first electric car that is able to travel 245 miles on a single charge. The price of a 2013 model is approximately \$90,000 (including tax and incentives).

Courtesy Tesla Motors

Suppose the supply and demand equations for this electric car are given by

$$P = 90{,}000 - 0.1x \quad \text{(Demand)}$$
$$P = 10{,}000 + 0.3x \quad \text{(Supply)}$$

where P is the price in dollars and x is the number of cars produced. Calculate the consumer surplus and the producer surplus for these two equations.

Solution:

Find the equilibrium point.

$$90{,}000 - 0.1x = 10{,}000 + 0.3x$$
$$0.4x = 80{,}000$$
$$x = 200{,}000$$

Let $x = 200{,}000$ in either the supply or the demand equation.

$$P = 90{,}000 - 0.1(200{,}000) = 70{,}000$$
$$P = 10{,}000 + 0.3(200{,}000) = 70{,}000$$

According to these models, if the price of a Tesla Motors Roadster is \$70,000, then 200,000 cars will be sold and there will be no surplus.

Write the systems of linear inequalities that correspond to consumer surplus and producer surplus.

CONSUMER SURPLUS	PRODUCER SURPLUS
$P \leq 90{,}000 - 0.1x$	$P \geq 10{,}000 + 0.3x$
$P > 70{,}000$	$P < 70{,}000$
$x \geq 0$	$x \geq 0$

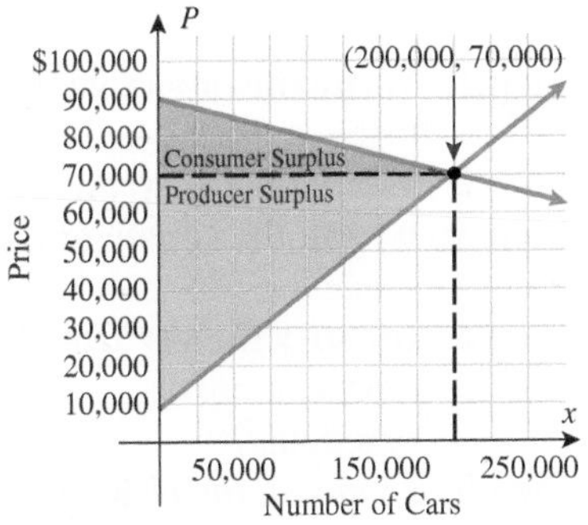

The consumer surplus is the area of the red triangle. $A = \frac{1}{2}bh$

$= \frac{1}{2}(200{,}000)(20{,}000)$

The consumer surplus is two billion dollars. $= 2{,}000{,}000{,}000$

The producer surplus is the area of the blue triangle. $A = \frac{1}{2}bh$

$= \frac{1}{2}(200{,}000)(60{,}000)$

The producer surplus is six billion dollars. $= 6{,}000{,}000{,}000$

The graph of the systems of linear inequalities in Example 6 are said to be **bounded**, whereas the graphs of the systems of linear inequalities in Examples 3–5 are said to be **unbounded**. Any points that correspond to boundary lines intersecting are called **corner points** or **vertices**. In Example 6, the vertices corresponding to the consumer surplus are the points (0, 90,000), (0, 70,000), and (200,000, 70,000), and the vertices corresponding to the producer surplus are the points (0, 70,000), (0, 10,000), and (200,000, 70,000).

8.7.3 The Linear Programming Model

8.7.3 SKILL

Solve the optimization problem, which combines minimizing or maximizing a function subject to constraints, using linear programming.

8.7.3 CONCEPTUAL

Understand that linear programming is a graphical method for solving optimization problems in which vertices represent maxima or minima.

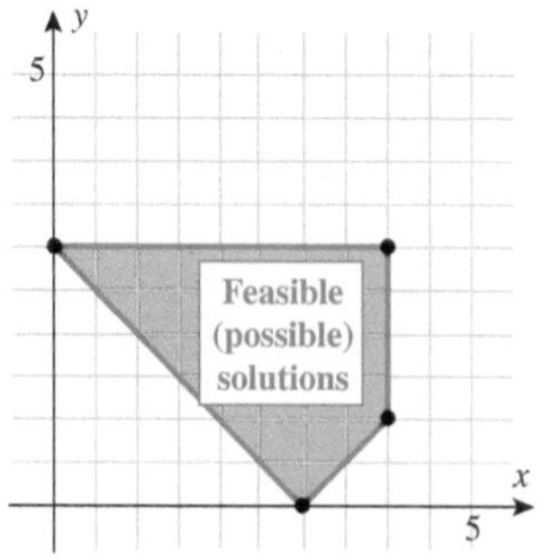

Often we seek to maximize or minimize a function subject to constraints. This process is called **optimization**. When the function we seek to minimize or maximize is linear and the constraints are given in terms of linear inequalities, a mathematical method to approach such problems is called **linear programming**. In linear programming, we start with a linear equation, called the **objective function**, that represents the quantity that is to be maximized or minimized.

The goal is to minimize or maximize the objective function $z = Ax + By$ subject to *constraints*. In other words, find the points (x, y) that make the value of z the largest (or smallest). The **constraints** are a system of linear inequalities, and the common shaded region represents the **feasible** (possible) **solutions**.

If the constraints form a bounded region, the maximum or minimum value of the objective function will occur using the coordinates of one of the vertices. If the region is not bounded, then if an optimal solution exists, it will occur at a vertex. A procedure for solving linear programming problems is outlined below.

SOLVING AN OPTIMIZATION PROBLEM USING LINEAR PROGRAMMING

Step 1: Write the objective function. This expression represents the quantity that is to be minimized or maximized.

Step 2: Write the constraints. This is a system of linear inequalities.

Step 3: Graph the constraints. Graph the system of linear inequalities and shade the common region, which contains the feasible solutions.

Step 4: Identify the vertices. The corner points (vertices) of the shaded region represent possible solutions for maximizing or minimizing the objective function.

Step 5: Evaluate the objective function for each vertex. For each corner point of the shaded region, substitute the coordinates into the objective function and list the value of the objective function.

Step 6: Identify the optimal solution*. The largest (maximum) or smallest (minimum) value of the objective function in Step 5 is the optimal solution.

*If unbounded shaded region, then a solution may not exist.

EXAMPLE 7 Maximizing an Objective Function

Find the maximum value of $z = 2x + y$ subject to the following constraints:

$$x \geq 1 \quad x \leq 4 \quad x + y \leq 5 \quad y \geq 0$$

Solution:

STEP 1 Write the objective function. $z = 2x + y$

STEP 2 Write the constraints.

$x \geq 1$
$x \leq 4$
$y \leq -x + 5$
$y \geq 0$

STEP 3 Graph the constraints.

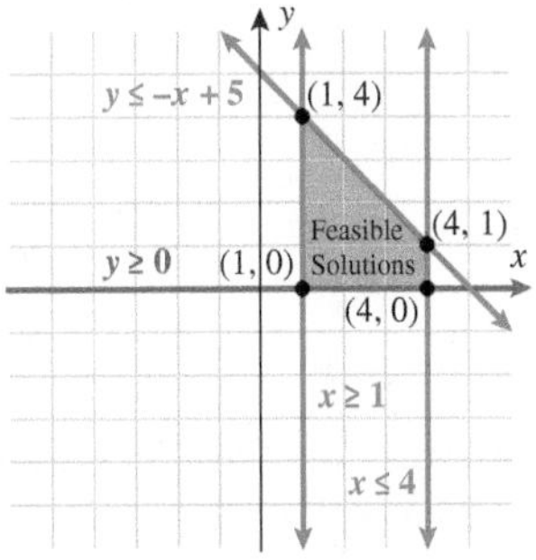

Note: Since the feasible region is bounded, a maximum will exist.

STEP 4 Identify the vertices. (1, 4), (4, 1), (1, 0), (4, 0)

STEP 5 Evaluate the objective function for each vertex.

VERTEX	x	y	OBJECTIVE FUNCTION: $z = 2x + y$
(1, 4)	1	4	$2(1) + 4 = \mathbf{6}$
(4, 1)	4	1	$2(4) + 1 = \mathbf{9}$
(1, 0)	1	0	$2(1) + 0 = \mathbf{2}$
(4, 0)	4	0	$2(4) + 0 = \mathbf{8}$

STEP 6 The maximum value of z is **9**, subject to the given constraints when $x = 4$ and $y = 1$.

YOUR TURN Find the maximum value of $z = x + 3y$ subject to these constraints:

$$x \geq 1 \quad x \leq 3 \quad y \leq -x + 3 \quad y \geq 0$$

STUDY TIP

The bounded region is the region that satisfies *all* of the constraints. Only vertices of the bounded region correspond to possible solutions. Even though $y = -x + 5$ and $y = 0$ intersect at $x = 5$, that point of intersection is outside the shaded region and therefore is *not* one of the vertices.

[CONCEPT CHECK]

In Example 7, the point (5, 1) would correspond to a z-value of 11 (which is greater than 9). Why is the point (5, 1) not a maximum in Example 7?

ANSWER Because (5, 1) does not satisfy the constraints.

ANSWER

The maximum value of z is **7**, which occurs when $x = 1$ and $y = 2$.

EXAMPLE 8 Minimizing an Objective Function

Find the minimum value of $z = 4x + 5y$ subject to the following constraints:

$$x \geq 0 \qquad 2x + y \leq 6 \qquad x + y \leq 5 \qquad y \geq 0$$

Solution:

STEP 1 Write the objective function. $z = 4x + 5y$

STEP 2 Write the constraints.

$$x \geq 0$$
$$y \leq -2x + 6$$
$$y \leq -x + 5$$
$$y \geq 0$$

> **STUDY TIP**
> Maxima or minima of objective functions only occur at the vertices of the shaded region corresponding to the constraints.

STEP 3 Graph the constraints.

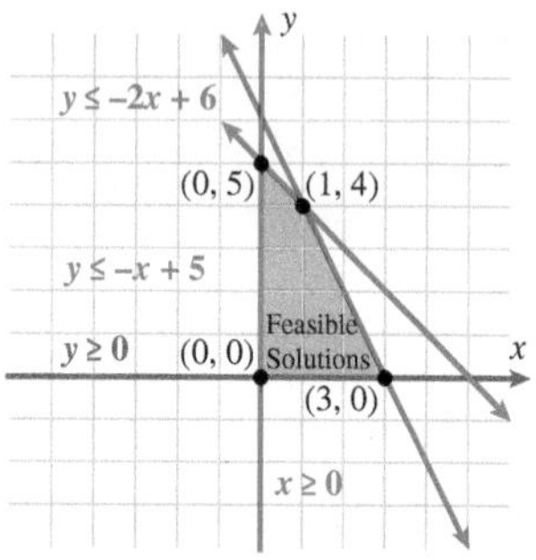

Note: Since the feasible region is bounded, a maximum will exist.

STEP 4 Identify the vertices. (0, 0), (0, 5), (1, 4), (3, 0)

STEP 5 Evaluate the objective function for each vertex.

VERTEX	x	y	OBJECTIVE FUNCTION: $z = 4x + 5y$
(0, 0)	0	0	$4(0) + 5(0) = \mathbf{0}$
(0, 5)	0	5	$4(0) + 5(5) = \mathbf{25}$
(1, 4)	1	4	$4(1) + 5(4) = \mathbf{24}$
(3, 0)	3	0	$4(3) + 5(0) = \mathbf{12}$

STEP 6 The minimum value of z is **0**, which occurs when $x = 0$ and $y = 0$.

YOUR TURN Find the minimum value of $z = 2x + 3y$ subject to these constraints:

$$x \geq 1 \qquad 2x + y \leq 8 \qquad x + y \geq 4$$

ANSWER

The minimum value of z is **8**, which occurs when $x = 4$ and $y = 0$.

EXAMPLE 9 Solving an Optimization Problem Using Linear Programming: Unbounded Region

Find the maximum value and the minimum value of $z = 7x + 3y$ subject to the following constraints:

$$y \geq 0 \qquad -2x + y \leq 0 \qquad -x + y \geq -4$$

Solution:

STEP 1 Write the objective function. $z = 7x + 3y$

STEP 2 Write the constraints.

$$y \geq 0$$
$$y \leq 2x$$
$$y \geq x - 4$$

STEP 3 Graph the constraints.

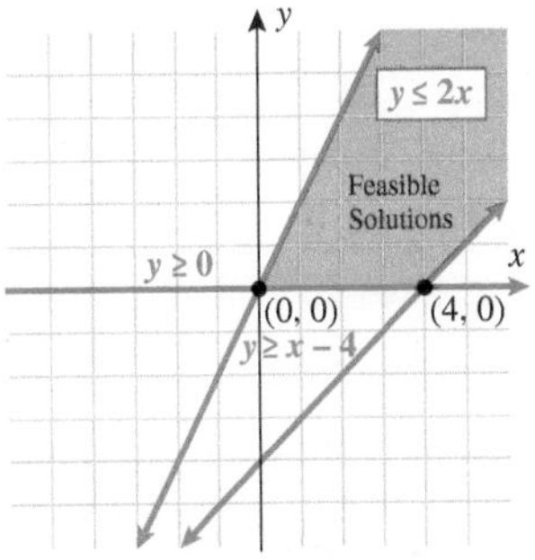

Note: Since the feasible region is unbounded, a maximum or minimum value may or may not exist.

STEP 4 Identify the vertices. (0, 0), (4, 0)

STEP 5 Evaluate the objective function for each vertex.

VERTEX	x	y	OBJECTIVE FUNCTION: $z = 7x + 3y$
(0, 0)	0	0	$7(0) + 3(0) = \mathbf{0}$
(4, 0)	4	0	$7(4) + 3(0) = \mathbf{28}$

STEP 6 The minimum value of z is **0**, which occurs when $x = 0$ and $y = 0$.
There is no maximum value, because if we select a point in the shaded region, say (3, 3), the objective function at (3, 3) is equal to 30, which is greater than 28.

When the feasible solutions are contained in a bounded region, then a maximum and a minimum exist, and each is located at one of the vertices. If the feasible solutions are contained in an unbounded region, then if a maximum or a minimum exists, it is located at one of the vertices.

[SECTION 8.7] SUMMARY

Graphing a Linear Inequality

1. Change the inequality sign to an equal sign.
2. Draw the line $y = mx + b$. (Dashed for strict inequalities and solid for nonstrict inequalities.)
3. Test a point. (Select a point in one half-plane, and test the inequality. Repeat this step for the other half-plane.)
4. Shade the half-plane that satisfies the linear inequality.

Graphing a System of Linear Inequalities

- Draw the individual linear inequalities.
- The overlapped shaded region, if it exists, is the solution.

Linear Programming Model

1. Write the objective function.
2. Write the constraints.
3. Graph the constraints.
4. Identify the vertices.
5. Evaluate the objective function for each vertex.
6. Identify the optimal solution if it exists.

[SECTION 8.7] EXERCISES

• SKILLS

In Exercises 1–4, match each linear inequality with the correct graph.

1. $y > x$ **2.** $y \geq x$ **3.** $y < x$ **4.** $y \leq x$

a.

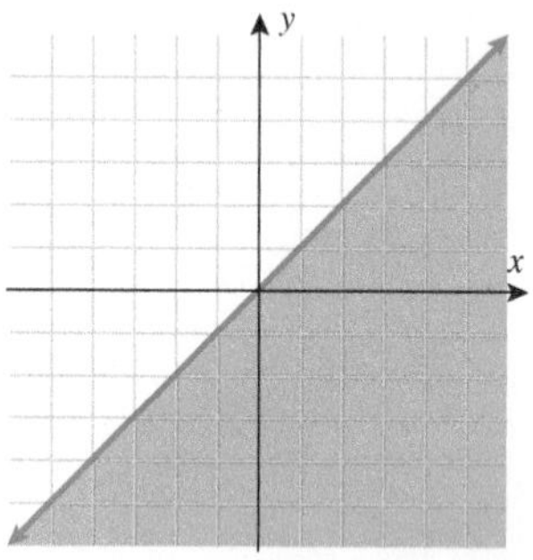

b.

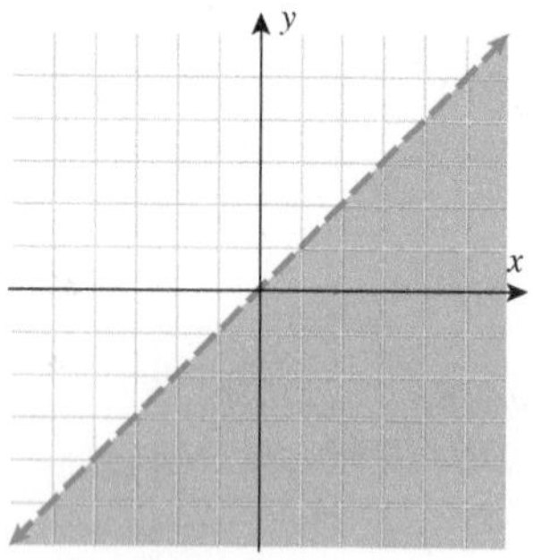

c.

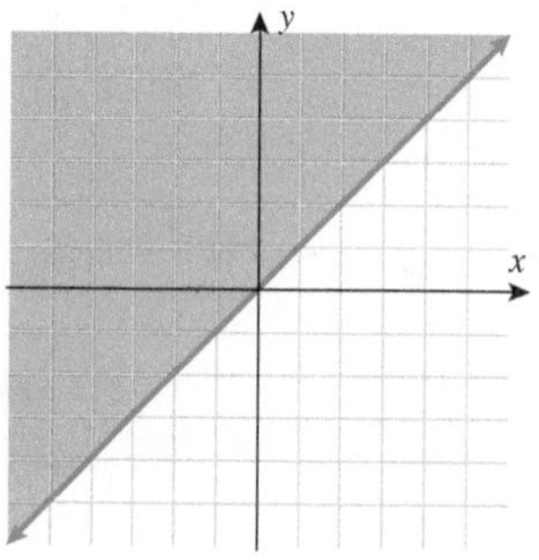

d.

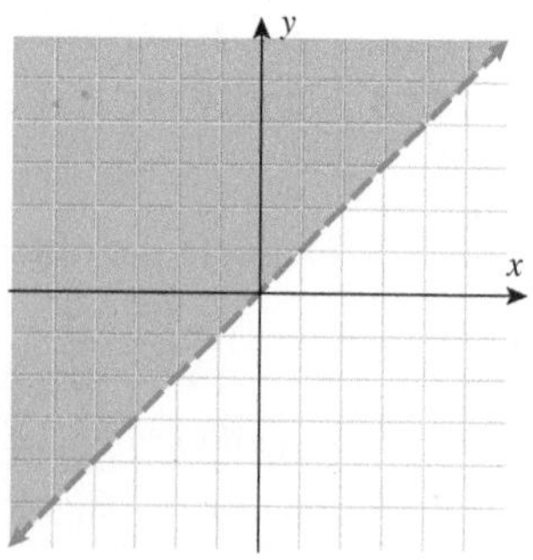

In Exercises 5–20, graph each linear inequality.

5. $y > x - 1$ **6.** $y \geq -x + 1$ **7.** $y \leq -x$ **8.** $y > -x$

9. $y \leq -3x + 2$ **10.** $y < 2x + 3$ **11.** $y \leq -2x + 1$ **12.** $y > 3x - 2$

13. $3x + 4y < 2$ **14.** $2x + 3y > -6$ **15.** $5x + 3y < 15$ **16.** $4x - 5y \leq 20$

17. $4x - 2y \geq 6$ **18.** $6x - 3y \geq 9$ **19.** $6x + 4y \leq 12$ **20.** $5x - 2y \geq 10$

In Exercises 21–50, graph each system of inequalities or indicate that the system has no solution.

21. $y \geq x - 1$
$y \leq x + 1$

22. $y > x + 1$
$y < x - 1$

23. $y > 2x + 1$
$y < 2x - 1$

24. $y \leq 2x - 1$
$y \geq 2x + 1$

25. $y \geq 2x$
$y \leq 2x$

26. $y > 2x$
$y < 2x$

27. $x > -2$
$x < 4$

28. $y < 3$
$y > 0$

29. $x \geq 2$
$y \leq x$

30. $y \leq 3$
$y \geq x$

31. $\begin{array}{l} y > x \\ x < 0 \\ y < 4 \end{array}$

32. $\begin{array}{l} y \le x \\ x \ge 0 \\ y \le 1 \end{array}$

33. $\begin{array}{r} x + y > 2 \\ y < 1 \\ x > 0 \end{array}$

34. $\begin{array}{r} x + y < 4 \\ x > 0 \\ y \ge 1 \end{array}$

35. $\begin{array}{r} -x + y > 1 \\ y < 3 \\ x > 0 \end{array}$

36. $\begin{array}{r} x - y > 2 \\ y < 4 \\ x \ge 0 \end{array}$

37. $\begin{array}{r} x + 3y > 6 \\ y \le 1 \\ x \ge 1 \end{array}$

38. $\begin{array}{r} x + 2y > 4 \\ y < 1 \\ x \ge 0 \end{array}$

39. $\begin{array}{l} y \ge x - 1 \\ y \le -x + 3 \\ y < x + 2 \end{array}$

40. $\begin{array}{l} y < 4 - x \\ y > x - 4 \\ y > -x - 4 \end{array}$

41. $\begin{array}{r} x + y > -4 \\ -x + y < 2 \\ y \ge -1 \\ y \le 1 \end{array}$

42. $\begin{array}{l} y < x + 2 \\ y > x - 2 \\ y < -x + 2 \\ y > -x - 2 \end{array}$

43. $\begin{array}{r} y < x + 3 \\ x + y \ge 1 \\ y \ge 1 \\ y \le 3 \end{array}$

44. $\begin{array}{r} y \le -x + 2 \\ y - x \ge -3 \\ y \ge -2 \\ y \le 1 \end{array}$

45. $\begin{array}{r} y + x < 2 \\ y + x \ge 4 \\ y \ge -2 \\ y \le 1 \end{array}$

46. $\begin{array}{r} y - x < 3 \\ y + x > 3 \\ y \le -2 \\ y \ge -4 \end{array}$

47. $\begin{array}{r} 2x - y < 2 \\ 2x + y > 2 \\ y < 2 \end{array}$

48. $\begin{array}{r} 3x - y > 3 \\ 3x + y < 3 \\ y < -2 \end{array}$

49. $\begin{array}{r} x + 4y > 5 \\ x - 4y < 5 \\ x > 6 \end{array}$

50. $\begin{array}{r} 2x - 3y < 6 \\ 2x + 3y > 6 \\ x < 4 \end{array}$

In Exercises 51–54, find the value of the objective function at each of the vertices. What is the maximum value of the objective function? What is the minimum value of the objective function?

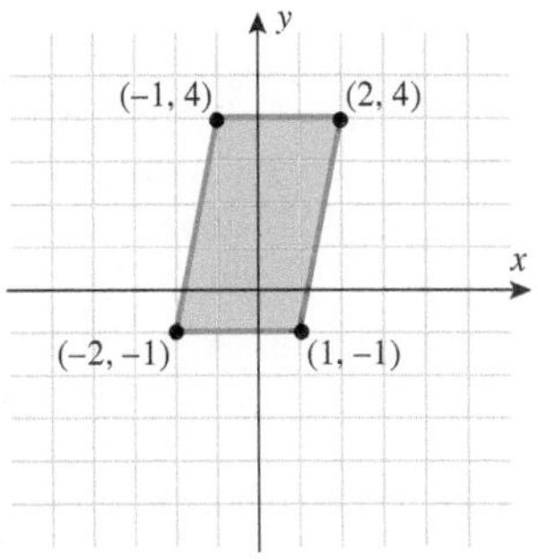

51. Objective function: $z = 2x + 3y$

52. Objective function: $z = 3x + 2y$

53. Objective function: $z = 1.5x + 4.5y$

54. Objective function: $z = \frac{2}{3}x + \frac{3}{5}y$

In Exercises 55–62, minimize or maximize each objective function subject to the given constraints.

55. Minimize $z = 7x + 4y$ subject to
$x \ge 0 \quad y \ge 0 \quad -x + y \le 4$

56. Maximize $z = 3x + 5y$ subject to
$x \ge 0 \quad y \ge 0 \quad -x + y \ge 4$

57. Maximize $z = 4x + 3y$ subject to
$x \ge 0 \quad y \le -x + 4 \quad y \ge -x$

58. Minimize $z = 4x + 3y$ subject to
$x \ge 0 \quad y \ge 0$
$x + y \le 10 \quad x + y \ge 0$

59. Minimize $z = 2.5x + 3.1y$ subject to
$x \ge 0 \quad y \ge 0 \quad x \le 4$
$-x + y \le 2 \quad x + y \le 6$

60. Maximize $z = 2.5x - 3.1y$ subject to
$x \ge 1 \quad y \le 7 \quad x \le 3$
$-x + y \ge 2 \quad x + y \ge 6$

61. Maximize $z = \frac{1}{4}x + \frac{2}{5}y$ subject to
$x + y \ge 5 \quad x + y \le 7$
$-x + y \le 5 \quad -x + y \ge 3$

62. Minimize $z = \frac{1}{3}x - \frac{2}{5}y$ subject to
$x + y \ge 6 \quad x + y \le 8$
$-x + y \le 6 \quad -x + y \ge 4$

• APPLICATIONS

For Exercises 63–66, employ the following supply and demand equations:

Demand:	$P = 80 - 0.01x$
Supply:	$P = 20 + 0.02x$

where P is the price in dollars when x units are produced.

63. Consumer Surplus. Write a system of linear inequalities corresponding to the consumer surplus.

64. Producer Surplus. Write a system of linear inequalities corresponding to the producer surplus.

65. Consumer Surplus. Calculate the consumer surplus given the supply and demand equations.

66. Producer Surplus. Calculate the producer surplus given the supply and demand equations.

67. Hurricanes. After back-to-back-to-back-to-back hurricanes (Charley, Frances, Ivan, and Jeanne) in Florida in the summer of 2004, FEMA sent disaster relief trucks to Florida. Floridians mainly needed drinking water and generators. Each truck could carry no more than 6000 pounds of cargo or 2400 cubic feet of cargo. Each case of bottled water takes up 1 cubic foot of space and weighs 25 pounds. Each generator takes up 20 cubic feet and weighs 150 pounds. Let x represent the number of cases of water and y represent the number of generators, and write a system of linear inequalities that describes the number of generators and cases of water each truck can haul to Florida.

68. Hurricanes. Repeat Exercise 67 with a smaller truck and different supplies. Suppose the smaller trucks that can haul 2000 pounds and 1500 cubic feet of cargo are used to haul plywood and tarps. A case of plywood takes up 60 cubic feet and weighs 500 pounds. A case of tarps takes up 10 cubic feet and weighs 50 pounds. Letting x represent the number of cases of plywood and y represent the number of cases of tarps, write a system of linear inequalities that describes the number of cases of tarps and plywood each truck can haul to Florida. Graph the system of linear inequalities.

69. Hurricanes. After the 2004 hurricanes in Florida, a student at Valencia Community College decided to create two T-shirts to sell. One T-shirt said, "I survived Charley on Friday the Thirteenth," and the second said, "I survived Charley, Frances, Ivan, and Jeanne." The Charley T-shirt costs him \$7 to make and he sold it for \$13. The other T-shirt cost him \$5 to make and he sold it for \$10. He did not want to invest more than \$1000. He estimated that the total demand would not exceed 180 T-shirts. Find the number of each type of T-shirt he needed to make to yield maximum profit.

70. Hurricanes. After Hurricane Charley devastated central Florida unexpectedly, Orlando residents prepared for Hurricane Frances by boarding up windows and filling up their cars with gas. It took 5 hours of standing in line to get plywood, and lines for gas were just as time-consuming. A student at Seminole Community College decided to do a spoof of the "Got Milk?" ads and created two T-shirts: "Got Plywood?" showing a line of people in a home improvement store, and "Got Gas?" showing a street lined with cars waiting to pump gasoline. The "Got Plywood?" shirts cost \$8 to make, and she sold them for \$13. The "Got Gas?" shirts cost \$6 to make, and she sold them for \$10. She decided to limit her costs to \$1400. She estimated that demand for these T-shirts would not exceed 200 T-shirts. Find the number of each type of T-shirt she should have made to yield maximum profit.

71. Health. A diet must be designed to provide at least 275 units of calcium, 125 units of iron, and 200 units of vitamin B. Each ounce of food A contains 10 units of calcium, 15 units of iron, and 20 units of vitamin B. Each ounce of food B contains 20 units of calcium, 10 units of iron, and 15 units of vitamin B.

a. Find a system of inequalities to describe the different quantities of food that may be used (let $x =$ the number of ounces of food A and $y =$ the number of ounces of food B).

b. Graph the system of inequalities.

c. Using the graph found in part (b), find two possible solutions (there are infinitely many).

72. Health. A diet must be designed to provide at least 350 units of calcium, 175 units of iron, and 225 units of vitamin B. Each ounce of food A contains 15 units of calcium, 25 units of iron, and 20 units of vitamin B. Each ounce of food B contains 25 units of calcium, 10 units of iron, and 10 units of vitamin B.

a. Find a system of inequalities to describe the different quantities of food that may be used (let $x =$ the number of ounces of food A and $y =$ the number of ounces of food B).

b. Graph the system of inequalities.

c. Using the graph found in part (b), find two possible solutions (there are infinitely many).

73. Business. A manufacturer produces two types of computer mouse: a USB wireless mouse and a Bluetooth mouse. Past sales indicate that it is necessary to produce at least twice as many USB wireless mice than Bluetooth mice. To meet demand, the manufacturer must produce at least 1000 computer mice per hour.

a. Find a system of inequalities describing the production levels of computer mice. Let x be the production level for the USB wireless mouse, and let y be the production level for Bluetooth mouse.

b. Graph the system of inequalities describing the production levels of computer mice.

c. Use your graph in part (b) to find two possible solutions.

74. Business. A manufacturer produces two types of mechanical pencil lead: 0.5-millimeter and 0.7-millimeter lead. Past sales indicate that it is necessary to produce at least 50% more 0.5-millimeter lead than 0.7-millimeter lead. To meet demand, the manufacturer must produce at least 10,000 pieces of pencil lead per hour.

a. Find a system of inequalities describing the production levels of pencil lead. Let x be the production level for 0.5-millimeter pencil lead and y be the production level for 0.7-millimeter pencil lead.

b. Graph the system of inequalities describing the production levels of pencil lead.

c. Use your graph in part (b) to find two possible solutions.

• CATCH THE MISTAKE

In Exercises 75 and 76, explain the mistake that is made.

75. Graph the inequality $y \geq 2x + 1$.

Solution:

Graph the line $y = 2x + 1$ with a solid line.

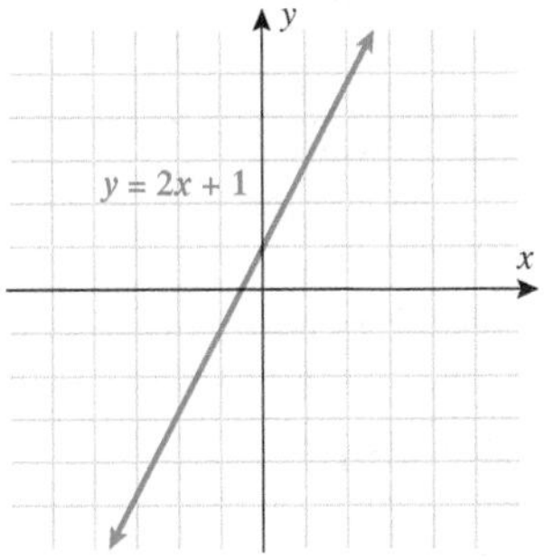

Since the inequality is $\geq$, shade to the *right*.

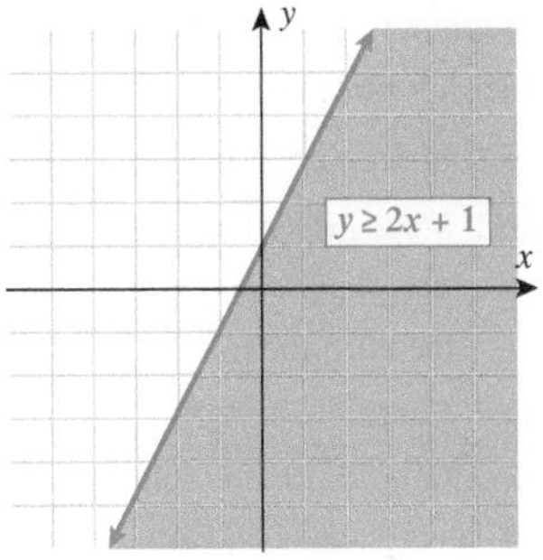

This is incorrect. What mistake was made?

76. Graph the inequality $y < 2x + 1$.

Solution:

Graph the line $y = 2x + 1$ with a solid line.

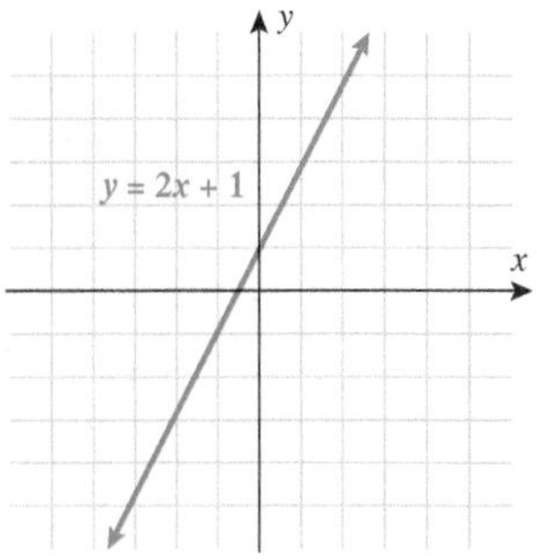

Since the inequality is $<$, shade *below*.

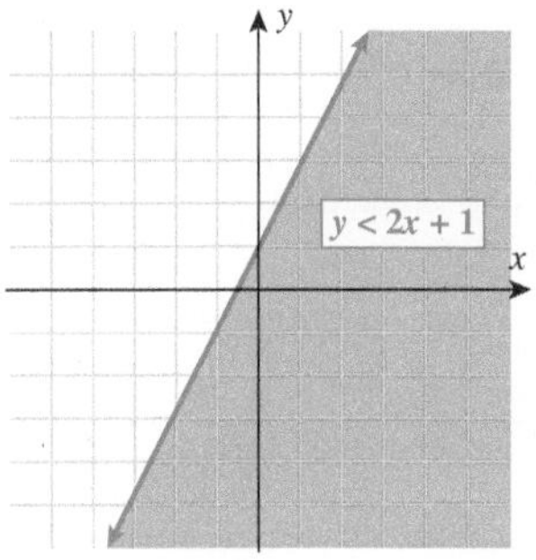

This is incorrect. What mistake was made?

• CONCEPTUAL

In Exercises 77–82, determine whether each statement is true or false.

77. A linear inequality always has a solution that is a half-plane.

78. A dashed curve is used for strict inequalities.

79. A solid curve is used for strict inequalities.

80. A system of linear inequalities always has a solution.

81. An objective function always has a maximum or minimum.

82. An objective function subject to constraints that correspond to a bounded region always has a maximum and a minimum.

• CHALLENGE

In Exercises 83 and 84, for the system of linear inequalities, assume *a*, *b*, *c*, and *d* are real numbers.

$$\begin{aligned} x &\geq a \\ x &< b \\ y &> c \\ y &\leq d \end{aligned}$$

83. Describe the solution when $a < b$ and $c < d$.

84. What will the solution be if $a > b$ and $c > d$?

For Exercises 85 and 86, use the following system of linear inequalities:

$$\begin{aligned} y &\leq ax + b \\ y &\geq -ax + b \end{aligned}$$

85. If a and b are positive real numbers, graph the solution.

86. If a and b are negative real numbers, graph the solution.

87. Maximize the objective function $z = 2x + y$ subject to the following conditions, where $a > 2$.

$$\begin{aligned} ax + y &\geq -a \\ -ax + y &\leq a \\ ax + y &\leq a \\ -ax + y &\geq -a \end{aligned}$$

88. Maximize the objective function $z = x + 2y$ subject to the following conditions, where $a > b > 0$.

$$\begin{aligned} x + y &\geq a \\ -x + y &\leq a \\ x + y &\leq a + b \\ -x + y &\geq a - b \end{aligned}$$

• PREVIEW TO CALCULUS

In calculus, the first steps when solving the problem of finding the area enclosed by a set of curves are similar to those for finding the feasible region in a linear programming problem.

In Exercises 89–92, graph the system of inequalities and identify the vertices—that is, the points of intersection of the given curves.

89. $y \leq x + 2$
$y \geq x^2$

90. $x \leq 25$
$x \geq y^2$

91. $y \leq x^2$
$y \geq x^3$
$x \geq 0$

92. $y \geq x^3$
$y \leq -x$
$y \geq x + 6$

[CHAPTER 8 REVIEW]

SECTION	CONCEPT	KEY IDEAS/FORMULAS
8.1	**Systems of linear equations in two variables**	$A_1x + B_1y = C_1$ $A_2x + B_2y = C_2$
	Solving systems of linear equations in two variables	**Substitution method** Solve for one variable in terms of the other, and substitute that expression into the other equation. **Elimination method** Eliminate a variable by adding multiples of the equations. **Graphing method** Graph the two lines. The solution is the point of intersection. Parallel lines have no solution, and identical lines have infinitely many solutions.
	Three methods and three types of solutions	One solution, no solution, infinitely many solutions.
8.2	**Systems of linear equations in three variables**	Planes in a three-dimensional coordinate system.
	Solving systems of linear equations in three variables	Step 1: Reduce the system to two equations and two unknowns. Step 2: Solve the system resulting from Step 1. Step 3: Substitute solutions found in Step 2 into any of the equations to find the third variable. Step 4: Check.
	Types of solutions	One solution (point), no solution, or infinitely many solutions (line or the same plane).
8.3	**Systems of linear equations and matrices**	
	Matrices	$A_{m\times n} = \begin{bmatrix} a_{11} & a_{12} & \cdots & a_{1n} \\ a_{21} & a_{22} & \cdots & a_{2n} \\ \vdots & & & \vdots \\ a_{m1} & a_{m2} & \cdots & a_{mn} \end{bmatrix}$
	Augmented matrices	$\begin{aligned} a_1x + b_1y + c_1z &= d_1 \\ a_2x + b_2y + c_2z &= d_2 \\ a_3x + b_3y + c_3z &= d_3 \end{aligned} \Rightarrow \left[\begin{array}{ccc\|c} a_1 & b_1 & c_1 & d_1 \\ a_2 & b_2 & c_2 & d_2 \\ a_3 & b_3 & c_3 & d_3 \end{array}\right]$
	Row operations on a matrix	1. $R_i \leftrightarrow R_j$ Interchange row i with row j. 2. $cR_i \to R_i$ Multiply row i by the constant c. 3. $cR_i + R_j \to R_j$ Multiply row i by the constant c and add to row j, writing the results in row j.
	Row–echelon form of a matrix	A matrix is in **row–echelon form** if it has all three of the following properties: 1. Any rows consisting entirely of 0s are at the bottom of the matrix. 2. For each row that does not consist entirely of 0s, the first (leftmost) nonzero entry is 1 (called the leading 1). 3. For two successive nonzero rows, the leading 1 in the higher row is farther to the left than the leading 1 in the lower row. If a matrix in row–echelon form has the following additional property, then the matrix is in **reduced row–echelon form**: 4. Every column containing a leading 1 has zeros in every position above and below the leading 1.

SECTION	CONCEPT	KEY IDEAS/FORMULAS
	Gaussian elimination with back-substitution	Step 1: Write the system of equations as an augmented matrix. Step 2: Apply row operations to transform the matrix into row–echelon form. Step 3: Apply back-substitution to identify the solution.
	Gauss–Jordan elimination	Step 1: Write the system of equations as an augmented matrix. Step 2: Apply row operations to transform the matrix into *reduced* row–echelon form. Step 3: Identify the solution.
	Inconsistent and dependent systems	No solution or infinitely many solutions
8.4	**Matrix algebra**	$\begin{array}{c} \\ \text{Row } 1 \\ \text{Row } 2 \\ \vdots \\ \text{Row } i \\ \vdots \\ \text{Row } m \end{array} \begin{array}{c} \begin{array}{ccccccc} \text{Column 1} & \text{Column 2} & \cdots & \text{Column } j & \cdots & \text{Column } n \end{array} \\ \begin{bmatrix} a_{11} & a_{12} & \cdots & a_{1j} & \cdots & a_{1n} \\ a_{21} & a_{22} & \cdots & a_{2j} & \cdots & a_{2n} \\ \vdots & \vdots & \cdots & \vdots & \cdots & \vdots \\ a_{i1} & a_{i2} & \cdots & a_{ij} & \cdots & a_{in} \\ \vdots & \vdots & \cdots & \vdots & \cdots & \vdots \\ a_{m1} & a_{m2} & \cdots & a_{mj} & \cdots & a_{mn} \end{bmatrix} \end{array}$
	Equality of matrices	The orders must be the same: $A_{m \times n}$ and $B_{m \times n}$ and corresponding entries are equal.
	Matrix addition and subtraction	The orders must be the same: $A_{m \times n}$ and $B_{m \times n}$. Perform operation entry by entry.
	Scalar and matrix multiplication	*All* of the entries are multiplied by the scalar. For matrix multiplication ■ The orders must satisfy the relationship: $A_{m \times n}$ and $B_{n \times p}$, resulting in $(AB)_{m \times p}$. ■ Perform multiplication row by column. ■ Matrix multiplication is not commutative: $AB \neq BA$.
	Matrix equations	Linear system: $AX = B$. *Front* (left) multiply both sides of the equation by A^{-1} (provided A^{-1} exists), which results in $X = A^{-1}B$.
	Finding the inverse of a square matrix	Only square matrices, $n \times n$, can have inverses, $A^{-1}A = I_n$. Note: not all square matrices will have an inverse. Step 1: Form the matrix $[A \mid I_n]$. Step 2: Use row operations to transform this matrix to $[I_n \mid A^{-1}]$.
	Solving systems of linear equations using matrix algebra and inverses of square matrices	$AX = B$ Step 1: Find A^{-1}. Step 2: $X = A^{-1}B$.

SECTION	CONCEPT	KEY IDEAS/FORMULAS
8.5	**The determinant of a square matrix and Cramer's rule**	Cramer's rule can be used only to solve a system of linear equations with a unique solution.
	Determinant of a 2×2 matrix	$\begin{vmatrix} a & b \\ c & d \end{vmatrix} = ad - bc$
	Determinant of an $n \times n$ matrix	Let A be a square matrix of order $n \times n$. Then: ■ The **minor** M_{ij} of the element a_{ij} is the determinant of the $(n-1) \times (n-1)$ matrix obtained when the ith row and jth column of A are deleted. ■ The **cofactor** C_{ij} of the element a_{ij} is given by $C_{ij} = (-1)^{i+j}M_{ij}$. $\begin{bmatrix} 1 & 3 & 2 \\ 4 & -1 & 0 \\ 5 & -2 & 3 \end{bmatrix}$ $M_{11} = \begin{vmatrix} -1 & 0 \\ -2 & 3 \end{vmatrix} = -3 - 0 = -3$ $C_{11} = (-1)^{1+1}M_{11} = (1)(-3) = -3$ Sign pattern of cofactors for the determinant of a 3×3 matrix: $\begin{bmatrix} + & - & + \\ - & + & - \\ + & - & + \end{bmatrix}$ If A is a 3×3 matrix, the determinant can be given by $\det(A) = a_{11}C_{11} + a_{12}C_{12} + a_{13}C_{13}$. This is called **expanding the determinant by the first row**. (Note that any row or column can be used.) $\begin{vmatrix} a_1 & b_1 & c_1 \\ a_2 & b_2 & c_2 \\ a_3 & b_3 & c_3 \end{vmatrix} = a_1\begin{vmatrix} b_2 & c_2 \\ b_3 & c_3 \end{vmatrix} - b_1\begin{vmatrix} a_2 & c_2 \\ a_3 & c_3 \end{vmatrix} + c_1\begin{vmatrix} a_2 & b_2 \\ a_3 & b_3 \end{vmatrix}$
	Cramer's rule: Systems of linear equations in two variables	The system $a_1x + b_1y = c_1$ $a_2x + b_2y = c_2$ has the solution $x = \frac{D_x}{D} \quad y = \frac{D_y}{D} \quad \text{if } D \neq 0$ where $D = \begin{vmatrix} a_1 & b_1 \\ a_2 & b_2 \end{vmatrix} \quad D_x = \begin{vmatrix} c_1 & b_1 \\ c_2 & b_2 \end{vmatrix} \quad D_y = \begin{vmatrix} a_1 & c_1 \\ a_2 & c_2 \end{vmatrix}$
	Cramer's rule: Systems of linear equations in three variables	The system $a_1x + b_1y + c_1z = d_1$ $a_2x + b_2y + c_2z = d_2$ $a_3x + b_3y + c_3z = d_3$ has the solution $x = \frac{D_x}{D} \quad y = \frac{D_y}{D} \quad z = \frac{D_z}{D} \quad \text{if } D \neq 0$ where $D = \begin{vmatrix} a_1 & b_1 & c_1 \\ a_2 & b_2 & c_2 \\ a_3 & b_3 & c_3 \end{vmatrix} \quad D_x = \begin{vmatrix} d_1 & b_1 & c_1 \\ d_2 & b_2 & c_2 \\ d_3 & b_3 & c_3 \end{vmatrix}$ $D_y = \begin{vmatrix} a_1 & d_1 & c_1 \\ a_2 & d_2 & c_2 \\ a_3 & d_3 & c_3 \end{vmatrix} \quad D_z = \begin{vmatrix} a_1 & b_1 & d_1 \\ a_2 & b_2 & d_2 \\ a_3 & b_3 & d_3 \end{vmatrix}$

SECTION	CONCEPT	KEY IDEAS/FORMULAS
8.6	**Partial fractions**	$\frac{n(x)}{d(x)}$ where $\frac{n(x)}{d(x)}$ is proper.
	Performing partial-fraction decomposition	Factor $d(x)$ Write $\frac{n(x)}{d(x)}$ as a sum of partial fractions: *Case 1:* Distinct (nonrepeated) **linear** factors *Case 2:* Repeated **linear** factors *Case 3:* Distinct **irreducible quadratic** factors *Case 4:* Repeated **irreducible quadratic** factors. **Distinct linear factors** $\frac{n(x)}{d(x)} = \frac{A}{(ax+b)} + \frac{B}{(cx+d)} + \cdots$ **Repeated linear factors** $\frac{n(x)}{d(x)} = \frac{A}{(ax+b)} + \frac{B}{(ax+b)^2} + \cdots + \frac{M}{(ax+b)^m}$ **Distinct irreducible quadratic factors** $\frac{n(x)}{d(x)} = \frac{Ax+B}{ax^2+bx+c}$ **Repeated irreducible quadratic factors** $\frac{n(x)}{d(x)} = \frac{A_1x+B_1}{ax^2+bx+c} + \frac{A_2x+B_2}{(ax^2+bx+c)^2} + \frac{A_3x+B_3}{(ax^2+bx+c)^3} + \cdots + \frac{A_mx+B_m}{(ax^2+bx+c)^m}$
8.7	**Systems of linear inequalities in two variables**	
	Linear inequalities in two variables	■ $\leq$ or $\geq$ use solid lines. ■ $<$ or $>$ use dashed lines.
	Systems of linear inequalities in two variables	Solutions are determined graphically by finding the common shaded region.
	The linear programming model	Finding optimal solutions Minimizing or maximizing a function subject to constraints (linear inequalities)

[CHAPTER 8 REVIEW EXERCISES]

8.1 Systems of Linear Equations in Two Variables

Solve each system of linear equations.

1. $r - s = 3$
   $r + s = 3$

2. $3x + 4y = 2$
   $x - y = 6$

3. $-4x + 2y = 3$
   $4x - y = 5$

4. $0.25x - 0.5y = 0.6$
   $0.5x + 0.25y = 0.8$

5. $x + y = 3$
   $x - y = 1$

6. $3x + y = 4$
   $2x + y = 1$

7. $4c - 4d = 3$
   $c + d = 4$

8. $5r + 2s = 1$
   $r - s = -3$

9. $y = -\frac{1}{2}x$
   $y = \frac{1}{2}x + 2$

10. $2x + 4y = -2$
    $4x - 2y = 3$

11. $1.3x - 2.4y = 1.6$
    $0.7x - 1.2y = 1.4$

12. $\frac{1}{4}x - \frac{3}{4}y = 12$
    $\frac{1}{2}y + \frac{1}{4}x = \frac{1}{2}$

13. $5x - 3y = 21$
    $-2x + 7y = -20$

14. $6x - 2y = -2$
    $4x + 3y = 16$

15. $10x - 7y = -24$
    $7x + 4y = 1$

16. $\frac{1}{3}x - \frac{2}{9}y = \frac{2}{9}$
    $\frac{4}{5}x + \frac{3}{4}y = -\frac{3}{4}$

Match each system of equations with its graph.

17. $2x - 3y = 4$
    $x + 4y = 3$

18. $5x - y = 2$
    $5x - y = -2$

19. $x + 2y = -6$
    $2x + 4y = -12$

20. $5x + 2y = 3$
    $4x - 2y = 6$

a.

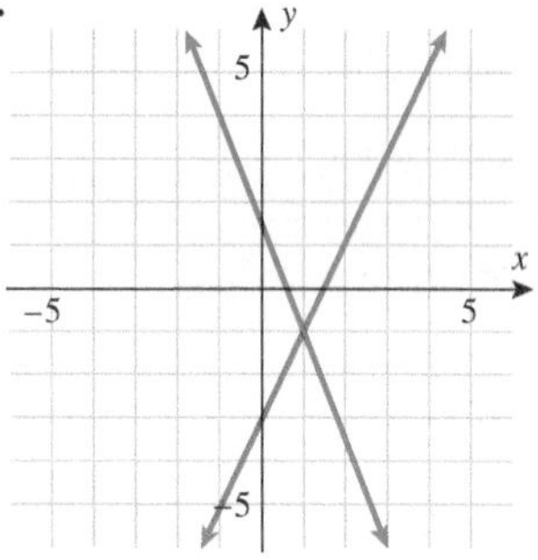

b.

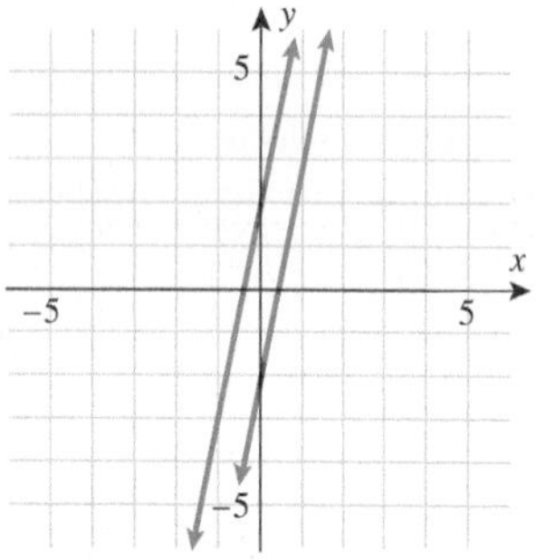

c.

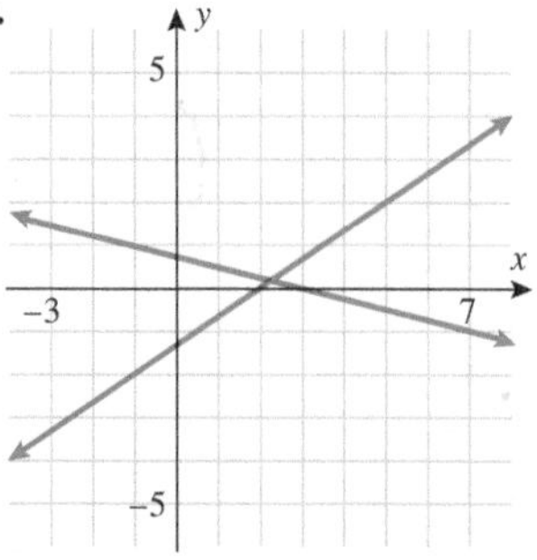

d.

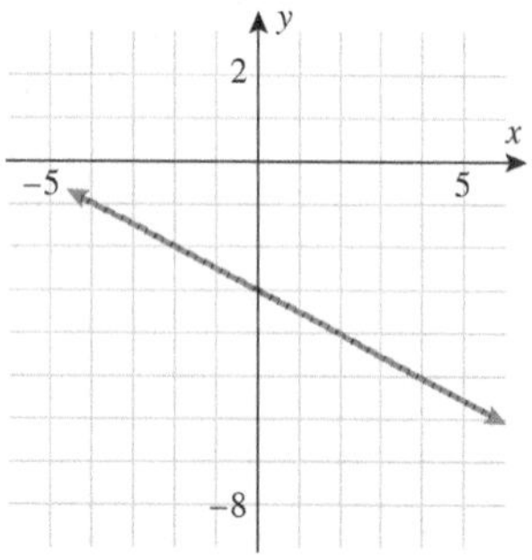

Applications

21. **Chemistry.** In chemistry lab, Alexandra needs to make a 42-milliliter solution that is 15% NaCl. All that is in the lab is 6% and 18% NaCl. How many milliliters of each solution should she use to obtain the desired mix?

22. **Gas Mileage.** A Nissan Sentra gets approximately 32 mpg on the highway and 18 mpg in the city. Suppose 265 miles were driven on a full tank (12 gallons) of gasoline. Approximately how many miles were driven in the city and how many on the highway?

8.2 Systems of Linear Equations in Three Variables

Solve each system of linear equations.

23. $x + y + z = 1$
    $x - y - z = -3$
    $-x + y + z = 3$

24. $x - 2y + z = 3$
    $2x - y + z = -4$
    $3x - 3y - 5z = 2$

25. $x + y + z = 7$
    $x - y - z = 17$
    $y + z = 5$

26. $x + z = 3$
    $-x + y - z = -1$
    $x + y + z = 5$

Applications

27. **Fitting a Curve to Data.** The average number of flights on a commercial plane that a person takes per year can be modeled by a quadratic function $y = ax^2 + bx + c$, where $a < 0$, and x represents age: $16 \leq x \leq 65$. The following table gives the average number of flights per year that a person takes on a commercial airline. Determine a quadratic function that models this quantity. *Note:* Coefficients will be approximate.

AGE	NUMBER OF FLIGHTS PER YEAR
16	2
40	6
65	4

28. **Investment Portfolio.** Danny and Paula decide to invest \$20,000 of their savings. They put some in an IRA account earning 4.5% interest, some in a mutual fund that has been averaging 8% a year, and some in a stock that earned 12% last year. If they put \$4000 more in the IRA than in the mutual fund, and the mutual fund and stock have the same growth in the next year as they did in the previous year, they will earn \$1525 in a year. How much money did they put in each of the three investments?

8.3 Systems of Linear Equations and Matrices

Write the augmented matrix for each system of linear equations.

29. $\begin{aligned} 5x + 7y &= 2 \\ 3x - 4y &= -2 \end{aligned}$

30. $\begin{aligned} 2.3x - 4.5y &= 6.8 \\ -0.4x + 2.1y &= -9.1 \end{aligned}$

31. $\begin{aligned} 2x - z &= 3 \\ y - 3z &= -2 \\ x + 4z &= -3 \end{aligned}$

32. $\begin{aligned} 2y - x + 3z &= 1 \\ 4z - 2y + 3x &= -2 \\ x - y - 4z &= 0 \end{aligned}$

Indicate whether each matrix is in row–echelon form. If it is, state whether it is in *reduced* row–echelon form.

33. $\left[\begin{array}{cc|c} 1 & 1 & 0 \\ 0 & 1 & 2 \end{array}\right]$

34. $\left[\begin{array}{cc|c} 1 & 2 & 0 \\ 0 & 0 & 1 \end{array}\right]$

35. $\left[\begin{array}{ccc|c} 2 & 0 & 1 & 1 \\ 0 & -2 & 0 & 2 \\ 0 & 0 & 2 & 3 \end{array}\right]$

36. $\left[\begin{array}{cccc|c} 1 & 0 & 1 & 0 & 2 \\ 0 & 0 & 1 & 1 & -3 \\ 0 & 1 & 0 & 0 & 2 \\ 0 & 0 & 0 & 1 & 1 \end{array}\right]$

Perform the indicated row operations on each matrix.

37. $\left[\begin{array}{cc|c} 1 & -2 & 1 \\ 0 & -2 & 2 \end{array}\right] \quad \frac{-1}{2}R_2 \to R_2$

38. $\left[\begin{array}{cc|c} 1 & 4 & 1 \\ 2 & -2 & 3 \end{array}\right] \quad R_2 - 2R_1 \to R_2$

39. $\left[\begin{array}{ccc|c} 1 & -2 & 0 & 1 \\ 0 & -2 & 3 & -2 \\ 0 & 1 & -4 & 8 \end{array}\right] \quad R_2 + R_1 \to R_1$

40. $\left[\begin{array}{cccc|c} 1 & 1 & 1 & 6 & 0 \\ 0 & 2 & -2 & 3 & -2 \\ 0 & 0 & 1 & -2 & 4 \\ 0 & -1 & 3 & -3 & 3 \end{array}\right] \quad \begin{array}{l} -2R_1 + R_2 \to R_1 \\ R_4 + R_3 \to R_4 \end{array}$

Apply row operations to transform each matrix to reduced row–echelon form.

41. $\left[\begin{array}{cc|c} 1 & 3 & 0 \\ 3 & 4 & 1 \end{array}\right]$

42. $\left[\begin{array}{ccc|c} 1 & 2 & -1 & 0 \\ 0 & 1 & -1 & -1 \\ -2 & 0 & 1 & -2 \end{array}\right]$

43. $\left[\begin{array}{ccc|c} 4 & 1 & -2 & 0 \\ 1 & 0 & -1 & 0 \\ -2 & 1 & 1 & 12 \end{array}\right]$

44. $\left[\begin{array}{ccc|c} 2 & 3 & 2 & 1 \\ 0 & -1 & 1 & -2 \\ 1 & 1 & -1 & 6 \end{array}\right]$

Solve the system of linear equations using augmented matrices.

45. $\begin{aligned} 3x - 2y &= 2 \\ -2x + 4y &= 1 \end{aligned}$

46. $\begin{aligned} 2x - 7y &= 22 \\ x + 5y &= -23 \end{aligned}$

47. $\begin{aligned} 5x - y &= 9 \\ x + 4y &= 6 \end{aligned}$

48. $\begin{aligned} 8x + 7y &= 10 \\ -3x + 5y &= 42 \end{aligned}$

49. $\begin{aligned} x - 2y + z &= 3 \\ 2x - y + z &= -4 \\ 3x - 3y - 5z &= 2 \end{aligned}$

50. $\begin{aligned} 3x - y + 4z &= 18 \\ 5x + 2y - z &= -20 \\ x + 7y - 6z &= -38 \end{aligned}$

51. $\begin{aligned} x - 4y + 10z &= -61 \\ 3x - 5y + 8z &= -52 \\ -5x + y - 2z &= 8 \end{aligned}$

52. $\begin{aligned} 4x - 2y + 5z &= 17 \\ x + 6y - 3z &= -\tfrac{17}{2} \\ -2x + 5y + z &= 2 \end{aligned}$

53. $\begin{aligned} 3x + y + z &= -4 \\ x - 2y + z &= -6 \end{aligned}$

54. $\begin{aligned} 2x - y + 3z &= 6 \\ 3x + 2y - z &= 12 \end{aligned}$

Applications

55. **Fitting a Curve to Data.** The average number of flights on a commercial plane that a person takes a year can be modeled by a quadratic function $y = ax^2 + bx + c$, where $a < 0$ and x represents age: $16 < x < 65$. The table below gives the average number of flights per year that a person takes on a commercial airline. Determine a quadratic function that models this quantity by solving for a, b, and c using matrices and compare with Exercise 27. *Note:* Coefficients will be approximate.

AGE	NUMBER OF FLIGHTS PER YEAR
16	2
40	6
65	4

56. **Investment Portfolio.** Danny and Paula decide to invest \$20,000 of their savings in investments. They put some in an IRA account earning 4.5% interest, some in a mutual fund that has been averaging 8% a year, and some in a stock that earned 12% last year. If they put \$3000 more in the mutual fund than in the IRA, and the mutual fund and stock have the same growth in the next year as they had in the previous year, Danny and Paula will earn \$1877.50 in a year. How much money did they put in each of the three investments?

8.4 Matrix Algebra

Calculate the given expression, if possible.

$$A = \begin{bmatrix} 2 & -3 \\ 0 & 1 \end{bmatrix} \quad B = \begin{bmatrix} 1 & 5 & -1 \\ 3 & 7 & 2 \end{bmatrix} \quad C = \begin{bmatrix} 5 & 0 & 1 \\ 2 & -1 & 4 \\ 0 & 3 & 6 \end{bmatrix}$$

$$D = \begin{bmatrix} 5 & 2 \\ 9 & 7 \end{bmatrix} \quad E = \begin{bmatrix} 2 & 0 & 3 \\ 4 & 1 & -1 \end{bmatrix}$$

57. $A + C$ **58.** $B + A$ **59.** $B + E$

60. $A + D$ **61.** $2A + D$ **62.** $3E + B$

63. $2D - 3A$ **64.** $3B - 4E$ **65.** $5A - 2D$

66. $5B - 4E$ **67.** AB **68.** BC

69. DA **70.** AD **71.** $BC + E$

72. DB **73.** EC **74.** CE

Determine whether B is the multiplicative inverse of A using $AA^{-1} = I$.

75. $A = \begin{bmatrix} 6 & 4 \\ 4 & 2 \end{bmatrix} \quad B = \begin{bmatrix} -0.5 & 1 \\ 1 & -1.5 \end{bmatrix}$

76. $A = \begin{bmatrix} 1 & -2 \\ 2 & -4 \end{bmatrix} \quad B = \begin{bmatrix} 1 & 2 \\ 2 & -2 \end{bmatrix}$

77. $A = \begin{bmatrix} 1 & -2 & 6 \\ 2 & 3 & -2 \\ 0 & -1 & 1 \end{bmatrix} \quad B = \begin{bmatrix} -\frac{1}{7} & \frac{4}{7} & 2 \\ \frac{2}{7} & -\frac{1}{7} & -2 \\ \frac{2}{7} & -\frac{1}{7} & -1 \end{bmatrix}$

78. $A = \begin{bmatrix} 0 & 7 & 6 \\ 1 & 0 & -4 \\ -2 & 1 & 0 \end{bmatrix} \quad B = \begin{bmatrix} 1 & 1 & 1 \\ -2 & -2 & -2 \\ 2 & 0 & 6 \end{bmatrix}$

Find A^{-1}, if it exists.

79. $A = \begin{bmatrix} 1 & 2 \\ -3 & 4 \end{bmatrix}$ **80.** $A = \begin{bmatrix} -2 & 7 \\ -4 & 6 \end{bmatrix}$

81. $A = \begin{bmatrix} 0 & 1 \\ -2 & 0 \end{bmatrix}$ **82.** $A = \begin{bmatrix} 3 & -1 \\ -2 & 2 \end{bmatrix}$

83. $A = \begin{bmatrix} 1 & 3 & -2 \\ 2 & 1 & -1 \\ 0 & 1 & -3 \end{bmatrix}$ **84.** $A = \begin{bmatrix} 0 & 1 & 0 \\ 4 & 1 & 2 \\ -3 & -2 & 1 \end{bmatrix}$

85. $A = \begin{bmatrix} -1 & 1 & 0 \\ -2 & 1 & 2 \\ 1 & 2 & 4 \end{bmatrix}$ **86.** $A = \begin{bmatrix} -4 & 4 & 3 \\ 1 & 2 & 2 \\ 3 & -1 & 6 \end{bmatrix}$

Solve the system of linear equations using matrix algebra.

87. $\begin{aligned} 3x - y &= 11 \\ 5x + 2y &= 33 \end{aligned}$ **88.** $\begin{aligned} 6x + 4y &= 15 \\ -3x - 2y &= -1 \end{aligned}$

89. $\begin{aligned} \tfrac{5}{8}x - \tfrac{2}{3}y &= -3 \\ \tfrac{3}{4}x + \tfrac{5}{6}y &= 16 \end{aligned}$ **90.** $\begin{aligned} x + y - z &= 0 \\ 2x - y + 3z &= 18 \\ 3x - 2y + z &= 17 \end{aligned}$

91. $\begin{aligned} 3x - 2y + 4z &= 11 \\ 6x + 3y - 2z &= 6 \\ x - y + 7z &= 20 \end{aligned}$ **92.** $\begin{aligned} 2x + 6y - 4z &= 11 \\ -x - 3y + 2z &= -\tfrac{11}{2} \\ 4x + 5y + 6z &= 20 \end{aligned}$

8.5 The Determinant of a Square Matrix and Cramer's Rule

Evaluate each 2 × 2 determinant.

93. $\begin{vmatrix} 2 & 4 \\ 3 & 2 \end{vmatrix}$ **94.** $\begin{vmatrix} -2 & -4 \\ -3 & 2 \end{vmatrix}$

95. $\begin{vmatrix} 2.4 & -2.3 \\ 3.6 & -1.2 \end{vmatrix}$ **96.** $\begin{vmatrix} -\frac{1}{4} & 4 \\ \frac{3}{4} & -4 \end{vmatrix}$

Employ Cramer's rule to solve each system of equations, if possible.

97. $\begin{aligned} x - y &= 2 \\ x + y &= 4 \end{aligned}$ **98.** $\begin{aligned} 3x - y &= -17 \\ -x + 5y &= 43 \end{aligned}$

99. $\begin{aligned} 2x + 4y &= 12 \\ x - 2y &= 6 \end{aligned}$ **100.** $\begin{aligned} -x + y &= 4 \\ 2x - 6y &= -5 \end{aligned}$

101. $\begin{aligned} -3x &= 40 - 2y \\ 2x &= 25 + y \end{aligned}$ **102.** $\begin{aligned} 3x &= 20 + 4y \\ y - x &= -6 \end{aligned}$

Evaluate each 3 × 3 determinant.

103. $\begin{vmatrix} 1 & 2 & 2 \\ 0 & 1 & 3 \\ 2 & -1 & 0 \end{vmatrix}$ **104.** $\begin{vmatrix} 0 & -2 & 1 \\ 0 & -3 & 7 \\ 1 & -10 & -3 \end{vmatrix}$

105. $\begin{vmatrix} a & 0 & -b \\ -a & b & c \\ 0 & 0 & -d \end{vmatrix}$ **106.** $\begin{vmatrix} -2 & -4 & 6 \\ 2 & 0 & 3 \\ -1 & 2 & \frac{3}{4} \end{vmatrix}$

Employ Cramer's rule to solve each system of equations, if possible.

107. $\begin{aligned} x + y - 2z &= -2 \\ 2x - y + z &= 3 \\ x + y + z &= 4 \end{aligned}$ **108.** $\begin{aligned} -x - y + z &= 3 \\ x + 2y - 2z &= 8 \\ 2x + y + 4z &= -4 \end{aligned}$

109. $\begin{aligned} 3x + 4z &= -1 \\ x + y + 2z &= -3 \\ y - 4z &= -9 \end{aligned}$ **110.** $\begin{aligned} x + y + z &= 0 \\ -x - 3y + 5z &= -2 \\ 2x + y - 3z &= -4 \end{aligned}$

8.6 Partial Fractions

Write the form of each partial-fraction decomposition. Do not solve for the constants.

111. $\dfrac{4}{(x-1)^2(x+3)(x-5)}$

112. $\dfrac{7}{(x-9)(3x+5)^2(x+4)}$

113. $\dfrac{12}{x(4x+5)(2x+1)^2}$

114. $\dfrac{2}{(x+1)(x-5)(x-9)^2}$

115. $\dfrac{3}{x^2+x-12}$

116. $\dfrac{x^2+3x-2}{x^3+6x^2}$

117. $\dfrac{3x^3+4x^2+56x+62}{(x^2+17)^2}$

118. $\dfrac{x^3+7x^2+10}{(x^2+13)^2}$

Find the partial-fraction decomposition for each rational function.

119. $\dfrac{9x+23}{(x-1)(x+7)}$

120. $\dfrac{12x+1}{(3x+2)(2x-1)}$

121. $\dfrac{13x^2+90x-25}{2x^3-50x}$

122. $\dfrac{5x^2+x+24}{x^3+8x}$

123. $\dfrac{2}{x^2+x}$

124. $\dfrac{x}{x(x+3)}$

125. $\dfrac{5x-17}{x^2+4x+4}$

126. $\dfrac{x^3}{(x^2+64)^2}$

8.7 Systems of Linear Inequalities in Two Variables

Graph each linear inequality.

127. $y \geq -2x+3$

128. $y < x-4$

129. $2x+4y > 5$

130. $5x+2y \leq 4$

131. $y \geq -3x+2$

132. $y < x-2$

133. $3x+8y \leq 16$

134. $4x-9y \leq 18$

Graph each system of inequalities or indicate that the system has no solution.

135. $y \geq x+2$, $y \leq x-2$

136. $y \geq 3x$, $y \leq 3x$

137. $x \leq -2$, $y > x$

138. $x+3y \geq 6$, $2x - y \leq 8$

139. $3x-4y \leq 16$, $5x+3y > 9$

140. $x+y > -4$, $x-y < 3$, $y \geq -2$, $x \leq 8$

Minimize or maximize the objective function subject to the constraints.

141. Minimize $z = 2x + y$ subject to

$$x \geq 0 \quad y \geq 0 \quad x+y \leq 3$$

142. Maximize $z = 2x + 3y$ subject to

$$x \geq 0 \quad y \geq 0$$
$$-x+y \leq 0 \quad x \leq 3$$

143. Minimize $z = 3x - 5y$ subject to

$$2x+y > 6 \quad 2x-y < 6 \quad x > 0$$

144. Maximize $z = -2x + 7y$ subject to

$$3x+y < 7 \quad x-2y > 1 \quad x \geq 0$$

Applications

For Exercises 145 and 146, refer to the following:

An art student decides to hand-paint coasters and sell sets at a flea market. She decides to make two types of coaster sets: an ocean watercolor and black-and-white geometric shapes. The cost, profit, and time it takes her to paint each set are summarized in the table below.

	OCEAN WATERCOLOR	GEOMETRIC SHAPES
Cost	\$4	\$2
Profit	\$15	\$8
Hours	3	2

145. Profit. If the student's costs cannot exceed \$100 and she can spend a total of only 90 hours painting the coasters, determine the number of each type she should make to maximize her profit.

146. Profit. If the student's costs cannot exceed \$300 and she can spend only 90 hours painting, determine the number of each type she should make to maximize her profit.

[CHAPTER 8 PRACTICE TEST]

Solve each system of linear equations using elimination and/or substitution methods.

1. $x - 2y = 1$
$-x + 3y = 2$

2. $3x + 5y = -2$
$7x + 11y = -6$

3. $x - y = 2$
$-2x + 2y = -4$

4. $3x - 2y = 5$
$6x - 4y = 0$

5. $x + y + z = -1$
$2x + y + z = 0$
$-x + y + 2z = 0$

6. $6x + 9y + z = 5$
$2x - 3y + z = 3$
$10x + 12y + 2z = 9$

In Exercises 7 and 8, write the system of linear equations as an augmented matrix.

7. $6x + 9y + z = 5$
$2x - 3y + z = 3$
$10x + 12y + 2z = 9$

8. $3x + 2y - 10z = 2$
$x + y - z = 5$

9. Perform the following row operations.

$$\begin{bmatrix} 1 & 3 & 5 \\ 2 & 7 & -1 \\ -3 & -2 & 0 \end{bmatrix} \quad \begin{matrix} R_2 - 2R_1 \to R_2 \\ R_3 + 3R_1 \to R_3 \end{matrix}$$

10. Rewrite the following matrix in reduced row–echelon form.

$$\left[\begin{array}{ccc|c} 2 & -1 & 1 & 3 \\ 1 & 1 & -1 & 0 \\ 3 & 2 & -2 & 1 \end{array}\right]$$

In Exercises 11 and 12, solve the systems of linear equations using augmented matrices.

11. $6x + 9y + z = 5$
$2x - 3y + z = 3$
$10x + 12y + 2z = 9$

12. $3x + 2y - 10z = 2$
$x + y - z = 5$

13. Multiply the matrices, if possible.

$$\begin{bmatrix} 1 & -2 & 5 \\ 0 & -1 & 3 \end{bmatrix} \begin{bmatrix} 0 & 4 \\ 3 & -5 \\ -1 & 1 \end{bmatrix}$$

14. Add the matrices, if possible.

$$\begin{bmatrix} 1 & -2 & 5 \\ 0 & -1 & 3 \end{bmatrix} + \begin{bmatrix} 0 & 4 \\ 3 & -5 \\ -1 & 1 \end{bmatrix}$$

15. Find the inverse of $\begin{bmatrix} 4 & 3 \\ 5 & -1 \end{bmatrix}$, if it exists.

16. Find the inverse of $\begin{bmatrix} 1 & -3 & 2 \\ 4 & 2 & 0 \\ -1 & 2 & 5 \end{bmatrix}$, if it exists.

17. Solve the system of linear equations with matrix algebra (inverses).

$$\begin{aligned} 3x - y + 4z &= 18 \\ x + 2y + 3z &= 20 \\ -4x + 6y - z &= 11 \end{aligned}$$

Calculate the determinant.

18. $\begin{vmatrix} 7 & -5 \\ 2 & -1 \end{vmatrix}$

19. $\begin{vmatrix} 1 & -2 & -1 \\ 3 & -5 & 2 \\ 4 & -1 & 0 \end{vmatrix}$

In Exercises 20 and 21, solve the system of linear equations using Cramer's rule.

20. $x - 2y = 1$
$-x + 3y = 2$

21. $3x + 5y - 2z = -6$
$7x + 11y + 3z = 2$
$x - y + z = 4$

22. A company has two rubrics for scoring job applicants based on weighting education, experience, and the interview differently.

Matrix A:

	Rubric 1	Rubric 2
Education	0.4	0.6
Experience	0.5	0.1
Interview	0.1	0.3

Applicants receive a score from 1 to 10 in each category (education, experience, and interview). Two applicants are shown in the matrix B.

Matrix B:

	Education	Experience	Interview
Applicant 1	4	7	3
Applicant 2	6	5	4

What is the order of BA? What does each entry in BA tell us?

Write each rational expression as a sum of partial fractions.

23. $\dfrac{2x + 5}{x^2 + x}$

24. $\dfrac{3x - 13}{(x - 5)^2}$

25. $\dfrac{5x - 3}{x(x^2 - 9)}$

26. $\dfrac{1}{2x^2 + 5x - 3}$

Graph the inequalities.

27. $-2x + y < 6$

28. $4x - y \geq 8$

In Exercises 29 and 30, graph the system of inequalities.

29. $x + y \leq 4$
$-x + y \geq -2$

30. $x + 3y \leq 6$
$2x - y \leq 4$

31. Minimize the function $z = 5x + 7y$ subject to the constraints

$$x \geq 0 \quad y \geq 0 \quad x + y \leq 3 \quad -x + y \geq 1$$

32. Find the maximum value of the objective function $z = 3x + 6y$ given the constraints

$$x \geq 0 \qquad y \geq 0$$
$$x + y \leq 6 \qquad -x + 2y \leq 4$$

[CHAPTERS 1–8 CUMULATIVE TEST]

1. Evaluate $g[f(-1)]$, with $f(x) = \sqrt{2x + 11}$ and $g(x) = x^3$.
2. Use interval notation to express the domain of the function $G(x) = \dfrac{9}{\sqrt{1 - 5x}}$.
3. Using the function $f(x) = x^2 - 3x + 2$, evaluate the difference quotient $\dfrac{f(x + h) - f(x)}{h}$.
4. Find all the real zeros (and state the multiplicity) of $f(x) = -4x(x - 7)^2(x + 13)^3$.
5. Find the vertex of the parabola $f(x) = -0.04x^2 + 1.2x - 3$.
6. Factor the polynomial $P(x) = x^4 + 8x^2 - 9$ as a product of linear factors.
7. Find the vertical and horizontal asymptotes of the function $f(x) = \dfrac{5x - 7}{3 - x}$.
8. Approximate e^{π} using a calculator. Round your answer to two decimal places.
9. Evaluate $\log_5 0.2$ exactly.
10. Solve $5^{2x-1} = 11$ for x. Round the answer to three decimal places.
11. Evaluate $\log_2 6$ using the change-of-base formula. Round your answer to three decimal places.
12. Solve $\ln(5x - 6) = 2$. Round your answer to three decimal places.
13. Give the exact value of $\cos 30°$.
14. How much money should you put now in a savings account that earns 4.7% a year compounded weekly, if you want to have \$65,000 in 17 years?
15. The terminal side of angle θ in standard position passes through the point $(-5, 2)$. Calculate the exact values of the six trigonometric function for angle θ.
16. Find all values of θ, where $0° \leq \theta \leq 360°$, when $\cos\theta = -\dfrac{\sqrt{3}}{2}$.
17. Graph the function $y = \tan(\frac{1}{4}x)$ over the interval $-2\pi \leq x \leq 2\pi$.
18. Verify the identity $\cos(3x) = \cos x(1 - 4\sin^2 x)$.
19. State the domain and range of the function $y = 5\tan\left(x - \dfrac{\pi}{2}\right)$.
20. Simplify the trigonometric expression $\dfrac{\sec^4 x - 1}{\sec^2 x + 1}$.
21. Use the half-angle identities to find the exact value of $\tan\left(-\dfrac{3\pi}{8}\right)$.
22. Write the product $7\sin(-2x)\sin(5x)$ as a sum or difference of sines and/or cosines.
23. Solve the triangle $\beta = 106.3°$, $\gamma = 37.4°$, $a = 76.1$ m.
24. Find the angle (rounded to the nearest degree) between the vectors $\langle 2, 3\rangle$ and $\langle -4, -5\rangle$.
25. Find all complex solutions to $x^3 - 27 = 0$.
26. Graph $\theta = -\dfrac{\pi}{4}$.
27. Given
$$A = \begin{bmatrix} 3 & 4 & -7 \\ 0 & 1 & 5 \end{bmatrix} \quad B = \begin{bmatrix} 8 & -2 & 6 \\ 9 & 0 & -1 \end{bmatrix} \quad C = \begin{bmatrix} 9 & 0 \\ 1 & 2 \end{bmatrix}$$
find CB.
28. Solve the system using Gauss–Jordan elimination.
$$\begin{aligned} x - 2y + 3z &= 11 \\ 4x + 5y - z &= -8 \\ 3x + y - 2z &= 1 \end{aligned}$$
29. Use Cramer's rule to solve the system of equations.
$$\begin{aligned} 7x + 5y &= 1 \\ -x + 4y &= -1 \end{aligned}$$
30. Write the matrix equation, find the inverse of the coefficient matrix, and solve the system using matrix algebra.
$$\begin{aligned} 2x + 5y &= -1 \\ -x + 4y &= 7 \end{aligned}$$
31. Graph the system of linear inequalities.
$$\begin{aligned} y &> -x \\ y &\geq -3 \\ x &\leq 3 \end{aligned}$$

CHAPTER 9

Conics, Systems of Nonlinear Equations and Inequalities, and Parametric Equations

© Photodisc/Age Fotostock America, Inc.

Health Korvola/Getty Images, Inc.

We will now study three types of conic sections, or conics: the parabola, the ellipse, and the hyperbola. The trajectory of a basketball is a *parabola*, Earth's orbit around the Sun is an *ellipse*, and the shape of a cooling tower is a *hyperbola*.

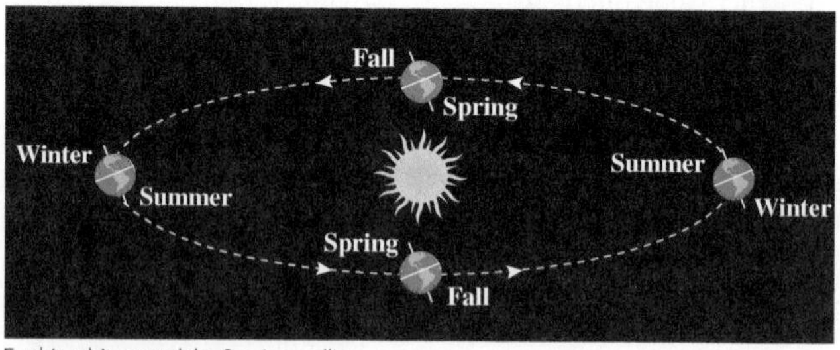

Earth's orbit around the Sun is an *ellipse*.

LEARNING OBJECTIVES

- Determine whether a general second-degree equation in two variables corresponds to a parabola, an ellipse, or a hyperbola.
- Graph a parabola in rectangular coordinates.
- Graph an ellipse in rectangular coordinates.
- Graph a hyperbola in rectangular coordinates.
- Solve systems of nonlinear equations, and interpret some graphically in terms of conics.

[IN THIS CHAPTER]

We define the three conic sections: the parabola, the ellipse, and the hyperbola. Algebraic equations and the graphs of these conics are discussed. We solve systems of nonlinear equations and inequalities involving parabolas, ellipses, and hyperbolas. We then will determine how rotating the axes changes the equation of a conic, and with our results we will be able to identify the graph of a general second-degree equation as one of the three conics. We will discuss the equations of the conics first in rectangular coordinates and then in polar coordinates. Finally, we will look at parametric equations, which give orientation along a plane curve.

CONICS, SYSTEMS OF NONLINEAR EQUATIONS AND INEQUALITIES, AND PARAMETRIC EQUATIONS

9.1 CONIC BASICS	9.2 THE PARABOLA	9.3 THE ELLIPSE	9.4 THE HYPERBOLA	9.5 SYSTEMS OF NONLINEAR EQUATIONS	9.6 SYSTEMS OF NONLINEAR INEQUALITIES	9.7 ROTATION OF AXES	9.8 POLAR EQUATIONS OF CONICS	9.9 PARAMETRIC EQUATIONS AND GRAPHS
• Three Types of Conics	• Parabola with a Vertex at the Origin • Parabola with a Vertex at the Point (h, k) • Applications	• Ellipse Centered at the Origin • Ellipse Centered at the Point (h, k) • Applications	• Hyperbola Centered at the Origin • Hyperbola Centered at the Point (h, k) • Applications	• Solving a System of Nonlinear Equations	• Nonlinear Inequalities in Two Variables • Systems of Nonlinear Inequalities	• Rotation of Axes Formulas • The Angle of Rotation Necessary to Transform a General Second-Degree Equation into a Familiar Equation of a Conic	• Equations of Conics in Polar Coordinates	• Parametric Equations of a Curve • Applications of Parametric Equations

- Solve systems of nonlinear inequalities, and interpret some graphically in terms of conics.
- Graph general second-degree polynomial functions by rotation of axes.
- Graph parabolas, ellipses, and hyperbolas in polar coordinates.
- Use parametric equations to describe orientation along a plane curve.

9.1 CONIC BASICS

SKILLS OBJECTIVE

- Classify a conic as an ellipse, a parabola, or a hyperbola.

CONCEPTUAL OBJECTIVE

- Understand that a conic is a graph that corresponds to a second-degree equation in two variables.

9.1.1 Three Types of Conics

Names of Conics

9.1.1 SKILL

Classify a conic as an ellipse, a parabola, or a hyperbola.

9.1.1 CONCEPTUAL

Understand that a conic is a graph that corresponds to a second-degree equation in two variables.

The word *conic* is derived from the word *cone*. Let's start with a (right circular) **double cone** (see the figure below).

Conic sections are curves that result from the intersection of a plane and a double cone. The four conic sections are a **circle**, an **ellipse**, a **parabola**, and a **hyperbola**. **Conics** is an abbreviation for conic sections.

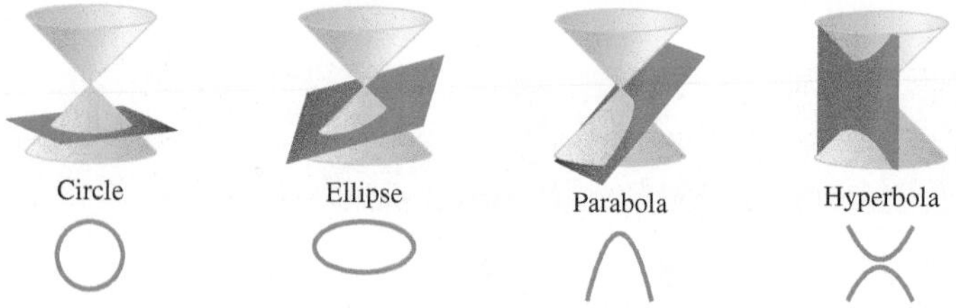

STUDY TIP

A circle is a special type of ellipse. All circles are ellipses, but not all ellipses are circles.

In Section 0.5, circles were discussed, and we will show that a circle is a particular type of an ellipse. Now we will discuss parabolas, ellipses, and hyperbolas. There are two ways in which we usually describe conics: graphically and algebraically. An entire section will be devoted to each of the three conics, but here we will summarize the definitions of a parabola, an ellipse, and a hyperbola and show how to identify the equations of these conics.

Definitions

You already know that a circle consists of all points equidistant (at a distance equal to the radius) from a point (the center). Ellipses, parabolas, and hyperbolas have similar definitions in that they all have a constant distance (or a sum or difference of distances) to some reference point(s).

A **parabola** is the set of all points that are **equidistant from both a line and a point**. An **ellipse** is the set of all points the **sum of whose distances to two fixed points is constant**. A **hyperbola** is the set of all points the **difference of whose distances to two fixed points is constant**.

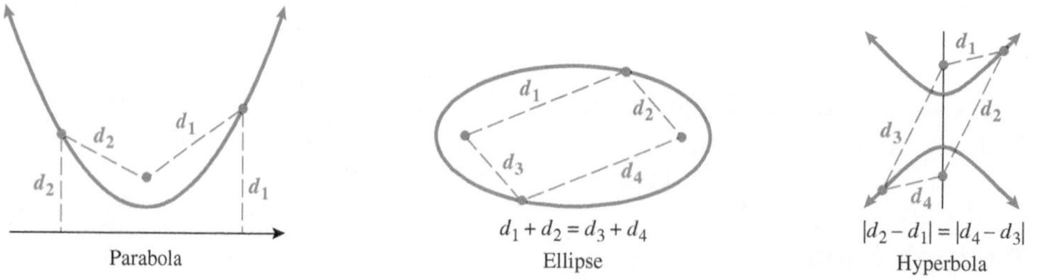

The **general form of a second-degree equation in two variables**, x and y, is given by

$$Ax^2 + Bxy + Cy^2 + Dx + Ey + F = 0$$

If we let $A = 1, B = 0, C = 1, D = 0, E = 0$, and $F = -r^2$, this general equation reduces to the equation of a circle centered at the origin: $x^2 + y^2 = r^2$. In fact, all three conics (parabolas, ellipses, and hyperbolas) are special cases of the general second-degree equation.

Recall from Section 0.2 (Quadratic Equations) that the discriminant, $b^2 - 4ac$, determines what types of solutions result from solving a second-degree equation in one variable. If the discriminant is positive, the solutions are two distinct real roots. If the discriminant is zero, the solution is a real repeated root. If the discriminant is negative, the solutions are two complex conjugate roots.

The concept of discriminant is also applicable to second-degree equations in two variables. The discriminant $B^2 - 4AC$ determines the *shape* of the conic section.

CONIC	DISCRIMINANT
Ellipse	$B^2 - 4AC < 0$
Parabola	$B^2 - 4AC = 0$
Hyperbola	$B^2 - 4AC > 0$

STUDY TIP

All circles are ellipses since $B^2 - 4AC < 0$.

Using the discriminant to identify the shape of the conic will not work for degenerate cases (when the polynomial factors). For example, consider

$$2x^2 - xy - y^2 = 0$$

At first glance, one may think this is a hyperbola because $B^2 - 4AC > 0$, but this is a degenerate case.

$$(2x + y)(x - y) = 0$$

$$2x + y = 0 \quad \text{or} \quad x - y = 0$$

$$y = -2x \quad \text{or} \quad y = x$$

The graph is two intersecting lines.

We now identify conics from the general form of a second-degree equation in two variables.

CONCEPT CHECK

TRUE OR FALSE The graph of a third-degree equation in two variables is also a conic section.

ANSWER False

EXAMPLE 1 Determining the Type of Conic

Determine what type of conic section corresponds to each of the following equations:

a. $\dfrac{x^2}{a^2} + \dfrac{y^2}{b^2} = 1$ **b.** $y = x^2$ **c.** $\dfrac{x^2}{a^2} - \dfrac{y^2}{b^2} = 1$

Solution:

Write the general form of the second-degree equation:

$$Ax^2 + Bxy + Cy^2 + Dx + Ey + F = 0$$

a. Identify A, B, C, D, E, and F. $A = \dfrac{1}{a^2}, B = 0, C = \dfrac{1}{b^2}, D = 0, E = 0, F = -1$

Calculate the discriminant. $B^2 - 4AC = -\dfrac{4}{a^2b^2} < 0$

Since the discriminant is negative, the equation $\dfrac{x^2}{a^2} + \dfrac{y^2}{b^2} = 1$ is that of an **ellipse**.

Notice that if $a = b = r$, then this equation of an ellipse reduces to the general equation of a circle, $x^2 + y^2 = r^2$, centered at the origin, with radius r.

b. Identify A, B, C, D, E, and F. $A = 1, B = 0, C = 0, D = 0, E = -1, F = 0$

Calculate the discriminant. $B^2 - 4AC = 0$

Since the discriminant is zero, the equation $y = x^2$ is a **parabola.**

c. Identify A, B, C, D, E, and F. $A = \frac{1}{a^2}, B = 0, C = -\frac{1}{b^2}, D = 0, E = 0, F = -1$

Calculate the discriminant. $B^2 - 4AC = \frac{4}{a^2b^2} > 0$

Since the discriminant is positive, the equation $\frac{x^2}{a^2} - \frac{y^2}{b^2} = 1$ is a **hyperbola.**

ANSWER

a. ellipse

b. hyperbola

c. parabola

YOUR TURN Determine what type of conic corresponds to each of the following equations:

a. $2x^2 + y^2 = 4$ **b.** $2x^2 = y^2 + 4$ **c.** $2y^2 = x$

In the next three sections, we will discuss the standard forms of equations and the graphs of parabolas, ellipses, and hyperbolas.

[SECTION 9.1] SUMMARY

In this section, we defined the three conic sections and determined their general equations with respect to the general form of a second-degree equation in two variables:

$$Ax^2 + Bxy + Cy^2 + Dx + Ey + F = 0$$

The following table summarizes the three conics: ellipse, parabola, and hyperbola.

CONIC	GEOMETRIC DEFINITION: THE SET OF ALL POINTS	DISCRIMINANT
Ellipse	the sum of whose distances to two fixed points is constant	Negative: $B^2 - 4AC < 0$
Parabola	equidistant to both a line and a point	Zero: $B^2 - 4AC = 0$
Hyperbola	the difference of whose distances to two fixed points is constant	Positive: $B^2 - 4AC > 0$

It is important to note that a circle is a special type of ellipse.

[SECTION 9.1] EXERCISES

• SKILLS

In Exercises 1–12, identify each conic section as a parabola, ellipse, circle, or hyperbola.

1. $x^2 + xy - y^2 + 2x = -3$
2. $x^2 + xy + y^2 + 2x = -3$
3. $2x^2 + 2y^2 = 10$
4. $x^2 - 4x + y^2 + 2y = 4$
5. $2x^2 - y^2 = 4$
6. $2y^2 - x^2 = 16$
7. $5x^2 + 20y^2 = 25$
8. $4x^2 + 8y^2 = 30$
9. $x^2 - y = 1$
10. $y^2 - x = 2$
11. $x^2 + y^2 = 10$
12. $x^2 + y^2 = 100$

9.2 THE PARABOLA

SKILLS OBJECTIVES

- Find the equation of a parabola whose vertex is at the origin.
- Find the equation of a parabola whose vertex is at the point (h, k).
- Solve applied problems that involve parabolas.

CONCEPTUAL OBJECTIVES

- Understand that a parabola is the set of all points that are equidistant from a fixed line (the directrix) and a fixed point not on that line (the focus).
- Employ completing the square to transform an equation into the standard form of a parabola.
- Understand that the focus is the key to applications.

9.2.1 Parabola with a Vertex at the Origin

9.2.1 SKILL

Find the equation of a parabola whose vertex is at the origin.

9.2.1 CONCEPTUAL

Understand that a parabola is the set of all points that are equidistant from a fixed line (the directrix) and a fixed point not on that line (the focus).

Recall from Section 2.1 that the graphs of quadratic functions such as

$$f(x) = a(x - h)^2 + k \qquad \text{or} \qquad y = ax^2 + bx + c$$

were *parabolas* that opened either upward or downward. We now expand our discussion to *parabolas* that open to the right or left. We did not discuss these types of parabolas before because they are not functions (they fail the vertical line test).

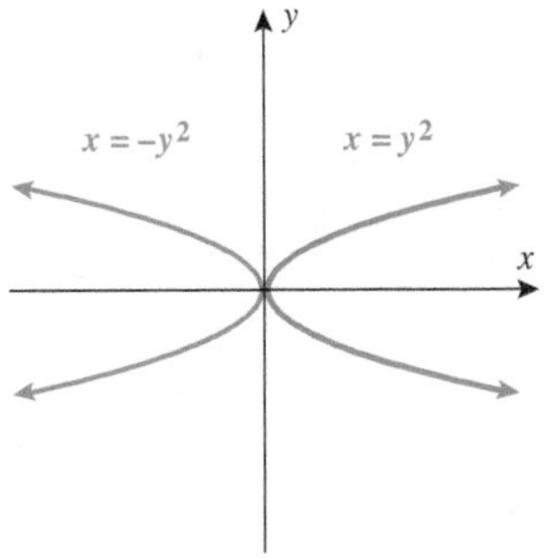

DEFINITION Parabola

A **parabola** is the set of all points in a plane that are equidistant from a fixed line, the **directrix**, and a fixed point not on the line, the **focus**. The line through the focus and perpendicular to the directrix is the **axis of symmetry**. The **vertex** of the parabola is located at the midpoint between the directrix and the focus along the axis of symmetry.

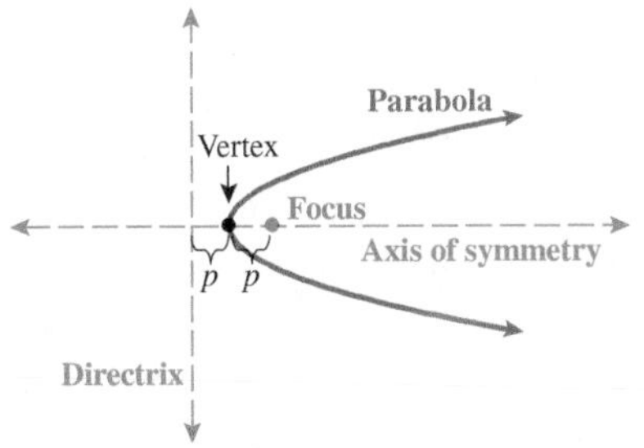

Here p is the distance along the axis of symmetry from the directrix to the vertex and from the vertex to the focus.

Let's consider a parabola with the vertex at the origin and the focus on the positive x-axis. Let the distance from the vertex to the focus be p. Therefore, the focus is located at the point $(p, 0)$. Since the distance from the vertex to the focus is p, the distance from the vertex to the directrix must also be p. Since the axis of symmetry is the x-axis, the directrix must be perpendicular to the x-axis. Therefore, the directrix is given by $x = -p$. Any point, (x, y), must have the same distance to the focus, $(p, 0)$, as to the point $(-p, y)$ of the directrix.

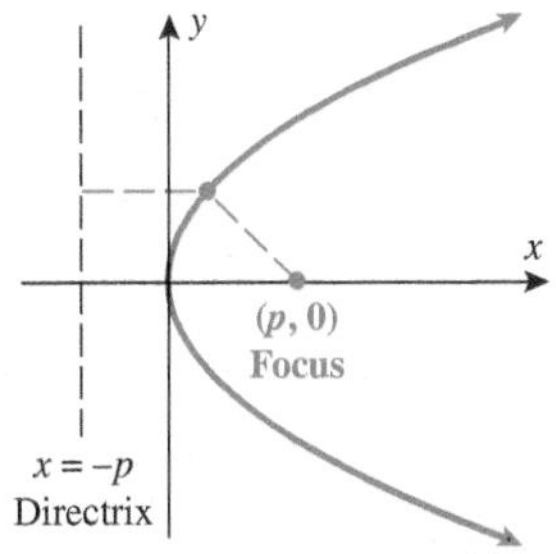

Derivation of the Equation of a Parabola

WORDS	MATH
Calculate the distance from (x, y) to $(p, 0)$ with the distance formula.	$\sqrt{(x-p)^2 + y^2}$
Calculate the distance from (x, y) to $(-p, y)$ with the distance formula.	$\sqrt{(x-(-p))^2 + 0^2}$
Set the two distances equal to one another.	$\sqrt{(x-p)^2 + y^2} = \sqrt{(x+p)^2}$
Recall that $\sqrt{x^2} = \lvert x \rvert$.	$\sqrt{(x-p)^2 + y^2} = \lvert x + p \rvert$
Square both sides of the equation.	$(x-p)^2 + y^2 = (x+p)^2$
Square the binomials inside the parentheses.	$x^2 - 2px + p^2 + y^2 = x^2 + 2px + p^2$
Simplify.	$\boxed{y^2 = 4px}$

The equation $y^2 = 4px$ represents a parabola opening right $(p > 0)$ with the vertex at the origin. The following box summarizes parabolas that have a vertex at the origin and a focus along either the x-axis or the y-axis.

[CONCEPT CHECK]

TRUE OR FALSE The directrix is perpendicular to the axis on which the focus of a parabola lies.

ANSWER True

EQUATION OF A PARABOLA WITH VERTEX AT THE ORIGIN

The standard (conic) form of the equation of a **parabola** with vertex at the origin is given by

EQUATION	$y^2 = 4px$	$x^2 = 4py$
VERTEX	$(0, 0)$	$(0, 0)$
FOCUS	$(p, 0)$	$(0, p)$
DIRECTRIX	$x = -p$	$y = -p$
AXIS OF SYMMETRY	x-axis	y-axis
$p > 0$	opens to the right	opens upward
$p < 0$	opens to the left	opens downward
GRAPH $(p > 0)$	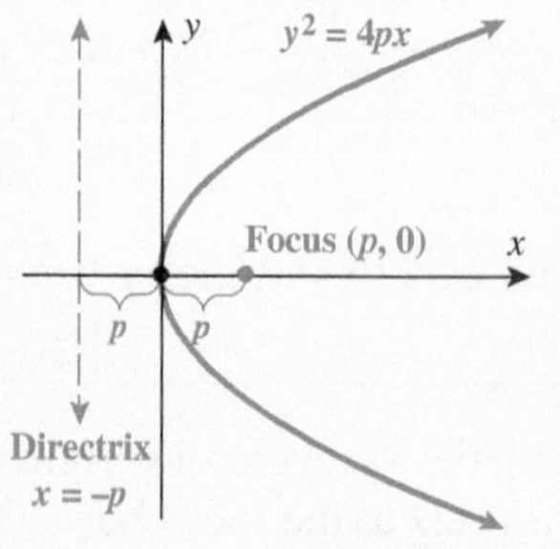	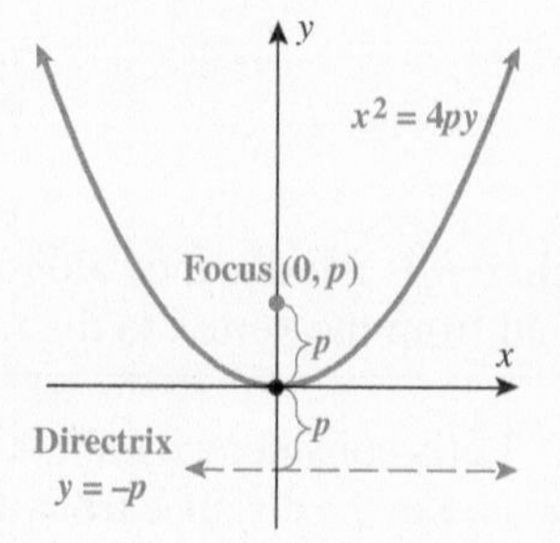

EXAMPLE 1 **Finding the Focus and Directrix of a Parabola Whose Vertex Is Located at the Origin**

Find the focus and directrix of a parabola whose equation is $y^2 = 8x$.

Solution:

Compare this parabola with the general equation of a parabola. $y^2 = 4px$

$y^2 = 8x$

Let $y^2 = 8x$. $4px = 8x$

Solve for p (assume $x \neq 0$). $4p = 8$

$p = 2$

The focus of a parabola of the form $y^2 = 4px$ is $(p, 0)$. $\boxed{\text{Focus } (2, 0)}$

The directrix of a parabola of the form $y^2 = 4px$ is $x = -p$. $\boxed{\text{Directrix } x = -2}$.

YOUR TURN Find the focus and directrix of a parabola whose equation is $y^2 = 16x$.

ANSWER

The focus is $(4, 0)$ and the directrix is $x = -4$.

Graphing a Parabola with a Vertex at the Origin

When a seamstress starts with a pattern for a custom-made suit, the pattern is used as a guide. The pattern is not sewn into the suit; rather, it is removed after being used to determine the exact shape and size of the fabric to be sewn together. The focus and directrix of a parabola are similar to the pattern used by a seamstress. Although the focus and directrix define a parabola, they do not appear on the graph of a parabola.

STUDY TIP

The focus and directrix define a parabola, but they do not appear on its graph.

We can draw an approximate sketch of a parabola whose vertex is at the origin with three pieces of information. We know that the vertex is located at $(0, 0)$. Additional information that we seek is the direction in which the parabola opens and approximately how wide or narrow to draw the parabolic curve. The direction toward which the parabola opens is found from the equation. An equation of the form $y^2 = 4px$ opens either left or right. It opens right if $p > 0$ and opens left if $p < 0$. An equation of the form $x^2 = 4py$ opens either up or down. It opens up if $p > 0$ and opens down if $p < 0$. How narrow or wide should we draw the parabolic curve? If we select a few points that satisfy the equation, we can use those as graphing aids.

In Example 1, we found that the focus of that parabola is located at $(2, 0)$. If we select the x-coordinate of the focus $x = 2$, and substitute that value into the equation of the parabola $y^2 = 8x$, we find the corresponding y-values to be $y = -4$ and $y = 4$. If we plot the three points $(0, 0)$, $(2, -4)$, and $(2, 4)$ and then connect the points with a parabolic curve, we get the graphs on the right.

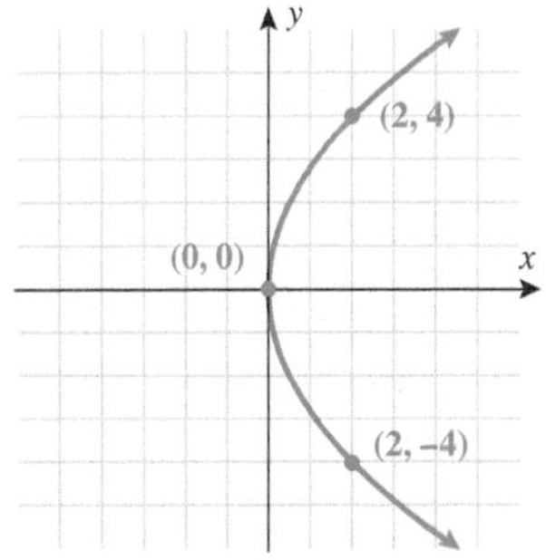

The line segment that passes through the focus $(2, 0)$, that is parallel to the directrix $x = -2$, and whose endpoints are on the parabola is called the **latus rectum**. The latus rectum in this case has length 8. The latus rectum is a graphing aid that assists us in determining how wide to draw the parabola.

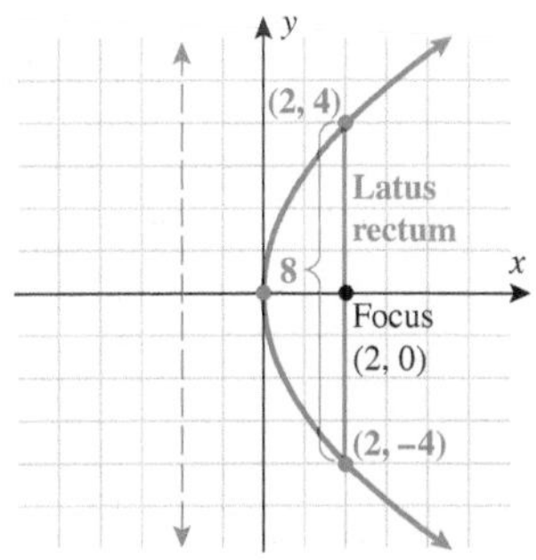

In general, the points on a parabola of the form $y^2 = 4px$ that lie above and below the focus $(p, 0)$ satisfy the equation $y^2 = 4p^2$ and are located at $(p, -2p)$ and $(p, 2p)$. The latus rectum will have length $4|p|$. Similarly, a parabola of the form $x^2 = 4py$ will have a horizontal latus rectum of length $4|p|$.

EXAMPLE 2 **Graphing a Parabola Whose Vertex Is at the Origin Using the Focus, Directrix, and Latus Rectum as Graphing Aids**

Determine the focus, directrix, and length of the latus rectum of the parabola $x^2 = -12y$. Employ these to assist in graphing the parabola.

Solution:

Compare this parabola with the general equation of a parabola. $\quad x^2 = 4py \quad x^2 = -12y$

Solve for p. $\quad 4p = -12$

$$p = -3$$

A parabola of the form $x^2 = 4py$ has focus $(0, p)$, directrix $y = -p$, and a latus rectum of length $4|p|$. For this parabola, $p = -3$; therefore, the focus is $\boxed{(0, -3)}$, the directrix is $\boxed{y = 3}$, and the length of the latus rectum is $\boxed{12}$.

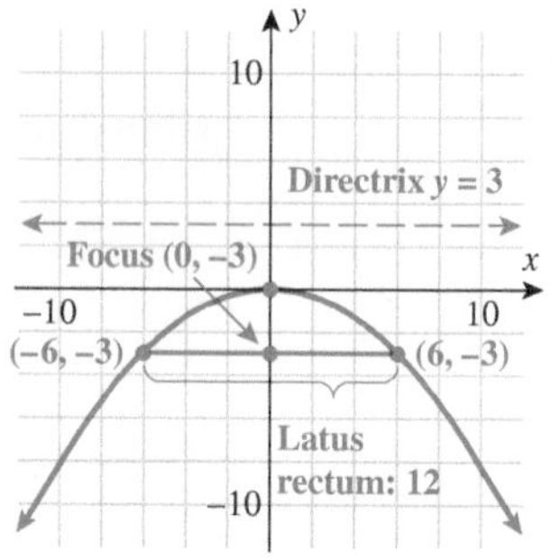

YOUR TURN Find the focus, directrix, and length of the latus rectum of the parabola $y^2 = -8x$, and use these to graph the parabola.

ANSWER

The focus is $(-2, 0)$.

The directrix is $x = 2$.

The length of the latus rectum is 8.

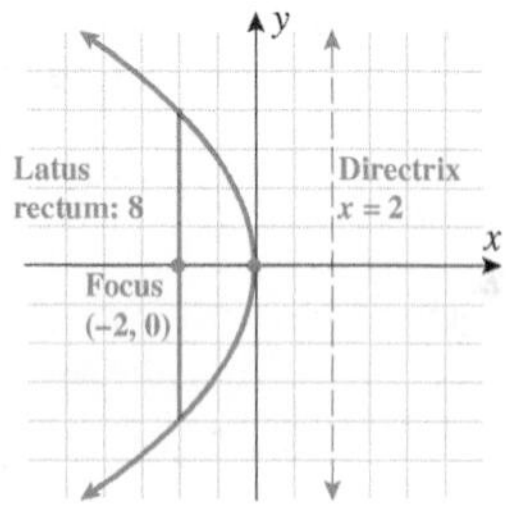

Finding the Equation of a Parabola with a Vertex at the Origin

Thus far we have started with the equation of a parabola and then determined its focus and directrix. Let's now reverse the process. For example, if we know the focus and directrix of a parabola, how do we find the equation of the parabola? If we are given the focus and directrix, then we can find the vertex, which is the midpoint between the focus and the directrix. If the vertex is at the origin, then we know the general equation of the parabola that corresponds to the focus.

EXAMPLE 3 **Finding the Equation of a Parabola Given the Focus and Directrix When the Vertex Is at the Origin**

Find the standard form of the equation of a parabola whose focus is at the point $\left(0, \frac{1}{2}\right)$ and whose directrix is $y = -\frac{1}{2}$. Graph the equation.

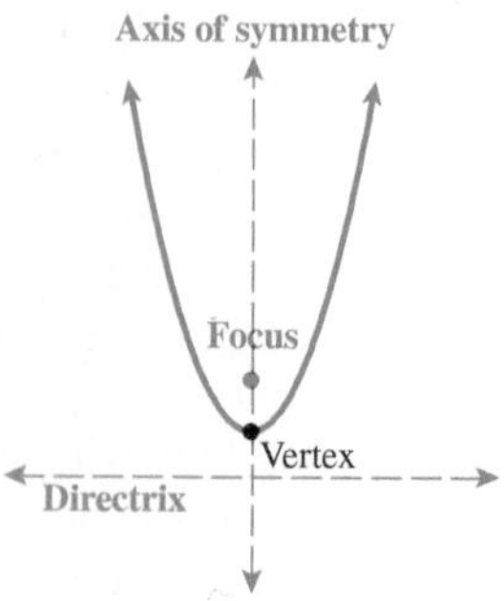

Solution:

The midpoint of the segment joining the focus and the directrix along the axis of symmetry is the vertex.

Calculate the midpoint between $\left(0, \frac{1}{2}\right)$ and $\left(0, -\frac{1}{2}\right)$.

$$\text{Vertex} = \left(\frac{0+0}{2}, \frac{\frac{1}{2} - \frac{1}{2}}{0}\right) = (0, 0).$$

A parabola with vertex at $(0, 0)$, focus at $(0, p)$, and directrix $y = -p$ corresponds to the equation $x^2 = 4py$.

Identify p given that the focus is $(0, p) = (0, \frac{1}{2})$. $\quad p = \dfrac{1}{2}$

Substitute $p = \frac{1}{2}$ into the standard equation of a parabola with vertex at the origin $x^2 = 4py$. $\quad x^2 = 2y$

Now that the equation is known, a few points can be selected, $(-2, 2)$ and $(2, 2)$, and the parabola can be point-plotted. Alternatively, the length of the latus rectum can be calculated to sketch the approximate width of the parabola.

To graph $x^2 = 2y$, first calculate the latus rectum. $\quad 4|p| = 4\left(\dfrac{1}{2}\right) = 2$

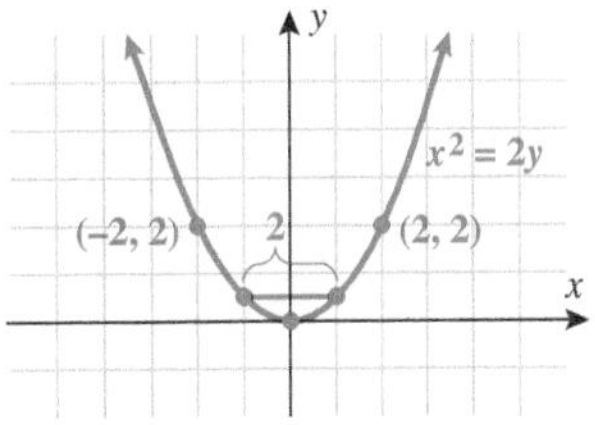

YOUR TURN Find the equation of a parabola whose focus is at the point $(-5, 0)$ and whose directrix is $x = 5$.

ANSWER

$y^2 = -20x$

Before we proceed to parabolas with general vertices, let's first make a few observations: The larger the latus rectum, the more rapidly the parabola widens. An alternative approach for graphing the parabola is to plot a few points that satisfy the equation of the parabola, which is the approach in most textbooks.

9.2.2 Parabola with a Vertex at the Point (h, k)

9.2.2 SKILL

Find the equation of a parabola whose vertex is at the point (h, k).

9.2.2 CONCEPTUAL

Employ completing the square to transform an equation into the standard form of a parabola.

Recall (Section 0.5) that the graph of $x^2 + y^2 = r^2$ is a circle with radius r centered at the origin, whereas the graph of $(x - h)^2 + (y - k)^2 = r^2$ is a circle with radius r centered at the point (h, k). In other words, the center is shifted from the origin to the point (h, k). This same translation (shift) can be used to describe parabolas whose vertex is at the point (h, k).

EQUATION OF A PARABOLA WITH VERTEX AT THE POINT (h, k)

The standard (conic) form of the equation of a parabola with vertex at the point (h, k) is given by

EQUATION	$(y - k)^2 = 4p(x - h)$	$(x - h)^2 = 4p(y - k)$
VERTEX	(h, k)	(h, k)
FOCUS	$(p + h, k)$	$(h, p + k)$
DIRECTRIX	$x = -p + h$	$y = -p + k$
AXIS OF SYMMETRY	$y = k$	$x = h$
$p > 0$	opens to the right	opens upward
$p < 0$	opens to the left	opens downward

STUDY TIP

When $(h, k) = (0, 0)$, the vertex of the parabola is located at the origin.

In order to find the vertex of a parabola given a general second-degree equation, first complete the square (Section 0.2) in order to identify (h, k). Then determine whether the parabola opens up, down, left, or right. Identify points that lie on the graph of the parabola. Intercepts are often the easiest points to find, since they are the points where one of the variables is set equal to zero.

[CONCEPT CHECK]

For the equation $y^2 + 4y - 5x - 5 = 0$, on which variable do you complete the square?

ANSWER y

EXAMPLE 4 Graphing a Parabola with Vertex (h, k)

Graph the parabola given by the equation $y^2 - 6y - 2x + 8 = 0$.

Solution:

Transform this equation into the form $(y - k)^2 = 4p(x - h)$, since this equation is of degree 2 in y and degree 1 in x. We know this parabola opens either to the left or to the right.

Complete the square on y: $y^2 - 6y - 2x + 8 = 0$

Isolate the y terms. $y^2 - 6y = 2x - 8$

Add 9 to both sides to complete the square. $y^2 - 6y + 9 = 2x - 8 + 9$

Write the left side as a perfect square. $(y - 3)^2 = 2x + 1$

Factor out a 2 on the right side. $(y - 3)^2 = 2\left(x + \frac{1}{2}\right)$

Compare with $(y - k)^2 = 4p(x - h)$ and identify (h, k) and p.

$$(h, k) = \left(-\frac{1}{2}, 3\right)$$

$$4p = 2 \Rightarrow p = \frac{1}{2}$$

The vertex is at the point $\left(-\frac{1}{2}, 3\right)$, and since $p = \frac{1}{2}$ is positive, the parabola opens to the right. Since the parabola's vertex lies in quadrant II and it opens to the right, we know there are two y-intercepts and one x-intercept. Apply the general equation $y^2 - 6y - 2x + 8 = 0$ to find the intercepts.

[STUDY TIP]

It is often easier to find the intercepts by converting to the general form of the equation.

Find the y-intercepts (set $x = 0$). $y^2 - 6y + 8 = 0$

Factor. $(y - 2)(y - 4) = 0$

Solve for y. $y = 2$ or $y = 4$

Find the x-intercept (set $y = 0$). $-2x + 8 = 0$

Solve for x. $x = 4$

Label the following points and connect them with a smooth curve:

Vertex:	$\left(-\frac{1}{2}, 3\right)$
y-intercepts:	$(0, 2)$ and $(0, 4)$
x-intercept:	$(4, 0)$

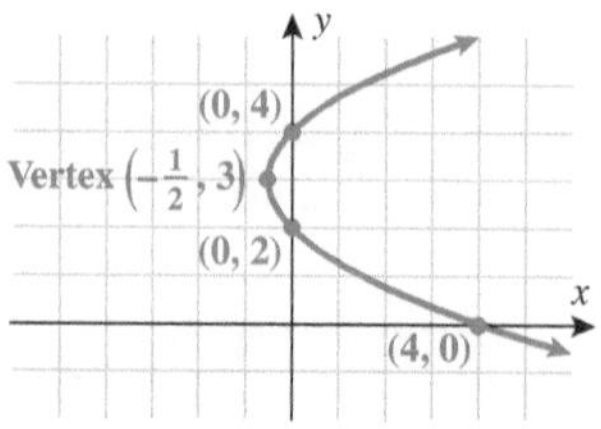

YOUR TURN For the equation $y^2 + 4y - 5x - 5 = 0$, identify the vertex and the intercepts, and graph.

ANSWER

Vertex: $\left(-\frac{9}{5}, -2\right)$

x-intercept: $x = -1$

y-intercepts: $y = -5$ and $y = 1$

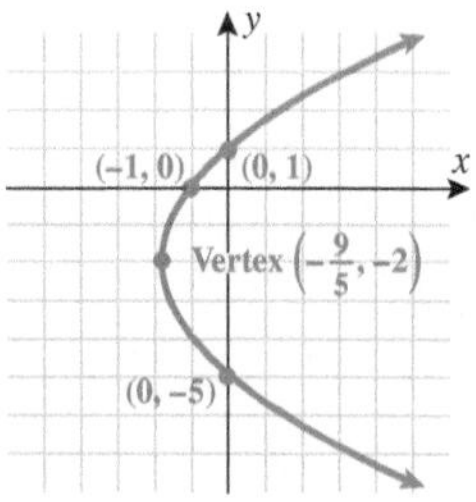

EXAMPLE 5 Graphing a Parabola with Vertex (h, k)

Graph the parabola given by the equation $x^2 - 2x - 8y - 7 = 0$.

Solution:

Transform this equation into the form $(x - h)^2 = 4p(y - k)$, since this equation is degree 2 in x and degree 1 in y. We know this parabola opens either upward or downward.

Complete the square on x: $\quad x^2 - 2x - 8y - 7 = 0$

Isolate the x terms. $\quad x^2 - 2x = 8y + 7$

Add 1 to both sides to complete the square. $\quad x^2 - 2x + 1 = 8y + 7 + 1$

Write the left side as a perfect square. $\quad (x - 1)^2 = 8y + 8$

Factor out the 8 on the right side. $\quad (x - 1)^2 = 8(y + 1)$

Compare with $(x - h)^2 = 4p(y - k)$ and identify (h, k) and p.

$$(h, k) = (1, -1)$$

$$4p = 8 \Rightarrow p = 2$$

The vertex is at the point $(1, -1)$, and since $p = 2$ is positive, the parabola opens upward. Since the parabola's vertex lies in quadrant IV and it opens upward, we know there are two x-intercepts and one y-intercept. Use the general equation $x^2 - 2x - 8y - 7 = 0$ to find the intercepts.

Find the y-intercept (set $x = 0$). $\quad -8y - 7 = 0$

Solve for y. $\quad y = -\frac{7}{8}$

Find the x-intercepts (set $y = 0$). $\quad x^2 - 2x - 7 = 0$

Solve for x. $\quad x = \frac{2 \pm \sqrt{4 + 28}}{2} = \frac{2 \pm \sqrt{32}}{2} = \frac{2 \pm 4\sqrt{2}}{2} = 1 \pm 2\sqrt{2}$

Label the following points and connect with a smooth curve:

Vertex: $(1, -1)$

y-intercept: $\left(0, -\frac{7}{8}\right)$

x-intercepts: $\left(1 - 2\sqrt{2}, 0\right)$ and $\left(1 + 2\sqrt{2}, 0\right)$

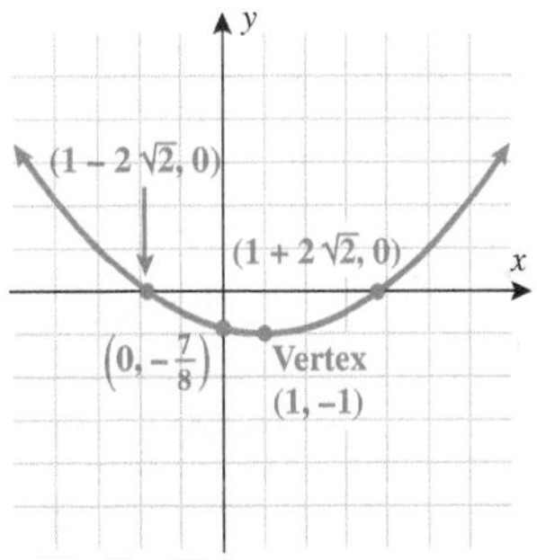

YOUR TURN For the equation $x^2 + 2x + 8y - 7 = 0$, identify the vertex and the intercepts, and graph.

ANSWER

Vertex: $(-1, 1)$

x-intercepts: $x = -1 \pm 2\sqrt{2}$

y-intercept: $y = \frac{7}{8}$

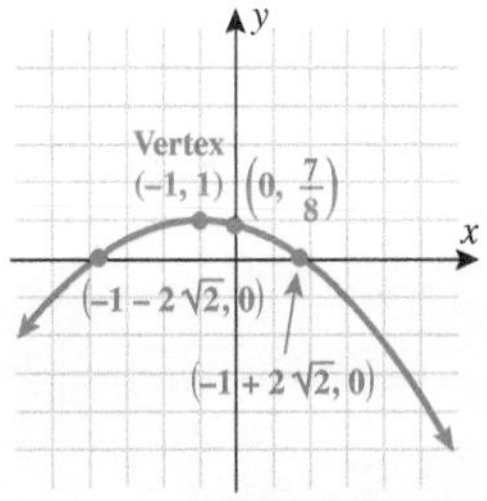

EXAMPLE 6 **Finding the Equation of a Parabola with Vertex (h, k)**

Find the general form of the equation of a parabola whose vertex is located at the point $(2, -3)$ and whose focus is located at the point $(5, -3)$.

Solution:

Draw a Cartesian plane and label the vertex and focus. The vertex and focus share the same axis of symmetry, $y = -3$, and indicate a parabola opening to the right.

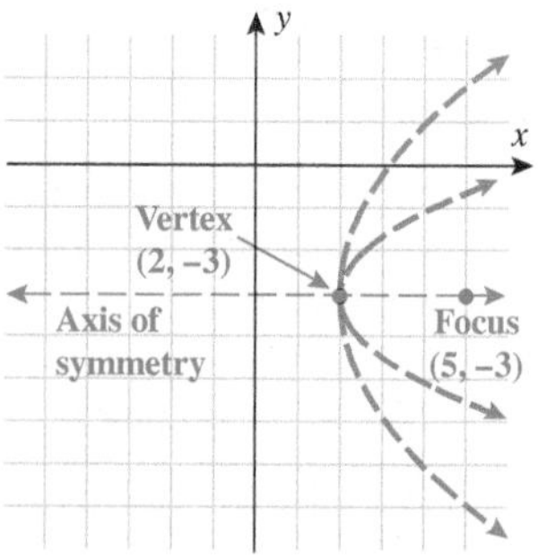

Write the standard (conic) equation of a parabola opening to the right. $(y - k)^2 = 4p(x - h) \quad p > 0$

Substitute the vertex $(h, k) = (2, -3)$ into the standard equation. $[y - (-3)]^2 = 4p(x - 2)$

Find p.

The general form of the vertex is (h, k) and the focus is $(h + p, k)$.

For this parabola, the vertex is $(2, -3)$ and the focus is $(5, -3)$.

Find p by taking the difference of the x-coordinates. $p = 3$

Substitute $p = 3$ into $[y - (-3)]^2 = 4p(x - 2)$. $(y + 3)^2 = 4(3)(x - 2)$

Eliminate parentheses. $y^2 + 6y + 9 = 12x - 24$

Simplify. $\boxed{y^2 + 6y - 12x + 33 = 0}$

YOUR TURN Find the equation of the parabola whose vertex is located at $(2, -3)$ and whose focus is located at $(0, -3)$.

ANSWER

$y^2 + 6y + 8x - 7 = 0$

9.2.3 Applications

9.2.3 SKILL

Solve applied problems that involve parabolas.

9.2.3 CONCEPTUAL

Understand that the focus is the key to applications.

If we start with a parabola in the xy-plane and rotate it around its axis of symmetry, the result will be a three-dimensional paraboloid. Solar cookers illustrate the physical property that the rays of light coming into a parabola are reflected to the focus. A flashlight reverses this process in that its light source at the focus illuminates a parabolic reflector to direct the beam outward.

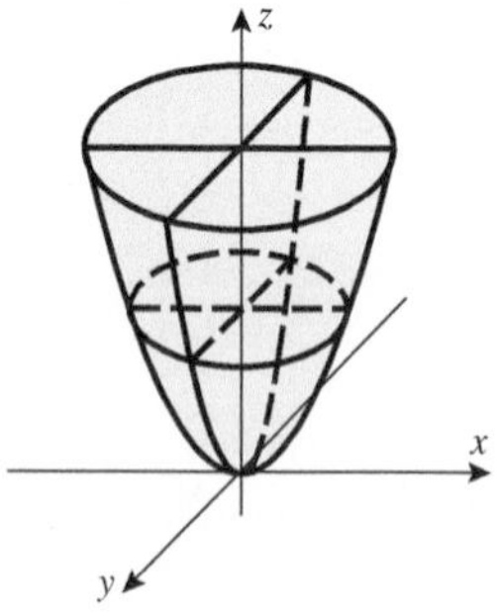

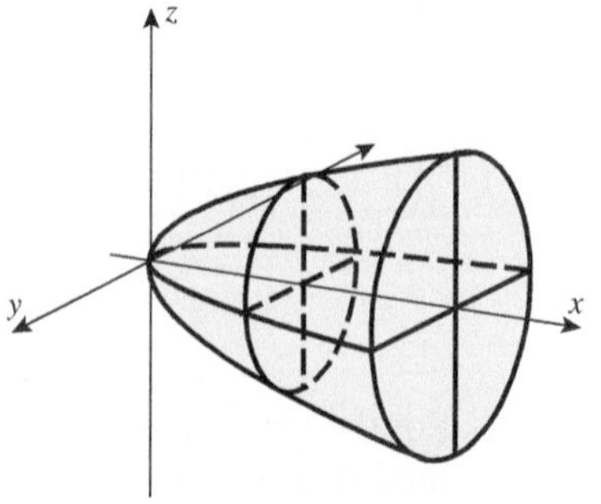

Satellite dish

A satellite dish is in the shape of a paraboloid. Functioning as an antenna, the parabolic dish collects all of the incoming signals and reflects them to a single point, the focal point, which is where the receiver is located. In Examples 7 and 8, and in the Applications Exercises, the intention is not to find the three-dimensional equation of the paraboloid, but rather to find the equation of the plane parabola that's rotated to generate the paraboloid.

EXAMPLE 7 **Finding the Location of the Receiver in a Satellite Dish**

A satellite dish is 24 feet in diameter at its opening and 4 feet deep in its center. Where should the receiver be placed?

Solution:

Draw a parabola with a vertex at the origin representing the center cross section of the satellite dish.

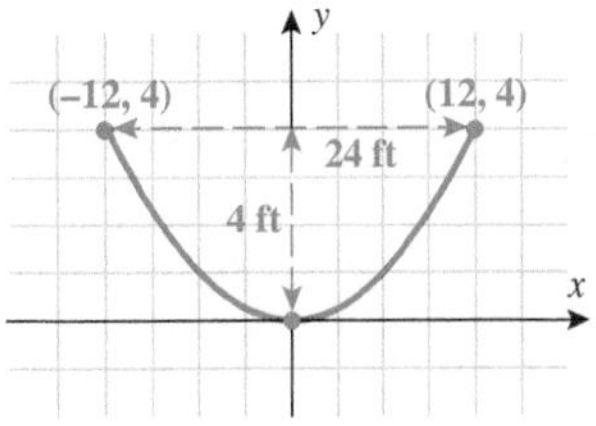

Write the standard equation of a parabola opening upward with vertex at (0, 0). $x^2 = 4py$

The point (12, 4) lies on the parabola, so substitute (12, 4) into $x^2 = 4py$. $(12)^2 = 4p(4)$

Simplify. $144 = 16p$

Solve for p. $p = 9$

Substitute $p = 9$ into the focus $(0, p)$. focus: (0, 9)

The receiver should be placed 9 feet from the vertex of the dish.

[CONCEPT CHECK]

The more concave the parabolic dish, the (closer/farther) the focus is from the vertex.

ANSWER Closer

Parabolic antennas work for sound as well as for light. Have you ever wondered how the sound of the quarterback calling audible plays is heard by the sideline crew? The crew holds a parabolic system with a microphone at the focus. All of the sound in the direction of the parabolic system is reflected toward the focus, where the microphone amplifies and records the sound.

Francis Specker/Icon SMI/NewsCom

EXAMPLE 8 **Finding the Equation of a Parabolic Sound Dish**

If the parabolic sound dish the sideline crew is holding has a 2-foot diameter at the opening and the microphone is located 6 inches from the vertex, find the equation that governs the center cross section of the parabolic sound dish.

Solution:

Write the standard equation of a parabola opening to the right with the vertex at the origin (0, 0). $x = 4py^2$

The focus is located 6 inches ($\frac{1}{2}$ foot) from the vertex. $(p, 0) = \left(\frac{1}{2}, 0\right)$

Solve for p. $p = \frac{1}{2}$

Let $p = \frac{1}{2}$ in $x = 4py^2$. $x = 4\left(\frac{1}{2}\right)y^2$

Simplify. $x = 2y^2$

[SECTION 9.2] SUMMARY

In this section, we discussed parabolas whose vertex is at the origin.

EQUATION	$y^2 = 4px$	$x^2 = 4py$
VERTEX	$(0, 0)$	$(0, 0)$
FOCUS	$(p, 0)$	$(0, p)$
DIRECTRIX	$x = -p$	$y = -p$
AXIS OF SYMMETRY	x-axis	y-axis
$p > 0$	opens to the right	opens upward
$p < 0$	opens to the left	opens downward
GRAPH	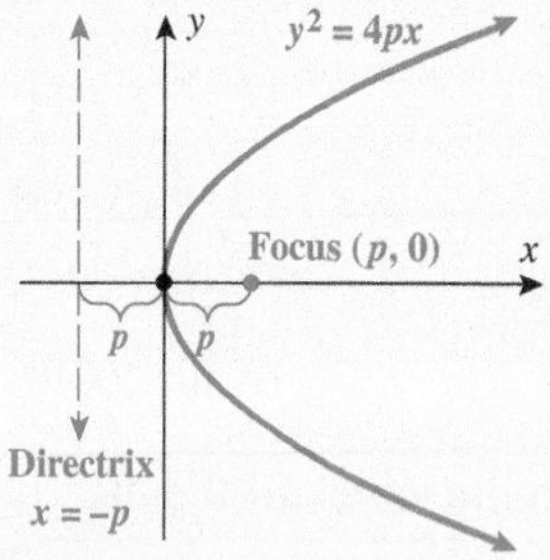	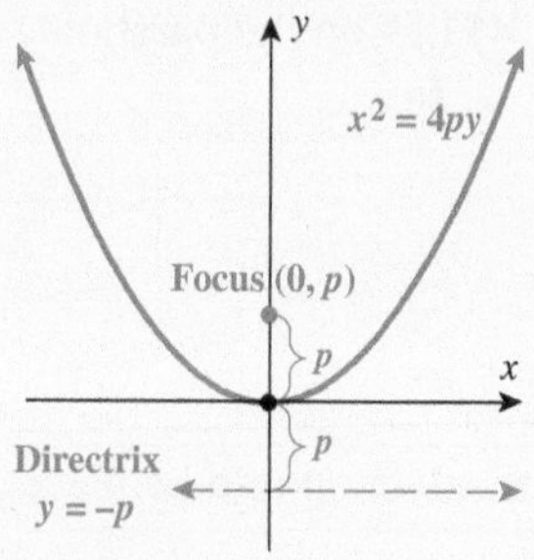

For parabolas whose vertex is at the point (h, k):

EQUATION	$(y - k)^2 = 4p(x - h)$	$(x - h)^2 = 4p(y - k)$
VERTEX	(h, k)	(h, k)
FOCUS	$(p + h, k)$	$(h, p + k)$
DIRECTRIX	$x = -p + h$	$y = -p + k$
AXIS OF SYMMETRY	$y = k$	$x = h$
$p > 0$	opens to the right	opens upward
$p < 0$	opens to the left	opens downward

[SECTION 9.2] EXERCISES

• SKILLS

In Exercises 1–4, match each equation to the corresponding parabola.

1. $y^2 = 4x$ **2.** $y^2 = -4x$ **3.** $x^2 = -4y$ **4.** $x^2 = 4y$

a.

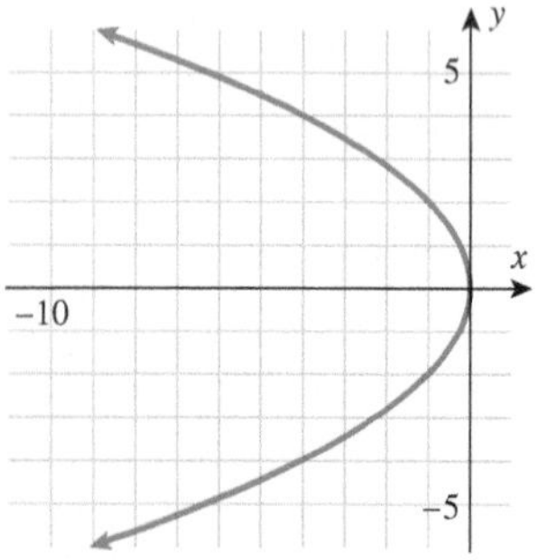

b.

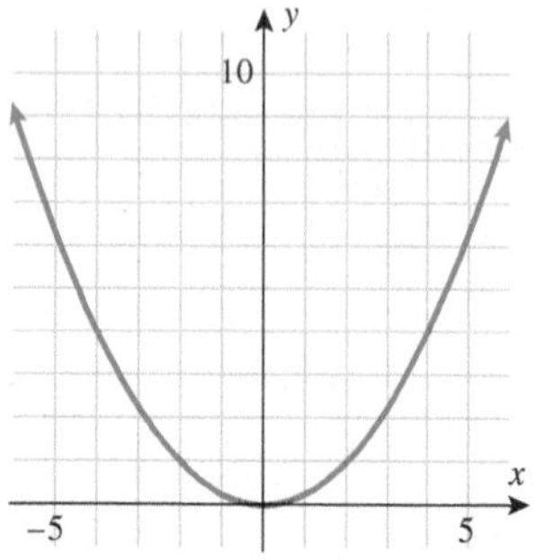

c.

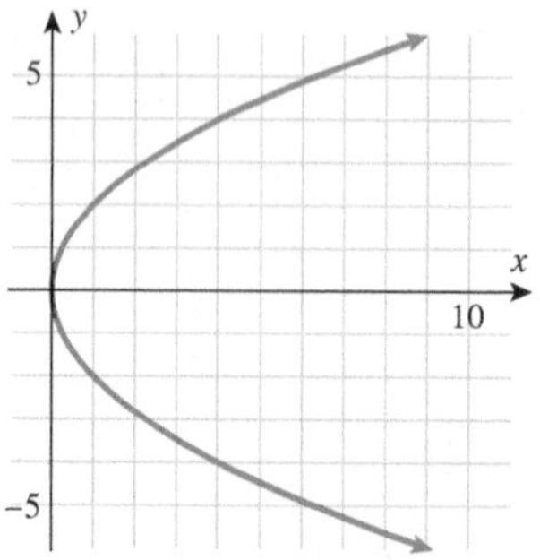

d.

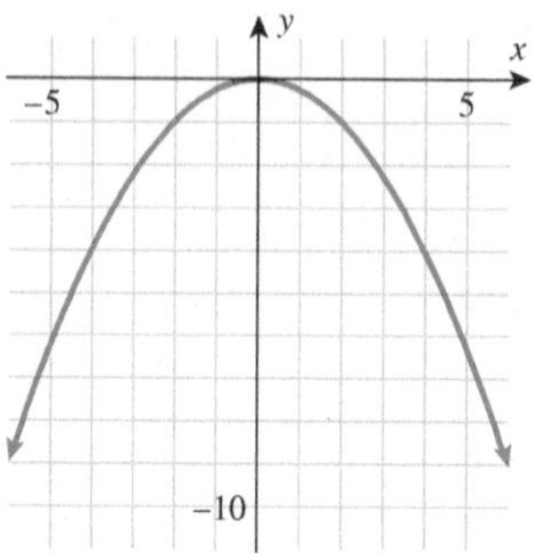

In Exercises 5–8, match each equation to the corresponding parabola.

5. $(y - 1)^2 = 4(x - 1)$ **6.** $(y + 1)^2 = -4(x - 1)$ **7.** $(x + 1)^2 = -4(y + 1)$ **8.** $(x - 1)^2 = 4(y - 1)$

a.

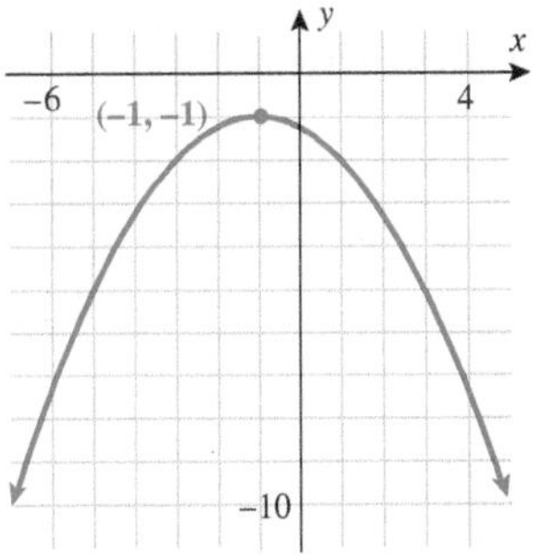

b.

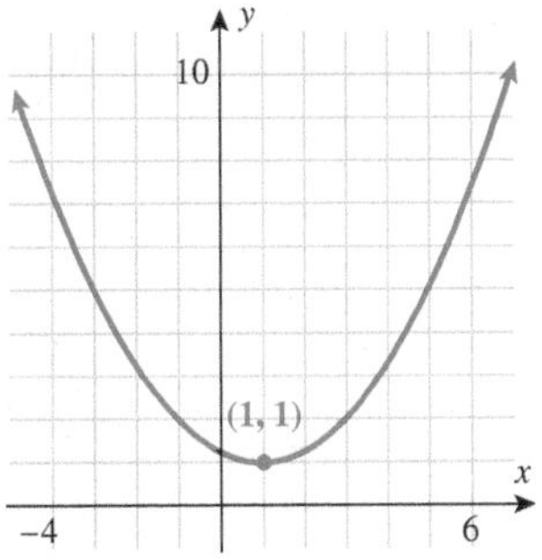

c.

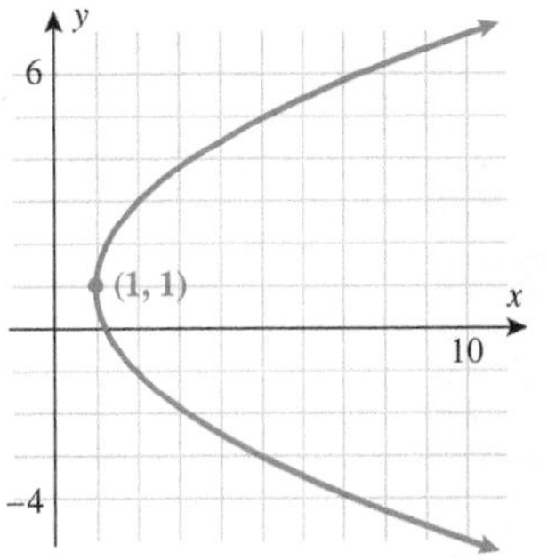

d.

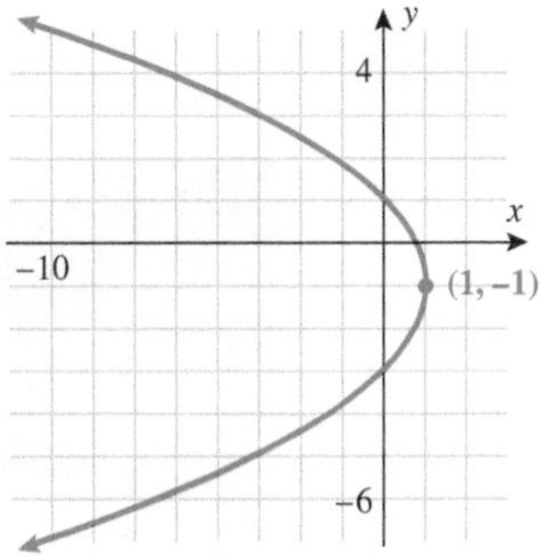

In Exercises 9–20, find an equation for the parabola described.

9. Vertex at $(0, 0)$; focus at $(0, 3)$

10. Vertex at $(0, 0)$; focus at $(2, 0)$

11. Vertex at $(0, 0)$; focus at $(-5, 0)$

12. Vertex at $(0, 0)$; focus at $(0, -4)$

13. Vertex at $(3, 5)$; focus at $(3, 7)$

14. Vertex at $(3, 5)$; focus at $(7, 5)$

15. Vertex at $(2, 4)$; focus at $(0, 4)$

16. Vertex at $(2, 4)$; focus at $(2, -1)$

17. Focus at $(2, 4)$; directrix at $y = -2$

18. Focus at $(2, -2)$; directrix at $y = 4$

19. Focus at $(3, -1)$; directrix at $x = 1$

20. Focus at $(-1, 5)$; directrix at $x = 5$

In Exercises 21–24, write an equation for each parabola.

21.

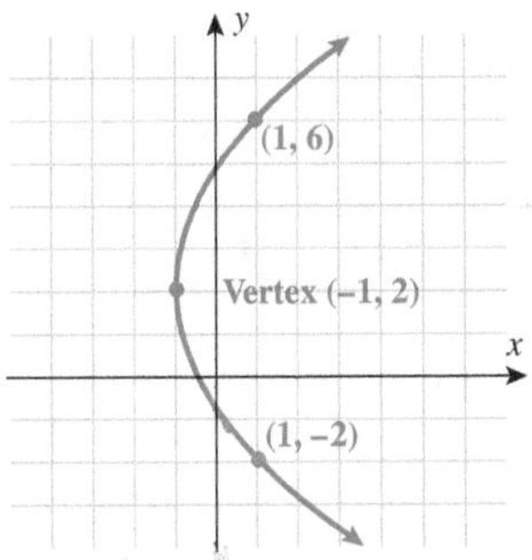

22.

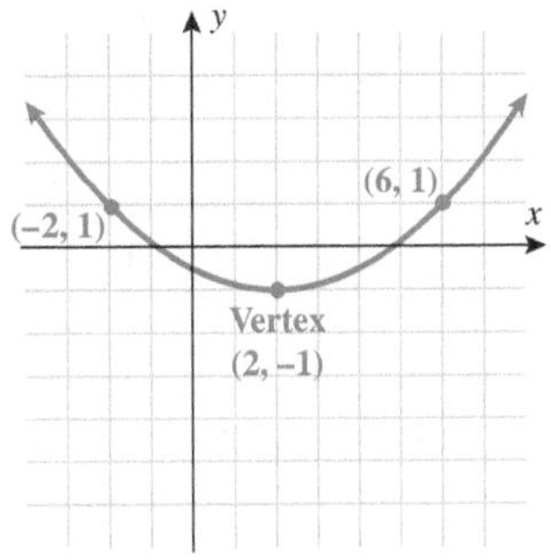

23.

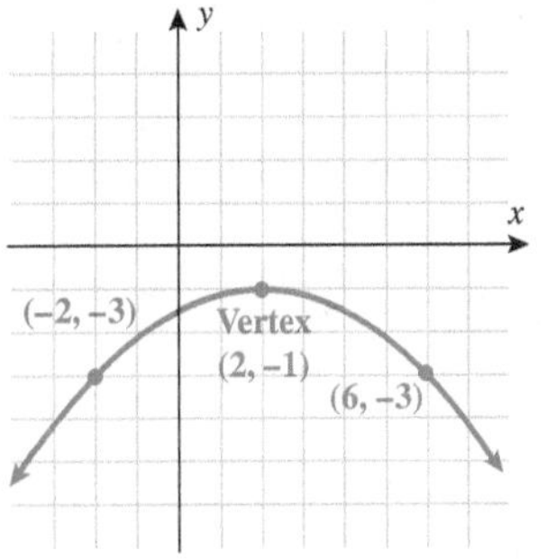

24.

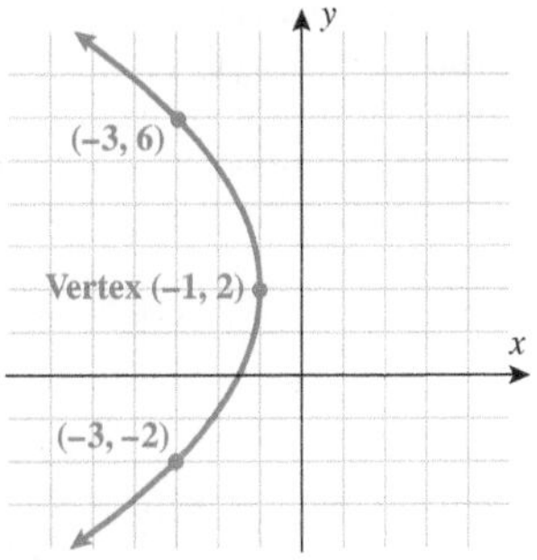

In Exercises 25–32, find the focus, vertex, directrix, and length of latus rectum and graph the parabola.

25. $x^2 = 8y$ **26.** $x^2 = -12y$ **27.** $y^2 = -2x$ **28.** $y^2 = 6x$

29. $x^2 = 16y$ **30.** $x^2 = -8y$ **31.** $y^2 = 4x$ **32.** $y^2 = -16x$

In Exercises 33–44, find the vertex and graph the parabola.

33. $(y - 2)^2 = 4(x + 3)$ **34.** $(y + 2)^2 = -4(x - 1)$ **35.** $(x - 3)^2 = -8(y + 1)$ **36.** $(x + 3)^2 = -8(y - 2)$

37. $(x + 5)^2 = -2y$ **38.** $y^2 = -16(x + 1)$ **39.** $y^2 - 4y - 2x + 4 = 0$ **40.** $x^2 - 6x + 2y + 9 = 0$

41. $y^2 + 2y - 8x - 23 = 0$ **42.** $x^2 - 6x - 4y + 10 = 0$ **43.** $x^2 - x + y - 1 = 0$ **44.** $y^2 + y - x + 1 = 0$

• APPLICATIONS

45. Satellite Dish. A satellite dish measures 8 feet across its opening and 2 feet deep at its center. The receiver should be placed at the focus of the parabolic dish. Where is the focus?

46. Satellite Dish. A satellite dish measures 30 feet across its opening and 5 feet deep at its center. The receiver should be placed at the focus of the parabolic dish. Where is the focus?

47. Eyeglass Lens. Eyeglass lenses can be thought of as very wide parabolic curves. If the focus occurs 2 centimeters from the center of the lens and the lens at its opening is 5 centimeters, find an equation that governs the shape of the center cross section of the lens.

48. Optical Lens. A parabolic lens focuses light onto a focal point 3 centimeters from the vertex of the lens. How wide is the lens 0.5 centimeter from the vertex?

Exercises 49 and 50 are examples of solar cookers. Parabolic shapes are often used to generate intense heat by collecting sun rays and focusing all of them at a focal point.

49. **Solar Cooker.** The parabolic cooker MS-ST10 is delivered as a kit, handily packed in a single carton, with complete assembly instructions and even the necessary tools.

Solar cooker, Ubuntu Village, Johannesburg, South Africa

Thanks to the reflector diameter of 1 meter, it develops an immense power: 1 liter of water boils in significantly less than half an hour. If the rays are focused 40 centimeters from the vertex, find the equation for the parabolic cooker.

50. **Le Four Solaire at Font-Romeu "Mirrors of the Solar Furnace."** There is a reflector in the Pyrenees Mountains that is eight stories high. It cost \$2 million and took 10 years to build. Made of 9000 mirrors arranged in a parabolic formation, it can reach 6000°F just from the Sun hitting it!

Solar furnace, Odellio, France

If the diameter of the parabolic mirror is 100 meters and the sunlight is focused 25 meters from the vertex, find the equation for the parabolic dish.

51. **Sailing under a Bridge.** A bridge with a parabolic shape has an opening 80 feet wide at the base (where the bridge meets the water), and the height at the center of the bridge is 20 feet. A sailboat whose mast reaches 17 feet above the water is traveling under the bridge 10 feet from the center of the bridge. Will it clear the bridge without scraping its mast? Justify your answer.

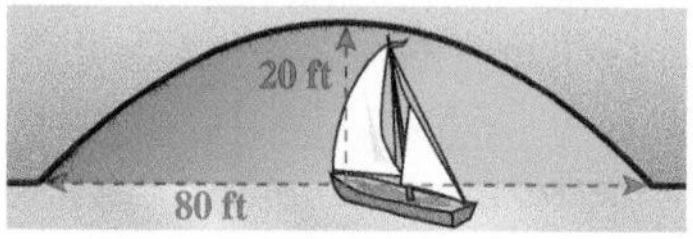

52. **Driving under a Bridge.** A bridge with a parabolic shape reaches a height of 25 feet at the center of the road, and the width of the bridge opening at ground level is 20 feet combined (both lanes). If an RV is 10 feet tall and 8 feet wide, it won't make it under the bridge if it hugs the center line. Will it clear the bridge if it straddles the center line? Justify your answer.

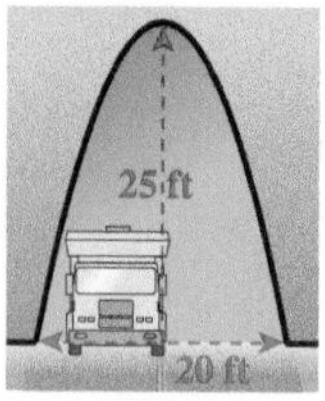

53. **Parabolic Telescope.** The Arecibo radio telescope in Puerto Rico has an enormous reflecting surface, or radio mirror. The huge "dish" is 1000 feet in diameter and 167 feet deep and covers an area of about 20 acres. Using these dimensions, determine the focal length of the telescope. Find the equation for the dish portion of the telescope.

54. **Suspension Bridge.** If one parabolic segment of a suspension bridge is 300 feet and if the cables at the vertex are suspended 10 feet above the bridge, whereas the height of the cables 150 feet from the vertex reaches 60 feet, find the equation of the parabolic path of the suspension cables.

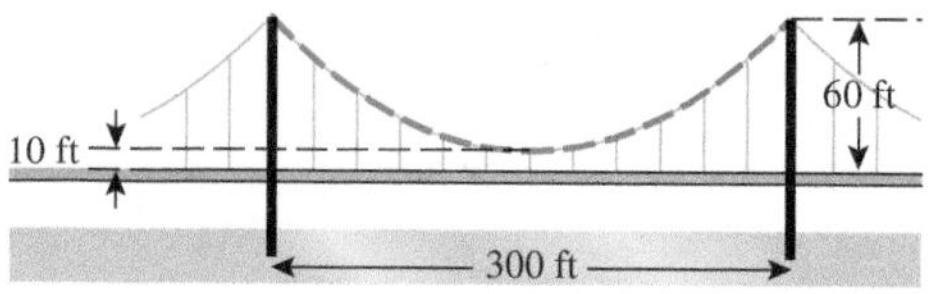

55. **Health.** In a meditation state, the pulse rate (pulses per minute) can be modeled by $p(t) = 0.18t^2 - 5.4t + 95.5$, where t is in minutes. What is the minimum pulse rate according to this model?

56. **Health.** In a distress situation, the pulse rate (pulses per minute) can be modeled by $p(t) = -1.1t^2 + 22t + 80$, where t is the time in seconds. What is the maximum pulse rate according to this model?

57. **Business.** The profit, in thousands of dollars, for a product is $P(x) = -x^2 + 60x - 500$, where x is the production level in hundreds of units. Find the production level that maximizes the profit. Find the maximum profit.

58. **Business.** The profit, in thousands of dollars, for a product is $P(x) = -x^2 + 80x - 1200$, where x is the production level in hundreds of units. Find the production level that maximizes the profit. Find the maximum profit.

• CATCH THE MISTAKE

In Exercises 59 and 60, explain the mistake that is made.

59. Find an equation for a parabola whose vertex is at the origin and whose focus is at the point (3, 0).

Solution:

Write the general equation for a parabola whose vertex is at the origin.	$x^2 = 4py$
The focus of this parabola is $(p, 0) = (3, 0)$.	$p = 3$
Substitute $p = 3$ into $x^2 = 4py$.	$x^2 = 12y$

This is incorrect. What mistake was made?

60. Find an equation for a parabola whose vertex is at the point (3, 2) and whose focus is located at (5, 2).

Solution:

Write the equation associated with a parabola whose vertex is (3, 2).	$(x - h)^2 = 4p(y - k)$
Substitute (3, 2) into $(x - h)^2 = 4p(y - k)$.	$(x - 3)^2 = 4p(y - 2)$

The focus is located at (5, 2); therefore, $p = 5$.

Substitute $p = 5$ into $(x - 3)^2 = 4p(y - 2)$.	$(x - 3)^2 = 20(y - 2)$

This is incorrect. What mistake(s) was(were) made?

• CONCEPTUAL

In Exercises 61–64, determine whether each statement is true or false.

61. The vertex lies on the graph of a parabola.

62. The focus lies on the graph of a parabola.

63. The directrix lies on the graph of a parabola.

64. The endpoints of the latus rectum lie on the graph of a parabola.

In Exercises 65 and 66, use the following equation:

$$\frac{(y - k)^2}{(x - h)} = 4$$

65. Find the directrix of the parabola.

66. Determine whether the parabola opens to the right or to the left.

In Exercises 67 and 68, use the following information about the graph of the parabola:

Axis of symmetry: $x = 6$

Directrix: $y = 4$

Focus: (6, 9)

67. Find the vertex of the parabola.

68. Find the equation of the parabola.

• CHALLENGE

69. Derive the standard equation of a parabola with its vertex at the origin, opening upward, $x^2 = 4py$. [Calculate the distance d_1 from any point on the parabola (x, y) to the focus $(0, p)$. Calculate the distance d_2 from any point on the parabola (x, y) to the directrix $(-p, y)$. Set $d_1 = d_2$.]

70. Derive the standard equation of a parabola opening right, $y^2 = 4px$. [Calculate the distance d_1 from any point on the parabola (x, y) to the focus $(p, 0)$. Calculate the distance d_2 from any point on the parabola (x, y) to the directrix $(x, -p)$. Set $d_1 = d_2$.]

71. Two parabolas with the same axis of symmetry, $y = 6$, intersect at the point (4, 2). If the directrix of one of these parabolas is the y-axis and the directrix of the other parabola is $x = 8$, find the equations of the parabolas.

72. Two parabolas with the same axis of symmetry, $x = 9$, intersect at the point $(6, -5)$. If the directrix of one of these parabolas is $y = -11$ and the directrix of the other parabola is $y = 1$, find the equations of the parabolas.

73. Find the points of intersection of the parabolas with foci $\left(0, \frac{3}{2}\right)$ and $\left(0, -\frac{3}{4}\right)$, and directrices $y = \frac{1}{2}$ and $y = -\frac{5}{4}$, respectively.

74. Find two parabolas with focus $(1, 2p)$ and vertices $(1, p)$ and $(1, -p)$ that intersect each other.

• PREVIEW TO CALCULUS

In calculus, to find the area between two curves, we need first to find the point of intersection of the two curves. In Exercises 75–78, find the points of intersection of the two parabolas.

75. Parabola I: vertex: $(0, -1)$; directrix: $y = -\frac{5}{4}$
Parabola II: vertex: (0, 7); directrix: $y = \frac{29}{4}$

76. Parabola I: vertex: (0, 0); focus: (0, 1)
Parabola II: vertex: (1, 0); focus: (1, 1)

77. Parabola I: vertex: $\left(5, \frac{5}{3}\right)$; focus: $\left(5, \frac{29}{12}\right)$
Parabola II: vertex: $\left(\frac{13}{2}, \frac{289}{24}\right)$; focus: $\left(\frac{13}{2}, \frac{253}{24}\right)$

78. Parabola I: focus: $\left(-2, -\frac{35}{4}\right)$; directrix: $y = -\frac{37}{4}$
Parabola II: focus: $\left(2, -\frac{101}{4}\right)$; directrix: $y = -\frac{99}{4}$

9.3 THE ELLIPSE

SKILLS OBJECTIVES

- Find the equation of an ellipse centered at the origin.
- Find the equation of an ellipse centered at the point (h, k).
- Solve applied problems that involve ellipses.

CONCEPTUAL OBJECTIVES

- Understand that an ellipse is the set of all points in the plane the sum of whose distances from two fixed points (foci) is constant.
- Employ completing the square to transform an equation into the standard form of an ellipse.
- Understand that the endpoints and the foci are important for application problems involving ellipses.

9.3.1 Ellipse Centered at the Origin

Definition of an Ellipse

9.3.1 SKILL

Find the equation of an ellipse centered at the origin.

9.3.1 CONCEPTUAL

Understand that an ellipse is the set of all points in a plane the sum of whose distances from two fixed points (foci) is constant.

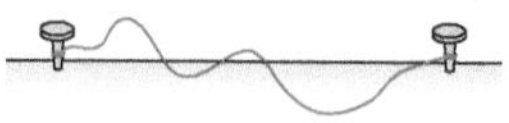

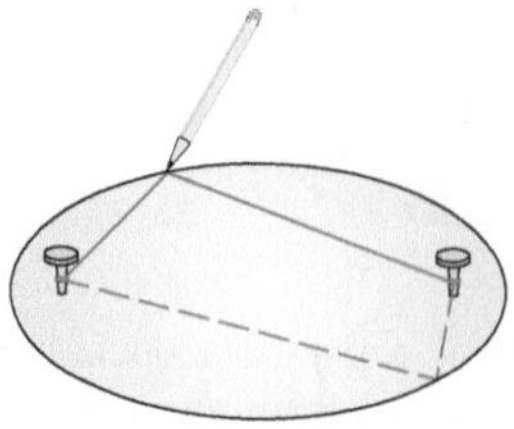

If we were to take a piece of string, tie loops at both ends, and tack the ends down so that the string had lots of slack, we would have the picture in the margin. If we then took a pencil and pulled the string taut and traced our way around for one full rotation, the result would be an ellipse (See the second figure in the margin).

DEFINITION Ellipse

An **ellipse** is the set of all points in a plane the sum of whose distances from two fixed points is constant. These two fixed points are called **foci** (plural of focus). A line segment through the foci called the **major axis** intersects the ellipse at the **vertices**. The midpoint of the line segment joining the vertices is called the **center**. The line segment that intersects the center, joins two points on the ellipse, and is perpendicular to the major axis is called the **minor axis**.

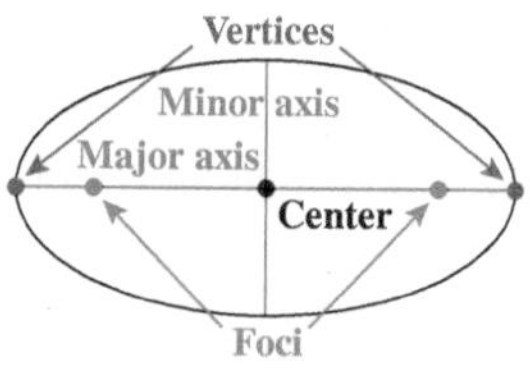

Let's start with an ellipse whose center is located at the origin. Using graph-shifting techniques, we can later extend the characteristics of an ellipse centered at a point other than the origin. Ellipses can vary in shape from circular to something quite elongated, either horizontally or vertically, that resembles the shape of a racetrack. We say that the ellipse has either greater (elongated) or lesser (circular) *eccentricity*; as we will see, there is a simple mathematical definition of *eccentricity*. It can be shown that the standard equation of an ellipse with its center at the origin is given by one of two forms, depending on whether the orientation of the major axis of the ellipse is horizontal or vertical. For $a > b > 0$, if the major axis is horizontal, then the equation is given by $\frac{x^2}{a^2} + \frac{y^2}{b^2} = 1$, and if the major axis is vertical, then the equation is given by $\frac{x^2}{b^2} + \frac{y^2}{a^2} = 1$.

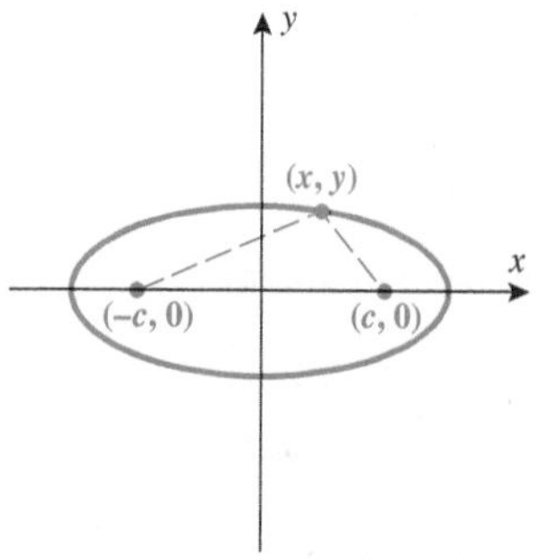

Let's consider an ellipse with its center at the origin and the foci on the x-axis. Let the distance from the center to the focus be c. Therefore, the foci are located at the points $(-c, 0)$ and $(c, 0)$. The line segment containing the foci is called the major axis, and it lies along the x-axis. The sum of the two distances from the foci to any point (x, y) must be constant.

Derivation of the Equation of an Ellipse

WORDS	MATH
Calculate the distance from (x, y) to $(-c, 0)$ by applying the distance formula.	$\sqrt{[x-(-c)]^2+y^2}$
Calculate the distance from (x, y) to $(c, 0)$ by applying the distance formula.	$\sqrt{(x-c)^2+y^2}$
The sum of these two distances is equal to a constant ($2a$ for convenience).	$\sqrt{[x-(-c)]^2+y^2}+\sqrt{(x-c)^2+y^2}=2a$
Isolate one radical.	$\sqrt{[x-(-c)]^2+y^2}=2a-\sqrt{(x-c)^2+y^2}$
Square both sides of the equation.	$(x+c)^2+y^2=4a^2-4a\sqrt{(x-c)^2+y^2}+(x-c)^2+y^2$
Square the binomials inside the parentheses.	$x^2+2cx+c^2+y^2=4a^2-4a\sqrt{(x-c)^2+y^2}+x^2-2cx+c^2+y^2$
Simplify.	$4cx-4a^2=-4a\sqrt{(x-c)^2+y^2}$
Divide both sides of the equation by -4.	$a^2-cx=a\sqrt{(x-c)^2+y^2}$
Square both sides of the equation.	$(a^2-cx)^2=a^2[(x-c)^2+y^2]$
Square the binomials inside the parentheses.	$a^4-2a^2cx+c^2x^2=a^2(x^2-2cx+c^2+y^2)$
Distribute the a^2 term.	$a^4-2a^2cx+c^2x^2=a^2x^2-2a^2cx+a^2c^2+a^2y^2$
Group the x and y terms together, respectively, on one side and constants on the other side.	$c^2x^2-a^2x^2-a^2y^2=a^2c^2-a^4$
Factor out the common factors.	$(c^2-a^2)x^2-a^2y^2=a^2(c^2-a^2)$
Multiply both sides of the equation by -1.	$(a^2-c^2)x^2+a^2y^2=a^2(a^2-c^2)$
We can make the argument that $a > c$ in order for a point to be on the ellipse (and not on the x-axis). Thus, since a and c represent distances and therefore are positive, we know that $a^2 > c^2$, or $a^2 - c^2 > 0$. Hence, we can divide both sides of the equation by $a^2 - c^2$, since $a^2 - c^2 \neq 0$.	$x^2+\dfrac{a^2y^2}{(a^2-c^2)}=a^2$
Let $b^2 = a^2 - c^2$.	$x^2+\dfrac{a^2y^2}{b^2}=a^2$
Divide both sides of the equation by a^2.	$\boxed{\dfrac{x^2}{a^2}+\dfrac{y^2}{b^2}=1}$

The equation $\dfrac{x^2}{a^2} + \dfrac{y^2}{b^2} = 1$ represents an ellipse with its center at the origin with the foci along the x-axis, since $a > b$. The following box summarizes ellipses that have their center at the origin and foci along either the x-axis or the y-axis.

[CONCEPT CHECK]

TRUE OR FALSE In an ellipse, the distance from the foci to the center is always less than the distance from the vertices to the center.

ANSWER True

EQUATION OF AN ELLIPSE WITH CENTER AT THE ORIGIN

The **standard form of the equation of an ellipse** with its center at the origin is given by

ORIENTATION OF MAJOR AXIS	Horizontal (along the x-axis)	Vertical (along the y-axis)
EQUATION	$\dfrac{x^2}{a^2} + \dfrac{y^2}{b^2} = 1 \quad a > b > 0$	$\dfrac{x^2}{b^2} + \dfrac{y^2}{a^2} = 1 \quad a > b > 0$
FOCI	$(-c, 0)$ and $(c, 0)$ where $c^2 = a^2 - b^2$	$(0, -c)$ and $(0, c)$ where $c^2 = a^2 - b^2$
VERTICES	$(-a, 0)$ and $(a, 0)$	$(0, -a)$ and $(0, a)$
OTHER INTERCEPTS	$(0, b)$ and $(0, -b)$	$(b, 0)$ and $(-b, 0)$

GRAPH

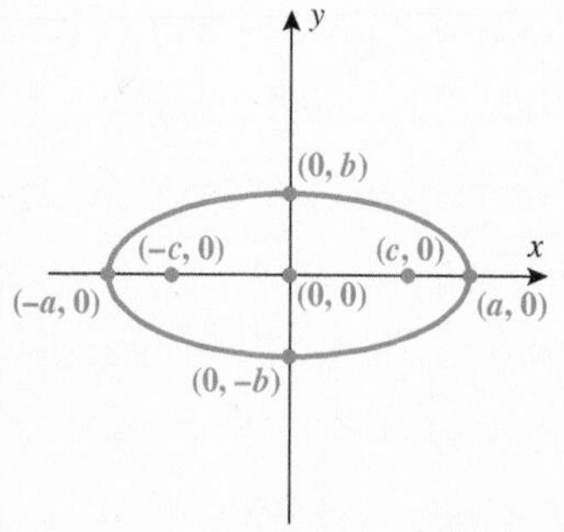

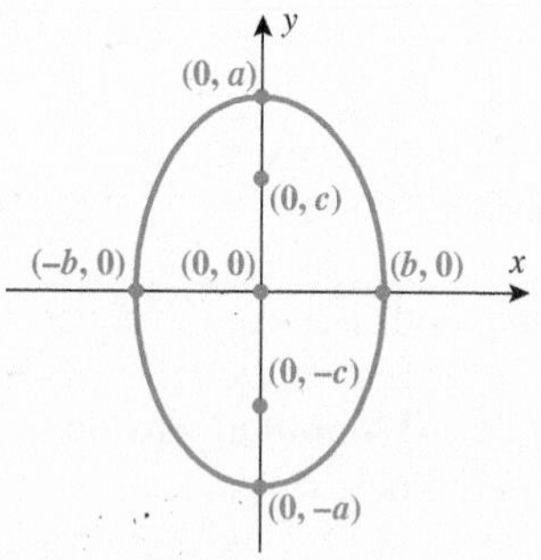

In both cases, the value of c, the distance along the major axis from the center to the focus, is given by $c^2 = a^2 - b^2$. The length of the major axis is $2a$ and the length of the minor axis is $2b$.

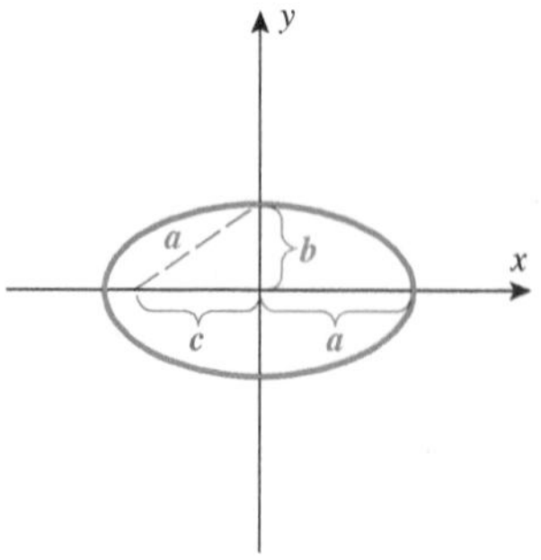

Notice that when $a = b$, the equation $\dfrac{x^2}{a^2} + \dfrac{y^2}{b^2} = 1$ simplifies to $\dfrac{x^2}{a^2} + \dfrac{y^2}{a^2} = 1$ or $x^2 + y^2 = a^2$, which corresponds to a circle. The vertices correspond to intercepts when an ellipse is centered at the origin. One of the first things we notice about an ellipse is its *eccentricity*. The **eccentricity**, denoted e, is given by $e = \dfrac{c}{a}$, where $0 < e < 1$. The circle is a limiting form of an ellipse, $c = 0$. In other words, if the eccentricity is close to 0, then the ellipse resembles a circle, whereas if the eccentricity is close to 1, then the ellipse is quite elongated, or eccentric.

Graphing an Ellipse with Center at the Origin

The equation of an ellipse in standard form can be used to graph an ellipse. Although an ellipse is defined in terms of the foci, the foci are not part of the graph. It is important to note that if the divisor of the term with x^2 is larger than the divisor of the term with y^2, then the ellipse is elongated horizontally.

EXAMPLE 1 Graphing an Ellipse with a Horizontal Major Axis

Graph the ellipse given by $\frac{x^2}{25} + \frac{y^2}{9} = 1$.

Solution:

Since $25 > 9$, the major axis is horizontal. $\quad a^2 = 25$ and $b^2 = 9$

Solve for a and b. $\quad a = 5$ and $b = 3$

Identify the vertices: $(-a, 0)$ and $(a, 0)$. $\quad (-5, 0)$ and $(5, 0)$

Identify the endpoints (y-intercepts) on the minor axis: $(0, -b)$ and $(0, b)$. $\quad (0, -3)$ and $(0, 3)$

Graph by labeling the points $(-5, 0)$, $(5, 0)$, $(0, -3)$, and $(0, 3)$ and connecting them with a smooth curve.

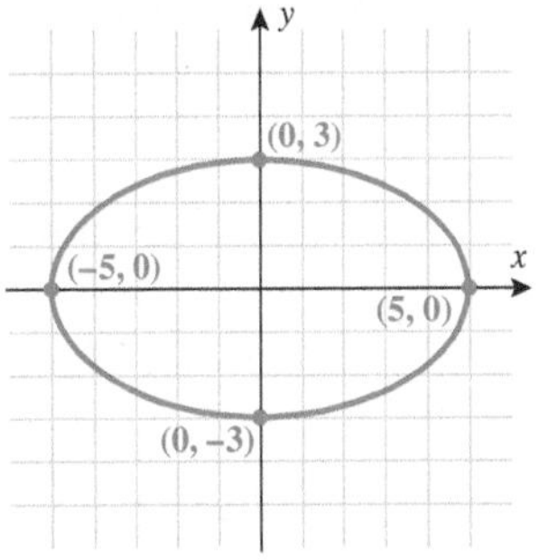

> **STUDY TIP**
> If the divisor of x^2 is larger than the divisor of y^2, then the major axis is horizontal along the x-axis, as in Example 1. If the divisor of y^2 is larger than the divisor of x^2, then the major axis is vertical along the y-axis, as you will see in Example 2.

If the divisor of x^2 is larger than the divisor of y^2, then the major axis is horizontal along the x-axis, as in Example 1. If the divisor of y^2 is larger than the divisor of x^2, then the major axis is vertical along the y-axis, as you will see in Example 2.

EXAMPLE 2 Graphing an Ellipse with a Vertical Major Axis

Graph the ellipse given by $16x^2 + y^2 = 16$.

Solution:

Write the equation in standard form by dividing by 16. $\quad \frac{x^2}{1} + \frac{y^2}{16} = 1$

Since $16 > 1$, this ellipse is elongated vertically. $\quad a^2 = 16$ and $b^2 = 1$

Solve for a and b. $\quad a = 4$ and $b = 1$

Identify the vertices: $(0, -a)$ and $(0, a)$. $\quad (0, -4)$ and $(0, 4)$

Identify the x-intercepts on the minor axis: $(-b, 0)$ and $(b, 0)$. $\quad (-1, 0)$ and $(1, 0)$

Graph by labeling the points $(0, -4)$, $(0, 4)$, $(-1, 0)$, and $(1, 0)$ and connecting them with a smooth curve.

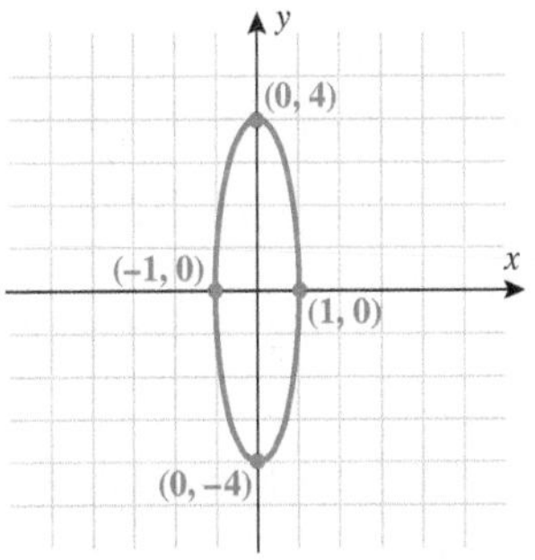

YOUR TURN Graph the ellipses:

a. $\frac{x^2}{9} + \frac{y^2}{4} = 1$ **b.** $\frac{x^2}{9} + \frac{y^2}{36} = 1$

ANSWER

a.

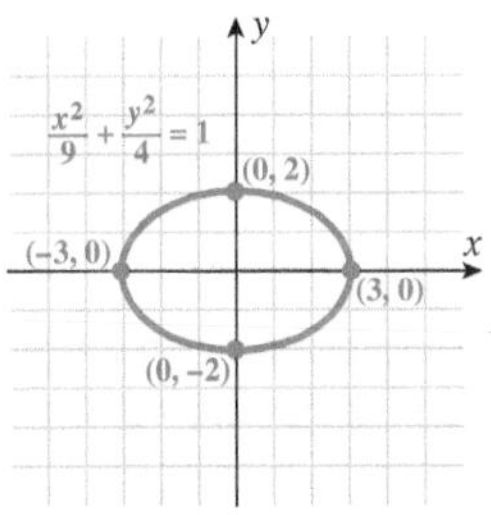

b.

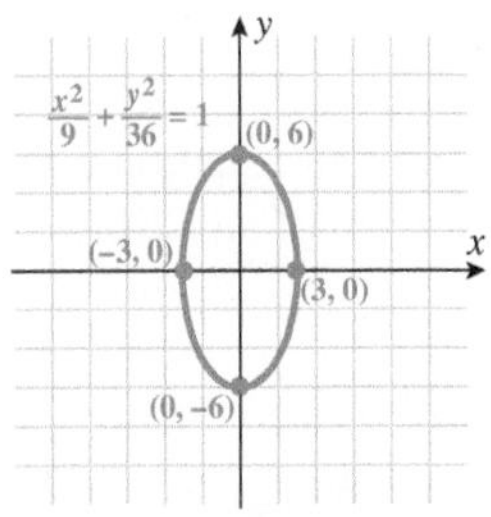

Finding the Equation of an Ellipse with Center at the Origin

What if we know the vertices and the foci of an ellipse and want to find the equation to which it corresponds? The axis on which the foci and vertices are located is the major axis. Therefore, we will have the standard equation of an ellipse, and a will be known (from the vertices). Since c is known from the foci, we can use the relation $c^2 = a^2 - b^2$ to determine the unknown b.

EXAMPLE 3 **Finding the Equation of an Ellipse Centered at the Origin**

Find the standard form of the equation of an ellipse with foci at $(-3, 0)$ and $(3, 0)$ and vertices $(-4, 0)$ and $(4, 0)$.

Solution:

The major axis lies along the x-axis, since it contains the foci and vertices.

Write the corresponding general equation of an ellipse. $\frac{x^2}{a^2} + \frac{y^2}{b^2} = 1$

Identify a from the vertices:

Match vertices $(-4, 0) = (-a, 0)$ and $(4, 0) = (a, 0)$. $a = 4$

Identify c from the foci:

Match foci, $(-3, 0) = (-c, 0)$ and $(3, 0) = (c, 0)$. $c = 3$

Substitute $a = 4$ and $c = 3$ into $b^2 = a^2 - c^2$. $b^2 = 4^2 - 3^2$

Simplify. $b^2 = 7$

Substitute $a^2 = 16$ and $b^2 = 7$ into $\frac{x^2}{a^2} + \frac{y^2}{b^2} = 1$. $\frac{x^2}{16} + \frac{y^2}{7} = 1$

The equation of the ellipse is $\boxed{\frac{x^2}{16} + \frac{y^2}{7} = 1}$.

YOUR TURN Find the standard form of the equation of an ellipse with vertices at $(0, -6)$ and $(0, 6)$ and foci $(0, -5)$ and $(0, 5)$.

ANSWER

$\frac{x^2}{11} + \frac{y^2}{36} = 1$

9.3.2 Ellipse Centered at the Point (h, k)

9.3.2 SKILL

Find the equation of an ellipse centered at the point (h, k).

9.3.2 CONCEPTUAL

Employ completing the square to transform an equation into the standard form of an ellipse.

We can use graph-shifting techniques to graph ellipses that are centered at a point other than the origin. For example, to graph $\frac{(x - h)^2}{a^2} + \frac{(y - k)^2}{b^2} = 1$ (assuming h and k are positive constants), start with the graph of $\frac{x^2}{a^2} + \frac{y^2}{b^2} = 1$ and shift the graph to the right h units and up k units. The center, the vertices, the foci, and the major and minor axes all shift. In other words, the two ellipses are identical in shape and size, except that the ellipse $\frac{(x - h)^2}{a^2} + \frac{(y - k)^2}{b^2} = 1$ is centered at the point (h, k).

The following table summarizes the characteristics of ellipses centered at a point other than the origin.

EQUATION OF AN ELLIPSE WITH CENTER AT THE POINT (h, k)

The **standard form of the equation of an ellipse** with its center at the point (h, k) is given by

ORIENTATION OF MAJOR AXIS	Horizontal (parallel to the x-axis)	Vertical (parallel to the y-axis)
EQUATION	$\frac{(x-h)^2}{a^2} + \frac{(y-k)^2}{b^2} = 1$	$\frac{(x-h)^2}{b^2} + \frac{(y-k)^2}{a^2} = 1$
GRAPH	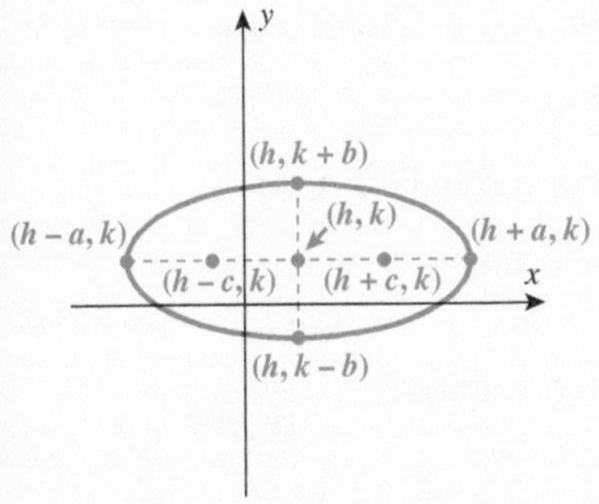	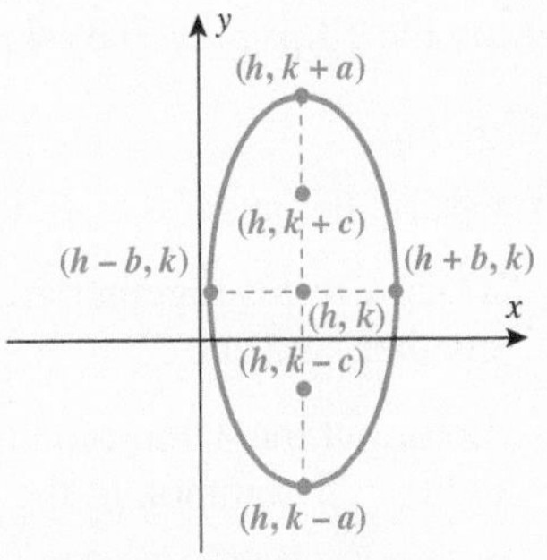
FOCI	$(h - c, k)$ and $(h + c, k)$	$(h, k - c)$ and $(h, k + c)$
VERTICES	$(h - a, k)$ and $(h + a, k)$	$(h, k - a)$ and $(h, k + a)$

In both cases, $a > b > 0$, $c^2 = a^2 - b^2$, the length of the major axis is $2a$, and the length of the minor axis is $2b$.

EXAMPLE 4 Graphing an Ellipse with Center (h, k) Given the Equation in Standard Form

Graph the ellipse given by $\frac{(x-2)^2}{9} + \frac{(y+1)^2}{16} = 1$.

Solution:

Write the equation in the form $\frac{(x-h)^2}{b^2} + \frac{(y-k)^2}{a^2} = 1$. $\quad \frac{(x-2)^2}{3^2} + \frac{[y-(-1)]^2}{4^2} = 1$

Identify a, b, and the center (h, k). $\quad a = 4$, $b = 3$, and $(h, k) = (2, -1)$

Draw a graph and label the center: $(2, -1)$.

Since $a = 4$, the vertices are up four units and down four units from the center: $(2, -5)$ and $(2, 3)$.

Since $b = 3$, the endpoints of the minor axis are to the left and right three units: $(-1, -1)$ and $(5, -1)$.

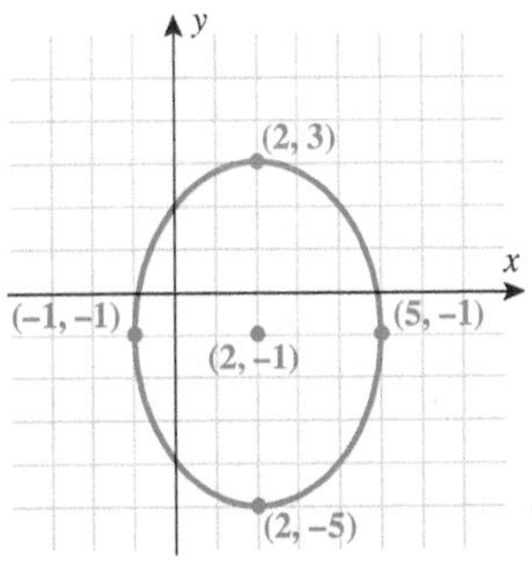

YOUR TURN Graph the ellipse given by $\frac{(x+1)^2}{9} + \frac{(y-3)^2}{1} = 1$.

ANSWER

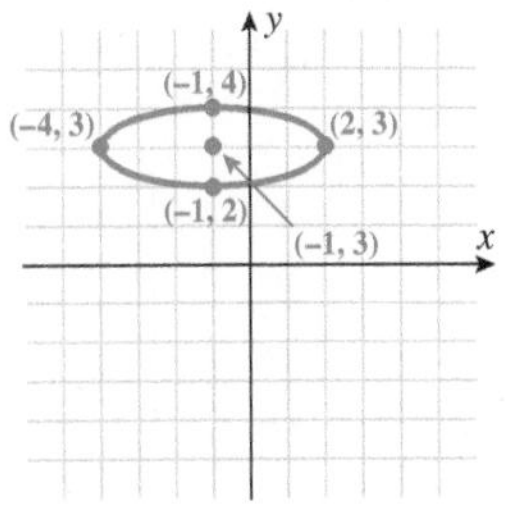

[CONCEPT CHECK]

An ellipse of the form $Ax^2 + Bx + Cy^2 - Dy - E = 0$, where A, B, C, D, and E are all positive constants, has a center that lies in which quadrant?

ANSWER quadrant II

All active members of the Lambda Chi fraternity are college students, but not all college students are members of the Lambda Chi fraternity. Similarly, all circles are ellipses, but not all ellipses are circles. When $a = b$, the standard equation of an ellipse simplifies to a standard equation of a circle. Recall that when we are given the equation of a circle in general form, we first complete the square in order to express the equation in standard form, which allows the center and radius to be identified. We use that same approach when the equation of an ellipse is given in a general form.

EXAMPLE 5 Graphing an Ellipse with Center (h, k) Given an Equation in General Form

Graph the ellipse given by $4x^2 + 24x + 25y^2 - 50y - 39 = 0$.

Solution:

Transform the general equation into standard form.

Group x terms together and y terms together, and add 39 to both sides. $\quad (4x^2 + 24x) + (25y^2 - 50y) = 39$

Factor out the 4 common to the x terms and the 25 common to the y terms. $\quad 4(x^2 + 6x) + 25(y^2 - 2y) = 39$

Complete the square on x and y. $\quad 4(x^2 + 6x + 9) + 25(y^2 - 2y + 1) = 39 + 4(9) + 25(1)$

Simplify. $\quad 4(x + 3)^2 + 25(y - 1)^2 = 100$

Divide by 100. $\quad \dfrac{(x + 3)^2}{25} + \dfrac{(y - 1)^2}{4} = 1$

Since $25 > 4$, this is an ellipse with a horizontal major axis.

Now that the equation of the ellipse is in standard form, compare to $\dfrac{(x - h)^2}{a^2} + \dfrac{(y - k)^2}{b^2} = 1$ and identify a, b, h, k. $\quad a = 5, b = 2$, and $(h, k) = (-3, 1)$

Since $a = 5$, the vertices are five units to the left and right of the center. $\quad (-8, 1)$ and $(2, 1)$

Since $b = 2$, the endpoints of the minor axis are up and down two units from the center. $\quad (-3, -1)$ and $(-3, 3)$

Graph.

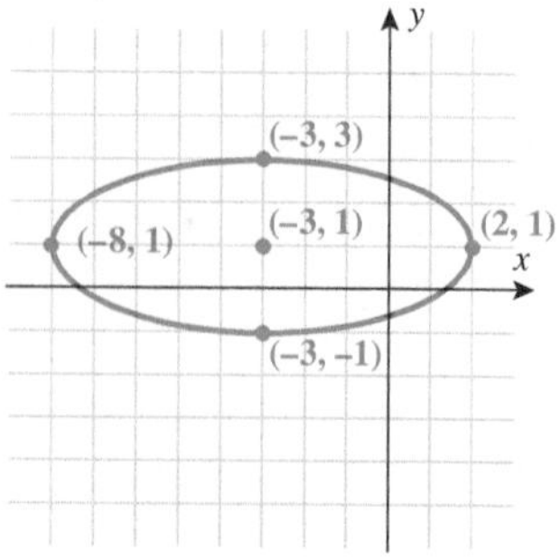

YOUR TURN Write the equation $4x^2 + 32x + y^2 - 2y + 61 = 0$ in standard form. Identify the center, vertices, and endpoints of the minor axis, and graph.

ANSWER

$\dfrac{(x + 4)^2}{1} + \dfrac{(y - 1)^2}{4} = 1$

Center: $(-4, 1)$

Vertices: $(-4, -1)$ and $(-4, 3)$

Endpoints of minor axis: $(-5, 1)$ and $(-3, 1)$

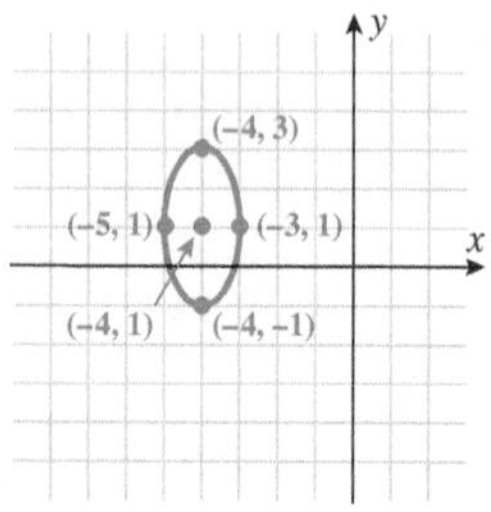

9.3.3 Applications

There are many examples of ellipses all around us. On Earth we have racetracks, and in our solar system, the planets travel in elliptical orbits with the Sun as a focus. Satellites are in elliptical orbits around Earth. Most communications satellites are in a *geosynchronous* (GEO) orbit—they orbit Earth once each day. In order to stay over the same spot on Earth, a *geostationary* satellite has to be directly above the equator; it circles Earth in exactly the time it takes Earth to turn once on its axis, and its orbit has to follow the path of the equator as Earth rotates. Otherwise, from Earth the satellite would appear to move in a north–south line every day.

If we start with an ellipse in the *xy*-plane and rotate it around its major axis, the result is a three-dimensional ellipsoid.

9.3.3 SKILL

Solve applied problems that involve ellipses.

9.3.3 CONCEPTUAL

Understand that the endpoints and the foci are important for application problems involving ellipses.

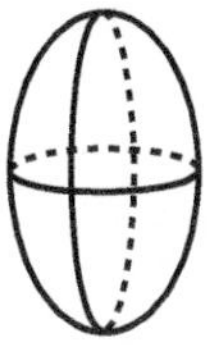

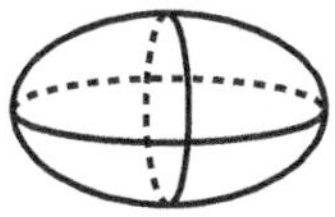

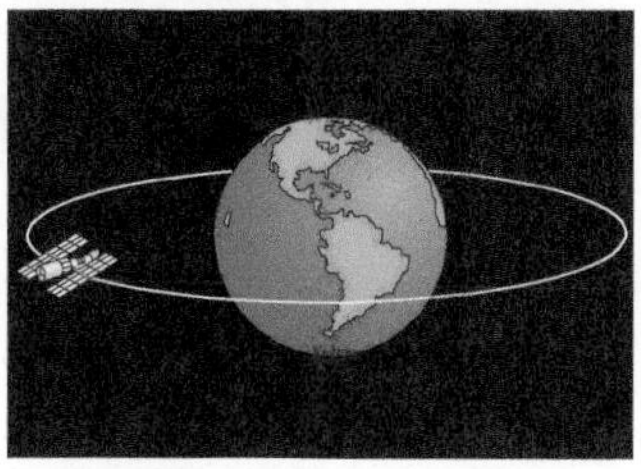

A football and a blimp are two examples of ellipsoids. The ellipsoidal shape allows for a more aerodynamic path.

ManuKro/iStock/ Getty Images

Peter Phipp/Age Fotostock America, Inc.

EXAMPLE 6 **An Official NFL Football**

A longitudinal section (that includes the two vertices and the center) of an official Wilson NFL football is an ellipse. The longitudinal section is approximately 11 inches long and 7 inches wide. Write an equation governing the elliptical longitudinal section.

Solution:

Locate the center of the ellipse at the origin and orient the football horizontally.

Write the general equation of an ellipse centered at the origin. $\frac{x^2}{a^2} + \frac{y^2}{b^2} = 1$

The length of the major axis is 11 inches. $2a = 11$

Solve for *a*. $a = 5.5$

The length of the minor axis is 7 inches. $2b = 7$

Solve for *b*. $b = 3.5$

Substitute $a = 5.5$ and $b = 3.5$ into $\frac{x^2}{a^2} + \frac{y^2}{b^2} = 1$. $\boxed{\frac{x^2}{5.5^2} + \frac{y^2}{3.5^2} = 1}$

[CONCEPT CHECK]

The foci of a football would be closer to the (center/vertices) than the foci of a basketball would be.

ANSWER vertices

[SECTION 9.3] SUMMARY

In this section, we first analyzed ellipses that are centered at the origin.

<table>
<tr><td>ORIENTATION OF MAJOR AXIS</td><td>Horizontal
along the x-axis</td><td>Vertical
along the y-axis</td></tr>
<tr><td>EQUATION</td><td>$\frac{x^2}{a^2} + \frac{y^2}{b^2} = 1 \quad a > b > 0$</td><td>$\frac{x^2}{b^2} + \frac{y^2}{a^2} = 1 \quad a > b > 0$</td></tr>
<tr><td>FOCI*</td><td>$(-c, 0)$ and $(c, 0)$</td><td>$(0, -c)$ and $(0, c)$</td></tr>
<tr><td>VERTICES</td><td>$(-a, 0)$ and $(a, 0)$</td><td>$(0, -a)$ and $(0, a)$</td></tr>
<tr><td>OTHER INTERCEPTS</td><td>$(0, -b)$ and $(0, b)$</td><td>$(-b, 0)$ and $(b, 0)$</td></tr>
<tr><td>GRAPH</td><td>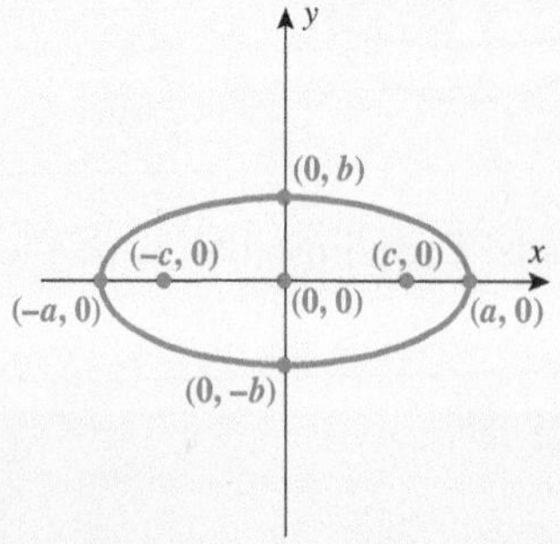
</td><td>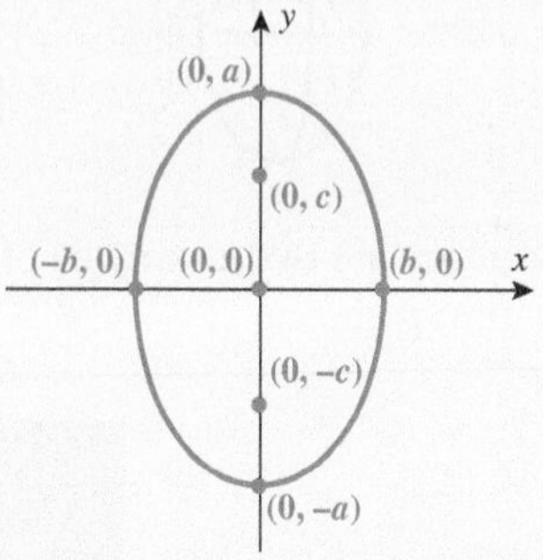
</td></tr>
</table>

$*c^2 = a^2 - b^2$

For ellipses centered at the origin, we can graph an ellipse by finding all four intercepts.

For ellipses **centered at the point (h, k),** the major and minor axes and endpoints of the ellipse all shift accordingly. When $a = b$, the ellipse is a circle.

<table>
<tr><td>ORIENTATION OF MAJOR AXIS</td><td>Horizontal
(parallel to the x-axis)</td><td>Vertical
(parallel to the y-axis)</td></tr>
<tr><td>EQUATION</td><td>$\frac{(x-h)^2}{a^2} + \frac{(y-k)^2}{b^2} = 1$</td><td>$\frac{(x-h)^2}{b^2} + \frac{(y-k)^2}{a^2} = 1$</td></tr>
<tr><td>GRAPH</td><td>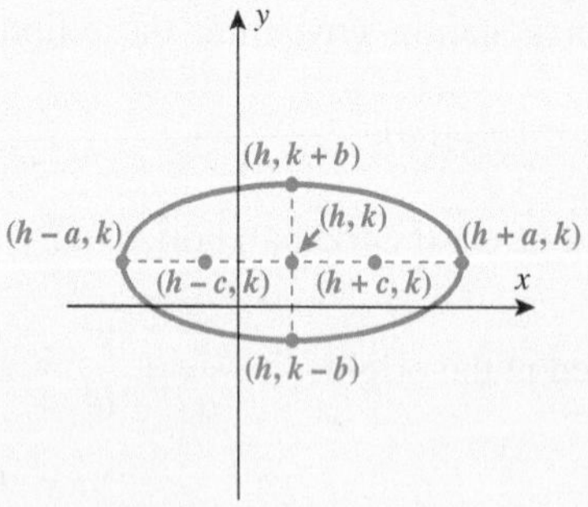
</td><td>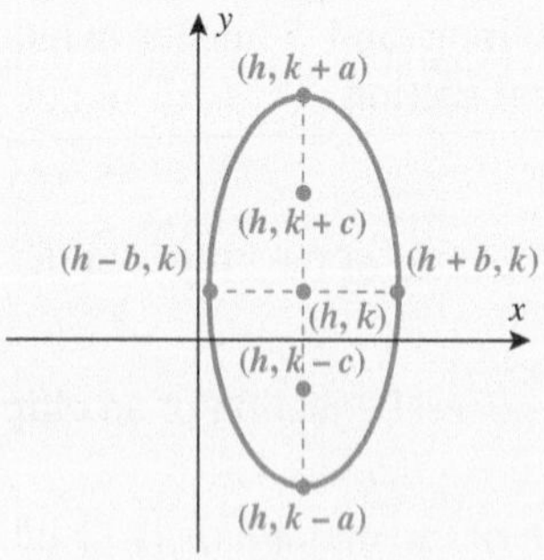
</td></tr>
<tr><td>FOCI</td><td>$(h - c, k)$ and $(h + c, k)$</td><td>$(h, k - c)$ and $(h, k + c)$</td></tr>
<tr><td>VERTICES</td><td>$(h - a, k)$ and $(h + a, k)$</td><td>$(h, k - a)$ and $(h, k + a)$</td></tr>
</table>

$*c^2 = a^2 - b^2$

[SECTION 9.3] EXERCISES

• SKILLS

In Exercises 1–4, match each equation with the corresponding ellipse.

1. $\dfrac{x^2}{36} + \dfrac{y^2}{16} = 1$

2. $\dfrac{x^2}{16} + \dfrac{y^2}{36} = 1$

3. $\dfrac{x^2}{8} + \dfrac{y^2}{72} = 1$

4. $4x^2 + y^2 = 1$

a.

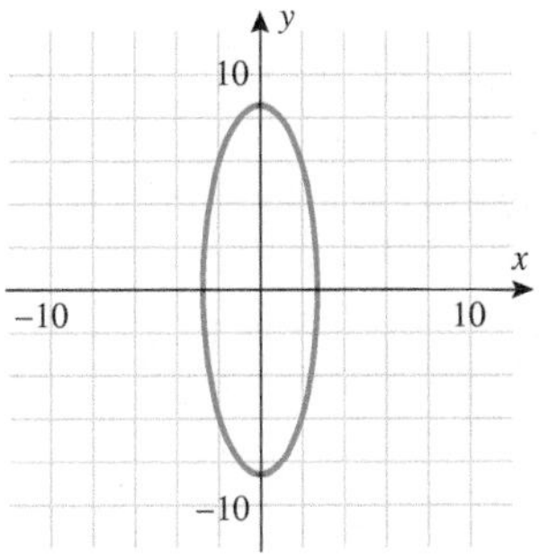

b.

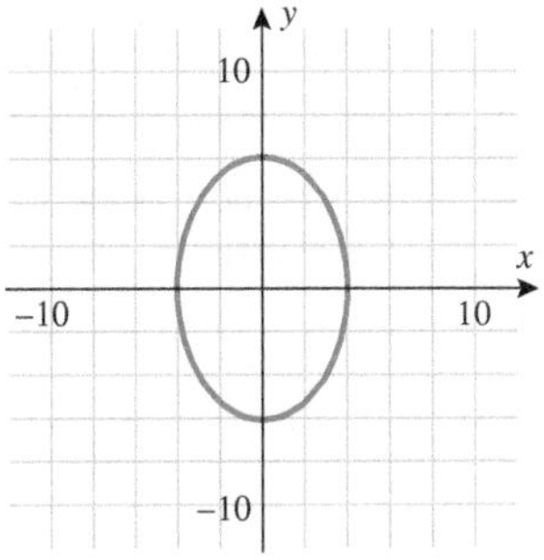

c.

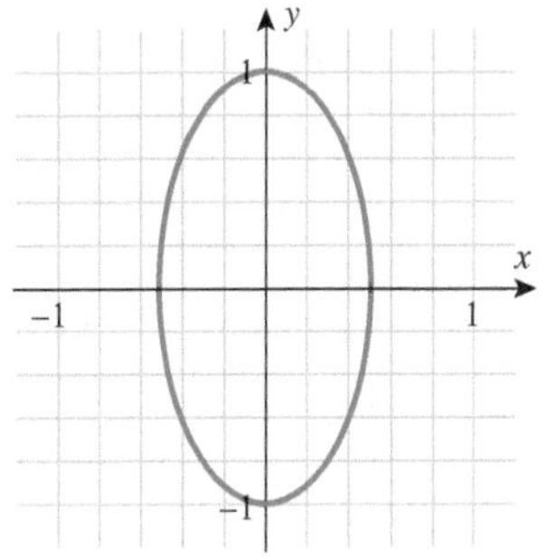

d.

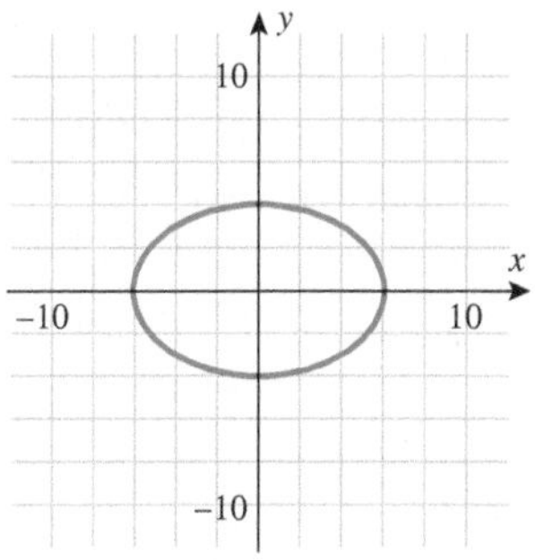

In Exercises 5–16, graph each ellipse. Label the center and vertices.

5. $\dfrac{x^2}{25} + \dfrac{y^2}{16} = 1$

6. $\dfrac{x^2}{49} + \dfrac{y^2}{9} = 1$

7. $\dfrac{x^2}{16} + \dfrac{y^2}{64} = 1$

8. $\dfrac{x^2}{25} + \dfrac{y^2}{144} = 1$

9. $\dfrac{x^2}{100} + y^2 = 1$

10. $9x^2 + 4y^2 = 36$

11. $\dfrac{4}{9}x^2 + 81y^2 = 1$

12. $\dfrac{4}{25}x^2 + \dfrac{100}{9}y^2 = 1$

13. $4x^2 + y^2 = 16$

14. $x^2 + y^2 = 81$

15. $8x^2 + 16y^2 = 32$

16. $10x^2 + 25y^2 = 50$

In Exercises 17–24, find the standard form of the equation of an ellipse with the given characteristics.

17. Foci: $(-4, 0)$ and $(4, 0)$ Vertices: $(-6, 0)$ and $(6, 0)$

18. Foci: $(-1, 0)$ and $(1, 0)$ Vertices: $(-3, 0)$ and $(3, 0)$

19. Foci: $(0, -3)$ and $(0, 3)$ Vertices: $(0, -4)$ and $(0, 4)$

20. Foci: $(0, -1)$ and $(0, 1)$ Vertices: $(0, -2)$ and $(0, 2)$

21. Major axis vertical with length of 8, minor axis length of 4, and centered at $(0, 0)$

22. Major axis horizontal with length of 10, minor axis length of 2, and centered at $(0, 0)$

23. Vertices $(0, -7)$ and $(0, 7)$ and endpoints of minor axis $(-3, 0)$ and $(3, 0)$

24. Vertices $(-9, 0)$ and $(9, 0)$ and endpoints of minor axis $(0, -4)$ and $(0, 4)$

In Exercises 25–28, match each equation with its graph.

25. $\dfrac{(x-3)^2}{4} + \dfrac{(y+2)^2}{25} = 1$

26. $\dfrac{(x+3)^2}{4} + \dfrac{(y-2)^2}{25} = 1$

27. $\dfrac{(x-3)^2}{25} + \dfrac{(y+2)^2}{4} = 1$

28. $\dfrac{(x+3)^2}{25} + \dfrac{(y-2)^2}{4} = 1$

a.

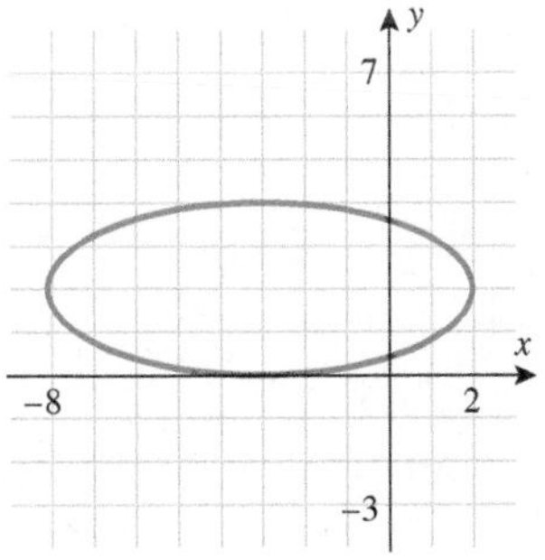

b.

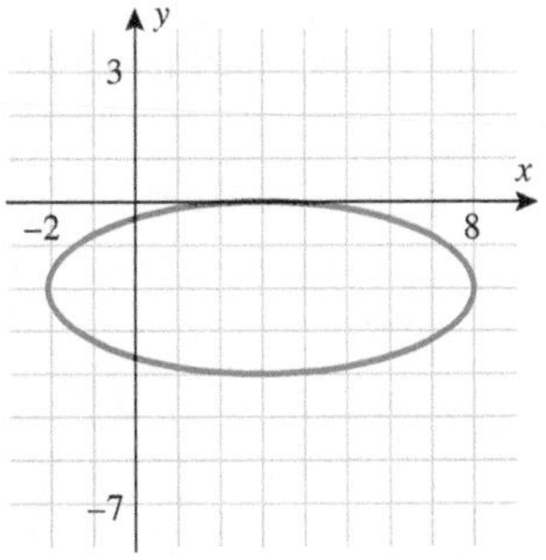

c.

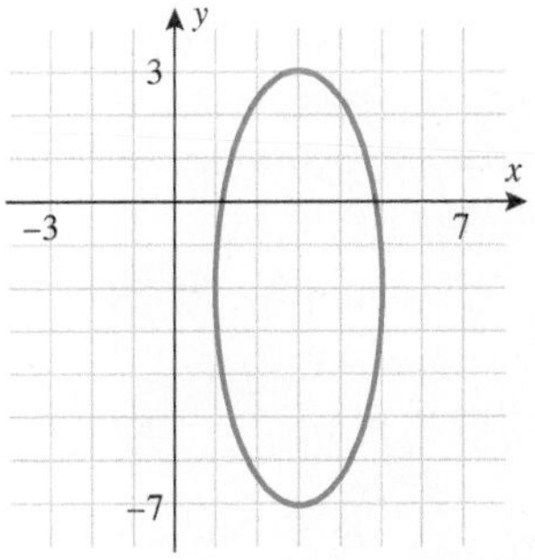

d.

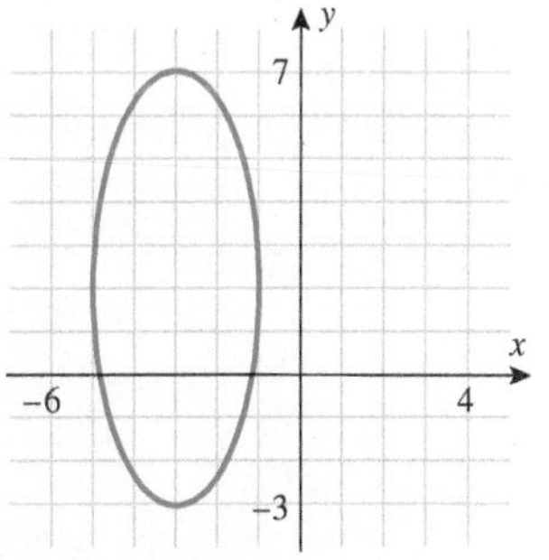

In Exercises 29–38, graph each ellipse. Label the center and vertices.

29. $\dfrac{(x-1)^2}{16} + \dfrac{(y-2)^2}{4} = 1$

30. $\dfrac{(x+1)^2}{36} + \dfrac{(y+2)^2}{9} = 1$

31. $10(x+3)^2 + (y-4)^2 = 80$

32. $3(x+3)^2 + 12(y-4)^2 = 36$

33. $x^2 + 4y^2 - 24y + 32 = 0$

34. $25x^2 + 2y^2 - 4y - 48 = 0$

35. $x^2 - 2x + 2y^2 - 4y - 5 = 0$

36. $9x^2 - 18x + 4y^2 - 27 = 0$

37. $5x^2 + 20x + y^2 + 6y - 21 = 0$

38. $9x^2 + 36x + y^2 + 2y + 36 = 0$

In Exercises 39–46, find the standard form of the equation of an ellipse with the given characteristics.

39. Foci: $(-2, 5)$ and $(6, 5)$ Vertices: $(-3, 5)$ and $(7, 5)$

40. Foci: $(2, -2)$ and $(4, -2)$ Vertices: $(0, -2)$ and $(6, -2)$

41. Foci: $(4, -7)$ and $(4, -1)$ Vertices: $(4, -8)$ and $(4, 0)$

42. Foci: $(2, -6)$ and $(2, -4)$ Vertices: $(2, -7)$ and $(2, -3)$

43. Major axis vertical with length of 8, minor axis length of 4, and centered at $(3, 2)$

44. Major axis horizontal with length of 10, minor axis length of 2, and centered at $(-4, 3)$.

45. Vertices $(-1, -9)$ and $(-1, 1)$ and endpoints of minor axis $(-4, -4)$ and $(2, -4)$

46. Vertices $(-2, 3)$ and $(6, 3)$ and endpoints of minor axis $(2, 1)$and $(2, 5)$

• APPLICATIONS

47. **Carnival Ride.** The Zipper, a favorite carnival ride, maintains an elliptical shape with a major axis of 150 feet and a minor axis of 30 feet. Assuming it is centered at the origin, find an equation for the ellipse.

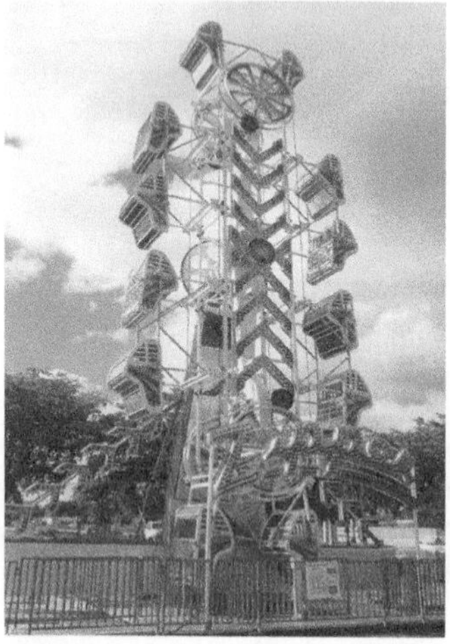

Zipper

Courtesy Chance Morgan, Inc.

48. **Carnival Ride.** A Ferris wheel traces an elliptical path with both a major and a minor axis of 180 feet. Assuming it is centered at the origin, find an equation for the ellipse (circle).

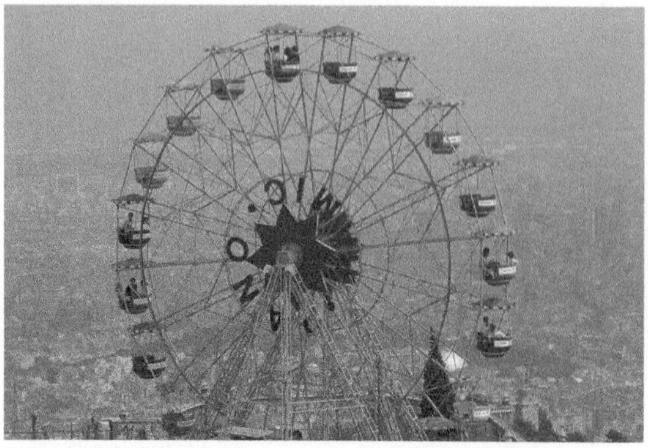

Ferris wheel, Barcelona, Spain

Tina Buckman/Index Stock

For Exercises 49 and 50, refer to the following information:

A high school wants to build a football field surrounded by an elliptical track. A regulation football field must be 120 yards long and 30 yards wide.

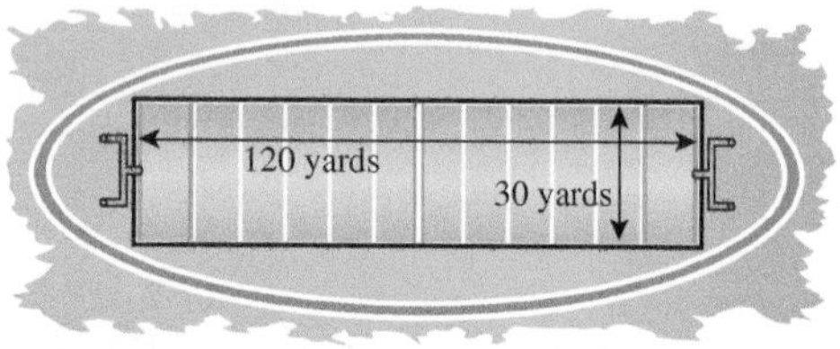

49. **Sports Field.** Suppose the elliptical track is centered at the origin and has a horizontal major axis of length 150 yards and a minor axis length of 40 yards.
    a. Write an equation for the ellipse.
    b. Find the width of the track at the end of the field. Will the track completely enclose the football field?

50. **Sports Field.** Suppose the elliptical track is centered at the origin and has a horizontal major axis of length 150 yards. How long should the minor axis be in order to enclose the field?

For Exercises 51 and 52, refer to orbits in our solar system:

The planets have elliptical orbits with the Sun as one of the foci. Pluto (orange), the planet farthest from the Sun, has a very elongated, or flattened, elliptical orbit, whereas Earth (royal blue) has an almost circular orbit. Because of Pluto's flattened path, it is not always the planet farthest from the Sun.

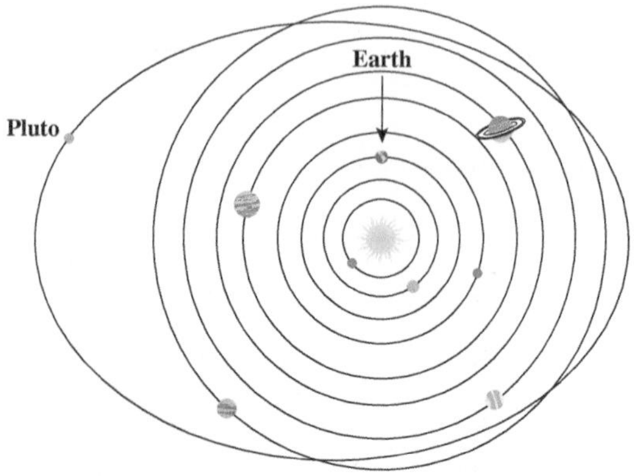

51. **Planetary Orbits.** The orbit of the dwarf planet Pluto has approximately the following characteristics (assume the Sun is the focus):

- The length of the major axis $2a$ is approximately 11,827,000,000 kilometers.
- The perihelion distance from the dwarf planet to the Sun is 4,447,000,000 kilometers.

Determine the equation for Pluto's elliptical orbit around the Sun.

52. **Planetary Orbits.** Earth's orbit has approximately the following characteristics (assume the Sun is the focus):

- The length of the major axis $2a$ is approximately 299,700,000 kilometers.
- The perihelion distance from Earth to the Sun is 147,100,000 kilometers.

Determine the equation for Earth's elliptical orbit around the Sun.

For Exercises 53 and 54, refer to the following information:

Asteroids orbit the Sun in elliptical patterns and often cross paths with Earth's orbit, making life a little tense now and again. A few asteroids have orbits that cross Earth's orbit—called "Apollo asteroids" or "Earth-crossing asteroids." In recent years, asteroids have passed within 100,000 kilometers of Earth!

53. **Asteroids.** Asteroid 433, or Eros, is the second largest near-Earth asteroid. The semimajor axis is 150 million kilometers and the eccentricity is 0.223, where eccentricity is defined as $e = \sqrt{1 - \frac{b^2}{a^2}}$, where a is the semimajor axis or $2a$ is the major axis, and b is the semiminor axis or $2b$ is the minor axis. Find the equation of Eros's orbit. Round a and b to the nearest million kilometers.

54. **Asteroids.** The asteroid Toutatis is the largest near-Earth asteroid. The semimajor axis is 350 million kilometers and the eccentricity is 0.634, where eccentricity is defined as $e = \sqrt{1 - \frac{b^2}{a^2}}$, where a is the semimajor axis or $2a$ is the major axis, and b is the semimajor axis or $2b$ is the minor axis. On September 29, 2004, it missed Earth by 961,000 miles. Find the equation of Toutatis's orbit.

55. **Halley's Comet.** The eccentricity of Halley's Comet is approximately 0.967. If a comet had e almost equal to 1, what would its orbit appear to be from Earth?

56. **Halley's Comet.** The length of the semimajor axis is 17.8 AU (astronomical units) and the eccentricity is approximately 0.967. Find the equation of Halley's Comet. (Assume 1 AU = 150 million km.)

• CATCH THE MISTAKE

In Exercises 57 and 58, explain the mistake that is made.

57. Graph the ellipse given by $\frac{x^2}{6} + \frac{y^2}{4} = 1$.

Solution:

Write the standard form of the equation of an ellipse. $\frac{x^2}{a^2} + \frac{y^2}{b^2} = 1$

Identify a and b. $a = 6, b = 4$

Label the vertices and the endpoints of the minor axis, $(-6, 0)$, $(6, 0)$, $(0, -4)$, $(0, 4)$, and connect them with an elliptical curve.

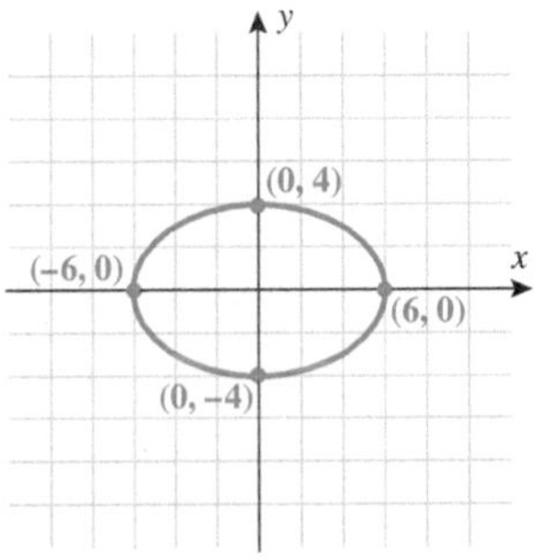

This is incorrect. What mistake was made?

58. Determine the foci of the ellipse $\frac{x^2}{16} + \frac{y^2}{9} = 1$.

Solution:

Write the general equation of a horizontal ellipse. $\frac{x^2}{a^2} + \frac{y^2}{b^2} = 1$

Identify a and b. $a = 4, b = 3$

Substitute $a = 4, b = 3$ into $c^2 = a^2 + b^2$. $c^2 = 4^2 + 3^2$

Solve for c. $c = 5$

Foci are located at $(-5, 0)$ and $(5, 0)$.

The points $(-5, 0)$ and $(5, 0)$ are located outside of the ellipse.

This is incorrect. What mistake was made?

• CONCEPTUAL

In Exercises 59–62, determine whether each statement is true or false.

59. If you know the vertices of an ellipse, you can determine the equation for the ellipse.

60. If you know the foci and the endpoints of the minor axis, you can determine the equation for the ellipse.

61. Ellipses centered at the origin have symmetry with respect to the x-axis, the y-axis, and the origin.

62. All ellipses are circles, but not all circles are ellipses.

63. How many ellipses, with major and minor axes parallel to the coordinate axes, have focus $(-2, 0)$ and pass through the point $(-2, 2)$?

64. How many ellipses have vertices $(-3, 0)$ and $(3, 0)$?

65. If two ellipses intersect each other, what is the minimum number of intersection points?

66. If two ellipses intersect each other, what is the maximum number of intersection points?

• CHALLENGE

67. The eccentricity of an ellipse is defined as $e = \frac{c}{a}$. Compare the eccentricity of the orbit of Pluto to that of Earth (refer to Exercises 51 and 52).

68. The eccentricity of an ellipse is defined as $e = \frac{c}{a}$. Since $a > c > 0$, then $0 < e < 1$. Describe the shape of an ellipse when

a. e is close to zero

b. e is close to one

c. $e = 0.5$

69. Find the equation of an ellipse centered at the origin that contains the points $(1, 3)$ and $(4, 2)$.

70. Find the equation of an ellipse centered at the origin that contains the points $\left(1, \frac{6\sqrt{5}}{5}\right)$ and $\left(-\frac{5}{3}, 2\right)$.

71. Find the equation of an ellipse centered at $(2, -3)$ that passes through the points $(1, -\frac{1}{3})$ and $(5, -3)$.

72. Find the equation of an ellipse centered at $(1, -2)$ that passes through the points $(1, -4)$ and $(2, -2)$.

• PREVIEW TO CALCULUS

In calculus, the derivative of a function is used to find its maximum and minimum values. In the case of an ellipse, with major and minor axes parallel to the coordinate axes, the maximum and minimum values correspond to the y-coordinate of the vertices that lie on its vertical axis of symmetry.

In Exercises 73–76, find the maximum and minimum values of each ellipse.

73. $4x^2 + y^2 - 24x + 10y + 57 = 0$

74. $9x^2 + 4y^2 + 72x + 16y + 124 = 0$

75. $81x^2 + 100y^2 - 972x + 1600y + 1216 = 0$

76. $25x^2 + 16y^2 + 200x + 256y - 176 = 0$

9.4 THE HYPERBOLA

SKILLS OBJECTIVES

- Find the equation of a hyperbola centered at the origin.
- Find the equation of a hyperbola centered at the point (h, k).
- Solve applied problems that involve hyperbolas.

CONCEPTUAL OBJECTIVES

- Understand that a hyperbola is the set of all points in the plane the difference of whose distances from two fixed points (foci) is a positive constant.
- Employ completing the square to transform an equation into the standard form of a hyperbola.
- Understand that it is the difference in time of signals remaining constant that enables ships to navigate along a hyperbolic curve to shore.

9.4.1 Hyperbola Centered at the Origin

9.4.1 SKILL

Find the equation of a hyperbola centered at the origin.

9.4.1 CONCEPTUAL

Understand that a hyperbola is the set of all points in the plane the difference of whose distances from two fixed points (foci) is a positive constant.

The definition of a hyperbola is similar to the definition of an ellipse. An ellipse is the set of all points the *sum* of whose distances from two points (the foci) is constant. A *hyperbola* is the set of all points the *difference* of whose distances from two points (the foci) is constant. What distinguishes their equations is a minus sign.

Ellipse centered at the origin: $$\frac{x^2}{a^2} + \frac{y^2}{b^2} = 1$$

Hyperbola centered at the origin: $$\frac{x^2}{a^2} - \frac{y^2}{b^2} = 1$$

DEFINITION Hyperbola

A **hyperbola** is the set of all points in a plane the difference of whose distances from two fixed points is a positive constant. These two fixed points are called **foci.** The hyperbola has two separate curves called **branches**. The two points where the hyperbola intersects the line joining the foci are called **vertices**. The line segment joining the vertices is called the **transverse axis of the hyperbola**. The midpoint of the transverse axis is called the **center**.

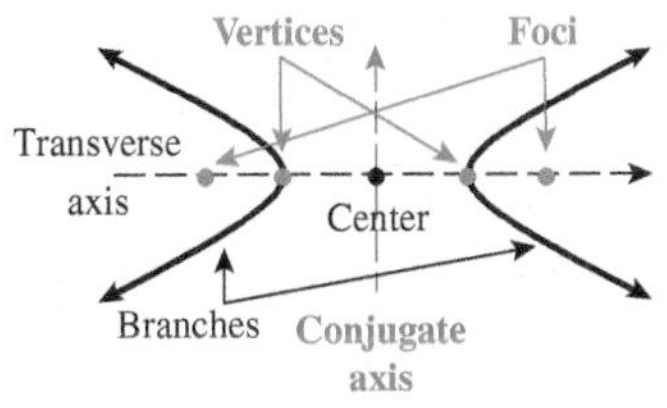

Let's consider a hyperbola with the center at the origin and the foci on the x-axis. Let the distance from the center to the focus be c. Therefore, the foci are located at the points $(-c, 0)$ and $(c, 0)$. The difference of the two distances from the foci to any point (x, y) must be constant. We then can follow an analysis similar to that applied with an ellipse.

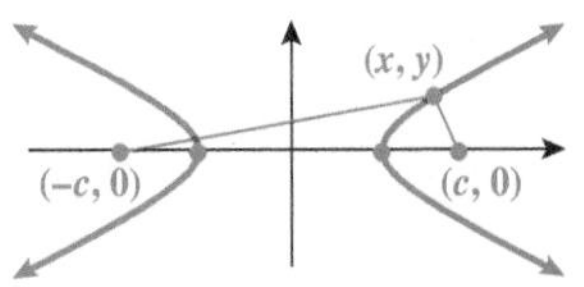

Derivation of the Equation of a Hyperbola

WORDS	MATH
The difference of these two distances is equal to a constant (2a for convenience).	$\sqrt{[x-(-c)]^2+y^2}-\sqrt{(x-c)^2+y^2}=\pm 2a$
Following the same procedure that we used with an ellipse leads to:	$(c^2-a^2)x^2-a^2y^2=a^2(c^2-a^2)$
We can make the argument that $c > a$ in order for a point to be on the hyperbola (and not on the x-axis). Therefore, since a and c represent distances and therefore are positive, we know that $c^2 > a^2$, or $c^2 - a^2 > 0$. Hence, we can divide both sides of the equation by $c^2 - a^2$, since $c^2 - a^2 \neq 0$.	$x^2-\dfrac{a^2y^2}{(c^2-a^2)}=a^2$
Let $b^2 = c^2 - a^2$.	$x^2-\dfrac{a^2y^2}{b^2}=a^2$
Divide both sides of the equation by a^2.	$\dfrac{x^2}{a^2}-\dfrac{y^2}{b^2}=1$

The equation $\frac{x^2}{a^2}-\frac{y^2}{b^2}=1$ represents a hyperbola with its center at the origin and the foci along the x-axis. The following box summarizes hyperbolas that have their center at the origin and foci along either the x-axis or the y-axis.

[CONCEPT CHECK]

TRUE OR FALSE In a hyperbola, the foci are always closer to the center than the vertices.

ANSWER False

EQUATION OF A HYPERBOLA WITH CENTER AT THE ORIGIN

The **standard form of the equation of a hyperbola** with its center at the origin is given by

ORIENTATION OF TRANSVERSE AXIS	Horizontal (along the x-axis)	Vertical (along the y-axis)
EQUATION	$\dfrac{x^2}{a^2}-\dfrac{y^2}{b^2}=1$	$\dfrac{y^2}{a^2}-\dfrac{x^2}{b^2}=1$
FOCI	$(-c, 0)$ and $(c, 0)$ where $c^2 = a^2 + b^2$	$(0, -c)$ and $(0, c)$ where $c^2 = a^2 + b^2$
ASYMPTOTES	$y=\dfrac{b}{a}x$ and $y=-\dfrac{b}{a}x$	$y=\dfrac{a}{b}x$ and $y=-\dfrac{a}{b}x$
VERTICES	$(-a, 0)$ and $(a, 0)$	$(0, -a)$ and $(0, a)$
TRANSVERSE AXIS	Horizontal length $2a$	Vertical length $2a$
GRAPH	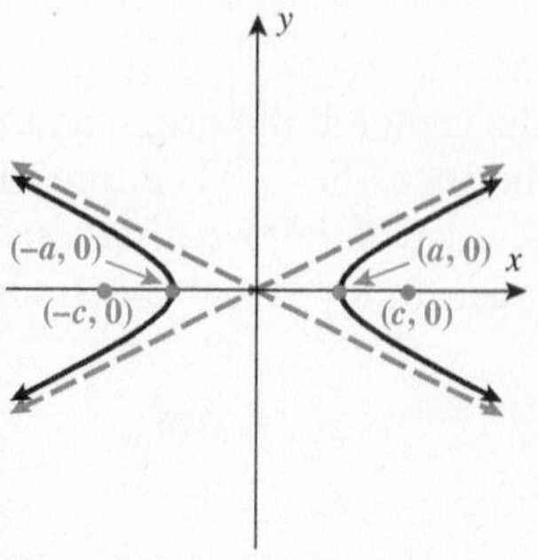	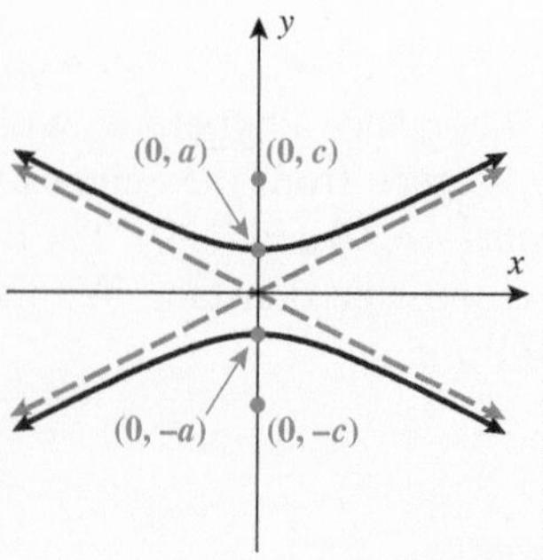

Note that for $\frac{x^2}{a^2} - \frac{y^2}{b^2} = 1$, if $x = 0$, then $-\frac{y^2}{b^2} = 1$, which yields an imaginary number for y. However, when $y = 0$, $\frac{x^2}{a^2} = 1$, and therefore $x = \pm a$. The vertices for this hyperbola are $(-a, 0)$ and $(a, 0)$.

EXAMPLE 1 Finding the Foci and Vertices of a Hyperbola Given the Equation

Find the foci and vertices of the hyperbola given by $\frac{x^2}{9} - \frac{y^2}{4} = 1$.

Solution:

Compare to the standard equation of a hyperbola, $\frac{x^2}{a^2} - \frac{y^2}{b^2} = 1$. $a^2 = 9, b^2 = 4$

Solve for a and b. $a = 3, b = 2$

Substitute $a = 3$ into the vertices, $(-a, 0)$ and $(a, 0)$. $(-3, 0)$ and $(3, 0)$

Substitute $a = 3, b = 2$ into $c^2 = a^2 + b^2$. $c^2 = 3^2 + 2^2$

Solve for c. $c^2 = 13$

$c = \sqrt{13}$

Substitute $c = \sqrt{13}$ into the foci, $(-c, 0)$ and $(c, 0)$. $(-\sqrt{13}, 0)$ and $(\sqrt{13}, 0)$

The vertices are $\boxed{(-3, 0)}$ and $\boxed{(3, 0)}$, and the foci are $\boxed{(-\sqrt{13}, 0)}$ and $\boxed{(\sqrt{13}, 0)}$.

YOUR TURN Find the vertices and foci of the hyperbola $\frac{y^2}{16} - \frac{x^2}{20} = 1$.

ANSWER

Vertices: $(0, -4)$ and $(0, 4)$
Foci: $(0, -6)$ and $(0, 6)$

EXAMPLE 2 Finding the Equation of a Hyperbola Given Foci and Vertices

Find the standard form of the equation of a hyperbola whose vertices are located at $(0, -4)$ and $(0, 4)$ and whose foci are located at $(0, -5)$ and $(0, 5)$.

Solution:

The center is located at the midpoint of the segment joining the vertices. $\left(\frac{0+0}{2}, \frac{-4+4}{2}\right) = (0, 0)$

Since the foci and vertices are located on the y-axis, the standard equation is given by: $\frac{y^2}{a^2} - \frac{x^2}{b^2} = 1$

The vertices $(0, \pm a)$ and the foci $(0, \pm c)$ can be used to identify a and c. $a = 4, c = 5$

Substitute $a = 4, c = 5$ into $b^2 = c^2 - a^2$. $b^2 = 5^2 - 4^2$

Solve for b. $b^2 = 25 - 16 = 9$

$b = 3$

Substitute $a = 4$ and $b = 3$ into $\frac{y^2}{a^2} - \frac{x^2}{b^2} = 1$. $\boxed{\frac{y^2}{16} - \frac{x^2}{9} = 1}$

YOUR TURN Find the equation of a hyperbola whose vertices are located at $(-2, 0)$ and $(2, 0)$ and whose foci are located at $(-4, 0)$ and $(4, 0)$.

ANSWER

$\frac{x^2}{4} - \frac{y^2}{12} = 1$

Graphing a Hyperbola Centered at the Origin

To graph a hyperbola, we use the vertices and asymptotes. The asymptotes are found by the equations $y = \pm\frac{b}{a}x$ or $y = \pm\frac{a}{b}x$, depending on whether the transverse axis is horizontal or vertical. An easy way to draw these graphing aids is to first draw the rectangular box that passes through the vertices and the points $(0, \pm b)$ or $(\pm b, 0)$. The **conjugate axis** is perpendicular to the transverse axis and has length $2b$. The asymptotes pass through the center of the hyperbola and the corners of the rectangular box.

$$\frac{x^2}{a^2} - \frac{y^2}{b^2} = 1$$

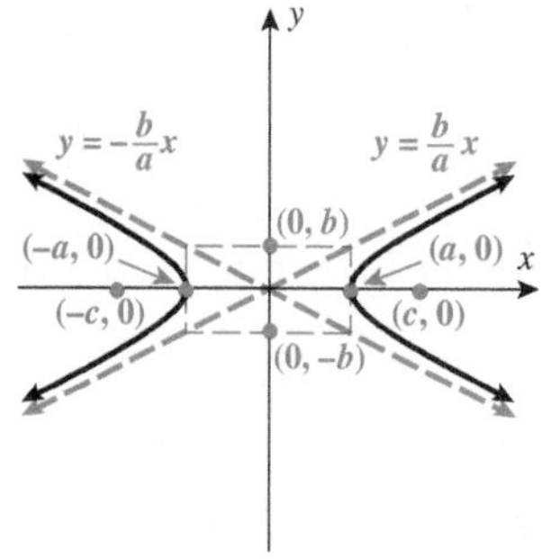

$$\frac{y^2}{a^2} - \frac{x^2}{b^2} = 1$$

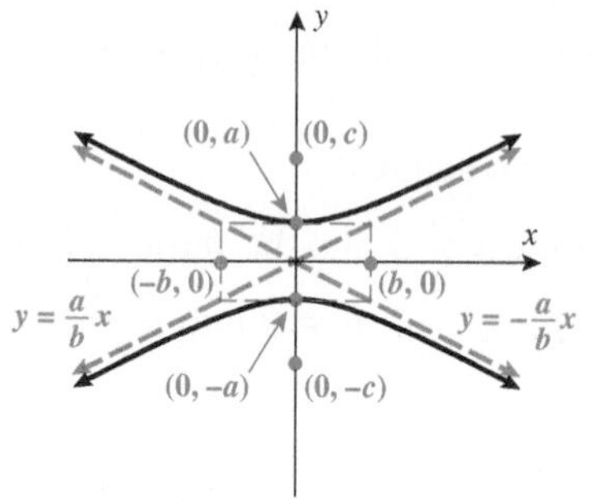

EXAMPLE 3 **Graphing a Hyperbola Centered at the Origin with a Horizontal Transverse Axis**

Graph the hyperbola given by $\frac{x^2}{4} - \frac{y^2}{9} = 1$.

Solution:

Compare $\frac{x^2}{2^2} - \frac{y^2}{3^2} = 1$ to the general equation $\frac{x^2}{a^2} - \frac{y^2}{b^2} = 1$.

Identify a and b. $a = 2$ and $b = 3$

The transverse axis of this hyperbola lies on the x-axis.

Label the vertices $(-a, 0) = (-2, 0)$ and $(a, 0) = (2, 0)$ and the points $(0, -b) = (0, -3)$ and $(0, b) = (0, 3)$. Draw the rectangular box that passes through those points. Draw the asymptotes that pass through the center and the corners of the rectangle.

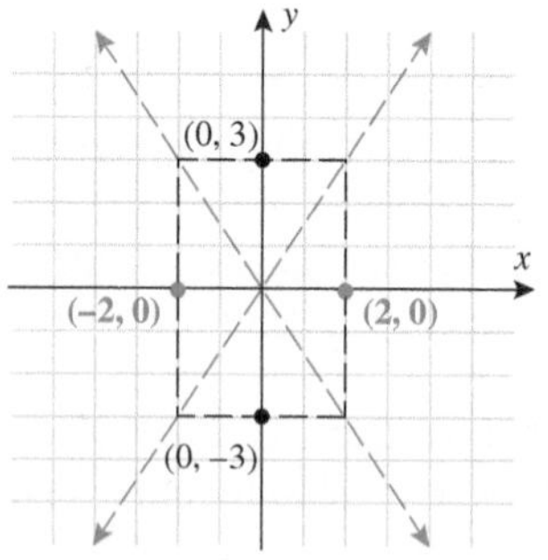

Draw the two branches of the hyperbola, each passing through a vertex and guided by the asymptotes.

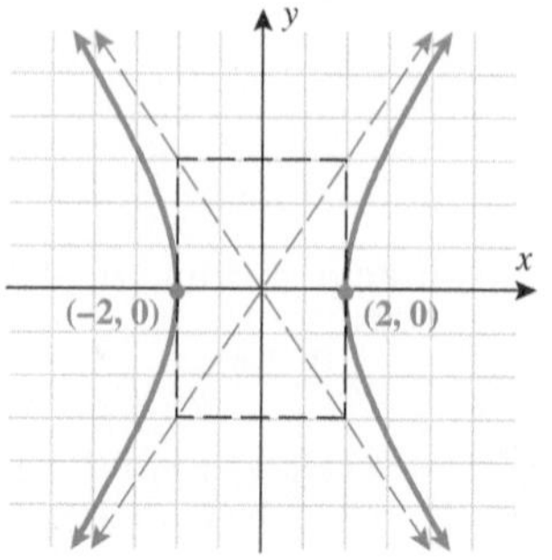

In Example 3, if we let $y = 0$, then $\frac{x^2}{4} = 1$ or $x = \pm 2$. Thus the vertices are $(-2, 0)$ and $(2, 0)$, and the transverse axis lies along the x-axis. Note that if $x = 0$, then $y = \pm 3i$.

EXAMPLE 4 Graphing a Hyperbola Centered at the Origin with a Vertical Transverse Axis

Graph the hyperbola given by $\frac{y^2}{16} - \frac{x^2}{4} = 1$.

Solution:

Compare $\frac{y^2}{4^2} - \frac{x^2}{2^2} = 1$ to the general equation $\frac{y^2}{a^2} - \frac{x^2}{b^2} = 1$.

Identify a and b. $a = 4$ and $b = 2$

The transverse axis of this hyperbola lies along the y-axis.

Label the vertices $(0, -a) = (0, -4)$ and $(0, a) = (0, 4)$ and the points $(-b, 0) = (-2, 0)$ and $(b, 0) = (2, 0)$. Draw the rectangular box that passes through those points. Draw the **asymptotes** that pass through the center and the corners of the rectangle.

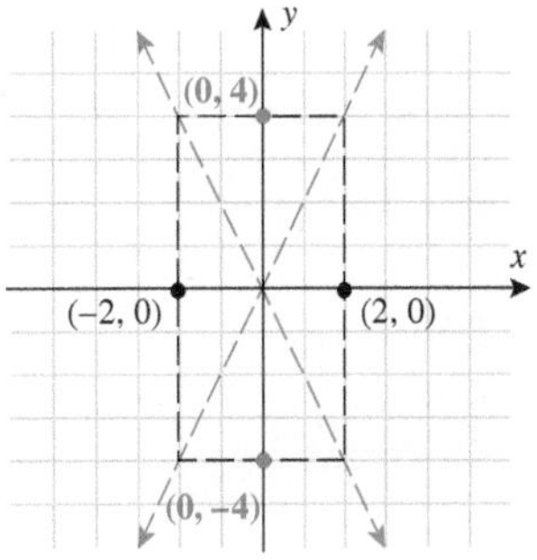

Draw the two **branches** of the hyperbola, each passing through a vertex and guided by the asymptotes.

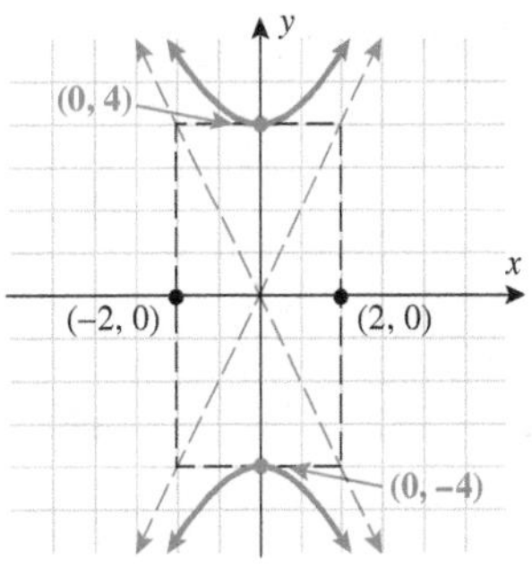

YOUR TURN Graph the hyperbolas:

a. $\frac{y^2}{1} - \frac{x^2}{4} = 1$ **b.** $\frac{x^2}{4} - \frac{y^2}{1} = 1$

ANSWER

a.

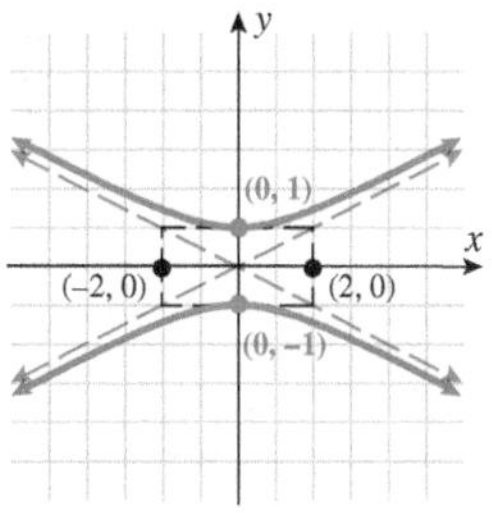

b.

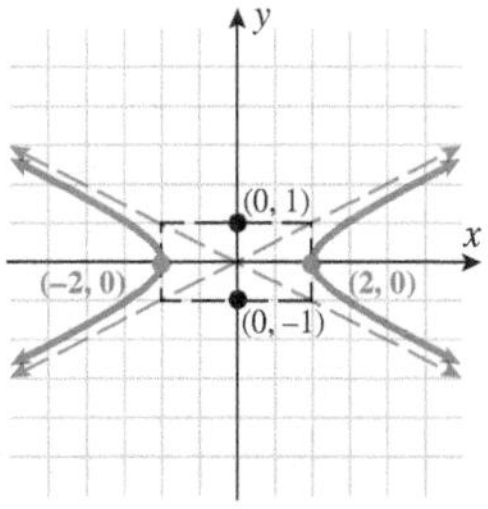

9.4.2 Hyperbola Centered at the Point (h, k)

9.4.2 SKILL

Find the equation of a hyperbola centered at the point (h, k).

9.4.2 CONCEPTUAL

Employ completing the square to transform an equation into the standard form of a hyperbola.

We can use graph-shifting techniques to graph hyperbolas that are centered at a point other than the origin—say, (h, k). For example, to graph $\frac{(x-h)^2}{a^2} - \frac{(y-k)^2}{b^2} = 1$, start with the graph of $\frac{x^2}{a^2} - \frac{y^2}{b^2} = 1$ and shift to the right h units and up k units. The center, the vertices, the foci, the transverse and conjugate axes, and the asymptotes all shift. The following table summarizes the characteristics of hyperbolas centered at a point other than the origin.

EQUATION OF A HYPERBOLA WITH CENTER AT THE POINT (h, k)

The **standard form of the equation of a hyperbola** with its center at the point (h, k) is given by

ORIENTATION OF TRANSVERSE AXIS	Horizontal (parallel to the x-axis)	Vertical (parallel to the y-axis)
EQUATION	$\frac{(x-h)^2}{a^2} - \frac{(y-k)^2}{b^2} = 1$	$\frac{(y-k)^2}{a^2} - \frac{(x-h)^2}{b^2} = 1$
VERTICES	$(h-a, k)$ and $(h+a, k)$	$(h, k-a)$ and $(h, k+a)$
FOCI	$(h-c, k)$ and $(h+c, k)$ where $c^2 = a^2 + b^2$	$(h, k-c)$ and $(h, k+c)$ where $c^2 = a^2 + b^2$
GRAPH	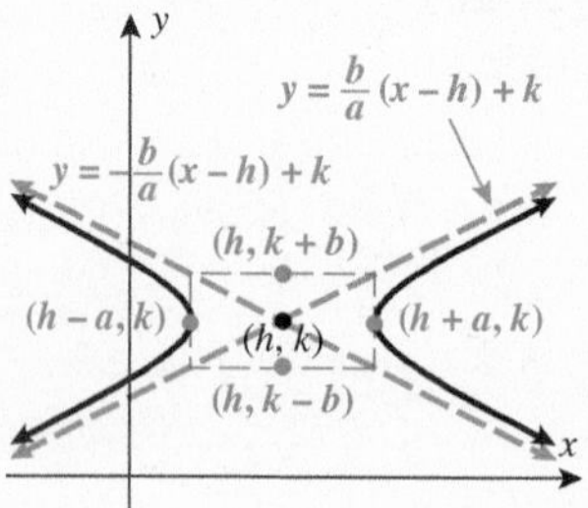	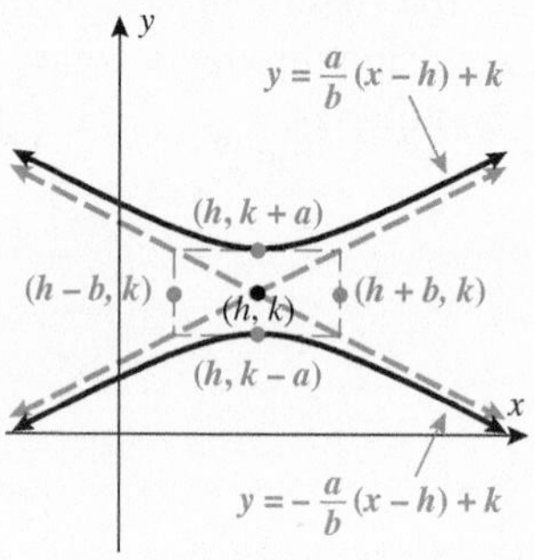

EXAMPLE 5 Graphing a Hyperbola with Center Not at the Origin

Graph the hyperbola $\frac{(y-2)^2}{16} - \frac{(x-1)^2}{9} = 1$.

Solution:

Compare $\frac{(y-2)^2}{4^2} - \frac{(x-1)^2}{3^2} = 1$ to the general equation $\frac{(y-k)^2}{a^2} - \frac{(x-h)^2}{b^2} = 1$.

Identify a, b, and (h, k). $a = 4, b = 3$, and $(h, k) = (1, 2)$

The transverse axis of this hyperbola lies along $x = 2$, which is parallel to the y-axis.

Label the vertices $(h, k - a) = (1, -2)$ and $(h, k + a) = (1, 6)$ and the points $(h - b, k) = (-2, 2)$ and $(h + b, k) = (4, 2)$. Draw the rectangular box that passes through those points. Draw the **asymptotes** that pass through the center $(h, k) = (1, 2)$ and the corners of the rectangle. Draw the two **branches** of the hyperbola, each passing through a vertex and guided by the asymptotes.

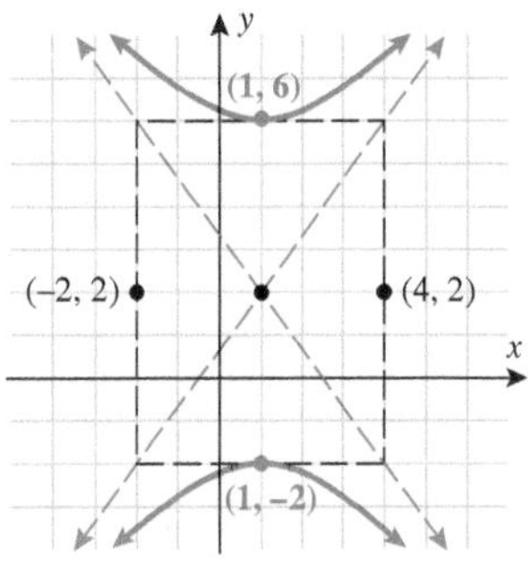

EXAMPLE 6 Transforming an Equation of a Hyperbola to Standard Form

Graph the hyperbola $9x^2 - 16y^2 - 18x + 32y - 151 = 0$.

Solution:

Complete the square on the x terms and y terms, respectively. $9(x^2 - 2x) - 16(y^2 - 2y) = 151$

$$9(x^2 - 2x + 1) - 16(y^2 - 2y + 1) = 151 + 9 - 16$$

$$9(x-1)^2 - 16(y-1)^2 = 144$$

$$\frac{(x-1)^2}{16} - \frac{(y-1)^2}{9} = 1$$

Compare $\frac{(x-1)^2}{16} - \frac{(y-1)^2}{9} = 1$ to the general form $\frac{(x-h)^2}{a^2} - \frac{(y-k)^2}{b^2} = 1$.

Identify a, b, and (h, k). $a = 4, b = 3$, and $(h, k) = (1, 1)$

The transverse axis of this hyperbola lies along $y = 1$.

Label the vertices $(h - a, k) = (-3, 1)$ and $(h + a, k) = (5, 1)$ and the points $(h, k - b) = (1, -2)$ and $(h, k + b) = (1, 4)$. Draw the rectangular box that passes through these points. Draw the **asymptotes** that pass through the center $(1, 1)$ and the corners of the box. Draw the two **branches** of the hyperbola, each passing through a vertex and guided by the asymptotes.

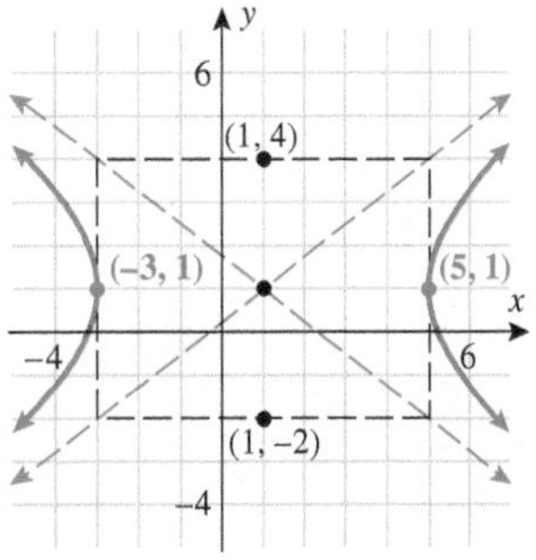

[CONCEPT CHECK]

A hyperbola of the form $Ax^2 - Bx - Cy^2 + Dy - E = 0$, where A, B, C, D, and E are all positive constants, has a center that lies in which quadrant?

ANSWER quadrant I

9.4.3 Applications

9.4.3 SKILL

Solve applied problems that involve hyperbolas.

9.4.3 CONCEPTUAL

Understand that it is the difference in time of signals remaining constant that enables ships to navigate along a hyperbolic curve to shore.

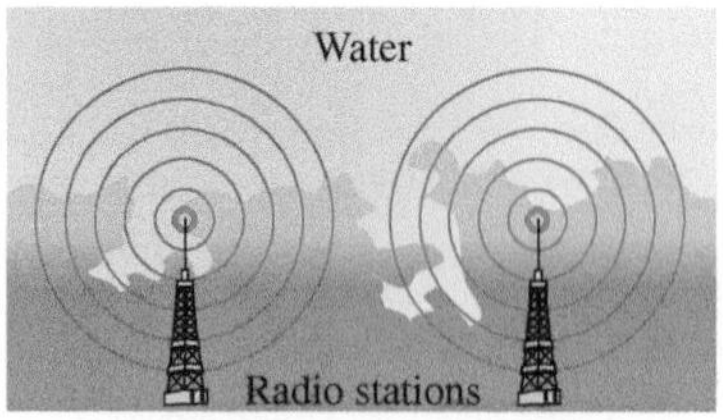

Nautical navigation is assisted by hyperbolas. For example, suppose that two radio stations on a coast are emitting simultaneous signals. If a boat is at sea, it will be slightly closer to one station than to the other station, which results in a small time difference between the received signals from the two stations. Recall that a hyperbola is the set of all points whose differences in the distances from two points (the foci—or the radio stations) are constant. Therefore, if the boat follows the path associated with a constant time difference, that path will be hyperbolic.

The synchronized signals would intersect one another in associated hyperbolas. Each time difference corresponds to a different path. The radio stations are the foci of the hyperbolas. This principle forms the basis of a hyperbolic radio navigation system known as *LORAN* (**LO**ng-**RA**nge **N**avigation).

There are navigational charts that correspond to different time differences. A ship selects the hyperbolic path that will take it to the desired port, and the LORAN chart lists the corresponding time difference.

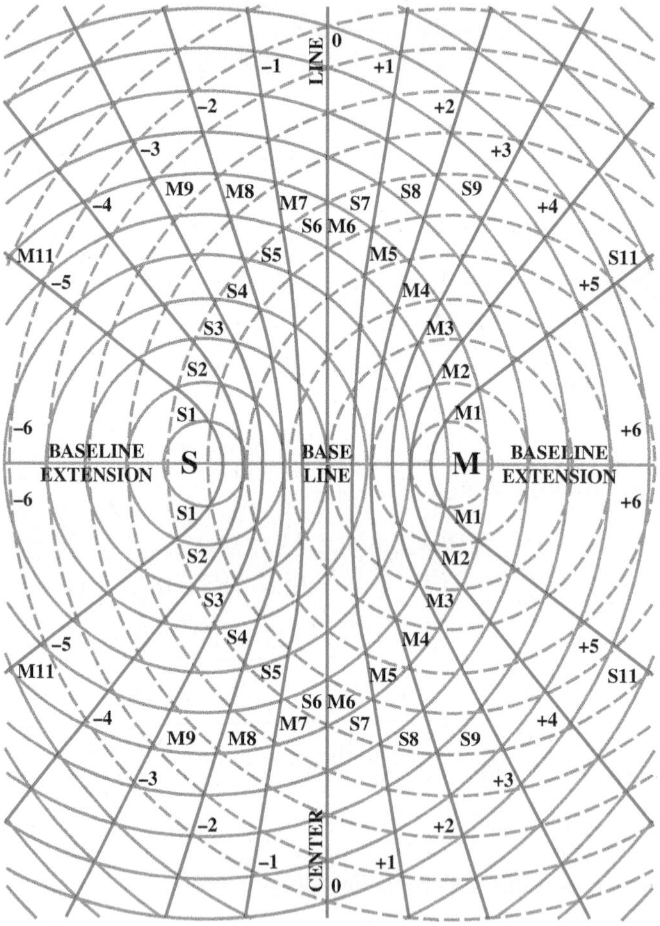

[CONCEPT CHECK]

TRUE OR FALSE In LORAN systems, the foci correspond to the radio stations.

ANSWER True

EXAMPLE 7 **Nautical Navigation Using LORAN**

Two LORAN stations are located 200 miles apart along a coast. If a ship records a time difference of 0.00043 second and continues on the hyperbolic path corresponding to that difference, where does it reach shore? Assume that the speed of the radio signal is 186,000 miles per second.

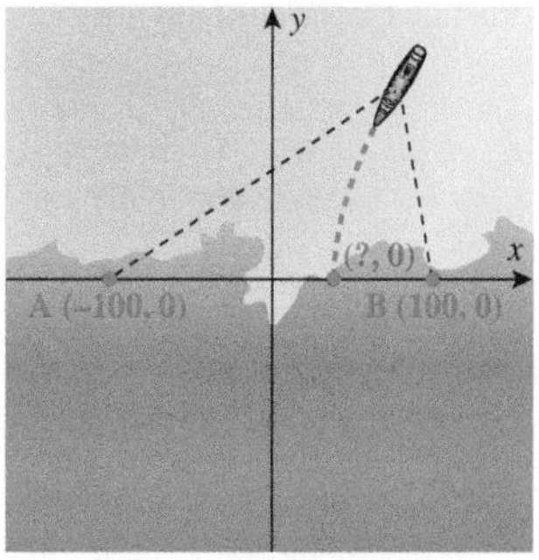

Solution:

Draw the xy-plane and the two stations corresponding to the foci at $(-100, 0)$ and $(100, 0)$. Draw the ship somewhere in quadrant I.

The hyperbola corresponds to a path where the difference in the distances between the ship and the respective stations remains constant. The constant is $2a$, where $(a, 0)$ is a vertex. Find that difference by using $d = rt$.

Substitute $r = 186{,}000$ miles/second and $t = 0.00043$ second into $d = rt$.

$$d = (186{,}000 \text{ miles/second})(0.00043 \text{ second}) \approx 80 \text{ miles}$$

Set the constant equal to $2a$. $\qquad 2a = 80$

Find a vertex $(a, 0)$. $\qquad (40, 0)$

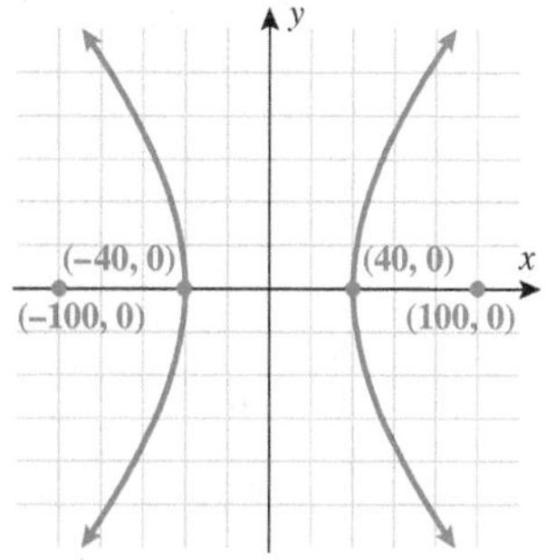

The ship reaches shore between the two stations, 60 miles from station B and 140 miles from station A.

[SECTION 9.4] SUMMARY

In this section, we discussed hyperbolas centered at the origin.

EQUATION	$\frac{x^2}{a^2} - \frac{y^2}{b^2} = 1$	$\frac{y^2}{a^2} - \frac{x^2}{b^2} = 1$
TRANSVERSE AXIS	Horizontal (x-axis), length $2a$	Vertical (y-axis), length $2a$
CONJUGATE AXIS	Vertical (y-axis), length $2b$	Horizontal (x-axis), length $2b$
VERTICES	$(-a, 0)$ and $(a, 0)$	$(0, -a)$ and $(0, a)$
FOCI	$(-c, 0)$ and $(c, 0)$ where $c^2 = a^2 + b^2$	$(0, -c)$ and $(0, c)$ where $c^2 = a^2 + b^2$
ASYMPTOTE	$y = \frac{b}{a}x$ and $y = -\frac{b}{a}x$	$y = \frac{a}{b}x$ and $y = -\frac{a}{b}x$
GRAPH	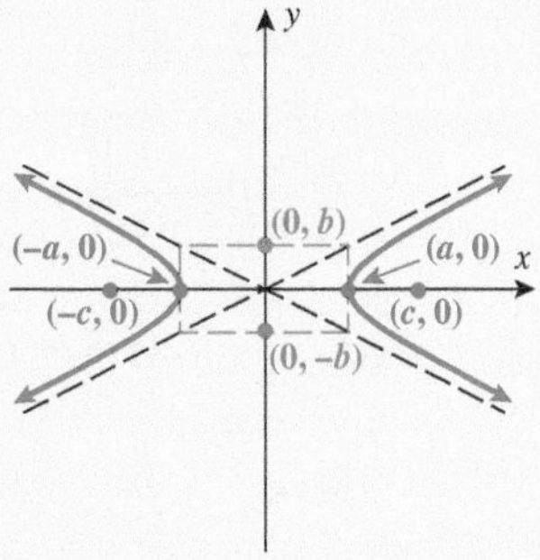	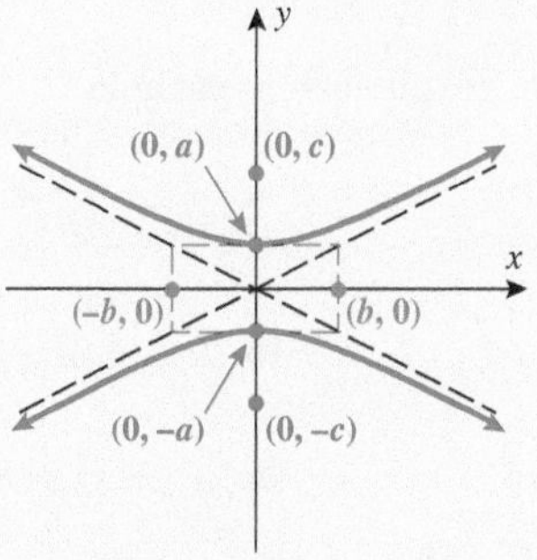

For a hyperbola centered at (h, k), the vertices, foci, and asymptotes all shift accordingly.

ORIENTATION OF TRANSVERSE AXIS	Horizontal (parallel to the x-axis)	Vertical (parallel to the y-axis)
EQUATION	$\frac{(x-h)^2}{a^2} - \frac{(y-k)^2}{b^2} = 1$	$\frac{(y-k)^2}{a^2} - \frac{(x-h)^2}{b^2} = 1$
VERTICES	$(h-a, k)$ and $(h+a, k)$	$(h, k-a)$ and $(h, k+a)$
FOCI	$(h-c, k)$ and $(h+c, k)$ where $c^2 = a^2 + b^2$	$(h, k-c)$ and $(h, k+c)$ where $c^2 = a^2 + b^2$
GRAPH	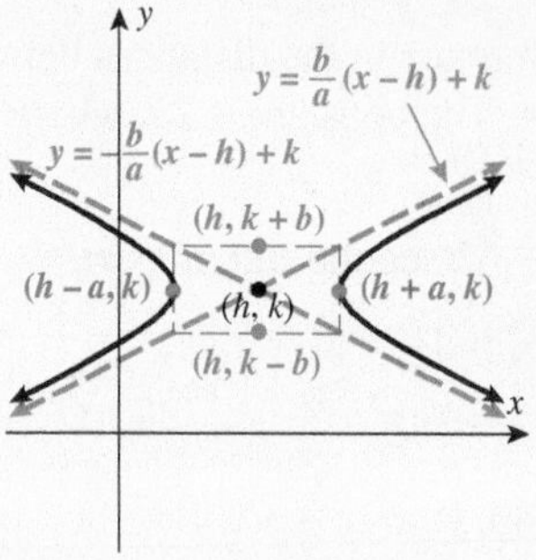	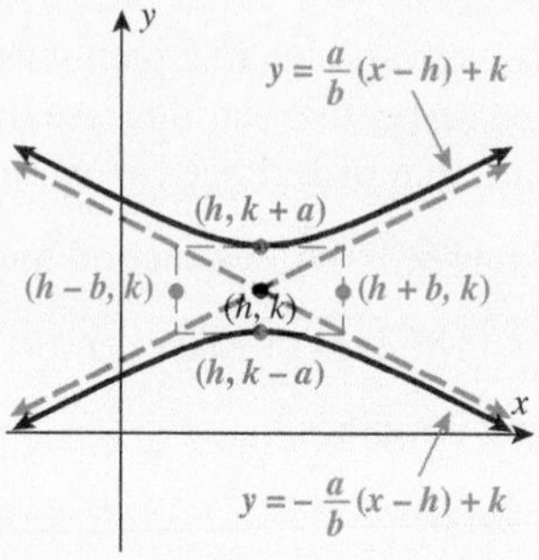

[SECTION 9.4] EXERCISES

• SKILLS

In Exercises 1–4, match each equation with the corresponding hyperbola.

1. $\frac{x^2}{36} - \frac{y^2}{16} = 1$
2. $\frac{y^2}{36} - \frac{x^2}{16} = 1$
3. $\frac{x^2}{8} - \frac{y^2}{72} = 1$
4. $4y^2 - x^2 = 1$

a.

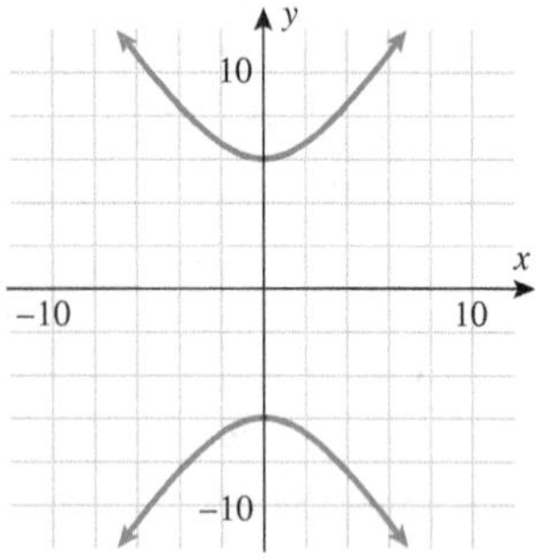

b.

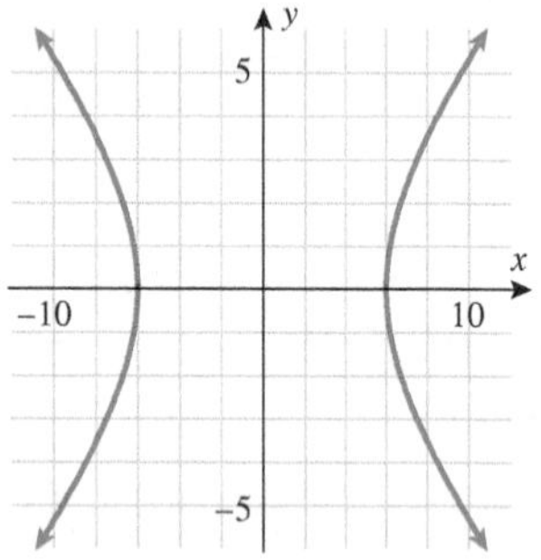

c.

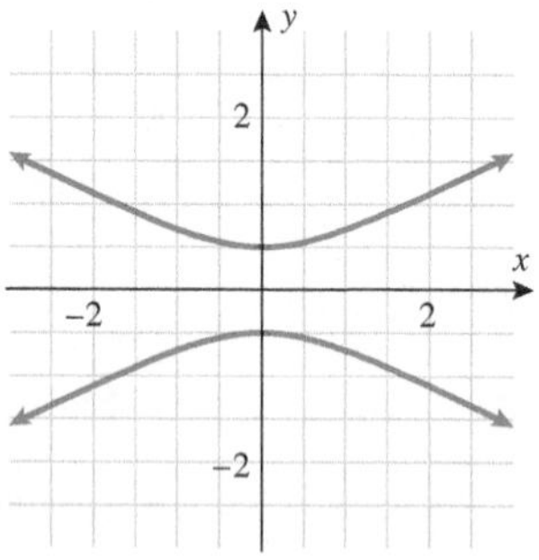

d.

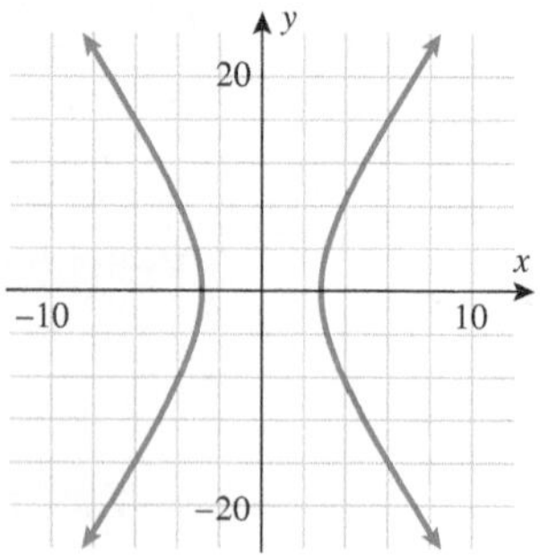

In Exercises 5–16, graph each hyperbola.

5. $\frac{x^2}{25} - \frac{y^2}{16} = 1$
6. $\frac{x^2}{49} - \frac{y^2}{9} = 1$
7. $\frac{y^2}{16} - \frac{x^2}{64} = 1$
8. $\frac{y^2}{144} - \frac{x^2}{25} = 1$
9. $\frac{x^2}{100} - y^2 = 1$
10. $9y^2 - 4x^2 = 36$
11. $\frac{4y^2}{9} - 81x^2 = 1$
12. $\frac{4}{25}x^2 - \frac{100}{9}y^2 = 1$
13. $4x^2 - y^2 = 16$
14. $y^2 - x^2 = 81$
15. $8y^2 - 16x^2 = 32$
16. $10x^2 - 25y^2 = 50$

In Exercises 17–24, find the standard form of an equation of the hyperbola with the given characteristics.

17. Vertices: $(-4, 0)$ and $(4, 0)$ Foci: $(-6, 0)$ and $(6, 0)$

18. Vertices: $(-1, 0)$ and $(1, 0)$ Foci: $(-3, 0)$ and $(3, 0)$

19. Vertices: $(0, -3)$ and $(0, 3)$ Foci: $(0, -4)$ and $(0, 4)$

20. Vertices: $(0, -1)$ and $(0, 1)$ Foci: $(0, -2)$ and $(0, 2)$

21. Center: $(0, 0)$; transverse: x-axis; asymptotes: $y = x$ and $y = -x$

22. Center: $(0, 0)$; transverse: y-axis; asymptotes: $y = x$ and $y = -x$

23. Center: $(0, 0)$; transverse axis: y-axis; asymptotes: $y = 2x$ and $y = -2x$

24. Center: $(0, 0)$; transverse axis: x-axis; asymptotes: $y = 2x$ and $y = -2x$

In Exercises 25–28, match each equation with the corresponding hyperbola.

25. $\frac{(x-3)^2}{4} - \frac{(y+2)^2}{25} = 1$

26. $\frac{(x+3)^2}{4} - \frac{(y-2)^2}{25} = 1$

27. $\frac{(y-3)^2}{25} - \frac{(x+2)^2}{4} = 1$

28. $\frac{(y+3)^2}{25} - \frac{(x-2)^2}{4} = 1$

a.

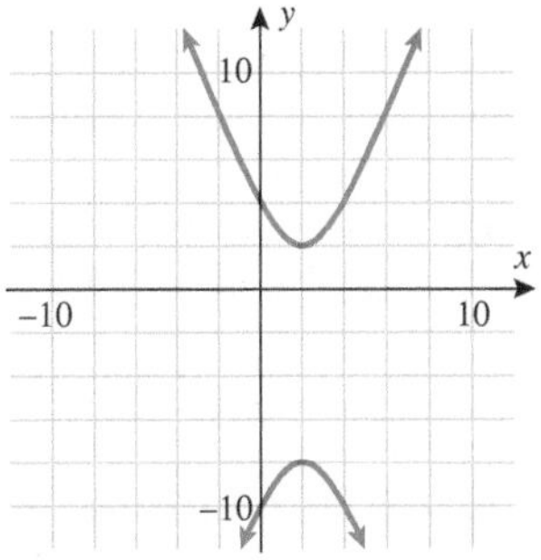

b.

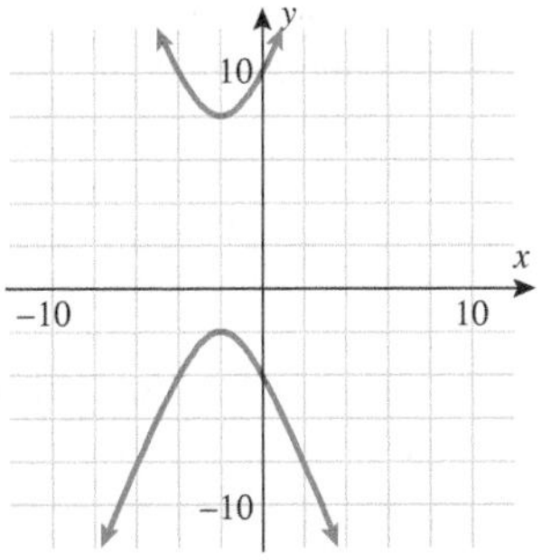

c.

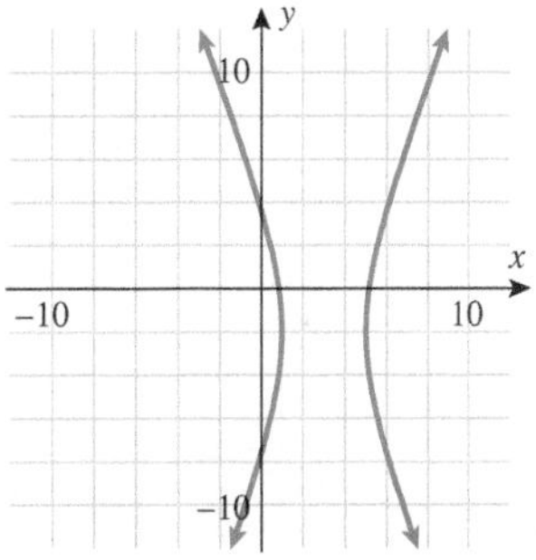

d.

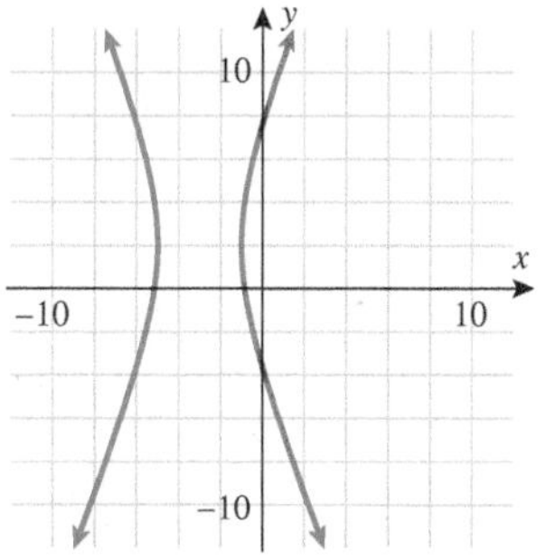

In Exercises 29–38, graph each hyperbola.

29. $\frac{(x-1)^2}{16} - \frac{(y-2)^2}{4} = 1$

30. $\frac{(y+1)^2}{36} - \frac{(x+2)^2}{9} = 1$

31. $10(y+3)^2 - (x-4)^2 = 80$

32. $3(x+3)^2 - 12(y-4)^2 = 36$

33. $x^2 - 4x - 4y^2 = 0$

34. $-9x^2 + y^2 + 2y - 8 = 0$

35. $-9x^2 - 18x + 4y^2 - 8y - 41 = 0$

36. $25x^2 - 50x - 4y^2 - 8y - 79 = 0$

37. $x^2 - 6x - 4y^2 - 16y - 8 = 0$

38. $-4x^2 - 16x + y^2 - 2y - 19 = 0$

In Exercises 39–42, find the standard form of the equation of a hyperbola with the given characteristics.

39. Vertices: $(-2, 5)$ and $(6, 5)$ Foci: $(-3, 5)$ and $(7, 5)$

40. Vertices: $(1, -2)$ and $(3, -2)$ Foci: $(0, -2)$ and $(4, -2)$

41. Vertices: $(4, -7)$ and $(4, -1)$ Foci: $(4, -8)$ and $(4, 0)$

42. Vertices: $(2, -6)$ and $(2, -4)$ Foci: $(2, -7)$ and $(2, -3)$

• APPLICATIONS

43. Ship Navigation. Two LORAN stations are located 150 miles apart along a coast. If a ship records a time difference of 0.0005 second and continues on the hyperbolic path corresponding to that difference, where will it reach shore?

44. Ship Navigation. Two LORAN stations are located 300 miles apart along a coast. If a ship records a time difference of 0.0007 second and continues on the hyperbolic path corresponding to that difference, where will it reach shore? Round to the nearest mile.

45. Ship Navigation. If the captain of the ship in Exercise 43 wants to reach shore between the stations and 30 miles from one of them, what time difference should he look for?

46. Ship Navigation. If the captain of the ship in Exercise 44 wants to reach shore between the stations and 50 miles from one of them, what time difference should he look for?

47. Light. If the light from a lamp casts a hyperbolic pattern on the wall due to its lampshade, calculate the equation of the hyperbola if the distance between the vertices is 2 feet and the foci are half a foot from the vertices.

48. **Special Ops.** A military special ops team is calibrating its recording devices used for passive ascertaining of enemy location. They place two recording stations, alpha and bravo, 3000 feet apart (alpha is due east of bravo). The team detonates small explosives 300 feet west of alpha and records the time it takes each station to register an explosion. The team also sets up a second set of explosives directly north of the alpha station. How many feet north of alpha should the team set off the explosives if it wants to record the same difference in times as on the first explosion?

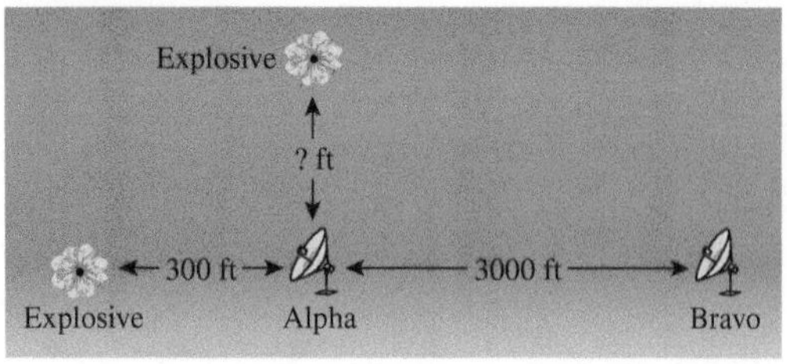

For Exercises 49 and 50, refer to the following:

Nuclear cooling towers are typically built in the shape of a hyperboloid. The cross section of a cooling tower forms a hyperbola. The cooling tower pictured is 450 feet tall and modeled by the equation $\frac{x^2}{8100} - \frac{y^2}{16{,}900} = 1$.

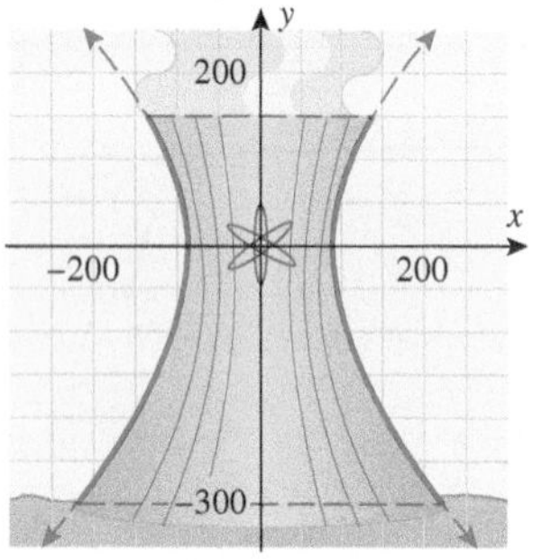

49. **Engineering/Design.** Find the diameter of the top of the cooling tower to the nearest foot.

50. **Engineering/Design.** Find the diameter of the base of the tower to the nearest foot.

In Exercises 51–54, refer to the following:

The navigation system LORAN (long-range navigation) uses the reflection properties of a hyperbola. Two synchronized radio signals are transmitted at a constant speed by two distant radio stations (foci of the hyperbola). Based on the order of arrival and the interval between the signals, the location of the craft along a branch of a hyperbola can be determined. The distance between the radio stations and the craft remains constant. With the help of a third station, the location of the craft can be determined exactly as the intersection of the branches of two hyperbolas.

51. **LORAN Navigation System.** Two radio stations, located at the same latitude, are separated by 200 kilometers. A vessel navigates following a trajectory parallel to the line connecting *A* and *B*, 50 kilometers north of this line. The radio signal transmitted travels at 320 m/μs. The vessel receives the signal from *B*, 400 μ s after receiving the signal from *A*. Find the location of the vessel.

52. **LORAN Navigation System.** Two radio stations, located at the same latitude, are separated by 300 kilometers. A vessel navigates following a trajectory parallel to the line connecting *A* and *B*, 80 kilometers north of this line. The radio signals transmitted travel at 350 m/μs. The vessel receives the signal from *B*, 380 μs after receiving the signal from *A*. Find the location of the vessel.

53. **LORAN Navigation System.** Two radio stations, located at the same latitude, are separated by 460 kilometers. A vessel navigates following a trajectory parallel to the line connecting *A* and *B*, 60 kilometers north of this line. The radio signals transmitted travel at 420 m/μs. The vessel receives the signal from *B*, 500 μs after receiving the signal from *A*. Find the location of the vessel.

54. **LORAN Navigation System.** Two radio stations, located at the same latitude, are separated by 520 kilometers. A vessel navigates following a trajectory parallel to the line connecting *A* and *B*, 40 kilometers north of this line. The radio signals transmitted travel at 500 m/μs. The vessel receives the signal from *B*, 450 μs after receiving the signal from *A*. Find the location of the vessel.

• CATCH THE MISTAKE

In Exercises 55 and 56, explain the mistake that is made.

55. Graph the hyperbola $\frac{y^2}{4} - \frac{x^2}{9} = 1$.

Solution:

Compare the equation to the standard form and solve for *a* and *b*.	$a = 2, b = 3$
Label the vertices $(-a, 0)$ and $(a, 0)$.	$(-2, 0)$ and $(2, 0)$
Label the points $(0, -b)$ and $(0, b)$.	$(0, -3)$ and $(0, 3)$

Draw the rectangle connecting these four points, and align the asymptotes so that they pass through the center and the corner of the boxes. Then draw the hyperbola using the vertices and asymptotes.

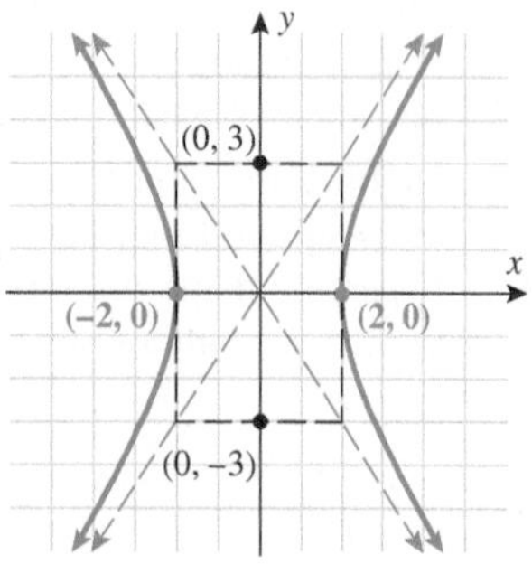

This is incorrect. What mistake was made?

56. Graph the hyperbola $\frac{x^2}{1} - \frac{y^2}{4} = 1$.

Solution:

Compare the equation to the general form and solve for *a* and *b*.	$a = 2, b = 1$
Label the vertices $(-a, 0)$ and $(a, 0)$.	$(-2, 0)$ and $(2, 0)$
Label the points $(0, -b)$ and $(0, b)$.	$(0, -1)$ and $(0, 1)$

Draw the rectangle connecting these four points, and align the asymptotes so that they pass through the center and the corner of the boxes. Then draw the hyperbola using the vertices and asymptotes.

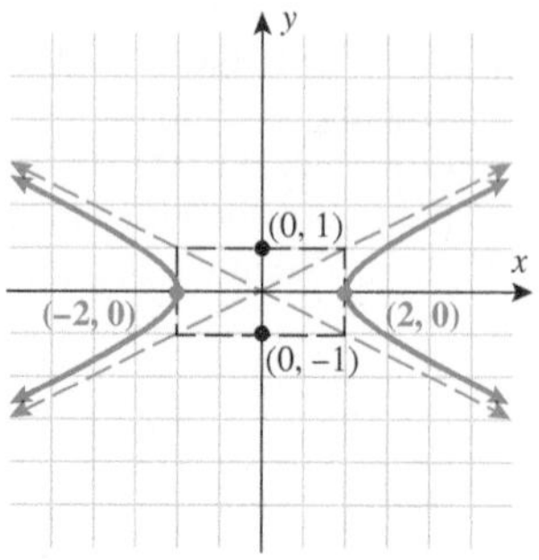

This is incorrect. What mistake was made?

• CONCEPTUAL

In Exercises 57–60, determine whether each statement is true or false.

57. If you know the vertices of a hyperbola, you can determine the equation for the hyperbola.

58. If you know the foci and vertices, you can determine the equation for the hyperbola.

59. Hyperbolas centered at the origin have symmetry with respect to the x-axis, y-axis, and the origin.

60. The center and foci are part of the graph of a hyperbola.

61. If the point (p, q) lies on the hyperbola $\frac{x^2}{a^2} - \frac{y^2}{b^2} = 1$, find three other points that lie on the hyperbola.

62. Given the hyperbola $\frac{x^2}{4} - \frac{y^2}{b^2} = 1$, find b such that the asymptotes are perpendicular to each other.

63. A vertical line intersects the hyperbola $\frac{x^2}{9} - \frac{y^2}{4} = 1$ at the point (p, q), and intersects the hyperbola $\frac{x^2}{9} - \frac{y^2}{16} = 1$ at the point (p, r). Determine the relationship between q and r. Assume p, r, and q are positive real numbers.

64. Does the line $y = \frac{2b}{a}x$ intersect the hyperbola $\frac{x^2}{a^2} - \frac{y^2}{b^2} = 1$?

• CHALLENGE

65. Find the general equation of a hyperbola whose asymptotes are perpendicular.

66. Find the general equation of a hyperbola whose vertices are $(3, -2)$ and $(-1, -2)$ and whose asymptotes are the lines $y = 2x - 4$ and $y = -2x$.

67. Find the asymptotes of the graph of the hyperbola given by $9y^2 - 16x^2 - 36y - 32x - 124 = 0$.

68. Find the asymptotes of the graph of the hyperbola given by $5x^2 - 4y^2 + 20x + 8y - 4 = 0$.

69. If the line $3x + 5y - 7 = 0$ is perpendicular to one of the asymptotes of the graph of the hyperbola given by $\frac{x^2}{a^2} - \frac{y^2}{b^2} = 1$ with vertices at $(\pm 3, 0)$, find the foci.

70. If the line $2x - y + 9 = 0$ is perpendicular to one of the asymptotes of the graph of the hyperbola given by $\frac{y^2}{a^2} - \frac{x^2}{b^2} = 1$ with vertices at $(0, \pm 1)$, find the foci.

• PREVIEW TO CALCULUS

In Exercises 71 and 72, refer to the following:

In calculus, we study hyperbolic functions. The hyperbolic sine is defined by $\sinh u = \frac{e^u - e^{-u}}{2}$; the hyperbolic cosine is defined by $\cosh u = \frac{e^u + e^{-u}}{2}$.

71. If $x = \cosh u$ and $y = \sinh u$, show that $x^2 - y^2 = 1$.

72. If $x = \frac{e^u + e^{-u}}{e^u - e^{-u}}$ and $y = \frac{2}{e^u - e^{-u}}$, show that $x^2 - y^2 = 1$.

In Exercises 73 and 74, refer to the following:

In calculus, we use the difference quotient $\frac{f(x + h) - f(x)}{h}$ to find the derivative of the function f.

73. Find the derivative of $y = f(x)$, where $y^2 - x^2 = 1$ and $y < 0$.

74. Find the difference quotient of $y = f(x)$, where $4x^2 + y^2 = 1$ and $y > 0$.

9.5 SYSTEMS OF NONLINEAR EQUATIONS

SKILLS OBJECTIVE

- Solve systems of nonlinear equations.

CONCEPTUAL OBJECTIVE

- Understand the types of solutions to systems of nonlinear equations—distinct number of solutions, no solutions, and infinitely many solutions—and interpret the solutions graphically.

9.5.1 Solving a System of Nonlinear Equations

9.5.1 SKILL

Solve systems of nonlinear equations.

9.5.1 CONCEPTUAL

Understand the types of solutions to systems of nonlinear equations—distinct number of solutions, no solutions, and infinitely many solutions—and interpret the solutions graphically.

In Chapter 8, we discussed solving systems of *linear* equations. We applied elimination and substitution to solve systems of linear equations in two variables, and we employed matrices to solve systems of linear equations in three or more variables. Recall that a system of linear equations in two variables has one of three types of solutions:

One solution	Two lines that intersect at one point	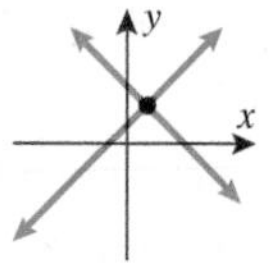
No solution	Two parallel lines (never intersect)	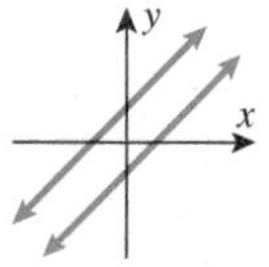
Infinitely many solutions	Two lines that coincide (same line)	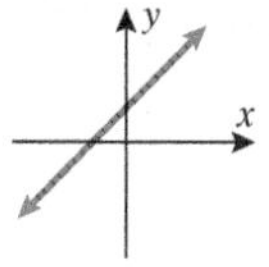

Notice that systems of *linear* equations in two variables always corresponded to *lines*. Now we turn our attention to systems of *nonlinear* equations in two variables. If any of the equations in a system of equations is nonlinear, then the system is a nonlinear system. The following are systems of nonlinear equations:

$$\begin{Bmatrix} y = x^2 + 1 \text{ (Parabola)} \\ y = 2x + 2 \text{ (Line)} \end{Bmatrix} \quad \begin{Bmatrix} x^2 + y^2 = 25 \text{ (Circle)} \\ y = x \text{ (Line)} \end{Bmatrix} \quad \begin{Bmatrix} \dfrac{x^2}{9} + \dfrac{y^2}{4} = 1 \text{ (Ellipse)} \\ \dfrac{y^2}{16} - \dfrac{x^2}{25} = 1 \text{ (Hyperbola)} \end{Bmatrix}$$

To find the solutions to these systems, we ask the question, "At what point(s)—if any—do the graphs of these equations intersect?" Since some nonlinear equations represent conics, this is a convenient time to discuss systems of nonlinear equations.

How many points of intersection do a line and a parabola have? The answer depends on which line and which parabola. As we see in the following graphs, the answer can be one, two, or none.

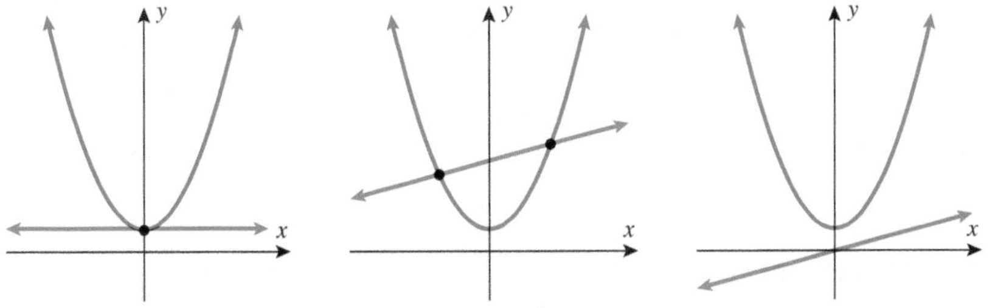

One solution **Two solutions** **No solution**

How many points of intersection do a parabola and an ellipse have? One, two, three, four, or no points of intersection correspond to one solution, two solutions, three solutions, four solutions, or no solution, respectively.

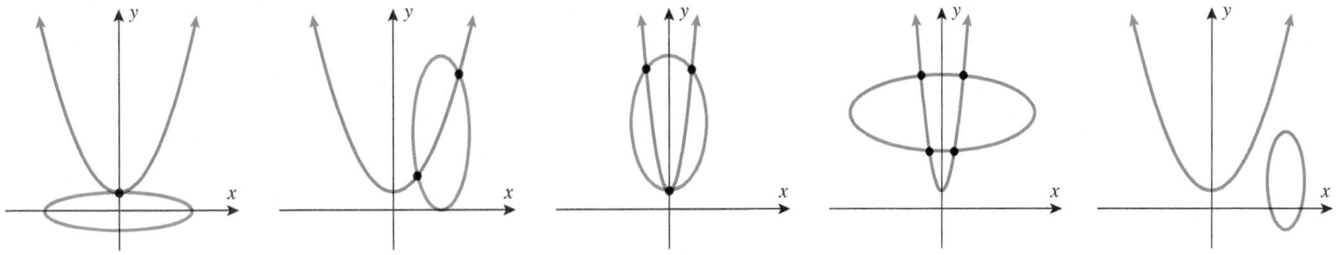

One solution **Two solutions** **Three solutions** **Four solutions** **No solution**

How many points of intersection do a parabola and a hyperbola have? The answer depends on which parabola and which hyperbola. As we see in the following graphs, the answer can be one, two, three, four, or none.

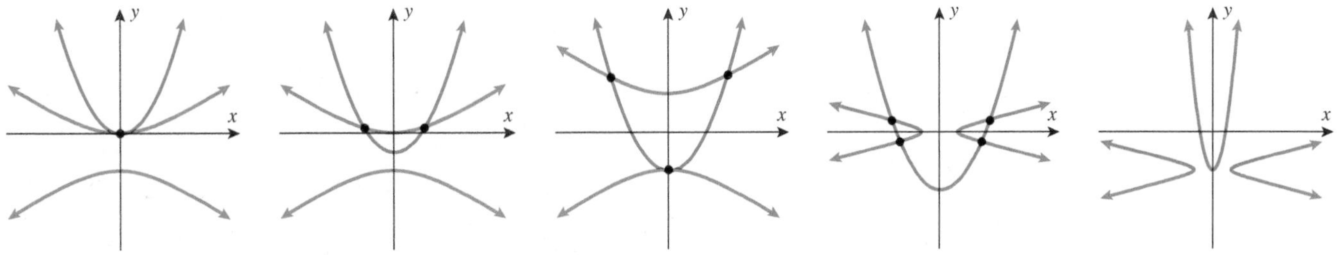

One solution **Two solutions** **Three solutions** **Four solutions** **No solution**

Using Elimination to Solve Systems of Nonlinear Equations

The first three examples in this section use elimination to solve systems of two nonlinear equations. In linear systems, we can eliminate either variable. In nonlinear systems, the variable to eliminate is the one that is raised to the same power in both equations.

EXAMPLE 1 **Solving a System of Two Nonlinear Equations by Elimination: One Solution**

Solve the system of equations, and graph the corresponding line and parabola to verify the answer.

Equation (1): $2x - y = 3$

Equation (2): $x^2 - y = 2$

Solution:

Equation (1): $2x - y = 3$

Multiply both sides of Equation (2) by -1. $-x^2 + y = -2$

Add. $2x - x^2 = 1$

Gather all terms to one side. $x^2 - 2x + 1 = 0$

Factor. $(x - 1)^2 = 0$

Solve for x. $x = 1$

Substitute $x = 1$ into original Equation (1). $2(1) - y = 3$

Solve for y. $y = -1$

The solution is $x = 1, y = -1$, or $(1, -1)$.

Graph the line $y = 2x - 3$ and the parabola $y = x^2 - 2$ and confirm that the point of intersection is $(1, -1)$.

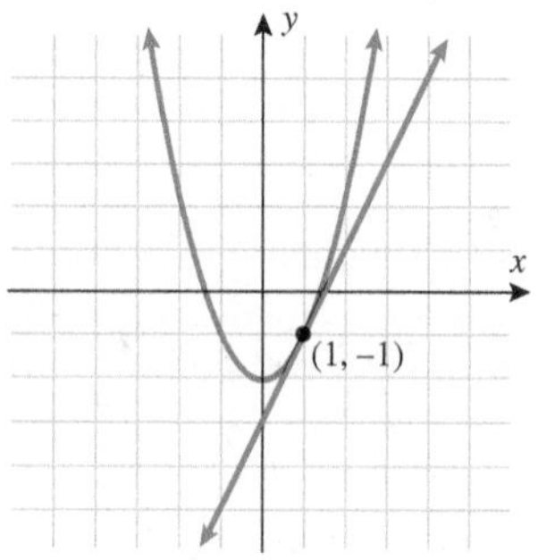

EXAMPLE 2 Solving a System of Two Nonlinear Equations with Elimination: More Than One Solution

Solve the system of equations, and graph the corresponding parabola and circle to verify the answer.

Equation (1): $-x^2 + y = -7$

Equation (2): $x^2 + y^2 = 9$

Solution:

Equation (1):	$-x^2 + y = -7$
Equation (2):	$x^2 + y^2 = 9$
Add.	$y^2 + y = 2$
Gather all terms to one side.	$y^2 + y - 2 = 0$
Factor.	$(y + 2)(y - 1) = 0$
Solve for *y*.	$y = -2$ or $y = 1$
Substitute $y = -2$ into Equation (2).	$x^2 + (-2)^2 = 9$
Solve for *x*.	$x = \pm\sqrt{5}$
Substitute $y = 1$ into Equation (2).	$x^2 + (1)^2 = 9$
Solve for *x*.	$x = \pm\sqrt{8} = \pm 2\sqrt{2}$

There are four solutions: $(-\sqrt{5}, -2)$, $(\sqrt{5}, -2)$, $(-2\sqrt{2}, 1)$, and $(2\sqrt{2}, 1)$

Graph the parabola $y = x^2 - 7$ and the circle $x^2 + y^2 = 9$ and confirm the four points of intersection.

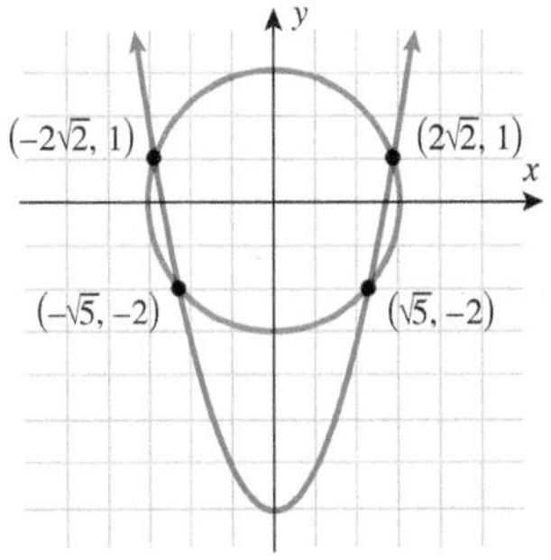

EXAMPLE 3 **Solving a System of Two Nonlinear Equations with Elimination: No Solution**

Solve the system of equations, and graph the corresponding parabolas to verify the answer.

$$\text{Equation (1):} \quad x^2 + y = 3$$
$$\text{Equation (2):} \quad -x^2 + y = 5$$

Solution:

Equation (1):	$x^2 + y = 3$
Equation (2):	$-x^2 + y = 5$
Add.	$2y = 8$
Solve for y.	$y = 4$
Substitute $y = 4$ into Equation (1).	$x^2 + 4 = 3$
Simplify.	$x^2 = -1$

$x^2 = -1$ has no real solution.

There is **no solution** to this system of nonlinear equations.

Graph the parabola $y = -x^2 + 3$ and the parabola $y = x^2 + 5$ and confirm that there are no points of intersection.

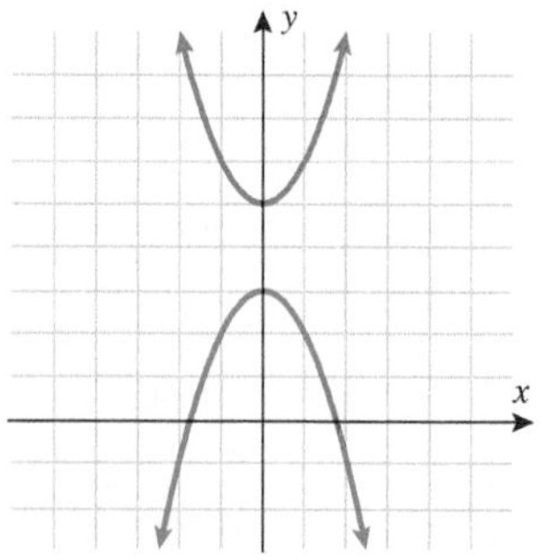

EXAMPLE 4 **Solving a System of Nonlinear Equations with Elimination**

Solve the system of nonlinear equations with elimination.

$$\text{Equation (1):} \quad \frac{x^2}{4} + y^2 = 1$$

$$\text{Equation (2):} \quad x^2 - y^2 = 1$$

Solution:

Add Equations (1) and (2) to eliminate y^2.

$$\frac{x^2}{4} + y^2 = 1$$
$$x^2 - y^2 = 1$$
$$\frac{5}{4}x^2 = 2$$

Solve for x.

$$x^2 = \frac{8}{5}$$
$$x = \pm\sqrt{\frac{8}{5}}$$

Let $x = \pm\sqrt{\frac{8}{5}}$ in Equation (2).

$$\left(\pm\sqrt{\frac{8}{5}}\right)^2 - y^2 = 1$$

Solve for y.

$$y^2 = \frac{8}{5} - 1 = \frac{3}{5}$$
$$y = \pm\sqrt{\frac{3}{5}}$$

There are four solutions:

$$\left(-\sqrt{\frac{8}{5}}, -\sqrt{\frac{3}{5}}\right), \left(-\sqrt{\frac{8}{5}}, \sqrt{\frac{3}{5}}\right), \left(\sqrt{\frac{8}{5}}, -\sqrt{\frac{3}{5}}\right), \text{ and } \left(\sqrt{\frac{8}{5}}, \sqrt{\frac{3}{5}}\right)$$

A calculator can be used to approximate these solutions:

$$\sqrt{\frac{8}{5}} \approx 1.26$$

$$\sqrt{\frac{3}{5}} \approx 0.77$$

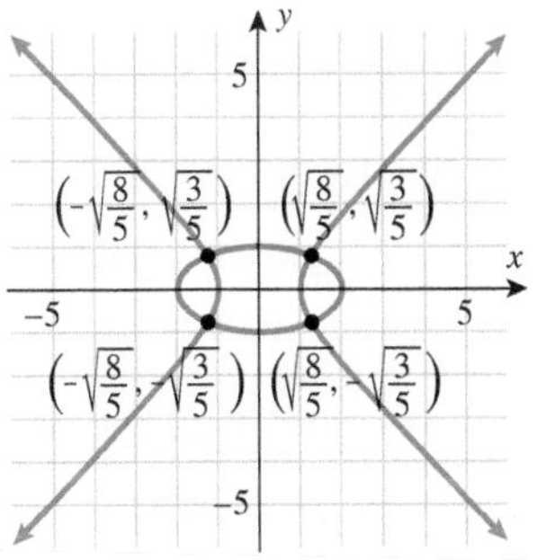

YOUR TURN Solve the following systems of nonlinear equations:

a. $-x + y = 3$, $x^2 - y = -1$

b. $x^2 + y = 2$, $-x + y = 3$

c. $\dfrac{x^2}{9} + \dfrac{y^2}{4} = 1$, $\dfrac{y^2}{9} - \dfrac{x^2}{16} = 1$

ANSWER

a. $(-1, 2)$ and $(2, 5)$

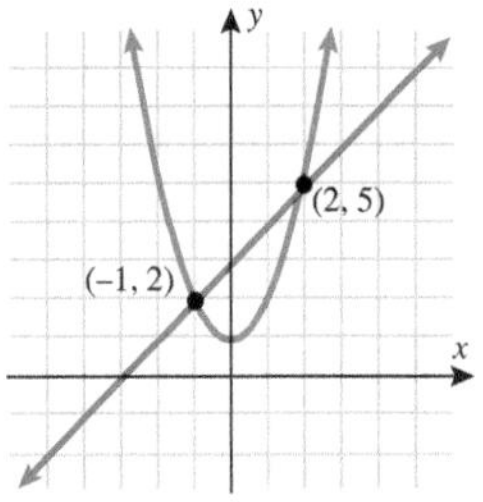

b. no solution

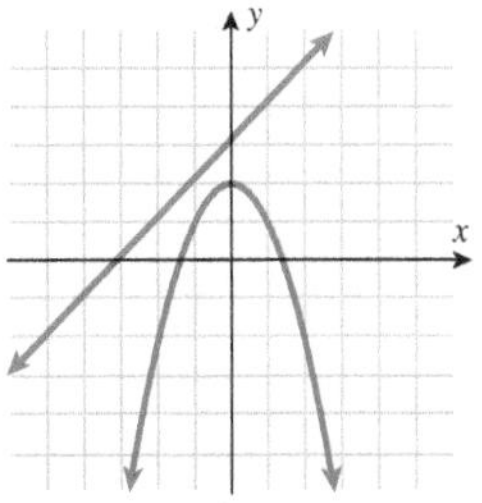

c. no solution

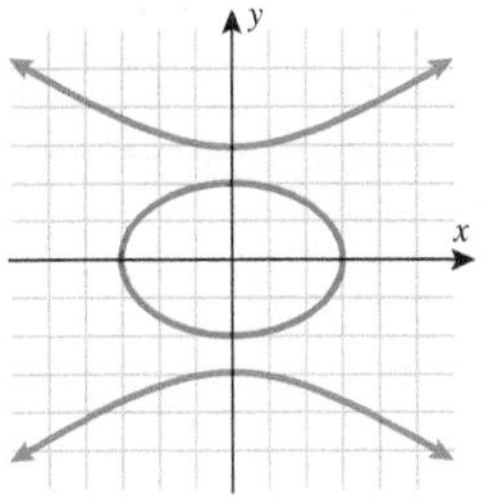

Using Substitution to Solve Systems of Nonlinear Equations

STUDY TIP

Extraneous solutions are possible when you have one equation with a linear (or odd) power and one equation with a second-degree (or even) power.

Elimination is based on the idea of eliminating one of the variables and solving the remaining equation in one variable. This is not always possible with nonlinear systems. For example, a system consisting of a circle and a line

$$x^2 + y^2 = 5$$
$$-x + y = 1$$

cannot be solved with elimination, because both variables are raised to different powers in each equation. We now turn to the substitution method. It is important to always check solutions, because extraneous solutions are possible.

EXAMPLE 5 **Solving a System of Nonlinear Equations with Substitution**

Solve the system of equations, and graph the corresponding circle and line to verify the answer.

Equation (1): $x^2 + y^2 = 5$

Equation (2): $-x + y = 1$

Solution:

Rewrite Equation (2) with y isolated.

Equation (1):	$x^2 + y^2 = 5$
Equation (2):	$y = x + 1$
Substitute Equation (2), $y = x + 1$, into Equation (1).	$x^2 + (x + 1)^2 = 5$
Eliminate the parentheses.	$x^2 + x^2 + 2x + 1 = 5$
Gather like terms.	$2x^2 + 2x - 4 = 0$
Divide by 2.	$x^2 + x - 2 = 0$
Factor.	$(x + 2)(x - 1) = 0$
Solve for x.	$x = -2$ or $x = 1$
Substitute $x = -2$ into Equation (1).	$(-2)^2 + y^2 = 5$
Solve for y.	$y = -1$ or $y = 1$
Substitute $x = 1$ into Equation (1).	$(1)^2 + y^2 = 5$
Solve for y.	$y = -2$ or $y = 2$

There appear to be four solutions: $(-2, -1)$, $(-2, 1)$, $(1, -2)$, and $(1, 2)$, but a line can intersect a circle in no more than two points. Therefore, at least two solutions are *extraneous*. All four points satisfy Equation (1), but only $(-2, -1)$ and $(1, 2)$ also satisfy Equation (2).

The answer is $\boxed{(-2, -1) \text{ and } (1, 2)}$.

Graph the circle $x^2 + y^2 = 5$ and the line $y = x + 1$ and confirm the two points of intersection.

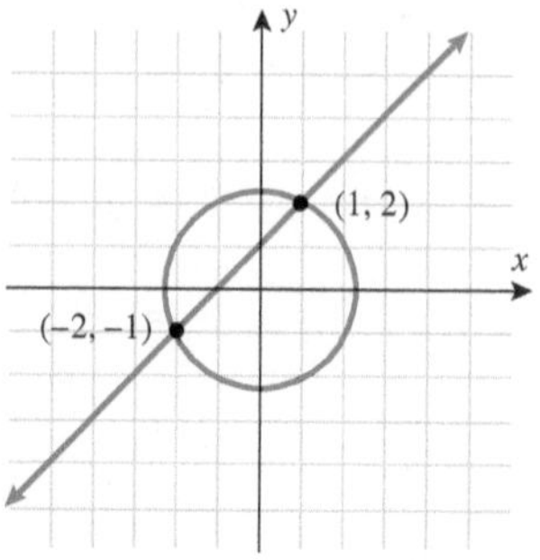

Note: After solving for x, had we substituted back into the linear Equation (2) instead of Equation (1), extraneous solutions would not have appeared. In general, **substitute back into the lowest-degree equation, and always check solutions.**

STUDY TIP

Substitute back into the lowest-degree equation, and always check solutions.

YOUR TURN Solve the system of equations $x^2 + y^2 = 13$ and $x + y = 5$.

ANSWER

(2, 3) and (3, 2)

In Example 6, the equation $xy = 2$ can also be shown to be a rotated hyperbola (Section 9.7). For now, we can express this equation in terms of a reciprocal function $y = \frac{2}{x}$, a topic we discussed in Section 1.2.

EXAMPLE 6 Solving a System of Nonlinear Equations with Substitution

Solve the system of equations.

Equation (1): $x^2 + y^2 = 5$

Equation (2): $xy = 2$

Solution:

Since Equation (2) tells us that $xy = 2$, we know that neither x nor y can be zero.

Solve Equation (2) for y. $\quad y = \frac{2}{x}$

Substitute $y = \frac{2}{x}$ into Equation (1). $\quad x^2 + \left(\frac{2}{x}\right)^2 = 5$

Eliminate the parentheses. $\quad x^2 + \frac{4}{x^2} = 5$

Multiply by x^2. $\quad x^4 + 4 = 5x^2$

Collect the terms to one side. $\quad x^4 - 5x^2 + 4 = 0$

Factor. $\quad (x^2 - 4)(x^2 - 1) = 0$

Solve for x. $\quad x = \pm 2 \quad \text{or} \quad x = \pm 1$

Substitute $x = -2$ into Equation (2), $xy = 2$, and solve for y. $\quad y = -1$

Substitute $x = 2$ into Equation (2), $xy = 2$, and solve for y. $\quad y = 1$

Substitute $x = -1$ into Equation (2), $xy = 2$, and solve for y. $\quad y = -2$

Substitute $x = 1$ into Equation (2), $xy = 2$, and solve for y. $\quad y = 2$

Check to see that there are four solutions: $(-2, -1), (-1, -2), (2, 1)$, and $(1, 2)$.

Note: It is important to check the solutions either algebraically or graphically (see the graph on the left).

[CONCEPT CHECK]

TRUE OR FALSE A system of nonlinear equations that corresponds to the intersection of a hyperbola and an ellipse can have five solutions.

ANSWER False

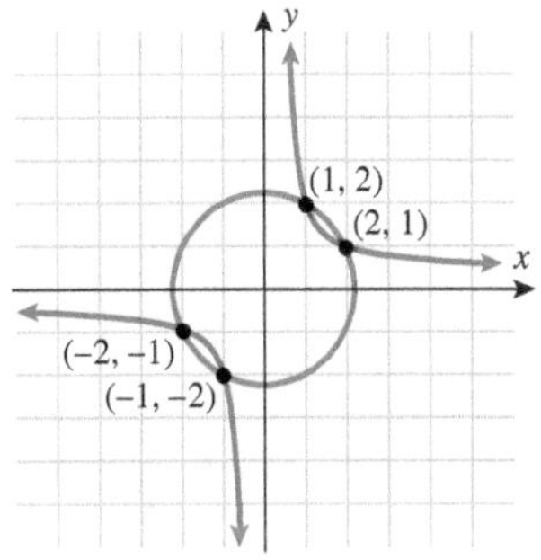

YOUR TURN Solve the system of equations $x^2 + y^2 = 2$ and $xy = 1$.

ANSWER

$(-1, -1)$ and $(1, 1)$

Applications

EXAMPLE 7 Calculating How Much Fence to Buy

A couple buy a rectangular piece of property advertised as 10 acres (approximately 400,000 square feet). They want two fences to divide the land into an internal grazing area and a surrounding riding path. If they want the riding path to be 20 feet wide, one fence will enclose the property and one internal fence will sit 20 feet inside the outer fence. If the internal grazing field is 237,600 square feet, how many linear feet of fencing should they buy?

Solution:

Use the five-step procedure for solving word problems from Section 0.1, and use two variables.

STEP 1 **Identify the question.**

How many linear feet of fence should they buy? Or, what is the sum of the perimeters of the two fences?

STEP 2 **Make notes or draw a sketch.**

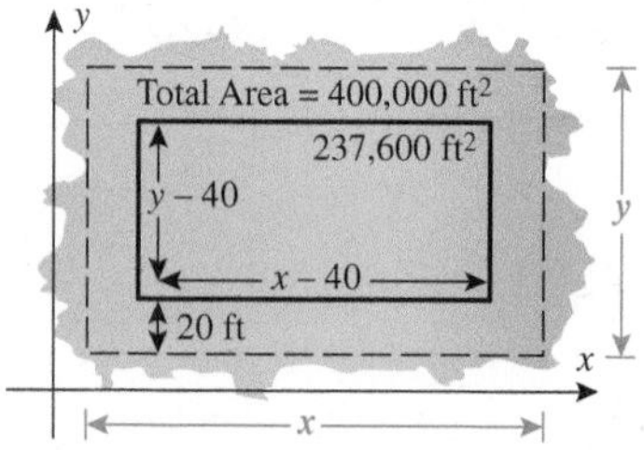

STEP 3 **Set up the equations.**

$x =$ length of property $\qquad x - 40 =$ length of internal field

$y =$ width of property $\qquad y - 40 =$ width of internal field

Equation (1): $\qquad xy = 400{,}000$

Equation (2): $\qquad (x - 40)(y - 40) = 237{,}600$

STEP 4 **Solve the system of equations.**

Substitution Method

Since Equation (1) tells us that $xy = 400{,}000$, we know that neither x nor y can be zero.

Solve Equation (1) for y. $\qquad y = \dfrac{400{,}000}{x}$

Substitute $y = \dfrac{400{,}000}{x}$ into Equation (2). $\qquad (x - 40)\left(\dfrac{400{,}000}{x} - 40\right) = 237{,}600$

Eliminate the parentheses. $\qquad 400{,}000 - 40x - \dfrac{16{,}000{,}000}{x} + 1600 = 237{,}600$

Multiply by the LCD, x. $\qquad 400{,}000x - 40x^2 - 16{,}000{,}000 + 1600x = 237{,}600x$

Collect like terms on one side. $\qquad 40x^2 - 164{,}000x + 16{,}000{,}000 = 0$

Divide by 40. $\qquad x^2 - 4100x + 400{,}000 = 0$

Factor. $\qquad (x - 4000)(x - 100) = 0$

Solve for x. $\qquad x = 4000 \quad \text{or} \quad x = 100$

Substitute $x = 4000$ into the original Equation (1). $\quad 4000y = 400{,}000$

Solve for y. $\quad y = 100$

Substitute $x = 100$ into the original Equation (1). $\quad 100y = 400{,}000$

Solve for y. $\quad y = 4000$

The two solutions yield the same dimensions: 4000×100. The inner field has the dimensions 3960×60. Therefore, the sum of the perimeters of the two fences is

$$2(4000) + 2(100) + 2(3960) + 2(60) = 8000 + 200 + 7920 + 120 = 16{,}240$$

The couple should buy 16,240 linear feet of fencing.

STEP 5 **Check the solution.**

The point (4000, 100) satisfies both Equation (1) and Equation (2).

It is important to note that some nonlinear equations are not conic sections (they could be exponential, logarithmic, or higher degree polynomial equations). These systems of linear equations are typically solved by the substitution method (see the exercises).

[SECTION 9.5] SUMMARY

In this section, systems of two equations wherein at least one of the equations is nonlinear (e.g., conics) were discussed. The substitution method and elimination method can *sometimes* be applied to nonlinear systems. When the two equations are graphed, the points of intersection are the solutions of the system. Systems of nonlinear equations can have more than one solution. Also, extraneous solutions can appear, so it is important to always check solutions.

[SECTION 9.5] EXERCISES

• SKILLS

In Exercises 1–12, solve the system of equations by applying the elimination method.

1. $x^2 - y = -2$, $-x + y = 4$

2. $x^2 + y = 2$, $2x + y = -1$

3. $x^2 + y = 1$, $2x + y = 2$

4. $x^2 - y = 2$, $-2x + y = -3$

5. $x^2 + y = -5$, $-x + y = 3$

6. $x^2 - y = -7$, $x + y = -2$

7. $x^2 + y^2 = 1$, $x^2 - y = -1$

8. $x^2 + y^2 = 1$, $x^2 + y^2 = -1$

9. $x^2 + y^2 = 3$, $4x^2 + y = 0$

10. $x^2 + y^2 = 6$, $-7x^2 + y = 0$

11. $x^2 + y^2 = -6$, $-2x^2 + y = 7$

12. $x^2 + y^2 = 5$, $3x^2 + y = 9$

In Exercises 13–24, solve the system of equations by applying the substitution method.

13. $x + y = 2$
$x^2 + y^2 = 2$

14. $x - y = -2$
$x^2 + y^2 = 2$

15. $xy = 4$
$x^2 + y^2 = 10$

16. $xy = -3$
$x^2 + y^2 = 12$

17. $y = x^2 - 3$
$y = -4x + 9$

18. $y = -x^2 + 5$
$y = 3x - 4$

19. $x^2 + xy - y^2 = 5$
$x - y = -1$

20. $x^2 + xy + y^2 = 13$
$x + y = -1$

21. $2x - y = 3$
$x^2 + y^2 - 2x + 6y = -9$

22. $x^2 + y^2 - 2x - 4y = 0$
$-2x + y = -3$

23. $4x^2 + 12xy + 9y^2 = 25$
$-2x + y = 1$

24. $-4xy + 4y^2 = 8$
$3x + y = 2$

In Exercises 25–40, solve the system of equations by applying any method.

25. $x^3 - y^3 = 63$
$x - y = 3$

26. $x^3 + y^3 = -26$
$x + y = -2$

27. $4x^2 - 3xy = -5$
$-x^2 + 3xy = 8$

28. $2x^2 + 5xy = 2$
$x^2 - xy = 1$

29. $2x^2 - xy = 28$
$4x^2 - 9xy = 28$

30. $-7xy + 2y^2 = -3$
$-3xy + y^2 = 0$

31. $4x^2 + 10y^2 = 26$
$-2x^2 + 2y^2 = -6$

32. $x^3 + y^3 = 19$
$x^3 - y^3 = -35$

33. $\log_x(2y) = 3$
$\log_x(y) = 2$

34. $\log_x(y) = 1$
$\log_x(2y) = \frac{1}{2}$

35. $\frac{1}{x^3} + \frac{1}{y^2} = 17$
$\frac{1}{x^3} - \frac{1}{y^2} = -1$

36. $\frac{2}{x^2} + \frac{3}{y^2} = \frac{5}{6}$
$\frac{4}{x^2} - \frac{9}{y^2} = 0$

37. $2x^2 + 4y^4 = -2$
$6x^2 + 3y^4 = -1$

38. $x^2 + y^2 = -2$
$x^2 + y^2 = -1$

39. $2x^2 - 5y^2 + 8 = 0$
$x^2 - 7y^2 + 4 = 0$

40. $x^2 + y^2 = 4x + 6y - 12$
$9x^2 + 4y^2 = 36x + 24y - 36$

In Exercises 41 and 44, graph each equation and find the point(s) of intersection.

41. The parabola $y = x^2 - 6x + 11$ and the line $y = -x + 7$

42. The circle $x^2 + y^2 - 4x - 2y + 5 = 0$ and the line $-x + 3y = 6$

43. The ellipse $9x^2 - 18x + 4y^2 + 8y - 23 = 0$ and the line $-3x + 2y = 1$.

44. The parabola $y = -x^2 + 2x$ and the circle $x^2 + 6x + y^2 - 4y + 12 = 0$.

• APPLICATIONS

45. Numbers. The sum of two numbers is 10, and the difference of their squares is 40. Find the numbers.

46. Numbers. The difference of two numbers is 3, and the difference of their squares is 51. Find the numbers.

47. Numbers. The product of two numbers is equal to the reciprocal of the difference of their reciprocals. The product of the two numbers is 72. Find the numbers.

48. Numbers. The ratio of the sum of two numbers to the difference of the two numbers is 9. The product of the two numbers is 80. Find the numbers.

49. Geometry. A rectangle has a perimeter of 36 centimeters and an area of 80 square centimeters. Find the dimensions of the rectangle.

50. Geometry. Two concentric circles have perimeters that add up to 16π and areas that add up to 34π. Find the radii of the two circles.

51. Horse Paddock. An equestrian buys a 5-acre rectangular parcel (approximately 200,000 square feet) and is going to fence in the entire property and then divide the parcel into two halves with a fence. If 2200 linear feet of fencing is required, what are the dimensions of the parcel?

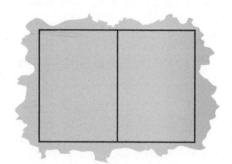

52. **Dog Run.** A family moves into a new home and decides to fence in the yard to give its dog room to roam. If the area that will be fenced in is rectangular and has an area of 11,250 square feet, and the length is twice as great as the width, how many linear feet of fence should the family buy?

53. **Footrace.** Your college algebra professor and Jeremy Wariner (2004 Olympic Gold Medalist in the men's 400 meter) decided to race. The race was 400 meters. Jeremy gave your professor a 1-minute head start and still crossed the finish line 1 minute 40 seconds before your professor. If Jeremy ran five times faster than your professor, what was each person's average speed?

54. **Footrace.** You decided to race Jeremy Wariner for 800 meters. At that distance, Jeremy runs approximately twice as fast as you. He gave you a 1-minute head start and crossed the finish line 20 seconds before you. What were each of your average speeds?

55. **Velocity.** Two cars start moving simultaneously in the same direction. The first car moves at 50 miles per hour; the speed of the second car is 40 miles per hour. A half-hour later, another car starts moving in the same direction. The third car reaches the first one 1.5 hours after it reached the second car. Find the speed of the third car.

56. **Design.** Two boxes are constructed to contain the same volume. In the first box, the width is 16 centimeters larger than the depth, and the length is five times the depth. In the second box, both the length and the width are 4 centimeters shorter and the depth is 25% larger than in the first box. Find the dimensions of the second box.

57. **Numbers.** Find a number consisting of four digits such that

- the sum of the squares of the thousands and the units is 13.
- the sum of the squares of the hundreds and the tens is 85.
- the hundreds is one more than the tens.
- the thousands is one more than the units.
- when 1089 is subtracted from the number, the result has the same digits but in inverse order.

58. **Numbers.** Find a number consisting of three digits such that

- the sum of the cubes of the hundreds and the units is 9.
- the tens is one more than twice the hundreds.
- the hundreds is one more than the units.

• CATCH THE MISTAKE

In Exercises 59 and 60, explain the mistake that is made.

59. Solve the system of equations: $\begin{aligned} x^2 + y^2 &= 4 \\ x + y &= 2 \end{aligned}$

Solution:

Multiply the second equation by (-1) and add to the first equation. $x^2 - x = 2$

Subtract 2. $x^2 - x - 2 = 0$

Factor. $(x+1)(x-2) = 0$

Solve for x. $x = -1$ and $x = 2$

Substitute $x = -1$ and $x = 2$ into $x + y = 2$. $-1 + y = 2$ and $2 + y = 2$

Solve for y. $y = 3$ and $y = 0$

The answer is $(-1, 3)$ and $(2, 0)$.

This is incorrect. What mistake was made?

60. Solve the system of equations: $\begin{aligned} x^2 + y^2 &= 5 \\ 2x - y &= 0 \end{aligned}$

Solution:

Solve the second equation for y. $y = 2x$

Substitute $y = 2x$ into the first equation. $x^2 + (2x)^2 = 5$

Eliminate the parentheses. $x^2 + 4x^2 = 5$

Gather like terms. $5x^2 = 5$

Solve for x. $x = -1$ and $x = 1$

Substitute $x = -1$ into the first equation. $(-1)^2 + y^2 = 5$

Solve for y. $y = -2$ and $y = 2$

Substitute $x = 1$ into the first equation. $(1)^2 + y^2 = 5$

Solve for y. $y = -2$ and $y = 2$

The answers are $(-1, -2)$, $(-1, 2)$, $(1, -2)$, and $(1, 2)$.

This is incorrect. What mistake was made?

• CONCEPTUAL

In Exercises 61–64, determine whether each statement is true or false.

61. A system of equations representing a line and a parabola can intersect in at most three points.

62. A system of equations representing a line and a cubic function can intersect in at most three places.

63. The elimination method can always be used to solve systems of two nonlinear equations.

64. The substitution method always works for solving systems of nonlinear equations.

65. A circle and a line have at most two points of intersection. A circle and a parabola have at most four points of intersection. What is the greatest number of points of intersection that a circle and an nth-degree polynomial can have?

66. A line and a parabola have at most two points of intersection. A line and a cubic function have at most three points of intersection. What is the greatest number of points of intersection that a line and an nth-degree polynomial can have?

• CHALLENGE

67. Find a system of equations representing a line and a parabola that has only one real solution.

68. Find a system of equations representing a circle and a parabola that has only one real solution.

In Exercises 69–72, solve each system of equations.

69. $x^4 + 2x^2y^2 + y^4 = 25$
$x^4 - 2x^2y^2 + y^4 = 9$

70. $x^4 + 2x^2y^2 + y^4 = 169$
$x^4 - 2x^2y^2 + y^4 = 25$

71. $x^4 + 2x^2y^2 + y^4 = -25$
$x^4 - 2x^2y^2 + y^4 = -9$

72. $x^4 + 2x^2y^2 + y^4 = -169$
$x^4 - 2x^2y^2 + y^4 = -25$

• PREVIEW TO CALCULUS

In calculus, when finding the derivative of equations in two variables, we typically use implicit differentiation. A more direct approach is used when an equation can be solved for one variable in terms of the other variable.

In Exercises 73–76, solve each equation for y in terms of x.

73. $x^2 + 4y^2 = 8, y < 0$

74. $y^2 + 2xy + 4 = 0, y > 0$

75. $x^3y^3 = 9y, y > 0$

76. $3xy = -x^3y^2, y < 0$

9.6 SYSTEMS OF NONLINEAR INEQUALITIES

SKILLS OBJECTIVES

- Graph a nonlinear inequality in two variables.
- Graph a system of nonlinear inequalities in two variables.

CONCEPTUAL OBJECTIVES

- Understand that a nonlinear inequality in two variables may be represented by either a bounded or an unbounded region.
- Interpret an overlapping shaded region as a solution.

9.6.1 Nonlinear Inequalities in Two Variables

9.6.1 SKILL

Graph a nonlinear inequality in two variables.

9.6.1 CONCEPTUAL

Understand that a nonlinear inequality in two variables may be represented by either a bounded or an unbounded region.

Linear inequalities are expressed in the form $Ax + By \leq C$. Specific expressions can involve either of the strict or either of the nonstrict inequalities. Examples of **nonlinear inequalities in two variables** are

$$9x^2 + 16y^2 \geq 1 \quad x^2 + y^2 > 1 \quad y \leq -x^2 + 3 \quad \text{and} \quad \frac{x^2}{20} - \frac{y^2}{81} < 1$$

We follow the same procedure as we did with linear inequalities. We change the inequality to an equal sign, graph the resulting nonlinear equation, test points from the two regions, and shade the region that makes the inequality true. For strict inequalities, $<$ or $>$, we use dashed curves, and for nonstrict inequalities, $\leq$ or $\geq$, we use solid curves.

EXAMPLE 1 Graphing a Strict Nonlinear Inequality in Two Variables

Graph the inequality $x^2 + y^2 > 1$.

Solution:

STEP 1 Change the inequality sign to an equal sign. $x^2 + y^2 = 1$

The equation is the equation of a circle.

STEP 2 Draw the graph of the circle.

The center is $(0, 0)$ and the radius is 1.

Since the inequality $>$ is a strict inequality, draw the circle as a **dashed** curve.

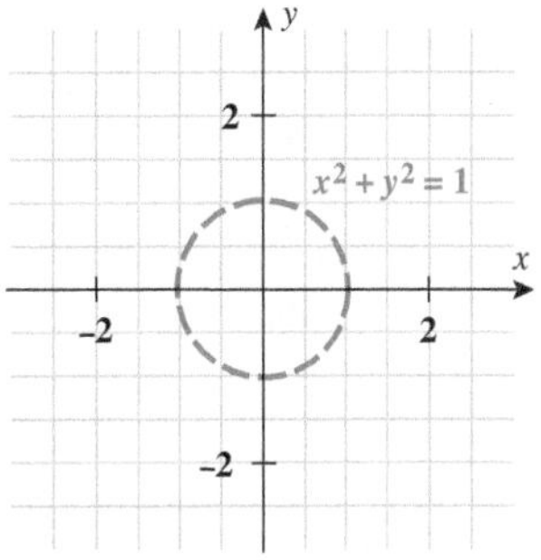

STEP 3 Test points in each region (outside the circle and inside the circle).

Substitute $(2, 0)$ into $x^2 + y^2 > 1$. $4 \geq 1$

The point $(2, 0)$ satisfies the inequality.

Substitute $(0, 0)$ into $x^2 + y^2 > 1$. $0 \geq 1$

The point $(0, 0)$ does not satisfy the inequality.

STEP 4 Shade the region containing the point $(2, 0)$.

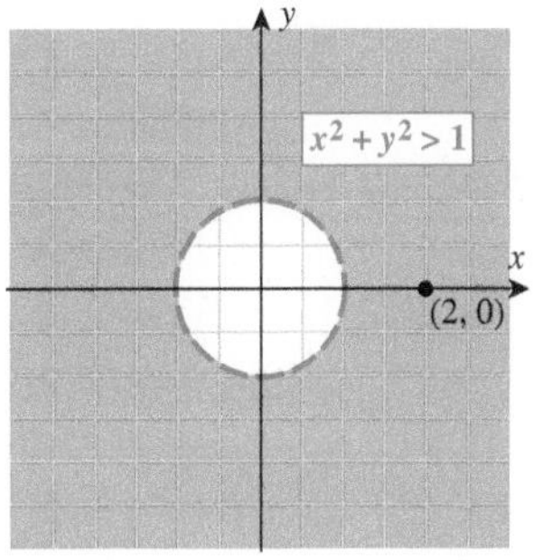

[CONCEPT CHECK]

TRUE OR FALSE A nonlinear inequality with an ellipse as a boundary can have a bounded or an unbounded region for a solution, depending on the inequality.

ANSWER True

EXAMPLE 2 Graphing a Nonstrict Nonlinear Inequality in Two Variables

Graph the inequality $y \leq -x^2 + 3$.

Solution:

STEP 1 Change the inequality sign to an equal sign. $y = -x^2 + 3$

The equation is that of a parabola.

STEP 2 Graph the parabola.

Reflect the base function, $f(x) = x^2$, about the x-axis and shift up three units. Since the inequality $\leq$ is a nonstrict inequality, draw the parabola as a **solid** curve.

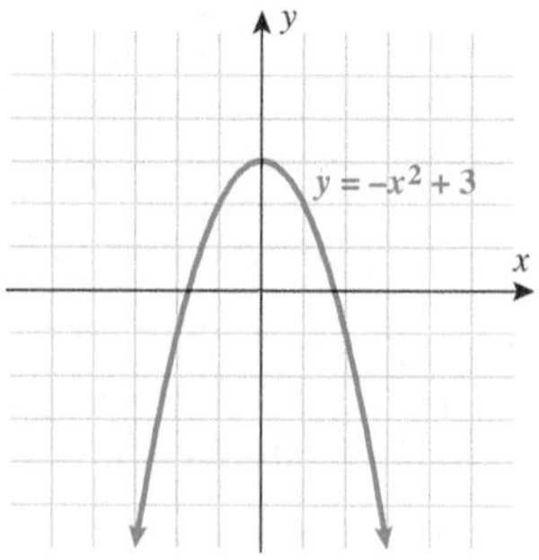

STEP 3 Test points in each region (inside the parabola and outside the parabola).

Substitute $(3, 0)$ into $y \leq -x^2 + 3$. $0 \leq -6$

The point $(3, 0)$ does not satisfy the inequality.

Substitute $(0, 0)$ into $y \leq -x^2 + 3$. $0 \leq 3$

The point $(0, 0)$ does satisfy the inequality.

STEP 4 Shade the region containing the point $(0, 0)$.

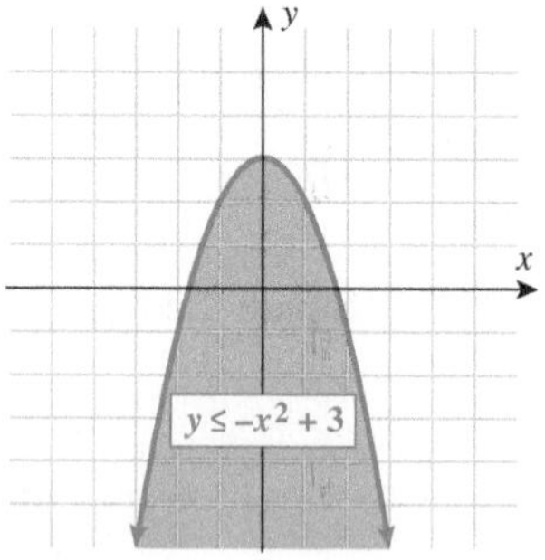

YOUR TURN Graph the following inequalities:

a. $x^2 + y^2 \leq 9$ **b.** $y > -x^2 + 2$

ANSWER

a.

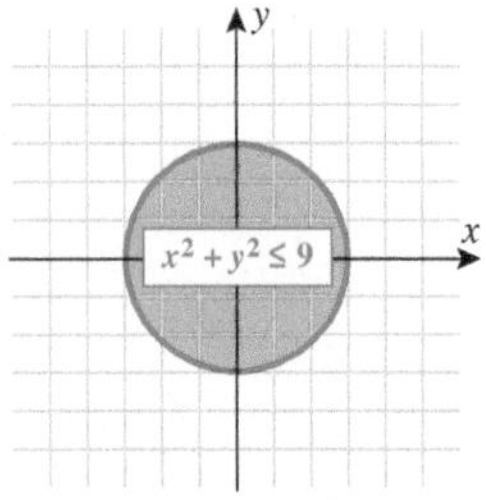

b.

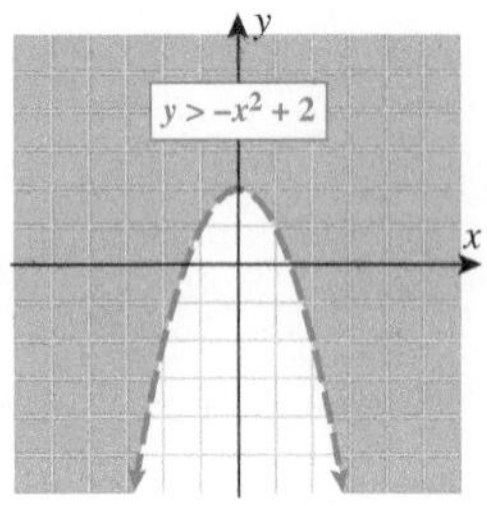

9.6.2 Systems of Nonlinear Inequalities

9.6.2 SKILL

Graph a system of nonlinear inequalities in two variables.

9.6.2 CONCEPTUAL

Interpret an overlapping shaded region as a solution.

To solve a system of inequalities, first graph the inequalities and shade the region containing the points that satisfy each inequality. The overlap of all the shaded regions is the solution.

EXAMPLE 3 Graphing a System of Inequalities

Graph the solution to the system of inequalities: $y \geq x^2 - 1$
$y < x + 1$

Solution:

STEP 1 Change the inequality signs to equal signs. $y = x^2 - 1$
$y = x + 1$

STEP 2 The resulting equations represent a parabola (to be drawn solid) and a line (to be drawn dashed). Graph the two equations.

To determine the points of intersection, set the y-values equal to each other. $x^2 - 1 = x + 1$

Write the quadratic equation in standard form. $x^2 - x - 2 = 0$

Factor. $(x - 2)(x + 1) = 0$

Solve for x. $x = 2$ or $x = -1$

Substitute $x = 2$ into $y = x + 1$. $(2, 3)$

Substitute $x = -1$ into $y = x + 1$. $(-1, 0)$

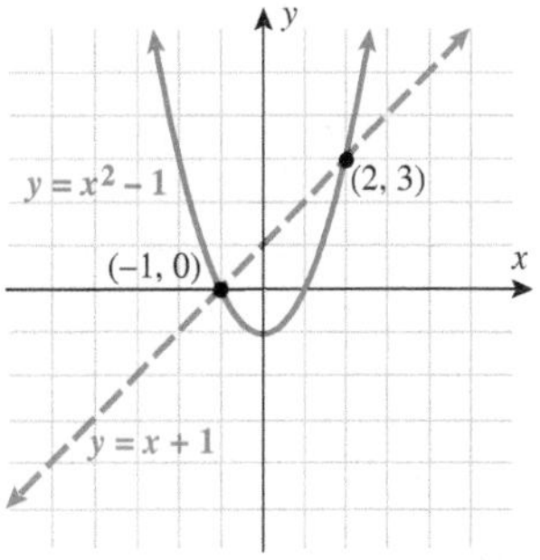

STEP 3 Test points and shade the regions.

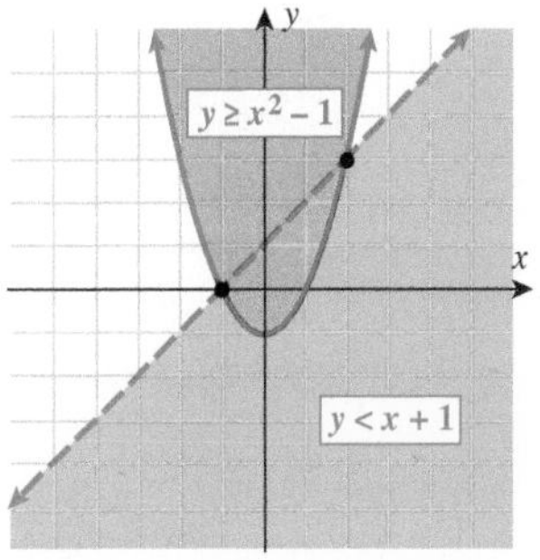

STUDY TIP

The points of intersection correspond to the vertices of the bounded region.

STEP 4 Shade the common region.

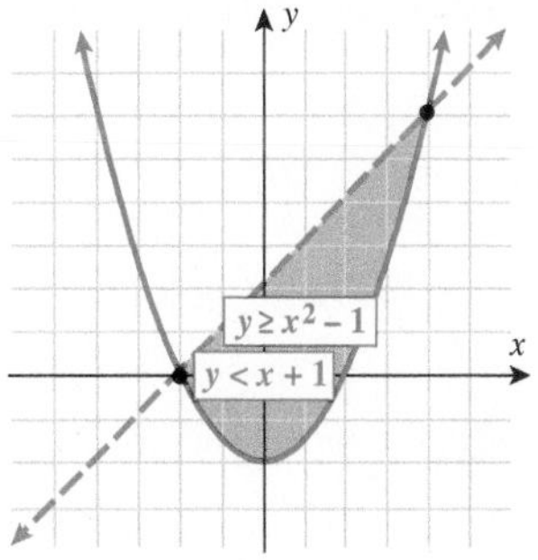

YOUR TURN Graph the solution to the system of inequalities: $x^2 + y^2 < 9$
$y > 0$

ANSWER

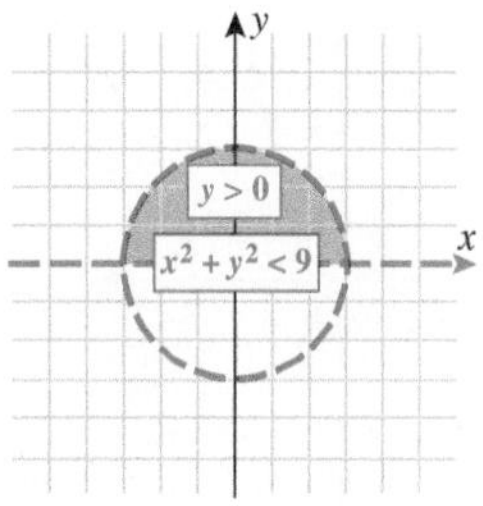

[CONCEPT CHECK]

A system of nonlinear inequalities corresponding to $y > x^2 + A$ and $y < x^2 - A$, where $A > 0$, has no solution.

ANSWER True

EXAMPLE 4 Solving a System of Nonlinear Inequalities

Solve the system of inequalities:
$$x^2 + y^2 < 2$$
$$y \geq x^2$$

Solution:

STEP 1 Change the inequality signs to equal signs.
$$x^2 + y^2 = 2$$
$$y = x^2$$

STEP 2 The resulting equations correspond to a circle (to be drawn dashed) and a parabola (to be drawn solid). Graph the two inequalities.

To determine the points of intersection, solve the system of equations by substitution.
$$x^2 + \underbrace{(x^2)}_{y}{}^2 = 2$$
$$x^4 + x^2 - 2 = 0$$

Factor.
$$(x^2 + 2)(x^2 - 1) = 0$$

Solve for x.
$$\underbrace{x^2 = -2}_{\text{no solution}} \quad \text{or} \quad \underbrace{x^2 = 1}_{x = \pm 1}$$

The points of intersection are $(-1, 1)$ and $(1, 1)$.

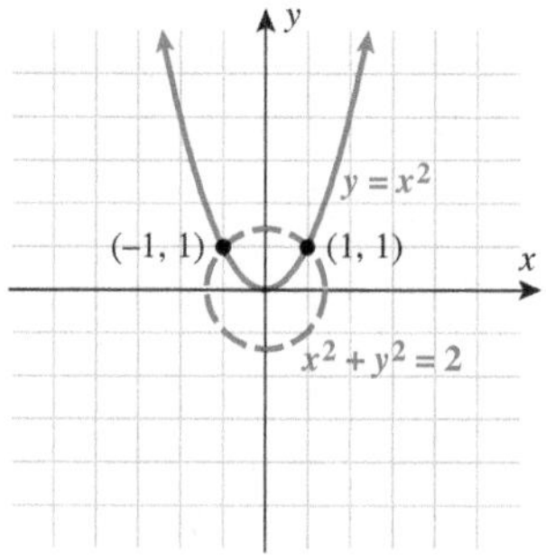

STEP 3 Test points and shade the regions.

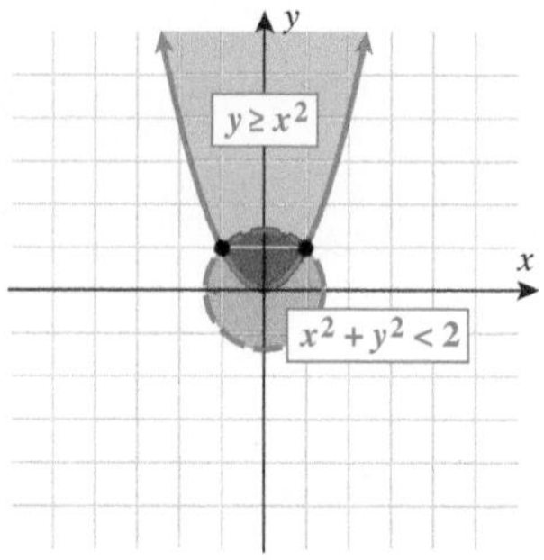

STEP 4 Identify the common region as the solution.

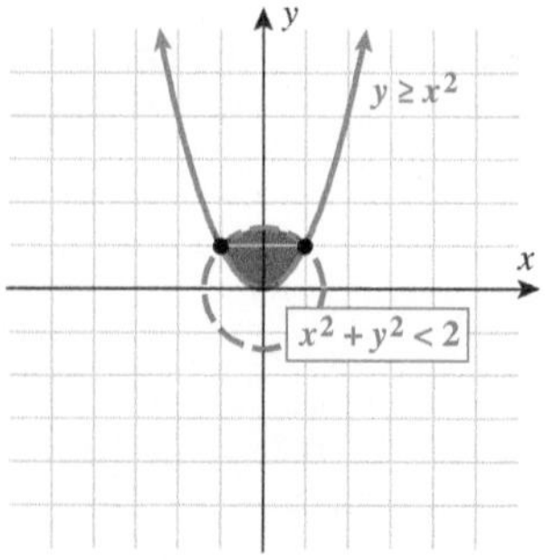

YOUR TURN Solve the system of inequalities:
$$x^2 + y^2 < 2$$
$$y < x^2$$

ANSWER

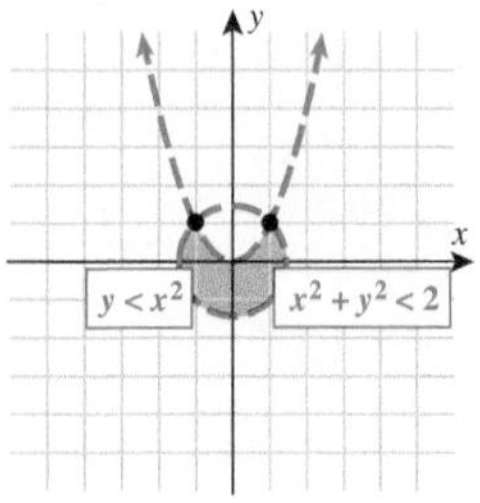

It is important to note that any inequality based on an equation whose graph is not a line is considered a nonlinear inequality.

EXAMPLE 5 Solving a System of Nonlinear Inequalities

Solve the system of inequalities: $(x-1)^2 + \frac{y^2}{4} < 1$

$$y \geq \sqrt{x}$$

Solution:

STEP 1 Change the inequality signs to equal signs.

$$(x-1)^2 + \frac{y^2}{4} = 1$$
$$y = \sqrt{x}$$

STEP 2 The resulting equations correspond to an ellipse (to be drawn dashed) and the square-root function (to be drawn solid). Graph the two inequalities.

To determine the points of intersection, solve the system of equations by substitution. $(x-1)^2 + \frac{\overbrace{(\sqrt{x})^2}^{y}}{4} = 1$

Multiply by 4. $4(x-1)^2 + x = 4$

Expand the binomial squared. $4(x^2 - 2x + 1) + x = 4$

Distribute. $4x^2 - 8x + 4 + x = 4$

Combine like terms and gather terms to one side. $4x^2 - 7x = 0$

Factor. $x(4x - 7) = 0$

Solve for x. $x = 0$ and $x = \frac{7}{4}$

The points of intersection are $(0, 0)$ and $\left(\frac{7}{4}, \sqrt{\frac{7}{4}}\right)$.

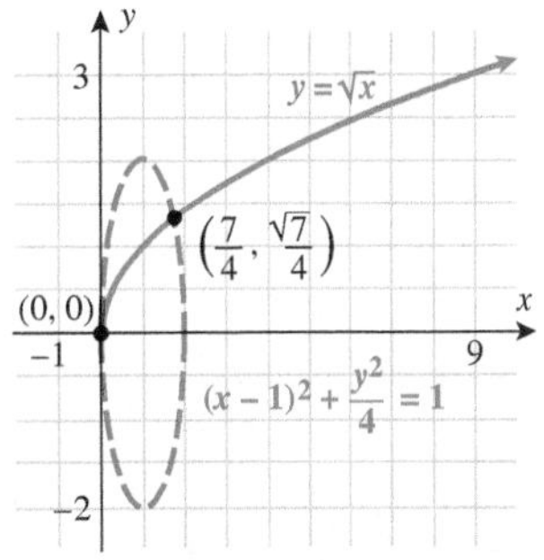

STEP 3 Shade the solution.

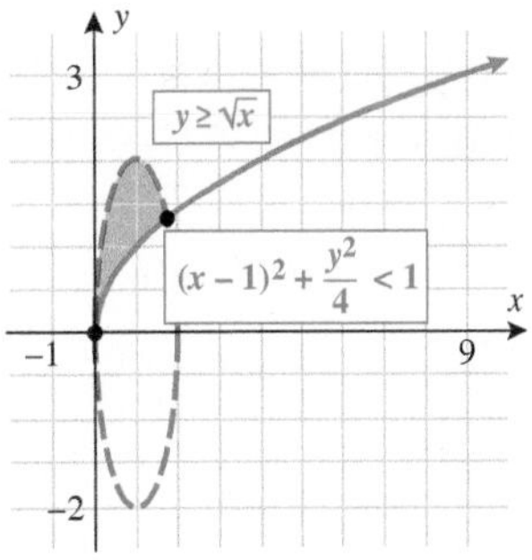

[SECTION 9.6] SUMMARY

In this section, we discussed nonlinear inequalities in two variables. Sometimes these result in bounded regions (e.g., $x^2 + y^2 \leq 1$), and sometimes these result in unbounded regions (e.g., $x^2 + y^2 > 1$). When solving systems of inequalities, we first graph each of the inequalities separately and then look for the intersection (overlap) of all shaded regions.

[SECTION 9.6] EXERCISES

• SKILLS

In Exercises 1–12, match the nonlinear inequality with the correct graph.

1. $x^2 + y^2 < 25$
2. $x^2 + y^2 \leq 9$
3. $\dfrac{x^2}{9} + \dfrac{y^2}{16} \geq 1$
4. $\dfrac{x^2}{4} + \dfrac{y^2}{9} > 1$
5. $y \geq x^2 - 3$
6. $x^2 \geq 16y$
7. $x \geq y^2 - 4$
8. $\dfrac{x^2}{9} + \dfrac{y^2}{25} \geq 1$
9. $9x^2 + 9y^2 < 36$
10. $(x - 2)^2 + (y + 3)^2 \leq 9$
11. $\dfrac{x^2}{4} - \dfrac{y^2}{9} \geq 1$
12. $\dfrac{y^2}{16} - \dfrac{x^2}{9} < 1$

a.

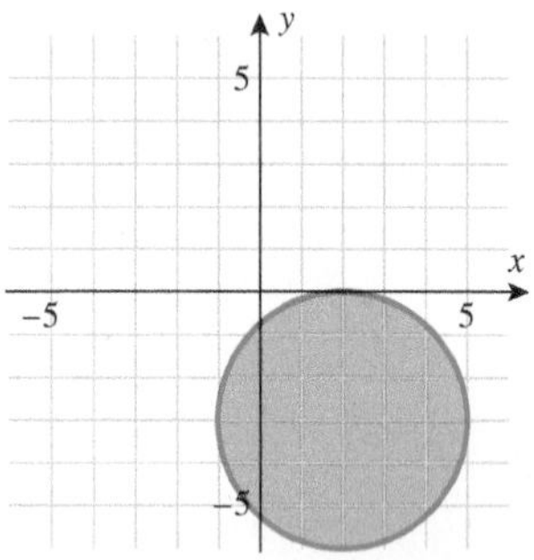

b.

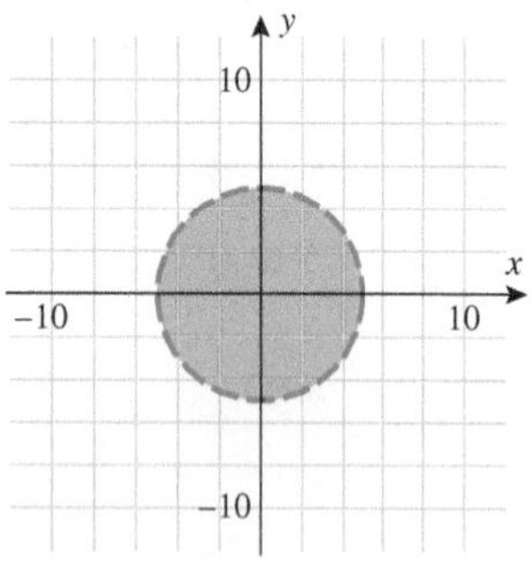

c.

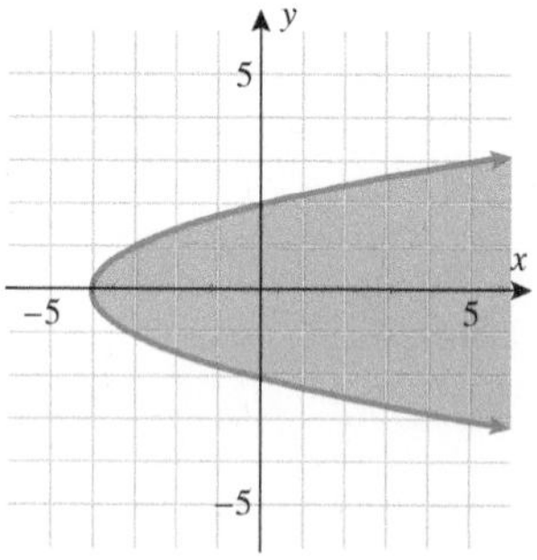

d.

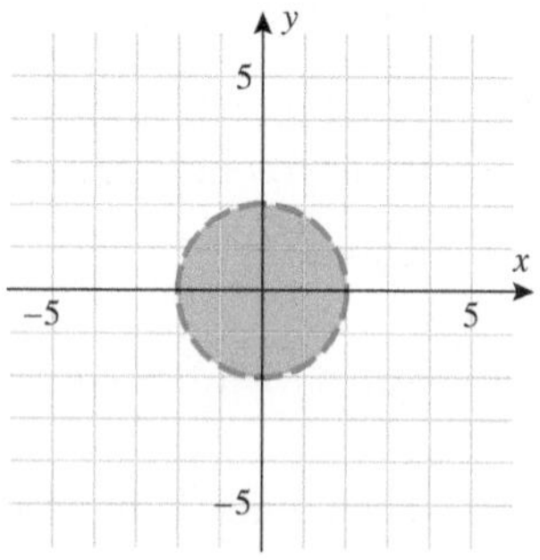

e.

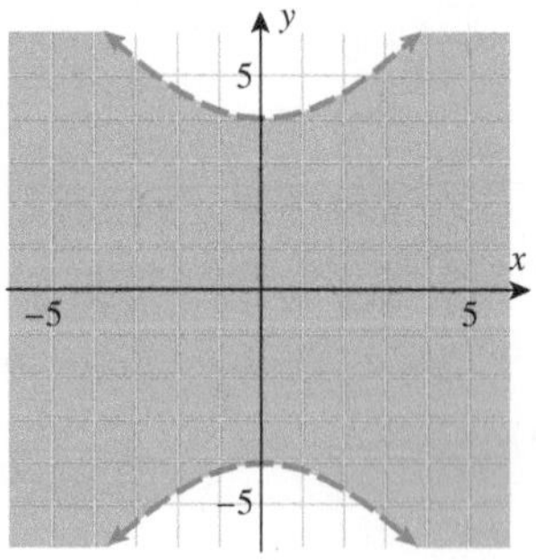

f.

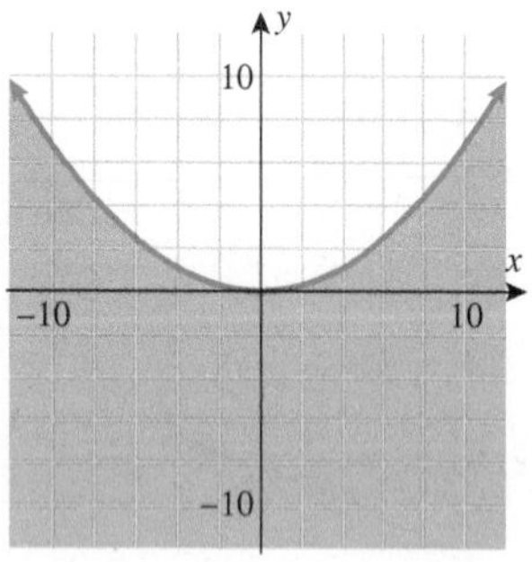

g.

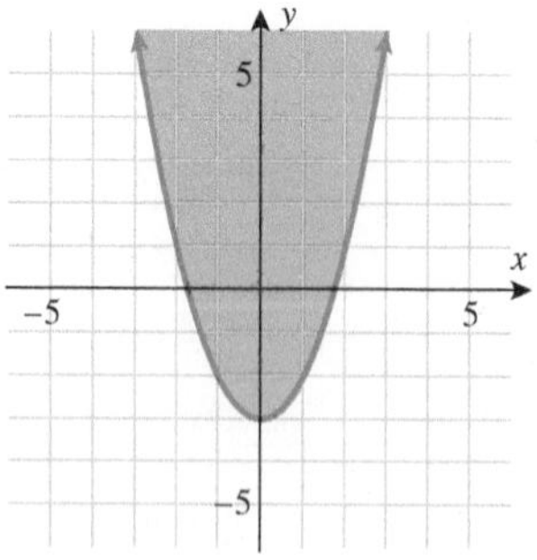

h.

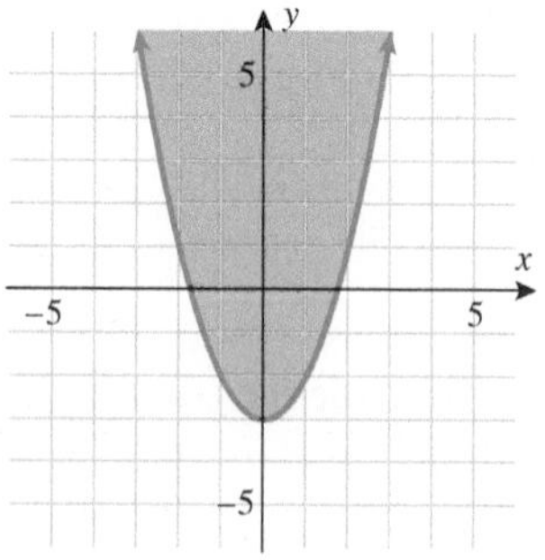

i.

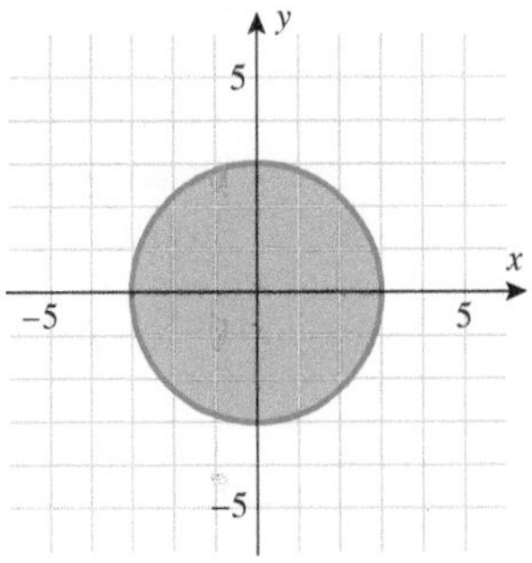

j.

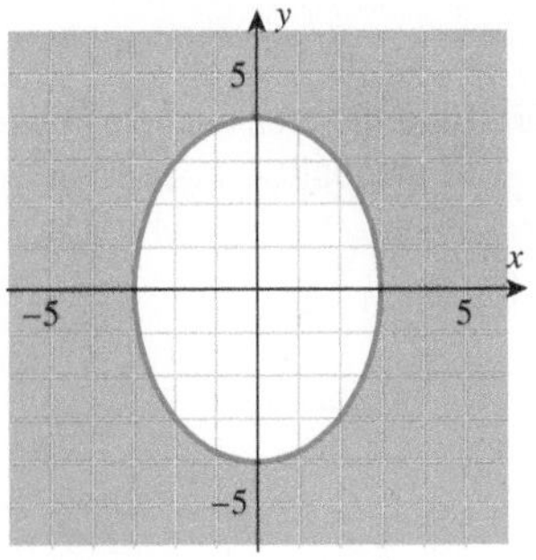

k.

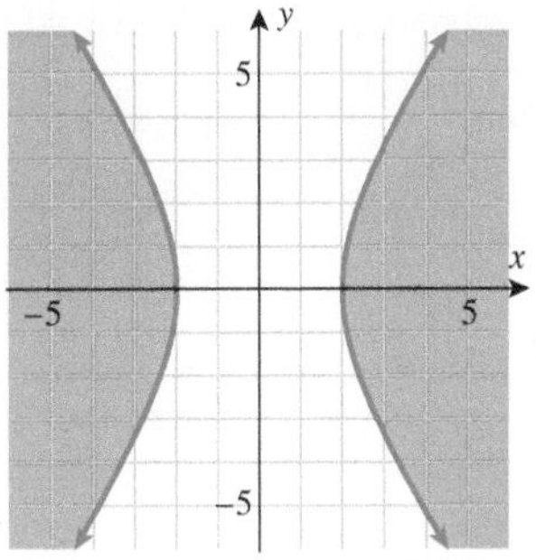

l.

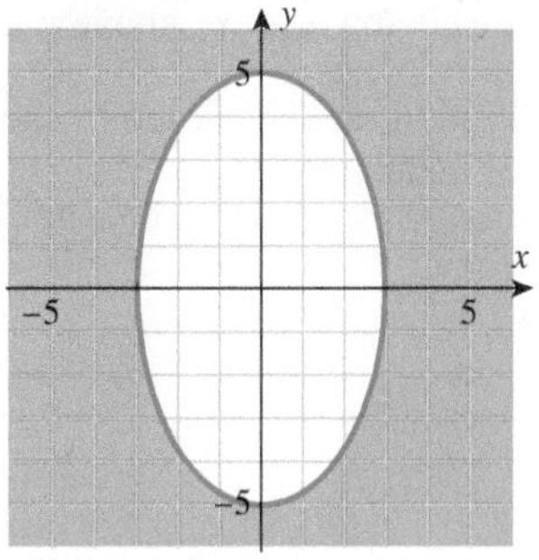

In Exercises 13–30, graph the nonlinear inequality.

13. $y \leq x^2 - 2$

14. $y \geq -x^2 + 3$

15. $x^2 + y^2 > 4$

16. $x^2 + y^2 < 16$

17. $x^2 + y^2 - 2x + 4y + 4 \geq 0$

18. $x^2 + y^2 + 2x - 2y - 2 \leq 0$

19. $3x^2 + 4y^2 \leq 12$

20. $\dfrac{(x-2)^2}{9} + \dfrac{(y+1)^2}{25} > 1$

21. $9x^2 + 16y^2 - 18x + 96y + 9 > 0$

22. $\dfrac{(x-2)^2}{4} - \dfrac{(y+3)^2}{1} \geq 1$

23. $9x^2 - 4y^2 \geq 26$

24. $\dfrac{(y+1)^2}{9} - \dfrac{(x+2)^2}{16} < 1$

25. $36x^2 - 9y^2 \geq 324$

26. $25x^2 - 36y^2 + 200x + 144y - 644 \geq 0$

27. $y \geq e^x$

28. $y \leq \ln x$

29. $y < -x^3$

30. $y > -x^4$

In Exercises 31–50, graph each system of inequalities or indicate that the system has no solution.

31. $y < x + 1$
$y \leq x^2$

32. $y < x^2 + 4x$
$y \leq 3 - x$

33. $y \geq 2 + x$
$y \leq 4 - x^2$

34. $y \geq (x-2)^2$
$y \leq 4 - x$

35. $y \leq -(x+2)^2$
$y > -5 + x$

36. $y \geq (x-1)^2 + 2$
$y \leq 10 - x$

37. $-x^2 + y > -1$
$x^2 + y < 1$

38. $x < -y^2 + 1$
$x > y^2 - 1$

39. $y \geq x^2$
$x \geq y^2$

40. $y < x^2$
$x > y^2$

41. $x^2 + y^2 < 36$
$2x + y > 3$

42. $x^2 + y^2 < 36$
$y > 6$

43. $x^2 + y^2 < 25$
$y \geq 6 + x$

44. $(x-1)^2 + (y+2)^2 \leq 36$
$y \geq x - 3$

45. $x^2 + y^2 \leq 9$
$y \geq 1 + x^2$

46. $x^2 + y^2 \geq 16$
$x^2 + (y-3)^2 \leq 9$

47. $x^2 - y^2 < 4$
$y > 1 - x^2$

48. $\dfrac{x^2}{4} - \dfrac{y^2}{9} \leq 1$
$y \geq x - 5$

49. $y < e^x$
$y > \ln x \quad x > 0$

50. $y < 10^x$
$y > \log x \quad x > 0$

• APPLICATIONS

51. Find the area enclosed by the system of inequalities.
$x^2 + y^2 < 9$
$x > 0$

52. Find the area enclosed by the system of inequalities.
$x^2 + y^2 \leq 5$
$x \leq 0$
$y \geq 0$

In Exercises 53 and 54, refer to the following:

The area enclosed by the ellipse $\dfrac{x^2}{a^2} + \dfrac{y^2}{b^2} = 1$ is given by $ab\pi$.

53. Find the area enclosed by the system of inequalities.
$4x^2 + y^2 \leq 16$
$x \leq 0$
$y \geq 0$

54. Find the area enclosed by the system of inequalities.
$9x^2 + 4y^2 \geq 36$
$x^2 + y^2 \leq 9$

In Exercises 55 and 56, refer to the following:

The area below $y = x^2$, above $y = 0$, and between $x = 0$ and $x = a$ is $\frac{a^3}{3}$.

55. Find the area enclosed by the system of inequalities.

$$\begin{aligned} y &\le x^2 \\ x &\ge 0 \\ x &\le 6 \\ y &\ge x - 6 \end{aligned}$$

56. Find the area enclosed by the system of inequalities.

$$\begin{aligned} y &\le x^2 + 4 \\ y &\ge x \\ x &\ge -3 \\ x &\le 3 \end{aligned}$$

• CATCH THE MISTAKE

In Exercises 57 and 58, explain the mistake that is made.

57. Graph the system of inequalities: $x^2 + y^2 < 1$
$x^2 + y^2 > 4$

Solution:

Draw the circles $x^2 + y^2 = 1$ and $x^2 + y^2 = 4$.

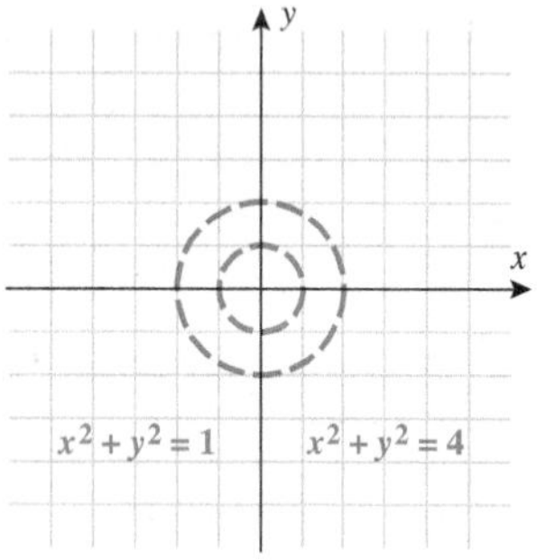

Shade outside $x^2 + y^2 = 1$ and inside $x^2 + y^2 = 4$.

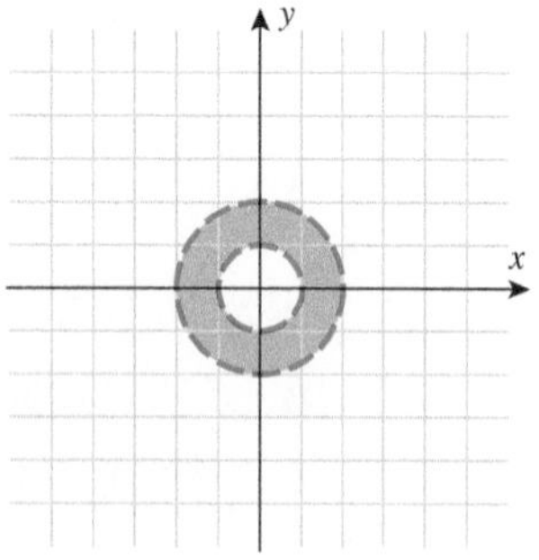

This is incorrect. What mistake was made?

58. Graph the system of inequalities: $x > -y^2 + 1$
$x < y^2 - 1$

Solution:

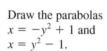

Draw the parabolas $x = -y^2 + 1$ and $x = y^2 - 1$.

Shade the region between the curves.

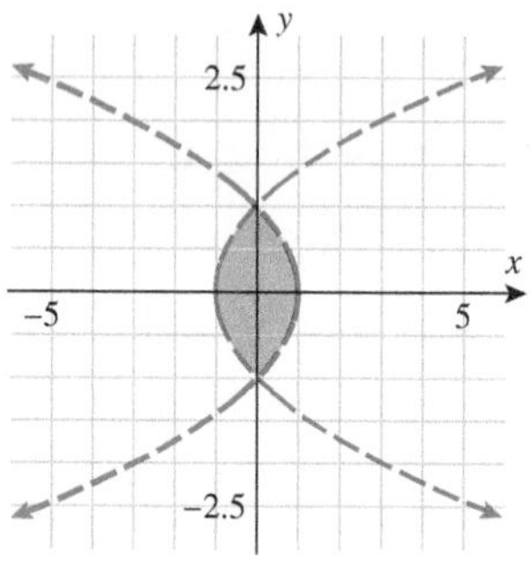

This is incorrect. What mistake was made?

• CONCEPTUAL

In Exercises 59–66, determine whether each statement is true or false.

59. A nonlinear inequality always represents a bounded region.

60. A system of inequalities always has a solution.

61. The solution to the following system of equations is symmetric with respect to the y-axis:

$$\frac{x^2}{a^2} - \frac{y^2}{b^2} \le 1$$
$$y \ge x^2 - 2a$$

62. The solution to the following system of equations is symmetric with respect to the origin:

$$\frac{x^2}{a^2} - \frac{y^2}{b^2} \le 1$$
$$y \ge \sqrt[3]{x}$$

63. The solution to the following system of equations is symmetric with respect to the origin:

$$\frac{x^2}{a^2} - \frac{y^2}{b^2} \ge 1$$
$$\frac{x^2}{4a^2} + \frac{y^2}{a^2} \le 1$$

64. The solution to the following system of equations is bounded:

$$\frac{x^2}{a^2} - \frac{y^2}{b^2} \le 1$$
$$x \ge -2a$$
$$x \le 2a$$

65. The following systems of inequalities have the same solution:

$$16x^2 - 25y^2 \geq 400 \quad x \geq -6 \quad x \leq 6$$

$$\frac{y^2}{25} - \frac{x^2}{16} \geq 1 \quad y \geq -6 \quad y \leq 6$$

66. The solution to the following system of inequalities is unbounded:

$$\frac{x^2}{a^2} - \frac{y^2}{b^2} \leq 1$$

$$\frac{y^2}{a^2} - \frac{x^2}{b^2} \leq 1$$

• CHALLENGE

67. For the system of nonlinear inequalities $\begin{matrix} x^2 + y^2 \geq a^2 \\ x^2 + y^2 \leq b^2 \end{matrix}$, what restriction must be placed on the values of a and b for this system to have a solution? Assume that a and b are real numbers.

68. Can $x^2 + y^2 < -1$ ever have a real solution? What types of numbers would x and/or y have to be to satisfy this inequality?

69. Find a positive real number a such that the area enclosed by the curves is the same.

$$x^2 + y^2 = 144 \quad \text{and} \quad \frac{x^2}{a^2} + \frac{y^2}{4^2} = 1$$

70. If the areas of the regions enclosed by $x^2 + y^2 = 1$ and $\frac{x^2}{a^2} + \frac{y^2}{b^2} = 1$ are equal, what can you say about a and b?

71. If the solution to

$$4x^2 + 9y^2 \leq 36$$
$$(x - h)^2 \leq 4y$$

is symmetric with respect to the y-axis, what can you say about h?

72. The solution to

$$\frac{x^2}{a^2} + \frac{y^2}{b^2} \leq 1$$
$$y \geq x$$

is located in quadrants I, II, and III. If the sections in quadrants I and III have the same area, what can you say about a and b?

• PREVIEW TO CALCULUS

In calculus, the problem of finding the area enclosed by a set of curves can be seen as the problem of finding the area enclosed by a system of inequalities.

In Exercises 73–76, graph the system of inequalities.

73. $y \leq x^3 - x$
$y \geq x^2 - 1$

74. $y \leq x^3$
$y \geq 2x - x^2$

75. $y \geq x^3 - 2x^2$
$y \leq x^2$
$y \leq 5$

76. $y \leq \sqrt{1 - x^2}$
$y \geq x^2$
$y \leq 2x$

9.7 ROTATION OF AXES

SKILLS OBJECTIVES

- Transform general second-degree equations into recognizable equations of conics by analyzing rotation of axes.
- Determine the angle of rotation that will transform a general second-degree equation into a familiar equation of a conic section.

CONCEPTUAL OBJECTIVES

- Understand how the equation of a conic section is altered by rotation of axes.
- Understand how the angle of rotation formula is derived.

9.7.1 Rotation of Axes Formulas

9.7.1 SKILL

Transform general second-degree equations into recognizable equations of conics by analyzing rotation of axes.

9.7.1 CONCEPTUAL

Understand how the equation of a conic section is altered by rotation of axes.

In Sections 9.1 through 9.4, we learned to recognize equations of parabolas, ellipses, and hyperbolas that were centered at any point in the Cartesian plane and whose vertices and foci were aligned either along or parallel to either the x-axis or the y-axis. We learned, for example, that the equation of an ellipse centered at the origin takes the form

$$\frac{x^2}{a^2} + \frac{y^2}{b^2} = 1$$

where the major and minor axes are, respectively, either the x- or the y-axis, depending on whether a is greater than or less than b. Now let us look at an equation of a conic section whose graph is *not* aligned with the x- or y-axis: the equation $5x^2 - 8xy + 5y^2 - 9 = 0$.

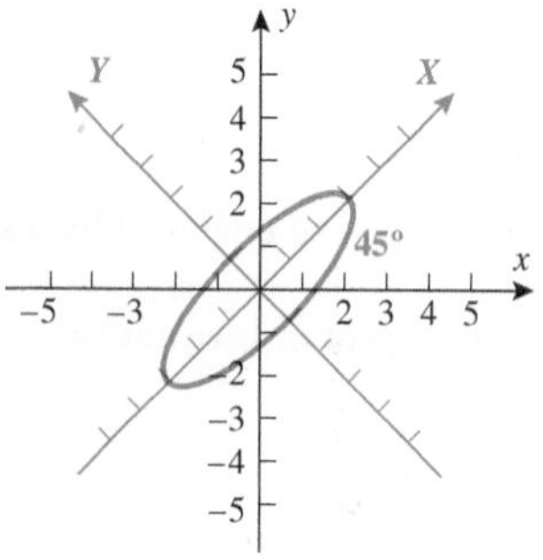

This graph can be thought of as an ellipse that started with the major axis along the x-axis and the minor axis along the y-axis and then was rotated counterclockwise 45°. A new XY-coordinate system can be introduced that has the same origin but is rotated by a certain amount from the standard xy-coordinate system. In this example, the major axis of the ellipse lies along the new X-axis, and the minor axis lies along the new Y-axis. We will see that we can write the equation of this ellipse as

$$\frac{X^2}{9} + \frac{Y^2}{1} = 1$$

We will now develop the *rotation of axes formulas*, which enables us to transform the generalized second-degree equation in xy, that is, $Ax^2 + Bxy + Cy^2 + Dx + Ey + F = 0$, into an equation in XY of a conic that is familiar to us.

WORDS

Let the new XY-coordinate system be displaced from the xy-coordinate system by rotation through an angle θ. Let P represent some point a distance r from the origin.

MATH

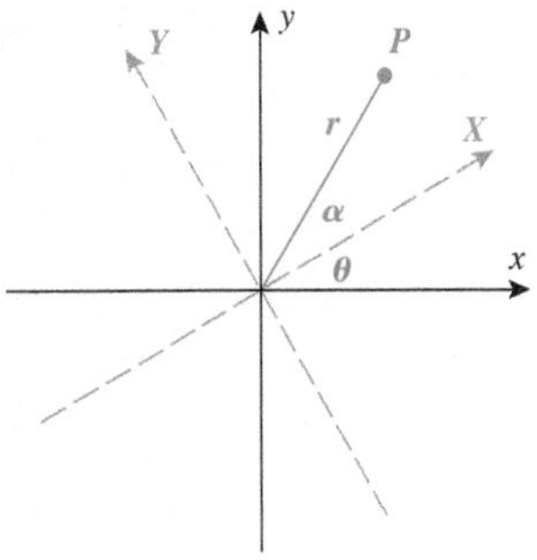

We can represent the point P as either the point (x, y) or the point (X, Y).

We define the angle α as the angle r makes with the X-axis, and $\alpha + \theta$ as the angle r makes with the x-axis.

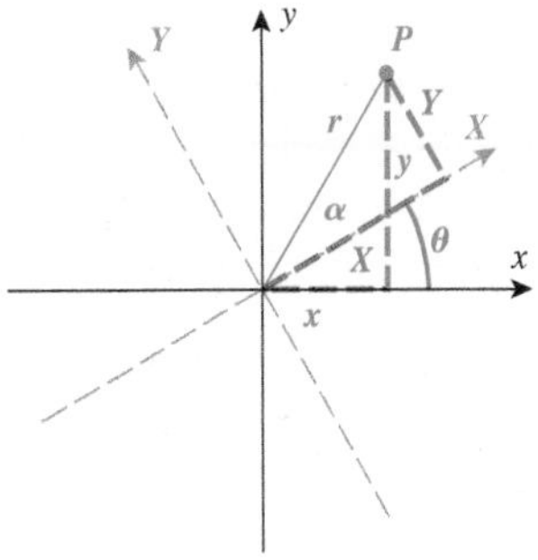

We can represent the point P in polar coordinates using the following relationships:

$$x = r\cos(\alpha + \theta)$$
$$y = r\sin(\alpha + \theta)$$
$$X = r\cos\alpha$$
$$Y = r\sin\alpha$$

Let us now derive the relationships between the two coordinate systems.

WORDS	MATH
Start with the x term and write the cosine identity for a sum.	$x = r\cos(\alpha + \theta)$ $= r(\cos\alpha\cos\theta - \sin\alpha\sin\theta)$
Eliminate the parentheses and group r with the α terms.	$x = (r\cos\alpha)\cos\theta - (r\sin\alpha)\sin\theta$
Substitute according to the relationships $X = r\cos\alpha$ and $Y = r\sin\alpha$.	$\boxed{x = X\cos\theta - Y\sin\theta}$
Start with the y term and write the sine identity for a sum.	$y = r\sin(\alpha + \theta)$ $= r(\sin\alpha\cos\theta + \cos\alpha\sin\theta)$
Eliminate the parentheses and group r with the α terms.	$y = (r\sin\alpha)\cos\theta + (r\cos\alpha)\sin\theta$
Substitute according to the relationships $X = r\cos\alpha$ and $Y = r\sin\alpha$.	$\boxed{y = Y\cos\theta + X\sin\theta}$

By treating the boxed equations for x and y as a system of linear equations in X and Y, we can then solve for X and Y in terms of x and y. The results are summarized in the following box.

ROTATION OF AXES FORMULAS

Suppose that the x- and y-axes in the rectangular coordinate plane are rotated through an acute angle θ to produce the X- and Y-axes. Then the coordinates (x, y) and (X, Y) are related according to the following equations:

$$x = X\cos\theta - Y\sin\theta \qquad\qquad X = x\cos\theta + y\sin\theta$$
$$\text{or}$$
$$y = X\sin\theta + Y\cos\theta \qquad\qquad Y = -x\sin\theta + y\cos\theta$$

EXAMPLE 1 **Rotating the Axes**

If the xy-coordinate axes are rotated 60°, find the XY-coordinates of the point $(x, y) = (-3, 4)$.

Solution:

Start with the rotation formulas.

$$X = x\cos\theta + y\sin\theta$$
$$Y = -x\sin\theta + y\cos\theta$$

Let $x = -3$, $y = 4$, and $\theta = 60°$.

$$X = -3\cos 60° + 4\sin 60°$$
$$Y = -(-3)\sin 60° + 4\cos 60°$$

Simplify.

$$X = -3\underbrace{\cos 60°}_{\frac{1}{2}} + 4\underbrace{\sin 60°}_{\frac{\sqrt{3}}{2}}$$

$$Y = 3\underbrace{\sin 60°}_{\frac{\sqrt{3}}{2}} + 4\underbrace{\cos 60°}_{\frac{1}{2}}$$

$$X = -\frac{3}{2} + 2\sqrt{3}$$

$$Y = \frac{3\sqrt{3}}{2} + 2$$

The XY-coordinates are $\boxed{\left(-\frac{3}{2} + 2\sqrt{3}, \frac{3\sqrt{3}}{2} + 2\right)}$.

YOUR TURN If the xy-coordinate axes are rotated 30°, find the XY-coordinates of the point $(x, y) = (3, -4)$.

ANSWER

$\left(\frac{3\sqrt{3}}{2} - 2, -\frac{3}{2} - 2\sqrt{3}\right)$

EXAMPLE 2 Rotating an Ellipse

Show that the graph of the equation $5x^2 - 8xy + 5y^2 - 9 = 0$ is an ellipse aligning with coordinate axes that are rotated by 45°.

Solution:

Start with the rotation formulas. $x = X\cos\theta - Y\sin\theta$

$y = X\sin\theta + Y\cos\theta$

Let $\theta = 45°$. $x = X\underbrace{\cos 45°}_{\frac{\sqrt{2}}{2}} - Y\underbrace{\sin 45°}_{\frac{\sqrt{2}}{2}}$

$y = X\underbrace{\sin 45°}_{\frac{\sqrt{2}}{2}} + Y\underbrace{\cos 45°}_{\frac{\sqrt{2}}{2}}$

Simplify. $x = \frac{\sqrt{2}}{2}(X - Y)$

$y = \frac{\sqrt{2}}{2}(X + Y)$

Substitute $x = \frac{\sqrt{2}}{2}(X - Y)$ and $y = \frac{\sqrt{2}}{2}(X + Y)$ into $5x^2 - 8xy + 5y^2 - 9 = 0$.

$$5\left[\frac{\sqrt{2}}{2}(X - Y)\right]^2 - 8\left[\frac{\sqrt{2}}{2}(X - Y)\right]\left[\frac{\sqrt{2}}{2}(X + Y)\right] + 5\left[\frac{\sqrt{2}}{2}(X + Y)\right]^2 - 9 = 0$$

Simplify. $\frac{5}{2}(X^2 - 2XY + Y^2) - 4(X^2 - Y^2) + \frac{5}{2}(X^2 + 2XY + Y^2) - 9 = 0$

$$\frac{5}{2}X^2 - 5XY + \frac{5}{2}Y^2 - 4X^2 + 4Y^2 + \frac{5}{2}X^2 + 5XY + \frac{5}{2}Y^2 = 9$$

Combine like terms. $X^2 + 9Y^2 = 9$

Divide by 9. $\boxed{\frac{X^2}{9} + \frac{Y^2}{1} = 1}$

This (as discussed earlier) is an ellipse whose major axis is along the X-axis.

The vertices are at the points $(X, Y) = (\pm 3, 0)$.

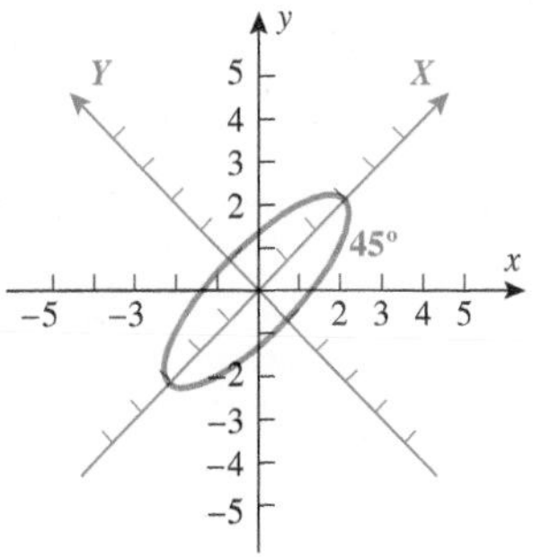

[CONCEPT CHECK]

TRUE OR FALSE If the angle of rotation, θ, is equal to 180°, then the new points (X, Y) are related to the original points (x, y) by $(X, Y) = (-x, -y)$.

ANSWER True

9.7.2 The Angle of Rotation Necessary to Transform a General Second-Degree Equation into a Familiar Equation of a Conic

9.7.2 SKILL

Determine the angle of rotation that will transform a general second-degree equation into a familiar equation of a conic section.

9.7.2 CONCEPTUAL

Understand how the angle of rotation formula is derived.

In Section 9.1, we stated that the general second-degree equation

$$Ax^2 + Bxy + Cy^2 + Dx + Ey + F = 0$$

corresponds to a graph of a conic. Which type of conic it is depends on the value of the discriminant, $B^2 - 4AC$. In Sections 9.2–9.4, we discussed graphs of parabolas, ellipses, and hyperbolas with vertices along either the axes or lines parallel (or perpendicular) to the axes. In all cases the value of B was taken to be zero. When the value of B is nonzero, the result is a conic with vertices along the new XY-axes (or, respectively, parallel and perpendicular to them), which are the original xy-axes rotated through an angle θ. If given θ, we can determine the rotation equations as illustrated in Example 2, but how do we find the angle θ that represents the *angle of rotation*?

To find the angle of rotation, let us start with a general second-degree polynomial equation:

$$Ax^2 + Bxy + Cy^2 + Dx + Ey + F = 0$$

We want to transform this equation into an equation in X and Y that does not contain an XY-term. Suppose we rotate our coordinates by an angle θ and use the rotation equations

$$x = X\cos\theta - Y\sin\theta \qquad y = X\sin\theta + Y\cos\theta$$

in the general second-degree polynomial equation; then the result is

$$A(X\cos\theta - Y\sin\theta)^2 + B(X\cos\theta - Y\sin\theta)(X\sin\theta + Y\cos\theta)$$
$$+ C(X\sin\theta + Y\cos\theta)^2 + D(X\cos\theta - Y\sin\theta) + E(X\sin\theta + Y\cos\theta) + F = 0$$

If we expand these expressions and collect like terms, the result is an equation of the form

$$aX^2 + bXY + cY^2 + dX + eY + f = 0$$

where

$$a = A\cos^2\theta + B\sin\theta\cos\theta + C\sin^2\theta$$

$$b = B(\cos^2\theta - \sin^2\theta) + 2(C - A)\sin\theta\cos\theta$$

$$c = A\sin^2\theta - B\sin\theta\cos\theta + C\cos^2\theta$$

$$d = D\cos\theta + E\sin\theta$$

$$e = -D\sin\theta + E\cos\theta$$

$$f = F$$

WORDS	MATH
We do not want this new equation to have an XY-term, so we set $b = 0$.	$B(\cos^2\theta - \sin^2\theta) + 2(C - A)\sin\theta\cos\theta = 0$
We can use the double-angle formulas to simplify.	$\underbrace{B(\cos^2\theta - \sin^2\theta)}_{\cos(2\theta)} + (C - A)\underbrace{2\sin\theta\cos\theta}_{\sin(2\theta)} = 0$
Subtract the $\sin(2\theta)$ term from both sides of the equation.	$B\cos(2\theta) = (A - C)\sin(2\theta)$
Divide by $B\sin(2\theta)$.	$\dfrac{B\cos(2\theta)}{B\sin(2\theta)} = \dfrac{(A - C)\sin(2\theta)}{B\sin(2\theta)}$
Simplify.	$\boxed{\cot(2\theta) = \dfrac{A - C}{B}}$

ANGLE OF ROTATION FORMULA

To transform the equation of a conic

$$Ax^2 + Bxy + Cy^2 + Dx + Ey + F = 0$$

into an equation in X and Y without an XY-term, rotate the xy-axes by an acute angle θ that satisfies the equation

$$\cot(2\theta) = \frac{A - C}{B} \quad \text{or} \quad \tan(2\theta) = \frac{B}{A - C}$$

Notice that the trigonometric equation $\cot(2\theta) = \dfrac{A - C}{B}$ or $\tan(2\theta) = \dfrac{B}{A - C}$ can be solved exactly for some values of θ (Example 3) but will have to be approximated with a calculator for other values of θ (Example 4).

EXAMPLE 3 **Determining the Angle of Rotation I: The Value of the Cotangent Function Is That of a Known (Special) Angle**

Determine the angle of rotation necessary to transform the following equation into an equation in X and Y with no XY term:

$$3x^2 + 2\sqrt{3}xy + y^2 + 2x - 2\sqrt{3}y = 0$$

Solution:

Identify the A, B, and C parameters in the equation.	$\underset{A}{\underline{3}}x^2 + \underset{B}{\underline{2\sqrt{3}}}\,xy + \underset{C}{\underline{1}}y^2 + 2x - 2\sqrt{3}y = 0$
Write the rotation formula.	$\cot(2\theta) = \dfrac{A - C}{B}$
Let $A = 3$, $B = 2\sqrt{3}$, and $C = 1$.	$\cot(2\theta) = \dfrac{3 - 1}{2\sqrt{3}}$
Simplify.	$\cot(2\theta) = \dfrac{1}{\sqrt{3}}$
Apply the reciprocal identity.	$\tan(2\theta) = \sqrt{3}$

From our knowledge of trigonometric exact values, we know that $2\theta = 60°$ or $\boxed{\theta = 30°}$.

EXAMPLE 4 **Determining the Angle of Rotation II: The Argument of the Cotangent Function Needs to Be Approximated with a Calculator**

Determine the angle of rotation necessary to transform the following equation into an equation in X and Y with no XY term. Round to the nearest tenth of a degree.

$$4x^2 + 2xy - 6y^2 - 5x + y - 2 = 0$$

Solution:

Identify the A, B, and C parameters in the equation. $\underset{A}{4x^2} + \underset{B}{2xy} - \underset{C}{6y^2} - 5x + y - 2 = 0$

Write the rotation formula. $\cot(2\theta) = \dfrac{A - C}{B}$

Let $A = 4, B = 2,$ and $C = -6$. $\cot(2\theta) = \dfrac{4 - (-6)}{2}$

Simplify. $\cot(2\theta) = 5$

Apply the reciprocal identity. $\tan(2\theta) = \dfrac{1}{5} = 0.2$

Write the result as an inverse tangent function. $2\theta = \tan^{-1}(0.2)$

With a calculator, evaluate the right side of the equation. $2\theta \approx 11.31°$

Solve for θ and round to the nearest tenth of a degree. $\boxed{\theta = 5.7°}$

Special attention must be given when evaluating the inverse tangent function on a calculator, because the result is always in quadrant I or IV. If 2θ turns out to be negative, then 180° must be added so that 2θ is in quadrant II (as opposed to quadrant IV). Then θ will be an acute angle lying in quadrant I.

Recall that we stated (without proof) in Section 9.1 that we can identify a general equation

$$Ax^2 + Bxy + Cy^2 + Dx + Ey + F = 0$$

as that of a particular conic depending on the discriminant.

Parabola	$B^2 - 4AC = 0$
Ellipse	$B^2 - 4AC < 0$
Hyperbola	$B^2 - 4AC > 0$

EXAMPLE 5 Graphing a Rotated Conic

For the equation $x^2 + 2xy + y^2 - \sqrt{2}x - 3\sqrt{2}y + 6 = 0$:

a. Determine which conic the equation represents.

b. Find the rotation angle required to eliminate the *XY* term in the new coordinate system.

c. Transform the equation in *x* and *y* into an equation in *X* and *Y*.

d. Graph the resulting conic.

Solution (a):

Identify *A*, *B*, and *C*. $\underset{A}{1}x^2 + \underset{B}{2}xy + \underset{C}{1}y^2 - \sqrt{2}x - 3\sqrt{2}y + 6 = 0$

$$A = 1, B = 2, C = 1$$

Compute the discriminant. $B^2 - 4AC = 2^2 - 4(1)(1) = 0$

Since the discriminant equals zero, the equation represents a **parabola**.

[CONCEPT CHECK]

TRUE OR FALSE The rotation angle may be acute or obtuse.

ANSWER False

Solution (b):

Write the rotation formula. $\cot(2\theta) = \dfrac{A - C}{B}$

Let $A = 1, B = 2$, and $C = 1$. $\cot(2\theta) = \dfrac{1 - 1}{2}$

Simplify. $\cot(2\theta) = 0$

Write the cotangent function in terms of the sine and cosine functions. $\dfrac{\cos(2\theta)}{\sin(2\theta)} = 0$

The numerator must equal zero. $\cos(2\theta) = 0$

From our knowledge of trigonometric exact values, we know that $2\theta = 90°$ or $\boxed{\theta = 45°}$.

Solution (c):

Start with the equation $x^2 + 2xy + y^2 - \sqrt{2}x - 3\sqrt{2}y + 6 = 0$, and use the rotation formulas with $\theta = 45°$.

$$x = X\cos 45° - Y\sin 45° = \frac{\sqrt{2}}{2}(X - Y)$$

$$y = X\sin 45° + Y\cos 45° = \frac{\sqrt{2}}{2}(X + Y)$$

Find x^2, xy, and y^2.

$$x^2 = \left[\frac{\sqrt{2}}{2}(X - Y)\right]^2 = \frac{1}{2}(X^2 - 2XY + Y^2)$$

$$xy = \left[\frac{\sqrt{2}}{2}(X - Y)\right]\left[\frac{\sqrt{2}}{2}(X + Y)\right] = \frac{1}{2}(X^2 - Y^2)$$

$$y^2 = \left[\frac{\sqrt{2}}{2}(X + Y)\right]^2 = \frac{1}{2}(X^2 + 2XY + Y^2)$$

Substitute the values for x, y, x^2, xy, and y^2 into the original equation.

$$x^2 + 2xy + y^2 - \sqrt{2}x - 3\sqrt{2}y + 6 = 0$$

$$\frac{1}{2}(X^2 - 2XY + Y^2) + 2\frac{1}{2}(X^2 - Y^2) + \frac{1}{2}(X^2 + 2XY + Y^2) - \sqrt{2}\left[\frac{\sqrt{2}}{2}(X - Y)\right] - 3\sqrt{2}\left[\frac{\sqrt{2}}{2}(X + Y)\right] + 6 = 0$$

Eliminate the parentheses and combine like terms.

$$2X^2 - 4X - 2Y + 6 = 0$$

Divide by 2.

$$X^2 - 2X - Y + 3 = 0$$

Add Y.

$$Y = (X^2 - 2X) + 3$$

Complete the square on X.

$$Y = (X - 1)^2 + 2$$

Solution (d):

This is a parabola opening upward in the XY-coordinate system shifted to the right one unit and up two units.

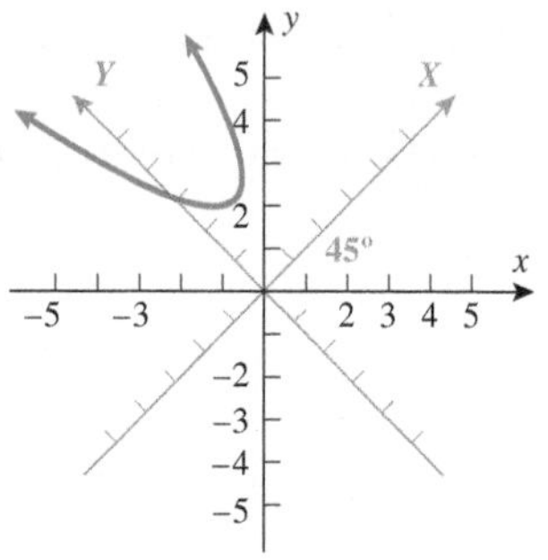

[SECTION 9.7] SUMMARY

In this section, we found that the graph of the general second-degree equation

$$Ax^2 + Bxy + Cy^2 + Dx + Ey + F = 0$$

can represent conics in a system of rotated axes.

The following are the rotation formulas relating the xy-coordinate system to a rotated coordinate system with axes X and Y.

$$x = X\cos\theta - Y\sin\theta$$
$$y = X\sin\theta + Y\cos\theta$$

where the rotation angle θ is found from the equation

$$\cot(2\theta) = \frac{A - C}{B} \quad \text{or} \quad \tan(2\theta) = \frac{B}{A - C}$$

[SECTION 9.7] EXERCISES

• SKILLS

In Exercises 1–8, the coordinates of a point in the *xy*-coordinate system are given. Assuming that the *XY*-axes are found by rotating the *xy*-axes by the given angle θ, find the corresponding coordinates for the point in the *XY* system.

1. $(2, 4), \theta = 45°$
2. $(5, 1), \theta = 60°$
3. $(-3, 2), \theta = 30°$
4. $(-4, 6), \theta = 45°$
5. $(-1, -3), \theta = 60°$
6. $(4, -4), \theta = 45°$
7. $(0, 3), \theta = 60°$
8. $(-2, 0), \theta = 30°$

In Exercises 9–24, (a) identify the type of conic from the discriminant, (b) transform the equation in *x* and *y* into an equation in *X* and *Y* (without an *XY* term) by rotating the *x*- and *y*-axes by the indicated angle θ to arrive at the new *X*- and *Y*-axes, and (c) graph the resulting equation (showing both sets of axes).

9. $xy - 1 = 0, \theta = 45°$
10. $xy - 4 = 0, \theta = 45°$
11. $x^2 + 2xy + y^2 + \sqrt{2}x - \sqrt{2}y - 1 = 0, \theta = 45°$
12. $2x^2 - 4xy + 2y^2 - \sqrt{2}x + 1 = 0, \theta = 45°$
13. $y^2 - \sqrt{3}xy + 3 = 0, \theta = 30°$
14. $x^2 - \sqrt{3}xy - 3 = 0, \theta = 60°$
15. $7x^2 - 2\sqrt{3}xy + 5y^2 - 8 = 0, \theta = 60°$
16. $4x^2 + \sqrt{3}xy + 3y^2 - 45 = 0, \theta = 30°$
17. $3x^2 + 2\sqrt{3}xy + y^2 + 2x - 2\sqrt{3}y - 2 = 0, \theta = 30°$
18. $x^2 + 2\sqrt{3}xy + 3y^2 - 2\sqrt{3}x + 2y - 4 = 0, \theta = 60°$
19. $7x^2 + 4\sqrt{3}xy + 3y^2 - 9 = 0, \theta = \frac{\pi}{6}$
20. $37x^2 + 42\sqrt{3}xy + 79y^2 - 400 = 0, \theta = \frac{\pi}{3}$
21. $7x^2 - 10\sqrt{3}xy - 3y^2 + 24 = 0, \theta = \frac{\pi}{3}$
22. $9x^2 + 14\sqrt{3}xy - 5y^2 + 48 = 0, \theta = \frac{\pi}{6}$
23. $x^2 - 2xy + y^2 - \sqrt{2}x - \sqrt{2}y - 8 = 0, \theta = \frac{\pi}{4}$
24. $x^2 + 2xy + y^2 + 3\sqrt{2}x + \sqrt{2}y = 0, \theta = \frac{\pi}{4}$

In Exercises 25–38, determine the angle of rotation necessary to transform the equation in *x* and *y* into an equation in *X* and *Y* with no *XY* term.

25. $x^2 + 4xy + y^2 - 4 = 0$
26. $3x^2 + 5xy + 3y^2 - 2 = 0$
27. $2x^2 + \sqrt{3}xy + 3y^2 - 1 = 0$
28. $4x^2 + \sqrt{3}xy + 3y^2 - 1 = 0$
29. $2x^2 + \sqrt{3}xy + y^2 - 5 = 0$
30. $2\sqrt{3}x^2 + xy + 3\sqrt{3}y^2 + 1 = 0$
31. $\sqrt{2}x^2 + xy + \sqrt{2}y^2 - 1 = 0$
32. $x^2 + 10xy + y^2 + 2 = 0$
33. $12\sqrt{3}x^2 + 4xy + 8\sqrt{3}y^2 - 1 = 0$
34. $4x^2 + 2xy + 2y^2 - 7 = 0$
35. $5x^2 + 6xy + 4y^2 - 1 = 0$
36. $x^2 + 2xy + 12y^2 + 3 = 0$
37. $3x^2 + 10xy + 5y^2 - 1 = 0$
38. $10x^2 + 3xy + 2y^2 + 3 = 0$

In Exercises 39–48, graph the second-degree equation. (*Hint:* Transform the equation into an equation that contains no *xy* term.)

39. $21x^2 + 10\sqrt{3}xy + 31y^2 - 144 = 0$
40. $5x^2 + 6xy + 5y^2 - 8 = 0$
41. $8x^2 - 20xy + 8y^2 + 18 = 0$
42. $3y^2 - 26\sqrt{3}xy - 23x^2 - 144 = 0$
43. $3x^2 + 2\sqrt{3}xy + y^2 + 2x - 2\sqrt{3}y - 12 = 0$
44. $3x^2 - 2\sqrt{3}xy + y^2 - 2x - 2\sqrt{3}y - 4 = 0$
45. $37x^2 - 42\sqrt{3}xy + 79y^2 - 400 = 0$
46. $71x^2 - 58\sqrt{3}xy + 13y^2 + 400 = 0$
47. $x^2 + 2xy + y^2 + 5\sqrt{2}x + 3\sqrt{2}y = 0$
48. $7x^2 - 4\sqrt{3}xy + 3y^2 - 9 = 0$

• CONCEPTUAL

In Exercises 49–52, determine whether each statement is true or false.

49. The graph of the equation $x^2 + kxy + 9y^2 = 5$, where k is any positive constant less than 6, is an ellipse.
50. The graph of the equation $x^2 + kxy + 9y^2 = 5$, where k is any constant greater than 6, is a parabola.
51. The reciprocal function is a rotated hyperbola.
52. The equation $\sqrt{x} + \sqrt{y} = 3$ can be transformed into the equation $X^2 + Y^2 = 9$.

• CHALLENGE

53. Determine the equation in X and Y that corresponds to $\frac{x^2}{a^2} + \frac{y^2}{b^2} = 1$ when the axes are rotated through

    a. 90° b. 180°

54. Determine the equation in X and Y that corresponds to $\frac{x^2}{a^2} - \frac{y^2}{b^2} = 1$ when the axes are rotated through

    a. 90° b. 180°

55. Identify the conic section with equation $y^2 + ax^2 = x$ for $a < 0$, $a > 0$, $a = 0$, and $a = 1$.

56. Identify the conic section with equation $x^2 - ay^2 = y$ for $a < 0$, $a > 0$, $a = 0$, and $a = 1$.

• PREVIEW TO CALCULUS

In calculus, when finding the area between two curves, we need to find the points of intersection of the curves.

In Exercises 57–60, find the points of intersection of the rotated conic sections.

57. $x^2 + 2xy = 10$
    $3x^2 - xy = 2$

58. $x^2 - 3xy + 2y^2 = 0$
    $x^2 + xy = 6$

59. $2x^2 - 7xy + 2y^2 = -1$
    $x^2 - 3xy + y^2 = 1$

60. $4x^2 + xy + 4y^2 = 22$
    $-3x^2 + 2xy - 3y^2 = -11$

9.8 POLAR EQUATIONS OF CONICS

SKILLS OBJECTIVE

■ Express equations of conics in polar form and graph them.

CONCEPTUAL OBJECTIVE

■ Define all conics in terms of a focus and a directrix.

9.8.1 Equations of Conics in Polar Coordinates

9.8.1 SKILL

Express equations of conics in polar form and graph them.

9.8.1 CONCEPTUAL

Define all conics in terms of a focus and a directrix.

In Section 9.1, we discussed parabolas, ellipses, and hyperbolas in terms of geometric definitions. Then, in Sections 9.2–9.4, we examined the rectangular equations of these conics. The equations for ellipses and hyperbolas when their centers are at the origin were simpler than when they were not (when the conics were shifted). In Section 7.5, we discussed polar coordinates and graphing of polar equations. In this section, we develop a more unified definition of the three conics in terms of a single focus and a directrix. You will see in this section that if the *focus* is located at the origin, then equations of conics are simpler when written in polar coordinates.

Alternative Definition of Conics

Recall that when we work with rectangular coordinates, we define a parabola (Sections 9.1 and 9.2) in terms of a fixed point (focus) and a line (directrix), whereas we define an ellipse and hyperbola (Sections 9.1, 9.3, and 9.4) in terms of two fixed points (the foci). However, it is possible to define all three conics in terms of a single focus and a directrix.

The following alternative representation of conics depends on a parameter called *eccentricity*.

ALTERNATIVE DESCRIPTION OF CONICS

Let D be a fixed line (the **directrix**), F be a fixed point (a **focus**) not on D, and e be a fixed positive number (**eccentricity**). The set of all points P such that the ratio of the distance from P to F to the distance from P to D equals the constant e defines a conic section.

$$\frac{d(P, F)}{d(P, D)} = e$$

- If $e = 1$, the conic is a **parabola**.
- If $e < 1$, the conic is an **ellipse**.
- If $e > 1$, the conic is a **hyperbola**.

When $e = 1$, the result is a parabola, described by the same definition we used previously in Section 9.1. When $e \neq 1$, the result is either an ellipse or a hyperbola. The major axis of an ellipse passes through the focus and is perpendicular to the directrix. The transverse axis of a hyperbola also passes through the focus and is perpendicular to the directrix. If we let c represent the distance from the focus to the center and let a represent the distance from the vertex to the center, then eccentricity is given by

$$e = \frac{c}{a}$$

In polar coordinates, if we locate the focus of a conic at the pole, and the directrix is either perpendicular or parallel to the polar axis, then we have four possible scenarios:

- The directrix is *perpendicular* to the polar axis and p units to the *right* of the pole.
- The directrix is *perpendicular* to the polar axis and p units to the *left* of the pole.
- The directrix is *parallel* to the polar axis and p units *above* the pole.
- The directrix is *parallel* to the polar axis and p units *below* the pole.

Let us take the case in which the directrix is perpendicular to the polar axis and p units to the right of the pole.

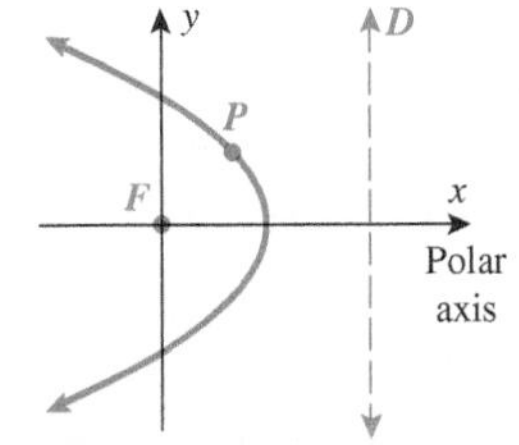

In polar coordinates (r, θ), we see that the distance from the focus to a point P is equal to r, that is, $d(P, F) = r$, and the distance from P to the closest point on the directrix is $d(P, D) = p - r\cos\theta$.

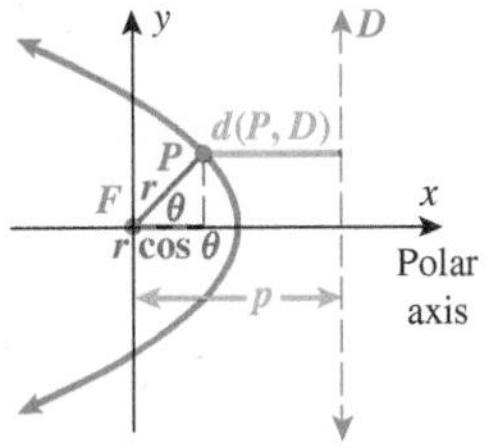

WORDS	MATH
Substitute $d(P, F) = r$ and $d(P, D) = p - r\cos\theta$ into the formula for eccentricity, $\frac{d(P, F)}{d(P, D)} = e$.	$\frac{r}{p - r\cos\theta} = e$
Multiply the result by $p - r\cos\theta$.	$r = e(p - r\cos\theta)$
Eliminate the parentheses.	$r = ep - er\cos\theta$
Add $er\cos\theta$ to both sides of the equation.	$r + er\cos\theta = ep$
Factor out the common r.	$r(1 + e\cos\theta) = ep$
Divide both sides by $1 + e\cos\theta$.	$\boxed{r = \frac{ep}{1 + e\cos\theta}}$

We need not derive the other three cases here, but note that if the directrix is perpendicular to the polar axis and p units to the *left* of the pole, the resulting polar equation is

$$r = \frac{ep}{1 - e\cos\theta}$$

If the directrix is parallel to the polar axis, the directrix is either above $(y = p)$ or below $(y = -p)$ the polar axis and we get the sine function instead of the cosine function, as summarized in the following box:

POLAR EQUATIONS OF CONICS

The following polar equations represent conics with one focus at the origin and with eccentricity e. It is assumed that the positive x-axis represents the polar axis.

EQUATION	DESCRIPTION
$r = \frac{ep}{1 + e\cos\theta}$	The directrix is *vertical* and p units to the *right* of the pole.
$r = \frac{ep}{1 - e\cos\theta}$	The directrix is *vertical* and p units to the *left* of the pole.
$r = \frac{ep}{1 + e\sin\theta}$	The directrix is *horizontal* and p units *above* the pole.
$r = \frac{ep}{1 - e\sin\theta}$	The directrix is *horizontal* and p units *below* the pole.

ECCENTRICITY	THE CONIC IS A(N) ______	THE ______ IS PERPENDICULAR TO THE DIRECTRIX
$e = 1$	Parabola	Axis of symmetry
$e < 1$	Ellipse	Major axis
$e > 1$	Hyperbola	Transverse axis

EXAMPLE 1 **Finding the Polar Equation of a Conic**

Find a polar equation for a parabola that has its focus at the origin and whose directrix is the line $y = 3$.

Solution:

The directrix is horizontal and above the pole. $r = \dfrac{ep}{1 + e\sin\theta}$

A parabola has eccentricity $e = 1$, and we know that $p = 3$. $\boxed{r = \dfrac{3}{1 + \sin\theta}}$

YOUR TURN Find a polar equation for a parabola that has its focus at the origin and whose directrix is the line $x = -3$.

[CONCEPT CHECK]

TRUE OR FALSE The polar equation for a parabola with a vertical directrix is $r = \dfrac{p}{1 \pm \cos\theta}$.

ANSWER True

ANSWER

$r = \dfrac{3}{1 - \cos\theta}$

EXAMPLE 2 **Identifying a Conic from Its Equation**

Identify the type of conic represented by the equation $r = \dfrac{10}{3 + 2\cos\theta}$.

Solution:

To identify the type of conic, we need to rewrite the equation in this form: $r = \dfrac{ep}{1 \pm e\cos\theta}$

Divide the numerator and denominator by 3. $r = \dfrac{\frac{10}{3}}{\left(1 + \frac{2}{3}\cos\theta\right)}$

Identify e in the denominator. $= \dfrac{\frac{10}{3}}{\left(1 + \underbrace{\frac{2}{3}}_{e}\cos\theta\right)}$

The numerator is equal to ep. $= \dfrac{\underbrace{5}_{p}\cdot\overbrace{\frac{2}{3}}^{e}}{\left(1 + \underbrace{\frac{2}{3}}_{e}\cos\theta\right)}$

Since $e = \frac{2}{3} < 1$, the conic is an $\boxed{\text{ellipse}}$. The directrix is $x = 5$, so the major axis is along the x-axis (perpendicular to the directrix).

YOUR TURN Identify the type of conic represented by the equation

$$r = \frac{10}{2 - 10\sin\theta}$$

ANSWER

hyperbola, $e = 5$, with transverse axis along the y-axis

In Example 2 we found that the polar equation $r = \dfrac{10}{3 + 2\cos\theta}$ is an ellipse with its major axis along the x-axis. We will graph this ellipse in Example 3.

EXAMPLE 3 Graphing a Conic from Its Equation

The graph of the polar equation $r = \dfrac{10}{3 + 2\cos\theta}$ is an ellipse.

a. Find the vertices.

b. Find the center of the ellipse.

c. Find the lengths of the major and minor axes.

d. Graph the ellipse.

Solution (a):

From Example 2 we see that $e = \frac{2}{3}$, which corresponds to an ellipse, and $x = 5$ is the directrix.

The major axis is perpendicular to the directrix. Therefore, the major axis lies along the polar axis. To find the vertices (which lie along the major axis), let $\theta = 0$ and $\theta = \pi$.

$\theta = 0$: $\quad r = \dfrac{10}{3 + 2\cos\theta} = \dfrac{10}{5} = 2$

$\theta = \pi$: $\quad r = \dfrac{10}{3 + 2\cos\pi} = \dfrac{10}{1} = 10$

The vertices are the points $\boxed{V_1 = (2, 0)}$ and $\boxed{V_2 = (10, \pi)}$.

Solution (b):

The vertices in rectangular coordinates are $V_1 = (2, 0)$ and $V_2 = (-10, 0)$.

The midpoint (in rectangular coordinates) between the two vertices is the point $(-4, 0)$, which corresponds to the point $\boxed{(4, \pi)}$ in polar coordinates.

Solution (c):

The length of the major axis, $2a$, is the distance between the vertices. $\quad \boxed{2a = 12}$

The length $a = 6$ corresponds to the distance from the center to a vertex.

Apply the formula $e = \dfrac{c}{a}$ with $a = 6$ and $e = \frac{2}{3}$ to find c. $\quad c = ae = 6\left(\dfrac{2}{3}\right) = 4$

Let $a = 6$ and $c = 4$ in $b^2 = a^2 - c^2$. $\quad b^2 = 6^2 - 4^2 = 20$

Solve for b. $\quad b = 2\sqrt{5}$

The length of the minor axis is $\boxed{2b = 4\sqrt{5}}$.

Solution (d):

Graph the ellipse.

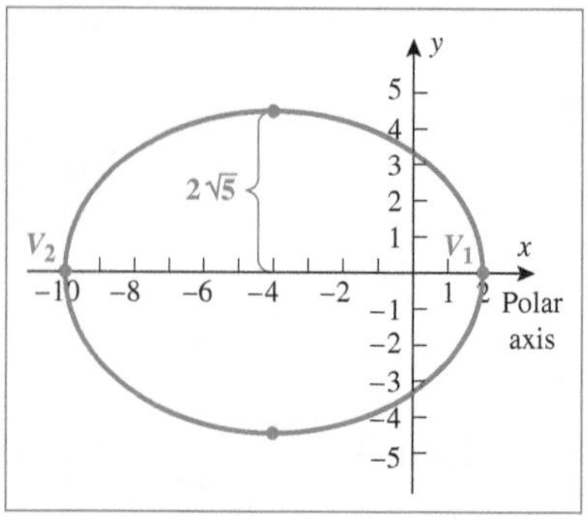

EXAMPLE 4 **Identifying and Graphing a Conic from Its Equation**

Identify and graph the conic defined by the equation $r = \dfrac{2}{2 + 3\sin\theta}$.

Solution:

Rewrite the equation in the form $r = \dfrac{ep}{1 + e\sin\theta}$.

$$r = \frac{2}{2 + 3\sin\theta} = \frac{\overbrace{\left(\frac{2}{3}\right)}^{p}\overbrace{\left(\frac{3}{2}\right)}^{e}}{1 + \underbrace{\left(\frac{3}{2}\right)}_{e}\sin\theta}$$

The conic is a *hyperbola* since $e = \frac{3}{2} > 1$.

The directrix is horizontal and $\frac{2}{3}$ unit above the pole (origin).

To find the vertices, let $\theta = \dfrac{\pi}{2}$ and $\theta = \dfrac{3\pi}{2}$.

$\theta = \dfrac{\pi}{2}$: $$r = \frac{2}{2 + 3\sin\left(\frac{\pi}{2}\right)} = \frac{2}{5}$$

$\theta = \dfrac{3\pi}{2}$: $$r = \frac{2}{2 + 3\sin\left(\frac{3\pi}{2}\right)} = \frac{2}{-1} = -2$$

The vertices in polar coordinates are $\left(\frac{2}{5}, \frac{\pi}{2}\right)$ and $\left(-2, \frac{3\pi}{2}\right)$.

The vertices in rectangular coordinates are $V_1 = \left(0, \frac{2}{5}\right)$ and $V_2 = (0, 2)$.

The center is the midpoint between the vertices: $\left(0, \frac{6}{5}\right)$.

The distance from the center to a focus is $c = \frac{6}{5}$.

Apply the formula $e = \dfrac{c}{a}$ with $c = \dfrac{6}{5}$ and $e = \dfrac{3}{2}$ to find a.

$$a = \frac{c}{e} = \frac{\frac{6}{5}}{\frac{3}{2}} = \frac{4}{5}$$

Let $a = \frac{4}{5}$ and $c = \frac{6}{5}$ in $b^2 = c^2 - a^2$.

$$b^2 = \left(\frac{6}{5}\right)^2 - \left(\frac{4}{5}\right)^2 = \frac{20}{25}$$

Solve for b.

$$b = \frac{2\sqrt{5}}{5}$$

The asymptotes are given by $y = \pm\dfrac{a}{b}(x - h) + k$, where $a = \dfrac{4}{5}$, $b = \dfrac{2\sqrt{5}}{5}$, and $(h, k) = \left(0, \dfrac{6}{5}\right)$.

$$y = \pm\frac{2}{\sqrt{5}}x + \frac{6}{5}$$

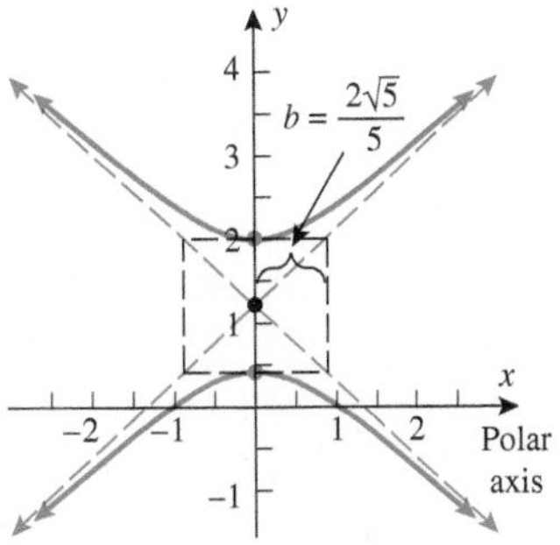

It is important to note that although we relate specific points (vertices, foci, etc.) to rectangular coordinates, another approach to making a rough sketch is to simply point-plot the equation in polar coordinates.

EXAMPLE 5 Graphing a Conic by Point-Plotting in Polar Coordinates

Sketch a graph of the conic $r = \dfrac{4}{1 - \sin\theta}$.

Solution:

STEP 1 The conic is a parabola because the equation is in the form

$$r = \frac{(4)(1)}{1 - (1)\sin\theta}$$

Make a table with key values for θ and r.

θ	$r = \dfrac{4}{1 - \sin\theta}$	(r, θ)
0	$r = \dfrac{4}{1 - \sin 0} = \dfrac{4}{1} = 4$	$(4, 0)$
$\dfrac{\pi}{2}$	$r = \dfrac{4}{1 - \sin\dfrac{\pi}{2}} = \dfrac{4}{1 - 1} = \dfrac{4}{0}$	undefined
π	$r = \dfrac{4}{1 - \sin\pi} = \dfrac{4}{1} = 4$	$(4, \pi)$
$\dfrac{3\pi}{2}$	$r = \dfrac{4}{1 - \sin\dfrac{3\pi}{2}} = \dfrac{4}{1 - (-1)} = \dfrac{4}{2} = 2$	$\left(2, \dfrac{3\pi}{2}\right)$
2π	$r = \dfrac{4}{1 - \sin(2\pi)} = \dfrac{4}{1} = 4$	$(4, 2\pi)$

STEP 2 Plot the points on a polar graph and connect them with a smooth parabolic curve.

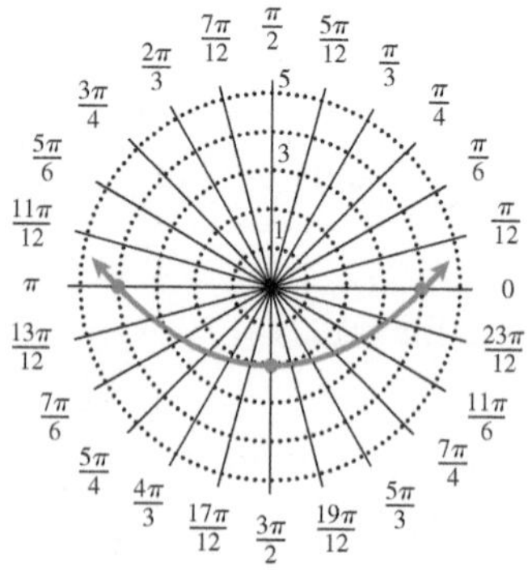

[SECTION 9.8] SUMMARY

In this section, we found that we could graph polar equations of conics by identifying a single focus and the directrix. There are four possible equations in terms of eccentricity e:

EQUATION	DESCRIPTION
$r = \dfrac{ep}{1 + e\cos\theta}$	The directrix is *vertical* and p units to the *right* of the pole.
$r = \dfrac{ep}{1 - e\cos\theta}$	The directrix is *vertical* and p units to the *left* of the pole.
$r = \dfrac{ep}{1 + e\sin\theta}$	The directrix is *horizontal* and p units *above* the pole.
$r = \dfrac{ep}{1 - e\sin\theta}$	The directrix is *horizontal* and p units *below* the pole.

[SECTION 9.8] EXERCISES

• SKILLS

In Exercises 1–14, find the polar equation that represents the conic described (assume that a focus is at the origin).

	Conic	Eccentricity	Directrix
1.	Ellipse	$e = \frac{1}{2}$	$y = -5$
2.	Ellipse	$e = \frac{1}{3}$	$y = 3$
3.	Hyperbola	$e = 2$	$y = 4$
4.	Hyperbola	$e = 3$	$y = -2$
5.	Parabola	$e = 1$	$x = 1$
6.	Parabola	$e = 1$	$x = -1$
7.	Ellipse	$e = \frac{3}{4}$	$x = 2$
8.	Ellipse	$e = \frac{2}{3}$	$x = -4$
9.	Hyperbola	$e = \frac{4}{3}$	$x = -3$
10.	Hyperbola	$e = \frac{3}{2}$	$x = 5$
11.	Parabola	$e = 1$	$y = -3$
12.	Parabola	$e = 1$	$y = 4$
13.	Ellipse	$e = \frac{3}{5}$	$y = 6$
14.	Hyperbola	$e = \frac{8}{5}$	$y = 5$

In Exercises 15–26, identify the conic (parabola, ellipse, or hyperbola) that each polar equation represents.

15. $r = \dfrac{4}{1 + \cos\theta}$

16. $r = \dfrac{3}{2 - 3\sin\theta}$

17. $r = \dfrac{2}{3 + 2\sin\theta}$

18. $r = \dfrac{3}{2 - 2\cos\theta}$

19. $r = \dfrac{2}{4 + 8\cos\theta}$

20. $r = \dfrac{1}{4 - \cos\theta}$

21. $r = \dfrac{7}{3 + \cos\theta}$

22. $r = \dfrac{4}{5 + 6\sin\theta}$

23. $r = \dfrac{40}{5 + 5\sin\theta}$

24. $r = \dfrac{5}{5 - 4\sin\theta}$

25. $r = \dfrac{1}{1 - 6\cos\theta}$

26. $r = \dfrac{5}{3 - 3\sin\theta}$

In Exercises 27–42, for the given polar equation: (a) identify the conic as either a parabola, an ellipse, or a hyperbola; (b) find the eccentricity and vertex (or vertices); and (c) graph.

27. $r = \dfrac{2}{1 + \sin\theta}$

28. $r = \dfrac{4}{1 - \cos\theta}$

29. $r = \dfrac{4}{1 - 2\sin\theta}$

30. $r = \dfrac{3}{3 + 8\cos\theta}$

31. $r = \dfrac{2}{2 + \sin\theta}$

32. $r = \dfrac{1}{3 - \sin\theta}$

33. $r = \dfrac{1}{2 - 2\sin\theta}$

34. $r = \dfrac{1}{1 - 2\sin\theta}$

35. $r = \dfrac{4}{3 + \cos\theta}$

36. $r = \dfrac{2}{5 + 4\sin\theta}$

37. $r = \dfrac{6}{2 + 3\sin\theta}$

38. $r = \dfrac{6}{1 + \cos\theta}$

39. $r = \dfrac{2}{5 + 5\cos\theta}$

40. $r = \dfrac{10}{6 - 3\cos\theta}$

41. $r = \dfrac{6}{3\cos\theta + 1}$

42. $r = \dfrac{15}{3\sin\theta + 5}$

• APPLICATIONS

For Exercises 43 and 44, refer to the following:

Planets travel in elliptical orbits around a single focus, the Sun. Pluto (orange), the dwarf planet farthest from the Sun, has a pronounced elliptical orbit, whereas Earth (royal blue) has an almost circular orbit. The polar equation of a planet's orbit can be expressed as

$$r = \frac{a(1 - e^2)}{(1 - e\cos\theta)}$$

where e is the eccentricity and $2a$ is the length of the major axis. It can also be shown that the perihelion distance (minimum distance from the Sun to a planet) and the aphelion distance (maximum distance from the Sun to the planet) can be represented by $r = a(1 - e)$ and $r = a(1 + e)$, respectively.

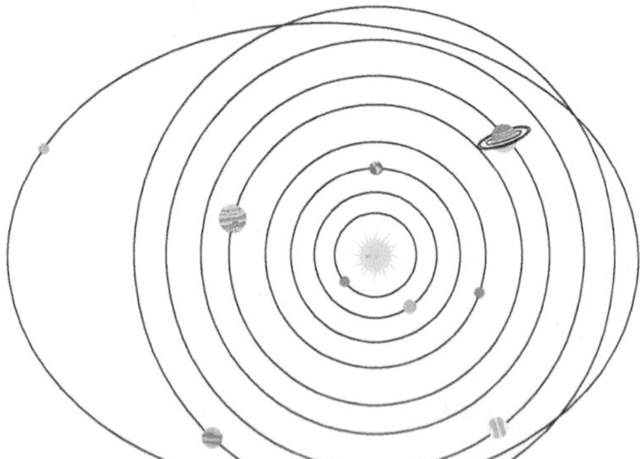

43. **Planetary Orbits.** Pluto's orbit is summarized in the picture below. Find the eccentricity of Pluto's orbit. Find the polar equation that governs Pluto's orbit.

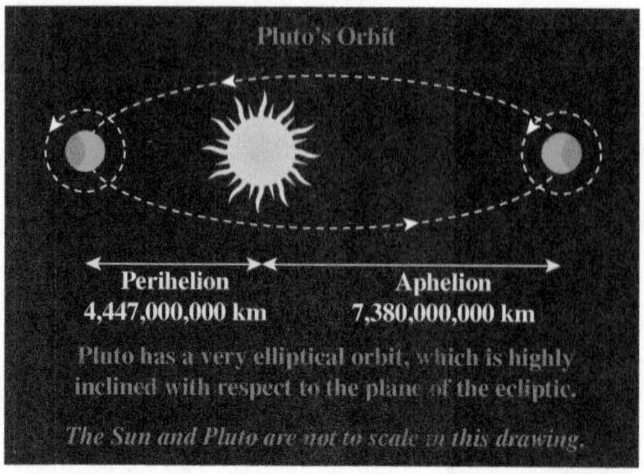

44. **Planetary Orbits.** Earth's orbit is summarized in the picture below. Find the eccentricity of Earth's orbit. Find the polar equation that governs Earth's orbit.

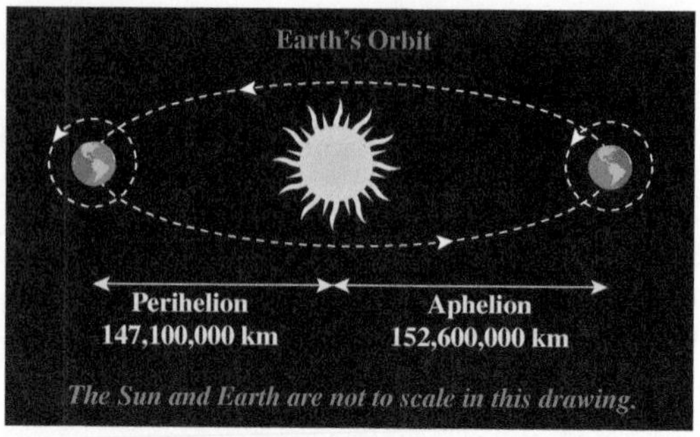

For Exercises 45 and 46, refer to the following:

Asteroids, meteors, and comets all orbit the Sun in elliptical patterns and often cross paths with Earth's orbit, making life a little tense now and again. Asteroids are large rocks (bodies under 1000 kilometers across), meteors range from sand particles to rocks, and comets are masses of debris. A few asteroids have orbits that cross Earth's orbits—called Apollos or Earth-crossing asteroids. In recent years, asteroids have passed within 100,000 kilometers of Earth!

45. **Asteroids.** The asteroid 433 or Eros is the second largest near-Earth asteroid. The semimajor axis of its orbit is 150 million kilometers and the eccentricity is 0.223. Find the polar equation of Eros's orbit.

46. **Asteroids.** The asteroid Toutatis is the largest near-Earth asteroid. The semimajor axis of its orbit is 350 million kilometers and the eccentricity is 0.634. On September 29, 2004, it missed Earth by 961,000 miles. Find the polar equation of Toutatis's orbit.

47. **Earth's Orbit.** A simplified model of Earth's orbit around the Sun is given by $r = \dfrac{1}{1 + 0.0167\cos\theta}$. Find the center of the orbit in

    a. rectangular coordinates

    b. polar coordinates

48. **Uranus's Orbit.** A simplified model of Uranus's orbit around the Sun is given by $r = \dfrac{1}{1 + 0.0461\cos\theta}$. Find the center of the orbit in

    a. rectangular coordinates

    b. polar coordinates

49. Orbit of Halley's Comet. A simplified model of the orbit of Halley's Comet around the Sun is given by $r = \frac{1}{1 + 0.967\sin\theta}$. Find the center of the orbit in rectangular coordinates.

50. Orbit of the Hale–Bopp Comet. A simplified model of the orbit of the Hale–Bopp Comet around the Sun is given by $r = \frac{1}{1 + 0.995\sin\theta}$. Find the center of the orbit in rectangular coordinates.

• CONCEPTUAL

51. When $0 < e < 1$, the conic is an ellipse. Does the conic become more elongated or elliptical as e approaches 1 or as e approaches 0?

52. Show that $r = \frac{ep}{1 - e\sin\theta}$ is the polar equation of a conic with a horizontal directrix that is p units *below* the pole.

53. Convert from rectangular to polar coordinates to show that the equation of a hyperbola, $\frac{x^2}{a^2} - \frac{y^2}{b^2} = 1$, in polar form is $r^2 = -\frac{b^2}{1 - e^2\cos^2\theta}$.

54. Convert from rectangular to polar coordinates to show that the equation of an ellipse, $\frac{x^2}{a^2} + \frac{y^2}{b^2} = 1$, in polar form is $r^2 = \frac{b^2}{1 - e^2\cos^2\theta}$.

• CHALLENGE

55. Find the major diameter of the ellipse with polar equation $r = \frac{ep}{1 + e\cos\theta}$ in terms of e and p.

56. Find the minor diameter of the ellipse with polar equation $r = \frac{ep}{1 + e\cos\theta}$ in terms of e and p.

57. Find the center of the ellipse with polar equation $r = \frac{ep}{1 + e\cos\theta}$ in terms of e and p.

58. Find the length of the latus rectum of the parabola with polar equation $r = \frac{p}{1 + \cos\theta}$. Assume that the focus is at the origin.

• PREVIEW TO CALCULUS

In calculus, when finding the area between two polar curves, we need to find the points of intersection of the two curves. In Exercises 59–62, find the values of θ where the two conic sections intersect on $[0, 2\pi]$.

59. $r = \frac{2}{2 + \sin\theta}$, $r = \frac{2}{2 + \cos\theta}$

60. $r = \frac{1}{3 + 2\sin\theta}$, $r = \frac{1}{3 - 2\sin\theta}$

61. $r = \frac{1}{4 - 3\sin\theta}$, $r = \frac{1}{-1 + 7\sin\theta}$

62. $r = \frac{1}{5 + 2\cos\theta}$, $r = \frac{1}{10 - 8\cos\theta}$

9.9 PARAMETRIC EQUATIONS AND GRAPHS

SKILLS OBJECTIVES

- Graph parametric equations.
- Graph cycloids and the curves representing projectile motion.

CONCEPTUAL OBJECTIVES

- Understand that the results of increasing the value of the parameter reveal the orientation of a curve or the direction of motion along it.
- Use time as a parameter in parametric equations such as those representing cycloids and projectile motion.

9.9.1 Parametric Equations of a Curve

9.9.1 SKILL

Graph parametric equations.

9.9.1 CONCEPTUAL

Understand that the results of increasing the value of the parameter reveal the orientation of a curve or the direction of motion along it.

Thus far we have talked about graphs in planes. For example, the equation $x^2 + y^2 = 1$, when graphed in a plane, is the unit circle. Similarly, the function $f(x) = \sin x$, when graphed in a plane is, a sinusoidal curve. Now, we consider the **path along a curve**. For example, if a car is being driven on a circular racetrack, we want to see the movement along the circle. We can determine where (position) along the circle the car is, at some time t, using *parametric equations*. Before we define *parametric equations* in general, let us start with a simple example.

Let $x = \cos t$ and $y = \sin t$ and $t \geq 0$. We then can make a table of some corresponding values.

t SECONDS	$x = \cos t$	$y = \sin t$	(x, y)
0	$x = \cos 0 = 1$	$y = \sin 0 = 0$	$(1, 0)$
$\frac{\pi}{2}$	$x = \cos\left(\frac{\pi}{2}\right) = 0$	$y = \sin\left(\frac{\pi}{2}\right) = 1$	$(0, 1)$
π	$x = \cos \pi = -1$	$y = \sin \pi = 0$	$(-1, 0)$
$\frac{3\pi}{2}$	$x = \cos\left(\frac{3\pi}{2}\right) = 0$	$y = \sin\left(\frac{3\pi}{2}\right) = -1$	$(0, -1)$
2π	$x = \cos(2\pi) = 1$	$y = \sin(2\pi) = 0$	$(1, 0)$

If we plot these points and note the correspondence to time (by converting all numbers to decimals), we will be tracing a *path* counterclockwise along the unit circle.

TIME (SECONDS)	$t = 0$	$t = 1.57$	$t = 3.14$	$t = 4.71$
POSITION	$(1, 0)$	$(0, 1)$	$(-1, 0)$	$(0, -1)$

Notice that at time $t = 6.28$ seconds we are back to the point $(1, 0)$.

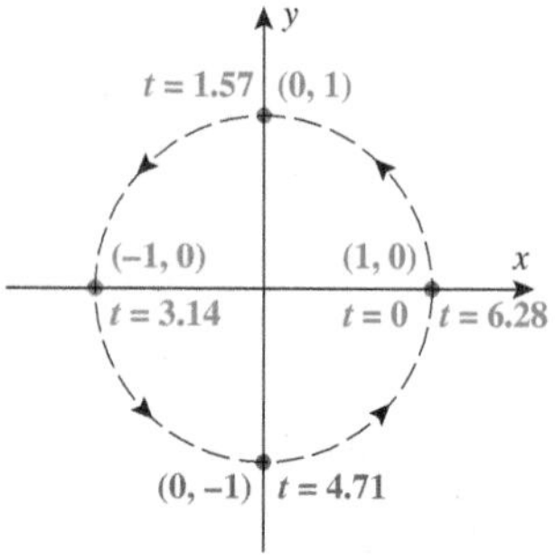

We can see that the path represents the unit circle, since $x^2 + y^2 = \cos^2 t + \sin^2 t = 1$.

DEFINITION **Parametric Equations**

Let $x = f(t)$ and $y = g(t)$ be functions defined for t on some interval. The set of points $(x, y) = [f(t), g(t)]$ represents a **plane curve**. The equations

$$x = f(t) \qquad \text{and} \qquad y = g(t)$$

are called **parametric equations** of the curve. The variable t is called the **parameter**.

Parametric equations are useful for showing movement along a curve. We insert arrows in the graph to show **direction**, or **orientation**, along the curve as t increases.

EXAMPLE 1 Graphing a Curve Defined by Parametric Equations

Graph the curve defined by the parametric equations

$$x = t^2 \qquad y = (t - 1) \qquad t \text{ in } [-2, 2]$$

Indicate the orientation with arrows.

Solution:

STEP 1 Make a table and find values for t, x, and y.

t	$x = t^2$	$y = (t - 1)$	(x, y)
$t = -2$	$x = (-2)^2 = 4$	$y = (-2 - 1) = -3$	$(4, -3)$
$t = -1$	$x = (-1)^2 = 1$	$y = (-1 - 1) = -2$	$(1, -2)$
$t = 0$	$x = 0^2 = 0$	$y = (0 - 1) = -1$	$(0, -1)$
$t = 1$	$x = 1^2 = 1$	$y = (1 - 1) = 0$	$(1, 0)$
$t = 2$	$x = 2^2 = 4$	$y = (2 - 1) = 1$	$(4, 1)$

STEP 2 Plot the points in the xy-plane.

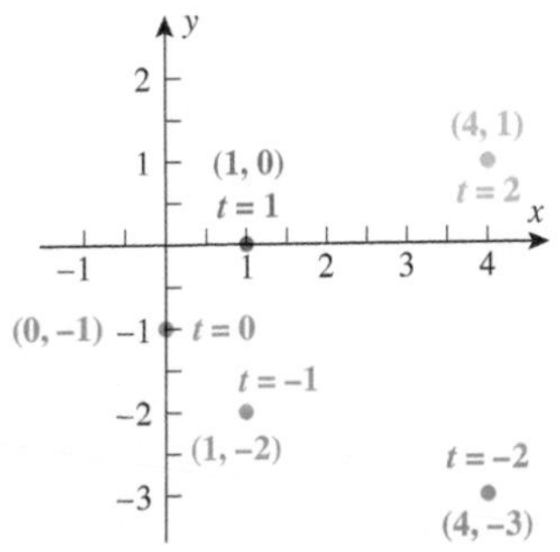

STEP 3 Connect the points with a smooth curve and use arrows to indicate direction.

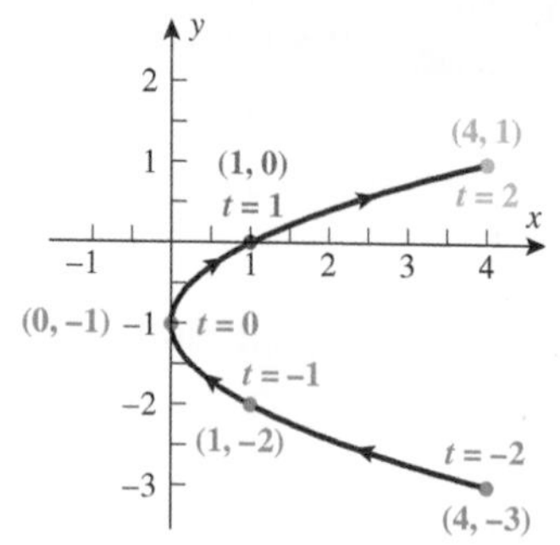

The shape of the graph appears to be a parabola. The parametric equations are $x = t^2$ and $y = (t - 1)$. If we solve the second equation for t, getting $t = y + 1$, and substitute this expression into $x = t^2$, the result is $x = (y + 1)^2$. The graph of $x = (y + 1)^2$ is a parabola with vertex at the point $(0, -1)$ and opening to the right.

YOUR TURN Graph the curve defined by the parametric equations

$$x = t + 1 \qquad y = t^2 \qquad t \text{ in } [-2, 2]$$

Indicate the orientation with arrows.

ANSWER

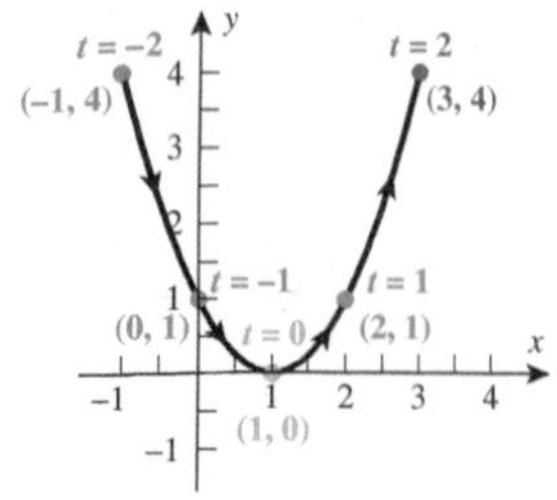

Sometimes it is easier to show the rectangular equivalent of the curve and eliminate the parameter.

EXAMPLE 2 Graphing a Curve Defined by Parametric Equations by First Finding an Equivalent Rectangular Equation

Graph the curve defined by the parametric equations

$$x = 4\cos t \qquad y = 3\sin t \qquad t \text{ is any real number}$$

Indicate the orientation with arrows.

Solution:

One approach is to point-plot as in Example 1. A second approach is to find the equivalent rectangular equation that represents the curve.

We apply the Pythagorean identity. $\sin^2 t + \cos^2 t = 1$

Find $\sin^2 t$ from the parametric equation for y. $y = 3\sin t$

Square both sides. $y^2 = 9\sin^2 t$

Divide by 9. $\sin^2 t = \dfrac{y^2}{9}$

Similarly, find $\cos^2 t$. $x = 4\cos t$

Square both sides. $x^2 = 16\cos^2 t$

Divide by 16. $\cos^2 t = \dfrac{x^2}{16}$

Substitute $\sin^2 t = \dfrac{y^2}{9}$ and $\cos^2 t = \dfrac{x^2}{16}$ into $\sin^2 t + \cos^2 t = 1$. $\dfrac{y^2}{9} + \dfrac{x^2}{16} = 1$

The curve is an ellipse centered at the origin and elongated horizontally.

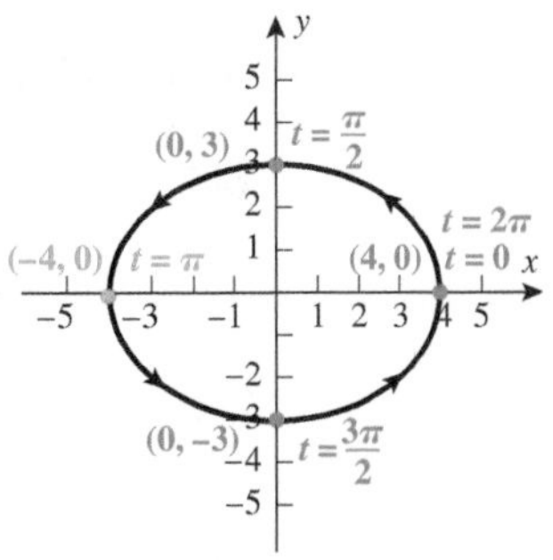

The orientation is counterclockwise. For example, when $t = 0$, the position is $(4, 0)$; when $t = \frac{\pi}{2}$, the position is $(0, 3)$; and when $t = \pi$, the position is $(-4, 0)$.

[CONCEPT CHECK]

For any curve defined by the parametric equations $x = a\cos t$, $y = b\sin t$ where t is any real number, the graph is an ellipse, and the path travelled around the ellipse is periodic with period ______

ANSWER 2π

STUDY TIP

For open curves the orientation can be determined from two values of t. However, for closed curves three points should be chosen to be sure whether the orientation is clockwise or counterclockwise.

9.9.2 Applications of Parametric Equations

Parametric equations can be used to describe motion in many applications. Two that we will discuss are the *cycloid* and a *projectile*. Suppose that you paint a red X on a bicycle tire. As the bicycle moves in a straight line, if you watch the motion of the red X, you will see that it follows the path of a **cycloid**.

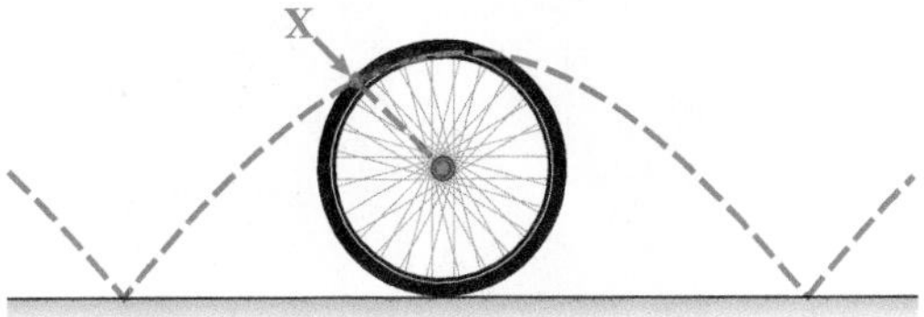

9.9.2 SKILL

Graph cycloids and the curves representing projectile motion.

9.9.2 CONCEPTUAL

Use time as a parameter in parametric equations such as those representing cycloids and projectile motion.

The parametric equations that define a cycloid are

$$x = a(t - \sin t) \quad \text{and} \quad y = a(1 - \cos t)$$

where t is any real number.

STUDY TIP

A cycloid is a curve that does not have a simple rectangular equation. The only convenient way to describe its path is with parametric equations.

EXAMPLE 3 Graphing a Cycloid

Graph the cycloid given by $x = 2(t - \sin t)$ and $y = 2(1 - \cos t)$ for t in $[0, 4\pi]$.

Solution:

STEP 1 Make a table and find key values for t, x, and y.

t	$x = 2(t - \sin t)$	$y = 2(1 - \cos t)$	(x, y)
$t = 0$	$x = 2(0 - 0) = 0$	$y = 2(1 - 1) = 0$	$(0, 0)$
$t = \pi$	$x = 2(\pi - 0) = 2\pi$	$y = 2[1 - (-1)] = 4$	$(2\pi, 4)$
$t = 2\pi$	$x = 2(2\pi - 0) = 4\pi$	$y = 2(1 - 1) = 0$	$(4\pi, 0)$
$t = 3\pi$	$x = 2(3\pi - 0) = 6\pi$	$y = 2[1 - (-1)] = 4$	$(6\pi, 4)$
$t = 4\pi$	$x = 2(4\pi - 0) = 8\pi$	$y = 2(1 - 1) = 0$	$(8\pi, 0)$

STEP 2 Plot points in a plane and connect them with a smooth curve.

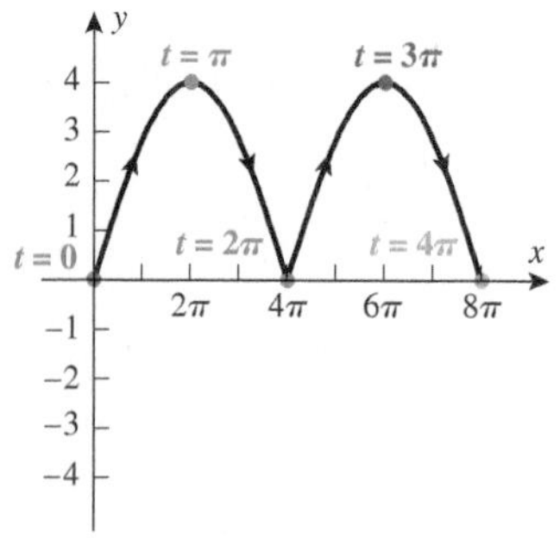

Another example of parametric equations describing real-world phenomena is *projectile motion*. The accompanying photo of a golfer hitting a golf ball presents an example of a projectile.

Fitzer/Getty Images

Let v_0 be the initial velocity of an object, θ be the initial angle of inclination with the horizontal, and h be the initial height above the ground. Then the parametric equations describing the **projectile motion** (which will be developed in calculus) are

$$\boxed{x = (v_0 \cos\theta)t} \quad \text{and} \quad \boxed{y = -\tfrac{1}{2}gt^2 + (v_0 \sin\theta)t + h}$$

where t is the time and g is the constant acceleration due to gravity (9.8 meters per square second or 32 feet per square second).

EXAMPLE 4 Graphing Projectile Motion

Suppose a golfer hits his golf ball with an initial velocity of 160 feet per second at an angle of 30° with the ground. How far is his drive, assuming the length of the drive is from the tee to where the ball first hits the ground? Graph the curve representing the path of the golf ball. Assume that he hits the ball straight off the tee and down the fairway.

Solution:

STEP 1 Find the parametric equations that describe the path of the golf ball that the golfer drove.

First, write the parametric equations for projectile motion.

$$x = (v_0 \cos\theta)t \quad \text{and} \quad y = -\tfrac{1}{2}gt^2 + (v_0 \sin\theta)t + h$$

Let $g = 32 \text{ ft/sec}^2$, $v_0 = 160 \text{ ft/sec}$, $h = 0$, and $\theta = 30°$.

$$x = (160 \cdot \cos 30°)t \quad \text{and} \quad y = -16t^2 + (160 \cdot \sin 30°)t$$

Evaluate the sine and cosine functions and simplify.

$$x = 80\sqrt{3}t \quad \text{and} \quad y = -16t^2 + 80t$$

STEP 2 Graph the projectile motion.

t	$x = 80\sqrt{3}t$	$y = -16t^2 + 80t$	(x, y)
$t = 0$	$x = 80\sqrt{3}(0) = 0$	$y = -16(0)^2 + 80(0) = 0$	$(0, 0)$
$t = 1$	$x = 80\sqrt{3}(1) \approx 139$	$y = -16(1)^2 + 80(1) = 64$	$(139, 64)$
$t = 2$	$x = 80\sqrt{3}(2) \approx 277$	$y = -16(2)^2 + 80(2) = 96$	$(277, 96)$
$t = 3$	$x = 80\sqrt{3}(3) \approx 416$	$y = -16(3)^2 + 80(3) = 96$	$(416, 96)$
$t = 4$	$x = 80\sqrt{3}(4) \approx 554$	$y = -16(4)^2 + 80(4) = 64$	$(554, 64)$
$t = 5$	$x = 80\sqrt{3}(5) \approx 693$	$y = -16(5)^2 + 80(5) = 0$	$(693, 0)$

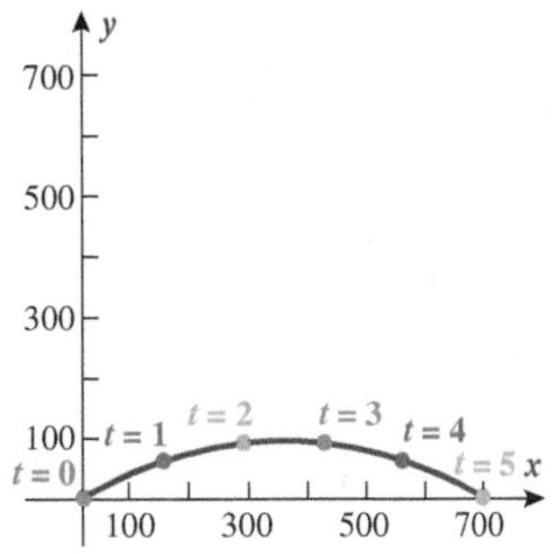

We can see that we selected our time increments well (the last point, $(693, 0)$, corresponds to the ball hitting the ground 693 feet from the tee).

STEP 3 Identify the horizontal distance from the tee to where the ball first hits the ground.

Algebraically, we can determine the distance of the tee shot by setting the height y equal to zero. $y = -16t^2 + 80t = 0$

Factor out the common term, $-16t$. $-16t(t - 5) = 0$

Solve for t. $t = 0$ or $t = 5$

The ball hits the ground after 5 seconds.

Let $t = 5$ in the horizontal distance, $x = 80\sqrt{3}t$. $x = 80\sqrt{3}(5) \approx 693$

The ball hits the ground 693 feet from the tee.

With parametric equations, we can also determine when the ball lands (5 seconds).

[CONCEPT CHECK]

TRUE OR FALSE In Example 4, the curve does extend beyond $t = 5$, but it would-correspond to $y < 0$, which is non-physical.

ANSWER True

[SECTION 9.9] SUMMARY

Parametric equations are a way of describing, as a function of t, the parameter, the path an object takes along a curve in the xy-plane. Parametric equations have equivalent rectangular equations. Typically, the method of graphing a set of parametric equations is to eliminate t and graph the corresponding rectangular equation. Once the curve is found, orientation along the curve can be determined by finding points corresponding to different t-values. Two important applications are cycloids and projectiles, whose paths we can trace using parametric equations.

[SECTION 9.9] EXERCISES

• SKILLS

In Exercises 1–30, graph the curve defined by the parametric equations.

1. $x = t + 1,\ y = \sqrt{t},\ t \geq 0$
2. $x = 3t,\ y = t^2 - 1,\ t$ in $[0, 4]$
3. $x = -3t,\ y = t^2 + 1,\ t$ in $[0, 4]$
4. $x = t^2 - 1,\ y = t^2 + 1,\ t$ in $[-3, 3]$
5. $x = t^2,\ y = t^3,\ t$ in $[-2, 2]$
6. $x = t^3 + 1,\ y = t^3 - 1,\ t$ in $[-2, 2]$
7. $x = \sqrt{t},\ y = t,\ t$ in $[0, 10]$
8. $x = t,\ y = \sqrt{t^2 + 1},\ t$ in $[0, 10]$
9. $x = (t + 1)^2,\ y = (t + 2)^3,\ t$ in $[0, 1]$
10. $x = (t - 1)^3,\ y = (t - 2)^2,\ t$ in $[0, 4]$
11. $x = e^t,\ y = e^{-t},\ -\ln 3 \leq t \leq \ln 3$
12. $x = e^{-2t},\ y = e^{2t} + 4,\ -\ln 2 \leq t \leq \ln 3$
13. $x = 2t^4 - 1,\ y = t^8 + 1,\ 0 \leq t \leq 4$
14. $x = 3t^6 - 1,\ y = 2t^3,\ -1 \leq t \leq 1$
15. $x = t(t - 2)^3,\ y = t(t - 2)^3,\ 0 \leq t \leq 4$
16. $x = -t\sqrt[3]{t},\ y = -5t^8 - 2,\ -3 \leq t \leq 3$
17. $x = 3 \sin t,\ y = 2 \cos t,\ t$ in $[0, 2\pi]$
18. $x = \cos(2t),\ y = \sin t,\ t$ in $[0, 2\pi]$
19. $x = \sin t + 1,\ y = \cos t - 2,\ t$ in $[0, 2]\pi$
20. $x = \tan t,\ y = 1,\ t$ in $\left[-\frac{\pi}{4}, \frac{\pi}{4}\right]$
21. $x = 1,\ y = \sin t,\ t$ in $[-2\pi, 2\pi]$
22. $x = \sin t,\ y = 2,\ t$ in $[0, 2\pi]$
23. $x = \sin^2 t,\ y = \cos^2 t,\ t$ in $[0, 2\pi]$
24. $x = 2\sin^2 t,\ y = 2\cos^2 t,\ t$ in $[0, 2\pi]$
25. $x = 2\sin(3t),\ y = 3\cos(2t),\ t$ in $[0, 2\pi]$
26. $x = 4\cos(2t),\ y = t,\ t$ in $[0, 2\pi]$
27. $x = \cos\left(\frac{t}{2}\right) - 1,\ y = \sin\left(\frac{t}{2}\right) + 1,\ -2\pi \leq t \leq 2\pi$
28. $x = \sin\left(\frac{t}{3}\right) + 3,\ y = \cos\left(\frac{t}{3}\right) - 1,\ 0 \leq t \leq 6\pi$
29. $x = 2\sin\left(t + \frac{\pi}{4}\right),\ y = -2\cos\left(t + \frac{\pi}{4}\right),\ -\frac{\pi}{4} \leq t \leq \frac{7\pi}{4}$
30. $x = -3\cos^2(3t),\ y = 2\cos(3t),\ -\frac{\pi}{3} \leq t \leq \frac{\pi}{3}$

In Exercises 31–40, the given parametric equations define a plane curve. Find an equation in rectangular form that also corresponds to the plane curve.

31. $x = \frac{1}{t},\ y = t^2$
32. $x = t^2 - 1,\ y = t^2 + 1$
33. $x = t^3 + 1,\ y = t^3 - 1$
34. $x = 3t,\ y = t^2 - 1$
35. $x = t,\ y = \sqrt{t^2 + 1}$
36. $x = \sin^2 t,\ y = \cos^2 t$
37. $x = 2\sin^2 t,\ y = 2\cos^2 t$
38. $x = \sec^2 t,\ y = \tan^2 t$
39. $x = 4(t^2 + 1),\ y = 1 - t^2$
40. $x = \sqrt{t - 1},\ y = \sqrt{t}$

• APPLICATIONS

For Exercises 41–50, recall that the flight of a projectile can be modeled with the parametric equations

$$x = (v_0 \cos\theta)t \qquad y = -16t^2 + (v_0 \sin\theta)t + h$$

where t is in seconds, v_0 is the initial velocity, θ is the angle with the horizontal, and x and y are in feet.

41. **Flight of a Projectile.** A projectile is launched from the ground at a speed of 400 feet per second at an angle of 45° with the horizontal. After how many seconds does the projectile hit the ground?

42. **Flight of a Projectile.** A projectile is launched from the ground at a speed of 400 feet per second at an angle of 45° with the horizontal. How far does the projectile travel (what is the horizontal distance), and what is its maximum altitude?

43. **Flight of a Baseball.** A baseball is hit at an initial speed of 105 miles per hour and an angle of 20° at a height of 3 feet above the ground. If home plate is 420 feet from the back fence, which is 15 feet tall, will the baseball clear the back fence for a home run?

44. **Flight of a Baseball.** A baseball is hit at an initial speed of 105 miles per hour and an angle of 20° at a height of 3 feet above the ground. If there is no back fence or other obstruction, how far does the baseball travel (horizontal distance), and what is its maximum height?

45. **Bullet Fired.** A gun is fired from the ground at an angle of 60°, and the bullet has an initial speed of 700 feet per second. How high does the bullet go? What is the horizontal (ground) distance between the point where the gun is fired and the point where the bullet hits the ground?

46. **Bullet Fired.** A gun is fired from the ground at an angle of 60°, and the bullet has an initial speed of 2000 feet per second. How high does the bullet go? What is the horizontal (ground) distance between the point where the gun is fired and the point where the bullet hits the ground?

47. **Missile Fired.** A missile is fired from a ship at an angle of 30°, an initial height of 20 feet above the water's surface, and a speed of 4000 feet per second. How long will it be before the missile hits the water?

48. **Missile Fired.** A missile is fired from a ship at an angle of 40°, an initial height of 20 feet above the water's surface, and a speed of 5000 feet per second. Will the missile be able to hit a target that is 2 miles away?

49. **Path of a Projectile.** A projectile is launched at a speed of 100 feet per second at an angle of 35° with the horizontal. Plot the path of the projectile on a graph. Assume that $h = 0$.

50. **Path of a Projectile.** A projectile is launched at a speed of 150 feet per second at an angle of 55° with the horizontal. Plot the path of the projectile on a graph. Assume that $h = 0$.

• CATCH THE MISTAKE

In Exercises 51 and 52, explain the mistake that is made.

51. Find the rectangular equation that corresponds to the plane curve defined by the parametric equations $x = t + 1$ and $y = \sqrt{t}$. Describe the plane curve.

Solution:

Square $y = \sqrt{t}$. $\quad y^2 = t$

Substitute $t = y^2$ into $x = t + 1$. $\quad x = y^2 + 1$

The graph of $x = y^2 + 1$ is a parabola opening to the right with its vertex at $(1, 0)$.

This is incorrect. What mistake was made?

52. Find the rectangular equation that corresponds to the plane curve defined by the parametric equations $x = \sqrt{t}$ and $y = t - 1$. Describe the plane curve.

Solution:

Square $x = \sqrt{t}$. $\quad x^2 = t$

Substitute $t = x^2$ into $y = t - 1$. $\quad y = x^2 - 1$

The graph of $y = x^2 - 1$ is a parabola opening up with its vertex at $(0, -1)$.

This is incorrect. What mistake was made?

• CONCEPTUAL

In Exercises 53 and 54, determine whether each statement is true or false.

53. Curves given by equations in rectangular form have orientation.

54. Curves given by parametric equations have orientation.

55. Determine what type of curve the parametric equations $x = \sqrt{t}$ and $y = \sqrt{1 - t}$ define.

56. Determine what type of curve the parametric equations $x = \ln t$ and $y = t$ define.

• CHALLENGE

57. Prove that $x = a\tan t$, $y = b\sec t$, $0 \le t \le 2\pi$, $t \neq \frac{\pi}{2}, \frac{3\pi}{2}$ are parametric equations for a hyperbola. Assume that a and b are nonzero constants.

58. Prove that $x = a\csc\left(\frac{t}{2}\right)$, $y = b\cot\left(\frac{t}{2}\right)$, $0 \le t \le 4\pi$, $t \neq \pi, 3\pi$ are parametric equations for a hyperbola. Assume that a and b are nonzero constants.

59. Consider the parametric curve $x = a\sin^2 t - b\cos^2 t$, $y = b\cos^2 t + a\sin^2 t$, $0 \le t \le \frac{\pi}{2}$. Assume that a and b are nonzero constants. Find the Cartesian equation for this curve.

60. Consider the parametric curve $x = a\sin t + a\cos t$, $y = a\cos t - a\sin t$, $0 \le t \le 2\pi$. Assume that a is not zero. Find the Cartesian equation for this curve.

61. Consider the parametric curve $x = e^{at}$, $y = be^t$, $t > 0$. Assume that a is a positive integer and b is a positive real number. Determine the Cartesian equation.

62. Consider the parametric curve $x = a\ln t$, $y = \ln(bt)$, $t > 0$. Assume that b is a positive integer and a is a positive real number. Determine the Cartesian equation.

• PREVIEW TO CALCULUS

In calculus, some operations can be simplified by using parametric equations. Finding the points of intersection (if they exist) of two curves given by parametric equations is a standard procedure.

In Exercises 63–66, find the points of intersection of the given curves given that *s* and *t* are any real numbers.

63. Curve I: $x = t$, $y = t^2 - 1$
Curve II: $x = s + 1$, $y = 4 - s$

64. Curve I: $x = t^2 + 3$, $y = t$
Curve II: $x = s + 2$, $y = 1 - s$

65. Curve I: $x = 100t$, $y = 80t - 16t^2$
Curve II: $x = 100 - 200t$, $y = -16t^2 + 144t - 224$

66. Curve I: $x = t^2$, $y = t + 1$
Curve II: $x = 2 + s$, $y = 1 - s$

[CHAPTER 9 REVIEW]

SECTION	CONCEPT	KEY IDEAS/FORMULAS
9.1	**Conic basics**	
	Three types of conics	**Parabola, ellipse, and hyperbola:** **Parabola:** Distances from a point to a reference point (focus) and a reference line (directrix) are equal. **Ellipse:** Sum of the distances between the point and two reference points (foci) is constant. **Hyperbola:** Difference of the distances between the point and two reference points (foci) is constant.
9.2	**The parabola**	
	Parabola with a vertex at the origin	See figures below
	Parabola with a vertex at the point (h, k)	See table below
	Applications	Antenaes
9.3	**The ellipse**	
	Ellipse centered at the origin	See figures below

Parabola with a vertex at the origin:

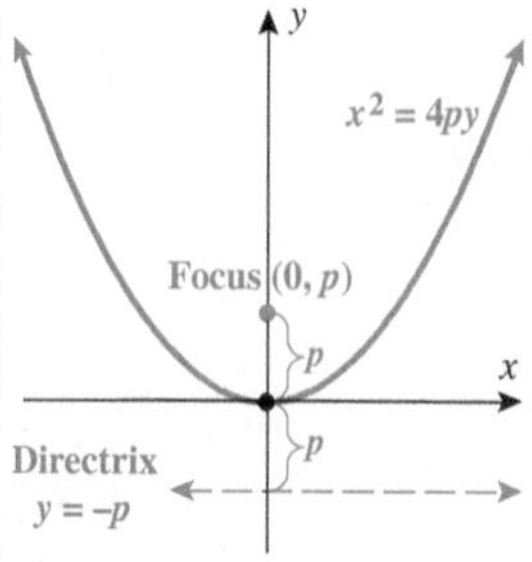

Up: $p > 0$ Down: $p < 0$

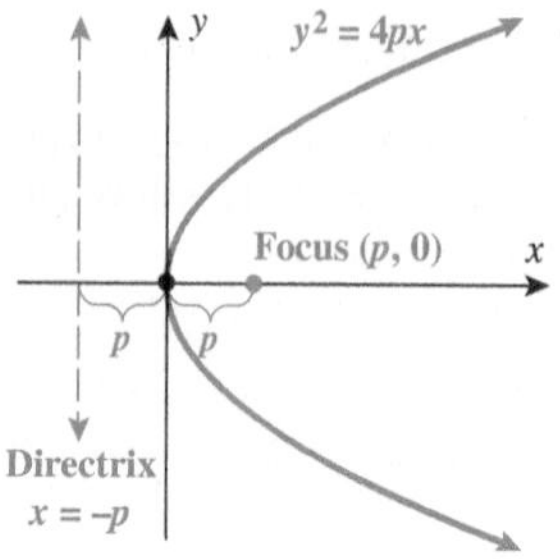

Right: $p > 0$ Left: $p < 0$

Parabola with a vertex at the point (h, k):

EQUATION	$(y - k)^2 = 4p(x - h)$	$(x - h)^2 = 4p(y - k)$
VERTEX	(h, k)	(h, k)
FOCUS	$(p + h, k)$	$(h, p + k)$
DIRECTRIX	$x = -p + h$	$y = -p + k$
AXIS OF SYMMETRY	$y = k$	$x = h$
$p > 0$	opens to the right	opens upward
$p < 0$	opens to the left	opens downward

Ellipse centered at the origin:

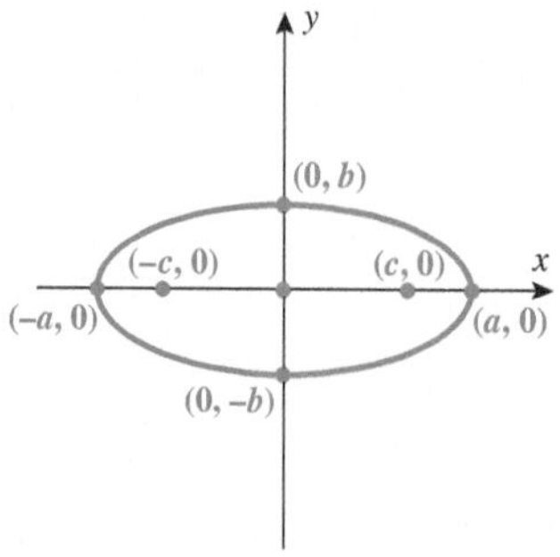

$$\frac{x^2}{a^2} + \frac{y^2}{b^2} = 1$$
$$c^2 = a^2 - b^2$$

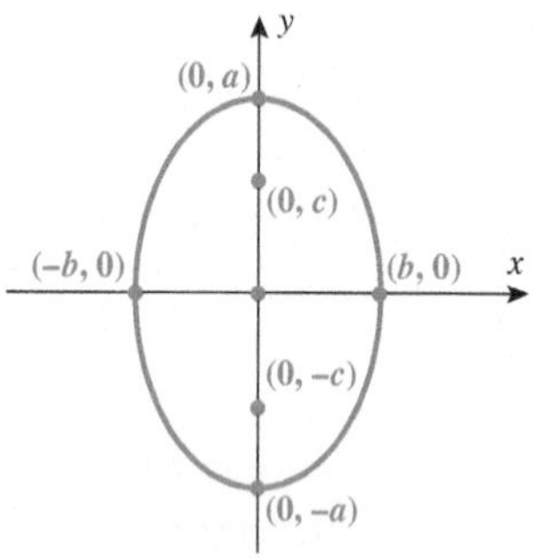

$$\frac{x^2}{b^2} + \frac{y^2}{a^2} = 1$$
$$c^2 = a^2 - b^2$$

SECTION	CONCEPT	KEY IDEAS/FORMULAS
	Ellipse centered at the point (h, k)	See table below

ORIENTATION OF MAJOR AXIS	Horizontal (parallel to the x-axis)	Vertical (parallel to the y-axis)
EQUATION	$\dfrac{(x-h)^2}{a^2} + \dfrac{(y-k)^2}{b^2} = 1$	$\dfrac{(x-h)^2}{b^2} + \dfrac{(y-k)^2}{a^2} = 1$
GRAPH	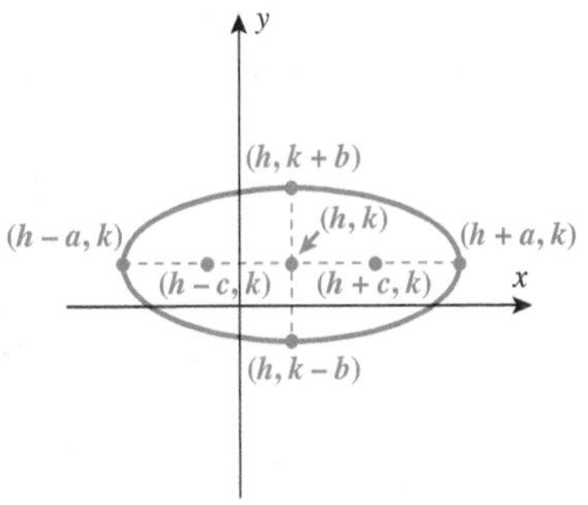	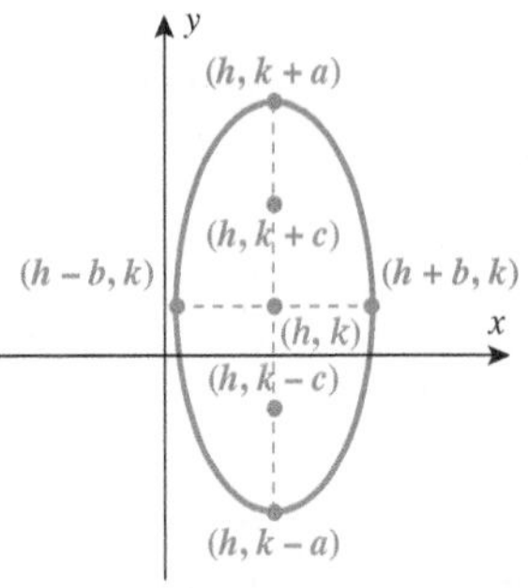
FOCI	$(h - c, k)$ and $(h + c, k)$	$(h, k - c)$ and $(h, k + c)$
VERTICES	$(h - a, k)$ and $(h + a, k)$	$(h, k - a)$ and $(h, k + a)$

SECTION	CONCEPT	KEY IDEAS/FORMULAS
	Applications	Orbits
9.4	**The hyperbola**	
	Hyperbola centered at the origin	See graphs below

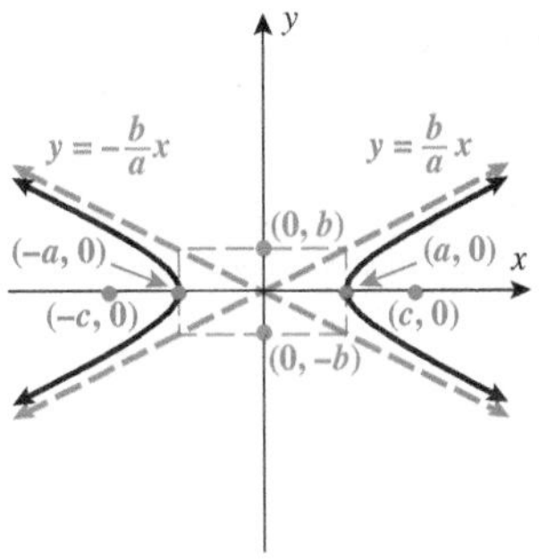

$$\frac{x^2}{a^2} - \frac{y^2}{b^2} = 1$$
$$c^2 = a^2 + b^2$$

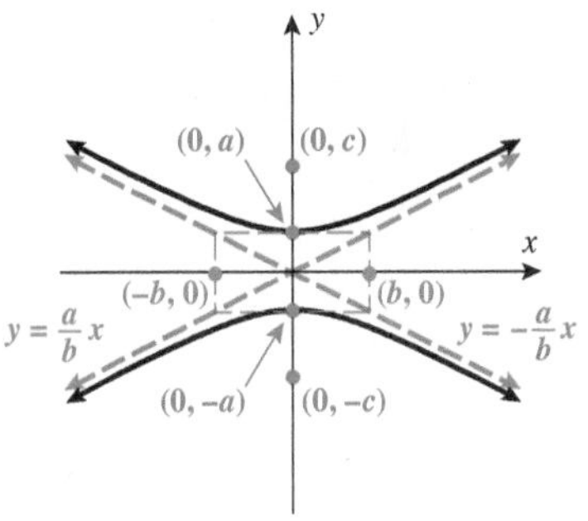

$$\frac{y^2}{a^2} - \frac{x^2}{b^2} = 1$$
$$c^2 = a^2 + b^2$$

Hyperbola centered at the point (h, k)

ORIENTATION OF TRANSVERSE AXIS	Horizontal (parallel to the x-axis)	Vertical (parallel to the y-axis)
EQUATION	$\dfrac{(x-h)^2}{a^2} - \dfrac{(y-k)^2}{b^2} = 1$	$\dfrac{(y-k)^2}{a^2} - \dfrac{(x-h)^2}{b^2} = 1$
VERTICES	$(h - a, k)$ and $(h + a, k)$	$(h, k - a)$ and $(h, k + a)$
FOCI	$(h - c, k)$ and $(h + c, k)$ where $c^2 = a^2 + b^2$	$(h, k - c)$ and $(h, k + c)$ where $c^2 = a^2 + b^2$
GRAPH	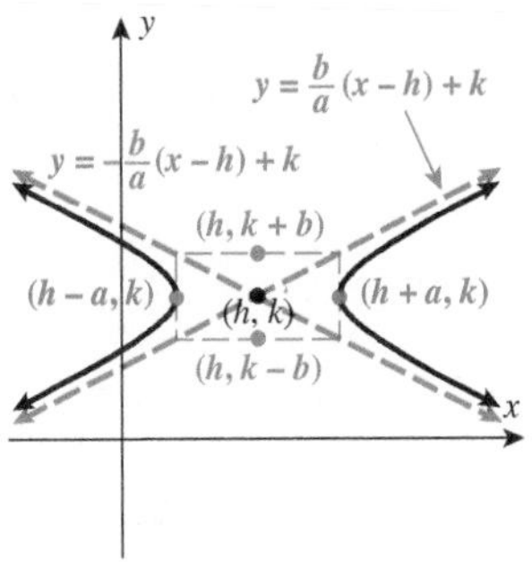	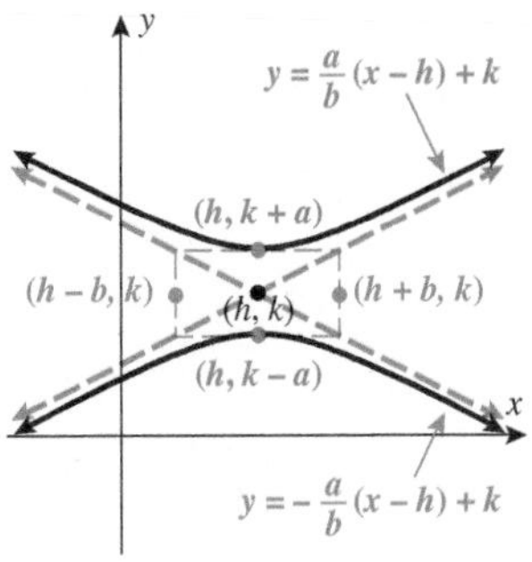

SECTION	CONCEPT	KEY IDEAS/FORMULAS
	Applications	LORAN

CHAPTER 9 REVIEW

SECTION	CONCEPT	KEY IDEAS/FORMULAS
9.5	**Systems of nonlinear equations**	There is no procedure guaranteed to solve nonlinear equations.
	Solving a system of nonlinear equations	**Elimination** Eliminate a variable by either adding one equation to the other or subtracting one equation from the other. **Substitution** Solve for one variable in terms of the other and substitute into the second equation.
9.6	**Systems of nonlinear inequalities**	Solutions are determined graphically by finding the common shaded regions. ■ $\leq$ or $\geq$ Use solid curves. ■ $<$ or $>$ Use dashed curves.
	Nonlinear inequalities in two variables	Step 1: Rewrite the inequality as an equation. Step 2: Graph the equation. Step 3: Test points. Step 4: Shade.
	Systems of nonlinear inequalities	Graph the individual inequalities and the solution in the common (overlapping) shaded region.
9.7	**Rotation of axes**	
	Rotation of axes formulas	$x = X\cos\theta - Y\sin\theta$ $y = X\sin\theta + Y\cos\theta$
	The angle of rotation necessary to transform a general second-degree equation into a familiar equation of a conic	$\cot(2\theta) = \frac{A - C}{B}$ or $\tan(2\theta) = \frac{B}{A - C}$
9.8	**Polar equations of conics**	All three conics (parabolas, ellipses, and hyperbolas) can be defined in terms of a single focus and a directrix.
	Equations of conics in polar coordinates	The directrix is *vertical* and p units to the *right* of the pole. $r = \frac{ep}{1 + e\cos\theta}$ The directrix is *vertical* and p units to the *left* of the pole. $r = \frac{ep}{1 - e\cos\theta}$ The directrix is *horizontal* and p units *above* the pole. $r = \frac{ep}{1 + e\sin\theta}$ The directrix is *horizontal* and p units *below* the pole. $r = \frac{ep}{1 - e\sin\theta}$
9.9	**Parametric equations and graphs**	
	Parametric equations of a curve	Parametric equations: $x = f(t)$ and $y = g(t)$ Plane curve: $(x, y) = (f(t), g(t))$
	Applications of parametric equations	Cycloids and projectiles

[CHAPTER 9 REVIEW EXERCISES]

9.1 Conic Basics

Determine whether each statement is true or false.

1. The focus is a point on the graph of the parabola.
2. The graph of $y^2 = 8x$ is a parabola that opens upward.
3. $\frac{x^2}{9} - \frac{y^2}{1} = 1$ is the graph of a hyperbola that has a horizontal transverse axis.
4. $\frac{(x+1)^2}{9} + \frac{(y-3)^2}{16} = 1$ is a graph of an ellipse whose center is $(1, 3)$.

9.2 The Parabola

Find an equation for the parabola described.

5. Vertex at $(0, 0)$; Focus at $(3, 0)$
6. Vertex at $(0, 0)$; Focus at $(0, 2)$
7. Vertex at $(0, 0)$; Directrix at $x = 5$
8. Vertex at $(0, 0)$; Directrix at $y = 4$
9. Vertex at $(2, 3)$; Focus at $(2, 5)$
10. Vertex at $(-1, -2)$; Focus at $(1, -2)$
11. Focus at $(1, 5)$; Directrix at $y = 7$
12. Focus at $(2, 2)$; Directrix at $x = 0$

Find the focus, vertex, directrix, and length of the latus rectum, and graph the parabola.

13. $x^2 = -12y$
14. $x^2 = 8y$
15. $y^2 = x$
16. $y^2 = -6x$
17. $(y+2)^2 = 4(x-2)$
18. $(y-2)^2 = -4(x+1)$
19. $(x+3)^2 = -8(y-1)$
20. $(x-3)^2 = -8(y+2)$
21. $x^2 + 5x + 2y + 25 = 0$
22. $y^2 + 2y - 16x + 1 = 0$

Applications

23. **Satellite Dish.** A satellite dish measures 10 feet across its opening and 2 feet deep at its center. The receiver should be placed at the focus of the parabolic dish. Where should the receiver be placed?
24. **Clearance under a Bridge.** A bridge with a parabolic shape reaches a height of 40 feet in the center of the road, and the width of the bridge opening at ground level is 30 feet combined (both lanes). If an RV is 14 feet tall and 8 feet wide, will it make it through the tunnel?

9.3 The Ellipse

Graph each ellipse.

25. $\frac{x^2}{9} + \frac{y^2}{64} = 1$
26. $\frac{x^2}{81} + \frac{y^2}{49} = 1$
27. $25x^2 + y^2 = 25$
28. $4x^2 + 8y^2 = 64$

Find the standard form of an equation of the ellipse with the given characteristics.

29. Foci: $(-3, 0)$ and $(3, 0)$ Vertices: $(-5, 0)$ and $(5, 0)$
30. Foci: $(0, -2)$ and $(0, 2)$ Vertices: $(0, -3)$ and $(0, 3)$
31. Major axis vertical with length of 16, minor axis length of 6, and centered at $(0, 0)$
32. Major axis horizontal with length of 30, minor axis length of 20, and centered at $(0, 0)$

Graph each ellipse.

33. $\frac{(x-7)^2}{100} + \frac{(y+5)^2}{36} = 1$
34. $20(x+3)^2 + (y-4)^2 = 120$
35. $4x^2 - 16x + 12y^2 + 72y + 123 = 0$
36. $4x^2 - 8x + 9y^2 - 72y + 147 = 0$

Find the standard form of an equation of the ellipse with the given characteristics.

37. Foci: $(-1, 3)$ and $(7, 3)$ Vertices: $(-2, 3)$ and $(8, 3)$
38. Foci: $(1, -3)$ and $(1, -1)$ Vertices: $(1, -4)$ and $(1, 0)$

Applications

39. **Planetary Orbits.** Jupiter's orbit is summarized in the picture. Utilize the fact that the Sun is a focus to determine an equation for Jupiter's elliptical orbit around the Sun. Round to the nearest hundred thousand kilometers.

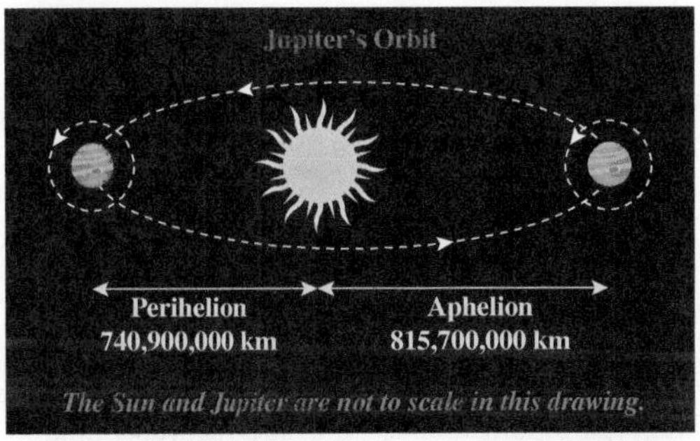

40. Planetary Orbits. Mars's orbit is summarized in the picture that follows. Utilize the fact that the Sun is a focus to determine an equation for Mars's elliptical orbit around the Sun. Round to the nearest million kilometers.

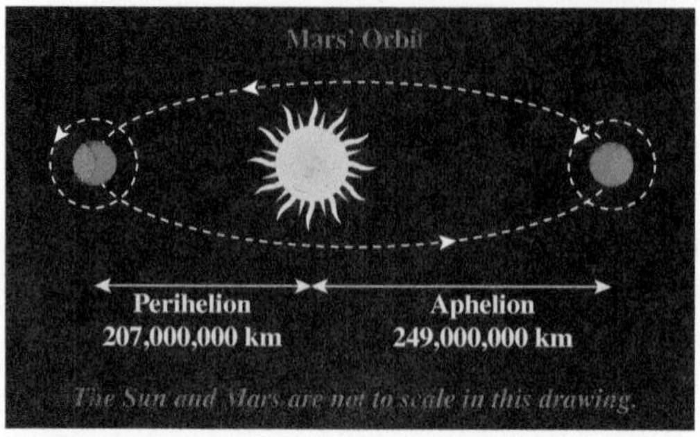

Mars' Orbit

Perihelion
207,000,000 km

Aphelion
249,000,000 km

The Sun and Mars are not to scale in this drawing.

9.4 The Hyperbola

Graph each hyperbola.

41. $\dfrac{x^2}{9} - \dfrac{y^2}{64} = 1$ **42.** $\dfrac{x^2}{81} - \dfrac{y^2}{49} = 1$

43. $x^2 - 25y^2 = 25$ **44.** $8y^2 - 4x^2 = 64$

Find the standard form of an equation of the hyperbola with the given characteristics.

45. Vertices: $(-3, 0)$ and $(3, 0)$ Foci: $(-5, 0)$ and $(5, 0)$

46. Vertices: $(0, -1)$ and $(0, 1)$ Foci: $(0, -3)$ and $(0, 3)$

47. Center: $(0, 0)$; Transverse: y-axis; Asymptotes: $y = 3x$ and $y = -3x$

48. Center: $(0, 0)$; Transverse axis: y-axis; Asymptotes: $y = \frac{1}{2}x$ and $y = -\frac{1}{2}x$

Graph each hyperbola.

49. $\dfrac{(y - 1)^2}{36} - \dfrac{(x - 2)^2}{9} = 1$

50. $3(x + 3)^2 - 12(y - 4)^2 = 72$

51. $8x^2 - 32x - 10y^2 - 60y - 138 = 0$

52. $2x^2 + 12x - 8y^2 + 16y + 6 = 0$

Find the standard form of an equation of the hyperbola with the given characteristics.

53. Vertices: $(0, 3)$ and $(8, 3)$ Foci: $(-1, 3)$ and $(9, 3)$

54. Vertices: $(4, -2)$ and $(4, 0)$ Foci: $(4, -3)$ and $(4, 1)$

Applications

55. Ship Navigation. Two LORAN stations are located 220 miles apart along a coast. If a ship records a time difference of 0.00048 second and continues on the hyperbolic path corresponding to that difference, where will it reach shore? Assume that the speed of radio signals is 186,000 miles per second.

56. Ship Navigation. Two LORAN stations are located 400 miles apart along a coast. If a ship records a time difference of 0.0008 second and continues on the hyperbolic path corresponding to that difference, where will it reach shore?

9.5 Systems of Nonlinear Equations

Solve the system of equations with the elimination method.

57. $\begin{aligned} x^2 + y &= -3 \\ x - y &= 5 \end{aligned}$ **58.** $\begin{aligned} x^2 + y^2 &= 4 \\ x^2 + y &= 2 \end{aligned}$

59. $\begin{aligned} x^2 + y^2 &= 5 \\ 2x^2 - y &= 0 \end{aligned}$ **60.** $\begin{aligned} x^2 + y^2 &= 16 \\ 6x^2 + y^2 &= 16 \end{aligned}$

Solve the system of equations with the substitution method.

61. $\begin{aligned} x + y &= 3 \\ x^2 + y^2 &= 4 \end{aligned}$ **62.** $\begin{aligned} xy &= 4 \\ x^2 + y^2 &= 16 \end{aligned}$

63. $\begin{aligned} x^2 + xy + y^2 &= -12 \\ x - y &= 2 \end{aligned}$ **64.** $\begin{aligned} 3x + y &= 3 \\ x - y^2 &= -9 \end{aligned}$

Solve the system of equations by applying any method.

65. $\begin{aligned} x^3 - y^3 &= -19 \\ x - y &= -1 \end{aligned}$ **66.** $\begin{aligned} 2x^2 + 4xy &= 9 \\ x^2 - 2xy &= 0 \end{aligned}$

67. $\begin{aligned} \dfrac{2}{x^2} + \dfrac{1}{y^2} &= 15 \\ \dfrac{1}{x^2} - \dfrac{1}{y^2} &= -3 \end{aligned}$ **68.** $\begin{aligned} x^2 + y^2 &= 2 \\ x^2 + y^2 &= 4 \end{aligned}$

9.6 Systems of Nonlinear Inequalities

Graph the nonlinear inequality.

69. $y \geq x^2 + 3$ **70.** $x^2 + y^2 > 16$

71. $y \leq e^x$ **72.** $y < -x^3 + 2$

73. $y \geq \ln(x - 1)$ **74.** $9x^2 + 4y^2 \leq 36$

Solve each system of inequalities and shade the region on a graph, or indicate that the system has no solution.

75. $\begin{aligned} y &\geq x^2 - 2 \\ y &\leq -x^2 + 2 \end{aligned}$ **76.** $\begin{aligned} x^2 + y^2 &\leq 4 \\ y &\leq x \end{aligned}$

77. $\begin{aligned} y &\geq (x + 1)^2 - 2 \\ y &\leq 10 - x \end{aligned}$ **78.** $\begin{aligned} 3x^2 + 3y^2 &\leq 27 \\ y &\geq x - 1 \end{aligned}$

79. $\begin{aligned} 4y^2 - 9x^2 &\leq 36 \\ y &\geq x + 1 \end{aligned}$ **80.** $\begin{aligned} 9x^2 + 16y^2 &\leq 144 \\ y &\geq 1 - x^2 \end{aligned}$

9.7 Rotation of Axes

The coordinates of a point in the xy-coordinate system are given. Assuming the X- and Y-axes are found by rotating the x- and y-axes by the indicated angle θ, find the corresponding coordinates for the point in the XY system.

81. $(-3, 2)$, $\theta = 60°$ **82.** $(4, -3)$, $\theta = 45°$

Transform the equation of the conic into an equation in X and Y (without an XY term) by rotating the x- and y-axes through the indicated angle θ. Then graph the resulting equation.

83. $2x^2 + 4\sqrt{3}xy - 2y^2 - 16 = 0$, $\theta = 30°$

84. $25x^2 + 14xy + 25y^2 - 288 = 0$, $\theta = \dfrac{\pi}{4}$

Determine the angle of rotation necessary to transform the equation in x and y into an equation in X and Y with no XY term.

85. $4x^2 + 2\sqrt{3}xy + 6y^2 - 9 = 0$
86. $4x^2 + 5xy + 4y^2 - 11 = 0$

Graph the second-degree equation.

87. $x^2 + 2xy + y^2 + \sqrt{2}x - \sqrt{2}y + 8 = 0$
88. $76x^2 + 48\sqrt{3}xy + 28y^2 - 100 = 0$

9.8 Polar Equations of Conics

Find the polar equation that represents the conic described.

89. An ellipse with eccentricity $e = \frac{3}{7}$ and directrix $y = -7$
90. A parabola with directrix $x = 2$

Identify the conic (parabola, ellipse, or hyperbola) that each polar equation represents.

91. $r = \dfrac{6}{4 - 5\cos\theta}$
92. $r = \dfrac{2}{5 + 3\sin\theta}$

For the given polar equations, find the eccentricity and vertex (or vertices), and graph the curve.

93. $r = \dfrac{4}{2 + \cos\theta}$
94. $r = \dfrac{6}{1 - \sin\theta}$

9.9 Parametric Equations and Graphs

Graph the curve defined by the parametric equations.

95. $x = \sin t,\ y = 4\cos t$ for t in $[-\pi, \pi]$
96. $x = 5\sin^2 t,\ y = 2\cos^2 t$ for t in $[-\pi, \pi]$
97. $x = 4 - t^2,\ y = t^2$ for t in $[-3, 3]$
98. $x = t + 3,\ y = 4$ for t in $[-4, 4]$

The given parametric equations define a plane curve. Find an equation in rectangular form that also corresponds to the plane curve.

99. $x = 4 - t^2,\ y = t$
100. $x = 5\sin^2 t,\ y = 2\cos^2 t$
101. $x = 2\tan^2 t,\ y = 4\sec^2 t$
102. $x = 3t^2 + 4,\ y = 3t^2 - 5$

[CHAPTER 9 PRACTICE TEST]

Match each equation to the corresponding graph.

1. $x = 16y^2$

2. $y = 16x^2$

3. $x^2 + 16y^2 = 1$

4. $x^2 - 16y^2 = 1$

5. $16x^2 + y^2 = 1$

6. $16y^2 - x^2 = 1$

a.

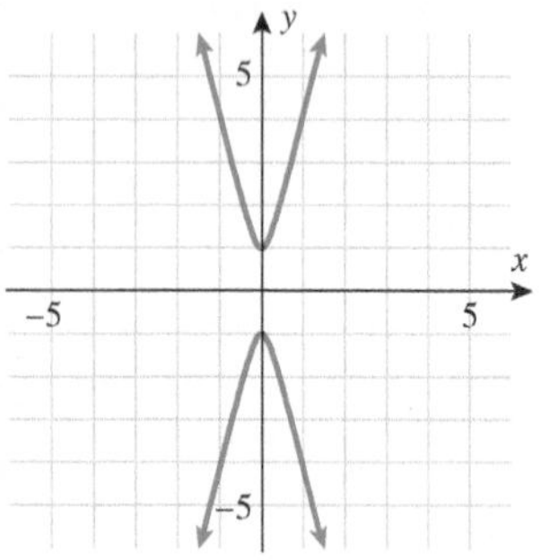

b.

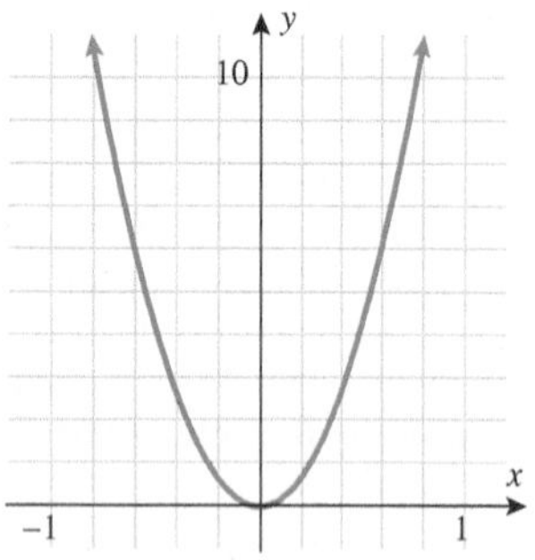

c.

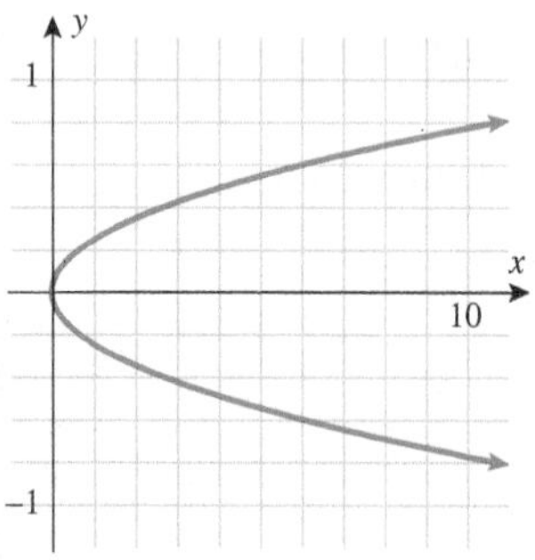

d.

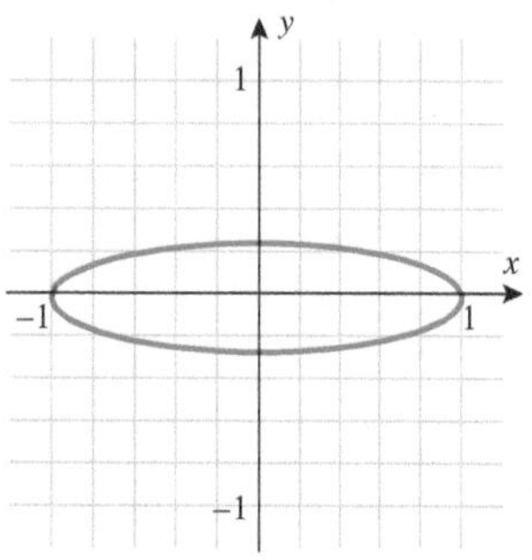

e.

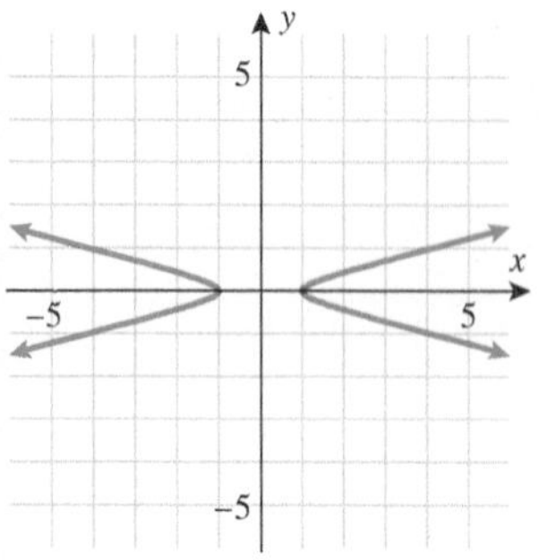

f.

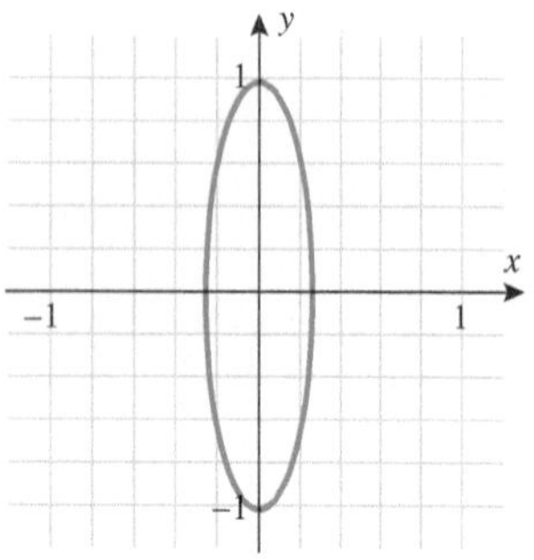

Find the equation of the conic with the given characteristics.

7. Parabola vertex: $(0, 0)$ focus: $(-4, 0)$

8. Parabola vertex: $(0, 0)$ directrix: $y = 2$

9. Parabola vertex: $(-1, 5)$ focus: $(-1, 2)$

10. Parabola vertex: $(2, -3)$ directrix: $x = 0$

11. Ellipse center: $(0, 0)$; vertices: $(0, -4), (0, 4)$; foci: $(0, -3), (0, 3)$

12. Ellipse center: $(0, 0)$; vertices: $(-3, 0), (3, 0)$; foci: $(-1, 0), (1, 0)$

13. Ellipse vertices: $(2, -6), (2, 6)$; foci: $(2, -4), (2, 4)$

14. Ellipse vertices: $(-7, -3), (-4, -3)$; foci: $(-6, -3), (-5, -3)$

15. Hyperbola vertices: $(-1, 0)$ and $(1, 0)$; asymptotes: $y = -2x$ and $y = 2x$

16. Hyperbola vertices: $(0, -1)$ and $(0, 1)$; asymptotes: $y = -\frac{1}{3}x$ and $y = \frac{1}{3}x$

17. Hyperbola foci: $(2, -6), (2, 6)$; vertices: $(2, -4), (2, 4)$

18. Hyperbola foci: $(-7, -3), (-4, -3)$; vertices: $(-6, -3), (-5, -3)$

Graph the following equations:

19. $9x^2 + 18x - 4y^2 + 16y - 43 = 0$

20. $4x^2 - 8x + y^2 + 10y + 28 = 0$

21. $y^2 + 4y - 16x + 20 = 0$

22. $x^2 - 4x + y + 1 = 0$

23. Eyeglass Lens. Eyeglass lenses can be thought of as very wide parabolic curves. If the focus occurs 1.5 centimeters from the center of the lens, and the lens at its opening is 4 centimeters across, find an equation that governs the shape of the lens.

24. Planetary Orbits. The planet Uranus's orbit is described in the following picture with the Sun as a focus of the elliptical orbit. Write an equation for the orbit.

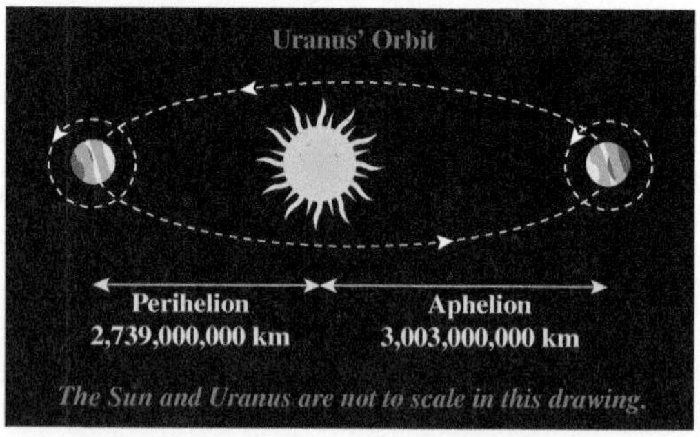

Graph the following nonlinear inequalities:

25. $y < x^3 + 1$

26. $y^2 \geq 16x$

Graph the following systems of nonlinear inequalities:

27. $y \leq 4 - x^2$
$16x^2 + 25y^2 \leq 400$

28. $y \leq e^{-x}$
$y \geq x^2 - 4$

29. Identify the conic represented by the equation $r = \dfrac{12}{3 + 2\sin\theta}$. State the eccentricity.

30. Use rotation of axes to transform the equation in x and y into an equation in X and Y that has no XY term: $6\sqrt{3}x^2 + 6xy + 4\sqrt{3}y^2 = 21\sqrt{3}$. State the rotation angle.

31. A golf ball is hit with an initial speed of 120 feet per second at an angle of 45° with the ground. How long will the ball stay in the air? How far will the ball travel (horizontal distance) before it hits the ground?

32. Describe (classify) the plane curve defined by the parametric equations $x = \sqrt{1 - t}$ and $y = \sqrt{t}$ for t in $[0, 1]$.

[CHAPTERS 1–9 CUMULATIVE TEST]

1. Solve for x: $(x+2)^2 - (x+2) - 20 = 0$.
2. Find an equation of a circle centered at $(5, 1)$ and passing through the point $(6, -2)$.
3. Evaluate the difference quotient $\frac{f(x+h) - f(x)}{h}$ for the function $f(x) = 8 - 7x$.
4. Write an equation that describes the following variation: I is directly proportional to both P and t, and $I = 90$ when $P = 1500$ and $t = 2$.
5. Find the quadratic function that has vertex $(7, 7)$ and goes through the point $(10, 10)$.
6. **Compound Interest.** How much money should you put now in a savings account that earns 4.7% interest a year compounded weekly if you want to have $65,000 in 17 years?
7. Solve the logarithmic equation exactly: $\log x^2 - \log 16 = 0$.
8. In a 30°-60°-90° triangle, if the shortest leg has length 8 inches, what are the lengths of the other leg and the hypotenuse?
9. Use a calculator to evaluate $\cot(-27°)$. Round your answer to four decimal places.
10. **Sound Waves.** If a sound wave is represented by $y = 0.007\sin(850\pi t)$ cm, what are its amplitude and frequency?
11. For the trigonometric expression $\tan\theta(\csc\theta + \cos\theta)$, perform the operations and simplify. Write the answer in terms of $\sin\theta$ and $\cos\theta$.
12. Find the exact value of $\cos\left(-\frac{11\pi}{12}\right)$.
13. Solve the trigonometric equation $4\cos^2 x + 4\cos 2x + 1 = 0$ exactly over the interval $0 \le \theta \le 2\pi$.
14. **Airplane Speed.** A plane flew due north at 450 miles per hour for 2 hours. A second plane, starting at the same point and at the same time, flew southeast at an angle of 135° clockwise from due north at 375 miles per hour for 2 hours. At the end of 2 hours, how far apart were the two planes? Round to the nearest mile.
15. Find the vector with magnitude $|\mathbf{u}| = 15$ and direction angle $\theta = 110°$.
16. Given $z_1 = 5(\cos 15° + i\sin 15°)$ and $z_2 = 2(\cos 75° + i\sin 75°)$, find the product $z_1 z_2$ and express it in rectangular form.
17. At a food court, 3 medium sodas and 2 soft pretzels cost $6.77. A second order of 5 medium sodas and 4 soft pretzels costs $12.25. Find the cost of a soda and the cost of a soft pretzel.
18. Find the partial-fraction decomposition for the rational expression $\frac{3x+5}{(x-3)(x^2+5)}$.
19. Graph the system of inequalities or indicate that the system has no solution.

$$y \ge 3x - 2$$
$$y \le 3x + 2$$

20. Solve the system using Gauss–Jordan elimination.

$$\begin{aligned} x - 2y + z &= 7 \\ -3x + y + 2z &= -11 \end{aligned}$$

21. Given $A = \begin{bmatrix} 3 & 4 & -7 \\ 0 & 1 & 5 \end{bmatrix}$, $B = \begin{bmatrix} 8 & -2 & 6 \\ 9 & 0 & -1 \end{bmatrix}$, and $C = \begin{bmatrix} 9 & 0 \\ 1 & 2 \end{bmatrix}$, find $2B - 3A$.
22. Use Cramer's rule to solve the system of equations.

$$\begin{aligned} 25x + 40y &= -12 \\ 75x - 105y &= 69 \end{aligned}$$

23. Find the standard form of the equation of an ellipse with foci $(6, 2)$ and $(6, -6)$ and vertices $(6, 3)$ and $(6, -7)$.
24. Find the standard form of the equation of a hyperbola with vertices $(5, -2)$ and $(5, 0)$ and foci $(5, -3)$ and $(5, 1)$.
25. Solve the system of equations.

$$\begin{aligned} x + y &= 6 \\ x^2 + y^2 &= 20 \end{aligned}$$

Answers to Odd-Numbered Exercises*

CHAPTER 0

Section 0.1

1. $m = 2$ 3. $t = \frac{7}{5}$ 5. $x = -10$

7. $n = 2$ 9. $x = 12$ 11. $t = -\frac{15}{2}$

13. $x = -1$ 15. $p = -\frac{9}{2}$ 17. $x = \frac{1}{4}$

19. $x = -\frac{3}{2}$ 21. $a = -8$ 23. $x = -15$

25. $c = -\frac{35}{13}$ 27. $m = \frac{60}{11}$ 29. $x = 36$

31. $p = 8$ 33. $y = -2$ 35. $p = 2$

37. no solution 39. 12 mi 41. 270 units

43. $r_1 = 3$ ft, $r_2 = 6$ ft 45. 5.25 ft

47. \$20,000 at 4%, \$100,000 at 7%

49. \$3000 at 10%, \$5500 at 2%, \$5500 at 40%

51. 70 ml of 5% HC1, 30 ml of 15% HC1

53. 9 min 55. 233 ml 57. 2.3 mph

59. walker: 4 mph, jogger: 6 mph

61. bicyclist: 6 min, walker: 18 min

63. 22.5 hr 65. 2.4 hr

67. 2 field goals, 6 touchdowns

69. 3.5 ft from the center

71. Should have subtracted $4x$ and added 7 to both sides; $x = 5$

73. $x = \dfrac{c - b}{a}$ 75. $\dfrac{P - 2l}{2} = w$ 77. $\dfrac{2A}{b} = h$

79. $\dfrac{A}{l} = w$ 81. $\dfrac{V}{lw} = h$

83. Janine's average speed is 58 mph, Tricia's average speed is 70 mph.

Section 0.2

1. $x = 3$ or $x = 2$ 3. $p = 5$ or $p = 3$

5. $x = -4$ or $x = 3$ 7. $x = -\frac{1}{4}$

9. $y = \frac{1}{3}$ 11. $y = 0$ or $y = 2$

13. $p = \frac{2}{3}$ 15. $x = -3$ or $x = 3$

17. $x = -6$ or $x = 2$ 19. $p = -5$ or $p = 5$

21. $x = -2$ or $x = 2$ 23. $p = \pm 2\sqrt{2}$

25. $x = \pm 3i$ 27. $x = -3, 9$

29. $x = \dfrac{-3 \pm 2i}{2}$ 31. $x = \dfrac{2 \pm 3\sqrt{3}}{5}$

33. $x = -2, 4$ 35. $x = -3, 1$

37. $t = 1, 5$ 39. $y = 1, 3$

41. $p = \dfrac{-4 \pm \sqrt{10}}{2}$ 43. $x = \frac{1}{2}, 3$

45. $x = \dfrac{4 \pm 3\sqrt{2}}{2}$ 47. $t = \dfrac{-3 \pm \sqrt{13}}{2}$

49. $s = \dfrac{-1 \pm i\sqrt{3}}{2}$ 51. $x = \dfrac{3 \pm \sqrt{57}}{6}$

53. $x = 1 \pm 4i$ 55. $x = \dfrac{-7 \pm \sqrt{109}}{10}$

57. $x = \dfrac{-4 \pm \sqrt{34}}{3}$ 59. $v = -2, 10$

61. $t = -6, 1$ 63. $x = -7, 1$

65. $p = 4 \pm 2\sqrt{3}$ 67. $w = \dfrac{-1 \pm i\sqrt{167}}{8}$

69. $p = \dfrac{9 \pm \sqrt{69}}{6}$ 71. $t = \dfrac{10 \pm \sqrt{130}}{10}$

73. $x = -0.3, 0.4$

75. $t = 8$ (Aug. 2003) and $t = 12$ (Dec. 2003)

77. 31,000 units 79. \$1 per bottle 81. 3 days

83. **a.** 55.25 sq in.
    b. $4x^2 + 30x + 55.25$
    c. $4x^2 + 30x$ represents the increase in usable area of the paper.
    d. $x \approx 0.2$ in.

85. 17, 18 87. Length: 15 ft, width: 9 ft

89. Base: 6, height: 20 91. Impact with ground in 2.5 sec

93. 21.2 ft 95. 5 ft × 5 ft 97. 10 days

99. The problem is factored incorrectly. The correction would be $t = -1, 6$.

101. false 103. true 105. $x^2 - 2ax + a^2 = 0$

107. $t = \pm\sqrt{\dfrac{2s}{g}}$ 109. $c = \pm\sqrt{a^2 + b^2}$

111. $\dfrac{-b}{2a} + \dfrac{\sqrt{b^2 - 4ac}}{2a} - \dfrac{b}{2a} - \dfrac{\sqrt{b^2 - 4ac}}{2a} = \dfrac{-2b}{2a} = \dfrac{-b}{a}$

113. $x^2 - 6x + 4 = 0$ 115. 250 mph

117. $ax^2 - bx + c = 0$

119. Small jet: 300 mph, 757: 400 mph

Section 0.3

1. $x \neq 2$, no solution 3. $p \neq 1$, no solution

5. $x \neq -2$, $x = -10$ 7. $n \neq -1,0$, no solution

9. $a \neq 0, -3$, no solution 11. $n \neq 1$, $n = \frac{53}{11}$

---

*Answers that require a proof, graph, or otherwise lengthy solution are not included.

13. $x \neq -\frac{1}{5}, \frac{1}{2}, x = -3$ **15.** $t \neq 1$, no solution

17. $x = 3$ or $x = 4$, $x \neq 0$ **19.** $x = -\frac{3}{4}$ or $x = 2$, $x \neq 0$, $x \neq 3$

21. no solution **23.** $x = 5$

25. $y = -\frac{1}{2}$ **27.** $x = 5$

29. $x = -9$ or $x = 7$ **31.** $x = 4$

33. $y = 0, 25$ **35.** $s = 3, 6$

37. $x = -3, -1$ **39.** $x = 0$

41. $x = 1$ and $x = 5$ **43.** $x = 7$

45. $x = -3$ and $x = -\frac{15}{4}$ **47.** $x = \frac{5}{2}$

49. no solution **51.** $x = 1$

53. $x = 4$ and $x = -8$ **55.** $x = 1, 5$

57. $x = 7$ **59.** $x = 4$

61. $x = 0, x = -8$ **63.** $x = \pm 1, x = \pm\sqrt{2}$

65. $x = \dfrac{\pm i\sqrt{6}}{2}, x = \pm i\sqrt{2}$ **67.** $t = \frac{5}{4}, t = 3$

69. $x = \pm 1, \pm i, x = \pm\frac{1}{2}, \pm\frac{1}{2}i$

71. $y = -\frac{3}{4}, y = 1$ **73.** $z = 1$

75. $t = -27, t = 8$ **77.** $x = -\frac{4}{3}, x = 0$

79. $u = \pm 8, u = \pm 1$ **81.** $x = 0, -3, 4$

83. $p = 0, \pm\frac{3}{2}$ **85.** $u = 0, \pm 2, \pm 2i$

87. $x = \pm 3, 5$ **89.** $y = -2, 5, 7$

91. $x = 0, 3$ **93.** $t = \pm 5$

95. $y = 2{,}3$ **97.** $p = 10$ or $p = 4$

99. $y = 5$ or $y = 3$ **101.** $t = 4$ or $t = 2$

103. $x = 8$ or $x = -1$ **105.** $y = 0$ or $y = \frac{2}{3}$

107. $x = -\frac{23}{14}$ or $x = \frac{47}{14}$ **109.** $x = 13$ or $x = -3$

111. $p = 7$ or $p = -13$ **113.** $y = 9$ or $y = -5$

115. $x = \pm\sqrt{5}$ or $x = \pm\sqrt{3}$

117. $x = \pm 2$ or $x = \pm i\sqrt{6}$ **119.** January and September

121. 162 cm **123.** 7.5 cm in front of lens

125. Object distance = 6 cm
image distance = 3 cm

127. 25 cm **129.** no solution

131. Cannot cross multiply—must multiply by LCD first; $p = \frac{6}{5}$

133. false **135.** $x = \dfrac{a-b}{c}$

137. $x = -2$

139. $x = \dfrac{by}{a - y - cy}, x \neq 0, -\dfrac{b}{c+1}$

Section 0.4

1. $[-2, 3)$ 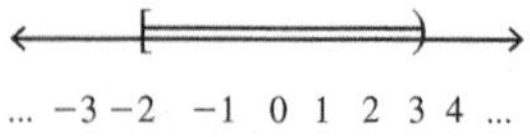

3. $(-3, 5]$ 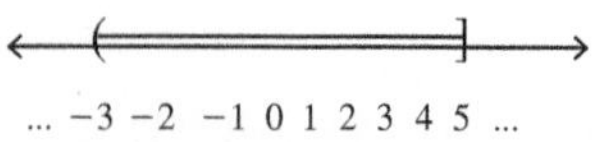

5. $[4, 6]$ 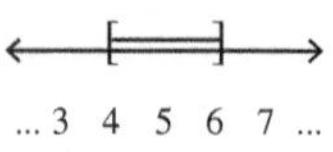

7. $[-8, -6]$ 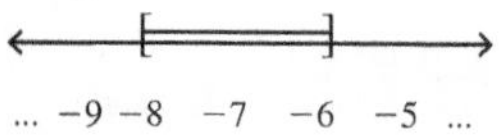

9. $\varnothing$ 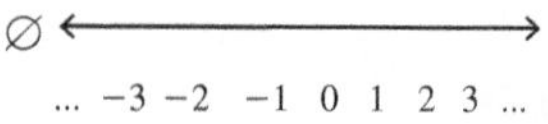

11. $[1, 4)$ 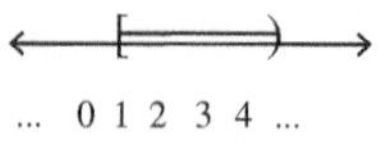

13. $[-1, 2)$ 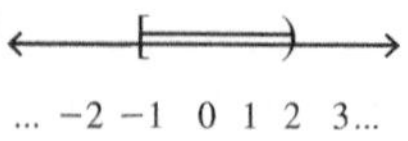

15. $(-\infty, 4) \cup (4, \infty)$ 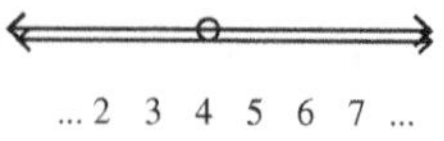

17. $(-\infty, -3] \cup [3, \infty)$ 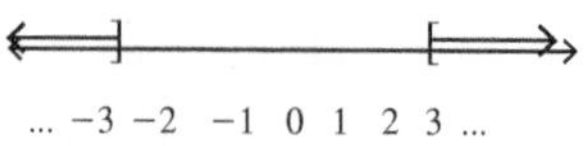

19. $(-3, 2]$ 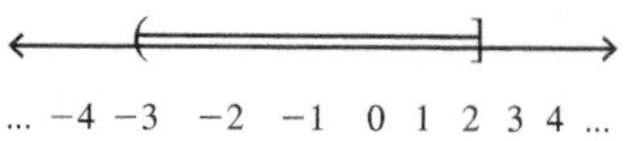

21. $(-3, \infty)$ **23.** $(-\infty, 6)$ **25.** $(-\infty, 1)$

27. $[-8, 4)$ **29.** $(-6, 6)$ **31.** $[\frac{1}{2}, \frac{5}{4}]$

33. $[-1, \frac{3}{2}]$ **35.** $(\frac{1}{3}, \frac{1}{2})$

37. $(-\infty, -\frac{1}{2}] \cup [3, \infty)$

39. $(-\infty, -1 - \sqrt{5}] \cup [-1 + \sqrt{5}, \infty)$

41. $(2 - \sqrt{10}, 2 + \sqrt{10})$ **43.** $(-\infty, 0] \cup [3, \infty)$

45. $(-\infty, -3) \cup (3, \infty)$ **47.** $(-\infty, -2] \cup [0, 1]$

49. $(0, 1) \cup (1, \infty)$ **51.** $(-\infty, -2) \cup [-1, 2)$

53. $(-\infty, -5] \cup (-2, 0]$ **55.** $(-2, 2)$

57. $\mathbb{R}$ (consistent) **59.** $[-3, 3) \cup (3, \infty)$

61. $(-3, -1] \cup (3, \infty)$ **63.** $(-\infty, -4) \cup (2, 5]$

65. $(-\infty, -2) \cup (2, \infty)$ **67.** $(-\infty, 2) \cup (6, \infty)$

69. $[3, 5]$ **71.** $\mathbb{R}$

73. $(-\infty, 2] \cup [5, \infty)$ **75.** $\mathbb{R}$

77. $(-\infty, -\frac{3}{2}] \cup [\frac{3}{2}, \infty)$ **79.** $(-\infty, -3) \cup (3, \infty)$

81. $[-3, 3]$ **83.** $\$5,156.25 \leq T \leq \$18,481$

85. 285,700 units

87. Between 33% and 71% intensities

89. Between 30 and 100 orders

91. For years 3–5, the car is worth more than you owe. In the first 3 years you owe more than the car is worth.

93. 75 sec

95. When the number of units sold was between 25 and 75 units.

97. Forgot to flip the sign when dividing by −3. Answer should be $[2, \infty)$.

99. Cannot divide by x $(-\infty, 0) \cup (3, \infty)$

101. true **103.** false

105. $\mathbb{R}$ **107.** no solution

Section 0.5

1. $d = 4, (3, 3)$ **3.** $d = 4\sqrt{2}, (1, 2)$

5. $d = 3\sqrt{10}, \left(-\frac{17}{2}, \frac{7}{2}\right)$ **7.** $d = 5, \left(-5, \frac{1}{2}\right)$

9. $d = 4\sqrt{2}, (-4, -6)$ **11.** $d = 5, \left(\frac{3}{2}, \frac{11}{6}\right)$

13.

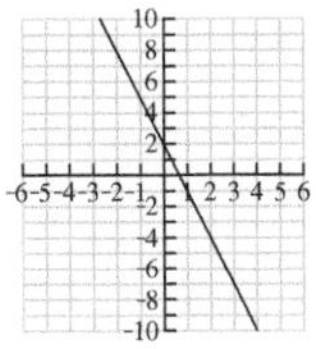

15.

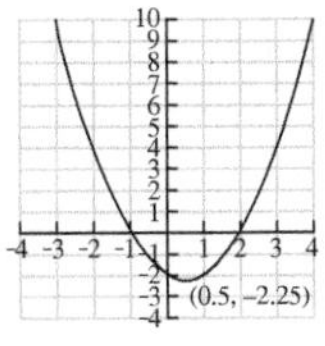

17.

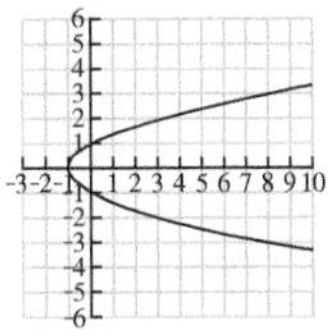

19. $(3, 0), (0, -6)$ **21.** $(4, 0)$, no y-intercept

23. $(\pm 2, 0), (0, \pm 4)$ **25.** x-axis

27. x-axis **29.** y-axis

31.

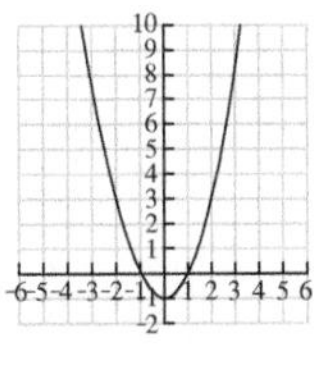

33.

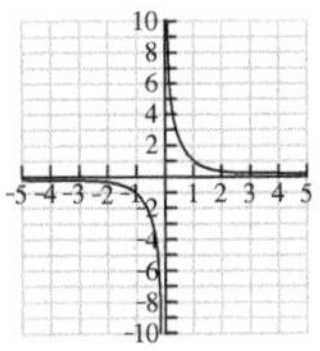

35.

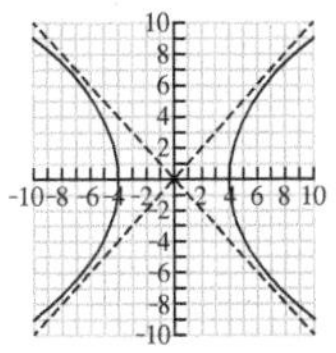

37. $(x - 5)^2 + (y - 7)^2 = 81$

39. $(x + 11)^2 + (y - 12)^2 = 169$

41. $(x - 5)^2 + (y + 3)^2 = 12$

43. $\left(x - \frac{2}{3}\right)^2 + \left(y + \frac{3}{5}\right)^2 = \frac{1}{16}$

45. $(2, -5), r = 7$ **47.** $(4, 9), r = 2\sqrt{5}$

49. $\left(\frac{2}{5}, \frac{1}{7}\right), r = \frac{2}{3}$ **51.** $(5, 7), r = 9$

53. $(1, 3), r = 3$ **55.** $(5, -3), r = 2\sqrt{3}$

57. $(3, 2), r = 2\sqrt{3}$ **59.** $\left(\frac{1}{2}, -\frac{1}{2}\right), r = \frac{1}{2}$

61.

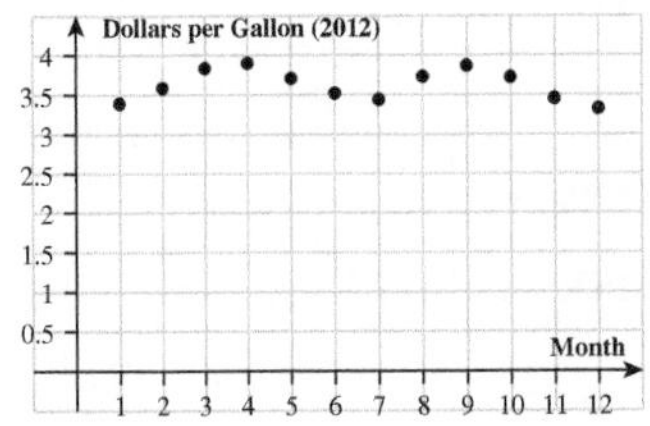

63. \$330 million **65.** $x^2 + y^2 = 2{,}250{,}000$

67. $x^2 + y^2 = 40{,}000$

69. The equation is not linear—you need more than two points to plot the graph.

71. The center should be $(4, -3)$.

73. false **75.** true **77.** single point $(-5, 3)$

79. origin **81.** $(x - 3)^2 + (y + 2)^2 = 20$

83. $4c = a^2 + b^2$

Section 0.6

1. 3 **3.** -2 **5.** $-\frac{19}{10}$ **7.** 2.379 **9.** -3

11. $(0.5, 0), (0, -1), m = 2$, increasing

13. $(1, 0), (0, 1), m = -1$, decreasing

15. none, $(0, 1), m = 0$, horizontal

17. $\left(\frac{3}{2}, 0\right), (0, -3)$

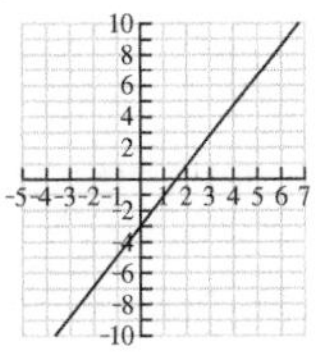

19. $(4, 0), (0, 2)$

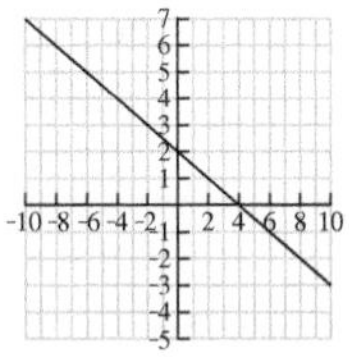

21. $(2, 0), \left(0, -\frac{4}{3}\right)$

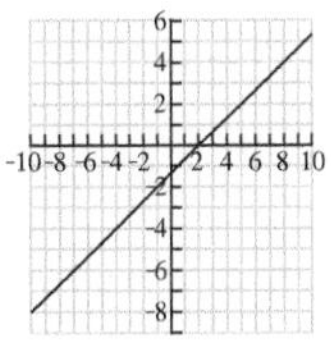

23. $(-2, 0), (0, -2)$

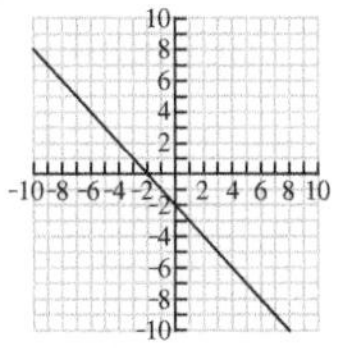

25. $(-1, 0)$, none

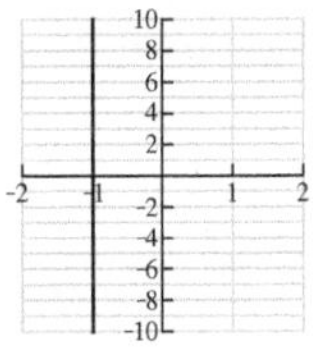

27. none, $(0, 1.5)$

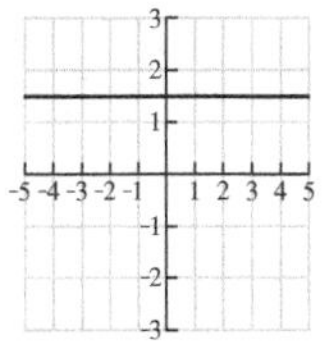

29. $\left(-\frac{7}{2}, 0\right)$, none

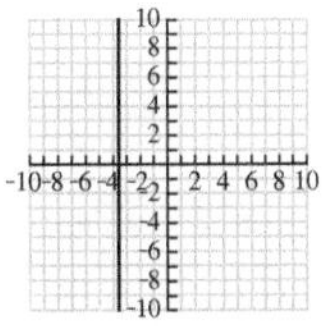

31. $y = \frac{2}{5}x - 2$ $m = \frac{2}{5}$ $y-$ intercept: $(0, -2)$

33. $y = -\frac{1}{3}x + 2$ $m = -\frac{1}{3}$ $y-$ intercept: $(0, 2)$

35. $y = 4x - 3$ $m = 4$ $y-$ intercept: $(0, -3)$

37. $y = -2x + 4$ $m = -2$ $y-$ intercept: $(0, 4)$

39. $y = \frac{2}{3}x - 2$ $m = \frac{2}{3}$ $y-$ intercept: $(0, -2)$

41. $y = -\frac{3}{4}x + 6$ $m = -\frac{3}{4}$ $y-$ intercept: $(0, 6)$

43. $y = 2x + 3$ **45.** $y = -\frac{1}{3}x$

47. $y = 2$ **49.** $x = \frac{3}{2}$

51. $y = 5x + 2$ **53.** $y = -3x - 4$

55. $y = \frac{3}{4}x - \frac{7}{4}$ **57.** $y = 4$

59. $x = -1$ **61.** $y = \frac{3}{5}x + \frac{1}{5}$

63. $y = -5x - 16$ **65.** $y = \frac{1}{6}x - \frac{121}{3}$

67. $y = -3x + 1$ **69.** $y = \frac{3}{2}x$ **71.** $x = 3$

73. $y = 7$ **75.** $y = \frac{6}{5}x + 6$ **77.** $x = -6$

79. $x = \frac{2}{5}$ **81.** $y = x - 1$ **83.** $y = -2x + 3$

85. $y = -\frac{1}{2}x + 1$ **87.** $y = 2x + 7$ **89.** $y = \frac{3}{2}x$

91. $y = 5$ **93.** $y = 2$ **95.** $y = \frac{3}{2}x - 4$

97. $y = \frac{5}{4}x + \frac{3}{2}$ **99.** $y = \frac{3}{7}x + \frac{5}{2}$

101. $C(h) = 1200 + 25h$; \$2000

103. \$375 **105.** 347 units

107. $F = \frac{9}{5}C + 32$, $-40°C = -40° F$

109. $\frac{1}{50}$ in./yr **111.** 0.06 oz/yr, 6 lb 12.4 oz

113. −0.35 in./yr, 2.75 in.

115. 2.4 plastic bags per year (in billions), 404 billion

117. The computations used to calculate the x- and y-intercepts should be reversed. So the x-intercept is (3, 0) and the y-intercept is (0, −2).

119. The denominator and numerator in the slope computation should be switched, resulting in the slope being undefined.

121. true **123.** false

125. Any vertical line is perpendicular to a line with slope 0.

127. $y = -\frac{A}{B}x + 1$ **129.** $y = \frac{B}{A}x + (2B - 1)$

131. $b_1 = b_2$

Section 0.7

1. $y = kx$ **3.** $V = kx^3$ **5.** $z = km$

7. $f = \frac{k}{\lambda}$ **9.** $F = \frac{kw}{L}$ **11.** $v = kgt$

13. $R = \frac{k}{PT}$ **15.** $y = k\sqrt{x}$ **17.** $d = rt$

19. $V = lwh$ **21.** $A = \pi r^2$ **23.** $V = \frac{\pi}{16}hr^2$

25. $V = \frac{400{,}000}{P}$ **27.** $F = \frac{2\pi}{\lambda L}$ **29.** $t = \frac{19.2}{s}$

31. $R = \frac{4.9}{I^2}$ **33.** $R = \frac{0.01L}{A}$ **35.** $F = \frac{0.025m_1m_2}{d^2}$

37. $W = 7.5H$ **39.** 1292 mph **41.** $F = 1.618H$

43. 24 cm **45.** \$37.50 **47.** 20,000

49. 600 w/m^2

51. Bank of America: 1.5%; Navy Federal Credit Union: 3%

53. $\frac{11}{12}$ or 0.92 atm

55. Should be y is inversely proportional to x

57. true **59.** b

61. $\sigma_{p_1}^2 = 1.23C_n^2 k^{7/6} L^{11/6}$

Chapter 0 Review

1. $x = \frac{16}{7}$ **3.** $p = -\frac{8}{25}$ **5.** $x = 27$

7. $y = -\frac{17}{5}$ **9.** $b = \frac{6}{7}$ **11.** $x = -\frac{6}{17}$

13. \$5000@20%; \$20,000@8%

15. 60 ml of 5%; 90 ml of 10%

17. $b = -3, 7$ **19.** $x = 0, 8$ **21.** $q = \pm 13$

23. $x = 2 \pm 4i$ **25.** $x = -2, 6$ **27.** $x = \frac{1 \pm \sqrt{33}}{2}$

29. $t = -1, \frac{7}{3}$ **31.** $f = \frac{1 \pm \sqrt{337}}{48}$ **33.** $q = \frac{3 \pm \sqrt{69}}{10}$

35. $x = -1, \frac{5}{2}$ **37.** $x = -3, \frac{2}{7}$ **39.** $h = 1$ ft, $b = 4$ ft

41. $x = \frac{6 \pm \sqrt{39}}{3}$ **43.** $t = -\frac{34}{5}, t \neq -4, 0$

45. $x = -\frac{1}{2}, x \neq 0$ **47.** $x = 6$

49. $x = 125$ **51.** no solution **53.** $x \cong -0.6$

55. $y = \frac{1}{4}, 1$ **57.** $x = -\frac{125}{8}, 1$ **59.** $x = -\frac{1}{8}, -1$

61. $x = \pm 2, \pm 3i$ **63.** $x = 0, -8, 4$ **65.** $p = \pm 2, 3$

67. $p = -\frac{1}{2}, \frac{5}{2}, 3$ **69.** $y = \pm 9$ **71.** no solution

73. $x \approx 0.9667, x = 1.7$

75. $(4, \infty)$

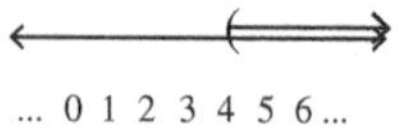

77. $[8, 12]$

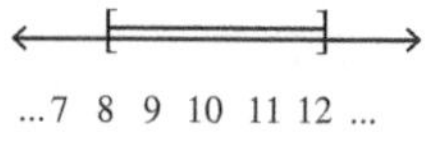

79. $(-\infty, \frac{5}{3})$ **81.** $(-\frac{3}{2}, \infty)$

83. $(4, 9]$ **85.** $[3, \frac{7}{2}]$

87. $[-6, 6]$ **89.** $(-\infty, 0] \cup [4, \infty)$

91. $(-\infty, -\frac{3}{4}) \cup (4, \infty)$ **93.** $(0, 3)$

95. $(-\infty, -6] \cup [9, \infty)$ **97.** $(-\infty, 2) \cup (4, 5]$

99. $(-\infty, -11) \cup (3, \infty)$ **101.** $(-\infty, -3) \cup (3, \infty)$

103. $\mathbb{R}$ **105.** $3\sqrt{5}$

107. $\sqrt{205}$ **109.** $(\frac{5}{2}, 6)$

111. (3.85, 5.3) **113.** $(\pm 2, 0), (0, \pm 1)$

115. $(\pm 3, 0)$, no y-intercepts

117. y-axis **119.** origin

121.

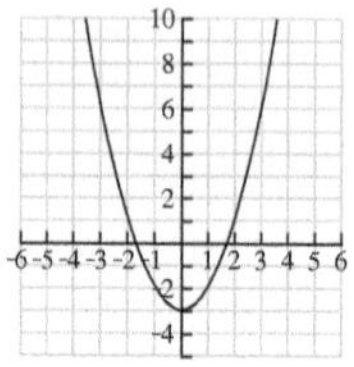

123.

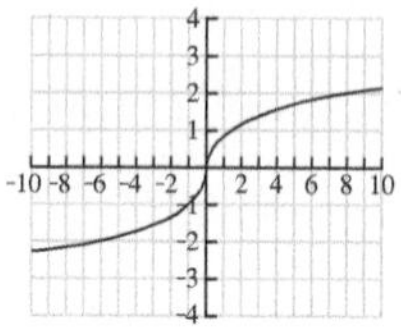

125.

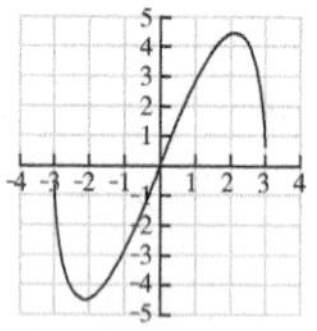

127. $(-2, -3), r = 9$

129. not a circle **131.** $y = -2x - 2$

133. $y = 6$ **135.** $y = \frac{5}{6}x + \frac{4}{3}$

137. $y = -2x - 1$ **139.** $y = \frac{2}{3}x + \frac{1}{3}$

141. $C = 2\pi r$ **143.** $A = \pi r^2$

Chapter 0 Practice Test

1. $p = -3$ **3.** $t = -4, 7$ **5.** $x = -\frac{1}{2}, \frac{8}{3}$

7. $y = -8$ **9.** $x = 4$ **11.** $y = 1$

13. $x = 0, 2, 6$ **15.** $(-\infty, 17]$ **17.** $(-\frac{32}{5}, -6]$

19. $(-\infty, -1] \cup [\frac{4}{3}, \infty)$

21. $(-\frac{1}{2}, 3]$

23. $\sqrt{82}$

25.

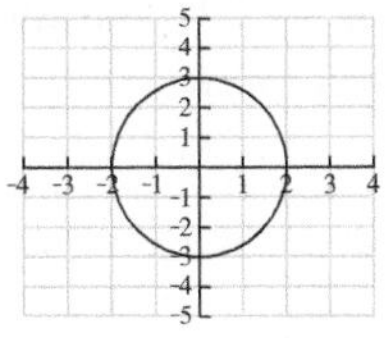

27. $(6, 0), (0, -2)$

29. $y = \frac{8}{3}x - 8$

31. $y = x + 5$

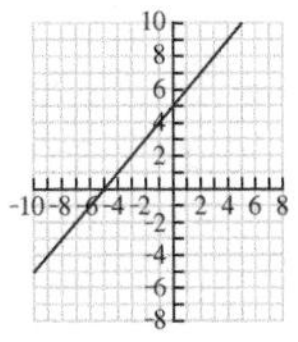

33. $y = -2x + 3$

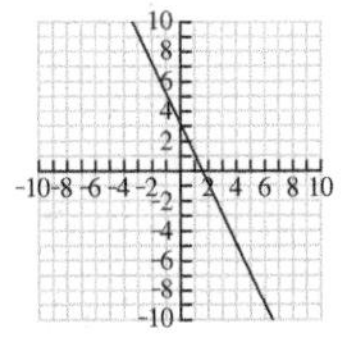

35. $F = \dfrac{30m}{P}$

CHAPTER 1

Section 1.1

1. not a function **3.** not a function

5. function **7.** not a function

9. not a function **11.** function

13. not a function **15.** function

17. not a function **19.** **a.** 5 **b.** 1 **c.** -3

21. **a.** 3 **b.** 2 **c.** 5 **23.** **a.** -5 **b.** -5 **c.** -5

25. **a.** 2 **b.** -8 **c.** -5 **27.** 1

29. -3 and 1 **31.** $[-4, 4]$

33. 6 **35.** -7 **37.** 6 **39.** -1

41. -33 **43.** $-\frac{7}{6}$ **45.** $\frac{2}{3}$ **47.** 4

49. $8 - x - a$ **51.** $(-\infty, \infty)$

53. $(-\infty, \infty)$ **55.** $(-\infty, 5) \cup (5, \infty)$

57. $(-\infty, -2) \cup (-2, 2) \cup (2, \infty)$

59. $(-\infty, \infty)$ **61.** $(-\infty, 7]$ **63.** $[-\frac{5}{2}, \infty)$

65. $(-\infty, -2] \cup [2, \infty)$ **67.** $(3, \infty)$

69. $(-\infty, \infty)$ **71.** $(-\infty, -4) \cup (-4, \infty)$

73. $(-\infty, \frac{3}{2})$ **75.** $(-\infty, -2) \cup (3, \infty)$

77. $(-\infty, -4] \cup [4, \infty)$ **79.** $(-\infty, \frac{3}{2})$

81. $(-\infty, \infty)$ **83.** $x = -2, 4$

85. $x = -1, 5, 6$ **87.** $T(6) = 64.8°F$, $T(12) = 90°F$

89. 27 ft, $[0, 2.8]$ **91.** $V(x) = x(10 - 2x)^2, (0, 5)$

93. E(4) ≈ 84 yen
E(7) ≈ 84 yen
E(8) ≈ 83 yen

95. 229 people

97. (1999, 2500), (2003, 3700), (2007, 4700), (2011, 5900), (2015, 6600)

99. **a.** $F(50) = 0$ **b.** $g(50) = 1000$ **c.** $H(50) = 2000$

101. Should apply the vertical line test to determine whether the relationship describes a function, which it does.

103. $f(x + 1) \neq f(x) + f(1)$, in general.

105. false **107.** true

109. $A = 2$ **111.** $C = -5, D = -2$

113. $(-\infty, -a) \cup (-a, a) \cup (a, \infty)$

115. $f'(x) = 3x^2 + 1$ **117.** $f'(x) = \dfrac{8}{(x + 3)^2}$

Section 1.2

1. neither **3.** odd **5.** even

7. even **9.** neither **11.** neither

13. neither **15.** neither

17. **a.** $(-\infty, \infty)$ **b.** $[-1, \infty)$ **c.** increasing: $(-1, \infty)$, decreasing: $(-3, -2)$, constant: $(-\infty, -3) \cup (-2, -1)$ **d.** 0 **e.** -1 **f.** 2

19. **a.** $[-7, 2]$ **b.** $[-5, 4]$ **c.** increasing: $(-4, 0)$, decreasing: $(-7, -4) \cup (0, 2)$, constant: nowhere **d.** 4 **e.** 1 **f.** -5

21. **a.** $(-\infty, \infty)$ **b.** $(-\infty, \infty)$ **c.** increasing: $(-\infty, -3) \cup (4, \infty)$, decreasing: nowhere, constant: $(-3, 4)$ **d.** 2 **e.** 2 **f.** 2

23. **a.** $(-\infty, \infty)$ **b.** $[-4, \infty)$ **c.** increasing: $(0, \infty)$, decreasing: $(-\infty, 0)$, constant: nowhere **d.** -4 **e.** 0 **f.** 0

25. **a.** $(-\infty, 0) \cup (0, \infty)$ **b.** $(-\infty, 0) \cup (0, \infty)$ **c.** increasing: $(-\infty, 0) \cup (0, \infty)$, decreasing: nowhere, constant: nowhere **d.** undefined **e.** 3 **f.** -3

27. **a.** $(-\infty, 0) \cup (0, \infty)$ **b.** $(-\infty, 5) \cup [7]$ **c.** increasing: $(-\infty, 0)$, decreasing: $(5, \infty)$, constant: $(0, 5)$ **d.** undefined **e.** 3 **f.** 7

29. $2x + h - 1$ **31.** $2x + h + 3$

33. $2x + h - 3$ **35.** $-6x - 3h + 5$

37. $3x^2 + 3xh + h^2 + 2x + h$

39. $\dfrac{-2}{(x + h - 2)(x - 2)}$

41. $\dfrac{-2}{\sqrt{1 - 2(x + h)} + \sqrt{1 - 2x}}$

43. $\dfrac{-4}{\sqrt{x(x + h)}(\sqrt{x} + \sqrt{x + h})}$

45. 13 **47.** 1 **49.** -2 **51.** -1

53. domain: $(-\infty, \infty)$ range: $(-\infty, 2]$ increasing: $(-\infty, 2)$ decreasing: nowhere constant: $(2, \infty)$

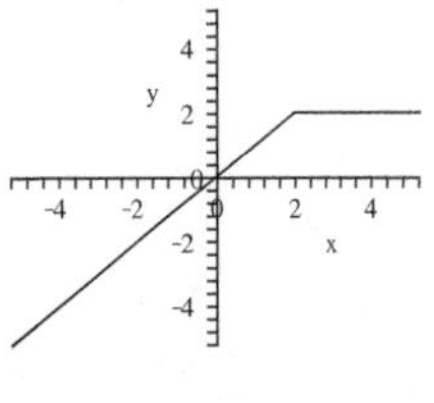

55. domain: $(-\infty, \infty)$ range: $[0, \infty)$ increasing: $(0, \infty)$ decreasing: $(-1, 0)$ constant: $(-\infty, -1)$

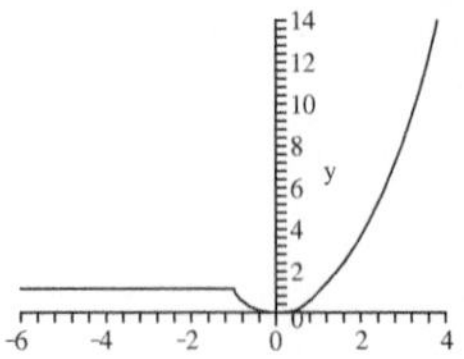

57. domain: $(-\infty, \infty)$ range: $(-\infty, \infty)$ increasing: $(-\infty, \infty)$ decreasing: nowhere constant: nowhere

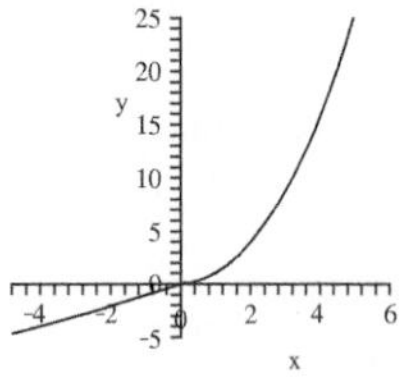

59. domain: $(-\infty, \infty)$ range: $[1, \infty)$ increasing: $(1, \infty)$ decreasing: $(-\infty, 1)$ constant: nowhere

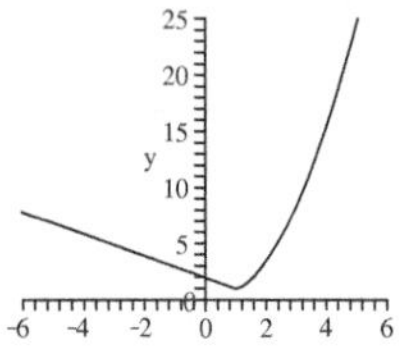

61. domain: $(-\infty, 2) \cup (2, \infty)$ range: $(1, \infty)$ increasing: $(2, \infty)$ decreasing: $(-\infty, 2)$

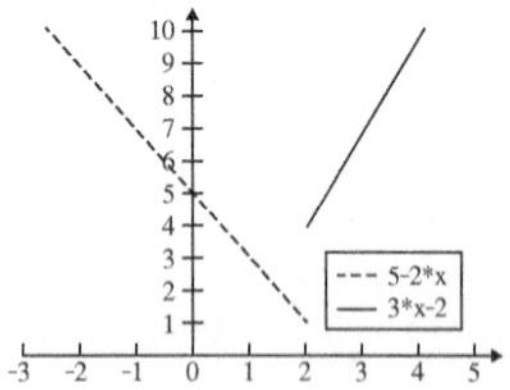

63. domain: $(-\infty, \infty)$ range: $[-1, 3]$ increasing: $(-1, 3)$ decreasing: nowhere constant: $(-\infty, -1) \cup (3, \infty)$

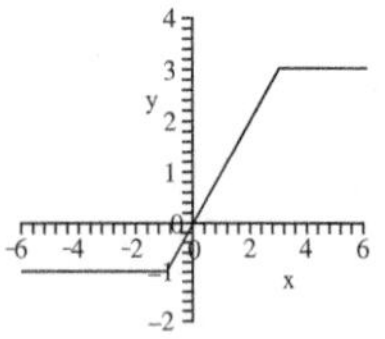

65. domain: $(-\infty, \infty)$ range: $[1, 4]$ increasing: $(1, 2)$ decreasing: nowhere constant: $(-\infty, 1) \cup (2, \infty)$

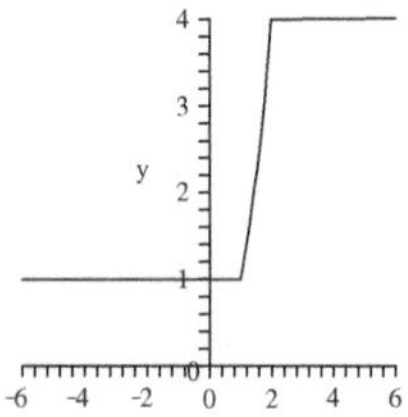

67. domain: $(-\infty, -2) \cup (-2, \infty)$ range: $(-\infty, \infty)$ increasing: $(-2, 1)$ decreasing: $(-\infty, -2) \cup (1, \infty)$ constant: nowhere

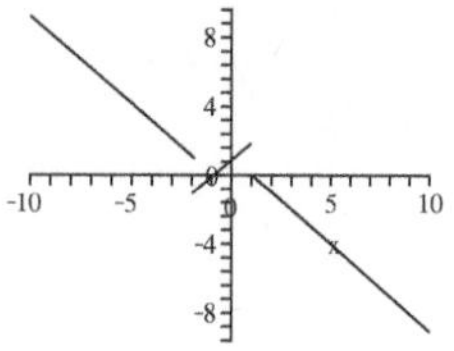

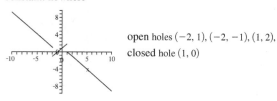

open holes $(-2, 1), (-2, -1), (1, 2)$, closed hole $(1, 0)$

69. domain: $(-\infty, \infty)$ range: $[0, \infty)$ increasing: $(0, \infty)$ decreasing: nowhere constant: $(-\infty, 0)$

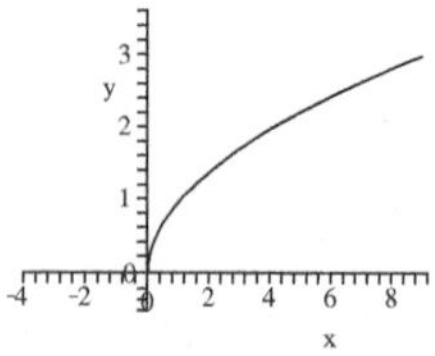

71. domain: $(-\infty, \infty)$ range: $(-\infty, \infty)$ increasing: nowhere decreasing: $(-\infty, 0) \cup (0, \infty)$ constant: nowhere

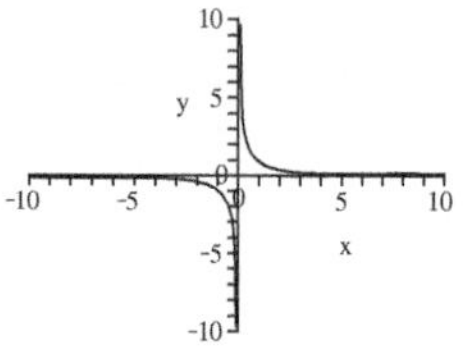

closed hole $(0, 0)$

73. domain: $(-\infty, 1) \cup (1, \infty)$ range: $(-\infty, -1) \cup (-1, \infty)$ increasing: $(-1, 1)$ decreasing: $(-\infty, -1) \cup (1, \infty)$ constant: nowhere

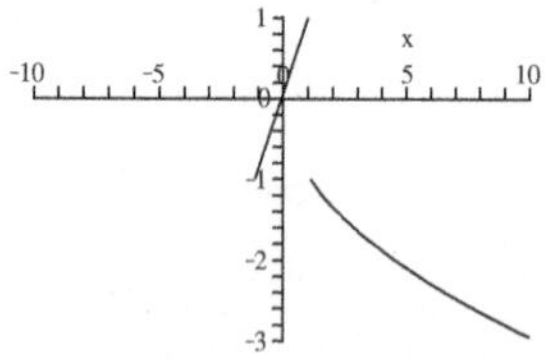

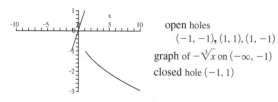

open holes $(-1, -1), (1, 1), (1, -1)$
graph of $-\sqrt[3]{x}$ on $(-\infty, -1)$
closed hole $(-1, 1)$

75. domain: $(-\infty, \infty)$ range: $(-\infty, 2) \cup [4, \infty)$ increasing: $(-\infty, -2) \cup (0, 2) \cup (2, \infty)$ decreasing: $(-2, 0)$ constant: nowhere

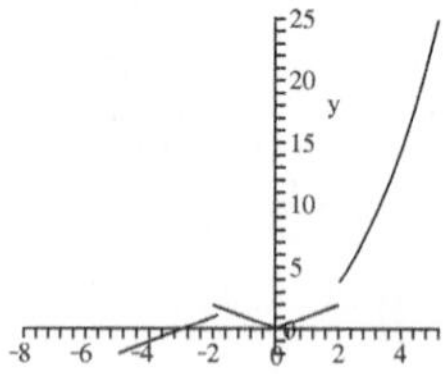

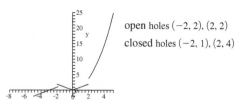

open holes $(-2, 2), (2, 2)$
closed holes $(-2, 1), (2, 4)$

77. domain: $(-\infty, 1) \cup (1, \infty)$
range: $(-\infty, 1) \cup (1, \infty)$
increasing: $(-\infty, 1) \cup (1, \infty)$
decreasing: nowhere constant: nowhere

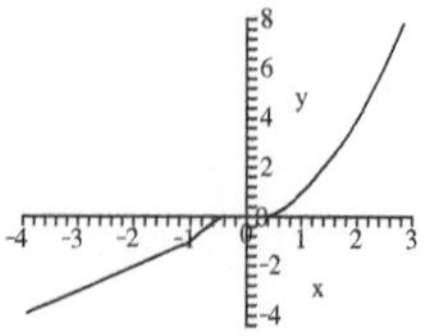

open hole $(1, 1)$

79. Profit is increasing from October through December and decreasing from January through October.

81. $C(x) = \begin{cases} 10x, & 0 \le x \le 50 \\ 9x, & 50 < x \le 100 \\ 8x, & x > 100 \end{cases}$

83. $C(x) = \begin{cases} 250x, & 0 \le x \le 10 \\ 175x + 750, & x > 10 \end{cases}$

85. $R(x) = \begin{cases} 50{,}000 + 3x, & 0 \le x \le 100{,}000 \\ -50{,}000 + 4x, & x > 100{,}000 \end{cases}$

87. $f(x) = 0.98 + 0.22[[x]], x \ge 0$

89. $f(t) = 3(-1)^{[t]}, t \ge 0$

91. **a.** 20 per yr **b.** 110 per yr

93. 0 ft/sec

95. Demand for the product is increasing at an approximate rate of 236 units over the first quarter.

97. The portion of $C(x)$ for $x > 30$ should be:

$15 + \underbrace{x - 30}_{\text{Number minutes beyond first 30}}$

99. false

101. yes, if $a = 2b$

103. yes, if $a = -4, b = -5$

105. $f'(x) = 0$

107. $f'(x) = 2ax + b$

Section 1.3

1. $y = |x| + 3$

3. $y = |-x| = |x|$

5. $y = 3|x|$

7. $y = x^3 - 4$

9. $y = (x + 1)^3 + 3$

11. $y = -x^3$

13.

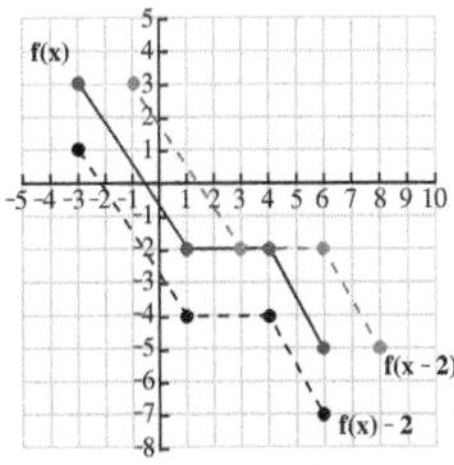

15.

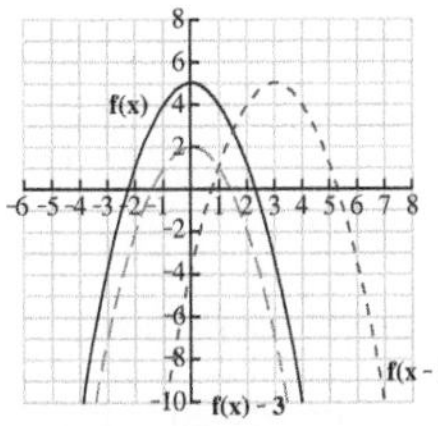

17.

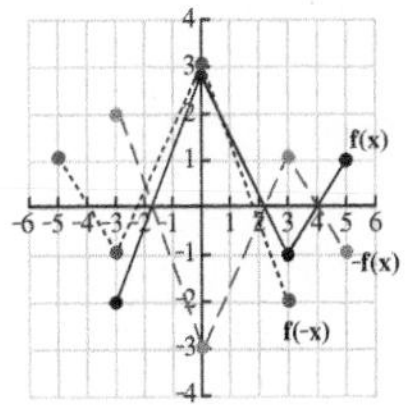

19.

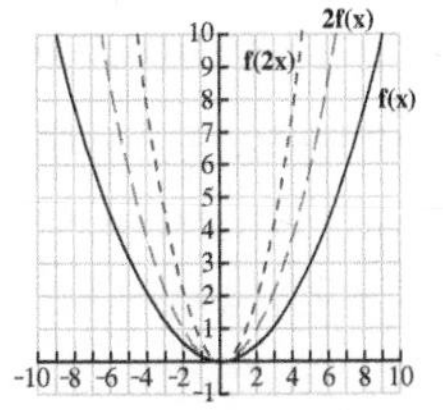

21.

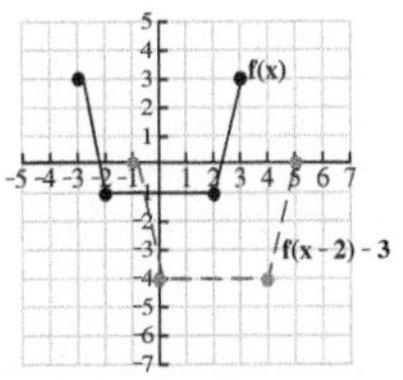

23.

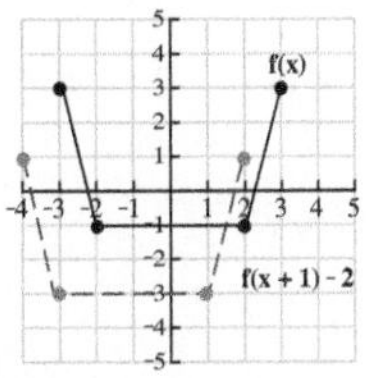

25.

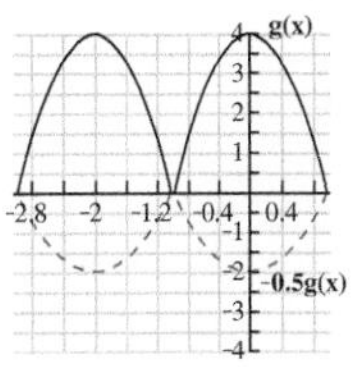

27.

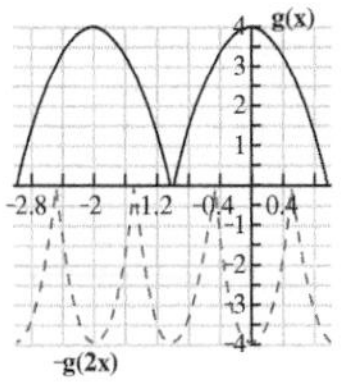

29.

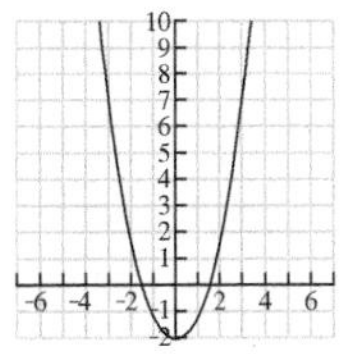

31.

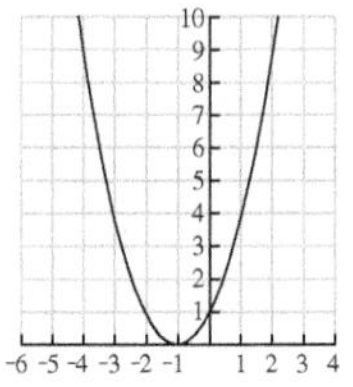

33.

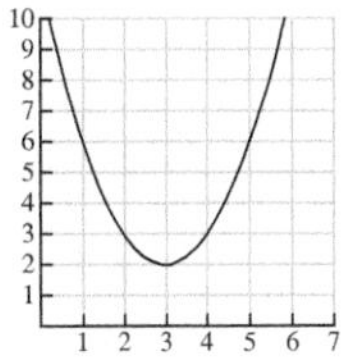

35.

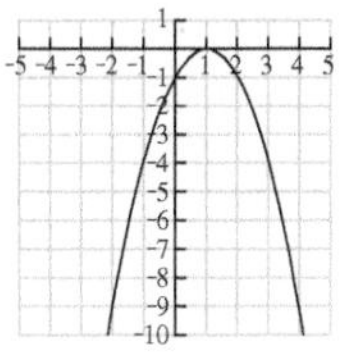

37.

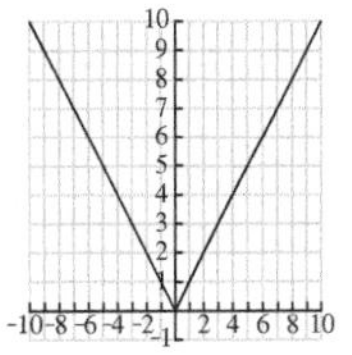

39.

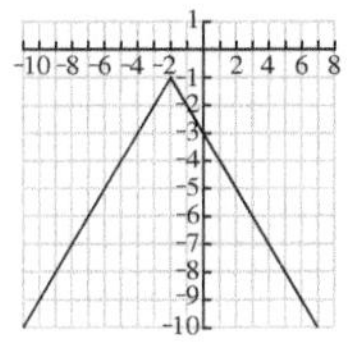

41.

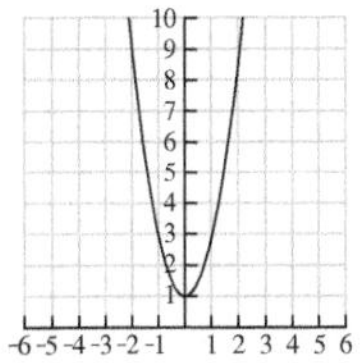

43.

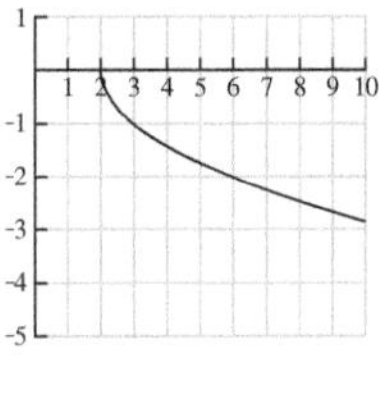

45.

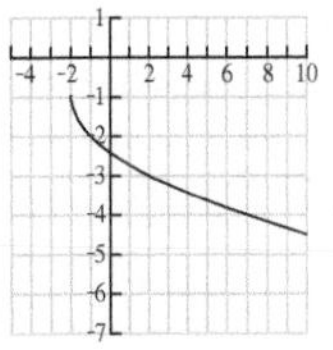

47.

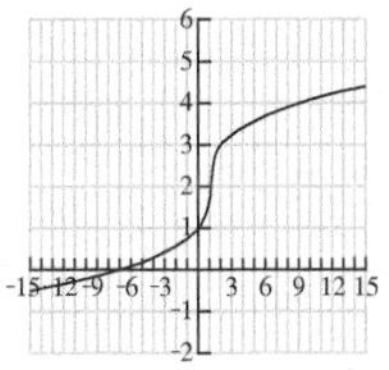

49.

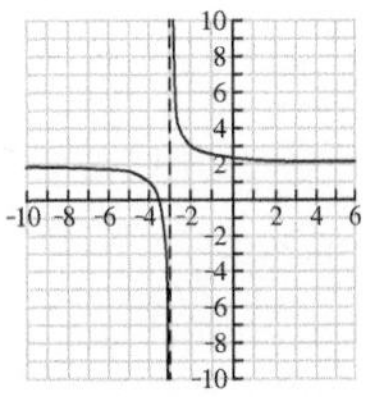

51.

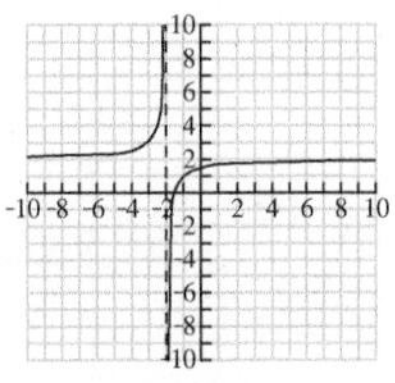

53. $f(x) = (x - 3)^2 + 2$

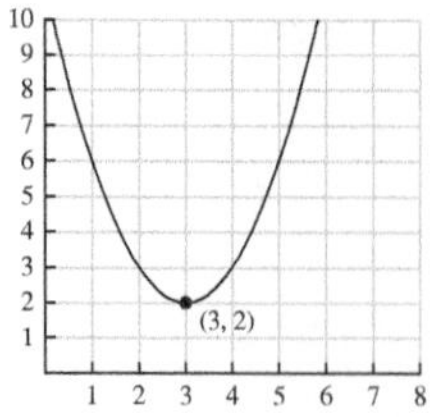

55. $f(x) = -(x + 1)^2 + 1$

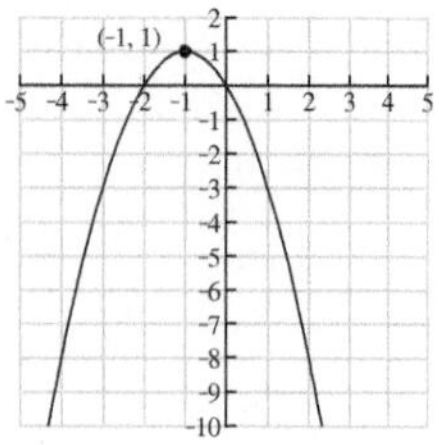

57. $f(x) = 2(x - 2)^2 - 5$

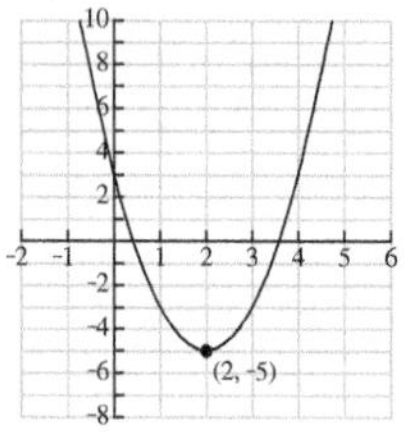

59. $S(x) = 10x$ and $S(x) = 10x + 50$

61. $T(x) = 0.33(x - 6500)$

63. $Q(t) = P(t + 50)$

65. a. $\text{BSA}(w) = \sqrt{\frac{900}{200}}$ **b.** $\text{BSA}(w - 3) = \sqrt{\frac{9(w-3)}{200}}$

67. (b) is wrong — shift right three units.

69. true **71.** true **73.** true

75. $(a + 3, b + 2)$ **77.** $(a - 1, 2b - 1)$

79. $f'(x) = 2x$, $g'(x) = 2(x - 1)$, g' is obtained by shifting f' to the right 1 unit.

81. $f'(x) = 2$, $g'(x) = 2$, f' and g' are the same.

Section 1.4

1.

$$\left.\begin{aligned} f(x) + g(x) &= x + 2 \\ f(x) - g(x) &= 3x \\ f(x) \cdot g(x) &= -2x^2 + x + 1 \end{aligned}\right\} \text{domain: } (-\infty, \infty)$$

$$\frac{f(x)}{g(x)} = \frac{2x + 1}{1 - x} \text{ domain: } (-\infty, 1) \cup (1, \infty)$$

3.

$$\left.\begin{aligned} f(x) + g(x) &= 3x^2 - x - 4 \\ f(x) - g(x) &= x^2 - x + 4 \\ f(x) \cdot g(x) &= 2x^4 - x^3 - 8x^2 + 4x \end{aligned}\right\} \text{domain: } (-\infty, \infty)$$

$$\frac{f(x)}{g(x)} = \frac{2x^2 - x}{x^2 - 4}$$

domain: $(-\infty, -2) \cup (-2, 2) \cup (2, \infty)$

5.

$$\left.\begin{aligned} f(x) + g(x) &= \frac{1 + x^2}{x} \\ f(x) - g(x) &= \frac{1 - x^2}{x} \\ f(x) \cdot g(x) &= 1 \\ \frac{f(x)}{g(x)} &= \frac{1}{x^2} \end{aligned}\right\} \text{domain: } (-\infty, 0) \cup (0, \infty)$$

7.

$$\left.\begin{aligned} f(x) + g(x) &= 3\sqrt{x} \\ f(x) - g(x) &= -\sqrt{x} \\ f(x) \cdot g(x) &= 2x \end{aligned}\right\} \text{domain: } [0, \infty)$$

$$\frac{f(x)}{g(x)} = \frac{1}{2} \text{ domain: } (0, \infty)$$

9.

$$\left.\begin{aligned} f(x) + g(x) &= \sqrt{4 - x} + \sqrt{x + 3} \\ f(x) - g(x) &= \sqrt{4 - x} - \sqrt{x + 3} \\ f(x) \cdot g(x) &= \sqrt{4 - x} \cdot \sqrt{x + 3} \end{aligned}\right\} \text{domain: } [-3, 4]$$

$$\frac{f(x)}{g(x)} = \frac{\sqrt{4 - x}\,\sqrt{x + 3}}{x + 3} \text{ domain: } (-3, 4]$$

11. $(f \circ g)(x) = 2x^2 - 5$ domain: $(-\infty, \infty)$
$(g \circ f)(x) = 4x^2 + 4x - 2$ domain: $(-\infty, \infty)$

13. $(f \circ g)(x) = \dfrac{1}{x + 1}$
domain: $(-\infty, -1) \cup (-1, \infty)$
$(g \circ f)(x) = \dfrac{2x - 1}{x - 1}$ domain: $(-\infty, 1) \cup (1, \infty)$

15. $(f \circ g)(x) = \dfrac{1}{|x - 1|}$ domain: $(-\infty, 1) \cup (1, \infty)$
$(g \circ f)(x) = \dfrac{1}{|x| - 1}$
domain: $(-\infty, -1) \cup (-1, 1) \cup (1, \infty)$

17. $(f \circ g)(x) = \sqrt{x + 4}$ domain: $[-4, \infty)$
$(g \circ f)(x) = \sqrt{x - 1} + 5$ domain: $[1, \infty)$

19. $(f \circ g)(x) = x$ domain: $(-\infty, \infty)$
$(g \circ f)(x) = x$ domain: $(-\infty, \infty)$

21. 15 **23.** 13 **25.** $26\sqrt{3}$

27. $\frac{110}{3}$ **29.** 11 **31.** $3\sqrt{2}$

33. undefined **35.** undefined **37.** 13

39. $f(g(1)) = \frac{1}{3}$ $g(f(2)) = 2$

41. $f(g(1)) =$ undefined $g(f(2)) =$ undefined

43. $f(g(1)) = \frac{1}{3}$ $g(f(2)) = 4$

45. $f(g(1)) = \sqrt{5}$ $g(f(2)) = 6$

47. $f(g(1)) =$ undefined $g(f(2)) =$ undefined

49. $f(g(1)) = \sqrt[3]{3}$ $g(f(2)) = 4$

51. $f(g(x)) = 2\left(\dfrac{x - 1}{2}\right) + 1 = x - 1 + 1 = x$

$g(f(x)) = \dfrac{(2x + 1) - 1}{2} = \dfrac{2x}{2} = x$

53. $f(g(x)) = \sqrt{(x^2 + 1) - 1} = \sqrt{x^2} = \underbrace{|x| = x}_{\text{Since } x \geq 1}$

$g(f(x)) = (\sqrt{x - 1})^2 + 1 = (x - 1) + 1 = x$

55. $f(g(x)) = \dfrac{1}{\frac{1}{x}} = x$ $g(f(x)) = \dfrac{1}{\frac{1}{x}} = x$

57. $f(g(x)) = 4\left(\frac{\sqrt{x+9}}{2}\right)^2 - 9$

$= 4\left(\frac{x+9}{4}\right) - 9 = x$

$g(f(x)) = \frac{\sqrt{(4x^2-9)+9}}{2}$

$= \frac{\sqrt{4x^2}}{2} = \frac{2x}{2} = x$

59. $f(g(x)) = \frac{1}{\frac{x+1}{x} - 1} = \frac{1}{\frac{x+1-x}{x}} = \frac{1}{\frac{1}{x}} = x$

$g(f(x)) = \frac{\frac{1}{x-1} + 1}{\frac{1}{x-1}} = \frac{\frac{1+x-1}{x-1}}{\frac{1}{x-1}} = \frac{\frac{x}{\cancel{x-1}}}{\frac{1}{\cancel{x-1}}} = x$

61. $f(x) = 2x^2 + 5x \quad g(x) = 3x - 1$

63. $f(x) = \frac{2}{|x|} \quad g(x) = x - 3$

65. $f(x) = \frac{3}{\sqrt{x} - 2} \quad g(x) = x + 1$

67. $F(C(K)) = \frac{9}{5}(K - 273.15) + 32$

69. **a.** $C(p) = 62{,}000 - 20p$

b. $R(p) = 600{,}000 - 200p$

c. $P(p) = 538{,}000 - 180p$

71. **a.** $C(n(t)) = -10t^2 + 500t + 1375$

b. $C(n(16)) = 6815$

The cost of production on a day when the assembly line was running for 16 hours is $6,815,000.

73. **a.** $A(r(t)) = \pi(10t - 0.2t^2)^2$

b. 11,385 sq mi

75. Must exclude -2 from the domain

77. $(f \circ g)(x) = f(g(x))$, not $f(x) \cdot g(x)$

79. Function notation, not multiplication

81. false **83.** true

85. $(g \circ f)(x) = \frac{1}{x}$ domain: $x \neq 0, a$

87. $(g \circ f)(x) = x$ domain: $[-a, \infty)$

89. $H'(x) = F'(x) + G'(x)$

91. $H'(x) \neq F'(x)G'(x)$

Section 1.5

1. not a function

3. function, not one-to-one

5. function, not one-to-one

7. function, one-to-one

9. function, not one-to-one

11. not one-to-one function

13. one-to-one function

15. not one-to-one function

17. one-to-one function

19.

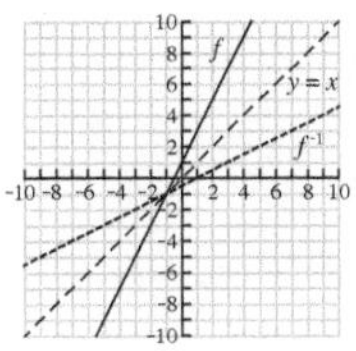

21.

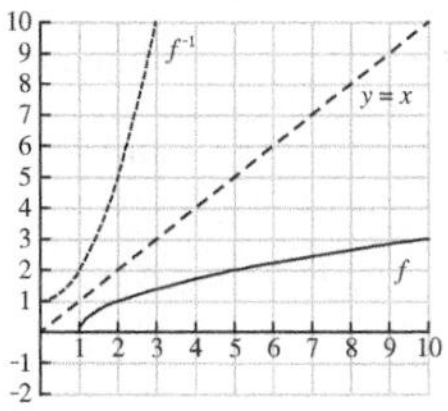

23.

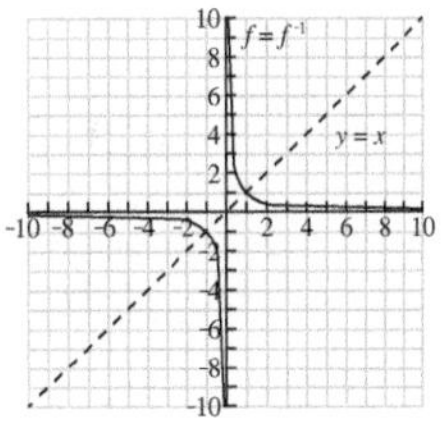

25

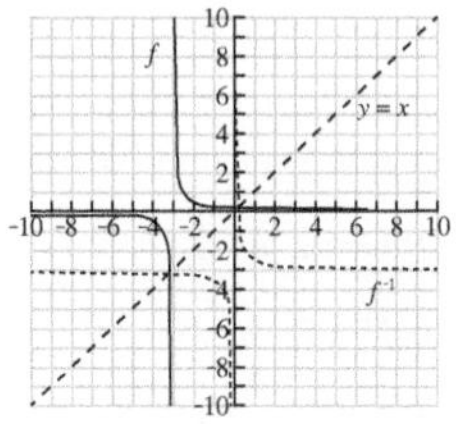

27.

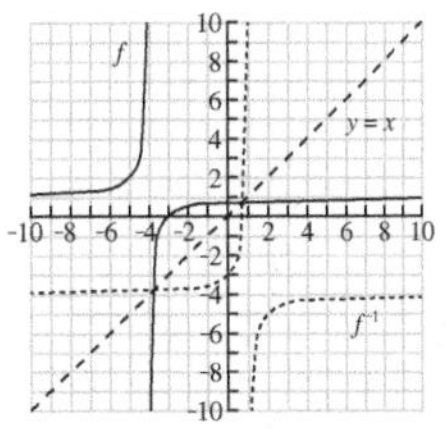

29.

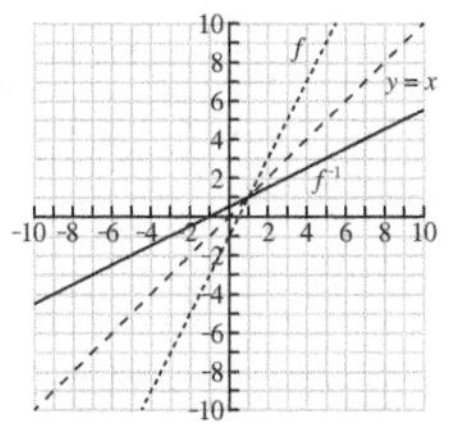

31.

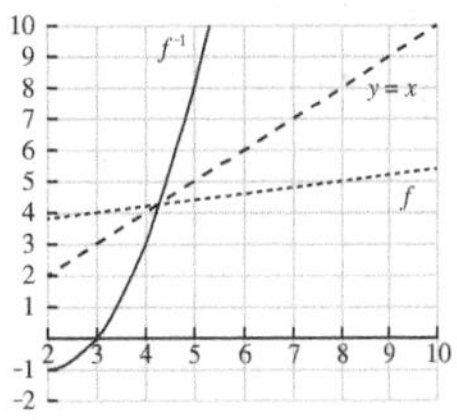

33.

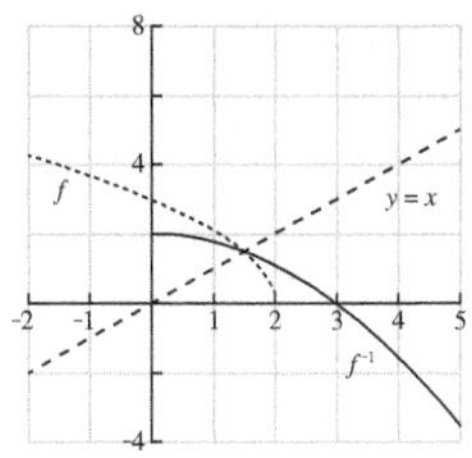

35.

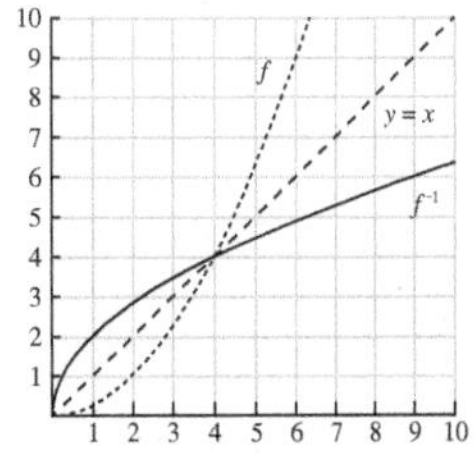

37. $f^{-1}(x) = -\frac{1}{3}x + \frac{2}{3}$

domain f: $(-\infty, \infty)$ domain f^{-1}: $(-\infty, \infty)$

range f: $(-\infty, \infty)$ range f^{-1}: $(-\infty, \infty)$

39. $f^{-1}(x) = \sqrt[3]{x - 1}$

domain f: $(-\infty, \infty)$ domain f^{-1}: $(-\infty, \infty)$

range f: $(-\infty, \infty)$ range f^{-1}: $(-\infty, \infty)$

41. $f^{-1}(x) = x^2 + 3$

domain f: $[3, \infty)$ domain f^{-1}: $[0, \infty)$

range f: $[0, \infty)$ range f^{-1}: $[3, \infty)$

43. $f^{-1}(x) = \sqrt{x + 1}$

domain f: $[0, \infty)$ domain f^{-1}: $[-1, \infty)$

range f: $[-1, \infty)$ range f^{-1}: $[0, \infty)$

45. $f^{-1}(x) = -2 + \sqrt{x + 3}$

domain f: $[-2, \infty)$ domain f^{-1}: $[-3, \infty)$

range f: $[-3, \infty)$ range f^{-1}: $[-2, \infty)$

47. $f^{-1}(x) = \dfrac{2}{x}$

domain f: $(-\infty, 0) \cup (0, \infty)$

range f: $(-\infty, 0) \cup (0, \infty)$

domain f^{-1}: $(-\infty, 0) \cup (0, \infty)$

range f^{-1}: $(-\infty, 0) \cup (0, \infty)$

49. $f^{-1}(x) = \dfrac{3x - 2}{x} = 3 - \dfrac{2}{x}$

domain f: $(-\infty, 3) \cup (3, \infty)$

range$f$: $(-\infty, 0) \cup (0, \infty)$

domain f^{-1}: $(-\infty ,0) \cup (0, \infty)$

range f^{-1}: $(-\infty, 3) \cup (3, \infty)$

51. $f^{-1}(x) = \dfrac{5x - 1}{x + 7}$

domain f: $(-\infty, 5) \cup (5, \infty)$

range f: $(-\infty, -7) \cup (-7, \infty)$

domain f^{-1}: $(-\infty, -7) \cup (-7, \infty)$

range f^{-1}: $(-\infty, 5) \cup (5, \infty)$

53. $f^{-1}(x) = \dfrac{1}{x^2}$

domain f = range f^{-1}: $(0, \infty)$

range f = domain f^{-1}: $(0, \infty)$

55. $f^{-1}(x) = \dfrac{2x^2 + 1}{x^2 - 1}$

domain f = range f^{-1}: $(-\infty, -1] \cup (2, \infty)$

range f = domain f^{-1}: $[0, 1) \cup (1, \infty)$

57. not one-to-one

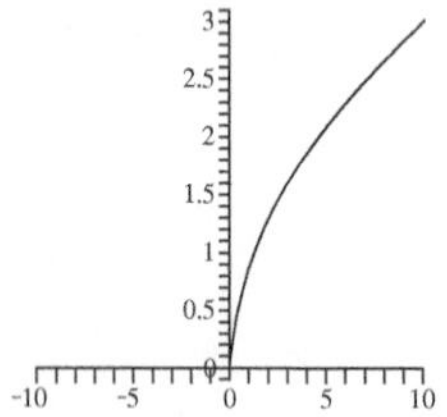

59. one-to-one

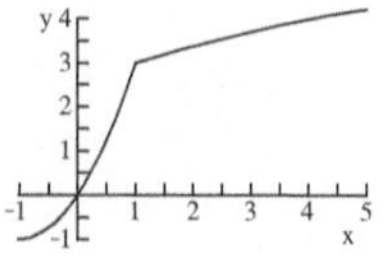

$$f^{-1}(x) = \begin{cases} x^3, x \le -1, \\ -1 + \sqrt{x+1}, -1 < x \le 1, \\ (x-2)^2, x > 1 \end{cases}$$

61. one-to-one

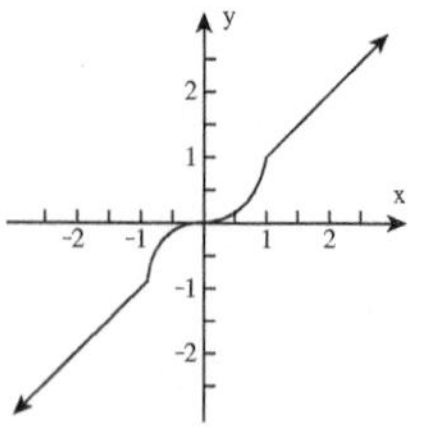

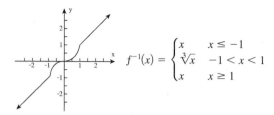

$$f^{-1}(x) = \begin{cases} x & x \le -1 \\ \sqrt[3]{x} & -1 < x < 1 \\ x & x \ge 1 \end{cases}$$

63. $f^{-1}(x) = \frac{5}{9}(x - 32)$ The inverse function represents the conversion from degrees Fahrenheit to degrees Celsius.

65. $C(x) = \begin{cases} 250x, & 0 \le x \le 10 \\ 2500 + 175(x - 10), & x > 10 \end{cases}$

$C^{-1}(x) = \begin{cases} \dfrac{x}{250}, & 0 \le x \le 2500 \\ \dfrac{x - 750}{175}, & x > 2500 \end{cases}$

67. $E(x) = 5.25x$, $E^{-1}(x) = \dfrac{x}{5.25}$, $x \ge 0$ The inverse function tells you how many hours you need to work to attain a certain take-home pay.

69. Domain: $[0, 24]$ Range: $[97.5528, 101.70]$

71. Domain: $[97.5528, 101.70]$ Range: $[0, 24]$

73. Not a function since the graph does not pass the vertical line test

75. false **77.** false **79.** $(b, 0)$

81. $f(x) = \sqrt{1 - x^2}, 0 \le x \le 1$,

$f^{-1}(x) = \sqrt{1 - x^2}, 0 \le x \le 1$

Domain and range of both are $[0, 1]$.

83. $m \ne 0$

85. $a = 4$, $f^{-1}(x) = \dfrac{1 - 2x}{x}$, $(-\infty, 0) \cup (0, \infty)$

87. **a.** $f^{-1}(x) = \dfrac{x - 1}{2}$ **b.** $f'(x) = 2$ **c.** $(f^{-1})'(x) = \dfrac{1}{2}$

89. **a.** $f^{-1}(x) = x^2 - 2, x \ge 0$ **b.** $f'(x) = \dfrac{1}{2\sqrt{x + 2}}$

c. $(f^{-1})'(x) = 2x$

Review Exercises

1. yes **3.** no **5.** yes **7.** no

9. **a.** 2 **b.** 4 **c.** $x = -3, 4$

11. **a.** 0 **b.** -2 **c.** $x \approx -5, 2$

13. 5 **15.** -665 **17.** -2 **19.** 4

21. $(-\infty, \infty)$ **23.** $(-\infty, -4) \cup (-4, \infty)$

25. $[4, \infty)$ **27.** $D = 18$ **29.** odd **31.** odd

33. **a.** $[-5, \infty)$ **b.** $[-3, \infty)$ **c.** increasing: $(-5, -3) \cup (3, \infty)$, decreasing: $(-1, 1)$, constant: $(-3, 1) \cup (1, 3)$ **d.** 2 **e.** 3 **f.** 1

35. **a.** $[-6, 6]$ **b.** $[0, 3] \cup \{-3, -2, -1\}$

c. increasing: $(0, 3)$, decreasing: $(0, 3)$,

constant: $(-6, -4) \cup (-4, -2) \cup (-2, 0)$

d. -1 **e.** -2 **f.** 3

37. $3x^2 + 3xh + h^2$ **39.** $1 - \dfrac{1}{x(x+h)}$ **41.** -2

43. domain: $(-\infty, \infty)$ range: $(0, \infty)$

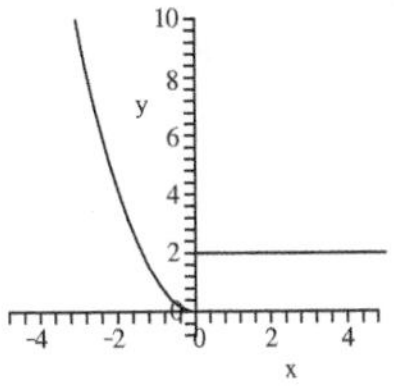

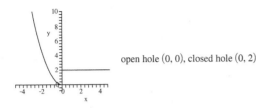

open hole $(0, 0)$, closed hole $(0, 2)$

45. domain: $(-\infty, \infty)$ range: $[-1, \infty)$

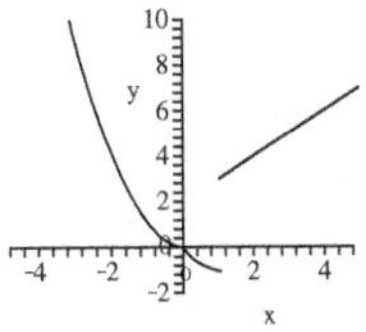

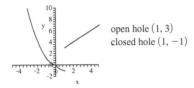

open hole $(1, 3)$
closed hole $(1, -1)$

47. \$29, 000 per year

49.

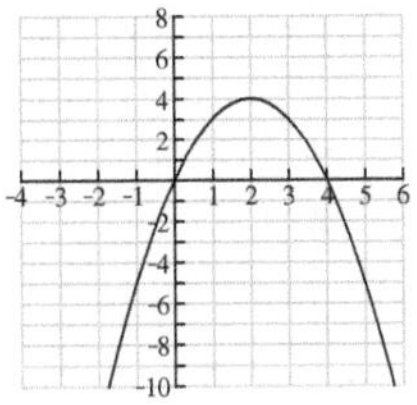

51.

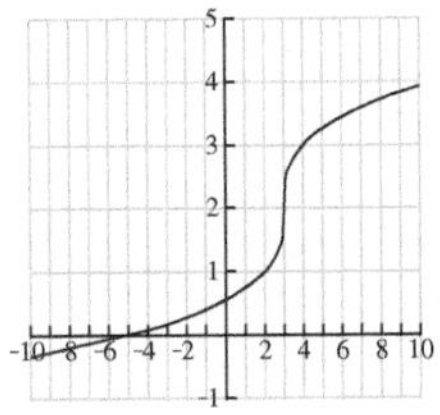

53.

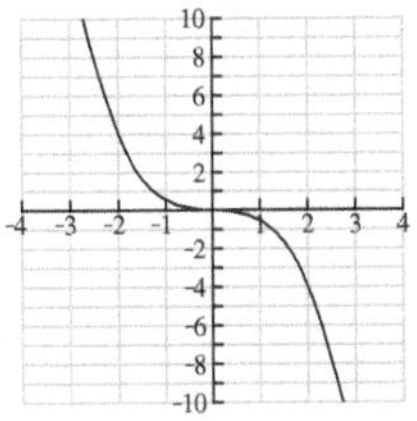

55.

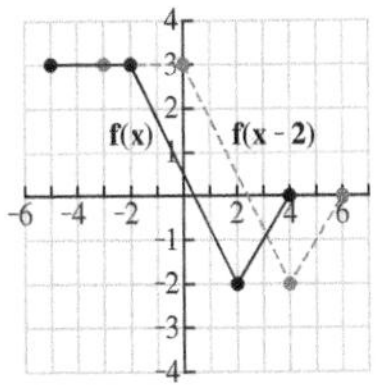

57.

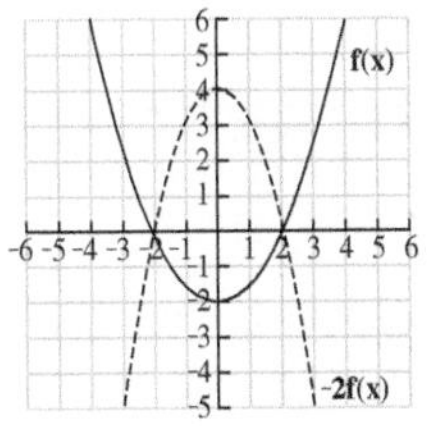

59. $y = \sqrt{x+3}$ domain: $[-3, \infty)$

61. $y = \sqrt{x-2} + 3$ domain: $[2, \infty)$

63. $y = 5\sqrt{x} - 6$ domain: $[0, \infty)$

65. $y = (x+2)^2 - 12$

67.

$$\left.\begin{aligned} g(x) + h(x) &= -2x - 7 \\ g(x) - h(x) &= -4x - 1 \\ g(x) \cdot h(x) &= -3x^2 + 5x + 12 \end{aligned}\right\} \text{domain: } (-\infty, \infty)$$

$$\frac{g(x)}{h(x)} = \frac{-3x - 4}{x - 3} \text{ domain: } (-\infty, 3) \cup (3, \infty)$$

69.

$$\left.\begin{aligned} g(x) + h(x) &= \frac{1}{x^2} + \sqrt{x} \\ g(x) - h(x) &= \frac{1}{x^2} - \sqrt{x} \\ g(x) \cdot h(x) &= \frac{1}{x^{3/2}} \\ \frac{g(x)}{h(x)} &= \frac{1}{x^{5/2}} \end{aligned}\right\} \text{domain: } (0, \infty)$$

71.

$$\left.\begin{aligned} g(x) + h(x) &= \sqrt{x-4} + \sqrt{2x+1} \\ g(x) - h(x) &= \sqrt{x-4} - \sqrt{2x+1} \\ g(x) \cdot h(x) &= \sqrt{x-4} \cdot \sqrt{2x+1} \end{aligned}\right\} \text{domain: } [4, \infty)$$

$$\frac{g(x)}{h(x)} = \frac{\sqrt{x-4}}{\sqrt{2x+1}}$$

73. $(f \circ g)(x) = 6x - 1$ domain: $(-\infty, \infty)$

$(g \circ f)(x) = 6x - 7$ domain: $(-\infty, \infty)$

75. $(f \circ g)(x) = \dfrac{8 - 2x}{13 - 3x}$

domain: $(-\infty, 4) \cup \left(4, \frac{13}{3}\right) \cup \left(\frac{13}{3}, \infty\right)$

$(g \circ f)(x) = \dfrac{x + 3}{4x + 10}$

domain: $(-\infty, -3) \cup \left(-3, -\frac{5}{2}\right) \cup \left(-\frac{5}{2}, \infty\right)$

77. $(f \circ g)(x) = \sqrt{(x-3)(x+3)}$

domain: $(-\infty, -3] \cup [3, \infty)$

$(g \circ f)(x) = x - 9$ domain: $[5, \infty)$

79. $f(g(3)) = 857, \quad g(f(-1)) = 51$

81. $f(g(3)) = \frac{17}{31}, \quad g(f(-1)) = 1$

83. $f(g(3)) = 12, \quad g(f(-1)) = 2$

85. $f(x) = 3x^2 + 4x + 7, \quad g(x) = x - 2$

87. $f(x) = \dfrac{1}{\sqrt{x}}, \quad g(x) = x^2 + 7$

89. $A(t) = 625\pi(t + 2)$ in^2

91. yes **93.** yes **95.** yes

97. not one-to-one **99.** one-to-one

101.

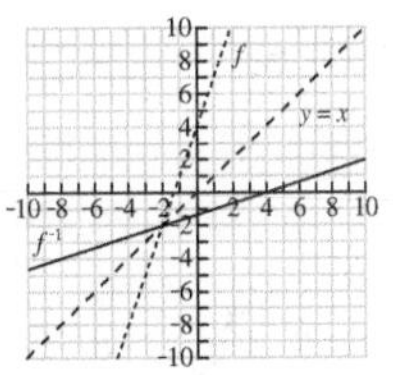

103.

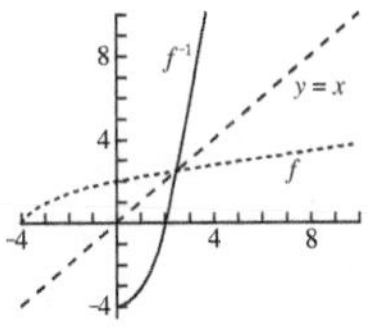

105. $f^{-1}(x) = \frac{1}{2}(x - 1) = \dfrac{x - 1}{2}$

domain f: $(-\infty, \infty)$ domain f^{-1}: $(-\infty, \infty)$

range f: $(-\infty, \infty)$ range f^{-1}: $(-\infty, \infty)$

107. $f^{-1}(x) = x^2 - 4$

domain f: $[-4, \infty)$ domain f^{-1}: $[0, \infty)$

range f: $[0, \infty)$ range f^{-1}: $[-4, \infty)$

109. $f^{-1}(x) = \dfrac{6 - 3x}{x - 1}$

domain f: $(-\infty, -3) \cup (-3, \infty)$

range f: $(-\infty, 1) \cup (1, \infty)$

domain f^{-1}: $(-\infty, 1) \cup (1, \infty)$

range f^{-1}: $(-\infty, -3) \cup (-3, \infty)$

111. $S(x) = 22,000 + 0.08x$,

$S^{-1}(x) = \dfrac{x - 22,000}{0.08}$, sales required to earn a desired income

Practice Test

1. b **3.** c

5. $\dfrac{\sqrt{x-2}}{x^2 + 11}$ domain: $[2, \infty)$

7. $x + 9$ domain: $[2, \infty)$ **9.** 4 **11.** neither

13. domain: $[3, \infty)$ range: $(-\infty, 2]$

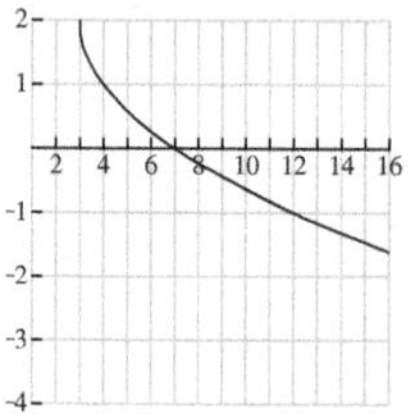

15. domain: $(-\infty, -1) \cup (-1, \infty)$ range: $[1, \infty)$

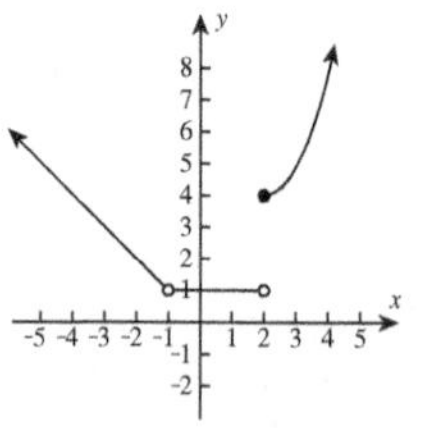

17. a. -2 **b.** 4 **c.** -3 **d.** $x = -3, 2$

19. $6x + 3h - 4$ **21.** -32

23. $f^{-1}(x) = x^2 + 5$

domain f: $[5, \infty)$ domain f^{-1}: $[0, \infty)$

range f: $[0, \infty)$ range f^{-1}: $[5, \infty)$

25. $f^{-1}(x) = \dfrac{5x - 1}{x + 2}$

domain f: $(-\infty, 5) \cup (5, \infty)$

range f: $(-\infty, -2) \cup (-2, \infty)$

domain f^{-1}: $(-\infty, -2) \cup (-2, \infty)$

range f^{-1}: $(-\infty, 5) \cup (5, \infty)$

27. $[0, \infty)$

29. $P(t) = \frac{9}{10}t + 10$

31. quadrant III, "quarter of unit circle"

33. $C(x) = \begin{cases} 15, & 0 \le x \le 30 \\ x - 15, & x > 30 \end{cases}$

CHAPTER 2

Section 2.1

1. b **3.** a **5.** b **7.** c

9.

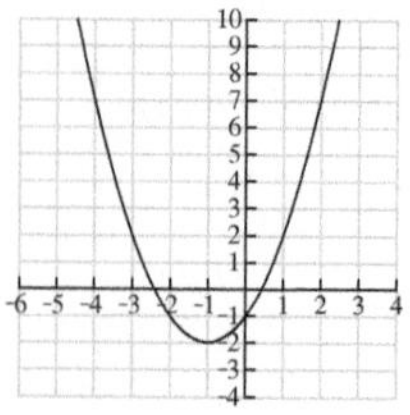

11.

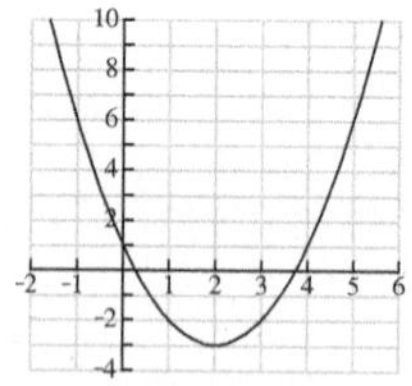

13.

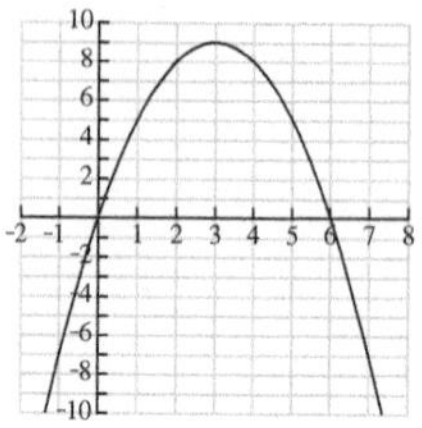

15.

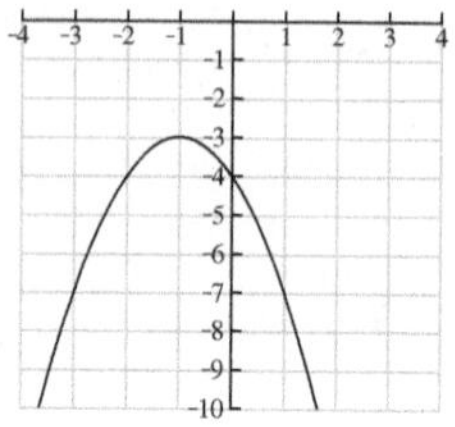

17.

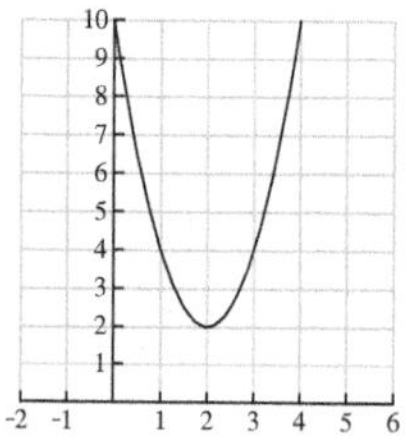

19.

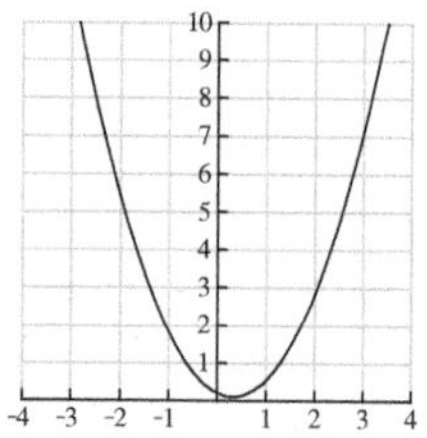

21. $f(x) = (x + 3)^2 - 12$ **23.** $f(x) = -(x + 5)^2 + 28$

25. $f(x) = 2(x + 2)^2 - 10$ **27.** $f(x) = -4(x - 2)^2 + 9$

29. $f(x) = (x + 5)^2 - 25$ **31.** $f(x) = \frac{1}{2}(x - 4)^2 - 5$

33.

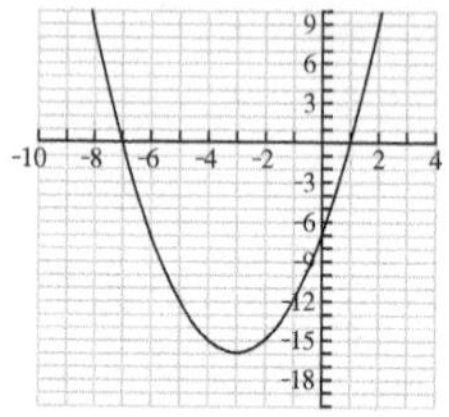

35.

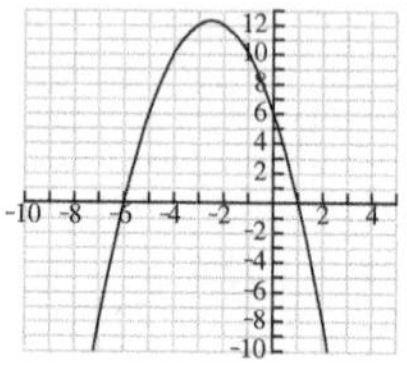

37.

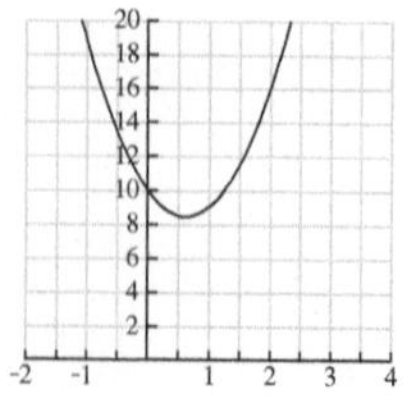

39.

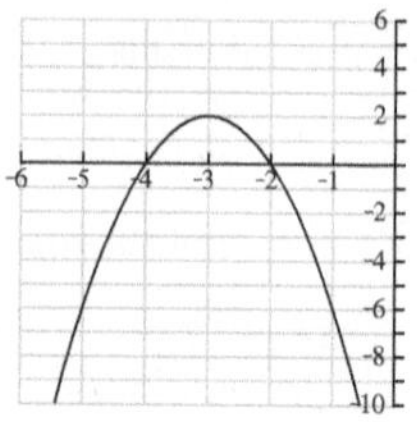

41. $\left(\frac{1}{33}, \frac{494}{33}\right)$ **43.** $\left(7, -\frac{39}{2}\right)$

45. $(21.67, -24.65)$ **47.** $y = -2(x + 1)^2 + 4$

49. $y = -5(x - 2)^2 + 5$ **51.** $y = \frac{5}{9}(x + 1)^2 - 3$

53. $y = 10(x + 2)^2 - 4$ **55.** $y = 12\left(x - \frac{1}{2}\right)^2 - \frac{3}{4}$

57. a. 350,000 units **b.** $12,262,500

59. He is gaining weight during January 2010 and losing weight from February 2010 to June 2011.

61. **a.** 120 ft **b.** 50 yd

63. 2,083,333 sq ft

65. **a.** 1 sec, 116 ft **b.** 3.69 sec

67. **a.** 26,000 ft **b.** 8944 ft

69. 15 to 16 or 64 to 65 units to break even.

71. **a.** $y = -0.01(t - 225)^2 + 400$ **b.** 425 min

73. Step 2 is wrong: Vertex is $(-3, -1)$. Step 4 is wrong: The x-intercepts are $(-2, 0)$, $(-4, 0)$. Should graph $y = (x + 3)^2 - 1$.

75. true **77.** false

79. $f(x) = a\left(x + \frac{b}{2a}\right)^2 + \frac{4ac - b^2}{4a}$

81. **a.** 62,500 sq ft **b.** 79,577 sq ft

83. $x = 5$

85. $\frac{(x - 0)^2}{9} + \frac{(y - 2)^2}{4} = 1$ ellipse

87. $(x + 3)^2 = 20\left(y + \frac{1}{5}\right)$ parabola

Section 2.2

1. polynomial; degree 5 **3.** polynomial, degree 7

5. not a polynomial **7.** not a polynomial

9. not a polynomial **11.** h

13. b **15.** e **17.** c

19.

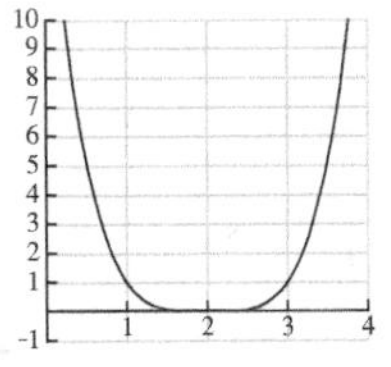

21.

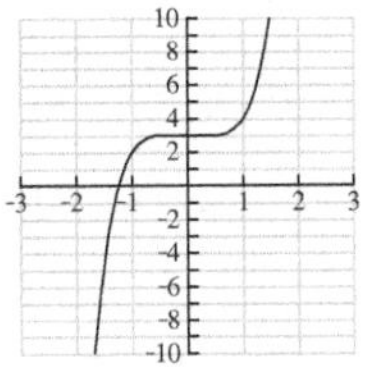

23.

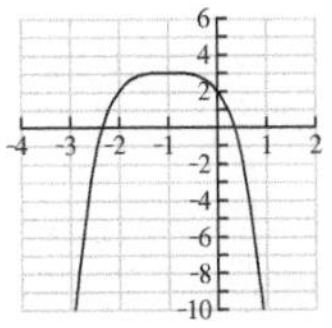

25. 3 (multiplicity 1), -4 (multiplicity 3)

27. 0 (multiplicity 2), 7 (multiplicity 2), -4 (multiplicity 1)

29. 0 (multiplicity 2), 1 (multiplicity 2)

31. 0 (multiplicity 1), $\frac{3}{2}$ (multiplicity 1), $-\frac{9}{4}$ (multiplicity 1)

33. $P(x) = x(x + 3)(x - 1)(x - 2)$

35. $P(x) = x(x + 5)(x + 3)(x - 2)(x - 6)$

37. $P(x) = (2x + 1)(3x - 2)(4x - 3)$

39. $P(x) = x^2 - 2x - 1$

41. $P(x) = x^2(x + 2)^3$

43. $P(x) = (x + 3)^2(x - 7)^5$

45. $P(x) = x^2(x + 1)(x + \sqrt{3})^2(x - \sqrt{3})^2$

47. $f(x) = (x - 2)^3$ **a.** 2 (multiplicity 3) **b.** crosses at 2 **c.** $(0, -8)$ **d.** falls left, rises right

e.

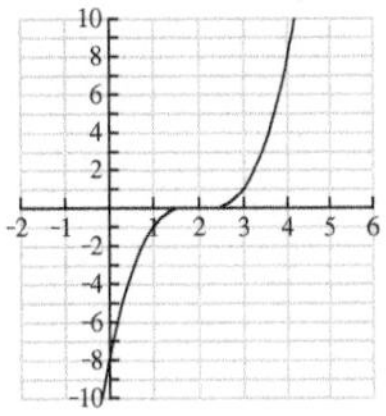

49. $f(x) = x(x - 3)(x + 3)$ **a.** 0, 3, -3 (multiplicity 1) **b.** crosses at each zero **c.** $(0, 0)$ **d.** falls left, rises right

e.

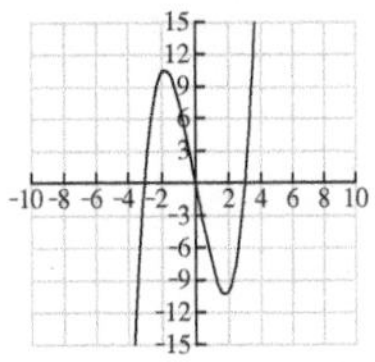

51. $f(x) = -x(x - 2)(x + 1)$ **a.** 0, 2, -1 (multiplicity 1) **b.** crosses at each zero **c.** $(0, 0)$ **d.** falls right, rises left

e.

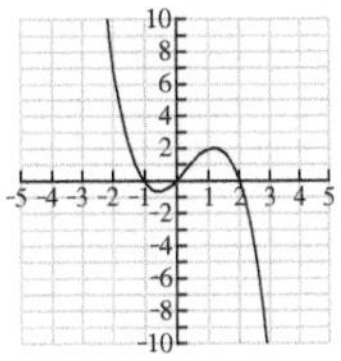

53. $f(x) = -x^3(x + 3)$ **a.** 0 (multiplicity 3), -3 (multiplicity 1) **b.** crosses at both 0 and -3 **c.** $(0, 0)$ **d.** falls left and right, without bound

e.

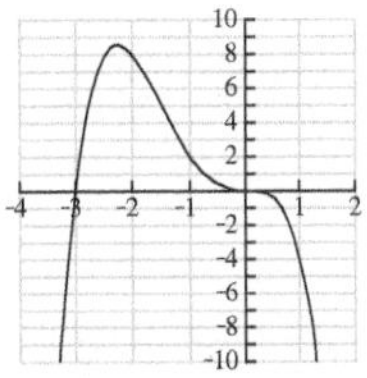

55. $f(x) = 12x^4(x - 4)(x + 1)$ **a.** 0 (multiplicity 4), 4 (multiplicity 1), -1 (multiplicity 1) **b.** touches at 0 and crosses at 4 and -1 **c.** (0,0) **d.** rises left and right, without bound

e.

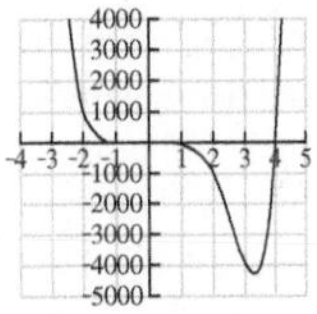

57. $f(x) = 2x^3(x - 4)(x + 1)$

a. 0 (multiplicity 3), 4(multiplicity 1), -1 (multiplicity 1)

b. crosses at each zero **c.** $(0, 0)$ **d.** falls left, rises right

e.

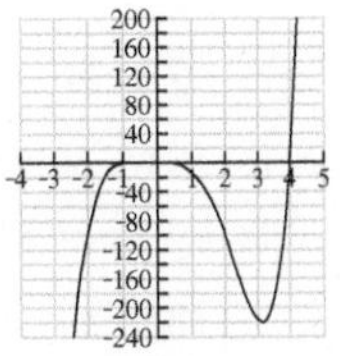

59. $f(x) = (x - 2)(x + 2)(x - 1)$ **a.** 1, 2, −2 (multiplicity 1)
b. crosses at each zero **c.** (0, 4)
d. falls left, rises right
e.
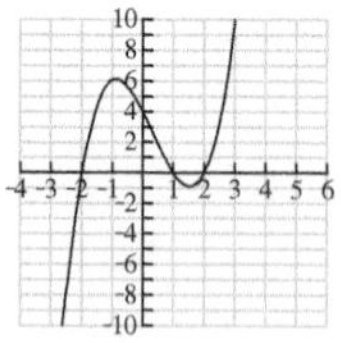

61. $f(x) = -(x + 2)^2(x - 1)^2$
a. −2 (multiplicity 2), 1 (multiplicity 2)
b. touches at both −2 and 1 **c.** (0, −4)
d. falls left and right, without bound
e.
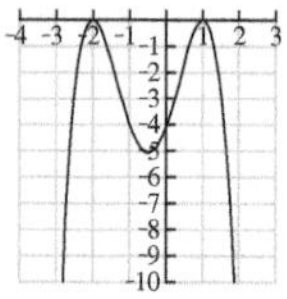

63. $f(x) = x^2(x - 2)^3(x + 3)^2$
a. 0 (multiplicity 2), 2 (multiplicity 3), −3 (multiplicity 2)
b. touches at both 0 and −3, and crosses at 2 **c.** (0, 0)
d. falls left, and rises right
e.
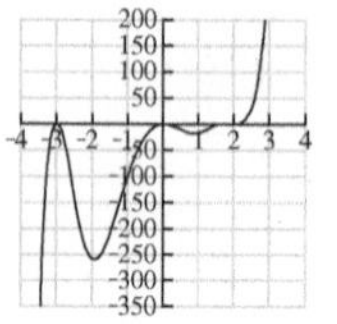

65. **a.** −3 (multiplicity 1), −1 (multiplicity 2), 2 (multiplicity 1)
b. even **c.** negative **d.** (0, 6)
e. $f(x) = -(x + 1)^2(x - 2)(x + 3)$

67. **a.** 0 (multiplicity 2), −2 (multiplicity 2), $\frac{3}{2}$ (multiplicity 1)
b. odd **c.** positive **d.** (0, 0)
e. $f(x) = x^2(2x - 3)(x + 2)^2$

69. **a.** Revenue for the company is increasing when advertising costs are less than \$400,000. Revenue for the company is decreasing when advertising costs are between \$400,000 and \$600,000.
b. The zeros of the revenue function occur when \$0 and \$600,000 are spent on advertising. When either \$0 or \$600,000 is spent on advertising, the company's revenue is \$0.

71. The velocity of air in the trachea is increasing when the radius of the trachea is between 0 and 0.45 cm and decreasing when the radius of the trachea is between 0.45 cm and 0.65 cm.

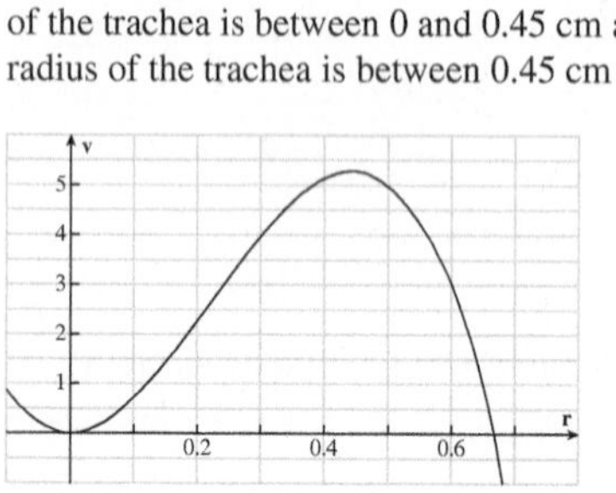

73. down **75.** 6th degree **77.** 4

79. If h is a zero of a polynomial, then $(x - h)$ is a factor of it, so in this case the function would be $P(x) = (x + 2)(x + 1)(x - 3)(x - 4)$.

81. false **83.** true **85.** n

87. $f(x) = (x + 1)^2(x - 3)^5$, $g(x) = (x + 1)^4(x - 3)^3$

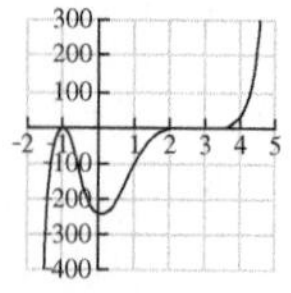
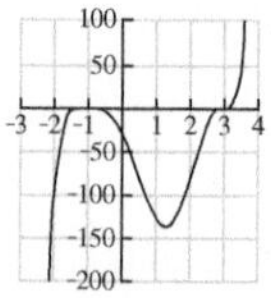

$h(x) = (x + 1)^6(x - 3)$

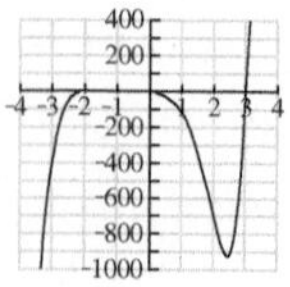

89. $0, a, -b$ **91.** $x = 1.154$

93. $x = -0.865, x = 1.363$

Section 2.3

1. $Q(x) = 3x - 3, \quad r(x) = -11$
3. $Q(x) = 3x - 28, \quad r(x) = 130$
5. $Q(x) = x - 4, \quad r(x) = 12$
7. $Q(x) = 3x + 5, \quad r(x) = 0$
9. $Q(x) = 2x - 3, \quad r(x) = 0$
11. $Q(x) = 4x^2 + 4x + 1, \quad r(x) = 0$
13. $Q(x) = 2x^2 - x - \frac{1}{2}, \quad r(x) = \frac{15}{2}$
15. $Q(x) = 4x^2 - 10x - 6, \quad r(x) = 0$
17. $Q(x) = -2x^2 - 3x - 9,$
$r(x) = -27x^2 + 3x + 9$
19. $Q(x) = x^2 + 1, \quad r(x) = 0$
21. $Q(x) = x^2 + x + \frac{1}{6}, \quad r(x) = -\frac{121}{6}x + \frac{121}{3}$
23. $Q(x) = 3x + 1, \quad r(x) = 0$
25. $Q(x) = 7x - 10, \quad r(x) = 15$
27. $Q(x) = -x^3 + 3x - 2, \quad r(x) = 0$
29. $Q(x) = x^3 - x^2 + x - 1, \quad r(x) = 2$
31. $Q(x) = x^3 - 2x^2 + 4x - 8, \quad r(x) = 0$
33. $Q(x) = 2x^2 - 6x + 2, \quad r(x) = 0$
35. $Q(x) = 2x^3 - \frac{5}{3}x^2 + \frac{53}{9}x + \frac{106}{27}, \quad r(x) = -\frac{112}{81}$
37. $Q(x) = 2x^3 + 6x^2 - 18x - 54, \quad r(x) = 0$
39. $Q(x) = x^6 + x^5 + x^4 - 7x^3 - 7x^2 - 4x - 4, \quad r(x) = -3$
41. $Q(x) = x^5 + \sqrt{5}x^4 - 44x^3 - 44\sqrt{5}x^2 - 245x - 245\sqrt{5},$
$r(x) = 0$
43. $Q(x) = 2x - 7, \quad r(x) = 0$
45. $Q(x) = x^2 - 9, \quad r(x) = 0$
47. $Q(x) = x + 6, \quad r(x) = -x + 1$
49. $Q(x) = x^4 - 2x^3 - 4x + 7, \quad r(x) = 0$
51. $Q(x) = x^4 + 2x^3 + 8x^2 + 18x + 36, \quad r(x) = 71$
53. $Q(x) = x^2 + 1, \quad r(x) = -24$
55. $Q(x) = x^6 + x^5 + x^4 + x^3 + x^2 + x + 1, \quad r(x) = 0$
57. $3x^2 + 2x + 1$ ft **59.** $x^2 + 1$ hr
61. Should have subtracted each term in the long division rather than adding them.

63. Forgot the "0" placeholder.

65. true **67.** false **69.** false **71.** yes

73. $Q(x) = x^{2n} + 2x^n + 1, \quad r(x) = 0$

75. $(2x - 5) + \dfrac{10}{x + 2}$

77. $(2x^2 - 2x + 3) - \dfrac{x - 3}{x^2 + x + 1}$

Section 2.4

1. $-4, 1, 3$; $P(x) = (x - 1)(x + 4)(x - 3)$

3. $-3, \frac{1}{2}, 2$; $P(x) = (2x - 1)(x + 3)(x - 2)$

5. $-3, 5$; $P(x) = (x^2 + 4)(x - 5)(x + 3)$

7. $-3, 1$; $P(x) = (x - 1)(x + 3)(x^2 - 2x + 2)$

9. $-2, -1$ (both multiplicity 2); $P(x) = (x + 2)^2(x + 1)^2$

11. $\pm 1, \pm 2, \pm 4$

13. $\pm 1, \pm 2, \pm 3, \pm 4, \pm 6, \pm 12$

15. $\pm\frac{1}{2}, \pm 1, \pm 2, \pm 4, \pm 8$

17. $\pm 1, \pm 2, \pm 4, \pm 5, \pm 10, \pm 20, \pm\frac{1}{5}, \pm\frac{2}{5}, \pm\frac{4}{5}$

19. $\pm 1, \pm 2, \pm 4, \pm 8$; rational zeros: $-4, -1, 2, 1$

21. $\pm 1, \pm 3, \pm\frac{1}{2}, \pm\frac{3}{2}$; rational zeros: $\frac{1}{2}, 1, 3$

23.

POSITIVE REAL ZEROS	NEGATIVE REAL ZEROS
1	1

25.

POSITIVE REAL ZEROS	NEGATIVE REAL ZEROS
1	0

27.

POSITIVE REAL ZEROS	NEGATIVE REAL ZEROS
2	1
0	1

29.

POSITIVE REAL ZEROS	NEGATIVE REAL ZEROS
1	1

31.

POSITIVE REAL ZEROS	NEGATIVE REAL ZEROS
2	2
0	2
2	0
0	0

33.

POSITIVE REAL ZEROS	NEGATIVE REAL ZEROS
4	0
2	0
0	0

35. a. Number of sign variations for $P(x)$: 0
Number of sign variations for $P(-x)$: 3

POSITIVE REAL ZEROS	NEGATIVE REAL ZEROS
0	3
0	1

b. possible rational zeros: $\pm 1, \pm 2, \pm 3, \pm 6$
c. rational zeros: $-1, -2, -3$
d. $P(x) = (x + 1)(x + 2)(x + 3)$

37. a. Number of sign variations for $P(x)$: 2
Number of sign variations for $P(-x)$: 1

POSITIVE REAL ZEROS	NEGATIVE REAL ZEROS
2	1
0	1

b. possible rational zeros: $\pm 1, \pm 7$
c. rational zeros: $-1, 1, 7$
d. $P(x) = (x + 1)(x - 1)(x - 7)$

39. a. Number of sign variations for $P(x)$: 1
Number of sign variations for $P(-x)$: 2

POSITIVE REAL ZEROS	NEGATIVE REAL ZEROS
1	2
1	0

b. possible rational zeros: $\pm 1, \pm 2, \pm 5, \pm 10$
c. rational zeros: $0, 1, -2, -5$
d. $P(x) = x(x - 1)(x + 2)(x + 5)$

41. a. Number of sign variations for $P(x)$: 4
Number of sign variations for $P(-x)$: 0

POSITIVE REAL ZEROS	NEGATIVE REAL ZEROS
4	0
2	0
0	0

b. possible rational zeros: $\pm 1, \pm 2, \pm 13, \pm 26$
c. rational zeros: $1, 2$
d. $P(x) = (x - 1)(x - 2)(x^2 - 4x + 13)$

43. a. Number of sign variations for $P(x)$: 2
Number of sign variations for $P(-x)$: 1

POSITIVE REAL ZEROS	NEGATIVE REAL ZEROS
2	1
0	1

b. possible rational zeros: $\pm 1, \pm\frac{1}{2}, \pm\frac{1}{5}, \pm\frac{1}{10}$
c. rational zeros: $1, -\frac{1}{2}, \frac{1}{5}$
d. $P(x) = (x - 1)(2x + 1)(5x - 1)$

45. **a.** Number of sign variations for $P(x)$: 1
Number of sign variations for $P(-x)$: 2

POSITIVE REAL ZEROS	NEGATIVE REAL ZEROS
1	2
1	0

b. possible rational zeros:

$\pm1, \pm2, \pm5, \pm10, \pm\frac{1}{2}, \pm\frac{1}{3}, \pm\frac{1}{6}, \pm\frac{2}{3},$

$\pm\frac{5}{2}, \pm\frac{5}{3}, \pm\frac{5}{6}, \pm\frac{10}{3}$

c. rational zeros: $-1, -\frac{5}{2}, \frac{2}{3}$

d. $P(x) = 6(x + 1)\left(x + \frac{5}{2}\right)\left(x - \frac{2}{3}\right)$

47. **a.** Number of sign variations for $P(x)$: 4
Number of sign variations for $P(-x)$: 0

POSITIVE REAL ZEROS	NEGATIVE REAL ZEROS
4	0
2	0
0	0

b. possible rational zeros: $\pm1, \pm2, \pm4$

c. rational zeros: 1

d. $P(x) = (x - 1)^2 (x^2 + 4)$

49. **a.** Number of sign variations for $P(x)$: 1
Number of sign variations for $P(-x)$: 1

POSITIVE REAL ZEROS	NEGATIVE REAL ZEROS
1	1

b. possible rational zeros:

$\pm1, \pm2, \pm3, \pm4, \pm6, \pm9, \pm12, \pm18, \pm36$

c. rational zeros: $-1, 1$

d. $P(x) = (x + 1)(x - 1)(x^2 + 9)(x^2 + 4)$

51. **a.** Number of sign variations for $P(x)$: 4
Number of sign variations for $P(-x)$: 0

POSITIVE REAL ZEROS	NEGATIVE REAL ZEROS
4	0
2	0
0	0

b. possible rational zeros:

$\pm1, \pm5, \pm\frac{1}{2}, \pm\frac{1}{4}, \pm\frac{5}{2}, \pm\frac{5}{4}$

c. rational zeros: $\frac{1}{2}$

d. $P(x) = (2x - 1)^2(x^2 - 4x + 5)$

53.

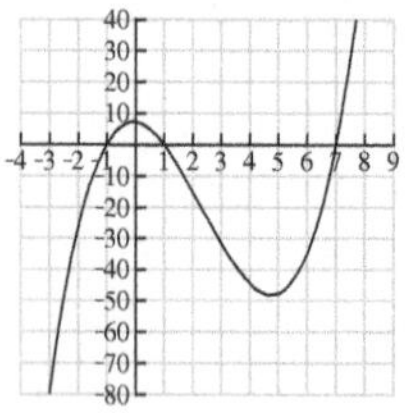

55.

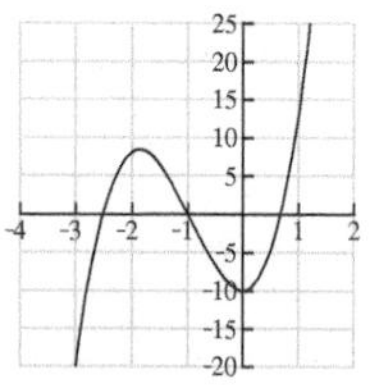

57. $x = 1.34$

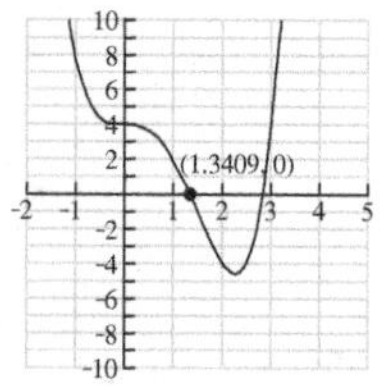

59. $x = 0.22$

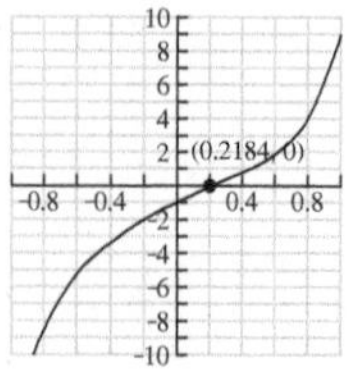

61. $x = -0.43$

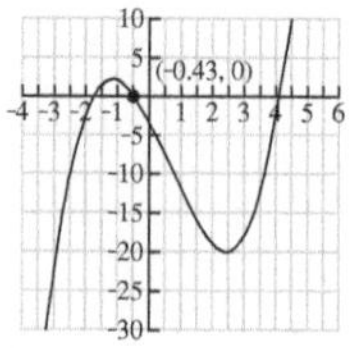

63. 6 in. × 8 in.

65. 30 cows

67. $P(x) = -0.0002x^2 + 8x - 1500$; 0 or 2 positive real zeros

69. 18 hr

71. It is true that one can get 5 negative zeros here, but there may be just 1 or 3.

POSITIVE REAL ZEROS	NEGATIVE REAL ZEROS
0	5
0	3
0	1

73. true **75.** false **77.** false **79.** b, c

81. a, c, and $-c$

83. $1, 5, -2; (-2, 1) \cup (5, \infty)$

85. $-\frac{1}{2}, 3, \pm\sqrt{2}; \left(-\sqrt{2}, -\frac{1}{2}\right) \cup \left(\sqrt{2}, 3\right)$

Section 2.5

1. $x = \pm 2i$; $P(x) = (x + 2i)(x - 2i)$

3. $x = 1 \pm i$; $P(x) = (x - (1 - i))(x - (1 + i))$

5. $x = \pm 2, \pm 2i$; $P(x) = (x - 2)(x + 2)(x - 2i)(x + 2i)$

7. $x = \pm\sqrt{5}, \pm i\sqrt{5}$;

$P(x) = (x - \sqrt{5})(x + \sqrt{5})(x - i\sqrt{5})(x + i\sqrt{5})$

9. $-i$

11. $-2i, 3 + i$

13. $1 + 3i, 2 - 5i$

15. $i, 1 + i$

17. $P(x) = x^3 - 2x^2 + 5x$

19. $P(x) = x^3 - 3x^2 + 28x - 26$

21. $P(x) = x^4 - 2x^3 + 11x^2 - 18x + 18$

23. $\pm 2i, -3, 5$; $P(x) = (x - 2i)(x + 2i)(x - 5)(x + 3)$

25. $\pm i, 1, 3$; $P(x) = (x - i)(x + i)(x - 3)(x - 1)$

27. $\pm 3i$, 1 (multiplicity 2); $P(x) = (x - 3i)(x + 3i)(x - 1)^2$

29. $1 \pm i, -1 \pm 2\sqrt{2}$;

$P(x) = (x - (1 + i))(x - (1 - i)) \cdot$

$(x - (-1 - 2\sqrt{2}))(x - (-1 + 2\sqrt{2}))$

31. $3 \pm i, \pm 2$;

$P(x) = (x - (3 + i))(x - (3 - i))(x - 2)(x + 2)$

33. $2 \pm i, 1, 4;$
$P(x) = (x - (2 + i))(x - (2 - i))(x - 1)(x - 4)$

35. $P(x) = (x + 3i)(x - 3i)(x - 1)$

37. $P(x) = (x + i)(x - i)(x - 5)$

39. $P(x) = (x + 2i)(x - 2i)(x + 1)$

41. $P(x) = (x - 3)(x - (-1 + i\sqrt{5}))(x - (-1 - i\sqrt{5}))$

43. $P(x) = (x + 3)(x - 5)(x + 2i)(x - 2i)$

45. $P(x) = (x + 1)(x - 5)(x + 2i)(x - 2i)$

47. $P(x) = (x - 1)(x - 2)(x - (2 - 3i))(x - (2 + 3i))$

49. $P(x) = -(x + 1)(x - 2)(x - (2 - i))(x - (-2 + i))$

51. $P(x) = (x - 1)^2 (x + 2i)(x - 2i)$

53. $P(x) = (x - 1)(x + 1)(x - 2i)(x + 2i)(x - 3i)(x + 3i)$

55. $P(x) = (2x - 1)^2 (x - (2 - i))(x - (2 + i))$

57. $P(x) = (x - 1)(x + 1)(3x - 2)(x - 2i)(x + 2i)$

59. Yes. In such a case, $P(x)$ is always above the x-axis since the leading coefficient is positive, indicating that the end behavior should resemble that of $y = x^{2n}$, for some positive integer n. Thus profit is always positive and increasing.

61. No. In such a case, it crosses the x-axis and looks like $y = -x^3$. Thus profit is decreasing.

63. Since the profit function is a third-degree polynomial, we know that the function has three zeros and at most two turning points. Looking at the graph, we can see there is one real zero where $t \leq 0$. There are no real zeros when $t > 0$, so the other two zeros must be complex conjugates. Therefore, the company always has a profit greater than approximately 5.1 million dollars, and in fact, the profit will increase toward infinity as t increases.

65. Since the concentration function is a third-degree polynomial, we know that the function has three zeros and at most two turning points. Looking at the graph, we can see there is one real zero at some time $t \geq 8$. The remaining zeros are a complex conjugate pair. Therefore, the concentration of the drug in the bloodstream will decrease to zero as the hours go by. Note that the concentration will not approach negative infinity since concentration is a nonnegative quantity.

67. Step 2 is an error. In general, the additive inverse of a real root need not be a root. This is being confused with the fact that complex roots occur in conjugate pairs.

69. false **71.** true

73. No. Complex zeros occur in conjugate pairs. Hence the collection of complex solutions contributes an even number of zeros, thereby requiring there to be at least one real zero.

75. $P(x) = x^6 + 3b^2x^4 + 3b^4x^2 + b^6$

77. $P(x) = x^6 + (2a^2 + b^2)x^4 + (a^4 + 2a^2b^2)x^2 + b^2a^4$

79. **a.** $f(x) = (x + 1)(x - i)(x + i)$

b. $f(x) = (x + 1)(x^2 + 1)$

81. **a.** $f(x) = (x + 2i)(x - 2i)(x + i)(x - i)$

b. $f(x) = (x^2 + 4)(x^2 + 1)$

Section 2.6

1. $(-\infty, -4) \cup (-4, 3) \cup (3, \infty)$

3. $(-\infty, -2) \cup (-2, 2) \cup (2, \infty)$

5. $(-\infty, \infty)$

7. $(-\infty, -2) \cup (-2, 3) \cup (3, \infty)$

9. HA: $y = 0$ VA: $x = -2$

11. HA: none VA: $x = -5$

13. HA: none VA: $x = \frac{1}{2}, x = -\frac{4}{3}$

15. HA: $y = \frac{1}{3}$ VA: none

17. $y = x + 6$ **19.** $y = 2x + 24$ **21.** $y = 4x + \frac{11}{2}$

23. b **25.** a **27.** e

29.

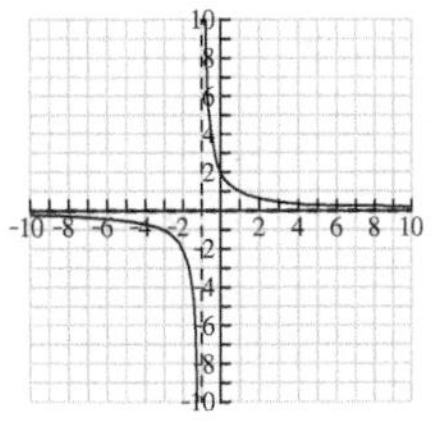

31.

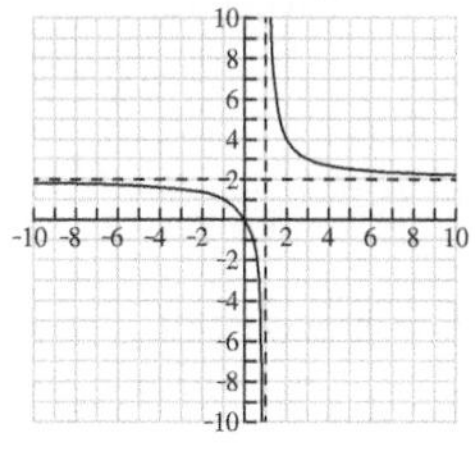

33.

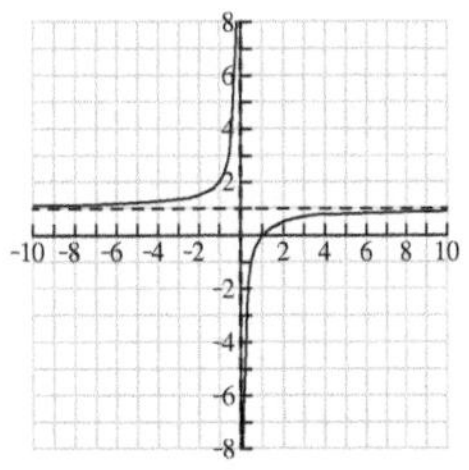

35.

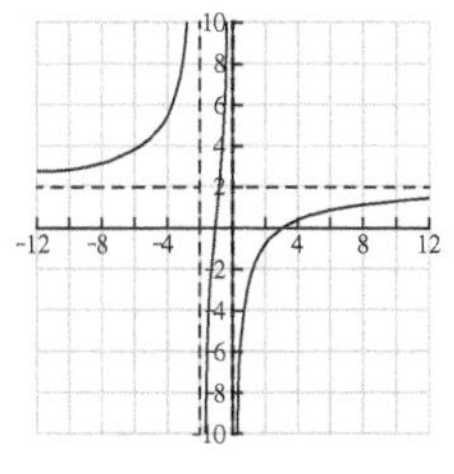

37.

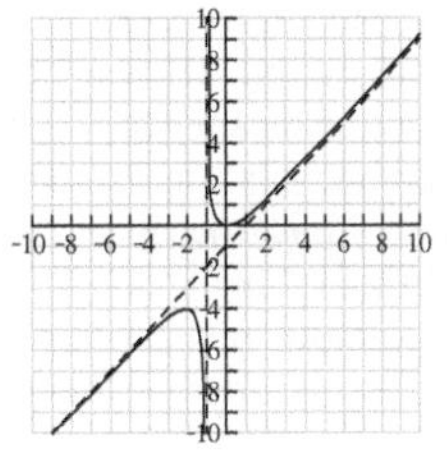

39.

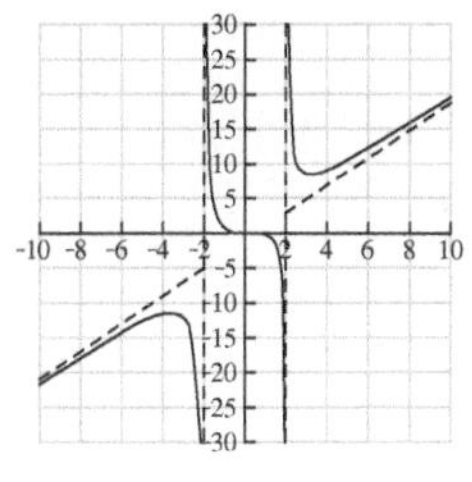

41.

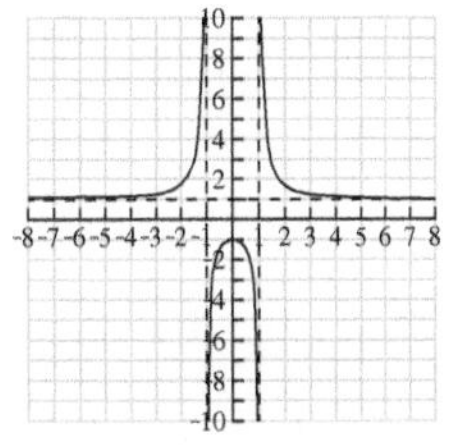

43.

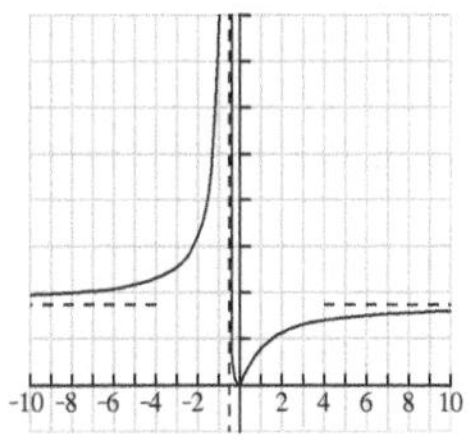

45.

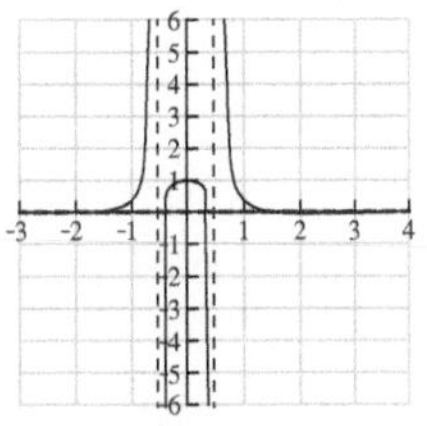

47.

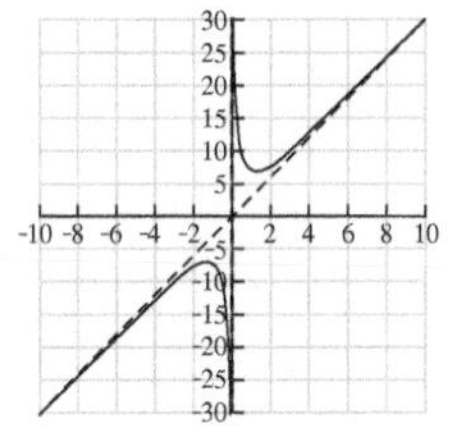

49.

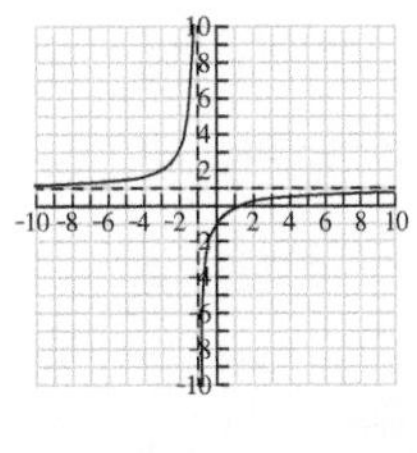

51.

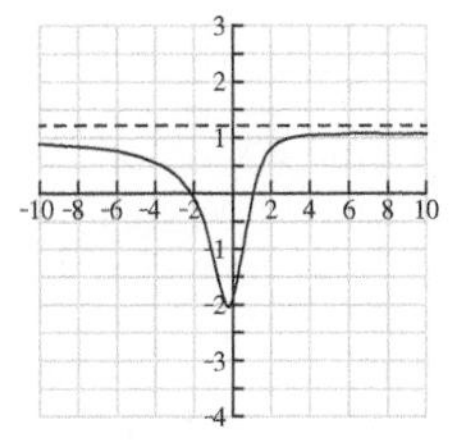

53.

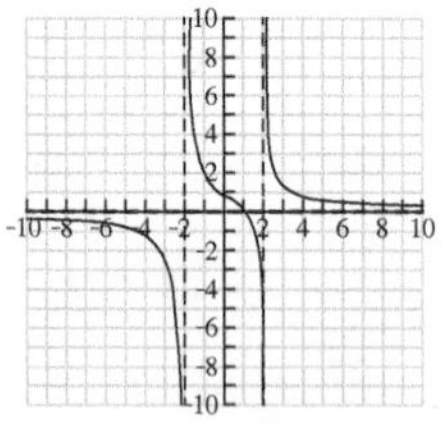

55. $y = \frac{1}{2}$

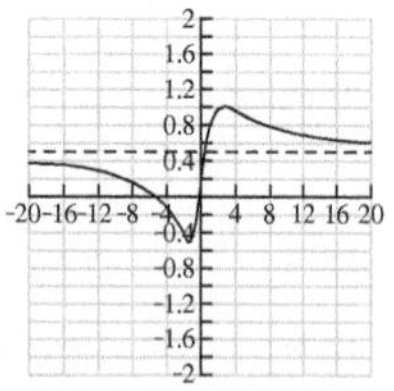

57. **a.** x-intercept: (2, 0); y-intercept: (0, 0.5)

b. HA: $y = 0$ VA: $x = -1, x = 4$

c. $f(x) = \dfrac{x-2}{(x+1)(x-4)}$

59. **a.** x-intercept: (0, 0); y-intercept: (0, 0)

b. HA: $y = -3$ VA: $x = -4, x = 4$

c. $f(x) = \dfrac{-3x^2}{(x+4)(x-4)}$

61. **a.** 4500 people **b.** 6 mo **c.** stabilizes around 9500

63. **a.** $C(1) \cong 0.0198$ **b.** $C(60) \cong 0.0324$ **c.** $C(300) \cong 0.0067$
d. $y = 0$; after several days, $C(t) \cong 0$

65. **a.** $N(0) = 52$ wpm **b.** $N(12) \cong 107$ wpm
c. $N(36) \cong 120$ wpm **d.** $y = 130$; 130 wpm

67. 2000 or 8000 units; average profit of $16 per unit.

69. The concentration of the drug in the bloodstream 15 hours after taking the dose is approximately 25.4 μg/mL. There are two times, 1 hour and 15 hours, after taking the medication at which the concentration of the drug in the bloodstream is approximately 25.4 μg/mL. The first time, approximately 1 hour, occurs as the concentration of the drug is increasing to a level high enough that the body will be able to maintain a concentration of approximately 25 μg/mL throughout the day. The second time, approximately 15 hours, occurs many hours later in the day as the concentration of the medication in the bloodstream drops.

71. $f(x) = \dfrac{x-1}{x^2-1} = \dfrac{\cancel{x-1}}{(\cancel{x-1})(x+1)} = \dfrac{1}{x+1}$ with a hole at $x = 1$, so $x = 1$ is not a vertical asymptote.

73. true **75.** false

77. HA: $y = 1$ VA: $x = c, x = -d$

79. Two possibilities: $y = \dfrac{4x^2}{(x+3)(x-1)}$ and $y = \dfrac{4x^5}{(x+3)^3(x-1)^2}$

81. $f(x) = \dfrac{x^3+1}{x^2+1}$

83. $x = -2, x = -1, x = 5$

85. $x = \frac{2}{3}, x = -\frac{1}{2}$

Review Exercises

1. b **3.** a

5.

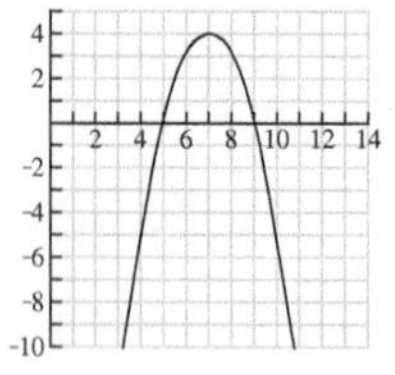

7.

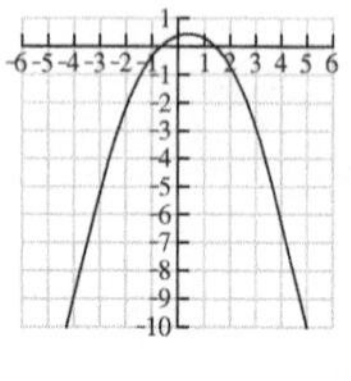

9. $f(x) = \left(x - \frac{3}{2}\right)^2 - \frac{49}{4}$

11. $f(x) = 4(x+1)^2 - 11$

13.

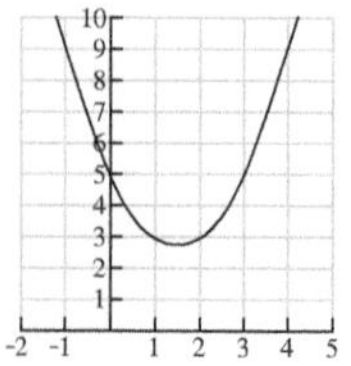

15.

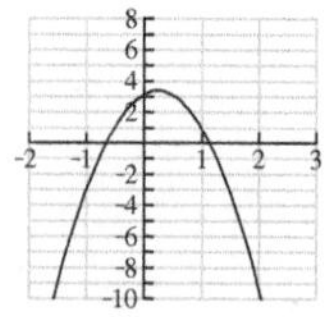

17. $\left(\frac{5}{26}, \frac{599}{52}\right)$ **19.** $\left(-\frac{2}{15}, \frac{451}{125}\right)$

21. $y = \frac{1}{9}(x+2)^2 + 3$

23. $y = 5.6(x - 2.7)^2 + 3.4$

25. **a.** $P(x) = -2x^2 + \frac{35}{3}x - 14$

b. $x \cong 4.1442433, 1.68909$

c.

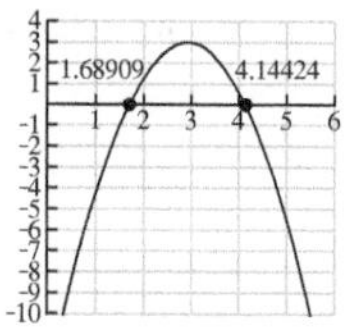

d. (1.6891, 4.144)

27. $A(x) = -\frac{1}{2}(x-1)^2 + \frac{9}{2}$, maximum at $x = 1$
base: 3 units, height: 3 units

29. yes, 6 **31.** no **33.** d **35.** a

37.

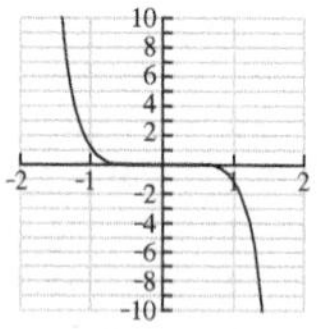

39.

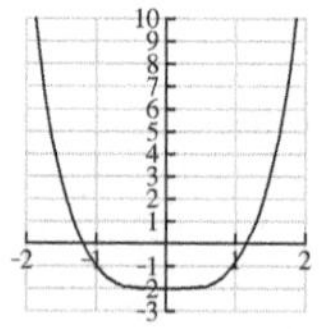

41. 6 (multiplicity 5), −4 (multiplicity 2)

43. 0, −2, 2, 3, −3, all multiplicity 1

45. $f(x) = x(x+3)(x-4)$

47. $f(x) = x(5x+2)(4x-3)$

49. $f(x) = x^4 - 2x^3 - 11x^2 + 12x + 36$

51. $f(x) = (x-7)(x+2)$ **a.** −2, 7 (both multiplicity 1)
b. crosses at −2, 7 **c.** (0, −14) **d.** rises right and left

e.

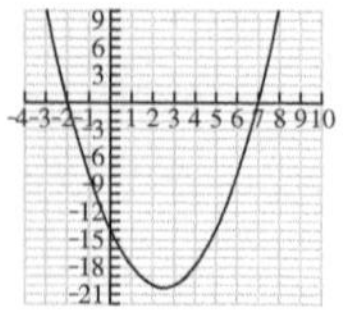

53. $f(x) = 6x^7 + 3x^5 - x^2 + x - 4$ **a.** (0.8748, 0) with multiplicity 1 **b.** crosses at its only real zero **c.** (0, −4)
d. falls left and rises right

e.

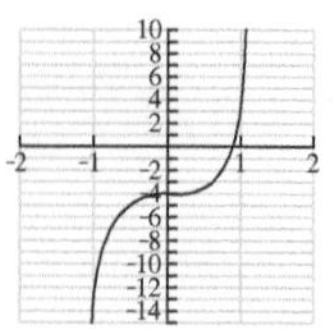

55. a.

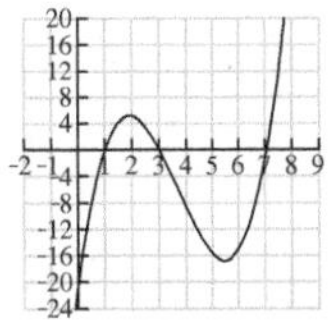

b. 1, 3, 7 (all with multiplicity 1)

c. between 1 and 3 hr, and more than 7 hr is financially beneficial

57. $Q(x) = x + 4, \quad r(x) = 2$

59. $Q(x) = 2x^3 - 4x^2 - 2x - \frac{7}{2}, \quad r(x) = -23$

61. $Q(x) = x^3 + 2x^2 + x - 4, \quad r(x) = 0$

63. $Q(x) = x^5 - 8x^4 + 64x^3 - 512x^2 + 4096x - 32{,}768,$

$r(x) = 262{,}080$

65. $Q(x) = x + 3, \quad r(x) = -4x - 8$

67. $Q(x) = x^2 - 5x + 7, \quad r(x) = -15$

69. $3x^3 + 2x^2 - x + 4$ ft **71.** $f(-2) = -207$

73. $g(1) = 0$ **75.** no **77.** yes

79. $P(x) = x(x + 2)(x - 4)^2$ **81.** $P(x) = x^2(x + 3)(x - 2)^2$

83.

POSITIVE REAL ZEROS	NEGATIVE REAL ZEROS
1	1

85.

POSITIVE REAL ZEROS	NEGATIVE REAL ZEROS
5	2
5	0
3	2
3	0
1	2
1	0

87. possible rational zeros: $\pm 1, \pm 2, \pm 3, \pm 6$

89. possible rational zeros: $\pm 1, \pm 2, \pm 4, \pm 8, \pm 16, \pm 32, \pm 64, \pm \frac{1}{2}$

91. possible rational zeros: $\pm 1, \pm \frac{1}{2}$; zeros: $\frac{1}{2}$

93. possible rational zeros:

$\pm 1, \pm 2, \pm 4, \pm 8, \pm 16$; zeros: $1, 2, 4, -2$

95. a.

POSITIVE REAL ZEROS	NEGATIVE REAL ZEROS
1	0

b. $\pm 1, \pm 5$

c. -1 is a lower bound, 5 is an upper bound.

d. none **e.** not possible

f.

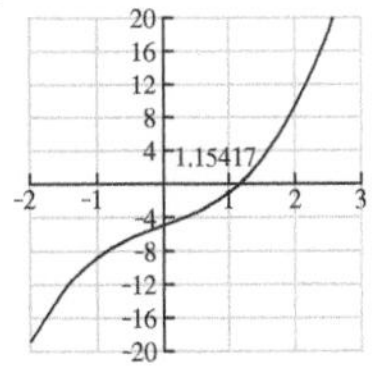

97. a.

POSITIVE REAL ZEROS	NEGATIVE REAL ZEROS
3	0
1	0

b. $\pm 1, \pm 2, \pm 3, \pm 4, \pm 6, \pm 12$

c. -1 is a lower bound, 12 is an upper bound.

d. 1, 2, 6 **e.** $P(x) = (x - 1)(x - 6)(x - 2)$

f.

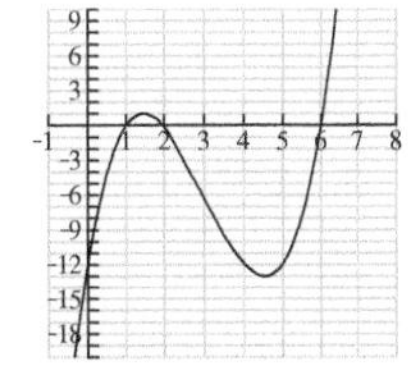

99. a.

POSITIVE REAL ZEROS	NEGATIVE REAL ZEROS
0	0
0	2
2	0
2	0

b. $\pm 1, \pm 2, \pm 3, \pm 4, \pm 6, \pm 8, \pm 12, \pm 24$

c. -4 is a lower bound, 8 is an upper bound.

d. $-2, -1, 1, 6$

e. $P(x) = (x - 2)(x + 1)(x + 2)(x - 6)$

f.

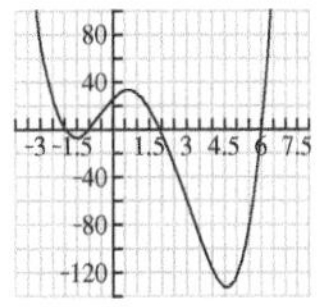

101. $P(x) = (x - 5i)(x + 5i)$

103. $P(x) = (x - (1 - 2i))(x - (1 + 2i))$

105. $2i, 3 - i$ **107.** $-i, 2 + I$

109. $P(x) = (x - i)(x + i)(x - 4)(x + 1)$

111. $P(x) = (x - 3i)(x + 3i)(x - (1 + i))(x - (1 - i))$

113. $P(x) = (x - 3)(x + 3)(x - 3i)(x + 3i)$

115. $P(x) = (x - 2i)(x + 2i)(x - 1)$

117. HA: $y = -1$ VA: $x = -2$

119. HA: none VA: $x = -1$ Slant: $y = 4x - 4$

121. HA: $y = 2$ VA: none

123.

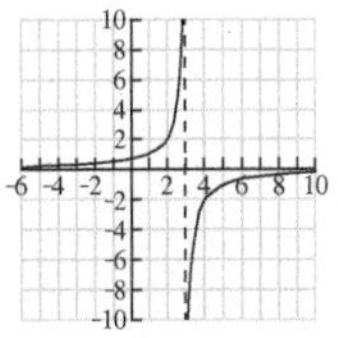

125.

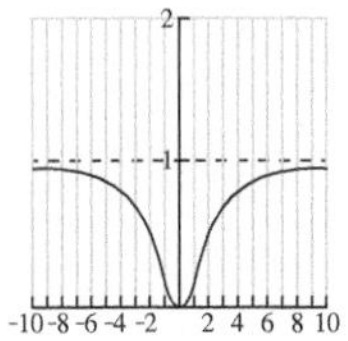

127.

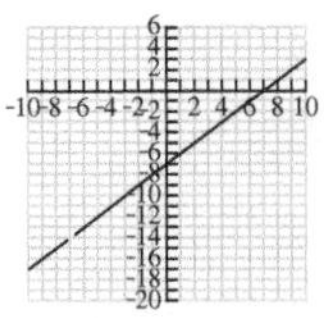

Practice Test

1.

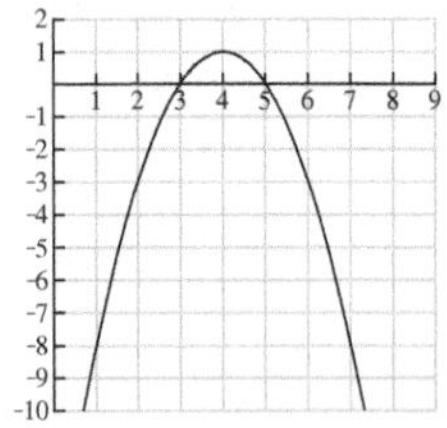

3. $\left(3, \frac{1}{2}\right)$

5. $f(x) = x(x-2)^3(x-1)^2$

7. $Q(x) = -2x^2 - 2x - \frac{11}{2}$, $r(x) = -\frac{19}{2}x + \frac{7}{2}$

9. yes

11. $P(x) = (x-7)(x+2)(x-1)$

13. yes, complex zero

15. possible rational zeros: $\pm 1, \pm 2, \pm 3, \pm 4, \pm 6, \pm 12, \pm\frac{1}{3}, \pm\frac{2}{3}, \pm\frac{4}{3}$

17. $\frac{3}{2}, \pm 2i$

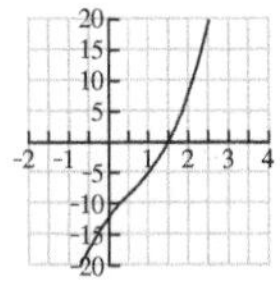

19. degree 3

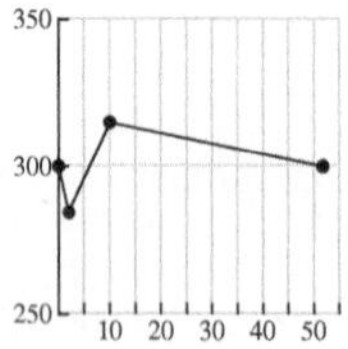

21. degree 3

23. **a.** x-intercept: (0, 0), y-intercept: (0, 0)

b. $x = \pm 2$ **c.** $y = 0$ **d.** none

e.

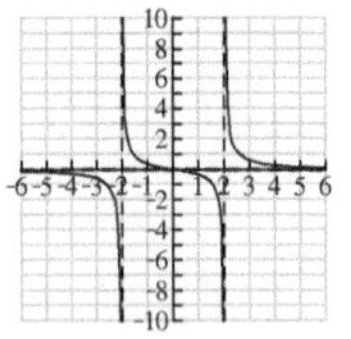

25. **a.** x-intercept: (3, 0), y-intercept: $\left(0, \frac{3}{8}\right)$

b. $x = -2, x = 4$ **c.** $y = 0$ **d.** none

e.

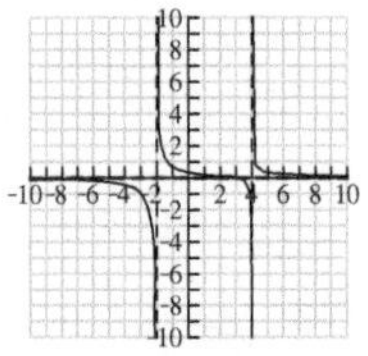

Cumulative Test

1. $f(2) = \frac{15}{2}$, $f(-1) = -5$, $f(1+h) = 4 + 4h - \dfrac{1}{\sqrt{h+3}}$,

$f(-x) = -4x - \dfrac{1}{\sqrt{2-x}}$

3. $f(-3) = \frac{7}{2}$, $f(0) = -\frac{5}{2}$, $f(4) = -\frac{7}{18}$, $f(1)$ is undefined.

5. $\dfrac{1}{\sqrt{x+h} + \sqrt{x}} + \dfrac{2x+h}{x^2(x+h)^2}$

7. **a.**

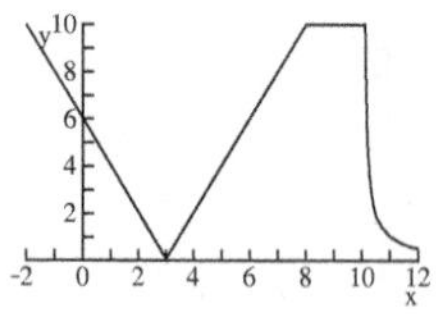

b. domain: $(-\infty, 10) \cup (10, \infty)$, range: $[0, \infty)$

c. increasing: (3, 8), decreasing: $(-\infty, 3) \cup (10, \infty)$, constant: (8,10)

9. $-\frac{1}{28}$

11. neither

13. right one unit and then up three units

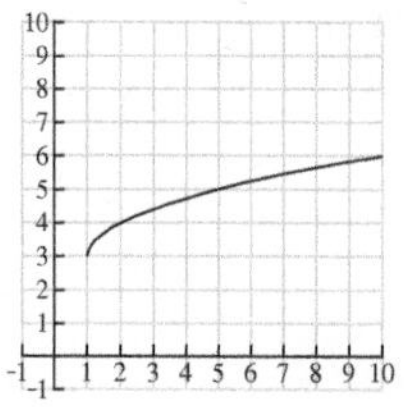

15. $g(f(-1)) = 0$

17. $f(x) = (x+2)^2 + 3$

19. $Q(x) = 4x^2 + 4x + 1$, $r(x) = -8$

21. possible rational zeros:

$\pm 1, \pm 2, \pm 3, \pm 6, \pm\frac{1}{2}, \pm\frac{1}{3}, \pm\frac{1}{4}, \pm\frac{1}{6}, \pm\frac{1}{12}, \pm\frac{2}{3}, \pm\frac{3}{2}, \pm\frac{3}{4}, \pm\frac{1}{4}$

zeros: $-2, -\frac{3}{4}, \frac{1}{3}$

23. $P(x) = (x+1)(x-2)(x-4)$

25. HA: $y = 0$ VA: $x = \pm 2$

CHAPTER 3

Section 3.1

1. $\frac{1}{25}$	**3.** 4	**5.** 27	**7.** 9.7385	
9. 7.3891	**11.** 0.0432	**13.** 27	**15.** 16	
17. 4	**19.** 19.81	**21.** f	**23.** e	**25.** b

27. y-intercept: (0, 1) HA: $y = 0$
domain: $(-\infty, \infty)$ range: $(0, \infty)$
other points: $\left(-1, \frac{1}{6}\right)$, (1, 6)

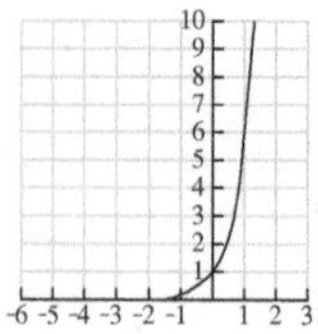

29. y-intercept: (0, 1) HA: $y = 0$
domain: $(-\infty, \infty)$ range: $(0, \infty)$
other points: (1, 0.1), (−1, 10)

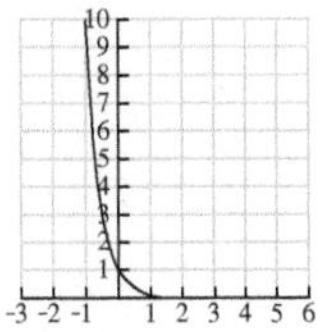

31. y-intercept: (0, 1) HA: $y = 0$
domain: $(-\infty, \infty)$ range: $(0, \infty)$
other points: $(1, e)$, $(2, e^2)$

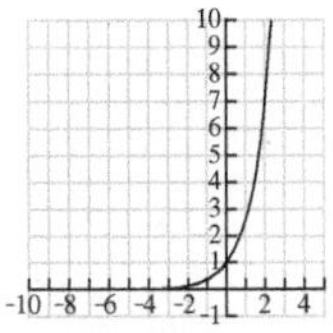

33. y-intercept: (0, 1) HA: $y = 0$
domain: $(-\infty, \infty)$ range: $(0, \infty)$
other points: $\left(1, \frac{1}{e}\right)$, $(-1, e)$

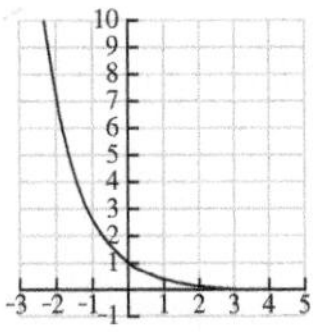

35. y-intercept: (0, 0) HA: $y = -1$
domain: $(-\infty, \infty)$ range: $(-1, \infty)$
other points: (2, 3), (1, 1)

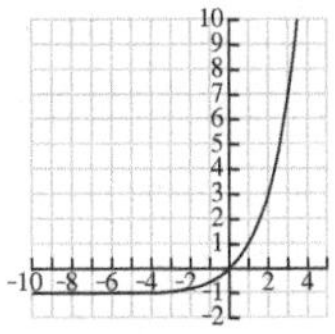

37. y-intercept: (0, 1) HA: $y = 2$
domain: $(-\infty, \infty)$ range: $(-\infty, 2)$
other points: $(1, 2 - e)$, $\left(-1, 2 - \frac{1}{e}\right)$

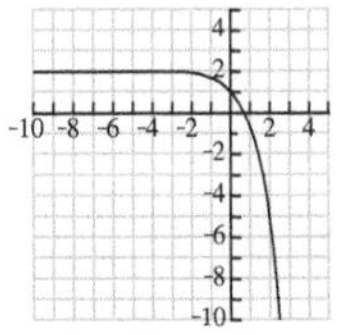

39. y-intercept: (0, 6) HA: $y = 5$
domain: $(-\infty, \infty)$ range: $(5, \infty)$
other points: (1, 5.25), (−1, 9)

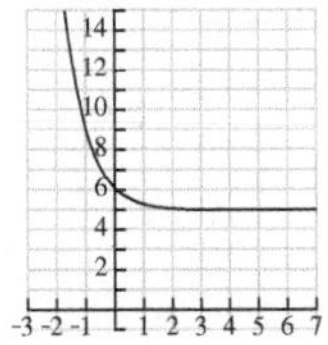

41. y-intercept: $(0, e - 4)$ HA: $y = -4$
domain: $(-\infty, \infty)$ range: $(-4, \infty)$
other points: $(-1, -3)$, $(1, e^2 - 4)$

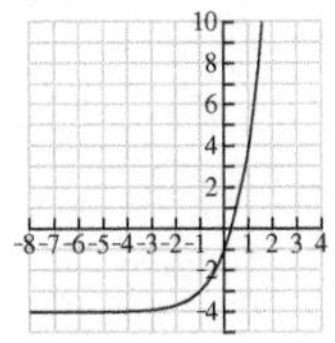

43. y-intercept: (0, 3) HA: $y = 0$
domain: $(-\infty, \infty)$ range: $(0, \infty)$
other points: $(2, 3e)$, $(1, 3\sqrt{e})$

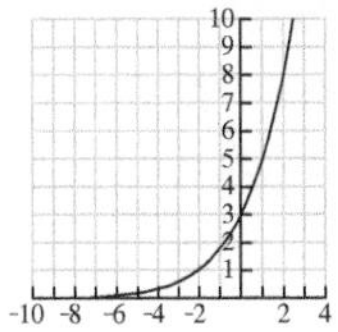

45. y-intercept: (0, 5) HA: $y = 1$
domain: $(-\infty, \infty)$ range: $(1, \infty)$
other points: (1, 3), (2, 2)

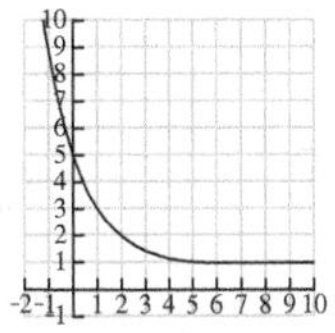

47. 10.4 million

49. $P(30) = 1500\left(2^{30/5}\right) = 96{,}000$

51. 168 mg

53. 2 mg

55. \$3448.42

57. \$13,011.03

59. \$4319.55

61. \$13,979.42

63. 3.4 mg/L

65. The mistake is that $4^{3/2} \neq \frac{4^3}{4^2}$. Rather,
$4^{3/2} = (\sqrt{4})^3 = 2^3 = 8.$

67. false

69. true

71.

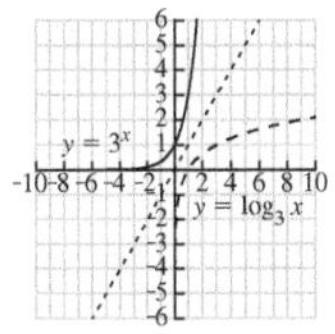

73.

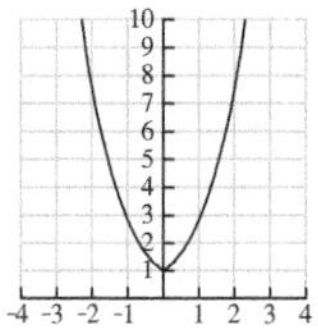

75. y-intercept: $(0, be - a)$ HA: $y = -a$

77. Domain: $(-\infty, \infty)$

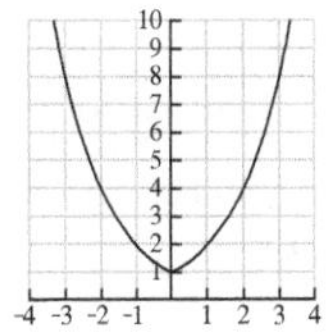

79.

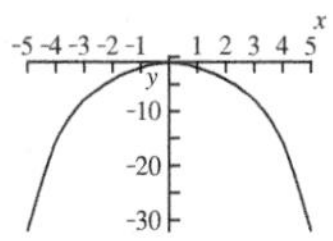

81. odd

Section 3.2

1. $81^{1/4} = 3$

3. $2^{-5} = \frac{1}{32}$

5. $10^{-2} = 0.01$

7. $10^4 = 10{,}000$

9. $\left(\frac{1}{4}\right)^{-3} = 64$

11. $e^{-1} = \frac{1}{e}$

13. $e^0 = 1$

15. $e^x = 5$

17. $x^z = y$

19. $y^x = x + y$

21. $\log(0.00001) = -5$

23. $\log_5 78{,}125 = 5^7$

25. $\log_{225}(15) = \frac{1}{2}$

27. $\log_{2/5}\left(\frac{8}{125}\right) = 3$

29. $\log_{1/27}(3) = -\frac{1}{3}$

31. $\ln 6 = x$

33. $\log_y x = z$

35. 0

37. 5

39. 7

41. −6

43. undefined **45.** undefined **47.** 1.46

49. 5.94 **51.** undefined **53.** −8.11

55. $(-5, \infty)$ **57.** $(-\infty, \frac{5}{2})$ **59.** $(-\infty, \frac{7}{2})$

61. $(-\infty, 0)\cup(0, \infty)$ **63.** $\mathbb{R}$ **65.** $(-2, 5)$

67. b **69.** c **71.** d

73. domain: $(1, \infty)$
range: $(-\infty, \infty)$

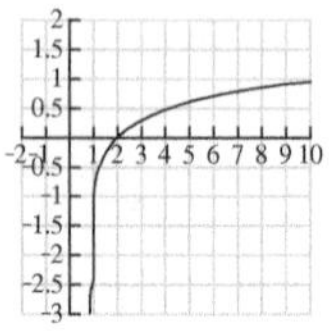

75. domain: $(-2, \infty)$
range: $(-\infty, \infty)$

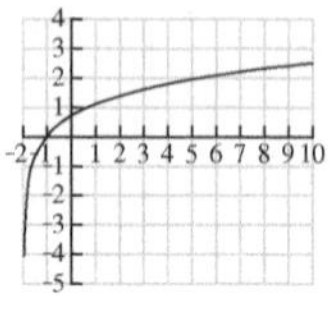

77. domain: $(-2, \infty)$
range: $(-\infty, \infty)$

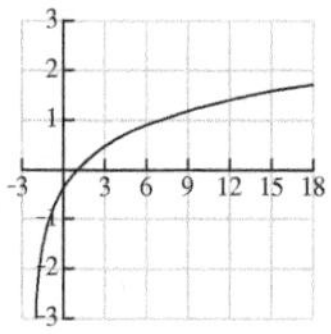

79. domain: $(0, \infty)$
range: $(-\infty, \infty)$

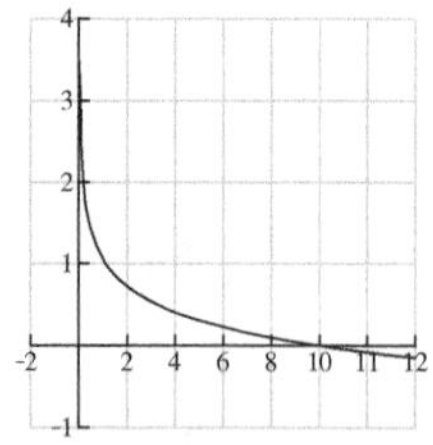

81. domain: $(-4, \infty)$
range: $(-\infty, \infty)$

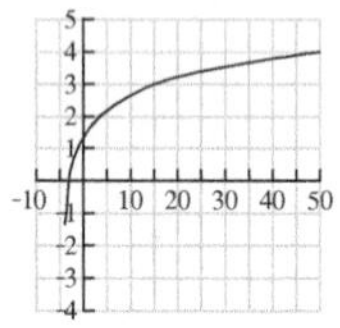

83. domain: $(0, \infty)$
range: $(-\infty, \infty)$

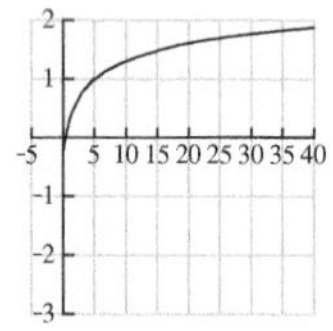

85. 60 dB **87.** 117 dB **89.** 8.5 **91.** 6.6 **93.** 3.3

95. Normal rainwater: 5.6
Acid rain/tomato juice: 4

97. 3.6 **99.** 13,236 yr **101.** 25 dB loss

103. a.

USAGE	WAVELENGTH	FREQUENCY
Super Low Frequency—Communication with Submarines	10,000,000 m	30 Hz
Ultra Low Frequency—Communication with Mines	1,000,000 m	300 Hz
Very Low Frequency—Avalanche Beacons	100,000 m	3000 Hz
Low Frequency—Navigation, AM Longwave Broadcasting	10,000 m	30,000 Hz
Medium Frequency—AM Broadcasts, Amateur Radio	1,000 m	300,000 Hz
High Frequency—Shortwave broadcasts, Citizens Band Radio	100 m	3,000,000 Hz
Very High Frequency—FM Radio, Television	10 m	30,000,000 Hz
Ultra High Frequency—Television, Mobile Phones	0.050 m	6,000,000,000 Hz

b.

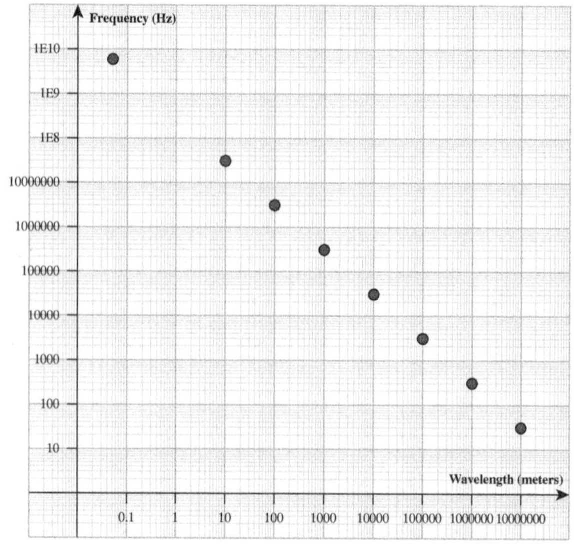

105. $\log_2 4 = x$ is equivalent to $2^x = 4$ (not $x = 2^4$).

107. The domain is the set of all real numbers such that $x + 5 > 0$, which is written as $(-5, \infty)$.

109. false **111.** true

113. domain: (a, ∞) range: $(-\infty, \infty)$
x-intercept: $(a + e^b, 0)$

115.

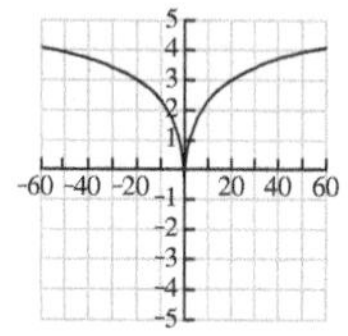

117. $f'(x) = e^x$ **119.** $(f^{-1})'(x) = \frac{1}{x}$

Section 3.3

1. 0 **3.** 1 **5.** 8 **7.** −3 **9.** $\frac{3}{2}$

11. 5 **13.** $x + 5$ **15.** 8 **17.** $\frac{1}{9}$ **19.** $\frac{7}{x^3}$

21. $3\log_b(x) + 5\log_b(y)$ **23.** $\frac{1}{2}\log_b(x) + \frac{1}{3}\log_b(y)$

25. $\frac{1}{3}\log_b(r) - \frac{1}{2}\log_b(s)$ **27.** $\log_b(x) - \log_b(y) - \log_b(z)$

29. $2\log x + \frac{1}{2}\log(x + 5)$

31. $3\ln(x) + 2\ln(x - 2) - \frac{1}{2}\ln(x^2 + 5)$

33. $2\log(x - 1) - \log(x - 3) - \log(x + 3)$

35. $\frac{1}{2}\ln(x + 5) - \frac{1}{2}\ln(x - 1)$

37. $\log_b(x^3y^5)$ **39.** $\log_b\left(\frac{u^5}{v^2}\right)$

41. $\log_b(x^{1/2}y^{2/3})$ **43.** $\log\left(\frac{u^2}{v^3z^2}\right)$

45. $\ln\left(\frac{x^2 - 1}{(x^2 + 3)^2}\right)$ **47.** $\ln\left(\frac{(x + 3)^{1/2}}{x(x + 2)^{1/3}}\right)$

49. 1.2091 **51.** −2.3219 **53.** 1.6599

55. 2.0115 **57.** 3.7856 **59.** 110 dB

61. 5.5 **63.** 0.0458 **65.** 16 times

67. $3\log 5 - \log 5^2 = 3\log 5 - 2\log 5 = \log 5$

69. Cannot apply the product and quotient properties to logarithms with different bases. Cannot reduce the given expression further without using the change-of-base formula.

71. true **73.** false **75.** false

79. $6\log_b x - 9\log_b y + 15\log_b z$

83. $f'(x) = \frac{1}{x} + \frac{1}{x} = \frac{2}{x}$ **85.** $f'(x) = -\frac{2}{x}$

Section 3.4

1. $x = \pm 2$ **3.** $x = -4$ **5.** $x = -\frac{3}{2}$

7. $x = -1$ **9.** $x = 3, 4$ **11.** $x = 0, 6$

13. $x = 1, 4$ **15.** $x = \dfrac{\log_2(27) + 1}{3} \approx 1.918$

17. $x = \ln 5 \approx 1.609$ **19.** $x = 10 \ln 4 \approx 13.863$

21. $x = \log_3(10) \approx 2.096$ **23.** $x = \dfrac{\ln(22) - 4}{3} \approx -0.303$

25. $x = \dfrac{\ln 6}{2} \approx 0.896$ **27.** 0.223

29. ± 2.282 **31.** $x = \ln\left(\dfrac{-7 + \sqrt{61}}{2}\right) \approx -0.904$

33. $x = 0$ **35.** $x = \ln 7 \approx 1.946$

37. $x = 0$ **39.** $x = \dfrac{\log_{10}(9)}{2} \approx 0.477$

41. $x = 40$ **43.** $x = \frac{9}{32}$ **45.** $x = \pm 3$

47. $x = 5$ **49.** $x = 6$ **51.** $x = -1$

53. no solution **55.** $x = \frac{25}{8}$ **57.** $x = -\frac{4}{5}$

59. $x = 47.5$ **61.** $x \approx \pm 7.321$ **63.** $x \approx -1.432$

65. $x \cong -1.25$ **67.** $x \approx 8.456$

69. $x = \dfrac{-3 + \sqrt{13}}{2} \cong 0.303$

71. $x \approx 3.646$

73. **a.** 151 beats per min
b. 7 min
c. 66 beats per min

75. 31.9 yr **77.** 19.74 yr **79.** 3.16×10^{15} J

81. 1 W/m^2 **83.** 4.61 hr **85.** 15.89 yr

87. $\ln(4e^x) \neq 4x$. Should first divide both sides by 4, then take the natural log:

$$4e^x = 9$$
$$e^x = \frac{9}{4}$$
$$\ln(e^x) = \ln\left(\frac{9}{4}\right)$$
$$x = \ln\left(\frac{9}{4}\right)$$

89. true **91.** false **93.** false

95. $x = \dfrac{1 + \sqrt{1 + 4b^2}}{2}$ **97.** $t = -5\ln\left(\dfrac{3000 - y}{2y}\right)$

99. $f^{-1}(x) = \ln\left(x + \sqrt{x^2 - 1}\right)$

101. $f^{-1}(x) = \ln\left(x + \sqrt{x^2 + 1}\right)$

103. $\ln y = x \ln 2$

Section 3.5

1. c (iv) **3.** a (iii) **5.** f (i)

7. 119 million **9.** 7.7 years, 2010

11. 2151.9 subscribers **13.** \$6,770,673 **15.** 332 million

17. 1.53 million **19.** 13.53 ml

21. **a.** $k = -\ln\left(\dfrac{8}{15}\right) \cong 0.6286$
b. 636,000 mp3 players

23. 7575 yr **25.** 131,158,556 years old

27. 105°F **29.** 3.8 hr before 7 A.M.

31. \$19,100

33. **a.** 84,520 **b.** 100,000 **c.** 100,000

35. 202,422 cases **37.** 1.89 yr

39. **a.** 18 yr **b.** 10 yr **41.** **a.** 30 yr **b.** \$328,120

43. $r = 0.07$, not 7 **45.** true

47. false **49.** more time

51. about 10.9 days **53.** $k_1 = k_2 + \ln\left(\frac{2 + c}{c}\right)$

55. $\dfrac{Pe^{kx}(e^{kh} - 1)}{h}$ **57.** $f'(x) = e^x + 1$

Review Exercises

1. 17,559.94 **3.** 5.52 **5.** 24.53

7. 5.89 **9.** 73.52 **11.** 6.25

13. b **15.** c

17. y-intercept: $(0, -1)$
HA: $y = 0$

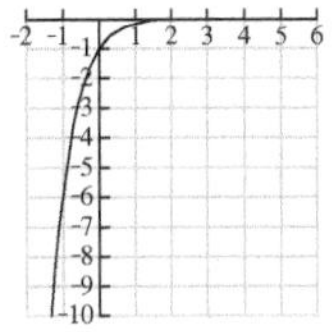

19. y-intercept: $(0, 2)$
HA: $y = 1$

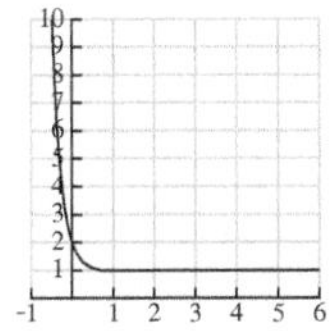

21. y-intercept: $(0, 1)$
HA: $y = 0$

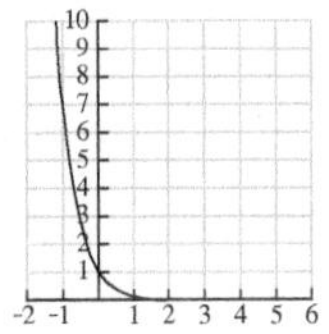

23. y-intercept: $(0, 3.2)$
HA: $y = 0$

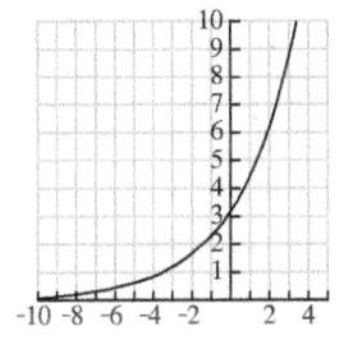

25. \$6144.68 **27.** \$23,080.29 **29.** $4^3 = 64$

31. $10^{-2} = \frac{1}{100}$ **33.** $\log_6 216 = 3$ **35.** $\log_{2/13}\left(\frac{4}{169}\right) = 2$

37. 0 **39.** -4 **41.** 1.51

43. -2.08 **45.** $(-2, \infty)$ **47.** $(-\infty, \infty)$

49. b **51.** d

53.

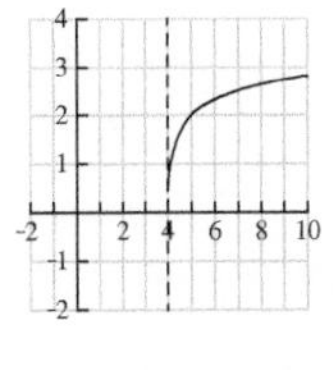

55.

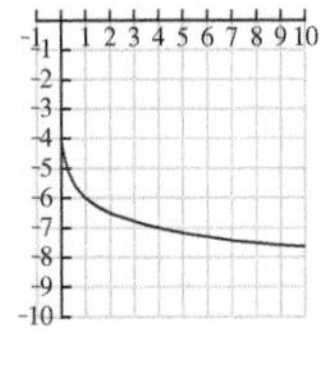

57. 6.5 **59.** 50 dB **61.** 1 **63.** 6

65. $a \log_c(x) + b \log_c(y)$ **67.** $\log_j(r) + \log_j(s) - 3\log_j(t)$

69. $\frac{1}{2}\log(a) - \frac{3}{2}\log(b) - \frac{2}{5}\log(c)$

71. 0.5283 **73.** 0.2939 **75.** $x = -4$

77. $x = \frac{4}{3}$ **79.** $x = -6$ **81.** $x \approx -0.218$

83. no solution **85.** $x = 0$ **87.** $x = \frac{100}{3}$

89. $x = 128\sqrt{2}$ **91.** $x \approx \pm 3.004$ **93.** $x \approx 0.449$

95. \$28,536.88 **97.** 16.6 yr **99.** 4.59 million

101. 6,250 bacteria **103.** 56 yr **105.** 16 fish

107. 343 mice

Practice Test

1. x^3 **3.** -4

5. $x = \pm\sqrt{1 + \ln 42} \approx \pm 2.177$

7. $x = \dfrac{-1 + \ln\left(\frac{300}{27}\right)}{0.2} \cong 7.04$

9. $x = 4 + e^2 \approx 11.389$

11. $x = e^e \approx 15.154$ **13.** $x = 9$

15. $x = \dfrac{-3 \pm \sqrt{9 - 4(-e)}}{2} \approx 0.729$

17. $x = \ln\left(\frac{1}{2}\right) \approx -0.693$ **19.** $(-1, 0) \cup (1, \infty)$

21. x-intercept: none
y-intercept: (0, 2)
HA: $y = 1$

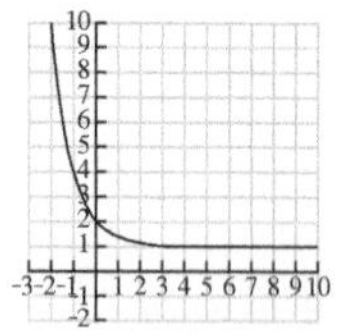

23. x-intercept: $\left(\dfrac{3 + \frac{1}{e}}{2}, 0\right)$
y-intercept: none
VA: $x = \frac{3}{2}$

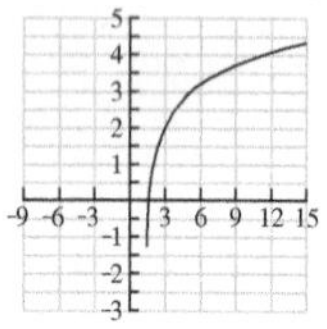

25. \$8051.62 **27.** 90 dB

29. $7.9 \times 10^{11} < E < 2.5 \times 10^{13}$ J

31. 7800 bacteria **33.** 3 days

Cumulative Test

1. domain: $(-\infty, -3) \cup (3, \infty)$; range: $(0, \infty)$

3. $g(x) = e^{2x}$ and $f(x) = \dfrac{1 - x}{1 + x}$ or

$g(x) = e^x$ and $f(x) = \dfrac{1 - x^2}{1 + x^2}$

5. $f(x) = -\frac{4}{9}x^2 - \frac{16}{9}x + \frac{11}{9}$ **7.** 2.197

9. **a.** 1 **b.** 5 **c.** 1 **d.** undefined

e. domain: $(-2, \infty)$ range: $(0, \infty)$

f. increasing: $(4, \infty)$, decreasing: $(0, 4)$, constant: $(-2, 0)$

11. yes **13.** $(1, -1)$

15. $Q(x) = -x^3 + 3x - 5$, $r(x) = 0$

17. HA: none VA: $x = 3$ Slant: $y = x + 3$

19.

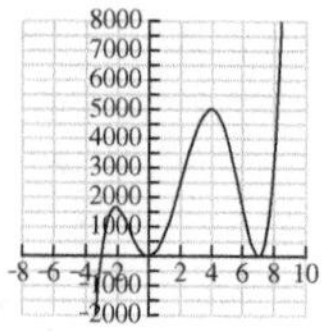

21. 5 **23.** $x = 0.5$ **25.** 8.62 yr

CHAPTER 4

Section 4.1

1. a. 72° **b.** 162° **3. a.** 48° **b.** 138°

5. a. 1° **b.** 91° **7.** 0.18

9. 0.02 **11.** 0.125 **13.** $\frac{\pi}{6}$ **15.** $\frac{\pi}{4}$

17. $\frac{7\pi}{4}$ **19.** $\frac{5\pi}{12}$ **21.** $\frac{17\pi}{18}$ **23.** $\frac{13\pi}{3}$

25. $-\frac{7\pi}{6}$ **27.** -20π **29.** 30° **31.** 135°

33. 67.5° **35.** 75° **37.** 1620° **39.** 171°

41. − 84° **43.** 229.18° **45.** 48.70° **47.** −160.37°

49. 198.48° **51.** 0.820 **53.** 1.95 **55.** 0.986

57. QII **59.** negative y-axis **61.** negative x-axis

63. I **65.** IV **67.** II **69.** 52°

71. 268° **73.** 330° **75.** $\frac{5\pi}{3}$ **77.** $\frac{11\pi}{9}$

79. 1.42 **81.** $\frac{2\pi}{3}$ ft **83.** $\frac{5}{2}$ in. **85.** $\frac{11\pi}{5}$ μm

87. $\frac{200\pi}{3}$ km **89.** 2.85 km² **91.** 8.621 cm²

93. 0.0236 ft² **95.** $\frac{2}{5}$ m/sec **97.** 272 km/hr

99. 9.8 m **101.** 1.5 mi **103.** $\frac{5\pi}{2}$ rad/sec

105. $\frac{2\pi}{9}$ rad/sec **107.** 6π in./sec **109.** $\frac{\pi}{4}$ mm/sec

111. 26.2 cm **113.** 653 in. or 54.5 ft

115. 1,440° **117.** 69.82 mph

119. 10.11 rad/sec = 1.6 rotations/sec

121. 7.8 cm **123.** 4.0 cm

125. Angular velocity must be expressed in radians (not degrees) per second. Use $\pi \frac{\text{rad}}{\text{sec}}$ in place of $\frac{180°}{\text{sec}}$.

127. true **129.** true **131.** 110° **133.** $\frac{15\pi}{2}$ units²

135. $\theta = \frac{\pi}{5}$ **137.** $\frac{\pi}{3}$

Section 4.2

1. $\frac{\sqrt{5}}{5}$ **3.** $\sqrt{5}$ **5.** 2 **7.** $\frac{2\sqrt{10}}{7}$

9. $\frac{7}{3}$ **11.** $\frac{3\sqrt{10}}{20}$ **13.** a **15.** b

17. c **19.** $\frac{\sqrt{3}}{3}$ **21.** $\sqrt{3}$ **23.** $\frac{2\sqrt{3}}{3}$

25. $\frac{2\sqrt{3}}{3}$ **27.** $\frac{\sqrt{3}}{3}$ **29.** $\sqrt{2}$ **31.** 0.6018

33. 0.1392 **35.** 0.2588 **37.** −0.8090 **39.** 1.3764

41. 0.4142 **43.** 1.0034 **45.** 0.7002 **47.** 18 ft

49. 5.50 mi **51.** 12 km **53.** 62°

55. $\beta = 58°, a \approx 6.4$ ft, $b \approx 10$ ft

57. $\alpha = 18°, b \approx 9.2$ mm, $a \approx 3.0$ mm

59. $\beta = 35.8°$; $c \approx 137$ mi; $b \approx 80.1$ mi

61. $\alpha \approx 56.0°$; $\beta \approx 34.0°$; $c \approx 51.3$ ft

63. $\alpha \approx 55.480°$; $\beta \approx 34.520°$; $b \approx 24{,}235$ km

65. $c \approx 27.0$ in.; $a \approx 24.4$ in.; $\alpha \approx 64.6°$

67. 75 ft 69. 260 ft 71. 80 ft

73. 170 m 75. 0.000016° 77. 4,414 ft

79. 136.69° 81. 3.5 ft 83. 4.7 in.

85. Opposite side has length 3, not 4.

87. true 89. false 91. 0

93. 0 95. $\frac{1}{2}$ 97. $\frac{6 - 2\sqrt{3}}{3}$

99. $\sqrt{3} - 1$

Section 4.3

1. $\sin\theta = \frac{2\sqrt{5}}{5}, \cos\theta = \frac{\sqrt{5}}{5}, \tan\theta = 2,$
$\csc\theta = \frac{\sqrt{5}}{2}, \sec\theta = \sqrt{5}, \cot\theta = \frac{1}{2}$

3. $\sin\theta = \frac{4\sqrt{41}}{41}, \cos\theta = \frac{5\sqrt{41}}{41}, \tan\theta = \frac{4}{5},$
$\csc\theta = \frac{\sqrt{41}}{4}, \sec\theta = \frac{\sqrt{41}}{5}, \cot\theta = \frac{5}{4}$

5. $\sin\theta = \frac{2\sqrt{5}}{5}, \cos\theta = -\frac{\sqrt{5}}{5}, \tan\theta = -2,$
$\csc\theta = \frac{\sqrt{5}}{2}, \sec\theta = -\sqrt{5}, \cot\theta = -\frac{1}{2}$

7. $\sin\theta = -\frac{7\sqrt{65}}{65}, \cos\theta = -\frac{4\sqrt{65}}{65}, \tan\theta = \frac{7}{4},$
$\csc\theta = -\frac{\sqrt{65}}{7}, \sec\theta = -\frac{\sqrt{65}}{4}, \cot\theta = \frac{4}{7}$

9. $\sin\theta = \frac{\sqrt{15}}{5}, \cos\theta = -\frac{\sqrt{10}}{5}, \tan\theta = -\frac{\sqrt{6}}{2},$
$\csc\theta = \frac{\sqrt{15}}{3}, \sec\theta = -\frac{\sqrt{10}}{2}, \cot\theta = -\frac{\sqrt{6}}{3}$

11. $\sin\theta = -\frac{\sqrt{6}}{4}, \cos\theta = -\frac{\sqrt{10}}{4}, \tan\theta = \frac{\sqrt{15}}{5},$
$\csc\theta = -\frac{2\sqrt{6}}{3}, \sec\theta = -\frac{2\sqrt{10}}{5}, \cot\theta = \frac{\sqrt{15}}{3}$

13. $\sin\theta = -\frac{2\sqrt{29}}{29}, \cos\theta = -\frac{5\sqrt{29}}{29}, \tan\theta = \frac{2}{5},$
$\csc\theta = -\frac{\sqrt{29}}{2}, \sec\theta = -\frac{\sqrt{29}}{5}, \cot\theta = \frac{5}{2}$

15. QIV 17. QII 19. QI 21. QI

23. QIII 25. $-\frac{4}{5}$ 27. $-\frac{60}{11}$ 29. $-\frac{84}{85}$

31. $\sqrt{3}$ 33. $-\frac{\sqrt{3}}{3}$ 35. $\frac{2\sqrt{3}}{3}$ 37. 1

39. -1 41. 0 43. 1 45. 1

47. possible 49. not possible

51. possible 53. possible 55. possible 57. $-\frac{1}{2}$

59. $-\frac{\sqrt{3}}{2}$ 61. $\frac{\sqrt{3}}{3}$ 63. 1 65. -2

67. 1 69. $\theta = 30°$ or $330°$

71. $\theta = 210°$ or $330°$ 73. $\theta = 90°$ or $270°$

75. $\theta = 270°$ 77. 110° 79. 143°

81. 322° 83. 140° 85. 340° 87. 1°

89. 335° 91. 1.3 93. 12°

95. 15°; The lower leg is bent at the knee in a backward direction at an angle of 15°.

97. 75.5°

99. Reference angle is measured between the terminal side and the x-axis, not the y-axis. The reference angle is 60°, $\sec 120° = -2$

101. true 103. false 105. false

107. true 109. $-\frac{3}{5}$

111. $y = (\tan\theta)(x - a)$ 113. $-\frac{a}{\sqrt{a^2 + b^2}}$

115. $-\frac{\sqrt{a^2 - b^2}}{b}$ 117. $\frac{12 + 3\sqrt{2} + \sqrt{3}}{6}$

119. $\frac{8}{3}$

Section 4.4

1. SSA 3. SSS 5. ASA

7. $\gamma = 75°, b \approx 12.2$ m, $c \approx 13.66$ m

9. $\beta = 62°, a \approx 163$ cm, $c \approx 215$ cm

11. $\beta = 116.1°, a \approx 80.2$ yd, $b \approx 256.6$ yd

13. $\gamma = 120°, a \approx 7$ m, $b \approx 7$ m

15. $\alpha = 97°, a \approx 118$ yd, $b \approx 52$ yd

17. $\beta_1 \approx 20°, \gamma_1 = 144°, c_1 \approx 9;$
$\beta_2 \approx 160°, \gamma_2 \approx 4°, c_2 \approx 1$

19. $\alpha = 40°, \beta = 100°, b \approx 18$

21. no triangle

23. $\beta = 90°, \gamma \approx 60°, c \approx 16$

25. $\beta \approx 23°, \gamma \approx 123°, c \approx 15$

27. $\beta_1 \approx 21.9°, \gamma_1 \approx 136.8°, c_1 \approx 11.36;$
$\beta_2 \approx 158.1°, \gamma_2 \approx 0.6°, c_2 \approx 0.17$

29. $\beta \approx 62°, \gamma \approx 2°, c \approx 0.275$

31. $\beta_1 \approx 77°, \alpha_1 \approx 63°, a_1 \approx 457;$
$\beta_2 \approx 103°, \alpha_2 \approx 37°, a_2 \approx 309$

33. $\alpha \approx 31°, \gamma \approx 43°, c \approx 2$

35. 1.7 mi 37. 1.3 mi 39. 26 ft 41. 270 ft

43. 17.1 m 45. 60.14 ft 47. 1.2 cm

49. The value of β is incorrect. Should be $\sin\beta = \frac{9\sin 120°}{7} = 1.113$ which there is no angle β that makes this true.

51. false 53. true 55. true

61. 27 in. 63. 22 m

Section 4.5

1. $b \approx 5, \gamma \approx 33°, \alpha \approx 47°$

3. $a \approx 5, \gamma \approx 6°, \beta \approx 158°$

5. $a \approx 2, \beta \approx 80°, \gamma \approx 80°$

7. $b \approx 5, \alpha \approx 43°, \gamma \approx 114°$

9. $b \approx 7, \alpha \approx 30°, \gamma \approx 90°$

11. $\alpha \approx 93°, \beta \approx 39°, \gamma \approx 48°$

13. $\gamma \approx 77°, \beta \approx 51.32°, \alpha = \beta \approx 51.32°$

15. $\alpha \approx 75°, \beta \approx 57°, \gamma \approx 48°$

17. no triangle

19. $\gamma = 90°, \beta \approx 23°, \alpha \approx 67°$

21. $\gamma = 105°, b \approx 5, c \approx 9$

23. $\beta \approx 12°, \gamma \approx 137°, c \approx 16$

25. $\beta \approx 77°, \alpha \approx 66°, \gamma \approx 37°$

27. $\gamma \approx 2°, \alpha \approx 168°, a \approx 13$

29. 55.4 **31.** 0.5 **33.** 23.6 **35.** 6.4

37. 4,408.4 **39.** 97.4 **41.** 25.0 **43.** 26.7

45. 111.64 **47.** 111,632,076 **49.** no triangle

51. 2710 mi **53.** 1280 mi **55.** 16 ft

57. 26.0 cm **59.** 83.07° **61.** 47,128 sq ft

63. 23.38 sq ft **65.** 8.73

67. Should have used the smaller angle β in Step 2

69. false **71.** true **73.** true

77. $\cos\left(\frac{x}{2}\right) = \sqrt{\dfrac{1 - \cos\left(2\cos^{-1}\left(\frac{1}{4}\right)\right)}{2}}$

81. 0.69 sq units **83.** 333 mi **85.** 129 m

Review Exercises

1. a. 62° **b.** 152° **3. a.** 55° **b.** 145°

5. a. 0.99° **b.** 90.99°

7. $\frac{3\pi}{4}$ **9.** $\frac{11\pi}{6}$ **11.** $\frac{6\pi}{5}$ **13.** 9π

15. 60° **17.** 225° **19.** 100° **21.** 1800°

23. 150° **25.** 754 in./min **27.** $\frac{2\sqrt{13}}{13}$

29. $\frac{\sqrt{13}}{2}$ **31.** $\frac{3}{2}$ **33.** b

35. b **37.** c **39.** 0.6691

41. 0.9548 **43.** 1.5399 **45.** 1.5477

47. 75 ft

49. $\sin\theta = -\frac{4}{5}, \cos\theta = \frac{3}{5}, \tan\theta = -\frac{4}{3},$
$\cot\theta = -\frac{3}{4}, \sec\theta = \frac{5}{3}, \csc\theta = -\frac{5}{4}$

51. $\sin\theta = \frac{\sqrt{10}}{10}, \cos\theta = -\frac{3\sqrt{10}}{10}, \tan\theta = -\frac{1}{3},$
$\cot\theta = -3, \sec\theta = -\frac{\sqrt{10}}{3}, \csc\theta = \sqrt{10}$

53. $\sin\theta = \frac{1}{2}, \cos\theta = \frac{\sqrt{3}}{2}, \tan\theta = \frac{\sqrt{3}}{3},$
$\cot\theta = \sqrt{3}, \sec\theta = \frac{2\sqrt{3}}{3}, \csc\theta = 2$

55. $\sin\theta = -\frac{\sqrt{5}}{5}, \cos\theta = \frac{2\sqrt{5}}{5}, \tan\theta = -\frac{1}{2},$
$\cot\theta = -2, \sec\theta = \frac{\sqrt{5}}{2}, \csc\theta = -\sqrt{5}$

57. $\sin\theta = -\frac{\sqrt{7.2}}{3}, \cos\theta = -\frac{\sqrt{7.2}}{6}, \tan\theta = 2,$
$\cot\theta = \frac{1}{2}, \sec\theta = -\frac{\sqrt{7.2}}{1.2}, \csc\theta = -\frac{\sqrt{7.2}}{2.4}$

59. $-\frac{1}{2}$ **61.** $-\frac{\sqrt{3}}{3}$ **63.** $-\frac{2\sqrt{3}}{3}$

65. $-\frac{\sqrt{2}}{2}$ **67.** $\sqrt{3}$ **69.** $-\sqrt{2}$

71. $-\frac{2\sqrt{3}}{3}$

73. $\gamma = 150°, b \approx 8, c \approx 12$

75. $\gamma = 130°, a \approx 1, b \approx 9$

77. $\beta = 158°, a = 11, b \approx 22$

79. $\beta = 90°, a = \sqrt{2}, c = \sqrt{2}$

81. $\beta = 146°, b \approx 266, c \approx 178$

83. $\beta_1 \approx 26°, \gamma_1 \approx 134°, c_1 \approx 15;$
$\beta_2 \approx 154°, \gamma_2 \approx 6°, c_2 \approx 2$

85. $\gamma_1 \approx 29°, \beta_1 \approx 127°, b_1 \approx 20;$
$\gamma_2 \approx 151°, \beta_2 \approx 5°, b_2 \approx 2$

87. no triangle

89. $\beta_1 \approx 15°, \gamma_1 \approx 155°, c_1 \approx 10;$
$\beta_2 \approx 165°, \gamma_2 \approx 5°, c_2 \approx 2$

91. $c \approx 46, \alpha \approx 42°, \beta \approx 88°$

93. $\gamma \approx 75°, \beta \approx 54°, \alpha \approx 51°$

95. $\gamma = 90°, \beta \approx 48°, \alpha \approx 42°$

97. $a \approx 4, \beta \approx 28°, \gamma \approx 138°$

99. $a \approx 11, \beta \approx 68°, \gamma \approx 22°$

101. $\gamma \approx 70°, \beta \approx 59°, \alpha \approx 51°$

103. $a \approx 26, \beta \approx 37°, \gamma \approx 43°$

105. $a \approx 28, \beta \approx 4°, \gamma \approx 166°$

107. no triangle

109. $\beta \approx 10°, \gamma \approx 155°, c \approx 10.3$

111. 141.8 **113.** 51.5 **115.** 89.8

117. 41.7 **119.** 5.2 in.

Practice Test

1. 6000 ft

3. exact value versus approximate value

5. QIV **7.** 585°

9. $\frac{15\pi}{4}$ in^2 **11.** $\gamma = 110°, a \approx 7.8, c \approx 14.6$

13. $\gamma \approx 96.4°, \beta \approx 48.2°, \alpha \approx 35.4°$

15. no triangle

17. $\gamma = 50°, b \approx 1.82, c \approx 4.08$

19. 57

Cumulative Test

1. $-\frac{5}{8}$ **3.** $-2x - h$

5. 1 **7.** $y = -2x^2 + 7$

9. VA: $x = 2$, HA: none,
SA: $y = x + 2$

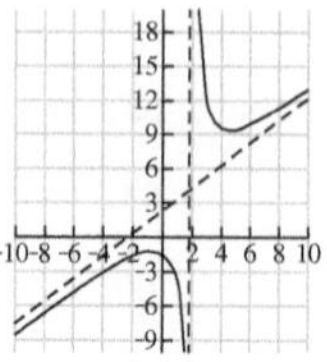

11. \$37,250 **13.** $x \approx 0.440$ **15.** $15\sqrt{2}$ ft

17. $\frac{12\pi}{5}$ **19.** $\sqrt{3}$ **21.** 1.6616

23. $\alpha = 138°, c \approx 8$ cm, $c \approx 9$ cm

CHAPTER 5

Section 5.1

1. $-\frac{\sqrt{3}}{2}$ **3.** $-\frac{\sqrt{3}}{2}$ **5.** $\frac{\sqrt{2}}{2}$ **7.** -1
9. $-\sqrt{2}$ **11.** $\sqrt{3}$ **13.** 2 **15.** $-\frac{\sqrt{3}}{2}$
17. $-\frac{\sqrt{3}}{2}$ **19.** $-\frac{\sqrt{2}}{2}$ **21.** $-\frac{\sqrt{3}}{2}$ **23.** $\frac{\sqrt{2}}{2}$
25. 1 **27.** $\frac{\sqrt{2}}{2}$ **29.** 0 **31.** -2
33. $\frac{\sqrt{3}}{3}$ **35.** $\theta = \frac{\pi}{6}, \frac{11\pi}{6}$ **37.** $\theta = \frac{4\pi}{3}, \frac{5\pi}{3}$
39. $\theta = 0, \pi, 2\pi, 3\pi, 4\pi$ **41.** $\theta = \pi, 3\pi$
43. $\theta = \frac{3\pi}{4}, \frac{7\pi}{4}$ **45.** $\theta = \frac{3\pi}{4}, \frac{5\pi}{4}$
47. $\theta = 0, \pi, 2\pi$ **49.** $\theta = \frac{\pi}{2}, \frac{3\pi}{2}$
51. $\theta = \frac{7\pi}{6}, \frac{11\pi}{6}$ **53.** $\theta = \frac{\pi}{6}, \frac{11\pi}{6}$
55. 22.9°F **57.** 99.1°F
59. 2.6 ft **61.** 135 lb
63. 10, 000 guests **65.** 10.7 μg/μL
67. 35°C
69. Should have used $\cos\left(\frac{5\pi}{6}\right) = -\frac{\sqrt{3}}{2}$ and $\sin\left(\frac{5\pi}{6}\right) = \frac{1}{2}$
71. true **73.** false **75.** true **77.** odd
79. $\theta = \frac{\pi}{4}, \frac{5\pi}{4}$ **81.** $\theta = \frac{\pi}{4}, \frac{3\pi}{4}, \frac{5\pi}{4}, \frac{7\pi}{4}$
83. $\theta = \frac{\pi}{3} + n\pi, \frac{2\pi}{3} + n\pi$
85. $\theta = \frac{\pi}{4}, \frac{3\pi}{4}, \frac{5\pi}{4}, \frac{7\pi}{4}$
87. 2 **89.** $\frac{3 - \sqrt{3}}{3}$

Section 5.2

1. c **3.** a **5.** h **7.** b **9.** e
11. $\frac{3}{2}; p = \frac{2\pi}{3}$ **13.** $1; p = \frac{2\pi}{5}$
15. $\frac{2}{3}; p = \frac{4\pi}{3}$ **17.** $3; p = 2$
19. $5; p = 6$

21.

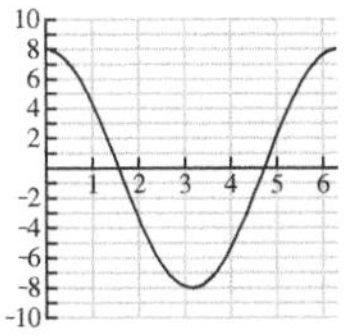

23.

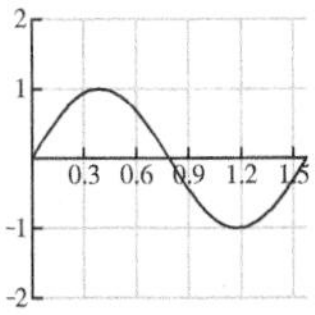

25.

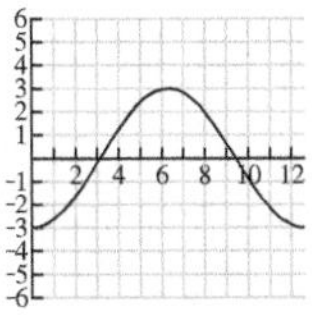

27.

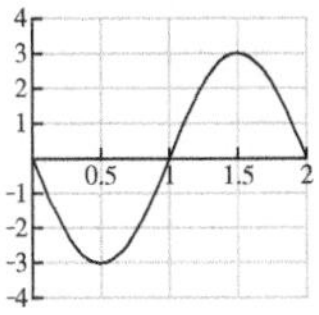

29.

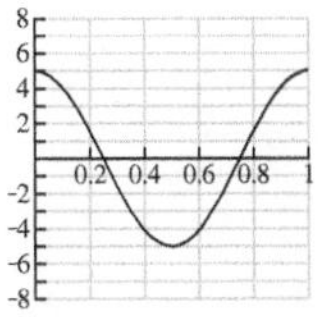

31.

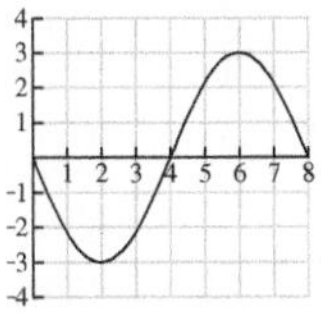

33.

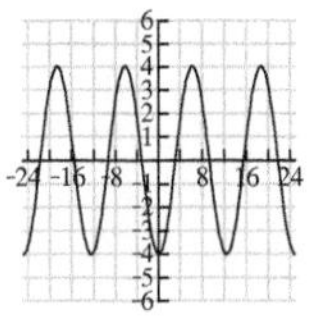

35.

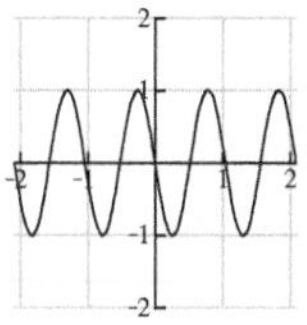

37.

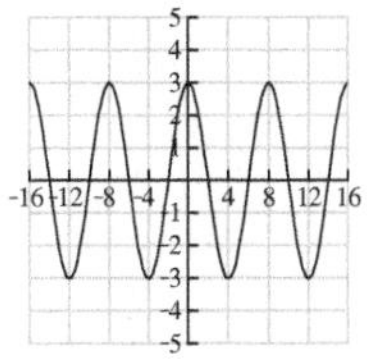

39.

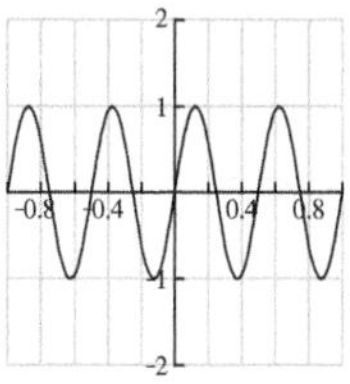

41. $y = -\sin(2x)$ **43.** $y = \cos(\pi x)$
45. $y = -2\sin\left(\frac{\pi}{2}x\right)$ **47.** $y = \sin(8\pi x)$

49. $2; 2; \frac{1}{\pi}$; right

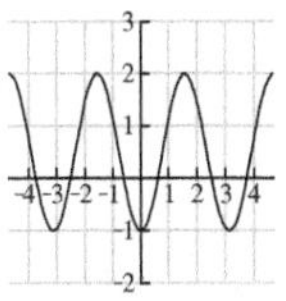

51. $5; \frac{2\pi}{3}; -\frac{2}{3}$; left

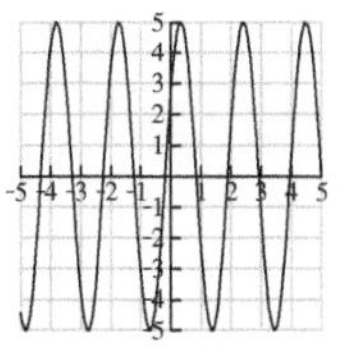

53. $6; 2; -2$; left

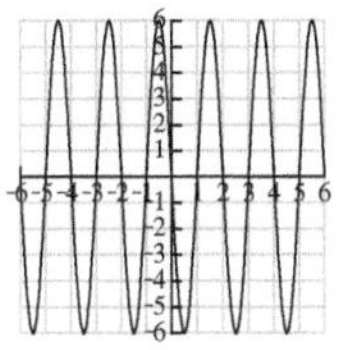

55. $3; \pi, -\frac{\pi}{2}$; left

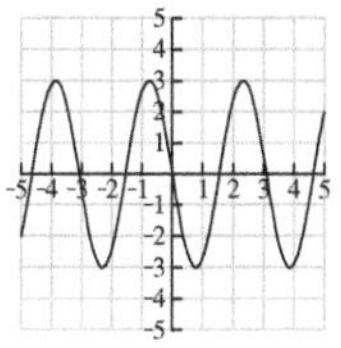

57. $\frac{1}{4}; 8\pi; 2\pi$; right

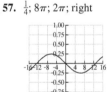

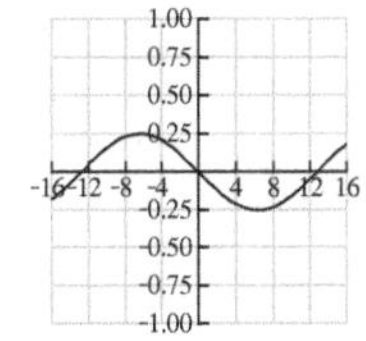

59. $2; 4; 4$; right

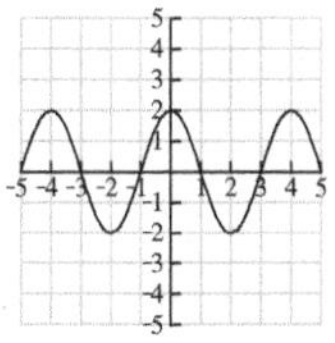

61.

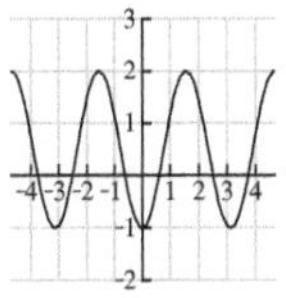

63.

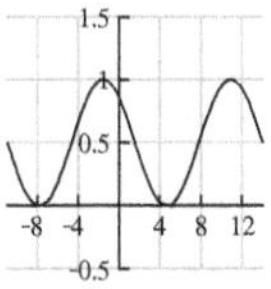

65.

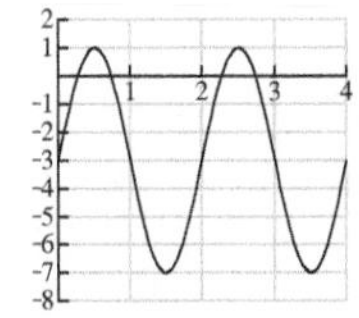

67.

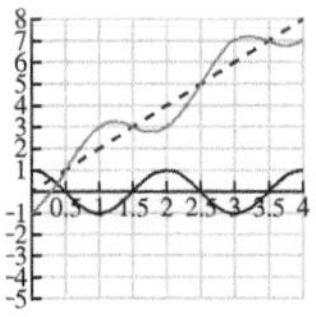

69.

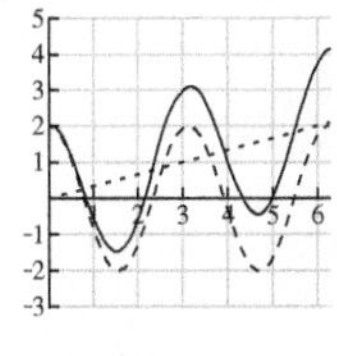

71.

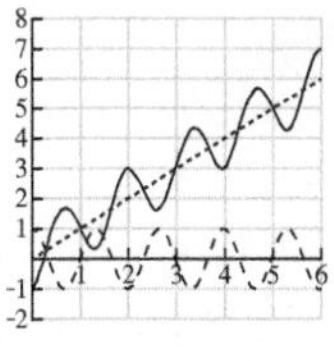

73.

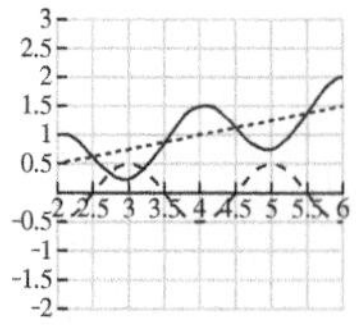

75.

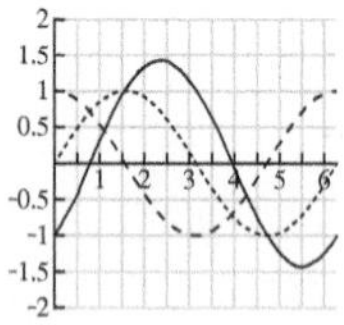

77.

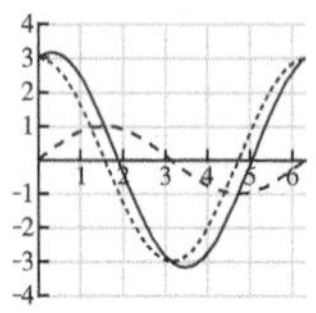

79.

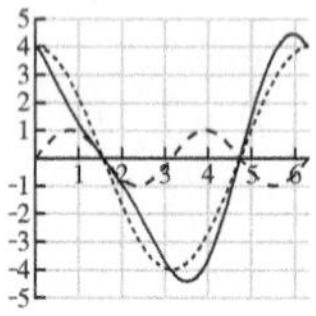

81.

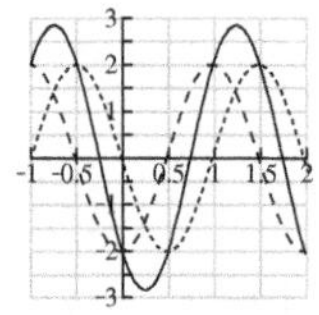

83.

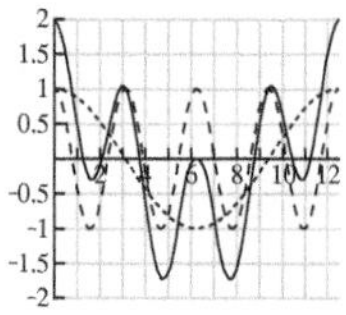

85.

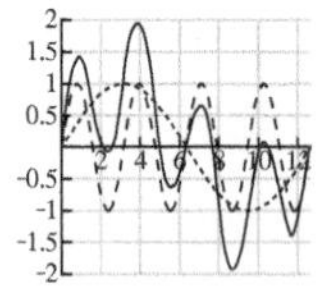

87.

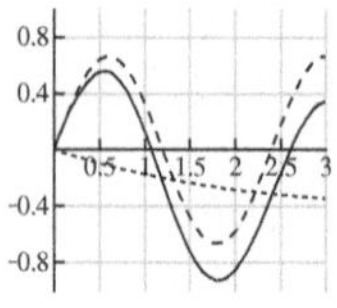

89.

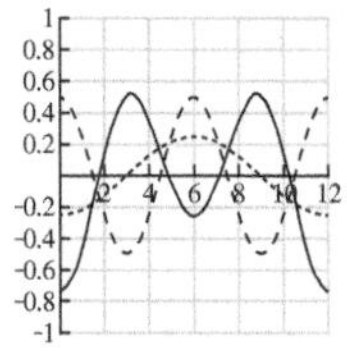

91.

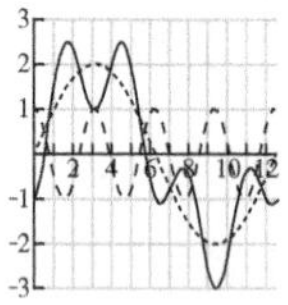

93.

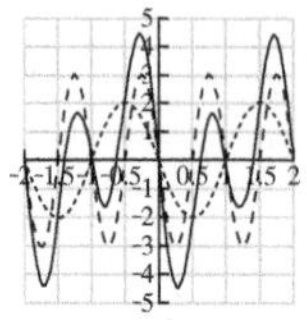

95. 3.5 or 3500 widgets **97.** 1 mg/L

99. 4 cm; 4 g **101.** $\frac{1}{4\pi}$ cycles/sec

103. 0.005 cm; 256 Hz **105.** 0.008 cm; 375 Hz

107. 660 m/sec **109.** 660 m/sec

111. The correct graph is reflected over the x-axis.

113. true **115.** false **117.** $(0, A)$

119. $x = \frac{n\pi}{B}$ **121.** $\left(0, -\frac{A}{2}\right)$ **123.** $\left(\frac{3\pi}{2B} + \frac{2n\pi}{B}, 0\right)$

125. $\left[-\frac{5A}{2}, \frac{3A}{2}\right]$

127. 2

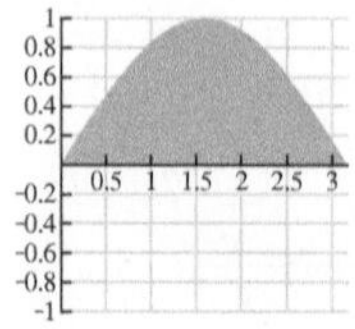

129. 1

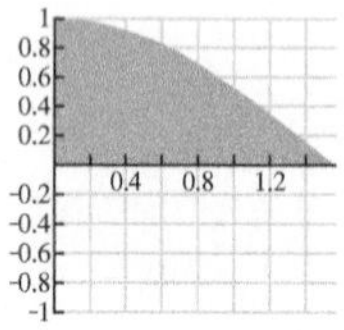

Section 5.3

1. b **3.** h **5.** c **7.** d

9.

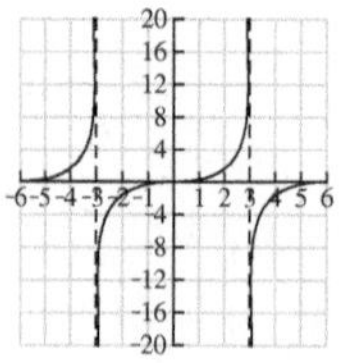

11.

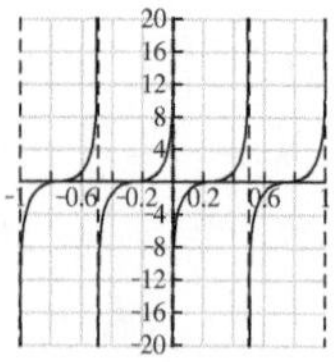

13.

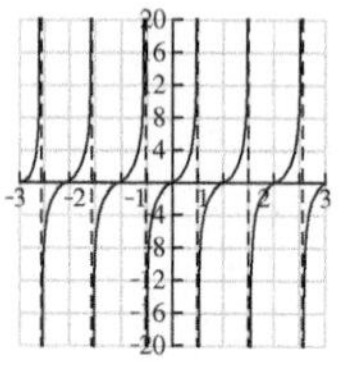

15.

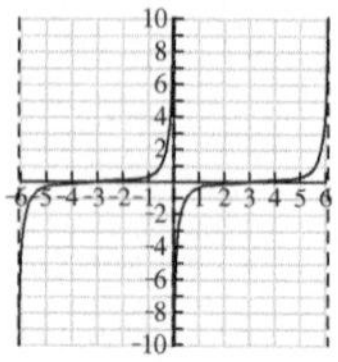

17.

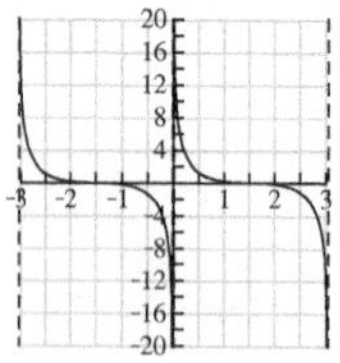

19.

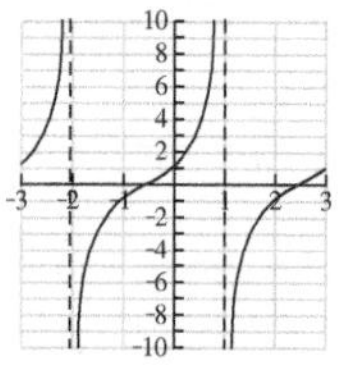

21.

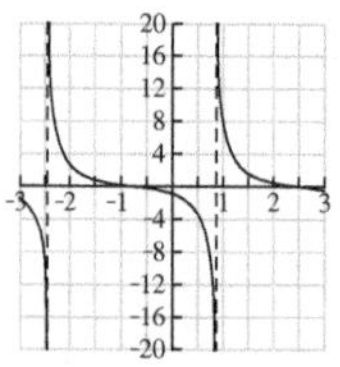

23.

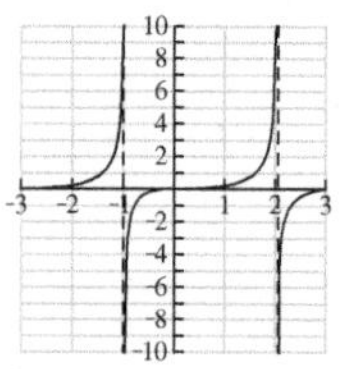

25.

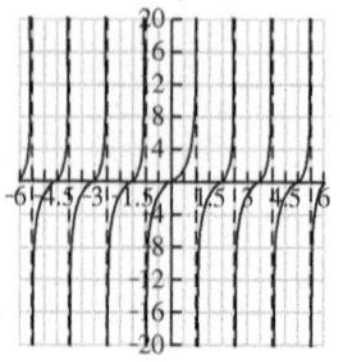

27.

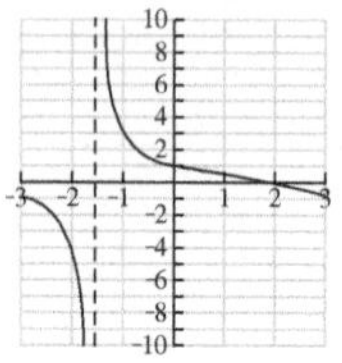

29.

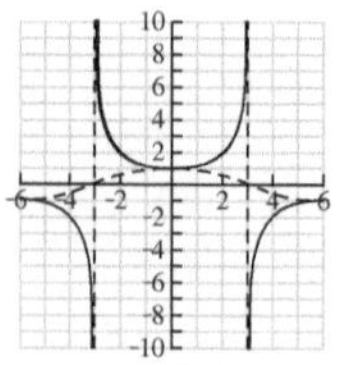

31.

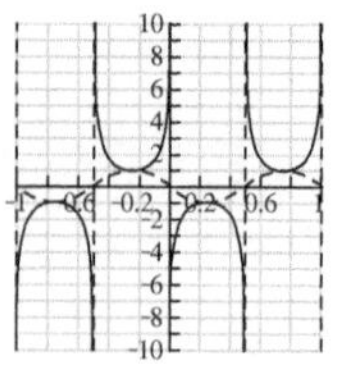

33.

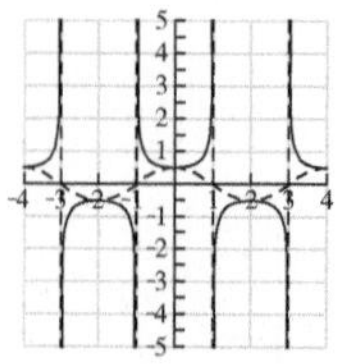

35.

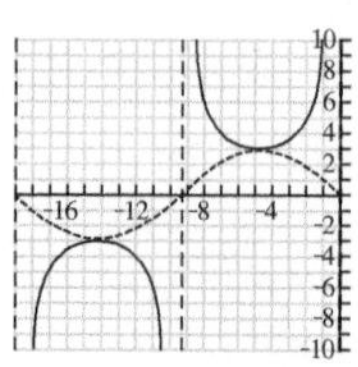

37.

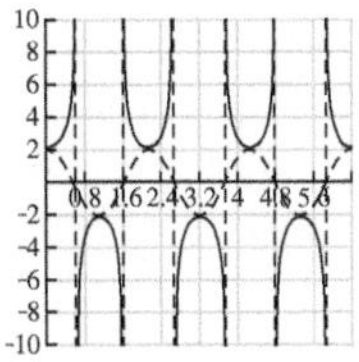

39.

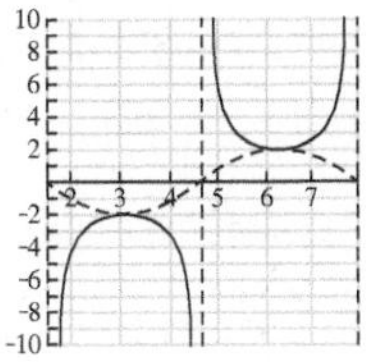

41.

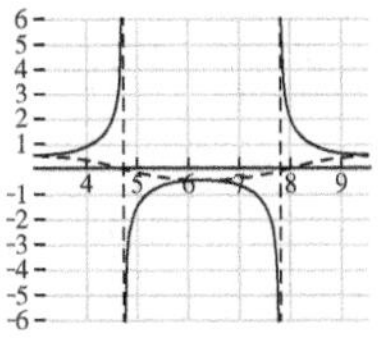

43.

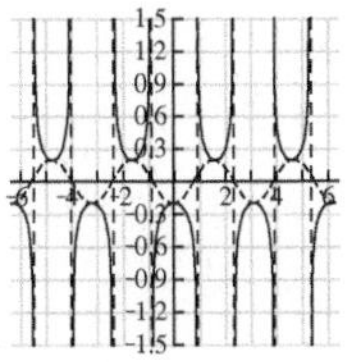

45.

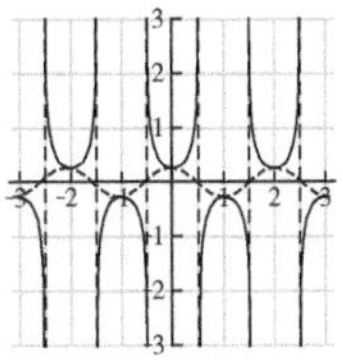

47.

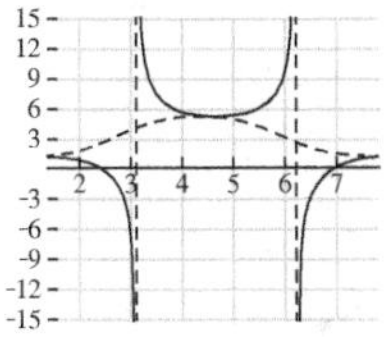

49.

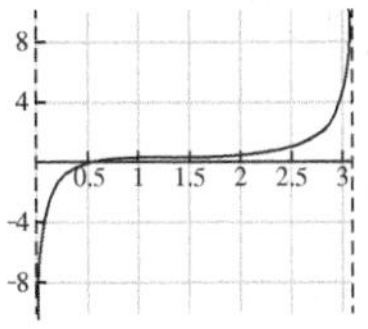

51.

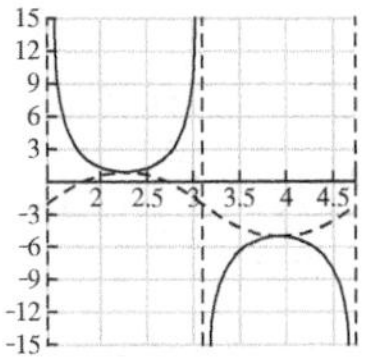

53.

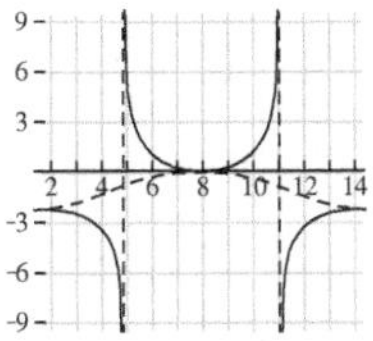

55.

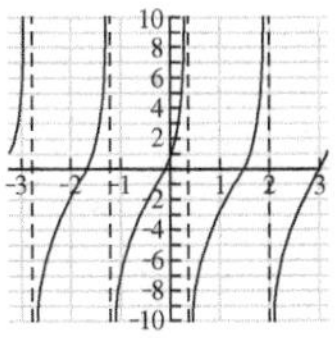

57. domain: $x \neq n$, n an integer range: $\mathbb{R}$

59. domain: $x \neq \frac{2n+1}{10}\pi$, n an integer
range: $(-\infty, -2] \cup [2, \infty)$

61. domain: $x \neq 2n\pi$, n an integer
range: $(-\infty, 1] \cup [3, \infty)$

63. domain: $x \neq 4n + 6$, n an integer range: $\mathbb{R}$

65. domain: $x \neq n$, n an integer
range: $\left(-\infty, -\frac{5}{2}\right] \cup \left[-\frac{3}{2}, \infty\right)$

67. 48 m

69. **a.** -5.2 mi **b.** -3 mi **c.** 0 **d.** 3 mi **e.** 5.2 mi

71. Forgot that the amplitude is 3, not 1. Guide function should have been $y = 3\sin(2x)$.

73. true

75. n, n an integer

77. $x = 0, \pm\frac{\pi}{2}, \pm\pi$

79. $x = \frac{n\pi - C}{B}$, n an integer

81. infinitely many solutions

83. $-\ln\frac{\sqrt{2}}{2}$

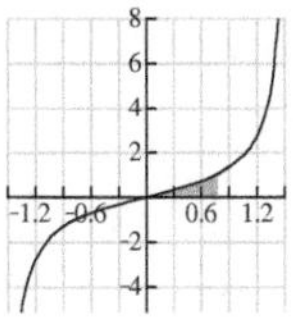

85. $\ln\left(\sqrt{2} + 1\right)$

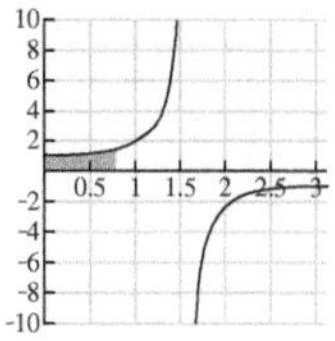

Review Exercises

1. $-\frac{\sqrt{3}}{3}$ **3.** $-\frac{1}{2}$ **5.** 1 **7.** -1

9. -1 **11.** $\frac{1}{2}$ **13.** $\frac{\sqrt{2}}{2}$ **15.** 1

17. $-\frac{\sqrt{3}}{2}$ **19.** $\frac{-\sqrt{3}}{3}$ **21.** 2π **23.** $y = 4\cos x$

25. 5 **27.** 2; $p = 1$ **29.** $\frac{1}{5}$; $p = \frac{2\pi}{3}$

31.

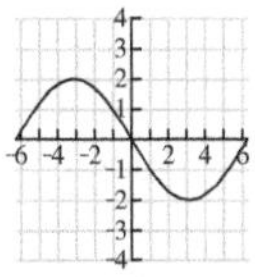

33.

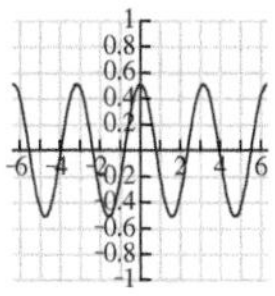

35. 3; 2π; $\frac{\pi}{2}$; 2 (up)

37. 4; $\frac{2\pi}{3}$; $-\frac{\pi}{4}$; -2 (down)

39. $\frac{1}{3}$; 2; $\frac{1}{2\pi}$; $\frac{1}{2}$ (down)

41.

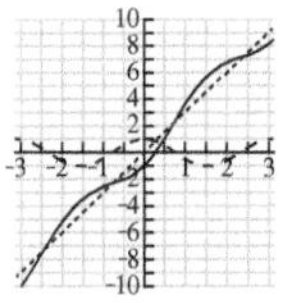

43.

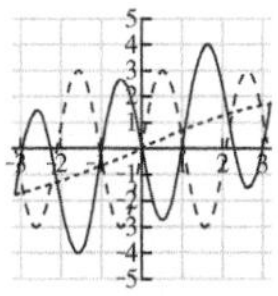

45. domain: $x \neq n\pi$, n an integer range: $\mathbb{R}$

47. domain: $x \neq \frac{2n+1}{4}\pi$, n an integer
range: $(-\infty, -3] \cup [3, \infty)$

49. domain: $x \neq \frac{6n+7}{6}$, n an integer
range: $\left(-\infty, -\frac{3}{4}\right] \cup \left[-\frac{1}{4}, \infty\right)$

51.

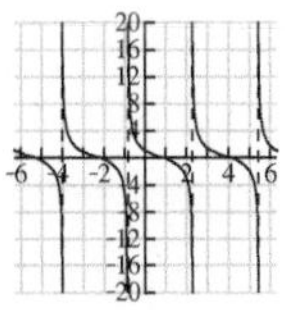

53.

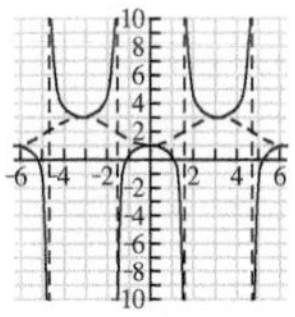

55.

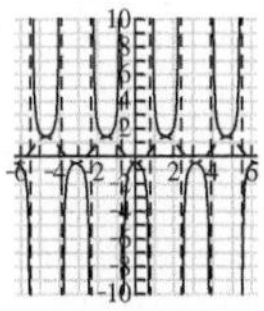

Practice Test

1. 5; $p = \frac{2\pi}{3}$

3.

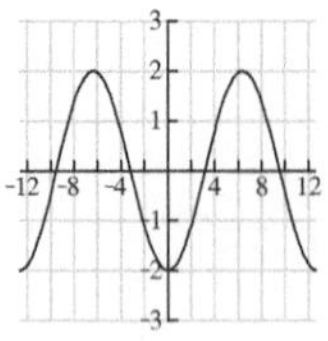

5.

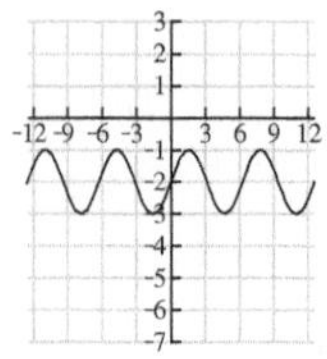

7.

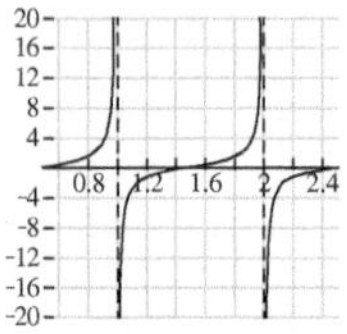

9. $x = \frac{n\pi}{2}$, n an integer

11. $(-\infty, -4] \cup [2, \infty)$

13.

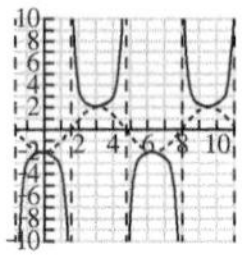

15. true

17. $y = 4\sin\left(2\left(x + \frac{3}{2}\right)\right) - \frac{1}{2}$

19.

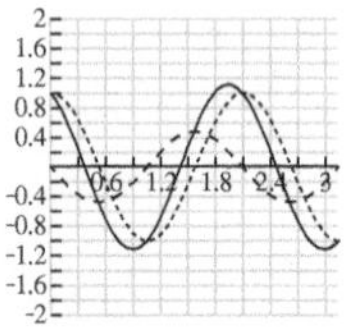

21. a. 4 b. 1

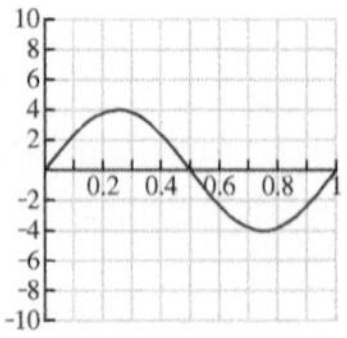

23. a. $y = 6 + 5\cos\left(2\left(x - \frac{\pi}{2}\right)\right)$

b. amplitude: 5, period: π, phase shift: $\frac{\pi}{2}$

c.

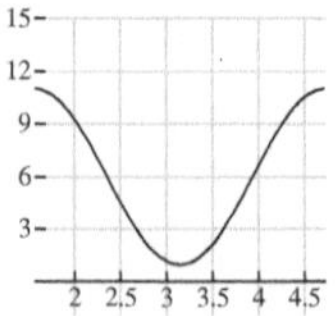

Cumulative Test

1. $(-5, \infty)$

3. $y = 2|x + 6| + 4$

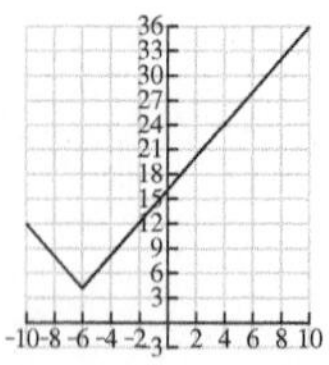

5. $f^{-1}(x) = \frac{5x + 2}{1 - 3x}$

domain f = range f^{-1}: $\left(-\infty, -\frac{5}{3}\right) \cup \left(-\frac{5}{3}, \infty\right)$

domain f^{-1} = range f: $\left(-\infty, \frac{1}{3}\right) \cup \left(\frac{1}{3}, \infty\right)$

7. $Q(x) = 3x^2 - \frac{5}{2}x + \frac{9}{2}$, $r(x) = \frac{9}{2}x + \frac{1}{2}$

9. $P(x) = (x - \sqrt{5})(x + \sqrt{5})(x - i)(x + i)$

11. \$3382

13. $3\ln a - 2\ln b - 5\ln c$

15. $x = 1$

17. $\alpha = 63°$, $b \approx 6.36$ in., $a \approx 12.47$ in.

19. $\beta \approx 71.17°$, $\gamma = 40.83°$, $c \approx 16.92$ m or $\beta = 108.83°$, $\gamma = 3.17°$, $c \approx 1.43$ m

21. $\cos\theta = -\frac{\sqrt{3}}{2}$, $\tan\theta = -\frac{\sqrt{3}}{3}$, $\cot\theta = -\sqrt{3}$, $\sec\theta = -\frac{2\sqrt{3}}{3}$, $\csc\theta = 2$

23. $f = \frac{2}{\pi}$

CHAPTER 6

Section 6.1

1. 30°
3. $90° - x$
5. 60°
7. $\cos(90° - x - y)$
9. $\sin(70° - A)$
11. $\tan(45° + x)$
13. $\sec(30° + \theta)$
15. 1
17. $\csc x$
19. -1
21. $\sec^2 x$
23. 1
25. $\sin^2 x - \cos^2 x$
27. $\sec x$
29. 1
31. $\sin^2 x$
33. $\csc^2 x$
35. $-\cos x$
37. 1
65. conditional
67. identity
69. conditional
71. conditional
73. conditional
75. identity
77. conditional
81. $|\sec\theta|$
83. Simplified the two fractions in Step 2 incorrectly
85. false
87. QI or QIV
89. QIII or QIV
91. no
93. no
95. $a^2 + b^2$
99. $\sec\theta$
101. $|a|\cos\theta$
103. $|a|\tan\theta$

Section 6.2

1. $\frac{\sqrt{6} - \sqrt{2}}{4}$
3. $\frac{\sqrt{6} - \sqrt{2}}{4}$
5. $-2 + \sqrt{3}$
7. $\frac{\sqrt{2} + \sqrt{6}}{4}$
9. $2 + \sqrt{3}$
11. $2 + \sqrt{3}$
13. $\sqrt{2} - \sqrt{6}$
15. $\sqrt{6} - \sqrt{2}$
17. $\cos x$
19. $-\sin x$
21. 0
23. $-2\cos(A - B)$
25. $-2\sin(A + B)$
27. $\tan(26°)$
29. $\frac{1 + 2\sqrt{30}}{12}$
31. $\frac{-6\sqrt{6} + 4}{25}$
33. $\frac{192 - 25\sqrt{15}}{-119}$
35. identity
37. conditional
39. identity
41. identity
43. identity
45. conditional
47. identity
49. identity
51. conditional

53. $y = \sin\left(x + \frac{\pi}{3}\right)$

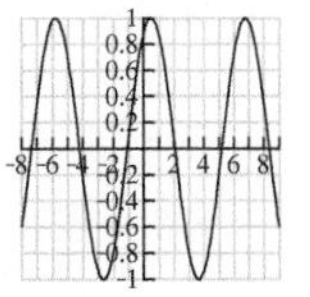

55. $y = \cos\left(x - \frac{\pi}{4}\right)$

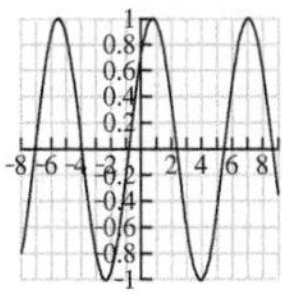

57. $y = -\sin 4x$

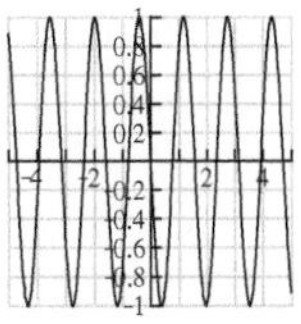

59. $y = \tan\left(x - \frac{\pi}{4}\right)$

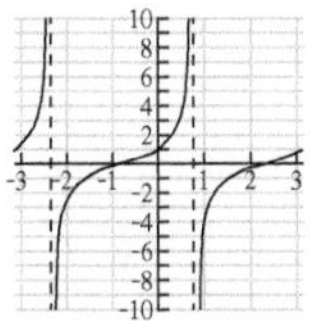

61. $y = \tan\left(x + \frac{\pi}{6}\right)$

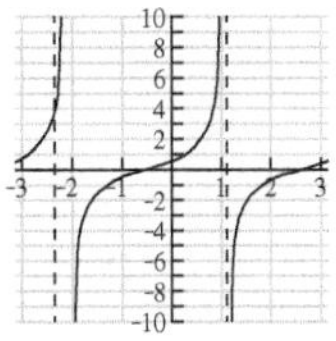

63. $\frac{\sqrt{2}}{2}\left(1 + x - \frac{x^2}{2!} - \frac{x^3}{3!} + \frac{x^4}{4!} + \frac{x^5}{5!} - - + + \dots\right)$

67. $E = A\cos(kz)\cos(ct)$ **69.** $T(t) = 38 - 2.5\sin\left(\frac{\pi}{6}t\right)$

71. $\tan(A + B) \neq \tan A + \tan B$. Should have used $\tan(A + B) = \dfrac{\tan A + \tan B}{1 - \tan A \tan B}$.

73. false **75.** false

79. $B = 2m\pi, \quad A = 2n\pi$; n, m integers

81. $\tan x = -\tan y$ **83.** $\tan x = \dfrac{2 - \tan y}{1 + 2\tan y}$

Section 6.3

1. $-\frac{4}{5}$ **3.** $\frac{120}{119}$ **5.** $\frac{120}{169}$ **7.** $-\frac{4}{3}$

9. $\frac{\sqrt{19}}{10}$ **11.** $\frac{119}{120}$ **13.** $\frac{\sqrt{3}}{3}$ **15.** $\frac{\sqrt{2}}{4}$

17. $\cos(4x)$ **19.** $-\frac{\sqrt{3}}{3}$ **21.** $-\frac{\sqrt{3}}{2}$ **23.** $-\frac{\sqrt{3}}{2}$

41.

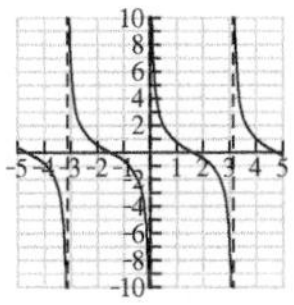

43.

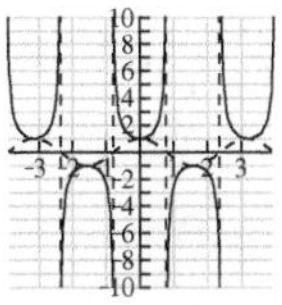

45.

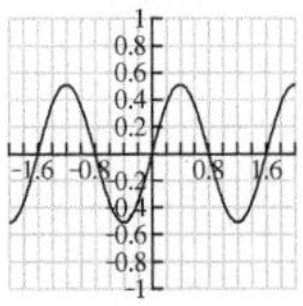

47.

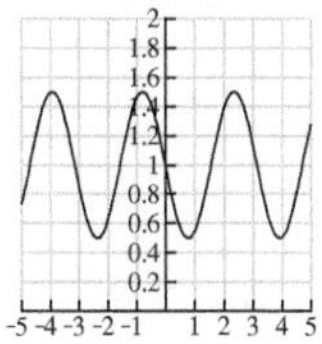

49.

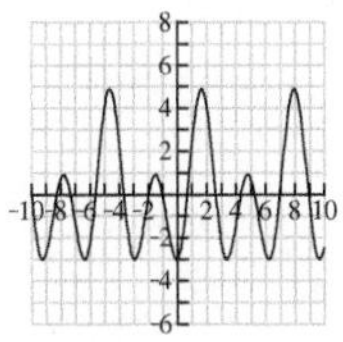

51. $\frac{\sqrt{2 - \sqrt{3}}}{2}$ **53.** $-\frac{\sqrt{2 + \sqrt{3}}}{2}$ **55.** $\frac{\sqrt{2 - \sqrt{3}}}{2}$

57. $\sqrt{3 + 2\sqrt{2}}$ **59.** $-\dfrac{2}{\sqrt{2 + \sqrt{2}}}$

61. $-\dfrac{1}{\sqrt{3 + 2\sqrt{2}}}$ or $1 - \sqrt{2}$ **63.** $-\dfrac{2}{\sqrt{2 - \sqrt{2}}}$

65. 1 **67.** $\frac{2\sqrt{13}}{13}$ **69.** $\frac{3\sqrt{13}}{13}$

71. $\frac{\sqrt{5} - 1}{2}$ or $\sqrt{\frac{3 - \sqrt{5}}{2}}$ **73.** $\sqrt{\frac{3 + 2\sqrt{2}}{6}}$

75. $-\frac{\sqrt{15}}{5}$ **77.** $\sqrt{\dfrac{1 - \frac{24}{\sqrt{601}}}{2}}$

79. $-\sqrt{\dfrac{1 - \sqrt{0.91}}{1 + \sqrt{0.91}}}$ **81.** $\sqrt{\frac{7}{3}}$ **83.** $\cos\left(\frac{5\pi}{12}\right)$

85. $\tan(75°)$ **87.** $-\tan\left(\frac{5\pi}{8}\right)$

101.

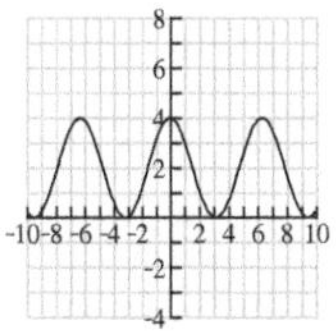

103.

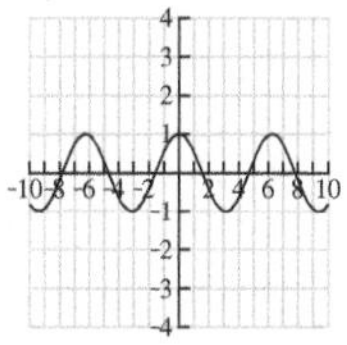

105.

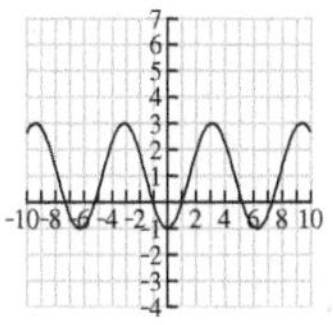

107.

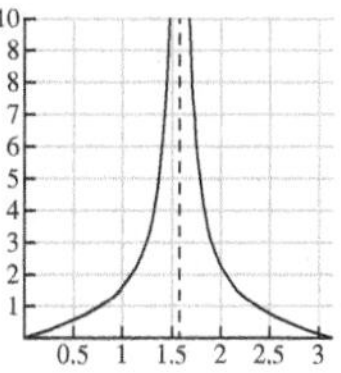

109. $C(t) = 2 + 10\cos(2t)$ **111.** 22,565,385 lb

115. $\sqrt{2}$ ft **117.** $\frac{1}{3}$

119. Should use $\sin x = -\frac{2\sqrt{2}}{3}$ because we are assuming that $\sin x < 0$.

121. false **123.** false **125.** false **127.** false

129. Cannot evaluate the identity at $A = \pi$

131. no **135.** $0 < x < \pi$

137. $\tan(2x)$ **139.** $\sin(3x)$

Section 6.4

1. $\frac{1}{2}[\sin(3x) + \sin x]$ **3.** $\frac{5}{2}[\cos(2x) - \cos(10x)]$

5. $2[\cos x + \cos(3x)]$ **7.** $\frac{1}{2}[\cos x - \cos(4x)]$

9. $\frac{1}{2}\left[\cos(2x) + \cos\left(\frac{2x}{3}\right)\right]$ **11.** $-\frac{3}{2}[\cos(1.9x) + \cos(1.1x)]$

13. $2[\sin(2\sqrt{3}x) - \sin(4\sqrt{3}x)]$

15. $2\cos(4x)\cos x$ **17.** $2\sin x\cos(2x)$

19. $-2\sin x\cos\left(\frac{3x}{2}\right)$ **21.** $2\cos\left(\frac{3}{2}x\right)\cos\left(\frac{5}{6}x\right)$

23. $2\sin(0.5x)\cos(0.1x)$ **25.** $-2\sin(\sqrt{5}x)\cos(2\sqrt{5}x)$

27. $2\cos\left(\frac{\pi}{24}x\right)\cos\left(\frac{5\pi}{24}x\right)$ **29.** $-\tan x$

31. $\tan(2x)$ **33.** $\cot\left(\frac{3x}{2}\right)$

43. $P(t) = \sqrt{3}\cos\left(\frac{\pi}{6}t + \frac{4}{3}\pi\right)$

45. $2\cos(886\pi t)\cos(102\pi t)$; 102 Hz; 443 Hz

47. $2\sin\left[\frac{2\pi tc}{2}\left(\frac{1}{1.55} + \frac{1}{0.63}\right)10^6\right] \cdot \cos\left[\frac{2\pi tc}{2}\left(\frac{1}{1.55} - \frac{1}{0.63}\right)10^6\right]$

49. $2\sin(1979\pi t)\cos(439\pi t)$

51. $\cos A \cos B \neq \cos(AB)$ and $\sin A \sin B \neq \sin(AB)$. Should have used the product-to-sum identities.

53. false **55.** true

57. $\frac{1}{4}[\sin(A - B + C) + \sin(C - A + B) - \sin(A + B + C) - \sin(A + B - C)]$

61.

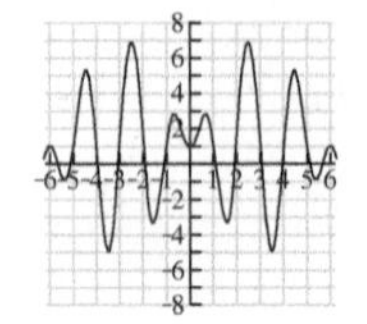

63.

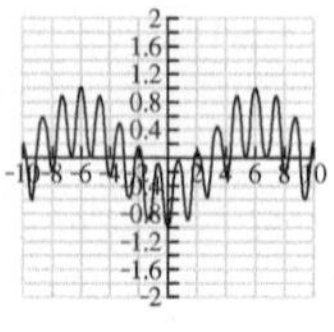

65. $\cos x = \cos y - \frac{2}{5}$ **67.** $2\sin y = \sec x$

Section 6.5

1. $\frac{\pi}{4}$ **3.** $-\frac{\pi}{3}$ **5.** $\frac{3\pi}{4}$ **7.** $\frac{\pi}{6}$

9. $\frac{\pi}{6}$ **11.** $-\frac{\pi}{3}$ **13.** 0 **15.** π

17. 60° **19.** 45° **21.** 120° **23.** 30°

25. −30° **27.** 135° **29.** −90° **31.** 90°

33. 57.10° **35.** 62.18° **37.** 48.10° **39.** −15.30°

41. 166.70° **43.** −0.63 **45.** 1.43 **47.** 0.92

49. 2.09 **51.** 0.31 **53.** $\frac{5\pi}{12}$ **55.** undefined

57. $\frac{\pi}{6}$ **59.** $\frac{2\pi}{3}$ **61.** $\sqrt{3}$ **63.** $\frac{\pi}{3}$

65. undefined **67.** 0 **69.** $-\frac{\pi}{4}$

71. not possible **73.** $\frac{2\pi}{3}$ **75.** $-\frac{\pi}{4}$

77. $\frac{\sqrt{7}}{4}$ **79.** $\frac{12}{13}$ **81.** $\frac{3}{4}$ **83.** $\frac{5\sqrt{23}}{23}$

85. $\frac{4\sqrt{15}}{15}$ **87.** $\frac{11}{60}$ **89.** $\frac{24}{25}$ **91.** $\frac{56}{65}$

93. $\frac{24}{25}$ **95.** $\frac{120}{119}$

97. $\sqrt{1 - u^2}$ **99.** $\frac{\sqrt{1 - u^2}}{u}$

101. April and October **103.** 3rd month

105. 0.026476 sec = 26 ms **107.** 173.4; June 22–23

109. 11 yr **111.** 0.70 m; 0.24 m

113. The identity $\sin^{-1}(\sin x) = x$ is valid only for x in the interval $\left[-\frac{\pi}{2}, \frac{\pi}{2}\right]$, not $[0, \pi]$.

115. In general, $\cot^{-1}x \neq \frac{1}{\tan^{-1}x}$.

117. false **119.** false

121. $\frac{1}{2}$ is not in the domain of the inverse secant function.

123. $\frac{\sqrt{6} - \sqrt{2}}{4}$ **125.** 0

127. a. $\left[\frac{\pi}{4}, \frac{5\pi}{4}\right]$

b. $f^{-1}(x) = \frac{\pi}{4} + \cos^{-1}(x - 3), [2, 4]$

129. $\sec^2 y = 1 + x^2$

131. $\sec y \tan y = x\sqrt{x^2 - 1}$

Section 6.6

1. $\frac{3\pi}{4}, \frac{5\pi}{4}$ **3.** $\frac{7\pi}{6}, \frac{11\pi}{6}, \frac{19\pi}{6}, \frac{23\pi}{6}$

5. $n\pi$, n an integer **7.** $\frac{7\pi}{12}, \frac{11\pi}{12}, \frac{19\pi}{12}, \frac{23\pi}{12}$

9. $\frac{7\pi}{3} + 4n\pi, \frac{11\pi}{3} + 4n\pi$, n an integer

11. $\frac{\pi}{6}, \frac{2\pi}{3}, \frac{7\pi}{6}, \frac{5\pi}{3}, -\frac{\pi}{3}, -\frac{5\pi}{6}, -\frac{4\pi}{3}, -\frac{11\pi}{6}$

13. $-\frac{2\pi}{3}, -\frac{4\pi}{3}$

15. $\frac{\pi(2 + 3n)}{12}$, n an integer **17.** $\frac{(2n + 1)\pi}{3}$, n an integer

19. $-\frac{\pi}{2}, -\frac{7\pi}{6}, -\frac{11\pi}{6}$ **21.** $\frac{\pi}{6}, \frac{\pi}{3}, \frac{7\pi}{6}, \frac{4\pi}{3}$

23. $\frac{\pi}{12}, \frac{7\pi}{12}, \frac{13\pi}{12}, \frac{19\pi}{12}$ **25.** $\frac{\pi}{3}, \frac{2\pi}{3}, \frac{4\pi}{3}, \frac{5\pi}{3}$

27. $\frac{2\pi}{3}$ **29.** $\frac{\pi}{4}, \frac{3\pi}{4}, \frac{5\pi}{4}, \frac{7\pi}{4}$

31. $\frac{\pi}{2}, \frac{3\pi}{2}, \frac{\pi}{3}, \frac{5\pi}{3}$ **33.** $\frac{7\pi}{6}, \frac{11\pi}{6}, \frac{3\pi}{2}$

35. $\frac{\pi}{2}$ **37.** $0, \pi$

39. $\frac{\pi}{12}, \frac{5\pi}{12}, \frac{7\pi}{12}, \frac{11\pi}{12}, \frac{13\pi}{12}, \frac{17\pi}{12}, \frac{19\pi}{12}, \frac{23\pi}{12}$

41. 115.83°, 295.83°, 154.17°, 334.17°

43. 333.63° **45.** 29.05°, 209.05°

47. 200.70°, 339.30° **49.** 41.41°, 318.59°

51. 56.31°, 126.87°, 236.31°, 306.87°

53. 101.79°, 281.79°, 168.21°, 348.21°, 9.74°, 189.74°, 80.26°, 260.26°

55. 80.12°, 279.88°

57. 64.93°, 121.41°, 244.93°, 301.41°

59. 15°, 45°, 75°, 105°, 135°, 165°, 195°, 225°, 255°, 285°, 315°, 345°

61. $\frac{\pi}{4}, \frac{5\pi}{4}$ **63.** π **65.** $\frac{\pi}{6}$ **67.** $\frac{\pi}{3}$

69. $\frac{\pi}{4}, \frac{3\pi}{4}, \frac{5\pi}{4}, \frac{7\pi}{4}$ **71.** $\frac{\pi}{2}, \frac{3\pi}{2}$

73. $0, \pi, \frac{\pi}{4}, \frac{7\pi}{4}$ **75.** $\frac{\pi}{6}, \frac{5\pi}{6}, \frac{3\pi}{2}, \frac{\pi}{2}, \frac{7\pi}{6}, \frac{11\pi}{6}$

77. $\frac{\pi}{6}, \frac{\pi}{3}, \frac{7\pi}{6}, \frac{4\pi}{3}$ **79.** $\frac{\pi}{6}, \frac{5\pi}{6}, \frac{7\pi}{6}, \frac{11\pi}{6}$

81. $\frac{3\pi}{2}$ **83.** $\frac{2\pi}{3}, \frac{4\pi}{3}$

85. $\frac{\pi}{3}, \frac{5\pi}{3}, \pi$

87. $\frac{\pi}{24}, \frac{5\pi}{24}, \frac{13\pi}{24}, \frac{17\pi}{24}, \frac{25\pi}{24}, \frac{29\pi}{24}, \frac{37\pi}{24}, \frac{41\pi}{24}$

89. 57.47°, 122.53°, 216.38°, 323.62°

91. 30°, 150°, 199.47°, 340.53°

93. 14.48°, 165.52°, 270°

95. 111.47°, 248.53° **97.** 60°, 300°

99. 4th quarter of 2008, 2nd quarter of 2009, and 4th quarter of 2010

101. 9 P.M. **103.** March **105.** 2001

107. 24° **109.** $\frac{3}{4}$ sec

111. $(0, 1), \left(\frac{\pi}{3}, \frac{3}{2}\right), \left(\frac{5\pi}{3}, \frac{3}{2}\right), (\pi, -3), (2\pi, 1)$

113. March and September

115. 1 A.M. and 11 A.M.

117. The value $\theta = \frac{3\pi}{2}$ does not satisfy the original equation.

$$\sqrt{2 + \sin\left(\frac{3\pi}{2}\right)} = \sqrt{2 - 1} = 1,$$

while $\sin\left(\frac{3\pi}{2}\right) = -1$. So this value of θ is an extraneous solution.

119. Cannot divide by $\cos x$ because it could be zero. Factor as $2\cos x(3\sin x - 1) = 0$.

121. false **123.** true

125. $\frac{\pi}{6}, \frac{5\pi}{6}, \frac{7\pi}{6}, \frac{11\pi}{6}$ **127.** $\frac{\pi}{6}$ or 30°

129. no solution **131.** $5 + 2n$, n an integer

133. $x = 0, 2\pi$ **135.** $x = 0, \frac{\pi}{3}, -\frac{\pi}{3}$

Review Exercises

1. 60° **3.** 45° **5.** 60° **7.** $\sec^2 x$

9. $\sec^2 x$ **11.** $\cos^2 x$ **13.** $-(4 + 2\csc x + \csc^2 x)$

21. identity **23.** conditional **25.** identity

27. $\frac{\sqrt{2} - \sqrt{6}}{4}$ **29.** $\sqrt{3} - 2$ **31.** $\sin x$

33. $\tan x$ **35.** $\frac{117}{44}$ **37.** $-\frac{897}{1025}$

39. identity

41.

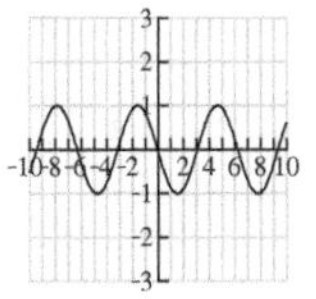

43.

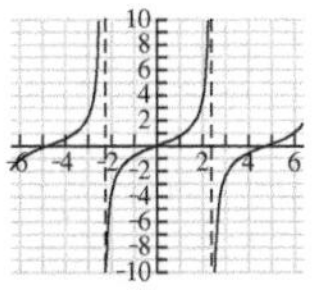

45. $\frac{7}{25}$ **47.** $\frac{671}{1800}$ **49.** $\frac{336}{625}$

51. $\frac{\sqrt{3}}{2}$ **53.** $\frac{3}{2}$ **61.** $-\frac{\sqrt{2 - \sqrt{2}}}{2}$

63. $\frac{1}{\sqrt{3 + 2\sqrt{2}}}$ **65.** $\frac{2}{\sqrt{2 + \sqrt{3}}}$ **67.** $\frac{7\sqrt{2}}{10}$

69. $-\frac{5}{4}$ **71.** $\sin\left(\frac{\pi}{12}\right)$

77.

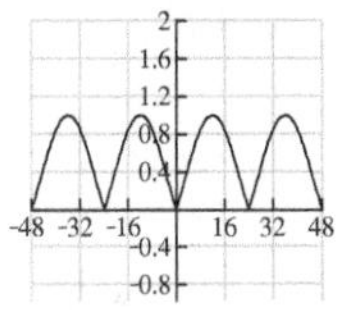

79.

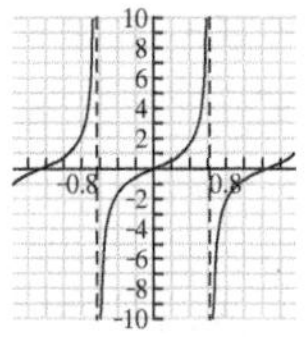

81. $3[\sin(7x) + \sin(3x)]$ **83.** $-2\sin(4x)\sin(x)$

85. $2\sin\left(\frac{x}{3}\right)\cos x$ **87.** $\cot(3x)$

93. $\frac{\pi}{4}$ **95.** $\frac{\pi}{2}$ **97.** $\frac{\pi}{6}$ **99.** −90°

101. 60° **103.** −60° **105.** −37.50° **107.** 22.50°

109. 1.75 **111.** −0.10 **113.** $-\frac{\pi}{4}$ **115.** $-\sqrt{3}$

117. $\frac{\pi}{3}$ **119.** $\frac{60}{61}$ **121.** $\frac{7}{6}$ **123.** $\frac{6\sqrt{35}}{35}$

125. $\frac{2\pi}{3}, \frac{5\pi}{3}, \frac{5\pi}{6}, \frac{11\pi}{6}$ **127.** $-\frac{\pi}{2}, -\frac{3\pi}{2}$ **129.** $\frac{9\pi}{4}, \frac{21\pi}{4}$

131. $\frac{\pi}{3}, \frac{2\pi}{3}, \frac{4\pi}{3}, \frac{5\pi}{3}$ **133.** $\frac{3\pi}{8}, \frac{11\pi}{8}, \frac{7\pi}{8}, \frac{15\pi}{8}$

135. $0, \pi, 2\pi, \frac{3\pi}{4}, \frac{7\pi}{4}$

137. 80.46°, 260.46°, 170.46°, 350.46°

139. 90°, 270°, 138.59°, 221.41°

141. 17.62°, 162.38° **143.** $\frac{\pi}{4}, \frac{5\pi}{4}$

145. $\pi, \frac{\pi}{3}$ **147.** $0, \pi, 2\pi, \frac{\pi}{6}, \frac{11\pi}{6}$

149. $\frac{3\pi}{2}$ **151.** π

153. $\frac{\pi}{2}, \frac{3\pi}{2}$ **155.** 90°, 270°, 135°, 315°

157. 0°, 360° **159.** 90°, 270°, 60°, 300°

Practice Test

1. $x = \frac{(2n + 1)\pi}{2}$, n an integer **3.** $-\frac{\sqrt{2 - \sqrt{2}}}{2}$

5. $\frac{\sqrt{30}}{10}$ **7.** $\cos(10x)$

9. $\cos\left(\frac{a + b}{2}\right)$ **11.** $20\cos x \cos 3$

13. $\theta = \frac{4\pi}{3} + 2n\pi, \frac{5\pi}{3} + 2n\pi$, n an integer

15. 14.48°, 165.52°, 90°, 270° **17.** conditional

19. $-\frac{\sqrt{26}}{26}$ **21.** $\cot\left(\frac{\pi}{6}x + \frac{\pi}{8}\right)$

23. $\left[c - \frac{1}{2}, c\right) \cup \left(c, c + \frac{1}{2}\right]$;
$f^{-1}(x) = \frac{1}{\pi}\csc^{-1}\left(\frac{x - a}{b}\right) - \frac{c}{\pi}$

25. $\frac{8}{3} + 8n, \frac{16}{3} + 8n$, n an integer

27. $\frac{\pi}{2} + 6n\pi, \frac{7\pi}{2} + 6n\pi$, n an integer

Cumulative Test

1. a. $\frac{\sqrt{3}}{2}$ **b.** $\sqrt{3}$ **c.** −2

3. a. $\frac{2\pi}{3}$ **b.** $-\frac{\pi}{6}$ **c.** $\frac{5\pi}{6}$

5. even **7.** $\frac{1}{x^3} - 1; (-\infty, 0) \cup (0, \infty)$

9. $\left(-\frac{6}{5}, -\frac{3}{5}\right)$

11. $Q(x) = 5x - 4$, $r(x) = -5x + 7$

13. HA: $y = 0.7$; VA: $x = -2, x = 3$

15. $(-3, \infty)$ **17.** 4 **19.** 0.4695

21. $-\frac{7\pi}{12}$ **23.** conditional **25.** $\frac{5}{12}$

CHAPTER 7

Section 7.1

1. $\sqrt{13}$ **3.** $5\sqrt{2}$ **5.** 25

7. $\sqrt{73}$, 69.4° **9.** $\sqrt{26}$, 348.7° **11.** $\sqrt{17}$, 166.0°

13. 8, 180° **15.** $2\sqrt{3}$, 60° **17.** $\langle -2, -2 \rangle$

19. $\langle -12, 9 \rangle$ **21.** $\langle 0, -14 \rangle$ **23.** $\langle -36, 48 \rangle$

25. $\langle 6.3, 3.0 \rangle$ **27.** $\langle -2.8, 15.8 \rangle$ **29.** $\langle 2.6, -3.1 \rangle$

31. $\langle 8.2, -3.8 \rangle$ **33.** $\langle -1, 1.7 \rangle$ **35.** $\left\langle -\frac{5}{13}, -\frac{12}{13} \right\rangle$

37. $\left\langle \frac{60}{61}, \frac{11}{61} \right\rangle$ **39.** $\left\langle \frac{24}{25}, -\frac{7}{25} \right\rangle$ **41.** $\left\langle -\frac{3}{5}, -\frac{4}{5} \right\rangle$

43. $\left\langle \frac{\sqrt{10}}{10}, \frac{3\sqrt{10}}{10} \right\rangle$ **45.** $7\vec{i} + 3\vec{j}$ **47.** $5\vec{i} - 3\vec{j}$

49. $-\vec{i} + 0\vec{j}$ **51.** $2\vec{i} + 0\vec{j}$ **53.** $-5\vec{i} + 5\vec{j}$

55. $7\vec{i} + 0\vec{j}$ **57.** H: 1905 ft/sec; V: 1100 ft/sec

59. 2801 lb

61. 11.7 mph, 31° west of due north

63. 52.41° east of due north, 303 mph

65. 250 lb

67. V: 51.4 ft/sec; H: 61.3 ft/sec

69. 29.93 yd **71.** 10.9° **73.** 1156 lb

75. 23.75°, 351.16 **77.** $5\sqrt{2}$, 5 **79.** 8.97 N-m

81. 31.95 N-m

83. 8.67, 18.05° counterclockwise of south

85. 1611 N; 19°

87. Magnitude cannot be negative. Observe that
$|\langle -2, -8 \rangle| = \sqrt{(-2)^2 + (-8)^2} = \sqrt{68} = 2\sqrt{17}$.

89. false **91.** true **93.** vector

95. $\sqrt{a^2 + b^2}$ **103.** 1 **105.** $\langle 1, 2t + h\rangle$

Section 7.2

1. 2 **3.** -3 **5.** 42 **7.** 11

9. $-13a$ **11.** -1.4 **13.** 98° **15.** 109°

17. 3° **19.** 30° **21.** 105°

23. 180° **25.** not orthogonal **27.** orthogonal

29. not orthogonal **31.** orthogonal **33.** orthogonal

35. orthogonal **37.** 400 ft-lb **39.** 80,000 ft-lb

41. 1299 ft-lb **43.** 148 ft-lb **45.** 1607 lb

47. 694,593 ft-lb **49.** \$49,300; total cost

53. **a.** $\cos\beta = \frac{v_1}{\sqrt{v_1^2 + v_2^2}}$, $\sin\beta = \frac{v_2}{\sqrt{v_1^2 + v_2^2}}$,

$\cos\alpha = \frac{w_1}{\sqrt{w_1^2 + w_2^2}}$, $\sin\alpha = \frac{w_2}{\sqrt{w_1^2 + w_2^2}}$

55. $\vec{n} = \langle r, 0\rangle$, $\vec{u}\cdot\vec{n} = |\vec{u}|r$ **57.** -2

59. The dot product of two vectors is a scalar, not a vector.

61. false **63.** true **65.** 17

73. **a.** $\text{proj}_{-\vec{u}}\, 2\vec{u} = -2\vec{u}$ **b.** $\text{proj}_{-\vec{u}}\, c\vec{u} = -c\vec{u}$

75. $\vec{u}$ is perpendicular to $\vec{v}$, $\theta = 90°$

77. 6, -6 **79.** $2t^2 - 3t^3$ **81.** 1.456 radi

Section 7.3

1.–8.

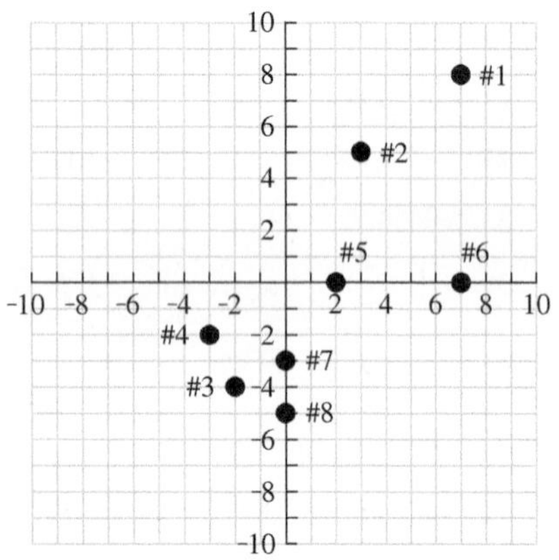

9. $\sqrt{2}[\cos(\frac{7\pi}{4}) + i\sin(\frac{7\pi}{4})] =$
$\sqrt{2}[\cos(315°) + i\sin(315°)]$

11. $2[\cos(\frac{\pi}{3}) + i\sin(\frac{\pi}{3})] =$
$2[\cos(60°) + i\sin(60°)]$

13. $4\sqrt{2}[\cos(\frac{3\pi}{4}) + i\sin(\frac{3\pi}{4})] =$
$4\sqrt{2}[\cos(135°) + i\sin(135°)]$

15. $2\sqrt{3}[\cos(\frac{5\pi}{3}) + i\sin(\frac{5\pi}{3})] =$
$2\sqrt{3}[\cos(300°) + i\sin(300°)]$

17. $3[\cos(0) + i\sin(0)] =$
$3[\cos(0°) + i\sin(0°)]$

19. $\frac{\sqrt{2}}{2}[\cos(\frac{5\pi}{4}) + i\sin(\frac{5\pi}{4})] =$
$\frac{\sqrt{2}}{2}[\cos(225°) + i\sin(225°)]$

21. $2\sqrt{3}\left[\cos\left(\frac{5\pi}{4}\right) + i\sin\left(\frac{5\pi}{4}\right)\right] =$
$2\sqrt{3}[\cos(225°) + i\sin(225°)]$

23. $5\sqrt{2}\left[\cos\left(\frac{3\pi}{4}\right) + i\sin\left(\frac{3\pi}{4}\right)\right] =$
$5\sqrt{2}[\cos(135°) + i\sin(135°)]$

25. $\sqrt{58}[\cos(293.2°) + i\sin(293.2°)]$

27. $\sqrt{61}[\cos(140.2°) + i\sin(140.2°)]$

29. $13[\cos(112.6°) + i\sin(112.6°)]$

31. $10[\cos(323.1°) + i\sin(323.1°)]$

33. $\frac{\sqrt{13}}{4}[\cos(123.7°) + i\sin(123.7°)]$

35. $5.59[\cos(24.27°) + i\sin(24.27°)]$

37. $\sqrt{17}[\cos(212.84°) + i\sin(212.84°)]$

39. $4.54[\cos(332.31°) + i\sin(332.31°)]$

41. -5 **43.** $\sqrt{2} - \sqrt{2}i$

45. $-2 - 2\sqrt{3}i$ **47.** $-\frac{3}{2} + \frac{\sqrt{3}}{2}i$

49. $1 + i$ **51.** $-3\sqrt{2} + 3\sqrt{2}i$

53. $2.1131 - 4.5315i$ **55.** $-0.5209 + 2.9544i$

57. $5.3623 - 4.4995i$ **59.** $-2.8978 + 0.7765i$

61. $0.6180 - 1.9021i$ **63.** $-0.87 - 4.92i$

65. **a.** 59.7 mi **b.** $59.7[\cos(68.8°) + i\sin(68.8°)]$
c. 6.8°

67. **a.** $\overrightarrow{AB} = B - A = -2i$, $\overrightarrow{BC} = C - B = 3 - 3i$,
$\overrightarrow{CD} = D - C = -i$
b. $3\sqrt{5}[\cos(297°) + i\sin(297°)]$

69. $z = 2\sqrt{13}[\cos(56.31°) + i\sin(56.31°)]$

71. The point is in QIII, not QI. Add 180° to $\tan^{-1}(\frac{8}{3})$.

73. true **75.** true **77.** 0°

79. $\sqrt{b^2} = |b|$

81. $a\sqrt{5}[\cos(296.6°) + i\sin(296.6°)]$

83. $-\frac{\pi}{2} - \frac{\pi\sqrt{3}}{2}i$

85. $8.79[\cos(28°) + i\sin(28°)]$

87. $-z = r[\cos(\theta + \pi) + i\sin(\theta + \pi)]$

89. $r = 5$ **91.** $r = 2\sin\theta$

Section 7.4

1. $-6 + 6\sqrt{3}i$ **3.** $-4\sqrt{2} - 4\sqrt{2}i$

5. $0 + 8i$ **7.** $\frac{9\sqrt{2}}{2} + \frac{9\sqrt{2}}{2}i$

9. $0 + 12i$ **11.** $\frac{3}{2} + \frac{3\sqrt{3}}{2}i$

13. $-\sqrt{2} + \sqrt{2}i$ **15.** $0 - 2i$

17. $\frac{3}{2} + \frac{3\sqrt{3}}{2}i$ **19.** $-\frac{5}{2} - \frac{5\sqrt{3}}{2}i$

21. $4 - 4i$ **23.** $-64 + 0i$

25. $-8 + 8\sqrt{3}i$ **27.** $1{,}048{,}576 + 0i$

29. $-1{,}048{,}576\sqrt{3} - 1{,}048{,}576i$

31. $2[\cos(150^\circ) + i\sin(150^\circ)]$,
$2[\cos(330^\circ) + i\sin(330^\circ)]$

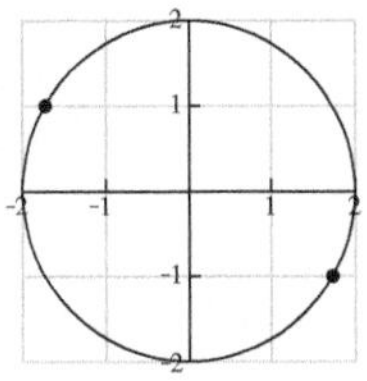

33. $\sqrt{6}[\cos(157.5^\circ) + i\sin(157.5^\circ)]$,
$\sqrt{6}[\cos(337.5^\circ) + i\sin(337.5^\circ)]$

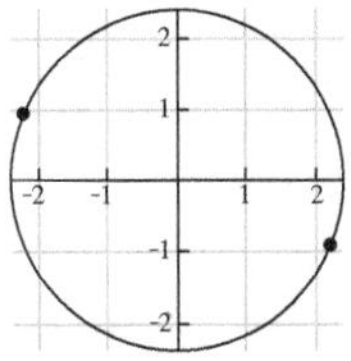

35. $2[\cos(20^\circ) + i\sin(20^\circ)]$,
$2[\cos(140^\circ) + i\sin(140^\circ)]$,
$2[\cos(260^\circ) + i\sin(260^\circ)]$

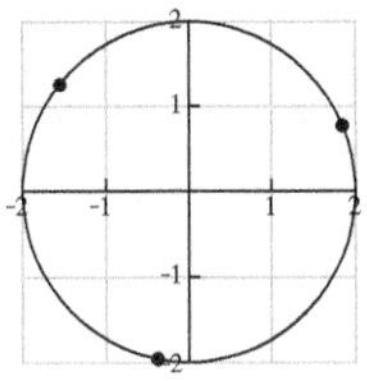

37. $\sqrt[3]{2}[\cos(110^\circ) + i\sin(110^\circ)]$,
$\sqrt[3]{2}[\cos(230^\circ) + i\sin(230^\circ)]$,
$\sqrt[3]{2}[\cos(350^\circ) + i\sin(350^\circ)]$

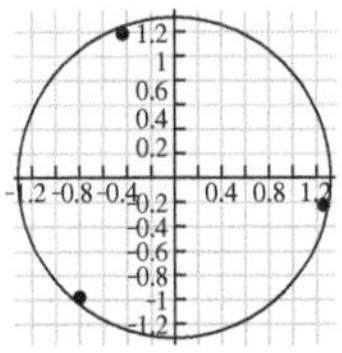

39. $2[\cos(78.75^\circ) + i\sin(78.75^\circ)]$,
$2[\cos(168.75^\circ) + i\sin(168.75^\circ)]$,
$2[\cos(258.75^\circ) + i\sin(258.75^\circ)]$,
$2[\cos(348.75^\circ) + i\sin(348.75^\circ)]$

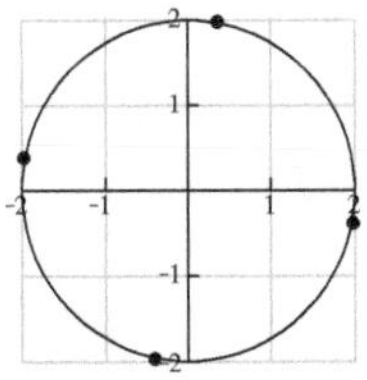

41. $\pm 2, \pm 2i$

43. $-2, 1 - \sqrt{3}i, 1 + \sqrt{3}i$

45. $\sqrt{2} + \sqrt{2}i, -\sqrt{2} + \sqrt{2}i,$
$-\sqrt{2} - \sqrt{2}i, \sqrt{2} - \sqrt{2}i$

47. $1, \frac{1}{2} + \frac{\sqrt{3}}{2}i, -\frac{1}{2} + \frac{\sqrt{3}}{2}i,$
$-1, -\frac{1}{2} - \frac{\sqrt{3}}{2}i, \frac{1}{2} - \frac{\sqrt{3}}{2}i$

49. $-\frac{\sqrt{2}}{2} + \frac{\sqrt{2}}{2}i, \frac{\sqrt{2}}{2} - \frac{\sqrt{2}}{2}i$

51. $\sqrt[4]{2}[\cos(\frac{\pi}{8}) + i\sin(\frac{\pi}{8})]$,
$\sqrt[4]{2}[\cos(\frac{5\pi}{8}) + i\sin(\frac{5\pi}{8})]$,
$\sqrt[4]{2}[\cos(\frac{9\pi}{8}) + i\sin(\frac{9\pi}{8})]$,
$\sqrt[4]{2}[\cos(\frac{13\pi}{8}) + i\sin(\frac{13\pi}{8})]$

53. $2[\cos(\frac{\pi}{5}) + i\sin(\frac{\pi}{5})]$,
$2[\cos(\frac{3\pi}{5}) + i\sin(\frac{3\pi}{5})]$,
$2[\cos(\pi) + i\sin(\pi)]$
$2[\cos(\frac{7\pi}{5}) + i\sin(\frac{7\pi}{5})]$,
$2[\cos(\frac{9\pi}{5}) + i\sin(\frac{9\pi}{5})]$

55. $\pi^2[\cos(\frac{\pi}{14}) + i\sin(\frac{\pi}{14})]$,
$\pi^2[\cos(\frac{5\pi}{14}) + i\sin(\frac{5\pi}{14})]$,
$\pi^2[\cos(\frac{9\pi}{14}) + i\sin(\frac{9\pi}{14})]$
$\pi^2[\cos(\frac{13\pi}{14}) + i\sin(\frac{13\pi}{14})]$,
$\pi^2[\cos(\frac{17\pi}{14}) + i\sin(\frac{17\pi}{14})]$,
$\pi^2[\cos(\frac{21\pi}{14}) + i\sin(\frac{21\pi}{14})]$
$\pi^2[\cos(\frac{25\pi}{14}) + i\sin(\frac{25\pi}{14})]$

57. $[\cos(45^\circ) + i\sin(45^\circ)]$,
$[\cos(117^\circ) + i\sin(117^\circ)]$
$[\cos(189^\circ) + i\sin(189^\circ)]$,
$[\cos(261^\circ) + i\sin(261^\circ)]$,
$[\cos(333^\circ) + i\sin(333^\circ)]$

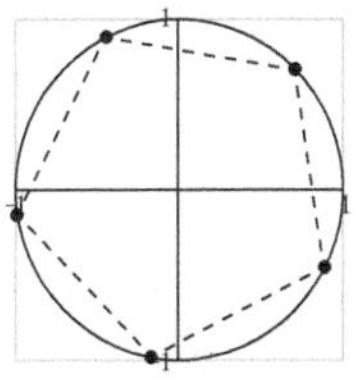

59. $[\cos(50^\circ + 60^\circ k) + i\sin(50^\circ + 60^\circ k)]$,
$k = 0, 1, 2, 3, 4, 5$

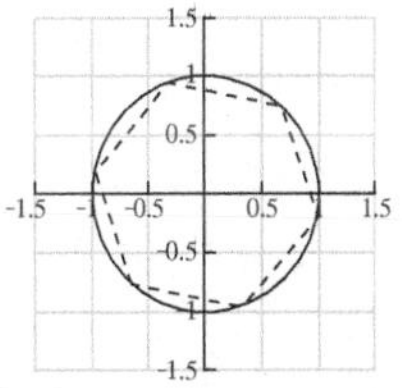

61. Reversed order of angles being subtracted.

63. Should use De Moivre's formula. In general $(a + b)^6 \neq a^6 + b^6$.

65. true

67. false

69. true

71. true

79. $\cos(3x) = 4\cos^3 x - 3\cos x$

81. $2^{\frac{n+m}{2}} e^{\frac{\pi}{4}(m-n)i}$

Section 7.5

1. – 10.

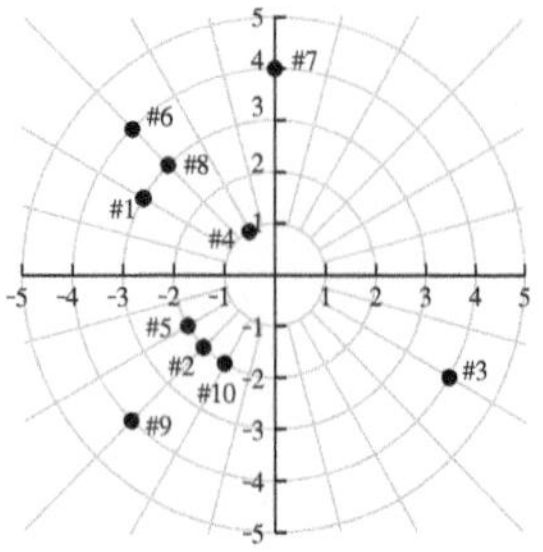

11. $\left(4, \frac{\pi}{3}\right)$ **13.** $\left(2, \frac{4\pi}{3}\right)$ **15.** $\left(4\sqrt{2}, \frac{3\pi}{4}\right)$

17. $(3, 0)$ **19.** $\left(2, \frac{7\pi}{6}\right)$ **21.** $(2, -2\sqrt{3})$

23. $\left(\frac{\sqrt{3}}{2}, -\frac{1}{2}\right)$ **25.** $(0, 0)$ **27.** $(-1, -\sqrt{3})$

29. $\left(\frac{\sqrt{2}}{2}, -\frac{\sqrt{2}}{2}\right)$ **31.** d **33.** a

35.

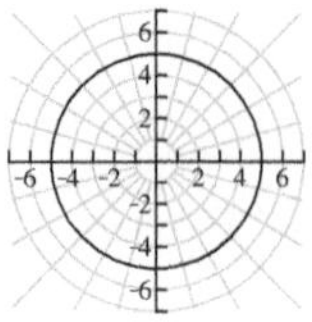

37.

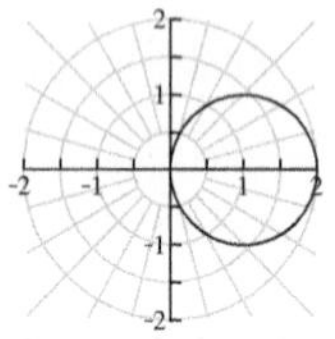

39.

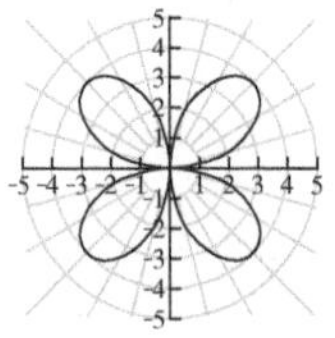

41.

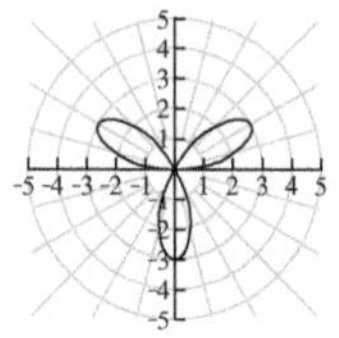

43.

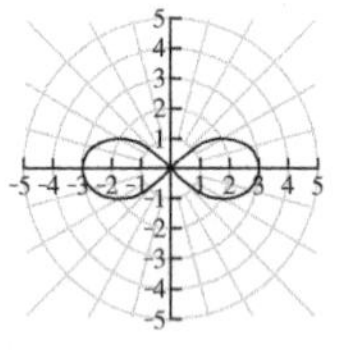

45.

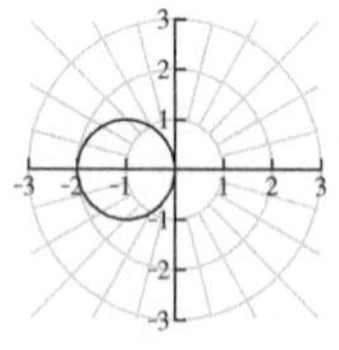

47.

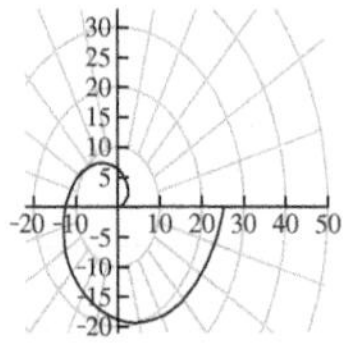

49.

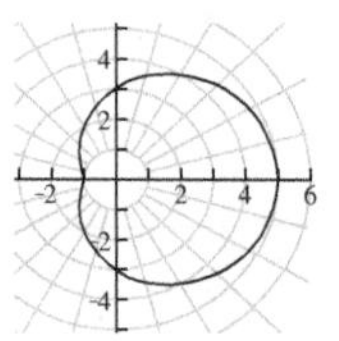

51. $y = -2x + 1$, line **53.** $(x - 1)^2 + y^2 = 9$, circle

55.

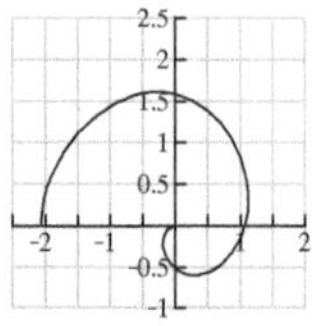

57.

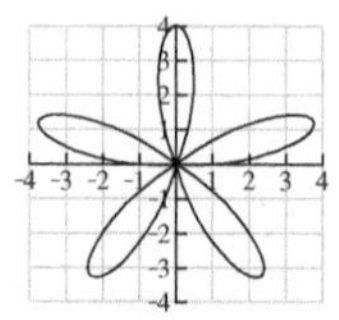

59.

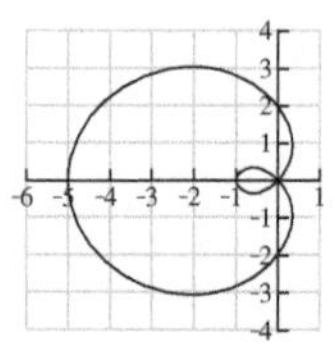

61.

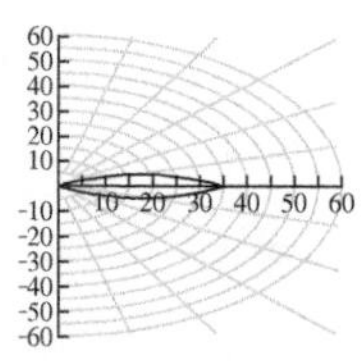

63. $r = \sqrt{\theta}$ more tightly wound than graph of $r = \theta$

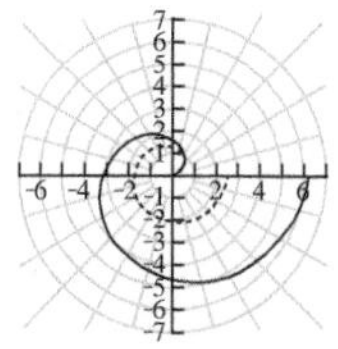

65. $r^2 = \frac{1}{4}\cos(2\theta)$ much closer to the origin than graph of $r^2 = 4\cos(2\theta)$

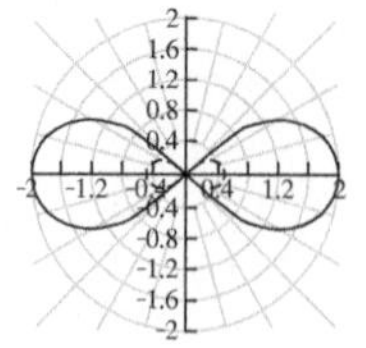

67.

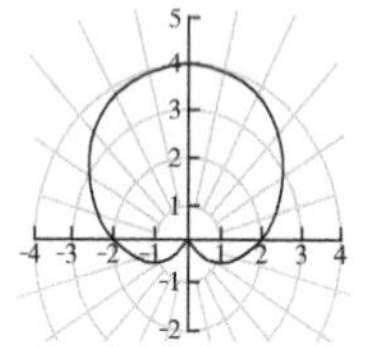

69. a.–c. All three graphs are figure eights. Extending the domain in (b) results in movement twice as fast; doing so in (c) results in movement four times as fast.

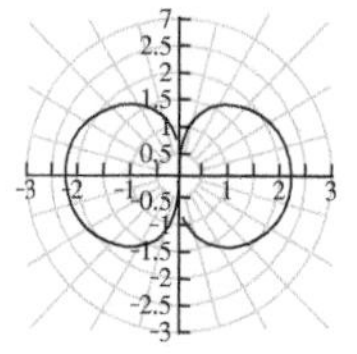

71. a. $r = 8\sin(3\theta), 0 \leq \theta \leq 2\pi$ **b.** 50 times

73. The point is in QIII, so needed to add π to the angle.

75. true **77.** $r = \frac{a}{\cos\theta}$

79. $(-a, \theta \pm 180°)$

81. $\left(2, \frac{\pi}{3}\right), \left(2, \frac{5\pi}{3}\right)$

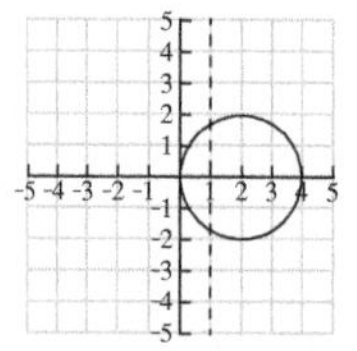

83. $x^3 - y^3 - 2axy = 0$

85. circle with radius a centered at (a, b)

87. $\left(2\sqrt{2}, \frac{\pi}{4}\right), \left(-2\sqrt{2}, \frac{5\pi}{4}\right)$ **89.** $\left(\frac{2-\sqrt{2}}{2}, \frac{3\pi}{4}\right), \left(\frac{2+\sqrt{2}}{2}, \frac{7\pi}{4}\right)$

Review Exercises

1. 13 **3.** 13 **5.** 26, 112.6°

7. 20, 323.1° **9.** $\langle 2, 11\rangle$ **11.** $\langle 38, -7\rangle$

13. $\langle 2.6, 9.7\rangle$ **15.** $\langle -3.1, 11.6\rangle$ **17.** $\left\langle \frac{\sqrt{2}}{2}, -\frac{\sqrt{2}}{2}\right\rangle$

19. $5\vec{i} + \vec{j}$ **21.** -6 **23.** -9

25. 16 **27.** 59° **29.** 49°

31. 166°

33. not orthogonal

35. orthogonal

37. not orthogonal

39. not orthogonal

41. – 42.

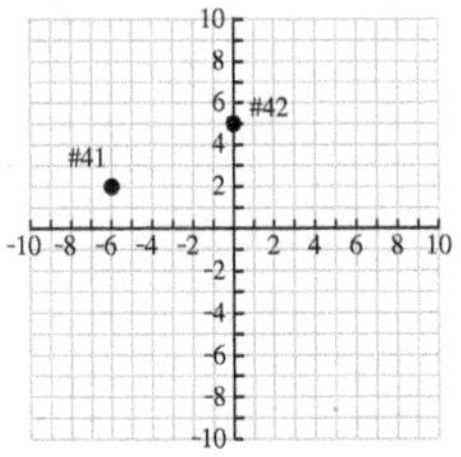

43. $2[\cos(315°) + i\sin(315°)]$

45. $8[\cos(270°) + i\sin(270°)]$

47. $61[\cos(169.6°) + i\sin(169.6°)]$

49. $17[\cos(28.1°) + i\sin(28.1°)]$

51. $3 - 3\sqrt{3}i$

53. $-1 + i$

55. $-3.7588 - 1.3681i$

57. $-12i$

59. $-\frac{21}{2} - \frac{21\sqrt{3}}{2}i$

61. $-\frac{\sqrt{3}}{2} + \frac{1}{2}i$

63. -6

65. -324

67. $16 - 16\sqrt{3}i$

69. $2[\cos(30°) + i\sin(30°)]$,
$2[\cos(210°) + i\sin(210°)]$

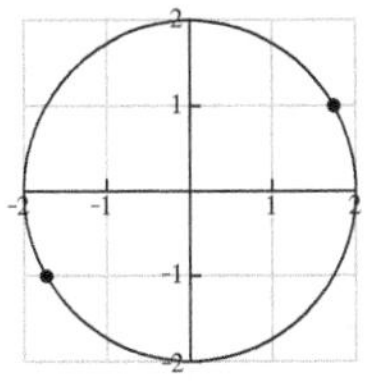

71. $4[\cos(45°) + i\sin(45°)]$,
$4[\cos(135°) + i\sin(135°)]$,
$4[\cos(225°) + i\sin(225°)]$,
$4[\cos(315°) + i\sin(315°)]$

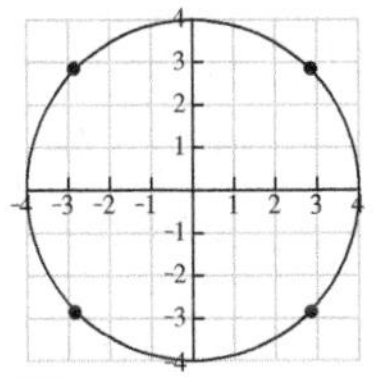

73. $3 + 3\sqrt{3}i, -6, 3 - 3\sqrt{3}i$

75. $\frac{\sqrt{2}}{2} + \frac{\sqrt{2}}{2}i, -\frac{\sqrt{2}}{2} + \frac{\sqrt{2}}{2}i, -\frac{\sqrt{2}}{2} - \frac{\sqrt{2}}{2}i, \frac{\sqrt{2}}{2} - \frac{\sqrt{2}}{2}i$

77. $\left(2\sqrt{2}, \frac{3\pi}{4}\right)$

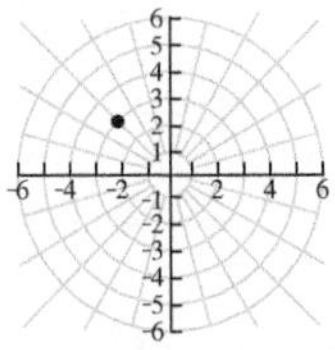

79. $\left(10, \frac{7\pi}{6}\right)$

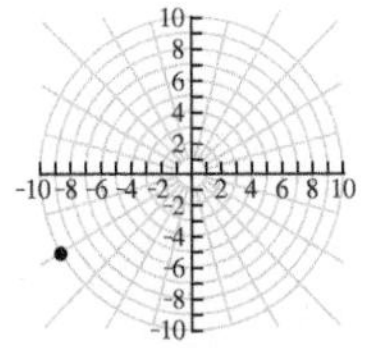

81. $\left(2, \frac{3\pi}{2}\right)$

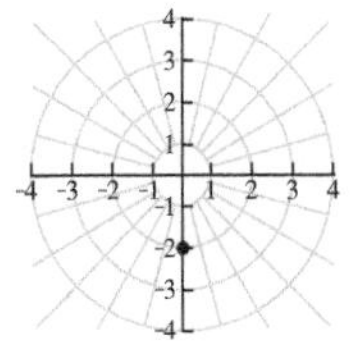

83. $\left(-\frac{3}{2}, \frac{3\sqrt{3}}{2}\right)$

85. $(1, \sqrt{3})$

87. $\left(-\frac{1}{2}, -\frac{\sqrt{3}}{2}\right)$

89.

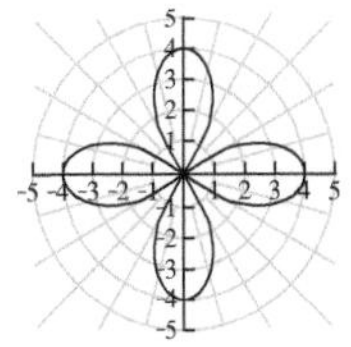

91.

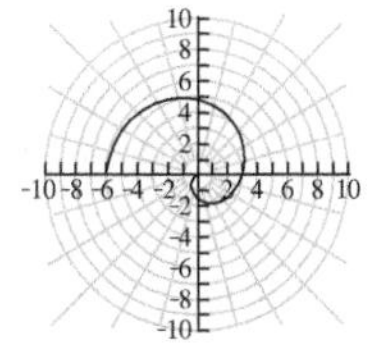

Practice Test

1. 13, 112.6°

3. **a.** $\langle -14, 5\rangle$ **b.** -16

5. 9

7. $32{,}768[-1 + \sqrt{3}i]$

9. $\left(-\frac{3\sqrt{3}}{2}, -\frac{3}{2}\right)$

11. $(15\sqrt{5}, 333.4°)$

13.

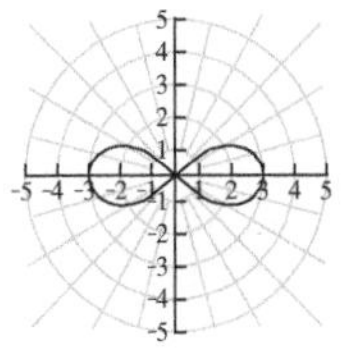

17. -20

19. $\sqrt{2}$

21. 50,769 lb, $\alpha \approx 12°$

23. $4[\cos(67.5° + 90°k) + i\sin(67.5° + 90°k)]$,
$k = 0, 1, 2, 3$

Cumulative Test

1. $(f \circ g)(x) = \dfrac{-12x - 19}{3x + 5}$,
domains: $f = (-\infty, \infty)$, $g = f \circ g = \left(-\frac{5}{3}, \infty\right)$

3. $y = -\frac{1}{3}(x + 1)^2 + 2 = -\frac{1}{3}x^2 - \frac{2}{3}x + \frac{5}{3}$

5. no HA, VA: $x = 1$, slant: $y = x - 1$

7. $\log_{625} 5 = \frac{1}{4}$

9. $\sin\theta = \frac{3}{8}$, $\cos\theta = \frac{\sqrt{55}}{8}$, $\tan\theta = \frac{3\sqrt{55}}{55}$
$\cot\theta = \frac{\sqrt{55}}{3}$, $\sec\theta = \frac{8\sqrt{55}}{55}$, $\csc\theta = \frac{8}{3}$

11. $c \approx 13.1$ m, $\alpha \approx 56.1°$, $\beta = 73.9°$

13. Amplitude $= \frac{1}{3}$, Period $= \frac{\pi}{2}$, Phase shift $= \frac{\pi}{4}$ (right),
Vertical shift $= 4$ (up)

15. $\frac{25\sqrt{3} - 48}{11}$

CHAPTER 8

Section 8.1

1. $(8, -1)$ **3.** $(1, -1)$ **5.** $(1, 2)$

7. $u = \frac{32}{17}, v = \frac{11}{17}$ **9.** no solution

11. infinitely many solutions

13. infinitely many solutions

15. $(1, 3)$ **17.** $(6, 8)$ **19.** $(-6.24, -2.15)$

21. $(2, 5)$ **23.** $(-3, 4)$ **25.** $(1, -\frac{2}{7})$

27. $(\frac{19}{7}, \frac{11}{35})$ **29.** infinitely many solutions

31. $(4, 0)$ **33.** $(-2, 1)$ **35.** $(3, -2)$

37. $(\frac{75}{32}, \frac{7}{16})$ **39.** $(4.2, -3.5)$

41. C **43.** d

45. $(0, 0)$

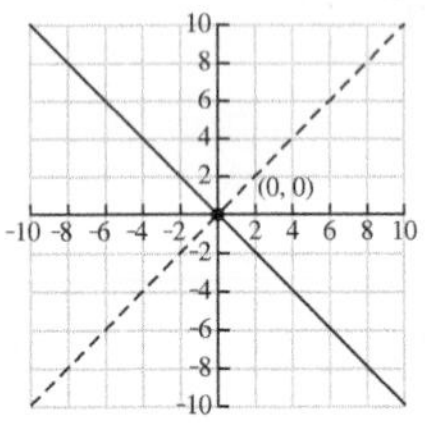

47. $(-1, -1)$

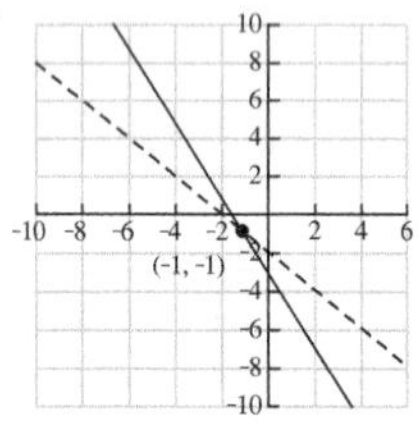

49. $(0, -6)$

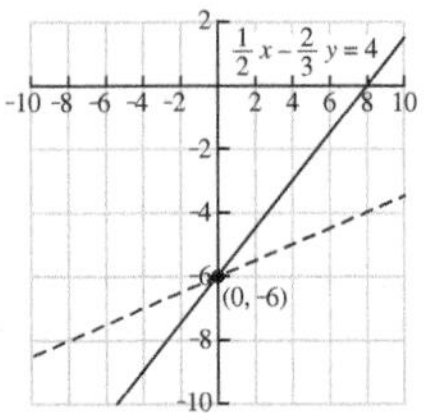

51. no solution

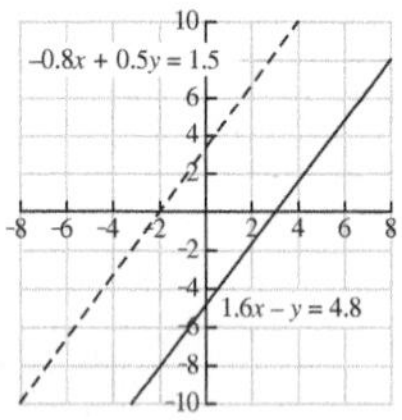

53. $(3, 1)$ **55.** $(1, 0)$

57. Infinitely many solutions:
$\left(x, \frac{125 - 2x}{5}\right)$

59. 15.86 ml of 8% HCl, 21.14 ml of 15% HCl

61. $300,000 of sales

63. 169 highway miles, 180.5 city miles

65. plane speed: 450 mph, wind speed: 50 mph

67. 10% stock: $3500, 14% stock: $6500

69. 8 CD players

71. males: 8,999,215; females: 9,329,125

73. Not every term in the first equation is multiplied by -1 correctly. The equation should be $-2x - y = 3$, and the resulting solution should be $x = 11, y = -25$.

75. false **77.** false

79. $A = -4, B = 7$

81. 2% drink: 8 cups, 4% drink: 96 cups

83. $(-1, 2)$ **85.** $(2, 6)$

87. $(\sqrt{3}, -2), (\sqrt{3}, 2), (-\sqrt{3}, -2), (-\sqrt{3}, 2)$

89. $A = \frac{3}{2}, B = -\frac{1}{2}$ **91.** $A = \frac{4}{5}, B = \frac{1}{5}$

Section 8.2

1. $x = -\frac{3}{2}, y = -3, z = \frac{9}{2}$

3. $x = -2, y = \frac{9}{2}, z = \frac{1}{2}$

5. $x = 5, y = 3, z = -1$

7. $x = \frac{90}{31}, y = \frac{103}{31}, z = \frac{9}{31}$

9. $x = -\frac{13}{4}, y = \frac{1}{2}, z = -\frac{5}{2}$

11. $x = -2, y = -1, z = 0$

13. $x = 2, y = 5, z = -1$

15. no solution **17.** no solution

19. $x = 1 - a, y = -(a + \frac{1}{2}), z = a$

21. $x = 41 + 4a, y = 31 + 3a, z = a$

23. $x_1 = -\frac{1}{2}, x_2 = \frac{7}{4}, x_3 = -\frac{3}{4}$

25. no solution

27. $x_1 = 1, x_2 = -1 + a, x_3 = a$

29. $x = \frac{2}{3}a + \frac{8}{3}, y = -\frac{1}{3}a - \frac{10}{3}, z = a$

31. $x = a, y = \frac{20}{3} - \frac{13}{3}a, z = 5 - 3a$

33. 100 basic widgets, 100 midprice widgets, and 100 top-of-the-line widgets produced

35. 6 chicken sandwiches
3 tuna sandwiches
5 roast beef sandwiches

37. $h_0 = 0, v_0 = 52, a = -32$

39. $y = -0.0625x^2 + 5.25x - 50$

41. money market account: $10,000,
mutual fund: $4000, stock: $6000

43. 33 regular model skis, 72 trick skis, 5 slalom skis

45. game 1: 885 points, game 2: 823 points, game 3: 883 points

47. Equation (2) and Equation (3) must be added correctly – should be $2x - y + z = 2$. Also, should begin by eliminating one variable from Equation (1).

49. true **51.** false

53. $x^2 + y^2 + 4x - 2y - 4 = 0$

55. $a = -\frac{55}{24}, b = -\frac{1}{4}, c = \frac{223}{24}, d = \frac{1}{4}, e = 44$

57. no solution

59. $x_1 = -2, x_2 = 1, x_3 = -4, x_4 = 5$

61. $A = 0, B = 1, C = 1, D = 0$

63. $A = 2, B = 3, C = -4$

65. $A = \frac{4}{3}, B = -1, C = -\frac{1}{3}$

Section 8.3

1. 2×3 **3.** 1×4 **5.** 1×1

7. $\left[\begin{array}{cc|c} 3 & -2 & 7 \\ -4 & 6 & -3 \end{array}\right]$

9. $\left[\begin{array}{ccc|c} 2 & -3 & 4 & -3 \\ -1 & 1 & 2 & 1 \\ 5 & -2 & -3 & 7 \end{array}\right]$

11. $\left[\begin{array}{ccc|c} 1 & 1 & 0 & 3 \\ 1 & 0 & -1 & 2 \\ 0 & 1 & 1 & 5 \end{array}\right]$

13. $\left[\begin{array}{ccc|c} -4 & 3 & 5 & 2 \\ 2 & -3 & -2 & -3 \\ -2 & 4 & 3 & 1 \end{array}\right]$

15. $\begin{cases} -3x + 7y = 2 \\ x + 5y = 8 \end{cases}$

17. $\begin{cases} -x = 4 \\ 7x + 9y + 3z = -3 \\ 4x + 6y - 5z = 8 \end{cases}$

19. $\begin{cases} x = a \\ y = b \end{cases}$

21. not reduced form

23. reduced form

25. not reduced form

27. reduced form

29. reduced form

31. $\left[\begin{array}{cc|c} 1 & -2 & -3 \\ 0 & 7 & 5 \end{array}\right]$

33. $\left[\begin{array}{ccc|c} 1 & -2 & -1 & 3 \\ 0 & 5 & -1 & 0 \\ 3 & -2 & 5 & 8 \end{array}\right]$

35. $\left[\begin{array}{cccc|c} 1 & -2 & 5 & -1 & 2 \\ 0 & 1 & 1 & -3 & 3 \\ 0 & -2 & 1 & -2 & 5 \\ 0 & 0 & 1 & -1 & -6 \end{array}\right]$

37. $\left[\begin{array}{cccc|c} 1 & 0 & 5 & -10 & -5 \\ 0 & 1 & 2 & -3 & -2 \\ 0 & 0 & -7 & 6 & 3 \\ 0 & 0 & 8 & -10 & -9 \end{array}\right]$

39. $\left[\begin{array}{cccc|c} 1 & 0 & 4 & 0 & 27 \\ 0 & 1 & 2 & 0 & -11 \\ 0 & 0 & 1 & 0 & 21 \\ 0 & 0 & 0 & 1 & -3 \end{array}\right]$

41. $\left[\begin{array}{cc|c} 1 & 0 & -8 \\ 0 & 1 & 6 \end{array}\right]$

43. $\left[\begin{array}{ccc|c} 1 & 0 & 0 & -2 \\ 0 & 1 & 0 & -1 \\ 0 & 0 & 1 & 0 \end{array}\right]$

45. $\left[\begin{array}{ccc|c} 1 & 0 & 0 & 2 \\ 0 & 1 & 0 & 5 \\ 0 & 0 & 1 & -1 \end{array}\right]$

47. $\left[\begin{array}{ccc|c} 1 & 0 & -2 & 1 \\ 0 & 1 & -2 & 2 \end{array}\right]$

49. $\left[\begin{array}{ccc|c} 1 & 0 & 1 & 1 \\ 0 & 1 & 1 & -\frac{1}{2} \\ 0 & 0 & 0 & 0 \end{array}\right]$

51. $x = -7, y = 5$

53. $x = 2a - 3, y = a$

55. no solution

57. $x = 4a + 41, y = 31 + 3a, z = a$

59. $x_1 = -\frac{1}{2}, x_2 = \frac{7}{4}, x_3 = -\frac{3}{4}$

61. no solution

63. $x_1 = 1, x_2 = a - 1, x_3 = a$

65. $x = \frac{2}{3}(a + 4), y = -\frac{1}{3}(a + 10), z = a$

67. no solution

69. $x_1 = -2, x_2 = 1, x_3 = -4, x_4 = 5$

71. $(1, -2)$

73. no solution

75. $(-2, 1, 3)$

77. $(3, -2, 2)$

79. no solution

81. $x = \frac{a}{4} + 3, y = \frac{7a}{4} + 1, z = a$

83. $x = \frac{72 - 11a}{14}, y = \frac{13a + 4}{14}, z = a$

85. $x = 1, y = 2, z = -3, w = 1$

87. 960 red dwarfs, 8 blue stars, 2,880,000 yellow stars

89. 2 chicken, 2 tuna, 8 roast beef, 2 turkey bacon

91. initial height: 0 ft, initial velocity: 50 ft/sec
acceleration: -32 ft/sec^2

93. $y = -0.053x^2 + 4.58x - 34.76$

95. about 88 ml of the 1.5% solution and 12 ml of the 30% solution

97. money market account: \$5500, mutual fund: \$2500, stock: \$2000

99. product x: 25 units, product y: 40 units, product z: 6 units

101. $a = -\frac{22}{17}, b = -\frac{44}{17}, c = -\frac{280}{17}$

103. Need to line up a single variable in a given column before forming the augmented matrix. The correct matrix is

$\left[\begin{array}{ccc|c} -1 & 1 & 1 & 2 \\ 1 & 1 & -2 & -3 \\ 1 & 1 & 1 & 6 \end{array}\right]$; after reducing, $\left[\begin{array}{ccc|c} 1 & 0 & 0 & 2 \\ 0 & 1 & 0 & 1 \\ 0 & 0 & 1 & 3 \end{array}\right]$.

105. Row 3 is not inconsistent. It implies $z = 0$.

107. false **109.** true **111.** false **113.** false

115. $f(x) = -\frac{11}{6}x^4 + \frac{44}{3}x^3 - \frac{223}{6}x^2 + \frac{94}{3}x + 44$

117. 35 hr

119. $(-1, 2)$, $(2, 5)$, and $(3, -1)$

121. $c_1 = \frac{3}{4}, c_2 = -\frac{3}{4}$

123. $c_1 = 2, c_2 = -3, c_3 = 1$

Section 8.4

1. 2×3

3. 2×2

5. 3×3

7. 4×4

9. $x = -5, y = 1$

11. $x = -3, y = -2, z = 3$

13. $x = 6, y = 3$

15. $\begin{bmatrix} -1 & 5 & 1 \\ 5 & 2 & 5 \end{bmatrix}$

17. $\begin{bmatrix} -2 & 4 \\ 2 & -2 \\ -1 & 3 \end{bmatrix}$

19. not defined

21. not defined

23. $\begin{bmatrix} -2 & 12 & 3 \\ 13 & 2 & 14 \end{bmatrix}$

25. $\begin{bmatrix} 8 & 3 \\ 11 & 5 \end{bmatrix}$

27. $\begin{bmatrix} -3 & 21 & 6 \\ -4 & 7 & 1 \\ 13 & 14 & 9 \end{bmatrix}$

29. $\begin{bmatrix} 3 & 6 \\ -2 & -2 \\ 17 & 24 \end{bmatrix}$

31. not defined

33. $\begin{bmatrix} 0 & 60 \end{bmatrix}$

35. $\begin{bmatrix} -6 & 1 & -9 \end{bmatrix}$

37. $\begin{bmatrix} 7 & 10 & -8 \\ 0 & 15 & 5 \\ 23 & 0 & -7 \end{bmatrix}$

39. $\begin{bmatrix} 12 & 20 \\ 30 & 42 \end{bmatrix}$

41. $\begin{bmatrix} -4 \\ -4 \\ -16 \end{bmatrix}$

43. not defined

45. yes

47. yes

49. yes

51. $\begin{bmatrix} 0 & -1 \\ 1 & 2 \end{bmatrix}$

53. $\begin{bmatrix} -\frac{1}{13} & \frac{8}{39} \\ \frac{20}{39} & -\frac{4}{117} \end{bmatrix}$

55. $\begin{bmatrix} \frac{1}{2} & \frac{1}{2} & 0 \\ \frac{1}{2} & 0 & \frac{1}{2} \\ 0 & -\frac{1}{2} & -\frac{1}{2} \end{bmatrix}$

57. A^{-1} does not exist.

59. $\begin{bmatrix} -\frac{1}{2} & -\frac{1}{2} & \frac{5}{2} \\ \frac{1}{2} & \frac{1}{2} & -\frac{3}{2} \\ 0 & -1 & 1 \end{bmatrix}$

61. $\begin{bmatrix} \frac{1}{2} & \frac{1}{2} & 0 \\ \frac{3}{4} & \frac{1}{4} & -\frac{1}{2} \\ \frac{1}{4} & \frac{3}{4} & -\frac{1}{2} \end{bmatrix}$

63. $x = 2, y = -1$

65. $x = \frac{1}{2}, y = \frac{1}{3}$

67. $x = 0, y = 0, z = 1$

69. A^{-1} does not exist.

71. $x = -1, y = 1, z = -7$

73. $x = 3, y = 5, z = 4$

75. $A = \begin{bmatrix} 0.70 \\ 0.30 \end{bmatrix}, B = \begin{bmatrix} 0.89 \\ 0.84 \end{bmatrix}$

a. $46A = \begin{bmatrix} 32.3 \\ 13.8 \end{bmatrix}$, out of 46 million people, 32.2 million said that they had tried to quit smoking, while 13.8 million said that they had not.

b. $46B = \begin{bmatrix} 40.94 \\ 38.64 \end{bmatrix}$, out of 46 million people, 40.94 million believed that smoking would increase the chance of getting lung cancer, and 38.64 million believed that smoking would shorten their lives.

77. $A = \begin{bmatrix} 0.589 & 0.628 \\ 0.414 & 0.430 \end{bmatrix}, B = \begin{bmatrix} 100M \\ 110M \end{bmatrix}$

$AB = \begin{bmatrix} 127.98M \\ 88.7M \end{bmatrix}$ 127.98 million registered voters; of those, 88.7 million actually vote

79. $A = \begin{bmatrix} 0.45 & 0.50 & 1.00 \end{bmatrix}$

$B = \begin{bmatrix} 7{,}523 \\ 2{,}700 \\ 15{,}200 \end{bmatrix}$ $AB = [19{,}935.35]$

81. $AB = \begin{bmatrix} 0.228 \\ 0.081 \\ 0.015 \end{bmatrix}$, total cost per mile to run each type of automobile

83. $N = \begin{bmatrix} 2 \\ 1 \\ 0 \end{bmatrix}$ $XN = \begin{bmatrix} 10 \\ 16 \\ 20 \end{bmatrix}$

The nutritional content of the meal is 10 g of carbohydrates, 16 g of protein, and 20 g of fat.

85. $N = \begin{bmatrix} 200 \\ 25 \\ 0 \end{bmatrix}$ $XN = \begin{bmatrix} 9.25 \\ 13.25 \\ 15.75 \end{bmatrix}$

Company 1 would charge \$9.25, Company 2 would charge \$13.25, and Company 3 would charge \$15.75 for 200 minutes of talking and 25 text messages. The better cell phone provider for this employee would be Company 1.

87. JAW **89.** LEG **91.** EYE

93. $X = \begin{bmatrix} 8 & 4 & 6 \\ 6 & 10 & 5 \\ 10 & 4 & 8 \end{bmatrix}^{-1} \begin{bmatrix} 18 \\ 21 \\ 22 \end{bmatrix} = \begin{bmatrix} 1 \\ 1 \\ 1 \end{bmatrix}$

The combination of one serving each of foods A, B, and C will create a meal of 18 g carbohydrates, 21 g of protein, and 22 g of fat.

95. Not multiplying correctly. It should be

$$\begin{bmatrix} 3 & 2 \\ 1 & 4 \end{bmatrix} \cdot \begin{bmatrix} -1 & 3 \\ -2 & 5 \end{bmatrix} = \begin{bmatrix} -7 & 19 \\ -9 & 23 \end{bmatrix}$$

97. A is not invertible because the identity matrix was not reached.

99. false **101.** true **103.** false

105. $\begin{bmatrix} a_{11}^2 + a_{12}a_{21} & a_{11}a_{12} + a_{12}a_{22} \\ a_{21}a_{11} + a_{22}a_{21} & a_{22}^2 + a_{21}a_{12} \end{bmatrix}$

107. $x = 9$

109. $A = \begin{bmatrix} 1 & 1 \\ 1 & 1 \end{bmatrix}, A^2 = \begin{bmatrix} 2 & 2 \\ 2 & 2 \end{bmatrix}, A^3 = 2^{n-1}A, n \geq 1$

111. must have $m = p$

113.
$$A \cdot A^{-1} = \begin{bmatrix} a & b \\ c & d \end{bmatrix} \cdot \left(\frac{1}{ad - bc} \begin{bmatrix} d & -b \\ -c & a \end{bmatrix} \right)$$
$$= \frac{1}{ad - bc} \left(\begin{bmatrix} a & b \\ c & d \end{bmatrix} \cdot \begin{bmatrix} d & -b \\ -c & a \end{bmatrix} \right)$$
$$= \frac{1}{ad - bc} \begin{bmatrix} ad - bc & 0 \\ 0 & ad - bc \end{bmatrix}$$
$$= \begin{bmatrix} \frac{ad - bc}{ad - bc} & 0 \\ 0 & \frac{ad - bc}{ad - bc} \end{bmatrix} = \begin{bmatrix} 1 & 0 \\ 0 & 1 \end{bmatrix} = I$$

115. $ad - bc = 0$

117. $\begin{bmatrix} \frac{1}{4x} & \frac{1}{4x} \\ \frac{1}{4y} & -\frac{1}{4y} \end{bmatrix}$

119. $\begin{bmatrix} \cos\theta & -\sin\theta \\ \sin\theta & \cos\theta \end{bmatrix}$

Section 8.5

1. -2 **3.** 31 **5.** -28 **7.** -0.6 **9.** 0

11. $x = 5, y = -6$ **13.** $x = -2, y = 1$

15. $x = -3, y = -4$ **17.** $x = -2, y = 5$

19. $x = 2, y = 2$

21. $D = 0$, inconsistent or dependent system

23. $D = 0$, inconsistent or dependent system

25. $x = \frac{1}{2}, y = -1$ **27.** $x = 1.5, y = 2.1$

29. $x = 0, y = 7$ **31.** 7

33. -25 **35.** -180 **37.** 0 **39.** 238

41. 0 **43.** $x = 2, y = 3, z = 5$

45. $x = -2, y = 3, z = 5$ **47.** $x = 2, y = -3, z = 1$

49. $D = 0$, inconsistent or dependent system

51. $D = 0$, inconsistent or dependent system

53. $x = -3, y = 1, z = 4$ **55.** $x = 2, y = -3, z = 5$

57. $x = -2, y = \frac{3}{2}, z = 3$ **59.** yes

61. 6 units^2 **63.** 6 units^2

65. $y = 2x$ **67.** $I_1 = \frac{7}{2}, I_2 = \frac{5}{2}, I_3 = 1$

69. The second determinant should be subtracted; that is, it should be $-1\begin{vmatrix} -3 & 2 \\ 1 & -1 \end{vmatrix}$.

71. In D_x and D_y, the column $\begin{bmatrix} 6 \\ -3 \end{bmatrix}$ should replace the column corresponding to the variable that is being solved for in each case. More specifically, D_x should be $\begin{vmatrix} 6 & 3 \\ -3 & -1 \end{vmatrix}$ and D_y should be $\begin{vmatrix} 2 & 6 \\ -1 & -3 \end{vmatrix}$.

73. true **75.** false **77.** abc **79.** -419

81. $-b_1\begin{vmatrix} a_2 & c_2 \\ a_3 & c_3 \end{vmatrix} + b_2\begin{vmatrix} a_1 & c_1 \\ a_3 & c_3 \end{vmatrix} - b_3\begin{vmatrix} a_1 & c_1 \\ a_2 & c_2 \end{vmatrix}$

$= -b_1[(a_2)(c_3) - (a_3)(c_2)] + b_2[(a_1)(c_3) - (a_3)(c_1)]$
$\quad -b_3[(a_1)(c_2) - (a_2)(c_1)]$

$= -a_2b_1c_3 + a_3b_1c_2 + a_1b_2c_3 - a_3b_2c_1 - a_1b_3c_2 + a_2b_3c_1$

85. r **87.** $-\rho^2 \sin\varphi$

Section 8.6

1. d **3.** a **5.** b

7. $\frac{A}{x-5} + \frac{B}{x+4}$ **9.** $\frac{A}{x-4} + \frac{B}{x} + \frac{C}{x^2}$

11. $2x - 6 + \frac{3x+33}{x^2+x+5}$ **13.** $\frac{Ax+B}{x^2+10} + \frac{Cx+D}{(x^2+10)^2}$

15. $\frac{1}{x} - \frac{1}{x+1}$ **17.** $\frac{1}{x-1}$

19. $\frac{2}{x-3} + \frac{7}{x+5}$ **21.** $\frac{3}{x-1} + \frac{4}{(x-1)^2}$

23. $\frac{4}{x+3} - \frac{15}{(x+3)^2}$ **25.** $\frac{3}{x+1} + \frac{1}{x-5} + \frac{2}{(x-5)^2}$

27. $\frac{-2}{x+4} + \frac{7x}{x^2+3}$ **29.** $\frac{-2}{x-7} + \frac{4x-3}{3x^2-7x+5}$

31. $\frac{x}{x^2+9} - \frac{9x}{(x^2+9)^2}$ **33.** $\frac{2x-3}{x^2+1} + \frac{5x+1}{(x^2+1)^2}$

35. $\frac{1}{x-1} + \frac{1}{2(x+1)} + \frac{-3x-1}{2(x^2+1)}$

37. $\frac{3}{x-1} + \frac{2x+5}{x^2+2x-1}$ **39.** $\frac{1}{x-1} + \frac{1-x}{x^2+x+1}$

41. $\frac{1}{d_o} + \frac{1}{d_i} = \frac{1}{f}$ **43.** $-\frac{11}{4}e^{2t} + \frac{7}{4}e^{-2t}$

45. The form of the decomposition is incorrect. It should be $\frac{A}{x} + \frac{Bx+C}{x^2+1}$. Once this correction is made, the correct decomposition is $\frac{1}{x} + \frac{2x+3}{x^2+1}$.

47. false **49.** true **51.** false

53. $\frac{1}{x-1} - \frac{1}{x+2} + \frac{1}{x-2}$ **55.** $\frac{1}{x} + \frac{1}{x+1} - \frac{1}{x^3}$

57. $\frac{x}{x^2+1} - \frac{2x}{(x^2+1)^2} + \frac{x+2}{(x^2+1)^3}$

59. $\frac{3}{k} - \frac{3}{k+3}$ **61.** $\frac{1}{k^2} - \frac{1}{(k+1)^2}$

Section 8.7

1. d **3.** b

5.

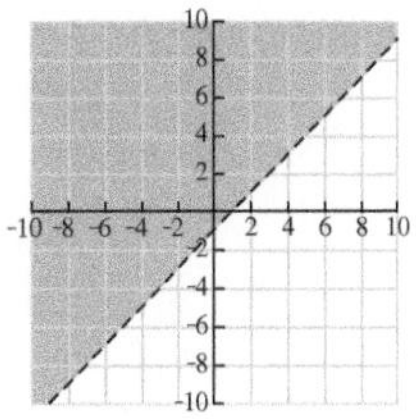

7.

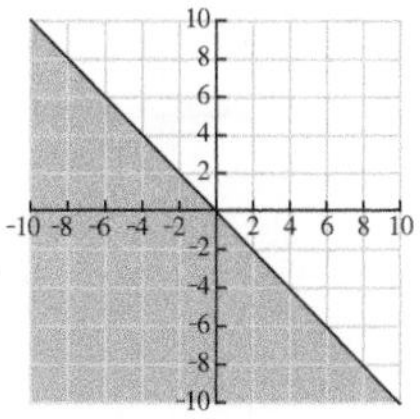

9.

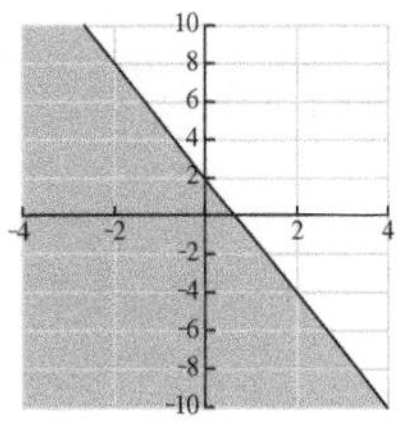

11.

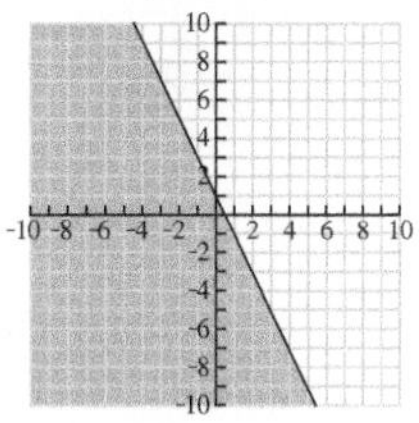

13.

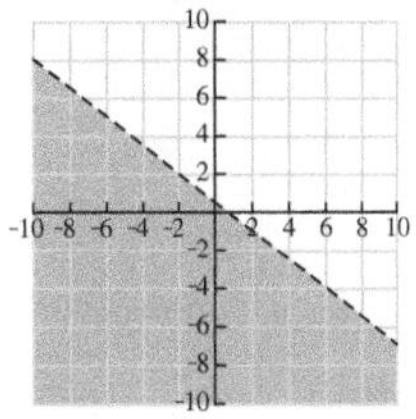

15.

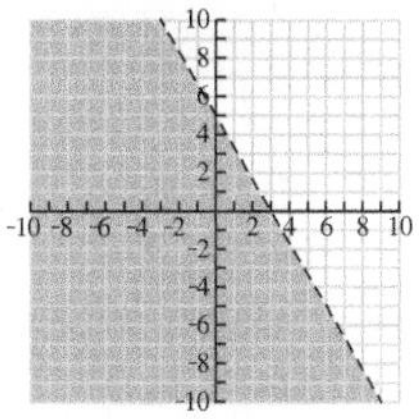

17.

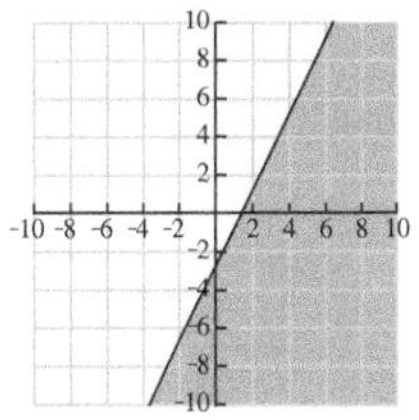

19.

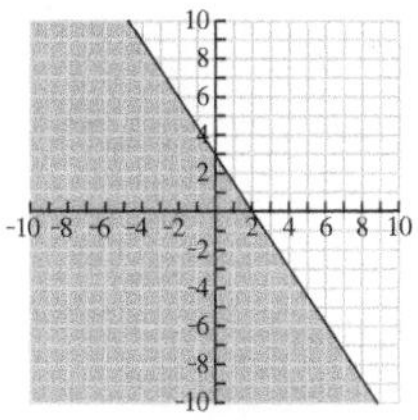

21.

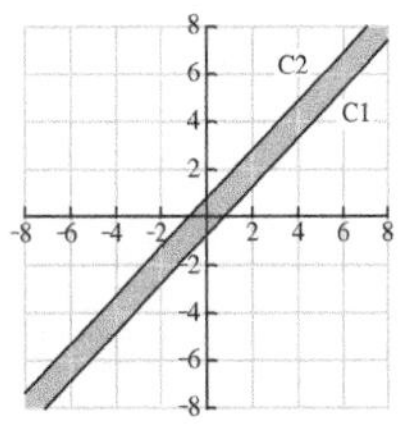

23.

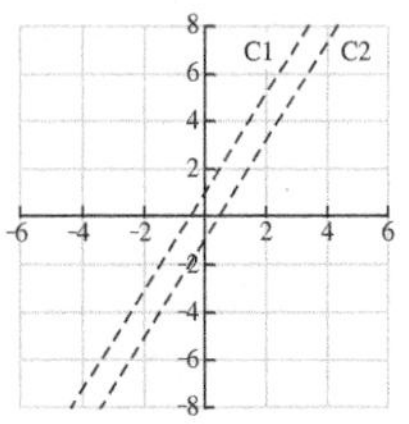

25.

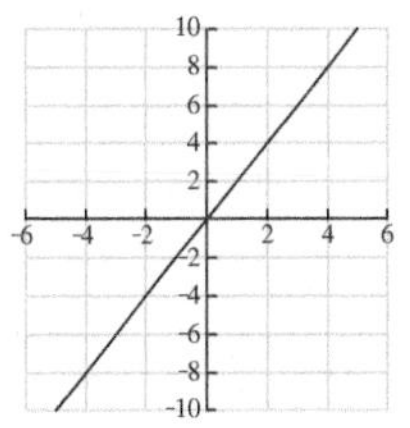

27.

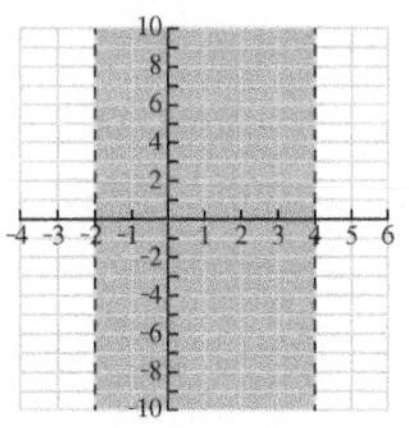

29.

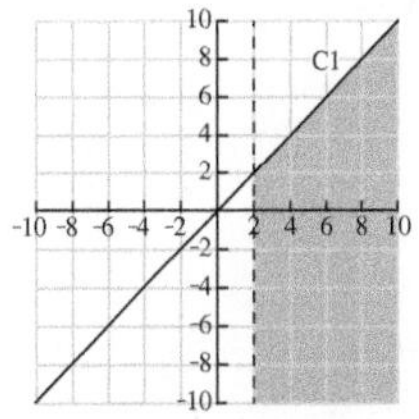

31.

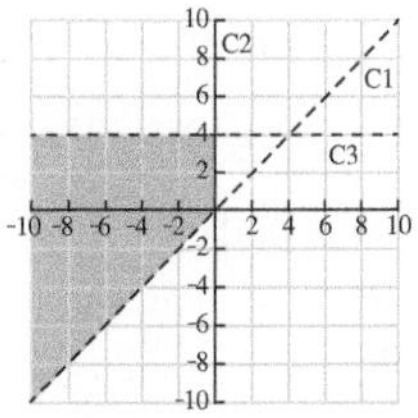

33.

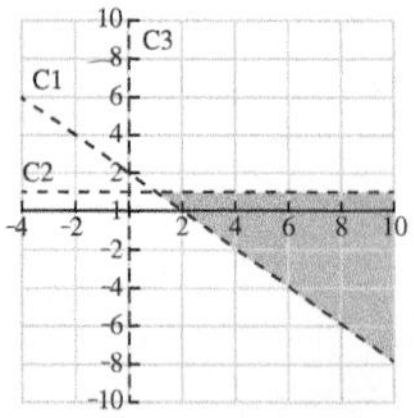

35.

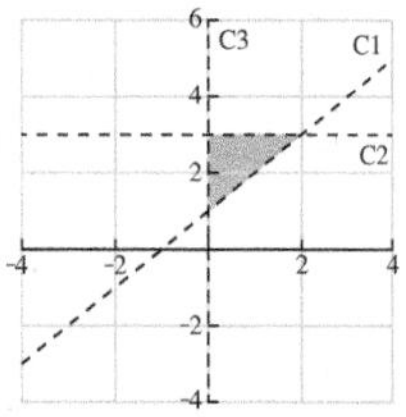

37.

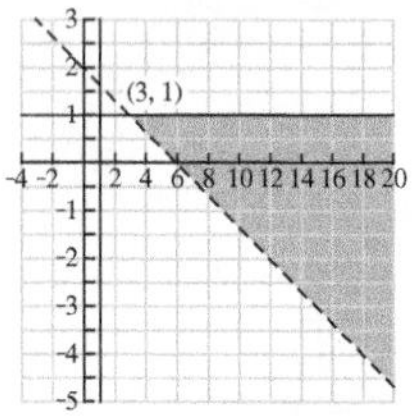

39.

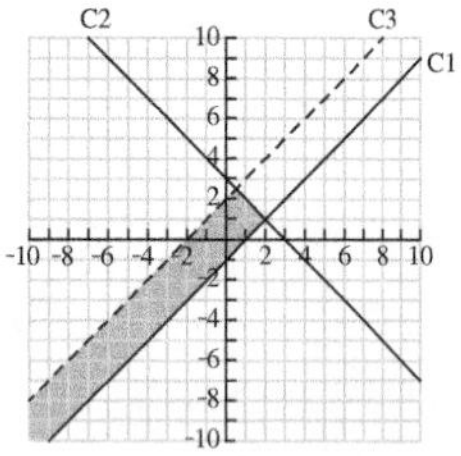

41.

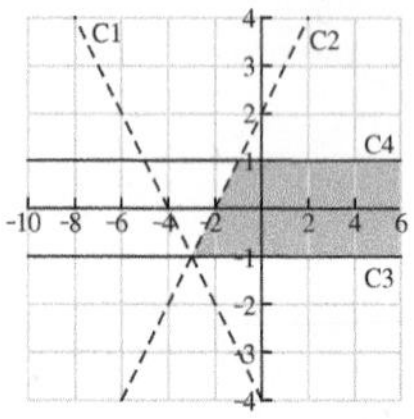

43.

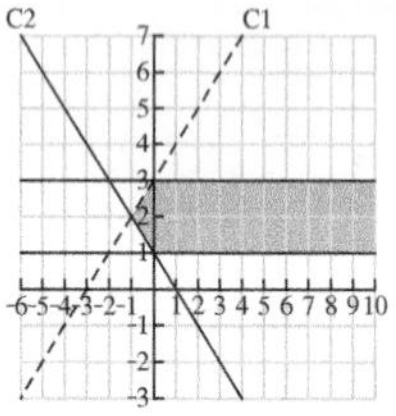

45. no solution

47.

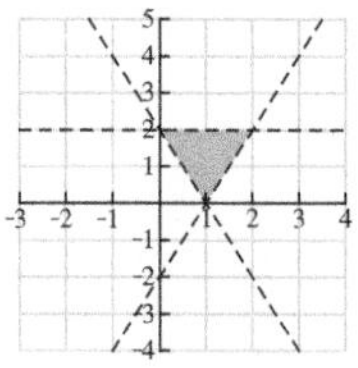

49.

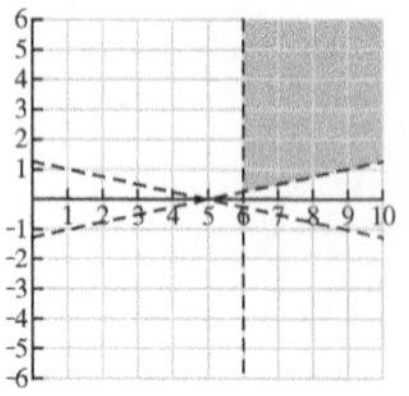

51. $f(x, y) = z = 2x + 3y$
$f(-1, 4) = 10$
$f(2, 4) = 16$ (MAX),
$f(-2, -1) = -7$ (MIN),
$f(1, -1) = -1$

53. $f(x, y) = z = 1.5x + 4.5y$
$f(-1, 4) = 16.5$
$f(2, 4) = 21$ (MAX)
$f(-2, -1) = -7.5$ (MIN)
$f(1, -1) = -3$

55. minimize at $f(0, 0) = 0$

57. no maximum

59. minimize at $f(0, 0) = 0$

61. maximize at $f(1, 6) = \frac{53}{20} = 2.65$

63. $\begin{cases} P \leq 80 - 0.01x \\ P \geq 60 \\ x \geq 0 \end{cases}$

65. 20,000 units^2

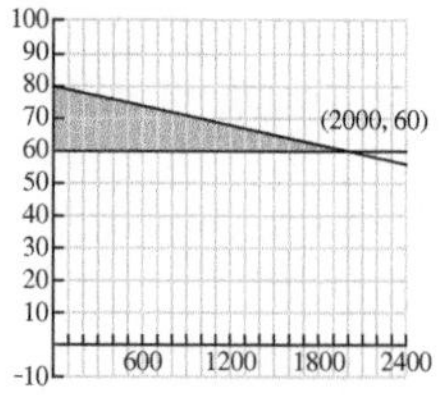

67. $\begin{cases} x \geq 0, y \geq 0 \\ x + 20y \leq 2400 \\ 25x + 150y \leq 6000 \end{cases}$

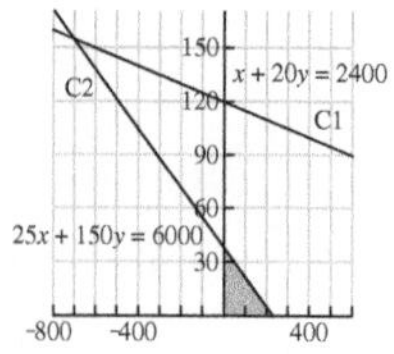

69. Francis T-shirts: 130
Charley T-shirts: 50 (profit \$950)

71. **a.**

$275 \leq 10x + 20y$
$125 \leq 15x + 10y$
$200 \leq 20x + 15y$
$x \geq 0, y \geq 0$

b.

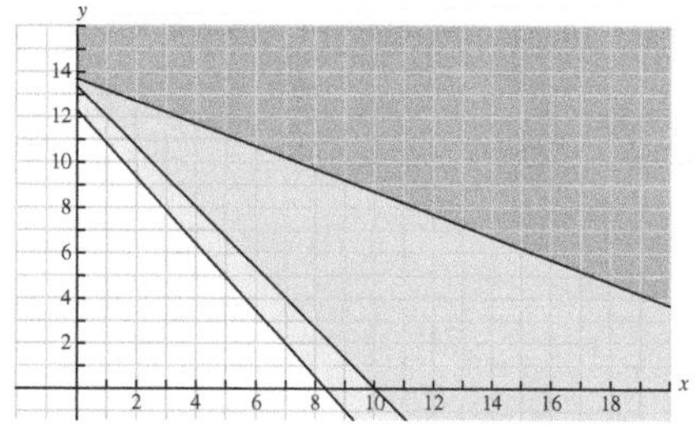

c. Two possible diet combinations are 2 oz of food A and 14 oz of food B or 10 oz of food A and 10 oz of food B.

73. **a.**

$x \geq 2y$
$x + y \geq 1000$
$x \geq 0, y \geq 0$

b.

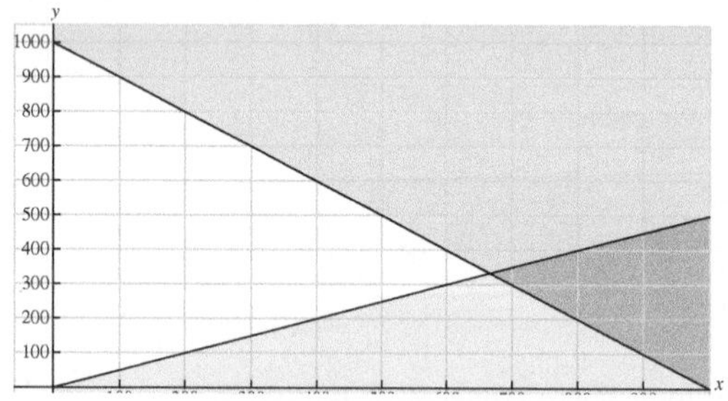

c. Two possible solutions would be for the manufacturer to produce 700 USB wireless mice and 300 Bluetooth mice or 800 USB wireless mice and 300 Bluetooth mice.

75. The shading should be above the line.

77. true

79. false

81. false

83. shaded rectangle

85.

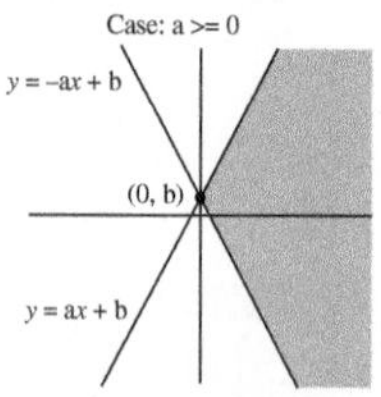

87. maximum at $(0, a)$ and is a

89.

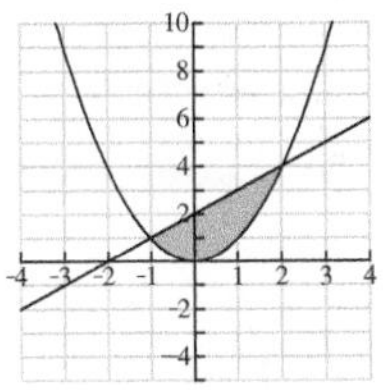

91.

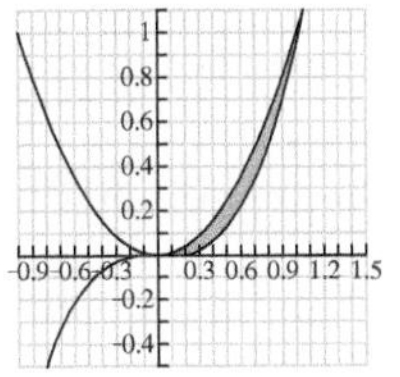

Review Exercises

1. $(3, 0)$ **3.** $\left(\frac{13}{4}, 8\right)$ **5.** $(2, 1)$ **7.** $\left(\frac{19}{8}, \frac{13}{8}\right)$

9. $(-2, 1)$

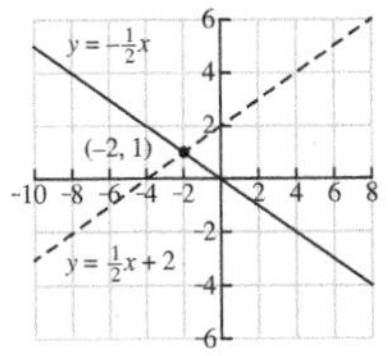

11. $(12, 5.8\overline{3})$

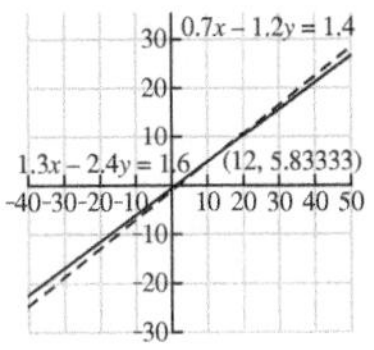

13. $(3, -2)$ **15.** $(-1, 2)$ **17.** c **19.** d

21. 6% NaCl: 10.5 ml, 18% NaCl: 31.5 ml

23. $x = -1, y = -a + 2, z = a$

25. no solution

27. $y = -0.0050x^2 + 0.4486x - 3.8884$

29. $\left[\begin{array}{cc|c} 5 & 7 & 2 \\ 3 & -4 & -2 \end{array}\right]$ **31.** $\left[\begin{array}{ccc|c} 2 & 0 & -1 & 3 \\ 0 & 1 & -3 & -2 \\ 1 & 0 & 4 & -3 \end{array}\right]$

33. no **35.** no

37. $\left[\begin{array}{cc|c} 1 & -2 & 1 \\ 0 & 1 & -1 \end{array}\right]$ **39.** $\left[\begin{array}{ccc|c} 1 & -4 & 3 & -1 \\ 0 & -2 & 3 & -2 \\ 0 & 1 & -4 & 8 \end{array}\right]$

41. $\left[\begin{array}{cc|c} 1 & 0 & \frac{3}{5} \\ 0 & 1 & -\frac{1}{5} \end{array}\right]$ **43.** $\left[\begin{array}{ccc|c} 1 & 0 & 0 & -4 \\ 0 & 1 & 0 & 8 \\ 0 & 0 & 1 & -4 \end{array}\right]$

45. $x = \frac{5}{4}, y = \frac{7}{8}$ **47.** $x = 2, y = 1$

49. $x = -\frac{74}{21}, y = -\frac{73}{21}, z = -\frac{3}{7}$

51. $x = 1, y = 3, z = -5$

53. $x = -\frac{3}{7}a - 2, y = \frac{2}{7}a + 2, z = a$

55. $y = -0.005x^2 + 0.45x - 3.89$

57. not defined **59.** $\begin{bmatrix} 3 & 5 & 2 \\ 7 & 8 & 1 \end{bmatrix}$

61. $\begin{bmatrix} 9 & -4 \\ 9 & 9 \end{bmatrix}$ **63.** $\begin{bmatrix} 4 & 13 \\ 18 & 11 \end{bmatrix}$

65. $\begin{bmatrix} 0 & -19 \\ -18 & -9 \end{bmatrix}$ **67.** $\begin{bmatrix} -7 & -11 & -8 \\ 3 & 7 & 2 \end{bmatrix}$

69. $\begin{bmatrix} 10 & -13 \\ 18 & -20 \end{bmatrix}$ **71.** $\begin{bmatrix} 17 & -8 & 18 \\ 33 & 0 & 42 \end{bmatrix}$

73. $\begin{bmatrix} 10 & 9 & 20 \\ 22 & -4 & 2 \end{bmatrix}$ **75.** yes

77. yes **79.** $\begin{bmatrix} \frac{2}{5} & -\frac{1}{5} \\ \frac{3}{10} & \frac{1}{10} \end{bmatrix}$

81. $\begin{bmatrix} 0 & -\frac{1}{2} \\ 1 & 0 \end{bmatrix}$ **83.** $\begin{bmatrix} -\frac{1}{6} & \frac{7}{12} & -\frac{1}{12} \\ \frac{1}{2} & -\frac{1}{4} & -\frac{1}{4} \\ \frac{1}{6} & -\frac{1}{12} & -\frac{5}{12} \end{bmatrix}$

85. $\begin{bmatrix} 0 & -\frac{2}{5} & \frac{1}{5} \\ 1 & -\frac{2}{5} & \frac{1}{5} \\ -\frac{1}{2} & \frac{3}{10} & \frac{1}{10} \end{bmatrix}$ **87.** $x = 5, y = 4$

89. $x = 8, y = 12$ **91.** $x = 1, y = 2, z = 3$

93. -8 **95.** 5.4

97. $x = 3, y = 1$ **99.** $x = 6, y = 0$

101. $x = 90, y = 155$ **103.** 11

105. $-abd$ **107.** $x = 1, y = 1, z = 2$

109. $x = -\frac{15}{7}, y = -\frac{25}{7}, z = \frac{19}{14}$

111. $\dfrac{A}{x-1} + \dfrac{B}{(x-1)^2} + \dfrac{C}{x+3} + \dfrac{D}{x-5}$

113. $\dfrac{A}{x} + \dfrac{B}{4x+5} + \dfrac{C}{2x+1} + \dfrac{D}{(2x+1)^2}$

115. $\dfrac{A}{x-3} + \dfrac{B}{x+4}$ **117.** $\dfrac{Ax+B}{x^2+17} + \dfrac{Cx+D}{(x^2+17)^2}$

119. $\dfrac{4}{x-1} + \dfrac{5}{x+7}$ **121.** $\dfrac{1}{2x} + \dfrac{15}{2(x-5)} - \dfrac{3}{2(x+5)}$

123. $\dfrac{-2}{x+1} + \dfrac{2}{x}$ **125.** $\dfrac{5}{x+2} - \dfrac{27}{(x+2)^2}$

127.

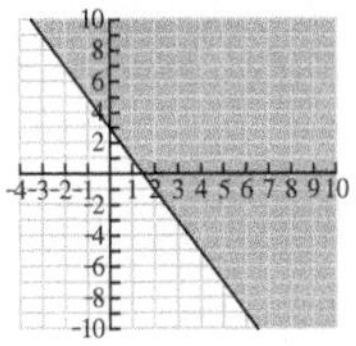

129.

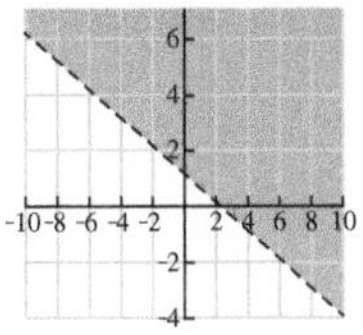

131.

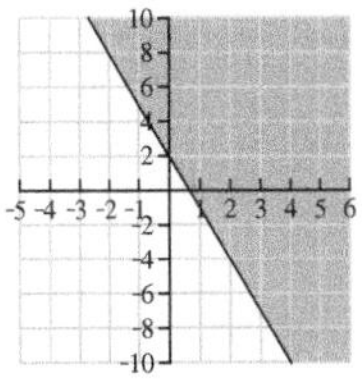

133.

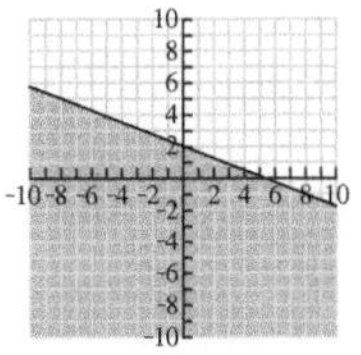

135. no solution

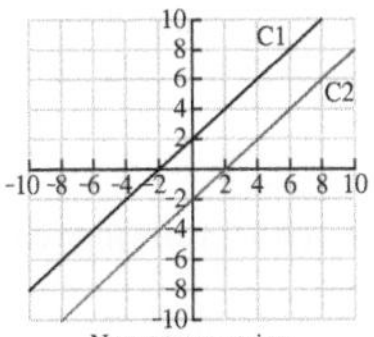

No common region.

137.

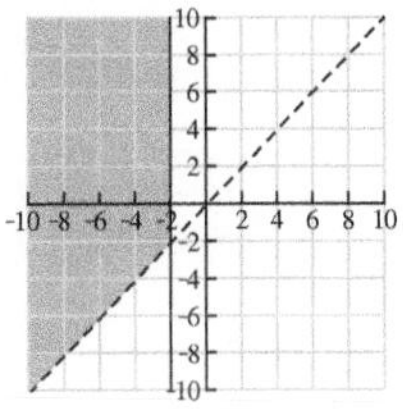

139.

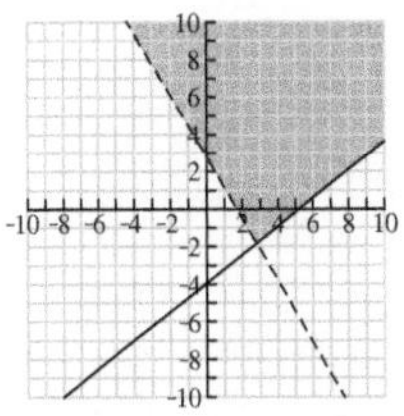

141. minimum value of z: 0, occurs at $(0, 0)$

143. minimum value of z: -30, occurs at $(0, 6)$

145. ocean watercolor: 10
geometric shape: 30 (profit \$390)

Practice Test

1. (7, 3)
3. $x = a, y = a - 2$
5. $x = 1, y = -5, z = 3$
7. $\begin{bmatrix} 6 & 9 & 1 & \vert & 5 \\ 2 & -3 & 1 & \vert & 3 \\ 10 & 12 & 2 & \vert & 9 \end{bmatrix}$
9. $\begin{bmatrix} 1 & 3 & 5 \\ 0 & 1 & -11 \\ 0 & 7 & 15 \end{bmatrix}$
11. $x = -\frac{1}{3}a + \frac{7}{6}, y = \frac{1}{9}a - \frac{2}{9}, z = a$
13. $\begin{bmatrix} -11 & 19 \\ -6 & 8 \end{bmatrix}$
15. $\begin{bmatrix} \frac{1}{19} & \frac{3}{19} \\ \frac{5}{19} & -\frac{4}{19} \end{bmatrix}$
17. $x = -3, y = 1, z = 7$
19. -31
21. $x = 1, y = -1, z = 2$
23. $\frac{5}{x} - \frac{3}{x+1}$
25. $\frac{1}{3x} + \frac{2}{3(x-3)} - \frac{1}{x+3}$
27.

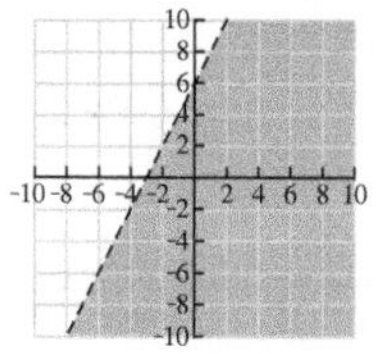

29.

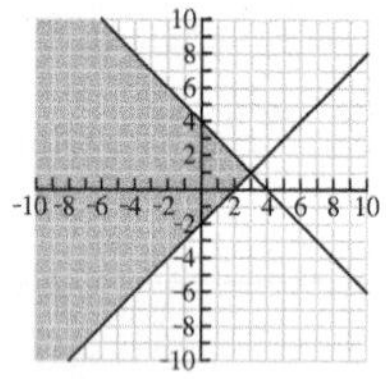

31. minimum value of z: 7, occurs at (0, 1)

Cumulative Test

1. 27
3. $2x + h - 3$
5. (15, 6)
7. VA: $x = 3$, HA: $y = -5$
9. -1
11. 2.585
13. $\frac{\sqrt{3}}{2}$
15. $\sin\theta = \frac{2\sqrt{29}}{29}, \cos\theta = \frac{-5\sqrt{29}}{29}, \tan\theta = \frac{-2}{5}$
$\cot\theta = -\frac{5}{2}, \sec\theta = -\frac{\sqrt{29}}{5}, \csc\theta = \frac{\sqrt{29}}{2}$
17.

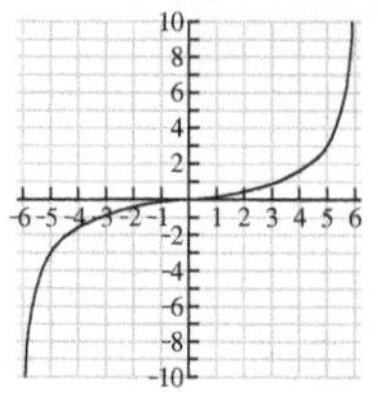

19. domain: $x \neq \frac{(2n+1)\pi}{2} + \frac{\pi}{2} = \frac{(2n+2)\pi}{2} = (n+1)\pi$, n any integer, range: all reals
21. 1
23. $\alpha = 36.3°, b \approx 123.4$ m, $c \approx 78.1$ m
25. $-2, 1 - \sqrt{3}i, 1 + \sqrt{3}i$
27. $\begin{bmatrix} 72 & -18 & 54 \\ 26 & -2 & 4 \end{bmatrix}$
29. $x = \frac{3}{11}, y = -\frac{2}{11}$
31.

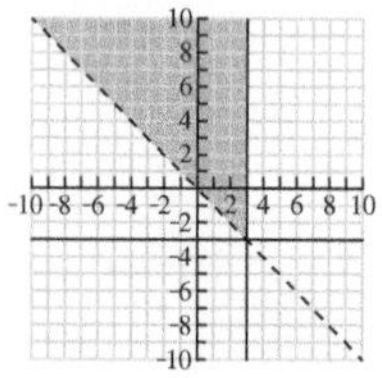

CHAPTER 9

Section 9.1

1. hyperbola
3. circle
5. hyperbola
7. ellipse
9. parabola
11. circle

Section 9.2

1. c
3. d
5. c
7. a
9. $x^2 = 12y$
11. $y^2 = -20x$
13. $(x - 3)^2 = 8(y - 5)$
15. $(y - 4)^2 = -8(x - 2)$
17. $(x - 2)^2 = 4(3)(y - 1) = 12(y - 1)$
19. $(y + 1)^2 = 4(1)(x - 2) = 4(x - 2)$
21. $(y - 2)^2 = 8(x + 1)$
23. $(x - 2)^2 = -8(y + 1)$
25. vertex: (0, 0) focus: (0, 2)
directrix: $y = -2$
length of latus rectum: 8

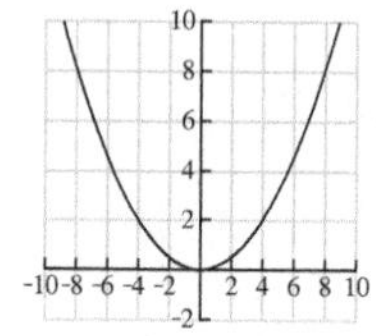

27. vertex: (0, 0) focus: $\left(-\frac{1}{2}, 0\right)$
directrix: $x = \frac{1}{2}$
length of latus rectum: 2

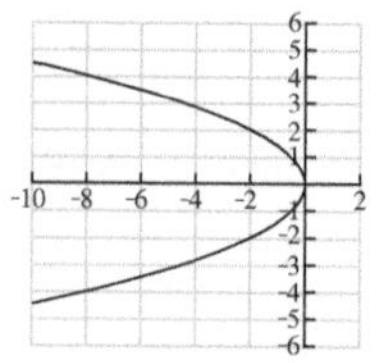

29. vertex: (0, 0) focus: (0, 4)
directrix: $y = -4$
length of latus rectum: 16

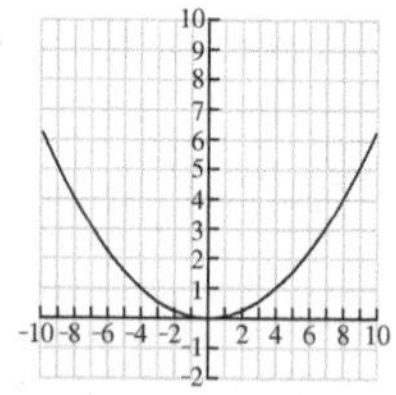

31. vertex: (0, 0) focus: (1, 0)
directrix: $x = -1$
length of latus rectum: 4

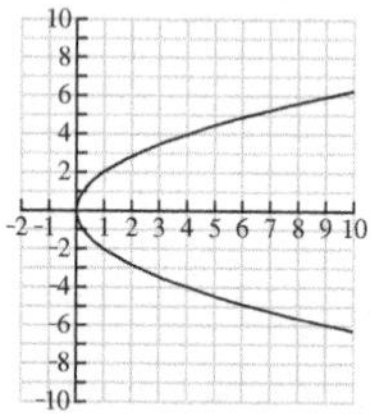

33. vertex: $(-3, 2)$

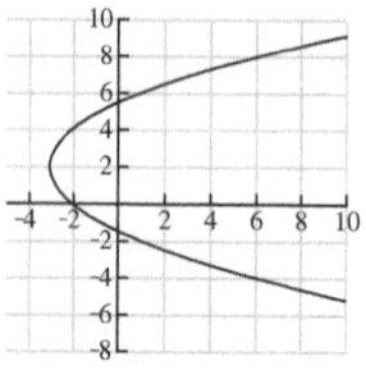

35. vertex: $(3, -1)$

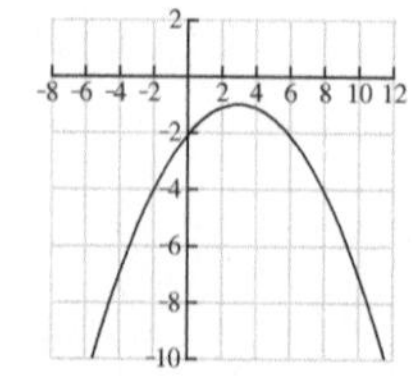

37. vertex: $(-5, 0)$

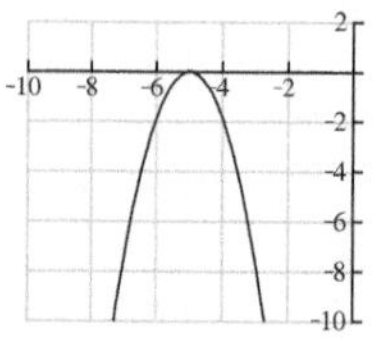

39. vertex: (0, 2)

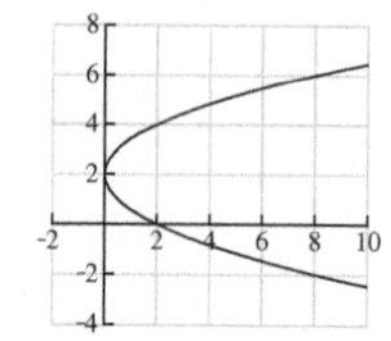

41. vertex: $(-3, -1)$

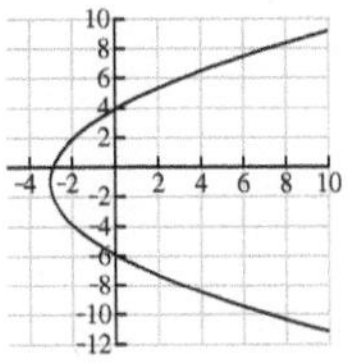

43. vertex: $\left(\frac{1}{2}, \frac{5}{4}\right)$

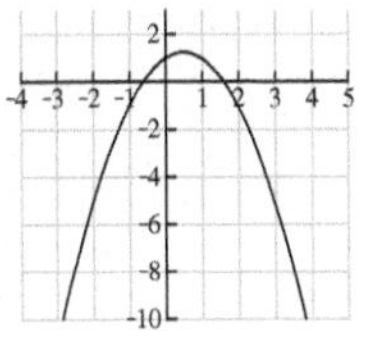

45. $(0, 2)$, receiver placed 2 ft from vertex

47. opens up: $y = \frac{1}{8}x^2$, for any x in $[-2.5, 2.5]$

opens right: $x = \frac{1}{8}y^2$, for any y in $[-2.5, 2.5]$

49. $x^2 = 4(40)y = 160y$

51. yes, opening height 18.75 ft, mast 17 ft

53. 374.25 ft, $x^2 = 1497y$

55. 55 pulses per min

57. The maximum profit of \$400,000 is achieved when 3000 units are produced.

59. If the vertex is at the origin and the focus is at $(3, 0)$, then the parabola must open to the right. The general equation is $y^2 = 4px$, for some $p > 0$.

61. true

63. false

65. $x = h - 1$

67. $\left(6, \frac{13}{2}\right)$

69. Equate d_1 and d_2 and simplify:

$$\sqrt{(x-0)^2 + (y-p)^2} = |y + p|$$
$$x^2 = 4py$$

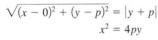

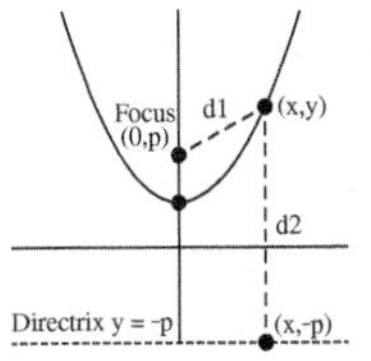

71. $(y-6)^2 = 8(x-2)$, $(y-6)^2 = -4(x-6)$

73. $(2, 3), (-2, 3)$

75. $(2, 3), (-2, 3)$

77. $(1, 7), (10, 10)$

Section 9.3

1. d

3. a

5. center: $(0, 0)$
vertices: $(\pm 5, 0), (0, \pm 4)$

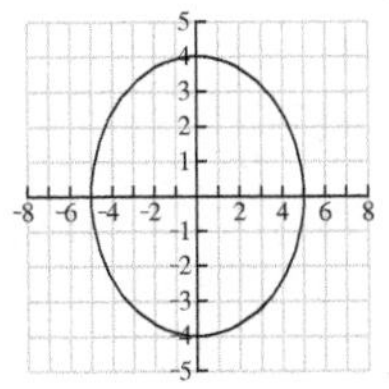

7. center: $(0, 0)$
vertices: $(\pm 4, 0), (0, \pm 8)$

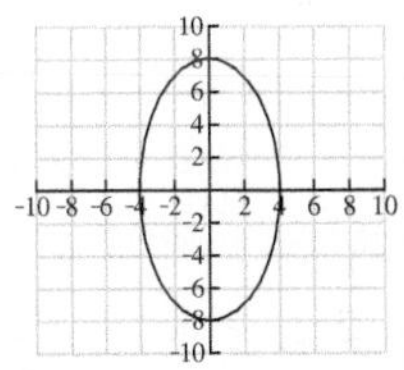

9. center: $(0, 0)$
vertices: $(\pm 10, 0), (0, \pm 1)$

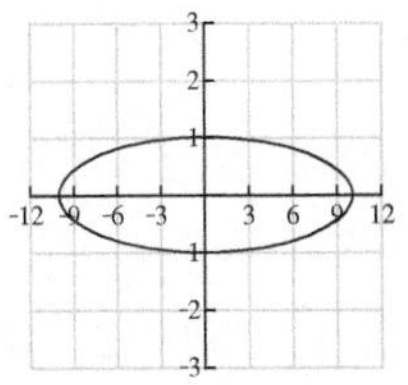

11. center: $(0, 0)$
vertices: $\left(\pm\frac{3}{2}, 0\right), \left(0, \pm\frac{1}{9}\right)$

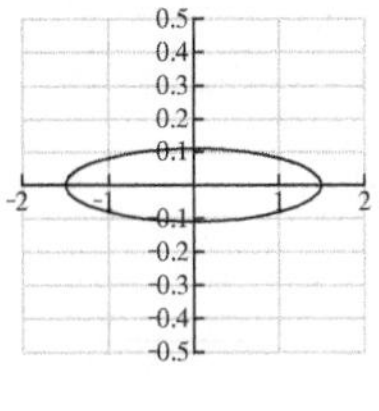

13. center: $(0, 0)$
vertices: $(\pm 2, 0), (0, \pm 4)$

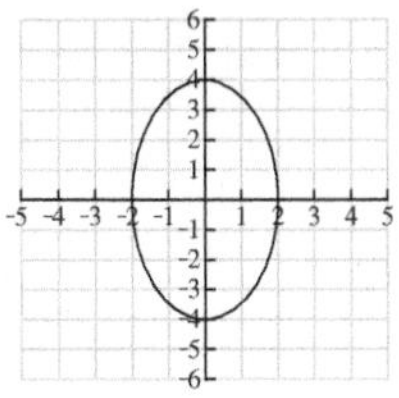

15. center: $(0, 0)$
vertices: $(\pm 2, 0), (0, \pm\sqrt{2})$

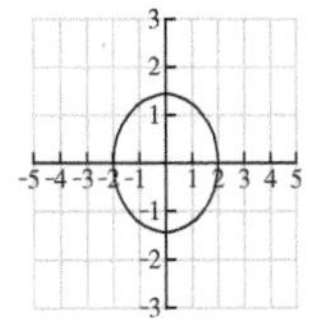

17. $\frac{x^2}{36} + \frac{y^2}{20} = 1$

19. $\frac{x^2}{7} + \frac{y^2}{16} = 1$

21. $\frac{x^2}{4} + \frac{y^2}{16} = 1$

23. $\frac{x^2}{9} + \frac{y^2}{49} = 1$

25. c

27. b

29. center: $(1, 2)$
vertices: $(-3, 2), (5, 2), (1, 0), (1, 4)$

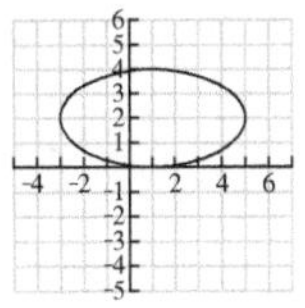

31. center: $(-3, 4)$
vertices: $(-2\sqrt{2} - 3, 4), (2\sqrt{2} - 3, 4)$, $(-3, 4 + 4\sqrt{5}), (-3, 4 - 4\sqrt{5})$

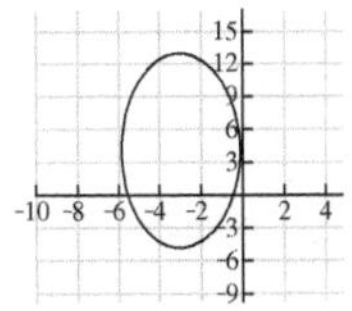

33. center: $(0, 3)$
vertices: $(-2, 3), (2, 3), (0, 2), (0, 4)$

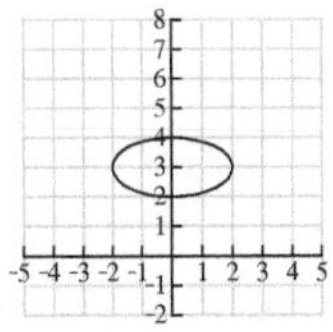

35. center: $(1, 1)$
vertices: $(1 \pm 2\sqrt{2}, 1), (1, 3), (1, -1)$

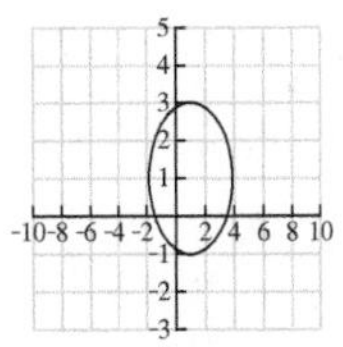

37. center: $(-2, -3)$
vertices: $(-2 \pm \sqrt{10}, -3), (-2, -3 \pm 5\sqrt{2})$

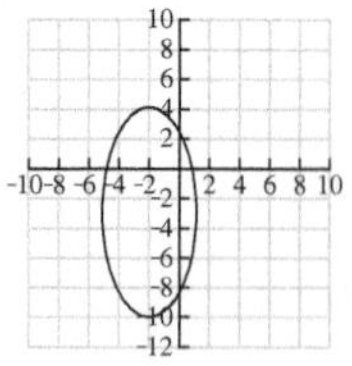

39. $\frac{(x-2)^2}{25} + \frac{(y-5)^2}{9} = 1$ **41.** $\frac{(x-4)^2}{7} + \frac{(y+4)^2}{16} = 1$

43. $\frac{(x-3)^2}{4} + \frac{(y-2)^2}{16} = 1$ **45.** $\frac{(x+1)^2}{9} + \frac{(y+4)^2}{25} = 1$

47. $\frac{x^2}{225} + \frac{y^2}{5625} = 1$

49. **a.** $\frac{x^2}{5625} + \frac{y^2}{400} = 1$ **b.** width at end of field is 24 yd; no, because football field is 30 yd wide

51. $\frac{x^2}{5{,}914{,}000{,}000^2} + \frac{y^2}{5{,}729{,}000{,}000^2} = 1$

53. $\frac{x^2}{150{,}000{,}000^2} + \frac{y^2}{146{,}000{,}000^2} = 1$

55. straight line

57. It should be $a^2 = 6, b^2 = 4$, so that $a = \pm\sqrt{6}, b = \pm 2$.

59. false **61.** true

63. three ellipses **65.** one point

67. Pluto: $e \cong 0.25$ Earth: $e \cong 0.02$

69. $x^2 + 3y^2 = 28$

71. $8x^2 + 9y^2 - 32x + 54y + 41 = 0$

73. maximum: -3, minimum: -7

75. maximum: 1, minimum: -17

Section 9.4

1. b **3.** d

5.

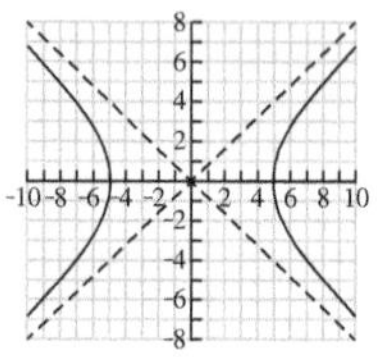

7.

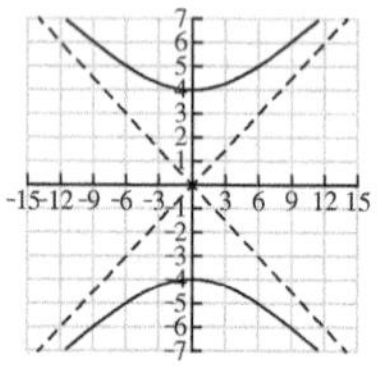

9.

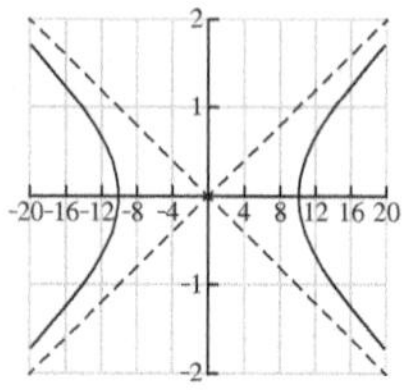

11.

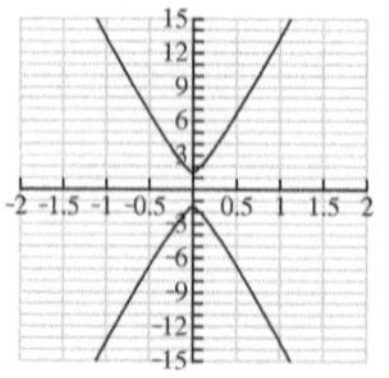

13.

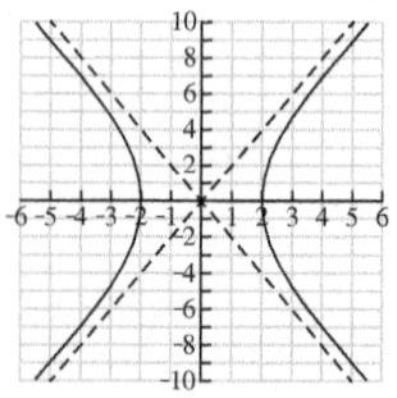

15.

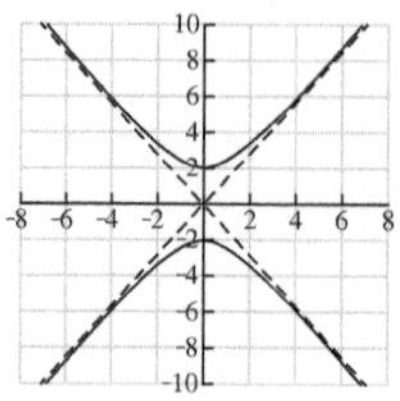

17. $\frac{x^2}{16} - \frac{y^2}{20} = 1$ **19.** $\frac{y^2}{9} - \frac{x^2}{7} = 1$

21. $x^2 - y^2 = a^2$ **23.** $\frac{y^2}{4} - x^2 = b^2$

25. c **27.** b

29.

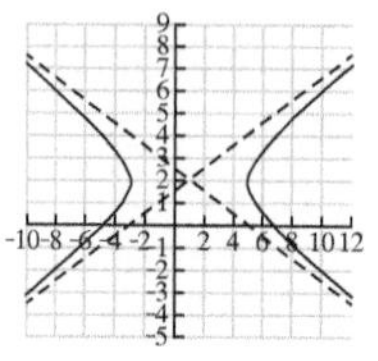

31.

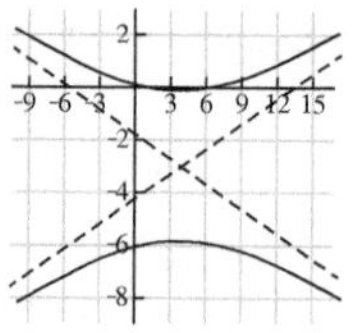

33.

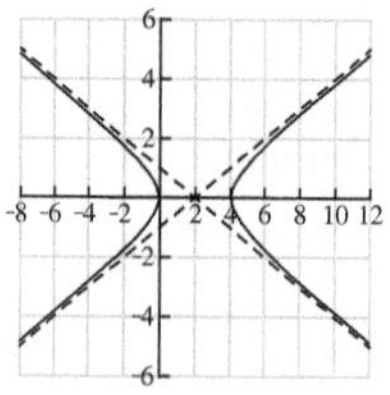

35.

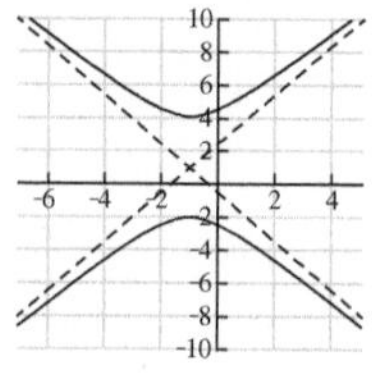

37.

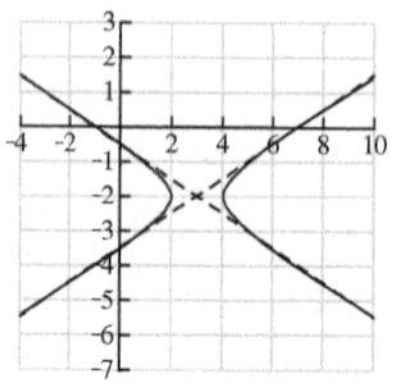

39. $\frac{(x-2)^2}{16} - \frac{(y-5)^2}{9} = 1$ **41.** $\frac{(y+4)^2}{9} - \frac{(x-4)^2}{7} = 1$

43. Ship will come ashore between the two stations 28.5 mi from one and 121.5 mi from the other.

45. 0.000484 sec **47.** $y^2 - \frac{4}{5}x^2 = 1$

49. 275 ft **51.** (76, 50)

53. (109.4, 60)

55. The transverse axis should be vertical. The points are $(3, 0), (-3, 0)$ and the vertices are $(0, 2), (0, -2)$.

57. false **59.** true

61. $(p, -q), (-p, q)$ and $(-p, -q)$

63. $r > q$

65. $\frac{x^2}{a^2} - \frac{y^2}{b^2} = 1$, which is equivalent to $x^2 - y^2 = a^2$

67. $y = -\frac{4}{3}x + \frac{2}{3}, y = \frac{4}{3}x + \frac{10}{3}$

69. $(\pm\sqrt{34}, 0)$ **73.** $\frac{-(2x+h)}{\sqrt{1+(x+h)^2} + \sqrt{1+x^2}}$

Section 9.5

1. $(2, 6), (-1, 3)$ **3.** $(1, 0)$

5. no solution **7.** $(0, 1)$

9. $(0.63, -1.61), (-0.63, -1.61)$

11. no solution **13.** $(1, 1)$

15. $(2\sqrt{2}, \sqrt{2}), (-2\sqrt{2}, -\sqrt{2}),$
$(\sqrt{2}, 2\sqrt{2}), (-\sqrt{2}, -2\sqrt{2})$

17. $(-6, 33), (2, 1)$ **19.** $(3, 4), (-2, -1)$

21. $(0, -3), \left(\frac{2}{5}, -\frac{11}{5}\right)$

23. $(-1, -1), \left(\frac{1}{4}, \frac{3}{2}\right)$

25. $(-1, -4), (4, 1)$

27. $(1, 3), (-1, -3)$

29. $(-4, -1), (4, 1)$

31. $(-2, -1), (-2, 1), (2, -1), (2, 1)$

33. $(2, 4)$

35. $\left(\frac{1}{2}, \frac{1}{3}\right), \left(\frac{1}{2}, -\frac{1}{3}\right)$

37. no solution

39. no solution

41.

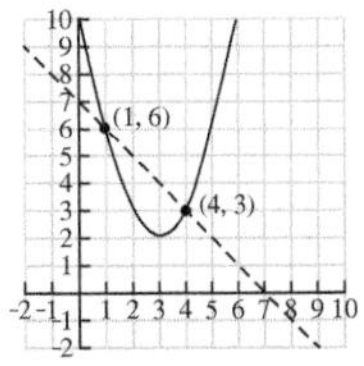

43.

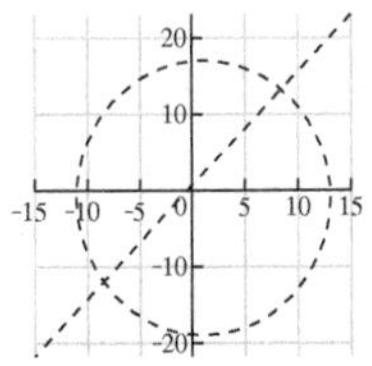

45. 3 and 7

47. 8 and 9, −8 and −9

49. 8 cm × 10 cm

51. 400 ft × 500 ft or $\frac{1000}{3}$ ft × 600 ft

53. professor: 2 m/sec, Jeremy: 10 m/sec

55. 60 mph

57. 4763

59. In general, $y^2 - y \neq 0$. Must solve this system using substitution.

61. false

63. false

65. $2n$

67. Consider $\begin{cases} y = x^2 + 1 \\ y = 1 \end{cases}$. Any system in which the linear equation is the tangent line to the parabola at its vertex will have only one solution.

69. $(1, 2), (-1, 2), (1, -2), (-1, -2)$

71. no solution

73. $y = \sqrt{\frac{8 - x^2}{4}}$

75. $y = \frac{3}{x^{3/2}}$

Section 9.6

1. b **3.** j **5.** h **7.** c **9.** d **11.** k

13.

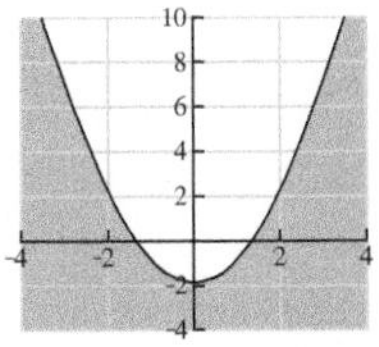

15.

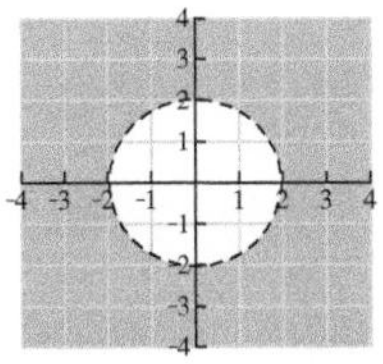

17.

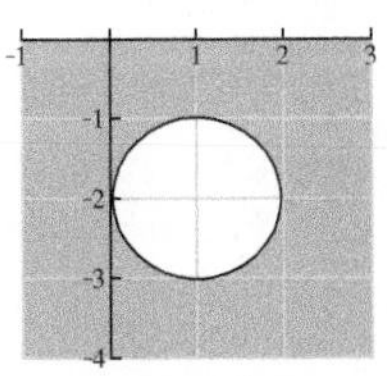

19.

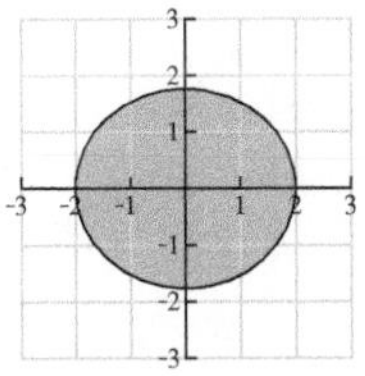

21.

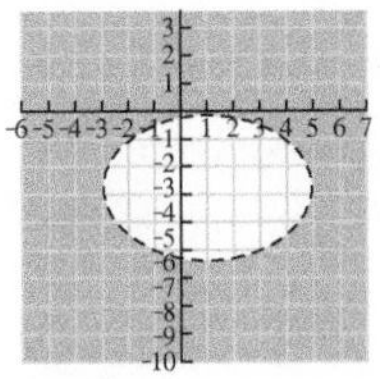

23.

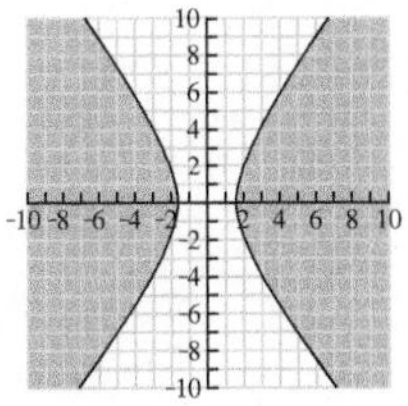

25.

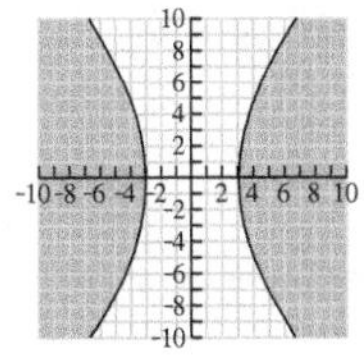

27.

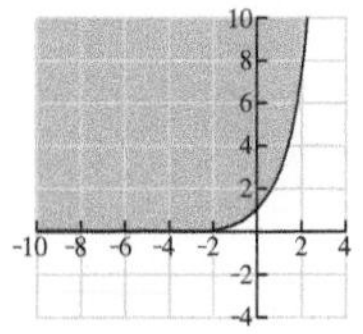

29.

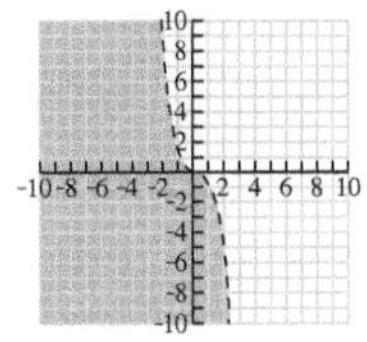

31.

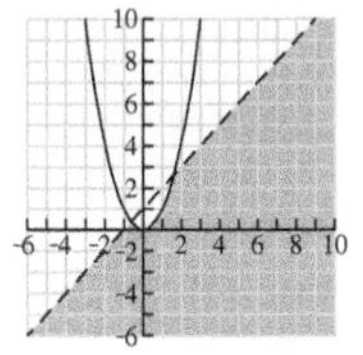

33.

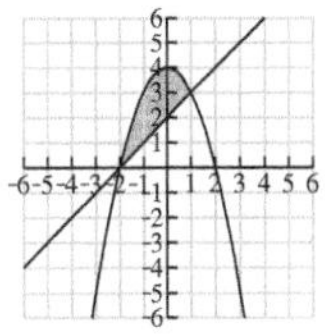

35.

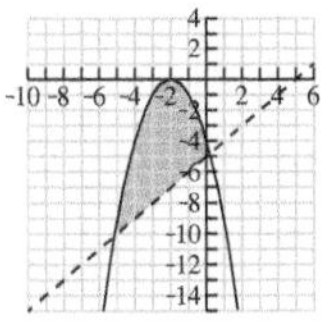

37.

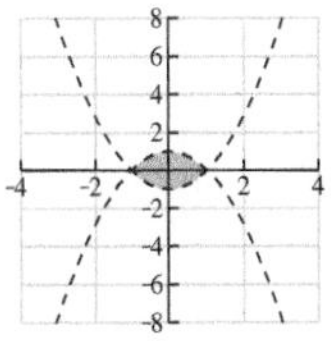

39.

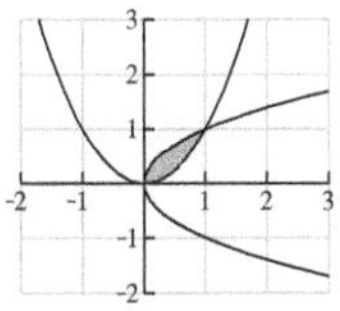

41.

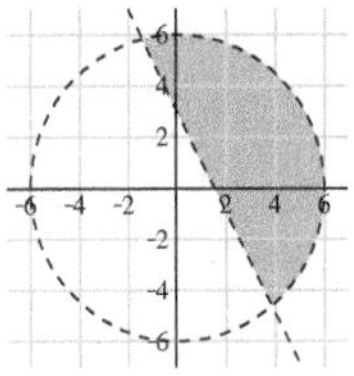

43.

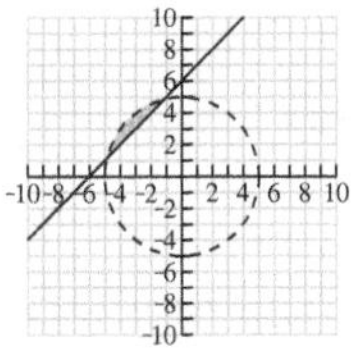

45.

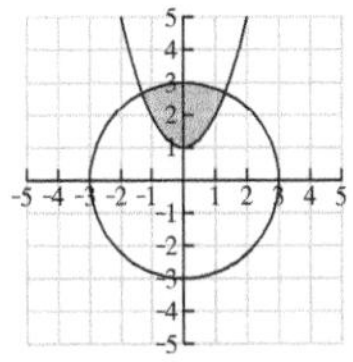

47.

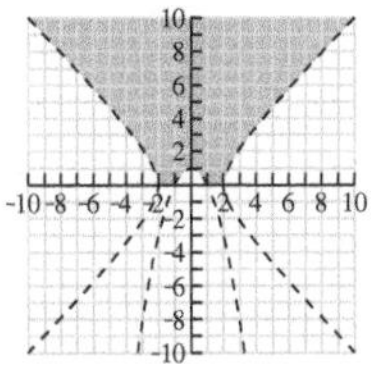

49.

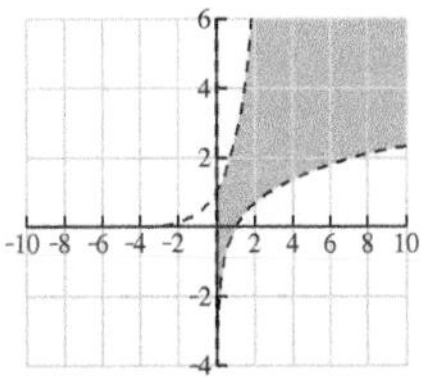

51. $\frac{9}{2}\pi$ units^2

53. 2π units^2

55. 90 units^2

57. There is no common region here–it is empty, as is seen in the graph below:

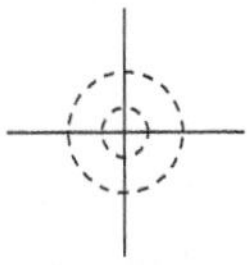

No common region.

59. false **61.** true **63.** true

65. false **67.** $0 \le a \le b$ **69.** $a = 36$

71. $h = 0$

73.

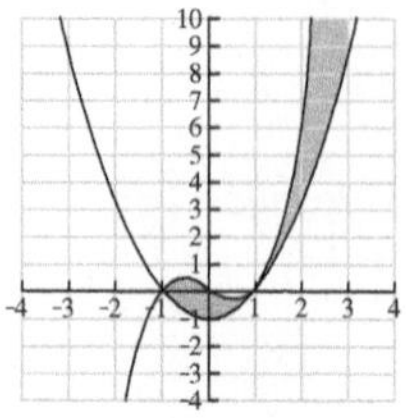

75.

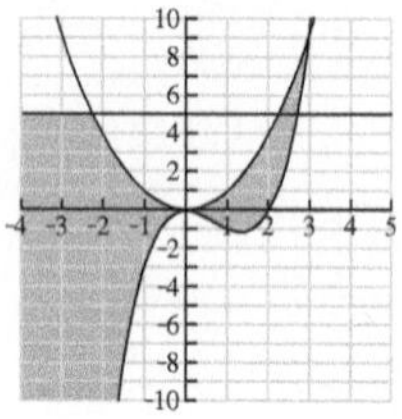

Section 9.7

1. $(3\sqrt{2}, \sqrt{2})$

3. $\left(-\frac{3\sqrt{3}}{2} + 1, \frac{3}{2} + \sqrt{3}\right)$

5. $\left(-\frac{1 + 3\sqrt{3}}{2}, \frac{\sqrt{3} - 3}{2}\right)$

7. $\left(\frac{3\sqrt{3}}{2}, \frac{3}{2}\right)$

9. **a.** hyperbola **b.** $\frac{X^2}{2} - \frac{Y^2}{2} = 1$

c.

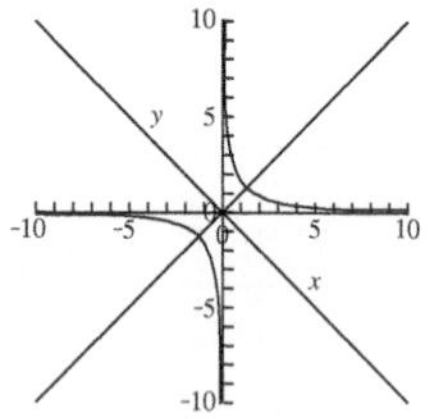

11. **a.** parabola **b.** $2X^2 - 2Y - 1 = 0$

c.

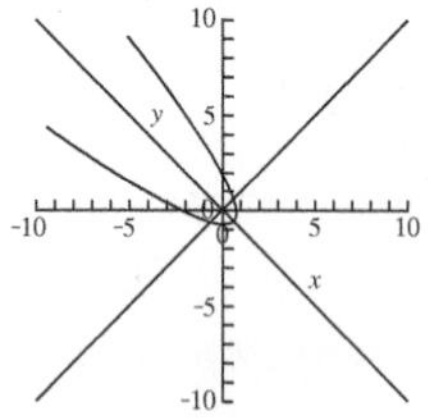

13. **a.** hyperbola **b.** $\frac{X^2}{6} - \frac{Y^2}{2} = 1$

c.

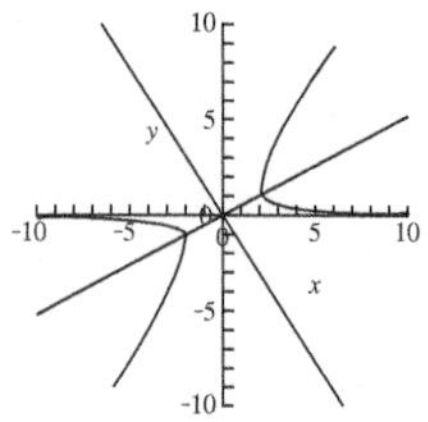

15. **a.** ellipse **b.** $\frac{X^2}{2} + \frac{Y^2}{1} = 1$

c.

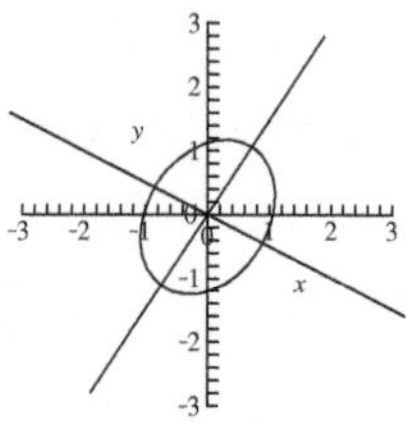

17. **a.** parabola **b.** $2X^2 - 2Y - 1 = 0$

c.

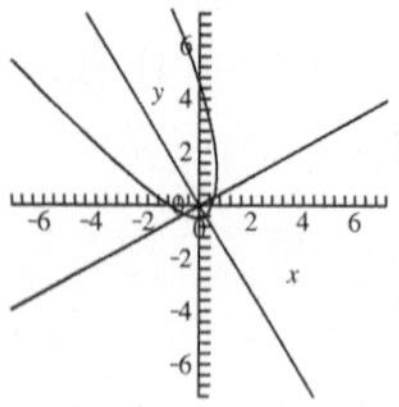

19. **a.** ellipse **b.** $\frac{X^2}{1} + \frac{Y^2}{9} = 1$

c.

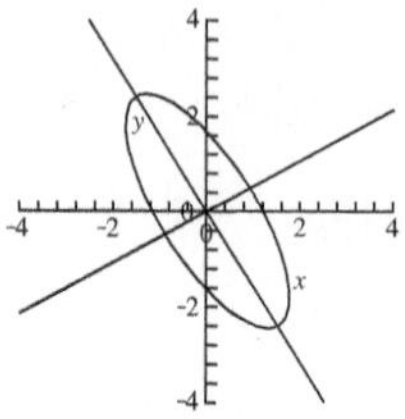

21. **a.** hyperbola **b.** $\frac{X^2}{3} - \frac{Y^2}{2} = 1$

c.

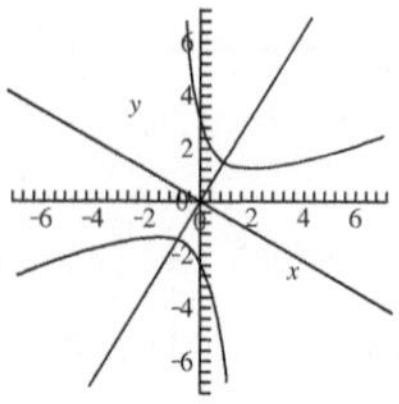

23. **a.** parabola **b.** $Y^2 - X - 4 = 0$

c.

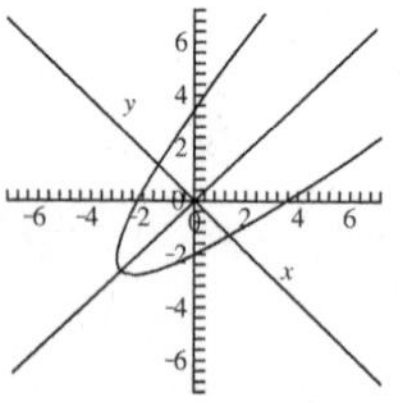

25. 45° **27.** 60° **29.** 30°

31. 45° **33.** 15° **35.** 40.3°

37. 50.7°

39.

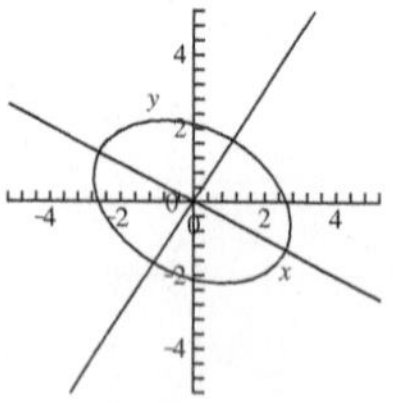

41.

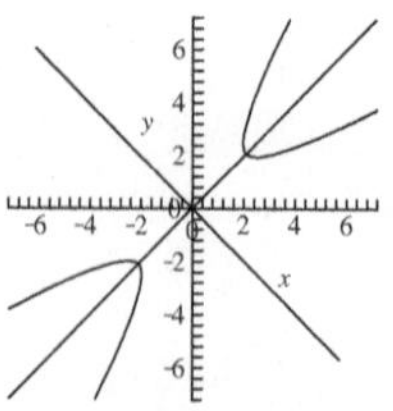

43.

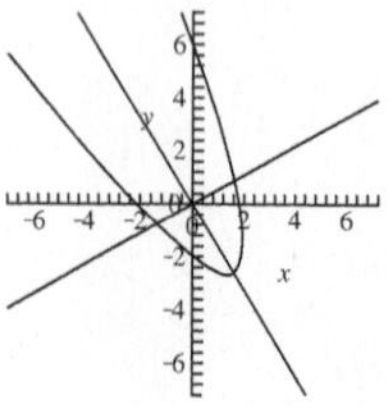

45.

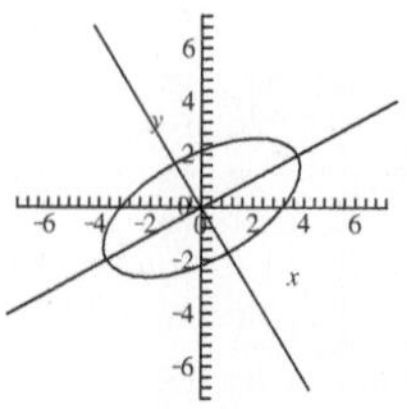

47.

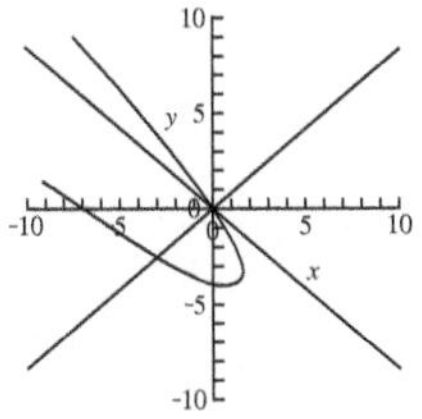

49. true

51. true

53. **a.** $\frac{x^2}{b^2} + \frac{y^2}{a^2} = 1$ **b.** The original equation

55. $a < 0$: hyperbola; $a = 0$: parabola; $a > 0$: ellipse; $a = 1$: circle

57. $(-\sqrt{2}, -2\sqrt{2}), (\sqrt{2}, 2\sqrt{2})$

59. $(-1, 0), (1, 0), (3, 1), (-3, -1)$

Section 9.8

1. $r = \dfrac{5}{2 - \sin\theta}$

3. $r = \dfrac{8}{1 + 2\sin\theta}$

5. $r = \dfrac{1}{1 + \cos\theta}$

7. $r = \dfrac{6}{4 + 3\cos\theta}$

9. $r = \dfrac{12}{3 - 4\cos\theta}$

11. $r = \dfrac{3}{1 - \sin\theta}$

13. $r = \dfrac{18}{5 + 3\sin\theta}$

15. parabola

17. ellipse

19. hyperbola

21. ellipse

23. parabola

25. hyperbola

27. **a.** parabola **b.** $e = 1, (0, 1)$

c.

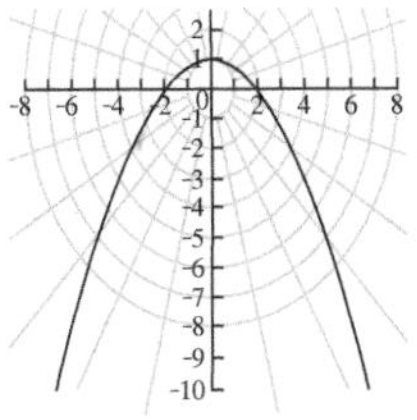

29. **a.** hyperbola **b.** $e = 2, (0, -4), (0, -\frac{4}{3})$

c.

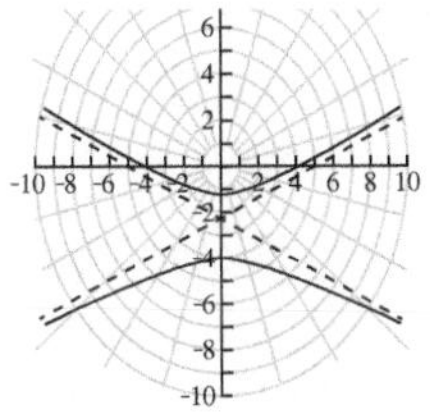

31. **a.** ellipse **b.** $e = \frac{1}{2}, (0, \frac{2}{3}), (0, -2)$

c.

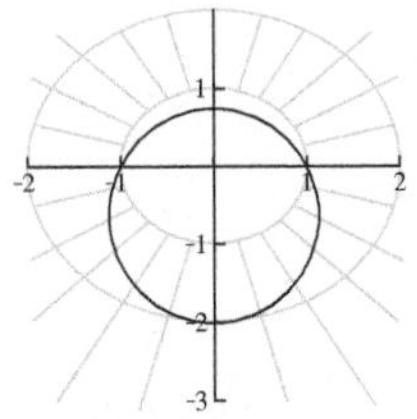

33. **a.** parabola **b.** $e = 1, (0, -\frac{1}{4})$

c.

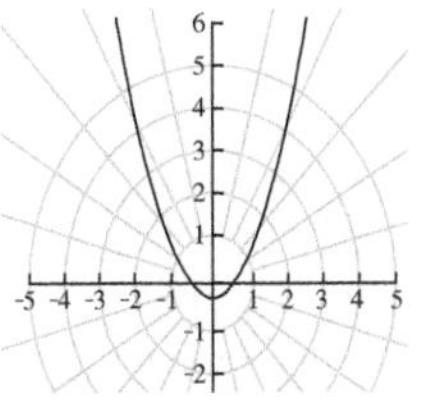

35. **a.** ellipse **b.** $e = \frac{1}{3}, (1, 0), (-2, 0)$

c.

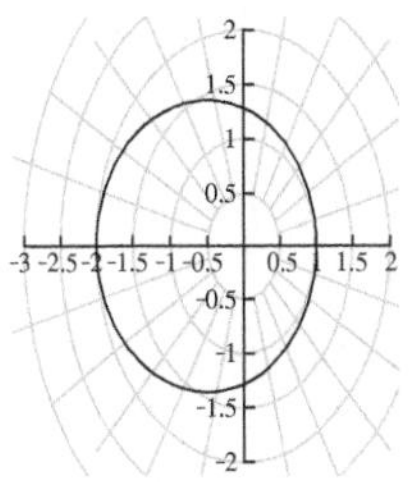

37. **a.** hyperbola **b.** $e = \frac{3}{2}, (0, \frac{6}{5}), (0, 6)$

c.

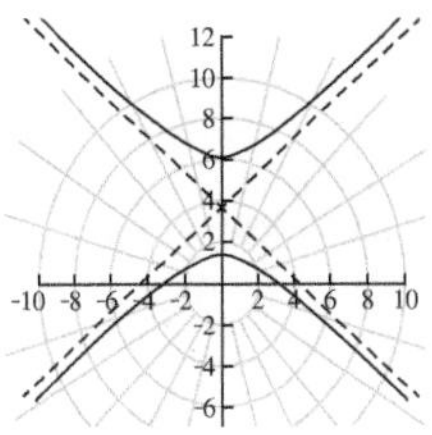

39. **a.** parabola **b.** $e = 1, (0, \frac{1}{5})$

c.

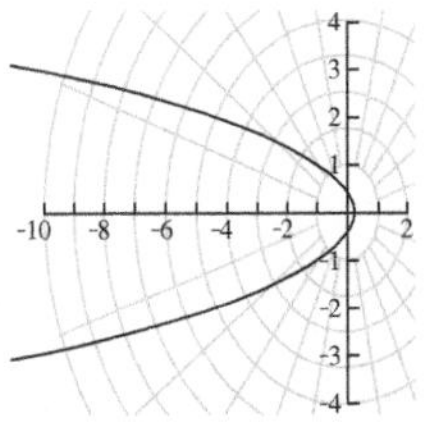

41. **a.** hyperbola **b.** $e = 3, (\frac{3}{2}, 0), (3, 0)$

c.

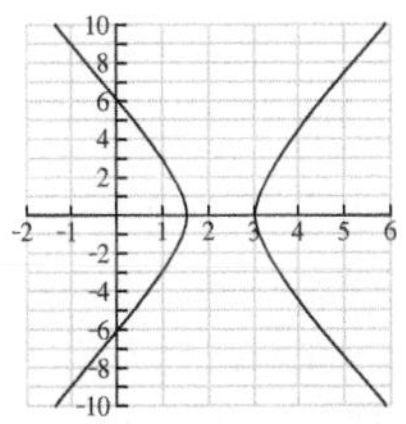

43. $0.248, r = \dfrac{5{,}913{,}500{,}000(1 - 0.248^2)}{1 - 0.248\cos\theta}$

45. $r = \dfrac{150{,}000{,}000(1 - 0.223^2)}{1 - 0.223\cos\theta}$

47. **a.** $(-0.0167, 0)$ **b.** $(0.0167, \pi)$

49. $(0, -15.406)$

51. $e \to 1$: more elliptical, $e \to 0$: more circular

55. $\frac{2ep}{1-e^2}$

57. $\left(-\frac{\frac{ep}{1+e}-\frac{ep}{1-e}}{2}, \pi\right)$

59. $\theta = \frac{\pi}{4}, \frac{5\pi}{4}$

61. $\theta = \frac{\pi}{6}, \frac{5\pi}{6}$

Section 9.9

1.

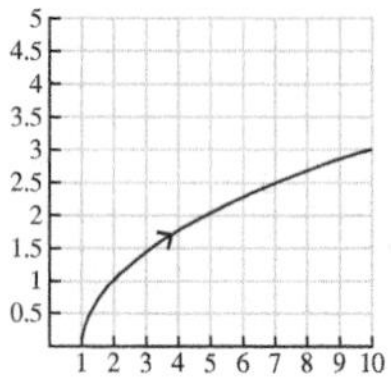

3.

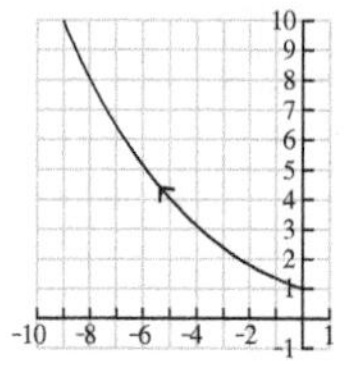

5.

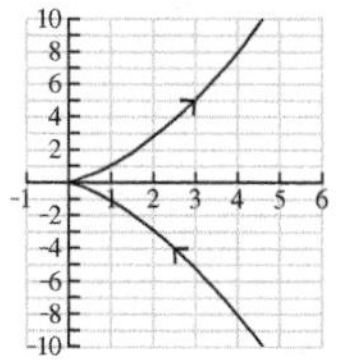

7.

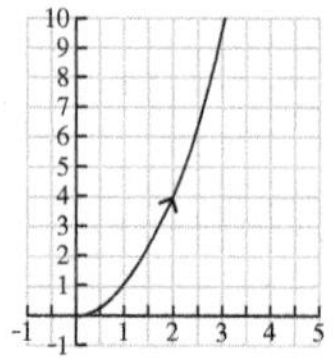

9.

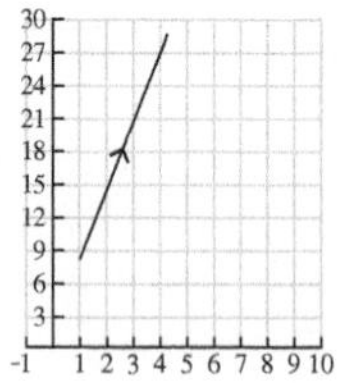

11.

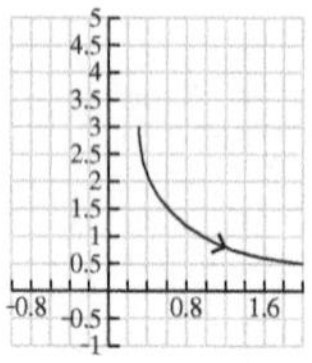

13.

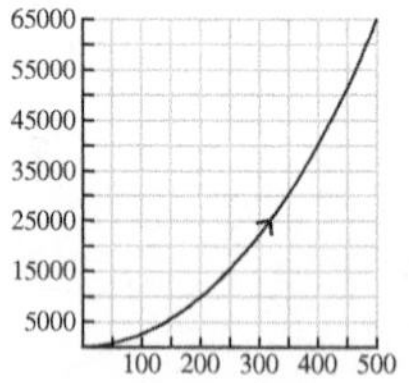

15.

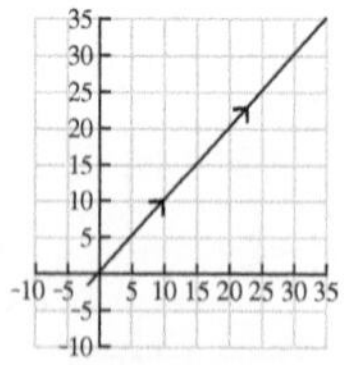

17.

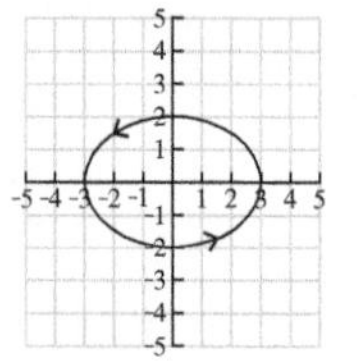

19.

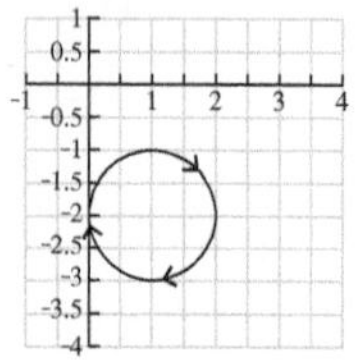

21.

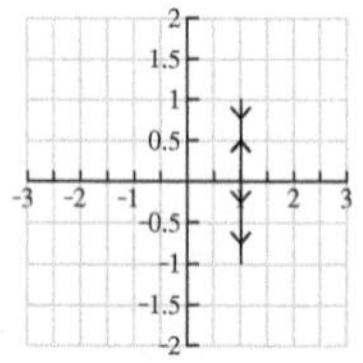

23.

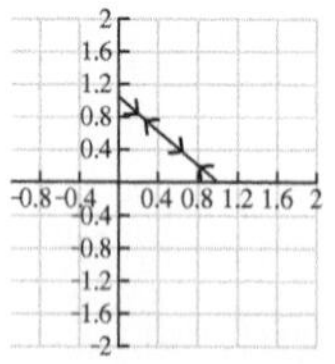

25.

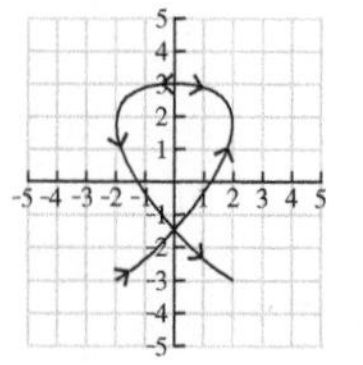

27.

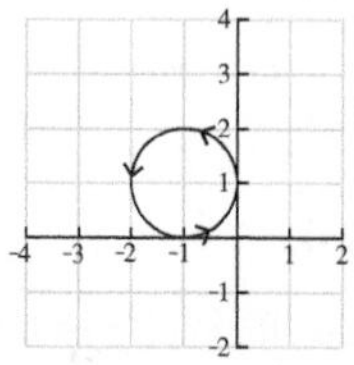

29.

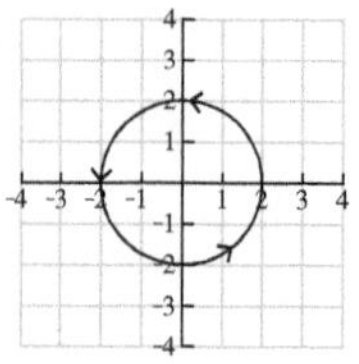

31. $y = \frac{1}{x^2}$

33. $y = x - 2$

35. $y = \sqrt{x^2 + 1}$

37. $x + y = 2$

39. $x + 4y = 8$

41. 17.7 sec

43. yes

45. distance: 13, 261 ft; max height: 5742 ft

47. 125 sec

49.

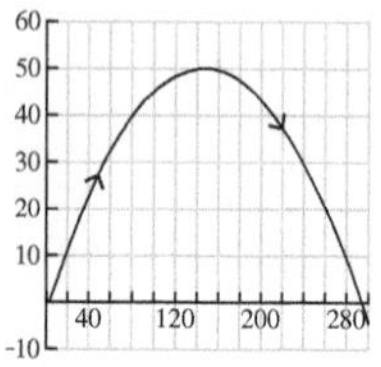

51. The original domain must be $t \geq 0$. Only the portion of the parabola where $y \geq 0$ is part of the plane curve.

53. false

55. quarter circle in QI

59. $y = \frac{a-b}{a+b}x + \frac{2ab}{a+b}$

61. $y = bx^{1/a}$

63. $(-3, 8), (2, 3)$

65. $(-100, -96), (1300, -1664)$

Review Exercises

1. false

3. true

5. $y^2 = 12x$

7. $y^2 = -20x$

9. $(x-2)^2 = 8(y-3)$

11. $(x-1)^2 = -4(y-6)$

13. F: $(0, -3)$, V: $(0, 0)$, D: $y = 3$, LR:12

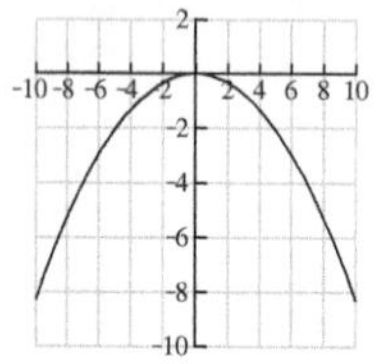

15. F: $(\frac{1}{4}, 0)$, V: $(0, 0)$, D: $x = -\frac{1}{4}$, LR: 1

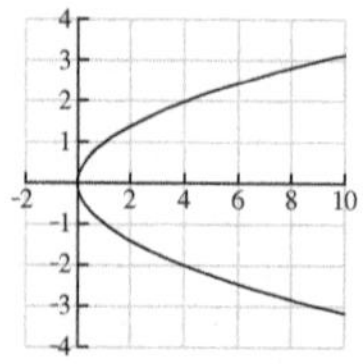

17. F: $(3, -2)$, V: $(0, 0)$, D: $x = 1$, LR: 4

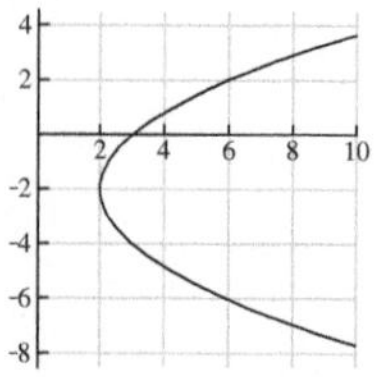

19. F: $(-3, -1)$, V: $(-3, 1)$, D: $y = 3$, LR: 8

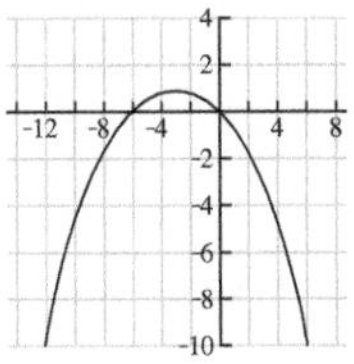

21. F: $\left(-\frac{5}{2}, -\frac{79}{8}\right)$, V: $\left(-\frac{5}{2}, -\frac{75}{8}\right)$, D: $y = -\frac{71}{8}$, LR: 2

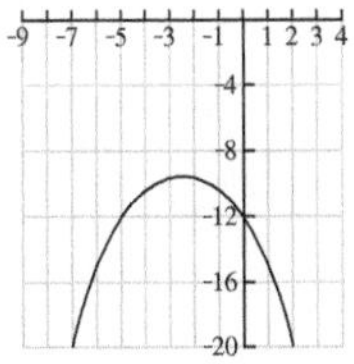

23. 3.125 ft from center

25.

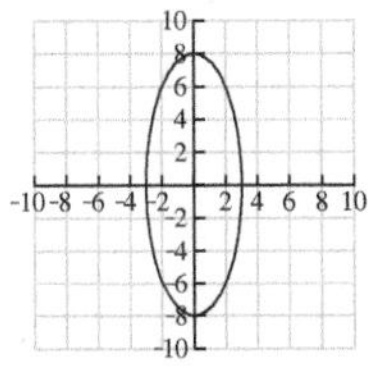

27.

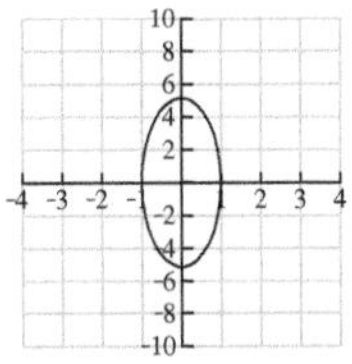

29. $\frac{x^2}{25} + \frac{y^2}{16} = 1$

31. $\frac{x^2}{9} + \frac{y^2}{64} = 1$

33.

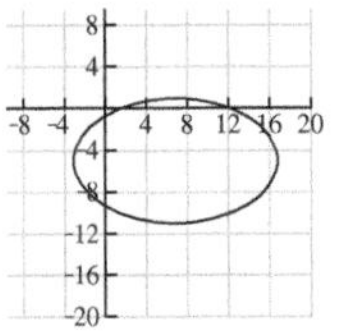

35.

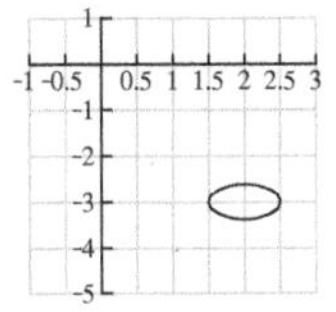

37. $\frac{(x-3)^2}{25} + \frac{(y-3)^2}{9} = 1$

39. $\frac{(x-(3.74 \times 10^7))^2}{6.058 \times 10^{17}} + \frac{(y-0)^2}{6.044 \times 10^{17}} = 1$

41.

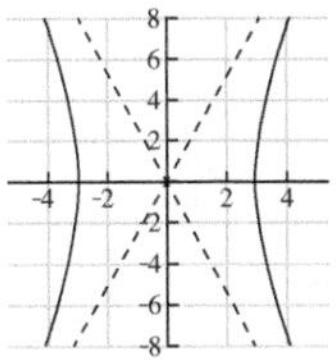

43.

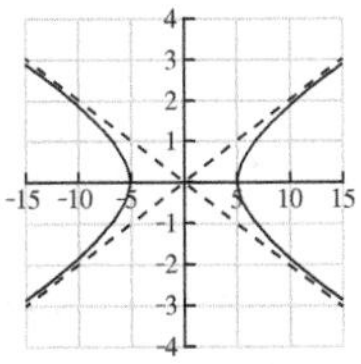

45. $\frac{x^2}{9} - \frac{y^2}{16} = 1$

47. $\frac{y^2}{9} - x^2 = 1$

49.

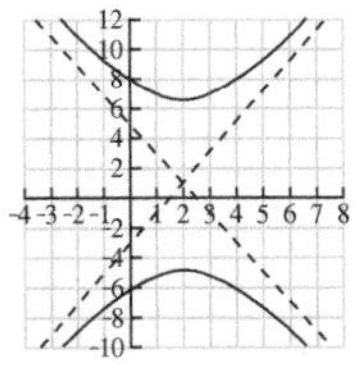

51.

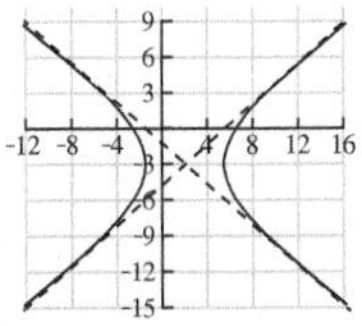

53. $\frac{(x-4)^2}{16} - \frac{(y-3)^2}{9} = 1$

55. between the stations: 65.36 mi from one, 154.64 mi from the other

57. $(-2, -7), (1, -4)$

59. $(1, 2), (-1, 2)$

61. no solution

63. no solution

65. $(2, 3), (-3, -2)$

67. $\left(\frac{1}{2}, \frac{1}{\sqrt{7}}\right), \left(-\frac{1}{2}, \frac{1}{\sqrt{7}}\right), \left(\frac{1}{2}, -\frac{1}{\sqrt{7}}\right), \left(-\frac{1}{2}, -\frac{1}{\sqrt{7}}\right)$

69.

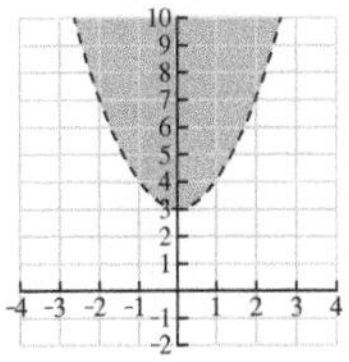

71.

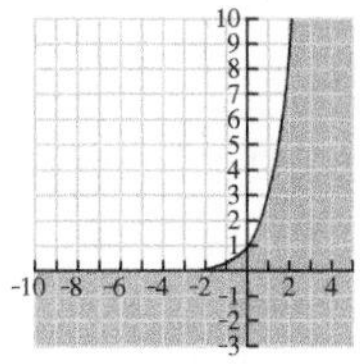

73.

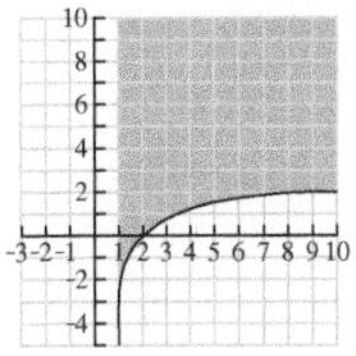

75.

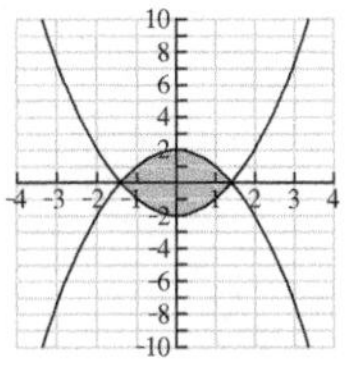

77.

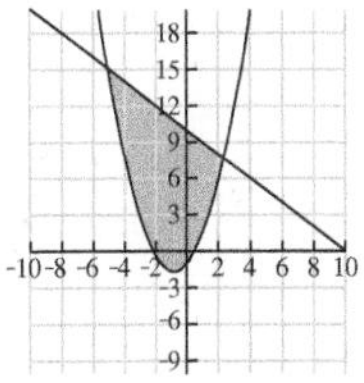

79.

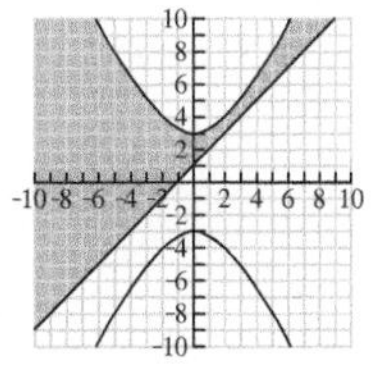

81. $\left(-\frac{3}{2} + \sqrt{3}, \frac{3\sqrt{3}}{2} + 1\right)$

83. $\frac{x^2}{4} - \frac{y^2}{4} = 1$

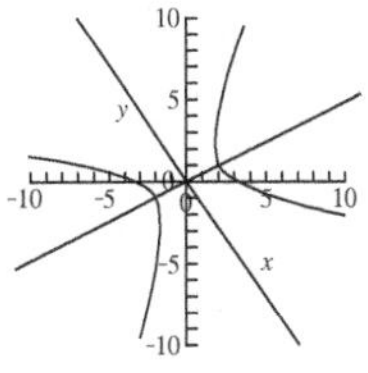

85. 60°

87.

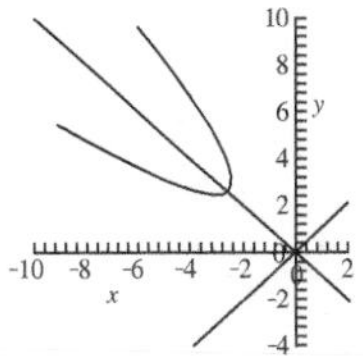

89. $r = \dfrac{21}{7 - 3\sin\theta}$

91. hyperbola

93. $e = \frac{1}{2}, \left(\frac{4}{3}, 0\right), (-4, 0)$

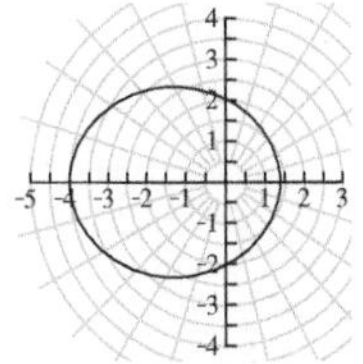

95.

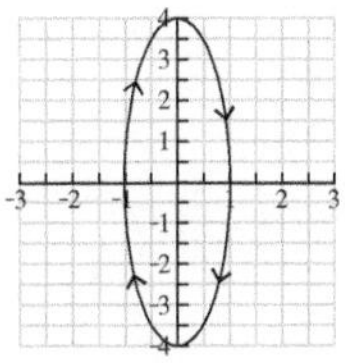

97.

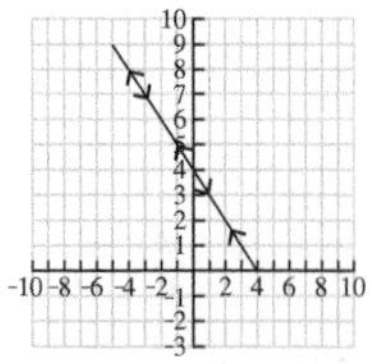

99. $x = 4 - y^2$

101. $y = 2x + 4$

Practice Test

1. c

3. d

5. f

7. $y^2 = -16x$

9. $(x + 1)^2 = -12(y - 5)$

11. $\frac{x^2}{7} + \frac{y^2}{16} = 1$

13. $\frac{(x-2)^2}{20} + \frac{y^2}{36} = 1$

15. $x^2 - \frac{y^2}{4} = 1$

17. $\frac{y^2}{16} - \frac{(x-2)^2}{20} = 1$

19.

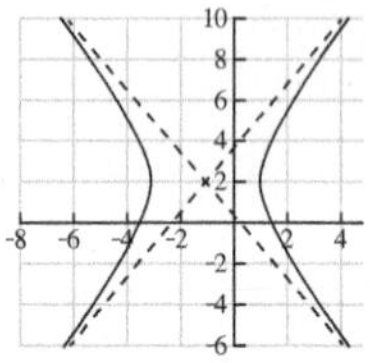

21.

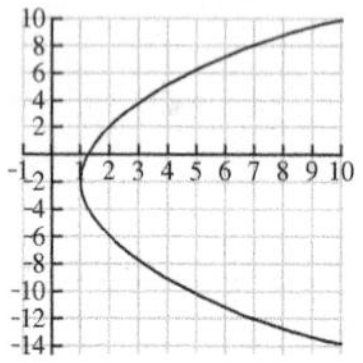

23. $x^2 = 6y$

25.

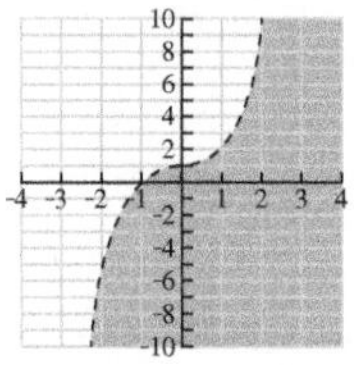

27.

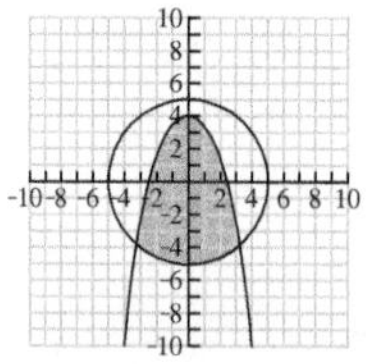

29. ellipse, $e = \frac{2}{3}$

31. 5.3 sec, 450 ft

Cumulative Test

1. $-6, 3$

3. -7

5. $y = \frac{1}{3}(x - 7)^2 + 7$

7. 4

9. 1.9626

11. $\frac{1}{\cos\theta} + \sin\theta$

13. $\frac{\pi}{3}, \frac{2\pi}{3}, \frac{4\pi}{3}, \frac{5\pi}{3}$

15. $\langle -5.13, 14.10 \rangle$

17. soda: $1.29, soft pretzel: $1.45

19.

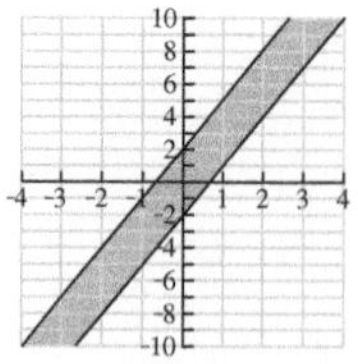

21. $\begin{bmatrix} 7 & -16 & 33 \\ 18 & -3 & -17 \end{bmatrix}$

23. $\frac{(x-6)^2}{9} + \frac{(y+2)^2}{25} = 1$

25. $(2, 4), (4, 2)$

Applications Index

Subject Index

Definitions, Rules, Formulas, and Graphs

Exponents and Radicals

$a^0 = 1, a \neq 0$

$a^{-x} = \dfrac{1}{a^x}$

$a^x a^y = a^{x+y}$

$\dfrac{a^x}{a^y} = a^{x-y}$

$(a^x)^y = a^{xy}$

$(ab)^x = a^x b^x$

$\left(\dfrac{a}{b}\right)^x = \dfrac{a^x}{b^x}$

$\sqrt{a} = a^{1/2}$

$\sqrt[n]{a} = a^{1/n}$

$\sqrt[n]{a^m} = a^{m/n} = \left(\sqrt[n]{a}\right)^m$

$\sqrt[n]{ab} = \sqrt[n]{a}\sqrt[n]{b}$

$\sqrt[n]{\left(\dfrac{a}{b}\right)} = \dfrac{\sqrt[n]{a}}{\sqrt[n]{b}}$

Quadratic Formula

If $ax^2 + bx + c = 0$, then

$$x = \frac{-b \pm \sqrt{b^2 - 4ac}}{2a}$$

Inequalities

If $a < b$ and $b < c$, then $a < c$.
If $a < b$, then $a + c < b + c$.
If $a < b$ and $c > 0$, then $ca < cb$.
If $a < b$ and $c < 0$, then $ca > cb$.

Absolute Value

1. $|x| = \begin{cases} x & \text{if } x \geq 0 \\ -x & \text{if } x < 0 \end{cases}$
2. If $|x| = c$, then $x = c$ or $x = -c$. $(c > 0)$
3. If $|x| < c$, then $-c < x < c$. $(c > 0)$
4. If $|x| > c$, then $x < -c$ or $x > c$. $(c > 0)$

Special Factorizations

1. *Difference of two squares:*
   $A^2 - B^2 = (A + B)(A - B)$
2. *Perfect square trinomials:*
   $A^2 + 2AB + B^2 = (A + B)^2$
   $A^2 - 2AB + B^2 = (A - B)^2$
3. *Sum of two cubes:*
   $A^3 + B^3 = (A + B)(A^2 - AB + B^2)$
4. *Difference of two cubes:*
   $A^3 - B^3 = (A - B)(A^2 + AB + B^2)$

Properties of Logarithms

1. $\log_b(MN) = \log_b M + \log_b N$
2. $\log_b\left(\dfrac{M}{N}\right) = \log_b M - \log_b N$
3. $\log_b M^p = p \log_b M$
4. $\log_b M = \dfrac{\log_a M}{\log_a b} = \dfrac{\ln M}{\ln b} = \dfrac{\log M}{\log b}$
5. $\log_b b^x = x; \ln e^x = x$
6. $b^{\log_b x} = x; e^{\ln x} = x, x > 0$

Symmetry

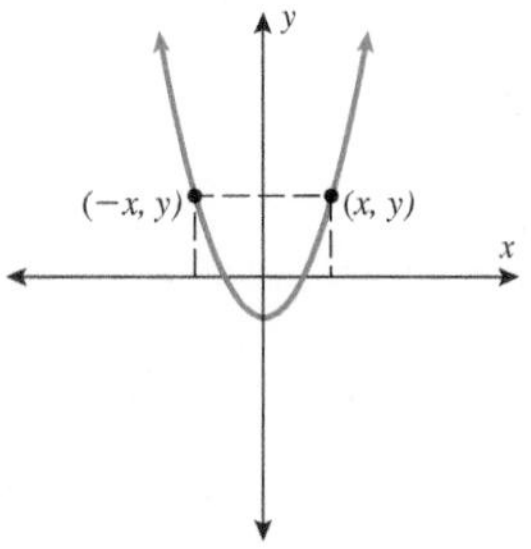

y-Axis Symmetry

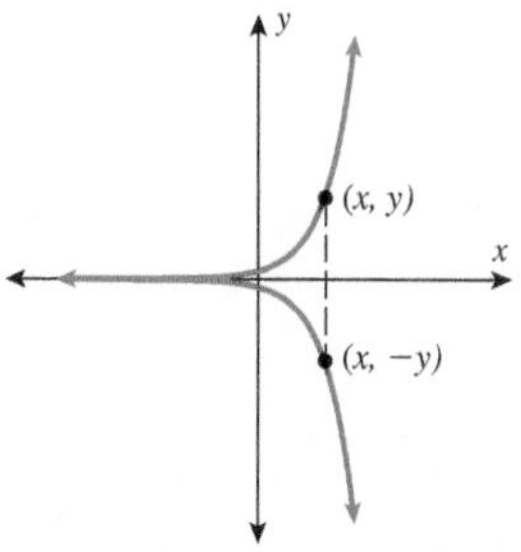

x-Axis Symmetry

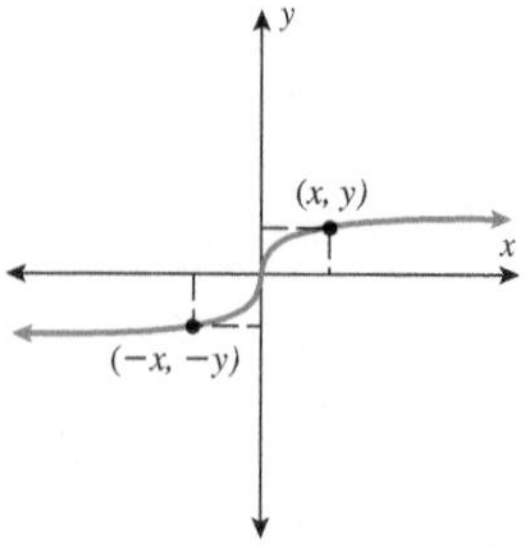

Origin Symmetry

Formulas/Equations

Distance Formula

The distance from (x_1, y_1) to (x_2, y_2) is $\sqrt{(x_2 - x_1)^2 + (y_2 - y_1)^2}$.

Midpoint Formula

The midpoint of the line segment with endpoints (x_1, y_1) and (x_2, y_2) is $\left(\frac{x_1 + x_2}{2}, \frac{y_1 + y_2}{2}\right)$.

Standard Equation of a Circle

The standard equation of a circle of radius r with center at (h, k) is $(x - h)^2 + (y - k)^2 = r^2$.

Slope Formula

The slope m of the line containing the points (x_1, y_1) and (x_2, y_2) is

$$\text{slope } (m) = \frac{\text{change in } y}{\text{change in } x} = \frac{y_2 - y_1}{x_2 - x_1} \quad (x_1 \neq x_2)$$

where m is undefined if $x_1 = x_2$.

Slope-Intercept Equation of a Line

The equation of a line with slope m and y-intercept (b) is $y = mx + b$.

Point-Slope Equation of a Line

The equation of a line with slope m containing the point (x_1, y_1) is $y - y_1 = m(x - x_1)$.

Quadratic Formula

The solutions of the equation $ax^2 + bx + c = 0$, $a \neq 0$, are $x = \dfrac{-b \pm \sqrt{b^2 - 4ac}}{2a}$.

If $b^2 - 4ac > 0$, there are two unequal real solutions.

If $b^2 - 4ac = 0$, there is a repeated real solution.

If $b^2 - 4ac < 0$, there are two complex solutions (complex conjugates).

Geometry Formulas

Circle

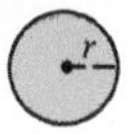

$r =$ Radius, $A =$ Area, $C =$ Circumference

$A = \pi r^2 \quad C = 2\pi r$

Triangle

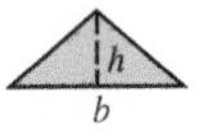

$b =$ Base, $h =$ Height (Altitude), $A =$ Area

$A = \frac{1}{2}bh$

Rectangle

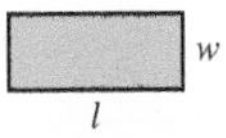

$l =$ Length, $w =$ Width, $A =$ Area, $P =$ Perimeter

$A = lw \quad P = 2l + 2w$

Rectangular Box

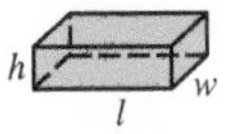

$l =$ Length, $w =$ Width, $h =$ Height, $V =$ Volume, $S =$ Surface area

$V = lwh \quad S = 2lw + 2lh + 2wh$

Sphere

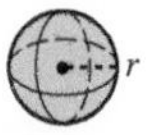

$r =$ Radius, $V =$ Volume, $S =$ Surface area

$V = \frac{4}{3}\pi r^3 \quad S = 4\pi r^2$

Right Circular Cylinder

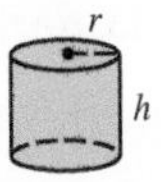

$r =$ Radius, $h =$ Height, $V =$ Volume, $S =$ Surface area

$V = \pi r^2 h \quad S = 2\pi r^2 + 2\pi rh$

Conversion Table

1 centimeter ≈ 0.394 inch	1 joule ≈ 0.738 foot-pound	1 mile ≈ 1.609 kilometers
1 meter ≈ 39.370 inches	1 gram ≈ 0.035 ounce	1 gallon ≈ 3.785 liters
≈ 3.281 feet	1 kilogram ≈ 2.205 pounds	1 pound ≈ 4.448 newtons
1 kilometer ≈ 0.621 mile	1 inch ≈ 2.540 centimeters	1 foot-lb ≈ 1.356 joules
1 liter ≈ 0.264 gallon	1 foot ≈ 30.480 centimeters	1 ounce ≈ 28.350 grams
1 newton ≈ 0.225 pound	≈ 0.305 meter	1 pound ≈ 0.454 kilogram

FUNCTIONS

Constant Function	$f(x) = b$
Linear Function	$f(x) = mx + b$, where m is the slope and b is the y-intercept
Quadratic Function	$f(x) = ax^2 + bx + c,\ a \neq 0$ or $f(x) = a(x - h)^2 + k$ parabola, vertex (h, k)
Polynomial Function	$f(x) = a_n x^n + a_{n-1}x^{n-1} + \cdots + a_1 x + a_0$
Rational Function	$R(x) = \dfrac{n(x)}{d(x)} = \dfrac{a_n x^n + a_{n-1}x^{n-1} + \cdots + a_1 x + a_0}{b_m x^m + b_{m-1}x^{m-1} + \cdots + b_1 x + b_0}$
Exponential Function	$f(x) = b^x,\ b > 0,\ b \neq 1$
Logarithmic Function	$f(x) = \log_b x,\ b > 0,\ b \neq 1$

GRAPHS OF COMMON FUNCTIONS

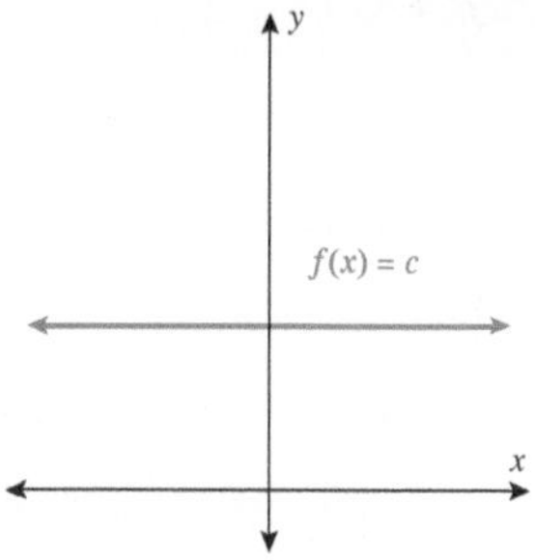

Constant Function

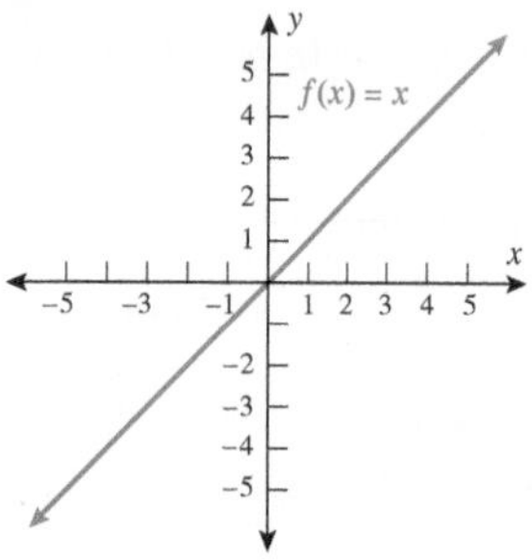

Identity Function

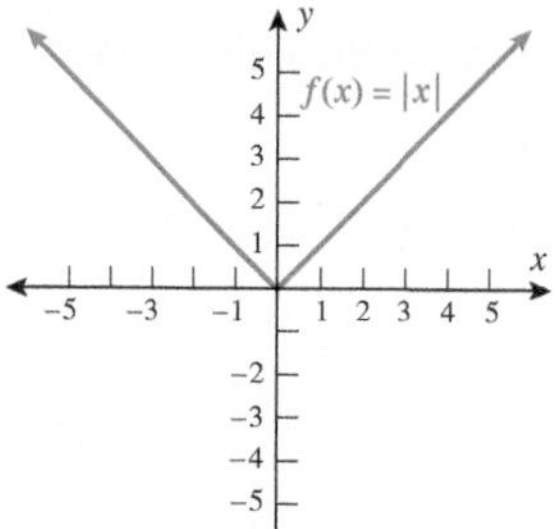

Absolute Value Function

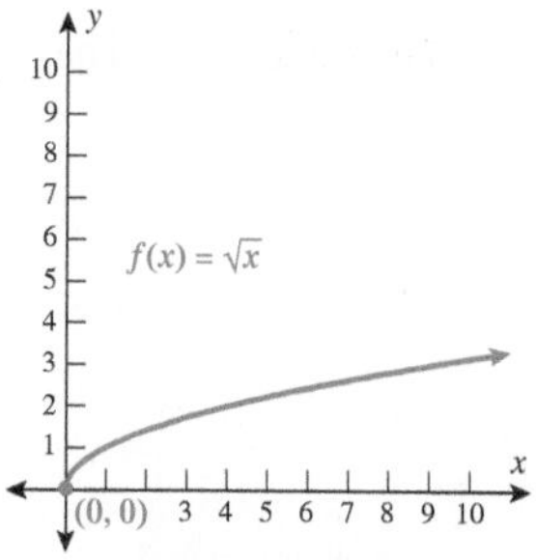

Square Root Function

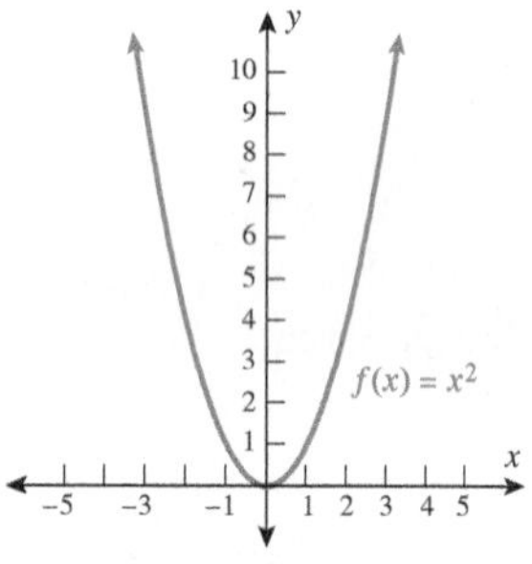

Square Function

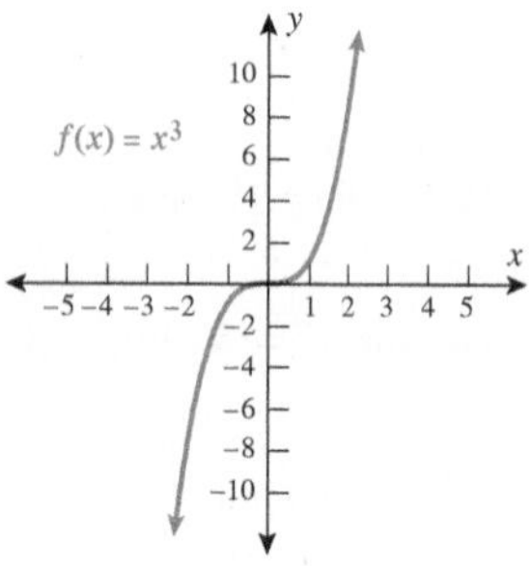

Cube Function

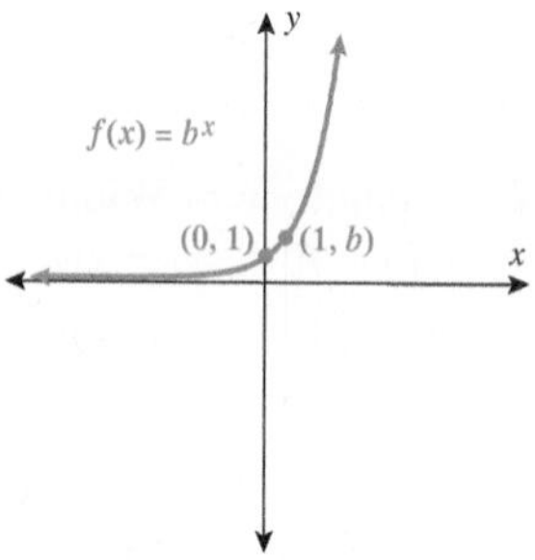

Exponential function

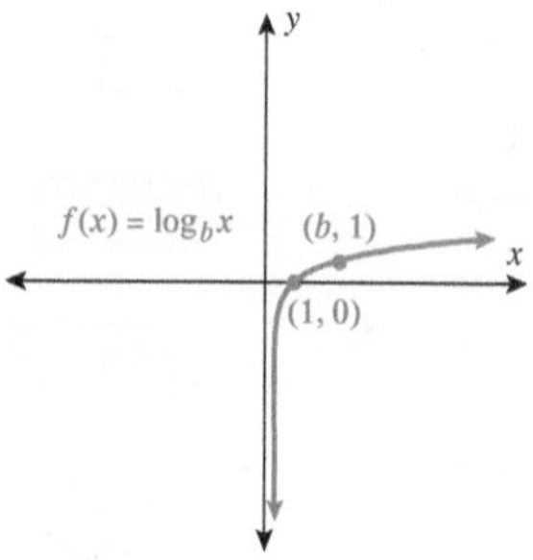

Logarithmic Function

TRANSFORMATIONS

In each case, c represents a positive real number.

Function		**Draw the graph of f and:**
Vertical translations	$y = f(x) + c$	Shift f upward c units.
	$y = f(x) - c$	Shift f downward c units.
Horizontal translations	$y = f(x - c)$	Shift f to the right c units.
	$y = f(x + c)$	Shift f to the left c units.
Reflections	$y = -f(x)$	Reflect f about the x-axis.
	$y = f(-x)$	Reflect f about the y-axis.

HERON'S FORMULA FOR AREA

If the semiperimeter, s, of a triangle is

$$s = \frac{a + b + c}{2}$$

then the area of that triangle is

$$A = \sqrt{s(s - a)(s - b)(s - c)}.$$

Conic Sections

Parabola

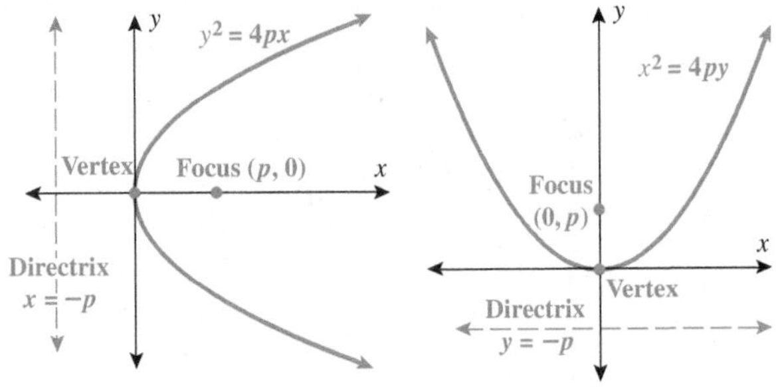

Ellipse

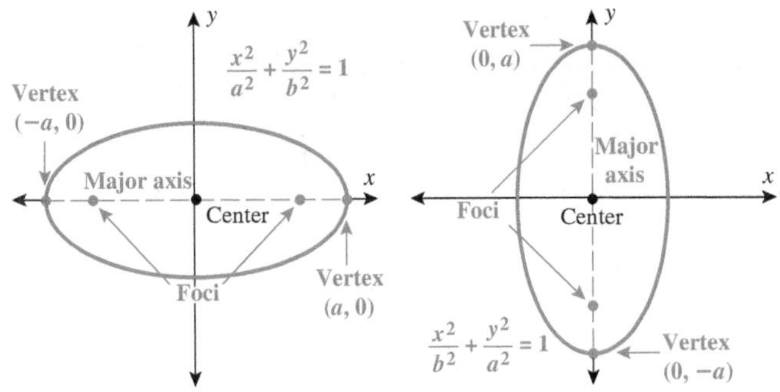

Hyperbola

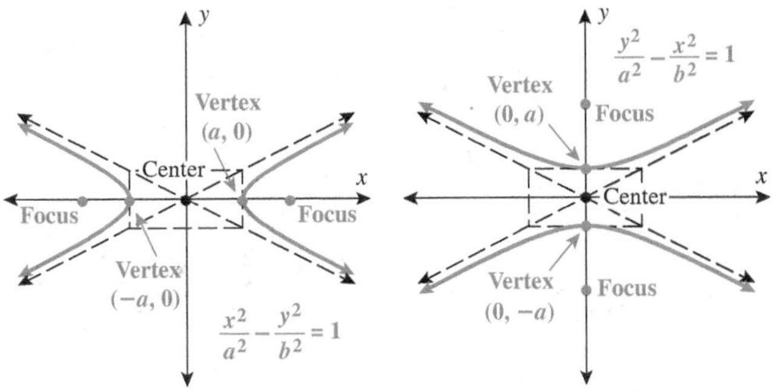

Sequences

1. Infinite Sequence:

$$\{a_n\} = a_1, a_2, a_3, \ldots, a_n, \ldots$$

2. Summation Notation:

$$\sum_{i=1}^{n} a_i = a_1 + a_2 + a_3 + \cdots + a_n$$

3. nth Term of an Arithmetic Sequence:

$$a_n = a_1 + (n - 1)d$$

4. Sum of First n Terms of an Arithmetic Sequence:

$$S_n = \frac{n}{2}(a_1 + a_n)$$

5. nth Term of a Geometric Sequence:

$$a_n = a_1 r^{n-1}$$

6. Sum of First n Terms of a Geometric Sequence:

$$S_n = \frac{a_1(1 - r^n)}{1 - r} \quad (r \neq 1)$$

7. Sum of an Infinite Geometric Series with $|r| < 1$:

$$S = \frac{a_1}{1 - r}$$

The Binomial Theorem

1. $n! = n(n-1)(n-2)\cdots 3 \cdot 2 \cdot 1;$
$1! = 1; 0! = 1$

2. $\binom{n}{r} = \frac{n!}{r!(n-r)!}$

3. Binomial theorem:

$$(a + b)^n = \binom{n}{0}a^n + \binom{n}{1}a^{n-1}b + \binom{n}{2}a^{n-2}b^2 + \cdots + \binom{n}{n}b^n$$

Permutations, Combinations, and Probability

1. ${}_nP_r$, the number of permutations of n elements taken r at a time, is given by

$${}_nP_r = \frac{n!}{(n-r)!}.$$

2. ${}_nC_r$, the number of combinations of n elements taken r at a time, is given by

$${}_nC_r = \frac{n!}{(n-r)!r!}.$$

3. *Probability of an Event:* $P(E) = \frac{n(E)}{n(S)}$, where

$n(E)$ = the number of outcomes in event E and

$n(S)$ = the number of outcomes in the sample space.

Inverse Trigonometric Functions

$y = \sin^{-1}x$	$x = \sin y$	$-\dfrac{\pi}{2} \le y \le \dfrac{\pi}{2}$	$-1 \le x \le 1$
$y = \cos^{-1}x$	$x = \cos y$	$0 \le y \le \pi$	$-1 \le x \le 1$
$y = \tan^{-1}x$	$x = \tan y$	$-\dfrac{\pi}{2} < y < \dfrac{\pi}{2}$	x is any real number
$y = \cot^{-1}x$	$x = \cot y$	$0 < y < \pi$	x is any real number
$y = \sec^{-1}x$	$x = \sec y$	$0 \le y \le \pi,\ y \ne \dfrac{\pi}{2}$	$x \le -1$ or $x \ge 1$
$y = \csc^{-1}x$	$x = \csc y$	$-\dfrac{\pi}{2} \le y \le \dfrac{\pi}{2},\ y \ne 0$	$x \le -1$ or $x \ge 1$

Graphs of the Inverse Trigonometric Functions

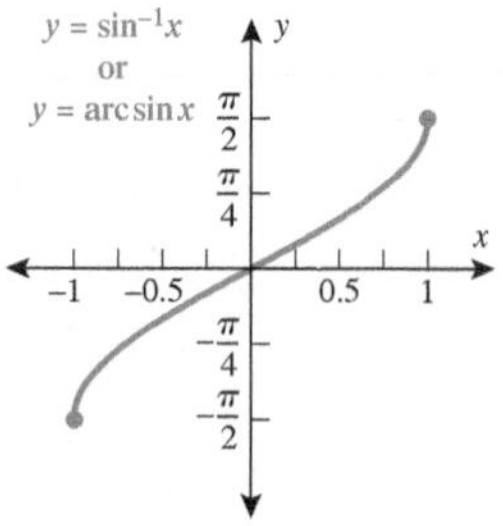

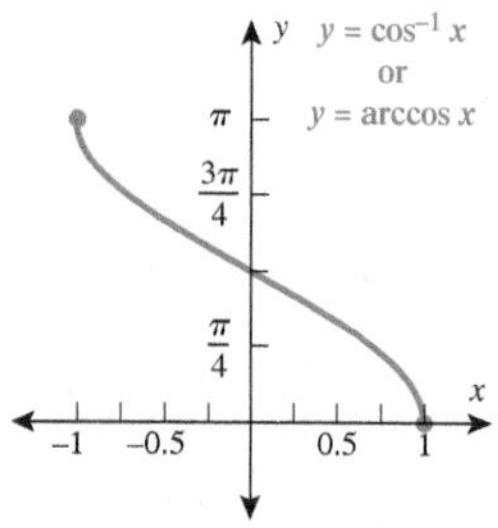

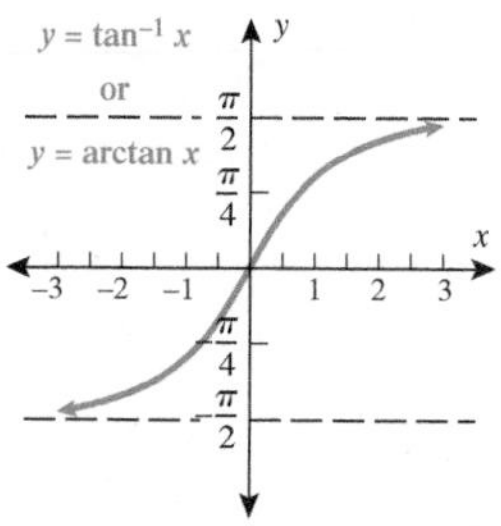

Vectors

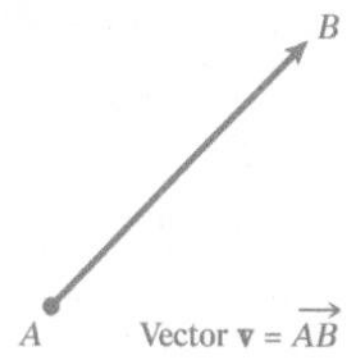

For vectors $\mathbf{u} = \langle a, b\rangle$ and $\mathbf{v} = \langle c, d\rangle$, and real number k,

$$\mathbf{u} = a\mathbf{i} + b\mathbf{j}$$

$$|\mathbf{u}| = \sqrt{a^2 + b^2}$$

$$\mathbf{u} + \mathbf{v} = \langle a + c, b + d\rangle$$

$$k\mathbf{u} = \langle ka, kb\rangle$$

$$\mathbf{u} \cdot \mathbf{v} = ac + bd$$

$$\cos\theta = \frac{\mathbf{u} \cdot \mathbf{v}}{|\mathbf{u}||\mathbf{v}|}$$

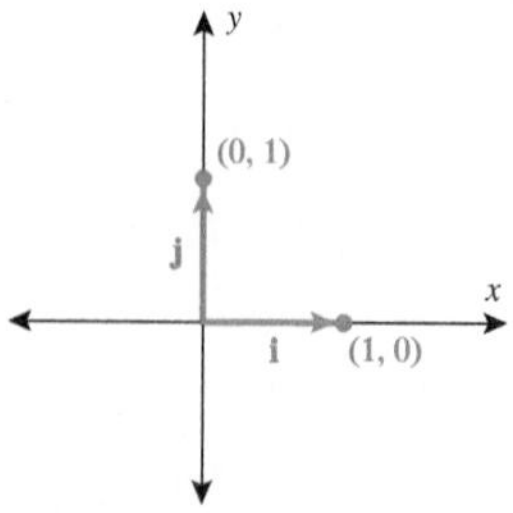

Vector Addition

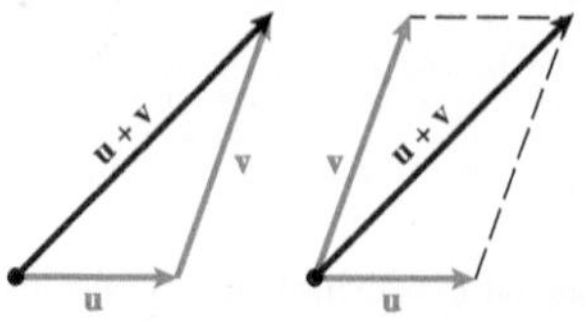

Scalar Multiplication

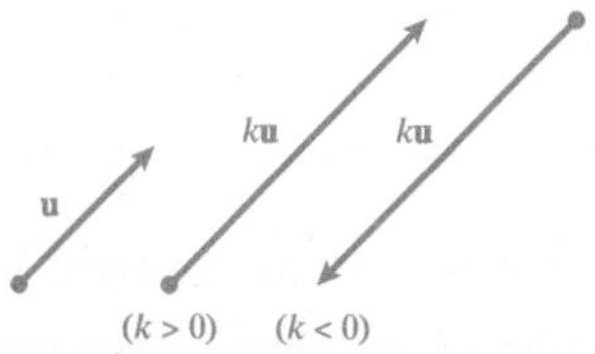

$$\text{Comp}_{\mathbf{v}}\,\mathbf{u} = |\mathbf{u}|\cos\theta = \frac{\mathbf{u} \cdot \mathbf{v}}{|\mathbf{v}|}$$

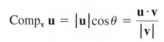

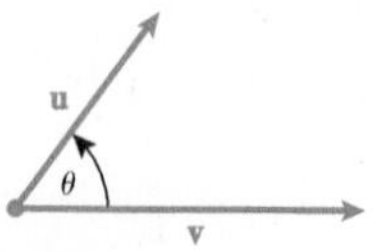

Graphs of the Trigonometric Functions

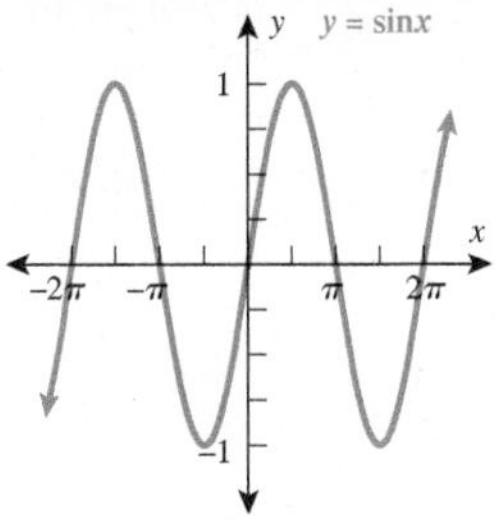

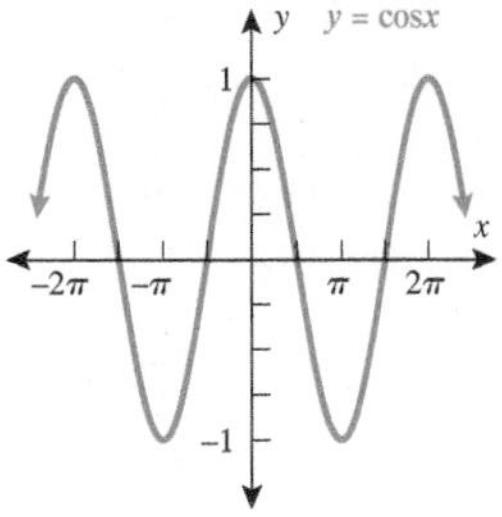

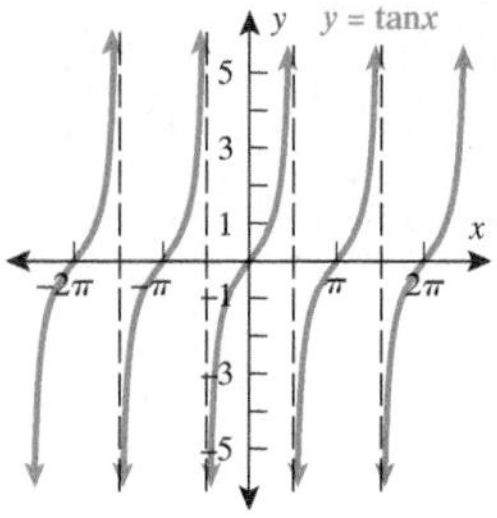

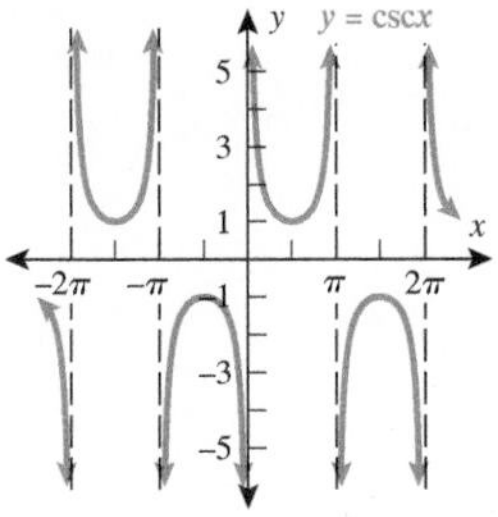

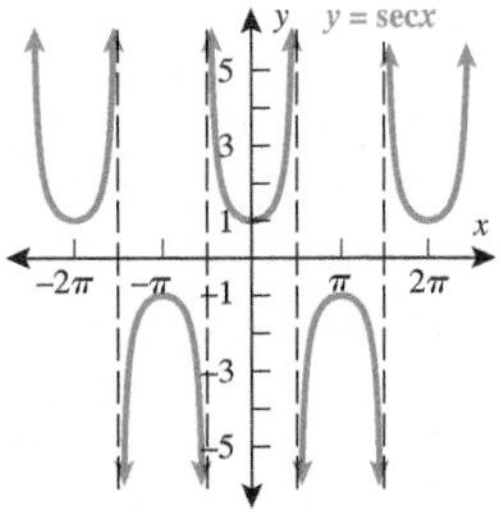

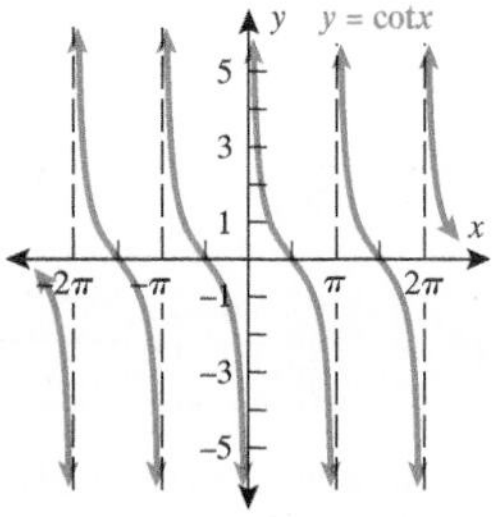

Amplitude, Period, and Phase Shift

$y = A\sin(Bx + C)$ $\qquad$ $y = A\cos(Bx + C)$

$$\text{Amplitude} = |A| \qquad \text{Period} = \frac{2\pi}{B}$$

$$\text{Phase shift} = \frac{C}{B}\begin{cases} \text{left} & \text{if } C/B > 0 \\ \text{right} & \text{if } C/B < 0 \end{cases}$$

$y = A\tan(Bx + C)$ $\qquad$ $y = A\cot(Bx + C)$

$$\text{Period} = \frac{\pi}{B}$$

$$\text{Phase shift} = \frac{C}{B}\begin{cases} \text{left} & \text{if } C/B > 0 \\ \text{right} & \text{if } C/B < 0 \end{cases}$$

Polar Coordinates

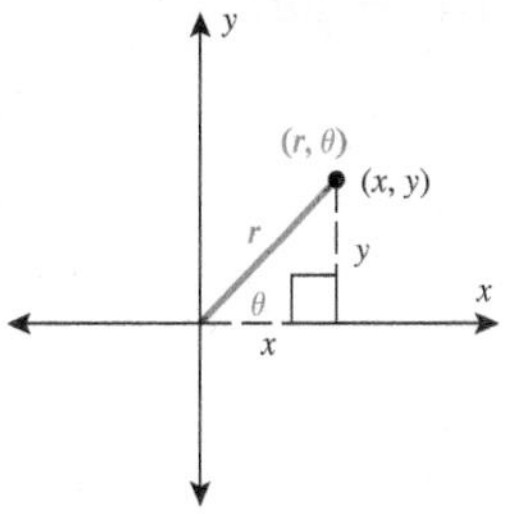

$$x = r\cos\theta$$

$$y = r\sin\theta$$

$$r^2 = x^2 + y^2$$

$$\tan\theta = \frac{y}{x}$$

Complex Numbers

For the complex number $z = a + bi$:

the **conjugate** is $\bar{z} = a - bi$

the **modulus** is $|z| = \sqrt{a^2 + b^2}$

the **argument** is θ, where $\tan\theta = b/a$

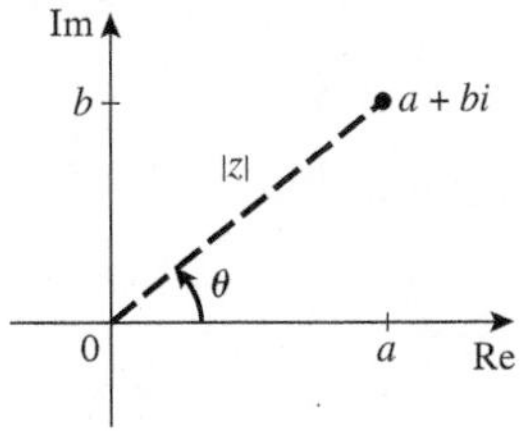

Polar (Trigonometric) form of a complex number

For $z = a + bi$, the polar form is

$$z = r(\cos\theta + i\sin\theta)$$

where $r = |z|$ is the modulus of z, and θ is the argument of z.

De Moivre's Theorem

$$z^n = [r(\cos\theta + i\sin\theta)]^n = r^n(\cos n\theta + i\sin n\theta)$$

***n*th Root Theorem**

$$z^{1/n} = [r(\cos\theta + i\sin\theta)]^{1/n}$$

$$= r^{1/n}\left(\cos\frac{\theta + 2k\pi}{n} + i\sin\frac{\theta + 2k\pi}{n}\right)$$

where $k = 0, 1, 2, \ldots n - 1$

Rotation of Axes

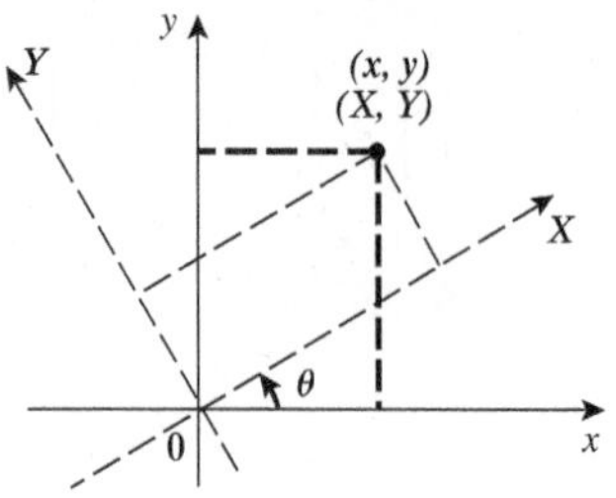

Rotation of axes formulas

$x = X\cos\theta - Y\sin\theta$

$y = X\sin\theta + Y\cos\theta$

Angle-of-rotation formula for conic sections

$$\cot(2\theta) = \frac{A - C}{B} \text{ or}$$

$$\tan(2\theta) = \frac{B}{A - C}$$

Sums of Powers of Integers

$$\sum_{k=1}^{n} 1 = n \qquad \sum_{k=1}^{n} k = \frac{n(n+1)}{2}$$

$$\sum_{k=1}^{n} k^2 = \frac{n(n+1)(2n+1)}{6} \qquad \sum_{k=1}^{n} k^3 = \frac{n^2(n+1)^2}{4}$$

The Derivative of a Function

The **average rate of change** of f between a and b is

$$\frac{f(b) - f(a)}{b - a}$$

The **derivative** of f at a is

$$f'(a) = \lim_{x \to a} \frac{f(x) - f(a)}{x - a}$$

$$f'(a) = \lim_{h \to 0} \frac{f(a+h) - f(a)}{h}$$

The Area Under the Graph a Curve

The **area under the graph of f** on the interval $[a, b]$ is the limit of the sum of the areas of approximating rectangles

$$A = \lim_{n \to \infty} \sum_{k=1}^{n} \overbrace{\underbrace{f(x_k)}_{\text{height}}\underbrace{\Delta x}_{\text{width}}}^{\text{Area of rectangle, } R_k}$$

where

$$\Delta x = \frac{b - a}{n}$$

$$x_k = a + k\Delta x$$

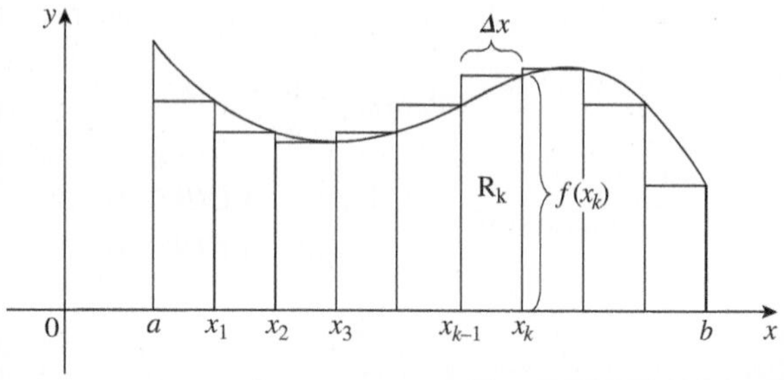

Right Triangle Trigonometry

$$\sin\theta = \frac{\text{opp}}{\text{hyp}} \qquad \csc\theta = \frac{\text{hyp}}{\text{opp}}$$

$$\cos\theta = \frac{\text{adj}}{\text{hyp}} \qquad \sec\theta = \frac{\text{hyp}}{\text{adj}}$$

$$\tan\theta = \frac{\text{opp}}{\text{adj}} \qquad \cot\theta = \frac{\text{adj}}{\text{opp}}$$

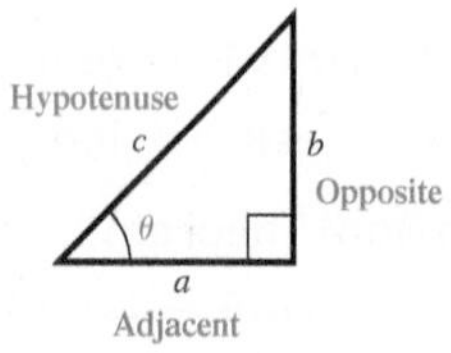

Trigonometric Function in the Cartesian Plane

$$\sin\theta = \frac{y}{r} \qquad \csc\theta = \frac{r}{y}$$

$$\cos\theta = \frac{x}{r} \qquad \sec\theta = \frac{r}{x}$$

$$\tan\theta = \frac{y}{x} \qquad \cot\theta = \frac{x}{y}$$

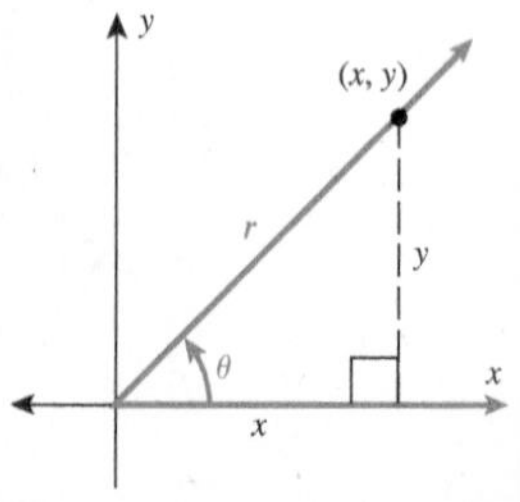

Exact Values of Trigonometric Functions

x degrees	x radians	$\sin x$	$\cos x$	$\tan x$
$0°$	0	0	1	0
$30°$	$\frac{\pi}{6}$	$\frac{1}{2}$	$\frac{\sqrt{3}}{2}$	$\frac{\sqrt{3}}{3}$
$45°$	$\frac{\pi}{4}$	$\frac{\sqrt{2}}{2}$	$\frac{\sqrt{2}}{2}$	1
$60°$	$\frac{\pi}{3}$	$\frac{\sqrt{3}}{2}$	$\frac{1}{2}$	$\sqrt{3}$
$90°$	$\frac{\pi}{2}$	1	0	—

Angle Measurement

π radians $= 180°$

$s = r\theta \quad A = \frac{1}{2}r^2\theta \quad (\theta \text{ in radians})$

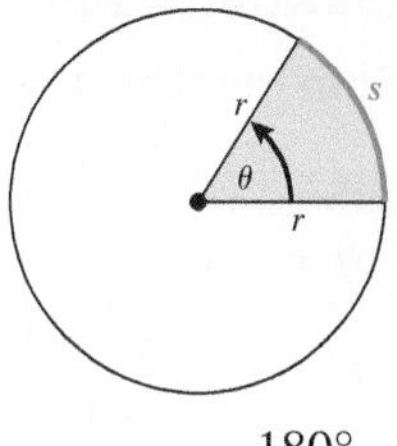

To convert from degrees to radians, multiply by $\frac{\pi}{180°}$.

To convert from radians to degrees, multiply by $\frac{180°}{\pi}$.

Oblique Triangles

Law of Sines

In any triangle,

$$\frac{\sin\alpha}{a} = \frac{\sin\beta}{b} = \frac{\sin\gamma}{c}.$$

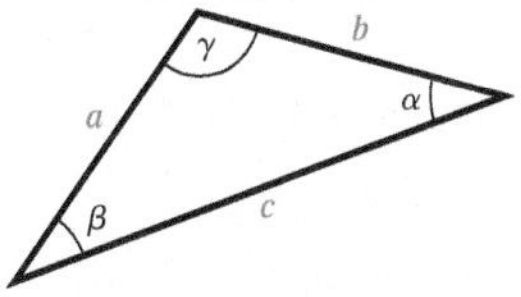

Law of Cosines

$$a^2 = b^2 + c^2 - 2bc\cos\alpha$$
$$b^2 = a^2 + c^2 - 2ac\cos\beta$$
$$c^2 = a^2 + b^2 - 2ab\cos\gamma$$

Circular Function $(\cos\theta, \sin\theta)$

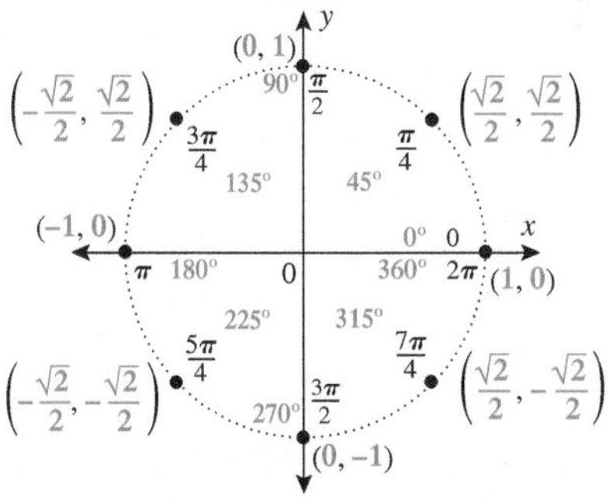

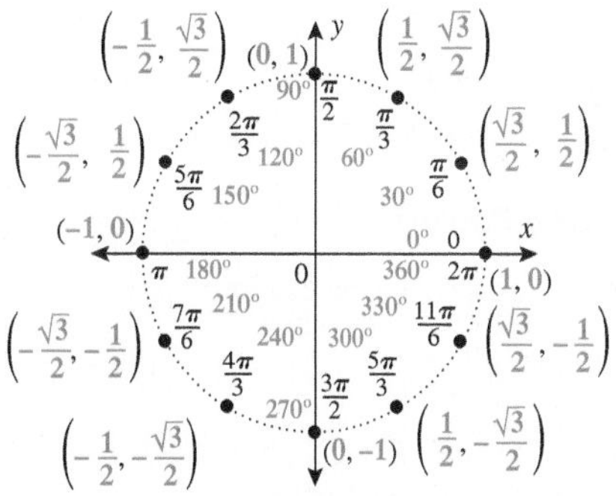

Trigonometric Identites

Sum Identities

$\sin(x + y) = \sin x \cos y + \cos x \sin y$

$\cos(x + y) = \cos x \cos y - \sin x \sin y$

$$\tan(x + y) = \frac{\tan x + \tan y}{1 - \tan x \tan y}$$

Difference Identities

$\sin(x - y) = \sin x \cos y - \cos x \sin y$

$\cos(x - y) = \cos x \cos y + \sin x \sin y$

$$\tan(x - y) = \frac{\tan x - \tan y}{1 + \tan x \tan y}$$

Double-Angle Identities

$\sin 2x = 2\sin x \cos x$

$$\cos 2x = \begin{cases} \cos^2 x - \sin^2 x \\ 1 - 2\sin^2 x \\ 2\cos^2 x - 1 \end{cases}$$

$$\tan 2x = \frac{2\tan x}{1 - \tan^2 x} = \frac{2\cot x}{\cot^2 x - 1} = \frac{2}{\cot x - \tan x}$$

Half-Angle Identities

Sign $(+/-)$ is determined by quadrant in which $x/2$ lies

$$\sin\left(\frac{x}{2}\right) = \pm\sqrt{\frac{1 - \cos x}{2}}$$

$$\cos\left(\frac{x}{2}\right) = \pm\sqrt{\frac{1 + \cos x}{2}}$$

$$\tan\left(\frac{x}{2}\right) = \frac{1 - \cos x}{\sin x} = \frac{\sin x}{1 + \cos x} = \pm\sqrt{\frac{1 - \cos x}{1 + \cos x}}$$

Identities for Reducing Powers

$$\sin^2 x = \frac{1 - \cos 2x}{2} \qquad \cos^2 x = \frac{1 + \cos 2x}{2}$$

$$\tan^2 x = \frac{1 - \cos 2x}{1 + \cos 2x}$$

Cofunction Identities

(Replace $\pi/2$ with $90°$ if x is in degree measure.)

$$\sin\left(\frac{\pi}{2} - x\right) = \cos x \qquad \cos\left(\frac{\pi}{2} - x\right) = \sin x$$

$$\tan\left(\frac{\pi}{2} - x\right) = \cot x \qquad \cot\left(\frac{\pi}{2} - x\right) = \tan x$$

$$\sec\left(\frac{\pi}{2} - x\right) = \csc x \qquad \csc\left(\frac{\pi}{2} - x\right) = \sec x$$

Product–Sum Identities

$\sin x \cos y = \frac{1}{2}[\sin(x + y) + \sin(x - y)]$

$\cos x \sin y = \frac{1}{2}[\sin(x + y) - \sin(x - y)]$

$\sin x \sin y = \frac{1}{2}[\cos(x - y) - \cos(x + y)]$

$\cos x \cos y = \frac{1}{2}[\cos(x + y) + \cos(x - y)]$

Sum–Product Identities

$$\sin x + \sin y = 2\sin\left(\frac{x + y}{2}\right)\cos\left(\frac{x - y}{2}\right)$$

$$\sin x - \sin y = 2\cos\left(\frac{x + y}{2}\right)\sin\left(\frac{x - y}{2}\right)$$

$$\cos x + \cos y = 2\cos\left(\frac{x + y}{2}\right)\cos\left(\frac{x - y}{2}\right)$$

$$\cos x - \cos y = -2\sin\left(\frac{x + y}{2}\right)\sin\left(\frac{x - y}{2}\right)$$

Basic Trigonometric Identites

Reciprocal Identities

$$\csc x = \frac{1}{\sin x} \qquad \sec x = \frac{1}{\cos x} \qquad \cot x = \frac{1}{\tan x}$$

Quotient Identities

$$\tan x = \frac{\sin x}{\cos x} \qquad \cot x = \frac{\cos x}{\sin x}$$

Identities for Negatives

$\sin(-x) = -\sin x \qquad \cos(-x) = \cos x$

$\tan(-x) = -\tan x$

Pythagorean Identities

$\sin^2 x + \cos^2 x = 1 \qquad \tan^2 x + 1 = \sec^2 x$

$1 + \cot^2 x = \csc^2 x$